THE ROUGH GUIDE TO

The USA

This eleventh edition updated by

Nick Edwards, Max Grinnell, Charles Hodgkins, Steven
Horak, Sarah Hull, Stephen Keeling, Todd Obolsky,
Andrew Rosenberg, Claus Vogel and Greg Ward

**ROUGH
GUIDES**

roughguides.com

Contents

Introduction to
The USA

As the world's only superpower and biggest economy by a huge margin, almost everyone on the planet knows something about the USA, even if they've never been. The Statue of Liberty, the Empire State, the Hollywood sign, Las Vegas neon, Golden Gate and the White House have long been global icons, and American brands and images are familiar everywhere, from Apple computers and Levi's to Coca-Cola and hot dogs. Yet first-time visitors should expect some surprises. Though its cities draw the most tourists – New York, New Orleans, Miami, Los Angeles and San Francisco are all incredible destinations in their own right – America is above all a land of stunningly diverse and achingly beautiful landscapes. In one nation you have the mighty Rockies and spectacular Cascades, the vast, mythic desert landscapes of the Southwest, the endless, rolling plains of Texas and Kansas, the tropical beaches and Everglades of Florida, the giant redwoods of California and the sleepy, pristine villages of New England. You can soak up the mesmerizing vistas in Crater Lake, Yellowstone and Yosemite national parks, stand in awe at the Grand Canyon, hike the Black Hills, cruise the Great Lakes, paddle in the Mississippi, surf the gnarly breaks of Oahu and get lost in the vast wilderness of Alaska. Or you could easily plan a trip that focuses on the out-of-the-way hamlets, remote prairies, eerie ghost towns and forgotten byways that are every bit as "American" as its showpiece icons and monuments.

The sheer size of the country prevents any sort of overarching statement about the typical American experience, just as the diversity of its people undercuts any notion of the typical American. Icons as diverse as Mohammed Ali, Louis Armstrong, Sitting Bull, Hillary Clinton, Michael Jordan, Madonna, Martin Luther King, Abraham Lincoln, Elvis Presley, Mark Twain, John Wayne and Walt Disney continue to inspire and entertain the world, and everyone has heard of the blues, country and western,

ABOVE GRAND CANYON **RIGHT** GUGGENHEIM MUSEUM, NYC

jazz, rock 'n' roll and hip-hop – all American musical innovations. There are Irish Americans, Italian Americans, African Americans, Chinese Americans and Latinos, Texan cowboys and Bronx hustlers, Seattle hipsters and Alabama pastors, New England fishermen, Las Vegas showgirls and Hawaiian surfers. Though it often sounds clichéd to foreigners, the only thing that holds this bizarre federation together is the oft-maligned "**American Dream**". While the USA is one of the world's oldest still-functioning democracies and the roots of its European presence go back to the 1500s, the palpable sense of newness here creates an odd sort of optimism, wherein anything seems possible and fortune can strike at any moment.

Indeed, aspects of American culture can be difficult for many visitors to understand, despite the apparent familiarity: its obsession with guns; the widely held belief that "government" is bad; the real, genuine pride in the American Revolution and the US Constitution, two hundred years on; the equally genuine belief that the USA is the "greatest country on earth"; the wild grandstanding of its politicians (especially at election time); and the bewildering contradiction of its great liberal and open-minded traditions with laissez-faire capitalism and extreme cultural and religious conservatism. That's America: diverse, challenging, beguiling, maddening at times, but always entertaining and always changing. And while there is no such thing as a typical American person or landscape, there can be few places where strangers can feel so confident of a warm reception.

NATIONAL PARK ABBREVIATIONS

National Forest	N.F.
National Historic Park	N.H.P.
National Monument	N.M.
National Park	N.P.
National Preserve	N.PR.
National Recreation Area	N.R.A.
National Seashore	N.S.
National Volcanic Monument	N.V.M.
National Wildlife Refuge	N.W.R.
State Park	S.P.

PACIFIC STANDARD TIME

MOUNTAIN STANDARD TIME

Vancouver

Seattle

WASHINGTON

Portland

OREGON

Boise

IDAHO

MONTANA

Butte

Helena

NORTH DAKOTA

Bismarck

SOUTH DAKOTA

Rapid City

MOUNT RUSHMORE

YELLOWSTONE NATIONAL PARK

WYOMING

Cheyenne

Reno

NEVADA

Salt Lake City

UTAH

Denver

COLORADO

San Francisco

YOSEMITE NATIONAL PARK

Las Vegas

CALIFORNIA

GRAND CANYON NATIONAL PARK

Flagstaff

ARIZONA

Albuquerque

Santa Fe

Amarillo

Los Angeles

Phoenix

NEW MEXICO

TEXAS

San Diego

Tucson

PACIFIC OCEAN

El Paso

BIG BEND NATIONAL PARK

MEXICO

ALASKA

CANADA

Anchorage

Juneau

ALASKAN STANDARD TIME

HAWAII-ALEUTIAN STANDARD TIME

Kauai

Oahu

Molokai

Honolulu

Maui

HAWAII

Big Island

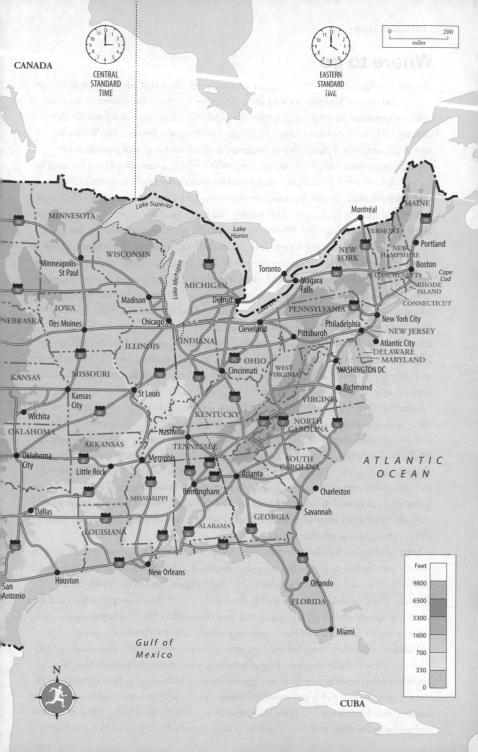

Where to go

The most invigorating American expeditions are often those that take in more than one region. You do not, however, have to cross the entire continent from shore to shore in order to appreciate its amazing diversity; it would take a long time to see the whole country, and the more time you spend simply travelling, the less time you'll have to savour the small-town pleasures and backroad oddities that may well provide your strongest memories. Unless you're travelling to and within a centralized location such as New York City, you'll need a **car** – that mandatory component of life in the USA.

The obvious place to start for most people is **New York City** – international colossus of culture and finance, with a colourful history and numerous skyscrapers to prove its status as the essential American city. While you could easily spend weeks exploring the place, just a little more effort will take you into the deeper reaches of the **Mid-Atlantic** region to the north. Here, whether in upstate New York, New Jersey or Pennsylvania, major cities such as Philadelphia and Pittsburgh border a landscape of unexpected charm and beauty, from the bucolic hamlets of Amish country and the wilderness of the Adirondack Mountains to iconic sights such as Niagara Falls and holiday favourites like the Catskills. Next door, **New England** has a similarly varied appeal; most visitors know it for the colonial and history-rich city of Boston, but there's much to be said for its rural byways, leading to centuries-old villages in Vermont and New Hampshire, bayside Massachusetts and the rugged individualism of the lobster-catching harbours and mountains of Maine – which take up nearly half the region.

Seven hundred miles west lie the **Great Lakes**, on the whole the country's most underappreciated region; vigorous cities including Chicago and Minneapolis, isolated and evocative lakeshores in Michigan and Minnesota, and rousing college towns such as Madison, Wisconsin, reward any visitor with more than a few days to explore. Bordering Ohio to the east, the nearby **Capital Region** is the home of Washington DC, capital of the nation and centrepiece for its grandest museums and monuments. Nearby Baltimore is one of the region's few other big cities, and to the south the old tobacco country of Virginia holds a fair share of American history while coal-mining West Virginia has a scattering of curious natural treasures.

Although Virginia is technically part of the **South**, for the purest experience you'll need to venture even further to get the feel of its charismatic churches, BBQ dinners, country music and lively cities such as Atlanta and Memphis. The "deepest" part of the South lies in Georgia, Alabama and Mississippi, and in these states – with their huge plantations and long history of slavery – you'll get a very different view of American life than anywhere else in the country. Other Southern states have their own unique cultures: **Florida** is a mix of old-fashioned Southern manners and backwater swamps leavened with ultra-modern cities including Miami, Latino culture, miles of tempting beaches and the lustrous Keys islands; **Louisiana** offers more atmospheric swamps and "Cajun" culture, with New Orleans one of the few spots in the USA with a strongly Catholic, yet broadly indulgent culture of drinking, dancing and debauchery; and **Texas** is the country's capital for oil-drilling, BBQ-eating and right-wing-politicking, with huge expanses of land, equally big cities and plenty of history.

The **Great Plains**, which sit in the geographical centre of the country, are often overlooked by visitors, but include many of America's most well-known sights, from Mount Rushmore in South Dakota to the Gateway Arch in St Louis and the Wild West town of Dodge City in Kansas. To the west rise the great peaks of the **Rockies**, and with them a melange of exciting cities such as Denver, beautiful mountain scenery like Montana's Glacier National Park, the geysers of Yellowstone and great opportunities for

AMERICA: THE MUSICAL MELTING POT

Some of the world's greatest musical genres took root in cities and small towns across America, products of the collisions of European, African and indigenous cultures.

The **blues** was forged from a combination of African and gospel sounds into a simple twelve-bar form during the late nineteenth century. You can still catch Mississippi blues in Delta juke joints (p.463), and electrified urban blues in the gritty clubs of Chicago (p.292).

Jazz took root in the Creole culture of New Orleans, blending African traditions with western techniques to create a distinctly American art form. Jazz is still dance music in New Orleans (p.555); cooler urban stylings can be enjoyed in clubs in New York (p.96).

Nashville remains synonymous with **country and western** (p.448); outside the cities, rural Appalachia brims with backwoods fiddlers (p.363) and Louisiana's sleepy bayous are alive with Cajun and zydeco (p.560).

Rock 'n' roll has come a long way since its blues-based infancy, when young trucker Elvis Presley shook up white country with raw R&B in 1950s Memphis (p.441). Spiky New York punk, quirky Ohio industrial, furious LA hardcore, slacker Seattle grunge, and spaced-out neo-psychedelia are but a few of the rock genres that continue to thrive in the USA.

In the 1960s, the heartfelt **soul** of masters like Otis Redding preceded the explosion of talent that came to define the Motown era, born in Detroit (p.262).

Loaded with attitude, street-style and political savvy, **hip-hop** was born on the streets of New York (p.96), and later LA. Today any city with a major black population has a distinctive rap scene, including in the so-called "Dirty South", where rappers play on the raw call-and-response stylings of early blues.

Modern dance music had its genesis in Chicago **house** (p.292), New York **garage** (p.96) and Detroit **techno** (p.264), though club culture is now a global phenomenon.

skiing throughout at places like Idaho's Sun Valley. Bordering the southern side of the Rockies, the desert **Southwest** region is also rich with astounding natural beauty – whether in the colossal chasm of the Grand Canyon, striking national parks at Zion and Canyonlands or the Native American heart of the Four Corners region – along with a handful of charming towns and less interesting big cities.

The country's most populous state is, of course, **California**, synonymous with the idea of "the West Coast" and its freewheeling culture of surfing, libertine lifestyles and self-worship. However, the further from the water you get, the less the stereotypes hold, especially in the lava beds and redwoods of the far north, the ghost towns and magnificent Yosemite in the Sierras and the intriguing deserts of Death Valley. To the state's north, Oregon and Washington – the rain-soaked pair making up the **Pacific Northwest** – offer pleasantly progressive towns such as Seattle and Portland and some of the most striking scenery anywhere in the USA: the stunning landscape of the Columbia River Gorge, the pristine islands of the San Juans, the snowy peaks of the Cascades and more.

Beyond the lower 48 states, **Alaska** is a winter wonderland of great mountains and icy spires, with few roads and people, but much to offer anyone with a zest for the outdoors and the unexpected. **Hawaii** is the country's holiday paradise, a handful of splendid islands in the central Pacific with remote jungle settings and roaring volcanoes.

When to go

The continental US is subject to dramatically shifting weather patterns, most notably produced by westerly winds sweeping across the continent from the Pacific. The **Northeast**, from Maine down to Washington DC, experiences low precipitation as a rule, but temperatures can range from bitterly cold in winter to uncomfortably hot and humid in the summer. **Florida**'s temperatures are not dramatically high in summer, but humidity is a problem; in the winter, the state is warm and sunny enough to attract many visitors.

The **Great Plains** are alternately exposed to seasonal icy Arctic winds and humid tropical airflows from the Gulf of Mexico. Winters around the Great Lakes and Chicago can be abjectly cold, and it can freeze or even snow in winter as far south as Texas, though spring and autumn get progressively longer and milder further south through the Plains. **Tornadoes** (or "twisters") are a frequent local phenomenon, tending to cut a narrow swath of destruction in the wake of violent spring or summer thunderstorms.

In the **South**, summer is the wettest season, with high humidity, and the time when thunderstorms are most likely to strike. One or two **hurricanes** each year rage across Florida and/or the Gulf of Mexico states between August and October. The winter is mild for the most part and the two shoulder seasons usually see warm days and fresher nights.

Temperatures in the **Rockies** correlate closely with altitude, so nights can be cold even in high summer. Beyond the mountains in the south lie the extensive arid deserts of the **Southwest**. In cities such as Las Vegas and Phoenix, the mercury regularly soars above

OPPOSITE FROM TOP SURFING IN OAHU; THE STRIP, LAS VEGAS; THE EVERGLADES

100°F, though the atmosphere is not usually humid enough to be as enervating as that might sound and air conditioning is ubiquitous.

West of the Cascades, the **Pacific Northwest** is the only region where winter is the wettest season, and outside summer the climate is wet, mild and seldom hot. Further south, **California**'s weather more or less lives up to the popular idyllic image, though the climate is markedly hotter and drier in the south than in the north, where there's enough snow to make the mountains a major skiing destination from November to April. San Francisco and the northern coast is kept milder and colder than the inland region by its propensity to attract sea fog.

AVERAGE TEMPERATURE (°F) AND RAINFALL

To convert °F to °C, subtract 32 and multiply by 5/9

	Jan	Feb	Mar	Apr	May	Jun	Jul	Aug	Sep	Oct	Nov	Dec
ANCHORAGE												
Max/min temp	19/5	27/9	33/13	44/27	54/36	62/44	65/49	64/47	57/39	43/29	30/15	20/6
Days of rain	7	6	5	4	5	6	10	15	14	12	7	6
CHICAGO												
Max/min temp	32/18	34/20	43/29	55/40	65/50	75/60	81/66	79/65	73/58	61/47	47/34	36/23
Days of rain	11	10	12	11	12	11	9	9	9	9	10	11
HONOLULU												
Max/min temp	76/69	76/67	77/67	78/68	80/70	81/72	82/73	83/74	83/74	82/72	80/70	78/69
Days of rain	14	11	13	12	11	12	14	13	13	13	13	15
LAS VEGAS												
Max/min temp	60/29	67/34	72/39	81/45	89/52	99/61	103/68	102/66	95/57	84/47	71/36	61/30
Days of rain	2	2	2	1	1	1	2	2	1	1	1	2
LOS ANGELES												
Max/min temp	65/46	66/47	67/48	70/50	72/53	76/56	81/60	82/60	81/58	76/54	73/50	67/47
Days of rain	6	6	6	4	2	1	0	0	1	2	3	6
MIAMI												
Max/min temp	74/61	75/61	78/64	80/67	84/71	86/74	88/76	88/76	87/75	83/72	78/66	76/62
Days of rain	9	6	7	7	12	13	15	15	18	16	10	7
NEW ORLEANS												
Max/min temp	62/47	65/50	71/55	77/61	83/68	88/74	90/76	90/76	86/73	79/64	70/55	64/48
Days of rain	10	12	9	7	8	13	15	14	10	7	7	10
NEW YORK CITY												
Max/min temp	37/24	38/24	45/30	57/42	68/53	77/60	82/66	80/66	79/60	69/49	51/37	41/29
Days of rain	12	10	12	11	11	10	12	10	9	9	9	10
SAN FRANCISCO												
Max/min temp	55/45	59/47	61/48	62/49	63/51	66/52	65/53	65/53	69/55	68/54	63/51	57/47
Days of rain	11	11	10	6	4	2	0	0	2	4	7	10
SEATTLE												
Max/min temp	45/36	48/37	52/39	58/43	64/47	69/52	72/54	73/55	67/52	59/47	51/41	47/38
Days of rain	18	16	16	13	12	9	4	5	8	13	17	19
WASHINGTON DC												
Max/min temp	42/27	44/28	53/35	64/44	75/54	83/63	87/68	84/66	78/58	67/48	55/38	45/29
Days of rain	11	10	12	11	12	11	11	11	8	8	9	10

OPPOSITE FROM TOP *66 DINER*, ALBUQUERQUE; WHALE-WATCHING IN CALIFORNIA; BRIDGEPORT BREWING, PORTLAND, OREGON

Author picks

Our hard-travelling authors have visited every corner of this vast, magnificent country. Here are their personal highlights.

Most scenic highways US-1 blazes a mesmerizing path across the Florida Keys (p.493) while California's Hwy-1 takes in the best of the Californian coast (p.868) and Going-to-the-Sun Road (p.720) is an astonishing route through Glacier National Park. Blue Ridge Parkway (p.357) winds through the heart of rural Appalachia.

Best microbreweries Since the 1990s America has been experiencing a craft beer revolution, led by the likes of Lost Coast Brewery in Eureka, CA (p.914); Boulevard Brewing Company, Kansas City, MO (p.626); and iconic Brooklyn Brewery in NYC (p.95). The environmentally conscious Great Lakes Brewing, Cleveland, OH, makes a selection of great beers (p.248), while Full Sail Brewing Co, Hood River, OR (p.957) offers spectacular views. Oregon's oldest craft brewery is Bridgeport Brewing in Portland (p.955), an especially rich area for microbreweries.

Classic diners Few American icons are so beloved as the roadside diner, where burgers, apple pie and strong coffee are often served 24/7. The *South Street Diner* in Philadelphia is a buzzing 24hr spot with a huge menu and great daily specials (p.134). In Chicago, there's *Lou Mitchell's* (p.290), while LA boasts *Rae's Diner*, seen in many films (p.844), and *Pann's*, one of the all-time great Googie diners (p.844). *Waylan's Ku-Ku Burger* in Miami, OK, right on Rte-66, is a real classic in the heart of the Midwest (p.630), while *66 Diner* in Albuquerque, NM (p.749) is a classic Fifties throwback.

Top wildlife spots The USA is incredibly rich in wildlife, with national parks such as Yellowstone (p.697) and Grand Teton (p.703) especially good at preserving herds of elk and deer, moose and giant grizzlies, while reserves such as Boundary Waters in Minnesota (p.312) hold wolves and white-tailed deer. Visit the Florida Everglades for alligators and birdlife (p.527), or the Black Hills in South Dakota for buffalo (p.651). Whales can be spotted off the coast of Washington (p.934) or California (p.912), while gentle manatees bask along the coast of Florida (p.519).

Our author recommendations don't end here. We've flagged up our favourite places – a perfectly sited hotel, an atmospheric café, a special restaurant – throughout the guide, highlighted with the ★ symbol.

30
things not to miss

It's not possible to see everything that the USA has to offer in one trip – and we don't suggest you try. What follows is a selective and subjective taste of the country's highlights: unforgettable cities, spectacular drives, magnificent parks, spirited celebrations and stunning natural phenomena. All entries have a page reference to take you straight into the Guide, where you can find out more. Coloured numbers refer to chapters in the Guide.

1

1 **REDWOOD NATIONAL PARK, CA**

Page 914

Soak up the quiet majesty of the world's biggest trees, wide enough to drive through and soaring upwards like skyscrapers.

2 **GLACIER NATIONAL PARK, MT**

Page 719

Montana's most spectacular park holds not only fifty glaciers, but also two thousand lakes, a thousand miles of rivers and the exhilarating Going-to-the-Sun highway.

3 **SWEET AUBURN, ATLANTA, GA**

Page 415

This historic district holds the birthplace of Dr Martin Luther King, Jr and other spots honouring his legacy.

4 **THE NATIONAL MALL, WASHINGTON DC**

Page 319

From the Lincoln Memorial and the White House to the US Capitol by way of the towering Washington Monument – this grand parkway is an awesome showcase of American culture and history.

5 WALT DISNEY WORLD, ORLANDO, FL

Page 510

Though each of Orlando's theme parks strives to outdo the rest, Walt Disney World remains the one to beat.

6 FRESH LOBSTER, MAINE

Page 224

The picture-perfect towns and harbours of Maine are a rich source of crab and lobster, best eaten freshly boiled at a local fish shack.

7 SKIING IN THE ROCKY MOUNTAINS

Pages 678, 682 & 700

The Rockies make for some of the best skiing anywhere, with their glitzy resorts and atmospheric mining towns.

8 GOING TO A BASEBALL GAME

Pages 170 & 285

America's summer pastime is a treat to watch wherever you are, from Chicago's ivy-clad Wrigley Field to Boston's Fenway Park, the oldest ballpark in the country.

9 YELLOWSTONE NATIONAL PARK, WY

Page 697

The national park that started it all has it all, from steaming fluorescent hot springs and spouting geysers to sheer canyons and meadows filled with wild flowers and assorted beasts.

10 LAS VEGAS, NV

Page 795

From the Strip's erupting volcanoes, Eiffel Tower and Egyptian pyramid to its many casinos, Las Vegas will blow your mind as well as your wallet.

11

12

13

18

19

20

21

25 ROCK AND ROLL HALL OF FAME, OH
Page 246

Housed inside this striking glass pyramid is an unparalleled collection of rock music's finest mementoes, recordings, films and exhibitions.

26 VENICE BEACH, LA, CA
Page 836

Combines wacky LA culture with Muscle Beach, surfing, sand and good food, all a short drive from the glitz of Beverly Hills and Hollywood.

27 ANCESTRAL PUEBLOAN SITES
Page 742

Scattered through desert landscapes such as New Mexico's magnificent Bandelier National Monument, the dwellings of the Ancestral Puebloans afford glimpses of an ancient and mysterious world.

28 MIAMI'S ART DECO, FL
Page 482

This flamboyant city is deservedly famed for the colourful pastel architecture of its restored South Beach district.

29 MARDI GRAS, NEW ORLEANS, LA
Page 556

Crazy, colourful, debauched and historic – this is the carnival to end them all.

30 CRATER LAKE, OR
Page 964

Formed from the blown-out shell of volcanic Mount Mazama, this is one of the deepest and bluest lakes in the world, and offers some of the most mesmerizing scenery anywhere.

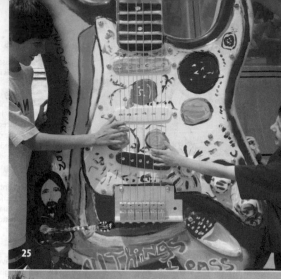

25

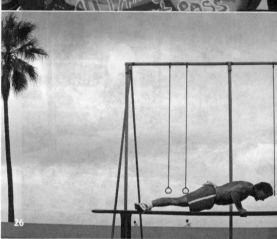

26

27

28

29

30

Itineraries

The following itineraries span the entire length of this incredibly diverse country, from the historic cities of the east, to the deserts of the Southwest and the jaw-dropping Rocky Mountains. Given the vast distances involved, you may not be able to cover everything, but even picking a few highlights will give you a deeper insight into America's natural and historic wonders.

CLASSIC COAST-TO-COAST

This three-week tour gives a taster of the USA's iconic landscapes and cities from the East to West coasts, travelling from New York to Los Angeles along sections of historic Rte-66.

❶ New York, NY America's biggest city is home to Times Square, the Statue of Liberty, the Met, Madison Square Garden, the Empire State, Harlem, Brooklyn Bridge and Jay-Z. **See p.56**

❷ Chicago, IL America's third city boasts some serious skyscrapers, top museums, live blues, the Cubs and the Bears, and those deep-dish pizzas. See p.276

❸ Springfield, IL Immerse yourself in all things Abraham Lincoln at the Illinois state capital, now a virtual shrine to the great American president. See p.294

❹ St Louis, MO Head south to this old city on the Mississippi, and take the train to the top of the Gateway Arch, a momentous feat of engineering. **See p.619**

❺ Route 66 Travelling southwest from St Louis to Oklahoma City be sure to take the Americana-rich remaining stretches of the most iconic US highway. **See p.630**

❻ Santa Fe, NM As you continue west on I-40 across New Mexico, detour to the state capital, a glorious ensemble of Spanish adobe and baroque. **See p.737**

❼ Grand Canyon I-40 cuts across Arizona via Flagstaff, gateway to one of the grandest, most mind-blowing natural wonders in the world. **See p.766**

❽ Las Vegas, NV Around four hours' drive west of the Grand Canyon lies America's playground, a confection of mega-casinos and pool parties in the middle of the desert. **See p.795**

❾ Los Angeles, CA You've made it: watch the sun set over the Pacific Ocean at Santa Monica Pier or wacky Venice Beach before soaking up the sights in Hollywood. **See p.822**

THE DEEP SOUTH AND FLORIDA

Hot, sultry, rich in history, culture and some of the greatest music made in America, the Deep South is perhaps the most beguiling part of the USA. Take two or three weeks to see the highlights, travelling by car or by bus, and end up on the beaches of south Florida.

❶ New Orleans, LA It's impossible not to fall in love with this gorgeous city, with its romantic French Quarter, indulgent food, jazz heritage and famously ebullient citizens. **See p.536**

❷ Mississippi Delta Soak up the blues heritage in Clarksdale, Mississippi, a five-hour drive north of New Orleans, before leaving the state via Tupelo, the home of Elvis. **See p.463 & p.466**

ABOVE LITTLE BIGHORN BATTLEFIELD NATIONAL MONUMENT, MT; BADLANDS NATIONAL PARK, SD

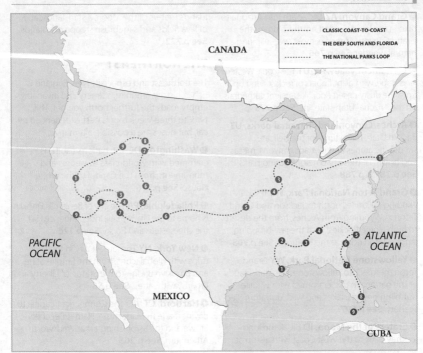

❸ Montgomery, AL Continue east to the fascinating capital of Alabama, laced with monuments to Martin Luther King, Civil Rights and Hank Williams. **See p.459**

❹ Atlanta, GA Make the short journey northeast to the buzzing capital of the South, birthplace of Martin Luther King and home to US icons CNN and Coca-Cola. **See p.413**

❺ Charleston, SC Over in South Carolina, this is perhaps the finest old town in all America, enriched by the culture of the nearby Sea Islands. **See p.405**

❻ Savannah, GA Cut back into Georgia to absorb the charms of Charleston's raffish but equally ravishing cousin, a city of moss-tangled squares and historic homes. **See p.424**

❼ St Augustine, FL Drop south into Florida to see the oldest town in America, founded by the Spanish in 1565. **See p.506**

❽ Miami, FL The Florida coast is studded with great beaches and attractions such as the Kennedy Space Center, but it's hard to top Miami and fabulous, Art Deco South Beach. **See p.482**

❾ Key West, FL End up travelling spectacular US-1 across the Keys to America's party-hard Caribbean outpost. **See p.496**

THE NATIONAL PARKS LOOP

Only when you traverse the American West will you begin to grasp just how big – and rich in natural beauty – this nation is. Come in summer to enjoy the sunshine and take three to four weeks to complete this trip, making a loop from San Francisco by car.

❶ Yosemite National Park, FL Just a 3hr 30min drive from San Francisco, you won't forget your first tantalizing glimpse of the rocky domes, peaks and waterfalls of Yosemite Valley. **See p.860**

❷ Death Valley, CA Leave the snowy Sierras for the lowest, hottest and driest area in North America, with vast dunes and flaming red rocks. **See p.851**

❸ Zion National Park, UT Cross over into Utah to explore this spectacular park, with a fifteen-mile canyon hemmed in by reddish walls of sandstone. **See p.780**

❹ Grand Canyon, AZ Dip south into Arizona to take in the less crowded northern rim of the Grand Canyon, America's most awe-inspiring natural wonder. **See p.766**

❺ Monument Valley, AZ/UT The iconic Western landscape, with giant fingers of rock soaring up from the dusty desert floor like ancient cathedrals on the Arizona–Utah state line. **See p.773**

❻ Arches/Canyonlands national parks, UT Back in Utah, make time for the delicate sandstone arches and myriads canyons, mesas and buttes of these two neighbouring parks. **See p.787 & p.788**

❼ Grand Teton National Park, WY It's a winding 500 miles north to Jackson and Grand Teton in Wyoming from Arches; from the desert to high alpine Rockies, with the jaw-dropping, jagged Teton ridge at the forefront. **See p.703**

❽ Yellowstone National Park, WY Grand Teton merges into Yellowstone, the granddaddy of the national parks, crammed with wildlife, bubbling geysers, lakes and wild, untrammelled scenery. **See p.697**

❾ Craters of the Moon, ID Break the long journey back to the West Coast with a stop at Idaho's Craters of the Moon, a stark landscape of lava fields and sagebrush steppe grasslands. **See p.722**

THE NORTHEAST

The northeast and especially New England is rich in history, stunning scenery and invariably empty roads the further north you get. This two- to three-week tour is best experienced by car, but buses are a possible alternative.

❶ Washington DC The nation's capital is crammed with world-class museums and monuments, from the Capitol to the White House. **See p.316**

❷ Philadelphia, PA The city of Benjamin Franklin is home to the Liberty Bell, Independence Hall, the cheesesteak and Rocky. **See p.126**

❸ New York, NY The largest city in the USA drips with global icons, from the Empire State and Brooklyn Bridge to the Statue of Liberty and Broadway theatres. **See p.56**

❹ Hartford, CT Visit the Connecticut capital to pay homage to Mark Twain, Harriet Beecher Stowe and the astonishing art at Wadsworth Atheneum. **See p.205**

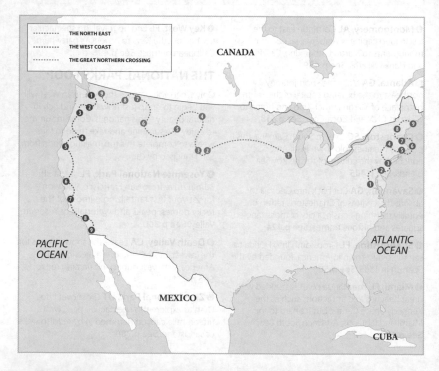

THE NORTH EAST
THE WEST COAST
THE GREAT NORTHERN CROSSING

CANADA

PACIFIC OCEAN

ATLANTIC OCEAN

MEXICO

CUBA

❺ **Nantucket, MA** Take the ferry to the "Little Gray Lady", a once great whaling community still redolent of the era of Moby-Dick. **See p.193**

❻ **Provincetown and Cape Cod, MA** Take a day or two to explore the historic towns, tranquil beaches and fish shacks of this hook-shaped peninsula. **See p.188**

❼ **Boston, MA** New England's lively capital drips with colonial history, but also boasts enticing restaurants, top art museums and some of the USA's best sports teams. **See p.161**

❽ **White Mountains, NH** Across into New Hampshire the mountains become bigger and wilder, perfect for hiking and biking, and culminating in mighty Mount Washington. **See p.221**

❾ **Acadia National Park, ME** Maine's coastline of wooded bays and small villages snakes northeast to this pristine section of rolling, mist-shrouded hills, fir forests and lobster pounds. **See p.234**

THE WEST COAST

The north–south journey along the Pacific starts in the rainy, forested northwest and ends at the southern deserts of California (with extensions to Tijuana and Vancouver at either end). You could travel by trains and buses as well as by car.

❶ **Seattle, WA** The home of grunge, Microsoft and Starbucks is now a booming city, with Pike Place Market, the stunning Chihuly Garden, huge salmon and gourmet coffee. **See p.923**

❷ **The Cascades, WA & OR** Travel inland through the Cascade Mountains, where the giant, snow-capped volcanic cones of Mount Rainier, Mount St Helens and Mount Hood loom over the horizon. **See p.945, p.946 & p.957**

❸ **Portland, OR** Rent a bike and cycle Oregon's hip capital, soaking up the art, organic food, microbrews and kooky shows. **See p.949**

❹ **Crater Lake, OR** Achingly beautiful national park, a vast, waterlogged crater surrounded by a spectacular snowy rim. **See p.964**

❺ **Redwood National Park, CA** Travel south along the Californian coastline, taking in these giant natural beauties. **See p.914**

❻ **San Francisco, CA** One of America's most appealing cities: historic, progressive, beautifully sited and home to the Golden Gate and Alcatraz. **See p.875**

❼ **Big Sur and Hwy-1, CA** The coastal road between San Francisco and Los Angeles is a scenic, surprisingly wild route of misty cliffs and untouched beaches. **See p.868**

❽ **Los Angeles, CA** Take your pick of iconic 'hoods: Hollywood, Beverly Hills, Malibu, Santa Monica and Venice Beach – or just hit Disneyland and Magic Mountain. **See p.822**

❾ **San Diego, CA** Visit the zoo, SeaWorld or simply hang out at the beach at California's laidback southern capital, the gateway to Baja. **See p.814**

THE GREAT NORTHERN CROSSING

Cross the country on the lesser travelled – but blissfully untouched – northern route, taking at least two weeks to drive between Chicago and Seattle.

❶ **Madison, WI** The capital of Wisconsin also happens to be the most attractive college town in the USA, just 2hr 30min drive northwest of Chicago. **See p.302**

❷ **Badlands National Park, SD** It's a long day of driving across the Great Plains to the Badlands, a truly desolate, magical place, especially at sunrise. **See p.650**

❸ **Black Hills, SD** Forested mountain plateau rising above the plains, home to Mount Rushmore and the equally monumental Crazy Horse Mountain. **See p.651**

❹ **Theodore Roosevelt National Park, ND** Drive into North Dakota to explore the wild, untouched and multicoloured badlands created by the Little Missouri. **See p.658**

❺ **Little Bighorn, MT** Cross into Montana to visit one of America's most poignant battlefields, where Custer's 7th Cavalry were trounced by Sitting Bull and Crazy Horse. **See p.709**

❻ **Butte, MT** This shabby old mining town in central Montana is a treasure trove of once grand architecture, old diners and even Cornish pasties. **See p.713**

❼ **Glacier National Park, MT** Northern Montana is dominated by this sensational preserve of glaciers, snowy peaks, alpine lakes and historic lodges. **See p.719**

❽ **Idaho Panhandle** I-90 cuts across this narrow section of Idaho, laced with inviting hiking and biking trails and home to the genuine Western town of Wallace. **See p.727**

❾ **Cascade Loop, WA** End up in Washington, touring the peaks and valleys of the mighty Cascade Mountains before arriving at Seattle and the Pacific Ocean. **See p.944**

KATZ'S DELI, NEW YORK CITY

Basics

Getting there

Anyone travelling to the USA from abroad should start by deciding which area to explore first; the country is so vast that it makes a huge difference which airport you fly into. Once you've chosen whether to hit the swamps of Florida, the frozen tundra of Alaska, the summer heat of the South or the splendour of the Rockies and Southwest, you can then buy a flight to the nearest hub city.

In general, ticket prices are highest from July to September, and around Easter, Thanksgiving and Christmas. Fares drop during the shoulder seasons – April to June, and October – and even more so in low season, from November to March (excluding Easter, Christmas and New Year). Prices depend more on when Americans want to head overseas than on the demand from foreign visitors. Flying at weekends usually costs significantly more; prices quoted below assume midweek travel and include taxes.

Flights from the UK and Ireland

More than twenty US cities are accessible by **nonstop** flights from the **UK**. At these gateway cities, you can connect with onward domestic flights. **Direct** services (which may land once or twice on the way, but are called direct if they keep the same flight number throughout their journey) fly from Britain to nearly every other major US city.

Nonstop flights to Los Angeles from London take eleven or twelve hours; the London to Miami flight takes eight hours; and flying time to New York is seven or so hours. Following winds ensure that return flights take an hour or two less. One-stop direct flights to destinations beyond the East Coast add time to the journey but can work out cheaper than nonstop flights.

Four airlines run nonstop scheduled services to the USA from **Ireland**. Flights depart from both Dublin and Shannon airports, and the journey times are very similar to those from London.

As for **fares**, Britain remains one of the best places in Europe to obtain flight bargains, though prices vary widely. In low or shoulder season, you should be able to find a return flight to East Coast destinations such as New York for around £490, or to California for around £580, while high-season rates can easily double. These days the fares available on the airlines' own websites are often just as good as those you'll find on more general travel websites.

With an **open-jaw** ticket, you can fly into one city and out of another, though if you're renting a car remember that there's usually a high drop-off fee for returning a rental car in a different state than where you picked it up (see p.34). An **air pass** can be a good idea if you want to see a lot of the country. These are available only to non-US residents, and must be bought before reaching the USA (see p.33).

Flights from Australia, New Zealand and South Africa

For passengers travelling **from Australasia** to the USA, the most expensive time to fly has traditionally been during the northern summer (mid-May to end Aug) and over the Christmas period (Dec to mid-Jan), with shoulder seasons covering March to mid-May and September, and the rest of the year counting as low season. Fares no longer vary as much across the year as they used to, however.

Instead, fares on the regular Air New Zealand, Qantas and United flights from eastern Australian cities to **Los Angeles**, the main US gateway airport, tend to start at around Aus$1175 in low season, or more like Aus$1900 in summer. Flying from Western Australia can add around Aus$400–500, while throughout the year, flying all the way through to New York tends to cost another Aus$200–250 extra.

From New Zealand, the cost of flying from Auckland or Christchurch to LA or San Francisco ranges from roughly NZ$1800–3200 across the year, or more like NZ$2200–3800 to New York.

From South Africa, transatlantic flights from Cape Town or Johannesburg are fairly pricey, costing around ZAR24,000–28,000 to New York or

A BETTER KIND OF TRAVEL

At Rough Guides we are passionately committed to travel. We believe it helps us understand the world we live in and the people we share it with – and of course tourism is vital to many developing economies. But the scale of modern tourism has also damaged some places irreparably, and climate change is accelerated by most forms of transport, especially flying. All Rough Guides' flights are carbon-offset, and every year we donate money to a variety of environmental charities.

PACKAGES AND TOURS

Although independent travel is usually cheaper, countless flight and accommodation **packages** allow you to bypass all the organizational hassles. A typical package from the UK might be a return flight plus mid-range Midtown hotel accommodation for three nights in New York City, starting at around £700 per person in low season and more like £950 at peak periods.

Fly-drive deals, which give cut-rate car rental when a traveller buys a transatlantic ticket from an airline or tour operator, are always cheaper than renting on the spot, and give great value if you intend to do a lot of driving. They're readily available through general online booking agents such as Expedia and Travelocity, as well as through specific airlines. Several of the operators listed here also book accommodation for **self-drive tours**.

A simple and exciting way to see a chunk of America's great outdoors is to take a specialist touring and **adventure package**, which includes transport, accommodation, food and a guide. Companies such as TrekAmerica carry small groups around on minibuses and use a combination of budget hotels and camping. Most concentrate on the West – ranging from Arizona to Alaska, and lasting from seven days to five weeks; cross-country treks and adventures that take in New York or Florida are also available. Typical rates for a week – excluding transatlantic flights – range from £620 in low season up to £930 in midsummer. Trips to Alaska cost a good bit more.

---

other East Coast cities and ZAR26,000–31,000 to LA or San Francisco, depending on the time of year.

Various add-on fares and air passes valid in the continental US are available with your main ticket, allowing you to fly to destinations across the States. These must be bought before you go.

AIRLINES

Aer Lingus ⓦ aerlingus.com
Air Canada ⓦ aircanada.com
Air New Zealand ⓦ airnewzealand.com
Air Pacific ⓦ airpacific.com
Alaska Airlines ⓦ alaskaair.com
American Airlines ⓦ aa.com
British Airways ⓦ ba.com
Continental Airlines ⓦ continental.com
Delta Airlines ⓦ delta.com
Frontier Airlines ⓦ frontierairlines.com
Hawaiian Airlines ⓦ hawaiianair.com
JAL (Japan Airlines) ⓦ jal.com
KLM ⓦ klm.com
Kuwait Airways ⓦ kuwait-airways.com
Qantas Airways ⓦ qantas.com.au
Singapore Airlines ⓦ singaporeair.com
Southwest ⓦ southwest.com
United Airlines ⓦ united.com
US Airways ⓦ usair.com
Virgin Atlantic ⓦ virgin-atlantic.com
WestJet ⓦ westjet.com

AGENTS AND OPERATORS

Adventure World Australia ⓦ adventureworld.com.au, New Zealand ⓦ adventureworld.co.nz
American Holidays Ireland ⓦ americanholidays.com
Bon Voyage UK ⓦ bon-voyage.co.uk

Creative Tours Australia ⓦ creativeholidays.com
Exodus UK ⓦ exodus.co.uk
Explore Worldwide UK ⓦ explore.co.uk
Funway Holidays UK ⓦ funwayholidays.co.uk
Jetsave UK ⓦ jetsave.com
North America Travel Service UK ⓦ northamericatravelservice .co.uk
North South Travel UK ⓦ northsouthtravel.co.uk
STA Travel UK ⓦ statravel.co.uk, Australia ⓦ statravel.com.au, New Zealand ⓦ statravel.co.nz, South Africa ⓦ statravel.co.za
Titan HiTours UK ⓦ titantravel.co.uk
Trailfinders UK & Ireland ⓦ trailfinders.com
travel.com.au Australia ⓦ travel.com.au
Travelsphere UK ⓦ travelsphere.co.uk
TrekAmerica UK ⓦ trekamerica.co.uk
Virgin Holidays UK ⓦ virginholidays.co.uk

Getting around

Distances in the USA are so great that it's essential to plan in advance how you'll get from place to place. Amtrak provides a skeletal but often scenic rail service, and there are usually good bus links between the major cities. Even in rural areas, with advance planning, you can usually reach the main points of interest without too much trouble by using local buses and charter services.

That said, travel between cities is almost always easier if you have a **car**. Many worthwhile and memorable US destinations are far from the cities: even if a bus or train can take you to the general vicinity of one of the great national parks, for

HISTORIC RAILROADS

While Amtrak has a monopoly on long-distance rail travel, a number of historic or **scenic railways**, some steam-powered or running along narrow-gauge mining tracks, bring back the glory days of train travel. Many are purely tourist attractions, doing a full circuit through beautiful countryside in two or three hours, though some can drop you off in otherwise hard-to-reach wilderness areas. Fares vary widely according to the length of your trip. We've covered the most appealing options in the relevant Guide chapters.

example, it would be of little use when it comes to enjoying the great outdoors.

By rail

Travelling on the national Amtrak network (☎800 872 7245, ⓦamtrak.com) is rarely the fastest way to get around, though if you have the time it can be a pleasant and relaxing experience. As you will note from our map (see p.32), the Amtrak system isn't comprehensive – East Coast states from Virginia northward are well covered with rail routes but some Western states are left out altogether. What's more, the cross-country routes tend to be served by one or at most two trains per day, so in large areas of the nation the only train of the day passes through at three or four in the morning. A number of small local train services connect stops on the Amtrak lines with towns and cities not on the main grid. Amtrak also runs the coordinated, but still limited, Thruway bus service that connects some cities that their trains don't reach

For any one specific journey, the train is usually more **expensive** than taking a Greyhound bus, or even a plane – the standard rail fare from New York to Los Angeles, for example, starts at around $220 one way with advance online booking – though special deals, especially in the off-peak seasons (Sept–May, excluding Christmas), can bring the cost of a coast-to-coast return trip down to around $220–300. Money-saving **passes** are also available (see box, p.33).

Even with a pass, you should always **reserve** as far in advance as possible; all passengers must have seats, and some trains, especially between major East Coast cities, are booked solid. Sleeping compartments start at around $400 per night,

including three full meals, in addition to your seat fare, for one or two people. However, even standard Amtrak quarters are surprisingly spacious compared to aeroplane seats, and there are additional dining cars and lounge cars (with full bars and sometimes glass-domed 360° viewing compartments). Finally, if you want to make your journey in the Northeast in a hurry, hop aboard the speedy Acela service, which can shave anywhere from thirty minutes to an hour off your trip, though tends to cost from $25 100 more than a fare on a standard Amtrak train.

By bus

If you're travelling on your own and plan on making a lot of stops, **buses** are by far the cheapest way to get around. The main long-distance operator, **Greyhound** (☎800 231 2222, ⓦgreyhound.com, international customers without toll-free access can also call ☎214 849 8100 from 5am–1am CST), links all major cities and many towns. Out in the country, buses are fairly scarce, sometimes appearing only once a day, if at all. However, along the main highways, buses run around the clock to a full timetable, stopping only for meal breaks (almost always fast-food chains) and driver changeovers.

To avoid possible hassle, travellers should take care to sit as near to the driver as possible, and to arrive during daylight hours – many bus stations are in dodgy areas. In many smaller places, the post office or a petrol station doubles as the bus stop and ticket office. Reservations can be made in

GREEN TORTOISE

One alternative to long-distance bus torture is the fun, countercultural **Green Tortoise**, whose buses, complete with foam cushions, bunks, fridges and rock music, mostly ply the West and the Northwest of the country, but can go as far as New Orleans, Washington DC and New York. Highlights include the California Cruiser (11 days; $505), the coast-to-coast USA Explorer (34 days; $2816), and the gung-ho Alaska Expedition (27 days; $2500); food and park admissions cost extra. There are more than thirty seductive options, each allowing plenty of stops for hiking, river-rafting, bathing in hot springs and the like.

Green Tortoise's main office is in San Francisco (☎415 956 7500 or ☎800 867 8647, ⓦgreentortoise.com).

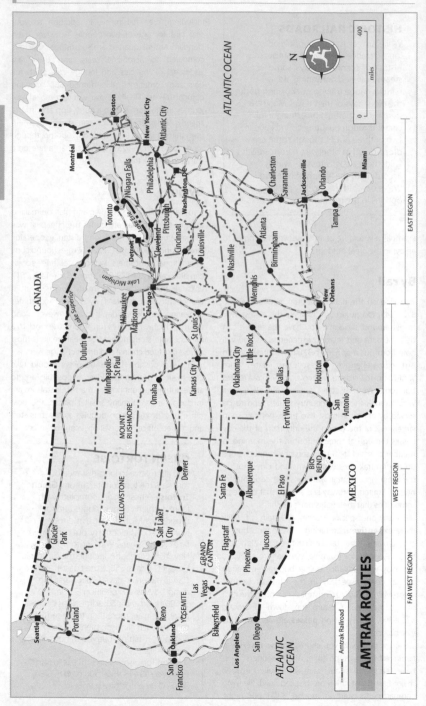

AMTRAK ROUTES

···· Amtrak Railroad

person at the station, online or on the toll-free number. Oddly they do not guarantee a seat, so it's wise to join the queue early – if a bus is full, you may have to wait for the next one, although Greyhound claims it will lay on an extra bus if more than ten people are left behind. **Fares** on shorter journeys average out at about 25¢ per mile, but for longer hauls there are plenty of savings available – check the website's discounts page.

Other operators include **Trailways** (☎800 776 7581, ⓦtrailways.com), whose regional divisions cover some parts of the country more comprehensively, **Megabus** (☎877 462 6342, ⓦus.megabus .com), whose low-cost service covers the Northeast and Midwest, Northeast operator **Peter Pan** (☎800 343 9999, ⓦpeterpanbus.com) and the alternative **Green Tortoise** (see box, p.31).

By plane

Despite the presence of good-value discount airlines – most notably Southwest and JetBlue – **air travel** is a much less appealing way of getting around the country than it used to be. With air fuel costs escalating even faster than petrol costs, and airlines cutting routes, demanding customers pay for routine services and jacking up prices across the board, the days of using jet travel as a spur to vacation adventuring are long gone. To get any kind of break on price, you'll have to reserve well ahead of time (at least three weeks), preferably not embark in the high season, and be firm enough in your plans to buy a "non-refundable" fare – which if changed can incur costs of $100 or more. Nonetheless, flying can still cost less than the train – though still more than

the bus. In those examples where flying can make sense for short local hops, we mention such options wherever appropriate throughout this Guide. Otherwise, phone the airlines or visit their websites to find out routes and schedules.

By car

For many, the concept of cruising down the highway, preferably in a convertible with the radio blasting, is one of the main reasons to set out on a tour of the USA. The romantic images of countless road movies are not far from the truth, though you don't have to embark on a wild spree of drinking, drugs and sex to enjoy **driving** across America. Apart from anything else, a car makes it possible to choose your own itinerary and to explore the astonishing wide-open landscapes that may well provide your most enduring memories of the country.

Driving in the cities, on the other hand, is not exactly fun, and can be hair-raising. Yet in larger places a car is by far the most convenient way to make your way around, especially as public transport tends to be spotty outside the major cities. Many urban areas, especially in the West, have grown up since cars were invented. As such, they sprawl for so many miles in all directions – Los Angeles and Houston are classic examples – that your hotel may be fifteen or twenty miles from the sights you came to see, or perhaps simply on the other side of a freeway that can't be crossed on foot.

Renting a car

To **rent a car**, you must have held your licence for at least one year. Drivers under 25 may encounter

---

PRE-TRIP PLANNING FOR OVERSEAS TRAVELLERS

AMTRAK PASSES

The **USA Rail Pass** (15-day/8 segments/$489; 30-day/12 segments/$669; 45-day/18 segments/$859) covers the entire Amtrak network for the designated period, though you are restricted to a set number of individual journeys. The **California Rail Pass** buys you seven days' travel in a 21-day period within that state for $159. Passes can be bought from the Amtrak website (ⓦamtrak.com).

AIR PASSES

The main American airlines offer **air passes** for visitors who plan to fly a lot within the USA. These must be bought in advance and are often sold with the proviso that you cross the Atlantic with the same airline or group of airlines (such as Star Alliance). Each deal will involve the purchase of a certain number of flights, air miles or coupons. Other plans entitle foreign travellers to discounts on regular US domestic fares, again with the proviso that you buy the ticket before you leave home. Check with the individual airlines to see what they offer and the overall range of prices. However you do it, flying within the USA is only a wise choice for travel in regions where fares are low anyway; flights within Florida, for example, are very expensive.

DRIVING FOR FOREIGNERS

Foreign nationals from English-speaking countries can drive in the USA using their **full domestic driving licences** (International Driving Permits are not always regarded as sufficient). Fly-drive deals are good value if you want to **rent** a car (see pp.33–34), though you can save up to fifty percent simply by booking in advance with a major firm. If you choose not to pay until you arrive, be sure you take a written confirmation of the price with you. Remember that it's safer not to drive right after a long transatlantic flight – and that most standard rental cars have **automatic transmissions**.

---

problems and have to pay higher than normal insurance premiums. Rental companies expect customers to have a credit card; if you don't, they may let you leave a cash deposit (at least $500), but don't count on it. All the major **rental companies** have outlets at the main airports but it can often be cheaper to rent from a city branch. Reservations are handled centrally, so the best way to shop around is either online, or by calling their national toll-free numbers. Potential variations are endless; certain cities and states are consistently cheaper than others, while individual travellers may be eligible for corporate, frequent-flier or AAA discounts. In low season you may find a tiny car (a "subcompact") for as little as $150 per week, but a typical budget rate would be more like $35–40 per day or around $220 per week including taxes. You can get some good deals from strictly local operators, though it can be risky as well. Make reading up on such inexpensive vendors part of your pre-trip planning.

Even between the major operators – who tend to charge $50–100 per week more than the local competition – there can be a big difference in the quality of cars. Industry leaders like Alamo, Hertz and Avis tend to have newer, lower-mileage cars and more reliable breakdown services. Always be sure to get **unlimited mileage** and remember that leaving the car in a different city to the one where you rented it can incur a drop-off charge of $200 or more.

HITCHHIKING

Hitchhiking in the United States is a **bad idea**, making you a potential victim both inside (you never know whom you're travelling with) and outside the car, as the odd fatality may occur from hitchers getting a little too close to the highway lanes. At a minimum, in the many states where the practice is illegal, you can expect a steep fine from the police and, on occasion, an overnight stay in the local jail.

Small print and insurance

When you rent a car, read the small print carefully for details on **Collision Damage Waiver** (CDW), sometimes called **Liability Damage Waiver** (LDW). This form of insurance specifically covers the car that you are driving yourself – you are in any case insured for damage to other vehicles. At $12–20 a day, it can add substantially to the total cost, but without it you're liable for every scratch to the car – even those that aren't your fault. Increasing numbers of states are requiring that this insurance be included in the weekly rental rate and are regulating the amounts charged to cut down on rental-car company profiteering. Some credit card companies offer automatic CDW coverage to customers using their card; contact your issuing company for details. Alternatively, European residents can cover themselves against such costs with a reasonably priced annual policy from Insurance4CarHire (Ⓦ insurance4carhire.com).

The **American Automobile Association**, or AAA (☎ 800 222 4357, Ⓦ aaa.com), provides free maps and assistance to its members and to members of affiliated associations overseas, such as the British AA and RAC. If you **break down** in a rented car, call one of these services if you have towing coverage, or the emergency number pinned to the dashboard.

CAR RENTAL AGENCIES

Alamo USA ☎ 800 462 5266, Ⓦ alamo.com
Avis USA ☎ 800 230 4898, Ⓦ avis.com
Budget USA ☎ 800 527 0700, Ⓦ budget.com
Dollar USA ☎ 800 800 3665, Ⓦ dollar.com
Enterprise USA ☎ 800 261 7331, Ⓦ enterprise.com
Hertz USA ☎ 800 654 3131, Ⓦ hertz.com
Holiday Autos USA ☎ 866 392 9288, Ⓦ holidayautos.com
National USA ☎ 800 227 7368, Ⓦ nationalcar.com
Thrifty USA & Canada ☎ 800 847 4389, Ⓦ thrifty.com

Cycling

Cycling is another realistic mode of transport. An increasing number of big cities have cycle lanes and local buses equipped to carry bikes (strapped to the outside), while in country areas, roads have wide shoulders and fewer passing motorists. Unless you plan to cycle a lot and take your own bike, however, it's not especially cheap. Bikes can be rented for $15–50 per day, or at discounted weekly rates, from outlets that are usually found close to beaches, university campuses and good cycling areas. Local visitor centres have details.

The national nonprofit **Adventure Cycling Association**, based in Missoula, Montana (☎406 721 1776 or ☎800 755 2453, ⓦadventurecycling .org), publishes maps of several lengthy routes, detailing campgrounds, motels, restaurants, bike shops and places of interest. Many individual states issue their own cycling guides; contact the state tourist offices (see p.53). Before setting out on a long-distance cycling trip, you'll need a good-quality, multispeed bike, panniers, tools and spares, maps, padded shorts and a helmet (legally required in many states and localities). Plan a route that avoids interstate highways (on which cycling is unpleasant and usually illegal) and sticks to well-maintained, paved rural roads. Of problems you'll encounter, the main one is traffic: RVs, huge eighteen-wheelers and logging trucks can create intense backdraughts capable of pulling you out into the middle of the road.

Backroads Bicycle Tours (☎800 462 2848, ⓦbackroads.com), and the HI-AYH hostelling group (see p.36) arrange multiday cycle tours, with camping or stays in country inns; where appropriate we've also mentioned local firms that offer this.

Greyhound, Amtrak and major airlines will carry passengers' bikes – dismantled and packed into a box – for a small fee.

Accommodation

The cost of accommodation is significant for any traveller exploring the USA, especially in the cities, but wherever you travel, you're almost certain to find a good-quality, reasonably priced motel or hotel. If you're prepared to pay a little extra, wonderful historic hotels and lodges can offer truly memorable experiences.

The prices we give in the Guide represent the cheapest double room in high season. Typical rates in motels and hotels start at $45 per night in rural areas, more like $80 in major cities, though discounts are available at slack times. Unsurprisingly, the sky's the limit for luxury hotels, where exclusive suites can easily run into four figures. Many hotels will set up a third single bed for around $15–25 extra, reducing costs for three people sharing. For lone travellers, on the other hand, a "single room" is usually a double at a slightly reduced rate at best. A dorm bed in a hostel usually costs $20–35 per night, but standards of cleanliness and security can be low, and for groups of two or more the saving compared to a motel is often minimal. In certain parts of the USA, **camping** makes a cheap – and exhilarating – alternative (see p.44). Alternative methods of finding a room online are through ⓦairbnb.com and the free hosting site ⓦcouchsurfing.org.

Wherever you stay, you'll be expected to pay in advance, at least for the first night and perhaps for further nights, too. Most hotels ask for a credit card imprint when you arrive, but some still accept cash or US dollar travellers' cheques. Reservations – essential in busy areas in summer – are held only until 6pm, unless you've said you'll be arriving late. Note that some cities – probably the ones you most want to visit – tack on a **hotel tax** that can raise the total tax for accommodation to as much as fifteen percent.

Note that as well as the local numbers we give in the Guide, many hotels have **freephone** numbers (found on their websites), which you can use within the USA.

Hotels and motels

The term **"hotels"** refers to most accommodation in the Guide. **Motels**, or "motor hotels", tend to be found beside the main roads away from city centres, and are thus much more accessible to drivers. Budget hotels or motels can be pretty basic, but in general standards of comfort are uniform – each room comes with a double bed (often two), a TV, phone and usually a portable coffeemaker, plus an attached bathroom. You don't get a much better deal by paying, say, $80 instead of $55. Above $80 or so, the room and its fittings simply get bigger and include more amenities, and there may be a swimming pool and added amenities such as irons and ironing boards, or premium cable TV (HBO, Showtime, etc). Most hotels and motels now offer wi-fi, albeit sometimes in the lobby only.

The least expensive properties tend to be family-run, independent "mom 'n' pop" motels, but these are rarer nowadays, in the big urban areas at least. When you're driving along the main interstates there's a lot to be said for paying a few dollars more to stay in **motels** belonging to the national chains. These range from the ever-reliable and cheap *Super 8* and *Motel 6* (from $45) through to the mid-range *Days Inn* and *La Quinta* (from $60) up to the more commodious *Holiday Inn Express* and *Marriott* (from $80).

During off-peak periods, many motels and hotels struggle to fill their rooms, so it's worth bargaining to get a few dollars off the asking price. Staying in the same place for more than one night may bring further reductions. Also, look for discount coupons, especially in the free magazines distributed by local visitor centres and welcome centres near the borders between states. These can offer amazing value – but read the small print first. **Online rates** are also usually cheaper, sometimes considerably so.

Few budget hotels or motels bother to compete with the ubiquitous diners by offering full breakfasts, although most will provide free self-service coffee, pastries and if you are lucky, fruit or cereal, collectively referred to as "continental breakfast".

B&Bs

Staying in a **B&B** is a popular, sometimes luxurious, alternative to conventional hotels. Some B&Bs consist of no more than a couple of furnished rooms in someone's home, and even the larger establishments tend to have fewer than ten rooms, sometimes without TV or phone, but often laden with potpourri, chintzy cushions and an assertively precious Victorian atmosphere. If this cosy, twee setting appeals to you, there's a range of choices throughout the country, but keep a few things in mind. For one, you may not be an anonymous guest as you would in a chain hotel, but may be expected to chat with the host and other guests, especially during breakfast. Also, some B&Bs enforce curfews, not allowing or appreciating their guests to stumble in long after midnight after a heady night of drunken partying. The only way to know the policy for certain is to check each B&B's policy online – there's often a lengthy list of do's and don'ts.

The **price** you pay for a B&B – which varies from around $80 to $275 for a double room – always includes breakfast (sometimes a buffet on a sideboard, but more often a full-blown cooked meal). The crucial determining factor is whether each room has an en-suite bathroom; most B&Bs provide private bath facilities, although that can damage the authenticity of a fine old house. At the top end of the spectrum, the distinction between a "boutique hotel" and a "bed-and-breakfast inn" may amount to no more than that the B&B is owned by a private individual rather than a chain.

In many areas, B&Bs have united to form central booking agencies, making it much easier to find a room at short notice; we've given contact information for these where appropriate.

Historic hotels and lodges

Throughout the country, but especially out West, many towns still hold **historic hotels**, whether dating from the arrival of the railroads or from the heyday of Route 66 in the 1940s and 1950s. So long as you accept that not all will have up-to-date facilities to match their period charm, these can make wonderfully ambient places to spend a night or two. Those that are exceptionally well preserved or restored may charge $200 or more per room, but a more typical rate for a not overly luxurious but atmospheric, antique-furnished room would be more like $100–150.

In addition, several **national parks** feature long-established and architecturally distinguished hotels, traditionally known as **lodges**, that can be real bargains thanks to their federally controlled rates. The only drawback is that all rooms tend to be reserved far in advance. Among the best are *El Tovar* and *Grand Canyon Lodge* on the South and North rims, respectively, of the Grand Canyon; the *Old Faithful Inn* in Yellowstone; and *Glacier Park Lodge* in Glacier.

Hostels

Hostel-type accommodation is not as plentiful in the USA as it is in Europe, but provision for backpackers and low-budget travellers does exist. Unless you're travelling alone, most **hostels** cost about the same as motels; stay in them only if you prefer their youthful ambience, energy and sociability. Many are not accessible on public transport, or convenient for sightseeing in the towns and cities, let alone in rural areas.

These days, most hostels are independent, with no affiliation to the HI-AYH (Hostelling International-American Youth Hostels; ☎240 650 2100, ⓦhiusa .org) network. Many are no more than converted motels, where the "dorms" consist of a couple of sets of bunk beds in a musty room, which is also let out as a private unit on demand. Most expect guests to bring sheets or sleeping bags. Rates range from $20 to about $35 for a dorm bed, and from $40–60 for a double room, with prices in the major cities at the higher end. Those few hostels that do belong to HI-AYH tend to impose curfews and limit daytime access hours, and segregate dormitories by sex.

Food and drink

The USA is not all fast food. Every state offers its own specialities, and regional cuisines are distinctive and delicious. In addition, international food turns up regularly – not only in the big cities, but also in more unexpected places. Many farming and ranching regions – Nevada and central California in particular – have a number of Basque restaurants; Portuguese restaurants, dating from whaling days, line the New England coast; and old-fashioned Welsh pasties can be found in the mining towns of Montana.

In the big cities, you can pretty much eat whatever you want, whenever you want, thanks to the ubiquity of restaurants, 24-hour diners, and bars and street carts selling food well into the night. Also, along all the highways and on virtually every town's main street, **restaurants**, fast-food joints and cafés try to outdo one another with bargains and special offers. Whatever you eat and wherever you eat, service is usually prompt, friendly and attentive – thanks in large part to the institution of **tipping**. Waiters depend on tips for the bulk of their earnings; fifteen to twenty percent is the standard rate, with anything less sure to be seen as an insult.

Regional cuisines

Many regions have developed their own cuisines, combining available ingredients with dishes and techniques of local ethnic groups. It's perfectly possible to create a fabulous US road-trip itinerary by tracking the nation's **regional cuisines** – much of it dished up in humble roadside restaurants packed full of locals. Broadly, **steaks** and other cuts of beef are prominent in the Midwest, the Rockies, the South and Texas, while **fish** and seafood dominate the menus in Florida, Louisiana, along the "low country" coast of the Carolinas and Georgia, around Chesapeake Bay in Maryland, and in the Pacific Northwest. **Shellfish**, such as the highly rated Dungeness crab and the Chesapeake's unique soft-shell crab, highly spiced and eaten whole, is the dish of choice on the East Coast; Maine lobsters and steamers (clams), eaten whole or mixed up in a chowder, are reason alone to visit New England. Although the Hawaiian islanders consume more than half the **Spam** eaten in the nation, they also dish up delicious fresh fish and sushi as a matter of course, with tasty local varieties including *mahi-mahi* (dorado) and *ono* (which

---

> ## VEGETARIAN EATING
>
> In the big US cities at least, being a **vegetarian** – or even a vegan – presents few problems. However, don't be too surprised in rural areas if you find yourself restricted to a diet of eggs, grilled-cheese sandwiches and limp salads. In the South, most soul food cafés offer great-value vegetable plates (four different veggies, including potatoes), but many dishes will be cooked with pork fat, so ask before tucking in. Similarly, baked beans nationwide, and the nutritious-sounding red beans and rice dished up in Louisiana, usually contain bits of diced pork.

---

translates as "delicious"). Even in the carnivorous Deep South, catfish provides a delicious alternative, slathered in butter and "blackened" with spices.

Cajun food, country French-inspired cooking that originated in the bayous of Louisiana as a way to finish up leftovers, uses a lot of pork – chitlins (pork intestines), and the spicy sausages known as boudin and chaurice abound. Sausages are also prepared with seafood like crawfish, or even alligator. **Creole** cuisine, its urban cousin, found mainly in New Orleans, is the product of a number of cultures: spicy, fragrant jambalayas, po-boys and gumbos are cooked as often in local homes as they are in restaurants. The distinction between Cajun and Creole cooking is often misunderstood (see p 552)

Southern cooking, or **soul food**, is delicious and very fattening – everything from grits to collard greens, from crispy fried chicken to teeth-rotting pralines. **BBQ** is also very popular in the South, especially in Tennessee and in particular in Memphis, where every neighbourhood has its own classic 'cue hut, offering anything from dry-rub ribs to sweetly smoky BBQ spaghetti (generally, the more ramshackle the restaurant, the better the BBQ). Other BBQ centres outside the South include Kansas City and Chicago. In the Southwest, indigenous **Native American** communities continue to cook their traditional food; you will see Navajo frybread everywhere, a kind of fried taco dished up with minced beef.

At the other end of the spectrum, in a region where butter is despised and raw food diets abound, **California cuisine** is geared toward health and aesthetics. It grew out of French nouvelle cuisine and was pioneered in the 1970s, utilizing a wide mix of fresh, local, seasonal ingredients. Portions are small but beautifully presented, with accompanying high prices: expect to pay $50 a head (or much more) for a full dinner with wine. **New American cuisine** applies the same principles to different regional food, generally presenting healthier versions of local favourites.

Finally, there are also regional variations on **American staples**. You can get plain old burgers and hot dogs anywhere, but for a truly American experience, grab a piping-hot **Philly cheesesteak** sandwich, gooey with cheese and thin-sliced beef from a diner in eastern Pennsylvania, or one of New York's signature **Coney Island hot dogs** – or the LA version of the **frankfurter**, rolled in a tortilla and stuffed with cheese and chilli. Almost every eastern state has at least one spot claiming to have invented the **hamburger**, and regardless of where you go, you can find a good range of authentic diners where the buns are fresh, the patties are large, handcrafted and tasty, and the dressings and condiments are inspired.

Other cuisines

In the cities, in particular, where centuries of settlement have created distinctive local neighbourhoods, each community offers its own take on the cuisine of its homeland. San Francisco has its Chinatown, New York its Jewish delis, Boston its Italian restaurants, Miami its Cuban coffeeshops. **Mexican food** is so common it might as well be an indigenous cuisine, especially in border territories of southern California, Texas and the Southwest. The food is different from that found south of the border, focusing more on frying and on a standard set of staples. The essentials, however, are the same: lots of rice and black or pinto beans, often served refried (boiled, mashed and fried), with variations on the tortilla, a thin corn or flour pancake that can be wrapped around fillings and eaten by hand (a burrito); folded and filled (a taco); rolled, filled and baked in sauce (an enchilada); or fried flat and topped with a stack of filling (a tostada).

Italian food is widely available, too; the top-shelf restaurants in major cities tend to focus on the northern end of the boot, while the tomato-heavy, gut-busting portions associated with southern Italian cooking are usually confined to lower-end, chequered-tablecloth diners with massive portions and pictures of Frank and Dino on the walls. Pizza restaurants occupy a similar range from high-end gourmet places to cheap and tasty dives – New Yorkers and Chicagoans can argue for days over which of their respective cities makes the best kind, either Gotham's shingle-flat "slices" or the Windy City's overstuffed wedges that actually resemble slices of meat pie.

When it comes to **Asian** eating, Indian cuisine is usually better in the cities, though there are increasing exceptions as the resident population grows. When eaten in the Chinatown neighbourhoods of major cities Chinese cooking will be top-notch, and often inexpensive – beware, though, of the dismal-tasting "chop suey" and "chow mein" joints in the suburbs and small towns. Japanese, once the preserve of the coasts and sophisticated cities, has become widely popular, with sushi restaurants in all price ranges and chain teriyaki joints out on the freeways. Thai and Vietnamese restaurants, meanwhile, provide some of the best and cheapest ethnic food available, sometimes in diners mixing the two, and occasionally in the form of "fusion" cooking with other Asian cuisines (or "pan-Asian", as it's widely known).

Drink

New York, Baltimore, Chicago, New Orleans and San Francisco are the consummate **boozing towns** – filled with tales of famous, plastered authors indulging in famously bad behaviour – but almost anywhere you shouldn't have to search very hard for a comfortable place to drink. You need to be 21 years old to buy and consume alcohol in the USA, and it's likely you'll be asked for ID if you look under 30.

"Blue laws" – archaic statutes that restrict when, where and under what conditions alcohol can be purchased – are held by many states, and prohibit the sale of alcohol on Sundays; on the extreme end of the scale, some counties (known as "**dry**") don't allow any alcohol, ever. The famous whiskey and bourbon distilleries of Tennessee and Kentucky, including Jack Daniel's (see p.452), can be visited – though maddeningly, several are in dry counties, so they don't offer samples. A few states – Vermont, Oklahoma and Utah (which, being predominantly Mormon, has the most byzantine rules) – restrict the alcohol content in beer to just 3.2 percent, almost half the usual strength. Rest assured, though, that in a few of the more liberal parts of the country (New York City, for one), alcohol can be bought and drunk any time between 6am and 4am, seven days a week, while in the cities of New Orleans and Savannah you are even permitted to drink alcohol on the streets.

Note that if a bar is advertising a happy hour on "**rail drinks**" or "well drinks" that these are cocktails made from the liquors and mixers the bar has to hand (as opposed to top-shelf, higher-quality brands).

Beer

The most popular American **beers** may be the fizzy, insipid lagers from national brands, but there is no lack of alternatives. The craze for microbreweries started in northern California several decades ago, and even today Anchor Steam – once at the vanguard – is still an excellent choice for sampling. The West Coast continues to be, to a large extent, the centre of the microbrewing movement, and even the smaller towns have their own share of decent handcrafted beers. Portland, Oregon, abounds in breweries, with enthusiasts from around the world making the trip to sample draughts. Los Angeles, San Diego, Seattle, the Bay Area, Denver and other western cities rank up there, too, and you can even find excellent brews in tiny spots such as Whitefish, Montana, where the beers of Great Northern Brewing are well worth seeking out, or Asheville, North Carolina, where the number of excellent craft breweries grows each year.

On the East Coast look for Boston-based Samuel Adams and its mix of mainstream and alternative brews. Check out, the top-notch offerings of Pennsylvania's Victory Brewing too, or stop in at Washington DC's great beer-tasting spot, the Bier Baron, to sample a broad array of the country's finest potables – some eight hundred different kinds. Elsewhere, the Texas brand Lone Star has its dedicated followers, Indiana's best beverages come from Three Floyds Brewing and Pete's Wicked Ales in Minnesota can be found throughout the USA. Indeed, microbreweries and brewpubs can now be found in virtually every sizeable US city and college town. Almost all serve a wide range of good-value, hearty food to help soak up the drink. For more on craft beers, see Ⓦ craftbeer.com.

Wine

California and, to a lesser extent, Oregon, Washington, and a few other states, are famous for their **wines**. In California, it's the Napa and Sonoma valleys that boast the finest grapes, and beefy reds such as Merlot, Pinot Noir and Cabernet Sauvignon as well as crisp or buttery whites like Chardonnay and Sauvignon Blanc all do very well. Many tourists take "wine-tasting" jags in the California vineyards, where you can sip (or slurp) at sites ranging from down-home country farms with tractors and hayrides to upper-crust estates thick with modern art and yuppies in designer wear. Elsewhere, Oregon's Willamette Valley and other areas in the state are known for excellent vino, especially pinot noir, while Washington state has its prime vineyards in places like the Yakima Valley, Columbia River

Gorge and the Walla Walla area, among others. Beyond this, a broad variety of states from Arizona to Virginia have established wineries, typically of varying quality, though there are always a few standouts in each state that may merit a taste while you're on your journey. You'll find details of tours and tastings throughout the Guide.

Festivals

In addition to the main public holidays – on July 4, Independence Day, the entire country takes time out to picnic, drink, salute the flag, and watch or participate in fireworks displays, marches, beauty pageants, eating contests and more, to commemorate the signing of the Declaration of Independence in 1776 – there is a diverse multitude of engaging local events in the USA: arts-and-crafts shows, county fairs, ethnic celebrations, music festivals, rodeos, sandcastle-building competitions, chilli cook-offs and countless others.

Certain festivities, such as Mardi Gras in New Orleans, are well worth planning your holiday around but obviously other people will have the same idea, so visiting during these times requires an extra amount of advance effort, not to mention money. **Halloween** (Oct 31) is also immensely popular. No longer just the domain of masked kids running around the streets banging on doors and demanding "trick or treat", in some bigger cities Halloween has evolved into a massive celebration. In LA's West Hollywood, New York's Greenwich Village, New Orleans's French Quarter and San Francisco's Castro district, for example, the night is marked by colourful parades, mass cross-dressing, huge block parties and wee-hours partying. **Thanksgiving Day**, on the fourth Thursday in November, is more sedate. Relatives return to the nest to share a meal (traditionally, roast turkey and stuffing, cranberry sauce, and all manner of delicious pies) and give thanks for family and friends. Ostensibly, the holiday recalls the first harvest of the Pilgrims in Massachusetts, though Thanksgiving was a national holiday before anyone thought to make that connection.

Annual festivals and events

For further details of the festivals and events listed overleaf, including more precise dates, see the relevant page of the Guide, or access their websites. The state tourist boards (see p.53) can provide more complete calendars for each area.

JANUARY

Cowboy Poetry Gathering Elko, NV Ⓦ westernfolklife.org. See p.806.
Sundance Film Festival Park City, UT Ⓦ sundance.org/festival.
Winter Carnival St Paul, MN Ⓦ winter-carnival.com. See p.308.

FEBRUARY

Daytona 500 Daytona Beach, FL Ⓦ daytonainternationalspeedway .com. See p.505.
Groundhog Day Punxsutawney, PA Ⓦ groundhog.org.
Mardi Gras New Orleans, LA (the six weeks before Lent) Ⓦ mardigrasneworleans.com. See p.556.

MARCH

Academy Awards (the "Oscars") Los Angeles, CA Ⓦ oscars.org. See p.827.
Ice Alaska Fairbanks, AK Ⓦ icealaska.com. See p.994.
St Joseph's Day and the Mardi Gras Indians' "Super Sunday" New Orleans, LA Ⓦ mardigrasindians.com. See p.557.
South by Southwest Music Festival Austin, TX Ⓦ sxsw.com. See p.583.
Ultra Music Festival Miami, FL Ⓦ ultramusicfestival.com. See p.486.
World Championship Crawfish Étouffée Cook-off Eunice, LA Ⓦ eunice-la.com. See p.560.

APRIL

Arkansas Folk Festival Mountain View, AR Ⓦ arkansas.com/events. See p.474.
Coachella Music & Arts Festival Coachella, CA Ⓦ coachella.com. See p.849.
Festival International de Louisiane Lafayette, LA Ⓦ festivalinternational.com. See p.560.
Fiesta San Antonio San Antonio, TX Ⓦ fiesta-sa.org. See p.596.
French Quarter Festival New Orleans, LA Ⓦ fqfi.org. See p.557.
Gathering of Nations Pow Wow Albuquerque, NM Ⓦ gatheringofnations.com.
Jazz and Heritage Festival (Jazz Fest) New Orleans, LA (into May) Ⓦ nojazzfest.com. See p.557.

MAY

Crawfish Festival Breaux Bridge, LA Ⓦ bbcrawfest.com. See p.560.
Folk Festival Kerrville, TX (into June) Ⓦ kerrvillefolkfestival.com.
Indianapolis 500 Indianapolis, IN Ⓦ indy500.com. See p.273.
Kentucky Derby Louisville, KY Ⓦ kentuckyderby.com. See p.435.
Leaf Festival (also Oct) Black Mountain, NC Ⓦ theleaf.com. See p.403.
Memphis in May International Festival Memphis, TN Ⓦ memphisinmay.org. See p.441.
Merrie Monarch Hilo, HI Ⓦ merriemonarch.com.

Spoleto Festival Charleston, SC (into June) Ⓦ spoletousa.org.
Tejano Conjunto Festival San Antonio, TX Ⓦ guadalupe culturalarts.org.

JUNE

Bluegrass Festival Telluride, CO Ⓦ bluegrass.com. See p.690.
CMA Music Festival Nashville, TN Ⓦ cmafest.com. See p.450.
Little Bighorn Days Hardin, MT Ⓦ custerslaststand.org.
Texas Folklife Festival San Antonio, TX Ⓦ texasfolklifefestival.org.

JULY

Cheyenne Frontier Days Cheyenne, WY Ⓦ cfdrodeo.com. See p.692.
Essence Music Festival New Orleans, LA Ⓦ essencemusicfestival .com.
Hopi Festival of Arts and Culture Flagstaff, AZ Ⓦ musnaz.org.
National Basque Festival Elko, NV Ⓦ elkobasque.com. See p.805.
National Cherry Festival Traverse City, MI Ⓦ visit.cherryfestival .org. See p.267.
Newport Folk Festival Newport, RI Ⓦ newportfolkfest.net. See p.202.
World Eskimo-Indian Olympics Fairbanks, AK Ⓦ weio.org. See p.994.

AUGUST

Augusta Festival of Appalachian Culture Elkins, WV Ⓦ augusta heritage.com.
Burning Man Black Rock City, NV (into Sept) Ⓦ burningman.com. See p.805.
Elvis Week (Anniversary of Elvis's death) Memphis, TN Ⓦ elvis.com. See p.445.
Indian Market Santa Fe, NM Ⓦ swaia.org. See p.737.
Inter-Tribal Indian Ceremonial Gallup, NM Ⓦ theceremonial.com. See p.751.
Iowa State Fair Des Moines, IA Ⓦ iowastatefair.com.
Maine Lobster Festival Rockland, ME Ⓦ mainelobsterfestival .com. See p.231.
Mountain Dance and Folk Festival Asheville, NC Ⓦ folkheritage .org.
Newport Jazz Festival Newport, RI Ⓦ newportjazzfest.net. See p.202.
Satchmo SummerFest New Orleans, LA Ⓦ fqfi.org.
Southwest Louisiana Zydeco Festival Opelousas, LA Ⓦ zydeco .org. See p.560.

SEPTEMBER

Bluegrass and Chili Festival Claremore, OK Ⓦ claremore.org.
Buffalo Roundup Custer State Park, SD Ⓦ southdakota.com.
Bumbershoot Seattle, WS Ⓦ bumbershoot.org. See p.932.
Detroit International Jazz Festival Detroit, MI Ⓦ detroit jazzfest.com. See p.261.
Festa di San Gennaro New York, NY Ⓦ sangennaro.org.
Fiestas de Santa Fe Santa Fe, NM Ⓦ santafefiesta.org. See p.737.
International Balloon Fiesta Albuquerque, NM Ⓦ balloon fiesta.com.

Mississippi Delta Blues & Heritage Festival Greenville,
MS Ⓦ deltablues.org. See p.464.

Moja Arts Festival Charleston, SC (into Oct) Ⓦ mojafestival.com.

Monterey Jazz Festival Monterey, CA Ⓦ montereyjazzfestival.org.

Panhandle South Plains Fair Lubbock, TX Ⓦ southplainsfair.com.

Pendleton Round-Up Pendleton, OR Ⓦ pendletonroundup.com.
See p.966.

Southern Decadence New Orleans, LA Ⓦ southerndecadence.net.
See p.557.

OCTOBER

Arkansas Blues and Heritage Festival Helena, AR Ⓦ bluesand
heritagefest.com.

Art & Pumpkin Festival Half Moon Bay, CA Ⓦ miramarevents
.com/pumpkinfest/.

Festivals Acadiens et Créoles Lafayette, LA Ⓦ festivalsacadiens
.com. See p.560.

Great American Beer Festival Denver, CO Ⓦ greatamericanbeer
festival.com.

Helldorado Days Tombstone, AZ Ⓦ helldoradodays.com.
See p.759.

NOVEMBER

Ozark Folk Festival Eureka Springs, AR Ⓦ ozarkfolkfestival.com.
See p.475.

Voodoo Experience New Orleans, LA Ⓦ worshipthemusic.com.
See p.557.

DECEMBER

Art Basel Miami, FL Ⓦ artbasel.com/Miami-Beach. See p.488.

The outdoors

Coated by dense forests, cut by deep canyons and capped by great mountains, the USA is blessed with fabulous backcountry and wilderness areas. Even the heavily populated East Coast has its share of open space, notably along the Appalachian Trail, which winds from Mount Katahdin in Maine to the southern Appalachians in Georgia – some two thousand miles of untrammelled woodland. To experience the full breath-taking sweep of America's wide-open stretches, however, head west: to the Rockies, the red-rock deserts of the South-west or right across the continent to the amazing wild spaces of the West Coast. On the downside, be warned that in many coastal areas, the shoreline can be disappointingly hard to access, with a high proportion under private ownership.

National parks and monuments

The **National Park Service** administers both national parks and national monuments. Its rangers do a superb job of providing information and advice to visitors, maintaining trails and organizing such activities as free guided hikes and campfire talks.

In principle, a **national park** preserves an area of outstanding natural beauty, encompassing a wide range of terrain and prime examples of particular landforms and wildlife. Thus Yellowstone has boiling geysers and herds of elk and bison, while Yosemite offers towering granite walls and cascading water falls. A **national monument** is usually much smaller, focusing perhaps on just one archeological site or geological phenomenon, such as Devil's Tower in Wyoming. Altogether, the national park system comprises around four hundred units, including national seashores, lakeshores, battle-fields and other historic sites.

While national parks tend to be perfect places to **hike** – almost all have extensive trail networks – all are far too large to tour entirely on foot (Yellow-stone, for example, is bigger than Delaware and Rhode Island combined). Even in those rare cases where you can use public transport to reach a park, you'll almost certainly need some sort of vehicle to explore it once you're there. The Alaska parks are mostly howling wilderness, with virtually no roads or facilities for tourists – you're on your own.

Most parks and monuments charge **admission fees**, ranging from $5 to $25, which cover a vehicle and all its occupants for up to a week. For anyone on a touring vacation, it may well make more sense to buy the **Inter-agency Annual Pass**, also known as the "America the Beautiful Pass". Sold for $80 at all federal parks and monuments, or online at Ⓦ store.usgs.gov/pass, this grants unrestricted access for a year to the bearer, and any accompanying passen-gers in the same vehicle, to all national parks and monuments, as well as sites managed by such agencies as the US Fish and Wildlife Service, the Forest Service and the BLM (see p.44). It does not, however, cover or reduce additional fees like charges for camping in official park campgrounds, or permits for backcountry hiking or rafting.

> The Park Service website, Ⓦ **nps.gov**, details the main attractions of the national parks, plus opening hours, the best times to visit, admission fees, hiking trails and visitor facilities.

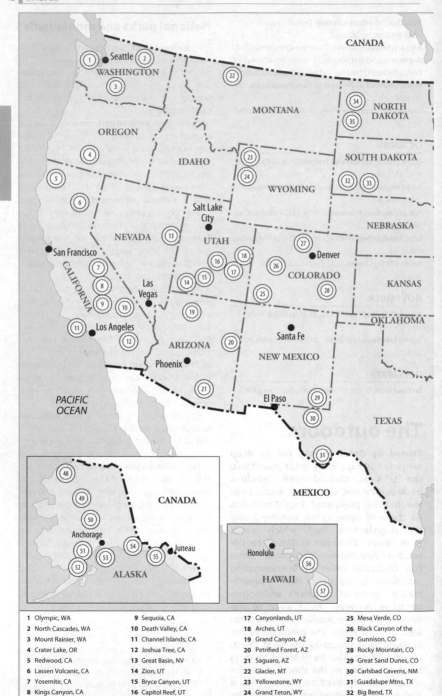

1 Olympic, WA	**9** Sequoia, CA	**17** Canyonlands, UT	**25** Mesa Verde, CO
2 North Cascades, WA	**10** Death Valley, CA	**18** Arches, UT	**26** Black Canyon of the
3 Mount Rainier, WA	**11** Channel Islands, CA	**19** Grand Canyon, AZ	**27** Gunnison, CO
4 Crater Lake, OR	**12** Joshua Tree, CA	**20** Petrified Forest, AZ	**28** Rocky Mountain, CO
5 Redwood, CA	**13** Great Basin, NV	**21** Saguaro, AZ	**29** Great Sand Dunes, CO
6 Lassen Volcanic, CA	**14** Zion, UT	**22** Glacier, MT	**30** Carlsbad Caverns, NM
7 Yosemite, CA	**15** Bryce Canyon, UT	**23** Yellowstone, WY	**31** Guadalupe Mtns, TX
8 Kings Canyon, CA	**16** Capitol Reef, UT	**24** Grand Teton, WY	**32** Big Bend, TX

US NATIONAL PARKS

33 Badlands, SD	**41** Great Smoky Mtns, TN	**49** Gates of the Arctic, AK
34 T. Roosevelt (north), ND	**42** Congaree, SC	**50** Denali, AK
35 T. Roosevelt (south), ND	**43** Shenandoah, VA	**51** Lake Clark, AK
36 Voyageurs, MN	**44** Acadia, ME	**52** Katmai, AK
37 Isle Royale, MI	**45** Everglades, FL	**53** Kenai Fjords, AK
38 Hot Springs, AR	**46** Biscayne, FL	**54** Wrangell-St Elias, AK
39 Mammoth Cave, KY	**47** Dry Tortugas, FL	**55** Glacier Bay, AK
40 Cuyahoga Valley, OH	**48** Kobuk Valley, AK	**56** Haleakala, HI
		57 Hawaii Volcanoes, HI

Two further passes, obtainable at any park but not online, grant **free access** for life to all national parks and monuments, again to the holder and any accompanying passengers, and also provide a fifty percent discount on camping fees. The **Senior Pass** is available to any US citizen or permanent resident aged 62 or older for a one-time fee of $10, while the **Access Pass** is issued free to blind or permanently disabled US citizens or permanent residents. While hotel-style **lodges** are found only in major parks, every park or monument tends to have at least one well-organized **campground**. Often, a cluster of motels can be found not far outside the park boundaries. With appropriate permits – subject to restrictions in popular parks – backpackers can also usually camp in the backcountry (a general term for areas inaccessible by road).

Other public lands

National parks and monuments are often surrounded by tracts of **national forest** – also federally administered but much less protected. These too usually hold appealing rural campgrounds but, in the words of the slogan, each is a "Land Of Many Uses", and usually allows logging and other land-based industry (thankfully, more often ski resorts than strip mines).

Other government departments administer wildlife refuges, national scenic rivers, recreation areas and the like. The **Bureau of Land Management** (BLM) has the largest holdings of all, most of it open rangeland, such as in Nevada and Utah, but also including some enticingly out-of-the-way reaches. Environmentalist groups engage in endless running battles with developers, ranchers and the extracting industries over uses – or alleged misuses – of federal lands.

While **state parks** and **state monuments**, administered by individual states, preserve sites of more limited, local significance, many are explicitly intended for recreational use, and thus hold better campgrounds than their federal equivalents.

Camping and backpacking

The ideal way to see the great outdoors – especially if you're on a low budget – is to tour by car and **camp** in state and federal campgrounds. Typical public campgrounds range in price from free (usually when there's no water available, which may be seasonal) to around $30 per night. Fees at the generally less scenic commercial campgrounds – abundant near major towns, and often resembling open-air hotels, complete with shops and restaurants – are more like $20–35. If you're camping in high season, either reserve in advance or avoid the most popular areas.

Backcountry camping in the national parks is usually free, by permit only. Before you set off on anything more than a half-day hike, and whenever you're headed for anywhere at all isolated, be sure to inform a ranger of your plans, and ask about weather conditions and specific local tips. Carry sufficient food and drink to cover emergencies, as well as all the necessary equipment and maps. Check whether fires are permitted; even if they are, try to use a camp stove in preference to local materials. In wilderness areas, try to camp on previously used sites. Where there are no toilets, bury human waste at least six inches into the ground and 100ft from the nearest water supply and campground.

Health issues

Backpackers should never drink from rivers and streams; you never know what acts people – or animals – have performed further upstream. **Giardia** – a water-borne bacteria that causes an intestinal disease characterized by chronic diarrhoea, abdominal cramps, fatigue and weight loss – is a serious problem. Water that doesn't come from a tap should be boiled for at least five minutes, or cleansed with an iodine-based purifier or a giardia-rated filter.

Hiking at lower elevations should present few problems, though near water **mosquitoes** can drive you crazy; Avon Skin-so-Soft or anything containing DEET are fairly reliable repellents. **Ticks** – tiny beetles that plunge their heads into your skin and swell up – are another hazard. They sometimes leave their heads inside, causing blood clots or infections, so get advice from a ranger if you've been bitten. One species of tick causes **Lyme Disease**, a serious condition that can even affect the brain. Nightly inspections of your skin are strongly recommended.

Beware, too, of **poison oak**, which grows throughout the west, usually among oak trees. Its leaves come in groups of three (the middle one on a short stem) and are distinguished by prominent veins and shiny surfaces. If you come into contact with it, wash your skin (with soap and cold water) and clothes as soon as possible – and don't scratch. In serious cases, hospital emergency rooms can give antihistamine or adrenaline shots. A comparable curse is **poison ivy**, found throughout the country. For both plants, remember the sage advice, "Leaves of three, let it be".

Mountain hikes

Take special care hiking at higher elevations, for instance in the 14,000ft peaks of the Rockies, or in California's Sierra Nevada (and certainly in Alaska). Late snows are common, and in spring avalanches are a real danger, while meltwaters make otherwise simple stream crossings hazardous. Weather conditions can also change abruptly. **Altitude sickness** can affect even the fittest of athletes: take it easy for your first few days above 7000ft. Drink lots of water, avoid alcohol, eat plenty of carbohydrates and protect yourself from the sun.

Desert hikes

If you intend to hike in the **desert**, carry plentiful extra food and water, and never go anywhere without a map. Cover most of your ground in early morning: the midday heat is too debilitating. If you get lost, find some shade and wait. So long as you've registered, the rangers will eventually come looking for you.

At any time of year, you'll stay cooler during the day if you wear full-length sleeves and trousers, while a wide-brimmed hat and good sunglasses will spare you the blinding headaches that can result from the desert light. You may also have to contend with **flash floods**, which can appear from nowhere. Never camp in a dry wash, and don't attempt to cross flooded areas until the water has receded.

It's essential to carry – and drink – large quantities of **water** in the desert. In particular, hiking in typical summer temperatures requires drinking a phenomenal amount. Loss of the desire to eat or drink is an early symptom of heat exhaustion, so it's possible to become seriously dehydrated without feeling thirsty. Watch out for signs of dizziness or nausea; if you feel weak and stop sweating, it's time to get to the doctor. Check whether water is available on your trail; ask a ranger, and carry plenty with you even if it is.

When **driving** in the desert, carry ample water in the car, take along an emergency pack with flares, a first-aid kit and snakebite kit, matches and a compass. A shovel, tyre pump and extra petrol are always a good idea. If the engine overheats, don't turn it off; instead, try to cool it quickly by turning the front end of the car towards the wind. Carefully pour some water on the front of the radiator, and turn the air conditioning off and the heat up full blast. In an emergency, never panic and leave the car: you'll be harder to find wandering around alone.

Adventure travel

The opportunities for **adventure travel** in the USA are all but endless, whether your tastes run towards whitewater rafting down the Colorado River, mountain biking in the volcanic Cascades, canoeing down the headwaters of the Mississippi River, horseback riding in Big Bend on the Rio Grande in Texas or Big Wall rock climbing on the sheer granite monoliths of Yosemite Valley.

While an exhaustive listing of the possibilities could fill a huge volume, certain places have an especially high concentration of adventure opportunities, such as Moab, Utah (see p.790) or New Hampshire's White Mountains (see p.221). Throughout the text we recommend guides, outfitters and local adventure-tour operators.

Skiing

Downhill **ski** resorts can be found all over the USA. The eastern resorts of Vermont and New York State, however, pale by comparison with those of the Rockies, such as Vail and Aspen in Colorado, and the Sierra Nevada in California. Expect to pay $45–100 per day (depending on the quality and popularity of the resort) for lift tickets, plus another $30 or more per day to rent equipment.

A cheaper alternative is **cross-country skiing**, or ski touring. Backcountry ski lodges dot mountainous areas along both coasts and in the Rockies. They offer a range of rustic accommodation, equipment rental and lessons, from as little as $20 a day for skis, boots and poles, up to about $200 for an all-inclusive weekend tour.

Wildlife

Watch out for bears, deer, moose, mountain lions and rattlesnakes in the backcountry, and consider the effect your presence can have on their environment.

Other than in a national park, you're highly unlikely to encounter a **bear**. Even there, it's rare to stumble across one in the wilderness. If you do, don't run, just back away slowly. Most fundamentally, it will be after your food, which should be stored in airtight containers when camping. Ideally, hang both food and garbage from a high but slender branch some distance from your camp. Never attempt to feed bears, and never get between a mother and her young. Young animals are cute; their irate mothers are not.

Snakes and creepy-crawlies

Though the deserts in particular are home to a wide assortment of poisonous creatures, these are rarely aggressive towards humans. To avoid trouble, observe obvious precautions. Don't attempt to handle wildlife; keep your eyes open as you walk, and watch where you put your hands when scrambling over obstacles; shake out shoes, clothing and bedding before use; and back off if you do spot a creature, giving it room to escape.

If you are bitten or stung, current medical thinking rejects the concept of cutting yourself open and attempting to suck out the venom. Whether snake, scorpion or spider is responsible, apply a cold compress to the wound, constrict the area with a tourniquet to prevent the spread of venom, drink lots of water and bring your temperature down by resting in a shady area. Stay as calm as possible and seek medical help immediately.

Sports

As well as being good fun, catching a baseball game at Chicago's Wrigley Field on a summer afternoon or joining the screaming throngs at a Steelers football game in Pittsburgh can give visitors an unforgettable insight into a town and its people. Professional teams almost always put on the most spectacular shows, but big games between college rivals, Minor League baseball games and even Friday night high-school football games provide an easy and enjoyable way to get on intimate terms with a place.

Specific details for the most important teams in all the sports are given in the various city accounts in this Guide. They can also be found through the Major League websites: Ⓦmlb.com (baseball); Ⓦnba.com (basketball); Ⓦnfl.com (football); Ⓦnhl.com (ice hockey); and Ⓦmlssoccer.com (soccer).

Major spectator sports

Baseball, because the Major League teams play so many games (162 in the regular season, usually at least five a week from April to September, plus the October playoffs), is probably the easiest sport to catch when travelling. The ballparks – such as Boston's historic Fenway Park, New York's famed Yankee Stadium, LA's glamorous Dodger Stadium or Baltimore's evocative Camden Yards – are great places to spend time. It's also among the cheapest sports to watch (from around $10–15 a seat for the bleachers), and tickets are usually easy to come by.

Pro football, the American variety, is quite the opposite. Tickets are exorbitantly expensive and almost impossible to obtain (if the team is any good), and most games are played in huge, fortress-like stadiums far out in the suburbs; you'll do better stopping in a bar to watch it on TV.

College football is a whole lot better and more exciting, with chanting crowds, cheerleaders and cheaper tickets, which can be hard to obtain in football-crazed college towns in parts of the South and Midwest. Although New Year's Day games such as the Rose Bowl or the Orange Bowl are all but impossible to see live, big games like USC vs UCLA, Michigan vs Ohio State or Notre Dame vs anybody are not to be missed if you're anywhere nearby.

Basketball also brings out intense emotions. The protracted pro playoffs run well into June. The men's month-long college playoff tournament, called "March Madness", is acclaimed by many as the nation's most exciting sports extravaganza, taking place at venues spread across the country in many small to mid-sized towns.

Ice hockey, usually referred to simply as hockey, was long the preserve of Canada and cities in the far north of the USA, but now penetrates the rest of the country, with a concentration around the East Coast and Great Lakes. Tickets, particularly for successful teams, are hard to get and not cheap.

Other sports

Soccer remains much more popular as a participant sport, especially for kids, than a spectator one, and those Americans that are interested in it usually follow foreign matches like England's Premier League, rather than their home-grown talent. The good news for international travellers is that any decent-sized city will have one or two pubs where you can catch games from England, various European countries or Latin America; check out Ⓦlivesoccertv.com for a list of such establishments and match schedules.

Golf, once the province of moneyed businessmen, has attracted a wider following in recent decades due to the rise of celebrity golfers such as Tiger Woods and the construction of numerous municipal and public courses. You'll have your best access at these, where a round of golf may cost from $15 for a beaten-down set of links to around $50 for a chintzier course. Private golf courses have varying standards for allowing non-members to play (check their websites) and steeper fees – over $100 a person for the more elite courses.

The other sporting events that attract national interest involve four legs or four wheels. The **Kentucky Derby**, held in Louisville on the first Saturday in May (see p.435), is the biggest date on the horse-racing calendar. Also in May, the NASCAR **Indianapolis 500**, the world's largest motor-racing event, fills that city with visitors throughout the month, with practice sessions and carnival events building up to the big race.

Travel essentials

Costs

When it comes to **average costs** for travelling expenses, much depends on where you've chosen to go. A road trip around the backroads of Texas and the Deep South won't cost you much in accommodation, dining or souvenir-buying, but **petrol prices** will add to the expense – these vary from state to state, but at the time of writing average between $3.50 and $4 per gallon. By contrast, getting around a city such as Boston, New York or Chicago will be relatively cheap, but you'll pay much more for your hotel, meals, sightseeing and shopping. Most items you buy will be subject to some form of state – not federal – **sales tax**, anywhere from less than three percent (in Colorado) to more than eight percent (in California). In addition, varying from state to state, some counties and cities may add on another point or two to that rate. Alaska, Delaware, Montana, New Hampshire and Oregon have no state sales tax, but goods may be liable to some other form of tax from county to county.

Unless you're camping or staying in a hostel, **accommodation** will be your greatest expense while in the USA. A detailed breakdown is given in the Accommodation section (see p.35) but you can reckon on at least $30–50 per day, based on sharing, more or less double that if travelling solo. Unlike accommodation, prices for good **food** don't automatically take a bite out of your wallet, and you can indulge anywhere from the lowliest (but still scrumptious) burger shack to the choicest restaurant helmed by a celebrity chef. You can get by on as little as $20 a day, but realistically you should aim for more like $40.

Where it exists, and where it is useful (which tends to be only in the larger cities), **public transport** is usually affordable, with many cities offering good-value travel passes. **Renting a car**, at $150–220 per week, is a far more efficient way to explore the broader part of the country, and, for a group of two

or more, it could work out cheaper. Drivers staying in larger hotels in the cities should factor in the increasing trend towards charging even for **self-parking**; this daily fee may well be just a few dollars less than that for valet parking.

For attractions in the Guide, prices are quoted for adults, with children's rates listed if they are significantly lower or when the attraction is aimed primarily at youngsters; at some spots, kids get in for half-price, or for free if they're under 6.

Tipping

In the USA, waiters earn most of their income from tips, and not leaving a fair amount is seen as an insult. Waiting staff expect tips of at least fifteen percent, and up to twenty percent for very good service. When sitting at a bar, you should leave at least a dollar per round for the barkeeper; more if the round is more than two drinks. Hotel porters and bellhops should receive at least $2 per piece of luggage, more if it has been lugged up several flights of stairs. About fifteen percent should be added to taxi fares; round up to the nearest 50¢ or dollar, as well.

Crime and personal safety

No one could pretend that America is crime-free, although away from the urban centres **crime** is often remarkably low. Even the lawless reputations of Miami, Detroit or Los Angeles are far in excess of the truth and most parts of these cities, by day at least, are safe; at night, however, some areas are completely off-limits. All the major tourist areas and the main nightlife zones in cities are invariably brightly lit and well policed. By planning carefully and taking good care of your possessions, you should, generally speaking, have few problems.

Car crime

Crimes committed against tourists driving rented **cars** aren't as common as they once were, but it still pays to be cautious. In major urban areas, any car you rent should have nothing on it – such as a particular licence plate – that makes it easy to spot as a rental car. When driving, under no circumstances should you stop in any unlit or seemingly deserted urban area – and especially not if someone is waving you down and suggesting that there is something wrong with your car. Similarly, if you are accidentally rammed by the driver behind you, do not stop immediately, but proceed on to the nearest well-lit, busy area and call ☎911 for assistance. Hide any valuables out of sight, preferably locked in the trunk or in the glove compartment.

Electricity

Electricity runs on 110V AC. All plugs are two-pronged and rather insubstantial. Some travel plug adapters don't fit American sockets.

Entry requirements

Citizens of 35 countries – including the UK, Ireland, Australia, New Zealand and most Western European countries – can enter under the Visa Waiver Program if visiting the United States for a period of less than ninety days. To obtain authorization, you must apply online for ESTA (Electronic System for Travel Authorization) approval before setting off. This is a straightforward process – simply go to the ESTA **website** (Ⓦesta.cbp.dhs.gov), fill in your info and wait a very short while (sometimes just minutes, but it's best to leave at least 72hr before travelling to make sure) for them to provide you with an authorization number. You will not generally be asked to produce that number at your port of entry, but it is as well to keep a copy just in case, especially in times of high-security alerts – you will be denied entry if you don't have one. This ESTA authorization is valid for up to two years (or until your passport expires, whichever comes first) and costs $14, payable by credit card when applying. When you arrive at your port of entry you will be asked to confirm that your trip has an end date, that you have an onward ticket and that you have adequate funds to cover your stay. The customs official may also ask you for your address while in the USA; the hotel you are staying at on your first night will suffice. Each traveller must also undergo the US-VISIT process at immigration, where both index fingers are digitally scanned and a digital headshot is also taken for file. All passports need to be **machine readable**; any issued after October 2006 must include a digital **chip** containing biometric data (most countries issue these automatically nowadays, but check).

Prospective visitors from parts of the world not mentioned above require a valid passport and a non-immigrant **visitor's visa** for a maximum ninety-day stay. How you'll obtain a visa depends on what country you're in and your status when you apply; check Ⓦtravel.state.gov. Whatever your nationality, visas are not issued to convicted felons and anybody who owns up to being a communist, fascist or drug dealer. On arrival, the date stamped on your passport is the latest you're legally allowed to stay. The Department of Homeland Security (DHS) has toughened its stance on anyone violating this rule, so even **overstaying** by a few days can result in a protracted interrogation from officials. Overstaying may also cause you to be turned away next time you try to enter the USA. To get an **extension** before your time is up, apply at the nearest Department of Homeland Security office, whose address will be under the Federal Government Offices listings at the front of the phone book. INS officials will assume that you're working in the USA illegally, and it's up to you to convince them otherwise by providing evidence of ample finances. If you can, bring along an upstanding American citizen to vouch for you. You'll also have to explain why you didn't plan for the extra time initially.

FOREIGN EMBASSIES IN THE USA

Australia 1601 Massachusetts Ave NW, Washington DC 20036 ☎ 202 797 3000, Ⓦ austemb.org
Canada 501 Pennsylvania Ave NW, Washington DC 20001 ☎ 202 682 1740, Ⓦ canadianembassy.org
Ireland 2234 Massachusetts Ave NW, Washington DC 20008 ☎ 202 462 3939, Ⓦ embassyofireland.org
New Zealand 37 Observatory Circle NW, Washington DC 20008 ☎ 202 328 4800, Ⓦ nzembassy.com
South Africa 4301 Connecticut Ave NW, Suite 220, Washington DC 20008 ☎ 202 232 4400, Ⓦ saembassy.org
UK 3100 Massachusetts Ave NW, Washington DC 20008 ☎ 202 588 6500, Ⓦ ukinusa.fco.gov.uk

Gay and lesbian travellers

The **gay scene** in America is huge, albeit heavily concentrated in the major cities. San Francisco, where between a quarter and a third of the voting population is reckoned to be gay or lesbian, is arguably the world's premier gay city. New York runs a close second, and up and down both coasts gay men and women enjoy the kind of visibility and influence those in other places can only dream about. Gay public officials and police officers are no longer a novelty. Resources, facilities and organizations are endless.

Virtually every major city has a predominantly gay area and we've tried to give an overview of local resources, bars and clubs in each large urban area. In the rural heartland, however, life can look more like the Fifties – homosexuals are still oppressed and commonly reviled. Gay travellers need to watch their step to avoid hassles and possible aggression.

National **publications** are available from any good bookstore. Bob Damron in San Francisco (Ⓦdamron .com) produces the best and sells them at a discount online. These include the *Men's Travel Guide*, a pocket-sized yearbook listing hotels, bars, clubs and resources for gay men ($18.36); the *Women's Traveller*, which provides similar listings for lesbians ($15.16); the *Damron City Guide*, which details lodging and entertainment in major cities ($18.36); and *Damron Accommodations*, with 1000 accommodation listings for gays and lesbians worldwide ($19.16).

Gayellow Pages in New York (Ⓦgayellowpages .com) publishes a useful directory of businesses in the USA and Canada ($25, CD-ROM edition $10), plus regional directories for New England, New York and the South. *The Advocate*, based in Los Angeles ($3; Ⓦadvocate.com) is a bimonthly national gay news magazine, with features, general info and classified ads. Finally, the International Gay & Lesbian Travel Association in Fort Lauderdale, FL (☎954 776 2626, Ⓦiglta.org), is a comprehensive, invaluable source for gay and lesbian travellers.

Health

If you have a serious accident while in the USA, emergency medical services will get to you quickly and charge you later. For **emergencies** or ambulances, dial ☎911, the nationwide emergency number.

Should you need to see a doctor, consult the *Yellow Pages* telephone directory under "Clinics" or "Physicians and Surgeons". The basic consultation fee is $50–100, payable in advance. Tests, X-rays etc are much more. Medications aren't cheap either – keep all your receipts for later claims on your insurance policy.

Foreign visitors should bear in mind that many pills available over the counter at home – most codeine-based painkillers, for example – require a prescription in the USA. Local brand names can be confusing; ask for advice at the pharmacy in any drugstore.

In general, inoculations aren't required for entry to the USA.

MEDICAL RESOURCES FOR TRAVELLERS

CDC Ⓦ cdc.gov/travel. Official US government travel health site.
International Society for Travel Medicine Ⓦ istm.org. Full listing of travel health clinics.

Insurance

In view of the high cost of medical care in the USA, all travellers visiting from overseas should be sure to buy some form of **travel insurance**. American and Canadian citizens should check that they are already covered – some homeowners' or renters' policies are valid on holiday, and credit cards such as American Express often include some medical or other insurance, while most Canadians are covered for medical mishaps overseas by their provincial health plans. If you only need trip cancellation/interruption coverage (to supplement your existing plan), this is generally available at a cost of about six percent of the trip value.

Internet

With most American homes now online, **cyber-cafés**, where you can get plugged in for around $3–5 an hour on a terminal in the café, are not as common as they were. Most hotels and many coffeeshops offer free wi-fi for guests and nearly all **public libraries** provide free internet access, but often there's a wait and machine time is limited. A useful website – Ⓦkropla.com – has information on how to plug in a laptop when abroad, as well as handy worldwide communications info.

Mail

Post offices are usually open Monday to Friday from 9am to 5pm, and Saturday from 9am to noon, and there are blue mailboxes on many street corners. At time of publication, first-class **mail** within the USA costs 46¢ for a letter weighing up to 28 grams (an ounce), $1.10 for the rest of the world. Airmail between the USA and Europe may take a week.

In the USA, the last line of the address includes the city or town and an abbreviation denoting the state ("CA" for California; "TX" for Texas, for example).

ROUGH GUIDES TRAVEL INSURANCE

Rough Guides has teamed up with WorldNomads.com to offer great **travel insurance** deals. Policies are available to residents of over 150 countries, with cover for a wide range of **adventure sports**, 24hr emergency assistance, high levels of medical and evacuation cover and a stream of **travel safety information**. Roughguides.com users can take advantage of their policies online 24/7, from anywhere in the world – even if you're already travelling. And since plans often change when you're on the road, you can extend your policy and even claim online. Roughguides.com users who buy travel insurance with WorldNomads.com can also leave a positive footprint and donate to a community development project. For more information go to Ⓦ**roughguides.com/travel-insurance**.

OPENING HOURS AND PUBLIC HOLIDAYS

Government offices (including post offices) and banks will be closed on the following national **public holidays**:

Jan 1 New Year's Day

Third Mon in Jan Martin Luther King, Jr's Birthday

Third Mon in Feb Presidents' Day

Last Mon in May Memorial Day

July 4 Independence Day

First Mon in Sept Labor Day

Second Mon in Oct Columbus Day

Nov 11 Veterans' Day

Fourth Thurs in Nov Thanksgiving Day

December 25 Christmas Day

The last line also includes a five-digit number – the **zip code** – denoting the local post office. It is very important to include this, though the additional four digits that you will sometimes see appended are not essential. You can check zip codes on the US Postal Service website, at ⓦusps.com.

Rules on sending **parcels** are very rigid: packages must be in special containers bought from post offices and sealed according to their instructions, which are given at the start of the *Yellow Pages*. To send anything out of the country, you'll need a green customs declaration form, available from a post office.

Maps

The free **road maps** distributed by each state through its tourist offices and welcome centres are usually fine for general driving and route planning.

Rand McNally produces maps for each state, bound together in the *Rand McNally Road Atlas*, and you're apt to find even cheaper state and regional maps at practically any petrol station along the major highways for around $3–7. Britain's best source for maps is Stanfords, at 12–14 Long Acre, London WC2E 9LP (☎020 7836 1321, ⓦstanfords. co.uk), which also has a mail-order service.

The American Automobile Association, or AAA ("Triple A"; ☎877 244 9790, ⓦaaa.com) provides free maps and assistance to its members, as well as to British members of the AA and RAC. Call the main number to get the location of a branch near you; bring your membership card or at least a copy of your membership number.

If you're after really **detailed maps** that go far beyond the usual fold-out, try Thomas Guides ($20–40; ⓦmapbooks4u.com). Highly detailed **park, wilderness** and **topographical maps** are available through the Bureau of Land Management for the West (ⓦblm.gov) and for the entire country through the Forest Service (ⓦfs.fed.us/maps). The best supplier of detailed, large-format map books for travel through the American backcountry is **Benchmark Maps** (ⓦbenchmarkmaps.com), whose elegantly designed depictions are easy to follow and make even the most remote dirt roads look appealing.

Money

The US dollar comes in $1, $5, $10, $20, $50 and $100 **denominations**. One dollar comprises one hundred cents, made up of combinations of one-cent pennies, five-cent nickels, ten-cent dimes and 25-cent quarters. You can check current exchange rates at ⓦxe.com/ucc; at the time of writing one pound sterling will buy $1.50–1.55 and a euro $1.30–1.35.

Bank hours generally run from 9am to 5pm Monday to Thursday, and until 6pm on Friday; the big bank names are Wells Fargo, US Bank and Bank of America. With an **ATM card**, you'll be able to withdraw cash just about anywhere, though you'll be charged $2–4 per transaction for using a different bank's network. Foreign cash-dispensing cards linked to international networks, such as Plus or Cirrus, are also widely accepted – ask your home bank or credit card company which branches you can use. To find the location of the nearest ATM, call AmEx (☎800 227 4669); Cirrus (☎800 424 7787); Accel/The Exchange (☎800 519 8883); or Plus (☎800 843 7587).

Credit and **debit cards** are the most widely accepted form of payment at major hotels, restaurants and retailers, even though some smaller merchants still do not accept them. You'll be asked to show some plastic when renting a car, bike or other such item, or to start a "tab" at hotels for incidental charges; in any case, you can always pay the bill in cash when you return the item or check out of your room.

US **travellers' cheques** are the safest way for overseas visitors to carry their money, and the better-known cheques, such as those issued by American Express and Visa, are treated as cash in most shops.

Phones

The USA currently has well over one hundred **area codes** – three-digit numbers that must precede the seven-figure number if you're calling from abroad (following the 001 international access code) or from a different area code, in which case you prefix the ten digits with a 1. It can get confusing, especially as certain cities have several different area codes within their boundaries; for clarity, in this Guide, we've included the local area codes in all telephone numbers. Note that some cities require you to dial all ten digits, even when calling within the same code. Numbers that start with the digits 800 – or increasingly commonly 888, 877 and 866 – are **toll-free**, but these can only be called from within the USA itself.

Unless you can organize to do all your calling online via Skype (ⓦskype.com), the cheapest way to make **long-distance** and **international** calls is to buy a **prepaid phonecard**, commonly found in newsagents or grocery stores, especially in urban areas. These are cheaper than the similar cards issued by the big phone companies, such as AT&T, that are usually on sale in pharmacy outlets and chain stores, and will charge only a few cents per minute to call from the USA to most European and other western countries. Such cards can be used from any touchpad phone but there is usually a surcharge for using them from a payphone (which, in any case, are increasingly rare). You can also usually arrange with your local telecom provider to have a **chargecard** account with free phone access in the USA, so that any calls you make are billed to your home. This may be convenient, but it's more expensive than using prepaid cards.

CALLING HOME FROM THE USA

For country codes not listed below, dial 0 for the operator, consult any phone directory or log onto ⓦcountry callingcodes.com.

Australia 011 + 61 + area code minus its initial zero.

New Zealand 011 + 64 + area code minus its initial zero.

Republic of Ireland 011 + 353 + area code minus its initial zero.

South Africa 011 + 27 + area code.

UK 011 + 44 + area code minus its initial zero.

If you are planning to take your **mobile phone** (more often called cell phones in America) from outside the USA, you'll need to check with your service provider whether it will work in the country: you will need a **tri-band** or **quad-band** phone that is enabled for international calls. Using your phone from home will probably incur hefty **roaming charges** for making calls and charge you extra for incoming calls, as the people calling you will be paying the usual rate. Depending on the length of your stay, it might make sense to rent a phone or buy compatible prepaid SIM cards from US providers; check ⓦtriptel.com or ⓦplanetomni .com. Alternatively, you could pick up an inexpensive pay-as-you-go phone from one of the major electrical shops.

Senior travellers

Anyone aged over 62 (with appropriate ID) can enjoy a vast range of **discounts** in the USA. Both Amtrak and Greyhound offer (smallish) percentage reductions on fares to older passengers, and any US citizen or permanent resident aged 62 or over is entitled to free admission for life to all national parks, monuments and historic sites using a Senior Pass (issued for a one-time fee of $10 at any such site). This free admission applies to all accompanying travellers in the same vehicle and also gives a fifty percent reduction on park user fees, such as camping charges.

For discounts on accommodation, group tours and vehicle rental, US residents aged 50 or over should consider joining the AARP (American Association of Retired Persons; ☎888 687 2277, ⓦaarp.org) for an annual $16 fee; the website also offers lots of good travel tips and features. Road Scholar (☎800 454 5768, ⓦroadscholar.org), runs an extensive network of educational and activity programmes for people over 60 throughout the USA, at prices broadly in line with those of commercial tours.

Shopping

Not surprisingly, the USA has some of the greatest **shopping** opportunities in the world – from the luxury-lined blocks of Fifth Avenue in New York, the Miracle Mile in Chicago and Rodeo Drive in Beverly Hills, to the local markets found in cities both big and small, offering everything from fruit and vegetables to handmade local crafts.

When buying clothing and accessories, international visitors will need to convert their sizes

CLOTHING AND SHOE SIZES

WOMEN'S CLOTHING

American	4	6	8	10	12	14	16	18
British	6	8	10	12	14	16	18	20
Continental	34	36	38	40	42	44	46	48

WOMEN'S SHOES

American	5	6	7	8	9	10	11
British	3	4	5	6	7	8	9
Continental	36	37	38	39	40	41	42

MEN'S SHIRTS

American	14	15	15.5	16	16.5	17	17.5	18
British	14	15	15.5	16	16.5	17	17.5	18
Continental	36	38	39	41	42	43	44	45

MEN'S SHOES

American	7	7.5	8	8.5	9	9.5	10	10.5	11	11.5
British	6	7	7.5	8	8.5	9	9.5	10	11	12
Continental	39	40	41	42	42.5	43	44	44	45	46

MEN'S SUITS

American	34	36	38	40	42	44	46	48
British	34	36	38	40	42	44	46	48
Continental	44	46	48	50	52	54	56	58

into American equivalents (see box above). For almost all purchases, state taxes will be applied (see p.47).

Time

The continental US covers four **time zones**, and there's one each for Alaska and Hawaii as well. The Eastern zone is five hours behind Greenwich Mean Time (GMT), so 3pm London time is 10am in New York. The Central zone, starting approximately on a line down from Chicago and spreading west to Texas and across the Great Plains, is an hour behind the east (10am in New York is 9am in Dallas). The Mountain zone, which covers the Rocky Mountains and most of the Southwest, is two hours behind the East Coast (10am in New York is 8am in Denver). The Pacific zone includes the three coastal states and Nevada, and is three hours behind New York (10am in the Big Apple is 7am in San Francisco). Lastly, most of Alaska (except for the St Lawrence Islands, which are with Hawaii) is nine hours behind GMT (10am in New York is 6am in Anchorage), while Hawaii is ten hours behind GMT (10am in New York is 5am in Honolulu). The USA puts its clocks forward to daylight saving time on the second Sunday in March and turns them back on the first Sunday in November.

Tourist information

Each state has its own **tourist office** (see box opposite). These offer prospective visitors a colossal range of free maps, leaflets and brochures on attractions from overlooked wonders to the usual tourist traps. You can either contact the offices before you set off, or, as you travel around the country, look for the state-run "welcome centres", usually along main highways close to the state borders. In heavily visited states, these often have piles of discount coupons for cut-price accommodation and food. In addition, visitor centres in most towns and cities – often known as the "Convention and Visitors Bureau", or CVB, and listed throughout this Guide – provide details on the area, as do local Chambers of Commerce in almost any town of any size.

Travelling with children

Children under 2 years old go free on domestic flights and for ten percent of the adult fare on international flights – though that doesn't mean they get a seat, let alone frequent-flier miles. Kids aged between 2 and 12 are usually entitled to half-price tickets. Discounts for train and bus travel are broadly similar. Car-rental companies usually

STATE TOURISM INFORMATION

Alabama ☎ 800 252 2262, ⓦ alabama.travel

Alaska ☎ 800 862 5275, ⓦ travelalaska.com

Arizona ☎ 866 275 5816, ⓦ arizonaguide.com

Arkansas ☎ 800 628 8725, ⓦ arkansas.com

California ☎ 800 862 2543, ⓦ visitcalifornia.com

Colorado ☎ 800 265 6723, ⓦ colorado.com

Connecticut ☎ 888 288 4748, ⓦ ctvisit.com

Delaware ☎ 866 284 7483, ⓦ visitdelaware.com

Florida ☎ 888 735 2872, ⓦ visitflorida.com

Georgia ☎ 800 847 4842, ⓦ exploregeorgia.org

Hawaii ☎ 800 464 2924, ⓦ gohawaii.com

Idaho ☎ 800 847 4843, ⓦ visitidaho.org

Illinois ☎ 800 226 6632, ⓦ enjoyillinois.com

Indiana ☎ 888 365 6946, ⓦ visitindiana.com

Iowa ☎ 800 345 4692, ⓦ traveliowa.com

Kansas ☎ 800 252 6727, ⓦ travelks.com

Kentucky ☎ 800 225 8747, ⓦ kentuckytourism.com

Louisiana ☎ 800 994 8626, ⓦ louisianatravel.com

Maine ☎ 888 624 6345, ⓦ visitmaine.com

Maryland ☎ 800 634 7386, ⓦ visitmaryland.org

Massachusetts ☎ 800 227 6277, ⓦ massvacation.com

Michigan ☎ 888 784 7328, ⓦ michigan.org

Minnesota ☎ 800 657 3700, ⓦ exploreminnesota.com

Mississippi ☎ 866 733 6477, ⓦ visitmississippi.org

Missouri ☎ 800 519 2100, ⓦ visitmo.com

Montana ☎ 800 847 4868, ⓦ visitmt.com

Nebraska ☎ 800 228 4307, ⓦ visitnebraska.gov

Nevada ☎ 800 237 0774, ⓦ travelnevada.com

New Hampshire ☎ 800 386 4664, ⓦ visitnh.gov

New Jersey ☎ 800 847 4865, ⓦ visitnj.org

New Mexico ☎ 800 545 2070, ⓦ newmexico.org

New York ☎ 800 456 8369, ⓦ iloveny.com

North Carolina ☎ 800 847 4862, ⓦ visitnc.com

North Dakota ☎ 800 435 5663, ⓦ ndtourism.com

Ohio ☎ 800 282 5393, ⓦ discoverohio.com

Oklahoma ☎ 800 652 6552, ⓦ travelok.com

Oregon ☎ 800 547 7842, ⓦ traveloregon.com

Pennsylvania ☎ 800 847 4872, ⓦ visitpa.com

Rhode Island ☎ 800 556 2484, ⓦ visitrhodeisland.com

South Carolina ☎ 888 727 6453, ⓦ discoversouthcarolina.com

South Dakota ☎ 800 732 5682, ⓦ travelsd.com

Tennessee ☎ 800 462 8366, ⓦ tnvacation.com

Texas ☎ 800 888 8839, ⓦ traveltex.com

Utah ☎ 800 882 4386, ⓦ utah.com

Vermont ☎ 800 837 6668, ⓦ vermontvacation.com

Virginia ☎ 800 847 4882, ⓦ virginia.org

Washington ☎ 800 544 1800, ⓦ experiencewa.com

Washington DC ☎ 800 422 8644, ⓦ washington.org

West Virginia ☎ 800 225 5982, ⓦ wvtourism.com

Wisconsin ☎ 800 432 8747, ⓦ travelwisconsin.com

Wyoming ☎ 800 225 5996, ⓦ wyomingtourism.org

---

provide kids' car seats – which are required by law for children under the age of 4 – for around $10 a day. You would, however, be advised to check, or bring your own; they are not always available. Recreational vehicles (RVs) are a particularly good option for families. Even the cheapest motel will offer inexpensive two-bed rooms as a matter of course, which is a relief for non-US travellers used to paying a premium for a "family room", or having to pay for two rooms.

Virtually all tourist attractions offer **reduced rates** for kids. Most large cities have natural history museums or aquariums, and quite a few also have hands-on children's museums; in addition most state and national parks organize children's activities. All the national restaurant chains provide highchairs and special kids' menus; and the trend for more upmarket family-friendly restaurants to provide crayons with which to draw on paper tablecloths is still going strong.

For a database of kids' attractions, shops and activities all over the USA, check the useful site ⓦ gocitykids.parentsconnect.com.

Travellers with disabilities

By international standards, the USA is exceptionally accommodating for travellers with mobility concerns or other physical disabilities. By law, all public buildings, including hotels and restaurants, must be wheelchair accessible and provide suitable toilet facilities. Most street corners have dropped curbs (less so in rural areas), and most public transport systems include subway stations with elevators and buses that "kneel" to let passengers in wheelchairs board.

Getting around

The Americans with Disabilities Act (1990) obliges all air carriers to make the majority of their services accessible to travellers with disabilities, and airlines will usually let attendants of more seriously disabled people accompany them at no extra charge.

Almost every Amtrak train includes one or more coaches with accommodation for handicapped passengers. Guide dogs travel free and may accompany blind, deaf or disabled passengers. Be sure to give 24 hours' notice. Hearing-impaired passengers can get information on ☎ 800 523 6590 (TTY/TDD).

Greyhound, however, has its challenges. Buses are not equipped with lifts for wheelchairs, though staff will assist with boarding (intercity carriers are required by law to do this), and the "Helping Hand" policy offers two-for-the-price-of-one tickets to passengers unable to travel alone (carry a doctor's certificate). The American Public Transportation Association, in Washington DC (☎ 202 496 4800, ⓦ apta.com), provides information about the accessibility of public transportation in cities.

The American Automobile Association (contact ⓦ aaa.com for phone number access for each state) produces the *Handicapped Driver's Mobility Guide*, while the larger car-rental companies provide cars with hand controls at no extra charge, though only on their full-sized (ie most expensive) models; reserve well in advance.

Resources

Most state tourism offices provide **information** for disabled travellers (see p.53). In addition, SATH, the Society for Accessible Travel and Hospitality, in New York (☎ 212 447 7284, ⓦ sath.org), is a not-for-profit travel-industry group of travel agents, tour operators, hotel and airline management, and people with disabilities. They pass on any enquiry to the appropriate member, though you should allow plenty of time for a response. Mobility International USA, in Eugene, OR (☎ 541 343 1284, ⓦ miusa.org), offers travel tips and operates exchange programmes for disabled people. They also serve as a national information centre on disability.

The "America the Beautiful Access Pass", issued without charge to permanently disabled or blind US citizens, gives free lifetime admission to all national parks. It can only be obtained in person at a federal area where an entrance fee is charged; you'll have to show proof of permanent disability, or that you are eligible for receiving benefits under federal law.

Women travellers

A woman travelling alone in America is not usually made to feel conspicuous, or liable to attract unwelcome attention. Cities can feel a lot safer than you might expect from recurrent media images of demented urban jungles, though particular care must be taken at night: walking through unlit, empty streets is never a good idea, and, if there's no bus service, take a taxi.

In the major urban centres, if you stick to the better parts of town, going into bars and clubs alone should pose few problems: there's generally a pretty healthy attitude toward women who do so, and your privacy will be respected.

However, small towns may lack the same liberal or indifferent attitude toward lone women travellers. People seem to jump immediately to the conclusion that your car has broken down, or that you've suffered some strange misfortune. If your vehicle does break down on heavily travelled roads, wait in the car for a police or highway patrol car to arrive. If you don't already have one, you should also rent a mobile phone with your car, for a small charge.

Women – as well as men – should never hitchhike in the USA. Similarly, you should never pick up anyone who's trying to hitchhike. If someone is waving you down on the road, ostensibly to get help with a broken-down vehicle, just drive on by or call the highway patrol to help them.

Avoid travelling at night by public transport – deserted bus stations, if not actually threatening, will do little to make you feel secure. Where possible, team up with a fellow traveller. On Greyhound buses, sit near the driver.

Should disaster strike, all major towns have some kind of rape counselling service; if not, the local sheriff's office will arrange for you to get help and counselling, and, if necessary, get you home. The

National Organization for Women (☎ 202 628 8669, ⓦ now.org) has branches listed in local phone directories and on its website, and can provide information on rape crisis centres, counselling services and feminist bookstores.

RESOURCES AND SPECIALISTS

Gutsy Women Travel Anaheim, CA ☎ 866 464 8879, ⓦ gutsywomentravel.com. International agency that provides practical support and organizes trips for lone female travellers.

Womanship Annapolis, MD ☎ 800 342 9295, ⓦ womanship.com. Live-aboard, learn-to-sail cruises for women of all ages. Destinations may include Chesapeake Bay, Florida, the Pacific Northwest and Mystic, Connecticut.

The Women's Travel Group Bloomfield, NJ ☎ 646 309 5607, ⓦ thewomenstravelgroup.com. Arranges luxury and unusual vacations, itineraries, room-sharing and various activities for women.

Working in the USA

Permission to **work** in the USA can only be granted by the Immigration and Naturalization Service in the USA itself. Contact your local embassy or consulate for advice on current regulations, but be warned that unless you have relatives or a prospective employer in the USA to sponsor you, your chances are at best slim. Students have the best chance of prolonging their stay, while a number of **volunteer** and **work** **programmes** allow you to experience the country less like a tourist and more like a resident.

STUDY, VOLUNTEER AND WORK PROGRAMMES

American Field Service Intercultural Programs ⓦ afs.org, ⓦ afs.org.au, ⓦ afsnzl.org.nz, ⓦ afs.org/southafrica. Global UN-recognized organization running summer student exchange programmes to foster international understanding.

American Institute for Foreign Study ⓦ aifs.com. Language study and cultural immersion, as well as au pair and Camp America programmes.

BTCV (British Trust for Conservation Volunteers) ⓦ tcv.org.uk. One of the largest environmental charities in Britain, with a programme of unusual working holidays (as a paying volunteer) – around £300 for two months wilderness camping while restoring the deserts in Nevada, for example.

BUNAC (British Universities North America Club) ⓦ bunac.com. Working holidays in the USA for international students.

Camp America ⓦ campamerica.co.uk. Well-known company that places young people as counsellors or support staff in US summer camps, for a minimum of nine weeks.

Council on International Educational Exchange (CIEE) ⓦ ciee.org. Leading NGO offering study programmes and volunteer projects around the world.

Earthwatch Institute ⓦ earthwatch.org. Long-established international charity with environmental and archeological research projects worldwide.

New York City

VIEW OF MANHATTAN FROM THE ROCKEFELLER CENTER

1

New York City

The cultural and financial capital of the USA, if not the world, New York City is an adrenaline-charged, history-laden place that holds immense romantic appeal for visitors. Its past is visible in the tangled lanes of Wall Street and tenements of the Lower East Side; meanwhile, towering skyscrapers serve as monuments of the modern age. Street life buzzes round the clock and shifts markedly from one area to the next. The waterfront, redeveloped in many places, and the landscaped green spaces – notably Central Park – give the city a chance to catch its breath. Iconic symbols of world culture – the neon of Times Square, the sculptures at Rockefeller Center – always seem just a stone's throw away. For raw energy, dynamism and social diversity, you'd be hard-pressed to top it; simply put, there's no place quite like it.

New York City comprises the central island of **Manhattan** and the four outer boroughs – **Brooklyn**, **Queens**, the **Bronx** and **Staten Island**. Manhattan, to many, *is* New York; certainly, this is where you're likely to stay and spend most of your time. Though you could spend weeks here and still barely scratch the surface, there are some key attractions and pleasures that you won't want to miss. These include the different **ethnic neighbourhoods**, like Chinatown, and the more artsy concentrations of Soho and the East and West villages. Of course, there is also the celebrated **architecture** of Midtown and the Financial District, as well as many fabulous **museums**. In between sightseeing, you can **eat** just about anything, at any time, cooked in any style; you can **drink** in any kind of company; and enjoy any number of obscure **movies**. The more established arts – **dance**, **theatre** and **music** – are superbly presented. For the avid consumer, the choice of **shops** is almost numbingly exhaustive.

Manhattan is a hard act to follow, though **Brooklyn** is a worthy rival: there's the ragged glory of Coney Island, the trim brownstones of Brooklyn Heights, the foodie destinations in South Brooklyn and the hip nightlife of Williamsburg. The rest of the outer boroughs also have their draws, namely the innovative museums of **Long Island City** and **Astoria**, both in Queens; and the renowned **Bronx Zoo** and adjacent botanical gardens in the Bronx. Last but not least, a free trip on the **Staten Island Ferry** is a sea-sprayed, refreshing good time.

Brief history

The first European to see Manhattan Island, then inhabited by the Lenape, was the Italian navigator Giovanni da Verrazano, in 1524. Dutch colonists established the settlement of **New Amsterdam** exactly one hundred years later. The first governor, Peter Minuit, was the man who famously bought the island for a handful of trinkets. Though we don't know for sure who "sold" it (probably a northern branch of the Lenni Lenape), the other side of the story was that the concept of owning land was utterly alien to Native Americans – they had merely agreed to support Dutch claims to use the land. By the time the British laid claim to the area in 1664, the heavy-handed rule of governor **Peter Stuyvesant** had so alienated its inhabitants that the Dutch relinquished control without a fight.

CENTRAL PARK

Highlights

❶ National September 11 Memorial & Museum One of a few sights clustered by the new One World Trade Center that honours the victims of 9/11. **See p.65**

❷ Walking the Brooklyn Bridge In one direction, you'll move toward pretty Brooklyn Heights; the other way, it's to the downtown skyline. **See p.67**

❸ The High Line The most innovative walkway around, on a disused railroad line above Chelsea and the Meatpacking District. **See p.71**

❹ Empire State Building Enjoy the mind-blowing views from the top of

the most iconic skyscraper in the city. **See p.74**

❺ Central Park A massive, gorgeous, green space, filled with countless bucolic amusements. **See p.77**

❻ The Metropolitan Museum of Art The museum's mammoth collection could keep you busy for days. **See p.78**

❼ Coney Island Stroll the boardwalk, scream on the Cyclone and savour the most famous hot dogs in America at this beachside amusement park. **See p.84**

HIGHLIGHTS ARE MARKED ON THE MAP ON P.60

Renamed **New York**, the city prospered and grew, its population reaching 33,000 by the time of the American Revolution. The opening of the **Erie Canal** in 1825 facilitated trade farther inland, spurring the city to become the economic powerhouse of the nation, the base later in the century of **tycoons** such as Cornelius Vanderbilt and **financiers** like J.P. Morgan. The **Statue of Liberty** arrived from France in 1886, a symbol of the city's role as the gateway for generations of immigrants, and the early twentieth century saw the sudden proliferation of Manhattan's extraordinary **skyscrapers**, which cast New York as the city of the future in the eyes of an astonished world.

Almost a century later, the events of **September 11, 2001**, which destroyed the World Trade Center, shook New York to its core. Yet the Financial District bounced back with a new array of glitzy skyscrapers (as well as some moving memorials) to reassert the neighbourhood's preeminence. It was hit again, along with many low-lying waterfront areas, by 2012's destructive Hurricane Sandy, but the city is well on its way to recovering from that blow too.

Manhattan

The island can be loosely divided into three areas: **Downtown** (below 14th St), **Midtown** (14th St to Central Park/59th St) and **Uptown** (north of 59th St), though each is made up of neighbourhoods of very individual character. The patchwork below 14th Street is one of the most vibrant, exciting parts of the city. Downtown's interest actually begins in New York Harbor, which holds the compulsory attractions of the **Statue of Liberty** and **Ellis Island**. On land, the southernmost neighbourhood is the **Financial District**, with Wall Street at its centre. The buildings of the **Civic Center** transition into the jangling streetlife of **Chinatown**, which has encroached upon touristy **Little Italy**. East of here, the one-time immigrant-heavy **Lower East Side** is a trendy spot full of chic bars and restaurants. **Soho** and **Tribeca** are expensive residential and shopping districts. North of Houston Street, the activity picks up even more in the **West Village** (also known as Greenwich Village) and **East Village**, two former bohemian enclaves that remain great fun despite ongoing gentrification.

North of the East Village, across 14th Street, busy **Union Square** is always great for people watching, elegant **Gramercy Park**, the **Flatiron District** and emerging **NoMad** (north of Madison Square Park), base of the new Museum of Mathematics, spread north from there. Their West Side counterparts include **Chelsea**, home to art galleries, a large gay continent and the popular High Line park; and the tiny **Garment District**, which doesn't have much to see. Around 42nd Street along Broadway, the **Theater District** heralds a cleaned-up, frenetic area of entertainment that culminates at **Times Square**. East of here lies **Midtown East**, where much of the business of Manhattan takes place.

Central Park provides a breath of fresh air in the middle of the island; it's where the city comes to play and escape the crowds. It's bordered by the distinguished **Upper East Side**

CITY STREETS AND ORIENTATION

The first part of Manhattan to be settled was what is now Downtown; this is why the streets here have names (as opposed to numbers) and are somewhat randomly arranged. Often you will hear of places referred to as being either on the **West Side** or the **East Side**; this refers to whether the place lies west or east of **Fifth Avenue**, which begins at the arch in Washington Square Park and runs north to cut along the east side of Central Park. On the East Side above Houston Street (pronounced "Howstun"), and on the West Side above 14th, the streets follow a **grid pattern**, progressing northward one by one. When looking for a specific **address**, keep in mind that on streets, house numbers increase as you walk away from Fifth in either direction; on avenues, house numbers increase as you move north.

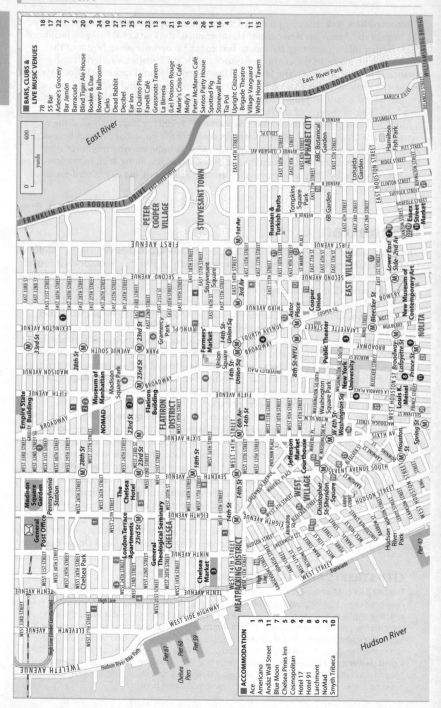

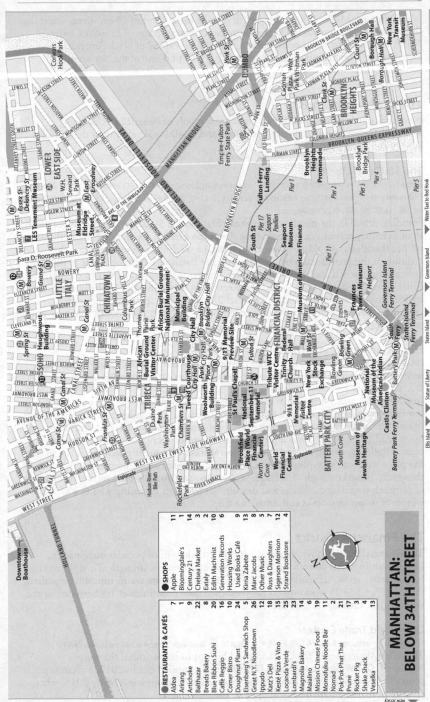

MANHATTAN: BELOW 34TH STREET

● RESTAURANTS & CAFÉS

Aldea	7
Arirang	1
Artichoke	9
Balthazar	22
Breads Bakery	8
Blue Ribbon Sushi	20
Caffe Reggio	16
Corner Bistro	10
Doughnut Plant	24
Eisenberg's Sandwich Shop	5
Great N.Y. Noodletown	26
Ippudo	12
Katz's Deli	18
Keste Pizza & Vino	15
Locanda Verde	25
Lombardi's	23
Magnolia Bakery	14
Maialino	6
Mission Chinese Food	19
Momofuku Noodle Bar	11
Nomad	2
Pok Pok Phat Thai	21
Prune	17
Rocket Pig	3
Shake Shack	4
Veselka	13

● SHOPS

Apple	11
Bloomingdale's	1
Century 21	14
Chelsea Market	3
Eataly	2
Edith Machinist	10
Generation Records	6
Housing Works	4
Used Books Café	9
Kirna Zabete	13
Marc Jacobs	8
Other Music	5
Russ & Daughters	7
Sigerson Morrison	12
Strand Bookstore	4

1

– its "Museum Mile" running along Fifth Avenue from 82nd to 104th streets – and the **Upper West Side**, home to the high-culture performance spaces of Lincoln Center. North of these neighbourhoods, **Harlem**, the cultural capital of black America, is experiencing a new renaissance; further north, you'll find one of the city's most intriguing museums – **the Cloisters** and its medieval arts collection.

The Harbour Islands

New York City's harbour holds two powerful symbols of America's welcome to immigrants: the **Statue of Liberty** and **Ellis Island**, traditional gateway to the so-called land of the free.

The Statue of Liberty

Statue Daily 9.30am–5pm • Free with ferry ticket (extra $3 for crown ticket; book ahead) • ☎ 212 363 3200, ⓦ nps.gov/stli **Statue Cruises ferry** Services leave from the pier in Battery Park daily every 30–45min, 9am–4.45pm • $17 return, tickets from Castle Clinton, in the park • ☎ 201 604 2800, ⓦ statuecruises.com

Standing proud in the middle of New York Harbor, the **Statue of Liberty** has for more than a century served as a symbol of the American Dream. Depicting Liberty throwing off her shackles and holding a beacon to light the world, the monument was the creation of the French sculptor Frédéric Auguste Bartholdi, in recognition of fraternity between the French and American people. The statue, designed by Gustave Eiffel, of Eiffel Tower fame, was built in Paris between 1874 and 1884 and formally dedicated by President Grover Cleveland on October 28, 1886. The standard tour grants entrance to the museum at the base and the pedestal observation deck (168 steps up); it's 354 steps up to the crown.

Ellis Island Immigration Museum

Ellis Island Immigration Museum Daily 9.30am–5.15pm • Free with ferry ticket • ☎ 212 363 3200, ⓦ nps.gov/elis **Statue Cruises ferry** Services leave from the pier in Battery Park daily every 30–45min, 9am–4.45pm • $17 return, tickets from Castle Clinton, in the park • ☎ 201 604 2800, ⓦ statuecruises.com

Just across the water from the Statue of Liberty, **Ellis Island** was the first stop for more than twelve million prospective immigrants. It became an immigration station in 1892, mainly to handle the massive influx from southern and eastern Europe, and remained open until 1954, when it was left to fall into an atmospheric ruin. In the turreted central building, the **Ellis Island Immigration Museum** eloquently recaptures the spirit of the place with artefacts, photographs, maps and personal accounts that tell the story of those who passed through. The huge, vaulted **Registry Room** on the second floor, scene of so much trepidation, elation and despair, has been left imposingly bare, with just a couple of inspectors' desks and American flags.

The Financial District

The **Financial District** is synonymous with the Manhattan of popular imagination, its tall buildings and powerful skyline symbols of economic strength. Though the city had an active securities market by 1790, the **Stock Exchange** wasn't officially organized until 1817, when 28 stockbrokers adopted their own constitution. It's been one of the world's great financial centres ever since.

One World Trade Center

72 Vesey St • ⓦ onewtc.com • Subway A, C, #2, #3, #4, #5 to Fulton St; E to World Trade Center; R to Cortland St; #1 to Rector St

The tallest skyscraper in the US (and third highest in the world, if the spire is included), **One World Trade Center** (1776ft) finally topped out in 2012, a gleaming pinnacle of glass and steel. The tower is expected to be complete in early 2015, when an enclosed **observation deck** will open to the public.

SEPTEMBER 11 AND ITS AFTERMATH

Completed in 1973, the Twin Towers of the **World Trade Center** were an integral part of New York's legendary skyline, and a symbol of the city's social and economic success. At 8.46am on September 11, 2001, a hijacked airliner slammed into the north tower; seventeen minutes later another hijacked plane struck the south tower. As thousands looked on in horror – in addition to hundreds of millions viewing on TV – the south tower collapsed at 9.50am, its twin at 10.30am. In all, 2995 people perished at the WTC and the simultaneous attack on Washington DC.

In 2003, Polish-born American architect Daniel Libeskind was named the winner of a competition to design the new World Trade Center, though his plans were initially plagued with controversy and he's had little subsequent involvement with the project. In 2006 a modified design, still incorporating Libeskind's original 1776ft-high Freedom Tower, was finally accepted and construction is now nearing completion. In addition to the sights mentioned here – One World Trade Center, the September 11 Memorial and the Tribute WTC Center – you can check out **St Paul's Chapel** (Mon–Sat 10am–6pm, Sun 7am–3pm; free), at Fulton Street and Broadway, dating from 1766; the main attraction inside is "Unwavering Spirit", a poignant exhibition on 9/11.

National September 11 Memorial & Museum

Entrance at Albany St and Greenwich St • Daily: mid-March to mid-Sept 10am–8pm (last entry 7pm); mid-Sept to mid-March 10am–6pm (last entry 5pm) • Free, with a reserved visitor pass (see website) • ☎ 212 312 8800, ⓦ 911memorial.org • Subway A, C, #2, #3, #4, #5 to Fulton St; E to World Trade Center; R to Cortland St; #1 to Rector St

The incredibly moving **National September 11 Memorial & Museum** was dedicated on September 11, 2011 to commemorate the ten-year anniversary of the 9/11 attacks. The two memorial pools, representing the footprints of the original towers, are each around one acre in size, with 30ft waterfalls tumbling down their sides. The names of the 9/11 victims – some women listed with their "unborn children" – are inscribed on bronze parapets surrounding the pools, while the contemplative eight-acre Memorial Plaza is filled with nearly four hundred oak trees. The underground **9/11 Memorial Museum**, in between the two pools, should be open sometime in 2014.

Tribute WTC Visitor Center

120 Liberty St, between Greenwich and Church sts • Mon–Sat 10am–6pm, Sun 10am–5pm (last ticket sold 30min before closing) • $15; tours Mon–Fri & Sun 11am, noon, 1pm, 2pm & 3pm, Sat 11am, noon, 1pm, 2pm, 3pm & 4pm; $10 ($20 with Tribute Center admission) • ☎ 1866 737 1184, ⓦ tributewtc.org • Subway A, C, #2, #3, #4, #5 to Fulton St; E to World Trade Center; R to Cortland St; #1 to Rector St

The poignant **Tribute WTC Visitor Center** houses five small galleries that commemorate the attacks of September 11, beginning with a model of the Twin Towers and a moving section about that chilling day, embellished with video and taped accounts of real-life survivors. A handful of items found on the site – a pair of singed high-heeled shoes, pieces of twisted metal – make heart-rending symbols of the tragedy. The centre also offers daily walking **tours** (1hr 15min) of the National September 11 Memorial (includes memorial pass).

Wall Street and around

The narrow canyon of **Wall Street** gained its name from the Dutch stockade built in the 1650s to protect New Amsterdam from the English colonies to the north. Today, behind the Neoclassical mask of the **New York Stock Exchange**, at Broad and Wall streets, the purse strings of the world are pulled. Due to security concerns, however, the public can no longer observe the frenzied trading on the floor of the exchange.

Federal Hall

26 Wall St, at Nassau St • Mon–Fri 9am–5pm • Free • ☎ 212 825 6990, ⓦ nps.gov/feha • Subway #2, #3, #4, #5 to Wall St

The Greek Revival **Federal Hall** was built in 1842 as the US Customs House, but the exhibits inside relate to the headier days of 1789, when George Washington was sworn in as president from a balcony on this site. There's a monumental statue of Washington outside.

1

Trinity Church

75 Broadway, between Rector and Church sts · Mon–Fri 7am–6pm, Sat 8am–4pm, Sun 7am–4pm · Free · Subway #4, #5 to Wall St

At Wall Street's western end, **Trinity Church** is a knobbly neo-Gothic structure erected in 1846, and was the city's tallest building for fifty years. The place has the air of an English church, especially in its sheltered graveyard, which is the resting place of early luminaries including the first Secretary of the Treasury Alexander Hamilton, who was killed in a duel by then-Vice President Aaron Burr.

National Museum of the American Indian

1 Bowling Green · Daily 10am–5pm, Thurs till 8pm · Free · ☎ 212 514 3700, ⓦ nmai.si.edu · Subway R to Whitehall St; #1 to South Ferry; #4, #5 to Bowling Green

Broadway comes to a gentle end at **Bowling Green Park**, an oval of turf used for the game by eighteenth-century colonial Brits, in the shadow of Cass Gilbert's 1907 **US Custom House**. The Custom House contains the superb **National Museum of the American Indian**, a fascinating assembly of artefacts from almost every tribe native to the Americas, including large wood-and-stone carvings from the Pacific Northwest and elegant featherwork from Amazonia.

Battery Park and Castle Clinton

Battery Place and State and Whitehall sts · **Park** Daily sunrise–1am · Free · ☎ 212 344 3491, ⓦ thebattery.org **Castle Clinton** Daily 8.30am–5pm · Free · ☎ 212 344 7220, ⓦ nps.gov/cacl · Subway R to Whitehall St; #1 to South Ferry; #4, #5 to Bowling Green

Downtown Manhattan lets out its breath in **Battery Park**, where the nineteenth-century **Castle Clinton** once protected the southern tip of Manhattan and now sells ferry tickets to the Statue of Liberty and Ellis Island (see p.64). The spruced-up park stretches for blocks up the west side and is dotted with piers and some inventive landscaping; the fortress, however, was badly damaged by Hurricane Sandy in 2012.

The Museum of Jewish Heritage

36 Battery Place · Mon, Tues, Thurs & Sun 10am–5.45pm, Wed 10am–8pm, Fri 10am–5pm; Oct–March museum closes at 3pm on Fri; closed Jewish holidays · $12 or $17 with audio guide; free Wed 4–8pm · ☎ 646 437 4202, ⓦ mjhnyc.org · Subway R to Whitehall St; #4, #5 to Bowling Green

Just a few feet from the Hudson River, the **Museum of Jewish Heritage** is essentially a memorial of the Holocaust, and has three floors of exhibits on twentieth-century Jewish history. The moving and informative collection features objects from everyday Eastern European Jewish life, prison garb that survivors wore in Nazi concentration camps, photographs, personal belongings and multimedia presentations.

Fraunces Tavern Museum

54 Pearl St, at Broad St · Daily noon–5pm · $7 · ☎ 212 425 1778, ⓦ frauncestavernmuseum.org · Subway R to Whitehall St; #1 to South Ferry; #4, #5 to Bowling Green

For a window into eighteenth-century Manhattan, check out partly reconstructed **Fraunces Tavern**. Here, on December 4, 1783, with the British conclusively beaten, a weeping George Washington took leave of his assembled officers, intent on returning to rural life in Virginia. Today there's a quirky museum of Revolutionary artefacts

---

STATEN ISLAND FERRY

The **Staten Island ferry** (☎ 718 727 2508, ⓦ siferry.com) sails from a modern terminal on the east side of Battery Park, built directly above the South Ferry subway station. Departures are frequent, from every 15–20 minutes during weekday rush hours (7–9am and 5–7pm), to every 60 minutes late at night (the ferry runs 24hr). The 25-minute ride is New York's best bargain: it's absolutely free, offering wide-angle views of the city and the **Statue of Liberty** that become more spectacular as you retreat. Most visitors get the next boat straight back to Manhattan, as there's not much to detain you on **Staten Island** itself.

upstairs, including a lock of Washington's hair, preserved like a holy relic. The restaurant/bar downstairs was closed but looking to reopen at the time of writing.

South Street Seaport
Fulton St and South St • Subway A, C, J, #2, #3, #4, #5 to Fulton St

The touristy **South Street Seaport** was once New York's bustling sail-ship port; it's now crammed with pubs, restaurants and well-known chain stores. The **South Street Seaport Museum**, 12 Fulton St (Jan–March Thurs–Sun 10am–5pm; April–Dec Tues–Sun 10am–6pm; $10; ☎212 748 8600, ⓦsouthstreetseaportmuseum.org), housed in a series of restored warehouses, offers exhibits on maritime art and history.

The Brooklyn Bridge
From just about anywhere in the seaport you can see the much-loved **Brooklyn Bridge**, which was the world's largest suspension bridge when it opened in 1883. The beauty of the bridge itself and the spectacular views of Manhattan it offers make a walk across its wooden planks an essential part of any New York trip; you'll find the pedestrian walkway at the top of Park Row, opposite City Hall.

City Hall Park and around
City Hall: Free tours Thurs 10am (must reserve in advance at ☎ 212 788 2656, ⓦ nyc.gov/html/artcom) & Wed noon (sign up at the NYC information kiosk, opposite the Woolworth Building; Mon–Fri 9am–6pm, Sat & Sun 10am–5pm) • Subway J, Z to Chambers St; R to City Hall; #2 or #3 to Park Place; #4, #5 or #6 to Brooklyn Bridge–City Hall

Immediately north of St Paul's Chapel, Broadway and Park Row form the apex of **City Hall Park**, a brightly flowered triangle now worthy of its handsome setting. At the top of the park is stately **City Hall**, which was completed in 1812. Inside, it's an elegant meeting of arrogance and authority, with the sweeping spiral staircase delivering you to the precise geometry of the Governor's Room.

The Woolworth Building
233 Broadway, between Barclay St and Park Place • Subway J, Z to Chambers St; R to City Hall; #2 or #3 to Park Place; #4, #5 or #6 to Brooklyn Bridge–City Hall

Cass Gilbert's 1913 **Woolworth Building** is a venerable onlooker over City Hall Park, with its soaring lines fringed with Gothic decoration. Frank Woolworth made his fortune from "five and dime" stores and, true to his philosophy, he paid cash for his skyscraper (the lobby and interior are closed to sightseers).

African Burial Ground National Monument and Visitor Center
Monument Duane St, at Elk St • Daily 9am–5pm • Free • ☎ 212 637 2019, ⓦ nps.gov/afbg **Visitor Center** 290 Broadway • Tues–Sat 10am–4pm, closed federal holidays • Subway A, C, J, Z to Chambers St; R to City Hall

The **African Burial Ground National Monument** occupies a tiny portion of a cemetery that between the 1690s and 1794 was the only place Africans could be buried in the city (as it was then actually outside the city boundaries). It was uncovered in 1991 during the construction of a federal office building. To learn more, head to the nearby **Visitor Center**, where a video and interactive exhibition explain the site's significance.

Chinatown
Manhattan's most thriving ethnic neighbourhood, **Chinatown** has in recent decades pushed north across Canal Street into Little Italy and northeast into the Lower East Side. There aren't many sights; rather, the appeal of the neighbourhood lies simply in its unbridled energy, in the hordes of people coursing the streets all day long – and, of course, in its excellent **Chinese food**. Today, **Mott Street** is the most vibrant thoroughfare, and the streets around – Canal, Pell, Bayard, Doyers and Bowery – host a positive

1

glut of restaurants, tea and rice shops, grocers and vendors selling everything from jewellery to toy robots.

Little Italy

On the north side of Canal Street, **Little Italy** is light years away from the solid ethnic enclave of old. Originally settled by the huge nineteenth-century influx of Italian immigrants, the neighbourhood has far fewer Italians living here now and the restaurants (of which there are plenty) tend to have high prices and a touristy feel. However, some original bakeries and *salumerias* (speciality food stores) do survive, and you can still indulge yourself with a good cappuccino and a tasty pastry.

Nolita

North of Little Italy, **Nolita** runs from Grand to Houston streets, between Bowery and Lafayette Street. Brimming with chic boutiques and restaurants, the district surrounds **St Patrick's Old Cathedral** (on Mulberry and Prince sts), once the spiritual heart of Little Italy and the oldest Catholic cathedral in the city.

New Museum of Contemporary Art

235 Bowery, opposite Prince St • Wed & Fri–Sun 11am–6pm, Thurs 11am–9pm • $14, free for age 18 and under & Thurs 7–9pm; Free guided tours Wed–Fri 12.30pm, Sat & Sun 12.30pm & 3pm; free audio tours available for download on the website • ☎ 212 219 1222, ⓦ newmuseum.org • Subway N, R to Prince St; #6 to Spring St; F to Second Ave

To see a powerful symbol of the rebirth of the **Bowery** – the city's original skid row – check out the **New Museum of Contemporary Art**. The building itself, a stack of seven shimmering aluminium boxes designed by Japanese architects, is as much of an attraction as the avant-garde work inside.

The Lower East Side

Below the eastern stretch of Houston Street, the **Lower East Side** began life toward the end of the nineteenth century as an insular slum for roughly half a million Jewish immigrants. Since then it has changed considerably, with many Dominican and Chinese inhabitants, followed by a recent influx of well-off students, artists, designers and the like. It's all made the neighbourhood quite cool, and a hotbed for trendy shops, bars and restaurants, with **Stanton** and **Clinton streets** as the epicentre. You can still **buy** just about anything cut-price in the Lower East Side, especially on Sunday mornings, when **Orchard Street** is filled with stalls and stores selling discounted clothes and accessories.

Lower East Side Tenement Museum

97 Orchard St • Accessible only by themed guided tours (every 15–30min, 10.30am–5pm; 1hr); for tickets, go to the museum's visitor centre at 103 Orchard St (daily 10am–6pm) • Tours $22 • ☎ 212 431 0233, ⓦ tenement.org • Subway B, D to Grand St; F, J, M, Z to Delancey St/Essex St

The excellent **Lower East Side Tenement Museum**, which is housed in a nineteenth-century tenement, provides a good synopsis for delving into the neighbourhood's past. This will probably be your only chance to see the claustrophobic, crumbling interior of the type of building that housed so many immigrants in former times; tours begin and end at the visitor centre at 103 Orchard St.

Museum at Eldridge Street

12 Eldridge St, just south of Canal St • Mon–Thurs & Sun 10am–5pm, Fri 10am–3pm; guided tours only (every 30min, last tour 4pm; 1hr) • $10, free Mon • ☎ 212 219 0888, ⓦ eldridgestreet.org • Subway B, D to Grand St; F to East Broadway

To get a feel for the Lower East Side's Jewish roots, make for the absorbing **Museum at Eldridge Street**. Built in 1887 as the first synagogue constructed by Eastern European Orthodox Jews in the city (and still a functioning house of worship), the site opened as a museum in 2007. Tours take you upstairs to the main sanctuary and provide a thorough introduction to the history of the building.

Soho and Tribeca

Since the early 1980s, **Soho**, the grid of streets that runs south of Houston Street, has been all about fashion chic, urbane shopping and cosmopolitan art galleries. For the first half of the twentieth century, this area was a wasteland of manufacturers and warehouses, but as rising rents drove artists out of Greenwich Village in the 1940s and 1950s, Soho suddenly became "in". In the 1960s, largely due to the area's magnificent cast-iron architecture, Soho was declared a historic district. Following this, yuppification set in, bringing the fashionable boutiques, hip restaurants and tourist crowds that are Soho's signature today. The flamboyant **Haughwout Building** can be found at the northeast corner of Broome Street and Broadway. You should also check out **72–76 Greene Street**, a neat extravagance whose Corinthian portico stretches up the building's whole five storeys, all in painted metal, and the strongly composed elaborations of its sister building at nos. 28–30.

Tribeca (the triangle below Canal St), south of Soho and west of City Hall, is a former wholesale-food district that's now an enclave of urban style; mixed in among the spacious loft apartments are upmarket restaurants, tiny parks and the odd gallery.

The West Village

For many visitors, the **West Village** (also known as Greenwich Village, or simply "the Village") is the most-loved neighbourhood in New York, despite having lost any radical edge long ago. It still sports many attractions that brought people here in the first place: a busy streetlife, particularly along main drag **Bleecker Street**, that lasts later than in many other parts of the city; more restaurants per head than anywhere else; bars cluttering every corner; and beautiful brownstone-filled blocks like those of Bedford and Grove streets.

Greenwich Village grew up as a rural retreat from the early and frenetic nucleus of New York City. Refined Federal and Greek Revival townhouses lured some of the city's highest society names, and later, at the start of World War I, the Village proved fertile ground for struggling artists and intellectuals, who were attracted to the area's cheap rents and growing community of freethinking residents. This continued to grow after World War II, laying the path for rebellious, countercultural groups and activities in the 1960s, particularly **folk music**, with Bob Dylan a resident for much of his early career.

Washington Square Park

Fifth Ave, Waverly Place, W 4th St and MacDougal St • Daily 6am–midnight • Free • ☎ 212 998 6780, ⓦ nycgovparks.org • Subway A, B, C, D, E, F, M to West 4th St

The natural heart of the Village, renovated **Washington Square Park** retains its northern edging of red-brick rowhouses – the "solid, honorable dwellings" of Henry James's novel *Washington Square* – and Stanford White's imposing **Washington Memorial Arch**, built in 1892 to commemorate the centenary of George Washington's inauguration. The park is also the heart of New York University: in warm weather, it becomes a space for sports, performance, protest and socializing.

Christopher Street

Subway #1 to Christopher St-Sheridan Square

The spiritual heart of gay New York, **Christopher Street** joins Seventh Avenue at **Sheridan Square**, home of the *Stonewall Inn*'s gay bar where, in 1969, a police raid precipitated a siege that lasted the best part of an hour. The **Annual Gay Pride Parade**, typically held on the last Sunday in June (starting at 5th Ave and 52nd St, and ending around Sheridan Square), honours this turning point in the struggle for equal rights.

1

The East Village

The **East Village**, sandwiched between 14th and Houston streets, to the east of Broadway – though its heart is east of Third Avenue – differs quite a bit from its western counterpart. Once, like the adjacent Lower East Side, the neighbourhood was a refuge for immigrants and solidly working-class people. Home to New York's nonconformist intelligentsia in the early twentieth century, it later became the haunt of **the Beats** – Kerouac, Burroughs, Ginsberg et al – punk rockers and struggling artists. In the past two decades, a flourishing culinary and bar scene has taken root, rents have risen and things seem rather tame – albeit with the occasional indie flourish.

St Mark's Place

Subway #6 to Astor Place

The East Village's main drag, the vaudevillian **St Mark's Place** (8th St), is still one of Downtown's more vibrant strips, even if the thrift shops, panhandlers and political hustlers have given way to more sanitized forms of rebellion. Noodle bars, hippie-chick boutiques and the odd chain restaurant have taken hold.

Tompkins Square Park

Aves A to B, and E 7 to E 10 sts • Daily 6am–midnight • Free • ☎ 212 674 6377, Ⓦ nycgovparks.org • Subway L to First Ave; #6 to Astor Place

Tompkins Square Park has long been a focus for the East Village community, and was the scene of the notorious 1988 riots that partly inspired the musical *Rent*. These days things are far more relaxed, and the surrounding area sports some of the most enticing bars and restaurants in the city. Jazz legend **Charlie Parker** lived at 151 Ave B (closed to the public) on the east side of the park from 1950 until his death in 1954; the free **Charlie Parker Jazz Festival** features concerts in the park on the last weekend in August.

Union Square

Downtown Manhattan ends at 14th Street, which slices across from the housing projects of the East Side through rows of cut-price shops to the meatpacking warehouses on the Hudson River. In the middle is **Union Square**, its shallow steps enticing passers-by to sit and watch the motley assortment of skateboarders, Whole Foods shoppers and NYU students or to stroll the cool, tree-shaded paths and lawns. The shopping that once dominated the stretch of **Broadway** north of here, formerly known as Ladies' Mile for its fancy stores and boutiques, has been moved to Fifth Avenue.

Gramercy Park

Between 20th and 21st streets, where Lexington Avenue becomes Irving Place, Manhattan's clutter suddenly breaks into the ordered, open space of **Gramercy Park**. This former swamp, reclaimed in 1831, is one of the city's best parks, its centre tidily planted and, most noticeably, completely empty for much of the day – principally because the only people who can gain access are those rich enough to live here and possess keys to the gate. Guests at the *Gramercy Park Hotel* are also allowed in.

Madison Square

Broadway and Fifth Avenue meet at 23rd Street at **Madison Square**, with a serene, well-manicured **park**. Most notable among the elegant structures nearby is the **Flatiron Building**, 175 Fifth Ave, between 22nd and 23rd streets; the 1902 Beaux Arts structure is known for its unusual narrow corners and 6.5ft-wide rounded tip.

Museum of Mathematics

11 E 26th St, between Fifth and Madison aves • Daily 10am–5pm • $15, kids 12 and under $9 • ☎ 212 542 0566, ⓦ momath.org • Subway N, R, #6 to 23rd St or 28th St

Somewhere between a high-minded institution and an interactive romper room, the **Museum of Mathematics** debuted in late 2012 with the goal of making maths fun and accessible to kids – and adults. Featuring roughly thirty exhibits on two floors, the gallery puts a focus on experience and engagement over understanding, with the idea that the latter will naturally follow.

Chelsea and the Meatpacking District

Home to a thriving **gay community**, and considered the heart of the New York art market because of its many renowned **art galleries** (check out West 24th St, between Tenth and Eleventh aves), the centre of **Chelsea** lies west of Broadway between 14th and 23rd streets. During the nineteenth century, this was New York's theatre district. Nothing remains of that now, but the hotel that put up all the actors, writers and attendant entourages – the **Hotel Chelsea** – remains a (closed to the public) landmark. Mark Twain and Tennessee Williams lived here, Dylan Thomas staggered in and out and Sid Vicious, of the Sex Pistols, stabbed his girlfriend Nancy Spungen to death in their suite in October 1978, a few months before he died of a heroin overdose.

Creating a buffer between the West Village and Chelsea proper, the **Meatpacking District** between Gansevoort Street and West 15th Street, west of Ninth Avenue, has seen the majority of its working slaughterhouses converted to French bistros, late-night clubs, wine bars and fancy shops.

The High Line

Gansevoort St to 34th St, between Tenth and Eleventh aves; entrances at Gansevoort, 14th, 16th, 18th, 20th, 23rd, 26th, 28th and 30th sts • Daily: spring & summer 7am–11pm; autumn 7am–10pm; winter 7am–7pm; stargazing April to early Sept Tues at dusk, weather permitting • Free, though some tours $15 • ☎ 212 500 6035, ⓦ thehighline.org • Subway A, C, E, to 14th St; L to Eighth Ave; C, E to 23rd St

Beginning in the Meatpacking District, though running mostly through West Chelsea, the **High Line** is an ambitious regeneration programme and perhaps the city's most unique park, slicing through buildings and past factories and apartments on a former elevated rail line. It's been opened in three stages, the last of which, the High Line at the West Rail Yards, is slated for completion in 2014; all are popular spots for a stroll and a picnic lunch.

In addition, the **Whitney Museum of American Art** (see p.79) has broken ground on a new indoor-outdoor exhibition space designed by Renzo Piano, near the southern terminus, due to open in 2015.

The Garment District

The ever-diminishing **Garment District**, a loosely defined patch north of Chelsea between 34th and 42nd streets and Sixth and Eighth avenues, still produces a high percentage of all the women's and children's clothes in America. Retail stores abound: **Macy's**, the largest department store in the world, is on **Herald Square** at 34th Street and Seventh Avenue. Dominant landmarks nearby include the **Penn Station** and **Madison Square Garden** complex, which swallows up millions of commuters in its train station (see p.86) and accommodates various pro sports teams (see p.101).

Midtown East

Midtown East is what most people think of as New York City's Midtown, with the grand **Fifth Avenue** having along its flanks prestigious buildings like the **Empire State Building**, **Grand Central Terminal** and the **Rockefeller Center**, major shopping stops such

1

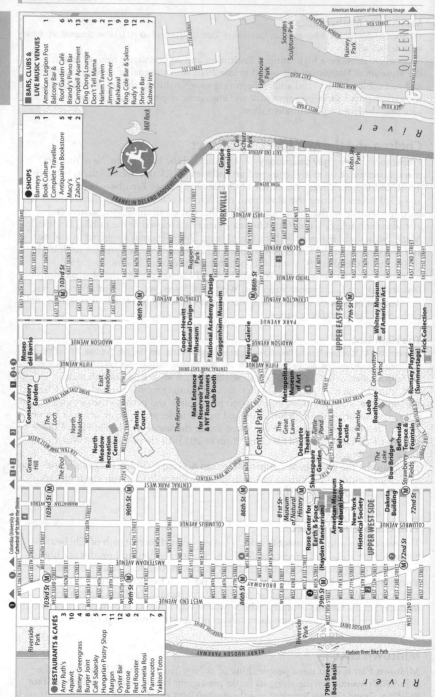

● RESTAURANTS & CAFÉS

Amy Ruth's	3
Aquavit	10
Barney Greengrass	4
Burger Joint	8
Café Sabarsky	5
Hungarian Pastry Shop	1
Margon	11
Oyster Bar	12
Penrose	6
Red Rooster	2
Salumeria Rosi	7
Parmacotto	
Yakitori Totto	9

● SHOPS

Barneys	3
Book Culture	1
Complete Traveller Antiquarian Bookstore	5
Macy's	4
Zabar's	2

■ BARS, CLUBS & LIVE MUSIC VENUES

American Legion Post	1
Balcony Bar & Roof Garden Café	6
Brandy's Piano Bar	13
Campbell Apartment	4
Ding Dong Lounge	8
Don't Tell Mama	2
Harlem Tavern	11
Jimmy's Corner	9
Kashkaval	10
King Cole Bar & Salon	12
Rudy's	3
Shrine Bar	7
Subway Inn	

American Museum of the Moving Image

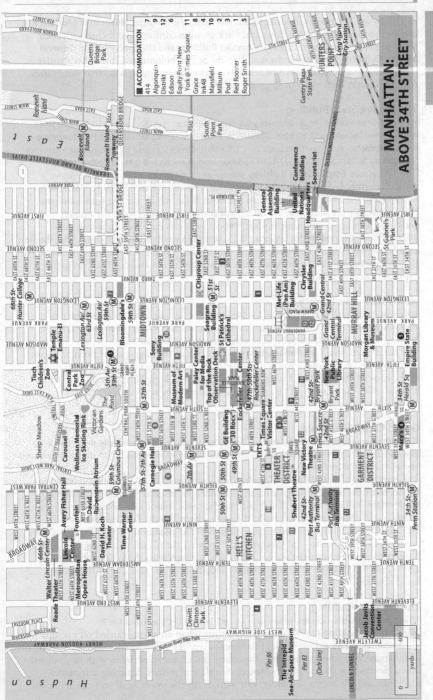

MANHATTAN:
ABOVE 34TH STREET

■ ACCOMMODATION	
414	7
Algonquin	9
Distrikt	12
Edison	6
Equity Point New York @ Times Square	11
Grace	8
Ink48	4
Mansfield	10
Milburn	2
Pod	3
Red Rooster	1
Roger Smith	5

1

as Tiffany and Bergdorf Goodman and, not least, the essential **Museum of Modern Art**; east of there, Lexington, Madison and Park avenues continue the theme with their share of skyscrapers, including the **Chrysler Building** and the spiky-topped **General Electric Building**, 570 Lexington Ave, behind St Bartholomew's Church, its slender shaft rising to a meshed crown of abstract sparks and lightning bolts that symbolizes the radio waves used by its original owner, RCA.

The Empire State Building

350 Fifth Ave, between 33rd and 34th sts • Observatory Daily 8am–2am, last trip 1.15am • $25, ages 6–12 $19, kids under 5 and military personnel free; audio tour $8; buy tickets online or, for an extra $20, express to skip lines • ☎ 212 736 3100, ⓦ esbnyc.com • **New York Skyride** Daily 8am–10pm • Tickets bought online $29, youths and seniors $19; more at box office; combined tickets for New York Skyride and the Observatory $47 • ☎ 212 279 9777, ⓦ skyride.com • Subway B, D, F, M, N, Q, R to 34th St-Herald Square

The 102-storey **Empire State Building** stands as perhaps the most evocative and muscular symbol of New York, as it has since it was completed in 1931. An elevator takes you to the main **observatory** on the 86th floor, which was the summit of the building before the radio and TV mast was added. The views from the outside walkways here are as stunning as you'd expect (you can continue up to the tiny 102nd-floor **observatory** for an extra $15, but the view is about the same). For the best experience, you should try to time your visit so that you'll reach the top at sunset; note that during peak times, waits to ascend can be upwards of an hour (buy online, or express, tickets to skip the lines).

New York Public Library

Fifth Ave and 42nd St • Mon & Thurs–Sat 10am–6pm, Tues & Wed 10am–8pm, Sun 1–5pm (except summer); tours start at the information desk in Astor Hall, the main lobby (1hr; Mon–Sat 11am & 2pm, Sun 2pm; free) • ☎ 212 930 0800 or ☎ 917 275 6975, ⓦ nypl.org • Subway B, D, F, M to 42nd St-Bryant Park; #7 to Fifth Ave; #4, #5, #6, #7, S to Grand Central ˜

The Beaux Arts **New York Public Library** boasts one of the largest collections of books in the world. Leon Trotsky worked occasionally in the large coffered Reading Room at the back of the building during his brief sojourn in New York, just prior to the 1917 Russian Revolution. It's worth going inside just to appreciate its reverent, church-like atmosphere.

Grand Central Terminal

87 E 42nd St, between Lexington and Vanderbilt aves • Tours Wed 12.30pm, $10 suggestion donation, run by the Municipal Arts Society (ⓦ mas.org), and Fri 12.30pm, free, run by the Grand Central Partnership (ⓦ grandcentralpartnership.com) • ⓦ grandcentralterminal.com • Subway S, #4, #5, #6, #7 to Grand Central-42nd St

The huge bulk of **Grand Central Terminal** was completed in 1913 around a basic iron frame, but features a dazzling Beaux Arts facade; its immense size is now dwarfed by the **MetLife** Building behind it. Regardless, the main station's **concourse** is a sight to behold – 470ft long and 150ft high, it boasts a barrel-vaulted ceiling speckled like a Baroque church with a painted representation of the winter night sky. The 2500 stars are shown back to front – "as God would have seen them", the painter is reputed to have explained. You can explore on your own, perhaps with the aid of a self-guided audio tour (GCT tour window on main concourse; $7) or take one of the tours listed above.

The Chrysler Building

405 Lexington Ave, at 42nd St • Lobby Mon–Fri 8am–6pm • Subway S, #4, #5, #6, #7 to Grand Central-42nd St

The **Chrysler Building** (1930) dates from a time when architects carried off prestige with grace and style. For a short while, this was the world's tallest building; today, it's one of Manhattan's best-loved structures. The lobby, once a car showroom, with its opulently inlaid elevators, walls covered in African marble and murals depicting aeroplanes, machines and the brawny builders who worked on the tower, is all you can see inside.

CLOCKWISE FROM TOP GRAND CENTRAL STATION (P.86); CONEY ISLAND (P.84); HUDSON RIVER WITH EMPIRE STATE BUILDING (P.74) >

1

The United Nations Headquarters

First Ave, between 45th and 46th sts • Guided tours Mon–Fri 9.45am–4.45pm; tours last 45min • $16, kids 5–12 $9; bring ID and call ahead to see if anything is off-limits that day • ☎ 212 963 8687, Ⓦ visit.un.org • Subway S, #4, #5, #6, #7 to Grand Central-42nd St

The **United Nations** complex comprises the glass-curtained **Secretariat**, the curving sweep of the **General Assembly**, and, connecting them, the low-rising **Conference Wing**. Guided **tours** leave from the General Assembly lobby and take in the UN conference chambers and its constituent parts; itineraries depend on official room usage.

Rockefeller Center

Taking up the blocks between Fifth and Sixth aves and 48th and 51st sts • Leaflets for self-guided tours available from GE Building lobby desk or online • ☎ 212 332 6868 or ☎ 212 632 3975, Ⓦ rockefellercenter.com • Subway B, D, F, M to 47–50th sts-Rockefeller Center

At the heart of Fifth Avenue's glamour is **Rockefeller Center**, built between 1932 and 1940 by John D. Rockefeller Jr, son of the oil magnate. One of the finest pieces of urban planning anywhere, the Center balances office space with cafés, a theatre, underground concourses and rooftop gardens; many visitor attractions are housed in the GE Building, or 30 Rock (see box below).

The Museum of Modern Art

11 W 53rd St, just off Fifth Ave • Daily 10.30am–5.30pm, Fri till 8pm • $25, free for kids 16 and under and for all Fri 4–8pm • ☎ 212 708 9400, Ⓦ moma.org • Subway E, M to Fifth Ave-53rd St, B, D, F, M to 47–50th Sts-Rockefeller Center

Founded in 1929 by three wealthy women (including a Rockefeller), the **Museum of Modern Art** offers the finest collection of late nineteenth- and twentieth-century art anywhere, making for an essential stop. Most of the interest is in the Painting and Sculpture galleries on the fourth and fifth floors; rooms are set up in roughly chronological order (gallery 1 on the fifth floor starts things off with a post-Impressionist survey). Nineteenth-century highlights include Van Gogh's *Starry Night* and Munch's *The Scream*, while the modern period is represented by works such as Picasso's *Demoiselles d'Avignon*, Jasper Johns' *Flag*, Barnett Newman's "zips" and Warhol's soup cans. Matisse gets an entire room, and Dalí's familiar *Persistence of Memory* (the one with the drooping clocks), while often out on loan, is worth a long look if it's at home. There's plenty more – Cartier-Bresson photographs, a survey of interior design, provocative contemporary pieces by the likes of Jeff Koons and an excellent film programming series, to name a few.

Times Square and the Theater District

Forty-second Street meets Broadway at the southern margin of **Times Square**, centre of the **Theater District** and a top tourist attraction. Traditionally a melting pot of debauchery, depravity and fun, Times Square was cleaned up in the 1990s and turned

---

ROCKEFELLER CENTER ATTRACTIONS

The GE Building ("30 Rock") 30 Rockefeller Plaza, Subway B, D, F, M to 47–50th sts-Rockefeller Center. Among the offices in this 1930s building are the NBC Studios – free tickets to show recordings are available from the mezzanine lobby or out in the street, and tours ($19.25) are given too. In winter, the recessed area of the Lower Plaza becomes an ice rink and a huge tree is displayed at Christmas time.

Top of the Rock 30 Rockefeller Plaza ☎ 212 698 2000, Ⓦ topoftherocknyc.com; Subway B, D, F, M to 47–50th sts-Rockefeller Center. This observation deck offers completely unobstructed views over Manhattan. Daily 8am–midnight, last elevator at 11pm; $25, kids 6–12 $16.

Radio City Music Hall 1260 Sixth Ave ☎ 212 307 7171 (tickets) or ☎ 212 247 4777 (tour info), Ⓦ radiocity.com; Subway B, D, F, M to 47–50th sts-Rockefeller Center. The last word in 1930s luxury, best known for the Rockettes, whose Christmas shows and kicklines have dazzled the masses since 1932. Stage Door" guided tours (1hr), daily 11am–3pm every 30min; $23.70.

into a largely sanitized universe of popular consumption, with refurbished theatres and blinking signage – best experienced as a rush of neon and energy after dark.

Carnegie Hall

57th St, at 7th Ave (there are separate entrances for the box office, museum and Zankel Hall) • Tours Oct–May only, typically Mon–Fri 11.30am, 12.30pm, 2pm & 3pm, Sat 11.30am & 12.30pm, Sun 12.30pm, though call or check web for current schedule, as it frequently changes; 1hr • $10 • Tours ☎ 212 903 9765, concert tickets ☎ 212 247 7800, ⓦ carnegiehall.org • Subway N, Q, R to 57th St

Stately **Carnegie Hall** is one of the world's great concert venues. Tchaikovsky conducted the programme on opening night and Mahler, Rachmaninov, Toscanini, Frank Sinatra and Judy Garland have played here. Even if you don't have time for a show, it's worth taking the tour to admire the vast interior.

Central Park

Five visitor centres, most open daily 10am–5pm • ☎ 212 310 6600, ⓦ centralparknyc.org • Rent bikes (April–Nov daily 10am–6pm; $9–15/hr, $45–50/day) or boats (daily 10am until dusk weather permitting; ☎ 212 517 2233; $12 for the first hour, $2.50/15min thereafter; $20 refundable cash deposit required) at the Loeb Boathouse, on the eastern bank of the lake near the park's centre

Completed in 1876, smack in the middle of Manhattan, **Central Park** extends from 59th to 110th streets, and provides residents (and street-weary visitors) with a much-needed refuge from big-city life. The poet and newspaper editor William Cullen Bryant had the idea for an open public space in 1844 and spent seven years trying to persuade City Hall to carry it out. Eventually, 840 desolate and swampy acres north of the city limits were set aside. The two architects commissioned, **Frederick Law Olmsted** and **Calvert Vaux**, planned a complete illusion of the countryside in the heart of Manhattan – which was already growing at a fantastic rate. Even today, the sense of captured nature survives.

It's easy to get around **on foot**, along the many paths that crisscross the park. There's little chance of getting lost, but to know exactly where you are, find the nearest lamppost: the first two figures signify the number of the nearest street. After dark, however, you'd be well advised not to enter on foot.

The southern park

Subway A, B, C, D, #1 to 59th St–Columbus Circle

Most places of interest in the park lie in its southern reaches. At 64th Street and Fifth Avenue, the **Central Park Zoo** tries to keep caging to a minimum and the animals as close to the viewer as possible (April–Oct Mon–Fri 10am–5pm, Sat & Sun 10am–5pm; Nov–March daily 10am–4.30pm; $12, kids 3–12, $7; ☎212 439 6500). Beyond here, the **Dairy**, once a ranch building intended to provide milk for nursing mothers, now houses a **visitor centre** (Tues–Sun 10am–5pm; ☎212 794 6564).

Nearby, the Trump-owned **Wollman Rink** (ice skating Nov–April Mon & Tues 10am–2.30pm, Wed & Thurs 10am–10pm, $11; Fri & Sat 10am–11pm, Sun 10am–9pm, $17; ☎212 439 6900, ⓦwollmanskatingrink.com) is a lovely place to skate in winter; in the warmer months it becomes a small amusement park, **Victoria Gardens**. From the rink, swing west past the restored **Sheep Meadow**, a dust bowl in the 1970s, now emerald green; then move north up the formal Mall to the terrace, with the sculptured birds and animals of **Bethesda Fountain** below, edging the lake. West is **Strawberry Fields**, a tranquil, shady spot dedicated to John Lennon by his widow, Yoko Ono, and the **Imagine mosaic** – both are near where he was killed in 1980 (see p.80).

Mid-park and the northern park

Subway B, C to 81st, 86th or 96th sts; #6 to 86th, 96th or 103rd sts

At 81st Street, near the West Side, stands the mock citadel of **Belvedere Castle** (daily 10am–5pm), another visitor centre that has nature exhibits and boasts great views of the park from its terraces. Next to the castle, the **Delacorte Theater** is home to

1

Shakespeare in the Park performances in the summer (tickets are free, though they go very quickly; visit ⓦ publictheater.org for details), while the immense **Great Lawn** is a preferred sprawling ground for sun-loving New Yorkers. Beginning at 86th Street, the track around the **Jacqueline Onassis Reservoir** is a favoured place for joggers; however, the one can't-miss in the northern part of the park is the lush **Conservatory Garden** (East 104th–106th sts along Fifth Ave, with entrance at 105th; daily 8am–dusk).

The Metropolitan Museum of Art

1000 Fifth Ave, at 82nd St • Mon–Thurs & Sun 10am–5.30pm, Fri & Sat 10am–9pm • Suggested donation $25, seniors $17, students $12 includes same-day admission to The Cloisters • ☎ 212 535 7710, ⓦ metmuseum.org • Subway #4, #5 or #6 to 86th St-Lexington Ave

One of the world's great art museums, the **Metropolitan Museum of Art** (usually referred to as just "the Met") juts into Central Park. Its all-embracing collection amounts to more than two million works of art, spanning America and Europe as well as China, Africa, the Far East and the classical and Islamic worlds. You could spend weeks here and not see everything.

If you make just one visit, head for the **European Painting** galleries. Of the early (fifteenth- and sixteenth-century) **Flemish and Dutch paintings**, the best are by Jan van Eyck, who is generally credited with having started the tradition of north European realism. The **Italian Renaissance** is less spectacularly represented, but a worthy selection includes an early *Madonna and Child Enthroned with Saints* by Raphael and Duccio's sublime masterpiece *Madonna and Child*. Don't miss the **Spanish** galleries, which include Goya's widely reproduced portrait of a toddler in a red jumpsuit, *Don Manuel Osorio Manrique de Zuniga*, and a room of freaky, dazzling canvases by El Greco.

The **nineteenth-century galleries** house a startling array of **Impressionist** and **post-Impressionist** art, showcasing Manet and Monet among others, and the compact twentieth-century collection features Picasso's portrait of Gertrude Stein and Gauguin's masterly *La Orana Maria*, alongside works by Klee, Hopper and Matisse. The **Medieval Galleries** are no less exhaustive, with displays of sumptuous Byzantine metalwork and jewellery donated by J.P. Morgan, while the **Asian Art galleries** house plenty of murals, sculptures and textile art from Japan, China, Southeast and Central Asia and Korea. Close to being a museum in its own right, the **American Wing** is a thorough introduction to the development of fine art in America; the spectacular **courtyard** reopened in 2009, studded with sculpture from the likes of Daniel Chester French and Augustus Saint-Gaudens. Other highlights include the imposing **Temple of Dendur** in the Egyptian section, and the **Greek** and **Roman** sculpture galleries, magnificently restored less than a decade ago.

The Upper East Side

A two-square-mile grid, the **Upper East Side** has wealth as its defining characteristic, as you'll appreciate if you've seen any of the many Woody Allen (a longtime resident) movies set here. The area's stretch of **Fifth Avenue** has been the upper-class face of Manhattan since the opening of Central Park attracted the Carnegies, Astors and Whitneys to migrate north and build fashionable residences. **Grand Army Plaza**, at Central Park South and Fifth Avenue, flanked by the extended chateau of the swanky **Plaza Hotel**, and glowing with the gold statue of the Civil War's General William Tecumseh Sherman, serves as the introduction.

The Frick Collection

1 E 70th St, at 5th Ave • Tues–Sat 10am–6pm, Sun 11am–5pm • $18, pay what you wish Sun 11am–1pm • ☎ 212 288 0700, ⓦ frick.org • Subway #6 to 68th St

The robber-baron Henry Clay Frick lived in a sumptuous mansion on the corner of 70th Street, a handsome spread that now holds the **Frick Collection**. Perhaps the most enjoyable of the big New York galleries, it is made up of the art treasures hoarded by Frick during his years as a ruthless moneymaker. The collection includes paintings by Rembrandt, Reynolds, Hogarth, Gainsborough (*St James's Park*) and Bellini, whose *St Francis* suggests his vision of Christ by means of pervading light, a bent tree and an enraptured stare. Opposite *St Francis*, El Greco's *St Jerome* reproachfully surveys the riches all around, looking out to the South Hall, where two early Vermeers hang – *Officer and Laughing Girl*, a masterful play on light, and *Girl at Her Muse*.

The Whitney Museum of American Art

945 Madison Ave, at E 75th St • Wed, Thurs, Sat & Sun 11am–6pm, Fri 1–9pm • $18, pay what you wish Fri 6–9pm • ☎ 800 944 8639, ⓦ whitney.org • Subway #6 to 77th St

The **Whitney Museum of American Art** is best known for its biennial show of contemporary American art, always an exercise in provocation. When that's not on, enjoy the prominent Abstract Expressionists collection, with great works by high priests Pollock and De Kooning, leading on to Rothko and the Colour Field painters, and the later pop art works of Warhol, Johns and Oldenburg. The museum is especially strong on Hopper, O'Keeffe and Calder. Note, however, that the museum is planning to relocate to new digs near the High Line in 2015 (see p.71); the Madison Avenue location will be used for exhibitions put on by the Met.

The Guggenheim Museum

1071 Fifth Ave, at E 89th St • Mon–Wed, Fri & Sun 10am–5.45pm, Sat 10am–7.45pm • $22, pay what you wish Sat 5.45–7.45pm; multimedia tours free; free apps for iPhone and iPodTouch; guided tours daily 11am & 1pm (free) • ☎ 212 423 3500, ⓦ guggenheim.org • Subway #4, #5, #6 to 86th St

The **Guggenheim Museum** is better known for the building than its collection. Designed by Frank Lloyd Wright, this unique, curving structure caused a storm of controversy when it was unveiled in 1959. Its centripetal spiral ramp, which wends all the way to the top floor or, alternatively, from the top to the bottom, is still thought by some to favour Wright's talents over those of the exhibited artists. Much of the building is given over to temporary exhibitions, but the permanent collection includes work by Chagall, the major Cubists and, most completely, Kandinsky. Additionally, there are some late nineteenth- and early twentieth-century paintings, not least the exquisite Degas' *The Rehearsal*, Cezanne's *Man with Crossed Arms* and Picasso's haunting *Woman Ironing*.

Cooper-Hewitt, National Design Museum

2 E 91st St, at 5th Ave • ☎ 212 849 8400, ⓦ cooperhewitt.org • Subway #6 to 96th St

Housed in an elegant mansion built for Andrew Carnegie, the Smithsonian-run **Cooper-Hewitt, National Design Museum** is expected to reopen in 2014 after a redevelopment programme. This wonderful institution is the only museum in the USA devoted exclusively to historic and contemporary design; the core permanent exhibition, "What Is Design?", will draw on the 200,000 items in the collection.

Museo del Barrio

1230 Fifth Ave, at E 104th St • Wed–Sat 11am–6pm • Suggested donation $9, free every third Sat of month and Wed 6–9pm • ☎ 212 831 7272, ⓦ elmuseo.org • Subway #6 to 103rd St

The **Museo del Barrio** showcases Latin American and Caribbean art and culture, including rare **Taíno** artefacts, from the pre-Columbian civilization that flourished in Puerto Rico and other Caribbean islands. The museum takes its name from **El Barrio** or Spanish Harlem, which collides head-on with the affluence of the Upper East Side around here.

Gracie Mansion

East End Ave, at E 88th St • 45min tours Wed 10am, 11am, 1pm & 2pm • $7, reservations required • ☎ 311 or ☎ 212 570 4751, ⓦ nyc.gov • Subway #4, #5, #6 to 86th St

Overlooking the East River, **Gracie Mansion** is one of the best-preserved colonial buildings in the city. Built in 1799, it has been the official residence of the mayor of

1

New York City since 1942, when Fiorello LaGuardia, "man of the people" that he was, reluctantly set up house here – though "mansion" is a bit overblown for what's a rather cramped clapboard cottage.

The Upper West Side

North of 59th Street, Manhattan's West Side transitions from the hustle of Columbus Circle to the grandeur of Lincoln Center's cultural institutions, before morphing into a lively residential area. This is the **Upper West Side**, now one of the city's more desirable addresses, though in truth an area long favoured by artists and intellectuals.

Lincoln Center for the Performing Arts

Between 62nd and 66th sts, bordered by Amsterdam and Columbus aves and Broadway • 2–5 tours daily 10.30am–4.30pm, leaving from the David Rubinstein Atrium, Broadway • Tours $17 • ☎ 212 875 5350, ⓦ lc.lincolncenter.org • Subway #1 to 66th St-Lincoln Center

Occupying a four-block plot west of Broadway between 62nd and 66th streets, the **Lincoln Center for the Performing Arts** is a marble assembly of buildings put up in the early 1960s on the site of some of the city's worst slums. Home to the Metropolitan Opera, the New York Philharmonic, the prestigious Juilliard School and a host of other companies (see p.98), the centre is worth seeing even if you don't catch a performance. At the centre of the complex, the marble-and-glass **Metropolitan Opera House** showcases murals by Marc Chagall behind each of its high front windows.

The Dakota

1 W 72nd St, at Central Park West • Subway B, C to 72nd St

The most famous of the monumental apartment buildings of **Central Park West** is the **Dakota**, a grandiose Renaissance-style mansion completed in 1884. Over the years, tenants have included Lauren Bacall and Leonard Bernstein, and in the late 1960s the building was used as the setting for Roman Polanski's film *Rosemary's Baby*. Now most people know it as the former home of **John Lennon**, who was killed out front – and (still) of his wife Yoko Ono, who owns a number of the apartments. There's a Lennon memorial in nearby Central Park (see p.77).

New-York Historical Society

170 Central Park West, at 77th St • Tues–Thurs & Sat 10am–6pm, Fri 10am–8pm, Sun 11am–5pm • $15, kids 5–13 $5, pay what you wish Fri 6–8pm • ☎ 212 873 3400, ⓦ nyhistory.org • Subway B, C to 81st St-Museum of Natural History

The often-overlooked **New-York Historical Society** is more a museum of American than of New York history. Its collection includes watercolours by naturalist James Audubon; a broad sweep of nineteenth-century American portraiture; Hudson River School landscapes, most notably Thomas Cole's metaphorical Course of America series; and a glittering display of Tiffany glass lamps; downstairs the **DiMenna Children's History Museum** illuminates the role of kids in NYC's history.

The American Museum of Natural History

Central Park West, between 77th and 81st sts, main entrance to museum on Central Park West at 79th St and to Rose Center on 81st St • Daily 10am–5.45pm, Rose Center open until 8.45pm on first Fri of month • Suggested admission $19, kids 2–12 $10.50, with additional charges for IMAX films, certain special exhibits and Hayden Planetarium shows ($33/$20.50 for an all-in pass) • ☎ 212 769 5100, ⓦ amnh.org • Subway B, C to 81st St-Museum of Natural History

The **American Museum of Natural History**, the largest museum of its kind in the world, is a strange architectural blend of heavy Neoclassical and rustic Romanesque styles covering four city blocks. The museum boasts superb nature dioramas and anthropological collections, interactive and multimedia displays and an awesome assemblage of bones, fossils and models.

Top attractions include the **Dinosaur Exhibit**, the massive totems in the **Hall of African Peoples**, the taxidermic marvels in **North American Mammals** (including a vividly staged bull and moose fight), and the two thousand gems in the **Hall of Meteorites**. The **Hall of Ocean Life** features a replica of, among other aquatic beings, a 94ft-long blue whale.

The **Rose Center for Earth and Space**, comprising the **Hall of the Universe** and the **Hayden Planetarium**, boasts all the latest technology and an innovative design, with open construction, spiral ramps and dramatic glass walls on three sides of the facility. The Planetarium screens the dramatic thirty-minute "Journey to the Stars", narrated by Whoopi Goldberg.

Columbia University

114th and 121st sts, between Amsterdam Ave and Morningside Drive • Tours Mon–Fri 11am & 3pm • Free • Subway #1 to 116th St

The grand Riverside Drive makes the most pleasant route up from the Upper West Side to prestigious **Columbia University**, in Morningside Heights. Regular guided **tours** start from the visitor centre, in room 213 of the stately Low Library, in the heart of the campus

Cathedral Church of St John the Divine

1047 Amsterdam Ave, at 112th St • Mon–Sat 7.30am–6pm, Sun 7.30am–7pm • Free, though regular guided ($6) and vertical tours ($15) available • ☎ 212 316 7540, ⓦ stjohndivine.org • Subway #1 to Cathedral Parkway-110th St

The **Cathedral Church of St John the Divine** rises up with a solid kind of majesty. A curious, somewhat eerie mix of Romanesque and Gothic styles, the church was begun in 1892, though building stopped with the outbreak of war in 1939 and only resumed, sporadically, from the late 1970s into the late 1990s; today, with no ongoing construction, it's barely two-thirds finished.

Harlem

Home to a culturally and historically rich black community, **Harlem** is a neighbourhood on the rise. Up until recently, because of a near-total lack of support from federal and municipal funds, Harlem formed a self-reliant and inward-looking community. Today, the fruits of a cooperative effort involving businesses, residents and City Hall are manifest in new housing, retail and community projects. But while brownstones triple in value, there remain problems of how to deal with the area's evolution and gentrification, as well as the poverty and unemployment still in evidence. The streets are generally safe for visitors, especially during the day.

The Apollo Theater

253 W 125th St, at Frederick Douglass Blvd • ☎ 212 531 5300, ⓦ apollotheater.org • Subway A, B, C, D, #2, #3 to 125th St

Harlem's working centre, 125th Street, between Broadway and Fifth Avenue, is anchored by the famous **Apollo Theater**, for many years the nexus of black entertainment in the Northeast. Almost all the great jazz, blues and soul figures played here – James Brown recorded his seminal *Live at the Apollo* album in 1962 – though a larger attraction today is Amateur Night (March–Oct Wed 7.30pm; $20–32).

Studio Museum in Harlem

144 W 125th St, at Malcolm X Blvd • Thurs & Fri noon–9pm, Sat 10am–6pm, Sun noon–6pm • $7, free Sun • ☎ 212 864 4500, ⓦ studiomuseum.org • Subway #2, #3 to 125th St

The absorbing **Studio Museum in Harlem** has more than 60,000 square feet of exhibition space dedicated to contemporary African American painting, photography and sculpture. The permanent collection is displayed on a rotating basis and includes works by Harlem Renaissance-era photographer James Van Der Zee, as well as paintings and sculptures by postwar artists.

National Jazz Museum

104 E 126th St, suite 2D • Mon–Fri 10am–4pm • Free • ⓦ jazzmuseuminharlem.org • Subway #4, #5, #6 to 125th St

Harlem – along with New Orleans – is one of the cradles of **jazz**. Duke Ellington, Thelonious Monk, Charlie Parker, Count Basie, John Coltrane and Billie Holiday all

1

got their start here, yet there is surprisingly little to show for this musical heritage. The **National Jazz Museum** is a rare exception, though for now it is more of an organizational body than a conventional museum; the plan is to eventually open a full-scale jazz museum opposite the Apollo Theater on West 125th Street (the target is 2015), but for now its main function is to arrange jazz-related programmes, classes and live events (check the website).

Washington Heights

North of Harlem, starting from West 145th Street or so, is the neighbourhood of **Washington Heights**, an area that evolved from poor farmland to highly sought-after real estate in the early part of the twentieth century. Today, the area is home to the largest Dominican population in the US; it's worth coming for the food, though the area is probably best known as the stomping ground of New York's pioneer **graffiti** artists, such as **TAKI 183**.

The Morris–Jumel Mansion

65 Jumel Terrace, at W 160th St and Edgecombe Ave • Wed–Sun 10am–4pm • $5 • ☎ 212 923 8008, ⓦ morrisjumel.org • Subway C to 163rd St

The **Morris–Jumel Mansion**, the oldest house in Manhattan, comes as a surprise. With its proud Georgian outlines (faced by a later Federal portico), it was built as a rural retreat in 1765 by Colonel Roger Morris and served briefly as George Washington's headquarters. Later, wine merchant Stephen Jumel bought the mansion and refurbished it for his wife Eliza, formerly a prostitute and his mistress. When Jumel died in 1832, Eliza married ex-vice president Aaron Burr, twenty years her senior; the second floor holds her bedroom and boudoir, as well as the couple's bedroom, done up in period style.

The Cloisters

99 Margaret Corbin Drive, Fort Tryon Park • Daily: March–Oct 10am–5.15pm; Nov–Feb 10am–4.45pm • Suggested donation $25, includes same-day admission to the Metropolitan Museum of Art • ☎ 212 923 3700, ⓦ metmuseum.org • Subway A to 190th St–Fort Washington Ave, from where #M4 bus runs to the Cloisters (but can take 1hr 30min); a taxi from Midtown will cost $25–30

It's worth heading up to the northern tip of Manhattan for **The Cloisters** in Fort Tryon Park. This reconstructed monastic complex houses the pick of the Metropolitan Museum's (see p.78) medieval collection. Among its larger artefacts are a monumental Romanesque Hall made up of French remnants and a frescoed Spanish Fuentidueña Chapel, both from the thirteenth century, as well as the famed "Unicorn Tapestries".

Brooklyn

Until the early 1800s, **Brooklyn** was no more than a group of autonomous towns and villages, but Robert Fulton's steamship service across the East River changed all that, starting with the establishment of a leafy retreat at Brooklyn Heights. What really transformed things, though, was the opening of the Brooklyn Bridge on May 24, 1883. Thereafter, development spread deeper inland, as housing was needed to service a more commercialized Manhattan. By 1900, Brooklyn was fully established as part of the newly incorporated New York City, and its fate as Manhattan's perennial kid brother was sealed.

Brooklyn Heights

Subway #2, #3, #4, #5, R to Court St-Borough Hall, or simply walk from Manhattan over the Brooklyn Bridge

Brooklyn Heights, one of New York City's most beautiful neighbourhoods, has little in common with the rest of the borough. Begin your tour at the **Esplanade** – more commonly known as the **Promenade** – with its fine Manhattan views across the water. **Pierrepoint** and **Montague** streets, the Heights' main arteries, are studded with

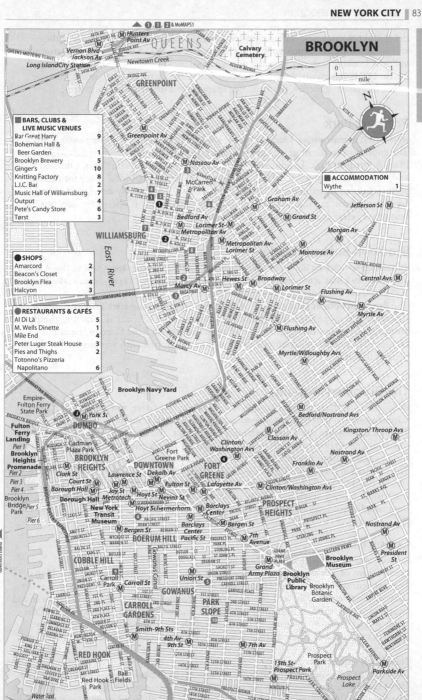

BROOKLYN

0 ——————— 1
mile

■ BARS, CLUBS & LIVE MUSIC VENUES

Bar Great Harry	9
Bohemian Hall & Beer Garden	1
Brooklyn Brewery	5
Ginger's	10
Knitting Factory	8
L.I.C. Bar	2
Music Hall of Williamsburg	7
Output	4
Pete's Candy Store	6
Tørst	3

■ ACCOMMODATION

Wythe	1

● SHOPS

Amarcord	2
Beacon's Closet	1
Brooklyn Flea	4
Halcyon	3

● RESTAURANTS & CAFÉS

Al Di Là	5
M. Wells Dinette	1
Mile End	4
Peter Luger Steak House	3
Pies and Thighs	2
Totonno's Pizzeria Napolitano	6

1

delightful brownstones, restaurants, bars and shops. Below the Esplanade is the still-in-development **Brooklyn Bridge Park**, where Piers 1, 5 and 6 have playgrounds, volleyball courts, waterparks and a pop-up pool looking out on the waterfront. Just north, **DUMBO** is an artsy neighbourhood where the factories have mostly become condos; it boasts galleries, performance spaces and a lovely waterfront strip.

Prospect Park

☏ 718 965 8951, ⓦ prospectpark.org • Subway #2, #3 to Grand Army Plaza; B, Q to Prospect Park; F to Seventh Ave/9th St

The enormous swath of green that rolls forth from behind the arch at Grand Army Plaza is **Prospect Park**. Landscaped in the early 1890s by the same duo, Olmsted and Vaux, who designed Central Park, the sward remains an ideal place for exercise, picnics and family gatherings. There's a zoo, carousel and newly developed Lakeside recreational area, among other attractions. During the day it's perfectly safe, but it's best to stay clear of the park at night.

Brooklyn Botanic Garden

900 Washington Ave • March–Oct Tues–Fri 8am–6pm, Sat & Sun 10am–6pm; Nov–Feb Tues–Fri 8am–4.30pm, Sat 10am–4.30pm • $10, under-12s free, free Tues and Sat before noon, also free winter weekdays • ☏ 718 623 7200, ⓦ bbg.org • Subway #2, #3 to Eastern Pkwy; #4, #5 to Franklin Ave

The **Brooklyn Botanic Garden**, one of the city's most enticing park and garden spaces, is smaller and more immediately likeable than its more celebrated cousin in the Bronx. Sumptuous but not overplanted, its 52 acres comprise a Rose Garden, Japanese Garden, Shakespeare Garden and delightful lawns draped with weeping willows and beds of flowering shrubs.

The Brooklyn Museum

200 Eastern Pkwy • Wed 11am–6pm, Thurs 11am–10pm, Fri–Sun 11am–6pm, first Sat of every month (except Sept) until 11pm • Suggested donation $12 • ☏ 718 638 5000, ⓦ brooklynmuseum.org • Subway #2, #3 to Eastern Pkwy

Though doomed to stand in the shadow of the Met, the **Brooklyn Museum** is a major museum and a good reason to forsake Manhattan for an afternoon. Highlights include the Egyptian antiquities on the third floor and, on the fourth floor, Judy Chicago's *The Dinner Party* and the American period rooms. A floor up, works by Charles Sheeler and Georgia O'Keeffe head the American Identities exhibition, but just as fascinating is the Visible Storage section, an array of Americana objects behind glass that are part of the museum holdings but not in normal rotation.

Coney Island

ⓦ coneyislandusa.com • Subway D, F, N, Q to Coney Island-Stillwell Ave

Generations of working-class New Yorkers have come to relax at one of Brooklyn's farthest points, **Coney Island**. Undeniable highlights include the 1927 wooden roller coaster, the **Cyclone** ($8), and the 90-year-old **Wonder Wheel** ($6). The beach, a broad swath of golden sand, is beautiful, although it is often crowded on hot days and the water might be less than clean. In late June, catch the **Mermaid Parade**, one of the country's oddest and glitziest small-town fancy-dress parades, which culminates here.

New York Aquarium

Surf Ave and W 8th St • June–Aug Mon–Fri 10am–6pm, Sat & Sun 10am–7pm; Sept, Oct, April & May Mon–Fri 10am–5pm, Sat & Sun 10am–5.30pm; Nov–March daily 10am–4.30pm • $9.95 • ☏ 718 265 3474, ⓦ nyaquarium.com • Subway F, Q to West 8th St-NY Aquarium

The **New York Aquarium** on the boardwalk opened in 1896 and recently weathered the effects of Hurrican Sandy; it's still only partially reopened, though with a brand-new shark exhibit and also its prize recent acquisition, Mitul the baby walrus, rescued off the coast of Alaska in 2012.

Brighton Beach

Subway Q to Brighton Beach Ave

Brighton Beach, or "Little Odessa", is a walkable stretch east of Coney Island and home to the country's largest community of Russian émigrés. Its main drag, Brighton Beach Avenue, runs underneath the Q subway line in a hodgepodge of food shops and appetizing restaurants.

Queens

Named in honour of the wife of Charles II of England, **Queens** was one of the rare places where postwar immigrants could buy their own homes and establish their own communities (**Astoria**, for example, holds the world's largest concentration of Greeks outside Greece). It's worth going to Long Island City and Astoria for the restaurants, bars and scattered art scene or to Flushing for another version of an NYC Chinatown (or to see the Mets play baseball); otherwise, must-see sights are thin on the ground.

American Museum of the Moving Image

36-01 35th Ave, between 36th and 37th sts · Tues–Thurs 10.30am–5pm, Fri 10.30am–8pm, Sat & Sun 11.30am–7pm · $12, kids 3–18 $6, free Fri 4–8pm · ☎ 718 777 6888, ⓦ movingimage.us · Subway M, R to Steinway St; N, Q to 36th Ave-31st St

In the Astoria's old Paramount complex, the **American Museum of the Moving Image** devotes its space to the history of film, video and TV. The core exhibit, "Behind the Screen", contains more than 125,000 objects, including old movie cameras and special-effects equipment; early televisions; all kinds of costumes and props, plus enough *Star Wars* action figures to make an obsessed fan drool with envy. There's a real focus on interactivity, too, as you have the opportunity to create a short animated film, make a soundtrack and see how live television is edited.

MoMA PS 1 Contemporary Art Center

22–25 Jackson Ave, at 46th Ave · Mon & Thurs–Sun noon–6pm · $10 suggested donation, free with MoMA ticket · ☎ 718 784 2084, ⓦ momaps1.org · Subway #7 to 45th Rd-Court Square; E, M to 23rd St-Ely Ave; G to Long Island City-Court Square

The renowned **MoMA PS 1 Contemporary Art Center** occupies a hundred-room nineteenth-century brick schoolhouse. Founded in 1971, PS 1 became affiliated with the **Museum of Modern Art** in 2000. It has no real permanent collection of its own; however, one of the long-term installations, James Turrell's *Meeting*, is as surprising and provocative a piece as you'll find.

The Bronx

The city's northernmost and only mainland borough, **The Bronx** has a reputation of being tough and crime-ridden. In fact, it's not much different from the other outer boroughs, though geographically it has more in common with Westchester County to the north than it does with the island regions of New York City: steep hills, deep valleys and rocky outcroppings to the west, and marshy flatlands along Long Island Sound to the east. Settled in the seventeenth century by the Swede Jonas Bronk, it became part of New York proper around the end of the nineteenth century. Its main thoroughfare, **Grand Concourse**, was lined with luxurious Art Deco apartment houses; many, though greatly run-down,

1

still stand. Just off the Grand Concourse, **Yankee Stadium**, at 161st Street and River Avenue (☎718 293 4300, ⓦnewyork.yankees.mlb.com), is home to the most successful team in professional sports, 27-time World Series champs the New York Yankees.

The Bronx Zoo

Bronx River Pkwy, at Fordham Rd • April–Oct Mon–Fri 10am–5pm, Sat, Sun & holidays 10am–5.30pm; Nov–March daily 10am–4.30pm • $16.95, kids 3–12 $11.95, additional charges for some rides and exhibits; Wed donation • ☎718 367 1010, ⓦbronxzoo.org • Subway #2, #5 to West Farms Square-East Tremont Ave; bus #BxM11 express ($5.50) from Madison Ave to Bronx River Gate B

The largest urban zoo in the USA, the **Bronx Zoo** is better than most; it was one of the first institutions of its kind to realize that animals both looked and felt better out in the open. The "Wild Asia" exhibit is an almost-forty-acre wilderness through which tigers, elephants and deer roam relatively free, visible from a monorail (May–Oct; $4). Look in also on the colobus monkeys and baboons in the "Congo Gorilla Forest"; "Himalayan Highlands", with endangered species such as the red panda and snow leopard; and "Tiger Mountain", which allows visitors the opportunity to get up close and personal with Siberian tigers.

New York Botanical Garden

2900 Southern Blvd, at Fordham Rd and Bronx River Pkwy • Tues–Sun 10am–6pm, until 5pm mid-Jan to Feb • $25 all-access, kids 12 and under $10; $10 grounds only, kids 12 and under $2, free Wed; parking $12 • ☎718 817 8700, ⓦnybg.org • Subway B, D, #4 to Bedford Park, then a 20min walk; Metro-North Harlem Line to Botanical Garden Station

Across the road from the Bronx Zoo's main entrance is the back turnstile of the **New York Botanical Garden**, in parts as wild as anything you're likely to see upstate. Don't miss its Enid A. Haupt Conservatory, a turn-of-the-century crystal palace featuring a stunning 90ft dome, beautiful reflecting pool, lots of tropical plants and seasonal displays.

ARRIVAL AND DEPARTURE | NEW YORK CITY

BY PLANE

New York City is served by three major airports: John F. Kennedy, or JFK, in Queens; LaGuardia, also in Queens; and Newark, in New Jersey.

JFK From JFK, the NYC Airporter (☎718 777 5111, ⓦnyc airporter.com) runs buses to Grand Central Terminal, Port Authority Bus Terminal and Penn Station (every 20–30min 5am–11.30pm; 45–60min; $16 one-way, $29 return). The AirTrain (24hr daily; $5; ⓦpanynj.gov/airtrain) runs between JFK and the Jamaica and Howard Beach subway stations in Queens; at Jamaica you can connect to the subway lines E, J or Z, and at Howard Beach, to the A subway line, into Manhattan (from both stations: 1hr; $2.75). Alternatively, the Long Island Railroad runs trains from the Jamaica station to Penn Station (20min; $7 off-peak, $9.59 peak).

La Guardia From LaGuardia, NYC Airporter buses take 45–60min to get to Grand Central and Port Authority Bus Terminal (every 20–30min 5am–11pm; $13 one-way, $23 return). Alternatively, for $2.75, you can take the #M60 bus to 106th St in Manhattan, where you can transfer to Downtown-bound subway lines.

Newark From Newark, Newark Airport Express (☎877 863 9275, ⓦcoachusa.com) runs buses to Grand Central Station, Port Authority Bus Terminal and Penn Station (every 15–30min 4.45am–1.45am; $16 one-way, $28 return). You can also use the AirTrain service, which essentially runs for

free (fare included in NJ Transit or Amtrak tickets) between all Newark terminals, car parks and the Newark Airport Train Station, where you can connect with NJ Transit or Amtrak trains into New York Penn Station. It usually takes about 20min, and costs $15 one way (every 20–30min 6am–midnight).

Airport taxis Taxis are pricey from the airports; reckon on paying $25 to $37 from LaGuardia to Manhattan, a flat rate of $52 from JFK, and $55 to $70 from Newark; you'll also be responsible for the turnpike and tunnel tolls – an extra $8–13 or so – as well as a fifteen- to twenty-percent tip for the driver. You should only use official yellow taxis that wait at designated ranks – just follow the signs out of the terminal.

BY BUS

Greyhound buses pull in at the Port Authority Bus Terminal, 42nd St and Eighth Ave. From here various subway lines will take you where you want to go.

Destinations Boston (14 daily; 4hr 30min); Philadelphia (20 daily; 2hr–2hr 35min); Washington DC (20 daily; 4hr 20min–6hr 5min)

BY TRAIN

Amtrak trains come in to Penn Station, at Seventh Ave and 33rd St. Multiple subway lines converge here, making it easy to get elsewhere in the city.

Destinations Boston (19 daily; 3hr 40min–5hr 20min); Philadelphia (48 daily; 1hr 5min–1hr 30min); Washington DC (38 daily; 2hr 45min–3hr 40min).

BY CAR

Routes Arriving by car, you have a range of options: Rte-495 transects Midtown Manhattan from New Jersey through the Lincoln Tunnel ($13) and from the east through the Queens–Midtown Tunnel ($7.50). From the southwest, I-95 (the New Jersey Turnpike) and I-78 serve Canal and Spring sts (near Soho) via the Holland Tunnel ($13). From the north, I-87 (New York State Thruway) and I-95 serve Manhattan's loop roads. Be prepared for delays at tunnels and bridges.

Parking You might get lucky with street parking depending on where you stay; otherwise, ⊚ nyc.bestparking.com gives garage maps and price comparisons. It won't be cheap.

GETTING AROUND

Few cities equal New York for sheer street-level stimulation, and **walking** is the most exciting way to explore. However, it's also exhausting, so at some point you'll need to use some form of public transport. Citywide subway and bus system maps – the subway map is especially invaluable – are available from all subway station booths, tourist information centres (see below), the concourse office at Grand Central or online at ⊚ mta.info.

BY SUBWAY

The fastest way to get from point A to point B in Manhattan and the boroughs is the subway (⊚ mta.info), open 24hr. A number or letter identifies each train and route; every trip, whether on the express lines, which stop only at major stations, or the locals, which stop at all stations, costs $2.50 (there's a 25¢ surcharge for single standalone tickets). All riders must use a MetroCard, available at station booths or credit/debit/ATM card-capable vending machines. Metro-Cards can be purchased in any amount from a $2.75 single ride (if purchased on its own; otherwise, $2.50) to $112; a $20 purchase provides $21 worth of rides; there's a $1 surcharge for each new MetroCard you buy. Unlimited rides are available with a seven or thirty-day pass ($30/$112).

BY BUS

New York's bus system (again, ⊚ mta.info) is clean, efficient and fairly frequent. The big advantage is that you can see where you're going and hop off more or less when you want; on the downside, it can be extremely slow – in peak hours almost down to walking pace – though it can be your best bet for travelling crosstown. Buses leave their route terminal points at 5–10min intervals, and stop every two or three blocks. The $2.50 fare is payable on entry with a MetroCard (the same one used for the subway) or in cash, but with exact change only; you can transfer for free (continuing in the same direction) within 2hr of swiping your MetroCard.

BY TAXI

Taxis are relatively good value for short journeys (fares start at $2.50, plus surcharges), convenient and can be caught just about anywhere; there's a maximum of four passengers per cab. You should only use official yellow taxis.

INFORMATION

NYC & Company 810 Seventh Ave at 53rd St (Mon–Fri 8.30am–6pm, Sat & Sun 9am–5pm; ☎ 212 484 1222, ⊚ nycgo.com). The best visitor centre in New York, with leaflets on what's going on in the arts, bus and subway maps, and information on accommodation – though it can't actually book anything for you.

ACCOMMODATION

Prices for **accommodation** in New York are well above the norm for the USA as a whole. Most hotels charge more than $200 a night (although exceptions for under $100 a night do exist), and for anything better than four stars you'll be lucky to pay less than $400. Most of New York's **hotels** are in Midtown Manhattan, though more and more chic spots are being built downtown. Booking ahead is strongly advised; at certain times of the year – May, June, September, October and the run-up to Christmas and New Year, for example – everything is likely to be full. **Hostels** offer savings, and run the gamut in terms of quality, safety and amenities. It pays to do research ahead of time to ensure satisfaction upon arrival. Average hostel rates range from $30 to $60.

FINANCIAL DISTRICT, TRIBECA AND SOHO

Andaz Wall Street 75 Wall St ☎ 212 590 1234, ⊚ andaz.com; subway #2, #3, #4, #5 to Wall St; map pp.62–63. Spacious, stylish rooms, with a host of generous extras: 24hr tea and coffee (posh Italian espresso, no less) in the lobby, free happy hour daily 6–8pm and free snacks and soft drinks at any time. $418

Cosmopolitan 95 W Broadway, at Chambers St ☎ 212 566 1900, ⊚ cosmohotel.com; subway A, C, #1, #2, #3 to Chambers St; map pp.62–63. A great Tribeca location plus smart, well-maintained rooms and relatively low prices make this a good deal. $379

1

CITY TOURS

Countless businesses and individuals compete to help you make sense of the city, offering all manner of guided tours; even if you don't need the assistance, you might appreciate the background they provide.

BUS AND BOAT TOURS

Circle Line Ferry Pier 83 at West 42nd St and Twelfth Ave ☎ 212 563 3200, ⓦ circleline42.com. Circumnavigate Manhattan while listening to live commentary; the 3hr tour runs year-round ($34).

Gray Line Port Authority Bus Terminal ☎ 800 669 0051, ⓦ newyorksightseeing.com. Double-decker bus tours offering an unlimited hop-on, hop-off service, taking in the main sights of Manhattan, for around $45. If you're not happy with your tour guide (quality can vary), you can hop off the bus and wait another 15min for the next one.

WALKING TOURS

Big Onion Walking Tours ☎ 212 439 1090, ⓦ bigonion.com. Guided by history grad students

from local universities, the venerable Big Onion specializes in tours with an ethnic and historical focus: pick one, or take the "Immigrant New York" tour and learn about everyone. Cost is $20; the food-included "Multi-Ethnic Eating Tour" is $25. Tours last about 2hr.

Harlem Heritage Tours ☎ 212 280 7888, ⓦ harlem heritage.com. Local Neal Shoemaker runs cultural tours of this historic neighbourhood, ranging from Harlem Gospel ($39) to Harlem Renaissance-themed walking tours ($25). The tours sometimes include food, a cultural performance, film clips and/or bus service.

Municipal Arts Society ☎ 212 935 3960, ⓦ mas.org /tours. Opinionated, incredibly detailed historical and architectural tours in Manhattan, Brooklyn, Queens and the Bronx ($20). They also offer free tours of Grand Central Terminal (Wed 12.30pm; from the information booth).

★ **Smyth Tribeca** 85 W Broadway, between Warren and Chambers sts ☎ 212 587 7000, ⓦ thompsonhotels .com; subway A, C, #1, #2, #3 to Chambers St; map pp.62–63. One of the best boutiques in this part of town, with plush, contemporary design and furnishings with Classical and Art Deco touches; iPod docking station, plasma TV and large bathroom (with Kiehl products) included. **$413**

LOWER EAST SIDE, EAST VILLAGE AND WEST VILLAGE

★ **Blue Moon** 100 Orchard St, between Delancey and Broome sts ☎ 212 533 9080, ⓦ bluemoon-nyc.com; subway F to Delancey St; J, M, Z to Essex St; map pp.62–63. Lower East Side tenement transformed into a luxurious boutique, with rooms named after 1930s and 40s celebrities and decked out with period iron-frame beds and the odd antique – rooms on the upper floors also come with fabulous views across the city. Continental breakfast and iPod docks included. **$275**

Hotel 91 91 E Broadway ☎ 646 438 6600, ⓦ hotel91 .com; subway F to East Broadway; map pp.62–63. Funky Lower East Side boutique, with a slight Asian theme – orchids grace every room, and a statue of Buddha sits in the lobby. Rooms are compact but well equipped, with LCD TVs and plush marble bathrooms – this is a real bargain for this area, but ask for a room away from the Manhattan Bridge if you're a light sleeper. **$220**

Larchmont 27 W 11th St, between Fifth and Sixth aves ☎ 212 989 9333, ⓦ larchmonthotel.com; subway F, L to 14th St; map pp.62–63. A budget hotel, in a terrific location on a tree-lined street in Greenwich Village. Rooms are

small but homely and clean (with TV and a/c). A robe and slippers are provided so you can traipse down the hall to the shared bathroom. Includes continental breakfast. **$119**

UNION SQUARE, FLATIRON DISTRICT AND CHELSEA

Ace 20 W 29th St at Broadway ☎ 212 679 2222, ⓦ ace hotel.com; subway N, R to 28th St; map pp.62–63. A whole host of different room styles (including bunks), with muted tones, artwork and the odd retro-style fridge or guitar dotted around. It's also something of a foodie hotbed, with its acclaimed on-site restaurants. **$399**

Americano 518 W 27th St, between Tenth and Eleventh aves ☎ 212 216 0000, ⓦ hotel-americano.com; subway #1 to 28th St; map pp.62–63. The eye-catching *Americano* sits right on the High Line, with 56 rooms and a sleek, modern style all its own. Japanese-style platform beds, showers that look out onto the skyline and separate elevators for guest and public use. **$395**

★ **Chelsea Pines Inn** 317 W 14th St, between Eighth and Ninth aves ☎ 212 929 1023 or ☎ 888 546 2700, ⓦ chelseapinesinn.com; subway A, C, E to 14th St; map pp.62–63. Housed in an old brownstone on the Greenwich Village/Chelsea border, this super-friendly hotel offers a personalized experience and has clean, comfortable, "shabby chic" rooms, all done with a movie motif and recently renovated. Long popular with a gay and lesbian clientele. Best to book in advance. **$289**

Hotel 17 225 E 17th St, between Second and Third aves ☎ 212 475 2845, ⓦ hotel17ny.com; subway #4, #5, #6, L, N, Q, R to 14th St-Union Square; map pp.62–63.

Seventeen's rooms have basic amenities and many share baths, but it's clean, friendly and nicely situated on a leafy street minutes from Union Square and the East Village. $149

★ **NoMad** 1170 Broadway, at W 28th St ☎ 212 796 1500, ⊛ thenomadhotel.com; subway #6 to 28th St; map pp.62–63. A competitor for the same crowd as the nearby *Ace* (see p.88), the welcoming *NoMad* offers stylish, spacious rooms with damask patterns, Iranian rugs, clawfoot tubs, king-size beds and a mishmash of tasteful art on the walls – different in each space. A cut above. $425

MIDTOWN EAST

Algonquin 59 W 44th St, between Fifth and Sixth aves ☎ 212 840 6800, ⊛ algonquinhotel.com; subway B, D, F, M, #7 to 42nd St-Bryant Park; map pp.72–73. New York's oldest continuously operated hotel and one of the city's famed literary hangouts has retained its old-club atmosphere and decor from the days of the Round Table, though the rooms have been refurbished to handsome effect. Ask about summer and weekend specials. $519

★ **Mansfield** 12 W 44th St, between Fifth and Sixth aves ☎ 212 277 8700, ⊛ mansfieldhotel.com; subway B, D, F, M to 42nd St; map pp.72–73. One of the nicest little hotels in the city, the *Mansfield* has a clubby library lounge and an inviting bar – with live jazz during the week – that lend an affable air. Rooms are trim and nicely appointed. $399

★ **Pod** 230 E 51st St, between Second and Third aves ☎ 212 355 0300, ⊛ thepodhotel.com; subway #6 to 51st St; map pp.72–73. This pleasant hotel is one of the best deals in Midtown. All 370 pods (solo, double, bunk, queen and "double double", all redolent of a colourful ship's quarters) come with a/c, iPod docks and flat-screen TVs, though single and bunk rooms are shared-bath. The open-air roof-deck bar is a bonus. There's another location at 145 E 39th St. $255

Roger Smith 501 Lexington Ave, at E 47th St ☎ 212 755 1400, ⊛ rogersmith.com; subway #6 to 51st St; map pp.72–73. Lots of personality: individually decorated rooms, a great restaurant, helpful service and artwork on display in public spaces. Breakfast is included. $349

MIDTOWN WEST AND UPPER WEST SIDE

★ **414** 414 W 46th St, between Ninth and Tenth aves ☎ 212 399 0006, ⊛ 414hotel.com; subway C, E to 50th St; map pp.72–73. Popular with Europeans, this guesthouse, with larger-than-ordinary rooms across two townhouses, makes a nice camp a bit removed from Times Square's bustle. The backyard garden is a wonderful place to enjoy your morning coffee. $250

★ **Distrikt** 342 W 40th St, between Eighth and Ninth aves ☎ 212 706 6100, ⊛ distrikthotel.com; subway A, C, E to 42nd St–Port Authority; map pp.72–73. The welcoming, city-neighbourhood-themed *Distrikt* has rooms done in classy muted browns and beiges, with black

and white accents; choose one of the upper floors ("Harlem") for the best views. $399

Edison 228 W 47th St, between Broadway and Eighth Ave; ☎ 212 840 5000, ⊛ edisonhotelnyc.com; subway N, Q, R to 49th St; #1 to 50th St; map pp.72–73. The most striking thing about the 1000-room *Edison* is its beautifully restored Art Deco lobby. The rooms, while not fancy, are clean and recently renovated and the prices are reasonable for Midtown. If you want a big hotel right on Broadway, look no further. $265

Equity Point New York @ Times Square 206 W 41st St, between Seventh and Eighth aves ☎ 212 703 8600, ⊛ equity-point.com; subway A, C, E to 42nd St–Port Authority; N, Q, R, S, #1, #2, #3, #7 to Times Square-42nd St; map pp.72–73. A brightly coloured lobby and rooms makes this hostel, right in the middle of the madness, a decent low-cost alternative. Rooms come with high-speed internet access and free continental breakfasts. Dorms $70, doubles $280

Grace 125 W 45th St, between Sixth and Seventh aves ☎ 212 354 2323, ⊛ grace.room-matehotels.com; subway B, D, F, M to 42nd St-Bryant Park; map pp.72–73. You won't find many hotels like this one, with a lobby that more closely resembles a concession stand; a tiny glassed-in pool overlooked by a louche loungey bar; different, funky retro wallpaper on each floor; and ultra-modern (and pet-friendly) rooms, with platform beds and, in some rooms, bunks (great if you've got a small group). $359

★ **Ink48** 653 Eleventh Ave, between 47th and 48th sts ☎ 212 757 0088, ⊛ ink48.com; subway C, E to 50th St; map pp.72–73. On a strip of car-related businesses (petrol stations, dealers, repair shops), this old printing press has been remade into a dashing hotel; all the spacious rooms face out, many to the Hudson, for splendid views, and have modern decor, (typically) king beds and lofty ceilings; there's a rooftop bar too. Dog-friendly. $519

Milburn 242 W 76th St, between Broadway and West End ☎ 212 362 1006, ⊛ milburnhotel.com; subway #1 to 79th St; map pp.72–73. Once you're beyond the classic-feel lobby, the rooms (all with kitchenettes) and suites are a little less showy but on the large side for the neighbourhood. Great for families; free continental breakfasts, too. $249

BROOKLYN

★ **Wythe** 80 Wythe Ave, at N 11th St, Williamsburg ☎ 718 460 8000, ⊛ wythehotel.com; subway L to Bedford St; map p.83. This old factory has been smartly converted into a chic boutique hotel; various industrial touches have been preserved and emphasized, whether exposed brick or floor-to-ceiling warehouse-style windows. "Baby queens" offer a good deal, though you may want to upgrade for the extra space and the Brooklyn or Manhattan-side views on the higher floors. $200

1

EATING

New Yorkers take their food very seriously, and are obsessed with new cuisines, new dishes and new restaurants. Certain areas hold pockets of ethnic restaurants, especially in the outer boroughs, but you can generally find whatever you want, wherever (and whenever) you want. The following section groups together top cafés and restaurants; you can also find examples of a recent trend, the **food truck**, scattered all around town, serving lobster rolls, Korean tacos and much more. Check @nycfoodtruck on Twitter locations.

FINANCIAL DISTRICT, TRIBECA AND SOHO

Balthazar 80 Spring St, between Crosby St and Broadway ☎ 212 965 1414, ⓦ balthazarny.com; subway #6 to Spring St; map pp.62–63. At Keith McNally's popular bistro, the tastefully ornate Parisian decor keeps your eyes busy until the food arrives; then all you can do is savour the moules frites ($22), exquisite pastries and everything in between. Main dishes $19–36. Mon–Thurs 7.30am–midnight, Fri 7.30am–1am, Sat 8am–1am, Sun 8am–midnight.

Blue Ribbon Sushi 119 Sullivan St, between Prince and Spring sts ☎ 212 343 0404, ⓦ blueribbonrestaurants .com; subway C, E to Spring St; map pp.62–63. Widely considered one of the best sushi restaurants in New York, with fish flown in daily from Japan and and sushi master Toshi Ueki at the helm. Sushi platters from $25.50. Daily noon–2am.

Locanda Verde 377 Greenwich St, at N Moore St ☎ 212 925 3797, ⓦ locandaverdenyc.com; subway #1 to Franklin St; map pp.62–63. This casual Italian taverna is a showcase for star chef Andrew Carmellini's exceptional creations; try the porchetta sandwich ($17), stuffed mountain trout ($26) or his fabulous pastas ($17–19). Mon–Fri 7am–3pm & 5.30–11pm, Sat & Sun 8am–3pm & 5.30–11pm.

CHINATOWN AND LOWER EAST SIDE

Doughnut Plant 379 Grand St, between Essex and Clinton sts ☎ 212 505 3700; subway F, J, M, Z to Delancey–Essex St; map pp.62–63. Serious (and seriously delicious) doughnuts ($2.75–3.25); be sure to sample the seasonal flavours and glazes, including chestnut cake, pumpkin and passion fruit. Second location in the *Chelsea Hotel*, at 220 W 23rd St (Mon–Fri 7am–10pm, Sat & Sun 8am–10pm). Cash only. Daily 6.30am–8pm.

★ **Great N.Y. Noodletown** 28 Bowery, at Bayard St ☎ 212 349 0923, ⓦ greatnynoodletown.com; subway J, N, Q, R, Z, #6 to Canal St; map pp.62–63. *Noodletown* is best during soft-shell crab season (May–Aug), when the crustaceans are crispy, salty and delicious (priced seasonally). The Cantonese-style roast meats, *lo mein* (noodles; $5.25) and soups ($4.95) are good year-round. Daily 9am–3.30am.

★ **Katz's Deli** 205 E Houston St, at Ludlow St ☎ 212 254 2246, ⓦ katzsdelicatessen.com; subway F to Lower East Side–Second Ave; map pp.62–63. Jewish stalwart (opened in 1888), *Katz's* offers overstuffed pastrami and corned beef sandwiches that should keep you going for about a week (sandwiches $15.45–16.75). The famous faux-gasm scene from *When Harry Met Sally* was shot here. Mon–Wed 8am–10.45pm, Thurs 8am–2.45am, Fri

8am–Sun 10.45pm.

Mission Chinese Food 154 Orchard St, between Rivington and Stanton sts ☎ 212 529 8800, ⓦ mission chinesefood.com/ny; subway F to Lower East Side–Second Ave; map pp.62–63. Cultish San Francisco Chinese fusion joint with a menu of small dishes such as *char siu* pig ear terrine ($9) and tea-poached chilled greens ($6.50), and large dishes such as thrice-cooked bacon and spicy *mapo tofu* (both $12.50). Oh, and there's free beer while you wait for a table. Daily noon–3pm & 5.30pm–midnight.

Pok Pok Phat Thai 137 Rivington St, between Suffolk and Norfolk sts ☎ 212 447 1299, ⓦ pokpokphatthai .com; subway F to Delancey St; J, M, Z to Essex St; map pp.62–63. *Phat Thai* specialist (the original hails from Portland, Oregon), with a fabulous regular version ($9.50), nicely accompanied by Pok Pok Som drinking vinegars in various fruity flavours ($4.50). Daily noon–11pm.

EAST VILLAGE

Artichoke 328 E 14th St, between First and Second aves ☎ 212 228 2004; subway L to First Ave; map pp.62–63. Fabulous late-night pizza slices to take away, with just four choices: sumptuous cheese-laden Sicilian ($4), Margherita ($4), crab ($4.50) or the trademark artichoke-spinach, topped with a super-creamy sauce ($4.50). Also in the West Village at 111 MacDougal St (between W 3rd and Bleecker sts). Daily 10am–5am.

Ippudo 65 Fourth Ave, between E 9th and E 10th sts ☎ 212 388 0088, ⓦ ippudony.com; subway #6 to Astor Place; map pp.62–63. The first overseas outpost of Fukuoka-based "ramen king" Shigemi Kawahara, this popular ramen shop offers steaming bowls of classic *tonkotsu*-style noodles for $17 in booths and at communal wooden tables, as well as tasty pork buns and roast chicken appetizers. Be prepared to wait (no reservations). Mon–Thurs 11am–3.30pm & 5–11.30pm, Fri & Sat 11am–3.30pm & 5–12.30pm, Sun 11am–10.30pm.

★ **Momofuku Noodle Bar** 171 First Ave, between E 10th and E 11th sts ☎ 212 387 8487, ⓦ momofuku .com; subway #6 to Astor Place; map pp.62–63. Celebrated chef David Chang's first restaurant, where his simplest creations are still the best: silky steamed pork buns, laced with hoisin sauce and pickled cucumbers ($10), or steaming bowls of chicken and pork ramen noodles ($12–16). Mon–Thurs noon–4.30pm & 5.30–11pm, Fri noon–4.30pm & 5.30pm–2am, Sat noon–4pm & 5.30pm–2am, Sun noon–4pm & 5.30–11pm.

1

Prune 54 E 1st St, between First and Second aves ☎ 212 677 6221, ⊕ prunerestaurant.com; subway F to Lower East Side-Second Ave; map pp.62–63. This Mediterranean-influenced American bistro still delivers one of the city's most exciting dining experiences, serving dishes such as sweetbreads wrapped in bacon, wild striped bass with cockles and ricotta ice cream with salted caramel chunks (dinner mains $23–32). Mon–Fri 11.30am–3.30pm & 5.30–11pm, Sat & Sun 10am–3.30pm & 5.30–11pm.

WEST VILLAGE

Caffè Reggio 119 MacDougal St, between Bleecker and W 3rd sts ☎ 212 475 9557; subway A, B, C, D, E, F, M to W 4th St; map pp.62–63. This historic Village coffeehouse dates back to 1927 and is embellished with all sorts of Italian antiques, paintings and sculpture. Tennessee Williams sipped espresso here (now $2.75) and scenes from *Godfather II* were filmed inside. Mon–Thurs 8am–3am, Fri & Sat 8am–4.30am, Sun 9am–3am.

★ **Corner Bistro** 331 W 4th St, at Jane St ☎ 212 242 9502, ⊕ cornerbistrony.com; subway A, C, E, L to 14th St; map pp.62–63. A pub with cavernous cubicles, paper plates and one of the better burgers in town ($6.75). It's a long-standing haunt for West Village literary and artsy types. Mon–Sat 11.30am–4am, Sun noon–4am.

★ **Kesté Pizza & Vino** 271 Bleecker St, between Jones and Cornelia sts ☎ 212 243 1500, ⊕ kestepizzeria.com; subway A, B, C, D, E, F, M to W 4th St; #1 to Christopher St; map pp.62–63. The Neapolitan-designed wood-fired oven turns out perfect pizzas; try the original Mast'nicola (*lardo*, Pecorino Romano and basil; $9) or lip-smacking Pizza del Papa (butternut squash cream, smoked mozzarella and artichoke; $19). No reservations. Mon–Sat noon–3.30pm & 5–11pm, Sun noon–3.30pm & 5–10pm.

Magnolia Bakery 401 Bleecker St, at W 11th St ☎ 212 462 2572; subway #1 to Christopher St; map pp.62–63. Everyone comes for the heavenly and deservedly famous multicoloured cupcakes (celebrated in both *Sex and the City* and *Saturday Night Live*), $2.75 each. Queues can stretch around the block. Mon–Thurs & Sun 9am–11.30pm, Fri & Sat 9am–12.30am.

The Spotted Pig 314 W 11th St, at Greenwich St ☎ 212 620 0393, ⊕ thespottedpig.com; subway #1 to Christopher St; map pp.62–63. New York's best gastropub, courtesy of British chef April Bloomfield. The menu is several steps above most bar food – think crispy pig's ear salad with lemon caper dressing ($15) or smoked haddock chowder ($16) – and the wine list is excellent. Mon–Fri noon–3pm & 5.30pm–2am, Sat & Sun 11am–3pm & 5.30pm–2am.

UNION SQUARE, FLATIRON DISTRICT AND CHELSEA

★ **Aldea** 31 W 17th St, between Fifth and Sixth aves ☎ 212 675 7223, ⊕ aldearestaurant.com; subway F, M to 14th St; map pp.62–63. In a cool, relaxed dining room, Portuguese-accented dishes come exquisitely prepared and full of flavour. For this kind of refined seasonal cooking – say, duck confit with crisped duck skin and chorizo, or sea-salted cod with poached egg and ramps – prices are high but not too high (mains $27–36) and a three-course *prix-fixe* lunch ($25) seals the deal. Mon 11.30am–2pm & 5.30–10pm, Tues–Thurs 11.30am–2pm & 5.30–11pm, Fri 11.30am–2pm & 5.30pm–midnight, Sat 5.30pm–midnight.

★ **Eisenberg's Sandwich Shop** 174 Fifth Ave, at W 22nd St ☎ 212 675 5096; subway N, R to 23rd St; map pp.62–63. A colourful luncheonette, this shop has been serving cheesy Reubens ($10), great tuna sandwiches ($7.25), matzoh-ball soup ($4) and old-fashioned fountain sodas at a well-worn counter since 1930. Mon–Fri 6.30am–8pm, Sat 9am–6pm, Sun 9am–5pm.

★ **Maialino** Gramercy Park Hotel, 2 Lexington Ave ☎ 212 777 2410, ⊕ maialinonyc.com; subway #6 to 23rd St; map pp.62–63. Much of the focus at this Roman trattoria is on the hog (which gives the place its name) – there's excellent cured *salumi* ($9–17), pasta with *guanciale* ($17) or suckling pig ragù ($23) – but everything's well prepared and desserts are exceptional. Reservations essential. Mon–Thurs 7.30–10am, noon–2pm & 5.30–10.30pm, Fri 7.30–10am, noon–2pm & 5.30–11pm, Sat 10am–2pm & 5.30–11pm, Sun 10am–2pm & 5.30–10.30pm, bar open throughout until midnight.

Rocket Pig 463 W 24th St, between W Ninth and Tenth aves, Chelsea ☎ 212 645 5660; subway C, E to 23rd St; map pp.62–63. They do one thing – a messy, smoked-pork sandwich ($14), whose accoutrements (red onion jam, for one) have helped make it one of the city's newest signature sandwiches. Mon–Sat 11am–6pm.

Shake Shack Madison Square Park, near E 23rd St and Madison Ave, multiple other locations ☎ 212 889 6600; subway N, R to 23rd St; map pp.62–63. Danny Meyer's leafy food kiosk in the centre of Madison Square Park is wildly popular, with long queues for the perfectly grilled burgers and frozen-custard shakes. You can also buy beer and wine to sip outside, with nearly every item around $7 or less. Daily 11am–11pm.

MIDTOWN EAST

Aquavit 65 E 55th St, between Madison and Park aves ☎ 212 307 7311, ⊕ aquavit.org; subway E, M to Fifth Ave–53rd St; map pp.72–73. Go for a blowout in the main dining room ($85 for four courses, $135 tasting menu, dishes also à la carte) or relax over Swedish meatballs and a variety of the eponymous drink in the bar-lounge. Reserve ahead. Mon–Fri 11.45am–2.30pm & 5.30–10.30pm, Sat 5.30–10.30pm.

Arirang 32 W 32nd St, between Fifth and Sixth aves ☎ 212 967 5088, ⊕ koreanrestaurantnyc.com; subway B, D, F, M, N, Q, R to 34th St-Herald Square; map pp.62–63.

1

Up three flights of stairs (or an elevator) – but worth seeking out for the chicken soups – with handmade dough flakes ($9.99) or ginseng ($18.99), seafood pancake ($13.99) and, if you're with two or three friends, chicken casserole ($54.99). Daily 10am–midnight.

★ **Oyster Bar** Lower level, Grand Central Terminal, at E 42nd St and Park Ave ☎ 212 490 6650, ⓦ oysterbarny .com; subway #4, #5, #6, #7 to 42nd St–Grand Central; map pp.72–73. This wonderfully distinctive place, down in the vaulted dungeons of Grand Central, attracts plenty of Midtown office-workers for lunch – she-crab bisque ($6.95), steamed Maine lobster (priced by the pound) and sweet Kumamoto oysters ($3.25 each) top the list. Mon–Sat 11.30am–9.30pm.

TIMES SQUARE AND THEATER DISTRICT

★ **Burger Joint** 119 W 56th St, between Sixth and Seventh aves, in Le Parker Meridien; another location at 33 W 8th St ☎ 212 708 7414, ⓦ burgerjointny.com; subway F, N, Q, R to 57th St; map pp.72–73. Though the secret has long been out on this greasy hamburger stand incongruously located in a swish Midtown hotel, it still makes for good fun, good value and, most important, good eating. You might have to wait for a table. Mon–Thurs & Sun 11am–11.30pm, Fri & Sat 11am–midnight.

Margon 136 W 46th St, between Sixth and Seventh aves ☎ 212 354 5013; subway B, D, F, M to 47–50th sts–Rockefeller Center; N, Q, R to 49th St; map pp.72–73. This narrow Cuban lunch counter is nearly always packed, but the jostling is worth it; savoury Cuban sandwiches ($9 with rice and beans), garlicky *pernil* (Wed special, $8.75) and, best of all, brightly seasoned octopus salad ($10) are the top choices. Mon–Sat 7am–5pm.

★ **Yakitori Totto** 251 W 55th St (second floor), between Broadway and Eighth Ave ☎ 212 245 4555, ⓦ tottonyc.com; subway A, B, C, D, #1 to 59th St–Columbus Circle; N, Q, R to 57th St; B, D, E to Seventh Ave; map pp.72–73. This hideaway is perfect for late-night snacking. Skewers of grilled chicken heart, skirt steak and chicken thigh with spring onions all burst with flavour; a fistful (most $3–5 each) with some sides and a cold Sapporo make a nice meal. Mon–Fri 11.30am–2pm & 5.30pm–midnight, Sat 5.30pm–1am, Sun 5.30–11pm.

UPPER EAST SIDE

Café Sabarsky in the Neue Galerie 1048 Fifth Ave, at E 86th St ☎ 212 288 0665; subway #4, #5, #6 to 86th St; map pp.72–73. Sumptuous decor that harkens back to Old Vienna fills the handsome parlour of the former Vanderbilt mansion. The menu reads like that of an upscale Central European Kaffeehaus; it includes superb pastries, including Linzertorte and strudels ($9), and small sandwiches ($14–16), many made with cured meats. Mon & Wed 9am–6pm, Thurs–Sun 9am–9pm.

Penrose 1590 Second Ave, between E 82nd and E 83rd sts ☎ 212 203 2751, ⓦ penrosebar.com; subway #4, #5, #6 to 86th St; map pp.72–73. This popular new gastropub makes an excellent lunch diversion from Museum Mile; highlights include the mighty Pat La Frieda Penrose burger, worth every morsel at $12, and the beer-battered and fried Irish sausages with smoky sauce ($6). Mon–Thurs 3pm–4am, Fri 1pm–4am, Sat & Sun 11am–4am.

UPPER WEST SIDE

★ **Barney Greengrass** 541 Amsterdam Ave, between 86th and 87th sts; subway #1 to 86th St; map pp.72–73. The "sturgeon king" is an Upper West Side fixture; the deli (and restaurant) have been around since time began. The smoked-salmon section is a particular treat. Deli: Tues–Sun 8am–6pm; restaurant: Tues–Fri 8.30am–4pm, Sat & Sun 8.30am–5pm.

Hungarian Pastry Shop 1030 Amsterdam Ave, between W 110th and W 111th sts ☎ 212 866 4230; subway #1 to 110th St; map pp.72–73. This simple, no-frills coffeehouse is a favourite with Columbia University affiliates. You can sip your espresso and read Proust all day if you like (madeleines, anyone?); the only problem is choosing between the pastries, cookies and cakes, all made on the premises. Mon–Fri 7.30am–11.30pm, Sat 8.30am–11.30pm, Sun 8.30am–10.30pm.

★ **Salumeria Rosi Parmacotto** 283 Amsterdam Ave, between 73rd and 74th sts ☎ 212 877 4801, ⓦ salumeriarosi.com; subway #1, #2, #3 to 72nd St; map pp.72–73. On your left as you enter is a deli counter with a dizzying array of gorgeous cured meats; on your right, the slender dining room, where you can order lots of small plates: a selection of *salumi* ($6–9 each, sampling $18–27) and some cheeses ($8 each, sampling $17), crisp Brussels sprouts ($12) and a pasta or two ($14–15). Mon–Fri noon–10/11pm, Sat & Sun 11am–10pm.

HARLEM

Amy Ruth's 113 W 116th St, between Malcolm X and Powell blvds ☎ 212 280 8779, ⓦ amyruthsharlem.com; subway #2, #3 to 116th St; map pp.72–73. The barbecue chicken ($13.95), named in honour of President Obama, is more than enough reason to visit this small, casual family restaurant, but waffle breakfasts (from $7.95) and desserts (think peach cobbler and banana pudding; $5) are equally enticing. Mon 11.30am–11pm, Tues–Thurs 8.30am–11pm, Fri 8.30am–5.30am, Sat 7.30am–5.30am, Sun 7.30am–11pm.

★ **Red Rooster** 310 Malcolm X Blvd, between W 125th and W 126th sts ☎ 212 792 9001, ⓦ redroosterharlem .com; subway #2, #3 to 125th St; map pp.72–73. Marcus Samuelsson's restaurant opened in 2011, bringing a sophisticated take on Southern comfort food. Sandwiches are $15–17, while mains such as lamb and sweet potato hash are $18–29 (lunch is cheaper). Leave room for the Rooster mud pie ($11). Mon–Thurs 11.30am–3pm & 5.30–10.30pm, Fri 11.30am–3pm & 5.30–11.30pm, Sat 10am–3pm & 5–11.30pm, Sun 10am–3pm & 5–10pm.

BROOKLYN

★ **Al Di Là** 248 Fifth Ave, at Carroll St, Park Slope ☎718 783 4565, ⓦaldilatrattoria.com; subway R to Union St–Fourth Ave; map p.83. Venetian country cooking at its finest at this husband-and-wife-run trattoria. Standouts include beet and ricotta ravioli ($12), a delicate *malfatti* (spinach gnocchi; $15), the daily risotto (price varies) and braised rabbit with polenta ($26). Early or late, expect at least a 45min wait. Mon–Thurs noon–3pm & 6–10.30pm, Fri noon–3pm & 6–11pm, Sat 11am–3.30pm & 5.30–11pm, Sun 11am–3.30pm & 5–10pm.

Mile End 97A Hoyt St, between Pacific St and Atlantic Ave, Boerum Hill ☎718 852 7510, ⓦmileenddeli.com; subway F, G to Bergen St; A, C, G to Hoyt–Schermerhorn St; map p.83. This Montréal-style deli attracts long lunch queues for its *poutine* (fries with curds and gravy; $8/$12) and smoked-meat sandwich: a peppery pile on rye bread with mustard ($14). Breakfast and dinner are no slouch, either. Mon & Tues 8am–4pm, Wed–Sat 8am–4pm & 6–11pm, Sun 10am–4pm & 6–10pm.

Peter Luger Steak House 178 Broadway, at Driggs Ave, Williamsburg ☎718 387 7400, ⓦpeterluger.com; subway J, M, Z to Marcy Ave; map p.83. Catering to carnivores since 1887, *Peter Luger* may just be the city's finest steakhouse. The service is surly and the decor plain, but the porterhouse steak – the only cut served – is divine (roughly $50/person); the lunchtime-only burger ($12) is a great deal. Cash only; reservations required. Mon–Thurs 11.45am–9.45pm, Fri & Sat 11.45am–10.45pm, Sun 12.45–9.45pm.

Pies and Thighs 166 S 4th St, at Driggs Ave, Williamsburg ☎347 529 6090, ⓦpiesnthighs.com; subway J, M, Z to Marcy Ave; map p.83. Great chicken biscuits ($6), expertly fried chicken ($13 with a side) and a rotating list of pies (slices $4.50–5.50). Mon–Fri 9am–4am & 5pm–midnight, Sat & Sun 10am–4pm & 5pm–midnight.

Totonno's Pizzeria Napolitano 1524 Neptune Ave, between 15th and 16th sts, Coney Island ☎718 372 8606, ⓦtotonnos.com; subway D, F, N, Q to Coney Island–Stillwell Ave; map p.83. The coal-oven-fired pizzas at this ancient (circa 1924), no-frills spot inspire devotion among pizza lovers for their sweet, fresh mozzarella and crispy crusts. The basic starts at $19.50; add on toppings from there. No slices; cash only. Wed–Sun noon–8pm.

QUEENS

M. Wells Dinette 22–25 Jackson Ave, between 46th Rd and 46th Ave, in MoMA PS1 (see p.85), Long Island City ☎718 786 1800; subway G, #7 to Court Square; E, M to Court Square-Ely; map p.83. Cheekily modelled on a classroom (MoMA PS1's building used to be a school), *M. Wells Dinette* is like no school cafeteria you've known. The menu changes, but expect dishes such as foie gras and oats, braised tongue with tarragon and other daring, cholesterol-rich exercises. Mon & Thurs–Sun noon–6pm.

DRINKING

New York's best **bars** are, generally speaking, in Downtown Manhattan – the West and East villages, Soho and the Lower East Side – and in outer-borough hoods like Williamsburg, Red Hook and Long Island City. Most of the places listed below serve food of some kind and have happy hours sometime between 4pm and 8pm during the week. See also the bars listed in "Gay New York" (p.99).

FINANCIAL DISTRICT, SOHO AND TRIBECA

Dead Rabbit 30 Water St, between Broad St and Coenties Slip ☎646 422 7906, ⓦdeadrabbitnyc.com; subway R to Whitehall St; map pp.62–63. Housed in a gorgeous old space, with a menu of classic cocktails ($12), bottled punches ($10), highballs ($11), wine, beer and a vast range of whiskey; the bar menu features fish and chips, stews and meat pies. Tap room daily 11am–4am; parlour Mon–Wed 5pm–2am, Thurs–Sat 5pm–3am.

Ear Inn 326 Spring St, between Washington and Greenwich sts ☎212 226 9060, ⓦearinn.com; subway C, E to Spring St; #1 to Houston St; map pp.62–63. "Ear" as in "Bar" with half the neon "B" blacked out. This historic pub, a stone's throw from the Hudson River, opened in 1890 (the building dates from 1817). Its creaky (and some claim, haunted) interior is as cosy as a Cornish inn, with a good mix of beers on tap ($6.50) and basic, reasonably priced American food. Free, old-school jazz every Sunday (8–11pm). Daily noon–4am.

Fanelli Café 94 Prince St, at Mercer St ☎212 226 9412; subway N, R to Prince St; map pp.62–63. Established in 1922 (the building dates from 1853), the relaxed *Fanelli* is a favourite destination of the not-too-hip after-work crowd, with a small dining room at the back (mains $11–15). Mon–Wed & Sun 10am–2am, Thurs–Sat 10am–4am.

LOWER EAST SIDE AND EAST VILLAGE

7B 108 Ave B, at E 7th St ☎212 473 8840; subway L to First Ave; map pp.62–63. This quintessential East Village hangout has often been used as the sleazy set in films and commercials. It features deliberately crazy bartenders, cheap pitchers of beer and one of the best punk and rock 'n' roll jukeboxes in the East Village. Daily noon–4am.

★ **Booker & Dax** 207 Second Ave, at E 13th St ☎212 254 3500, ⓦmomofuku.com/new-york/booker-and-dax; subway #6 to Bleecker St; map pp.62–63.

1

Manhattans and plenty of creative bar theatrics: drinks made with hot pokers ("friend of the devil") and lots of liquid nitrogen knocking around. Mon–Thurs & Sun 6pm–2am, Fri & Sat 6pm–3am.

Decibel 240 E 9th St, between Second and Third aves ☎212 979 2733, ⍟sakebardecibel.com; subway #6 to Astor Place; map pp.62–63. A rocking atmosphere (with good tunes) pervades this beautifully decorated underground sake bar. The inevitable wait for a wooden table will be worth it. Daily 6pm–3am, Sun until 1am.

★ **Grassroots Tavern** 20 St Mark's Place, between Second and Third aves ☎212 475 9443; subway #6 to Astor Place; map pp.62–63. This wonderful, roomy underground den has dirt-cheap pitchers (from $7), free popcorn, an extended happy hour and at least three of the manager's pets roaming around at all hours of the day or night. Daily 4pm–4am.

WEST VILLAGE

55 Bar 55 Christopher St, between Sixth and Seventh aves ☎212 929 9883, ⍟55bar.com; subway #1 to Christopher St; map pp.62–63. A gem of an underground dive bar that's been around since 1919, with a great jukebox, congenial clientele and live jazz and blues nightly (including guitarist Mike Stern; sets $10). Daily 3pm–3am.

Blind Tiger Ale House 281 Bleecker St, at Jones St; ☎212 462 4682, ⍟blindtigeralehouse.com; subway A, B, C, D, E, F, M to W 4th St; #1 to Christopher St; map pp.62–63. This wood-panelled pub is the home of serious ale connoisseurs, with 28 rotating draughts (primarily US microbrews such as Sixpoint and Smuttynose for around $6.50), a couple of casks and loads of bottled beers – they also serve cheese plates from *Murray's* (see p.101). The prime location means it tends to get packed. Daily 11.30am–4am.

White Horse Tavern 567 Hudson St, at W 11th St ☎212 243 9260; subway #1 to Christopher St; map pp.62–63. A Greenwich Village institution, which opened in 1880: Dylan Thomas supped his last here before being taken to hospital with alcohol poisoning (check out the portrait and plaque inside), while Norman Mailer and Hunter S. Thompson were also regulars. Daily 11am–3am.

UNION SQUARE AND CHELSEA

Bar Jamón 125 E 17th St, at Irving Place ☎212 253 2773, ⍟casamononyc.com; subway L, N, Q, R, #4, #5, #6 to 14th St–Union Square; map pp.62–63. A superb place to sip on sherry and nosh on Spanish tapas (most $3–10). Be warned though: there are just fourteen stools. Mon–Fri 5pm–2am, Sat & Sun 2pm–2am.

★ **El Quinto Pino** 401 W 24th St, at 9th Ave ☎212 206 6900, ⍟elquintopinonyc.com; subway C, E to 23rd St; map pp.62–63. There are relatively few seats in this elegant Chelsea tapas bar, so come early for pork cracklings

($6) and an uncanny sea urchin sandwich ($15), paired with a good selection of Spanish wines. Mon–Thurs 5pm–midnight, Fri & Sat 5pm–1am, Sun 5–11pm.

La Birreria Eataly, 200 Fifth Ave, at W 23rd St ☎212 937 8910, ⍟eatalyny.com/birreria; subway N, R, #6 to 23rd St; map pp.62–63. A sprawling rooftop bar above the insanely popular Eataly market, *Birreria* is a modern twist on the beer garden – you'd expect nothing less than the handcrafted ales and home-made sausages considering the foodie haven below. Mon–Wed & Sun 11.30am–10pm, Thurs–Sat 11.30am–11pm.

Molly's 287 Third Ave, between E 22nd and E 23rd sts ☎212 889 3361, ⍟mollysshebeen.com; subway #6 to 23rd St; map pp.62–63. While the city veers from throwback cocktails and nouveau speakeasies to local microbrew palaces, the friendly bartenders at *Molly's* are content to pour some of the best pints of Guinness around. Sawdust floor included. Daily 11am–4am.

Peter McManus Café 152 Seventh Ave, at 19th St ☎212 929 9691; subway #1 to 18th St; map pp.62–63. Unlike many Irish pubs in the city, this is the real deal, and it's been so since 1936. The worn oak bar adds character, along with the tasty in-house McManus Ale and two old-style telephone booths inside. Mon–Sat 11am–4am, Sun noon–4am.

Tia Pol 205 Tenth Ave, between 22nd and 23rd sts ☎212 675 8805; subway C, E to 23rd St; map pp.62–63. This popular tapas bar frequently fills up its narrow space – come early if you want to miss the crowds. You can graze on bar snacks or construct a meal; wash it all back with the easy-drinking house-made sangria ($9 glass). Mon 5.30–11pm, Tues–Thurs noon–11pm, Fri noon–midnight, Sat 11am–midnight, Sun 11am–10.30pm.

MIDTOWN EAST

Campbell Apartment Southwest balcony, Grand Central Terminal ☎212 953 0409; subway #4, #5, #6, #7 to 42nd St–Grand Central; map pp.72–73. Once home to businessman John W. Campbell, who oversaw the construction of Grand Central, this majestic space – built to look like a Florentine palace – was sealed up for years. Now it's one of New York's most distinctive cocktail bars. Go early and don't wear trainers (or a T-shirt, ripped jeans or baseball cap). Mon–Thurs noon–1am, Fri & Sat noon–2am, Sun noon–midnight.

King Cole Bar and Salon 2 E 55th St, between Fifth and Madison aves, in the St Regis hotel ☎212 753 4500, ⍟kingcolebar.com; subway E, M to Fifth Ave–53rd St; map pp.72–73. The reputed birthplace of the Bloody Mary has recently been refurbished and reborn as a bar-restaurant meant to evoke a 1920s jazz lounge. Fortunately, the grand Maxfield Parrish mural remains in its proper spot, right above the bar. Ask about the secret in the painting while sipping on a cocktail and sampling small or large plates of refined, upscale cuisine. Daily until late.

TIMES SQUARE AND THEATER DISTRICT

★ **Jimmy's Corner** 140 W 44th St, between Broadway and Sixth Ave ☎ 212 221 9510; subway B, D, F, M to 42nd St-Bryant Park; N, Q, R, #1, #2, #3 to Times Square-42nd St; map pp.72–73. You'd be hard pressed to find a more atmospheric watering hole anywhere in the city – or a better jazz/R&B jukebox. Mon–Fri 11am–4am, Sat noon–4pm, Sun 3pm–4am.

Kashkaval 856 Ninth Ave, between W 55th and W 56th sts ☎ 212 581 8282, ⓦ kashkavalfoods.com; subway A, B, D, #1 to 59th St–Columbus Circle; map pp.72–73. Tucked in the back of a cheese shop, this cosy wine bar serves up tasty bites, including excellent cheese and meat plates, cold *meze* (the beetroot *skordalia* is good) and an array of fondues. Daily 11am–midnight.

★ **Rudy's** 627 Ninth Ave, between W 44th and W 45th sts ☎ 646 707 0890, ⓦ rudysbarnyc.com; subway A, C, E to 42nd St-Port Authority; map pp.72–73. One of New York's cheapest, friendliest and liveliest bars, a favourite with local actors and musicians. *Rudy's* offers free hot dogs, a backyard that's great in summer and some of the cheapest pitchers of beer in the city ($7–16). Daily 8am–4am.

UPPER EAST SIDE

★ **Balcony Bar & Roof Garden Café** Metropolitan Museum of Art, 1000 Fifth Ave, at E 82nd St ☎ 212 535 7710, ⓦ metmuseum.org; subway #4, #5, #6 to 86th St; map pp.72–73. It's hard to imagine a more romantic spot to sip a glass of wine and kick off the evening, whether on the *Roof Garden Café*, with some of the best views in the city, or in the *Balcony Bar* overlooking the Great Hall. Café: May–Oct Tues–Thurs & Sun 10am–4.30pm, Fri & Sat 10am–8pm; bar: year-round Fri & Sat 4–8.30pm.

Subway Inn 143 E 60th St, at Lexington Ave ☎ 212 223 8929; subway N, R, #4, #5, #6 to Lexington Ave–59th St; map pp.72–73. This neighbourhood dive bar, across from Bloomingdale's, has been serving customers since 1937 and is great for a late-afternoon beer. Mon–Fri 10am–4am, Sat & Sun 11am–4am.

UPPER WEST SIDE

Ding Dong Lounge 929 Columbus Ave, between W 105th and W 106th sts ☎ 212 663 2600, ⓦ dingdong lounge.com; subway B, C to 103rd St; map pp.72–73. This punk bar with a DJ and occasional live bands attracts a vibrant mix of drinkers. Happy hour 4–8pm, with $4 draught beer and $5 cocktails. Daily 4pm–4am.

HARLEM

Harlem Tavern 2153 Frederick Douglass Bvld, at W 116th St ☎ 212 866 4500, ⓦ harlemtavern.com; subway B, C, #2, #3 to 116th St; map pp.72–73. Restaurant, bar and enticing beer garden (excellent seasonal beer selection), with live jazz and weekend brunches ($14.95). Mon–Fri noon–2am, Sat & Sun 11am–2am.

BROOKLYN

Bar Great Harry 280 Smith St, at Sackett St, Carroll Gardens ☎ 718 222 1103, ⓦ bargreatharry.com; subway F, G to Carroll St; map p.83. An essential stop on any Carroll Gardens pub crawl, with a vast list of microbrews and select imports (20 on tap, 70 in bottles). Beers $5–8. Daily 2pm–4am (though can shut earlier).

Brooklyn Brewery 1 Brewers Row, 79 N 11th St, Williamsburg ☎ 718 486 7422, ⓦ brooklynbrewery .com; subway L to Bedford Ave; map p.83. New York's best-known microbrewery, where you can sample a variety of the label's beers ($5) – including some not available elsewhere – in a bar setting. Fri 6–11pm, Sat noon–8pm, Sun noon–6pm.

Pete's Candy Store 709 Lorimer St, between Frost and Richardson sts, Williamsburg ☎ 718 302 3770, ⓦ petes candystore.com; subway L to Lorimer St; G to Metro-politan Ave; map p.83. This terrific little spot was once a real sweet shop. There's free live music every night, a reading series, Scrabble and Bingo nights, pub quizzes and some well-poured cocktails. Mon–Wed & Sun 5pm–2am, Thurs–Sat 5pm–4am.

★ **Tørst** 615 Manhattan Ave, between Nassau and Driggs aves, Greenpoint; subway G to Nassau Ave; map p.83. A shiny new temple for beer-drinkers, *Tørst* boasts reclaimed wood and a sleek metal bar, behind which 21 draughts sit hooked up to the "flux capacitor", which allows bartenders to monitor and adjust the gas and carbonation without descending to the kegs below. Mon–Wed & Sun noon–midnight, Thurs–Sat noon–2am.

QUEENS

Bohemian Hall and Beer Garden 29-19 24th Ave, between 29th and 30th sts, Astoria ☎ 718 274 4925, ⓦ bohemianhall.com; subway N, Q to Astoria Blvd; map p.83. This 100-year-old Czech bar is the real deal, catering to old-timers and serving a good selection of pilsners, among other offerings. Out back there's a very large beer garden, complete with picnic tables, trees, free-flowing pitchers, grills for burgers and sausages, and a bandstand for polka groups. Mon–Thurs 5pm–1am, Fri 3pm–2am, Sat noon–2am, Sun noon–1am.

L.I.C. Bar 45–58 Vernon Blvd, at 46th Ave, Long Island City ☎ 718 786 5400, ⓦ longislandcitybar.com; subway #7 to Vernon Blvd–Jackson Ave or 45th Rd–Courthouse Square; G to 21st St; map p.83. A friendly, atmospheric place for a beer, burger and some free live music (Mon, Wed, Sat & Sun); hunker down at the old wooden bar or out in the pleasant garden. Mon–Thurs & Sun 4pm–2am, Fri & Sat 2pm–4am.

1

NIGHTLIFE

You'll never be at a loss for something fun or culturally enriching to do while in New York. The **live music** scene, in particular, well reflects New York's diversity: on any night of the week, you can hear pretty much any type of music, from thumping hip-hop to raging punk, and, of course, plenty of jazz. There are also quite a few **dance clubs**, where you can move to hard-hitting house or cheesy tunes from the 1970s and 80s.

Tickets For advance tickets, go to the venue's box office or (at least for bigger venues) visit Ticketmaster (☎ 212 307 4100 or ☎ 800 755 4000 outside NY, ⓦ ticketmaster.com) or Ticketweb (ⓦ ticketweb.com).

Listings Check out *Time Out New York* ($4.99; available from newsstands citywide or online at ⓦ timeout.com) or a free-sheet like *The Village Voice* (free; available in newspaper boxes and many other spots around town) or *The Onion* (whose cultural listings are excellent; ⓦ theonion.com). Useful websites include ⓦ ohmyrockness.com (for indie rock) and ⓦ themagazine.com (indie-ish, but covers many genres).

ROCK, POP AND MULTI-GENRE

Arlene's Grocery 95 Stanton St, between Ludlow and Orchard sts ☎ 212 473 9831, ⓦ arlenesgrocery.net; subway F to Lower East Side–Second Ave; map pp.62–63. An intimate, erstwhile *bodega* (hence the name) that hosts nightly gigs by local, reliably good indie bands. Go on Mon nights (free) after 10pm for punk and heavy-metal karaoke, with live band backing. Tues–Thurs & Sun cover $8, Fri & Sat $10. Daily 6pm–4am.

Bowery Ballroom 6 Delancey St, at Bowery ☎ 212 533 2111, ⓦ boweryballroom.com; subway J, Z to Bowery; B, D to Grand St; map pp.62–63. No attitude, great acoustics and even better views have earned this venue praise from both fans and bands. Major labels test their up-and-comers here. Most shows cost $15–35. Daily 7pm till late.

Knitting Factory 361 Metropolitan Ave, at Havemeyer St, Williamsburg ☎ 347 529 6696, ⓦ bk.knittingfactory .com; subway L to Bedford Ave; G, L to Metropolitan Ave; map p.83. This intimate showcase for indie rock and underground hip-hop moved to Brooklyn in 2009, but has maintained a loyal following and quality acts. Most tickets $5–15. Daily shows from 6pm or 7pm till late.

★ **(Le) Poisson Rouge** 158 Bleecker St, at Thompson St ☎ 212 505 3474, ⓦ lepoissonrouge.com; subway A, B, C, D, E, F, M to W 4th St; map pp.62–63. Mix of live rock, folk, pop and electronica at 7pm ($10–15), with dance parties most weekends Fri and Sat (often free). Daily 5pm–2am, Fri & Sat until 4am.

Music Hall of Williamsburg 66 N 6th St, between Wythe and Kent aves, Williamsburg ☎ 718 486 5400, ⓦ musichallofwilliamsburg.com; subway L to Bedford Ave; map p.83. A large performance space with excellent acoustics, set in an old factory – one of Brooklyn's best venues. From 6pm until the opening band starts, all drinks are $3. Tickets $10–20. Shows 8/9pm till late.

JAZZ VENUES

★ **American Legion Post (Col. Charles Young #398)** 248 W 132nd St, between Powell and Frederick Douglass blvds ☎ 212 283 9701; subway #2, #3 to W 135th St; map pp.72–73. This veterans' club hosts one of the best deals in Harlem, the free Sun evening jam sessions (7pm– midnight); the headliner is Seleno Clarke on his classic Hammond B-3 organ. Sun 4pm–midnight, jazz nights also Wed, Thurs & every other Sat 8pm–midnight.

Shrine Bar 2271 Powell Blvd, between W 133rd and W 134th sts ☎ 212 690 7807, ⓦ shrinenyc.com; subway B, #2, #3 to 135th St; map pp.72–73. Named for Fela Kuti's legendary joint in Lagos, this cosy bar and performance space features African decor and walls lined with album sleeves. Shows start at 6pm most nights, and there's flavoursome Israeli and West African food from the owners. Daily 4pm–4am.

Village Vanguard 178 Seventh Ave, between Perry and W 11th sts ☎ 212 255 4037, ⓦ villagevanguard.com; subway #1, #2, #3 to 14th St; map pp.62–63. An NYC jazz landmark since 1935, with a regular roster of big names. Cover $25 per set, plus a one-drink minimum. Daily 7.30pm–1am.

CLUBS AND DISCOS

The action is spread out, with the Lower East Side, the East and West villages and Brooklyn offering as many venues as "hot" nightlife hubs like the Meatpacking District. Cover charges range from $15 to $50, though most average out at around $20; always bring photo ID.

Cielo 18 Little W 12th St, between Washington St and Ninth Ave ☎ 212 645 5700, ⓦ cieloclub.com; subway L to Eighth Ave; A, C, E to 14th St; map pp.62–63. Expect velvet rope-burn at this super-exclusive see-and-be-seen place: there's only room for 250 people. The Monday-night reggae and dub party Deep Space from François K gets the most hype. Best sound system in the city. Cover $20–25. Mon & Wed–Sat 10pm–4am.

Output 78 Wythe Ave, at N 12th St ☎ 212 645 5700, ⓦ outputclub.com; subway L to Bedford Ave, Williamsburg; map p.83. The "official club of Williamsburg" opened with much fanfare in 2013, with a smallish, industrial warehouse space, big sound system and a focus on dancing, not posing. Lots of techno and ambient. Cover $15–20 (advance). Wed–Sat 10pm–5am.

Santos Party House 96 Lafayette St, between Canal and Walker sts ☎ 212 584 5492, ⓦ santospartyhouse .com; subway J, N, Q, R, Z, #6 to Canal St; map pp.62–63.

1

Two-floor club and art space, with wild hip-hop, Latin and house most Thursdays to Saturdays; check the website for the current schedule. Cover usually $10–15. Daily 7pm–4am.

PERFORMING ARTS AND FILM

Home to Broadway and 42nd Street, New York is one of the world's great **theatre** centres. Even if you're not normally a theatre buff, going to see a play or a musical while here is virtually de rigueur. The various theatre venues are referred to as Broadway, Off-Broadway or Off-Off Broadway, representing a descending order of ticket price, production polish, elegance and comfort. **Classical music**, **opera** and **dance** are all very well represented, too. As for **film**, you couldn't hope for better pickings: the city has several large indie theatres, assorted revival and arthouse cinemas and countless Hollywood-blockbuster multiplexes. Last but not least, NYC has many excellent **comedy** clubs.

Tickets Expect to shell out $150 or so for orchestra seats at the hottest Broadway shows, though prices can be cut considerably if you can wait in line on the day of the performance at the TKTS booth in Times Square (Mon, Thurs & Fri 3–8pm, Tues 2–8pm, Wed & Sat 10am–2pm & 3–8pm, Sun 11am–7pm); there are also booths at the Seaport and downtown Brooklyn. If you're prepared to pay full price, go directly to the theatre box office or use Telecharge (☎212 239 6200 or ☎800 43 7250 outside NY, ⓦtelecharge.com) or Ticketmaster; expect to pay a $7 surcharge per ticket. For Off-Broadway shows, Ticket Central (☎212 279 4200, ⓦticketcentral.com) sells tickets online and at its offices at 416 W 42nd St, between Ninth and Tenth avenues (daily noon–8pm; ☎212 279 4200).

THEATRE, CABARET AND COMEDY

Don't Tell Mama 343 W 46th St, at 9th Ave ☎212 757 0788, ⓦdonttellmamanyc.com; subway A, C, E to 42nd St-Port Authority. Lively and convivial Midtown West piano bar and cabaret featuring rising stars and singing waitresses. Cover free to $30 plus two-drink minimum.

La Mama E.T.C. (Experimental Theater Club) 74A E 4th St, at 2nd Ave ☎212 475 7710, ⓦlamama.org; subway F to Second Ave. A real gem with three different auditoria, known for politically and sexually charged material as well as visiting dance troupes from overseas.

Playwrights Horizons 416 W 42nd St, at 9th Ave ☎212 564 1235 (admin) or ☎279 4200 (tickets), ⓦplaywrightshorizons.org; subway A, C, E, #7 to 42nd St-Port Authority; N, Q, R, S, #1, #2, #3 to Times Square-42nd St. This well-respected drama-centric space is located right by Times Square, though its mission remains the same as it was when it was founded in a YMCA in 1971 – championing works by undiscovered playwrights.

The Public Theater 425 Lafayette St ☎212 539 8500, ⓦpublictheater.org; subway #6 to Astor Place. The city's primary presenter of the Bard's plays. In summer, it produces the free Shakespeare in the Park series at the open-air Delacorte Theater in Central Park; year-round it delivers thought-provoking Off-Broadway productions.

Upright Citizens Brigade Theatre 307 W 26th St, between Eighth and Ninth aves ☎212 366 9176, ⓦucbtheatre.com; subway C, E to 23rd St; #1 to 28th St. Consistently hilarious sketch-based and improv comedy, seven nights a week. You can sometimes catch *Saturday Night Live* cast members in the ensemble. Cover $5–10, though free some nights.

CLASSICAL MUSIC, OPERA AND DANCE

Alice Tully Hall Lincoln Center, Broadway and W 65th St ☎212 671 4050, ⓦlc.lincolncenter.org; subway #1 to 66th St. A smaller Lincoln Center hall for the top chamber orchestras, string quartets and instrumentalists. The weekend chamber series is deservedly popular. Tickets are mostly in the $30–70 range.

Avery Fisher Hall Lincoln Center, Broadway and W 65th St ☎212 875 5030, ⓦlc.lincolncenter.org or ⓦnyphil .org; subway #1 to 66th St. The permanent home of the New York Philharmonic. Ticket prices for the Philharmonic range $30–150. The open rehearsals (9.45am on the first day of new concert weeks, usually Wed or Thurs) are a great bargain; tickets are $18.

Brooklyn Academy of Music 30 Lafayette Ave, Brooklyn ☎718 636 4100, ⓦbam.org; subway #2, #3, #4, #5, N, R to Atlantic Ave-Barclays Center. The BAM Opera House is the perennial home of Philip Glass operatic premieres and Laurie Anderson performances. It also hosts a number of contemporary imports from Europe and China, often with a modern-dance component.

Carnegie Hall 154 W 57th St, at 7th Ave ☎212 247 7800, ⓦcarnegiehall.org; subway N, Q, R to 57th St–Seventh Ave. The greatest names from all schools of music have performed here, from Tchaikovsky (who conducted the hall's inaugural concert) and Toscanini to Gershwin and, um, Lady Gaga. The stunning acoustics lure big-time performers at sky-high prices. Check the website for up-to-date admission rates and schedules.

Metropolitan Opera House Lincoln Center, Columbus Ave, at 64th St ☎212 362 6000, ⓦmetoperafamily.org; subway #1 to 66th St. More popularly known as the Met, New York's premier opera venue is home to the world-renowned Metropolitan Opera Company from Sept/early Oct to late April/early May. Tickets are expensive (up to $310) and can be well-nigh impossible to snag, though 175 standing-room tickets go on sale at 10am on day of performance ($17–35) and 200 "rush-tickets" for orchestra

1

seats go on sale at 6pm ($25). The limit is one ticket per person, and the queue has been known to form at dawn.

FILM

★ **Film Forum** 209 W Houston St, between Sixth and Seventh aves ☎ 212 727 8110, ⓦ filmforum.org; subway #1 to Houston St; A, B, C, D, E, F, M to W 4th St. The cosy three-screen Film Forum has an eccentric but

famously popular programme of new independent movies, documentaries and foreign films, as well as a repertory programme specializing in silent comedy, camp classics and cult directors.

Landmark Sunshine Cinema 143 E Houston St, at 1st Ave ☎ 212 260 7289, ⓦ landmarktheatres.com; subway F to Second Ave. This former Yiddish vaudeville house is the best place in town to see indie films.

GAY NEW YORK

There are few places in America where **gay culture** thrives as it does in New York. **Chelsea** (centred on Eighth Ave, between 14th and 23rd sts), the **East Village** and **Hell's Kitchen** have replaced the **West Village** as the hubs of gay New York, although a strong presence still lingers around Christopher Street. There's Brooklyn's **Park Slope**, too, though perhaps more for women than for men. The free weekly *Gay City News, Next* and *GO* have listings.

RESOURCES

Bluestockings 172 Allen St, between Stanton and Rivington sts ☎ 212 777 6028, ⓦ bluestockings.com; subway F to Second Ave or Delancey St. Fairtrade café and lefty bookstore that's an informal centre of the lesbian and bi community. Daily 11am–11pm.

Gay Men's Health Crisis (GMHC) 446 W 33rd St, between Ninth and Tenth aves ☎ 212 367 1000, ⓦ gmhc.org. Despite the name, this incredible organization – the oldest and largest not-for-profit AIDS organization in the world – provides testing, information and referrals to everyone: gay, straight and transgender.

The Lesbian, Gay, Bisexual & Transgender Community Services Center 208 W 13th St, west of Seventh Ave ☎ 212 620 7310, ⓦ gaycenter.org. The Center houses well over a hundred groups and organizations, and sponsors workshops, movie nights and lots more.

BARS AND CLUBS

Barracuda 275 W 22nd St, between Seventh and Eighth aves ☎ 212 645 8613; subway C, E, #1 to 23rd St; map pp.62–63. A favourite spot in New York's gay scene, and pretty laidback for Chelsea. Two-for-one happy hour 4–9pm

during the week, crazy drag shows, karaoke nights and a look that changes several times a year. Daily 4pm–4am.

Brandy's Piano Bar 235 E 84th St, between Second and Third aves ☎ 212 744 4949, ⓦ brandyspianobar .com; subway #4, #5, #6 to 86th St; map pp.72–73. Handsome uptown cabaret/piano bar with a crazy, mixed and generally mature clientele. Definitely worth a visit; note there's a two-drink minimum during the nightly sets (which start at 9.30pm). Daily 4pm–3.30am.

Ginger's 363 Fifth Ave, between 5th and 6th sts, Park Slope, Brooklyn ☎ 718 788 0924, ⓦ gingersbarbklyn .com; subway F, G, R to Fourth Ave–9th St; map p.83. The best lesbian bar in New York is this dark, laidback Park Slope joint with a pool table, outdoor space and plenty of convivial company. Mon–Fri 5pm–4am, Sat & Sun 2pm–4am.

Stonewall Inn 53 Christopher St, between Waverly Place and Seventh Ave S ☎ 212 488 2705, ⓦ thestonewall innnyc.com; subway #1 to Christopher St–Sheridan Square; A, B, C, D, E, F, M to W 4th St; map pp.62–63. Yes, that Stonewall, site of the seminal 1969 riot, mostly refurbished and flying the pride flag like they own it – which, one could say, they do. Daily 2pm–4am.

SHOPPING

When it comes to consumerism, New York leaves all other cities behind. **Midtown Manhattan** is mainstream territory, with the department stores, big-name clothes designers and larger chains. Downtown plays host to a wide variety of more offbeat stores – **SoHo** is perhaps the most popular shopping neighbourhood in these parts, and generally the most expensive. Affordable alternatives for the young and trendy are available in the **Lower East Side**; good vintage clothing can be found there, in the East Village and in Williamsburg, Brooklyn.

BOOKS

Complete Traveller Antiquarian Bookstore 199 Madison Ave, at E 35th St ☎ 212 685 9007, ⓦ ctrarebooks .com; subway #6 to 33rd St; map pp.72–73. An extensive collection of rare travel tomes, including the entire Baedeker series, WPA guides, old books on NYC and maps. Mon–Fri 9.30am–6.30pm, Sat 10am–6pm, Sun noon–5pm.

Housing Works Bookstore Café 126 Crosby St,

between Houston and Prince sts ☎ 212 334 3324, ⓦ housingworks.org; subway B, D, F, M to Broadway–Lafayette; N, R to Prince St; #6 to Bleecker St; map pp.62–63. Excellent selection of very cheap and second-hand books. With a small espresso and snack bar and comfy chairs, it's a great place to spend an afternoon. Proceeds benefit those with HIV and AIDS and the homeless. Mon–Fri 10am–9pm, Sat & Sun 10am–5pm.

1

★ **Strand Bookstore** 828 Broadway, at E 12th St ☎ 212 473 1452, ⓦ strandbooks.com; subway N, R, Q, L, #4, #5, #6 to Union Square; map pp.62–63. Yes, it's hot and crowded, and the staff seem to resent working here, but with "18 miles of books" and a stock of more than 2.5 million titles, this is the largest discount book store in the city. Mon–Sat 9.30am–10.30pm, Sun 11am–10.30pm.

MUSIC

Generation Records 210 Thompson St, between Bleecker and W 3rd sts ☎ 212 254 1100, ⓦ generation records.com; subway A, B, C, D, E, F, M to W 4th St; map pp.62–63. The focus here is on hardcore, metal and punk with some indie. New CDs and vinyl upstairs, used goodies downstairs. Mon–Thurs & Sun 11am–10pm, Fri & Sat 11am–11pm.

Halcyon 57 Pearl St, at Water St, DUMBO, Brooklyn ☎ 718 260 9299, ⓦ halcyontheshop.com; subway F to York St; map p.83. A trusted source for dance music, but offers stuff ranging from jazz to techno. Radio shows, listening parties and a general air of music-nerd community make this a top pick. Mon, Wed & Sat noon–8pm, Tues, Thurs & Fri noon– 9pm, Sun noon–6pm.

Other Music 15 E 4th St, between Broadway and Lafayette St ☎ 212 477 8150, ⓦ othermusic.com; subway #6 to Astor Place; map pp.62–63. This homespun place is an excellent spot for "alternative" CDs, both old and new, that can otherwise be hard to find. Everfriendly and knowledgeable staff. Mon–Fri 11am–9pm, Sat noon–8pm, Sun noon–7pm.

FASHION

★ **Amarcord** 252 Lafayette St, between Prince and Spring sts ☎ 212 431 4161, ⓦ amarcordvintagefashion.com; subway N, R to Prince St; #6 to Spring St; map p.83. Also 223 Bedford Ave, between N 4th and N 5th sts, Williamsburg (daily noon–8pm). A real find. The owners make regular trips through their home country of Italy in search of discarded Dior, Gucci, Yves Saint Laurent and so forth from the 1940s onward. The Williamsburg store carries menswear. Mon–Sat noon–7.30pm, Sun noon–7pm.

Beacon's Closet 88 N 11th St, between Berry St and Wythe Ave, Williamsburg, Brooklyn ☎ 718 486 0816, ⓦ beaconscloset.com; subway L to Bedford Ave; map pp.62–63. Also 10 W 13th St between Fifth and Sixth aves, West Village. Vast 5500-square-foot usedclothing paradise, specializing in modern fashions and vintage attire. Williamsburg: Mon–Fri 11am–9pm, Sat & Sun 11am–8pm; West Village: Daily 11am–8pm.

Edith Machinist 104 Rivington St, at Ludlow St ☎ 212 979 9992; subway F to Delancey St; J, M, Z to Essex St; map pp.62–63. Very popular with the trendy vintage set, this used-clothing emporium holds some amazing finds

(particularly shoes) for those willing to sift through the massive stock. Tues–Sat noon–7pm, Sun noon–6pm.

Kirna Zabête 96 Greene St, between Prince and Spring sts ☎ 212 941 9656, ⓦ kirnazabete.com; subway N, R to Prince St; map pp.62–63. The best of the downtown shops, this is a concept store that stocks hand-picked highlights from designers such as Jason Wu, Rick Owens and Proenza Schouler. Mon–Sat 11am–7pm, Sun noon–6pm.

Marc Jacobs 163 Mercer St, between Houston and Prince sts ☎ 212 343 1490, ⓦ marcjacobs.com; subway N, R to Prince St; map pp.62–63. Marc Jacobs rules the New York fashion world like a Cosmopolitan-sipping colossus. Women from all walks of life come here to blow the nest egg on his latest "it" bag or pair of boots. Mon–Sat 11am–7pm, Sun noon–6pm.

Sigerson Morrison 28 Prince St, at Mott St ☎ 212 219 3893, ⓦ sigersonmorrison.com; subway N, R to Prince St; map pp.62–63. Kari Sigerson and Miranda Morrison make timeless, simple and elegant shoes for women. A required pilgrimage for shoe worshippers. Daily 8am–6pm.

DEPARTMENT STORES

Barneys New York 660 Madison Ave, at E 61st St ☎ 212 826 8900, ⓦ barneys.com; subway N, R to Fifth Ave–59th St; map pp.72–73. This temple to designer fashion is the best place to find cutting-edge labels or next season's hot item. The younger Co-op section was such a hit that it spawned several standalone Barneys Co-op stores. Mon–Fri 10am–8pm, Sat 10am–7pm, Sun 11am–6pm.

Bloomingdale's Lexington Ave and E 59th St (officially 1000 Third Ave) ☎ 212 705 2000, ⓦ bloomingdales.com; subway N, R, #4, #5, #6 to Lexington Ave–59th St; map pp.72–73. It has the atmosphere of a large, bustling bazaar, packed with concessions offering perfumes and designer clothes. Mon, Tues & Thurs 10am–8.30pm, Wed, Fri & Sat 10am–10pm, Sun 11am–7pm.

Century 21 22 Cortlandt St, between Broadway and Church St ☎ 212 227 9092, ⓦ c21stores.com; subway R to Cortlandt St or Rector St; #1 to Rector St; #4, #5 to Wall St; map pp.62–63. The granddaddy of designer discount department stores, where all the showrooms send their samples to be sold at the end of the season, usually at up to sixty percent off. Mon–Wed 7.45am–9pm, Thurs & Fri 7.45am–9.30pm, Sat 10am–9pm, Sun 11am–8pm.

Macy's 151 W 34th St, on Broadway at Herald Square ☎ 212 695 4400, ⓦ macys.com; subway B, D, F, M, N, Q, R to 34th St–Herald Square; map pp.72–73. Spread across two buildings, two million square feet of floor space and ten floors, Macy's until recently held the title of largest department store in the world. A highlight is the Cellar, the housewares department in the basement. If you're not American, head to the visitor centre to receive a ten percent discount card (bring your passport). Mon–Sat 10am–9.30pm, Sun 11am–8.30pm.

SPORTS IN NEW YORK

Seeing either of New York's two **baseball** teams involves a trip to the outer boroughs. The **Yankees** play in the Bronx, at **Yankee Stadium**, between 161st and 164th streets and River Avenue (☎ 718 293 6000, ⊛ newyorkyankees.mlb.com). Get there on the #4, B or D subway lines direct to the 161st Street station. The **Mets** are based in Queens, at **Citi Field**, 126th Street and Roosevelt Avenue, Willets Point, Queens (☎ 718 507 8499, ⊛ newyorkmets.mlb.com). Take the #7 train, direct to Willets Point. Tickets for games run $15–30.

New York's football teams – the **Jets** and **Giants** – play at the **Metlife Stadium**, East Rutherford, New Jersey (☎ 201 935 8500, ⊛ metlife.com). Buses from the Port Authority Bus Terminal (see p.86), serve the stadium. Tickets for both teams are always officially sold out well in advance, but you can often get seats (legally) from websites such as ⊛ stubhub.com.

There are three New York pro teams: the NBA **Knicks** (⊛ nba.com/knicks) and the WNBA **Liberty** (⊛ wnba.com/liberty), both of which play at **Madison Square Garden**, West 33rd Street at Seventh Avenue (☎ 212 465 6741, ⊛ thegarden.com); and the **Brooklyn Nets** (⊛ nba.com/nets), who call Barclays Center, 620 Atlantic Ave, at Flatbush Ave (☎ 917 618 6700, ⊛ barclayscenter.com) home. Tickets for the Knicks are very expensive, and, due to impossibly high demand, available in only limited numbers, if at all. Nets tickets are easier to score, while the women's games are fairly exciting and cheaper (starting at a little over $10, though they can be much more).

New York's **hockey** team, the **Rangers** (⊛ rangers.nhl.com), also plays at Madison Square Garden; tickets range from $50 to $370. Starting in 2015–16, the New York Islanders (⊛ islanders.nhl.com) will skate at the Barclays Center. The area **soccer** team, the **New York Red Bulls** (☎ 877 727 6223, ⊛ newyorkredbulls.com; tickets $23–73), play over in Harrison, New Jersey; a second pro team, New York City FC, starts play in 2015.

FOOD

Chelsea Market 75 Ninth Ave, between W 15th and W 16th sts ☎ 212 243 6005, ⊛ chelseamarket.com; subway A, C, E to 14th St; map pp.62–63. A complex of eighteen former industrial buildings, among them the old Nabisco Cookie Factory. A true smorgasbord of stores, including Fat Witch Bakery, Morimoto, Ronnybrook Dairy and the Lobster Place. Mon–Sat 7am–9pm, Sun 8am–7pm.

Eataly 200 Fifth Ave, at W 23rd St ☎ 212 229 2560, ⊛ eatalyny.com; subway N, R to 8th St; #6 to Astor Place; map pp.62–63. This wildly popular Mario Batalli venture is part Italian café/restaurant complex, part food market, with an incredible range of wine, cheese, meat, breads and seafood, sourced locally or flown in from Italy. Market daily 10am–11pm.

Murray's Cheese Shop 254 Bleecker St, at Cornelia St ☎ 212 243 3289, ⊛ murrayscheese.com; subway A, B, C, D, E, F, M to W 4th St; #1 to Christopher St; map pp.62–63. More than three hundred fresh cheeses and excellent panini sandwiches, all served by a knowledgeable staff. Mon–Sat 8am–8pm, Sun 10am–7pm.

★ **Russ & Daughters** 179 E Houston St, between Allen and Orchard sts ☎ 212 475 4880; subway F to Lower East Side–Second Ave; map pp.62–63. The original Manhattan gourmet shop, dating back to 1914, sells caviar, *halvah*, pickled vegetables, fine cheeses and amazing hand-rolled bagels with smoky lox (from $8.75). Mon–Fri 8am–8pm, Sat 9am–7pm, Sun 8am–5.30pm.

Zabar's 2245 Broadway, at W 80th St ☎ 212 787 2000, ⊛ zabars.com; subway #1 to 79th St; map pp.72–73. Perhaps the city's top gourmet shop, with an astonishing variety of cheeses, olives, meats, salads, freshly baked breads and croissants and prepared dishes. Avoid weekend afternoons, when tour buses turn the modest-sized store into Dante's seventh circle of hell. Mon–Fri 8am–7.30pm, Sat 8am–8pm, Sun 9am–6pm.

MISCELLANEOUS

Apple Store 103 Prince St, at Greene St ☎ 212 226 3126, ⊛ apple.com; subway N, R to Prince St; map pp.62–63. Other locations in Grand Central Terminal; 767 Fifth Ave; 401 W 14th St; and 1981 Broadway. The original Apple gadget store in Manhattan gets extremely crowded, but the latest in laptops, iPads, iPhones and iPods are all here for as cheap as you'll get them anywhere. Mon–Sat 9am–9pm, Sun 9am–7pm.

★ **Brooklyn Flea** 176 Lafayette Ave, between Clermont and Vanderbilt aves, Fort Greene (Sat); East River State Park, at N 7 St, Williamsburg (Sun) ☎ 212 243 5343, ⊛ brooklynflea.com; subway G to Clinton–Washington aves; C to Lafayette Ave (Sat); L to Bedford Ave (Sun); map p.83. The "flea" epithet is a bit of a misnomer, as this is as much a high-quality outdoor arts and crafts fair as secondhand fair, with two hundred stalls and superb artisan food. In winter (Dec–March), it moves indoors – check the website for locations. A food-related offshoot at the Williamsburg site, Smorgasburg, is equally worthwhile. Sat & Sun 10am–5pm.

The Mid-Atlantic

GETTYSBURG NATIONAL MILITARY PARK

The Mid-Atlantic

The three mid-Atlantic states – New York, Pennsylvania and New Jersey – stand at the heart of the most populated and industrialized corner of the US. Although dominated in the popular imagination by the grey smokestacks of New Jersey and steel factories of Pennsylvania, these states actually encompass beaches, mountains, islands, lakes, forests, rolling green countryside and many worthwhile small cities and towns.

European settlement here was characterized by considerable shifts and turns: the **Dutch**, who arrived in the 1620s, were methodically squeezed out by the **English**, who in turn fought off the **French** challenge to secure control of the region by the mid-eighteenth century. The Native American population, including the **Iroquois Confederacy** and Lenni Lenape, had sided with the French against the English and were soon confined to reservations or pushed north into Canada. At first, the economy depended on the fur trade, though by the 1730s English **Quakers**, along with **Amish** and **Mennonites** from Germany, plus a few Presbyterian **Irish**, had made farming a significant force, their holdings extending to the western limits of the region.

All three states were important during the **Revolution**: more than half the battles were fought here, including major American victories at **Trenton** and **Princeton** in New Jersey. Upstate New York was geographically crucial, as the British forces knew that American control of the Hudson River would effectively divide New England from the other colonies. After the Revolution, industry became the region's prime economic force, with **mill towns** springing up along the numerous rivers. By the mid-1850s the large **coalfields** of northeast Pennsylvania were powering the smoky steel mills of Pittsburgh and the discovery of high-grade **crude oil** in 1859 marked the beginning of the automobile age. Though still significant, especially in the regions near New York City, heavy industry has now largely been replaced by tourism as the economic engine.

Although many travellers to the East Coast do not venture much further than New York City itself, the region offers varied attractions, from the crashing Atlantic surf of **Long Island**, through the wooded **Catskill Mountains** and the imposing **Adirondacks**, occupying a quarter of the state, to the cultured and pastoral **Finger Lakes**. In the northwest corner of the state, beyond the **Erie Canal cities** along I-90, awesome **Niagara Falls** and artsy post-industrial **Buffalo** hug the Canadian border. **Pennsylvania** is best known for the fertile **Pennsylvania Dutch** country and the two great cities of **Philadelphia** and **Pittsburgh. New Jersey**, often pictured as one big industrial carbuncle, offers shameless tourist pleasures along the shore – from the boardwalk and casinos of **Atlantic City** to the small-town charm of **Cape May**.

The entire region is well covered by **public transport**, and metropolitan areas have good local transport systems that radiate out to outlying areas, meaning that only in the wilder forest and mountain areas do you really need a car. **Car rental** is expensive out of New York City, so better done from one of the other cities.

FRANK LLOYD WRIGHT'S BUILDING, FALLINGWATER, NEAR PITTSBURGH, PA

Highlights

❶ The Adirondacks, NY A vast and rugged alpine wilderness offering superb hiking, skiing, fishing and mountain-climbing opportunities. **See p.115**

❷ The Finger Lakes, NY With charming Ithaca, famed for its Ivy League university, as its hub, this delightful region brims with lakes, rolling hills, wineries and waterfalls. **See p.116**

❸ Niagara Falls, NY Take the memorable *Maid of the Mist* boat trip, or visit the Cave of the Winds and stand close enough to feel the spray from these majestic falls. **See p.122**

❹ History in Philadelphia, PA See the Liberty Bell and trace the steps of Benjamin Franklin in the city of brotherly love, where the Declaration of Independence was signed. **See p.126**

❺ Art and architecture, Pittsburgh, PA The Warhol Museum, Cathedral of Learning and two outlying Frank Lloyd Wright houses lend a surprising cultural flair to the so-called Steel City. **See p.140**

❻ Cape May, NJ The cultured end of the Jersey shore is exemplified by the Victorian architecture, quaint B&Bs and swish restaurants of this pleasant resort town. **See p.153**

HIGHLIGHTS ARE MARKED ON THE MAP ON P.106

New York State

However much exists to attract visitors, the vast state of **NEW YORK** stands inevitably in the shadow of America's most celebrated city. The words "New York" bring to mind soaring skyscrapers and congested streets, not the beaches of **Long Island** to the east or 50,000 square miles of rolling dairy farmland, colonial villages, workaday towns, lakes, waterfalls and towering mountains that fan out north and west from New York City and constitute **upstate New York.** Just an hour's drive north of Manhattan, the valley of the **Hudson River**, with the moody **Catskill Mountains** rising stealthily from the west bank, offers a respite from the intensity of the city. Much wilder and more rugged are the peaks of the vast **Adirondack Mountains** further north, which hold some of eastern America's most enticing scenery. To the west, the slender **Finger Lakes** and endless miles of dairy farms and vineyards occupy the central portion of the state. Of the larger cities, only **Buffalo** and **Rochester** hold much of interest, but some of the smaller towns, like Ivy League **Ithaca** and the spa town of **Saratoga Springs**, can be quite captivating.

In the seventeenth and eighteenth centuries semi-feudal **Dutch landowning dynasties** held sway upstate. Their control over tens of thousands of tenant farmers was barely affected by the transfer of colonial power from Holland to Britain or even by American Independence. Only with the completion of the **Erie Canal** in 1825, linking New York City with the Great Lakes, did the interior start to open up.

HIGHLIGHTS

1 The Adirondacks, NY

2 The Finger Lakes, NY

3 Niagara Falls, NY

4 History in Philadelphia, PA

5 Art and architecture, Pittsburgh, PA

6 Cape May, NJ

THE MID-ATLANTIC

2

GREAT REGIONAL DRIVES
Riverside Drive Follow US-9 and its subsidiary routes as they intertwine with the majestic Hudson River, all the way from NYC to the Adirondacks.
Coastal Route South of metropolitan New York, Rte-36 bends round with the New Jersey shoreline and merges with Rte-35, passing the most spectacular beaches.
Across Pennsylvania Take the leisurely route on US-30 from Philadelphia, via Amish country and Gettysburg, all the way to Pittsburgh.

Long Island

Just east of New York City, **Long Island** unfurls for 125 miles of lush farmland and broad sandy beaches, and is most often explored as an excursion from the metropolis. Its western end abuts the urban boroughs of Brooklyn and Queens but further east the settlements begin to thin out and the countryside gets surprisingly wild. The **north** and **south shores** differ greatly – the former is more immediately beautiful, its cliffs topped with luxurious mansions and estates, while the latter is fringed by almost continuous sand, interspersed with vacation spots such as **Jones Beach** and **Fire Island**. At its far end, Long Island splits in two, the **North Fork** retaining a marked rural aspect while the **South Fork** includes the **Hamptons**, an enclave of New York's richest and most famous.

ARRIVAL AND DEPARTURE   LONG ISLAND

By train The quickest way to reach Long Island is via the reliable Long Island Railroad (☎ 718 330 1234, ⓦ mta.info) from Penn Station.

By ferry You can also arrive via ferry from New England: Cross Sound Ferry connects New London, CT to Orient Point, Long Island (☎ 860 443 5281 in New England, ☎ 631 323 2525 on Long Island, ⓦ longislandferry.com).

By bus Numerous bus services (operated by the usual major companies, as well as Hampton Jitney; ☎ 800 936 0440, ⓦ hamptonjitney.com) cover most destinations.

By car If you're driving to Long Island, you'll take the Brooklyn–Queens Expressway (the BQE) to I-495 East. Parking permits during summer for most of Long Island's beaches are issued only to local residents.

GETTING AROUND

By ferry In many cases, ferries are the best means of travelling. For Fire Island there are various crossings, which you must use, as driving between the two road access points at either end of the island is restricted to island business owners: Fire Island Ferries (30–45min; $9 one-way; ☎ 631 665 3600, ⓦ fireislandferries.com) run from Bay Shore, the Sayville Ferry Service (25–45min; $7–13.50 one-way; ☎ 631 589 0810, ⓦ sayvilleferry.com) from Sayville, and

Davis Park Ferries (25–35min; $8.50 one-way; ☎ 631 475 1665, ⓦ davisparkferry.com) from Patchogue. Regular ferries connect the North Fork at Greenport (pedestrians $2 one-way; cars including driver $10 one-way; ☎ 631 749 0139, ⓦ northferry.com) with pleasant Shelter Island (ⓦ shelter-island.org) and on to the South Fork (pedestrians $1 one-way; cars including passengers $14 one-way; ☎ 631 749 1200, ⓦ southferry.com).

The South Shore

Long Island's **South Shore** merges gently with the wild Atlantic, with shallow, creamy sand beaches and rolling dunes – two of the most popular options are **Long Beach** and **Jones Beach**, which together run along fifty miles of seashore, getting less crowded the further east you go. **Ocean Parkway** leads along the narrow offshore strand from Jones Beach to **Captree**, from where the **Robert Moses Causeway** crosses back to **Bay Shore**, or heads south to pristine **Robert Moses State Park**, at the western tip of Fire Island. This way you can bypass the sprawling mess of **Amityville**, famous for its 1974 "horror"; the house in which a mysterious supernatural force is said to have victimized the occupants still stands as a private residence at 108 Ocean Ave.

Fire Island

A slim spit of land parallel to the South Shore, **Fire Island** is in many ways a microcosm of New York City and on summer weekends half of Manhattan seems to be holed up in its tiny settlements, including the primarily gay enclaves of **Cherry Grove** and **The Pines**, lively **Ocean Beach**, exclusive **Point O'Woods** and **Sunken Forest** (aka Sailor's Haven), which attracts a mixed crowd.

ACCOMMODATION   FIRE ISLAND

Fire Island Hotel & Resort 25 Cayuga Walk, Ocean Bay Park ☎ 631 583 8000, ⓦ fireislandhotel.com. Offering a range of rooms, suites, apartments and cabins, all decorated in a colourful modernist style, this popular hotel also has a pool, a lounge and a lively bar. $229

Grove Hotel Bayview Walk and Holly Walk, Cherry Grove ☎ 631 597 6600, ⓦ grovehotel.com. Fire Island's largest hotel, with compact but comfortable rooms in three price ranges, this place has especially good off-peak deals. $75

EATING AND DRINKING

Flynn's 1 Cayuga St, Ocean Beach ☎ 631 583 5000, ⓦ flynnsfireislandny.com. This vibrant restaurant offers pricey mains such as pan-seared scallops in the $25–30 range but is also known for riotous club nights. Mid-May to Sept daily noon–11pm; club till 2am.

Matthew's 935 Bay Walk, Ocean Beach ☎ 631 583 8016, ⓦ matthewsseafood.com. Famed for its terrific fish specials like the crispy fried jumbo shrimp for around $30, Matthew's also offers a good few tasty starters. Mon–Sat noon–4pm & 5.30–10.30pm.

The North Shore

Along the rugged **North Shore**, Long Island drops to the sea in a series of bluffs, coves and wooded headlands. The expressway beyond Queens leads straight onto the ultra-exclusive **Gold Coast**, where **Great Neck** was F. Scott Fitzgerald's West Egg in *The Great Gatsby*. In Old Westbury, at 71 Old Westbury Rd, **Old Westbury Gardens** comprise a Georgian mansion with beautiful, well-tended gardens and some pleasant works of art, including a few Gainsboroughs (late April to Oct Mon & Wed–Sun 10am–5pm; $10; ☎ 516 333 0048, ⓦ oldwestburygardens.org).

Sagamore Hill, on the coast road in Oyster Bay, twelve miles north of Old Westbury, is where **Teddy Roosevelt** lived for thirty-odd years (May–Sept daily 10am–5pm; Oct–April Wed–Sun 10am–5pm; hourly tours $5; ☎ 516 922 4788, ⓦ nps.gov/sahi). Its 23 rooms are adorned with hunting trophies, while the Old Orchard Museum (same days 9am–5pm; free), in the same gorgeous grounds, recounts Teddy's political and personal life. Nearby **COLD SPRING HARBOR** grew up as a whaling port; a fully equipped whaleboat and a 400-piece assembly of scrimshaw work help its **Whaling Museum** (June–Aug daily 11am–5pm; Sept–May closed Mon; $6; ☎ 631 367 3418, ⓦ cshwhalingmuseum.org) to recapture that era.

The North Fork

Less touristy than the North Shore, the **North Fork** – once an independent colony – boasts typical wild Atlantic coastal scenery. In **GREENPORT**, its most picturesque town, a spacious wooden boardwalk encloses a harbour pierced by the masts of visiting yachts. At the west end there's the small **East End Seaport Museum and Marine Foundation** (July & Aug 1–5pm; Sept–June Sat & Sun 1–5pm; donation; ☎ 631 477 2100, ⓦ eastendseaport.org), which displays a variety of nautical equipment and memorabilia, and maintains a working blacksmith shop.

ACCOMMODATION AND EATING   THE NORTH FORK

Bartlett House Inn 503 Front St, Greenport ☎ 631 477 0371, ⓦ bartletthouseinn.com. An extremely spacious and attractive Victorian B&B containing eight delightfully appointed rooms and two luxury suites. $219
Chowder Pot Pub 102 3rd St, Greenport ☎ 631 477

1345. Right opposite the ferry terminal, this friendly family seafood restaurant does plenty of fish and some meat dishes for $20–25 to follow its eponymous chowder. July & Aug daily 11am–10pm; Sept–June closed Mon–Wed.

The South Fork

The US holds few wealthier quarters than the small towns of Long Island's **South Fork**, where huge mansions lurk among the trees or stand boldly on the flats behind the dunes. The area also has a wider selection of facilities than the wilder North Fork.

The Hamptons

Nowhere is consumption as deliberately conspicuous as in the **Hamptons**, among the oldest communities in the state. Long association with the smart set has left **SOUTHAMPTON** unashamedly upper class, its streets lined with galleries and clothing and jewellery stores. **EAST HAMPTON** is the trendiest of the Hamptons, filled with the mansions of celebrities like Renée Zellweger, Jerry Seinfeld and Steven Spielberg.

Sag Harbor

Historic **SAG HARBOR**, in its heyday a port second only to that of New York, was designated first Port of Entry to the New Country by George Washington; the **Old Custom House** (May & Sept Sat & Sun 10am–5pm; June–Aug Tues–Sun 10am–5pm; $5; ☎ 631 692 4664) dates from this era. The **Whaling Museum** on Main Street (mid-May to mid-Oct Mon–Sat 10am–5pm, Sun 1–5pm; $5; ☎ 631 725 0770, ⊕ sagharborwhaling museum.org) commemorates the town's brief whaling days with guns and scrimshaw. The windmill where John Steinbeck once lived serves as a **visitor centre** (see below).

Montauk

Blustery, wind-battered **MONTAUK**, on the furthest tip of Long Island, isn't chic or quaint. Real people actually live here and it provides access to the rocky wilds of **Montauk Point**. A **lighthouse** – New York State's oldest, dating from 1796 – forms an almost symbolic finale to this stretch of the American coast.

INFORMATION	THE SOUTH FORK

Chamber of Commerce 76 Main St, Southampton (Mon–Fri 10am–4pm, Sat & Sun 11am–3pm; ☎ 631 283 0402, ⊕ southamptonchamber.com).
Visitor centre The Windmill, Sag Harbor (July & Aug daily 10am–4pm; May, June, Sept & Oct Fri–Sun 10am–4pm; ☎ 631 725 0011, ⊕ sagharborchamber.com).
Listings To see what's on in the Hamptons, pick up *Dan's Hamptons* (⊕ danshamptons.com).

ACCOMMODATION AND EATING

SOUTHAMPTON

Barrister's 36 Main St ☎ 631 283 6206, ⊕ barrister southampton.com. Marvellous fresh seafood and other delights are served up here – try the crisp-roast Long island duckling with apricot-hazelnut liquor sauce for $24. Daily 11.30am–10.30pm.
★ **Southampton Publick House** 40 Bowden Square ☎ 631 283 2800, ⊕ publick.com. This brewpub-restaurant has a fine selection of ales and lagers with which to wash down its snacks and burgers or pricier mains such as braised pork shank ($22). Daily 11am–10pm, bar till 1am.

SAG HARBOR

American Hotel 49 Main St ☎ 631 725 3535, ⊕ the americanhotel.com. Housed in an attractive 1846 building, the hotel has classily furnished rooms, while the restaurant does splendid French-influenced meals for around $20. **$225**
Baron's Cove Inn 31 W Water St ☎ 631 725 2100, ⊕ baronscove.com. This rather well-heeled hotel offers reasonable rates and peaceful harbour views from its comfortable rooms, which are nicely designed with bright fabrics. **$145**

★ **Sen** 23 Main St ☎ 631 725 1774, ⊕ senrestaurant .com. The seaside offshoot of a renowned NYC sushi bar, this is the best place on the whole island for authentic, high-quality Japanese cuisine; a seven-course tasting menu costs $28. Mon–Thurs & Sun 5.30–9.30pm, Fri & Sat 5.30–10.30pm.

MONTAUK

Gurney's Inn 290 Old Montauk Hwy ☎ 631 668 2345, ⊕ gurneysinn.com. Sleek modern interiors and expansive sea views are the order of the day at this plush resort with a sea-water spa and quality seafood restaurant. **$240**
★ **The Lobster Roll** 1980 Montauk Hwy (Rte-27) ☎ 631 267 3740, ⊕ lobsterroll.com. The ultimate Montauk dining experience of excellent fresh seafood is to be found halfway back towards East Hampton; the famous lobster roll itself goes for $20.95. May–Oct daily 11.30am–9.30pm.
Sands Motel Corner of Montauk Hwy (Rte-27) and S Emerson Ave ☎ 631 668 5100, ⊕ montauksands.com. Fairly standard motel but crisp and clean, with some of the best rates on the island, especially off peak, and good weekly deals. **$95**

The Hudson Valley

You only need to travel a few miles north of Manhattan before the **Hudson River Valley** takes on a Rhine-like charm, with prodigious historic homes rising from its steep and thickly wooded banks. Few of the cities along the Hudson, including the large but lacklustre state capital of **Albany**, hold much to attract the visitor, though many of the small towns are worth checking out, such as **Tarrytown**, abode of novelist Washington Irving, and the regional historic and culinary hot spot **Hyde Park**.

Tarrytown and Irvington

A mere 25 miles north of central New York City on US-9, leafy **TARRYTOWN** and the village of **IRVINGTON** were the original settings for Washington Irving's tales of *Rip Van Winkle* and *The Legend of Sleepy Hollow*. You can tour the farm cottage on West Sunnyside Lane, off Broadway/US-9, which the author rebuilt and renamed **Sunnyside** (tours early May to mid-Nov Wed–Sun 10.30am, noon, 1.30pm & 3pm; $12; ☎914 591 8763, ⓦhudsonvalley.org). Irvington's riverside **Hudson Park** makes for a scenic picnic.

Ossining

About ten miles north of Tarrytown along US-9, the town of **OSSINING** holds two impressive mid-Victorian creations: one is a huge bridge carrying the **Old Croton Aqueduct**, New York City's first water supply; the other, just south of town, is **Sing Sing Prison**, which for more than 150 years has been the place where New York City criminals get sent "up the river".

Hyde Park

HYDE PARK, set on a peaceful plateau some forty miles further up the Hudson's east bank from Ossining, is worth a stop for the homes of **Franklin D.** and **Eleanor Roosevelt**. Well signposted off US-9, these homes, a **Vanderbilt mansion** and a couple of minor attractions all come under the aegis of the **Henry A. Wallace Visitor and Education Center** (daily: April–Oct 8.45am–6.30pm; Nov–March 8.45am–5.30pm). The grounds of all three homes are open from dawn to dusk at no charge.

The Roosevelt complex

US-9 • **House and museum** Daily 9am–5pm • Tours $14 • ☎ 845 486 7770, ⓦ nps.gov/hofr **Val-Kill** May–Oct daily 9am–5pm; Nov–April Mon & Thurs–Sun 9am–5pm • Tours $8 • ⓦ nps.gov/elro

The **house** where the "New Deal" president was born and spent much of his adult life is preserved here along with a library and a good **museum**, containing extensive letters, photos and artefacts. FDR lies buried in the Rose Garden, beside his wife (and distant cousin) Eleanor, one of the first women to play a prominent role in American politics. After FDR's death in 1945, Eleanor moved to **Val-Kill**, the nearby cottage retreat where she carried on her work until her death in 1962.

The Vanderbilt Mansion

Daily 9am–5pm • $8 • ⓦ nps.gov/vama

A three-mile-long cliff-top **path** along the Hudson from the Roosevelt complex winds up at the Beaux Arts **Vanderbilt Mansion**. This virtual palace is, believe it or not, the smallest of the family's residences. The furnishings are quite garish but the formal gardens are very pretty and offer a fine view of the Hudson River.

The Culinary Institute of America

Beyond its mansions, Hyde Park has one other huge tourist draw: the fascinating campus of the **Culinary Institute of America**, the most prestigious cooking school in the country, which stands along US-9, south of Hyde Park at 1946 Campus Drive. The outstanding restaurants here (see opposite) have trained some of America's best chefs; classes and **tours** (Mon 10am & 4pm, Wed & Thurs 4pm; $5; ⓦciachef.edu) can also be booked.

Culinary Institute of America South 1946 Campus Drive ☎845 471 6608, ⓦciachef.edu. There are two high-class restaurants – one American, the other Italian – plus two cafés on the premises, where some of the country's best chefs cut their teeth. Hours vary.

Golden Manor Motel US-9 almost opposite the Roosevelt complex ☎845 229 2157, ⓦgoldenmanor hydepark.com. This humble but perfectly adequate motel provides just about the only budget accommodation on this stretch of the river. **$65**

Rhinebeck

Six miles north of Hyde Park, **RHINEBECK** is the location of **America's oldest hotel** in continuous operation (see below), housed in a lovely, white colonial building. The small, unhurried town is also home to the New Agey **Omega Institute for Holistic Studies**, which runs a spa and offers a wide range of health and wellness workshops at a large campus east of town on Lake Drive (☎800 944 1001, ⓦeomega.org).

★ **Beekman Arms** 6387 Mill St (US-9) ☎845 876 7077, ⓦbeekmandelamaterinn.com. This venerable establishment has been hosting and feeding travellers in its warm, wood-panelled rooms since 1766. There is also a classy restaurant, serving quality meat and fish dishes for $20–30, and the larger *Delamater Inn*, run by the same people, a block away. **$165**

Calico Restaurant & Patisserie 6384 Mill St (US-9) ☎845 876 2749, ⓦcalicorhinebeck.com. The menu here reveals Italian and French influences, with dishes such as bouillabaise going for $25 and an extensive wine list. Wed–Sat 11am–2pm & 5.15–8pm, Sun brunch 11am–2pm.

Foster's Coachhouse Tavern 6411 Montgomery St ☎845 876 8052, ⓦfosterscoachhouse.com. Large, family-friendly, all-American restaurant, serving huge and tasty burgers and sandwiches – try the salmon burger for $9 – plus desserts such as banana pie. Tues–Sun 11am–11pm, Fri & Sat 11am–midnight.

Woodstock

Around twenty miles northwest of Rhinebeck, on the other side of the Hudson, Hwy-28 meanders into the Catskills, looping past the lovely Ashokan Reservoir where Hwy-375 branches off to **WOODSTOCK**. The village, carved out of the lush deciduous woodlands and cut by fast-rushing creeks, was not actually the venue of the famed **psychedelic picnic** of August 1969. That was some sixty miles southwest in Bethel, where a monument at Herd and West Shore roads marks the festival site on the farm owned by Max Yasgur. However, Woodstock has enjoyed a bohemian reputation since the foundation in 1903 of the **Byrdcliffe Arts Colony** (which runs summer residency courses; ☎845 679 2079, ⓦwoodstockguild.org), and during the 1960s it was a favourite stomping ground for the likes of Dylan, Hendrix and Van Morrison. The town still trades on its **hippie** past with shops selling crystals and tie-dyed T-shirts. Woodstock's galleries and craft shops command a regional reputation and the village is also a hub for the performing arts: the **Maverick Concert** series (late June to Aug; $25–40, students $5; ☎845 679 8217, ⓦmaverickconcerts.org) has played host to some of the world's finest chamber musicians since 1906.

By bus Services from New York City's Port Authority Bus Terminal (3–4 daily; 2hr 30min; Adirondack Trailways; ☎800 858 8555, ⓦtrailwaysny.com) pull in at Woodstock's terminal at 4 Mill Hill Rd.

Chamber of Commerce Rock City Rd, just off the village green (☎845 679 6234, ⓦwoodstockchamber.com).

ACCOMMODATION

Getaway-on-the-Falls 5 Waterfall Way ☎845 679 2568, ⓦgetawayonthefalls.com. Delightful guesthouse with a few studios, an apartment and a log cabin, all set in grounds landscaped by the horticulturalist owner. **$140**

Rip Van Winkle Campgrounds 149 Blue Mountain Rd, Saugerties ☎845 246 8334, ⓦripvanwinkle campgrounds.com. Well signposted off Rte-212, this high-quality campground in 160 acres of woodland has plenty of tent pitches and lots of RV spaces, plus a swimming pool. May–Oct. **$35**

2

Twin Gables 73 Tinker St ☎ 845 679 9479, ⓦ twingables woodstockny.com. The village's oldest guesthouse is cute, cosy and central, with brightly decorated rooms, including a couple of economy singles. Breakfast is included. **$119**

EATING

Bear Café Two miles west on Rte-212, Bearsville ☎ 845 679 5555, ⓦ bearcafe.com. This rural spot perhaps surprisingly serves excellent international and French cuisine, such as filet mignon for $34. Mon, Wed & Thurs 5–9pm, Fri & Sat 5–10pm, Sun 11am–2.30pm & 5–9pm.

Joshua's 51 Tinker St ☎ 845 679 5533, ⓦ joshuascafe .com. The village's favourite place to eat packs plenty of people into a small space to enjoy its Middle Eastern and world cuisine, such as Bedouin mixed grill for $27. 11am–10pm; closed Wed.

★ **New World Home Cooking Company** Towards Saugerties at 1411 Rte-212 ☎ 845 246 0900, ⓦ ricorlando.com. Top chef Ric Orlando places an emphasis on sustainable food with recipes from around the world such as Thai BBQ organic chicken for $26. Mon–Sat 5–10pm, Sun 3–10pm.

The Catskill Mountains

Rising above the west bank of the Hudson River, the magnificent crests of the **Catskills**, cloaked with maple and beech that turn orange, ochre and gold each autumn, have a rich and absorbing beauty. This dislocated branch of the Appalachians is inspiring country, filled with amenities – campgrounds, hiking, fishing and, especially, skiing.

Mount Tremper

Seven miles west of Woodstock, in the quiet hamlet of **MOUNT TREMPER**, the **Emerson Place Kaleidoscope** (Mon–Thurs & Sun 10am–5pm, Fri & Sat 10am–7pm; $8) claims to be the world's largest, created by a local hippie artist in a 60ft-high converted grain silo. It plays ten-minute sound and light shows on request throughout the day and is part of the vast *Emerson Resort & Spa* (see below).

Phoenicia and around

As you continue along Hwy-28, the picturesque village of **PHOENICIA**, in a hollow to the right of the road, is an ideal resting place and a great base for hiking trails in the area. For a scenic loop back to I-87, continue west on Hwy-49A and return via Hwy-23A and Hwy-23, halting for a breathtaking view of the dramatic **gorge** between the villages of Hunter and Catskill. The area's premier **ski runs** are on Hunter Mountain (☎ 518 263 4223, ⓦ huntermtn.com), where daredevils can try out the exhilarating zip-line during other seasons. A fun way to see some of the best mountain scenery is to catch the circular **Catskill Mountain Railroad** from Phoenicia (late May to late Sept Fri–Sun & hols 11am, 1pm & 2.50pm; $14 return; ☎ 845 688 7400, ⓦ catskillmtrailroad.com) through scenic Esopus Creek.

ACCOMMODATION AND EATING — THE CATSKILL MOUNTAINS

MOUNT TREMPER

★ **The Emerson Resort & Spa** 146 Mt Pleasant Rd ☎ 845 688 2828, ⓦ emersonresort.com. Vast upmarket resort, with spacious modern rooms and suites, two restaurants and a café. The spa offers soothing holistic treatments. **$179**

PHOENICIA AND AROUND

Phoenicia Belle 73 Main St ☎ 845 688 7226, ⓦ phoeniciabelle.com. A welcoming B&B with a pretty, blue-painted clapboard exterior. All the rooms are comfortably fitted out in true rustic fashion and the cheaper ones share bathrooms. **$115**

Phoenicia Diner 5681 Hwy-28 ☎ 845 688 9957, ⓦ phoeniciadiner.com. Excellent old-style diner that serves large helpings of breakfast all day and filling lunch items including fried catfish sandwich for $10. Thurs–Mon 7am–5pm.

Red Ranch Motel 4555 Rte-32, Catskill ☎ 518 678 3380, ⓦ redranchmotel.com. The proximity to the mountains make the spruce rooms here a much better budget option than the motels nearer the Thruway at Saugerties. Italian restaurant on site too. April–Nov. **$68**

Scribner Hollow Lodge 13 Scribner Hollow Rd (Hwy-23A), Hunter ☎ 518 263 4211, ⓦ scribnerhollow.com. Only half a mile from the slopes, this smart place boasts deluxe rooms, a fine-dining restaurant with great views and a multipool swimming grotto. **$120**

Albany

Founded by Dutch fur-trappers in the early seventeenth century, **ALBANY** made its money by controlling trade along the Erie Canal, and its reputation by being capital of the state. It's not an unpleasant town, just rather boring, though there are a few livelier areas on the fringes. A good place to start a tour is the **Quackenbush House**, the city's oldest building, built along the river in 1736 and now serving as part of the **Albany Urban Culture Park**. The adjacent visitor centre (see below) has details of **tours** of the imposing Neoclassical **Capitol** and the downtown area, where a number of Revolutionary-era homes survive.

Uphill from the waterfront, the ugly complex of Nelson A. Rockefeller's **Empire State Plaza** has one redeeming feature: the view from **Corning Tower**'s 42nd-floor observation deck (daily 10am–2.30pm; free) looks out far across the state, beyond the twisting Hudson River to the Adirondack foothills, the Catskills and the Berkshires in Massachusetts. It also peers down on the neighbouring Performing Arts Center, known locally as "**The Egg**" (☎518 478 1845, ⊛theegg.org) – which adds the only curves to the Plaza's harsh angularity. The **New York State Museum** (daily 9.30am–5pm; free; ☎518 474 5877, ⊛nysm.nysed.gov), one level down at the south end of the plaza, reveals everything you could want to know about New York State in imaginative exhibits, including the original set of *Sesame Street*.

The most engaging part of Albany is the few blocks west of the plaza, a neighbourhood full of nineteenth-century brick-built Victorian houses. The **Albany Institute of History and Art**, 125 Washington Ave (Wed–Sat 10am–5pm, Sun noon–5pm; $10; ☎518 463 4478, ⊛albanyinstitute.org), has a good range of Hudson River School paintings.

ARRIVAL AND INFORMATION   ALBANY

By bus Greyhound and Adirondack Trailways (see p.111) use the bus station just downhill from the heart of downtown.

By train The Amtrak station is a 2-mile local bus ride across the river.

Visitor centre 25 Quackenbush Square, corner of Broadway and Clinton (Mon–Fri 9am–4pm, Sat 10am–3pm, Sun 11am–3pm; ☎518 434 0405, ⊛albany.org).

ACCOMMODATION

Hampton Inn & Suites 25 Chapelk St ☎518 432 7000, ⊛hamptoninn.com. One of the better-value chain hotels that predominate here, with smartly furnished, reasonably spacious rooms and suites, plus a passable buffet breakfast. **$115**

The Morgan State House Inn 393 State St ☎518 427 6063, ⊛statehouse.com. This classy, ivy-clad converted Victorian offers just about the only atmospheric accommodation in town, with elegantly designed and extremely comfortable rooms. **$176**

EATING AND DRINKING

Although there are a few places to eat or drink in downtown Albany, another fruitful area to search for nightlife is in the college town of **Troy**, directly across the river.

Justin's 301 Lark St ☎518 436 7008, ⊛justinsalbany .com. The subdued lighting and plain brick interior provide a suitable ambience in which to enjoy Jamaican jerk chicken or pork tenderloin for $19, or to drink the night away. Mon–Fri 11.30am–1am, Sat & Sun 10.30am–1am; bar till 4am.

Lark Tavern 453 Madison Ave ☎518 463 7875, ⊛lark tavern.com. Lively haunt, renovated and renamed to

indicate that it is more than just a typical Irish pub, with regular live music, as well a good range of bar food. Mon–Sat 11am–4am, Sun noon–4am.

Mamoun's 206 Washington Ave ☎518 434 3901, ⊛mideasterndining.com. This popular place specializes in Lebanese and Syrian cuisine, with great lamb, chicken and vegetarian dishes for $15–20. Mon–Fri 11.30am–3pm & 5–10pm, Sat & Sun noon–10pm.

Saratoga Springs

Saratoga was fast, man, it was real fast. It was up all night long.   Hattie Gray, founder of *Hattie's* restaurant

For well over a century, **SARATOGA SPRINGS**, just 42 miles north of Albany on I-87, was very much the place to be seen for the Northeast's richest and most glittering

2

names. At first, the town's curative waters were the main attraction; then John Morrisey, an Irish boxer, transformed things by opening a **racetrack** and **casino** here during the 1860s. During the August horse-racing season, Saratoga Springs retains the feel of an exclusive vintage resort – but for the rest of the summer it is accessible, affordable and fun.

Broadway, the main axis, and the few blocks just east of it are where you'll find most of the action. The carefully cultivated **Congress Park**, off South Broadway, remains a shady retreat from town-centre traffic. Three of the original mineral springs still flow up to the surface here, funnelled out into drinking fountains. Also here is the original **casino**, which when built formed part of a whole city block. The **racetrack** (late July to early Sept, post time 1pm; $3–5; ☎518 584 6200, ⓦnyra.com) still functions in a rather grand, old-fashioned manner, though the dress code is no longer as strict as it once was. There's no such pretension at the **harness track**, aka the Equine Sports Center, on nearby Crescent Avenue (evening races several times a week May–Nov; $2; ☎518 584 2110). If you can't get to either, visit the array of paintings, trophies and audiovisual displays at the **National Museum of Racing and Hall of Fame**, on Union Avenue at Ludlow Street (late March to Oct Mon–Sat 10am–4pm, Sun noon–4pm; Nov closed Mon & Tues; Dec & Jan closed Mon–Wed; during race meet daily 8am–5pm; $7; ☎518 584 0400, ⓦracingmuseum.org).

Saratoga Spa State Park and around
Daily 8am–dusk • $8/car • ☎518 584 2000, ⓦsaratogaspastatepark.org

On the southern edge of town, green **Saratoga Spa State Park** presents opportunities to swim in great old Victorian pools, picnic, hike or even "take the waters" – in other words, have a hot bath in the tingly, naturally carbonated stuff and receive a variety of spa treatments. The nearby **Saratoga Performing Arts Center** (June to early Sept; ☎518 587 3330, ⓦspac.org) – or SPAC – is home to the New York City Ballet in July, the Philadelphia Orchestra in August and hosts other quality festivals.

ARRIVAL AND INFORMATION
SARATOGA SPRINGS

By bus and train Long-distance buses use the Amtrak station at 26 Station Lane, some 2 miles west of downtown.

Visitor centre 97 Broadway (daily 8.30am–5pm; ☎518 584 3255, ⓦsaratoga.org).

ACCOMMODATION

Gideon Putnam Hotel 24 Gideon Putnam Rd ☎518 584 3000, ⓦgideonputnam.com. This large, venerable hotel in the heart of Saratoga Spa State Park offers high-quality rooms and suites, while its grand, leather lounge furniture oozes class. **$177**

Saratoga Arms 497 Broadway ☎888 242 2390, ⓦsaratogaarms.com. Extremely pleasant boutique hotel with floral-patterned rooms and linens, furniture carefully

designed in period style, free spa water and complimentary gourmet breakfasts. **$189**

Turf and Spa 140 Broadway ☎518 584 2550, ⓦsaratogaturfandspa.com. Good central motel with bright, fairly large rooms and a decent-sized open-air swimming pool. Prices spike sharply during race season but are very reasonable otherwise. **$80**

EATING, DRINKING AND NIGHTLIFE

9 Maple Avenue 9 Maple Ave ☎518 583 2582, ⓦ9mapleave.com. Very intimate jazz bar with just forty seats. It offers live jazz and blues until the early hours and specializes in a huge range of quality whiskies and martinis. Daily 4pm till late.

Caffé Lena 47 Phila St ☎518 583 0022, ⓦcaffelena .org. This popular non-profit venue is where Don McLean first inflicted *American Pie* on the world. It continues to host folk and spoken-word events; entry $3–30. Wed–Sun 6pm–midnight.

★ **Hattie's** 45 Phila St ☎518 584 4790, ⓦhatties restaurant.com. Huge helpings of tasty Southern and Louisiana cuisine such as farm-raised catfish and Jasper's mac and cheese cost $14–18 at this friendly spot, an institution since 1938. Daily 5–11pm.

Wheat Fields 440 Broadway ☎518 587 0534, ⓦwheatfields.com. Good salads, pasta and main courses like sautéed shrimp and spinach for $23 are served on an outdoor patio. Mon–Thurs 4–9pm, Fri & Sat 11am–10pm, Sun 11.30am–9pm.

The Adirondacks

The **Adirondacks**, which covers an area larger than Connecticut and Rhode Island combined, are said by locals to be named after an Iroquois insult for enemies they'd driven into the forests and left to become "bark eaters". For sheer grandeur, the region is hard to beat: 46 peaks reach to more than 4000ft; in summer the purple-green mountains span far into the distance in shaggy tiers, in autumn the trees form a russet-red kaleidoscope.

Until recent decades this vast northern region between Albany and the Canadian border was almost the exclusive preserve of loggers, fur trappers and a few select New York millionaires; these days mountaineers, skiers and dedicated hikers form the majority of visitors. Outdoor pursuits are certainly the main attractions in the rugged wilderness of the **Adirondack Mountains**, though a few small resorts, especially the former Winter Olympic venue of **Lake Placid** and its smaller neighbour **Lake Saranac**, offer creature comforts in addition to breathtaking scenery.

2

GETTING AROUND AND INFORMATION	THE ADIRONDACKS

By bus and by car Though Adirondack Trailways buses serve the area you'll find it hard-going without a car.
Visitor information Adirondack Region tourist office

(☎800 487 6867, ⓦ visitadirondacks.com); Adirondack Mountain Club (☎518 668 4447, ⓦ adk.org).

Lake Placid

The winter sports centre of **LAKE PLACID**, twice the proud host of the Winter Olympics, lies thirty miles west of I-87 on Hwy-73. In winter there's thrilling alpine skiing at imposing Whiteface Mountain and all manner of Nordic disciplines at Mount Van Hoevenberg; in summer you can watch luge athletes practise on refrigerated runs, freestyle skiers somersaulting off dry slopes into swimming pools and top amateur ice hockey games. The mountain slopes also provide challenging terrain for hikers and cyclists. At the **Olympic Sports Complex** on Mount Van Hoevenburg (☎518 523 4436), you can do a bloodcurdling bobsled run ($70) or bike the extensive trail network ($35/ day rental; $6 trail pass).

The town itself is set on two lakes: **Mirror Lake**, which you can sail on in summer and skate on in winter, and larger **Lake Placid**, just to the west, on which you can take a narrated **cruise** in summer ($15; ☎518 523 9704, ⓦlakeplacidmarina.com). Other attractions include the **Olympic Center** at 2634 Main St, which houses four ice rinks, and the informative **1932 and 1980 Lake Placid Winter Olympic Museum** (self-guided audio tour $5; ☎518 523 1655).

John Brown Farm State Historic Site

115 John Brown Rd • **House** May–Oct Mon & Wed–Sun 10am–5pm • $2 • ☎518 523 3900

Outside the village on Hwy-73, the **John Brown Farm State Historic Site** was where the famous abolitionist brought his family in 1849 to aid a small colony of black farmers and where he conceived his ill-fated raid on Harper's Ferry in an attempt to end slavery. The house is less interesting than his story (see p.359); the grounds, which include Brown's grave, are open year-round.

INFORMATION AND ACTIVITIES	LAKE PLACID

Visitor centre Olympic Sports Complex (☎518 523 2445, ⓦ lakeplacid.com).
Activities Good mountain bikes, maps of local trails, and guided tours are available from High Peaks Cyclery, 2733 Main St (☎518 523 3764, ⓦ highpeakscyclery.com). The

Olympic Sites Passport ($32; ☎518 523 1655, ⓦ whiteface .com) allows you on the chairlift to the top of the 393ft ski jump and 8 miles up the sheer Whiteface Mountain toll road and back again, on the Whiteface gondola, and into the Olympic museum (see above).

ACCOMMODATION	

Alpine Air Motel 2050 Saranac Ave ☎518 523 3821, ⓦalpineairmotel.com. Beautifully located by the Chubb

River, with picnic tables and a heated outdoor pool, this place has hotel-standard rooms at motel prices. **$90**

★ **Keene Valley Hostel** Fifteen miles southeast in Keene Valley ☎518 576 2030, ⓦkeenevalleyhostel .com. With clean bathrooms, a full kitchen, wi-fi and a music system, this hostel-cum-campground is a great base for all the best hiking trails. Dorms $25, camping $15

Mirror Lake Inn Resort & Spa 77 Mirror Lake Drive ☎518 523 2544, ⓦmirrorlakeinn.com. Casually elegant

resort with more than 120 rooms, the best of them palatial, and an array of facilities, most notably the high-quality spa. $215

Stagecoach Inn 3 Stagecoach Way ☎518 523 9698, ⓦlakeplacidstagecoachinn.com. Exuding rustic charm, this 1820s country house has been converted into a fine B&B, with well-appointed rooms and lush grounds. $169

EATING, DRINKING AND NIGHTLIFE

Bluesberry Bakery 2436 Main St ☎518 523 4539, ⓦbluesberrybakery.com. The town's best bakery makes a great selection of sandwiches, turnovers, muffins and scones, but is most renowned for its delicious apple strudel. Thurs–Sun 7.30am–5pm.

Hunan Oshaka 2436 Main St ☎518 523 1558. This simple, unpretentious restaurant offers a unique choice of Chinese, Japanese and Mexican cuisine. Try the Adirondack spicy dragon roll for $15.95. Daily 11.30am–10pm.

★ **Station Street Bar & Grille** 1 Station St ☎518 523 996. This well-established restaurant-bar is undoubtedly the friendliest place for a night out with the locals and serves delicious ribs and other dishes for around $15. Daily 11am–2am.

Zig Zags Pub 2528 Main St ☎518 523 8221. This buzzing nightspot is the main place for live music at the weekend, showcasing an eclectic range of mostly local bands. Hours vary.

Saranac Lake

SARANAC LAKE, ten miles northwest of Lake Placid, is a smaller, more laidback and cheaper base for the region. The tranquil lakeshore is lined with lovely gingerbread cottages, most of them built during the late 1800s, when this was a popular middle-class retreat and spa. **Robert Louis Stevenson** spent the winter of 1888 in a small cottage on the east side of town at 44 Stevenson Lane; it's now preserved as a **museum** (July–Sept Tues–Sun 9.30am–noon & 1–4.30pm; Oct–June by appointment; $5; ☎518 891 1462, ⓦrobertlouisstevensonmemorialcottage.org).

ACCOMMODATION AND EATING   SARANAC LAKE

★ **Eat-n-Meet** 139 Broadway ☎518 891 3149, ⓦeatnmeet.com. Quirky, colourful and laidback place serving meals made from mostly organic ingredients, such as Harmony Hills pork liver and onions with mash for $12. Mon–Thurs noon–9pm, Fri & Sat noon–10pm, Sun noon–8pm.

Hotel Saranac 100 Main St ☎518 891 2200, ⓦhotel

saranac.com. The rather austere-looking red-brick exterior conceals a range of bright, appealing rooms, including some new whirlpool suites. There is also a friendly bar. $85

★ **Saranac Club & Inn** 371 Park Ave ☎518 891 7212. Set in quiet manicured grounds, this spacious B&B offers friendly service and far better value than its Lake Placid equivalents. $120

The Finger Lakes

At the heart of the state, southwest of Syracuse on the far side of the Catskills from New York City, are the eleven **Finger Lakes**, narrow channels gouged out by glaciers that have left telltale signs in the form of drumlins, steep gorges and a number of waterfalls. With the exception of progressive, well-to-do **Ithaca** and tiny **Skaneateles**, few towns compete with the lakeshore scenery. That said, the area as a whole is relaxing and enjoys a growing reputation for quality **wineries**. It also has another area of exceptional natural beauty at the western end of the lakes in **Letchworth State Park**.

Skaneateles

SKANEATELES (pronounced "Skinny-Atlas"), crouching at the neck of Skaneateles Lake, is perhaps the prettiest Finger Lakes town. It's also the best place to go swimming in the region: just a block from the town centre, and lined by huge resort homes, the appealing bay sports a **beach** (summer daily; $3) and the **Skaneateles Marina**, where you can rent watersports equipment (☎315 685 5095) and take boat trips, from Mid-Lakes Navigation ($12 for 50min; ☎315 685 8500, ⓦmidlakesnav.com); they also offer various meal cruises.

Auburn

Seven miles west of Skaneateles, **AUBURN** is the largest town at the northern end of the lakes. There are a number of imposing nineteenth-century buildings in and around downtown, most notably the well-preserved **Seward House Historic Museum** at 33 South St (Tues–Sat 10am–5pm, Sun 1–5pm; $8; ☎315 252 1283, ☎sewardhouse.org), tours of which chronicle the life of its former owner, William Seward. A prominent member of Abraham Lincoln's cabinet, Seward was instrumental in the abolition of slavery and also negotiated the purchase of Alaska (see p.1032). The **Cayuga Museum & Case Research Lab**, 203 Genesee St (Feb–Dec Tues–Sun noon–5pm; free; ☎315 253 8051, ☎cayugamuseum.org), celebrates the work of Auburn native Theodore Willard Case, who first invented sound for movies here in the 1920s.

Seneca Falls

At **SENECA FALLS**, just west of the northern tip of Cayuga Lake and around fifteen miles west of Skaneateles, Elizabeth Cady Stanton and a few colleagues held the first Women's Rights Convention in 1848 – well before female suffrage in 1920. On the site of the **Wesleyan Chapel**, 136 Fall St, where the first campaign meeting was held, is the terrific **Women's Rights National Historical Park** (daily 9am–5pm; ☎315 568 2991, ☎nps.gov/wori), which sets the early and contemporary women's movements in their historical contexts, emphasizing the connection with the African American civil rights movements. A block east, at 76 Fall St, the **National Women's Hall of Fame** (Feb–Dec Wed–Sat 10am–4pm, June–Aug also Sun noon–4pm; $3; ☎315 568 8060, ☎greatwomen.org), honours about two hundred pioneering women, including Emily Dickinson and Sojourner Truth.

The Cayuga Wine Trail

The area on either side of the stretch of Hwy-89 that runs between Seneca Falls and Ithaca has been dubbed the **Cayuga Wine Trail**, with dozens of small wineries operating along the west shore of the largest of the Finger Lakes. Two of the best are **Sheldrake Point**, in the hamlet of Ovid (Jan–March Mon & Fri–Sun 11am–5pm; April–Dec daily 10am–5.30pm; ☎607 532 9401, ☎sheldrakepoint.com), and **Thirsty Owl** (daily 11.30am–5pm; ☎607 869 5851, ☎thirstyowl.com); both offer tastings for a nominal fee and the latter also conducts tours.

Ithaca

Cayuga Lake comes to a halt at its southern end at picturesque **ITHACA**, piled like a diminutive San Francisco above the lakeshore and culminating in the towers, sweeping lawns and shaded parks of Ivy League **Cornell University**. On campus, which is cut by striking gorges, creeks and lakes, the sleek, I.M. Pei-designed **Herbert F. Johnson Museum of Art** (Tues–Sun 10am–5pm; free; ☎607 255 6464, ☎museum.cornell.edu), across the street from the gorge-straddling **suspension bridge**, merits a visit more for its fifth-floor view of the town and lake than for the moderate collection of Asian and contemporary art. Adjacent to campus lie the **Cornell Plantations** (daily dawn–dusk; free; ☎607 255 2400, ☎plantations.cornell.edu), the extensive botanical gardens and arboretum run by the university.

The pick of the countless **waterfalls** within a few miles of town are the slender **Taughannock Falls**, ten miles north just off Hwy-89 and with a swimming beach; at a height of 215ft, they are taller than Niagara.

Letchworth State Park

Hours vary • $8/car • ☎585 493 3600, ☎nysparks.com

Less than ten miles west of the westernmost Finger, undeveloped Conesus Lake, **Letchworth State Park** bills itself as the "Grand Canyon of the East". Despite this being a rather bold claim, the park is undoubtedly a regional highlight that well deserves a detour. The long, narrow park covers more than fourteen thousand acres on either side of the **Genesee River**, with the centrepieces being the impressive canyons carved by the river, a huge dam at the southern end and two sets of waterfalls. There are seventy miles of trails with plenty of recreational facilities and campgrounds.

ARRIVAL, INFORMATION AND GETTING AROUND   THE FINGER LAKES

By bus and train The only long-distance bus route into the area is with Greyhound to Ithaca, whose terminal is at W State and N Fulton. Otherwise you can take Greyhound or Amtrak to Syracuse, from where Centro buses (☎315 442 3400, ⓦcentro.org) operate a service to Auburn via Skaneateles.
By car To see the Finger Lakes properly you really need a car and a vehicle is essential to access most lakes, the Wine Trail or Letchworth State Park.

Visitor centres Cayuga County Office of Tourism, 131 Genesee St, Auburn (Mon–Fri 9am–5pm; ☎315 255 1658, ⓦtourcayuga.com); 904 East Shore Drive, off Hwy-34 N, Ithaca (Mon–Fri 9am–5pm, Sat 10am–5pm, Sun 10am–4pm, longer in summer; ☎607 272 1313, ⓦvisitithaca.com).
Listings For news of what's on, pick up the free *Ithaca Times* (ⓦithaca.com).

ACCOMMODATION

SKANEATELES
★ **1899 Lady of the Lake** 2 W Lake St ☎888 685 7997, ⓦladyofthelake.net. Overlooking the lake, this attractive Victorian B&B offers three quaintly decorated rooms with striped wallpaper and floral linens. $185
Colonial Motel 4239 E Genesee St (Hwy-20) ☎315 685 5751, ⓦcolonialmotelonline.com. On the east side of town, this better than average motel has rooms with fridges and microwaves, plus an outdoor pool and picnic area. $80
Sherwood Inn 26 W Genesee St ☎315 685 3405, ⓦthesherwoodinn.com. The lavish rooms in this hotel, which originates from 1807, are more city chic than pastoral, and there's a good dining room and tavern. $215

AUBURN
★ **Tuskill House** 5 Tuskill Square ☎315 252 0055, ⓦtuxillhouse.com. Just round the corner from the Seward House, this delightful B&B has extremely cosy rooms, some with shared bathrooms, and a spacious lounge with cable TV and a selection of DVDs. Gourmet breakfasts, such as cheese soufflé, are served. $79

SENECA FALLS
Hubbell House 42 Cayuga St ☎315 568 9690, ⓦhubbellhousebb.com. Set on the wooded banks of tiny Van Cleef Lake, yet an easy walk into town, this splendid

1855 mansion has opulent rooms and fine breakfasts. $155

ITHACA
Inn on Columbia 228 Columbia St ☎607 272 0204, ⓦcolumbiabb.com. Located in a leafy street close to the Commons, with good-value rooms in the main house and more lavish accommodation in two neighbouring properties. $125
Statler Hotel 130 Statler Drive ☎800 541 2501, ⓦstatlerhotel.cornell.edu. Within the Cornell campus proper, this smart modern hotel offers all conveniences – from its huge, lavishly designed rooms and suites to business and fitness centres and a fine taverna. $230

LETCHWORTH STATE PARK
Country Inn & Suites 130 N Main St, Mt Morris ☎585 658 4080, ⓦcountryinns.com. Less than a mile from the northern park entrance, the modern chain franchise extends a rural welcome and feels more personal than corporate. $105
Glen Iris Inn Letchworth State Park ☎585 493 2622, ⓦglenirisinn.com. Right in the heart of the park, the founder's former residence has been converted into a wonderful inn, with charmingly furnished rooms and an excellent restaurant. $100

EATING, DRINKING AND NIGHTLIFE

SKANEATELES
★ **Doug's Fish Fry** 8 Jordan St ☎315 685 3288, ⓦdougsfishfry.com. Local institution famed for its filling $10 fish dinners but also offering lobster, oysters, chicken, gumbo and shakes. Daily 11am–9pm.
Rosalie's Cucina 841 W Genesee St ☎315 685 2200, ⓦrosaliescucina.com. Good place for Tuscan family recipes, such as *rigatoni della cucina* for $24.50, with a great bakery at the back too. May–Oct Mon–Thurs & Sun 5–8.30pm, Fri & Sat 5–9pm; Nov–April closed Sun.

AUBURN
Bambino's 105 Genesee St ☎315 255 3385, ⓦbambinosbistro.com. Very popular Italian bistro decorated in warm rustic colours, where you can enjoy delights such as the lobster-rich *ravioli di aragosta* for $16.95. Daily 11.30am–10pm.

SENECA FALLS
Parker's Grille & Tap House 86 Fall St ☎315 568 1614, ⓦparkersgrille.com. This bustling restaurant-bar serves

a decent range of snacks, salads, sandwiches, burgers and Mexican dishes for $5–15, as well as quality draft beers. Daily 11am–midnight, bar till 2am.

ITHACA
The Haunt 702 Willow Ave ☎607 275 3477, ⓦthe haunt.com. One of the town's liveliest venues hosts an eclectic mixture of club nights and live acts, mostly obscure but with the odd star like Jonathan Richman. Also does fine BBQ for $15–20. Tues–Sun 11am–1am or later.
★ **Ithaca Ale House** 111 N Aurora St ☎ 607 256 7977, ⓦithacaalehouse.com. There's a great selection of craft beers to sample and you can stuff yourself on a variety of pizzas, salads and original sandwiches for $10–15. Mon–

Sat 11am–1am, Sun 10am–10.30pm.
Moosewood 215 N Cayuga St ☎607 273 9610, ⓦmoosewoodcooks.com. This top-rated vegetarian restaurant of cookbook fame does unique creations such as roasted russets with chipotle aioli, mostly $10–20. Mon–Thurs 11.30am–3pm & 5.30–8.30pm, Fri & Sat 11.30am–3pm & 5.30–9pm, Sun 5.30–8.30pm.

LETCHWORTH STATE PARK
Questa Lasagna 55 Main St, Mt Morris ☎585 658 3761, ⓦquestalasagna.com. The home-made pasta can be bought uncooked, while the delicious seafood lasagne costs $9.50 for lunch, $16 for dinner. Mon–Wed 11am–8pm, Thurs & Fri 11am–9pm, Sat noon–9pm, Sun noon–8pm.

Cooperstown

Seventy miles west of Albany, sitting gracefully on the wooded banks of tranquil Otsego Lake, is pleasant **COOPERSTOWN**, christened "Glimmerglass" by novelist James Fenimore Cooper, son of the town's founder. The birth of baseball, said to have originated here on Doubleday Field, is commemorated by the inspired and spacious **National Baseball Hall of Fame**, on Main Street (daily: June–Aug 9am–5pm; Sept–May 9am–9pm; $19.50; ☎607 547 7200, ⓦbaseballhall.org), enjoyable even for the uninitiated. The delightful **Fenimore Art Museum**, just north of town on Lake Road/Rte-80 (April to mid-May & mid-Oct to Dec Tues–Sun 10am–4pm; mid-May to mid-Oct daily 10am–5pm; $12; ☎888 547 1450, ⓦfenimoreartmuseum.org), has innovative special exhibits and a fine collection of folk and Native North American art. In summer, Cooperstown hosts **classical concerts** and the **Glimmerglass Opera** at Alice Busch Opera Theater, north on Rte-80 by the lake ($12–90; ☎607 547 5704, ⓦglimmerglass.org).

GETTING AROUND AND INFORMATION   COOPERSTOWN

Tram (trolley) In summer, park in one of the free car parks on the edge of town and take the tram around the sights (8am–9pm; $3 all-day pass).
Visitor centre 31 Chestnut St (June–Aug daily 9am–6pm;

Sept–May Mon–Sat 9am–5pm; ☎607 547 9983, ⓦcooperstownchamber.org); the website is an excellent way to arrange accommodation.

ACCOMMODATION AND EATING

Blue Mingo Grill 6098 Rte-90 ☎607 547 7496, ⓦblue mingogrill.com. The wonderful location on Otsego Lake and $20–25 fusion and New American dishes, which

change nightly, make this one of the area's best and most creative restaurants. Late May to Oct daily 11am–10pm.
★ **Cooperstown Diner** 136½ Main St ☎607 547

THE ERIE CANAL

Until the advent of the railways, the **Erie Canal**, which runs for 363 miles between Albany and Buffalo, was the main means for transporting goods between the Atlantic coast via the Hudson to the Great Lakes. These days it is used more for pleasure trips, providing boaters with the opportunity to get to grips with some of its 36 locks. The section of the river around Rochester retains the most character in this sense. The fertile farming country on either side comprises the **agricultural heartland** of New York State. The eastern parts, also known as Central Leatherstocking after the protective leggings worn by the area's first settlers, are well off the conventional tourist trails, with the exception of the lovely village of Cooperstown. Meanwhile, the industrial college town of Syracuse only merits a visit for the **Erie Canal Museum** (Mon–Sat 10am–5pm, Sun 10am–3pm; free; ☎315 471 0593, ⓦeriecanalmuseum.org), housed in an 1850s weighing station at 318 E Erie Blvd.

2

9201, ⓦcooperstowndiner.com. For a quick but filling bite in town, try the all-day breakfasts, fine sandwiches and burgers, or specials like pot roast and prime rib, mostly $10–15. Daily 6am–8pm.

The Inn At Cooperstown 16 Chestnut St ⓣ607 547 5756, ⓦinnatcooperstown.com. This grand, centrally located 1874 mansion offers a range of high-quality rooms and suites, as well as an excellent complimentary gourmet breakfast. **$150**

Lake 'N Pines 7182 Rte-80 ⓣ607 547 2790, ⓦlake npinesmotel.com. The best of the lakeside motels offers superb value off-season for its neat, spacious rooms and larger cottages. Indoor and outdoor pools. April–Nov. **$130**

Rochester

In contrast to its sprawling suburbs, downtown **ROCHESTER** is a salubrious place, with its central office-block area sitting astride the Genesee River and bordered by well-heeled mansions on spacious boulevards. High-tech companies such as Bausch & Lomb, Xerox and Kodak have created a thriving local economy throughout the years, despite national and regional economic downturns.

The high-tech **Rochester Museum & Science Center** at 657 East Ave (Mon–Sat 9am–5pm, Sun 11am–5pm; $12; ⓣ585 271 4320, ⓦrmsc.org) houses interesting interactive displays on science, natural history, Native Americans and local history. Nearby at 500 University Ave, the **Memorial Art Gallery** (Wed–Sun 11am–5pm, Thurs 11am–9pm; $10; ⓣ585 473 7720, ⓦmag.rochester.edu) houses a surprisingly extensive collection that includes three Monets and a Rembrandt. Aurasma technology has also been applied to a number of the paintings.

One important former Rochester resident is celebrated at the **Susan B. Anthony House**, 17 Madison St (Tues–Sun 11am–5pm; $6; ⓣ585 235 6124, ⓦsusanbanthony house.org), where this renowned suffragette lived from 1866 to 1906.

The International Museum of Photography

900 East Ave • Tues–Sat 10am–5pm, Sun 11am–5pm • $12 • ⓣ585 271 3361, ⓦeastmanhouse.org

Kodak's (and its founder, George Eastman's) legacies throughout the metropolitan area include Kodak Park, the Eastman Theater and, above all, the **International Museum of Photography** at George Eastman House, two miles from downtown. In the modern annexe, a first-rate exhibition of photographic history ranges from high-quality Civil War prints to modern experimental works. There's also a space for temporary exhibitions and an arthouse cinema, but the house itself is surpassed in glory by its superbly maintained gardens.

Strong National Museum of Play

Manhattan Square • Mon–Thurs 10am–5pm, Fri & Sat 10am–8pm, Sun noon–5pm • $13, under 2s free, butterfly garden $4 • ⓣ585 263 2700, ⓦmuseumofplay.org

An obsessive collector of anything and everything, local bigwig Margaret Woodbury Strong (1897–1969) bequeathed her estate to the city and today it is the **Strong National Museum of Play**. Half devoted to a history of the American family and half obsessed with a history of American children's pop culture, it features interactive exhibits such as a history of *Sesame Street* and a fully working 1920s carousel. The best feature is a stunning butterfly garden, where colourful lepidoptera flitter among beautiful orchids and tropical plants in an enclosed conservatory.

ARRIVAL, GETTING AROUND AND INFORMATION   ROCHESTER

By bus The Greyhound station is at Broad and Chestnut sts. Destinations Buffalo (9 daily; 1hr 25min–1hr 50min); New York (8 daily; 5hr 55min–7hr 45min).

By train The Amtrak station, 320 Central Ave, is on the north side beyond the I-490 inner loop road. Destinations Albany (5 daily; 4hr 18min–4hr 58min);

Buffalo (3 daily; 1hr 20min); New York (4 daily; 7hr 17min–8hr 27min).

Local buses Regional Transit Service (RTS) public buses (ⓣ585 288 1700, ⓦrgrta.com) serve greater Rochester.

Visitor centre 45 East Ave (Mon–Fri 8.30am–5pm, Sat 10am–3pm; ⓣ800 677 7282, ⓦvisitrochester.com).

ACCOMMODATION

428 Mt Vernon 428 Mt Vernon Ave ☎716 271 0792, ⊚428mtvernon.com. At the entrance to lush Highland Park, this welcoming B&B has pleasantly decorated guest rooms, a lovely parlour and relaxing grounds. $140

Radisson Hotel Rochester Riverside 120 E Main St ☎585 546 6400, ⊚radisson.com. This high rise is as central as it gets. The rooms are large and smart; those on the upper floors offer sweeping views across the river and city beyond. $130

Red Roof Inn 4820 W Henrietta Rd, off I-90 exit 46 ☎585 359 1100, ⊚redroof.com. Reliable budget chain that provides somewhat more than budget quality, with flat-screen TVs and spacious, comfortable rooms. Great for the price. $70

EATING AND DRINKING

Beale St Café 689 South Ave ☎585 271 4650, ⊚thebealegrille.com. This northern outpost of the South serves fine helpings of New Orleans cuisine, such as Bourbon Street fried chicken for $13, complemented by live blues at weekends. Mon 11am–10pm, Tues–Thurs 11am–1pm, Fri & Sat 11am–11pm, Sun 2-10pm.

Esan 696 Park Ave ☎585 271 2271, ⊚esanparkave .com. A great place for authentically spicy and inexpensive Thai food, such as the delicious red stir-fry *pad pet* for $8.95, in the heart of the university area. Mon–Thurs 11.15am–9.30pm, Fri & Sat 11.15am–10.30pm, Sun 3.30–9.30pm.

★ **Next Door** 3220 Monroe Ave ☎585 249 4575, ⊚nextdoorbarandgrill.com. Owned by the famous Wegman's grocery, this superb suburban restaurant has a classy ambience and serves upmarket meals like Long Island duck breast for $31, as well as fine desserts and wines. Mon–Sat 11.30am–2.30pm & 5.30–10pm, bar till later.

Nick Tahou Hots 320 W Main St ☎585 436 0184, ⊚garbageplate.com. Famous for its $5–6 "garbage plate", a local hodgepodge of meats, eggs and vegetables, *Nick's* is a local institution, though the idea may not appeal to all. Mon–Sat 8am–8pm.

Buffalo

As I-90 sweeps down into the state's second largest city, **BUFFALO**, downtown looms up in a cluster of Art Deco spires and glass-box skyscrapers. The city's early twentieth-century prosperity is reflected in such architecturally significant structures as the towering 1932 **City Hall** (free observation deck on the top floor) and the deep-red terracotta relief of Louis Sullivan's **Guaranty Building** on Church Street. Just west of downtown, the massive abandoned grain elevators form part of the ongoing redevelopment of **Canalside** into a major entertainment and shopping hub. Renowned as a blue-collar city, Buffalo also loves its professional **sports** teams: football's Bills (☎877 228 4257, ⊚buffalobills.com) and ice hockey's Sabres (☎888 467 2273, ⊚sabres.nhl.com) both draw huge crowds.

Immediately north of downtown lie **Allentown** and **Elmwood Village**, Buffalo's most bohemian neighbourhoods. At 641 Delaware Ave, the **Theodore Roosevelt Inaugural National Historic Site** (Mon–Fri 9am–5pm, Sun noon–5pm; $10; ☎716 884 0095, ⊚trsite.org) allows you to tour the house where Teddy took the oath of office after President Mckinley's assassination in 1901.

Beyond Elmwood Village at 1300 Elmwood Ave, the airy new **Burchfield Penney Art Center** (Tues–Sat 10am–5pm, Thurs until 9pm, Sun 1–5pm; $10; ☎716 878 6011, ⊚burchfieldpenney.org) displays works by local artists. The area nearby around **Delaware Park** features several homes designed by **Frank Lloyd Wright**, most notably the Darwin D. Martin House Complex (tour times and lengths vary; $12.50–41; ☎716 947 9217, ⊚darwinmartinhouse.org).

Albright-Knox Art Gallery

1285 Elmwood Ave • Tues, Thurs, Sat & Sun noon–5pm, Fri noon–10pm • $13 • ☎716 882 8700, ⊚ albrightknox.org

That Buffalo's wealthy merchants were a cultured lot is apparent in the excellent **Albright-Knox Art Gallery**, two miles north of downtown amid the green spaces of the Frederick Law Olmsted-designed Delaware Park. One of the top modern collections in the world, it's especially strong on recent American and European art with works by Pollock, Rothko, Warhol and Rauschenberg. Other highlights are a Surrealism collection and pieces by earlier artists such as Matisse, Picasso and Monet. There are also a refreshing number of interactive exhibits.

ARRIVAL, GETTING AROUND AND INFORMATION

By plane Buffalo's airport (☎716 630 6020, ⓦbuffalo airport.com) is 8 miles from town; it is well connected with major cities in the northeast and some further afield.

By bus Greyhound, Metro Bus and Metro Rail, the city's tramway (both Metros ☎716 855 7211, ⓦnfta.com/metro), all operate from the downtown depot at Ellicott and N Division sts. Several local routes go to Niagara Falls.

By train Amtrak trains stop some six blocks from the bus station, at Exchange St, as well as in the eastern suburb of Depew, close to the airport.

By taxi Buffalo Taxi Cab (☎716 822 3030, ⓦbuffalotaxi cab.com).

Visitor centre 617 Main St (Mon–Fri 9am–5pm, Sat 10am–2pm; ☎716 852 2356).

ACCOMMODATION

★ **Elmwood Village Inn** 893 Elmwood Ave ☎716 886 2397, ⓦelmwoodvillageinn.com. Set in a gaily painted Victorian house, with colour extending throughout, and lovely rooms themed on different parts of the world; great breakfasts included too. **$110**

Hampton Inn & Suites 220 Delaware Ave ☎716 855 2223, ⓦhamptoninn3.hilton.com. A safe bet in the heart of downtown with smart, spacious suites, fitness and business centres, and adequate complimentary breakfasts. **$100**

HI-Buffalo Hostel 667 Main St ☎716 852 5222, ⓦhostelbuffalo.com. Very central hostel in a classy old building, with clean dorms and a few private rooms. Best budget option for the Buffalo/Niagara area. No lockout. Dorms **$25**, doubles **$65**

The Mansion on Delaware Avenue 414 Delaware Ave ☎716 886 3300, ⓦmansionondelaware.com. Centrally located luxury inn, whose rooms are superbly furnished and have fireplaces. Evening cocktails and gourmet breakfasts are served. **$195**

EATING, DRINKING AND NIGHTLIFE

The majority of downtown's theatres, venues and restaurants are handily grouped along Chippewa and Main; Allentown, Elmwood Village and Hartel Avenue are other trendy areas for food and drink. For details of what's on, pick up the free weekly *Art Voice* (ⓦartvoice.com) or the gay and lesbian *Outcome* (ⓦoutcomebuffalo.com).

Anchor Bar 1047 Main St ☎716 886 8920, ⓦanchor bar.com. The city's speciality of Buffalo (spicy chicken) wings with blue cheese and celery dressing is said to have been invented here. Mon–Thurs 11am–10pm, Fri 11am–midnight, Sat noon–midnight, Sun noon–10pm.

Asbury Hall 341 Delaware Ave ☎716 852 3835, ⓦbabevillebuffalo.com. Inside local recording artist Ani DiFranco's *Babeville*, which occupies an imposing deconsecrated church, this hip performance space hosts left-field gigs and other events. Hours vary.

Bacchus Wine Bar & Restaurant 54 W Chippewa St ☎716 854 9463, ⓦultimaterestaurants.com/bacchus. A good bar and restaurant, where you can enjoy dishes such as pecan-crusted Atlantic salmon for $24, accompanied by jazz, blues, folk and world music. Tues–Thurs 5–11pm, Fri & Sat 5pm–midnight.

Cole's 1104 Elmwood Ave ☎716 886 1449, ⓦcoles buffalo.com. Lively place that does imaginative burgers, such as Vietnamese *bahn mi* pork for $11, plus an array of appetizers, salads and chicken dishes, as well as decent beers. Mon–Thurs 11am–11pm, Fri & Sat 11am–midnight, Sun 11am–3pm.

★ **Nietzsche's** 248 Allen St ☎716 886 8539, ⓦnietzsches.com. Bar with friendly staff and cheap drinks, hosting a wide variety of live acts seven days a week, including regular open mics; there's room for dancing in the back. Free–$12. Daily 6pm–late.

Saigon Café 1098 Elmwood Ave ☎716 883 1252, ⓦthesaigoncafe.com. Simple Thai and Vietnamese place, which churns out delights like marinated pork chops and dancing seafood for $10–16. Mon–Thurs 11am–10pm, Fri 11am–11pm, Sat noon–11pm, Sun noon–9pm.

Niagara Falls

Every second almost three-quarters of a million gallons of water explode over the knife-edge **NIAGARA FALLS**, right on the border with Canada some twenty miles north of Buffalo on I-190. This awesome spectacle is made even more impressive by the variety of methods laid on to help you get closer to it. At night the falls are lit up and the coloured waters tumble dramatically into blackness, while in winter the whole scene changes as the fringes of the falls freeze to form gigantic razor-tipped icicles.

Some visitors will, no doubt, find the whole experience a bit too gimmicky, although the green fringes of the state park provide some bucolic getaways. Don't expect too much from the touristy towns of **Niagara Falls, New York** or even more developed

Niagara Falls, Ontario. Once you've seen the falls from as many different angles as you can manage and traced the **Niagara Gorge**, you'll have a better time heading back to Buffalo.

Niagara Falls comprises three distinct cataracts. The tallest are the **American** and **Bridal Veil falls** on the American side, separated by tiny Luna Island and plunging over jagged rocks in a 180ft drop; the broad **Horseshoe Falls**, which curve their way over to Canada, are far more majestic. Together, they date back a mere twelve thousand years, when the retreat of melting glaciers allowed water trapped in Lake Erie to gush north to Lake Ontario. Back then the falls were seven miles downriver, but constant erosion has cut them back to their present site.

Views of the falls

The best views on the American side are from the **Observation Tower** (daily 10am–5pm; $1, free in winter), and from the area at its base where the water rushes past. In the middle of the river, Terrapin Point on **Goat Island** has similar views of Horseshoe Falls. Near here, the nineteenth-century tightrope-walker Blondin crossed the Niagara repeatedly, and even carried passengers across on his back. The sheer power of the falls is most evident when you approach the towering cascade on the not-to-be-missed **Maid of the Mist** boat trip, which leaves from the foot of the observation tower (mid-April to Oct daily 9.15am–7.30pm every 15min; $15.50, kids $9; ☎716 284 8897, ⓦmaidofthemist.com). Another excellent way to see the falls is on the **Cave of the Winds** tour (mid-May to late Oct daily 9am–5pm, until 9pm July & Aug; $11, kids $9; ☎716 278 1730, ⓦniagarafallsstatepark.com), which leads from Goat Island by elevator down to the base of the falls. A "**Discovery Pass**" for these and other attractions costs $53.50 for adults and $34 for children at the visitor centre but only $33/$26 online.

For a bird's-eye view, Rainbow Air Inc **helicopter** tours, 454 Main St (9am–dusk; from $100; ☎716 284 2800, ⊛rainbowairinc.com), are breathtaking but brief. To check out the superior view from Niagara, Ontario, it's a fifteen-minute walk across the **Rainbow Bridge** to the Canadian side (pedestrians 50¢, cars $3.25; passports required). Driving across is inadvisable: even discounting the toll, parking on the other side is expensive and increased security checks make delays more likely.

ARRIVAL, GETTING AROUND AND INFORMATION   NIAGARA FALLS

By bus All buses stop downtown at 303 Rainbow Blvd, a 10min walk from the falls.

By train Amtrak trains stop 2 miles from downtown at 27th St and Lockwood Rd.

Destinations New York City (3 daily; 9hr 10min–9hr 45min); Toronto (3 daily; 3hr).

By car Arriving by car, follow the signs to one of the National Park car parks, which cost $10 (free off-season); some street parking is also available.

Local buses Local Metro Transit System buses ($2 base fare, day pass $5; ☎716 285 9319, ⊛nfta.com) run to all areas of the city and to Buffalo.

Niagara Scenic Trolley Getting around Niagara Falls State Park is easy, thanks to this twee but convenient tram ($2; free off-season) which connects all car parks and the major sightseeing points.

Niagara Tourism & Convention Corporation 10 Rainbow Blvd (daily: June to mid-Sept 8.30am–7pm; mid-Sept to May 9am–5pm; ☎716 282 8992, ⊛niagara-usa.com).

Niagara Falls State Park Visitors' Center Near the falls (daily 9am–5pm, longer hours in summer; ☎716 278 1796, ⊛niagarafallsstatepark.com).

ACCOMMODATION

Staying in central Niagara can be quite expensive if you don't plan ahead, but huge competition keeps rates down overall. US-62 (Niagara Falls Blvd), east of I-190, is lined with inexpensive motels; some are rather tacky honeymoon spots.

HI-Niagara Falls 1101 Ferry Ave ☎716 282 3700, ⊜niagarahostel@gmail.com. Friendly, well-run hostel with clean and spacious dorms, good-value singles and a few larger rooms. Preference is given to HI members and reservations are necessary in summer. Dorms $25, doubles $60

Niagara Falls Campground & Lodging 2405 Niagara Falls Blvd ☎716 731 3434, ⊛niagarafallscampground .net. Six miles from downtown, the closest campground to the falls has good facilities, clean bathrooms and free wi-fi. Open April–Oct. $35

Park Place B&B 740 Park Place ☎716 282 4626,

⊛parkplacebb.com. Comfortable spot near downtown, with quaintly decorated rooms, full breakfast and afternoon pastries. Good off-season rates. $119

Red Coach Inn 2 Buffalo Ave ☎716 282 1459, ⊛redcoach.com. Popular, well-appointed mock-Tudor B&B with rooms, suites and views of the falls. The restaurant is pretty good, too. $149

Seneca Niagara Casino & Hotel 310 4th St ☎716 299 1100, ⊛senecaniagaracasino.com. Luxury pad whose interiors are about as garish as the flashy neon entrance. Rates vary considerably – look out for online promotions. Several highly rated restaurants on the premises. $135

EATING AND DRINKING

Chu's Dining Lounge 1019 Main St ☎716 285 7278, ⊛chusdining.com. Pleasant restaurant, specializing in Cantonese and Szechuan cuisine. Try the triple delight with shrimp chicken and beef in spicy garlic sauce for $10.95. Daily 11am–11pm.

Como Restaurant 2200 Pine Ave ☎716 285 9341, ⊛comorestaurant.com. A good option, with huge portions of Italian cuisine and a reasonably priced deli. Two-course specials go for $11.95. Mon–Thurs & Sun 11.30am–9pm, Fri & Sat 11.30am–10pm.

Top Of The Falls Goat Island, Niagara Falls State Park ☎716 278 0340, ⊛niagarafallsstatepark.com. The food is adequate standard American fare but the setting is unrivalled. Floor-to-ceiling windows ensure everyone gets

a great view across the falls. April–Oct daily 11am–4pm, later in peak season.

Wine On Third 501 3rd St ☎716 285 9463, ⊛wineon third.com. New American cuisine such as seared Chilean sea bass with pepper purée ($30) is supplemented by an extensive wine list at this smart restaurant. Mon–Wed 4pm–midnight, Thurs 4pm–1am, Fri & Sat 4pm–2am, Sun 4–10pm.

Zaika Indian Cuisine 421 3rd St ☎716 804 0444, ⊛anindianzaika.com. Authentic and welcoming curry house with an emphasis on north Indian dishes, such as lamb *achari* for $16.95. Also does good-value buffets. Daily 11.30am–10pm.

CLOCKWISE FROM TOP ATLANTIC CITY, NJ (P.151); NIAGARA FALLS, NY (P.122); LIBERTY BELL, PHILADELPHIA, PA (P.128) >

Pennsylvania

2

PENNSYLVANIA was explored by the Dutch in the early 1600s, settled by the Swedes forty years later, and claimed by the British in 1664. Charles II of England, who owed a debt to the Penn family, rid himself of the potentially troublesome young **William Penn**, an enthusiastic advocate of religious freedom, by granting him land in the colony in 1682. Penn Jr immediately established a "holy experiment" of "brotherly love" and tolerance, naming the state after his father and setting a good example by signing a peaceful cohabitation treaty with the Native Americans. Most of the early agricultural settlers were religious refugees, Quakers like Penn himself and Mennonites from Germany and Switzerland, to be joined by Irish Catholics during the potato famines of the nineteenth century.

"The Keystone State" was crucial in the development of the United States. Politicians and thinkers like **Benjamin Franklin** congregated in Philadelphia – home of both the Declaration of Independence and the Constitution – and were prominent in articulating the ideas behind the Revolution. Later, the battle in Gettysburg, in south Pennsylvania, marked a turning point in the Civil War. Pennsylvania was also vital industrially: Pittsburgh, in the west, was the world's leading steel producer in the nineteenth century, and nearly all the nation's anthracite coal is still mined here.

The two great urban centres of **Philadelphia** and **Pittsburgh**, both lively and vibrant tourist destinations, are at opposite ends of the state. The three hundred miles between them, though predominantly agricultural, are topographically diverse. There are more than one hundred state parks, with green rolling countryside in the east and brooding forests in the west. **Lancaster County**, home to traditional Amish farmers, the **Gettysburg** battlefield and the **Hershey** chocolate factory, minutes away from state capital **Harrisburg**, draw visitors by the thousands. Finally, in the far northwest, **Lake Erie** provides the state's only waterfront, centred upon the eponymous town.

Philadelphia

The original capital of the nation, **PHILADELPHIA** was laid out by William Penn Jr in 1682, on a grid system that was to provide the pattern for most American cities. Just a few blocks away from the noise and crowds of downtown, shady cobbled alleys stand lined with red-brick colonial houses, while the peace and quiet of huge Fairmount Park make it easy to forget you're in a major metropolis. Settled by **Quakers**, Philadelphia prospered swiftly on the back of trade and commerce, becoming the second largest city in the British Empire by the 1750s. Economic power fuelled strong revolutionary feeling, and the city was the hub for most of the **War of Independence** and the US capital until 1800, while Washington DC was being built. The **Declaration of Independence** was written, signed, and first publicly read here in 1776, as was the **US Constitution** ten years later. Philadelphia was also a hotbed of new ideas in the arts and sciences, as epitomized by the scientist, philosopher, statesman, inventor and printer **Benjamin Franklin**.

Philadelphia, which means "City of Brotherly Love" in Greek, is in fact one of the most **ethnically mixed** US cities, with substantial communities of Italians, Irish, Eastern Europeans and Asians living side-by-side among the large **African American** population. Many of the city's black residents are descendants of the migrants who flocked here after the Civil War when Philadelphia was seen as a bastion of tolerance and liberalism. Philly also retains its Quaker heritage, with large "meetings" or congregations of **The Society of Friends**. Having ditched its erstwhile tag of "Filthydelphia", Philadelphia's strength today is its great energy in the face of economic adversity.

Central Philadelphia stretches for about two miles from the **Schuylkill** (pronounced "school-kill") **River** on the west to the **Delaware River** on the east; the metropolitan area extends for many miles in all directions, but everything you're likely to want to see is right in the central swath. The city's central districts are compact, walkable and readily accessible from each other; Penn's sensibly planned grid system makes for easy sightseeing.

PHILADELPHIA

▲ Fishtown & Northern Liberties

● RESTAURANTS

Amada	6
Bistro Romano	10
Buddakan	5
City Tavern	7
London Grill	2
Ocean City	3
Osteria	1
Parc	8
Pat's King of Steaks	12
The Prime Rib	9
Rangoon	4
South Street Diner	11

■ ACCOMMODATION

Apple Hostel	3
Club Quarters	4
La Reserve Center	7
Morris House Hotel	5
Penn's View Hotel	8
Philadelphia Bella Vista	6
Rittenhouse 1715	2
The Windsor Suites	1

■ BARS & LIVE MUSIC VENUES

Dirty Frank's	10
Good Dog Bar	9
Johnny Brendas	1
Khyber Pass	2
Kraftwork Bar	3
Painted Bride Art Center	4
Standard Tap	11
Theater of Living Arts	8
Tin Angel	6
Tria	7
Trocadero	5

Delaware River

Benjamin Franklin Bridge

Independence Seaport

Penn's Landing

Eastern State Penitentiary

Philadelphia Museum of Art

Rodin Museum

Free Library

The Franklin Institute

Academy of Natural Sciences

Please Touch Museum

Mütter Museum

Rosenbach Museum

Pennsylvania Academy of the Fine Arts

Painted Bride Art Center

Betsy Ross House

Christ Church

National Constitution Center

Free Quaker Meeting House

Jewish History Museum

First Bank of the US

African American Museum

Convention Center

Reading Terminal Market

Independence Mall

Liberty Bell Center

Independence Hall & Congress Hall

Philosophical Hall

INHP Visitor Center

Independence National Historic Park

Physick House

Theatre of Living Arts

Head House Square

Pennsylvania Academy of the Fine Arts

City Hall

CENTER CITY

CHINATOWN

Trocadero

OLD CITY

SOCIETY HILL

Franklin Square

Washington Square

Rittenhouse Square

Drexel University

University of Pennsylvania

Fairmount Park

Schuylkill River

Spring Garden

Zoo

Museum of Archeology & Anthropology

Subway station

0   400
yards

FAIRMOUNT AVENUE
WALLACE STREET
MT. VERNON STREET
GREEN STREET
SPRING GARDEN STREET
CALLOWHILL STREET
VINE STREET
RACE STREET
ARCH STREET
MARKET STREET
CHESTNUT STREET
SANSOM STREET
WALNUT STREET
LOCUST STREET
SPRUCE STREET
PINE STREET
LOMBARD STREET
SOUTH STREET

JUNIPER STREET
BROAD STREET
15th St
City Hall

Italian Market

2ND STREET
3RD STREET
4TH STREET
5TH STREET
6TH STREET
7TH STREET
8TH STREET
9TH STREET
10TH STREET
11TH STREET
12TH STREET
13TH STREET
15TH STREET
16TH STREET
17TH STREET
18TH STREET
19TH STREET
20TH STREET
21ST STREET
22ND STREET
23RD STREET
24TH STREET
25TH STREET
26TH ST
30th Street
23 ST STREET
24 ST STREET
25 ST STREET

N COLUMBUS BLVD
FRONT STREET

PENNSYLVANIA AVENUE
JOHN F. KENNEDY BOULEVARD
BENJAMIN FRANKLIN PARKWAY
VINE STREET EXPRESSWAY
FAIRMOUNT AVENUE
SPRING GARDEN STREET
CALLOWHILL STREET

2

Independence National Historic Park

All INHP sites (unless otherwise specified) are open 365 days a year; hours usually 9am–5pm, sometimes longer in summer • Free • ☎ 215 597 8974, Ⓦ nps.gov/inde

Any tour of Philadelphia should start with **Independence National Historic Park**, or **INHP**, "America's most historic square mile". Though the park covers a mere four blocks just west of the Delaware River, between Walnut and Arch streets, it can take more than a day to explore in full. The solid red-brick buildings here, not all of which are open to the public, epitomize the Georgian (and after the Revolution, Federalist) obsession with balance and symmetry.

Free **tours** set off from the rear of the east wing of Independence Hall, the single most important site. Throughout the day, costumed actors perform patchy but informative skits in various locations – *The Gazette* free newsletter has listings and a useful map.

Independence Hall

In peak season, free tickets must be obtained at the Independence Visitor Center (see p.132)

It's best to reach **Independence Hall** early, to avoid the hordes of tourists and school parties. Built in 1732 as the Pennsylvania State House, this was where the Declaration of Independence was prepared, signed and, after the pealing of the Liberty Bell, given its first public reading on July 8, 1776.

The **Liberty Bell** itself hung in Independence Hall from 1753, ringing to herald vital announcements such as victories and defeats in the Revolutionary War. Stories as to how it received its famous crack vary, but it's undisputed that it rang publicly for the very last time on George Washington's birthday in 1846. It later acquired the name Liberty Bell because of its inscription from Leviticus, advocating liberty, which made it an anti-slavery symbol. After the Civil War, the silent bell was adopted as a symbol of freedom and reconciliation and embarked on a national rail tour. The iconic lump of metal now rests in a shrine-like space in the new multimedia **Liberty Bell Center** in INHP.

Congress Hall

Next door to Independence Hall, **Congress Hall**, built in 1787 as Philadelphia County Courthouse, is where members of the new United States Congress first took their places, and where all the patterns for today's US government were established. The original seating and podium are still in place.

First Bank of the United States

3rd and Chestnut sts • Access to displays Tues–Sun 10am–4pm

The **First Bank of the United States** was established in 1797 to formalize the new union's currency. In 1774, delegates of the first Continental Congress – predecessor of the US Congress – chose defiantly to meet at Carpenter's Hall, 320 Chestnut St, to air their grievances against the English king. Today the building exhibits early tools and furniture.

Franklin Court and the B Free Franklin Post Office

Directly north of the first Bank of the United States, **Franklin Court**, 313 Market St, is a tribute to Benjamin Franklin on the former site of his home. An underground museum has hilarious dial-a-quote recordings of his pithy sayings and the musings of his

---

THE PHILADELPHIA PASS

Although the attractions of Independence National Historic Park are free, most of Philadelphia's other museums and places of interest have hefty entrance fees, so it is worth considering buying the good-value **Philadelphia Pass** (valid 1–5 days; $49–115; Ⓦ philadelphiapass.com), which allows entry to more than thirty city attractions. It is available at a discount online or at various locations, including the Independence Visitor Center (see p.132).

contemporaries, as well as a working printshop. The **B Free Franklin Post Office**, 316 Market St, sells stamps and includes a small postal museum.

Old City

Immediately north of INHP lies **Old City**, Philadelphia's earliest commercial area, above Market Street near the riverfront. Washington, Franklin and Betsy Ross all worshipped at **Christ Church**, on 2nd Street just north of Market, which dates from 1727. The church's official burial ground, two blocks west at 5th and Arch (tour times vary; ☎215 922 1695, ⓦchristchurchphila.org), includes gravestones of signatories to the Declaration of Independence, among them **Benjamin Franklin**. At 239 Arch St, the **Betsy Ross House** (daily 10am–5pm; $5; ☎215 686 1252, ⓦbetsyrosshouse.org), by means of unimpressive wax dummies, salutes the woman credited, probably apocryphally, with making the first American flag.

Elfreth's Alley

The claim of **Elfreth's Alley** – a pretty little cobbled way off 2nd Street between Arch and Race streets – to be the "oldest street in the United States" is somewhat dubious, though it has been in continuous residential use since 1727; its thirty houses, notable for their wrought-iron gates, water pumps, wooden shutters and attic rooms, date from later in the eighteenth century. At no. 126 is the **Elfreth's Alley Museum** (Wed–Sat 10am–5pm, Sun noon–5pm; $5, guided tour $5; ☎215 574 0560, ⓦelfrethsalley.org); the house was built by blacksmith Jeremiah Elfreth in 1762.

National Constitution Center

525 Arch St • Mon–Fri 9.30am–5pm, Sat 9.30am–6pm, Sun noon–5pm • $14.50 • ☎215 409 6600, ⓦconstitutioncenter.org

The area north of Market Street holds three excellent museums. The must-see **National Constitution Center** is a modern, interactive and provocative museum dedicated to the nation's best-known document, offering a wealth of information. Highlights include a 360° theatrical production called *Freedom Rising* and Signers Hall, where you can add your signature to the Constitution alongside 42 life-size bronze figures of the Founding Fathers.

National Museum of American Jewish History

101 S Independence Mall E • Tues–Fri 10am–5pm (until 8pm June–Aug), Sat & Sun 10am–5.30pm • $12 • ☎215 923 3811, ⓦnmajh.org

The permanent state-of-the-art displays at the **National Museum of American Jewish History** chronicle the history of Judaism in America, starting on the fourth floor and working down, with a **Hall of Fame** on the ground floor lauding prominent Jews such as Albert Einstein, Steven Spielberg and Barbra Streisand. Revolving special exhibitions occupy the fifth floor.

African American Museum in Philadelphia

7th and Arch sts • Wed–Sat 10am–5pm, Sun noon–5pm • $14 • ☎215 574 0380, ⓦaampmuseum.org

The emotive and politically informed **African American Museum in Philadelphia** tells the stories of the thousands of blacks who migrated north to Philadelphia after Reconstruction and in the early twentieth century. The museum's most interesting aspect in many ways is its exploration of the cultural impact of African Americans through their influence in spheres such as music, sport and politics.

Penn's Landing

Just east of Old City along the Delaware River, where William Penn stepped off in 1682, spreads the huge and heavily industrialized port of Philadelphia. Along the port's southern reaches, on the river-side of the I-95 freeway, the old docklands have been renovated as part of the **Penn's Landing** development, the most interesting feature of which is the **Independence Seaport Museum** (daily 10am–5pm; $13.50; ☎215 925

5439, ⓦphillyseaport.org). Admission includes entry onto two **historical ships**: the flagship USS *Olympia* and the World War II submarine *Becuna*. All along the riverfront promenade are food stalls, landscaped pools and fountains; regular outdoor concerts and festivals are held here. The seasonal Riverlink **ferry** crosses the Delaware (May–Sept hourly 10am–6pm; from $6 return; ❶215 925 5465, ⓦriverlinkferry.org) to the down-at-heel town of **Camden**, where the main attraction is the **Adventure Aquarium** (daily 10am–5pm; $24.95; ❶856 365 3300, ⓦadventureaquarium.com), only worthwhile if you have kids in tow.

Society Hill

Society Hill, an elegant residential area west of the Delaware and directly south of INHP, spreads between Walnut and Lombard streets. Though it is indeed Philadelphia's high society that lives here now, the area was named after its first inhabitants, the Free Society of Traders. After falling into disrepair, the Hill itself was flattened in the early 1970s to provide a building site for I.M. Pei's twin skyscrapers, Society Hill Towers. Luckily, the rest of the neighbourhood has been restored to form one of the city's most picturesque districts: cobbled gas-lit streets are lined with immaculately kept colonial, Federal and Georgian homes, often featuring the state's namesake keystones on their window frames. One of the few buildings open to the public is the **Physick House**, 321 S 4th St, home to Dr Philip Syng Physick, "the Father of American Surgery", and filled with eighteenth- and nineteenth-century decorative arts (Thurs–Sat noon–4pm, Sun 1–4pm; $5; ❶215 925 7866, ⓦphilalandmarks.org).

Center City

Center City, Philadelphia's main business and commercial area, stretches from 8th Street west to the Schuylkill River, dominated by the endearing baroque wedding cake of **City Hall** and its 37ft bronze statue of Penn. Before ascending thirty storeys to the **observation deck** (Mon–Fri 9.30am–4.15pm; $5) at Penn's feet, check out the quirky sculptures and carvings around the building, including the cats and mice at the south entrance. A couple of blocks north, at Broad and Cherry streets, the **Pennsylvania Academy of the Fine Arts** (Tues–Sat 10am–5pm, Sun 11am–5pm; $15; ❶215 972 7600, ⓦpafa.org), housed in an elaborate, multicoloured Victorian pile, exhibits three hundred years of American art, including works by Mary Cassatt, Thomas Eakins and Winslow Homer.

Beginning at 8th Street, **Chinatown**, marked by the gorgeous 40ft Friendship Gate at 10th and Arch, has some of the best budget food in the city. A few blocks over on 12th Street is the century-old **Reading Terminal Market** (daily 9am–4pm; ❶215 922 2317, ⓦreadingterminalmarket.org), where many Amish farmers come to the city to sell their produce. It's always good for a lively time and makes a great lunch spot.

Rittenhouse Square

Grassy **Rittenhouse Square**, one of Penn's original city squares, is in a very fashionable part of town. On one side it borders chic Walnut Street, on the other a residential area of solid brownstones with beautifully carved doors and windows. The red-brick 1860 **Rosenbach Museum**, 2010 Delancey Place, holds more than thirty thousand rare books, as well as James Joyce's original hand-scrawled manuscripts of *Ulysses* (Tues & Fri noon–5pm, Wed & Thurs noon–8pm, Sat & Sun noon–6pm; $10, including house tour; ❶215 732 1600, ⓦrosenbach.org). On summer evenings there are free outdoor jazz and R&B concerts in the square.

Fairmount Park

The mile-long Benjamin Franklin Parkway, known as Museum Row, sweeps northwest from City Hall to the colossal Museum of Art in **Fairmount Park**, an area of countryside annexed by the city in the nineteenth century. Spanning nine hundred scenic acres on both sides of the Schuylkill River, this is one of the world's largest landscaped city parks, with jogging, biking and hiking trails, early-American homes, an all-wars memorial to the state's black soldiers, and the country's first **zoo** at 3400 W Girard Ave (March–Oct 9.30am–5pm; $20; Nov–Feb 9.30am–4pm; $18; ☎215 243 1100, ⓦphillyzoo.org). In the late 1960s, local resident **Joe Frazier** and **Muhammad Ali** all but brought the city to a standstill with the announcement one afternoon that they were heading to Fairmount for an informal slug-out.

Philadelphia Museum of Art

Franklin Parkway and 26th St • Tues–Sun 10am–5pm, Wed & Fri until 8.45pm • $20, donation first Sun of month & Wed after 5pm • ☎215 763 8100, ⓦphilamuseum.org

The steps of the **Philadelphia Museum of Art** were immortalized by **Sylvester Stallone** in the film *Rocky*, an event commemorated by the **Rocky statue**. Inside are some of the finest treasures in the US, with a twelfth-century French cloister, **Renaissance** art, a complete Robert Adam interior from a 1765 house in London's Berkeley Square, **Rubens** tapestries, Pennsylvania Dutch crafts and Shaker furniture, a strong **Impressionist** collection and the world's most extensive **Marcel Duchamp** collection.

Rodin Museum

Franklin Parkway and 22nd St • Wed–Mon 10am–5pm • $8 suggested donation • ☎215 763 8100, ⓦrodinmuseum.org

A few blocks back towards Center City from the Philadelphia Museum of Art, the exquisite **Rodin Museum**, marble-walled and set in a shady garden with a green pool, holds the largest collection of Rodin's Impressionistic sculptures and casts outside of Paris, including *The Burghers of Calais*, *The Thinker* and *The Gates of Hell*.

The Franklin Institute and around

The vast edifice of the **Franklin Institute**, N 20th Street and Benjamin Franklin Parkway (daily 9.30am–5pm; $16.50, $22.50 including one IMAX show; ☎215 448 1200, ⓦfi.edu), houses a Planetarium, the Tuttleman IMAX Theater (film only $9), and the Mandell Futures Center, which concentrates on technological developments. Continuing the educational theme, the nearby **Academy of Natural Sciences**, 1900 Benjamin Franklin Parkway, exhibits dinosaurs, mummies and gems (Mon–Fri 10am–4.30pm, Sat & Sun 10am–5pm; $15; ☎215 299 1000, ⓦansp.org). Among the rare items at the **Free Library of Philadelphia**, 19th and Vine streets (Mon–Wed 9am–9pm, Thurs–Sat 9am–5pm, Sun 1–5pm; tours at 11am; free; ☎215 686 5322, ⓦlibrary.phila.gov), are cuneiform tablets from 3000 BC, medieval manuscripts and first editions of Dickens and Poe.

Eastern State Penitentiary

2027 Fairmount Ave • Daily 10am–5pm, last entry 4pm • $14 • ☎215 236 3300, ⓦeasternstate.org

Just a short walk northeast of the Philadelphia Museum of Arts, occupying two full blocks of Fairmount Avenue between 20th and 22nd streets, stand the gloomy Gothic fortifications of the **Eastern State Penitentiary**, one of Philadelphia's most significant historic sites, which embodies a complete history of attitudes toward crime and punishment in the US. After a period of decay following its closure in 1970, the bulk of the Panopticon-style radial prison has been restored. Informative **audio tours** point out the prison's many novel architectural features, as well as its old synagogue and the upmarket cell where Al Capone cooled his heels.

West Philadelphia

Across the Schuylkill River, **West Philadelphia** is home to the Ivy League **University of Pennsylvania**, where Franklin established the country's first medical school. The compact but extremely pleasant campus has some great museums: the small **Institute of Contemporary Art**, 118 S 36th St (Wed 11am–8pm, Thurs & Fri

11am–6pm, Sat & Sun 11am–5pm; free; **☎**215 898 5911, **ⓦ**icaphila.org) displays cutting-edge travelling exhibitions in an airy space; the intriguing **Arthur Ross Gallery**, 220 S 34th St (Tues–Fri 10am–5pm, Sat & Sun noon–5pm; free; **☎**215 898 2083, **ⓦ**upenn.edu/ARG) features changing exhibits, particularly of international and colourful, innovative artwork.

Museum of Archeology and Anthropology

3260 South St • Tues–Sun 10am–5pm, Wed till 8pm • $12 • **☎** 215 898 4000, **ⓦ** penn.museum

The superlative **Museum of Archeology and Anthropology** is the university's top draw. Regarded by experts as one of the world's finest science museums, its exhibits span all the continents and their major epochs – from Nigerian Benin bronzes to Chinese crystal balls. Most astonishing is the priceless twelve-ton granite Sphinx of Rameses II, c.1293–1185 BC, in the Lower Egyptian Gallery.

South Philadelphia

Staunchly blue-collar **South Philadelphia**, centre of Philadelphia's black community since the Civil War, is also home to many of the city's Italians; opera singer **Mario Lanza** and pop stars Fabian and Chubby Checker grew up here. It's also where to come for an authentic – and very messy – **Philly cheesesteak** (see opposite), and to rummage through the wonderful **Italian Market** (another *Rocky* location), which runs along 9th Street south from Christian Street. One of the last surviving urban markets in the USA, it features wooden market stalls packed to overflowing with bric-a-brac and various produce – most famously, mozzarella. **South Street**, the original boundary of the city, is now one of Philadelphia's main **nightlife** districts, with dozens of cafés, bars, restaurants and nightclubs lined up along the few blocks west from Front Street; there are also many good book, record and clothing **shops** for browsing by day or evening.

ARRIVAL AND DEPARTURE | PHILADELPHIA

By plane Philadelphia's International Airport (**☎**215 937 6800, **ⓦ**phl.org) is 7 miles southwest of the city off I-95. Taxis into town cost $30–35 (try Yellow Cab; **☎**215 829 4222), and SEPTA, the South East Pennsylvania Transit Authority (see below) runs trains from the airport every 30min (4.30am–11.30pm; $7) to five downtown stations.

By bus The Greyhound station is downtown at 1001 Filbert St.

Destinations Baltimore (8 daily; 1hr 55min–2hr 45min); Harrisburg (5 daily; 1hr 55min–2hr 50min); New York City (20 daily; 2–3hr); Pittsburgh (8 daily; 5hr 45min–9hr

45min); Washington DC (8 daily; 3hr 20min–4hr 25min).

By train The grand 30th Street Amtrak station is just across the Schuylkill River in the university area (free transfer downtown on SEPTA). SEPTA connects to NJ Transit, and between the two commuter rail systems you can travel to the Jersey shore, Princeton, suburban Pennsylvania and New York City for a fraction of the price of Amtrak.

Destinations New York City (10 daily; 1hr 12min–1hr 37min); Pittsburgh (1 daily; 7hr 23min); Washington DC (10 daily; 1hr 35min–2hr 17min).

GETTING AROUND

By bus SEPTA (**☎**215 580 7800, **ⓦ**septa.org) runs an extensive bus system. The handiest route is #76, which runs from Penn's Landing and the Independence Hall area out along Market St past City Hall to the museums and Fairmount Park. Buses require exact fares of $2 (tokens, purchased in batches of two or more, cost only $1.55); day passes, also good for the airport, go for $7. Bright purple

PHLASH buses run a handy downtown loop in summer (June–Oct daily 10am–8pm; $2, day pass $5; **☎**215 474 5274, **ⓦ** phillyphlash.com).

By subway SEPTA also has a subway system: the most useful lines cross the city east–west (Market–Frankford line) and north–south (Broad St line). Ticketing works in the same way as for the buses.

INFORMATION

Visitor centres The excellent Independence Visitor Center, 1 Independence Mall W (daily 8.30am–6pm; **☎**215 965 7676, **ⓦ**phlvisitorcenter.com), contains a staggering wealth

of information and should be the first stop on any visitor's itinerary. There is a smaller visitor centre downtown in City Hall, room 121 (Mon–Fri 9am–5pm; **☎**215 686 2840).

TOURS

Big Bus Company ☎ 215 389 8687, ⓦ phillytour.com. A useful hop-on, hop-off tour aboard open-topped double-deckers and trams (trolleys), with commentary on the major sites. 24hr pass $27.

Ghosts of Philadelphia ☎ 215 413 1997, ⓦ ghosttour .com. Morbidly fascinating historical tours every evening from next to Independence Hall. Late March–Nov, hours vary; $17, kids $10.

Mural Arts Program ☎ 215 389 8687, ⓦ muralarts .org. Among services offered are 2hr tram ($30) and walking ($20) tours of the city's extensive neighbourhood murals. Hours vary.

ACCOMMODATION

Hotels anywhere downtown or near the historic area tend to be prohibitively expensive, though at weekends there's a chance of getting a reduced rate. Parking is always expensive. The Independence Visitor Center is a great resource for accommodation discounts; B&Bs are a good option here, but usually need to be booked in advance.

Apple Hostel 32 S Bank St ☎ 215 922 0222, ⓦ apple hostels.com. Friendly hostel wedged between Independence Hall National Park and Old City, with bunk beds, some private rooms and free games, tea and coffee. No curfews. Dorms __$37__, doubles __$83__

Club Quarters 1628 Chestnut St ☎ 215 282 5000, ⓦ clubquarters.com. Sleekly designed rooms in a red-brick building in midtown. This full-service hotel offers better rates if you join its membership scheme. __$175__

★ **La Reserve Center City B&B** 1804 Pine St ☎ 215 735 1137, ⓦ lareservebandb.com. Lovely rooms, of which the two cheapest share a bathroom. The welcoming owner dishes up a modest-sized gourmet breakfast and dispenses loads of information. __$80__

★ **Morris House Hotel** 225 S 8th St ☎ 215 922 2446, ⓦ morrishousehotel.com. Luxury boutique hotel in a 1787 Society Hill mansion with a lovely courtyard, cleverly refurbished to maintain its historical feel. Ample continental breakfast included. __$239__

Penn's View Hotel Front and Market sts ☎ 215 922 7600, ⓦ pennsviewhotel.com. Exceptional service and clean, comfortable rooms in Old City, in this lavishly decorated and furnished hotel. There's a very fine wine bar next to the lobby. Continental breakfast included. __$185__

Philadelphia Bella Vista 752 S 10th St ☎ 215 238 1270, ⓦ philadelphiabellavistabnb.com. Cute little gaily painted place with comfy, compact rooms that constitute some of the best deals in town. Handy both for downtown and the buzzing South St area. __$95__

Rittenhouse 1715 1715 Rittenhouse Square St ☎ 215 546 6500, ⓦ rittenhouse1715.com. Classing itself as a boutique hotel, this central B&B offers a range of rooms, all with marble bathrooms, and a few truly palatial suites. __$224__

The Windsor Suites 1700 Benjamin Franklin Pkwy ☎ 215 981 5678, ⓦ thewindsorsuites.com. Circular, modern high-rise, handily located for Museum Row and midtown, whose rooms are sharply designed, the suites containing fully equipped kitchens. __$150__

EATING

Eating out in Philadelphia is a real treat: the ubiquitous **street stands** sell soft pretzels with mustard for 50¢, Chinatown and the Italian Market are good for ethnic food, while Reading Terminal Market offers bargain lunches of various cuisines. South Street has plenty of good, if rather touristy, places, while pricier, trendier restaurants cluster along S 2nd Street in the Old City. The **South Philly cheesesteak**, a hot sandwich of wafer-thin roast beef topped with melted cheese (aka Cheez Whiz), varies from place to place around town.

★ **Amada** 217 Chestnut St ☎ 215 625 2450, ⓦ amada restaurant.com. A dash of Spanish inspiration in Old City, with more than sixty tapas dishes at around $10, great paella and fine sangria. Daily 11.30am–2.30pm, plus Mon–Thurs 5–10pm, Fri & Sat 5–11pm.

Bistro Romano 120 Lombard St ☎ 215 925 8880, ⓦ bistroromano.com. Quality Italian food is served in a converted eighteenth-century granary, with authentic pastas and other dishes costing around $20, and a piano bar on Friday and Saturday evenings. Mon–Thurs 4.30–10pm, Fri & Sat 4.30–11pm, Sun 4–9pm.

Buddakan 325 Chestnut St ☎ 215 574 9440, ⓦ buddakan.com. Delicious pan-Asian fusion mains such as five spice duck breast cost around $20. Admire the 10ft-high gilded Buddha while dining. Mon–Thurs 11.30am–2.30pm & 5–11pm, Fri 11.30am–2.30pm & 5pm–midnight, Sat 5pm–midnight, Sun 4–10pm.

City Tavern 138 S 2nd St ☎ 215 413 1443, ⓦ citytavern .com. Reconstructed 1773 tavern in INHP, originally frequented by John Adams. Chef Walter Staib cooks and costumed staff serve "olde style" food to a harpsichord accompaniment – dinner mains such as braised rabbit are mostly well over $20. Daily 11.30am–10.30pm.

London Grill 2301 Fairmount Ave ☎ 215 978 4545, ⓦ londongrill.com. This sophisticated establishment in the museum district serves delicious American and European cuisine at fair prices, with dishes such as horseradish-crusted salmon going for $19. Mon 4pm–2am, Tues–Fri 11am–2am, Sat & Sun 10am–2am.

Ocean City 234-6 N 9th St ☎ 215 829 0688. Huge Chinatown space specializing in fresh seafood, which is on display in tanks; also excellent dim sum for a few bucks each before 3pm. Daily 11am–10pm.

Osteria 640 N Broad St ☎ 215 763 0920, ⓦ osteriaphilly.com. Award-winning Italian restaurant with a good selection of pizzas and antipasti, mains such as wild halibut for $25–30 and delicious desserts. Mon–Thurs & Sun 5–10pm, Fri & Sat 5–11pm.

Parc 227 S 18th St ☎ 215 545 2262, ⓦ parc-restaurant.com. Excellent French bistro right opposite ritzy Rittenhouse Square. Mains such as skate grenobloise go for $20–30. Also a long wine list, plus of bottled beers and absinthe. Mon–Thurs 7.30am–11pm, Fri 7.30am–midnight, Sat 10am–midnight, Sun 10am–10pm.

★ **Pat's King of Steaks** 1237 E Passyunk Ave ☎ 215

468 1546, ⓦ patskingofsteaks.com. The cheesesteaks at this delightfully decrepit, outdoor-seating-only cheesesteak joint are the real deal. Daily 24hr.

The Prime Rib 1701 Locust St ☎ 215 772 1701, ⓦ theprimerib.com. The place for real steaks, not cheesesteaks; truly prime cuts of beef cost around $50 at this classy restaurant, whose wine list and decor are equally opulent. Daily 4.30–11pm.

Rangoon 112 N 9th St ☎ 215 829 8939, ⓦ rangoonrestaurant.com. Friendly and intimate Burmese joint, serving an authentic selection of curries, rice and noodle dishes at $10–12; try the cheap lunch specials. Daily 11am–10.30pm.

South Street Diner 140 South St ☎ 215 627 5258, ⓦ southstreetdinerphilly.com. The huge menu, including great burgers, sandwiches, wraps and quesadillas for $7–15, make this place perpetually busy, even in the wee hours. Daily 24hr.

DRINKING AND NIGHTLIFE

The most popular areas for bar-hopping are South Street and around 2nd Street in the Old City, although the Northern Liberties and Fishtown areas, a little further north, beyond the flyovers, have established reputations for trendy bars and clubs. Local brews are popular and inexpensive; try any ale by Yards, or Yuengling if you prefer lager.

★ **Dirty Frank's** 347 S 13th St ☎ 215 732 5010. Popular with a very mixed crowd, this Philly institution touts itself as "one of the few places in the world where you can drink a $3 pint of Yuengling underneath oil paintings by nationally recognized artists". Daily 11am–2am.

Good Dog Bar 224 S 15th St ☎ 215 985 9600, ⓦ gooddogbar.com. Laidback and friendly bar that has a revolving range of cheap beers including Brooklyn Summer Ale for $5, as well as wines, cocktails and tasty burgers. Daily 11.30am–2am.

★ **Khyber Pass Pub** 56 S 2nd St ☎ 215 238 5888, ⓦ khyberpasspub.com. Offering more than twenty beers on tap or cask, with tempting names like Rogue Old Crustacean, this bar is one of the best watering holes in this lively strip. Daily 11am–2am.

Kraftwork Bar 531 E Girard Ave ☎ 215 739 1700,

ⓦ kraftworkbar.com. Unpretentious and friendly sports bar in Fishtown, which offers dollar dogs on Phillies game days and beers by Two Brothers Brewing. Mon–Fri noon–2am, Sat & Sun 10.30am–2am.

Standard Tap 901 N 2nd St ☎ 215 922 0522, ⓦ standardtap.com. Popular Northern Liberties bar, located in a fine house, with a range of beers from regional breweries like Flying Fish and River Horse on tap, as well as filling bar food. Mon–Fri 4pm–2am, Sat & Sun 11am–2am.

Tria 123 S 18th St ☎ 215 972 8742, ⓦ triacafe.com. As the name suggests, this trendy bar-café concentrates on three areas of fermentation, in this case beer, wine and cheese. Educational classes too. There's another location at 1123 Spruce St. Daily noon–late.

LIVE MUSIC AND ENTERTAINMENT

Few reminders are left of the 1970s "Philadelphia Sound". Instead, in recent times the city has produced the likes of Pink, while its active underground scene features psych bands like Bardo Pond, The Asteroid #4 and Fern Knight. The world-famous **Philadelphia Orchestra** performs at the smart modern Kimmel Center for the Performing Arts (☎ 215 790 5800, ⓦ kimmelcenter.org). Philadelphia's other great strength is its **theatre** scene, where small venues abound: visit the Theatre Alliance website at ⓦ theatrealliance.org, which features the StageTix discount ticket programme. **Listings** for all events can be found in the free *City Paper* (ⓦ citypaper.net) or *Philadelphia Weekly* (ⓦ philadelphiaweekly.com) newspapers.

Johnny Brendas 1201 N Frankford Ave ☎ 215 739 9684, ⓦ johnnybrendas.com. Underground establishment that showcases mostly unknown local and national rock and indie bands. Free–$20. Hours vary.

Painted Bride Art Center 230 Vine St ☎ 215 925 9914, ⓦ paintedbride.org. Avant-garde art gallery with live jazz, dance and theatre performances after dark. Hours vary.

Theater of Living Arts 334 South St ☎ 215 922 1011, ⓦ thetla.com. Converted movie palace that's one of the best places to catch mid-sized rock bands. Tickets mostly $15–25. Hours vary.

Tin Angel 20 S 2nd St ☎ 215 928 0770, ⓦ tinangel .com. Intimate upstairs bar and coffeehouse, featuring top

local and nationally known folk, jazz, blues and acoustic acts. Free–$25. Hours vary.

Trocadero 1003 Arch St ☎ 215 922 6888, ⓦ thetroc .com. Downtown music venue in a converted 1870 theatre, sometimes featuring big-name alternative bands. ID is essential; tickets mostly $20–50. Hours vary.

Lancaster County: Pennsylvania Dutch Country

Lancaster County stretches for about 45 miles from **Coatesville**, which is forty miles west of Philadelphia on US-30, to the Susquehanna River in the west. Although tiny, uncosmopolitan Lancaster, ten miles east of the river, was US capital for a day in September 1777, the region is famed more for its preponderance of agricultural religious communities, known collectively as the **Pennsylvania Dutch**. They actually have no connection to the Netherlands; the name is a mistaken derivation of Deutsch (German). A touristy place even before it was brought to international fame by the movie *Witness*, most of Lancaster County has maintained its natural beauty in the face of encroaching commercialization. It is a region of gentle countryside and fertile farmlands, eccentric-sounding place names such as **Intercourse**, horse-drawn buggies, tiny roadside bakeries and Amish children wending their way between immaculate, flower-filled farmhouses and one-room schoolhouses.

However, attempting to live a simple life away from the pressures of the outside world has proved too much for many Pennsylvania Dutch. A few (mainly Mennonites) have succumbed to commercial need by offering rides in their buggies and meals in their homes, while members of the stricter orders have moved away to communities in less touristic mid-Western states. When visiting, remember that Sunday is a day of rest for the Amish, so many attractions, restaurants and other amenities will be closed.

Though useful for a general overview and historical insight, the attractions that interpret Amish culture tend toward overkill. It's far more satisfying just to explore the countryside for yourself. Here, among the streams with their covered bridges and fields striped with corn, alfalfa and tobacco, the reality hits you – these aren't actors recreating an ancient lifestyle, but real people, part of a living, working community.

Pennsylvania Dutch Country sights

Among the widely spread formal attractions, the **Ephrata Cloister**, 632 W Main St, Ephrata, at the junction of US-272 and 322 (April–Oct Mon–Sat 9am–5pm, Sun noon–5pm; Nov–Dec & March closed Mon, Jan & Feb closed Mon & Tues; $10;

THE PENNSYLVANIA DUTCH

The people now known as the Pennsylvania Dutch originated as **Anabaptists** in sixteenth-century Switzerland, under the leadership of Menno Simons. His unorthodox advocacy of adult baptism and literal interpretation of the Bible led to the order's persecution; they were invited by William Penn to settle in Lancaster County in the 1720s. Today the twenty or so orders of Pennsylvania Dutch include the "plain" Old Order **Amish** (a strict order that originally broke away from Simons in 1693) and freer-living **Mennonites**, as well as the "fancy" **Lutheran** groups (distinguished by the colourful circular "hex" signs on their barns). Living by an unwritten set of rules called Amish Ordnung, which includes absolute pacifism, the Amish are the strictest and best known: the men with their wide-brimmed straw hats and beards (but no "military" moustaches), the women in bonnets, plain dresses (with no fripperies like buttons) and aprons. Shunning electricity and any exposure to the corrupting influence of the outside world, the Amish power their farms with generators, and travel (at roughly 10mph) in handmade horse-drawn buggies. For all their insularity, the Amish are very friendly and helpful; resist the temptation to photograph them, however, as the making of "graven images" offends their beliefs.

2

☎717 733 6600, ⓦephratacloister.org), re-creates the eighteenth-century settlement of German Protestant celibates that acted, among other things, as an early publishing and printing centre. Further south, about three miles northeast of Lancaster, the **Landis Valley Museum**, 2451 Kissell Hill Rd (Mon–Sat 9am–5pm, Sun noon–5pm; $12; ☎717 569 0401, ⓦlandisvalleymuseum.org), is a living history museum of rural life, with demonstrations of local crafts. The oldest building in the county, the **Hans Herr House**, 1849 Hans Herr Drive, five miles south of downtown Lancaster off US-222 (April–Nov Mon–Sat 9am–4pm; $8; ☎717 464 4438, ⓦhansherr.org), is a 1719 Mennonite church with a pretty garden and orchard, a medieval German facade and exhibits on early farm life.

ARRIVAL, DEPARTURE AND GETTING AROUND   LANCASTER COUNTY

By train and bus Amtrak, Greyhound and Capital Trailways buses (☎717 397 4861) all arrive at 53 McGovern Ave, Lancaster.

By car The best route through the concentrated Amish communities is US-30, which runs east–west, but the backroads are the most interesting.

By bike The most fun way to see the area is to ride a bike, which gives the benefits of all that fresh air and shows more consideration for the ubiquitous horse-drawn buggies. For self-guided bike tours, contact Lancaster Bicycle Club in Lancaster (ⓦlancasterbikeclub.org).

INFORMATION

Pennsylvania Dutch CVB 501 Greenfield Rd, Lancaster (daily 9am–4pm, until 6pm June–Aug; ☎717 299 8901, ⓦpadutchcountry.com). This place does an excellent job of providing orientation and advice on accommodation.

Mennonite Information Center 2209 Millstream Rd,

Lancaster (April–Oct Mon–Sat 8am–5pm; Nov–March Mon–Sat 8.30am–4.30pm; ☎717 299 0954, ⓦmennoniteinfoctr .com). Screens a short film entitled *Who Are the Amish?* and sorts lodging with Mennonite families. If you call at least 2hr ahead, a guide can take you on a 2hr, $49 tour in your car.

TOURS

Bus tours The Amish Experience, on US-340 between Intercourse and Bird-in-Hand at Plain & Fancy Farm (☎717 768 3600 ext 210, ⓦamishexperience.com), offer 2hr bus tours (March–Nov daily 10am, noon, 2pm & 4pm; Dec–Feb Sat & Sun 10am, noon & 2pm; $27.95); some accommo-

dation options offer a similar service for free.

Buggy rides AAA Buggy Rides offer lolloping 4-mile countryside excursions for $14 (☎717 989 2829, ⓦaaabuggyrides.com) from the Kitchen Kettle Village in Intercourse.

ACCOMMODATION

Accommodation options in Pennsylvania Dutch Country range from reasonably priced hotels and B&Bs, which can be arranged through a central agency (☎800 552 2632, ⓦauthenticbandb.com), to farm vacations ask at the CVB; (see above) – and campgrounds.

Cameron Estate Inn & Restaurant 1855 Mansion Lane, Mount Joy ☎717 492 0111, ⓦcameronestateinn .com. Out-of-the-way gay-friendly inn on 15 acres with sparkling, comfortable rooms (one with jacuzzi), free full breakfast and a restaurant. **$149**

Countryside Motel 134 Hartman Bridge Rd (Hwy-896), Ronks ☎717 687 8431, ⓦcountrysidemotelpa .com. Clean and simple place with decent-sized rooms, set amid undulating farmland 6 miles east of Lancaster. **$75**

Village Inn & Suites 2695 Old Philadelphia Pike, Bird-in-Hand ☎800 914 2473, ⓦbird-in-handvillageinn .com. Excellent old inn with modern amenities, large breakfasts, deck, lawn and back pasture. Price includes 2hr tour of Amish Country and use of the adjacent motel's pool. Book ahead. **$129**

White Oak Campground 372 White Oak Rd, Quarryville ☎717 687 6207, ⓦwhiteoakcampground .com. Overlooking the heart of the Dutch farmlands, this 25-acre site has plenty of shade and good facilities. **$30**

EATING, DRINKING AND ENTERTAINMENT

Lancaster County food is delicious, Germanic and served in vast quantities. There are no Amish-owned restaurants, but Amish roadside stalls sell fresh home-made root beer, jams, pickles, breads and pies. The huge "all-you-can-eat" tourist restaurants on US-30 and US-340 may look off-putting, all pseudo-rusticism with costumed waitresses, but most serve good meals for around $20 "family-style" – you share long tables with other out-of-towners. Typical fare includes fried chicken, hickory-smoked ham, *schnitz und knepp* (apple, ham and dumpling stew), sauerkraut, pickles, cottage cheese and apple butter, shoo-fly pie and the like. None stays open past 8pm, though a few regular diners in busier areas do open later.

Central Market 23 N Market St, Lancaster ☏ 717 785 6390, ⓦcentralmarketlancaster.com. Housed in a huge Victorian red-brick building, the town's oldest market sells fresh local farm produce and lunch to loyal Lancastrians and tourists alike. Tues & Fri 6am–4pm, Sat 6am–2pm.

Good 'n' Plenty East Brook Rd, US-896, Smoketown ☏ 717 394 7111, ⓦgoodnplenty.com. Not Amish-owned, though Amish women cook and serve food in this, the best of the family-style restaurants. Early Feb to mid-Dec Mon–Sat 11.30am–8pm.

Lancaster Brewing Co. 302 N Plum St, Lancaster ☏ 717 391 6258, ⓦlancasterbrewing.com. Brewpub serving good New American cuisine for $15–25 and five different microbrews. Restaurant daily 11.30am–10pm,

bar till midnight or 2am.

Lancaster Dispensing Co. 33–35 N Market St, Lancaster ☏ 717 299 4602, ⓦdispensingco.com. Downtown Lancaster's trendiest, friendliest bar, with live weekend jazz and blues, plus overstuffed sandwiches for $7–9. Mon–Sat 11am–2am, Sun noon–2am.

Molly's Pub 253 E Chestnut St, Lancaster ☏ 717 396 0225, ⓦmollyspub.com. Neighbourhood bar with lively atmosphere and good burgers, sandwiches and salads for $8–12. Mon–Sat 11.30am–2am, Sun 3pm–2am.

Plain and Fancy 3121 Old Philadelphia Pike (US-340), Bird-in-Hand ☏ 717 768 4400, ⓦplainandfancyfarm .com. Standard family-style restaurant offering hearty $20 country meals; the only one in the area open on Sunday. Daily 11.30am–8pm.

Harrisburg

HARRISBURG, Pennsylvania's capital, lies on the Susquehanna River thirty or so miles northwest of Lancaster. It's a surprisingly attractive small city, its lush waterfront lined with shuttered colonial buildings, and is amusingly complemented by its kitschy Chocolatetown neighbour **Hershey**. Harrisburg is also known as the site of the **Three Mile Island** nuclear facility, which suffered a famous meltdown in the 1970s and stands along the river on the east side of town.

The ornate, attractive Italian Renaissance **capitol** at Third and State streets has a dome modelled on St Peter's in Rome (tours Mon–Fri 8.30am–4pm, Sat & Sun 9am, 11am, 1pm & 3pm; free; ☏ 800 868 7672, ⓦpacapitol.com). The complex includes the four-floor **State Museum of Pennsylvania** at Third and North (Wed–Sat 9am–5pm, Sun noon–5pm; $5; ☏ 717 787 4980, ⓦstatemuseumpa.org), a cylindrical building that holds a planetarium (Sat & Sun only), archeological and military artefacts, decorative arts, tools and machinery.

National Civil War Museum

1 Lincoln Circle • Mon–Sat 10am–5pm, Wed until 8pm, Sun noon–5pm • $10 • ☏ 717 260 1861, ⓦnationalcivilwarmuseum.org

Undoubtedly, Harrisburg's real attraction is the excellent **National Civil War Museum**, roughly two miles east of downtown at the summit of hilly Reservoir Park, with fine city views. Almost 730,000 Americans were killed in the Civil War – more than in all other conflicts since the Revolution combined – and the museum offers an intelligent analysis of the reasons for, and results of, the war. Especially evocative are the fictionalized monologues, playing on video screens in every gallery, which focus on the human cost of the conflict.

ARRIVAL AND INFORMATION   HARRISBURG

By bus Greyhound and other buses stop at 411 Market St.
By train The Amtrak station is located at Fourth and Chestnut sts.

Visitor centre Not open to walk-ins, but can be contacted for good local and regional information (☏ 717 231 7788, ⓦvisithhc.com).

ACCOMMODATION AND EATING

★ **Appalachian Brewing Co.** 50 N Cameron St ☏ 717 221 1080, ⓦabdbrew.com. Flagship branch of a small mid-PA brewery, which serves multicuisine bar

food in the $7–18 range, as well as beautifully crafted ales. Mon–Thurs & Sun 11am–11pm, Fri & Sat 11am–midnight.

City House B&B 915 N Front St ☎717 903 2489, ⓦcityhousebb.com. With its lovely riverside location, grand fireplaces, stained-glass windows and hardwood features, this is a fine choice. Great breakfast too. $125

Delhi Kabab House 17 S Second St ☎717 234 7011, ⓦdelhikababhouse.com. Excellent north Indian restaurant, which specializes in tenderly cooked kebabs and various curries for around $15. It also has hookahs. Tues–Thurs 6–10pm, Fri & Sat 6–11pm.

Radisson Penn Harris 1150 Camp Hill Bypass, Camp Hill ☎717 763 7117, ⓦradisson.com. Set in a tranquil location across the river from downtown, this reliable chain offers remarkably good value with its spacious, pleasant rooms. $119

Hershey

HERSHEY, ten miles east of Harrisburg, was built in 1903 by candy magnate Milton S. Hershey for his chocolate factory – so it has streets named Chocolate and Cocoa avenues and streetlamps in the shape of Hershey's Chocolate Kisses. In summer thousands flock here for **Hersheypark**, 100 W Hersheypark Drive (mid-May to Sept, hours vary; $57.95; ☎717 534 3090 or ☎800 437 7439, ⓦhersheypark.com), a hugely popular amusement park, with stomach-churning roller coasters and various other rides; cheaper special events take place for Halloween and Christmas. South of the park at 63 W Chocolate Ave, the **Hershey Story** (daily 9am–5pm, later in summer; $10; ☎717 534 3439, ⓦhersheystory .org) tells the Milton S. Hershey story in great detail and has revolving exhibits.

Hershey Chocolate World

251 Park Blvd · Daily 9am–5pm, later in summer · Prices to different attractions vary; combination tickets are available · ☎717 534 4900, ⓦhersheyschocolateworld.com

The most diverting year-round attraction is **Hershey's Chocolate World**, which offers a free mini-train ride through a romanticized simulated chocolate factory, the 4-D **Hershey's Great Chocolate Factory Mystery** show ($6.95), the **Tasting Adventure** ($9.95) and the cheesy musical/historical **Trolley Works Tour** around town ($12.95). The newest and best feature is **Build Your Own Candy Bar** ($14.95), where you get kitted up in a plastic hat and pinafore to custom-build your own chocolate bar and design the wrapper, both by computer.

ARRIVAL AND DEPARTURE   HERSHEY

By bus Greyhound buses stop by request at 337 W Chocolate St. Local Lebanon Transit buses (☎717 273 3058, ⓦlebanontransit.org) run into Harrisburg and around Lebanon County.

ACCOMMODATION, EATING AND DRINKING

Hershey Park Camping Resort 1200 Sweet Rd, Hummelstown ☎717 534 8999, ⓦhersheyparkcamping resort.com. The best campground in the region, with lush camping sites, RV hookups and some neat log cabins. Sites from $45, cabins $101

Hotel Hershey 100 Hotel Rd ☎717 533 2171, ⓦthe hotelhershey.com. Palatial resort hotel offering 276 luxury rooms, a range of quality boutiques and an on-site spa offering chocolate-based beauty treatments. $359

Howard Johnson Inn 845 E Chocolate Ave ☎717 533 9157, ⓦhowardjohnsonhershey.com. Standard chain hotel offering fair rates for such a touristic spot. The restaurant does good meat and fish mains, mostly under $20. $120

★ **The Inn at Westwynd Farm** 1620 Sand Beach Rd, Hummelstown ☎717 533 6764, ⓦwestwyndfarminn .com. Delightful rustic B&B on a working horse farm, with extremely cosy rooms, some with jacuzzis and the smallest with shared bathrooms. $60

Troegs Brewing Company 200 E Hershey Park Drive ☎717 534 1297, ⓦtroegs.com. The welcoming tasting room here serves filling sandwiches and mains such as duck confit for $14, as well as its own highly quaffable brews. Mon–Wed & Sun 11am–9pm, Fri & Sat 11am–10pm.

Gettysburg

The small town of **GETTYSBURG**, thirty miles south of Harrisburg near the Maryland border, gained tragic notoriety in July 1863 for the cataclysmic **Civil War** battle in which fifty thousand men died. There were more casualties during these three days than in any American battle before or since – a full third of those who fought were killed or wounded – and entire regiments were wiped out when the tide finally turned against the South.

Four months later, on November 19, Abraham Lincoln delivered his **Gettysburg Address** at the dedication of the National Cemetery. His two-minute speech, in memory of all the soldiers who died, is acknowledged as one of the most powerful orations in American history. Gettysburg, by far the most baldly commercialized of all the Civil War sites, is overwhelmingly geared toward **tourism**, relentlessly replaying the most minute details of the battle. Fortunately, it is perfectly feasible to avoid the crowds and commercial overkill and explore for yourself the rolling hills of the battlefield (now a national park) and the tidy town streets with their shuttered historic houses.

Gettysburg National Military Park

Park Daily 6am–10pm • Free **Visitor centre** daily: June–Aug 8am–7pm; Sept–May 8am–6pm • $12.50 • ☏ 717 334 1124, ⊚ nps.gov/gett

It takes most of a day to see the 3500-acre **Gettysburg National Military Park**, which surrounds the town. The stunning new **visitor centre**, just over a mile south of downtown at 1175 Baltimore Pike now rivals Harrisburg's (see p.137) as the best Civil War **museum** in the state, possibly the country. It is beautifully designed, with tons of memorabilia such as photos, guns, uniforms, surgical and musical instruments, tents and flags, as well as exhaustive written information. Five repeating ten-minute videos, interspersed throughout the chronological sequence of the museum, chronicle the early part of the war, the three days of the battle and the war's conclusion. The star exhibit is the moving **Cyclorama**, a 356ft circular painting of Pickett's Charge, the suicidal Confederate thrust across open wheatfields in broad daylight. This is also the place to pick up details of a self-guided **driving route**, or a **guide** will join you in your car for a personalized two-hour tour ($65).

Not far from the visitor centre, the **Gettysburg National Cemetery** contains thousands of graves arranged in a semicircle around the Soldiers' National Monument, on the site where Lincoln gave the Gettysburg Address. Most stirring of all are the hundreds of small marble gravestones marked only with numbers. A short walk away, the battlegrounds themselves, golden fields reminiscent of an English country landscape, are peaceful now except for their names: **Valley of Death**, **Bloody Run**, **Cemetery Hill**. Uncanny statues of key figures stand at appropriate points, while heavy stone monuments honour different regiments.

Other attractions

Star billing in the town centre goes to the impressive new 800-square-foot 3-D **diorama** of the battle at the **Gettysburg History Center**, 241 Steinwehr Ave (Mon–Thurs & Sun 9am–6pm, Fri & Sat 9am–8pm, until 10pm in summer; $7; ☏717 334 6408, ⊚gettysburgdiorama.com). The only other sight worth a peek in town, at 528 Baltimore St, is the **Jennie Wade House** (daily 9am–5pm; $7.75; ☏717 334 4100), the former home of the only civilian to die in the battle, killed by a stray bullet as she made bread for the Union troops in her sister's kitchen. To the west of the park, President Eisenhower, who retired to Gettysburg, is commemorated at the **Eisenhower National Historic Site** (daily 9am–4pm, closes 2pm Jan & Feb; $7.50; ☏717 338 9114, ⊚nps.gov/eise), where his Georgian-style mansion holds an array of memorabilia. The site is accessible only on shuttle-bus tours from the National Park visitor centre (see below).

GETTING AROUND, INFORMATION AND TOURS
GETTYSBURG

By car There is no public transport to Gettysburg, and although the town is compact and easy to walk around, a car is essential when touring the huge battlefield.

Visitor centre 102 Carlisle St (daily 8.30am–5pm; ☏717 334 6274, ⊚gettysburg.travel).

Bus tours Two-hour double-decker Battlefield Bus Tours, running through the town and making numerous stops, depart from 778 Baltimore St (up to 8 tours daily; $26 for audio, $30 for live guide; ☏717 334 6296, ⊚gettysburgbattlefieldtours.com).

ACCOMMODATION

Artillery Ridge Resort 610 Taneytown Rd ☎717 334 1288, ⓦartilleryridge.com. In addition to providing shady camping places on the verdant ridges, this place organizes horseriding and other activities. April–Oct. $35
Baladerry Inn 40 Hospital Rd ☎717 337 1342, ⓦbaladerryinn.com. Historic hospital, built in 1830, converted into a smart B&B, with ten very well-appointed en-suite rooms. The ample country breakfasts are served on the terrace in summer. $155
★ **Doubleday Inn** 104 Doubleday Ave ☎717 334 9119, ⓦdoubledayinn.com. A very welcoming, memorabilia-packed luxury B&B – the only one within the battlefield itself

– offering cosy rooms full of character, and gourmet breakfasts. Hosts regular historic talks. $140
Gettysburg Travelodge 613 Baltimore St ☎717 334 9281, ⓦtravelodge.com. This standard motel between downtown and the battlefield has inflated rates because of its location but still offers the cheapest rooms around. $110
Historic Farnsworth House Inn 401 Baltimore St ☎717 334 8838, ⓦfarnsworthhouseinn.com. An 1810 townhouse, used as Union HQ in the war and still riddled with bullet holes. Includes ten rooms, a tavern and a theatre. $170

EATING, DRINKING AND ENTERTAINMENT

Blue Parrot Bistro 35 Chambersburg St ☎717 337 3739, ⓦblueparrotbistro.com. Pasta, seafood and steaks with a good choice of sauces go for $25–30 in this attractive restaurant with a Mock Tudor design. Tues–Thurs 11.30am–2pm & 5–9pm, Fri & Sat 11.30am–2pm & 5–9.30pm.
★ **Dobbin House Tavern** 89 Steinwehr Ave ☎717 334 2100, ⓦdobbinhouse.com. This former hide-out for escaped slaves dating from 1776 actually contains two restaurants: the candlelit *Alexander* offers meat, poultry and fish dishes for $25–40, while the *Springhouse Tavern* serves lighter and cheaper snacks. Tavern daily 11.30am–8.30pm, Alexander daily 5–8.30pm.
Garryowen Irish Pub 126 Chambersburg St ☎717 337

2719, ⓦgarryowenirishpub.net. The town's liveliest spot hosts open-mic and other live music nights, some trad Irish, which you can sip a Guinness to. Also has world soccer on TV. Daily noon–1am.
Mayflowers 533 Steinwehr Ave ☎717 337 3377. Huge modern Chinese restaurant that does a high-quality evening buffet for little over $10, while the à la carte menu includes sushi. Daily 11.30am–10pm.
Thai Classic IV 51 Chambersburg St ☎717 334 6736, ⓦthaiclassiconline.com. Imaginatively decorated in bright colours, this branch of a small chain rustles up favourites such as *pad prik King* and green curry for around $10. Mon–Thurs 11am–9.30pm, Fri & Sat 11am–10.30pm, Sun noon–8pm.

Pittsburgh

The appealing ten-block district known as the **Golden Triangle**, at the heart of downtown **PITTSBURGH**, stands at the confluence of the Monongahela, Allegheny and Ohio rivers; this area was once bitterly fought over as the gateway to the West. The French built Fort Duquesne on the site in 1754, only for it to be destroyed four years later by the British, who replaced it with **Fort Pitt**. Industry began with the development of iron foundries in the early 1800s and by the time of the Civil War, Pittsburgh was producing half of the iron and one third of the glass in the US. Soon after, the city became the world's leading producer of steel, thanks to the vigorous expansion programmes of **Andrew Carnegie**, who by 1870 was the richest man in the world. Present-day Pittsburgh is dotted with his cultural bequests, along with those of other wealthy forefathers, including the Mellon bankers, the Frick coal merchants and the Heinz food producers.

The city has gradually ditched its Victorian reputation for dirt and pollution since its transformation began in the 1960s and has now established itself as one of America's most attractive and most liveable cities. The face-lift involved large-scale demolition of abandoned steel mills, which freed up much of the downtown waterfront to make way for sleek skyscrapers and green spaces. Each of Pittsburgh's close-knit neighbourhoods – the **South Side** and **Mount Washington**, across the Monongahela River from the Golden Triangle, the **North Side** across the Allegheny River and the **East End** – has a distinct flavour.

Downtown: the Golden Triangle

The *New York Times* once described Pittsburgh as "the only city with an entrance" – and, true enough, the view of the **Golden Triangle** skyline on emerging from the tunnel on the Fort Pitt Bridge is undeniably breathtaking. Surrounded by water and steel bridges, the Triangle's imaginative contemporary architecture stands next to gothic churches and red-brick warehouses. Philip Johnson's magnificent postmodern concoction, the black-glass gothic **PPG Place** complex, looms incongruously over the old **Market Square**, lined with restaurants and shops. **Point State Park**, at the peak of the Triangle, is where it all began. The site of five different forts during the French and Indian War, it still contains the 1764 **Fort Pitt Blockhouse**, the city's oldest structure. The park itself is now a popular gathering area, boasting a 150ft fountain with a pool, and is a great place to view sunsets and an excellent venue for the city's free outdoor festivals.

History is most apparent on the faded buildings along Liberty Avenue, with 1940s and 1950s fronts left in place during successive interior renovations. At the flat end of the Triangle, the modernist new steel-and-glass edifice of the **CONSOL Energy Center** hosts large concerts and exhibitions and is home to the successful **Pittsburgh Penguins** ice hockey team (☎ 412 642 7367, ⓦpenguins.nhl.com). Northeast of downtown, along Penn Avenue past the vast new Convention Center, the characterful **Strip District** has a bustling early-morning fresh produce market, as well as bargain shops by day and

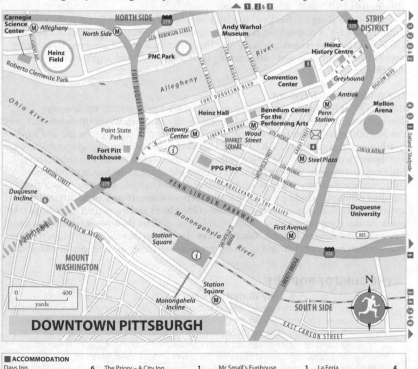

DOWNTOWN PITTSBURGH

lively night-time venues. The seven-floor **Senator John Heinz Pittsburgh Regional History Center**, at 1212 Smallman St (daily 10am–5pm; $15; ☎412 454 6000, ⊛heinzhistorycenter.org), does a good job of telling the city's story, paying particular attention to immigrants of various eras.

The South Side
In the nineteenth century, 400ft **Mount Washington**, across the Monongahela River, was the site of most of the city's coal mines. No longer dominated by belching steel mills and industry, the **South Side**, banked by the green "mountain", is an area of many churches, colourful houses nestled on steep hills and old neighbourhoods. The 1877 **Duquesne Incline**, from 1197 W Carson St to 1220 Grandview Ave, is a working cable-car system ($2.50 one-way; ☎412 381 1665, ⊛duquesneincline.org) whose upper station contains a small **museum**. The outdoor observation platform is a prime spot for **views** over the Golden Triangle and beyond, especially awesome after dark.

The best way to get to the South Side is across the 1883 blue-and-cream **Smithfield Street Bridge**, the oldest of fifteen downtown bridges and notable for its elliptical "fish-eye" truss. Just to the west of the bridge stands red-brick **Station Square**, a food and shopping complex converted from old railroad warehouses. In front stands the jetty for the enjoyable hour-long narrated Just Ducky Tours **river cruises** (April–Oct daily 10.30am–6pm; Nov Sat & Sun 10.30am–6pm, $22, kids $15; tours every 90min; ☎412 402 3825, ⊛justduckytours.com).

Heading east along the banks of the Monongahela, **East Carson Street** is the main commercial drag of South Side, where a long-standing community of Polish and Ukrainian steelworkers has gradually absorbed an offbeat mix of artsy residents, along with the attendant cafés and bars, making it far and away Pittsburgh's most vibrant **nightlife** centre (see p.145).

The Andy Warhol Museum
117 Sandusky St • Tues, Thurs, Sat & Sun 10am–5pm, Fri 10am–10pm • $10, Fri 5–10pm $5 • ☎412 237 8300, ⊛ warhol.org

The star attraction on the **North Side** is undoubtedly the **Andy Warhol Museum**, just over the Seventh Street Bridge from downtown. The museum documents the life and work of Pittsburgh's most celebrated son (see box below) over seven floors of a spacious Victorian warehouse; it claims to be the largest museum in the world devoted to a single artist. Although the majority of Warhol's most famous pieces are in the hands of private collectors, the museum boasts an impressive and ever-changing selection of over five hundred exhibits, including iconic pop art and portraiture. It pays equal attention to archival material, there are informative **self-guided tours** and occasional workshops take place. At any given time, two or three non-Warhol exhibits show work related in some way to Warhol themes. During "**Good Fridays**" (5–10pm) there is free entrance to the lobby, which has a cash bar, and often buzzes with live bands or other performance arts.

THE GURU OF POP ART
Born in Pittsburgh in 1928, **Andy Warhol** (born Andrew Warhola, the youngest son of working-class Slovakian immigrants) moved to New York City at the age of 21, after graduating from Carnegie-Mellon University. After a decade as a successful commercial artist, by the early 1960s he was leading the vanguard of the new Pop Art movement, shooting 16mm films such as *Chelsea Girls*, and by 1967 had developed the "Exploding Plastic Inevitable" multimedia show, featuring erotic dancers and music by The Velvet Underground, whom he managed. After founding *Interview* magazine in 1969, Warhol became transfixed by the rich and famous and, up until his death in 1987, was perhaps best known for his celebrity portraits and his appearances at society events. Ironically, he always disowned his gritty hometown, which didn't fit with NYC cool, and would probably turn in his grave that his main shrine is located back there, as are his mortal remains, in Bethel cemetery, Bethel Park (☎412 835 8538).

PNC Park and Heinz Field

West of the Andy Warhol Museum stands **PNC Park**, the home of the **Pittsburgh Pirates** baseball team (☎800 289 2827, ⓦpirates.com). The stadium is beautifully constructed so that from most seats you get a sweeping view of the Allegheny and downtown, and it's a real treat to watch a game here on a balmy summer night, even though the team is a laughing stock. Further west, the gargantuan edifice of **Heinz Field** is home to football's **Pittsburgh Steelers** (☎412 323 1200, ⓦsteelers.com), the only team to have won six Superbowls, most recently in 2009.

Carnegie Science Center

1 Allegheny Ave • Daily 10am–5pm, Sat until 7pm • $17.95, kids $11.95 • ☎ 412 237 3400, ⓦ carnegiesciencecenter.org

Heading northwest along the river, you come to the huge, state-of-the-art **Carnegie Science Center**, predominantly aimed at children, with an interactive engineering playspace, a miniature railroad and a planetarium. The centre contains an impressive OMNIMAX theatre ($8 for one show, $13 for two). Admission also includes entry to the **USS Requin**, a 1945 submarine out beside the river.

Other North Side attractions

The North Side's post-industrial revitalization centres around the intriguingly named **Mexican War Streets**, on the northern edge of Allegheny Commons, a tree-lined area of nineteenth-century grey-brick and limestone terraces. The excellent and highly unusual **Mattress Factory**, 500 Sampsonia Way (Tues–Sat 10am–5pm, Sun 1–5pm; $15; ☎412 231 3169, ⓦmattress.org), has contemporary installations by top mixed-media artists, and is a must on any visit to the city. The **National Aviary**, Allegheny Commons West (daily 10am–5pm; $13; ☎412 323 7235, ⓦaviary.org), is a huge indoor bird sanctuary with more than two hundred species, including foul-mouthed parrots, fluttering inside a 30ft glass dome. Nearby, **The Children's Museum of Pittsburgh**, 10 Children's Way, Allegheny Square (daily 10am–5pm; $13, kids $12; ☎412 322 5058, ⓦpittsburghkids. org), offers a plethora of games, events and special exhibitions.

Oakland

Anchoring the extensive **East End** of Pittsburgh, **Oakland**, the city's university area, is totally dominated by the campuses of **Carnegie-Mellon University**, the **University of Pittsburgh** (always known as "Pitt"), and several other colleges. At Fifth Avenue and Bigelow Boulevard, the 42-storey, 2529-window Gothic Revival **Cathedral of Learning** is a university building with a difference: among its classrooms the 26 **Nationality Rooms** are furnished with antiques and specially crafted items donated by the city's different ethnic groups, from Lithuanian to Chinese. These can be visited on ninety-minute **guided tours** (Mon–Sat 9am–2.30pm, Sun 11am–2.30pm; $4; ☎412 624 6000, ⓦpitt.edu/~natrooms). On the grounds behind the Cathedral of Learning is the French Gothic **Heinz Memorial Chapel** (Mon–Fri 9am–5pm, Sun 1–5pm; free; ☎412 624 4157, ⓦheinzchapel.pitt.edu), notable for its long, narrow, stained-glass windows depicting political, literary and religious figures.

Across from the cathedral at 4400 Forbes Ave, the **Carnegie** cultural complex holds two great museums – the **Museum of Natural History**, famed for its extensive dinosaur relics and sparkling gems, and the **Museum of Art**, with Impressionist, post-Impressionist and American regional art, as well as an excellent modern collection (both museums Tues–Sat 10am–5pm, Thurs until 8pm, Sun noon–5pm; $17.95; ☎412 622 3131, ⓦcarnegiemuseums.org). Nearby, Schenley Park includes the colourful flower gardens of **Phipps Conservatory** (daily 9.30am–5pm, Fri until 10pm; $15; ☎412 622 6814, ⓦphipps.conservatory.org) and wild wooded areas beyond.

Shadyside and Squirrel Hill

The stretch of Fifth Avenue from the Cathedral of Learning up to **Shadyside** is lined with important and architecturally beautiful academic buildings, places of worship and the

2

former mansions of the early industrialists. Other buildings of note include the exquisite external mural of the Byzantine Catholic **Church of the Holy Spirit** and the humble broadcasting complex of **WQED** (⊕ wqed.org) opposite, notable for being the first publicly funded TV station when it opened in April 1954. Shadyside itself is an upmarket, trendy neighbourhood containing the particularly chic commercial section of Walnut Street. Continuing along Fifth Avenue, you come to the **Pittsburgh Center for the Arts**, at no. 6300, in the corner of Mellon Park, which showcases innovative Pittsburgh art in various media (Tues–Sat 10am–5pm, Thurs until 7pm, Sun noon–5pm; $5; ☎ 412 361 0873, ⊕ pittsburgharts.org). A short way to the southeast, **Squirrel Hill** is another lively area, housing a mixture of students and the city's largest Jewish community, with a fine selection of shops and restaurants lining Murray and Forbes avenues.

The outer East End

A mile east of Squirrel Hill, the most notable feature at the **Frick Art and Historical Center** complex, 7227 Reynolds St (Tues–Sun 10am–5pm; free; ☎ 412 371 0600, ⊕ thefrickpittsburgh.org), is the **Frick Art Museum**, which displays Italian, Flemish and French art from the fifteenth to the nineteenth centuries, as well as two of Marie Antoinette's chairs. Just over two miles north, bordering the Allegheny River, the green expanse of **Highland Park** contains the nicely landscaped and enjoyable **Pittsburgh Zoo and PPG Aquarium** (daily: summer 9.30am–6pm; spring & autumn 9am–5pm; winter 9am–4pm; $14, winter $10; ☎ 412 665 3640, ⊕ zoo.pgh.pa.us), which has the distinction of owning a Komodo dragon and having successfully bred two baby elephants.

ARRIVAL AND DEPARTURE | PITTSBURGH

By plane Pittsburgh International Airport is 15 miles west of downtown (☎ 412 472 3525, ⊕ pitairport.com). The local PAT (see below) route #28X runs roughly every 20min between the airport and twelve downtown and Oakland locations (daily 5am–midnight; $3.75).

By bus Greyhound buses pull in downtown at 55 11th St.
Destinations Cleveland (5 daily; 2hr 25min–3hr 30min); Erie (2 daily; 3hr 20min); New York City (13 daily; 8hr 25min–13hr 35min); Philadelphia (8 daily; 5hr 45min–9hr 55min).

By train The attractive Amtrak train station is at 1100 Liberty Ave.
Destinations Chicago (1 daily; 9hr 46min); Cleveland (1 daily; 2hr 54min); New York (1 daily; 9hr 20min); Philadelphia (1 daily; 7hr 25min); Washington DC (1 daily; 7hr 50min).

GETTING AROUND AND INFORMATION

Transport information PAT, the combined transport authority (☎ 412 442 2000, ⊕ portauthority.org), has a downtown service centre at 534 Smithfield St (Mon–Thurs 7.30am–5.30pm, Fri 7.30am–5pm), where you can pick up timetables.

By bus There is an extensive and efficient bus service around the city (free downtown–$3).

By subway The small "T" subway system (free downtown–$4.10) goes to the South Hills.
By taxi Yellow Cab (☎ 412 665 8100).
Visitor centre Liberty Ave, downtown (Mon–Fri 8am–4pm, Sat 9am–5pm, Sun 10am–3pm; ☎ 412 281 7711, ⊕ visit pittsburgh.com); subsidiary branches at the airport and at the Senator John Heinz Pittsburgh Regional History Center.

ACCOMMODATION

Pittsburgh's hotels and few B&Bs are generally pricey, although weekend packages at luxury downtown hotels can bring rates down to not too much above $100. You can check out all of the Pittsburgh area's B&Bs at ⊕ pittsburghbnb.com.

Days Inn 2727 Mosside Blvd, Monroeville ☎ 800 225 3297, ⊕ daysinn.com. Handily placed for the east side and downtown, 12 miles west via the Parkway, the rooms here are adequate and functional. **$70**
Doubletree Hotel Pittsburgh City Center One Bigelow Square ☎ 412 281 5800, ⊕ doubletree.com. Convenient downtown high-rise chain hotel offering suites

with kitchens; look for advance internet rates. **$190**
★ **The Inn on the Mexican War Streets** 604 W North Ave ☎ 412 231 6544, ⊕ innonthemexicanwar streets.com. Eight tastefully refurbished rooms in a unique Gothic-style mansion in this trendy North Side neighbourhood. The less expensive rooms are great value. **$139**
The Inn on Negley 703 S Negley Ave, Shadyside ☎ 412

661 0631, @innonnegley.com. Friendly, upmarket establishment with eight elegantly furnished rooms and suites, several with jacuzzi. As well as the complimentary gourmet breakfasts, quality teas and sweets are served noon–4pm. $180

The Priory – A City Inn 614 Pressley St @412 231 3338, @thepriory.com. Restored 1880s inn, originally built to house travelling Benedictine monks. Room rates include continental breakfast, evening wine, weekday limo service and use of the fitness room. $155

The Westin Convention Center Pittsburgh 1000 Penn Ave @412 281 3700, @westin.com. Flashy downtown tower with luxuriously furnished rooms, swimming pool, gym and other top amenities. $260

EATING

Downtown is rather deserted at night, so it's better to head for the Strip District or along East Carson Street on the South Side. Station Square and Mount Washington are more upmarket, while Oakland is home to various cheap student hangouts. The other East End neighbourhoods have a number of good cheap and mid-priced places.

★ **The Church Brew Works** 3525 Liberty Ave @412 688 8200, @churchbrew.com. Housed in a grand, converted old church where vats have replaced the organ, this vast restaurant serves American cuisine for $18–34, along with fine ales brewed on site. Mon–Thurs 11.30am–4pm, Fri & Sat 11.30am–11pm, Sun noon–9pm.

Grandview Saloon 1212 Grandview Ave @412 431 1400, @thegrandviewsaloon.com. Relaxed Mount Washington restaurant, where you can enjoy fantastic views and $10 burgers at lunchtime or much more expensive American dinner mains. Mon–Thurs & Sun 11.30am–9pm, Fri & Sat 11.30am–10pm.

Kaya 2000 Smallman St @412 261 6565. Stylish Caribbean restaurant in the Strip District with star dishes like tropical paella for $24, as well as a huge range of beers, rums and cocktails. Mon–Wed 11.30am–10pm, Thurs–Sat 11.30am–11pm, Sun 11am–9pm.

La Feria 5527 Walnut St @412 682 4501, @laferia .net. Colourful upstairs Peruvian shop-cum-restaurant in Shadyside, offering a limited but tasty selection of inexpensive specials from the Andes for around $10. BYOB. Mon–Sat 10am–8.30pm, Sun 10am–3pm.

Lulu's Noodles/Yumwok 400 S Craig St @412 687 7777. Combined Oakland establishment serving filling noodles and good standard pan-Asian cuisine for less than $10. Justifiably popular with students. BYOB. Daily 11am–9.30pm.

Mallorca 2228 E Carson St @412 488 1818, @mallorcarestaurantpgh.com. This smart South Side restaurant serves excellent paella and Mediterranean dishes for $12–35, as well as fine sangria. Mon–Thurs 11.30am–10.30pm, Fri & Sat 11.30am–11.30pm, Sun noon–10pm.

★ **Salt Of The Earth** 5523 Penn Ave @412 441 7258, @saltpgh.com. Not quite as humble as the name suggests, this slick new upscale restaurant serves main courses such as hangar steak with collard greens for $27 and has a great wine list. Mon–Sat 5pm–midnight.

Yo Rita 1120 E Carson St @412 904 3557, @yorita southside.com. Offering a refreshingly imaginative take on tacos, such as the chorizo taco with dippy egg, asadero cheese and maple-arbol chilli sauce for a mere $7. Mon–Sat 4–11pm.

NIGHTLIFE AND ENTERTAINMENT

Pittsburgh's nightlife offers rich pickings in everything from the classics to jazz and alternative rock. The *City Paper*, a free weekly newspaper published on Wednesdays (@pghcitypaper.com), has extensive **listings**.

BARS AND LIVE MUSIC VENUES

★ **Brillobox** 4104 Penn Ave @412 621 4900, @brillobox.net. Two prodigal Pittsburghers returning from New York created this unique bar, which is both chic and a fun local spot for watching sports. There's a good jukebox downstairs and a performance space for mostly obscure acts above. Tues–Sun 5pm–2am.

Club Café 56–58 S 12th St @412 431 4950, @clubcafe live.com. Laidback South Side club of intimate size, with regular live music, including rock, folk and salsa. Hours vary.

Mr Small's Funhouse 400 Lincoln Ave, Millvale @800 594 8499, @mrsmalls.com. Several miles northeast of downtown off US-28, this converted church hosts most of the mid-sized US and foreign indie rock acts. Hours vary.

Piper's Pub. 1828 E Carson St @412 431 6757, @piperspub.com. Convivial South Side bar, which is the place for soccer, rugby and Gaelic football on TV. Imported and US beers are available and the food is decent, especially the $8–10 breakfasts. Mon–Fri 11am–midnight, Sat & Sun 8.30am–midnight.

PERFORMING ARTS VENUES

Benedum Center for the Performing Arts 719 Liberty Ave @412 456 6666, @pgharts.org. The city's main downtown venue for ballet, dance and opera companies occupies a rather grand building.

City Theatre 1300 Bingham St @412 431 4400, @citytheatrecompany.org. The nationally regarded City

Theatre Company puts on ground-breaking productions in a converted South Side church.
Heinz Hall 600 Penn Ave ☎ 412 392 4900, ⊛ pittsburgh symphony.org. This classy downtown edifice is the home base of the widely travelled Pittsburgh Symphony Orchestra.
Rex Theater 1602 E Carson St ☎ 412 381 6811, ⊛ rextheater.com. This former cinema hosts mainly rock shows, often of national and international standing.

Around Pittsburgh

Just over an hour southeast of Pittsburgh, the **Laurel Highlands** takes in seventy miles of rolling wooded hills and valleys. The main reasons to come this way down Hwy-381 are to see one of Frank Lloyd Wright's most unique creations, **Fallingwater**, and to take advantage of some prime outdoor opportunities around the small town of **Ohiopyle**.

Fallingwater

Signposted off Hwy-381, some 20 miles south of I-70 • Mid-March to late Nov daily except Wed 10am–4pm; Dec & early March Fri–Sun 11.30am–3pm • Tour $23, in advance $20 • ☎ 724 329 8501, ⊛ fallingwater.org

You don't need to be an architecture buff to appreciate Frank Lloyd Wright's **Fallingwater**, which was built in the late 1930s for the Kaufmann family, owners of Pittsburgh's premier department store. Set on Bear Run Creek in the midst of the gorgeous deciduous forest of Bear Run Nature Reserve, it is the only one of Wright's buildings to be on display exactly as it was designed, which makes sense as it's built right into a set of cliffside waterfalls. Wright used a cantilever system to make the multitiered structure "cascade down the hill like the water down the falls". The house's almost precarious position is truly stunning, and it is remarkable how well its predominantly rectangular shapes blend in with nature's less uniform lines. Among the house's pioneering features is a lack of load-bearing walls, which gives an extra sense of space, and natural skylights.

Ohiopyle

Five miles south of Fallingwater, tiny **OHIOPYLE** is the most convenient base from which to enjoy the wilds of **Ohiopyle State Park** or activities like whitewater rafting on the **Youghiogheny River** – White Water Adventurers, at 6 Negley St (equipment rental $25; ☎ 800 992 7238, ⊛ wwaraft.com) is one of several outfits that rent equipment and give instruction. The park fans out around the town and river, offering a maze of trails for hiking or biking, and natural delights such as **Cucumber Falls** and the unique habitat of the **Ferncliff Peninsula**, known for its wild flowers.

ACCOMMODATION AND EATING · OHIOPYLE

Ohiopyle House Café 144 Grant St ☎ 724 329 1122, ⊛ ohiopylehousecafe.com. This homely establishment serves up tasty dishes such as lobster ravioli for $10–15, plus sweet treats like caramel pudding. Daily 8am–10pm.
Yough Plaza Motel Sherman St ☎ 800 992 7238, ⊛ wwaraft.com. Run by White Water Adventurers, this slightly overpriced motel has reasonable standard units and studio apartments, the only rooms in the park area. $110

Allegheny National Forest

Occupying more than half a million acres and a sizeable portion of four counties, the pristine **Allegheny National Forest** affords a bounty of opportunities for engaging in outdoor pursuits like hiking, fishing, snowmobiling and, best of all, admiring the **autumn foliage**, which rivals any in New England. In the north, there are several points of interest within easy access of Hwy-6, the major route through the forest. Just north of the highway, it is worth a stop to admire the views from the **Kinzua Viaduct** railroad bridge, the highest and longest in the world when constructed in 1882. The dominant feature of the forest's northern section is the huge **Kinzua Reservoir**, created by a dam at the southern end. Swimming is possible at **Kinzua** and **Kiasutha beaches** or you can enjoy a picnic at **Rimrock Overlook** or at **Willow Bay** in the very north.

| INFORMATION AND ACCOMMODATION | ALLEGHENY NATIONAL FOREST |

Visitor centre The summer-only Kinzua Point Information Center on Hwy-59 (☎ 814 726 1291) has details on trails, private cabins and campgrounds around the forest.
Camping Allegheny National Forest ☎ 877 444 6777,

ⓦ reserveusa.com. You can camp in any of the twenty state-run camping sites, all of which enjoy splendid natural locations. **$30**

Erie

The focal point of Pennsylvania's forty-mile slice of Lake Erie waterfront is the pleasant city of **ERIE** itself. It bears no resemblance to the major urban centres of Pittsburgh or Philadelphia, being entirely low-rise and extremely leafy. There are several places of cultural interest in the city, all within walking distance of the square, including the Neoclassical **Court House** and several **museums** devoted to history, art and science.

Erie Maritime Museum

150 E Front St • April–Oct Mon–Sat 9am–5pm, Sun noon–5pm; Nov–March closed Mon–Wed • $10 • ☎ 814 452 2744, ⓦ flagshipniagara.org

Erie's most absorbing museum is the **Erie Maritime Museum** in the Bayfront Historical District, which has a fascinating display on the geological and ecological development of the Great Lakes, and also focuses on warships of different periods; the elegant **US Flagship Niagara**, usually moored outside, is part of the museum.

Presque Isle State Park

Can be reached by water taxi from Dobbins Landing on the bayfront (late May to mid-Oct Mon noon–6pm, Tues–Sun 10am–6pm; $8 return; ☎ 814 881 2502, ⓦ porterie.org)

Undoubtedly, Erie's main attraction is the elongated comma-shaped peninsula of **Presque Isle State Park**, which bends east from its narrow neck three miles west of downtown until it almost touches the city's northernmost tip. The park is maintained as a nature preserve and has wide sandy **beaches** good for swimming, backed by thick woods offering a series of trails.

| ARRIVAL AND INFORMATION | ERIE |

By bus Regular Greyhound services pull in at the Intermodal Transit Terminal, at 208 E Bayfront Drive.
Destinations Buffalo (4 daily; 1hr 55min); Cleveland (4 daily; 1hr 40min–2hr 5min); Pittsburgh (2 daily; 3hr 20min).
By train The Amtrak station is centrally located at 125 W 14th St.
Destinations Buffalo (1 daily; 1hr 38min); Cleveland (2 daily;

1hr 51min); New York City (1 daily; 11hr 13min).
Visit Erie Intermodal Transit Terminal, 208 E Bayfront Drive (Mon–Fri 8.30am–5pm; ☎ 814 454 1000, ⓦ visit erlepa.com).
Stull Interpretive Center and Nature Shop Presque Isle (daily: June–Aug 10am–5pm; Sept–Nov & March–May 10am–4pm; ☎ 814 836 9107, ⓦ presqueisle.org).

| ACCOMMODATION | |

It is worth noting that accommodation rates can more than double in the peak of high season. Apart from the places listed below, numerous functional motels also line Peninsula Drive on the approach to Presque Isle.

Bayfront Inn 2540 W 8th St ☎ 814 838 2081, ⓦ bayfrontinnerie.com. This smart modern place with colourful decor and furnishings provides particularly good off-season bargains. Has a salt-water pool and breakfast is included in summer. **$80**
Boothby Inn B&B 311 W 6th St ☎ 814 456 1888, ⓦ theboothyinn.com. Elegant, centrally located inn on

Erie's Millionaire Row, whose cosy rooms make for a very pleasant stay. The breakfast is simple continental. **$100**
Sara's Campground 50 Peninsula Drive ☎ 814 833 4560, ⓦ sarascampground.com. Conveniently located just before the entrance to Presque Isle, this campground has lots of shade, good facilities and organizes various activities. April–Oct. **$25**

EATING

Khao Thai 36 N Park Row ☎814 454 4069, ⓦkhaothaionline.com. Good place for freshly spiced Thai food, such as the seafood house special Thai Rama and other favourite dishes for $12–15, all served with a smile. Mon–Sat 11am–9pm.

★ **The Pufferbelly** 414 French St ☎814 455 1557, ⓦthepufferbelly.com. Surprisingly good-value fine-dining restaurant, where you can sample classy mains such as maple-mustard glazed pork chops for $19 and desserts including peanut butter pie. Mon–Thurs 11.30am–8pm, Fri & Sat 11.30am–10.30pm, Sun 11am–8pm.

Sara's 25 Peninsula Drive ☎814 833 1957, ⓦsaras andsallys.com. This classic 50s-style diner at the entrance to Presque Isle serves up hearty burgers, hot dogs, salads and sandwiches, all well under $10. April–Oct daily 10.30am–9pm, till 10pm in summer.

New Jersey

The skinny coastal state of **NEW JERSEY** has been at the heart of US history since the Revolution, when a battle was fought at **Princeton**, and George Washington spent two bleak winters at Morristown. As the Civil War came, the state's commitment to an industrial future ensured that, despite its border location along the Mason–Dixon Line, it fought with the Union.

That commitment to industry has doomed New Jersey in modern times; most travellers only see "the Garden State", so called for the rich market garden territory at the state's heart, from the stupendously ugly New Jersey Turnpike toll road, which is always heavy with truck traffic. Even the songs of **Bruce Springsteen**, **Asbury Park**'s golden boy, paint his home state as a gritty urban wasteland of empty lots, grey highways, lost dreams and blue-collar heartache. The majority of the refineries and factories actually hug only a mere fifteen-mile-wide swath along the turnpike, but bleak cities like **Newark**, home to the major airport, and Trenton, the forgettable capital, reinforce the dour image. But there is more to New Jersey than factories and pollution. Alongside its revolutionary history, the northwest corner near the Delaware Water Gap is traced with picturesque lakes, streams and woodlands, while in the south, the town of **Princeton** adds architectural elegance to the interior with the grand buildings of its Ivy League university.

Best of all, the Atlantic shore, which suffered some of the worst damage during Hurricane Sandy (see box below) offers a 130-mile stretch of almost uninterrupted **resorts** – some rowdy, some run-down, some undeveloped and peaceful. The beaches, if occasionally crowded, are safe and clean: sandy, broad and lined by characteristic wooden **boardwalks**, some of them charge admission during the summer, in an attempt to maintain their condition. The rowdy, sleazy glitz of **Atlantic City** is perhaps the shore's best-known attraction, though there are also quieter resorts like **Spring Lake** and Victorian **Cape May**.

Princeton

Self-satisfied **PRINCETON**, which began its days inauspiciously as Stony Brook in the late 1600s, lies on US-206 eleven miles north of Trenton. It rose to fame as home to **Princeton University**, the nation's fourth oldest, which broke away from overly religious

---

HURRICANE SANDY

In October 2012 a huge section of the northeastern seaboard from the Carolinas to southern New England was ravaged by **Hurricane Sandy**, which had already left a trail of destruction in parts of the Caribbean. With wind speeds of 74mph and 13ft storm surges, it caused 125 deaths and $62 billion worth of damage in the USA, much of it to the coastal areas of New Jersey and New York. At the height of the storm, more than 7.5 million people lost their electricity, and in some cases it took weeks to restore. The devastation is still evident in many of these areas, which will take years to recover completely.

Yale in 1756. In January 1777, a week after Washington's triumph against the British at Trenton, the **Battle of Princeton** occurred southwest of town, another turning point in the revolutionary effort. After the war, in 1783, the **Continental Congress**, fearful of potential attack from incensed unpaid veterans in Philadelphia, met here for four months; the leafy, well-kept town was then left in peace to follow its academic pursuits. Alumni of Princeton University include actor James Stewart, Jazz Age writer F. Scott Fitzgerald, actress Brooke Shields and presidents Wilson and Madison.

Mercer Street

Mercer Street, the long road that sweeps southwest past the university campus to Nassau Street, is lined with elegant colonial houses, graced with shutters, columns and wrought-iron fences. The simple house at no. 112 is where **Albert Einstein** lived while teaching at the Institute of Advanced Study; unfortunately, the house is not open to the public. The **Princeton Battlefield State Park**, a mile and a half south of downtown, includes the 1772 **Thomas Clarke House** at no. 500, a Quaker farmhouse that served as a hospital during the battle.

The university campus

Princeton University's tranquil and shaded campus is a beautiful place for a stroll. Just inside the main gates on Nassau Street, **Nassau Hall**, a vault-like historic building containing numerous portraits of famous graduates and one of King George II, was the largest stone building in the nation when constructed in 1756; its 26in-thick walls, now patterned with plaques and patches of ivy placed by graduating classes, withstood American and British fire during the Revolution. It was also the seat of government during Princeton's brief spell as national capital in 1783. The 1925 **chapel**, based on one at King's College, Cambridge University, in England, has stained-glass windows showing scenes from works by Dante, Shakespeare and Milton, and from the Bible. Across campus, the **Prospect Gardens**, a flowerbed in the shape of the university emblem, are a blaze of orange in summer. Somewhat smug student-led **tours** (during term Mon–Sat 10am, 11am, 1.30pm & 3.30pm, Sun 1.30pm & 3.30pm; hours vary during holidays; free; ☎609 258 1766, ⊛princeton.edu) take you to all of these sights, leaving from the Frist Campus Center.

In the middle of the campus, fronted by the Picasso sculpture *Head of a Woman*, the **University Art Museum** is well worth a look for its collection from the Renaissance to the present, including works by Modigliani, Van Gogh and Warhol, as well as Asian and pre-Columbian art (Tues–Sat 10am–5pm, Sun 1–5pm; free; ☎609 258 3788, ⊛princetonartmuseum.org).

ARRIVAL, INFORMATION AND TOURS
PRINCETON

By plane The Olympic Airporter shuttle bus makes the run to and from Newark airport (daily: times vary; 1hr 30min trip; $27–40 one-way; ☎609 587 6600, ⊛olympic-limo.com).

By bus Coach USA buses from New York's Port Authority bus station (☎800 222 0492, ⊛suburbantransit.com) run every 30min to Palmer Square.

By train Amtrak and NJ Transit trains stop at Princeton Junction, 3 miles south of Princeton. You can buy a transfer in advance for the SEPTA shuttle service to downtown and the campus (☎215 580 7800, ⊛septa.com).

Frist Campus Center At the university (hours vary; ☎609 258 1766, ⊛princeton.edu/frist).

Chamber of Commerce 9 Vandeventer Ave (Mon–Fri 8.30am–5pm; ☎609 924 1776, ⊛princetonchamber.org).

Walking tours The Historical Society Museum, 158 Nassau St (Tues–Sun noon–4pm; ☎609 921 6748, ⊛princetonhistory.org), organizes 2hr walking tours through town (Sun 2pm; $7) and also provides maps so you can guide yourself.

ACCOMMODATION

Nassau Inn 10 Palmer Square E ☎609 921 7500, ⊛nassauinn.com. Ersatz-colonial mansion on beautifully landscaped grounds, with period furniture in all the spacious rooms and suites. Gourmet breakfast included. $315

Peacock Inn 20 Bayard Lane ☎609 924 1707, ⊛peacockinn.com. Tucked in a quiet and leafy spot, this

2

small boutique hotel has meticulously designed rooms and a fine-dining restaurant. **$275**

Red Roof Inn Princeton 3203 Brunswick Pike, Lawrenceville ☎ 609 896 3388, ⓦ redroof.com. Best of the budget motels in this southern suburb, with bright, functional rooms, furnished in contemporary style, and including new flat-screen TVs. **$70**

EATING AND DRINKING

Elements 163 Baynard Lane ☎ 609 252 9680, ⓦ elementsprinceton.com. Upmarket, elegant restaurant that serves fish and meat dishes such as Griggstown chicken with egg and sherry for $34. Mon–Thurs 5.30–9pm, Fri 5.30–10pm, Sat 5–10pm, Sun 5–8pm.

Teresa Caffe 23 Palmer Square E ☎ 609 921 1974, ⓦ teresacaffe.com. This welcoming place dishes up handsome portions of creative, good-value Italian food for $14–23. Mon–Thurs 11am–11pm, Fri 11am–midnight, Sat 9am–midnight, Sun 3–10pm.

Triumph Brewery 138 Triumph St ☎ 609 942 7855, ⓦ triumphbrewing.com. Popular brewpub that makes good ales, serves food such as fish and chips for $16, and draws a mixed crowd. Mon–Sat 11am–midnight, Sun noon–midnight, bar till 2am.

Yankee Doodle Tap Room Nassau Inn, 10 Palmer Square E ☎ 609 921 7500, ⓦ nassauinn.com. Well-established hotel bar that is usually full of ancient revellers drinking, reminiscing and enjoying live jazz. Daily noon–1am.

Spring Lake and Asbury Park

SPRING LAKE, an elegant Victorian resort about twenty miles from Princeton down the Jersey coast, is one of the smallest, most uncommercial communities on the shore, a gentle respite on the road south to Atlantic City. You can walk the undeveloped two-mile **boardwalk** and watch the crashing ocean from battered gazebos, swim and bask on the white beaches (in summer, compulsory beach tags cost a small fee), or sit in the shade by the town's namesake, **Spring Lake** itself. Wooden footbridges, swans, geese and the grand St Catharine Roman Catholic Church on the banks of the lake give it the feel of a country village. What little activity there is centres on the upmarket shops of Third Avenue.

Bruce Springsteen fans are better off using Spring Lake as a base for visiting nearby **ASBURY PARK**, a decaying old seaside town where the Boss lived for many years and played his first gigs. Almost nothing remains of the carousels and seaside arcades that Springsteen wrote about on early albums such as his debut, *Greetings from Asbury Park*.

ARRIVAL AND INFORMATION

SPRING LAKE AND ASBURY PARK

By car or bus Spring Lake is accessible by US-34 from the New Jersey Turnpike and served by New Jersey Transit (☎ 973 275 5555, ⓦ njtransit.com) from New York City.

Chamber of Commerce 302 Washington Ave (Mon–Sat 11am–3pm; ☎ 732 449 0577, ⓦ springlake.org); can help with lodging, especially on summer weekends.

ACCOMMODATION

SPRING LAKE

Chateau Inn & Suites 104 Warren Ave ☎ 732 974 2000, ⓦ chateauinn.com. This fancy inn offers luxury rooms and the Brighton Room breakfast lounge, with leather chairs and a library. **$229**

Spring Lake Inn 104 Salem Ave ☎ 732 449 2010, ⓦ springlakeinn.com. Just a couple of blocks in from the sea, this delightful B&B, nicely painted in contrasting pastel shades, is one of the more modest places in terms of pricing. **$149**

EATING, DRINKING AND ENTERTAINMENT

SPRING LAKE

★ **Whispers** 200 Monmouth Ave ☎ 732 974 9755, ⓦ whispersrestaurant.com. For a blowout, this top-notch establishment serves superb fresh fish, such as grilled Scottish salmon in pistachio coconut red curry sauce for $31, as well as quality cuts of meat. Daily 5.30–10.30pm.

Who's On Third 1300 Third Ave ☎ 732 449 4233. No-nonsense café serving filling breakfasts with lots of egg, sausage, bacon and pancakes, plus sandwiches and more ample meals for lunch; most items under $10. Daily 8am–5pm.

ASBURY PARK

★ **The Stone Pony** 913 Ocean Ave ☎ 732 502 0600, ⓦ stoneponyonline.com. Famous as the place where Springsteen played dozens of times in the mid-1970s and has returned occasionally since, it's still going strong and is an obligatory stop for devotees. Ticket prices vary. Hours vary.

Atlantic City

What they wanted was Monte Carlo. They didn't want Las Vegas. What they got was Las Vegas. We always knew that they would get Las Vegas. Stuart Mendelson, *Philadelphia Journal*

ATLANTIC CITY, on Absecon Island just off the midpoint of the Jersey shoreline, has been a tourist magnet since 1854, when Philadelphia speculators created it as a rail terminal resort. In 1909, at the peak of the seaside town's popularity, Baedeker wrote "there is something colossal about its vulgarity" – a glitzy, slightly monstrous quality that it sustains today. The real-life model for the modern version of the board game **Monopoly**, it has an impressive **popular history**, boasting the nation's first **boardwalk** (1870), the world's first **Ferris wheel** (1892), the first colour **postcards** (1893) and the first **Miss America Beauty Pageant** (1921 – it only moved to Las Vegas in 2006). During Prohibition and the Depression, Atlantic City was a centre for rum-running, packed with speakeasies and illegal gambling dens. Thereafter, in the face of increasing competition from Florida, it slipped into a steep decline, until desperate city officials decided in 1976 to open up the decrepit resort to legal **gambling**, now its mainstay. The city also has a huge **Latino** population.

2

The boardwalk and piers

Atlantic City's wooden **boardwalk** was originally built as a temporary walkway, raised above the beach so that vacationers could take a seaside stroll without treading sand into the grand hotels. Alongside the brash 99¢ shops and exotically named palm-readers, a few beautiful Victorian buildings that survived the wrecking ball invoke a former elegance, despite the fact that many now house fast-food joints. The **Central Pier** offers all the fun of a fair, with rides and old-fashioned games. A few blocks south, another pier has been remodelled into an ocean-liner-shaped shopping centre. The small and faded **Atlantic City Arts Center** (summer daily 10am–4pm, closed Mon off-season; free; ☎609 347 5837, ⓦacartcenter.org), on the Garden Pier at the quiet northern end of the boardwalk, has a free collection of seaside memorabilia, postcards, photos and a special exhibit on Miss America, and also hosts travelling art shows.

Note that it's unwise to stray further from the five-mile boardwalk along the ocean than the parallel Pacific, Atlantic and Arctic avenues, as other parts of the city can be dangerous at night and are not that savoury by day.

THE CASINOS OF ATLANTIC CITY

Each of Atlantic City's dozen **casinos**, which also act as luxury hotels, conference centres and concert halls, has a slightly different image, though you might not guess it among the apparent uniformity of vast, richly ornamented halls, slot machines, relentless flashing lights, incessant noise, chandeliers, mirrors and a disorienting absence of clocks or windows. The casinos are divided into four areas: **uptown**, **midtown** and **downtown** occupy the north, central and south sections of the boardwalk respectively, while the **marina** enclave towers over a spit of land in the northwest of the city.

The most outwardly ostentatious, unsurprisingly, is Donald Trump's **Taj Mahal**. Occupying nearly twenty acres and more than forty storeys high, dotted with glittering minarets and onion domes, this gigantic but oddly anticlimactic piece of Far Eastern kitsch stands uptown, opposite the arcade-packed Steel Pier. **Bally's** charmingly garish midtown Wild West Casino is much more outlandish and fun, and also offers complete access to the games and memberships of adjacent Roman-themed **Caesars**, the smaller **Showboat** uptown and **Hilton** downtown, although flashy **Tropicana** is the more amusing of the two casinos down at that end. All casinos are **open 24 hours**, including holidays, and have a strict minimum **age requirement**, so be prepared to show ID that proves you're 21 or older. Oddly, the slot machines now only take notes (minimum $5).

2

Absecon Lighthouse
July & Aug daily 10am–5pm; Sept–June Mon & Thurs–Sun 11am–4pm · $7 · ☏ 609 449 1360, ⓦ absteconlighthouse.org

A block off the boardwalk, where Pacific and Rhode Island avenues meet, and at the heart of some of the city's worst deprivation, stands the **Absecon Lighthouse**. Active until 1933, it's now fully restored and offers a terrific view from its 167ft tower.

The beaches
Atlantic City's **beach** is free, family-filled and surprisingly clean considering its proximity to the boardwalk. Beaches at well-to-do **Ventnor**, a Jitney ride away, are quieter, while three miles south of Atlantic City, New Jersey's beautiful people pose on the beaches of **Margate** (both beaches charge a nominal fee), watched over by **Lucy the Elephant** at 9200 Atlantic Ave. A 65ft wood-and-tin Victorian oddity, Lucy was built as a seaside attraction in 1881 and used variously as a tavern and a hotel. Today, her huge belly contains a museum (mid-June to early Sept Mon–Sat 10am–8pm, Sun 10am–5pm; early Sept to Dec & April to mid-June days and hours vary; $8; ☏ 609 823 6473, ⓦ lucytheelephant.org) filled with Atlantic City memorabilia, as well as photos and artefacts from her own history.

ARRIVAL AND DEPARTURE

By plane Atlantic City International Airport in Pomona (☏ 609 645 7895, ⓦ acairport.com) has direct flights to Philadelphia; cabs cost around $30 to downtown.
By bus The bus terminal at Atlantic and Michigan is served by NJ Transit and Greyhound.
By train NJ Transit trains stop next to the Convention Center, at 1 Miss America Way, and are connected by a free shuttle service to all casinos.

GETTING AROUND AND INFORMATION

By bus or minibus Ventnor and Margate, to the south on Absecon Island, are served by buses along Atlantic Ave. Pale blue Jitneys ($2.50, exact change required; ☏ 609 344 8642, ⓦ jitneys.net) run 24hr along Pacific Ave.
By bicycle or rolling chair Along the boardwalk, various bike rental stands and rickshaw-like rolling chairs (☏ 609 347 7148) provide alternative means of transport.
By taxi Atlantic City Cab Service (☏ 609 822 7900).
Visitor centre Inside Boardwalk Hall at 2314 Pacific Ave (summer Mon–Fri 9.30am–5.30pm, Thurs–Sun until 8pm; winter Mon & Thurs–Sun 9.30am–5.30pm; ☏ 609 449 7130, ⓦ atlanticcitynj.com).

ACCOMMODATION

Though you will not find the same bargains as in Las Vegas, the recession has forced accommodation rates at the casinos down for most of the year, although they still rise at weekends and in summer. Advance online booking is likely to yield good discounted package deals even then, with $200 suites going for around half-price. Alternatively, cheap motels line the main highways into town such as US-30 in Absecon, 6 miles northwest, and hotel prices are cheaper in quiet Ocean City, a family resort around ten miles south.

Bally's Atlantic City Park Place and Boardwalk ☏ 609 340 2000, ⓦ harrahs.com. One of the big midtown theme casinos, *Bally's* offers a full-service spa, fifteen restaurants and four bars, not to mention multiple gambling opportunities, all under one roof. $79
EconoLodge Beach & Boardwalk 3001 Pacific Ave ☏ 609 344 2925, ⓦ econolodge.com. Standard chain motel with compact but comfortable rooms, just behind the boardwalk and close to the *Trump Taj Mahal* casino. $51
The Irish Pub Inn 164 St James Place ☏ 609 344 9063, ⓦ theirishpub.com. Basic, cheap rooms above one of the town's best bars (see opposite), so not the place to stay if you're sensitive to noise. Great single rates from $25. $55
Resorts Atlantic City Casino Hotel 1133 Boardwalk ☏ 800 336 6378, ⓦ resortsac.com. The most pleasant and most reasonably priced of the huge casino hotels, with a swimming pool and spa, plus the full gamut of bars and restaurants. $119
Rodeway Inn 124 S North Carolina Ave ☏ 609 345 0155, ⓦ choicehotels.com. Two-storey motel with basic but clean and reasonably priced rooms close to the boardwalk, not far from the pier. $68

EATING, DRINKING AND NIGHTLIFE

The boardwalk is lined with pizza, burger and sandwich joints, while the diners on Atlantic and Pacific avenues serve soul food and cheap breakfasts. All the large casinos boast several restaurants, ranging in price and menu but all of average quality, as well as all-you-can-eat buffets – most cost around $15 for lunch, and around $20 for dinner. **Nightlife** centres on the casinos, where big-name entertainers perform regularly, but you'll be lucky to find tickets for much under $100. The free *Atlantic City Weekly* (ⓦ atlanticcityweekly.com) has full listings.

Hunan Chinese Restaurant 2323 Atlantic Ave ☏ 609 348 5946. Reasonably priced Chinese food two blocks from the boardwalk. Combination plates cost $8–12 and seafood is a speciality. Daily noon–10pm.

The Irish Pub 164 St James Place ☏ 609 344 9063, ⓦ theirishpub.com. For a convivial night away from the casinos, try this friendly, dark-panelled pub, which serves bar food for well under $10 and often has live Irish music. Daily 11.30am–3am.

Los Amigos 1926 Atlantic Ave ☏ 609 344 2293, ⓦ losamigosrest.com. Great for cheap, late-night food, this pleasant and colourful Mexican restaurant and bar across from the bus station churns out decent burritos, tacos and so on. Mon–Thurs 11.30am–10pm, Fri & Sat 11.30am–11pm, Sun 3–9pm.

White House Sub Shop 2301 Arctic Ave ☏ 609 345 1564. This bright and super-efficient Atlantic City institution is where the submarine sandwich was born; definitely worth a visit. Mon–Thurs & Sun 9.30am–10pm, Fri & Sat 9.30am–4am.

Cape May

CAPE MAY was founded in 1620 by the Dutch Captain Mey, on the small hook at the very southern tip of the Jersey coast, jutting out into the Atlantic and washed by the Delaware Bay on the west. Though the town began its day as a whaling and farming community, in 1745 the first advertisement for Cape May's restorative air and fine accommodation appeared in the Philadelphia press, heralding a period of great prosperity through tourism, aided by the town's superb **beaches**.

The Victorian era was Cape May's finest, when Southern plantation owners flocked to the fashionable boarding houses of this genteel "resort of Presidents". Nearly all its gingerbread architecture dates from a mass rebuilding after a severe fire in 1878. Today, the whole town is a National Historic Landmark, with more than six hundred **Victorian buildings**, tree-lined streets, beautifully kept **gardens** and a lucrative B&B industry.

Cape May's brightly coloured houses were built by nouveau riche Victorians with a healthy disrespect for subtlety. Cluttered with cupolas, gazebos, balconies and "widow's walks", the houses follow no architectural rules except excess. They were known as "patternbook homes", with designs and features chosen from catalogues and thrown together in accordance with the owner's taste.

The Emlen Physick Estate

1048 Washington St • Tour hours vary • $18 • ☏ 609 884 5404, ⓦ capemaymac.org

The Victorian obsession with the Near East is everywhere in Cape May: Moorish arches and onion domes sit comfortably next to gingerbread- and Queen Anne-style turrets. This fascination reaches its apogee at the **Emlen Physick Estate**, which was built by the popular Philadelphia architect Frank Furness. It has been restored to its 1879 glory, with whimsical "upside-down" chimneys, a mock-Tudor half-timbered facade and much original furniture.

Cape May Lighthouse

April–Nov daily; Dec–March Sat & Sun; hours vary • $8 • ☏ 609 884 5404, ⓦ capemaymac.org

West of town, where the Delaware Bay and the ocean meet, the 1859 **Cape May Lighthouse**, visible from 25 miles out at sea, offers great views from a gallery below the lantern (199 steps up) and a small exhibit on its history at ground level. Be prepared to get dizzy as you climb up the tight spiral.

The beaches

Cape May's excellent **beaches** literally sparkle with quartz pebbles. Beach tags ($6/day, $10/3-day, $15/week, $28 for a seasonal pass) must be worn from 10am until 6pm in the summer and are available at the beach, from official vendors or from **City Hall**, 643 Washington St (☏ 609 884 9525, ⓦ capemaycity.com).

2

WILDWOOD

The traditionally blue-collar resort of **Wildwood**, near Cape May on a barrier island east of Rte-47, offers a counterpoint to the pretty but often pretentious olde-worlde charm of Cape May. Its 1950s architecture, left lovingly intact, includes dozens of gaudy and fun-looking hotels with names like *Pink Orchid*, *Waikiki* and *The Shalimar*, all still featuring plastic palm trees, kidney-shaped swimming pools and plenty of aqua, orange and pink paint. To best appreciate the town's brash charm, take a stroll along the boardwalk and stop on the wide, throbbing, free beaches. Additionally, check out the local amusement rides and water parks, such as Morey's Piers, Raging Waters and Splash Zone.

ARRIVAL AND INFORMATION
CAPE MAY

By bus New Jersey Transit runs an express bus to Cape May from Philadelphia and the south Jersey coast, as well as services from New York and Atlantic City. Greyhound also stops at the terminal, opposite the corner of Lafayette and Ocean Sts.

By ferry Ferries connect the town to Lewes, Delaware ($8–10/person, $30–44/car; schedules on ☎ 800 643 3779, ⓦ capemaylewesferry.com).

Visitor centre Attached to the bus terminal (daily 9am–4.30pm; ☎ 609 884 9562, ⓦ capemaynj.com).

TOURS AND ACTIVITIES

Cycling You can rent a bike from the Village Bike Shop at 609 Lafayette ($5/hr, $12/day, $40/week; ☎ 609 884 8500, ⓦ villagebikescapemay.com).

Whale- and dolphin-watching The Cape May Whale Watcher, at Second Ave and Wilson Drive (☎ 609 884 5445 or ☎ 800 786 5445, ⓦ capemaywhalewatcher.com), offers various trips (daily March–Dec) around Cape May Point, including two dolphin-watches (2hr; 10am & 6.30pm; $30) and a whale and dolphins voyage (3hr; 1pm; $50).

ACCOMMODATION

Many of Cape May's pastel Victorian homes have been converted to pricey B&Bs, which get oversubscribed on summer weekends. During July and August even old motor inns can command more than $100 a night; June and September rates are often around half that.

Cape Harbor Motor Inn 715 Pittsburgh Ave ☎ 609 884 0018, ⓦ capeharbormotorinn.com. Comfortable motel, situated in a residential street seven blocks from the beach; cheaper than most places but rates soar in August especially. **$98**

★ The Chalfonte 301 Howards St ☎ 609 884 8409, ⓦ chalfonte.com. The oldest continually operating B&B, set in an 1876 mansion three blocks from the beach, with wraparound columned verandas and tastefully designed rooms, the cheaper ones with shared bathrooms. **$90**

Inn of Cape May 7 Ocean St ☎ 609 884 5555, ⓦ innofcapemay.com. This once-fashionable Victorian shorefront hotel has been fully refurbished so all rooms are unique,

with private bathrooms. Breakfast included. Open daily April–Oct, weekends only late Oct to Dec. **$175**

Queen Victoria 102 Ocean St ☎ 609 884 8702, ⓦ queenvictoria.com. Thirty-five rooms, all named after British people and places, in four expertly restored buildings. Rates include bicycle loans, beach chairs, breakfast (in bed, if desired) and afternoon tea. **$240**

Seashore Campgrounds 720 Seashore Rd ☎ 609 884 4010, ⓦ seashorecampgrounds.com. Well-organized campground with a huge range of facilities, including a heated pool, tennis court, mini-golf, billiards and arcade games. Good off-season discounts. Open mid-April to Oct. **$56**

EATING

Cape May lacks the usual boardwalk snack bars, but it has plenty of cheap lunch places. Dinner, however, is far more expensive. Cape May's liquor laws are stringent, which means that many restaurants are BYO – call to check.

The Black Duck on Sunset 1 Sunset Blvd ☎ 609 898 0100, ⓦ blackduckonsunset.com. A fine nouvelle cuisine restaurant, whose delights include honey roast half duck for $29 and orange almond salad for $9. Daily 11.30am–10pm.

Depot Market Café 409 Elmira St ☎ 609 884 8030. Opposite the bus terminal, this intimate café offers filling sandwiches, salads and hoagies, as well as some more substantial meals for $10 or a little more. Daily 10am–10pm.

★ **Gecko's** Carpenters Square Mall, 31 Perry St ☎ 609 898 7750, ⓦcapemaygeckos.com. A good lunch stop with a tasty Southwestern and Mexican menu – try the crab enchiladas New Mexico for $10.50. Patio seating available. Thurs–Sun 11am–9pm.

Le Verandah Hotel Alcott, 107 Grant St ☎ 609 884 5868, ⓦhotelalcott.com. The French chef at this elegant hotel bistro makes sure that creations such as the $30 imperial seafood galette are the real thing. Daily noon–10pm.

Mad Batter 19 Jackson St ☎ 609 884 5970, ⓦ mad batter.com. Splash out on meat and fresh fish dishes, served by candlelight in the garden. Lunch is $11–16, dinner mains up to $33. Live jazz and blues some nights. Daily 8am–midnight.

NIGHTLIFE AND ENTERTAINMENT

Cape May is a friendly and laidback place to be after dark; the day-trippers have gone home and the bars and music venues are enjoyed by locals and tourists alike. For something a bit livelier, head a few miles north to the raucous nightclubs of Wildwood (see box opposite).

Cabanas 429 Beach Ave ☎ 609 884 4800, ⓦcabanas onthebeach.com. Two-level bar-restaurant that often hosts live music downstairs, as well as serving decent food; upstairs is a low-key cocktail lounge. Mon–Fri 11.30am–2am, Sat & Sun 9am–2am.

Carney's 411 Beach Ave ☎ 609 884 4424, ⓦcarneys capemaynj.com. Spacious and very informal Irish bar in an appealing Victorian with ornate wooden arches. Features raucous live music on weekend nights. Daily 11am–2am.

Ugly Mug Washington St Mall and Decatur St ☎ 609 884 3459, ⓦuglymugcapemay.com. This friendly bar is a local favourite and serves chowder, sandwiches and seafood to soak up the speciality cocktails and martinis. Daily noon–2am.

New England

SWAN BOATS IN BOSTON PUBLIC GARDENS

New England

The states of Massachusetts, Rhode Island, Connecticut, Vermont, New Hampshire and Maine – collectively known as New England – exemplify America at its most nostalgic: country stores that brim with cider and gourds, snow-dusted hillsides, miles of blazing autumn foliage, clam shacks, cranberry bogs and an unruly ocean that distinguishes and defines it all. Scratch just beneath the surface, and you'll also uncover fiercely independent locals, innovative chefs, some of the country's best contemporary art museums and a profound sense of history.

Boston especially is celebrated as the birthplace of American independence – so many seminal events took place here, or nearby at Lexington and Concord. New England was also home to many of the preeminent figures of American literature, from Mark Twain and Henry Thoreau to Emily Dickinson and Jack Kerouac. The **Ivy League** colleges – Harvard, Yale, Brown, Dartmouth et al – are the oldest in the country and remain hugely influential, continually channelling new life into towns like Cambridge and New Haven and setting a decidedly liberal tone throughout the region.

To the east, the peninsula of **Cape Cod** flexes off **Massachusetts** like a well-tanned arm. Here you will find three hundred miles of shoreline, sea roses, tumbling sand dunes and the fantastic isles of **Nantucket** and **Martha's Vineyard**. In the western part of the state, the tranquil **Berkshires** offer the best in summer festivals as well as fascinating art museums. The sights of **Connecticut** and **Rhode Island** tend to be urban, but away from I-95 you'll find plenty of tranquil pockets, particularly in the way of Newport and Block Island, fifty miles south of Providence. **Boston** is a vibrant and enchanting city from which to set off north, where the population begins to thin out (and the **seafood** gets better as you go). The rest of **Massachusetts** is rich in historical and literary sights, while further inland, the lakes and mountains of **New Hampshire** and **Maine** offer rural wildernesses to rival any in the nation. Maine is especially known for its coastline, dotted with lighthouses and wild blueberry bushes. The beloved country roads of **Vermont** offer pleasant wandering through rural towns and serene forests; during your travels, be sure to pick up some maple syrup, a local delicacy, for your pancakes back home.

The best time to visit New England is in late September and October, when visitors flock to see the magnificent **autumn foliage**. Particularly vivid in Vermont, it's an event that's not to be missed.

ACADIA NATIONAL PARK, ME

Highlights

❶ Boston, MA Revolutionary history comes to life around every corner in one of America's most chronicled, walkable cities. See p.161

❷ Provincetown, MA Wild beaches, lovely flower-filled streets, and an alternative vibe on the outer reaches of Cape Cod. See p.188

❸ Historic "summer cottages", Newport, RI Conspicuous consumption gone crazy in this yachtie resort. **See p.201**

❹ Burlington, VT In a complete contrast to Vermont's profusion of perfect villages, this is a genuine city, with a waterfront, a vibrant downtown and the state's best restaurants and nightlife. See p.215

❺ White Mountains, NH Ski, hike or just soak up the scenery on Mount Washington or Franconia Notch. **See p.221**

❻ Acadia National Park, ME Remote mountains and lakes, stunning cliffs and the chance to catch the sunrise before anyone else in the USA. **See p.234**

HIGHLIGHTS ARE MARKED ON THE MAP ON P.160

Massachusetts

The state of **MASSACHUSETTS** was established with a lofty aim: to become, in the words of seventeenth-century governor John Winthrop, a utopian "**City upon a hill**". This Puritan clarity of thought and forcefulness of purpose can be traced from the foundation of Harvard College in 1636, through the intellectual impetus behind the Revolutionary War and the crusade against slavery, to the nineteenth-century achievements of **writers** such as Melville, Emerson, Hawthorne and Thoreau.

NEW ENGLAND

HIGHLIGHTS

1 Boston, MA

2 Provincetown, MA

3 Historic "summer cottages", Newport, RI

4 Burlington, VT

5 White Mountains, NH

6 Acadia National Park, ME

0   100

miles

GREAT REGIONAL DRIVES

Rte-100, VT Vermont is famed far and wide for its spectacular autumn foliage. Easy-going Rte-100 cuts through the heart of the state and skirts the perimeter of the Green Mountain Forest.

Acadia's Park Loop Road, ME Craggy granite cliffs, crisp ocean air and melancholy stands of fir and spruce are hallmarks of this breathtaking national park in the eastern corner of the country.

Kancamagus Hwy, NH Easily driven in a day, but pleasant enough to be savoured for weeks, "the Kanc" – set in the White Mountains – has enough hiking trails, campgrounds and tumbling waterfalls to satisfy the most discerning nature lover.

Spending a few days in **Boston** is strongly recommended. Perhaps America's most historic city, and certainly one of its most elegant, it offers a great deal of modern life as well, thanks in part to the presence of **Cambridge**, the home of Harvard University and MIT (Massachusetts Institute of Technology), just across the river. Several historic towns are within easy reach – **Salem** to the north, known for its "witch" sights, **Concord** and **Lexington**, just inland, richly imbued with Revolutionary War history, and **Plymouth**, to the south, the site of the Pilgrims' first settlement (1620). Alternative **Provincetown**, a ninety-minute ferry ride across the bay at the tip of Cape Cod, is great fun, known for its gay scene, sunbathing and bike riding galore. The rest of the Cape, particularly its two islands – **Nantucket** and **Martha's Vineyard** – offer old sea-salted towns, excellent shellfish and lovely beaches. **Western Massachusetts** is best known for the beautiful **Berkshires**, which host the celebrated **Tanglewood** summer music festival and boast museum-filled towns such as **North Adams** and **Williamstown** – both in the far northwest corner of the state, at the end of the incredibly scenic **Mohawk Trail**. **Amherst** and **Northampton** are stimulating college towns in the verdant **Pioneer Valley**, with all the cafés, restaurants and bookstores you could want.

Boston

A modern American city that proudly trades on its colonial past, **BOSTON** is about as close to the Old World as the New World gets. This is not to say it lacks contemporary attractions: its cafés, museums, neatly landscaped public spaces and diverse neighbourhoods are all as alluring as its historic sites. Boston has grown up around **Boston Common**, a utilitarian chunk of green established for public use and "the feeding of cattell" in 1634. A good starting point for a tour of the city, it is also one of the links in the string of nine parks called the **Emerald Necklace**. Another piece is the lovely **Public Garden**, across Charles Street from the Common, where Boston's iconic swan boats paddle the main pond. Grand boulevards such as

---

THE FREEDOM TRAIL

Delineated by a 2.5-mile-long red-brick (or paint) stripe in the sidewalk, the **Freedom Trail** (ⓦ thefreedomtrail.org) stretches from Boston Common to Charlestown, linking sixteen points "significant in their contribution to this country's struggle for freedom". About half the sights on the trail are related to the Revolution itself; the others are more germane to other times and topics.

Though some of the touches intended to accentuate the trail's appeal move closer to tarnishing it (the costumed actors outside some of the sights, the pseudo-antique signage), the Freedom Trail remains the easiest way to orient yourself downtown, and is especially useful if you'll only be in Boston for a short time, as it does take in many "must-see" sights. Detailed National Park Service **maps** of the trail can be picked up from the visitor centre (see p.174). Thrifty travellers take note: most stops on the trail are either **free** or inexpensive to enter.

3

3

BOSTON

Ⓣ 'T' Station

Charles River

RESTAURANTS & CAFÉS

Chacarero	10
Douzo	18
flour bakery + café	7/17/20
Galleria Umberto	3
Gourmet Dumpling House	13
Island Creek Oyster Bar	22
Maria's Pastry	5
Mike & Patty's	15
Mike's Pastry	1
Myers + Chang	16
Neptune Oyster	4
Paramount	14
Pizzeria Regina	2
Scampo	11
Silvertone	9
Taiwan Café	12
Toro	21
Trident Booksellers & Café	19
Zo	6/8

0   400
        yards

Museum of Fine Arts & Isabella Stewart Gardner Museum

Commonwealth Avenue lead west from the Public Garden into **Back Bay**, where Harvard Bridge crosses into **Cambridge**. The beloved **North End**, adjacent to the waterfront, is Boston's Little Italy, its narrow streets chock-a-block with excellent bakeries and restaurants. Behind the Common rises the **State House** and lofty **Beacon Hill**, every bit as dignified as when writer Henry James called Mount Vernon Street "the most prestigious address in America".

Massachusetts State House

Corner of Beacon and Park sts • Mon–Fri 8.45am–5pm, guided tours Mon–Fri 10am–3.30pm • Free • ☎ 617 727 3676, ⓦ sec.state.ma.us/trs • Park St T

Behind Boston Common rises the large gilt dome of the **Massachusetts State House**, completed in 1798 and still the seat of Massachusetts' government. Its most famous fixture, a carved fish dubbed the "Sacred Cod", symbolizes the wealth Boston accrued from maritime trade. Politicos take this symbol so seriously that when Harvard pranksters stole it in the 1930s the House of Representatives didn't reconvene until it was recovered.

54th Massachusetts Regiment Monument

Beacon St, on the edge of Boston Common • Free • Park St T

Across from the State House is a majestic monument honouring the **54th Massachusetts Regiment**, the first all-black company to fight in the Civil War, and its leader, Robert Gould Shaw, scion of a moneyed Boston Brahmin clan. Isolated from the rest of the Union army, the regiment performed bravely; most of its members, including Shaw, were killed in a failed attempt to take Fort Wagner from the Confederates in 1863. Augustus Saint-Gaudens' outstanding 1897 bronze sculpture depicts the regiment's farewell march down Beacon Street.

Beacon Hill

Charles St T

No visit to Boston would be complete without an afternoon spent strolling around delightful **Beacon Hill**, a dignified stack of red brick rising over the north side of Boston Common. This is the Boston of wealth and privilege, one-time home to numerous historical and literary figures – including John Hancock, John Quincy Adams, Louisa May Alcott and Oliver Wendell Holmes. As you walk, keep an eye out for the **purple panes** in some of the townhouses' windows (such as nos. 63 and

---

THE BLACK HERITAGE TRAIL

Massachusetts was the first state to declare slavery illegal, in 1783 – partly as a result of black participation in the Revolutionary War – and a large community of free blacks and escaped slaves swiftly grew in the North End and on Beacon Hill. The **Black Heritage Trail** traces the neighbourhood's key role in local and national black history and is the most important historical site in America devoted to pre-Civil War African American history and culture.

Pick up the trail at 46 Joy St, where the **Abiel Smith School** – the first public building in the country established for the purpose of educating black children – contains a **Museum of African American History** (Mon–Sat 10am–4pm; $5; ☎ 617 725 0022, ⓦ afroammuseum.org). Adjacent, the **African Meeting House** was built in 1806 as the country's first African American church; Frederick Douglass issued his call here for all blacks to take up arms in the Civil War. The trail continues around Beacon Hill, including a glimpse of the **Lewis and Harriet Hayden House**. Once a stop on the famous "Underground Railroad", the home was owned by the Haydens who sheltered legions of runaway slaves from bounty hunters in pursuit.

The best way to experience the trail is by taking a ninety-minute National Park Service **walking tour** (late May to early Sept Mon–Sat 10am, noon & 2pm; mid-Sept to Nov 2pm only; free; ☎ 617 742 5415, ⓦ nps.gov/boaf; Park St T).

64 Beacon St). At first an irritating accident, they were eventually regarded as the definitive Beacon Hill status symbol due to their prevalence in the windows of Boston's most prestigious homes.

Park Street Church

Corner of Park and Tremont sts • Office hours Mon–Fri 8.30am–4.30pm • Free • ☎ 617 523 3383 • Park St T

Although the 1809 **Park Street Church** is a simple mass of bricks and mortar, its 217ft-tall white telescoping **steeple** is undeniably impressive. The church's reputation rests not on its size, however, but on the events that took place inside: this is where abolitionist William Lloyd Garrison delivered his first public address calling for the nationwide abolition of slavery, and where the song *America* ("My country 'tis of thee…") was first sung, on July 4, 1831.

Granary Burying Ground

Tremont St, between Park and School sts • Daily 9am–5pm • Free • ☎ 617 523 3383 • Park St T

Adjacent to the Park Street Church, the atmospheric **Granary Burying Ground** includes the Revolutionary remains of Paul Revere, Samuel Adams and John Hancock, although, as the rangers will tell you, "the stones and the bones may not match up".

The Boston Athenæum

10½ Beacon St • Mon–Wed 9am–8pm, Thurs & Fri 9am–5.30pm, Sat 9am–4pm; art and architecture tour Tues & Thurs 3pm (reservations required) • Free • ☎ 617 227 0270 (ext 279 for tour reservations), ⓦ bostonathenaeum.org • Park St T

Around the block from the Granary Burying Ground, the venerable **Boston Athenæum** is one of Boston's most alluring and yet least-visited sights. Established in 1807, it's one of the oldest independent research libraries in the country, and counts among its holdings books from the private library of George Washington. Additionally, the library's **ornate interior** and impressive array of **artworks**, including paintings by John Singer Sargent and Gilbert Stuart, rival those of the Museum of Fine Arts (see p.170).

The Athenæum is not exactly welcoming to guests (perhaps explaining its lack of visitors); non-members are confined to the first floor, and everyone has to leave bags and coats at the **front desk** – it's all very formal Beacon Hill.

King's Chapel Burying Ground

58 Tremont St • **Burying Ground** June–Sept Mon–Sat 10am–4pm, Sun 1–4pm • Free **Music recitals** Tues 12.15–12.50pm; $3 suggested donation • ☎ 617 523 1749 • Park St T

The ethereal **King's Chapel Burying Ground** is the final resting place for seventeenth-century luminaries such as Mary Chilton, woman of the *Mayflower* (see p.182), and Boston's first governor, John Winthrop. One of the chief pleasures here is examining the ancient tombstones, many beautifully etched with winged skulls and wistful seraphim. On Tuesday afternoons, be sure to stop by the chapel for a taste of jazz, folk or chamber music.

Old South Meeting House

310 Washington St • Daily: April–Oct 9.30am–5pm; Nov–March 10am–4pm • $6, kids $1 • ☎ 617 482 6439, ⓦ oldsouthmeetinghouse.org • Downtown Crossing T

On the morning of December 16, 1773, nearly five thousand locals met at **Old South Meeting House**, awaiting word from **Governor Thomas Hutchinson** on whether he would permit the withdrawal of three ships in Boston Harbor containing taxed tea. When a message was received that the ships would not be removed, Samuel Adams announced, "This meeting can do no more to save the country!". His simple declaration triggered the **Boston Tea Party**. Considered to be the first major act of rebellion preceding the Revolutionary War, it was a carefully planned event wherein one hundred men, some dressed in Native American garb, solemnly threw enough British tea into the harbour to make 24 million cuppas.

3

Old State House

206 Washington St • Daily: Oct–April 9am–5pm; May–Sept 9am–6pm • $8.50 • ☎ 617 720 1713, ⓦ bostonhistory.org • State St T

That the graceful, three-tiered tower of the red-brick **Old State House** is dwarfed by skyscrapers amplifies rather than diminishes its colonial-era dignity. Built in 1712, this was the seat of colonial government, and from its balcony the Declaration of Independence was first publicly read in Boston on July 18, 1776; two hundred years later, Queen Elizabeth II made a speech from the same balcony. Inside is a neat **museum** of Boston history that includes a dapper jacket belonging to John Hancock. Outside, a circle of cobblestones set on a traffic island at the intersection of Devonshire and State streets marks the site of the **Boston Massacre** on March 5, 1770, when British soldiers fired on a crowd that was pelting them with stone-filled snowballs, and killed five, including Crispus Attucks, a former slave.

Faneuil Hall

Faneuil Hall Square • Daily 9am–5pm • Free • ☎ 617 242 5642, ⓦ nps.gov/bost • State St T

Inside **Faneuil Hall**, a four-storey brick building and former colonial marketplace, Revolutionary firebrands such as Samuel Adams and James Otis whipped up popular support for independence by protesting British tax legislation. Head upstairs to the impressive second floor: its focal point is a massive canvas depicting an embellished version of "The Great Debate", during which Daniel Webster argued, in 1830, for the concept of the United States as one nation.

Quincy Market

In front of Faneuil Hall • Mon–Sat 10am–9pm, Sun noon–6pm • Free • ☎ 617 523 1300, ⓦ faneuilhallmarketplace.com • State St T

The three oblong markets just behind Faneuil Hall were built in the early eighteenth century to contain the trade that outgrew the hall. The centre building, known as **Quincy Market**, holds a super-extended corridor lined with stands vending a variety of takeaway treats – it's the mother of mall food courts.

New England Holocaust Memorial

98 Union St • Daily 24hr • Free • ☎ 617 457 8755, ⓦ nehm.org • Haymarket T

Just north of Faneuil Hall are six tall hollow glass pillars erected as a memorial to victims of the Holocaust. Built to resemble smokestacks, the columns of the **New England Holocaust Memorial** are etched with six million numbers, recalling the tattoos the Nazis gave their victims. Steam rises from grates beneath the pillars to accentuate their symbolism, an effect that's particularly striking at night.

The North End

Haymarket T

Hemmed in nearly all around by Boston Harbor, the small, densely populated **North End** is Boston's **Little Italy**. Though the above-ground highway that once separated the area from downtown has been removed (replaced by the landscaped Rose Kennedy Greenway), the area still has a bit of a detached feeling, making it all the more charming.

Paul Revere House

19 North Square • Mid-April to Oct daily 9.30am–5.15pm; Nov, Dec & early to mid-April daily 9.30am–4.15pm; Jan, Feb & March Tues–Sun 9.30am–4.15pm • $3.50 • ☎ 617 523 2338, ⓦ paulreverehouse.org • Haymarket T

The little triangular wedge of cobblestones and gaslights known as **North Square** is among the most historic and attractive pockets of the city, home to the **Paul Revere House**, the oldest residential address in downtown Boston. Revere, a silversmith who fathered sixteen children, gained immortality on April 18, 1775, when he headed out on his now-legendary "midnight ride" to Lexington (see p.179), successfully warning

SWEET WAVE

The granite **Copp's Hill Terrace**, on Charter Street across from the Copp's Hill Burying Ground's northern side, was the place from which British cannons bombarded Charlestown during the Battle of Bunker Hill. Just over a century later, in 1919, a 2.5 million-gallon tank of molasses exploded nearby, creating a syrupy tidal wave 30ft high that engulfed entire buildings and drowned 21 people and a score of horses. Old North Enders claim you can still catch a whiff of the stuff on exceptionally hot days.

John Hancock and Samuel Adams (and anyone else within earshot) of the impending British march.

Old North Church

193 Salem St • **Church** Jan & Feb Tues–Sun 10am–4pm; March–May daily 9am–5pm; June–Oct daily 9am–6pm; Nov & Dec daily 10am–5pm • Free **Behind the Scenes tour** (gives access to steeple and crypt) Daily: March 10 & 11am, 1–2pm, April–Oct 10 & 11am, 1–4pm, Nov & Dec 10 & 11am, 1–3pm • $5 • ☎ 617 523 6676, ⊚ oldnorth.com • Haymarket T

Few places in Boston have as emblematic a quality as the simple yet noble **Old North Church**. Built in 1723, it's easily recognized by its gleaming 191ft **steeple** – though it was a pair of lanterns that secured the structure's place in history. The church sexton, Robert Newman, is said to have hung both of them inside on the night of April 18, 1775, to signal the movement of British forces "by sea" from Boston Common (which then bordered the Charles River) to Lexington–Concord (see p.179). The interior is spotlessly white and well lit, thanks to the Palladian windows behind the pulpit. Below your feet are 37 basement-level crypts (viewable on the "Behind the Scenes" tour).

Copp's Hill Burying Ground

Hull St • Daily dawn–dusk • Free

Up Hull Street from Old North Church, **Copp's Hill Burying Ground**, with eerily tilting slate tombstones and stunning harbour views, holds the highest ground in the North End. You'll notice that many gravestones have chunks missing, the consequence of British soldiers using them for target practice during the 1775 Siege of Boston; the grave of one Captain Daniel Malcolm bears particularly strong evidence of this. As you exit the cemetery, keep an eye out for the **narrowest house** at 44 Hull St; a private residence merely 10ft wide.

All Saints' Way

Between nos. 4 and 8 Battery St • Free • Haymarket T

At the northern end of Hanover Street, the North End's main byway, sits **All Saints' Way**. Squeezed in between two homes, it's a narrow brick alley decked out with reverential images of saints and serene cherubim. A celebrated neighbourhood landmark, it offers a unique bit of local flavour.

Charlestown

To get here, cross over the Charlestown Bridge (follow the Freedom Trail), or take the short ferry trip (☎ 617 227 4321, ⊚ mbta.com; $3) from Long Wharf to the Charlestown Navy Yard

Across Boston Harbor from the North End, historic **Charlestown** ("Chucktown" to residents) is a very pretty, quietly affluent neighbourhood that stands considerably isolated from the city. Most visitors only make it over this way for the historic frigate the **USS Constitution** (if at all), which is a shame, because the neighbourhood's narrow, hilly byways, lined with antique gaslights and Colonial- and Federal-style rowhouses, make for pleasant exploration and offer great views of Boston. As you make the uphill climb to the **Bunker Hill Monument** – Charlestown's other big sight – look toward the water for jaw-dropping vistas.

USS Constitution and Museum

Constitution Wharf • **USS Constitution** April–Sept Tues–Sun 10am–6pm; Oct 10am–4pm; March Thurs–Sun 10am–4pm; lower deck only accessible on a 30min guided tour • Free • ☎ 617 242 5601, ⓦ history.navy.mil/ussconstitution **Museum** Building 22 • Daily: April–Oct 9am–6pm; Nov–March 10am–5pm • $5 donation • ☎ 617 426 1812, ⓦ ussconstitutionmuseum.org • North Station T

The celebrated **USS Constitution**, also known as "Old Ironsides", is the oldest commissioned warship afloat in the world. Launched in Boston in 1797, she earned her nickname during the War of 1812, when advancing cannonballs bounced off her hull; she subsequently saw 33 battles without ever losing one. Across the way, the **USS Constitution Museum** houses sophisticated displays on the history of the ship; upstairs is more fun, with hands-on sailorly exhibits testing your ability to balance on a footrope and determining whether your comrades have scurvy or gout.

Bunker Hill Monument and Museum

43 Monument Square • Daily: July & Aug 9am–5.30pm; Sept–June 9am–4.30pm; museum open 30min longer than monument • Free • ☎ 617 242 7275, ⓦ nps.gov/bost

A grey, dagger-like obelisk that's visible from just about anywhere in Charlestown, the **Bunker Hill Monument** sits on Breed's Hill, the actual site of the battle fought on June 17, 1775, which, while technically won by the British, invigorated the patriots, whose strong showing felled nearly half the British troops. A spiral staircase of 294 steps leads to sweeping views at the top; a new **museum** at the base has interesting exhibits on the battle as well as the history of Charlestown.

The waterfront and Seaport District

Boston's **waterfront** has recently seen major revitalization efforts, making this prime strolling territory. Wisteria-laden **Columbus Park**, next to the *Marriott Long Wharf Hotel*, is a pretty place to picnic. Faneuil Hall originally stood at the head of **Long Wharf**, which stuck out nearly 2000ft into the harbour. Later, a 1000ft expanse of the waterfront was filled in, and the **Custom House Tower**, 3 McKinley Square, once the tallest skyscraper in New England, was erected to mark the end of the wharf. Though it too now finds itself inland, its observation deck offers terrific harbour views (**tours** daily except Fri 2pm [$4] and 6pm [$7.50, with beverage]; ☎ 617 310 6300). Long Wharf is also the base for **ferries** to the Cape, Salem, MA, and the Harbor Islands.

New England Aquarium

Central Wharf • July & Aug Mon–Thurs & Sun 9am–6pm, Fri & Sat 9am–7pm; Sept–June Mon–Fri 9am–5pm, Sat & Sun 9am–6pm • $24.95; kids (3–11) $17.95 • ☎ 617 973 5200, ⓦ neaq.org • Aquarium T

Next door to Long Wharf is the waterfront's main draw, the **New England Aquarium**. Inside, a colossal, three-storey glass cylindrical tank is packed with giant sea turtles, moray eels and sharks as well as a range of other ocean exotica that swim by in unsettling proximity. Near the ticket counter, brave visitors can pat scratchy bonnethead sharks and velvety cownose rays as they swim through a mangrove-themed touch tank that opened in 2011. The Aquarium also runs **whale-watching** trips and houses a **3-D IMAX theatre**.

Boston Children's Museum

308 Congress St • Mon–Thurs, Sat & Sun 10am–5pm, Fri 10am–9pm • $14, Fri 5–9pm $1 • ☎ 617 426 6500, ⓦ bostonchildrensmuseum.org • South Station T

It's hard to miss the larger-than-life 1930s-era **Hood Milk Bottle** model, across the Congress Street bridge from downtown. Just behind the bottle, the expanded **Boston Children's Museum** comprises three floors of educational exhibits craftily designed to trick kids into learning about topics from musicology to the engineering of a humungous bubble. Before heading out, be sure to check out the Recycle Shop, where industrial leftovers are transformed into appealing craft fodder.

Institute of Contemporary Art

100 Northern Ave • Tues, Wed, Sat & Sun 10am–5pm, Thurs & Fri 10am–9pm • $15, free Thurs 5–9pm; kids (17 and under) free; free for families last Sat of the month • ☎ 617 478 3100, ⊕ icaboston.org • Courthouse Station T

Looking like a tremendous, glimmering ice cube perched above Boston Harbor, the **Institute of Contemporary Art**, located in the Seaport District, offers a show before you've even crossed the threshold. Complementing the museum's collection of avant-garde artworks is the building's dramatic cantilever shape, which juts 80ft over the water. From the interior, this extended section functions as the "Founders Gallery", a meditative ledge where, if you look down, you'll find yourself standing directly above the water.

The Museum of Science

1 Science Park • July to early Sept Mon–Thurs 9am–7pm, Fri 9am–9pm; mid-Sept to June Mon–Thurs 9am–5pm, Fri 9am–9pm • $22, kids (3–11) $19; IMAX $10, kids $8; 3-D Theater $5, kids $4 • ☎ 617 723 2500, ⊕ mos.org • Science Park T

At the northern end of the waterfront, clear across the Boston peninsula from the Children's Museum, the beloved **Museum of Science** has several floors of interactive exhibits illustrating basic principles of natural and physical science. An impressive IMAX cinema takes up the full height of one end of the building, and the museum's **3-D Theater** provides a chance to wear those retro-cool 3-D glasses.

Back Bay and beyond

Beginning in 1857, the spacious boulevards and elegant houses of **Back Bay** were fashioned along gradually filled-in portions of former Charles River marshland. Thus a walk through the area from east to west provides an impressive visual timeline of Victorian architecture. One of the most architecturally significant of its buildings is the Romanesque **Trinity Church**, 206 Clarendon St (Mon, Fri & Sat 9am–5pm, Tues–Thurs 9am–6pm, Sun 1–6pm; $7, includes guided tour; ☎617 536 0944, ⊕ trinitychurchboston.org; Copley T), whose stunning interior was designed to feel like "walking into a living painting". Towering over the church is Boston's signature skyscraper, the **John Hancock Tower**, an elegant wedge designed by I.M. Pei. Nearby **Newbury Street** is famed for its swanky boutiques, cafés and art galleries.

Boston Public Library

700 Boylston St • Mon–Thurs 9am–9pm, Fri & Sat 9am–5pm • Free • ☎ 617 536 5400, ⊕ bpl.org • Copley T

The handsome **Boston Public Library** (1895) faces Trinity Church and iconic Copley Square. Beyond the marble staircase and signature lions are a series of impressive murals. You can also check out the imposing **Bates Reading Room**, with its barrel-vaulted ceiling and oak panelling. Seek out the top floor's **Sargent Hall**, covered with seventeen remarkable murals painted by John Singer Sargent.

Public Garden

Bounded by Beacon, Arlington, Boylston and Charles sts • **Swan boats** April to late June daily 10am–4pm; late June to early Sept daily 10am–5pm; early to mid-Sept Mon–Fri noon–4pm, Sat & Sun 10am–4pm • $3 • ☎ 617 522 1966, ⊕ swanboats.com • Arlington T

Boston's most beautiful outdoor space, the **Public Garden** is a 24-acre botanical park first earmarked for public use in 1859. Of the garden's 125 types of trees, most impressive are the weeping willows that ring the picturesque man-made **lagoon**, around which you can take a fifteen-minute ride in a **swan boat**. These elegant, pedal-powered conveyances have been around since 1877, long enough to have become a Boston institution.

Christian Science complex

200 Massachusetts Ave • Mapparium Tues–Sat 10am–4pm • $6 • ☎ 617 450 7000, ⊕ marybakereddylibrary.org • Hynes T

The **Christian Science Center** is the "Mother Church" of the First Church of Christ, Scientist, and the home of the *Christian Science Monitor* newspaper. Its campus houses the marvellous **Mapparium**, a curious, 30ft stained-glass globe through which you can walk on a footbridge. The sphere's best feature is its lack of sound absorption, which enables a tiny whisper spoken at one end of the bridge to be easily heard by someone at the other.

South End
Back Bay T

The residential **South End**, extending below Back Bay from Massachusetts Avenue to I-93 and the Mass Pike (I-90), is both quaint and stylish in equal measure. This posh enclave boasts a spectacular concentration of **Victorian architecture**, adorned with fanciful "Rinceau" **ironwork**. Details like these have made the area quite popular with upwardly mobile Bostonians, among them a strong gay and lesbian contingent. Here you will find some of the liveliest **streetlife**, and the best restaurants, in town.

Museum of Fine Arts
465 Huntington Ave • Mon, Tues, Sat & Sun 10am–4.45pm, Wed–Fri 10am–9.45pm • $25 (good for two visits in a ten-day period), Wed after 4pm admission by donation; kids $10, under-17s free at weekends and after 3pm weekdays • ☎ 617 267 9300, ⓦ mfa.org • Museum T

Beyond the boundaries of Back Bay is the **Museum of Fine Arts**. From its magnificent collections of Asian and ancient Egyptian art onwards, the MFA (as it's known) holds sufficient marvels to detain you all day. In 2010, the museum completed an ambitious expansion that saw the addition of a magnificent new Art of the Americas wing, 53 galleries, a state-of-the-art auditorium and a glass pavilion for the central courtyard. High points include Renoir's *Dance at Bougival*; Gauguin's sumptuous display of existential angst *Where do we come from? What are we? Where are we going?*; a saxophone made by Adolphe Sax himself (Musical Instruments room); and Gilbert Stuart's George Washington portraits (one of which is famously replicated on the dollar bill).

Isabella Stewart Gardner Museum
280 The Fenway • Daily 11am–5pm, Thurs till 9pm; tours all week, times vary • $15; $2 off with MFA ticket stub (within two days of use); free for anyone under 18, celebrating a birthday or named "Isabella"; **tours** free • ☎ 617 566 1401, ⓦ gardnermuseum.org • Museum T

Less broad in its collection, but more distinctive and idiosyncratic than the MFA, the **Isabella Stewart Gardner Museum** is one of the city's jewels. Styled after a fifteenth-century Venetian villa, the Gardner brims with a dazzling collection of works meant to "fire the imagination". Best known for its spectacular central courtyard, the museum's show-stopping pieces by John Singer Sargent – including a famous portrait of Isabella – are another highlight. In 2012, the Gardner unveiled a new glass-and-copper **entrance wing**, which has greenhouses, a special exhibition gallery and an information centre called "The Living Room", dedicated to the museum's own intriguing life story as the work of a single individual. Classical concerts are held on select Thursday nights as well as on Sunday afternoons from September to May (tickets $27; includes museum admission).

Fenway Park
4 Yawkey Way • 50min tours daily 9am–4pm (till 5pm in summer), on the hour but call ahead as times vary according to game schedule • Tours $16, kids $12; game tickets $12–135 • ☎ 617 226 6666 (tours), ☎ 877 733 7699 (game tickets), ⓦ redsox.com • Kenmore or Fenway T

Home to Boston's beloved **Red Sox** baseball team, **Fenway Park** was constructed in 1912 in a tiny, asymmetrical space just off Brookline Avenue, resulting in its famously awkward dimensions. The 37ft left-field wall, aka the **Green Monster**, is its most distinctive quirk (it was originally built because home runs were breaking local windows); that it is so high makes up for some of the park's short distances.

Tours of the ballpark are fun and deservedly popular, but your best bet is to come to see a game. The season runs from April to October, and **tickets** are reasonable.

364.4 SMOOTS (+ 1 EAR)

If you walk from Back Bay to Cambridge via the scenic **Harvard Bridge** (which leads directly into MIT's campus), you might wonder about the peculiar marks partitioning the sidewalk. These units of measure, affectionately known as "Smoots", represent the height of **Oliver R. Smoot**, an MIT Lambda Chi Alpha fraternity pledge in 1958. As the shortest pledge, part of Smoot's initiation included the use of his body as a tape measure, all down the **Harvard Bridge** – resulting in the conclusive "364.4 Smoots (+ 1 Ear)" at the bridge's terminus. While the marks continue to be repainted each year by LCA, the "Smoot" itself has gone global and even appears on a Google conversion calculator.

Cambridge

Harvard or Central T

The excursion across the Charles River to **Cambridge** merits at least half a day, and begins with a fifteen-minute ride on the Red T line to **Harvard Square**. Walk down almost any street here, and you will pass monuments and plaques honouring literati and revolutionaries who lived in the area as early as the seventeenth century. But Cambridge also vibrates with energy: it's filled with students from nearby Harvard University and MIT, and in warm weather, street musicians. Feel free to wander into **Harvard Yard** and around the core of the university, founded in 1636; its enormous Widener Library (named for a victim of the *Titanic* disaster) boasts a Gutenberg Bible and a first folio of Shakespeare.

Harvard Art Museums

32 Quincy St • Currently closed; check website for hours and admission • ☎ 617 495 9400, ⓦ harvardartmuseums.org • Harvard T

Cambridge has several first-class museums, with a few engaging exhibits of note. Unfortunately, the **Harvard Art Museums** are currently closed for a major renovation and slated to reopen as a single museum in the autumn of 2014. Once unveiled, this will encompass more than 150,000 works of art, including highlights of Harvard's substantial collection of Western art, a small yet excellent selection of German Expressionists and Bauhaus works, and sensuous Buddhas and gilded bodhisattvas from its Asian and Islamic art collection.

Harvard Museum of Natural History

26 Oxford St • Daily 9am–5pm • $12, includes entry to the Peabody Museum • ☎ 617 495 3045, ⓦ hmnh.harvard.edu • Harvard T

A few blocks north of the Harvard Art Museums is the **Harvard Museum of Natural History**, a nineteenth-century Victorian building with curio-style exhibits. The galleries feature a number of gloriously huge dinosaur fossils as well as a stunning collection of flower models constructed entirely from glass.

MIT Museum

265 Massachusetts Ave • Daily 10am–5pm • $10 • ☎ 617 253 5927, ⓦ web.mit.edu/museum • Central T

A couple of miles southeast of Harvard Square is the **Massachusetts Institute of Technology** (MIT). The small but compelling **MIT Museum**, near Central Square, has standout displays including "Holography: the Light Fantastic", a seriously cool collection of eye trickery. The best exhibit, however, is Arthur Ganson's "Gestural Engineering", a hypnotizing ensemble of imaginative mini-machines, such as a walking wishbone.

ARRIVAL AND DEPARTURE   BOSTON

By plane Just 3 miles from downtown, Logan International Airport (☎ 800 235 6426, ⓦ massport.com), has four terminals (A, B, C and E), connected by shuttle buses. Taxis will take you downtown for around $30, or you can take the subway (daily 5am–midnight; Blue or Silver lines; $2.50; ☎ 800 392 6100, ⓦ mbta.com). A fun alternative is a water taxi (Mon–Sat 7am–10pm, Sun 7am–8pm; $10; ☎ 617 422 0392, ⓦ citywatertaxi.com)

3

across the harbour; courtesy bus #66 will take you to the pier.

By bus Boston's major bus hub is South Station, in the southeast corner of downtown at Summer St and Atlantic Ave; the subway (Red Line), takes you to the centre of town or to Cambridge. Greyhound, Mega Bus (☎ 877 462 6342, ⓦ megabus.com) and Peter Pan (☎ 800 343 9999, ⓦ peterpanbus.com) offer national service, including frequent direct routes to New York City and Washington DC.

Destinations Concord, NH (1 daily; 1hr 45min); Hartford, CT (12 daily; 2hr 30min); New York City (15 daily; 4hr 20min); Portland, ME (2 daily; 2hr).

By train As with the buses, the main terminus is South Station. Some Amtrak services make an extra stop at Back Bay Station, 145 Dartmouth St, on the Orange subway line near Copley Square. North Station, at 135 Causeway St, is used by northerly commuter trains and Amtrak's Downeaster.

Destinations Dover, NH (1hr 25min; 5 daily); Durham, NH (1hr 20min; 5 daily); Freeport, ME (3hr 10min; 2 daily); Portland, ME (2hr 30min; 5 daily).

By ferry The Inner Harbor ferry connects Long Wharf with the Charlestown Navy Yard (every 15min: Mon–Fri 6.30am–8pm, Sat & Sun 10am–6pm; $3; ☎ 800 392 6100, ⓦ mbta.com).

GETTING AROUND

Much of the pleasure of visiting Boston comes from being in a city that was built long before cars were invented. Walking around town can be a joy; conversely, driving is a nightmare. All **public transport** in the area is run by the Massachusetts Bay Transport Authority (☎ 800 392 6100, ⓦ mbta.com).

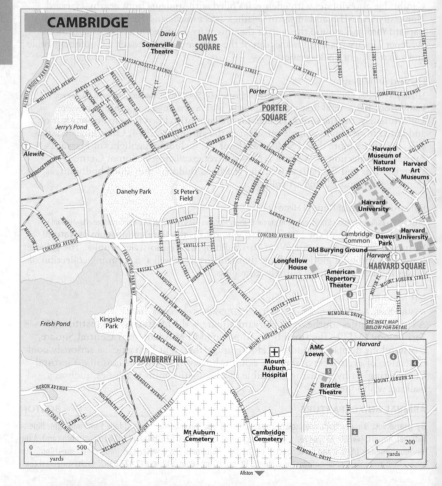

BY SUBWAY

Boston's subway, known as the "T", is the oldest in the USA. Its first station, Park Street, remains its centre (any train marked "inbound" is headed here). Four lines – Red, Green, Blue and Orange – operate daily from 5am until 12.30am, although certain routes begin to shut down earlier. The four lines are supplemented by a bus rapid transit (BRT) route, the Silver Line.

TICKETS AND FARES

Boston has a somewhat confusing system for subway fares. Within the city, the standard fare is $2.50, payable by the purchase of a "CharlieTicket", bought at ATM-like machines in the station. If you pick up a "CharlieCard" – with more of a credit card thickness and a longer lifespan – from a station attendant your fare begins at only $2 per ride. The simplest bet is the LinkPass which seamlessly covers all subway and local bus journeys (as well as the ferry to Charlestown) for $11/day or $18/week.

BY BUS

The MBTA manages a whopping 170 bus routes around the city. Fares are $2 with a CharlieTicket, $1.50 with a CharlieCard. Most buses run from 5.30am to 1am.

BY BIKE

In and around Boston are some 80 miles of bike trails. Rent from Urban AdvenTours, in the North End at 103 Atlantic Ave ($35/day; ☎ 800 9/9 3370, ⓦ urban adventours.com; Haymarket T); Community Bicycle Supply, in the South End at 496 Tremont St ($25/day; ☎ 617 542 8623, ⓦ communitybicycle.com; Back Bay T); and Back Bay Bicycles, 366 Commonwealth Ave ($35/day, cash only; ☎ 617 247 2336, ⓦ papa-wheelies.com; Hynes T).

3

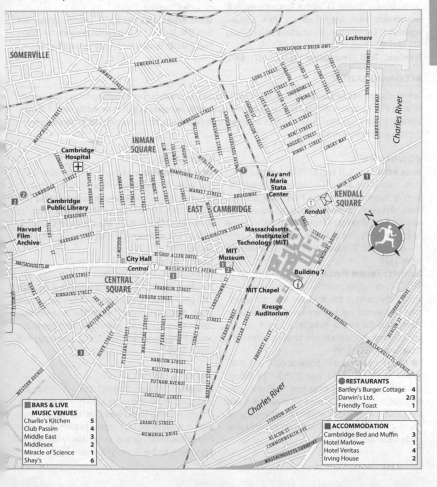

● RESTAURANTS	
Bartley's Burger Cottage	4
Darwin's Ltd.	2/3
Friendly Toast	1

■ ACCOMMODATION	
Cambridge Bed and Muffin	3
Hotel Marlowe	1
Hotel Veritas	4
Irving House	2

■ BARS & LIVE MUSIC VENUES	
Charlie's Kitchen	5
Club Passim	4
Middle East	3
Middlesex	2
Miracle of Science	1
Shay's	6

3

INFORMATION

Boston Common Visitor Center 139 Tremont St (daily 3am–5pm; ☎ 617 426 3115; Park St T). The main tourist office, with loads of maps and brochures, information on historical sights, cultural events, accommodation, restaurants and bus trips.

National Park Service visitor centre 15 State St, across from the Old State House (daily 9am–5pm; ☎ 617 242 5642, ⓦ nps.gov/bost; State St T). Chock-full of maps, facts and helpful park rangers who lead fascinating free history tours (see box below).

Cambridge Office of Tourism Harvard Square (Mon–Fri 9am–5pm, Sat & Sun 9am–1pm; ☎ 617 441 2884, ⓦ cambridgeusa.org; Harvard T). Kiosk outside the subway station.

Advance information The best sources are the Greater Boston Convention & Visitors Bureau (GBCVB; ⓦ bostonusa .com) and the Boston Globe (ⓦ boston.com).

TOURS

Boston Duck Tours ☎ 617 267 3825, ⓦ bostonduck tours.com. Excellent tours that take to the streets and the Charles River in restored World War II amphibious landing vehicles. Tours depart March to Nov every 30min from the Prudential Center (53 Huntington Ave) and the Museum of Science (1 Science Park); abbreviated, summer-only tours leave from the New England Aquarium (1 Central Wharf). Reservations advised. Tours $33.99 ($30.99 from aquarium).

Freedom Trail Foundation ☎ 617 357 8300, ⓦ thefreedomtrail.org. Lively 90min tours ($13) of Freedom Trail highlights led by costumed guides.

Harvard Tours ☎ 617 674 7788, ⓦ harvardtour.com. A boisterous 70min tour of the Harvard campus ($8.95 online, $10 in person) led by undergrads in intentionally misspelled "Hahvahd" T-shirts.

Urban Adventours (see p.173). Leisurely themed bike tours (2hr 30min; $50) which pedal alongside the Charles River and take in sights like Fenway Park and Back Bay.

ACCOMMODATION

Good-quality, inexpensive accommodation is hard to find in Boston – any hotel room within walking distance of downtown for under $175 has to be considered a bargain. Room rates range wildly depending on the season and the day – if the rates below seem high, it's worth calling to check the current price. On the plus side, the city has a number of good hostels, and there are some well-priced B&Bs.

DOWNTOWN

Ames Hotel 1 Court St ☎ 617 979 8100, ⓦ ameshotel .com; State St T; map pp.162–163. One of Boston's "it" spots, a contemporary boutique hotel inside the city's oldest skyscraper. Luxurious interiors are furnished in whites and greys (with the odd citrus burst), and enhanced by flat-screen TVs, iPod docks and great views. The lively on-site restaurant, *Woodward*, feels like a chic museum of curios. $305

Marriott's Custom House 3 McKinley Square ☎ 617 310 6300, ⓦ marriott.com; Aquarium T; map pp.162–163. All the rooms at this downtown landmark-turned-hotel are high-end, one-bedroom suites with spectacular views. While the exterior embodies a bygone era, the interior is modern and plush, with luxurious linens and a small kitchen set-up. $299

★ **Omni Parker House** 60 School St ☎ 617 227 8600, ⓦ omnihotels.com; Park T; map pp.162–163. Though the present building only dates from 1927, the lobby, decorated in dark oak with carved gilt mouldings, recalls the splendour of the original nineteenth-century property. Rooms are on the small side, but come equipped with modern amenities. $245

BEACON HILL

John Jeffries House 14 David G. Mugar Way ☎ 617 367 1866, ⓦ johnjeffrieshouse.com; Charles/MGH T; map pp.162–163. This little gem has some of the best prices in town, and clean and tasteful rooms to match. Set at the foot of Beacon Hill, it offers Victorian-style decor, cable TV and kitchenettes in most rooms. Singles $125, doubles $150

Liberty Hotel 215 Charles St ☎ 617 224 4000, ⓦ libertyhotel.com; Charles/MGH T; map pp.162–163. The *Liberty Hotel* has taken over the labyrinthine digs of an 1851 prison and fashioned it with stylish furniture and lush details. Prepare to be wowed by its 90ft lobby, phenomenal skyline views and unique architecture. The property also houses *Scampo* restaurant (see p.176) and the trendy *Alibi* lounge. $299

THEATER DISTRICT

HI-Boston 19 Stuart St ☎ 617 536 9455, ⓦ boston hostel.org; Hynes T; map pp.162–163. Straddling the Chinatown-Theater District border, this eco-friendly hostel is set in a handsome brick historic building. Rooms are bright, clean and stylish, with on-site laundry facilities and a community kitchen. Dorms $50, doubles $150

THE NORTH END

★ **La Cappella Suites** 290 North St ☎617 699 2331, ⓦlacappellasuites.com; Haymarket T; map pp.162–163. The three cosy, modern rooms at this inn in the heart of the North End come with cable TV and a nice public seating area. Two of the rooms have private balconies. Be prepared for a five-floor walkup (with great views as a pay-off). **$150**

THE WATERFRONT

Harborside Inn 185 State St ☎617 723 7500, ⓦharborsideinnboston.com; State St T; map pp.162–163. This small hotel is housed in a renovated 1890s mercantile warehouse across from Faneuil Hall. The rooms – with exposed brick, hardwood floors and cherry furniture – are a welcome surprise for this part of town. They also have an excellent sister property, the *Charlesmark Hotel*, in Back Bay (see p.169). **$149**

BACK BAY

★ **Charlesmark Hotel** 655 Boylston St ☎617 247 1212, ⓦthecharlesmark.com; Copley T; map pp.162–163. Forty small, contemporary rooms with cosy beechwood furniture, good rates, a lively bar and modern amenities including CD/DVD players and a hooked-up speaker system that lets you sing in the shower. Nice location too, across from the library (see p.169). **$139**

★ **Inn @ St. Botolph** 99 St. Botolph St ☎617 236 8099, ⓦinnatstbotolph.com; Back Bay T; map pp.162–163. Fall through the rabbit hole at this designer's dream on the cusp of the South End. The sixteen oversized suites run wild with black and brown stripes, houndstooth and zebra zig-zags. The inn has kitchenettes throughout, an on-site laundry, gym and free continental breakfast. **$250**

Newbury Guest House 261 Newbury St ☎617 670 6000, ⓦnewburyguesthouse.com; Copley T; map pp.162–163. This big, popular Victorian brownstone in a really great location fills up frequently, so call ahead. The 32 rooms range from spacious bay-windowed quarters with hardwood floors to tiny digs ideal for the discerning economic traveller. Rooms can be noisy, however. Continental breakfast included. **$209**

THE SOUTH END

40 Berkeley 40 Berkeley St ☎617 375 2524, ⓦ40berkeley.com; Back Bay T; map pp.162–163. Clean, simple hostel with private rooms (no dorm beds) in a convenient South End location; full breakfast included. Singles **$106**, doubles **$116**, triples **$126**

★ **Clarendon Square Inn** 198 W Brookline St ☎617 536 2229, ⓦclarendonsquare.com; Prudential T; map pp.162–163. Gorgeous three-room B&B on a residential side street with lavish design details such as chandeliers and wainscotting, an inspired art collection and pampering

extras including heated bathroom tiles, a private garden and a 24hr roof-deck hot tub. **$225**

★ **Encore B&B** 116 W Newton St ☎617 247 3425, ⓦencorebandb.com; Back Bay T; map pp.162–163. Relax and rejuvenate at this cheerful, modern four-room B&B set in a nineteenth-century Victorian townhouse. Guestrooms have postcard-perfect views, and the daily continental breakfast is served in a sunlit nook. **$215**

AROUND FENWAY PARK

Gryphon House 9 Bay State Rd ☎617 375 9003, ⓦinnboston.com; Kenmore T; map pp.162–163. This hotel-cum-B&B around the corner from Fenway has eight wonderfully appointed suites equipped with working gas fireplaces, cable TV, a handy DVD library, continental breakfast and free parking (a huge plus in Boston). **$225**

★ **Hotel Commonwealth** 500 Commonwealth Ave ☎617 933 5000, ⓦhotelcommonwealth.com; Kenmore T; map pp.162–163. Old-world charm paired with modern decor make this a welcome addition to Boston's luxury hotel scene, with nice touches including L'Occitane products, cool linens and access to the *Hawthorne* and *Eastern Standard* bars (see p.178). **$299**

CAMBRIDGE

Cambridge Bed and Muffin 267 Putnam Ave ☎617 576 3166, ⓦbedandmuffin.com; Central or Harvard T; map pp.172–173. Just a block from the river and close to Harvard and Central squares, this tranquil B&B has a friendly owner and endearing little rooms with polished pine floors. No en-suite bathrooms and no TVs, but plenty of books and quiet. **$120**

★ **Hotel Marlowe** 25 Edwin H Land Blvd ☎617 868 8000, ⓦhotelmarlowe.com; Lechmere or Kendall/MIT T; map pp.172–173. The decor at this hotel is cosy, plush and hip with faux-leopard-print couches in the lobby and bold furniture in the guestrooms. There's an evening wine hour, fitness centre and free kayak and bicycle use. Pet friendly. **$200**

★ **Hotel Veritas** 1 Remington St ☎617 520 5000, ⓦthehotelveritas.com; Harvard T; map pp.172–173. A chic, 31-room European-style boutique hotel right in Harvard Square. The landscaped patio, silk drapes and cocktails are all welcome amenities, plus return guests are greeted with artisanal chocolates. Rooms are on the small side, however. **$250**

Irving House 24 Irving St ☎617 547 4600, ⓦirving house.com; Harvard T; map pp.172–173. Excellent, friendly, popular option near Harvard Square that falls somewhere between an inn, a hostel and a B&B. Laundry facilities (coin-operated), limited parking and generous breakfasts are included. It has a sister facility, *Harding House*, at 288 Harvard St. Singles **$135**, doubles **$165**

EATING

Boston is loaded with excellent **restaurants**. While boiled lobster, shucked oysters and clam chowder are local favourites, the city's dining scene also mirrors the increasing diversity of its population, with a rainbow of Indian, Mexican, Greek and assorted Asian cuisines. Studenty Cambridge has the best budget eats, while the historic North End is king of Italian – some of its bakeries and pizzerias are nearly a century old. Tremont Street, in the stylish South End, is known as "Restaurant Row", beloved of foodies.

BOSTON COMMON

★ **Chacarero** 101 Arch St ☎ 617 542 0392, ⓦ chacarero.com; Downtown Crossing T; map pp.162–163. Fabulous and fresh, the *chacarero* is a Chilean sandwich ($7.75) built on warm, soft bread and filled with avocado, chicken or beef, green beans, muenster cheese and hot sauce; good veggie version ($6.70), too. Cash only. Other locations. Mon–Fri 8am–6pm.

Silvertone 69 Bromfield St ☎ 617 338 7887, ⓦ silvertonedowntown.com; Park St T; map pp.162–163. Nostalgia runs high at this bustling basement bar and restaurant serving standout comfort foods such as mashed potatoes and meatloaf ($12) and a super-cheesy macaroni cheese ($9). Also has cocktails and a good selection of beer on tap. Mon–Fri 11.30am–11pm, Sat 5–11pm.

FANEUIL HALL

★ **Zo** 92 State St ☎ 617 227 0101, ⓦ zoboston.com; State St T; map pp.162–163. During weekday lunch hours *Zo* serves up Boston's best gyro sandwiches – succulent pork, juicy tomatoes, onion, and home-made tzatziki on warm flatbread ($8). There's another branch behind the massive Center Plaza building. Mon–Fri 11am–3pm.

CHINATOWN

Gourmet Dumpling House 52 Beach St ☎ 617 338 6222; Chinatown T; map pp.162–163. Tables fill up quickly at this Chinese restaurant known for its dumplings (try the mini variety with pork; $6.50) and extensive, authentic menu. Daily 11am–midnight.

Taiwan Café 34 Oxford St ☎ 617 426 8181; Chinatown T; map pp.162–163. Busy, authentic Taiwanese spot serving sautéed watercress with garlic ($11), stewed minced pork over rice ($2.75) and pan-fried dumplings done just right ($7). Daily 11am–1am.

BEACON HILL

Paramount 44 Charles St ☎ 617 720 1152, ⓦ paramount boston.com; Charles/MGH T; map pp.162–163. Dating from 1937, the Hill's neighbourhood diner serves banana and caramel French toast ($8) and omelettes ($6–9) to brunch regulars by day, and American standards such as hamburgers ($11) and steak tips (grilled cuts of sirloin; $19) by night. Expect long queues at weekends. Mon–Thurs 7am–10pm, Fri 7am–11pm, Sat 8am–11pm, Sun 8am–10pm.

Scampo 215 Charles St (in the Liberty Hotel) ☎ 617 536 2100, ⓦ scampoboston.com; Charles/MGH T; map pp.162–163. An Italian restaurant helmed by star chef

Lydia Shire. The imaginative menu includes a "mozzarella bar" (six different riffs on caprese salad; $14–27), handmade pasta dishes and eclectic pizzas. Mon–Wed & Sun 11.30am–10pm, Thurs–Sat 11.30am–11pm.

NORTH END

★ **Galleria Umberto** 289 Hanover St ☎ 617 227 5709; Haymarket T; map pp.162–163. North End nirvana. There are fewer than a dozen items on the menu, inclusing perfect pizza slices and savoury *arancini* (fried and stuffed rice balls). Lunch only, and get there early as they almost always sell out. Cash only. Mon–Sat 10.45am–2.30pm.

★ **Maria's Pastry** 46 Cross St ☎ 617 523 1196, ⓦ mariaspastry.com; Haymarket T; map pp.162–163. The best pastries in the North End. Maria's chocolate *cannoli* with fresh ricotta filling will make your day. Mon–Sat 7am–7pm, Sun 7am–5pm.

Mike's Pastry 300 Hanover St ☎ 617 742 3050, ⓦ mikespastry.com; Haymarket T; map pp.162–163. In many ways *Mike's* is the North End, and lining up for the twine-wrapped boxes of eclairs, *cannoli*, marzipan, *gelato* and the like is a quintessential Boston experience. Mon, Tues & Sun 8am–10pm, Wed & Thurs 8am–10.30pm, Fri & Sat 8am–11.30pm.

★ **Neptune Oyster** 63 Salem St ☎ 617 742 3474, ⓦ neptuneoyster.com; Haymarket T; map pp.162–163. Snazzy little raw bar serving excellent shucked shellfish and best-in-town lobster rolls (served hot with butter or cold with mayo; $25). If you can only make it to one of Boston's seafood restaurants, let this be the one. Mon–Fri 11.30am–10pm, Sat & Sun 11.30am–11pm.

Pizzeria Regina 11½ Thacher St ☎ 617 227 0765, ⓦ reginapizzeria.com; Haymarket T; map pp.162–163. Visit this North End legend for tasty, cheap pizza, served in a neighbourhood feed station where the wooden booths haven't budged since the 1920s. Don't be fooled by spin-offs bearing the *Regina* label in other parts of town – this is the original, vastly superior location. Be prepared for a wait. Mon–Thurs & Sun 11am–11.30pm, Fri & Sat 11.30am–12.30am.

THE WATERFRONT AND SEAPORT DISTRICT

★ **flour bakery + café** 12 Farnsworth St ☎ 617 338 4333, ⓦ flourbakery.com; South Station T; map pp.162–163. This first-rate café is just around the corner from the Children's Museum (see p.168). Bursting with fantastic pastries, sandwiches and salads, it's best known for its BLTs and raspberry seltzer (with carbonated water). Top off your meal with a home-made pop tart or peanut butter Oreo cookie. Other branches. Mon–Fri 7am–8pm, Sat 8am–6pm, Sun 9am–5pm.

BACK BAY

Douzo 131 Dartmouth St ☎ 617 859 8886, ⓦ douzosushi .com; Back Bay T; map pp.162–163. Sexy, modern decor coupled with standout sushi make this an enjoyable option along the Back Bay-South End border. Easy to find – it's just outside the T station. Daily 11.30am–11.30pm.

★ **Mike & Patty's** 12 Church St ☎ 617 423 3447, ⓦ mikeandpattys.com; Arlington T; map pp.162–163. Located in Bay Village, a residential satellite of Back Bay, this teensy breakfast and lunch spot serves the best sandwiches in Boston. While it's not on the road to any major sights, those who make the trek out will feel amply rewarded by the pork torta with sweet potato and avocado ($8) and grilled banana sandwich with cinnamon honey butter ($7). Tues–Sun 8am–2pm.

Trident Booksellers & Café 338 Newbury St ☎ 617 267 8688, ⓦ tridentbookscafe.com; Hynes T; map pp.162–163. Divine little bookshop/café, with a "perpetual breakfast" and tasty, vegetarian-friendly lunches and dinners. Free wi-fi. Daily 8am–midnight.

SOUTH END

★ **Myers + Chang** 1145 Washington St ☎ 617 542 5200, ⓦ myersandchang.com; Broadway T; map pp.162–163. This "indie diner" with an open kitchen serves Asian fusion dishes such as chicken with ginger-sesame waffles ($18), *nasi goreng* (Indonesian fried rice with shrimp, pineapple and fried egg; $14) and an awesome scorpion bowl for two ($18). Your bill comes with coconut macaroons. Mon–Thurs & Sun 11.30am–10pm, Fri & Sat 11.30am–11pm.

★ **Toro** 1704 Washington St ☎ 617 536 4300, ⓦ toro-restaurant.com; Back Bay T; map pp.162–163. This superlative tapas bar shakes up sassafras mojitos ($10), and serves octopus ceviche ($9) and mouth-watering grilled corn with *queso* ($8) to a buzzing, stylish crowd. On weekend nights, waiting times can be obscene (no reservations are taken); get there as early as possible. Mon–Thurs noon–3pm & 5.30–10.15pm, Fri noon–3pm & 5.30–11.45pm, Sat 5–11.45pm, Sun 10.30am–2.30pm & 5–10.15pm.

AROUND FENWAY PARK

Island Creek Oyster Bar 500 Commonwealth Ave, in the Hotel Commonwealth ☎ 617 532 5300, ⓦ island creekoysterbar.com; Kenmore T; map pp.162–163. Swish shellfish restaurant busy with plates of lobster roe noodles ($32), buttermilk biscuits ($4) and the region's freshest oysters. The ultra-modern interior is distinguished by high ceilings and walls of discarded seashells. Extremely popular; reservations highly recommended. Mon–Sat 4pm–1am, Sun 10.30am–1am.

CAMBRIDGE

Bartley's Burger Cottage 1246 Massachusetts Ave ☎ 617 354 6559, ⓦ mrbartley.com; Harvard T; map pp.172–173. A must-visit since 1960: Boston's best burgers, washed down with raspberry lime rickeys. The names of the dishes poke fun at politicians of the hour, and noisy servers shout out your order. Good veggie burgers, too. Sometimes they close on a whim. Cash only. Mon–Sat 11am–9pm.

Darwin's Ltd 148 Mt Auburn St (☎ 617 354 5233, ⓦ darwinsltd.com) and 1629 Cambridge St (☎ 617 491 2999); both Harvard T; map pp.172–173. Two locations, both offering wonderfully inventive sandwich combinations (such as roast beef, sprouts and apple slices) on freshly baked bread. A Harvard institution. Cash only. Mon–Sat 6.30am–9pm, Sun 7am–9pm.

Friendly Toast 1 Hampshire St ☎ 617 621 1200, ⓦ thefriendlytoast.net; Kendall/MIT T; map pp.172–173. A riot of 1950s kitsch, vinyl seating and lime green walls, this breakfast-all-day funhouse serves pumpkin pancakes with whipped cream ($8.50) and "King Cakes" in honour of Elvis (banana and chocolate-chip pancakes with peanut butter in between; $11). Expect a long wait at weekends. Mon, Tues & Sun 8am–10pm, Wed & Thurs 8am–11pm, Fri & Sat 8am–1am.

DRINKING AND NIGHTLIFE

Boston has a vibrant nightlife scene that offers everything from tried-and-true neighbourhood taverns to young, trendy lounges. The live music is dominated by the very best local and touring indie bands. The free weeklies *Boston Phoenix* (ⓦ thephoenix.com) and *Dig Boston* (ⓦ digboston.com) are the foremost sources for up-to-date listings. Note that most establishments are officious in demanding ID.

BARS

Bleacher Bar 82A Lansdowne St, Kenmore Square ☎ 617 262 2424, ⓦ bleacherbarboston.com; Kenmore T; map pp.162–163. Beneath the bleachers in centre field is the newest addition to Fenway Park, and you don't need a ticket to get in. Here, you'll find a pub festooned with vintage memorabilia and a window with a direct view of the diamond – quite thrilling on game night. Mon–Wed & Sun 11am–1am, Thurs–Sat till 2am.

Bukowski Tavern 50 Dalton St, Back Bay ☎ 617 437 9999, ⓦ bukowskitavern.net; Hynes T; map pp.162–163. Arguably Boston's best dive bar, with views over the Mass

3

Pike and such a vast beer selection that a home-made "wheel of indecision" is spun by staff when patrons can't decide. Cash only. Mon–Sat 11.30am–2am, Sun noon–2am.

Charlie's Kitchen 10 Eliot St, Cambridge ☎ 617 492 9646, ⓦ charlieskitchen.com; Harvard T; map pp.172–173. Downstairs is a well-loved burger joint, upstairs is a buzzing bar – with eighteen beers on tap, a rocking jukebox and a good mix of patrons – at its rowdiest on Tuesday karaoke nights. There's an outdoor beer garden, too. Mon–Wed & Sun 11am–1am, Thurs–Sat 11am–2am.

★ **Drink** 348 Congress St, Fort Point Channel ☎ 617 695 1806, ⓦ drinkfortpoint.com; South Station or World Trade Center T; map pp.162–163. A subterranean hot spot with a zigzagging bar and painstakingly constructed cocktails (they even chip their own ice). Don't be fooled by the limited menu – expert bartenders can concoct you the perfect customized beverage. It's a bit of a hike from downtown; take a taxi. Expect a long wait at weekends. Daily 4pm–1am.

★ **Eastern Standard** 528 Commonwealth Ave, in the Hotel Commonwealth, Kenmore Square ☎ 617 532 9100, ⓦ easternstandardboston.com; Kenmore T; map pp.162–163. Set inside a gorgeous, high-ceilinged dining room, this Boston favourite pulls in a nicely mixed crowd. Knowledgeable bartenders, great comfort food and a landscaped patio in summer. Mon–Thurs & Sun 7am–midnight, Fri & Sat 7am–1am.

★ **The Hawthorne** 500A Commonwealth Ave, in the Hotel Commonwealth, Kenmore Square ☎ 617 532 9150, ⓦ thehawthornebar.com; Kenmore T; map pp.162–163. Enchanting craft cocktail bar run by dressy bartending wizards. Pair a drink here with a game at Fenway Park (see p.170) and dinner at neighbouring *Island Creek* (see p.177) and you've got a great night out on the town. Daily 5pm–2am.

Lower Depths Taproom 476 Commonwealth Ave, Kenmore Square ☎ 617 266 6662, ⓦ thelowerdepths .com; Kenmore T; map pp.162–163. A down-home addition to the ballpark scene, this attractive pub is known for its extensive beer selection (17 on tap, plus 160 in bottles), home-made pretzels ($4) and $1 hot dogs. Cash only; beer and wine only. Daily 11.30am–1am.

Lucky's 355 Congress St, Fort Point Channel ☎ 617 357 5825, ⓦ luckyslounge.com; South Station or World Trade Center T; map pp.162–163. Over the water in the Fort Point neighbourhood, and quite a walk from the subway, this underground lounge is one of Boston's best-kept secrets (there's no sign out front). Inside is a 1950s pad complete with martini-swilling patrons and live jazz; on Sundays, Frank Sinatra impersonators get the locals swinging. Mon–Fri 11am–2am, Sat & Sun 10am–2am.

Middlesex 315 Massachusetts Ave, Cambridge ☎ 617 868 6739, ⓦ middlesexlounge.us; Central T; map pp.172–173. A slightly hipper-than-thou vibe, but the

gorgeous space (exposed brick, pale wood panelling) makes you want to dress to impress. There are queues out the door for its nights of electro-retro dance (cover free to $10). Mon–Wed 5pm–1am, Thurs–Sat 5pm–2am, Sun check online calendar.

★ **Miracle of Science Bar & Grill** 321 Massachusetts Ave, Cambridge ☎ 617 868 2866, ⓦ miracleofscience .us; Central T or #1 bus; map pp.172–173. Surprisingly hip despite its status as an MIT hangout, this popular bar has a science-themed decor and a laidback, unpretentious crowd, though it can get quite crowded on weekend nights. The bar stools will conjure up memories of high school chemistry class. Mon–Fri 11am–1am, Sat & Sun 9am–1am.

Shay's 58 JFK St, Cambridge ☎ 617 864 9161, ⓦ shays pubandwinebar.com; Harvard T; map pp.172–173. Unwind with grad students over wine and quality beer at this relaxed hideaway with a welcome little outdoor patio and plates overflowing with nachos. Mon–Sat 11am–1am, Sun noon–1am.

LIVE MUSIC VENUES

The Beehive 541 Tremont St, in the Boston Center for the Arts, South End ☎ 617 423 0069, ⓦ beehiveboston .com; Back Bay T; map pp.162–163. With chandeliers dripping from the ceiling, a red-curtained stage and knock-you-down cocktails, the *Beehive* exudes a vaudeville vibe, complete with jazz, cabaret or burlesque shows nearly every night. No cover. Mon–Wed 5pm–1am, Thurs & Fri 5pm–2am, Sat & Sun 10am–1am.

Club Passim 47 Palmer St, Cambridge ☎ 617 492 7679, ⓦ clubpassim.org; Harvard T; map pp.172–173. Legendary folkie hangout where Joan Baez and Suzanne Vega got their starts. Acoustic music, folk, blues and jazz in a windowed basement setting. Cover around $15. Daily 6–11pm.

Middle East 472 Massachusetts Ave, Cambridge ☎ 617 864 3278, ⓦ mideastclub.com; Central T; map pp.172–173. Local and regional bands of every sort – rock to mambo to hardcore – stop in regularly at this Cambridge institution. Bigger acts are hosted downstairs; smaller ones ply their trade in a tiny upstairs space. A third venue, the *Corner*, has shows nightly that are usually free, with belly dancing every Sunday. Check online for performance times.

Paradise Rock Club 967 Commonwealth Ave, Allston ☎ 617 562 8800, ⓦ thedise.com; Pleasant St T; map pp.162–163. One of Boston's classic venues – having hosted Blondie, Elvis Costello and Tom Waits, to name a few – and as popular as it was 35 years ago. Tickets around $20. Check online for performance times.

Scullers DoubleTree hotel, 400 Soldiers Field Rd, Allston ☎ 617 562 4111, ⓦ scullersjazz.com; Central T; map pp.162–163. Genteel jazz club that draws five-star acts. You'll need to hop in a taxi to get here, as the walk along the river at night can be risky. Cover varies wildly – anything from $20 to $45. Check online for performance times.

BOSTON SPECTATOR SPORTS

Boston is undeniably a sports town. Ever since the Boston Red Stockings scored their first run in 1871, the city's devotion to baseball has raged to a nearly religious fervour. There's no shortage of **Patriots** football (ⓦpatriots.com), **Bruins** ice hockey (ⓦbruins.nhl.com) or **Celtics** basketball (ⓦnba.com/celtics) fans either. Baseball is treated with reverence in Boston, so it's appropriate that the city's team, the **Red Sox** (ⓦredsox.com), plays in one of the country's most celebrated ballparks, **Fenway Park** (see p.170). Though they compete in a stadium a long drive away, seeing a Patriots game live is a rare treat for non-season ticket holders. Both the Celtics and Bruins light up massive TDBanknorth Garden, a stadium in Boston's West End.

★ **Wally's Cafe** 427 Massachusetts Ave, Roxbury ☎617 424 1408, ⓦwallyscafe.com; Massachusetts Ave T; map pp.162–163. Founded in 1947, this jazz club is one of Boston's best assets. Refreshingly unhewn, it hosts lively jazz and blues shows nightly, drawing a diverse crowd. No cover. Mon–Sat 11am–1.30am, Sun noon–2am.

ENTERTAINMENT

Boston prides itself on being a sophisticated city, and nowhere does that show up more than in its proliferation of **orchestras** and **choral groups**. The city's **theatre scene** divides into the traditionally mainstream productions of the Theater District (often Broadway offshoots) and more experimental companies in Cambridge. There is also a healthy independent film scene, largely clustered in Cambridge.

BosTix Half-price, day-of-show ticket booth with two outlets: Copley Square, at the corner of Dartmouth and Boylston sts, and Faneuil Hall Marketplace (both Tues–Sat 10am–6pm, Sun 11am–4pm; ☎617 262 8632 ext 229, ⓦbostix.org).

Brattle Theatre 40 Brattle St, Cambridge ☎617 876 6837, ⓦbrattlefilm.org; Harvard T. A historic indie cinema that pleasantly looks its age. Hosts themed film series plus occasional author appearances and readings; beer and wine are served alongside hot popcorn.

Citi Performing Arts Center 270 Tremont St ☎617 482 9393, ⓦciticenter.org; Boylston T. Two classic venues have been rebranded under the Citi Center moniker: the

Wang is the biggest performance centre in Boston, a movie house of palatial proportions; the Shubert, dubbed the "Little Princess" has been restored to its pretty, early 1900s appearance. Both host large-scale dance performances, theatre productions and rock shows.

Symphony Hall 301 Massachusetts Ave ☎888 266 1492 (event information) or ☎888 266 1200 (box office), ⓦbso.org; Symphony T. The dignified, acoustically perfect venue for the prestigious Boston Symphony Orchestra. The famous Boston Pops concerts happen in May and June (as well as their signature show on July 4); in July and Aug, the BSO retreats to Tanglewood, in the Berkshires (see p.196).

Lexington and Concord

On the night of April 18, 1775, **Paul Revere** rode down what is now Massachusetts Avenue from Boston, racing through Cambridge and Arlington on his way to warn the American patriots gathered at **Lexington** (14 miles to the west) of an impending British attack. Close behind him was a force of more than seven hundred British soldiers, intent on seizing supplies hoarded by the local militia. Today, Revolutionary War history is evoked here in a piecemeal but enthusiastic fashion in the **Minute Man National Historical Park**, with scale models, remnant musketry and the odd preserved bullet hole. **Concord** (where the Patriots' supplies were held) continues the Independence theme, though the town's literary associations are just as much, if not more, of a draw.

Minuteman National Historical Park

Buckman Tavern 1 Bedford St • Daily April–Oct 10am–4pm; guided tour every 30min • ☎781 862 5598 **Hancock-Clarke House** 36 Hancock St • April–May call for hours; June–Oct daily 10am–4pm, guided tours hourly • ☎781 861 0928 **Munroe Tavern** 1332 Massachusetts Ave • April–May, call for hours; June–Oct daily noon–4pm, guided tours hourly • ☎781 862 0295 • All three sites can all be visited on a joint ticket for $12; otherwise admission to each one is $7 • ⓦlexingtonhistory.org

Although much of Revere's route has been turned into major thoroughfares, the various settings of the first military confrontation of the Revolutionary War – "the shot heard 'round the world" – remain much as they were then. The triangular **Town Common** at Lexington was where the British encountered their first opposition. Captain John Parker ordered his 77 American "**Minutemen**" to "stand your ground. Don't fire unless fired upon, but if they mean to have a war let it begin here". No one knows who fired the first shot, but the eight soldiers who died are buried beneath an affecting memorial at the northwestern end of the park. Guides in period costume lead tours of the **Buckman Tavern**, where the Minutemen waited for the British to arrive; the **Hancock-Clarke House**, a quarter of a mile north, where Samuel Adams and John Hancock were awakened by Paul Revere, is now a museum. The **Munroe Tavern** served as a field hospital for British soldiers, though only for ninety minutes. It now houses the **Museum of the British Redcoats**, which gives a British perspective on the events of April 19, 1775.

By the time the British soldiers marched on Concord, on the morning after the encounter in Lexington, the surrounding countryside was up in arms, and the Revolutionary War was in full swing. In running battles in the town itself, and along the still-evocative **Battle Road** leading back toward Boston, 73 British soldiers and 49 colonials were killed over the next two days.

3

Orchard House

399 Lexington Rd, Concord • Tours: April–Oct Mon–Sat 10am–4.30pm, Sun 1–4.30pm; Nov–March Mon–Fri 11am–3pm, Sat 10am–4.30pm, Sun 1–4.30pm • $10 • ☎ 978 369 4118, ⊛ louisamayalcott.org

Just outside Concord, the area's rich **literary heritage** is the focus at **Orchard House**, where Louisa May Alcott lived from 1858 to 1877 and wrote *Little Women*. The guided tour is well worth your time; although it focuses heavily on the differences between Alcott's life and her most famous book, it is also the best way to get a good understanding of the area's strong nineteenth-century literary, intellectual and liberal activist community.

Walden Pond State Reservation

South of Concord on Rte-126 • Daily sunrise to sunset • Parking $5 • ☎ 978 369 3254, ⊛ mass.gov

Walden Pond was where Henry David Thoreau conducted the experiment in solitude and self-sufficiency described in his 1854 book *Walden*. The site where his log cabin once stood is marked with stones, and at dawn you can still watch the pond "throwing off its nightly clothing of mist" (at midday, it's a great spot for swimming and hiking). Thoreau is interred, along with Ralph Waldo Emerson, Nathaniel Hawthorne and Louisa May Alcott, atop a hill in **Sleepy Hollow Cemetery**, just east of the centre of Concord.

ARRIVAL, INFORMATION AND TOURS

LEXINGTON AND CONCORD

By bus Buses run to Lexington from Alewife Station (15min; $2), at the northern end of the Red T line.

By train Trains from Boston's North Station pull in at Concord Depot (40–45min; $8.50 one-way), a stiff 1.5-mile walk from the centre.

Visitor centre 250 North Great Rd (Rte-2A), Lincoln (daily: April–Oct 9am–5pm; Nov 9am–4pm; ☎ 978 369 6993,

⊛ nps.gov/mima). The headquarters for the Minuteman National Historical Park offers the best orientation on the area.

Tours Liberty Ride (June–Oct daily 10am–4pm; April & May Sat & Sun only; $25 for two days; ☎ 781 862 0500 ext. 260, ⊛ libertyride.us) operates a hop-on, hop-off service, stopping at all the main sights.

EATING AND DRINKING

80 Thoreau 80 Thoreau St, Concord ☎ 978 318 0008, ⊛ 80thoreau.com. While Concord may be long on Revolutionary War heroes, historically it has been short on culinary trailblazers. Enter *80 Thoreau*, an epicurean favourite drawing foodies all the way from restaurant-mad Boston. Mains $20–31. Mon–Thurs 5.30–10.30pm, Fri & Sat 5.30–11.30pm.

La Provence 105–107 Thoreau St, Concord ☎ 978 371 7428, ⊛ laprovence.us. Authentic French cooking in a colourful, casual dining room with friendly counter service.

The chicken Provence sandwich ($6.80) has a tangy mustard kick, and makes a nice accompaniment to the red bliss potato salad ($6.95/lb). There's also an exquisite on-site bakery. Mon–Fri 7am–7pm, Sat 7am–5.30pm.

Royal India Bistro 7 Meriam St, Lexington ☎ 781 861 7350, ⊛ bistroroyalindia.com. Top-notch Indian food and stellar service in a cosy, central, family-run place near the Town Common. Mains cost about $13. Mon–Thurs & Sun 11.30am–10.30pm, Fri & Sat 11.30am–11pm.

Salem

SALEM is remembered less as the site where the colony of Massachusetts was first established than as the place where, sixty years later, Puritan self-righteousness reached its apogee in the horrific **witch trials** of 1692. Nineteen Salem women were hanged as witches (and one man, Giles Corey, was pressed to death with a boulder), thanks to a group of impressionable teenage girls who reported as truth a garbled mixture of fireside tales told by a West Indian slave, Tituba, and scare stories published by Cotton Mather, a pillar of the Puritan community. In the eighteenth and nineteenth centuries, Salem hit its stride as a flourishing seaport, and the remnants from this era only add to the town's historic ambience – with abandoned wharves, rows of stately sea captains' homes and an astounding display of riches at the **Peabody Essex Museum**.

Salem Witch Museum

19 1/2 Washington Square N • Daily: July & Aug 10am–7pm; Sept–June 10am–5pm • $9 • ☎ 978 744 1692, ⓦ salemwitchmuseum.com

The **Salem Witch Museum** provides some entertaining, if kitschy, orientation on the witch trials. Really just a sound-and-light show that uses wax figures to depict the events, it's still better than the other "museums" in town. In front of the house is an imposing statue of a caped **Roger Conant**, founder of Salem's first Puritan settlement.

Peabody Essex Museum

161 Essex St • Tues–Sun 10am–5pm, third Thurs of the month till 9.30pm • $15 • ☎ 978 745 9500, ⓦ pem.org

Salem's crown jewel is the **Peabody Essex Museum**, whose vast, modern space incorporates more than thirty galleries filled with remarkable *objets* brought home by voyaging New Englanders. Founded by a ship captain in 1799, the museum has stellar Oceanic, African, contemporary art and Asian displays, most notably the **Yin Yu Tang** ($5 extra), a stunning sixteen-room Qing dynasty merchant's house reassembled here in Salem.

Salem Maritime National Historic Site

Main visitor centre 2 New Liberty St • Mon–Fri & Sun 10am–5pm, Sat 9am–5pm • **Tours** Daily $5 • ☎ 978 740 1650, ⓦ nps.gov/sama

The remnants of Salem's original waterfront have been preserved as the **Salem Maritime National Historic Site**. The chief sights – opulent Derby House and the imposing Custom House, where writer Nathaniel Hawthorne once worked as a surveyor – can only be visited on daily one-hour tours.

House of Seven Gables

115 Derby St • Daily: July–Oct 10am–7pm; Nov–June 10am–5pm, closed first half of Jan • $12.50 • ☎ 978 744 0991, ⓦ 7gables.org

The **House of Seven Gables**, the star of Hawthorne's eponymous novel, is a rambling old mansion beside the sea. Tours of the 1668 house – the oldest surviving wooden mansion in New England – cover the building's history and architecture. The author's birthplace, a small, burgundy, c.1750 structure, was moved here from Union Street in 1958.

WHALE-WATCHING ON CAPE ANN

As you head north out of Boston, you pass through a succession of rich little ports that have been all but swallowed up by the suburbs. One of the most popular and exhilarating activities along this stretch of coast is **whale-watching**: trips depart from Gloucester, Salem and Newburyport to whale feeding grounds, where an abundance of plankton and small fish provide sufficient calories (around one million a day) to keep 50ft, 25-ton **humpbacks** happy. Gloucester whale-watching companies include the Yankee Fleet, 37 Commercial St (☎ 800 942 5464, ⓦ yankeefleet.com); Captain Bill & Sons (☎ 800 339 4253, ⓦ captbillandsons.com) at 24 Harbor Loop; and Cape Ann Whale Watch, at 415 Main St (☎ 800 877 5110, ⓦ seethewhales .com). During July and August, each company offers two daily trips (around $48; May, June & Sept Mon–Fri 1 daily, Sat & Sun 2 daily; Oct 1 daily).

ARRIVAL AND DEPARTURE

By bus There's a regular MBTA bus (50min; $4.50) from Haymarket in Boston.

By train MBTA commuter trains run hourly (30min; $6.75 one-way) between Boston's North Station and Salem.

By ferry A high-speed ferry (late May to Oct; $27 return;

SALEM

☎617 227 4321, ⓦbostonharborcruises.com), runs from Long Wharf in Boston to Salem's Blaney Street dock. Advance purchase is recommended. It's advisable to take the ferry or train in October, as the roads get very congested due to Halloween festivities.

ACCOMMODATION AND EATING

Hawthorne Hotel 18 Washington Square W ☎978 744 4080, ⓦhawthornehotel.com. Right in the heart of things, this full-service hotel is a Salem landmark with reasonable prices and a respectable restaurant and pub. Built in 1925, it has 89 rooms furnished with eighteenth-century reproduction furniture, iPod docks and flat-screen TVs. **$129**

★ **Northey Street House Bed and Breakfast** 30

Northey St ☎978 397 1582, ⓦnortheystreethouse .com. Big, blue 1809 Federal house with three comfortable rooms and one apartment for four. The Garden Room has modern, Asian-inspired decor and opens onto a garden with raspberries, Japanese maples and a little koi fishpond. The affable host encourages a no-indoor-shoes policy, with slippers provided. Doubles **$160**, apartment **$210**

EATING

62 Restaurant 62 Wharf St ☎978 744 0062, ⓦ62restaurant.com. Contemporary Italian trattoria renowned for its outstanding service, with home-made pasta dishes and small plates (try the mozzarella-stuffed *arancini*; $7) alongside pricier mains such as pan-roasted duck with grilled peaches ($26). Save room for the warm toffee pudding ($8). Tues–Sat 5–10pm (bar till midnight), Sun 5–9pm (bar till 10pm).

★ **A&J King Artisan Bakers** 48 Central St ☎978 744 4881, ⓦajkingbakery.com. Hidden on a side street with terrible parking, this to-die-for bakery has gooey sticky

buns, crusty loaves of bread and plump little carrot cakes. You can also pick up artisanal sandwiches, such as smoked salmon with crème fraîche and alfalfa sprouts ($7.75). Mon–Fri 7am–6pm, Sat & Sun 7am–4pm.

Life Alive 281 Essex St ☎978 594 4644, ⓦlifealive .com. A few blocks from the train station, this regional favourite is part café and part health store, with a huge range of smoothies and tasty organic and vegetarian meals such as "The Goddess" wrap, a blend of carrots, beets, broccoli, tofu, ginger sauce and brown rice ($9). Mon–Sat 8am–10pm, Sun 11am–8pm.

Plymouth

PLYMOUTH, America's so-called "hometown", is best known for being the first permanent settlement established by the English **Pilgrims** in 1620. The town is mostly given over to commemorating their landing, and needs only be visited by people with a real interest in the story. Its attractions lie in the centre, along the waterfront or in the historic district.

Plymouth Rock

The most famous sight in town is **Plymouth Rock**, on the waterfront at North and Water streets, and sheltered by a pseudo-Greek temple on the seashore where the Pilgrims are said to have first touched land. It is really of symbolic importance only: the rock was identified in 1741, no one can be sure where exactly they did land, and the Pilgrims had in fact already spent several weeks on Cape Cod before coming here.

Mayflower II

Docked at the State Pier on Water St • Daily 9am–5pm • $10, combined ticket with Plimoth Plantation $29.95 • ☎508 746 1622, ⓦplimoth.org

The best sight in Plymouth is the **Mayflower II**, a replica of the original *Mayflower*. This version meticulously reproduces the brown hull and red strapwork that were typical of a seventeenth-century merchant vessel – which is what the original was, before being "outfitted" for passengers prior to its horrendous 66-day journey across the Atlantic. On board, role-playing "interpreters" in period garb, meant to represent the Pilgrim passengers, field questions.

Plimoth Plantation

137 Warren Ave • Daily 9am–5pm • $25.95, combined ticket with Mayflower II $29.95 • ☎ 508 746 1622, ⊛ plimoth.org

Similar to the *Mayflower II* in approach and authenticity is the **Plimoth Plantation**, three miles south of town off Rte-3. Here, a recreation of "Plimoth" c.1627, as well as a Wampanoag settlement, have been built using traditional techniques. At the English village, visitors are expected to participate in a charade and pretend to have stepped back into the seventeenth century – which, depending on your mood, can be quite enjoyable. Exchanges in the Wampanoag village are less structured, with the Native American staff wearing traditional clothes (but not role-playing) and happy to chat about native customs.

ARRIVAL AND INFORMATION   PLYMOUTH

By bus Plymouth & Brockton buses (☎ 508 746 0378, ⊛ p-b.com) run from Boston ($20), stopping at the Park and Ride lot at exit 5 off Rte-3, where a local shuttle makes stops around town before heading to Plimoth Plantation (May–Aug Fri–Sun; $15 all-day re-boarding pass).

Visitor centre 130 Water St (daily: June–Aug 8am–8pm; Sept–May 9am–5pm; ☎ 508 747 7525, ⊛ seeplymouth .com).

ACCOMMODATION, EATING AND DRINKING

Best Western Cold Spring 180 Court St ☎ 508 746 2222, ⊛ bestwestern.com. This appealing hotel, comprised of a set of small buildings on a leafy campus, has clean, modern rooms with flat-screen TVs, a swimming pool with views of Cape Cod bay, laundry facilities and a complimentary breakfast. __$150__

Blue Blinds Bakery 7 North St ☎ 508 747 0462, ⊛ blueblindsbakery.com. "Just a block from the Rock", and set in a bygone-era house with a wide porch and an antique cash register, this café has a small but delectable breakfast and lunch menu (pancakes, granola with yogurt, sandwiches and soups) and irresistible baked goods. Mon–Thurs 6am–9pm, Fri 6am–3pm, Sun 7am–3pm.

Blue-Eyed Crab 170 Water St ☎ 508 747 6776, ⊛ blue-eyedcrab.com. This merry seafood favourite has a cheerful, tropical-themed menu and ambience. The scallop salad comes with mesclun greens, mango and jicama ($12.95), while the crab burger is topped with avocado and pickled jalapeños ($12.95). Dinner mains are around $23. Mon–Thurs & Sun 11.30am–9pm, Fri 11.30am–10pm, Sat noon–10pm.

By the Sea 22 Winslow St ☎ 508 830 9643, ⊛ bytheseabedandbreakfast.com. Close to Plymouth Rock, this B&B offers three spacious, newly renovated suites with harbour views. The hosts serve a "jumpstart" in the morning (coffee and pastries), and give breakfast vouchers redeemable at area businesses, one of which is the lovely *Blue Blinds* (see above). __$175__

New Bedford

The old whaling port of **NEW BEDFORD**, 55 miles due south of Boston, was immortalized at the start of Herman Melville's *Moby Dick*, and is still home to one of the nation's most active fishing fleets. Much of the downtown and working waterfront area is preserved within the **New Bedford Whaling National Historic Park** (visitor centre at 33 Williams St, daily 9am–5pm; ☎ 508 996 4095, ⊛ nps.gov/nebe), the centrepiece of which is the impressive **New Bedford Whaling Museum** at 18 Johnny Cake Hill (May–Sept daily 9am–5pm; Oct–April Tues–Sat 9am–4pm, Sun 11am–4pm; every second Thurs of the month till 8pm; $14; ☎ 508 997 0046, ⊛ whalingmuseum.org), featuring a 66ft blue whale skeleton, collections of scrimshaw and harpoons, and an evocative half-sized whaling vessel replica. More affecting is the **Seamen's Bethel** directly opposite (late May to mid-Oct daily 10am–4pm; free; ☎ 508 992 3295, ⊛ portsociety.org); the chapel really does have the ship-shaped pulpit described in *Moby Dick*, though this one was rebuilt after a fire in 1866.

Audubon's Birds of America

613 Pleasant St • Tues & Wed 1–5pm, Thurs 1–5pm & 6–9pm, Fri 9am–12.30pm, Sat 9am–1pm & 2–5pm, also open by appointment • Free • ☎ 508 991 6275

One of New Bedford's most exceptional attractions is **Audubon's Birds of America**, housed in the city's handsome nineteenth-century public library. John James Audubon, a famed ornithologist and artist, composed this collection of 435 **engravings** between

1827 and 1839. To create the works, he developed a groundbreaking technique wherein he studied each bird's habits and positions out in the field (before shooting them); the resulting prints were hand-painted and the true-to-life images mailed in sets to subscribers. New Bedford's library is one of just 119 institutions in the world with a complete folio, stored here in the third-floor art room. At any given time, ten of the huge prints are out on display (viewable only with a staff member present); if there's a specific bird you'd like to see, however, **call ahead** and helpful librarians will have it ready.

ACCOMMODATION AND EATING NEW BEDFORD

Antonio's 267 Coggeshall St ☎508 990 3636, ⓦantoniosnewbedford.com. Authentic Portuguese dishes at a popular restaurant a mile outside downtown. Cash only. Mon–Thurs & Sun 11.30am–9.30pm, Fri & Sat 11.30am–10pm.

Brick Pizzeria Napoletana 163 Union St ☎508 999 4943, ⓦpizzeriabrick.com. Sumptuous brick-oven pizzas sprinkled with toppings such as hot salami and olives ($10) or prosciutto, artichokes and goat's cheese ($12). They're ready in minutes. Mon–Sat 11am–9pm, Sun noon–8pm.

No Problemo 813 Purchase St ☎508 984 1081, ⓦnoproblemotaqueria.com. Whale-sized burritos, *taquitos* and zesty sangria are served up by tattooed staff at this hip taqueria and bar with Day of the Dead decor. Cash only. Mon–Wed 11am–9pm, Thurs–Sat 11am–10pm, Sun noon–8pm.

Orchard Street Manor 139 Orchard St ☎508 984 3475, ⓦthe-orchard-street-manor.com. In a nineteenth-century whaling captain's home, this atmospheric B&B has Moroccan accoutrements, antique chandeliers, a vintage pool table and great breakfasts. **$125**

Cape Cod and the islands

One of the most celebrated slices of real estate in America, **Cape Cod** boasts a dazzling, three-hundred-mile coastline with some of the best beaches in New England. A slender, crooked peninsula, it's easily accessed from the region's snug villages, many of which have been preserved as they were a hundred or more years ago.

Cape Cod was named by Bartholomew Gosnold in 1602, on account of the prodigious quantities of cod caught by his crew off Provincetown. Less than twenty years later the Pilgrims landed nearby, before moving on to Plymouth. Today, much of the land on the Cape, from its salt marshes to its ever-eroding dunes, is considered a fragile and endangered ecosystem, and once you head north to the **Outer Cape**, past the spectacular dunes of **Cape Cod National Seashore**, you get a feeling for why this narrow spit of land still has a reputation as a seaside wilderness. **Provincetown**, at the very tip of Cape Cod, is a popular gay resort and summer destination for bohemians, artists and fun-seekers lured by the excellent beaches, art galleries and welcoming atmosphere.

Just off the south coast of Cape Cod, the relatively unspoiled islands of **Martha's Vineyard** and **Nantucket** have long been some of the most popular and prestigious vacation destinations in the USA. Both mingle an easy-going cosmopolitan atmosphere and some of the best restaurants and B&Bs on the East Coast. Nantucket is usually considered the more highfalutin' of the pair, teased for its preppy fashions; Martha is more expansive and laidback, known for its elaborate gingerbread-style houses, wild moorlands and perfect beaches.

ARRIVAL AND DEPARTURE CAPE COD AND THE ISLANDS

By car When the Cape Cod Canal was finally completed at the start of the twentieth century, it turned the Cape Cod peninsula into an island. Now all traffic bottlenecks at two enormous bridges across the waterway – Bourne on Hwy-28 and Sagamore on Hwy-6 – and you may regret trying to drive there on a summer Friday (or back on a Sun).

By plane A number of airlines go direct to Cape Cod, including Cape Air (☎800 352 0714, ⓦcapeair.com), which flies to Hyannis and Provincetown from Boston several times a day.

By bus Peter Pan Bus Lines subsidiary Bonanza (☎888 751 8800, ⓦpeterpanbus.com) operates services from Boston (one-way $27) and New York (one-way $65) to Woods Hole and Falmouth, while Plymouth & Brockton (☎508 746 0378, ⓦp-b.com) has a more complete set of Cape destinations (one-way Boston to Hyannis $19, to Provincetown $29).

By ferry Ferries from Boston (see p.172) take 90min to cross to Provincetown; there are boats to the various islands (see box, p.192).

The Cape's southern coast

From the Bourne Bridge, **Rte-28** runs south to Falmouth then hugs the Nantucket Sound until it merges with routes 6 and 6A in Orleans. Pleasant Falmouth makes a diverting jump-off point for ferries to Martha's Vineyard. Further up, Hyannis, the commercial hub of Cape Cod, is quite commercialized and ferry-oriented, although it does have a number of good beaches and watering holes.

Falmouth and Woods Hole

Boasting more coastline than any other Cape Cod town, **Falmouth** has no fewer than fourteen harbours among its eight villages. At the centre of these is **Falmouth Village**, with a prim central green surrounded by Federal and Greek Revival homes. The small town of **Woods Hole**, four miles southwest, owes its name to the water passage, or "hole", between Penzance Point and Nonamesset Island. Most people come here for the ferry to Martha's Vineyard (see box, p.192), as it's little more than picture-perfect Nobska Point Lighthouse and a few restaurants.

Hyannis

It stands to reason that **HYANNIS** – the largest port on the Cape, and its main commercial hub – would be a little less charming than Falmouth and Woods Hole. Nevertheless, it still sparkles a bit from the glamour it earned when the **Kennedy compound** at Hyannisport placed it at the centre of world affairs. Hence the existence of the **John F. Kennedy Museum** (mid-April to late May Mon–Sat 10am–4pm, Sun noon–4pm; June–Oct Mon–Sat 9am–5pm, Sun noon–5pm; Nov Fri & Sat 10am–4pm, Sun noon–4pm; mid-Feb to early April Thurs–Sat 10am–4pm, Sun noon–4pm; $8; ☏ 508 790 3077, ⓦ jfkhyannismuseum.org), which shows photographs, news clippings and film footage of the days JFK spent on the Cape.

3

ACCOMMODATION	THE CAPE'S SOUTHERN COAST

FALMOUTH

Captain's Manor Inn 27 W Main St ☏ 508 388 7336, ⓦ captainsmanorinn.com. Dating from 1849, this gorgeously restored sea captain's home is done up with Greek Revival accents – intended to please the original owner's Southern bride. The obliging hosts provide lots of pampering perks including home-made snacks and a nightly turndown service. **$230**

Inn on the Sound 313 Grand Ave ☏ 508 457 9666, ⓦ innonthesound.com. A stunning location (45ft above the bay), mesmerizing views and gourmet food make this posh B&B a real treat, with luxury linens and a well-stocked library. **$225**

WOODS HOLE

Woods Hole Inn 28 Water St ☏ 508 495 0248, ⓦ woods holeinn.com. In an unbeatable location just steps from the ferry terminal, this eco-friendly inn has fourteen colourful quarters artfully done up with luxury linens and iPod docks. Parking and home-made breakfast is included. **$235**

HYANNIS

HI-Hyannis 111 Ocean St ☏ 508 775 7990, ⓦ hiusa .org/hyannis. Directly across from the ferry docks, this inviting hostel has 37 beds (mainly dorms) in a spacious shingled house. Free continental breakfast and internet access. Open late May to mid-Oct. Dorms **$35**

Sea Coast Inn 33 Ocean St ☏ 800 466 4100, ⓦ sea coastcapecod.com. Clean and functional motel-style accommodation close to the ferry docks; the helpful owners throw in free breakfast and internet. Open May–Oct. **$128**

EATING

FALMOUTH

The Glass Onion 37 N Main St ☏ 508 540 3730, ⓦ theglassoniondining.com. Swish New American restaurant firing off some of the Cape's best cuisine. Order the seared sea scallop salad with cucumber noodles ($25) for entry into seafood heaven. Mon–Sat 5pm–late.

★ **The Pickle Jar** 170 Main St ☏ 508 540 6760, ⓦ picklejarkitchen.com. They cure their pastrami in-house, smoke their salmon and spice their own pickles at this superb breakfast and lunch spot just off the town green. Breakfast sees griddle cakes ($8) and granola and yogurt parfaits ($9), lunch has chicken sandwiches with boursin cheese, cucumber and dill aioli ($9). Don't miss the fried pickle chips ($7). 7am–3pm; closed Tues.

WOODS HOLE

Pie in the Sky Bakery 10 Water St ☎ 508 540 5475, ⓦ woodshole.com/pie. Right by the ferry terminal. Stock up here before heading over to Martha's Vineyard: puffy popovers, "wonder bars" baked with chocolate, giant cookies, fresh sandwiches, soups and salads are all on offer. It's a tiny place, packed with colourful glass bottles and art in a wooden alcove overlooking the harbour. Daily 5am–10pm.

HYANNIS

Brazilian Grill 680 Main St ☎ 508 771 0109, ⓦ braziliangrill-capecod.com. Be sure to indulge in the full *rodizio* ($31.95) at this *churrascaria* – a carnivore's paradise where mouth-watering meats are delivered straight from hand-held skewers to diners' plates. There's also an overflowing buffet with plenty of vegetarian options. Mon–Fri 11.30am–9pm, Sat & Sun 11.30am–10pm.

★ **Four Seas Ice Cream** 360 S Main St, Centerville ☎ 508 775 1394. Since 1934, this scoop shop near Craigville Beach has been the place to go for unbeatable ice cream cones. Mid-May to mid-Sept daily 9am–9.30pm (until 10.30pm in July & Aug).

Raw Bar 230 Ocean St ☎ 508 775 8800. Next to the ferry dock, this crowd-pleaser serves up plenty of raw shellfish in addition to a mean lobster roll and Jamaican jerk chicken wings. Good views from the spacious porch. Daily 11am–11pm.

The Mid-Cape

The middle stretch of Cape Cod holds some of its prettiest, most unspoiled places. Timeworn fishing communities such as Wellfleet and Chatham, along with dozens of carefully maintained, mildly touristy hamlets along the many winding roads, are what most people hope to find when they come to the Cape. Cutting across the middle, the **Cape Cod Rail Trail** follows a paved-over railroad track from Dennis to Eastham, through forests and cranberry bogs. It makes a good **cycling** trip; bikes can be rented in all the main towns.

The genteel, whitewashed town of **CHATHAM** is tucked away in a protected harbour between Nantucket Sound and the open Atlantic Ocean. Hang out at the **Fish Pier** on Shore Road and wait for the fleet to come in during the mid-afternoon, or head a mile south on Hwy-28 to **Chatham Light**, one of many lighthouses built to protect mariners from the treacherous shoals.

ACCOMMODATION AND EATING   **THE MID-CAPE**

The Captain's House Inn 369–377 Old Harbor Rd, Chatham ☎ 508 945 0127, ⓦ captainshouseinn.com. Sumptuously renovated 1839 Greek Revival whaling captain's home; most rooms have fireplaces, and rates include delicious breakfasts and afternoon tea with freshly baked scones. **$270**

Chatham Pier Fish Market 45 Barcliff Ave Ext, Chatham ☎ 508 945 3474, ⓦ chathampierfishmarket .com. Order lobster rolls and inexpensive plates of delectable fried seafood while fishermen unload their catch and seals bob just beyond. May–Oct daily 10am–8pm.

★ **Marion's Pie Shop** 2022 Main St (Rte-28), Chatham ☎ 508 432 9439. Delicious sweet apple pies, savoury chicken pies and yummy breakfast cinnamon rolls. Note that "misbehaving children will be made into pies". June–Aug Mon–Sat 8am–6pm, Sun 8am–4pm; Sept–May Tues–Sat 8am–5pm, Sun 8am–4pm.

Pleasant Bay Village Resort Motel 1191 Orleans Rd, Chatham ☎ 508 945 1133, ⓦ pleasantbayvillage.com. Among the more affordable digs in town, with spacious, clean motel rooms (suites available), a pool and jacuzzi, and stunning gardens tucked inside six acres of woodlands. Open May–Oct. **$155**

Cape Cod National Seashore

After the bustle of Cape Cod's towns, the **Cape Cod National Seashore** really does come as a proverbial breath of fresh air. These protected lands, spared by President Kennedy from the development further south, take up virtually the entire Atlantic side of the Cape, from Chatham north to Provincetown. Most of the way you can park by the road, and strike off across the dunes to windswept, seemingly endless beaches.

Displays and movies at the main **Salt Pond Visitor Center**, on US-6 just north of Eastham (daily 9am–4.30pm, till 5pm July & Aug; ☎ 508 255 3421, ⓦ nps.gov/caco), trace the geology and history of the Cape. A road and a hiking and cycling trail head east to the sands of **Coast Guard Beach** and **Nauset Light Beach**, both of which offer excellent swimming.

ACCOMMODATION   CAPE COD NATIONAL SEASHORE

HI-Truro 111 N Pamet Rd, Truro ☎508 349 3889, ⓦ hiusa.org. One of the east coast's best hostels: 42 dorm beds in a capacious former Coast Guard station that's a stone's throw from the beach. Dorms **$39**

Provincetown

The compact fishing village of **PROVINCETOWN** (or, as it's popularly known, "P-Town") is a gorgeous place, with silvery clapboard houses and gloriously unruly gardens lining the town's tiny, winding streets. Bohemians and artists have long flocked here for the quality of light and vast beaches; in 1914 Eugene O'Neill (see p.204) established the Provincetown Playhouse here in a small hut. Since the Beatnik 1950s, the town has also been a **gay** centre, and today its population of five thousand rises tenfold in the summer. Commercialism, though quite visible along the main drags, tends to be countercultural: gay, environmental and feminist gift shops join arty galleries, restaurants and bars on the aptly named **Commercial Street**. However, strict zoning ensures that there are few new buildings in town. Albeit crowded and raucous from July through to September, P-Town remains a place where history, natural beauty and, above all, difference, are respected and celebrated.

Provincetown lies 120 miles from Boston by land, but less than fifty miles by sea, nestled in the New England coast's largest natural harbour. Its tiny core is centred on

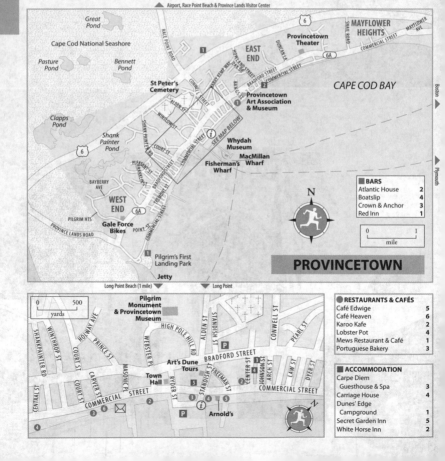

the three narrow miles of **Commercial Street**. **MacMillan Pier**, always busy with charters, yachts and fishing boats (which unload their catch each afternoon), splits the town in half. East of the centre (but still on Commercial St), are scores of quaint art galleries, as well as the delightful **Provincetown Art Association and Museum** (late May to Sept Mon–Thurs 11am–8pm, Fri 11am–10pm, Sat & Sun 11am–5pm; Oct to mid-May Thurs–Sun noon–5pm; $10; ☎508 487 1750, ⓦpaam.org), which rotates works from its two-thousand-strong collection.

Pilgrim Monument and Provincetown Museum

High Pole Hill Rd • Daily: April to mid-May & mid-Sept to Nov 9am–5pm; late May to early Sept 9am–7pm • $12 • ☎508 487 1310, ⓦpilgrim-monument.org

Looming above the centre of P-Town, the **Pilgrim Monument and Provincetown Museum** has permanent exhibits giving a fairly romantic account of the Pilgrim story and subsequent history of the town, along with a 252ft granite tower with an observation deck (accessible by 116 stairs) that looks out over the whole of the Cape.

The beaches

A little way beyond the town's narrow strip of sand, undeveloped **beaches** are marked only by dunes and a few shabby beach huts. You can swim in the clear water from the uneven rocks of the two-mile breakwater, or find blissful isolation on undeveloped beaches nearby. West of town, **Herring Cove Beach**, easily reached by bike or through the dunes, is more crowded, but never unbearably so. In the wild **Province Lands**, at the Cape's northern tip, vast sweeping moors and bushy dunes are buffeted by Cape Cod's deadly sea, the site of one thousand known shipwrecks. The **visitor centre** (May–Oct daily 9am–5pm; ☎508 487 1256), in the middle of the dunes on Race Point Road, has videos and displays highlighting the exceptionally fragile environment here.

3

ARRIVAL AND DEPARTURE   PROVINCETOWN

By ferry By far the nicest way to arrive is on one of the passenger ferries. Bay State Cruise Company (☎877 783 3779, ⓦbaystatecruisecompany.com) runs an express ferry in the summer three times a day from Boston's World Trade Center pier (90min express return $85), and a standard ferry (Sat only; return $46; 3hr), while Boston Harbor Cruises (☎617 227 4321, ⓦbostonharborcruises.com), offers express service from Boston's Long Wharf (May–Oct; 90min; return $85). By far the cheapest option is the Plymouth to Provincetown ferry (90min; return $43; ☎508 747 2400, ⓦp-townferry.com).

By bus A slower option is the Plymouth & Brockton bus, which runs to Provincetown four times daily from Boston via Hyannis ($29 one way from Boston; 3hr 45min; $10 one way from Hyannis; ☎508 746 0378, ⓦp-b.com).

GETTING AROUND

By bike It couldn't be easier to walk around tiny P-Town, though many visitors prefer to cycle the narrow streets, hills and the undulating Province Lands bike trail, an enchanting 6-mile route with great vistas. For rentals, Arnold's, 329 Commercial St (☎508 487 0844), right in the centre of town, is open from mid-April to mid-Oct, as is Gale Force Bikes, close to the bike trail at 144 Bradford St Ext (☎508 487 4849, ⓦgaleforcebikes.com). Bikes at both are about $20/day.

By bus The Cape Cod Regional Transit Authority (☎800 352 7155, ⓦcapecodtransit.org) runs frequent Flex route buses (daily 6.30am–10pm) connecting P-Town with other villages on the Cape; simply flag them down on the side of the road (except for Rte-6, for safety reasons) and cough up $2.

INFORMATION AND TOURS

Visitor centre In the Chamber of Commerce at the end of the wharf, 307 Commercial St (May–Oct daily 9am–5pm; Nov–April limited hours; ☎508 487 3424, ⓦptown chamber.com).

Dune tours Art's Dune Tours amble about the dunes in 4WD vehicles (4 Standish St; April–Oct 10am–dusk; $27;

☎508 487 1950, ⓦartsdunetours.com).

Whale-watching tours Dolphin Fleet, 132 Bradford St (April–Oct; $44; ☎508 240 3636, ⓦwhalewatch.com), is the best company for whale-watching, with 3–4hr cruises leaving frequently from MacMillan Pier.

ACCOMMODATION

Many of the most picturesque cottages in town are **guesthouses**, some with spectacular bay views – unsurprisingly, many are run by gay couples and are generally **gay-friendly**. The best area to be is the quiet West End, though anything on Bradford Street will also be removed from the summertime racket.

Carpe Diem Guesthouse & Spa 12–14 Johnson St ☎800 487 0132, ⓦcarpediemguesthouse.com. Friendly, accommodating owners, beautifully appointed rooms with a bit of an Eastern vibe, horseback riding, a spa and an afternoon wine and cheese hour at this B&B on a quiet side street. $249
Carriage House 7 Central St ☎800 309 0248, ⓦthe carriaghse.com. Fabulously maintained rooms, some with private decks, and all with DVD and CD players; gourmet breakfasts and a hot tub and sauna add soothing extras. $195
Dunes' Edge Campground Rte-6 just east of the central traffic lights ☎508 487 9815, ⓦdunesedge .com. Close to the beach and near to town, this campground has wooded sites, laundry facilities and hot showers. Open May–Sept. $42

Secret Garden Inn 300A Commercial St ☎508 487 9027, ⓦsecretgardenptown.com. This 1830s captain's house is a relative bargain, with seven quaint rooms done up in country furnishings, but with modern touches such as TVs and a/c. The inn has a veranda and splendid garden; country breakfast included. $119
White Horse Inn 500 Commercial St ☎508 487 1790. An eclectic art-strewn space in the quiet East End neighbourhood; some rooms have shared bathrooms. There are also family-sized apartments with kitchens. It's bygone-era Provincetown: no TVs or wi-fi, but there's a private strip of beach, a delightful owner and a beatnik vibe. Cash or cheque only. Open May–Sept. Rooms $70, apartments $185

EATING

Café Edwige 333 Commercial St ☎508 487 4020, ⓦedwigeatnight.com. Breakfast is the thing at this popular second-floor restaurant; try the home-made Danish pastries and fresh-fruit pancakes. Creative bistro food at dinner (mains $20–34). Daily 9am–10pm.
Café Heaven 199 Commercial St ☎508 487 9639. Massive breakfast plates (served through the afternoon), baguette sandwiches and local art make this a popular daytime choice, but it's the juicy hamburgers that really stand out. There's usually a wait to get in. Daily 8am–2pm & 6–10pm.
Karoo Kafe 338 Commercial St ☎508 487 6630, ⓦkaroorestaurants.com. Tasty, inexpensive South African food. Order the Cape Malay stew (curry, coconut milk and veggies over rice; $14) at the counter and enjoy it on sunny, zebra-striped seating. Daily 11am–9pm.
Lobster Pot 321 Commercial St ☎508 487 0842, ⓦptownlobsterpot.com. Its landmark neon sign is like

a beacon for those who come from far and wide for the ultra-fresh crustaceans. Affordable (lobster ravioli $11; clam chowder $5–6) and family-oriented, with a great outdoor deck. April–Nov daily 11.30am–10pm.
Mews Restaurant & Café 429 Commercial St ☎508 487 1500, ⓦmews.com. Since opening in 1961, this unassuming restaurant has served everyone from Judy Garland to Marc Jacobs, garnering rave reviews for its rotating fusion cuisine (think pork vindaloo or almond-crusted cod; both $26) and extensive vodka bar (286 and counting). Daily 6pm–late.
Portuguese Bakery 299 Commercial St ☎508 487 1803. This old stand-by is the place to come for cheap breakfasts and baked goods, particularly the tasty *malasadas* (fried dough) and *rabanada*, akin to French toast. Also good for an egg sandwich at breakfast; ask for it on a Portuguese muffin. Late April to Sept Mon–Fri 7am–7pm, Sat & Sun 7am–8/9pm; call for Oct hours.

NIGHTLIFE AND ENTERTAINMENT

On summer weekends, boatloads of revellers come to P-Town in search of its notoriously **wild nightlife**, which is heavily geared towards a **gay** clientele. Some establishments have terrific waterfront locations, making them ideal for a drink at sunset.

Atlantic House 6 Masonic Place, behind Commercial St ☎508 487 3821, ⓦahouse.com. The "A-House" – a dark drinking hole favoured by Tennessee Williams and Eugene O'Neill – now has a trendy gay dance club and bar. Daily noon–1am.
Boatslip 161 Commercial St ☎508 487 1669, ⓦboatslip resort.com. The daily tea dances (4–7pm) at this resort are legendary; you can either dance away on a long wooden deck overlooking the water, or cruise inside under a disco ball and flashing lights. June–Aug daily 4–7pm; May,

Sept & Oct Sat & Sun 4–7pm.
Crown & Anchor 247 Commercial St ☎508 487 1430, ⓦonlyatthecrown.com. A massive complex housing several bars, including *The Vault*, a leather bar, *Wave*, a video-karaoke bar and *Paramount*, a massive nightclub. Hours vary according to venue.
Red Inn 15 Commercial St ☎508 487 7334, ⓦthered inn.com. For a complete change of nightlife pace, head to the *Red Inn's* teensy bar, where you can sip martinis on the porch of a historic house by the sea. Daily 5.30pm–close.

Martha's Vineyard

The largest offshore island in New England, twenty-mile-long **MARTHA'S VINEYARD** encompasses more physical variety than Nantucket, with hills and pastures providing scenic counterpoints to the beaches and wild, windswept moors on the separate island of **Chappaquiddick**.

Martha's Vineyard's most genteel town is **Edgartown**, all prim and proper with its freshly painted, white clapboard colonial homes, museums and manicured gardens. The other main settlement, **Vineyard Haven**, is more commercial and one of the island's ferry ports. **Oak Bluffs**, in between the two (and the other docking point for ferries), has an array of fanciful wooden gingerbread cottages and inviting restaurants. Be aware of island terminology: heading "Up-Island" takes you southwest to the cliffs at **Aquinnah** (formerly known as Gay Head); conversely, "Down-Island" refers to the triumvirate of easterly towns mentioned above.

Aquinnah lighthouse

9 Aquinnah Circle • Mid-June to mid-Oct daily 10am–5pm; June & July also Fri & Sat 7–9pm; Aug & Sept also Fri & Sat 6–8pm • $5

Trips around the west side of the island are decidedly bucolic, with nary a peep of the water beyond the rolling hills and private estates; however, you do eventually come to the **lighthouse** at **Aquinnah**, where the multicoloured clay was once the main source of paint for the island's houses – now, anyone caught removing any clay faces a sizeable fine. From Moshup beach below, you can get great views of this spectacular formation.

The beaches

Martha's Vineyard is clustered with beautiful **beaches**. Highlights include the secluded, gorgeous Wasque, at the end of Wasque Road in Chappaquiddick, and South Beach, at the end of Katama Road south of Edgartown, known for its "good waves and good bodies". The gentle State Beach, along Beach Road between Oak Bluffs and Edgartown, is more family-oriented.

GETTING AROUND   MARTHA'S VINEYARD

By bus The island has a bus system that connects the main towns and villages (daily 7am–12.45am; $1/town, $7/day; ☎ 508 639 9440, ⓦ vineyardtransit.com).

By car Bringing a car over on the ferry is expensive, and often impossible on summer weekends without reserving well in advance. Another alternative is to rent a car from Budget, in Vineyard Haven, Oak Bluffs or the airport (☎ 508 693 1911, ⓦ budget.com), or from Adventure Rentals in

Vineyard Haven (☎ 508 693 1959, ⓦ islandadventuresmv .com) or Oak Bluffs (☎ 508 696 9147).

By bike You can easily get around by bike; pick one up at the rental places lined up by the ferry dock ($25/day). The best bike ride is along the State Beach Park between Oak Bluffs and Edgartown, with the dunes to one side and marshy Sengekontacket Pond to the other; purpose-built cycle routes continue to the youth hostel at West Tisbury.

ACCOMMODATION

Edgartown Inn 56 N Water St, Edgartown ☎ 508 627 4794, ⓦ edgartowninn.com. This eighteenth-century home is a quintessential New England inn with colourful rooms that evoke another era (read: none has a TV). The Garden House and Barn out back have shared bathrooms (and the least expensive rooms). $125

HI-Martha's Vineyard 525 Edgartown–West Tisbury Rd, West Tisbury ☎ 508 693 2665, ⓦ capecod.hiusa .org; easily accessed by the #6 bus route. Pleasant setting, 78 dorm beds and a full kitchen. It is a bit off the beaten track, but there are bike rental deals and free bike delivery. Open April to mid-Nov. Dorms $29

Madison Inn 18 Kennebec Ave, Oak Bluffs ☎ 508 693 2760, ⓦ madisoninnmv.com. Run by the masterminds

behind the landmark *Nashua House* (see p.192), this fourteen-room inn is gussied up with floral linens, iPod docks, flat-screen TVs and cheerfully painted chambers. Within easy walking distance of the beach, the ferry terminal and restaurants. $229

Martha's Vineyard Family Campground 569 Edgartown Rd, Edgartown ☎ 508 693 3772, ⓦ campmv .com. Come nightfall, you can roast s'mores on an open fire at this full-shade campground tucked inside an oak forest. Open late May to mid-Oct. $50

Menemsha Inn & Cottages and Beach Plum Inn North Rd, Menemsha ☎ 508 645 2521, ⓦ menemsha inn.com and ⓦ beachpluminn.com. Beautifully maintained adjacent properties within walking distance

3

FERRIES TO MARTHA'S VINEYARD AND NANTUCKET

Unless otherwise specified, all the **ferries** below run several times daily in midsummer (mid-June to mid-Sept). Most have fewer services from May to mid-June, and between mid-September and October. There is at least a skeleton service to each island year-round, though not on all routes. To discourage clogging of the roads, round-trip costs for cars are prohibitively high in the peak season (mid-May to mid-Sept; Woods Hole ferry only), while costs for bikes are just $6 each way. Be sure to make reservations in advance as spaces do sell out.

TO MARTHA'S VINEYARD

Falmouth to Oak Bluffs (about 35min). The *Island Queen* (cash or travellers' cheque only; ☎508 548 4800, ⓦislandqueen.com). Passengers ($20), bikes ($8) or kayaks ($12).
Falmouth to Edgartown (1hr). Falmouth Ferry Service ($50, $10 for bikes; ☎508 548 9400, ⓦfalmouthedgartownferry.com).
Hyannis to Oak Bluffs. Hy-Line (☎800 492 8082, ⓦhylinecruises.com). High-speed ferry (50min; $72) or traditional (1hr 40min; $45), both passengers only.
New Bedford to Vineyard Haven or Oak Bluffs (1hr). New England Fast Ferry ($68; ☎866 683 3779, ⓦnefastferry.com). Passengers only.
Woods Hole to both Vineyard Haven and Oak Bluffs (45min). Steamship Authority ($137 high season or $87 low season/car, not including passengers, who must pay $8 each way; ☎508 477 8600, ⓦsteamshipauthority.com). Car ferry, year-round. Reservations required to bring a car on summer weekends and holidays – you can bring a car stand-by all other times, though the wait can be long.
Quonset Point, Rhode Island, to Oak Bluffs (1hr 30min). Vineyard Fast Ferry ($79; ☎401 295 4040, ⓦvineyardfastferry.com). Passengers only. Good for those travelling from Connecticut or New York; Quonset is south of Providence and Warwick. Shuttles are provided to Kingston Amtrak station ($22) and Providence airport ($15).

TO NANTUCKET

From Hyannis: pedestrians $35 (2hr15min journey); pedestrians $69 (1hr journey); May–Oct vehicles $400; off-season vehicles $280 (Steamship Authority ☎508 477 8600 for auto reservations, ☎508 495 3278 for pedestrians, ⓦsteamshipauthority.com). Also Hy-Line Cruises, pedestrians only; 2hr journey $45 return; 1hr journey $77 return (☎800 492 8082, ⓦhylinecruises.com).

In summer, the Hy-Line ferry company runs a **connecting service** between Oak Bluffs, Martha's Vineyard and Nantucket (one departure daily; pedestrians only; $36 one-way; ☎800 492 8082). The trip takes 1hr 10min.

---

of the Menemsha beach, but also with access to private town beaches on the north shore. The *Beach Plum Inn* is better for young adults, while the cottages at *Menemsha* suit families. Open May–Nov; book early. **$215**, cottages/ week from **$2200**

Nashua House Hotel 30 Kennebec Ave, Oak Bluffs ☎508 693 0043, ⓦnashuahouse.com. Small rooms, all with shared bathrooms, but this friendly, central Victorian is an easy walk from the ferry, and one of the least expensive choices on the island. **$129**

EATING AND DRINKING

Eating is one of the principal pleasures of Martha's Vineyard; fresh lobster, fish and quahogs (large clams) are particularly abundant. Only in Edgartown, Vineyard Haven and Oak Bluffs can you order alcohol with meals, but elsewhere you can bring your own.

Back Door Donuts 5 Post Office Square, behind MV Gourmet Café and Bakery, Oak Bluffs ☎508 693 3688, ⓦmvbakery.com. Local institution knocking out crispy doughnuts in honey-dipped, Boston cream and cinnamon and sugar varieties – all warm, delicious and $1.50 or less each. Try the apple fritter. Daily 7.30pm–12.30am.

The Bite 29 Basin Rd, Menemsha ☎508 645 9239, ⓦthebitemenemsha.com. Classic New England clam shack with a few outdoor tables and some of the juiciest fried belly clams you'll ever taste (from $14) – they also do mussels, fish and chips, squid and quahog chowder ($4). Cash only. Late May to Sept daily 11am–sunset.

Chilmark Chocolates 19 State Rd, Chilmark ☏ 508 645 3013. Lines snake out the door for *Chilmark*'s island-grown berries dipped in organic chocolate and other home-made sweets. Thurs–Sun 11.30am–5.30pm.

Détente Nevin Square, on Winter St, Edgartown ☏ 508 627 8810, ⓦ detentemv.com. Of the fancier restaurants on the island, this one's your best bet. Seasonal menus use local ingredients, ranging from halibut to lamb shank – it also has a fabulous wine list. Dinner only, mains from $33. June–Aug daily 5.30–10pm; Sept–May call for hours.

Larsen's Fish Market 56 Basin Rd, Menemsha ☏ 508 645 2680, ⓦ larsensfishmarket.com. Primarily selling fresh fish and lobster to take away (great for picnics), this

much-loved shack also knocks out excellent lobster rolls – freshly caught, boiled and crammed into a hot-dog bun ($12). May–Oct daily 9am–7pm.

Offshore Ale Company 30 Kennebec Ave, Oak Bluffs ☏ 508 693 2626, ⓦ offshoreale.com. This friendly local brewpub has wooden booths, live shows almost nightly in season, great pizzas and comfort food. Daily 11.30am–late.

Slice of Life 50 Circuit Ave, Oak Bluffs ☏ 508 693 3838, ⓦ sliceoflifemv.com. Relax on the sunny porch of this casual café/bakery and enjoy a stack of buttermilk pancakes with Vermont maple syrup, or try the house speciality, a fried-green tomato BLT. Tues–Sun 8am–9pm.

Nantucket

The thirty-mile, two-hour sea crossing to **NANTUCKET** may not be an ocean odyssey, but it does set the "Little Gray Lady" apart from her larger, shore-hugging sister, Martha. Nantucket's smaller size adds to its palpable sense of identity, as does the architecture; the "gray" epithet refers not only to the winter fogs, but to the austere grey clapboard and shingle applied uniformly to buildings across the island. The tiny cobbled carriageways of **Nantucket Town** itself, once one of the largest cities in Massachusetts, were frozen in time by economic decline 150 years ago. Today, this area of delightful old restored houses – the town has more buildings on the National Register of Historic Places than Boston – is very much the island hub. Surrounding the ferry exit is a plethora of bike rental places and tour companies. **Straight Wharf** leads directly onto **Main Street**, with its shops and restaurants.

Whaling Museum

13 Broad St, at the head of Steamboat Wharf • Feb to early April Sat & Sun 11am–4pm; mid-April to May daily 11am–4pm; June–Oct daily 10am–5pm; early to mid-Nov Sat & Sun 11am–4pm, last week in Nov daily 10am–5pm; Dec Fri–Sun 10am–5pm • $20 • ☏ 508 228 1894, ⓦ nha.org

The excellent **Whaling Museum** houses an outstanding collection of seafaring exotica, including a gallery of delicately carved scrimshaw and a 46ft sperm whale skeleton that washed ashore in 1998. Look for the rotted tooth on its jaw; officials believe it was an infection that brought about the whale's demise.

The beaches

Beyond the town, Nantucket remains surprisingly wild, a mixture of moors, marshes and heathland, though the main draw remains its untrammelled sandy **beaches**. One of the best can be found at **Siasconset** (pronounced "Sconset"), seven flat, bike-friendly miles east of the town, where venerable cottages stand literally encrusted with salt.

INFORMATION   NANTUCKET

Chamber of Commerce Zero Main St, second floor (Mon–Fri 9am–5pm; ☏ 508 228 1700, ⓦ nantucket chamber.org).

Nantucket Visitor Services 25 Federal St (April–Dec daily 9am–5pm; Jan–March Mon–Sat 9am–5pm; ☏ 508 228 0925, ⓦ nantucket-ma.gov/visitor).

ACCOMMODATION

HI-Nantucket Surfside Beach 31 Western Ave ☏ 508 228 0433, ⓦ hiusa.org. Dorm beds a stone's throw from Surfside Beach in an 1873 lifesaving station, just over 3 miles south of Nantucket Town. Very close to a shuttle stop. Dorms **$39**

Martin House Inn 61 Centre St ☏ 508 228 0678, ⓦ martinhouseinn.com. Thirteen lovely rooms, some with working fireplaces, offer good value in this romantic 1803 seaman's house, with inviting common areas and a spacious veranda – local art and antiques feature throughout. Singles $125, doubles $220

Union Street Inn Union Street Inn 7 Union St ☎ 888 517 0707, ⓦ unioninn.com. This luxurious B&B boasts a central location, hearty breakfasts and dazzling rooms, with stylish rugs, drapes and patterned wallpaper – it's pricey, and much better value off-season. $345

Veranda House 3 Step Lane ☎ 508 228 0695, ⓦ theverandahouse.com. The theme at this boutique hotel is "retro chic", bringing a refreshingly contemporary addition to the island's traditional Victorian-style B&Bs; rooms are stylishly designed, most with harbour views, and come with gourmet breakfast. $339

EATING AND DRINKING

Nantucket abounds in first-rate restaurants, most of them located in or around Nantucket Town. If you're having dinner out, though, be prepared for the bill: **prices** are often comparable to those in Manhattan.

Black Eyed Susan's 10 India St ☎ 508 325 0308, ⓦ black-eyedsusans.com. Popular Southern-influenced breakfast and brunch place (and also dinner Mon–Sat), serving big delicious omelettes and grits with cheese for $9–10. Dinner mains from $27. Cash only. Mon–Sat 7am–1pm & 6–10pm, Sun 7am–1pm.

Cisco Brewers 5 Bartlett Farm Rd ☎ 508 325 5929, ⓦ ciscobrewers.com. More of an alfresco bar than a tour-giving brewery (although they do have those), *Cisco* peddles sample flights of home-made beer, wine and liquor in a leafy courtyard; patrons are encouraged to bring comestibles. The location, 2.5 miles from town, is the only drawback – take a cab, as getting here by bike is a little hairy. Mon–Sat 10am–7pm, Sun noon–6pm.

Sayle's Seafood 99 Washington St Ext ☎ 508 228 4599, ⓦ saylesseafood.com. The closest thing in town to a classic clam shack, serving chowder ($3.50), fresh lobster and fried clams (at market prices) – take out for a picnic or enjoy on the porch. Mon–Sat 10am–8pm, Sun noon–8pm.

Something Natural 50 Cliff Rd ☎ 508 228 0504, ⓦ somethingnatural.com. Handy deli-bakery on the way to Madaket, with home-made bread stuffed with the likes of avocado, cheddar and chutney ($9.50). Find a spot at a picnic table and wash down your meal with Nantucket Nectar's "Matt Fee Tea" – named after the owner. April to mid-Oct Mon–Thurs 8am–4pm, Fri–Sun 8am–5.30pm.

Straight Wharf 6 Harbor Square ☎ 508 228 4499, ⓦ straightwharfrestaurant.com. Superb New American restaurant serving bluefish pâté and watermelon salad in an airy, waterfront dining room. The bar shifts to more of an Animal House vibe come nightfall. Reservations recommended. Daily 11.30am–2pm & 5.30–10pm.

Amherst and Northampton

North of Springfield, the **Pioneer Valley** is a verdant corridor created by the Connecticut River, home to the college towns of **AMHERST** and **NORTHAMPTON**. The region is an excellent choice for those who like to hike, bike, hang out in cafés and browse bookshops.

Emily Dickinson Museum

280 Main St, Amherst • March–May & Sept–Dec Wed–Sun 11am–4pm; June–Aug daily except Tues 10am–5pm • Full tours (hourly according to season; 1hr 30min) $12; Homestead tours (hourly; 45min) $10 • ☎ 413 542 8161, ⓦ emilydickinsonmuseum.org

As the former home of one of America's greatest poets, the **Emily Dickinson Museum** acts as a poignant tribute to the writer and throws light on her famously secluded life here in the nineteenth century. The museum comprises **The Homestead**, Dickinson's birthplace and home, and **The Evergreens** next door, home of her brother Austin and his family. The two beautifully preserved houses can only be visited on **guided tours**.

ARRIVAL AND DEPARTURE   AMHERST AND NORTHAMPTON

By bus Greyhound and Peter Pan buses from Amherst and Springfield arrive at 1 Roundhouse Plaza (☎ 413 586 1030) in Northampton; in Amherst, buses from Northampton and Springfield drop off at 8 Main St (at Amherst Books).

By train Amtrak's Vermonter train runs once a day between Burlington, VT and New York via Amherst, pulling into town at 13 Railroad St, just off Main St.

ACCOMMODATION, EATING AND DRINKING

Amherst Brewing Company 24 N Pleasant St, Amherst ☎ 413 253 4400, ⓦ amherstbrewing.com. The brass bar and exposed brick give a touch of class to this decent brewpub. Live music – mostly jazz – and a street terrace are added attractions. Mon–Sat 11.30am–1am, Sun 11am–1am.

Black Walnut Inn 1184 N Pleasant St, Amherst ☎413 549 5649, ⓦblackwalnutinn.com. This attractive 1821 Federal-style B&B is shaded by tall black walnut trees, its gorgeous rooms decorated with period antiques and super-comfy beds. It's the huge, scrumptious breakfasts, though, that really win five stars. **$135**

★ **Herrell's Ice Cream** 8 Old South St, Northampton ☎413 586 9700, ⓦherrells.com. Home base for a small but illustrious regional chain of ice cream stores; original owner Steve Herrell was apparently the first to grind up candy bars and add them to his concoctions. Mon–Thurs & Sun noon–11pm, Fri & Sat noon–11.30pm.

Sylvester's 111 Pleasant St, Northampton ☎413 586 5343, ⓦsylvestersrestaurant.com. Housed in the former home of Sylvester Graham, inventor of the graham cracker, *Sylvester's* serves up delightful treats such as banana-bread French toast (two for $7.50) and waffles ($6.50). Daily 7am–2.30pm.

The Berkshires

A rich cultural history, world-class summer arts festivals and a bucolic landscape of forests and verdant hills make the **Berkshires**, at the extreme western edge of Massachusetts, an especially enticing region.

Stockbridge

Just south of I-90 and fifty miles west of Springfield, the spotless main street of **STOCKBRIDGE** is classic Berkshires, captured by the work of artist **Norman Rockwell**, who lived here for 25 years until his death in 1978.

Magnificent houses in the hills around Stockbridge include **Chesterwood**, at 4 Williamsville Rd (daily: late May to Aug 10am–5pm; Sept to mid-Oct 11am–4pm; $16; ☎413 298 3579, ⓦchesterwood.org), the Colonial Revival mansion and studio of Daniel Chester French, sculptor of the Lincoln Memorial, and the gorgeously whimsical **Naumkeag**, at 5 Prospect Hill Rd, Rte-7 (late May to mid-Oct daily 10am–5pm; $15; ☎413 298 3239, ⓦthetrustees.org), built in 1886 as a summer home for the prosperous attorney Joseph Hodges Choate.

Norman Rockwell Museum

9 Rte-183 (3 miles west of Stockbridge) • May to mid-Nov daily 10am–5pm (July & Aug Thurs till 7pm); mid-Nov to April Mon–Fri 10am–4pm, Sat & Sun 10am–5pm • $16 • ☎413 298 4100, ⓦnrm.org

The most comprehensive of several tributes to the artist in New England, the **Norman Rockwell Museum** displays some 574 of his original paintings and drawings, most of which were *Saturday Evening Post* covers. Despite Rockwell's penchant for advertising endorsements, and the idealism that infused much of his work, it's hard not to be drawn in by the artist's obsessive attention to detail, and his simple but clever ideas – see *Girl Reading the Post*, *Four Freedoms* and the witty *Triple Self-Portrait*.

ACCOMMODATION AND EATING | STOCKBRIDGE

Red Lion Inn 30 Main St ☎413 298 1690, ⓦredlioninn .com. This grandmotherly inn, which also offers accommodation in historic cottages all over town, is for many the quintessential New England inn, with a vast range of rooms. Repair to the *Lion's Den*, its atmospheric cellar tavern, to get down with the rest of the town. **$155**

OLD STURBRIDGE VILLAGE

Halfway between Worcester and Springfield on US-20, near the junction of I-90 and I-84, the restored and reconstructed **Old Sturbridge Village** (April to mid-Oct daily 9.30am–5pm; late Oct to March Tues–Sun 9.30am–4pm; $24; ☎508 347 3362, ⓦosv.org), made up of preserved buildings brought from all over the region, gives a somewhat idealized but engaging portrait of a small New England town in the 1830s. Costumed interpreters act out roles – working in blacksmiths' shops, planting and harvesting vegetables, tending cows and the like – but they pull it off in an unusually convincing manner. The 200-acre site itself, with mature trees, ponds and dirt footpaths, is very pretty, and worth a half-day visit.

PERFORMING ARTS IN LENOX

Lenox is home to some of the Berkshires' most popular festivals: the summer season of **Shakespeare & Company** (70 Kemble St; ☎413 637 1199, ⓦshakespeare.org) and **Tanglewood**, the summer home of the Boston Symphony Orchestra (297 W St/Rte-183; advance tickets Sept–May ☎617 266 1492; otherwise ☎413 637 1600, ⓦbso.org; it's cheaper and arguably more enjoyable to sit on the grass [tickets from \$23.50]. On Rte-20 between Becket and Lee, **Jacob's Pillow** (mid-June to Aug Wed–Sun; ☎413 243 0745, ⓦjacobspillow .org) puts on one of the best contemporary dance festivals in the country.

Lenox and around

Roughly five miles north of Stockbridge on US-7, tourists flock to **LENOX** each year for its summer performing arts festivals (see box above), but there are also a couple of literary attractions hereabouts worth checking out. In 1902, writer **Edith Wharton** (1862–1937) joined a long list of artists summering in the Berkshires when she moved into **The Mount**, 2 Plunkett St, US-7 (May–Oct daily 10am–5pm; \$18; ☎413 551 5111, ⓦedithwharton.org), an elegant country house she designed. Guided tours (45min) of the house provide a mine of information.

Author **Herman Melville** moved to **Arrowhead**, 780 Holmes Rd (late May to late Oct daily 9.30am–5pm; tours hourly 10am–4pm; \$13; ☎413 442 1793, ⓦmobydick.org), near Pittsfield, north of Lenox, in 1850, finishing *Moby Dick* here soon after. Guided tours (45min) of his creaking wooden home – which dates from 1796 – add colour to his life and work (it's the only museum dedicated to Melville in the USA).

Hancock Shaker Village

1843 W Housatonic St (Rte-20 at Rte-41) • Daily: mid-April to June 10am–4pm; July–Oct 10am–5pm • \$18 • ☎413 443 0188, ⓦhancockshakervillage.org

From 1790 until 1960, the **Hancock Shaker Village**, eleven miles northwest of Lenox, was an active **Shaker community**, and today offers an illuminating insight into this remarkable Christian sect. A branch of the Quakers that had fled England to America in 1774, the Shakers were named for the convulsive fits of glee they experienced when worshipping. Hancock retains one of the biggest collections of Shaker furniture in the country and is home to eighteen preserved clapboard buildings.

ACCOMMODATION AND EATING

LENOX

⭐ **Bistro Zinc** 56 Church St ☎413 637 8800, ⓦbistro zinc.com. Popular with power-lunchers on mobile phones, when the tasty French food is reasonably priced; dinner is considerably more expensive (mains \$18–29). Daily 11.30am–3pm & 5.30–10pm (July & Aug till midnight). **Church Street Café** 65 Church St ☎413 637 2745, ⓦchurchstreetlenox.com. The tasty New England offerings, from sautéed Maine crab cakes to maple- and cider-glazed pork chops, win accolades for this place – more restaurant than café – in the centre of Lenox. Mid-May to Oct daily 11.30am–2.30pm & 5–11pm.

Garden Gables Inn 135 Main St ☎413 637 0193, ⓦgardengablesinn.com. Stylish, luxurious B&B set in a farm that dates back to 1780; all rooms come with iPod docks, LCD TVs, DVD players, afternoon sherry and working fireplaces. Huge breakfast buffet included. Also boasts the largest pool in the Berkshires. **\$199**
⭐ **Hampton Terrace** 91 Walker St ☎800 203 0656, ⓦhamptonterrace.com. This elegant 1852 gem offers deluxe rooms with clawfoot tubs, antique furniture and all the extras – the swimming pool is a real bonus in summer. **\$229**

North Adams and Williamstown

In the northwest corner of the Berkshires, sleepy **NORTH ADAMS** and bucolic **WILLIAMSTOWN** are the unlikely locations of the region's premier art showcases. The former is home to the glorious **Mass MoCA** (Massachusetts Museum of Contemporary Art), 287 Marshall St (July & Aug daily 10am–6pm; Sept–June Mon & Wed–Sun 11am–5pm; \$15; ☎413 662 2111, ⓦmassmoca.org), a sprawling collection of modern installations (including **Sol LeWitt**'s mind-bending work), videos and upside-down trees in a captivating old textile mill.

In Williamstown, the highlight of **The Clark**, 225 South St (July & Aug daily 10am–5pm; Sept–June closed Mon; June–Oct $15, Nov–May free; ☎413 458 2303, ⓦclarkart.edu), is its 32-strong collection of Renoirs, while the ravishing **Williams College Museum of Art**, at 15 Lawrence Hall Drive (Tues–Sat 10am–5pm, Sun 1–5pm; free; ☎413 597 2429, ⓦwcma.williams.edu), specializes in American art from the late eighteenth century onwards, including the world's largest repository of work by brothers **Maurice** and **Charles Prendergast**.

ACCOMMODATION AND EATING	NORTH ADAMS AND WILLIAMSTOWN

The Guest House at Field Farm 554 Sloan Rd, Williamstown ☎413 458 3135, ⓦthetrustees.org /field-farm. Six stylish bedrooms, each with private bath, in a 1948 Bauhaus-inspired country home littered with modern art and surrounded by more than 300 acres of meadows and woodlands. Open May–Dec. **$195**

Mezze 777 Cold Spring Rd (US-7), Williamstown ☎413 458 0123, ⓦmezzerestaurant.com. Urban contemporary meets rural gentility. The seasonal and locally sourced menu features Mediterranean, Moroccan and American-influenced dishes such as braised rabbit and home-made pasta, sesame-seared organic tofu and lamb with thyme. Mains $14–30. Mon, Tues, Thurs & Sun 5–9pm, Fri & Sat 5–10pm.

★ **The Porches Inn** 231 River St, North Adams ☎413 664 0400, ⓦporches.com. Just across the street from Mass MoCA, this is an ultra-modern hotel with a hot tub and sauna, laptop rentals and free breakfast buffet. It occupies a row of houses formerly lived in by mill workers. **$189**

Rhode Island

A mere 48 miles long by 37 miles wide, **RHODE ISLAND** is the smallest state in the Union, yet it had a disproportionately large influence on national life: in 1652 it enacted the first law against slavery in North America, and just over ten years later it was the first to guarantee religious freedom – in the eighteenth century it also saw the beginning of the **Industrial Revolution** in America. Today, Rhode Island is a prime tourist destination, boasting nearly four dozen National Historic Landmarks and four hundred miles of spectacular coastline.

More than thirty tiny islands make up the state, including Hope, Despair and the bay's largest, Rhode Island (also known by its Native American name "Aquidneck"), which gives the state its name. **Narragansett Bay** has long been a determining factor in Rhode Island's economic development and strategic military importance, as the **Ocean State** developed through sea trade, whaling and smuggling before shifting to manufacturing in the nineteenth century. Today, the state's principal destinations are its two original ports: the colonial college town of **Providence**, and well-heeled **Newport**, home to extravagant mansions that once belonged to America's most prominent families, and still a major yachting centre.

Providence

Spread across seven hills on the Providence and Seekonk rivers, **PROVIDENCE** was Rhode Island's first settlement, founded in 1636 "in commemoration of God's providence" on land granted to Roger Williams by the Narragansett tribe.

The state's **capital** since 1790, today Providence is the third largest city in New England, with a vibrant arts scene, excellent restaurants and lots of students, drawn by the city's prestigious higher education institutions, Ivy League **Brown University** and the **Rhode Island School of Design** (RISD, or "Rizdee"). Just as enticing are the city's historic **neighbourhoods**: west of Downcity, the vibrant Italian community on **Federal Hill** boasts some exceptional restaurants, while east of the river lies **College Hill**, the oldest part of town, with many historic buildings – in fact, the city holds one of the finest collections of colonial and early Federal buildings in the nation.

Downcity and around

The hub of downtown ("**Downcity**") is the transport centre at Kennedy Plaza, surrounded by new, modern buildings, with the notable exception of the 1878 **City Hall** at its western end. Nearby **Westminster Street** is especially good for independent shops and cafés.

Just north of Downcity at the top of Constitution Hill, the **State Capitol** (Mon–Fri 8.30am–4.30pm; free; call ahead for guided tours ☏401 222 2357, ⊛sos.ri.gov /publicinfo/tours) dominates the city skyline with a vast dome constructed between 1895 and 1904 by noted architects McKim, Mead & White.

Just across the Providence River from the State Capitol, the **Roger Williams National Memorial** (daily: mid-May to mid-Oct 9am–5pm; mid-Oct to mid-May 9am–4.30pm; free; ☏401 521 7266, ⊛nps.gov/rowi) was the site of the original settlement of Providence in 1636. It's now a four-acre park honouring the life of the founder of Rhode Island – there's not much to see in the park itself, but the small **visitors' centre** at the north end includes replicas of Williams' personal effects.

College Hill and around

Much of Providence's historic legacy can be found across the river from Downcity in the **College Hill** area, an attractive tree-lined district of colonial buildings, museums and **Brown University**. The white clapboard **First Baptist Meeting House** (Mon–Fri 10am–noon & 1–3pm; $2; ☏401 454 3418, ⊛firstbaptistchurchinamerica.org), at the foot of the hill at 75 N Main St, dates from 1638, and testifies to the state's origins as a "lively experiment" in religious freedom. Founded in 1764 (and moved here six years later), the leafy, historic campus of **Brown University** is a rich trove of historic buildings and

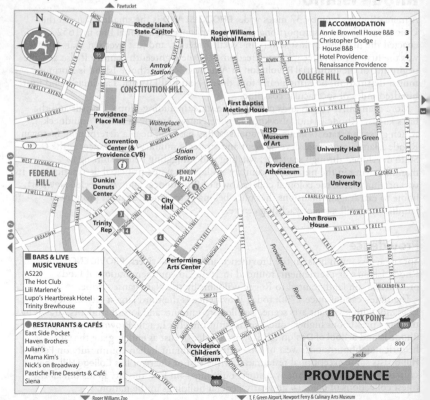

■ ACCOMMODATION	
Annie Brownell House B&B	3
Christopher Dodge House B&B	1
Hotel Providence	4
Renaissance Providence	2

■ BARS & LIVE MUSIC VENUES	
AS220	4
The Hot Club	5
Lili Marlene's	1
Lupo's Heartbreak Hotel	2
Trinity Brewhouse	3

● RESTAURANTS & CAFÉS	
East Side Pocket	1
Haven Brothers	3
Julian's	7
Mama Kim's	2
Nick's on Broadway	6
Pastiche Fine Desserts & Café	4
Siena	5

PROVIDENCE

libraries; free guided tours are offered on weekdays and select Saturdays from the Welcome Center at 75 Waterman St (☎401 863 2378, ⓦbrown.edu).

RISD Museum of Art
224 Benefit St, second entrance at 20 N Main St • Tues–Sun 10am–5pm (Thurs till 9pm) • $12, free Sun & third Thurs of the month (5–9pm) • ☎401 454 6500, ⓦrisdmuseum.org

Providence's second major college is the prestigious **Rhode Island School of Design**, founded in 1877. The school's impressive **Museum of Art** houses over 80,000 works in 45 galleries, a skilfully melded hodgepodge of five industrial buildings and houses between Benefit and Main streets. The collection covers everything from ancient Egypt to Asian arts and European paintings from just about every period – though quality varies, everything is superbly presented and the galleries are small enough to be easily absorbed.

Federal Hill
Federal Hill, west of Downcity, is Providence's **Little Italy**, greeting visitors with the traditional symbol of welcome, a bronze pine cone, on the entrance arch on Atwells Avenue. Settled by Italian immigrants in the 1910s and 1920s, this area is now one of the friendliest in the city, alive with cafés, delis, bakeries and bars, and with a lively piazza around the Italianate fountain in **DePasquale Square**.

ARRIVAL AND DEPARTURE   PROVIDENCE

By plane T.F. Green Airport (☎888 268 7222, ⓦpvd airport.com) in Warwick, 9 miles south of downtown, is served by most US carriers. RIPTA bus #14 and #20 ($2) run to downtown (Kennedy Plaza). Taxis should be around $32.

By train The train station, 100 Gaspee St, is served by Amtrak services from Boston and New York, and the MBTA commuter rail from Boston. Taxis meet most trains.

Destinations Boston (20 daily; 50min); New Haven (18 daily; 1hr 25min); New York City (19 daily; around 3hr).
By bus Greyhound and Peter Pan buses stop downtown at the Kennedy Plaza hub.
Destinations Boston (3 daily; 1hr); New Haven (3 daily; 2hr 45min); New London (3 daily; 1hr 45min); New York City (3 daily; 5hr 25min).

GETTING AROUND, INFORMATION AND TOURS

By bus Local RIPTA buses are easy to use and convenient (Kennedy Plaza ticket window Mon–Fri 7am–6pm, Sat 9am–noon & 1–5pm; $2/trip, $6/24hr pass; ☎401 781 9400, ⓦripta.com).
Rhode Island Convention Center 1 Sabin St (Mon–Sat

9am–5pm; ☎401 751 1177 or ☎800 233 1636, ⓦgoprovidence.com).
Historical tours The Rhode Island Historical Society (☎401 331 8575, ⓦrihs.org) leads walking tours through the city.

ACCOMMODATION

Annie Brownell House B&B 400 Angell St ☎401 454 2934, ⓦanniebrownellhouse.com. Four rooms in a lovely 1899 Colonial Revival clapboard house near Thayer St, with rooms furnished in late Victorian style. Full, delicious hot breakfasts and friendly host. **$140**
Christopher Dodge House B&B 11 W Park St ☎401 351 6111, ⓦprovidence-hotel.com. Small boutique hotel in an Italianate townhouse dating from 1858, boasting 11ft ceilings, marble fireplaces and full breakfasts. Standard rooms are simply but comfortably decked out with cable TV; superior rooms are a lot bigger. **$149**

Hotel Providence 139 Mathewson St ☎800 861 8990, ⓦhotelprovidence.com. Newish luxury hotel with eighty plush and colourful rooms themed on classic novels from the likes of Tolstoy and Dumas, and a trendy restaurant downstairs. **$229**
★ **Renaissance Providence** 5 Avenue of the Arts ☎401 919 5000, ⓦmarriott.com. Luxurious downtown hotel on the site of a former Masonic temple, with 272 comfortable, well-appointed rooms, some overlooking the State House. A 5min walk from the train station. **$199**

EATING

Providence boasts excellent **food** options. Thayer Street is lined with inexpensive places popular with students, while nearby Wickenden Street has a more mature clientele. Rhode Island is the proud home of several unique (and sickeningly sweet) beverages, the most famous of which is the state drink, **coffee milk**, made with syrup and served all over Providence; a "**coffee cabinet**" is a milkshake prepared by blending ice cream with milk and said syrup.

3

3

WATERFIRE

Throughout the summer months, the spectacular event known as **WaterFire** (select Sat evenings May–Oct; free; ⓦ waterfire.org) enthralls visitors and locals alike with one hundred bonfires set at sunset along the centre of the Providence River. Tended by gondoliers and accompanied by suitably inspiring music, the fires burn until just past midnight, while entertainers and food vendors keep the crowds happy.

★ **East Side Pocket** 278 Thayer St ☏401 453 1100, ⓦeastsidepocket.com. Bulging falafel sandwiches ($5) and other Middle Eastern "pockets" served hot, fresh and cheap at this popular student hangout. Mon–Thurs 10am–1am, Fri & Sat 10am–2am, Sun 10am–10pm.

Haven Brothers Next to City Hall, Fulton St. This diner-on-wheels has pitched up here nightly since 1888, serving classic hot dogs, burgers and fries (from $5). Daily 5pm–4am.

Julian's 318 Broadway ☏401 861 1770, ⓦjulians providence.com. One of a new wave of innovative contemporary restaurants, serving everything from house corned beef ($15) to vegan seitan vindaloo curry ($18) and plum-and-ginger-glazed monkfish ($20). Mon–Fri 9am–11pm, Sat & Sun 9am–2pm & 5–11pm (bar open till 1am).

★ **Mama Kim's** College Hill or Kennedy Plaza (call or follow on Twitter for real-time hours and location) ☏401 787 8977, ⓦmamakims.us. This Korean pioneer of the city's food truck movement fires up beef bulgogi sliders ($3), seafood Pajun (traditional pancakes; $6) and plump

dumplings stuffed with the region's best kimchi ($3). Mon–Fri 11am–2pm & 5–8pm, Sat 12.30–3.30pm.

Nick's on Broadway 500 Broadway ☏401 421 0286, ⓦnicksonbroadway.com. Though it's a fair hike from anything else (it's in the West End), brunch lovers flock here for the best-in-town breakfast specials (from $7) and brioche French toast ($8). Wed–Sat 7am–3pm & 5.30–10pm, Sun 8am–3pm.

Pastiche Fine Desserts & Café 92 Spruce St ☏401 861 5190, ⓦpastichefinedesserts.com. This blue clapboard cottage on Federal Hill offers fabulous home-baked lemon custard tarts, mascarpone torte, banana creams and more. Tues–Thurs 8.30am–11pm, Fri & Sat 8.30am–11.30pm, Sun 10am–10pm.

★ **Siena** 238 Atwells Ave ☏401 521 3311, ⓦsienari .com. The current trendsetter in Federal Hill, with a sparkling Tuscan menu featuring wood-fired pizzas ($12–13), superb pastas ($15–19) and luscious wood-grilled meats ($19–29). Mon–Thurs 5–11pm, Fri 5pm–midnight, Sat 4.30pm–midnight, Sun 3–9pm.

NIGHTLIFE

The city's nightlife bustles around Empire and Washington streets, south of Kennedy Plaza in Downcity, and along Thayer Street near Brown University during term-time.

AS220 115 Empire St ☏401 831 9327, ⓦas220.org. Hip, lively, anti-establishment café/bar/gallery, with eclectic local art and diverse nightly performances; check the website to find out about its other galleries and events. Hours vary.

The Hot Club 575 S Water St ☏401 272 4945, ⓦhotclubprov.com. More of a bar than a club, where you can sip drinks and enjoy free popcorn on an outdoor terrace right on the river. Cash only. Mon–Thurs & Sun noon–1am, Fri & Sat noon–2am.

Lili Marlene's 422 Atwells Ave ☏401 751 4996. Dark, spacious yet intimate venue with burgundy booths, a pool table and late-night snacks. Tucked out of the way in Federal Hill, this locals' haunt draws its crowd by word of mouth.

Mon–Thurs & Sun 3pm–1am, Fri & Sat 3pm–2am.

Lupo's Heartbreak Hotel 79 Washington St ☏401 272 5876, ⓦlupos.com. This is *the* spot in town to see nationally recognized bands perform. Tickets generally $12–20 in advance, $30-plus for big names. Box office Mon–Fri noon–6pm.

Trinity Brewhouse 186 Fountain St ☏401 453 2337, ⓦtrinitybrewhouse.com. The interior of this hip brewhouse-meets-sports-bar feels a bit like the dining hall of Harry Potter's Hogwarts – all oversized chandeliers, wood-panelled walls and cathedral windows. Everything on tap has been brewed in-house; try the Rhode Island IPA ($4.75). Mon–Thurs 11.30am–1am, Fri 11.30am–2am, Sat noon–2am, Sun noon–1am.

Newport

With its gorgeous location on Aquidneck Island, fleets of polished yachts, rose-coloured sunsets and long-standing association with America's fine and fabulous, **NEWPORT** is straight out of a fairy tale. The Kennedys were married here (Jackie was a local girl); and though F. Scott Fitzgerald set his novel **The Great Gatsby** in Long Island, it's no surprise that the iconic 1974 movie version was filmed in Newport. Indeed, many of the town's opulent *fin-de-siècle* mansions – former summer homes of the likes of the Astors and Vanderbilts – are still owned by America's current crop of mega-wealthy.

Stroll beyond the extravagant facades, though, and you'll find much more. The streets are laden with history, and sights commemorate everything from the town's pioneering role in religious freedom in America to the landing of French forces during the Revolutionary War. Newport's prime seaside location also means that the views are often, if not always, free – a short drive and you're greeted by unrivalled shores, with rugged seascapes and long swaths of sand.

The Newport mansions

Daily: April to mid-Nov 10am–6pm; Marble House, The Elms & The Breakers also mid-Nov to Jan daily 10am–5pm • $14.50 single entry (Breakers $19.50); combined ticket to any five Society mansions is $31.50; the Breakers plus one other property is $24.50 (you can easily walk between these properties, but parking is also available at all of them) • ☎ 401 847 1000, ⓦ newportmansions.org

When sociologist Thorstein Veblen visited Newport at the turn of the twentieth century, he was so horrified by the extravagance that he coined the phrase "conspicuous consumption". From the 1880s, this had been the summer playground of the New York elite, with wealthy families competing to outdo each other with lavish **mansions** and annual parties. The Gilded Age lasted just a few decades; beginning with the introduction of US income tax in 1913, by the early 1940s most of the mansions had closed for good; the **Preservation Society of Newport County** maintains the bulk of the dozen or so houses open for public viewing today.

The mansions each boast their own version of Gilded Age excess: **Marble House**, built in 1892 for William Vanderbilt with its golden ballroom and adjacent Chinese teahouse; **Rosecliff**, with a colourful rose garden and heart-shaped staircase; the ornate French **The Elms**, known for its gardens; and Cornelius Vanderbilt II's **The Breakers**, an Italian Renaissance-style palace overlooking the ocean and the grandest of the lot. Besides those, a number of earlier, smaller houses, including the quirky Gothic Revival cottage **Kingscote**, built in 1841, may well make for a more interesting excursion. Note that many houses can only be seen on hourly tours; unless you're a mansion nut, viewing one or two should suffice to get a glimpse of the opulence.

One way to see the mansions on the cheap is to peer in the back gardens from the **Cliff Walk**, which begins on Memorial Boulevard where it meets First (Easton) Beach. This spectacular three-and-a-half-mile oceanside path alternates from pretty stretches lined by jasmine and wild roses to rugged rocky passes.

ARRIVAL AND GETTING AROUND   NEWPORT

By bus Peter Pan buses and RIPTA bus #60 from Providence arrive at the visitor centre downtown. From here, RIPTA bus #67 ($2) runs every 15–20min (Mon–Sat 8am–8pm, Sun 9.40am–8pm) downtown along Bellevue Ave, past most of the mansions, ending beyond Rough Point at the end of the Cliff Walk.

By bike Rent bikes at Ten Speed Spokes, 18 Elm St (Tues–Fri 10am–6pm, Sat 10am–5pm; May–Oct also Mon & Sun noon–5pm; $35/day; ☎ 401 847 5609, ⓦ tenspeed spokes.com).

INFORMATION AND TOURS

Visitor centre 23 America's Cup Ave (daily 9am–5pm; ☎ 401 845 9123, ⓦ gonewport.com).
Walking tours Newport Historical Society (☎ 401 841 8770, ⓦ newporthistorytours.org) runs a range of themed walking tours (from $12) through downtown.
Cruises Easily the most relaxing way to see Newport is on

a cruise; try Classic Cruises of Newport (☎ 401 847 0298, ⓦ cruisenewport.com), which offers trips from Bannister's Wharf on the beautiful 72ft schooner *Madeleine* (5 daily in summer; 1hr 30min; $28) and motor yacht *Rum Runner II* (4 daily in summer; 1hr 15min; $20).

ACCOMMODATION

Newport contains almost one hundred inns and B&Bs, while cheaper chain **motels** are a few miles north in Middletown. If you're stuck, **Bed & Breakfast Newport** (☎ 800 800 8765, ⓦ bbnewport.com) can help find something affordable.

NEWPORT'S FESTIVALS

There's always something afoot in Newport, particularly in August for the **Newport Folk Festival** (where Bob Dylan got his start in 1963; ☎401 848 5055, ⓦnewportfolkfest.net) as well as the high-profile **Jazz Festival** (ⓦnewportjazzfest.net). The **Newport Music Festival** (☎401 849 0700, ⓦnewportmusic.org) in July boasts classical music performed at the mansions, while the **Waterfront Irish Festival** in September is one of the region's biggest Irish events (ⓦnewportwaterfrontevents.com).

★ **Hilltop** 2 Kay St, at Bellevue Ave ☎401 846 03902, ⓦhilltopnewport.com. Newport's most popular B&B occupies a gorgeous house completed in 1910. The five rooms all have comfy Victorian interiors, LCD TVs with generous bathrooms and quality breakfasts. Enjoy the afternoon tea (daily 3–5pm), and home-made cakes and port left out in the evenings. $275

★ **Ivy Lodge** 12 Clay St ☎401 849 6865, ⓦivylodge.com. Boasting a stunning 33ft gothic entry hall with wraparound balconies, this B&B beauty has eight rooms filled with antique reproduction furniture and modern amenities including flat-screen TVs, DVR and whirlpool tubs. Prices plummet in the off-season. $219

Marshall Slocum Guest House 29 Kay St ☎401 841 5120, ⓦmarshallslocuminn.com. Five comfortable period-style rooms in a historic 1855 B&B near Bellevue Ave, with gardens and gourmet breakfasts – but no TV. Excellent value. $155

★ **Rose Island Lighthouse** Rose Island, Narragansett Bay ☎401 847 4242, ⓦroseislandlighthouse.org. Worth it for the sheer novelty of staying in a lighthouse (a museum during the day), and for the magical sunset views. It's a bit like camping, with an outdoor shower, a bring-your-own food policy and limited water. Leave your car in Newport (the hotel arranges a car permit) and you'll be taken over by ferry. $185

William Gyles Guesthouse 16 Howard St ☎401 369 0243, ⓦnewporthostel.com. Newport's only hostel is welcoming and comfortable, with basic breakfast, shared kitchen and free internet terminals and wi-fi. Winter rates are usually lower. Open April–Dec. Dorms $45 weekdays, $69 weekends, doubles $138

EATING

★ **Belle's Cafe** Newport Shipyard, 1 Washington St ☎401 846 6000, ⓦnewportshipyard.com. At this well-kept secret, tucked away from the downtown bustle, you can grab two delicious lobster rolls for $18.75 and paninis (from $9.25) in the company of the world's finest yachts. Mon–Sat 7am–3pm.

Black Pearl Bannister's Wharf ☎401 846 5264, ⓦblackpearlnewport.com. Harbourside institution famous for its clam chowder; opt for more formal options in the Commodore's Room (*escargots bourguignon*) and less formal ones in the Tavern (*escargots* with garlic butter). Feb–Dec daily 11.30am–1am.

★ **Flo's Clam Shack** 4 Wave Ave ☎401 847 8141, ⓦflosclamshack.net. Hugely popular joint across from First Beach. At $4.50 for a bowl of clam chowder and $5.25 for a dozen clam cakes, it's worth the wait. Cash only. April–Dec Thurs–Sun 11am–9pm (June–Aug daily).

Mamma Luisa 673 Thames St ☎401 848 5257, ⓦmammaluisa.com. The best Italian restaurant in Newport, with fabulous home-made pastas (from $13.95) and refreshing fruit sorbets ($6.95). Daily except Wed 5–10pm.

Salvation Café 140 Broadway ☎401 847 2620, ⓦsalvationcafe.com. Hip spot off the main drag, with exotic concoctions such as oxtail bolognese ($19) and salmon belly dumplings ($7). Daily 5–11pm, Sun brunch 11am–2.30pm.

★ **Tallulah On Thames** 464 Thames St ☎401 849 2433, ⓦtallulahonthames.com. Hot farm-to-table restaurant, with seasonal ingredients sourced from local suppliers: think Aquidneck Farm "slow egg" with pork belly and toast ($16), and Bell & Evans roast chicken ($35). Feb–Dec Wed–Sun 5.30–11pm; May–Sept also Mon.

Connecticut

Just ninety miles long by 55 miles wide, **CONNECTICUT** is New England's southernmost state and the most influenced by New York City; thousands of commuters make the trip each day, and many of the opulent mansions are owned by Wall Street bankers. As a result, tourism here is of a sophisticated sort, with art galleries, vineyards, historical houses, museums and increasingly eclectic cuisine on offer, while the state's lesser-known natural offerings along the densely populated coast make for some pleasant surprises.

The coast is studded with enticing small towns, from the colonial charms of **Mystic** and **Stonington** to hip **New London** and intellectual **New Haven**, home of Yale University. Further inland, the state capital at **Hartford** is a real surprise, with a gradually regenerating downtown and a trio of attractions.

Mystic

Thanks to Julia Roberts, **MYSTIC** is best-known throughout the USA for its pizza joint, but this elegant New England town offers far more than that – a host of independent stores and galleries, the intriguing maritime re-creations of **Mystic Seaport** and the beluga whales at **Mystic Aquarium**. Most of the attractions lie in the **historic downtown** area, a major shipbuilding centre in the nineteenth century, while **Old Mystic** comprises a couple of quaint streets a few miles north. The two are divided by I-95 (exit 90) and **Olde Mistick Village**, a slightly kitsch shopping mall.

Mystic Aquarium & Institute for Exploration

3

55 Coogan Blvd, I-95 exit 90 • Daily: April–Oct 9am–5pm; Nov & March 9am–4pm; Dec–Feb 10am–4pm • $29.95, kids 3–17 $21.95 • ☎ 860 572 5955, ⓦ mysticaquarium.org

The outstanding **Mystic Aquarium & Institute for Exploration** is home to more than four thousand marine specimens, including penguins, sea lions, sharks, stingrays, piranhas and the only **beluga whales** in New England – specially designed tanks allow close-up encounters with these three graceful snow-white creatures (albeit through reinforced glass).

Mystic Seaport

75 Greenmanville Ave • April–Oct daily 9am–5pm; Nov daily 10am–4pm; Dec & mid-Feb to March Thurs–Sun 10am–4pm • $24, kids 6–17 $15 • ☎ 888 973 2767, ⓦ mysticseaport.org

The **Museum of America & the Sea**, or just **Mystic Seaport**, north of downtown, is one of the nation's largest and most enjoyable maritime museums. Founded in 1929 on a nineteen-acre wedge of riverfront once occupied by shipyards, the site is roughly divided into three parts: the **Preservation Shipyard** is primarily dedicated to the restoration of the 1841 *Charles W. Morgan*, while further along, more than sixty buildings housing old-style workshops and stores reflect life in a seafaring **village** c.1876. The final section contains a series of more formal **exhibit halls**, including the absorbing **Voyages** gallery, with multimedia displays covering the whole span of American maritime history.

ARRIVAL AND INFORMATION

MYSTIC

By bus Peter Pan runs services to Mystic from New York, Boston and Providence; note that the bus stops at the SEAT bus shelter near The Kite Shop in Olde Mistick Village, which is not especially convenient for downtown.

By train Amtrak services from New York and Boston pull in at 2 Roosevelt Ave off US-1 downtown (no ticket office; buy at platform kiosks or on the train).

Visitor centres Mystic's main information office lies in Olde Mistick Village, off I-95 (Mon–Sat 9.30am–5pm, Sun 10am–5pm; ☎ 860 536 1641, ⓦ mystic.org), and can help with finding hotels. There's a smaller welcome centre (Mon–Fri 9am–4.30pm, Sat & Sun 10am–4pm; ☎ 860 572 9578, ⓦ mysticchamber.org) at the train station.

ACCOMMODATION AND EATING

★ **Bravo Bravo** 20 E Main St ☎ 860 536 3228, ⓦ bravobravoct.com. This Italian seafood specialist is the best place for a gourmet splurge in Mystic. Feast on lobster ravioli, linguine with clams or seafood stew ($17–30). Tues–Thurs 11.30am–2pm & 5–9pm, Fri & Sat 11.30am–2pm & 5–10pm, Sun 5–9pm.

Mystic Pizza 56 W Main St ☎ 860 536 3700, ⓦ mysticpizza.com. The tourists outside this otherwise ordinary family-run pizza place are here because of the eponymous 1988 Julia Roberts movie, largely filmed in the area – business boomed in the 1990s as a result, and though things have calmed down since then, plenty of pilgrims still come to taste a "slice of heaven"; huge, tasty pizzas (slices from $2.29).

Mon–Thurs & Sun 10am–1pm, Fri & Sat 10am–10.30pm.

★ **S&P Oyster Co** 1 Holmes St ☎860 536 2674, ⓦsp-oyster.com. Fine seafood on the waterfront overlooking the drawbridge – the best place to enjoy Mystic in the summer. Try the incredibly fresh Stonington scallops ($25.95), lobster tacos ($19.95) or a tilapia sandwich ($9.25). No reservations. Mon–Thurs & Sun 11.30am–10pm, Fri & Sat 11.30am–11pm.

★ **Steamboat Inn** 73 Steamboat Wharf ☎860 536 8300, ⓦsteamboatinnmystic.com. A luxurious downtown option, whose eleven elegant rooms overlook the water and are furnished in a modern, country-inn style with cable TV and DVD players. **$200**

Whaler's Inn 20 E Main St ☎860 536 1506, ⓦwhalersinnmystic.com. Right in the heart of downtown Mystic, near the drawbridge over the river, this is the most central choice and Mystic's best hotel (as opposed to B&B). Comprises five historic buildings – Hoxie House rooms have the best river views. Parking included. **$140**

Stonington

Tucked away on the coast near the state's eastern border, **STONINGTON** is a gorgeous old fishing village, originally settled in 1649. Its main road, **Water Street**, is dotted with restaurants and shops, while parallel **Main Street** contains some dazzling examples of colonial and Federal clapboard architecture. At 7 Water St, the **Old Lighthouse Museum** (May–Oct daily except Wed 10am–5pm; $9; ☎860 535 1440, ⓦstoningtonhistory.org) recounts town life through the centuries, with exhibits on seal-hunting, a collection of local salt-glazed ceramics from the short-lived Stonington potteries and trinkets from Asia brought back by the town's notable seafarers. Museum admission includes access to the Italianate **Captain Nathaniel B. Palmer House**, 40 Palmer St (May–Oct Thurs–Sun 1–5pm; $9; ☎860 535 8445), at the north end of town, celebrating Stonington's premier seafarer (credited with one of the earliest sightings of Antarctica in 1820).

ACCOMMODATION AND EATING | STONINGTON

Inn at Stonington 60 Water St ☎860 535 2000, ⓦtheinnatstonington.com. Right in the heart of Stonington's historic centre, this charming hotel is actually fairly new, despite appearances – all eighteen rooms come with views of the harbour or village, with fireplaces, jacuzzis and polished stone tiles. **$225**

★ **Noah's Restaurant** 113 Water St ☎860 535 3925, ⓦnoahsfinefood.com. This place is known for its superb home-style cooking, with an eclectic menu featuring everything from Korean pancakes to something conjured up from that day's local catch (dinner mains $16.95–26.95). Tues–Thurs & Sun 7.45am–9pm, Fri & Sat 7.45am–9.30pm.

Orchard Street Inn 41 Orchard St ☎860 535 2681, ⓦorchardstreetinn.com. Five elegant rooms, some with garden patio, in a quiet clapboard cottage. The owners will pick you up for free from Mystic or New London train stations, and provide free bikes once you arrive. **$220**

New London

A booming **whaling port** in the nineteenth century, **NEW LONDON** is a lively, multicultural working city, with two absorbing attractions on its outskirts. The town relied heavily on military-base revenue in the twentieth century, but struggled in the 1990s due to spending cuts. Though parts of town remain edgy, New London is reviving today, thanks largely to the presence of Connecticut College, the US Coast Guard Academy and pharmaceutical giant Pfizer's R&D headquarters in nearby Groton.

Monte Cristo Cottage

325 Pequot Ave • June–Aug Thurs–Sat noon–4pm, Sun 1–3pm • $7 • ☎860 443 5378 ext 290, ⓦtheoneill.org

Two miles south of downtown, the **Monte Cristo Cottage** faithfully preserves the memory of **Eugene O'Neill** (1888–1953), one of America's most acclaimed playwrights and winner of the Nobel Prize for Literature in 1936. His summer house is full of period fittings and furnishings (some original), and enthusiastic guides fill in the biographical details.

US Coast Guard Academy

Academy 31 Mohegan Ave, I-95 exit 83 • Tours Mon, Fri & Wed 1pm; self-guided tours daily 9am–4.30pm; cadet drill autumn and spring Fri 4pm • Free, ID required • ☎ 860 444 8500, ⓦ cga.edu **US Coast Guard Museum** 15 Mohegan Ave (Waesche Hall) • Sept–May Mon–Fri 9am–4pm, Sat 10am–4pm, Sun 1–4pm; June–Aug Mon–Fri 9am–4pm • Free • ☎ 860 444 8511

The **US Coast Guard Academy**, just off I-95 (1.5 miles north of downtown), spreads out on a leafy 103-acre, red-brick campus built in the 1930s and overlooking the Thames. Visitors are welcome to explore the grounds and the **US Coast Guard Museum**, charting two centuries of Coast Guard history and housing the figurehead from the USS *Eagle*, a 295ft barque launched in 1936.

ARRIVAL AND INFORMATION   NEW LONDON

By bus Greyhound buses stop downtown at 45 Water St, connecting New London with Boston via Providence, and New York via New Haven.

By train Trains serve New London's Union Station, at 35 Water St (☎ 800 872 7245), right in the heart of downtown and conveniently close to the ferry docks.

By ferry The New London Ferry Dock, 2 Ferry St, hosts ferries to Orient Point on Long Island via the Cross Sound Ferry (hourly; 1hr 20min; $15 one-way, $54 with vehicle; ☎ 860 443 5281, ⓦ longislandferry.com) and one to Block Island, RI (Block Island Express; June–Sept up to 4/day; 1hr 15min; $25 one-way, $45 same-day return; ☎ 860 444 4624, ⓦ goblockisland.com).

EATING

Fred's Shanty 272 Pequot Ave ☎ 860 447 1301, ⓦ freds-shanty.com. This classic food shack has been knocking out tasty hot dogs, fries, shakes and burgers since 1972. Overlooks the Thames River, south of downtown. March–Oct daily 11.30am–9pm.

★ **Mangetout** 140 State St ☎ 860 444 2066, ⓦ mangetoutorganic.com. Contemporary organic and vegetarian place (though it does serve fish), with fresh breakfasts and lunches (tofu and walnut burgers from $7.65), and yummy desserts including ginger pavlova and hummingbird cake ($4.75). Daily 11am–4pm.

Hartford

The town that former resident Mark Twain once described as "the best built and handsomest ... I have ever seen" is today hardly recognizable as such. Rather, the modern capital of Connecticut, **HARTFORD**, is best known as the insurance centre of the United States. Though the city itself has fallen on rather hard times, the old architecture scattered around town continues to tell many a history. Highlights include the gold-domed **State Capitol** at 210 Capitol Ave (Sept–June 1hr tours hourly Mon–Fri 9.15am–1.15pm; July & Aug additional tour at 2.15pm; free; ☎ 860 240 0222, ⓦ cga .ct.gov/capitoltours), an 1878 concoction of styles. By contrast, down by the river the cutting-edge **Connecticut Science Center** (Sept–June Tues–Sun 10am–5pm; July & Aug daily; $19, kids 4–17 $14; ☎ 860 520 2116, ⓦ CTSciencecenter.org) is a magnet for families, with mind-boggling (and wildly entertaining) interactive exhibits.

Wadsworth Atheneum

600 Main St • Wed–Fri 11am–5pm, Sat & Sun 10am–5pm • $10 • ☎ 860 278 2670, ⓦ wadsworthatheneum.org

Hartford's pride and joy is the Greek Revival **Wadsworth Atheneum**, founded by Daniel Wadsworth in 1842 and the nation's oldest continuously operating public art museum. The world-class collection, spanning more than five thousand years, includes a precious ensemble of 160 **Hudson River School** paintings, Renaissance and Baroque masterpieces and a significant contemporary collection.

Mark Twain House and Museum

351 Farmington Ave • April–Dec Mon–Sat 9.30am–5.30pm, Sun noon–5.30pm; Jan–March closed Tues • $16 • ☎ 860 247 0998, ⓦ marktwainhouse.org • CT Transit buses #60, #62, #64, #66 from downtown Hartford

A mile west of downtown, the hilltop community known as Nook Farm was home in the 1870s to next-door neighbours Mark Twain and Harriet Beecher Stowe. The bizarrely ornate **Mark Twain House and Museum** was where the giant of American literature penned many of his classic works between 1874 and 1891. Tours offer tantalizing insights into the author's life, and also draw attention to the lavish and somewhat eccentric way the house was furnished – black-and-orange brickwork, whimsical carvings and the only domestic Tiffany interior open to the public. Twain's legendary wit and innovative writing style are highlighted by exhibits of his work and the engrossing Ken Burns biographical documentary shown in the **museum**.

Harriet Beecher Stowe Center

77 Forest St • May–Oct Mon–Sat 9.30am–5pm, Sun noon–5pm; Nov–April closed Mon & Tues • $10 • ☎ 860 522 9258, ⓦ harrietbeecherstowecenter.org

In 1852, **Harriet Beecher Stowe** made history with *Uncle Tom's Cabin*, her groundbreaking and best-selling anti-slavery novel. As a woman of the nineteenth century Stowe had no right to vote, yet she was able to turn public opinion decisively against slavery and became hugely influential. The **Harriet Beecher Stowe Center** serves as a poignant memorial to the author, and includes the white Victorian Gothic home she bought in 1873.

ARRIVAL AND INFORMATION

By plane Bradley International Airport (☎ 860 292 2000, ⓦ bradleyairport.com), 12 miles north of the city, is served by the hourly CT Transit Bradley Flyer ($1.25; ☎ 860 525 9181, ⓦ cttransit.com) to Union Station and Old State House in downtown Hartford. Taxis are also available outside (around $36 to downtown).

By bus Long-distance buses pull into the Union Station terminal.

Destinations Boston (12 daily; 1hr 50min–2hr 40min); Brattleboro, VT (1 daily; 2hr 20min); New Haven (6 daily; 1hr); New York City (26 daily; 2hr 30min–3hr); Providence,

RI (2 daily; 2hr 15min).

By train Union Station is at 1 Union Place, just off I-84, exit 48/49, on the western edge of downtown Hartford. Taxis tend to charge $10 for trips within the centre.

Destinations New Haven (6 daily; 47–58min); New York City (2 daily; around 3hr); Springfield, MA (7 daily; 40–50min).

Visitor centre 100 Pearl St (Mon–Fri 9am–5pm; ☎ 860 244 0253, ⓦ letsgoarts.org). There's also information at the Old State House.

HARTFORD

EATING

Abyssinian 533 Farmington Ave ☎ 860 218 2231, ⓦ getinjera.com. Authentic Ethiopian and Eritrean stews, salads, fish dishes and breads, with plentiful vegetarian options (mains $12.95–16.95); enjoy them all with the spongy *injera* bread made on site. Mon–Sat 5–10pm.

First & Last Tavern 939 Maple Ave ☎ 860 956 6000, ⓦ hartford.firstandlasttavern.com. Local favourite, no-frills Italian diner since 1936, with great pasta (try the exquisite clam sauce) and brick-oven pizzas – mediums (15-inch) $15–23. Mon–Wed 11.30am–9pm, Thurs 11.30am–9.30pm, Fri 11.30am–10.30pm, Sat noon–10.30pm, Sun noon–9pm.

★ **Mozzicato De Pasquale's Bakery & Pastry Shop** 329 Franklin Ave ☎ 860 296 0426, ⓦ mozzicatobakery .com. Historic old-time Italian café combining the DePasquale Bakery founded in 1908 with the pastry shop opened by Italian immigrant Gino Mozzicato in 1973. Serves delicious coffee and pastries – try the whipped cream cakes. Daily 7am–9pm.

★ **Rein's Deli** 435 Hartford Turnpike, 11 miles north in Vernon (exit 65 off I-84) ☎ 860 875 1344, ⓦ reinsdeli .com. Since 1973, road-weary souls have made the pilgrimage to this New York-style deli for its bulging pastrami sandwiches and addictive home-made pickles. Daily 7am–midnight.

New Haven

One of Connecticut's founding colonies, **NEW HAVEN** is best known for the idyllic Ivy League campus of **Yale University**, quality **pizza** joints and two world-class **art galleries**. It also offers some of the best restaurants, most exciting nightspots and most diverting cultural festivals in all of New England. Founded in 1638 by a group of wealthy Puritans from London, New Haven became the seat of Yale University in 1716, the third oldest college in the nation. Today, its leafy campus and magnificent Gothic architecture continue to exert a veritable historic presence. Tensions between the city and the university once made New Haven an uneasy place, though an active symbiosis has thrived since the early 2000s. Residents are encouraged to take advantage of the university's cultural and public offerings, and more than half of the student body volunteers in some sort of local outreach programme. The city is undergoing significant **development** in the downtown area, with vacant spaces around George Street slowly being transformed into new residential, cultural and commercial spaces.

The Green

Downtown, centred on the **Green**, retains a historic atmosphere. Laid out in 1638, the Green was the site of the city's original settlement and also functioned as a meeting area and burial ground. In its centre, the crypt of the 1814 **Center Church** (April–Oct Thurs & Sat 11am–1pm; free; ☎203 787 0121, ⓦnewhavencenterchurch.org) holds tombs dating back to 1687. Surrounding the Green are a number of stately government buildings and the student-filled **Chapel Street district**, a lively area filled with bookshops, independent stores, cafés and bars.

Yale University campus

Yale Visitor Information Center, 149 Elm St • Tours Mon–Fri 10.30am & 2pm, Sat & Sun 1.30pm • Free • ☎ 203 432 2300, ⓦ yale.edu/visitor

Founded in 1701, **Yale University** is one of the world's great seats of learning, with some 11,000 students and one of the largest libraries in the USA. You can visit most of the major buildings (just north of the Green) on self-guided tours, but to get inside one of the twelve colleges and learn about contemporary life at Yale, take a **guided tour** from the **visitor centre** (the oldest house in New Haven, built in 1767), conducted by students. Tour highlights include the cobbled courtyards of **Old Campus**, 216ft **Harkness Tower** and cathedral-like **Sterling Memorial Library**.

Yale Center for British Art

1080 Chapel St • Tues–Sat 10am–5pm, Sun noon–5pm • Free • ☎ 203 432 2800, ⓦ britishart.yale.edu

The Louis Kahn-designed **Yale Center for British Art** contains an exceptional collection of British paintings and sculpture, donated to Yale by Paul Mellon in 1966. The highlights reside in the fourth floor galleries of pre-1850 work, with special sections on **Turner**, **Hogarth** and **Constable**.

Yale University Art Gallery

1111 Chapel St • Tues–Fri 10am–5pm, Sat & Sun 11am–5pm; guided tours Sat 1.30pm • Free • ☎ 203 432 0600, ⓦ artgallery.yale.edu

The beautifully presented work on display at the **Yale University Art Gallery** has to be one of the best culture-vulture bargains in New England. The collection now has more than 185,000 objects dating from ancient Egyptian times to the present. Highlights include the exquisite **Italian Renaissance** collection, with pieces from Sienese School masters such as **Duccio**, and vivid Dutch portraits by **Frans Hals** and **Rubens**.

Yale Peabody Museum of Natural History

170 Whitney Ave • Mon–Sat 10am–5pm, Sun noon–5pm • $9 • ☎ 203 432 5050, ⓦ peabody.yale.edu

Yale's **Peabody Museum of Natural History** is easily recognizable by the huge bronze statue of a *Torosaurus latus* out front, a good indication of what's inside – a gasp-inducing collection of complete **dinosaur fossils**. The museum offers plenty more, however; skeletons of giant mastodons and sabre-tooth cats, early human fossils and rare Native American artefacts, including Red Cloud's feathered headdress.

ARRIVAL AND INFORMATION   NEW HAVEN

By bus Union Station, six blocks southeast of the Yale downtown campus, is home to Peter Pan and Greyhound services.

Destinations Boston (3 daily; 4hr); Hartford (6 daily; 1hr); New York (9 daily; 1hr 50min).
By train Union Station serves Amtrak trains and

Metro-North (☎ 800 638 7646, ⓦ mta.info/mnr), which serve all the stations between here and New York City at 30min intervals (up to 10min intervals during rush hours). If you arrive at night, grab a taxi to your hotel; Metro Taxi (☎ 203 777 7777) has a good reputation.

Destinations Boston (17 daily; 2hr 30min); New London (11 daily; 50min); New York (20 daily; 1hr 35min).

Visitor centre Just off the Green at 1000 Chapel St (Mon–Wed 10am–9pm, Thurs–Sat 10am–10pm, Sun noon–5pm; ☎ 203 773 9494, ⓦ infonewhaven.com).

ACCOMMODATION

Make sure to book well in advance if you intend to visit around Yale graduation in June, before the beginning of the term in September, and during Parents' Weekend in October. Cheaper **motels** are available along the I-91 corridor.

Courtyard New Haven at Yale 30 Whalley Ave ☎ 203 777 6221, ⓦ courtyard.com. Conveniently located just west of Yale campus, with 207 plush, modern rooms; some good weekend deals. $149

Farnum Guesthouse 616 Prospect St ☎ 203 562 7121, ⓦ farnamguesthouse.com. Best B&B option, with eight charming rooms close to Yale Divinity School. Full breakfast included. $109

New Haven Hotel 229 George St ☎ 203 498 3100, ⓦ newhavenhotel.com. Stylish hotel offering luxurious,

modern rooms equipped with huge flat-screen TVs, DVD players and iPod docks. There's also a handy 24hr laundry and gym. $159

★ **The Study at Yale** 1157 Chapel St ☎ 203 503 3900, ⓦ studyatyale.com. This relatively new boutique hotel is unquestionably New Haven's top spot, with iPod docks, flat-screen TVs and large workspaces in every stylish room. Its oversized windows have postcard-perfect views of the Yale campus, and there's great coffee and reading material in the lobby. $199

EATING

New Haven offers an eclectic range of restaurants, many located around the Green and on Chapel and College streets. Savour this university town's intellectual atmosphere at one of many fine downtown cafés, and don't leave without trying the pizza, available at the family-run Italian restaurants in Wooster Square. In warm weather months, more than forty food carts (Thai, Italian, Chinese, Greek, Mexican, soul food, cupcakes) set up shop at the intersection of York and Cedar streets.

Atticus Bookstore Café 1082 Chapel St ☎ 203 776 4040, ⓦ atticusbookstorecafe.com. Artisan breads, sandwiches, scones and great breakfast plates of applewood-smoked bacon, cranberry pecan toast and gruyère cheese ($5–7), all served in a relaxed bookshop. Mon–Thurs 7am–9pm, Fri & Sat 7am–10pm, Sun 8am–9pm.

Caseus 93 Whitney Ave ☎ 203 624 3373, ⓦ caseus newhaven.com. *Caseus* means cheese in Latin, and this popular fromagerie and bistro zealously exalts its moniker. It's a little pricey, but head here for charcuterie boards ($14), beet and cashew salad ($15) and divine grilled cheese sandwiches ($12), served on the sun-dappled patio. Reservations recommended. Mon & Tues 11.30am–2.30pm, Wed & Thurs 11.30am–2.30pm & 5.30–9pm, Fri & Sat 11.30am–2.30pm & 5.30–9.45pm.

★ **Frank Pepe's Pizzeria** 157 Wooster St ☎ 203 865 5762, ⓦ pepespizzeria.com. A Wooster St institution since 1925, drawing crowds with its coal-fired pizzas. Order the white clam pizza ($12.75–26.25) for the full experience. Daily 11.30am–10pm.

Louis' Lunch 261–263 Crown St ☎ 203 562 5507, ⓦ louislunch.com. This small, dark, ancient burger landmark allegedly served America's first hamburger, c.1900. It's still served on slices of toasted flat bread, with strictly no ketchup ($5.25) – cheese, tomato and onion are the only acceptable garnishes. Cash only. Tues & Wed 11am–3.45pm, Thurs–Sat noon–2am.

Sally's Apizza 237 Wooster St ☎ 203 624 5271, ⓦ sallysapizza.com. *Sally's* is the connoisseur's pizza choice (it only serves pizza, soda and beer), with fresh, zesty sauces and perfectly baked coal-fired pizzas (from $7.50). The downside: you sometimes wait more than an hour to get your food (get in line before 5pm). Wed–Fri 5–10pm, Sat & Sun 5–11pm.

Union League Café 1032 Chapel St ☎ 203 562 4299, ⓦ unionleaguecafe.com. Superb but pricey French brasserie specializing in fresh, seasonal produce (some sourced from the Yale Sustainable Garden Project). Dishes might include roasted Long Island duck or pan-seared swordfish (mains $23.75–36). Mon–Thurs 11.30am–2.30pm & 5–9.30pm, Fri 11.30am–2.30pm & 5–10pm, Sat 5–10pm.

NIGHTLIFE AND ENTERTAINMENT

★ **Bar** 254 Crown St ☎ 203 495 8924, ⓦ barnightclub .com. A simple name for a not-so-simple spot that's a combination pizzeria, brewery, bar and stylish nightclub. Mon & Tues 4pm–1am, Wed & Thurs 11.30am–2.30pm

& 4pm–1am, Fri–Sun 11.30am–1am.

Cafe Nine 250 State St ☎ 203 789 8281, ⓦ cafenine .com. Intimate club with live music every night, from punk to jazz to R&B. Cover $5–10. Daily 7pm–1am.

Owl Shop 268 College St ☎ 203 624 3250, ⓦ owlshop cigars.com. Smoky, old-school cigar bar (it dates to 1934) enhanced by good scotch and frequent jazz. Mon–Thurs 10am–1am, Fri & Sat 10am–2am, Sun noon–1am.
Rudy's 1227 Chapel St ☎ 203 865 1242, ⓦ rudysnew haven.com. A favourite local dive bar since 1934, despite being booted to this newish location in 2011 (the famous wood tables and wall panels, smothered in carvings, were preserved). Legendary Belgian-style *frites*, too. Mon–Thurs 11.30am–1am, Fri & Sat 11.30am–2am, Sun 10.30am–1am.

Shubert Performing Arts Center 247 College St ☎ 203 562 5666, ⓦ shubert.com. Founded in 1914, this gorgeous historic theatre has staged many world premieres, including *The King and I*, *Oklahoma!* and *The Sound of Music*, and it still hosts top-quality musicals and plays. Box office Mon–Fri 9.30am–5.30pm, Sat 10am–3pm.
Toad's Place 300 York St ☎ 203 562 5589, ⓦ toadsplace .com. Mid-sized live music venue where Bruce Springsteen and the Stones used to "pop in" to play impromptu gigs. Hosts regular dubstep nights ($5–25). Opening times vary according to events (usually 6–10pm).

Vermont

With its white churches and red barns, covered bridges and clapboard houses, snowy woods and maple syrup, **VERMONT** comes closer than any other New England state to fulfilling the quintessential image of small-town Yankee America. Much of the state is smothered by verdant, mountainous forests; indeed, the name Vermont supposedly comes from the French *vert mont*, or green mountain.

    This was the last area of New England to be settled, early in the eighteenth century. The leader of the New Hampshire settlers, the now-legendary **Ethan Allen**, formed his **Green Mountain Boys** in 1770, and during the Revolutionary War, this all-but-autonomous force helped to win the decisive Battle of Bennington. In 1777, Vermont declared itself an independent republic, with the first constitution in the world explicitly forbidding slavery and granting universal (male) suffrage; in 1791 it became the first state admitted to the Union after the original thirteen colonies. A more recent example of Vermont's progressive attitude occurred in 2000, when former governor Howard Dean signed the **civil union** bill into law, making the state the first in the USA to sanction marital rights for same-sex couples. Today, Vermont remains liberal when it comes to politics: the state continually attracts a mix of hippies, environmentalists and professionals escaping the rat race, most of them aspiring to an eco-friendly philosophy best epitomized by **Ben & Jerry's** additive-free, locally produced ice cream.

    With the occasional exception, such as the extraordinary assortment of Americana at the **Shelburne Museum** near **Burlington** (a lively city worth visiting in any case), there are few specific sights. Tourism here is more activity-oriented, and though the state's rural charms can be enjoyed year-round, most visitors come during two well-defined seasons: to see the spectacular **autumn foliage** in the first two weeks of October, and to **ski** in the depths of winter, when resorts such as **Killington** and **Stowe** spring to life.

The Green Mountains

North of western Massachusetts, the Berkshires roll into the much higher **Green Mountains**, Vermont's forested backbone. Most visitors begin their explorations of the area at **Brattleboro**, a lively college town with plenty of enticing stores and bars, or **Bennington**, forty miles on the other side of the hills and home to a smattering of historic attractions. From either town routes lead north through a hinterland of traditional Vermont villages – **Grafton**, **Chester** and **Weston** – to the ski resort at **Killington**.

Bennington

Little has happened in **BENNINGTON** to match the excitement of the days when Ethan Allen's Green Mountain Boys were based here more than two hundred years ago. A 306ft hilltop obelisk (mid-April to Oct daily 9am–5pm; $3) commemorates the 1777 **Battle of Bennington**, in which the Boys were a crucial factor in defeating the British

---

THE LONG TRAIL

Running along the ridge of Vermont's Green Mountains, 272 miles from the Massachusetts border to Québec, the **Long Trail** is one of America's premier **hiking routes**. Those planning on hiking its entire length should count on it taking between 25 and 30 days. The most conventional way of accomplishing this feat is to hike from shelter to shelter, maintained during summer and usually no more than a gentle day's hike apart. A moderate fee is charged at sites with caretakers (usually $5), and availability is on a first-come, first-served basis; if the shelter itself is full, you'll have to camp, so unless you plan to arrive early you'll need to carry a tent. All shelters are on the primitive side (no electricity or running water). Contact the Green Mountain Club (☎ 802 244 7037, ⓦ greenmountainclub.org) for more information.

---

under General Burgoyne (though the battle itself was fought just across the border in New York). Nearby, acclaimed New England poet **Robert Frost** (see p.220) was buried in the cemetery of Old First Church on Main St (Rte-9) in 1963. You should also check out the **Bennington Museum**, 75 Main St (July–Oct daily 10am–5pm; Feb–June & Nov–Dec closed Wed; $10; ☎ 802 447 1571, ⓦ benningtonmuseum.org), which contains a memorable array of Americana and the largest collection of paintings by folk artist Grandma Moses.

ACCOMMODATION, EATING AND DRINKING　　　　　BENNINGTON

★ **Blue Benn Diner** 314 North St (US-7) ☎ 802 442 5140. This authentic, 1940s-era diner draws a diverse crowd of hard-boiled locals and artsy students. In addition to the usual comfort foods, vegetarian dishes also feature on the menu. Mon & Tues 6am–5pm, Wed–Fri 6am–8pm, Sat & Sun 6am–4pm.

★ **Harwood Hill Motel** 864 Harwood Hill Rd (Rte-7A) ☎ 802 442 6278, ⓦ harwoodhillmotel.com. If you don't mind staying out of town, this friendly motel is a superb deal, with spacious, immaculate rooms tucked into the base of the mountains. **$81**

Madison Brewing Co 428 Main St ☎ 802 442 7397, ⓦ madisonbrewingco.com. Fun, stylish brewpub with hearty burgers (from $8.99) and six varieties of in-house beer ($4.25–6.75). Live blues most nights. Daily 11.30am–2am.

Brattleboro

Home to yoga studios, vintage record shops and bookstores catering to the town's youthful population, **BRATTLEBORO** is essentially a red-brick college town with little in the way of conventional sights – instead, it boasts a cosmopolitan art and live music scene, as well as tubing, kayaking and river skating and **ice-fishing** in winter. Just outside the centre at 400 Linden St (Rte-30), visit the excellent local fromagerie and wine shop at **Grafton Cheese** (daily 10am–6pm; free; ☎ 800 472 3866, ⓦ graftonvillagecheese.com).

ACCOMMODATION, EATING AND DRINKING　　　　　BRATTLEBORO

Chelsea Royal Diner 487 Marlboro Rd (Rte-9), W Brattleboro (exit 2, I-91) ☎ 802 254 8399, ⓦ chelsea royaldiner.com. Great local diner, offering $5.99 breakfast plates and pot roast for just $9.99 on Sunday. Home of the "original Cajun skillet" ($7.99). Daily 5.30am–9pm.

★ **Flat Street Brew Pub** 6 Flat St ☎ 802 257 1911, ⓦ flatstreet.net/pub. This bar is an ale-lover's paradise, with twenty beers on tap and good pub grub (grass-fed burger; $10). Charming ambience, too. Mon–Thurs & Sun 4pm–11pm, Fri & Sat 4pm–12.30am.

★ **Forty Putney Road B&B** 192 Putney Rd ☎ 802 254 6268, ⓦ fortyputneyroad.com. Superb B&B in a grand French Baronial-style house dating from 1929 (when it really was no. 40), with plush, contemporary-style rooms. Grab a pint by the fire in the cosy tavern, stroll the gardens or relax with a book in the gazebo. **$159**

Mocha Joe's 82 Main St ☎ 802 257 7794, ⓦ mochajoes .com. Good espresso in a stylish basement with exposed beams and slate floors – they roast their own beans. Free wi-fi. Mon–Thurs 7am–8pm, Fri 7am–10pm, Sat 7.30am–10pm, Sun 7.30am–8pm.

Grafton and Chester

Heading north from Brattleboro, routes 30 and 35 offer a less-travelled alternative into central Vermont. Few places come closer to the iconic image of rural New England than **GRAFTON**, a truly gorgeous ensemble of brilliant white clapboard buildings, shady trees and a bubbling brook in the centre. Further north, sleepy **CHESTER** blends prototypical Vermont clapboard houses with more ornate, Victorian architecture, laid out charmingly where Rte-11 runs along a narrow green.

ACCOMMODATION AND EATING
GRAFTON AND CHESTER

★ **Grafton Inn** 92 Main St, Grafton ☎800 843 1801, ⓦgraftoninnvermont.com. Around since 1801, this luxurious inn and restaurant has accommodated everyone from Rudyard Kipling to Teddy Roosevelt. The old carriage house is now a cosy pub, *Phelps Barn* (Tues–Sun 4–10pm). **$165**

Inn Victoria 321 Main St, Chester ☎802 875 4288, ⓦinnvictoria.com. Built in 1851, this elegant B&B goes to town on the Victorian theme with its eight ornate and comfortable rooms (albeit with flat-screen TVs, DVD players and iPod docks). **$140**

Weston

One of the prettiest villages along scenic Rte-100 (running north along the Green Mountains from Wilmington, almost halfway between Brattleboro and Bennington) is **WESTON**, which spreads out beside a little river and centres on an idyllic green. Most of the action revolves around the labyrinthine **Vermont Country Store** (daily 8.30am–6pm; ⓦvermontcountrystore.com), and the smaller but more authentic **Weston Village Store**, established in 1891 across the road at 660 Main St (daily 9am–6pm; ☎802 824 5477, ⓦwestonvillagestore.com). Both sell a range of vaguely rural and domestic articles, such as locally produced maple syrup and cheeses.

ACCOMMODATION AND EATING
WESTON

Bryant House 657 Main St ☎802 824 6287. A magnificent soda fountain dominates the 1885 mahogany bar of this restaurant. The menu includes classic New England fare such as chicken pie and "johnnycakes", made with cornbread and topped with molasses, as well as burgers and sandwiches (mains $14–18), May–Oct Mon–Wed 11am–3.30pm, Thurs–Sun 11am–9pm.

Colonial House Inn & Motel 287 Rte-100 ☎802 824 6286, ⓦcohoinn.com. Gorgeous old house dating back to 1790, with relatively cheap motel rooms in newer wings,

and what has to be one of the tastiest and most filling breakfasts in the state. **$85**

Inn at Weston 630 Main St (Rte-100) ☎802 824 6789, ⓦinnweston.com. This inviting, centrally located place offers the best accommodation in town, with a main building dating back to 1848 and cheaper rooms in the Coleman House annexe; check out the greenhouse, with around one thousand orchids, or relax on the deck or in the gazebo. **$185**

Calvin Coolidge State Historic Site

3780 Rte-100A, Plymouth Notch • Late May to mid-Oct daily 9.30am–5pm • $8 • ☎802 672 3773, ⓦhistoricsites.vermont.gov

Former president **Calvin Coolidge** was born in **Plymouth Notch** in 1872 (and buried in the local cemetery in 1933), and most of the village is now preserved as the immaculate **Calvin Coolidge State Historic Site**. Coolidge never lost ties to Plymouth Notch, conducting a "Summer White House" here during his presidency (1923–29). All of the buildings in which Coolidge's life played out have been kept more or less the way they were; the humble timber Birthplace (1845), the more comfortable Homestead (1876) where he grew up (preserved as it was when Coolidge was sworn in as President here in 1923) and his father's general store (1855).

Killington

Rte-100 eventually winds its way to **KILLINGTON**, a sprawling resort nine miles north of Plymouth Notch/Calvin Coolidge State Historic Site, that, since 1958, has grown from sleepy wilderness to become the most popular ski destination in the state. Other than a small collection of stores and motels on US-4, you'll find most of the action along **Killington Road**, which starts just before the northern intersection of US-4 and Rte-100. **Killington Resort** (4763 Killington Rd; Lift tickets $88 Sat & holidays, $80 Mon–Fri; ☎800 621 6867, ⓦkillington.com) itself sits at the top of the road, which terminates at the *K-1 Lodge*; in **summer** the focus is on **hiking** and **mountain biking**, with 45 miles of trails (basic park access $5; with K-1 Gondola rides $35/ day; bike rentals $70/day). You can also take the **K-1 Express Gondola** (July, Aug & Oct daily 10am–5pm; Sept Sat & Sun 10am–5pm; $10 one-way, $15 return) from the *K-1 Lodge* to the summit of **Killington Peak** (4241ft) and hike down.

ACCOMMODATION, EATING AND DRINKING | KILLINGTON

★ **Birch Ridge Inn** 37 Butler Rd ☎ 802 775 1010, ⓦ birchridge.com. This extra-cosy B&B offers classic, old-fashioned Vermont hospitality in a modern alpine ski lodge, with rooms in various styles and home-baked breads and muffins. $109

Inn at Long Trail 709 US-4, Sherburne Pass ☎ 802 775 7181, ⓦ innatlongtrail.com. After several nights spent in primitive shelters, hikers on the Long Trail will appreciate the comfort of this family-run B&B with tree-trunk beams and a stone fireplace. $105

Pickle Barrel 1741 Killington Rd ☎ 802 422 3035, ⓦ picklebarrelnightclub.com. A rowdy three-level bar and nightclub that gets crazy on winter weekends. Sept–April Thurs–Sat 8pm–close.

★ **Wobbly Barn Steakhouse** 2229 Killington Rd ☎ 802 422 6171, ⓦ wobblybarn.net. Some sort of lively entertainment every weekend, but the draw since 1963 has really been the beef and prime rib (broiled, mesquite-grilled and barbecued). Come for Tuesday's "Wild Game Night" (elk, venison, buffalo), or "Lynchburg Southern Barbecue Sundays". Mains from $25. Nov–April Mon–Wed & Sun 4.30–11pm, Thurs–Sat 4.30pm–1.30am.

Woodstock and around

Since its settlement in the 1760s, beautiful **WOODSTOCK**, a few miles west of the Connecticut River up US-4, has been one of Vermont's more refined centres (not to be confused with Woodstock, New York, namesake of the 1969 music festival). Its distinguished houses cluster around an oval green, now largely taken over by art galleries and tearooms.

Marsh-Billings-Rockefeller National Historical Park

54 Elm St (Rte-12), 1 mile north of Woodstock • Late May to Oct daily 10am–5pm; tours run every 30min–1hr • $8 (includes tour), kids under 15 free; combined ticket with Billings Farm $17 • ☎ 802 457 3368, ⓦ nps.gov/mabi

Hard to imagine today, but thanks to intensive logging, the leafy hills of Vermont were virtually stripped bare by the 1860s. The **Marsh-Billings-Rockefeller National Historical Park** encompasses the nineteenth-century mansion of three generations of groundbreaking conservationists who managed to reverse this trend. Illuminating one-hour ranger **tours** (the only way to visit) provide plenty of context. You can also explore 553 acres of forest around the site, which contain a twenty-mile network of **hiking trails** across Mount Tom (1359ft). Park your car and reserve a tour at the Billings Farm and Museum (see below) across the road.

Billings Farm and Museum

5302 River Rd (off Rte-12), 1 mile north of Woodstock • May–Oct daily 10am–5pm; Nov–Feb Sat & Sun 10am–3.30pm • $12, kids (5–15) $6, kids 3–4 ($3), combined ticket with Marsh-Billings-Rockefeller National Historical Park $17 • ☎ 802 457 2355, ⓦ billingsfarm.org

Across the street from the Marsh-Billings-Rockefeller National Historical Park lies the **Billings Farm and Museum**, the working part of the former Billings and Rockefeller property, established in 1871. Exhibits in the barn cover various aspects of farm life, as well as the history of the site. In the grounds are various sheds and displays, but the real crowd-pleaser is **milking time** in the cowshed (daily 3.15–5pm), and especially for kids, the chance to pet horses and Jersey calves.

ACCOMMODATION AND EATING | WOODSTOCK AND AROUND

Applebutter Inn 7511 Happy Valley Rd (just off US-4) in Taftsville, 4 miles east of Woodstock ☎ 802 457 4158, ⓦ applebutterinn.com. Cosy B&B in an 1854 gabled house, with comfortable beds, personable proprietors and huge breakfasts kicking off with tasty home-made granola. $100

Bentley's 1 Elm St ☎ 802 457 3232, ⓦ bentleysof woodstock.com. Superior versions of traditional bistro food (tequila and lime chicken, duck quesadillas, garlic and Guinness mussels) and a good range of microbrews. Casual and moderately priced (sandwiches from $9.95, main courses $19.95–25.95). Mon–Thurs 11.30am–9.30pm, Fri & Sat 11am–10pm, Sun 11am–9.30pm.

Braeside Motel 432 Woodstock Rd (US-4) ☎ 802 457 1366, ⓦ braesidemotel.com. Spacious, clean and simple family-owned motel a mile east of the village, with friendly owners and a pool. **$98**

Mountain Creamery 33 Central St ☎ 802 457 1715, ⓦ mountaincreameryvt.com. Filling country breakfasts and lunch served daily, as well as some fine home-made ice cream downstairs. Daily 7am–3pm.

★ **Woodstock Inn and Resort** 14 The Green ☎ 802 457 1100, ⓦ woodstockinn.com. The largest, fanciest and best place to stay in the area, with sumptuous rooms, manicured grounds dotted with Adirondack chairs, an eighteen-hole golf course and four gourmet restaurants. It's also got a winter sports facility and a fitness centre with a spa. **$260**

Quechee

Six miles east of Woodstock, **QUECHEE** is off the main US-4 highway, a combination of quaint Vermont village and expensive new condos. The main highlight here lies on US-4 itself, **Quechee Gorge State Park**, which preserves the splendours of the **Quechee Gorge**. A delicate bridge spans the 165ft chasm of the Ottauquechee River, and hiking trails lead down from the **visitor centre** (daily: May–Oct 9am–5pm; Nov–April 10am–4pm; ☎ 802 295 6852).

The river spins the turbines of the **Simon Pearce Glass Mill** (daily 10am–9pm; ☎ 802 295 2711, ⓦ simonpearce.com), housed in a former wool mill along Main Street back in Quechee. Here, you can watch glass bowls and plates being blown, and then eat from them at the superb on-site **restaurant** (see below).

ACCOMMODATION AND EATING | QUECHEE

Quality Inn at Quechee Gorge 5817 Woodstock Rd, (US-4) ☎ 802 295 7600, ⓦ qualityinnquechee.com. Standard motel accommodation and the area's least expensive hotel, with indoor heated pool and continental breakfast included. **$125**

★ **Simon Pearce Glass** 1760 Main St ☎ 802 295 1470, ⓦ simonpearce.com. Inventive New American-type main courses ($19–35), as well as occasional no-nonsense beef and Guinness stew and shepherd's pie. Daily 11.30am–2.45pm & 6–9pm.

Montpelier

Some 55 miles north of Quechee on I-89, **MONTPELIER** is the smallest state capital in the nation, with fewer than ten thousand inhabitants. Surrounded by leafy gardens, the golden-domed **Vermont State House** at 115 State St (Nov–June Mon–Fri 7.30am–4.15pm; July–Oct also Sat 11am–3pm; free; free guided tours every 30min July–Oct Mon–Fri 10am–3.30pm, Sat 11am–2.30pm; ☎ 802 828 2228, ⓦ vtstatehouse.org) is well worth a peek for its marble-floored and mural-lined hallways.

INFORMATION | MONTPELIER

Visitor centre 134 State St (Mon–Fri 6am–5pm, Sat & Sun 9am–5pm; ☎ 802 828 5981, ⓦ vermontvacation.com). Offers plenty of information on local and statewide attractions.

ACCOMMODATION AND EATING

Capital Plaza Hotel 100 State St ☎ 802 274 5252, ⓦ capitolplaza.com. The best hotel in downtown Montpelier offers comfortable and spacious digs across from the Art Deco Capitol Theatre, though note that you are paying a premium for the location. **$152**

Coffee Corner 83 Main St, at State St ☎ 802 229 9060, ⓦ coffeecorner.com. A Montpelier standard for more than sixty years, where you can scarf down cheap diner food at Formica tables or rub elbows with

Vermont's political potentates at the lunch counter. Daily 6.30am–3pm.

La Brioche Bakery & Cafe 89 Main St ☎ 802 229 0443, ⓦ neci.edu/labrioche. Cheerful, well-designed bakery run by New England Culinary Institute students. The "1/2 Bag Lunch" will get you half a sandwich, a small but interesting salad or soup and a cookie (try the "Vermont Crunchy": a peanut butter oatmeal cookie with chocolate chips and nuts). Mon–Fri 7am–5pm, Sat 7am–3pm.

Ben & Jerry's Ice Cream Factory

1281 Waterbury–Stowe Rd (Rte-100) • Tours every 30min daily: July to mid-Aug 9am–8pm; mid-Aug to late Oct 9am–6pm; late Oct to June 10am–5pm; store and "scoop shop" close 1hr later • $4, kids (under 12) free • ☎ 802 882 1240, ⓦ benjerry.com

Few people paid much attention to **WATERBURY** before 1985, when Ben Cohen and Jerry Greenfield (whose ice-cream-making history began in 1978, in a renovated Burlington gas station) decided to locate their new manufacturing facility in the tiny town. Today **Ben & Jerry's Ice Cream Factory** is nestled one mile north of I-89 in the village of Waterbury Center. Tours of the production factory, where (weekdays only) machines turn cream, sugar and other natural ingredients into more than fifty flavours, are followed by a free mini-scoop of the stuff – you can buy more at the gift shop and ice cream counter outside.

Stowe

At the foot of Vermont's highest mountain, **Mount Mansfield** (4393ft), there is still a beautiful nineteenth-century village at the heart of **STOWE**, with its white-spired meeting house and town green. Though it has been a popular summer destination since before the Civil War, what really put the town on the map was the arrival of the **Von Trapp family** in 1941, whose story inspired *The Sound of Music*. While most of historic Stowe village lies along Rte-100 (Main St), Rte-108 (Mountain Rd) is Stowe's primary thoroughfare, stretching from the main village on Rte-100 up to the **Stowe Mountain Resort** (daily 8am–4pm; lift tickets $92/day; summer day passes $80; ☎802 253 3000, ⓦ stowe.com), and on through the mountain gap known as **Smugglers' Notch**.

Mount Mansfield

Rte-108 • ☎ 802 253 7311, ⓦ stowe.com

Ascending to the peak of **Mount Mansfield**, the highest point in Vermont, is a challenge no matter how you do it, but you'll be rewarded by dizzying views that go all the way to Canada. Weather permitting, the easiest approach is to drive up the **Toll Road**, a winding 4.5-mile ascent of mostly dirt track that begins seven miles up from Stowe village on Mountain Road (late May to mid-Oct daily 9am–4pm; $28/car). The road ends at a tiny **visitor centre** (3850ft); from here it's a short scramble to the ridge that runs along the mountain top, and around 1.5 miles to the peak, known as "the Chin" (4393ft). Alternatively, you can take the **Gondola Skyride** (late-June to mid-Oct daily 10am–4.30pm; $19, $25 return), which affords jaw-dropping views and ends at **Cliff House** (3660ft).

GETTING AROUND AND INFORMATION   STOWE

Bike rental In summer, when the crowds thin out considerably, Stowe's cross-country skiing trails double as mountain bike routes. AJ's Ski & Sports, 350 Mountain Rd, rents bikes from $24/day (daily 9am–6pm; ☎802 253 4593, ⓦ ajssports.com).

Visitor centre 51 Main St, at Depot Rd (June–Aug Mon–Sat 9am–8pm, Sun 9am–5pm; Sept–May hours vary; ☎802 253 7321, ⓦ gostowe.com).

ACCOMMODATION

★ **Green Mountain Inn** 1 Main St ☎802 253 7301, ⓦ greenmountaininn.com. Gorgeous hotel built in 1833, centrally located and amply outfitted – options range from opulent suites with jacuzzi tubs and fireplaces to plush rooms. Offers two good restaurants, free health club use, free tea and cookies (daily 4–5pm) and a heated pool. **$159**

Stowe Mountain Lodge 7412 Mountain Rd ☎802 253 3560, ⓦ stowemountainlodge.com. The pride of Stowe Mountain Resort stands right next to the Spruce Peak ski area, offering real luxury; floor-to-ceiling windows make the most of the scenery, while rooms boast designer furnishings and contemporary art. LCD TVs, iPod docks and stone-frame fireplaces are standard. **$263**

Trapp Family Lodge 42 Trapp Hill Rd ☎802 253 8511, ⓦ trappfamily.com. Austrian-themed ski resort (as fancy as it is expensive) on the site of the original Trapp family house, also the first cross-country ski centre in America. Rates include cross-country ski passes and access to skiing and hiking trails. **$275**

EATING, DRINKING AND ENTERTAINMENT

★ **Blue Moon Café** 25 School St ☎802 253 7006, ⓦbluemoonstowe.com. Inventive New American fare (mains $16–31) featuring local game (braised venison and the like) and seafood; Stowe's best all-round dining choice. Good wine list. Tues–Sun 6–9pm.

DeliBakery 42 Trapp Hill Rd ☎802 253 5705, ⓦtrappfamily.com. The Trapp family bakery serves up Austrian *wurst*, meat and cheese boards and all sorts of pastries from $6. Daily 7am–8pm.

Matterhorn 4969 Mountain Rd ☎802 253 8198, ⓦmatterhornbar.com. The region's best bands have been coming here for years – you can enjoy live music in the nightclub most weekends, or listen from the downstairs wood-panelled dining room (specializing in, oddly, pizzas and sushi). Tues–Sun 5pm–midnight.

★ **McCarthy's** 2043 Mountain Rd ☎802 253 8626, ⓦmccarthysrestaurantstowe.com. Irish-themed joint, but especially noted for its huge, all-American breakfasts: Mansfield Valley eggs, Vermont maple bacon, corned beef hash and thick pancakes (plates $6–9). It's been a local favourite since 1974 – expect long queues at the weekend. Daily 6.30am–2.30pm.

Burlington and around

Lakeside **BURLINGTON**, Vermont's largest city, with a population near forty thousand, is one of the most enjoyable destinations in New England. Renowned for its liveability and green development, it's home to a hip, eclectic community that fuses urbanism with rural Vermont values. The city faces 150-mile-long **Lake Champlain**, which forms the natural boundary between Vermont and New York State. Burlington's founders included Revolutionary War hero Ethan Allen and his family; Ethan's brother Ira founded the University of Vermont. Home to five colleges and universities, the area has blossomed as a youthful and outward-looking college town. Its downtown is easily strolled by foot, notably around the **Church Street Marketplace**.

The waterfront

In the summertime, locals and visitors alike stroll leisurely along the pedestrian boardwalks that line Burlington's **waterfront**, taking in gorgeous views of the Adirondack Mountains (in wintertime, they may be strolling *on* Lake Champlain, which often freezes over in February). The highly interactive **ECHO Lake Aquarium and Science Center** (1 College St; daily 10am–5pm; $12.50, kids 3–17 $9.50; ☎802 864 1848, ⓦechovermont.org), situated at the water's edge, is an excellent place to bring young children. Burlington's annual waterfront **Winter Festival** (first week in Feb) boasts fabulous ice sculptures, carved on the premises. If you're looking to get onto Lake Champlain, opt for the convivial *Spirit of Ethan Allen III* (May–Oct; 1hr narrated cruises from $16.21; ☎802 862 8300, ⓦsoea.com), which sets out from the Burlington Boathouse at 1 College St.

The Shelburne Museum

6000 Shelburne Rd (US-7), Shelburne (7 miles south of Burlington) • Mid-May to Oct daily 10am–5pm; Nov & Dec Tues–Sun 10am–5pm • $22, valid for two successive days • ☎ 802 985 3346, ⓦ shelburnemuseum.org

It takes a whole day, if not more, to take in the fabulous 45-acre collection of unalloyed Americana gathered at the **Shelburne Museum**, seven miles south of Burlington. More than thirty buildings dot the beautifully landscaped grounds, from the 80ft-diameter **McClure Round Barn** and horseshoe-shaped **Circus Building** to the enormous, 892-ton steam paddlewheeler **Ticonderoga**.

Shelburne Farms

1611 Harbor Rd, Shelburne (7 miles south of Burlington) • Daily: mid-May to mid-Oct 9am–5.30pm; mid-Oct to mid-May 10am–5pm • $8; with guided tour $11 • ☎ 802 985 8686, ⓦ shelburnefarms.org

Next to the Shelburne Museum, **Shelburne Farms** is a working farm reborn as a nonprofit environmental education centre; activities include cow milking, egg collection and rabbit-petting. The hilly landscape is peppered with three massive buildings: the main house, a coach barn and a horseshoe-shaped farm barn. You can get some exercise by walking the 4.5-mile Farm Trail, which circles the property, or the half-mile Lone Tree Hill trail and numerous side paths diverging from the roadways.

ARRIVAL AND DEPARTURE

BURLINGTON AND AROUND

By plane Burlington International Airport (☏ 802 863 1889, ⓦ burlingtonintlairport.com) is a few miles east of downtown along US-2 (bus #12 to downtown runs every 30min 6.30am–10pm; $1.25). Taxis to downtown cost around $15.
By bus Greyhound buses drop off at the airport.
Destinations Boston (4 daily; 4hr 25min–5hr 25min); Montpelier (4 daily; 45min); Montréal (4 daily; 2hr 30min).

By train Amtrak's *Vermonter* trains arrive at 29 Railroad Ave, Essex Junction, an inconvenient 5 miles northeast of town (connecting buses $1.25). Note that the station only opens twice a day (for the two trains) and there is no ticket office.
Destinations Brattleboro (1 daily; 3hr 7min); Montpelier (1 daily; 38min); Springfield, MA (5hr 13min); Waterbury (1 daily; 25min); Windsor (1 daily; 2hr 5min).

GETTING AROUND AND INFORMATION

By bus The local CCTA bus ($1.25; ☏ 802 864 0211, ⓦ cctaride.org) connects points all over the downtown area, and travels to the nearby towns of Winooski, Essex and Shelburne. You can get route maps and schedules at the main downtown terminal on the corner of Cherry and Church sts. CCTA also operates the very convenient (free) College Street Shuttle between the University of Vermont

and the waterfront, with stops at the Fleming Museum and the Church Street Marketplace (every 15–30min: Mon–Fri 6.30am–7pm; late May to June & Sept to mid-Oct also Sat & Sun 9am–9pm; no services July & Aug).
Chamber of Commerce 60 Main St (mid-May to Aug Mon–Fri 8am–5pm, Sat & Sun 9am–5pm; Sept to mid-May Mon–Fri 8am–5pm; ☏ 877 686 5253, ⓦ vermont.org).

ACCOMMODATION

Bel Aire Motel 111 Shelburne Rd ☏ 802 863 3116, ⓦ belairevt.com. This no frills, old-fashioned roadside motel makes a cheap alternative to the numerous chains in the area, with basic but clean doubles and decent cable TV. **$79**
Courtyard Burlington Harbor 25 Cherry St ☏ 802 864 4700, ⓦ marriott.com. The best hotel downtown, with a fabulous location near the waterfront and newish, luxurious rooms and amenities; buffet breakfast, indoor pool and LCD TVs included. Parking $8/day. **$229**
North Beach Campground 60 Institute Rd ☏ 802 862

0942, ⓦ enjoyburlington.com. Less than 2 miles north of town on the shores of Lake Champlain, with 137 sites and various other facilities (including plenty for the kids), and access to a sandy beach. Open May to mid-Oct. **$26**, hookups **$36**
★ **Willard Street Inn** 349 S Willard St ☏ 802 651 8710, ⓦ willardstreetinn.com. The large rooms at this distinctive 1881 Queen Anne are brilliantly restored (but not frilly). You'll get lots of home-baked goodies, excellent breakfasts served in a glass sunroom and a lush, relaxing English garden. **$150**

EATING AND DRINKING

American Flatbread 115 St Paul St ☏ 802 861 2999, ⓦ americanflatbread.com. Wildly popular pizza place, especially at weekends, for its organic wheat dough and all-natural toppings, including local cheeses and sausage (from $11.50 for a large). Mon–Thurs & Sun 11.30am–2.30pm & 5–10pm, Fri & Sat 11.30am–2.30pm & 5–11pm.
Farmhouse Tap & Grill 160 Bank St ☏ 802 859 0888, ⓦ farmhousetg.com. Built on the heap of a former *McDonald's*, with a beer garden with a huge list of brews and a restaurant with gourmet burgers and locally sourced pub grub. Fun tip: check out the old *McD's* tiles on the dining room floor. Mon–Thurs & Sun 11.30am–10pm, Fri & Sat 11.30am–11pm.
Leunig's Bistro 115 Church St ☏ 802 863 3759, ⓦ leunigsbistro.com. Sleek, modern bistro serving contemporary French cuisine; dinner mains range from $21–32, but the lunch plates are better value ($12–15). Outdoor dining when the weather permits. Mon–Thurs 11am–10pm, Fri 11am–11pm, Sat 9am–11pm, Sun 9am–10pm.

Muddy Waters 184 Main St ☏ 802 658 0466. A popular coffee house whose crazy interior is lined with used furniture, thrift-store rejects, plants and rough-hewn panelled walls. Extremely potent caffeinated beverages. Mon 7.30am–6pm, Tues–Thurs 7.30am–11pm, Fri & Sat 7.30am–midnight, Sun 8.30am–10pm.
★ **Myer's Bagel Bakery** 377 Pine St ☏ 802 863 5013. Get a taste of Montréal-style bagels at this local early-morning favourite; the Montréal Spice bagel is an addictive treat (the "spice" is steak seasoning). Don't be put off by the out-of-the-way location. Plain bagels from $1, cash only. Daily 4am–1pm.
★ **Penny Cluse Café** 169 Cherry St ☏ 802 651 8834, ⓦ pennycluse.com. All-day breakfast nook famed for its gingerbread pancakes ($7) and biscuits doused in herb gravy ($3.50). Lunchtime offerings include grilled chicken with orzo ($9.75) and beer-battered fish tacos ($10.75). Expect queues at the weekend. Mon–Fri 6.45am–3pm, Sat & Sun 8am–3pm.

Trattoria Delia 152 St Paul St • 802 864 5253, ⦿ trattoriadelia.com. Traditional regional Italian fare that goes beyond the usual pasta dishes – try the wild boar served over soft polenta – and a tempting wine list, at reasonable prices (pastas from $14.50, main courses from $21). A great date spot. Daily 5–10pm.

New Hampshire

"Live Free or Die" is the official motto of **NEW HAMPSHIRE**, summing up a deeply held belief in rugged individualism and independence that goes back to colonial times. The state boasts densely forested mountains, whitewater rivers and challenging ski resorts, making it the premier state in the region for outdoor activities

New Hampshire's short Atlantic coastline is a stretch of mellow, sun-drenched beaches capped by **Portsmouth**, a well-preserved colonial town with a crop of excellent restaurants and stylish inns. Inland, there are more than 1300 lakes; the largest, **Lake Winnipesaukee**, is ringed with both tourist resorts and quiet villages. The magnificent **White Mountains** spread across northern New Hampshire, culminating in the highest peak in New England, formidable **Mount Washington**.

Portsmouth

New Hampshire's most urbane city, **PORTSMOUTH**, just off I-95 at the mouth of the Piscataqua River, blends small-town accessibility with a dash of sophistication. It has always been an important port – it was state capital until 1808 – but retains the feel of a New England village, with the spire of **North Church** in the central **Market Square**, dating from 1854, remaining the tallest structure in town. Having endured the cycles of prosperity and hardship typical of many New England cities, Portsmouth has found its most recent triumphs in the cultural arena, attracting artists, musicians, writers and, notably, gourmet chefs. In addition to a wealth of tantalizing restaurants, Portsmouth's unusual abundance of well-preserved colonial buildings makes for an absorbing couple of days.

Moffatt-Ladd House

154 Market St • June to late Oct Mon–Sat 11am–5pm, Sun 1–5pm • $6 • 603 436 8221, ⦿ moffattladd.org

Of the grand old mansions in Portsmouth, the **Moffatt-Ladd House** is one of the most impressive. Completed in 1763, the building is particularly notable for its Great Hall, which occupies more than a quarter of the first floor. Using inventories left by Captain John Moffatt, who designed the home, historians have transformed the **Yellow Chamber** (also on the second floor) into one of the best-documented eighteenth-century American rooms.

John Paul Jones House

43 Middle St • May–Oct daily 11am–5pm • $6 • 603 436 8420, ⦿ portsmouthhistory.org

Home to the Portsmouth Historical Society's museum, the 1758 Georgian **John Paul Jones House** was where the US's first great naval commander boarded in 1777 while his ships were outfitted in the Langdon shipyards. Inside the boxy yellow structure you can view some of his naval memorabilia and lavish period-furnished rooms. Upstairs there's an incredibly detailed exhibit on the **1905 Portsmouth Peace Treaty** between Russia and Japan.

Strawbery Banke Museum

14 Hancock St • May–Oct daily 10am–5pm • $17.50 • 603 433 1100, ⦿ strawberybanke.org

Portsmouth was officially founded by English Settlers (led by Captain Walter Neal) in 1630, but was known as **Strawbery Banke** until 1653 for the abundance of wild strawberries in the area. The **Strawbery Banke Museum** is a collection of 37 meticulously restored and maintained historic wooden buildings, including the **Shapley Drisco House**: half of the house is outfitted as from the 1790s, the other half, from the 1950s. The 1766 **Pitt Tavern** holds the most historic significance, having acted as a meeting place for patriots and loyalists during the Revolution, while one of the most intriguing exhibits occupies the **Shapiro House** (1795), twentieth-century home of a Russian-Jewish immigrant family. The stained-wood **Sherburne House** is a rare survivor from 1695 – its interior focuses on seventeenth-century architecture.

ARRIVAL, INFORMATION AND TOURS

By bus C&J Trailways (☎ 800 258 7111, 🌐 ridecj.com) has frequent daily services from Boston/Logan Airport and New York that terminate at its Portsmouth Transportation Center, 185 Grafton Drive (☎ 603 430 1100), on the outskirts of town at exit 3A I-95. Greyhound buses arrive at 55 Hanover St, a short walk from Market Square.

Chamber of Commerce 500 Market St (Mon–Fri 8.30am–5pm; ☎ 603 610 5510, 🌐 portsmouthchamber

PORTSMOUTH

.org), a 15min walk from Market Square (parking on site). It also operates an information kiosk in Market Square (May–Oct daily 10am–5pm). See also 🌐 portsmouthnh .com.

Tours Portsmouth Harbor Cruises at Ceres Street Dock offer several trips and have a full bar on every boat (90min harbour cruise $18, 1hr evening cruise $14; call ☎ 603 436 8084 for departure times, 🌐 portsmouthharbor.com).

ACCOMMODATION

⭐ **Ale House Inn** 121 Bow St ☎ 603 431 7760, 🌐 ale houseinn.com. Portsmouth's only waterfront inn, above the town's theatre (free tickets for guests), is a truly luxurious treat – a contemporary boutique hotel with each room equipped with a flat-screen TV and an iPad. The ten cosy rooms occupy a remodelled brick brewery warehouse dating from 1880. Free parking and use of mountain bikes. **$199**

Inn at Strawbery Banke 314 Court St ☎ 603 436

7242, 🌐 innatstrawberybanke.com. Seven bright, relaxing rooms, several with four-poster beds, in a sumptuous colonial home built in the early 1800s near the waterfront. Reservations strongly recommended. **$160**

Port Inn 505 US-1 Bypass, at the traffic circle ☎ 603 436 4378, 🌐 theportinn.com. These good-value, comfortable and clean rooms, some with microwaves and refrigerators, are among the cheapest in Portsmouth. **$125**

EATING

The Friendly Toast 113 Congress St ☎ 603 430 2154, 🌐 thefriendlytoast.com. Kitschy thrift-store decor with an interesting selection of breakfasts, sandwiches and omelettes (from $7.75), a huge menu of mixed drinks, shakes, beers and coffees and an equally eclectic crowd. The portions are enormous. Mon–Thurs 7am–10pm, Fri 7am–Sun 9pm (24hr).

⭐ **Jumpin' Jay's Fish Café** 150 Congress St ☎ 603 766 3474, 🌐 jumpinjays.com. Hands down the best seafood in Portsmouth (and probably the state), with an amazing raw bar, dishes such as lobster mac and cheese and fish

tacos and a "fresh catches" menu, which might offer Florida *mahi-mahi* and Atlantic scallops. Mains $19–31. Mon–Thurs 5.30–9.30pm (winter closes at 9pm), Fri & Sat 5–10pm, Sun 5–9pm.

Ristorante Massimo 59 Penhallow St ☎ 603 436 4000, 🌐 ristorantemassimo.com. Intimate, smart Italian restaurant, with fresh pasta ($12–33) and plenty of seafood main courses ($23–35), such as olive oil-poached monkfish risotto. Service is exceptional. Reservations essential. Mon–Sat 5–10pm.

DRINKING AND NIGHTLIFE

Music Hall 28 Chestnut St ☎ 603 436 2400, 🌐 themusic hall.org. Portsmouth's largest performance space hosts well-known, nationally touring folk, rock, jazz and blues bands, classical concerts, plus dance, theatre and other performances every day of the year. The Beaux Arts building dates from 1878. Box office Mon–Sat noon–6pm.

Portsmouth Brewery 56 Market St ☎ 603 431 1115, 🌐 portsmouthbrewery.com. More like a restaurant than

a pub, with most of the interior taken up by wait-staffed tables – cosy up to the bar if you just want to sample their range of exceptional beers. Daily 11.30am–12.30am.

Press Room 77 Daniel St ☎ 603 431 5186, 🌐 press roomnh.com. Popular for its nightly live jazz, blues, folk and bluegrass performances. Also serves decent microbrews, inexpensive salads, burgers (from $9.95) and pizza ($8.95) in a casual pub-style setting. Mon 5pm–1am, Tues–Thurs & Sun 4pm–1am, Fri & Sat noon–1am.

The Merrimack Valley

The financial and political heartland of New Hampshire is the **Merrimack Valley**, home to the state capital, **Concord** (pronounced "conquered"), with its elegant, gold-domed

State House (107 N Main St; Mon–Fri 8am–4.15pm; free; ☎603 271 2154, ⓦnh.gov), and with a few worthy detours off I-93, the main highway through the region.

Canterbury Shaker Village

288 Shaker Rd, Canterbury (I-93 exit 18) • Mid-May to Oct daily 10am–5pm • $17, good for two consecutive days • ☎603 783 9511, ⓦshakers.org

About twenty minutes north of Concord, **Canterbury Shaker Village** is New England's premier museum of Shaker life. In 1792, this tranquil village became the sixth Shaker community in the USA and, at its zenith in the mid-nineteenth century, there were some three hundred people living on the grounds; the last Shaker living in Canterbury died in 1992 aged 96. You can take several engrossing one-hour **tours** of the site, which introduce the Shaker ideals, day-to-day life and architecture (there are 25 perfectly restored buildings in the village).

Robert Frost Farm

122 Rockingham Rd (Rte-28; exit 4 from I-93), Derry • May, June & Sept to mid-Oct Wed–Sun 10am–4pm; July & Aug daily 10am–4pm • Gardens and barn free, farmhouse $5 • ☎603 432 3091, ⓦrobertfrostfarm.org

South of Concord, on the outskirts of Derry, the **Robert Frost Farm** is the most illuminating New England memorial to the great poet, and the only one he himself wished to preserve (Frost lived here with his young family between 1900 and 1909). Fans should visit for the optional **free guided tours** as much as the house itself, entertaining hour-long introductions to Frost's life, character and poetry.

The Lakes Region

Of the literally hundreds of lakes occupying the state's central corridor, the biggest by far is **Lake Winnipesaukee**, which forms the centre of the holiday-oriented **Lakes Region**. Long segments of its three-hundred-mile shoreline, especially in the east, consist of thick forests sweeping down to waters dotted with little islands, disturbed only by pleasure craft. The most sophisticated of the towns along the shoreline is **Wolfeboro**; the most fun has to be **Weirs Beach**. To get on the water consider a trip on **M/S Mount Washington**, a 230ft monster of a boat that departs from the dock in the centre of Weirs Beach several times a day to sail to Wolfeboro (mid-May to Oct; from $29; ☎603 366 5531, ⓦcruisenh.com).

Wolfeboro

Because Governor Wentworth of New Hampshire built his summer home nearby in 1768, tiny **WOLFEBORO** claims to be "the oldest summer resort in America". Sandwiched between lakes Winnipesaukee and Wentworth, it's certainly the most attractive town in the region – access to the **waterfront**, with wide, fine views, is one of the best reasons to stay.

Weirs Beach

The short boardwalk at **WEIRS BEACH**, the very essence of seaside tackiness (even if it is 50 miles inland), is the social centre of the Lakes Region in the summer. Its little wooden jetty throngs with vacationers, the amusement arcades jingle with cash and there's even a neat little crescent of sandy beach, suitable for family swimming. A quieter diversion here is the **Winnipesaukee Railroad** (June to late Oct; $14/1hr, $16/2hr; ☎603 279 5253, ⓦhoborr.com), which operates scenic trips along the lakeshore between Weirs Beach and Meredith, four miles north.

ACCOMMODATION AND EATING	THE LAKES REGION

WOLFEBORO

123 North Main Bed & Breakfast 123 N Main St (Rte-109) ☎603 569 9191, ✉rbranscombe@juno.com. Cosy, 1854 colonial-style inn close to the lake and town. Rooms are tastefully furnished and full breakfast is included. **$125**

★ **Bailey's Bubble** 5 Railroad Ave ☎ 603 569 3612, ⓦ baileysbubble.com. Luscious ice cream in the centre of town; try "Maine Black Bear" (raspberry, chocolate chips and truffles) or "Moose Tracks" (vanilla, fudge and peanut butter cups). $3–3.75 a scoop. Late May to early Sept daily 11am–10pm.

★ **Wolfeboro Inn** 90 N Main St (Rte-109) ☎ 603 569 3016, ⓦ wolfeboroinn.com. Built in 1812, this historic inn is on the waterfront with its own beach and some of the best restaurants in town. It has 44 elegant rooms, some dating back to the inn's foundation – some have private balconies overlooking the lake. $159

★ **Wolfe's Tavern** 90 N Main St (Rte-109) ☎ 603 569 3016, ⓦ wolfeboroinn.com. Enticing restaurant offering several dining areas; the fancy *1812 Room* serves fine, expensive New England-style cuisine, while the old tavern

section is a dark pub-like place and much better value. Enjoy one of its 72 beers on tap. Daily 7am–9pm (10pm in summer).

WEIRS BEACH

Cozy Inn, Lakeview House & Cottages 12 Maple St ☎ 603 366 4310, ⓦ cozyinn-nh.com. Multisite property comprising the charming 1880s inn with basic but comfy rooms, the hilltop 1860 house with larger rooms and sixteen rustic cottages – shared-bath rooms go for as low as $59 in summer. $115

Half Moon Motel & Cottages 28 Tower St ☎ 603 366 4494, ⓦ weirsbeach.com/halfmoon/motel. This old motel might look like an army barracks, but its rooms were remodelled in 2011 and the views of the lake are jaw-dropping. $119

The White Mountains

Thanks to their accessibility from both Montréal and Boston, the enchanting **WHITE MOUNTAINS** have become a year-round tourist destination. It's a commercialized region, with quite a lot of development flanking the main highways, but the great granite massifs retain much of their majesty. **Mount Washington**, at 6288ft the highest peak in the entire Northeast, claims some of the most severe weather in the world. Much of the region is protected within the **White Mountains National Forest**, established in 1918 and covering almost 1250 square miles today.

Piercing the range are a few high passes, called "**notches**", and the roads through these gaps, such as the **Kancamagus Highway** between **Lincoln** and **Conway**, make for enjoyably scenic routes. However, you won't really have made the most of the White Mountains unless you also set off on foot, bike or skis across the long expanses of thick evergreen forest that encircles them.

Franconia Notch

Ten miles beyond **Lincoln**, I-93 passes through **Franconia Notch State Park**, a slender valley crammed between two great walls of stone. From the **Flume Visitor Center** (May to late Oct daily 9am–5pm; ☎ 603 745 8391), you can walk along a two-mile boardwalk-cum-nature trail to the Pemigewasset River as it rages through the narrow, rock-filled Flume gorge (entry $15). Alternatively, take a $15 cable-car ride up the sheer granite face of

---

HIKING, SKIING AND CYCLING IN THE WHITE MOUNTAINS

Hiking in the White Mountains is coordinated by the **Appalachian Mountain Club** or "AMC" (ⓦ outdoors.org), whose chain of information centres, hostels and huts along the Appalachian Trail, traversing the region from northeast to southwest, is detailed below. Call ☎ 603 466 2721 for trail and weather information before you attempt any serious expedition.

Downhill and cross-country **skiers** can choose from several resorts that double up as summertime activity centres. The Waterville Valley Resort (☎ 603 236 8311, ⓦ waterville.com) and Loon Mountain (☎ 603 745 8111, ⓦ loonmtn.com), both just east of I-93, are good for downhill, while Jackson (☎ 603 383 9355, ⓦ jacksonxc.org), about fifteen miles north of Conway on Rte-16, has some of the finest cross-country skiing trails in the northeast. General information on the skiing centres is available from Ski NH (☎ 603 745 9396, ⓦ skinh.com).

In the summer, the cross-country skiing trails can make for strenuous but exhilarating **biking** (you can take lifts up the slopes and ride back down). Both Waterville and Loon have bikes for rent on site for around $34 per day; Loon also runs a zip-line ($26).

Cannon Mountain (late May to mid-Oct daily 9am–5pm; ☎ 603 823 8800, ⓦcannonmt .com), or hike the various, well-marked trails up to panoramic views for free.

Frost Place

Ridge Rd, off Bickford Hill Rd, Franconia • June Thurs–Sun 1–5pm; July & Aug daily except Tues 1–5pm; Sept & Oct daily except Tues 10am–5pm • Suggested donation $5 • ☎ 603 823 5510, ⓦ frostplace.org

One mile south of the friendly village of **FRANCONIA**, **Frost Place** is another former home of poet Robert Frost (see p.210), memorable largely for the inspiring panorama of mountains in its backdrop. Frost lived here from 1915 to 1920, and the house is now a "Center for Poetry and the Arts", with a poet-in-residence, readings, workshops and a small display of Frost memorabilia, such as signed first editions and photographs.

Mount Washington

From the awe-inspiring peak of 6288ft-high **Mount Washington** you can, on a clear day, see all the way to the Atlantic and into Canada. But the real interest in making the ascent lies in the extraordinary severity of the weather here, which results from the summit's position right in the path of the principal storm tracks and air-mass routes affecting the northeastern USA. Winds exceed hurricane strength on more than a hundred days of the year, and in 1934 they reached the highest speed ever recorded anywhere in the world – 231mph. You can ascend the mountain via a number of **hiking trails**, but most visitors opt for the easier option of driving via **Mount Washington Auto Road**, or taking the train along the **Mount Washington Cog Railway**.

Mount Washington Auto Road

Great Glen Trails Outdoor Center (Rte-16, 3 miles north of Pinkham Notch) • Early May to late Oct – weather permitting – 7.30am–6pm in peak season; call to check • $26 for private cars and driver (plus $8 for each additional adult and $6 for kids 5–12) • ☎ 603 356 0300, ⓦ mtwashingtonautoroad.com

The drive up **Mount Washington Auto Road** isn't quite as spine-tingling as you may expect, although the hairpin bends and lack of guard-rails certainly keep you alert. The toll includes a "This car climbed Mt. Washington" bumper sticker and a short audio-tour CD. Driving takes thirty or forty minutes under normal conditions.

Specially adapted **minibuses**, still known as "stages" in honour of the twelve-person horse-drawn carriages that first used the road, give narrated tours (daily 8.30am–5pm; $35, kids 5–12 $12; 2hr return) as they carry groups of tourists up the mountain.

Mount Washington Cog Railway

3168 Base Station Rd, Marshfield Station • Trains run late April to Dec; check website for dates and times • $64 • ☎ 603 278 5404, ⓦ thecog.com

A three-hour return trip on the **Mount Washington Cog Railway** (with a scant 20min at the summit) is a truly momentous experience, inching up the steep wooden trestles while avoiding descending showers of coal smut, though anyone who's not a train aficionado might find it not really worth the money.

The summit

Assuming the weather cooperates (and be prepared to be disappointed), the views from the summit of Mount Washington are gasp-inducing, but look closer and you'll see the remarkable spectacle of buildings actually held down with great chains. The utilitarian **Sherman Adams Summit Building** (daily: mid-May to Aug 8am–6pm; Sept 8am–5pm; Oct 8am–4.30pm; free; ☎ 603 466 3347) serves as the headquarters of Mount Washington State Park and contains a cafeteria, restrooms and a gift shop, as well as the **Mount Washington Weather Observatory**. The observatory's various findings, exhibits on the environment and history of the mountain, videos and an electronic "weather wall" are displayed at the **Mount Washington Museum** downstairs (mid-May to mid-Oct daily 9am–6pm; free for Auto Road or Cog Railway users, otherwise $3; ☎ 603 356 2137, ⓦmountwashington.org). You can also climb the few remaining feet to the actual (and humble-looking) summit point, or visit nearby **Tip Top House**; erected in 1853, this is the only original building to survive the devastating fire of 1908. Its saloon-like interior has been preserved, frozen in time (usually open late May to mid-Oct daily 10am–4pm; free).

North Conway

Surrounded on all sides by shopping malls, factory outlets and fast-food chains, **NORTH CONWAY** is a major resort town and can be fairly depressing, with the strip south towards Conway particularly over-developed. Fortunately, there is some relief in the centre, a village core that manages to maintain a hint of rustic backcountry appeal – you'll also find plenty of **budget accommodation** and **places to eat** here.

The Kancamagus Highway

The **Kancamagus Highway** (Hwy-112), connecting North Conway and Lincoln, is the least busy road through the mountains, and makes for a very pleasant 34-mile drive. Several campgrounds are situated in the woods to either side, and various walking trails are signposted. The half-mile hike to **Sabbaday Falls**, off to the south roughly halfway along the highway, leads up a narrow rocky cleft in the forest to a succession of idyllic waterfalls. If you plan on a picnic, though, take note: there is no food or gas available along the highway.

3

GETTING AROUND AND INFORMATION

THE WHITE MOUNTAINS

By bus You'll need a car to make the most of the White Mountains, but the AMC runs a hiker shuttle bus service (June–early Sept daily; early Sept to mid-Oct Sat & Sun) with stops at many of the trailheads and AMC lodges throughout the Mount Washington region (call ☎603 466 2727 or visit ⓦoutdoors.org for information, reservations strongly recommended; one-way trips $22; $18 for AMC members; $10 for any stop 10min apart or less).

Visitor centre In Lincoln on Rte-112, just off I-93 at exit 32 (daily: July–Sept 8.30am–6pm; Oct–June 8.30am–5.30pm; ☎603 745 8720, ⓦvisitwhitemountains .com); has a small exhibit on the region, gives lodging advice and sells compulsory parking passes ($3/day, $5/week) and maps.

ACCOMMODATION

Thanks to the influx of young hikers and skiers to the White Mountains, there's a relative abundance of budget accommodation in the area. Keep in mind, too, that rates vary dramatically between seasons, and even from weekday to weekend. **Campers** can pitch their tents anywhere below the tree line and away from the roads in the White Mountains National Forest, provided they show consideration for the environment. There are also numerous official campgrounds, particularly along the Kancamagus Highway ($20–22/night).

AMC LODGES

Highland Center Lodge at Crawford Notch Rte-302, Bretton Woods ☎603 278 4453, ⓦoutdoors.org. Great choice year-round: lodging in dorms or double rooms (cheapest with shared bathroom). Hearty alpine breakfasts and family-style dinners are included, as are activities including guided hikes and game nights. Dorms $50, doubles $98

Joe Dodge Lodge Pinkham Notch, 361 Rte-16 ☎603 466 2721, ⓦoutdoors.org. Popular with walkers aiming to get a full day's hike in around Pinkham Notch – unless you camp, this is the only choice for miles around. All rooms are simple, and dressed throughout with pine wood finish: double rooms with private bathroom and meals, or bunks with a shared bathroom. No TVs, but access to wi-fi. Dorms $64, doubles $146

AMC LODGES

The Appalachian Mountain Club (☎617 523 0655, ⓦoutdoors.org) operates eight delightfully remote **mountain huts** in New Hampshire along a 56-mile stretch of the **Appalachian Trail**, each about a day's hike apart. Generally offering full service in season (June to mid-Oct, exceptions noted below), including mixed bunkrooms (blankets but no sheets), toilets, cold water and two hot meals per day for $106–141, they are a fairly popular choice – reservations are required (call ☎603 466 2727). Carter Notch, Lonesome Lake and Zealand Falls huts are open out of season (without heat, running water or food) for $30.

3

MOTELS, HOTELS AND B&BS

Omni Mount Washington Resort 310 Mt Washington Hotel Rd, Bretton Woods ☎ 603 278 1000, ⌨ omni hotels.com. One of the grandest hotels in the state, with lavish rooms to match. **$199**

School House Motel 2152 White Mountain Hwy (Rte-16), North Conway ☎ 603 356 6829, ⌨ schoolhouse motel.com. Probably the cheapest place in town, with basic but adequate rooms, all with cable TV and free morning coffee. **$78**

★ **Sugar Hill Inn** 116 Rte-117, Sugar Hill ☎ 603 823 5621, ⌨ sugarhillinn.com. This posh secluded inn, set in a converted eighteenth-century farmhouse, is ideal for romantic getaways, with antique-filled rooms, fireplaces and mountain views. Gourmet breakfasts (included) show off local produce; there's also a guest-only tavern menu and exquisite fine dining. **$150**

Thayer's Inn 111 Main St, Littleton ☎ 603 444 6469, ⌨ thayersinn.com. A creaky but comfortable local landmark established in 1843, having hosted the likes of Richard Nixon and Ulysses S. Grant. Rooms are dressed in Victorian style (with floral, period wallpaper) and there's breakfast included. **$90**

EATING AND DRINKING

Chef's Market 2724 Main St (Rte-16), North Conway ☎ 603 356 4747, ⌨ chefsmarketnorthconway.com. This cosy café has great sandwiches (from $7), pasta salads and smoothies for lunch, with more substantial dinners such as pesto scallops ($28.95) and tomato-basil beef lasagne ($21.95). 11am–11pm; closed Tues.

★ **Littleton Diner** 145 Main St, Littleton ☎ 603 444 3994, ⌨ littletondiner.com. Open since 1930, this landmark diner has heaps of character. Best known for its delicious buckwheat pancakes and local maple syrup, the kitchen also cranks out New England comfort food (think roast turkey with cranberry sauce; $10), sandwiches and pie. Cash only. Daily 6am–8pm.

Miller's Café & Bakery Littleton Grist Mill, 16 Mill St, Littleton ☎ 603 444 2146, ⌨ millerscafeandbakery .com. Great daily selection of soup, salad and panini deals, with a pot roast sandwich (stuffed with garlic potatoes, green apples and horseradish mayo; $7.49), plus quiche and home-made baked goods. June–Aug Tues–Sat 7am–3pm.

★ **Polly's Pancake Parlor** 672 Rte-117 (I-93 exit 38), Sugar Hill ☎ 603 823 5575, ⌨ pollyspancakeparlor .com. Polly's might be in the middle of nowhere, but it's a scenic nowhere and well worth the trip if you love pancakes ($7.99 for six). Add blueberries, choc chips, coconut or walnuts and it's $9.29. Mid-May to Oct Mon–Fri 7am–2pm, Sat & Sun 7am–3pm; March to mid-May & Nov Sat & Sun 7am–2pm.

★ **Wildcat Inn & Tavern** 94 Main St (Rte-16A), Jackson ☎ 603 383 4245, ⌨ wildcattavern.com. Gourmet country cuisine in the dining room and garden, with cheaper sandwiches (from $7) and appetizers in the less formal couch-filled tavern, which often hosts a lively après-ski scene. Mon–Fri 5–11.30pm, Sat & Sun noon–11.30pm.

Maine

Celebrated as "the way life should be", **MAINE** more than lives up to its unofficial motto. Filled with lobster shacks, dense forests, scenic lakes and seaside enclaves, the state offers ample opportunities for exploring, or for just lounging in Adirondack chairs and watching the leaves change colour – there's a little something for everyone here. As large as the other five New England states combined, Maine has barely the year-round population of Rhode Island. In theory, therefore, there's plenty of room for all the visitors who flood the state in summer; in practice, though, most people head straight for the extravagantly corrugated coast.

At the southern end of the coastline, the beach towns of **Ogunquit** and **Old Orchard Beach** quickly lead up to Maine's most cosmopolitan city, **Portland**. The **Mid-Coast**, between Brunswick and Bucksport, is characterized by its craggy shores, windswept peninsulas and sheltered inlets, though the towns of **Boothbay Harbor** and **Camden** are certainly busy enough. Beyond the idyllic Blue Hill Peninsula, **Down East** Maine is home to **Acadia National Park**, the state's most popular outdoor escape, in addition to the bustling summer retreat of **Bar Harbor**. Farther north, you'll find foggy weather and exhilarating scenery, capped by the candy-striped lighthouse at **Quoddy Head**, the easternmost point in the United States.

Inland, you'll really begin to appreciate the size and space of the state, where vast tracts of mountainous forest are dotted with lakes and barely pierced by roads. This region is ideal territory for hiking and canoeing, particularly in **Baxter State Park**, site of the northern terminus of the Appalachian Trail.

Maine's climate is famously harsh. In **winter**, the state is covered in snow, and often ice, while even in what is officially **summer** temperatures don't really start to rise until June or even July. This is Maine's most popular season, its start heralded by sweet corn and the re-opening of lobster shacks, and its end marked by the wild blueberry harvest. Brilliant **autumn colours** begin to spread from the north in late September, when, unlike elsewhere in New England, off-season prices apply, and the cool weather is great for apple-picking, leaf gaping or simply curling up with a blanket and a book.

The Maine coast

Although the water is chilly, Maine's **beaches** are unequivocally beautiful, and there are plenty of rocky coastal footpaths and harbour villages to explore. The liveliest destinations are **Portland** and arty **Rockland**; there's a wide choice of smaller seaside towns, such as **Bath** and **Blue Hill**, if you're looking for a more peaceful base. **Beaches** are more common (and the sea warmer) further south, for example at **Ogunquit**.

The best way to see the coast itself is by **boat**: ferries and excursions operate from even the smallest harbours, with major routes including the ferries to Canada from Portland and Bar Harbor, shorter trips to **Monhegan** island via Port Clyde, Boothbay Harbor and New Harbor and **Vinalhaven** via Rockland.

Ogunquit and around

The three-mile spit that shields gay-friendly **OGUNQUIT** from the open ocean is one of Maine's finest **beaches** ($25 parking), a long stretch of sugary sand and calm surf that is ideal for leisurely strolls.

Ogunquit Museum of American Art

543 Shore Rd • May–Oct daily 10am–5pm • $10 • ☎ 207 646 4909, ⊛ ogunquitmuseum.org

The compact **Ogunquit Museum of American Art** is endowed with a strong collection of nineteenth- and twentieth-century American art, such as seascapes by Marsden Hartley and Rockwell Kent. Displays are enhanced by the building's spectacular ocean views. In the garden, grinning animal sculptures mingle with serene marble women.

Perkins Cove and Marginal Way

Perkins Cove, a pleasant knot of restaurants and shops a few miles south of downtown, is best reached by walking along **Marginal Way**, a winding path that traces the crescent shoreline from Ogunquit Beach. The 1.5-mile trail offers unspoilt views of the Atlantic coast, particularly stunning in autumn.

ACCOMMODATION AND EATING | OGUNQUIT AND AROUND

It's worth paying a bit more to **stay** near the centre of town, as Ogunquit traffic can snarl (you'll also save on hefty beach parking fees).

Bread and Roses Bakery 246 Main St ☎ 207 646 4227, ⊛ breadandrosesbakery.com. A community hub with tempting displays of eclairs, "mousse bombs", whoopie pies, fruit tarts and cupcakes. Daily 7am–11pm; closed Jan & Feb.

Footbridge Lobster 108 Perkins Cove Rd ☎ 207 251 4217. Right in Perkins Cove, this charming takeaway stand is the place in town to get an outstanding lobster roll. The fisherman-owner catches all his own crustaceans. Late May to mid-Oct daily 7am–9pm.

Gazebo Inn 527 Main St (Rte-1) ☎ 207 646 3733, ⊛ gazeboinnogt.com. Within walking distance of Footbridge Beach, this Ogunquit favourite has fifteen modern rooms – including four suites in a renovated barn – that seem to overflow with amenities: rain showers, heated floors, fireplaces and posh linens. There is also a pool, hot tub, library with internet stations and massage room. Full breakfast included. **$159**

Ogunquit Beach Inn 67 School St ☎ 207 646 1112, ⊛ ogunquitbeachinn.com. On a quiet side street close to

the action, the five rooms in this gay-friendly B&B date from the 1920s and are lined with knotted pine and Ogunquit art. Sample the owner's addictive chocolate chip banana bread. April–Oct only. **$165**
Wells-Ogunquit Resort Motel 203 Post Rd (Rte-1),

1.5 miles north in Moody ☎207 646 8588, ⓦwells -ogunquit.com. Impeccably kept modern motel rooms have cable TV and refrigerators, and there's a pool and barbecue set-ups. Breakfast showcases great-grandma's recipe for sugar baked beans. May–Oct only. **$104**

Kennebunkport

There's a reason former presidents **George Herbert Walker Bush** (known locally as "41") and **George "W" Bush** summer in genteel **Kennebunkport** – it's beautiful, historical and full of places to eat that even Barbara applauds.

The best beach in these parts is **Goose Rocks**, about three miles north of **Dock Square** (the town centre) on King's Highway (off Dyke Rd via Rte-9). It's a premium stretch of expansive sand, though you will need a permit to park here ($12 daily, $50 weekly; call the Kennebunkport police ☎207 967 2454). Neighbouring **Kennebunk** is home to a trio of attractive beaches; permits for these ($16 daily, $52 weekly) can be purchased at HB Provisions (15 Western Ave, Kennebunk; ☎207 967 5762), which also has a deli.

ACCOMMODATION   KENNEBUNKPORT

Bufflehead Cove Inn Bufflehead Cove Rd (off Rte-35), Kennebunk ☎207 967 3879, ⓦbuffleheadcove.com. Accessed by a private woodland road, this forested 1880s inn has a blissful setting: the Kennebunk River winds right in front of the house. Five guestrooms with nice perks including private balconies, fresh flowers and an afternoon wine and cheese hour; the hosts are famed for their breakfasts. May–Oct only. **$165**
The Colony Hotel 140 Ocean Ave, Kennebunkport ☎207 967 3331, ⓦthecolonyhotel.com. This mean-dering old resort dates from 1914, with 125 rooms spread between three buildings and two houses. Rooms are

delightfully old-fashioned – those in the main property don't have TVs or a/c – with stunning ocean views and access to the hotel's heated saltwater pool, eighteen-hole putting green and private slip of beach. Pet-friendly. Mid-May to Oct only. **$199**
Franciscan Guest House 26 Beach Ave, Kennebunk ☎207 967 4865, ⓦfranciscanguesthouse.com. In the gardened grounds of a monastery (of all things), the *Franciscan* has rates that simply cannot be beat. Guestrooms, located in what were once school classrooms, are basic, with no daily maid service. Still, the property is pleasant, with a saltwater pool, full breakfasts and a fun return crowd. **$99**

EATING AND NIGHTLIFE

Bandaloop 2 Dock Square, Kennebunkport ☎207 967 4994, ⓦbandaloop.biz. You can choose your own dining adventure, where one of eight proteins – free-range chicken, hormone-free steak, tofu etc – is paired with your pick of sauces, such as a garlicky gravy or a fruity balsamic reduction ($17–29). The emphasis is on organic produce, and vegetarians will be well pleased. Daily 5–10pm.
Clam Shack 2 Western Ave, just before the Kennebunkport Bridge, Kennebunk ☎207 967 3321,

ⓦtheclamshack.net. The mighty, mini *Clam Shack* lives up to the hype with fried clams endorsed by Barbara Bush and celebrity chef Rachael Ray, whoopie pies favoured by Martha Stewart and takeaway fried fish and lobster rolls. Mid-May to Oct daily 11am–9pm.
The Ramp 77 Pier Rd, Cape Porpoise ☎207 967 8500. Head below deck to this lively little bar with ocean views and a decor that evokes the belly of a ship. Great pub food too. Summer daily 11.30am–9pm; call for hours rest of year.

Portland

The largest city in Maine, **PORTLAND** was founded in 1632 in a superb position on the Casco Bay Peninsula, and quickly prospered, building ships and exporting great inland pines for use as masts. A long line of wooden **wharves** stretched along the seafront, with the merchants' houses on the hillside above.

From its earliest days, Portland was a cosmopolitan city. When the **railroads** came in the 1840s, the Canada Trunk Line had its terminus right on Portland's quayside, bringing the produce of Canada and the Great Plains one hundred miles closer to Europe than it would have been at any other major US port. **Custom House Wharf** remains much as it must have looked when novelist Anthony Trollope passed through in 1861 and said, "I doubt whether I ever saw a town with more evident signs of prosperity".

As with much of New England, the good times didn't last through the mid-twentieth century. Grand Trunk Station was torn down in 1966, and downtown Portland appeared to be in terminal decline – until, that is, a group of committed residents undertook the energetic redevelopment of the area now known as the **Old Port**. Their success has revitalized the city, keeping it at the heart of Maine life – though you shouldn't expect a hive of energy. Portland is quite simply a pleasant, sophisticated and very attractive town, where you can experience the benefits of a large city at a lesser cost and without the hassle of crowds.

Portland Museum of Art

7 Congress Square • Tues–Thurs, Sat & Sun 10am–5pm, Fri 10am–9pm; June to mid-Oct also Mon 10am–5pm • $10, Fri free 5–9pm • ☎ 207 775 6148, ⓦ portlandmuseum.org

Portland's single best destination, the **Portland Museum of Art** was designed in 1983 by I.M. Pei and Partners. Modernist works, scenes of Maine and stirring seascapes are prevalent, exemplified by Winslow Homer's colossal *Weatherbeaten*, the centrepiece of the collection. An earthy alternative to the maritime pieces is *Woodsmen in the Woods of Maine* by Waldo Peirce. Rich and dark, it was commissioned by the Westbrook Post Office in 1937 and is displayed here with the clouded-glass mailroom door still intact.

Wadsworth-Longfellow House/Maine Historical Society

485–489 Congress St • Guided tours on the hour May–Oct Mon–Sat 10am–5pm, Sun noon–5pm; last tour leaves at 4pm • $12 • ☎ 207 774 1822, ⓦ mainehistory.org

The **Wadsworth-Longfellow House/Maine Historical Society** was Portland's first brick house when built in 1785 by Revolutionary War hero Peleg Wadsworth. More famously, it was the boyhood home of Wadsworth's grandson, the poet Henry Wadsworth Longfellow. Next door, the **Historical Society Museum** has changing displays of state history and art.

The Old Port and waterfront

The restored **Old Port** near the quayside, between Exchange and Pearl streets, can be quite entertaining, with all sorts of red-brick antiquarian shops, bookstores, boutique clothing spots (especially on Exchange Street) and other diversions. Several companies operate **boat trips** (see box, p.228) from the nearby wharves.

If you follow Portland's waterfront to the end of the peninsula, you'll come to the **Eastern Promenade**, a remarkably peaceful two-mile harbour trail that culminates in a small beach, below the headland.

ARRIVAL AND DEPARTURE   **PORTLAND**

By car Both I-95 and Rte-1 skirt the peninsula of Portland, within a few miles of the city centre, while I-295 goes through it.

By plane Portland International Jetport (☎ 207 774 7301, ⓦ portlandjetport.org) abuts I-95, and is connected with downtown by the city bus (#5; limited Sun service; $1.50;

WINSLOW HOMER'S STUDIO

In 2006, the Portland Museum of Art acquired **Winslow Homer's** studio in Prouts Neck – a coastal summer colony located in Scarborough, twelve miles south of Portland. Lauded as one of America's greatest nineteenth-century painters, Homer (1836–1910) kicked off his art career at 21 working as an illustrator for *Harper's Weekly* magazine. He moved into Prouts Neck in 1883, where he completed many of the majestic seascapes that are the hallmarks of his work, such as *Weatherbeaten* and *The Gulf Stream*. Opened in September 2012 after extensive renovations, the refurbished studio gives visitors an intimate peek into the life of a master painter. Those who make the trip will also enjoy the view of the pounding Atlantic from the studio's porch – gallery-worthy in its own right. For more information on tours of the studio (2hr 30min; $55), contact PMA (see above).

BOAT TRIPS FROM PORTLAND

Several companies operate **boat trips** from the wharves near the Old Port: the Portland Schooner Co. (daily in summer; 2hr trip $35, overnight trips $240; T 207 766 2500, W portlandschooner.com) has two vintage schooners that sail around the harbour and to the Casco Bay islands and lighthouses from the Maine State Pier, adjacent to Casco Bay Lines on Commercial Street. With Lucky Catch Cruises, at 170 Commercial St ($25; T 207 761 0941, W luckycatch.com) shellfish fans don a pair of lobsterman overalls and head out to catch their very own lobster. Casco Bay Lines runs a twice-daily mailboat all year, and additional cruises in summer, to eight of the innumerable **Calendar Islands** in Casco Bay, from its terminal at 56 Commercial St at Franklin (return fares to one island $7.70–11.55, scenic cruises $13.25–24; T 207 774 7871, W cascobaylines.com). **Long, Chebeague** and **Peaks islands** have accommodation or camping facilities.

T 207 774 0351, W gpmetrobus.net).

By bus Concord Coach Lines (T 207 828 1151, W concord coachlines.com), also at the Transportation Center, is the principal bus operator along the coast, with frequent service from Boston and Bangor. Greyhound runs to Montréal, New Hampshire and Vermont, as well as destinations within Maine; the station is at 950 Congress St, on the eastern edge of downtown.

By train Amtrak's *Downeaster* arrives five times daily at the Portland Transportation Center (100 Thompson's Point Rd, 3 miles from downtown) from Boston's North Station. Destinations Boston (5 daily; 2hr); Dover, NH (5 daily; 1hr); Exeter, NH (5 daily; 1hr 20min).

3

GETTING AROUND, INFORMATION AND TOURS

By bike CycleMania, at 59 Federal St (T 207 774 2933, W cyclemania1.com), rents bicycles for $25/day, which you can ride around the city's hundreds of acres of undeveloped land.

Visitor centre 14 Ocean Gateway Pier, via Commercial St (April–June Mon–Sat 9.30am–4.30pm; July–Oct Mon–Fri 9am–5pm, Sat & Sun 9am–4pm; Nov–March Mon–Fri 9am–3pm, Sat 10am–3pm; T 207 772 5800, W visit portland.com); also staffs an information office at the Jetport (T 207 775 5809).

Land and sea tours The amphibious World War II vehicles of Downeast Duck Adventures, 94 Commercial St (May–Oct; 1hr; $25; reservations recommended; T 800 979 3370, W downeastducktours.com), cavort through the Old Port and then plunk into Casco Bay for a glimpse of the Calendar Islands. Portland Discovery, 170 Commercial St (May–Oct; 90min; $40; T 207 774 0808, W portland discovery.com), runs entertaining tours that combine a tram ride with a "lighthouse lover's cruise", where you'll spot four of the coastline's iconic beacons.

ACCOMMODATION

The Chadwick 140 Chadwick St T 207 774 5141, W thechadwick.com. Tucked away in Portland's West End, this 1891 Victorian has four guestrooms that are a tasteful marriage of antiques and modern design. You'll find gourmet breakfasts, a garden with a hammock for two, a welcoming host and happy guests. $225

Danforth 163 Danforth St T 207 879 8755, W danforthinn.com. This 1823 Federal-style mansion overflows with architectural delights: opaque windows in the billiard room (a holdover from Prohibition days), nineteenth-century galleries and a rooftop cupola with harbour views. Many of the ten rooms have working fireplaces, and all feature richly patterned textiles, posh soaps and original art. $279

Inn at St John 939 Congress St T 207 773 6481, W innatstjohn.com. Just outside downtown, in a slightly dodgy area near the Greyhound station, this creaky yet charming 1897 Victorian offers reasonably priced, comfortable rooms, some with shared baths. Breakfast included, no elevator. Shared bath $110, en-suite $139

Inn on Carleton 46 Carleton St T 207 775 1910, W innoncarleton.com. Nineteenth-century Victorian with six stylish rooms done up in a soothing colour palette and furnished with four-poster beds and fireplaces. Located in the West End, a few minutes' walk from downtown. The heavenly breakfasts can be taken in the English garden. $195

Marriott Residence Inn 145 Fore St T 207 761 1660, W marriott.com. A slinky hotel garnering rave reviews for its smart waterfront location and 179 suites stocked with fridge, microwave and dishwasher. On-site laundry facilities, a pool, jacuzzi, fitness centre and free continental breakfast are among the many perks. $279

EATING

Portland is famed for its outstanding restaurants, and most of its bars (see opposite) serve good food as well. The bountiful Farmers' Market, in Monument Square (May–Nov Wed 7am–2pm) offers the perfect opportunity to sample local produce.

Caiola's 58 Pine St ☎207 772 1110, ⓦcaiolas.com. Cosy West End restaurant with a rotating menu of upscale comfort food – think orange-marinated swordfish, juicy burgers, paella with chicken and chorizo, and excellent desserts. Sunday brunch is more affordable but displays the same good taste. Reservations recommended. Mon–Thurs 5.30–9.30pm, Fri & Sat 5.30–10pm, Sun 9am–2pm.

Duckfat 43 Middle St ☎207 774 8080, ⓦduckfat.com. Unassuming sandwich shop where local spuds are cut and fried in duck fat, salted and served with a choice of home-made dipping sauces. Singing with flavour, these humble *pommes frites* ($5) give this outwardly modest restaurant best-in-town status. Daily 11am–10pm.

Eventide Oyster Co. 86 Middle St ☎207 774 8538, ⓦeventideoysterco.com. Sleek oyster *boîte* with just a few tables and a handful of stools hugging the marble bar. In addition to raw shellfish ($15 for six), you'll find excellent (though small) lobster rolls ($12). The "clam bake" – steamed clams, mussels, potatoes, pork and a hard-boiled egg – is a superb New England feast (serves 2–3; $32). Daily 11am–midnight.

★ **Lobster Shack at Two Lights** 225 Two Lights Rd, 9 miles south in Cape Elizabeth ☎207 799 1677, ⓦlobstershacktwolights.com. Perhaps the best seafood-eating scenery in all of Maine: lighthouse to the left, unruly ocean to the right, and a lobster roll overflowing on the plate in front of you. April–Oct daily 11am–8pm (8.30pm July & Aug).

★ **Miyake** 468 Fore St ☎207 871 9170, ⓦmiyake restaurants.com. Formerly an insider hole-in-the-wall, this Portland favourite has moved into stylish new digs. Serving renowned sushi with a French flair, the menu garners quite a buzz for its four-course tasting menu ($50), fresh *uni* (sea urchins) and scallop rolls with spicy mayonnaise ($15). The chef-owner harvests his own clams and has a farm with pigs, chickens and veggies. Mon–Sat 11.30am–2.30pm & 5.30–10pm.

Otto Pizza 576 Congress St ☎207 773 7099, ⓦottoportland.com. New York-style, thin-crust pizza made with flatbread dough and creating toppings such as mashed potatoes and bacon ($21). Set in a hip storefront by the art museum, with another branch at 225 Congress St (☎207 358 7870). Mon–Thurs & Sun 11.30am–11pm, Fri & Sat 11.30am–2am.

Standard Baking Co. 75 Commercial St ☎207 773 2112, ⓦforestreet.biz. Pre-eminent French-inspired bakery serving devilishly good croissants, sticky buns, olive bread, macaroons, madeleines, butter cookies and more. Mon–Fri 7am–6pm, Sun 7am–5pm.

Street and Co. 33 Wharf St ☎207 775 0887, ⓦstreetandcompany.net. A great special-occasion seafood spot where the cuts are grilled, blackened or broiled to perfection and served in an intimate dining room. There are a few good non-fish items as well. Reservations recommended. Mon–Thurs 5.30–9.30pm, Fri & Sat 5.30–10pm, Sun 5.30–9pm.

NIGHTLIFE AND ENTERTAINMENT

Portland's bar scene is rowdier than you might expect, with fun seekers packing the pubs every weekend. Portland Parks and Recreation (☎207 756 8275, ⓦportlandmaine.com) sponsors free outdoor noon and evening jazz and blues concerts during the summer.

Gritty McDuff's 396 Fore St ☎207 772 2739, ⓦgrittys.com. Portland's first brewpub, making Portland Head Pale Ale and Black Fly Stout. Food, folk music, long wooden benches and a friendly atmosphere, which can get rowdy on Saturday nights. Daily 11am–late.

★ **Novare Res Bier Café** 4 Canal Plaza, Suite 1 (enter through alleyway on lower Exchange St, by KeyBank sign) ☎207 761 2437, ⓦnovareresbiercafe.com. A little tricky to find, this very cool Old Port beer spot has more than 500 brews with 25 on tap, outdoor and indoor picnic tables and tasty charcuterie and cheese plates. Mon–Thurs 4pm–1am, Fri 3pm–1am, Sat & Sun noon–1am.

SPACE Gallery 538 Congress St ☎207 828 5600, ⓦspace538.org. Artsy space that displays contemporary artworks and always has something interesting going on, whether it's films, music, art shows or local bands. Sometimes a cover ($7–18).

Freeport

Much of the current prosperity of **FREEPORT**, fifteen miles north of Portland, rests on the invention by Leon L. Bean, in 1912, of a funky-looking rubber-soled fishing boot. That original boot is still selling (there's now an enormous replica at the entrance), and **L.L. Bean** has grown into a multinational clothing conglomerate, with a mammoth store on Main Street that literally never closes. Originally, this was so pre-dawn hunting expeditions could stock up; all the relevant equipment is available for rent or sale, and the store runs regular workshops to teach backcountry activities and survival skills. In practice, though, the late-night hours seem more geared toward high school students, who attempt to fall asleep in the tents without being noticed by store personnel. L.L. Bean is now more of a fashion emporium and Freeport has expanded to include a mile-long stretch of top-name **factory outlets**. To get away from the shops, head a mile south of Freeport to the sea. The very green promontory visible just across the water as you drive is **Wolfe's Neck Woods State Park**. In summer, for $3, you can follow hiking and nature trails along the unspoiled fringes of the headland (daily 9am–sunset; ☎207 865 4465).

ARRIVAL AND DEPARTURE   FREEPORT

By train Amtrak's *Downeaster* arrives twice daily from Boston's North Station at 36 Depot St, in the heart of downtown.

Destinations Boston (2 daily; 3hr 10min); Exeter, NH (2 daily; 2hr); Dover, NH (2 daily; 1hr 30min).

ACCOMMODATION AND EATING

Applewood Inn 8 Holbrook St ☎207 865 9705, ⓦapplewoodusa.com. Welcoming B&B with artful decor in a great location just behind L.L. Bean (next door to Mr. Bean's former house, no less). Some rooms are fancier and have jacuzzis, and there is one lovely suite that sleeps eight. The charming hosts moonlight as hot-dog vendors. $165, suite $300

Broad Arrow Tavern Harraseeket Inn, 162 Main St ☎207 865 9377, ⓦharaseeketinn.com. Gourmet pizzas, pulled-pork sandwiches and a great lunch buffet served in a lodge-style dining room with an open kitchen and a roaring fire. Daily 11.30am–10.30pm.

★ **Conundrum Wine Bistro** 117 Rte-1 (by the wooden Indian sculpture), 3 miles south of downtown ☎207 865 0303, ⓦconundrumwinebistro.com. The best food in Freeport. Most people come for the swanky martinis, then get hooked on the fresh, eclectic mains ($12–20), such as butternut squash ravioli with sage cream sauce. Tues–Thurs 4.30–10pm, Fri & Sat 4.30pm–midnight.

Harraseeket Inn 162 Main St ☎207 865 9377, ⓦharaseeketinn.com. After a day spent chasing down outlet sales, retreat to this renowned clapboard inn with some eighty rooms, two good restaurants (see above) and an indoor pool. Genteel quarters are spruced up with posh linens, canopy beds and antiques; deluxe rooms include fireplaces and jacuzzi tubs. $185

Bath

The charming small town of **BATH**, seventeen miles northeast of Freeport, has an exceptionally long history of **shipbuilding**: the first vessel to be constructed and launched here was the *Virginia* in 1607, by Sir George Popham's short-lived colony. **Bath Iron Works**, founded in 1833, continues to produce ships – during World War II, more destroyers were built here than in all Japan. At the superb **Maine Maritime Museum**, 243 Washington St (daily 9.30am–5pm; $15 for two days; ☎207 443 1316, ⓦmainemaritimemuseum.org), you can take a tram (trolley) tour of the Iron Works (reservations recommended; $27), explore several visiting historic vessels or browse the museum's intriguing collection of ship-related paintings, photographs and artefacts.

ACCOMMODATION AND EATING   BATH

Beale Street Barbeque and Grill 215 Water St ☎207 442 9514, ⓦmainebbq.com. Hickory-smoked Memphis barbecue in an airy, modern dining room. Mon–Sat 11am–10pm, Sun noon–10pm.

The Cabin 552 Washington St ☎207 443 6224, ⓦcabinpizza.com. Enjoy some of Maine's best pizza in dark, wooden booths near the maritime museum. Cash only. Mon–Thurs & Sun 10am–10pm, Fri & Sat 10am–11pm.

Coveside B&B 6 Gotts Cove Lane, 13 miles south in Georgetown ☎207 371 2807, ⓦcovesidebandb.com. This idyllic hideaway, tucked between a boat-filled cove and a beautiful garden, has seven stylish rooms, friendly hosts, kayaking opportunities and phenomenal breakfasts.

Open late May to Oct. $160

Kismet Inn 44 Summer St ☎207 443 3399, ⓦkismetinnmaine.com. Five brightly painted rooms in a turreted Queen Anne house, with yoga classes, spa services and organic meals. A unique retreat for tranquillity and rejuvenation: sink into one of *Kismet's* luxurious soaking tubs and let the world fall away. $255

Solo Bistro 128 Front St ☎207 443 3373, ⓦsolobistro.com. Hip bistro with colourful, contemporary seating, exposed brick and dangling white lamps. Dinner is a seasonal, upscale affair with the likes of pan-seared scallops with pistachio pesto (mains $16–25). There's a cute wine bar downstairs. Mon–Sat 11.30am–2pm & 5pm–late, Sun 5pm–late.

Boothbay Harbor

BOOTHBAY HARBOR, at the southern tip of Hwy-27, twelve miles south from Rte-1, is a crowded, yet undeniably pretty, waterfront resort town. The dock lays on **boat trips** of all kinds, including Balmy Days Cruises (☎207 633 2284, ⓦbalmydayscruises.com), which offers all-day trips to Monhegan Island for $34, and harbour tours for $16. One of the state's most beloved attractions, the **Coastal Maine Botanical Gardens** (call for directions; daily 9am–5pm; $14; ☎207 633 4333, ⓦmainegardens.org) is honeycombed by well-tended trails and twelve winsome gardens.

ACCOMMODATION AND EATING   BOOTHBAY HARBOR

Baker's Way 89 Townsend Ave (Rte-27) ☎207 633 1119. This unassuming storefront belies a marvellous culinary hybrid: a doughnut shop that moonlights as a Vietnamese restaurant. Early morning sees muffins and croissants; after 11am, bowls of piping hot *pho*, tofu curry and steamed dumplings are served at tables in the back garden. Daily 6.30am–9pm.

Cabbage Island Clam Bakes Pier 6 at the Fisherman's Wharf Inn ☎207 633 7200, ⓦcabbageislandclambakes .com. Lobster nirvana: head out on a scenic harbour cruise (complete with full bar), then disembark at 5.5-acre Cabbage Island for an authentic clambake of steamed shellfish, chowder, corn on the cob and blueberry cake ($59.95). Daily departures late June to early Sept.

Hodgdon Island Inn 374 Barters Island Rd, 4 miles north in Boothbay ☎207 633 7474, ⓦboothbaybb .com. Close to the Botanical Gardens, the nine rooms at

this waterfront Italianate mansion have a fresh, cheerful look. There's also a heated pool, full breakfasts and homemade desserts in the evening. **$159**

Ports of Italy 47 Commercial St ☎207 633 1011, ⓦportsofitaly.com. Authentic northern Italian food – such as fettuccine with local scallops – served in a candlelit dining room. There's also a polished mahogany bar, just right for swilling one of the perfect Cabernets. Mains $18–23. Reservations recommended. Late May to mid-Oct daily 4.30–9pm.

★ **Topside Inn** 60 McKown St ☎207 633 5404, ⓦtopsideinn.com. Perched on top of a steep hill, this former sea captain's home boasts Boothbay's most spectacular vantage point. The chic rooms are the best in town and breakfast is served in a sunny dining room. Open May to mid-Oct. **$165**

Rockland

ROCKLAND, where Rte-1 reaches Penobscot Bay, has historically been Maine's largest lobster distributor, and boasts the state's busiest working harbour. It's a hip enclave with a strong arts and cultural scene, endowed with some remarkable museums and a happening Art Deco theatre. Rockland's cultural centrepiece is the outstanding **Farnsworth Art Museum**, 16 Museum St (10am–5pm: June–Oct daily; Nov, Dec, April & May Tues–Sun; Jan–March Wed–Sun; $12; ☎207 596 6457, ⓦfarnsworthmuseum .org). Its collection spans two centuries of American art, much of it Maine-related, and spreads over several buildings; the **Wyeth Center**, a beautiful gallery in a converted old church, holds two floors' worth of works by Jamie and N.C. Wyeth.

ACCOMMODATION   ROCKLAND

★ **LimeRock Inn** 96 Limerock St ☎207 594 2257, ⓦlimerockinn.com. Elegant rooms with striped wallpaper and antique cherry furniture in a turreted Queen Anne mansion. Chat with the lovely hosts on the

wraparound porch. Excellent breakfasts. **$159**

Ripples Inn at the Harbor 16 Pleasant St ☎207 594 5771, ⓦripplesinnattheharbor.com. Endearing little Victorian with five cheerful rooms and nice design

---

ROCKLAND FESTIVALS

In the first weekend of August, up to 100,000 visitors descend on Rockland's Harbor Park for the annual **Maine Lobster Festival** (☎207 596 0376, ⓦmainelobsterfestival.com) – some 20,000 pounds of lobster is consumed over the course of the five-day celebration, which also sees the coronation of the "Maine Sea Goddess". The **North Atlantic Blues Festival** (mid-July; ☎207 596 6055, ⓦnorthatlanticbluesfestival.com) is another popular event, a two-day jamboree held on the waterfront and boasting top-billed performers.

3

details including antique wash stands, wainscoting and hand-painted walls. Run by a gem of a proprietor.

EATING AND ENTERTAINMENT

★ **Home Kitchen Café** 650 Main St ☎ 207 596 2449, ⓦ homekitchencafe.com. Breakfast-all-day joint with wittily named menu items – the "pig's boogie" omelette is made with bacon and red peppers ($8.95). Don't miss the justly famous cinnamon buns ($3.75) and fish tacos ($9.75). Mon 7am–3pm, Wed–Sat 7am–3pm & 5–9pm, Sun 8am–2pm.

Miller's Lobster Co. 83 Eagle Quarry Rd (off Rte-73), 9 miles south in Spruce Head ☎ 207 594 7406, ⓦ millerslobster.com. This lobster landmark cooks its crustaceans in sea water and serves them on a dock that's bounded by water on three sides. Family-owned since 1977. Mid-June to early Sept daily 11am–7pm.

Primo 2 S Main St (Rte-73) ☎ 207 596 0770, ⓦ primorestaurant.com. This fittingly named farm-to-table bigwig is one of Maine's top-rated restaurants. The menu is dictated by what's fresh outside – all of its veggies and animals are raised on-site – and served in a rambling Victorian house. There's fine dining downstairs, but the second floor, which has a copper bar and velvet banquettes, is livelier. Mains $30–40. Reservations required downstairs. July & Aug daily 5.30–9.30pm; Sept–June call for hours.

Strand Theatre 345 Main St ☎ 207 594 0070, ⓦ rocklandstrand.com. One of Rockland's star attractions is this grand, 1920s Art Deco venue. Shows run the gamut from theatre performances and comedy acts to live bands and arthouse films. Hours vary.

Monhegan Island

Deliberately low-key **Monhegan Island**, eleven miles from the mainland, has long attracted a hardy mix of artists and fishermen. It also pulls its fair share of tourists, but for good reason: it's the most worthwhile jaunt away from the mainland along the entirety of the Maine coast.

On this rocky outcrop, **lobsters** are the main business, though the stunning cliffs and isolated coves have also drawn artists, including Edward Hopper and Rockwell Kent. The small village huddles around the tiny harbour, protected by Manana and Smutty Nose islands. Other than a few old hotels and some good restaurants, there's not much urbanity. Seventeen miles of **hiking trails** twist through the wilderness and past a magnificent 1824 lighthouse.

ARRIVAL AND DEPARTURE   MONHEGAN ISLAND

By boat You can access Monhegan from Port Clyde (18 miles south of Rockland), Boothbay Harbor, New Harbor and Muscongus. From Port Clyde, it takes about 1hr via Monhegan Boat Lines (May–Oct daily; Nov–April Mon, Wed & Fri; three sailings a day in summer, fewer at other times; $35 return; ☎ 207 372 8848, ⓦ monheganboat .com). Reservations recommended. Sailing time from other ports: Boothbay Harbor (90min), New Harbor (70min), Muscongus (6hr).

ACCOMMODATION

Island Inn ☎ 207 596 0371, ⓦ islandmonhegan.com. This sea-salted 1816 summer inn is quintessentially Maine. Its 28 updated rooms (and four suites) have painted floors, oak furniture and bright white beds, but the best amenity is the view. Open late May to mid-Oct. Shared bath **$170**, en-suite **$235**

Trailing Yew ☎ 207 596 0440, ⓦ trailingyew.com. Eclectic, old-fashioned but well-regarded abode, with 33 rooms (some singles; $140) spread among several buildings; many rooms do not have heat or electricity. Open May–Oct. **$240**

Camden and Rockport

The adjacent communities of **CAMDEN** and **ROCKPORT** split into two separate towns in 1891, in a dispute over who should pay for a new bridge over the Goose River between them. Rockport is now a quiet working port, among the prettiest on the Maine coast, home to lobster boats, pleasure cruisers and little else; Camden has clearly won the competition for visitors. One essential regional stop is **Camden Hills State Park**, two miles north of Camden ($4.50; ☎207 236 3109), where you can hike or drive up to a tower that affords one of the best views of the Maine coastline; on a clear day it's possible to see as far as Acadia National Park.

Don't underestimate the magnetism of the Belted Galloway cows at **Aldermere Farm**, at 70 Russell Ave in Rockport (☎207 236 2739, ⊛aldermere.org). These endearing "Oreo cows" (so named for their black-white-black stripe pattern) have been amusing passers-by for ages. The farm offers year-round educational programming, but most people just pop by for a glimpse of the belties.

ACCOMMODATION   CAMDEN AND ROCKPORT

The Belmont 6 Belmont Ave, Camden ☎207 236 8053, ⊛thebelmontinn.com. Decorated with conservative elegance, this 1891 Victorian sits on a quiet residential street just beyond the commercial district. Rooms are gussied up in soothing tones of white and forest green, and there's a wraparound porch. Breakfast (included) is an event. **$189**

Ducktrap Motel 12 Whitney Rd, Lincolnville ☎207 789 5400, ⊛ducktrapmotel.com. Cute, basic budget option just north of Camden. It also has an ocean-view

cottage and two larger, family-sized rooms. Doubles **$95**, family rooms **$105**, cottage **$115**

Whitehall Inn 52 High St (Rte-1), Camden ☎207 236 3391, ⊛whitehall-inn.com. It's tough to beat the 1901 *Whitehall* for local history: the film *Peyton Place* was shot here, and writer Edna St Vincent Millay was "discovered" in 1912 when she read a poem to partygoers in the lobby. A gracious clapboard inn, it has forty rooms with Frette linens and flat-screen TVs that manage to retain a vintage Maine look. Open mid-May to late Oct. **$170**

EATING AND DRINKING

Boynton-McKay 30 Main St, Camden ☎207 236 2465, ⊛boynton-mckay.com. Order a tall stack of pancakes or eggs over-easy at this one-time apothecary that retains its original fixtures and is famed for its breakfasts. Tues–Sat 7am–5pm, Sun 8am–4pm; July & Aug open daily.

★ **Long Grain** 31 Elm St, Camden ☎207 236 9001. Remarkable Asian cuisine – a sampling of Thai, Vietnamese and Korean fare – that's very well priced (mains average $11). While the ambience is laidback, the kitchen skill level

is serious – the chef was a James Beard semi-finalist. Don't skip dessert. Tues–Sat 11.30am–3pm & 4.30–9pm.

Shepherd's Pie 18 Central St, Rockport ☎207 236 8500, ⊛shepherdspierockport.com. This neighbourly pub with a pressed tin ceiling and burnished wood floors is *the* place to dine or drink in Rockport. The renowned chef cranks out upscale delights such as roast duck breast with pears ($22) and chicken liver toasts ($5). Daily 5–10pm.

Mount Desert Island

Considering that two million visitors come to **MOUNT DESERT ISLAND** each year, and that it boasts not only a genuine fjord but also the highest headland on the entire Atlantic coast north of Rio de Janeiro, it is an astonishingly small place, measuring just fifteen miles by twelve. One among innumerable rugged granite islands along the Maine coast, it is the most accessible, linked to the mainland by bridge since 1836, and has the best facilities. It's also breathtakingly beautiful – a glorious melding of ocean-battered cliffs, cool, hushed forests, stocky lupine flowers and marvellous sunrises.

OUT TO SEA

In high season, more than twenty different **sea trips** set off each day from Bar Harbor, for purposes ranging from deep-sea fishing to cocktail cruises. Among the most popular are the **whale-watching**, puffin and seal trips run by Bar Harbor Whale Watch Company, 1 West St (3hr; $59; ☎207 288 2386, ⊛barharborwhales.com). If you're travelling with children, don't miss **Diver Ed's** Dive-In Theater (leaving from the *College of Atlantic*, 105 Eden St; $40; ☎207 288 3483, ⊛divered.com); Ed documents his madcap undersea adventures with a live, on-boat broadcast, then surfaces with a wealth of creatures. Lulu Lobster Boat Rides (2hr; $30; ☎207 963 2341, ⊛lululobsterboat.com) offers authentic **lobstering** trips with Captain John, who raises traps, spots seals and charms riders with nautical folklore.

The social centre, **Bar Harbor**, has accommodation and restaurants to suit all wallets, while you'll find lower-key communities, such as **Southwest Harbor**, all over the island. **Acadia National Park**, which covers much of the region, offers active travellers plenty of outdoor opportunities.

Bar Harbor

The town of **BAR HARBOR** began life as an exclusive resort, summer home to the Vanderbilts and the Astors; the great fire of October 1947 that destroyed their opulent "cottages" changed the direction of the town's growth. It's now firmly geared towards tourists, though it's by no means downmarket.

Abbe Museum

26 Mount Desert St • Late May to early Nov daily 10am–5pm; early Nov to Dec & Feb to late May Thurs–Sat 10am–4pm • $6, admission includes Sieur de Monts location, off the Park Loop Rd • ☎ 207 288 3519, ⓦ abbemuseum.org

The native Wabanaki heritage – and current happenings – are maintained by the **Abbe Museum**, which has gorgeously constructed exhibit spaces full of light and pale wood panelling. Although the opening displays on Wabanaki culture are well put together, the Abbe's knockout piece is the "Circle of the Four Directions", a contemplative, circular space built of cedar panels that span upward into an arced skylight.

Acadia National Park

Park Open all year • $20/vehicle or $5/motorcycle or bike; good for seven days **Hulls Cove visitor centre** Just off Rte-3 at the entrance to Park Loop Rd • Mid-April to Oct daily 9am–5pm • ☎ 207 288 3338, ⓦ nps.gov/acad **Park headquarters** (for out-of-season info) 20 McFarland Hill Drive • Nov & Dec daily 8am–4.30pm; Jan & Feb Mon–Fri 8am–4.30pm

Stretched out over most of Mount Desert Island, **ACADIA NATIONAL PARK** is the most visited natural place in Maine. It's visually stunning, with all you could want in terms of mountains and lakes for secluded rambling, and **wildlife** such as seals, beavers and bald eagles. The two main geographical features are the narrow fjord of **Somes Sound**, which almost splits the island in two, and lovely **Cadillac Mountain**, 1530ft high, which offers tremendous ocean views. The summit can be reached either by a moderately strenuous climb or by a very leisurely drive up a low-gradient road.

The one and only sizeable beach, five miles south of Bar Harbor, is a stunner: called simply **Sand Beach**, it's a gorgeous strand bounded by twin headlands, with restrooms, a car park and a few short hiking trails. The water, unfortunately, is usually arctic.

ARRIVAL AND DEPARTURE   MOUNT DESERT ISLAND

By plane Flights into Bar Harbor are relatively infrequent and expensive – Bar Harbor/Hancock County Airport (☎ 207 667 7329, ⓦ bhairport.com), on Rte-3 in Trenton, has a limited service run by Cape Air and PenAir. It's more feasible to fly to Bangor International Airport (☎ 866 359 2264, ⓦ flybangor.com), 45 miles away, and get the shuttle bus to Bar Harbor ($40 one-way; ☎ 207 479 5911,

ⓦ barharborbangorshuttle.com).
By bus West's Coastal Connections Buses ($27 one-way; ☎ 207 546 2823, ⓦ westbusservice.com) travel between Bangor and the border town of Calais via Ellsworth.
By car Mount Desert is easy enough to get to from Rte-1 via Rte-3, although in summer roads on the island itself get congested.

GETTING AROUND AND INFORMATION

By shuttle bus Public transport is minimal outside of Bar Harbor, though once you get there, take advantage of the free Island Explorer shuttle buses (ⓦ exploreacadia.com), with eight routes that loop back to Bar Harbor.
By bike Three companies rent bikes for less than $30/day: Bar Harbor Bicycle Shop, 141 Cottage St on the edge of town (☎ 207 288 3886, ⓦ barharborbike.com); Coastal Kayak & Acadia Bike, across from the post office at 48 Cottage St (☎ 800 526 8615, ⓦ acadiabike.com); and Southwest Cycle,

at 370 Main St in Southwest Harbor (☎ 207 244 5856, ⓦ southwestcycle.com). All provide excellent maps and are good at suggesting routes. Carry water, as there are very few refreshment stops inside the park.
Visitor centres Bar Harbor's main tourist information office is at 1201 Bar Harbor Rd (Rte-3) in Trenton just before you cross the bridge to Mount Desert Island (☎ 800 345 4617, ⓦ barharborinfo.com). In summer, there's another in the Municipal Building at 2 Cottage St (☎ 207 288 5103).

ACCOMMODATION

Hwy-3 into and out of Bar Harbor (which becomes Main St on the way south) is lined with budget motels to satisfy the enormous demand for accommodation. Many places are open May to October only, and rates increase drastically in July and August. Lots book up early, so call ahead to check for availability.

BAR HARBOR

2 Cats 130 Cottage St ☎207 288 2808, ⊛2cats barharbor.com. Three spacious rooms, sweetly furnished with four-poster beds, sitting areas, hardwood floors and big bathtubs. The inn doubles as the best breakfast spot in town (see below), and breakfast is included in the rate. **$165**

Seacroft Inn 18 Albert Meadow ☎800 824 9694, ⊛seacroftinn.com. No-frills B&B with welcoming hosts, quilted bedspreads and affordable rooms, one with a bath down the hall ($40 cheaper). Great central location, and a continental breakfast in the morning. Open mid-May to Oct. **$149**

★ **Ullikana** 16 The Field ☎207 288 9552, ⊛ullikana .com. Artfully decorated rooms that pop with colour and character. The location – on a private byway just off Main St – is tops, and the sumptuous breakfasts are served on a terrace overlooking the water. Open late May to Oct. **$195**

SOUTHWEST AND NORTHEAST HARBOR

The Claremont 22 Claremont Rd, Southwest Harbor ☎800 244 5036, ⊛theclaremonthotel.com. One of Maine's most beautiful properties, this classic old-fashioned hotel has tennis and croquet, boating and an excellent shorefront. On Friday nights, fine dining is accompanied by live piano music. Open late May to mid-Oct. **$215**

★ **Harbourside Inn** 48 Harborside Rd (Rte-198), Northeast Harbor ☎207 276 3272, ⊛harboursideinn .com. Nineteenth-century woodland inn with patterned wallpaper, clawfoot tubs and working fireplaces. The inn is right on the edge of azalea gardens and hiking trails, and there's an organic breakfast. No TVs, but lots of tranquillity. Family-owned and operated. Open June to mid-Sept. **$150**

CAMPING IN ACADIA NATIONAL PARK

Blackwoods Near Seal Harbor ☎207 288 3274, ⊛recreation.gov. Administered by the National Park Service, this tranquil, all-season campground takes reservations up to a year in advance. **$20**

Echo Lake Camp Rte-102, south of Somesville ☎207 244 3747, ⊛amcecholakecamp.org. The Appalachian Mountain Club maintains this popular lakefront property with tent sites, a dining room, kitchens, bathhouses and canoes; rates include three family-style meals a day. Open July to early Sept; cash or cheque only. Per week **$663**

Seawall Off Rte-102A, near Bass Harbor ☎207 244 3600, ⊛nps.gov/acad. Lovely forested campsites, only half of which are reservable. Open late May to Sept. **$14**

EATING AND NIGHTLIFE

BAR HARBOR

2 Cats 130 Cottage St ☎207 288 2808, ⊛2cats barharbor.com. The town's best breakfast place. All the baked goods are made in-house, the herbs are home-grown, and the coffee – which comes in enormous mugs – is Fairtrade. Nice outdoor patio, but expect to queue for it. The owners run an adjacent inn (see above). Daily 7am–1pm.

Lompoc Café & Brew Pub 36 Rodick St ☎207 288 9392, ⊛lompoccafe.com. Eclectic, affordable menu in a woodsy outdoor dining room with bocce ball. Order the bang bang sandwich (fried chicken, spicy slaw, hot sauce and honey; $10.50), and the mussels in Dijon sauce ($9) and wash it down with a regional beer. Live music every weekend. May to mid-Oct daily 4.30pm–1am.

Mount Desert Island Ice Cream 325 Main St ☎207 801 4006, ⊛mdiic.com. Not your average scoop – foodies wax poetic about the varieties here: salt caramel, blueberry basil sorbet and Thai chilli head a long list of exceptional and ever-changing flavours. There's another location at 7 Firefly Lane (☎207 801 4007) and one in Portland.

June–Aug daily 11am–10.30pm; April & May & Sept & Oct, call for hours.

Reel Pizza Cinerama 33 Kennebec Place, on the Village Green ☎207 288 3828 takeaway, ☎207 288 3811 movie info, ⊛reelpizza.net. Eat pizza, drink beer and watch arty or blockbuster films on the big screen – it's fun when your order comes up on the bingo board. Movie tickets $6. Daily 4.30pm–late.

Side Street Café 49 Rodick St ☎207 801 2591, ⊛sidestreetbarharbor.com. The beating heart of Bar Harbor, *Side Street* pairs pitchers of tangy margaritas with tempting comfort foods such as lobster stew ($9.95), crab quesadillas ($16) and mac and cheese with avocado ($9). Expect a wait at peak times. Daily 11am–midnight.

SOUTHWEST HARBOR

Beal's Lobster Pier 182 Clark Point Rd ☎207 244 3202, ⊛bealslobster.com. Fresh seafood for under $14 on a rickety wooden pier. You can pick out your own lobster from a tank, or choose from a small menu of other seafood choices. Late May to mid-Oct daily 11am–8pm.

3

ACADIA NATIONAL PARK
Jordan Pond Park Loop Rd ☎207 276 3316, ⓦthejordanpondhouse.com. Light meals, ice cream and popovers (puffy egg muffins) in the heart of the park, between Bar Harbor and Northeast Harbor. Afternoon tea, an Acadia tradition, is served in the lakeside garden (11.30am–5.30pm; reservations recommended). Mid-May to late Oct daily 11.30am–9pm.

Downeast Maine: the coast to Canada

Few travellers venture into the hundred miles of Maine lying east beyond Acadia National Park, mainly because it is almost entirely unpopulated, windswept and remote. In summer, though, the weather is marked by mesmerizing fogs, and the coastal drive is exhilarating – it runs next to the Bay of Fundy, home to the highest tides in the nation. **Downeast Maine** is also characterized by its wild **blueberry** crops – ninety percent of the nation's harvest comes from this corner of the state.

A short way northeast of Acadia, a loop road leads from Rte-1 to the rocky outcrop of **Schoodic Point**, which offers good birdwatching, great views and a splendid sense of solitude. Each village has one or two B&Bs and well-priced restaurants, such as **Machias**, known for its best-in-state blueberry pie at *Helen's* (see below). Close to Canada, you'll find the salt-of-the-earth communities of **Lubec** and **Eastport**, tiny enclaves with marvellous ocean scenery.

EATING   DOWNEAST MAINE

Helen's 111 Main St/Rte-1, Machias ☎207 255 8433, ⓦhelensrestaurantmachias.com. Make sure you don't leave town without trying the blueberry pie at this landmark restaurant – it's considered the finest in the state, if not the world. Everything on the comfort food-filled menu is delicious. Mon–Sat 6am–8pm, Sun 6am–7.30pm.

West Quoddy Head and around

With a distinctive, candy-striped **lighthouse** dramatically signalling its endpoint, **WEST QUODDY HEAD** is the easternmost point of the USA, jutting defiantly into the stormy Atlantic. Just beyond the turnoff for Quoddy Head, tiny **LUBEC** was once home to more than twenty sardine-packing plants. They're all gone now, but the restored McCurdy's Fish Company, on Water Street, now gives tours ($3); you might spot a seal as you stroll the main drag. Lubec also hosts the dynamic adult music camp The Summer Keys (ⓦsummerkeys.com).

Campobello Island

Lubec is the gateway to **CAMPOBELLO ISLAND**, in New Brunswick, Canada, where Franklin D. Roosevelt summered from 1909 to 1921, and to which he occasionally returned during his presidency. His barn-red cottage, furnished just as the Roosevelts left it, is now open to the public as the **Roosevelt Campobello International Park** (mid-May to mid-Oct daily 9am–5pm; free; ☎877 851 6663, ⓦfdr.net). The rest of the park, located on Canadian soil but held jointly with the United States, is good for a couple of hours' wandering – the coastal trails and the drive out to **Liberty Point** are worth the effort. Remember that you will need a valid passport to cross the border.

The Quoddy Loop

The border between the United States and Canada weaves through the centre of Passamaquoddy Bay; the towns to either side get on so well that they refused to fight against each other in the War of 1812, and promote themselves jointly to tourists as the **Quoddy Loop** (ⓦquoddyloop.com). It's perfectly feasible to take a "two-nation vacation", but each passage through customs and immigration between **Calais** (pronounced "callous") in the States (50 miles north of Lubec) and **St Stephen** in Canada does take a little while – and be aware, also, that the towns are in different time zones.

INLAND AND WESTERN MAINE

The vast expanses of the **Maine interior**, stretching up into the cold far north, consist mostly of evergreen forests of pine, spruce and fir, interspersed with the white birches and maples responsible for the spectacular autumn colours. Distances here are large. Once you get away from the two biggest cities – **Augusta** and **Bangor** – it's roughly two hundred miles by road to the northern border at **Fort Kent**, while to drive between the two most likely inland bases, **Greenville** and **Rangeley**, takes three hours or more. Driving (there's no public transport) through this mountainous scenery can be a great pleasure – it smells like Christmas trees as you go – but be aware that beyond Millinocket some roads are access routes belonging to the lumber companies: gravel-surfaced and vulnerable to bad weather. This is great territory in which to **hike** – the **Appalachian Trail** culminates its two-thousand-mile course up from Georgia at the top of Mount Katahdin – or raft on the **Allagash Wilderness Waterway**.

Eastport

If you have the driving stamina, **EASTPORT**, some forty miles up the road from the Quoddy Loop, is one of the most spectacular places you'll ever see, with an edge-of-the-earth feel and stunning views of the Canadian shoreline. **Raye's Mustard**, at 83 Washington St (Mon–Fri 8.30am–5pm, Sat & Sun 10am–5pm; ☎ 207 853 4451, ⓦ rayesmustard.com), is the country's last surviving stone mustard mill and has been producing its 25 varieties of "liquid gold" for more than a century.

ACCOMMODATION AND EATING

Inn on the Wharf 69 Johnson St, Lubec ☎ 207 733 4400, ⓦ theinnonthewharf.com. Contemporary white rooms with occasional splashes of colour in a renovated sardine factory overlooking the ocean, with an on-site restaurant serving fresh crustaceans. Kayak and bike rental available too. **$100**

Katie's on the Cove 9 Katie Lane, Robbinston (8 miles north of Eastport on Rte-1) ☎ 207 454 8446, ⓦ katiesonthecove.com. Local institution doling out unbelievably good confections from a canary-yellow house covered in painted flowers. Try the "needhams", an old-fashioned Maine delicacy crafted from chocolate

WEST QUODDY HEAD AND AROUND

and mashed potatoes – you'll be hooked after one bite. Call for hours.

Peacock House 27 Summer St, Lubec ☎ 207 733 2403, ⓦ peacockhouse.com. A fantastic place to stay: charming proprietors, country-chic guestrooms, quilts and patterned wallpaper in a rambling clapboard house. Open May–Oct. **$98**

Quoddy Bay Lobster 7 Sea St, Eastport ☎ 207 853 6640. Feast on ultra-fresh lobster rolls, chowder and clams at this seaside favourite, owned by lobstermen and with a picnic table ambience. July & Aug daily 10am–6pm; call for hours May, June, Sept & Oct.

Baxter State Park and the far north

On a clear day in serenely unspoiled **BAXTER STATE PARK** ($14/car; ☎ 207 723 5140, ⓦ baxterstateparkauthority.com), the 5268ft peak of **Katahdin** (or "greatest mountain", in the language of the Penobscot tribe) is visible from afar. Forests here – the park is an enormous 200,000 acres – are home to deer, beaver, a few bears, some recently introduced caribou and plenty of **moose**. These endearingly gawky creatures are virtually blind and tend to be seen at early morning or dusk; you may spot them feeding in shallow water. They do, however, cause major havoc on the roads, particularly at night. Aim to be at your destination before the sun sets – each year sees a significant number of moose-related collisions.

INFORMATION AND ACCOMMODATION

Arrival Plan to arrive at the park early in the day, as only a limited number of visitors are permitted access to Katahdin trailheads. The park headquarters is located at 64 Balsam Drive (next to *McDonald's*) in Millinocket (☎ 207 723 5140, ⓦ baxterstateparkauthority.com). There is another centre

BAXTER STATE PARK

at Togue Pond, the southern entrance to the park.

Camping There are ten designated campgrounds in Baxter (☎ 207 723 5140), providing an array of options from basic tent sites to cabins equipped with beds, heating stoves, and gas lighting. From **$11**

The Great Lakes

ROCK AND ROLL HALL OF FAME, CLEVELAND, OH

The Great Lakes

The five interconnected Great Lakes (Superior, Ontario, Michigan, Erie and Huron) are impressive enough taken singly. Taken as a whole, the Great Lakes form the largest body of fresh water in the world; Lake Superior alone is more than three hundred miles from east to west. The shores of these inland seas can rival any coastline: Superior and the northern reaches of Lake Michigan offer stunning rocky peninsulas, craggy cliffs, tree-covered islands, mammoth dunes and deserted beaches. Such natural amenities and marvels stand in contrast to the areas along Lake Erie, and the southern environs of lakes Michigan and Huron, where sluggish waters lap against massive conurbations and ports that have seen better days.

To varying degrees, the principal states that line the American side of the lakes – **Ohio, Michigan, Indiana, Illinois, Wisconsin** and **Minnesota** – share this mixture of natural beauty and heavy industry. Cities such as **Chicago** and **Detroit**, for all their pros and cons, do not characterize the entire region, although the former's magnificent architecture, museums, music and restaurants make it a worthy destination. Within the first hundred miles or so of the lakeshores, especially in Wisconsin and Minnesota, tens of thousands of smaller lakes and tumbling streams are scattered through a luxuriant rural wilderness; beyond that, you are soon in the heart of the **Corn Belt**, where you can drive for hours and encounter nothing more than a succession of crossroads communities, grain silos and giant barns.

Getting around the Great Lakes region can be a challenge without a car, but with a little planning it can be fairly manageable, with frequent air and bus connections between the main cities and Amtrak passing through most larger places, if only once daily.

Brief history

The first foreigner to reach the Great Lakes, the French explorer Champlain, found the region in 1603 inhabited mostly by tribes of Huron, Iroquois and Algonquin. France soon established a network of military forts, Jesuit missions and fur-trading posts here, which entailed treating the native people as allies rather than subjects. After the **French and Indian War** with Britain from 1754 to 1761, however, the victorious British felt under no constraints to deal equitably with the Native Americans, and things grew worse with large-scale American settlement after Independence. The **Black Hawk War** of 1832 put a bloody end to traditional Native American life.

Settlers from the east were followed to Wisconsin and Minnesota by waves of **Scandinavians** and **Germans**, while the lower halves of Illinois and Indiana attracted **Southerners**, who attempted to maintain slavery here and resisted Union conscription during the Civil War. As regards culture and ideological inclinations, these areas still have more in common with neighbouring Kentucky and Tennessee than with the industrial cities of their own states.

Highlights

❶ Rock and Roll Hall of Fame and Museum, Cleveland, OH From rockabilly to Motown to punk – it's all here inside this striking museum. **See p.246**

❷ The Henry Ford Museum, Detroit, MI Home to such oddities as the chair Abraham Lincoln was sitting in when he was assassinated. **See p.263**

❸ Pictured Rocks National Lakeshore, MI Multihued sandstone cliffs, spectacular sand dunes and picturesque waterfalls dot this remote corner of Michigan's Upper Peninsula. **See p.269**

❹ Chicago architecture, IL Take a boat tour on the Chicago River or plan a walking tour to see the Second City's diverse architectural heritage. **See p.276**

❺ Wrigley Field, Chicago, IL Soak in the sun with a cold beer and a hot dog at this historic ivy-covered ballpark. **See p.285**

❻ State Street, Madison, WI From one end to another, this mile-long pedestrian paradise is replete with boutique stores, fine pubs, live music venues and a celebrated farmers' market. **See p.303**

❼ Boundary Waters Canoe Area Wilderness, MN Canoe, hike or just marvel at more than one million acres of lakes, rivers and forest. **See p.312**

HIGHLIGHTS ARE MARKED ON THE MAP ON P.242

THE GREAT LAKES

HIGHLIGHTS

1. Rock and Roll Hall of Fame and Museum, Cleveland, OH
2. The Henry Ford Museum, Detroit, MI
3. Pictured Rocks National Lakeshore, MI
4. Chicago architecture, IL
5. Wrigley Field, Chicago, IL
6. State Street, Madison, WI
7. Boundary Waters Canoe Area Wilderness, MN

GREAT REGIONAL DRIVES

Ohio route Drive from Cleveland west along the shore of Lake Erie on Rte-3 to Sandusky, then south on rural Rte-4 to Columbus and on to Cincinnati via scenic Rte-3.

North Shore Scenic Drive Jump on Hwy-61 in Duluth to follow a trail of tiny shoreline towns along the coast of Lake Superior. The autumn foliage is top-notch and there are seven state parks along the way.

Door County Coastal Byway North of Milwaukee, this road takes motorists along the Door County Peninsula, and includes jaunts by the rocky coastline and the towns of Sister Bay and Egg Harbor.

Rockford to Galena Take US-20 west from Rockford, Illinois out to Galena. In a state that is quite flat, the rolling hills and valleys along this route make for some rather fine vistas.

The demands of the Civil War encouraged the growth of **industry** in the region, with its abundant supplies of ores and fuel, as well as efficient transport by water and rail. As lakeshore cities like Chicago, Detroit and Cleveland grew in the early twentieth century, their populations swelled with hundreds of thousands of European immigrants and poor blacks from the South. But a lack of planning, inadequate housing and mass lay-offs at times of low demand bred conditions led to the riots of the late 1960s and continuing inner-city deprivation. Depression in the 1970s ravaged the economy – especially the **automobile** industry, on which so much else depended – and gave the area the unpleasant title of "**Rust Belt**". Since then, cities such as **Cleveland** have revived their fortunes to some degree, although the current economic crisis has hit the region especially hard. Times have remained tough for **Detroit**, and the city declared bankruptcy in 2013, making it the largest American city to do so.

Ohio

OHIO, the easternmost of the Great Lakes states, lies to the south of shallow Lake Erie. This is one of the nation's most industrialized regions, but the industry is largely concentrated in the east, near the Ohio River. To the south the landscape becomes less populated and more forested.

Enigmatic traces of Ohio's earliest inhabitants exist at the **Great Serpent Mound**, a grassy state park sixty miles east of Cincinnati, where a cleared hilltop high above a river was reshaped to look like a giant snake swallowing an egg, possibly by the Adena Indians around 800 BC. When the French claimed the area in 1699, it was inhabited by the **Iroquois**, in whose language Ohio means "something great". In the eighteenth century, the territory's prime position between Lake Erie and the Ohio River made it the subject of fierce contention between the French and British. Once the British acquired control of most land east of the Mississippi, settlers from New England began to establish communities along both the Ohio River and the Iroquois War Trail paths on the shores of the lake.

During the Civil War, Ohio was at the forefront of the struggle, producing two great Union generals, **Ulysses Grant** and **William Tecumseh Sherman**, and sending more than twice its quota of volunteers to fight for the North. Its progress thereafter has followed the classic "Rust Belt" pattern: rapid industrialization, aided by its natural resources and crucial location, followed by 1970s post-industrial gloom and a period of steady revitalization that has been stopped in its tracks by the current credit crunch.

Although the state is dominated by its triumvirate of "C" towns (**Cleveland**, **Columbus** and **Cincinnati**), the **Lake Erie Islands** are its most visited holiday destination, attracting thousands of partying mainlanders. Cincinnati and Cleveland have both undergone major face-lifts and are surprisingly attractive, as is the comparatively unassuming state capital of Columbus.

Cleveland

It's a long time since the great industrial port of **CLEVELAND** – for decades the butt of jokes after the heavily polluted Cuyahoga River caught fire in 1969 – has been considered the "Mistake on the Lake". Although parts of the city have been hit by the latest recession, the most revitalized areas remain hubs of energy. Cleveland boasts a sensitive restoration of the Lake Erie and Cuyahoga River waterfront, a superb constellation of museums, a growing culinary scene and modern downtown super-stadiums. What with the now well-established **Rock and Roll Hall of Fame**,

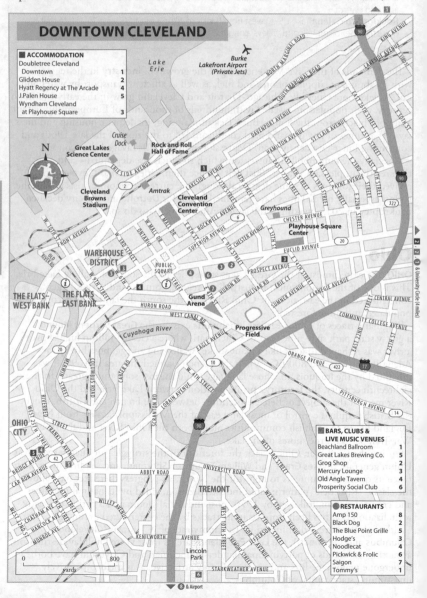

DOWNTOWN CLEVELAND

ACCOMMODATION
Doubletree Cleveland Downtown	1
Glidden House	2
Hyatt Regency at The Arcade	4
J.Palen House	5
Wyndham Cleveland at Playhouse Square	3

BARS, CLUBS & LIVE MUSIC VENUES
Beachland Ballroom	1
Great Lakes Brewing Co.	5
Grog Shop	2
Mercury Lounge	3
Old Angle Tavern	4
Prosperity Social Club	6

RESTAURANTS
Amp 150	8
Black Dog	2
The Blue Point Grille	5
Hodge's	3
Noodlecat	4
Pickwick & Frolic	6
Saigon	7
Tommy's	1

there's an unmistakeable buzz about the place, augmented by the city hosting the 2014 Gay Games.

Founded in 1796, thirty years later Cleveland profited greatly from the opening of the **Ohio Canal** between the Ohio River and Lake Erie. During the city's heyday, which began with the Civil War and lasted until the 1920s, its vast iron and coal supplies made it one of the most important **steel** and **shipbuilding centres** in the world. **John D. Rockefeller** made his billions here, as did the many others whose restored old mansions line "Millionaires' Row".

Outside of the lively **downtown**, trendy **Ohio City**, just to the southwest, and the cultural institutions of **University Circle**, some distance east of the river, are the most rewarding areas to explore.

Downtown and around

Downtown Cleveland is a bustling place and its redevelopment has seen the emergence of several distinct subsections. Its main streets congregate on the stately nineteenth-century Beaux Arts **Public Square**, which is dominated in its southwestern corner by the landmark **Terminal Tower**. **Ontario Street**, which runs north–south through the Square, divides the city into east and west. Among the banks and corporate headquarters stand a couple of glamorous shopping malls: the **Avenue at Tower City** is located in the Terminal Tower. Another, the **Arcade**, is a skylit hall built in 1890.

The Gateway District

At the southern end of downtown is the **Gateway District**, where new restaurants and bars surround **Progressive Field** stadium, home of the Indians baseball team (☎216 420 4487, ⍟indians.com), and the equally modern, multipurpose **Quicken Loans Arena** (☎888 894 9424, ⍟theqarena.com), aka "The Q", which hosts the Cavaliers basketball team, along with other major sporting and entertainment events.

The riverfront

Northwest of The Q, at the **riverfront**, one of the nation's busiest waterways shares space with excellent bars, clubs and restaurants, all strung out along a boardwalk. On the west bank of the Cuyahoga River, the **Flats**, long known for its nightlife, has an atmospheric, still industrial setting, set among some remaining grimy buildings and no less than fourteen bridges.

The Warehouse District

A short but steady climb east from the river leads to the historic **Warehouse District**, a pleasant stretch of nineteenth-century commercial buildings between West Third and West Ninth streets, given over to shops, galleries, cafés and trendy restaurants.

North Coast Harbor

North of the busy Cleveland Memorial Shoreway (Hwy-2), the waters of Lake Erie lap gently into **North Coast Harbor**, a showpiece of Midwest regeneration, whose centrepiece is the iconic **Rock and Roll Hall of Fame** (see box, p.246). Next door to the Rock Hall – as Clevelanders refer to it – is the giant **Great Lakes Science Center** (daily 10am–5pm; $14.95, $19 OMNIMAX combo-ticket; ☎216 696 4941, ⍟greatscience .com), one of America's largest interactive science museums, which cleverly outlines the interdependency of science, technology and the environment, with emphasis on the lakes region. Across the road, the futuristic, 72,000-seat **Cleveland Browns Stadium** is the home of the Browns pro football team (☎440 891 5000, ⍟clevelandbrowns.com).

Ohio City

To the west of the river, **Ohio City** is one of Cleveland's more hip neighbourhoods, with junk stores, exotic restaurants, Victorian clapboard houses and the busy **West Side Market**, at Lorain Ave and W 25th St (Mon & Wed 7am–4pm, Fri & Sat 7am–6pm), which sells all manner of ethnic foods. It's easily spotted by its red-brick clock tower. To the east, **Tremont** is another up-and-coming area.

University Circle and around

Four miles east of downtown, **University Circle** is a cluster of more than seventy cultural and medical institutions and is also home to several major performing arts companies (see p.248), as well as Frank Gehry's twisted-steel Weatherhead School of Management building at Case Western University. Adjacent to University Circle, **Murray Hill** is Cleveland's Little Italy; beyond this attractive area of brick streets, small delis and galleries is the trendy neighbourhood of **Coventry Village**.

University Circle museums and galleries

The eclectic **Museum of Art**, fronted by a lagoon at 11150 East Blvd (Tues, Thurs, Sat & Sun 10am–5pm, Wed & Fri 10am–9pm; free; ☎216 421 7340, ⓦclevelandart.org) has a collection that ranges from Renaissance armour to African art, with a good café. One of the area's newest attractions is **MOCA**, 11400 Euclid Ave (Tues–Sun 11am–5pm, Thurs till 9pm; $8; ☎216 421 8671, ⓦmocacleveland.org), an interactive modern art museum, featuring revolving exhibitions and housed in a stunning glass-and-steel polygonal structure. Also notable is the **Museum of Natural History**, Wade Oval (Mon–Sat 10am–5pm, Sun noon–5pm, Wed until 10pm; $12, planetarium $4; ☎800 317 9155, ⓦcmnh.org), with exhibits on dinosaurs and Native American culture.

4

THE ROCK AND ROLL HALL OF FAME

Cleveland, not the most obvious candidate, convincingly won a hotly contested bid to host the **Rock and Roll Hall of Fame** largely because **Alan Freed**, a local disc jockey, popularized the phrase "rock and roll" here back in 1951. Since then, Cleveland has hardly produced a roll call of rock icons – Joe Walsh, Pere Ubu and Nine Inch Nails are the biggest names. Ignoring criticism that it bought victory by stumping up most cash, the city embraced the idea of the museum with enthusiasm and few now argue with the choice.

The museum's octogenarian architect – **I.M. Pei** – wanted the building "to echo the energy of rock and roll". A trademark Pei tinted-glass pyramid (he also designed the larger Louvre one), this white structure of concrete, steel and glass strikes a bold pose on the shore of Lake Erie, especially when illuminated at night. The base of the pyramid extends into an impressive entrance plaza shaped like a turntable, complete with a stylus arm attachment.

The museum is much more than an array of **mementos** and artefacts. Right from the start, with the excellent twelve-minute **films** *Mystery Train* and *Kick Out the Jams*, the emphasis is on the contextualization of rock. The exhibits chart the art form's evolution and progress, acknowledging influences ranging from the blues singers of the Delta to the hillbilly wailers of the Appalachians. Elsewhere in the subterranean main exhibition hall, there's an in-depth look at seven crucial **rock genres** through the cities that spawned them: rockabilly (Memphis), R&B (New Orleans), Motown (Detroit), psychedelia (San Francisco), punk (London and New York), hip-hop (New York) and grunge (Seattle). Much space is taken up by exhibits on what the museum sees as the key rock artists of all time, including Elvis Presley, the Beatles, Jimi Hendrix, the Rolling Stones and U2. All inductees to the hall are selected annually by an international panel of rock "experts", but only performers who have released a record 25 years prior to their nomination are eligible.

Escalators lead to a level devoted to Freed, **studio techniques** and a great **archive** of rare live recordings, which you can listen to on headphones. The third floor houses the **Hall of Fame** itself, where an hourly video presentation of all inductees unfolds on three vast screens; the upper storeys contain the museum's **temporary exhibitions** and a **3-D film** of U2 in concert (extra $3).

The museum is at North Coast Harbor (daily 10am–5.30pm, Wed & summer Sat until 9pm; $22; reservations ☎216 781 7625, ⓦrockhall.com). Weekends get very crowded and are best avoided.

University Circle gardens

The **Cleveland Botanical Garden**, 11030 East Blvd (Tues–Sat 10am–5pm, Sun noon–5pm; May–Sept Wed till 9pm; $9.50; ☎216 721 1600, ⍟cbgarden.org), has a glasshouse that features a cloudforest, a desert ecosystem, free-roaming chameleons and butterflies, a waterfall and a treetop walkway. Meanwhile, dotted along East and Martin Luther King Jr boulevards in Rockefeller Park, 24 small landscaped cultural **gardens** are dedicated to and tended by Cleveland's diverse ethnic groups, including Croatians, Estonians and Finns.

Cleveland Metroparks Zoo

3900 Wildlife Way • June–Aug Mon–Fri 10am–5pm, Sat & Sun 10am–7pm; Sept–May daily 10am–5pm • April–Oct 12.25; Nov–March $8.25 • ☎216 661 6500, ⍟clemetzoo.com • By car, exit at W 25th or Fulton Rd; during summer, RTA runs special buses from downtown to the zoo

Five miles southwest of downtown via I-71, the **Cleveland Metroparks Zoo** features a "Wolf Wilderness", while the spectacular 164-acre **RainForest** building is populated by some seven thousand plants and 118 species of animals, including orang-utans, American crocodiles and Madagascan hissing cockroaches.

ARRIVAL AND DEPARTURE
CLEVELAND

By plane Cleveland Hopkins International Airport is 10 miles southwest of downtown. The 20min taxi ride into town costs around $20, but the Regional Transit Authority (RTA; ☎216 621 9500, ⍟riderta.com) train is only $3.50 and takes just 10min longer.

By bus Greyhound arrives at 1465 Chester Ave, at the back of Playhouse Square.

Destinations Chicago (6 daily; 6hr 40min–10hr 30min); Cincinnati (5 daily; 4hr 45min–5hr 55min); Columbus (6 daily; 2hr 25min–2hr 50min); New York (10 daily; 9hr 10min–13hr 55min); Pittsburgh (6 daily; 2hr 25min–3hr 30min).

By train The Amtrak station is on the lakefront at 200 Cleveland Memorial Shoreway NE.

Destinations Chicago (3 daily; 7hr); New York (2 daily; 12hr 45min); Pittsburgh (1 daily; 3hr 27min).

GETTING AROUND, INFORMATION AND TOURS

By bus The RTA runs an efficient bus service ($2.25 one-way or $5 for an unlimited day pass) and a small train line ($2.25), known locally as "the Rapid", until about 12.30am.

By light rail A light rail system – the Waterfront Line – connects Terminal Tower, the Flats, the Rock and Roll Hall of Fame and other downtown sights (every 15min, 6.15am– midnight; $2.25).

By tram (trolley) There are four free trams that cover different parts of downtown (Mon–Fri 7am–7pm).

Visitor centre Positively Cleveland, 334 Euclid Ave (June–Aug daily 9am–5pm; Sept–May Mon–Fri 9am–5pm; ☎216 875 6680, ⍟positivelycleveland.com); or try the booth on the baggage level of the airport (hours vary).

Tours *Goodtime III* (☎216 861 5110, ⍟goodtimeiii.com) runs 2hr boat cruises (from $17) from the dock at East Ninth Street Pier.

ACCOMMODATION

Travellers without cars tend to stay at the downtown hotels, whose room-only prices are not cheap, but many of which offer packages that include admission to the Rock and Roll Hall of Fame or other attractions. B&Bs can be booked through ⍟positivelycleveland.com.

Doubletree Cleveland Downtown 1111 Lakeside Ave ☎216 241 5100, ⍟doubletree1.hilton.com. Good online deals, great lake views from the upper storeys and proximity to the Rock and Roll Hall of Fame make this reliable chain franchise a popular choice. **$164**

Glidden House 1901 Ford Drive, University Circle ☎216 231 8900, ⍟gliddenhouse.com. Sixty very comfortable and brightly coloured rooms and suites are housed in an imposing Gothic mansion. Large continental breakfast is included. **$175**

Hyatt Regency at The Arcade 420 Superior Ave, University Circle ☎216 575 1234, ⍟cleveland.hyatt.com.

Set behind the imposing facade of the Arcade, a historic landmark, this hotel provides all the usual upscale comforts and services. **$259**

★ **J. Palen House** 2708 Bridge Ave, Ohio City ☎216 664 0813, ⍟jpalenhouse.com. Extremely attractive and conveniently located Victorian house with a conical turret, oak beams, lavishly furnished rooms and a gourmet three-course breakfast. **$159**

Wyndham Cleveland at Playhouse Square 1260 Euclid Ave ☎216 615 7500, ⍟wyndham.com. The best option in the downtown theatre district, Playhouse Square, providing luxury accommodation at mid-range prices. **$140**

4

EATING

The city has a range of culinary delights, many of them ethnic. The excellent West Side Market (Mon & Wed 7am–4pm, Fri & Sat 7am–6pm) in Ohio City abounds with cheap, unusual picnic food, while there are some excellent fine-dining restaurants around town. Little Italy and Coventry Village are worth exploring for authentic Italian food and coffee bars, respectively.

★ **Amp 150** 4277 W 150th St ☎ 216 706 8787, ⓦ amp150.com. The airport *Marriott* hotel might seem an unlikely location, but it's worth the trip for top chef Dean Max's imaginative creations such as duck confit nuggets and beef delmonico. Four-course dinner $35. Mon–Fri 6am–midnight, Sat & Sun 7am–midnight.

Black Dog 850 Euclid Ave ☎ 216 862 6268, ⓦ blackdog kitchenandbar.com. Relaxed and welcoming bar-restaurant, which serves a range of burgers for around $11, pricier mains such as seafood-rich diavolo pasta, and good beer. Mon–Thurs 11am–midnight, Fri & Sat 11am–2am, Sun 10am–10pm.

The Blue Point Grille 700 W St Clair Ave ☎ 216 875 7827, ⓦ bluepointgrille.com. Warehouse District favourite, serving the best seafood in town, with specials such as Nag's Head grouper with lobster mashed potatoes for $32. Mon–Fri 11am–3pm & 5–10pm, Sat 5–11pm, Sun 4–9pm.

Hodge's 668 Euclid Ave ☎ 216 771 4000, ⓦ hodges cleveland.com. Huge slick restaurant where you can enjoy dishes such as pan-seared Alaskan halibut for £26 or try the hodgepodge fixed three-course dinner for $30.

Mon–Fri 11.30am–10pm, Sat 4–11pm, Sun 4–9pm.

Noodlecat 234 Euclid Ave ☎ 216 589 0007, ⓦ noodle cat.com. A Japanese-American noodle house, serving ramen, udon and soba noodles for around $10–15. Also features exclusive sakes and rare teas. Daily 11am–11pm.

Pickwick & Frolic 2035 E 4th St ☎ 216 241 7425, ⓦ pickwickandfrolic.com. Cavernous restaurant with champagne lounge and martini bar. You can enjoy cabaret and stand-up comedy while dining on a huge range of pizza or rustic American cuisine for $20–30. Daily noon–11pm.

★ **Saigon** 2061 E 4th St ☎ 216 344 2020, ⓦ saigon cleveland.com. Great-value place, with most of the exquisite Vietnamese items such as salt-baked squid costing around $10 or less. Mon–Thurs 11am–10pm, Fri 11am–11pm, Sat 5–11pm.

Tommy's 1824 Coventry Rd ☎ 216 321 7757, ⓦ tommys coventrycleveland.com. Great-value food, much of it Middle Eastern and vegetarian, dished up in a trendy, bright setting in lively Coventry Village. Try the famous shakes too. Mon–Thurs & Sun 9am–9pm, Fri 9am–10pm, Sun 7.30am–10pm.

NIGHTLIFE AND ENTERTAINMENT

The Warehouse District and East 4th Street boast the greatest conglomeration of drinking, live music and dancing venues, although those in the know head across the river to more bohemian Ohio City and Tremont. Less than 5 miles east, both University Circle and youthful Coventry Village have good bars. The free weekly, the *Cleveland Scene* (ⓦ clevescene.com), has listings of alternative music, cinema and other events.

BARS, CLUBS AND LIVE MUSIC VENUES

Beachland Ballroom 15711 Waterloo Rd ☎ 216 383 1124, ⓦ beachlandballroom.com. It's more than 10 miles east of downtown, but this buzzing venue in a former Croatian social club draws the top indie and rock bands. Hours vary.

★ **Great Lakes Brewing Co.** 2516 Market Ave, Ohio City ☎ 216 771 4404, ⓦ greatlakesbrewing.com. At this famous old joint, Cleveland's best brewpub, the huge mahogany bar still bears the bullet holes made during a 1920s shoot-out involving lawman Elliot Ness. Mon–Thurs 11.30am–midnight, Fri & Sat 11.30am–1am.

Grog Shop 2785 Euclid Heights Blvd, Cleveland Heights ☎ 216 321 5588, ⓦ grogshop.gs. Near Coventry Village, the *Grog Shop* is a fun, sweaty, collegiate punk and alternative venue, with bands on every night. Hours vary.

Mercury Lounge 1392 W 6th St ☎ 216 566 8840, ⓦ themercurylounge.com. In the Warehouse District, this hip martini lounge and dance club tends to attract Cleveland's fashionable set. Daily 5pm–late.

Old Angle Tavern 1848 W 25th St, Ohio City ☎ 216 861 5643, ⓦ oldangletavern.com. Friendly pub with multiple screens for international sporting fixtures, decent pub grub, a selection of ales and lively music at night. Daily 10am–2am.

Prosperity Social Club 1109 Starkweather Ave ☎ 216 937 1938, ⓦ prosperitysocialclub.com. Located in a 1938 ballroom in Tremont, this is a hip hangout, with a great jukebox, live music and a huge range of beers. Mon, Tues & Sun 4pm–midnight, Wed–Sat 4pm–2am.

PERFORMING ARTS VENUES

Playhouse Square 1501 Euclid Ave ☎ 216 241 6000, ⓦ playhousesquare.com. Within this impressive complex of four renovated old theatres the small Ohio Theater, with its gorgeous starlit-sky lobby ceiling, is home to the Cleveland Opera and Ballet, as well as comedy, musicals, concerts and the Great Lakes Theatre Festival. The Allen Theater is where the prestigious Cleveland Play House company performs drama.

Severance Hall 11001 Euclid Ave, University Circle ☎ 216 231 1111, ⓦ clevelandorchestra.com. This grand Neoclassical venue is home to the well-respected Cleveland Orchestra, when they are not on tour.

The Lake Erie Islands

The **LAKE ERIE ISLANDS** – **Kelleys Island** and the three **Bass Islands** further north – were early stepping stones for the **Iroquois** on the route to what is now Ontario. French attempts to claim the islands in the 1640s met with considerable hostility, and they were left more or less in peace until 1813, when the Americans established their control over the Great Lakes by destroying the entire English fleet in the **Battle of Lake Erie**. A boom in **wine production** brought the islands prosperity in the 1860s, but last century they were hit successively by Prohibition, the emergence of the California wineries, an increase in motoring vacations and the lake's appalling pollution. Thankfully, the cleanup of recent decades has worked; today the islands are again a popular summer destination, with fishing, swimming and partying as the main attractions. **Sandusky** and nearby **Port Clinton** act as the main jump-off points to the islands.

The mainland

The large coal-shipping port of **SANDUSKY**, fifty miles west of Cleveland on US-2, is probably the most visited of the lakeshore towns, thanks to **Cedar Point Amusement Park**, five miles southeast of town (early May to Aug daily hours vary; Sept to early Nov weekends only; from $44.99; ☎419 627 2350, ⍉cedarpoint.com). The largest ride park in the nation – and considered by many to be the best in the world – Cedar Point boasts no less than seventeen roller coasters. The neighbouring **Soak City** water park (June–Aug daily 10am–8pm; from $32.99) is owned by Cedar Point and provides a good way to cool off, with eighteen acres of water slides and a wave pool. Aquatic fun continues through the winter a few miles further southeast at **Kalahari Waterpark** (daily 10am, closing times vary; $46, after 5pm $39; ☎877 525 2477, ⍉kalahariresorts.com), America's largest indoor water park; there's even a surf-making pool. The smaller resort town of **PORT CLINTON**, twelve miles west across the Sandusky Bay Bridge, is another departure point for the islands. Its pleasant lakefront is dotted with decent cafés and jet-ski rental outlets.

ARRIVAL AND INFORMATION
THE MAINLAND

By bus Greyhound buses stop way out at 6513 Milan Rd (US-250).

By train Amtrak trains pass through Sandusky once daily en route between Chicago and the east coast. The unstaffed station, at North Depot and Hayes aves, is in a dodgy area.

Visitor centre 4424 Milan Rd, Sandusky (June–Aug Mon–Fri 8am–8pm, Sat 9am–8pm, Sun 10am–4pm; Sept–May Mon–Fri 8.30am–5.30pm; ☎419 625 2984, ⍉shoresandislands.com).

ACCOMMODATION AND EATING

Kalahari 7000 Kalahari Drive, Sandusky ☎855 875 7774, ⍉kalahariresorts.com. The luxury resort that includes the water park has huge rooms with jacuzzis and all mod cons, as well as a top tropical restaurant and a host of other facilities. $249

KOA 2311 Cleveland Rd, Sandusky ☎419 625 7906, ⍉mhdcorp.com. Upscale campground with superb facilities such as a huge store, heated swimming pool and sports grounds. Cabins available as well as plenty of tent and RV spaces. Camping $32.50, cabins $63.50

★ **The Original Margaritaville** 212 Fremont Ave, Sandusky ☎419 627 8903, ⍉themargaritavilleonline .com. Ribs and steaks for under $20 supplement the wide Mexican menu in this fun spot with an on-site waterfall and live music at weekends. Daily 11am–2am.

Sunnyside Tower 3612 NW Catawba Rd, Port Clinton ☎419 797 9315, ⍉sunnysidetower.com. Set on two lush acres, this Victorian-style B&B offers beautifully designed rooms and suites, plus a spacious lounge for socializing. $134

Kelleys Island

About nine miles north of Sandusky, **KELLEYS ISLAND** lies in the western basin of Lake Erie. Seven miles across at its widest, it's the largest American island on the lake, but it's also one of the most peaceful and picturesque, home to less than two hundred permanent residents. With few buildings less than a century old, the whole island is a National Historic District. Its seventy-plus archeological sites include **Inscription Rock**,

4

a limestone slab carved with 400-year-old pictographs; you can find it east of the dock on the southern shore. The **Glacial Grooves State Memorial**, on the west shore, is a 400ft trough of solid limestone, scoured with deep ridges by the glacier that carved out the Great Lakes.

Settled in the 1830s, Kelleys was initially a working island, its economy based on lumber, then wine, and later limestone quarrying. All but the last have collapsed, though a steady **tourist industry** has developed.

ARRIVAL AND INFORMATION
KELLEYS ISLAND

By plane Daily flights with Griffing Flying Service (☎419 626 5161, ⓦgriffingflyingservice.com) leave daily from Sandusky and Port Clinton and cost $45 one way.

By ferry Kelleys Island Ferry Boat Line ($9.50 one-way, bikes $3, cars $15; ☎419 798 9763, ⓦkelleysislandferry.com) operate from Main St in Marblehead year-round, when weather permits, as frequently as every 30min at peak times.

By catamaran Jet Express ($14.99 one-way; ☎800 245 1538, ⓦjet-express.com) runs summer services from its dock at 101 W Shoreline Drive, Sandusky to Kelleys Island.

Chamber of Commerce Division St, straight up from the dock (June–Aug daily 10am–5pm; ☎419 746 2360, ⓦkelleysislandchamber.com).

Website There is plenty of info at ⓦkelleysisland.com.

GETTING AROUND

By bike or golf cart Getting around the island is easy; cars are heavily discouraged and most people, when not strolling, use bikes ($4/hr or $24/day) or golf carts ($11/hr or $67/day), available from Caddy Shack Square (☎419 746 2221, ⓦcaddyshacksquare.com).

ACCOMMODATION AND EATING

The Inn on Kelleys Island 317 W Lakeshore Drive ☎866 878 2135, ⓦkelleysisland.com/theinn. A restored nineteenth-century Victorian home with a great lake view and a private beach. The cosy rustic rooms are very relaxing. $95

Kelleys Island Brewery 504 W Lakeshore Drive ☎419 746 2314, ⓦkelleysislandbrewpub.com. Fine brewhouse that serves its own delicious ales for $5 and dinners such as Lake Erie perch with soup or salad and fries for $19, plus filling breakfasts and sandwiches. April–Oct daily 8am–2am.

State Park Campground 920 Division St ☎419 746 2546. The first-come, first-served state park on the north bay near the beach has more than 100 sites. Fairly basic but a lovely location. Pitches $31

Village Pump 103 W Lakeshore Drive ☎419 746 2281, ⓦvillagepumpki.com. Lively place that serves good homestyle food – T-Bone steak for just $14.45 – and drink; try its signature brandy Alexander. March–Dec daily 11am–2am.

South Bass Island

SOUTH BASS ISLAND is the largest and southernmost of the Bass Island chain, three miles from the mainland and northwest of Kelleys Island; the island's name derives from the excellent bass fishing in the surrounding waters. Also referred to as **Put-in-Bay** after its one and only village, this is the most visited of the American Lake Erie Islands, its permanent population of 450 growing tenfold in the summer.

Just a year after its first white settlers arrived, British troops invaded the island during the War of 1812. The Battle of Lake Erie, which took place off the island's southeastern edge, is commemorated by **Perry's Victory and International Peace Memorial**, set in a 25-acre park. You can see the distant battle site from an observation deck near the top of the 352ft stone column (May–Oct daily 10am–7pm; $3). All this history is well documented at the **Lake Erie Islands Historical Society**, 441 Catawba Ave (daily: May–Oct 10am–5pm, July & Aug until 6pm; $2; ☎419 285 2804, ⓦleihs.org), which features dozens of model ships, memorabilia and exhibits on the shipping and fishing industries.

ARRIVAL AND INFORMATION
SOUTH BASS ISLAND

By plane Daily flights with Griffing Flying Service (see above) leave from Sandusky and Port Clinton and cost $45 one way.

By catamaran Jet Express (see above) runs summer services to Put-in-Bay from its dock at 101 W Shoreline

Drive, Sandusky ($19.50 one-way), and from 5 N Jefferson St, Port Clinton ($14.99 one-way).

By ferry South Bass Island is served by Miller Ferry (☎ 800 500 2421, ⓦ millerferry.com; $7 one-way, bikes $2, cars

$15) from late March to late Nov.

Visitor centre Harbor Square, just next to the northern dock, Put-in-Bay (June–Aug daily 9am–6pm; Sept–May hours vary; ☎ 419 285 2832, ⓦ visitputinbay.com).

GETTING AROUND

By bike or golf cart You can rent bikes ($4/hr or $16/day) and golf carts (from $11/hr or $60/day) from Park Bike Rental on Hartford Ave, Put-in-Bay (☎ 419 285 2113,

ⓦ parkbikerental.com).

By shuttle bus A service runs between the northern dock and the state park ($1).

ACCOMMODATION

Arbor Inn B&B 511 Trenton Ave ☎ 419 285 2306, ⓦ arborinnpib.com. Set amid woods, this pleasantly chilled B&B has manicured gardens, which you can enjoy from the porch, and very comfortable rooms. **$95**

Commodore Resort 272 Delaware Ave ☎ 419 285 3101, ⓦ commodoreresort.com. With an attractive pool

area and decent bar-cum-grill, this cheerful resort offers competitive rates for its nicely designed rooms. **$80**

Fox's Den Campground Langram Rd ☎ 419 285 5001. This centrally located and well-equipped private campground is the only alternative to camping in the State Park. **$32**

EATING, DRINKING AND NIGHTLIFE

Beer Barrel Saloon Put-in-Bay ☎ 419 285 2337, ⓦ beerbarrelpib.com. Claims to have the longest uninterrupted bar in the world, complete with 160 bar stools, and provides booze, bar food and regular live music to partying holidaymakers. April–Nov daily 11am–2am.

The Boardwalk 341 Bayview Ave ☎ 419 285 3695, ⓦ the-boardwalk.com. Actually a set of three restaurants sharing the harbour boardwalk: the *Main Deck* and

Upper Deck do sandwiches, meat and seafood for $10–20, while *Rita's Cantina* serves Mexican. June–Sept daily 11am–11pm.

Round House Put-in-Bay ☎ 419 285 4595, ⓦ theroundhousebar.com. Named after the rotund shape of its roof, this buzzing bar features daily live bands and DJs, plus a full range of drinks and snacks. May–Oct daily noon–late.

Columbus

Officially Ohio's largest city, although Cleveland's metropolitan area is greater, **COLUMBUS** is a likeable place to visit. State capital and home to the massive Ohio State University, the city's position in the rural heart of the state also makes it the only centre of culture for a good two-hour drive in any direction. Ohio became a state in 1803 and legislators designated this former patch of rolling farmland, on the high east bank of the Scioto River, its capital in 1812. The fledgling city was built from scratch, and its considered town planning is evident today in broad thoroughfares and green spaces.

Though Columbus has more people, it always seems to lag behind Cincinnati or Cleveland in terms of public recognition. As such, the place is best enjoyed for what it is – a lively college city with some good **museums**, gorgeous Germanic **architecture** and a particularly vibrant **nightlife**. Surprisingly, it boasts one of the country's most active **gay scenes**.

Downtown Columbus

The spacious, orderly and easy-going **downtown** area holds several attractions. In the northwest corner of downtown, the area surrounding the impressive Nationwide Arena, home to NHL's Columbus Blue Jackets (☎ 800 645 2637, ⓦ bluejackets.com), dubbed the **Arena District**, has attracted a number of restaurants and nightspots. Just above it, left off High Street, is the restored Victorian warehouse of **North Market** (see p.253), while on the right side the strikingly deconstructivist **Greater Columbus Convention Center** is a massive pile of angled blocks designed by Peter Eisenman and completed in 1993.

4

Ohio Statehouse

1 Capitol Square • Mon–Fri 7am–6pm, Sat & Sun 11am–5pm • Hourly tours Mon–Fri 10am–3pm, Sat & Sun noon–3pm • Free • ☎ 888 644 6123, ⓦ ohiotatehouse.org

The **Ohio Statehouse** is a grand colonnaded edifice, pleasantly set in ten acres of park at the intersection of Broad and High streets, the two main downtown arteries. The highlights of this 1839 Greek Revival structure – one of the very few state capitols without a dome – are the ornate Senate and House chambers. A statue of Ohio native President William McKinley proudly stands outside the main entrance.

COSI

333 W Broad St • Mon–Sat 10am–5pm, Sun noon–6pm • $17.95, kids $12.95 • ☎ 614 228 2674, ⓦ cosi.org

Housed in a streamlined structure across the river from the capitol, **COSI** (Center of Science and Industry) boasts more than 300,000 square feet of exhibit space. Most of it is geared toward familiarizing children with science, covering broad topics such as life, progress, space, the ocean and gadgets. It shows related movies ($7.50), as well as putting on live shows (prices vary).

Columbus Museum of Art

480 E Broad St • Tues–Sun 10am–5.30pm, Thurs until 8.30pm • $12, free Sun • ☎ 614 221 6801, ⓦ columbusmuseum.org

About a mile east of High Street (US-23), a giant Henry Moore sculpture stands at the entrance to the inviting **Columbus Museum of Art**. Indoors, this airy space holds particularly good collections of Western and modernist art. There is also an admirable interactive element, allowing visitors to display their own creativity. The restructured new wing should be complete by 2015.

The German Village

Just six blocks south of the Statehouse, I-70 separates downtown from the delightful **German Village** neighbourhood. During the mid-nineteenth century, thousands of German immigrants settled in this part of Columbus, building neat red-brick homes, the most lavish of which surround the 23-acre **Schiller Park**. Their descendants gradually dwindled in numbers by the 1950s and the area became increasingly run-down until it won a place on the National Register of Historic Places. The best way to explore its brick-paved streets, corner bars, old-style restaurants, Catholic churches and grand homes is to stop in at the **German Village Meeting Haus**, 588 S 3rd St (Mon–Fri 9am–4pm, Sat 10am–2pm; ☎ 614 221 8888, ⓦ germanvillage.com), where popular walking tours ($10) run by the German Village Society start with a twelve-minute video presentation. The Society also oversees the immensely popular Haus und Garten Tour on the last Sunday in June and the Oktoberfest celebrations in late September. Book-lovers will adore the **Book Loft**, 631 S 3rd St (daily 10am–11pm; ☎ 614 464 1774), whose books, many of them discounted, are crammed into 32 rooms of one grand building.

The Brewery District

Just west of High Street (US-23) are the warehouses of the **Brewery District**, where, until Prohibition, the German immigrants brewed beer by traditional methods. Many of the original buildings still stand, but today the beer is produced by just a couple of microbreweries. These brewpubs are typical of the area's more mainstream **nightlife**.

Short North Arts District

Across Nationwide Boulevard at the top end of downtown is the **Short North Arts District** (ⓦ shortnorth.org), a former red-light district that's now Columbus's most vibrant enclave. Standing on either side of High Street – the main north–south thoroughfare – its entrance is marked by the iron gateways of the Cap at Union Station. Thereafter starts the trail of galleries, bars and restaurants that makes the area so popular with locals; it is also the heart of the gay community. The first Saturday of each month sees the **Gallery Hop**, when local art-dealers throw open their doors – complementing the artworks with wine, snacks and occasional performance pieces – and the socializing goes on well into the evening.

The university campus

Businesses beyond the Short North Arts District, become a little more low-rent for a mile before High Street cuts through the **university campus** and suddenly sprouts cheap eating places and funky shopping. For bargain vinyl, head to Used Kids Records, 1980 N High St (☎614 421 9455). On the other side of the road, the **Wexner Center for the Arts**, North High St at 15th Ave (Tues, Wed & Sun 11am–6pm, Thurs–Sat 11am–8pm; free; ☎614 292 3535, ⊛wexarts.org), is another Eisenman construction, even more extreme than the Convention Center (see p.251).

ARRIVAL, GETTING AROUND AND INFORMATION
COLUMBUS

By plane Port Columbus International Airport is 7 miles northeast of downtown. Central Ohio Transit Authority's (COTA; ☎614 228 1776, ⊛cota.com) express route bus #52 runs from there through downtown for $2.75, while taxis cost around $25.

By bus Greyhound stops at 111 E Town St. Destinations Cincinnati (6 daily; 1hr 55min–2hr 55min);

Cleveland (6 daily; 2hr 25min–2hr 50min).

Local buses COTA's citywide bus service costs $2 for a one-way ride and $4.50 for a day pass.

Visitor centre 277 W Nationwide Blvd (Mon–Fri 8am–5pm, Sat & Sun 10am–4pm; ☎614 221 6623, ⊛experiencecolumbus.com).

ACCOMMODATION

Compared with other cities in the region, Columbus offers a good choice of convenient mid-range places to stay. Downtown rates are good, while even more savings can be had by staying in the German Village area.

50 Lincoln-Short North 50 E Lincoln St, Short North ☎614 299 5050, ⊛columbus-bed-breakfast.com. Enjoy a warm welcome and lavish furnishings in one of the seven rooms of this grand Short North house, now a delightful B&B. $130

Drury Inn and Suites Convention Center 88 E Nationwide Blvd ☎614 221 7008, ⊛druryhotels.com. Smart and comfortable chain hotel within walking distance of downtown and Short North. It offers a decent breakfast and happy hour. $119

German Village Inn 920 S High St ☎614 443 6506,

⊛germanvillageinn.net. This family-run motel, on the south edge of the German Village/Brewery District, has simple but smart rooms and is one of the best deals going. $54

★ **The Lofts Hotel** 55 E Nationwide Blvd ☎614 461 2663, ⊛55lofts.com. Luxury New York-style loft conversions, within easy walking distance of the Arena and the downtown areas. Great online deals. $209

The Westin Great Southern 310 S High St ☎614 228 3800, ⊛westincolumbus.com. Columbus's grand red-brick Victorian hotel, with surprisingly moderate rates for some rooms, all of which are of high quality. $189

EATING

The Short North and German Village neighbourhoods are crammed with places to eat, be they bottom-dollar snack bars or stylish and adventurous bistros. For a wide range of ethnic and organic snacks during the day, try the North Market, downtown at 59 Spruce St (Tues–Fri 9am–7pm, Sat 8am–5pm, Sun noon–5pm; ☎614 463 9664), which also sells fresh produce.

Haiku 800 N High St, Short North ☎614 294 8168, ⊛haikushortnorth.com. Excellent Japanese restaurant with a huge range of sushi, noodle and rice dishes for $10–15. Also hosts art and entertainment events. Mon–Thurs 11am–11pm, Fri & Sat 11am–midnight, Sun 4–10pm.

Katzinger's 475 S 3rd St, German Village ☎614 228 3354, ⊛katzingers.com. A mesmerizing range of gut-busting sandwiches for around $10, plus Jewish delicacies and cheesecakes, are available at this slightly upmarket deli. Mon–Fri 8.30am–8.30pm, Sat & Sun 9am–8.30pm.

Marcella's 615 N High St, Short North ☎614 223 2100. Buzzing Italian restaurant with a lively bar. The food is a range of moderately upmarket pizzas, pasta, salads and main dishes such as veal saltimbocca for $21.95. Mon–Thurs & Sun 6–10pm, Fri & Sat 6pm–midnight.

Schmidt's 240 E Kossuth St, German Village ☎614 444 6808, ⊛schmidthaus.com. This Columbus landmark (since 1886) serves a range of sausages, schnitzel and strudel in a former slaughterhouse, served by waitresses in German garb. Mains $10–15. Mon–Thurs & Sun 11am–10pm, Fri & Sat 11am–11pm.

4

★ **Surly Girl Saloon** 1126 N High St, Short North ☎614 294 4900, ⓦsurlygirlsaloon.com. Heapings of Tex-Mex, Cajun and other cuisines only cost around $10 in this quirky joint where Western bordello meets *Pirates of the Caribbean*. Fine microbrews on tap help the place get rowdy late on. Daily 11am–2am.

NIGHTLIFE

This youthful university town is a rich source of local bands, from country revivalists to experimental alternative acts. The main nightlife areas are the bohemian Short North Arts District, also the gay hub, and the more mainstream Brewery District on the south side of the centre. The weekly *Outlook* (ⓦoutlookweekly.net) has complete listings. The *Other Paper* (ⓦtheotherpaper.com) provides fuller free details of what's happening around town.

Axis Night Club 775 N High St ☎614 291 4008, ⓦaxisonhigh.com. Very popular gay nightspot that gets steamier as the night wears on, as people gyrate to the latest disco and trance vibes. Cover on club nights varies. Hours vary.

Basement 391 Neil Ave, Arena District ☎614 461 5483, ⓦpromowestlive.com. One of the city's hottest new music venues, where you are likely to hear upcoming bands of different genres. Good sound system. Hours vary.

Oldfield's On High 2590 N High St ☎614 784 0477. Campus bar with live music across a broad range of genres. No cover most nights. Mon–Sat 6pm–2am.

Short North Tavern 674 N High St, Short North ☎614 221 2432. The oldest bar in the neighbourhood, with live bands playing at the weekend dressed in German garb. Daily 6pm–2.30am.

★ **Skully's Music-Diner** 1151 N High St, Short North ☎614 291 8856, ⓦskullys.org. Classic 1950s-style diner whose happy hour (4–9pm) is often followed by cool indie-rock shows. Mon–Fri 11am–2.30am, Sat noon–2.30am, Sun 1pm–2.30am.

Sloppy Donkey Sports Bar 2040 N High St ☎614 297 5000. Extremely popular student hangout with cheapish drinks, large screens and bar games. Daily noon–2am.

4

Cincinnati

CINCINNATI, just across the Ohio River from Kentucky, is a dynamic commercial metropolis with a definite European flavour and a sense of the South. Its tidy centre, rich in architecture and culture, lies within walking distance of the attractive **riverfront**, the lively **Over-the-Rhine** district to the north and arty **Mount Adams**.

The city was founded in 1788 at the point where a Native American trading route crossed the river. Its name comes from a group of Revolutionary War admirers of the Roman general Cincinnatus, who saved Rome in 458 BC and then returned to his small farm, refusing to accept any reward. Cincinnati quickly became an important supply point for pioneers heading west on flatboats and rafts, and its population skyrocketed with the establishment of a major steamboat **riverport** in 1811. Tens of thousands of **German** immigrants poured in during the 1830s.

Loyalties were split by the **Civil War**. Despite the loss of some important markets, the city decided that its future lay with the Union. In the prosperous postwar decade, Cincinnati acquired Fountain Square and the country's first professional baseball team, the **Reds** (ⓦreds.com) they, along with the **Bengals** football team (ⓦbengals.com), remain a great source of pride.

Downtown Cincinnati

Downtown Cincinnati rolls back from the Ohio River to fill a flat basin area ringed by steep hills. During the city's emergent industrial years, the filth, disease and crime drove the middle classes from downtown en masse. Nowadays, however, attractive stores, street vendors, restaurants, cafés, open spaces and gardens occupy the area. The city's rich blend of architecture is best appreciated **on foot**. Over, among and even right through the hotel plazas, office lobbies and retail areas, the **Skywalk** network of air-conditioned passages spans sixteen city blocks. A mile-long **riverside walk** begins at **Public Landing**, at the bottom of Broadway, and stretches east past painted showboats and the **Bicentennial Commons**, a 200th-birthday present from the city to itself in 1988.

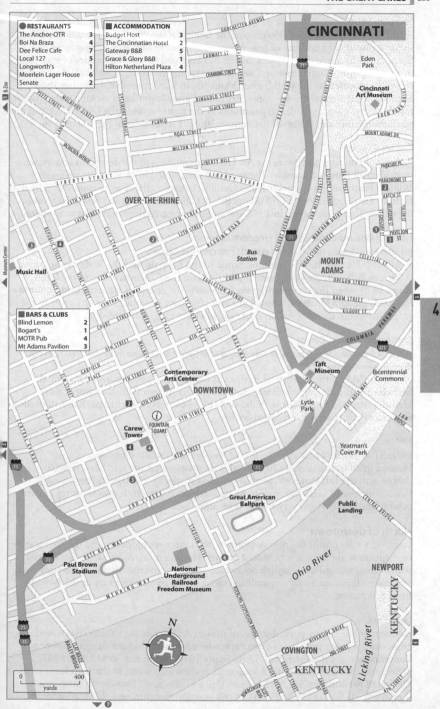

CINCINNATI

RESTAURANTS
The Anchor-OTR	3
Boi Na Braza	4
Dee Felice Cafe	7
Local 127	5
Longworth's	1
Moerlein Lager House	6
Senate	2

ACCOMMODATION
Budget Host	3
The Cincinnatian Hotel	2
Gateway B&B	5
Grace & Glory B&B	1
Hilton Netherland Plaza	4

BARS & CLUBS
Blind Lemon	2
Bogart's	1
MOTR Pub	4
Mt Adams Pavilion	3

Fountain Square

At the geographic centre of downtown, the **Genius of the Waters** in **Fountain Square** sprays a cascade of hundreds of jets, meant to symbolize the city's trading links. Surrounded by a tree-dotted plaza and all but enclosed by soaring facades of glass and steel, it's a popular lunch spot and venue for daytime concerts, as well as the second largest **Oktoberfest** in the world, after Munich's, in late September. Looming above Fifth and Vine streets, the 48-storey, Art Deco **Carew Tower** has a viewing gallery on its top floor that gives a wonderful panorama of the tight bends of the Ohio River and the surrounding hillsides (Mon–Thurs 9am–5.30pm, Fri 9am–6pm, Sat 10am–7pm; $3).

Procter & Gamble HQ

Just east of Fountain Square are the Art Deco headquarters of the detergents and hygiene-product giant **Procter & Gamble**. The company was formed in 1837 by candle-maker William Procter and soap-maker James Gamble, to exploit the copious supply of animal fat from the slaughterhouses of "Porkopolis", as Cincinnati was then known. By sponsoring radio's *The Puddle Family* in 1932, the company created the world's first **soap opera**.

National Underground Railroad Freedom Museum

50 E Freedom Way • Tues–Sat 11am–5pm • $12 • ☎ 513 333 7500, ⓦ freedomcenter.org

South of I-71, Paul Brown Stadium, home of the Bengals, and the Reds' Great American Ballpark, are giant cement additions on the Cincinnati side of the Ohio River. In between the two sporting venues stands the engaging **National Underground Railroad Freedom Museum**, whose light and airy space chronicles the city's role in the emancipation of slaves as well as other worldwide struggles for freedom.

Contemporary Arts Center

Sixth and Walnut sts • Mon 10am–9pm, Wed–Fri 10am–6pm, Sat & Sun 11am–6pm • $7.50, free Mon after 5pm • ☎ 513 345 8400, ⓦ contemporaryartscenter.org

The left-field, multimedia art exhibitions at the superb **Contemporary Arts Center**, housed in a stunning new building designed by Iraqi-born British architect Zaha Hadid, often lead to run-ins with the city's more conservative citizens. Exhibits occupy four floors and revolve every few months.

Taft Museum

316 Pike St • Wed–Fri 11am–4pm, Sat & Sun 11am–5pm • $10, free on Sun • ☎ 513 241 0343, ⓦ taftmuseum.org

Housed in an immaculate 1820 Federal-style mansion on the northeast fringe of downtown, the **Taft Museum** contains priceless works by the likes of Rembrandt, Goya, Turner and Gainsborough in its permanent collection. It also hosts temporary exhibitions that change every two or three months.

North of downtown

Just over a mile northeast from downtown, the land rises suddenly and the streets start to conform to the contours of **Mount Adams**. Here, century-old townhouses coexist with avant-garde galleries, stylish boutiques, international restaurants and trendy bars. To explore these and enjoy unparalleled views of the river, take a taxi or the #49 bus from downtown.

Eden Park

Adjacent to the tightly packed streets of Mount Adams are the rolling lawns, verdant copses and scenic overlooks of **Eden Park**, where you will find the delightful **Krohn Conservatory** at 1501 Eden Park Drive (daily 10am–5pm; free; ☎ 513 421 5707, ⓦ cincinnatiparks.com/krohn). A loop road at the western end of the park leads to the **Cincinnati Art Museum**, on Art Museum Drive (Tues–Sun 11am–5pm; June–Aug till 9pm on Wed; free; ☎ 513 639 2984, ⓦ cincinnatiartmuseum.org). Its one hundred labyrinthine galleries span five thousand years, taking in an excellent Islamic collection as well as a solid selection of European and American paintings by the likes of Matisse, Monet, Picasso, Edward Hopper and Grant Wood.

Museum Center

1301 Western Ave • Mon–Sat 10am–5pm, Sun 11am–6pm • Museums $8.50 each, all three $12.50, OMNIMAX $7.50, discount with museum entry • ☎ 513 287 7000, ⓦ cincymuseum.org

Northwest from downtown, Cincinnati's three-in-one **Museum Center** is housed in the magnificent Art Deco **Union Terminal**, approached via a stately driveway off Ezzard Charles Drive. Highlights of the **Museum of Natural History** are dioramas of Ice Age Cincinnati and "the Cavern", which houses a living bat colony. The **Historical Society** holds a succession of well-presented, short-term exhibitions and the **Cinergy Children's Museum** has a two-storey treehouse and eight other interactive exhibit areas.

Covington

Covington, directly across the Ohio River on the Kentucky side, is regarded as the southern side of Cincinnati. It can be reached from downtown Cincinnati by walking over the bright blue, 1057ft-long **John A. Roebling Suspension Bridge**, at the bottom of Walnut Street, which was built in 1867 and served as a prototype for the Brooklyn Bridge. A ten-minute walk southwest of the bridge brings you to the attractive, narrow, tree-lined streets and nineteenth-century houses of **MainStrasse Village**. It's a Germanic neighbourhood of antique shops, bars and restaurants that plays host to the lively **Maifest** on the third weekend of each May and is the centrepiece of the citywide **Oktoberfest** on the weekend after Labor Day. At 6th and Philadelphia streets, 21 mechanical figures accompanied by glockenspiel music toll the hour on the German Gothic **Carroll Chimes Bell Tower**.

Creation Museum

Mon–Fri 10am–6pm, Sat 9am–6pm, Sun noon–6pm • $29.95, discounts online and Tues & Wed • ☎ 888 582 4253, ⓦ creationmuseum.org

South of MainStrasse Village, en route to the airport off I-275, one of the area's newest attractions is the multimillion-dollar **Creation Museum**. A truly "only in America" experience, the state-of-the-art dioramas, video show and planetarium ($7) argue an uncompromising creationist case and make Darwin out to be little short of Lucifer himself. There is also a **petting zoo**.

Newport

Across the Licking River from Covington, the subdued town of **Newport** has become a lot livelier since the opening of a large shopping complex and the impressive **Newport Aquarium**, 1 Aquarium Way (daily 9am–7pm; $23; ☎ 859 261 7444 or ☎ 800 406 3474, ⓦ newportaquarium.com). Clear underwater tunnels and see-through floors allow visitors to be literally surrounded by sharks and snapping gators.

ARRIVAL AND DEPARTURE   CINCINNATI

By plane Cincinnati-Northern Kentucky International Airport is 12 miles south of downtown, in Covington, Kentucky. Taxis to the city centre (☎ 859 586 5236) cost $32–35.

By bus The Greyhound station is on the eastern fringe of the city centre, just off Broadway at 1005 Gilbert Ave. Destinations Cleveland (5 daily; 4hr 40min–5hr 15min);

Columbus (6 daily; 1hr 55min); Indianapolis (2hr 5min–3hr); Lexington (1hr 25min); Louisville (5 daily; 1hr 45min).
By train Amtrak trains arrive a mile northwest of downtown at the Union Terminal museum complex.
Destinations Chicago (1 daily; 9hr 40min); Indianapolis (1 daily; 3hr 30min); New York (4 weekly; 18hr 30min); Washington DC (4 weekly; 14hr 40min).

GETTING AROUND AND INFORMATION

By bus The Metro bus network ($1.75–4.25; ☎ 513 621 4455, ⓦ go-metro.com) covers routes within the city and

neighbouring Ohio counties. Buses on the Kentucky side are run by TANK ($1.50; ☎ 859 331 8265, ⓦ tankbus.org), including shuttle buses across to Cincinnati.

Visitor centre Fountain Square (Wed–Sun 11am–5pm; ☎ 513 534 5877); or contact the Cincinnati USA Regional Tourism Network (☎ 859 589 2260, ⓦ cincinnatiusa.com).

ACCOMMODATION

Although Cincinnati's quality hotels are reasonable by big-city standards, budget travellers may have problems finding affordable downtown rooms. Uptown motels – over 2 miles north – are much cheaper, but you'll need a car to get around safely at night.

Budget Host 3356 Central Pkwy ☎ 513 559 1600, ⓦ budgethost.com. Just about the cheapest place in uptown Cincinnati, though the adequate doubles vary greatly in price according to demand. Three miles from downtown. **$70**

The Cincinnatian Hotel 601 Vine St ☎ 513 381 3000, ⓦ cincinnatianhotel.com. Exuding pure class with its marble lobby and wood-panelled rooms, this 1882 building houses the city's prime independent luxury hotel. **$209**

Gateway B&B 326 E 6th St, Newport, Kentucky ☎ 859 581 6447, ⓦ gatewaybb.com. Comfortable, affordable Victorian place with cosy rooms, 5min from downtown Cincinnati and Covington, Kentucky. **$129**

Grace & Glory B&B 3539 Shaw Ave ☎ 513 321 2824, ⓦ graceandglorybb.com. This small, welcoming place with comfortable rooms and common lounge, 5 miles east of downtown, is a good option if you have a car. The Glory Suite Extension room is a super bargain. **$59**

Hilton Netherland Plaza 35 W 5th St ☎ 513 421 9000, ⓦ hilton.com. One of the classier *Hilton* franchises, located in a National Historic Landmark building, with a sumptuous Art Deco lobby, gym and well-furnished rooms. Rates vary wildly. **$150**

EATING

Cincinnati boasts excellent homegrown gourmet and continental restaurants. It's also famous for **Cincinnati chilli**, a combination of spaghetti noodles, meat, cheese, onions and kidney beans, served at chains such as *Skyline Chili*, who have more than forty locations, including one at Vine and 7th streets, downtown.

The Anchor-OTR 1401 Race St, Over-the-Rhine ☎ 513 421 8111, ⓦ theanchor-otr.com. Snazzy yet casual, this new restaurant and oyster bar does a range of delicious seafood, such as an exceptionally creamy chowder and main courses for around $20. Tues–Thurs 11.30am–2.30pm & 5–10pm, Fri & Sat 11.30am–2.30pm & 5–11pm.

Boi Na Braza 441 Vine St ☎ 513 421 7111, ⓦ boinabraza .com. Carnivores can feast on the unlimited *rodizio*-style Brazilian meat cuts for $39.95, while the sumptuous salad bar costs $19.95 per person. Mon–Thurs 5–10pm, Fri 11am–2pm & 5–10pm, Sat 5–10.30pm, Sun 5–9pm.

Dee Felice Cafe 529 Main St, Covington, Kentucky ☎ 859 261 2365, ⓦ deefelicecafe.com. This small and atmospheric spot specializes in Cajun cuisine, with lots of fresh seafood dishes, and doubles as a jazz venue Wed–Sun. Daily 5–11pm.

Local 127 127 W 4th St ☎ 513 721 1345, ⓦ mylocal127 .com. Excellent restaurant serving New American cuisine in chic surroundings. Duck breast with rhubarb and sugar snap peas goes for $29. Mon–Thurs 11.30am–9pm, Fri 11.30am–10pm, Sat noon–10pm.

Longworth's 1108 St Gregory St, Mount Adams ☎ 513 651 2253, ⓦ longworths-mtadams.com. Good hamburgers, sandwiches, salads and pizzas at attractive prices in a delightful garden setting. Daily 11am–2.30am, food till midnight.

★ **Moerlein Lager House** 115 Joe Nuxhall Way ☎ 513 421 2337, ⓦ moerleinlagerhouse.com. Large airy place with a deck overlooking the river, serving tempting seafood appetizers and main dishes such as prime rib for $23, as well as a fine range of beers brewed on-site. Mon–Thurs 11am–midnight, Fri & Sat 11am–1am, Sun 11am–11pm.

★ **Senate** 1212 Vine St, Over-the-Rhine ☎ 513 421 2020, ⓦ senatepub.com. This pristine diner-style spot dishes up gourmet hot dogs such as Korean or Japanese-style, as well as oysters, mussels and other delights for $10–30. Great draught ales too. Tues–Thurs 11.30am–2pm & 4.30–11pm, Fri & Sat 11.30am–2pm & 4.30pm–1am.

NIGHTLIFE AND ENTERTAINMENT

After dark, the hottest area with the widest appeal is the **Over-the-Rhine** district, which fans out from Main Street around 12th and 14th streets, and buzzes every night. The next liveliest areas are ritzier **Mount Adams** and more collegiate **Corryville**, a 5min drive northwest from downtown. Entertainment **listings** for the whole city can be found in the free *Cincinnati CityBeat* (ⓦ citybeat.com).

BARS AND CLUBS

Blind Lemon 936 Hatch St, Mount Adams ☎ 513 241 3885, ⓦ theblindlemon.com. Beyond the intimate, low-ceilinged bar, you'll find a relaxed patio crowd. Live music (mostly acoustic) nightly. Mon–Fri 5.30pm–2.30am, Sat & Sun 3pm–2.30am.

Bogart's 2621 Vine St, Corryville ☎ 513 281 8400, ⓦ bogarts.com. Established indie acts play this mid-sized venue a couple of miles north of downtown. It also hosts club nights and special events. Hours vary.

★ **MOTR Pub** 1345 Vine St, Over-the-Rhine ☎ 513 381 6687, ⓦ motrpub.com. One of the hippest joints in this increasingly trendy area, with a well-stocked bar and regular live music. Mon 5pm–midnight, Tues–Thurs 5pm–2am, Fri & Sat 5pm–2.30am, Sun 10am–midnight.

Mt Adams Pavilion 949 Pavilion St, Mount Adams ☎ 513 744 9200, ⓦ mountadamspavilion.com. From its terraced outdoor deck, you'll have great views of the city and the Ohio River. Great Bloody Marys. Stages various club nights. Mon–Sat 4pm–2.30am, Sun 4pm–midnight.

PERFORMING ARTS VENUES

Cincinnati Playhouse in the Park Eden Park ☎ 513 421 3888, ⓦ cincyplay.com. This established company puts on drama, musicals and comedies, with performances throughout the year.

Music Hall 1243 Elm St, Over-the-Rhine ☎ 513 744 3344, ⓦ cincinnatiarts.org. This 1870s conglomeration of spires, arched windows and cornices, is said to have near-perfect acoustics. Home to Cincinnati's Opera and Symphony Orchestra, it also hosts the May Festival of choral music.

Michigan

Mention **MICHIGAN** and most people will immediately think of the automotive industry and the grit and (faded) glory of Detroit. Those who've visited will also know of the diverse beaches, dunes and cliffs scattered along the 3200-mile shoreline of its two vividly contrasting **peninsulas**.

The mitten-shaped **Lower Peninsula** is dominated from its southeastern corner by the industrial giant of **Detroit**, surrounded by satellite cities heavily devoted to the automotive industry. In the west, the scenic 350-mile Lake Michigan shoreline drive passes through likeable little ports before reaching the stunning **Sleeping Bear Dunes** and resort towns such as **Traverse City**, in the peninsula's balmy northwest corner. The desolate, dramatic and thinly populated **Upper Peninsula**, reaching out from Wisconsin like a claw to separate lakes Superior and Michigan, is a dramatic departure from the cosmopolitan south.

In the mid-seventeenth century, **French explorers** forged a successful trading relationship with the Chippewa, Ontario and other Native American tribes. The **British**, who acquired control after 1763, were far more brutal. Governor Henry Hamilton, the "Hair Buyer of Detroit", advocated taking scalps rather than prisoners. Ever since, Michigan's economy has developed in waves, the eighteenth-century fur, timber and copper booms culminating in the state establishing itself at the forefront of the nation's manufacturing capacity, thanks to its abundant raw materials, good transport links and the genius of innovators such as **Henry Ford**. Today the state is attempting to reinvent itself as a "creative hub" for new technologies, as the automotive industry continues to decline.

Detroit

DETROIT is the poster child for urban blight in the United States, despite many attempts to overcome this negative imagery, and in some cases, a rather stark reality. It is a city which boasts a billion-dollar downtown development, ultra-modern motor-manufacturing plants, some excellent museums and one of the nation's biggest art galleries – but since the 1960s, media attention has dwelt instead on its huge tracts of urban wasteland, where for block after block there's nothing but the occasional heavily fortified loan shop or unpleasant-looking grocery store. Crippled with debt, the city itself admitted defeat and in 2013 filed the largest municipal **bankruptcy** in US history. And yet, there are signs that things are improving, with local business promoters pointing to the bustle around **Greektown** at night and the **Detroit Historical Museum** as signs of a renaissance of sorts.

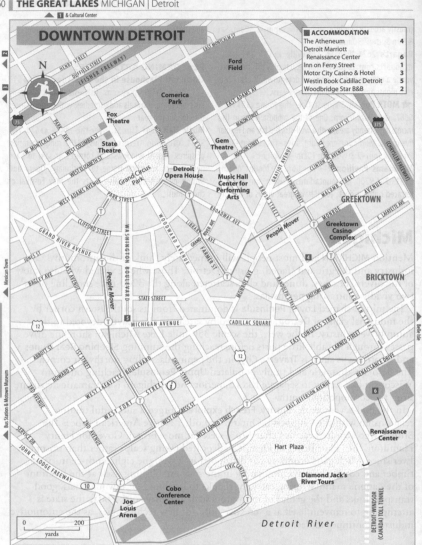

DOWNTOWN DETROIT

ACCOMMODATION	
The Atheneum	4
Detroit Marriott Renaissance Center	6
Inn on Ferry Street	1
Motor City Casino & Hotel	3
Westin Book Cadillac Detroit	5
Woodbridge Star B&B	2

As for orientation, it makes sense to think of Detroit as a region rather than a concentrated city – and, with some planning and wheels, it holds plenty to see and do. Futuristic glass-box office buildings and a tastefully revamped park in downtown overlook the glass-green Detroit River, but for the most part it's rather empty, even in the middle of the day. Other interesting areas include the huge **Cultural Center**, freewheeling **Royal Oak**, posh **Birmingham** and the Ford-town of **Dearborn**.

Brief history

Founded in 1701 by **Antoine de Mothe Cadillac**, as a trading post for the French to do business with the Chippewa, Detroit was no more than a medium-sized port two hundred years later. Then **Henry Ford**, **Ransom Eli Olds**, the **Chevrolets** and the

Dodge brothers began to build their automobile empires. Thanks to the introduction of the mass assembly line, Detroit boomed in the 1920s, but the auto barons sponsored the construction of segregated neighbourhoods and shed workers during times of low demand. Such policies created huge ghettos, resulting, in July 1967, in the bloodiest **riot** in the USA in fifty years. More than forty people died and thirteen hundred buildings were destroyed. The **inner city** was left to fend for itself, while the all-important motor industry was rocked by the oil crises and Japanese competition. Today, though scarred and bruised, Detroit is not the mess some would have it, and suburban residents have started to return to the city's festivals, theatres, clubs and restaurants.

The Renaissance Center

Free tours start from the PURE DETROIT/GM Collection Store • Mon–Fri noon & 2pm

Most of downtown's offices and stores are squeezed into the six gleaming towers of the **Renaissance Center (RenCen)**, a virtual city within a city. Rising up 73 storeys from the riverbank, the towers offer a great view of the metropolis from their free observation deck (open as part of the free tours). It's an attractive public space and the soaring glass atrium known as the "Winter Garden" is particularly impressive.

Hart Plaza and around

The urban breathing space of **Hart Plaza** rolls down to the river in the shade of the RenCen and hosts free lunchtime concerts and lively weekend ethnic festivals all summer long; the US leg of the annual **Detroit International Jazz Festival**, the world's largest free jazz festival, takes place here over Labor Day weekend. Across the plaza is the **Joe Louis Arena**, home of the beloved Red Wings hockey team (see p.265).

The Theater District

Ten blocks north of the RenCen up Woodward Avenue is the **Theater District**, downtown's prime nightlife spot. Highlights are the magnificently restored Siamese-Byzantine **Fox Theatre** (see p.265) a huge old movie palace that is the city's top concert, drama and film venue, and the grand Italian Renaissance **State Theatre** next door. This area is at the centre of the city's **Columbia Street** redevelopment project, home to Ford Field and Comerica Park (see p.265), as well as microbreweries, coffeehouses and the inevitable themed restaurants.

Belle Isle Park

Diamond Jack's River Tours (June–Aug; 2hr; $17; ☎ 313 843 9376, ⓦ diamondjack.com), depart from Hart Plaza downtown, or take DOT bus #25 and transfer at MacArthur Bridge to the #12

Three miles east of the RenCen, **Belle Isle Park** is an inner-city island retreat with twenty miles of paths, sports facilities, and free attractions including an aquarium and elaborate gardens. It's also home to the annual **Detroit Grand Prix** Indy car race.

The Detroit Cultural Center

Three miles northwest of downtown, next to Wayne State University, the top-class museums of the **Detroit Cultural Center** are clustered within easy walking distance of one another.

Detroit Institute of Arts

5200 Woodward Ave • Wed & Thurs 9am–4pm, Fri 9am–10pm, Sat & Sun 9am–5pm • $8 • ☎ 313 833 7900, ⓦ dia.org

One of America's most prestigious art museums, the colossal **Detroit Institute of Arts** traces the history of civilization through one hundred galleries. Most notable are the Chinese, Persian, Egyptian, Greek, Roman, Dutch and American collections – not to mention the largest Italian collection outside of Italy. The museum has masterpieces such as a Van Gogh self-portrait and John Singer Sargent's *Mosquito Nets*, as well as Diego Rivera's enormous, show-stealing, 1933 *Detroit Industry* mural. The DIA also presents live music every Friday (6–10pm; free with museum admission).

Charles H. Wright Museum of African American History

315 E Warren St • Tues–Sat 9am–5pm, Sun 1–5pm • $8 • ☎ 313 494 5800, ⓦ thewright.org

The impressive **Charles H. Wright Museum of African American History** is the largest African American museum in the world. Its massive core exhibit covers six hundred years of history in eight distinct segments, starting with a chilling sculpture of a slave boat, before moving through the Civil War, the Great Depression and the work of Dr Martin Luther King, Jr and Malcolm X.

Detroit Historical Museum

5401 Woodward Ave • Tues–Fri 9.30am–4pm, Sat & Sun noon–5pm • $6 • ☎ 313 833 1805, ⓦ detroithistorical.org

The **Detroit Historical Museum** was completely redesigned and reopened in 2012. The new interactive exhibits deal with the city's role in mobilizing the USA for World War II, and it helped transport slaves to Canada before the Civil War. The **Gallery of Innovation** is predictably hands-on, while the **Allesee Gallery of Culture** and the **Kid Rock Music Lab** lets folk young and old experiment with musical innovation.

The Motown Museum

2648 W Grand Blvd • July–Aug Mon–Fri 10am–6pm, Sat 10am–8pm; Sept–June Tues–Sat 10am–6pm • $10 • ☎ 313 875 2264, ⓦ motownmuseum.org

Unlike cities such as Memphis, Nashville and New Orleans, Detroit is devoid of the bars, clubs and homes of its musical heroes. The golden age of Motown was very much confined to a specific time and place, and, disappointingly, only at the **Motown Museum** can Tamla fans pay homage to one of the world's most celebrated record labels. The museum, run as a not-for-profit organization, is housed in the small white-and-blue clapboard house, Hitsville USA, which served as Motown's recording studio from 1959 to 1972. On the ground floor, Studio A remains just as it was left: battered instruments stand piled up against the nicotine-stained acoustic wall-tiles and

---

THE MOTOWN SOUND

The legend that is Tamla Motown started in 1959 when Ford worker and part-time songwriter **Berry Gordy Jr** borrowed $800 to set up a studio. From his first hit onward – the prophetic *Money (That's What I Want)* – he set out to create a crossover style, targeting his records at white and black consumers alike.

Early Motown hits were pure formula. Gordy softened the blue notes of most contemporary black music in favour of a more danceable, poppy beat, with **gospel**-influenced singing and clapping. Prime examples of the early approach featured all-female groups such as the **Marvelettes** (*Needle in a Haystack*), the **Supremes** (*Baby Love*) and **Martha Reeves and the Vandellas** (*Nowhere to Run*), as well as the all-male **Miracles** (*Tracks of My Tears*), featuring the sophisticated love lyrics of lead singer **Smokey Robinson**. Gordy's "Quality Control Department" scrutinized every beat, playing all recordings through speakers modelled on cheap transistor radios before the final mix.

The Motown organization was an intense, close-knit community: **Marvin Gaye** married Gordy's sister, while "Little" **Stevie Wonder** was the baby of the family. The label did, however, move with the times, utilizing such innovations as the wah-wah pedal and synthesizer. By the late 1960s its output had acquired a harder sound, crowned by the acid soul productions of Norman Whitfield with the versatile **Temptations**. In 1968 the organization outgrew its premises on Grand Avenue; four years later it abandoned Detroit altogether for LA. Befitting the middle-of-the-road tastes of the 1970s, the top sellers were then the high-society soul of **Diana Ross** and the ballads of the **Commodores**. This saw many top artists, dissatisfied with Gordy's constant intervention, leave the label, although the crack songwriting team of Holland-Dozier-Holland, responsible for most of the **Four Tops'** hits, stayed in Detroit to produce the seminal **Chairmen of the Board** (*Gimme Just A Little More Time*), along with **Aretha Franklin** and **Jackie Wilson**. Today, Motown is owned by the giant **Universal Music Group**.

a well-scuffed Steinway piano all but fills the room. Upstairs are the former living quarters of label founder **Berry Gordy**, while in the adjoining room record sleeves, gold and platinum discs and other memorabilia are displayed.

The Henry Ford Museum

20900 Oakwood Blvd, Dearborn • Daily 9.30am–5pm• $15 • ☎ 313 271 6001, ⓦ thehenryford.org • Accessible on SMART bus routes #200 and #250

The enormous **Henry Ford Museum**, ten miles from downtown in Dearborn, pays fulsome tribute to its founder as a brilliant industrialist and do-gooder. The former is certainly true. The inventor of the assembly line didn't succeed by being a philanthropist, however, and was indeed dubbed "an industrial fascist – the Mussolini of Detroit" by the *New York Times* in 1928. He only grudgingly allowed the United Auto Workers (UAW) into his factories in 1943, and was less than welcoming to his black employees, banning them from the model communities he built for his white workers and forcing them instead into a separate town sardonically named "Inkster".

Ford was an inveterate collector of Americana. In addition to the massive "**The Automobile in American Life**" exhibit, ranging from early Ford models and postal carriages to NASCAR vehicles and electric cars, the twelve-acre museum amounts to a giant curiosity shop, holding planes, trains and row upon row of domestic inventions. Real oddities include the chair Lincoln was sitting in and the car Kennedy was riding in when each was shot, the bus Rosa Parks was riding when she refused to give up her seat, and even a test tube holding Edison's last breath. One pertinent item not on view is the Iron Cross that Hitler presented to Ford (a notorious anti-Semite) in 1938.

Down the street from the main museum complex, **Greenfield Village** (daily 9.30am–5pm; $2) is a collection of homes owned by famous Americans, including the Wright Brothers' bicycle shop. Amid these curious surroundings, costumed hosts demonstrate everything from weaving to puncture-repair.

Automotive Hall of Fame

21400 Oakwood Blvd • May–Oct daily 9am–5pm; Sept–April closed Mon & Tues • $8 • ☎ 313 240 4000, ⓦ automotivehalloffame.org

Directly next door to the Ford sprawl, the **Automotive Hall of Fame** is more interesting than it might at first sound. In paying homage to the innovators and inventors of the global (not just the Detroit) auto industry, the interactive exhibits let you see how you might have handled problems encountered by Buick, Honda and the like. There's also a replica of the world's first petrol-powered automobile and an elaborate "Hall of Honor" featuring a vast mural celebrating all things vehicular.

ARRIVAL AND DEPARTURE   DETROIT

By plane Detroit Metropolitan Wayne County Airport is in Romulus, 18 miles southwest of downtown and a hefty taxi ride; Metro Airport Taxi (☎ 800 745 5191) charges $41 while Checker Sedan Taxis (☎ 800 351 5466) is $55. The SMART bus #125 ($1.50; ☎ 866 962 5515, ⓦ smartbus.org) goes downtown from Smith terminal.

By bus Greyhound buses pull in at 1001 Howard Ave, a dodgy area.

Destinations Chicago (8 daily; 6hr); Cleveland (7 daily; 4hr); New York City (4 daily; 17hr).

By train Amtrak has a station in the city proper at 11 W Baltimore Ave, an area best avoided late at night, and another 10 miles out at 16121 Michigan Ave, Dearborn, near the Henry Ford Museum. Three trains a day head to Chicago (5hr).

GETTING AROUND AND INFORMATION

By elevated railway Downtown, the People Mover elevated railway loops around thirteen art-adorned stations (Mon–Thurs 6.30am–midnight, Fri 6.30am–2am, Sat 9am–2am, Sun noon–midnight; 50¢).

By bus SMART serves the entire metro region, while DDOT

buses ($1.50; ☎ 313 933 1300, ⓦ detroitmi.gov/ddot) offer a patchier inner-city service.

Visitor centre Tenth floor, 211 W Fort St, downtown (Mon–Fri 9am–5pm; ☎ 313 202 1800, ⓦ visitdetroit.com).

ACCOMMODATION

The Atheneum 1000 Brush St ☎313 962 2323, ⓦatheneumsuites.com. Fancy hotel in the Greektown neighbourhood, with skyline views from the rooms and luxurious in-room soaking tubs. $149

Detroit Marriott Renaissance Center Renaissance Center ☎313 568 8000, ⓦmarriotthotels.com. A fun place to stay in the RenCen, towering over the city by the river – ask for a room on the upper floors. $179

Inn on Ferry Street 84 E Ferry St ☎313 871 6000, ⓦinnonferrystreet.com. This fine hotel over in the Midtown neighbourhood is made up of four Victorian homes, with a total of forty rooms. A nice place to spend a bit of time away from downtown proper, and close to the Detroit Institute of Arts and other cultural attractions. $139

Motor City Casino & Hotel 2901 Grand River Ave ☎866 782 9622, ⓦmotorcitycasino.com. Two miles from downtown, *Motor City* is a city unto itself. With six different restaurants, including *Iridescence* (below), a spa and a massive gaming emporium, it's Vegas-style luxury at a reasonable price. $119

Westin Book Cadillac Detroit 1114 Washington Blvd ☎313 442 1600, ⓦbookcadillacwestin.com. Listed on the National Registry of Historic Places, the *Book* was renovated and taken over by the *Westin* chain. It offers elegant rooms and a full range of amenities. $189

Woodbridge Star B&B 3985 Trumbull Ave ☎313 831 9668. A friendly, affordable option, with good-value rooms just west of the Theater District. $75

EATING

Detroit's ethnic restaurants dish up the best (and least expensive) food in the city. **Greektown**, basically one block of Monroe Avenue between Beaubien and St Antoine streets, is crammed with authentic Greek places. Less commercial, but offering just as high a standard, are the bakeries, bars and cantinas of **Mexican Town**, west of downtown. Royal Oak, 10 miles north, has a wide range of vaguely alternative wholefood places and is the liveliest suburban hangout in this sprawling metropolis.

★ **Atwater Block Brewery** 237 Joseph Campau St ☎313 393 2073. This spacious Rivertown brewpub serves up excellent beer-battered fish, mussels, wings and whatever else the chefs can think of. Mon 9am–5pm, Tues–Fri 9am–noon, Sat 3pm–1.30am.

★ **Fishbone's Rhythm Kitchen Café** 400 Monroe Ave, Greektown ☎313 965 4600. This noisy, fun and often packed chain restaurant is a Cajun joint with whiskey ribs, crawfish, gumbo, sushi and lots more. Mon–Thurs 11am–midnight, Fri & Sat 11am–2am.

Iridescence Motor City Casino & Hotel, 2901 Grand River Ave ☎877 777 0711. On the hotel's top floor, this warm lavender-coloured restaurant is *the* place for a romantic dinner in Detroit. The wine list has won awards, and the mains include coldwater lobster tails and striped sea bass. It's expensive (dinner for two will run around $100–150 with wine), but worth it. Wed & Thurs 5–10pm, Fri & Sat 5–11pm, Sun 5–10pm.

Slows Bar BQ 2138 Michigan Ave ☎313 962 9828. A lively, affordable restaurant and bar that brings the Southern flavour north, with the best mac and cheese around. Daily 11am–2am.

NIGHTLIFE AND ENTERTAINMENT

There's a lot to do at night in Detroit – the city where the **techno** beat originated and is still going strong. The bars and clubs of the **Theater District** are ever popular, while the **Rivertown** area is renowned for its chic bistros and hip jazz and blues bars. The suburbs of upmarket **Birmingham** and youthful **Royal Oak** are good places to hang out, while there are a couple of fun establishments in the blue-collar neighbourhood of **Hamtramck**. Way up on the northern fringe, once-deserted **Pontiac** now has a range of well-attended rock venues, clubs and lounges. Most of Detroit's major arts venues are conveniently grouped together in the northwest section of downtown. For event **listings** in Detroit and Ann Arbor, pick up the free weekly *Metro Times*.

BARS, CLUBS AND LIVE MUSIC VENUES

★ **Baker's Keyboard Lounge** 20510 Livernois Ave, Royal Oak ☎313 345 6300. Mostly local jazz musicians jam in what claims to be the world's oldest jazz club. When there's no live music, the jukebox provides ample reason to get up and dance. Cover $5–10. Mon–Thurs 8pm–2am, Fri 11am–2am, Sat 4pm–2am.

Gusoline Alley 309 S Center St, Royal Oak ☎248 545 2235. Cramped and dark with a loaded jukebox, this is a legend among Detroit bars, serving beers from all over the globe. Go early for a seat; the melange of different people

makes it great for people-watching. Daily 10am–2am.

★ **Saint Andrew's Hall/Shelter** 431 E Congress St ☎313 961 6358. This cramped downtown club promotes top bands on the alternative circuit. It only holds 800 people, so get a ticket in advance. Downstairs is the *Shelter* club, with lesser-known touring bands followed by dance music. Cover $10–25. Daily 8pm–1am.

PERFORMING ARTS VENUES

Detroit Opera House 1526 Broadway ☎313 237 SING, ⓦdetroitoperahouse.com. Sumptuous venue, its main

DETROIT SPECTATOR SPORTS

Detroit is one of the few cities with franchises competing at the professional level in all four major team sports. **Hockey**'s Red Wings are arguably the town favourites, and tickets are hard to get; they play downtown at the Joe Louis Arena (☎313 983 6606, ⓦdetroitredwings.com). **Baseball**'s Tigers (☎313 962 4000, ⓦdetroit.tigers.mlb.com) call the snazzy Comerica Park, or COPA, home, while the Lions play **football** at adjacent Ford Field (☎313 262 2003, ⓦdetroitlions.com). Lastly, the Pistons (☎248 377 0100, ⓦnba.com/pistons) play **basketball** in the Palace of Auburn Hills, 25 miles north.

entrance dominated by a sweeping staircase and giant chandeliers. It's the home of the Michigan Opera Theatre, and works by Wagner and the like dominate, but it also host dance shows and various spectaculars.

Fox Theatre 2211 Woodward Ave ☎313 983 6611, ⓦolympiaentertainment.com. This gorgeous venue is the biggest draw in the Theater District, hosting big Broadway shows. Tickets can be costly, though, at $25–125.

Gem Theatre 333 Madison Ave ☎313 963 9800, ⓦgemtheatre.com. Well worth a visit – shows here include small jazz combos and performances in its Colony Club dining room.

Max M. Fisher Music Center 3711 Woodward Ave ☎313 576 5111, ⓦdetroitsymphony.com. The main group to hold court here is the Detroit Symphony Orchestra, conducted by Leonard Slatkin.

Music Hall Center for Performing Arts 350 Madison Ave ☎313 887 8500, ⓦmusichall.org. The city's primary dance venue, though it also hosts rock concerts, youth theatre and Broadway shows. Its Jazz Café is a hidden gem, and it's worth checking out a show there.

Ann Arbor

4

With a population of just over 114,000, **ANN ARBOR**, 45 minutes' drive west of Detroit along I-94, offers a greater choice of restaurants, live music venues and cultural activities than most towns ten times its size. The **University of Michigan** has shaped the economy and character of the town ever since it was moved here from Detroit in 1837, providing the city with a very conspicuous progressive edge.

The best thing to do in Ann Arbor is to stroll around downtown and the campus, which meet at South State and Liberty streets. Downtown's twelve blocks of brightly painted shops and street cafés offer all you would expect from a college town, with forty bookshops and more than a dozen record stores.

ARRIVAL AND INFORMATION

ANN ARBOR

By bus The frequent Greyhound services from Detroit stop at 116 W Huron St.

Destinations Chicago (3 daily; 4hr); Detroit (4 daily; 1hr).

By train Amtrak is on the north edge of downtown at 325 Depot St.

Destinations Chicago (3 daily; 4hr); Detroit (3 daily; 1hr).

Visitor centre 120 W Huron St (Mon–Fri 8.30am–5pm; ☎734 995 7281, ⓦannarbor.org).

ACCOMMODATION AND EATING

Burnt Toast Inn 415 W William St ☎734 669 6685, ⓦburnttoastinn.com. This place is as warm and welcoming as a B&B should be; highlights include plush robes and yoga mats, and the breakfasts are made with locally sourced ingredients. **$125**

Dahlmann Campus Inn 615 E Huron St ☎734 769 2200, ⓦcampusinn.com. The choice place to stay in Ann Arbor, in by far the best most convenient location, and with friendly staff on the premises. **$199**

The Original Cottage Inn 512 E William St ☎734 663 3379. The pizza here is top-notch and the *Gemütlichkeit* is excellent. Mon–Thurs 11am–11pm, Fri & ssSat 11am–midnight, Sun 11am–10pm.

★ **Zingerman's** 422 Detroit St ☎734 663 DELI. An excellent (if expensive) deli. The sandwich offerings are prodigious and they can accommodate gluten-free diners, vegans and just about anyone else. Daily 7am–10pm.

NIGHTLIFE AND ENTERTAINMENT

Ann Arbor's live music scene enjoys a nationwide reputation. Unlike many college towns, the place doesn't go to sleep during the summer, either. For news of gigs, grab a copy of the free, monthly *Current*.

The Ark 316 S Main St ☎734 761 1451, ⓦa2ark.org. Lovers of folk, roots and acoustic music will not be disappointed here. Tickets $11–30. Daily 8pm–midnight.
Blind Pig 208 S First St ☎734 996 8555, ⓦblindpig music.com. The best place in town to watch live rock, alternative and blues ($7–12). Jimi Hendrix, Iggy Pop and MC5 have all graced the stage here. Daily 9pm–1am.

Michigan Theater 603 E Liberty St ☎734 668 TIME, ⓦmichtheater.org. There's something for everyone at this beautiful Art Deco venue, with first-run movies, repertory programming and big-name music acts from around the world – Ben Folds, Ladysmith Black Mambazo and U2 have all played sets. Tickets $8–35. Times vary.

Lake Michigan's eastern shoreline

From Ann Arbor, you'll travel a little over 150 miles west along I-94 before you reach Lake Michigan and the quaint town of **St Joseph**, just the first of many small ports along the lake's 350-mile eastern shoreline. North from St Joseph along Hwy-31, the northwest reaches of the lower peninsula attract sportspeople and tourists from all over the Midwest. Here, out on the unspoiled **Leelanau Peninsula** you'll find the beautiful **Sleeping Bear Dunes**, as well as the charming towns of **Harbor Springs** and **Petoskey**; all are within striking distance of larger **Traverse City**. On its way north from Traverse City, scenic Hwy-31 skims along Lake Michigan through Charlevoix and other pretty lakeside towns. At the northern tip of the lower peninsula, revitalized **Mackinaw City** is the departure point for the state's major tour-bus attraction, Old-World **Mackinac Island**.

St Joseph

Less than thirty miles north of Indiana, **ST JOSEPH** lies just north of "Harbor Country" – a string of adorable small towns offering good swimming, boating and fishing opportunities. St Joseph's tidy and compact downtown perches on a high bluff, from which steep steps lead down to sandy Silver Beach and two lighthouses atop two piers.

Holland and Grand Haven

Fifty miles north of St Joseph, **HOLLAND** was settled in 1847 by Dutch religious dissidents. Today's residents lose no opportunity to let visitors know of their roots: tens of thousands of tulips brighten the town in early summer, while the Holland museum, a Dutch village, a clog factory and the inevitable windmill attract those with even the slightest interest in ersatz Dutch-American culture.

Twenty miles up the shoreline, **GRAND HAVEN** boasts one of the largest and most appealing sandy beaches on the Great Lakes, best seen on a leisurely stroll along the one-and-a-half-mile, largely concrete boardwalk.

Ludington

Just under one hundred miles north of Holland, a string of pleasant small villages starts with **LUDINGTON**, where a long stretch of public beach precedes **Ludington State Park**, eight miles north on Hwy-116, which offers great hiking, camping (see below) and sightseeing amid sweeping sand dunes and virgin pine forests; admission is $8 per car.

ACCOMMODATION AND EATING   LUDINGTON

House of Flavors 402 W Ludington Ave ☎231 845 5785. A chrome-heavy diner with breakfasts, burgers and a huge range of ice-cream flavours, including black cherry and the curiously titled "blue moon". Daily 7am–9pm.
Ludington State Park 8800 W M-116, Ludington ☎301 784 9090. There's camping in some beautiful sites

in the state park, though summer spots tend to fill up a year in advance. $29
Snyder's Shoreline Inn 903 W Ludington Ave ☎231 845 1261, ⓦsnydersshoreinn.com. This rather scenic property is the only one downtown with uninterrupted views of the lakeshore. Open May–Oct. $79

Sleeping Bear Dunes National Lakeshore

The southwestern edge of the heavily wooded **Leelanau Peninsula** is occupied by the **Sleeping Bear Dunes National Lakeshore** (ⓦsleepingbeardunes.com), a constantly resculptured area of towering dunes and precipitous 400ft drops; admission is $10 per car. The area was named by the Chippewa, who saw the mist-shrouded North and South Manitou islands as the graves of two drowned bear cubs, and the massive mainland dune, covered with dark trees, as their grieving mother. Fierce winds off Lake Michigan cause the dunes to edge inland, burying trees that reappear years later stripped of foliage. Stunning overlooks can be had along the hilly, nine-mile loop of the **Pierce Stocking Scenic Drive**, off Hwy-109. You can also clamber up the strenuous but enjoyable **Dune Climb**, four miles farther north on Hwy-109.

Traverse City

Smooth beaches and striking bay views help make lively **TRAVERSE CITY** the favourite in-state resort for Michigan natives and for those escaping Chicago as well. A town of fifteen thousand year-round residents, it was saved from the stagnation that overtook many communities when their lumber mills closed down, because the stripped fields proved to be ideal for fruit-growing. Today, the area's claim to be "**Cherry Capital of the World**" is no idle boast. Thousands of acres of cherry orchards envelop the town, their wispy, pink blossoms bringing a delicate beauty each May. At the **National Cherry Festival**, held during the first full week in July, visitors can watch parades, fireworks and concerts, while sampling every cherry product imaginable.

Traverse City's neat **downtown** rests along the bottom of the west arm of **Grand Traverse Bay**, below the Old Mission Peninsula. This slender seventeen-mile strip of land, which divides the bay into two inlets, makes for a pleasant short driving tour along narrow roads with tremendous views of the bay on either side. Five sandy public beaches and a small harbour can be found around the town itself. Various companies offer boat, windsurfer, jet-ski and mountain bike rental. There are eighteen **golf courses** in the immediate area, as well – some of them among the most beautiful in the country.

ARRIVAL AND INFORMATION   TRAVERSE CITY

By bus Greyhound buses stop near downtown at 115 Hall St; there's a daily service to Detoit (7hr).
Visitor centre 101 Grandview Pkwy, downtown (Mon–Fri 9am–6pm, Sat 9am–3pm; June–Sept also Sun 9am–3pm; 𝕋 231 947 1120, 𝕎 visittraversecity.com).

ACCOMMODATION, EATING AND DRINKING

Blue Tractor Cook Shop 423 S Union St 𝕋 231 922 9515. This downtown spot is distinguished by its elaborate burgers and its six varieties of mac and cheese. Daily 11am–11pm.

Country Inn & Suites 420 Munson Ave 𝕋 231 941 0208, 𝕎 countryinns.com/traverse-city-hotel-mi-49686/usatcmi. A rather nice outpost of this well-known chain, complete with a free continental breakfast and a well-kept pool. $79

North Peak Brewing Company 400 W Front St 𝕋 231 941 7325. This fine bar serves up excellent salmon and burgers; its beers are made on the premises and range from oatmeal stouts to malty ambers. Mon–Thurs 11am–11pm, Fri & Sat 11am–midnight, Sun noon–11pm.

Omelette Shoppe & Bakery 124 Cass St 𝕋 231 946 0912. The portions at this Traverse City breakfast staple are generous, to say the least. Mon–Fri 6.30am–3pm, Sat & Sun 7.30am–3pm.

Traverse City State Park 1132 US-31 N 𝕋 231 922 5270. A solid choice for those who like the great outdoors, and the best budget option, this campground has complete hookups, access to a nearby beach and a small store. $27

Petoskey and around

In **PETOSKEY**, high above Lake Michigan sixteen miles north of Traverse City along US-31, grand Victorian houses encircle the downtown's nicely restored **Gaslight District**. Ernest Hemingway spent many of his teenage summers here and alludes to the town in his novel *The Torrents of Spring*.

Twelve miles up Hwy-119, **HARBOR SPRINGS** is a favourite with the Midwestern elite. The charming Main Street and small shaded beach of this "Cornbelt Riviera" resort are certainly captivating. From here, the "**Tunnel of Trees**" scenic drive follows a section of Hwy-119 to Mackinaw City. Along this narrow winding road, occasional breaks in the overhanging trees afford views of Lake Michigan and Beaver Island. It's perhaps one of the best drives in the Wolverine State, and you may find yourself winding back again for a second look.

ACCOMMODATION AND EATING   PETOSKEY AND AROUND

Jesperson's 312 Howard St, Petoskey ☎ 231 347 3601. They do great pies and sandwiches here, but be prepared to wait. March–Dec Mon–Sat 11am–8pm.

Roast & Toast Café & Coffee 309 Lake St, Petoskey ☎ 231 347 7767. This eclectic coffeeshop and café serves soups and sandwiches and home-made potpies.

Daily 7am–9pm.

Stafford's Perry Hotel Bay and Lewis sts, Petoskey ☎ 231 347 4000, ☜ staffords.com. This centrally located place offers old-school glamour from another age, complete with a reading library. **$159**

Mackinaw City

Forty miles northeast of Petoskey, **MACKINAW CITY** has long enjoyed a steady tourist trade as the major embarkation point for Mackinac Island and, though the streets have been landscaped and visitors flock to **Mackinaw Crossings**, a mall-cum-entertainment zone on South Huron Street, that remains its real *raison d'être*.

ACCOMMODATION   MACKINAW CITY

Clarion Hotel Beachfront 905 S Huron Ave ☎ 231 436 5539, ☜ clarionhotel.com. The hotel features a 300ft private sandy beach, a free hot breakfast bar and rooms with a view of Mackinac Island. **$110**

Lamplighter Motel 303 E Jamet St ☎ 231 436 5350,

☜ lamplightermotel.com. This budget independent motel is a bit of a 1960s throwback, but it's well kept and has some fun theme rooms, such as the Lighthouse and Somewhere in Time, which pays homage to the cult film classic. Open May–Nov. **$99**

Mackinac Island

Viewed from an approaching boat, the tree-blanketed rocky limestone outcrop of **MACKINAC ISLAND** (pronounced "Mackinaw"), suddenly thrusting out from the swirling waters, is an unforgettable sight. As you near the harbour, large Victorian houses come into view, dappling the hillsides with white and pastel. On disembarking, you'll see rows of horses and buggies (all motorized transport is banned from the island, except for emergency vehicles) and inhale the omnipresent smell of fresh manure. Also ubiquitous on the island is **fudge**, relentlessly marketed as a Mackinac "delicacy".

Mackinac's crowded **Main Street** can get irritating, but the island is worth visiting, not least for the ferry ride over and the chance to cycle along the hilly backroads. Underneath the tourist trimmings is a rich history. French priests established a mission to the Huron Indians here during the winter of 1670–71. The French built a fort in 1715, but within fifty years had lost control of the island to the British. The government acknowledged the island's beauty by designating it as the country's second national park, two years after Yellowstone in 1875, though it was handed over to the state of Michigan twenty years later. To get a feel for the history, hike or cycle up to the whitewashed stone **Fort Mackinac**, a US Army outpost until 1890. Its ramparts afford a great view of the village and lake below, though admission is a steep $11 (May to mid-Oct daily 9.30am–4.30pm).

ARRIVAL AND INFORMATION   MACKINAC ISLAND

By catamaran Arnold Transit (May–Oct, schedule varies; ☎ 906 847 3351, ☜ arnoldline.com) and Shepler's Ferry (late April to mid-Oct, schedule varies; ☎ 231 436 5023, ☜ sheplers ferry.com); both companies offer high-speed catamaran

crossings from the ferry terminal in Mackinaw City ($23/ pedestrian, $8/bike) and do not require reservations.

Information kiosk Main St (daily 9am–5pm; ☎ 906 847 3783, ☜ mackinac.com).

ACCOMMODATION, EATING AND NIGHTLIFE

Grand Hotel ☎ 906 847 3331, ☜ grandhotel.com. This is the island's grand behometh and it is priced accordingly. Sightseers be warned: it costs $10 just to set

foot in the lobby. **$289**

Horn's Gaslight Bar ☎ 906 847 6154. The place for live music on the island, seven nights a week starting at 9pm. Daily 8pm–1am.

Murray Hotel ☎ 906 847 3360, ⓦ 4mackinac.com. Decorated with plenty of chintz and carefully selected antiques, this hotel offers a large continental breakfast buffet. **$195**

Pink Pony Bar & Grill ☎ 906 847 3341. Fun atmosphere (raucous at times) and a great view of the harbour. Mon–Sat 11am–2am, Sun noon–2am.

The Upper Peninsula

From the map, it would seem logical for Michigan's **Upper Peninsula**, separated from the rest of the state by the **Mackinac Straits**, to be part of Wisconsin. However, when Michigan entered the Union in 1837, its legislators, eyeing the peninsula's huge mineral wealth, incorporated it into their new state before Wisconsin existed.

Previously the "UP" (pronounced "You-p"), as it's commonly known, figured prominently in French plans to create an empire in North America. Father Jacques Marquette and other missionaries made peace with the native people and established settlements, including the port of Sault Ste Marie in 1688. The French hoped to press further south, but before they could get much past Detroit, the British inflicted a severe military defeat in 1763.

Vast, lonesome and wild, the UP is full of stunning landmarks, exemplified by the **Pictured Rocks National Lakeshore**. Most of the eastern section is marked by low-lying, sometimes swampy land between softly undulating limestone hills. Infamous for its bitter winters, the northwest corner is the most desolate, especially the rough and broken **Keweenaw Peninsula** and **Isle Royale National Park**, fifty miles offshore. The UP's only real city is **Marquette**, a college town with a quiet buzz that makes a good base for exploration.

Until 1957 you could get to the UP from lower Michigan only by ferry. Today, the five-mile **Mackinac Bridge** ($3.50 toll), lit up beautifully at night, stretches elegantly across the bottleneck Mackinac Straits.

4

Pictured Rocks National Lakeshore

The **Pictured Rocks National Lakeshore** offers a splendid array of multicoloured cliffs, rolling dunes and secluded sandy beaches. Over the millennia rain, wind, ice and sun have carved and gouged arches, columns and caves into the face of the lakeshore, all stained different hues. Hiking trails run along the clifftops, and Hwy-58 takes you close to the water, but the best way to see the cliffs is by **boat** (see below). Those in a hurry can get a glimpse of the cliffs by visiting the **Miners Castle Overlook**, twelve miles east of Munising, or **Munising Falls**, one of a half-dozen nearby waterfalls, near the village's well-signposted visitor centre.

INFORMATION AND TOURS

Visitor centre Munising (Mon–Fri 9am–5pm; ☎ 906 387 2138, ⓦ munising.org).

Tours Pictured Rocks Cruises offers a 3hr narrated tour that leaves from the City Pier in Munising (late May to early Oct 2–5 trips daily; $36; ☎ 906 387 3386, ⓦ picturedrocks.com).

PICTURED ROCKS NATIONAL LAKESHORE

Shipwreck Tours, less than a mile farther along the lake, at 1204 Commercial St, gives 2hr narrated cruises in a glass-bottomed boat, with surprisingly clear views of three shipwrecks – one intact (June to early Oct 2–3 trips daily; $32; ☎ 906 387 4477, ⓦ shipwrecktours.com).

ACCOMMODATION AND EATING

Scotty's Motel 415 Cedar St ☎ 906 387 2449. A very basic mid-twentieth-century classic family-run property – essentially, a serviceable motel in the late 1950s fashion and truly no-frills. **$79**

Sydney's 400 Cedar St ☎ 906 387 1555. A solid supper club-style establishment with local perch, steaks and a Friday night special known as the "Seafood Spectacular Buffet". Mon–Thurs 6am–11pm, Fri & Sat 6am–2am, Sun 6am–10pm.

Marquette

Forty miles west of Munising is the unofficial capital of the UP, the low-key college town of **MARQUETTE**, also the centre of the area's massive ore industry. Premier among Marquette's sights is rugged **Presque Isle Park**, north of town on Lakeshore Boulevard, almost completely surrounded by Lake Superior and with stunning views of the lake. Back in town, at East Ridge Street and Lakeshore, the **Marquette Maritime Museum and Lighthouse** (mid-May to late Oct daily 10am–5pm; $5; ☎906 226 2006, ⓦmqtmaritimemuseum.com) has exhibits on the fishing and freighting industries, as well as a video about the fabled Superior wrecking of the *Edmund Fitzgerald*. The area's most curious sight is the **Superior Dome**, on Northern Michigan University's campus at 1401 Presque Isle Ave, the largest wooden dome in the world.

ACCOMMODATION, EATING AND DRINKING   MARQUETTE

Landmark Inn 230 N Front St ☎906 228 2580, ⓦthelandmarkinn.com. Rooms overlooking the lake are the real highlight here and the atmosphere is quite peaceful. Some of the rooms have modest historic importance, having played host to Amelia Earhart and Abbott and Costello, among others. **$149**

Remie's Bar 111 Third St ☎906 226 9133. A little bit rowdy, with a dozen beers on tap and music on Wednesdays to fuel the mayhem. Daily 11am–2am.
The Vierling 119 S Front St ☎906 228 3533. One of Michigan's first microbreweries and a place for everything from whitefish bites to filet mignon. Daily 11am–11pm.

Isle Royale National Park

Much closer to Canada than to the USA, the 45-mile sliver of **Isle Royale National Park**, fifty miles out in Lake Superior, is geographically and culturally very, very far from Detroit. All cars are banned and, instead of freeways, 166 miles of hiking trails lead past windswept trees, swampy lakes and grazing moose. Aside from other outdoors types, the only traces of human life you're likely to see are ancient mineworks, possibly two millennia old, shacks left behind by commercial fishermen in the 1940s, and a few lighthouses and park buildings. Hiking, canoeing, fishing and scuba-diving among shipwrecks are the principal leisure activities.

Before you leave the mainland, visit the park headquarters in Houghton (see below) for advice on water purity, mosquitoes and temperatures that can drop well below freezing even in summer.

ARRIVAL, INFORMATION AND ACCOMMODATION   ISLE ROYALE NATIONAL PARK

Access The park is open mid-May to Sept. Entry is $4/person.
By ferry Ferries to Isle Royale leave from Copper Harbor ($65 one-way; ☎906 289 4437, ⓦisleroyale.com), Houghton ($63 one-way; ☎906 482 0984, ⓦnps.gov/isro) and Grand Portage, Minnesota ($67 one-way; ☎715 392 2100, ⓦgrand-isle-royale.com).
By plane You can hop over by plane with the Isle Royale Seaplane Service in Houghton ($299 return; ☎906 482 8850, ⓦroyaleairservice.com).

Park headquarters 800 E Lakeshore Drive, Houghton (Mon–Fri 8am–4.30pm; ☎906 482 0984, ⓦnps.gov/isro).
Rock Harbor Lodge ☎906 337 4993 (Oct–April ☎866 644 2003), ⓦisleroyaleresort.com. The only formal accommodation in the park features rooms with gorgeous views of the lake, along with Adirondack chairs that are perfect for relaxing in. The management also rents canoes and kayaks for $41/day and offers cruises for $41. **$271**

Indiana

Thanks to an influx of northward migrants early in the nineteenth century – including the family of Abraham Lincoln, who lived for fourteen years near the present-day village of Santa Claus before moving to Illinois – much of **INDIANA** bears the influence of the easy-going South. Unlike the abolitionist Lincolns, many former Southerners brought slaves to this new territory, and thousands rioted against being drafted into the Union army when the Civil War broke out. However, massive industrialization throughout the northwest corner of the state since the late nineteenth century firmly integrated Indiana into the regional economy. On a national level, this sports-happy state is best known these days for automobile racing and high school basketball.

CLOCKWISE FROM TOP STATE ST, MADISON, WI (P.303); KENNEDY'S LIMOUSINE, HENRY FORD MUSEUM, DEARBORN, MI (P.263); LOOP ARCHITECTURE IN DOWNTOWN CHICAGO, IL (P.276) >

"Kennedy Car"
1961 Lincoln

Despite some beautiful dunes and beaches, the most lasting memories provided by Indiana's fifty-mile lakeshore (by far the shortest of the Great Lakes states) are of the grimy steel mills and poverty-stricken neighbourhoods of towns like Gary and East Chicago. In northern Indiana, the area in and around Elkhart and Goshen contains one of the nation's largest **Amish settlements**. The central plains are characterized by small market towns, except for the sprawling capital, **Indianapolis**, which makes a nice enough stopover. **Bloomington**, the home of Indiana University (and its perennial standout college basketball team), is the state's premier college town. Hilly southern Indiana, at its most appealing in the autumn, is a welcome contrast to the central cornbelt, boasting several quaint towns such as **Jasper**, while thriving **Columbus** exhibits a great array of contemporary architecture for such a small city.

Indianapolis

INDIANAPOLIS began life in 1821, when a tract of barely inhabited marshes was designated the state capital. While its location in the middle of Indiana's rich farmland bore immense commercial advantages, the absence of a navigable river prohibited the transportation of bulky materials such as coal and iron to sustain heavy industry. Though home to more than sixty car manufacturers by 1910, the city never seriously threatened Detroit's supremacy. Today the city's economic wellbeing is centred around the food, paper and pharmaceutical industries, including the giant Eli Lilly Corporation and massive healthcare facilities such as the Indianapolis Medical Center.

Although Indianapolis continues its focus on sports – in recent years, it has constructed several world-class sports arenas, including the retro-styled **Conseco Fieldhouse** downtown – there is more to the city than could perhaps once have been said. Along with new hotels, a gaggle of fine museums and a zoo, its old downtown landmarks have become cultural, shopping and dining complexes. No longer is it (quite) true that nothing happens here except for the glamorous **Indianapolis 500 car race** each May.

Downtown Indianapolis

The core of Indianapolis's spacious, relaxed downtown is the reasonably tasteful **Circle Centre** shopping and entertainment complex. Suspended over the busy Washington and Illinois intersection, the spectacular **Indianapolis Artsgarden** is an eight-storey glass rotunda illuminated with twinkling lights. A performance and exhibition space, it doubles as a walkway to Circle Centre and several downtown hotels. One block north, streets radiate from **Monument Circle**, the starting point for a lengthy series of memorials and plazas dedicated to war veterans. You can climb the 330 steps of the renovated 284ft **Soldiers and Sailors Monument** (daily 10am–7pm; walk up free, elevator $2).

Lockerbie Square Historic District

Starting at New York and East streets, the serene, tree-shaded **Lockerbie Square Historic District** (ⓦlockerbiesquare.org) is a small enclave of picturesque residences that were home to nineteenth-century artisans and business leaders. Small wood-frame cottages line the cobblestone streets, many of them painted in bright pinks, blues and yellows, and fronted by ornately carved porches.

Indiana State Museum

650 W Washington St • Mon–Sat 9am–5pm, Sun 11am–5pm • $9.50 • ☎ 317 232 1637, ⓦ indianamuseum.org

Several blocks west of Monument Circle, the **Indiana State Museum** gives a useful insight into the state's history through exhibits on everything from geology to sport. Highlights include "Enterprise Indiana", which features a 100ft-long "assembly line"

THE INDIANAPOLIS 500

Seven miles northwest of downtown, the **Indianapolis Motor Speedway** stages three events each year; one is the legendary **Indianapolis 500**, held on the last Sunday in May, the others are July's prestigious NASCAR Brickyard 400 and August's Red Bull Indianapolis GP.

The Indy 500 is preceded by two weeks of qualification runs that whittle the hopeful entrants down to a final field of 33 drivers, one of whom will scoop the million-dollar first prize. The two-and-a-half-mile circuit was built as a test track for the city's motor manufacturers. The first five-hundred-mile race – held in 1911 and won in a time of 6hr 42min, at an average speed of 74.6mph – was a huge success, vindicating the organizers' belief that the distance was the optimum length for spectators' enjoyment. Cars now hit 235mph, though the official times of the winners are reduced by delays caused by accidents. While the technology is marvellous, the true legends in the eyes of their fans are such championship drivers as A.J. Foyt, Mario Andretti and members of the Unser dynasty. The big race crowns one of the nation's largest festivals, attended by almost half a million spectators. Seats for the race usually sell out well in advance ($75–95; ☎800 822 4639, ⓦsecurebrickyard.com), but you may gain admittance to the infield ($40), for a tailgate-style, rowdy atmosphere and limited viewing.

carrying products made in the state, along with blockbuster special exhibitions on *Star Wars* ephemera and such.

Eiteljorg Museum of American Indians and Western Art

500 W Washington St, on the western edge of downtown • Mon–Sat 10am–5pm, Sun noon–5pm; tours at 1pm • $10 • ☎317 636 9378, ⓦeiteljorg.org

Harrison Eiteljorg, an Indianapolis industrialist who went West in the 1940s to speculate in minerals, fell so deeply in love with the art of the region that he brought as much of it back with him as possible, especially from Taos, New Mexico. On display in the **Eiteljorg Museum of American Indians and Western Art** are works by Frederic Remington, Charles M. Russell and Georgia O'Keeffe, as well as tribal artefacts from all over North America and a 38ft Haida totem pole.

White River State Park

801 W Washington St • Mon–Sat 9am–7pm, Sun 11am–7pm; tours at 1pm • $10 • ☎317 233 2434, ⓦwhiteriverstatepark.org

The Eiteljorg Museum stands amid the rolling greenery of **White River State Park**, which is also home to the sizeable **Indianapolis Zoo** (June–Sept Mon–Thurs 9am–5pm, Fri–Sun 9am–6pm; Oct–May daily 9am–4pm; $14.95; ☎317 630 2001, ⓦindyzoo.com). In the park's southeast corner stands the superb **Victory Field**, home of the Indianapolis Indians (☎317 269 3545), the feeder team for baseball's Cincinnati Reds.

Indianapolis Museum of Art

1200 W 38th St • Tues, Wed & Sat 11am–5pm, Thurs & Fri 11am–9pm, Sun noon–5pm • Free • ☎317 923 1331, ⓦimamuseum.org

Opposite the cemetery, more than 150 lush wooded acres accommodate the capacious **Indianapolis Museum of Art**. The main building is surrounded by a lake, botanical garden, sculpture courtyard and a concert terrace. Inside, the exceptional displays include the largest collection of Turner paintings outside Britain and travelling exhibits such as a well-curated collection of modern Japanese prints and African textiles.

Children's Museum of Indianapolis

3000 N Meridian St • Daily 10am–5pm; closed Mon late Sept to late Feb • $18.50, under-18s $13.50 • ☎317 334 3322, ⓦchildrensmuseum.org

The **Children's Museum of Indianapolis**, four miles north of downtown off I-65, is one of the best of its kind. Its most popular exhibit is the Dinosphere, in which visitors can dig for genuine fossils, while All Aboard! is an entertaining romp through the Age of Steam, and Mr Bear's Playhouse is an adorable way for the very young to learn about birds' nests and the uses of water.

ARRIVAL AND INFORMATION

By plane Indianapolis International Airport is 10 miles southwest of downtown, on the #8 IndyGo bus route ($1.75; ☎ 317 635 3344) – IndyGo's Green Line Downtown/Airport Express route provides nonstop service from the airport to downtown and the Convention Center (daily 5am–9pm; $10). A taxi into the centre costs around $38; try Yellow Cabs (☎ 317 487 7777).

INDIANAPOLIS

By bus or train Both Greyhound buses and Amtrak trains arrive at 350 S Illinois St (☎ 317 267 3071), next to the fairly central Union Station complex.

Visitor centres 201 S Capitol St, beside the RCA Dome (Mon–Fri 8.30am–5.30pm; ☎ 800 323 4639, ⊛ indy.org); in the glass pavilion at 100 W Washington St (Mon–Sat 10am–9pm, Sun noon–6pm; ☎ 317 624 2563).

ACCOMMODATION

Indianapolis has plenty of quality places to stay, with budget options about 5 miles from downtown near the interstate. Prices can double during the race months of May, August and September.

★ **The Alexander** 333 S Delaware St ☎ 317 624 8200, ⊛ thealexander.com. Every room in this hotel, which opened in 2013, contains recently commissioned works of art, along with a mid-twentieth-century styling that's more SoCal than central Indiana. **$199**

★ **Canterbury Hotel** 123 S Illinois St ☎ 317 204 2569, ⊛ canterburyhotel.com. Much the classiest downtown option, this landmark hotel was rebuilt in 1928 and offers a hundred opulent and expensive rooms. **$169**

Indy Hostel 4903 Winthrop Ave ☎ 317 727 1696, ⊛ indyhostel.us. Appealing small-scale hostel in a former family home, located in a friendly neighbourhood 6 miles

from downtown. Bike rental available. Dorms **$32**, rooms **$58**

Staybridge Suites 535 S West St ☎ 317 536 7500, ⊛ ichotelsgroup.com. This hotel is right next to Lucas Oil Stadium, and it features a complimentary hot breakfast buffet, an afternoon cocktail reception during the week and free laundry services. **$151**

The Villa Inn 1456 N Delaware St ☎ 317 916 8500, ⊛ thevillainn.com. Castellated six-room luxury B&B inn with the feel of a hotel, 2 miles north of downtown, and offering a spa and restaurant. The same owners run two other local B&Bs. **$200**

EATING

The swish Circle Centre mall houses dozens of places to eat, but most are chains. You'd do better to stick to the more established restaurants downtown or head up to Broad Ripple Village (bus #17) at College Ave and 62nd St, which is packed with bars and cafés (along with galleries and shops).

★ **3 Sisters Café** 334 N Guilford Ave ☎ 317 257 5556. Stop in for a laidback atmosphere and a healthy dose of vegetarian food. Mon–Sat 8am–9pm, Sun 8am–4pm.

Bazbeaux 6360 Massachusetts Ave, downtown ☎ 317 636 7662 and 811 E Westfield Blvd, Broad Ripple Village ☎ 317 255 5711. The best (thin-crust) pizzas in town, with a range of exotic toppings. Mon–Thurs & Sun 11am–9pm, Fri & Sat 11am–10pm.

★ **H20 Sushi** 1912 Broad Ripple Ave ☎ 317 254 0677. This restaurant and sushi bar has successfully married a traditional mix of sushi with a more modern choice of savoury

combos. Tues–Thurs 5.30–9pm, Fri & Sat 5.30–10pm.

★ **Shapiro's** 808 S Meridian St ☎ 317 631 4041. Landmark deli just a few blocks off downtown, where you can fill up on lox, tongue and other specialities in an old-style cafeteria atmosphere for around $10. Leave room for the huge desserts. Daily 8am–6pm.

Yat's Cajun and Creole 885 Massachusetts Ave ☎ 317 686 6380 and 5463 N College Ave ☎ 317 253 8817. Wildly popular Louisiana-flavoured cafeteria, offering a changing menu of inexpensive daily specials in two locations (mains $5.50–8). Mon–Sat 11am–9pm, Sun 11am–7pm.

NIGHTLIFE AND ENTERTAINMENT

The **nightlife** area in downtown is Massachusetts Avenue, where good bars and restaurants are easy to come by. Further afield is the chic **Broad Ripple Village**. Check the free weekly *NUVO* (⊛ nuvo.net) "Indy's alternative voice", for full details of gigs and events.

BARS AND PUBS

★ **Chatterbox** 435 Massachusetts Ave ☎ 317 636 0584, ⊛ chatterboxjazz.com. Ever-busy local bar, hosting live jazz nightly for the past 25 years. Mon–Fri 4pm–2am, Sat & Sun 6pm–2am.

★ **Rathskeller Restaurant** 401 E Michigan St

☎ 317 636 0396. German beer hall in the basement of the historic Athenaeum building, offering food, live music and a *biergarten*. Mon–Thurs & Sun 11am–9pm, Fri & Sat 11am–10pm.

Slippery Noodle Inn 372 S Meridian St ☎ 317 631 6974. Indiana's oldest bar, established in 1850, next to

Union Station, with cheap beer (Mon & Tues), and live blues nightly from 8.30pm. Mon–Fri 11am–3am, Sat noon–3am, Sun 4pm–3am.

Vogue 6259 N College Ave ☎ 317 259 7029, ⓦ thevogue .com. Popular Broad Ripple rock and indie venue in a former cinema, also featuring retro club nights. Wed, Fri & Sat 9pm–2am.

PERFORMING ARTS VENUES

Indiana Symphony Orchestra 45 Monument Circle ☎ 317 639 4300, ⓦ indyorch.org. This venerable institution performs weekly Sept–May, and also puts on the "Symphony on the Prairie" series outdoors at the Conner Prairie, 6 miles north of Indianapolis.

Madame Walker Theatre Center 617 Indiana Ave ☎ 317 236 2099, ⓦ walkertheatre.com. Black cultural and heritage centre putting on "Jazz on the Avenue" every fourth Friday, plus regular dance events, plays and concerts.

Murat Centre 502 N New Jersey St ☎ 317 231 0000, ⓦ murat.com. This former Masonic shrine hosts headliners and Broadway musicals.

Bloomington

College town **BLOOMINGTON**, just 45 miles southwest of Indianapolis on Hwy-37, is by far the liveliest small city in Indiana and owes its vibrancy to the main campus of Indiana University, east of downtown. The I.M. Pei-designed **Indiana University Art Museum** on E Seventh Street (Tues–Sat 10am–5pm, Sun noon–5pm; free) holds a fine international collection of painting and sculpture and a collection of unique musical instruments. Across the street from the pastoral campus, Indiana native and law student, Hoagy Carmichael composed the TinPan Alley gem *Stardust* on the piano of a popular hangout.

ARRIVAL AND INFORMATION   **BLOOMINGTON**

By bus Bloomington Shuttle, 3200 Venture Blvd (☎ 812 332 6004), runs between here and Indianapolis.

Visitor centre 2855 N Walnut St (Mon–Fri 8.30am–5pm,

Sat 9am–4pm; ☎ 812 334 8900, ⓦ visitbloomington .com).

ACCOMMODATION, EATING AND DRINKING

Brewpub at Lennie's 1795 E Tenth St ☎ 812 339 2256. The liveliest drinking spot around with different cream ales and IPA on tap. Mon–Thurs & Sun 11am–midnight, Fri & Sat 11am–1am

FARMbloomington 108 E Kirkwood Ave ☎ 812 323 0002. Real food right from the farm, such as bone-in pork chops and *puttanesca* with locally grown vegetables. Tues–Sun 11am–3pm & 5–10pm.

Grant Street Inn 310 N Grant St ☎ 812 334 2353, ⓦ grantstreetinn.com. This pleasant B&B offers fine

rooms decorated in a variety of styles from Victorian to upscale modern. $179

Hampton Inn 2100 N Walnut St ☎ 812 334 2100. Centrally located, this mainstay chain hotel is a friendly, clean choice. $89

Laughing Planet 322 E Kirkwood ☎ 812 323 2233. This casual favourite is renowned for its burritos, which can be customized with more than thirty ingredients, such as baked tofu and kale. Daily 11am–9pm.

Illinois

While there is plenty more to **ILLINOIS** than just the Windy City, much of the cultural and social identity of this state revolves around **Chicago**, the largest and most exciting city in the Great Lakes region. Perched in the state's northeastern corner, on the shores of **Lake Michigan**, Chicago has a distinguished skyline, top-rated museums, restaurants, cafés and dozens of nightspots.

Illinois was first explored and settled by the French, though in 1763 the territory was sold to the English. Granted statehood in 1818, Illinois remained a distant frontier until the mid-1830s; only once the native **Sauk** were subjugated, after a series of uprisings, did settlers arrive in sizeable numbers. One early immigrant was young **Abraham Lincoln**, who practised law from 1837 onward in **Springfield**, now the state capital and home to a wide range of Lincolniana, including his monumental tomb.

Chicago

CHICAGO is in many ways the nation's last great city. Sarah Bernhardt called it "the pulse of America" and, though long eclipsed by Los Angeles as the nation's second most populous city after New York, Chicago really does have it all, with less hassle and fewer infrastructural problems than its coastal rivals.

Most visitors to Chicago are immediately bowled over by its magnificent urban **skyline**, adorned with one of the world's finest assemblages of **modern architecture**, ranging from Mies van der Rohe's masterpieces on the campus of the Illinois Institute of Technology to the 110-storey **Willis Tower** (more commonly known by its former name, Sears Tower). The city is also rightly quite proud of the wonderful Millennium Park and the extraordinary treasures of the **Art Institute of Chicago**, as well as several other excellent **museums**. The city's strongest suit is **live music**, with a phenomenal array of **jazz** and **blues** clubs packed into the back rooms of its amiable bars and cafés. The **rock** scene is also healthy, having spawned such bands as Smashing Pumpkins and Wilco during the 1990s and R&B stars R. Kelly, Kanye West and Lupe Fiasco in recent years. And almost everything is noticeably less expensive than in other US cities – **eating out**, for example, costs much less than in New York or LA, but is every bit as good.

Brief history

Founded in the early 1800s, Chicago had a population of just fifty in 1830. Its expansion was triggered first by the opening of the Erie Canal in 1825, and then by the arrival of the first locomotive in 1848; by 1860 it was the largest railroad centre in the world, serving as the main connection between the established East Coast cities and the frontier that stretched more than two thousand miles west to the Pacific Ocean. That position on the sharp edge between civilization and wilderness made it a crucible of innovation. Many aspects of modern life, from skyscrapers to suburbia, had their start, and perhaps their finest expression, here on the shores of Lake Michigan.

The Great Chicago Fire and new arrivals

The furious pace of development was briefly halted in 1871 when the **Great Chicago Fire** destroyed much of the urban fabric. Chicago boomed thereafter, doubling in population every decade. The nickname "Windy City" was coined by a New York newspaper editor in the 1890s to describe the boastful claims of the city's promoters when attempting to lure investors from the eastern United States. By 1900 the city was home to more than two million people, many of whom made their way on crowded ships from Ireland and Eastern Europe. In the early years of the twentieth century, it cemented its reputation as a place of apparently limitless opportunity, with jobs aplenty for those not averse to strenuous physical labour and largely monotonous tasks in factories, stockyards and railroad facilities. The attraction was strongest among **blacks** from the Deep South: African Americans poured into the city, with more than 75,000 arriving during the war years of 1916–18 alone.

The 1920s to today

During the Roaring Twenties, Chicago's self-image as a no-holds-barred free market was pushed to the limit by a new breed of entrepreneur. Criminal syndicates, ruthlessly

---

CHICAGO ORIENTATION

Chicago's visitor-friendly street grid is numbered from **State Street** – "that great street" in Sinatra's song – at zero east and west, and **Madison Street** at zero north and south. **Lake Michigan**, which gives the city some of its most attractive open space, makes a clear point of reference to the east of the urban grid. **Michigan Avenue** is the main thoroughfare.

The **Chicago River**, which cuts through the heart of downtown, separates the business district from the shopping and entertainment areas of the North Side.

CHICAGO'S CITYPASS

For significant **discounts** at five of the city's major tourist and cultural attractions – the Hancock Observatory (or Skydeck Observatory at the Willis Tower), the Field Museum, Shedd Aquarium, Adler Planetarium & Astronomy Museum and the Museum of Science and Industry – you can purchase a **CityPass** ($89, ages 3–11 $79; ☎ 888 330 5008, ⓦ citypass.com). Valid for nine days, it lets you skip most queues and save money (up to $84, if you visit all five sights). CityPasses are sold at each of the attractions, or via the website.

---

run by the likes of **gangsters** such as Al Capone and Bugs Moran, took advantage of Prohibition to sell bootleg alcohol. Shootouts in the street between sharp-suited, Tommy-gun-wielding mobsters were not as common as legend would have it, but the backroom dealing and iron-handed control they pioneered was later perfected by politicians such as former mayor **Richard J. Daley** who ran Chicago single-handedly from the 1950s until his death in 1976. Today's mayor, former President Obama staffer Rahm Emanuel, with his slightly abrasive and heavy-handed approach, seems to be continuing the tradition.

Millennium Park

Until the late 1990s, the area that is downtown's **Millennium Park** was a rather dreary-looking, albeit well-located, slice of real estate. Thanks to a highly ambitious (and hugely expensive, to the tune of $475 million) renovation project that long overran its original 2000 completion date, it's a showcase for public art, landscape design and performing arts. Its twin artistic centrepieces are equally compelling. First is a stunning, seamless, stainless-steel sculpture officially titled **Cloud Gate** but universally known as "the Bean", by British-based artist Anish Kapoor. Inspired by liquid mercury, it invites viewers to walk around, beside and even underneath it to enjoy spectacular and endlessly intriguing reflections of both the city and the sky above it. Nearby, **Crown Fountain** by Jaume Plensa consists of two glass-brick towers set either side of a black granite plaza; giant video images of the faces of ordinary Chicagoans play across them both, and water spurts from them in summer at unexpected intervals to form a lake that's usually filled with playing children. Further back, the **Jay Pritzker Pavilion** is an amazing open-air auditorium designed by Frank Gehry, who used mighty swirls and flourishes of steel to improve its acoustics. Finally the **Lurie Garden** features more than 26000 plants in total, representing more than 250 varieties native to the Illinois prairie.

Downtown Chicago: The Loop

Downtown Chicago offers a masterclass in **modern architecture** with buildings that range from the prototype skyscrapers of the 1890s (such as the Monadnock Building) to Mies van der Rohe's "less is more" modernist masterpieces, and the ninth tallest building in the world, the quarter-of-a-mile-high **Willis Tower**.

The compact heart of Chicago is known as **the Loop**, because it's circled by the elevated tracks of the CTA "L" trains. The best way to get your bearings downtown is on one of the many excellent **city tours** (see p.288); whether you take a river cruise, ride the "L" or join a walking tour, you'll get a sense of the major architectural landmarks and their assorted histories.

Chicago Cultural Center

The **Chicago Cultural Center** at 77 E Randolph St not only holds the city's main visitor centre (see p.289), but is worth admiring in its own right. Built in 1897 as the original Chicago Public Library, it's a splendid Beaux Arts palace filled with opulent detail, including the 38ft Tiffany Dome on the fourth floor. The first-floor "Landmark Chicago" exhibit has photographs of dozens of notable Chicago architectural treasures.

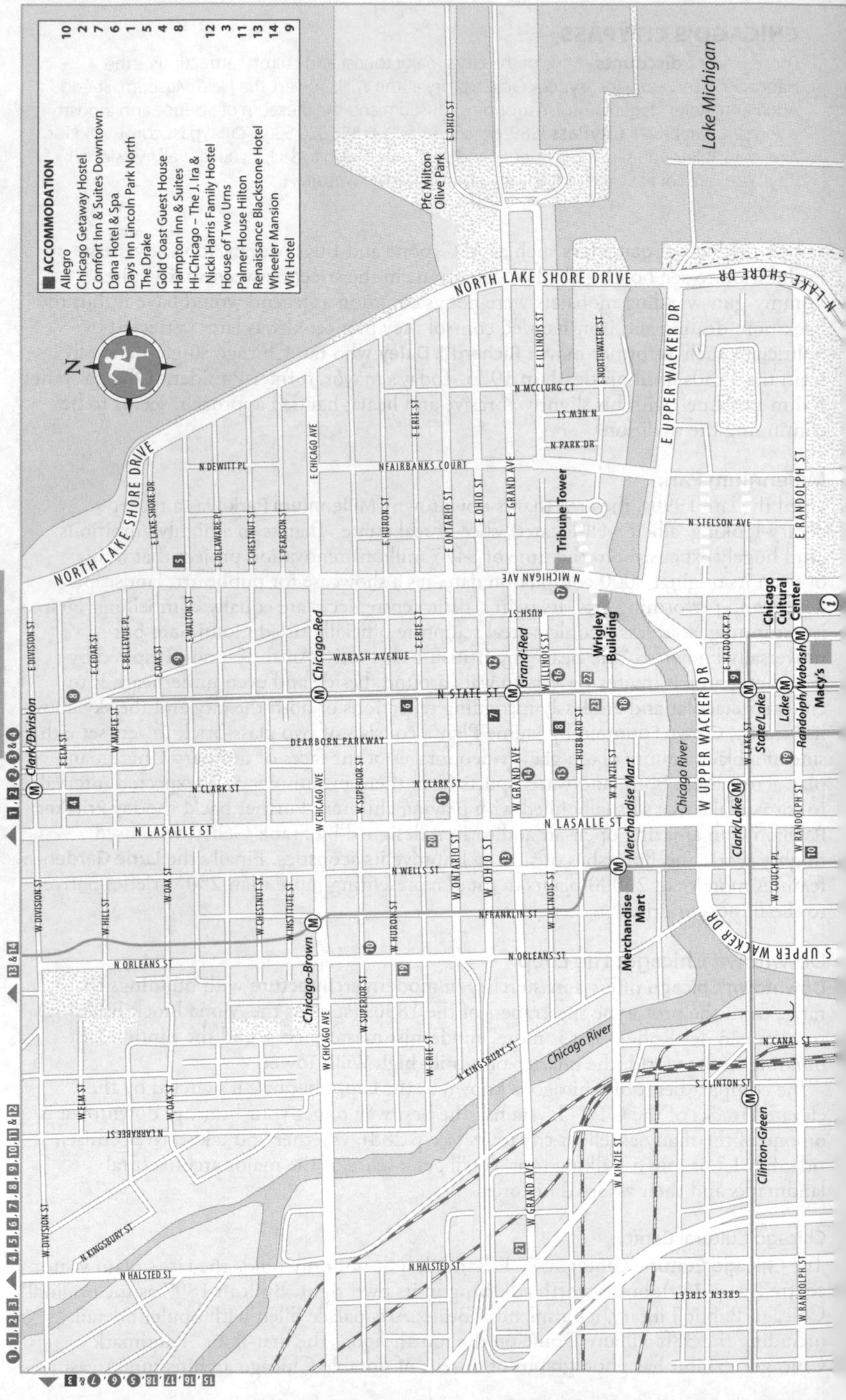

ACCOMMODATION
Allegro 10
Chicago Getaway Hostel 2
Comfort Inn & Suites Downtown 7
Dana Hotel & Spa 6
Days Inn Lincoln Park North 1
The Drake 5
Gold Coast Guest House 4
Hampton Inn & Suites 8
HI-Chicago – The J. Ira & Nicki Harris Family Hostel 12
House of Two Urns 3
Palmer House Hilton 11
Renaissance Blackstone Hotel 13
Wheeler Mansion 14
Wit Hotel 9
N
Lake Michigan
Pfc Milton Olive Park
NORTH LAKE SHORE DRIVE
N LAKE SHORE DR
E UPPER WACKER DR
W UPPER WACKER DR
S UPPER WACKER DR
Chicago River
Tribune Tower
Wrigley Building
Chicago Cultural Center
Macy's
Merchandise Mart
Clark/Division
Chicago-Red
Grand-Red
Chicago-Brown
Merchandise Mart
Clark/Lake
State/Lake
Lake
Randolph/Wabash
Clinton-Green
N MICHIGAN AVE
WABASH AVENUE
N STATE ST
DEARBORN PARKWAY
N CLARK ST
N LASALLE ST
N WELLS ST
N FRANKLIN ST
N ORLEANS ST
N KINGSBURY ST
N HALSTED ST
N LARRABEE ST
GREEN STREET
N CANAL ST
S CLINTON ST
1, 2, 3 & 4
13 & 14
1, 2, 3, 4, 5, 6, 7, 8, 9, 10, 11 & 12
15, 16, 17, 18, 5, 6, 7 & 8

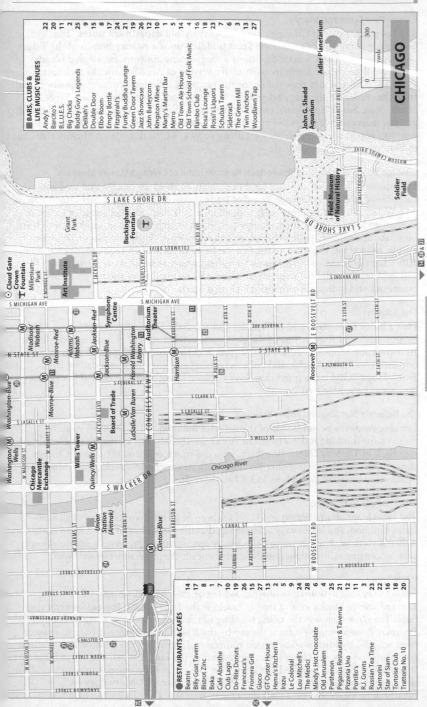

CHICAGO

BARS, CLUBS & LIVE MUSIC VENUES

Andy's	22
Barcito's	20
B.L.U.E.S.	11
Big Chicks	2
Buddy Guy's Legends	25
Delilah's	9
Double Door	15
Elbo Room	8
Empty Bottle	17
Fitzgerald's	24
Funky Buddha Lounge	21
Green Door Tavern	19
Jazz Showcase	26
John Barleycorn	12
Kingston Mines	10
Marty's Martini Bar	1
Metro	5
Old Town Ale House	14
Old Town School of Folk Music	4
Rainbo Club	16
Rosa's Lounge	18
Rossi's Liquors	23
Schubas Tavern	7
Sidetrack	6
The Green Mill	3
Twin Anchors	13
Woodlawn Tap	27

RESTAURANTS & CAFÉS

Beatrix	14
Billy Goat Tavern	17
Bistrot Zinc	8
Boka	1
Café Absinthe	7
Club Lago	10
Do-Rite Donuts	19
Francesca's	26
Frontera Grill	15
Gioco	27
GT Oyster House	13
Hema's Kitchen II	2
Irazu	5
Le Colonial	9
Lou Mitchell's	24
The Medici	28
Mindy's Hot Chocolate	6
Old Jerusalem	4
Parthenon	25
Pegasus Restaurant & Taverna	21
Pizzeria Uno	12
Portillo's	11
R.J. Grunts	3
Russian Tea Time	23
Santorini	22
Star of Siam	16
Tortoise Club	18
Trattoria No. 10	20

4

Carson Pirie Scott and Macy's

The Loop holds two of Chicago's grandest century-old **department stores**. The best-looking, the 1899 **Carson Pirie Scott** building (now a swanky branch of the Target all-purpose store), at 1 S State St, boasts a magnificent ironwork facade that blends botanic and geometric forms in an intuitive version of Art Moderne. Its architect, Louis Sullivan, was also responsible for the gorgeous spherical bronze clocks suspended from the corners of the **Macy's** department store (Mon–Thurs 10am–8pm, Fri & Sat 10am–9pm, Sun 11am–7pm), two blocks north at State and Washington. The ho-hum exterior masks one of the world's great stores, with seven floors of merchandise. Make sure you pop in to see the elaborate Tiffany ceiling, which is made up of more than one million pieces of iridescent glass.

Chicago Board of Trade and the Federal Reserve Bank of Chicago Money Museum

Half the world's wheat and corn (and pork-belly futures) are bought and sold amid the cacophonic roar of the **Chicago Board of Trade,** housed in a gorgeous Art Deco tower at 141 W Jackson Blvd, appropriately topped by a 30ft stainless steel statue of Ceres, the Roman goddess of grain. It's no longer possible to watch the action inside, but to learn more about monetary policy, the value of the American dollar and macroeconomic trends, head across the street to the **Federal Reserve Bank of Chicago's Money Museum**, 230 S LaSalle St (Mon–Fri 8.30am–5pm; free),where there's a short introductory film and exhibits that tell how the Federal Reserve helps the flow of money going to businesses and individuals around the United States.

The Rookery

Half a block from the Board of Trade at 209 S LaSalle St, the **Rookery**, built in 1886 by Burnham and Root, is one of the city's most celebrated and photographed edifices. Its forbidding Moorish-gothic exterior gives way to a wonderfully airy lobby, decked out with cool Italian marble and gold leaf during a major 1905 remodelling by Frank Lloyd Wright; the spiral cantilever staircase rising from the second floor must be seen to be appreciated.

The Reliance Building and Fisher Building

Looking up at the proud facade of the **Reliance Building**, 32 N State St, you'd be forgiven for thinking it dates from the Art Deco Thirties, but it was in fact completed way back in 1895 by Daniel Burnham, who did much to shape the face of Chicago through his buildings. His **Fisher Building**, with its tongue-in-cheek, aquatic-inspired ornamental terracotta, stands at 343 S Dearborn St.

The Manhattan Building

The 1890 **Manhattan Building** at 431 S Dearborn St was the world's first tall all-steel-frame building, and is generally acknowledged as the progenitor of the modern curtain-walled skyscraper. Now converted into luxury apartments, it preserves some noteworthy exterior ornament, including impish figures beneath the projecting bay windows.

Willis Tower

S Wacker Drive and Adams St • **Skydeck Observatory** Daily: April–Sept 9am–10pm; Oct–March 9am–8pm • $18

Located several blocks west of the "L" tracks is the 1451ft **Willis Tower** (formerly the Sears Tower), which was the tallest building in the world until 1998, when Malaysia's Petronas Towers nudged it from the top by the length of an antenna; both have since been eclipsed by further construction projects in Taiwan and the Middle East. Various companies occupy the tower (Sears moved out in the early 1990s), and it's so huge that it has more than one hundred elevators. Two ascend, in little more than a minute, from the ground-level shopping mall to the 103rd-floor **Skydeck Observatory** for breathtaking views that on a clear day take in four states – Illinois, Michigan,

Wisconsin and Indiana. Visitors can also peer down onto the city from one of the elaborate glass boxes that hang off the side of the Skydeck. Look east for the distinctive triangular **Metropolitan Detention Center**, where prisoners exercise on the grassy roof beneath wire netting to ensure they don't get whisked away by helicopter.

The Chicago River

The Loop is usually said to end at the "L" tracks, but the blocks beyond this core, to either side of the Chicago River, hold plenty of interest. Broad, double-decked **Wacker Drive**, parallel to the water, was designed as a sophisticated promenade, lined by benches and obelisk-shaped lanterns, by Daniel Burnham in 1909. Though never completed, and despite the almost constant intrusion of construction works, it makes for a nice extended walk. The direction of the river itself was reversed a century ago, in an engineering project more extensive than the digging of the Panama Canal. As a result, rather than letting its sewage and industrial waste flow east into Lake Michigan, Chicago now sends it all south into the Corn Belt.

A **boat tour** from beneath the Michigan Avenue Bridge gives magnificent views of downtown (see p.277). However, half an hour's walk, especially at lunchtime when the office workers are out in force, will do the trick nearly as well. Burnham's promenade runs along both sides of the river, crossing back and forth over the twenty-odd drawbridges that open and close to let barges and the occasional sailboat pass. The **State Street Bridge** makes a superb vantage point. On the south bank, at 35 E Wacker Drive, the elegant Beaux Arts **Jewelers Building** was built in 1926 and is capped on the seventeenth floor by a domed rotunda that once housed Al Capone's favourite speakeasy.

330 North Wabash Building

Across the river stands what's commonly considered Ludwig Mies van der Rohe's masterpiece – the 1971 **330 North Wabash Building** (formerly known as the IBM Building). The gentle play of light and shadow across the detailed bronze and smoked-glass facade has been the model for countless other less considered copies worldwide. The building is so huge that it acts as a funnel for winter winds off Lake Michigan, and heavy ropes sometimes must be tied across the broad plaza at its base to protect people from getting blown away.

333 West Wacker Drive

Perhaps Chicago's most successful and acclaimed building of recent years stands at **333 West Wacker Drive**. Towering over a broad bend in the river, and bowed to follow its curve, the green glass facade reflects the almost fluorescent green of the river (now upgraded from "toxic" to merely "very polluted"). On the lower floors, a more classically detailed stone base actively addresses its stalwart elder neighbours.

The Art Institute of Chicago

111 S Michigan Ave • Mon–Wed & Fri 10.30am–5pm, Thurs 10.30am–8pm, Sat & Sun 10.30am–5pm • Suggested donation $23 • ☎ 312 443 3600, Ⓦ artic.edu

The **Art Institute of Chicago** ranks as one of the greatest art museums in the world, thanks to a magnificent collection that includes, and extends way beyond, Impressionist and Post-Impressionist paintings, Asian art, photography and architectural drawings. While the Neoclassical facade of the main entrance does its best to look dignified, the numerous added-on wings can make it hard to find your way around. In 2009, the museum also opened its new Modern Wing, designed by "starchitect" Renzo Piano.

The Impressionists and early Moderns

Most visitors head straight upstairs to the Impressionist works, which include a wall full of Monet's *Haystacks* captured in various lights, next to Seurat's immediately familiar Pointillist *Sunday Afternoon on La Grande Jatte*. A handful of Post-Impressionist masterpieces by Van Gogh, Gauguin and Matisse are arrayed nearby. Beyond these masterworks, other highlights include the pitchfork-holding farmer of Grant Wood's oft-parodied *American Gothic*, which he painted as a student at the Art Institute school, and sold to the museum for $300 in 1930; El Greco's 1577 *Assumption of the Virgin*; Edward Hopper's lonely *Nighthawks*; Pablo Picasso's melancholy *Old Guitarist*, one of the definitive masterpieces of his Blue Period; a tortured, tuxedoed self-portrait that was Max Beckmann's last Berlin painting before fleeing the Nazis; canvases by Jackson Pollock and Mark Rothko; and several works by Georgia O'Keeffe, such as a 1926 depiction of New York's *Shelton Hotel*, where she was living.

Other attractions

Moving on, be sure to look for the beautiful pre-Columbian ceramics from what's now the Southwest USA; the ornate carved stone used for the coronation of the Aztec ruler Moctezuma II on July 15, 1503; and the delightful seventh-century Indonesian-sculptured stone monkeys in the Southeast Asia collections, displayed around the McKinlock Court Garden, which in summer is employed as an **open-air café**. Also here, in the east end of the complex, is the immaculately reconstructed Art Moderne trading room of the Chicago Stock Exchange, designed by Louis Sullivan in 1893 and moved here in the 1970s.

The graceful lines of the recently opened Modern Wing include contemporary arts and early twentieth-century European masterworks and a diverse, regularly rotated set of sculptures and installations. Finally, the Art Institute's high-quality **shop** is well worth perusing.

Grant Park

East of the Art Institute toward Lake Michigan, **Grant Park** is an urban oasis that's become a bit overshadowed by the high-profile Millennium Park (see p.277) immediately northwest. In any case, wandering through the park requires traversing some busy roads, so casual rambling can be frustrating. The major attractions are gathered in its landscaped southern half, known as the **Museum Campus**.

Field Museum of Natural History

1200 S Lake Shore Drive, at Roosevelt Rd • Daily 9am–5pm; last admission always 4pm • $15, plus extra for temporary exhibitions • ⓦ fieldmuseum.org

The extensive and engaging **Field Museum of Natural History** is ten minutes' walk south of the Art Institute, in a huge, marble-clad, Daniel Burnham-designed Greek temple. It's quite an erratic sort of institution, in which the exhibits vary enormously in their age and sophistication. "Natural history" is taken to include anything non-white and non-European, so as well as a hall of stupendous dinosaurs, including "Sue", the most complete *T.rex* fossil ever found, the permanent collection ranges from Egyptian tombs – the entire burial chamber of the son of a Fifth Dynasty pharaoh was brought here in 1908 – to the man-eating lions of Tsavo and some fascinating displays on the islands of the Pacific. Best of all for young kids is the "Underground Adventure", a simulated environment that "shrinks" visitors to a hundredth of their normal size and propels them into a world of giant animatronic spiders and crayfish.

John G. Shedd Aquarium

1200 S Lake Shore Drive • June–Aug daily 9am–6pm; Sept–May Mon–Fri 9am–5pm, Sat, Sun & holidays 9am–6pm; arrive early to beat the long queues and school groups • $37.95, kids $28.95 • ☎ 312 939 2438, ⓦ sheddaquarium.org

On the shores of Lake Michigan, the **John G. Shedd Aquarium** proclaims itself the largest indoor aquarium in the world. The 1920s structure is rather old-fashioned, but the light-hearted displays are informative and entertaining. The central exhibit, a 90,000-gallon recreation of a coral reef, complete with eels, sea turtles and thousands of tropical fish, is surrounded by more than a hundred smaller habitats. Highlights include the **Wild Reef** exhibit, featuring floor-to-ceiling living reefs, tropical fish, sharks and rays. The **Oceanarium** provides an enormous contrast, with its modern lakeview home for marine mammals such as Pacific white-sided dolphins and beluga whales. In this gorgeous amphitheatre, you can watch demonstrations of the animals' natural behaviours and learn how their trainers' positive reinforcement can be used with pets at home. Performances are held four to six times daily; at other times, watch from underwater galleries as the animals cruise around the tank, and listen to the clicks, beeps and whistles they use to communicate with each other.

Adler Planetarium

1300 S Lake Shore Drive • Daily: May–Aug 9.30am–6pm; Sept–April 9.30am–4.30pm • Basic pass $22, premium pass with two 45min star programmes $28 • ☎ 312 922 7827, ⓦ adlerplanetarium.org

Looking like a heavily stylized temple, the Art Deco **Adler Planetarium** is the oldest planetarium in the Western Hemisphere. First-time visitors should head directly into "Our Solar System", which includes interactive stations displaying moon rocks and a fantastical globe that simulates the wayward motions of clouds on various gas-filled planets like Jupiter and Saturn. The real highlight here is the **Grainger Sky Theater**, where the unmissable "Cosmic Wonder" (5 daily) show probes the cosmos through remarkable images of the Crab Nebula, star formations and Orion the Hunter.

The Near North Side

While Chicago's **Near North Side** has few show-stopping attractions, it's great for simply wandering around, chancing upon odd **shops**, neighbourhood bars and historic sites and just people-watching, particularly along Michigan Avenue and Wells Street.

The Magnificent Mile

When the Michigan Avenue Bridge was built over the Chicago River in 1920, the warehouse district along its north bank quickly changed into one of the city's most upmarket quarters, now known as the **Magnificent Mile**, famed for its fashionable shops and department stores. Throughout the Roaring Twenties one glitzy tower after another appeared along Michigan Avenue, including at no. 400 the white terracotta, wedding-cake colossus of the **Wrigley Building**, built by the Chicago-based chewing-gum magnate (now headquarters of the online offer retailer Groupon and spectacularly lit up at night). This was eclipsed almost immediately by the "Mag Mile's" most famous structure, the **Tribune Tower**. Still housing the editorial offices of Chicago's morning newspaper, as well as, on the ground floor, the studios of its main AM radio station, WGN (you can peer in from the street and watch the DJs in action), the tower was completed in 1925. Its flying buttresses and gothic detailing turn their back on the then-prevalent Moderne style. Look closely at its lower floors and you'll see embedded chunks of historic buildings – like the Parthenon and the Great Pyramid – "borrowed" from around the world by *Tribune* staffers.

The John Hancock Center

875 N Michigan Ave • **Observatory** Daily 9am–11pm • $18

While the Tribune Tower anchors its southern end, the Mag Mile's northern reaches are dominated by the cross-braced steel **John Hancock Center**. Though it's about 325ft shorter than the Willis Tower, the 360-degree panorama on a clear day from its 94th-floor **Skydeck Observatory** is unforgettable. It's worth pointing out that taking the elevator to the swanky *Signature Lounge* on the 96th floor costs nothing, and you can use that extra money to buy a cocktail of your choice.

The Shopping District

At ground level, you're right at the heart of Chicago's prime **shopping district**. Stores like Neiman-Marcus and Tiffany & Co front onto Michigan Avenue, but most of the shops are enclosed within multistorey complexes, or "vertical shopping malls".

The oldest of these – and still the best – is **Water Tower Place**, 835 N Michigan Ave, with more than a hundred stores on seven floors, plus a bustling food court.

Across from Water Tower Place, at the centre of this consumer paradise, stands the **Historic Water Tower** – a whimsically gothic stone castle, topped by a 100ft tower, which was built in 1869 and is one of the very few structures to have survived the 1871 fire. Inside the Water Tower is a tiny yet compelling gallery of rotating photographic exhibits by Chicago-based artists.

Museum of Contemporary Art

220 E Chicago Ave • Tues 10am–8pm, Wed–Sun 10am–5pm • $12 • ☎ 312 280 2660, ⊚ mcachicago.org

The **Museum of Contemporary Art**, one block east of the Historic Water Tower, is a spare space that holds photography, video and installation works on everything from "selfies" to cartoons, as well as a permanent collection featuring pieces by Chuck Close, Louise Bourgeois, Andy Warhol and others. At the rear is a lake-view patio where a Wolfgang Puck café serves good coffee and bistro food.

Navy Pier

600 E Grand Ave • Mon–Thurs & Sun 10am–10pm, Fri & Sat 10am–noon • ☎ 312 595 7437, ⊚ navypier.com

Opened in 1995, **Navy Pier** was originally a facility for the United States Navy and then a branch of the University of Illinois (colloquially known as "Harvard on the Rocks") until 1965. After a few decades of intermittent use, it was completely overhauled and reopened in 1995. Today, more than eight million visitors a year flock to its shops, chain restaurants, IMAX theatre and giant Ferris wheel. Three floors are taken up by the imaginative interactive exhibits of the **Chicago Children's Museum** (Mon–Wed, Fri & Sun 10am–5pm, Thurs & Sat 10am–8pm; mid-June to Aug also Fri 5–8pm; $10, no reduction for children; free Thurs 5–8pm and first Sun of month; ☎ 312 527 1000, ⊚ chichildrensmuseum.org). The pier also serves as a venue for concerts and weekend festivals in summer, and an embarkation point for several boat tours.

The Gold Coast

As its name suggests, the **Gold Coast**, stretching north from the Magnificent Mile along the lakeshore, is one of Chicago's wealthiest and most desirable neighbourhoods. This residential district is primarily notable for Chicago's most central (and style-conscious) beach. The broad strand of **Oak Street Beach** is accessible via a walkway under Lake Shore Drive, across from the *Drake Hotel*. After dark, the summertime crowds are apt to be found in the myriad bars of Rush and Division streets. The more northerly reaches of the Gold Coast, approaching Lincoln Park, are also its most exclusive, especially in the stretch of Astor Street running south from the park.

Old Town

Old Town, west of LaSalle Street to either side of North Avenue, has a lived-in look, in part due to the mix of small cottages built after the Great Fire and its modest apartment buildings. Originally a German immigrant community based around the 1873 **St Michael's Church**, it now boasts a broad ethnic and cultural mix. **Wells Street**, the main drag, emerged in the late 1960s as a mini-Haight-Ashbury. All signs of that era have vanished, leaving only the *Second City* comedy club (see p.293). The rest of the neighbourhood is packed with bars, galleries and BBQ joints, and makes for a diverting afternoon's wander. Especially noteworthy is the House of Glunz, 1206 N Wells St, a wine shop dating from 1888 that is known for its wine-tasting programmes.

Lincoln Park

In summer, Chicago's largest green space, **Lincoln Park**, provides a much-needed respite from the gridded pavements of the rest of the city. Unlike Grant Park to the south, it's packed with leafy nooks and crannies, monuments and sculptures, and has a couple of friendly, family-oriented **beaches** at the eastern ends of North and Fullerton avenues. Near the small **zoo** at the heart of the park (late May to Oct Mon–Fri 9am–6pm, Sat & Sun 9am–7pm; Nov–May daily 9am–4.30pm; free), renowned for its menagerie of African apes and curious red pandas, you can rent paddleboats or bikes. If the weather's bad, head for the pleasantly humid **conservatory**, 2400 N Stockton Drive (daily 9am–5pm; free), or bone up on Chicago's captivating past at the **Chicago History Museum**, at the south end of the park at 1601 N Clark St (Mon–Sat 9.30am–4.30pm, Sun noon–5pm; $14; ☎312 642 4600, ⒲chicagohistory.org), with comprehensive displays on regional and national history, including some rather twee dioramas depicting the Great Fire of 1871 and the World's Columbian Exposition.

The Lincoln Park neighbourhood, inland from the lake, centres on **Lincoln Avenue** and **Clark Street**, which run diagonally from near the Historical Society Museum; **Halsted Street**, with its blues bars, nightclubs and myriad restaurants, runs north–south through the district's heart. Any of these main roads merits an extended stroll, with forays into the many book- and record stores. Look for the **Biograph Theatre** movie house (now a live theatre stage), 2433 N Lincoln Ave, where **John Dillinger** was ambushed and killed by the FBI in 1934, thanks to a tip from his companion, the legendary Lady in Red.

Wrigleyville

In the 1800s thousands of German immigrants settled in what was then the separate enclave of Lakeview, which was annexed to the city formally in 1889. This area is now called **Wrigleyville** in honour of **Wrigley Field**, 1060 W Addison St at N Clark St, the ivy-covered 1920s stadium of baseball's much-loved Cubs, and one of the best places to get a real feel for the game. There are few more pleasant and relaxing ways to spend an afternoon than drinking beer, eating hot dogs and watching a ballgame in the sunshine, among the Cubs' faithful. Two-hour **field tours** run from May through September on select days (every 30min 10am–4pm), and cost $25 (see p.294).

Wicker Park/Bucktown

Three miles northwest of the Loop, **Wicker Park/Bucktown** is Chicago's newest neighbourhood. Once a Polish and German community referred to as the "Polish Gold Coast", it is now a trendy, upmarket enclave of shops, hipster bars and Victorian mansions. Stylish health-food cafés, galleries, tattoo parlours, boutiques and alternative bookstores follow Damen Street north to Bucktown.

The West Side

West of the Chicago River, Chicago's **West Side** was where the **Great Fire of 1871** started, though the urban myth that it was due to Mrs O'Leary's cow kicking over a lantern is patently untrue. Regardless, the flames spread quickly east to engulf the entire central city, which was built of wood and fed the fire for three full days. Ironically, the O'Leary cottage is now the site of the Chicago Fire Department training academy. The West Side also saw 1886's **Haymarket Riots**, when striking workers assembled at the old city market at Desplaines and Randolph streets; after a peaceful demonstration, as police began to break up the crowd, a bomb exploded, killing an officer. Six more policemen and four workers died in the resulting panic. Four labour leaders were later found guilty of murder and hanged, although none had been present at the event. Today the West Side of the city remains plagued with poverty and antisocial behaviours, though the Little Italy community (anchored by the vast University of Illinois at Chicago campus) remains stable.

Oak Park

Visitor centre 1010 Lake St (daily 10am–5pm; ☎708 848 1500, ⒲ visitoakpark.com) • Take the Green Line west to the Harlem Ave stop

Nine miles west of the Loop, the affluent and well-designed nineteenth-century suburb of **Oak Park** is easily accessible by public transport. The area's **visitor centre**, just over two blocks east of the station, provides an excellent architectural **walking tour map**.

Hemingway's Birthplace and Museum

Birthplace 339 N Oak Park Ave **Museum** 200 N Oak Park Ave • Mon–Fri & Sun 1–5pm, Sat 10am–5pm • $10 • ☎ 708 848 2222, ⓦ ehfop.org

Ernest Hemingway was born and raised in Oak Park, editing his high-school newspaper and living a normal middle-class life. His birthplace, where he lived until the age of 6, is now preserved as a shrine to the author, and run in conjunction with a **museum** of his life, two blocks south, displaying, among other exhibits, his childhood diary.

Unity Temple

875 Lake St • Mon–Fri 10.30am–4.30pm, Sat 10am–2pm, Sun 1–4pm • $10 • ☎ 708 383 8873, ⓦ unitytemple-utrf.org

In 1889, a decade before Hemingway's birth, an ambitious young architect named **Frank Lloyd Wright** arrived in Oak Park, which he used for the next twenty years as a testing ground for his innovative design theories. Most of the 25 buildings he put up here are in keeping with conventional Victorian design, and few are open to the public; fortunately, however, his most interesting and groundbreaking edifices are maintained as monuments. His ideal of an "organic architecture", in which all aspects of the design derive from a single unifying concept – quite at odds with the fussy and rather busy "gingerbread" style popular at the time – is exemplified by the **Unity Temple**. Though the simplicity of this angular, reinforced-concrete structure was largely dictated by economics, its unembellished surfaces contribute to a masterful manipulation of space, especially in the skylit interior, where the subtle interplay of overlapping planes creates a dynamic spatial flow.

Wright home and studio

951 Chicago Ave, at Forest Ave • Guided 45min tours Mon–Fri 11am, 1pm & 3pm, Sat & Sun every 20min 11am–3.30pm • Tours $15 • ☎ 708 848 1976, ⓦ gowright.org

Wright built his small, brown-shingled **home and studio** aged 22 in 1889, and remodelled it repeatedly for the next twenty years. It shows all his hallmarks: large fireplaces to symbolize the heart of the home and family; free-flowing, open-plan rooms; and the visual linking of interior and exterior spaces. The furniture of the kitchen and dining rooms is Wright's own design; he added a two-storey studio in 1898, with a mezzanine drafting area suspended by chains from the roof beams. You can see the house itself on a guided tour (see p.288). Lengthier, self-guided audio walking tours ($15) take in the dozen other Wright-designed houses within a two-block radius.

The South Side

In contrast to the wealth and prosperity of the North Side, Chicago's **South Side**, a vast jumble of neighbourhoods stretching from Roosevelt Road all the way to the border with Indiana, contains some very stark contrasts between the very wealthy and the tremendously poor.

Much of the heavy industry in the city was historically concentrated here, in the sprawling **Chicago Stockyards**, the slaughterhouses and meatpackers that Upton Sinclair exposed in his 1906 novel *The Jungle*, and whose oppressive odours covered most of the South Side until the 1950s. Parts of the South Side failed to benefit from the economic uplift of the 1990s and early 2000s, but there remain a number of thriving districts: not just the **Prairie Avenue** and **Hyde Park** districts, but also the buzzing **Chinatown** around Wentworth Avenue and 22nd Street; the artsy, predominantly Mexican **Pilsen** district, a few blocks north and west; and the largely Irish, blue-collar **Bridgeport**, formerly known by the evocative name "Hardscrabble", which was the nucleus of Mayor Daley's old fiefdom, and also served as the home of baseball's White Sox (see p.294).

Prairie Avenue

Two blocks east of Michigan Avenue, a mile from the Loop and only a quarter of a mile from the lake, **Prairie Avenue** started life as an exclusive suburb. It's best reached by taxi, bus or train, as the walk south from the Loop just isn't that interesting. As the one part of Chicago to remain unscathed in the Great Fire of 1871, this area had a brief moment of glory as the city's finest address. However, by 1900 the railroads had cut it off from Lake Michigan, and the wealthy fled back to their traditional North Side haunts. One of the few structures to have survived is the Romanesque 1887 **Glessner House**, Chicago's last H.H. Richardson-designed house, standing sentry at Prairie Avenue and 18th. Behind the forbidding stone facade, the house opens onto a garden court, its interior filled with Arts and Crafts furniture, and swathed in William Morris fabrics and wall coverings. The Chicago Architecture Foundation gives guided tours (Wed–Sun 1pm & 3pm; $10, free Wed on a first-come, first-served basis; ⓣ312 326 1480, ⓦglessnerhouse.org).

Hyde Park and the university

Six miles south of the Loop, **Hyde Park**, the most attractive and sophisticated South Side neighbourhood, is also one of Chicago's more racially integrated areas. Of course, these days, the neighbourhood has received additional attention for being the home of President Barack Obama prior to his arrival in the White House. The **University of Chicago**, endowed by Rockefeller in 1892, has encouraged a college-town atmosphere, with bookshops and cafés along East 57th Street in close proximity to its compact campus. On the campus itself, two buildings are well worth searching out: the massive Collegiate gothic pile of the **Rockefeller Memorial Chapel**, 59th Street and Woodlawn Avenue (daily 9am–4pm; free), and the Prairie-style, Frank Lloyd Wright-designed **Robie House**, two blocks north at 5757 S Woodlawn Ave (tours Thurs–Sun 11am–3pm; $15; ⓦwrightplus.org).

The Midway

Washington Park wraps around the south side of the campus to join the long green strip of the **Midway** – one of the few reminders that Chicago was the site of the **World's Fair Columbian Exposition**. Attracting some thirty million spectators in the summer of 1893 (at the time, 45 percent of the US population), the Midway was then filled with full-sized model villages from around the globe, including an Irish market town and a mock-up of Cairo, complete with belly dancers. Today, these vast spaces contain a children's garden, a roller/ice skating rink and playing fields.

Museum of Science and Industry

57th St, at Lake Shore Drive • Daily: June–Aug 9.30am–5.30pm; Sept–May 9.30am–4pm • $18 • ⓣ773 684 1414, ⓦmsichicago.org

A short stroll east of the Midway, in the north end of Jackson Park, the cavernous **Museum of Science and Industry** was Chicago's single most popular tourist destination until it started charging admission in 1991. Besides interactive computer displays, the best of which explores the inner workings of the brain and heart, exhibits include a captured German U-boat, a trip down a replica coal mine, and a fairy castle created by silent film star Colleen Moore, which contains several hundred miniatures including a book crafted by Walt Disney. The complex also hosts a giant OMNIMAX movie dome; admission to that is $9 extra.

East of the museum, **Promontory Point** juts into Lake Michigan and gives great views of the Chicago skyline, including a close-up look at Mies van der Rohe's first high-rise, the Promontory Apartments at 5530 S Lake Shore Drive.

ARRIVAL AND DEPARTURE — CHICAGO

BY PLANE

O'Hare International Airport Chicago's O'Hare International Airport (ⓦohare.com), the national headquarters for United, American and several other airlines, is 17 miles northwest of downtown. It is connected to the city centre by 24hr CTA (Blue Line) trains from the station under Terminal 4 (around 40min; $5). Taxis into town from O'Hare cost up to $45 (there's also a ride-share programme with a flat rate of $22), and take 30min–1hr.

Midway Airport Smaller than O'Hare and primarily used by domestic airlines, Midway is 11 miles southwest of downtown, and you can take one of CTA's Midway (Orange Line) trains from right outside the terminal (30min; $2.25). The taxi fare into town is about $30 and the journey time 20–40min.

Airport shuttles Another option is the Airport Express bus and van service between the airports and downtown hotels (around $32 from O'Hare, $27 from Midway; ☎ 888 284 3826, ⓦ airportexpress.com).

BY BUS

Greyhound and a number of regional bus companies pull into the large 24hr bus station at 630 W Harrison St (☎ 312 408 5800), three blocks southwest of Union Station.
Destinations Detroit (6 daily; 5hr); Milwaukee (10 daily; 1hr 30min); St Louis (7 daily; 5hr).

BY TRAIN

Chicago is the hub of the Amtrak rail system, and almost every cross-country route passes through Union Station, west of the Loop at Canal and Adam sts.

Destinations Detroit (3 daily; 4hr); Milwaukee (7 daily; 1hr 30min); St Louis (5 daily; 5hr)

BY CAR

Arriving in Chicago by car, racing towards the gleaming glass towers of the Loop, can be memorable. Bear in mind, though, that traffic on the expressways to and from downtown can be bumper-to-bumper during rush hours.
Parking Parking can be a problem, though the fare boxes of parking meters accept credit cards, which is helpful. Check street signs for restrictions, which are rigidly enforced – violations may result in your car being towed and impounded. Perhaps the best place to leave a car in the downtown area is in the garage under Grant Park, at Columbus St and Monroe Drive, close to the east side of the Art Institute ($34/24hr).

GETTING AROUND

The **Chicago Transit Authority** (CTA; ☎ 312 836 7000, ⓦ transitchicago.com) operates a system of elevated trains 24hr a day. Pick up a CTA system map, available at most subway stations and visitor centres, or from CTA headquarters west of the Chicago River at 567 W Lake St.

Fares and passes CTA riders will need to buy a "Chicago card" (available in all "L" stations) and add value to it. One ride costs $2.25; taking two more rides within 2hr costs just 25¢. Passes good for one ($10), three ($20) or seven ($28) days of unlimited rides on both buses and the "L" are sold at O'Hare and Midway airports as well as Union Station, the visitor centre and other locations. Due to a quirk of CTA policy, rides originating at O'Hare cost $5.
By bus Buses run every 5–15min during rush hours and every 8–20min at other times.
The "L" Rapid transit trains run every 5–15min during the day and every 15min–1hr all night. Lines are colour-coded

and denoted by route rather than destination. The Howard–Dan Ryan is the Red Line; Lake–Englewood–Jackson Park is the Green Line; the O'Hare–Congress–Douglas is the Blue Line; the Ravenswood is the Brown Line (whose trains circle the Loop, giving the area its name); the Evanston Express is the Purple Line; the Midway–Loop is the Orange Line; the Pink Line runs from the Loop to suburb of Cicero; and the Skokie Swift is the Yellow Line.
By commuter train Metra Commuter Trains run from various points downtown to and from the suburbs and outlying areas, including Oak Park and Hyde Park. Fares range from $2.75–9.25.

CHICAGO GUIDED TOURS

The best **guided tours** of Chicago are those offered by the **Chicago Architecture Foundation**, based in the Archicenter in the Santa Fe Building at 224 S Michigan Ave (☎ 312 922 3432, ⓦ architecture.org). Expert guides point out the city's many architectural treasures and explain their role in Chicago's history and development. Most popular of all are the superb Architecture River Cruises along the Chicago River that leave from Michigan Avenue and Lower Wacker Drive (90min; late April to early June Mon–Fri 6 daily, Sat & Sun 8 daily; early June to Sept Mon–Fri 10 daily, Sat & Sun 13 daily; Oct Mon–Fri 6 daily, Sat & Sun 11 daily; Nov Mon–Fri 3 daily, Sat & Sun 6 daily; $37.85). The Foundation also runs several **walking tours** of the Loop, departing from the Archicenter on a complicated schedule of at least two different two-hour tours daily throughout the year ($17 each), and a daily 45-minute, $5 lunchtime tour of downtown landmarks at 12.15pm.

For a free and personalized tour, the Chicago Greeter programme (ⓦ chicagogreeter.com) is an excellent choice. Tours leave from the lobby of the Chicago Cultural Center and you can set up a tour beforehand by contacting the website several weeks in advance. Alternately, you can just show up and take advantage of the "Instagreeter" programme. The tours are led by a trained greeter and cover about 25 different neighbourhoods, or you can pick one of the forty themed tours such as "Gay & Lesbian Chicago" or "Green Chicago".

By taxi Chicago's taxis cost $3.25 at the drop of the flag, and $1.80/mile. They can be hailed anytime in the Loop and other central neighbourhoods; otherwise call Yellow (☎312 829 4222) or Checker taxis (☎312 243 2537).

By bike You can rent bikes ($30/day) at Millennium Park's multilevel bike park at 239 E Randolph St.

INFORMATION

Visitor centres Chicago Office of Tourism, in the lobby of the Chicago Cultural Center, 77 E Randolph St (Mon–Thurs 9am–6pm, Fri & Sat 9am –6pm, Sun 10am–5pm; ☎800 877 CHICAGO, ⍵ explorechicago.org). There are also information centres in the Historic Water Tower, 800 N Michigan Ave (Mon–Thurs 9am–7pm, Fri & Sat 9am–6pm, Sun 10am–5pm) and in the Northwest Exelon Pavilion at Millennium Park (daily 9am–5pm).

ACCOMMODATION

Most central accommodation is oriented toward business and convention trade rather than tourism, but there are still plenty of moderately priced rooms in and around the Loop, to say nothing of the myriad of establishments that are scattered alongside major interstates. Even top-class downtown hotels are, comparatively, not that expensive. Note, however, that a room tax of 16.4 is added to all bills, while overnight parking can cost $2 at a modest downtown hotel, and as much as $47 at a fancy one. If you're stuck, try Hot Rooms, a reservation service offering hotel rooms at discount rates (☎773 468 7666, ⍵ hotrooms.com). While they're not as prominent as elsewhere, B&B rooms are available from around $90/night; the Chicago B&B Association maintains full listings (⍵ chicago-bed-breakfast.com).

★ **Allegro** 179 W Randolph St ☎312 236 0123, ⍵ allegrochicago.com. With a colourful, updated Art Deco design, this boutique hotel is sure to delight. Luxury amenities throughout, and a wine reception from 5–6pm. $189

Chicago Getaway Hostel 616 W Arlington Place ☎773 929 5380, ⍵ getawayhostel.com. Easy-going hostel close to loads of good bars and eats on nearby Clark St. Oh yes, they also have free guitars for general use. Open 24hr. Dorms $255, private rooms $65

Comfort Inn & Suites Downtown 15 E Ohio St ☎312 894 0900, ⍵ chicagocomfortinn.com. This high-rise chain hotel is given considerable charm by its restored Art Deco lobby. The rooms are well equipped, and complemented by fitness and sauna facilities. Rates include continental breakfast. $149

Dana Hotel & Spa 660 N State St ☎312 202 6000, ⍵ danahotelandspa.com. Each room has an elaborate balcony overlooking the surrounding urban milieu, and the interior touches include natural wood finishes and carved stone tables. There's also a sky lounge with outdoor fire pits and a seemingly endless wine list. $229

Days Inn Lincoln Park North 644 W Diversey Pkwy at Clark ☎773 525 7010, ⍵ lpndaysinn.com. This good, friendly motel is popular with visiting musicians and a convenient base for North Side nightlife. Free continental breakfast. $99

The Drake 140 E Walton Place ☎312 787 2200, ⍵ thedrakehotel.com. Chicago's society hotel, just off the Magnificent Mile, has been modernized without sacrificing its sedate charms, and its well-appointed rooms have jacuzzis. You can always just pop in for a drink at the elegant *Coq d'Or*, which also features piano singalongs. $189

★ **Gold Coast Guest House** 113 W Elm St ☎312 337 0361, ⍵ bbchicago.com. Inconspicuous 1870s rowhouse that's been beautifully converted to offer four high-class en-suite B&B rooms, with a friendly atmosphere and an excellent full breakfast. $149

Hampton Inn & Suites 33 W Illinois Ave ☎312 832 0330, ⍵ hamptoninnchicago.com. Clean high-rise chain hotel (built in 1988 but "Frank-Lloyd-Wright-inspired") in a good River North location, and with a rather nice pool. $199

★ **HI-Chicago – The J. Ira & Nicki Harris Family Hostel** 24 E Congress St ☎312 360 0300, ⍵ hichicago .org. Huge, very central hostel complete with a games room, luggage storage and laundry facilities. Open 24hr, with internet access, full kitchen, and free continental breakfast. As well as dorm beds, there are semiprivate rooms with shared living room. Dorms $30, rooms $80

★ **House of Two Urns** 1239 N Greenview Ave, Wicker Park ☎773 235 1408, ⍵ twourns.com. This rambling, artist-owned B&B, three blocks from the "L" and close to Wicker Park, is filled with contemporary art; the five guest rooms have a quirky flair, but some share facilities. Parking is available and an elaborate breakfast is also included. Three- and four-room apartments are also available. Doubles $99, apartments $149

Palmer House Hilton 17 E Monroe St ☎312 726 7500, ⍵ chicagohilton.com/hotels_palmer.aspx. One of the city's most historic hotels, the *Palmer House* is in the centre of the Loop, and perfect for visits to Millennium Park and the Art Institute of Chicago. $129

Renaissance Blackstone Hotel 636 S Michigan Ave ☎312 447 0955, ⍵ blackstonerenaissance.com. The *Blackstone* is part of American political legend. It was here that Warren G. Hardin was selected as the Republican Party presidential nominee in one of its famous "smoke-filled rooms". Today, it remains a luxurious choice and the rooms feature plush sofas and a banquet of pillows. $169

4

Wheeler Mansion 2020 S Calumet Ave ☎312 945 2020, ⓦwheelermansion.com. A very grand mansion that's been converted into a plush, formal, but romantic B&B that's a hit with business travellers. In the Prairie Avenue Historic District, close to Soldier Field. **$279**

Wit Hotel 201 N State St ☎312 467 0200, ⓦthewithotel .com. Contemporary Chicago hotel design calls for expansive glass exteriors, and the *Wit* does not disappoint. The rooms have soaking tubs, marine- and pastel-coloured interiors, and floor-to-ceiling windows. **$209**

EATING

Chicago's cosmopolitan make-up is reflected in its plethora of ethnic restaurants. **Italian** food, ranging from hearty **deep-dish pizza** – developed in 1943 at *Pizzeria Uno* (see opposite) – to delicately crafted creations presented at stylish trattorias, continues to dominate a very dynamic scene. In recent years there's been a surge of popularity for **New American** cuisine. **Thai** restaurants still thrive, as do ones with a broad **Mediterranean** slant, many of which serve tapas; and there are still plenty of opportunities to sample more long-standing Chicago cuisines – Eastern European, German, Mexican, Chinese, Indian, even Burmese and Ethiopian. Of course, a number of establishments serve good old-fashioned **BBQ ribs**, a legacy of Chicago's days as the nation's meatpacker. And no visit is complete without sampling a messy Italian beef sandwich, or a Chicago-style hot dog, laden with tomatoes, onions, celery salt, hot peppers and a pickle. The largest concentration of restaurants is found north and west of the **Loop**. To the west, **Greektown**, around Halsted Street at Jackson Boulevard, and **Little Italy**, on and around Taylor Street, are worth a look, while the **Near North** and **River North** areas harbour a good number of upmarket places.

THE LOOP
Beatrix 519 N Clark St ☎312 284 1377. Equal parts 1960s modish airline terminal and contemporary casual, *Beatrix* does breakfast, lunch and dinner quite well. Standouts here include freshly squeezed juices, a warm pot roast sandwich and the chilli- and chocolate-glazed salmon. Daily 8am–midnight.

★ **Billy Goat Tavern** 430 N Michigan Ave, at Hubbard St ☎312 222 1525. This legendary journalists' haunt opens early and closes late, serving the "cheezborgers" made famous by John Belushi's comedy skit. Very reasonable. Mon–Fri 6am–2am, Sat & Sun 10am–2am.

Do Rite Donuts 50 W Randolph St ☎312 488 2483. An attractive, small doughnut shop with some fine offerings, include pistachio-Meyer lemon, vanilla bean and the outstanding Boston Creme. They close when they sell out, so come early. Mon–Fri 6.30am–2pm, Sat & Sun 7am–1pm.

GT Oyster House 531 N Wells St ☎312 929 3501. Delightful, expensive seafood restaurant most popular for dinner, when the tuna poke or a snapper ceviche are recommended. There's a bar where you can enjoy mussels or caviar. Mon–Fri 11.30am–11pm, Sat & Sun 10am–midnight.

Lou Mitchell's 565 W Jackson Ave, at Clinton St ☎312 939 3111. Near Union Station, *Lou's* has been around since 1923, serving terrific omelettes, waffles and hash browns all day long. Try the pecan-laden cookies. Mon–Sat 5.30am–3pm, Sun 7am–3pm.

★ **Russian Tea Time** 77 E Adams St, at Michigan Ave ☎312 360 0000. This Midwestern nod to New York's exclusive *Russian Tea Room* offers a (pricey) sampling of authentic fare from the former Soviet empire. Mon–Thurs 11am–9pm, Fri & Sat 11am–midnight.

Tortoise Club 350 N State St ☎312 755 1700. Dark and warm, this is the type of place you want to sit in and drink a Manhattan or twelve, whilst feasting on the likes of wild pheasant pie, steak tartare and crab cake. Mon–Thurs 11.30am–10.30pm, Fri 11.30am–11.30pm, Sat & Sun 5–9pm.

Trattoria No. 10 10 N Dearborn St ☎312 984 1718. This charming surprise, in a series of underground rooms, serves up delicious ravioli, grilled sea scallops and risotto. Mon–Thurs 11.30am–9pm, Fri 11.30am–10pm, Sat 5–10pm.

THE WEST SIDE: GREEKTOWN AND LITTLE ITALY
Francesca's on Taylor 1400 W Taylor St ☎312 829 2828. Assorted Francesca-family restaurants dot Chicago. This relatively subdued example offers some of the best Italian food in the city, including a rather nice chicken parmigiana. Don't be surprised to find a crowd here all day. Mon 11.30am–9pm, Tues–Thurs 11.30am–10pm, Fri & Sat 11.30am–11pm, Sun 4–9pm.

Parthenon 314 S Halsted St, at Jackson Blvd ☎312 726 2407. One of the oldest places in Greektown, but still deservedly popular: *saganaki* (fried cheese doused with Metaxa brandy and ignited) was invented here. Daily 11am–midnight.

Pegasus Restaurant & Taverna 130 S Halsted St, at Adams St ☎312 226 3377. Lively Greek option, where true hospitality and evocative wall murals add to the appeal. Stuffed squid and *pustitsio* (macaroni, meat and cheese casserole) are recommended. The rooftop garden has a superb view of the Loop skyline. Mon–Thurs 11am–11pm, Fri 11am–midnight, Sat noon–midnight, Sun noon–10pm.

★ **Santorini** 800 W Adams St, at S Halsted St ☎312 829 8820. The decor recreates a Greek island village, and the food is beguiling, too; grilled octopus and lamb *exohiko* (wrapped in filo pastry and fried) are highlights. Mon–Fri 11am–10pm, Sat & Sun 11am–midnight.

SOUTH LOOP AND THE SOUTH SIDE

Gioco 1312 S Wabash Ave, at 13th St ☎312 939 3870. Immensely popular (and somewhat expensive) place, whose classic, meticulously prepared Italian cuisine is drawing a hip crowd to the rapidly gentrifying South Loop district. Mon–Thurs 11.30am–2pm & 5–10pm, Fri & Sat–11.30pm, Sun 5–10pm.

★ **The Medici** 1327 E 57th St ☎773 667 7394. Hyde Park institution close to the University of Chicago, serving up a mix of salads, pizza and quality hamburgers. Next door is its in-house bakery, which is a solid choice for pain au chocolat and the like. Mon–Thurs 7am–1pm, Fri 7am–11pm, Sat 9am–11pm, Sun 9am–10pm.

NEAR NORTH SIDE AND RIVER NORTH

★ **Bistrot Zinc** 1131 N State St, at Elm St ☎312 337 1131. Very friendly, intimate neighbourhood bistro, offering a quintessential French menu prepared and served just the way it should be, at good prices. Mon–Thurs 11.30am–10pm, Fri 11.30am–11pm, Sat 10am–3pm & 5–11pm, Sun10am–3pm & 5–9pm.

Club Lago 331 W Superior St, at N Orleans St ☎312 337 9444. Best described as a post-World War II American take on Northern Italian, this low-key restaurant is a good place for a drink or a plate of baked clams. Mon–Thurs 11am–10pm, Fri & Sat 11am–11pm.

★ **Frontera Grill & Topolobampo** 445 N Clark St, at Illinois St ☎312 661 1434. Wildly imaginative Mexican food: *Frontera Grill* is crowded and boisterous; *Topolobampo* is more refined and pricier. The front door and bar are shared between the two and going here for margaritas is the only way to start and finish the evening. Mon–Thurs 11.30am–2.30pm & 5–11pm, Fri & Sat 11.30am–2.30pm & 5pm–midnight, Sun 11.30am–2.30pm & 5–10pm.

★ **Le Colonial** 937 N Rush St, at Walton St ☎312 255 0088. This atmospheric evocation of some colonial outpost in Indochina, with its palm trees and rattan furniture, serves zestful French-influenced Vietnamese food at reasonable prices, and has outdoor seating in summer. Mon–Thurs 11.30am–2.30pm & 5–11pm, Fri & Sat 11.30am–2.30pm & 5pm–midnight, Sun 11.30am–2.30pm & 5–10pm.

Pizzeria Uno 29 E Ohio St, at Wabash Ave ☎312 321 1000. The original outlet of the chain that put Chicago deep-dish pizza on the map. It's in an old nineteenth-century mansion, which makes things even more compelling. Mon–Fri 11am–1am, Sat 11am–2am, Sun 11am–11pm.

Portillo's 100 W Ontario St, at La Salle St ☎312 587 8930. Much-loved local chain that serves delicious Chicago hot dogs and the best Italian beef sandwich in the city. The interior has a slew of ersatz Chicago-themed ephemera, including a recreated tenement and banners from the long-gone Chicago Stadium. Mon–Thurs 10.30am–11pm, Fri & Sat 10.30am–midnight, Sun 11am–11pm.

Star of Siam 11 E Illinois St, at State St ☎312 670 0100. Terrific Thai food served in a spacious, inviting setting. The tom yum soup, pad thai and curries are top-notch. Mon–Thurs 11am–10pm, Fri & Sat 11am–11pm.

LINCOLN PARK AND OLD TOWN

★ **Boka** 1729 N Halsted St ☎773 337 6070. Stylish option close to the Steppenwolf Theatre, serving inventive and tasty dishes from around the world on a changing weekly menu that offers small ($8–12) and large ($21–37) portions, depending on your appetite. Mon–Thurs 5–9.30pm, Fri & Sat 5–10.30pm.

Hema's Kitchen II 2411 N Clark St ☎773 529 1705. Bustling Indian restaurant that's well regarded for its garlic naan, curried fish and tandoori chicken. BYO beer or wine. Daily noon–11pm.

Old Jerusalem 1411 N Wells St, at Evergreen Ave ☎312 944 3304. This long-time favourite serves reasonable Middle Eastern dishes; the falafel is great. BYO beer or wine. Daily 11am–10pm.

RJ Grunts 2056 Lincoln Park W, at Clark St ☎773 929 5363. Check out the great burgers and a top-notch salad bar – purported to be the nation's first – in a casual neighbourhood atmosphere. The well-stocked *tableau de verdure* (salad buffet) contains more than 100 items, all fresh, all well selected. Mon–Fri 11.30am–noon, Sat 10am–2am, Sun 10am–9pm.

WICKER PARK

Café Absinthe 1954 W North Ave, at Milwaukee Ave ☎773 278 4488. Fine French dining in a romantic, casual setting. One of the city's best restaurants, with prices to match. Tues–Thurs 5.30–10pm, Fri & Sat 5.30–11pm, Sun 5.30–9pm.

★ **Irazu** 1865 N Milwaukee Ave ☎773 252 5687. Very cheap but wonderful Costa Rican diner, serving great burritos plus a small selection of authentic main courses. Mon–Sat 11.30am–9pm.

★ **Mindy's Hot Chocolate** 1747 N Damen Ave ☎773 489 1747. With a mix of sweet and savoury offerings, the weekend brunch at *Mindy's* is a good bet, and its chocolate desserts are miniature masterpieces. Tues 5.30–10pm, Wed & Thurs 11.30am–2pm & 5–10pm, Fri & Sat 10am–2pm & 5.30pm–midnight, Sun 10am–2pm.

4

DRINKING

Chicago is a consummate boozer's town, and one of the best US cities for **bars**, catering to just about every group and interest, with many open until 3, 4 or even 5am. The city's drinking areas include the touristy **Division Street**, the post-college melange that is **Wrigleyville** and a clutch of places in bookish **Hyde Park**. **Wicker Park** is the trendiest hangout zone, while

Halsted Street between Belmont and Addison is known as **Boystown** for its gay bars and clubs. The hundred-plus **cafés and coffeehouses** across the city may not have taken the place of the traditional taverns, but they're a growing alternative.

PUBS AND BARS

⭐ **Barcito's** 151 W Erie ☎ 312 274 1111. Tucked into a larger restaurant, this swanky Mexican bar has a happy hour of sorts, with $1 oysters and free tapas with the purchase of an alcoholic beverage. Mon–Thurs 3pm–midnight, Fri–Sun 3pm–1am.

⭐ **Delilah's** 2771 N Lincoln Ave ☎ 773 472 2771. Choose from a great selection of beers (150) and whiskeys at this dimly lit bar (playing underground records – from rock to alt-country – at night, along with an eclectic mix of kung fu and blaxploitation movies). Mon–Fri & Sun 4pm–2am, Sat 4pm–3am.

Green Door Tavern 678 N Orleans St ☎ 312 664 5496. In an unlikely spot near the galleries of River North, this historic place is chock-full of Chicago memorabilia: some pure kitsch, others genuine antiques. Drink at the long bar or settle into a cosy back room to sample home-style cooking. Mon–Fri 11am–2am, Sat 10am–3am, Sun 10am–2am.

John Barleycorn 658 W Belden Ave ☎ 773 348 8899. A dimly lit Lincoln Park pub dating to 1890. This former speakeasy and John Dillinger haunt has retained many of its original nautical-themed fixtures. The lovely garden is open in summer. Tues–Fri 4pm–2am, Sat 11am–3am, Sun 9am–2am.

⭐ **Old Town Ale House** 219 W North Ave ☎ 312 944 7020. An eclectic crowd of scruffy regulars and yuppies mingle in this convivial haunt, complete with a pinball machine and a library of paperbacks. Mon–Fri & Sun noon–4am, Sat 11am–5am.

Rainbo Club 1150 N Damen Ave ☎ 773 489 5999. Busy Wicker Park bar and hangout for indie-rock types. A photo booth keeps things interesting in the wee small hours. Mon–Fri & Sun 4pm–2am, Sat 4pm–3am.

⭐ **Rossi's Liquors** 412 N State St ☎ 312 644 5775. Amid the sleek modern new buildings of River North, *Rossi's* is a low-down dive bar with a great jukebox and lots of local colour. Worth a stop. Mon–Fri 7am–2am, Sat 7am–3am, Sun 11am–2am.

Twin Anchors 1655 N Sedgwick St, at North Ave ☎ 312 266 1616. You'll wait for a seat in this neighbourhood spot, famed for its BBQ ribs, but the interesting clientele and 1950s-style bar make it worthwhile. Mon–Fri 5–11pm, Sat noon–midnight, Sun noon–10.30pm.

⭐ **Woodlawn Tap** 1172 E 55th St, at Woodlawn Ave ☎ 773 643 5516. In the centre of Hyde Park, this place features cheap cold beer and conversation that alternates between Chicago politics and Plato. Jazz on Sunday evenings (from 9pm). Mon–Fri 10.30am–2am, Fri & Sat 11am–3am, Sun 11am–2am.

GAY AND LESBIAN BARS

⭐ **Big Chicks** 5024 N Sheridan Rd, Andersonville ☎ 773 728 5511. A friendly place for a mixed crowd, with a no-charge jukebox and free BBQs outside on summer Sundays. Cash only. Mon–Thurs & Sun 5pm–midnight, Fri & Sat 5–10pm.

Marty's Martini Bar 1511 W Balmoral Ave ☎ 773 561 6425. Tightly packed place, with a fun crowd fuelled by the martinis both classic and contemporary – a stellar spot in which to spend the violet hour. Mon–Fri 5pm–2am, Sat 5pm–3am.

Sidetrack 3349 N Halsted St ☎ 773 477 9189. One of the most popular bars along Halsted's gay strip in Lakeview. Theme nights include Sunday, which is dedicated to showtunes. Mon–Thurs, Sat & Sun 3pm–2am, Fri 3pm–3am.

NIGHTLIFE AND ENTERTAINMENT

From its earliest frontier days, Chicago has had some of the best **nightlife** in the USA. Blues fans who celebrate Chicago as the birthplace of Muddy Waters' **urban blues** will not be disappointed. The city remains proud of its blues traditions, while continuing to innovate in other genres, such as the energetic dance beat of 1980s **house music** as well as the groundbreaking **jazz** of the Art Ensemble of Chicago. There are **nightclubs** aplenty all over town, especially along Halsted Street, Lincoln Avenue and Clark Street on the North Side. **Uptown**, at the intersection of North Broadway and Lawrence, has a couple of excellent venues for jazz and rock. The best **gay clubs** congregate in the Boystown area, which is a mile north of Lincoln Park. Highbrow pursuits are also well provided for: Chicago's **classical music**, **dance** and **theatre** are world-class. For **listings**, Chicagoans pick up free weeklies including the excellent *Chicago Reader* (available Thurs afternoon and online at ⓦ chicagoreader.com), the *New City* and the gay and lesbian *Windy City Times*. The Friday issues of the *Chicago Sun-Times* and the *Chicago Tribune* are useful, while *Time Out Chicago* (online only; ⓦ timeoutchicago.com) has good arts, music, theatre and movie listings.

BLUES

B.L.U.E.S. 2519 N Halsted St ☎ 773 528 1012, ⓦ chicagobluesbar.com. Opened in the 1970s, *B.L.U.E.S.* is still going strong, though it's a bit touristy. The tiny stage

has been graced by all the greats. Cover $10. Mon–Fri & Sun 8pm–2am, Sat 8pm–3am.

⭐ **Buddy Guy's Legends** 700 S Wabash Ave ☎ 312 427 1190, ⓦ buddyguys.com. South Loop club owned by veteran bluesman Buddy Guy, with great acoustics and atmosphere, aiming to present the very best local and national acts. Cover $10–20. Daily 9.30pm–12.45am.

Kingston Mines 2548 N Halsted St ⓣ773 477 4646. Top-notch local and national acts on two stages play to an up-for-it, partying crowd. College students get in for free with a valid ID. Cover $12–15. Mon–Thurs 8pm–4am, Fri 7pm–4am, Sat 7pm–5am, Sun 6pm–4am.

★ **Rosa's Lounge** 3420 W Armitage Ave ⓣ773 342 0452, ⓦrosaslounge.com. Run by Mama Rosa and her son, this West Side club is undoubtedly the friendliest blues joint around. For real aficionados. Cover $7–10. Tues–Sat 8pm–midnight.

JAZZ

★ **Andy's** 11 E Hubbard St ⓣ312 642 6805. Very popular with the after-work crowd; informal with moderate prices. Cover $8–20. Daily 9pm–1am.

★ **The Green Mill** 4802 N Broadway ⓣ773 878 5552. One of the best – and most beautiful – rooms for local and national talent, including the fabulous pianist Patricia Barber and slam poetry innovator Marc Smith. Located in the Uptown neighbourhood, and proud of its chequered Prohibition-era past. Cover $4–15. Sat & Sun 7pm–3am.

Jazz Showcase 806 S Plymouth Court ⓣ312 360 0234, ⓦjazzshowcase.com. A classy, dressed-up room that hosts premier jazz by top names. Cover $20–25. Sat & Sun 8pm–midnight.

ROCK

★ **Double Door** 1572 N Milwaukee Ave ⓣ773 489 3160, ⓦdoubledoor.com. Former biker bar turned hip music venue in the Wicker Park/Bucktown neighbourhood. Indie bands, DJ collectives and soul ensembles are mainstays here. Cover $15–20. Tues–Sat 8.30pm–1am.

Elbo Room 2871 N Lincoln Ave ⓣ773 549 5549, ⓦelboroomchicago.com. Easy-going venue specializing in emerging bands, whether indie, pop, funk or ska. Cover $5–9. Sat & Sun 9pm–2am.

★ **Empty Bottle** 1035 N Western Ave ⓣ773 276 3600, ⓦemptybottle.com. Loud hole-in-the-wall club where you might hear just about anything: experimental jazz, alternative rock, hip-hop, house, dub and progressive country. Its block parties are the stuff of legend. Cover $7–15. Daily 8pm–2am.

Metro 3730 N Clark St ⓣ773 549 0203, ⓦmetrochicago.com. Arguably the top spot in the city, this club, in an old cinema building, regularly hosts young British bands trying to break the States, plus DJ mixes. Cover $17–23. Wed–Sun 9pm–1am.

FOLK, COUNTRY AND WORLD MUSIC

★ **Fitzgerald's** 6615 W Roosevelt, Berwyn ⓣ708 788 2118, ⓦfitzgeraldsnightclub.com; accessible by the CTA's Blue Line. In the western suburb of Berwyn, an excellent venue for alt-country, Americana, Cajun and zydeco. Tickets $10–30. Daily 8pm–midnight.

Old Town School of Folk Music 4544 N Lincoln Ave ⓣ773 728 6000. Established in 1959, this place presents about eighty concerts a year, including just about every type of folk and world music, and also offers great classes. Tickets $18–30. Wed–Sun 2–10pm.

★ **Schubas Tavern** 3159 N Southport Ave, Lakeview ⓣ773 525 2508, ⓦschubas.com. A quirky roster of up-and-coming acts, from rock to alt-country or roots, appear at this intimate, all-but-perfect neighbourhood venue. Tickets $10–25. Tues–Sun 8pm–midnight.

CLUBS, THEATRE AND COMEDY

While it was once every Chicago actor and playwright's ambition to end up in New York, many are now perfectly happy to remain here. The city supports numerous theatre companies, several of which boast reputations as good as any in the USA. Comedy, too, is particularly vibrant; Chicago's improvisational scene is considered the best in the nation.

Court Theatre 5535 S Ellis St ⓣ773 753 4472, ⓦcourttheatre.org. Based on the campus of the University of Chicago, the Court Theatre takes on a little bit of everything; recent successes have included dramatic interpretations of Martin Luther King, Jr's last night and *The Iliad*.

Goodman Theatre 170 N Dearborn St ⓣ312 443 3800, ⓦgoodman-theatre.org. Right in the Loop, the Goodman is Chicago's traditional big-production house and yearly staples include *A Christmas Carol* and a musical or two.

Second City 1616 N Wells St ⓣ312 337 3992, ⓦsecondcity.com. This band of comedic improvisers spreads its activities across three separate auditoriums in its Old Town digs. Greats including Stephen Colbert, John Belushi and Chris Farley have made merry here over the past fifty years.

Steppenwolf Theatre 650 N Halsted St ⓣ312 335 1650, ⓦsteppenwolf.org. This prestigious ensemble, with alumni including John Malkovich and Gary Sinise, got its start in a church basement more than thirty years ago and it continues to draw rave reviews. A must-see while in Chicago.

4

CLASSICAL MUSIC, OPERA AND DANCE

Civic Opera House 20 N Wacker Drive ⓣ312 332 2244, ⓦlyricopera.org. Based in the sumptuous Civic Opera House, the Lyric Opera of Chicago has recently mounted productions of *Otello*, *Turandot* and *Parsifal*.

Hubbard Street Dance Chicago 1147 W Jackson Blvd ⓣ312 850 9744, ⓦhubbardstreetdance.com. Edgy productions by this terpsichorean ensemble whose performances incorporate jazz, hip-hop and other styles.

Joffrey Ballet 10 E Randolph St ⓣ312 739 0120, ⓦjoffrey.com. This company performs a range of classic works, such as *The Nutcracker* and *Le Sacre Du Printemps*.

CHICAGO SPECTATOR SPORTS

Chicagoans are, for better or worse, loyally supportive of their teams. The city's most successful outfit in recent memory was the **Bulls** basketball team, helmed by Michael Jordan and winner of six NBA championships in the 1990s (☎312 455 4000, ⓦnba.com/bulls). Now, though, with the Jordan era long gone, Bulls fans have little to cheer about, though the team's fortunes have improved in recent years. They play in the modern and severe United Center, 1901 W Madison St, as do hockey's **Blackhawks**, who triumphed in 2010 and 2013 to become the Stanley Cup champions (☎312 455 4000, ⓦchicagoblackhawks.com). The **Bears** football team (☎312 455 7000, ⓦchicagobears.com) can be seen at the 61,500-capacity Soldier Field, 425 E McFetridge Drive, at the south end of Grant Park. As for baseball, neither Chicago team had won a World Series since 1917 until the **White Sox** finally broke the streak in 2005. They play their contests at the distinctly nondescript US Cellular Field stadium, at 333 W 35th St on the South Side (☎312 674 1000, ⓦchicago.whitesox.mlb.com). The long-suffering **Cubs** still call grand old Wrigley Field home (☎773 404 CUBS, ⓦchicago.cubs.mlb.com).

Ravinia Festival 418 Sheridan Rd, Highland Park ☎847 266 5100, ⓦravinia.org. The bucolic grounds here provide the summer home of the Chicago Symphony Orchestra and they are supplemented by touring pop, country and jazz acts.

Symphony Center 220 S Michigan Ave ☎312 294 3000, ⓦchicagosymphony.org. Main performance space of the world-renowned Chicago Symphony Orchestra, which also spends part of the year on tour.

4 Springfield

Two hundred miles south of Chicago, the Illinois state capital of **SPRINGFIELD** spreads out from a neat, downtown grid. There is one primary reason people make a pilgrimage to this rather generic city: Abraham Lincoln. The sixteenth president of the United States honed his legal and political skills here, and his old homes, haunts and final resting place illuminate not only the life of this conflicted and contrary individual, but also the uncertainty and turmoil of a nation on the brink of civil war.

Lincoln Home Visitor Center

426 S Seventh St • Daily 8.30am–5pm • Free • ☎217 492 4241, ⓦnps.gov/liho

The number-one Lincoln attraction is the only house he ever owned, and which he shared with his wife, Mary Todd, from 1844 to 1861. For a free narrated tour, pick up tickets at the **Lincoln Home Visitor Center**. The excellent display "What a Pleasant Home Abe Lincoln Has" offers perspective on the neighbourhood as Lincoln knew it and a brief film titled *Abraham Lincoln: A Journey to Greatness* will help pass the time while you wait for the next available tour.

Abraham Lincoln Presidential Library and Museum

212 N Sixth St • Daily 9am–5pm • Library free; museum $12 • ☎217 782 5764, ⓦalplm.org

Four blocks north of the Lincoln Home Visitor Center, the **Abraham Lincoln Presidential Library and Museum** is a state-of-the-art new facility that covers Lincoln's career in exhaustive detail, with fascinating original documents and interactive displays. In lesser hands, life-sized reproductions of Lincoln sitting in front of a fireplace studying his books would be maudlin and trite, but it all seems to work quite well. The core of the museum contains the Treasures gallery, which contains dozens of original Lincoln family items.

Old State Capitol

Sixth and Adams sts • Mid-April to Aug daily 9am–5pm; Sept to mid-April Tues–Sat same hours; 30min tours available • Free • ☎217 785 7960

In the restored Greek Revival **Old State Capitol**, Lincoln attended at least 240 Supreme Court hearings, and proclaimed in 1858, "A house divided against itself cannot stand.

I believe this government cannot endure permanently, half slave and half free". Objects, busts and papers relating to Lincoln and the Democrat Stephen A. Douglas, whom he debated (and subsequently lost to) in Illinois' 1858 US Senate election, and whom he defeated in the 1860 presidential race, can be found throughout the building. The optional thirty-minute tour gives more details on the building's architecture and Lincoln's activities here.

Lincoln's Tomb

1500 Monument Ave • March, April, Sept & Oct Tues–Sat 9am–5pm; May–Aug daily 9am–5pm; Nov–Feb Tues–Sat 9am–4pm • Free

Lincoln's Tomb, an 117ft-tall obelisk, stands in beautiful Oak Ridge Cemetery on the north side of town. The vault, adorned with busts and statuettes, is open to the public. Inside are inscribed the words, "Now he belongs to the ages". Other memorials abound, including the Vietnam Veterans Memorial, which features five black granite walls engraved with the names of three thousand Illinoisians who were killed in battle or who remain missing in action.

Dana-Thomas House

301 E Lawrence Ave • Tours Wed–Sun 9am–4pm (every 20min) • $10 • ☎ 217 782 6776

Completed in 1904, the **Dana-Thomas House** survives as the best-preserved and most completely furnished example of **Frank Lloyd Wright**'s early Prairie houses, with more than four hundred pieces of glasswork, original art and light fixtures. A seven-minute film provides a great introduction and the gift shop is a dream for architecture and design enthusiasts.

ARRIVAL AND INFORMATION

By plane Abraham Lincoln Capital Airport (☎ 217 788 1060, ⓦ flyspi.com) currently has two major airlines serving Springfield (United Airlines and American Airlines).

By bus Greyhound buses drop off 2 miles east of downtown at 2815 S Dirksen Pkwy.

Destinations Chicago (4 daily; 3hr); St Louis (4 daily; 2hr).

SPRINGFIELD

By train Amtrak trains roll in at Third and Washington sts downtown.

Destinations Chicago (5 daily; 4hr); St Louis (5 daily; 2hr).

Visitor centre 109 N Seventh St (Mon–Fri 8.30am–4.30pm; ☎ 217 789 2360, ⓦ visit-springfieldillinois.com).

ACCOMMODATION AND EATING

Augie's Front Burner 109 S Fifth St ☎ 217 544 6979. This place serves up good California-style and vegetarian meals, such as black bean cakes. Mon–Fri 11am–2.30pm & 5–9.30pm, Sat 5–9.30pm.

Cozy Dog Drive-In 2935 S Sixth St ☎ 217 525 1992. Claims to be the birthplace of the Cozy Dog (also known as the corn dog), a deep-fried, batter-drenched hot dog on a stick. Mon–Sat 8am–8pm.

D'Arcy's Pint Restaurant 661 W Stanford Ave ☎ 217 492 8800. Serves up the ultimate Horseshoe, a regional speciality comprised of thick-sliced bread topped with hamburger along with French fries and a so-called "secret" cheese sauce. Mon–Sat 11am–1am.

The Inn at 835 835 S Second St ☎ 217 523 4466, ⓦ innat835.com. A charming ten-room B&B converted from a 1909 downtown apartment block. **$165**

Galena

The charming town of **GALENA**, in the far northwest corner of Illinois, has changed little since its nineteenth-century heyday when, thanks to its sheltered location just a few miles up the Galena River, it was a major port of call for Mississippi River steamboats. These days, the main foot traffic comes from weekend travellers who step back in time strolling along the gentle crescent of Main Street. Its impeccable red-brick facades and graceful skyline of spires and crosses place it among the most attractive river towns in the USA.

Galena's most celebrated resident was **Ulysses S. Grant**, the noted Union army Civil War general. Grant moved to the town in 1860, working with his brothers as a clerk in a leather store owned by his father. His West Point education encouraged the townspeople to appoint him as colonel when they raised the 21st Illinois regiment on the outbreak of war. When he came home, in August 1865, it was as commander of the victorious Union army.

Grant's house

500 Bouthillier St • Wed–Sun 9am–4.45pm • Suggested donation $5 • It's best to phone before arriving on ☎ 815 777 0248

The grateful citizens of Galena presented Ulysses S. Grant with a **house**, a couple of blocks up Bouthillier Street on the far side of the river. It was there, in the drawing room, that he received the news of his election as president in 1868. Although he went on to serve two terms, he is commonly agreed to have been a better general than president. His administrations were plagued by scandal, and he lost all his own money through unwise investments. Here an interpreter (dressed in period costume in summer) will give you a tour of this Italianate home, and tell you about the daily goings-on of the Grant family.

INFORMATION   GALENA

Visitor centre The 1857 Railroad Museum, across the river from the town proper at 101 Bouthillier St, serves as the local visitor centre (Mon–Sat 9am–5pm, Sun 10am–4pm; ☎ 815 777 4390, ⊛ galena.org).

ACCOMMODATION AND EATING

Cloran Mansion Bed & Breakfast 1237 Franklin St ☎ 815 777 0583, ⊛ cloranmansion.com. Locally known for being quite pet-friendly, this Italiante mansion offers rooms with a very distinct feel, complemented by the lovely outdoor fire-pit patio and beautiful gardens. **$145**
Farmers' Guest House 334 Spring St ☎ 815 777 3456, ⊛ galenabedandbreakfast.com. A 5min walk from downtown, this B&B has top-notch full breakfasts and warm hospitality provided by owner Susan Steffan. The complimentary wine hour begins at 5pm, a good way to start the evening. **$159**

Fried Green Tomatoes 213 N Main St ☎ 815 777 3938. A mix of Italian food here that ranges from the steak martini appetizer (mashed potatoes and steak tips) to a decadent espresso-encrusted salmon fillet. Mon–Thurs & Sun 5–10pm, Fri & Sat 4.30–10pm.
Fritz and Frites 317 Main St ☎ 815 777 2004. A German and French bistro mash-up that serves schnitzel, steak frites and garlic-roasted chicken. Tues–Sun 11.30am–9pm.
Little Tokyo 300 N Main St St ☎ 815 777 8883. An unexpected sushi gem, with fine crab tempura and spicy yellowtail rolls. Daily 11am–10pm.

Wisconsin

Nearly as many cows as humans call **WISCONSIN** home; more than five million of each reside in this rich, rolling farmland. However, America's self-proclaimed "Dairyland" is more than just one giant pasture. Beyond the massive hills, red barns and silvery silos lie endless pine forests, some fifteen thousand sky-blue lakes, postcard-pretty valleys and dramatic bluffs. The state, whose Ojibway name means "gathering of the waters", is bordered by Lake Michigan to the east, Lake Superior in the north and, to the west, the Mississippi and St Croix rivers.

The **history** of Wisconsin is a familiar one in the American narrative of westward expansion. Seventeenth-century French and British explorers began by trading with the Native Americans and soon ousted them from their land. The European settlers who followed – predominantly Germans, Scandinavians and Poles – tended to be liberal and progressive; such major national social programmes as labour laws for women and children, assistance for the elderly and the disabled, and unemployment compensation found their first manifestation in the USA right here.

Wisconsin today is best known for its liquids. The **milk** from all those cattle yields cheeses of all kinds, while the **beer**, as the song says, is what made **Milwaukee** famous. Sparkling **Madison** apart, Wisconsin's other cities can veer toward the quiet and tame side, but they're also safe and amiable.

Milwaukee

Just ninety miles north of Chicago, bustling **MILWAUKEE** is the largest city in Wisconsin and is a combination of the rural Midwest and its stylish urban counterparts. Visually it's a mix of elegant architecture, rambling Victorian warehouses and revamped waterfront developments. Its prime position on the shores of Lake Michigan, at the confluence of three rivers, made it a meeting place for Native American groups long before white settlers moved in, while the opulent mansions lining the lake commemorate the industrialists who helped make this Wisconsin's economic and manufacturing capital. By 1850, less than two decades old and with a population of twenty thousand, Milwaukee already had a dozen breweries and 225 saloons.

   Downtown Milwaukee, split north to south by the Milwaukee River, is just a mile long and a few blocks wide. Handsome old buildings and gleaming, modern steel-and-glass structures are comfortably corralled together on three sides by spaghetti-like strands of freeway, with Lake Michigan forming the fourth boundary. To bolster the allure of downtown, the city has successfully poured millions into its **Riverwalk** development along the Milwaukee River, now something of a nightlife centre and the site of many public entertainment events.

Milwaukee Art Museum

700 N Art Museum Drive • Tues–Sun 10am–5pm, Thurs till 8pm • $15 • ☎ 414 224 3200, ⓦ mam.org

East of the river on the lakefront, the **Milwaukee Art Museum** contains works by European masters and twentieth-century Americans. One wing – with stunning views of the lake – is devoted to a comprehensive collection of Post-Impressionist paintings. Recent special exhibitions have grappled with tattoo art and recent triumphs in animated films. Architect Santiago Calatrava's spectacular expansion is an attraction in itself, the white wings of the building flapping up and down three times each day to reduce heat gain and glare.

Milwaukee Public Museum

800 W Wells St • **Museum** Daily 9am–5pm, Thurs until 8pm• $14 • ☎ 414 278 2702, ⓦ mpm.edu **Dome Theater** Show times vary • $8 • ☎ 414 319 4629, ⓦ mpm.edu/imax

At the **Milwaukee Public Museum**, the intertwined histories and mysteries of the earth, nature and humankind are imaginatively presented through dioramas such as "A Sense of Wonder" and a trip back in time (presented via old storefronts and memorabilia) to nineteenth-century Milwaukee. The **Humphrey IMAX Dome Theater**, with its giant, wraparound screen, shows elaborate films on the solar system's weather and the world of dinosaurs.

Pabst Mansion

2000 W Wisconsin Ave • Feb–Nov Mon–Sat 10am–4pm, Sun noon–4pm; mid-Jan to Feb closed Mon • $10 • ☎ 414 931 0808, ⓦ pabstmansion.com

West of downtown, the 37-room **Pabst Mansion** was completed in 1893 as the castle of local beer baron Captain Frederick Pabst, and is a knockout example of ornate Flemish Renaissance architecture, featuring exquisite wood-, glass- and ironwork. Not surprisingly, the folks at the mansion offer a wide range of beer-related tours.

MILWAUKEE'S FESTIVALS

The eleven-day **Summerfest** (late June to early July), also known as "the Big Gig", is an extravaganza of music and entertainment available for one general admission ticket price of $17 each day. In the past, acts on stage here have included the Dropkick Murphys, Billy Idol, Lewis Black and John Mayer. The **Wisconsin State Fair** (early Aug) takes place in nearby West Allis, west of the city, and it features everything from country music stars to a vast range of deep-fried culinary offerings. Details on both festivals from the visitor centre (see opposite).

Best Place at the Historic Pabst Brewery

901 W Juneau Ave • Tours Mon, Wed & Thurs 2 & 4pm, Fri–Sun noon, 1pm & 2pm • $8 • ☎ 414 630 1609, ⊛ bestplacemilwaukee.com

The Pabst Brewery in Milwaukee closed up shop in the 1990s, but the **Best Place at the Historic Pabst Brewery**, a clutch of historic structures, keeps the spirit of this brewery alive. A visit starts with a 25-minute tour through Milwaukee brewing history, complete with old TV adverts, a bit of a singalong and an introduction to the beautiful murals in the main lobby created by Chicagoan Edgar Miller. Of course, there's plenty of Pabst Blue Ribbon beer to be had along the way.

Harley-Davidson Museum

400 Canal St • Daily 9am–6pm, till 8pm on Thurs • $18 • ☎ 877 436 8738, ⊛ hdmuseum.com

The shiny new museum responsible for one of Milwaukee's legendary brand names, **Harley-Davidson**, is geared squarely toward Harley devotees; for those more interested in Harley chic, there's ample opportunity to purchase all kinds of merchandise at the shop or throughout Milwaukee.

ARRIVAL AND DEPARTURE

MILWAUKEE

By plane Mitchell airport, 8 miles south of downtown at 5300 S Howell Ave, is connected with the city centre by bus #80 ($2.25), and by shared-ride van service ($15). A taxi will set you back about $30.

By bus Greyhound (☎ 414 272 2156) and Wisconsin Coach (☎ 262 542 8864, ⊛ wisconsincoach.com), serving south-eastern Wisconsin, operate out of the same terminal at

606 N James Lovell Drive. Badger Bus (☎ 414 276 7490, ⊛ badgerbus.com), across the street at no. 635, runs to Madison and points between (6 daily; $38 return).

By train Amtrak is at 433 W St Paul Ave.

Destinations Chicago (7 daily; 1hr 30min); Minneapolis/St Paul (1 daily; 5hr).

GETTING AROUND AND INFORMATION

By public transport Getting around Milwaukee is easy and inexpensive via the county's extensive transport system (flat fare $2.25; 24hr info ☎ 414 344 6711, ⊛ ridemcts.com).

On the Milwaukee Loop The Milwaukee Loop is a

special tram (trolley) service connecting 25 stops in the city centre (June–Aug Thurs–Sat 11am–9pm; $1).

Visitor centre 400 W Wisconsin Ave (daily 8am–5pm; ☎ 414 273 7222, ⊛ visitmilwaukee.org).

ACCOMMODATION

★ **Aloft Hotel** 1230 N Old World Third St ☎ 414 226 0122, ⊛ aloftmilwaukeedowntown.com. With its close proximity to some of Milwaukee's "Old World" brewpubs and its modish jet-set-style interiors, this hotel is a good bet for those who want to be close to the nightlife. $119

★ **The Brewhouse Inn & Suites** 1215 N 10th St ☎ 414 810 3350, ⊛ brewhousesuites.com. For beer aficionados, this hotel is truly a dream come true. Located in the historic Pabst Brewery (see above), it's all a bit steampunk – they've kept the six brew kettles on hand as decorative elements. The rooms are quite nice, and there's an enormous stained-glass window etched with a picture of King Gambrinus, the patron saint of beer. $119

★ **Brumder Mansion** 3046 W Wisconsin Ave ☎ 414 342 9767, ⊛ brumdermansion.com. Fabulously decorated,

enormous B&B with an in-house theatre, just minutes from downtown. Rooms include antiques, marble, rich draperies and stained glass. $99

★ **Hotel Metro** 411 E Madison St ☎ 414 272 1937, ⊛ hotelmetro.com. This retro Art Deco hotel has an historic feeling with a modern twist. Updated and eco-friendly, it's worth the extra cash for the fireplace and jacuzzi that sit in the centre of the room. $179

The Pfister Hotel 424 E Wisconsin Ave ☎ 414 273 8222, ⊛ pfisterhotel.com. This hotel sits nestled like a Victorian Grande Dame in the heart of downtown. Replenish yourself in the spa or visit the 23rd-floor martini lounge. There is even a world-class Victorian art collection. Rack rates are pricey, but often you can grab a special package for considerably less. $219

EATING

The Germans who first settled in Milwaukee determined its eating style – heavy on bratwurst, rye bread and beer. Subsequent immigrants threw the collective kitchen wide open, making for a culinary cornucopia. With Lake Michigan lapping the city's feet, freshwater fish can hardly be overlooked, especially on a Friday night when legendary fish fries break out all over the place.

4

★ **Bacchus** 925 E Wells ☎ 414 765 1166. Located in the historic Cudahy Tower and featuring fresh seafood and handmade pastas, this place drips with taste and style. Mon–Thurs 5.30–9pm, Fri & Sat 5.30–10pm.

★ **Cafe Benelux** 346 N Broadway ☎ 414 501 2500. With Dutch-style *pannenkoeken*, along with mussels and spicy Dutch meatballs, this is an extravagant place for a Low Country lunch or dinner. In warmer months, eat on the outdoor deck. Mon–Thurs 7am–midnight, Fri 7am–1am, Sat 8am–1am, Sun 8am–midnight.

Carnevor 724 N Milwaukee St ☎ 414 223 2200. The art of fine dining and outstanding cuts of meat are in full swing at this chic and contemporary steakhouse. Mon–

Wed 5–10pm, Thurs–Sat 5–11pm.

Eddie Martini's 8612 W Watertown Plank Rd ☎ 414 771 6680. Inventive takes on American classics served in a highly energetic atmosphere. Mon–Sat 11.30am–2pm & 5–9pm.

Rudy's 1122 N Edison St ☎ 414 223 1122. Family-friendly and affordable Mexican place. Try the house special combo platters, which include lobster mac and cheese and tuna crudo. Daily 11am–11pm.

★ **Trocadero** 1758 N Water St ☎ 414 272 0205. Parisian-styled eastside spot that serves small plates and great continental dishes such as grilled tuna and saffron shrimp. Mon–Fri 11am–10pm, Sat & Sun 9am–10pm.

NIGHTLIFE AND ENTERTAINMENT

The concept of neighbourhoods is vital to Milwaukee's nightlife. On the east side, Brady Street, a counterculture haven in the 1960s, is now filled with Italian restaurants and bars. Walker's Point, on the edge of downtown, has all sorts of watering holes, while the Polish locals can be found farther south. Downtown gets busy on the weekend, especially either side of the river on Water and Old World Third streets between Juneau and State. The Third Ward, a restored warehouse district on the edge of downtown full of shops and cafés, is also worth checking out.

PUBS AND BARS

Milwaukee Ale House 233 N Water St ☎ 414 226 BEER. Milwaukee's sole all-grain, old-style brewpub serves filling food and its own beer, such as the fine Sheepshead Stout. Mon 4pm–midnight, Tues, Wed & Sun 11am–midnight, Thurs–Sat 11am–2am.

★ **Old German Beer Hall** 1009 N Old World Third St ☎ 414 226 2728. This Old World favourite is distinguished by its excellent hot pretzels, sausages and a charming game in the back room that involves pounding nails into a massive tree stump. It should not be missed. Daily 11am–2am.

Safe House 779 N Front St ☎ 414 271 2007, ⓦ safe -house.com. This unique, tongue-in-cheek nightclub seems to have come straight out of a spy film. Hint: enter through the "International Exports Ltd" office. Mon–Thurs 11.30am–1.30am.

Up and Under Pub 1216 E Brady St ☎ 414 276 2677. Milwaukee's top blues bar – the Wednesday karaoke is some of the best around. Cover $7–15. Daily 5pm–2am.

Von Trier 2235 N Farwell Ave ☎ 414 272 1775. Black Forest decor and lots of imported beers – the Weises is a house speciality. Mon–Thurs 3pm–2am, Fri–Sun 2pm–2.30am.

PERFORMING ARTS VENUES

Marcus Center for the Performing Arts 929 N Water St ☎ 414 273 7121, ⓦ marcuscenter.org. The biggest venue in town, home to the Milwaukee Symphony, the Milwaukee Ballet and the well-regarded children's theatre group, First Stage.

Milwaukee Repertory Theater 108 E Wells St ☎ 414 224 9490, ⓦ milwaukeerep.com. This place has a reputation for staging risk-taking productions in addition to classics.

Pabst Theater 144 E Wells St ☎ 414 286 3663. This historic, well-appointed venue features a melange of pop, rock, comedy and folk performances. Tickets $20–90.

Riverside Theater 116 W Wisconsin Ave ☎ 414 286 3663. A place to see big-name acts in town; recent guests have included Bob Dylan, Eddie Vedder and Sheryl Crow.

Green Bay

GREEN BAY was an important location for seventeenth-century French explorers, but for the past nine decades it has been most well known for the Green Bay Packers, one of the United States' most beloved professional football teams.

Green Bay Packer Hall of Fame

1265 Lombardi Ave • Daily 8am–9pm • $10 • ☎ 920 569 7512

The **Green Bay Packer Hall of Fame** celebrates the dynastic years of the 1960s when the Pack won Superbowls I and II, as well as more recent stars such as Reggie White and Aaron Rodgers. Stuffed with hands-on displays, cinemas and memorabilia, the museum offers more than enough to satisfy any football fan. The Hall of Fame is located in an atrium inside the Packers' **Lambeau Field** stadium, which you can also tour (times vary; $11, or $19 combination ticket with Hall of Fame; ⓦpackers.com).

EATING AND DRINKING   GREEN BAY

Kavarna 143 N Broadway ⓣ 920 430 3200. A bit of a sleeper hit in a town known for beers and brats, this vegetarian/vegan fave serves BBQ black bean burgers, veggie wraps and locally roasted coffee. Mon–Fri 7am–9pm, Sat 9am–9pm, Sun 9am–6pm.

Titletown Brewing Company 200 Dousman St ⓣ 920 437 2337. A great setting for drinks in a former railroad depot downtown and stellar beers. Mon–Thurs & Sun 11am–9.30pm, Fri & Sat 11am–10.30pm.

Door County

From Sturgeon Bay, 140 miles north of Milwaukee, **Door County** sticks into Lake Michigan like a gradually tapering candle for 42 miles. A charming collection of small towns, tiny villages and an island, its three hundred miles of shoreline smacks more of New England than the Midwest. A journey here provides access to a small sliver of America largely devoid of tacky billboards, sloppy diners, bland chain motels and banal amusements. Activities include browsing around galleries and attending arts festivals, as well as hiking, fishing and boating. Winter is considerably quieter, with ice fishing, cross-country skiing and snowmobiling being the predominant outdoor activities.

Peninsula State Park

Over on the western side of Door County, biking and hiking trails traverse the thickly forested hills of **Peninsula State Park** (situated between tiny Fish Creek and enchanting **Ephraim**, with its picturesque white-clapboard architecture). Peninsula Park is one of the most popular parks in Wisconsin and summer camping reservations usually get booked up in January. Just outside it on Hwy-42, the old-fashioned Skyway Drive-In movie theatre (ⓣ920 854 9938) offers a couple of hours' diversion on a warm night.

Washington Island and Rock Island

Washington Island, off the peninsula's northern tip, is a tiny dollop of land that offers a different cultural perspective. During Prohibition, the Icelandic community here convinced authorities that (40 percent alcohol) bitters were an ancient cure for rheumatism and dyspepsia. Cases of the stuff were shipped in, and the habit stuck; drop into the historic *Nelsen's Hall Bitters Pub and Restaurant* (ⓣ920 847 2496), about two miles from the Detroit Harbor dock, for a taste. **Motel rooms** are available on Washington, but there's no such luxury on the primitive neighbouring 950-acre **Rock Island**. Once the private estate of a millionaire, it's dotted with stark, stone buildings; no cars are allowed, so see it by foot or bike.

GETTING AROUND AND INFORMATION   DOOR COUNTY

By ferry The islands are served by the Washington Island Ferry from Northport at the tip of the peninsula (daily; $13 return, cars $26, bikes $4; ⓣ920 847 2546, ⓦwisferry.com) and the Rock Island Ferry out of Jackson Harbor (May to mid-Oct daily; $13 return for foot traffic only; ⓣ920 847 3322).
By bike Renting a bicycle gives you the chance to follow an excellent cycle trail; Fish Creek's Nor Door Cyclery (ⓣ920

868 2275, ⓦnordoorsports.com), on Hwy-42 just north of the entrance to Peninsula State Park (see above), has the best models.
Visitor centre Hwy-42/57 upon entering Sturgeon Bay (lobby open 24hr, staffed times vary; ⓣ920 743 4456, ⓦdoorcounty.com); you can pick up road and trail maps here and phone local lodgings for free.

ACCOMMODATION

Birchwood Lodge 337 Hwy-57, Sister Bay ⓣ920 854 7195, ⓦbirchwoodlodge.com. A pleasant lodge with a variety of accommodation options, including European-

designed suites with a modern touch. $139
★ **French Country Inn** 3052 Spruce Lane, Ephraim ⓣ920 854 4001. This charming B&B close to the water

offers seven rooms (two with private baths) in the summer and four in the winter. Breakfast features organic, local produce when possible. $90

Path of Pines County Rd F off Hwy-42, near Fish Creek ☎920 868 3332. A privately owned campground, the property is very well maintained and it's a bit less cramped than some of the publicly owned campsites in the area. Open mid-May to mid-Oct. $30

Peninsula State Park Campground 9462 Shore Rd, Fish Creek ☎920 868 3258. This is one of the best-maintained campgrounds in the state; amenities include boat rental, a store and showers. Note that as well as the camping fee, you need to pay a $9.70 reservation fee and $7 daily admission (or $10 for out-of-state residents) to enter the park. $20

Settlement Courtyard Inn & Lavender Spa 9126 Hwy-42, Fish Creek ☎920 868 3524, ⓦsettlementinn .com. The *Settlement's* location on a 200-acre estate makes it an ideal year-round destination with four miles of trails for biking, hiking or cross-country skiing. Clean and comfortable, breakfast included. $199

White Gull Inn 4225 Main St, Fish Creek ☎920 868 3517, ⓦwhitegullinn.com. The county's crown jewel, this elegant old inn, next to delightful Sunset Park, was built in 1896. Rooms are decorated in antiques, and some have fireplaces and double whirlpools. The inn is also known for its good restaurant (breakfast is included) and fish boil (see below) every night in summer. $219

EATING

One reward of a midsummer visit to Door County is the chance to sample the cherry in all its guises. Another traditional treat is the fish boil, a delicious outdoor ritual involving whitefish steaks, potatoes and onions cooked in a cauldron over a wood fire. Rounded off with coleslaw and cherry pie, it's widely available for between $12 and $18.

★ **136 Restaurant & Wine Bar** 136 S 3rd Ave, Sturgeon Bay ☎920 746 1100. It's cosy here and the well-rounded wine selection complements the seafood well, which usually includes haddock, scallops and salmon. Mon–Wed 11am–9pm, Thurs–Sat 11am–10pm.

★ **Al Johnson's Swedish Restaurant** Hwy-42, Sister Bay ☎920 854 2626. Swedish pancakes, meatballs and other fine Scandinavian dishes make this spot worth a look. Be sure and look up to see goats grazing atop the sod roof. Daily 6am–8pm.

Bluefront Cafe 86 W Maple St, Sturgeon Bay ☎920 743 9218. Eclectic fare is on offer at this low-key café; highlights include a ham and pretzel roll sandwich and a vegetarian portobello Reuben. Tues–Sat 11am–2.30pm & 5–8.30pm, Sun 10am–2pm.

Madison

MADISON is best known for playing host to the University of Wisconsin and the state government. As a bastion of progressive politics and culture in the Badger State, its splendid setting on an isthmus continues to attract students and others from Portland to Pakistan. Today this stimulating, youthful metropolis is home to a clutch of compelling museums, great restaurants and a student-fuelled nightlife scene.

Capitol Square and around

Downtown is neatly laid out on an isthmus between lakes Mendota and Monona, with the white-granite **State Capitol** (tours Mon–Sat 9am–3pm excluding noon, Sun 1–3pm; ☎608 266 0382) sitting on a hill at its centre, surrounded by shady trees, lawns and park benches. The State Capitol square is the site of a nationally renowned **farmers' market** (late April to early Nov Sat 6am–2pm), where you can browse the local produce and arts and crafts. Nearby, the glassy and well-regarded **Overture Center**, 201 State St (box office ☎608 258 4141, ⓦovereturecenter.com), hosts touring musicians, Broadway plays and other cultural events; inside, the **Madison Museum of Contemporary Art** 227 State St (Tues–Thurs 11am–5pm, Fri noon–8pm, Sat 10am–8pm, Sun noon–5pm; free; ☎608 257 0158, ⓦmmoca.org), features touring exhibits.

Frank Lloyd Wright buildings

Frank Lloyd Wright designed the **Unitarian Meeting House**, 900 University Bay Drive, in the late 1940s. Its sweeping, dramatically curved ceiling and triangle motif are definitely worth a look (May–Oct Mon–Fri tours at 10.30am & 2.30pm, Sun 9am & 11am; Nov–April Sun 9am & 11am; $10). The lakeside **Monona Terrace Community and Convention Center**, 1 John Nolen Drive, is a more recently realized example of Wright's grand vision (daily tours at 1pm; $3). Surprisingly intimate and full of architectural detail, the Center, with its curves, arches and domes, echoes the State Capitol building just a few blocks away.

The University campus

If the Capitol is the city's governmental heart, the 46,000-student **University of Wisconsin** is its spirited, liberal-thinking head, now mellowed since its protest heyday in the late 1960s. The **Memorial Union**, 800 Langdon St (☎608 262 1583), holds a cafeteria and pub, the *Rathskeller*, with tables strewn beneath huge, vaulted ceilings and live music most nights. Outside, the spacious **UW Terrace** offers beautiful sunset views over Lake Mendota. After time on the terrace, a walk down the tree-lined **Lakeshore Path** is a nice way to relax and burn off a few calories post-*Rathskeller*. Capitol and campus are connected by State Street, a welcoming eight-block-long pedestrian mall surrounded by restaurants, cafés, bars and stores.

ARRIVAL AND INFORMATION

MADISON

By plane Van Galder/Coach USA buses depart from the Memorial Union to Chicago's O'Hare Airport (10 daily; $29 one-way, $58 return; ☎608 752 5407, ☎coachusa.com /vangalder). Madison also has a recently renovated airport (☎608 246 3380), offering flights all over the Midwest and further afield.

By bus Greyhound buses run regularly to Milwaukee, Green Bay and beyond, while Badger Coaches makes

eight trips daily from downtown Milwaukee ($19 one-way, $38 return; ☎608 255 6771, ☎badgerbus.com). Both leave from in front of the Chazen Museum of Art, 750 University Ave.

Visitor centre 452 State St (Mon & Tues 11am–2pm, Wed & Thurs 11am–5pm, Fri 11am–6pm, Sat 9am–6pm, Sun noon–4pm; ☎608 262 4636, ☎visitmadison.com).

ACCOMMODATION

Best Western Inn on the Park 22 S Carroll St ☎608 257 8811. Every room has a nice view and it's the closest hotel to all of the events on the square. **$109**

HI-Madison 141 S Butler St ☎608 441 0144, ☎hiusa .org/madison.org. Hostel with thirty beds, five private rooms and all the usual amenities: kitchen, laundry, internet access, storage and lockers. Dorms **$26**, doubles **$61**

Madison Concourse Hotel 1 W Dayton St ☎608 257 6000, ☎concoursehotel.com. Spacious, well-appointed rooms just steps from State Street. **$139**

Mansion Hill Inn 424 Pinckney St ☎608 255 0172, ☎mansionhillinn.com. The hosts here provide a relaxed setting within a restored 1857 Romanesque Revival mansion located close to the campus. **$199**

EATING, DRINKING AND ENTERTAINMENT

State Street is a veritable smorgasbord of food and drink, and the Capitol Square and King Street areas have also seen a spate of great new restaurants open in recent years. For details of what's on, check the free weekly *Isthmus* (☎thedailypage.com), which comes out on Thursdays and carries full listings.

★ **Graze** 1 S Pickney St ☎608 251 2700. The locally sourced dishes here include whitefish cakes, designer mac and cheese and a beet and walnut burger. Mon–Wed 11am–10pm, Thurs & Fri 11am–11pm, Sat 7am–11pm, Sun 9.30am–3pm.

Great Dane Pub & Brewing Co 123 E Doty St ☎608 284 0000. Billiards and brews complement fresh hearty food (think fried fish and cheese dips) in this inviting pub. Mon–Thurs 11am–2am, Fri & Sat 11am–2.30am.

★ **Marigold Kitchen** 118 S Pinckney St ☎608 661 5559. Charming, sunny spot serving delicious, creative

breakfast and lunch dishes – such as *challah* French toast and chilli poached eggs – focusing on local, organic ingredients. Mon–Fri 7am–3pm, Sat 7am–2pm, Sun 8am–2pm.

★ **The Old Fashioned** 23 N Pinckney St ☎608 310 4545, ☎theoldfashioned.com. Named for the state's signature brandy cocktail, this homely restaurant serves the traditional food that made Wisconsin famous, such as fried cheese curds and a killer version of its eponymous cocktail. Mon & Tues 7.30am–10.30pm, Wed–Fri 7.30am–2am, Sat 9am–2am, Sun 9am–11pm.

4

Spring Green

During his seventy-year career, Wisconsin-born architect and social philosopher **Frank Lloyd Wright** designed such monumental structures as New York's spiralling Guggenheim Museum and Tokyo's earthquake-proof *Imperial Hotel*. Three miles south of **SPRING GREEN**, itself forty miles west of Madison on Hwy-14, stand more intimate examples of his work: Wright's magnificent former residence, **Taliesin**, and his **Hillside Home School**. His studio is imposing, and there's also a theatre space on the estate. Extensive and varied tours are available of the house and the school (May–Oct daily; reservations recommended; $16–80). Tours leave from the **Frank Lloyd Wright Visitor Center** (☎608 588 7900, ⓦtaliesinpreservation.org), which was designed by Wright in 1953 as a restaurant; it now features displays, a café and a bookstore. Among numerous other Wright-influenced buildings in Spring Green are the bank and the pharmacy.

House on the Rock

Hwy-23 • Mid-March to Nov daily 9am–5pm •$12.50 per section or $28.50 for all three; Nov & Dec Christmas tours Mon & Thurs–Sun 9am–5pm • $19.95 • ☎ 800 947 2799, ⓦ thehouseontherock.com

From 1944 onward, Alex Jordan built the **House on the Rock**, six miles south of Taliesin on Hwy-23, on and out of a natural, 60ft, chimney-like rock – for no discernible reason. He certainly never lived in it, nor did he intend it to become Wisconsin's number-one tourist attraction. The first section of this multilevel series of furnished nooks and chambers includes the Gate House Ensemble (a Rube Goldberg-like jukebox that replicates the sound of a chamber orchestra) and the original house, whose interior design is Frank Lloyd Wright meets *The Flintstones*. The second section plays host to a chaotic tribute to aviation (with hundreds of model planes), more music machines and one of the world's largest fireplaces. The third section has a massive circus display and the world's largest carousel. Taken as one riotous and bizarre experience, the net effect is overwhelming and disorienting, great fun and ghastly.

ACCOMMODATION AND EATING	SPRING GREEN

The Shed 123 N Lexington St ☎608 588 9049. The Friday fish fry here is not to be missed, and the salad bar is a healthy and welcome option. Mon–Thurs & Sun 10am–9pm, Fri & Sat 10am–10pm.

Spring Green Motel Hwy 14 E ☎608 588 2141. In an area where the price of lodging can be quite steep, this well-kept motel is most welcome. The rooms are small but pleasant, and the fire pit and gazebos offer a place to gather and relax. **$109**

Minnesota

Though **MINNESOTA** is more than a thousand miles from either coast, it's virtually a seaboard state, thanks to **Lake Superior**, connected to the Atlantic via the St Lawrence Seaway. The glaciers that, millions of years ago, flattened all but its southeast corner also gouged out more than fifteen thousand **lakes**, and major **rivers** run along the eastern and western borders. Ninety-five percent of the population lives within ten minutes of a body of water, and the very name Minnesota is a Sioux word meaning "land of sky-tinted water".

French explorers in the sixteenth century encountered prairies to the south and, in the north, dense forests whose abundant waterways were an ideal breeding ground for beavers and muskrats. Admitted to the Union in 1858, the new state of Minnesota was at first settled by Germans and Scandinavians, who farmed in the west and south. Other ethnic groups followed, many drawn by the massive **iron ore** deposits of north central Minnesota, which are expected to hold out for two more centuries.

More than half of all Minnesotans live in the southeast, around the Twin Cities of **Minneapolis** and **St Paul**. Together these two cities function as the Midwest's great civic double act for their combined cultural, recreational and business opportunities.

Smaller cities include the northern shipping port of **Duluth**, the gateway to the Scenic Hwy-61 lakeshore drive.

Minneapolis and St Paul

Commonly known as the **Twin Cities**, **MINNEAPOLIS** (a hybrid Sioux/Greek word meaning "water city") and **ST PAUL** are competitive yet complementary. Fraternally rather than identically twinned, they may be even better places to live than they are to visit, thanks to their cleanliness, cultural activity, social awareness and relatively low crime rates.

Only a twenty-minute expressway ride separates the respective downtowns, but each has its own character, style and strengths. **St Paul**, the state capital – originally called Pig's Eye, after a scurrilous French-Canadian fur trader who sold whiskey at a Mississippi River landing in the 1840s – is the staid, slightly older sibling, careful to preserve its buildings and traditions. The compact but stately downtown is built, like Rome, on seven hills: the **Capitol** and the **Cathedral** occupy one each, both august monuments that keep the city mindful of its responsibilities.

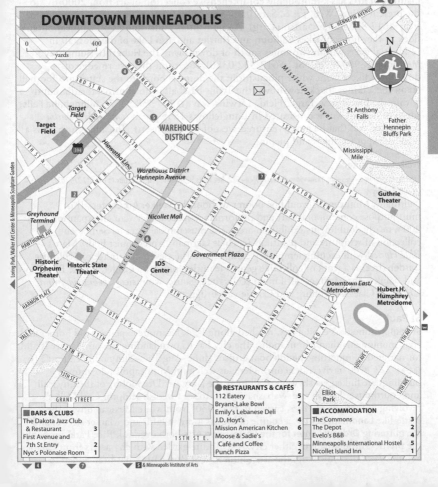

DOWNTOWN MINNEAPOLIS

RESTAURANTS & CAFÉS	
112 Eatery	5
Bryant-Lake Bowl	7
Emily's Lebanese Deli	1
J.D. Hoyt's	4
Mission American Kitchen	6
Moose & Sadie's Café and Coffee	3
Punch Pizza	2

BARS & CLUBS	
The Dakota Jazz Club & Restaurant	3
First Avenue and 7th St Entry	2
Nye's Polonaise Room	1

ACCOMMODATION	
The Commons	3
The Depot	2
Evelo's B&B	4
Minneapolis International Hostel	5
Nicollet Island Inn	1

Minneapolis, founded on money generated by the Mississippi's hundreds of flour-and sawmills, is livelier, artier and more modern, with up-to-date architecture and an upbeat attitude. The residents are spread over wider ground than in St Paul, and dozens of lakes and parks underscore the city's appeal.

Minneapolis

Downtown Minneapolis is laid out on a simple grid. The riverfront, dubbed the **Mississippi Mile**, continues to be developed as a place for strolling, dining and entertainment. The vast Third Avenue Bridge makes an ideal vantage point for viewing **St Anthony Falls**, a controlled torrent in a wide stretch of the river.

Downtown's major stores line up along the pedestrianized **Nicollet Mall**, which runs along Nicollet Avenue between Washington Avenue S and 13th Street S. Hennepin Avenue, the other main drag, is a block west. The area is anchored by the beautifully restored **Orpheum** and **State theatres**, twin hosts to top-quality Broadway shows and concerts. The ultra-modern **Guthrie Theater**, 818 S Second St (☎612 377 2224, ⓦguthrietheater.org), opened in 2006 on the riverfront.

One mile south from downtown, at 2400 Third Ave S, the huge **Minneapolis Institute of Arts** has a thoroughly comprehensive collection of art from 2000 BC to the present (Tues, Wed, Fri & Sat 10am–5pm, Thurs 10am–9pm, Sun 11am–5pm; free; ☎612 870 3200, ⓦartsmia.org). Arctic winters aside, hordes of Minneapolitans flock to the shores of lakes **Calhoun** and **Harriet** and also **Lake of the Isles**, all in residential areas within two miles south of downtown. The **Hubert H. Humphrey Metrodome**, 900 S Fifth St (☎612 332 0386), squats on the eastern edge of downtown like a giant white pincushion; the dome is home to the state's pro football team, the Vikings. Back downtown the Twins baseball team controls the diamond within the brand-new Target Field, 1 Twins Way (☎800 338 9467). **Minnehaha Falls,** south of downtown, was featured in Longfellow's 1855 poem *Song of Hiawatha* despite the fact that he never ventured west of Massachusetts. The adjacent park is a favourite spot for hikes and picnics.

Walker Art Center

1750 Hennepin Ave S • Tues–Sun 11am–5pm, Thurs till 9pm • $12, free Thurs 5–9pm and first Sat of month • ☎ 612 375 7622, ⓦ walkerart.org

Culturally, Minneapolis would be poorer without the **Walker Art Center**. This multipurpose contemporary art and performance space underwent an expansion in 2005, nearly doubling its exhibition area. The museum balances its permanent collection of sculpture and paintings (such as German Expressionist Franz Marc's *Blue Horses*) with exciting temporary exhibitions. The eleven-acre outdoor **Sculpture Garden** (free) is a work of collective genius featuring pieces by Calder, Louise Bourgeois and Frank Gehry. Its most striking piece is the gigantic, whimsical *Spoonbridge and Cherry* by Claes Oldenburg and Coosje van Bruggen.

St Paul

St Paul, Minnesota's capital city, reached along I-94, has more expensive old homes and civic monuments than Minneapolis. The city has its own landing site on Harriet Island for narrated summertime **paddleboat** cruises (June–Aug Tues–Sun noon & 2pm; $16; ☎651 227 1100, ⓦriverrides.com). Here, as well as in Minneapolis, downtown buildings are linked via skyways. Call in at the jazzy Art Deco lobby of the **City Hall and Courthouse,** Fourth and Wabasha streets, to see Swedish sculptor Carl Milles' revolving 36ft *Vision of Peace*, carved in the 1930s from white Mexican onyx. The castle-like **Landmark Center,** a couple of blocks away at Fifth and Market streets, and the glittering **Ordway Center for the Performing Arts** both overlook Rice Park, probably the prettiest little square in either city. A sculpture garden with characters from Charles Schulz's *Peanuts* comic strip, the artist himself a St Paul native, has been added to

DOWNTOWN ST PAUL

N

RESTAURANTS & CAFÉS

Downtowner Woodfire Grill	2
Mickey's Dining Car	4
Saint Paul Grill	6
Sakura	1
Trattoria DaVinci	3
W.A. Frost	5

BARS & CLUBS

| Muddy Pig | 2 |
| Tom Reid's Hockey City Pub | 1 |

ACCOMMODATION

Best Western Bandana Square	1
The Covington Inn	3
The Saint Paul Hotel	2

Schulz Park next to the Landmark Center. A few blocks east, **Town Square Park** is a lush, multilevel indoor garden in a shopping complex at Minnesota and Sixth streets.

Kellogg Boulevard

The broad and well-landscaped **Kellogg Boulevard** is the front yard of the gorgeous granite and limestone **Minnesota History Center**, at no.345 (Tues 10am–8pm, Wed–Sat 10am–5pm, Sun noon–5pm; holidays open Mon 10am–5pm; $11; ☎651 259 3000, ⓦmnhs.org), which with its extensive research facilities and some inventive exhibits for the more casual visitor, is the best place to grasp the state's story. An immense steel iguana is the doorkeeper at the exciting hands-on **Science Museum of Minnesota**, 120 W Kellogg Blvd (daily 9.30am–9.30pm; $20; ☎651 221 9444, ⓦsmm.org), which also has a domed Omnitheater (entry included in ticket) for giant-screen films.

Summit Avenue

A well-preserved five-mile Victorian boulevard, **Summit Avenue**, leads away from downtown. **F. Scott Fitzgerald**, who was born close by, finished his first success, *This Side of Paradise*, in 1918 while living in a modest rowhouse at no. 599. He disparaged

> **FESTIVALS IN ST PAUL**
>
> Annual celebrations in St Paul include the **Taste of Minnesota** (tons of food, live entertainment, rides and fireworks) running from late June to July 4 on Harriet Island, and the nation's largest **State Fair** (end Aug to early Sept). The **Winter Carnival** (late Jan to early Feb) is a frosty gala designed to make the most of the season with ice and snow sculpting, hot-air ballooning, team sports, parades and more. The visitor centre (see below) has details of all events.

the avenue as a "museum of American architectural failures". Look for the coffin atop no. 465, once the home of an undertaker, and visit the **James J. Hill House** at no. 240, a railroad baron's sumptuous mansion from around 1891 (tours every 30min Wed–Sat 10am–3.30pm, Sun 1–3.30pm; $9; reservations recommended; ☎651 297 2555).

Another good bet is the venerable and picturesque **Como Park Zoo and Marjorie McNeely Conservatory** (daily: April–Sept 10am–6pm; Oct–March 10am–4pm; $3 donation requested; ☎651 487 8200), reached by taking I-94 to the Lexington Avenue exit, then continuing north on Lexington for about three miles. Highlights here include a herd of rambunctious bison and an eye-opening exhibit dedicated to frogs, appropriately titled "Ribbit Zibit".

The Mall of America

I-494 at 24th Ave, Bloomington • Mon–Sat 10am–9.30pm, Sun 11am–7pm • ☎952 883 8800, ⊛mallofamerica.com • 20min south of the cities – take bus #54M from St Paul's West Sixth Street at Cedar, the #5E bus or the light rail from downtown Minneapolis; catch the train from 5th St on Nicollet Mall

Shopping addicts make the pilgrimage to the **Mall of America** from all over the Midwest – and far beyond. Opened in 1992, this mind-boggling 4.2-million-square-foot, four-storey monument to consumerism incorporates more than five hundred stores, with a seven-acre Nickelodeon Universe theme park. Featured rides include **UnderWater Adventures** ($18.99), with 1.2 million gallons of water and amazing Gulf of Mexico and Caribbean aquariums. Evidence of the Mall's all-under-one-roof convenience is provided by the **Chapel of Love** retail store, where more than five thousand couples have legitimately tied the knot.

ARRIVAL AND DEPARTURE   MINNEAPOLIS AND ST PAUL

By plane Twin Cities International Airport lies about 10 miles south of either city in suburban Bloomington. Super Shuttle Minneapolis (☎612 827 7777) takes travellers between the airport and major hotels for around $18, while some lodgings provide their own transport. Taxis to Minneapolis will set you back close to $43, and to St Paul $32. You can also take the Hiawatha light rail system (☎612 373 3333, ⊛metrotransit.org) into Minneapolis (daily 4am–1am: $1.75–2.25), or bus #54 to St Paul (same hours: $1.75–2.25).

By bus The Greyhound bus terminals, both in convenient downtown locations, are at 950 Hawthorne Ave (☎612 371 3325) in Minneapolis and the Union Depot, 214 4th St E (☎651 222 0507) in St Paul.
Destinations Chicago (5 daily; 9hr); Milwaukee (7 daily; 6hr).
By train The Amtrak train station is conveniently located at the grand old Union Depot at 214 E 4th St.
Destinations Chicago (1 daily; 7hr); Milwaukee (1 daily; 5hr).

GETTING AROUND AND INFORMATION

By light rail The 12-mile-long Hiawatha Light Rail line is a nice way to explore Minneapolis and calls at the Mall of America, Target Field and Nicollet Mall.
By bus Metro Transit buses (☎612 373 3333) make both cities relatively easy to explore without a car.

Minneapolis visitor centre 250 Marquette Ave (Mon–Fri 8am–5pm; ☎612 767 8000, ⊛minneapolis.org).
St Paul visitor centre 75 W 5th St (Mon–Fri 8am–5pm; ☎651 265 4900, ⊛visitsaintpaul.com).

ACCOMMODATION

You're likely to pay more for lodgings downtown than in the suburbs, where dozens of cheap motels line I-494 near the airport, though some of the pricier central hotels offer reduced rates and special package deals on weekends. The pretty riverside community of Stillwater, 25 miles from St Paul via I-35 N and Hwy-36 E, has many grand old B&Bs and motels

(☎ 651 439 4001 for information). For B&B options in the Twin Cities, consult ⊛ bedandbreakfast.com, as many B&Bs do not have their own websites.

MINNEAPOLIS

The Commons 615 Washington Ave SE ☎ 612 379 8888, ⊛ commonshotel.com. Tucked right next to the University of Minnesota's campus, this property is good value and convenient for those with university business. **$109**

★ **The Depot** 225 Third Ave S ☎ 612 375 1700, ⊛ thedepotminneapolis.com. The historic *Depot* building recently underwent massive renovations and now boasts an enormous indoor water park, luxury accommodation, dining and even an ice rink. Check for packages or specials to keep the cost down. **$159**

Evelo's B&B 2301 Bryant Ave S ☎ 612 374 9656. Three comfortable rooms in a well-preserved Victorian home near bus lines, lakes and downtown. Non-smoking only. **$85**

★ **Minneapolis International House** 2400 Stevens Ave ☎ 612 874 0407, ⊛ minneapolishostel.com. This conveniently situated independent hostel has private rooms and dorm beds. Dorms **$28**, rooms **$60**

Nicollet Island Inn 95 Merriam St ☎ 612 331 1800, ⊛ nicolletislandinn.com. Pricey, mid-river establishment with the edge on other downtown hotels because of its delightful location and excellent restaurant. **$179**

ST PAUL

Best Western Bandana Square 1010 Bandana Blvd W ☎ 651 647 1637, ⊛ bestwestern.com. Straightforward rooms and a nice indoor pool and sauna housed in a former railroad car repair shop. **$145**

The Covington Inn Pier 1, Harriet Island ☎ 651 292 1411, ⊛ covingtoninn.com. A one-of-a-kind B&B in a converted towboat facing downtown. **$180**

★ **The Saint Paul Hotel** 350 Market St ☎ 651 292 9292, ⊛ stpaulhotel.com. This grand, 1910 establishment is Minnesota's top hotel. Rooms tend to be smaller than those of other luxury hotels, but the staff and atmosphere make up for it. The *St Paul Grill* provides some of the city's finest dining, while the classy bar has tons of great scotches and cognacs. **$219**

EATING

Preconceptions of Midwestern blandness are swiftly put to rest by an almost bewildering array of restaurants in the Twin Cities. In Minneapolis, head for the downtown warehouse district, the southerly Nicollet neighbourhood, the funky Uptown and Lyn-Lake areas, or the university's Dinkytown. In St Paul, try Galtier Plaza downtown, the Asian restaurants on University Avenue or the horde of ethnic options along Grand Avenue.

MINNEAPOLIS

112 Eatery 112 N 3rd St ☎ 612 343 7696. This small, upscale café serves an inventive mix of American and continental dishes, from pork tenderloin to sautéed sweetbreads. Mon–Thurs 5pm–midnight, Fri & Sat 5pm–1am, Sun 5–10pm.

★ **Bryant-Lake Bowl** 810 W Lake St ☎ 612 825 3737. Bowling and fantastic food rarely go hand-in-hand, but this Lyn-Lake institution manages to do both well, turning out such creative dishes as organic chicken wings and a pulled pork sandwich that could hold its own in North Carolina. Daily 8am–2am.

Emily's Lebanese Deli 641 University Ave NE ☎ 612 379 4069. Friendly, low-cost local place for Lebanese staples. Mon, Wed, Thurs & Sun 9am–9pm, Fri & Sat 9am–10pm.

J.D. Hoyts 301 Washington Ave N ☎ 612 338 1560. A traditional supper club serving down-home food at good prices. The grilled catfish is quite good and the grilled bananas are worth a try. Mon–Sat 4pm–1am, Sun 10am–1am.

★ **Mission American Kitchen** 77 S 7th St ☎ 612 339 1000. A great choice for lunch and dinner, serving delicious and creative starters such as truffle cream cheese wontons

and devilled eggs. Mon–Fri 11am–2.30pm & 5–10pm, Sat 5–10pm.

★ **Moose & Sadie's Café and Coffee** 212 3rd Ave ☎ 612 371 0464. This great breakfast and lunch spot in the warehouse district has yummy baked goods and soups including coconut milk curry. Mon–Fri 7am–8pm, Sat & Sun 9am–2pm.

Punch Pizza 210 Hennepin Ave ☎ 612 623 8114. Popular Neapolitan pizzas are produced in the stylish wood-fired oven here. Daily 11am–10pm.

ST PAUL

★ **Downtowner Woodfire Grill** 253 W 7th St ☎ 651 228 9500. This neighbourhood restaurant is ideal if you plan to catch a local football game or just enjoy dinner. Weekends have live jazz music starting at 8pm. Mon 7am–10pm, Tues–Thurs 7am–10.30pm, Fri & Sat 7am–11pm, Sun 8am–9pm.

Mickey's Dining Car 36 W 7th St ☎ 651 698 0259. A landmark, always-open diner in a 1930s dining car. Daily 24hr.

St Paul Grill 350 Market St ☎ 651 224 7455. Traditional American dishes are on the menu in this classic downtown hotel. Daily 11am–2pm & 5.30–10pm.

4

★ **Sakura** 350 St Peter St ☎651 224 0185. Fresh sushi in a relaxing environment, with a great long sushi bar and a smooth vibe. Mon–Sat 11.30am–2.30pm & 5.30–10.30pm, Sun noon–2.30pm & 4–9.30pm.

Trattoria DaVinci 400 Sibley St ☎651 222 4050. Exceptional Northern Italian cuisine served in an Italian Renaissance-inspired setting. Tues–Thurs 11am–9pm, Fri 11am–10pm, Sat 5–10pm.

★ **W.A. Frost** 374 Selby Ave and Western Ave ☎651 224 5715. This former pharmacy and F. Scott Fitzgerald hangout has been converted into a plush restaurant with a garden patio. The menu spans Mediterranean, Asian and Middle Eastern cuisines and features dishes such as mushroom Wellington and squash ravioli; the wine cellar stocks some 3000 bottles. Mon–Thurs 11am–11.30pm, Fri 11am–12.30am, Sat 10.30am–12.30am, Sun 10.30am–11.30pm.

NIGHTLIFE AND ENTERTAINMENT

Unusually, nightlife in Minneapolis (and, to a lesser extent, St Paul) hasn't been siphoned off by suburbia – 100,000 students ensure a vibrant club scene. The Greater Twin Cities have been dubbed a "cultural Eden on the prairie", where 2.5 million people support upwards of one hundred theatre companies, more than forty dance troupes, twenty classical music ensembles and more than a hundred art galleries. Sir Tyrone Guthrie began the theatrical boom back in 1963, enrolling large-scale local assistance to establish the classical repertory company named for him. The cities now have more theatres per capita than anywhere in the USA apart from New York City. For complete entertainment information and listings, check out the ubiquitous free weekly *City Pages*.

MINNEAPOLIS BARS AND CLUBS

★ **The Dakota Jazz Club and Restaurant** 1010 Nicollet Mall ☎612 332 1010, ⓦdakotacooks.com. Gourmet Midwestern food and great local and national jazz acts downtown. Cover $15–25. Mon–Sat 11.30am–11pm, Sun 5.30–9pm.

First Avenue and 7th St Entry 701 1st Ave ☎612 338 8388 or ☎612 332 1775, ⓦfirst-avenue.com. The landmark rock venue where Prince's *Purple Rain* was shot still packs them in with top bands and dance music. Cover $5–15. Daily 8pm–1am.

Nye's Polonaise Room 112 E Hennepin Ave ☎651 379 2021. Experience old-European atmosphere at the piano and polka bars and in the Polish-American restaurant. The karaoke is without equal in the Twin Cities. Mon–Thurs 4pm–2am, Fri & Sat 11am–2am, Sun 4pm–1am.

ST PAUL BARS

Muddy Pig 162 N Dale St ☎651 254 1030. A hip neighbourhood joint with good bar food and a wide selection of microbrews. Mon–Thurs 11.3am–1am, Fri & Sat 11.30am–2am.

Tom Reid's Hockey City Pub 258 W 7th St ☎651 292 9916. This pre- and post-game hangout is where locals gather to honour the state's favourite sport. Daily 11am–2am.

THEATRES

Chanhassen Dinner Theater 501 W 78th St, Chanhassen (24 miles west of Minneapolis) ☎952 934 1525. Mainstream musicals, popular comedies and drama on four stages, plus meals, 30min from downtown.

Fitzgerald Theater 10 E Exchange St, St Paul ☎651 290 1200, ⓦfitzgeraldtheater.org. Best known as the venue for Garrison Keillor's weekly *A Prairie Home Companion* recording, it also hosts other concerts and lectures.

Great American History Theater 30 E 10th St, St Paul ☎651 292 4323, ⓦhistorytheatre.com. Original plays deal with events and personalities from the region's past, such as productions based on Vietnam War oral histories and swing music showcases.

Park Square 20 W 7th Place, St Paul ☎651 291 7005, ⓦparksquaretheatre.org. The venue for well-executed classic and contemporary plays.

Penumbra 270 N Kent St, St Paul ☎651 224 3180, ⓦpenumbratheatre.org. African American theatre company focusing, not surprisingly, on works by African American playwrights.

Duluth

DULUTH, at the western extremity of Lake Superior, 150 miles north of Minneapolis and St Paul, forms a long crescent at the base of the **Arrowhead**, the northeastern stretch of Minnesota poking into Lake Superior. Named for a seventeenth-century French officer, Daniel Greysolon, Sieur du Luth (1636–1710), the town cascades down from the granite bluffs surrounding **Skyline Drive** (an exhilarating 30-mile route) to a busy **harbour**, shared with Superior, Wisconsin. Together these "twin ports" constitute the largest inland harbour in the USA.

In the 1980s, Duluth went through a rebuilding period and began to encourage tourism. The main drawback is that it's bitingly **cold** here. The seaway is frozen through the winter, and even spring and autumn evenings can be chilly. Temperatures are always significantly cooler near the lake – the location of nearly all the attractions and activities.

From the visitor centre (see below), a short walk down Lake Avenue leads to the free **Marine Museum** (June to early Oct daily 10am–9pm; early Oct to June times vary; ☎ 218 727 2497, ⊛ lsmma.com) in Canal Park, a vantage point for watching big boats from around the world pass under the delightfully archaic Aerial Lift Bridge. Originating at Canal Park, Duluth's **Lakewalk** is the free way to take in the view and it's a great way to get a sense of the surrounding marine industrial landscape. Also worthwhile is a visit to the stately lakeside Jacobean Revival mansion **Glensheen**, 3300 London Rd (May–Oct daily 9.30am–4pm; Nov–April Sat & Sun 11am–2pm; $15; ☎ 218 726 8910). The vast interior features finely crafted original furnishings, and the grounds are immaculate.

At 506 W Michigan St, the **Depot** complex (daily June–Aug 9.30am–6pm; Sept–May 10am–5pm; $12) houses the Lake Superior Railroad Museum, a children's museum, cultural heritage centre and an art museum, and is the starting point for some local rail excursions (see below); at night, it's home to performing arts companies.

ARRIVAL, INFORMATION AND ACTIVITIES   DULUTH

By bus Greyhound buses pull in 4 miles south of town just off I-35 at 4426 Grand Ave.

Visitor centre 21 W Superior St suite 100 (Mon–Fri 8.30am–5pm; ☎ 218 722 4011, ⊛ visitduluth.com).

Activities VistaFleet operates 90min harbour cruises

(May–Oct; $14; ☎ 218 722 6218, ⊛ vistafleet.com). The North Shore Scenic Railroad Company runs rail excursions along the Superior shoreline to the busy Two Harbors community, departing from the Depot complex (early May to mid-Oct Fri–Sun; $15; ☎ 218 722 1273).

ACCOMMODATION AND EATING

Charles Weiss Inn 1615 E Superior St ☎ 218 724 7016, ⊛ acweissinn.com. A nice Victorian-styled B&B in a quiet residential neighbourhood. $109

Edgewater Resort and Waterpark 2400 London Rd ☎ 218 728 3601, ⊛ duluthwaterpark.com. This place boasts an elaborate indoor water park, complete with several splash pools. The rooms are family friendly, and they all include pull-out cots. $129

Fitger's Brewhouse Brewery and Grille 600 E Superior St ☎ 218 279 2739. A brewhouse where the pale ale is quite fine and the Lake Superior smoked fish wrap makes an uncommonly good accompaniment. Mon & Sun 11am–midnight, Tues 11am–1am, Wed–Sat

11am–2am.

Indian Point West off Hwy-23, at 75th St and Grand Ave ☎ 218 624 5637. A rather basic, but well-kept campground with summer bayside tent sites and full hookups also available. A small store on the premises also provides basic sundries and camping supplies. Tents $37, RV hookups $45

Northern Waters Smokehaus 394 S Lake Ave ☎ 218 724 7307. Smoked fish is quite big in Duluth and this place has perhaps the best offerings in town. They don't just do smoked fish, as you'll notice In sandwiches such as the Silence of the Lambwich and the Pastrami Mommy. Mon–Sat 10am–8pm, Sun 10am–6pm.

Highway 61 and around

Memorialized on vinyl by Minnesota native Bob Dylan, stunning **Scenic Highway 61** follows Lake Superior for 150 miles northeast from Duluth to the US/Canadian border, its precipitous cliffs interspersed with pretty little ports and picture-postcard picnic sites.

At **Gooseberry River State Park**, forty miles along from Duluth, the river splashes over volcanic rock through waterfalls and cascades to its outlet in Lake Superior. Like all but one of the seven other state parks along Hwy-61, it provides access to the rugged three-hundred-mile **Superior Hiking Trail** (☎ 218 834 2700), divided into easily manageable segments for day-trekkers.

THE GUNFLINT TRAIL

The unpaved sixty-mile **Gunflint Trail** from Grand Marais cuts the wilderness in two; otherwise there are no roads in this backcountry, let alone electricity or telephones. Most lakes remain motor-free, and stringent rules limit entry to the wilderness. For those who don't want to rough it, several rustic lodges lie strung out along the trail; contact the Gunflint Trail Association (☎ 218 387 3191, ⓦ gunflint-trail.com) for more information.

Just beyond **Cascade River State Park**, the road dips into the somnolent little port of **GRAND MARAIS**, where a walk around the photogenic Circular Harbor will soon cure car-stiff legs. The **visitor centre** here (see below) has lists of **outfitters** for those heading west into the **Boundary Waters Canoe Area Wilderness**, a paradise for canoeing, backpacking and fishing. It's one of the most heavily used wilderness areas in the country; overland trails, or "portages", link more than a thousand lakes and in winter you can ski and dogsled cross-country.

The town of **GRAND PORTAGE**, just below the Canadian border, is at the lake end of the historic Eight-and-a-half-mile portage route – so vital to the nineteenth-century fur trade – now preserved in the form of **Grand Portage National Monument**, where a clutch of fur-trade-era buildings has been superbly reconstructed. In town, residents of the Grand Portage Indian Reservation operate a **casino**. In summer, ferries run daily to remote **Isle Royale National Park** (see p.270).

INFORMATION AND ACCOMMODATION   HIGHWAY 61 AND AROUND

Visitor centre 13 N Broadway, Grand Marais (☎ 218 387 2524, ⓦ grandmarais.com).

Camping To camp at any of the state parks along here, reserve on ☎ 866 857 2757.

Voyageurs National Park

Set along the border lakes between Minnesota and Canada, **VOYAGEURS NATIONAL PARK** is like no other in the US national park system. To see it properly, or indeed to grasp its immense beauty at all, you need to leave your car behind and venture into the wild by boat. Once out on the lakes, you're in a great, silent world. Kingfishers, osprey and eagles swoop down for their share of the abundant walleye; moose and bear stalk the banks.

The park's name comes from the intrepid eighteenth-century French-Canadian trappers, who needed almost a year to get their pelts back to Montréal in primitive birch bark canoes. Their "customary waterway" became so established that the treaty of 1783 ending the American Revolution specified it as the international border.

You can't do Voyageurs justice on a day-trip, though daily cruises from the Rainy Lake visitor centre (see opposite) do at least allow a peek at the lake country. If you're here for a few days, rent a **boat** (figure on $50 a day) and camp out. It's easy to get lost in this maze of islands and rocky outcrops, and unseen sandbanks lurk beneath the surface. If you're at all unsure, hire a guide from one of the resorts for the first day (around $250/8hr day). During **freeze-up** – usually from December until March – the park takes on a whole new aura as a prime destination for skiers and snowmobilers.

Once inside the park, you need to take a few **precautions**. Check (natural) mercury levels in fish before eating them, don't pick wild rice (only Native Americans may do this), be wary of Lyme Disease (a tick-induced gastric illness), boil drinking water and watch out for bears. Discuss such matters, along with customs procedures, in case you plan to paddle into Canadian waters, with a ranger before venturing out.

ARRIVAL AND INFORMATION

By car Most travellers access Voyageurs from Hwy-53, which runs northwest from Duluth. After just over 100 miles, at Orr, it intersects with Rte-23, which runs northeast toward Crane Lake, at the eastern end of the park.

Visitor centres About 28 and 31 miles beyond Hwy-53's junction with Rte-23, highways 129 and 122 lead, respectively, to the visitor centres at Ash River (May–Sept

VOYAGEURS NATIONAL PARK

daily 9am–5pm; ☎ 218 374 3221) and Kabetogama Lake (same hours; ☎ 218 875 2111). Another prime visitor centre is at Rainy Lake, at the westernmost entrance, 36 miles farther on via International Falls (daily mid-May to Sept 9am–5pm; Oct to mid-May Wed–Sun same hours; from $12–20 for a range of tours; ☎ 218 286 5258, ⓦ nps.gov/voya).

ACCOMMODATION

Camping You can camp on one of the many scattered islands, most plentiful around Crane Lake. There are also first-come, first-served state-owned campgrounds on the mainland at Ash River and Woodenfrog, near Kabetogama. $12

Kettle Falls Hotel 12977 Chippewa Trail, Kabetogama ☎ 218 240 1724 (May–Oct) or ☎ 218 875 2070 (Nov–April), ⓦ kettlefallshotel.com. A perfectly rustic way to experience Voyageurs, with a wide range of lodging options, day-trips and boat rentals. From $80

4

The Capital Region

NATIONAL GALLERY OF ART EAST BUILDING,
WASHINGTON DC

5

The Capital Region

The city of Washington, in the District of Columbia, and the four surrounding states of Virginia, West Virginia, Maryland and Delaware are collectively known as the Capital Region. Since the days of the first American colonies, US history has been shaped here, from the Jamestown landings to agitation for Independence, to the battles of the Revolutionary and Civil wars to 1960s Civil Rights milestones and protest movements on issues including war, abortion and gay rights.

Early in the seventeenth century, the first British settlements began to take root along the rich estuary of the **Chesapeake Bay**; the colonists hoped for gold but found their fortunes instead in tobacco. Virginia, the first settlement, was the largest and most populous. Half of its people were **slaves**, brought from Africa to do the backbreaking work of harvesting the "noxious weed" of tobacco. Despite its central position on the East Coast, almost all the region lies below the Mason-Dixon Line – the imaginary line between North and South, drawn up in 1763 to resolve a border dispute, but which became the symbolic boundary between free and unfree states. Slaves helped build the Capitol, and until the Civil War one of the country's busiest slave markets was just two blocks from the White House.

Tensions between North and South finally erupted into the **Civil War**, of which traces are still visible everywhere. The hundred miles between the capital of the Union – Washington DC – and that of the Confederacy – Richmond, Virginia – were a constant and bloody battleground for four long years between 1861 and 1865.

Washington DC itself, with its magnificent monuments and terrific museums, is an essential stop on any tour of the region, or of the country. **Virginia**, to the south, is home to hundreds of historic sites, from the estates of revolutionary leaders and early politicians to the Colonial capital of **Williamsburg**, as well as the narrow forested heights of **Shenandoah National Park** along the crest of the Blue Ridge Mountains. Much greater expanses of wilderness, crashing whitewater rivers and innumerable backwoods villages await you in far less-visited **West Virginia**. Most tourists come to **Maryland** for the maritime traditions of Chesapeake Bay, though many of its quaint old villages have been gentrified by weekend pleasure-boaters. **Baltimore** is full of character, enjoyably unpretentious if a bit ramshackle, while **Annapolis**, the pleasant state capital, is linked by bridge and ferry to the Eastern Shore. **New Castle**, across the border in **Delaware**, is a well-preserved colonial-era town; nearby are some of the East Coast's best (and least crowded) beaches.

Washington DC

WASHINGTON, DISTRICT OF COLUMBIA (the boundaries of the two are identical) can be unbearably hot and humid in summer, and bitterly cold in winter. It was chosen as the site of the **capital** of the newly independent United States of America because of a

Great regional drives p.319
Smithsonian essentials p.325
Spectator sports in Washington DC p.338

Tickets for Colonial Williamsburg p.347
Chincoteague's Pony Swim p.352

Highlights

❶ National Gallery of Art, Washington DC
One of the country's premier Institutions for art
and culture, laid out in spacious, elegant
surroundings on the National Mall. **See p.326**

❷ Georgetown, Washington DC Though now
part of Washington, this eighteenth-century
neighbourhood long predates the capital and
draws visitors with its architecture, dining and
shopping. **See p.331**

❸ Colonial Williamsburg, VA This reconstruction of colonial America, apothecaries and all,
makes for a fun and interesting trip. **See p.347**

❹ Monticello, VA Thomas Jefferson's home is
as much an architectural icon as it is a symbol of
democracy. **See p.353**

❺ New River Gorge, WV A spectacular river
canyon with a 1000ft chasm carved in steep-
walled limestone cliffs – one of the country's
outstanding natural attractions. **See p.362**

❻ The Du Pont mansions, DE Wilmington is
the site of some of the East Coast's greatest,
most palatial mansions, once owned by the
industrialist Du Pont family, and now open to
the public. **See p.377**

HIGHLIGHTS ARE MARKED ON THE MAP ON P.318

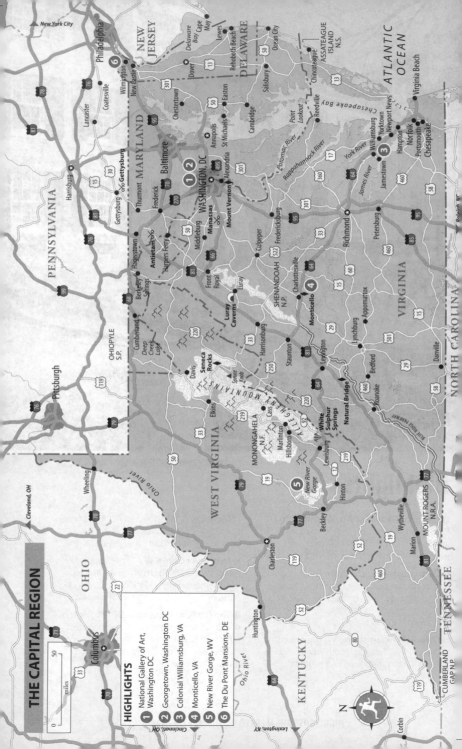

GREAT REGIONAL DRIVES

Blue Ridge Pkwy/Skyline Drive, VA Autumn is a particularly fine (and popular) time to travel the 215 miles of the Virginia piece of the Parkway (it goes for another 250 miles through North Carolina), or connect with the Drive for another one-hundred-plus miles along the length of Shenandoah National Park.

New River Gorge, WV Gatewood Road or State Rte-25 provides vertigo-inducing views, as does the photogenic bridge 267m above the river, in this mountainous area.

Chesapeake Bay Bridge-Tunnel, VA Try the salty over-under route on US-13 from Cape Charles on the DelMarVa peninsula into Virginia Beach.

compromise between the northern and southern states and, basically, because George Washington wanted it there – sixteen miles upstream from his Mount Vernon estate. The other side of DC, with a majority black population, is run as a virtual colony of Congress, where residents have only non-voting representation and couldn't vote in presidential elections until the 23rd amendment was passed in 1961 – the city's official licence plate reads "Taxation Without Representation".

The best times to come are during April's National Cherry Blossom Festival and the more temperate months (May, June & Sept). The nation's capital puts on quite a display for its guests, and, best of all, admission to all major attractions on the **National Mall** is always free; the most famous sites include the White House, memorials to four of the greatest presidents and the superb museums of the Smithsonian Institution. Between the Mall and the main spine of **Pennsylvania Avenue** – the route that connects Capitol Hill to the **White House** – the Neoclassical buildings of the **Federal Triangle** are home to agencies forming the hub of the national bureaucracy. In recent years, even the once-blighted area known as **Old Downtown** (north of the eastern side of the Mall), has had a dramatic uptick in visitors and nightlife around its **Penn Quarter**, centred around 7th and F streets. West of the White House, **Foggy Bottom** is another cornerstone of the federal bureaucracy.

Further northwest is the city's oldest area, **Georgetown**, where popular bars and restaurants line M Street and Wisconsin Avenue above the **Potomac River**. Other neighbourhoods to check out – especially for hotels, restaurants and bars – are **Dupont Circle** at Massachusetts, Connecticut and New Hampshire avenues, and the gentrifying community of **Adams Morgan**, a favoured destination of the weekend party crowd. More gung-ho visitors may also want to follow the Red Line Metro out to the genteel precinct of **Upper Northwest**, which offers some interesting historical neighbourhoods, along with the National Zoo. Most tourists also walk or take the short Metro ride to **Arlington** in nearby Virginia to visit the National Cemetery, burial place of John F. Kennedy.

With the US Capitol as the centre of the street grid, the District is divided into four **quadrants** – northeast, northwest, southeast and southwest. Dozens of broad **avenues**, named after states, run diagonally across a standard grid of **streets**, meeting up at monumental traffic circles like Dupont Circle. Almost all the most famous sights are on **Capitol Hill** or, running two miles west, the broad, green **National Mall**.

Brief history

Once the site of the national capital was chosen, Maryland and Virginia ceded sovereignty of a diamond-shaped tract to the federal government (though a half-century later, Virginia demanded its land back). Although George Washington's baroque, radial plan of the city was laid out in 1791 by **Pierre L'Enfant**, few buildings were erected, apart from the actual houses of government, until well into the next century. Charles Dickens, visiting in 1842, found "spacious avenues that begin in nothing and lead nowhere". After the **Civil War**, thousands of Southern blacks arrived in search of a sanctuary from racial oppression; to some extent, they found one. By the 1870s African Americans made up more than a third of the population of 150,000, but as poverty and squalor became endemic, official **segregation** was reintroduced in 1920.

5

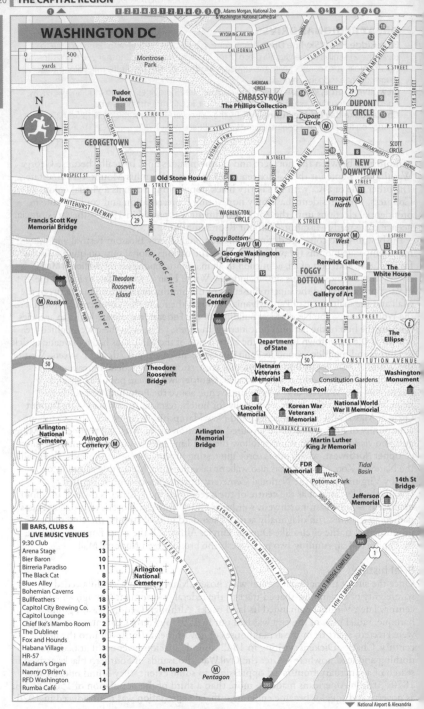

WASHINGTON DC

0   500
yards

Montrose Park

Tudor Palace

GEORGETOWN

Old Stone House

EMBASSY ROW
The Phillips Collection

Dupont Circle

DUPONT CIRCLE

NEW DOWNTOWN

SCOTT CIRCLE

Farragut North

Francis Scott Key Memorial Bridge

Foggy Bottom-GWU

George Washington University

Farragut West

Renwick Gallery

The White House

FOGGY BOTTOM

Corcoran Gallery of Art

Rosslyn

Theodore Roosevelt Island

Potomac River

Little River

Kennedy Center

The Ellipse

Department of State

Theodore Roosevelt Bridge

Vietnam Veterans Memorial

Constitution Gardens

Washington Monument

Reflecting Pool

National World War II Memorial

Arlington National Cemetery

Arlington Cemetery

Lincoln Memorial

Korean War Veterans Memorial

Arlington Memorial Bridge

Martin Luther King Jr Memorial

FDR Memorial

West Potomac Park

Tidal Basin

14th St Bridge

Jefferson Memorial

Arlington National Cemetery

Pentagon

Pentagon

■ BARS, CLUBS & LIVE MUSIC VENUES

9:30 Club	7
Arena Stage	13
Bier Baron	10
Birreria Paradiso	11
The Black Cat	8
Blues Alley	12
Bohemian Caverns	6
Bullfeathers	18
Capitol City Brewing Co.	15
Capitol Lounge	19
Chief Ike's Mambo Room	2
The Dubliner	17
Fox and Hounds	9
Habana Village	3
HR-57	16
Madam's Organ	4
Nanny O'Brien's	1
RFD Washington	14
Rumba Café	5

Adams Morgan, National Zoo & Washington National Cathedral

National Airport & Alexandria

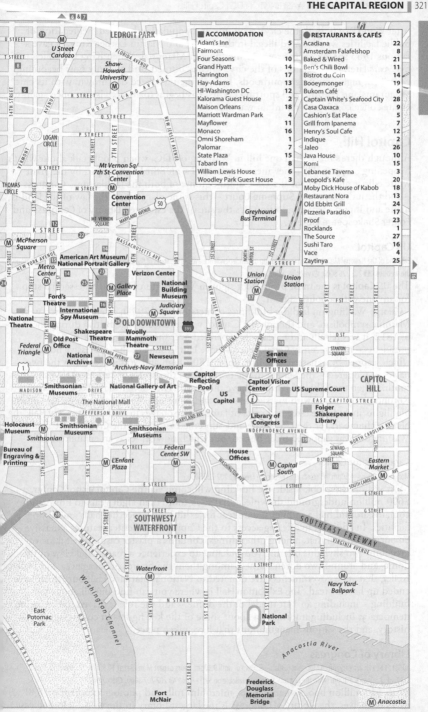

■ ACCOMMODATION	
Adam's Inn	5
Fairmont	9
Four Seasons	10
Grand Hyatt	14
Harrington	17
Hay-Adams	13
HI-Washington DC	12
Kalorama Guest House	2
Maison Orleans	18
Marriott Wardman Park	4
Mayflower	11
Monaco	16
Omni Shoreham	1
Palomar	7
State Plaza	15
Tabard Inn	8
William Lewis House	6
Woodley Park Guest House	3

● RESTAURANTS & CAFÉS	
Acadiana	22
Amsterdam Falafelshop	8
Baked & Wired	21
Ben's Chili Bowl	11
Bistrot du Coin	14
Booeymonger	19
Bukom Café	6
Captain White's Seafood City	28
Casa Oaxaca	9
Cashion's Eat Place	5
Grill from Ipanema	7
Henry's Soul Cafe	12
Indique	2
Jaleo	26
Java House	10
Komi	15
Lebanese Taverna	3
Leopold's Kafe	20
Moby Dick House of Kabob	18
Restaurant Nora	13
Old Ebbitt Grill	24
Pizzeria Paradiso	17
Proof	23
Rocklands	1
The Source	27
Sushi Taro	16
Vace	4
Zaytinya	25

After **World War II**, both the city's economy and population boomed. Segregation of public facilities was declared illegal in the 1950s, and Martin Luther King, Jr gave a famous 1963 speech on the steps of the Lincoln Memorial. When King was killed just five years later, large sections of the city's ghettos burned, and are only now becoming gentrified, high-rent neighbourhoods. Indeed, the revitalized downtown, with its chic restaurants and cultural and sporting events, has begun to attract visitors once again to an area once considered an urban wasteland.

Capitol Hill

Although there's more than one hill in Washington DC, when people talk about what's happening on "**The Hill**", they mean **Capitol Hill** – an 88ft knoll topped by the giant white edifice and dome of the US Capitol. Home of both the legislature – **Congress** – and the judiciary – the **Supreme Court** – this is the place where the law of the land is made and interpreted; in addition, it's the site of the esteemed **Library of Congress** and **Folger Shakespeare Library**.

US Capitol

East end of the National Mall, between Constitution and Independence aves • Free tours of the building require prior reservations through the website • ☎ 202 226 8000, ⓦ visitthecapitol.gov

The **US Capitol** is the most prominent sight in Washington DC and an essential stop for anyone with a political bent.

George Washington laid the building's cornerstone in 1793 in a ceremony rich with Masonic symbolism, and though the Capitol was torched by the British during the War of 1812, it was rebuilt and repeatedly expanded over the ensuing centuries. Ten presidents – most recently Gerald Ford – have lain in state in the impressive **Rotunda**, which, capped by a massive cast-iron dome 180ft high and 96ft across, links the two halves of Congress – the **Senate** in the north wing, the **House of Representatives** in the south. When the "Tholos" lantern above the dome is lit, Congress is in session. The Rotunda is decorated with massive frescoes and paintings of national heroes, and other highlights include the esteemed casts of famous personages in **National Statuary Hall**; the **historic chambers** for the US Senate and Supreme Court; and the **Crypt** where George Washington was supposed to be buried, but which now serves as an exhibition hall.

Capitol Visitor Center

Mon–Sat 8.30am–4.30pm (no reservation needed) • Free • ☎ 202 226 8000

Most visitors' first look inside the building will come via the **Capitol Visitor Center**, a $600 million underground showpiece that took more than eight years to finish and contains around half a million square feet for exhibitions, meeting halls and dining facilities. In addition to offering access to the Capitol, the Center features a massive **Emancipation Hall** that, among other things, contains a plaster cast of the Statue of Freedom, two skylights offering you a chance to experience a magisterial view of the dome, and around two dozen statues, among them the figures of Sacagawea and Helen Keller, that state governments have donated to National Statuary Hall but which have ended up here instead. The **Exhibition Hall** is where you can find out all about the building – including an 11ft model of the dome – and the role it played in the nation's democracy, including information about some of the key figures in congressional history, and the various inaugurations that have taken place.

Library of Congress

10 1st St SE • Hours vary: often Mon–Sat 8.30am–4.30pm or until 9.30pm; tours depart Mon–Sat at 10.30am, 11.30am, 12.30pm, 1.30pm, 2.30pm & 3.30pm (with the last tour time not available on Sat) • Free • ☎ 202 707 8000, ⓦ loc.gov

With 140 million books, manuscripts, microfilm rolls and photographs kept on 530 miles of shelves, the **Library of Congress** is the largest library in the world. Housed east of the Capitol in the Jefferson, Madison and John Adams buildings, it was set up to serve members of Congress in 1800. In 1870, the library became the national copyright repository, and in time it outgrew its original home. The exuberantly eclectic **Thomas Jefferson Building** opened in 1897, complete with a domed octagonal **Reading Room** and hundreds of mosaics, murals and sculptures in its stunning Great Hall. The library's huge collection is showcased on the second floor in the **main gallery**, where periodic exhibitions are based around broad subjects. You must sign up to do **research** in the collection, since this is a non-circulating library; free tours are also available.

Supreme Court

1st St NE and E Capitol St NE • Mon–Fri 9am–4.30pm • Free • ☎ 202 479 3211, ⓦ supremecourt.gov

The **Supreme Court**, which makes its judgements in a building across from the US Capitol, is the nation's final arbiter of what is and isn't legal. The federal judiciary dates to 1787, but the court didn't receive its own building until 1935, when Cass Gilbert – architect of New York's Woolworth Building – designed this Greek Revival masterpiece. From the start of October to the end of April, oral arguments are heard every Monday, Tuesday and Wednesday from 10am to noon, and 1pm to 3pm on occasion. The sessions, which almost always last an hour per case, are open to the public on a first-come, first-served basis; arrive by 8.30am if you really want one of the 150 seats.

Folger Shakespeare Library

201 E Capitol St • Mon–Sat 10am–5pm; tours Mon–Fri 11am & 3pm, Sat 11am & 1pm • Free • ☎ 202 544 4600, ⓦ folger.edu

The renowned **Folger Shakespeare Library**, on the south side of the Supreme Court, was founded in 1932 and today holds more than 600,000 items including books, manuscripts, paintings and engravings, many of them related to Shakespeare's work and background – although most are off-limits unless you're a registered researcher. The dark-oak Great Hall – with its carved lintels, stained glass, Tudor roses and sculpted ceiling – displays public exhibitions about the playwright and Elizabethan themes, and the reproduction Elizabethan Theater hosts lectures and readings as well as medieval and Renaissance music concerts. An Elizabethan garden on the east lawn grows herbs and flowers common in the sixteenth century.

The National Mall west: monuments

The elegant, two-mile-long **National Mall** stretches between the Capitol and the Lincoln Memorial and is DC's most popular green space, used for summer softball games and Fourth of July concerts. When there's a protest gesture to be made, the Mall is the place to make it. What the Mall is perhaps best known for, however, is its quartet of presidential **monuments**, along with the **White House** and the powerful **memorials** to veterans of the twentieth century's various wars.

Washington Monument

15th St NW and Constitution Ave • Daily 9am–5pm; late May to early Sept until 10pm • Free • ☎ 202 426 6841, ⓦ nps.gov/wamo

The Mall's most prominent feature, the **Washington Monument**, is an unadorned marble obelisk built in memory of George Washington. At 555ft, it's the tallest all-masonry structure in the world, towering over the city from its hilltop perch. To visit the monument pick up a ticket from the 15th Street kiosk, just south of Constitution Avenue on Madison Drive (8am–4.30pm), which allows you to turn up at a fixed time later in the day. The kiosk is first-come, first-served; tickets run out early during the peak season. You can also book a ticket in advance with the National Park Service ($1.50; ☎ 877 444 6777). Once you gain access, a seventy-second **elevator ride** whisks you past the honorary stones in the (closed) stairwell and deposits you at a level where the views are, of course, tremendous (though the windows could use some cleaning).

5

The White House

1600 Pennsylvania Ave NW • Tues–Thurs 7.30–11am, Fri 7.30am–noon, Sat 7.30am–1pm • Free • ☎ 202 456 7041, ⓦ nps.gov/whho

For nearly two hundred years, the **White House** has been the residence and office of the President of the United States. Standing at the edge of the Mall, due north from the Washington Monument at America's most famous address, this grand, Neoclassical edifice was completed in 1800 by Irish immigrant James Hoban, who modelled it on the Georgian manors of Dublin. Security at the White House is tight but somewhat looser than during the lockdown years of the Bush administration. Self-guided **tours** are offered at least one month in advance (and no more than six) on a first-come, first-served system. US citizens should submit a request through their Congressional representative, while foreign visitors should consult their embassy; the personal information you give must exactly match that on the photo ID you're required to show for entry. If you're interested in the history of the place and its occupants, walk a few blocks southeast to the **visitor centre** at 1450 Pennsylvania Ave (daily 7.30am–4pm; ☎ 202 208 1631).

Lincoln Memorial

Constitution Ave, between French and Bacon sts • Daily 24hr, staffed 9.30am–11.30pm • Free • ☎ 202 426 6841, ⓦ nps.gov/linc

The **Lincoln Memorial**, with its stately Doric columns, anchors the west end of the Mall. It's a fitting tribute to the sixteenth US president, who preserved the Union through the Civil War and provided the first step towards ending slavery in the country with his Emancipation Proclamation in 1863. During the Civil Rights March on Washington in 1963, Martin Luther King, Jr delivered his epic "I Have a Dream" speech here, and on-site protests against the Vietnam War in the 1960s fuelled the growing anti-war feeling in the country. Inside the monument, an enormous, craggy likeness of Lincoln sits firmly grasping the arms of his throne-like chair, deep in thought. Inscriptions of his two most celebrated speeches – the Gettysburg Address and the Second Inaugural Address – are carved on the south and north walls.

Rev. Martin Luther King, Jr. Memorial

1964 Independence Ave • Daily 24hr, staffed 9am–10pm • Free • ☎ 202 737 5420, ⓦ mlkmemorial.org

This rather stern-looking, full-length representation of **Martin Luther King, Jr.** met with a bit of controversy on its unveiling in October 2011. Design choices were questioned, from the stone used to Dr. King's forbidding facial expression and cross-armed stance. A quote of his, chiselled into the base, was abbreviated and inadvertently given a somewhat arrogant meaning; it was later removed. Nonetheless, it's a striking 30ft-tall portrait of the man who dreamed of a colourblind nation.

National World War II Memorial

17th St NW, at Independence Ave • Daily 24hr, staffed 9.30am–11.30pm • Free • ☎ 202 426 6841, ⓦ nps.gov/nwwm

Just west of the Washington Monument, the **National World War II Memorial** comprises two arcs around a fountain with a combined 56 stone pillars (representing the number of US states and territories at the time of the war) decorated with bronze wreaths. Quotes from FDR and Eisenhower are chiselled on the walls, and a concave wall of four thousand golden stars reminds you of the 400,000 fallen US soldiers.

Vietnam Veterans Memorial

Constitution Ave and 21st St NW • Daily 24hr, staffed 9.30am–11.30pm • Free • ☎ 202 426 6841, ⓦ nps.gov/vive

The striking wedge of black granite slashed into the green lawn of the Mall that makes up **Vietnam Veterans Memorial** serves as a sombre and powerful reminder of the 58,000 US soldiers who died in Vietnam. The pathway that slopes down from the grass forms a gash in the earth, its increasing depth symbolizing the increasing involvement of US forces in the war. The polished surface is carved with the names of every soldier who died, in chronological order from 1959 to 1975, and you can often find family members taking paper rubbings of the names of the departed.

Korean War Veterans Memorial

Independence Ave and 21st St SW • Daily 24hr, staffed 8am–11.45pm • Free • ☎ 202 426 6841, ⓦ nps.gov/kwvm

On the opposite side of the Vietnam memorial, southeast of the Lincoln Memorial, the **Korean War Veterans Memorial** has as its centrepiece a Field of Remembrance, featuring nineteen life-sized, armed combat troops sculpted from stainless steel.

Jefferson Memorial

Tidal Basin, south bank • Daily 24hr, staffed 9.30am–11.30pm • Free • ☎ 202 426 6841, ⓦ nps.gov/thje

The shallow dome of the **Jefferson Memorial**, just south of the Mall near 14th Street SW and Ohio Drive, hovers over a huge bronze statue of Thomas Jefferson, the author of the Declaration of Independence and the third US president. Just out front, the picturesque **Tidal Basin** stretches up to the Mall and offers one of the best places in town to take a break from sightseeing (or view the bright blooms of **Japanese cherry trees** in early to mid-April).

FDR Memorial

West Basin Drive SW at Ohio Drive • Daily 24hr, staffed 9.30am–11.30pm • Free • ⓦ nps.gov/fdrm

Across the Tidal Basin, the **FDR Memorial** spreads across a seven-acre site made up of a series of interlinking granite outdoor galleries – called "rooms" – punctuated by waterfalls, statuary, sculpted reliefs, groves of trees, shaded alcoves and plazas.

The National Mall east: museums

In contrast to the memorials and monuments of its western half, the **National Mall**'s eastern side is dominated by museums, most of which are part of the spectacular **Smithsonian Institution**. The Smithsonian was endowed in 1846 by Englishman James Smithson; the Institution's original home, a 1855 fantasy-medieval structure known as the **Castle**, at 1000 Jefferson Drive SW, is a commanding presence in the centre of the Mall's south side.

National Museum of American History

14th St NW and Constitution Ave • Daily 10am–5.30pm; late May to early Sept until 7.30pm or 8pm • Free • ☎ 202 633 1000, ⓦ americanhistory.si.edu

One of the prime repositories of US cultural artefacts is the **National Museum of American History**, which was imaginatively renovated in 2008. A wide common area off the lobby is lined with "**artefact walls**" that show off some of the items that the museum previously had to keep in storage – from 200-year-old tavern signs and toy chests, to the **John Bull**, the nation's oldest functioning steam locomotive, dating from 1831. Elsewhere in the museum, you're apt to find anything from George Washington's wooden teeth to Jackie Kennedy's designer dresses to Judy Garland's ruby slippers from *The Wizard of Oz*. You could easily spend a full day poking around the displays, but three to four hours would be a reasonable compromise – and to stick to this time frame, you'll have to be selective. The museum's biggest draw is the battered red, white and blue flag that inspired the US national anthem – the **Star-Spangled Banner** itself, which survived the British bombardment of Baltimore Harbor during the War of 1812 (see p.1027). Until the new **National Museum of African American History and Culture** opens on the Mall (due in 2015; ⓦ nmaahc.si.edu) exhibits from its collection are on display here.

SMITHSONIAN ESSENTIALS

The Castle acts as the main **visitor centre** (daily 8.30am–5.30pm; ☎ 202 633 1000) for the Smithsonian museums. Unless otherwise stated, all Smithsonian museums and galleries are **open daily** all year (except Dec 25) from 10am until 5.30pm, with summer hours until 7.30 or 8pm, and admission is **free**. For details on current exhibitions and events, call the visitor centre or visit the Smithsonian's website at ⓦ si.edu.

5

National Museum of Natural History
10th St NW and Constitution Ave • Daily 10am–5.30pm; late May to early Sept until 7.30pm or 8pm • Free • ☎ 202 633 1000, ⓦ mnh.si.edu

On the north side of the Mall lies the imposing, three-storey entrance rotunda of the **National Museum of Natural History**, which traces evolution from fossilized four-billion-year-old plankton to dinosaurs' eggs and beyond. In fact, the "Dinosaurs" section is the most popular part of the museum, with hulking skeletons reassembled in imaginative poses. The museum also boasts a truly exceptional array of gemstones, including the legendary 45-carat Hope Diamond, which once belonged to Marie Antoinette, and the **Gem and Mineral Hall**, which features natural and reconstructed environments, interactive exhibits and hands-on specimens. Elsewhere, the museum has some three hundred replicas focusing on mostly fur-wearing, milk-producing creatures, and the 25,000-square-foot **Ocean Hall** uses hundreds of displays and specimens – among them, a 50ft-long whale model – to explain the world of the sea. All this makes the museum an incredible educational institution, so be prepared to handle the hundreds of children scampering about.

National Gallery of Art
Constitution Ave, between 3rd and 4th sts NW • Mon–Sat 10am–5pm, Sun 11am–6pm • Free • ☎ 202 737 4215, ⓦ nga.gov

The visually stunning **National Gallery of Art** is one of the most important museums in the USA, though not part of the Smithsonian per se. The original Neoclassical gallery, opened in 1941, is now called the **West Building** and holds the bulk of the permanent collection. Galleries to the west on the main floor display major works by early- and high-Renaissance and Baroque masters, arranged by nationality: half a dozen Rembrandts fill the **Dutch** gallery, including a glowing, mad portrait of *Lucretia*; Van Eyck and Rubens dominate the **Flemish**; and El Greco, Goya and Velázquez face off in the **Spanish**. In the voluminous **Italian** galleries, there's the only da Vinci in the Americas, the 1474 *Ginevra de' Benci*, painted in oil on wood; Titian's vivid image of *Saint John the Evangelist on Patmos* and *Venus with a Mirror*; and Raphael's renowned *Alba Madonna* (1510). The other half of the West Building holds an exceptional collection of **nineteenth-century paintings** – a couple of Van Goghs, some Monet studies of Rouen Cathedral and water lilies, Cézanne still lifes and the like. For **British art**, you can find genteel portraits by Gainsborough and Reynolds, and even more evocative hazy land- and waterscapes by J.M.W. Turner. Augustus St Gaudens' magisterial battle sculpture *Memorial to Robert Gould Shaw and the Massachusetts 54th Regiment* takes up a whole room to itself.

The East Building
The National Gallery's **East Building** (same hours and admission) was opened in 1978 with an audaciously modern I.M. Pei design, dominated by a huge atrium. **European** highlights of the permanent collection include Pablo Picasso's Blue Period pieces *The Tragedy* and *Family of Saltimbanques*, along with his Cubist *Nude Woman*, and Henri Matisse's exuberant *Pianist and Checker Players*. Andy Warhol's works are as familiar as they come, with classic serial pieces *32 Soup Cans*, *Let Us Now Praise Famous Men* and *Green Marilyn*. Notable **Abstract Expressionist** works include large, hovering slabs of blurry colour by Mark Rothko, *The Stations of the Cross* by Barnett Newman and Jackson Pollock's *Number 1, 1950 (Lavender Mist)*. There's also Robert Rauschenberg's splattered, stuffed-bird sculpture known as *Canyon*, and Jasper Johns's *Targets*, which is among his most influential works.

National Air and Space Museum
Independence Ave, at 6th St SW • Daily 10am–5.30pm; late May to early Sept until 7.30pm or 8pm • Free • ☎ 202 633 1000, ⓦ nasm.si.edu

The **National Air and Space Museum** is DC's most popular attraction, and a huge draw for families of all ages. Here you can see all kinds of flying machines, rockets, satellites and assorted aeronautic gizmos, highlighted by Charles Lindbergh's **Spirit of St Louis**. Elsewhere, the "Space Race" exhibit traces the development of space flight, including an array of spacesuits from different eras, while nearby, "Rocketry and Space Flight" outlines the history of rocketry. The whimsically labelled "Wright Cycle Co." is devoted to the siblings who pioneered aeronautics; the focus is the handmade *Wright Flyer*, in which the Wrights made the first powered flight in December 1903. However, "Apollo to the Moon" is the most popular and crowded room in the museum, centring on the **Apollo 11** (1969) and **17** (1972) missions, the first and last US flights to the moon.

National Museum of the American Indian

Independence Ave, at 4th St SW • Daily 10am–5.30pm; late May to early Sept until 7.30pm or 8pm • Free • ☎ 202 633 1000, ⊛ nmai.si.edu

Skirting the Capitol Reflecting Pool along Jefferson Drive is the Smithsonian's **National Museum of the American Indian**, with undulating walls the colour of yellow earth. The collection reaches back thousands of years and incorporates nearly a million objects from all over North America and beyond – featuring fascinating ceramics, textiles and other artefacts from civilizations such as the Olmec, Maya and Inca.

Hirshhorn Museum

Independence Ave, at 7th St SW • Daily 10am–5.30pm; late May to early Sept until 7.30pm or 8pm • Free • ☎ 202 633 1000, ⊛ hirshhorn.si.edu

With its concrete facade and monumental scale, the **Hirshhorn Museum** is strongest for its modern sculpture: bronzes by Henri Matisse, masks and busts by Pablo Picasso and Brancusi's *Torso of a Young Man*, resembling a cylindrical brass phallus. The Hirshhorn's cache of modern paintings has several strengths (de Kooning, Bacon) and starts with figurative paintings from the late nineteenth and early twentieth centuries, winding its way toward Abstract Expressionism and Pop Art.

National Museum of African Art

950 Independence Ave SW • Daily 10am–5.30pm; late May to early Sept until 7.30pm or 8pm • Free • ☎ 202 633 4600, ⊛ nmafa.si.edu

The domed **National Museum of African Art** holds more than six thousand sculptures and artefacts from sub-Saharan Africa. The permanent collection has a wide range and there are plenty of rotating exhibits, which may include headrests, mostly carved from wood using an adze (cutting tool), as well as assorted ivory snuff containers, carved drinking horns, combs, pipes, spoons, baskets and cups.

National Museum of Asian Art

Arthur M. Sackler Gallery 1050 Independence Ave SW **Freer Gallery** Jefferson Drive at 12th St NW • Both galleries daily 10am–5.30pm; late May to early Sept until 7.30pm or 8pm • Free • ☎ 202 633 1000, ⊛ asia.si.edu

The two buildings that hold the collection of the **National Museum of Asian Art** are consistently fascinating. The angular and pyramidal **Arthur M. Sackler Gallery** features 3000-year-old Chinese bronzes, ritual wine containers decorated with the faces and tails of dragons, intricate jade pendants, remarkably well-preserved carved wooden cabinets and book stands, and Qing imperial porcelain embellished with symbolic figures and motifs. Hindu temple sculpture from India includes bronze, brass and granite representations of Brahma, Vishnu and Shiva; there's also a superb thirteenth-century stone carving of the elephant-headed Ganesha.

The companion **Freer Gallery** also offers a fine array of Asian art – Chinese jades and bronzes, Byzantine illuminated manuscripts, Buddhist wall sculptures and Persian metalwork. The highlight, though, is the collection of more than one thousand prints, drawings and paintings by London-based American artist James McNeill Whistler – the largest collection of his works anywhere – featuring the magnificent **Peacock Room**, with a ceiling covered with imitation gold leaf and walls painted with blue and gold peacocks. Among other works are pieces by Whistler's contemporaries, Winslow Homer and John Singer Sargent.

5

United States Holocaust Memorial Museum

100 Raoul Wallenburg Place SW • Daily 10am–6.30pm • Free; tickets for specific entry times are available free of charge from 10am each day at the 14th St entrance; you can also reserve in advance • ☎ 202 488 0400, ⓦ ushmm.org

Just off the Mall, the most important institution is the sizeable **United States Holocaust Memorial Museum**, which recalls the persecution and murder of six million Jews by the Nazis and personalizes the suffering of individual victims. Newspapers and newsreels documenting Nazi activities from the early 1930s through to the "Final Solution" are on display, plus replicas and, in many cases, actual relics, of Warsaw Ghetto streets, railroad cattle-cars and other artefacts on the top floors.

Bureau of Engraving and Printing

300 14th St SW • Access by tour only (free): Mon–Fri every 15min 9–10.45am & 12.30–2pm; arrive early for tickets March–Aug • Free • ☎ 202 874 2330, ⓦ moneyfactory.gov

The **Bureau of Engraving and Printing** is the federal agency that designs and prints all US currency, government securities and postage stamps. It's one of DC's most popular tours, netting half a million visitors annually.

Corcoran Gallery of Art

17th St NW and New York Ave • Wed–Sun 10am–5pm, Thurs closes 9pm • $10 • ☎ 202 639 1700, ⓦ corcoran.org

Just north of the Mall, the **Corcoran Gallery of Art** is one of the oldest and most respected art museums in the USA, featuring masterpieces by Frederic Edwin Church and Albert Bierstadt, and portraits by John Singer Sargent, Thomas Eakins and Mary Cassatt, among others. The mid-level paintings by Degas, Renoir, Monet, Sisley and Pissarro, however, aren't as eye-catching as the **Salon Doré** (Gilded Room), an eighteenth-century Parisian interior that's been re-created to stunning effect, with floor-to-ceiling hand-carved panelling, gold-leaf decor and ceiling murals.

Downtown and around

Those whose patience grows thin with the hordes of people on the Mall may enjoy a trip through Washington DC's **downtown** district, which in the last fifteen years has seen new boutiques, restaurants and hotels spring up in the so-called **Penn Quarter**. Adjacent to downtown is the wedge-shaped **Federal Triangle**, home to countless government agencies and the National Archives, while, to the northwest, the **New Downtown** area, known for its lobbyist-rich K Street, has swanky shops and restaurants.

National Archives

700 Pennsylvania Ave NW • Mon, Tues, Sat & Sun 10am–5.30pm, Wed–Fri 10am–9pm • Free • ☎ 202 357 5000, ⓦ archives.gov

On display at the **National Archives** are the three short texts upon which the United States was founded: the **Declaration of Independence**, the **Constitution** and the **Bill of Rights** – three original sheets of parchment secured in bomb-proof, argon-filled, glass-and-titanium containers. The impressive Neoclassical Greek building also houses temporary exhibitions with fascinating documents such as the Louisiana Purchase, the Marshall Plan, Nixon's resignation letter, the Emancipation Proclamation and the Japanese surrender from World War II. As the official repository of all US national records – census data, treaties, passport applications – the Archives also attract thousands of visitors who come here each year in search of their own genealogical, military or other records. Among the holdings are seven million pictures; 125,000 reels of film; 200,000 sound recordings; eleven million maps and charts; and a quarter of a million other artefacts.

National Portrait Gallery

8th St, at F St NW • Daily 11.30am–7pm • Free • ☎ 202 633 8300, ⓦ npg.si.edu

In the centre of the Penn Quarter, the **Old Patent Office** – a Neoclassical gem dating from 1836 – houses two of the city's major art displays: the Smithsonian's **National**

Portrait Gallery and American Art Museum. In the Portrait Gallery, striking images of figures from the performing arts include Paul Robeson as Othello; photographs of Gloria Swanson and Boris Karloff; and a rough-hewn wooden head of Bob Hope. Also worth a look are the presidential portraits – one for every man to occupy the office, from Gilbert Stuart's George Washington, an imperial study of an implacable leader, to Norman Rockwell's overly flattering portrait of Richard Nixon.

American Art Museum

American Art Museum 8th St, at F St NW • Daily 10am–5.30pm • Free • ☎ 202 633 7970, ⓦ americanart.si.edu Renwick Gallery 17th St and Pennsylvania Ave • Daily 10am–5.30pm • Free • ☎ 202 633 2850

The **American Art Museum**, in the Old Patent Office building, holds one of the more enduring of the city's art collections, which dates back to the early nineteenth century. The museum contains almost four hundred paintings by George Catlin, who spent six years touring the Great Plains, painting portraits and scenes of Native American life as well as lush landscapes. There are also notable twentieth-century modern pieces – items by Robert Motherwell, Willem de Kooning, Robert Rauschenberg, Clyfford Still, Ed Kienholz and Jasper Johns – but none more vibrant than Nam June Paik's jaw-dropping **Electronic Superhighway**, a huge, neon-outlined map of the USA. Another branch of the American Art Museum, the **Renwick Gallery**, located near the White House, offers overflow space for the museum's treasures, as well as rotating exhibits focusing on the decorative arts.

International Spy Museum

800 F St NW • Daily: usually June–Aug 9am–7pm; Sept–May 10am–6pm • $19.95 • ☎ 202 393 7798, ⓦ spymuseum.org

The **International Spy Museum** is a hugely popular DC attraction – tickets sell out days in advance during the high season – celebrating espionage in all forms, including feudal Japan's silent and deadly ninjas, surveillance pigeons armed with cameras from World War I, and infamous modern-day CIA moles such as Aldrich Ames. The museum's standouts are undoubtedly its artefacts from the height of the Cold War in the 1950s and 1960s, including tiny pistols disguised as lipstick holders, cigarette cases, pipes and torches; invisible-ink writing kits and a Get Smart!-styled shoe phone; a colourful and working model of James Bond's Aston Martin spy car; and a rounded capsule containing a screwdriver, razor and serrated knife – ominously marked "rectal tool kit".

Ford's Theatre National Historic Site

511 10th St NW • Daily 9am–5pm, closed during rehearsals and matinees • Free, advance tickets are required for entry; either turn up when the site opens to reserve them, or call ☎ 202 397 7328 • Information on ☎ 202 347 4833, ⓦ nps.gov/foth

A beautiful restoration of the nineteenth-century playhouse, **Ford's Theatre National Historic Site** continues to stage regular productions of contemporary and period drama (see p.338). It was here, on April 14, 1865, a mere five days after the end of the Civil War, that **Abraham Lincoln** was shot by the actor and Confederate zealot John Wilkes Booth during a performance of *Our American Cousin*. A grand renovation has brought the site back to vivid life, and you can see the damask-furnished presidential box, in which Lincoln sat in his rocking chair, and eye-opening items like the actual murder weapon (a .44 Derringer), a bloodstained piece of Lincoln's overcoat and Booth's knife, keys, compass, boot and diary. After he was shot, the mortally wounded president was carried across the street to the **Petersen House**, where he died the next morning. That, too, is open to the public (daily 9.30am–5.30pm; free; ☎ 202 426 6924), who troop through its gloomy parlour rooms to see a replica of Lincoln's deathbed.

National Museum of Women in the Arts

1250 New York Ave NW • Mon–Sat 10am–5pm, Sun noon–5pm • $10 • ☎ 202 783 5000, ⓦ nmwa.org

Housed in a converted Masonic Temple is the country's only major museum dedicated to female artists. The collection is arranged chronologically, starting with works from the Renaissance, on to twentieth-century works that include the classical sculpture of

5

Camille Claudel, the paintings of Georgia O'Keeffe and Tamara de Lempicka, linocuts by Hannah Höch and, most boldly, a cycle of prints depicting the hardships of working-class life by the socialist Käthe Kollwitz.

Newseum

555 Pennsylvania Ave NW • Daily 9am–5pm • $21.95 • ⓦ newseum.org

The popuar **Newseum** is an "edutainment" colossus that provides a flashy look at the greatest hits of the news biz, spread over 250,000 square feet and seven levels. You'll see how modern news is gathered and transmitted, witness pivotal moments in journalism through re-enactments, bone up on the freedoms of speech and press and get a look at the history of news as provided by the News Corporation, owner of **FOX News**.

National Building Museum

401 F St NW • Mon–Sat 10am–5pm, Sun 11am–5pm • Free • ⓦ nbm.org

The **National Building Museum** is a stirring museum of architecture. Its best feature, though, is the majestic **Great Hall**, one of the most impressive interior spaces anywhere in DC. The eight supporting columns are 8ft across at the base and more than 75ft high; each is made up of 70,000 bricks, plastered and painted to resemble Siena marble.

Dupont Circle to Upper Northwest

Beyond downtown, Washington's other key attractions are spaced out among various neighbourhoods, but they are nevertheless worth taking the time to visit. Many lie near Connecticut Avenue, running from the swanky shopping and dining area of **Dupont Circle** up to the elite precinct of **Upper Northwest** – both areas conveniently accessed by subway. Just to the northeast is the hip urban district of **Adams Morgan** – a draw for its diners, clubs and bars.

Phillips Collection

1600 21st St NW • Tues, Wed, Fri & Sat 10am–5pm, Thurs 10am–8.30pm, Sun 11am–6pm • Free admission weekdays, $10 weekends, $12 special exhibitions • ☎ 202 387 2151, ⓦ phillipscollection.org

The oldest part of the Georgian Revival brownstone housing the **Phillips Collection**, just northwest of Dupont Circle, is one of DC's key museums, and has expanded considerably in the last several years. On display are works by everyone from Renoir to Rothko (and several by non-modern artists such as Giorgione and El Greco). Highlights include signature pieces by Willem de Kooning and Richard Diebenkorn, Blue Period Picassos, Matisse's *Studio, Quai St-Michel*, a Cézanne still life, and no fewer than four van Goghs, including the powerful *Road Menders*. Top billing generally goes to Renoir's *The Luncheon of the Boating Party*.

Embassy Row

The intriguing strip that is **Embassy Row** starts in earnest a few paces northwest up Massachusetts Avenue from Dupont Circle, where the **Indonesian Embassy** at no. 2020 (closed to the public) occupies the magnificent Art Nouveau Walsh-McLean House, built in 1903 for gold baron Thomas Walsh. It's a superb building – with colonnaded loggia and intricate, carved windows – and saw regular service as one of Washington society's most fashionable venues.

Anderson House

2118 Embassy Row (Massachusetts Ave NW) • Free guided tours Tues–Sat 1.15pm, 2.15pm & 3.15pm • Free • ☎ 202 785 2040

The **Anderson House** was finished in 1905 with a grey-stone exterior sporting twin arched entrances, heavy wooden doors and colonnaded portico. Inside there's a grand ballroom, and original furnishings include cavernous fireplaces, inlaid marble floors, Flemish tapestries and diverse murals.

5

The National Zoo

3001 Connecticut Ave NW • Buildings daily: April–Oct 10am–6pm; Nov–March 10am–4.30pm; grounds daily: April–Oct 6am–8pm; Nov–March 6am–6pm • Free; parking $10 • ☎ 202 873 4800, ⊛ natzoo.si.edu

Located in the hilly district of Upper Northwest, the Smithsonian's **National Zoo** was founded back in 1889, and provides plenty of interest to animal enthusiasts. **Amazonia** is a re-creation of a tropical river and rainforest habitat – piranhas included – while the **Small Mammal House** showcases some of the zoo's lovable oddballs including golden tamarind monkeys, armadillos, meerkats and porcupines. Further along, orang-utans are encouraged to leave the confines of the **Great Ape House** and commute to the "**Think Tank**", where scientists and four-legged primates come together to hone their communication skills. If all else fails, there are always the **giant pandas**, who have been amusing visitors since their arrival in 1972. Nearby, the **Asia Trail** displays such curious beasts as the sloth bear, a fishing cat, a somewhat grotesque Japanese giant salamander and the formidable clouded leopard.

Washington National Cathedral

3101 Wisconsin Ave NW • Daily 10am–5.30pm • $5 donation • ☎ 202 537 6200, ⊛ cathedral.org/cathedral

The twin towers of **Washington National Cathedral**, the world's sixth largest, are visible long before you reach the heights of Mount St Alban where the church sits, a good walk from the subway line in Upper Northwest. Built from Indiana limestone in the medieval English Gothic style, the Episcopal cathedral took 83 years to build and measures more than a tenth of a mile from the west end of the nave to the high altar at the opposite end. Among other things, you'll find the sarcophagus of **Woodrow Wilson**, the only president to be buried in the District – though presidents including Ford and Reagan have lain in state here – and the **Space Window** commemorating the flight of *Apollo 11*, whose stained glass incorporates a sliver of moon rock.

Georgetown

Although it is a mile from the nearest subway stop – taking the DC Circulator helps (see p.334) – **Georgetown** is the quintessential DC neighbourhood, enlivened by a main drag (M Street) where chic restaurants and boutiques are housed in 200-year-old buildings, and the historic **C&O Canal** runs parallel to the south (tour info at ⊛ nps.gov/CHOH).

The Old Stone House

3051 M St NW • Daily noon–5pm • Free • ⊛ nps.gov/olst

The **Old Stone House** is the only surviving pre-Revolutionary home in the city. Built in 1765 by a Pennsylvania carpenter, it retains its rugged, rough-hewn appearance, the craggy rocks used for the 3ft-thick walls being quarried from blue fieldstone.

Tudor Place

1644 31st St NW • Tours on the hour Tues–Sat 10am–3pm, Sun noon–3pm • $10 • ☎ 202 965 0400, ⊛ tudorplace.org

Tudor Place, which definitely merits a visit, was once the estate of Martha Washington's granddaughter. Its Federal-style architecture and Classical domed portico has remained virtually untouched since its 1816 construction, and many of the furnishings and objects inside belonged to George and Martha.

Dumbarton Oaks

1703 32nd St NW • **Gardens** Tues–Sun: mid-March to Oct 2–6pm; Nov to early March 2–5pm • $8 • ☎ 202 339 6409 **Museum** Tues–Sun 2–5pm • Free • ☎ 202 339 6401, ⊛ doaks.org

Dumbarton Oaks encompasses a marvellous red-brick Georgian mansion surrounded by **gardens** and woods. In 1944, this was the site of a meeting that led to the founding of the United Nations the following year. Its **museum** is excellent for its pre-Columbian gold, jade and polychromatic carvings, sculpture and pendants, as well as ceremonial

5

axes, jewellery made from spondylus shells, stone masks of unknown significance and sharp jade "celts", possibly used for human sacrifice.

Arlington National Cemetery

Daily: April–Sept 8am–7pm; Oct–March 8am–5pm • Free; ANC tours $8.75, kids $4.50 • ☎ 877 907 8585, ⓦ arlingtoncemetery.mil •
You can walk here from the Lincoln Memorial, across the Arlington Bridge, or take the Blue Line Metro

Across the Potomac River west of the National Mall, the vast sea of identical white headstones on the hillsides of Virginia's **Arlington National Cemetery** stand on land that once belonged to Confederate general **Robert E. Lee**. Some 350,000 US soldiers and others – from presidents to Supreme Court justices – now lie here. An eternal flame marks the grave of **President John F. Kennedy**, who lies next to his wife, Jacqueline Kennedy Onassis, and a short distance from his brother, Robert (the only grave marked with a simple white cross). At the **Tomb of the Unknowns** (more commonly known as the Tomb of the Unknown Soldier), visitors can watch a solemn Changing of the Guard ceremony (April–Sept every 30min; Oct–March hourly). The cemetery's prominent Neoclassical **Arlington House** (same hours as cemetery; free) is Lee's modest mansion, which his family was forced to sell after the war as the proximity of the nation's war dead created a less than ideal setting for the country home.

Unless you have strong legs, stamina and lots of time, the best way to see the vast cemetery is on one of the frequent ANC Tours buses that leave continuously from the visitor centre (see p.334).

Marine Corps and Air Force memorials

Beyond the gates of the cemetery are notable **memorials** to the **Marine Corps**, on Arlington Blvd at Meade St (daily 24hr; ⓦ nps.gov/gwmp/usmc.htm), based around the Iwo Jima Statue, which commemorates the bloody World War II battle where 6800 lives were lost; and to the **Air Force**, on Columbia Pike off Washington Blvd (Mon–Fri 10am–5pm, Sat 10am–2pm; ⓦ airforcememorial.org), recognizable by its three giant steel arcs twisting 270ft out into the sky.

ARRIVAL AND DEPARTURE   **WASHINGTON DC**

BY PLANE

Washington DC is served by three major airports: Dulles International Airport, 26 miles west in northern Virginia (IAD; ☎ 703 572 2700, ⓦ mwaa.com/dulles); Baltimore-Washington International Airport, halfway between DC and Baltimore (BWI; ☎ 410 859 7111, ⓦ bwiairport.com); and the conveniently central Ronald Reagan Washington National Airport, west across the Potomac River from the Mall (DCA; ☎ 703 417 8000, ⓦ metwashairports.com), mostly used by domestic flights.

Taxis and shuttles You can take a taxi downtown from BWI or Dulles ($60), while SuperShuttle (☎ 800 BLUE VAN, ⓦ supershuttle.com) offers door-to-door service from Dulles (45min; $34) and National (15min; $15). Cheaper are the express buses that run every 30min from both airports to nearby Metro subway stations. From Dulles, take the Washington Flyer Express Bus (☎ 888 WASH FLY, ⓦ washfly .com) to the West Falls Church Metro station (30min; $10, return $18), from which you can access downtown. From BWI, a free shuttle service connects the airport with the BWI rail terminal (10–15min). The most economical choice

is the southbound Penn Line of the Maryland Rail Commuter Service (MARC; $6 one-way; ☎ 410 539 5000, ⓦ mta .maryland.gov), providing frequent peak-hour departures to Washington's Union Station, a 40min trip. The station is also reached from BWI by the quicker daily Amtrak trains ($14 regular, $34 express, which take 30min). National Airport conveniently has its own subway stop and is just a short ride from the city centre. A taxi downtown from National costs around $26.

BY BUS

Greyhound and other buses stop at a modern terminal at 1005 First St NE, in a fairly dodgy part of the city, a few blocks north of the Union Station Metro; take a cab, especially at night.

BY TRAIN

By train, you arrive amid the gleaming, Neoclassical spectre of Union Station, 50 Massachusetts Ave NE, three blocks north of the US Capitol and with a connecting Metro station.

5

BY CAR

Driving into DC is a sure way to experience some of the worst traffic on the East Coast – the main I-95 and I-495 freeways that circle Washington on the Beltway are jammed 18hr a day.

GETTING AROUND

Getting around DC is easy. The most prominent sights, including the museums, monuments and White House, are within walking distance of each other, and an excellent public transport system reaches outlying sights and neighbourhoods.

By Metro subway The expansive Metro (☎ 202 637 7000, ⓦ wmata.com) is clean and efficient (trains Mon–Thurs 5am–midnight, Fri 5am–3am, Sat 7am–3am, Sun 7am–midnight). Single fares start at $1.70; during rush hours it's $2.10 (5am–9.30am & 3–7pm); and if you're going out to the suburbs the one-way fare can be up to $4.50. Day passes cost $8.30 and are valid weekdays (from 9.30am) and all day on weekends.

By bus The standard fare on the extensive bus network is $1.80, or $4 for express buses.

By taxi In the downtown core, most journeys are around $10 and most cross-town fares are no more than $20. There are taxi stands at major hotels and transport terminals (including Union Station). For more information, call the DC Taxicab Commission on ☎ 855 484 4966 or visit ⓦ dctaxi.dc.gov.

By tourist shuttle bus The special "DC Circulator" (☎ 202 962 1423, ⓦ dccirculator.com) covers major sights on five routes via shuttle bus for a fare of $1.

INFORMATION

DC Chamber of Commerce Visitor Center 1213 K St NW (Mon–Fri 9am–4.30pm; ☎ 866 324 7386, ⓦ dcchamber.org); can help with maps, tours, bookings and information.

White House Visitor Information Center 1450 Pennsylvania Ave NW (daily 7.30am–4pm; ☎ 202 208 1631, ⓦ nps.gov/whho); supplies free maps and handy guides to museums and attractions.

ACCOMMODATION

Washington DC is one of the most expensive places to stay in America outside of New York. Most DC hotels cater to business travellers and political lobbyists, and during the week are quite expensive. At weekends, however, many cut their rates by up to fifty percent. Alternatively, if you really want to save money, numerous chain hotels on the suburban outskirts have affordable rates and Metro access. For a list of vacancies, call WDCA Hotels (☎ 800 503 3330, ⓦ wdcahotels.com), which provides a hotel reservation and travel-planning service. Similarly, a number of B&B agencies offer comfortable doubles starting from $60 in the low season: try Capitol Reservations (ⓦ capitolreservations.com) or Bed & Breakfast Accommodations, Ltd (☎ 877 893 3233, ⓦ bedandbreakfastdc.com). Wherever you go, make sure the facility has air conditioning; DC can be unbearably stifling in summer.

Adam's Inn 1744 Lanier Place NW, Adams Morgan ☎ 202 745 3600, ⓦ adamsinn.com. Three adjoining Victorian townhouses with simple B&B rooms near the zoo. No in-room TVs, but continental breakfast, garden patio and laundry. Sharing a bathroom saves you $30. **$159**

Fairmont 2401 M St NW ☎ 202 429 2400, ⓦ fairmont .com. Classy oasis with comfortable rooms, pool, health club, whirlpool and garden courtyard. Just north of Washington Circle, midway between Foggy Bottom and Georgetown. **$330**

Four Seasons 2800 Pennsylvania Ave NW, Georgetown ☎ 202 342 0444, ⓦ fourseasons.com. This modern red-brick pile is one of DC's most luxurious and expensive hotels. Service is superb, and there's a pool, fitness centre and full-service spa. **$345**

Grand Hyatt 1000 H St NW, downtown ☎ 202 582 1234, ⓦ grandwashington.hyatt.com. Smart corporate hotel with an eye-opening twelve-storey atrium and lagoon, waterfalls and glass elevators, plus tasteful rooms and an on-site café, restaurant and sports bar. Adjacent Metro connection. **$290**

Harrington 1100 E St NW, downtown ☎ 202 628 8140, ⓦ hotel-harrington.com. One of the old and basic downtown hotels, dating from 1914, in a prime location near Pennsylvania Ave. Though pretty worn around the edges, rooms (singles to quads) have a/c and TV, plus prices are tough to beat for the area. **$175**

★ **Hay-Adams** 800 16th St NW, Foggy Bottom ☎ 202 638 6600, ⓦ hayadams.com. From the gold-leaf and walnut lobby to the sleek modern rooms, the *Hay-Adams* is one of DC's finest hotels. Upper floors have great views of the White House across the square. Breakfast is served in one of the District's better spots for early-morning power dining. **$369**

HI-Washington DC 1009 11th St NW ☎ 202 737 2333, ⓦ hiwashingtondc.org. Large (270 beds), clean, downtown hostel with free continental breakfast and wi-fi, plus kitchen, lounge, laundry, luggage storage and organized activities. Dorms **$55**

5

Kalorama Guest House 2700 Cathedral Ave NW, Woodley Park ☎ 202 588 8188, ⓦ kaloramaguesthouse .com. Spacious Victorian accommodation in Upper North-west, filled with antiques, with free continental breakfast (but no TV). Booking is essential – single rooms can be as cheap as $85, though prices spike in the high season. **$175**

Maison Orleans 414 5th St SE ☎ 202 544 3694, ⓦ bnblist.com/dc/maisonorleans. Historic 1902 rowhouse that's now a pleasant B&B offering continental breakfast, plus a trio of functional rooms, patio with fountains, and small garden, within easy reach of the Capitol. **$180**

Marriott Wardman Park 2660 Woodley Rd NW ☎ 202 328 2000, ⓦ marriott.com. Woodley Park's historic monument manages to be the largest hotel in DC, with two pools, a health club and restaurants with cracking staff. Convention business keeps rooms full most of the year. **$250**

Mayflower 1127 Connecticut Ave NW, New Downtown ☎ 202 347 3000, ⓦ renaissancehotels.com/WASSH. Sumptuous Washington classic featuring a promenade – a vast, imperial hall – and smart rooms with subtle, tasteful furnishings; the terrific *Café Promenade* restaurant is much in demand. **$265**

★ **Monaco** 700 F St NW, downtown ☎ 202 628 7177, ⓦ monaco-dc.com. Grand, Neoclassical former post office that today houses ultra-chic accommodation. Features include sophisticated modern rooms, minimalist contemporary decor, public spaces with marble floors and columns, and striking spiral stairways. Weekday rates can double. **$270**

Omni Shoreham 2500 Calvert St NW, Upper Northwest ☎ 202 234 0700, ⓦ omnihotels.com. Plush institution bursting with history and overlooking Rock Creek Park.

Offers swanky, comfortable rooms, many with a view of the park, plus an outdoor pool, tennis courts and the *Marquee Bar* for drinks. **$200**

Palomar 2121 P St NW, Dupont Circle ☎ 202 448 1800, ⓦ hotelpalomar-dc.com. Excellent boutique accommodation with flat-screen TVs and CD players in the rooms, an on-site pool, fitness centre, stylish lounge and location close to the Circle. **$270**

State Plaza 2117 E St NW, Foggy Bottom ☎ 202 861 8200, ⓦ stateplaza.com. Commodious suites with fully equipped kitchens and a dining area, plus a rooftop sun-deck, health club and good café. Peak periods require three-night minimum stay. **$150**

Tabard Inn 1739 N St NW ☎ 202 785 1277, ⓦ tabardinn.com. Three converted Victorian townhouses near Dupont Circle, with forty unique, antique-stocked rooms. Old fixtures and furnishings are far from sleek and modern (no elevators or TVs), but affordable rates include breakfast and a pass to the nearby YMCA. Shared bath **$130**, en suite **$180**

William Lewis House 1309 R St NW ☎ 202 462 7574, ⓦ wlewishous.com. Elegantly decorated, gay-friendly B&B set in two century-old townhouses north of Logan Circle. All ten antique-filled rooms have shared bath and net access. Outside there's a roomy porch and a garden with a hot tub. Rates include breakfast. It's ultra-cheap for what you get, so reservations are essential. **$119**

Woodley Park Guest House 2647 Woodley Rd NW, Upper Northwest ☎ 202 667 0218, ⓦ woodleypark guesthouse.com. Sixteen cosy rooms (the cheapest share facilities) that come with free continental breakfast. Close to the zoo, the Metro and plenty of good restaurants. **$165**

EATING

Restaurants come and go more quickly in Washington DC than in similarly sized cities in the USA. Certain neighbourhoods – Connecticut Avenue around Dupont Circle, 18th Street and Columbia Road in Adams Morgan, M Street in Georgetown and downtown's Seventh Street and Chinatown – always seem to hold a satisfying range of dining options. Otherwise, the cafés in the main museums are good for downtown lunch breaks. Likewise, you'll find convenient food courts in Union Station and at the Old Post Office.

DOWNTOWN

Acadiana 901 New York Ave NW ☎ 202 408 8848, ⓦ arcadianarestaurant.com. Chic Cajun spot that serves up mid-priced muffulettas, po-boys and crawfish for lunch, then saves the big-ticket scallops and bacon, veal medal-lions with grits, and grilled swordfish for dinner. Mon–Thurs 11.30am–10.30pm, Fri 11.30am–11pm, Sat 5.30–11pm, Sun 11am–9.30pm.

Captain White's Seafood City 1100 Maine Ave SW ☎ 202 484 2722, ⓦ captainwhitesseafood.com. South of downtown at the Fish Wharf, a fine vendor hawking catfish, oysters, crab and other delicious choices, which you can get fresh to go or fried up in a tasty platter or sandwich. Daily 7am–9pm.

Jaleo 480 7th St NW ☎ 202 628 7949, ⓦ jaleo.com. Smart tapas bar-restaurant with tempting selections such as sautéed shrimp, chicken fritters and patatas bravas, plus supreme paella. Limited reservation policy makes for long waits during peak hours. Mon & Sun 11.30am–10pm, Tues–Thurs 11.30am–11pm, Fri & Sat 11.30am–midnight.

Old Ebbitt Grill 675 15th St NW ☎ 202 347 4801, ⓦ ebbitt.com. One of DC's biggest names: a plush re-creation of a nineteenth-century tavern, with mahogany bar (serving microbrews), gas chandeliers, leather booths and gilt mirrors. Offers everything from burgers to oysters. Mon–Thurs 7.30am–2am, Fri 7.30am–3am, Sat 8.30am–3am, Sun 8.30am–2am.

5

Proof 775 G St NW ☎202 737 7663, ⓦproofdc.com. A delicious, upper-end grab bag of flavours and styles, with a fine wine selection to boot. Try the charcuterie plates to start, and move on to a huge range of cheeses, sashimi, ceviche and salmon or sablefish. Mon 5.30–10pm, Tues–Fri 11.30am–2pm & 5.30–10pm, Sat 5.30–11pm, Sun 5.30–9pm.

The Source 575 Pennsylvania Ave NW ☎202 637 6100, ⓦwolfgangpuck.com. LA-based wunder-chef Wolfgang Puck takes DC by the lapels with this expensive fusion place – doling out curiosities from pork-belly dumplings to "lacquered" Chinese duckling – and attracts a range of celebrities, including President Obama himself. Tues–Sat 11.30am–2pm & 5.30–10pm.

Zaytinya 701 9th St NW ☎202 638 0800, ⓦzaytinya .com. Stylish mid-priced Turkish and Middle Eastern place that serves a range of inventive meze plates, ranging from Lebanese beef tartare to pork-and-orange-rind sausage and veal cheeks. Good cheeses, too. Mon & Sun 11.30am–10pm, Tues–Thurs 11.30am–11pm, Fri & Sat 11.30am–midnight.

DUPONT CIRCLE

Bistrot du Coin 1738 Connecticut Ave NW ☎202 234 6969, ⓦbistroducoin.com. Classic bistro with a superb bar, boisterous atmosphere and genuine, affordable French food – goat cheese salad, foie gras, tartines and rabbit stew, among other offerings. Mon–Wed & Sun 11.30am–11pm, Thurs–Sat 11.30am–1am.

Java House 1645 Q St NW ☎202 387 6622, ⓦjava housedc.com. A local favourite serving the neigh-bourhood's best coffee. A good spot to read a book, have an afternoon chat or fire up the laptop for wi-fi access. Desserts, bagels, salads and sandwiches are on offer, too. Daily 7am–9.40pm.

★ **Komi** 1509 17th St NW ☎202 332 9200, ⓦkomirestaurant.com. One of the city's top restaurants, for which you should reserve well in advance. Enjoy pricey, rotating, fixed-price ($135) selections that may include suckling pig, pasta and *spanakopita* – though you really never know. Tues–Sat 6–11pm.

Moby Dick House of Kabob 1300 Connecticut Ave NW ☎202 833 9788, ⓦmobysonline.com. Delicious and cheap Middle Eastern fare featuring spicy and savoury gyros, chicken and lamb sandwiches, boneless chicken in pomegranate sauce, braised beef with aubergine and other cheap delights. Mon–Thurs 11am–10pm, Fri 11am–4am, Sat noon–4am.

Pizzeria Paradiso 2003 P St NW ☎202 223 1245, ⓦeatyourpizza.com. Supreme pizzeria, with famously tasty pizzas such as the enormous Siciliana, potato-and-pesto Genovese, and ultra-peppery, spicy Atomica. Expect to wait in line. Mon–Thurs 11.30am–10pm, Fri & Sat 11am–midnight, Sun noon–10pm.

Restaurant Nora 2132 Florida Ave NW ☎202 462 5143, ⓦnoras.com. Top-notch restaurant with prices to match. The all-organic fare includes Spanish octopus, Amish pork roast and veal osso buco. Mon–Sat 5.30–10pm.

Sushi Taro 1503 17th St NW ☎202 462 8999, ⓦsushitaro.com. Plenty of fine sushi, sashimi, tempura and teriyaki, with moderate to expensive prices. If raw fish isn't your thing, choose from the selection of steak and pork cutlets. Mon–Fri 11.30am–2pm & 5.30–10pm, Sat 5.30–10pm.

ADAMS MORGAN AND SHAW

★ **Amsterdam Falafelshop** 2425 18th St NW ☎202 234 1969, ⓦfalafelshop.com. Among the finest falafel spots in the country, this unassuming place doles out piping-hot, seriously yummy falafel with a broad range of garnishes, and pretty good brownies and fries, too. Mon & Sun 11am–midnight, Tues–Thurs 11.30am–2.30am, Fri & Sat 11.30am–4am.

Ben's Chili Bowl 1213 U St NW, Shaw ☎202 667 0909, ⓦbenschilibowl.com. A favourite of the president's, and well worth the trip for the legendary chilli dogs, milk-shakes and cheese fries. Mon–Thurs 6am–2am, Fri 6am–4am, Sat 7am–4am, Sun 11am–midnight.

Bukom Café 2442 18th St NW, Adams Morgan ☎202 265 4600, ⓦbukom.com. Serves delicious West African dishes such as spicy "beer meat", oxtail or okra soup, *egusi*, a broth of goat meat with ground melon seeds and spinach, and chicken yassa, with onions and spices, for $10–12. Daily 4pm–2am.

Casa Oaxaca 2106 18th St NW ☎202 387 2272, ⓦoaxaca indc.com. Not as flashy as some other Latin joints in the area, but among the best – great for its wide range of mole dishes, grilled steak and sautéed shrimp, at mid-range prices. Mon–Thurs & Sun 5–10.30pm, Fri & Sat 5–11.30pm.

Cashion's Eat Place 1819 Columbia Rd NW, Adams Morgan ☎202 797 1819, ⓦcashionseatplace.com. New Southern cuisine, offering hickory-smoked lamb, rabbit meatloaf, corn cakes, grits, sweet potatoes and fruit and nut pies – at mid- to high prices. Brunch dishes are about half the price. Tues–Fri 5.30–10pm, Sat 10.30am–2.30pm & 5.30–11pm, Sun 10.30am–2.30pm.

Grill from Ipanema 1858 Columbia Rd NW, Adams Morgan ☎202 986 0757, ⓦthegrillfromipanema.com. Brazilian staples highlighted by meat stews, shrimp dishes and a scrumptious weekend brunch. Try the mussels and watch your caipirinha intake. Mon–Fri 4.30–10.30pm, Sat noon–11.30pm, Sun noon–10pm.

Henry's Soul Cafe 1704 U St NW, Shaw ☎202 265 3336, ⓦhenryssoulcafe.com. Authentic soul food: the chicken wings, fried trout, meatloaf, ribs, beef liver and sweet potato pie give a savoury and heavy taste of the Deep South for $10. Mon & Sun 11.30am–10pm, Tues–Thurs 11.30am–11pm, Fri & Sat 11.30am–midnight.

GEORGETOWN

Baked & Wired 1052 Thomas Jefferson St NW ☎ 202 333 2500, ⓦ bakedandwired.com. Among the city's finest bakeries, where you can sample great pies, coffee cakes, brownies, cookies and especially delicious cupcakes, plus a good selection of coffee and tea. Mon–Thurs 7am–8pm, Fri 7am–9pm, Sat 8am–9pm, Sun 9am–8pm.

Booeymonger 3265 Prospect St NW ☎ 202 333 4810, ⓦ booeymonger.com. Crowded deli-coffeeshop, excellent for its inventive sandwiches like the Gatsby Arrow (roast beef and Brie) and the Patty Hearst (turkey and bacon with Russian dressing). Daily 8am–midnight.

Leopold's Kafe 3315 M St NW ☎ 202 965 6005, ⓦ kafeleopolds.com. European café that features mid- to high-priced continental fare such as sweet onion tarts, veal schnitzel, bratwurst, smoked fish and delicious desserts and pastries. Breakfast can be particularly good here. Mon–Sat 11am–10pm, Sun 11am–9pm.

Rocklands 2418 Wisconsin Ave NW ☎ 202 333 2558, ⓦ rocklands.com. A bit north of the main action, but still worth the trek to enjoy some of DC's best pork sandwiches, ribs, beans, sausages and other staples of the barbecue scene, all for low prices. Mon–Fri 4.30–10.30pm, Sat noon–11.30pm, Sun noon–10pm.

UPPER NORTHWEST

Indique 3512 Connecticut Ave NW ☎ 202 244 6600, ⓦ Indique.com. Recipes from all over India come together with a modern twist at this stylish and affordable restaurant. Don't miss the tasty curries including seafood masala and a piquant lamb vindaloo. Daily 5.30–10.15pm.

Lebanese Taverna 2641 Connecticut Ave NW ☎ 202 265 8681. Solid Middle Eastern joint with an assortment of kebabs, grilled-meat platters and leg of lamb. Part of a local chain. Mon–Thurs & Sun 11.30am–10pm, Fri & Sat 11.30am–11pm.

Vace 3315 Connecticut Ave NW ☎ 202 363 1999, ⓦ vaceitaliandeli.com. Grab a slice of the excellent designer or traditional pizzas – some of DC's best – and tasty sub sandwiches, focaccia and pasta, or pack a picnic from the selection of sausages, salads and olives, then head to the zoo. Mon–Fri 9am–9pm, Sat 9am–8pm, Sun 10am–5pm.

NIGHTLIFE AND ENTERTAINMENT

Peak times for drinking in DC tend to be during rush hour, but for solid late-night imbibing, the well-worn haunts of collegiate Georgetown, yuppified Dupont Circle and boisterous Adams Morgan will do nicely – and in the suit-and-tie spots on Capitol Hill, you can even spy a politician or two. For clubs, expect to pay a cover of $5 to $25 (highest on weekends); ticket prices for most gigs run to the same amount, unless you're seeing a major name. Check the free weekly *CityPaper* (ⓦ washingtoncitypaper.com) for up-to-date listings of music, theatre and other events, in addition to alternative features and reporting. Gay and lesbian life is centred on Dupont Circle.

BARS

Bier Baron 1523 22nd St NW, Dupont Circle ☎ 202 293 1887, ⓦ bierbarondc.com. Formerly the renowned *Brickskeller*, this brick-lined basement saloon still serves a whopping, 600-strong beer selection. Worth a visit for its convivial atmosphere. Mon–Thurs 4pm–midnight, Fri & Sat 4pm–2am, Sun noon–2am.

Birreria Paradiso 2003 P St NW ☎ 202 223 1245. Downstairs at Dupont Circle's *Pizzeria Paradiso* (see opposite), this is a supreme touchstone for beer lovers, who come to sample US and European brews, among them excellent Belgian ales, lambics, stouts and porters. Mon–Thurs 11.30am–10pm, Fri & Sat 11am–midnight, Sun noon–10pm.

Bullfeathers 410 1st St SE ☎ 202 484 0228, ⓦ bullfeathersdc.com. Politician-watchers just may catch a sighting at this old-time Hill favourite, a dark and clubby spot with affordable beer, which was named for one of Teddy Roosevelt's favourite euphemisms during his White House years. Mon–Thurs & Sun 11am–11pm, Fri & Sat 11am–2am.

Capitol City Brewing Co. 1100 New York Ave NW ☎ 202 628 2222, ⓦ capcitybrew.com. Prominent microbrewing spot near Union Station, highlighted by a good range of ales and porters, but only adequate food. Part of a small local chain. Mon–Thurs 11am–midnight, Fri & Sat 11am–1am, Sun 11am–10pm.

Capitol Lounge 231 Pennsylvania Ave SE ☎ 202 547 2098, ⓦ capitolloungedc.com. Signature brick-walled saloon on the Hill for drinking and partying, with pool tables, inexpensive beer, three bars on two levels and a bevy of Congressional staffers looking to get plastered. Mon–Wed 4pm–2am, Thurs 11am–2am, Fri 11am–3am, Sat & Sun 10.30am–3am.

The Dubliner 4 F St NW, in the Phoenix Park Hotel ☎ 202 737 3773, ⓦ dublinerdc.com. A wooden-vaulted, good-time Irish pub with draft Guinness, boisterous conversation and live Irish music. The patio is a solid summer hangout. Mon–Thurs & Sun 11am–1.30am, Fri & Sat 11am–2.30am.

Fox and Hounds 1537 17th St NW, Dupont Circle ☎ 202 232 6307, ⓦ triofoxandhounds.com. This easy-going bar draws a diverse crowd, all here to enjoy the stiff and cheap rail drinks and the solid jukebox. Mon–Thurs 4pm–2am, Fri & Sat 11am–3am, Sun 11am–2am.

Nanny O'Brien's 3319 Connecticut Ave NW, Upper

5

Northwest ☎202 686 9189, ⓦnannyobriens.com. An authentic Irish pub with live music from (or in the style of) the Emerald Isle, several nights a week. Mon–Thurs noon–2am, Fri & Sat noon–3am.

RFD Washington 810 7th St NW ☎202 289 2030, ⓦlovethebeer.com. The leader in downtown DC microbreweries, with hundreds of bottled beers and dozens of locally crafted brews on tap. Centrally located near the Verizon Center, so watch for heavy post-game crowds. Daily 11am–2am.

CLUBS AND LIVE MUSIC VENUES

9:30 Club 815 V St NW, Shaw ☎202 265 0930, ⓦ930 .com. Top musicians love to play at this spacious yet intimate club, deservedly famous as DC's best venue for live acts, from indie rock and pop to reggae and rap. Show nights door 7pm.

★ **The Black Cat** 1811 14th St NW, Shaw ☎202 667 7960, ⓦblackcatdc.com. One of the top venues in town, part-owned by Dave Grohl, this indie institution provides a showcase for rock, punk and garage bands and veteran alternative acts alike. Cash only. Mon–Thurs & Sun 8pm–2am, Fri & Sat 7pm–3am.

Blues Alley 1073 Wisconsin Ave NW (rear) Georgetown ☎202 337 4141, ⓦbluesalley.com. Small, celebrated Georgetown jazz bar, in business for more than forty years, which attracts top names. Cover can run up to $45, with a $12 food/drink minimum at tables. Book in advance. Daily 6pm–midnight.

★ **Bohemian Caverns** 2001 11th St NW, Shaw ☎202 299 0800, ⓦbohemiancaverns.com. Legendary DC jazz supper club, set in a basement grotto below the stylish ground-level restaurant. A limited number of reserved tickets for bigger acts. Mon–Thurs 7pm–midnight, Fri & Sat 7.30pm–2am, Sun 6pm–midnight.

Chief Ike's Mambo Room 1725 Columbia Rd NW, Adams Morgan ☎202 332 2211, ⓦchiefikes.com. Ramshackle mural-clad bar that draws the college crowd for live bands playing rock, reggae and r'n'b, or DJs hosting theme nights. Mon 6pm–2am Tues–Thurs 5pm–2am, Fri & Sat 5pm–3am.

Habana Village 1834 Columbia Rd NW ☎202 462 6310, ⓦhabanavillage.com. Intoxicating Latin dance joint (tango and salsa lessons are available) infused with an eclectic spirit. A good downstairs bar serves a fine mojito. Mon–Fri 4.30–10.30pm, Sat noon–11.30pm, Sun noon–10pm.

★ **HR-57** 1007 H St NE ☎202 253 0044, ⓦhr57.org. Small but authentic club where jazz in various manifestations – classic, hard bop, free and cool – is performed by ardent professionals as well as up-and-comers. Cover usually around $15. Wed, Fri & Sat 6.30pm–1am, Thurs 6.30–11pm, Sun 5–10pm.

IOTA 2832 Wilson Blvd, Arlington, VA ☎703 522 8340, ⓦiotaclubandcafe.com. Fine warehouse-style music joint with nightly performances by local and national indie, folk and blues bands. Has a great bar, and attached restaurant, too. Mon–Fri 11am–late, Sat 8am–late.

Madam's Organ 2461 18th St NW, Adams Morgan ☎202 667 5370, ⓦmadamsorgan.com. Hip spot known for showcasing a variety of driving live blues, grinding raw funk and the odd bluegrass band; also offers solidly rib-sticking soul food and generous cocktails. Mon–Thurs & Sun 5pm–2am, Fri & Sat 5pm–3am.

Rumba Café 2443 18th St NW, Adams Morgan ☎202 588 5501, ⓦrumbacafe.com. This Latin oasis is a good bet for a night of sipping caipirinhas and grooving to live Brazilian bossa nova and Afro-Cuban rhythms. Mon–Wed 4.30pm–1.30am, Thurs–Sun 11am–1.30am.

Wolf Trap Farm Park 1645 Trap Rd, Vienna, VA ☎703 255 1868, tickets on ☎877 965 3872, ⓦwolftrap.org. Great spot to see American music in all its native forms – bluegrass, jazz, ragtime, Cajun, zydeco etc. Enquire about public transport to and from performances.

PERFORMING ARTS VENUES

Arena Stage 1101 6th St NW ☎202 544 9066, ⓦarenastage.org. Highly regarded, often pioneering site that puts on contemporary pieces.

Ford's Theatre 511 10th St NW, downtown ☎202 347 4833, ⓦfordstheatre.org. Historic venue with a family-friendly programme of mainstream musicals and dramas,

---

SPECTATOR SPORTS IN WASHINGTON DC

Tickets to Washington Redskins **football** games at FedEx Field in Landover, Maryland (☎301 276 6050, ⓦredskins.com), are almost impossible to get unless you have a connection. Much easier to obtain are tickets to DC's Washington Nationals **baseball** team, which plays at Nationals Park on the Anacostia waterfront; tickets $5–170 (☎202 675 6287, ⓦnationals.mlb .com). East of Capitol Hill, at RFK Stadium, is the DC United **soccer** squad; tickets $15–50 (☎202 587 5000, ⓦdcunited.com), which plays in the pro MLS league. The huge downtown Verizon Center (ⓦverizoncenter.com) hosts home games of the men's pro **basketball** Washington Wizards; tickets $15–190 (☎202 661 5050, ⓦnba.com/wizards) and women's Mystics; tickets $10–85 (☎202 397 7328, ⓦwnba.com/mystics), as well as the pro **hockey** Capitals (tickets $15–100; ☎202 397 7328, ⓦcapitals.nhl.com).

frequently historical in nature.

Kennedy Center 2700 F St NW, ☎202 467 4600, ⓦkennedy-center.org. The performing arts heavyweight in town, the Kennedy Center hosts most of the capital's highbrow cultural events, including National Symphony Orchestra and Washington National Opera performances.

National Theatre 1321 Pennsylvania Ave NW, downtown ☎202 628 6161, ⓦnationaltheatre.org. Offers big-name touring musicals and other crowd-pleasers.

Shakespeare Theatre 450 7th St NW, downtown ☎202 547 1122, ⓦshakespearetheatre.org. Celebrated troupe stages six productions per year of work by the Bard and others, plus free summer performances in Rock Creek Park.

Woolly Mammoth Theatre 641 D St NW, downtown ☎202 289 2443, ⓦwoollymammoth.net. Experimental theatre showcasing budget and mid-priced contemporary and off-the-wall plays.

Virginia

VIRGINIA is the oldest American colony: its recorded history began at **Jamestown**, just off the Chesapeake Bay, with the establishment in 1607 of the first successful British colony in North America. Though the first colonists hoped to find gold, it was **tobacco** that made their fortunes – as Native Americans were driven off their land and **slaves** were imported from Africa to work the plantations. Many of the wealthy Virginian planters had an enormous impact on the foundation of the United States: Thomas Jefferson, George Washington and James Madison among them. Later, as the confrontation between North and South over slavery and related issues grew more divisive, Virginia was caught in the middle, but joined the Confederacy when the **Civil War** broke out, providing the Confederate capital, Richmond, and its military leader, General Robert E. Lee. Four long years later, Virginia was ravaged, its towns and cities wrecked, its farmlands ruined and most of its youth dead.

Richmond itself was largely destroyed in the war; today it's a small city with some good museums, the best ones historical in nature. The bulk of the colonial sites are concentrated just east, in what is known as the **Historic Triangle**, where **Jamestown**, the original colony, **Williamsburg**, the restored colonial capital, and **Yorktown**, site of the final battle of the Revolutionary War, lie within half an hour's drive of each other on the Colonial Parkway. Another historic centre, **Charlottesville** – famously home to Thomas Jefferson's Monticello – sits at the foot of the gorgeous **Blue Ridge Mountains**, an hour west of Richmond. It's also within easy reach of the natural splendour of **Shenandoah National Park** and the little towns of the western valleys. **Northern Virginia**, a short hop from Washington DC, holds well-preserved estates, cottages, churches, barns and taverns tucked away along the quiet backroads, in addition to the antique architecture of **Alexandria**, **Manassas**, the scene of two important Civil War battles, and the very popular longtime home of George Washington, **Mount Vernon**.

Alexandria

Extending a good half-mile west of the Potomac, the Old Town of **ALEXANDRIA** was originally an important colonial trading post and a busy port named after the pioneer John Alexander. The town was part of the District of Columbia in 1800, but Virginia demanded it and the surrounding land back in 1846. Nestled on the Potomac River just beyond the limits of the nation's capital (but not beyond its Metro system), Alexandria seems at least two centuries removed from the modern political whirl.

Gadsby's Tavern

134 N Royal St • Tours: April–Oct Mon & Sun 1–5pm, Tues–Sat 10am–5pm; Nov–March Wed–Sat 11am–4pm, Sun 1–4pm • $5 • ☎703 548 1288, ⓦgadsbystavern.org

In earlier days, George Washington maintained close ties with Alexandria, owning property here and attending gatherings at the famous **Gadsby's Tavern**, which occupies

5

two stately Georgian buildings dating from 1792 and 1785. Downstairs, there's a working restaurant, complete with colonial food and costumed staff.

Old Town sights

Among the restored buildings open to the public are **Carlyle House**, 121 N Fairfax St (tours Tues–Sat 10am–4pm, Sun noon–4pm; $5; ☎703 549 2997, ⍵carlylehouse.org), a 1752 sandstone manor that was home to five royal governors, and **Lee-Fendall House**, 614 Oronoco St (Wed–Sat 10am–4pm, Sun 1–4pm; $5; ☎703 548 1789, ⍵leefendallhouse.org), a splendid clapboard mansion built in 1785 by Phillip Fendall, a cousin of General Lee's father. South of King Street, the **Lyceum**, 201 S Washington St (Mon–Sat 10am–5pm, Sun 1–5pm; $2; ☎703 746 4994, ⍵alexandriahistory.org), houses the town's history museum in a magisterial, 1839 Greek Revival building, designed to be a centrepiece for Alexandria's cultural affairs.

Another eye-catcher is the **Stabler-Leadbeater Apothecary Museum**, 105 S Fairfax St (April–Oct Mon & Sun 1–5pm, Tues–Sat 10am–5pm; Nov–March Wed–Sat 11am–4pm, Sun 1–4pm; $5; ☎703 746 3852, ⍵apothecarymuseum.org), which was founded in 1792 and remained in business until the 1930s. It still displays herbs, potions and medical paraphernalia – some eight thousand items in all.

The waterfront

Down on the waterfront, a former munitions factory houses the **Torpedo Factory Art Center**, 105 N Union St (daily 10am–5pm; free; ☎703 838 4565, ⍵torpedofactory.org), where you can watch artists at work in their studios and browse numerous galleries. In the same building, the **Alexandria Archaeology Museum** (Tues–Fri 10am–3pm, Sat 10am–5pm, Sun 1–5pm; free; ☎703 746 4399, ⍵alexandriaarchaeology.org) displays aspects of 250 years of the town's history and prehistory.

George Washington National Masonic Memorial

101 Callahan Drive • Mon–Sat 10am–4pm, Sun noon–4pm • Free • ☎ 703 683 2007, ⍵ gwmemorial.org

Next to the Amtrak and King Street Metro station stands the 333ft obelisk of the **George Washington National Masonic Memorial**, where you'll find a 17ft bronze **statue** of the founding father, sundry Masonic memorabilia and dioramas depicting events from his life.

ARRIVAL AND INFORMATION
ALEXANDRIA

By Metro subway The Metro station for Old Town Alexandria is King Street (25min from downtown DC; yellow and blue lines), a mile or so from most of the sights. You can pick up the local DASH bus ($1.60; ☎703 746 DASH, ⍵dashbus.com), which runs down King St and throughout Old Town, or, if you prefer, you can make the 20min walk from the station instead.

Visitor centre Ramsay House, 221 King St (daily: Jan–March 10am–5pm; April–Dec 10am–8pm; ☎703 746 3301, ⍵funside.com); has details on walking tours.

ACCOMMODATION AND EATING

Hard Times Café 1404 King St ☎703 837 0050, ⍵hardtimescafe.com. At the cheaper end of the spectrum, this place doles out four styles of fiery chilli, from classic Texas to spicy-as-hell Terlingua, plus a veggie option. Good wings, rings, fries and savoury microbrews, too. Daily 11am–2am.

Hotel Monaco 480 King St ☎703 549 6080, ⍵monaco -alexandria.com. Boasting stylish decor, wine tastings and chic rooms and suites that variously offer jetted tubs, flat-screen TVs and in-room bars. **$189**

The Majestic 911 King St ☎703 837 9117, ⍵majestic cafe.com. The upmarket diner offerings here include chowder, ribs, chops, meatloaf and calf's liver. Mon–Fri 11.30am–2.30pm & 5.30–10pm, Sat & Sun 1–9pm.

Morrison House 116 S Alfred St ☎703 838 8000, ⍵morrisonhouse.com. A Federal-style townhouse (built in 1985) with modern boutique comforts and designer furnishings. **$209**

★ **Restaurant Eve** 110 S Pitt St ☎703 706 0450, ⍵restauranteve.com. An elite, nouveau-American bistro offering expensive multicourse meals drawn from a rotating menu of seafood, game and beef ($110–150). Mon–Fri 11.30am–2.30pm & 5.30–10pm, Sat 5.30–10pm.

Mount Vernon and around

3200 George Washington Memorial Pkwy • Daily: April–Aug 8am–5pm; March, Sept & Oct 9am–5pm; Nov–Feb 9am–4pm • $17 • ☎ 703 780 2000, ⓦ mountvernon.org • From downtown DC (15 miles away), it can be reached by the Fairfax Connector bus #101 from the Huntington Metro station (hourly; $1.60; ⓦ fairfaxcounty.gov/connector)

Set on a bluff overlooking the Potomac River, eight miles south of Alexandria, **Mount Vernon** is **George Washington**'s five-hundred-acre country estate, which has been restored to the year 1799, the last year of the general's life.

In the house itself, the furnishings and decoration reflect Washington's sense of simple, spartan style. The items on display include a reading chair with a built-in fan and a key to the destroyed Bastille, presented by Thomas Paine on behalf of Lafayette. The four-poster bed upon which Washington died stands in an upstairs bedroom. Outside are the renovated **slave quarters**, built to house the ninety slaves who lived and worked on the grounds. Washington and his wife, Martha, are buried in a simple tomb on the south side of the house. For the full background on Mount Vernon, the fancy modern **Reynolds Museum** on the plantation site has interactive displays, models of Washington and assorted short films. It also traces Washington's ancestry and displays porcelain from the house, medals, weapons, silver and a series of striking miniatures.

The grist mill

Rte-235 S • April–Oct daily 10am–5pm • $4, or $2 extra with Mount Vernon admission

Three miles away from Mount Vernon stands the restored **grist mill** that Washington built as a water-powered testament to the future of American industry. Today colonial re-enactors go about the laborious work of crushing grain into flour and cornmeal. A **distillery** features copper stills, a boiler and mash tubs, and a short movie about Washington's role in the whiskey-making process.

Manassas National Battlefield Park

6511 Sudley Rd • Daily 8.30am–5pm• $3 • ☎ 703 361 1339, ⓦ nps.gov/mana

Manassas National Battlefield Park extends over grassy hills at the western fringes of the Washington DC suburbs, just off I-66. The first major land battle of the Civil War – known in the North as the **Battle of Bull Run** – was fought here on the morning of July 21, 1861. Expecting an easy victory, some 25,000 Union troops attacked a Confederate detachment that controlled a vital railroad link to the Shenandoah Valley. But the rebels proved powerful opponents, and their strength in battle earned their commander, Thomas J. Jackson, his famous nickname (see p.356). He and General Lee also masterminded a second, even more demoralizing Union loss here in late August 1862, the battle of "Second Manassas", that came close to the high point of Confederate ascendancy. The **visitor centre** at the entrance describes how the battles took shape, and details other aspects of the war.

Fredericksburg

Only a mile off the I-95 highway, halfway to Richmond from Washington DC, **FREDERICKSBURG** is one of Virginia's prettiest historic towns, where elegant downtown streets are backed by residential avenues lined with white picket fences. In colonial days, this was a busy inland port, in which tobacco and other plantation commodities were loaded onto boats that sailed down the Rappahannock River. Dozens of stately early American buildings along the waterfront now hold antique stores and boutiques.

In the 1816 town hall, the **Fredericksburg Area Museum**, 907 Princess Anne St (Mon–Sat 10am–5pm, Sun noon–5pm; $7; ☎ 540 371 3037, ⓦ famcc.org), has a range of displays tracing local history, from Native American settlements to the wartime era.

5

The **Rising Sun Tavern**, 1304 Caroline St, was built as a home in 1760 by George Washington's brother, Charles. As an inn, it became a key meeting place for patriots and a hotbed of sedition. It is now a small **museum** (March–Oct Mon–Sat 10am–5pm, Sun noon–4pm; Nov–Feb Mon–Sat 11am–4pm, Sun noon–4pm; $5; ☎540 373 1559), showcasing antique decor and a collection of pub games and pewter. Guides are also on hand to explain eighteenth-century medicine at **Hugh Mercer's Apothecary Shop**, 1020 Caroline St (same hours as above; $5), which often involved treating patients with the likes of leeches and crab claws. If you're more interested in George Washington, you can venture out to his family's **Ferry Farm**, 268 Kings Hwy (daily: March–Oct 10am–5pm; Nov–Feb 10am–4pm; $8; ☎540 370 0732, ⓦkenmore.org), where he grew up and which still has a bucolic setting and maintains gardens appropriate for the era.

Fredericksburg's Battlefields

Fredericksburg and Spotsylvania National Battlefield Park Hours vary, often Mon–Fri 9am–5pm, Sat & Sun 9am–6pm • Free • ⓦ nps.gov/frsp

Fredericksburg's strategic location made it vital during the Civil War, and the land around the town was heavily contested. More than 100,000 men lost their lives in the major battles and countless bloody skirmishes. The **visitor centre** (see below) can lead you out to **Fredericksburg and Spotsylvania National Battlefield Park**, south of town. Contact the centre or the website for information on the other major battlefields, **Wilderness** and **Chancellorsville**, both west of town, as well as the various manors and shrines in the area.

ARRIVAL AND INFORMATION
FREDERICKSBURG

By bus Greyhound buses pull in at the station at 1400 Jefferson Davis Hwy.

By train The Amtrak station is at 200 Lafayette Blvd.

Visitor centre 702 Caroline St (Mon–Sat 9am–5pm; Sun 11am–5pm; ☎540 373 1776, ⓦvisitfred.com). There are informative exhibits here, while for information about the dozens of other key historical and cultural treasures in the region contact Preservation Virginia (ⓦapva.org).

ACCOMMODATION AND EATING

Basilico 2577 Cowan Blvd ☎540 370 0355, ⓦbasilico deli.com. A fine Italian deli with rib-sticking pizzas, pastas and sandwiches. Mon–Sat 9am–9pm, Sun 11am–4pm.

Colonial Tavern 406 Lafayette Blvd ☎540 373 1313, ⓦirishbrigadetavern.com. The place to fill up on Irish food, music and beer. Mon–Sat 11am–2am, Sun 11am–midnight.

Inn at the Olde Silk Mill 1707 Princess Anne St ☎540 371 5666, ⓦinnattheoldesilkmill.com. A worthwhile motel, known for its antique-stocked rooms. $99

Richard Johnston Inn 711 Caroline St ☎540 899 7606, ⓦtherichardjohnstoninn.com. A good, old-fashioned B&B, this elegant, eighteenth-century establishment offers plush rooms and some jetted tubs. $150

Sammy T's 801 Caroline St ☎540 371 2008. A popular bar and diner with substantial sandwiches, salads, wraps and pastas, and a good range of bottled beers. Daily 11.30am–9.30pm.

Richmond

Founded in 1737 at the farthest navigable point on the James River, **RICHMOND** remained a small outpost until Virginians, realizing that their capital at Williamsburg was open to British attack, shifted it fifty miles further inland. When war broke out it was named the **capital of the Confederacy**. After the war, Richmond was devastated, but today's town maintains an extensive inventory of architecturally significant older buildings alongside its modern office towers, and **tobacco** is still a major industry. Richmond's **downtown** centres on a few blocks rising up from the James River to either side of Broad Street. Up the hill in the **Court End District**, dozens of well-preserved antebellum homes provide a suitable backdrop for some important museums and historic sites.

Virginia State Capitol

910 Capitol St • Tours Mon–Sat 9am–4pm, Sun 1–4pm • Free • ☎ 804 698 1788, ⓦ virginiageneralassembly.gov

The **Virginia State Capitol** houses the oldest legislative body still in existence in the USA; the site has been in continuous use since 1788 as the state (and, briefly, Confederate) legislature. Thomas Jefferson had a hand in the design, and the domed central rotunda holds the only marble statue of George Washington modelled from life (by master sculptor Jean-Antoine Houdon), as well as busts of Jefferson and the seven other Virginia-born US presidents.

Governor's Mansion and around

Governor's Mansion 901 E Grace St • Tours Tues–Thurs 10am–noon & 2–4pm • Free • ☎ 804 371 2642

On Capitol Square is the Federal-style **Governor's Mansion**, which, like the Capitol, is the oldest of its kind in the USA, dating to 1813. Much less reserved, across from Capitol Square, is the huge Victorian **Old City Hall**, 1001 E Broad St, designed in 1894 in a Gothic Revival style and so visually busy it makes your head spin.

Museum and White House of the Confederacy

1201 E Clay St • Mon–Sat 10am–5pm, Sun noon–5pm • Museum $9, White House $10; combo ticket $15 • ⓦ moc.org

Two blocks north of the Capitol, the **Museum of the Confederacy** covers the history of the Civil War through weapons, uniforms and personal effects of Confederate leaders, including J.E.B. Stuart's plumed hat, the tools used to amputate General Stonewall Jackson's arms at Chancellorsville (he died regardless), and General Robert E. Lee's revolver and the pen he used to sign the surrender.

The **White House of the Confederacy** is an 1818 Neoclassical mansion where Jefferson Davis lived as Confederate president. After he absconded when the South fell in 1865, Abraham Lincoln famously visited the house and even sat briefly in Davis's office chair.

Valentine Richmond History Center

1015 E Clay St • Tues–Sat 10am–5pm, Sun noon–5pm • $8 • ☎ 804 649 0711, ⓦ richmondhistorycenter.com

The 1812 **Wickham House** now forms part of the excellent **Valentine Richmond History Center**. This Federal-style monolith houses a small local history museum focusing on the experience of working-class and black Americans, as well as an extensive array of furniture and pre-Civil War clothing such as whalebone corsets and other **Victorian** apparel.

Jackson Ward

West of the Convention Center on Sixth Street is a neighbourhood of early nineteenth-century houses, **Jackson Ward**, filling a dozen blocks around First and Clay streets. This National Historic Landmark District has been the centre of Richmond's African American community since well before the Civil War, when the city had the largest free black population in the USA. As well as covering local history, the **Maggie L. Walker House**, 110 E Leigh St (Mon–Sat 9am–5pm; free; ☎ 804 771 2017, ⓦ nps.gov/mawa), traces the working life of the physically disabled, black Richmond resident who, during the 1920s, became the first woman in the USA to found and run a bank, now the Consolidated Bank and Trust.

Canal Walk

A nice example of urban revitalization is the landscaping of a 1.25-mile stretch of waterfront into **Canal Walk**, which runs between downtown and Shockoe Bottom. **Canal boat rides** depart from around 14th and Virginia streets (hours vary, often Fri & Sat noon–7pm, Sun noon–5pm; $8; ☎ 804 649 2800), providing a leisurely and pleasant thirty-minute jaunt.

5

American Civil War Center and around

490 Tredegar St • Daily 9am–5pm • Free • ☎ 804 771 2145, ⓦ nps.gov/rich

For insight into the Confederate period, you can start or end your stroll at the **American Civil War Center** at the refurbished **Tredegar Iron Works**, a munitions plant whose foundry churned out tons of Confederate materiel. The centre has multimedia presentations about Civil War history and three floors of compelling exhibits. Tredegar is also the main visitor centre for **Richmond National Battlefield Park**, which describes the dozens of Civil War sites in the area that can be accessed on an eighty-mile drive. Those who weren't so lucky ended up just west of Tredegar at **Hollywood Cemetery**, 412 S Cherry St (daily 8am–5pm; free tours April–Oct Mon–Sat 10am; ☎ 804 648 8501, ⓦ hollywoodcemetery.org), where a 90ft-tall granite **pyramid** commemorates the 18,000 Confederate troops killed nearby.

Shockoe Bottom

Split down the middle by the raised I-95 freeway, the gentrified riverfront warehouse district of **Shockoe Bottom** still holds a few reminders of Richmond's industrial past among the restaurants and nightclubs on its cobblestone streets. From **Shockoe Slip**, an old wharf rebuilt in the 1890s after being destroyed in the Civil War, Cary Street runs east along the waterfront, lined by a wall of brick warehouses – many of which have been converted into lofts and condos – known as **Tobacco Row**.

The Edgar Allan Poe Museum

1914 E Main St • Tues–Sat 10am–5pm, Sun 11am–5pm • $6 • ☎ 804 648 5523, ⓦ poemuseum.org

On Main Street, Richmond's oldest building, an appropriately gloomy 250-year-old flagstone house, holds the **Edgar Allan Poe Museum**, commemorating the dark poet who grew up here. Showcased within are memorabilia and relics such as his walking stick and a lock of his hair, plus a model of Richmond as it was in Poe's time.

Church Hill

Church Hill, a few blocks northeast of the Edgar Allan Poe Museum, is one of Richmond's oldest surviving districts, its decorative eighteenth-century houses looking out over the James River. Capping the hill at the heart of the neighbourhood, the 1741 **St John's Church**, 2401 E Broad St (tours Mon–Sat 10am–3.30pm, Sun 1–3.30pm; $7; ⓦ historicstjohnschurch.org), is best known as the place where, during a 1775 debate, future state governor and firebrand **Patrick Henry** proclaimed, "Give me liberty or give me death!". His speech, along with the debate itself, is re-created by actors in period dress every Sunday at 2pm in summer.

The Fan District

The **Fan District**, so named because its tree-lined avenues fan out at oblique angles, spreads west from the downtown area, beyond Belvidere Street (US-1), and its centrepiece, **Monument Avenue**, which is lined with garish Victorian and Historic Revival mansions from the turn of the twentieth century.

Virginia Museum of Fine Arts

2800 Grove Ave • Mon–Wed, Sat & Sun 10am–5pm, Thurs & Fri 10am–9pm • $5 donation • ⓦ vmfa.museum

South of Monument Avenue stands the **Virginia Museum of Fine Arts**, newly remodelled into a grand and inspiring modern space to house its extensive collection of Impressionist and post-Impressionist paintings, among them American works ranging from Charles Willson Peale's acclaimed portraits to George Catlin's romantic images of Plains Indians to the Pop Art creations of Roy Lichtenstein and Claes Oldenburg. Other galleries contain such items as Frank Lloyd Wright furniture, Lalique jewellery,

Hindu and Buddhist sculpture from the Himalayas and jewel-encrusted Fabergé eggs, crafted in the 1890s for the Russian tzars.

ARRIVAL AND GETTING AROUND   RICHMOND

By plane The airport, 10 miles east of downtown, is served by a half-dozen national carriers and has a small visitor centre (Mon–Fri 9.30am–4.30pm; ☎ 804 226 3000, ⓦ flyrichmond.com) in the arrivals terminal.

By car Richmond is 2hr by car from Washington DC, via I-95, which cuts through the east side of downtown.

By train Amtrak trains pull into 1500 E Main St (there's

another station further out at 7519 Staples Mill Rd).

By bus The Greyhound bus station, just off I-64 at 2910 N Blvd, is a good way from the centre of town.

Local buses Much of Richmond is compact enough to walk around, but to get to outlying places you can take a GRTC bus; $1.50, $2 express routes (☎ 804 358 4782, ⓦ ridegrtc.com).

ACCOMMODATION

The Berkeley 1200 E Cary St ☎ 804 780 1300, ⓦ berkeleyhotel.com. Elegant small hotel with boutique touches and suites with private terraces, on the historic Shockoe Slip. $182

Grace Manor Inn 1853 W Grace St ☎ 804 353 4334, ⓦ thegracemanorinn.com. Stately B&B housing three tasteful suites in a grand 1910 building. Rooms are rich with antique decor; some have fireplaces and clawfoot tubs. Breakfast can be quite good, too. $150

Henry Clay Inn 114 N Railroad Ave, Ashland ☎ 804 798 3100, ⓦ henryclayinn.com. Though it's 11 miles out of town, this is a pleasant B&B with fourteen

antique-filled rooms. Some are suites with jacuzzis and fridges. $95

★ **The Jefferson** 101 W Franklin St ☎ 804 788 8000, ⓦ jeffersonhotel.com. Grand hotel with a marble-columned lobby, marble baths and stylish rooms. Smart and sizeable suites also available. $385

Linden Row Inn 100 E Franklin St ☎ 804 783 7000, ⓦ lindenrowinn.com. A chic row of red-brick Georgian terraced houses has been converted into a comfortable modern hotel with antique furnishings. However, unless you get a swanky Parlor Suite, the rooms can be on the drab side. $239

EATING AND DRINKING

The Black Sheep 901 W Marshall St, near Jackson Ward ☎ 804 648 1300. Eclectic restaurant whipping up fantastic hashes and French toast for breakfast, as well as chicken and dumplings, mushroom bucatini and lamb kebabs – a hodgepodge of flavours and prices. Tues–Sat 10am–10pm, Sun 9am–9pm.

Julep's 1719 E Franklin St, Shockoe Bottom ☎ 804 377 3968, ⓦ juleps.net. New Southern dining at its best, with many great mid-priced to expensive dishes, among them onion-crusted salmon, sweetwater crab soup and duck breast with pancetta. Mon–Sat 5.30–10pm.

★ **Mamma Zu** 501 S Pine St, south of downtown ☎ 804 788 4205. Italian food in the South can often be awful, but this is one big exception: a terrific upper-end restaurant that serves up delicious oyster soup, veal marsala and calamari, among other savoury choices. Mon–Fri 11am–2pm & 5.30–10pm, Sat 5.30–11pm.

Millie's Diner 2603 E Main St ☎ 804 643 5512, ⓦ milliesdiner.com. Worth a trip out beyond Shockoe

Bottom to enjoy expensive but delicious seafood and steak, plus rack of lamb and vegetarian risotto, and there's also a nice range of brews. Tues–Fri 11am–2pm & 5.30–10pm, Sat 10am–3pm & 5.30–10pm, Sun 9am–3pm & 5.30–9.30pm.

Penny Lane Pub 421 E Franklin St, downtown ☎ 804 780 1682, ⓦ pennylanepub.com. British-style joint with substantial grilled food and other affordable pub grub, including a mean steak-and-Guinness pie, plus a full range of English and other beers, and European soccer on TV. Mon–Fri 11am–2am, Sat 10am–2am, Sun call for hours.

Strawberry Street Café 421 N Strawberry St ☎ 804 353 6860, ⓦ strawberrystcafe.com. Casual and comfortable Fan District café offering mainly inexpensive quiches, pasta and salads, but also mid-priced jambalaya and crab cakes, and a salad bar nestled in an old bathtub. Mon–Thurs 11.30am–10pm, Fri 11.30am–11pm, Sat 10am–11pm, Sun 10am–10pm.

NIGHTLIFE AND ENTERTAINMENT

Richmond's main **nightlife** spots are concentrated around the **Shockoe Slip** and **Shockoe Bottom** areas, just east of downtown. For details on music and events, check the free *Style Weekly* newspaper or ⓦ arts.richmond.com.

Barksdale Theatre 1601 Willow Lawn Drive ☎ 804 282 2620, ⓦ barksdalerichmond.org. A good bet for mainstream theatre.

Chamberlayne Actors Theatre 319 N Wilkinson Rd, Henrico ☎ 804 262 9760, ⓦ cattheatre.com. Offers fringe works that are daring and contemporary.

5 The Historic Triangle

Besides Boston, the **Historic Triangle**, on the peninsula that stretches southeast of Richmond between the James and York rivers, holds the richest concentration of colonial-era sites in the USA. **Jamestown**, founded in 1607, was Virginia's first settlement; **Williamsburg** is a detailed replica of the colonial capital; and **Yorktown** was the site of the climactic battle in the Revolutionary War. All are within a scenic hour's drive from Richmond, and Williamsburg is accessible by Amtrak **train**.

Although I-64 is the quickest way to cover the fifty miles from Richmond to Williamsburg, a far more pleasing drive along US-5 rolls through plantation country, where many eighteenth-century mansions are open to the public. Once you're in the Historic Triangle, the best way to get around is along the wooded Colonial Parkway, which winds west to Jamestown and east to Yorktown, twenty miles in all. Most of the area's numerous tourist facilities are to be found around Williamsburg.

Jamestown

Site Daily 9am–5pm · Seven-day pass $10/car, includes Yorktown battlefield · ☎ 757 229 1733, ⓦ nps.gov/jame **Visitor centre** Colonial Pkwy

Jamestown was England's first successful stab at a New World colony, after earlier efforts to the south failed. Built as a trading and military outpost, its lore and legend are still being celebrated four hundred years later, with recent archeological discoveries adding new insights and perspectives. You'll want to visit both the original location and the re-created site by taking the scenic Colonial Parkway, or highways 5 and 31 from Williamsburg. Protected within the **Jamestown National Historic Site** on Jamestown Island, the one bit of seventeenth-century Jamestown to survive the ravages of time and a 1698 fire is the 50ft tower of the first brick church, built around 1650 – one of the oldest extant English structures in the USA.

The area is roughly divided into two sections: the **New Towne** is where the colonists relocated after the 1620s to erect businesses, establish permanent residences, build livestock pens and so on. Much of what's visible are replicas of the original brick foundations buried below (to protect from weather damage). More interesting is the site of the **Old Towne**, which includes ruins from the original triangular 1607 fort. Here you'll see dozens of archeologists working behind a perimeter, and you can also drop in on the **Archaearium**, where some of the many treasures discovered here – everything from glassware to utensils to the skeleton of a colonist who died a violent death – are on display (also online at ⓦhistoricjamestowne.org).

At the end of the Colonial Parkway, the **visitor centre** (see above), features drawings and audiovisual exhibits that conjure up the past, and, closer to the park entrance, you can watch artisans making old-fashioned **glasswork** (some of it for sale), as well as see the brick remnants of a seventeenth-century kiln.

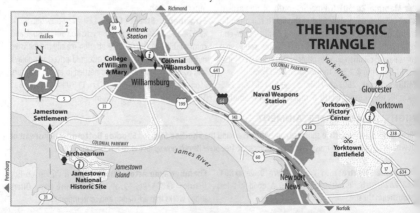

Jamestown Settlement

2110 Jamestown Rd, Rte-31S • Daily 9am–5pm • $16, $20.50 with Yorktown Victory Center • ☎ 757 253 4838, ⍟ historyisfun.org

If looking at dusty artefacts isn't enough for you, head to the adjacent **Jamestown Settlement** for a more family-friendly, somewhat simplified look at the early colony. This complex of museums and full-size replicas provides a colourful view of what went on here, its reconstructed buildings staffed by guides in period costume weaving, making pottery and so on. Replicas of the three **ships** that carried the first settlers are moored on the James River.

Colonial Williamsburg

The splendid re-creation of **Colonial Williamsburg** is an essential tourist experience for anyone with a flair for American history. While you have to buy a pricey ticket to look inside the restored buildings, the grounds are open all the time, and you can wander freely down the cobblestone streets and across the green commons.

From the Wren Building on the William and Mary campus, separated from Colonial Williamsburg by a mock-historic shopping centre, **Duke of Gloucester Street** runs east through the historic area to the old Capitol. The first of its eighteenth-century buildings is the Episcopalian **Bruton Parish Church**, where all the big names of the Revolutionary period were known to visit, and which has served as a house of worship for nearly three hundred years. Behind the church, the broad **Palace Green** spreads north to the Governor's Palace (see p.348). West of the church, the 1771 **courthouse** and the octagonal **powder magazine**, protected by a guardhouse, face each other in the midst of Market Square. Further along, **Chowning's Tavern**, a reconstruction of an alehouse that stood here in 1766, is a functioning pub with lively entertainment.

The Capitol

The real architectural highlight is the **Capitol**, a monumental edifice at the east end of Duke of Gloucester Street. The current building, a 1945 reconstruction of the 1705 original, has an open-air ground-floor **arcade** linking two keyhole-shaped wings. One wing housed the elected, legislative body of the Colonial government, the **House of Burgesses**, while the other held the chambers of the **General Court** – where alleged felons, including thirteen of Blackbeard's pirates, were tried.

Duke of Gloucester Street

The "merchants" of **Duke of Gloucester Street** have been done up as eighteenth-century apothecaries, cobblers and silversmiths, and the docents inside are an excellent source of historical information on their respective crafts; taking part in a casual conversation or working demonstration can be an excellent way to get into the spirit of things

---

TICKETS FOR COLONIAL WILLIAMSBURG

Although it's pleasant enough to stroll about the open spaces of Colonial Williamsburg, to set foot inside any of the buildings that have been restored or rebuilt you need to buy a **ticket**, either from the main **visitor centre** (101 Visitor Center Drive; daily 9am–5pm; ☎ 888 965 7254, ⍟ history.org), north of the centre off the Colonial Parkway, or from a smaller office at the west end of Duke of Gloucester Street. Most buildings in the park are open daily from 9am to 5pm, but about a third of them may have special hours and days they're open; check the website for details. Day-pass **tickets** are $42 (kids $21) and include access to the merchant shops and the Capitol, and admission to on-site museums devoted to folk art and the decorative arts, or $50 (kids $25) to include a Governor's Mansion tour and an extra day. Aside from these, there are additional charges for the special programmes and events offered by Colonial Williamsburg, such as staged courthouse trials, holiday spectacles and candlelit walking tours.

5

– learning about anything from making bullets and saddles to printing presses and wigs. The **Raleigh Tavern** along Gloucester Street was where the Independence-minded colonial government reconvened after being dissolved by the loyalist governors in 1769 and again in 1774; the original burned down in 1859.

The Governor's Palace

The imposing two-storey **Governor's Palace**, at the north end of Palace Green, has a grand ballroom and opulent furnishings, and must have served as a telling declaration of royal power, no doubt enforced by the startling display of swords, muskets and other deadly weaponry interlaced on the walls of the foyer.

Yorktown

Site Daily 9am–5pm • $10/car for seven-day pass, good also for admission to Jamestown National Historic Site • ☎ 757 898 2410, ⓦ nps.gov/yonb **Visitor centre** 200 Water St, Rte-1020

YORKTOWN, along the York River on the north side of the peninsula, gave its name to the decisive final major battle of the **Revolutionary War**, when, on October 18, 1781, overwhelmed and besieged British (and German mercenary) troops under the command of Charles, Lord Cornwallis, surrendered here to the joint American and French forces commanded by George Washington. At the heart of the namesake battlefield that surrounds the town, a **visitor centre** has interpretive displays, including a replica, walk-through fighting ship and military artefacts, and also provides several guided tours of the area. A dozen original buildings survive from the era, along with the earthworks. The **Siege Line Overlook** (at the visitor centre) has good views of strategic points, while maps and an audio tour are available if you want to explore in detail.

Note that, as at Jamestown, the state of Virginia and National Park Service have constructed a mini theme park nearby – this time a re-created Continental Army encampment – as part of the **Yorktown Victory Center** (daily 9am–5pm; $9.75, $20.50 with Jamestown Settlement; ⓦ historyisfun.org), west of the battlefield on US-17. The museum covers both sides of the conflict, and two outdoor museums portray life on a middle-class farm and in a Revolutionary War camp.

ARRIVAL AND DEPARTURE   THE HISTORIC TRIANGLE

By car Of the three main sites, only Williamsburg is easily reached without a car, and it's the hub of accommodation and dining.

By train or bus Amtrak trains and Greyhound buses stop at 468 N Boundary St, Williamsburg, two blocks from the Governor's Palace.

GETTING AROUND

By bike The Colonial Pkwy makes an excellent, scenic cycling route to Jamestown (12 miles from Williamsburg) or Yorktown (14 miles); rent a bike from Bikes Unlimited at 141 Monticello Ave in Williamsburg ($25/day; ☎ 757 229 4620, ⓦ bikewilliamsburg.com).

By shuttle bus In Colonial Williamsburg, ticket-holders

can use the hop-on, hop-off shuttle buses (daily 9am–10pm) that leave from the visitor centre and stop at convenient points in the historic area. You can also pick up the free Historic Triangle Shuttle, which stops at all the major attractions (mid-March to Nov daily every 30min, 9.30am–4pm).

ACCOMMODATION

For accommodation, the Williamsburg Hotel/Motel Association (☎ 757 220 3330, ⓦ gowilliamsburg.com) can find you a bed at no extra charge. West of the centre, US-60 is lined with endless motels, and there are also several cheap options just a few blocks east of the Capitol.

Bassett Motel 800 York St, Williamsburg ☎ 757 229 5175, ⓦ bassettmotel.com. The basic but clean and well-sited *Bassett Motel* is just east of the Capitol. **$79**

Duke of York Motel 508 E Water St, Yorktown ☎ 757 898 3232, ⓦ dukeofyorkmotel.com. This option has beachfront units, some with kitchenettes, fridges and jacuzzis, along the York River. **$119**

Marriott's Manor Club at Ford's Colony 101 St Andrews Drive, 4 miles outside Yorktown ☎ 757 258 5705, ⓦmarriott.com. Expensive villas as well as entry-level units with DVD players, fireplaces and patios. $149

EATING AND DRINKING

The various restaurants and taverns along Duke of Gloucester Street in Colonial Williamsburg feature good (if overpriced) pub food; some operate on a seasonal basis only (often April–Oct).

★ **Cheese Shop** 410 W Duke of Gloucester St, Colonial Williamsburg ☎ 757 220 0298, ⓦcheeseshop williamsburg.com. Great deli sandwiches – try the Virginia ham – but expect a wait during peak hours. Mon–Sat 10am–8pm, Sun 11am–6pm.

Green Leafe Café 765 Scotland St, Colonial Williamsburg ☎ 757 220 3405, ⓦgreenleafe.com. Near the William and Mary campus, the *Green Leafe Café* offers solid chilli, burgers, pizza and pasta, and dozens of brews on tap. Daily 11am–2am.

Trellis Café Merchants Square mall, 403 W Duke of Gloucester St, Colonial Williamsburg ☎ 757 229 8610, ⓦthetrellis.com. West of the historic area, the excellent *Trellis Café* serves pricey seafood and steak mains for dinner, but affordable sandwiches and burgers for lunch. Daily 8–10am, 11am–3pm & 5–9pm.

The Atlantic coast

One of the busiest of the East Coast ports, **Norfolk** sits midway along the coast at the point where the Chesapeake Bay empties into the Atlantic Ocean. As Virginia's only heavy industrial centre, it's not pretty, but it does hold a rich maritime and naval heritage, as well as the Chrysler Museum, one of the region's best art galleries, and provides access to historic **Portsmouth**, a short ferry ride away. Fifteen miles east of Norfolk, along the open Atlantic, **Virginia Beach** draws summer sun-seekers to the state's busiest seashore.

The rest of Virginia's Atlantic coast is on its isolated and sparsely populated **Eastern Shore**, where the attractive little island town of **Chincoteague** serves as the headquarters of a wildlife refuge that stretches to the Maryland border as part of the Assateague Island National Seashore.

Norfolk

Along with Hampton Roads and Newport News on the north side of the James River, **NORFOLK** is home to the largest US naval base, with all manner of grey-steel behemoths cruising past regularly.

Nauticus: The National Maritime Center

1 Waterside Drive • June–Aug daily 10am–5pm; Sept–May Tues–Sat 10am–5pm, Sun noon–5pm • $16 • ☎ 757 664 1000, ⓦnauticus.org

The waterfront features Norfolk's premier attraction, **Nauticus: The National Maritime Center**, which has oceanography displays, shallow pools for touching tidal creatures and horseshoe crabs, bigger aquariums, large-screen films, interactive naval exhibits and a deep-sea submersible. On the second floor, the **Hampton Roads Naval Museum** (Tues–Sat 10am–5pm, Sun noon–5pm; free; ⓦhrnm.navy.mil) documents historical naval operations in the area; across from the centre, you can tour the decks of the **USS Wisconsin** (daily 10am–4.45pm; included in Nauticus admission).

Hermitage Foundation Museum

7637 N Shore Rd • Mon, Tues, Fri & Sat 10am–5pm, Sun 1–5pm • Museum tours $5, garden tours $6 • ☎ 757 423 2052, ⓦhermitagefoundation.org

An extraordinary array of Asian antiquities is displayed in the intimate Tudor-style home, now known as the **Hermitage Foundation Museum**, by the Lafayette River. It's really a hodgepodge, encompassing everything from Persian rugs, medieval tapestries and ancient Chinese ceremonial vessels to European Christian icons and hand-painted stained glass. There are also tours of the gardens ($6) and of some of the related buildings on the site (summer, by reservation only).

5

Chrysler Museum

245 W Olney Rd, at Mowbray Arch • Wed 10am–9pm, Thurs–Sat 10am–5pm, Sun noon–5pm • Free • ☎ 757 664 6200, ⓦ chrysler.org

The city's biggest-name institution, the **Chrysler Museum**, half a mile north of the Norfolk waterfront, holds another eclectic collection, this one belonging to car magnate Walter Chrysler Jr, comprising ancient Greek statuary, French Impressionist paintings, Franz Klein abstractions and Maya funerary objects, as well as world-class Tiffany and Lalique glassware.

Moses Myers House and around

323 E Freemason St • Wed–Sun noon–5pm • Free • ☎ 757 333 1087

For a glimpse of bourgeois life in the area c.1800, check out the Chrysler Museum's **Moses Myers House**, the elegant home of one of Norfolk's most prominent Jewish residents, adorned with portraits by Gilbert Stuart and Thomas Sully, and carefully restored to its early nineteenth-century flair. The associated **Norfolk History Museum**, 601 E Freemason St (tours only, Wed–Sun noon & 2pm; free; ☎ 757 441 1526), has a predictable array of historical objects and antiques but is most interesting for the sturdy 1794 Georgian manor it's housed in.

ARRIVAL, GETTING AROUND AND INFORMATION   NORFOLK

By plane Norfolk Airport Shuttle (☎ 757 963 0433, ⓦ jamesrivertrans.com) connects downtown Norfolk with Norfolk International Airport ($21), 5 miles northeast.

By bus Amtrak bus connections from Newport News, across the James River on the north shore, stop at W Bute St at York St, and Greyhound stops at 701 Monticello Ave.

Local buses HRT buses ($1.50) provide transport around downtown (Mon–Fri 6.30am–11pm, Sat noon–midnight, Sun noon–8pm; ⓦ norfolk.gov/Visitors/net.asp).

Visitor centre 9401 Fourth View St, exit 273 off I-64 (daily 9am–5pm; ☎ 757 441 1852).

ACCOMMODATION AND EATING

Bardo 430 W 21st St ☎ 757 622 7362, ⓦ bardoeats .com. Inexpensive seafood with an Asian edge – seared tuna, ginger dumplings and fried shrimp. Mon–Fri 11am–2am, Sat & Sun 5pm–2am.

★ **Doumar's** 1919 Monticello Ave ☎ 757 627 4163, ⓦ doumars.com. For an inexpensive taste of Americana, stop by this 1950s-era drive-in restaurant where white-hatted waitstaff bring the food to your car; it's tops for barbecue, burgers and waffle-cone ice cream. Mon–Thurs

8am–11pm, Fri–Sun 8am–12.30am.

Freemason Inn 411 W York St ☎ 757 963 7000, ⓦ freemasoninn.com. A pleasant four-unit B&B whose rooms offer fireplaces and jacuzzi tubs, with free on-site wine and cheese. $159

Governor Dinwiddie 506 Dinwiddie St ☎ 757 392 1330, ⓦ governordinwiddiehotel.com. Good-value place in Portsmouth, whose rooms and suites variously offer DVD players, kitchens and in-room bars. $169

Portsmouth

A small **paddlewheel ferry** (hours vary, often Mon–Fri 7.15am–11.30pm, Sat & Sun 10.15am–11.45pm; $1.50; ⓦ hrtransit.org) shuttles from Waterside Park in **Norfolk** across the harbour to the historic city of **PORTSMOUTH**. Here, if you're sufficiently fired up by all the military hardware on view, drop by the **Norfolk Naval Shipyard Museum**, 2 High St, on the waterfront (Tues–Sat 10am–5pm, Sun 1–5pm; $3; ☎ 757 393 8591, ⓦ portsnavalmuseums.com), whose tourable highlight is a century-old **lightship** (same hours, but closed Dec–Feb), which once acted as a floating lighthouse for the harbour. Away from the docks, Portsmouth's brick-lined streets are flanked by charming early American houses and the fetching 1846 Colonial Revival **courthouse**, now an art gallery (Tues–Sat 9am–5pm, Sun 11am–5pm; $5; ⓦ courthousegalleries.com).

Virginia Beach

The massive resort of **VIRGINIA BEACH** has grown to become the largest city in the state, with nearly half a million people. Although the oceanfront commercial activity can be a monument to tackiness, the relaxed atmosphere actually leads some to stay longer than planned.

The city's focus is its long, sandy **beach**, lined with hotels and motels, and backed by a boardwalk strip of bars, restaurants and nightclubs. Virginia Beach is also a major **surf centre**, hosting the **East Coast Surfing Championships** in late August (☎800 861 7873, ☯surfecsc.com). The beach is the site of dozens of high-spirited annual **festivals**, few better than the **American Music Festival** (☎757 491 7866, ☯beachstreetusa.com), which draws big-name artists to jam on the sands over Labor Day weekend. Away from the beach, most of the action is along Atlantic Avenue, the main drag.

Virginia Aquarium and Marine Science Center

717 General Booth Blvd • Daily 9am–5pm • $22, $28 with IMAX show, kids $15/$21 • ☎757 385 FISH, ☯virginiaaquarium.com

High-tech exhibits and an IMAX theatre are featured at the **Virginia Aquarium and Marine Science Center**, which explores all things aquatic, including tanks devoted to sharks, rays, sea turtles and jellyfish in different climatically themed environments, a short, pleasant nature trail through the **Owls Creek salt marsh** and an aviary displaying dozens of native species. The museum also organizes **dolphin-watching** expeditions (April–Oct; $19; 90min) and **whale-watching** cruises (late Dec to mid-March; $28; 2hr 30min), for which you should reserve in advance.

Association for Research and Enlightenment

215 67th St, at Atlantic Ave • Mon–Fri 8am–5pm • Free • ☎800 333 4499, ☯edgarcayce.org

The eccentric Association for Research and Enlightenment focuses on **Edgar Cayce** (1877–1945), known as "the sleeping prophet" because of his alleged ability, while in a trance, to diagnose and heal the ailments of individuals anywhere in the world. Willing visitors can use an enormous metaphysical library, take in a lecture on various New Age subjects or test their own personal ESP.

First Landing State Park

With an entrance five miles west of Virginia Beach off Hwy-60/Shore Drive, the woodland of **First Landing State Park** was the site where the first English settlers touched land in 1607 before moving on to Jamestown; it's Virginia's most popular state park, good for boating, cycling and camping, with a beach on the Chesapeake Bay.

Adam Thoroughgood House

1636 Parish Rd • Tues–Sat 9am–5pm, Sun 11am–5pm • $4 • ☎757 460 7588, ☯museumsvb.org

About eight miles inland from First Landing State Park is one of the city's many historic relics (for the various others, enquire at the visitor centre), the **Adam Thoroughgood House**, the squat brick home of a man who came to the New World as a servant and ended up as a colonial leader and militiaman; his story, and that of the era, is told through the 1636 building's antiques and displays.

The coast

A few miles up and down the coast from Virginia Beach are some beautiful and peaceful stretches of golden sand. To the south lies the nine-thousand-acre, four-mile-long **Back Bay National Wildlife Refuge** (daily dawn–dusk; $5/car, $2/hiker or cyclist; ☯fws.gov/backbay), an avian preserve for snow geese, falcons and bald eagles (and the occasional sea turtle), where you can walk, bike or fish (but not swim), and **False Cape State Park**, a mile-wide barrier spit that connects to North Carolina and is one of the region's last undisturbed coastlines – though you'll have to arrive by foot, bike or boat (cars are banned on False Cape).

ARRIVAL, GETTING AROUND AND INFORMATION   VIRGINIA BEACH

By bus Greyhound stops at 1017 Laskin Rd, off 31st St. Destinations Charlottesville, VA (3 daily; 6hr 30min–13hr 30min); New York City (3 daily; 11hr 35min–13hr 5min);

Williamsburg, VA (2 daily; 2hr–2hr 30).
By train The Amtrak bus connection from Newport News train station arrives at 19th St and Pacific Ave.

5

Destinations Baltimore, MD (2 daily; 7hr 45min–8hr 45min); Norfolk, VA (2 daily; 40min).
Trams (trolleys) and local buses Beach trams called The Wave (May–Sept daily 8am–2am; $1; ☎757 222 6100, ⊛hrtransit.org) are the easiest way to get around

(buses cost the same); the most useful route is up and down Atlantic Ave (#30).
Visitor centre 2100 Parks Ave, at the east end of I-264, half a mile west of the beach at 21st St (daily: June–Aug 9am–7pm; Sept–May 9am–5pm; ☎800 822 3224, ⊛vbfun.com).

ACCOMMODATION

Barclay Cottage 400 16th St ☎757 422 1956, ⊛barclay cottage.com. A tasteful B&B in a century-old homestead, whose rooms offer the usual quaint Victorian decor, with some jetted tubs. Shared bath $190, en suite $215
The Capes Ocean Resort 2001 Atlantic Ave ☎757 428 5421, ⊛capeshotel.com. This place offers a broad range

of rooms, though all come with oceanfront balconies and fridges. Open March–Oct. $179
Four Sails 3301 Atlantic Ave ☎757 491 8100, ⊛four sails.com. A seaside tower with amenities such as sauna, pool and sundeck, in a central location, with widely varying rates depending on the season. $199

EATING AND DRINKING

Baja Cantina 206 23rd St ☎757 437 2920, ⊛baja cantina.com. A friendly bar featuring serviceable Mexican food at low prices. Daily 11.30am–2am.
Catch 31 3001 Atlantic Ave ☎757 213 3472, ⊛catch31 .com. On the main drag, the choices are inconsistent, but at *Catch 31* you'll find decent burgers and surf-and-turf, with a waterside view. Mon–Fri 6am–2am, Sat 7am–2am.

★ **Terrapin** 3102 Holly Rd ☎757 321 6688, ⊛terrapinvirginiabeach.com. Among the best restaurants in town, a moderate to upper-end place with delicious specialities such as veal shank, truffle mac and cheese, and spicy sea scallops. Mon–Thurs 5.30–9.30pm, Fri & Sat 5.30–10pm, Sun 5–9pm.

The Eastern Shore

Virginia's longest and least-visited stretch of Atlantic coastline, the **Eastern Shore**, lies separated from the rest of the state. On the distant side of the Chesapeake Bay, and with its fishing and farming culture, it has developed fairly independently over the centuries. Only the southernmost segment of what's known as the Delmarva Peninsula actually belongs to Virginia, by which point it has narrowed to become a flat spit of sand protected by a fringe of low-lying islands.

US-13, which runs down the centre of the peninsula and provides a handy short cut from Philadelphia or points north, crosses seventeen miles of open sea at the mouth of the Chesapeake Bay via the **Chesapeake Bay Bridge-Tunnel** ($13/car one way, $18 one way within 24hr; ⊛cbbt.com). For most of its 23-mile length, the roadway runs just a few yards above the water, twice burrowing beneath the surface, before reaching its southern extremity halfway between Norfolk and Virginia Beach. To either side of US-13, a few hamlets and fishing harbours such as Nassawadox, Assawoman and Accomac are tucked away on rambling backroads.

Chincoteague and around

The most appealing destination on the Eastern Shore, **CHINCOTEAGUE** occupies a beautiful seven-mile-long barrier island just south of the Maryland border. Little more than a village, the town is attracting new migrants, but still makes a relaxed base for exploring **Assateague Island National Seashore** (hours vary, often 6am–8pm; $15 week-long vehicle pass, $5/day, walkers and cyclists free; ☎757 336 6577, ⊛nps.gov/asis), whose northern half holds several good hiking trails and can only be reached from Maryland.

CHINCOTEAGUE'S PONY SWIM

If you're in Chincoteague on the last Wednesday and Thursday of July, don't miss the annual **Pony Swim**, when the 150 wild ponies that roam Assateague Island to the north are herded together and directed on a swim through the channel to Chincoteague Memorial Park. Here the foals are sold by auction to help the local community. Note that it is only possible to cross the island's state border on foot – you must return to the mainland for vehicular access.

The southern half of the seashore, just a mile onwards from Chincoteague, is taken up by the 14,000 acre **Chincoteague National Wildlife Refuge** (daily: May–Sept 5am–10pm; March, April & Oct 6am–8pm; Nov–Feb 6am–6pm; $10 seven-day vehicle pass, daily pass $5; ⓦfws.gov/northeast/chinco), notable for fine birdwatching and a range of animals from bats and otters to wild ponies. Call in at the **visitor centre** (☏757 336 6122) for information on the fifteen miles of trails through the dunes and marshes or the pleasant beach at **Tom's Cove**.

ACCOMMODATION AND EATING | CHINCOTEAGUE AND AROUND

Assateague Island Campgrounds ☏410 641 3030, ⓦfnps.gov/assa. There are several types of first-come, first-served campgrounds available on the Maryland side of the national seashore, on the bay or oceanfront. $20

Bill's Seafood 4040 Main St ☏757 336, 5831, ⓦbills seafoodrestaurant.com. The best of the local seafood places, a fine restaurant serving delicious crab, oysters, clams and shrimp at moderate prices, plus steaks and chops. Daily 6am–close.

Cedar Gables Seaside Inn 6095 Hopkins Lane ☏888 491 2944, ⓦcedargable.com. A homely B&B whose four suites have fireplaces, jacuzzis, CD players and fridges, with

excellent breakfasts, too. $190

Island Creamery 6243 Maddox Blvd ☏757 336 6236, ⓦislandcreamery.com. A great ice cream outlet, known for its broad range of tasty flavours. Mon–Thurs & Sun 11am–9pm, Fri & Sat 11am–10pm.

Island Manor House 4160 Main St ☏800 852 1505, ⓦislandmanor.com. A smart, antique-furnished B&B with eight quaint rooms. $155

Refuge Inn 7058 Maddox Blvd ☏757 336 5511, ⓦrefugeinn.com. An assortment of charming rooms and suites with patios and balconies, plus a swimming pool. $165

Charlottesville

Seventy miles west of Richmond, **CHARLOTTESVILLE**, at the geographical centre of the state, holds some of the finest examples of early American architecture, set around a compact, low-rise centre, crisscrossed by magnolia-shaded streets, which make for a pleasant stroll along the pedestrianized blocks of **Main Street**. The most compelling attraction is Thomas Jefferson's home and memorial, **Monticello**, which sits atop a hill just east of town, overlooking the beautiful Neoclassical campus of the University of Virginia, which he also designed.

The University of Virginia

1215 Lee St • 45min guided tours of the campus begin from the Rotunda (daily 10am, 11am, 2pm, 3pm & 4pm, except during holidays • Free • ☏434 924 0311, ⓦvirginia.edu

Though he wrote the Declaration of Independence and served as the third US president, Thomas Jefferson took more pride in having established the **University of Virginia** than in any of his other achievements, as he designed every building down to the most minute detail, planned the curriculum and selected the faculty.

The centrepiece of the campus, called by Jefferson an "academical village", is the red-brick, white-domed **Rotunda**, modelled on the Pantheon and completed in 1826 to house the library and classrooms. A basement gallery tells the history of the university, while upstairs a richly decorated central hall links three elliptical classrooms. A staircase winds up to the **Dome Room**, where paired Corinthian columns rise to an ocular skylight. Twin colonnades stretch along either side of a lushly landscaped quadrangle – the **Lawn** – linking single-storey student apartments with ten taller pavilions in which professors live and hold tutorials.

Monticello

931 Thomas Jefferson Pkwy • Daily 9am–5pm • $24 mid-March to Oct; $18 Jan to mid-March, Nov & Dec; includes 40min house tour; free entry for grounds; speciality guided tours (various programmes) $42–55; reserve ahead • ☏434 984 9822, ⓦmonticello.org

One of America's most familiar buildings – it graces the back of the nickel – **Monticello**, three miles southeast of Charlottesville on Hwy-53, was the home of Thomas Jefferson for most of his life. Its symmetrical brick facade, cantered upon a white Doric portico, is

5

surrounded by acres of beautiful hilltop grounds, which once made up an enormous plantation, with fine views out over the Virginia countryside.

From the outside, Monticello looks like an elegant, Palladian-style country estate, but as soon as you enter the domed entrance hall, with its animal hides, native craftworks, and fossilized bones and elk antlers (from Lewis and Clark's epic 1804 journey across North America, which Jefferson sponsored as president), you begin to see a different side of the man. His love of gadgets is evidenced by an elaborate dual-pen device he used to make automatic copies of all his letters, and by a weather vane over the front porch, connected to a dial so he could measure wind direction without stepping outside. In his **private chambers**, he slept in a cramped alcove that linked his dressing room and his study – he would get up on the right side of the bed if he wanted to make late-night notes, on the left if he wanted to get dressed.

With the price of a tour ticket you can also visit the **gardens**, in which extensive flower and vegetable gardens spread to the south and west, while other parts of the plantation site focus on the remains of **Mulberry Row**, Monticello's slave quarters. Despite calling slavery an "abominable crime", Jefferson owned almost two hundred slaves and recent research indicates he probably had one or more children with one of them, Sally Hemings. At the south end of Mulberry Row, a grove of ancient hardwood trees surrounds Jefferson's gravesite, marked by a simple stone **obelisk**; the epitaph, which lists his major accomplishments, does not mention his having been president.

ARRIVAL AND DEPARTURE   CHARLOTTESVILLE

By bus Greyhound buses pull in at 310 W Main St. Destinations Baltimore, MD (3 daily; 4hr 15min–5hr 45min); Washington DC (2 daily; 3hr 10min).
By train Amtrak trains stop at 810 W Main St.

Destinations Washington DC (3 daily; 2hr 45min–3hr 30min); Wilmington, DE (3 daily; 4hr 30min–5hr).
Visitor centre 610 E Main St (daily 9am–5pm; ☎ 434 293 6789, ⊛ charlottesville.org).

ACCOMMODATION

200 South Street Inn 200 South St ☎ 434 979 0200, ⊛ southstreetinn.com. Good-value B&B rooms are available at these two restored, antique-laden houses, some of whose two dozen units have fireplaces and whirlpool tubs. $173
English Inn 2000 Morton Drive ☎ 434 971 9900, ⊛ englishinncharlottesville.com. A large, mock-Tudor

motel with clean and functional rooms, some equipped with fridges and microwaves, plus a pool, sauna and gym. $120
Inn at Court Square 410 E Jefferson St ☎ 434 295 2800, ⊛ innatcourtsquare.com. This handsome place offers nine rooms in two houses as well as excellent Southern cuisine. $159

EATING AND DRINKING

The Bluegrass Grill & Bakery 313 2nd St SE ☎ 434 295 9700. A good morning stop for tasty pancakes, hash, biscuits and blintzes. Mon–Sat 7am–2pm, Sun 8.30am–2pm.
C&O Restaurant 515 E Water St ☎ 434 971 7044, ⊛ candorestaurant.com. Housed in an old railroad engineers' building, this place offers high-end cuisine from braised veal to pan-fried trout, on a rotating menu of New Southern favourites. Mon–Thurs & Sun 5–10pm, Fri &

Sat 5–11pm. Late-night menu till 1am.
★ **Tastings** 502 E Market St ☎ 434 293 3663, ⊛ tastingsofcville.com. Just north of the downtown mall the upmarket *Tastings* offers upper-end steak, fricassees, crab cakes and lobster bisque, plus a fine selection of wine – including many from local vineyards. Tues & Wed 11.30am–2.30pm, Thurs–Sat 11.30am–2.30pm & 6–9pm.

Appomattox Court House

113 National Park Drive • Daily 8.30am–5pm •$3–5 according to season • ⊛ nps.gov/apco

Set amid the rolling hills of central Virginia, some sixty miles south of Charlottesville on US-460 and Hwy-24, the village of **APPOMATTOX COURT HOUSE** was the site where Ulysses S. Grant blocked General Lee's retreating Confederate army and forced a surrender, on April 9, 1865, that effectively ended the Civil War after four bloody years. Final papers were signed in the home of the **McLean family**, who, ironically, had moved here to get away from the war after the first major battle – Bull Run – was fought on their property in Manassas. Details of the surrender are given in **Appomattox Court House National Historical Park**. The village has been handsomely restored and the McLean home is now a museum.

Shenandoah National Park

The dark forests, rocky ravines and lovely waterfalls of **SHENANDOAH NATIONAL PARK**, far from being untouched wilderness, were created when hundreds of small family farms and homesteads were condemned by the state and federal governments during the Depression, and the land was left to revert to its natural state. With this history, it's no surprise that Shenandoah, meaning "river of high mountains", has one of the most scenic byways in the US, **Skyline Drive**, a thin, 105-mile ribbon of pavement curving along the crest of the Blue Ridge Mountains. It starts just off I-66 near the town of **Front Royal**, 75 miles west of DC, and winds south through the park, giving great views over the area. However, the road was constructed using the latest in 1930s technology and it can be quite narrow at points for modern vehicles. Some of the vertiginous slopes alongside, combined with wildlife such as deer and smaller mammals that cross over the road, also make a trip on the Drive a bit hazardous in places – hence the 35 mph limit in force throughout the route.

Any time of year you can get the best of what the park has to offer by following one of the many **hiking trails** that split off from the ridge; most are two to six miles long. One begins near Byrd visitor centre and winds along to tumbling **Dark Hollow Falls**; another trail, leaving Skyline Drive at mile marker 45, climbs up a treacherous incline to the top of **Old Rag Mountain** for panoramic views out over the whole of Virginia and the Allegheny Mountains in the west. More ambitious hikers, or those who want to spend the night out in the backcountry, should head for the **Appalachian Trail**.

INFORMATION   SHENANDOAH NATIONAL PARK

Entry Week-long admission to the park is $15/car and $8/pedestrian, valid for seven days ($10 and $5 respectively in winter).

Visitor centres Details on any of the park's hiking trails,

and free overnight camping permits, can be picked up at the following visitor centres: Dickey Ridge, milepost 4.7, Harry F. Byrd Sr, milepost 51, and Loft Mountain, milepost 79 (daily 8.30am–5pm; ☏ 540 999 3500, ⊚ nps.gov/shen).

ACCOMMODATION

Big Meadows Lodge Milepost 51.2 ☏ 888 896 3833, ⊚ visitshenandoah.com. Comfortable, welcoming rooms in a gorgeous location with a good communal room for post-hike mingling. **$100**

Campgrounds ☏ 877 444 6777, ⊚ recreation.gov. There are four campgrounds in the park. **$15**

Lewis Mountain Cabin Milepost 57.5 ☏ 888 896 3833,

⊚ visitshenandoah.com. Cosy, rustic cabin accommodation. **$110**

Skyland Resort Milepost 41.7 ☏ 888 896 3833, ⊚ goshenandoah.com. The 1894 *Skyland Resort* offers cabins and hotel rooms as well as a large restaurant with panoramic views. **$110**

The Shenandoah Valley

Many of the small towns of the **SHENANDOAH VALLEY** were left in ruins after the Civil War – the region changed hands more than seventy times at a cost of some 100,000 dead or maimed. Numerous monuments and cemeteries line the backroads, now surrounded by horse farms and apple orchards. Some eight major battlefields can be found here, and the region is marked as an official **National Historic Area**; for more details on following the military campaigns on foot or by car, visit ⊚ shenandoahatwar.org.

Luray Caverns

970 Hwy 211 W • Daily: April–Oct 9am–6pm; Nov–March 9am–5pm • $24, kids $12 • ⊚ luraycaverns.com

Besides its martial history, the northern Shenandoah Valley also holds half a dozen of Virginia's many **limestone caverns**, which tend to be privately owned and touristy and

5

cost between $15–25 to explore. One of the largest is **Luray Caverns**, twelve miles east of New Market off Hwy-211, featuring an underground "organ" with stalagmites as "pipes".

Frontier Culture Museum

1290 Richmond Rd, Staunton • Daily: mid-March to Nov 9am–5pm; Dec to mid-March 10am–4pm • $10 • ⓦ frontiermuseum.org

South of Luray Caverns, off Hwy-250 northwest of the town of **STAUNTON**, the **Frontier Culture Museum** showcases eight different kinds of immigrant farms, including buildings that were mostly imported from Europe. It's more a historic theme park than an authentic cultural experience, but still worth a look to see how backbreaking it must have once been to live the rural life.

Woodrow Wilson Presidential Library

18–24 N Coalter St • Mon–Sat 9am–5pm, Sun noon–5pm • $14, kids $5 • ⓦ woodrowwilson.org

The **Woodrow Wilson Presidential Library** commemorates the 28th president of the USA with exhibits on how he led the country into World War I and into various moral crusades, with a look at his chic Pierce-Arrow presidential limousine and his birthplace next door.

Lexington and around

With horse-drawn carriages moving along its quiet, brick-lined streets, the small valley town of **LEXINGTON** offers a few key historical sites, and is also a good place to visit for its dozens of fine old homes; pick up a walking-tour map at the **visitor centre**.

Lee Chapel and Museum

100 N Jefferson St • Mon–Sat 9am–5pm, Sun 1–5pm, closes 4pm in winter • Free • ☎ 434 458 8768, ⓦ chapelapps.wlu.edu

The sombre **Lee Chapel and Museum** is on the colonnaded campus of **Washington and Lee University**, north of the town centre. General Robert E. Lee taught here after the war – when it was known as Washington University – and, along with his family, is interred in the chapel's crypt; his famed horse, Traveler, is buried just outside.

George C. Marshall Museum

1600 VMI Parade • Tues–Sat 11am–4pm • $5 • ☎ 540 463 7103, ⓦ marshallfoundation.org

East of Lee chapel, on the far end of the parade ground of the **Virginia Military Institute**, the **George C. Marshall Museum** documents the life of World War II US General, and later Secretary of State, George C. Marshall, whose Marshall Plan helped rebuild Europe after the war.

Stonewall Jackson House

8 E Washington St • March–Dec Mon–Sat 9am–5pm, Sun 1–5pm • $8 • ⓦ stonewalljackson.org

In the town centre, the **Stonewall Jackson House** is where the Confederate general and VMI professor lived before he rode off to war and died at the Battle of Chancellorsville. His spartan 1801 brick townhouse is furnished as it was when he lived there. Nearby, Jackson is buried, with 144 other Confederates, in the **Stonewall Jackson Memorial Cemetery**, on S Main Street at White Street (daily dawn–dusk; free).

Cyrus McCormick's Farm and Virginia Horse Center

Farm Daily 8.30am–5pm • Free • ☎ 540 377 2255 **Horse Center** Mon–Fri 8.30am–5pm • Free, but $5–20 for some events (advance booking required) • ☎ 540 464 2950, ⓦ horsecenter.org

For a break from military history, take a trip fifteen miles north of town, off Rte-606, to **Cyrus McCormick's Farm**, where the famed inventor of the industrial reaper is honoured in an antique setting that includes a grist mill, blacksmith's forge, smokehouse and museum. For a further taste of the bucolic life, the **Virginia Horse Center**, a few miles north of town on Rte-39 sits on six hundred acres, with eight barns and eighteen rings and arenas for displays of equine gallantry. There's a full schedule of events, including rodeos, riding clinics and the Rockbridge Regional Fair: some are free, others require advance tickets.

The Natural Bridge

15 Appledore Lane • Daily 8am until dark • $21, kids $12; $29/$17 with caverns • ☎ 800 533 1410, ⓦ naturalbridgeva.com

Twenty miles south of Lexington on US-11 is the spectacular **Natural Bridge**, a 215ft limestone arch slowly carved by a creek (and there are **caverns** here as well). George Washington allegedly carved his initials into the rock (though it takes a keen eye to see them) and Thomas Jefferson was so impressed that he bought the site to preserve it and owned it for fifty years.

INFORMATION	LEXINGTON AND AROUND

Visitor centre 106 E Washington St (☎ 540 463 3777, ⓦ lexingtonvirginia.com).

ACCOMMODATION

Historic Country Inns ☎ 877 283 9680, ⓦ lexington historicinns.com. A range of appealing B&Bs spread over three stately old structures with 31 rooms and twelve suites, some with fireplaces, jacuzzis and in-room bars. **$127**

Hummingbird Inn 30 Wood Lane ☎ 540 997 9065, ⓦ hummingbirdinn.com. Just a few miles north of town, the *Hummingbird Inn* has five quaint rooms, with the

added appeal of a renovated c.1780 farmhouse with fine dining, a solarium and veranda. **$159**

Magnolia House Inn 501 S Main St ☎ 540 463 2567, ⓦ magnoliahouseinn.com. The 1868 inn was built by the architect of the Lee Chapel and has five comfortable units with tasteful furnishings in a pleasant garden setting. **$166**

EATING

Bistro on Main 8 N Main St ☎ 540 464 4888, ⓦ bistro -lexington.com. For delicious shrimp and grits, catfish and duck breast at moderate prices, this is a reliable choice. Tues–Sat 11.30am–2.30pm & 5–9pm, Sun 11am–2pm.

★ **Sheridan Livery Inn** 35 N Main St ☎ 540 464 1887, ⓦ sheridanliveryinn.com. Some of the best food around, from the barbecued shrimp and crab-cake sandwiches to the succulent strip steak and chilli-braised pork shoulder.

Mon–Thurs & Sun 11am–9pm, Fri & Sat 11am–9.30pm.

Southern Inn Restaurant 37 S Main St ☎ 540 463 3612, ⓦ southerninn.com. Right in the centre of town, the *Southern Inn* has good, affordable sandwiches, steak and seafood, with pricier New Southern offerings such as shad roe and roasted guinea hen. Mon–Sat 11.30am– 10pm, Sun 10am–9pm.

Blue Ridge Parkway

Once it wends its way out of Shenandoah National Park, Skyline Drive becomes the **Blue Ridge Parkway**, a beautiful route heading southwest along the crest of the Appalachians. However, **I-81**, sweeping along the flank of the mountains, is a more efficient way of getting from Virginia to North Carolina and on to the Great Smoky Mountains (see p.453).

ACCOMMODATION	THE BLUE RIDGE PARKWAY

Campgrounds ☎ 828 271 4779, ⓦ nps.gov/blri. Call for information on the various campgrounds and visitor centres along the Parkway. **$16**

Rocky Knob Cabins Milepost 174 ☎ 540 593 3503, ⓦ blueridgeresort.com. Offers a memorable stay in the idyllic Meadows of Dan, with units dating from the

Depression featuring kitchenettes and fireplaces. Open May–Nov. **$59**

Peaks of Otter Lodge Twenty miles north of Roanoke, at Milepost 86 ☎ 800 542 5927, ⓦ peaksofotter.com. This handsome place is open year-round, with clean, simple rooms and lake views. **$144**

Roanoke

Of the towns near the Blue Ridge Parkway, **ROANOKE**, between I-81 and the Parkway, is the largest in western Virginia. It's known for its historic **farmers' market**, dating

5

from 1882, on Campbell Ave at Market St (daily 8am–3pm; ☎540 342 2028), along with the **Taubman Museum**, 110 Salem Ave SE (Tues–Sat 10am–5pm; free; ☎540 342 5760, ⊚taubmanmuseum.org), whose sweeping, ultra-modern steel-and-glass structure was designed by an associate of Frank Gehry. The art is no less interesting, focusing on oddball folk and outsider art, local artists and eye-opening conceptual and minimalist pieces.

Fascinating items are on view at the **History Museum of Western Virginia**, 1 Market Square (Tues–Fri 10am–4pm, Sat 10am–5pm, Sun 1–5pm; $3; ⊚history-museum .org), which records settlement of the region and holds everything from Victorian fashions to documents signed by Thomas Jefferson and war relics, and at the **Virginia Museum of Transportation**, 303 Norfolk Ave (Mon–Sat 10am–5pm, Sun 1–5pm; $8; ⊚vmt.org), home to the South's largest collection of diesel locomotives, plus antique buggies, buses and fire trucks. The visitor centre (see below) has walking-tour maps of the town and information on historic homes, plantations and other tourable sites. Finally, for sweeping views of the valley, make the fifteen-minute drive from the farmers' market up Mill Mountain to the **Roanoke Star**, an 89ft, neon-lit star built in 1949 (ask at the visitor centre for directions), which gives the town its nickname, "Star City".

INFORMATION   ROANOKE

Visitor centre 101 Shenandoah Ave NE (daily 9am–5pm; ☎540 342 6025, ⊚visitroanokeva.com).

ACCOMMODATION AND EATING

202 Market 202 Market Square ☎540 343 6644, ⊚202market.net. A sizeable spot for drinking and live music that also boasts fine high-class cuisine such as seafood, ribs and some Asian offerings. Daily 11.30am–2am.

Grace's Place, 1316 Grandin Rd ☎540 981 1340, ⊚starwoodhotels.com. A savoury array of pizzas, pastas and sandwiches for affordable prices. Mon–Thurs & Sun 11am–9pm, Fri & Sat 11am–10pm.

★ **Hotel Roanoke** 110 Shenandoah Ave ☎540 985 5900, ⊚hotelroanoke.com. Unlike many towns in the region, Roanoke boasts one fine hotel, an upmarket,

mock-Tudor structure built in 1882, whose units now feature smart decor and flat-screen TVs, plus on-site pools and a fitness centre. $139

Sheraton Roanoke 2801 Hershberger Rd ☎540 563 9300, ⊚starwoodhotels.com. The *Sheraton* has a pool, gym, sauna and quality rooms. $159

Texas Tavern 114 W Church Ave ☎540 342 4825, ⊚texastavern-inc.com. A longtime, open-all-hours diner favourite where you can load up on gut-busting egg and ham sandwiches, burgers and, of course, great chilli. Daily 24hr.

West Virginia

Mostly poor and rural, **WEST VIRGINIA** is known for its timber and coal mining industries, which thrive thanks to the state's rich natural resources. Nicknamed "the Mountain State", it boasts the longest whitewater rivers and most extensive wilderness in the eastern USA; for these reasons, the state has become a popular destination for hikers and outdoors enthusiasts, the moonshiners of old replaced by ski instructors and mountain-bike guides.

Back when the state was part of Virginia proper, the small-plot farmers here had little in common with the slave-holding tidewater planters of eastern Virginia. When the Civil War broke out, the area voted to set up a rival Virginia government, loyal to the Union; **statehood** was formalized by Congress in 1863. But mostly the state's been known for its **mining** – one of America's most powerful unions, the United Mine Workers, sprang from here, and the mining companies themselves are responsible for resource extraction despoiling much of the landscape, including the "mountaintop removal" that has rendered much of the majestic scenery a cleaved and scarred wasteland.

The state's most popular destination, the restored 1850s town of **Harpers Ferry**, barely in West Virginia at all, stands just across the broad rivers that form its Maryland and

Virginia borders. To the west, the **Allegheny Mountains** stretch for more than 150 miles, their million-plus acres of hardwood forest rivalling New England's for brilliant autumnal colour. West Virginia's oldest town, **Lewisburg**, sits just off I-64 at the mountains' southern foot, while the capital, **Charleston**, lies in the comparatively flat Ohio River Valley of the west.

Harpers Ferry and around

The ruggedly sited eighteenth-century town of **HARPERS FERRY**, now restored as a **national historic park**, clings to steep hillsides above the rocky confluence of the Potomac and Shenandoah rivers. After suffering the ravages of the Civil War and torrential floods in the late 1800s and the 1930s, the town was all but abandoned, but has since been reconstructed (though the official population stands at less than 300 people).

The place is most identified with **John Brown**, the zealous antebellum-era abolitionist and possible lunatic who seized a federal arsenal here in 1859 in hopes of raising a national black insurrection against slavery. It didn't work, and Brown's scattered forces were routed by US troops commanded by none other than Robert E. Lee.

Shuttle buses drop off at the end of gaslit Shenandoah Street in the heart of the restored **Lower Town**, or Old Town, whose buildings include a blacksmith's shop, clothing and dry-goods stores, tavern and boarding house – as well as the **Master Armorer's House**, once occupied by the chief gunsmith. Museums housing exhibits on the Civil War and black history line both sides of High Street as it climbs away from the river. Nearby, a set of stone steps leads to the 1782 **Harper House**, the oldest in town.

A footpath continues uphill, past overgrown churchyards hemmed in by dry-stone walls, to **Jefferson Rock**, a huge grey boulder affording a great view over the two rivers. For a longer hike, several trails lead onwards into the surrounding forest: the **Appalachian Trail** – linking Maine to Georgia – continues from Jefferson Rock across the Shenandoah River into the Blue Ridge Mountains of Virginia, while the **Maryland Heights Trail** makes a six-mile round-trip around the headlands of the Potomac River. You can also float down the Shenandoah in a **raft** or inner-tube provided by one of the many outfitters along the rivers east and south of town.

ARRIVAL AND INFORMATION
HARPERS FERRY AND AROUND

By train Harpers Ferry makes a popular excursion from Washington DC and is served by several trains daily on the Maryland Rail Commuter network ($11 one-way; ☎ 800 325 7245, ⓦ mtamaryland.com) and by one daily Amtrak service, the *Capitol Limited*, which stops at the corner of Potomac and Shenandoah sts.

By car and shuttle bus Parking is virtually banned in the central area, though you can arrive via the shuttle

buses that run from the large park visitor centre on US-340 (see below).

Park entry The park is open daily 8am–5pm; entry is $4/person, $6/car.

Visitor centres The large park visitor centre is on US-340 (daily 8am–5pm; ☎ 304 535 6029, ⓦ nps.gov/hafe). The Jefferson County tourist bureau is at 37 Washington Court (☎ 304 535 2627, ⓦ hello-wv.com).

ACCOMMODATION AND EATING

The Angler's Inn 867 W Washington St ☎ 340 535 1239, ⓦ theanglersinn.com. An 1880 Victorian dwelling provides the requisite B&B amenities, plus the opportunity to go on a full-day fishing expedition on local rivers (combo packages start at $600). **$140**

Canal House 1225 W Washington St ☎ 304 535 2880, ⓦ canalhousecafe.com. Eating choices in town are limited, though the *Canal House* is a reliable option for its coffee and sandwiches. Mon, Thurs & Fri 5–9pm, Sat

noon–9pm, Sun noon–7pm.

Harpers Ferry Hostel 19123 Sandy Hook Rd, Knoxville, Maryland ☎ 301 834 7652, ⓦ harpersferryhostel.org. Hostel 7 miles east of town that offers by far the cheapest night's sleep around. Dorms **$24**

Laurel Lodge 844 E Ridge St ☎ 304 535 2886, ⓦ laurel lodge.com. Cosy, charming Craftsman bungalow with three rooms featuring smart antique decor. **$140**

5

Charles Town

CHARLES TOWN, four miles south of Harpers Ferry on US-340, is where John Brown was tried and hanged; the **Jefferson County Museum**, at Washington and Samuel streets (March–Dec Tues–Sat 11am–4pm; $3; ☎304 725 8628, ⓦjeffctywvmuseum.org), tells the story of his trial, which took place at the still-functional, 1836 Greek Revival **Jefferson County Courthouse**, 100 E Washington St (Mon–Fri 9am–5pm), as well as his conviction and execution, which deepened animosity between North and South, and helped lead to the Civil War in 1861. Drop by the museum for walking tours of the town's fetching antique homes, which include a half-dozen owned by the family of George Washington.

Sheperdstown

SHEPHERDSTOWN, a cosy village along the Potomac, ten miles to the north Charles Town, is great for wandering, with quaint shops and cafés looking across the river to Maryland's infamous **Antietam Battlefield** (see p.372), casualties from which lay scattered throughout the town during and after the fighting. Sited in a 1786 red-brick edifice with plenty of Victorian furnishings and antiques, the **Historic Shepherdstown Museum**, 129 E German St (April–Oct Sat 11am–5pm, Sun 1–4pm; $4; ⓦhistoricshepherdstown.com), displays war relics and a replica of the 1787 steamboat that James Rumsey designed as a prototype, two decades before Robert Fulton got the official credit.

Berkeley Springs

BERKELEY SPRINGS (also known as Bath) is preserved as a state historic park, thirty miles west of Harpers Ferry on Hwy-9 and seven miles south of I-70, and was a favourite summer retreat of George Washington. Assorted massage and steam-bath treatments are still available. You can take a soak in the old **Roman Baths**, 2 S Washington St (daily 10am–6pm; $30/30min soak or $45 with massage; ☎304 258 2711 for reservations, ⓦberkeleyspringssp.com), in active use since 1815; the spring's waters are 74°F year-round but heated to 102°F for bathers. The town's leafy and green **central square** has footpaths fanning out in all directions; one of these climbs the hill up to the medieval-looking **Berkeley Castle**, a private estate built in 1885.

ACCOMMODATION   **BERKELEY SPRINGS**

★ **Highlawn Inn** 171 Market St ☎304 258 5700, ⓦhighlawninn.com. Among the better B&Bs in Berkeley Springs, spread over four buildings, including some rooms with whirlpool tubs featuring the area's famed waters. $98

Manor Inn 234 Fairfax St ☎304 258 1552, ⓦbathmanorinn.com. A good option where the three simple rooms are affordable and quaint. $105

The Allegheny Mountains

The **Allegheny Mountains**, West Virginia's segment of the Appalachian chain, are spread along a 140-mile crest protected as part of the **Monongahela National Forest**, within which numerous state parks contain the most spectacular sights and a variety of wildlife, including deer, turkey, bear and otters. There are no cities and few towns, and public transport is nonexistent, but if you like to backpack, hike, cycle, climb or canoe, the Alleghenies merit a lengthy visit.

The Northern Monongahela

Some of the most beautiful stretches of the Monongahela National Forest are in the **northern** part of the state, where the thundering torrents of the **Blackwater Falls**, near the town of Davis, pour over a 60ft limestone cliff before crashing down through a steeply walled canyon, its water amber from the presence of tannins. South from here spreads the dense forest of broad **Canaan Valley**, while to the east rise the highlands of the **Dolly Sods Wilderness**, vividly marked with rocky topography and murky bogs.

Rising up at the south end of the Canaan Valley, the state's highest point, 4861ft **Spruce Knob**, stands out over the headwaters of the Potomac River – you can actually drive all the way to the summit, which is crowned with a squat observation tower. Even more impressive views can be had from the top of the notched and craggy **Seneca Rocks**, some twenty miles to the northeast, whose 1000ft cliffs offer the most challenging rock climb on the East Coast. If you want to take the easy way up to the top, a good trail leads in around the back of the North Peak, and takes well under an hour.

Near the *Smoke Hotel Resort* (see below) is the **Smoke Hole Canyon**, whose river has cut a nearly half-mile-deep chasm into the sheer rock walls, out of which sometimes rise mist and fog in a truly spellbinding sight. For the hardy, the **North Fork Mountain Trail** follows the canyon for 24 miles.

The Southern Monongahela

The **southern half** of the Monongahela National Forest is, like most of the Alleghenies, a mountainous, semi-inaccessible region – two roads, US-219 and Hwy-92, wind north to south, with a handful of minor roads twisting between them – offering outstanding recreation as well as great scenic vistas.

One signature sight is the state-run **Cass Scenic Railroad**, a restored, steam-powered logging railroad built in 1902, which carries visitors on a five-hour trip up to the top of 4842ft Bald Knob (schedule varies; $24–32; ☏304 456 4300, ⍟cassrailroad.com), starting at the old lumber-mill-company town of **CASS**, five miles west of Hwy-28 (near the town of Green Bank), now preserved in its entirety as a historic park. You can **stay the night** in one of thirteen rail-employees' two-storey cottages built in 1902 (see p.362) or rent a historic 1920s train carriage, with basic furnishings, for a trip up the mountain and an overnight stay ($119/person, bring non-tent camping supplies).

A rigorous five-mile walk downhill from Cass leads along the tracks to the start of the bicycle-friendly **Greenbrier River Trail** (⍟greenbrierrivertrail.com), which follows the river and the railroad for 79 miles, coming out near Lewisburg (see p.362). You can also rent a **mountain bike** or take part in a fishing, cycling or skiing tour, from Elk River Touring Center (☏866 572 3771, ⍟ertc.com), fifteen miles north of Marlinton, off US-219 in the hamlet of **Slatyfork**. Five miles west of the junction between the Cass Scenic Road and exquisite Highland Scenic Highway (Hwy-150), is **Cranberry Glades Botanical Area**, where a half-mile boardwalk is set out around a patch of peat bog swamp – one of four such bogs occupying 750 acres. Further along, the **Highland Scenic Highway** (April–Oct only) merits a leisurely trip to explore its 43 miles of eye-catching views, several fine **campgrounds** and 150 miles of hiking trails that branch off from it.

INFORMATION

THE ALLEGHENY MOUNTAINS

Monongahela National Forest Supervisor 200 Sycamore St, Elkins, West Virginia (Mon–Fri 8am–4.45pm; ☏304 636 1800, ⍟fs.fed.us/r9/mnf).

Seneca Rocks Discovery Center Near the junction of Hwy-33 and Hwy-55, Northern Monongahela (April–Oct Fri–Sun 9am–4.30pm; ☏304 567 2827).

Marlinton visitor centre 301 8th St, Marlinton, Southern Monongahela (☏800 336 7009, ⍟pocahontascountywv.com).

Marlinton Ranger District (☏304 799 4334); information on access and activities.

ACCOMMODATION

THE NORTHERN MONONGAHELA

Big Bend Campground ☏304 257 4488. Sites available seasonally (April–Oct). **$16**

Smoke Hotel Resort 10min north of the rocks on Hwy-55 ☏800 828 8478, ⍟smokehole.com. Of the limited lodging options, thus is the most reliable, with modern, family-size log cabins, cottages and motel rooms. Doubles **$69**, cottages **$139**, cabins **$199**

THE SOUTHERN MONONGAHELA

Campgrounds ☎ 304 846 2695 or ☎ 303 799 4334, ⓦ fs.usda.gov. The 43-mile length of theHighland Scenic Hwy has several fine campgrounds: Summit Lake, Day Run and Tea Creek, all with drinking water available and vault toilets. First come, first served. Open April–Nov.

Cass Scenic Railroad ☎ 304 456 4300, ⓦ cassrailroad .com. The cottages of former railroad workers have been converted into self-catering accommodation with fully equipped kitchens and sleep six to twelve people. Call or check website for prices and availability.

Elk River Inn US 219, Slatyfork ☎ 304 572 3771, ⓦ elkriverinnandrestaurant.com. The neat property here operates friendly lodging in an inn, farmhouse and four cabins with more amenities. There's a restaurant on the premises, and a full breakfast is included. The hosts also provide a shuttle service for hiking and biking, and offer fishing packages as well. Weekends require a two-night stay. Farmhouse $50, inn $75, cabins $80

Lewisburg and White Sulphur Springs

Just off I-64, south of the Monongahela National Forest, **LEWISBURG** offers a collection of handsome, brick-faced, early-nineteenth-century houses and makes for pleasant wandering, especially along **Washington Street**. It's also known for its somewhat touristy **Lost World Caverns**, off Fairview Road outside of town (hours vary, often daily 9am–5pm; $12; ⓦlostworldcaverns.com), where you can join 45min self-guided tours through dramatic cave formations, as well as a guided, four-hour spelunking tour ($70; two-person minimum) into the darker, more claustrophobia-inducing recesses of the site. Just east of Lewisburg, **WHITE SULPHUR SPRINGS** is a historic town mainly known for its sprawling resort.

INFORMATION   LEWISBURG AND WHITE SULPHUR SPRINGS

Visitor centre 540 N Jefferson St (☎ 800 833 2068, ⓦ greenbrierwv.com); hands out walking tour maps and can suggest driving tours around Greenbrier Valley.

ACCOMMODATION AND EATING

General Lewis Inn 301 E Washington St ☎ 304 645 2600, ⓦ generallewisinn.com. This cosy hotel is one of the better-value quarters in town, offering two dozen comfortable Victorian rooms and a fine, moderately priced restaurant serving all-American cuisine. $135

★ **Greenbrier Hotel and Resort** 300 W Main St ☎ 304 536 1110, ⓦ greenbrier.com. The grandest hotel in the state, with a pillared entrance hall, 6500 lush acres, 850 units, golf courses and fine restaurants. Two dozen US presidents have stayed here, perhaps thanks in part to the hotel's extensive, deep-underground Cold War-era bunker, which, having been decommissioned, is now open for fascinating 90min tours (hours vary; $30). $550

The New River Gorge

Perhaps West Virginia's most spectacular river canyon, the **NEW RIVER GORGE** lies thirty miles west of Lewisburg along I-64. Stretching for more than fifty miles, and protected as a national park, the 1000ft chasm was carved through the limestone mountains by the New River – ironically one of the oldest in North America. There's no easy access to most of the gorge; to see it in full, you have to get out on the water. Any of the three visitor centres (see opposite) can provide full details on all the cycling, climbing, hiking and rafting options available. The Canyon Rim centre sits near the **New River Gorge Bridge**, dramatically suspended 900ft above the river.

 HINTON, at the southern end of the gorge (and another Amtrak stop), is an almost perfectly preserved company town, beautifully sited, with brick-lined streets angling up from the water, lined by dozens of grand civic buildings as well as rows of old worker housing.

ARRIVAL AND INFORMATION   THE NEW RIVER GORGE

By train One Amtrak train a day in each direction connects Hinton, Prince and Thurmond stations in the New River Gorge to Indianapolis and Chicago going west, and to DC, Baltimore, Philadelphia and New York going northeast.

Park access The New River Gorge is open 24hr, and

admission is free. Aside from the visitor centres, find information at ⓦ nps.gov/neri.

Visitor centres There are three visitor centres along the gorge's borders: in Sandstone, where Hwy-64 crosses the river (daily 9am–5pm; ☎304 466 0417); at Canyon Rim,

7 miles north of Oak Hill on Hwy-19 (June–Aug daily 10am–5pm; ☎304 574 2115); and in Hinton at 206 Temple St (Tues–Sat 10am–2pm; ☎304 466 5420), which also offers walking tour maps and an old railroad museum to boot.

ACCOMMODATION

New River Falls Lodge 110 Cliff Island Drive ☎304 466 5710, ⓦnewriverfallslodge.com. The property offers two attractive options: lodge-style rooms with

hardwood floors and satellite TVs, or four two-bedroom cottages with kitchens and fireplaces. Doubles **$125**, cottages **$225**

Charleston

CHARLESTON, West Virginia's capital and largest city, holds few major attractions, but does have a nice selection of Victorian-era buildings, which you can see on a walking tour provided by the **visitor centre**. The riverfront **State Capitol**, 1900 Kanawha Blvd (Mon–Fri 7am–7pm, Sat & Sun 11am–7pm; ☎304 558 4839), designed by Lincoln Memorial and US Supreme Court architect Cass Gilbert, is a stately Renaissance Revival structure from 1932 that has an impressively large, gold-leafed dome. The **West Virginia Cultural Center** (Tues–Sat 9am–5pm, Sun noon–5pm; free; ☎304 558 0220, ⓦwvculture.org), in the same complex, has useful displays on coal mining, geology, forestry, war and state history, but much more extensive is the unexpectedly modern **Clay Center for the Arts & Sciences of West Virginia**, 1 Clay Square (Wed–Sat 10am–5pm, Sun noon–5pm; $13.50; ☎304 561 3570, ⓦtheclaycenter.org), a huge one-stop shop for everything scientific and artistic, with kid-friendly science-exhibit halls, a planetarium, concert stages for theatre and musical performances, an art gallery for regional artists and various cafés and gift shops. Finally, the town hosts the **Vandalia Festival**, Appalachia's largest celebration of arts and crafts, held on Memorial Day weekend and featuring lively bluegrass and folk music as well as tall-tale contests.

INFORMATION   CHARLESTON

Visitor centre 200 Civic Center Drive (Mon–Fri 9am–5pm; ☎304 344 5075, ⓦcharlestonwv.com).

ACCOMMODATION AND EATING

★ **The Bluegrass Kitchen** 1600 Washington St E ☎304 346 2871, ⓦbluegrasswv.com. Top-notch, mid-priced New Southern fare such as bourbon trout and grits, butternut squash pasta and a nice brisket reuben. Mon–Thurs 11am–9pm, Fri & Sat 11am–10pm, Sun 10am–3pm.

Brass Pineapple 1611 Virginia St E ☎304 344 0748,

ⓦbrasspineapple.com. If you want distinctive accommodation in Charleston, try the *Brass Pineapple*, a Victorian-styled B&B with plenty of antique, flowery decor. **$169**

Embassy Suites 300 Court St ☎304 347 8700, ⓦembassysuites.com. Most lodging choices in Charleston are of the chain variety. The *Embassy Suites* is among the most reliable, with a gym, pool and business centre. **$189**

Maryland

Founded as the sole Catholic colony in strongly Protestant America, and, in the nineteenth century, one of the most contentious slave states in the Union, **MARYLAND** has always been unique. Within its small, irregularly shaped geometry, its attractions range from the frantic boardwalk beaches of **Ocean City** to the sleepy fishing villages of the **Chesapeake Bay** and the little-known hamlets of the **Eastern Shore**. The Chesapeake Bay's legendary **blue crabs** and sweet rockfish, served by roadside places in the Bay's colonial-era towns, are additional reasons to drop in.

Maryland's largest city is the busy port of **Baltimore**, a quirky metropolis with a revitalized urban waterfront, a thriving cultural scene and eclectic neighbourhoods.

5

Western Maryland stretches over a hundred miles to the Appalachian foothills, its rolling farmlands notable chiefly for the Civil War killing grounds at **Antietam**. Just twenty miles south of Baltimore, picturesque **Annapolis** has served as Maryland's capital since 1694 and is best known for its national naval academy. Some of the state's most worthwhile spots are across the Chesapeake Bay on the Eastern Shore, connected to the rest of the state by the US-50 bridge but still a world apart.

Baltimore

Thanks to TV's potent *The Wire*, **BALTIMORE** has a reputation as a city in deep decline, its glory days of port industry distant, and rife with criminals fighting desperate wars of survival. While it's true that there are crime-ridden places in town worth avoiding, Baltimore is still among the more enjoyable stops on the East Coast, and its closely knit neighbourhoods and historic quarters provide an engaging backdrop to many diverse attractions, especially those along its celebrated **waterfront**. The city, home to everyone from writers Edgar Allan Poe and H.L. Mencken to civil rights icons Frederick Douglass and Thurgood Marshall, also boasts top-rated **museums**, which cover everything from fine arts to black history and urban archeology.

Downtown Baltimore

The re-emergent core of **downtown Baltimore** makes for a pleasant stroll along the brick-lined waterfront and features a bevy of nautical and science-oriented attractions. It's also within walking distance of the two sports stadiums, which makes it a convenient spot for fans to meet for dinner or a drink.

The main cluster of **restaurants and cafés** is found west of **Charles Street**, in Baltimore's original shopping district. One landmark here, dating from 1782, is the oldest and loudest of the city's covered markets, **Lexington Market**, 400 W Lexington St (Mon–Sat 8.30am–6pm; ☎410 685 6169, ⓦlexingtonmarket.com), with more than a hundred food stalls, including **Faidley's** (see p.370). Safe during the day, the area can be a bit dodgier after dark.

Westminster Church

519 W Fayette St • Mon–Fri 8.30am–5pm • Free • ☎410 706 2072

Just south of the market, **Westminster Church** was built in 1852 atop the main Baltimore cemetery. Its most famous resident is **Edgar Allan Poe**, who lived in town for three years in the 1830s before moving on to Richmond, Virginia. In 1849, while passing through Baltimore, Poe was found incoherent near a polling place and died soon after. In 1875, his remains were moved from a pauper's grave and entombed within the stone memorial that stands along Green Street on the north side of the church.

Oriole Park at Camden Yards

333 West Camden St • Tours generally Mon–Sat 10am, 11am, noon & 1pm, Sun noon, 1pm, 2pm & 3pm excluding game days • Tickets $9–60, tours $9 • ☎888 848 BIRD, ⓦtheorioles.com

Despite the notoriety of the Poe site, most visitors come to visit **Oriole Park at Camden Yards**, five blocks south, the baseball stadium of the Baltimore Orioles. Open-faced, with steel trusses and bricked arches, the park, opened in 1992, was one of the first to reintroduce a historic flair to stadium design, in contrast to the concrete boxes that had dominated pro sports for a generation.

Just next door, resembling a newly landed alien spaceship, is the 68,400-seat **M&T Bank Stadium**, home to the **Baltimore Ravens** football team, who were named after Edgar Allan Poe's most (in)famous character ($85–175 tickets; ☎410 547 SEAT, ⓦbaltimoreravens.com).

CLOCKWISE FROM TOP LINCOLN MEMORIAL, WASHINGTON DC (P.324); NEW RIVER GORGE BRIDGE, WV (P.362); STATUE OF THOMAS JEFFERSON AT MONTICELLO, CHARLOTTESVILLE, VA (P.353) >

5

The Inner Harbor

The **Inner Harbor** is a success story of urban revitalization. The rotting wharves and derelict warehouses that stood here through the 1970s were replaced by the sparkling steel-and-glass **Harborplace** mall (Mon–Sat 10am–9pm, Sun noon–6pm; ☎410 332 4191, ⓦharborplace.com), though the businesses inside aren't too different from those you'll find in any other consumer zone. Sweeping views of the entire city and beyond can be admired from the 27th-storey Top of the World observation deck at Baltimore's **World Trade Center**, on the north pier (hours vary, often Wed & Thurs 10am–6pm, Fri & Sat 10am–7pm, Sun 11am–6pm; $5; ☎410 837 8439, ⓦviewbaltimore.org).

Historic Ships of Baltimore

Pier 1, 301 E Pratt St · Hours vary, often daily 10am–4.30 or 5.30pm · One-ship tour $11, two ships $14, four ships $18 · ☎410 539 1797, ⓦhistoricships.org

Nothing in the Inner Harbor dates from before its rebuilding, but to lend an air of authenticity, a handful of historic ships float here as part of the Baltimore Maritime Museum's rebranding as **Historic Ships of Baltimore**. Although the four boats on view are rather eclectic – a Coast Guard cutter that survived Pearl Harbor, a Chesapeake Bay lightship and a World War II diesel submarine – the highlight for most is the USS *Constellation*, the only Civil War-era vessel still afloat and the last all-sail warship built by the US Navy. It was constructed in 1854 and restored in 1999.

National Aquarium

501 E Pratt St · Hours vary, often Mon–Thurs & Sun 9am–5pm, Fri 9am–8pm, Sat 9am–6pm · $25, or $28 with dolphin show · ☎410 576 3800, ⓦaqua.org

Far and away the biggest tourist attraction in Baltimore, the **National Aquarium** is an essential sight for anyone with an affection for jellyfish, sharks, rays, sea turtles and other oceanic creatures, which dart around before visitors in their own enclosed tanks and pools. It is, of course, as much theme park as scientific institution, so it's no surprise the aquarium's **Dolphin Amphitheater** is very much in the style of SeaWorld.

Federal Hill and around

A short walk south of the Inner Harbor, the **Federal Hill** district is a great place to escape from the crowds. Lined with captivating shops, restaurants and galleries, its main thoroughfare, **Light Street**, leads to the indoor **Cross Street Market**, which opened in 1875 and has two blocks of open-air vendors boasting excellent delis, seafood bars and fruit sellers. **Federal Hill Park** in the northeast is a quiet public space with fine views over the harbour and the downtown cityscape.

In the northern part of the district, by the harbour at 601 Light St, the glass, steel and concrete **Maryland Science Center** (Mon–Fri 10am–5pm, Sat 10am–6pm, Sun 11am–5pm; $17, kids $14, IMAX show $8; ☎410 685 5225, ⓦmdsci.org) is mainly aimed at kids, with interactive displays on themes ranging from dinosaurs to space travel.

American Visionary Art Museum

800 Key Hwy · Tues–Sun 10am–6pm · $16 · ☎410 244 1900, ⓦavam.org

The **American Visionary Art Museum**, east of Federal Hill Park, is devoted to the works of untrained or amateur artists, with thousands of pieces by American "visionaries", crafted with everything from glass and porcelain to toothpicks and tinfoil. Some of the more notable pieces include an obsessively intricate sculpture of Coney Island's boardwalk and eerie Bosch-like paintings of alien abductions.

Mount Vernon

Baltimore's most elegant quarter is just north of downtown on the shallow rise known as **Mount Vernon**. Adorned with eighteenth-century brick townhouses, this district

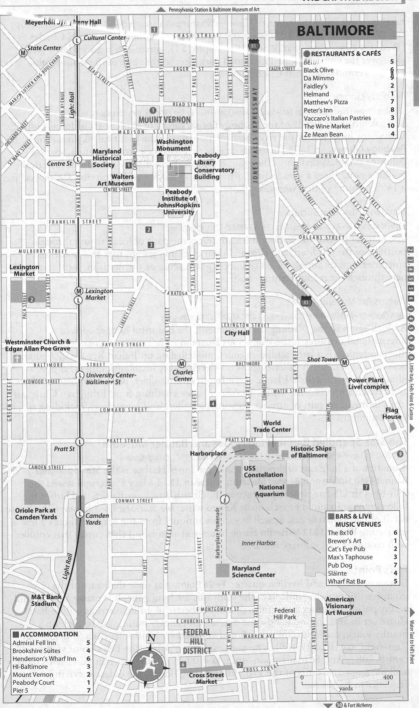

▲ Pennsylvania Station & Baltimore Museum of Art

BALTIMORE

● RESTAURANTS & CAFÉS

Berili	5
Black Olive	6
Da Mimmo	9
Faidley's	2
Helmand	1
Matthew's Pizza	7
Peter's Inn	8
Vaccaro's Italian Pastries	3
The Wine Market	10
Ze Mean Bean	4

■ BARS & LIVE MUSIC VENUES

The 8x10	6
Brewer's Art	1
Cat's Eye Pub	2
Max's Taphouse	3
Pub Dog	7
Sláinte	4
Wharf Rat Bar	5

■ ACCOMMODATION

Admiral Fell Inn	5
Brookshire Suites	4
Henderson's Wharf Inn	6
HI-Baltimore	3
Mount Vernon	2
Peabody Court	1
Pier 5	7

Meyerhoff Jji Tiony Hall

State Center

Cultural Center

MOUNT VERNON

Maryland Historical Society

Washington Monument

Walters Art Museum

Peabody Library Conservatory Building

Peabody Institute of JohnsHopkins University

Lexington Market

Westminster Church & Edgar Allan Poe Grave

City Hall

University Center-Baltimore St

Charles Center

Shot Tower

Power Plant Live! complex

Flag House

World Trade Center

Harborplace

Historic Ships of Baltimore

USS Constellation

National Aquarium

Oriole Park at Camden Yards

Camden Yards

Inner Harbor

Maryland Science Center

M&T Bank Stadium

Harborplace Promenade

American Visionary Art Museum

FEDERAL HILL DISTRICT

Federal Hill Park

Cross Street Market

N

0 400

yards

◀ Greyhound Bus Station

Water Taxi to Fell's Point ▶

▼ ⑩ & Fort McHenry

2 | 3 | 4 | 5 | 6 | 9 | 4 | 0 | 7 | 8, Little Italy, Fells Point & Canton ▶

5

takes its name from the home of George Washington (see p.341), whose likeness tops the 178ft marble column of the central **Washington Monument** at 699 N Charles St (Wed–Fri 10am–4pm, Sat & Sun 10am–5pm; $1), where 228 steps lead to a great view over the city. It's located in a small park next to the spire of the sham-Gothic Mount Vernon Methodist Church.

Peabody Library

17 E Mount Vernon Place • Tues–Thurs 9am–5pm, Fri 9am–3pm • Free • ☏ 410 234 4943, ⓦ guides.library.jhu.edu

The solemn stone facade of the **Peabody Conservatory of Music**, part of Johns Hopkins University, hides one of the city's best interior spaces: the beautiful, skylit atrium of the **Peabody Library**, an 1878 Victorian delight rich with cast-iron balconies, soaring columns and glass skylights. The ground floor features displays of various historical books, among them a wonderful illustrated 1555 edition of Boccaccio's *Decameron* and a 1493 printing of the *Nuremburg Chronicles*.

Maryland Historical Society

201 W Monument St • Wed–Sun 10am–5pm • $9 • ☏ 410 685 3750, ⓦ mdhs.org

The **Maryland Historical Society** museum traces the path of local history through portraits of the old Maryland elite and their clothing, jewels, toys and household amenities, and its antique-filled chambers give a sense of the maritime wealth created here through nineteenth-century trade.

Walters Art Museum

600 N Charles St • Wed–Sun 10am–5pm • Free • ☏ 410 547 9000, ⓦ thewalters.org

A block south of the Washington Monument, the beautiful hodgepodge of international treasures at the **Walters Art Museum** is well deserving of a lengthy visit. The centrepiece is a large sculpture court, modelled on an Italian Renaissance palazzo, beyond which modern galleries show off Greek and Roman antiquities, European illuminated manuscripts, Islamic ceramics, Byzantine silver, pre-Columbian artefacts and French Impressionist works. You're apt to see anything from Ethiopian Christian icons to medieval suits of armour, Egyptian jewellery and sarcophagi, including an intact mummy.

The Star-Spangled Banner Flag House and Banner Museum

844 E Pratt St • Tues–Sat 10am–4pm; last tour at 3.30pm • $8 • ☏ 410 837 1793, ⓦ flaghouse.org

A quarter of a mile east of downtown and the Inner Harbor is the **Star-Spangled Banner Flag House and Banner Museum** where in 1813 Mary Pickersgill sewed the 30ft-by-45ft US flag, whose presence at the British attack on Baltimore Harbor the following year inspired Francis Scott Key to write *The Star-Spangled Banner*. The house is full of patriotic tributes, as well as various antiques from the era, and there's a less interesting **War of 1812 Museum** (same hours and admission) that covers that conflict with costumes and military relics.

Fell's Point

Baltimore's oldest and liveliest quarter, **Fell's Point**, was once the heart of the city's extensive shipbuilding industry. The shipyards are long gone, but many old bars and earthy pubs have hung on to form one of the better nightlife districts on the East Coast, set in and around handsome nineteenth-century buildings. To pick up a healthy snack, duck into the area's **Broadway Market**, 1640 Aliceanna St (Mon–Sat 7am–6pm; ☏410 685 6169), a favourite stopping point. The Fell's Point **visitor centre**, 808 S Ann St (daily noon–4pm; ☏410 675 6750), provides good self-guided walking maps and tours of the 1765 **Robert Long House**, the oldest surviving urban residence in Baltimore.

Canton and Greektown

East of Fell's Point and two miles southeast of downtown, **Canton** is another district full of historic rowhouses, some of which date back to the Civil War, and is being revitalized with new restaurants and nightlife. A mile east, **Greektown** is still a thriving Hellenic community, after almost a century, and boasts its share of authentic bakeries, diners and groceries.

Fort McHenry National Monument

2400 E Fort Ave • Daily: June–Aug 9am–8pm; Sept–May 9am–5pm • $7 seven-day pass • ☎ 410 962 4290, ⓦ nps.gov/fomc

Linked by water taxi from Fell's Point, but on the opposite side of the harbour, **Fort McHenry National Monument** is a star-shaped fort that the British bombed during the War of 1812 to penetrate the harbour and attack Baltimore. The attack failed, and when he saw "the bombs bursting in air", Francis Scott Key was moved to write the poem *The Star-Spangled Banner*, first known as "The Defense of Fort McHenry". Over the next century, the fort was used as a prison for Confederate soldiers and political prisoners. You can tour the fort's old barracks, officers' and enlisted men's quarters and guardhouse, and see military hardware and relics of different eras. The Banner itself, however, is housed in the National Museum of American History (see p.325) in Washington, DC.

Baltimore Museum of Art

10 Art Museum Drive • Wed–Fri 10am–5pm, Sat & Sun 11am–6pm • Free • ☎ 443 573 1700, ⓦ artbma.org

Two miles north of downtown, the **Charles Village** district is enjoyable for its early twentieth-century rowhouses and walkable streets. Here you can find the **Baltimore Museum of Art**, as good a venue as you're likely to find for viewing classic art in the area. As well as Italian and Dutch works by Botticelli, Raphael, Rembrandt and Van Dyck, the museum holds Chardin's *A Game of Knucklebones*, played by a smiling scamp, drawings by Dürer and Goya and photographs from Weston, Stieglitz and others. The highlight is the **Cone Collection** of works by Delacroix, Degas, Cézanne and Picasso, as well as more than a hundred drawings and paintings by Matisse, among them his signature *Large Reclining Nude* and *Seated Odalisque*.

ARRIVAL AND DEPARTURE | BALTIMORE

By plane Baltimore-Washington International Airport (BWI; ☎410 859 7111, ⓦ bwiairport.com) is 10 miles south of the city centre and also serves as a key airport for Washington, DC. The cheapest way to get into the city is on the MTA commuter rail system (25min; $1.60; ☎410 539 5000, ⓦ mta.maryland.gov), which connects BWI to the restored Pennsylvania Station, half a mile north of downtown, at 1515 N Charles St. Shuttle vans from the airport go to downtown Baltimore (around $13–18), and Inner Harbor ($20–25) including Super Shuttle (20min; $13–23 one-way; ☎ 800 258 3826, ⓦ supershuttle.com).

By bus Greyhound buses stop south of downtown, at 2110 Haines St, though this is in a grim area; take a taxi downtown. Destinations Charlottesville, VA (3 daily; 4hr 25–5hr 55min); Norfolk, VA (5 daily; 6hr 5min–10hr 50min); Raleigh, NC (5 daily; 7hr 50min–8hr 50min).

By train Penn Station is also the arrival point of Amtrak trains; because it's in a dicey neighbourhood, you should either take a cab downtown or get on the Penn-Camden light rail shuttle (Mon–Sat 5am–11pm, Sat 6am–11pm, Sun 11am–7pm; $1.60 one-way), which stops downtown. Destinations Alexandria, VA (11 daily; 1hr 20min–2hr); New York City (10 daily; 2hr 40–3hr 20min); Richmond, VA (9 daily; 3hr–3hr 30min); Washington DC (8 daily; 35min).

GETTING AROUND AND INFORMATION

By bus The MTA's bus, subway and light rail lines ($1.60, day-pass $3.50; ☎410 539 5000, ⓦ mta.maryland.gov) cover many locations, though the subway and light rail are limited to one main route each, connecting at Lexington Market. Have exact change ready.

By water taxi Water taxis link the Inner Harbor and 16 citywide attractions, including the National Aquarium, Fell's Point and Fort McHenry (daily: schedule varies, often Mon–Thurs & Sun 10am–8pm, Fri & Sat 10am–11pm; $12 all-day pass; ☎410 563 3901, ⓦ thewatertaxi.com).

Visitor centre 401 Light St, near the Maryland Science Center (mid-March to mid-Nov daily 9am–5pm; mid-Nov to mid-March Wed–Sun 10am–4pm; ☎410 837 7024, ⓦ baltimore.org); also has booths at the airport and train station.

5

ACCOMMODATION

Baltimore has the usual chain hotels available downtown, along with a few local institutions, while the B&Bs clustered around the historic waterfront area of Fell's Point make for a pleasant alternative. The visitor centre (see p.369) can help with reservations.

★ **Admiral Fell Inn** 888 S Broadway ☎410 522 7377, ⓦharbormagic.com. Chic historic hotel spread over seven buildings (some dating from the 1770s) in the heart of Fell's Point. Rooms have vaulted ceilings and fireplaces; some have jacuzzis and balconies as well. __$239__

Brookshire Suites 120 E Lombard St ☎410 625 1300, ⓦharbormagic.com. Arty boutique rooms define this stylish establishment at the Inner Harbor, with modern decor in its suites, a business centre, drinks in the *Cloud Club* and fine waterside views. __$249__

Henderson's Wharf Inn 1000 Fell St ☎410 522 7087, ⓦhendersonswharf.com. Prominent harbourside spot with modern rooms that include boutique furnishings and fridges. Continental breakfast and on-site gym, as well. __$279__

HI-Baltimore 17 W Mulberry St ☎410 576 8880 ⓦbaltimorehostel.org. Set in a sturdy 1850s brownstone, this boasts nearly fifty dorm beds, with antiques, deck and patio, free wi-fi, karaoke and laundry, plus movie screenings. Dorms __$60__

Mount Vernon 24 W Franklin St ☎410 727 2000, ⓦmountvernonbaltimore.com. This ultra-cheap hotel offers clean rooms with complimentary breakfast, plus a central location. __$113__

Peabody Court 612 Cathedral St ☎410 727 7101, ⓦpeabodycourthotel.com. A handsome, converted 1928 apartment building in a historic neighbourhood, with marble bathrooms and tasteful decor. Pet-friendly. __$209__

Pier 5 711 Eastern Ave ☎410 539 2000, ⓦharbormagic .com. Centrally located, upmarket boutique hotel with plenty of snazzy style, offering smart rooms with CD players, and suites with fridges, microwaves and in-room bars. __$319__

EATING

Baltimore's restaurants tend to be good value and reasonably priced, with particularly appealing fresh seafood places offering top-notch steamed crabs, as well as the usual diners and more than a dozen good restaurants side by side in Little Italy. Fell's Point boasts numerous vegetarian, seafood and other options.

Bertha's 734 S Broadway ☎410 327 5795, ⓦberthas .com. Classic, affordable seafood restaurant, tucked away behind a tiny Fell's Point bar. Known for its delicious mussels, crab cakes and high tea, and nightly live blues, jazz and Dixieland. Mon–Thurs 11.30am–10pm, Fri & Sat 11am–11pm, Sun 10.30am–10pm.

Black Olive 814 S Bond St, Fell's Point ☎410 276 7141, ⓦtheblackolive.com. Expensive but succulent Mediterranean food, including affordable meze (small plates) such as grilled octopus salad and calamari, as well as pricier mains including rack of lamb, crab-cake platters and lobster tail. Daily noon–2pm & 5–10pm.

Da Mimmo 217 S High St ☎410 727 6876, ⓦdamimmo .com. Intimate, upmarket Little Italy café, with a wide-ranging menu that includes clams, *saltimbocca*, gnocchi and lobster tetrazzini. Live piano music and a romantic ambience. Mon–Thurs & Sun 11.30am–10.30pm, Fri & Sat 11.30am–midnight.

★ **Faidley's** 203 N Paca, downtown ☎410 727 4898. Located in Lexington Market, the best and cheapest of many outlets serving oysters, clams and other catches from the Chesapeake Bay, including terrific crab cakes – a business dating back to 1886. Stand-up dining only. Mon–Sat 9am–5pm.

Helmand 806 N Charles St ☎410 752 0311, ⓦhelmand.com. Mid-priced, dinner-only Afghan restaurant in Mount Vernon, with savoury dishes such as *aushak* (leek-filled vegetarian ravioli), *koufta challow* (lamb and beef meatballs) and the delicious *kaddo borawni* (a fried pumpkin appetizer). Mon–Thurs & Sun 5–10pm, Fri & Sat 5–11pm.

Matthew's Pizza 3131 Eastern Ave, west of Greektown ☎410 276 8755, ⓦmatthewspizza.com. Old-style hole in the wall that still boasts the city's best slices – rich and tangy, with a solid crust and traditional ingredients, or toppings like crab and home-made meatballs. Mon–Thurs 11am–10pm, Fri & Sat 11am–11pm, Sun noon–9pm.

Peter's Inn 504 S Ann St, Fell's Point ☎410 675 7313, ⓦpetersinn.com. Top-notch restaurant with a fine, rotating menu, where you can get anything from shrimp grits to mushroom risotto to veal.cheeks, for moderate to high prices. Also has an enjoyable bar on site. Tues–Thurs 6.30–10pm, Fri & Sat 6.30–11pm.

Vaccaro's Italian Pastries 222 Albemarle St, Little Italy ☎410 685 4905, ⓦvaccarospastry.com. Great spot to load up on cheesecakes, cannoli, cookies and other sweets, and to indulge in the kind of delicious gelato they make in the Old Country. Part of a local chain. Mon–Thurs & Sun 9am–10pm, Fri & Sat 9am–midnight.

The Wine Market 921 E Fort Ave, south of Federal Hill ☎410 244 6166, ⓦwinemarketbistro.com.

Innovative, mid- to upper-end cuisine that throws together a melange of curious dishes – anything from Korean short ribs and potstickers to mac and cheese and fried oysters – often successfully. Mon–Thurs 11am–11pm, Fri 11am–midnight, Sat 9am–midnight, Sun 9am–11pm.

Ze Mean Bean 1739 Fleet St, Fell's Point ☎410 675 5999, ⓦzemeanbean.com. Rib-stuffing Slavic place where you can get your fill of rich and tasty potato dumplings, pierogi, goulash and even chicken Kiev, most for affordable prices, though the service can be spotty. Mon–Fri 11am–11pm, Sat 9.30am–11pm, Sun 9am–10pm.

NIGHTLIFE AND ENTERTAINMENT

Baltimore has plenty of places to drink and Fell's Point may well have the most. One bar after another lines up along Broadway and the many smaller side streets, and almost all feature some sort of entertainment. For a rundown of what's on, pick up a copy of the excellent and free *City Paper* (ⓦcitypaper.com) or check out ⓦBaltimore.org.

BARS AND LIVE MUSIC VENUES

The 8x10 10 E Cross St, Federal Hill ☎410 625 2000, ⓦthe8x10.com. Enjoyable bar and live music venue that features good beer and cocktails and an eclectic mix of bands, from jazz to indie rock and electronica, often for a cover charge of $5–15. Tues–Sun 4pm–2am.

★ **Brewer's Art** 1106 N Charles St, Mount Vernon ☎410 547 6925, ⓦthebrewersart.com. The place anyone with a yen for microbrews must visit – a local landmark for beer-making that's tops for its Belgian-style Ozzy, dark Proletary Ale and good old Charm City Sour Cherry. Daily 4pm–1.45am.

Cat's Eye Pub 1730 Thames St, Fell's Point ☎410 276 9085, ⓦcatseyepub.com. Cosy, crowded bar, offering forty beers on tap and live music nightly, from blues and rock to jazz, bluegrass and folk. Daily noon–2am.

Max's Taphouse 737 S Broadway ☎410 675 6297, ⓦmaxs.com. Huge corner venue with a very long bar known for its prime domestic and European ales –with some 500 kinds in bottles, and up to 100 on tap – pool tables, and, upstairs, a leather-upholstered cigar lounge. Daily 11am–2am.

Pub Dog 200 E Cross St, Federal Hill ☎410 727 6077, ⓦpubdog.net. Baltimore has countless places to drink

and this is among the best, with a great atmosphere, doling out a range of handcrafted brews from the Irish stout Black Dog to the various fruity Berry Dogs, and some serviceable burgers and pizza as well. Daily 5pm–2am.

Sláinte 1700 Thames St ☎410 563 6600, ⓦslaintepub .com. Free-spirited Irish pub in Fell's Point where you can knock back the requisite Guinness and indulge in hearty meals such as bangers and mash, potato pancakes and fish and chips. Daily 7am–2am.

Wharf Rat Bar 801 S Ann St, Fell's Point ☎410 276 9034, ⓦthewharfrat.com. This friendly bar, well stocked with English ales, other European imports and regional microbrews, packs in a trendy and discerning crowd. Daily 11am–2am.

MAJOR VENUES

Meyerhoff Symphony Hall 1212 Cathedral St ☎410 783 8000, ⓦbsomusic.org. The city's highbrow culture is concentrated northwest of the centre, in the Mount Royal Avenue area, centred around Meyerhoff Symphony Hall.

Power Plant Live! 34 Market Place ☎410 727 5483, ⓦpowerplantlive.com. Complex next to the Inner Harbor offering dining and mainstream entertainment. Daily 11am–2am.

Frederick

One of the first towns settled in northwestern Maryland, **FREDERICK**, less than an hour west of Baltimore, at the junction of I-70 and I-270, was laid out in 1745 by German farmers and grew to become a main stopover on the route west to the Ohio Valley; the bulk of today's tidy town survives from the early 1800s. Frederick is also a good base for exploring Antietam (see p.372) and Harpers Ferry (see p.359).

The **visitor centre** (see p.372) has walking tour maps of the town highlights, some of which include the **Schifferstadt House**, just off US-15 (April to mid-Dec Tues–Sun noon–4pm; $5; ☎301 668 6088), a stone-walled farmhouse built in 1756 and largely unaltered since; the **Roger Taney House**, 121 S Bentz St (April to mid-Dec Sat & Sun 1–4pm; $6; ☎301 663 1188), owned by the US Supreme Court chief justice best known for presiding over the infamous **Dred Scott** case; and the **Barbara Fritchie House**, 154 W Patrick St (tours by appointment at ☎301 698 8992), where 95-year-old Barbara Fritchie was said to have defiantly waved the US flag while Confederate soldiers marched past. Although this story is mythical, the house is a well-preserved piece of Americana, with a historic flag still hanging from the pitched roof. A short

5

walk east, the **National Museum of Civil War Medicine**, 48 E Patrick St (Mon–Sat 10am–5pm, Sun 11am–5pm; $7.50; ☎301 695 1864, ⓦcivilwarmed.org) offers intriguing exhibits on mid-nineteenth-century military medicine, including grisly amputation tools and battlefield triage.

In the outskirts north of Frederick, **Cunningham Falls State Park** (daily 8am–sunset) and the **Catoctin Mountain Park** (daily dawn–dusk; free) hold seemingly endless hardwood forests – great for autumn colour – in the midst of which are preserved remnants of early homesteads and industrial operations such as a sawmill, ironworks and whiskey still. Pick up details on hiking and camping at the main **visitor centre** (see below).

INFORMATION FREDERICK

Visitor centre 19 E Church St (☎301 600 2888, ⓦfredericktourism.org).

Catoctin Mountain Park visitor centre Hwy-77,

2 miles west of US-15 (Fri 9.30am–7pm, Sat & Sun 8.30am–7pm; ☎301 663 9330, ⓦnps.gov/cato).

ACCOMMODATION

Cunningham Falls State Park There are 56 campsites spread between two areas, 41 with electric hookups. Open April–Oct. **$20**

Hill House 12 W Third St ☎301 682 4111, ⓦhillhousefrederick.com. Has rooms artfully decorated in Victorian

and early American design that feature antiques and balconies. **$145**

Hollerstown Hill 4 Clarke Place ☎301 228 3630, ⓦhollerstownhill.com. Four pleasant rooms in historic buildings from the late nineteenth century. **$175**

EATING AND DRINKING

Barley & Hops 5473 Urbana Pike ☎301 668 5555, ⓦbarleyandhops.net. This place is worthwhile for its sandwiches and surf-and-turf main, with good microbrewed pale ales and stouts. Mon–Thurs & Sun 11am–10pm, Fri & Sat 11am–11pm.

Brewer's Alley 124 N Market St ☎301 631 0089, ⓦbrewers-alley.com. A nice range of handcrafted beer on tap, from Kolsch to oatmeal stout. Mon–Thurs

11.30am–midnight, Fri & Sat 11.30am–12.30am, Sun noon–11.30pm.

Monocacy Crossing 4424 Urbana Pike ☎301 846 4204, ⓦmonocacycrossing.com. Fine sandwiches and seafood at lunchtime, or somewhat expensive ribs, crab cakes, duck étouffée and other top-shelf cuisine for dinner. Tues–Thurs 11.30am–9pm, Fri 11.30am–10pm, Sat 3–10pm, Sun noon–8pm.

Antietam National Battlefield

The site of the single bloodiest battle in the Civil War – which caused more American deaths than on any other day in US history – **Antietam National Battlefield** spreads over unaltered farmlands outside the village of **Sharpsburg**, fifteen miles west of Frederick. Here, on the morning of September 17, 1862, forty thousand Confederate troops faced a Union army twice that number. Hours later, 23,000 men from both sides lay dead or dying.

For all the carnage, the battle wasn't tactically decisive and the South would invade the North the following year, but the Confederates' lack of success lost them the support of their would-be ally Great Britain, while the Union performance encouraged Lincoln to issue the Emancipation Proclamation.

INFORMATION ANTIETAM NATIONAL BATTLEFIELD

Entry $4 three-day pass, $6 per family.

Visitor centre A mile north of Sharpsburg off Hwy-65

(hours vary, usually daily 8.30am–5pm; ☎301 432 5124, ⓦnps.gov/anti); stocks driving tour maps of the park.

ACCOMMODATION

Jacob Rohrbach Inn 138 W Main St, Sharpsburg ☎301 432 5079, ⓦjacob-rohrbach-inn.com. This excellent, 200-year-old homestead has four well-appointed rooms

and one detached cottage. Guests are treated to a gourmet breakfast, made in part with veggies and herbs from the inn's own garden. **$170**

Cumberland and the C&O Canal

5

The only large town in the far west of Maryland, sandwiched between West Virginia and Pennsylvania in a part of the state only eight miles wide, **CUMBERLAND** was a noteworthy town in early America. It started life as a coal-milling centre in the late 1700s, before becoming the eastern terminus of the **National Road**, one of the country's first graded, modern **turnpikes** (for horse-drawn cargo), and was later made the terminus of the **C&O (Chesapeake & Ohio) Canal**, an impressive engineering feat begun in 1813 and completed in 1850.

There are six **visitor centres** along the canal (see below), all with information on hiking, cycling, canoeing and camping – invaluable if you're interested in travelling the entire 184.5 miles along the **canal towpath**, one of the longest and loveliest contiguous trails in the USA. In summer, the historic trains of the **Western Maryland Scenic Railroad** leave from here to make the three-hour trip to Frostburg, to the west, through the surrounding mountains (May–Dec, hours vary; $33, kids $15; ☏301 759 4400, ⓦwmsr.com). Look for the tiny black-and-white log cabin where George Washington served his first commission in the 1750s, standing directly opposite the station on the other side of the canal.

ARRIVAL AND INFORMATION

CUMBERLAND AND THE C&O CANAL

By train The Cumberland Amtrak train station is at 201 E Harrison St, at Queen City St.
Park entry $3/pedestrian, $5/car for three days.

Visitor centres There are six visitor centres along the canal: the westernmost is in Cumberland, at 13 Canal St (daily 9am–5pm; ☏301 722 8226, ⓦnps.gov/choh).

ACCOMMODATION

Bruce House Inn 201 Fayette St ☏301 777 8860, ⓦbrucehouseinn.com. This 1840 charmer appeals for its fine breakfasts and four B&B rooms with stylish modern and early American furnishings. **$119**

Annapolis

Maryland's capital since 1694, **ANNAPOLIS** has changed little in size and appearance over the centuries, its charmingly narrow, time-worn streets making it among the more engaging small US cities.

Maryland State House

100 State Circle • Daily 9am–5pm • Free curators' tours (donation requested) by appointment on ☏410 260 6445

At the centre of Annapolis, overlooking the town's dense web of streets, stands the stately Georgian beauty that is the **Maryland State House**. The structure was completed in 1779, and for six months between 1783 and 1784 it served as the official Capitol of the USA; it remains the nation's oldest statehouse still in use. The **Old Senate Chamber**, off the grand entrance hall, is where the Treaty of Paris was ratified in 1784, officially ending the Revolutionary War. A statue of George Washington stands here on the spot where, three weeks before the treaty signing, he resigned his commission as head of the Continental Army. Also on the grounds of the State House is the cottage-sized **Old Treasury**, built in 1735 to hold colonial Maryland's currency reserves.

Historic houses

Many grand post-revolutionary brick homes line the streets of Annapolis. Among the best are the red-brick **Hammond-Harwood House**, two blocks west of the State House at 19 Maryland Ave, off King George St (April–Oct Tues–Sun noon–5pm, last tour 4pm; Nov–March closes 1hr earlier; $7; ☏410 263 4683, ⓦhammondharwoodhouse.org), which was built in 1774 and is notable for its beautiful woodwork and intricate front doorway; the 1774 **Chase-Lloyd House**, 22 Maryland Ave (donation; Mon–Sat 2–4pm; ☏410 263 2723), a three-storey Georgian brick townhouse with grand stairway, interior Ionic columns and intricate ornamentation; and the 1765

5

William Paca House and Gardens, 186 Prince George St (Mon–Sat 10am–5pm, Sun noon–5pm, tours often hourly 10.30am–3.30pm; $10, $7 gardens only; ☎410 267 7619), named for one of the state's governors and signers of the Declaration of Independence. Its splendid formal garden has French-styled geometry and lovely topiary and boasts a nice viewing pavilion. Besides such elite manors, dozens of eighteenth-century clapboard cottages and warehouses fill the narrow streets that run down to the waterfront. The **Historic Annapolis Foundation**, housed in a c.1715 tavern at 18 Pinkney St (☎410 267 7619, ⓦannapolis.org), can provide information on self-guided tours of many of them.

Banneker-Douglass Museum

84 Franklin St • Tues–Sat 10am–4pm • Free • ☎410 216 6180, ⓦbdmuseum.com

For a different insight into Maryland history, stop by the **Banneker-Douglass Museum**, a few blocks northeast of the Capitol, named after two of the most prominent black figures of early America and home to the state's largest holding of African American art and artefacts.

The waterfront and US Naval Academy

Few historic sites survive on the **Chesapeake Bay waterfront** save the 1850s dockside **Market House** at 25 Market Place, a replacement of a colonial Revolutionary army warehouse that is home to a handful of food vendors, still struggling today after a 2003 hurricane and ownership lawsuits. Among the boat-supply shops and harbourside bars, the grey-stone walls of the **US Naval Academy** house four thousand "plebes" who spend four rigid years here before embarking on careers as naval officers. Superb guided tours leave from **Armel-Leftwich Visitor Center** ($10; call for hours at ☎410 293 8687, ⓦnavyonline.com) in Halsey Field House, through Gate 1 at the end of King George St, and take in the elaborate crypt and marble sarcophagus of early American naval hero John Paul Jones, as well as cannons, a space capsule and other oddments.

ARRIVAL AND INFORMATION   ANNAPOLIS

By car It's only about 30min from Washington DC (via US-50) or Baltimore (via I-97).

By bus Greyhound buses stop at 308 Chinquapin Round Rd.

Destinations Virginia Beach, VA (1 daily; 13hr 20min); Wilmington, DE (1 daily; 2hr 15min).

By train You can access Amtrak and MARC trains (☎866 743 3682, ⓦmta.maryland.gov) at BWI Airport via the North Star (C-60) Route on Annapolis's ADOT bus system ($4; ☎410 263 7964).

Visitor centre 26 West St (☎410 280 0445, ⓦvisit -annapolis.org).

ACCOMMODATION

Annapolis Inn 144 Prince George St ☎410 295 5200, ⓦannapolisinn.com. Three supremely elegant suites, with fireplaces in two of them and luxury throughout. **$259**

Flag House Inn 26 Randall St ☎410 280 2721, ⓦflaghouseinn.com. Some of the best reasons to book at *Flag House* are the helpful owners and the full hot breakfast in the morning. **$190**

Historic Inns of Annapolis 58 State Circle ☎410 263 2641, ⓦhistoricinnsofannapolis.com. Three stylish buildings provide smart accommodation options in classic Georgian structures. **$170**

Royal Folly 65 College Ave ☎410 263 3999, ⓦroyal folly.com. Sizeable modern suites variously come with fireplaces, jacuzzis, patios, flat-screen TVs and iPod docks. **$275**

EATING

Chick and Ruth's Delly 165 Main St ☎410 269 6737, ⓦchickandruths.com. A worthwhile, no-frills place, good for an energy boost with its gut-busting breakfasts and huge sandwiches. Mon–Thurs & Sun 6.30am–11.30pm, Fri & Sat 6.30am–12.30am.

Sam's on the Waterfront 2020 Chesapeake Harbour

Drive E ☎410 263 3600, ⓦsamsonthewaterfront.com. A primo marina-side place with a range of delicious offerings from lamb sirloin and lobster-rice noodles to tuna tartare. Tues–Thurs 11.30am–9pm, Fri & Sat 11.30am–10pm, Sun 10.30am–9pm.

The Eastern Shore

The rambling backroads of Maryland's **Eastern Shore** cross over half of the broad Delmarva (Delaware, Maryland, Virginia) peninsula that protects the Chesapeake from the open Atlantic, its country lanes passing the odd wooden farmhouse or dilapidated tobacco barn. It's accessible via the US-50 bridge, built across the Chesapeake Bay in the early 1960s. Branching off from US-50 as the highway races down to the beach resort of **Ocean City**, quiet country lanes lead to 200-year-old bayside towns like **Chestertown** and **St Michaels**.

Chestertown

A prime Chesapeake port in colonial days, **CHESTERTOWN** stretches west along High Street from the Chester River, hosting fine old riverfront homes and a courthouse square lined with ornate wooden cottages. Although the town is rich with historic edifices, like the grand 1769 Georgian mansion **Widehall**, 101 N Water St, the only house regularly open to the public is the contemporaneous **Geddes-Piper House**, 101 Church Alley (Tues–Fri 10am–4pm; tours May–Oct Sat 1–4pm; $4; ☎410 778 3499), a Federal-style brick structure that has a good collection of kitchen tools and eighteenth-century furnishings.

ACCOMMODATION AND EATING   CHESTERTOWN

Brooks Tavern 870 High St ☎410 810 0012, ⓦbrookstavern.com. A little off the usual tavern track, this spot does a mean crab-cake sandwich, plus upper-end seafood, steak, duck ragu and BBQ crêpes. Tues–Thurs 11.30am–9pm, Fri & Sat 11.30am–10pm, Sun 10.30am–9pm.

Great Oak Manor 10568 Cliff Rd ☎800 504 3098, ⓦgreatoakmd.com. A refined and elegant place, with expensive rooms, some of which come with fireplaces and antique decor. $229

Imperial Hotel 208 High St ☎410 778 5000, ⓦimperialchestertown.com. Has a central location with eleven rooms and a pair of suites. Its *Front Room* restaurant serves "eclectic contemporary" meals, centring on fine steak and seafood. Restaurant Tues–Fri 11.30am–3pm & 4–9pm, Sat 4–9pm, Sun 4–8pm. $160

Widow's Walk Inn 402 High St ☎410 778 6455, ⓦchestertown.com/widow. Many of Chestertown's old houses have been converted into charming B&Bs, among them *Widow's Walk Inn*, with its five dainty, rather twee rooms. $110

St Michaels

The fetching harbour of **ST MICHAELS**, twelve miles west of US-50 on Hwy-33, is one of the Chesapeake Bay's oldest ports. Founded during the mid-1600s, it grew into one of colonial America's prime shipbuilding centres. Since the 1960s, it has been revitalized, its old buildings now gentrified into art galleries, boutiques and cosy B&Bs.

St Mary's Square, the old town green, sits a block east of Talbot Street on Mulberry Street, while north along the docks is the extensive and modern **Chesapeake Bay Maritime Museum** at 213 N Talbot St (daily: April–Oct 9am–5pm; Nov–March 10am–4pm; $13; ☎410 745 2916, ⓦcbmm.org), which hosts a number of restored old vessels on its premises, as well as exhibits on the oyster industry and talks on working-class life on the Bay. The complex also focuses on the restored 1879 **Hooper Strait Lighthouse**, at the foot of which float several Chesapeake Bay sailboats making the most of the bay's shallow waters.

ACCOMMODATION AND EATING   ST MICHAELS

★ **Bistro St Michaels** 403 S Talbot St ☎410 745 9111, ⓦbistrostmichaels.com. This place serves some of the best steamed mussels, salmon and shrimp around, at a premium price. Mon, Thurs & Sun 5–9pm, Fri & Sat 5–10pm.

Cherry Street Inn 103 Cherry St ☎410 745 6309, ⓦcherrystreetinn.com. The excellent *Cherry Street Inn's* two lovely suites are well appointed, and there's a tasty breakfast on offer, too. $155

Key Lime Cafe 207 N Talbot St ☎410 745 3158, ⓦkeylime-café.com. Tops for its succulent clams, oysters, duck salad and ribs, with a nice selection of fresh fish, too. Mon & Thurs 8am–3pm, Fri & Sat 8am–4pm, Sun 8am–2pm.

5

Parsonage Inn 210 N Talbot St ☎410 745 8383, Ⓦparsonage-inn.com. One of number of very nice B&Bs in town, this 1883 Victorian splendour has rooms with graceful period decor, some with fireplaces. **$170**

Ocean City

With more than ten miles of broad Atlantic beach and hordes of visitors, **OCEAN CITY** is Maryland's number one summer resort, accessible across the Eastern Shore via US-50. There's a lively, three-mile-long **beach boardwalk**, along which are numerous fast-food and trinket vendors hawking their wares, and a pair of amusement parks with the usual carnival-style thrill rides.

ACCOMMODATION, EATING AND DRINKING   **OCEAN CITY**

Commander Hotel Boardwalk, at 14th St ☎410 289 6166, Ⓦcommanderhotel.com. This place offers a variety of rooms, suites and apartments. **$175**

The Crystal Beach Hotel 2500 N Baltimore Ave ☎866 BEACH 21, Ⓦcrystalbeachhotel.com. Has rooms with kitchenettes and balconies. **$169**

PGN Crab House 2906 N Philadelphia Ave ☎410 289 8380. Good eating options amid the national chains include the *PGN Crab House* for its succulent crab cakes.

Daily 11am–11pm.
Sea Hawk Motel 12410 Coastal Hwy ☎800 942 9042, Ⓦseahawkmotel.com. Clean and reliable units, some with fridges and microwaves. **$136**

Shenanigan's 309 N Atlantic ☎410 289 7181, Ⓦocshenanigans.com. Open in season, this Irish pub offers a full menu of seafood, shepherd's pie and burgers, and live music. Call for hours.

Delaware

Founded in 1631, **DELAWARE** was once part of neighbouring Pennsylvania – Philadelphia is only ten miles north – until separating in 1776. In 1787 it was also the first original former colony to ratify the Constitution and become a state. Much of Delaware's prosperity can be traced to its lax incorporation laws that have allowed countless multinational corporations to take up official residence near the state capital, **Wilmington**, and also to the wealthy **Du Pont family**, who set up shop nearby (see opposite). Delaware's perfectly preserved old colonial capital, **New Castle**, lies on the Delaware Bay, five miles south of I-95. Further south, **Dover**, the capital, may not detain you long, but beyond it, the small and amiable resorts of **Lewes** and **Rehoboth Beach** mark the northern extent of more than twenty miles of mostly unspoiled Atlantic beaches.

Wilmington

Pleasant **WILMINGTON** boasts decent art museums and some pretty waterside parks, and the surrounding Brandywine Valley holds the manor homes and gardens (and factories) of the Du Ponts. The two main streets, Market and King, run north for about a mile to the Brandywine River, lined with stores and other businesses, as well as a handful of restored eighteenth-century structures including the **Old Town Hall**, 500 Market St (by appointment; ☎302 655 7161 for details), a graceful 1798 Federal mansion. Nearby is the **Delaware History Museum**, 504 Market St (Wed–Fri 11am–4pm, Sat 10am–4pm; $6, free first Fri; ☎302 656 0637, Ⓦdehistory.org), offering three storeys of exhibits on the history, life and folk art of the state. A short walk north of the downtown commercial district, at the top end of Market Street, **Brandywine Park** is filled with grassy knolls lining both banks of the Brandywine River. The nearby **Delaware Art Museum**, 2301 Kentmere Pkwy (Wed–Sat 10am–4pm, Sun noon–4pm; $12, free Sun; ☎302 571 9590, Ⓦdelart.org), focuses on Pre-Raphaelites such as Dante Rossetti, and on American artists from the nineteenth and twentieth centuries including Frederic Church, Winslow Homer, Edward Hopper and Augustus Saint Gaudens. For those with a yen for the archly modern, the **Delaware Center for the Contemporary Arts**, downtown at 200 S Madison St (Tues & Thurs–Sat 10am–5pm, Wed & Sun noon–5pm; free; ☎302 656 6466, ⊛thedcca.org), is best known for its dozens of yearly rotating exhibits that showcase regional and national artists.

Around the waterfront
Most of Wilmington's colonial sites are hidden away amid the shambling, industrialized waterfront east of downtown. These include the **Hendrickson House Museum**, at 606 Church St, a c.1690 pinewood residence with furnishings from various eras, and **Old Swedes Church**, one of the oldest houses of worship in the USA, built in 1698 (both April–Dec Wed–Sat 10am–4pm; $4; ☎302 652 5629, ⊛oldswedes.org). Several miles north, near I-95 in Rockwood Park, the Gothic Revival **Rockwood Mansion**, 610 Shipley Rd (park and gardens daily 6am–10pm; mansion tours Wed–Sat 10am–3pm, Sun noon–3pm; $10 tours; ⊛rockwood.org), was built in 1854 in the style of a rural English estate, its elegant rooms now restored to their resplendent Gilded Age appearance.

ARRIVAL, GETTING AROUND AND INFORMATION   WILMINGTON

By bus Greyhound buses arrive at 101 N French St, on the dodgy south side of the city.
Destinations Alexandria, VA (1 daily; 7hr 25min); New York City (10 daily; 2hr 15min–6hr 45min).
By train Amtrak trains pull in at 100 S French St.
Destinations Alexandria, VA (11 daily; 2hr 10min–2hr 45min); Baltimore, MD (11 daily; 50min–1hr 5min); Boston,

MA (5 daily; 6hr 35min–8hr 10min); Charlottesville, VA (1 daily; 4hr 50min).
Local buses The DART bus system runs around the county; tickets $1.15 (☎800 652 3278, ⊛dartfirststate.com).
Visitor centre 100 W 10th St, Suite 20 (Mon–Fri 9am–5pm; ☎800 489 6664, ⊛visitwilmingtonde.com); has walking and driving tour maps.

ACCOMMODATION AND EATING

Hotel du Pont 100 W 11th St ☎302 594 3100, ⊛hotel dupont.com. Easily the best option, this choice is splendidly ornate, with well-appointed rooms and suites that are the height of contemporary chic. **$439**
Inn at Wilmington 1300 Rocky Run Pkwy ☎302 479 7900, ⊛innatwilmington.com. The rooms and suites here, with CD players and microwaves, are appropriately affordable. **$120**
Moro 1307 N Scott St ☎302 777 1800, ⊛moro

restaurant.net. For upmarket Atlantic cuisine such as wine-braised rabbit, veal chops and pan-seared scallops, this dining room, in the happening Trolley Square area northwest of downtown, is a winner. Tues–Sat 5–11pm.
Washington Street Ale House 1206 Washington St ☎302 658 2537, ⊛wsalehouse.com. This tap room has serviceable pasta and seafood, but the main draw is its copious microbrew selection. Mon–Sat 11am–1am, Sun 10am–1am.

The Du Pont mansions
Pierre Samuel du Pont de Nemours and his family arrived in Delaware in 1800, fleeing the wrath of revolutionary France, and set up a gunpowder mill that became the main supplier of conventional explosives to the US government. The family built several huge mansions in the **Brandywine Valley** north of Wilmington.

Bellevue State Park
800 Carr Rd • Daily 8am–dusk • Free
A short distance up I-95 from the Rockwood Mansion, the first of the **Du Pont mansions** is accessible in **Bellevue State Park**. William du Pont Jr converted a Gothic Revival mansion into his own version of James Madison's Neoclassical home and called it **Bellevue Hall**. You can't get inside, but can visit the grounds and see the charming ponds, woodlands, gardens and tennis courts.

The Hagley Museum
200 Hagley Rd • Mid-March to Dec daily 9.30am–4.30pm • $14 • ⊛hagley.org
The **Hagley Museum**, off Hwy-141 just north of Wilmington, showcases the Du Pont family's 1802 founding of a small water-powered gunpowder mill, which grew over the

5

next century to include larger steam- and electricity-powered factories – most of which are still in working order. Be sure to tour the luxurious Du Pont mansion, Eleutherian Mills, the centrepiece of the 235-acre estate.

Nemours Mansion

Hwy-141 (Powder Mill Drive) and Alapocas Rd • Guided mansion tours Tues–Sat 9.30am, noon & 3pm, Sun noon & 3pm • $15 • ☎ 800 651 6912, ⓦ nemoursmansion.org

The enormous, dusty-pink **Nemours Mansion** was built by Alfred du Pont in 1910 and named for the family's ancestral home in France, and is surrounded by a 300-acre, French-style garden. Inside the mansion, you'll find plenty of lavish rooms (including ones devoted to fitness, bowling and ice-making) and a collection of early twentieth-century automobiles.

Winterthur

5105 Kennett Pike • March–Nov Tues–Sun 10am–5pm; last tickets sold at 3.15pm for 3.30pm tour • Tours $18–40 • ⓦ winterthur.org

Off Hwy-52, the one-time Du Pont family estate of **Winterthur** now displays American decorative arts from 1640 to 1860, each of its 175 rooms showcasing styles ranging from a simple Shaker cottage to a beautiful three-storey elliptical staircase taken from a North Carolina plantation. Separately, the estate galleries present a selection of furniture, textiles, ceramics, paintings and glass in a museum setting.

New Castle

Delaware's original capital, **NEW CASTLE**, fronts the broad Delaware River, just six miles south of Wilmington via Hwy-141. Founded in the 1650s by the Dutch and taken over by the British in 1664, New Castle has managed to survive intact, its quiet cobbled streets and immaculate eighteenth-century brick houses shaded by ancient hardwood trees.

The heart of New Castle is the tree-filled **town square** that spreads east from the shops of Delaware Street, dominated by the stalwart tower of the **Immanuel Episcopal Church**, built in 1703 and bordered by tidy rows of eighteenth-century gravestones. On the west edge of the green, the **Old Court House**, 211 Delaware St (Wed–Sat 10am–3.30pm, Sun 1.30–4.30pm; free), was built in 1732 and served as the first state capitol until 1881. Its dainty cupola provided the vista from which surveyors determined the state's arcing northern border, drawn up when Delaware seceded from Pennsylvania (and Great Britain) in 1776.

The colonial houses

The fine collection of colonial houses fill the blocks around the town green. The largest is the **George Read II House**, two blocks south along the river at 42 The Strand (Jan–March Sat 10am–4pm, Sun 11am–4pm; April–Dec Wed–Sun 11am–4pm; $7; ☎302 322 8411, ⓦwww.hsd.org/read.htm), a sumptuous replica of a c.1800 house, with marble fireplaces, elaborately carved woodwork, Federal-style plaster ornament and picturesque gardens. A collection of classic edifices lies several blocks north along Third and Fourth streets: the **Amstel House**, 2 E Fourth St (April–Dec Wed–Sat 10am–4pm, Sun noon–4pm; $5, $9 for combo with Dutch House; ☎302 322 2794, ⓦnewcastlehistory.org), a 1730 early Georgian mansion that hosted prominent Revolutionary-era figures; the hexagonal brick **Old Library Museum**, 40 E Third St (March–Dec Sat & Sun 1–4pm; free), housing the historical society's collection; and the **Dutch House**, 32 E Third St (May–Dec Wed–Sat 10am–4pm, Sun noon–4pm; $5, $9 for combo with Amstel House), a simple c.1700 residence with decor and artefacts including a cherry-wood cupboard, duck-footed wooden chairs and polychromed Delft ceramics.

5

Jessop's Tavern 114 Delaware St ☎302 322 6111, ⓦjessops-tavern.com.com. The popular and well-reviewed *Jessop's Tavern* serves colonial-style food, such as crabs, clams and shepherd's pie. Mon–Thurs & Sun 11.30am–10pm, Fri & Sat 11.30am–late.

Terry House 130 Delaware St ☎302 322 2505, ⓦterryhouse.com. There's only one B&B left in New Castle, and it's just as well that it's the *Terry House*, a stately townhouse dating from the Civil War with four simple, tastefully decorated rooms. **$100**

Dover

Located in Delaware's mostly agricultural centre, just west of US-13, the capital **DOVER** is a small town hemmed in by suburbia. South of **Lockerman Street**, the main route through town, the 1791 **Old State House** is the state's one-time judicial and legislative chambers, now a museum furnished with early American antiques (Mon–Sat 9am–4.30pm, Sun 1.30–4.30pm; free; ☎302 744 5055, ⓦhistory.delaware.gov). To the west, around the oval **town green**, lawyers and corporations have taken over a number of eighteenth- and nineteenth-century buildings.

In the same building as the **visitor centre** (see below), at 406 Federal St, the impressive **Biggs Museum of American Art** (Tues–Sat 9am–4.30pm, Sun 1.30–4.30pm; free; ☎302 674 2111, ⓦbiggsmuseum.org) has a wealth of historical and decorative art, including colonial-era furniture, paintings by the likes of Benjamin West and Gilbert Stuart, silver and porcelain services and heroic landscapes from Albert Bierstadt and Thomas Cole.

Nearby, **First State Heritage Park**, 102 S State St (ⓦdestateparks.com), not only hosts the current statehouse and state archives, but also includes a smattering of museums.

Spence's Bazaar

550 S New St • Tues & Fri 7.30am–6.30pm • Free • ☎302 734 3441

For more than fifty years, **Spence's Bazaar** has hosted a **flea market** that all of Dover turns out for, including dozens of local **Amish**, who ride here in their old horse-drawn buggies to sell home-grown fruits and vegetables.

John Dickinson Plantation

340 Kitts Hummock Rd • Wed–Sat 10am–3.30pm • Free • ☎302 739 3277

A few miles outside town, the eighteen-acre **John Dickinson Plantation**, off Rte-9, is where costumed re-enactors of colonial residents, including slaves, go about farming, cooking and gardening; both the estate's grounds and 1740 brick mansion are viewable on various tours, lasting ninety minutes to two hours.

ARRIVAL AND INFORMATION DOVER

By bus Greyhound buses pull in at 716 S Governors Ave.
Visitor centre Corner of Duke of York and Federal sts

(Tues–Sat 9am–4.30pm, Sun 1.30–4.30pm; ☎302 744 5055, ⓦcityofdover.com).

ACCOMMODATION AND EATING

Franco's 1708 E Lebanon Rd ☎302 677 1946, ⓦfrancospizzainc.com. A good place for affordable pizza and pasta dishes. Mon–Sat 11am–10pm, Sun noon–9pm.
Kirby and Holloway 656 N Dupont Hwy ☎302 734 7133. Slightly out of town and known for its filling steaks, burgers, chicken and dumplings and turkey platters, most

below $10. Mon–Sat 6am–9pm, Sun 6am–8pm.
State Street Inn 228 N State St ☎302 734 2294, ⓦstatestreetinn.com. Comfortable rooms – two with whirlpool tubs – in a cosy inn with a parlour, exercise room and even a putting green. **$110**

The Delaware coast

The thirty-mile-long **Delaware coast** is one of the little-known jewels of the East Coast, aside from the brash summer resort of **Rehoboth Beach**. The historic fishing

5

community of **Lewes** is an attractive stopover, but what set the area apart are the long, isolated stretches of sand. Much has been preserved as open space, most extensively at **Delaware Seashore State Park**, which stretches south to the Maryland border.

Lewes

Accessible via Hwy-1, the natural harbour at the mouth of Delaware Bay at **LEWES** has attracted seafarers ever since a Dutch whaling company set up a small colony here in 1631, a history outlined in the mock-Dutch **Zwaanendael Museum**, 102 Kings Hwy (April–Oct Tues–Sat 10am–4.30pm, Sun 1.30–4.30pm; Nov–March Wed–Sat only; free; ☎302 645 1148). The tourist office next door (see below), housed inside a gambrel-roofed 1730s farmhouse, has walking tour maps of the town and its numerous eighteenth-century homes. Don't miss the **Lewes Historic Complex**, three blocks north at 110 Shipcarpenter St (Mon–Sat 11am–4pm; $5, various tours $10; ☎302 645 7670, ⓦhistoriclewes.org), twelve classic properties dating from the early colonial to late Victorian eras, including a crude plank-house, doctor's office, store and boathouse. On Front Street, the 1812 **Memorial Park** is decorated by an array of cannons, and commemorates a British attack that resulted in spotty cannonball damage around town.

There's a popular, extensive **beach** along the Delaware Bay at the foot of town, while 3000-acre, four-mile-long **Cape Henlopen State Park** (daily 8am–dusk; ☎302 645 8983), where the bay meets the open ocean just a mile east of town, boasts the biggest sand dunes north of Cape Hatteras and some appealing hiking trails, including one to a World War II-era observation tower.

ARRIVAL, GETTING AROUND AND INFORMATION   LEWES

By ferry Taking the open-water route, you can depart (or arrive) via ferry across Delaware Bay from beside the state park to Cape May, NJ (times vary by day and season; 1hr 25min; $32–36/car, $8–10/person; ☎800 64 FERRY, ⓦcmlf.com).

By bike You can walk to most places in town, or rent a bike from Lewes Cycle Sports, 526 Savannah Rd ($25/day; ☎302 645 4544).

Visitor centre 120 Kings Hwy (June–Sept Mon–Fri 10am–4pm, Sat 9am–3pm, Sun 10am–2pm; ☎302 645 8073, ⓦleweschamber.com).

ACCOMMODATION AND EATING

Blue Water House 407 E Market St ☎302 645 7832, ⓦlewes-beach.com. A B&B with eight stylish rooms and a suite, all with watersports rentals. Two-night minimum. **$185**

The Buttery 102 2nd St, at Savannah Rd ☎302 645 7755, ⓦbutteryrestaurant.com. A fine French bistro that has mid-priced crab cakes, burgers and seafood sandwiches for lunch, and pricey steak and rack of lamb for dinner. Mon–Fri 11.30am–close, Sat & Sun 10.30am–close.

Cafe Azafran 109 Market St ☎302 644 4446, ⓦcafeazafran.com. This place offers a nice assortment of tapas (including seafood items) for a range of prices. Mon & Tues 7am–3.30pm, Wed–Sun 7am–3.30pm & 5pm–close.

Cape Henlopen State Park The park's campgrounds offer the chance to sleep beside sand dunes, with some six-person cabins also available. Tent sites **$33**, cabins **$82**

Hotel Blue 110 Anglers Rd ☎302 645 4880, ⓦhotelblue.info. The modern rooms and suites here come with flat-screen TVs, boutique decor and fireplaces. **$229**

Rehoboth Beach

A nonstop parade of motels and malls along the six miles of Hwy-1 links Lewes with **REHOBOTH BEACH**, Delaware's largest beach resort. The town's wooden **boardwalk** is one of the last left on the East Coast, stretching along the Atlantic to either side of Rehoboth Avenue – **"the Avenue"** – which acts as the main drag. With its novelty and trinket shops, carnival-style amusements and various tourist traps, the town has no sights to speak of, but it can be enjoyable if you just want to mingle with the crowds or worship the sun with the other beachgoers.

South of Rehoboth, **Delaware Seashore State Park** (daily 8am–dusk; ☎302 227 2800, ⓦdestateparks.com) stretches for miles along a thin, sandy peninsula, split by Hwy-1 and bounded by the ocean and freshwater marshlands, and good for its fishing and surfing.

ACCOMMODATION AND EATING   REHOBOTH BEACH

Crosswinds 312 Rehoboth Ave ☎302 227 7997, ⓦcrosswindsmotel.com. Three blocks from the beach, this is the best of Rehoboth's motels (very pricey in July and Aug), with clean rooms with fridges. **$195**

Dogfish Head Brewing 320 Rehoboth Ave ☎302 226 2739, ⓦdogfish.com. Best for its fine microbrews, weekend live bands and on-site distillery. Mon–Thurs & Sun noon–11pm, Fri & Sat noon–1am.

Planet X Cafe 35 Wilmington Ave ☎302 226 1928, ⓦplanetxcafe.com. One of Rehoboth's better restaurants, serving appealing, expensive Asian fusion cuisine such as ahi tuna fillets, peanut-crusted shrimp and, of course, lump crab cakes. Daily 4.30–10pm.

Rehoboth Guest House 40 Maryland Ave ☎302 227 4117, ⓦrehobothguesthouse.com. Gay-friendly B&B with porch and shaded backyard, and basic rooms (add about $40 for private bath). **$125**

The South

FORSYTH PARK, SAVANNAH, GA

The South

Mark Twain put it best, as early as 1882: "In the South, the [Civil] war is what AD is elsewhere; they date everything from it". Several generations later, the legacies of slavery and "The War Between the States" remain evident throughout the southern heartland states of North Carolina, South Carolina, Georgia, Kentucky, Tennessee, Alabama, Mississippi and Arkansas. It's impossible to travel through the region without experiencing constant reminders of the two epic historical clashes that have shaped its destiny: the Civil War, and the civil rights movement of the 1950s and 1960s.

For many travellers, the most exciting aspect of a visit to the South has to be its **music**. Fans flock to the homelands of Elvis Presley, Hank Williams, Robert Johnson, Dolly Parton and Otis Redding, heading to the country and blues hot spots of **Nashville** and **Memphis**, or seeking out backwoods barn dances in Appalachia and blues juke joints in the Mississippi Delta. The South gave the world rock'n'roll, and its contribution to music in general cannot be overstated.

The Southern experience is also reflected in a rich regional **literature**, documented by the likes of William Faulkner, Carson McCullers, Eudora Welty, Margaret Mitchell and Harper Lee. Major destinations include the elegant coastal cities of **Charleston** and **Savannah**, college towns **Athens** and **Chapel Hill**, and the historic Mississippi River ports of **Natchez** and **Vicksburg**. Away from the urban areas, perfumed with delicate magnolia trees, the classic Southern scenery consists of fertile but sun-baked farmlands, with undulating hillsides dotted with wooden shacks and rust-red barns and broken by occasional forests. Highlights include the misty Appalachian **mountains** of Kentucky, Tennessee and North Carolina; the subtropical **beaches** and tranquil **barrier islands** along the Atlantic and Gulf coasts of Georgia and South Carolina; and the river road through the tiny, time-warped settlements of the flat **Mississippi Delta**. In July and August, the daily high **temperature** is mostly a very humid 90°F, and while almost every public building is air-conditioned, the heat can be debilitating. May and June are more bearable, and tend to see a lot of local festivals, while the autumn colours in the mountains – just as beautiful and a lot less expensive and congested than New England – are at their headiest during October.

BLUE RIDGE PARKWAY, NC

Highlights

❶ **Blue Ridge Parkway, NC** A slow, circuitous but exhilarating wilderness highway that makes a destination in itself. **See p.400**

❷ **Martin Luther King Birth Home, Atlanta, GA** Engaging tours take you around King's childhood home, in the South's most dynamic city. **See p.416**

❸ **Savannah, GA** With its impossibly romantic garden squares, gorgeous architecture and bustling old waterfront, this atmospheric town also has a hip edge, partly due to its art school. **See p.424**

❹ **Memphis, TN** This sleepy city on the Mississippi is especially thrilling for music fans: you could spend days checking out Beale Street, Sun Studio, the Stax Museum, Al Green's church and, of course, Graceland. **See p.438**

❺ **Country Music Hall of Fame, Nashville, TN** At once a fascinating interactive museum and a treasure trove of memorabilia, including Elvis's gold Cadillac. **See p.447**

❻ **The Mississippi Delta, MS** The birthplace of the blues holds an irresistible appeal, with funky little Clarksdale as the obvious first port of call. **See p.462**

HIGHLIGHTS ARE MARKED ON THE MAP ON PP.386–387

As a rule, public transport in rural areas is poor and you will see far more, and be able get out to the backwaters – the Blue Ridge Parkway, the Outer Banks of North Carolina, the Ozarks and the Mississippi Delta to mention but a few – if you **rent a car**. In any case, it's best to take things at your own pace – you'll find things to see and do in the most unlikely places. Incidentally, if you harbour fantasies of travelling through the South by boat along the Mississippi, note that only luxury craft make the trip these days.

Gulf of Mexico

Brief history

The British dominated the region from the seventeenth century onwards, establishing increasingly successful agricultural colonies in the Carolinas and Georgia. Both climate and soil favoured staple crops, and massive labour-intensive plantations sprang up, predominantly growing tobacco prior to independence, and then increasingly shifting to cotton. Eventually, the big landowners turned to slavery as the most profitable

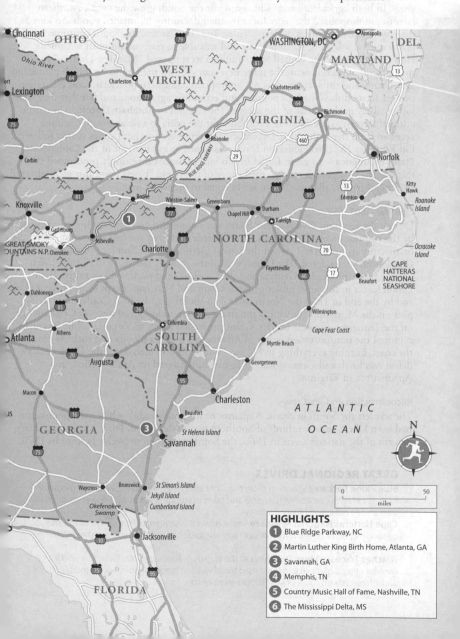

HIGHLIGHTS

1. Blue Ridge Parkway, NC
2. Martin Luther King Birth Home, Atlanta, GA
3. Savannah, GA
4. Memphis, TN
5. Country Music Hall of Fame, Nashville, TN
6. The Mississippi Delta, MS

source of labour. Millions of blacks were brought across from Africa, most arriving via the port of Charleston.

Early nineteenth-century

Although the South prospered until the middle of the nineteenth century, there was little incentive to diversify its economy. As a result, the Northern states began to surge ahead in both agriculture and industry; while the South grew the crops, Northern factories monopolized the more lucrative manufacturing of finished goods. So long as there were equal numbers of slave-owning and "free" states, the South continued to play a central role in national politics, and was able to resist **abolitionist** sentiment. However, the more the United States fulfilled its supposed "Manifest Destiny" to spread across the continent, the more new states joined the Union for which plantation agriculture, and thus slavery, was not appropriate. Southern politicians and plantation owners accused the North of political and economic aggression, and felt that they were losing all say in the future of the nation. The election of **Abraham Lincoln**, a longtime critic of slavery, as president in 1860 brought the crisis to a head. South Carolina **seceded** from the Union that December, and ten more southern states swiftly followed. On February 18, 1861, Jefferson Davis was sworn in as president of the **Confederate States of America** – an event for which his vice president shockingly proclaimed that this was the first government in the history of the world "based upon this great physical and moral truth…that the Negro is not equal to the white man".

Civil War (1861–65)

During the resultant **Civil War**, the South was outgunned and ultimately overwhelmed by the vast resources of the North. The Confederates fired the first shots and scored the first victory in April 1861, when the Union garrison at Fort Sumter (outside Charleston) surrendered. The Union was on the military defensive until mid-1862, when its navy blockaded Georgia and the Carolinas and occupied key ports. Then Union forces in the west, under generals Grant and Sherman, swept through Tennessee, and by the end of 1863 the North had taken Vicksburg, the final Confederate-held port on the Mississippi, as well as the strategic mountain-locked town of Chattanooga on the Tennessee–Georgia border. Grant proceeded north to Virginia, while Sherman captured the transportation nexus of Atlanta and began a bloody and ruthless march to the coast, burning everything in his way. With 258,000 men dead, the Confederacy's defeat was total, and General Robert E. Lee **surrendered** on April 9, 1865, at Appomattox in Virginia.

Reconstruction and Jim Crow

The war left the South in chaos. A quarter of the South's adult white male population had been killed, and two thirds of Southern wealth destroyed. From controlling thirty percent of the nation's assets in 1860, the South was down to twelve percent in 1870,

---

GREAT REGIONAL DRIVES

Blue Ridge Parkway Spanning more than four hundred miles, this spectacular mountain route links North Carolina with Virginia and takes in stunning vistas, wild-flower-studded hiking trails and Appalachian bluegrass shows.

Cape Hatteras National Seashore Snake down this slender coastal barrier island and you'll be sandwiched between forty miles of ravishing beaches and saltwater marshes, with sunbathing opportunities galore.

Natchez Trace Parkway Stretching all the way from Natchez to Nashville, this verdant corridor offers a glimpse into what road travel was like before petrol stations and billboards, and intersects with some of Mississippi's most historic towns.

while the spur the war gave to industrialization meant that the North was booming. For a brief period of **Reconstruction**, when the South was occupied by Union troops, newly freed Southern blacks were able to vote, and black representatives were elected to both state and federal office. However, unrepentant former Confederates, spurred in part by allegations of profiteering by incoming Northern Republican "carpetbaggers", thwarted any potential for change, and by the end of the century the Southern states were firmly back under white Democratic control. As Reconstruction withered away, "**Jim Crow**" segregation laws were imposed, backed by the not-so-secret terror of the **Ku Klux Klan**, and poll taxes, literacy tests and property qualifications disenfranchised virtually all blacks. Many found themselves little better off as **sharecroppers** – in which virtually all they could earn from raising crops went to pay their landlords – than they had been as slaves, and there were mass migrations to cities like Memphis and Atlanta, as well as to the North.

6

School desegregation and the Civil Rights movement

Not until the landmark 1954 Supreme Court ruling in **Brown vs Topeka Board of Education** outlawed segregation in schools was there any sign that the federal authorities in Washington might concern themselves with inequities in the South. Even then, individual states proved extremely reluctant to effect the required changes. In the face of institutionalized white resistance, nonviolent black protestors coalesced to form the **Civil Rights movement**, and broke down segregation through a sustained programme of mass action. After tackling such issues as public transport – most famously in the Montgomery bus boycott and the Freedom Rides – and segregated dining facilities, with lunch-counter sit-ins reaching their apex in Greensboro, North Carolina, the campaign eventually culminated in restoring full black voter registration – not without the loss of many protestors' lives. One fulfilling itinerary through the Southern states today is to trace the footsteps of **Dr Martin Luther King, Jr**, from his birthplace in Atlanta through his church in Montgomery to the site of his assassination in Memphis.

North Carolina

NORTH CAROLINA, the most industrialized of the Southern states, breaks down into three distinct areas – the coast, the Piedmont and the mountains. The **coast** promises stunning beaches, beautiful landscapes and a fascinating history – the world's first powered flight took place here. The inner coast consists largely of the less developed **Albemarle Peninsula**, with colonial **Edenton** nearby. The central **Piedmont** is less appealing, dominated by manufacturing cities and the academic institutions of the prestigious "Research Triangle": **Raleigh**, the state capital, is home to North Carolina State University; **Durham** has Duke; and the University of North Carolina is in trendy **Chapel Hill**. **Winston-Salem** combines tobacco culture and Moravian heritage, while the boomtown of **Charlotte** is distinguished by little but its downtown skyscrapers. In the **Appalachian Mountains**, alternative **Asheville** makes a hugely enjoyable stop along the spectacular **Blue Ridge Parkway**.

The Albemarle Peninsula

The huge **Albemarle Peninsula** remains largely unexploited. Local towns try to make much of their **colonial history** – but often there's not a lot left to see. The area is rewarding to explore if you like to travel off the beaten path, its sleepy old towns and remote plantations set in wide swathes of rural farmland. The first stop is **Edenton**, a bayside town with a relaxed ambience.

6

> ## DOWN-HOME SOUTHERN COOKING
>
> The region's varied **cuisine** ranges from creamy, cheese-topped grits (maize porridge) to highly calorific, irresistible soul food: fried chicken, smothered pork chops and the like, along with collard greens, sweet potatoes, macaroni and all manner of tasty vegetables. Barbecue – a deep source of regional pride and cultural identity – is king here, particularly in Memphis, but each state has its own smoked-meat variations and closely guarded recipes. Seafood is also exemplary, from catfish to the wonderful Low Country Boils – fish stews served with rice, traditionally prepared on the sea islands of the Carolinas and Georgia.

Edenton

EDENTON, set along the majestic Albemarle Sound waterfront, was established as North Carolina's first state capital in 1722 and was a major centre of unrest in the American Revolution. Nowadays, it makes a nice, peaceful little base for explorations of the coast, with some good B&Bs and restaurants, and a nostalgic small-town feel. Strolling along the town's main road, **Broad Street**, lined with colonial facades and old-fashioned stores, brings you to the visitor centre.

Among other historic figures, Edenton was home to **Harriet Jacobs**, a runaway slave who hid for seven years in her grandmother's attic. In 1842, she finally escaped to the North through such ruses as disguising herself as a sailor, and was eventually reunited in Boston with the two children she had with a white man in Edenton. She wrote her autobiography as *Incidents in the Life of a Slave Girl*, one of the most famous published slave narratives of the nineteenth century.

ACCOMMODATION AND EATING   EDENTON

309 Bistro & Spirits 309 S Broad St ☎ 252 482 0997. Right in the heart of things, this gussied-up café with original art and a cheerful striped awning is the regional hub for tangy martinis and New American food such as blackened tuna salad ($10). Mon 11am–2pm, Tues & Thurs 11am–2.30pm & 5–9pm, Fri & Sat 11am–9pm.

Nothin' Fancy Café and Market 701 N Broad St ☎ 252 482 1909. Down-home joint in a small shopping complex half a mile from downtown. Delicious plates of meatloaf ($8.25), cornbread ($2.75) and tomato pudding ($2.25) are

served at vinyl booths on checkerboard floors amid antique, craft and book stalls. Mon & Sun 11am–3pm, Tues–Fri 11am–8pm, Sat 8am–8pm.

The Pack House Inn 103 E Albemarle St ☎ 252 482 3641, ⊚ thepackhouse.com. Grand old inn with three unique properties: an eight-room Victorian mansion, a tobacco packing house (dating to 1915) and a nineteenth-century cottage that's great for families. Three-course breakfast included in the rate; other perks include lavish antiques and coal-burning fireplaces. **$109**

Somerset Place State Historic Site

Creswell, 28 miles southeast of Edenton on US-64 • April–Oct Mon–Sat 9am–5pm, Sun 1–5pm; Nov–March Mon–Sat 10am–4pm, Sun 1–4pm • Free • ☎ 252 797 4560, ⊚ nchistoricsites.org/somerset

A vivid picture of slave life is painted by **Somerset Place State Historic Site**. The museum here tells the history of the plantation, from its origins in the 1780s to its growth by 1865 into a 100,000-acre enterprise, and its demise after the Civil War. Exhibits detail the accumulation of more than eight hundred enslaved Africans and the work they did; on the grounds, a sweeping waterfront vista of lowland fields and huge oaks, you can walk through reconstructions of the plantation hospital and two typical slave houses.

The southern shore

The southern shore of the Albemarle Peninsula holds less to see, though the marshy country roads make for a pleasant drive. **Lake Mattamuskeet Wildlife Refuge** (☎ 252 926 4021, ⊚ fws.gov/mattamuskeet) is an amazing sight in winter (particularly Dec & Jan), when thousands of swans migrate here from Canada. The entrance is on Hwy-94, about a mile north of its intersection with US-264.

The Outer Banks

The **OUTER BANKS**, a string of skinny barrier islands, the remnants of ancient sand dunes, stretch about 180 miles from the Virginia border to Cape Lookout. Easily navigable by bridges, seafood shack-lined avenues and lonely highways, it's a great region to meander, with wonderful wild beaches, otherworldly marshes and attractive small towns such as **Kitty Hawk**, **Kill Devil Hills** and **Nags Head**. **Roanoke Island**, site of the first English settlement in the USA – which vanished inexplicably in 1590 – has obvious historical interest; its village, **Manteo**, is perhaps the nicest on the Outer Banks. There is no public transport other than the ferries between Ocracoke and the mainland (see p.393).

Kitty Hawk, Kill Devil Hills and Nags Head

A melding of salt marshes, beaches and estuaries, the main towns of the Outer Banks are in parts beautifully unspoiled, yet at times quite touristy. In **Nags Head**, **Jockey's Ridge State Park** (ⓦjockeysridgestatepark.com) boasts the largest sand dunes on the east coast – beautiful at sunset. Walking downhill is like clomping through a warm snowbank – a surreal and highly enjoyable experience.

Wright Brothers National Memorial

1000 N Croatan Hwy (US-158) • Daily 9am–5pm • $4 • ☎ 252 473 2111, ⓦ nps.gov/wrbr

The main feature of the **Wright Brothers National Memorial**, just off the main road at **Kill Devil Hills**, is the Wright Brothers Monument, a 60ft granite fin atop a 90ft dune (which is in fact *the* Kill Devil Hill). The memorial commemorates Orville Wright's **first powered flight**, on December 17, 1903. (Most histories say the flight took place at **Kitty Hawk**, 8 miles north, but that was just the name of the nearest post office.) A boulder next to the memorial's **visitor centre** marks where Orville's first aircraft took off, and numbered markers show the distance of the brothers' four subsequent landings. Exhibits in the visitor centre record their various outlandish experiments.

INFORMATION
KITTY HAWK, KILL DEVIL HILLS AND NAGS HEAD

Visitor centre 5230 N Croatan Hwy (US-158), Kitty Hawk (daily 9am–5.30pm; ☎ 252 261 4644, ⓦ outerbanks.org).

ACCOMMODATION AND EATING

KILL DEVIL HILLS

Flying Fish Café 2003 S Croatan Hwy (US-158) ☎ 252 441 6894, ⓦ flyingfishcafeobx.com. One of the fancier dinner spots (though it retains a relaxed beach ambience), boasting top-notch Mediterranean-influenced cuisine and knowledgeable waiters. Daily 5–10pm.

Kill Devil Grill 2008 S Virginia Dare Trail ☎ 252 449 8181, ⓦ thekilldevilgrill.com. Part 1930s diner car (complete with tabletop jukeboxes), part snug dining room with vinyl booths, this retro favourite dishes up mouth-watering house-roasted chicken ($13), fish-of-the-day sandwiches ($9.50), and decadent key lime pie ($6). Tues–Sat 11.30am–10pm.

NAGS HEAD

Blue Moon Beach Grill 4104 S Virginia Dare Trail (in Surfside Plaza) ☎ 252 261 2583, ⓦ bluemoonbeachgrill.com. Located in an unprepossessing mall, this tiny seafood restaurant with jazzy decor draws crowds for its fish and chips ($14) and fried calamari ($9) – easily the best squid in town. Great beer selection, too. Daily 11.30am–9pm.

First Colony Inn 6715 S Croatan Hwy (US-158) ☎ 252 441 2343, ⓦ firstcolonyinn.com. Luxurious inn in a 1930s beach hotel, with wraparound verandas and a pool. The airy rooms are filled with antique furniture and have a crisp white colour palette. Continental breakfast is included, and there's free access to the water park and exercise rooms of the nearby YMCA. **$199**

Nags Head Beach Inn 303 E Admiral St ☎ 800 441 8466, ⓦ nagsheadbeachinn.com. Genial eight-room inn that backs onto the beach and is stocked with beach chairs, umbrellas, bikes and coolers. There's a nice modern style, too. A breakfast buffet is included. Open May–Aug. **$199**

Surfin' Spoon 2408 S Virginia Dare Trail ☎ 252 441 7873, ⓦ surfinspoon.com. This hip, self-serve frozen yogurt shop scoops up ingenious flavours including strawberry lemonade and tart plain, with a vast range of toppings. Tues–Sat noon–11pm.

Tortugas' Lie 3014 S Virginia Dare Trail ☎ 252 441 7299, ⓦ tortugaslie.com. Rowdy little Caribbean spot with surfboards, licence plates and chilli lights dangling over the tables and horseshoe-shaped bar. The creamy fish tacos, crammed with jack cheese and cabbage, are superb ($13.50), while the "shark attack" cocktail (vodka lemonade), comes with a plastic fish full of grenadine. Mon–Thurs & Sun 11.30am–10.15pm, Fri & Sat 11.30am–10.30pm, bar open later.

Roanoke Island

ROANOKE ISLAND, between the mainland and Bodie Island, is accessible from both by bridges. This was the location of the **first English settlement** in North America, founded in 1585, and makes much of its status as Sir Walter Raleigh's so-called "Lost Colony" (see box below). **Manteo**, the island's commercial centre, is a quaint waterfront village with clapboard cottages clustered under delicate magnolia trees, and a downtown dotted with restaurants, kite shops, parks and art galleries.

Fort Raleigh National Historic Site

Three miles north of Manteo off US-64 • **Site** Daily 9am–5pm • Free • ☎ 252 473 2111, ⓦ nps.gov/fora **Elizabethan Gardens** Daily, times vary with season • $9 • ⓦ elizabethangardens.org

Nothing authentic survives of the Roanoke settlement, though **Fort Raleigh National Historic Site** contains a tiny reconstruction of the colonists' earthwork fort, set in a wooded glade. A fascinating museum covers the history of the expeditions and colonization, and an outdoor amphitheatre on the ocean hosts performances of *The Lost Colony* and other productions (June–Aug; $10–45; ⓦ thelostcolony.org). Adjacent to the fort, the **Elizabethan Gardens** are elegantly landscaped with walkways and statues.

Roanoke Island Festival Park

1 Festival Park • March–Dec daily 9am–5pm • $10 tickets valid for two consecutive days • ☎ 252 475 1500, ⓦ roanokeisland.com

Across a small footbridge from **Manteo**, the **Roanoke Island Festival Park** has a slew of historical attractions. Highlights include the **adventure museum**, an interactive exhibit on the history of the Outer Banks, the **settlement site**, a living museum peopled with "Elizabethan" soldiers and craftsmen and the *Elizabeth II*, a reconstruction of a sixteenth-century English ship.

ACCOMMODATION AND EATING — ROANOKE ISLAND

Full Moon Café & Brewery 208 Queen Elizabeth St ☎ 252 473 6666, ⓦ thefullmooncafe.com. Casual, friendly spot in the centre of town that brews its own beer and serves comfort food such as chowder ($5), gourmet sandwiches and warm Brie salad with apples and almonds ($11). Nice outdoor seating, too. Mon–Thurs & Sun

---

ROANOKE: THE LOST COLONY

According to popular myth, the first English attempt to settle in North America – Sir Walter Raleigh's colony at Roanoke – remains an unsolved mystery, in which the "Lost Colony" disappeared without a trace. In 1587, 117 colonists set off from England, intending to farm a fertile site beside Chesapeake Bay; however, after tensions grew between the privateers and their passengers, the ships dumped them at Roanoke Island. Their leader, **John White**, was stranded in England when war broke out with Spain. When White finally managed to persuade a reluctant sea captain to carry him back to Roanoke in 1590, he found the island abandoned. Even so, he was reassured by the absence of the agreed distress signal (a carved Maltese cross), while the word "**Croatoan**" inscribed on a tree seemed a clear message that the colonists had moved south to the eponymous island. However, fearful of both the Spanish and of the approaching hurricane season, White's crew refused to take him any further. There the story usually ends, with the colonists never seen again. In fact, twenty years later, several reports reached the subsequent, more durable colony of Jamestown (in what's now Virginia), of English settlers being dispersed as slaves among the Native American tribes of North Carolina. Rather than admit their inability to rescue their fellow countrymen, and thus expose a vulnerability that might deter prospective settlers or investors, the Jamestown colonists seem simply to have written their predecessors out of history.

11am–8pm, Fri & Sat 11am–9pm.

Roanoke Island Inn 305 Fernando St ☎ 252 473 5511, ⓦ roanokeislandinn.com. Perched on the bay and steps from the town boardwalk, this 1860s cottage makes a nice retreat with sailing, bike use and ample home-made baked goods. Eight spacious rooms are outfitted with antique headboards and cosy quilts; there's also a bungalow and three-bedroom cottage. Breakfast is included. **$228**

Cape Hatteras National Seashore

CAPE HATTERAS NATIONAL SEASHORE stretches south from South Nags Head on Bodie Island to **Hatteras** and **Ocracoke** islands, with forty miles of unspoiled beaches on its seaward side. Even in high season you can pull off the road and walk across the dunes to deserted beaches. The salt marshes on the western side are also beautiful. At the northern end of Hatteras Island, the **Pea Island National Wildlife Refuge** (ⓦ fws.gov/peaisland) offers guided canoe tours (☎ 252 475 4180), trails and observation platforms for birdwatching.

Since the sixteenth century, around a thousand ships have been wrecked along this treacherous stretch of coast. At the south end of Hatteras Island, near the early nineteenth-century black-and-white-striped **Cape Hatteras Lighthouse**, a visitor centre (see below) has exhibits on the island's maritime history; you can climb the 208ft (around twelve-storey) lighthouse (mid-April to mid-Oct; $8).

Further south at the village of **Frisco**, the **Native American Museum** is a loving collection of arts and crafts from around the USA, including a drum from a Hopi *kiva*. It also offers several acres of forested nature **trails** (Tues–Sun 10.30am–5pm; $5; ☎ 252 995 4440, ⓦ nativeamericanmuseum.org).

In Hatteras, next to the Ocracoke ferry landing, the **Graveyard of the Atlantic Museum** (April–Oct Mon–Sat 10am–4pm; Nov–March Mon–Fri 10am–4pm; free; ☎ 252 986 2995, ⓦ graveyardoftheatlantic.com) tells the stories of the explorers, pirates and Civil War blockade-runners who perished along this wild stretch of coast.

INFORMATION
CAPE HATTERAS NATIONAL SEASHORE

Visitor centre Cape Hatteras Lighthouse (daily: June–Aug 9am–6pm; Sept–May 9am–5pm; ☎ 252 473 2111, ⓦ nps.gov/caha).

ACCOMMODATION AND EATING

Cape Hatteras Motel 46556 Hwy-12, Buxton ☎ 800 995 0711, ⓦ capehatterasmotel.com. About a mile from the lighthouse, this faded beach motel has a spectacular location, basic, slightly outdated decor, good rates and a pool. **$158**

Diamond Shoals 46843 Hwy-12, next to Lighthouse Rd, Buxton ☎ 252 995 5217, ⓦ diamondshoals.net. It's a good seafood rule of thumb that if a restaurant has its own fish market, only the freshest crustaceans will make it to your plate. A longtime Hatteras favourite, *Diamond Shoals* adheres to this principle. Mains come with hush puppies (fried balls of cornmeal), and there's great sushi too – rare in these parts. Daily 6.30am–2.30pm & 5–9pm.

National Park Service campgrounds ☎ 252 441 0882, ⓦ nps.gov/caha. The NPS operates first-come, first-served campgrounds at Frisco and Oregon Inlet on Bodie Island (early April to mid-Oct); and at Cape Point near Buxton (late May to Sept). **$20**

Ocracoke Island

Peaceful **OCRACOKE ISLAND**, a sixteen-mile ribbon of land forty minutes by free ferry from Hatteras, is even more beautiful than its neighbour. Despite the tourist crowds in the tiny village of **Ocracoke**, the southern tip of the island has hung onto its atmosphere and it's easy to find yourself a deserted patch of beach.

ARRIVAL AND DEPARTURE
OCRACOKE ISLAND

By ferry In summer, free ferries run between Hatteras and Ocracoke (40min). There's room for just thirty cars, and it's loaded on a first-come, first-served basis. Ferries from Ocracoke also head south down the coast to Cedar Island on the mainland (2hr 15min; $1/pedestrian, $15/car) and to Swan Quarter on the Albemarle Peninsula (2hr 30min; same fares). Both require reservations in summer, preferably a day or two in advance. For further information contact ☎ 800 293 3779 or ⓦ ncferry.org.

6

ACCOMMODATION AND EATING

Dajio 305 Irvin Garrish Hwy ☎ 252 928 7119, ⓦ dajio restaurant.com. Candlelit cottage set back among spindly oak trees, with a patio and outdoor bar. The New American cuisine is a dream: crab dip with crostini ($14), chicken and prosciutto linguine ($18) and local scallops in coriander pesto ($22). Happy hour (3–5pm), with $6 baskets of peel-and-eat shrimp, is highly enjoyable. March–Nov daily 8am–9.30pm.

Eduardo's Taco Stand 950 Irvin Garrish Hwy ☎ 252 588 0202. Mouth-watering Mexican food truck with authentic fare like steak *asada* sandwiches ($10), and Americanized riffs like a "gringa" taco stacked with cheesy pork, pineapple, guacamole and *pico de gallo* ($4). Seating

consists of a handful of picnic tables. Cash only. Mon–Fri 7am–9pm, Sat 6am–9pm, Sun 6am–7pm.

Edward's 226 Old Beach Rd ☎ 800 254 1359, ⓦ edwardsofocracoke.com. Within walking distance of all the village's restaurants and sights, this low-key place on a quiet side street offers simple, 1950s-style rooms and cottages with outdoor space. $90

Ocracoke Campground 4352 Irvin Garrish Hwy ☎ 877 444 6777, ⓦ nps.gov/caha. Ocracoke's NPS campground tends to be the first of the Outer Banks sites to fill up; unlike the others, it accepts reservations. There are toilets, cold showers and grills; a quick jaunt over the dunes and you'll be on the beach. Open April–Oct. $23

Cape Lookout National Seashore

The mainland between Cedar Island and Beaufort is a rural backwater, sparsely settled and barely touched by tourists. There are no hotels, and the most likely reason to pass through is to get to the all-but-deserted **CAPE LOOKOUT NATIONAL SEASHORE**, a narrow ribbon of sand stretching south of Ocracoke Island along three Outer Banks with no roads or habitation. The seashore is only accessible by **ferry** or private boat (see p.394) and its few visitors share a total of around 56 miles of beach along all three islands.

At the northern tip of the first island, **North Core Banks**, stand the eerie ruins of the abandoned village of **Portsmouth**, whose last two residents left in 1971. To get to the peaceful **Shackleford Banks**, inhabited by wild mustangs since the early 1500s, when they are thought to have swum ashore from shipwrecks, you can catch ferries from Beaufort (see below).

ARRIVAL AND INFORMATION

CAPE LOOKOUT NATIONAL SEASHORE

By ferry Ferries arrive at Portsmouth Village from Ocracoke (Portsmouth Island Boat Tours; ☎ 252 928 4361, ⓦ portsmouthnc.com). The ferry from Atlantic, south of Cedar Island on the mainland (Morris Marina ferry service; ☎ 252 225 4261, ⓦ portsmouthislandfishing.com), lands at Long Point, 17 miles south of Portsmouth, which you can only reach on foot. South Core Banks is served by private

ferry from Davis (south of Atlantic on the mainland), Beaufort and Harkers Island; see ⓦ nps.gov/calo. Ferries run April–Nov.

Visitor centre The visitor centre is at the eastern end of the mainland settlement of Harkers Island (Mon–Fri 9am–5pm; ☎ 252 728 2250, ⓦ nps.gov/calo).

ACCOMMODATION

National Park Service cabins ☎ 877 444 6777, ⓦ nps .gov/calo. There are two sets of cabins on the island, one apiece on North and South Core. As you'd expect, amenities are sparse (neither has a fridge, one requires a carry-in

generator for electricity), though you're rewarded with total isolation on a stunning, melancholy beach. Cabins sleep at least six. There's also primitive camping available. Open mid-March to Nov. $101

Beaufort and around

BEAUFORT, about 150 miles southeast of Raleigh, is one of North Carolina's most alluring coastal towns. A good base for visiting the nearby beaches, it has an attractive waterfront that's lively at night. North Carolina's third oldest town, Beaufort also has an appealing twelve-block **historical district**, centring on Turner Street, off the waterfront. Here you'll find handsome old houses, an apothecary and the city jail.

The beaches

South of Beaufort, the **beaches** along the twenty-mile offshore **Bogue Banks** are always pretty crowded, especially **Atlantic Beach** at the east end, with **Emerald Isle**, to the west, marginally less so. On **Bear Island** to the south – (ferries May & Sept Wed–Sun, April & Oct Fri–Sun) – the stunning **Hammocks Beach State Park** has high dunes, a wooded shore and perfect beaches.

ARRIVAL AND ACTIVITIES

By ferry and boat taxis Ferries (15min; $15) to Shackleford Banks (see opposite) are run by Island Ferry Adventures (☏ 252 728 7555, ⓦ islandferryadventures.com) and Outer Banks Ferry Service (☏ 252 728 4129, ⓦ outerbanksferry .com), both of which are on the waterfront. Bear Island

BEAUFORT AND AROUND

can be reached from Swansboro by boat taxi or ferry ($5; ⓦ ncparks.gov).
Kayaking Beaufort Inlet Watersports (☏ 252 728 7607, ⓦ beaufortwatersports.com) offers kayak rental ($10/hr) and tours (from $25).

ACCOMMODATION

Cedars Inn 305 Front St ☏ 252 838 1463, ⓦ cedarsinn .com. Built for a shipwright's son in 1768, this waterfront B&B has six guest quarters, all renovated in 2013. The light and airy rooms, some with fireplaces, are done up with a tasteful blend of modern textiles and antique fixtures. From the front steps, you can take a quick stroll into town, or watch the sailboats bobbing in the harbour. $150
Hammocks Beach State Park 1572 Hammocks Beach Rd, Swansboro ☏ 910 326 4881, ⓦ ncparks.gov.

Accessible only by boat, this pristine campground is fringed by seagrass, tidal pools and the glorious ocean. From late May to Aug, you might spot loggerhead turtles coming ashore to lay their eggs. $10
Inlet Inn 601 Front St ☏ 252 728 3600, ⓦ inlet-inn .com. In the heart of the historic district, this harbourfront hotel has large balcony rooms and rocking chairs on the deck, with a complimentary breakfast basket delivered to your room each morning. $130

EATING, DRINKING AND NIGHTLIFE

Beaufort Grocery Co. 117 Queen St ☏ 252 728 3899, ⓦ beaufortgrocery.com. Inventive Southern food – try the signature pimento cheese dip ($9) or a crab sandwich with spicy remoulade ($12) – made from superbly fresh ingredients. In the heart of downtown, it fills up quickly with locals, especially at lunch. The bourbon pecan pie is out of this world. Daily except Tues 11.30am–2.30pm & 5.30pm–close.
Blue Moon 119 Queen St ☏ 252 728 5800, ⓦ blue moonbistro.biz. Divine locally sourced bistro food in a little 1820s house with pressed tin ceilings, posies on the

table and eye-catching art. The menu rotates; recent offerings have included shrimp risotto with prosciutto and chèvre ($23) and spinach, apple and radish salad ($9). Reservations recommended. Tues–Sat 5.30pm–close.
★ **Island Grille** 401 Money Island Drive, Atlantic Beach, 7 miles southwest of Beaufort ☏ 252 240 0000, ⓦ igrestaurant.net. Tropical fans whir over patrons dining on stuffed filet mignon ($33) and shrimp and scallops ($26) at this sophisticated but unintimidating Caribbean-style gem by the beach. Reservations essential (it's tiny). Mon, Tues, Fri & Sat 5–9pm, Wed, Thurs & Sun 5.30–9pm.

Wilmington and around

Even though it's the largest town on North Carolina's coast, **WILMINGTON**, set back along the **Cape Fear River**, fifty miles short of the state's southern border, retains a laidback, attractive air. The location for a number of movies and TV shows (including, notably, *Dawson's Creek* and *One Tree Hill*), it has earned the nickname "Wilmywood", and the influx of creative types has led to a certain style that feels very different from the rest of the coast. It's particularly lively after dark, when the tiny riverfront downtown takes on an edgy energy that belies the town's size.

While Wilmington's extravagant houses, ornate **City Hall** and lovely **Thalian Hall theatre** demonstrate its former wealth as a port – and the **Cape Fear Museum**, 814 Market St (Mon–Sat 9am–5pm, Sun 1–5pm; $7; ☏ 910 798 4350, ⓦ capefearmuseum.com) gives a lively account of local history – the three or four blocks parallel to the river, and in particular the weathered, boardwalked **waterfront**, dotted with bars and restaurants, are the real draw.

The beaches

Wilmington makes a great base for a number of **beaches**: broad and bustling Wrightsville Beach, just nine miles east; Carolina Beach, fifteen miles south, which is also good for hiking; and the laidback white sands of Kure Beach, a popular fishing destination. Local celebs and starlets hang out on rarefied and lovely **Bald Head Island**, around an hour's drive from Wilmington south on Hwy-17.

Carolina Beach State Park

1010 State Park Rd, Carolina Beach (15 miles south of Wilmington) • Daily: Nov–Feb 8am–6pm; March, April, Sept & Oct 8am–8pm; May–Aug 8am–10pm • Free • ☎ 910 458 8206, ⓦ ncparks.gov

Honeycombed with wooded trails, the riverfront preserve of **Carolina Beach State Park** is home to a cache of botanical gems: within a 65-mile radius of Wilmington, you'll find the only native-growing Venus flytraps in the world, many right here among the longleaf pines and turkey oaks. The park sustains a number of other splendidly named carnivorous plants; meandering around the grounds, you may stumble upon butterworts, bladderworts, pitcher plants or sundews. The bug-eating flytraps are smaller and more inconspicuous than you'd expect; to make sure you spot them, take a ranger-led tour.

ARRIVAL, INFORMATION AND TOURS WILMINGTON AND AROUND

By bus Greyhound (☎ 910 791 8040) buses stop at 505 Cando St, 4 miles east of downtown.

Visitor centre 505 Nutt St (Mon–Fri 8.30am–5pm, Sat 9am–4pm, Sun 1–4pm; ☎ 877 406 2356, ⓦ wilmington andbeaches.com); there's also an information booth at the foot of Market St by the water.

Tours At the base of Market St, in the small Riverfront Park, you can pick up a horse-drawn carriage tour ($12; ☎ 910 251 8889, ⓦ horsedrawntours.com); a harbour cruise

(from $17; ☎ 910 343 1611, ⓦ cfrboats.com); or a water taxi (late May to early Oct; $5 return) to the battleship USS *North Carolina* (daily: June–Aug 8am–8pm; rest of year 8am–5pm; $12; ☎ 910 251 5797, ⓦ battleshipnc.com), which participated in every naval offensive in the Pacific during World War II. Wrightsville Beach Scenic Tours runs superb shelling trips ($35) to pristine Masonboro Island, in addition to birding, environmental and party cruises (☎ 910 200 4002, ⓦ wrightsvillebeachscenictours.com).

ACCOMMODATION

Graystone Inn 100 S Third St ☎ 888 763 4773, ⓦ graystoneinn.com. Genteel B&B with posh comforts including evening turndown service and a wine and cheese hour. Peruse books in the library or linger on the veranda; if you do choose to venture out, it's just a few blocks to downtown. **$159**

Palm Air Cottages 133 Fort. Fisher Blvd N, Kure Beach, 18 miles south of Wilmington ☎ 910 458 5269, ⓦ palmaircottages.com. Cheerfully painted cottages, a stone's throw from Kure Beach. Clustered around a swimming pool, the immaculate little abodes have been

updated with new a/c units and cable TV. Bookable by the week only. **$450**

TownePlace Suites 305 Eastwood Rd ☎ 910 332 3326, ⓦ marriott.com. Though the setting won't win any style awards (it's on a highway, sandwiched between strip development), this exceedingly accommodating hotel is conveniently placed halfway between Wrightsville Beach and downtown Wilmington. Rooms are a compact version of a stylish modern apartment: fluffy beds, flat-screen TVs and kitchens outfitted with dishwashers, fridges and stovetops. **$119**

EATING, DRINKING AND NIGHTLIFE

Catalan 224 S Water St ☎ 910 815 0200, ⓦ lecatalan .com. Great for a chilled Sauvignon Blanc and a small plate, this French-style café/wine bar has a superb location on the boardwalk. Tues–Sat 11.30am–close.

Copper Penny 109 Chestnut St ☎ 910 762 1373, ⓦ copperpennync.com. Convivial English pub with excellent bar food – nachos (piled high with steak and sautéed veggies; $10), juicy burgers ($11) and overstuffed sandwiches – served amid wooden booths and sports paraphernalia. Mon–Sat 11am–late, Sun noon–late.

Dock Street Oyster Bar 12 Dock St ☎ 910 762 2827, ⓦ dockstreetoysterbar.net. Fun, casual joint specializing

in raw oysters, crab claws and seafood. Belly up to the bar – strung with buoys and mermaid paintings – for a heady bloody Mary, or duck out back for dinner on the deck. Mon–Thurs 3–10pm, Fri–Sun 11am–10pm.

The Wayfarer 110 S Front St ☎ 910 762 4788, ⓦ wayfarerdeli.com. Tiny, atmospheric sandwich shop with scuffed wood floors, exposed brick walls and a world-travelling sandwich menu. The "Cuban revolution" presses pork and Swiss cheese together on ciabatta ($10.50), while the meatloaf sandwich is dressed with chipotle ketchup and rocket (arugula; $9.50). Be sure to order a side of the heavenly s'mac and cheese. Tues–Sat 11am–5pm.

Raleigh and around

Founded as North Carolina's capital in 1792, **RALEIGH**, part of the "Triangle" along with Durham and Chapel Hill, focuses on the central **Capitol Square**, where the **North Carolina Museum of History**, 5 E Edenton St (Mon–Sat 9am–5pm, Sun noon–5pm; free; ☎919 807 7900, ⓦncmuseumofhistory.org), provides a far-reaching chronology. Opposite, the **North Carolina Museum of Natural Sciences**, 11 W Jones St (same hours and admission; ☎919 707 9800, ⓦnaturalsciences.org), looks at local geology, as well as animal and plant life dating back to the dinosaur age.

City Market

South of the capitol, the four-block **City Market**, a lamplit, cobbled enclave at Blount and Martin streets, holds a number of good shops and restaurants. Check out the local artists at work in **Artspace**, 201 E Davie St (Tues–Sat 10am–6pm; ☎919 821 2787, ⓦartspacenc.org).

North Carolina Museum of Art

2110 Blue Ridge Rd • Tues–Thurs, Sat & Sun 10am–5pm, Fri 10am–9pm • Free • ☎919 839 6262, ⓦncartmuseum.org

Eight miles northwest of the city (accessed via Rte-1), the **North Carolina Museum of Art** has an eclectic display from the ancient world, Africa, Europe and the USA, along with a smart restaurant, *Iris*. It's surrounded by 160 bucolic acres that are crisscrossed with nature trails and peppered with fanciful sculptures.

ARRIVAL AND INFORMATION

RALEIGH AND AROUND

By plane Raleigh-Durham airport is off I-40, 15min northwest of town. A taxi into town costs around $30, while a circuitous shuttle service (☎919 599 8100, ⓦskyshuttleride.com) will set you back $25.

By bus The Greyhound station is in a seedy area at 314 W Jones St (☎919 834 8275).

By train Amtrak stops at 320 W Cabarrus St.

Visitor centre 500 Fayetteville St (Mon–Sat 9am–5pm; ☎919 834 5900, ⓦvisitraleigh.com).

ACCOMMODATION AND EATING

42nd St Oyster Bar 508 W Jones St ☎919 831 2811, ⓦ42ndstoysterbar.com. This downtown restaurant has been a popular spot for fresh fish and seafood since the 1930s, and retains many of its original fixtures – the signature neon sign dates to the 1950s, and legend has it that, when in use, the boiler in the lobby cooked more oysters than any other in the country. Mon–Thurs 4.30–11pm, Fri & Sat 4.30pm–1am, Sun 4.30–10pm.

Big Ed's 220 Wolfe St ☎919 836 9909, ⓦbigedscity market.com. Classic Southern cooking done right at this City Market breakfast hub, with molasses on the table, monstrous pancakes and just-like-mom's biscuits and gravy. The ceiling is a jumble of dangling lamps, hams, baskets and jugs. Mon–Fri 7am–2pm, Sat 7am–noon, Sun 8am–1pm.

★ **Cameron Park Inn** 211 Groveland St ☎919 835 2171, ⓦcameronparkinn.com. Beautifully restored 1912 Victorian B&B on a residential street, set between dignified oak trees and an English garden. Rooms are full of gorgeous design details including cathedral windows, clawfoot tubs and hand-carved fireplace mantles. **$149**

Neomonde 3817 Beryl Rd ☎919 828 1628, ⓦneomonde.com. Just off Hillsborough St, the epicentre of Raleigh's student scene, *Neomonde* is a superb Middle Eastern café, bakery and market serving stuffed pitta sandwiches and fava bean salad. Daily 10am–9pm.

The Pit 328 W Davie St ☎919 890 4500, ⓦthepit -raleigh.com. North Carolina is famed for its barbecue – particularly smoked pork – and this lively landmark wins accolades for its fried pimento cheese ($6), beef brisket ($16) and of course, chopped pork ($13), pit-cooked overnight. Mon–Thurs 11am–10pm, Fri & Sat 11am–11pm, Sun 11am–9pm.

Durham

Twenty miles northwest of Raleigh, **DURHAM** found itself at the centre of the nation's tobacco industry after farmer Washington Duke came home from the Civil War with the idea of producing cigarettes. By 1890 he and his three sons had formed the **American Tobacco Company**, one of the nation's most powerful businesses.

6

In 1924, the Duke family's $40 million endowment to Trinity College enabled it to expand into a world-respected medical research facility that became **Duke University**. On campus, the **Nasher Museum of Art** at 2001 Campus Drive (Tues, Wed, Fri & Sat 10am–5pm, Thurs 10am–9pm, Sun noon–5pm; $5; ☎919 684 5135, ⓦnasher.duke .edu) has good African, pre-Columbian, medieval and contemporary collections.

Duke Homestead Historic Site
North of I-85 at 2828 Duke Homestead Rd • Tues–Sat 9am–5pm • Free • ☎919 477 5498, ⓦnchistoricsites.org

The **Duke Homestead Historic Site** is an absorbing living museum covering the social history of tobacco farming, with demonstrations of early farming techniques and tobacco-rolling. It centres on the former home of Washington Duke (see p.397), a modest pine farmhouse that he built in 1852. After serving in the Civil War, Duke walked 135 miles to return to his country home.

Historic Stagville
5828 Old Oxford Rd (10 miles north of downtown) • Hourly tours Tues–Sat 10am–4pm • Free • ☎919 620 0120, ⓦstagville.org

The fascinating **Historic Stagville** illustrates North Carolina plantation life, in particular the slave experience, from the early 1800s to Reconstruction. The grounds have preserved the small two-storey homes of its residents, as well as the plantation owners' house and a colossal barn built by skilled slave carpenters.

ARRIVAL AND INFORMATION
DURHAM

By bus Greyhound buses (☎919 687 4800) stop at 515 W Pettigrew St.

Visitor centre 101 E Morgan St (Mon–Fri 8.30am–5pm, Sat 10am–2pm; ☎919 687 0288, ⓦdurham-nc.com).

ACCOMMODATION AND EATING

Arrowhead Inn 106 Mason Rd ☎919 477 8430, ⓦarrowheadinn.com. Dating from 1775, this inviting B&B pampers with fresh flowers, whirlpool tubs and a fireplace in every room. If you're feeling flush, book a night in the delightfully modern log cabin, surrounded by gardens. Doubles $160, cabin $299

Dame's Chicken & Waffles 317 W Main St ☎919 682 9235, ⓦdameschickenwaffles.com. Leave your diet at the door for this Durham favourite specializing in a truly American, culinary hybrid: sweet, syrupy waffles (try the gingerbread variety) topped with savoury fried chicken. Wait times can be outrageous (upwards of an hour), and reservations are a must. Mon 11am–3pm, Tues–Thurs 11am–9pm, Fri 11am–10pm, Sat 10am–10pm, Sun 10am–3pm.

Parker & Otis 112 S Duke St ☎919 683 3200, ⓦparkerandotis.com. At the heart of an upbeat shopping area, stylish *Parker & Otis* serves organic gourmet sandwiches, salads and breakfasts using local ingredients. Mon–Sat 7.30am–7pm, Sun 10am–3pm.

Chapel Hill

CHAPEL HILL, on the southwest outskirts of Durham, is a liberal little college town with a strong music scene – having given birth to bands like Superchunk and Archers of Loaf, and musicians including Ben Folds, not to mention James "*Carolina on My Mind*" Taylor, it's a regular on the indie band tour circuit. It's a pleasant place to hang out, joining the students in the bars and cafés along **Franklin Street**, which fringes the north side of campus. Franklin continues west into the community of **Carrboro**, where it becomes **Main Street**; bars and restaurants here have a slightly hipper, post-collegiate edge.

The University of North Carolina

The **University of North Carolina**, dating from 1789, was the nation's first state university. On campus, the splendid **Morehead Planetarium**, 250 E Franklin St (Tues–Sat 10am–3.30pm, Sun 1am–4.30pm; $7.25; ☎919 843 7997, ⓦmoreheadplanetarium.org), served as an early NASA training centre, while the **Ackland Art Museum**, 101 S Columbia St (Wed, Fri & Sat 10am–5pm, Thurs 10am–8pm, Sun 1–5pm; free; ☎919 966 5736, ⓦackland.org) is strong on Asian art and antiquities.

ACCOMMODATION

Carolina Inn 211 Pittsboro St ☎919 933 2001, ⓦcarolinainn.com. Of the few places to stay downtown, one of the most popular is the historic, university-owned

Carolina Inn, with tasteful rooms, near Franklin St, on the northwestern side of campus. **$200**

EATING, DRINKING AND NIGHTLIFE

Cat's Cradle 300 E Main St, Carrboro ☎919 967 9053, ⓦcatscradle.com. Legendary Triangle music venue that got its start in the folkie heyday of the 1960s, and has since hosted everyone from Iggy Pop to Lucinda Williams. Check online for show times.

Lantern 423 W Franklin St, Chapel Hill ☎919 969 8846, ⓦlanternrestaurant.com. Though its menu is distinctly Pacific Rim, *Lantern* honours its roots by sourcing local ingredients. There's an upmarket dining room with sage-coloured walls, a bordello-style bar with glowing red lanterns, and a leafy back garden. Try the salt-and-pepper shrimp and the crispy chickpeas. Reservations recommended. Mon–Sat 5.30–10pm, bar till 2am.

Orange County Social Club 108 E Main St, Carrboro ☎919 933 0669, ⓦorangecountysocialclub.com. Hip,

laidback bar with vintage decor, a pool table, a top-notch jukebox and a garden. Daily 4pm–2am.

Sandwhich 407 W Franklin St, Chapel Hill ☎919 929 2114, ⓦsandwhich.biz. Moroccan-influenced Southern fusion food, with gourmet sandwiches and tagines. Order at the counter, then relax on the patio with a mint-and sage iced tea. Mon 11am–4pm, Tues–Sat 11am–9pm.

Sunrise Biscuit Kitchen 1305 E Franklin St, Chapel Hill, 2 miles east of downtown ☎919 933 1324. Buttery breakfast heaven: huge biscuit sandwiches crammed with golden-fried chicken and gooey cheddar cheese. Excellent cinnamon rolls too. Though you can order inside (it's mainly a drive-through), there's no seating. Mon–Sat 6am–2.30pm, Sun 7am–2.30pm.

Winston-Salem

Though synonymous with the brand name of its cigarettes, **WINSTON-SALEM**, eighty miles west of Chapel Hill, owes its spot on the tourist itinerary to **Old Salem**, a well-preserved twenty-block area that honours the heritage of the city's first Moravian settlers. Escaping religious persecution in what is now the Czech Republic, the first Moravians settled in the Piedmont in the mid-eighteenth century. They soon established trading links with the frontier settlers and founded the town of Salem on a communal basis – they permitted only those of the same religious faith to live here. Demand for their crafts helped establish the adjacent community of Winston, which, accruing tremendous wealth from tobacco, soon outgrew the older town. The two merged in 1913 to form Winston-Salem.

Old Salem Museums and Gardens

900 Old Salem Rd • Tues–Sat 9.30am–4.30pm, Sun 1–4.30pm • $23, $26 for two days, $15 for two buildings of your choice • ☎336 721 7300, ⓦoldsalem.org

Old Salem is a living history museum, with costumed craftspeople demonstrating nineteenth-century skills, including paper-cutting and pottery, in a number of **restored buildings** and seasonal gardens growing Moravian crops. Admission includes entrance to the far-reaching **Museum of Early Southern Decorative Arts**, which houses a dignified collection of folk art, paintings and textiles.

ARRIVAL AND INFORMATION

By bus Greyhound buses (☎336 724 1429) stop at 100 W 5th St.

Visitor centre 200 Brookstown Ave, three blocks from Old

Salem (Mon–Fri 8.30am–5pm, Sat 10am–4pm; Jan & Feb closed Sat; ☎336 728 4200, ⓦvisitwinstonsalem.com).

ACCOMMODATION AND EATING

Augustus T Zevely Inn 803 S Main St ☎336 748 9299, ⓦwinstonsalembandb.com. Painstakingly restored to its nineteenth-century appearance, this handsome brick pile stands at the heart of Old Salem, and is named after

the Moravian doctor who lived here in 1845. Continental breakfast included. **$105**

Sweet Potatoes 529 N Trade St ☎336 727 4844, ⓦsweetpotatoes.ws. Located in Winston-Salem's burgeoning Arts District, hospitable *Sweet Potatoes* dishes up top-notch Southern comfort food such as fried green tomatoes and okra ($9), shrimp and grits ($11) and of course, sweet potato pie. Tues–Sat 11am–3pm & 5–10pm, Sun 10.30am–3pm.

Charlotte

The prosperous banking centre of **CHARLOTTE**, where I-77 and I-85 meet near the South Carolina border, is the largest city in the state. It's also a transport hub, with direct flights from Europe, and some fine museums to divert anyone in transit.

The museums

Downtown (more commonly called "uptown" or "center city"), an unlovely mass of skyscrapers and commerce focused on **Tryon Street**, boasts the kids-oriented **Discovery Place**, 301 N Tryon St, with an aquarium and an IMAX theatre (Mon–Fri 9am–4pm, Sat 10am–6pm, Sun noon–5pm; $12, kids $10; ☎704 372 6261, ⓦdiscoveryplace.org) and the **Bechtler Museum**, 420 S Tryon St (Mon & Wed–Sat 10am–5pm, Sun noon–5pm; $8; ☎704 353 9200, ⓦbechtler.org) whose quality collection of mid-twentieth-century art includes pieces by Picasso, Warhol and Miró. Arts, crafts and modern design are displayed at the stylish new **Mint Museum Uptown**, 500 S Tryon St (Wed 11am–9pm, Thurs–Sat 11am–6pm, Sun 1–5pm; $10; ☎704 337 2000, ⓦmintmuseum.org), while the **Gantt Center**, 551 S Tryon St, focuses on African American art and photography (Tues–Sat 10am–5pm, Sun 1–5pm; $8; ☎704 547 3700, ⓦganttcenter.org). A few blocks away, the excellent **Levine Museum of the New South**, 200 E Seventh St (Mon–Sat 10am–5pm, Sun noon–5pm; $8; ☎704 333 1887, ⓦmuseumofthenewsouth.org), looks at the growth of the region from Reconstruction onwards.

ARRIVAL AND INFORMATION   CHARLOTTE

By plane Charlotte/Douglas International Airport, 7 miles west of town, is a $25 taxi ride from uptown.

By train or bus Greyhound stops (☎704 375 3332) at 601 W Trade St, while Amtrak pulls in at 1914 N Tryon St. Destinations Atlanta, GA (6 daily; 4hr 15min); Wilmington, NC (2 daily; 8hr 25min); Winston Salem, NC (5 daily; 1hr 40min).

Visitor centre 330 S Tryon St (Mon–Fri 8.30am–5pm, Sat 9am–3pm, Sun noon–4pm; ☎704 331 2700, ⓦcharlottesgotalot.com); there are smaller branches in the Levine Museum of the New South and at the airport.

ACCOMMODATION, EATING AND NIGHTLIFE

Dunhill Hotel 237 N Tryon St ☎704 332 4141, ⓦdunhill hotel.com. Uptown's 1929 *Dunhill* possesses a faded, old-fashioned charm. Perks include frequent home-made cookies, an evening turndown service and a smart restaurant. $225

Halcyon Flavors from the Earth 500 S Tryon St, in the Mint Museum Uptown ☎704 910 0865, ⓦhalcyonflavors.com. Fitting for an art museum restaurant, this farm-to-table hot spot has impeccable design sense: sky-blue ceilings, stylishly patterned chairs and chandeliers that look like giant bird's nests. Head here for sophisticated small plates and some of the state's best cocktails. Tues–Sat 11am–10pm, Sun 11am–3pm.

Blue Ridge Parkway

The best way to see the **mountains** of North Carolina is from the exhilarating **Blue Ridge Parkway**, which runs across the northwest of the state from Virginia to the **Great Smoky Mountains National Park**. It's a delight to drive; the vast panoramic expanses of forested hillside, with barely a settlement in sight, may astonish travellers fresh from the crowded centres of the east coast. This rural region has been a breeding ground since the early twentieth century for **bluegrass** music, which is still performed regularly; laidback, liberal **Asheville** is a good place to see the edgier stylings of "newgrass".

The peak tourist season for the **Blue Ridge Parkway** is October, when the leaves of the deciduous trees turn vivid shades of yellow, gold and red. Year-round, however, this twisting mountain road – largely built in the 1930s by President Roosevelt's Civilian

THE BLUE RIDGE PARKWAY MOUNTAIN ACTIVITIES

Organized **outdoor pursuits** available along the Blue Ridge Parkway include **whitewater rafting** and **canoeing**, most of it on the Nolichucky River near the Tennessee border, south of Johnson City, Tennessee, but also on the Watauga River and Wilson Creek. Companies running trips include Nantahala Outdoor Center (☎888 905 7238, ⓦnoc.com) and High Mountain Expeditions (☎800 262 9036, ⓦhighmountainexpeditions.com), who also offer biking, hiking and tubing trips. Expect to pay around $85 per person for a full day of rafting.

Winter sees **skiing** at a number of slopes and resorts, particularly around **Banner Elk**, sixteen miles southwest of Boone. Resort accommodation is expensive, ski passes less so. Appalachian Ski Mountain (ⓦappskimtn.com) is near Blowing Rock and Ski Beech (ⓦbeech mountainresort.com); the highest ski area in the east, is at Beech Mountain. You can pick up full listings at visitor centres, or check ⓦhighcountryhost.com.

6

Conservation Corps – is a worthwhile destination in itself, peppered with state-run campgrounds, short hiking trails and dramatic overlooks. Although the Parkway is closed to commercial vehicles, the constant curves make it hard to average anything approaching the 45mph speed limit.

Boone

Friendly **BOONE** is the most obvious northern base for exploring the mountains. Just a few miles off the Parkway, it has the feel of a Western frontier town, spiced up with a bit of Appalachian music heritage: guitarist Doc Watson traced his roots here, and other bluegrass musicians still ply their trade in the area. The town's main drag, **King Street**, is a picturesque stretch of nineteenth-century brick buildings, sharply framed by the forested mountains.

INFORMATION

BOONE

Visitor centre 1700 Blowing Rock Rd (Mon–Sat 9am–5pm, Sun 9am–3pm; ☎800 438 7500, ⓦhighcountryhost.com).

ACCOMMODATION AND EATING

Hidden Valley Motel 8275 Hwy-105, 8 miles west of town ☎828 963 4372, ⓦhiddenvalleymotel.com. You'll get clean, comfortable rooms at this wonderfully friendly motel, nestled at the base of the mountains and surrounded by a pretty garden. $60

Hob Knob Farm Café 506 W King St ☎828 262 5000, ⓦhobknobfarmcafe.com. Most of the dishes on the long, globally influenced menu here are organic and locally sourced. Wed–Sun 10am–10pm.

★ **Vidalia** 831 W King St ☎828 263 9176, ⓦvidalia ofboonenc.com. Across from the courthouse, this lovely little restaurant with an open kitchen serves inventive New Southern food fired up with fresh local produce. Reservations recommended. Mon & Sat 5–9pm, Tues–Fri & Sun 11am–2pm & 5–9pm.

Blowing Rock and around

Hwy-321 • Jan & Feb Fri–Sun 10am–5pm; March–May daily 9am–6pm; June & July daily 8.30am–7pm; Aug & Sept Mon–Thurs & Sun 9am–6pm, Fri & Sat 8.30am–7pm; Oct daily 8.30am–7pm; Nov & Dec daily 9am–5pm • $6 • ☎828 295 7111, ⓦtheblowingrock.com

Eight miles south of Boone, **BLOWING ROCK** is a pleasant, if touristy, resort just south of the Blue Ridge Parkway. The "Blowing Rock" itself, a high cliff from which light objects thrown over the side will simply blow back up, is nowhere near as impressive as photos suggest.

Grandfather Mountain

2050 Blowing Rock Hwy, in Linville • Daily: spring & autumn 9am–6pm; summer 8am–7pm; winter 9am–5pm • $18 • ☎828 733 4337, ⓦgrandfather.com

The privately owned nature preserve of **Grandfather Mountain** (5964ft), fifteen miles south of Blowing Rock, with access at milepost 305, offers nature trails and alpine

6

HIKING AROUND LINVILLE GORGE WILDERNESS

Rough Ridge, at milepost 302.8, is one of several access points to the 13.5-mile **Tanawha Trail**, which runs along the ridge above the Parkway from Beacon Heights to Julian Price Park, looking out over the dense forests to the east. Another good hiking destination is the **Linville Gorge Wilderness**, at milepost 316.4, a couple of miles outside **Linville Falls village**. There are two main trails; one is a steep, 1.6-mile round-trip climb to the top of the high and spectacular **Linville Falls** themselves. Breathtaking views from either side of the gorge look down 2000ft to the **Linville River** below. An easier walk leads to the base of the falls. You can also climb **Hawksbill** or **Table Rock** mountains from the nearest forest road, which leaves Hwy-181 south of the village of Jonas Ridge (signposted "Gingercake Acres", with a small, low sign to Table Rock).

Linville Falls Campground Gurney Franklin Rd, via Hwy-221 ☎ 828 765 2681, ⓦ linvillefalls.com. This friendly campground in amiable Linville Falls village is shaded by mountain laurel and offers laundry facilities, grills and hot showers. Open May–Sept. $20
Linville Falls Lodge 48 Hwy-183 ☎ 800 634 4421, ⓦ linvillefallslodge.com. Peaceful, family-owned mountain lodge with nine cosy quarters and a restaurant, *Spears Grill*, which serves microbrews and good country cooking, including fresh trout and hickory-smoked pork BBQ. Open April–Nov. $95

hiking paths, as well as ranger-led programmes. The price may be high, but the owners make a genuine attempt to protect this unique environment.

Asheville

Relaxed **ASHEVILLE**, in a pretty spot roughly one hundred miles southwest of Boone, is both an outdoors sports hub and a vibrant arts community, with a strong student presence from UNC and superb restaurants, microbreweries, galleries, boutique stores and live music venues. Retaining an appealing 1920s downtown core, it's a nice place to walk around, with handsome **Art Deco** buildings and intriguing local crafts. Twentieth-century novelist Thomas Wolfe memorialized the town in the autobiographical novel, *Look Homeward, Angel*. **Wolfe's childhood home**, a yellow Victorian pile that also served as a boarding house called Old Kentucky Home, has been preserved at 52 N Market St (tours Tues–Sat 9am–5pm; $5; ☎ 828 253 8304, ⓦ wolfememorial.com).

Biltmore Estate

1 Lodge St • Hours and prices vary wildly: typically June–Aug daily; Sept–May closed Sat • $44–69; buy in advance for a discount • ☎ 800 411 3812, ⓦ biltmore.com

Asheville's big attraction, two miles south of town, is the **Biltmore Estate**, the largest private mansion in the USA, with 250 rooms. Built in the late nineteenth century by George Vanderbilt – the youngest son of the wealthy industrialist family – and loosely modelled on a Loire chateau, it's a wild piece of nouveau riche folly, from the Victorian chic of the indoor palm court to the gardens designed by Frederick Law Olmsted, he of New York's Central Park. At the time it was built it took a week simply to travel the estate on horseback; today you can easily fill a day or more taking a tour, enjoying tastings at the winery, renting a bike to explore the 8000 acres of grounds, hopping on a river raft or a kayak and eating at its restaurants; there's even a 213-room inn.

ARRIVAL, INFORMATION AND TOURS   ASHEVILLE

By bus Asheville's Greyhound terminal (☎ 828 253 8451) is 2 miles out of downtown at 2 Tunnel Rd, a highway lined with motels.
Visitor centre 36 Montford Ave, reached via exit 4C off I-240 (daily 9am–5pm; ☎ 828 258 6101, ⓦ explore asheville.com).
Bus tour For a madcap, but informed, historical overview,

join a LaZoom comedy bus tour, which depart from 90 Biltmore Ave ($24; ☎ 828 225 6932, ⓦ lazoomtours.com).
Walking tour The city has created a treasure hunt-style walking tour denoting 1.7 miles of historic markers and creative works, dubbed the Urban Trail. You can print a guide out at ⓦ ashevillenc.gov, or hop on a 2hr tour with Brenda Seright Williams ($20; ⓦ urbantrailasheville.com).

ACCOMMODATION

Biltmore Village Inn 119 Dodge St ☎828 274 8707, ⓦbiltmorevillageinn.com. Former residence of George Vanderbilt's lawyer, who helped the tycoon secure Biltmore (see opposite), this spectacular 1892 Victorian offers the consummate B&B experience: posh rooms, caring staff, sweeping scenery and chef-driven meals. **$255**

Campfire Lodgings 116 Old Marshall Hwy, 7 miles north of town via Hwy-26 ☎828 658 8012, ⓦcampfire lodgings.com. Set in tranquil forest 10min north of Asheville, this friendly outfitter offers campgrounds, cabins

sleeping four ($160) and luxurious yurts ($115). Tents **$38**, cabins **$160**, yurts **$115**

★ **Inn at Wintersun** 1 Wintersun Lane, 12 miles east of town via Hwy-74A ☎828 628 9979, ⓦinnat wintersun.com. Stunning hilltop B&B surrounded by 117 acres filled with horse pastures and hiking trails. The lavish guestrooms are furnished with antique armoires, rich textiles, working fireplaces and Bose radios; the best amenity, however, is the picture-perfect view of the Blue Ridge Mountains. **$175**

EATING, DRINKING AND NIGHTLIFE

12 Bones 5 Riverside Drive, 2 miles southwest of downtown ☎828 253 4499, ⓦ12bones.com. Queues snake onto the pavement for the outrageously good barbecue, cornbread and jalapeno grits at this smokehouse. Order at the counter, sit under the covered deck and prepare to get messy with the home-made sauce. Mon–Fri 11am–4pm.

Corner Kitchen 3 Boston Way, 3 miles south of downtown ☎828 274 2439, ⓦthecornerkitchen.com. Exceptional New American cuisine in a century-old house close to the Biltmore Estate, with oodles of character. Though the menu rotates, at breakfast you might find a salad of spinach, bacon, blue cheese, pecans and eggs ($9), come dinner, pork belly with watermelon relish ($22). Mon–Fri 7.30am–3pm & 5–9pm, Sat & Sun 9am–3pm & 5–9pm.

★ **Cúrate** 11 Biltmore Ave ☎828 239 2946, ⓦcuratetapasbar.com. In a city of excellent restaurants, this tapas hot spot stands out with its pre-eminent Spanish cuisine, modern dining room with a huge marble bar and top-notch service. Sample small plates of *jamón ibérico* (served on pig-shaped cutting boards; $20), potato and onion omelettes ($6), lamb skewers ($12) and sangria mixed tableside ($30 a pitcher). Reservations highly

recommended. Tues–Thurs & Sun 11.30am–10.30pm, Fri & Sat 11.30am–11pm.

Jack of the Wood 95 Patton Ave ☎828 252 5445, ⓦjackofthewood.com. Asheville has a lively nightlife scene, with lots of places to drink craft beer and listen to live music. This enjoyable Celtic bar has hand-brewed beer and regular bluegrass, folk and newgrass shows. Mon–Thurs 3pm–1am, Fri–Sun noon–2am.

Tupelo Honey 12 College St ☎828 255 4863, ⓦtupelohoneycafe.com. Landmark sidewalk café with great people watching and a breakfast-all-day menu boasting delicious sweet potato pancakes ($6) and eggs benedict with goat's cheese grits ($10); you'll also find salads, sandwiches and sophisticated dinner mains such as caper-studded trout in beurre blanc ($21). Meals come with a basket of warm biscuits and home-made jam. Daily 9am–10pm.

★ **White Duck Taco Shop** 1 Roberts St, Suite 101, 1 mile west of downtown ☎828 258 1660, ⓦwhite ducktacoshop.com. Bright, cheerful *taqueria* with ingenious variations such as Bangkok shrimp ($3.45) and Thai peanut chicken with tropical salsa ($3.45). There's often a queue, but it moves quickly. Nice alfresco seating, too. Mon–Sat 11.30am–9pm.

Chimney Rock

431 Main St, Chimney Rock • Daily: hours vary • $15 • ☎800 277 9611, ⓦchimneyrockpark.com

Twenty-five miles southeast of the Parkway on US-64/74A, the natural granite tower of **Chimney Rock** protrudes from the almost-sheer side of Hickory Nut Gorge. After taking the elevator 26 storeys up through the body of the mountain, you can walk along protected walkways above the impressive cliffs. Many of the climactic moments of *The Last of the Mohicans* were filmed here; you may recognize the mighty **Hickory Nut Falls**, which tumble 400ft from the western end of the gorge.

LEAF FESTIVAL

Laidback **Black Mountain**, sixteen miles east of Asheville on I-40, hosts the hugely enjoyable **Leaf Festival** (ⓦtheleaf.org), a folk music and arts and crafts gathering, held in mid-May and October. Showcasing Appalachian and world folk music, it attracts major European and African musicians. There's little to do here otherwise, but the town has a few good **music** venues, restaurants and coffee shops.

South Carolina

The relatively small state of **SOUTH CAROLINA** remains, with Mississippi, one of the most impoverished and rural in the USA. **Politics** in the first state to secede from the Union in 1860 have traditionally been conservative, particularly following the Civil War during the tumultuous period of **Reconstruction** and **Jim Crow** segregation. The region's main fascination lies in the subtropical coastline, also called the **Low Country**, and its **sea islands**. Wild beaches, swampy marshes and lush palmetto groves preserve traces of a virtually independent black culture (featuring the unique patois, "Gullah"), dating back to the start of the Civil War when enslaved Africans stayed put but area plantation owners fled the scene. There are no interstates along the coast, so journeys take longer than you might expect, the views are pretty and the pace of life definitely feels slower. Beyond the grand old peninsular port of **Charleston** – one of the most elegant towns in the nation with its pastel-coloured old buildings, appealing waterfront and Caribbean ambience – restored plantations stretch as far north as **Georgetown**, en route toward tacky **Myrtle Beach**.

Myrtle Beach

MYRTLE BEACH is an unmitigated stretch of commercial seaside development twenty miles down the coast from the North Carolina border. Predominantly a golf centre and family resort, it's packed during mid-term vacations with students drinking and partying themselves into a frenzy. Fans of elaborate water parks, factory outlet malls, funfairs and parasailing will be in heaven. The widest stretch of sand is at **North Myrtle Beach**, a chain of small communities centring on Ocean Boulevard. South of Myrtle Beach lies **Murrells Inlet**, a fishing port with lots of good seafood restaurants and **Pawleys Island**, a secluded resort once favoured by plantation owners and today retaining a slower pace than its neighbours.

Georgetown and around

The peaceful waterfront community of **GEORGETOWN** – the first town in forty miles beyond Myrtle Beach that's anything more than a resort – makes a nice contrast to the northerly commercialism (though when the wind is blowing in the wrong direction, the fragrance from the monstrous paper works on the opposite bank can be off-putting). It's hard to imagine today, but in the eighteenth century Georgetown was the centre of a thriving network of Low Country rice plantations; by the 1840s the area produced nearly half the rice grown in the United States. While Front Street, the main street, has a time-warped, late-1950s feel, Georgetown's 32-block **historic district** features many fine eighteenth-century and antebellum houses.

The **Rice Museum**, in the Clock Tower at 633 Front St (Mon–Sat 10am–4.30pm; $7; ☎843 546 7423, ⓦricemuseum.org), tells of the Low Country's long history of rice cultivation and its dependence on a constant supply of enslaved Africans brought over from the Windward coast for their expertise. There are also displays on local heroes such as Ruby Forsythe, who taught at the region's little one-room schoolhouse for 53 years.

Hopsewee Plantation

494 Hopsewee Rd, 13 miles south of Georgetown on US-17 • Tours Feb–Nov Tues–Fri 10am–4pm, Sat noon–4pm • $17.50 • ☎843 546 7891, ⓦhopsewee.com

The grand 1740 mansion home of Thomas Lynch, a signatory of the Declaration of Independence, **Hopsewee Plantation** is set in Spanish-moss-draped grounds. The estate was once a profitable rice-growing enterprise; in 1850 alone Hopsewee churned out 560,000lb of the crop. Nowadays, it's known for its gorgeous tearoom, set with gilded china and white tablecloths and pouring plenty of cuppas.

Hampton Plantation State Historic Site

Two miles off US-17 on Hwy-857, 16 miles south of Georgetown • House tours Mon, Tues, Sat & Sun 1pm, 2pm & 3pm; grounds daily 9am–5pm • House $7.50, grounds free • ☎ 803 734 0156, ⓦ southcarolinaparks.com

Tours of the **Hampton Plantation State Historic Site** concentrate on the history of slavery. The grounds are lovely, but the house is most impressive. An eighteenth-century Neoclassical monolith built by Huguenots, the inside is relatively bare. The plantation itself is isolated in the heart of the dense **Francis Marion National Forest**, a heavily African American area particularly known for its sweetgrass basket-weaving, which originated with slaves from West Africa.

6

INFORMATION AND TOURS

Visitor centre 531 Front St (Mon–Sat 9am–5pm; ☎ 843 546 8436, ⓦ georgetownchamber.com).
Boat tours Hop on the *Carolina Rover* (1 tour daily; 3hr;

GEORGETOWN AND AROUND

$33, reservations recommended; ☎ 843 546 8822, ⓦ roverboattours.com) for a cruise of the coast, including a spell shelling on a nearby barrier island.

ACCOMMODATION AND EATING

Keith House Inn 1012 Front St ☎ 843 485 4324, ⓦ thekeithhouseinn.com. Dating from 1825, this central B&B marries nineteenth-century details with chic modern design sense, evident in the spa-like bathrooms and bold colour scheme. Take breakfast in the sunroom, where creeping fig vine grows upon the walls. **$149**
Kudzu Bakery 120 King St ☎ 843 546 1847, ⓦ kudzu bakery.com. Just off the main drag and located in a beautiful brick building (and one-time stable), this primo bakery doles out muffins, breads, cookies and pies and boasts a small deli and wine shop. Mon–Fri 9am–5.30pm, Sat 9am–2pm.

Mansfield Plantation 1776 Mansfield Rd ☎ 866 717 1776, ⓦ mansfieldplantation.com. One of the best places in the state to experience a plantation stay. Hauntingly authentic, *Mansfield* dates from 1718 and retains its original slave quarters, chapel, schoolhouse and plantation home. Guest rooms, spread amongst the historic structures, are tastefully done up, and the ground's thousand acres, dripping with Spanish moss, invite exploration on foot or by boat. **$150**
Wildfish Grill 619 Front St ☎ 843 527 3250. Central seafood restaurant with plenty of personality (the decor is a riot of nautical art and fish netting) and a delicious menu of fish tacos, burgers and great daily specials. Daily 11am–10pm.

Charleston

CHARLESTON, one of the finest-looking towns in the USA, is a compelling place, its **historic district** lined with tall, narrow houses of peeling, multicoloured stucco, adorned with wooden shutters and wide piazzas (porches). The palm trees and tropical climate give the place a Caribbean air, while the hidden gardens, leafy patios and ironwork balconies evoke the romance of New Orleans.

Charleston's **historic district** is a predominantly residential area of leaning lines, weathered colours and exquisite courtyards bounded by Calhoun Street to the north and East Bay Street by the river. The further south of Broad you head, the posher and more residential the streets become. The district is best taken in by strolling at your own pace – though that pace can get pretty slow in high summer, when the heat is intense. Attractive spots to pause in the shade include the elegantly landscaped **Waterfront Park**, a greenway with fountains and boardwalks leading out over the river and **White Point Garden**, by the Battery on the tip of the peninsula, where the breezy, flower-filled lawns have good views across the water.

Charleston's historic houses

Many of the city's fine **houses** are available for **tours**. The late nineteenth-century **Calhoun Mansion**, 14–16 Meeting St, is fabulously over-the-top, with ornate plaster and woodwork and hand-painted porcelain ballroom chandeliers (daily 11am–5pm, every 30min; $15; ☎ 843 722 8205, ⓦ calhounmansion.net). Nearby, the antebellum **Edmondston-Alston House**, one of the first houses built on the Battery (in 1825), overlooks the harbour at 21 E Battery St (Mon & Sun 1.30–4.30pm, Tues–Sat 10am–4.30pm; $12; ☎ 843 722 7171, ⓦ middletonplace.org). The elegant Neoclassical

6

Nathaniel-Russell House, 51 Meeting St (Mon–Sat 10am–5pm, Sun 2–5pm; $10, $16 with the Aiken-Rhett House; ☎843 722 3405, ☜historiccharleston.org), is noted for its flying staircase, which soars unsupported for three floors.

The Charleston Museum's $22 combination ticket gets you into the 1803 **Joseph Manigault House**, a lovely structure built by descendants of Huguenot settlers, and the 1772 **Heyward-Washington House**, at the south end of the peninsula at 87 Church St, which was built by Thomas Heyward, a rice baron and signatory of the Declaration of Independence. Admission to each separately is $10 (Mon–Sat 10am–5pm, Sun 1–5pm; ☎843 722 2996, ☜charlestonmuseum.org). North of downtown, the antebellum urban plantation **Aiken-Rhett House**, 48 Elizabeth St, retains not only its original decor and furnishings but also the work-yard and slave quarters (Mon–Sat 10am–5pm, Sun 2–5pm; $10, $16 with the Nathaniel-Russell House; ☎843 722 3405, ☜historiccharleston.org).

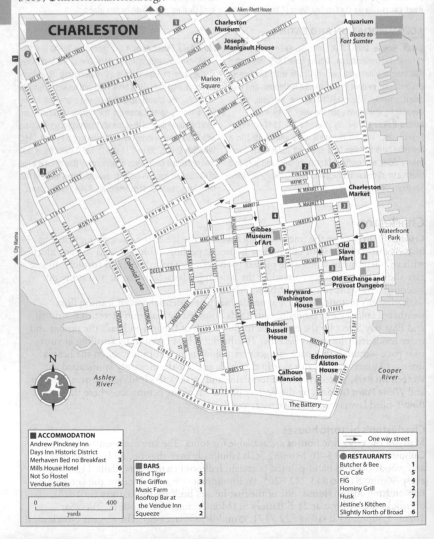

CHARLESTON

Aiken-Rhett House

Charleston Museum

Joseph Manigault House

Aquarium

Boats to Fort Sumter

Marion Square

Charleston Market

Gibbes Museum of Art

Old Slave Mart

Waterfront Park

Old Exchange and Provost Dungeon

Heyward-Washington House

Nathaniel-Russell House

Edmonston-Alston House

Calhoun Mansion

The Battery

Ashley River

Cooper River

City Marina

Colonial Lake

N

MURRAY BOULEVARD

SOUTH BATTERY

One way street

■ **ACCOMMODATION**

Andrew Pinckney Inn	2
Days Inn Historic District	4
Merhaven Bed no Breakfast	3
Mills House Hotel	6
Not So Hostel	1
Vendue Suites	5

0   400
yards

■ **BARS**

Blind Tiger	5
The Griffon	3
Music Farm	1
Rooftop Bar at the Vendue Inn	4
Squeeze	2

● **RESTAURANTS**

Butcher & Bee	1
Cru Café	5
FIG	4
Hominy Grill	2
Husk	7
Jestine's Kitchen	3
Slightly North of Broad	6

The Old Exchange and Provost Dungeon

122 E Bay St • Daily 9am–5pm, downstairs accessible by guided tour only (included in admission price) • $8 • ☎ 843 727 2165, ⓦ oldexchange.com

Built in 1771 as the Customs House and used as a prison during the Revolutionary War, the **Old Exchange and Provost Dungeon** is a hugely significant colonial structure. The upper floors feature exhibits on the history of the building and of Charleston; the tone changes in the dank confines below, however, where spotlit dummies recount tales of revolutionaries, gentlemen pirates and all manner of derring-do.

The Old Slave Mart

6 Chalmers St • Mon–Sat 9am–5pm • $7 • ☎ 843 958 6467, ⓦ oldslavemart.org

Following Charleston's inception in 1670, one third of the nation's enslaved Africans passed through the city. The **Old Slave Mart** was built in 1856 for the express purpose of buying and selling African slaves. The detailed exhibits in this compact, haunting place document the reach and effects of the trans-Atlantic slave trade, and include rare personal audio recordings from ex-slaves. Upstairs, the "Triumph over Slavery" exhibit delineates and celebrates African American history.

The market area and around

Charleston's **market area** runs from Meeting Street to East Bay Street, focusing on a long, narrow line of enclosed, low-roofed, nineteenth-century sheds. Undeniably touristy, packed with hard-headed "basket ladies" weaving sweetgrass crafts, this is one of the liveliest spots in town, selling knick-knacks, spices, tacky T-shirts, jewellery and rugs.

Gibbes Museum of Art

135 Meeting St • Tues–Sat 10am–5pm, Sun 1–5pm • $9 • ☎ 843 722 2706, ⓦ gibbesmuseum.org

The intriguing **Gibbes Museum of Art** places a strong emphasis on Charleston itself, providing a quick history of the city through art. The first floor holds eighteenth- and nineteenth-century oil paintings, including an engaging collection of miniature portraits with frames of velvet, gold and pearls. The second and third floors display rotating and contemporary exhibits.

The Charleston Museum

360 Meeting St • Mon–Sat 9am–5pm, Sun 1–5pm • $10, $16 with the Joseph Manigault House or the Heyward-Washington House, $22 with both • ☎ 843 722 2996, ⓦ charlestonmuseum.org

The vast **Charleston Museum**, opposite the visitor centre, is filled with a wealth of city memorabilia, and has videos on subjects from rice-growing to the Huguenots and strong sections on Native Americans, architecture and the devastation of the Civil War.

South Carolina Aquarium

100 Aquarium Wharf • Daily: March–Aug 9am–5pm; Sept–Feb 9am–4pm • $24.95, kids $14.95 • ☎ 843 720 1990, ⓦ scaquarium.org

At the end of Calhoun Street, overlooking the harbour, you'll find Charleston's splendid **Aquarium**. With a 40ft-deep tank at the core, its open, eye-level exhibits recreate South Carolina's various watery habitats – including the Piedmont, swamps, salt marshes and ocean – and their indigenous aquatic, plant and animal life. The porch-like terrace, with wide benches, is a nice place to catch the river breezes; watch out for schools of dolphins playing in the water below.

Fort Sumter National Monument

Fort Five miles offshore • Accessed by boat tour; 2–3 daily • $18 • ☎ 843 722 2628, ⓦ fortsumtertours.com **Visitor centre** 340 Concord St • Daily 8.30am–5pm • Free • ☎ 843 888 3123, ⓦ nps.gov/fosu

The first shots of the Civil War were fired on April 12, 1861, at **Fort Sumter**, a redoubtable federal garrison that occupied a small artificial island at the entrance to Charleston Harbor. After secession, the federal government had to decide whether to reprovision its forts in the south. When a relief expedition was sent to Fort Sumter,

6

Confederate General Pierre Beauregard demanded its surrender. After a relentless barrage, the garrison gave in the next day.

Fort Sumter may only be seen on regular **boat tours** that leave near the Aquarium at the eastern end of Calhoun Street. Just one of the fort's original three storeys is left, thanks not to the assault that started the war, but to its subsequent siege and bombardment by Union troops, who finally reoccupied it on Good Friday 1865, the very day Lincoln was assassinated. Exhibits in the mainland **visitor centre** cover not only the fort but also the history of Charleston and the build-up to the conflict.

ARRIVAL AND DEPARTURE   CHARLESTON

By plane Charleston International Airport is 12 miles north of downtown, off I-526 (wchs-airport.com); the airport shuttle (☎843 767 1100) costs $12, while a Charleston Green taxi (☎843 819 0846) is around $30.
By bus The Greyhound station (☎843 744 4247) is at 3610 Dorchester Rd, a disreputable spot near I-26. There's a daily

service to Savannah, GA (2hr 10min).
By train The Amtrak station is in a dodgy area at 4465 Gaynor Ave, 8 miles north of downtown.
Destinations Atlanta, GA (2 daily; 4hr 40min); Savannah, GA (2 daily; 1hr 45min).

GETTING AROUND, INFORMATION AND TOURS

By bus or tram (trolley) CARTA buses ($1.75; ☎843 724 7420, wridecarta.com) cover most areas, including nearby beaches, and there are three useful tram routes, the Downtown Area Shuttles (DASH; $1.75). Passes ($6/day, $12/three-day, $14/ten rides) cover both.
Visitor centre 375 Meeting St (daily 8.30am–5pm; ☎843 853 8000, wcharlestoncvb.com).
Horse and carriage rides These provide a lively and

leisurely overview; Old South Carriage Co leaves regularly from 14 Anston St (1hr; $22, kids $15; ☎843 723 9712, woldsouthcarriagetours.com).
Walking tours Charleston is a lovely place to stroll around; the visitor centre has details of walking tours covering everything from pirates through architecture to black history, as well as discount coupons, maps and bus/tram passes.

ACCOMMODATION

To enjoy the best of Charleston it's worth budgeting to stay within walking distance of **downtown**, where many homes in the historic district serve as pricey B&Bs. Further out, the usual **motels** cluster around US-17 in West Ashley and Mount Pleasant and along I-26 in North Charleston.

Andrew Pinckney Inn 40 Pinckney St ☎843 937 8800, wandrewpinckneyinn.com. Stylish, Caribbean-style rooms in this boutique hotel beside the historic market. Continental breakfast served on the rooftop terrace overlooking the city. **$159**
Days Inn Historic District 155 Meeting St ☎843 722 8411, wdaysinn.com. This two-storey motel lacks the charm of the B&Bs, but rooms are spacious and comfortable, with attractive wrought-iron balconies and an unbeatable location. The pool and free off-street parking are a bonus. **$125**
Merhaven Bed no Breakfast 16 Halsey St ☎843 577 3053. Two simply elegant rooms, with shared bath and, obviously, no breakfast, in an artist-owned Arts and Crafts home with a pretty, shady courtyard. No credit cards. **$140**

Mills House Hotel 115 Meeting St ☎843 577 2400, wmillshouse.com. Large, smart, very central hotel, in business since 1853. Guestrooms combine elegant period furnishings with modern comfort. **$230**
Not So Hostel 156 Spring St ☎843 722 8383, wnotso hostel.com. Appealing, very friendly hostel in a double-porched 1850 house on the northern edge of downtown. Rates include free parking and a full breakfast. An annexe a few blocks away has simple rooms. Dorms **$26**, doubles **$62**
Vendue Suites 30 Vendue Range ☎843 723 2228, wvenduesuites.com. Three stylish, spick-and-span suites and a friendly atmosphere at this lovely, superbly located boutique hotel. Free snacks and in-room breakfast provided. **$195**

EATING

Historic Charleston's elegant ambience lends itself very well to classy, superbly executed **New Southern cooking** served up in a variety of innovative restaurants. There are also plenty of **ethnic restaurants** and cafés along Market and King streets.

Butcher & Bee 654 King St ☎843 619 0202, wbutcher andbee.com. An out-of-the-way artisanal sandwich shop with a sleek, industrial-style setting. Order at the counter,

then make new friends at the communal table. On weekends, it's great for late-night grub. Mon–Wed & Sun 11am–3pm, Thurs 11am–3pm & 6pm–midnight,

Fri & Sat 11am–3pm & 11pm–3am.

★ **Cru Café** 18 Pinckney St ☎ 843 534 2434, ⓦ crucafe.com. Cosy, pretty restaurant in an eighteenth-century house with a porch, dishing up satisfying, sophisticated food that puts a modern global twist on local staples. Try the pan-roasted local trigger fish with green tomatoes. Tues–Thurs 11am–3pm & 5–10pm, Fri & Sat 11am–3pm & 5–11pm.

★ **FIG** 232 Meeting St ☎ 843 805 5900, ⓦ eatatfig.com. Minimalist neighbourhood bistro with a focus on fresh Low Country ingredients. Menus change seasonally, but the fish stews, green garlic soup and shrimp with polenta are good bets and the farm-fresh veggies are wonderful. Mon–Thurs 5.30–10.30pm, Fri & Sat till 11pm.

Hominy Grill 207 Rutledge Ave ☎ 843 937 0930, ⓦ hominygrill.com. This neighbourhood restaurant has built up such a reputation for its comforting Low Country cooking that it's almost impossible to get a seat at lunch. Come for dinner instead and try the fried green tomato BLT ($9) or catfish Creole with crispy okra ($15). Mon–Fri 7.30am–9pm, Sat 9am–9pm, Sun 9am–3pm.

Husk 76 Queen St ☎ 843 577 2500, ⓦ huskrestaurant.com. This highly regarded restaurant marries scrupulously sourced local ingredients with culinary wizardry – think lacquered duck legs with toasted peanuts ($30) and water-melon salad with bourbon-smoked salt ($12). Though it's housed in a dignified 1893 Queen Anne, the ambience is markedly unfussy. Mon–Thurs 11.30am–2.30pm & 5.30–10pm, Fri & Sat 11.30am–2.30pm & 5.30–11pm, Sun 10am–2.30pm & 5.30–10pm.

Jestine's Kitchen 251 Meeting St ☎ 843 722 7224. Straightforward Low Country cooking, served in a simple, tourist filled dining room in the heart of downtown. Go for the fried chicken, meat loaf or collard greens and finish off with Coca-Cola cake. Tues–Thurs 11am–9.30pm, Fri & Sat 11am–10pm, Sun 11am–9pm.

Slightly North of Broad 192 E Bay St ☎ 843 723 3424, ⓦ mavericksouthernkitchens.com. One of the smart, buzzy nouvelle Southern bistros that Charleston specializes in – crab-stuffed flounder, crispy chicken livers with grits and the like. It's lively at lunchtime, when they offer an $11 *prix fixe* menu. Mon–Fri 11.30am–3pm & 5.30pm–close, Sat & Sun 5.30pm–close.

NIGHTLIFE AND ENTERTAINMENT

Charleston has a vibrant nightlife, though downtown bars tend to be touristy. For **listings**, see the free weekly *City Paper* (ⓦ charlestoncitypaper.com). Chief among the city's many **festivals** is Spoleto (ⓦ spoletousa.org), an extraordinarily rich extravaganza of international arts held in late May/early June.

Blind Tiger 38 Broad St ☎ 843 577 0342, ⓦ blindtiger charleston.com. Popular downtown drinking hole with a hidden entrance, a busy deck hung with lanterns and ferns, good bar food, cheap beer and regular live music. Mon–Sat 11.30am–2am, Sun 11am–2am.

The Griffon 18 Vendue Range ☎ 843 723 1700, ⓦ griffoncharleston.com. Cosy tavern, serving craft ales as well as tasty English-style fish and chips. Every inch of its bar, walls and ceiling beams is covered with scribbled-on dollar bills. Mon–Fri 11am–2am, Sat noon–2am.

Music Farm 32 Ann St ☎ 843 577 6969, ⓦ musicfarm.com. This warehouse-like building alongside the visitor centre is the best place in Charleston to see regional and national touring bands. Check online for performance times.

Rooftop Bar at the Vendue Inn 19 Vendue Range ☎ 843 577 7970, ⓦ vendueinn.com. Enjoyable and elegant cocktail bar and restaurant with dramatic views over the harbour, the historic district and out to Fort Sumter. Daily 11.30am–midnight.

★ **Squeeze** 213 E Bay St ☎ 843 937 6210, ⓦ squeeze-bar.com. Tiny bar (hence the name) with an unpretentious, friendly atmosphere, craft cocktails, good tunes and striking decor. Sadly, *Squeeze* sustained fire damage in 2013; at the time of writing, locals were hopeful it would be quickly up and running. Daily 5pm–2am.

Around Charleston

The **river road**, Hwy-61, leads **west** from Charleston along the Ashley River past a series of opulent **plantations**. An easy jaunt from the city, these country estates make for a diverting afternoon's visit.

Drayton Hall

3380 Ashley River Rd • Mon–Sat 9am–3.30pm, Sun 11am–3.30pm • $18 • ☎ 843 769 2600, ⓦ draytonhall.org

Drayton Hall is an elegant Georgian mansion with handcarved wood and plasterwork; there is little furniture on show, and the guided tours (on the half hour) concentrate on the fine architecture. At 10.45am, 12.45pm and 2.45pm, talks, elucidated by photographs and artefacts, emphasize the role of **African Americans** in the Low Country, tracing the story of slavery and emancipation and how it relates to Drayton Hall.

Magnolia Plantation and Gardens

3550 Ashley River Rd • Daily: March–Oct 8am–5.30pm; Nov–Feb 9am–4.30pm • $15 • ☎ 800 367 3517, ⓦ magnoliaplantation.com

The **Magnolia Plantation and Gardens** is famed for its stunning ornamental gardens, particularly in spring when the azaleas are blooming. Admission gives you access to the grounds, which include a tropical greenhouse, a petting zoo, a maze and a wildlife observation tower, but you have to pay extra ($8 each) for **house tours**, the "**Slavery to Freedom**" tour, a visit to the **Audubon Swamp**, complete with alligators and lush plant life, "nature train" tour of the grounds or a "nature boat" tour of the swamp.

Charles Towne Landing

1500 Old Towne Rd • Daily 9am–5pm • $7.50 • ☎ 843 852 4200, ⓦ friendsofcharlestownelanding.org

West of the Ashley River Bridge, **Charles Towne Landing** is a 663-acre state park on the site where in 1670 the English colonists established the first permanent settlement in the Carolinas. As well as the landing site itself, you can see a living history settlement, a replica of a seventeenth-century merchant ship and a zoo, home to creatures the colonists would have encountered when they landed here – pumas, bison, alligators, black bears and otters.

The beaches

East of Charleston, **beaches** such as **Isle of Palms** and **Sullivan's Island** are heavily used by locals on weekends. The further from town, the more likely you are to find a peaceful stretch. South of the city, the waves of **Folly Beach** are rated highly by surfers.

The sea islands

South of Charleston toward Savannah, the coastline dissolves into small, marshy **Sea islands** peppered with oyster beds and prickly palmetto groves. Along this romantic strand, icy drinks are sipped on bayfront verandas, century-old oak trees take up whole streets, and a West African dialect that pre-dates America is spoken.

Edisto Island

On pretty **Edisto Island**, south of US-17 on Hwy-174, live oaks festooned with drapes of Spanish moss form canopies over the roads, bright green marshes harbour rich birdlife and fine beaches line the seaward side. There are no motels, but **Edisto Beach State Park** (daily 8am–6pm; $5; ☎ 843 869 2156, ⓦ southcarolinaparks.com) has a **campground** (see below).

ACCOMMODATION   EDISTO ISLAND

Edisto Beach State Park campground 8377 State Cabin Rd ☎ 843 869 2156, ⓦ southcarolinaparks.com. Inviting campground near a beach lined with palmetto trees and other semitropical plants. The park also maintains seven a/c cabins (sleeping four) – which fill up months in advance – and come complete with utensils, linens and TVs. Tents **$38**, cabins **$130**

Beaufort

The largest town in the area, **BEAUFORT** (pronounced "Byoofert") has a lovely historic district, brought to life in novels by writer and resident Pat Conroy, and in films such as *Forrest Gump* and *The Big Chill*. Despite being a vanguard of the secessionist movement, this tidal village was one of the first taken by Union troops at the start of the Civil War. Hoping to prevent the destruction of their homes, cotton and indigo planters fled town (in what was dubbed "The Great Skedaddle") at the beginning of the conflict. The thousands of West African slaves that were left behind – isolated on islands with no bridge to the mainland – thrived, and their community's language (known as "Gullah"), customs and culture remain preserved to this day.

FROM TOP PERFORMERS AT THE JUKE JOINT FESTIVAL, CLARKSDALE, MS (P.463); MARTIN LUTHER KING JR NATIONAL HISTORIC SITE, ATLANTA, GA (P.415) >

6

By bus The Greyhound station (☎ 843 524 4646) is 2 miles north of town on US-21.

Visitor centre 713 Craven St (Mon–Sat 9am–5pm, Sun noon–5pm; ☎ 843 525 8500, ⓦ beaufortsc.org); offers details of local tours and discount coupons for the motels out on US-21.

Kayaking tours Get out on the water by renting a kayak (from $25) with knowledgeable Lands End Tours (☎ 615 243 4684, ⓦ beaufortlandsendtours.com), who also do guided trips.

ACCOMMODATION AND EATING

Cuthbert House Inn 1203 Bay St ☎ 843 521 1315, ⓦ cuthberthouseinn.com. General Sherman himself stayed at this esteemed B&B, where, inside the fireplace, Union soldiers etched their names in elegant penmanship. Overlooking the bay, the inn offers nine spacious guestrooms, free bike use, access to a DVD library and happy hour on a veranda filled with rocking chairs. **$190**

★ **Old Bull Tavern** 205 West St ☎ 843 379 2855. Central, arty gastropub that feels like it could have been airlifted from Manhattan, yet its setting – between tidal marshes and antebellum homes – only adds to its charm. Dimly lit by Edison bulbs, the bar mixes a mean cocktail, while the kitchen dishes up sophisticated fare such as ricotta gnocchi with wild shrimp ($12) and addictive rosemary cashews ($3). Check out the witty, rotating sayings above the bar. Tues–Sat 5pm–midnight.

Sergeant White's 1908 Boundary St ☎ 843 522 2029. Destination barbecue restaurant where you choose a "meat and three" ($8.99) – pulled pork, roast chicken, candied yams, collard greens, fried okra and more – from the delicious smorgasbord at the front, then dine on checkerboard tablecloths in a dining room filled with knick-knacks. Mon–Fri 11am–3pm.

St Helena Island

Across the bridge southeast of Beaufort, **ST HELENA ISLAND**, dotted with small shrimp- and oyster-fishing communities, is among the least spoiled of the eastern sea islands. The further south you go the more gorgeous the **landscape** gets: amazing Spanish moss hangs from ancient oaks, while enormous, wide views stretch out across vibrant green marshes patterned with small salt creeks.

The Penn Center

16 Penn Center Circle W, off US-21 • Mon–Sat 9am–4pm • Museum $5, grounds free • ☎ 843 838 2474, ⓦ penncenter.com

St Helena Island is a region of strong **black communities**, descended from slaves who acquired parcels of land after they were freed by the Union army; their Gullah dialect is an Afro-English patois with many West African words. The **Penn Center** houses the **school** started for freed slaves in 1862 by Laura Towne, a white teacher from Pennsylvania. During the 1960s, this remote campus was the only place in South Carolina where interracial groups could safely convene, and, as such, served as an important retreat for civil rights leaders. Grab a map at the administrative office, then be sure to take a look at the **Gantt Center**, a humble wooded cottage with an astounding history – it was once home to Martin Luther King, Jr, and handwritten drafts of his "I Have a Dream" speech were uncovered here. The Penn Center also houses the small **York W. Bailey Museum**, with historic photos and island artefacts.

Red Piano Too Gallery

870 Sea Island Pkwy (US-21) • Mon–Sat 10am–5pm, Sun 1–4.30pm • Free • ☎ 843 838 2241, ⓦ redpianotoo.com

A bright beacon perched at the intersection of US-21 and MLK Drive, the remarkable **Red Piano Too Gallery** showcases a strong collection of regional paintings, sculpture and folk art, hung from every nook and cranny and conjuring the sea islands in all their vibrant beauty.

Hunting Island State Park

2555 Sea Island Pkwy (US-21) • Daily: June–Aug 6am–9pm; Sept–May 6am–6pm • $5, lighthouse $2 • ☎ 843 838 2011, ⓦ southcarolinaparks.com

St Helena's main **beach**, at **Hunting Island State Park**, can get crowded, but it's ravishing: soft white sand, wide and gently shelving, scattered with shards of pearly shells and fringed with a mature maritime forest of palmettos, palm trees and sea oats. Pelicans come here to feed, particularly in the early morning; it's also a turtle-nesting site. Tackling the 175 steps of the little black-and-white lighthouse, you're rewarded with views that extend forty miles.

ACCOMMODATION	ST HELENA ISLAND
Hunting Island State Park campground 2555 Sea Island Pkwy ☎ 843 838 2011, ⓦ southcarolinaparks .com. Lodgings next to the lighthouse in one weather-beaten cabin (sleeping six), although you need to reserve well in advance. There's also a large campground near the water. Tents **$38**, cabin **$210**	**Sweetgrass Restaurant** 100 Marina Drive, Dataw Island Marina ☎ 843 838 2151, ⓦ sweetgrassdataw.com. Dine on salmon seared in tequila-lime sauce ($21) and Frogmore stew, thick with shrimp and sausage ($19) at this upmarket favourite in the marina of a gated community. Mon & Tues 5–9pm, Thurs–Sat 5–9pm, Sun 11.30am–9pm.

Georgia

Compared to the rest of **GEORGIA**, the largest of the Southern states, the bright lights of its capital Atlanta are a wild aberration. Apart from some beaches and towns on the highly indented coastline, this rural state is composed of slow, easy-going settlements where the best, and sometimes the only, way to enjoy your time is to sip iced tea and have a chat on the porch.

Settlement in Georgia, the thirteenth British colony (named after King George II), started in 1733 at Savannah, intended as a haven of Christian principles for poor Britons, with both alcohol and slavery banned. However, under pressure from planters, **slavery** was introduced in 1752 and by the time of the **Civil War** almost half the population were African slaves. Little fighting took place on Georgia soil until Sherman's troops advanced from Tennessee, burned Atlanta to the ground, and, in the infamous "March to the Sea", laid waste to all property on the way to the coast.

Today, bustling **Atlanta** stands as the unofficial capital of the South. The city where **Dr Martin Luther King, Jr** was born, preached and is buried bears little relation to *Gone With the Wind* stereotypes and its forward-thinking energy is upheld as a role model for the "New South". The state's main tourist destination, though, is the **coast**, stretching south from beautiful old **Savannah** via the **sea islands** to the semitropical **Okefenokee Swamp**, inland near Florida. In the **northeast**, the **Appalachian foothills** are fetching in autumn, while the college town of **Athens** is known for its offbeat rock heroes R.E.M. and the B-52s.

Atlanta

At first glance, **ATLANTA** is a typical large American city and one that suffers particularly badly from urban sprawl: the population of the entire metropolitan area exceeds 5.5 million. It is also undeniably upbeat and progressive, with little interest in lamenting a lost Southern past, and since electing the nation's first black mayor, the late Maynard Jackson, in 1974, it has remained the most conspicuously **black-run** city in the USA. As if to counterbalance the alienating sprawl, the city maintains plenty of active, prettily landscaped green spaces (most notably, the 22-mile **BeltLine**), and its neighbourhoods have distinct, recognizable identities; quaint **Virginia Highlands** is just a short drive away from trendy **Inman Park** and grungier, punky **Little Five Points**, for example, but the three have little in common. Once you accept the driving distances and the roaring freeways, dynamic Atlanta has plenty to offer, with must-see attractions from sites associated with Dr King to cultural institutions including the **High Museum of Art** and **Atlanta History Center**. At time of writing, the **National Center for Civil and Human Rights** (ⓦ cchrpartnership.org) was gearing up to open in Centennial Park, between the aquarium and World of Coca-Cola.

6

ATLANTA

Ⓜ MARTA Station

— BeltLine

Buckhead ▲   ▲ Amtrak Station

Arts Center Ⓜ

High Museum of Art

Piedmont Park

Atlanta Botanical Garden

■ **BARS & LIVE MUSIC VENUES**
Blind Willie's	2
Clermont Lounge	3
The EARL	8
Manuel's Tavern	4
Northside Tavern	1
The Porter Beer Bar	7
Star Community Bar	6
The Vortex	5

Midtown Ⓜ

Margaret Mitchell House

MIDTOWN

Fox Theatre
North Avenue Ⓜ

Civic Center Ⓜ

National Center for Civil and Human Rights

Georgia Aquarium

World of Coca-Cola

Centennial Olympic Park

Georgia Dome

CNN Center

Vine City

Dome/GWCC/ Phillips/CNN

Peachtree Center Ⓜ

MARTIN LUTHER KING JR. HISTORIC DISTRICT

King Center

NPS Visitor Center

MLK Jr. Birth Home

Ebenezer Baptist Church

DOWNTOWN

Five Points Ⓜ

ⓘ

Garnett Ⓜ

Georgia State Ⓜ

Georgia State Capitol

King Memorial Ⓜ

Oakland Cemetery

N

Turner Field

Grant Park

Cyclorama

Zoo Atlanta

0   800
yards

▲ Hartsfield International Airport

6

ATLANTA ORIENTATION

Atlanta's layout is confusing, with its roads following old Native American trails rather than a logical grid. An unbelievable number of streets are named "Peachtree"; be sure to determine whether you're looking for Avenue, Road or Boulevard and pay special attention to whether it's "NW", "W" or so forth. The most important, **Peachtree Street**, cuts a long north–south swath through the city. Note also that the city is split into three urban centres: Downtown (home to major attractions like the **World of Coca-Cola**), Midtown (the arts district) and Buckhead (fancy suburbia). Sights are scattered, but relatively easy to reach by car or on the subway. Most neighbourhoods, including **downtown**, the Martin Luther King Jr Historic District along **Auburn Avenue** and trendy **Little Five Points**, are easy to explore on foot.

The CNN Center

190 Marietta St NW • Tours daily 9am–5pm • $15, reservations recommended • ☎ 404 827 2300, ⓦ cnn.com/tour

In the heart of downtown, the **CNN Center** is the headquarters of the largest news broadcaster in the world. A variety of energetic guided tours rush you past frazzled producers and toothy anchorpersons. You'll also learn some of the nitty-gritty of television production, such as how dialogue prompts get posted into cameras; one lucky tour-taker will get to don an invisible cloak via a "green screen" – used when reporting the weather forecast.

Georgia Aquarium

225 Baker St NW • Mon–Fri & Sun 10am–5pm, Sat 9am–6pm • $35, kids $29, various passes available • ☎ 404 581 4000, ⓦ georgiaaquarium.org

On the north side of **Centennial Olympic Park**, the city's most beloved open space, the **Georgia Aquarium** is a state-of-the-art facility that is so popular you should probably book in advance. Highlights include the biggest tank in the world, filled with sharks and manta rays and recreations of Georgia habitats; it's also the only aquarium outside Asia to have whale sharks.

World of Coca-Cola

121 Baker St NW • Mon–Thurs from 10am, Fri–Sun from 9am; closing times vary • $16 • ☎ 404 676 5151, ⓦ worldofcoca-cola.com

Next to the aquarium, the **World of Coca-Cola** is a shiny, happy slice of modern Americana. Pushed by its relentlessly smiley guides as an "entertainment experience", it's stuffed with high-tech displays and hokey memorabilia illustrating the iconic brand's extraordinary journey from Atlanta soda fountain to world domination. Above all, it's an eye-opening study of genius marketing, peaking in the "Taste it" room, where kids and parents alike excitedly slurp Coke drinks from around the world – best avoid Italy's bitter "Beverly" – a hyper feeding frenzy that pumps visitors full of sugar before siphoning them off to the gift store.

Martin Luther King, Jr National Historic Site

Visitor centre: 450 Auburn Ave NE • Daily 9am–5pm • Free • ☎ 404 331 6922, ⓦ nps.gov/malu

One and a half miles east of Centennial Park, **Auburn Avenue** stands as a monument to Atlanta's black history. During its heyday in the 1920s, "**Sweet Auburn**" was a prosperous, progressive area of black-owned businesses and jazz clubs, but it went into a decline with the Depression from which it has never truly recovered. Several blocks have been designated as the **Martin Luther King, Jr National Historic Site**, in honour of Auburn's most cherished native son. This short stretch of road is the most visited attraction in all Georgia and it's a moving experience to watch the crowds of school kids waiting in turn to take photographs. Head first for the park service's **visitor centre** where an exhibition covers King's life and campaigns. If you're looking for a broader account of the civil rights years, the museum in Memphis is much more comprehensive (see p.439), but this provides a powerful summary, culminating with the mule-drawn wagon used in King's funeral procession in Atlanta on April 9, 1968.

6

REVEREND DR MARTIN LUTHER KING, JR (1929–68)

Martin Luther King, Jr was born at 501 Auburn Ave, Atlanta, on January 15, 1929. The house was then home to his parents and his grandparents; both his maternal grandfather, Rev A.D. Williams, and his father, Martin Luther King, Sr, served as pastor of **Ebenezer Baptist Church** nearby. Young Martin was ordained at 19 and became co-pastor at Ebenezer with his father, but continued his studies at Crozer Theological Seminary in Pennsylvania, where he was profoundly influenced by the ideas of Mahatma Gandhi, and at Boston University. Returning to the South, King became pastor of Dexter Avenue Baptist Church in **Montgomery**, Alabama, in 1954, where his leadership during the bus boycott a year later (see p.459) brought him to national prominence. A visit to India in 1959 further cemented his belief in nonviolent resistance as the means by which racial segregation could be eradicated. He returned to Atlanta in 1960, becoming co-pastor at Ebenezer once more, but also taking on the presidency of the **Southern Christian Leadership Conference**. As such, he became the figurehead for the civil rights struggle, planning strategy for future campaigns, flying into each new trouble spot, and commenting to the news media on every latest development. His apotheosis in that role came in August 1963, when he addressed the **March on Washington** with his "I Have a Dream" speech. He was awarded the **Nobel Peace Prize** in 1964. Despite King's passionate espousal of nonviolence, J. Edgar Hoover's **FBI** branded him "the most dangerous and effective Negro leader in the country", and persistently attempted to discredit him over his personal life. King himself became more overtly politicized in his final years. Challenged by the stridency of Malcolm X and the radicalism of urban black youth, he came to see the deprivation and poverty of the cities of the North as affecting black and white alike, and only solvable by tackling "the triple evils of racism, extreme materialism, and militarism". In the South, he had always been able to appeal to the federal government as an (albeit often reluctant) ally; now, having declared his opposition to the war in **Vietnam**, he faced a sterner and lonelier struggle. In the event, his **Poor People's Campaign** had barely got off the ground before King was assassinated (see p.439) in Memphis on April 4, 1968.

Birth Home

501 Auburn Ave NE • Daily 10am–4.30pm • Free • ☎ 404 331 6922, ⊛ nps.gov/malu

You should check in at the visitor centre for a free tour of King's **Birth Home**, a short walk east. As only fifteen people can visit at a time and school groups often visit en masse, you may have to settle for a "virtual tour", using the computers at the visitor centre. The house itself is a fourteen-room Queen Anne-style shotgun, restored to its prosperous 1930s appearance. Home to King until he was 12 (he was born in an upstairs bedroom), it remained in his family until 1971.

King Center

449 Auburn Ave NE • Daily: May to early Sept 9am–6pm; early Sept to May 9am–5pm • Free • ☎ 404 526 8900, ⊛ thekingcenter.org

Across from the visitor centre, the **King Center** is privately run by King's family. Chiefly a research facility, it features artefacts such as his travelling case and the hotel key from the room at the *Lorraine Motel* where he was assassinated (see p.439), as well as tiny rooms devoted to Mahatma Gandhi and Rosa Parks. King's mortal remains, along with those of his wife, Coretta, who died in 2006, are held in a plain marble **tomb** inscribed with the words "Free at last, Free at last, thank God Almighty I'm Free at last", which stands, guarded by an eternal flame, in the shallow Reflecting Pool outside.

Ebenezer Baptist Church

101 Jackson St • Daily 9am–5pm • Free • ☎ 404 331 6922, ⊛ nps.gov/malu

Next door to the King Center, the **Ebenezer Baptist Church**, where both King's baptism and funeral took place – and where his mother was assassinated while playing the organ in 1974 – has been carefully restored. During the 1960s, King worked as a pastor here with his father. Inside, you can listen to King's speeches (they're piped in on a loop) from the same pews where his congregants sat. It will give you chills.

x Theatre
50 Peachtree St NE • Tours Mon, Thurs & Sat on the hour from 10am–1pm • $18 • ☎ 404 881 2100, ⓦ foxtheatre.org

Nestled among the glass skyscrapers, the flamboyant Art Deco **Fox Theatre**, with its strong Moorish theme, is a rare and gorgeous remnant of old Atlanta. If you're not attending one of its fairly mainstream shows, you can see the lovely interior on an organized tour.

Margaret Mitchell House
990 Peachtree St NE • Mon–Sat 10am–5.30pm, Sun noon–5.30pm • $13 • ☎ 404 249 7015, ⓦ margaretmitchellhouse.com

Three blocks north of the Fox Theatre, the only brick home left on Peachtree Street is the **Margaret Mitchell House**. Mitchell and her husband lived in the small apartment she called "the dump" during the ten years she took to write the best-selling novel of all time, *Gone With the Wind*. Published in 1936, it took just six weeks to sell enough copies to form a tower fifty times higher than the Empire State Building; the 1939 movie scaled further peaks of popularity. Lively guided tours tell the fascinating tale.

High Museum of Art
1280 Peachtree St NE • Tues, Wed, Fri & Sat 10am–5pm, Thurs 10am–8pm, Sun noon–5pm • $19.50 • ☎ 404 733 4444, ⓦ high.org

Part of the **Woodruff Arts Center**, an umbrella organization that houses the city's symphony orchestra and **Alliance Theatre**, Atlanta's splendid **High Museum of Art**, in stunning, airy premises designed by Renzo Piano and Richard Meier, is world-class. Permanent collections include idiosyncratic folk art by Howard Finster and Mose Tolliver, some fabulous mid-century American furniture and extensive European galleries covering five centuries from Renaissance Italy to the French Impressionists.

Atlanta Botanical Garden
1345 Piedmont Ave NE • Tues–Sun: April 9am–7pm; May–Oct 9am–7pm (Thurs 9am–10pm); Nov–March 9am–5pm • $19 • ☎ 404 876 5859, ⓦ atlantabotanicalgarden.org

With its leafy trails, playgrounds, tennis courts, boardwalk and public pool, elegant **Piedmont Park** has provided a lot of pulse to Atlanta since its construction in 1904. The highlight of the park, however, is the wonderfully landscaped **Atlanta Botanical Garden**. In addition to its manicured gardens and vast conservatories of gorgeous orchids and tropical plants, the garden hosts summer-long sculpture exhibitions and big-name concerts.

Atlanta History Center
30 W Paces Ferry Rd NW • Mon–Sat 10am–5.30pm, Sun noon–5.30pm • $16.50 • ☎ 404 814 4000, ⓦ atlantahistorycenter.com

Tucked away in the west, the **Atlanta History Center** offers a superb run-through of the factors that led to the city's relentless growth and is strong on African American and women's history. A Civil War exhibit features an extraordinary number of artefacts; even if the military minutiae don't captivate you, the human stories will, and the whole combines to provide a clear history of the war. You can also tour two houses on the pretty grounds: the 1920s mock-Classical mansion **Swan House** and the rustic **Tullie Smith Farm**.

THE BELTLINE
An excellent way to sightsee in Atlanta is via the **BeltLine** (ⓦ beltline.org), a 22-mile train corridor that has been transformed into an appealing green space and massive bike loop. Encircling the city, the path skirts Piedmont Park, and comes quite close to Zoo Atlanta. With or without an itinerary, though, it's great for ambling, with plenty of entrance points and restaurants close at hand. Atlanta Beltline Bicycle (☎ 404 588 9930, ⓦ atlantabeltlinebicycle.com) has friendly staff and **rents bikes** for $15/day.

6

The Wren's Nest

1050 Ralph David Abernathy Blvd SW • Tues–Sat 10am–2.30pm, storytelling Sat 1pm • $5 • ☎ 404 753 7735, ⓦ wrensnest.org

Historically an African American neighbourhood, the **West End**, southwest of downtown, remains so today: a more upbeat counterpoint to Sweet Auburn. The **Wren's Nest** is the former home of Joel Chandler Harris, the white author of *Br'er Rabbit*. The house remains much as Harris left it upon his death in 1908, while a short film explains that he first heard the Uncle Remus stories from slaves when he trained as a printer on a plantation newspaper. On Saturday afternoon, storytelling sessions take place in the peaceful, untamed garden.

Atlanta Cyclorama and Civil War Museum

800 Cherokee Ave SE • Tues–Sat 9.15am–4.30pm • $10 • ☎ 404 658 7625, ⓦ atlantacyclorama.org

A mile southeast of downtown, in **Grant Park** – named for a Confederate defender of Atlanta, not the victorious Union general – a theatre houses the **Cyclorama**, a huge circular painting, executed in 1885–86, depicting the Battle of Atlanta. Cycloramas were popular entertainments in the days before movies; you sit inside the circle of the painting while the whole auditorium slowly rotates. In part to mask deterioration of the canvas, a 3-D diorama has been built in front that makes it hard to see where the painting ends and the mannequins begin. The accompanying **museum** treats the war from the viewpoint of the average soldier, interspersing distressing statistics with photos and memorabilia.

Zoo Atlanta

800 Cherokee Ave SE • Mon–Fri 9.30am–5.30pm, Sat & Sun 9.30am–6.30pm • $22 • ☎ 404 624 5600, ⓦ zooatlanta.org

Next to the Cyclorama, **Zoo Atlanta** features a pair of giant pandas from Chengdu, gorillas, kangaroos, otters and flamingos plus recreations of various habitats. It'll cost you just $3 for the thrill of feeding a gentle giraffe.

Oakland Cemetery

248 Oakland Ave SE • Daily dawn–dusk • Free • ☎ 404 688 2107, ⓦ oaklandcemetery.com

The city's oldest and largest burial ground, **Oakland Cemetery** is the resting place of famous Atlanta citizens, including Margaret Mitchell; walking tours are available. Built in the "garden cemetery" tradition, its sweeping 88 acres are beautifully landscaped with dogwood trees, delicate magnolias and ornate headstones and mausoleums.

Little Five Points and around

Northeast of Auburn Avenue, around Euclid and Moreland avenues, the youthful, if gentrifying, **Little Five Points** district is a tangle of thrift stores, hip restaurants, body-piercing parlours, bars and clubs. Home to some of the city's best nightlife, it's equally diverting when the sun is up – pop into a record store, or spend the afternoon with coffee and a book.

Northeast, beyond the upmarket **Virginia-Highland** restaurant district, the trek to **Emory University**'s campus is rewarded by the lovely **Michael C. Carlos Museum** (571 S Kilgo Circle; Tues–Fri 10am–4pm, Sat 10am–5pm, Sun noon–5pm; $8; ☎ 404 472 4282, ⓦ carlos.emory.edu), which hosts a splendid collection of fine art and antiquities from all six inhabited continents.

Jimmy Carter Presidential Library and Museum

441 Freedom Pkwy • Mon–Sat 9am–4.45pm, Sun noon–4.45pm • $8 • ☎ 404 865 7100, ⓦ jimmycarterlibrary.org

On the hill where Sherman is said to have watched Atlanta burn, the **Jimmy Carter Presidential Library and Museum** is devoted to the peanut farmer who rose to become Georgia state governor and the 39th president of the USA; look out for 12-year-old Jimmy's school essay on health, in which he earnestly urges readers to keep their teeth clean.

ARRIVAL AND DEPARTURE

ATLANTA

By plane The huge Hartsfield-Jackson International Airport (☎ 800 897 1910, ⓦ atlanta-airport.com) is 10 miles south of downtown Atlanta, just inside I-285 ("the perimeter"). It's the southern terminus of the north/south lines of the subway (see below), a 15min trip from downtown, and is also served by the Atlanta Airport Shuttle buses (every 15min, daily 6am–midnight; $16.50 to downtown; ☎ 404 941 3440, ⓦ taass.net) and Su-Taxi (☎ 404 255 6333; $30 to downtown).

By bus Greyhound buses (☎ 404 584 1728) arrive south of downtown at 232 Forsyth St, near the Garnett subway station.

Destinations Birmingham, AL (5 daily; 2hr 50min); Chattanooga, TN (9 daily; 2hr 10min); Macon, GA (9 daily; 1hr 40min); Montgomery, AL (5 daily; 4hr); Nashville, TN (8 daily; 4hr 30min); Savannah, GA (4 daily; 4hr 35min).

By train Atlanta's Amtrak station, 1688 Peachtree St NW, is at the north end of Midtown, just under a mile north of the nearest subway station, Arts Center.

Destinations Birmingham, AL (1 daily; 4hr 15min); Savannah, GA (2 daily; 4hr 40min).

GETTING AROUND, INFORMATION AND TOURS

By subway The useful MARTA subway system has four lines, two east/west and two north/south, which intersect downtown at Five Points (Mon–Fri 5am–1am, Sat & Sun 6am–1am; one-way fare $2.50, one-day pass $9, seven-day pass $23.75; ☎ 404 848 5000, ⓦ itsmarta.com).

Visitor centre 65 Upper Alabama St (Mon–Sat 10am–6pm,

Sun noon–6pm; ☎ 404 521 6600, ⓦ atlanta.net).

Walking tours The Atlanta Preservation Center leads lively historical walking tours of different neighbourhoods (90min; $10, cash only; ☎ 404 688 3353, ⓦ atlanta preservationcenter.com).

ACCOMMODATION

The most economical accommodation options in downtown Atlanta are the chains, but even these aren't particularly inexpensive; **weekend rates** can be better, but just to park costs at least $20 per night (and up to twice that for valet parking). Midtown can be cheaper, and puts you nearer the nightlife.

Artmore Hotel 1302 W Peachtree St ☎ 404 876 6100, ⓦ artmorehotel.com. Cool independent hotel in a refurbished historic building, with a pretty candlelit courtyard, near the High Museum of Art. **$139**

The Ellis 176 Peachtree St NE ☎ 404 523 5155, ⓦ ellishotel.com. Central, stylish hotel close to Centennial Park and the aquarium. The modern rooms, which are on the small side, have iPod docks and marble bathrooms. There's an on-site restaurant, and an enjoyable breakfast buffet ($15). **$199**

Hampton Inn and Suites Downtown 161 Spring St NW ☎ 404 589 1111, ⓦ hamptoninn.hilton.com. Located in a handsome brick building that dates from 1927, this downtown chain has comfortable rooms and is within walking distance of many attractions, making it one of the

best-value central options. Rates include breakfast. **$149**

Highland Inn 644 N Highland Ave ☎ 404 874 5756, ⓦ thehighlandinn.com. Hipsters flock to this cool, slightly tatty, hotel near Little Five Points and Virginia Highlands. It's a lively place, with an adjacent café, and a fun historic set-up – dating from 1927, it once held a bowling alley and swimming pool, now converted to a courtyard and lounge. **$80**

Twelve Centennial Park 400 W Peachtree St ☎ 404 418 1212, ⓦ twelvehotels.com. If you want to live like a (moneyed) local, book one of these beautifully designed urban lofts right by the Civic Center metro downtown. The suites are vast, modern and well equipped, with balconies and kitchens, while the good sushi/steak restaurant, *Room*, and lively bar downstairs enhance the buzzy atmosphere. **$209**

EATING AND DRINKING

Atlanta has scores of good restaurants to suit all budgets and tastes. The most popular neighbourhoods (such as Inman Park and Virginia-Highland) each tend to have their own community bistro with an upcoming chef. Most Midtown options are upmarket, while **Southern soul food** is best around Auburn Avenue.

El Taco 1186 N Highland Ave NE, Virginia-Highland ☎ 404 873 4656, ⓦ eltaco-atlanta.com. Boisterous Tex-Mex place distinguished by its gorgeous mural depicting Frida Kahlo, tequila-swilling party-goers and a *lucha libre* wrestler. Underneath lanterns shaped like stars, a hip clientele enjoys frozen margaritas, fried chicken tacos with grilled corn ($3.50) and marinated steak fajitas ($16). Mon–Thurs 5–10pm, Fri 5–11pm,

Sat 11.30am–11pm, Sun 11.30am–10pm.

Empire State South 999 Peachtree St, Midtown ☎ 404 541 1105, ⓦ empirestatesouth.com. Close to diverting Piedmont Park. A great Midtown itinerary would begin with brunch at this sophisticated Southern bistro – regulars wax poetic about the poached "farm egg" on crispy rice ($12) – and continue with a stroll beside the dogwood trees and oaks of this historic green space. It's also fun for cocktails,

6

bocce ball and charcuterie "jars" of devilled ham, pickles and peanut hummus, savoured on the terrace. Mon–Fri 7am–11pm, Sat 5.30–11pm, Sun 10.30am–11pm.

★ **Fox Bros. Bar-B-Q** 1238 Dekalb Ave, Little Five Points ☎404 577 4030. Atlanta's best barbecue, a few blocks from the heart of Little Five Points. It makes little difference if you choose a plateful of Texas-style ribs, juicy pulled pork or tangy fried pickles – everything is delicious. Parking can be tricky, and there's often a queue to get in. Mon–Thurs & Sun 11am–10pm, Fri & Sat 11am–11pm.

Highland Bakery 655 Highland Ave NE, Old Fourth Ward ☎404 586 0772, ⍟highlandbakery.com. Pre-eminent breakfast joint with unbeatable peanut butter French toast ($9) and tall stacks of sweet potato pancakes, dotted with toasted pecans ($8). Great on-site bakery, too. Mon–Fri 7am–4pm, Sat & Sun 8am–4pm.

Manuel's Tavern 602 N Highland Ave NE, Poncey-Highland ☎404 525 3447, ⍟manuelstavern.com. Memorabilia lines the walls of this classic neighbourhood bar in Poncey-Highland, a favourite watering hole for journalists, writers and politicians. Jimmy Carter announced his run for governor here in 1970. Superb pub food served until late. Mon 11am–midnight, Tues–Fri 11am–1am, Sat 9.30am–1pm, Sun 9.30am–noon.

The Optimist 914 Howell Mill Rd, West Midtown ☎404 477 6260, ⍟theoptimistrestaurant.com. Lively, pricey seafood hideaway (mains about $25) whose airy white decor has the fine lines of a classy yacht. Getting a reservation can be tough; fortunately, there are two inviting bars, one for small plates and shucked oysters, the other with pinstriped seating and a full menu. Mon–Thurs 11.30am–2.30pm & 5–10pm, Fri 11.30am–2.30pm &

5–11pm, Sat 5–11pm, Sun 5–10pm.

★ **The Porter Beer Bar** 1156 Euclid Ave NE, Little Five Points ☎404 223 0393, ⍟theporterbeerbar.com. Stocking an international line-up of more than eight hundred beers, this buzzing bar turns out fantastic gastropub food such as goat's cheese fritters with honey ($6.75), garlicky steamed mussels ($9.25) and divine salt-and-vinegar popcorn ($3.50). Great location at the centre of Little Five Points. Mon–Thurs 11.30am–midnight, Fri 11.30am–2.30am, Sat 11am–2.30am, Sun 11am–midnight.

Ria's Bluebird 421 Memorial Drive SE, Grant Park ☎404 521 3737, ⍟riasbluebird.com. Queues snake out of the door for Ria's hearty and healthy daily breakfast and lunch specials – buttermilk pancakes, overfilled burritos, tempeh Reuben sandwiches – in this cosy, friendly diner opposite Oakland Cemetery. Daily 8am–3pm.

Sweet Auburn Curb Market 209 Edgewood Ave SE, Sweet Auburn ☎404 659 1665, ⍟sweetauburncurb market.com. Bustling indoor fresh produce market, with stands serving cheap soul food, gourmet burritos, Caribbean food, healthy smoothies, deli sandwiches and fresh coffee. Mon–Sat 8am–6pm.

The Vortex 438 Moreland Ave, Little Five Points ☎404 688 1828, ⍟thevortexbarandgrill.com. Stepping into this riotous bar and grill is like entering He-Man's castle – the property is fronted by an enormous 20ft skull with spinning neon eyes. An Atlanta legend, famed for its gut-busting burgers (try the "Elvis", stacked with bacon, peanut butter and fried bananas; $10). The interior is a wild display of shark and alligator heads, memorabilia and flying skeletons. Smoking is permitted; patrons must be 18 or older. Mon–Thurs & Sun 11am–midnight, Fri & Sat 11am–2am.

NIGHTLIFE

The main nightlife areas are Virginia-Highland, Little Five Points and Midtown, the centre of Atlanta's thriving gay and lesbian scene. For **listings**, check the free weekly *Creative Loafing* (⍟clatl.com). **AtlanTIX** (⍟atlantaperforms.com), with a booth in the visitor centre (see p.419), sells half-price (usually same-day) tickets for local events and performances.

Blind Willie's 828 N Highland Ave NE, Virginia Highland ☎404 873 2583, ⍟blindwilliesblues.com. One of the more casual joints in Virginia-Highland, this laidback blues bar has live music, strong drinks and a small dance floor. Occasional big-name acts. Cover $3–12. Mon–Sat 7pm–late.

Clermont Lounge 789 Ponce de Leon Ave NE, Poncey-Highland ☎404 874 4783, ⍟clermontlounge.net. The oldest strip club in the city, the *Clermont* is at once a ramshackle dive bar, a jolting and unusual attraction, a source of community and an Atlanta institution. Charismatic women, some in their 60s, strut their stuff on a tiny bar to a melting pot of nervous tourists, enthusiastic regulars and celebrities. You must be 21 or older to enter. Mon–Sat 1pm–3am.

★ **The EARL** 488 Flat Shoals Ave SE, East Atlanta ☎404 522 3950, ⍟badearl.com. Part welcoming dive bar, part top-notch rock venue, the *EARL* cooks up great

pub food and pulls a nice crowd of devotees. All shows are 21-up. Occasionally a cover; generally around $12 but it can reach $60. Mon–Sat 11.30am–2.30am, Sur 11.30am–midnight.

★ **Northside Tavern** 1058 Howell Mill Rd NW Westside ☎404 874 3950, ⍟northsidetavern.com. In business since 1972, this wonderful, scruffy dive blues ba with cheap drinks and a smoky ambience gets the local swinging with its soulful performances. Mon–Thurs n cover, $10 cover Fri & Sat. Daily noon–2.30am.

Star Community Bar 437 Moreland Ave NE, Little Five Points ☎404 681 9018, ⍟starbar.net. Enjoyable, hi Little Five Points bar, in a former bank bursting with Elvi memorabilia, offering live Americana, funk, country an rockabilly. Many shows are free; covers run about $8. Mor & Wed–Sat 8pm–3am, Tues 9pm–3am.

Dahlonega

DAHLONEGA, in the Appalachian foothills 65 miles northeast of Atlanta on US-19, owes its origins to the first-ever **Gold Rush** in the USA. Benjamin Parks discovered gold at Hall County, three miles south, in 1828; Dahlonega was established five years later as the seat of Lumpkin County. Soon enough gold had been excavated for Dahlonega to acquire its own outpost of the US Mint, which, by the time production was terminated by the Civil War, had produced over $6 million of gold coin. The story is recounted in the lively **Gold Museum** on the main square (Mon–Sat 9am–5pm, Sun 10am–5pm; $6; ☎706 864 2257, ⓦgastateparks.org). From May to October, Saturday afternoons see bluegrass jams on the museum grounds; the town also hosts **Gold Rush Days**, a down-home hoedown, in October.

ACCOMMODATION AND EATING

DAHLONEGA

★ **Cedar House Inn and Yurts** 6463 US-19 ☎706 867 9446, ⓦgeorgiamountaininn.com. This warm and cosy eco-lodge has three wood-panelled rooms with quilted bedspreads and sixteen modernized yurts with microwaves and fridges. A delicious veggie breakfast is included. Rooms $115, yurts $135

Wolf Mountain Vineyards 180 Wolf Mountain Trail ☎706 867 9862, ⓦwolfmountainvineyards.com. Wine buffs, foodies and nature lovers alike will enjoy a visit to this gorgeous family-owned vineyard and café, tucked between grapevines and the Southern Appalachian Mountains. Lunch and brunch only, reservations required. Wine tastings start at $10. Open March–Dec. Thurs–Sun noon–5pm.

Amicalola Falls State Park

Twenty miles west of Dahlonega on Hwy-52, **Amicalola Falls State Park** (daily 7am–10pm; $5/vehicle; ☎706 265 4703, ⓦgastateparks.org/amicalolafalls) centres on a dramatic waterfall that cascades down a steep hillside. After driving to the overlook, continue another half-mile to the park's modern **lodge**, which has comfortable rooms and a restaurant with panoramic views. For even more seclusion, hike five miles toward the start of the **Appalachian Trail**, to reach the *Hike Inn*, accessible only on foot.

ACCOMMODATION

AMICALOLA FALLS STATE PARK

Amicalola Falls Lodge 418 Amicalola Falls Lodge Rd ☎800 573 9656, ⓦamicalolafallslodge.com. Though the decor is a bit outdated, you're coming to this scenic mountain lodge for tranquillity, not style. A quick walk from the eponymous falls, the property is in the heart of the forest, and hiking opportunities abound. $134

Hike Inn The 5-mile hike to the inn begins at the top of

Amicalola Falls ☎800 581 8032, ⓦhike-inn.com. Reached only by a mixed-terrain walk through the woods, this place has bunk beds, a lovely game room with a wood-burning stove and a porch for socializing. Blankets, towels, breakfast and lunch are included in the rate. Reservations essential. $150

Athens

Appealing **ATHENS**, almost seventy miles east of Atlanta, is home to the 30,000-plus students of the University of Georgia and has a liberal feel. Its compact downtown, north of campus, is alive with clubs, bars, restaurants, galleries and – of course – record stores; **Broad Street** in particular is lined with arty shops. The town is probably best known as the home of rock groups such as R.E.M., the B-52s and Widespread Panic, and remains one of the top college music towns in the nation.

The University of Georgia

405 College Station Rd • ☎706 542 3000, ⓦuga.edu

Established in 1785, the **University of Georgia** was the first state-chartered school in the nation and is now famed for its tailgate parties and Georgia Bulldogs football team. It's well worth meandering about the north end of campus, peppered with oak trees and stately columned buildings. Toward the southeast side, the marvellous **Georgia Museum of Art**, 90 Carlton St (Tues, Wed, Fri & Sat 10am–5pm, Thurs 10am–9pm, Sun

1–5pm; free; ☎706 542 4662, ⊛georgiamuseum.org) has a rich collection of modern works depicting twentieth-century American life.

State Botanical Garden of Georgia

2450 S Milledge Ave • Daily: April–Sept 8am–8pm; Oct–March 8am–6pm • Free • ☎706 542 1244, ⊛botgarden.uga.edu

South of the university, the **State Botanical Garden of Georgia** is a peaceful retreat. Five miles of nature trails loop around winsome flower beds, medicinal herbs and horticulture greenhouses. There's a nice alfresco coffee shop, too, with drinks sipped in the company of tropical palm fronds.

ARRIVAL, INFORMATION AND TOURS ATHENS

By bus Greyhound (☎706 549 2255, ⊛greyhound.com) arrives at 4020 Atlanta Hwy (US-78), 6 miles west of town.

Visitor centre Near campus at 280 E Dougherty St (Mon–Sat 10am–5pm, Sun noon–5pm; ☎706 353 1820, ⊛athenswelcomecenter.com).

Tours The visitor centre has details of tours covering everything from historic buildings to music heritage.

Listings For full what's-on listings, check the free weekly *Flagpole* (⊛flagpole.com).

ACCOMMODATION

Foundry Park Inn & Spa 295 E Dougherty St ☎706 549 7020, ⊛foundryparkinn.com. Spanning out from a nineteenth-century ironworks foundry (the university's iconic entry arch was cast here) the campus of this spacious hotel also includes the 1829 *Hoyt House* restaurant, a fitness centre, pool and the enjoyable *Melting Point* music venue (see below). Guest quarters have a country cottage look. **$120**

Hotel Indigo 500 College Ave ☎706 546 0430, ⊛indigoathens.com. Restorative, hip hotel within walking distance of all the shops and restaurants of downtown. The contemporary guestrooms are decked out with picture windows, pale wood furniture and modish shag rugs. Good restaurant, bar and café onsite, too. **$130**

EATING

Last Resort 174–184 W Clayton St ☎706 549 0810, ⊛lastresortgrill.com. Emblazoned with a lovely turnip and radish mural, this bustling New Southern bistro with scuffed floors, café tables and art-strewn walls dishes up delicious, affordable food including fried green tomatoes with bacon-vidalia dressing ($5.50) and black bean burgers with guacamole ($7). Don't skip dessert. Mon–Thurs & Sun 5–10pm, Fri & Sat 5–11pm.

Mama's Boy 197 Oak St, a mile east of downtown ☎706 548 6249, ⊛eatatmamasboy.com. The plain, unpromising exterior of this tiny breakfast-all-day favourite belies an interior of black and turquoise wallpaper and eye-catching chandeliers, one made out of mismatched mason jars. Head here for strawberry lemonade ($3) and biscuits topped with sausage-thyme gravy ($7). Daily 7am–3.30pm.

The National 232 W Hancock St ☎706 549 3450, ⊛thenationalrestaurant.com. Athens's foodie concourse, reborn from an old tyre plant (of all things) as a stylish Mediterranean restaurant with pressed tin ceilings, dainty framed prints and whitewashed walls. The "dinner and a movie" combo (Mon & Tues only; $29), is a fun way to experience the first-rate menu, and includes a ticket to Cine, the city's arthouse cinema. Mon–Thurs 11.30am–10pm, Fri & Sat 11.30am–late, Sun 5–10pm.

Weaver D's 1016 E Broad St ☎706 353 7797. R.E.M. fans head straight for this soul food café, whose motto, "Automatic for the People", inspired the band's 1992 album. A short walk east of downtown, it serves delicious fried chicken and veggies. Mon–Sat 7.30am–6pm.

DRINKING AND NIGHTLIFE

40 Watt Club 285 W Washington St ☎706 549 7871, ⊛40watt.com. You'll want to catch some live music in Athens. R.E.M. started out at this eclectic, now legendary rock venue, though it has moved from its original location. Check online for performance times.

Georgia Theatre 215 N Lumpkin St ☎706 850 7670, ⊛georgiatheatre.com. Rebuilt after a 2009 fire, this lovely old cinema is one of Athens's top music venues, and also sports a great rooftop bar. Check online for performance times.

The Melting Point 285 W Washington St, in the Foundry Park Inn ☎706 254 6909, ⊛meltingpointathens.com. Located in the *Foundry Park Inn* (see above), this handsome nineteenth-century building is an intimate venue for Americana and roots bands. Check online for performance times.

Trappeze Pub 269 N Hull St, Suite #6 ☎706 543 8997, ⊛trappezepub.com. Athens has a great beer scene, best experienced at this artisanal bar and restaurant which stocks a huge range of stouts, lagers, ales and ciders. Grab a barstool and order one of the excellent pints produced by

Terrapin, the city's local brewery. Mon–Sat 11am–2am, Sun 11am–midnight.

The World Famous 351 N Hull St ☎ 706 543 4002, ⓦ theworldfamousathens.com. Just down the block from *Trapeze* (see opposite). Start your night at the latter, then mosey on down to catch a show at this retro bar with great live music, fun cocktails, pinball machines and delicious comfort food such as chicken and waffle sandwiches ($9) and tofu lettuce wraps ($8). Mon–Sat noon–2am, Sun 3pm–midnight.

Macon

MACON (rhymes with "Bacon"), set along the **Ocmulgee River** eighty miles southeast of Atlanta, makes an attractive stop en route to Savannah, especially when its 300,000 **cherry trees** erupt with frothy blossoms, celebrated by a ten-day festival in March. Founded in 1823, and once a major cotton port, this sleepy place is permeated with music history: home to **Little Richard**, **Otis Redding** and the **Allman Brothers**, it was also where **James Brown** recorded his first smash, the epoch-making *Please Please Please*, in an unlikely-looking antebellum mansion at 830 Mulberry St. Otis is commemorated by a bronze statue beside the Otis Redding Memorial Bridge. Duane Allman and Berry Oakley, killed here in motorcycle smashes in 1971 and 1972 respectively, are buried in **Rose Hill Cemetery** on Riverside Drive, the inspiration for several of the band's songs.

Cherry Street, which looks little changed since Otis Redding's day, is downtown's main commercial strip.

Tubman African American Museum

340 Walnut St • Tues–Fri 9am–5pm, Sat 11am–5pm • $8 • ☎ 478 743 8544, ⓦ tubmanmuseum.com

The **Tubman African American Museum**, named for Underground Railroad leader Harriet Tubman, is dedicated to African American arts, culture and history. Exhibits range from African drums and textiles through to intricate quilts and dazzling avant-garde work. At press time, the museum had broken ground on a new facility, five times its current size, set to open on nearby Cherry Street in 2014.

Ocmulgee National Monument

1207 Emery Hwy • Daily 9am–5pm • Free • ☎ 478 752 8257, ⓦ nps.gov/ocmu

Between 900 and 1100 AD, a Native American group migrated from the Mississippi Valley to a spot overlooking the Ocmulgee River a couple of miles east of modern downtown Macon, where they levelled the site that is now **Ocmulgee National Monument**. Their settlement of thatched huts has vanished, though two grassy mounds, each thought to have been topped by a temple, still rise from the plateau. Near the visitor centre, you can enter the underground chamber of a ceremonial **earthlodge**, the clay floor of which holds a ring of moulded seats and a striking bird-shaped altar.

ARRIVAL, INFORMATION AND TOURS

MACON

By bus Greyhound (☎ 478 743 5411) pulls into town at 65 Spring St.

Visitor centre 450 Martin Luther King Jr Blvd (Mon–Sat 10am–5pm; ☎ 478 743 1074, ⓦ maconga.org).

Rock Candy Tours Created by a confectioner and the daughter of one of Capricorn Record's co-founders (the masterminds behind the Allman Brothers), this tour outfit offers music history walks imbued with incredible personal stories ($10; ☎ 478 955 5997, ⓦ rockcandytours.com).

ACCOMMODATION, EATING AND DRINKING

1842 Inn 353 College St ☎ 877 452 6599, ⓦ 1842inn .com. Though the interstate chains are cheaper, it's nicer to stay downtown. This luxurious antebellum inn offers a full Southern breakfast in its lovely courtyard. $189

★ **Dovetail** 543 Cherry St ☎ 478 238 4693, ⓦ dovetail macon.com. For a superb farm-to-table meal, head up a flight of stairs to this voguish gem, where you can eat in a barn-like dining room strung with Edison bulbs. Tues–Thurs 5.30–10pm, Fri & Sat 5.30–11pm.

Fountain of Juice 3045 Vineville Ave, 3 miles east of town ☎ 478 755 5000, ⓦ fountainofjuice.it. Fresh wraps and grilled sandwiches, crammed with creative fixings like bacon, Brie, lettuce and tomato ($8) and roast salmon with lemon aioli ($8). Great juice menu, too. Mon–Fri

11am–5pm, Sat 11am–3pm.

Grant's Lounge 576 Poplar St ☎ 478 746 9191, ⓦ grantslounge.com. For a living, breathing, whiskey-swilling piece of Southern rock history, head to this downtown dive bar and live music venue where the Allman Brothers and Lynyrd Skynyrd got their start. Tues–Sun 5pm–2am.

The Rookery 543 Cherry St ☎ 478 746 8658, ⓦ rookery macon.com. Dimly lit burger joint where the walls are covered in patrons' scribbles and meals are served in ancient wooden booths. Try the Jimmy Carter burger,

topped with peanut butter and bacon ($9.50) and wash it down with a pineapple upside-down shake ($5). Top-notch beer selection, too. Mon 11am–3pm, Tues–Thurs 11am–9.30pm, Fri & Sat 11am–10pm, Sun 11.30am–9.30pm.

Whistle Stop Café 443 McCrackin St in Juliette, 20 miles north of Macon ☎ 478 992 8886, ⓦ thewhistle stopcafe.com. This weathered clapboard restaurant, by the old railroad tracks, dishes up the (delicious) fried green tomatoes of book and film fame to a friendly Southern crowd straight out of Central Casting. Mon–Fri & Sun 11am–4pm, Sat 11am–8pm.

SHOPPING

Dreams to Remember 339 Cotton Ave ☎ 478 742 5737, ⓦ otisredding.com. Overseen by Otis Redding's daughter, this shop and mini-museum, open weekdays

only, sells a nice line in King of Soul memorabilia. Mon–Thurs 11am–5pm, Fri 1–5pm.

Savannah

American towns don't come much more beautiful than **SAVANNAH**, seventeen miles up the Savannah River from the ocean. The ravishing **historic district**, arranged around Spanish-moss-swathed garden squares, formed the core of the original city and boasts examples of just about every architectural style of the eighteenth and nineteenth centuries, while the cobbled **waterfront** on the Savannah River is edged by towering old cotton warehouses. Savannah's **historic district** is flanked by the river to the north, Martin Luther King Jr Boulevard to the west, Gaston Street to the south and Broad Street – which has long been replaced by the appealingly retro Broughton Street as downtown's main commercial thoroughfare – to the east. The main draw here is in wandering the side streets and admiring the shuttered Federal, Regency and antebellum houses, embellished with intricate iron balconies. More than twenty residential **squares**, shaded by canopies of ancient live oaks and ablaze with dogwood trees, azaleas and creamy magnolias, offer peaceful respite from the blistering summer heat, while subtropical **greenery** creeps its way through the ornate railings, cracks open the streets, casts cool shadows and fills the air with its warm, sensual fragrance.

Brief history

Savannah was founded in 1733 by **James Oglethorpe** as the first settlement of the new British colony of Georgia. His intention was to establish a haven for debtors, with no Catholics, lawyers or hard liquor – and, above all, no slaves. However, with the arrival of North Carolina settlers in the 1750s, plantation agriculture, based on slave labour, thrived. The town became a major export centre, at the end of important railroad lines by which **cotton** was funnelled from far away in the South. Sherman arrived here in December 1864 at the end of his March to the Sea; he offered the town to Abraham Lincoln as a Christmas gift, but at Lincoln's urging left it intact and set to work apportioning land to freed slaves. This was the first recognition of the need for "reconstruction", though such concrete economic provision for ex-slaves was rarely to occur again. After the Civil War, the plantations floundered, cotton prices slumped and Savannah went into decline. Not until the 1960s did local citizens start to organize what has been the successful restoration of their town. In the last three decades, the private **Savannah College of Art and Design** (SCAD) has injected even more vitality, attracting young artists and regenerating downtown by buying up a number of wonderful old buildings. Today it's a prosperous, relaxed place, more raffish than Charleston, less rowdy than New Orleans, but sharing their faded, melancholy beauty. Savannah acquired notoriety in the mid-1990s thanks to its starring role in John Berendt's est-selling *Midnight in the Garden of Good and Evil*; a compelling mix of cross-dressing, voodoo and murder that sums up this rather louche, very lovable place to a tee.

Cathedral of St John the Baptist

222 E Harris St • Daily 9am–5pm • Free • ☎ 912 233 4709, ⓦ savannahcathedral.org

The **Cathedral of St John the Baptist** is Savannah's pride and joy. Inside, 66ft-high ceilings soar dramatically, framing the organ's medallion-shaped stained-glass window and accenting the structure's exquisite ceiling murals. The towers of the French Gothic exterior, which dates from 1873, hold a mighty 4000lb steeple bell.

6

● ACCOMMODATION		● RESTAURANTS		Mrs. Wilkes'	7	● SHOPPING	
395 Inn	3	Back in the Day Bakery	9	The Olde Pink House	2	Savannah Bee	
zalea Inn	6	Gallery Espresso	5	Wiley's Championship BBQ	1	Company	1
ed and Breakfast Inn	5	Green Truck Pub	10				
arshall House	2	Gryphon Tea Room	6	■ BARS & LIVE MUSIC VENUES			
anters Inn	1	Lady and Sons	3	Hang Fire	2		
aunderbird Inn	4	Leopold's Ice Cream	4	Jazz'd Tapas Bar	3		
		Local 11 Ten	8	The Jinx	1		

6

House Museums
Most visitors take in a few **mansion tours**. The **Green-Meldrim House**, on Madison Square (Tues, Thurs & Fri 10am–3.30pm, Sat 10am–12.30pm; $8; ☎912 232 1251, ⓦstjohnsav.org), is the Gothic Revival mansion that General Sherman used as his headquarters. Its ironwork is a rare example of pre-Civil War craftsmanship; most iron in Savannah was melted down during the conflict. Literature fans will appreciate the **Flannery O'Connor Childhood Home** at 207 E Charlton St (daily except Thurs 1–4pm; $6; ☎912 233 6014, ⓦflanneryoconnorhome.org), where the legendary Southern Gothic writer lived from her birth in 1925 until 1938.

Massie Heritage Center
207 E Gordon St • Mon–Sat 10am–4pm, Sun noon–4pm • $7 • ⓦ massieschool.com

At the southern edge of the historic district, on Calhoun Square, the **Massie Heritage Center** is housed in Savannah's first public school. Today it's a simple, effective museum, illuminating Savannah's architecture with displays on its city plan, its neighbourhoods and its growth, and tracing influences from as far away as London and Egypt.

Telfair Museum of Art
Telfair Academy 121 Barnard St • $12 • Mon noon–5pm, Tues–Sat 10am–5pm, Sun 1–5pm **Jepson Centre** 207 W York St • Mon & Sun noon–5pm, Tues, Wed, Fri & Sat 10am–5pm, Thurs 10am–8pm • $12 **Owens-Thomas House** 124 Abercorn St • Mon noon–5pm, Tues–Sat 10am–5pm, Sun 1–5pm • $20 for entry to all three • ☎ 912 790 8800, ⓦ telfair.org

The **Telfair Academy**, a Regency mansion designed by English architect William Jay, forms the original core of the venerable **Telfair Museum of Art**, which now spreads across three sites. Its collection of nineteenth- and twentieth-century American and European art is missable (though it is nice to catch a glimpse of the wistful *Bird Girl*, moved here from Bonaventure Cemetery after being depicted on the cover of *Midnight in the Garden of Good and Evil*). More interesting are the Telfair's **Jepson Centre**, also on Telfair Square – a deliciously cool, light and airy modern structure that hosts changing contemporary exhibitions from photography to sculpture – and the **Owens-Thomas House** – designed by Jay when he was just 23. Tours here tell the history of the town through the history of the Regency-influenced building, which, rather than being all gussied up, reveals fascinating glimpses of its structure and workings.

The waterfront
Though the city squares are redolent of the Old South, Savannah's **waterfront**, at the foot of a steep little bluff below Bay Street and reached by assorted stone staircases and alleyways, resembles more an eighteenth-century European port and offers a rare evocation of early America. The main thoroughfare, River Street, loomed over by five-storey brick cotton warehouses, is cobbled with the ballast carried by long-vanished sailing ships. It's now a touristy stretch, lined with seafood restaurants and salty bars filled with partying crowds, but well worth a stroll.

First African Baptist Church
23 Montgomery St • Tues–Sat 11am & 2pm • $7 • ☎ 912 233 6597, ⓦ firstafricanbc.com

The 1775 **First African Baptist Church** is one of the oldest black churches in North America, built by slaves. The superbly informative tours point out the tribal carvings on the sides of the pews upstairs, and, downstairs, the diamond shapes made by holes in the floor – ventilation for slaves hiding in the 4ft subterranean crawl spaces while waiting to escape to safe havens via the Underground Railroad.

Ships of the Sea Maritime Museum
41 Martin Luther King Jr Blvd • Tues–Sun 10am–5pm • $8.50 • ☎ 912 232 1511, ⓦ shipsofthesea.org

Savannah's diverting little **Ships of the Sea Maritime Museum**, on the northwestern edge of the historic district, features painstakingly constructed ship models, beautifully displayed in glass and mahogany cases, scrimshaw, figureheads and other maritime art, all housed in a stunning 1819 Greek Revival mansion.

SCAD Museum of Art

601 Turner Blvd • Tues, Wed & Fri 10am–5pm, Thurs 10am–8pm, Sat & Sun noon–5pm • $10 • ☎ 912 525 7191, ⊕ scadmoa.org

Though not as compelling as the Telfair museums (see opposite), the contemporary works at sleek, small the **SCAD museum of art**, administered by the Savannah College of Art and Design, are worth a look, particularly the vibrant pieces of the African American collection and the glittery designs in the fashion gallery, named after *Vogue* icon André Leon Talley.

6

ARRIVAL AND DEPARTURE

By plane Savannah's airport (☎ 912 964 0514, ⊕ savannahairport.com) is 9 miles west of the city; a taxi to downtown costs around $28.

By bus The Greyhound bus station (☎ 912 232 2135)

is on the western edge of downtown at 610 W Oglethorpe Ave.

By train Amtrak trains pull in about 3 miles southwest of downtown, at 2611 Seaboard Coastline Drive.

GETTING AROUND, INFORMATION AND TOURS

By shuttle bus The historic district is best explored on foot, though Chatham Area Transit (CAT; ☎ 912 233 5767, ⊕ catchacat.org) operates the free CAT Shuttle service between downtown, the visitor centre, the waterfront and City Market, and a number of buses for destinations further afield ($1.50).

Visitor centre 301 Martin Luther King Jr Blvd (Mon–Fri 8.30am–5pm, Sat & Sun 9am–5pm; ☎ 912 944 0455, ⊕ visitsavannah.com). There's another small information office at River St on the waterfront (daily: Jan & Feb 9am–6pm; March–Dec 9am–8pm; ☎ 912 651 6662).

Tours The visitor centre has details of countless walking tours, and serves as the starting point for several different trolley tours (from around $20). Relaxing horse-and-carriage tours set off from the *Hyatt Regency*, next to City Hall on W Bay St ($20; ☎ 912 443 9333, ⊕ savannahcarriage.com), and you can buy tickets for lazy riverboat cruises at 9 E River St ($21.95; ☎ 800 786 6404, ⊕ savannahriverboat.com). Savannah Dan ($20; ☎ 912 398 3777, ⊕ savannahdan.com), sports full Southern regalia – seersucker suit, Panama hat and bow tie – when giving his superlative, no-nonsense walking tours of the historic district.

ACCOMMODATION

Ideally, you should budget to stay in the **historic district**, which is packed with gorgeous B&Bs and a few nice hotels. The usual chain **motels** can be found near the Greyhound station and further out on Ogeechee Road (US-17).

1895 Inn 126 E Oglethorpe Ave ☎ 912 231 8822, ⊕ the1895inn.net. Filled with art and antiques, this luxurious four-room B&B, in the heart of the historic district, is prevented from feeling stuffy by the friendliness of hosts Rob and Ed, who do everything to create a home away from home. Delicious breakfasts. **$175**

★ **Azalea Inn** 217 E Huntingdon St ☎ 912 236 080, ⊕ azaleainn.com. Charming, laidback B&B in a nineteenth-century mansion at the edge of the historic district near Forsyth Park, complete with adorable Yorkies, en bright, delightfully furnished rooms and a very welcome pool. Superb Southern breakfasts are served daily. **$225**

Bed and Breakfast Inn 117 W Gordon St ☎ 912 238 518, ⊕ savannahbnb.com. Great-value B&B with a variety of rooms in two 1853 townhouses and some carriage houses, on shady Chatham Square. **$159**

Marshall House 123 E Broughton St ☎ 912 644 7896, ⊕ marshallhouse.com. Savannah's oldest hotel, dating from 1851, is located on its hippest street. It was once a hospital for Civil War soldiers, but its rooms are decidedly plusher nowadays, with traditional decor, soft robes and a breakfast buffet. **$150**

Planters Inn 29 Abercorn St ☎ 800 544 1187, ⊕ plantersinnsavannah.com. A formal, welcoming, hotel rather than a B&B, in a lovely position in the historic district. Added perks include a nightly turndown service, wine and cheese hour and hand-delivered breakfasts. The excellent *Olde Pink House* restaurant (see p.428) is next door. **$125**

Thunderbird Inn 611 W Oglethorpe ☎ 866 324 2661, ⊕ thethunderbirdinn.com. Quirky vintage motel with retro fittings, opposite the Greyhound station. Free popcorn, Krispy Kremes and Moon Pies included. Very pet-friendly (they even have their own dog run). **$80**

EATING

Savannah has a lot of restaurants. City Market – four blocks of restored grain warehouses a few blocks back from the river – is downtown's prime dining and nightlife district; restaurants on the historic district squares are a little classier. Bustling Broughton Street also has a number of options, many of them in lovely restored Deco buildings.

Back in the Day Bakery 2403 Bull St, 2 miles south of downtown ☎912 495 9292, ⚲backinthedaybakery .com. Baby-blue, artisanal bakery with tempting trays of moist red velvet cupcakes and coconut macaroons, plus savoury treats such as the *jambon royal* panini, light lunches and espresso drinks. Tues–Sat 8am–5pm.

Gallery Espresso 234 Bull St ☎912 233 5348, ⚲galleryespresso.com. Overlooking verdant Chippewa Square, this slightly scruffy coffee shop has thrift-store decor, stout mugs of coffee and a community vibe. Mon–Fri 7.30am–10pm, Sat & Sun 8am–10pm.

Green Truck Pub 2430 Habersham St, 3 miles south of downtown ☎912 234 5885, ⚲greentruckpub.com. There are always queues for this venerable burger and fries joint that locally sources all its ingredients and makes everything – down to the delectable ketchup – from scratch. Tues–Sat 11am–11pm.

Gryphon Tea Room 337 Bull St ☎912 525 5880. There's a nice mix of art students, lecturers and ladies-that-lunch in this modish tearoom, housed in an old pharmacy with its original counter and a stunning stained-glass ceiling. Hundreds of special teas, genteel gourmet lunches and mouth-watering cakes; high tea is served throughout the day. Mon–Sat 11am–6pm.

Lady and Sons 102 W Congress St ☎912 233 2600, ⚲ladyandsons.com. The Southern restaurant of disgraced celebrity chef Paula Deen, who caused a media backlash in 2013 for using racial slurs, no longer sees queues around the block, but is still popular for its fried chicken and veg buffets ($15.99 lunch, $17.99 dinner), and à la carte dishes (crab cakes, chicken pot pie, fried green tomatoes and the like). Mon–Thurs 11am–9pm, Fri & Sat 11am–10pm, Sun 11am–5pm.

★ **Leopold's Ice Cream** 212 E Broughton St ☎912 234 4442, ⚲leopoldsicecream.com. Hollywood producer Stratton Leopold has revamped his family's traditional ice cream parlour, originally opened in 1919, and serves home-made ices, plus a full menu of sandwiches, salads and burgers. Mon–Thurs & Sun 11am–11pm, Fri & Sat 11am–midnight.

Local 11 Ten 1110 Bull St ☎912 790 9000, ⚲local 11ten.com. A hip, buzzy interpretation of Low Country, French and Italian food (pastas are made from scratch), with a small, seasonal menu using the freshest local ingredients and a thorough wine list. Daily 6–10pm.

★ **Mrs Wilkes'** 107 W Jones St ☎912 232 5997, ⚲mrswilkes.com. This local institution offers a real Southern experience, serving all-you-can-eat lunches for $18. Diners sit around communal tables helping themselves to delicious mounds of fried chicken, sweet potatoes, spinach, beans and pickled beets. There's no sign and no reservations; arrive early and join the line. Cash only. Mon–Fri 11am–2pm.

★ **The Olde Pink House** 23 Abercorn St ☎912 232 4286. With its pink Regency facade and effortlessly elegant upstairs dining room, the romantic *Pink House* is perfect for relaxed, special-occasion dining. You can also order its delicious Low Country food – crispy scored flounder, she-crab soup, Southern "sushi" – in the cheery, high-spirited tavern downstairs. Mon & Sun 5–10.30pm, Tues–Thurs 11am–10.30pm, Fri & Sat 11am–11pm.

Wiley's Championship BBQ 4700 Hwy-80, 7 miles east of downtown ☎912 201 3259, ⚲wileyschampionship bbq.com. On the way to Tybee Island, this tiny barbecue hut serves succulent ribs and pulled pork with devilishly good sides like sweet potato casserole and mac and cheese. Mon–Thur 11am–3pm & 5–8pm, Fri & Sat 11am–3pm & 5–9pm.

ENTERTAINMENT AND NIGHTLIFE

Savannah's nightlife is decidedly laidback, given energy by its large student population. Almost uniquely in the US (New Orleans is another exception) you can drink **alcohol** on the streets in open cups. For **listings**, pick up the free weekly *Connect* newspaper (⚲connectsavannah.com). **St Patrick's Day** (March 17) is a big deal in Savannah, with its large Irish population. Around a million visitors descend here to guzzle copious amounts of Guinness; many residents choose the weekend to leave town.

Hang Fire 37 Whitaker St ☎912 443 9956. A friendly, refreshingly ungrungy, little hipster bar downtown, where PBR flows freely and folk art lines the walls. It gets packed in the wee hours with a jovial 20- and 30-something crowd. Occasional DJs. Mon–Sat 5pm–3am.

Jazz'd Tapas Bar 52 Barnard St ☎912 236 7777, ⚲jazzdsavannah.com. Industrialist decor meets splashy folk art cheer at this buzzy basement martini bar/

restaurant, which has live, no-cover jazz or blues (Tues–Sun). The "tapas" (think Southern-style appetizer plates) are tasty and inexpensive. Mon–Thurs & Sun 4–10pm, Fri & Sat 4pm–midnight.

The Jinx 127 W Congress St (the sign says Velvet Elvis) ☎912 236 2281. Savannah's premier rock club, in City Market, which also puts on rock'n'roll bingo, karaoke and dance nights. Mon–Sat 4pm–3am.

SHOPPING

Savannah Bee Company 104 W Broughton St ☎912 233 7873, ⓦsavannahbee.com. No visit to Savannah would be complete without a trip to this honey purveyor's flagship store. There's a buffet of free samples and great gifts for lucky friends back home. Mon–Sat 10am–7pm, Sun 11am–5pm.

Brunswick

BRUNSWICK, the one sizeable settlement south of Savannah, is a hop-off point for the offshore **Golden Isles**. The town in itself is industrial, though there's a lovely old-fashioned downtown, and the shrimp docks can be quite interesting when the catch is brought in. To get a taste of local fishing culture, head out on a two-hour cruise with the *Lady Jane* ($40; ☎912 265 5711, ⓦshrimpcruise.com), a commercial shrimp trawler that's been outfitted for educational tours. Winding lazily among the creeks, you'll spot oyster beds and watch fiddler crabs skittering onshore. Up on deck, the crew catches and releases rays, horseshoe crabs, even rare sea turtles, while a biologist interprets everything to passengers. The best part, however, is when a trove of shrimp is hauled in and cooked right in front of you – some of the freshest crustaceans you'll ever lay your hands on. The whole experience is a Georgia coast must-do, especially if you're travelling with kids.

ACCOMMODATION AND EATING   BRUNSWICK

★ **Hostel in the Forest** Hwy-82, 10 miles west of Brunswick ☎912 264 9738, ⓦforesthostel.com. Reached via a muddy driveway, for $25 a person (three nights max; no credit cards) you'll get a rustic room in one of nine treehouses and a communal vegetarian dinner. Guests are expected to perform a small daily chore. **$25**

Indigo Coastal Shanty 1402 Reynolds St ☎912 265 2007, ⓦindigocoastalshanty.com. The worldly menu of this unassuming local café riffs on everything from Southern classics to Caribbean curries and Mexican sandwiches; try the jerk chicken with pineapple salsa ($10) or sample fresh local shrimp with a bowl of fisherman's soup ($11.50). Tues–Fri 11am–3pm, Fri & Sat 5–9pm.

The Golden Isles

Patterned with briny marshes, massive oak trees and perfect beaches, the **Golden Isles** make an appealing seashore break destination for inlanders. Comprised of a string of barrier islands linked by causeways, this idyllic retreat has great restaurants and a mellow pace.

Jekyll Island

A few miles south of Brunswick, **Jekyll Island** (reached by $6 toll road) was originally bought in 1887 for use as an exclusive "club" by a group of millionaires including the Rockefellers, the Pulitzers, the Macys and the Vanderbilts. Their opulent residences, known as "cottages", are still standing, surrounded by natural habitats that are legislated to remain forever wild. A small **Welcome Center** stands on the causeway (daily 9am–5pm; ☎912 635 3636, ⓦjekyllisland.com); the **Jekyll Island Museum**, in the old club stables on Stable Road (free; daily 9am–5pm) provides a good overview of the island's history and runs seasonally changing tours (daily 11am, 1pm & 3pm; $16). The island's tiny historic district centres on the rambling old original club building, which, as the *Jekyll Island Club Hotel*, now offers elegant **accommodation** (see p.430).

More than half of Jekyll Island is undeveloped, and activities including biking, swimming and horseback riding abound.

St Simons Island

Most of **St Simons Island**, reached via a causeway across a green marsh inhabited by wading birds, is still an evocative landscape of palms and live oaks covered with Spanish moss. The village is pleasantly quiet and the nearby beach is nice for **swimming** and strolling. Southeast Adventure Outfitters, 313 Mallory St (☎912 638 6732, ⓦsoutheastadventure.com), rents **kayaks** and runs bird- and dolphin-watching tours. **Fort Frederica National Monument**, five miles north of the causeway (daily 9am–5pm; $3; ☎912 638 3639, ⓦnps.gov/fofr), was built by General Oglethorpe in 1736 as the largest British fort in North America; it's now an atmospheric ruin.

Cumberland Island

To the south of St Simon's Island, **Cumberland Island** (☎912 882 4336, ⓦnps.gov/cuis) is a stunning wildlife refuge of marshes, beaches and semitropical forest roamed by wild horses, with the odd deserted planter's mansion. You can get here by ferry (see below) from the village of **St Mary's**, back on the mainland near the Florida border.

ARRIVAL AND DEPARTURE	THE GOLDEN ISLES
By car Jekyll and St Simons islands are easily reached by causeways; Jekyll Island has a $6 entrance fee ($28/week), while St Simons is free to visit.	**By ferry** Cumberland Island is only accessible by a 45min ferry, which docks in the town of St Mary's ($20; ☎877 860 6787, ⓦstmaryswelcome.com).

ACCOMMODATION AND EATING

Crabdaddy's 1217 Ocean Blvd, St Simons ☎912 634 1120, ⓦcrabdaddyseafood.com. Upmarket seafood restaurant with a casual ambience. Steak lovers will be well pleased with the Angus in coriander cream sauce ($25); shrimp and grits are another favourite. Reservations recommended. Daily 5–10pm.

Jekyll Island Club Hotel 371 Riverview Drive, Jekyll Island ☎855 535 9547, ⓦjekyllclub.com. Dating from 1888, this historic hotel, once the summer stomping ground of the country's elite, is now an expansive waterfront resort with rooms set in dignified old mansions and a huge turreted Victorian. **$210**

★ **Southern Soul Barbeque** 2020 Demere Rd, St Simons ☎912 638 7685, ⓦsouthernsoulbbq.com. Certainly the island's – and arguably the state's – best barbecue, fired up by hip, tattooed servers in a refurbished vintage petrol station. Seating is limited, but it's fun combining parties at the communal picnic tables. Mon–Sat 11am–10pm, Sun 11am–4pm.

Village Inn 500 Mallery St, St Simons ☎912 634 6056, ⓦvillageinnandpub.com. In the heart of St Simons, this 28-room inn has the welcoming ambience of a B&B but the quiet and seclusion of a boutique hotel. Densely shaded by towering live oaks, the property was endearingly constructed so that not one branch of these century-old trees would be broken or damaged. **$125**

Okefenokee Swamp

Hwy-177 off US-23/1 • Daily 9am–5.30pm • $15 • ☎912 283 0583, ⓦokeswamp.com

The dense **Okefenokee Swamp** stretches 684 square miles from a point roughly thirty miles southwest of Brunswick. Tucked away in its astonishing profusion of luxuriant plants and trees are some 20,000 alligators and more than thirty species of snake, as well as bears and pumas. You can enter at the **Okefenokee Swamp Park**, a private charity-owned concession at the northeast tip (Fargo and Folkston are the reserve's other access points). Admission grants access to a wildlife interpretive centre, observation tower and reconstructed pioneer buildings; $25 extra will get you **boat tours** through the swamp (slick yourself with bug repellent).

Kentucky

Both of the rival presidents during the Civil War, Abraham Lincoln and Jefferson Davis, were born in **KENTUCKY**, where acute divisions existed between slave-owning farmers and the merchants who depended on trade with the nearby cities of the industrial North. While the state remained officially neutral, more Kentuckians joined the Union army than the Confederates; after the war, however, Kentucky sided with the South in its hostility to Reconstruction and has tended to follow southern political trends.

Kentucky's rugged beauty is at its most appealing in the mountainous **east**, which suffers from acute rural poverty but boasts the fine scenery of the **Natural Bridge** and **Cumberland Gap** regions. Perhaps the most iconic area of the state is the **Bluegrass Downs**, home to bluegrass, bourbon and thoroughbred horses. The name comes from the unique steel-blue sheen of the buds in the meadows, only visible in early morning during April and May. The area centres on the reserved state capital **Lexington**, a major horse-breeding market, and holds some of the oldest towns west of the Alleghenies.

Hipper **Louisville**, however, home of the **Kentucky Derby**, lies eighty miles west and offers more reasons to linger. It is also a good access point to the bourbon country around **Bardstown**. Rural western Kentucky, where the Ohio River meets the Mississippi, is flat, heavily forested and generally less attractive. Meanwhile, in the **southern** hinterland, numerous small towns retain their tree-shaded squares and nineteenth-century townhouses – and their strict Baptist beliefs – while the endless caverns of **Mammoth Cave National Park** attract spelunkers and hikers in the thousands.

Lexington

Although the lack of a navigable river has always made its traders vulnerable to competition from Louisville, the productivity of the **bluegrass** fields has kept **LEXINGTON**'s economy ticking over since 1775, especially after its emergence as the world's largest **burley tobacco** market following World War I. However, its most conspicuous activity these days is the **horse** trade, with an estimated 450 farms in the vicinity. The glass office blocks, skywalks and shopping malls of Lexington's city centre, set in a dip on the Bluegrass Downs, crowd in on fountain-filled **Triangle Park**.

University of Kentucky Art Museum

405 Rose St • Tues–Sun noon–5pm, Fri until 8pm • Free • ⓦ uky.edu/ArtMuseum

One of Lexington's few non-equine-related attractions is the **University of Kentucky Art Museum**, in the Singletary Center for the Arts, which has a good permanent collection of contemporary American art and Native American artefacts. There are also frequent special exhibitions of international works, for which there is usually a charge.

LEXINGTON'S HORSES

Along **Paris** and **Ironworks pikes**, northeast of Lexington in an idyllic Kentucky landscape, sleek thoroughbred horses cavort in bluegrass meadows, often penned in by immaculate white-plank fences. To the west, you can watch the horses' early-morning workouts at **Keeneland** racetrack, 4201 Versailles Rd (April–Oct daily dawn–10am; $5; ☎859 254 3412, ⓦ keeneland.com). Dark-green grandstands emphasize the crisp white rails around the one-mile oval track, where **meetings** are held for three weeks in April (Wed–Sun 7.30pm) and three weeks in Oct (Wed–Sun 1pm). General admission is $5 and seats cost $8–20. There is a great canteen too.

The easiest way to see a farm is to take a guided bus tour out of Lexington; **Blue Grass Tours** (daily 9am & 1.30pm; $35; ☎859 252 5744, ⓦ bluegrasstours.com) offer a three-hour, fifty-mile itinerary that includes a stop at **Old Friends Farm** (ⓦ oldfriendsequine.org), plus a visit to Keeneland. Another of the few farms conducting its own tours is **Three Chimneys** (Tues–Sat by appointment; $10; book on ☎859 873 7053, ⓦ threechimneys.com) on Old Frankfort Pike, about fifteen minutes west of downtown. The **Thoroughbred Center**, 3380 Paris Pike (9am: April–Oct Mon–Sat; Nov–March Mon–Fri; $10; ☎859 293 1853, ⓦ thethoroughbredcenter.com), allows you to watch trainers at work. The enjoyable 1032-acre **Kentucky Horse Park**, a little further along at 4089 Ironworks Parkway (mid-March to Oct daily 9am–5pm; Nov to mid-March Wed–Sun 9am–5pm; $10–16; ⓦ kyhorsepark.com), features more than thirty different equine breeds, a working farm and guided **horseback rides** ($25); its fascinating **International Museum of the Horse** traces the use of horses throughout history. In nearby Georgetown, at **Whispering Woods**, experienced equestrians can canter unsupervised, while novices ride with a guide ($25 for 1hr; ⓦ whisperingwoodstrails.com).

ARRIVAL AND INFORMATION

LEXINGTON

By plane Lexington's airport is 6 miles west of town on US-60 W.

By bus Greyhound drops off about a mile northeast from downtown at 477 New Circle Rd, opposite the local bus station (bus #3 goes downtown).

Destinations Cincinnati (4 daily; 1hr 25min); Louisville (2 daily; 1hr 20min); Nashville (5hr 35min–7hr 50min).

Visitor centre 301 E Vine St (Mon–Fri 8.30am–5pm, Sat 10am–5pm, plus Sun May–Aug noon–5pm; ☎ 859 233 7299, ⓦ visitlex.com). Another useful resource is the free *ACE Weekly* (ⓦ aceweekly.com).

ACCOMMODATION

Clarion Hotel 1950 Newtown Pike ☎ 800 424 6423, ⓦ clarionhotellex.com. Vast upscale chain franchise northeast of downtown, with smart rooms, an indoor swimming pool and gym plus bars and restaurants. $104

Gratz Park Inn 120 W Second St ☎ 859 231 1777, ⓦ gratzparkinn.com. Downtown's oldest and most prestigious hotel, with rooms decorated in nineteenth-century style and a gourmet restaurant. $179

Horse Park 4089 Ironworks Parkway ☎ 859 233 4303, ⓦ kyhorsepark.com. The best and nearest campground to downtown, which has fine shared facilities and offers campers discounts to the Horse Park itself (see box, p.431). $25

La Quinta 1919 Stanton Way, junction I-64 & I-75, exit 115 ☎ 859 231 7551, ⓦ lq.com. Handily placed motel with compact but comfortable rooms and free continental breakfast. $99

Swann's Nest B&B 3463 Rosalie Lane ☎ 859 226 0095, ⓦ swannsnest.com. An appealing rural retreat, offering five comfortable guest suites in a stately colonnaded mansion on a thoroughbred farm with expansive grounds. $129

EATING AND DRINKING

Lexington's large student population means it has a fair selection of places to eat besides the **steakhouses** catering to the horse crowd and conventioneers. The streets around the junction of Broadway and Main Street hold a few lively bars.

Alfalfa Restaurant 141 E Main St ☎ 859 253 0014, ⓦ alfalfarestaurant.com. Hippyish café featuring a wide range of international food, mostly under $10, with an emphasis on vegetarian dishes and famous buckwheat pancakes. Regular art exhibitions. Mon & Tues 11am–2pm, Wed–Fri 11am–2pm & 5.30–9pm, Sat 9am–2pm & 5.30–9pm, Sun 9am–2pm.

Atomic Café 265 N Limestone St ☎ 859 254 1969, ⓦ atomiccafeky.com. Fun Caribbean ambience, with good spicy main courses for around $15 and potent cocktails. Live reggae Fri & Sat and a pleasant outdoor space. Tues–Thurs 4pm–1am, Fri & Sat 4pm–2.30am.

Horse & Barrel 101 N Broadway ☎ 859 259 3771, ⓦ deshahs.com. Affiliated with and adjoining *deSha's* restaurant, this bar specializes in a range of quality bourbons. Mon–Thurs 5pm–midnight, Fri & Sat 5pm–1am.

Le Deauville 199 N Limestone St ☎ 859 246 0999, ⓦ ledeauvillebistro.com. Enjoy a touch of Paris at this delightful bistro with pavement seating. Dishes such as bouillabaisse Marseillaise or filet mignon cost around $30–35. Mon–Thurs 5.30–10pm, Fri & Sat 5.30pm–12.30am.

Ramsey's Diner 496 E High St ☎ 859 259 2708, ⓦ ramseysdiners.com. Very popular and atmospheric diner, with three other outlets around town, all serving tasty sandwiches, burgers and meals for $7–15. Mon–Fri 11am–11pm, Sat & Sun 9am–11pm.

Around Lexington: Bluegrass Country

Other than the horse farms directly to the north, most places of interest near Lexington lie southwards, including the fine old towns of Danville and Harrodsburg, the restored **Shaker Village of Pleasant Hill** and **Berea College**. After about forty miles, the meadows give way to the striking **Knobs** – random lumpy outcrops, shrouded in trees and wispy low-hanging clouds, that are the eroded remnants of the Pennyrile Plateau.

The Shaker Village of Pleasant Hill

The utopian settlement of the **Shaker Village of Pleasant Hill**, hidden among the bluegrass hillocks near Harrodsburg, 26 miles southwest of Lexington, was established by **Shaker missionaries** from New England around 1805. Within twenty years, nearly five hundred villagers here were producing seeds, tools and cloth for sale as far away as New Orleans. During the Civil War, the pacifist Shakers were obliged to billet Union and Confederate troops alike. Numbers declined until the last member died in 1923, but a nonprofit organization has since returned the village to its nineteenth-century appearance.

The Shaker values of celibacy (they maintained their numbers through conversion and adoption of orphans), hygiene, simplicity and communal ownership have left their mark on the 34 grey and pastel-coloured dwellings, which women and men entered via different doors. Visitors can watch demonstrations of traditional handicrafts including broom-making and weaving (daily: April–Oct 10am–5pm; $15; Nov–March 10am–4pm; $7).

ACCOMMODATION AND EATING | THE SHAKER VILLAGE OF PLEASANT HILL

★ **The Inn at Shaker Village** 3501 Lexington Rd, Harrodsburg ☎859 734 5411, ⓦshakervillageky.org. The delightfully restored on-site inn offers good-value rustic rooms and also houses a superb restaurant specializing in boiled ham, lemon pie and other Kentucky favourites. **$100**

6

Berea

BEREA, thirty miles south of Lexington, just off I-75 in the foothills where Bluegrass Country meets Appalachia, is home to unique **Berea College**, which gives its 1500 mainly local students free tuition in return for work in crafts ranging from needlework to wrought ironwork. It was founded in 1855 by abolitionists as a vocational college for the young people of East Kentucky – both white and black, making it for forty years the only integrated college in the South. **Tours** of the campus and student craft workshops leave from the sumptuous *Boone Tavern Inn* (see below).

The college's reputation has also attracted many private art and craft galleries to little Berea; for details on these and a chance to buy local goods, visit the **Kentucky Artisan Center** at exit 77 off I-75 (daily 8am–8pm; free; ⓦkentuckyartisancenter.ky.gov).

EATING AND DRINKING | BEREA

Boone Tavern Inn 100 Main St N ☎859 985 3700, ⓦboonetavernhotel.com. You can get a taste of college life at this student-run inn, which offers neat, colourful rooms and a high-quality restaurant. **$116**

Daniel Boone National Forest

Almost the entire length of Kentucky east of Lexington is taken up by the steep slopes, narrow valleys and sandstone cliffs of the unspoiled **Daniel Boone National Forest**. Few Americans can have been so mythologized as **Daniel Boone**, who first explored the region in 1767 and thus ranks as one of Kentucky's earliest fur-trapping pioneers. Sadly, Boone failed to legalize his land claims and was forced to press further west to Missouri, where he died in 1820 at the age of 86.

ACCOMMODATION | DANIEL BOONE NATIONAL FOREST

Twin Knobs 5195 Twin Knobs Campground Rd, Salt Lick ☎877 444 6777, ⓦreserveamerica.com. At the north end of the forest, this is a good campground, with decent facilities and a great setting near Cave Run Lake. Open mid-March to Nov. **$24**

Natural Bridge State Resort Park

2135 Natural Bridge Rd, Slade • Open access • Free, chairlift $7 return • ☎606 663 2214, ⓦparks.ky.gov

The geological extravaganza of the **Red River Gorge**, sixty miles east of Lexington via the Mountain Parkway, is best seen by driving a thirty-mile loop from the **Natural Bridge State Resort Park** on Hwy-77, near the village of Slade. Natural Bridge itself is a large sandstone arch surrounded by steep hollows and exposed clifflines; for those reluctant to negotiate the half-mile climb, there is a chairlift. The park also offers hiking trails, canoeing, fishing and rock climbing.

ACCOMMODATION | NATURAL BRIDGE STATE RESORT PARK

Hemlock Lodge Natural Bridge State Resort Park ☎800 255 7275, ⓦparks.ky.gov. Weekends can be reserved a year in advance at this excellent rustic lodge with comfortable rooms and great views, not far from the bridge itself. Info on the park's two campgrounds is also available. **$110**

6

THE ORIGINAL FRIED CHICKEN

In 1940, "Colonel" Harland Sanders, so titled as a member of the Honorable Order of Kentucky Colonels, opened a small clapboard diner, the *Sanders Café*, alongside his motel and petrol station in tiny **Corbin**, ninety miles south of Lexington on I-75. His **Kentucky Fried Chicken** empire has since spread all over the world. The original hundred-seat restaurant, at 688 US-25 W (daily 10am–10pm; ☎ 606 528 2163), has been restored with 1940s decor and an immense amount of memorabilia. The food served is the usual *KFC*, but it's an atmospheric little spot.

Cumberland Gap National Historic Park

On the tri-state border of Kentucky, Tennessee and Virginia, the **Cumberland Gap National Historic Park**, a natural passageway used by migrating deer and bison, served as a gateway to the West for Boone and other pioneers. **Pinnacle Overlook**, a 1000ft lookout over the three states, is the finest spot to admire the extensive vista of forest and hills.

Louisville

LOUISVILLE, just south of Indiana across the Ohio River, is firmly embedded in the American national consciousness for its multimillion-dollar **Kentucky Derby**. Each May, the horse race attracts more than half a million fans to this cosmopolitan industrial city, which still bears the traces of the early French settlers who came upriver from New Orleans. Louisville also produces a third of the country's **bourbon**.

Besides a vibrant arts and festivals scene, the city boasts an excellent network of public parks. One native son who took advantage of the recreation facilities was three-times world heavyweight boxing champion **Muhammad Ali**, who would do his early-morning training in the scenic environs of Chickasaw Park.

Downtown Louisville rolls gently toward Main Street, then abruptly lunges to the river. **Riverfront Plaza**, between Fifth and Sixth streets, is a prime observation point for the natural **Falls of the Ohio** on the opposite side of the river. The new Big Four Bridge, accessed via the Louisville Waterfront Park a mile or so further east allows pedestrian and cycle access to Indiana. Away from the river, the **Historic District** around Central Park, which straddles Fourth Street, contains the highest concentration of Victorian houses in the country.

Muhammad Ali Center

144 N Sixth St • Tues–Sat 9.30am–5pm, Sun noon–5pm • $9 • ☎ 502 584 9254, ⊛ alicenter.org

The town's star attraction is the excellent **Muhammad Ali Center**, beside the river, which, apart from chronicling the local hero's boxing career with entertaining multimedia displays, provides insight into his political activism and Muslim faith, refreshingly presented in a positive light.

Louisville Slugger Museum

800 W Main St • Mon–Sat 9am–5pm, Sun 11am–5pm • $11 • ☎ 877 775 8443, ⊛ sluggermuseum.com

Even non-baseball fans will be impressed by the **Louisville Slugger Museum**, which is actually the factory of the country's prime baseball bat manufacturer. The guided tour is full of information on the history and process of bat making. All visitors receive a souvenir miniature bat at the end. You can also try your batting skills by facing ten pitches for an extra dollar.

Frazier History Museum

829 W Main St • Mon–Sat 9am–5pm, Sun noon–5pm • $10.50 • ☎ 502 753 5663, ⊛ fraziermuseum.org

Spread over three mildly diverting floors, the permanent collection of the **Frazier History Museum** includes a surprising wealth of treasure from the UK armouries and lots of displays on US history, while another section houses rotating special exhibitions.

Kentucky Derby Museum

Next to Churchill Downs at 704 Central Ave • Mid-March to Nov Mon–Sat 8am–5pm, Sun 11–5pm; Dec to mid-March Mon–Sat 9am–5pm, Sun 11am–5pm • $14 • ⓦ derbymuseum.org

The excellent hands-on **Kentucky Derby Museum** will appeal to horseracing enthusiasts and neophytes alike. Admission includes a magnificent audiovisual display that captures the Derby Day atmosphere on a 360° screen; you can take a Behind the Scenes tour of the stables and racecourse for an extra $11.

ARRIVAL AND GETTING AROUND

By plane Most major US airlines fly into Louisville International Airport, 5 miles south on I-65; it's around a $20 cab fare into town.

By bus The Greyhound terminus is fairly central at 720 W Muhammad Ali Blvd.

Destinations Cincinnati (5 daily; 1hr 45min); Indianapolis (4 daily; 2hr 10min); Lexington (2 daily; 1hr 20min); Memphis (2 daily; 8hr 25min–10hr 35min); Nashville (3hr–3hr 15min).

By tram (trolley) Downtown, you can hop on a TARC trolley (Mon–Fri 7.30am–8pm/10pm, Sat 7.30am–6pm; 50¢; ⓦ ridetarc.org).

INFORMATION AND TOURS

Visitor centre Fourth and Jefferson sts (Mon–Sat 10am–6pm, Sun noon–5pm; ☎ 502 379 6109, ⓦ goto louisville.com); offers discounts on some of the attractions.

Boat tours In summer, two sternwheelers, the Belle of Louisville and the Spirit of Jefferson, conduct lunchtime and dinnertime cruises from the wharf at 401 W River Rd (schedules vary; from $21; ☎ 502 574 2992, ⓦ belleof louisville.org).

ACCOMMODATION

21C Museum Hotel 700 W Main St ☎ 502 217 6300, ⓦ 21cmuseumhotels.com. This boutique hotel has luxuriously classy rooms and also houses an art museum and top-notch restaurant. Look out for the red penguins dotted around the property. $279

Central Park B&B 1353 S Fourth St ☎ 502 638 1505, ⓦ centralparkbandb.com. Opulent Victorian B&B in the heart of the Historic District with six quaintly decorated rooms in the main building and a converted carriage house. $135

Econo Lodge 401 S Second St ☎ 502 583 2841, ⓦ econo lodge.com. About as cheap as you'll find right downtown.

Most rooms are simple but perfectly adequate, while the priciest have hot tubs. $75

Galt House 140 N Fourth St ☎ 502 589 5200, ⓦ galt house.com. The official hotel of the Kentucky Derby is a massive high-rise right on the riverfront, with spacious and well-appointed rooms and a range of top facilities. $165

Hampton Inn Downtown Louisville 101 E Jefferson St ☎ 502 585 2200, ⓦ louisvilledowntown .hamptoninn.com. Comfortable standard chain rooms plus free buffet breakfast, indoor pool and fitness centre. $169

EATING AND DRINKING

Cumberland Brewery 1576 Bardstown Rd ☎ 502 458 8727, ⓦ cumberlandbrewery.com. Welcoming microbrewery that makes fine ales, as well as decent appetizers, salads, sandwiches and Mexican items, all around $10 or less. Mon–Thurs 4pm–midnight, Fri & Sat noon–midnight, Sun 1pm–midnight.

★ **Mayan Café** 813 E Market St ☎ 502 566 0651, ⓦ themayancafe.com. Traditional Maya dishes, such as rabbit in a corn-ginger sauce and salmon in creamy Mexican mushroom sauce, are served in a bright dining room for $15–20. Mon–Thurs 11am–2.30pm & 5–10pm, Fri 11am–2.30pm & 5–10.30pm, Sat 5–10.30pm.

THE KENTUCKY DERBY

The **Kentucky Derby** is one of the world's premier horse races; it's also, as Hunter S. Thompson put it, "decadent and depraved". Derby Day itself is the first Saturday in May, at the end of the two-week **Kentucky Derby Festival**. Since 1875, the leading lights of Southern society have gathered at **Churchill Downs**, three miles south of downtown Louisville, for an orgy of betting, haute cuisine and mint juleps in the plush grandstand, while tens of thousands of the beer-guzzling proletariat cram into the infield. Apart from the $40 infield tickets available on the day – offering virtually no chance of a decent view – all seats are sold out months in advance. The actual race, traditionally preceded by a mass drunken rendition of My Old Kentucky Home, is run over a distance of one and a quarter miles, lasts barely two minutes and offers around a million dollars in prize money.

Ramsi's Café on the World 1293 Bardstown Rd ☎ 502 451 0700, ⍟ramsiscafe.com. Atmospheric café offering eclectic, tasty selections from around the world such as Egyptian *kusheri* for $11. Mon–Thurs 11am–1am, Fri & Sat 11am–2am, Sun 10am–11pm.

Toast On Market 620 E Market St ☎ 502 569 4099, ⍟toastonmarket.com. Heaps of eggs and pancakes for breakfast or filling sandwiches and grilled cheese plus trimmings all go for under $10 here. Tues–Fri 7am–2pm, Sat & Sun 7am–3pm.

NIGHTLIFE AND ENTERTAINMENT

The two-mile strip around Bardstown Road and Baxter Avenue is punctuated by fun bars, while the best gay clubs are on the eastern edge of downtown. Check **listings** in the free *LEO* (Louisville Eccentric Observer; ⍟leoweekly.com) and *Velocity* (⍟louisville.metromix.com).

BARS, CLUBS AND LIVE MUSIC VENUES

Connection 130 S Floyd St ☎ 502 585 5752, ⍟the connection.net. The pick of Louisville's gay scene. At weekends, this giant club, complete with terrace garden, holds more than two thousand. Daily 8pm–2am.

Headliners 1386 Lexington Rd ☎ 502 584 8088, ⍟headlinerslouisville.com. Lively club that showcases local, national and even international indie bands, as well as cabaret acts. Hours vary.

Phoenix Hill Tavern 644 Baxter Ave ☎ 502 589 4957, ⍟phoenixhill.com. Big bar with four separate areas; occasionally hosts national touring acts and more regular theme nights. Wed–Sat 8pm–4am, Mon, Tues & Sun for special events.

Stevie Ray's Blues Bar 230 E Main St ☎ 502 582 9945, ⍟stevieraysbluesbar.com. As the name suggests, a loud, rocking blues bar, with live acts most nights. Cover free–$5. Daily 3pm–late.

PERFORMANCE VENUES

Actors' Theatre of Louisville 316 W Main St ☎ 502 584 1205, ⍟actorstheatre.org. The company that performs here has gained a national reputation for its new productions over fifty years of existence.

Kentucky Center for the Arts 501 W Main St ☎ 502 562 0100, ⍟kentuckycenter.org. Fronted by several outlandish sculptures, this place offers everything from dance lessons through rock and jazz to more highbrow shows.

Bourbon Country

Kentucky's much-vaunted **Bourbon Country**, centred on attractive **Bardstown**, forty miles south of Louisville on US-31 E, is the place to get acquainted with **bourbon whiskey**. The now world-famous tipple was created in early pioneer days, so the story goes, when Elijah Craig, a Baptist minister, added corn to the usual rye and barley. Named after Bourbon County near Lexington, Kentucky's whiskey soon gained a national reputation, thanks to crisp limestone water, strict laws concerning ingredients and the skills of small-scale distillers. Ironically, you can't drink the stuff in many counties, as they are dry. A good starting point is Bardstown's **Oscar Getz Museum of Whiskey History** in Spalding Hall, 114 N Fifth St (May–Oct Mon–Fri 10am–5pm, Sat 10am–4pm, Sun noon–4pm; Nov–April Tues–Sat 10am–4pm, Sun noon–4pm; free; ☎502 348 2999, ⍟whiskeymuseum.com).

The distilleries

Fourteen miles northwest of Bardstown at **Clermont**, the **Jim Beam's American Stillhouse** (526 Happy Hollow Rd; Mon–Sat 9am–5.30pm, Sun noon–4.30pm; $8 over 21, free under 21; ☎502 543 9877, ⍟americanstillhouse.com) has an informative tour of the distillery and home, followed by a tasting. At **Maker's Mark Distillery**, twenty miles south of Bardstown on Hwy-49 near **Loretto**, whiskey is still hand-crafted in an out-of-the-way collection of beautifully restored black, red and grey plankhouses (3350 Burkes Spring Rd; Mon–Sat 9.30am–3.30pm; March–Dec also Sun 11.30am–3.30pm; $7; ☎270 865 2881, ⍟makersmark.com).

Abraham Lincoln National Historic Site

Three miles south of Hodgenville, on US-31 E • Daily: June–Aug 8am–6.45pm; Sept–May closes 4.45pm • Free • ⍟ nps.gov/abli

On February 12, 1809, **Abraham Lincoln**, the sixteenth president of the USA, was born in a one-room log cabin in the frontier wilds, son of a wandering farmer and, if some accounts are to be believed, an illiterate and illegitimate mother. The **National Historic Site** has a symbolic cabin of his birth, enclosed in a granite and marble Memorial Building with 56 steps, one for each year of Lincoln's life.

The family moved ten miles northeast in 1811 to the **Knob Creek** area, where Lincoln's earliest memory was of slaves being forcefully driven along the road. Here you can visit another re-creation of his boyhood home (April–Oct daily varying hours; free).

ACCOMMODATION	ABRAHAM LINCOLN NATIONAL HISTORIC SITE
Nancy Lincoln Inn Abraham Lincoln National Historic Site ☎ 270 358 3845. Staying in one of the three log	cabins in the woods right next to old Abe's birthplace is a fairly spartan but highly atmospheric experience. **$70**

Mammoth Cave National Park

The 365 miles of labyrinthine passages (with an average of 5 new miles discovered each year) and domed caverns of **MAMMOTH CAVE NATIONAL PARK** lie around ninety miles south of Louisville. Its amazing geological formations, carved by acidic water trickling through limestone, include a bewildering display of stalagmites and stalactites, a huge cascade of flowstone known as **Frozen Niagara** and **Echo River**, 365ft below ground, populated by a unique species of colourless and sightless fish. Among traces of human occupation are Native American artefacts, a former saltpetre mine and the remains of an experimental tuberculosis hospital, built in 1843 in the belief that the cool atmosphere of the cave would help clear patients' lungs. You can take a limited-access self-guided tour, but by far the best way to appreciate the caves is to join one of the lengthy **ranger-guided tours** (see below) – keep in mind that the temperature in the caves is a constantly cool 54°F.

The park's attractions are by no means all subterranean. You can explore the scenic **Green River**, as it cuts through densely forested hillsides and jagged limestone cliffs, by following hiking trails or renting a canoe from Green River Canoeing (☎ 270 597 2031). The privately owned caves all around and the "attractions" in nearby Cave City and Park City are best ignored.

INFORMATION AND TOURS	MAMMOTH CAVE NATIONAL PARK
Visitor centre The on-site visitor centre is open daily (mid-April to Nov 8am–6.15pm; Dec to mid-April 9am–5pm; ⓦ nps.gov/maca).	**Tours** Tickets for ranger-guided tours (2–6hr; $10–48) are available from the visitor centre. You can check availability (ⓦ recreation.gov) in advance.

ACCOMMODATION	
Mammoth Cave Hotel Mammoth Cave National Park ☎ 270 758 2225, ⓦ mammothcavehotel.com. Spread across multiple units, the hotel contains motel-style rooms	and good-value cottages. Camping is free in the backcountry, though you'll need a permit from the visitor centre. **$61**

Tennessee

A shallow rectangle, just one hundred miles from north to south, **TENNESSEE** stretches 450 miles from the Mississippi to the Appalachians. The marshy **western** third of the state occupies a low plateau edging down toward the Mississippi. Only in the far southwest corner do the bluffs rise high enough to permit a sizeable riverside settlement – the exhilarating port of **Memphis**, the birthplace of urban **blues** and longtime home of **Elvis**. The plantation homes and dull, tidy towns of **middle Tennessee**'s rolling farmland reflect the comfortable lifestyle of its pioneers; smack in the heart of it sprawls hip **Nashville**, synonymous with **country music**. The mountainous **east** shares its top attraction with North Carolina – the peaks, streams and meadows of **Great Smoky Mountains National Park**.

6

Memphis

Perched above the Mississippi River, **MEMPHIS** is perhaps the single most exciting destination in the South – especially for music-lovers. Visitors flock to celebrate the city that gave the world **blues**, **soul** and **rock'n'roll**, and to chow down in the unrivalled **BBQ** capital of the nation. Memphis is both deeply atmospheric – with its faded downtown streets dotted with retro stores and diners and the sun setting nightly across the broad Mississippi – and invigorating, with a cluster of superb museums and fantastic restaurants. If it's the **Elvis** connection that appeals, you won't leave

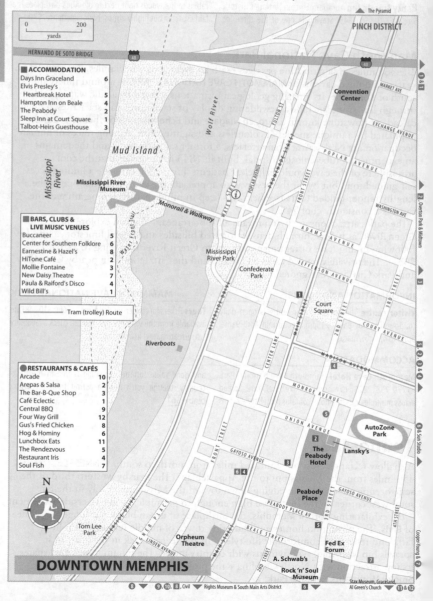

The Pyramid

PINCH DISTRICT

HERNANDO DE SOTO BRIDGE

■ **ACCOMMODATION**
Days Inn Graceland	6
Elvis Presley's Heartbreak Hotel	5
Hampton Inn on Beale	4
The Peabody	2
Sleep Inn at Court Square	1
Talbot-Heirs Guesthouse	3

Convention Center

MARKET AVE

EXCHANGE AVENUE

Mud Island

Wolf River

POPLAR AVENUE

Mississippi River

Mississippi River Museum

Monorail & Walkway

WASHINGTON AVE

■ **BARS, CLUBS & LIVE MUSIC VENUES**
Buccaneer	5
Center for Southern Folklore	6
Earnestine & Hazel's	8
HiTone Café	2
Mollie Fontaine	3
New Daisy Theatre	7
Paula & Raiford's Disco	4
Wild Bill's	1

ADAMS AVENUE

Mississippi River Park

Confederate Park

JEFFERSON AVENUE

Court Square

COURT AVENUE

—— Tram (trolley) Route

Riverboats

MADISON AVENUE

MONROE AVENUE

● **RESTAURANTS & CAFÉS**
Arcade	10
Arepas & Salsa	2
The Bar-B-Que Shop	3
Café Eclectic	1
Central BBQ	9
Four Way Grill	12
Gus's Fried Chicken	8
Hog & Hominy	6
Lunchbox Eats	11
The Rendezvous	5
Restaurant Iris	4
Soul Fish	7

UNION AVENUE

AutoZone Park

GAYOSO AVENUE

The Peabody Hotel

Lansky's

N

GAYOSO AVENUE

Peabody Place

PEABODY PLACE AV

Tom Lee Park

BEALE STREET

Orpheum Theatre

Fed Ex Forum

DOWNTOWN MEMPHIS

A. Schwab's

Rock 'n' Soul Museum

Stax Museum, Graceland, Al Green's Church

Rights Museum & South Main Arts District

disappointed – let alone empty-handed – but even the King represents just one small part of the rich musical heritage of the home of Sun and Stax studios.

Laidback and oddball, melancholy and determinedly nostalgic, Memphis has a friendly scale. **Downtown** still retains a healthy ensemble of buildings from the cotton era – best admired either along the riverfront or from the trolley down **Main Street** – along with a number of places that look unchanged since Elvis's day. Four miles southeast of downtown, the **Cooper-Young** intersection boasts a handful of hip restaurants and vintage stores.

Beale Street

Now a fabled blues corridor, **Beale Street** began life in the mid-nineteenth century as one of Memphis's most exclusive enclaves; within fifty years its elite residents had been driven out by yellow fever epidemics and the ravages of the Civil War to be replaced by a diverse mix of blacks, Greeks, Jews, Chinese and Italians. But it was **black culture** that gave the street its fame. Beale Street was where black roustabouts and travellers passing through Memphis immediately headed. In the Jim Crow era, it served as the centre for black businesses, financiers and professionals, and in its Twenties' heyday it was jammed with vaudeville theatres, concert halls, bars and juke joints (mostly white-owned). Although Beale still drew huge crowds in the Forties, the drift to the suburbs and, ironically, the success of the **civil rights** years in opening the rest of Memphis to black businesses, almost killed it off. The **bulldozers** of the late Sixties spared only the grand Orpheum Theatre, at 203 S Main St, and a few commercial buildings between Second and Fourth streets.

Beale Street has now been restored as a touristy **Historic District**. Its souvenir shops, music clubs, bars and cafés are bedecked with retro facades and neon signs, while a Walk of Fame honours musical greats such as B.B. King and Howlin' Wolf. Blues fans in particular will be drawn to its music venues, which showcase top regional talent. At Beale's western end, no. 126 – the former home of the iconic **Lansky's**, tailor to the Memphis stars – now lies dormant as a derelict nightclub; if you're looking to buy any of their gorgeous rock'n'roll threads, including Elvis's blue cable-knit "*Jailhouse Rock*" sweater, Lansky's continues to thrive in the historic *Peabody* hotel (see p.444).

A. Schwab's Dry Goods Store, at 163 Beale, looks much as it must have done when it opened in 1876, with an incredible array of voodoo paraphernalia – best-sellers include Mojo Hands and High John the Conqueror lucky roots – as well as 99¢ neckties and Sunday School badges.

Rock'n'Soul Museum

191 Beale St • Daily 10am–7pm, last admission 6.15pm • $11 • ☎ 901 205 2533, ⓦ memphisrocksnsoul.org

In the plaza of the enormous FedEx Forum, the appealing **Rock'n'Soul Museum** presents the story of the city's musical heritage scrapbook-style, making connections between migration, racism, civil rights and youth culture, with artefacts ranging from Elvis's stage gear and one of B.B. King's "Lucille" guitars to Isaac Hayes' diamond-encrusted "piano" watch.

The National Civil Rights Museum

450 Mulberry St • Wed–Sat 9am–6pm, Sun 1–6pm; Sept–May closes 5pm • $13 • ☎ 901 521 9699, ⓦ civilrightsmuseum.org

The **National Civil Rights Museum** provides the most rewarding and comprehensive history of the long and tumultuous struggle for civil rights to be had anywhere in the South. It's built around the shell of the former *Lorraine Motel*, where **Dr Martin Luther King, Jr** was assassinated by James Earl Ray on April 4, 1968. Dr King was killed by a single bullet as he stood on the balcony, the evening before he was due to lead a march in Memphis in support of a strike by black sanitation workers.

The *Lorraine* itself was one of the few places where blacks and whites could meet in Memphis during the segregation era; thus black singer Eddie Floyd and white guitarist Steve Cropper wrote soul classics such as *Knock on Wood* here, and Dr King was a regular guest. The facade of the motel is still all too recognizable from images of King's death, but

6

once inside visitors are faced with a succession of galleries that recount the major milestones of the movement, from A. Philip Randolph of the Brotherhood of Sleeping Car Porters, who originally called for a march on Washington in 1941, through to the Nation of Islam and the Black Panthers. There is some horrifying and very emotional footage, but by far the most affecting moment comes when you reach King's actual room, Room 306, still laid out as he left it, and see the spot where his life was cut short. Another wing, across from the motel, completes the story by incorporating the boarding house from which the fatal shot was fired. The bedroom rented that same day by James Earl Ray, and the sordid little bathroom that served as his sniper's nest, can be inspected behind glass, with the death site clearly visible beyond. King's own family remain highly sceptical as to whether Ray acted alone, and detailed panels lay out all sorts of conspiracy theories.

The South Main Arts District

A block west of the National Civil Rights Museum, the once flyblown South Main Street has been given a new lease of life. Spanning the nine or so blocks along Main between Vance and St Paul avenues, the **South Main Arts District** is a burgeoning stretch of galleries, stores and restaurants, complete with a crop of condos and lofts. It's particularly buzzing on the last Friday of the month, when the free "Art Trolley" (6–9pm) runs along Main and stores offer complimentary snacks and drinks.

Sun Studio

706 Union Ave • Daily 10am–6pm; tours (40min) depart on the half-hour • $12 • ☎ 800 441 6249, ⊕ sunstudio.com

Second only to Graceland, Memphis's principal shrine to the memory of Elvis is the hip little **Sun Studio**. This is where, in 1953, the shy 18-year-old trucker from Tupelo turned up with his guitar, claiming "I don't sound like nobody". The studio then went on to introduce rock'n'roll to the world with not only the King but also artists like Jerry Lee Lewis, Johnny Cash and Roy Orbison. Though Sun Records moved out of the building in 1960, the soundproofing remained in place through a variety of incarnations – including a brief, unlikely period as a scuba-diving store – making possible its restoration as a functioning studio in 1985 and retaining the eerie, almost spiritual atmosphere of the place. Tours start in an upstairs room where you can see B.B. King's chair and Elvis's high school diploma, before heading down into the studio. Measuring just 18 by 30ft, the shabby room fills with music as enthusiastic rockabilly guides play wild rock'n'roll recordings and tell choice anecdotes. Few visitors leave unmoved – or without posing for a photo with Elvis's original mic stand.

The Stax Museum of American Soul Music

926 E McLemore Ave • Tues–Sat 10am–5pm, Sun 1–5pm • $12 • ☎ 901 942 7685, ⊕ staxmuseum.com

In 1960, one of Memphis's most famous addresses, 926 E McLemore Ave, was occupied by the Capitol Theatre, a landmark in a neighbourhood where blacks had just started to outnumber whites. The theatre became the headquarters of the **Stax** record label, a veritable powerhouse of funky soul where over the next fourteen years artists such as Otis Redding, Isaac Hayes, Albert King and the Staples Singers cut fifteen US number-one hits and achieved 237 entries in the top 100. By the early 2000s, however, with Stax long since defunct, 926 E McLemore was just a derelict lot in a dodgy neighbourhood.

Now Stax has resurfaced, reconstructed larger than ever, with a music academy sitting next to the fabulous **Stax Museum of American Soul Music**, or **Soulsville**. Visits start with a film history of the label, using stunning footage to illuminate the triumphs and the tensions that arose from its all-but-unique status as a joint black-white enterprise in the segregated South. The first exhibit beyond, emphasizing soul music's gospel roots, is an entire African Methodist Episcopal Church, transported here from Mississippi. Among the wealth of footage and recordings, showpiece artefacts include Isaac Hayes's peacock-blue-and-gold Cadillac. The studio has been re-created in detail, featuring the two-track tape recorder used by Otis Redding to record *Mr Pitiful* and *Respect*.

6

THE SOUND OF MEMPHIS

Since the start of the twentieth century, Memphis has been a meeting place for black musicians from the Delta and beyond. During the Twenties, its downtown pubs, clubs and street corners were alive with the sound of the blues. After World War II, young musicians and radio DJs such as Bobby Bland and B.B. King experimented by blending the traditional blues sound with jazz, adding electrical amplification to create rhythm'n'blues. White promoter Sam Phillips started **Sun Records** in 1953, employing Ike Turner as a scout to comb the Beale Street clubs for new talent. Among those whom Turner helped introduce to vinyl were his own girlfriend, Annie Mae Bullock (later **Tina Turner**), Howlin' Wolf and Little Junior Parker, whose *Mystery Train* was Sun's first great recording. In 1953, the 18-year-old **Elvis Presley** hired the studio to record *My Happiness*, supposedly as a gift for his mother, and something prompted Phillips' assistant Marion Keisker to file away his recording. The next summer, Phillips called Elvis back to the studio to cut *That's All Right*, and thereby set out towards proving his much-quoted conviction that "If I could find a white man who had the Negro sound and the Negro feel, I could make a billion dollars". Phillips swiftly dropped his black artists and signed other white rockabilly singers like Carl Perkins and **Jerry Lee Lewis** to make classics such as *Blue Suede Shoes* and *Great Balls of Fire*. Elvis was soon sold on to RCA (for just $35,000), and didn't record in Memphis again until 1969, when at Chips Moman's American Studios he produced the best material of his later career, including *Suspicious Minds*.

In the Sixties and early Seventies, Memphis's **Stax Records** provided a rootsy alternative to the poppier sounds of Motown. This hard-edged Southern soul was created by a multiracial mix of musicians, Steve Cropper's fluid guitar complementing the blaring Memphis Horns. The label's first real success was *Green Onions* by studio band Booker T and the MGs; further hits followed from Otis Redding (*Try a Little Tenderness*), Wilson Pickett (*Midnight Hour*), Sam and Dave (*Soul Man*) and Isaac Hayes (*Shaft*). The label eventually foundered in acrimony; the last straw for many of its veteran soulmen was the signing of the British child star Lena Zavaroni for a six-figure sum.

The Pyramid

The northern boundary of downtown Memphis is marked by the astonishing 32-storey, 321ft **Pyramid** glinting in the sun over the mighty river. Completed in 1991, at two-thirds the size of Egypt's Great Pyramid, it was created to make a symbolic link with Egypt's Nile Delta. After years hosting major exhibitions and shows, it has since been overshadowed by downtown's FedEx Forum. A marvellous folly, at the time of writing, it was slated to become a Bass Pro Outdoor World store in late 2014.

Mud Island

125 N Front St • Mid-April to Oct Tues–Sun 10am–5pm • Park free, monorail $4 or free with $10 museum admission • ☎ 800 507 6507, ⓦ mudisland.com

From Riverside Drive, which runs south from the Pyramid, **monorail trains** and a walkway head across the Mississippi's Wolf Channel to **Mud Island**. Highlights of the island's slightly old-fashioned but enjoyable **Mississippi River Museum** include a full-sized reconstructed steamboat, a morbidly fascinating "Theater of Disasters", and salty tales of characters like keelboatman Mike Fink, who in 1830 styled himself "half horse, half alligator". **River Walk**, which runs to the southern tip of the island, is a scale replica of the lower Mississippi River; at the end, you can rent canoes and kayaks for a leisurely paddle around the nearby "Gulf of Mexico".

Mud Island hosts a variety of concerts and events: in summer, you can even bring a sleeping bag and join a mass camp-out where the tent, dinner, breakfast and entertainment is laid on.

Tom Lee Park

On the mainland, a walk via the waterfront Confederate and Mississippi River parks brings you to **Tom Lee Park**, a venue for major outdoor events including **Memphis in May** (see p.445). Stretching a mile along the river, it commemorates a black boatman who rescued 32 people from a sinking boat in 1925 – despite not being able to swim.

Graceland

3734 Elvis Presley Blvd, 10 miles south of downtown • Generally Mon–Sat 10am–4pm, but hours fluctuate wildly, check online for current opening hours • "Platinum" ticket to all attractions (allow 3hr) $37; house tours $33; parking $10; $70 VIP tour (barely worth it); reservations recommended • ☎ 901 332 3322, ⓦ elvis.com

In itself, Elvis Presley's **Graceland** was a surprisingly modest home for the world's most successful entertainer – it's certainly not the "mansion" you may have imagined. And while Elvis was clearly a man who indulged his tastes to the fullest, Graceland has none of the pomposity that characterizes so many other showpiece Southern residences. Visits are affectionate celebrations of the man; never exactly tongue-in-cheek, but not cloyingly reverential either.

Elvis was just 22 when he paid $100,000 for Graceland in 1957. Built in 1939, the stone-clad house was then considered one of the most desirable properties in Memphis, though today the neighbourhood is distinctly less exclusive, its main thoroughfare – **Elvis Presley Boulevard** – slightly dodgy and lined with discount liquor stores, ancient beauty parlours, used car lots and surprisingly few Elvis-related souvenir shops. Tours start opposite the house in **Graceland Plaza**; excited visitors, kitted out with headphones, are ferried across the road in minibuses, which depart every few minutes and sweep through the house's famous "musical gate", etched with musical notes and Elvis's silhouette. No stops are made at the perimeter "Wall of Love", scrawled with tens of thousands of messages from fans, but you are free to walk back there after the tour.

Inside the house

Audio tours, peppered with spoken memories from Priscilla Presley and Elvis's daughter, Lisa Marie, and rousing choruses from the King himself, allow you to spend as long as you wish, although upstairs is out of bounds. The interior is a jubilant tribute to the taste of the Seventies, each room reflecting Elvis's personal passions: highlights include the Hawaiian-themed **Jungle Room**, with its waterfall, tiki ornaments and green shag-carpeted ceiling, where Elvis recorded *Moody Blue* and other gems from his latter years; the **Pool Room**, whose walls and ceiling are covered in heavily pleated, paisley fabric suggesting a little-documented psychedelic phase; and the navy-and-lemon **TV Room**, mirrored and fitted with three screens that now show classic 1970s TV shows and Elvis's favourite movies.

Other buildings and memorial

In the **trophy building**, you parade past Elvis's platinum, gold and silver records, some of his wilder Vegas stage costumes and cases of intriguing clippings, photos and memorabilia; footage of early TV performances offers breathtaking reminders of just how charismatic the young Elvis was. The tour of the interior ends with the **racquetball building**, where he played on the morning he died. In the attached lounge, the piano where he sang for the last time (apparently *Unchained Melody*) stands eerily silent, while in the court itself his resplendent, bejewelled capes and jumpsuits stand sentinel beneath a huge monitor showing a late performance of *American Trilogy*. Here, perhaps more than anywhere else, you can feel the huge presence of the man who changed the face of music forever. Elvis (Jan 8, 1935–Aug 16, 1977), his mother, Gladys, his father, Vernon, and his grandmother, Minnie Mae, lie buried in the **meditation garden** outside, their graves strewn with flowers and soft toys sent from fans. Elvis's body was moved here two months after his death, when security problems at the local cemetery became unmanageable. There's often a log-jam here, as visitors crane to read the messages sent by fans, take moments to offer their own prayers and snap photos of the bronze memorial plaques. Graceland Plaza, resounding with nonstop Elvis hits, holds several extra attractions.

The King's toys

Don't miss Elvis's personal **aeroplanes**, including the *Lisa Marie*, customized with a 24-carat-gold washroom sink and velvet furnishings. Quite apart from his many cars

– among them a Harley-Davidson golf cart and super-sleek powder-pink 1955 Cadillac
– the enjoyable **Elvis Presley Automobile Museum** shows a wittily edited film of
action-packed and vaguely car-related clips from his movies. Finally, Graceland Plaza's
many **gift stores** will keep you occupied for hours, whether you're after an Elvis
toothbrush or a pair of blue suede shoes.

Overton Park

The centrepiece of wooded **Overton Park**, three miles or so east of downtown on Poplar
Avenue, is the **Memphis Zoo** (daily: March–Oct 9am–6pm; Nov–Feb 9am–5pm; last
admission 1hr before closing; $15, $5 parking; ☎901 333 6500, ⓦmemphiszoo.org).
If the usual array of gorillas, orang-utans and giraffes doesn't satisfy you, you can visit a
pair of giant pandas.

The park also holds the impressive **Memphis Brooks Museum of Art** (Wed & Fri
10am–4pm, Thurs 10am–8pm, Sat 10am–5pm, Sun 11am–5pm; $7; ☎901 544 6200,
ⓦbrooksmuseum.org), whose holdings feature a strong collection of medieval and
Renaissance works.

Pink Palace

3050 Central Ave • Mon–Sat 9am–5pm, Sun noon–5pm • $11.75 • ☎ 901 636 2362, ⓦ memphismuseums.org

A couple of miles southeast of Overton Park, the **Pink Palace** centres on the
marble mansion of Clarence Saunders, who founded America's first chain of
self-service **supermarkets**, Piggly-Wiggly, in 1916. Saunders went bankrupt in
1923 and never actually lived here; instead, the building became an appealingly
old-fashioned and quirky museum of Memphis history, with an adjacent IMAX
theatre and planetarium.

ARRIVAL AND DEPARTURE   MEMPHIS

By plane Memphis International Airport (☎901 922
8000, ⓦmscaa.com) is 12 miles south of downtown –
about 15min by taxi ($30).
By car Memphis is on I-40 as it runs east–west and I-55
from the south. Both join I-240, which loops around the
city, and cross the Mississippi River.
By bus Greyhound buses (☎901 395 8770) stop at 3033
Airways Blvd, about 2 miles from the airport, with

connections to local transport (☎901 274 6282,
ⓦmatatransit.com).
Destinations Birmingham, AL (2 daily; 4hr 30min);
Jackson, MS (1 daily; 4hr); Little Rock, AR (7 daily; 2hr
25min); Nashville, TN (5 daily; 4hr).
By train The Amtrak station, 545 S Main St, is on the
southern edge of downtown. There's a daily service to
Jackson (4hr 22min).

GETTING AROUND

By tram (trolley) The Memphis Area Transit Authority
(☎901 274 6282, ⓦmatatransit.com) runs a useful
downtown trolley along Main St and Riverside Drive,
connecting Beale St, the Civil Rights Museum and the
South Main Arts District ($1, day pass $3.50, 3-day pass $9;
available on board).
By shuttle bus Sun Studio provides a free daily shuttle

between Graceland, the studio and the Rock'n'Soul
Museum (hourly 10am–6pm; ☎800 441 6249, ⓦsun
studio.com); rides are dependent upon taking a Sun studio
tour, which is no hardship (see p.440).
By tour bus Memphis Hop runs a hop-on, hop-off shuttle
between the city's major attractions ($20; ☎901 577 5467,
ⓦmemphishop.com).

INFORMATION AND TOURS

Visitor centres The spacious Tennessee Welcome Center
is just off I-40 downtown at 119 N Riverside and Adams,
facing Mud Island at river level (daily: April–Sept 9am–
6pm; Oct–March 9am–5pm; ☎901 543 5333, ⓦmemphis
travel.com). There's another visitor centre at 3205 Elvis
Presley Blvd, on the way to Graceland.
Carriage tours Horse-drawn carriage tours (☎901 527
7542, ⓦcarriagetoursofmemphis.com) abound downtown

– prices vary but you're looking at around $50 for a
30min ride.
River cruises Another way to see the city is to float along
the mighty Mississippi: sternwheelers leave from the foot
of Beale St (March–Oct daily 2.30pm; May–Aug also 5pm
Sat & Sun; Nov Sat & Sun 2.30pm; 90min; $20; ☎901 527
2628, ⓦmemphisriverboats.net).

ACCOMMODATION

The most convenient place to stay is **downtown**, with a good choice of historic hotels and upscale chains. There are cheaper options near **Graceland**, on Elvis Presley Boulevard, to the south, though note that this area gets a bit dodgy at night. Wherever you stay, it's best to **book in advance** at busy times, such as the anniversary of Elvis's death in mid-August and during the Memphis in May festival (see p.445).

Days Inn Graceland 3839 Elvis Presley Blvd ☎ 901 346 5500, ⊛ daysinn.com. Good option within walking distance of Graceland, with lots of Elvis memorabilia and music, along with – bliss! – a guitar-shaped pool. Rates include continental breakfast. $\underline{$70}$

Elvis Presley's Heartbreak Hotel 3691 Elvis Presley Blvd ☎ 901 332 1000, ⊛ elvis.com. A nice choice for Elvis fans, this independent hotel – next to Graceland, and literally "down at the end of Lonely Street" – features a (small) heart-shaped pool, kitschy Elvis decor and peanut butter sandwiches in the *Jungle Room* lounge. Wild Elvis-themed suites sleep up to eight. There's a downtown shuttle ($10/ return) and free breakfast. Doubles $\underline{$140}$, suites $\underline{$600}$

Hampton Inn on Beale 175 Peabody Place ☎ 901 260 4000, ⊛ hamptoninn.hilton.com. In an unbeatable location just half a block from Beale St, with modern, immaculate rooms at reasonable prices, a pool and complimentary breakfast. Note that the building does get a bit of street noise. $\underline{$200}$

The Peabody 149 Union Ave ☎ 901 529 4000, ⊛ peabodymemphis.com. This opulent historic hotel near Beale St is famed for its legendary mascot ducks, who waddle from the elevator promptly at 11am, spend the day in the lobby fountain and then return to their penthouse at 5pm. Rooms are comfortably elegant, while the glorious lobby is an attraction in itself, with a friendly, relaxed bar and *Lansky's* boutique (see p.439), where you can pick up a pair of genuine blue suede shoes and other designs favoured by the King. $\underline{$335}$

Sleep Inn at Court Square 40 N Front St ☎ 901 522 9700, ⊛ sleepinn.com. Upmarket, good-value motel facing the river and backing onto Main St and the tram line. Rooms have fridges and microwaves, and rates include continental breakfast. $\underline{$115}$

★ **Talbot-Heirs Guesthouse** 99 S Second St ☎ 901 527 9772, ⊛ talbotheirs.com. Characterful, friendly and comfortable family-run place near Beale St. Each of the eight themed suites has a full kitchen, CD player and access to laundry facilities. Send them a list, and the kindly owners will stock your fridge for arrival. Continental breakfast included. $\underline{$150}$

EATING

Memphians love their food and justly proclaim their city to be the **pork BBQ** capital of the world. Fans should head for the **Memphis in May** festival (see p.445), when hundreds of teams compete in the World Championship Barbecue Contest. Soul food lovers, too, will be delighted at the choice and quality on offer. You'll have no problem finding somewhere good to eat downtown, from dives to sophisticated bistros, along **South Main**, or in the eclectic restaurants of **Cooper-Young**.

Arcade 540 S Main St, South Main Arts District ☎ 901 526 5757, ⊛ arcaderestaurant.com. Open since 1919, this landmark vintage diner – Elvis ate here! – was featured in Jim Jarmusch's movie *Mystery Train*, among many others. Come for big Southern breakfasts, pizzas and home cooking and heaps of atmosphere. Daily 7am–3pm.

Arepas & Salsa 662 Madison Ave, midtown ☎ 901 433 9980. A handy stopoff on the way to Sun Studio (three blocks away), this friendly Venezuelan café serves *tostones* sandwiches – beef, avocado, cabbage slaw and garlic sauce – crammed between rounds of toasted, squashed plantains. Don't miss the fresh mango juice, or the "UFOs", cheesy doughnuts made from ground maize. Mon–Thurs 11.30am–9pm, Fri & Sat 11.30am–11pm.

The Bar-B-Que Shop 1782 Madison Ave, midtown ☎ 901 272 1277, ⊛ dancingpigs.com. Past the door painted with dancing pigs, this atmospheric barbecue hut reels in locals and tourists alike and serves up succulent ribs, pulled pork on Texas toast (a thick slice of garlicky bread) and sweet, smoky BBQ spaghetti. Mon–Sat 11am–9pm.

★ **Café Eclectic** 603 N McLean Blvd, midtown ☎ 901 725 1718, ⊛ cafeeclectic.net. Delicious around-the-clock restaurant satisfying a nice range of appetites: wonderful for breakfast (try the French toast stuffed with Nutella; $6.25), they also do a mean cinnamon roll and blueberry pie, a top-notch latte and an excellent array of vegetarian and vegan dishes, including the "diablo" wrap with tofu, spinach, caramelized onions and spicy sauce ($10.50). Free wi-fi, so you might like to stay awhile. Mon–Sat 7am–10pm, Sun 9am–3pm.

Central BBQ 147 E Butler Ave, South Main Arts District ☎ 901 672 7760, ⊛ cbqmemphis.com. Just around the corner from the Civil Rights Museum, this is one of the city's best barbecue purveyors, with huge, lip-smacking plates of pulled pork ($9) and spiced beef brisket ($10). Its popularity has caused a number of locations to open up around town (the original restaurant is in Cooper-Young). Mon–Thurs & Sun 11am–9pm, Fri & Sat 11am–10pm.

Four Way Grill 998 Mississippi Blvd, South Memphis ☎ 901 507 1519, ⊛ fourwaymemphis.com. Convenient for the Stax museum, this spotless little soul food joint – a favourite haunt of Martin Luther King, Jr – dishes up unbeatable blue plate specials, including catfish, smothered chicken, green tomatoes and the like at low prices. Tues–Sat 11am–7pm, Sun 10am–5pm.

★ **Gus's Fried Chicken** 310 S Front St, downtown ☎ 901 527 4877, ⓦ gusfriedchicken.com. This tiny place near the South Main Arts District has caught the attention of the national press for its delicious, crackling-crisp and spicy chicken. Queues generally snake out the door, but it's worth the wait. Mon–Thurs & Sun 11am–9pm, Fri & Sat 11am–10pm.

Hog & Hominy 707 W Brookhaven Circle, East Memphis ☎ 901 207 7396, ⓦ hogandhominy.com. Hidden in a sea of chain development, this buzzed-about foodie delight marries exquisite Italian training with distinctively Southern flavours and whimsy. Coal-fired pizzas (around $15), short ribs with coriander and avocado ($14) and collards with pepper vinegar ($10) are doled out in a cool, pared-down dining room with chartreuse seating and a patio with bocce ball. There's a fun outdoor bar, too. Mon–Sat 11am–11pm (bar till 2am), Sun 11am–11pm.

Lunchbox Eats 288 S Fourth St, downtown ☎ 901 526 0820, ⓦ lunchboxeats.com. Conjuring up grade school memories, this classroom-themed lunch spot near the Rock'n'Soul Museum crafts inventive sandwiches such as smoked pork with mac and cheese and chicken on grids (waffles). Write your order out with a chubby pencil, and eat on cafeteria trays amid bright metal lunchboxes. Mon–Fri 10am–3pm, Sat noon–7pm.

The Rendezvous Charles Vergos Alley, behind 52 S Second St, downtown ☎ 901 523 2746, ⓦ hogsfly.com. Tucked away in a back alley, this touristy pork BBQ joint – famed for its superb herby dry-rub ribs rather than "wet" BBQ with sauce – is covered with charming memorabilia and is always very crowded. Tues–Thurs 4.30–10.30pm, Fri 11am–11pm, Sat 11.30am–11pm.

Restaurant Iris 2146 Monroe Ave, Midtown ☎ 901 590 2828, ⓦ restaurantiris.com. The menu at this French-Creole dreamboat rotates seasonally, but might include the lobster "knuckle sandwich" with tarragon ($14) or lamb sirloin with wilted arugula ($29). Reservations essential. Mon–Sat 5–10pm.

Soul Fish 562 S Cooper Ave, Cooper-Young ☎ 901 725 0722, ⓦ soulfishcafe.com. This big, stylishly bare-bones hot spot effortlessly combines trad and contemporary, dishing up phenomenal catfish and Southern sides (try the Cajun cabbage) to a fun, friendly crowd. Mon–Sat 11am–10pm, Sun 11am–9pm.

NIGHTLIFE AND ENTERTAINMENT

Memphis's thriving **music** scene can be tasted during the city's many **festivals**, especially **Memphis in May** (ⓦ memphisinmay.org), where big-name performances share space with BBQ contests, August's **Elvis Week** (ⓦ elvisweek .com), and the free **Memphis Music and Heritage festival**, staged downtown over Labor Day weekend. While the best **blues clubs** are beyond downtown and usually open at weekends only, at other times even touristy **Beale Street** has things to offer – especially *B.B. King's*, where B.B. himself appears once or twice a year. At the other end of the spectrum, the city's vibrant alternative scene sees garage **bands** playing holes-in-the-wall; head **midtown** for the hippest underground happenings. In Overton Park, the **Levitt Shell** (ⓦ levittshell.org) puts on more than fifty free, family-friendly concerts a year. On a Sunday, the **Rev Al Green's** gospel service is unmissable (see box below). The best source of **listings** is the free weekly *Memphis Flyer* (ⓦ memphisflyer.com). For all the latest on Memphis's music scene and oddball attractions, head on down to the wonderful Shangri-La Records, a treasure trove of Memphis music, midtown at 1916 Madison Ave (☎ 901 274 1916, ⓦ shangri.com), and pick up a copy of their regularly updated *Kreature Komforts* guide ($5).

BARS AND CLUBS

★ **Earnestine and Hazel's** 531 S Main St, South Main Arts District ☎ 901 523 9754. A legendary brothel-turned-juke joint, this spot was the haunt of everyone from Elvis to the Stax musicians. It's especially good late at night, when the Memphis jukebox blasts and the famed burgers start sizzling. Mon–Fri & Sun 11am–2am, Sat 11am–3am.

MEMPHIS GOSPEL: AL GREEN'S CHURCH

Memphis has been renowned for its **gospel** music since the Thirties, when Rev W. Herbert Brewster wrote **Mahalia Jackson**'s *Move On Up a Little Higher*. Following a religious revelation, the consummate soul stylist **Al Green**, who achieved chart success for **Hi Records** with hits including *Let's Stay Together* and *Tired of Being Alone*, has since the early 1980s ministered at his own **Full Gospel Tabernacle**, at 787 Hale Rd in the leafy suburb of Whitehaven. Visitors are welcome at the 11.30am Sunday services; continue a mile south of Graceland, then turn west (phone ahead to check he's in town; ☎ 901 396 9192, ⓦ algreenmusic.com). While they're very much church services rather than concerts, Green remains a charismatic performer and he does sing, backed by a smoking soul band.

Mollie Fontaine 679 Adams Ave, Victorian Village ☎901 524 1886, ⓦmolliefontainelounge.com. This rambling old Victorian house has been given an arty makeover, transforming it into the coolest nightspot in town. Order a muddled cocktail and drift through the enchanting rooms, dimly lit and decked out with bright pink furniture, zebra-print rugs, patterned wallpaper and haunting black-and-white photographs. Wed–Sat 5pm–3am.

Paula & Raiford's Disco 14 S Second St, downtown ☎901 521 2494, ⓦpaularaifords.com. Most definitely a disco and not a club, this old-school downtown hot spot – with a light-up dancefloor, dry ice, disco-balls, 40oz beers and a free limo service – is a Memphis institution, where hipsters of all persuasions get down after hours to the funkiest jams. $15 cover. Fri & Sat 10pm–4am.

LIVE MUSIC VENUES

Buccaneer 1368 Monroe Ave, midtown ☎901 278 0909. This grungy midtown venue – with a kind of pirate-themed junk-store ambience – is one of the city's best places to see local underground bands. Daily noon–2am.

Center for Southern Folklore 123 S Main St, downtown ☎901 525 3655, ⓦsouthernfolklore.com. A few blocks north of Beale St, this tiny venue celebrates the culture of the South, with a café, a store full of books, folk art and CDs and a stage for live performances. Mon–Fri 11am–5am, Sat 11am–6pm (later if there's a show).

HiTone Café 412–414 N Cleveland, midtown ☎901 278 8663, ⓦhitonememphis.com. From Memphis garage bands to indie rock to Elvis impersonators, this eclectic midtown bar/club is always worth checking out. Mon & Tues 5pm–1am, Wed & Thurs 5pm–2am, Fri & Sat 5pm–2.30am, Sun 11am–2am.

New Daisy Theatre 330 Beale St, downtown ☎901 525 8981, ⓦnewdaisy.com. Restored cinema at the east end of Beale that attracts a young, pierced crowd for its punk, metal and rock shows. Check online calendar for performance times.

Wild Bill's 1580 Vollintine Ave, Vollintine ☎901 726 5473. Juke joint 3 miles northeast of downtown where in-the-know tourists join locals at the long tables for live blues and soul at weekends. $10 cover. Fri & Sat 11pm–3am.

Nashville

Set on a bluff by the Cumberland River amid the gentle hills and farmlands of central Tennessee, big-hearted **NASHVILLE** attracts millions of visitors each year. The majority come for the **country music**, whether at mainstream showcases like the **Country Music Hall of Fame** and the **Grand Ole Opry**, or in the hipper honky-tonks and other live music venues found not only downtown but also in Nashville's many characterful neighbourhoods.

Behind the rhinestone glitter and showbiz exists a conservative, hard-working city. Nashville has been the leading settlement in middle Tennessee since **Fort Nashborough** was established in 1779, and state capital since 1843. It is now a major **financial** and **insurance** centre and a notably **religious** place: there are more churches per head here than anywhere else in the nation.

Downtown Nashville is spread along the Cumberland River, and while it looks much like any other regional business centre, "Lower Broad", along **Broadway** between 2nd and 5th avenues, is prime **country music** territory, lined with honky-tonks, bars, restaurants and gift stores. In addition to the venerable structures you'd expect in a state capital, downtown boasts many of the city's premier attractions, including the **Country Music Hall of Fame**, the **Ryman Auditorium** and the **Johnny Cash Museum**. Further afield, **Music Row**, which centres on Demonbreun Street a mile southwest of downtown, forms the heart of Nashville's recording industry, with companies including Warner Bros., Mercury and Sony operating out of plush office blocks.

The city has a number of hip little neighbourhoods ripe for discovery, particularly **East Nashville**, located across the river. It's a left-leaning place made up of aspiring musicians and young families, where quirky galleries rub elbows with thrift stores and stylish restaurants. East of Centennial Park, across West End Avenue, the campus of **Vanderbilt University** abuts the colourful **Hillsboro Village**, a four-block radius sliced through by 21st Avenue South and abounding in cafés and arty boutiques. Most visitors will enjoy themselves immensely by launching full-tilt into what "Nash Vegas" is best known for: the flash and fun of country music. If you're hankering for more local flavour, venture out of downtown to swill regional beer, browse oddball record stores and hunt for the perfect pair of cowboy boots.

Country Music Hall of Fame

Museum 222 5th Ave S • Daily 9am–5pm • $22, $35 including Studio B • ☎ 615 416 2001, ⓦ countrymusichalloffame.org **Hatch Show Print** 224 5th Ave S • Mon–Wed & Sun 9am–6pm, Thurs–Sat 9am–8pm • Free • ☎ 615 256 2805, ⓦ hatchshowprint.com

Everyone's first stop should be the superb **Country Music Hall of Fame**. A wealth of paraphernalia from countless stars, including all manner of gowns, guitars and battered leather boots, not to mention Elvis's gold Cadillac – combine with video footage, photos and, of course, lots and lots of music, to create a hugely enjoyable account of the genre from its earliest days. Songwriters and musicians give regular live performances and masterclasses

6

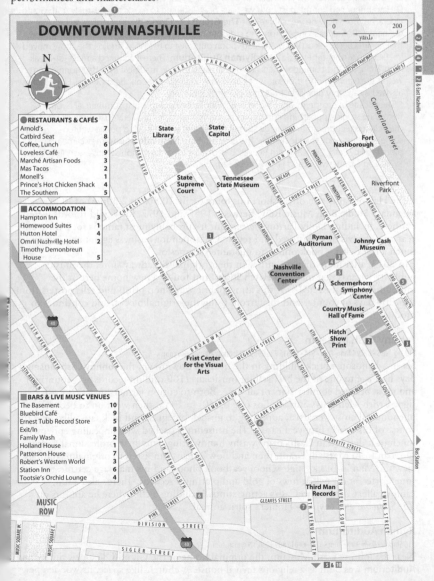

DOWNTOWN NASHVILLE

RESTAURANTS & CAFÉS

Arnold's	7
Catbird Seat	8
Coffee, Lunch	6
Loveless Café	9
Marché Artisan Foods	3
Mas Tacos	2
Monell's	1
Prince's Hot Chicken Shack	4
The Southern	5

ACCOMMODATION

Hampton Inn	3
Homewood Suites	1
Hutton Hotel	4
Omni Nashville Hotel	2
Timothy Demonbreun House	5

BARS & LIVE MUSIC VENUES

The Basement	10
Bluebird Café	9
Ernest Tubb Record Store	5
Exit/In	8
Family Wash	2
Holland House	1
Patterson House	7
Robert's Western World	3
Station Inn	6
Tootsie's Orchid Lounge	4

6

NASHVILLE COUNTRY

Country music is generally reckoned to have resulted from the interaction of British and Irish folk music, as brought by Tennessee's first Anglo settlers, with other ethnic music, including the spirituals and gospel hymns sung by African American slaves and their descendants. It first acquired its current form during the 1920s. As radios and record players became widely available, the **recording industry** took off and Nashville became the base for musicians of the mid-South. Local radio station **WSM** – "We Shield Millions", the slogan of its insurance-company sponsor – first broadcast on October 5, 1925, swiftly established itself as a champion of the country sound. Two years later, at the start of his *Barn Dance* show, compere George D. Hay announced "for the past hour we have been listening to music taken largely from Grand Opera, but from now on we will present **The Grand Ole Opry**". This piece of slang became the name of America's longest-running radio show, still broadcast live out to millions two to three nights per week on WSM-AM (650). Soon outgrowing the WSM studios, the show moved in 1943 to a former tabernacle – the **Ryman Auditorium**. There it acquired a make-or-break reputation; up-and-coming singers could only claim to have made it if they had gone down well at the Opry. Among thousands of hopefuls who tried to get on the show was Elvis Presley, advised by an Opry official in 1954 to stick to truck-driving.

The decade of prosperity after World War II witnessed country's first commercial boom. Recording studios, publishing companies and artists' agencies proliferated in Nashville and the major labels recognized that a large slice of the (white) record-buying public wanted something less edgy than rockabilly. The easy-listening **Nashville Sound** they came up with, pioneered by Patsy Cline and Jim Reeves, is kept alive today by million-selling artists like Taylor Swift, Carrie Underwood and Lady Antebellum.

The Hall of Fame also offers short **bus tours** (daily 10.30am–2.30pm) of RCA's legendary **Studio B** on Music Row. Between 1957 and 1977, forty gold records were cut here, including Dolly Parton's *Jolene*, but it's probably most famous for a thirteen-year run of Elvis hits. Restored and rewired, it's open for business again, and is very much a hot ticket – book online to guarantee a timeslot.

In 2013, after more than a century in their original Broadway store, the music publicity wizards that make up **Hatch Show Print** found a new home here at the museum. Established in 1879, this atmospheric workshop prints and sells posters from the early days of country and rock'n'roll, using the original blocks, and continues to produce new work.

Johnny Cash Museum

119 3rd Ave S • Daily 11am–7pm • $14 • ☎ 615 736 9909, ⊕ johnnycashmuseum.com

Set in a handsome brick building in the heart of downtown, the **Johnny Cash Museum** pays homage to one of the best-selling musicians (100 million records and counting) and most beloved country stars of all time. Born to cotton farmers in 1932, Cash signed with Memphis's Sun Studios (see p.440) in 1955, then went on to become a phenomenal crossover artist, appealing to gospel, bluegrass and rock fans alike over the course of his nearly fifty-year career. The museum is packed with appealing ephemera, much of it detailed in Cash's own swashy handwriting ("my first 'professional' guitar. On loan from Marshall Grant, then and now"). Fans can listen to original recordings, view the Man in Black's high-school yearbook photo and his marriage certificate to June Carter, and gawk at rows of gold and platinum records. There's also a fun, campy gallery devoted to Cash's acting stints, including a clip where he appears on *The Simpsons* as a coyote – Homer's spirit animal.

Ryman Auditorium

116 5th Ave • Daily 9am–4pm • $14 • ☎ 615 889 3060, ⊕ ryman.com

Near the Johnny Cash Museum, the original home of the Grand Ole Opry, the **Ryman Auditorium** was built as a religious revival house. A church-like space, its wooden pews illuminated by stained glass, it beautifully evokes the heyday of traditional country, with small exhibits on everything from Johnny and June to Hatch Show Print (see opposite). It's also a great venue for live gigs and musicals.

Frist Center for the Visual Arts

919 Broadway • Mon–Wed & Sat 10am–5.30pm, Thurs & Fri 10am–9pm, Sun 1–5.30pm • $10 • ☎ 615 244 3340, ⊛ fristcenter.org

Downtown has some non-music-related diversions. Housed in a gorgeous Art Deco building (and one-time post office), the **Frist Center for the Visual Arts** features everything from sculpture and photography to ancient art. If you have little ones in tow, don't miss the **ArtQuest Gallery**, where young Picassos can scribble, paint and sculpt to their hearts' delight.

Tennessee State Museum

505 Deaderick St • Tues–Sat 10am–5pm, Sun 1–5pm • Free • ☎ 615 741 2692, ⊛ tnmuseum.org

A few blocks northeast of the Frist Center, the **Tennessee State Museum** is strongest on Civil War history, highlighting the hardships suffered by soldiers on both sides, of whom 23,000 out of 77,000 died at Shiloh. One of the country's biggest museums, it has exhibits documenting regional life from prehistoric times through to the twentieth century.

Third Man Records

623 7th Ave S • Mon–Sat 10am–6pm, Sun noon–5pm • Free • ☎ 615 891 4393, ⊛ thirdmanrecords.com

Rock fans, particularly White Stripes aficionados, will enjoy a pilgrimage to Jack White's label and recording studio, **Third Man Records**, just south of downtown. A vibrant black, crimson and yellow brick pile, the studio also holds a tiny record shop and fun games such as the "voice-o-graph", where you can cut your very own vinyl record ($15) and mail it home in a specially made envelope.

The Parthenon

2500 West End Ave • **Museum** Tues–Sat 9am–4.30pm; Sun 12.30–4.30pm • $6 • ☎ 615 862 8431, ⊛ parthenon.org

In 1897, Tennessee celebrated its Centennial Exposition in **Centennial Park**, two miles southwest of downtown at West End and 25th avenues. Nashville honoured its nickname as the "Athens of the South" by constructing a full-sized wood-and-plaster replica of the **Parthenon**. That proved so popular that it was replaced by a permanent structure in 1931, which is now home to a minor **museum** of nineteenth-century American art. The upper hall is dominated by a gilded 42ft replica of Pheidias's statue of the goddess Athena – said to be the largest indoor statue in the Western hemisphere.

Cheekwood Botanical Garden and Museum of Art

1200 Forrest Park Drive, 8 miles south of downtown off Hwy-1 • Tues–Sat 9.30am–4.30pm, Sun 11am–4.30pm • $12, parking $3 • ☎ 615 356 8000, ⊛ cheekwood.org

Set on 55 stunning acres of wild flowers, rustling hickory trees and lawns dotted with art installations, **Cheekwood** is the meandering former estate of a Maxwell House Coffee scion. The 1932 Georgian mansion at its centre holds a dignified museum of American paintings and decorative objets.

ARRIVAL AND DEPARTURE   NASHVILLE

By plane Nashville International Airport (☎ 615 275 1600, ⊛ flynashville.com) is 8 miles – around a $25 taxi ride – southeast of downtown. The Gray Line shuttle (every 15–20min 6.30am–11pm; $14 one-way, $25 return; ☎ 615 275 1180, ⊛ graylinetn.com) drops off at most downtown hotels; you could also hop on a Metropolitan Transit Authority bus (hourly; $1.70; ☎ 615 862 5950,

⊛ nashvillemta.org).
By bus The Greyhound station is downtown at 709 5th Ave S (☎ 615 255 3556).
Destinations Asheville, NC (2 daily; 6hr); Atlanta, GA (8 daily; 4hr 30min); Birmingham, AL (5 daily; 3hr 50min); Memphis, TN (5 daily; 4hr)

INFORMATION AND TOURS

Visitor centre 5th Ave and Broadway, downtown (Mon–Sat 8am–5.30pm, Sun 10am–5pm; ☎615 259 4747, ⓦvisitmusiccity.com), In addition to its superb pre-planning website, the huge visitor centre has free wi-fi and features live music; the second branch, 150 4th Ave N (daily 8am–5pm; ☎615 259 4730), is also good.

Country music tours If you like your country music laid on with lots of campy fun, hop aboard the "Big Pink Bus" and let the singing Jugg Sisters of Nash-Trash Tours dish the dirt on all your favourite stars (90min; $35; adults only; reservations essential, as far in advance as possible; ☎615 226 7300, ⓦnashtrash.com).

ACCOMMODATION

Nashville has plenty of big-name chain hotels all around town and budget motels along the interstates and along **Briley Parkway** in Music Valley. Note that rates increase during the **CMA Music Festival** in June (see opposite).

Hampton Inn 310 4th Ave S ☎615 277 5000, ⓦhamptoninn.hilton.com. Perfectly situated across from the Country Music Hall of Fame, this upmarket chain has spotless, modern rooms, a gym and a whirlpool for relaxing after a day chasing down honky-tonks. Free hot breakfast included in the rate. $199
Homewood Suites 706 Church St ☎615 742 5550, ⓦhomewoodsuites.com. Set in a genteel, Renaissance-style building that dates from 1910, this central hotel is an all-suiter with a fridge, microwave, dishwasher and pull-out couch in every room. $215
Hutton Hotel 1808 West End Ave ☎615 340 9333, ⓦhuttonhotel.com. A mile west of downtown, it's all about style at this hip, independent hotel, well placed for the restaurants and bars of the West End. $239

Omni Nashville Hotel 250 5th Ave S ☎615 782 5300, ⓦomnihotels.com. New in 2013, this posh outpost of the *Omni* brand is poised to become Nashville's signature hotel. Connected by walkway to the Country Music Hall of Fame, its litany of perks includes a rooftop pool with skyline views, myriad on-site restaurants, a spa and flashy guestrooms with picture windows. Book a few months in advance for the cheapest rates. $199
Timothy Demonbreun House 746 Benton Ave ☎615 383 0426, ⓦtdhouse.com. Convivial B&B in a three-storey 1906 mansion located a mile from downtown. Guest quarters are named for wine varietals and outfitted with antiques and gas fireplaces; the enormous swimming pool is an afternoon delight. $150

EATING AND DRINKING

There are some delicious down-home southern joints **downtown**, though there are few good places to eat on Lower Broad. **East Nashville** is fast becoming a foodie destination, while the studenty **Hillsboro Village** and **Elliston Place** in the West End are the domain of hip, inexpensive cafés. Nashville has a burgeoning microbrewery scene, great places to be when tours are running and the taprooms flowing: try Yazoo (ⓦyazoobrew.com), Jackalope (ⓦjackalopebrew.com) and Blackstone (ⓦblackstonebrewery.com). Finally, keep an eye out for Googoo Clusters (ⓦgoogoo.com), a tantalizing confection of caramel, peanuts and milk chocolate that has been a Nashville favourite since 1912.

★ **Arnold's** 605 8th Ave S, downtown ☎615 256 4455. Classic canteen, just south of downtown, where locals wait in line for tasty meat-and-threes (meat, three veggies and buttery cornbread). The delicious soul food includes fried chicken, ham or pork chops served with sides for around $8. Get there early; weekday lunch only. Mon–Fri 6am–2.30pm.
Coffee, Lunch 300A 10th Ave S, downtown ☎615 678 8254, ⓦcoffeelunchnashville.com. Jumpstart your day with a mouth-watering steak, egg and cheddar biscuit ($4.50) from this hip little sandwicherie and gourmet coffee shop a few blocks west of the Country Music Hall of Fame. Mon–Fri 7am–5pm.
Holland House 935 W Eastland Ave, East Nashville ☎615 262 4190, ⓦhollandhousebarandrefuge.com. An assortment of chandeliers dangle from high ceilings at this popular cocktail bar and New American restaurant where popcorn is drizzled with truffle oil and drinks boast

creative ingredients such as grilled peaches and ginger ice cubes. Great happy hour. Mon–Thurs 5–10pm, Fri & Sat 5–11pm.
Loveless Café 8400 Hwy-100, 20 miles southwest of town ☎615 646 9700, ⓦlovelesscafe.com. This vintage roadhouse is a local institution for its country cooking. The fried chicken is amazing and breakfast superb: hunks of salty ham with gravy, eggs, toast and fluffy, secret-recipe biscuits. Daily 7am–9pm.
★ **Marché Artisan Foods** 1000 Main St, East Nashville ☎615 262 1111, ⓦmarcheartisanfoods.com. Impeccably fresh European-style food in a modern, airy space with artisanal meats, cheeses and antipasti to go; the home-made brioche and croissants make brunch particularly satisfying. The same people run the more upscale and equally wonderful *Margot* bistro (☎615 227 4668; dinner Tues–Sat, brunch Sun) around the corner at 1017 Woodland St. Tues–Sat 8am–9pm, Sun 9am–4pm.

★ **Mas Tacos** 732 McFerrin Ave, East Nashville ☎ 615 543 6271. A trip to East Nashville wouldn't be complete without a tortilla soup ($5), fried avocado taco ($3) and fresh watermelon juice ($2) from this slender *taqueria* with indigo walls, a chalkboard menu and a devout set of followers. Cash only. Tues–Thurs 11am–4pm, Fri 11am–9pm, Sat 11am–3pm.

Monell's 1235 6th Ave N, Germantown ☎ 615 248 4747, ⓦ monellstn.com. Superb Southern cooking – crispy fried chicken, corn pudding, buttery green beans and piping hot biscuits – served family style at communal tables. Gut-busting, affordable and utterly delicious. Mon 10.30am–2pm, Tues–Fri 10.30am–2pm & 5–8.30pm, Sat 8.30am–3pm & 5–8.30pm, Sun 8.30am–4pm.

Patterson House 1711 Division St, Midtown ☎ 615 636 7724. There's no sign hanging in front of this 1920s-style speakeasy, but it remains one of Music City's most popular – and exquisite – watering holes. Barkeeps here elevate cocktail making to an art; after being ushered past the velvet curtain, order a bacon-infused old-fashioned and savour this spicy elixir beside a wall lined with antique books. Upstairs is the *Catbird Seat* (☎ 615 810 8200), a foodie hot spot where a seven-course *prix fixe* ($100) is determined in advance for 32 lucky patrons (reservations required). Daily 5pm–3am.

Prince's Hot Chicken Shack 123 Ewing Drive, 8 miles north of downtown ☎ 615 226 9442. Nashville is famed for its tradition of "hot chicken" – wherein you choose your meal's level of spiciness – and this beloved hole-in-the-wall, in business for more than thirty years, is the place to try it. Be prepared to see stars if you order the hottest level of bird. Tues–Thurs noon–10pm, Fri 11.30am–4am, Sat 2pm–4am.

The Southern 150 3rd Ave S, downtown ☎ 615 724 1762, ⓦ thesouthernnashville.com. A great option just off Broadway (close to the Johnny Cash Museum), this snazzy steak and oyster joint offers great food around the clock, a bygone-era feel and a stunning patio with skyline views. Mon–Thurs 7.30am–10pm, Fri 7.30am–midnight, Sat 10am–midnight, Sun 10am–10pm.

ENTERTAINMENT

The two obvious ways to experience live country music in Nashville are either to head for the cluster of **honky-tonks** on Lower Broad or to buy a ticket for a **Grand Ole Opry** show, which will feature a mix of stars and newcomers (Thurs–Sat, sometimes Tues; ☎ 615 871 6779, ⓦ opry.com). However, it's worth making the effort to catch up-and-coming or more specialized acts at places like the *Bluebird Café* and the *Station Inn*; look out, too, for special events, including **bluegrass** nights, at Ryman Auditorium (see p.448). In the West End, studenty little Elliston Place boasts an inordinate number of nightlife options for its size, while musician-packed East Nashville is building a strong local scene. With its tacky clubs and vacant storefronts, Printers Alley, north of Broadway, is best avoided, excepting one fun karaoke dive bar, *Lonnie's*. For music at the other end of the spectrum, Nashville's Schermerhorn Symphony Center (ⓦ nashvillesymphony.org) has a world-class orchestra.

LISTINGS AND EVENTS

For listings, check the free weekly *Nashville Scene* (Thurs; ⓦ nashvillescene.com). In June, the huge four-day CMA Music Festival is one of country music's major events, packed with big-name concerts and opportunities to meet the stars (ⓦ cmafest.com).

LIVE MUSIC VENUES

The Basement 1604 8th Ave S, Music Row ☎ 615 254 8006, ⓦ thebasementnashville.com. Alt-country, rock and raw indie rule the roost in this tiny, rough-round-the-edges, smoke-free venue south of downtown. Check online for show times.

Bluebird Café 4104 Hillsboro Rd, Green Hills ☎ 615 383 1461, ⓦ bluebirdcafe.com. Having launched the careers of superstars including Garth Brooks and Taylor Swift, this intimate café, 6 miles west of downtown in the Green Hills district, is *the* place to see the latest country artists, and as a result makes frequent appearances on the popular TV show *Nashville*. The first of the two nightly shows tends to be open-mic or up-and-coming song-writers. Reservations recommended. Mon–Thurs & Sun 5–11.30pm, Fri & Sat 5.30pm–midnight.

Ernest Tubb Record Store Midnight Jamboree Texas Troubadour Theatre, 2414 Music Valley Drive, Opryland ☎ 615 889 2474, ⓦ etrecordshop.com. Old-time radio show, recorded every Saturday at 10pm, and broadcast from midnight to 1am, in a theatre adjoining the Music Valley branch of the Tubb store (the main store is on Broadway). Features promising newcomers as well as major Opry stars. Free. Sat midnight–1am.

Exit/In 2208 Elliston Place, West End ☎ 615 321 3340, ⓦ exitin.com. Venerable venue for rock, reggae and country, with the occasional big name. Mon–Sat 8pm–3am.

Family Wash 2038 Greenwood Ave, East Nashville ☎ 615 226 6700, ⓦ familywash.com. A friendly neighbourhood hub – part tavern, part café, part live music venue – with comfort food (they do a great shepherd's pie; $11) and eclectic unplugged music, from bluegrass through to folk and jazz. Tues–Sat 5pm–midnight.

★ **Robert's Western World** 416 Broadway, downtown ☎ 615 244 9552, ⓦ robertswesternworld.com. Some of the best country music on Broadway, plus

6

rockabilly and Western swing, in a lively honky-tonk that doubles as a cowboy boots store. No cover. Mon–Sat 11pm–3am, Sun noon–3am.

★ **Station Inn** 402 12th Ave S, Music Row ☎ 615 255 3307, ⊛ stationinn.com. Long-standing, intimate bluegrass, swing and acoustic venue near Music Row, with a euphoric crowd that sings along with popcorn and cheap beer. Shows 8pm and 9pm nightly; cover around $12. Daily 7pm–1am.

Tootsie's Orchid Lounge 422 Broadway, downtown ☎ 615 726 0463, ⊛ tootsies.net. Central, touristy, enjoyable honky-tonk, with a raucous atmosphere, plenty of memorabilia and good, gutsy live performers. No cover. Daily 9pm–2am.

Jack Daniel's Distillery

182 Lynchburg Hwy • Daily 9am–4.30pm • Free • ☎ 931 759 6357, ⊛ jackdaniels.com

The change-resistant village of **LYNCHBURG**, 75 miles southeast of Nashville, is home to **Jack Daniel's Distillery**. Founded in 1866, this is the oldest registered distillery in the country. **Tours** lead you through the sour-mash whiskey-making process; ironically, you can't order the stuff in town, as this is a dry county. Lynchburg itself is tiny, laid out around a neat town square with a red-brick courthouse and a number of old-fashioned stores.

Pigeon Forge and Sevierville

For anyone who loves kitschy themed **attractions**, there's plenty to do on the double-lane highway that makes up **Pigeon Forge** – ranging from Dollywood (see box below) through to "Jurassic Jungle" boat rides and the upside-down WonderWorks house; anyone else should arrive with low expectations. Neighbouring **Sevierville** has a more relaxed setting, and a key site on any **Dolly Parton** pilgrimage: a barefoot bronze statue of the superstar, set beside the nineteenth-century courthouse (125 Court Ave; ☎ 865 453 5502). This is Parton's hometown, and she has said that this local recognition is the monument of which she's the most proud.

EATING   **PIGEON FORGE AND SEVIERVILLE**

Applewood Farmhouse 240 Apple Valley Rd, Sevierville ☎ 865 428 1222, ⊛ applewoodfarmhouse restaurant.com. A Smokies institution, famed for its fritters, served warm with fresh apple butter and "juleps" (a mix of apple and pineapple juices) at the start of each meal. Good Southern cooking, too, served in a rambling house that dates to the 1920s. Daily 8am–9pm.

DOLLYWOOD

Born in 1946, one of twelve children with very limited means, music legend **Dolly Parton** was delivered in Locust Ridge, Tennessee by a doctor who arrived on horseback and left with a sack of homegrown cornmeal as compensation. As a child she sang every week on local radio, before leaving for Nashville the day after she finished at Sevier County High School. Her first success, duetting with Porter Wagoner, came to an end in the early Seventies, but she scored a major country hit in 1973 with *Jolene*. She then crossed over to a poppier sound, and, with her charismatic presence, was a natural in Hollywood films including *9 to 5* (the beat for whose theme song she came up with by tapping on her fingernails) and *The Best Little Whorehouse in Texas*. Always a strong-minded and inspirational figure, Dolly has sold more than 100 million records, written more than three thousand songs, and been awarded seven Grammys.

Dollywood, her "homespun fun" theme park at 2700 Dollywood Parks Blvd in Pigeon Forge (April–Dec, schedules vary; April–Oct $57, kids 4–11 $45; ☎ 800 365 5996, ⊛ dollywood.com), blends mountain heritage with roller coasters and the merriment of its celebrity shareholder. One section showcases Appalachian **crafts**; a museum looks at Dolly herself in entertaining detail; music shows are constantly on the go and the thrill rides offer plenty for adrenaline-junkies and kiddies alike. A water park, **Dolly's Splash Country** (late May to early Sept; $47, kids $42), is adjacent.

Gatlinburg

If you want to stay overnight, try **GATLINBURG**, squeezed amid the foothills of the Smokies a few miles south of Pigeon Forge on US-441. As well as being a fraction more upmarket than Pigeon Forge, it's more compact, with a walkable centre; that said, it's also bursting with overpriced, gimmicky tourist attractions. A couple of chairlifts sweep you up the surrounding peaks, one of them to the year-round Ober Gatlinburg **ski resort** and **amusement park** (ⓦ obergatlinburg.com).

ACCOMMODATION, EATING AND DRINKING   GATLINBURG   6

Mountain Lodge Restaurant 913 E Pkwy ☏ 865 436 2547. Popular local joint with straightforward country breakfasts – crisp strips of bacon, rich gravy, plump biscuits and pancakes served with molasses syrup – in a rustic cabin 2 miles east of the centre. Daily 7am–3pm.

★ **Ole Smoky Moonshine** 903 Pkwy ☏ 865 436 6995, ⓦ olesmokymoonshine.com. You can't pay a visit to Tennessee without sampling its famous moonshine. This, the state's first legal distillery, sells six flavours of liquor, including cherry and "white lightning", all born from family

recipes. We recommend the tangy apple pie, but you can try everything for free in the shop. Mon–Sat 10am–10pm, Sun noon–7pm.

Zoder's Inn & Suites 402 Pkwy ☏ 865 436 5681, ⓦ zoders.net. With Gatlinburg being the closest town to the Smokies, accommodation is relatively expensive. Central, good-value *Zoder's* has basic motel-style rooms with balconies that overlook a rushing stream, two swimming pools, and, come nightfall, milk and cookies. $123

Great Smoky Mountains National Park

Stretching for seventy miles along the Tennessee–North Carolina border, **GREAT SMOKY MOUNTAINS NATIONAL PARK** lies just two miles south of Gatlinburg on US-441. Don't expect immediate tranquillity, however: the roads, particularly in the autumn, can be lined almost bumper-to-bumper, and if you're not staying in Gatlinburg it's best to use the bypass rather than drive through the town.

Located within a day's drive of the major urban centres of the east coast and the Great Lakes – and of two thirds of the entire US population – the Smokies attract more than ten million visitors per year, more than twice as many as any other national park. These spectacularly corrugated peaks are named for the **bluish haze** that hangs over them, made up of moisture and hydrocarbons released by the lush vegetation – the park is home to the largest swath of old-growth forest left standing in the east, and is one of the most biodiverse places on earth. Since the Sixties, however,

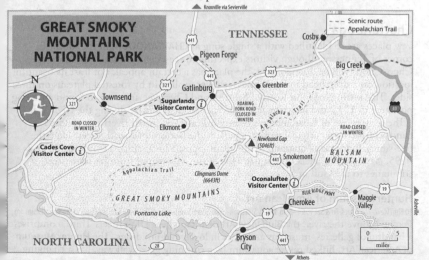

6

air pollution has been adding sulphates to the mix, which has cut back visibility by thirty percent. Sixteen peaks rise above 6000ft, their steep elevation accounting for dramatic changes in climate.

While late March to mid-May is a great time to visit for spring flowers, the **busiest periods** are midsummer (mid-June to mid-Aug), and, especially, October, when the hills are shrouded in a canopy of red, yellow and bronze. During June and July, rhododendrons blaze fiercely in the sometimes stifling summer heat. The best way to escape the crowds is to sample the park's eight hundred miles of **hiking** trails. Just inside the park on US-441, **Sugarlands Visitor Center** has details of hikes, driving tours and various ranger-led tours and activities (see below). Many visitors, however, do no more than follow **US-441**, here known as the Newfound Gap Road, all the way to North Carolina. From the gap itself, ten miles along on the state line, a spur road to the right winds for seven more miles up to **Clingman's Dome**, at 6643ft the highest point in Tennessee. A spiral walkway on top affords a panoramic view of the mountains.

Cades Cove

The main focus of visitor activity is in the **Cades Cove** area, which can be reached either by branching west at Sugarlands along the scenic **Little River Road**, or directly from Townsend via **Rich Mountain Road** (closed in winter). The eleven-mile driving loop here, jam-packed with cars in summer and autumn, passes deserted barns, homesteads, mills and churches that stand as a reminder of the farmers who carved out a living from this wilderness before National Park status was conferred in 1934. Halfway along, there's another **visitor centre** (see below). The loop is reserved for **cyclists** on Saturday and Wednesday mornings in summer.

INFORMATION AND TOURS

Sugarlands Visitor Center Two miles south of Gatlinburg on US-441 (daily: June–Aug 8am–7pm; April, May, Sept & Oct 8am–6pm; March & Nov 8am–5pm; Dec & Jan 9am–4.30pm; ☎ 865 436 1200, ⓦ nps.gov/grsm).
Cades Cove Visitor Center Midway along the Cades Cove Loop Rd (daily: April–Aug 9am–7pm; March, Sept & Oct 9am–6pm; Nov & Feb 9am–5pm; Dec & Jan 9am–4.30pm; ☎ 865 436 1200, ⓦ nps.gov/grsm).

GREAT SMOKY MOUNTAINS NATIONAL PARK

By bike Bikes can be rented at the Cades Cove Campground (☎ 865 448 9034).
Tours A Walk In the Woods (prices vary; ☎ 865 436 8283, ⓦ awalkinthewoods.com) offers exceptionally informed nature tours of the Smokies.
Camping The National Park Service administers ten campgrounds within the park. For details, check ⓦ nps .gov/grsm.

Chattanooga

Few places are so identified with a single song as **CHATTANOOGA**, in the southeast corner of Tennessee. Though visitors expecting to see Glenn Miller's "Chattanooga Choo-Choo" will be disappointed, the place has a certain appeal, not least its beautiful location on a deep bend in the **Tennessee River**, walled in by forested plateaus on three sides. This setting led John Ross, of Scottish and Cherokee ancestry, to found a trading post here in 1815 and its strategic importance made it a prize during the Civil War.

The centrepiece of Chattanooga's twenty miles of reclaimed riverfront is **Ross's Landing** (the town's original name), a park at the bottom of Broad Street. Here the five-storey **Tennessee Aquarium** (daily 10am–6pm; $24.95, kids $14.95; ☎ 800 262 0695, ⓦ tnaqua.org) traces the aquatic life of the Mississippi from its Tennessee tributaries to the Gulf of Mexico.

Hunter Museum of American Art

10 Bluff View • Mon, Tues, Fri & Sat 10am–5pm, Wed & Sun noon–5pm, Thurs 10am–8pm • $9.95 • ☎ 423 267 0968, ⓦ huntermuseum.org
Perched above the river, the **Bluff View Art District**, where High meets Third, comprises a handful of galleries, museums and cafés in lovely old buildings. The **Hunter Museum of American Art**, linked to the aquarium by a stunning glass walkway, has a changing

roster of exhibitions covering photography, painting, sculpture and folk art from the nineteenth century to the present.

Lookout Mountain

Tennessee Valley Railroad 4119 Cromwell Rd · June & July daily; check online for schedule rest of year as hours fluctuate wildly · $16 return · ☏ 423 894 8028, Ⓦ tvrail.com **Ruby Falls** 1720 S Scenic Hwy · Daily 8am–8pm · $17.95 · ☏ 423 821 2544, Ⓦ rubyfalls.com · Take Broad St south to Cummings Hwy

The name Chattanooga comes from a Creek word meaning "rock rising to a point"; the rock in question, the 2389ft **Lookout Mountain**, looms six miles south of downtown. To reach the top, either drive the whole way along a winding road or catch the world's steepest **incline railway**, which grinds its way up through a narrow gash in the forest from a base near the foot of the mountain, tackling gradients of up to 72.7 percent.

At the top, a short, steep walk through **Point Park** brings you to **Point Lookout**, which commands a view of the city and the Tennessee River below. This forms part of the **Chickamauga and Chattanooga National Military Park**, covering several sites around the city and in nearby Chickamauga, Georgia, that witnessed fierce Civil War fighting in 1863. Among the many memorials in Point Park is the only **statue** in the country to show Union and Confederate soldiers shaking hands.

Inside the mountain itself, **Ruby Falls**, a 145ft waterfall, is heralded by a mock-medieval castle entrance; a treetop obstacle course ($35) provides adrenaline-fuelled thrills.

Rock City

1400 Patten Rd · Daily: Jan to early March & Nov 8.30am–5pm; mid-March to May, Sept & Oct 8.30am–6pm; June–Aug 8.30am–8pm; Dec 8.30am–4pm · $21.95; combination ticket with Ruby Falls $34.90, combination with incline railway $47.90 · ☏ 706 820 2531, Ⓦ seerockcity.com

For a true Americana experience, join generations of road-trippers and "See Rock City" – the iconic sign, painted on roadside barns as far away as Georgia and Texas, was the result of an aggressive 1930s marketing campaign. **Rock City** itself is basically a walking trail along the top of Lookout Mountain that offers not only the pleasure of scrambling through narrow gaps and swinging on rope bridges, but also the weird **Fairyland Caverns**, carved into the rock and populated by grotesque characters that will delight kids and terrify adults.

ARRIVAL, INFORMATION AND TOURS

CHATTANOOGA

By bus Greyhound connections (☏ 423 892 1277) with Nashville and Atlanta arrive at 960 Airport Rd.

Visitor centre 1398 Market St (daily 10am–5pm; ☏ 800 322 3344, Ⓦ chattanoogafun.com).

Steam trains To ride a Chattanooga choo-choo, check out the authentic steam trains of the Tennessee Valley Railroad; they offer a variety of trips, from 55min local jaunts to a stunning 6-mile ride, crossing the river, running through deep tunnels and turning round on a giant turntable (from $16; ☏ 423 894 8028, Ⓦ tvrail.com).

River cruises The aquarium offers catamaran cruises into the Tennessee River Gorge (2–3hr; $29), while the more sedate *Southern Belle* riverboat cruises (from $14.95; ☏ 423 266 4488, Ⓦ chattanoogariverboat.com) leave from Pier 2.

ACCOMMODATION AND EATING

Big River Grille & Brewing Works 2020 Hamilton Place Blvd, 12 miles east of downtown ☏ 423 553 7723, Ⓦ bigrivergrille.com. Cavernous brewpub and restaurant that has great comfort food such as shrimp and grits ($16) and a stunning location overlooking the Tennessee River. Mon–Thurs 11am–10.30pm, Fri & Sat 11am–11.30pm.

Bluff View Inn 411 E 2nd St ☏ 800 725 8338, Ⓦ bluffviewartdistrict.com. Alluring B&B that offers a variety of rooms – some with lovely views – spread across three restored houses in the Bluff View Art District. $130

Crash Pad Hostel 29 Johnson St ☏ 423 648 8393, Ⓦ crashpadchattanooga.com. Nearly every hostel in the country could learn a thing or two from the eco-minded *Crash Pad*, where bunk beds are ingeniously outfitted with black-out curtains, outlets and reading lamps; there's also a stylish common area with poured concrete floors and stainless-steel appliances, great breakfasts and a gardened courtyard. $27

Easy Bistro 203 Broad St ☏ 423 266 1121, Ⓦ easybistro .com. For creative New Orleans-influenced cuisine, try this upmarket restaurant and cocktail bar located inside the first ever Coca-Cola bottling plant. Its menu is built upon locally sourced produce and seafood, and the decor is an arresting mix of high ceilings, black walls and white-leather banquettes. Mon–Fri 5–10pm, Sat 11am–10pm, Sun 11am–9pm.

Alabama

Just 250 miles from north to south, **ALABAMA** ranges from the fast-flowing rivers, waterfalls and lakes of the **Appalachian foothills** to the bayous and white sand beaches of the **Gulf Coast**. Away from the water's edge, agriculture, dominated by pecans, peaches and watermelons, flourishes on the gently sloping coastal plain. Industry is concentrated in the **north**, around **Birmingham** and **Huntsville**, first home of the nation's space programme, while the farmlands of middle Alabama envelop **Montgomery**, the state capital. Away from the French-influenced coastal strip around the pretty little town of **Mobile**, fundamentalist Protestant attitudes have traditionally backed right-wing demagogues, such as **George Wallace**, the four-time state governor who received ten million votes in the 1968 presidential election, and, more recently Alabama Chief Justice **Roy Moore**, who in the summer of 2003 was suspended for not obeying a federal court order to remove a monument of the Ten Commandments from the rotunda of the state judicial building in Montgomery. While times have moved on since the epic **civil rights** struggles in Montgomery, Birmingham and **Selma** – monuments and civic literature celebrate the achievements of the campaigners, and even Wallace renounced his racist views – a visit to Alabama offers a crucial reminder of just how recently those struggles were fought.

Birmingham

The rapid transformation of farmland into **BIRMINGHAM** began in 1870, with speculators attracted not by the scenery, but what lay under it – a mixture of iron ore, limestone and coal, perfect for the manufacture of iron and steel. The expansion of heavy industry was finally brought to an abrupt halt by the Depression and today iron and steel production account for just a few thousand jobs.

During the **civil rights** era Birmingham was renowned for the brutality of its police force. An intense civil rights campaign in 1963 was a turning point, setting Birmingham on the road to smoother race relations, and after 1979, under five-term black mayor Richard Arrington, the city slowly began to turn itself around. Today, the **Civil Rights Institute** near downtown memorializes the city's turbulent history of race relations. **Downtown Birmingham** extends north from the railroad tracks at Morris Avenue to 10th Avenue N, between 15th and 25th streets. The main interest is the powerful **Civil Rights Institute** and the **16th Street Baptist Church** (see box, p.458). **Five Points South**, its narrow streets packed with bars and restaurants, a mile or so south of the tracks on 20th Street and 11th Avenue S, is livelier, thanks to the presence of the university.

Alabama Jazz Hall of Fame

1631 4th Ave N • Tues–Sat 10am–5pm • $2 • ☎ 205 327 9424, ⓦ jazzhall.com

Be sure to call in at the **Carver Theatre for the Performing Arts**, where the **Alabama Jazz Hall of Fame** is a fond memorial to legends ranging from boogie-woogie maestro Clarence "Pinetop" Smith to jazzy space cadet Sun Ra.

Alabama Sports Hall of Fame

2150 Richard Arrington Blvd N • Mon–Fri 9am–5pm • $5 • ☎ 205 323 6665, ⓦ ashof.org

Northwest of downtown, the Birmingham-Jefferson Civic Center houses the **Alabama Sports Hall of Fame**, a tribute to greats including 1936 Olympic hero **Jesse Owens**, legendary Negro League pitcher **Le Roy "Satchel" Paige** and boxer **Joe Louis**.

BEALE STREET, MEMPHIS, TN (P.439) >

6

CIVIL RIGHTS IN BIRMINGHAM

In the first half of 1963, civil rights leaders chose Birmingham as the target of "Project C" (for confrontation), aiming to force businesses to integrate lunch counters and employ more blacks. Despite terrifying threats from Commissioner of Public Safety **Eugene "Bull" Connor**, pickets, sit-ins and marches went forward, resulting in mass arrests. More than two thousand protesters flooded the prisons; one was Dr Martin Luther King, Jr, who wrote his *Letter from a Birmingham Jail* after being branded an extremist by local white clergymen. Connor's use of high-pressure fire hoses, cattleprods and dogs against demonstrators acted as a potent catalyst of support. Pictures of snarling German Shepherds sinking their teeth into the flesh of schoolkids were transmitted around the world, and led to an agreement between civil rights leaders and businesses that June. Success in Birmingham sparked demonstrations in 186 other cities, which culminated in the 1964 Civil Rights Act prohibiting racial segregation. The headquarters for the campaign, the **16th Street Baptist Church**, on the corner of Sixth Avenue, was the site of a sickening Klan bombing on September 15, 1963, which killed four young black girls attending a Bible class. The three murderers were eventually jailed, though it took until 2002. Across the road, Kelly Ingram Park, site of the 1960s rallies, has a Freedom Walk diagramming the events through sculptures of menacing dogs, water cannons and youthful protestors. Next door, the admirable **Civil Rights Institute**, 520 16th St (Tues–Sat 10am–5pm, Sun 1–5pm; $12; ☎ 205 328 9696, ⓦ bcri.org), is an affecting attempt to interpret the factors that led to such violence and racial hatred. Exhibits re-create life in a segregated city, complete with a burned-out bus and heart-rending videos of bus boycotts and the March on Washington.

Birmingham Museum of Art

2000 Rev Abraham Woods Jr Blvd • Tues–Sat 10am–5pm, Sun noon–5pm • Free • ☎ 205 254 2565, ⓦ artsbma.org

On the northern outskirts of downtown, the **Birmingham Museum of Art** is strong on American landscapes, decorative arts and African American works and is surrounded by an expansive sculpture garden.

Sloss Furnaces

20 32nd St N • Tues–Sat 10am–4pm, Sun noon–4pm • Free • ☎ 205 324 1911, ⓦ slossfurnaces.com

The chimney stacks of **Sloss Furnaces**, which produced pig iron to feed the city's mills and foundries from 1882 until 1970, loom east of downtown. Fascinating self-guided **tours** through the boilers, stoves and casting areas vividly highlight the harsh working conditions endured by the ex-slaves, prisoners and immigrants who laboured here.

ARRIVAL AND INFORMATION
BIRMINGHAM

By plane Birmingham Airport (☎ 205 595 0533, ⓦ flybirmingham.com) is 5 miles from downtown; call Yellow Cabs (around $22) at ☎ 205 252 1131.

By bus The Greyhound station (☎ 205 252 7190) lies at 618 19th St N, between Sixth and Seventh aves. Destinations Atlanta, GA (5 daily; 3hr); Montgomery, AL (4 daily; 1hr 50min); Selma, AL (1 daily; 3hr 50min).

By train Amtrak pulls in downtown at 1819 Morris Ave.

Visitor centre Just off I-20/59 at 2200 Ninth Ave N (Mon–Fri 8.30am–5pm; ☎ 205 458 8000, ⓦ birminghamal.org).

Listings Birmingham has two free listings magazines: *Weld* (ⓦ weldbham.com) and the *Black and White* (ⓦ bwcitypaper.com).

ACCOMMODATION

Hampton Inn Downtown – Tutwiler 2021 Park Place ☎ 205 322 2100, ⓦ hamptoninn.hilton.com. Handsome restored 1920s hotel near the Civil Rights Institute. Each room has a unique layout, with huge windows looking out onto downtown. $159

Hotel Highland at Five Points South 1023 20th St S ☎ 205 933 9555, ⓦ thehotelhighland.com. Modern boutique hotel within walking distance of Five Points South,

offering comfortable suites, free continental breakfast and an inviting martini bar. $130

Westin Birmingham 221 Richard Arrington Jr Blvd ☎ 205 307 3600, ⓦ westinbirmingham.com. Across the street from the Sports Hall of Fame, the spacious guest quarters here have picture windows and a soothing colour palette; the rooftop pool is an added perk. $189

EATING, DRINKING AND NIGHTLIFE

Bottega 2240 Highland Ave S ☎205 939 1000, ⓦbottegarestaurant.com. Elegant 1920s clothing store in Five Points South that houses one of the city's classiest restaurants, serving luscious, garlic-rich Italian cuisine with mains at around $25; prices are lower in the adjoining café. Mon–Sat 5.30–10pm, café 11am–10pm.

Bottle Tree Cafe 3719 3rd Ave S ☎205 533 6288, ⓦthebottletree.com. Catch stellar indie bands at this wonderfully eclectic gallery/club/bar/café that serves creative finger food (try the "Viking funeral" fries topped with pimiento cheese and chilli; $10.50) and is decked out with comfy retro couches. Vegetarians will be well pleased with the menu. Mon 5pm–2am, Tues–Sat 11am–2am, Sun noon–3pm.

Chez Fonfon 2007 11th Ave S ☎205 939 3211, ⓦfonfonbham.com. Good French-influenced cooking in a romantic, Five Points South bistro with fixtures and furniture flown in all the way from Paris. Tues–Thurs 11am–10pm, Fri 11am–10.30pm, Sat 5–10pm.

Garage Cafe 2304 10th Terrace S ☎205 332 3220, ⓦgaragecafe.us. Hidden away on a short one-way street, this is a converted garage turned ephemera-strewn hip nightspot. Having a beer on its patio, dotted with trellises, trees and quirky statuary, is a Birmingham rite of passage. Cash only. Tues–Sat 11am–midnight, Mon & Sun 3pm–midnight.

Niki's West 223 Finley Ave W ☎205 252 5751, ⓦnikiswest.com. In business since 1957, this Birmingham institution falls somewhere between a Greek diner and a down-home Southern café. The speedy lunchtime buffet has delicious fried green tomatoes, butter beans and pork chops. Mon–Sat 6am–9.30pm.

Montgomery

MONTGOMERY's location, ninety miles south of Birmingham and 160 west of Atlanta, made it a natural political centre for the plantation elite, leading to its adoption as state capital in 1846 and temporary capital of the Confederacy fifteen years later. Today, motivated by a progressive mayor, Todd Strange, it's experiencing a resurgence, with artists and professionals moving into downtown's historic buildings, an inspiring urban farm (ⓦeatsouth.org) settling into its outskirts, and a brand-new stadium and baseball team (ⓦbiscuitsbaseball.com) in the heart of the city. Coupled with the community's incredible wealth of Civil Rights sights, this is a destination that should not be left off of any Southern itinerary.

Dexter Avenue King Memorial Baptist Church

Church 454 Dexter Ave • Tours (booked online) Tues–Fri 10am–4pm, Sat 10am–2pm • Free • ☎334 263 3970, ⓦdexterkingmemorial.org
Parsonage 309 S Jackson St • Same hours and website • ☎334 261 3270

Following the bus boycotts (see box below), Martin Luther King, Jr remained pastor at the **Dexter Avenue King Memorial Baptist Church**, in the shadow of the capitol, for a few years. The upstairs sanctuary, left much as it was during his ministry, contains his former pulpit. You can also tour the **Parsonage** where King lived with his family (and gawk at the small crater on the front porch where it was hit with a bomb in 1956) until their move back to his hometown of Atlanta in 1960.

CIVIL RIGHTS IN MONTGOMERY

In the 1950s, Montgomery's **bus system** was a miniature model of segregated society – as was the norm in the South. The regulation ordering blacks to give up seats to whites came under repeated attack from black organizations, culminating in the call by the Women's Political Council for a mass boycott after seamstress **Rosa Parks** was arrested on December 1, 1955, for refusing to give up her seat, stating that she was simply too tired. Black workers were asked to walk to work, while black-owned "rolling churches" carried those who lived farther away. The protest attracted huge support and the Montgomery Improvement Association (MIA), set up to coordinate activities, elected the 26-year-old pastor **Dr Martin Luther King, Jr** as its chief spokesperson. Despite personal hardships, bomb attacks and jailings, protestors continued to boycott the buses for eleven months, until in November 1956 the US Supreme Court declared segregation on public transport to be illegal.

The State Capitol

600 Dexter Ave • Mon–Fri 9am–4pm, Sat 9am–3pm • Free • ☎ 334 242 3935, ⓦ alabama.gov

On the front steps of the **State Capitol**, a bronze star marks the spot where Jefferson Davis was sworn in as president of the Confederacy on February 18, 1861. The Capitol's lovely Greek Revival facade was immortalized in photographs of the 1965 Voting Rights March, which culminated at its doorstep.

Civil Rights Memorial

Civil Rights Memorial Centre 400 Washington Ave • Mon–Fri 9am–4.30pm, Sat 10am–4pm • $2 • ☎ 334 956 8200, ⓦ splcenter.org

In front of the **Southern Poverty Law Center**, the moving **Civil Rights Memorial**, designed by Maya Lin (of Vietnam Veterans Memorial fame), consists of a cone-shaped black granite table. It's inscribed with a timeline of events structured around the deaths of forty civilians murdered by white supremacists and police; the circle ends with the assassination of Dr King. You can run your hands through the cool water that pumps evenly across it, softly touching the names while being confronted with your reflection. The wall behind, also running with water, is engraved with the quotation employed so often by Dr King: "(We will not be satisfied) until justice rolls down like waters and righteousness like a mighty stream". Displays in the **Civil Rights Memorial Centre** tell the stories of those killed during the movement.

Rosa Parks Museum

252 Montgomery St • Mon–Fri 9am–5pm, Sat 9am–3pm • $7.50 • ☎ 334 241 8615, ⓦ trojan.troy.edu

A few blocks west of the memorial, the exceptional **Rosa Parks Museum**, in front of the corner where Parks was arrested, commemorates "the mother of the Civil Rights movement". Exhibits cover the bus boycott and the resulting events that shook the nation.

Freedom Rides Museum

210 S Court St • Fri & Sat noon–4pm • Free • ☎ 334 242 3188, ⓦ preserveala.org

The small **Freedom Rides Museum** preserves the Greyhound bus terminal where, in 1961, an interracial group of 21 "freedom riders", attempting to desegregate private bus lines, was met with a violent mob of nearly a thousand.

Hank Williams Museum

118 Commerce St • Mon–Fri 9am–4.30pm, Sat 10am–4pm, Sun 1–4pm • $10 • ☎ 334 262 3600, ⓦ thehankwilliamsmuseum.net

Montgomery was jammed with mourners in 1954 for the funeral of 29-year-old country star **Hank Williams**, who died of heart failure on his way to a concert on New Year's Eve 1953. An Alabama native, Williams was as famous for his drink- and drug-fuelled lifestyle as he was for writing classics like *I'm So Lonesome I Could Cry*. Fans will thrill to the **Hank Williams Museum**, stashed with the singer's cowboy boots and hand-painted ties, personal notes (including a letter to Hank Williams Jr, imploring him to make a guitar "ring and talk in our good old family way") and the 1952 Cadillac in which he made his final journey. The **Hank Williams Memorial** dominates the Oakwood Cemetery Annex, at 1304 Upper Wetumpka Rd, near downtown.

Blount Cultural Park

Just off Woodmere Boulevard, ten miles southeast of the city, verdant, 300-acre **Blount Cultural Park** is home to the acclaimed **Alabama Shakespeare Festival** (ⓦ asf.net) and the slick **Montgomery Museum of Fine Arts** (Tues, Wed, Fri & Sat 10am–5pm, Thurs 10am–9pm, Sun noon–5pm; free; ☎ 334 240 4333, ⓦ mmfa.org), which spans more than two hundred years of American art and has an impressive collection of European masters.

ARRIVAL AND INFORMATION   **MONTGOMERY**

By plane Montgomery Airport (☎ 334 281 5040, ⓦ ifly montgomery.com) is 11 miles from downtown on US-80.

By bus The Greyhound station (☎ 334 286 0658) is at 950 W South Blvd.

Destinations Atlanta, GA (5 daily; 3hr); Birmingham, AL (4 daily; 1hr 50min); Selma, AL (3 daily; 1hr)
Visitor centre 300 Water St (Mon–Sat 8.30am–5pm, Sun noon–4pm; ☎ 334 262 0013, ⍟ visitingmontgomery.com); can provide information on tram (trolley) tours ($3).

ACCOMMODATION

Hampton Inn & Suites Downtown 100 Commerce St ☎ 334 265 1010, ⍟ hamptoninn.hilton.com. Clean, comfortable rooms and a substantial continental breakfast at this cheerful hotel in an historic building at the centre of town. $115
Lattice Inn 1414 S Hull St ☎ 334 263 1414, ⍟ thelattice inn.com. Lovingly restored 1906 house offering a relaxed

B&B, a pool, hot tub and lovely gardens a mile or so southeast of downtown in the Cloverdale neighbourhood. $95
Red Bluff Cottage 551 Clay St ☎ 334 264 0056, ⍟ redbluffcottage.com. Friendly B&B near the capitol, with comfortable, antique-laden rooms, a big porch with rocking chairs and delicious food. $110

EATING AND DRINKING

Montgomery's **downtown** has a good range of restaurants, a microbrewery and a handful of watering holes. A few minutes' drive southeast, suburban **Cloverdale** offers a selection of fancier restaurants and has a number of bars and jazz clubs.

Derk's Filet and Vine 431 Cloverdale Rd ☎ 334 262 8463, ⍟ filetandvine.com. Very popular neighbourhood deli/grocery/wine store serving hearty, varied lunches including pork chops or sweet potato casserole, deli sandwiches, wraps and salads. Mon–Fri 10am–7pm, Sat 7am–5pm.
Leroy 2752 Boultier Ave ☎ 334 356 7127, ⍟ leroylounge .com. Slender, hip, dimly lit drinking den in the Cloverdale neighbourhood with a retro feel, a nice selection of craft and import beers and a relaxed, starlit patio. Mon–Wed 3–11pm, Thurs–Sat 3pm–midnight, Sun 3pm–10am.

Railyard Brewing Company 12 W Jefferson St ☎ 334 262 0080. In the heart of downtown, this convivial gathering place fires off juicy burgers and brews its own beer. Order the fried pickles for an appetizer. Mon–Wed & Sun 11am–9pm, Thurs–Sat 11am–11pm.
True 503 Cloverdale Rd ☎ 334 356 3814, ⍟ true montgomery.com. Sublime, chef-driven New American cuisine with a rotating menu based on what's available locally. The cool, white-and-chrome dining room will make you want to dress up a bit. Tues–Fri 11am–2pm & 5–9pm, Sat 5.30–9pm, Sun 11am–2pm.

Selma

The market town of **SELMA**, fifty miles west of Montgomery, became the focal point of the civil rights movement in the early Sixties. Black demonstrations, meetings and attempts to register to vote were repeatedly met by police violence, before the murder of a black protester by a state trooper prompted the historic **march from Selma to Montgomery**, led by, among others, **Rev Martin Luther King, Jr**. Nowadays, Selma has fallen on hard times, but it's worth making a day-trip here from Montgomery to visit the fascinating **Voting Rights Museum** and take the historic walk across the Pettus bridge (see below).

National Voting Rights Museum

6 US Hwy-80 E · Mon–Thurs 10am–4pm, Fri–Sun by appt only · $6.50 · ☎ 334 418 0800, ⍟ nvrmi.com
On "Bloody Sunday", March 7, 1965, six hundred unarmed marchers set off across the steep incline of the imposing, narrow **Edmund Pettus Bridge**. As they went over the apex, a line of state troopers fired tear gas without warning, lashing out at the panic-stricken demonstrators with nightsticks and cattle prods. This violent confrontation, broadcast all over the world, is credited with having directly influenced the passage of the **Voting Rights Act** the following year. The full story – packed with personal testimony – is told in the **National Voting Rights Museum**, located beside the bridge.

Mobile

MOBILE (pronounced "Mo-beel") traces its origins to a French community founded in 1702 by Jean-Baptiste Le Moyne, who went on to establish the cities of Biloxi and

Nouvelle Orleans. These early white settlers brought with them **Mardi Gras**, which has been celebrated here since 1704, several years before New Orleans was even dreamed of. With its early eighteenth-century Spanish and colonial-style buildings, parallels with New Orleans are everywhere, from wrought-iron balconies to French street names, but there the comparisons end. It's a pretty place – especially in spring, when ablaze with delicate azaleas, camellias and dogwoods – but there's little to actually do.

A good starting point for exploring the town is **Fort Condé** at 150 S Royal St (daily 8am–5pm; free), a reconstruction of the city's 1724 French fort. Dioramas cover local history; don't miss the atmospheric old photos of carnival, the old city and local African American figures. North of the fort is the **Church Street Historic District**, full of pre-Civil War buildings.

The **Museum of Mobile**, across from Fort Condé at 111 S Royal St (Tues–Sat 9am–5pm, Sun 1–5pm; $7; ☎251 208 7569, ⓦmuseumofmobile.com), tells the story of the town from its earliest days, while the small **Carnival Museum**, 355 Government St (Mon, Wed, Fri & Sat 9am–4pm; $5; ☎251 432 3324, ⓦmobilecarnivalmuseum .com), set in a historic house embellished with an elaborate wrought-iron balcony, has quirky exhibits covering carnival's arcane rituals You can also tour the World War II battleship **USS Alabama** (daily: April–Sept 8am–6pm; Oct–March 8am–5pm; $15; ☎251 433 2703, ⓦussalabama.com), particularly fun if you're travelling with kids.

ARRIVAL AND INFORMATION   MOBILE

By bus The Greyhound station (☎251 478 6089) is centrally located at 2545 Government St.

Visitor centre Fort Condé, 150 S Royal St (daily 8am–4.30pm; ☎251 208 7569, ⓦmobile.org).

ACCOMMODATION AND EATING

Malaga Inn 359 Church St ☎251 438 4701, ⓦmalagainn.com. Comprised of two townhouses, this 1862 property has spacious rooms set around a pretty courtyard. Breakfast is included in the rate. __$104__

★ **Mediterranean Sandwich Co.** 274 Dauphin St ☎251 545 3161, ⓦmediterraneansandwich.com. Mouth-watering Greek sandwiches, salads and spreads crafted at a cheerful café in the centre of town. Some of the recipes have been deliciously Americanized, including the "Spartan" – toasted flatbread filled with roast beef and lamb, peppers, jack cheese and horseradish sauce ($7).

Mon–Wed 11am–9pm, Thurs 11am–2am, Fri & Sat 11am–3am.

NoJa 6 N Jackson St ☎251 433 0377, ⓦnojamobile .com. This worldly restaurant serves upmarket takes on Mediterranean and Asian cuisine (mains about $30). With its open kitchen, exposed brick walls and stylish scene, *NoJa* would be right at home in Manhattan's Greenwich Village, though its romantic Greek Revival exterior looks like it could have been airlifted from New Orleans. Don't miss the ginger doughnuts ($8). Tues–Sat 5.30–9.30pm.

Mississippi

Before the Civil War, when cotton was king and slavery remained unchallenged, **MISSISSIPPI** was the nation's fifth wealthiest state. Since the conflict, it has consistently been the poorest, its dependence on cotton a handicap that leaves it victim to the vagaries of the commodities market. The state has an undeniable pull, especially for **blues** fans, drawn to sleepy **Delta settlements** such as Alligator or Yazoo City – a land of scorching sun, parched earth, flooding creeks and thickets of bone-dry evergreens. **Clarksdale** is heaven for music fans, with its juke joints, festivals and atmospheric accommodation. South of the Delta, the rich woodlands and meadows of central Mississippi are heralded by steep loess bluffs, home to engaging historic towns. Driving is a pleasure, especially along the unspoiled Natchez Trace Parkway – devoid of trucks, buildings and neon signs. The largest city is the capital, **Jackson**, but there's little reason to stop here when you could stay in quaint river towns like **Vicksburg** and **Natchez** instead. In the north, literary **Oxford** has a lively college scene and should not be missed; Elvis fans should make a beeline for **Tupelo** and the King's humble birthplace.

Brief history

From Reconstruction onwards, Mississippi was known as the greatest bastion of segregation in the South. It witnessed some of the most notorious incidents of the **civil rights** era, from the lynching of Chicago teenager Emmett Till in 1955 to the murder of three activists during the "Freedom Summer" of 1964, which exposed the intimate connections between the Ku Klux Klan and the state's law enforcement officers. Not until the Seventies did the church bombings and murders end. The legalization of gambling in the 1990s stimulated the economy somewhat, with the hulking **casinos** of Biloxi and Tunica pulling considerable revenues across the state line from Tennessee and Alabama. The Gulf shoreline suffered appalling devastation from Hurricane Katrina in 2005, however, and though most of the casinos had reopened, the coast was still undergoing reconstruction when hit by the BP oil spill in 2010.

6

Clarksdale

CLARKSDALE, the first significant town south of Memphis, has an unquestionable right to claim itself as the **home of the blues**. It has a phenomenal roll call of former residents,

---

THE DELTA BLUES

As recently as 1900, much of the Mississippi Delta remained an impenetrable **wilderness** of cypress and gum trees, roamed by panthers and bears and plagued with mosquitoes. In 1903, **W.C. Handy**, often rather spuriously credited as "the Father of the Blues", but at that time the leader of a vaudeville orchestra, found himself waiting for a train in Tutwiler, fifteen miles southeast of Clarksdale. At some point in the night, a ragged black man carrying a guitar sat down next to him and began to play what Handy called "the weirdest music I had ever heard". Using a pocketknife pressed against the guitar strings to accentuate his mournful vocal style, the man sang that he was "Goin' where the Southern cross the Dog". This was the **Delta blues**, characterized by the interplay between words and music, with the guitar aiming to parallel and complement the singing rather than simply provide a backing.

The blues started out as young people's music; the old folk liked the banjo, fife and drum, but the younger generation were crazy for the wild showmanship of bluesmen such as **Charley Patton**. Born in April 1891, Patton was the classic itinerant bluesman, moving from plantation to plantation and wife to wife, and playing Saturday-night dances with a repertoire that extended from rollicking dance pieces to documentary songs such as *High Water Everywhere*, about the bursting of the Mississippi levees in April 1927. Another seminal artist, the enigmatic **Robert Johnson** was rumoured to have sold his soul to the Devil in return for a few brief years of writing songs such as *Love in Vain* and *Stop Breakin' Down*. His *Crossroads Blues* spoke of being stranded at night in the chilling emptiness of the Delta; themes carried to metaphysical extremes in *Hellhound on My Trail* and *Me and the Devil Blues* – "you may bury my body down by the highway side/So my old evil spirit can catch a Greyhound bus and ride."

In addition to towns such as Clarksdale and Helena in Arkansas (see p.469), blues enthusiasts may want to search out the following rural sites:

Stovall Farms Stovall Road, 7 miles northwest of Clarksdale. Where tractor-driver Muddy Waters was first recorded; a few cabins remain, though Muddy's own is now in the Clarksdale blues museum.

Sonny Boy Williamson II's grave Prairie Place, outside Tutwiler, 15 miles southeast of Clarksdale.

Parchman Farm Junction US-49 W and Hwy-32. Mississippi State penitentiary, immortalized in song by former prisoner Bukka White.

Dockery Plantation Hwy-8, between Cleveland and Ruleville. One of Patton's few long-term bases, also home to Howlin' Wolf and Roebuck "Pops" Staples.

Charley Patton's grave New Jerusalem Church, Holly Ridge, on Holly Ridge Rd off US-82 6 miles west of Indianola.

Robert Johnson's grave Little Zion Church, off Money Rd, roughly 4 miles northwest of Greenwood.

stretching from Son House, Muddy Waters, John Lee Hooker, Howlin' Wolf and Robert Johnson up to Ike Turner and Sam Cooke.

Clarksdale's music festivals are a major draw, among them the free **Sunflower River Blues and Gospel Festival** (ⓦsunflowerfest.org) in August, and the **Juke Joint festival** in April (ⓦjukejointfestival.com); for these you'll need to book accommodation months in advance. Some seventy miles south of Clarksdale, down-at-heel **Greenville**, the largest town on the Delta and an important riverport, hosts the **Mississippi Delta Blues & Heritage Festival** (ⓦdeltablues.org) in mid-September.

Music museums

Delta Blues Museum 1 Blues Alley · Mon–Sat: March–Oct 9am–5pm; Nov–Feb 10am–5pm · $7 · ☎ 662 627 6820, ⓦdeltabluesmuseum .org **Rock and Blues Museum** 113 E 2nd St · Tues–Sat 11am–5pm · $5 · ☎ 901 605 8662, ⓦblues2rock.com

Clarksdale's first-class music heritage is celebrated in the superb **Delta Blues Museum**, housed in the restored passenger depot of the Illinois Central Railroad, where many black Mississippians started their migration to the cities of the North.

Also well worth a look is the **Rock and Blues Museum**, a treasure trove of rare blues and rock memorabilia including a signed Chuck Berry guitar and original lithographs by John Lennon.

ACCOMMODATION   CLARKSDALE

Big Pink Guest House 312 Yazoo Ave ☎ 662 302 7500, ⓦbigpinkguesthouse.com. Offering some of the town's more upmarket digs, this converted ice cream parlour near the Delta Blues museum has huge rooms and fixtures – spiral staircase, 10ft doors and, remarkably, a two-storey courtyard with skylight and fountain – that were sent from New Orleans in the 1960s. $125

Riverside Hotel 615 Sunflower Ave ☎ 662 624 9163, ⓦcathead.biz/riverside.html. This iconic hotel offers basic, clean rooms (shared bath) in the old hospital building where Bessie Smith died after a car crash in 1937. The owner, daughter of previous innkeeper and local legend Frank "Rat" Ratliff, will happily recount to you the "true history of the blues". $70

★ **Shack Up Inn** 1 Commissary Circle, 4 miles south on US-49 ☎ 662 624 8329, ⓦshackupinn.com. This unique option, on the former Hopson cotton plantation, offers six old sharecroppers' cabins with kitchenette and porch, along with ten slightly plusher rooms in the cotton gin. It's hard to imagine a more evocative place to stay in the Delta. $70

EATING, DRINKING AND NIGHTLIFE

Abe's 616 State St ☎ 662 624 9947, ⓦabesbbq.com. Famed BBQ joint, in business since 1924, that's located at the iconic blues crossroads of Hwy-61 and 49. Mon–Fri 10am–8.30pm, Sat 10am–9pm, Sun 11am–2pm.

Ground Zero Blues Club Zero Blues Alley ☎ 662 621 9009, ⓦgroundzerobluesclub.com. Part-owned by Morgan Freeman, this venerable blues haunt – its walls packed with memorabilia and customer scribbles – is an excellent place to catch live music. The kitchen turns out solid Southern fare including pulled pork sandwiches and fried green tomatoes. Mon & Tues 11am–2pm, Wed & Thurs 11am–11pm, Fri & Sat 11am–1am.

★ **Red's** 395 Sunflower Ave ☎ 662 627 3166. Authentic juke joint and a Clarksdale must-do for soulful performances staged in a smoky, scruffy lounge. There's divine, slow-cooked BBQ fired up out front. Cover around $7. Thurs–Sat 8pm–2am, Sun 7pm–2am.

Indianola

Every summer **INDIANOLA**, 23 miles east of Greenville on US-82, has a "Homecoming" celebration for its most famous son, **B.B. King**, who plays along with other local blues bands. The **B.B. King Blues Museum**, at 400 2nd St (April–Oct Mon & Sun noon–5pm, Tues–Sat 10am–5pm; Nov–March closed Mon; $12; ☎662 887 9539, ⓦbbkingmuseum .org), tells a story of the blues by tracing King's sixty-year career from sharecropper in the cotton fields via Memphis to international success.

ACCOMMODATION, EATING AND NIGHTLIFE   INDIANOLA

The Blue Biscuit 501 2nd St ☎662 645 0258, ⓦthebluebiscuit.com. Across the street from the B.B. King Blues Museum, this down-home restaurant and juke joint has limited hours, but if you arrive on a weekend you're sure to find the beer flowing, the catfish frying and the live music hopping. The *Biscuit* also has rustic guest quarters spread between bungalows, a cottage and a 1929 farm office. Mon 11am–2pm & 5–9pm, Fri & Sat 5pm–1am, Sun 5–9pm.

The Crown 112 Front St ☎ 662 887 4522, ⓦ thecrownrestaurant.com. The name fits the bill at this superlative Southern café, which cooks up the region's best catfish dishes (order it poached with parmesan cheese; $10.50), gumbo and Mississippi fudge pie in a peach-coloured dining room with local art. Tues–Sat 11am–3pm.

Greenwood

Sleepy **GREENWOOD**, on the shady Yazoo River forty miles east of Indianola, is the country's second largest cotton exchange after Memphis. It has an odd atmosphere nowadays, the huge, aseptic surrounds of the Viking kitchen goods corporation and its associated **Alluvian** hotel and spa creating a wealthy enclave entirely out of keeping with the rest of the Delta. Legend has it that bluesman Robert Johnson died here after drinking a bottle of whiskey poisoned by an admirer's jealous husband.

ACCOMMODATION AND EATING
GREENWOOD

Crystal Grill 423 Carrollton Ave ☎ 662 453 6350, ⓦ crystalgrillms.com. Family-owned since 1932, this local favourite serves classic Delta fare like broiled catfish, veal cutlets and mile-high meringue pie in a 1900s dining room with its original tile floor. Tues–Sun 11am–10pm.

Delta Bistro 117 Main St ☎ 662 455 9575, ⓦ delta bistro.com. Arty, brick-walled spot with deliciously innovative takes on Southern classics: fried green tomato BLTs

($9), pimiento cheese sandwiches ($9) and black-eyed pea cakes with remoulade sauce ($8). Mon–Sat 11am–9pm.

Tallahatchie Flats 58458 Hwy-518 (Money Rd), 3 miles north of town ☎ 877 453 1854, ⓦ tallahatchie flats.com. You can stay in one of six renovated, appealingly dilapidated old Delta shacks here; porches look out over the river and nothing disturbs the peace but the whistle of the lonesome railroad. $85

Oxford

Nineteen thousand residents and 20,000 students enable **OXFORD**, an enclave of wealth in a predominantly poor region, to blend rural charm with a vibrant cultural life. Its central square is archetypal smalltown America, but the leafy streets have a vaguely European air – the town named itself after the English city as part of its (successful) campaign to persuade the **University of Mississippi**, known as Ole Miss, to locate its main campus here.

East of the university, in town, life revolves around the central **square**. Here you'll find Neilson's, the oldest department store in the south – little changed since 1897. You can pick up a cool pair of heels in one of the boutiques, have a quick lunch or join students sipping espresso on the peaceful balcony of the splendid **Square Books**.

Rowan Oak

Old Taylor Rd • Tues–Sat 10am–4pm, Sun 1–4pm • $5 • ☎ 662 234 3284, ⓦ rowanoak.com

From Ole Miss, a ten-minute walk through lush Bailey's Woods leads to secluded **Rowan Oak**, the lovely former home of novelist **William Faulkner**, preserved as it was

---

INTEGRATING OLE MISS

An appealing place today, in 1962 Oxford was the site of one of the bitterest displays of racial hatred seen in Mississippi – events that Bob Dylan responded to with his contemptuous *Oxford Town*. After eighteen months of legal and political wrangling, federal authorities ruled that **James Meredith** be allowed to enrol as the first black student at Ole Miss. The news that Meredith had been "sneaked" into college by federal troops sparked a riot that left two dead and 160 injured. Despite constant threats, Meredith graduated the following year, wearing a "NEVER" badge, the segregationist slogan of Governor Ross Barnett, upside down. A memorial commemorating his achievement was unveiled in September 2002, on the fortieth anniversary of his admission.

6

on the day he died in July 1962 (the day after the funeral, his wife added air conditioning to her bedroom, forbidden by Faulkner during his lifetime). Be sure to take a look into his office, where the writer scribbled the outline of *A Fable* directly onto the wall. The fictional Deep South town of Jefferson in Yoknapatawpha County, where the Nobel Prize-winner set his major works, was based heavily on Oxford and its environs.

INFORMATION

OXFORD

Visitor centre (Mon–Fri 8am–5pm, Sat 10am–4pm, Sun 1–4pm; ☎ 662 232 2447, ⓦ visitoxfordms.com); offers lots of information on William Faulkner and local events, and has offices in a cottage at 415 S Lamar Blvd.

ACCOMMODATION AND EATING

Ajax Diner 118 Courthouse Square ☎ 662 232 8880, ⓦ ajaxdiner.net. There's a great selection of places to eat on the square; this community hub with vinyl booths and a chequerboard floor serves huge plates of top-notch soul food. Mon–Sat 11.30am–10pm.

Big Bad Breakfast 719 N Lamar St ☎ 662 236 2666, ⓦ bigbadbreakfast.com. In a shopping centre a mile north of town, this wildly popular breakfast spot serves creative takes on traditional brunch items such as tabasco-cured bacon, skillets with crawfish and hash browns and biscuits with a herby tomato gravy. Mon–Fri 7am–1.30pm, Sat & Sun 8am–3pm.

Bottletree Bakery 923 Van Buren Ave ☎ 662 236 5000, ⓦ bottletreebakery.net. Just off the square, this friendly little café serves healthy breakfasts, scrumptious home-baked pastries – including its trademark humble pie – soups and sandwiches. Tues–Fri 7am–2.30pm, Sat 8am–2.30pm, Sun 8am–2pm.

City Grocery 152 Courthouse Square ☎ 662 232 8080, ⓦ citygroceryonline.com. For sophisticated Southern cuisine, head to this buzzy landmark, which has a balcony and upstairs bar. Mains cost about $28. Mon–Wed 11.30am–2pm & 6–10pm, Thurs–Sat 11.30am–2pm & 6–10.30pm.

Taylor Grocery Hwy-338 ☎ 662 236 1716, ⓦ taylor grocery.com. Just 15min south of Oxford, in tiny Taylor, this rickety old shack dishes up amazing catfish to a raucous crowd. Thurs–Sat 5–10pm, Sun 5–9pm.

Tupelo

On January 8, 1935, **Elvis Presley** and his twin brother Jesse were born in **TUPELO**, an industrial town in northeastern Mississippi. Jesse died at birth, while Elvis grew up to be a truck driver. Their parents, Gladys and Vernon Presley, who lived in poor, white East Tupelo, struggled to survive. The financial strain was bad enough that Elvis's sharecropper father, in a desperate attempt to raise cash, resorted to forgery and was given a three-year sentence. Their home was repossessed and the family moved to Memphis in 1948.

Surprisingly, for most of the year Tupelo doesn't go in for Elvis overkill; Main Street is a long, placid stretch of nondescript buildings, with nary a gift shop to be seen. The visitor centre has details of the enjoyable four-day **Elvis Festival**, held in June, when the town fills with jumpsuited tribute artists.

Elvis Presley Birthplace

306 Elvis Presley Drive • May–Sept Mon–Sat 9am–5.30pm, Sun 1–5pm; Oct–April Mon–Sat 9am–5pm, Sun 1–5pm • House $6, museum, church and house $15 • ☎ 662 841 1245, ⓦ elvispresleybirthplace.com

The actual **Elvis Presley Birthplace** is fascinating. A two-room shotgun house, built for $150 in 1934, it's been furnished to look as it did when Elvis was born; it's an undeniably moving experience to stand in this tiny building that the Presley family struggled so hard to keep.

Equally poignant is the adjacent family **church**, moved here from one block away; you sit in the pews as wraparound movie screens recreate the kind of barnstorming services that Elvis grew up with, ringing with speechifying, testifying and the emotional gospel music that the King always kept close to his heart. An unmissable small **museum** puts Elvis's early years in fascinating context, illustrating life in the prewar South with lots of old photos and memorabilia.

Neon Pig 1203 N Gloster St (Rte-145) ☎ 662 269 2533, ⓦ theneonpig.com. Don't be put off by the location (it's in a strip mall on the highway); inside, the *Pig* is loud, cosy and fun, with a small but tasty menu of custom-ground burgers, sandwiches and craft beer. There's also a little shop selling fresh veggies, shellfish and local meats. Mon–Sat 11am–9pm, Sun 11am–4pm.

Vicksburg

6

The historic port of **VICKSBURG** straddles a high bluff on a bend in the Mississippi, 44 miles west of Jackson. During the Civil War, its domination of the river halted Union shipping and led Abraham Lincoln to call Vicksburg the "key to the Confederacy". It was a crucial target for General Ulysses S. Grant, who eventually landed to the south in the spring of 1863, circled inland and attacked from the east. After a 47-day siege, the outnumbered Confederates surrendered on the Fourth of July – a holiday Vicksburg declined to celebrate for the next 81 years – and Lincoln was able to rejoice that "the Father of Waters again goes unvexed to the sea".

As the Mississippi has changed course since the 1860s, it's now the slender, canalized Yazoo River rather than the broad Mississippi that flows alongside the battlefield and most of downtown Vicksburg. The core of the city, a bare but attractive place of precipitous streets, steep terraces and wooded ravines, has changed little, however, despite the arrival of permanently moored riverfront **casinos**. Downtown, especially **Washington Street**, is being restored to its original late-Victorian appearance, though most of its finest buildings were destroyed during the siege.

Old Court House Museum

1008 Cherry St • June–Aug Mon–Sat 8.30am–5pm, Sun 1.30–5pm; Sept–May closes 4.30pm • $5 • ☎ 601 636 0741, ⓦ oldcourthouse.org

The fascinating **Old Court House Museum** covers the Civil War era in depth, even selling genuine miniè balls (bullets). Its catch-all exhibits include the tie Jefferson Davis wore at his inauguration, a wartime newspaper – printed on wallpaper because of the conflict – Confederate currency, and a weathered armchair favoured by (a likely very inebriated) General Grant during the siege. The second floor's court chamber feels like it could have been lifted from the set of *To Kill a Mockingbird*.

Biedenharn Candy Company

1107 Washington St • Mon–Sat 9am–5pm, Sun 1.30–4.30pm • $3.50 • ☎ 601 638 6514, ⓦ biedenharncoca-colamuseum.com

A small museum at the **Biedenharn Candy Company** marks the spot where Coca-Cola was first bottled, with vivid displays on how it all came about. Out back, you'll find an ancient 1900 soda fountain, dubbed "The Siberian Arctic", presumably because it kept beverages remarkably chilled.

Vicksburg National Military Park

3201 Clay St • Daily 8am–5pm • $8/vehicle, good for seven days • ☎ 601 636 0583, ⓦ nps.gov/vick

Entered via Clay Street (off US-80) just east of town, **Vicksburg National Military Park** preserves the main Civil War battlefield. A sixteen-mile loop drive through the rippling green hillsides traces every contour of the Union and Confederate trenches, punctuated by statues, refurbished cannon and more than 1600 state-by-state monuments. Nearby, in the **Vicksburg National Cemetery**, 13,000 of the 17,000 Union graves are marked simply "Unknown".

Mississippi Welcome Center Exit 1A beside the river (daily 8am–5pm; ☎ 601 638 4269).

Visitor centre Near exit 4, opposite the battlefield entrance on Clay St (June–Aug daily 8am–5.30pm; Sept–May Mon–Sat 8am–5pm, Sun 10am–5pm; ☎ 601 636 9421, ⓦ visitvicksburg.com).

6

ACCOMMODATION AND EATING

★ **Anchuca** 1010 First East St ☎ 888 686 0111, ⓦ anchucamansion.com. Housed in the town's first colonnaded mansion, this beautiful B&B boasts a pool and a very good restaurant with outdoor seating. $125

Deluxe Inn 2751 N Frontage Rd (just off I-20) ☎ 601 636 5121. The military park is the prime area for motels; this comfortable, mom-and-pop option offers clean, quiet rooms with freshly brewed coffee in the morning. $50

Rusty's 901 Washington St ☎ 601 638 2030, ⓦ rustys riverfront.com. Tables fill up quickly at this central

seafood and steak place with an open kitchen and superlative fried green tomatoes ($11), juicy rib eyes ($23) and airy coconut cream pie ($5). Tues–Fri 11am–2pm & 5–9.30pm, Sat 11am–9.30pm.

Walnut Hills 1214 Adams St ☎ 601 638 4910, ⓦ walnuthillsms.com. This restaurant whips up superb all-you-can-eat "round table" lunches ($22) of fried chicken and other Southern delicacies, served in an 1880s house. It also does à la carte. Mon & Wed–Sat 11am–9pm, Sun 11am–2pm.

Natchez

Seventy miles south of Vicksburg – at the end of the pretty Natchez Trace Parkway, the old Native American path that ran from here to Nashville – the river town of **NATCHEZ** is the oldest permanent settlement on the Mississippi River. By the time it first flew the Stars and Stripes in 1798, it had already been home to the Natchez people and their predecessors, as well as French, British and Spanish colonists. Unlike its great rival, Vicksburg, Natchez was spared significant damage during the Civil War, ensuring that its abundant Greek Revival antebellum mansions remained intact, complete with meticulous gardens. Interspersed among them are countless simpler but similarly attractive white clapboard homes, set along broad leafy avenues of majestic oaks, making Natchez one of the prettiest towns in the South. **Horse and carriage** tours (see opposite) explore downtown, while a number of individual mansions are open for tours.

Though Natchez proper perches well above the river, a small stretch of riverfront at the foot of the bluff constitutes **Natchez Under-the-Hill**. Once known as the "Sodom of the Mississippi", it now houses a handful of bars and restaurants, plus the 24-hour *Isle of Capri* riverboat **casino**.

Natchez's history of **slavery** is chronicled with a rather pitiful display at the **Forks of the Road monument**, a mile east of downtown on Liberty Road at St Catherine, on the site of the second largest slave market in the South.

Longwood

140 Lower Woodville Rd • Tours daily on the half hour 9am–5pm • $15 • ☎ 601 442 5193, ⓦ natchezpilgrimage.com

Fans of HBO's *True Blood* will recognize the elaborate, octagonal **Longwood**, with its huge dome and snow-white arches and columns, as the home of the vampire king of Mississippi. Such was their haste to get north at the start of the Civil War, the Philadelphia builders constructing this six-storey mansion left their tools behind (still on view). Only the first floor of Longwood was ever completed, and it's exciting to go from the elaborately furnished ground level to the raw, unfinished second storey, which spirals upward in an open, unvarnished wooden arc.

Melrose

1 Melrose Montebello Pkwy • Daily 8.30am–5pm • $10 • ☎ 601 446 5790, ⓦ nps.gov/natc

Unlike many of the town's house tours, which strive to present a Tara-like picture of life in antebellum Mississippi, the 1831 **Melrose** balances facts about the mansion's cotton planter homeowners with hard details on the lives of its slave population, whose quarters have been preserved.

William Johnson House and around

210 State St • Daily 9am–5pm • Free • ☎ 601 445 5345, ⓦ nps.gov/natc

Downtown, the fascinating **William Johnson House** relays the history of an African American barber whose sixteen-year diary offers a rare glimpse into the goings-on of a

Southern free person of colour. Born a slave in 1809, Johnson became a slaveholder himself during his adult years.

Nearby, at 400 State St, the chapel of the **First Presbyterian Church** (Mon–Sat 10am–4pm; $5 donation; ☎601 445 2581, ⓦfpcnatchez.org) holds an incredible collection of black-and-white photographs depicting all aspects of life in nineteenth-century, riverfront Natchez.

INFORMATION AND TOURS   NATCHEZ

Visitor centre 640 S Canal St (by the Mississippi River bridge; Mon–Sat 8.30am–5pm, Sun 9.30am–4pm; ☎601 446 6345, ⓦvisitnatchez.com); houses intriguing historical displays and overlooks the water.

Tours The visitor centre is the starting point for various tram (trolley), mansion and bus tours along with carriage rides (around $15).

Natchez Pilgrimage The mansions can also be seen during the twice-yearly pilgrimage tours (March & Oct; $30/three houses; ☎601 446 6631, ⓦnatchezpilgrimage.com), led by women trussed up in massive hoopskirts.

ACCOMMODATION AND EATING

★ **Carriage House** 401 High St, in Stanton Hall ☎601 445 5151, ⓦstantonhall.com. Sunday brunch is a must at this classic Southern restaurant, set on the grounds of an 1857 Greek Revival mansion. The buffet ($16) is a luscious cornucopia of crab and Brie soup, pork cheeks in grits, flaky biscuits and smothered mustard greens. Wed–Sun 11am–2pm.

Pig Out Inn 116 S Canal St ☎601 442 8050, ⓦpigoutinnbbq.com. Boasting "swine dining at its finest", this downtown haunt has soul records on the wall, barbecue smoking out back and oodles of pig paraphernalia throughout. Mon–Sat 11am–9pm, Sun 11am–3pm.

Slick Rick's 109 N Pearl St ☎601 445 9900, ⓦslickricksfoods.com. Artisanal sandwich shop with creative compilations such as the "bella", made with balsamic-infused mushrooms, spicy jack cheese and roasted pepper sauce ($9). Good vegan options, too. Mon–Fri 10am–6pm, Sat 10am–5pm.

Stone House Music Room 804 Washington St ☎601 445 7466, ⓦjosephstonehouse.com. This B&B offers something a little different from the other grand mansions; owned by a professional musician who gives free piano recitals to guests, it also has a billiards room and a store selling antique maps and prints. **$155**

Arkansas

Historically, **ARKANSAS** belongs firmly to the South. It sided with the Confederacy during the Civil War and its capital, **Little Rock**, was, in 1957, one of the most notorious flashpoints in the struggle for **civil rights**. Geographically, however, it marks the beginning of the Great Plains. Unlike the Southern states on the east side of the Mississippi River, Arkansas (the correct pronunciation, following a state law from 1881, is "Arkansaw") remained sparsely populated until the late nineteenth century. What's surprising about the eastern Arkansas delta lands is that they are far from totally flat: **Crowley's Ridge**, a narrow arc of windblown loess hills, breaks up the uniform smoothness, stretching 150 miles from southern Missouri to the sleepy river town of **Helena**, which is an important stop for **Delta blues** enthusiasts. In 1992 local boy **Bill Clinton's** accession to the presidency catapulted Arkansas to national prominence.

Though Arkansas encompasses the **Mississippi Delta** in the east, oil-rich timber lands in the south, and the sweeping **Ouachita** ("Wash-ih-taw") **Mountains** in the west, the cragged and charismatic **Ozark Mountains** in the north are its most scenic asset, abounding with parks, lakes, rivers and streams, and a couple of alternative little towns that make welcoming places to stay.

Helena

The small Mississippi port of **HELENA**, roughly sixty miles south of Memphis, was once the shipping point for Arkansas' cotton crop, when Mark Twain described it as

6

KING BISCUIT TIME SHOW

In 1941, Helena was the birthplace of the celebrated **King Biscuit Time Show**, broadcast on radio station KFFA (1360 AM). The first radio show in the nation to broadcast live Delta blues, it featured performances from legends including boogie pianist Pinetop Perkins and harmonica great **Sonny Boy Williamson II** ("Rice" Miller) – the local boy who featured Helena in intimate detail in many of his (usually extemporized) recordings. With a huge influence that belies its tiny size – musicians from B.B. King to Levon Helm cite it as a major inspiration – the show is the longest running in history, having been on air continuously ever since and hosted from 1950 onwards by living legend "Sunshine" Sonny Payne. **Broadcasts** are recorded from the foyer of the excellent Delta Cultural Center at 141 Cherry St (Tues–Sat 9am–5pm; broadcasts Mon–Fri 12.15–12.45pm; free; ☎870 338 4350, ⓦdeltaculturalcenter.com); observers are welcome. If you miss the show, make sure to stop by the centre's **music exhibit**.

occupying "one of the prettiest situations on the river". A compact **historic district** bordered by Holly, College and Perry streets reflects that brief period of prosperity, before the arrival of the railroad left most of the river towns obsolete, but nowadays it feels the strain of living in the shadow of the enormous casinos across the river. Most activity takes place along run-down **Cherry Street** on the levee.

The Depot

95 Missouri St • Tues–Sat 9am–5pm • Free • ☎ 870 338 4350, ⓦ deltaculturalcenter.com

The Delta Cultural Center (see box above) has another site, the Depot, a block south of the visitor centre, in a restored train depot. Exhibits cover all aspects of the region's history, from the first settlers of this soggy frontier to contemporary racism, with, of course, lots of good stuff about local musical heritage.

ACCOMMODATION AND EATING   HELENA

Edwardian Inn 317 Biscoe St, north of the Mississippi Bridge ☎870 338 9155, ⓦedwardianinn.com. This 1904 inn is an opulent, reasonably priced B&B with large oak-panelled rooms, slightly marred by its views over a chemical plant. **$90**

Granny Dee's 426 Cherry St ☎870 338 8862. Down-home soul food favourite with a great lunch buffet stocked with fried catfish, butter beans, bread pudding and the like. Tues–Sat 8am–3pm.

SHOPPING

Bubba Sullivan's Blues Corner 105 Cherry St ☎870 338 3501. Blues fans can buy a thrilling assortment of records at this legendary music shop. Bubba is a mine of information on local music, not least the town's superb

King Biscuit Blues Festival (ⓦkingbiscuitfestival.com), held every autumn, which attracts more than 60,000 visitors for its big-name blues, acoustic and gospel. Call ahead as hours fluctuate.

Little Rock

The geographical, political and financial centre of Arkansas, **LITTLE ROCK** is at the meeting point of the state's two major regions, the northwestern hills and the eastern Delta. Site of one of the key flashpoints of the civil rights era (see box opposite), the town today has a relaxed, open feel and maintains a certain cachet from the election of William J. Clinton to the presidency in 1992.

The library forms an anchor for the vibrant **River Market District**, with its splash of restaurants and bars, farmers' market and eclectic food hall. Along the Arkansas River, **Riverfront Park** runs for several blocks. A commemorative sign under the Junction Bridge marks the "little rock" for which the city is named (not particularly striking, but then the name gives that away).

William J. Clinton Presidential Library and Museum

1200 President Clinton Ave • Mon–Sat 9am–5pm, Sun 1–5pm • $7 • ☎ 501 374 4242, ⓦ clintonlibrary.gov

Bill is celebrated in the dazzling **William J. Clinton Presidential Library and Museum**, an elevated, glass-and-metal building glinting above the Arkansas River east of downtown. Spearheading the revitalization of a once-depressed district of abandoned warehouses, the environmentally friendly structure is now part of a campus of federally certified "green" buildings.

Old State House Museum

300 W Markham St • Mon–Sat 9am–5pm, Sun 1–5pm • Free • ☎ 501 324 9685, ⓦ oldstatehouse.com

Surrounded by smooth lawns and shaded by evergreens, the **Old State House Museum**, in the former capitol building, backs onto the river. The displays – everything from Civil War battle flags to African American quilts – do an admirable job of covering Arkansas history.

Historic Arkansas Museum

200 E 3rd St • Mon–Sat 9am–5pm, Sun 1–5pm • $2.50 • ☎ 501 324 9351, ⓦ historicarkansas.org

The **Historic Arkansas Museum**, a living museum of frontier life, includes the 1827 Hinderliter Grog Shop, Little Rock's oldest standing building. The institute is comprised of five antebellum houses, complete with costumed actors, and a handful of galleries devoted to local art, textiles and, intriguingly, knives, including the local weapon made famous by rapscallion Jim Bowie.

Arkansas Arts Center

MacArthur Park, 9th and Commerce sts • Tues–Sat 10am–5pm, Sun 11am–5pm • Free • ☎ 501 372 4000, ⓦ arkarts.com

The elegant **Arkansas Arts Center** has high-profile rotating shows, drawings dating from the Renaissance and a nice selection of contemporary crafts. The museum also houses a renowned children's theatre – try to catch a performance if you're travelling with kids.

CONFRONTATION AT CENTRAL HIGH

In 1957, Little Rock unexpectedly became the battleground in the first major conflict between state and federal government over **race relations**. At the time, the city was generally viewed as progressive by Southern standards. All parks, libraries and buses were integrated, a relatively high thirty percent of blacks were on the electoral register and there were black police officers. However, when the Little Rock School Board announced its decision to phase in **desegregation** gradually – the Supreme Court having declared segregation of schools to be unconstitutional – James Johnson, a candidate for governor, started a campaign opposing interracial education. Johnson's rhetoric began to win him support, and the incumbent governor, **Orval Faubus**, who had previously shown no interest in the issue, jumped on the bandwagon.

The first nine black students were due to enter **Central High School** that September. The day before school opened, Faubus, "in the interest of safety", reversed his decision to let blacks enrol, only to be overruled by the federal court. He ordered the National Guard to bar the black students anyway; soldiers with bayonets forced Elizabeth Eckford, one of the nine, from the school entrance into a seething crowd, from which she had to jump on a bus to escape. As legal battles raged during the day, at night blacks were subject to violent attacks by white gangs. Three weeks later, President Eisenhower reluctantly brought in the 101st Airborne Division, and, amid violent demonstrations, the nine entered the school. That year, they experienced intense intimidation; when one retaliated, she was expelled. The graduation of Ernest Green, the oldest, seemed to put an end to the affair, but Faubus, up for re-election, renewed his political posturing by closing down all Little Rock's public schools for the 1958–59 academic year – and thereby increased his majority. Today Central High School – an enormous brown, crescent-shaped structure at 1500 S Park Ave – is on the National Register of Historic Places and has been designated a National Park site. Across the street, at 2120 W Daisy L. Gatson Bates Drive, the **Central High Visitor Centre** (daily 9am–4.30pm; free; ☎ 501 374 1957, ⓦ nps.gov/chsc), on the spot from which reporters filed stories on the only public payphone in the neighbourhood, has a good exhibition about the crisis.

ARRIVAL AND INFORMATION

LITTLE ROCK

By bus Greyhound (☎ 501 372 3007) arrives at 118 E Washington Ave in North Little Rock, across the river. There are two daily services to Hot Springs, AR (1hr).

By train Amtrak is at Markham and Victory sts.

Visitor centre 615 E Capitol Ave (Mon–Sat 9am–5pm, Sun 1–5pm; ☎ 501 376 4781, ⓦ littlerock.com).

Listings For listings, check the free weekly *Arkansas Times* (ⓦ arktimes.com).

ACCOMMODATION, EATING AND NIGHTLIFE

Comfort Inn & Suites Downtown 707 I-30, near the Clinton Library ☎ 501 687 7700, ⓦ comfortinn.com. Good, centrally located budget option with large modern rooms, a swimming pool, complimentary airport shuttle and a hearty free breakfast. $90

Doe's Eat Place 1023 W Markham St ☎ 501 376 1195, ⓦ doeseatplace.net. This unpretentious landmark serves excellent steak and tamales; it's a long-time favourite of Clinton and still a hot spot for hungry politicos. Mon–Thurs 11am–2pm & 5.30–9.30pm, Fri 11am–2pm & 5.30–10pm, Sat 5.30–10pm.

River Market 400 President Clinton Ave ☎ 501 375 2552, ⓦ rivermarket.info/eat. The bustling market hall food court provides a wealth of places to eat, with stalls dishing up organic soups, Middle Eastern salads, BBQ, pad thai, artisan breads and coffee. Mon–Sat 7am–6pm.

The Root Café 1500 S Main St ☎ 501 414 0423, ⓦ therootcafe.com. A bit south of downtown, this earthy little place has a small farm-to-table menu with quirky items such as eggs "banh mi" (sprinkled with pickled carrots, daikon radish and coriander; $5.75), curry chicken salad sandwiches ($7.50), home-made bratwurst ($7.25) and vegan brownies. Tues–Fri 7am–2.30pm, Sat 8am–3.30pm, Sun 9am–2pm.

Rosemont B&B 515 W 15th St ☎ 501 374 7456, ⓦ rosemontoflittlerock.com. Bill Clinton was a regular visitor at this luxurious, powder-pink inn with sophisticated guest quarters, breakfasts made from locally sourced ingredients, a relaxing veranda and a manicured garden good for coffee and a paper. $99

Vino's 923 W 7th St ☎ 501 375 8466, ⓦ vinosbrewpub .com. You'll find good music at *Vino's*, a friendly brewpub/pizza joint with live indie and rock after dark. Mon–Thurs & Sun 11am–11pm, Fri & Sat 11am–midnight.

Hot Springs

Fifty miles southwest of Little Rock, the low-key, historic and somewhat surreal spa town of **HOT SPRINGS** nestles in the forested Zig Zag Mountains on the eastern flank of the Ouachitas. Its **thermal waters** have attracted visitors since Native Americans used the area as a neutral zone to mediate disputes. Early settlers fashioned a crude resort out of the wilderness, and after the railroads arrived in 1875 it became a European-style spa; its hot waters are said to cure rheumatism, arthritis, kidney disease and liver problems. The resort reached its glittering heyday during the Twenties and Thirties, when the mayor reputedly ran a gambling syndicate worth $30 million per annum, and players included Al Capone and Bugsy Siegel. Movie stars and politicians, aristocrats and prizefighters flocked, and Hot Springs became *the* place to see and be seen. The resort's popularity waned when new cures appeared during the Fifties; today its faded grandeur and small-town sleepiness give it a distinctive appeal.

Quite apart from its waters, Hot Springs prides itself on its small **galleries**, plenty of which line Central Avenue, along with some wonderfully weird Americana. The town hosts a prestigious documentary **film festival** each October (ⓦ hsdfi.org), and a well-known **classical music festival** in June (ⓦ hotmusic.org).

Fordyce Bathhouse

369 Central Ave • Feb–Dec daily 9am–5pm • Free • ☎ 501 620 6715, ⓦ nps.gov/hosp

Eight magnificent buildings behind a lush display of magnolia trees, elms and hedgerows make up the splendid **Bathhouse Row**. Between 1915 and 1962, the grandest of them all was the **Fordyce Bathhouse**, which reopened in 1989 as the visitor centre for **Hot Springs National Park**. Apart from the Buckstaff (see opposite), this is the only bathhouse you can actually enter: the interior, restored to its former radiance, is an atmospheric mixture of the elegant and the obsolete. The heavy use of veined Italian marble, mosaic-tile floors and stained glass lend it a decadent feel, while the gruesome hydrotherapy and electrotherapy equipment, including an electric shock massager, seem impossibly brutish.

Behind the Fordyce, two small **springs** have been left open for viewing. The **Grand Promenade** from here is a half-mile brick walkway overlooking downtown.

Buckstaff Bathhouse

509 Central Ave • March–Nov Mon–Sat 8am–11.45am & 1.30–3pm; Dec–Feb closed Sat afternoon • $30/1hr bath • ☎ 501 623 2308, ⓦ buckstaffbaths.com

It's still possible to take a "bath" – an hour-long process involving brisk rubdowns, hot packs, a thorough steaming and a needle shower – on Bathhouse Row. The only establishment still open for business is the 1912 **Buckstaff**, where a thermal mineral bath in a municipal, rather prosaic, atmosphere costs $30. Full bathing facilities are also available at several hotels. Hot Springs' water lacks the sulphuric taste often associated with thermal springs; fill a bottle at any of the drinking fountains near Central Avenue. Most of them pump out warm water – if you prefer it cold, head for the Happy Hollow Spring on Fountain Street.

Hot Springs Mountain

Trails of various lengths and severity lead up the steep slopes of **Hot Springs Mountain**. To reach the summit, take a short drive or any of several different trails, including a testing two-and-a-half-mile hike through dense woods of oak, hickory and short-leafed pine.

ARRIVAL AND INFORMATION · HOT SPRINGS

By bus Greyhound (☎ 501 623 5574) pulls in at 100 Broadway Terrace.

National Park Service visitor centre Located in Fordyce Bathhouse (see opposite).

ACCOMMODATION, EATING AND NIGHTLIFE

Alpine Motel 741 Park Ave (Hwy-7) ☎ 501 624 9164, ⓦ arlingtonhotel.com. At the budget end of the scale, a mile or so from Bathhouse Row, this option is a kitschy, clean mom-and-pop place. **$60**

Arlington Resort/Spa 239 Central Ave ☎ 501 623 7771, ⓦ arlingtonhotel.com. Dominating the centre, this quirky 1920s landmark oozes faded grandeur – Al Capone rented the entire fourth floor and President Clinton attended his junior and senior proms in the ballroom. **$88**

Gulpha Gorge Campground 305 Gorge Rd (Hwy-70B) ☎ 501 620 6715, ⓦ nps.gov/hosp. The nearest place to camp is the first-come, first-served spot in the national park, 2 miles northeast of town. **$10**

McClard's Bar-B-Q 505 Albert Pike, 3 miles south of downtown ☎ 501 623 9665, ⓦ mcclards.com. Famed barbecue joint where the mouth-watering ribs, slaw, beans and tamales are all prepared by hand; it's so good that Bill and Hillary stopped by on their wedding day. Tues–Sat 11am–8pm.

Rolando's 210 Central Ave ☎ 501 318 6054, ⓦ rolandosrestaurante.com. Hidden among the family restaurants along Central Ave, this festive *Nuevo Latino* place serves up tasty, creative food such as shrimp sautéed in a citrusy tequila sauce and topped with sweet peppers and onions. Mon–Thurs & Sun 11am–9pm, Fri & Sat 11am–10pm.

The Witness 1942 Millcreek Rd, at Panther Valley Ranch ☎ 501 623 9781, ⓦ witnessproductions.com. An outdoor musical of Christ's life as sung by the Apostle Peter, performed on weekends from June through October.

The Ozark Mountains

Although the highest peak fails to top 2000ft, the **Ozark Mountains**, extending beyond northern Arkansas into southern Missouri, are characterized by severe steep ridges and jagged spurs. Hair-raising roads weave their way over the precipitous hills, past rugged lakeshores and pristine rivers. When speculators poured into Arkansas in the 1830s, those who missed the best land etched out remote hill farms, much like those they'd left behind in Kentucky or Tennessee, and lived in isolation until the second half of the twentieth century. A massive tourism boom, while bringing much-needed cash, also created a string of cookie-cutter American towns; the Ozarks are now the fastest-growing rural section of the USA.

The word "Ozark" is everywhere, used to entice tourists into music shows, gift emporia and fast-food restaurants. With all the hype, it's difficult to tell what's genuine – a good reason to visit **Mountain View**, where traditional Ozark skills and music are preserved. The region's most visited town, **Eureka Springs**, just inside the Missouri border, is a pretty Victorian spa resort with a rootsy, bohemian scene.

Mountain View

Roughly sixty miles north of Little Rock, the state-run **Ozark Folk Centre**, two miles north of the town of **MOUNTAIN VIEW** on Hwy-14, is a good living history museum that attempts to show how life used to be in these remote hills, not reached by paved roads until the Fifties. Homestead skills are displayed in reconstructed log cabins, and folk musicians and storytellers perform throughout. In the evenings you can see Ozark and roots music **concerts** (early April to end Nov Tues–Sat 10am–5pm; crafts $12, concerts $12, combination ticket $19.50; ☎800 264 3655, ⓦozarkfolkcenter.com).

ACCOMMODATION AND EATING   MOUNTAIN VIEW

Buffalo Camping 1 Frost St, Gilbert ☎870 439 2888, ⓦgilbertstore.com. Near Pruitt Landing (see box below), this outfit administers a few log cabins, all of which sleep at least four and up to ten. **$109**

Folk Center 1032 Park Ave, Mountain View ☎800 264 3655, ⓦozarkfolkcenter.com. The Folk Center offers quiet, comfortable cabins year-round. **$67**

Inn at Mountain View 307 W Washington St ☎870 269 4200, ⓦinnatmountainview.com. This friendly inn is a pretty B&B owned by folk musicians; they serve a full country breakfast (minimum stay required at weekends and festivals). **$95**

Tommy's Famous W Main St (Hwy-66) and Famous Place ☎870 269 3278. Funky little place four blocks west of the town square that dishes up good pizza, ribs and BBQ. Note that Mountain View is a dry town. Daily 3–9pm.

Eureka Springs

Picturesque **EUREKA SPRINGS**, set on steep mountain slopes in Arkansas' northwestern corner, began life in the nineteenth century as a health resort. As that role diminished, its striking location turned it into a tourist destination, filled with Victorian buildings and streets linked by flights of stone stairs. Today it's a cool, progressive spot, with kitsch outdoor movie events, diversity weekends (ⓦeurekapride.com), and plenty of places offering alternative therapies.

Great Passion Play

935 Passion Play Rd • May–Oct • $25 • ☎800 882 7529, ⓦgreatpassionplay.org

Three miles east of town on US-62 E, a seven-storey **Christ of the Ozarks** – a statue of Jesus with a 60ft arm span – sets the tone for a jaw-dropping religious complex known as the **Great Passion Play**, the brainchild of Elna M. Smith, who worried that the holy sites of the Middle East would be destroyed by war, decided to build replicas in the Ozarks. The play itself re-enacts Christ's last days on earth with a cast of 250, including live animals, in a 4100-seat amphitheatre.

ACTIVITIES IN THE OZARK MOUNTAINS

In the **Ozark National Forest**, fifteen miles northwest of Mountain View off Hwy-14, you can tour the **Blanchard Springs Caverns** (times vary; $10; ☎870 757 2211, ⓦblanchardsprings .org), an eerily beautiful underground cave system with a crystal-clear swimming hole surrounded by towering rock bluffs. The **Buffalo River** – a prime destination for whitewater canoeing – flows across the state north of Mountain View. In the sweet little settlement of Gilbert, off Hwy-65 at the end of Hwy-333 E, **Buffalo Camping and Canoeing** (☎870 439 2888, ⓦgilbertstore.com) rents canoes for trips on the mid-section of the river, at its most spectacular around **Pruitt Landing**.

INFORMATION AND TOURS

Visitor centre Village Circle (daily 9am–5pm; ☎ 800 638 7352, ⓦeurekasprings.org).

Train tours Take a ride on the Eureka Springs and North Arkansas Railway, whose rolling stock includes a magnificent "cabbage-head" wood-burning locomotive; trips depart from the depot at 299 N Main St (April–Oct Tues–Fri 10.30am, noon & 2.30pm, Sat also 4pm; $14; ☎479 253 9623, ⓦesnarailway.com).

ACCOMMODATION, EATING AND NIGHTLIFE

Eureka Springs has lots of appealing places to stay; log cabins and B&Bs abound, many with staggering views. The town holds the fine Ozark folk festival in autumn (ⓦozarkfolkfestival.com), and the acclaimed blues festival in June (ⓦeurekaspringsblues.com).

6

Chelsea's Corner 10 Mountain St ☎479 253 6723, ⓦchelseascornercafe.com. This friendly local institution features live music most evenings. Mon–Sat 11am–9pm, Sun 9am–3pm.

Local Flavor Café 71 S Main St ☎479 253 9522, ⓦlocalflavorcafe.net. Dishes up tasty modern American cuisine, such as pear salad topped with pine nuts and parmesan cheese ($9), and has lovely balcony seating. Mon–Sat 11am–9pm, Sun 9am–3pm.

Mud Street Café 22 S Main St ☎479 253 6732, ⓦmudstreetcafe.com. This artsy café serves good espresso, light lunches and desserts. Thurs–Mon 8am–3pm.

★ **Sherwood Court** 248 W Van Buren ☎479 253 8920, ⓦsherwoodcourt.com. This welcoming inn offers individually decorated cottages and motel-style rooms around flower-filled courtyards. $̲4̲9̲

★ **Treehouse Cottages** 165 W Van Buren ☎479 253 8667, ⓦtreehousecottages.com. At this unique place, you can hide away in one of seven luxury cabins on stilts, set deep in the forest. $̲1̲4̲9̲

Florida

ALBION HOTEL, SOUTH BEACH, MIAMI

Florida

Brochure images of tanning tourists and Mickey Mouse give an inaccurate and incomplete picture of Florida. Although the aptly nicknamed "Sunshine State" is indeed devoted to the tourist trade, it's also among the least-understood parts of the USA. Away from its overexposed resorts lie forests and rivers, deserted strands filled with wildlife, and vibrant cities within reach of primeval swamps. Contrary to the popular retirement-community image, new Floridians tend to be a younger, more energetic breed, while Spanish-speaking enclaves provide close ties to Latin America and the Caribbean.

The essential stop is cosmopolitan, half-Latin **Miami**. A simple journey south from here brings you to the **Florida Keys**, a hundred-mile string of islands known for sport fishing, coral-reef diving and the sultry town of **Key West**, legendary for its sunsets and liberal attitude. Back on the mainland, west from Miami stretch the easily accessible **Everglades**, a water-logged sawgrass plain filled with alligators, a symbol of the state that can be found on college campuses (well, as a game mascot, anyway) and innumerable billboards. Much of Florida's **east coast** is heavily built-up – a side effect of the migration of so-called "sunbirds" seeking to escape the cold climes of the northeast USA. The residential stranglehold is loosened further north, where the **Kennedy Space Center** launches NASA shuttles. Further along, historical **St Augustine** stands as the longest continuously occupied European settlement in the US.

In **central Florida** the terrain turns green, though it's no rural idyll, thanks in mainly to **Orlando** and **Walt Disney World**, which sprawl out across the countryside. From here it's just a skip west to the towns and beaches of the **Gulf Coast**, and somewhat further north to the forests of the **Panhandle**, Florida's link with the Deep South.

Brief history

The **first European sighting** of Florida, just six years after Christopher Columbus reached the New World, is believed to have been made by John and Sebastian Cabot in 1498. At the time, the area's one hundred thousand inhabitants formed several distinct **tribes**: the Timucua across northern Florida, the Calusa around the southwest and Lake Okeechobee, the Apalachee in the Panhandle and the Tequesta along the southeast coast.

In 1513, a Spaniard, **Juan Ponce de León**, sighted land during *Pascua Florida*, Spain's Easter celebration; he named what he saw *La Florida*, or "Land of Flowers". Eight years later he returned, the first of several Spanish incursions prompted by rumours of gold hidden in the north of the region. When it became clear that Florida did not hold stunning riches, interest waned, and it wasn't until 1565 that conquistador Pedro Menéndez de Avilés founded **St Augustine**. In 1586, St Augustine was razed by a British naval bombardment led by Francis Drake, and the ensuing bloody confrontation for

SIGNPOST, KEY WEST

Highlights

❶ Ocean Drive, Miami South Beach's Art Deco showpiece, buzzing with cosmopolitan cafés, flashy vintage cars and beautiful people. See p.481

❷ Florida Keys Dive, snorkel or just admire the flaming sunsets off this chain of enticing islands. Alternatively, revel in the hedonistic culture of Key West at the end of the chain. See p.493

❸ Kennedy Space Center, Space Coast Take in some of the space-age technology here, just a stone's throw from the Merritt Island National Wildlife Refuge. See p.504

❹ St Augustine Sixteenth-century Spanish town packed with historic homes, an impressive living history museum and several nice beaches. See p.506

❺ Walt Disney World Pure entertainment, planned down to the last detail, for better or worse. See p.510

❻ Salvador Dalí Museum, St Petersburg The artist's Surrealist (and for some, scary) fantasies run amok in the state's unlikeliest art collection. See p.521

❼ Everglades National Park Trek through the vast sawgrass plains of the legendary Everglades, or canoe through alligator-filled mangrove swamps. See p.527

HIGHLIGHTS ARE MARKED ON THE MAP ON P.480

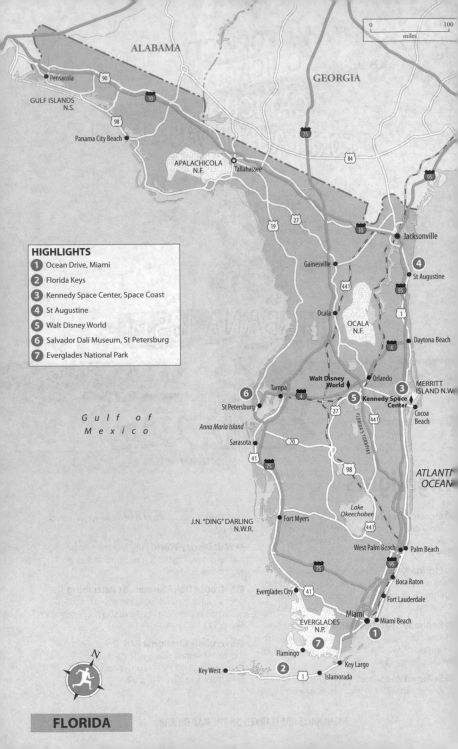

HIGHLIGHTS

1 Ocean Drive, Miami
2 Florida Keys
3 Kennedy Space Center, Space Coast
4 St Augustine
5 Walt Disney World
6 Salvador Dalí Museum, St Petersburg
7 Everglades National Park

WHEN TO GO: FLORIDA'S WEATHER

Warm sunshine and blue skies are almost always the norm in Florida. The state does, however, split into two **climatic zones**: subtropical in the south and warm temperate in the north. Orlando and points south have a mild season from October to April, with warm temperatures and low humidity – this is the **peak tourist season**, when prices are highest. Conversely, the southern summer (May–Sept) brings high humidity and afternoon storms; the rewards for braving the mugginess are lower prices and fewer tourists.

North of Orlando, winter is the off-peak period, even though daytime temperatures are generally comfortable (although snow has been known to fall on the Panhandle). During the northern Florida summer, the crowds arrive, and the days and nights are hot and very humid. Bear in mind that June to November is **hurricane season**, and there is a strong possibility of major storms throughout the entire state.

---

control was eventually settled when the British captured the crucial Spanish possession of Havana, Cuba; Spain willingly parted with Florida to get it back. By this point, indigenous Floridians had been largely wiped out by disease. The Native American population that was left largely comprised disparate tribes that had arrived from the north, collectively known as the **Seminoles**.

In the 1800s

Following American Independence, Florida once more reverted to Spain. In 1814, the US general (and future president) Andrew Jackson – with the intention of taking the region – marched south from Tennessee, killing hundreds of Native Americans and triggering the **First Seminole War**. Following the war, in 1819, Spain **ceded Florida** to the US, in return for American assumption of $5 million of Spanish debt. Not long after, Jackson was sworn in as Florida's first American governor, and Tallahassee selected as the new administrative centre.

Eleven years later, the **Act of Indian Removal** decreed that all Native Americans in the eastern US should be transferred to reservations in the Midwest. Most Seminole were determined to stay, which ignited the **Second Seminole War**; the Native Americans were steadily driven south, away from the fertile lands of central Florida and into the Everglades, where they eventually agreed to remain. Florida became the **27th state** on March 3, 1845, around the same time that the nascent railroad system first brought prosperity to the area.

Florida in the modern age

At the beginning of the twentieth century, the country's newspapers extolled the curative virtues of Florida's climate, and northern speculators invested their fortunes. These early efforts to promote Florida as a **tourist destination** brought in the wintering rich: the likes of Henry Flagler and Henry Plant extended their railroads and opened luxury resorts here. After World War I, everyone wanted a piece of Florida, and chartered trains brought in thousands of eager buyers. But most deals were only as solid as the paper they were written on, and in 1926 the banks began to default. The **Wall Street Crash** then made paupers of the millionaires whose investments had helped shape the state.

What saved Florida was **World War II**. During the war, thousands of troops arrived to guard the coastline, providing a taste of Florida that would entice many to return; postwar, the government expanded its facilities in and around Jacksonville, Tampa and Pensacola, bringing in thousands of residents and billions of investment dollars. Furthermore, in the mid-Sixties, the state government bent over backwards to help the Disney Corporation turn a sizeable slice of central Florida into **Walt Disney World**. Its enormous commercial success helped solidify Florida's place in the international tourist market.

Behind the optimistic facade, however, lie many **problems**. Gun laws remain notoriously lax, and the multimillion-dollar **drug trade** shows few signs of abating – at least a quarter of the cocaine entering the US is said to arrive via Florida. Recently, too, the environment along Florida's Gulf Coast was imperilled by 2010's Deepwater

7

Horizon **oil spill**. While the area has largely recovered from the disaster, the state filed suit against the oil company and its contractor in 2013, hoping to recoup some of the estimated billions of dollars it lost in tax income.

Miami

MIAMI is intoxicatingly beautiful, with palm trees swaying in the breeze and South Beach's famous Art Deco buildings glowing in the warm sunlight. Even so, it's the people – not the climate, the landscape or the cash – that make it so noteworthy. Two-thirds of the two-million-plus population are Hispanic, the majority of them **Cuban**, and Spanish is spoken here almost as often as English.

Miami has a range of districts that mirror its variegated cultural, economic and social divisions. Separated from the mainland by Biscayne Bay – and actually, a separate city – the most popular is **Miami Beach**, which is defined largely by the bacchanalian pursuits along **South Beach**. In addition to an enticing stretch of sand, this is home to much of the city's Art Deco architecture.

Back on the mainland, the towers of **downtown** herald Miami's proud status as the headquarters of many US corporations' Latin American operations. To the north, the art galleries and showrooms of **Wynwood** and the **Design District** are gradually starting to attract more visitors. Meanwhile, southwest of downtown, there's nowhere better for a Cuban lunch than **Little Havana**, which spreads out along 8th Street (also known as Calle Ocho). Immediately south, the spacious boulevards and ornate public buildings of **Coral Gables** are as impressive now as they were in the 1920s, when the district set new standards in town planning. Lastly, sun-worshippers should make time for **Key Biscayne**, a smart, secluded island community with some beautiful beaches, an easy five miles off the mainland. The Key had a "coloured-only" beach in the pre-civil rights era, and it is still significant in terms of local African American history.

Miami Beach

A long slender arm of land between Biscayne Bay and the Atlantic Ocean, **MIAMI BEACH**, three miles off the mainland, has been a headline-grabbing resort town for almost a hundred years. Until the 1910s – when its Quaker owner, John Collins, formed an unlikely partnership with a flashy entrepreneur, Carl Fisher – it was nothing more than an ailing fruit farm. With Fisher's money, Biscayne Bay was dredged, and the muck raised from its murky bed was used as landfill to transform this vegetated barrier island into a carefully sculptured landscape of palm trees, hotels and tennis courts. After a hurricane in 1926 devastated Miami (and especially the beach), damaged buildings were replaced by grander structures in the new Art Deco style, and Miami Beach as we know it appeared. More recently, the 1990s saw a renaissance spearheaded by a few savvy hoteliers and Miami's gay community.

MIAMI BEACH'S BEACHES

With twelve miles of calm waters, clean sands, swaying palms and candy-coloured lifeguard towers, you can't go wrong with Miami's cornucopia of **beaches**. The young and beautiful frequent those between 5th and 21st streets, a convenient hop from the juice bars and cafés on Ocean Drive. From 6th to 14th streets, **Lummus Park** – containing sand shipped in from the Bahamas – is the heart of the scene; there's an unofficial gay section roughly around 12th Street. North of 21st, things are more family-oriented, with a **boardwalk** running between the shore and the hotels up to 46th. To the south, **First Street Beach** and **South Pointe** are favoured by Cuban families, and are quite busy on weekends. For good **swimming**, head up to 85th, a quiet stretch that's usually patrolled by lifeguards.

South Beach

Occupying the southernmost three miles of Miami Beach is gorgeous **South Beach**, with its hundreds of dazzling pastel-coloured 1920s and 1930s Art Deco buildings. By day, the sun blares down on sizzling bodies on the sand, but it's worth braving an early-morning wake-up call to catch the dawn glow, which bathes the Deco hotels in pure, crystalline white light. By night, ten blocks of **Ocean Drive** become one of the

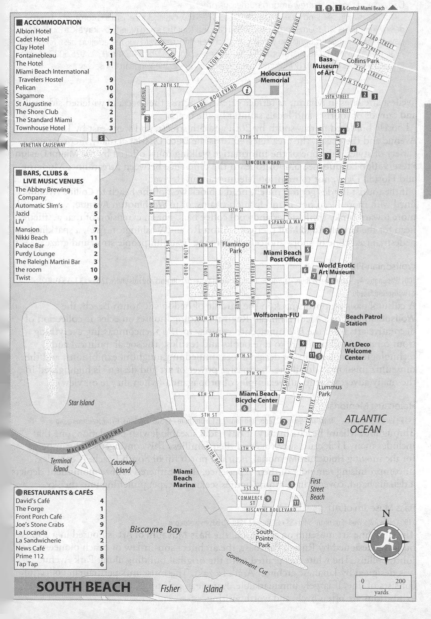

■ ACCOMMODATION

Albion Hotel	7
Cadet Hotel	4
Clay Hotel	8
Fontainebleau	1
The Hotel	11
Miami Beach International	
Travelers Hostel	9
Pelican	10
Sagamore	6
St Augustine	12
The Shore Club	2
The Standard Miami	5
Townhouse Hotel	3

■ BARS, CLUBS & LIVE MUSIC VENUES

The Abbey Brewing	
Company	4
Automatic Slim's	6
Jazid	5
LIV	1
Mansion	7
Nikki Beach	11
Palace Bar	8
Purdy Lounge	2
The Raleigh Martini Bar	3
the room	10
Twist	9

● RESTAURANTS & CAFÉS

David's Café	4
The Forge	1
Front Porch Café	3
Joe's Stone Crabs	9
La Locanda	7
La Sandwicherie	2
News Café	5
Prime 112	8
Tap Tap	6

SOUTH BEACH

0   200
yards

N

7

BISCAYNE BAY'S MILLION-DOLLAR MANSIONS

America's rich and famous have been coming to Miami for years, hiding away within ostentatious palm-smothered mansions on the keys. The only way to get a good look is to take a **boat tour** from Bayside Marketplace. These are unashamedly touristy, but provide fabulous views of the city, and include a narrated jaunt around some of the most exclusive areas. Guides will point out the opulent mansions of Shaquille O'Neal, Sean Combs (aka P Diddy or Puff Daddy), among numerous others.

Operators include Island Queen Cruises (☎305 379 5119, ⓦislandqueencruises.com), which runs daily 90min tours (10.30am–7pm) for $27. You can also tour the same islands by **kayak**, though it pays to take the boat tour first so you know which celebrity backyard you're paddling past. Try South Beach Kayak (Mon–Fri 10.30am–6pm, Sat & Sun 9am–6pm; $25/2hr, $40/4hr; ☎305 975 5087, ⓦsouthbeachkayak.com), 1771 Purdy Ave, Miami Beach, near the Venetian Causeway.

liveliest stretches in Miami, as terrace cafés spill across the specially widened sidewalk and crowds of tourists and locals saunter by the beach.

Loosely bordered north–south by 20th and 5th streets, and west–east by Lenox Avenue and the ocean, the area referred to as the **Deco District** actually incorporates a variety of styles: take one of the informative walking tours offered by the **Miami Design Preservation League** (see p.490) to learn the difference between Streamline, Moderne and Florida Deco, not to mention Mediterranean Revival.

If the tourist hordes get too much, head a block west of the beach to **Collins Avenue**, lined with more Deco hotels and fashion chains, or to **Washington Avenue**, which tends more toward funky thrift stores and cool coffee bars. For an extension of that aesthetic, head for the **Lincoln Road Mall** (between Alton Rd and Washington Ave), a sparkling pedestrianized zone of shops and cafés where the beautiful people stroll and graze.

Wolfsonian-FIU

1001 Washington Ave • Mon, Tues & Thurs–Sun noon–6pm, Fri noon–9pm • $7, students and kids under 12 $5 • ☎ 305 531 1001, ⓦ wolfsonian.fiu.edu

A cultural oasis plopped smack in the middle of hedonistic South Beach, the **Wolfsonian-FIU**, in a Mediterranean Revival building, houses an eclectic collection of decorative arts from the late nineteenth century to 1945, encompassing everything from ceramics and furniture to rare books and textiles. The social, political and technological implications of design are examined in thoughtful exhibitions, and the museum's mission to detail the "persuasive power of art and design" is highlighted in the many advertisements and examples of propaganda (when they're on view).

Holocaust Memorial

1933–1945 Meridian Ave • Daily 9am–9pm • $2 suggested donation for brochure • ☎ 305 538 1663, ⓦ holocaustmmb.org

Throughout Miami Beach's history, it has had a sizeable Jewish population, one that includes many Holocaust survivors and their families. This contingent is the impetus for the moving **Holocaust Memorial**, near the north tip of South Beach. A complex, uncompromising reminder of their experience, the weathered bronze monument depicts a defiant hand, covered in climbing figures seeking escape, punching into the sky.

Bass Museum of Art

2100 Collins Ave • Wed–Sun noon–5pm • $8 • ☎ 305 673 7530, ⓦ bassmuseum.org

The only fine art museum on the beach, the **Bass Museum of Art** is housed in a 1930s building designed by Russell Pancoast, the architect son-in-law of beach pioneer John Collins. The white box grafted onto the original building along Park Avenue was designed by Japanese architect Arata Isozaki. The museum's permanent collection consists of fine, if largely unremarkable, European paintings, although its temporary exhibitions are often lively and worth visiting.

World Erotic Art Museum

1205 Washington Ave • Mon–Thurs 11am–10pm, Fri–Sun 11am–midnight • $15 • ☎ 305 532 9336, ⓦ weam.com

Tucked into a rather innocuous-looking storefront on Washington Avenue is the **World Erotic Art Museum**. The expansive collection here includes thousands of posters, statues, paintings and decorative items that document erotic art traditions from across the globe. Unusual items include the phallus chair/sculpture from the film *A Clockwork Orange* and exhibit labels include "Fetish" and "Adam and Eve". It is definitely a stop for the emotionally mature, but it fits right in with the South Beach cultural milieu.

Downtown Miami

The chaotic and Latin-themed bustle of **Downtown Miami** that dominated the area for the past five decades is largely a memory today. The whole area, from Brickell in the

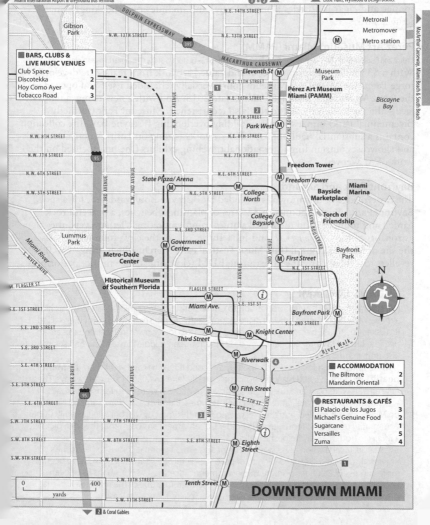

DOWNTOWN MIAMI

south to the Omni mall north of I-395, is being transformed by one of the largest construction booms in the United States. Vast, shimmering towers of glass and steel now line the waterfront, a mixture of offices, hotels and above all, pricey condos. The latter focus means that downtown, while retaining its commercial core, is becoming primarily an upscale residential area, though the recent financial meltdown has slowed this transformation. There's little to keep you here for long; vestiges of the centre's bustling heyday can be found on Flagler Street, now largely given over to cut-price electronics, clothes and jewellery stores.

HistoryMiami

Metro-Dade Cultural Center, 101 W Flagler St • Tues–Fri 10am–5pm, Sat & Sun noon–5pm • $8 • ☎ 305 375 1492, ⊛ historymiami.org

At the western end of NE 1st Street, the **Metro-Dade Cultural Center** contains **HistoryMiami**, which provides a comprehensive look at the region's history (tackling the early Native Americans, the role of Spain and Key West's "wrecking", sponge and cigar industries along the way) and includes two shockingly small refugee rafts.

Pérez Art Museum Miami (PAMM)

11th St and Biscayne Blvd • Tues–Sun 10am–6pm, Thurs until 9pm • $12 • ☎ 305 375 3000, ⊛ miamiartmuseum.org

With a $35 million infusion of cash and valued artwork from real estate developer Jorge Pérez, the Miami Art Museum controversially rebranded itself and opened as the **Pérez Art Museum Miami (PAMM)** in late 2013. And with a new name, a renovated face – the institution moved to the (also rechristened) Museum Park (formerly Bicentennial Park) into a stunning building overlooking Biscayne Bay. The collection contains a substantial haul of post-1940 artworks (strong on Latin American artists), and showcases outstanding international travelling exhibits (the first focused on the work of Ai Weiwei).

Bayfront Park and around

The eastern edge of downtown is bounded by Biscayne Boulevard and, for a spell, **Bayfront Park**, which amounts to 32 acres of plantings, benches, a peaceful rock garden and fountain, and memorial statues commemorating Vietnam vets, the astronauts of the *Challenger II*, and Julia Tuttle, one of the city's founders. It's also the site of Miami's colossal **Ultra Music Festival** each March, which brings 150,000 revellers to a three-day concert featuring EDM (electronic dance music) performers

CUBANS IN MIAMI

During the mid-1950s, when opposition to Cuba's Batista dictatorship began to assert itself, a trickle of Cubans started arriving in a predominantly Jewish section of Miami then called Riverside. The trickle became a flood when Fidel Castro took power in 1959, and the area became **Little Havana**, populated by the affluent Cuban middle classes who had the most to lose under communism.

These original immigrants were joined by a second influx in May 1980, when the **Mariel boatlift** brought 125,000 islanders from the port of Mariel to Miami in just a few days. These new arrivals were poor and uneducated, and a fifth of them were fresh from Cuban jails – incarcerated for criminal rather than political crimes. Bluntly, Castro had dumped his misfits on Miami. The city reeled, and then recovered from this mass arrival, but it left Miami's Cuban community utterly divided. Even today, older Cuban-Americans claim that they can pick out a *Marielito* from the way he or she walks.

That said, local division gives way to fervent agreement when it comes to Castro: he's universally detested. Despite failing to depose the dictator, Cuban-Americans have been far more successful at influencing the US government. Since the 1980s, Cubans have been vociferous supporters of the Republican Party, and therefore one of the main reasons that the US embargo of Cuba (imposed in 1962) remains in place, for now at least.

and international DJs (ⓦultramusicfestival.com). Adjacent is the **Bayside Marketplace**, a large pink shopping mall with pleasant waterfront views from its terrace – **boat tours** of Biscayne Bay depart from here (see box, p.484).

Across the boulevard, the striking **Freedom Tower**, at 600 Biscayne Blvd (ⓣ305 237 7816) built in 1925 and modelled on the bell tower in Seville, Spain, earned its name by housing the Cuban Refugee Center in the 1960s. It is now owned by nearby Miami-Dade Community College, and in recent years has hosted special exhibitions by locally based Cuban artists.

Wynwood and the Design District

North of downtown and NW 20th Street, the **Wynwood Art District** is home to one of the largest and most dynamic concentrations of **art galleries** in the nation. Though it's relatively safe to explore, galleries are spread out and the area is dodgy at night, so this is one part of Miami best experienced by car. Highlights include the **Rubell Collection**, 95 NW 29th St (Wed–Sat 10am–6pm, second Sat of month 10am–10pm; $10; ⓣ305 573 6090, ⓦrfc.museum), a massive modern art collection housed in a warehouse that formerly held drugs confiscated by the federal authorities. Further north, the **Design District** (ⓦmiamidesigndistrict.net), hemmed in by 36th and 41st streets between Miami Avenue and Biscayne Boulevard, is also worth a wander, crammed with hip restaurants and designer furniture stores. One standout studio here is **Locust Projects**, 155 NE 38th St #100 (Thurs–Sat noon–5pm; ⓣ305 576 8570, ⓦlocustprojects.org), a warehouse crammed with tantalizing multimedia installations.

Little Havana

The initial home of Miami Cubans was a few miles west of downtown in what became **LITTLE HAVANA**, whose streets, parks, memorials, shops and food reflect the Cuban experience in all its diversity. Note, though, that streets are much quieter than those of South Beach (except during the Little Havana Festival in early March), and today, many successful Cuban-Americans have moved elsewhere in the city, to be replaced by immigrants from parts of Central America, especially Nicaragua.

Make a beeline here for lunch at one of the many small restaurants on SW 8th Street, or **Calle Ocho**, the neighbourhood's main drag. Check out also **Cuban Memorial Boulevard**, the stretch of SW 13th Avenue just south of Calle Ocho, where a cluster of memorials underscores the Cuban-American presence in Miami. Here, the simple stone **Brigade 2506 Memorial** remembers those who died at the Bay of Pigs on April 17, 1961, during the abortive invasion of Cuba by US-trained Cuban exiles.

Coral Gables

All of Miami's constituent neighbourhoods are fast to assert their individuality, though none does it more definitively than **CORAL GABLES**, southwest of Little Havana. Twelve square miles of broad boulevards, leafy side streets and Spanish and Italian architecture form a cultured setting for a cultured community.

Coral Gables's creator was a northern transplant born in Pennsylvania, **George Merrick**, who raided street names from a Spanish dictionary to plan the plazas, fountains and carefully aged stucco-fronted buildings here. Unfortunately, Coral Gables was taking shape just as the Florida property boom ended. Merrick was wiped out, and died in 1942 as Miami's postmaster. But Coral Gables never lost its good looks, and it remains an impressive place to explore. Merrick wanted people to know they'd arrived somewhere special, and as such, eight grand **entrances** were planned on the main approach roads (though only four were completed). Three of these stand along the western end of Calle Ocho as you arrive from Little Havana.

HIGH ART

Introduced in Miami in 2002 as an offshoot of the eponymous Geneva festival, **Art Basel** has quickly become one of the city's biggest events. More than 50,000 gallery-owners, dealers, aficionados and art snobs – plus a startling number of fashionistas and celebs – descend over four days in the first week in December, keen to snap up a canvas or sculpture by an unknown, presumably in the hope it will be worth millions in a few years. Local and international galleries show paintings, photographs and varied media pieces from established art stars and emerging artists at the Miami Beach Convention Center, but discussions, film screenings, public showings and performance-art events are held all over South Beach and downtown: in hole-in-the-wall showrooms, local beaches and parks, and even, one year, on a minuscule island in the bay. For information, visit ⓦ artbasel.com/Miami-Beach.

The best way into Coral Gables is along SW 22nd Street, known as the **Miracle Mile**. Note the arcades and balconies here, and the spirals and peaks of the **Omni Colonnade Hotel**, at 180 Aragon Ave one block north, which were completed in 1926 to accommodate George Merrick's office.

Merrick House

907 Coral Way • Visits by 45min tour only on Sun & Wed 1pm, 2pm & 3pm • $5 • ☎ 305 460 5361

West of the Miracle Mile, the **Merrick House** was the entrepreneur George Merricks's boyhood home. In 1899, when he was 12, his family arrived here from New England to run a 160-acre farm, which was so successful that the house quickly grew from a wooden shack into an elegant dwelling of coral rock and gabled windows (thus inspiring the name of the future city).

Venetian Pool

2701 De Soto Blvd • Generally daily 11am–5pm but hours fluctuate wildly; call for schedule • $11.50, kids 3–12 $6.60 • ☎ 305 460 5306, ⓦ coralgables.com

While his property-developing contemporaries left ugly scars on the city from digging up the local limestone, George Merrick had the foresight to turn his biggest quarry into a sumptuous swimming pool. Opened in 1924, the **Venetian Pool** is an essential stop on a steamy Miami afternoon. Its pastel stucco walls hide a delightful spring-fed lagoon, with vine-covered loggias, fountains, waterfalls, coral caves and plenty of room to swim.

Biltmore Hotel

1200 Anastasia Ave • Free tours Sun 1.30pm & 2.30pm • ☎ 800 727 1926, ⓦ biltmorehotel.com

Wrapping its broad wings around the southern end of De Soto Boulevard, George Merrick's crowning achievement was the fabulous **Biltmore Hotel**. With a 26-storey tower visible across much of low-lying Miami, everything about the *Biltmore* is over-the-top: 20ft-tall fresco-coated walls, vaulted ceilings, immense fireplaces, custom-loomed rugs and a massive swimming pool, which hosted shows by such bathing belles and beaux as Esther Williams and original Tarzan Johnny Weissmuller. Today, it costs upward of $300 a night to stay here, but a fascinating free tour leaves from the lobby every Sunday at 1.30pm and 2.30pm; meet at the birdcages. You can also absorb some of the atmosphere by taking **afternoon tea** in the lobby for $25 (Mon–Fri 2pm & 3.30pm sittings; reservations recommended).

Vizcaya Museum and Gardens

3251 S Miami Ave • Daily except Tues 9.30am–4.30pm (last ticket sold), house closes at 5pm, gardens 5.30pm • $15, audio tours $5 extra; free house tours every hour 11.30am–2.30pm, subject to availability of voluntary tour guides • ☎ 305 250 9133, ⓦ vizcaya.org

In 1914, south of downtown, farm-machinery mogul James Deering spent $15 million on recreating a sixteenth-century Italian villa within the tropical jungle. A thousand-strong workforce completed his **Villa Vizcaya** in just two years. Deering's madly eclectic art collection, and his desire that the villa should appear to have been inhabited for four hundred years, result in a thunderous clash of Baroque, Renaissance, Rococo and Neoclassical fixtures and fittings. The fabulous landscaped **gardens**, with their many fountains and sculptures, are just as excessive.

Key Biscayne

A compact, immaculately manicured community, **KEY BISCAYNE**, five miles off mainland Miami, is a great place to live – if you can afford it. The only way onto the island is along the four-mile **Rickenbacker Causeway** ($1.75 one-way toll), which runs from SW 26th Road just south of downtown.

Crandon Park Beach, a mile along Crandon Boulevard (the continuation of the main road from the causeway), is one of the finest landscaped beaches in the city, with crystal-clear waters, BBQ grills and sports facilities (daily sunrise–sunset; $5/car; ☎ 305 361 5421). Three miles of yellow-brown beach fringe the park, and give access to a sand bar enabling knee-depth wading far from the shore.

Bill Baggs Cape Florida State Recreation Area

1200 S Crandon Blvd • Daily 8am–sunset • $8/car, $2/pedestrians and cyclists • ☎ 305 361 5811

Crandon Boulevard terminates at the entrance to the **Bill Baggs Cape Florida State Recreation Area**, four hundred wooded acres covering the southern extremity of Key Biscayne. An excellent swimming **beach** lines the Atlantic-facing side of the park and a boardwalk cuts around the wind-bitten sand dunes towards the 1820s **Cape Florida lighthouse**. Climb the 95ft-high structure for mesmerizing views of the whole island and downtown Miami. For more detailed information, take a ranger-led **tour** (Mon & Thurs–Sun 10am & 1pm; free; contact details as above) and check out the exhibits and video in the nearby **keeper's cottage**.

ARRIVAL AND DEPARTURE

MIAMI

By plane Miami International Airport (☎ 305 876 7000, ⊛ miami-airport.com) is 6 miles west of the city. A cab from the airport costs $24–52, depending on your destination, or the 24hr SuperShuttle minivans will deliver you to any address in Miami for $18–21/person (☎ 305 871 2000, ⊛ supershuttle.com). Via public transport, take the #7 Metrobus (☎ 305 770 3131) to downtown, a trip of 40–50min ($2; every 30min), or the #J Metrobus ($2; every 20–40min) to Miami Beach farther on. Shuttle buses also leave from the airport to the nearby Tri-Rail train station, with onward services to West Palm Beach.

By bus Miami's Greyhound bus station is at 4111 NW 27th St (☎ 305 871 1810), though services are scheduled to move to the MIC (see below) by mid-2014.

Destinations Daytona Beach (3 daily; 7hr–12hr 30min); Orlando (9 daily; 4hr 30min–10hr 30min); St Augustine (1 daily; 8hr 40min); St Petersburg (3 daily; 7hr 30min–9hr 30min); West Palm Beach (5 daily; 2hr).

By train By mid-2014, all trains will arrive and depart from the new Miami Intermodal Center (MIC) next to the airport, with transfer via the MIA Mover. For now, the Amtrak station is 7 miles northwest of the city, at 8303 NW 37th Ave. Tri-Rail Metrorail, with a service to downtown, has already been incorporated into the MIC.

Destinations Charleston, SC (1 daily; 14hr 45min); Fort Lauderdale (2 daily; 45min); Jacksonville (2 daily; 10hr 30min); New York City (2 daily; 27hr–31hr); Orlando (2 daily; 5hr–7hr 20min).

GETTING AROUND

On foot and by car Downtown and South Beach, the two main tourist areas, are eminently walkable – and, indeed, best enjoyed on foot. However, if you want to see more of the city, driving is the most practical option.

By public transport An integrated public transport network run by Metro-Dade Transit (☎ 305 770 3131, ⊛ miamidade.gov/transit) covers Miami, though night-time services are quite limited. Metrorail trains ($2) run along a single line between the northern suburbs and South Miami; useful stops are Government Center (for downtown), Vizcaya, Coconut Grove and Douglas Road or University (for Coral Gables). Downtown Miami is also ringed by the Metromover (free), a monorail that doesn't cover much ground but gives a great bird's-eye view. Metrobuses ($2, with a 50¢ surcharge for transfers) cover the entire city.

7

By taxi Taxis are abundant in Miami; either hail one on the street or call Central Cab (☎305 532 5555) or Metro Taxi (☎305 888 8888); meters start at $2.50.

By bike For bike rental, try the Miami Beach Bicycle Center, 601 5th St, South Beach (Mon–Sat 10am–7pm, Sun 10am–5pm; $8/hr, $24/24hr; ☎305 674 0150, ⓦbikemiamibeach.com).

INFORMATION AND TOURS

Visitor centres Head to the Downtown Welcome Center in the lobby of the Olympia Theater, 174 E Flagler St (Mon noon–5pm, Tues–Sat 10am–5pm; ☎305 379 7070, ⓦdowntownmiami.com); otherwise, try the Art Deco Welcome Center, 1001 Ocean Drive (daily 9.30am–7pm; ☎305 672 2014), a great source of information on the area's Art Deco hotels and walking tours (see below).

Tours Walking, bike, boat, coach and eco-history tours are offered by City Tours through History Miami (call for

schedule; no tours July & Aug; from $20; ☎305 375 1621, ⓦhistorymiami.org). In South Beach, don't miss the Miami Design Preservation League's 90min Art Deco Walking Tour (daily 10.30am, Thurs also 6.30pm; $20; ☎305 672 2014, ⓦmdpol.org), which starts at the Art Deco Welcome Center. The Center also offers a self-guided audio walking tour of the district (available daily 9.30am–5pm; 90min; $15) and several other speciality tours once a month.

ACCOMMODATION

Accommodation is rarely a problem in Miami – though you should expect rates to go up on weekends, holidays, festival weeks and in the main winter tourist season (Dec–April). Though it can be great fun to stay in one of the numerous Art Deco South Beach hotels, note that they were built in a different era, and, as such, rooms can be tiny.

SOUTH BEACH

Albion Hotel 1650 James Ave ☎877 RUBELLS, ⓦrubell hotels.com; map p.483. It's a sensitive conversion of a classic Nautical Deco building, and the rooms here are hip but simple; the raised pool – with portholes cut into its sides – is also a big draw. **$399**

★**Cadet Hotel** 1701 James Ave ☎305 672 6688, ⓦcadethotel.com; map p.483. Tranquil boutique hotel, with a peaceful patio reminiscent of a Jane Austen novel, in the South Beach fashion; the fresh strawberries and chocolate in the rooms upon arrival are nice touches. **$189**

Clay Hotel 1438 Washington Ave ☎800 379 2529, ⓦclayhotel.com; map p.483. This beautiful converted monastery serves as the city's best budget hotel (note it no longer operates as a hostel). **$88**

The Hotel 801 Collins Ave ☎305 531 2222, ⓦthehotel ofsouthbeach.com; map p.483. Designer Todd Oldham oversaw every element in the renovation of this hotel, and his colourful yet thoughtful makeover makes it one of the best options on the beach. Don't miss the rooftop, especially at night, when you can sip cocktails by the illuminated pool under the neon-clad spire touting the hotel's original name, *The Tiffany*. **$255**

★**Miami Beach International Travelers Hostel** 236 9th St ☎305 534 0268, ⓦhostelmiamibeach.com; map p.483. Friendly hostel with six-person dorms, a four-bed private room and several private twin rooms. Offers free breakfast, kitchen, laundry, a movie-lounge and free weekly English and Spanish classes. Dorms **$69**, four-bed rooms **$75**, twins/doubles **$145**

Pelican 826 Ocean Drive ☎305 673 3373, ⓦpelican hotel.com. Each room at this camp, quirky hotel is individually themed and named – try the tranquil "Love, Peace &

Leafforest" room, or if you're feeling slightly naughty, "Best Little Whorehouse" or "Me Tarzan, You Vain". **$355**

★**Sagamore** 1671 Collins Ave ☎305 535 8088, ⓦsagamorehotel.com; map p.483. This so-called "Art Hotel" sees itself as a gallery on the beach – indeed, the property is strewn with striking artworks in different media, and it's host to Art Basel events (see box, p.483) in season. The rooms, with kitchenettes, are large for South Beach; bathrooms come with jet tubs. **$480**

St Augustine 347 Washington Ave ☎305 532 0570, ⓦhotelstaugustine.com; map p.483. A spa-like mood prevails at this lovely place where multijet showers turn the bathrooms into steam cabins. It's located in a quieter part of town, too. **$254**

The Shore Club 1901 Collins Ave ☎305 695 3100, ⓦshoreclub.com; map p.483. Ultra-trendy hotel on the beach, with minimalist, brightly coloured rooms and several swanky bar-restaurants, such as the poolside *Sky Bar*. **$369**

★**Townhouse Hotel** 150 20th St ☎877 534 3800, ⓦtownhousehotel.com; map p.483. Small but stylish white rooms, great staff, free breakfast and squishy rooftop waterbeds – all at a fraction of most boutique hotel prices. **$195**

MIAMI BEACH

★**Fontainebleau** 4441 Collins Ave ☎800 548 8886, ⓦfontainebleau.com; map p.483. Five years after a $2 billion makeover, Miami Beach's original resort has large, bleached-white rooms, some with spacious balconies looking over the Atlantic. But access to amenities is key: there's a giant spa and more than a dozen restaurant, bar and nightclub options, including blingy club *LIV* (see p.493). **$559**

The Standard Miami 40 Island Ave, Miami Beach ☎ 305 673 1717, ⓦ standardhotels.com; map p.483. The Miami outpost of hip hotelier André Balazs's *Standard* chain has transformed a forlorn hotel on Belle Isle into spa accommodation complete with Turkish baths and a yoga centre. **$355**

DOWNTOWN AND CORAL GABLES
The Biltmore 1200 Anastacia Ave, Coral Gables ☎ 855 311 6903, ⓦ biltmorehotel.com; map p.485. A landmark Mediterranean-style hotel, opened in 1926, with rooms that are a little understated to be truly luxe. However, they are on the large side and come with European feather beds. The hotel evokes a large Spanish villa, and its huge, statue-ringed pool continues to impress. **$497**

Mandarin Oriental 500 Brickell Key Drive, downtown ☎ 305 913 8288, ⓦ mandarinoriental.com/miami; map p.485. The pick of the luxury chains downtown for its top-notch service and jaw-dropping views across Biscayne Bay. The spa, private beach, bar and restaurants are similarly world-class. **$479**

EATING

Miami does **Cuban food** best, and it's not limited to the traditional haunts in Little Havana. The hearty comfort food – notably rice and beans, fried plantains and shredded pork sandwiches – can be found in every neighbourhood, and you'll also want to try Cuban **coffee**: choose between *café Cubano*, strong, sweet and frothy, drunk like a shot with a glass of water, or *café cortadito*, a smaller version of a *café con leche* (with steamed milk). Cuban cooking is complemented by sushi bars and American home-style diners, as well as Haitian, Italian and New Floridian (a mix of Caribbean spiciness and fruity Florida sauces) restaurants, among a handful of other ethnic cuisines. Coral Gables, South Beach and the Design District are best for upmarket cafés and restaurants. **Seafood** is abundant: succulent grouper, yellowfin tuna and wahoo, a local delicacy, are among five hundred species of fish that thrive offshore. **Stone-crab claws** (served Oct–May), are another South Florida speciality.

SOUTH BEACH
★ **David's Café** 1058 Collins Ave ☎ 305 534 8736, ⓦ davidscafe.com; map p.483. Eat deep-fried delicacies and daily Cuban specials like chicken with rice and beans ($6) on the tables outside, wedged between businessmen and teens, or grab a *café Cubano* (95¢) at the takeaway window. There's also dining room-style seating. Try staples like Cuban sandwiches ($7.95) and pork chops ($12.45). Daily 24hr.

Front Porch Café 1418 Ocean Drive ☎ 305 531 8300, ⓦ frontporchoceandrive.com; map p.483. This local hangout is refreshingly low-key considering its location: the delicious, dinner-plate-sized pancakes will easily take care of both breakfast and lunch. Daily 7am–11pm.

Joe's Stone Crabs 11 Washington Ave ☎ 305 673 0365, ⓦ joesstonecrab.com; map p.483. Specializing in pricey but succulent stone crabs and always packed – if you're impatient, do as the locals do and head to the takeaway window. Crab cakes ($19), fresh fish and the crispy fried chicken basket ($10) are also good. Oct–July; hours vary.

La Locanda 413 Washington Ave ☎ 305 538 6277, ⓦ lalocandasobe.com; map p.483. Relax in the quieter part of town as gourmet pizza cooks right behind you in a huge stone pizza oven. A full roster of nicely sized antipasti, salads and pastas are also on offer. Mon–Thurs & Sun noon–midnight, Fri & Sat noon–1am.

La Sandwicherie 229 14th St ☎ 305 532 8934, ⓦ lasandwicherie.com; map p.483. Gigantic sandwiches stuffed with gourmet ingredients such as prosciutto and imported cheeses and starting at $5.20. Open until 6am on the weekend, it's a good choice for a post-clubbing refuel. Mon–Thurs 8am–5am, Fri & Sat 8am–6am.

News Café 800 Ocean Drive ☎ 305 538 6397, ⓦ newscafe.com; map p.483. This mid-priced street café (and local institution) has front-row seating for the South Beach promenade – although the food's undistinguished. Daily 24hr.

Prime 112 112 Ocean Drive ☎ 305 532 8112, ⓦ myles restaurantgroup.com; map p.483. Classy but not stuffy, this is Miami's meat temple – you get your indulgent dry-aged hunk of beef (from 8oz to 48oz cuts) with rich sauce options in an ultra-sleek setting. Mon–Fri noon–3pm & 5.30pm–midnight, Sat 5.30pm–1am, Sun 5.30pm–midnight.

Tap Tap 819 5th St ☎ 305 672 2898, ⓦ taptap restaurant.com; map p.483. Tasty, attractively presented and reasonably priced Haitian food. Most dishes cost less than $15 – the goat in a peppery tomato broth ($18) is a knockout. Daily noon–11pm.

MIAMI BEACH
The Forge 432 41st St ☎ 305 538 8533, ⓦ theforge .com; map p.483. A memorable, upmarket dining spot where the hearty traditional food and huge wine cellar combine appealingly with a vibrant atmosphere and eclectic clientele. Mains $31–50. Mon–Thurs & Sun 6–11pm, Fri & Sat 6pm–1am.

DOWNTOWN, THE DESIGN DISTRICT AND LITTLE HAVANA
★ **El Palacio de los Jugos** 5721 W Flagler Ave, Little Havana ☎ 305 264 8662; map p.485. A handful of tables at the back of a Cuban produce market, where the pork sandwiches and shellfish soup from the takeaway stand are the tastiest for miles. Also serving refreshing *jugos* (juices) from $2. Daily 6am–9pm.

★ **Michael's Genuine Food** 130 NE 40th St, Design District ☎ 305 573 5550, ⓦ michaelsgenuine.com;

7

map p.485. One of the hottest restaurants in town, with seasonal, local ingredients whipped into eclectic creations by lauded chef Michael Schwartz; sizes range from small to extra-large (medium and large mains $11–36). Favourites include the steak *au poivre* ($36) and the sweet and spicy pork belly ($14). Mon–Thurs 11.30am–3pm & 5.30–11pm, Fri & Sat 11.30am–3pm & 5.30pm–midnight, Sun 11am–2.30pm & 5.30–10pm.

★ **Sugarcane** 3252 NE 1st Ave, Design District ☎ 305 538 6277, ⓦ sugarcanerawbargrill.com; map p.485. Breezy large space with a plantation feel (and a charming outdoor terrace), a raw bar menu and an impressive range of tapas and *robata* (small grilled items). Order the $65 grand shellfish tower, relax with a caipirinha and imagine yourself on an island somewhere. Mon–Wed 11.30am–midnight, Thurs & Fri 11.30am–1am, Sat 10am–2am, Sun 10am–midnight.

Versailles 3555 SW 8th St, Little Havana ☎ 305 444 0240, ⓦ versaillesrestaurant.com; map p.485. Huge platters of inexpensive Cuban food amid a kitschy decor of chandeliers and mirrored walls (hence the name) and a buzzing neighbourhood atmosphere. Mon–Thurs 8am–1am, Fri 8am–3.30am, Sat 8am–4.30am, Sun 8am–2am.

Zuma 270 Biscayne Blvd Way, downtown ☎ 305 577 0277, ⓦ zumarestaurant.com; map p.485. Killer inventive sushi (plus grilled items, tempura and non-traditional Japanese specialities) in a soaring arty-industrial space. Open for brunch at weekends. Mon–Fri noon–3pm & 6pm–midnight, Sat 11.30am–2.30pm & 6pm–midnight, Sun 11.30am–2.30pm & 6–11pm.

NIGHTLIFE AND ENTERTAINMENT

Miami's **nightlife** is unsurpassed in Florida, and is among the best in the country. At the **clubs**, house and techno beats are the most popular, followed by salsa or merengue songs spun by Spanish-speaking DJs. Most of the action is centred in South Beach, with **cover charges** averaging around $20. Door policies are notoriously fierce at current in-spots; the places listed below include laidback local haunts as well as some of the hotter bars and clubs. The free *New Times* magazine (published Thurs), offers **listings** of what's going on where and when – including **gay and lesbian** info.

BARS AND LIVE MUSIC VENUES

★ **The Abbey Brewing Company** 1115 16th St, South Beach ☎ 305 538 8110; map p.483. Beer-lovers congregate here for the best beers on South Beach. Try the creamy Oatmeal Stout – their best and most popular brew. Daily 1pm–5am.

★ **Automatic Slim's** 1216 Washington Ave, South Beach ☎ 305 672 2220, ⓦ automatic-slims.com; map p.483. Raucous rock 'n' roll bar that's trashy fun, with neon-coloured shots in test tubes administered by naughty nurse bar girls and a blaring soundtrack. Tues–Sat 10pm–5am.

Hoy Como Ayer 2212 SW 8th St, Little Havana ☎ 305 541 2631, ⓦ hoycomoayer.us; map p.485. Despite the city's sizeable Cuban population, this dark, smoky joint is about the only place in Miami to hear decent Cuban music. Check website for schedule. Wed–Sat 9pm–3am.

Jazid 1342 Washington Ave, South Beach ☎ 305 673 9372, ⓦ jazid.net; map p.483. Fans of this crowded room are always fully into the experience, whatever the evening's genre (occasionally jazz, more likely reggae or alternative Latin; check the extensive schedule). Very anti-South Beach – laidback, no pretension. Cover $10 or less (or free). Daily 9pm–5am.

Palace Bar 1200 Ocean Drive, South Beach ☎ 305 531 7234, ⓦ palacesouthbeach.com; map p.483. Friendly, welcoming gay bar opposite the beach, with a diverse crowd of young and old, buff and not so much. Widely loved for its drag shows (Fri & Sat at 6pm). Mon–Thurs 11.30am–midnight, Fri–Sun 10am–2am.

★ **Purdy Lounge** 1811 Purdy Ave, South Beach ☎ 305 531 4622, ⓦ purdylounge.com; map p.483. An unheralded gem, this large neighbourhood bar on the less-touristed western side of South Beach pulls a loyal contingent of locals along with savvy out-of-towners. Mon–Fri 3pm–5am, Sat & Sun 6pm–5am.

The Raleigh Martini Bar Inside the Raleigh Hotel, 1775 Collins Ave, South Beach ☎ 305 534 6300, ⓦ raleighhotel.com; map p.483. This elegant 1940s hotel bar, with its lushly restored wood panelling, is a throwback to the heyday of cocktail culture. Daily 6pm–1am.

the room 100 Collins Ave, South Beach ☎ 305 531 6061, ⓦ theotherroom.com; map p.483. Low-lit Miami outpost of a minimalist NYC wine and beer bar – something low key, for a change. Daily 7pm–5am.

Tobacco Road 626 S Miami Ave, downtown ☎ 305 374 1198, ⓦ tobacco-road.com; map p.485. This friendly dive

---

THE SPORTING LIFE

Miami has a good local **sports** scene. The Marlins Major League **baseball** team hits from spring to early autumn at the stadium at 501 Marlins Way (☎ 305 480 2524, ⓦ marlins.com). The Dolphins, Miami's pro **football** team, plays throughout autumn at Dolphin Stadium, 2269 Dan Marino Blvd, sixteen miles northwest of downtown Miami (tickets, usually hard to come by, at ☎ 305 623 6100, ⓦ dolphinstadium.com; take bus #27 from the main bus station).

bar – Miami's oldest, from 1912 – is a favourite with locals for its exceptional live r'n'b. Come early (it's packed after 7pm), and check the website for the schedule of live acts. Daily 11.30am–5am.

CLUBS

Club Space 34 NE 11th St, downtown ☎ 305 375 0001, ⓦ clubspace.com; map p.485. This downtown pioneer has a rough-around-the-edge decor, with a type of illicit elegance: most people migrate here when the other venues shut down, for after-hours dancing until dawn – expect a friendly, loved-up, youngish crowd and big-name DJs. Fri 10pm–Sat 10am, Sat 10pm–Sun 4pm.

★ **Discotekka** 950 NE 2nd Ave, downtown ☎ 305 371 3773, ⓦ discotekka.com; map p.485. This sprawling club is a five-for-one deal, with distinct decor and music in each of its themed rooms, and is frequented by a somewhat younger crowd than most of Miami's dance venues. Fri & Sat 10pm–5am.

★ **LIV** Fontainebleau hotel, 4441 Collins Ave, Miami Beach ☎ 305 674 4680, ⓦ livnightclub.com; map p.483. The city's one-stop clubbing utopia, with all the expected trappings: throbbing beats, thousands of tiny lights pulsing over the dancefloor, short skirts, guys doused with cologne, and very expensive drinks. Wed–Sun 11pm–5am.

Mansion 1235 Washington Ave, South Beach ☎ 305 695 8411, ⓦ mansionmiami.com; map p.483. Sprawling theatre-cum-nightclub complex, with six VIP areas, nine bars and five dance floors, each with its own style of music; hip-hop and sets by big-name DJs are the most popular. Mon & Wed–Sat 11pm–5am.

Nikki Beach 1 Ocean Drive ☎ 305 538 1111, ⓦ nikki beach.com; map p.483. Right on the sand, this massive club, featuring loungers, beds and palm trees, offers an iconic South Beach experience. The food is passable, but the host of international and local DJs is the main reason to show up. Mon & Tues 11am–6pm, Wed–Sun 11am–11pm.

Twist 1057 Washington Ave, South Beach ☎ 305 538 9478, ⓦ twistsobe.com; map p.483. A South Beach institution, it's a party gone wild, with a maze of seven rooms (each with a different vibe), an outdoor terrace and two techno dance floors. There's also a separate building toward the back of the patio where go-go boys "dance" nightly. Daily 1pm–5am.

The Florida Keys

Folklore, films and widespread hearsay have given the **FLORIDA KEYS** – a hundred-mile chain of islands that runs to within ninety miles of Cuba – an image of glamorous intrigue they don't really deserve; at least, not now that the go-go days of the cocaine cowboys in the 1980s are long gone. The Keys can more accurately be described as an outdoor-lover's paradise, where fishing, snorkelling and diving dominate. Terrific untainted natural areas include the **Florida Reef**, a great band of living coral just a few miles off the coast. But for many, the various keys are only stops on the way to **Key West**. This self-proclaimed "Conch Republic" has vibrant, Caribbean-style streets with plenty of convivial bars in which to while away the hours, watching the spectacular **sunsets**.

Wherever you are on the Keys, you'll experience distinctive **cuisine**, served for the most part in hip little shacks where the food is fresh and the atmosphere laidback. **Conch**, a rich meaty mollusc, is a speciality, served in chowders and fritters. There's also **key lime pie**, a delicate, creamy concoction of special Key limes and condensed milk that bears little resemblance to the lurid green imposter pies served in the rest of the US.

GETTING AROUND   THE FLORIDA KEYS

By car Getting around the Keys could hardly be easier, provided you have a car. There's just one route all the way through to Key West: the Overseas Highway (US-1). The road is punctuated by mile markers (MM), starting with MM127 just south of Miami and finishing with MM0 in Key West, at the corner of Whitehead and Fleming streets. As per Keys convention, addresses are given by the closest mile marker, along with the appellation of either "Oceanside" or "Bayside", depending on whether the place in question faces the Atlantic Ocean or Florida Bay.

By bus Greyhound runs a shuttle bus twice a day from the Fort Lauderdale ($66) and Miami ($59) airports all the way to Key West.

Key Largo

The first and largest of the keys, **KEY LARGO**, is a bric-a-brac mix-up of petrol stations, shopping plazas and fast-food outlets. The town does, however, provide a fine opportunity to visit the Florida Reef, at the **John Pennekamp Coral Reef State Park**, at MM102.5-Oceanside (daily 8am–sunset; $8/car and up to 8 passengers, $4 for a single-occupant vehicle, $2 for pedestrians and cyclists; ☎305 451 1202, ⊛pennekamppark.com). This protected 78-square-mile section of living coral reef is rated as one of the most beautiful in the world. If you can, take the **snorkelling tour** (9am, noon & 3pm; 2hr 30min; $29.95, plus $9 for equipment), or the **guided scuba dive** (9.30am & 1.30pm; 1hr 30min; $60; diver's certificate required). The **glass-bottom boat tour** (9.15am, 12.15pm & 3pm; 2hr 30min; $24) is less demanding. For information and to make reservations for all of these tours, call ☎305 451 6300. On any of them, you're virtually certain to spot lobsters, angelfish, eels and jellyfish along the reef, and shoals of silvery minnows stalked by mean-looking barracuda. The reef itself is a delicate living thing, comprising millions of minute coral polyps extracting calcium from the sea water and growing from one to sixteen feet every thousand years.

ACCOMMODATION AND EATING   KEY LARGO

Ed & Ellen's Economy Efficiency MM103.5-Oceanside ☎888 333 5536, ⊛ed-ellens-lodgings.com. A terrific low-cost option, hidden by leafy sea grape trees, with basic but clean rooms, some with small kitchenettes and private bathrooms. $69

Harriette's MM95.7-Bayside ☎305 852 8689. Modest but cosy shack that's the best place for a filling, diner-style breakfast. Fans rave about the biscuits and muffins (key lime especially). Mon–Thurs 6am–8pm, Fri–Sun 8am–3pm.

Kona Kai Resort MM97.8-Bayside ☎800 365 7829, ⊛konakairesort.com. The huge, stylish chalets here have a luxurious feel, thanks in part to the tennis courts, orchid house and rather unique art gallery. $299

★ **Largo Lodge** MM101.5-Bayside ☎800 468 4378, ⊛largolodge.com. Gloriously quirky, adults-only vintage Keys option, with six large cottages and three plain rooms, where you can spy raccoons and iguanas in the garden. $349

★ **Snapper's** 4139 Seaside Ave, at end of Ocean View Ave at MM94.5-Oceanside ☎305 852 5956, ⊛snapperskeylargo.com. Delicious, fresh seafood – as well as chunks of alligator served like chicken nuggets ($9.29) – is available, served on the attractive deck. Plus, you can stay overnight at the tiny attached inn ($100). Daily 11am–10pm.

Islamorada

Comprising a twenty-mile strip of separate islands, including Plantation, Windley and Upper and Lower Matecumbe keys, **ISLAMORADA** (pronounced "eye-lah-more-RAH-da") is a much more welcoming place to dawdle than Key Largo. Most visitors come here to **fish** (you'll also see charter boats advertised all along the highway), but you can also explore **Indian Key Historic State Park**, one of many small, mangrove-skirted islands off Lower Matecumbe Key. Once a thriving settlement founded by wrecker Jacob Houseman, it now boasts a riot of exotic plants and evocative ruins. Kayak rentals ($20/hr, $50/day) are available from **Robbie's Marina** (☎305 664 9814) at MM77.5-Oceanside (there are no ferries).

ACCOMMODATION AND EATING   ISLAMORADA

Casa Morada MM82.2-Bayside ☎888 881 3030, ⊛casamorada.com. The tranquil *Casa Morada* has charm to spare. Traipse past the tropical garden and bocce court, over a tiny white bridge to a private bar on Florida Bay. A stay in one of the sixteen suites comes with a sizeable breakfast. $399

Hungry Tarpon MM77.5-Bayside ☎305 664 0535, ⊛hungrytarpon.com. The converted 1940s bait shop here serves excellent fresh fish as well as tasty breakfasts (like eggy burrito or French toast). Daily 6.30am–9pm.

Islamorada Fish Company 81532 Overseas Hwy ☎305 664 9271. Specialities (the way to go here) are a tad on the pricey side for the area ($21–24, fried baskets $13–22), but this spot (affiliated with Bass Pro Shops) is noted for its quality offerings and is often packed. Daily 11am–10pm.

Key Lantern/Blue Fin Inn MM82.1-Bayside ☎305 664 4572, ⊛keylantern.com. The very cheap lodgings here, with terrazzo floors and vintage pastel bathrooms, are typical mid-century Florida motel (the *Blue Fin* side was renovated more recently). Some rooms have kitchens (for $10 extra). $60

The Middle Keys

Once over Long Key Bridge, you're into **THE MIDDLE KEYS**. At the not-for-profit **Dolphin Research Center**, MM59-Bayside (daily 9am–4.30pm; ☏305 289 1121, ⍟dolphins.org), you can swim with the dolphins for $199 (reservations at ☏305 289 0002).

The largest of several islands in the Middle Keys, **Key Vaca** holds the nucleus of the area's major settlement, **Marathon**. Here you'll find great **fishing** and **watersports** opportunities, as well as a couple of small beaches. **Sombrero Beach**, along Sombrero Beach Road (off the Overseas Hwy near MM50-Oceanside), has good swimming waters and shaded picnic tables.

Opposite the turnoff to the beach at MM50.5-Bayside is the entrance to the 64-acre tropical forest of **Crane Point** (Mon–Sat 9am–5pm, Sun noon–5pm; $12.50; ☏305 743 9100, ⍟cranepoint.net). This includes the **Museum of Natural History of the Florida Keys**, which presents an excellent introduction to the history and ecology of the area. Follow the 1.5-mile **nature trail** past the hammock forest, an area of dense hardwood trees characteristic of the Keys, until you reach the end. Here, you'll find the hundred-year-old **Adderley House Historic Site**, established by settlers from the Bahamas.

7

ACCOMMODATION AND EATING THE MIDDLE KEYS

Banana Bay MM49.5-Bayside ☏305 743 3500, ⍟bananabay.com. There's a plantation feel to this greenery-strewn ten-acre property; a poolside tiki bar, bocce and tennis courts and a private beach make the place marvellous. $175

Castaway 15th St near MM47.5-Oceanside ☏305 743 6247. There's terrific seafood – including succulent beer-battered shrimp – at this no-nonsense spot, and every dinner comes with a trip to the salad bar and a basket of hot honey buns. Daily 11am–10pm.

★ **Seven Mile Grill** MM47.5-Bayside ☏305 743 4481. By the bridge of the same name, this tiny, laidback place serves delicious conch chowder and creamy key lime pie to locals, sea salts and tourists alike. Thurs–Tues 7am–4pm.

Stuffed Pig MM49-Bayside ☏305 743 4059. Aptly named breakfast hole whose lobster omelettes and crab Benedicts always wow diners. Cash only, and expect to wait at weekends. Daily 6am–2pm.

Tranquility Bay MM48.5-Bayside ☏888 755 7486, ⍟tranquilitybay.com. This unabashedly well-equipped option consists of 87 two- and three-bedroom beachhouses facing the bay, with white interiors and state-of-the-art kitchens. Good for families. $499

The Lower Keys

Starkly different from their neighbours to the north, **THE LOWER KEYS** are quiet, covered in dense vegetation and predominantly residential. Built on a limestone rather than a coral base, these islands have a flora and fauna all their own, most notably the elusive **Key deer** (see below).

The first place of consequence you'll hit after crossing the stunning **Seven Mile Bridge** is one of the Keys' prettiest spots: **Bahia Honda State Park**, at MM37-Oceanside (daily 8am–sunset; $8/car, pedestrians and cyclists $2; ☏305 872 2353, ⍟bahiahondapark .com). It has the best stretch of sand in the Keys by far, and pristine, two-tone ocean waters, which can be enjoyed on a leisurely **kayak ride** ($10/hr, $30/day). You can also take snorkelling trips out to the **Looe Key Marine Sanctuary** from here (daily 9.30am & 1.30pm; $29.95, $7 for equipment; ☏305 872 3210), a five-square-mile protected reef, easily the equal of the John Pennekamp Coral Reef State Park (see opposite). If you want to spend more time in the water, drive on to **Ramrod Key** and the Looe Key Dive Center (☏800 942 5397, ⍟diveflakeys.com), which offers daily five-hour scuba ($70) and snorkelling ($30) excursions to the sanctuary.

Delightfully tame Key deer amble around the **National Key Deer Refuge** on **Big Pine Key**, the main Lower Keys settlement. Visit the refuge centre (Mon–Fri 8am–5pm, park daily sunrise–sunset; ☏305 872 2239, ⍟nationalkeydeer.fws.gov), tucked away in a shopping mall off Key Deer Boulevard, just north of US-1 at MM30, to get a map of the best viewing spots.

Little Palm Island MM28.5-Oceanside, Little Torch Key ☎ 800 343 8567, ⊛ littlepalmisland.com. A stay on this idyllic, adults-only private islet with thatched cottages, set in lush gardens a few feet from the beach, constitutes a real splurge. $\overline{\underline{\$890}}$

Looe Key Reef Resort MM27.5-Oceanside ☎ 800 942 5397, ⊛ diveflakeys.com. The decor is early-80s, but the lodge is spotless and super value, and kayaks and snorkel gear are available for rent. An ideal base for visiting the marine sanctuary. $\overline{\underline{\$89}}$

Mangrove Mama's MM20-Bayside, Sugarloaf Key ☎ 305 745 3030. The friendly *Mama's* serves stupendous local cuisine in a cheery shack with a tropical garden. Daily 9am–10pm.

★ **No Name Pub** North Watson Blvd off MM30-Bayside ☎ 305 872 9115. Enjoy superb thin-crust pizza under a canopy of dollar bills suspended from the ceiling. Daily 11am–11pm.

Key West

Closer to Cuba than to mainland Florida, **KEY WEST** has a culture that is a bit contrary to the rest of the mainland US. Famed for their tolerant attitudes and laidback lifestyles, the thirty thousand islanders seem adrift in a great expanse of sea and sky, and – despite a million tourists a year – the place resonates with an individual spirit. In particular, liberal attitudes have stimulated a large **gay** influx, estimated at two out of five of the population. Although Key West today has been heavily transformed for tourists, the town has retained some of its offbeat character, especially away from the main drag of **Duval Street**, now a well-tended tourist strip of boutiques and beachwear shops (though it's still a pleasant place for a leisurely stroll).

Make sure to visit the **Bahamian Village**, centred on Thomas and Petronia streets. Originally settled by Cubans and African-Bahamians, this relatively unrestored, untouristy corner of town is an atmospheric patchwork of single-storey cigar-makers' cottages, Cuban groceries and ramshackle old churches, all covered by a rich green foliage.

Wreckers Museum

322 Duval St • Daily 10am–4pm • Free • ☎ 305 294 9502

Numerous **museums** in Key West concern themselves with "wrecking", or the salvaging of cargo from sunken vessels; it's the industry on which the town's earliest good times were based. The friendly little **Wreckers Museum** (also known as the Oldest House) illuminates the lives of the wreckers, portraying them as brave, uninsured heroes who risked all to save cargoes, ships and lives. Judging by the choice furniture that fills the house – lived in by the wrecker Captain Watlington during the 1830s – they did pretty well for their pains.

San Carlos Institute

516 Duval St • Fri–Sun noon–6pm • Free, $3 suggested donation • ☎ 305 294 3887

Near the top of Duval Street you'll find the **San Carlos Institute**, which has played a leading role in Cuban exile life since it opened in 1871. Financed by a grant from the Cuban government, the present two-storey building dates from 1924; Cuban architect Francisco Centurion designed it in the Cuban Baroque style of that period. Soil from Cuba's six provinces covers the grounds, and a cornerstone was taken from the tomb of Cuban independence campaigner José Martí. Don't forget to pick up the free Cuban Heritage Trail pamphlet here, which details sites of interest around town.

KEY WEST: THE END OF THE US

The **southernmost point** in Key West, and consequently in the continental US, is at the intersection of Whitehead and South streets. A daft-looking buoy marks the spot, and it is constantly mobbed by tourists. Back up and just west from the northern end of Duval Street is **Mallory Square**. In the early 1800s, thousands of dollars' worth of salvage was landed at the piers, stored in the warehouses and flogged at the auction houses here. At night there is usually some type of live music, which is really the main draw.

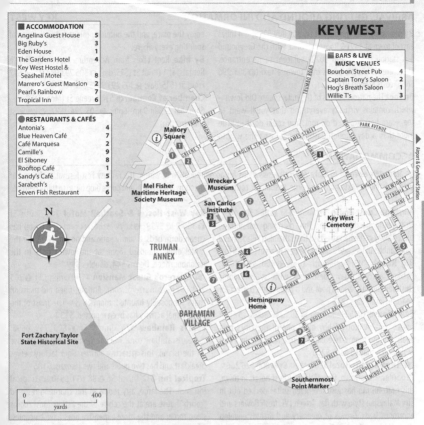

ACCOMMODATION

Angelina Guest House	5
Big Ruby's	3
Eden House	1
The Gardens Hotel	4
Key West Hostel & Seashell Motel	8
Marrero's Guest Mansion	2
Pearl's Rainbow	7
Tropical Inn	6

RESTAURANTS & CAFÉS

Antonia's	4
Blue Heaven Café	7
Café Marquesa	2
Camille's	9
El Siboney	8
Rooftop Café	1
Sandy's Café	5
Sarabeth's	3
Seven Fish Restaurant	6

BARS & LIVE MUSIC VENUES

Bourbon Street Pub	4
Captain Tony's Saloon	2
Hog's Breath Saloon	1
Willie T's	3

Mel Fisher Maritime Heritage Society Museum

200 Greene St • Mon–Fri 8.30am–5pm, Sat & Sun 9.30am–5pm • $12 • 📞 305 294 2633, 🌐 melfisher.org

The **Mel Fisher Maritime Heritage Society Museum** showcases the diamonds, pearls and daggers (as well as countless vases, an impressive emerald cross and the obligatory cannon) that Fisher pulled up from two seventeenth-century shipwrecks in the 1980s – a dazzling haul that's said to be worth at least $200 million.

Ernest Hemingway Home & Museum

907 Whitehead St • Daily 9am–5pm; tours leave every 10–30min and last approximately 30min • $12 • 📞 305 294 1136, 🌐 hemingway home.com

Toward the end of Whitehead Street, you'll find Key West's most popular tourist attraction: the **Ernest Hemingway Home & Museum**. Hemingway owned this large, vaguely Moorish house for thirty years, but lived in it for barely ten. Some of his most acclaimed novels, including *A Farewell to Arms* and *To Have and Have Not*, were written in the study (the hayloft of a carriage house, which the author entered by way of a rope bridge). Divorced in 1940, Hemingway boxed up his manuscripts and moved them to a back room at the original *Sloppy Joe's*, now *Captain Tony's* (see p.499), before heading off for a house in Cuba with his new wife, journalist Martha Gellhorn. Today, some sixty cats – many of them with six toes, traditionally employed as ships' mascots – pad contentedly around the gardens. Whatever the guides say, Hemingway kept his feline harem while living in Cuba, not Key West, so it's unlikely that these cats are in any way related to Papa's pets.

ARRIVAL, GETTING AROUND AND INFORMATION   KEY WEST

By plane or bus The airport (☎ 305 809 5200) is 4 miles east of town at 3491 S Roosevelt Blvd, with the Greyhound bus station (☎ 305 296 9072) adjacent to its entrance. There are no shuttle buses into town; a taxi (☎ 305 296 6666) costs around $18.

On foot The narrow streets of the mile-square Old Town – which contains virtually everything that you'll want to see – are best explored on foot. You could do it in little more than a day, though dashing about isn't the way to enjoy the place, and the humidity might get in the way of sprinting everywhere.

By bike Rent bikes from Adventure Scooter & Bicycle Rentals, at 1 Duval St ($15/day; ☎ 305 293 0441) and 617 Front St ($15/day; ☎ 305 293 9955).

Chamber of Commerce 510 Greene St (Mon–Fri 8am–6pm, Sat & Sun 9am–6pm; ☎ 305 294 2587, ⓦ keywestchamber.org).

ACCOMMODATION

It's absolutely essential to make advance reservations for accommodation in winter; the Fantasy Fest festival at the end of October is another extremely busy time. In summer, competition for rooms is less fierce, and prices drop by up to thirty percent.

Angelina Guest House 302 Angela St ☎ 888 303 4480, ⓦ angelinaguesthouse.com. This charming guesthouse, tucked away in the backstreets of the Bahamian Village, has a cool, Caribbean feel, and is one of the best deals in town. $119

Big Ruby's 409 Applerouth Lane ☎ 800 477 7829, ⓦ bigrubys.com. Gay guesthouse with stylish rooms clustered round a lagoon pool and a patio that's perfect for peaceful lounging. $215

Eden House 1015 Fleming St ☎ 305 296 6868, ⓦ edenhouse.com. A grotty lobby hides one of the city's best deals – large rooms, free parking, free happy hour every night and a shaded pool. $200

★ **The Gardens Hotel** 526 Angela St ☎ 800 526 2664, ⓦ gardenshotel.com. One of the swishest hotels in town, this graceful inn has just seventeen suites decked out in airy Malaysian style with flat-screen TVs, fresh flowers and enormous beds. Groves of greenery and orchids envelop the building and hide it from prying eyes. $240

Key West Hostel & Seashell Motel 718 South St ☎ 305 296 5719, ⓦ keywesthostel.com. The hostel has cheap dorm beds, a sunny patio and no curfew, while the motel offers standard rooms at the lowest rates in the neighbourhood. Dorms $44, doubles $99

★ **Marrero's Guest Mansion** 410 Fleming St ☎ 305 294 6977, ⓦ marreros.com. Antique-filled old mansion that's supposedly haunted; room 18 is where most of the paranormal activity has been reported. $130

Pearl's Rainbow 525 United St ☎ 800 749 6696, ⓦ pearlsrainbow.com. The one women-only guesthouse on the island, this attractive former cigar factory serves breakfast and has two pools and two jacuzzis. $185

Tropical Inn 812 Duval St ☎ 88 611 6510, ⓦ tropicalinn.com. The large, airy rooms in this charming restored "conch" house are at the centre of the action. Most rooms sleep three, and the more expensive ones have balconies. $255

EATING

There's no shortage of chic venues for fine French, Italian and Asian cuisine in Key West, but most menus, not surprisingly, feature fresh seafood. You should sample key lime pie and conch fritters – Key West specialities – at least once.

Antonia's 615 Duval St ☎ 305 294 6565, ⓦ antoniaskeywest.com. Expensive but excellent northern Italian cuisine served in a formal but friendly environment. Sit in the old front room rather than the characterless modern extension at the back. Daily 6–11pm.

★ **Blue Heaven Café** 729 Thomas St, at Petronia St ☎ 305 296 8666, ⓦ blueheavenkw.com. Sit in a dirt yard and enjoy yellowtail snapper, jerk chicken and fabulous lobster Benedict breakfasts as chickens peck around your feet. Daily 8am–10.30pm.

Café Marquesa Marquesa Hotel, 600 Fleming St ☎ 305 292 1244, ⓦ marquesa.com. This chichi restaurant with its imaginative and pricey New American menu (mains $25–38) is the town's best fine dining spot. Daily 6–10pm.

Camille's 1202 Simonton St ☎ 305 296 4811. Great, affordable breakfasts and brunches. The dinner menu changes every night, but usually features fresh fish and fancy steaks. Daily 8am–3pm & 6–10pm.

El Siboney 900 Catherine St ☎ 305 296 4184, ⓦ elsiboneyrestaurant.com. Come to this no-frills family diner for copious, inexpensive and good-quality Cuban dishes such as grilled pork tenderloin ($14.95) and breaded shrimp ($11.95). Daily 11am–9.30pm.

★ **Rooftop Café** 310 Front St ☎ 305 294 2042, ⓦ rooftopcafekeywest.com. "New Island" cuisine in a breezy, elegant, romantic setting (go for the "Before the Sunset" deal at $32 for three courses). It's also the insider's choice for key lime pie, served with a top layer of fluffy meringue and a gooey graham cracker crust (slices $8). Daily 11am–9.30pm.

★ **Sandy's Café** Inside the M&M Laundry, 1026 White St ☎ 305 295 0159. Dingy café offering cheap and

> ### KEY WEST'S FESTS
>
> The Chamber of Commerce can give precise dates for Key West's annual **festivals**, the best of which are the **Conch Republic Celebration** in April, **Hemingway Days** in July, and **Fantasy Fest** in late October, which plays like a gay Mardi Gras crossed with Halloween. A good source of information on LGBT celebrations and festivals is the Key West Business Guild, 513 Truman Ave (daily 9am–5pm; ☎ 305 294 4603, ✆ gaykeywestfl.com).

excellent Cuban sandwiches and the best *café con leche* this side of Miami. Daily 24hr.

Sarabeth's 530 Simonton St ☎ 305 293 8181, ✆ sarabethskeywest.com. Satisfying, home-style cooking in the appropriately welcoming setting of an old wooden clapboard house. Specials here include poached salmon salad ($14.95) and chicken pot pie ($19.50). Wed–Sun

8am–3pm & 6–9.30pm.

Seven Fish Restaurant 632 Olivia St ☎ 305 296 2777, ✆ 7fish.com. This little-known, mid-priced bistro, easy to miss in its tiny white corner building, serves some of the best food – shrimp scampi, meatloaf and the like – in town. There are just over a dozen tables, so it pays to call ahead. 6–10pm; closed Tues.

DRINKING, NIGHTLIFE AND ENTERTAINMENT

The anything-goes nature of Key West is exemplified by the convivial bars that make up the bulk of the island's **nightlife**: gregarious, rough-and-ready affairs, many stay open as late as 4am and feature regular live music. The most popular places are grouped around the northern end of Duval Street.

★ **Bourbon Street Pub** 724 Duval St ☎ 305 293 9800, ✆ bourbonstpub.com. This huge pub complex is the largest gay-friendly place to drink in the centre of town; there's a pleasant garden out the back, complete with a large hot tub. Daily 10am–4am.

★ **Captain Tony's Saloon** 428 Greene St ☎ 305 294 1838, ✆ capttonyssaloon.com. This rustic saloon was the original *Sloppy Joe's*, where Hemingway hung out (p.497). Today, it's one of the less cheesy choices for live music and the offerings are diverse. Daily 10am–1am.

Hog's Breath Saloon 400 Front St ☎ 305 296 4222, ✆ hogsbreath.com. One of the best places to catch live music in town, mostly for a nominal cover – just don't be put off by the boozed-up patrons circling its entrance. Daily 10am–2am.

Willie T's 525 Duval St ☎ 305 294 7674, ✆ williets.com. There's food here, but the selection of two dozen mojitos (two for $12 on Mon) is what distinguishes this watering hole. Great for people-watching, too. Daily 10am–2am.

The East Coast

Florida's **East Coast** presents a tremendously built-up mix of hotels, resorts, beaches and affluent developments north of Miami all the way to St Augustine. This is not to say this section of Florida is without merit, but it's a lot less laidback than the state's western Gulf Coast (see p.518). **Fort Lauderdale**, no longer the party town of popular imagination, is today a sophisticated cultural centre with a bubbling, increasingly upmarket social scene. To the north, **Boca Raton** and **Palm Beach** are quiet, exclusive communities, their Mediterranean Revival mansions inhabited almost entirely by multimillionaires. Beyond Palm Beach, the coast is less developed; even the **Space Coast**, anchored by the extremely popular **Kennedy Space Center**, is smack in the middle of a nature preserve. Just north, **Daytona Beach** attracts race car- and motorcycle-enthusiasts with its festivals and the Daytona International Speedway. Just south of the Georgia state line, **St Augustine** is the spot where Spanish settlers established the first permanent European foothold in North America.

By car, the scenic route along the coast is **Hwy-A1A**, which sticks to the ocean side of the **Intracoastal Waterway**, formed when the rivers dividing the mainland from the barrier islands were joined and deepened during World War II. When necessary, Hwy-A1A turns inland and links with the much less picturesque **US-1**. The speediest road in the region, **I-95**, runs about ten miles west of the coastline, and is only worthwhile if you're in a hurry.

Fort Lauderdale

Following the 1960 teen-exploitation movie *Where the Boys Are*, **FORT LAUDERDALE**, with its seven miles of palm-shaded white sands, instantly became the number-one Spring Break destination in the US. However, having fuelled its economic boom on underage drinking and lascivious excess, the city promptly turned its back on the revellers. By the end of the 1980s, it had imposed enough restrictions on boozing and wild behaviour to put an end to the bacchanal. Since then, Fort Lauderdale has transformed itself into a thriving pleasure port, catering to individual yacht-owners and major cruise liners alike. It's also one of the fastest-growing residential areas in the country, and has for years been known as one of **gay** America's favourite holiday haunts.

Downtown Fort Lauderdale

Downtown Fort Lauderdale focuses on a few blocks between E Broward and E Las Olas boulevards, which cross US-1 a couple of miles east of I-95. Heavily prettified with parks and promenades, it's a pleasant place for a stroll, especially if you follow the mile-long pedestrian **Riverwalk** along the north shore of the New River into the **historic district**. Las Olas Boulevard itself, the main **shopping district**, remains busy day and night, with boutiques, galleries, restaurants, bars and street cafés in abundance. It's also home to the stimulating **Museum of Art**, 1 E Las Olas Blvd (Mon–Wed, Fri & Sat 10am–5pm, Thurs 10am–7pm, Sun noon–5pm, closed Mon June–Sept; $14; ☎954 525 5500, ⓦmoafl.org), whose largely modern collection features the emotionally powerful expressionistic work of the CoBrA movement of artists from Copenhagen, Brussels and Amsterdam. Not far west, the stimulating interactive displays at the **Museum of Discovery & Science**, 401 SW 2nd St (Mon–Sat 10am–5pm, Sun noon–6pm; $14, $19 includes one IMAX film; ☎954 467 6637, ⓦmods.org), include a 12ft-tall Imperial mammoth in the Prehistoric Florida exhibit and Powerful You!, a series of pieces on the human body.

The beach

Although downtown has its charms and attractions, most visitors come to Fort Lauderdale for its broad, clean and undeniably beautiful **beach**. You'll find it by crossing the arching Intracoastal Waterway Bridge, about two miles along Las Olas Boulevard from downtown. Stretching out along the seafront, Fort Lauderdale Beach Boulevard once bore the brunt of Spring Break partying, though only a few remaining beachfront bars suggest the carousing of the past. Today, an attractive promenade draws a healthier crowd of joggers, in-line skaters and cyclists.

ARRIVAL, GETTING AROUND AND INFORMATION   FORT LAUDERDALE

By bus Greyhound buses pull in at 515 NE 3rd St (☎954 764 6551).
Destinations Jacksonville (5 daily; 7–13hr); Tallahassee (5 daily; 10hr–14hr 45min); Tampa (6 daily; 6hr 45min–8hr 25min).

By train The Amtrak and Tri-Rail train station is 2 miles west of town at 200 SW 21st Terrace – take free shuttle bus #FL-1 on weekdays, #FL-3 Sat & Sun.
Destinations Jacksonville (2 daily; 10hr); Orlando (2 daily;

4hr 20min–6hr 40min); West Palm Beach (2 daily; 1hr).

Local buses Broward County Transit bus #11 runs every 30min along Las Olas Blvd between downtown and the beach.

Water taxis You can travel by water taxi (all-day pass $20; ☎954 467 6677, ⓦwatertaxi.com) almost anywhere along Fort Lauderdale's many miles of waterfront.

Visitor centre 100 E Broward Blvd, Suite 200 (Mon–Fri 8.30am–5pm; ☎800 22 SUNNY, ⓦsunny.org).

ACCOMMODATION

The Atlantic Resort & Spa 601 N Fort Lauderdale Beach Blvd ☎954 567 8020, ⓦatlantichotelfl.com. The first of a projected series of luxury residence properties facing the ocean, this Mediterranean-style hotel features elegant rooms and suites, a spa, an oceanfront pool and

a superb restaurant. $347
The Bridge II Hostel 506 SE 16th St ☎954 522 6350, ⓦhostelfortlauderdale.com. Welcoming hostel with friendly staff, swimming pool and a job network for visitors looking to join a yacht crew. Dorms $25, doubles $53

Tropi Rock Resort 2900 Belmar St ☎800 888 2639, ⓦtropirock.com. Cool, family-owned hotel a block from the beach, where the good-value rates include use of tennis courts and a small gym. **$126**

EATING AND DRINKING

★ **Casablanca Café** 3049 Alhambra St ☎954 764 3500, ⓦcasablancacafeonline.com. An American piano bar in a Moroccan setting, serving a good, eclectic and moderately priced menu of Mediterranean-influenced American fare. Live music Wed nights. Daily 11.30am–11pm.

The Floridian 1410 E Las Olas Blvd ☎954 463 4041. Retro decor and outstanding diner food – especially the mammoth breakfasts – at rock-bottom prices. Daily 24hr.

★ **Seasons 52** 2428 E Sunrise Blvd at the Galleria Mall

☎954 537 1052, ⓦseasons52.com. Health-conscious regional restaurant chain where every one of the fresh and tasty seasonal dishes has less than 475 calories. Mon–Thurs & Sun 11.30am–10pm, Fri & Sat 11.30am–11pm.

Southport Raw Bar 1536 Cordova Rd ☎954 525 2526, ⓦsouthportrawbar.com. South of downtown, near Port Everglades, this boisterous local bar specializes in succulent crustaceans and well-prepared fish dishes. Mon–Wed 11am–midnight, Thurs & Sun 11am–2am, Fri & Sat 11am–3am.

Boca Raton

7

BOCA RATON (literally, "the mouth of the mouse"), twenty miles north of Fort Lauderdale, is noteworthy mostly for its abundance of **Mediterranean Revival architecture**. This style, prevalent here since the 1920s, has been kept alive in the downtown area by strict building codes. New structures must incorporate arched entranceways, fake bell towers and red-tiled roofs whenever possible, ensuring a consistent and distinctive "look".

The roots of this approach to architectural design originated with architect Addison Mizner, who swept into Boca Raton on the tide of the Florida property boom in 1925. Mizner was influenced by the medieval architecture he'd seen around the Mediterranean, and the few public buildings he completed (along with close to fifty homes) left an indelible mark on Boca Raton; his million-dollar *Cloister Inn*, for example, grew into the present-day **Boca Raton Resort** (see below).

Mizner's spirit is also invoked at **Mizner Park**, off US-1 between Palmetto Park Road and Glades Road, a stylish open-air shopping plaza adorned with palm trees and waterfalls. The park is home to the **Boca Raton Museum of Art**, 501 Plaza Real (Tues–Fri 10am–5pm, Sat & Sun noon–5pm; $8; ☎561 392 2500, ⓦbocamuseum.org), worth a stop for its drawings by modern European masters – Degas, Matisse and Picasso – and a formidable collection of West African tribal masks.

A mile north of Hwy-798 (which links downtown Boca Raton with the beach), at 1801 N Ocean Blvd/Hwy-A1A, the **Gumbo Limbo Nature Center** (Mon–Sat 9am–4pm, Sun noon–4pm; $5 donation; ☎561 544 8605, ⓦgumbolimbo.org) covers twenty acres inhabited by osprey, brown pelicans and sea turtles. Reserve well in advance for the night-time turtle-watching tours offered between May and July.

A couple of miles north of downtown at #3001 Hwy A1A, Boca Raton's most explorable **beachside** area is **Spanish River Park** (daily 8am–sunset; cars $16 Mon–Fri, $18 Sat & Sun, pedestrians and cyclists free). Most of these fifty acres of lush vegetation and high-rise greenery are only penetrable on trails through shady thickets.

ACCOMMODATION AND EATING

BOCA RATON

Boca Raton Resort 2501 E Camino Real ☎888 491 BOCA, ⓦbocaresort.com. Amenities abound at this pink palace of marble columns, sculptured fountains and carefully aged wood: two golf courses, thirty tennis courts, three fitness rooms and a half-dozen quality dining establishments. **$289**

Max's Grille 404 Plaza Real, Mizner Park ☎561 368 0080, ⓦmaxsgrille.com. Appealing American dishes with Asian influences, complemented by three dozen

wines offered by the glass. Mains $19–33. Mon–Thurs & Sun 9am–10pm, Fri & Sat 9am–11pm.

Ocean Lodge 531 N Ocean Blvd ☎561 395 7772, ⓦoceanlodgeflorida.com. This eighteen-room gem the beaches features suites with newish kitchenettes, screen TVs and a heated pool. Reasonable rates. **$209**

Towneplace Suites by Marriott 5110 NW 8th Av ☎561 994 7232, ⓦtowneplacebocaraton.com. Better than-average *Marriott*-related option, with a property shielded by lofty palms and comfortable, roomy suites with kitchenettes and living rooms. **$179**

Whale's Rib 2033 NE 2nd St, Deerfield Beach ☎954 421 8880, ⓦwhalesrib.com. Fresh *mahi-mahi* is the most popular order here (with the "whale fries", fresh-cooked crisps, a close second) and the rock shrimp, raw oysters and conch chowder keep flying out of the kitchen. Mon–Fri & Sun 11am–11pm, Sat 11am–midnight.

Palm Beach

A small island town of palatial homes and gardens, **PALM BEACH** is synonymous with new and old money of all sorts. The nation's wealthy began wintering here in the 1890s, after Henry Flagler brought his East Coast railroad south from St Augustine, building two luxury hotels on this then-secluded, palm-filled island. Since then, the rich and famous have flocked here to become part of the Palm Beach elite.

Lined with designer stores and high-class art galleries, **Worth Avenue**, close to the southern tip of the island, is a good place to see some of the town's Addison Mizner-inspired **architecture**: stucco walls, Romanesque facades, passageways leading to small courtyards and spiral staircases climbing to the upper levels.

Flagler Museum

1 Whitehall Way • Tues–Sat 10am–5pm, Sun noon–5pm • $18 • ☎561 655 2833, ⓦflagler.org

To the north, just off Cocoanut Row, white Doric columns front Whitehall, also known as the **Flagler Museum**. This, the most overtly ostentatious home on the island, was a $4 million wedding present from Henry Flagler to his third wife, Mary Lily Kenan. As in many of Florida's first luxury homes, the interior design was lifted from the great buildings of Europe: among the 73 rooms are an Italian library, a French salon and a Louis XV ballroom.

ARRIVAL AND INFORMATION   PALM BEACH

By train and bus Public transport options around Palm Beach are limited. The station that handles Amtrak, Tri-Rail and Greyhound (☎561 833 8534) is located at 205 S Tamarind Ave in West Palm Beach on the mainland. To get to Palm Beach, take any PalmTran bus ($1.50; ☎561 841 4BUS) terminating at Quadrille Blvd, and transfer to the #41 or the #42 (no Sun service).

Visitor centre 1555 Palm Beach Lakes Blvd, Suite 800 (Mon–Fri 8.30am–5.30pm; ☎561 233 3000, ⓦpalm beachfl.com).

ACCOMMODATION AND EATING

Charley's Crab 456 Ocean Blvd ☎561 659 1500, ⓦmuer.com. This appealing spot is the place to go for reasonably priced seafood in a lovely location overlooking the dunes. Dinner mains from $25. Mon–Sat 11.30am–10pm, Sun 11am–9pm.

Chesterfield 363 Cocoanut Row ☎561 659 5800, ⓦchesterfieldpb.com. Opulent boutique hotel, with antique-filled rooms, a popular nightclub on site and a traditional English tea every afternoon. **$385**

Hamburger Heaven 1 N Clematis St, W Palm Beach ☎561 655 5277, ⓦhamburgerheavenpb.com. Delicious burgers have been doled out by this restaurant (now in a new spot near the waterfront) since 1945, along with diner-style breakfasts, salads and sandwiches. Daily: June–Oct 7.30am–4pm; Nov–May 7.30am–8.30pm.

Palm Beach Historic Inn 365 S County Rd ☎561 832 4009, ⓦpalmbeachhistoricinn.com. This elaborate, handsomely furnished B&B offers some of the best rates in town (and a filling breakfast in bed), but you'll need to reserve early. **$129**

The Space Coast

About two hundred miles north of Palm Beach, the so-called **Space Coast** is the base of the country's space industry, with a focus on the government-sponsored endeavours in this area of exploration. The focal point is the much-visited **Kennedy Space Center**, which occupies a flat, marshy island bulging into the Atlantic. In stark contrast, the rest of the island is taken over by a sizeable nature preserve, the **Merritt Island National Wildlife Refuge**, offering great opportunities for seeing wildlife, especially birds.

CLOCKWISE FROM TOP CASTILLO DE SAN MARCOS, ST AUGUSTINE (P.507); MAGIC KINGDOM, WALT DISNEY WORLD (P.511); SEVEN MILE BRIDGE, FLORIDA KEYS (P.495) >

The Kennedy Space Center

Daily 9am–6pm, though thunderstorms may force some attractions to close • $43, kids $33 • ☎ 866 870 8025, ⓦ kennedyspacecenter.com • Take exit 212 off I-95 to Hwy-405, and follow the signs; you can also get here by connecting with Hwy-3 off Hwy-A1A

The **Kennedy Space Center** is the nucleus of the US space programme: it's here that space vehicles are developed, tested and blasted into orbit. **Merritt Island** has been the centre of NASA's activity since 1964, when the launch pads at Cape Canaveral US Air Force base, across the water, proved too small to cope with the giant new Saturn V rockets used to launch the Apollo missions. With the shuttle *Atlantis* in 2011, NASA concluded its manned launch programme for the foreseeable future; hundreds of workers were phased out and the area businesses that catered to them have taken a bit of a hit.

Crowds are thinnest at weekends and in May and September – but at any time, allow an entire day to see everything. The various exhibits in the **Visitor Complex** – mission capsules, spacesuits, lunar modules, a mock-up Space Shuttle flight deck – will keep anyone with the slightest interest in space exploration interested for a couple of hours. Afterwards, be sure to watch the two impressive IMAX movies and take a stroll around the open-air **Rocket Garden**, full of deceptively simple rockets from the 1950s, cleverly illuminated to show how they looked at blast-off. The newest attraction is the **Shuttle Launch Experience**, a simulation ride where passengers get to see what it's like to be an astronaut, vertically "launching" into space and orbiting Earth aboard the Space Shuttle. The remainder of the visit is comprised of a two-hour guided **bus tour**, which passes the 52-storey Vehicle Assembly Building (where Space Shuttles are prepared for launch), stops to view the launch pad and winds up with an opportunity to inspect a Saturn V rocket and witness a simulated Apollo countdown. For the dates and times of **real-life launches**, check the website, or sign up for event reminders by email.

Near the Space Center, on Hwy-405 in Titusville, the **Astronaut Hall of Fame** (included with regular admission) is one of Florida's most entertaining interactive museums, where exhibits allow you to experience G-force and a bumpy ride along the surface of Mars.

Merritt Island National Wildlife Refuge

Daily sunrise–sunset; visitor centre Tues–Sat 9am–4pm • Free; Black Point Wildlife Drive $5 • ☎ 321 861 0667, ⓦ fws.gov/merrittisland

NASA doesn't have Merritt Island all to itself: the agency shares it with the **Merritt Island National Wildlife Refuge**. Alligators, armadillos, raccoons, bobcats and an extravagant mix of birdlife live right up against some of the human world's most advanced hardware. Winter (Oct–March) is the best time to visit, when the skies are alive with birds migrating from the frozen north and mosquitoes aren't part of the equation. At any other time, especially in summer, the island's Mosquito Lagoon is worthy of its name: bring repellent.

Eight miles off I-95's exit 220, Hwy-406 leads to the seven-mile **Black Point Wildlife Drive**, which gives a solid introduction to the basics of the island's ecosystem; pick up the free leaflet at the entrance. Be sure to walk in the refuge, too: off the Wildlife Drive, the five-mile **Cruickshank Trail** weaves around the edge of the Indian River. Drive a few miles further east along Hwy-402 – branching from Hwy-406 just south of the Wildlife Drive and passing the **visitor centre** – and then hike the three-quarters-of-a-mile **Oak Hammock Trail** or the two-mile **Palm Hammock Trail**, both accessible from the visitor centre car park.

ACCOMMODATION AND EATING   **THE SPACE COAST**

The closest motels to the Kennedy Space Center are on the mainland along US-1 (in Titusville, for example) – or, if you're looking for a more picturesque location, try Cocoa Beach, a few miles south on a 10-mile strip of shore washed by some of the biggest surfing waves in Florida.

Fawlty Towers 3100 E Cocoa Beach Causeway ☎ 321 784 3870, ⓦ fawltytowersresort.com. The friendly, roomy pink-towered motel near the shore has a pool and tiki bar. Rooms are on the plain side, though the prices make up for it. **$59**

Luna Sea 3185 N Atlantic Ave ☎ 800 586 2732, ⓦ lunaseacocoabeach.com. This motel is a 1970s throwback; the decor is dated, but the rooms are neat, and stays come with free breakfast courtesy of the *Sunrise Diner* a mile north. $80

Sunset Café 500 W Cocoa Beach Causeway ☎ 321 783

8485. For great oysters and super riverfront views (and live entertainment nightly), trek here, but arrive early, as it's frequently mobbed. Daily 11am–10pm.

Daytona Beach

The consummate Florida beach town, with its T-shirt shops, amusement arcades and wall-to-wall motels, **DAYTONA BEACH** owes its existence to twenty miles of enticing light-brown sands. Once a favourite Spring Break destination, the town has tried to cultivate a more refined image in recent years. In a strange twist of fate, partying students have been replaced by bikers, as the town hosts three major annual events: the legendary **Daytona 500** stock-car race in February (tickets from $65; ☎877 306 RACE, ⓦ daytonainternationalspeedway.com); the massive **Bike Week**, in early March; and the relatively new, more family-friendly **Biketoberfest**, in October.

For all the excitement that racing generates, the best thing about Daytona is the seemingly limitless **beach**: it's 500ft wide at low tide, and fades dreamily off into the heat haze. Daytona is also one of the few beaches in Florida that you can drive on; pay $5 (Feb–Nov only) at the various entrances and follow the posted procedures.

Daytona International Speedway

1801 W International Speedway Blvd • All-access tour daily 10am–3pm, 90min; speedway tour daily 11.30am, 1.30pm, 3.30pm & 4pm, 30min; schedules for both subject to conditions and changes, so call ahead • All-access tour $23, kids 6–12 $17; speedway tour $16, kids 6–12 $10 • ☎ 877 306 RACE, ⓦ daytonainternationalspeedway.com • Bus #18 from Daytona Beach

The origin of Daytona's race-car and motorcycle obsession goes back to the early 1900s, when pioneering auto enthusiasts including Louis Chevrolet, Ransom Olds and Henry Ford came to Daytona's firm sands to race prototype vehicles beside the ocean. In fact, the world land speed record was smashed here five times by the British millionaire Malcolm Campbell. As increasing speeds made racing on the sands unsafe, the **Daytona International Speedway**, an ungainly configuration of concrete and steel holding 150,000 people, was opened in 1959 three miles west of downtown.

Though they can't capture the excitement of a race, **guided tram (trolley) tours** do provide a first-hand look at the fastest racetrack in the world. Speedway tours take in the track's infield and NASCAR (National Association of Stock Car Auto Racing) garages, while the all-access tour adds the drivers' meeting room, press box, an audience with the current winning Daytona 500 car, and a trip around the track (albeit a much slower one).

ARRIVAL AND GETTING AROUND   DAYTONA BEACH

By bus and tram (trolley) US-1 (called, in town, Ridgewood Ave) ploughs through mainland Daytona Beach, passing the Greyhound bus station at 138 S Ridgewood. Trams ($1.25) run the length of the beach until midnight (mid-Jan to early Sept).

Destinations Fort Lauderdale (2 daily; 6hr 10min–7hr 30min); Jacksonville (2 daily; 1hr 40min–2hr); Tampa (2 daily; 4hr 10min).

Visitor centre 126 E Orange Ave (Mon–Fri 9am–5pm; ☎ 800 854 1234, ⓦ daytonabeach.com).

ACCOMMODATION AND EATING

If you're going to be in Daytona during any of the big events, accommodation should be booked at least six months ahead; and expect minimum stays and prices to at least double. Any of the motels along the oceanfront Atlantic Avenue makes a good beach base.

Coquina Inn 544 S Palmetto Ave ☎386 254 4969, ⓦ coquinainn.com. Away from the beach but close to lively Beach St, this B&B (with bikes available for guests) occupies a grand mansion near the historic district. $119

Cove Motel 1306 N Atlantic Ave ☎800 828 3251, ⓦ motelcove.com. A family-friendly motel that is showing

its age a bit, but if you're looking for basic accommodation on the water, this is the place. $60

Daytona Diner 290 Beach St ☎386 258 8488, ⓦ thedaytonydiner.com. The decor is 1950s-style, but the breakfasts are modern-sized (huge) for about $6 a plate. Mon–Sat 7am–2pm.

7

Hidden Treasure Rum Bar & Grill 4940 S Peninsula Drive ☎386 761 9271, ⓦhiddentreasureonponceinlet.com. Nosh on fresh fish and shellfish at this Caribbean-coloured post next to the Ponce Inlet Lighthouse, on a deck built around sprawling tree trunks. Mon–Sat 11.30am–10pm, Sun 7.30am–9pm.

★ **Inlet Harbor** 133 Inlet Harbor Rd ☎386 767 5590, ⓦinletharbor.com. Enjoy shrimp umpteen different ways at this sizeable tropical-themed place overlooking a marina. Live music. Daily 11am–9pm.

★ **Tropical Manor** 2237 S Atlantic Ave ☎386 252 4920, ⓦtropicalmanor.com. This oceanfront motel is a gem, from the personal service to the lovingly maintained rooms touched up with charming handpainted foliage, flowers and fish. $103

▲ Vilano Beach

ST AUGUSTINE: THE OLD TOWN

N

0   100

yards

■ **BARS & LIVE-MUSIC VENUES**

A1A Aleworks	3
Mill Top Tavern	1
The Oasis	2

CASTILLO DRIVE

SAN MARCO AVENUE

City Gate

Castillo de San Marcos

ORANGE STREET

TOLOMATO LANE

Oldest Wooden Schoolhouse

COLONIAL QUARTER

Entrance

CORDOVA STREET

SPANISH STREET

ST GEORGE STREET

CUNA   STREET

AVENIDA MENENDEZ

SARAGOSSA STREET

CARRERA STREET

HYPOLITA STREET

CHARLOTTE STREET

Matanzas Bay

VALENCIA STREET

TREASURY STREET

Peña Peck House

Basilica Cathedral of St Augustine

AVENIDA MENENDEZ

BRIDGE OF LIONS

Flagler College

CATHEDRAL PLACE

PLAZA DE LA CONSTITUCIÓN

KING STREET

Lightner Museum

ARTILLERY LANE

Municipal Marina

CEDAR ST

GRANADA STREET

CORDOVA STREET

ST GEORGE STREET

AVILÉS STREET

LADIZ

CHARLOTTE STREET

MARINE STREET

BRAVO   ST

AVENIDA MENENDEZ

BRIDGE STREET

ONEIDA STREET

WASHINGTON ST

Oldest House

ST FRANCIS STREET

Greyhound Station & ①

① Beaches, Anastasia Island & St Augustine Beach

▼ 6

■ **ACCOMMODATION**		● **RESTAURANTS & CAFÉS**	
Carriage Way	2	95 Cordova	3
Casa Monica	5	Casa Maya	2
Casablanca Inn	3	Columbia	1
Kenwood Inn	6		
Pirate Haus Inn	4		
The Saragossa Inn	1		

St Augustine

Forty miles north of Daytona Beach, US-1 passes through the heart of charismatic **ST AUGUSTINE**. Eminently walkable, with a densely packed city centre and a Mediterranean feel, it bucks the daunting sprawl of much of Florida's East Coast. The oldest permanent settlement in the US, with much from its early days still intact along its narrow streets, it also offers two alluring lengths of **beach** just across Matanzas Bay.

Bordered on the west by St George Street – once the main thoroughfare and now a tourist-trampled, though genuinely historic, pedestrianized strip, its entrance anchored by the eighteenth-century City Gate – and on the south by Plaza de la Constitución, St Augustine's **Old Town** holds the well-tended evidence of the town's Spanish period. It may be small, but there's a lot to see: an early start, around 9am, will give you a lead on the tourist crowds, and should allow a good look at almost everything in one day.

Brief history

Though Ponce de León touched ground here in 1513, European settlement didn't begin until half a century later, when Spain's Pedro Menéndez de Avilés put ashore on St Augustine's Day in 1565. The town developed into a major social and administrative centre, soon to become the capital of east Florida. Subsequently, Tallahassee (see p.530) became the capital of a unified Florida, and St Augustine's fortunes waned. Since then, expansion has largely bypassed the town – a fact inadvertently facilitating the restoration programme that has turned this quiet community into a fine historical showcase.

Castillo de San Marcos National Monument

15 Castillo Drive • Daily 8.45am–4.45pm • $6 • Ⓦ nps.gov/casa

Given the fine state of the **Castillo de San Marcos National Monument**, on the northern edge of the Old Town beside the bay, it's difficult to believe that the fortress was built in the late 1600s. Its longevity is due to its design: a diamond-shaped rampart at each corner maximized firepower, and 14ft-thick walls reduced its vulnerability to attack. Inside, there are a number of great demonstrations (including one of historic weapons), while rambling along the 35ft-long ramparts reveals wonderful views across the city and the bay.

Oldest Wooden Schoolhouse

14 St George St • Mon–Thurs 9am–6pm, Fri–Sun 9am–8pm • $4.95 • ☎ 888 653 7245

You'll find a bunch of places called "The oldest…" in St Augustine; the **Oldest Wooden Schoolhouse**, set in lush gardens, is one of the most atmospheric – a restored wooden shack (containing period textbooks and artefacts) populated with animatronic wax dummies portraying nineteenth-century schoolchildren. It's perhaps unintentionally camp, but it all seems to work.

Colonial Quarter

33 St George St • Daily 9am–8pm, last ticket sold at 4.45pm • $12.99 • ☎ 904 342 2857

A fair-sized plot between Tolomato Lane and Cuna Street is taken up by the excellent **Colonial Quarter**. In its nine reconstructed homes and workshops, representing four different historic periods, volunteers dressed as Spanish settlers go about their business at anvils and foot-driven wood lathes. Tours of the quarter, musket drills and blacksmith demos are put on daily. Don't forget to stop by the candlelit *Taberna del Caballo* here for a glass of beer and some quality conversation – you might even end up singing old Spanish drinking songs with the servers.

Peña Peck House

143 St George St • Mon–Sat 10.30am–5pm, Sun 12.30–5pm • Donation requested • ☎ 904 829 5064

The **Peña Peck House** is thought to have originally been the Spanish treasury, but after the British took over in 1763 this was the home of the Governor. The property was acquired in 1837 by a Connecticut physician and his gregarious spouse, who turned the place into a high-society rendezvous. It's today run by the Woman's Exchange of St Augustine, whose members lead informative tours of the antique-filled house.

Plaza de la Constitución and around

In the sixteenth century, the Spanish king decreed that all colonial towns must be built around a central plaza; thus, St George Street runs into the **Plaza de la Constitución**, a marketplace from 1598. On the plaza's north side, the **Basilica Cathedral of St Augustine** (daily 7am–5pm; donation) adds a touch of grandeur, although it's largely a 1960s remodelling of the late eighteenth-century original.

Tourist numbers lessen as you cross south of the plaza into a web of quiet, narrow streets, all just as old as St George Street. West of the plaza along King Street, opposite Flagler College, the opulent **Lightner Museum** (daily 9am–5pm, last admission 4pm; $10; ☎ 904 824 2874, Ⓦ lightnermuseum.org) displays fine and decorative arts in the former building of one of the most fabulous resorts of the late nineteenth century.

Oldest House

14 St Francis St • Daily 9am–5pm, last admission 4.30pm • $8 • ☎ 904 824 2872

A substantial exploration of local history is available in the form of the fascinating **Oldest House**, which is indeed the oldest house in town, dating from the early 1700s. Its rooms are furnished to show how the house – and people's lives – changed as new eras unfolded. The house is managed by the St Augustine Historical Society; a ticket allows access to its range of related attractions, all old.

The beaches

Some fine **beaches** – busiest at weekends – lie just a couple of miles east from the Old Town. Crossing the bay via the Bridge of Lions, and continuing east on Hwy-A1A will bring you to the **Anastasia State Recreation Area**, on Anastasia Island (daily 8am–sunset; cars $8, cyclists and pedestrians $2), which offers a thousand protected acres of dunes, marshes and scrub, linked by nature walks. A few miles further south, **St Augustine Beach** is family terrain, with some good restaurants and a fishing pier.

ARRIVAL, GETTING AROUND, INFORMATION AND TOURS   ST AUGUSTINE

By bus The Greyhound station, 1711 Dobbs Rd, is a couple of miles from town, but drivers will drop you next to the Castillo if requested.

Destinations Jacksonville (1 daily; 1hr); Pensacola (1 daily; 11hr 30min); Sarasota (2 daily; 12hr 10min–18hr 45min).

By sightseeing train St Augustine is best seen on foot, though two sightseeing trains tour the main landmarks (both $23/3-day pass, kids $10): Ripley's (daily 8.30am–5pm; online discounts; ☎ 800 824 1906, ⓦ redtrains.com) and the Old Town Trolley (daily 8.30am–4.30pm; ☎ 888 910 8687, ⓦ trolleytours.com/st-augustine).

By taxi Ancient City Cabs (☎ 904 824 8161).

Visitor centre 10 Castillo Drive (daily 8.30am–5.30pm;

☎ 800 653 2489, ⓦ floridashistoriccoast.com). Shows a film on the history of the town, has recommendations for a variety of tours (see below) and provides information on numerous local festivals, including torchlit processions and a Menorcan Fiesta.

Guided tours Harbour cruises by Scenic Cruise (4–6 daily; $16.75; ☎ 800 542 8316, ⓦ scenic-cruise.com) leave from the Municipal Marina, near the foot of King St. The well-organized and informative City Walks ($12; ☎ 904 540 3476, ⓦ staugustinecitywalks.com) leads daily historical walking tours, while various spooky sites are visited on A Ghostly Experience evening tours (8pm; $15 walking tour, $26 tram (trolley) tour; ☎ 904 829 1122).

ACCOMMODATION

The Old Town has many excellent restored inns offering B&B, and there are cheaper chain hotels outside the centre of town along San Marco Avenue and Ponce de León Boulevard. Note that rates generally rise by $20–60 at weekends.

Carriage Way 70 Cuna St ☎ 800 908 9832, ⓦ carriage way.com. Canopy and four-poster beds, clawfoot tubs and antiques add to the period feel of this 1880s house. **$149**

★ **Casa Monica** 95 Cordova St ☎ 800 648 1888, ⓦ casa monica.com. Elegant, beautifully restored Spanish-style hotel that has hosted the king and queen of Spain. The rooms have wrought-iron beds and a certain sumptuous seaside charm. **$169**

Casablanca Inn 24 Av Menendez ☎ 904 829 0928, ⓦ casablancainn.com. This inn features many rooms with jacuzzis, whirlpool baths and a delightful cosy martini bar with live music. A good choice for those who want to be right in the mix of things. **$169**

Kenwood Inn 38 Marine St ☎ 904 824 2116,

ⓦ thekenwoodinn.com. Peacefully situated near the waterfront, this charming B&B has a pretty pool and offers complimentary use of bikes for guests. **$159**

Pirate Haus Inn 32 Treasury St ☎ 904 808 1999, ⓦ piratehaus.com. The town's only hostel accommodation, near the Plaza, is popular with backpackers. It has a giant kitchen, a common room stuffed with guidebooks, beds in a/c dorms and five private rooms. There's also a free, all-you-can-eat pancake breakfast. Dorms **$20**, doubles **$85**

★ **The Saragossa Inn** 34 Saragossa St ☎ 904 808 7384, ⓦ saragossainn.com. This lovely little pink cottage began life in 1924 as a Sears Craftsman bungalow and now holds four comfortable guest rooms and two suites, just a bit west of the beaten path. **$169**

EATING, DRINKING AND ENTERTAINMENT

Eating in the Old Town can be expensive, and a number of its cafés and restaurants are closed in the evening. Of those that stay open, several double as drinking spots and live music venues.

95 Cordova Casa Monica, 95 Cordova St ☎ 904 810 6810, ⓦ casamonica.com. This luxurious and elegant hotel restaurant's menu features expensive but masterful nouvelle continental cuisine. Mains $19–33. Daily 7.30am–2.30pm & 5–9pm, Fri & Sat till 10pm.

★ **A1A Aleworks** 1 King St ☎ 904 829 2977, ⓦ a1aaleworks.com. Nice brewpub that features fried lobster bites ($12) and mango BBQ shrimp skewers ($15).

The beers are quite good, and the higher-alcohol brews A Strange Stout and Porpoise Point Ale both come highly recommended. Daily 11am–midnight.

★ **Casa Maya** 17 Hypolita St ☎ 904 823 1739. Pleasant and healthy Maya-influenced food here, including corn tortilla *mahi-mahi* tacos and excellent brunch. Mon 8am–3.30pm, Wed & Thurs 10am–3.30pm & 5.30–9pm, Fri–Sun 8am–3.30pm & 5.30–9.30pm.

Columbia 98 St George St ☎ 904 824 3341, ⓦ columbiarestaurant.com. Enjoy paella, tapas and other traditional Spanish/Cuban food in a sumptuous setting of fountains and candlelight. Mon–Sat 11am–10pm, Sun noon–10pm.

★ **Mill Top Tavern** 19½ George St ☎ 904 829 2329, ⓦ milltop.com. There's a terrific atmosphere at the top of this nineteenth-century mill, where you'll hear live music and get a great, open-air view of the Castillo. Daily 11am–midnight.

The Oasis 4000 Ocean Trace Rd, St Augustine Beach ☎ 904 471 3424, ⓦ worldfamousoasis.com. This beach bar is famous for its massive menu and burgers with a multitude of tasty toppings, plus there's live music at dinner time. Mon–Thurs & Sun 6am–10pm, Fri & Sat 6am–11pm.

Jacksonville

Hunkered down between the great double loop of the St Johns River, **JACKSONVILLE** struggled for years to throw off its long-standing reputation as a dour industrial port city with a deeply conservative population. During the 1990s, the city gained some standing as a service industry centre, bringing a spate of construction projects and fresh homebuyers to the area. The sheer size of the city – at 841 square miles, the largest in the USA – serves to dilute its easy-going character, and it is quite difficult to get around without a car.

Museum of Contemporary Art

333 N Laura St • Tues, Wed, Fri & Sat 11am–5pm, Thurs 11am–9pm, Sun noon–5pm • $8, free Wed 5–9pm during Jacksonville's "Art Walk" event • ☎ 904 366 6911, ⓦ mocajacksonville.org

Jacksonville's **Museum of Contemporary Art** offers paintings, sculptures and photography of remarkable scope and depth, including large Ed Paschke and James Rosenquist canvases. The collection, amounting to more than 1000 pieces, also delves into printmaking and mixed media.

Cummer Museum of Art and Gardens

829 Riverside Ave • Tues 10am–9pm, Wed–Sat 10am–4pm, Sun noon–4pm • $10, free Tues 4–9pm • ☎ 904 366 6911, ⓦ cummer.org

Just south of the Fuller Warren River bridge (I-95), in the **Cummer Museum of Art and Gardens**, spacious rooms and sculpture-lined corridors contain works by prominent European and American masters. The two acres of lovely Italianate and English gardens that overlook the river are an added bonus.

The beaches

Travelling south from Jacksonville on I-95, then east on Hwy-202, you'll first hit **Ponte Vedra Beach**, whose crowd-free sands and million-dollar homes form one of the most exclusive communities in northeast Florida. A few miles north from here on Hwy-A1A is the much less snooty **Jacksonville Beach**. Two miles north of Jacksonville Beach's old pier, the more commercialized **Neptune Beach** blurs into the identical-looking **Atlantic Beach**; both are more family-oriented, and are best visited for eating and socializing.

ARRIVAL, GETTING AROUND AND INFORMATION JACKSONVILLE

By plane Jacksonville International Airport (ⓦ flyjacksonville.com) is 13 miles north of downtown. A cab into town costs $35–60, or you can opt for A9A Airport Transportation ($35–40; ☎ 877 399 8288, ⓦ skyjax.net). Local bus #CT3 departs for Jackson Landing every 60–90min ($1; reduced service Sat & Sun).

By bus It's an easy walk downtown from the Greyhound station at 10 N Pearl St.
Destinations Miami (2 daily; 9hr–9hr 50min); Tallahassee (3 daily; 3hr); Tampa (3 daily; 5hr 35min–6hr 20min).

By train The station is an awkward 6 miles northwest of downtown at 3570 Clifford Lane.
Destinations Orlando (2 daily; 3hr 10min); Savannah, GA (2 daily; 2hr 30min); Washington DC (2 daily; 15hr 15min); West Palm Beach (2 daily; 9hr).

By taxi Yellow Cab (☎ 904 260 1111); Gator City Taxi (☎ 904 355 8294).

Visitor centre 208 N Laura St, just south of Heming Plaza (Mon–Fri 9am–5pm; ☎ 904 421 9156, ⓦ visitjacksonville.com).

7

ACCOMMODATION

Fig Tree Inn 185 4th Ave S, Jacksonville Beach ☎904 246 8855, ⓦfigtreeinn.com. A pleasant stopover for a couple of days, this 1915 former beach house has six cheery rooms, individually themed and decorated, each with its own bath. **$149**

★ **The House on Cherry Street** 1844 Cherry St ☎904 384 1999, ⓦhouseoncherry.com. Both of the Victorian-themed rooms at this charming B&B in the Riverside-Avondale residential neighbourhood (near the Cummer Museum) have river views. Breakfast and after-noon tea are included. **$105**

Hyatt Regency Jacksonville Riverfront 225 Coastline Drive St ☎800 233 1234, ⓦjacksonville.hyatt.com. A great downtown riverfront location adds something to this otherwise corporate hotel that nonetheless has tons of amenities. **$199**

Sea Horse Oceanfront Inn 120 Atlantic Blvd, Neptune Beach ☎904 246 2175, ⓦseahorseoceanfrontinn.com. This modest, self-proclaimed "old-school" hotel near the beach won't win any style awards, but rooms are clean and uncrowded, and each offers a mini-fridge and balcony or private patio. **$129**

EATING AND DRINKING

Beach Hut Café 1281 S 3rd St, Jacksonville Beach ☎904 249 3516. Serves huge delicious breakfasts – think generous portions of biscuits and gravy or country-fried steak – with queues out the door. Daily 6am–2.30pm.

★ **Biscotti's** 3556 St Johns Ave ☎904 387 2060, ⓦbiscottis.net. One of the Riverside-Avondale area's more appealing spots – part coffeehouse, part restaurant, with Mediterranean specialities and a superb Sunday brunch. Mon–Thurs 10.30am–10pm, Fri 10.30am–midnight, Sat 8am–midnight, Sun 8am–9pm.

Ragtime Tavern Seafood Grill 207 Atlantic Blvd, Atlantic Beach ☎904 241 7877 ⓦragtimetavern.com. With an extensive seafood menu (mains from $18), this restaurant is popular with locals and visitors, and you can feast alfresco in the garden out back. Mon–Thurs & Sun 11am–midnight, Fri & Sat 11am–1am.

River City Brewing Co. 835 Museum Circle ☎904 398 2299, ⓦrivercitybrew.com. You'll find great steaks, home-brewed beer (from German and English malted barley) and lovely river views on offer here. Mon–Thurs 3–10pm, Fri & Sat 3pm–late, Sun 11am–6pm.

★ **Sun Dog Diner** 207 Atlantic Blvd, Neptune Beach ☎904 241 8221, ⓦsundogjax.com. Above-average creative diner fare, with specials such as pan-seared red snapper with corn salsa. Mon–Sat 11am–2am, Sun 10am–2am.

Orlando and the theme parks

Encompassing a broad and fertile expanse between the east and west coasts, most of Central Florida was farming and ranching country when vacation-mania first hit the state's coastal strips. From the 1970s on, this tranquil picture was shattered: no section of the state has been affected more dramatically by modern tourism. A clutter of highway interchanges, motels and billboards now arch around the sprawling city of **ORLANDO**, which welcomes more visitors than any other place in the state. The reason, of course, is **Walt Disney World**, the biggest and cleverest theme-park complex ever created, along with **Universal Orlando**, **SeaWorld Orlando** and a host of other attractions, though the downtown area still holds the city's best nightlife.

Walt Disney World

Take Osceola Pkwy to Disney exits, or I-4 West to exit 64 (Magic Kingdom, Disney Hollywood Studios), 65 (Animal Kingdom, Blizzard Beach) or 67 (Epcot, Typhoon Lagoon) • ☎407 939 6244, ⓦdisneyworld.com • See box, p.512

As significant as air conditioning in making the state what it is today, **WALT DISNEY WORLD** turned a wedge of Florida farmland into one of the world's most lucrative holiday destinations. The immense and astutely planned empire also pushed the state's media profile through the roof: from being a down-at-heel mix of cheap motels, retirement homes and alligator zoos, Florida became a showcase of modern international tourism overnight.

Disney World is the pacesetter among theme parks. It goes way beyond Disneyland (see p.837) – which opened in Anaheim, California, in 1955 – delivering escapism at its most technologically advanced and psychologically brilliant, across an area twice the size of Manhattan. Its four main theme parks are quite separate entities and, ideally, you should allow at least a full day for each. The **Magic Kingdom** is the Disney park of popular imagination, where Mickey mingles with the crowds – very much the park for kids, though at its high-tech best capable of captivating even the most jaded adult. Known for its giant, golfball-like geosphere, **Epcot** is Disney's celebration of science, technology and world cultures; this sprawling area involves a lot of walking, and young children may grow restless. The smaller **Disney's Hollywood Studios** takes its inspiration from movies, TV and music, offering some good thrill rides and live shows that will appeal to all ages. The newest of the four, **Disney's Animal Kingdom Park**, brings all manner of African and Asian wildlife to the theme-park setting.

Along with the main parks, other forms of entertainment have been created to keep people on Disney property for as long as possible. There are two excellent

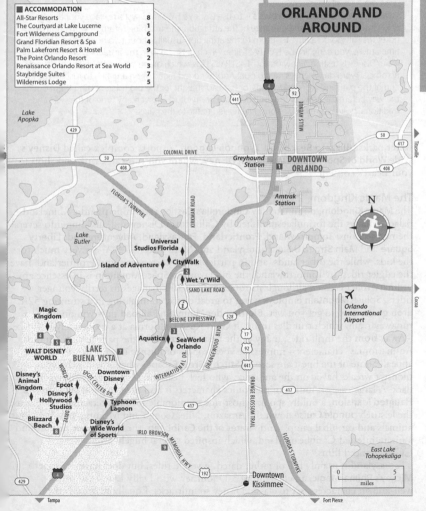

■ ACCOMMODATION	
All-Star Resorts	8
The Courtyard at Lake Lucerne	1
Fort Wilderness Campground	6
Grand Floridian Resort & Spa	4
Palm Lakefront Resort & Hostel	9
The Point Orlando Resort	2
Renaissance Orlando Resort at Sea World	3
Staybridge Suites	7
Wilderness Lodge	5

ORLANDO AND AROUND

7

7

INFORMATION, TICKETS AND HOW TO BEAT THE CROWDS

For general Disney World **information**, call ☎407 939 6244 or visit ⓦdisneyworld.com. **Tickets** cost $85 (children aged 3–9 $79), and allow unlimited access to all shows and rides in one park only, for that day only. The **Magic Your Way** ticket saves money if you spread your visit over a number of days – for example, a seven-day ticket would cost $267 (children 3–9 $248). You can buy a Magic Your Way ticket for a maximum of ten days and you can only visit one park per day. If you want to move from park to park in the same day, you must add the **Park Hopper** option for an additional flat fee of $57. The **Water Park Fun & More** option allows you to add from two to ten extra admissions (the exact number depends on the length of your basic Magic Your Way ticket) to Blizzard Beach and Typhoon Lagoon (see p.516), DisneyQuest and Disney's Wide World of Sports for a flat fee of $57. The **car parks** cost $14 a day, but are free if you're staying at a Walt Disney World resort.

Each park is generally **open** daily from 9am to between 6pm and 10pm, depending on the time of year; pick up the current schedule when you arrive. Note that Disney's Animal Kingdom Park closes at 5pm year-round. At their worst, waiting times for the most popular rides can be well over an hour.

The best way to **beat the crowds** is to use Disney's FASTPASS system. Place your admission ticket into a machine at the entrance of the attraction; the machine returns it with another ticket that gives you a time to return to the attraction, usually about two hours later. When that time arrives, you can join the FASTPASS line, which gets you in to the attraction with little or no wait. (Disney is testing a new option, FASTPASS Plus, which grants added flexibility, but there's no official word on when it's rolling out.) Another good tactic upon arrival is to rush to the far end of the park and work backwards, or to head straight for the big rides, getting them out of the way before the crowds arrive. Queues are pretty much a given any time of the year, and traditional holidays in the USA bring increased traffic to the parks.

---

water parks, **Blizzard Beach** and **Typhoon Lagoon**, a sports complex called **Disney's Wide World of Sports** and **Downtown Disney**, where you can eat, drink and shop to your heart's content.

The Magic Kingdom

The **Magic Kingdom**, dominated by **Cinderella's Castle**, a stunning pseudo-Rhineland palace, follows the formula established by California's Disneyland, dividing into several themed sections: **Tomorrowland**, **Frontierland**, **Fantasyland**, **Adventureland**, **Liberty Square** and **Main Street, U.S.A.** Fantasyland and Main Street, U.S.A. are very much for the kids, while the other lands, and in particular Tomorrowland and Frontierland, have the edgier rides. In Tomorrowland, the old favourite **Space Mountain** is in essence an ordinary roller coaster, although its total darkness still manages to terrify younger riders. **Splash Mountain** employs water to great effect, culminating in a stunning 52ft drop guaranteed to get you wet. **Big Thunder Mountain Railroad** puts you on board a runaway train, which trundles through Gold Rush California at a moderately fast pace.

Away from the thrill rides, many of the best attractions in the park rely on "Audio-Animatronics" characters – impressive vocal robots of Disney invention – for their appeal. Some of the finest are seen in **Stitch's Great Escape**, where the mischievous monster wreaks havoc on the audience, who feel, hear and smell strange things in the dark. A large cast of Audio-Animatronics characters is also used to good effect in the **Haunted Mansion**, a mildly spooky ghost ride memorable for its spectacular holograms; the leisurely **Jungle Cruise** down the Amazon, Nile, Congo and Mekong, past ferocious animals and cannibal camps; and **Pirates of the Caribbean**, the classic boat ride around a pirate-infested Caribbean island, which inspired several hugely profitable CGI-enhanced films.

Fantasyland is mainly full of rather dated, juvenile rides, but does have the superb **Mickey's PhilharMagic**, an enchanting 3-D journey with Daffy Duck and other well-known characters, set to classic Disney soundtracks. Equally magical is the

Wishes firework display, which takes place at park closing time, and which can't fail to excite even the most cynical visitors.

Epcot

Even before the Magic Kingdom opened, Walt Disney was developing plans for **Epcot** (Experimental Prototype Community of Tomorrow), conceived in 1966 as a real community experimenting with the new ideas and materials of the technologically advancing USA. However, the idea failed to shape up as Disney had envisioned: Epcot didn't open until 1982, when global recession and ecological concerns had put a dampener on the belief in the infallibility of science. One glaring drawback of this park is simply its immense size: it's twice as big as the Magic Kingdom, and very hard on the feet.

The Epcot Center is dominated by a 180ft geosphere that sits in the heart of **Future World**, which keeps close to Epcot's original concept of exploring the history and future of agriculture, transport, energy and communication. Future World is divided into several pavilions (including the geosphere, with its classic, recently modified **Spaceship Earth** ride), each corporate-sponsored and featuring its own rides, films, interactive exhibits and games. The best of the attractions are **Soarin'**, using the latest flight-simulator and IMAX movie technology to sweep you off on a breathtaking hang-glider ride over California; **Mission: SPACE**, a realistic re-creation of a mission to Mars, including real G-force on take-off; and **Test Track**, a roller-coaster-style ride where you test a high-performance car. Occupying the largest area in the park is **World Showcase**, with eleven different countries represented by recognizable national landmarks or stereotypical scenes. The **restaurants** here are among the best in Disney World; and it's a great place to watch the spectacular night-time sound-and-light show, **IllumiNations: Reflections of Earth**.

Disney's Hollywood Studios

After signing an agreement in the 1980s with Metro-Goldwyn-Mayer (MGM) to exploit MGM's many movie classics, Disney had an ample source of instantly recognizable images to mould into rides suitable for adults as much as for kids. The park opened in 1989 as Disney-MGM Studios, but since then, the addition of attractions encompassing music, television and theatre led to the decision to rename the park **Disney's Hollywood Studios** to reflect the broader focus on "entertainment".

THE WORLD OF WALT DISNEY

When the brilliant illustrator and animator Walt Disney devised the world's first theme park, California's **Disneyland** (see p.837), he left himself with no control over the hotels and restaurants that quickly engulfed it, preventing growth and erasing profits Disney felt were rightly his. Determined not to let that happen again, the Disney corporation secretly bought up 27,500 acres of central Florida farmland, acquiring by the late 1960s a site a hundred times bigger than Disneyland. With the promise of a jobs bonanza for Florida, the state legislature gave the corporation the rights of any major municipality (via a special jurisdiction called the Reedy Creek Improvement District), empowering it to lay roads, enact building codes and enforce the law with its own security force.

Walt Disney World's first "land", the Magic Kingdom, opened in 1971, and was a huge success. Unveiled in 1982, the far more ambitious Epcot represented the first major break from cartoon-based escapism – but its rose-tinted look at the future received a mixed response at the time. Partly due to this, and to some bad management decisions, the Disney empire (Disney himself died in 1966) faced bankruptcy by the mid-1980s. Since then, the corporation has sprung back from the abyss, and steers a tight and competitive ship that encompasses broadcast networks, publishing and movies – as well as a substantial merchandising arm. It may trade in fantasy, but when it comes to money, the Disney Corporation deals in the real world.

Most of the things to do at Disney's Hollywood Studios take the form of rides or shows, and there are fewer exhibit-style attractions than in the other Disney parks. Thrill-seekers will enjoy the gravity-defying drops (including moments of weightlessness) in the outstanding **The Twilight Zone Tower of Terror**, or the slightly more ordinary **Rock 'n' Roller Coaster** with its breakneck-speed launch.

Don't miss the thirty-minute behind-the-scenes **Studio Backlot Tour**, climaxing with the dramatic special effects on the *Catastrophe Canyon* movie set; the funny **Muppet Vision 3-D** show; and **The Great Movie Ride**, where Audio-Animatronics figures from famous movies interact with real-life actors.

Disney's Animal Kingdom Park

An animal-conservation theme park with Disney's patented over-the-top twist, **Disney's Animal Kingdom Park** was opened in 1998. The park, home to 250 species and some 1700 animals, is divided into seven "lands" – **Africa**, **Asia**, **Discovery Island**, **Oasis**, **Camp Minnie-Mickey**, **DinoLand U.S.A.** and **Rafiki's Planet Watch** – with Africa and Asia being the most visually impressive, each re-creating the natural landscapes and exotic atmosphere of these two continents with admirable attention to detail.

The best-realized attraction is Africa's **Kilimanjaro Safaris**, where a jeep takes you on what feels very much like a real African safari, to view giraffes, zebras, elephants, lions, gazelles and rhinos, as well as take part in anti-poacher manoeuvres. Elsewhere in Africa, the troop of lowland gorillas at the **Pangani Forest Exploration Trail** are definitely worth a look. Crossing over to **Asia**, you'll get an astounding up-close look at the healthiest-looking tigers in captivity at the **Maharajah Jungle Trek**. DinoLand U.S.A.'s **Dinosaur** is a slower but still exciting ride full of small drops and short stops in the dark while scary dinosaurs pop out of nowhere.

Universal Orlando

Off I-4, half a mile north of exits 74B or 75A • Park opens daily at 9am, closing times vary • One-day, one-park ticket $88, kids 3–9 $82, under-3s free; two-day, two-park ticket $110/$100; Universal Express Pass grants entry to any Express line for the day in one or both parks, $19.99–69.99 depending on season; parking $15 • ☎ 407 363 8000, ⓦ universalorlando.com

For some years, it seemed that TV and film production would move away from California to Florida, which, with its lower taxes and cheaper labour, was more amenable. The opening of Universal Studios in 1990 appeared to confirm that trend. So far, though, for various reasons, Florida has not proved to be a fully realistic alternative. Even so, this hasn't stopped the **Universal Studios** enclave here, known as **Universal Orlando**, from becoming a major player in the Orlando theme-park arena. Though Disney World still commands the lion's share of attention, Universal has siphoned off many visitors with its high-tech movie-themed attractions and the excellent thrill rides at **Islands of Adventure**. And with all the nightclubs at Disney now closed, **CityWalk** has become the main competition to downtown Orlando for nightlife dollars (see p.518). Furthermore, Universal has achieved fully fledged resort status with its three luxurious on-site **hotels** (see p.517).

Universal Studios Florida

Like its competitor Disney's Hollywood Studios, the four-hundred-acre **Universal Studios Florida** is a working production studio. The newest attraction, **The Simpsons Ride**,

---

THE ORLANDO FLEXTICKET

Universal Orlando, Sea World Orlando, Islands of Adventures and two water parks – Wet 'n Wild and Aquatica – have teamed together to create a pass that permits access to each park over a period of fourteen consecutive days. The **Orlando Flexticket** costs $294 (children 3–9 $274), or $334/$312 including Tampa's Busch Gardens (see p.520), with a free shuttle from Orlando.

combines cutting-edge flight-simulator technology with the irreverent humour of *The Simpsons*; it was enhanced by the introduction of a Springfield downtown area, complete with show-specific restaurants and products, in 2013. The park's newest roller coaster, **Hollywood Rip Ride Rockit**, reaches a height of 167ft and pulses to a soundtrack that you select beforehand. Don't miss **Shrek 4-D**, a delightful 3-D presentation brought even more to life by an overdose of superb "feelies" (including a few too many water sprays). Also worthwhile, **Disaster** gives you an intensely claustrophobic two minutes of terror as you experience what it's like to be caught on a subway train when an 8.0 Richter-scale quake hits.

Islands of Adventure

Islands of Adventure is Orlando's leader in state-of-the-art, edge-of-your-seat thrill rides: though there are plenty of diversions for the less daring, these rides are what brings the crowds. The park is divided into six sections – **Marvel Super Hero Island**, **The Lost Continent**, **Jurassic Park**, **Toon Lagoon**, **Seuss Landing** and the latest addition, opened in June 2010: **The Wizarding World of Harry Potter**. After five years of planning and consultation with author J.K. Rowling the last is an immersive experience, with permanent snow-cover on the gift shops, which feature postcards with Potter-themed stamps, magic wands and black school robes.

The real meat and potatoes of the Wizarding World, though are the rides, and they do not disappoint. The **Dragon Challenge** involves two speeding trains (separate lines for each) engineered to provide harrowing head-on near misses (the front-row seats are especially sought after), while **The Flight of the Hippogriff** is a fairly tame wicker-covered roller coaster that resembles the magical beast. For those willing to wait (and you will wait) in line, the **Forbidden Journey** is a kaleidoscope of virtual reality and extremely advanced **robotic technology** based around a recreation of Hogwarts.

The queues are a bit less intense over at **The Amazing Adventures of Spider-Man**, which uses every trick imaginable – HD 3-D, sensory stimuli, motion simulation and more – to spirit you into Spider-Man's battles with villains. Other park offerings for kids include **Dudley Do-Right's Ripsaw Falls** and **Popeye & Bluto's Bilge-Rat Barges**, both good for getting a midday drenching; and the whole of Seuss Landing, where everything is based on **Dr Seuss** characters. There's one **live performance** offered throughout the day: **The Eighth Voyage of Sinbad Stunt Show**, where the set, stunts and pyrotechnics are as good as the jokes are bad.

SeaWorld Orlando

Sea Harbor Drive, near the intersection of I-4 and the Beeline Expressway • Park opens daily at 9am, closing times vary • $79, kids 3–9 $71 ($10 discount for online purchases) • ☎ 407 351 3600, ⊚ seaworld.com

The cream of Florida's sizeable crop of marine parks, **SeaWorld Orlando** should not be missed: allocate a full day to see it all. The big event is *One Ocean* – thirty minutes of tricks performed by playful killer whales (you'll get drenched if you're sitting in the first fourteen rows of the stadium). Also, try not to miss the kid-orientated sea-lion extravaganza, *Clyde and Seamore Take Pirate Island*. The **Wild Arctic** complex, complete with artificial snow and ice, brings you close to beluga whales, walruses and polar bears, while a flight-simulator ride takes you on a stomach-churning helicopter flight through an Arctic blizzard.

The park's first thrill ride, **Journey to Atlantis**, travels on both water and rails, and has a 60ft drop (be prepared to get very wet). Much more exhilarating, however, is **Kraken**, a roller coaster that flings you around at speeds of up to 65 miles per hour, free-flying and looping-the-loop at great heights. The newest ride is the **Manta**, which takes its flat-lying riders on a steel roller coaster that emulates the movements of a manta ray.

7

ORLANDO'S WATER PARKS

Disney World has two excellent **water parks**. **Blizzard Beach**, north of the *All-Star Resorts* (see opposite) on World Drive (daily 9am–7pm; $52, kids 3–9 $44; ☎ 407 560 3400), is based on the fantasy that a hapless entrepreneur has opened a ski resort in Florida and the entire thing has started to melt. The star of the show is **Summit Plummet**, which shoots you off a 120ft vertical drop at more than fifty miles per hour. Gentler rides include toboggan-style slalom courses and raft rides. As well as the slides, **Typhoon Lagoon**, off Buena Vista Drive (daily 9am–7pm; $52, kids 3–9 $44; ☎ 407 939 5277), features a huge surfing pool and a shark reef where you can snorkel among tropical fish. Keen to get in on the act, SeaWorld Orlando has recently opened **Aquatica**, across the road from SeaWorld on International Drive (daily 9am–5pm, longer hours in summer; $55, kids 3–9 $50; ☎ 888 800 5447, ⓦ aquaticabyseaworld.com), which combines live animal attractions with wave pools, slides and beaches. Finally, **Wet 'n Wild**, 6200 International Drive (daily 10am–5pm, longer hours in summer; $55, children 3–9 $50; ☎ 800 992 9453, ⓦ wetnwildorlando.com), defends itself admirably in the face of the stiff competition, with a range of no-nonsense slides including the almost vertical **Der Stuka**.

With substantially less razzmatazz, plenty of smaller aquariums and displays offer a wealth of information about the underwater world. Among the highlights, the **Antarctica** region holds the popular **Penguin Encounter**, with scores of the birds scampering over an iceberg, and a new penguin chick-themed ride; **Turtle Trek** gives you a close-up look at these endangered mammals; and **Shark Encounter** includes a walk through an acrylic-sided tunnel.

ARRIVAL AND DEPARTURE

By plane The international airport is 9 miles south of downtown Orlando (☎ 407 825 2001). Local buses (see below) link the airport with downtown (#11 or #51) and International Drive (#42). Alternatively, shuttle buses operated by Mears Transportation (24hr; ☎ 407 423 5566) charge a flat fee of $18 to any hotel in downtown, $19 to International Drive, and $21 to Hwy-192. Those staying at Disney can take advantage of the free airport transfer offered by Disney's Magical Express Transportation (☎ 407 934 7639 or ☎ 866 599 0951). Taxis to these destinations cost $30–60.

GETTING AROUND AND INFORMATION

By bus You have to be determined to get to the theme parks without a car, but it can be done. Local Lynx buses (☎ 407 841 5969, ⓦ golynx.com) converge at the downtown Orlando terminal, 455 N Garland Ave. Route #50 heads to Walt Disney World, while route #8 or the limited-stop #38 go to International Drive (all rides are $2).

By tram (trolley) Along International Drive (including SeaWorld Orlando), the I-Ride Trolley (☎ 866 243 7483, ⓦ iridetrolley.com) operates every 20min daily

ORLANDO AND THE THEME PARKS

By bus The Greyhound terminal is downtown at 555 N John Young Pkwy (☎ 407 292 3424).
Destinations Sarasota (2 daily; 4hr); Tampa (6 daily; 1hr 40min–2hr 5min); West Palm Beach (6 daily; 3hr 20min–9hr).
By train The Amtrak station is at 1400 Sligh Blvd (☎ 407 843 7611).
Destinations Jacksonville (2 daily; 3hr 10min); Miami (2 daily; 5hr 30min–7hr 30min); Tampa (via Amtrak coach: 1 daily; 2hr).

8am–10.30pm, costing $1.50 one way.
By taxi Taxis are the best way to get around at night – try Diamond Cab (☎ 407 523 3333).
By car All the main rental firms have offices at or close to the airport.
Visitor centre 8723 International Drive (daily Mon–Fri 8am–5.30pm, Sat & Sun 9am–3pm; ☎ 407 363 5872, ⓦ visitorlando.com); the efficient official visitor centre with a plethora of brochures and discount coupons.

ACCOMMODATION

If you're on a budget, or want to spend time visiting the other parks, you'd do best to stay **outside Walt Disney World**. The chain hotels on **International Drive** are close to Universal Orlando and SeaWorld Orlando, with numerous restaurants and shops within walking distance. Plenty of hotels are dotted around Disney property in an area called **Lake Buena Vista**, while budget hotels – and even a hostel – line **Hwy-192** (also close to Disney). **Downtown** Orlando has a handful of charming, privately run hotels and B&Bs.

OUTSIDE THE PARKS

★ **The Courtyard at Lake Lucerne** 211 Lucerne Circle NE ☎ 407 648 5188, ⓦ orlandohistoricinn.com. Choose from Victorian- and Edwardian-era rooms or airy Art Deco suites at this charming downtown hotel. $117

Palm Lakefront Resort & Hostel 4840W Hwy-192 ☎ 407 396 1759, ⓦ orlandohostels.com. The obvious choice for backpackers, this resort-style hostel has six-bed, single-sex dorms, private rooms, a pool and a pleasant lakefront location. Dorms $19, doubles $36

The Point Orlando Resort 7389 Universal Blvd ☎ 866 994 6309, ⓦ thepointorlando.com. Conveniently located near the mix of Orlando's many theme parks, *The Point* is an ideal choice for families making an extended stay in the area. $119

Renaissance Orlando Resort at SeaWorld 6677 Sea Harbor Drive ☎ 800 327 6677, ⓦ renaissanceseaworld orlando.com. An upmarket hotel off International Drive directly opposite Sea World Orlando, with spacious rooms and an attractive atrium. $249

Staybridge Suites 8751 Stateside Drive, Lake Buena Vista ☎ 407 238 0777, ⓦ staybridge.com. Friendly and popular hotel smack in the middle of everything, with well-equipped suites, free shuttles to the parks, free internet and hot buffet breakfast. $156

WITHIN WALT DISNEY WORLD

Prices at the fabulously designed Disney World resorts (reservations for all: ☎ 407 939 7211 or ⓦ disneyworld .disney.go.com/resorts) scattered around Disney property are much higher than you'll pay elsewhere. However, the benefits (top-notch facilities, free airport transfers and parking, early access to the parks) can make it worth the extra cash. Though rooms may be available at short notice during the quieter times, you should reserve as far in advance as possible – nine months is not unreasonable.

All-Star Resorts W Buena Vista Drive, Lake Buena Vista ⓦ sborlando.com. Three resorts near the Blizzard Beach water park, with themes based on sports, music and movies. The most affordable options in Disney by far. $102

Animal Kingdom Lodge 2901 Osceola Pkwy, Lake Buena Vista. Wake up to see African wildlife grazing outside your window at one of Disney's most spectacular and luxurious resorts. $315

Fort Wilderness Campground 3520 N Fort Wilderness Trail, Orlando. Hook up your RV, pitch a tent or rent a six-person cabin on a lovely 700-acre forested site near the Magic Kingdom, complete with all the standard Disney privileges. RV hookup $77, tent pitches $54, cabins $67

Grand Floridian Resort & Spa 4401 Florida Way, Lake Buena Vista. Gabled roofs, verandas, crystal chandeliers and a full-service spa make this Disney's most elegant – and expensive – resort. $540

★ **Wilderness Lodge** 901 Timberline Trail, Orlando. This convincing representation of a luxury inn in Native American style features a soaring lobby and welcoming rooms. $325

WITHIN UNIVERSAL ORLANDO

Not to be outdone, Universal has achieved resort status with its three posh on-site hotels (reservations for all: ☎ 888 273 1311 or ⓦ universalorlando.com).

Hard Rock 5800 Universal Blvd, Orlando. Stuffed with rock artefacts, and with tunes blaring at the pool, this resort is far from tranquil, but very popular with the younger crowd. Rooms manage to be simple and stylish. $339

★ **Loews Portofino Bay** 5601 Universal Blvd, Orlando. A mostly successful re-creation of the Italian seaside village, with luxurious rooms tricked out in marble and high-end furnishings. $339

Royal Pacific Resort 6300 Hollywood Way, Orlando. The comfortable rooms here – more than 1000 of them – are decked out in bamboo to play up the tropical theme. There's a Wantilan Luau and dinner show every Saturday night ($70). $279

EATING

The pick of the locals' eating haunts are **downtown** and around; most visitors, however, head for **International Drive**'s inexpensive all-day buffets and gourmet restaurants. You are not allowed to take food into any of the theme parks, where the best restaurants are in **Epcot's World Showcase** – particularly the French- and Mexican-themed establishments.

Bahama Breeze 8849 International Drive ☎ 407 248 2499, ⓦ bahamabreeze.com. Decent Caribbean food ($15–20); the mains include a nice lobster and shrimp quesadilla. Daily 11am–1am.

★ **Café Tu Tu Tango** 8625 International Drive ☎ 407 248 2222, ⓦ cafetututango.com Original, imaginative dishes include spicy crab chopsticks ($8) and pumpkin pizza ($10). Mon, Wed, Thurs & Sun 11.30am–11pm, Tues, Fri & Sat 11.30am–midnight.

Dexter's of Thornton Park 808 E Washington St, downtown ☎ 407 648 2777, ⓦ dexwine.com. Trendy yet informal spot in downtown's hip Thornton Park neighbourhood. Moderately priced. Mon–Wed & Sun 7am–10pm, Thurs 7am–11pm, Fri & Sat 7am–midnight.

Ming Court 9188 International Drive ☎ 407 351 9988, ⓦ ming-court.com. An exceptional Chinese restaurant, with dim sum and sushi available. Not as costly as you might expect. Daily 11am–3pm & 4.30–11pm.

7

New Punjab 7451 International Drive ☎407 352 7887, ⓦpunjabindianrestaurant.com. Reasonably priced vegetable curries from $10.95–18.95, served in a lively, busily decorated room. Daily 11.30am–11pm.

★ **Roy's** 7760 W Sand Lake Rd, near International Drive ☎407 352 4844, ⓦroysrestaurant.com. Founded in Hawaii, *Roy's* specializes in Hawaiian fusion cuisine. Try

the $35 three-course menu for a mix of potstickers, meats and a dessert. Daily 5.30–10pm.

★ **White Wolf Café** 1829 N Orange Ave, downtown ☎407 895 9911, ⓦwhitewolfcafe.com. Down-to-earth café/antique store known for creative salads and sandwiches. Mon–Thurs 8am–9pm, Fri & Sat 8am–10pm, Sun 8am–3pm.

NIGHTLIFE AND ENTERTAINMENT

The closure of the nightclubs at Disney's shopping and entertainment complex, Downtown Disney, several years ago means that Orlando's nightspots are now concentrated in two main areas, each with a quite different atmosphere. **Citywalk**, part of Universal Orlando (6000 Universal Blvd; $11.95 for all-night access to every club, plus free parking after 6pm; ☎407 363 8000, ⓦcitywalkorlando.com), consists of thirty acres of restaurants, dance clubs and shops wedged between Universal Studios and Islands of Adventure. Away from the theme parks, **downtown** Orlando has a large, eclectic and much more appealing crop of bars, lounges and clubs. Most of the after-dark action happens along Orange Avenue.

The groove Citywalk ☎407 224 2165. Dance (or not) in this club designed to look like an old theatre, with multiple bars and three themed lounges. Daily 9pm–2am.
Imperial 1800 N Orange Ave, downtown ☎407 228 4992, ⓦimperialwinebar.com. This eclectic bar is housed in a former furniture import store, so you drink your microbrews and boutique wines surrounded by Asian art pieces. Mon–Thurs 5pm–midnight, Fri & Sat 5pm–2am.

Red Coconut Club Citywalk ☎407 224 2425. This self-billed "ultralounge" has plenty of retro couches, a people-watching-friendly balcony, live music and strong martinis. Mon–Thurs & Sun 8pm–2am, Fri & Sat 6pm–2am.
★ **The Social** 54 N Orange Ave, downtown ☎407 246 1419, ⓦthesocial.org. *The Social* is well known for its energetic live alternative rock, grunge and hip-hop performances. Check the website's calendar for shows, events and times. Hours vary.

The West Coast

In the three hundred miles from the state's southern tip to the junction with the Panhandle (see p.530), Florida's **West Coast** embraces all the extremes. Buzzing, youthful towns rise behind placid fishing hamlets; mobbed holiday strips lie just minutes from desolate swamplands; and a world-class art collection competes with a glitzy theme park. Surprises are plentiful, though the coast's one constant is proximity to the Gulf of Mexico – and sunset views rivalled only by those of the Florida Keys.

The west coast's largest city, **Tampa**, has more to offer than its corporate towers initially suggest – not least the lively nightlife scene in the Cuban enclave of **Ybor City**, and the **Busch Gardens** theme park. For the mass of visitors, though, the Tampa Bay area begins and ends with the **St Petersburg beaches**, whose miles of sea and sand are undiluted holiday territory. South of Tampa, a string of barrier-island beaches run the length of the Gulf (including those on beautiful Anna Maria Island), and the mainland towns that provide access to them – such as **Sarasota** and **Fort Myers** – have enough to warrant a stop.

Tampa

A small, stimulating city with an infectious, upbeat mood, **TAMPA**, the business hub of the west coast, is well worth your time. As one of the major beneficiaries of the flood of people and money into Florida, it boasts an impressive cultural infrastructure envied by many larger rivals. In addition to its fine **museums** and **Busch Gardens**, one of the most popular amusement parks in the state, the city holds, in **Ybor City**, just northeast of the city centre, the west coast's hippest and most culturally eclectic quarter.

Tampa began as a small settlement beside a US Army base that was built in the 1820s to keep an eye on the Seminoles. In the 1880s, the railroad arrived, and the

Hillsborough River, on which the city stands, was dredged to allow seagoing vessels to dock. Tampa became a booming port, simultaneously acquiring a major tobacco industry as thousands of Cubans moved north from Key West to the new cigar factories of neighbouring Ybor City. The Depression ended the economic surge, but the port remained one of the busiest in the country and tempered Tampa's postwar decline. Today, Tampa continues to draw on the strengths of its local culture, some historic attractions and a handful of universities.

Tampa Museum of Art

120 W Gasparilla Plaza • Mon–Thurs 11am–7pm, Fri 11am–8pm, Sat & Sun 11am–5pm • $10 • ☎ 813 274 8130, ⓦ tampamuseum.org

The highly regarded **Tampa Museum of Art** sits picturesquely next to the Hillsborough River in Curtis Hixon Waterfront Park. The museum specializes in classical antiquities and twentieth-century American art, and plays host to travelling exhibits such as noted collections of American Impressionist pieces and those of Caribbean artists. In the evenings, the building's outer skin glows and pulses, courtesy of LED lights hidden behind 13,000 square feet of perforated aluminium screens.

7

The old Tampa Bay Hotel and the Henry B. Plant Museum

401 W Kennedy Blvd • **Museum** Tues–Sat 10am–7pm, Sun noon–5pm • $10 • ☎ 813 254 1891, ⓦ plantmuseum.com

From the river, you'll see the silver minarets and cupolas on the far bank, sprouting from the main building of the University of Tampa. These neo-Moorish architectural ornaments adorn what was formerly the 500-room **Tampa Bay Hotel**. The structure, as bizarre a sight today as it was when it opened in 1891, was financed by steamship and railroad magnate Henry B. Plant. (To reach it, walk across the river on Kennedy Blvd and descend the steps into Plant Park.)

Since the Civil War, Plant had been buying up bankrupt railroads, steadily inching his way into Florida to meet his steamships unloading at Tampa's harbour. Eventually, he became rich enough to turn his fantasies of creating the world's most luxurious hotel into reality. However, lack of care for the fittings and Plant's death in 1899 hastened the hotel's transformation from the last word in comfort to a pile of crumbling plaster. The city bought it in 1904 and leased it to the University of Tampa in 1933. In one wing, the **Henry B. Plant Museum** holds what's left of the hotel's original furnishings plus some period artefacts.

Florida Aquarium

701 Channelside Drive • Daily 9.30am–5pm • $21.95, ecotour cruises $25.95, parking $6 • ☎ 813 273 4000, ⓦ flaquarium.org

In Tampa's dockland area, the splendid **Florida Aquarium** houses lavish displays of Florida's fresh- and saltwater habitats, from springs and swamps to beaches and coral reefs. Animal residents include an impressive variety of fish, birds, otters, turtles and alligators. For some extra excitement, join one of the ninety-minute Wild Dolphin Cruises that depart daily to spot the cetacean mammals and waterfowl (and, occasionally, a manatee) in their regular Tampa Bay environment.

Ybor City

In 1886, as soon as Henry Plant's ships had ensured a regular supply of Havana tobacco into Tampa, cigar magnate Don Vincente Martínez Ybor cleared a patch of scrubland three miles northeast of present-day downtown Tampa and laid the foundations of **Ybor City**. About twenty thousand migrants, mostly Cuban, settled here and created a Latin American enclave, producing the top-class, hand-rolled cigars that made Tampa the "**Cigar Capital of the World**" for a time. However, mass production, the popularity of cigarettes and the Depression proved a fatal combination for an industry built on skilled cigar-makers: as unemployment struck, Ybor City's tight-knit blocks of cobbled streets and red-brick buildings became surrounded by drab, low-rent neighbourhoods.

Ybor City today buzzes with tourists, and at night the atmosphere can get raucous, especially at weekends. The neighbourhood is trendy and culturally diverse, yet its Cuban roots are immediately apparent, and explanatory background texts adorn many buildings. The **Ybor City State Museum**, 1818 9th Ave (daily 9am–5pm; $4; ☎813 247 6323, ⊛ybormuseum.org), helps you grasp the finer points of Ybor City's history and its multi-ethnic make-up. The museum also offers occasional cigar-rolling demonstrations, and tours of a typical cigar worker's *casita* (every 30min, 10am–3pm; free with admission).

Busch Gardens

Two miles east of I-275, or 2 miles west of I-75, exit 54, at 3000 E Busch Blvd • Opening hours vary day to day but generally daily 10am–6pm • $85, kids $77, $10 discount with advance online purchase; parking $15 • ☎ 888 800 5447, ⊛ buschgardenstampabay.com

Busch Gardens is one of Florida's most popular theme parks, based on a recreation of colonial-era Africa and offering some of the fastest and most nerve-jangling roller coasters in the country. A sedate pseudo-steam-train or cable-car journey allows inspection of a variety of African wildlife, but by far the most popular of the twenty-odd rides are the roller coasters: **SheiKra**, with its terrifying 200ft, 90-degree dive; **Montu**, where your legs dangle precariously in mid-air; **Gwazi**, a giant wooden coaster; and **Kumba**, with plenty of high-speed loop-the-loops after an initial 135ft drop.

ARRIVAL AND DEPARTURE   TAMPA

By plane Tampa's airport (☎813 870 8700, ⊛tampaairport.com) is 5 miles northwest of downtown: local HART bus #30 is the least costly connection ($2). Taxis (try United ☎813 777 7777) can take you to downtown ($25) or a Busch Blvd motel (around $32); to St Petersburg or the beaches the journey costs $45–65.
By bus Greyhound buses arrive downtown at 610 Polk St (☎813 229 2174).

Destinations Fort Myers (2 daily; 3hr 50min); St Augustine (1 daily; 10hr 20min); St Petersburg (2 daily; 30min).
By train Amtrak trains arrive at 601 N Nebraska Ave (☎813 221 7600).
Destinations Fort Myers (Amtrak coach: 2 daily; 3hr 30min); Jacksonville (1 daily; 5hr 20min); St Petersburg (via Amtrak coach: 2 daily; 40min).

GETTING AROUND AND INFORMATION

By local bus Although both downtown Tampa and Ybor City are easily covered on foot, to travel between them without a car you'll need to use the HART local buses ($2, one-day pass $4; ☎813 254 4278, ⊛gohart.org); useful routes are #8 to Ybor City and #5 to Busch Gardens.
By streetcar The TECO Line Streetcar System ($2.50; ☎813 254 4278, ⊛tecolinestreetcar.org) operates replica

vintage streetcars (and one restored original) between downtown and Ybor City several times an hour.
Visitor centres Downtown at 401 East Jackson St, Ste 2100 (Mon–Fri 10am–5pm; ☎800 44 TAMPA, ⊛visittampabay.com); in Ybor City at 1600 E 8th Ave, suite B104 (Mon–Sat 10am–5pm, Sun noon–5pm; ☎813 241 8838, ⊛ybor.org).

ACCOMMODATION

Tampa is not generously supplied with low-cost accommodation right in town; you'll almost certainly save money by staying in St Petersburg (see opposite) or at the beaches (see p.522). There are some good deals, though, at the motels near Busch Gardens and the airport.

★ **Don Vincente de Ybor Historic Inn** 1915 Av Republica de Cuba ☎866 206 4545, ⊛donvicenteinn .com. A luxurious B&B in Ybor City, featuring sixteen beautifully restored suites and swing dancing on Tuesday nights. **$149**
Gram's Place 3109 N Ola Ave ☎813 221 0596, ⊛grams -inn-tampa.com. This quirky motel-cum-hostel offers private rooms – all themed in different musical styles – and rather tatty youth-hostel-style accommodation.

Dorms **$23**, doubles **$60**
Sheraton Tampa Riverwalk 200 N Ashley Drive ☎813 223 2222, ⊛sheratontampariverwalk.com. Very convenient downtown location, nicely situated on the banks of the Hillsborough River. **$349**
Wingate by Wyndham 3751 E Fowler Ave ☎813 979 2828, ⊛wingatetampa.com. With a free shuttle bus to Busch Gardens (5min away), great free breakfast, clean rooms and solicitous staff, you can't go wrong here. **$100**

EATING

★ **Bernini** 1702 7th Ave, Ybor City ☎ 813 248 0099, ⓦ berniniofybor.com. An Italian joint serving up wood-fired pizza and pasta in the lovely old Bank of Ybor City. Mon–Thurs 11.30am–10pm, Fri & Sat 11.30am–11pm, Sun 4–9pm.

★ **Bern's Steak House** 1208 S Howard Ave, Hyde Park ☎ 813 251 2421, ⓦ bernssteakhouse.com. An institution in Tampa, this high-end steakhouse has its own farm that supplies it with fruits and vegetables. It also has one of the world's largest wine cellars. Have dinner here and you'll feel like royalty. Impeccable service, and the dessert room upstairs is an experience as well. Mon–Thurs & Sun 5–10pm, Fri & Sat 5–11pm.

Café Dufrain 707 Harbour Post Drive, Harbour Island ☎ 813 275 9701, ⓦ cafedufrain.com. This great, moderately priced place overlooking the water on Harbour Island serves a variety of contemporary cuisine with mouth-watering meat and seafood dishes – try the gingered tuna ($25) or the flatiron steak ($28). Mon–Sat 11.30am–10pm.

Cephas 1701 E 4th Ave, Ybor City ☎ 813 247 9022, ⓦ cephashotshop.com. An appealing Jamaican restaurant offering jerk chicken and curried goat, chicken and fish. Mon–Sat 9am–8pm.

La Creperia Café 1729 E 7th Ave, Ybor City ☎ 813 248 9700, ⓦ lacreperiacafe.com. A wide choice of delicious sweet and savoury crêpes, plus free wi-fi. Also in St Petersburg at 2901 Central Ave (☎ 727 327 7400). Mon 10am–3pm, Tues–Thurs 10am–10pm, Fri & Sat 10am–11pm, Sun 9am–8pm.

Taco 913 E Hillsborough Ave ☎ 813 232 5889. Great tacos are made and served – from a parked bus – round the clock. The ingredients are fresh, and prices range from $2.75 to $7.50. Daily 24hr.

NIGHTLIFE AND ENTERTAINMENT

Ybor City's renowned **nightlife** tends to be younger and more raucous than in the city's other entertainment areas of Channelside, downtown next to the Florida Aquarium, and the International Plaza and Bay Street, near the airport at the junction of West Shore and Boy Scout boulevards. The free *Weekly Planet* (ⓦ weeklyplanet.com) has **listings**, as does Friday's *Tampa Tribune*.

Green Iguana 1708 E 7th Ave, Ybor City ☎ 813 248 9555, ⓦ greeniguana.com. Rock bands play nightly, and DJs keep the young crowd very much in the party mood. Kitchen open daily at 11am; closes 3am.

★ **New World Brewery** 1313 E 8th Ave, Ybor City ☎ 813 248 4969, ⓦ newworldbrewery.net. A very solid microbrew selection, and a patio for enjoying the beers as the sun sets. Mon–Thurs & Sun 11am–1am, Fri & Sat 11am–3am.

Skipper's Smokehouse 910 Skipper Rd ☎ 813 971 0666, ⓦ skipperssmokehouse.com. Blues and reggae rule at this family-oriented live music venue and restaurant that includes a regular Grateful Dead tribute band. Tues–Fri 11am–11pm, Sat 11am–midnight, Sun 5–9pm.

★ **Tampa Theatre** 711 Franklin St ☎ 813 274 8981, ⓦ tampatheater.org. Foreign-language, classic and cult films shown in an atmospheric 1920s theatre (twice-monthly tours $5). Tickets $10.

St Petersburg

Situated on the eastern edge of the Pinellas Peninsula, a bulky thumb of land poking between Tampa Bay and the Gulf of Mexico, **ST PETERSBURG** is a world away from Tampa, even though the two cities are just twenty miles apart. Declared the healthiest place in the US in 1885, St Petersburg wasted no time in wooing the recuperating and the retired, at one point putting five thousand green benches on its streets to take the weight off elderly feet. Today, St Petersburg's diverse selection of museums and plethora of art galleries have contributed to its emergence as one of Florida's richest cultural centres.

Salvador Dalí Museum

Corner of Bayshore Drive SE and 5th Ave SE • Mon–Wed, Fri & Sat 10am–5.30pm, Thurs 10am–8pm, Sun noon–5.30pm • $21 (includes free tour), Thurs after 5pm $10 • ☎ 727 823 3767, ⓦ salvadordalimuseum.org

The **Salvador Dalí Museum** lives in appropriately wild digs (a "bubble" constructed of hundreds of triangular pieces of glass, bursting out of a traditional rectangular shell), designed by noted architect Yann Weymouth. This impressive museum stores more than a thousand paintings, drawings, sketches and sculptures (only a fraction of which is on display) from the collection of a Cleveland industrialist, A. Reynolds Morse, who struck up a friendship with the artist in the 1940s. The hour-long tours that run continuously throughout the day trace a chronological path around the works, from Dalí's early experiments with Impressionism and Cubism to the seminal Surrealist canvas *The Disintegration of the Persistence of Memory*.

The pier

The town's quarter-of-a-mile-long **pier**, jutting from the end of 2nd Avenue North, is the main focal point for some visitors. The pier often hosts arts-and-crafts exhibitions, and the inverted-pyramid-like building at its head holds five storeys of restaurants, shops and fast-food counters. At the foot of the jetty, the **Museum of History**, 335 2nd Ave NE (Wed–Sat 10am–5pm, Sun 1–5pm; $12; ☎727 894 1052, ⦿spmoh.org), founded in 1920, recounts (using modest displays) St Petersburg's early-twentieth-century heyday as a winter resort.

Museum of Fine Arts

255 Beach Drive NE • Mon–Wed, Fri & Sat 10am–5pm, Thurs 10am–8pm, Sun noon–5pm • $17, including free guided tour • ☎727 896 2667, ⦿fine-arts.org

St Petersburg's **Museum of Fine Arts** holds a superlative collection ranging from pre-Columbian art through to Asian and African and the European Old Masters, as well as rotating exhibits in the airy and modern Hazel Hough wing, which more than doubles the museum's space. The MFA exposes its guests to aural wonders too, with summer series devoted to Chamber music and "Dinner & Jazz" in the conservatory overlooking the water (call for schedule).

ARRIVAL AND INFORMATION · ST PETERSBURG

By bus The Greyhound station is downtown at 180 9th St N (☎727 898 1496).
Destinations Fort Lauderdale (3 daily; 6hr 20min–9hr);

Orlando (2 daily; 2hr 50min).
Chamber of Commerce 100 2nd Ave N (Mon–Fri 8am–7pm, Sat 9am–7pm; ☎727 821 4715, ⦿stpete.com).

ACCOMMODATION, EATING AND DRINKING

★ **Ceviche** 10 Beach Drive ☎727 209 2299, ⦿ceviche .com. The tapas are tops at this buzzy choice and you can't go wrong with any of the *ceviche* options, though the *ceviche a la rusa* – oysters in lime juice, coriander (cilantro) and caviar and a shot of Russian vodka – for $11.95 is particularly wonderful. Mon 5–10pm, Tues, Wed & Sun 5pm–midnight, Thurs 5pm–2am, Fri & Sat 5pm–3am.
Dickens House 335 8th Ave NE ☎800 381 2022, ⦿dickenshouse.com. One of several charismatic B&Bs in the area, this restored Arts and Crafts cottage houses five classic rooms, and guests get a delicious gourmet breakfast. **$119**

Moon Under Water 332 Beach Drive NE ☎727 896 6160, ⦿themoonunderwater.com. This inexpensive British tavern is almost as well known for its cocktails and curries as for its prime waterfront vistas. Mon–Thurs & Sun 11am–11pm, Fri & Sat 11am–midnight.
Vinoy Renaissance 501 5th Ave NE ☎888 303 4430, ⦿renaissancehotels.com/tpasr. This pink hotel was undoubtedly simpler when it opened in 1925; the restored version's amenities are killer, with two pools, twelve tennis courts, a golf course, health spa and gourmet restaurants. **$199**

The St Petersburg beaches

Framing the Gulf side of the Pinellas Peninsula, a 35-mile chain of barrier islands forms the **St Petersburg Beaches**, one of Florida's busiest coastal strips. When the resorts of Miami Beach lost some of their allure during the 1970s, the St Petersburg beaches grew in popularity with Americans and other Floridians, and have since evolved into an established destination for package-holidaying Europeans. The beaches are beautiful, the sea warm and the sunsets fabulous.

The southern beaches

In twenty-odd miles of heavily touristed coast, only **Pass-a-Grille**, at the very southern tip of the barrier island chain, has the look and feel of a genuine community – two miles of tidy houses, cared-for lawns, small shops and a cluster of bars and restaurants. During the week, the town is blissfully quiet, while on weekends informed locals come here to enjoy one of the area's liveliest stretches of sand.

A mile and a half north of Pass-a-Grille, the painfully luxurious **Don CeSar Hotel** (see below) is a grandiose pink castle, filling seven beachside acres. Opened in 1928, and briefly busy with the likes of Scott and Zelda Fitzgerald, it enjoyed a short-lived glamour. During the Great Depression, part of the hotel was used as a warehouse, and later became the spring training base of the New York Yankees baseball team.

The northern beaches

Much of the northern section of **Sand Key**, the longest barrier island in the St Petersburg chain, and one of the wealthier portions of the coast, is taken up by stylish condos and time-share apartments. The island terminates in the pretty **Sand Key Park**, where tall palm trees frame a silky strip of shoreline. The park occupies one bank of **Clearwater Pass**, across which a belt of sparkling white sands marks the holiday town of **Clearwater Beach**, where a condo boom has all but obliterated the small-town feel.

7

GETTING AROUND   THE ST PETERSBURG BEACHES

By bus All buses ($2; ☎727 540 1900, ⊛psta.net) to the beaches originate in St Petersburg, at the Williams Park terminal, on 1st Ave N and 3rd St N; the information booth there has route details.

By tram (trolley) Linking all the St Petersburg beach communities, the Central Avenue trolley ($2) runs daily to St Pete Beach on Gulf Blvd. From here, you can change for the Suncoast Beach Trolley ($2), which links Passe-a-Grille in the extreme south to Sand Key and Clearwater Beach in the north.

ACCOMMODATION AND EATING

Barefoot Bay Motel 401 East Shore Drive, Clearwater Beach ☎727 447 1016, ⊛barefootbayresort.com. The staff here couldn't be friendlier, and the motel's clean, compact rooms are a 5min stroll from the beach. **$105**

★ **Fetishes** 6305 Gulf Blvd, St Petersburg Beach ☎727 363 3700, ⊛fetishesrestaurant.com. Upmarket and intimate dining experience, with classics like duck à l'orange ($32). Reservations advised as there are just eight tables. Mon–Sat 6–10pm.

Frenchy's Café 41 Baymont St, Clearwater Beach ☎727 446 3607, ⊛frenchysonline.com. This kitschy place cooks up solid "super grouper" sandwiches ($13) and seafood gumbo ($4.50 a bowl). Daily 11am–11pm.

Hurricane 807 Gulf Way, Pass-a-Grille ☎727 360 9558, ⊛thehurricane.com. Select from a well-priced menu of the freshest seafood possible while overlooking the Gulf of Mexico. Mon–Thurs & Sun 7am–11pm, Fri & Sat 7am–midnight.

Loews DonCeSar Hotel 3400 Gulf Blvd, St Petersburg Beach ☎727 360 1881, ⊛loewshotels.com/don-cesar-hotel. The slightly imposing Moorish pink turrets are in contrast with the rather relaxing, though average-size white-clad rooms (reminiscent of a Southern plantation, with indoor shutters and watery blue accents) and cheery common spaces. **$309**

Sheraton Sand Key 1160 Gulf Blvd, Sand Key ☎727 595 1611, ⊛sheratonsandkey.com. The 375 rooms here don't reflect much of a beach mentality, but being a *Sheraton*, the service is studied, and the quarters feature 37" flat-screen TVs and private balconies. **$230**

★ **Tortuga Inn and Beach Resort** 1325 Gulf Drive N, Bradenton Beach ☎877 TORTUGA, ⊛tortugainn.com. The charms of Anna Maria Island are within easy reach of this charming property that spreads over six different buildings. There's a well-kept pool (actually, three) and a relatively sedate private beach. **$200**

Sarasota

Rising on a gentle hillside beside the blue waters of Sarasota Bay, **SARASOTA**, 35 miles south of St Petersburg, is one of Florida's better-off and better-looking towns. It's also one of the state's leading cultural centres, home to numerous writers and artists, and the base of several respected performing arts companies. The community is far less stuffy than its wealth might suggest, and is fairly lively, with cafés, bars and restaurants complementing the excellent grouping of shops around the charming St Armand's Circle, located across the John Ringling Causeway.

The Ringling Museum Complex

5401 Bay Shore Rd • Daily 10am–5pm, Thurs till 8pm • $25 includes free guided tour, Thurs after 5pm $10 • ☎ 941 359 5700,
ⓦ ringling.org

During his lifetime, **John Ringling**, one of the owners of the fantastically successful
Ringling Brothers Circus, which started its complex train-powered stops across the US
in the 1880s, acquired a fortune estimated at $200 million. Recognizing Sarasota's
investment potential, he built the first causeway to the barrier islands and made this
the winter base for his circus. His greatest gift to the town, however, was a Venetian
Gothic-style mansion and an incredible collection of European Baroque paintings. If
you visit only one of the grand palatial homes in Florida, this should be it.

The **Ringling Museum Complex**, which includes the mansion, is three miles north of
downtown beside US-41. Begin your exploration by walking through the gardens to
the former winter residence of John and Mable Ringling, **Cà d'Zan** ("House of John",
in Venetian dialect), built in 1926 for $1.5 million, and furnished with New York
estate sale castoffs for an additional $400,000. A gorgeous piece of work and a triumph
of taste and proportion, it's serenely situated beside the bay. The artwork is displayed
in the spacious **museum**, built around a mock fifteenth-century Italian palazzo. Five
enormous paintings by Rubens, commissioned in 1625, and the painter's subsequent
Portrait of Archduke Ferdinand, are highlights, though there's also a wealth of talent
(El Greco, Van Dyck, Titian) from Europe's leading schools of the mid-sixteenth to
mid-eighteenth centuries.

The Sarasota beaches

Increasingly the stamping ground of European package tourists spilling south from the
St Petersburg beaches, the white sands of the **Sarasota beaches** are worth anybody's
time. The beaches are located on Lido Key and Siesta Key, and they are both accessible
from the mainland, though there is no direct link between them. A third island,
Longboat Key, is primarily residential.

The Ringling Causeway crosses the yacht-filled Sarasota Bay from the foot of
Sarasota's Main Street to **Lido Key**. The causeway flows into **St Armands Circle**, a
roundabout ringed by upmarket shops and restaurants dotted with some of Ringling's
replica classical statuary, including some that pay homage to great circus stars of the
past. Continuing south along Benjamin Franklin Drive, you come to the island's most
accessible beaches, ending after two miles at the attractive **Ted Sperling Park and South
Lido Beach** (daily 6am–11pm; free).

The bulbous northerly section of tadpole-shaped **Siesta Key**, reached by Siesta Drive
off US-41, about five miles south of downtown Sarasota, attracts a younger crowd. The
soft sand at the pretty but busy **Siesta Beach** (beside Beach Rd) has a sugary texture due
to its origins as quartz (not the more usual pulverized coral). To escape the crowds,
continue south past Crescent Beach and follow Midnight Pass Road for six miles to
Turtle Beach, a small, secluded stretch of sand.

ARRIVAL, GETTING AROUND AND INFORMATION   SARASOTA

By bus Greyhound buses stop downtown at 19 East Rd
(☎ 941 377 5658). The Amtrak bus from Tampa pulls in at
1993 Main St.
Destinations Fort Myers (via Amtrak bus; 2 daily; 1hr
40min); Jacksonville (1 daily; 7hr 40min); St Petersburg (2
daily; 45min); Tampa (via Amtrak bus; 2 daily; 2hr); West

Palm Beach (2 daily; 4hr 45min–6hr 40min).
Local buses The SCAT bus terminal (☎ 941 861 5000,
ⓦ scgov.net/scat) is at 1565 1st St (at Lemon Ave): catch
buses here for the Ringling estate or the beaches ($1.25).
Visitor centre 701 N Tamiami Trail (Mon–Sat 10am–5pm;
☎ 800 800 3906, ⓦ sarasotafl.org).

ACCOMMODATION AND EATING

★ **The Broken Egg** 140 Av Messina, Siesta Key ☎ 941
346 2750, ⓦ thebrokenegg.com. This place, decorated like
a schoolroom in primary colours, is extremely popular with

the locals for its all-American breakfasts (try the banana
walnut strudel French toast, or the "Eggseptionals" section)
and lunches. Daily 7.30am–2.30pm.

Hotel Ranola 118 Indian Place ☎941 951 0111, ⓦhotelranola.com. Small hip boutique hotel with nine rooms and excellent service. The stylish rooms come with hardwood floors, iPod docks and full kitchens and it's an easy walk to Main St. $179
Main Bar Sandwich Shop 1944 Main St ☎941 955 8733, ⓦthemainbar.com. Go for the lip-smacking,

reasonably priced sandwiches, not the uneven service, at this Sarasota staple. Mon–Sat 10am–4pm.
Two Señoritas 1355 Main St ☎941 366 1618, ⓦtwo senoritas.com. Excellent Tex-Mex favourites like quesadillas ($9–11) and made-to-order tangy guacamole in a restaurant with cutesy Mexican village decor. Mon–Thurs & Sun 11.30am–10.30pm, Fri & Sat noon–midnight.

Fort Myers

Fifty miles south of Sarasota, **FORT MYERS** may lack the same élan, but it's nonetheless one of the more upscale communities of Florida's southwest coast. Fortunately, most of its recent growth has occurred on the north side of the wide Caloosahatchee River, which the town straddles, allowing the traditional centre, along the waterway's south shore, to remain relatively unspoiled.

Once across the river, US-41 strikes **downtown** Fort Myers, picturesquely nestled on the water's edge. For a thorough insight into the town's history, head to the **Southwest Florida Museum of History**, 2031 Jackson St (Tues–Sat 10am–5pm; $9.50; ☎239 321 7430, ⓦmuseumofhistory.org), which has an eye-catching 84ft-long Pullman rail car and a series of exhibits on local industry and the native Calusa and Seminole peoples.

Edison Winter Estate

2350 McGregor Blvd • Daily 9am–5.30pm • $25 for guided homes and gardens tour, on the hour every hour; $20 for self-guided tour • ☎239 334 7419, ⓦefwefla.org

In 1885, six years after inventing the light bulb, **Thomas Edison** collapsed from exhaustion and was instructed by his doctor to find a warm working environment or face an early death. Vacationing in Florida, the 37-year-old Edison bought fourteen acres of land on the banks of the Caloosahatchee and cleared a section of it to spend his remaining winters. This became the **Edison Winter Estate**, a mile west of downtown. Tours begin in the gardens, planted with such exotics as African sausage trees and wild orchids. However, the house, which you can glimpse only through the windows, is an anticlimax. Its plainness is probably due to the fact that Edison spent most of his waking hours inside the **laboratory**, attempting to produce rubber from the latex-rich sap of *Solidago edisonii* (a strain of goldenrod weed he developed). However, when the tour reaches the engrossing **museum**, the full impact of Edison's achievements becomes apparent: you'll see several examples of the phonograph that Edison created in 1877, as well as some of the ungainly cinema projectors derived from Edison's Kinetoscope – which brought him a million dollars a year in royalties as early as 1907.

Next door, you can also traipse through the rather plain **Ford Winter Estate**, bought by Edison's close friend Henry Ford in 1915. Much more awe-inspiring is the enormous banyan tree outside the ticket office – the largest of its kind in the continental US.

Estero Island

The Fort Myers beaches on **Estero Island**, fifteen miles south of downtown, are quite cheerful, and appreciably different in character from the west coast's more commercialized beach strips. Accommodation is plentiful on and around Estero Boulevard – reached by San Carlos Boulevard – which runs the seven-mile length of the island. Most activity revolves around the short fishing pier and **Lynne Hall Memorial Park**, at the island's north end.

Estero Island becomes increasingly residential as you press south, Estero Boulevard eventually swinging over a slender causeway to **Lovers Key State Recreation Area** (daily 8am–sunset; $8/car, $2 for pedestrians and cyclists; ☎239 463 4588), where a footpath picks a trail over a couple of mangrove-fringed islands and several mullet-filled creeks

7

to **Lovers Key**, a secluded beach. If you don't fancy the walk, a free tram (trolley) will transport you between the park entrance and the beach.

Sanibel and Captiva

Reached only by crossing a causeway ($6 toll), the islands of **Sanibel** and **Captiva**, 25 miles southwest of Fort Myers, are virtually impossible to visit unless you have a car. However, they offer a wildlife refuge, mangroves and shell-strewn beaches – for which they are widely renowned. In contrast with the smooth beaches along the gulf side of Sanibel Island, the opposite edge comprises shallow bays and creeks, and a vibrant wildlife habitat under the protection of the **J.N. "Ding" Darling National Wildlife Refuge** (daily except Fri 7.30am–sunset; $5/car, $1 for cyclists and pedestrians; ☎239 472 1100). The main entrance and **information centre** are just off the Sanibel–Captiva road. If you intend to stay here for a night or two, contact the Fort Myers visitor centre beforehand for lodging ideas. Overnighting here, you'll be treated to a beach experience unlike those in most of Florida – lovely, yet with an acute sense of isolation.

7

ARRIVAL, GETTING AROUND AND INFORMATION   FORT MYERS

By bus and train Greyhound buses pull in at the Rosa Parks Transportation Center, 2250 Peck St, while daily Amtrak services from Tampa arrive at 6050 Plaza Drive, about 6 miles east of downtown.
Destinations Fort Lauderdale (3 daily; 3hr–4hr); Pensacola (1 daily; 21hr); St Augustine (1 daily; 11hr 15min); St Petersburg (via Amtrak bus; 2 daily; 3hr); Tallahassee (2 daily; 11hr 25min–14hr); Tampa (via Amtrak bus; 2 daily; 4hr).

Local buses Distances within Fort Myers, and from downtown to the beaches, are large, and you'll struggle without a car, though it is possible – just – to reach the beaches on local LeeTran buses ($1.25; ☎239 533 8726, ⬤rideleetran.com), which mostly leave from the Greyhound terminal.
Chamber of Commerce 2310 Edwards Drive (Mon–Fri 9am–4.30pm; ☎800 366 3622, ⬤fortmyers.org).

ACCOMMODATION

Accommodation costs in and around Fort Myers are low between May and December, when 30–60 percent gets lopped off the standard rates. However, in high season, prices skyrocket, and spare rooms are rare.

Casa Playa 510 Estero Blvd, Fort Myers Beach ☎800 569 4876, ⬤casaplayaresort.com. Each of the 35 rooms with kitchenettes and screened balconies in this 1950s-reminiscent hotel is uniquely decorated. **$199**
Outrigger Beach Resort 6200 Estero Blvd ☎239 463 3131, ⬤outriggerfmb.com. This friendly property on the Gulf has a picnic area, sundeck and tiki bar by the pool, if rather generic rooms. Good for families. **$125**
Red Coconut 3001 Estero Blvd, Fort Myers Beach ☎239 463 7200, ⬤redcoconut.com. The only one of the campgrounds right on the beach. Guests parked at one of the 41 sites (with full hookups) can take advantage of basic cable

and internet, a shower room and laundry facilities. **$66**
South Seas Island Resort 5400 Plantatin Rd, Captiva ☎239 472 5111, ⬤southseas.com. This sprawling, swanky collection of Polynesian-style villas and other lodgings at the tip of the island offers a handful of restaurants and activities galore (golf, tennis, kayak tours and fishing charters, for starters). **$239**
★**Tarpon Tale Inn** 367 Periwinkle Way, Sanibel ☎239 472 0939, ⬤tarpontale.com. Near both the bay and the Gulf, this bright, airy inn has five private bungalows outfitted in white wicker and antique oak, and beach bikes are available (two per cottage). **$149**

EATING

French Connection Café 2282 First St, Fort Myers ☎239 332 4443, ⬤frenchconnectioncafe.com. A convivial café perfect for inexpensive French staples including onion soup, crêpes and sandwiches. Mon–Thurs 11am–10pm, Fri & Sat 11am–midnight.
Traders Café 1551 Periwinkle Way, Sanibel ☎239 472 7242, ⬤traderssanibel.com. This airy restaurant and store is a local favourite specializing in American bistro food (mains $22–30). Homely pine walls add to the cosy

atmosphere. Daily 11.30am–2.30pm & 5–9pm; happy hour Sat 3–6pm.
★**The Veranda** 2122 Second St, Fort Myers ☎239 332 2065, ⬤verandarestaurant.com. Find the charm and elegance of the Old South dining here, amid a lush courtyard of mango trees, with a menu of regional specialities. Dinner is pricey, but lunch is much more reasonable. Reservations recommended. Mon–Fri 11am–4pm & 5.30–9pm, Sat 5.30–10pm.

Everglades National Park

One of the country's most celebrated natural areas, the **EVERGLADES NATIONAL PARK** is a vast, tranquil wildlife reserve, with a subtle, raw appeal that lies in stark contrast to America's more rugged national parks. The most dramatic sights are small pockets of trees poking above a completely flat sawgrass plain, yet these wide-open spaces resonate with life, forming part of an ever-changing ecosystem that evolved through a unique combination of climate, vegetation and wildlife.

Though it appears to be flat as a table-top, the limestone on which the Everglades stands tilts very slightly towards the southwest. For thousands of years, water from summer storms and the overflow of nearby Lake Okeechobee has moved slowly through the Everglades towards the coast. The water replenishes the sawgrass, which grows on a thin layer of soil formed by decaying vegetation. This gives birth to the algae at the base of a complex food chain that sustains much larger creatures – most importantly **alligators**. After the floodwaters have reached the sea, drained through the bedrock, or simply evaporated, the Everglades are barren except for the water

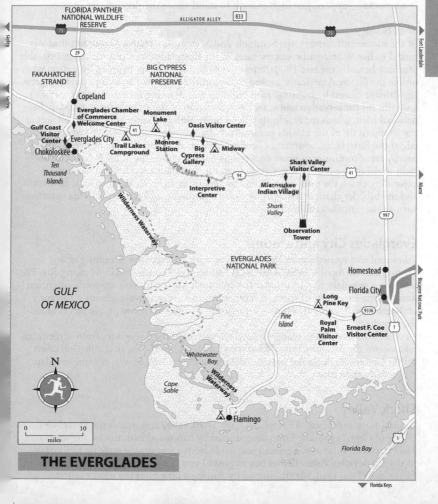

THE EVERGLADES

7

EVERGLADES ACTIVITIES AND TOURS

Around Shark Valley Visitor Center You can pedal down the loop road on a rented bike ($6.50/hr, must return by 4pm) or hop on the informative 2hr tram (trolley) tour (daily; $17.25; reservations on ☎ 305 221 8455), which stops frequently to view wildlife but won't allow you to linger in any particular place.

Around Everglades City There are several worthwhile boat trips; try the Everglades National Park Boat Tours, from $26.50 (☎ 239 695 2591), which depart

from the visitor centre, or Everglades Adventures (☎ 239 695 3299, ⓦ evergladesadventures.com) based at the Ivey House (see p.530). In addition, check the schedule on ⓦ nps.gov/ever for official park canoe trips and other activities.

Around Flamingo Watercraft and bike rentals are available from the marina store, and separate boats quietly glide through Florida Bay and the backcountry throughout the year ($32.25, kids 5–12 $16.13).

accumulated in ponds – or "gator holes" – created when an alligator senses water and clears the soil covering it with its tail. Sawgrass covers much of the Everglades, but where natural indentations in the limestone fill with soil, fertile tree islands – or "**hammocks**" – appear, just high enough to stand above the floodwaters.

Brief history

In the nineteenth century, the Seminole and Miccosukee **Native American tribes** were forced to live hunter-gatherer existences in the Everglades, and still maintain a sizeable presence here. By the late 1800s, a few towns had sprung up, peopled by settlers who, unlike the Native Americans, looked to exploit the land. As Florida's population grew, the damage caused by hunting, road building and draining for farmland gave rise to a significant **conservation** lobby. In 1947, a section of the Everglades was declared a national park, which today affords federal protection to a comparatively small area at the southern tip of the Florida peninsula. Urban development over the last century has edged the Everglades' boundaries further south, and unrestrained commercial use of nearby areas continues to upset the region's natural cycle. The 1200 miles of canals built to divert the flow of water away from the Everglades and toward the state's expanding cities, the poisoning caused by agricultural chemicals from local farmlands, and the broader changes wrought by global warming could yet turn Florida's greatest natural asset into a wasteland.

Everglades City and around

Purchased and named in the 1920s by an advertising executive dreaming of a subtropical metropolis, **EVERGLADES CITY**, three miles south off US-41 along Rte-29, now has a population of just under five hundred. Most who visit are solely intent on diminishing the stocks of sports fish living around the mangrove islands – the aptly christened **Ten Thousand Islands** – arranged like scattered jigsaw-puzzle pieces around the coastline.

For a closer look at the mangroves, which safeguard the Everglades from surge tides, take one of the park-sanctioned **boat trips** (see box above). The dockside **Gulf Coast Visitor Center** (see opposite) provides details on the cruises, as well as some excellent ranger-led **canoe trips**.

Shark Valley

Around forty miles east of Everglades City, **Shark Valley** epitomizes the Everglades' "River of Grass" moniker. From here, dotted by hardwood hammocks, the sawgrass plain stretches as far as the eye can see. Aside from a few simple walking trails close to the **Shark Valley Visitor Center** (see opposite) you can see Shark Valley only from a fifteen-mile loop road, ideally covered by renting a **bike** from the visitor centre.

The Miccosukee Indian Village

Mile Marker 70, US-41 • Daily 9am–5pm • $10 • ☎ 305 223 8380

You'll pass real Native American villages all along US-41, with most belonging to the **Miccosukee tribe**, descendants of the survivors of the last Seminole War (1858). Today the tribe runs a small but relatively prosperous reservation in the heart of the Everglades, though the kitschy souvenirs and displays at the **Miccosukee Indian Village** are rather contrived – grab some home-made chilli instead at nearby *Billie's Restaurant*.

Pine Island and Flamingo

The **Pine Island** section of the park – from the Coe Visitor Center entrance to Flamingo, perched at the end of the park road on Florida's southern tip – holds virtually everything that makes the Everglades tick. Spend a day or two in this southern portion of the park and you'll quickly grasp the fundamentals of its complex ecology.

Route-9336 (the only road in this section of the park) leads past the comprehensive **Ernest Coe Visitor Center** (see below) to the main park entrance. A mile further on, the **Royal Palm Visitor Center** (open 24hr) usually features ranger activities and events (but little information). The large numbers of park visitors who simply want to see an alligator are usually satisfied by walking the half-mile **Anhinga Trail** here: the notoriously lazy reptiles are easily seen during the winter, often splayed near the trail, looking like plastic props. All manner of birdlife can also be spotted, from snowy egrets to the bizarre, eponymous anhinga, an elegant black-bodied bird resembling an elongated cormorant. To beat the crowds, drop by the Anhinga Trail early; after that, peruse the adjacent, but very different, **Gumbo Limbo Trail**, a hardwood jungle hammock packed with exotic subtropical growths. At the 38-mile mark, **Flamingo** serves as a hub for deeper exploration of the park, with a visitor centre, a small boating supply store and a modest restaurant.

ARRIVAL AND INFORMATION

EVERGLADES NATIONAL PARK

By car There are three entrances to the park: Everglades City, at the northwestern corner; Shark Valley, at the northeastern corner; and another near the Ernest Coe Visitor Center, at the southeastern corner. US-41 skirts the northern edge of the park, providing the only land access to the Everglades City and Shark Valley entrances. There is no public transport along US-41, or to any of the park entrances.

Park admission Park entry is free at Everglades City, although from here you can travel only by boat or canoe. At the other entrances it's $10/car and $5 for pedestrians and cyclists. Entry tickets are valid for seven days.

When to visit The park is open year-round, but the most favourable time by far to visit is winter, when the receding floodwaters cause wildlife to congregate around gator holes, ranger-led activities are frequent and the mosquitoes are bearable. Visiting between seasons is also a good bet. But in summer, afternoon storms flood the prairies, park activities are substantially reduced and the mosquitoes are a severe annoyance, even as early as May.

Ernest Coe Visitor Center 40001 Rte-9336, Homestead (daily: mid-April to mid-Dec 9am–5pm; mid-Dec to mid-April 8am–5pm; ☎ 305 242 7700), Has a small giftshop and access to walking trails.

Flamingo Visitor Center End of Rte-9336, 38 miles from Ernest Coe centre (daily 8am–4.30pm; ☎ 305 695 2945). The only centre substantially inside the park provides access for campgrounds, backcountry permits and several boat tours and trips.

Gulf Coast Visitor Center 815 Oyster Bar Lane, Everglades City (daily: May–Oct 9am–4.30pm; Nov–April 8am–4.30pm; ☎ 239 695 3311). The dockside centre provides details on cruises, as well as the excellent ranger-led canoe trips and rentals.

Shark Valley Visitor Center 36000 SW 8th St, Miami (daily: May–Oct 9.15am–5.15pm; Nov–April 8.45am–5.15pm; ☎ 305 221 8776). Visitors can sign up for guided tram (trolley) tours, rent bikes, ply the two short walking trails or buy snacks.

ACCOMMODATION

A handful of places to stay exist in the towns just outside the park's perimeter, in Homestead (10 miles east of the park entrance at Ernest Coe), or Everglades City. In addition to the campgrounds listed below, there are many backcountry spots on the longer walking and canoe trails (permits are issued at the visitor centres – in season $10, plus $2/person free from around May to mid-Nov; check the park's website).

Chokoloskee Island Park 1150 Hamilton Lane, Chokoloskee ☎ 239 695 2414, ⊛ chokoloskee.com. This property on a marina holds spare but clean and functional efficiency units and RV/trailer sites (price includes electric, sewer, water and TV). Units $110, sites $49

Everglades International Hostel 20 SW 2nd Ave, Florida City ☎ 800 372 3874, ⊛ evergladeshostel.com. Besides its appeal for budget-minded travellers who don't want to camp, the hostel offers bike and boat rentals (canoes from $20, kayaks $28/afternoon; rates are higher for non-guests) and tours through Everglades Adventures (see box, p.528). Dorms $28, doubles $75

Flamingo Campground Near end of Rte-9336 in Flamingo ☎ 877 444 6777, ⊛ recreation.gov. Well-equipped grounds with 234 drive-in sites, some with water views, plus hot showers and picnic facilities. Tent sites are free May–Sept. Camping $16, RV sites $30

Ivey House 107 Camelia St, Everglades City ☎ 239 695 3299, ⊛ iveyhouse.com. The certified "green" property holding the three options here (cheery inn, more rustic lodge and cottage) got its start as a boarding house in the 1920s. Take advantage of the pool after a long day sweating in the swamp. Breakfast included. $89

Long Pine Key Campground Off Rte-9336, 6 miles from Ernest Coe Center ☎ 305 242 7873, ⊛ nps.gov /ever. Attractive campground with 108 sites for tents and RVs but no hookups or showers. No reservations, just follow posted instructions on bulletin board inside entrance. Tents sites are free May–Sept. Camping $16, RV sites $30

The Panhandle

Rubbing hard against Alabama in the west and Georgia in the north, the long, narrow **Panhandle** has much more in common with the states of the Deep South than with the rest of Florida. Hard to believe, then, that just over a century ago, the Panhandle *was* Florida. At the western edge, **Pensacola** was a busy port when Miami was still a swamp. Fertile soils lured wealthy plantation owners south, helping to establish **Tallahassee** as a high-society gathering place and administrative centre – a role which, as the state capital, it retains. But the decline of cotton, deforestation and the coming of the East Coast railroad eventually left the Panhandle high and dry. Much of the inland region still seems neglected, and the **Apalachicola National Forest** is perhaps the best place in Florida to disappear into the wilderness. The **coastal Panhandle**, on the other hand, is enjoying better times: despite rows of hotels, much is still untainted, boasting miles of blinding white sands.

Tallahassee

State capital it may be, but **TALLAHASSEE** is nevertheless a provincial city of oak trees and soft hills that won't take more than two days to explore in full. Around its small grid of central streets – where you'll find plenty of reminders of Florida's formative years – briefcase-clutching bureaucrats mingle with some of Florida State University's 35,000 students, who brighten the mood considerably and keep the city awake at night.

The Capitol Buildings

400 S Monroe St • **New Capitol** Mon–Fri 8am–5pm **Old Capitol** Mon–Fri 9.30am–4.30pm, Sat 10am–4.30pm, Sun noon–4.30pm • Free • ⊛ myfloridacapitol.com

A $50 million eyesore dominates the square mile of downtown Tallahassee: the vertical vents of the towering **New Capitol Building**, at Apalachee Parkway and Monroe Street. Florida's growing army of bureaucrats had previously been crammed into the more attractive **Old Capitol Building** dating from 1845, which stands in the shadow of its replacement.

Museum of Florida History

500 S Bronough St • Mon–Fri 9am–4.30pm, Sat 10am–4.30pm, Sun noon–4.30pm • Free • ☎ 850 245 6400, ⊛ museumoffloridahistory.com

For easily the fullest account of Florida's past anywhere in the state, visit the **Museum of Florida History**. Detailed accounts of Paleo-Indian settlements, and the significance of their burial and temple mounds, some of which have been found on the edge of Tallahassee, are valuable tools in comprehending Florida's prehistory. The colonialist crusades of the Spanish are outlined with copious finds, though there's little on the nineteenth-century Seminole Wars – one of the bloodier skeletons in Florida's closet. Railroads get ample attention; this makes sense, given the role they played in early tourism efforts and general boosterism throughout the state.

Black Archives Research Center and Museum

445 Gamble St • Mon–Fri 9am–5pm • Free • ☎ 850 599 3020

The **Black Archives Research Center and Museum** holds one of the largest and most important collections of African American artefacts in the nation, with oral histories and music stations, as well as some chilling Ku Klux Klan memorabilia. The museum is housed in the nineteenth-century Union Bank Building on the campus of **Florida A&M University**, which was established in 1887 as State Normal College for Colored Students; sporting legend Althea Gibson, the first African American to play professional international tennis, graduated from here in 1953.

ARRIVAL AND INFORMATION   TALLAHASSEE

By bus Tallahassee's Greyhound bus terminal is at 112 W Tennessee St (☎ 850 222 4249), within short walking distance of downtown, which can easily be explored on foot.
Destinations Atlanta, GA (4 daily; 6hr–14hr 30min);

Birmingham, AL (4 daily; 6hr 45min–16hr); Fort Lauderdale (6 daily; 10–14hr); Jacksonville (6 daily; 3–11hr); Orlando (4 daily; 4hr 40min–5hr 50min).
Visitor centre 106 E Jefferson St (Mon–Fri 8am–5pm; ☎ 800 628 2866, ⓦ visittallahassee.com).

ACCOMMODATION

Accommodation in Tallahassee is in short supply only during the sixty-day sitting of the state legislature, from early March, and on autumn weekends during home football games of the Florida State Seminoles and Florida A&M Rattlers. Hotels and motels on N Monroe Street, about 3 miles from downtown, are far cheaper than those downtown.

Comfort Suites 1026 Apalachee Pkwy ☎ 850 224 3200, ⓦ comfortsuites.com. The beds are heavenly at this comfortable, spotless motel, within walking distance of the capital. There's also a delicious, free continental breakfast. **$148**

★ **Governors Inn** 209 S Adams St ☎ 850 681 6855, ⓦ thegovinn.org. Every room in this splendid downtown inn is decorated with antique furniture reflecting the period of the governor each is named after. **$129**

EATING

Andrew's Capital Grill & Bar/Andrew's 228 228 S Adams St ☎ 850 222 3444, ⓦ andrewsdowntown.com. Casual grill and bar serving a variety of sandwiches and burgers all day; the chic downstairs *Andrew's 228* (dinner only) prepares delicious nouveau Italian dishes such as grouper *piccata* and gorgonzola cheesecake. Capital Grill: Mon–Thurs & Sun 11.30am–10pm, Fri & Sat 11.30am–11pm; Andrew's 228: Mon–Thurs 6–10pm, Fri & Sat 6–11pm.

★ **Barnacle Bill's** 1830 N Monroe St ☎ 850 385 8734, ⓦ barnaclebills.com. Inexpensive fresh fish and seafood served in a riotous atmosphere; occasional

live performances on the deck add to the festive air. Mon–Thurs & Sun 11.30am–10pm, Fri & Sat 11.30pm–11pm.

Mom and Dad's 4175 Apalachee Pkwy ☎ 850 877 4518. The delicious, authentic Italian food at this place, in business since 1963, is lovingly home-made by Mom and Dad (of course). Tues–Thurs 5–9pm, Fri & Sat 5–10pm.

Po' Boys Creole Café 19444 W Pensacola St ☎ 850 574 4144, ⓦ poboyswest.com. *Po'Boys* trades in a range of Creole delights such as shrimp remoulade and king crawfish (about $10), and mimosas are only $5 at Sunday brunch. Daily 11am–9.30pm.

Wakulla Springs State Park

Wakulla Springs State Park holds what is believed to be one of the biggest and deepest natural springs in the world. It pumps up half a million gallons of crystal-clear pure water from the bowels of the earth every day – though you'd never guess it from the calm surface.

It's refreshing to **swim** in the cool pool (in a small roped-off area – this is gator territory), but to learn more about the spring, take the thirty-minute **glass-bottom boat tour** ($8; depending on water conditions), and peer down to the swarms of fish hovering around the 180ft cavern through which the water flows. Fifty-minute **river cruises** ($8) let you glimpse some of the park's inhabitants: deer, turkeys, turtles, herons and egrets perched on bald cypress trees, and the ubiquitous alligators.

INFORMATION, ACCOMMODATION AND EATING   WAKULLA SPRINGS STATE PARK

Park entry The park is 15 miles south of Tallahassee, off Rte-61 on Rte-267. Opening hours are daily 8am–sunset. Admission is $6/car, or $2 for pedestrians and cyclists; for more information contact ☎850 926 0700.
Wakulla Springs Lodge 550 Wakulla Park Drive

☎850 421 2000, ⓦwakullasprings lodge.com. Built in 1937 beside the spring, the lovely wooden lodge is a serene hotel, with an excellent restaurant serving home-cooked country food. **$95**

7   The Apalachicola National Forest

With swamps, savannahs and springs dotted liberally about its half-million acres, the **Apalachicola National Forest**, which fans out southwest of Tallahassee, is the inland Panhandle at its natural best. Several roads enable you to drive through a good-sized chunk, with many undemanding spots for a rest and a snack. To see deeper into the forest you'll need to make more of an effort, by following one of the hiking trails, canoeing on the rivers or simply spending a night under the stars at one of the basic campgrounds. On the forest's southern edge, the large and forbidding **Tate's Hell Swamp** is a breeding ground for the deadly water moccasin snake; you're well advised to stay clear.

ARRIVAL, INFORMATION AND ACCOMMODATION APALACHICOLA NATIONAL FOREST

By car The main entrances to the forest (free) are off Hwy-20 and Hwy-319; four minor roads, routes 267, 375, 67 and 65, form cross-forest links between the two highways.
Ranger stations Apalachicola (☎850 643 2282) or Wakulla (☎850 926 3561).

Campgrounds There are five designated campgrounds with basic facilities (info on ☎850 643 2282); Camel Lake and Wright Lake ($10) have hot showers; the others (no running water) are free except for a $3 daily vehicle charge. Backcountry camping is free.

Pensacola and around

You might be inclined to overlook **PENSACOLA**, tucked away as it is at the western end of the Panhandle. The city, on the northern bank of the broad Pensacola Bay, is five miles inland from the nearest beaches, and its prime features are a naval aviation school and some busy dockyards. Pensacola is, however, rewarding, and the city centre has experienced something of a renaissance in the past few years. The nearby white beaches are relatively untouched, and it boasts a rich history, having been occupied by the Spanish as early as 1559. The town repeatedly changed hands between the Spanish, the French and the British before becoming the place where Florida was officially ceded by Spain to the US in 1821.

Pensacola was already a booming port by 1900, when the opening of the Panama Canal was expected to boost its fortunes still further. The many new buildings that appeared in the **Palafox District**, around the southerly section of Palafox Street, in the early 1900s – with their delicate ornamentation and attention to detail – still reflect the optimism of the era.

Historic Pensacola Village

Tues–Sat 10am–4pm • $6; buy tickets at Tivoli High House Shop, 205 E Zaragoza St • ☎850 595 5985, ⓦ historicpensacola.org
In earlier times, Native Americans, pioneer settlers and seafaring traders had gathered to swap, sell and barter on the waterfront of the **Seville District**, just east of Palafox

Street. Those who did well took up permanent residence here, and many of their homes remain in fine states of repair, forming – together with several museums – the **Historic Pensacola Village**. Tickets are valid for one week, and allow access to all of the museums and former homes in an easily navigated four-block area.

National Naval Aviation Museum

1750 Radford Blvd • Daily 9am–5pm • Free; IMAX movie $8.75 • ☏ 850 452 3604, ⓦ navalaviationmuseum.org

Inside the US naval base on Navy Boulevard, about eight miles southwest of central Pensacola, the **Museum of Naval Aviation** exhibits US naval aircraft. They range from the first flimsy seaplane, acquired in 1911, to Skyhawks later used by the Blue Angels flight team, to the Phantoms and Hornets of more recent times.

Gulf Islands National Seashore

$8/vehicle • ⓦ nps.gov/guis

An unsung gem in the area is the **Gulf Islands National Seashore** which contains historic fortifications (Fort Pickens), sumptuous white-sand beaches and ample wildlife-viewing opportunities. The park stretches across the states of Alabama and Florida, and the best access from Pensacola proper is via Hwy-292. The **Fort Barrancas Visitors Center** (Fri–Sun 9.30am–4.45pm) contains an informative short film, a gift shop and free brochures about what to see in this corner of the park.

Pensacola Beach

On the south side of the bay from the city, glistening beaches and windswept sand dunes fringe the fifty-mile-long **Santa Rosa Island**. On the island directly south of Pensacola, **PENSACOLA BEACH** has everything you'd want from a Gulf Coast beach: fine white sands, watersports rental outlets, a busy fishing pier and a sprinkling of motels, beachside bars and snack stands.

ARRIVAL, GETTING AROUND AND INFORMATION   PENSACOLA AND AROUND

By bus The Greyhound station is 7 miles north of the city centre, at 505 W Burgess Rd (☏ 850 476 4800); ECAT buses #44, #45 and #48 ($1.75; ☏ 850 595 3228, ⓦ goecat.com) link it to Pensacola proper.
Destinations Houston, TX (4 daily; 11hr 20min–12hr 35min); New Orleans, LA (4 daily; 4hr–6hr 45min); Tallahassee (4 daily; 3hr–5hr 30min).
Local buses ECAT buses serve the city, while #64 (The Beach

Jumper) goes to the beach twice daily; the main terminal is at 1515 W Fairfield Drive. Free trams (trolleys) trundle along the beach on summer afternoons and evenings.
Taxis Yellow Cab (☏ 850 433 3333).
Visitor centre 1401 E Gregory St, at the foot of the city side of the 3-mile Pensacola Bay Bridge (Mon–Fri 8am–5pm, Sat 9am–4pm, Sun 10am–4pm; ☏ 800 874 1234, ⓦ visitpensacola.com).

ACCOMMODATION AND EATING

Fish House 600 S Barracks St ☏ 850 470 0003, ⓦ good grits.com. Nicer than the name suggests, this spot features sushi and steaks along with the seafood. Daily 11am–late.
Noble Manor 110 W Strong St ☏ 850 434 9544, ⓦ noblemanor.com. A charming B&B in a handsome, restored 1905 mock-Tudor building, strewn with antiques and fine art prints. **$135**
Paradise Inn 21 Via De Luna Drive ☏ 850 932 2319,

ⓦ paradiseinn-pb.com. The inn, with affordable rooms, free breakfast, pool and private pier, can be downright fun, with live local talent playing its sometimes raucous bar from 6pm in summer. **$139**
Peg Leg Pete's 1010 Fort Pickens Rd ☏ 850 932 4139, ⓦ peglegpetes.com. The Pensacola institution is known for its Cajun food and its variety of oyster treatments (half-dozen $6–10). Daily 11am–late.

7

Louisiana

ALLIGATOR, PEARL RIVER

Louisiana

Swathed in the romance of pirates, voodoo and Mardi Gras, Louisiana is undeniably special. Its history is barely on nodding terms with the view that America was the creation of the Pilgrim Fathers; its way of life is proudly set apart. This is the land of the rural, French-speaking Cajuns (descended from the Acadians, eighteenth-century French-Canadian refugees), who live in the prairies and swamps in the southwest of the state, and the Creoles of jazzy, sassy New Orleans. (The term Creole was originally used to define anyone born in the state to French or Spanish colonists – famed in the nineteenth century for their masked balls, patois and distinct culture – as well as native-born, French-speaking slaves, but has since come to define anyone or anything native to Louisiana, and in particular its black population.)

Louisiana's distinctive, spicy cuisine, festivals and, above all, its music (jazz, R&B, Cajun and its bluesy black counterpart, zydeco) draw from all these cultures and more. Oddly enough, northern Louisiana – Protestant Bible Belt country, where old plantation homes stand decaying in vast cottonfields – feels more "Southern" than the marshy bayous, shaded by ancient cypress trees and laced with wispy trails of Spanish moss, of the Catholic south.

Visitors will find that the state has an enormous amount to offer. Whether you're canoeing along a cypress-clogged bayou, dining on spicy crawfish in a crumbling Creole cottage, or dancing on a steamy starlit night to the best live music in the world, Louisiana remains unique, a state that will get under your skin and stay there.

New Orleans

Infused with a dizzying jumble of cultures and influences, **NEW ORLEANS** is a bewitching place. Here, people dance at funerals and hold parties during hurricanes, world-class musicians make ends meet busking on street corners and hole-in-the-wall dives dish up gourmet Creole cuisine. There's a wistfulness here too, along with its famed *joie de vivre* – in the peeling facades of the old French Quarter, its filigree cast-iron balconies tangled with ferns and fragrant jasmine, and in the cemeteries lined with crumbling above-ground marble tombs. New Orleans's melancholy beauty – along with its ebullient spirit – has always come with an awareness of the fragility of life, due at least in part to its perilous geography.

It has become painfully clear to the rest of the world, too, since the events of August 2005, that there's a lot more to the "Big Easy" than its image as a nonstop

Highlights

❶ Swamp tours Watch out for alligators lurking in the ghostly, Spanish-moss-shaded bayous. See p.550 & p.565

❷ Napoleon House, New Orleans Steeped in old New Orleans elegance, this gorgeous family-owned bar has stayed the same for generations, complete with flickering lamps and a romantic subtropical courtyard. See p.554

❸ Mardi Gras From the masking and dancing of New Orleans's urban spectacular, to Cajun country's medieval customs, Louisiana's Fat Tuesday is unlike any other. See p.556 & p.560

❹ Maple Leaf on a Tuesday, New Orleans Rebirth Brass Band on the stage, smoke getting in everyone's clothes, and riotously happy music fans tearing the roof off this tumbledown neighbourhood bar. See p.557

❺ Laura plantation By far the River Road's most intriguing and illuminating account of Creole plantation life. See p.558

❻ Cajun and Creole festivals Celebrating anything from sweet potatoes to world music, these country festivals offer superb opportunities to enjoy Cajun and zydeco music, crafts and lots of delicious food. See p.560

❼ Angola prisoner rodeo An unbelievable spectacle, with lifers slugging it out for guts and glory in this notorious maximum-security prison. See p.566

HIGHLIGHTS ARE MARKED ON THE MAP ON P.538

party town. Even at the best of times this was a contradictory city, repeatedly revealing stark divisions between rich and poor (and, more explicitly, between white and black); years after **Katrina**, with the emotional and physical scars slowly healing, those contradictions remain. While you can still party in the French Quarter and the Marigny till dawn, dancing to great jazz and gorging on garlicky Creole food, just minutes away are neighbourhoods that are still struggling to rebuild. That's not to say that enjoying life is inappropriate in today's New Orleans – while it was let down not only by nature but also by federal and local government after Katrina, the city's vitality, courage and stubborn loyalty remain strong. The melange of cultures and races that built the city still gives it its heart; not "easy", exactly, but quite unlike anywhere else in the USA – or the world.

New Orleans is called the **Crescent City** because of the way it nestles between the southern shore of Lake Pontchartrain and a horseshoe bend in the Mississippi River. This unique location makes the city's layout confusing, with streets curving to follow the river, and shooting off at odd angles to head inland. Compass points are of little use – locals refer instead to **lakeside** (toward the lake) and **riverside** (toward the river), and, using Canal Street as the dividing line, **uptown** (or upriver) and **downtown** (downriver).

Brief history

New Orleans began life in 1718 as a **French-Canadian** outpost – an improbable, swampy setting in a prime location near the mouth of the **Mississippi River**.

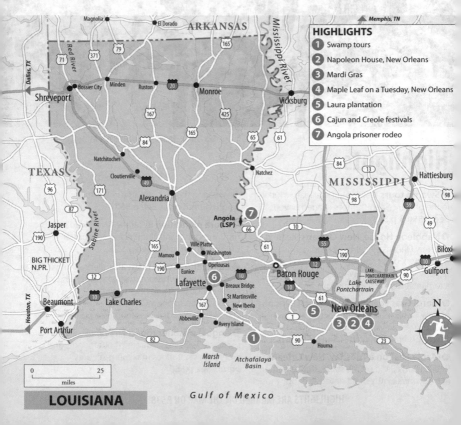

HIGHLIGHTS

1. Swamp tours
2. Napoleon House, New Orleans
3. Mardi Gras
4. Maple Leaf on a Tuesday, New Orleans
5. Laura plantation
6. Cajun and Creole festivals
7. Angola prisoner rodeo

LOUISIANA

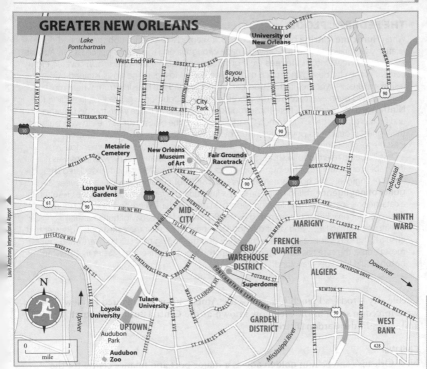

Development was rapid, and with the first mass importation of African **slaves**, as early as the 1720s, its unique demography took shape. The **Black Code**, drawn up by the French in 1685 to govern Saint-Domingue (today's Haiti) and established in Louisiana in 1724, gave slaves rights unparalleled elsewhere, including permission to marry, meet socially and take Sundays off.

In 1760, Louis XV secretly handed New Orleans, along with all French territory west of the Mississippi, to his **Spanish** cousin, Charles III, as a safeguard against British expansionism. Despite early resistance from its francophone population, the city benefited greatly from its period as a **Spanish** colony between 1763 and 1800: by the end of the eighteenth century, the **port** was flourishing, the haunt of smugglers, gamblers, prostitutes and pirates. Newcomers included Anglo-Americans escaping the American Revolution and aristocrats fleeing revolution in France. The city also became a haven for refugees – whites and **free blacks**, along with their slaves – escaping the slave revolts in Saint-Domingue (Haiti). As in the West Indies, the Spanish, French and free people of colour associated and formed alliances to create a distinctive **Creole** culture with its own traditions and ways of life, its own patois and a **cuisine** that drew influences from Africa, Europe and the colonies.

The Louisiana Purchase

Louisiana remained Spanish until it was ceded to Napoleon in 1801, under the proviso that it should never change hands again. Just two years later, however, Napoleon, strapped for cash to fund his battles with the British in Europe, struck a bargain with President Thomas Jefferson known as the **Louisiana Purchase**. This sneaky agreement handed over to the USA all French lands between Canada and Mexico, from the Mississippi to the Rockies, for just $15 million. Unwelcome in the

THE FEDERAL FLOOD

When **Hurricane Katrina** hit ground in 2005, it seemed at first as though the city had done relatively well in light of the full-scale damage wrought along the Mississippi coast. On August 29, however, New Orleans's **levees** were breached, and rising floodwaters soon covered eighty percent of the city, destroying much of it in their wake. Most damage was sustained by residential areas – whether in the suburban homes around the lakeside, from where most residents had been evacuated, to the less affluent neighbourhoods of the east, including the **Ninth Ward** and Gentilly, where those too poor or ill or old to move were trapped in attics and on rooftops for days. The French Quarter, which, as the oldest part of the city was built on the highest ground, was physically unhurt by the flooding, although the economic blow – not least the loss of a huge number of the neighbourhood's workforce – was tremendous.

Despite being referred to in shorthand as Katrina, the devastation of New Orleans was not an inevitable consequence of the hurricane: in November 2009, a federal judge declared the Corps of Engineers, the government body responsible for building New Orleans' levees, as **guilty of negligence**, ruling that "The Corps' lassitude and failure to fulfil its duties resulted in a catastrophic loss of human life and property in unprecedented proportions…Furthermore, the Corps not only knew, but admitted by 1988, that the Mr-Go [navigation channel] threatened human life… and yet it did not act in time to prevent the catastrophic disaster that ensued". The Corps appealed on a technicality, and the finding may still be overturned, but for most people, the case has been amply proven: the worst engineering disaster in American history could have been avoided.

Creole city – today's French Quarter – the Americans who migrated to New Orleans were forced to settle in the area now known as the **Central Business District** (or **CBD**) and, later, in the **Garden District**.

Civil War

New Orleans's antebellum **golden age** as a major port and finance centre for the cotton-producing South was brought to an abrupt end by the Civil War. Economically and socially ravaged by the conflict, Louisiana was almost brought to its knees by **Reconstruction**, with the once great city suffering a period of unprecedented lawlessness and racial violence. As the North industrialized and other Southern cities grew, the fortunes of New Orleans slipped.

Twentieth century

Jazz exploded into the bars and the bordellos around 1900, and, along with the evolution of **Mardi Gras** as a tourist attraction, breathed new life into the city. And though the Depression hit here as hard as it did the rest of the nation, it also – spearheaded by a number of local writers and artists – heralded the resurgence of the **French Quarter**, which had disintegrated into a slum. Even so, it was the less romantic duo of **oil** and **petrochemicals** that really saved the economy – until the slump of the 1950s pushed New Orleans well behind other US cities. The oil crash of the early 1980s gave it yet another battering, a gloomy start for near on two decades of high crime rates, crack deaths and widespread corruption.

Katrina and the current day

By the turn of the millennium things were improving, until **Hurricane Katrina** and its subsequent floods (see box above) ripped the place apart. In 2010 the Saints football team, amazingly, won the **Superbowl** (see p.547); so deeply emotional was this victory that the election of **Mitch Landrieu**, the black-majority city's first white mayor in thirty years, went barely noticed in even the local newspapers. A few months later, the sense of new beginnings was dealt a savage blow from the disastrous **BP oil spill** in the Gulf of Mexico and its long-term implications for the economy; if ever a city knew how to hold on and to fight back, however, New Orleans is it.

The French Quarter

The beautiful **French Quarter** is where New Orleans began in 1718. Today, battered and bohemian, decaying and vibrant, it remains the spiritual core of the city, its cast-iron balconies, hidden courtyards and time-stained stucco buildings exerting a fascination that has long caught the imagination of artists and writers. It's a wonderful place simply to wander; early morning, in the pearly light from the river, is a good time to explore.

The Quarter is laid out in a grid, unchanged since 1721. At just thirteen blocks wide – smaller than you might expect – it's easily walkable, bounded by the Mississippi River, Rampart Street, Canal Street and Esplanade Avenue, and centring on lively **Jackson Square**. Rather than French, the **architecture** is predominantly Spanish Colonial, with a strong Caribbean influence. Most buildings date from the late eighteenth century; much of the old city was devastated by fire in 1788 and 1794. Shops, restaurants and bars are concentrated between Decatur and Bourbon streets, while beyond Bourbon, up toward Rampart Street, and in the Lower Quarter, downriver from Jackson Square, things become more peaceful. Here, you'll find quiet, residential streets where the Quarter's **gay** community lives side by side with elegant dowagers, condo-dwellers and scruffy artists.

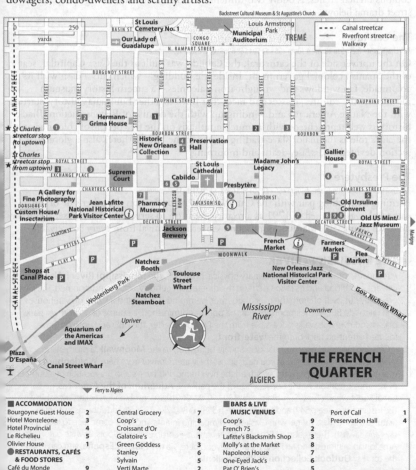

ACCOMMODATION				BARS & LIVE			
Bourgoyne Guest House	2	Central Grocery	7	MUSIC VENUES		Port of Call	1
Hotel Monteleone	3	Coop's	8	Coop's	9	Preservation Hall	4
Hotel Provincial	4	Croissant d'Or	4	French 75	2		
Le Richelieu	5	Galatoire's	1	Lafitte's Blacksmith Shop	3		
Olivier House	1	Green Goddess	3	Molly's at the Market	8		
RESTAURANTS, CAFÉS		Stanley	6	Napoleon House	7		
& FOOD STORES		Sylvain	5	One-Eyed Jack's	6		
Café du Monde	9	Verti Marte	2	Pat O' Brien's	5		

Jackson Square

Ever since its earliest incarnation as the Place d'Armes, a dusty parade ground used for public meetings and executions, **Jackson Square** has been at the heart of the Quarter. Presiding over it, an **equestrian statue** – the first in the nation, constructed by Clark Mills in 1856 – shows Andrew Jackson, the general whose victory in the 1815 **Battle of New Orleans**, the final battle in the War of 1812, finally secured American supremacy in the States. Portrayed here in a jaunty mode, waving his hat, Jackson went on to become US president. The hectoring inscription, "The Union Must and Shall be Preserved", was added by Union General "Beast" Butler during the Civil War occupation.

St Louis Cathedral

During the day, everyone passes by Jackson Square at some time or another, weaving their way through the tangle of artists, hot-dog vendors, palm readers and shambolic brass bands. A postcard-perfect backdrop for the Jackson statue, the 1794 **St Louis Cathedral** is the oldest continuously active cathedral in the United States. Dominated by three tall slate steeples, the facade, which marries Greek Revival symmetry with copious French arches, is oddly two-dimensional, like an elaborate stage prop for the street drama below.

The Cabildo

701 Chartres St • Tues–Sun 10am–4.30pm • $6 • ☎ 504 568 6968, ⓦ crt.state.la.us/museum

On the upriver side of the cathedral, the **Cabildo** was built as the Casa Capitular, seat of the Spanish colonial government. Inside the building – which cuts a dash with its colonnade, fan windows and wrought-iron balconies – a superb history **museum** illuminates the cultures, classes and races that bind together Louisiana's history, starting with the Native Americans and winding up with the demise of Reconstruction. Black history is well represented, with as much emphasis on the free people of colour as on the city's role as the major slave-trading centre of the South; there's also a gloomy section devoted to disease, death and mourning.

The Presbytère

751 Chartres St • Tues–Sun 10am–4.30pm • $6 • ☎ 504 568 6968, ⓦ crt.state.la.us/museum

Forming a matching pair with the Cabildo, the **Presbytère**, on the other side of the cathedral, was designed in 1791 as a rectory, went on to serve as a courthouse, and today holds an unmissable **Mardi Gras museum**. Covering carnival from every conceivable

---

THE MISSISSIPPI RIVER

A resonant, romantic and extraordinary physical presence, the **Mississippi River** is New Orleans's lifeblood and its *raison d'être*. In the nineteenth century, as the port boomed, the city gradually cut itself off from the river altogether, hemming it in behind a string of warehouses and railroads. But, as the importance of the port has diminished, a couple of downtown parks, plazas and riverside walks, accessible from the French Quarter, the CBD and uptown, have focused attention back onto the **waterfront**.

Crossing Decatur Street from Jackson Square brings you to the **Moonwalk**, a promenade where buskers serenade you as you gaze across the water. Upriver from here, **Woldenberg Park** makes a good place for a picnic, watching the river traffic drift by; it's also the location of a number of free music festivals. At the upriver edge of the park, the **Aquarium of the Americas**, near the Canal Street wharf (Tues–Sun 10am–5pm; $22.50, IMAX $10.50, combination tickets available with the Insectarium [see p.547] and the Zoo [see p.548]; ☎ 800 774 7394, ⓦ auduboninstitute.org), features a huge glass tunnel where visitors – rampaging infants, mostly – come face to face with rays and sawfish. There's also a Mississippi River habitat – complete with Spots, a white gator – an Amazonian rainforest and an IMAX theatre. Beyond here, via the **Plaza d'España**, you can enter the touristy **Outlook Collection at Riverwalk** mall.

angle, it's full of odd treasures such as jewel-encrusted costumes, primitive masks, posters and bizarre dance cards. You'll also find the outstanding **Katrina and Beyond**, which, using fascinating resident interviews, personal effects and multimedia displays, documents the searing path and aftermath of the 2005 hurricane (see box, p.540). In the entranceway, a piano that belonged to legendary R&B performer Fats Domino is shown upturned in the manner it was found after the storm – an evocative metaphor for a music mecca spun on its head. Elsewhere, a terrifying "hurricane room" gives visitors a taste of 160mph winds, and displays stun with statistics: you'll learn that during the crisis 35,000 evacuees were squeezed into the Superdome, a dozen police officers fired at civilians (killing two) and an astounding 65,000 people were trapped by floodwater.

Pharmacy Museum

514 Chartres St • Tues–Fri 10am–2pm, Sat 10am–5pm • $5 • ☎ 504 565 8027, ⊛ pharmacymuseum.org

The quirky **Pharmacy Museum**, in an old apothecary, offers great insights into the history of medicine. Huge hand-carved rosewood cabinets are cluttered with *gris-gris* (voodoo talismans said to bring luck), a fine range of Creole "tonics" used to cure "all the various forms of female weakness", dusty jars of leeches for blood-letting ("to remove irritability"), and various unpleasant-looking drills and corkscrews. Upstairs is mostly devoted to **women's medicine**, with a nineteenth-century sick room.

Jean Lafitte National Historical Park Visitor Center

419 Decatur St • Daily 9am–5pm • Free • ☎ 504 589 2636, ⊛ nps.gov/jela

Something of an anomaly among Upper Decatur's brassy T-shirt shops and theme restaurants, the **Jean Lafitte National Historical Park Visitor Center** is not only a starting point for excellent **walking tours** (see p.550), but also a great one-room introduction to Louisiana's delta region. Panels outline local history, architecture, cultural traditions, cuisine and ecology, while listening stations let you eavesdrop on natives expounding, in a variety of accents, on the meaning of local expressions. Touch-screen monitors feature classic footage of Louis Armstrong, Mahalia Jackson and Professor Longhair, among others.

A Gallery for Fine Photography

241 Chartres St • Mon & Thurs–Sun 10.30am–5.30pm • Free • ☎ 504 568 1313, ⊛ agallery.com

The unassuming exterior of **A Gallery for Fine Photography** belies such a fantastic collection of original prints that its pint-sized exhibit space seems nearly unbelievable. Works by the world's most renowned photographers are hung up to the rafters, with everyone from Diane Arbus to Henri Cartier-Bresson making an appearance.

The markets

Ursulines and N Peter sts • Free • Daily 9am–6pm

The speciality shops of the restored **French Market** – said to be on the site of a Native American trading area and certainly active since the 1720s – sell tourist knick-knacks; for stalls, head toward the old **Farmers' Market**, just off Decatur St, where fresh produce, spices, hot sauce and the like are sold throughout the day. Next door, a flea market abounds in trashy tack and bargain oddities; for vintage curiosities, head instead to the cavernous thrift stores across the way on Decatur.

New Orleans Jazz National Historical Park Visitor Center

916 N Peter St • Tues–Sun 9am–5pm • Free • ☎ 504 589 4841, ⊛ nps.gov/jazz

The **New Orleans Jazz National Historical Park Visitor Center**, tucked away between the French Market and the river, is a must for any music fan. Light, airy and intimate, it's a superb, informal place to attend regular free jazz concerts, talks, movies and workshops; afterwards, check out the photo displays, self-guided jazz walking tour brochures and small bookstore.

Old US Mint

400 Esplanade Ave • Tues–Sun 10am–4.30pm • $6 • ☎ 504 568 6968, ⓦ crt.state.la.us/museum

One of the outer boundaries of the Quarter, **Esplanade Avenue** is an exquisite, oak-shaded boulevard lined with crumbling nineteenth-century Creole mansions. Pre-Katrina, the **Old US Mint**, on the 400 block near the river, housed a fascinating **Jazz Museum** – featuring old instruments, sheet music, photos and personal effects – that has yet to reopen. In the meantime, the Mint hosts small shows of local interest (recent highlights have included a Napoleon exhibition and another on early jazz).

The Old Ursuline Convent

1112 Chartres St • Mon–Sat 10am–4pm • $5 • ☎ 504 525 9585, ⓦ stlouiscathedral.org

Built between 1745 and 1753, and established by nuns from Rouen, the tranquil **Old Ursuline Convent** is the oldest building in the Mississippi valley, and the only intact French Colonial structure in the city. Following the decisive Battle of New Orleans in 1815, General Andrew Jackson came here personally to thank the Ursuline sisters for their wartime prayers, claiming that "divine intervention" was what had saved him on the field. Inside, the hushed quarters are lined with wordy old information panels explaining the history of the convent; the real interest, however, is in the time-worn rooms, the spectacular gilded chapel and the lovely working herb garden at the back.

Gallier House

1132 Royal St • Hourly tours Mon, Thurs & Fri 10am, noon, 1pm & 2pm, Sat noon, 1pm, 2pm & 3pm • $12, $20 with the Hermann-Grima House (see opposite) • ☎ 504 525 5661, ⓦ hgghh.org

The handsome 1857 **Gallier House** is a fascinating little place. Prominent architect James Gallier Jr designed the structure for himself, with classic features, such as a carriageway leading to a courtyard and a parlour framed with cornices and gargoyles. Innovations included a cooling system and a flushing toilet, while the filigree cast-iron galleries were the last word in chic. Tours are superb, focusing as much on social history as fine furniture.

Madame John's Legacy

628 Dumaine St • Tues–Sun 10am–4.30pm • Free • ☎ 504 568 6968, ⓦ crt.state.la.us/museum

A rare example of the Quarter's early West Indies-style architecture, **Madame John's Legacy** was rebuilt after the fire of 1788 as an exact replica of the 1730 house that had previously stood on the site. Raised on stucco-covered pillars, it also features a distinctive, deep wraparound gallery that, cooler and airier than the indoor rooms, provided extra living space. There never was a real Madame John – the name was given to the house by nineteenth-century author George Washington Cable in his tragic short story *'Tite Poulette*, and it simply stuck, attracting hundreds of tourists to the city and spawning a nice line in Madame John souvenirs.

Historic New Orleans Collection

533 Royal St • Tues–Sat 9.30am–4.30pm, Sun 10.30am–4.30pm; guided tours Tues–Sat 10am, 11am, 2pm, & 3pm, Sun 11am, 2pm & 3pm • Front gallery free, tours $5 • ☎ 504 523 4662, ⓦ hnoc.org

Standing proud among Royal Street's antique stores and chichi art galleries is the splendid **Historic New Orleans Collection**. Entry to the streetfront gallery, which holds excellent temporary exhibitions, is free, but to see the bulk of the collection you'll need to take a guided tour. Tours might take in the galleries upstairs, where fascinating exhibits – including old maps, drawings and early publicity posters – fill a series of themed rooms, or they might venture into the neighbouring **Williams House**. The Williamses, prominent citizens in the 1930s (no relation to playwright Tennessee), filled their home with unusual, exotic objects, and the house is a must for anyone interested in design and decorative arts.

Bourbon Street

Though you'd never guess it from the hype, there are two faces to world-renowned **Bourbon Street**. The tawdry, touristy, booze-drenched stretch spans the seven stinky blocks from Canal to St Ann: a frat-pack cacophony of trashy daiquiri stalls, novelty shops and tired girlie bars. This enclave is best experienced after dark, when a couple – though by no means all – of its **bars** and **clubs** are worth a look, and the sheer mayhem takes on a bacchanalian life of its own. When the attraction of fighting your way through crowds of weekending drunks palls, however, it's easy to dip out again into the quieter parallel streets. If you do manage to make it as far as St Ann, you come to a distinct crossroads, marked by a gaggle of raucous gay clubs, beyond which Bourbon transforms into an appealing, predominantly gay, residential area.

Hermann-Grima House

820 St Louis St • Hourly tours Mon, Tues, Thurs & Fri 10am–2pm, Sat noon–3pm • $12, $20 with the Gallier House (see opposite) • ☎ 504 525 5661, ⓦ hgghh.org

Above Bourbon Street, tourists are outnumbered by locals walking their dogs, jogging or chatting on stoops. Half a block above Bourbon, the 1831 **Hermann-Grima House** does a nice job of illustrating the lifestyle of wealthy Creoles in antebellum New Orleans; otherwise, although these quiet streets are fringed by some of the Quarter's finest **vernacular architecture**, "sights" as such are few.

Rampart Street and around

Rampart Street, the run-down strip separating the Quarter from **Tremé**, is a boundary rarely crossed by tourists, and it can feel hairy at night. **Louis Armstrong Park**, meanwhile, is best avoided altogether except during its occasional **music festivals**, many of which, continuing its long tradition of black music and celebration, are held in **Congo Square**, the small paved area to the left of the entrance arch.

8

Tremé and Mid-City

In the 1800s, Tremé, the historic African American neighbourhood where **jazz** was developed in the bordellos of Storyville – long since gone – was a prosperous area, its shops, businesses and homes owned and frequented by New Orleans's free black population. By the late twentieth century, however, blighted by neglect and crime, Tremé had become a no-go zone. Despite this, its rich tradition of music, **jazz funerals** and **Second Lines** (loose, joyous street parades, led by funky brass bands and gathering dancing "Second Lines" of passers-by as they go) continued, and the turn of the millennium saw signs of gentrification. While many of its houses remain in bad shape post-Katrina, David *The Wire* Simon's HBO series *Tremé*, which premiered in 2010, brought the area appreciated visibility.

Backstreet Cultural Museum

1116 Henriette Delille St • Tues–Sat 10am–5pm • $8 • ☎ 504 522 4806, ⓦ backstreetmuseum.org

The best way to experience the financially poor but culturally rich neighbourhood of Tremé is to join a Second Line; to find out more about when you might catch one, make for the **Backstreet Cultural Museum**, in an old funeral parlour. This labour of love celebrates local street culture, including jazz funerals and the city's unique **Mardi Gras Indians** (see box, p.557), exhibiting lavish costumes and mementoes; it also acts as a social hub during the city's many festivals.

St Augustine's Church

210 Governor Nicholls St • Free • ☎ 504 525 5934, ⓦ staugustinecatholicchurch-neworleans.org

St Augustine's Church is one of the earliest African-American churches in the nation, active since 1842. Of major significance to the local black community, St Augustine's was at the centre of a hefty post-Katrina storm; when the Catholic Church, cash-strapped after the floods, announced St Augustine's closure in 2006, local protests – including an occupation – became national news; in 2009 the church was finally allowed to remain open. Today it welcomes tourists to occasional jazz masses and fundraising events. The spruce, light interior is peaceful, with stained-glass windows portraying French saints, and flags printed with affirmations (Unity, Creativity, Self-Determination, Purpose) in English and Swahili. In the garden, the affecting **Tomb of the Unknown Slave**, a toppled metal cross entwined with balls-and-chains and shackles, honours all African and Native American slaves buried in unmarked graves.

New Orleans Museum of Art

1 Collins C. Diboll Circle • Tues–Thurs 10am–6pm, Fri 10am–9pm, Sat & Sun 11am–5pm • $10 • ☎ 504 658 4100, ⓦ noma.org

Beyond Tremé, towards the lake, in the vast area known as **Mid-City**, New Orleans's 1500-acre **City Park** is a welcome green space, enlivened by pedal boats and an antique carousel, streaked with lagoons and shaded by centuries-old live oaks. The chief attraction, the excellent **New Orleans Museum of Art**, includes pre-Columbian pieces, African works, Asian ceramics and paintings, and contemporary art and photography. Its five-acre **sculpture garden** (free) is a must-see, its works – by Louise Bourgeois, Barbara Hepworth, Henry Moore and others – dotted among oaks, magnolias and lush gladioli.

The Marigny

Across Esplanade Avenue from the French Quarter, **Faubourg Marigny** (or "the Marigny") is a vibrant, mixed and low-rent area of Creole cottages and shotguns populated by artists, musicians and sundry bohemians. Its main drag and nightlife strip is **Frenchmen Street**, which boasts some of New Orleans's best spots to hear live music. Here, revellers spill out onto the streets, especially at the weekend and during festivals, to create a block party. Though the neighbourhood is gentrifying, and its gaggle of music venues, coffeeshops, bars and restaurants increasing, it's best **not to wander** too far away from the blocks around the district's main drag. Even Elysian Fields – where Stanley and Stella lived in Tennessee Williams's *A Streetcar Named Desire* – can feel distinctly dodgy, despite its heavenly name.

Bywater and Ninth Ward

Recently the Marigny's hipper – and hippier – credentials have been passed onto its neighbour, residential **Bywater**, another low-key, appealing artists' district. Bywater is officially part of the **Ninth Ward**, which, as one of the areas most drastically affected by the levee breaks and flooding, has become a byword for the very worst of Katrina's horrors. The **Lower Ninth** – downriver from the Industrial Canal – was particularly badly hit. Nowadays, valiant new builds, many of them financed by high-profile nonprofits – including Brad Pitt's Make It Right foundation – stand like sentinels of hope.

STAYING SAFE IN NEW ORLEANS

Although the heavily touristed French Quarter is comparatively safe, to wander unwittingly beyond it – even just a couple of blocks – can place your **personal safety** in serious jeopardy. While walking from the Quarter to the Marigny is usually safe enough during the day, it's not a good idea to stray far from the main drag of Frenchmen Street. Wherever you are, take the usual common-sense precautions, and at night always travel by cab when venturing any distance beyond the Quarter.

The CBD

Adjacent to the French Quarter, and bounded by the river, Canal Street, and the Ponchartrain Expressway, the Central Business District – or **CBD** – is New Orleans's civic-minded downtown. Due to its hustle-bustle ambience, it's less pleasing for a stroll than other Crescent City neighbourhoods, but some of its sights, particularly the **National World War II** and **Ogden** museums, will be of interest to visitors.

The Custom House and Insectarium

423 Canal St • **Insectarium** Tues–Sun 10am–5pm • $16.50, combination tickets available with the Aquarium (see p.542) and the Zoo (see p.548) • ☎ 504 581 4629, ⓦ auduboninstitute.org

Mark Twain had a point when he dismissed the foreboding Classical exterior of the **Custom House** as "inferior to a gasometer", but the dour granite colossus was key to New Orleans's grand antebellum building programme, a hymn to the city's optimism and aspirations. In summer 2008, the **Insectarium**, under the same auspices as the aquarium (see p.542) and zoo (see p.548) opened on the ground floor. It will mainly appeal to kids, but there's genuine interest in the exhibits on local breeds, and some exquisite beauty in the butterfly house.

The Superdome

The riverside edge of the CBD, a tangle of grey highways, is dominated by the colossal home of the New Orleans Saints NFL team, the **Superdome**. At 52 acres, with 27 storeys and a diameter of 680ft, this is one of the largest buildings on the planet, and has been etched upon the world's consciousness after housing more than thirty thousand Katrina evacuees in unthinkable conditions for six days. Though lurid tales of gang rapes, murders and suicides were later discovered to have been urban myths, the Superdome became a byword for the shocking neglect, chaos and human rights atrocities that New Orleans faced in the wake of the floods. Standing sentinel over the battered CBD for a year after Katrina, it finally reopened in autumn 2006 with a star-studded rock concert and a triumphant victory by the Saints over the Atlanta Falcons. The high-profile event marked a turning point in the city's sense of its own recovery; things reached an even higher emotional peak in January 2010 when the Saints defeated the Minnesota Vikings here to win their first ever place in the **Superbowl**. Even the team's eventual astonishing Superbowl victory over the Indiana-polis Colts – which gained the highest TV audience ever in the USA – could not quite match this moment; never had a game, a team, or a stadium, signified quite so much.

The Warehouse District

Spreading upriver from the foot of Canal Street, New Orleans's **Warehouse District**, part of the CBD, has a handful of attractions. Most sights are concentrated in the **Arts District**, the outcrop of galleries centred on Julia and Camp streets. The hub of the scene is the **Contemporary Arts Center**, at 900 Camp St (daily except Tues 11am–5pm; $5; ☎ 504 528 3805, ⓦ cacno.org).

National World War II Museum

945 Magazine St • Daily 9am–5pm • $22, $27 with Victory Theater • ☎ 504 528 1944, ⓦ nationalww2museum.org

The colossal **National World War II Museum** opened on June 6, 2000, the 56th anniversary of D-Day. After buying a ticket from the cordial volunteers (all ex-service personnel), you can weave your way through three floors of gnarly-looking weaponry, heartrending soldier keepsakes and media stations with oral histories. Though impressive, its gung-ho militarism can feel relentless. It's worth paying extra for the **Victory Theater**'s "Beyond All Boundaries" 4-D movie (hourly 10am–4pm), a sombre film overlaid with lighthearted super-effects such as shaking seats, billowing smoke and cascading snow (really soap bubbles).

8

Civil War Museum

929 Camp St, at Lee Circle • Tues–Sat 10am–4pm • $8 • ☎ 504 523 4522, ⓦ confederatemuseum.com

Near the World War II Museum, the **Civil War Museum** has its own, equally partisan, take on history. A rust-coloured Romanesque Revival hulk, designed in 1891 as a place for Confederate veterans to display their mementos, this so-called "Battle Abbey of the South" is a relic from a bygone age, full of bittersweet remembrances of long-lost Confederate generals and their forgotten families.

Ogden Museum of Southern Art

925 Camp St • Daily except Tues 10am–5pm, Thurs also 6–8pm with live music • $10 • ☎ 504 539 9600, ⓦ ogdenmuseum.org

A world away from the Civil War Museum but just next door, the superb **Ogden Museum of Southern Art** represents the South in all its complexity, strangeness and melancholy beauty. Its impressive collection runs the gamut from rare eighteenth-century watercolours to self-taught art, photography and modern sculpture.

Blaine Kern's Mardi Gras World

1380 Port of New Orleans Place • Daily 9.30am–5.30pm, last tour at 4.30pm • $19.95 • ☎ 504 229 3343 ⓦ mardigrasworld.com • Best reached via the free shuttle, with twenty downtown stops (call ☎ 504 361 7821 for pickup)

In the cavernous "dens" of **Blaine Kern's Mardi Gras World**, beyond the Convention Center, you can see artists constructing and painting the overblown, garish papier-mâché floats used in the official carnival parades. It's a surreal experience wandering past piles of dusty, grimacing has-beens from parades gone by.

8

The Garden District and uptown

Pride of uptown New Orleans, the **Garden District** drapes itself seductively across a thirteen-block area bounded by Magazine Street and St Charles, Louisiana and Jackson avenues. Two miles upriver from the French Quarter, it was developed as a residential neighbourhood in the 1840s by an energetic breed of Anglo-Americans who wished to display their accumulating cotton and trade wealth by building sumptuous mansions in huge gardens. Today, shaded by jungles of subtropical foliage, the glorious houses – some of them spick-and-span showpieces, others in ravishing ruin – evoke a nostalgic vision of the Deep South in a profusion of porches, columns and balconies. While it's a pleasure simply to wander around, you can pick up more details about the individual houses on any number of official or self-guided tours.

The historic **St Charles streetcar** (see p.550) is the nicest way to get to the Garden District and uptown, affording front-row views of "the Avenue" as St Charles is locally known. It's a popular Mardi Gras parade route; keep an eye out for the tossed beads and favours that missed outstretched hands and now adorn hundreds of tree branches here. Just before the streetcar takes a sharp turn at the river bend, it stops at peaceful **Audubon Park**, a lovely space shaded by Spanish-moss-swathed trees. You can also approach the Garden District and uptown via **Magazine Street**, the city's best shopping stretch, a six-mile string of clothing boutiques, restaurants and stores that runs parallel to St Charles riverside.

Audubon Zoo

6500 Magazine St • Tues–Fri 10am–4pm, Sat & Sun 10am–5pm • $17.50, combination tickets available with the Aquarium (see p.542) and the Insectarium (see p.547) • ☎ 504 861 2537, ⓦ auduboninstitute.org • A 10min walk or a free shuttle ride (every 15–25min) from the park's St Charles entrance

Audubon Park's top attraction, **Audubon Zoo**, boasts, among other habitats, a beautifully re-created **Louisiana swamp**, complete with Cajun houseboats, wallowing alligators (including the milky white, blue-eyed gators found in a local swamp), and knobbly cypress knees poking out of the emerald-green water.

ARRIVAL AND DEPARTURE

By plane Louis Armstrong New Orleans International Airport (MSY; ☎ 504 303 7500, ⓦ flymsy.com), 18 miles northwest of downtown on I-10, has an information booth (daily 9am–5pm; ☎ 504 303 7792) on the second floor in Concourse C. Flat-rate taxi fares into town (20–30min) are $33 for up to two people, or $14 each for three or more; shuttles can also take you to your hotel (every 30min; tickets sold 7am–last flight in the baggage claim area; $20 to downtown, $38 return; ☎ 504 522 3500, ⓦ airport shuttleneworleans.com).

By car Drivers approaching from either direction on I-10 should make sure not to stray onto I-610, which bypasses downtown altogether. For the CBD take exit 234C, following signs for the Superdome; for the French Quarter take 235B (signs for Vieux Carré) and for the Garden District take

the St Charles St exit. Using I-12 hooks you up with the Lake Pontchartrain Causeway – at 23 miles, one of the world's longest bridges – which enters the city from the northwest and connects with I-10.

By bus or train Greyhound buses (☎ 504 525 6075) and Amtrak trains arrive at Union Passenger Terminal, 1001 Loyola Ave, near the Superdome. This area, beneath the elevated Pontchartrain Expressway, is not great; book a cab in advance to take you to your lodgings. United Cabs is the best firm (☎ 504 522 9771).

Destinations (bus) Baton Rouge, LA (7 daily; 1hr 45min); Lafayette, LA (5 daily; 3hr 15min); Jackson, MS (1 daily; 5hr 35min).

Destinations (train) Greenwood, MS (1 daily; 6hr); Jackson, MS (1 daily; 4hr); Memphis, TN (1 daily; 8hr).

GETTING AROUND

The Regional Transit Authority (RTA) runs a network of buses and streetcars ($1.25, exact fare; ☎ 504 248 3900, ⓦ norta.com). "Jazzy" passes, valid on all services, cost $3/day, $9/3 days and $55/month; the RTA website lists vendors.

By bus The most useful bus routes include "Magazine" (#11), which runs between Canal St in the CBD and Audubon Park uptown, and "Jackson-Esplanade" (#91), from Rampart St on the edge of the Quarter to City Park.

By streetcar The handsome sage-green St Charles streetcar (a National Historic Monument, dating back around 150 years) rumbles a 13-mile loop from Carondelet St at Canal St, along St Charles Ave in the Garden District,

past Audubon Park to Carrollton uptown. Service is limited after dark. There are also two Canal St streetcars: the City Park service (#48, "City Park/Museum") starts by Harrah's Casino on Canal St, turns off at Carrollton and heads to City Park. The Carrollton Ave line (#47, "Cemeteries") travels the length of Canal St to where it meets City Park Ave; if you're heading to City Park, make sure to get off at Carrollton and transfer onto the #48. There's also a riverfront streetcar

---

CITY TOURS, RIVER CRUISES AND SWAMP VISITS

Walking tours are especially popular in New Orleans, with its wealth of gorgeous hidden courtyards and fine architectural details. The **Jean Lafitte National Historical Park Service** offers scholarly and accessible overviews of the Quarter (daily 9.30am; 1hr; free; collect tickets from the NPS visitor centre, 419 Decatur St, at 9am; ☎ 504 589 2636, ⓦ nps.gov/jela). **Le Monde Créole Tours** gives walking tours with a Creole spin, dipping into gardens, nineteenth-century homes and the Pharmacy Museum (daily 10.30am; 2hr; $24, cash only, reservations required; ☎ 504 568 1801, ⓦ mondecreole.com). For a greater understanding of New Orleans's beguiling "cities of the dead", take a stroll with **Save Our Cemeteries**; ticket proceeds go toward restoration work (1hr; $15; ☎ 504 525 3377, ⓦ saveourcemeteries.org). **Confederacy of Cruisers** runs excellent, low-impact bike tours around the city; rides have cocktail, culinary and Creole themes (check website for details as prices and times vary greatly; ☎ 504 400 5468, ⓦ confederacyofcruisers.com).

A lazy way to while away a steamy afternoon is on a **river cruise**. Leaving from the Toulouse Street wharf behind the Jackson Brewery mall, the *Natchez* steamboat heads seven miles or so downriver before looping back. The captain gives a running commentary while a jaunty Dixieland band plays in the dining room (daily 2.30pm, plus 11.30am at busy times; 2hr; $27.50, $38.50 with lunch; evening cruise 7pm, $43, $72.50 with dinner; ☎ 504 586 8777, ⓦ steamboatnatchez.com).

New Orleans's local **swamps** – many of them protected areas just a thirty-minute drive from downtown – are otherworldly enclaves that provide a wonderful contrast to the city itself. Dr Wagner's Honey Island Swamp Tours, based ten miles north of Lake Pontchartrain, venture onto the delta of the Pearl River, a wilderness occupied by nutrias, black bears and alligators, as well as ibis, great blue herons and snowy egrets (wildlife most abundant April, May & Sept–Nov; 2hr; $23, not including transport from downtown, reservations required; ☎ 985 641 1769, ⓦ honeyislandswamp.com).

between the Convention Center and Esplanade Ave.

By taxi Though New Orleans's most-visited neighbourhoods are easy to walk around, getting between them is not always simple on foot, and if you're travelling anywhere outside the Quarter after dark you should call a cab (see p.546).

By pedicab For short trips, pedicabs are a good solution, with better accessibility than taxis during heavily trafficked events (such as parades or Superdome games). Try NOLA Pedicabs ($1/block/person, about $28 for two from the Quarter to the Superdome; ☎504 274 1300, ⓦnola pedicabs.com).

INFORMATION

Visitor centre Jackson Square at 529 St Ann St in the French Quarter (daily 9am–5pm; ☎504 568 5661); a helpful place to pick up self-guided walking tours, free maps and discount vouchers.

Websites Before you arrive in town, check out ⓦnew orleanscvb.com or ⓦnola.com.

ACCOMMODATION

New Orleans has some lovely **places to stay**, from rambling old guesthouses seeping faded grandeur to stylish boutique hotels. **Room rates**, never low (you'll be pushed to find anything half decent for less than $100 a night), increase considerably for Mardi Gras and Jazz Fest, when prices can double and rooms are reserved months in advance. Most people choose to stay in the **French Quarter**, in the heart of things. Much of the accommodation here is in atmospheric **guesthouses**, most of them in old Creole townhouses. Outside the Quarter, the **Lower Garden District** offers a couple of budget options, while the **Marigny** specializes in B&Bs and the **Garden District** has a couple of gorgeous old hotels. The **CBD** is the domain of the city's upmarket chain and business hotels.

FRENCH QUARTER

Bourgoyne Guest House 839 Bourbon St ☎504 524 3621, ⓦbourgoynehouse.com. Good-value guesthouse in an 1830s Creole mansion. Five worn but cosy studios are set around a subtropical courtyard; fancier options include the lovely Green Suite, accessed by a sweeping staircase, and boasting two bedrooms, a kitchen, parlour and Bourbon St balcony. **$125**

★ **Hotel Monteleone** 214 Royal St ☎504 523 3341, ⓦhotelmonteleone.com. This handsome French Quarter landmark is the oldest hotel in the city, owned by the same family since 1886, and hosting a fine array of writers and luminaries since its inception. At sixteen storeys, it's something of a gentle giant on courtly Royal St, with an elegant Baroque facade, marble lobby, posh rooms, a rooftop pool and a splendid revolving bar tricked out like an antique carousel. **$189**

Hotel Provincial 1024 Chartres St ☎504 581 4995, ⓦhotelprovincial.com. This sprawling – yet somehow intimate – place is in a quiet part of the Quarter, with rooms around five peaceful, gaslit courtyards. All rooms are filled with antiques or period reproductions. Plus two nice outdoor pools, a bar and a fancy restaurant, *Stella!*, on site. **$149**

Le Richelieu 1234 Chartres St ☎504 529 2492, ⓦlerichelieuhotel.com. Handsome hotel in a restored factory and neighbouring townhouse. Though the old-world ambience of the lobby is not continued in the rather ordinary rooms, they are comfortable and clean. There's a small (unheated) outdoor pool and a little breakfast café. **$140**

★ **Olivier House** 828 Toulouse St ☎504 525 8456, ⓦolivierhousehotel.com. Though a bit dark in places, this atmospheric, quintessentially New Orleans guesthouse offers real character. The 41 rooms (and one cottage) vary widely, but most have quirky antique furniture and soaring windows. For the best view, ask for an upper-level room, many of which have balconies overlooking the tropical courtyard and small pool. **$139**

OUTSIDE THE FRENCH QUARTER

AAE Bourbon House 1660 Annunciation St, Lower Garden District ☎504 644 2199, ⓦaaebourbonhouse .com. This friendly hostel in the Lower Garden District has mixed and same-sex dorms and rooms sleeping one to eight. It's scruffy but clean enough, with a decent pancake breakfast and free daytime pickup from and drop-off to the train/bus stations (contact them in advance). Dorms **$20**

★ **Chimes B&B** 1146 Constantinople St, Garden District ☎504 899 2621, ⓦchimesneworleans.com. You're in a pretty part of the Garden District at this peaceful, casually stylish B&B. Each of the five rooms – all with their own entrance from the gorgeous courtyard – is light, airy and full of intriguing period detail. Great breakfast, too. Free off-street parking. **$158**

Columns Hotel 3811 St Charles Ave, Garden District ☎504 899 9308, ⓦthecolumns.com. Deliciously atmospheric uptown hotel in a stately 1883 mansion on the streetcar line. The whole place seeps louche bordello glamour, especially the faded Victorian bar (see p.554); the porch, with its namesake columns, is another nice spot for a drink. Some rooms come with a balcony, some are bordering on shabby. Rates include full breakfast, but it's not great. **$120**

★ **House of the Rising Sun B&B** 335 Pelican Ave, Algiers ☎504 231 6498, ⓦrisingsunbnb.com. Cross the Mississippi via the (free) 7min ferry from Canal St, and you're three blocks away from this charming 1896 "shotgun" cottage. Three spotless guestrooms have brocade bedspreads and access to a lush backyard with porch swing. The home-made breakfast is superb, and guests are entertained by Boudin "the wonder dog". Free parking. **$110**

India House Hostel 124 S Lopez St, Mid-City ☎504 821 1904, ⓦindiahousehostel.com. The location of this hip, run-down hostel is excellent for Jazz Fest and Voodoo Fest, and the Canal St streetcar is close by. It's the most sociable, and booziest, of the hostels, with the occasional jam session, crawfish boils and rowdy pool parties. Dorms plus a few basic rooms, some with bath. The area isn't great at night. Dorms **$17**

★ **Royal Street Inn** 1431 Royal St, Marigny ☎504 948 7499, ⓦroyalstreetinn.com. Modish lodging footsteps from Frenchmen St above the *R-Bar* (see p.555), and run by the same people. Quirky New Orleans style meets big-city boutique hip in the five suites (all with bath, and some with balcony) with their stripped floors, bare brick walls and leather sofas; all have DVD players and iPod docks. It's favoured by a young crowd who hang out in the bar, and can be noisy at weekends, but the comfort, location and price can't be beat. **$159**

EATING

New Orleans is a gourmand's dream. Restaurants here are far more than places to eat: from the haughtiest *grandes dames* of Creole cuisine right down to rough-and-ready po-boy shacks, they are fiercely cherished as the guardians of community, culture and heritage. Gratifyingly, prices are not high compared to other US cities – even at the swankiest places you can get away with $40 per head for a three-course feast with wine.

FRENCH QUARTER

Café du Monde 800 Decatur St ☎504 525 4544, ⓦcafedumonde.com. Open round the clock and famous for its *beignets* – in fact, it serves nothing else – this historic market coffeehouse is an unmissable stop while you're touring the French Quarter. Daily 24hr.

Central Grocery 923 Decatur St ☎504 523 1620. A New Orleans must-do since 1906. People queue down the street for this Italian merchant's muffulettas (see box below). A whole ($14.50) easily feeds two; the half sandwich is $7.50. Pair one with Zapp's chips for a blissful Jackson Square picnic. Tues–Sat 9am–5pm.

★ **Coop's** 1109 Decatur St ☎504 525 9053, ⓦcoopsplace.net. A merry fixture on the heavy-drinking, late-night, Lower Decatur bar scene, this dimly lit dive is a great bar, but the amazing surprise is the delicious food. This is gourmet stuff, at ridiculous prices – the "Taste of Coop's" gets you a seafood gumbo packed with fat oysters; shrimp Creole; a fantastic jambalaya; red beans and rice *and* spicy, crispy, fried chicken for an astonishing $14. Expect a wait at peak times. Mon–Thurs & Sun 11am–1am, Fri & Sat 11am–2am.

Croissant d'Or 617 Ursulines St ☎504 524 4663, ⓦcroissantdornola.com. Relax with a newspaper in the

---

NEW ORLEANS FOOD

New Orleans **food**, commonly defined as **Creole**, is a spicy, substantial – and usually very fattening – blend of French, Spanish, African and Caribbean cuisine, mixed up with a host of other influences including Native American, Italian and German. Some of the simpler dishes, like red beans and rice, reveal a strong West Indies influence, while others are more French, cooked with long-simmered sauces based on a **roux** (fat and flour heated together) and herby stocks. Many dishes are served **étouffée**, literally "smothered" in a tasty Creole sauce (a roux with tomato, onion and spices), on rice. Although there are some exceptions, what passes for **Cajun** food in the city tends to be a modern hybrid, tasty but not authentic; the "blackened" dishes, for example, slathered in butter and spices, made famous by chef Paul Prudhomme.

The mainstays of most menus are **gumbo** – a thick soup of seafood, chicken and vegetables – and **jambalaya**, a paella jumbled together from the same ingredients. Other specialities include **po-boys**, French-bread sandwiches overstuffed with oysters, shrimp or almost anything else, and **muffulettas**, the round Italian version, crammed full of aromatic meats and cheese and dripping with garlicky olive dressing. Along with **shrimp** and **soft-shell crabs**, you'll get famously good **oysters**; they're in season from September to April. **Crawfish**, or mudbugs (which resemble langoustines and are best between March and June), are served in everything from omelettes to bisques, or simply boiled in a spicy stock. Everyone should enjoy a *café au lait* and **beignet** (featherlight doughnuts, without a hole, cloaked in powdered sugar) at *Café du Monde* in the French Quarter (see p.541). And for another only-in-New-Orleans snack, look out for the absurd, giant, hot-dog-shaped **Lucky Dogs** carts set up throughout the Quarter. Featured in John Kennedy Toole's farcical novel *A Confederacy of Dunces*, they've become a beloved institution, though in truth the dogs themselves are nothing great.

courtyard at this daintily tiled French bakery and enjoy stout cups of café au lait and top-notch croissants, quiche and Danish pastries. Daily except Tues 6am–3pm.

Galatoire's 209 Bourbon St ☎504 525 2021, ⓦgalatoires.com. This grand Creole establishment – Tennessee Williams's favourite restaurant – is quintessential New Orleans with its mirror-lined dining room, and not at all stuffy. It's best for lunch, on Friday or Sunday especially, when you can join the city's old guard (gents in seersucker, Southern belles in pearls) spending long, convivial hours gorging on turtle soup ($7), oysters *en brochette* ($13), crabmeat sardou ($26) and filet mignon ($28). No reservations (except for the less characterful upstairs room), so expect a wait. Jacket and tie required after 5pm and all day Sun. Tues–Sat 11.30am–10pm, Sun noon–10pm.

★ **Green Goddess** 307 Exchange Place ☎504 301 3347, ⓦgreengoddessnola.com. Luscious Creole-Mediterranean-Southern fusion food at this teensy hole in the wall. Menus, using the freshest ingredients, vary seasonally, but don't miss the stupendous coconut seafood salad with avocado ($16) or sweet potato biscuits with orange honey butter ($4). It's also a lovely place to come for a glass of wine and an artisan cheese plate. Wed–Sun 11am–9pm.

Stanley 547 St Ann St ☎504 587 0093, ⓦstanley restaurant.com. Fresh and airy, with huge picture windows on Jackson Square and posies of fresh flowers on the marble-and-iron tables, this modern place with an unfussy retro feel offers a simple, creative menu of all-day breakfasts and brunches, salads and sandwiches. Daily 7am–10pm.

Sylvain 625 Chartres St ☎504 265 8123, ⓦsylvainnola .com. Hip gastropub with a pared-down, stylish interior – think framed antique maps, pressed tin ceilings and a subtropical courtyard. The food is a wonder: order the roasted beet bruschetta ($10) with the pan-fried pork shoulder ($22) or pappardelle bolognese ($16) for the perfect candlelit dinner. Mon–Thurs 5.30–11pm, Fri & Sat 11.30am–2.30pm & 5.30pm–midnight, Sun 10.30am–2.30pm & 5.30–10pm.

Verti Marte 1201 Royal St ☎504 525 4767. There is no better way to soak up a night of Bourbon Street booze than with an "All that Jazz" sandwich ($10) – grilled ham, turkey, shrimp, Swiss cheese, mushrooms and "wow" sauce – ordered over the counter at this cherished around-the-clock corner store. Don't be put off by the grubby exterior; this little deli cranks out some of the best po-boys in the city. Daily 24hr.

OUTSIDE THE FRENCH QUARTER

★ **Boucherie** 8115 Jeannette St, Uptown ☎504 862 5514, ⓦboucherie-nola.com. The Krispy Kreme bread pudding ($6) may be the headliner here, but all the creative, Southern dishes in this quaint cottage are fabulous, from the collard greens and "grit fries" ($7) to the smoked scallops with purple peas ($18). Tues–Sat 11am–3pm & 5.30–9.30pm.

Café Reconcile 1631 Oretha Castle Haley Blvd, Central City ☎504 568 1157, ⓦcafereconcile.org. Something special: a nonprofit venture, spearheaded by a Jesuit church, where local at-risk teens are trained for jobs in the hospitality industry. The bustling dining room, in the blighted but recovering neighbourhood of Central City, north of the Lower Garden District, is welcoming, prices are ridiculously low, and the food – fried chicken, catfish, pot roast, beans and rice – delicious. Mon–Fri 11am–2.30pm.

Casamento's 4330 Magazine St, Uptown ☎504 895 9761, ⓦcasamentosrestaurant.com. Spotless and old-fashioned, this prettily tiled oyster bar serves inexpensive ice-fresh oysters, fried crab claws and overstuffed trout "loaves" (sandwiches) to die for. Cash only. Tues & Wed 11am–2pm, Thurs–Sat 11am–2pm & 5.30–9pm; closed June–Aug.

★ **Cochon** 930 Tchoupitoulas St, CBD ☎504 588 2123, ⓦcochonrestaurant.com. Upscale but unintimidating CBD place, full of blissed-out diners – from businessmen to bearded hipsters – feasting on fine, authentic Cajun food: not spicy and stodgy, but flavoursome and complex. Everything, from the melt-in-the-mouth fried boudin balls ($8) to the boucherie plate ($14) and the tender rabbit and dumplings ($21), is utterly delicious. Mon–Thurs 11am–10pm, Fri & Sat 11am–11pm.

Commander's Palace 1403 Washington Ave, Garden District ☎504 899 8221, ⓦcommanderspalace.com. Established in 1880 so that Americans – new to the city and forging their own neighbourhood outside the Quarter – could have a place to break bread, this genteel restaurant with the famous striped awning and its name in lights is a New Orleans icon. Expect impeccable service – even water glasses are switched between courses – and exceptional takes on New Orleans cuisine. At lunch, don't miss the 25¢ martinis. No shorts or T-shirts allowed; jackets encouraged at dinner. Mon–Fri 11.30am–2pm & 6.30–10pm, Sat 11.30am–12.30pm & 6.30–10pm, Sun 10.30am–1.30pm & 6.30–10pm.

Jacques Imo's 8324 Oak St, Uptown ☎504 861 0886, ⓦjacques-imos.com. This cheery, noisy restaurant is the perfect place to fill up before a gig at the *Maple Leaf* (see p.557), and well worth a trip any time. The decor is funky-folksy, and the cooking, a delicious Creole-Cajun take on soul food, superb – from the fried green tomatoes ($9) and blackened redfish ($27) to the ambrosial alligator sausage cheesecake ($9). Reservations only for groups of five or more; get there early or expect to wait a while at the bar. Mon–Thurs 5–10pm, Fri & Sat 5–10.30pm.

Parkway Bakery & Tavern 538 Hagan Ave, Mid-City ☎504 482 3047, ⓦparkwaypoorboys.com. The city's oldest po-boy joint – dating to 1911 – and still its best. Join the line for roast beef sandwiches smothered in gravy

8

($9.80), and delicately fried shrimp po-boys "dressed" with lettuce, tomatoes and mayo ($11). Wash everything down with root beers served in old-timey glass bottles. Daily except Tues 11am–10pm.

★ **Upperline** 1413 Upperline St, Uptown ☎ 504 891 9822, ⓦ upperline.com. The Creole dishes are curated as

carefully as the fine art covering the walls of this uptown cottage, with an enchanting hostess who moonlights as a costume designer. A three-course *prix fixe* meal will set you back $40; try the perfect fried green tomatoes with shrimp remoulade and half-duckling with ginger peach sauce. Wed–Sun 5.30–9pm.

DRINKING

New Orleans's **drinking** scene, like the city itself, is unpretentious and inclusive: whether sipping Sazeracs in the golden glow of a 1930s cocktail bar or necking an Abita at dawn in a down-and-dirty dive, you'll more than likely find yourself in a high-spirited crowd of bohemian barflies. It is also legal to drink alcohol in the streets – for some visitors it's practically de rigueur – though not from a glass or bottle. Simply ask for a plastic "to go" cup in any bar and carry it with you. You'll be expected to finish your drink before entering another bar, however.

FRENCH QUARTER

French 75 Arnaud's, 815 Bienville St ☎ 504 523 5433, ⓦ arnaudsrestaurant.com. Hidden away in one of the city's old French-Creole restaurants, this is something of an in-the-know joint. The epitome of old New Orleans elegance with its dark mahogany walls, bevelled glass doors and etched-glass lamps, it's classy but unintimidating, just the place to dress up, settle back and sip on classic drinks. Be sure to take a break to peruse the little Mardi Gras museum upstairs (free). Daily 5.30–11pm.

Lafitte's Blacksmith Shop 941 Bourbon St ☎ 504 593 9761. Buzzing, tumbledown bar that's a favourite for tourists and locals alike. A front for pirate Lafitte's plottings, the building's practically unchanged since the 1700s – despite its exterior sprucing – and retains its beamed ceilings and blackened brick fireplace. Frequent live piano music. Mon–Wed & Sun 10am–2am, Thurs–Sat 10am–4am.

Molly's at the Market 1107 Decatur St ☎ 504 525 5169, ⓦ mollysatthemarket.net. Once famed as a haunt of politicos and media stars, *Molly's* is a French Quarter institution – remaining open through Katrina and the subsequent flooding – and pulls a rowdy crowd of locals, tourists, off-duty waiters and grungy street punks. Daily 10am–6am.

★ **Napoleon House** 500 Chartres St ☎ 504 524 9752, ⓦ napoleonhouse.com. If you visit just one bar in New Orleans, let this ravishing old place – all crumbling walls, classical music and shadowy corners – be it. Exuding a relaxed New Orleans elegance, the eighteenth-century building was the home of Mayor Girod, who schemed with notorious pirate Jean Lafitte to rescue Napoleon from exile, but since 1914 it has been owned and run by the same Italian family. Lamps flickering, its time-stained walls crammed with ancient oil paintings, it's atmospheric in the extreme, and on a warm night its tropical courtyard is one of the best places on earth to be. Bow-tied waiters serve café food, including warm muffulettas, gumbo and Mediterranean salads. Mon 11am–6pm, Tues–Sat 11am–midnight.

Pat O'Brien's 718 St Peter St ☎ 504 525 4823, ⓦ patobriens.com. Marked as a tourist magnet and

famed for its boozy, sippable rum punch (the "Hurricane"). What's surprising about this New Orleans legend is just how charming an evening here can be. The sprawling drinking environs range from an ebullient singalong piano bar to a fountain-laden patio. Don't forget to recoup the deposit on your glass. Mon–Thurs noon–midnight, Fri–Sun 10am–midnight.

Port of Call 838 Esplanade Ave ☎ 504 523 0120, ⓦ portofcallnola.com. Strung with rigging and life rings, this unpretentious drinking hole is haunted by a noisy crowd who put the world to rights around the large wooden bar or the small tables. Very strong drinks and great burgers, served with mushrooms or cheese and a buttery baked potato. Mon–Thurs & Sun 11am–midnight, Fri & Sat 11am–1am.

OUTSIDE THE FRENCH QUARTER

★ **Bacchanal** 600 Poland St, Bywater ☎ 504 948 9111, ⓦ bacchanalwine.com. *Bacchanal* may have the feel of a ramshackle, thrift store-cum-living room – bare brick walls, peeling stucco, wooden barrel seating and ancient, over-stuffed bookcases – but it's actually a very good, friendly wine bar in the style of a European bodega. Classy wines available by the glass, simple and delicious food, and occasional live bands in the courtyard. Daily 11am–midnight.

Columns Hotel 3811 St Charles Ave, Garden District ☎ 504 899 9308, ⓦ thecolumns.com. This gorgeous hotel bar (see p.551), on the fringes of the Garden District, oozes faded Southern grandeur; on warm evenings, make for the grand columned veranda, which overlooks the streetcar line. Mon–Thurs 3pm–midnight, Fri & Sat noon–2am, Sun noon–midnight.

Mimi's 2601 Royal St, Marigny ☎ 504 872 9868, ⓦ mimisinthemarigny.net. Time-worn corner bar populated by the coolest free spirits of Bywater and the Marigny. You'll find cheap and tasty tapas, pool and, endearingly, a Ms. Pac-Man game. Until a noise ordinance demanded its closure in 2013, *Mimi's* threw the best dance party in town, Saturday nights with DJ Soul Sister. At the time of writing, locals were rallying to reinstate the event;

8

check online for the latest. Daily 4pm–4am.

R-Bar 1431 Royal St, Marigny ☎504 948 7499, ⓦroyalstreetinn.com. Hip, smoky Marigny bar with funky thrift-store decor, a pool table and a great jukebox. It's popular with a youngish set, which includes visitors staying at the guesthouse upstairs (see p.552). On Fridays they host an ebullient crawfish boil. Daily 3pm–2am or later.

Snake and Jake's 7612 Oak St, Uptown ☎504 861 2802, ⓦsnakeandjakes.com. Dim, debauched and derelict, strewn with ancient Christmas tree lights, this quintessential New Orleans dive bar has a superb jukebox, with a playlist of New Orleans R&B and classic soul. Legend has it that if you get shot here, they'll give you free drinks for life. Go very late. Daily 7pm–7am.

ENTERTAINMENT AND NIGHTLIFE

New Orleans has long been one of the best places in the world to hear **live music**. **Jazz**, especially trad jazz, is **dance music** here – inclusive, joyous and sexy. You may or may not get to see world-famous names such as pianist Allen Toussaint or trumpeters Terence Blanchard and Nicholas Payton, but you will discover an astonishing range of local talents – one of the city's best-loved performers, trumpeter **Kermit Ruffins** can always be counted on for a good show. But there's far more to New Orleans than jazz alone. Though the "**New Orleans sound**", an exuberant, carnival-tinged hybrid of blues, parade music and R&B, had its heyday in the early 1960s, many of its stars are still gigging, from Al "Carnival Time" Johnson to Irma "It's Raining" Thomas. While **Cajun music** is not indigenous to the city, there are a couple of fantastic places to *fais-do-do* (the Cajun two-step) and dance to **zydeco**, its raunchier black relation. For something unique, scour the listings for **Mardi Gras Indians** (see box, p.557) such as the Wild Magnolias, whose rare gigs – you're most likely to catch them around Mardi Gras or Jazz Fest – are the most extraordinary performances you're ever likely to see.

LISTINGS

To decide where to go, check the free weekly *Gambit* (ⓦbestofneworleans.com) and the music monthly *Offbeat* (ⓦoffbeat.com). Fliers can be found in French Quarter record stores such as Louisiana Music Factory, 210 Decatur St (☎504 586 1094, ⓦlouisianamusicfactory.com), and the fabulous local radio station WWOZ (90.7 FM; listen online at ⓦwwoz.org) features regular gig information.

JAZZ VENUES

While the French Quarter has its share of venues (including Preservation Hall, the holy grail for trad jazz fans), there are plenty of good places elsewhere. Visitors who make a beeline for Bourbon Street, hoping to find it crammed with cool jazz clubs, will be disappointed. A better bet is Frenchmen Street, in the Marigny, lined with bars and music venues that get packed on the weekends.

Le Bon Temps Roulé 4801 Magazine St, Uptown ☎504 895 8117. A convivial mix of drinkers fills this smoky neighbourhood bar, complete with pool tables and good food. The weekly Soul Rebels gig (Thurs) has become an institution. No cover. Daily 5pm–2am.

★ **Preservation Hall** 726 St Peter St, French Quarter ☎504 522 2841, ⓦpreservationhall.com. This

8

NEW ORLEANS JAZZ

Jazz was born in New Orleans, shaped in the early twentieth century by the twin talents of Louis Armstrong and Joe "King" Oliver from a diverse heritage of African and Caribbean slave music, Civil War brass bands, plantation spirituals, black church music and work songs. In 1897, in an attempt to control the prostitution that had been rampant in the city since its earliest days, a law was passed that restricted the brothels to a fixed area bounded by Iberville and Basin streets. The area, which soon became known as **Storyville**, after the alderman who pronounced the ordinance, filled with newly arrived ex-plantation workers, seamen and gamblers, and, from the "mood-setting" tunes played in the brothels to bawdy saloon gigs, there was plenty of opportunity for musicians, in particular the solo piano players known as "professors", to develop personal styles. Nowadays jazz remains an evolving, organic art form, and you're spoilt for choice for places to hear it, whether in Second Lines (see p.545), at the city's many festivals, in dive bars or sophisticated lounges.

At the heart of it all are the **brass bands**. Although these have been integral to New Orleans's street music and parade culture since the nineteenth century, their resurgence in the 1990s led to an explosion of energy on the local jazz scene. Young, ragtag groups blast out a joyful, improvised and danceable cacophony of horns – a kind of homegrown party music that goes down as much of a storm in the student bars as on the backstreet parades. Favourites include ReBirth, the Soul Rebels and the Stooges, who mix trad brass stylings with hard funk, hip-hop, carnival music and reggae. The more traditional bands, meanwhile, whose line-up will typically include old hands and up-and-coming youngsters, play music that is just as danceable and equally popular.

MARDI GRAS AND OTHER NEW ORLEANS FESTIVALS

New Orleans's **carnival season** – which starts on Twelfth Night, January 6, and runs for the six weeks or so until Ash Wednesday – is unlike any other in the world. Though the name is used to define the entire season, **Mardi Gras** itself, French for "Fat Tuesday", is simply the culmination of a whirl of parades, parties, street revels and masked balls, all tied up with the city's labyrinthine social, racial and political structures.

Official carnival took its current form in 1857. At this time, the concept of the "**krewes**", or secret carnival clubs, was taken up enthusiastically by the New Orleans aristocracy, many of them white supremacists who, after the Civil War, used their satirical float designs and the shroud of secrecy to mock and undermine Reconstruction. Nowadays about fifty official krewes equip colourful floats, leading huge processions with different, often mythical, themes.

Each krewe is reigned over by a King and Queen, who go on to preside over the organization's closed, masked balls. There are women-only krewes, enormous "super krewes", and important African American groups. The best known and most significant of these is **Zulu**, established in 1909 when a black man mocked Rex, King of Carnival, by sporting a banana stalk sceptre and a tin can on his head. Today the Zulu parade on Mardi Gras morning is one of the most popular of the season (and the krewe's coconut throws [see below] some of the festival's most coveted). There are also many alternative, or **unofficial krewes**, including the anarchic **Krewe du Vieux** (from *Vieux Carré*, another term for the French Quarter), whose irreverent parade and "ball" (a polite term for a wild party, open to all) is a blast. The **gay** community plays a major part in Mardi Gras, particularly in the French Quarter, where the streets teem with strutting drag divas. And then there's the parade of the **Mystic Krewe of Barkus**, made up of dogs, hundreds of them, all spiffed up on some spurious theme.

Tourists are less likely to witness the spectacular **Mardi Gras Indians**, African American groups who gather on Mardi Gras morning to compete in chanting and dancing dressed in fabulous beaded and feathered costumes – sewed themselves over the previous year. For a chance of seeing the Indians, head to the Backstreet Cultural Museum in Tremé (see p.545) on Mardi Gras morning; this is also the meeting place for other black Mardi Gras groups including the "**skeleton**" gangs, who don bloody butcher's aprons and "wake the day" at dawn by beating bones on drums, and the **Baby Dolls**, grown women frolicking around in silky bonnets and bloomers.

Another New Orleans Mardi Gras ritual is the flinging of "**throws**". Teasing masked krewe members scatter beads, toys and doubloons (coins) from parade floats into the crowds, who beg, plead and scream for them.

tumbledown old building – with no bar, a/c or toilets, and just a few hard benches for seating – has long been lauded as the best place in New Orleans to hear trad jazz. The music is joyous, building steam as the night goes on – queues form well before the doors open. Thursday is brass band night. $15 cover. Cash only. Nightly sets every 45min 8–11pm.

Snug Harbor 626 Frenchmen St, Marigny ☎504 949 0696, ⓦsnugjazz.com. Sophisticated jazz club in an intimate, two-storey space. Regulars include Astral Project, who play cool modern jazz, clarinet maestro Dr Michael White and pianist Ellis Marsalis. Cover $15–25. Nightly shows 8pm & 10pm.

Spotted Cat 623 Frenchmen St, Marigny ☎504 943 3887, ⓦspottedcatmusicclub.com. With nightly roots music, the *Spotted Cat* has become the place to see the Cottonmouth Kings, whose high-octane twist on jubilant swing and trad is impossible not to dance to. No cover. Cash only. Mon–Thurs 4pm–2am, Sat & Sun 3pm–2am.

Three Muses 536 Frenchmen St, Marigny ☎504 252 4801, ⓦthethreemuses.com. Falling somewhere between a restaurant, a bar and a music venue, this kicking little jazz club has excellent tapas (try the lamb sliders with goat's cheese; $9), artisanal cocktails and terrific nightly live music. There's often a wait to get in. No cover, but a one-drink minimum. Mon, Wed & Sun 4–10pm, Thurs–Sat 4–11pm.

OTHER LIVE MUSIC

Chickie Wah Wah 2828 Canal St, Mid-City ☎504 304 4714, ⓦchickiewahwah.com. An intelligently selected mixed bag – folk, blues, brass and jazz – at this relatively upmarket club with retro folk art-meets-neon decor and a superb jukebox of local music. Unusually, many shows start early, at around 7 or 8pm. Cover varies. Mon–Thurs 11am–11pm, Fri & Sat 11am–1am.

Circle Bar 1032 St Charles Ave, CBD ☎504 588 2616, ⓦcirclebarneworleans.com. Painfully hip bar in a crumbling old house at Lee Circle. With an eclectic

The two weeks leading up to Mardi Gras are filled with processions, parties and balls. The fun starts early on Mardi Gras day, with **walking clubs** striding through uptown accompanied by raucous jazz on their ritualized bar crawls, and the skeletons (see above) gathering in Tremé. Zulu's big parade, in theory, sets off at 8.30am (but can be as much as 2hr late), followed by **Rex**. Across town, the Indians are gathering for their sacred Mardi Gras rituals, while the arty **St Ann walking parade** sets off from the Bywater to arrive in the Marigny at around 11am. Anyone is welcome to join them, as long as they are wearing something creative and/or surreal. The gay costume competition known as the **Bourbon Street awards** gets going at noon in the Quarter, while hipsters head back to the Marigny, where **Frenchmen Street** is ablaze with lavishly costumed carousers. The fun continues until midnight, when a siren wail heralds the arrival of a cavalcade of mounted police that sweeps through Bourbon Street and declares through megaphones that Mardi Gras is officially over.

OTHER NEW ORLEANS FESTIVALS

St Joseph's Day (March 19). Sicilian saint's day, at the midpoint of Lent. Altars of food are erected in churches all around town, and there's a parade. Celebrated in conjunction with the holiday, on the third Sunday in March ("Super Sunday") the Mardi Gras Indians (see p.555) take to the streets – their only official parade outside Mardi Gras.

French Quarter Festival (early April; ⓦfqfi.org). Superb free four-day music festival that rivals Jazz Fest for the quality and variety of music – and food – on offer.

Jazz Fest (two weekends, Fri–Sun & Thurs–Sun, end April/early May; ⓦnojazzfest.com). Enormous festival at the Fairgrounds Race Track, Mid-City, with stages hosting jazz, R&B, gospel, Afro-Caribbean, Cajun, blues and more, and evening performances in clubs all over town. Also features crafts and phenomenal food stands.

Southern Decadence (six days around Labor Day weekend; ⓦsoutherndecadence.net). Huge gay extravaganza, bringing around 100,000 party animals to the Quarter, with a costume parade of thousands on the Sunday afternoon.

Halloween (Oct 31). Thanks to the local passion for dressing up, New Orleans is a fabulous place to spend Halloween, with haunted houses, costume competitions, ghost tours and parades all over town.

Voodoo Experience (Halloween weekend; ⓦworshipthemusic.com). Three-day rock festival held in City Park with two hundred acts – from Nine Inch Nails to Calvin Harris, plus an eclectic span of local bands – performing to a mixed, high-spirited, Halloween-costumed crowd.

---

booking policy, from alt rock to bluegrass, it's renowned for resurrecting R&B legends from oblivion, and pulls a gorgeous, hard-partying crowd. Cover varies. Daily 4pm–2am.

Hi-Ho Lounge 2239 St Claude Ave ☎504 945 4446, ⓦhiholounge.net. On the fringes of Tremé, the Marigny and Bywater, this quirky place – vintage booths and an old Deco bar, domino games and table football – attracts a friendly crowd for everything from bluegrass jams to burlesque, hardcore punk, Mardi Gras Indians and old-school R&B. Cover varies. Daily 6pm–3am.

★ **Maple Leaf** 8316 Oak St, Uptown ☎504 866 9359, ⓦmapleleafbar.com. Legendary uptown bar with pressed-tin walls, a large dancefloor and a patio. It's a New Orleans favourite for really great blues, R&B, funk and brass bands; Rebirth's Tuesday-night gigs are a must. There's chess and pool, too. Cover varies. Daily 3pm–5am.

★ **One Eyed Jack's** 615 Toulouse St, French Quarter ☎504 569 8361, ⓦoneeyedjacks.net. Loosely conceived as a decadent cabaret lounge in old Bourbon St style, this hip bar and club presents a wide range of shows, including burlesque, trad jazz, rap battles, indie rock and punk to a friendly crowd. Cover varies. Check online for performance times.

★ **Rock 'n' Bowl** 3000 S Carrollton Ave, Mid-City ☎504 861 1700, ⓦrocknbowl.com. Its Mid-City location may be unprepossessing, but this eccentric and fun bowling alley-cum-music venue is an institution. Though it's especially heaving on Thursday – zydeco night ($12 cover) – it also books great local R&B, blues and swing, and the crowd is always lively. Bowling $24/hr per lane (up to six bowlers). Mon–Thurs & Sun 11.30am–midnight, Fri & Sat 11.30am–2am.

Tipitina's 501 Napoleon Ave, Uptown ☎504 895 8477, ⓦtipitinas.com. Legendary uptown venue, named after a Professor Longhair song, with a consistently good funk, R&B, brass, ska and reggae line-up. The Cajun *fais-do-do* (Sun 5–9pm; free lessons available) is fun, too. Cover $10–40. Check online for performance times.

8

The River Road and plantation country

The fastest roads out from New Orleans toward the west are speedy I-10 and US-61; you can also drive along the **River Road**, which hugs both banks of the Mississippi all the way to Baton Rouge, seventy miles upriver. It's not a particularly eventful drive, winding through flat, fertile farmland, but a series of bridges and ferries allows you to crisscross the water, stopping off and touring several restored antebellum **plantation homes** along the way.

Before the Civil War, these spectacular mansions were the focal points of the vast estates from where wealthy planters – or rather, their slaves – loaded cotton, sugar or indigo onto steamboats berthed virtually at their front doors. The superb Laura plantation excepted, **tours**, generally led by costumed guides, can skimp on details about the estates as a whole, and in particular their often vast slave populations. The cumulative effect can be overwhelming, so it's best to pick just one plantation or two.

Though you'd never guess it from the tourist brochures, hulking chemical plants dominate the River Road landscape. There are rural stretches where wide sugar-cane fields are interrupted only by moss-covered shacks – the prettiest views are around the small town of Convent, on the east bank of the – but you'll more often find yourself driving through straggling communities of boarded-up buildings.

San Francisco House

2646 Hwy-44 (River Rd), Garyville · Daily: April–Oct 9.30am–4.40pm; Nov–March 9am–4pm · $15 · ☎ 800 979 3370, ⓦ sanfranciscoplantation.org

In **Garyville**, 45 miles west of New Orleans, you'll come to the **San Francisco House**, on the north side of the river. Built in a style dubbed "Steamboat Gothic" by novelist Frances Parkinson Keyes, its rails, awnings and pillars evoke the graceful lines of a Mississippi showboat. The elaborate facade is matched by a gorgeous interior – a riot of pastoral trompe-l'oeils, floral motifs and Italian cherubs.

Laura plantation

2247 Hwy-18, Vacherie · Daily 10am–4pm; tours in French available · $20 · ☎ 888 799 7690, ⓦ lauraplantation.com

Crossing the river at **Lutcher**, the settlement a few miles beyond the San Francisco House, brings you to Vacherie and the fascinating **Laura plantation**. Rather than dwelling lovingly on priceless antiques, the tours here, which draw upon a wealth of historical documents – from **slave accounts** and photographs to private diaries – sketch a vivid picture of day-to-day plantation life in multicultural Louisiana.

Oak Alley

3645 Hwy-18, Vacherie · Nov–Feb Mon–Fri 9am–4.30pm, Sat & Sun 9am–5pm; March–Oct daily 9am–5pm · $20 · ☎ 800 442 5539, ⓦ oakalleyplantation.com

Four miles upriver from Laura, **Oak Alley**, the quintessential image of the antebellum plantation home, is an opulent Greek Revival mansion dating from 1839 – the magnificent oaks that form a canopy over the driveway are 150 years older, and rise up to 30ft in circumference.

Nottoway

31025 Hwy-1, White Castle · Daily 9am–4pm · $20, $8 grounds only · ☎ 800 979 3370, ⓦ nottoway.com

Twenty-seven miles south of Baton Rouge on the west bank, **Nottoway** (1859) is the largest surviving plantation home in the South, a huge, white Italianate edifice with

64 rooms. The interior is done up to the hilt, with twelve marble fireplaces, imposing antique furniture and a breathtaking ballroom with crystal chandeliers.

River Road African American Museum

406 Charles St, Donaldsonville • Wed–Sat 10am–5pm, Sun 1–5pm • $4 • ☎ 225 474 5553, ⊌ africanamericanmuseum.org

On the west bank, in the small town of **Donaldsonville**, the **River Road African American Museum** offers an alternative view of the region's history, highlighting its cuisine, music, the Underground Railroad, Reconstruction and the culture of the free blacks.

ARRIVAL AND TOURS	THE RIVER ROAD AND PLANTATION COUNTRY
By car To get to the River Road from New Orleans, take I-10 west to exit 220, turn onto I-310 and follow it to Hwy-48, on the east bank (above the river). This shortly becomes Hwy-44, or the River Road. For the west bank (below the river), cross Destrehan Bridge onto Hwy-18 rather than branching onto Hwy-48.	**By tour bus** A number of companies have regular shuttles from New Orleans to plantation country. Cajun Encounters (☎ 866 928 6877, ⊌ cajunencounters.com) and Cajun Pride (☎ 504 467 0758, ⊌ cajunprideswamptours.com) are two of the best.

Baton Rouge

When French explorers came upon the site of **BATON ROUGE** in 1699, they found poles smeared in animal blood to designate the hunting grounds of the Houma and Bayou Goula tribes. The area on these shallow bluffs therefore appeared on French maps as *Baton Rouge* – "red stick". Now capital of Louisiana and a key port, Baton Rouge is a relaxed city for its size. Even the presence of the state's largest **universities**, LSU and Southern, has done surprisingly little to raise the town anywhere much above "sleepy" status.

Surrounded by fifty acres of showpiece gardens, the magnificent Art Deco **Louisiana State Capitol** at 900 N 3rd St (daily 8am–4.30pm; free) serves as a monument to **Huey Long**, the "Kingfish", the larger-than-life populist Democratic governor who ordered its construction in 1930 and was assassinated in its corridors just five years later. Mark Twain referred to Baton Rouge's **Old State Capitol** (in use from 1850 to 1932), 100 North Blvd, as "that monstrosity on the Mississippi". A crenellated, pseudo-Gothic pile on a mound overlooking the river, it's worth a look for the **Museum of Political History** (Tues–Sat 9am–4pm; free, ☎ 800 488 2968, ⊌ louisianaoldstatecapitol.org), which illuminates Louisiana's scandal-ridden political past. The **LSU Rural Life Museum**, 4560 Essen Lane, just off I-10 southeast of downtown (daily 8am–5pm; $9; ☎ 225 765 2437, ⊌ rurallife.lsu.edu), re-creates pre-industrial Louisiana life through its restored buildings – among them a plantation house, slave cottages and a grist mill – spread over 25 sultry acres.

ARRIVAL, GETTING AROUND AND INFORMATION	BATON ROUGE
By bus Greyhound (☎ 225 383 3811), and connecting buses from New Orleans's Amtrak, come in at 1253 Florida St, a 15min walk from downtown.	**By cab** Try Bayou Taxi (☎ 225 274 0608). **Visitor centre** 359 3rd St, three blocks from the river (Mon–Fri 8am–5pm; ☎ 225 383 1825, ⊌ visitbatonrouge.com).

ACCOMMODATION AND EATING

Magpie Café 3205 Perkins Rd ☎ 225 366 6885. Sun-drenched coffee shop with colourful, wood-panelled walls, organic baked goods, pressed panini sandwiches and a hip clientele. The menu changes daily; think spicy carrot-ginger soup or turkey, brie and pear on a crusty ciabatta. Mon–Sat 7am–5.30pm.

Tony's Seafood 5215 Plank Rd ☎ 225 357 9669, ⊌ tonyseafood.com. Great local market with two perennially long queues: one for the region's freshest seafood (much of it still flipping its fins), the other for to-go boxes piled high with

8

red beans and rice, crawfish étouffée and superb boudin balls. Grab some hot sauce and beignet mix for friends back home before heading to the register. Mon–Thurs 8am–7.30pm, Fri & Sat 8am–8pm, Sun 8am–7pm.

The Stockade Bed and Breakfast 8860 Highland Rd

☎ 888 900 5430, ⓦ thestockade.com. Relaxed B&B with six traditional rooms set in a hacienda-style property that boasts exposed beams, 30 acres of woodland and an excellent art collection. A sumptuous daily breakfast is included in the rate. **$135**

Cajun country

Cajun country stretches across southern Louisiana from Houma in the east, via **Lafayette**, the hub of the region, into Texas. It's a region best enjoyed away from the larger towns, by visiting the many old-style hamlets that, despite modernization, can still be found cut off from civilization in soupy bayous, coastal marshes and inland swamps.

Cajuns are descended from the French colonists of Acadia, part of Nova Scotia, which was taken by the British in 1713. The Catholic **Acadians**, who had fished, hunted and farmed for more than a century, refused to renounce their faith and swear

---

CAJUN FESTIVALS

Held almost weekly it seems, **Cajun festivals** provide an enjoyable way to experience the food and music of the region. Note that for the larger events, it's a good idea to reserve a room in advance. The following is merely a sampler; for full details, check with any tourist office in the area.

Mardi Gras (Feb/March; ⓦ louisianatravel.com/cajun-mardi-gras). Cajun Carnival differs from its city cousin; although there are private balls, parties and formal parades, it is a far more countrified and very family-oriented affair. There's plenty of music and street dancing, of course, and villages like Eunice, Church Point and Mamou are the scene of the mischievous, somewhat surreal *Courir du Mardi Gras*.

Catfish Festival, Washington, near Opelousas (spring, but dates vary each year, so check the website; ⓦ townofwashingtonla.org). A lively weekend festival featuring arts, crafts, parades, catfish cookoffs and lots of zydeco.

World Championship Crawfish Étouffée Cookoff, Eunice (last Sun in March, or the third Sun, if Easter falls on the last one; ⓦ eunice-la.com). *The* place to taste the very best mudbugs, accompanied by great local music and a fierce spirit of competition among the scores of teams.

Festival International de Louisiane, Lafayette (last full week in April; ⓦ festivalinternational .com). Huge, free five-day festival with big-name participants from all over the French-speaking world, celebrating a wealth of indigenous music, culture and food.

Breaux Bridge Crawfish Festival, Breaux Bridge (first full weekend of May, Fri–Sun; ⓦ bbcrawfest.com). Crawfish-eating contests, étouffée cookoffs and mudbug races, along with music, craft stalls and dancing.

Opelousas Spice and Music Festival, Opelousas (June; ⓦ OpelousasSpiceAndMusicFestival .com). Two-day extravaganza of zydeco, fiddle jams and cookoffs.

Southwest Louisiana Zydeco Music Festival, Plaisance, near Opelousas (Sat before Labor Day; ⓦ zydeco.org). A month of zydeco-related events culminates in a full day of top zydeco performers playing turbo-fuelled "black Creole" music. Also regional cuisine, arts and crafts, talks, dancing and workshops.

Mamou Cajun Music Festival, Mamou (Fri & Sat in early Sept; ⓦ mamoucajunmusicfestival .com). Traditional live music, food, crafts, games and boudin-eating contests.

Festivals Acadiens et Créoles, Lafayette (late Sept or early Oct; ⓦ festivalsacadiens.com). Huge three-day festival, with Cajun, zydeco and traditional French bands, as well as indigenous crafts and food.

Louisiana Yambilee, Opelousas (last week in Oct; ⓦ yambilee.com). Opelousas celebrates the sweet potato in a big way, with food stalls, auctions, zydeco music, competitions and the marvelously named Lil' Miss Yum Yum beauty contest.

allegiance to the English king, and in 1755 the British expelled them all, separating families and burning towns. About 2500 ended up in French Louisiana, where they were given land to set up small farming communities, enabling them to rebuild the culture they had left behind. Hunting, farming and trapping, they lived in relative isolation until the 1940s, when major roads were built, immigrants from other states poured in to work in the **oil** business, and **Cajun music**, popularized by local musicians such as accordionist Iry Lejeune, came to national attention. Since then, the history of the Cajuns has continued to be one of struggle. The erosion of coastal wetlands threatens the existence of entire communities; the silting up of the Atchafalaya Basin is having adverse effects on fishing and shrimping; and not only are coastal towns in the firing line of devastating hurricanes, including **Katrina**, that hurtle up from the Gulf of Mexico, but also catastrophic oil spills, such as the **BP disaster** of 2010. After Roosevelt's administration decreed that all American children should speak English in schools, French was practically wiped out in Cajun country, and the local patois of the older inhabitants, with its strong African influences, was kept alive primarily by music. Since the 1980s, CODOFIL (the Council for Development of French in Louisiana) has been devoted to preserving the region's indigenous **language** and culture, and today you will find many signs, brochures and shopfronts written in French.

Cajun and zydeco **fais-do-dos** – dances, with live bands, held mostly on weekends – are great fun, and visitors will find plenty of opportunity to dance, whether at a restaurant, a club or one of the region's many **festivals**.

Lafayette and around

LAFAYETTE, 135 miles northwest of New Orleans on I-10, is geographically central in Cajun country, and the key city for its oil business. Originally named Vermilionville, after the orangey bayou nearby, it was renamed in 1844 in honour of the Marquis de Lafayette, the aristocratic French hero of the American Revolution. Today it's a sprawling city with a small-town feel, and is particularly vibrant during the superb **Festival International de Louisiane** and **Festivals Acadiens et Créoles** (see box opposite); at other times, you could use it as a base for exploring the swamps, bayous and dance halls of the region. There are plenty of smaller places nearby, especially in and around **Breaux Bridge**, that offer something a little more personal.

Cathedral of St John the Evangelist

914 St John St • Mon–Thurs 8.30am–4pm, Fri 8.30am–noon • Free • ☎ 337 232 1322, ⓦ saintjohncathedral.org

In the centre, such as it is, of Lafayette stands the Romanesque **Cathedral of St John the Evangelist**, and the old **cemetery**, where the crumbling, raised graves include that of Jean Mouton, the town's Cajun founder. Each of the magnificent branches of the 500-year-old **Cathedral Oak**, spreading over 200ft, weighs seventy tons.

Alexandre Mouton House and Lafayette Museum

1122 Lafayette St • Guided tours Tues–Sat 10am–4pm • $5 • ☎ 337 234 2208

Three blocks from the cathedral, the winsome **Alexandre Mouton House and Lafayette Museum** was the "Sunday home" – a townhouse used after Mass, before the family returned to their plantation – of Alexandre Mouton, Louisiana's first Democratic governor and the son of Lafayette's founder. It's now filled with family memorabilia, Civil War relics and Cajun Mardi Gras costumes.

Vermilionville

300 Fisher Rd, across from the airport • Tues–Sun 10am–4pm • $10 • ☎ 337 233 4077, ⓦ vermilionville.org

Lafayette has two excellent reconstructions of early Cajun communities. **Vermilionville** is the best, exploring the culture of the early Creoles as well as the Cajuns. Set in 23 attractive acres on the Bayou Vermilion, it's a living history site, filled with authentic old buildings occupied by craftspeople using traditional skills. A large replica of an old cotton gin serves as a **theatre** for noisy *fais-do-dos* and festivals. The **restaurant** cranks out good Cajun lunches, and offers cooking classes.

Acadian Cultural Center and Acadian Village

Next to Vermilionville, at 501 Fisher Rd, the **Acadian Cultural Center**, in the **Jean Lafitte National Historical Park and Preserve** (daily 8am–5pm; free; ☎337 232 0789, ⓦnps.gov/jela), offers good background on the Cajuns, with seasonal boat tours of the bayou. Further southwest, Lafayette's second folk-life museum, the smaller **Acadian Village**, 200 Greenleaf Drive (Mon–Sat 10am–4pm; $8; ☎337 981 2364, ⓦacadianvillage.org), depicts early nineteenth-century Cajun life along the bayous.

Breaux Bridge

You could easily drive through tiny **BREAUX BRIDGE**, eight miles east of Lafayette, and miss it, which would be a shame. Characterized by an old-fashioned main street, a crawfish-emblazoned steel bridge over the Bayou Teche, and a handful of B&Bs, restaurants and music venues, it makes an appealing base for **swamp tours** (see p.565), and for exploring the **Lake Martin nature reserve**, three miles south on Hwy-31, where there's an abundance of **birdlife** year-round – and the odd alligator.

ARRIVAL, GETTING AROUND AND INFORMATION   LAFAYETTE AND AROUND

By plane Lafayette's airport (☎337 266 4400, ⓦlftairport .com) is 3 miles southeast of town on Hwy-90. Public transport into the centre is limited; take a cab.

By bus and train Both Greyhound (☎337 235 1541) and Amtrak arrive at 100 Lee Ave.

By car To get the best from the area you'll need a car, as the dance halls, restaurants and hotels are spread out, and the local bus system is of little use to visitors.

By taxi Try Dixie Cab (☎337 235 7517).

Visitor centre 1400 NW Evangeline Thruway, off I-10 (Mon–Fri 8.30am–5pm, Sat & Sun 9am–5pm; ☎800 346 1958, ⓦlafayettetravel.com). The website is full of useful information on Cajun culture.

ACCOMMODATION

Chain hotels line Evangeline Thruway just south of I-10, US-90 and Hwy-182 toward New Iberia, but if you are after something with more character you'll need to head further out to the friendly hamlet of Breaux Bridge, just 8 miles east.

Bayou Cabins 100 W Mills Ave/Hwy-94, Breaux Bridge ☎337 332 6158, ⓦbayoucabins.com. Fourteen rustic cabins – most of which date from the nineteenth century – backing onto Bayou Teche, a 125-mile long waterway. It's run by the owners of *Bayou Boudin and Cracklin'* café, and rates include a fantastic Cajun breakfast. You're near the highway here, so there is some traffic noise. **$60**

Bayou Teche Bed and Breakfast 205 Washington St, Breaux Bridge ☎337 332 1049, ⓦaubayouteche bedandbreakfast.com. Overlooking the bayou, this historic guesthouse with plenty of personality has been welcoming travellers (many arriving from the waterway) since the 1850s. Though laden with antiques, the rooms feel cheerful and casual rather than fussy. There's zydeco on the radio, a huge communal table, fresh pastries at breakfast and a jug of wine to toast your arrival. **$95**

Blue Moon Guest House and Saloon 215 E Convent St, Lafayette ☎877 766 2583, ⓦbluemoonpresents .com. Cheerful hostel and guesthouse, in a nineteenth-century home on a nice street downtown, with two dorms, a two-bedroom bungalow and four private rooms. The main appeal is the back porch saloon, with regular Cajun, zydeco and bluegrass gigs and a full bar. Rates increase for festivals, when it's a gathering place for local musicians. Dorms **$18**, rooms **$70**, bungalow **$250**

Isabelle Inn 1130 Berard St, Breaux Bridge ☎337 412 0455, ⓦisabelleinn.com. Superb five-room B&B done up with silk drapes, posh linens and four-poster beds. After a day of *fais-do-do*, relax on the manicured grounds with a swimming pool, gardens and a swing dangling from the century-old live oak tree. **$175**

★ **Maison Madeleine** 1015 John D Hebert Drive, Breaux Bridge ☎337 332 4555, ⓦmaisonmadeleine .com. Dating to the 1840s, this woodland cottage done up with a designer's eye is tucked among the egret nests and occasional stray gator of Lake Martin reserve. The two lovely rooms pop with colour and art; breakfast sees a hearty American feast. There's a wide porch and a tropical courtyard. **$175**

EATING

Eating Cajun food is one of the big appeals of visiting the region. Although it bears resemblances to the Creole cuisine you'll find in New Orleans – lots of seafood, rice, rich tomatoey sauces and gumbos – this is more rustic, often spicy, and using plenty of pork. At lunchtime, takeaway boudin (spicy sausage made with rice) is a treat, as are rich pork cracklin' and salty hogshead cheese.

Blue Dog Café 1211 W Pinhook Rd, Lafayette ☎337 237 0005, ⓦbluedogcafe.com. Popular, touristy spot for Cajun-Creole food – the crabmeat au gratin is great – surrounded by the distinctive blue dog paintings of Cajun artist George Rodrigue. Mon–Thurs 11am–2pm & 5–9pm, Fri 11am–2pm & 5–10pm, Sat 5–10pm, Sun 10.30am–2pm (with music).

Buck & Johnny's 100 Berard St, Breaux Bridge ☎337 442 6630, ⓦbuckandjohnnys.com. Right in the heart of town, this chummy, brick-walled pizzeria fills up fast with locals munching on Cajun cobb salad (spinach, shrimp, crawfish, tomato, avocado and bacon; $10) and sizzling rounds of "bayou blast" pizza (alligator sausage, crawfish and shrimp; $10.50). Tues–Thurs & Sun 11am–2pm & 5–9pm, Fri & Sat 11am–2pm & 5–10pm.

★ **Café des Amis** 140 E Bridge St, Breaux Bridge ☎337 332 5273, ⓦcafedesamis.com. This friendly, arty restaurant is a buzzing community hub, and the Cajun-Creole food, with lots of creamy crawfish concoctions, is divine. Live music evenings (Wed), zydeco breakfasts (Sat 8.30–11.30am) and "mimosas & music" (Sun 11am–1pm). Tues 11am–2pm, Wed & Thurs 11am–9pm, Fri & Sat 7.30am–9pm, Sun 8am–2pm.

★ **The French Press** 214 E Vermilion St, Lafayette ☎337 233 9449, ⓦthefrenchpresslafayette.com. Wittily named – the building was originally a printing plant – this lively café fires off creative breakfasts such as the "baby breesus", three biscuit sliders crammed with

boudin and drizzled with cane syrup ($10.50). The ambience is stylish and airy, with peeling stucco walls, high ceilings and quirky oil paintings. Be prepared for a wait. Tues–Thurs 7am–2pm, Fri 7am–2pm & 5.30–9pm, Sat 9am–2pm & 5.30–9pm, Sun 9am–2pm.

Johnson's Boucaniere 1111 St John St, Lafayette ☎337 269 8878, ⓦjohnsonsboucaniere.com. Family-owned and operated since the 1930s, this is the place to come for mouthwatering boudin, smoked meats and impossibly tender barbecue. The grilled cheese, stuffed with pulled pork and brisket, is another tempting speciality. No indoor seating, but there's a covered patio and friendly service – a boon when handling the long lines. Tues–Thurs 10am–6pm, Fri 10am–9pm, Sat 7am–9pm.

Prejean's 3480 I-49 N, Lafayette ☎337 896 3247, ⓦprejeans.com. Barn-like, touristy restaurant offering delicious, gourmet Cajun food – try the shrimp sassafras and the gumbos – nightly live music (from 7pm), and dancing. Mon–Thurs & Sun 7am–9pm, Fri & Sat 7am–10pm.

Taco Sisters 407 Johnston St, Lafayette ☎337 234 8226, ⓦtacosisters.com. California-style taqueria, serving a healthy take on traditional fillings (all the tacos are stuffed with greens, chopped apples and carrots). The fish taco boasts house-smoked tuna; the brisket is another delicious bet. Drive-through only (though there are picnic tables); parking can be a pain. Mon–Fri 11am–6pm, Sat 11am–2pm.

North of Lafayette

North of Lafayette, the **Cajun prairie** has been described by folklorist Alan Lomax as the "Cajun cultural heartland". A patchwork of rice and soybean fields scattered with crawfish ponds, the region has a few tiny towns of interest.

Opelousas

Sleepy old **OPELOUSAS**, twenty miles north of Lafayette on I-49, was capital of Louisiana for a short period during the Civil War, and now has several claims to fame. It was the boyhood home of Jim Bowie, Texas Revolutionary hero and inventor of the Bowie knife; the birthplace of the great zydeco musician **Clifton Chenier**; and is the **yam** capital of the universe. It also hosts some good festivals (see box, p.560), and is a hub for zydeco music. You can find out more at the quirky **Opelousas Museum**, 315 N Main St (Mon–Fri 8am–4.30pm; free; ☎337 948 2589, ⓦcityofopelousas.com) – which tells stories such as how outlaw Clyde Barrow (of Bonnie and Clyde fame) got his last shave in town before being shot dead by the FBI in northern Louisiana.

Back in Time 123 W Landry St ☎337 942 2413. Right off the central square, this quaint café serves excellent salads, soups (try the corn-crab-shrimp variety; $6), and sandwiches named after film icons. The small dining room is jam-packed with with nostalgic knick-knacks. Service is very friendly. Mon–Sat 11am–2.30pm.

Eunice

To learn a little about the Cajun prairie, head for friendly **EUNICE**, about twenty miles west of Opelousas. The **Prairie Acadian Cultural Center** at the **Jean Lafitte National Historical Park**, 250 W Park Ave (Tues–Fri 8am–5pm, Sat 8am–6pm; free; ☎504 589 2133, ⓦnps.gov/jela), holds far-reaching displays on local life, with live Cajun music, dancing and cookery demonstrations. There's more music at the **Cajun Music Hall of Fame**, 240 S C.C. Duson Drive (Tues–Sat: late May to early Sept 9am–5pm; early Sept to late May 8.30am–4.30pm; free; ☎337 457 6534), which features accordions, steel guitars, fiddles and triangles among its memorabilia. If time is short, choose these two over the **Eunice Museum**, next to the Hall of Fame at 220 S C.C. Duson Drive (Tues–Sat 9am–5pm; free; ☎337 457 6540) – though this too has its charms; it's an old train depot crammed with a ragbag of local memorabilia.

CAJUN AND ZYDECO MUSIC VENUES

It's easy to "pass a good time" in Cajun country, especially if you're here at the weekend, when the *fais-do-dos* are traditionally held, or during any of its many festivals (see p.560). **Cajun music** is a jangling, infectious melange of nasal vocals backed by jumping accordion, violin and triangle, fuelled by traces of country, swing, jazz and blues. **Zydeco** is similar, but sexier, more blues-based, and usually played by black Creole musicians. Though songs are in French, the patois heard in both bears only a passing resemblance to the language spoken in France. Music is never performed without space for dancing; everyone can join in. As well as the popular restaurants *Café des Amis* and *Prejean's* (see p.563), plus the *Blue Moon Guest House* (see p.562), **venues** include record stores, river landings and the streets themselves. Sadly, old-time zydeco dance halls are dying out, but a few still exist. Check the music **listings** in the free weekly *Times of Acadiana* (ⓦtheadvertiser.com) or *Independent* (ⓦtheind.com); log onto ⓦzydecoonline.com, or simply look for signs saying "French dance here tonight".

Angelle's Whiskey River Landing 1365 Henderson Levee Rd, Henderson, Breaux Bridge ☎337 228 2277, ⓦwhiskeyriverlanding.net. Lively Cajun and zydeco parties on Sunday afternoons (4–8pm).

★ **Fred's Lounge** 420 6th St, Mamou, 10 miles north of Eunice ☎337 468 5411. Welcoming lounge presided over by the delightful Tante Sue, with live radio, dancing and lots of drinking. Mon–Thurs & Sun 11am–9pm, Fri & Sat 11am–10pm.

La Poussière 1301 Grand Pointe Ave, Breaux Bridge ☎337 332 1721, ⓦlapoussiere.com. The old folks' favourite, this venerable dance hall – where most people speak French – hosts *fais-do-dos* (Sat night & Sun afternoon).

Pont Breaux's 325 W Mills Ave, Breaux Bridge ☎337 332 4648, ⓦpontbreauxscajunrestaurant.com. You'll find great gumbo, live music and nightly dancing at this Cajun restaurant and classic haunt. Mon–Thurs & Sun 11am–9pm, Fri & Sat 11am–10pm.

Randol's 2320 Kaliste Saloom Rd, Lafayette ☎337 981 7080, ⓦrandols.com. Some call it a tourist trap, but if you want to hear live music any night of the week, this convivial seafood restaurant is a fun place to come and kick up your heels with a two-step. Mon–Thurs & Sun 5–9.30pm, Fri & Sat 5–10.30pm.

Rendezvous des Cajuns Liberty Center for Performing Arts, S 2nd St and Park Ave, Eunice ☎337 457 7389, ⓦeunice-la.com. Family-oriented and hugely popular live Cajun/zydeco radio and TV show, mostly in French. Cover $5. Sat 6–7.30pm.

★ **Savoy Music Center** 4413 Hwy-190 E, 3 miles east of Eunice ☎337 457 9563, ⓦsavoymusiccenter .com. The free jam sessions (Sat 9am–noon) at this Cajun record store and accordion workshop are a local institution. Store open Tues–Fri 9am–5pm.

Slim's Y-Ki-Ki 8393 Hwy-182 N, Opelousas ☎337 942 6242. Famed old locals' venue for zydeco music and dancing. Usually Fri & Sat but call to check.

SWAMP TOURS

Swamp tours are available from many landings in the **Atchafalaya Basin**; you'll pass numerous signs pinned to the old cypress trees along the roadside. The basin is an eerie place: in some places cars cut right across on the enormous concrete I-10 above, and old houseboats lie abandoned. The best tours take you further out, to the backwoods; wherever you go, you'll see scores of fishing boats and plenty of wildlife, including sunbathing alligators.

Bayou Teche Experience 317 E Bridge St, Breaux Bridge ☎ 337 366 0337, ⓦ bayoutechexperience.com. Glide through Lake Martin (see p.562) on a kayak ($40/half day); the silent craft get you close to the ample wildlife. Also offers biologist-led nature and birding tours (4hr; $100 for 5 people), Cajun heritage tours (4hr; $100 for 5 people), bike rental ($30) and kayak shuttle services ($10).

Cajun Country Swamp Tours 1209 Rookery Rd, Breaux Bridge ☎ 337 319 0010, ⓦ cajuncountryswamptours.com. Guides navigate small crawfish skiffs through the bird-rich Cypress Island Swamp – lots of opportunity for alligator-spotting (2hr; $20).

★ **Norbert LeBlanc** Rookery Rd, Breaux Bridge ☎ 337 654 1215. Led by a legendary Cajun octogenarian (and former alligator hunter), soft-spoken Norbert, who knows the swamp like the back of his hand and boasts an in-depth knowledge of its creatures and quirks. Tours (2hr; $20) are offered in both English and French.

ACCOMMODATION AND EATING   **EUNICE**

Allison's Hickory Pitt 501 W Laurel Ave (Hwy-190) ☎ 337 457 9218. Wonderful home-smoked barbecue, served in a tumbledown shack right off the highway. Hours vary; give them a call to double-check. Fri–Sun 11am–2pm.

★ **Le Village Guesthouse B&B** 121 Seale Lane ☎ 337 457 3573, ⓦ levillagehouse.com. Surrounded by lush foliage, this Cajun hideaway has immaculate guest quarters bedecked with patchwork quilts and cheery

antiques. The lovely owner cooks a mean breakfast and has great advice on local happenings. **$115**

Ruby's 123 S 2nd St ☎ 337 550 7665. Right downtown, *Ruby's* dishes up home-cooked Cajun food in a vintage setting. It's a great spot for plate lunches stacked high with stewed catfish, sweet carrots and creamed potatoes. Mon & Tues 6am–2pm, Wed & Thurs 6am–2pm & 5–9pm, Fri Thurs 6am–2pm & 5–10pm, Sat 5–10pm.

South of Lafayette

South of Lafayette, the towns are less immediately welcoming than those in the prairie, but the surroundings are undeniably atmospheric: this is **bayou country**, a marshy expanse of rivers and lakes dominated by the mighty Atchafalaya swamp, where the soupy green waters creep right up to the edges of the highway. The economy is based on fishing and shrimping, with hunting in the forests and sugar fields, but it's also a semi-industrial landscape, with a web of oil pipelines running beneath the waterways, and refineries and corrugated-iron shacks sharing space with white Catholic churches.

St Martinville

The main town of interest south of Lafayette is **ST MARTINVILLE**, off US-90 eighteen miles south of town. Settled in 1765 on the Bayou Teche, this was a major port of entry for exiled Acadians. The **Museum of the Acadian Memorial** (daily 10am–4.30pm; $3; ☎ 337 394 2258, ⓦ acadianmemorial.org) pays tribute to the thousands of refugees displaced from Canada to Louisiana between 1764 and 1788; part of the same complex, the **African American Museum** focuses on the arrival of enslaved Africans into southwest Louisiana during the 1700s, the emergence of free people of colour and the violence of Reconstruction.

ACCOMMODATION AND EATING   **ST MARTINVILLE**

Old Castillo 220 Evangeline Blvd ☎ 337 394 4010, ⓦ oldcastillo.com. Down by the bayou, this spacious, central B&B (dating to 1827) has sun-drenched rooms with

four-poster beds and hand-stitched quilts. The inn sits beside a majestic oak tree – the Evangeline Oak – immortalized in a poem by Henry Wadsworth Longfellow. **$80**

8

St. John Restaurant 211 E Bridge St ☏ 337 394 9994. Right in the heart of things, this little down-home Cajun restaurant has juicy steaks, checked tablecloths and walls lined with local art. The food is superb; be sure not to miss the crab cakes, a house speciality. Mon & Tues 11am–2pm, Wed–Fri 11am–2pm & 5–9pm, Sat 5–9pm.

Northern Louisiana

Northern Louisiana is at the heart of the region known as the **Ark-La-Tex**, where the cottonfields and soft vocal drawl of the Deep South Bible Belt merges with the ranches, oil and country music of Texas and the forested hills of Arkansas. Settled by the Scottish and Irish after the Louisiana Purchase, the area is strongly Baptist, with less of a penchant for fun than southern Louisiana, though it does share its profusion of **festivals**.

Angola Prison

Museum Tues–Fri 8am–4.30pm, Sat 9am–5pm • Free **Rodeos** Every Sun in Oct and during a two-day event in April • $15; reservations required • ⓦ angolarodeo.com

Isolated at the end of the long and lonely Hwy-60, hemmed in by the Tunica foothills and the Mississippi River sixty miles northwest of Baton Rouge, **Angola** – or "the farm" as it is commonly known – is the most famous maximum-security prison in the United States. Previously a byword for brutality and desperation, in 1995, the facility was transformed with the inauguration of warden Burl Cain into a model prison known for its strong religious slant. Famous inmates have included blues singer **Leadbelly**, who, as Huddy Ledbetter, served here in the 1930s; today, it holds about five thousand prisoners. Most of the men are lifers, and around a hundred of them are on Death Row. Outside the main gate, the **Angola Museum** offers a fascinating, if uncomfortable, insight into this complex place. Fading photos and newspapers reveal appalling prison conditions; the prodding sticks and belts used to beat convicts bring it closer to home. Since 1970, Angola has staged a **prisoner rodeo** every Sunday in October, a gladiatorial spectacle which draws thousands. These are extraordinary affairs, the crowds baying while lifers are flung, gored or trampled in their struggle for glory or just a simple change of scene.

Natchitoches and around

Tiny **NATCHITOCHES** (pronounced "Nakitish"), in the sleepy cottonfields of the Cane River, is the oldest European settlement in Louisiana, having begun life as a French trading post in 1714. With its lovingly restored Creole architecture, Natchitoches's **Front Street**, on the river, bears a passing resemblance to New Orleans's French Quarter – its lacy iron balconies, spiral staircases and cobbled courtyards complemented by old-style stores. Fleurs-de-lis on the **St Denis Walk of Honor** commemorate celebrities with local connections, such as John Wayne, Clementine Hunter (see opposite) and the cast of the movie *Steel Magnolias*, which was set and filmed here in 1988.

Cane River National Heritage Area

Hwy-119 • ☏ 318 356 5555, ⓦ nps.gov/crha

The **Cane River National Heritage Area**, a collection of restored plantation homes, churches and forts, stretches for 35 miles south from Natchitoches. Head first for the fascinating **Melrose Plantation**, on Hwy-119 (Tues–Sun 10am–5pm; $10), which was granted in 1794 to Marie Thérèse Coincoin, a freed slave, by her owner, Thomas Metoyer – the father of ten of her fourteen children. Coincoin expanded the original grounds into an 800-acre plantation; she was later able to buy freedom for two of her children and one of her grandchildren. Around 1900, enterprising Melrose owner

"Miss Cammie" Henry turned the crumbling plantation into an arts community, visited by painters and writers such as William Faulkner and John Steinbeck. In the 1940s, a black Melrose cook, **Clementine Hunter**, began to paint vivid images of life on and around the plantation; her works, many of which are on show here, have since become valuable pieces of folk art.

INFORMATION

NATCHITOCHES

Visitor centre 780 Front St (Mon–Sat 9am–5pm; ☎ 800 259 1714, ⓦ natchitoches.net); provides self-guided walking tours of historic downtown.

ACCOMMODATION AND EATING

Jefferson House 229 Second St, by the Cane River Lake ☎ 318 352 5834, ⓦ jeffersonhousebnb.com. Cosy, waterfront B&B with two spotless rooms furnished with antiques; nice extras include fireplaces and alfresco seating. Walkable to town. $120

Lasyone's 622 Second St ☎ 318 352 3353, ⓦ lasyones .com. The best place to eat in town, specializing in delicious meat pies, cream pies, red beans and sausage and fresh, crumbly cornbread. Mon–Sat 7am–3pm.

8

Texas

FORT WORTH

9 Texas

Still cherishing the memory that it was from 1836 to 1845 an independent nation, Texas stands proudly apart from the rest of the USA. While the sheer size of the state – 700 miles from east to west and more than 800 from top to bottom – gives it great geographical diversity, its 25 million residents are firmly bound together by a shared history and culture. Though the fervent state pride on show just about everywhere might seem a touch extreme to outsiders, Texas undeniably has a lot going for it.

The coastline of Texas curves southward more than 350 miles from Port Arthur, on the Louisiana border (a petrochemical town and birthplace of Janis Joplin) to the delta of the Rio Grande, which snakes northwest to form a 900-mile natural border with Mexico. Encompassed in this eastern section of the state is an interesting mix of big-city life and rural, backwoods culture.

The swampy, forested **east** is more like Louisiana than the pretty **Hill Country** or the agricultural plains of the northern **Panhandle**, while the tropical **Gulf Coast** has little in common with the mountainous **deserts** of the west. Changes in **climate** are dramatic: snow is common in the Panhandle, whereas the humidity of Houston is often unbearably thick.

There are 28 cities with a population of 100,000 or more, and each of the major tourist destinations is unique. Hispanic **San Antonio**, for example, with its Mexican population and rich history, has a laidback feel absent from commerce-driven **Houston** or **Dallas**, while trendy **Austin** revels in a lively music scene and an underground DIY ethos. One thing shared by the whole of Texas is **state pride**: Texas is a special place and its friendly residents know it.

Brief history

Early inhabitants of Texas included the Caddo in the east and nomadic Coahuiltecans further south. The **Comanche**, who arrived from the Rockies in the 1600s, soon found themselves at war when the **Spanish** ventured in looking for gold. In the 1700s, the Spanish began to build **missions** and **forts**, although these had minimal impact on the indigenous population's nomadic way of life. When Mexico won its independence from Spain in 1821, it took Texas as part of the deal. At first, the Mexicans were keen to open up their land and offered generous incentives to settlers. Stephen F. Austin established Anglo-American colonies in the Brazos and Colorado River valleys. However, the Mexican leader, Santa Anna, soon became alarmed by Anglo aspirations to autonomy, and his increasing restrictions led to the eight-month **Texas Revolution** of 1835–36.

The short-lived **Republic of Texas**, which included territory now in Oklahoma, Kansas, New Mexico, Colorado and Wyoming, served to define the state's identity. In 1845, Texas joined the Union on the understanding that it could secede whenever it wished; this antiquated provision has resurfaced in modern-day Texas politics. The influence, especially in the north and east, of settlers from the Southern states and their

MUSIC FESTIVAL, AUSTIN

Highlights

❶ The Rio Grande Valley Tiny, historic border towns dot one of the least-visited regions of the state. **See p.582**

❷ Catching a concert in Austin The live music capital of the US and a hotbed for Americana, outlaw country and the blues, with enough music venues to keep any visitor busy for weeks. **See p.588**

❸ San Antonio's River Walk Spend a few hours strolling along this scenic cobblestone path lined by many of the city's best restaurants and bars. **See p.592**

❹ Fort Worth From cattle drives in the rootin'-tootin' Stockyards, to world-class galleries in the Cultural District, Fort Worth is Texas' best-kept secret. **See p.601**

❺ Marfa An improbable minimalist arts community in the middle of the West Texas desert. **See p.609**

❻ Hiking in Big Bend National Park The Rio Grande rushes through astonishing canyons in this remote wilderness, crisscrossed by some of the best hiking trails in the USA. **See p.610**

HIGHLIGHTS ARE MARKED ON THE MAP ON P.572

9

attendant slave-centred cotton economy resulted in Texas joining the **Confederacy** during the Civil War (1860–65). During Reconstruction, settlers from both the North and the South began to pour in, and the phrase "Gone to Texas" was applied to anyone fleeing the law, bad debts or unhappy love affairs. This was also the period of the great **cattle drives**, when the longhorns roaming free in the south and west of Texas were rounded up and taken to the railroads in Kansas. The Texan – and national – fascination with the romantic myth of the **cowboy** has its roots in this. Today, his regalia – Stetson, boots and bandana – is virtually a state costume.

The twentieth century onwards

Along with ranching and agriculture, **oil** has been crucial. After the first big gusher in 1901, at Spindletop on the Gulf Coast, the focus of the Texas economy shifted almost overnight from agriculture toward rapid industrialization. Boom towns popped up as wildcatters chased the wells and millions of dollars were made as ranchers, who had previously thought their land only fit for cattle, sold out at vast profit. Today, Texas produces one-fifth of all the domestic oil in the United States, and the sight of nodding pump jacks is one of the state's most potent images. But the state's commitment to renewable energy is becoming a part of the landscape, too, as gleaming white **wind turbines** sprout up like mushrooms in the Panhandle-Plains region.

HIGHLIGHTS

1. The Rio Grande Valley
2. Catching a concert in Austin
3. San Antonio's River Walk
4. Fort Worth
5. Marfa
6. Hiking in Big Bend National Park

TEXAS

Houston

The fourth largest city in the United States, **HOUSTON** is an ungainly beast of a place, choked with successive rings of highways and high on humidity. Despite this, its sheer energy, its relentless Texas pride and, above all, its refusal to take itself totally seriously, lends it no small appeal. For visitors, its well-endowed museums, highly regarded performing arts scene and decent nightlife mean there is always something to do.

If you have just a short time, concentrate on the superb galleries of the **Museum District** and **Hermann Park**, which are linked to **downtown**, some five miles northeast, by tram (trolley). The city's human face is most evident in the **Montrose** area, which lies west of downtown and overlaps with the Museum District.

Uptown, also called the **Galleria** district after its massive upscale mall, is three miles west. Just outside the Loop, the Galleria's 300 or so shops and restaurants spread north along Post Oak Boulevard; there is little to do around here except shop and eat.

Brief history

The city's very existence has always depended on wild speculation and boom-and-bust excess. Founded on a muddy mire in 1837 by two real estate-booster brothers from New York – their dream was to establish it as the capital of the new Republic of Texas – Houston was soon superseded by the more promising site of Austin, even while somehow developing itself as a commercial centre.

Oil, discovered in 1901, became the foundation, along with cotton and real estate, of vast private fortunes, and over the next century wildly wealthy philanthropists poured cash into swanky galleries and showpiece skyscrapers. That colossal self-confidence helped Houston weather devastating oil crises in the 1980s, and more recently it endured the **Enron** corporate scandal. Houston has also developed a growing workforce eager to bring **alternative energy** to scale. Solar and wind projects offer the most promise in Texas; more than 25 percent of Houston's energy load, for instance, comes from wind.

Several **megachurches** headquartered downtown – with smooth-talking celebrity pastors like Joel Olsteen – have become powerful social, cultural and political forces, drawing as many as fifty thousand people to their Sunday services, which are open to the public.

Downtown Houston

Houston's skyline remains a dramatic monument to capitalism, ambition and glitz and nowhere is this more evident than **downtown**. The observation deck on the sixtieth floor of **Chase Tower**, 600 Travis St (Mon–Fri 7am–7pm; free), the state's highest building, offers staggering views of the sprawl. Also notable is the nearby Philip Johnson-designed **Penzoil Place**, 711 Louisiana St, while the lobby of the historic **JP Morgan Chase Building**, 712 Main St, is an Art Deco masterpiece.

Sam Houston Park

Daily dawn–dusk • **Museum** Tues–Sat 10am–4pm, Sun 1–4pm • Free; house tours $15

Nestled below the skyscrapers, **Sam Houston Park** is an appealing green space dotted with restored historic structures from all walks of nineteenth-century life, including a compact **museum** run by the Historical Society. House tours leave from 1100 Bagby St.

The Museum District and Montrose

Five miles southwest of downtown, the quiet oak-lined streets of the **Museum District** are enjoyable to explore on foot – a rarity for Houston. There are two main concentrations of exhibition spaces, with one entire complex dominated by the collections of oil millionaires **John and Dominique de Menil**. The Menil galleries and the Houston Center for Photography are in the **Montrose** district, which spreads west of downtown.

DOWNTOWN HOUSTON

5 , The Orange Show Monument & Galveston ▲

▲ I-10 & George Bush Intercontinental Airport

The Beer Can House ▲

■ ACCOMMODATION

Hotel ZaZa	6
La Colombe d'Or	5
La Maison in Midtown	3
The Lancaster	1
Magnolia Hotel	2
Morty Rich Hostel	4

● RESTAURANTS & CAFÉS

Breakfast Klub	4
Goode Company	5
Haven	6
Mi Sombrero	1
Pappas Bros. Steak House	3
RDG + Bar Annie	2

■ BARS, CLUBS & LIVE MUSIC VENUES

Anvil Bar & Refuge	4
AvantGarden	3
Catbird's	2
Continental Club	7
Etta's	5
Mugsy's	6
Notsuoh	1

Minute Maid Park

Discovery Green

THEATER DISTRICT

Wortham Theater

Bayou Place

Alley Theater

Angelika Film Center

City Hall

Texaco Plaza

Penzoil Place

Public Library

Baldwin Park

Mistown Park

Buffalo Bayou

Memorial Drive

Buffalo Bayou Park

Allen Pkwy

Montrose Blvd

Taft Street

Westheimer Road

Flora Street

Montrose Blvd

Yoakum Blvd

Graustark Street

Houston Center for Photography

Rothko Chapel

The Menil Collection

MONTROSE

Rice University & Hermann Park

Metrorail Tramline

0   yards   500

Shepherd Dr

N

Montrose is one of Houston's hippest neighbourhoods and **Westheimer**, the district's main drag, has enough tattoo parlours, vintage clothes stores, experimental art galleries and junk shops to feel refreshingly bohemian. Montrose has also long been the base of a very visible **gay community**, and a high concentration of gay bars and clubs remain. The district also extends south to pleasant **Hermann Park** and the appealing **Rice University** area, both accessible by the tram system. Just beyond **Mecom Fountain**, the park has a Japanese meditation garden and is a nice place to grab an ice cream and go for a stroll.

The Menil Collection

1533 Sul Ross St • Wed–Sun 11am–7pm • Free • ☎ 713 525 9400, ⓦ menil.org

A magnificent purpose-built gallery, designed by Renzo Piano, houses the private **Menil Collection**. Displayed in spacious, naturally lit white-walled rooms, the superb works range from Paleolithic carvings to Surrealist paintings. Artists with rooms to themselves include Picasso, Max Ernst and René Magritte. There's also a fine array of Alaskan Tlingit masks and an excellent bookstore, too.

Rothko Chapel

3900 Yupon St • Daily 10am–6pm • Free • ⓦ rothkochapel.org

The minimalist ecumenical **Rothko Chapel** contains fourteen sombre paintings commissioned by the de Menils from Mark Rothko shortly before his death. The artist, who worked with architect Philip Johnson in designing the chapel, considered these to be his most important works and their power in this tranquil space is undeniable. The broken obelisk in the small park outside is dedicated to Dr Martin Luther King, Jr. Check the website for talks and events hosted at the chapel, from Sufi dancing to meditations.

Byzantine Fresco Chapel Museum

4011 Yupon St • Wed–Sun 11am–6pm • Free

Designed by Francis de Menil and located on the edge of the Menil Collection campus, the **Byzantine Fresco Chapel Museum** houses a pair of thirteenth-century Cypriot frescoes – the only intact Byzantine frescoes in the Western hemisphere – in a simple contemporary structure.

Houston Center for Photography

1441 W Alabama St • Wed & Fri 11am–5pm, Thurs 11am–9pm, Sat & Sun noon–6pm • Free • ⓦ hcponline.org

The **Houston Center for Photography** features work from emerging American photographers. Although it doesn't have its own collection, the small space exhibits some of the most striking visual art produced in the Southwest. The centre also offers numerous excellent courses and workshops throughout the year.

Museum of Fine Arts

5601 Main St • Tues & Wed 10am–5pm, Thurs 10am–9pm, Fri & Sat 10am–7pm, Sun 12.15–7pm • $12; free Thurs • ⓦ mfah.org

At the intersection of Bissonet and Main streets, the expansive **Museum of Fine Arts** features an eclectic collection spanning a panoply of eras, filling its impressive buildings with everything from Renaissance art to rare African gold, with a couple of wings entirely devoted to decorative arts. Crane your neck upward from the Matisses and Rodins in the pine-shaded **Cullen Sculpture Garden** outside for a view of the downtown skyline.

Houston Museum of Natural Science

5555 Hermann Park Drive • Mon & Wed–Sun 9am–5pm, Tues 9am–8pm • $15; free Thurs 2–5pm • ⓦ hmns.org

At Hermann Park's **Houston Museum of Natural Science**, most exhibitions are geared toward kids. But at the museum's **Wiess Energy Hall**, you can pour crude oil over a cluster of clear marbles to learn, for example, that Middle Eastern light crude is similar in viscosity to West Texas intermediate crude. You can also decide for yourself which technologies – such as solar, wind and geothermal – are most likely to ease the world's

9

energy crunch. The museum's **Cockrell Butterfly Center** (daily 9am–5pm; $8)is a giant three-storey greenhouse where you can walk among exotic butterflies.

ARRIVAL AND DEPARTURE HOUSTON

By car Downtown Houston lies at the intersection of I-10 (San Antonio–New Orleans) and I-45 (Dallas–Galveston), with most of what you'll want to see encircled by Loop 610.

By plane George Bush Intercontinental Airport (☎ 281 230 3100), 23 miles north, is the main hub for Continental Airlines, while the smaller, domestic William P. Hobby Airport (☎ 713 640 3000), 7 miles southeast of downtown, is a major hub for Southwest. Taxis downtown cost about $50 from Intercontinental, $35 from Hobby. The SuperShuttle van (☎ 800 BLUE VAN, ⦿ supershuttle.com; starting at $25 from Intercontinental, $20 from Hobby) drops off at hotels

downtown and near the Galleria mall, west of downtown. METROBus (☎ 713 635 4000, ⦿ ridemetro.org) also offers routes into downtown from both airports.

By bus The Greyhound terminal is centrally located at 2121 Main St (☎ 713 759 6565).

Destinations Austin (4 daily; 3hr); Dallas (10 daily; 4hr 10min); El Paso (4 daily; 18hr 15min): Fort Worth (10 daily; 7hr); San Antonio (7 daily; 3hr 15min).

By train Amtrak arrives at 902 Washington Ave, on the western fringe of downtown. There's a daily service to San Antonio (5hr 10min).

GETTING AROUND AND INFORMATION

By car You'll need to rent a car to see the best of Houston, particularly since taxis are expensive; all the major companies are represented at the airports.

By tram (trolley) or bus Houston's public transport system is largely inadequate for a city of its size, but the downtown METRORail tram runs north–south for about 8 miles, mostly along Main and Fanin sts, between the University of Houston (UH) and Reliant Park; the Museum District stop is in the middle. Fares start at $1.25 and are based on zones; the downtown and surrounding area are in Zone 1. METRO also

operates dozens of bus routes, including the free and environmentally friendly GreenLink bus service (Mon–Fri 6.30am–6.30pm), which has eighteen stops downtown.

By bike Bikes can be placed on the front of city buses and are not a bad option. The Houston Bicycle Company at 404½ Westheimer ($25/day; ☎ 713 522 4622, ⦿ houston bicyclecompany.com) rents three-speeds.

Visitor centre First floor, City Hall, 901 Bagby St (Mon–Sat 9am–4pm; ☎ 713 437 5200, ⦿ visithoustontexas.com). There's a library branch on the other side of the plaza.

ACCOMMODATION

Inexpensive **hotels** are concentrated in three areas: near Reliant Stadium (southwest of downtown), and outside the Loop along either I-45 or I-10. Upmarket, business-oriented chains abound downtown and near the Galleria. **B&Bs** offer a welcome alternative in a city as potentially alienating as Houston, and there are a few **budget** options.

Hotel ZaZa 5701 Main St ☎ 888 880 3244, ⦿ hotel zazahouston.com. Trendy decor, with themed suites like the "Casablanca" wrapped around a sleek pool. There's a full range of amenities and the hotel boasts a fine position near Hermann Park and museums. $219

La Colombe d'Or 3410 Montrose Blvd ☎ 713 524 7999, ⦿ lacolombedor.com. With just six rooms and an ideal setting near the museums, this quaint but luxurious property is the smartest hotel in town. If you can't afford a room, sip a cocktail at the small, elegant bar. $295

★ **La Maison in Midtown** 2800 Brazos St ☎ 713 529 3600, ⦿ lamaisonmidtown.com. Central and exceedingly comfortable B&B with several handsome rooms and amenities including jacuzzis. $159

The Lancaster 701 Texas Ave ☎ 800 231 0336, ⦿ thelancaster.com. Lady Bird Johnson's Houston hotel of choice, in the heart of the Theater District. It's a sophisticated,

old-world option with a variety of rooms and suites, an included buffet breakfast and a restaurant serving upscale meals. $179

Magnolia Hotel 1100 Texas Ave ☎ 888 915 1110, ⦿ magnoliahotelhouston.com. A modern boutique hotel in an excellent downtown location. Most of the rooms are surprisingly spacious and all come with a wide range of amenities. There's a good-sized pool on the roof, but it's worth going up there for the views alone, which are spectacular, especially at night. $199

★ **Morty Rich Hostel** 501 Lovett Blvd, Montrose ☎ 713 636 9776, ⦿ hiusa.org/houston. Easily the best hostel in Houston: one look at its elegant facade and it's clear that this HI-affiliated hostel is a cut above the usual. Amenities include a swimming pool, a/c throughout, free wi-fi and a continental breakfast. Dorms $25

EATING

Breakfast Klub 3711 Travis St ☎ 713 528 8561. Obama campaign staffers favoured this popular breakfast spot

when their office was located across the street. Serves unique dishes like wings and waffles and catfish grits, as well as more traditional morning fare for around $10. Mon–Fri 7am–2pm, Sat & Sun 8am–2pm.

Goode Company 5109 Kirby Rd ☎ 713 522 2530. Good, reasonably priced BBQ joint, with big portions of beef brisket ($11.25), revered pecan pie ($4.75 a slice) and outdoor seating. This is the original location; there are a couple of others. Daily 11am–10pm.

★ **Haven** 2502 Algerian Way ☎ 713 581 6101. Certified "green" with locally sourced mains from about $20; try the bayou stew – catfish, oysters, shrimp and crawfish mixed with a delectable broth and rice ($25). Mon–Thurs 11am–10pm, Fri 11am–11pm, Sat 5–11pm, Sun 11am–2pm.

★ **Mi Sombrero** 3401 N Shepard Drive ☎ 713 862 7244. An authentic mom-and-pop Tex-Mex joint a few miles north of downtown that's been around since 1978. It's excellent

value, with dinner plates such as chicken tacos from about $5. Mon–Thurs & Sun 7am–9pm, Fri & Sat 7am–10pm.

Pappas Bros. Steak House 5839 Westheimer Rd ☎ 713 780 7352. Leather booths, marble columns, mahogany panelling and brass trim set the stage for you to devour an in-house, dry-aged slab of beef; filet mignons start at $44. Mon–Thurs 5–10pm, Fri & Sat 5–11pm.

RDG + Bar Annie 1800 Post Oak Blvd ☎ 713 840 1111. Innovative Southwestern cuisine from a menu designed by celebrated chef Robert del Grande. Dishes in the *RDG Grill Room* are a bit more extravagant, with prices to match; a braised short rib goes for $29. On the more moderate *Bar Annie* side, a shrimp and black bean tostada costs $18. Mon–Thurs 11.30am–4pm & 6–10pm, Fri 11.30am –4pm & 6–10.30pm, Sat 6–10.30pm, Sun 11am–2.30pm.

NIGHTLIFE AND ENTERTAINMENT

There's no shortage of things to do in the evening in Houston. While downtown has a few good **bars**, you'll find more lively offerings in **Montrose**, particularly along Westheimer Road. Downtown's much-trumpeted **Theater District** (🌐 houstontheaterdistrict.org), a seventeen-block area west of Milam Street between Congress and Capitol streets, holds most of the city's **performing arts**. For current listings, check the free *Houston Press* (🌐 houstonpress.com).

BARS, CLUBS AND LIVE-MUSIC VENUES

★ **Anvil Bar & Refuge** 1424 Westheimer Rd ☎ 713 523 1622, 🌐 anvilhouston.com. Smartly designed cocktail bar in an old tyre shop serving an assortment of expertly crafted drinks for around $10, plus a large selection of draughts. Though it's one of Houston's hipper establishments, it's rarely too packed. Daily 4pm–2am.

AvantGarden 411 Westheimer Rd ☎ 832 287 5577, 🌐 avantgardenhouston.com. Eclectic bar with a commitment to local live music; acts perform on a few stages in the three-storey house. Listen to local bands blow the roof off the joint or relax with a drink outside by the fountain constructed out of recycled Petron tequila bottles. Daily 7pm–2am.

★ **Catbird's** 1336 Westheimer Rd ☎ 713 523 8000. Laidback creative types swill cheap bottles of Lone Star Beer at this convivial dive bar with a pleasant patio and nightly specials. Daily 3pm–2am.

Continental Club 3700 Main St ☎ 713 529 9899, 🌐 continentalclub.com/houston.html. Cousin to the original in Austin, a classic live music venue on the tram line. Not for the claustrophobic (although there is an open patio out back), but it's worth it for acts that rarely disappoint. Standard bar drinks come at reasonable prices. Mon, Thurs & Fri 7pm–2am, Wed & Sat 8pm–2am.

Etta's 5120 Scott St ☎ 713 528 2611. Smokin' Sunday blues jams are the stuff of legend at this bar in a somewhat

rundown neighbourhood 3 miles east of downtown. Stay cool with cheap bottles of domestic beer (around $3) and gorge on fried chicken plates (around $8). Mon–Sat 11am–11.30pm.

Mugsy's 2239 Richmond Ave ☎ 713 522 7118. Relaxed joint in Upper Kirby with friendly clientele, good bartenders and a pleasant patio. Most cocktails go for around $5 while bottles of beer start at $2. Mon–Fri 4pm–2am, Sat 11am–2am, Sun noon–2am.

Notsuoh 314 Main St ☎ 713 409 4750. Young artists and hipsters congregate at this engaging downtown bar featuring live music, poetry readings and wi-fi. Look for the old neon sign outside that reads "The Home of EASY CREDIT". Daily 6pm–2am.

THEATRES

Alley Theatre 615 Texas Ave ☎ 713 220 5700, 🌐 alleytheatre.org. An independent theatre with a variety of shows on two stages.

Angelika Film Center 510 Texas Ave ☎ 713 225 1470, 🌐 angelikafilmcenter.com. Indie gem that shows arthouse movies and has a sister screen in New York City.

Wortham Theater Center 501 Texas Ave ☎ 713 237 1439, 🌐 worthamcenter.org. An elaborate home to Houston's opera and ballet companies, as well as hosting a steady stream of popular plays.

Around Houston

Navigating the sprawl around Houston is not an inviting prospect, but there are a few sights that make it worth bearing. Chief among these is **Space Center Houston**, north of

9

the city and long the focal point of the nation's space programme, and the **San Jacinto Battleground**, an important site in Texas' fight for independence from Mexico. At the outer edge of day-trip possibilities from Houston is the **Big Thicket National Preserve**, with forty miles of hiking trails through varied habitats.

Space Center Houston

1601 NASA Pkwy, 25 miles south of Houston off I-45 • Mon–Fri 10am–5pm, Sat & Sun 10am–6pm • $22.95; kids $18.95, parking $5 • ⓦ spacecenter.org

NASA has been controlling space flight from the **Johnson Space Center** at **Space Center Houston** here since the launch of *Gemini 4* in 1965 – locals love to point out that the first word spoken on the moon was "Houston". A working facility, the nerve centre of the International Space Station, it offers insight into modern space exploration, with tram (trolley) tours giving behind-the-scenes glimpses into various NASA compounds. The crowds can be overwhelming, however, and with all the kids running around, it feels a bit like Disney World.

San Jacinto Battleground

3523 Independence Pkwy S, 22 miles east of Houston off the La Porte Freeway • Daily 9am–6pm • Free

San Jacinto Battleground was the site of an eighteen-minute battle in 1836, when the Texans all but wiped out the superbly trained Mexican army. The fight is commemorated by the world's tallest stone-column **monument** (570ft, topped by a 34ft Lone Star). For $4, an elevator takes you to the observation floor, which provides views of the battlefield.

Big Thicket National Preserve

6102 Farm to Market Rd 420, 97 miles from Houston on US-69/287 • **Visitor centre** Daily 9am–5pm • Free • ☎ 409 951 6725, ⓦ nps.gov/bith

The **Big Thicket National Preserve** is a remarkable composite of natural elements from the Southwestern desert, central plains and Appalachian Mountains, with swamps and bayous to boot. The area once offered refuge for outlaws, runaway slaves and gamblers; now it just hides a huge variety of **plant** and **animal life**, including deer, alligators, armadillos, possums, hogs and panthers, and nearly two hundred species of birds.

Before entering the site, check in at the **visitor centre**, which has a wealth of information and brochures on the preserve's hiking, canoeing and backcountry camping possibilities. For an easy introduction to the varied habitats, drive 2.5 miles east of the visitor centre to the trailhead for the **Kirby Nature Trail**, a pleasant two-mile loop along the Village Creek.

The Gulf Coast

Look at the number of condo developments along the **Gulf Coast** and you will see that this is a major getaway destination. The climate ranges from balmy at **Galveston** to subtropical at the Mexican border. Devastating hurricanes in 1900 and again in 2008 all but levelled Galveston; recovery is ongoing, but the old, salty city still offers history, shopping and low-key relief from Houston. **Corpus Christi** makes the best base to explore the relatively unspoiled northern beaches of **Padre Island National Seashore**.

Galveston

In 1890, **GALVESTON** – on the northern tip of Galveston Island, the southern terminus of I-45 – was a thriving port, far larger than Houston fifty miles northwest; many newly arrived European immigrants chose to stay here in the so-called "Queen of the Gulf". However, the construction of Houston's Ship Canal, combined with the hurricane of 1900 that killed more than six thousand people (as told in Erik Larson's excellent book *Isaac's Storm*), left the coastal town to fade away. But thanks to its pretty historic district and its popularity with Houston residents seeking a summer escape, Galveston underwent a revitalization. Today, its pastel shotgun houses echo New Orleans, while its boozy bars and edgy beach bums bring to mind Jimmy Buffett songs about sailors and smugglers.

Downtown Galveston

Downtown, the historic **Strand** district has been fitted with gaslights, upmarket shops, restaurants and galleries. There are museums, too: the **Texas Seaport Museum**, for instance, in a complex of shops and restaurants on Pier 21, just off Water Street (daily 10am–5pm; $8), focuses on the port's role in trade and immigration during the nineteenth century; admission includes boarding the *Elissa*, an 1877 three-masted tall ship.

Between the Strand and the beaches to the south, Galveston boasts a profusion of historic homes open for guided tours. A standout is the ostentatious stone masterpiece **Bishop's Palace**, 1402 Broadway St (June–Aug Mon–Sat 11am–4pm, Sun noon–4pm; $10; guided tours daily 12.30pm & 3.30pm), with its stained glass, mosaics and marble.

The beaches

The downtown **beaches** of Seawall Boulevard are a bit rocky. They are hemmed in by a ten-mile-long seawall, which was constructed more than a century ago to protect Galveston from hurricanes. Slowly pedalling a **beach cruiser bike** along the seawall at sunset is a classic Galveston experience; contact Island Bicycle Company, 1808 Seawall Blvd, for rental options (☎409 762 2453, ⊛islandbicyclecompany.com; from $8/hr, $25/day). **Stewart Beach**, on the eastern edge of town, offers a wide range of services and plenty of space for families to soak up the sun. Fifteen miles west from downtown, **Jamaica Beach** is comparatively quiet and a locals' favourite.

Galveston Island State Park

14901 FM 3005 • Daily 24hr • $5 • ☎409 737 1222, ⊛tpwd.state.tx.us

Six miles west of downtown, **Galveston Island State Park** preserves 2000 acres of marshland that are a haven for several bird species, particularly during spring and autumn migrations. The park holds numerous easy trails that provide access to both the gulf and bay sides of the island. To really get a feel for the unique barrier island habitat, head out on a **kayak** along one of the generally calm water trails that surround the park; rent from Caribbean Breeze, 1723 61st St, in Galveston (☎409 740 0400; $30/half-day, $45/full-day).

Moody Gardens

I-45 off the 61st St exit • Daily 10am–6pm • Day pass $47

Brash and unabashedly touristy, **Moody Gardens** is Galveston's biggest attraction – for families, at least. The complex, on the west side of town, centres on three giant glass pyramids, and has an IMAX theatre, rainforest and an aquarium. Inclement weather makes a visit here much more appealing; otherwise it's hard to justify the costs and the hassle from the inevitable crowds.

ARRIVAL AND INFORMATION | GALVESTON

By car Driving from Houston to Galveston is straightforward: once it crosses over to the island, I-45 becomes Broadway, the town's main drag.

By bus Greyhound arrives at 714 25th St (a $6 taxi ride

from downtown). There is no Amtrak service.

Visitor centre 2328 Broadway (daily: June–Aug 9am–5pm; Sept–May 10am–5pm; ☎409 797 5000, ⊛galveston.com).

ACCOMMODATION

★ **Coastal Dreams** 3602 Ave P ☎409 770 0270, ⊛coastaldreamsbnb.com. The three rooms and one suite of this exceedingly charming and comfortable B&B all are

well appointed. The included breakfast is a real treat – it's worth staying here for that alone. **$119**

Gaido's Seaside Inn 3828 Seawall Blvd ☎409 762 9625,

9

ⓦ gaidosseaside.com. A clean, friendly, no-frills choice, with a good-sized outdoor pool and a free hot breakfast. **$79**

Galveston Island State Park Campground 14901 FM 3005 ☎ 409 737 1222, ⓦ tpwd.state.tx.us. The state park has a range of pleasant campgrounds to choose from; the gulf-side sites have services, while the bay-side ones have water but no electricity. Bay-side pitches **$15**, gulf side **$25**

Hotel Galvez 2024 Seawall Blvd ☎ 409 765 7721, ⓦ galveston.com/galvez. Far and away the most exclusive spot to stay on the island, this regal hotel, built in 1911, has a beautiful pool, a grand lobby, restaurant (see below) and lobby bar. Parking is $10 extra. **$269**

EATING, DRINKING AND ENTERTAINMENT

Brews Brothers Brew Pub 2404 Strand ☎ 417 230 6644. Huge selection of craft beers and a few of its own, as well as a bar that seems to go on forever. The staff are friendly and knowledgeable, there's a perennially smoke-filled cigar lounge out back and the whole place has an edgier feel to it than your typical brewpub. Daily noon–2am.

Galvez Bar and Grill Hotel Galvez, 2024 Seawall Blvd ☎ 409 765 7721, ⓦ galveston.com/galvez. This hotel's elegant and recently renovated restaurant serves well-executed dishes with a focus on surf and turf, such as a blackened red fish ($28). Its Sunday brunch is one of the most sought after in the state. Mon–Sat 6.30–11am, 11.30am–2pm & 5–10pm, Sun 6.30–10.30am, 11am–2pm & 5–10pm.

MOD Coffeehouse 2126 Postoffice St ☎ 409 765 5659. Friendly hipster downtown coffeeshop featuring Fairtrade and organic blends. There's free wi-fi and the menu is full of healthy eats such as hummus with pitta ($4.95). Daily 7am–10pm.

Mosquito Cafe 628 14th St ☎ 409 763 1010. A local favourite, this breezy breakfast and lunch joint serves tasty salads and iced teas. The Thai chicken salad ($10) is a good bet, and the grilled shrimp tacos ($12.99) do not disappoint. Tues–Thurs 11am–9pm, Fri & Sat 8am–9pm, Sun 8am–3pm.

★ **Old Quarter Acoustic Café** 413 20th St ☎ 409 762 9199, ⓦ old-quarter.com. A great venue for folk, alt-country and blues; the late Texas singer-songwriter Townes Van Zandt wrote *Rex's Blues* about the café's owner, musician Rex Bell. Cash only. Most shows start around 8pm. Wed–Sat, hours vary.

The Spot 3204 Seawall Blvd ☎ 409 621 5237. Lively bar and a nice family restaurant with a devoted following who come as much for the amazing Gulf views as for the four bars and three dozen TVs. The food is better than you might expect, with a grilled gulf shrimp dinner plate costing $14. Mon–Thurs & Sun 11am–11pm, Fri & Sat 11am–midnight.

Corpus Christi

Laidback **CORPUS CHRISTI** is reached along the coast on the two-lane Hwy-35 from Houston or Galveston, or on I-37 from San Antonio. Originally a rambunctious trading post, it too was hit by a fierce hurricane, in 1919, but recovered, transforming itself into a centre for naval air training, petroleum and shipping. The city is an outdoor destination – fishing, sailing, birding and watersports (mostly located across the channel on Padre Island) are all hugely popular here – but there are a few worthy cultural diversions. Corpus Christi's streets aren't all that compelling to wander, though the tranquil **Heritage Park** (Tues–Thurs 9am–5pm, Fri 9am–2pm, Sat 11am–2pm; free), at 1581 N Chaparral, is an impressive collection of twelve Victorian homes and gardens.

Art Museum of South Texas

1902 N Shoreline Blvd • Tues–Sat 10am–5pm, Sun 1–5pm • $68 • ⓦ artmuseumofsouthtexas.org

The impressive collection of the **Art Museum of South Texas** focuses on fine arts and crafts of the Americas. The bleach-white, Philip Johnson-designed building is stunning, with bright windows that give close-up views of freighters navigating Corpus Christi Bay; look for dolphins riding the bow wake. The museum also has an excellent small lunch spot, the *Dobson Café*.

The Selena Museum

5410 Leopard St • Mon–Fri 10am–4pm • $3

Much of Corpus Christi's population is Hispanic, and the community was devastated in 1995 when 23-year-old singer **Selena** was shot dead in a downtown *Days Inn* car park by the former president of her fan club. Selena was on the verge of becoming the first major crossover star of **Tejano** music, and 50,000 fans attended her funeral. The bizarre **Selena Museum** is stuffed with Selena memorabilia, from her extravagant gowns to her red Porsche.

ARRIVAL, GETTING AROUND AND INFORMATION   **CORPUS CHRISTI**

By plane Corpus Christi International Airport (☏ 361 289 0171) is about 10 miles west of the city's centre; a taxi into town is around $15.

By bus The Greyhound bus station is downtown at 702 N Chaparral St.

Local buses The CCRTA (☏ 361 289 2712, ⊛ ccrta.org) operates public transport in and around the city, including a good metro bus system (single fares 75¢). The website has detailed maps of the many routes.

Trams (trolleys) A daytime tram (Mon–Sat; $1.25, day pass $2) connects the major attractions with area hotels; look for the "B" signs that signal a tram stop.

Ferry From March to late Sept a pedestrian ferry operates from Peoples St to North Beach ($3 return).

Visitor centre 1823 N Chaparral St (Tues–Sat 9am–5pm; ☏ 800 766 BEACH, ⊛ corpuschristi-tx-cvb.org).

ACCOMMODATION, EATING AND DRINKING

Bayfront Inn 601 N Shoreline Blvd ☏ 800 456 2293, ⊛ bayfrontinncc.com. This basic downtown option has decent rooms, an outdoor swimming pool and a good location. **$60**

Executive Surf Club 309 N Water St ☏ 361 884 7873. Long-established bar and live music venue that serves decent burgers, too; the $5.75 shrimp burger is a steal. The nightly specials – like Tuesday's $2 pints – tend to draw crowds, though the local bands that play here are reason enough to drop in. Mon–Wed & Sun 11am–11pm, Thurs–Sat 11am–midnight.

House of Rock 511 Starr St ☏ 361 882 7625. A packed calendar of consistently stellar live music make this the best spot to catch a rock band, even if it's not always easy to stake out a comfortable spot. The bar side has a bit more room, a huge selection of beers and no cover charge.

Mon–Fri 3pm–2am, Sat 6pm–2am, Sun 9pm–2am.

V Boutique Hotel 701 N Water St ☏ 361 883 9200, ⊛ vhotelcc.com. With a prime location and more style than any other option around, the *V* is the best accommodation choice in town. Amenities include a fitness room and a creative Vietnamese restaurant (open for lunch and dinner). **$149**

Water Street Oyster Bar 309 N Water St ☏ 361 881 9448. Constantly buzzing, informal spot that serves traditional seafood dishes such as fried oyster and shrimp plates, crab cakes and shrimp po-boys ($7.95) and specialities including crawfish-stuffed chicken ($13.95). Mon–Thurs & Sun 11am–11pm, Fri & Sat 11am–midnight.

The Yardarm 4310 Ocean Drive ☏ 361 855 8157. A nautical-themed bayfront restaurant in a cute yellow house, with excellent seafood plates at reasonable prices, including a rich seafood stew ($24.50). Tues–Sat 5.30–10pm.

Padre Island National Seashore

Operated by the National Park Service, **Padre Island National Seashore** is not as unspoiled as its name suggests, with ranks of condos advancing steadily up the coast and a surprising amount of vehicular traffic on the beach itself. But it remains an excellent destination for **birdwatching** and waterborne activities, particularly **windsurfing** and **kayaking**. Any plans to head out on the water should include a stop in at **Worldwinds** (☏ 361 949 7472, ⊛ worldwinds.net), on Bird Basin Road 4.5 miles northwest of the visitor centre, which can provide suggestions on where and when to go as well as rent kayaks ($45/day) and boards (from $50/day).

Aside from exploring the coast in a boat or on a board or casting a reel, simply walking along the **miles of beaches** is the most popular island pastime. If you visit from autumn to spring, you'll stand a very good chance of spotting several **bird species** that migrate here by the thousands, including pelicans, terns and kestrels.

INFORMATION   **PADRE ISLAND NATIONAL SEASHORE**

Access and entry fees The entrance park is at 20420 Park Rd 22 and is open 24hr. Admission is $10/vehicle, $5/pedestrians and cyclists.

Visitor centre At the park entrance (daily 9am–5pm; ☏ 361 949 8068, ⊛ nps.gov/pais); can provide information on the release of sea turtle hatchlings (in season).

Port Isabel and South Padre Island

The graceful Queen Isabella Causeway, northeast of Brownsville, connects **PORT ISABEL**, home to one of the biggest commercial fishing fleets in Texas, to **SOUTH PADRE ISLAND**, one of the rowdiest Spring Break destinations in the USA. As you might expect, much of the island's activities don't extend beyond getting in the water, soaking up the sun's

9

rays and drinking a **beer** or three. Though this is enough for most visitors, Port Isabel itself holds a few engaging museums befitting a town proud of its nautical heritage. The best is the **Treasures of the Gulf Museum**, 317 E Railroad Ave (Tues–Sat 10am–4pm; $3; ☎956 943 7602), which tells the story of three sixteenth-century Spanish galleons that sank not far offshore. In the same building, the **Port Isabel Historical Museum** (same hours and fee), showcases numerous artefacts from the US-Mexican War.

ACCOMMODATION   PORT ISABEL AND SOUTH PADRE ISLAND

South Beach Inn 120 E Jupiter Lane ☎956 761 2471, ⓦsouthbeachtexas.com. This sedate choice, a few blocks from the beach, has a pool and decent rooms with kitchenettes. Its blindingly bright yellow exterior ensures it's easy enough to spot. **$69**

Southwind Inn 600 Davis St, Port Isabel ☎956 943 3392, ⓦsouthwindinn.com. A friendly, basic inn a couple of blocks from the water with a nice range of amenities, including kitchenettes, cable TV and a pool. Tends to fill up

much more quickly than any other spot in town; advance reservations are recommended. **$69**

Wanna Wanna 5100 Gulf Blvd, South Padre Island ☎956 761 7677, ⓦwannawanna.com. Beachfront place with fifteen mostly themed rooms that are clean, if dated; those on the second floor have ocean views. The friendly onsite beach bar (Mon–Thurs 11.30am–11pm, Fri–Sun 11.30am–midnight) is a popular local hangout and serves basic grilled dishes. **$129**

EATING AND DRINKING

Manuel's 313 E Maxan St, Port Isabel ☎956 943 1655. Though it's about as visually diverting as a hardware store, this nondescript Mexican spot draws crowds with monumental portions of simple meals such as sausage, egg and potato breakfast burritos ($5.25) that are every bit as good as they are oversized. Cash only. Tues–Sun 7am–2pm.

Palm Street Pier 204 W Palm St, South Padre Island ☎956 772 PALM, ⓦpalmstreetpier.com. Linger over a dramatic sunset at this secluded restaurant with west-facing views of the Laguna Madre. Stalwarts on the menu

include fried shrimp baskets ($14) and burgers ($8). Daily 11am–midnight.

Will and Jack's Burger Shack and Beer Garden 413 E Maxan St, Port Isabel ☎956 640 7440. Old-school burger joint tucked away behind the lighthouse with a menu that holds no surprises. Still, if you're craving red meat on a bun, you can't hope to find better; expect freshly grilled patties oozing juice and flavour in a variety of iterations (most around $8). The cosy beer garden out back occasionally hosts local bands. Cash only. Tues–Sun 11.30am–10pm.

Laredo and the Rio Grande Valley

LAREDO, population 200,000, is situated at the southern terminus of I-35 (the northern terminus is 1600 miles to the north in Duluth, MN). A busy bridge connects the USA to Mexico at the bottom of Convent Avenue, where a major Border Patrol presence exists. As battles between Mexican **drug cartels** have escalated in recent years, Laredo and its sister city across the border have garnered a violent reputation – most of the real risk is in Mexico though.

The focus of Laredo's main square is the pretty **St Augustin Cathedral**, a couple of blocks north of the Rio Grande at 200 St Augustin Ave, containing a modernist mural of the Crucifixion; there's a pleasant stone grotto outside. Otherwise, there's not much to do other than eat, drink and take in the atmosphere: this city, perhaps more than any other in Texas, reflects a strong **Latino influence**, evident in everything from the food to blaring hip-hop music.

The Rio Grande Valley

Heading southeast from Laredo down US-83 (called the **Zapata Hwy**) you pass through the **Rio Grande Valley**, a subtropical slice of South Texas decidedly well removed from the typical state itinerary. Actually a delta prone to flooding, the 180-mile-long valley contains few immediately identifiable sights, though a string of atmospheric farming communities, with tiny downtowns that have barely been touched in two hundred years, more than warrant a trip this far south.

★ **El Meson** 908 Grant St, Laredo ☎ 956 712 9009. Beloved, hard-to-find spot across the street from the cathedral that serves some of the best Mexican food in the state, with a daily menu and $5–7 meals such as chicken *flautas* with avocado, rice and beans. Mon–Sat 11.30am–4pm.

★ **La Posada Hotel** 1000 Zaragoza St, Laredo ☎ 956

722 1701, ⓦ laposada.com. On the main square, this historic and handsome place has recently been renovated and has spacious, well-appointed rooms, a lobby bar favoured by martini-drinking businessmen and two court-yard pools. The young Texas musician Ryan Bingham references the hotel in his song *Bread and Water*. **$114**

Austin

AUSTIN was a tiny community on the verdant banks of the (Texas) Colorado River when Mirabeau B. Lamar, president of the Republic of Texas, suggested in 1839 that it would make a better capital than swampy and disease-ridden Houston. Early building had to be done under armed guard, while angry Comanche watched from the surrounding hills. Despite this perilous location, Austin thrived.

Today the city wears its state capital status lightly. Since the 1960s, the laidback and progressive city – an anomaly in Texas – has been a haven for artists, musicians and writers, and many visitors come specifically for the **music**. And while complacency has crept in – its "alternative" edge being packaged as just another marketing tool – artists hungry for recognition are still attracted to this creative hotbed.

Due to a tech-fuelled population leap, brand-new towering condo complexes have shot up to threaten Austin's small-town vibe. Still, it remains the best city in the state for **cycling**, and the presence of the vast and pretty University of Texas campus adds to the pleasant atmosphere. Within the city limits a great park system offers numerous hiking and biking trails, plus a wonderful spring-fed swimming pool. In addition, Austin makes a fine base for exploring the green **Hill Country** that rolls away to the west.

Downtown Austin

Downtown Austin is a pleasant place to take a stroll; pick up a free self-guided walking tours leaflet from the visitor centre (see p.586). The prominent **Texas State Capitol** (Mon–Fri 7am–10pm, Sat & Sun 9am–8pm; free guided tours also available, call ☎ 512 305 8400 for schedule) is located in the middle of most of the popular sites and is a good visual reference; it's more than 300ft high, taller than the Capitol in Washington, with a sunset-red granite dome that accents the downtown skyline. The chandeliers, carpets and even the door hinges of this colossal building are emblazoned with Lone Stars and other Texas motifs. The dammed Colorado River – called Lady Bird Lake (formerly Town Lake) – borders downtown to the south.

SXSW

Austin's ten-day **SXSW festival** (South by Southwest; ⓦ sxsw.com), held in mid-March, has become the pre-eminent music and film conference in the nation – and quite a bit more besides. In recent years it's also morphed into one of the nation's foremost stages for tech companies to display their latest creations, reflecting Austin's surging stock in the industry. However, it's not cheap: passes for all film, music and interactive events cost $850 in advance, increasing to $1200 for a walk-up rate; a music-only pass is $550 ($650 walk-up).

Even if you can't afford to attend, the city is an exciting place to be during SXSW and there are literally hundreds of **unofficial gigs and events** open to all. To most locals, in fact, what's going on inside the conference is of secondary importance to the opportunity to catch some of the best acts on the planet in their favourite haunts.

9

Congress Avenue

Congress Avenue, an attractive, walkable stretch of shops and office buildings that slopes south from the Capitol down to Lady Bird Lake, is the heart of downtown. At no. 700 is **the Contemporary Austin** (Tues–Sat 11am–7pm, Sun noon–5pm; $5; ⓦthecontemporaryaustin.org), an attractive space to explore trends in modern art. It mostly showcases emerging artists, and the standard is generally pretty high.

At no. 419, the **Mexic-Arte Museum** (Mon–Thurs 10am–6pm, Fri & Sat 10am–5pm, Sun noon–5pm; $5; ⓦmexic-artemuseum.org) has a collection of traditional and

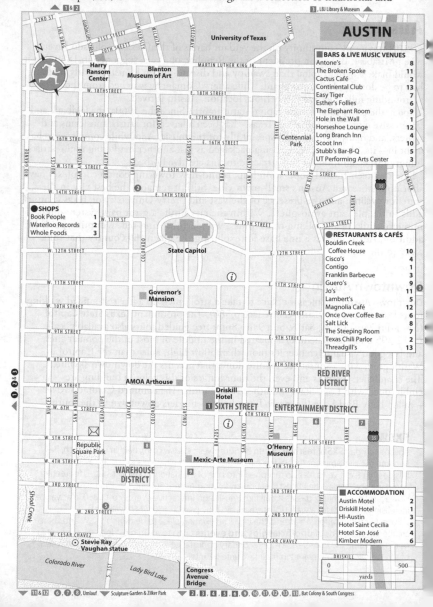

AUSTIN

■ BARS & LIVE MUSIC VENUES

Antone's	8
The Broken Spoke	11
Cactus Café	2
Continental Club	13
Easy Tiger	7
Esther's Follies	6
The Elephant Room	9
Hole in the Wall	1
Horseshoe Lounge	12
Long Branch Inn	4
Scoot Inn	10
Stubb's Bar-B-Q	5
UT Performing Arts Center	3

● SHOPS

Book People	1
Waterloo Records	2
Whole Foods	3

● RESTAURANTS & CAFÉS

Bouldin Creek Coffee House	10
Cisco's	4
Contigo	1
Franklin Barbecue	3
Guero's	9
Jo's	11
Lambert's	5
Magnolia Café	12
Once Over Coffee Bar	6
Salt Lick	8
The Steeping Room	7
Texas Chili Parlor	2
Threadgill's	13

■ ACCOMMODATION

Austin Motel	2
Driskill Hotel	1
HI-Austin	3
Hotel Saint Cecilia	5
Hotel San José	4
Kimber Modern	6

> ### THE CONGRESS AVENUE BRIDGE BATS
>
> If you're visiting between March and November, take a walk at dusk down to where Congress Avenue crosses Lady Bird Lake to watch 1.5 million **Mexican free-tailed bats** – the world's largest urban bat colony – emerge in an amorphous black cloud from their hangout under the bridge. While the views from the bridge are great, you do have to contend with traffic, crowds and the smell of guano; other options include viewing the mass exodus from below on a Capital Cruise tour boat (⊚ capitalcruises.com/bat-watching; $10) or from the *Austin American-Statesman*'s Bat Observation Center on the bridge's southeast side.

contemporary Latin American art. What it lacks in space it makes up for with its strong selection – most of which is of Mexican origin – and studied arrangement.

Sixth Street and around

Sixth Street crosses Congress and at night it is crowded with bar-hopping party people. If you're touring downtown during the day, cool off in the elegant lobby of the *Driskill Hotel*, at Sixth and Brazos, or visit the tiny **O. Henry Museum** at 409 E Fifth St (Wed–Sun noon–5pm; free; ⊚ austintexas.gov/department/o-henry-museum), a period home dedicated to one of the literary lions of Texas, William Sydney Porter (note the rosewood piano with mother-of-pearl inlay). On Saturday morning, it's worth perusing the city's excellent **farmers' market** (Sat 9am–1pm), at Republic Square Park, W 5th and Guadalupe streets.

West of downtown but within walking distance at the intersection of N Lamar Boulevard and Sixth Street, are **Waterloo Records** (600 N Lamar Blvd) and **Book People** (603 N Lamar Blvd), the best music store and bookstore, respectively in town. The flagship **Whole Foods** (525 N Lamar Blvd) grocery store is also at this intersection.

South Congress

Across the bridge from downtown, **South Congress** – or SoCo, as it's known – is a friendly neighbourhood of hip stores, bars and restaurants. With so many places that invite lingering, it's easy to whittle away an afternoon or evening here. Be sure to visit Uncommon Objects for unusual antiques, Allen's Boots for top-end Western wear and Friends of Sound for vintage vinyl. Several of this city's famous **food carts and trailers** parked streetside sell home-made snacks including cupcakes, tacos and BBQ sandwiches to keep you fuelled; check out ⊚ austinfoodcarts.com for a list.

Zilker Park and the Umlauf Sculpture Garden

2100 Barton Springs Rd **Barton Springs Pool** Late March to late Sept daily 5am–10pm • $3 **Umlauf Sculpture Garden** Wed–Fri 10am–4pm, Sat & Sun 1–4pm; $3.50 • ⊚ umlaufsculpture.org

Austin is blessed with many fine green spaces, perhaps none more appealing than the 350-acre **Zilker Park**, a perfect retreat on sultry Austin afternoons. One of its main attractions is the spring-fed, deliciously cool and expansive **Barton Springs Pool**; even if you choose not to take a dip, it's still a great spot to see the full spectrum of Austin's denizens. Another appealing outdoor space, south of the pool on Robert E. Lee Road, is the **Umlauf Sculpture Garden**, a tranquil, grassy enclave dotted with more than 100 works in bronze, terracotta, wood and marble.

The University of Texas

The campus is north of downtown and largely bounded by MLK Jr Blvd, Guadalupe St, Dean Keeton St and Red River St

The **University of Texas** – and its fiercely supported Longhorn football team, which plays on autumn Saturdays at 94,000-seat Darrell K. Royal-Texas Memorial Stadium – has a tangible,

9

almost defining, presence in Austin. You'll find most student activity in the inexpensive restaurants, vintage clothing shops and bookstores on the "Drag", the stretch of **Guadalupe Street** that runs along campus north from Martin Luther King Boulevard to 24th.

The campus

Oil has made "UT" one of the world's richest universities and its purchasing power is almost unmatched when it comes to rare and valuable books. The university's collection of manuscripts is available to scholars amid tight security in the **Harry Ransom Center**, in the southwest corner of campus, which houses a gallery (Tues, Wed & Fri 10am–5pm, Thurs 10am–7pm, Sat & Sun noon–5pm; free; ⓦhrc.utexas.edu) whose permanent collection includes a **Gutenberg Bible** and the **world's first photograph**. The quiet and beautiful **Battle Hall** houses UT's architecture library; note the stencilled open-truss ceiling. The best views in Austin are at sunset from the top of the **Texas Tower**, near the corner of 24th and Guadalupe (weekends and evenings only, depending on sunset times; $5; ⓸877 475 6633, ⓦutexas.edu/tower; reservations required).

LBJ Library and Museum

2313 Red River St • Daily 9am–5pm • $8 suggested donation • ⓦ lbjlibrary.org

The **LBJ Library and Museum**, on the eastern edge of the UT campus, traces the career of the brash and egotistical Lyndon Baines Johnson from his origins in the Hill Country to the House of Representatives, the Senate and the White House. Forty-five million documents are housed here and it's worth a visit. JFK is said to have made Johnson his vice president to avoid his establishing a rival power base; but in the aftermath of Kennedy's assassination, Johnson's administration (1963–69) was able to push through a radical social programme; indeed, Barack Obama's 2010 healthcare bill was hailed as the most meaningful domestic legislation since the civil rights advancements of the LBJ era. Johnson's nemesis, Vietnam, is presented here as an awful mess left by Kennedy for him to clear up, at the cost of great personal anguish.

ARRIVAL AND INFORMATION

By plane Flights arrive at the Austin-Bergstrom International Airport (⓸512 530 2242, ⓦaustintexas.gov /airport), 8 miles southeast of town. It's about 20min to downtown by taxi (Yellow Cab; around $30; ⓸512 452 9999) or by SuperShuttle van ($13 shared ride; ⓸512 258 3826, ⓦsupershuttle.com), while bus #100 runs every 20min (except late at night and early in the morning).
By bus The Greyhound station (⓸512 458 4463) is about 5 miles north of downtown at 916 E Koenig Lane.

Destinations Dallas (16 daily; 3hr 45min); Fort Worth (8 daily; 4hr); Houston (4 daily; 3hr); San Antonio (12 daily; 1hr 40min).
By train The Amtrak station (⓸512 476 5684) is at the western edge of downtown at 250 N Lamar Blvd.
Destinations Dallas (1 daily; 5hr 50min); Houston (2 daily; 3hr 25min); San Antonio (1 daily; 3hr 25min).
Visitor centre 209 E 6th St (Mon–Fri 9am–5pm, Sat & Sun 9.30am–5.30pm; ⓸866 GO AUSTIN, ⓦaustintexas.org).

GETTING AROUND

By bus The Capital METRO (⓸512 474 1200, ⓦcapmetro .org) runs buses downtown, crosstown and through the campus for a flat fare of $1, or $2.75 for express buses.
By MetroRail The commuter MetroRail route runs north 32 miles from downtown to the city of Leander.
On foot and by bike Austin is perfectly manageable on foot, as most of what you'll likely want to see is relatively close together. It also has one of the best networks of bike

paths in the USA. Rent from Bicycle Sport Shop, 517 S Lamar Blvd, just south of Barton Springs (Mon–Fri 10am–7pm, Sat 9am–6pm, Sun 11am–5pm; ⓸512 477 3472, ⓦbicycle sportshop.com); cruisers cost from $26/24hr, but you'll have to rent a lock as well. A downloadable city bike map is available from ⓦaustintexas.gov; the visitor centre and local bike shops have hard copies of it as well as of the excellent Town Lake Hike and Bike Trail.

ACCOMMODATION

★ **Austin Motel** 1220 S Congress Ave ⓸512 441 1157, ⓦaustinmotel.com. Basic rooms in a trendy old

motel in hip SoCo. A favourite with visiting musicians, it's across from the venerable *Continental Club*. **$83**

Driskill Hotel 604 Brazos St ☎ 800 252 9367, ⊚ driskill hotel.com. This handsome and historic downtown hotel is Austin's swankiest choice, with an opulent marble lobby and updated rooms. If you can't afford to stay, drop by the lobby bar for a mid-afternoon whiskey sour. **$229**

HI-Austin 2200 Lakeshore Blvd ☎ 800 725 2331, ⊚ hiaustin.org. Bargain rates right on the southern shore of Lady Bird Lake with clean rooms. No curfew and most of the young guests head out to Sixth St at night. Dorms **$22**

Hotel Saint Cecilia 112 Academy Drive ☎ 512 852 2400, ⊚ hotelsaintcecilia.com. This swanky SoCo boutique hotel, named after the patron saint of music and poetry, was created to inspire the best and brightest in the art world. Whether or not you're a rock star, director or painter, it's hard not to feel the call of the poolside bungalows and exceedingly hip

studios and suites. Studios **$460**, bungalows **$585**

Hotel San José 1316 S Congress Ave ☎ 512 444 7322, ⊚ sanjosehotel.com. Chic boutique hotel in the SoCo district. Restored from an old motel, it has a variety of minimalist rooms, some with shared bath, along with lovely gardens and a tiny pool and is adjacent to *Jo's* coffeeshop (see below). The courtyard happy hour attracts a local crowd for Micheladas, a spicy beer cocktail on the rocks. Rooms **$175**, courtyards suites **$360**

Kimber Modern 110 The Circle ☎ 512 912 1046, ⊚ kimbermodern.com. A stunning addition to an already thriving SoCo boutique hotel scene. The award-winning structure holds immaculate rooms marked by clean lines, abundant natural light and contemporary furnishings. Free breakfast. **$250**

EATING

CAFÉS

Jo's 1300 S Congress Ave ☎ 512 444 3800, ⊚ joscoffee .com. The original *Jo's* and still much beloved, this eclectic coffee spot serves drinks made from local roasts as well as a nice selection of filling sandwiches (most around $8.95) and baked goods. There's some outdoor seating, free wi-fi and a house band on Sundays. The downtown location is at 242 W 2nd St. Mon–Fri & Sun 7am–9pm, Sat 7am–10pm.

★ **Once Over Coffee Bar** 2009 S 1st St ☎ 512 326 9575, ⊚ onceovercoffeebar.com. *Once Over* takes its coffee seriously and it shows, with easily some of the best coffee east of Portland. There's no attitude, though, and a pleasant patio in the back. Mon–Sat 7am–9pm, Sun 8am–6pm.

★ **The Steeping Room** 4400 N Lamar Blvd ☎ 512 467 2663, ⊚ thesteepingroom.com. Austin has no shortage of knowledgeable coffeehouses, but comparatively few spots that treat tea with the same reverence; this is a clear exception. The attractive, sunny space in the neighbourhood of Rosedale boasts friendly service, an extensive tea list and plenty of healthy vegan and gluten-free dishes, such as the Buddha Bowl – the day's grain, tofu, beans and sweet potatoes ($10.95). Mon–Sat 8am–9pm, Sun 10am–5pm.

RESTAURANTS

Bouldin Creek Coffee House 1900 S 1st St ☎ 512 416 1601. Breakfast made from scratch is served all day at this buzzing vegetarian-only spot not far from SoCo. It has reasonable prices (a free-range, three-egg omelette with two sides costs $7.75) and friendly staff. Mon–Fri 7am–midnight, Sat & Sun 8am–midnight.

Cisco's 1511 E 6th St ☎ 512 478 2420. This second-generation Mexican family restaurant is open for breakfast and lunch. Order the *migas* (scrambled eggs with jalapeños, peppers, corn tortillas and biscuits; $7) to chase away your hangover. Daily 7am–2.30pm.

Contigo 2027 Anchor Lane ☎ 512 614 2260. Easy-going and popular restaurant in East Austin where you can settle in at a patio picnic table and enjoy dishes such as rabbit and dumplings ($15), sausage with sauerkraut ($11) and cauliflower gratin ($8). It's further out than most of the other options, but worth the trip. Mon, Tues, Thurs & Sat 5pm–midnight, Wed 5–11pm, Sun 10.30am–2pm.

★ **Franklin Barbecue** 900 E 11th St ☎ 512 653 1187. Long queues form well before this place opens – and it's easy to see why. Plates like brisket and pulled pork (both $12) exude more flavour than seems possible from mere meat and desserts like banana bourbon pie are a decadent end to a lunch that is every bit worth the wait. Tues–Sun 11am–2pm (though can closer earlier if it sells out).

Guero's 1412 S Congress Ave ☎ 512 447 7688. *Tacos al pastor* ($9.95) and *flautas* ($11) are specialities at this busy, sprawling restaurant across the bridge, south of downtown. Vegan and gluten-free options, too. Mon–Wed 11am–10pm, Thurs & Fri 11am–11pm, Sat & Sun 8am–11pm.

Lambert's 401 W 2nd St ☎ 512 494 1500. Exercise your taste buds at this self-described "fancy barbeque" restaurant that puts a modern twist on the old Texas staple. Produce and meats are sourced from local farms and ranches. The oak-smoked pork ribs ($18) are excellent, as is the jumbo shrimp and grits ($28). Daily 11am–2.30pm & 5.30–10pm.

Magnolia Café 1920 S Congress Ave ☎ 512 445 0000. A 24hr joint that's a local favourite for Tex-Mex and gingerbread pancake breakfasts ($5.50 for a full stack). A great place to refuel after a night living it up in SoCo. Daily 24hr.

★ **Salt Lick** 18300 FM 1826, Driftwood ☎ 512 858 4959, ⊚ saltlickbbq.com. A regular 30min pilgrimage for Austin's meat-lovers. This is the original location and the queues are every bit as long as they've always been; the brisket plates (from $13.95) are still the main reason why. The atmosphere is exceedingly friendly and the conversation between strangers flows freely. BYOB. Daily 11am–10pm.

9

Texas Chili Parlor 1409 Lavaca St ☎ 512 472 2828. Rub shoulders with politicians and their staffers at this venerable lunch spot downtown near the State Capitol. The chilli comes in bowls ($3.75–6.95) of several varieties; the XXX version is hot enough to melt Formica. Mon–Sat 11am–2am, Sun 11am–midnight.

Threadgill's 6416 N Lamar Blvd ☎ 512 451 5440, ⓦ threadgills.com. An Austin institution, north of downtown, established when Kenneth Threadgill was given the first licence to sell beer in the city after Prohibition. Bringing together hippies and rednecks in the 1960s, it was an incubator for the Austin sound and still features live bands, as well as basic Southern cuisine such as fried green tomatoes ($6.95) and pecan-crusted chicken ($12.95). Mon–Sat 11am–10pm, Sun 10am–9.30pm.

NIGHTLIFE AND ENTERTAINMENT

Austin's **live music scene** is legendary – and rightly so. Though the clubs and bars of Sixth Street are touristy and jammed with drunken 20-somethings, there are plenty of good places elsewhere downtown, and it's easy enough to hop in a cab to some of the further-flung classic joints. Many of the **bars** double as music venues. Two newspapers carry listings: the daily *Austin American-Statesman* (ⓦ austin360.com) and the alt-weekly *Austin Chronicle* (ⓦ austinchronicle.com). The website ⓦ billsmap.com pegs the venue of each night's shows on an endlessly helpful interactive map.

BARS

★ **Easy Tiger** 709 E 6th St ☎ 512 614 4972. Always-packed beer garden close to downtown that has a bakery, too. The stylish interior is marked by exposed brick walls and warm lighting, while outside there are ping pong tables and a creek running alongside. Thirty draught beers ($5–8) as well as an impressive whiskey list and pub food including home-made sausages in pretzel buns ($7). Daily: beer garden 11am–2am, bakery 7am–2am.

Hole in the Wall 2538 Guadalupe St ☎ 512 302 1470. Long-running dive near the UT campus with pool tables, live Americana music and dirt-cheap drinks ($2 for a PBR). Mon–Fri 11am–2am, Sat & Sun 3pm–2am.

Horseshoe Lounge 2034 S Lamar Blvd ☎ 512 442 9111. This beer joint is a survivor from a not-too-distant, rough-and-tumble South Austin past. Look for the red and green neon lights. A stream of often grizzled regulars line the horseshoe-shaped bar, with drinks at rock-bottom prices. Daily noon–2am.

★ **Long Branch Inn** 1133 E 11th St ☎ 512 472 5591. This dark, artsy dive smack in the middle of a quickly gentrifying neighbourhood has a small stage, a nice old wooden bar and slow-turning ceiling fans. Daily 3pm–2am.

Scoot Inn 1308 E 4th St ☎ 512 394 5486. Owned by the same folks who run the *Long Branch Inn*, this place attracts a similar but slightly younger crowd and has a nice outdoor beer garden and occasional live music. Daily 4pm–2am.

LIVE MUSIC

Antone's 2015 E Riverside Drive ☎ 512 800 4628, ⓦ antonesnightclub.com This historic Austin joint recently moved to its present location, but thankfully remains the best blues club in the city, a hot and sweaty haunt showcasing national and local acts. Daily 8.30pm–2am.

★ **The Broken Spoke** 3201 S Lamar Blvd ☎ 512 442 6189, ⓦ brokenspokeaustintx.com. Neighbourhood restaurant (good chicken-fried steak) and foot-stomping honky-tonk dance hall in South Austin. The barn-like dance floor attracts great country acts; it's a lot of fun. Tues–Fri 9am–midnight, Sat 9am–2am.

Cactus Café 2247 Guadalupe St ☎ 512 475 6515, ⓦ utexas.edu. A bar and folk-oriented live music venue in the UT student union building that's an excellent spot to catch acoustic acts. Mon–Thurs 11am–midnight, Fri 11am–2am, Sat 8pm–2am.

★ **Continental Club** 1315 S Congress Ave ☎ 512 441 2444, ⓦ continentalclub.com. This long-standing classic is the city's premier place to hear hard-edged country or

---

THE AUSTIN SOUND

Although Austin's folk revival in the 1960s attracted enough attention to propel Janis Joplin on her way from Port Arthur, Texas, to stardom in California, the city first achieved prominence in its own right as the centre of **outlaw country** music in the 1970s. **Willie Nelson** and **Waylon Jennings**, disillusioned with Nashville, spearheaded a movement that reworked country and western with an incisive injection of rock'n'roll. Venues like the now-closed *Armadillo World Headquarters*, far removed from the more conservative honky-tonks of the Plains, provided an environment that encouraged and rewarded risk-taking, experimentation and lots of sonic cross-breeding. These days the predominant **Austin sound** is a melange of country, folk and the blues, with strong psychedelic and alternative influences – but the scene is entirely eclectic. The tradition of black Texas bluesmen like Blind Lemon Jefferson and Blind Willie Johnson, as well as the rocking bar blues of Stevie Ray Vaughan, still lives on, with a top-notch **blues** club in the form of *Antone's*.

bluesy folk sung the Austin way. Mon 6pm–2am, Tues–Fri 4pm–2am, Sat & Sun 3pm–2am.

The Elephant Room 315 Congress Ave ☎512 473 2279, ⓦelephantroom.com. Austin's best spot for live jazz, this understated underground bar is dark and cramped, but consistently showcases stellar acts. Mon–Fri 4pm–2am, Sat & Sun 8pm–2am.

Stubb's Bar-B-Q 801 Red River St ☎512 480 8341, ⓦstubbsaustin.com. Indoor and outdoor stages feature eclectic bands of national repute – including a Sunday gospel brunch – which you can watch while chomping on great Texas-style brisket ($7.75), sausage ($6.95) and ribs ($14.95). Mon–Thurs 11am–10pm, Fri & Sat 11am–11pm, Sun 11am–9pm.

THEATRE AND CINEMA

★ **Alamo Drafthouse** 320 E 6th St ☎512 476 1230, ⓦdrafthouse.com. The Alamo Drafthouse has several locations, including this one in the heart of Sixth St, and offers one of the best cinematic experiences in the USA. The theatres feature everything from pre-movie, title-specific montages to award-winning documentaries – pints of local beer and made-to-order food are served right at your comfy seat.

Esther's Follies 525 E 6th St ☎512 320 0553, ⓦesthers follies.com. Austin's coolest cabaret spot combines spoofs of local and national politicians with Texas-style singing and dancing. Thurs 7–10.30pm, Fri & Sat 7–11.30pm.

UT Performing Arts Center 23rd St and Robert Dedman Drive ⓦutpac.org. The university's Performing Arts Center boasts a calendar filled with world-class events, from international dance troupes to plays and live music acts. As you might expect, the busiest times of the year coincides with term-time.

The Hill Country

The rolling hills, lakes and valleys of the **HILL COUNTRY**, north and west of Austin and San Antonio, were inhabited mostly by Apache and Comanche until after statehood in 1845, when German and Scandinavian settlers arrived. Many of the log-cabin farming communities they established are still here, such as **New Braunfels** (famous for its sausages and pastries, and, more recently, its watersports), **Fredericksburg** and **Luckenbach**. You may still hear German spoken, and the German influence is also felt in local food and music; *conjunto*, for example, is a blend of Tex-Mex and accordion music. The whole region is a popular retreat and resort area, with some wonderful hill views and lake swimming, and some good places to camp.

New Braunfels

NEW BRAUNFELS, thirty miles north of San Antonio on I-35, was founded by German immigrants – mostly artisans and artists – in 1845 and quickly became a trade centre. Nowadays, the community, along with its equally historic satellite, **Gruene**, just northeast, makes its living from tourism. The town's two rivers – the Comal and the Guadalupe – are ideal for easy **rafting** and **tubing**, making this a popular weekend destination. If outdoor activities don't appeal, head downtown; the historic district has enough antique stores, galleries and restored buildings to fill a couple of hours.

INFORMATION AND ACTIVITIES   NEW BRAUNFELS

Visitor centre Exit 187 off I-35 (Mon–Fri 8am–5pm; ☎800 572 2626, ⓦnbjumpin.com); provides a list of accommodation, as well as information on renting rafts and tubes.

Rafting and tubing The long-running Rockin' R, 1405 Gruene Rd (☎830 629 9999, ⓦrockinr.com), is one of the best outfits in town, offering raft and tube rentals and group tours (from 2hr 30min) of the Guadalupe River.

ACCOMMODATION, EATING, DRINKING AND ENTERTAINMENT

Gruene Hall 1281 Gruene Rd ☎830 606 1281, ⓦgruenehall.com. Top country stars have been performing for decades at the atmospheric clapboard *Gruene Hall*, and it's usually packed out. Drinks are cash only. Mon–Wed 11am–11pm, Thurs & Fri 11am–midnight, Sat 10am–1am, Sun 10am–9pm.

Heidelberg Lodges 1020 N Houston St ☎830 625 9967, ⓦheidelberglodges.com. The various rooms, suites and *casitas* on offer here are rustic, though their riverfront location on the Comal makes them a bargain. Suites **$149**, doubles **$124**

Huisache Grill 303 W San Antonio St ☎830 620 9001.

9

The *Huisache Grill* serves sophisticated, reasonably priced contemporary cuisine such as grilled Portobello sandwich ($10) for lunch and pecan-crusted pork tenderloin ($16) for dinner. Daily 11am–10pm.

Pat's Place 202 S Union Ave ☎830 625 9070. Popular with locals for its casual setting and rock-bottom prices, *Pat's* doles out basic crowd-pleasers including burgers ($4), cheese steaks ($7) and chicken nachos ($7). Mon–Thurs 11am–9pm, Fri & Sat 11am–10pm.

Fredericksburg

On weekends in **FREDERICKSBURG**, crowds of well-heeled day-trippers from San Antonio and Austin throng Main Street's cutesy speciality stores and fancy tearooms. Several original structures make up the **Pioneer Museum** at 325 W Main St, including a church and a store (Mon–Sat 10am–5pm, Sun noon–4pm; $5). A little more incongruous, the **National Museum of the Pacific War**, 340 E Main St (daily 9am–5pm; $14), features a Japanese garden of peace and lays out a historical trail past aircraft, tanks and heavy artillery. That a World War II museum commemorating ocean battles is located in landlocked Fredericksburg is due to the town being the birthplace of Admiral Charles W. Nimitz, who commanded the US Navy's Pacific fleet.

ACCOMMODATION, EATING AND DRINKING   FREDERICKSBURG

Full Moon Inn 3234 Luckenbach Rd ☎800 997 1124, ⊚fullmooninn.com. Attractive accommodation in rural cottages and cabins in the sleepy musical hamlet of Luckenbach, 10 miles southeast of Fredericksburg, immortalized in song by both Willie Nelson and Waylon Jennings. There are opportunities for swimming and fishing on the property's twelve acres, and breakfast is included. **$150**

Lady Bird Johnson RV Park Campground 432 Lady Bird Drive ☎830 997 7521. Field camping in the lovely surrounds of Lady Bird Johnson Municipal Park, 3 miles to the southwest off Hwy-16. **$10**

Sunday House 501 E Main St ☎800 274 3762, ⊚sundayhouseinn.com. Of the numerous budget hotels along E Main St, this stately place is one of the more luxurious. Amenities include an outdoor pool and flat-screen TVs. **$104**

EATING AND DRINKING

Becker Vineyards 464 Becker Farms Rd, Stonewall ☎830 644 2681, ⊚beckervineyards.com. The Hill Country is a booming wine region, and the best of the bunch is Becker Vineyards, in a stone barn 11 miles east of Fredericksburg, off Hwy-290. A bottle of Becker's merlot is a great buy at $17.95. Mon–Thurs 10am–5pm, Fri 10am–6pm, Sun noon–6pm.

Friedhelm's Bavarian Inn 905 W Main St ☎830 997 6300. You can eat substantially at this German-inspired old-school restaurant, which specializes in heaped plates of dumplings and sauerkraut (mains around $9) and steak. Tues–Sun 11am–10pm.

Opa's Smoked Meat 410 S Washington St ☎830 997 3358. If you're looking to stock up for a Hill Country picnic or day-trip, be sure to stop by *Opa's* first. There's a bewildering number of smoked meat varieties, including bratwurst (1lb; $7.95) and jalapeño beef (2.5lb; $19.95) as well as dense deli sandwiches (around $6) and German side dishes and baked goods. Mon–Fri 8am–5.30pm, Sat 8am–4pm.

San Antonio

With neither the modern skyline of an oil metropolis, nor the tumbleweed-strewn landscape of the Wild West, attractive and festive **SAN ANTONIO** looks nothing like the stereotypical image of Texas – despite being pivotal in the state's history. Standing at a geographical crossroads, it encapsulates the complex social and ethnic mixes of all of Texas. Although the Germans, among others, have made a strong cultural contribution, today's San Antonio is predominantly **Hispanic**. Now the seventh largest city in the USA, it retains an unhurried, organic feel and is one of the nicest places in Texas to spend a few days.

San Antonio is a delight to walk around, as its main attractions, including the pretty **River Walk**, the **Alamo**, **Market Square** and **HemisFair Park**, are all within strolling distance of each other. Slightly further out, but still accessible on foot, is the **King William Historic District** and the neighbouring **Blue Star Contemporary Arts Center**.

BIG BEND NATIONAL PARK (P.610) >

9

Brief history

Founded in 1691 by Spanish missionaries, San Antonio became a military garrison in 1718, and was settled by the Anglos in the 1720s and 1730s under Austin's colonization programme. It is most famous for the legendary **Battle of the Alamo**, in 1836, when General Santa Anna wiped out a band of ragtag Texas volunteers seeking independence from Mexico. After the Civil War, it became a hard-drinking, hard-fighting "sin city", at the heart of the Texas **cattle and oil empires**. Drastic floods in the 1920s wiped out much of the downtown area, but the sensitive **WPA programme** that revitalized two of the city's prettiest sites, **La Villita** and the **River Walk**, laid the foundations for its future as a major tourist destination. Recently several massive hotels (think Vegas) have been constructed to accommodate the booming tourism and convention industries. The **military** has a major presence in San Antonio, too, with four bases in the metropolitan area.

The River Walk

Since mission times, the **San Antonio River** has been vital to the city's fortunes. Destructive floods in the 1920s and subsequent oil drilling reduced its flow, leading to plans to pave the river over. Instead, a careful landscaping scheme, started in 1939 by the WPA, created

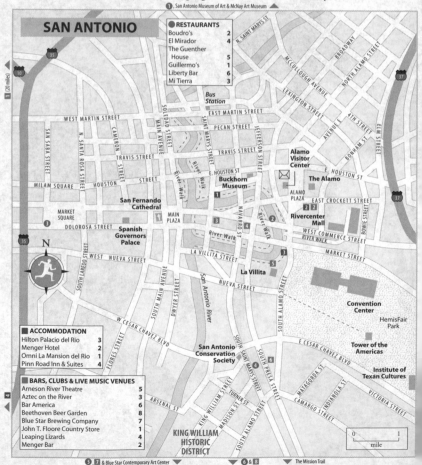

SAN ANTONIO

● **RESTAURANTS**
Boudro's	2
El Mirador	4
The Guenther House	5
Guillermo's	1
Liberty Bar	6
Mi Tierra	3

■ **ACCOMMODATION**
Hilton Palacio del Rio	3
Menger Hotel	2
Omni La Mansion del Rio	1
Pinn Road Inn & Suites	4

■ **BARS, CLUBS & LIVE MUSIC VENUES**
Arneson River Theatre	5
Aztec on the River	3
Bar America	6
Beethoven Beer Garden	8
Blue Star Brewing Company	7
John T. Floore Country Store	1
Leaping Lizards	4
Menger Bar	2

the Paseo del Rio, or **River Walk**, now the aesthetic and commercial focus of San Antonio. The walk, located below street level, is reached by steps from various spots along the main roads and crossed by humpbacked stone bridges. Cobbled paths, shaded by pine, cypress, oak and willow trees, wind for 2.5 miles beside the jade-green water, with much of the city's dining and entertainment options concentrated along the way.

La Villita
La Villita ("Little Town"), on the River Walk opposite HemisFair Park, was San Antonio's original settlement, occupied in the mid- to late eighteenth century by Mexican "squatters" with no titles to the land. Only when its elevation enabled it to survive fierce floods in 1819 did this rude collection of stone and adobe buildings become suddenly respectable. It is now a National Historic District, turned over to a dubious "arts community" consisting mostly of overpriced craft shops.

The Alamo
300 Alamo Plaza • Daily 9am–5.30pm • Free

San Antonio's most distinctive landmark, the **Alamo**, lies smack in the centre of downtown. Inextricably associated with the battle that took place here in 1836, a defining moment in the Texan struggle for independence against Mexico, the Alamo has been immortalized in movies and songs, and exists now as a rallying cry for Texas spirit.

Its fame, however, has little to do with its original purpose. It was built in the eighteenth century by the Spanish, the first in a trail of **Catholic missions** established along remote stretches of the San Antonio River. Each was laid out like a small fortified town, with the church as aesthetic and cultural focus. The goal was to strengthen Spanish control by "converting" the indigenous Coahuiltecans – in practice, using them as workforce and army. The missions flourished from 1745 to 1775, but couldn't survive the ravages of disease and attack from the Apache and Comanche, and fell into disuse early in the nineteenth century.

The infamous **Battle of the Alamo** occurred on March 6, 1836, when 5000 Mexican troops assaulted the mission, which was defended by just under 200 volunteers dreaming of Texan autonomy. Driven by the battle cry of "Victory or Death!" the besieged band – a few native Hispanic-Texans, adventurers like Davy Crockett and Jim Bowie, and aspiring colonists from other states – held out for thirteen days against the Mexicans before their demise.

The site
Considering its fame, the Alamo is surprisingly small. All that is left of the original complex is its **chapel**, fronted by a large arched sandstone facade, and the **Long Barracks**. A stream of bus tours makes visits crowded and hectic, but for anyone curious about the state's unique brand of pride and stubbornness, the Alamo is unmissable. No response but absolute reverence is permitted – effectively this is a shrine, and a sign insists visitors remove their hats. The grounds, with four acres of lush blooms, palms and cacti, are a haven from the commotion.

Buckhorn Saloon and Museum
318 E Houston St • Daily: June–Aug 10am–8pm; Sept–May 10am–5pm • Saloon free; upstairs museum $16.99 • ⓦ buckhornmuseum.com

For a jaw-dropping slice of kitsch Americana, the **Buckhorn Saloon and Museum** can't be beat. During San Antonio's heyday as a cowtown, cowboys, trappers and traders would bring their cattle horns to the original *Buckhorn Saloon* in exchange for a drink. The entire bar, a vast and lively Old West-themed space, has since been transplanted to this downtown location, where you can enjoy a mug of beer and a steak in the presence of hundreds of mounted horns and antlers. It is well worth exploring the extra floor,

9

which displays a staggering collection of wildlife trophies and includes an informative and entertaining museum of Texas history.

San Fernando Cathedral and Market Square

San Antonio's Hispanic heart beats strongly west of the river. Nowhere is this more visible than at the **San Fernando Cathedral**, 115 Main Plaza, established in 1731 and one of the oldest cathedrals in the USA. Mariachi Masses are held on Saturday at 5.30pm, when crowds overflow onto the plaza.

Market Square, a couple of blocks further northwest, dates from 1840. Its festive outdoor restaurants and stalls make it an appealing destination, especially during fiestas like Cinco de Mayo and the Day of the Dead. Fruit and vegetables are on sale early in the morning, while the shops are a compelling mix of colour and kitsch. **El Mercado**, an indoor complex, sells tourist-oriented gifts, jewellery and oddities.

HemisFair Park

200 S Alamo St • Daily dawn–dusk

It's a long walk on a hot day through the enormous **HemisFair Park** – a sprawling campus of administrative buildings with scant lawns – to the **Institute of Texan Cultures**, 801 E Durango Blvd (Mon–Sat 9am–5pm, Sun noon–5pm; $8), but it's worth the trip. Mapping the social histories of 26 diverse Texas cultures, this lively museum has especially pertinent African American and Native American sections. Also in the park, the touristy 750ft **Tower of the Americas** (Mon–Thurs & Sun 10am–10pm, Fri & Sat 10am–11pm) offers big views from its observation deck ($10.95).

King William Historic District

The 25-block **King William Historic District**, between the river and S Alamo Street, offers a different flavour to the city's more sleek pockets, its shady streets lined with the elegant late nineteenth-century homes of German merchants. It remains a fashionable residential area and has some stylish B&Bs; pick up **self-guided walking tours** outside the headquarters of the San Antonio Conservation Society, 107 King William St (☎210 224 6163).

The grassroots **Blue Star Contemporary Art Center** at 116 Blue Star St (☎210 227 6960, ⓦbluestarart.org) makes an appealingly rakish contrast to the rest of the neighbourhood, with its brewpub, workshops, galleries and crafts stores.

McNay Art Museum

6000 N New Braunfels Ave, at Austin Hwy • Tues, Wed & Fri 10am–4pm, Thurs 10am–9pm, Sat 10am–5pm, Sun noon–5pm • $15

Art lovers flock to the **McNay Art Museum**, easily one of the city's most beloved, as much for its exquisite exhibitions as for its striking architecture and the otherworldly escape it provides. This Moorish-style villa, complete with tranquil garden, was built in the 1950s to house the art collection of millionaire folk artist Marion Koogler McNay, and includes works from major players like Hopper and O'Keeffe.

ARRIVAL AND DEPARTURE   **SAN ANTONIO**

By plane San Antonio International Airport (☎210 207 3411, ⓦsanantonio.gov/aviation) is just north of the I-410 loop that encircles most of the sights. GO Airport Shuttle (☎210 281 9900, ⓦgoairportshuttle.com) makes the 20min journey downtown (every 15min, 7am–1.30am; $18 one-way, $34 return), while a taxi ride to downtown costs about $26 (Yellow Cab; ☎210 222 2222). All the major car-rental agencies have counters in Terminal A.

By bus Greyhound operates from 500 N St Mary's St (☎210 270 5815).

Destinations Austin (14 daily; 1hr 30min); Dallas (13 daily; 5hr); Fort Worth (7 daily; 7hr); Houston (10 daily; 3hr 30min).

By train Amtrak arrives centrally at 350 Hoefgen St. Destinations Austin (1 daily; 3hr 25min); Dallas (1 daily; 8hr 20min); Fort Worth (1 daily; 7hr); Houston (1 daily; 4hr 45min).

GETTING AROUND AND INFORMATION

By bus or streetcar In addition to a relatively good bus network, four downtown streetcar routes from Alamo Plaza serve the major attractions (every 10min; $1.20). A one-day pass ($4) available from the VIA Downtown Information Center, 211 W Commerce St (Mon–Fri 7am–6pm, Sat 9am–2pm; ☎ 210 475 9008, ⓦ viainfo.net) can be used on all buses and streetcars.

By bike Bikes can be rented from the Blue Star Bike Shop 1414 S Alamo St ($25/24hr; ☎ 210 858 0331, ⓦ bluestarbike shop; closed Tues) and are an excellent option for exploring neighbourhoods beyond the River Walk.

By car Driving in Texas' second largest city can be stressful and parking is expensive – thankfully, most of the main attractions are within walking distance of each other.

By boat San Antonio Cruises offer river tours that make a 35min circuit of the River Walk, departing from several locations (daily 9am–9pm; $8.25; ☎ 800 417 4139, ⓦ riosanantonio.com) as well as a boat taxi service ($5/ single ride or $10/day pass).

Visitor centre 317 Alamo Plaza (daily 9am–5pm; ☎ 800 447 3372, ⓦ visitsanantonio.com).

ACCOMMODATION

The pleasure of a moonlit amble along the River Walk back to your hotel is one of the joys of visiting San Antonio, so it's worth paying more to **stay in the centre**. Motels are clustered near Market Square on the west side of downtown; just north of Brackenridge Park on Austin Hwy; or on I-35 north toward Austin.

Hilton Palacio del Rio 200 S Alamo St ☎ 210 222 1400, ⓦ hilton.com. Modularly constructed for the 1968 World's Fair in just nine months, this hotel features spacious rooms with balconies overlooking the River Walk. A great value for the prime location, especially on the heels of a recent extensive renovation. $149

Menger Hotel 204 Alamo Plaza ☎ 210 223 4361, ⓦ mengerhotel.com. Bang by the Alamo, this atmospheric, historic hotel was a famous destination on the great cattle drives; Teddy Roosevelt recruited his "Rough Riders" here in 1898 for the Spanish-American War. The rooms don't quite live up to the glamour of the lobby, bar and communal areas. $149

★ **Omni La Mansion del Rio** 112 College St ☎ 210 518 1000, ⓦ omnihotels.com. Rooms at the nicest hotel property on the River Walk come with a full range of amenities and Spanish colonial decor, and some have courtyard access to the heated pool. $209

Pinn Road Inn & Suites 2327 Pinn Rd ☎ 210 670 1374, ⓦ pinnroadinn.com. Not the most central option, but a great deal for the rate (particularly the suites) and it's just a 10min drive to downtown. Rooms have charmingly dated decor, but all are clean and nicely furnished, with flat-screen TVs; the suites are larger and have kitchenettes. Doubles $70, suites $80

EATING

★ **Boudro's** 421 E Commerce St ☎ 210 224 8484. This stylish River Walk Tex-Mex bistro serves creative New American/Southwestern mains including mesquite-grilled quail ($28), a wonderful guacamole ($9) made at your table and killer prickly-pear margaritas. Mon–Thurs & Sun 11am–11pm, Fri & Sat 11am–midnight.

El Mirador 722 S St Mary's St ☎ 210 225 9444. Popular family-owned cantina serving very cheap Mexican breakfasts (around $4.25) and lunches ($6–9), and pricier Southwestern cuisine, such as grilled salmon in a citrus-based achiote sauce ($15) in the evening. Mon–Sat 6.30am–9pm, Sun 6.30am–2pm.

The Guenther House 205 E Guenther St ☎ 800 235 8186. An hour or two savouring the cookies and cakes in this airy flour-mill-cum-museum in the King William Historic District makes for a decadent outing, but for a real treat come early for scrumptious Southern-style breakfasts including biscuits and gravy ($5.25) and buttermilk pancakes ($6.25). Daily 7am–3pm.

Guillermo's 618 McCullough Ave ☎ 210 223 5587. Close to the River Walk, this cosy restaurant serves heaps of lovingly prepared Italian-American comfort food, including pizzas (from $11 for a large) and shrimp lasagne ($12). Mon–Sat 11am–9pm, Sun noon–8pm.

Liberty Bar 328 E Josephine St ☎ 210 227 1187. Popular, inexpensive restaurant and bar in a historic building dating back to the nineteenth century. Rotating menus feature specials such as pork sausage with sautéed cabbage ($12). Mon–Thurs & Sun 11am–9.30pm, Fri & Sat 11am–11pm.

★ **Mi Tierra** 218 Produce Row ☎ 210 225 1262. With its bedazzlement of *piñatas*, fairy lights and fiesta flowers, this festive 24hr institution is the highlight of Market Square, serving good, inexpensive Tex-Mex staples (mains around $11) and delicious sugary cakes at its *panadería*. Great bar, too. Daily 24hr.

9

NIGHTLIFE AND ENTERTAINMENT

Downtown, the River Walk offers rowdy **bars and clubs**. Somewhat less touristy, **Houston Street** is fast becoming a party strip with a crop of slick yuppie bars, while **S Alamo Street** has a smattering of great dives and live music joints. The year's biggest event is April's ten-day **Fiesta San Antonio** (ⓦfiesta-sa.org), marking Texas's victory in the Battle of San Jacinto with parades, cookouts and Latin music.

BARS

★ **Bar America** 723 S Alamo St ☎210 223 1285. Three pool tables, two rows of booths with well-worn orange vinyl seating and the best jukebox in town make this 30-year-old family-run dive a favourite for a cross-section of locals. Lone Star pounders cost $1.50. Daily 7.30pm–2am.

Beethoven Beer Garden 422 Pereida St ☎210 222 1521. Just off of S Alamo St in the King William District, this private club (regularly open to the public) is devoted to the preservation of German music and language. On the first Friday of each month from 5pm to midnight, stop by for cheap beer and huge dollops of delicious potato salad. Tues–Sat 4pm–2am.

Blue Star Brewing Company 1414 S Alamo St ☎210 212 5506, ⓦbluestarbrewing.com. Home brews (the cask-conditioned ale is an especially good bet; $5), food and live music – from Texas swing to Latin – in an airy arts complex in the King William District. Tues–Thurs 11am–11pm, Fri & Sat 11am–2am, Sun 11am–3pm.

Leaping Lizards 302 E Commerce ☎210 271 9494. At street level just a few steps up from the River Walk, this rowdy and youthful dive is frequented by local service-industry workers who flock here for the cheap drinks. Daily 2pm–2am.

Menger Bar 204 Alamo Plaza ☎210 223 4361. Cigar-smoking, top-shelf whiskey drinkers will feel right at home in this bar attached to the *Menger Hotel*, steps from the Alamo. Mon–Fri 11am–midnight, Sat & Sun 2pm–midnight.

LIVE MUSIC AND THEATRE

San Antonio's live music scene isn't terribly diverse, but there are plenty of places to catch an act. Just a short drive away in the Hill Country you'll find some great old rural dance halls, including *Gruene Hall* in New Braunfels (see p.589). For listings, check the free weekly *Current* (ⓦsacurrent.com).

Arneson River Theatre ☎210 207 8610, ⓦlavillita .com/arneson. At this outdoor venue on the River Walk opposite La Villita, you can watch Mexican folk music and dance on a stage separated from the audience by the river. Hours vary.

Aztec on the River 201 E Commerce St ☎210 481 1200, ⓦtheaztectheatre.com. An opulent, immaculate Art Deco theatre currently hosting short-run productions.

John T. Floore Country Store 14492 Old Bandera Rd, downtown Helotes ☎210 695 8827, ⓦliveatfloores.com. Old country dance hall 20 miles northwest of San Antonio, with great *tamales* (starchy, corn-based dough cooked in a leaf wrapper) and outdoor dancing at the weekend. The best bands in Texas play here regularly. Tues–Thurs 11am–4pm, Fri & Sat 11am–10pm, Sun 11am–9pm.

Dallas

Contrary to popular belief, there's no oil in status-conscious **DALLAS**. Since its founding in 1841 as a prairie trading post, by Tennessee lawyer John Neely Bryan and his Arkansas friend Joe Dallas, successive generations of **entrepreneurs** have amassed wealth here through trade and finance, using first cattle and later oil reserves as collateral. The power of **money** in Dallas was demonstrated in the late 1950s, when its financiers threw their weight behind integration – potentially racist restaurant owners and bus drivers were pressured not to resist the new policies and Dallas was spared major upheavals. The city's image, however, was tarnished by the **assassination** of President Kennedy in 1963 and it took the building of the Dallas/Fort Worth International Airport in the 1960s, and the twin successes of the *Dallas* TV show and the Cowboys football team in the 1970s, to restore confidence.

These days, the city's occasional stuffiness (**George W. Bush** moved here, to 10141 Daria Place, after vacating the White House) is tempered by a typically Texas delight in self-parody – this is, after all, the city that calls itself "Big D".

Downtown

Downtown Dallas is a paean to commerce. Studding the elegant modern skyline, many of its skyscrapers are landmarks themselves. The most noteworthy is **Fountain Place Tower**,

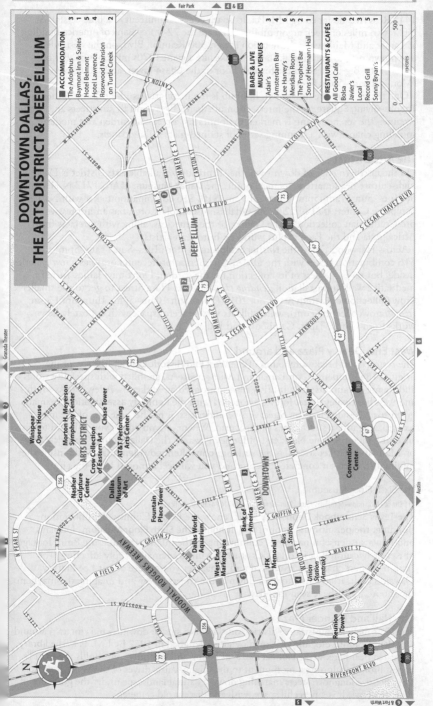

DOWNTOWN DALLAS, THE ARTS DISTRICT & DEEP ELLUM

■ ACCOMMODATION
The Adolphus	3
Baymont Inn & Suites	1
Hotel Belmont	5
Hotel Lawrence	4
Rosewood Mansion on Turtle Creek	2

■ BARS & LIVE MUSIC VENUES
Adair's	3
Amsterdam Bar	4
Lee Harvey's	6
Meridian Room	5
The Prophet Bar	2
Sons of Hermann Hall	1

● RESTAURANTS & CAFÉS
All Good Café	4
Bolsa	6
Javier's	2
Local	3
Record Grill	5
Sonny Bryan's	1

0   500

0   meters

N

▲ Fair Park   ▲ 4 & 5

▲ Granada Theater   ▲ 2

► Austin

► 6

▼ 5

▼ 6 & 8 Fort Worth

9

1445 Ross Ave, designed by I.M. Pei, its sharp edges reminiscent of a blue crystal. At night, two miles of green argon tubing delineate the 72-storey **Bank of America** building at Lamar and Main, while the **Reunion Tower**, 300 Reunion Blvd, on the west side of downtown next to the Amtrak station, looks like a giant 1970s microphone. For big views of the Big D, head to the fortieth floor of the **Chase Tower**, at 2200 Ross Ave (Mon–Fri 8am–5pm; free).

One refuge from the downtown hubbub is the incongruous Philip Johnson-designed **Thanks-Giving Square**, at the intersection of Akard, Ervay and Bryan streets and Pacific Avenue. The serene setting is marked by fountains, a pleasant garden and modern spiralling chapel with a stunning series of stained-glass ceiling panels.

The Arts District

On the northern edge of downtown, the surprisingly walkable **Arts District** is Dallas' high-culture headquarters. Its focal point, the **Dallas Museum of Art**, 1717 N Harwood St (Tues–Sun 11am–5pm, Thurs till 9pm; $10, $16 combination ticket with Nasher Sculpture Center; ☎214 922 1200, ⍵dallasmuseumofart.org), has an impressive pre-Columbian collection in the Gallery of the Americas, along with artefacts from Africa, Asia and the Pacific, plus works by European artists.

Across Harwood Drive, the **Nasher Sculpture Center** (Tues–Sun 11am–5pm; $10, $16 combination ticket with the DMA; ⍵nashersculpturecenter.org) has a few galleries inside, but saves the best of its collection for the garden. Don't miss James Turrell's meditative walk-in installation *Tending (Blue)*. Cross Flora Street to get to the smaller **Crow Collection of Eastern Art** at no. 2010 (Tues–Sun 10am–5pm, Thurs until 9pm; free; ⍵crowcollection.com), which fills its very peaceful space with delicately hewn works from China, Tibet, Cambodia and India.

West End, Dealey Plaza and around

The restored red-brick warehouses of the **West End Historic District**, the site of the original 1841 settlement on Lamar and Munger streets, are filled with speciality stores and theme restaurants; it's a touristy place, thronged at weekends. A few blocks south and west lies **Dealey Plaza**, forever associated with the **Kennedy assassination**. A small green space beside Houston Street's triple underpass, it has become one of the most recognizable urban streetscapes in the world. Whenever you come, you will find tourists snapping pictures. One block east of Dealey Plaza, in the **Dallas County Historical Plaza** on Main and Market streets, is the striking **John F. Kennedy Memorial**. Walk inside the minimalist, open-air concrete structure and you will feel removed from the city.

The Sixth Floor Museum

411 Elm St • Mon noon–6pm, Tues–Sun 10am–6pm • $16 • ☎214 747 6660, ⍵jfk.org

The **Texas Schoolbook Depository** itself is now the Dallas County Administration Building, the penultimate floor of which houses **the Sixth Floor Museum**. Displays build up a suspenseful narrative, culminating in the infamous juddering 8mm footage of Kennedy crumpling into Jackie's arms; the images remain deeply affecting. The "gunman's nest" has been re-created and, whatever you believe about Lee Harvey Oswald's guilt, it's chilling to look down at the streets below and imagine the mayhem the shooter must have seen that day.

City Hall and Pioneer Plaza

The city's main administrative district, on the south side of downtown, is focused around **City Hall**, a cantilevered upside-down pyramid designed in 1972 by I.M. Pei. The **library** is located near here, while **Pioneer Plaza**, at Young and Griffin streets, holds the world's largest bronze sculpture, a monument to the mighty cattle drives of the West. It depicts forty life-size longhorn steers marching down a natural landscape under the guidance of three cowboys. It is a peaceful space, with an adjacent old cemetery.

Dallas Heritage Village

1515 S Harwood St • Tues–Sat 10am–4pm, Sun noon–4pm • $9

Dallas's first park, **Old City Park**, is now both a recreational area and home to the **Dallas Heritage Village**, a living museum that charts the history of north Texas from 1840 to 1910. More than thirty buildings have been relocated to this bucolic spot south of I-30 from towns across the region, among them a farmhouse, a bank, a train station, a store, a church and a schoolhouse.

Deep Ellum

Deep Ellum – five blocks east of downtown between the railroad tracks and I-30 at Elm and Main streets – is the city's beguiling **alternative district**. Famous in the 1920s for its jazz and blues clubs (and supposedly named by Blind Lemon Jefferson, though it's more likely to stem from the Southern pronunciation of "elm"), the old warehouse district has fallen on tough times in recent years. Locals say it earned an undeserved violent reputation (partly because of misinformation peddled by the mayor) and people stayed away. It may have reached bottom, though, and its bars, music clubs, galleries and restaurants – including some of the best in the city – are once again luring the crowds back. It's walkable and best visited in the late afternoon or early evening, when a gallery tour can be combined with a night out.

Fair Park

Not far southeast of Deep Ellum, **Fair Park**, a gargantuan Art Deco plaza bedecked with endless Lone Stars, was built to house the Texas Centennial Exposition in 1936, and now hosts the annual **State Fair of Texas** (ⓦbigtex.com) for three weeks in October, the biggest event of its kind in the USA, with more than three million revellers. Its plethora of fine museums include the lively **Women's Museum** (Tues–Sun noon–5pm; $5; ⓦthewomens museum.org), full of intriguing facts and figures (women smile eight times a day more than men, apparently) and temporary exhibits exploring subjects as varied as Marilyn Monroe, female photographers and the lure of the shoe. The nearby **African American Museum** (Tues–Fri 11am–5pm, Sat 10am–5pm; free; ⓦaamdallas.org) is also terrific, with a superb collection of folk art. The **Museum of Nature and Science** (Mon–Sat 10am–5pm, Sun noon–5pm; $9.50; ⓦnatureandscience.org) boasts exhibits on everything from fossils to dental hygiene.

The centrepiece of the park is the magnificent **Hall of State Building**, an Art Deco treasure of bronze statues, blue tiles, mosaics and murals, with rooms decorated to celebrate the different regions of Texas (Tues–Sat 10am–5pm, Sun 1–5pm; free).

ARRIVAL AND DEPARTURE   DALLAS

By car Dallas proper is circled by Inner Loop 12 (or Northwest Hwy) and Outer Loop I-635 (which becomes LBJ Freeway).

By plane Dallas is served by two major airports. Dallas/Fort Worth (ⓣ972 574 8888, ⓦdfwairport.com) is around 17 miles west. You can catch one of a variety of different shuttle buses, such as SuperShuttle (ⓣ817 329 2000, ⓦsupershuttle .com), which costs $20 to get downtown; taxis cost around $45 (Yellow Cab; ⓣ214 426 6262). The other airport, Love Field (ⓣ214 670 6073, ⓦdallas-lovefield.com), used mostly by Southwest Airlines, lies about 9 miles northwest of Dallas. Taxis to downtown cost around $18, shuttles around $15.

By bus Greyhound is downtown at 205 S Lamar St.
Destinations Amarillo (3 daily; 6hr 50min); Austin (16 daily; 3hr 45min); El Paso (5 daily; 12hr 35min); Fort Worth (11 daily; 40min); Houston (10 daily; 4hr 10min); San Antonio (12 daily; 5hr).

By train Amtrak's 1916 Union Station is at 400 S Houston St. The Trinity Railway Express (ⓣ214 979 1111, ⓦtrinityrailway express.org) service runs regular commuter trains to Fort Worth for $5.
Destinations Austin (1 daily; 5hr 50min); San Antonio (1 daily; 10hr 10min).

GETTING AROUND AND INFORMATION

By light rail or bus DART, the Dallas Area Rapid Transit system (ⓣ214 979 1111, ⓦdart.org), is a light rail network that operates downtown and travels further afield to places including Mockingbird Station.

9

Day passes cost $4 and they're also good for the city's buses.

By tram (trolley) The McKinney Trolley (☎ 214 855 0006, ⓦ mata.org) runs north from the downtown Dallas Museum of Art up McKinney Ave to the West Village, a complex of restaurants and bars (every 30min, Mon–Fri 7am–midnight, Sat 10am–midnight; free).

Visitor centre Downtown in the "Old Red" Courthouse, 100 S Houston St (daily 9am–5pm; ☎ 214 571 1000, ⓦ visitdallas.com).

ACCOMMODATION

★ **The Adolphus** 1321 Commerce St ☎ 214 742 8200, ⓦ hoteladolphus.com. Stunning historic downtown hotel, decorated with antiques. Said to be the most beautiful building west of Venice, Italy, when it was built in 1912, it's a glamorous place to stay. **$170**

Baymont Inn & Suites 2370 W NW Hwy ☎ 214 350 5577, ⓦ baymontinndallas.com. Its location is anything but scenic, but the *Baymont* makes up for it with easy access to downtown and the airport, and comfortable accommodation at more than reasonable rates. Amenities include an indoor pool, gym and breakfast. **$79**

★ **Hotel Belmont** 901 Fort Worth Ave ☎ 866 870 8010, ⓦ belmontdallas.com. Renovated 1940s motel a short drive from downtown. Feels more like LA than Dallas, with a hip, casual bar and a pool with stunning city views. **$109**

Hotel Lawrence 302 S Houston St ☎ 877 396 0334, ⓦ hotellawrence.com. Central European-style hotel in a 1920s building. Small, comfortable rooms, a good continental breakfast, and milk and cookies every evening. **$139**

Rosewood Mansion on Turtle Creek 2821 Turtle Creek Blvd ☎ 214 559 2100, ⓦ mansiononturtlecreek .com. Situated in a leafy Dallas neighbourhood, this is the city's most exclusive and expensive hotel, with a wide variety of rooms and suites; all are exceedingly well appointed and stylish, with top-notch amenities including plush linens and large plasma TVs. It also features fine restaurants and a bar with terrace seating. **$330**

EATING

Dallas's restaurant scene is largely defined by its **neighbourhoods**. Downtown, the **West End Historic District** is lively, if touristy, with rowdy chains; in hipper **Deep Ellum** you can chow down on anything from sushi to Mexican. Uptown, chic **West Village**, accessible on the McKinney Trolley, is a squeaky-clean cluster of bars and restaurants catering to youthful loft-dwellers. Northeast of downtown, parallel to I-75, **Lower Greenville Avenue** has a more eclectic feel.

★ **All Good Café** 2934 Main St ☎ 214 742 5362, ⓦ allgoodcafe.com. Fresh home-style cooking at this cheery Deep Ellum haunt, which is more evocative of Austin than Dallas and transforms into a live Texas music venue in the evenings. Breakfast specials include the Hat Trick – *huevos rancheros* with peppered bacon and pancakes ($10.99) – while for dinner the meatloaf ($10.99) is unfussy, carnivorous bliss. Mon & Sun 9am–2pm, Tues–Sat 9am–9pm.

Bolsa 614 W Davis St ☎ 214 367 9367. Located in the (for Dallas) bohemian neighbourhood of Oak Cliff, this restaurant focuses on fresh, local ingredients and attracts a young, professional crowd. Much of the menu is seasonal, with regular dishes such as tasty flatbreads ($12–14) and a juicy pork loin with greens ($26). Mon–Fri 4–10.30pm, Sat 10am–11pm, Sun 10am–10pm.

Javier's 4912 Cole Ave ☎ 214 521 4211. At this handsome, long-running restaurant count on refreshingly traditional takes on Mexican food. It's not cheap, but the dishes are a revelation and include choices such as broiled shrimp with a BBQ, pineapple and almond sauce ($26.95) and beef tenderloin stuffed with cheese and butter ($28.95). Mon–Wed & Sun 5.30–10pm, Thurs–Sat 5.30–11pm.

Local 2936 Elm St ☎ 214 752 7500. Upscale but unpretentious modern restaurant in a historic Deep Ellum building. Mains ($20–35) include a cornflake-crusted sea bass; for dessert, the banana pudding ($7) is divine. Tues–Sat 5.30–10pm.

Record Grill 605 Elm St ☎ 214 742 1353. A small downtown greasy spoon wedged between a building and a car park. There's nothing in the way of atmosphere, but a double-meat bacon cheeseburger costs just $4.25. Not far from the Sixth Floor Museum. Mon–Fri 6am–3pm, Sat 6am–12.30pm.

Sonny Bryan's 2202 Inwood Rd ☎ 214 357 7120. The original location – it still looks like a shack – of this favourite local BBQ chain lies uptown. Get there in good time as the deliciously tender, smoky meat can be all snapped up by early afternoon. Daily 10am–9pm.

ENTERTAINMENT AND NIGHTLIFE

The best **nightlife** destinations in Dallas are Deep Ellum and Lower Greenville, and there is a small cluster of good **bars** on Perry Avenue near Fair Park. Full listings can be found in Thursday's free *Dallas Observer* (ⓦ dallasobserver.com) or in the *Dallas Morning News* (ⓦ dallasnews.com). The Arts District is the best spot to catch high-end plays and concerts, while Deep Ellum has no shortage of hip live music venues.

BARS

Adair's 2624 Commerce St ☎214 939 9900, ⓦadairs
saloon.com. This Deep Ellum hole-in-the-wall attracts both
old-timers and students with its hard-edged live honky-tonk
music, and shuffleboard and pool tables. Daily specials mean
drink prices are always manageable, particularly on Wed
when domestic pints go for $2. Mon 4pm–2am, Tues–Fri
11am–2am, Sat noon–2am, Sun 2pm–2am.

Amsterdam Bar 831 Exposition Ave ☎214 214 827
9933. The best of a cluster of great bars right next door to
Fair Park, with occasional live jazz, a large outdoor patio
and a good range of beers on tap. Daily 2.30pm–2am.

★ **Lee Harvey's** 1807 Gould St ☎214 428 1555,
ⓦleeharveys.com. PBR beer flows like water at this dive
situated between downtown and Deep Ellum with rows
of picnic tables on its patio and live music at weekends. A
local institution with little attitude and a low-key crowd.
Mon–Fri 11am–2am, Sat 3pm–2am, Sun 1pm–2am.

Meridian Room 3611 Parry Ave ☎214 826 8383. Popular
pub adjacent to Fair Park with an inviting, vintage decor and
a tasty Guinness steak sandwich ($9). It's not terribly roomy
so can get packed, but if you can find a table you'll want to
linger. Mon–Sat 4pm–2am, Sun noon–2am.

LIVE MUSIC VENUES AND THEATRES

AT&T Performing Arts Center 2100 Ross Ave ☎214
880 0202, ⓦattpac.org. This modern, four-venue

complex, designed by some of the world's pre-eminent
architects, is within walking distance of the Arts District
museums and hosts plays and big-name concerts.

Granada Theater 3524 Greenville Ave ☎214 824
9933, ⓦgranadatheater.com. Lovely old movie theatre
with a full slate of regional bands across all genres as
well as big-name acts, as well as Sunday-night watching
parties.

Morton H. Meyerson Symphony Center 2301 Flora
St ☎214 670 3600, ⓦdallassymphony.com. The Dallas
Symphony Orchestra performs in this showpiece Arts
District concert hall that also hosts regular performances
by local symphonies and choral groups.

The Prophet Bar 2548 Elm St ☎214 742 3667,
ⓦtheprophetbar.com. Venerable Deep Ellum live music
spot that hosts an eclectic mix of acts and nightly features,
including jam sessions and electronica DJs. Hours vary.

Sons of Hermann Hall 3414 Elm St ☎214 747 4422,
ⓦsonsofhermann.com. Delightfully old-school country
venue, just beyond Deep Ellum, where the Texas masters
come to play, and respectful young outfits pay tribute.
Plus swing lessons, open-mic nights and acoustic jams.
Tues & Wed 7pm–midnight, Thurs–Sat 7pm–2am.

Winspear Opera House 2403 Flora St ☎214 443 1000,
ⓦdallasopera.org. The bright-red, state-of-the-art
Winspear in the Arts District hosts performances by the
Dallas Opera.

Fort Worth

Often dismissed as some kind of poor relation to Dallas, friendly **FORT WORTH** in fact
has a buzz largely missing from its neighbour 35 miles to the east. Distinctly Western
in character and history, in the 1870s it was a stop on the great cattle drive to Kansas,
the **Chisholm Trail**, and when the railroads arrived it became a livestock market in its
own right. Cowboys and outlaws populated the city in its early years and much of that
character remains. But while the cattle trade is still a major industry and the **Stockyards**
provide a stimulating, atmospheric slice of Old West life, Fort Worth also prides itself
on excellent **museums** – the best in the state – and a compact, bustling and walker-
friendly **downtown**. Looking toward the future, the city is also undertaking the massive
Trinity River Master Plan, which will include one of the largest urban parks in the US,
and trails and greenways along the Trinity River.

Downtown

The chief focus of **downtown** Fort Worth is **Sundance Square**, a leafy, red-brick-paved
fourteen-block area of shops, restaurants and bars between First and Sixth streets. The
square is ringed by glittering skyscrapers and pervaded with a genuine enthusiasm for
the town's rich history.

Bass Performance Hall and around

525 Commerce St • Group tours Sat; 1hr 15min • ☎817 212 4215

Filling the block bounded by Commerce, Calhoun, Fourth and Fifth streets, **Bass
Performance Hall** (see p.604) is downtown's most arresting visual treat. A breathtaking

9

building that recalls the great opera houses of Europe, it's fronted by angels blowing golden trumpets. Elsewhere, notice the **trompe l'oeil murals** – especially the Chisholm Trail mural on Third Street between Main and Houston.

Sid Richardson Museum of Western Art

309 Main St • Mon–Thurs 9am–5pm, Fri & Sat 9am–8pm, Sun noon–5pm • Free • ⓦ sidrichardsonmuseum.org

Fans of cowboy art should head for the **Sid Richardson Museum of Western Art**, which has an excellent collection of late works by Frederic Remington, including some of his best black-and-white illustrations, and early elegiac cowboy scenes by Charles Russell; it also hosts temporary exhibitions.

The Cultural District

Fort Worth has the best galleries and museums in Texas, most of them concentrated in the **Cultural District**, two miles west of downtown on the #2 bus.

Kimbell Art Museum

3333 Camp Bowie Blvd • Tues–Thurs & Sat 10am–5pm, Fri noon–8pm, Sun noon–5pm • Free; special exhibits $16 • ⓦ kimbellart.org

The **Kimbell Art Museum** is one of the best small art museums in the US. The vaulted, naturally lit structure was designed by Louis Kahn, and the impeccable collection includes pre-Columbian and African pieces, with some noteworthy Maya funerary urns, unusual Asian antiquities, Pre-Columbian figures and a handful of Renaissance masterpieces.

Modern Art Museum

3200 Darnell St • Tues–Sat 10am–5pm, Sun 11am–5pm • $10, free Wed & first Sun of each month • ⓦ themodern.org

The **Modern Art Museum** is a Tadao Ando-designed modernist building whose light-flooded rooms hold the largest collection of modern art in the nation after New York's MoMA. Due to the vast nature of the permanent holdings, the exhibits rotate frequently, and the museum also regularly hosts theatre performances and film screenings.

Amon Carter Museum

3501 Camp Bowie Blvd • Tues, Wed, Fri & Sat 10am–5pm, Thurs 10am–8pm, Sun noon–5pm • Free • ⓦ cartermuseum.org

The **Amon Carter Museum**, just up the hill from the Modern Art Museum, concentrates on American art, with stunning photographs of Western landscapes, as well as a fine assortment of Remingtons and Russells, and works by Winslow Homer and Georgia O'Keeffe. The adjoining **library** complements the collection with a wide range of related subject matter and offers free wi-fi.

The Stockyards

With its wooden sidewalks, old storefronts, dusty rodeos and beer-soaked honky-tonks, the ten-block **Stockyards** area – centred on Exchange Avenue, two miles north of downtown – offers an evocation of the days when Fort Worth was "the richest little city in the world". There are daily **cattle drives**, a huffing, shuffling cavalcade of fifteen or so Texas Longhorns, that occur, weather permitting, at 11.30am. The cattle drives begin at the corrals behind the Livestock Exchange Building and the herd returns around 4pm.

Museums in the Stockyards have an appealing small-town feel. Try the **Stockyards Museum** (Mon–Sat 10am–5pm; donation suggested; ⓦ stockyardsmuseum.org), in the huge Livestock Exchange Building, offering a lovingly compiled jumble of local memorabilia including steer skulls, pre-Columbian pottery and rodeo posters.

Next door, the **Cowtown Coliseum** (ticket prices vary; ☏ 817 625 1025, ⓦ cowtown coliseum.com) holds rodeos, Wild West shows and country music hoedowns every weekend. It's fronted by a statue of Bill Pickett, the black rodeo star who invented the unsavoury but effective practice of "bulldogging" – stunning the bull by biting its lip.

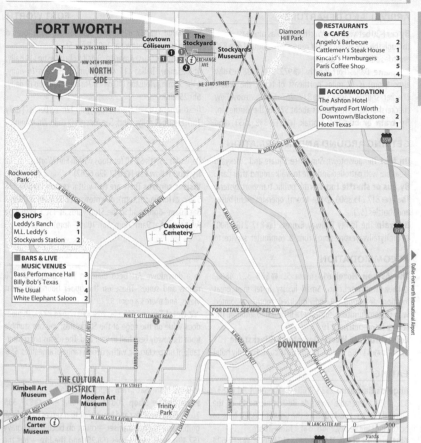

FORT WORTH

N

NORTH SIDE

NW 25TH STREET
NW 24TH STREET
NW 21ST STREET

Cowtown Coliseum
The Stockyards
Stockyards Museum
EXCHANGE AVE
NE 23RD STREET

Diamond Hill Park

Rockwood Park

N HENDERSON STREET

Oakwood Cemetery

N NORTHSIDE DRIVE
N MAIN STREET

W NORTHSIDE DRIVE

35W

Dallas-Fort Worth International Airport

● **RESTAURANTS & CAFÉS**
Angelo's Barbecue — 2
Cattlemen's Steak House — 1
Kincaid's Hamburgers — 3
Paris Coffee Shop — 5
Reata — 4

■ **ACCOMMODATION**
The Ashton Hotel — 3
Courtyard Fort Worth Downtown/Blackstone — 2
Hotel Texas — 1

● **SHOPS**
Leddy's Ranch — 3
M.L. Leddy's — 1
Stockyards Station — 2

■ **BARS & LIVE MUSIC VENUES**
Bass Performance Hall — 3
Billy Bob's Texas — 1
The Usual — 4
White Elephant Saloon — 2

WHITE SETTLEMENT ROAD

FOR DETAIL SEE MAP BELOW

DOWNTOWN

N UNIVERSITY DRIVE
CARROLL STREET
N HENDERSON STREET
COMMERCE STREET

THE CULTURAL DISTRICT
Kimbell Art Museum
Modern Art Museum
W 7TH STREET
Amon Carter Museum
CAMP BOWIE BOULEVARD
W LANCASTER AVENUE

Trinity Park

W LANCASTER AVE

0 — 500 yards

30

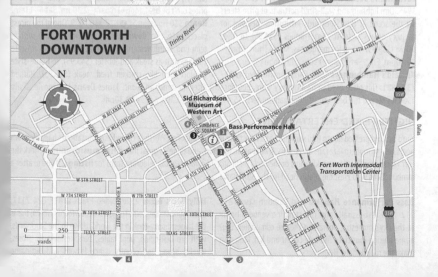

FORT WORTH DOWNTOWN

N

Trinity River

W BELKNAP STREET
W WEATHERFORD STREET
W 1ST STREET
W 2ND STREET

N FOREST PARK BLVD
N HENDERSON STREET
W BELKNAP STREET
W WEATHERFORD STREET
W 1ST STREET

Sid Richardson Museum of Western Art

SUNDANCE SQUARE
Bass Performance Hall

W 5TH STREET
W 6TH STREET
W 7TH STREET
W 10TH STREET
TEXAS STREET

THROCKMORTON STREET
HOUSTON STREET
COMMERCE STREET
TAYLOR STREET
LAMAR STREET
JENNINGS AVE

E 1ST STREET
E 2ND STREET
E 3RD STREET
E 4TH STREET
E 5TH STREET

Fort Worth Intermodal Transportation Center

E 9TH STREET
E 13TH STREET
E 15TH STREET
E 16TH STREET
E 18TH STREET

35W

Dallas

0 — 250 yards

9

ARRIVAL AND DEPARTURE

By car I-30 between Fort Worth and Dallas runs east–west through the city, while I-35W runs north–south. Loop 820 encircles all the major sights.

By plane Dallas/Fort Worth (☎972 574 8888, ⓦdfw airport.com) is 17 miles northeast of town; the Yellow Checker shuttle service (☎817 267 5150, ⓦgoyellow checkershuttle.com), charges about $25 for the journey in.

By train or bus The Amtrak (☎817 332 2931) and Greyhound (☎817 429 3089) stations are both located southeast of downtown at 1001 Jones St.

Destinations (bus) Amarillo (3 daily; 6hr); Austin (10 daily; 4hr 25min); Dallas (11 daily; 40min); El Paso (6 daily; 11hr 30min); Houston (10 daily; 7hr); San Antonio (9 daily; 6hr 25min).

Destinations (train) Austin (1 daily; 4hr 12min); Dallas (1 daily 1hr); El Paso (1 daily; 24hr); San Antonio (1 daily; 7hr 45min).

GETTING AROUND AND INFORMATION

On foot The downtown Sundance Square and Stockyard areas are well patrolled and safe to walk around after dark.

By bus or shuttle Fort Worth's public transport system, The T (☎817 215 8600, ⓦthe-t.com), operates useful buses and shuttles ($2).

By train The Trinity Railway Express (☎817 215 8600, ⓦtrinityrailwayexpress.org) runs a commuter service to Dallas for $5; it's $2.50 for stops within Fort Worth.

By taxi Yellow Cab (☎817 426 6262)

Visitor centres There are two visitor centres (☎800 433 5747, ⓦfortworth.com): downtown at 508 Main St (Mon–Sat 10am–6pm) and in the Stockyards at 130 E Exchange Ave (Mon–Sat 9am–6pm, Sun 10am–4pm).

ACCOMMODATION

The Ashton Hotel 610 Main St ☎866 327 4866, ⓦtheashtonhotel.com. Small luxury hotel in a great location, featuring 39 individualized rooms appointed with custom furniture; some feel a little dated, though. The service is top-notch. **$219**

Courtyard Fort Worth Downtown/Blackstone 601 Main St ☎817 885 8700, ⓦmarriott.com. Friendly hotel in a downtown Art Deco building with more than 200 rooms and suites. Those on the upper floor have great views, and there's a pool. **$229**

★ **Hotel Texas** 2415 Ellis Ave ☎817 624 2224. Tremendous value on the edge of the Stockyards; you can stumble from the rowdy beer hall to your bed. The rooms are comfortable, if unspectacular, with a decent range of amenities. **$89**

EATING

Angelo's Barbecue 2533 White Settlement Rd ☎817 332 0357. Venerable westside BBQ joint, north of the Cultural District. Locals declare the brisket ($8.95) here to be the best in the city. Mon–Sat 11am–10pm.

Cattlemen's Steak House 2458 N Main St ☎817 624 3945. Dim lighting and wall-sized portraits of prize steers set the scene at this Stockyards institution, beloved for its juicy steaks – from 16oz T-bones ($34.95) to 18oz sirloin ($39.95) – and icy margaritas. Mon–Thurs 11am–10.30pm, Fri & Sat 11am–11pm, Sun noon–9pm.

Kincaid's Hamburgers 4901 Camp Bowie Blvd ☎817 732 2881. This place used to be a grocery store, but since 1966 it's served the best unfussy 8oz hamburgers ($5.49) in Texas. Mon–Sat 11am–8pm, Sun 11am–3pm.

Paris Coffee Shop 700 W Magnolia Ave ☎817 335 2041. Busy breakfast and lunch spot that serves basic, fresh grub. There are no surprises – count on biscuits and gravy ($2.40), steak sandwiches ($8.25) and the like – but the prices can't be beat. Mon–Fri 6am–2.30pm, Sat 6–11am.

Reata 310 Houston St ☎817 336 1009. One of the nicest places to eat in downtown's Sundance Square, with a tempting Southwestern menu that ranges from upscale cuisine, such as steak and lobster ($43.95), to home-style comfort food like chicken fried steak ($16.95). Named after the ranch in *Giant*, James Dean's last movie. Daily 11am–2.30pm & 5–10.30pm.

NIGHTLIFE AND ENTERTAINMENT

You'd be hard pressed not to find something to your taste in after-dark Fort Worth, a city where roustabouts happily down beers next to modern jazz fans and bikers. **Bar crawling** is fun, and there's a great mix of **live music venues**. Check the *Fort Worth Weekly* (ⓦfwweekly.com) or the *Fort Worth Star-Telegram* (ⓦstar-telegram.com) for **listings**. If you're after a rambunctious Wild West night out, head for the Stockyards.

Bass Performance Hall 4th and Calhoun sts ☎817 212 4325, ⓦbasshall.com. This stunning venue is home to the city's orchestra, opera and theatre companies. Big-name touring musicians like Lyle Lovett and k.d. lang also make the rounds here. Hours vary.

Billy Bob's Texas 2520 Rodeo Plaza ☎817 624 7117, ⓦbillybobstexas.com. The jewel in cowtown's crown, this is the largest honky-tonk in the world, down in the Stockyards, with pro bull-riding, pool tables, bars, restaurants, stores, weekly swing and country dance lessons and big-name concerts. Mon–Wed 11am–midnight, Thurs 11am–2am, Fri 11am–5pm & 6pm–2am, Sat 11am–5pm & 6pm–midnight, Sun noon–2am.

★ **The Usual** 1408 W Magnolia Ave ☎817 810 0114. Sleek cocktail lounge exuding cool – and pleasantly devoid of pretension – serving well-conceived house creations as well as all of the classics. Has more of a mixed crowd than

you might expect and a steady line-up of quality DJs. Mon–Fri 4pm–2am, Sat & Sun 6pm–2am.

White Elephant Saloon 106 E Exchange Ave ☎817 624 8273, ⓦwhiteelephantsaloon.com. Notoriously wild and authentic old Stockyards saloon with a cowboy hat hall of fame and live acts nightly. Mon–Thurs & Sun noon–midnight, Fri & Sat noon–2am.

SHOPPING

Leddy's Ranch at Sundance 410 Houston St ☎817 336 0800. To stock up on top-of-the-line rhinestone Western wear or cowboy hats, head to Leddy's Ranch, which dresses some of the biggest acts in country music. Mon–Sat 9am–6pm.

M.L. Leddy's 2455 N Main St ☎888 565 2668. Venerable and well-respected hat, boot and saddle shop that also does a range of exquisite handmade buckles and equestrian

pieces. Mon–Sat 9am–6pm.

Stockyards Station 130 E Exchange Ave ☎817 625 9715, ⓦstockyardsstation.com. Large, open-air mall in the heart of the Stockyards with a collection of shops. It's undeniably touristy, but it houses the Ernest Tubb Record Shop (ⓦetrecordshop.com), which sells country music CDs. Daily 10am–8pm.

The Panhandle

Inhabitants of the **Panhandle**, the northernmost part of the state, call it "the real Texas". On a map, it appears as a rectangular appendix bordering Oklahoma and New Mexico. A starkly romantic agricultural **landscape** strewn with tumbleweeds and mesquite trees, it fulfils the fantasy of what Texas should look like. When Coronado's expedition passed this way in the sixteenth century, the gold-seekers drove stakes into the ground across the vast and unchanging vista, despairing of otherwise finding their way home – hence the name **Llano Estacado**, or staked plains, which persists today (the Panhandle is the southernmost portion of the Great Plains).

Once the buffalo – and the natives – had been driven away from what was seen as uninhabitable frontier country, the Panhandle in the 1870s began to yield great **natural resources**. Helium, especially in Amarillo, as well as oil and agriculture, have brought wealth to the region, which is also home to large **ranches**.

The Panhandle holds few actual tourist attractions – its real appeal is its barren, rural beauty. But **music** has deep roots in the area, too. Songwriters such as Bob Wills, Buddy Holly, Roy Orbison, Waylon Jennings, Terry Allen, Joe Ely, Jimmie Dale Gilmore and Natalie Maines of the Dixie Chicks all grew up here.

Lubbock

With its faceless block buildings and simple homes, **LUBBOCK**, the largest city in the Panhandle, is at first glance unremarkable. Dig a little deeper, though, and you will find a complex city, one that accommodates Southern Baptism, the high-scoring Texas Tech university's Red Raiders football team and a songwriting history unmatched in the state, led by Buddy Holly.

You can get an interesting overview of local history at the university's **Ranching Heritage Center** (Mon–Sat 10am–5pm, Sun 1–5pm; free; ⓦnrhc.ttu.edu), northwest of downtown, where 38 original buildings illustrate the evolution of ranch life. Highlights include a one-room schoolhouse, a limestone and sandstone house built to protect a pioneer family from attacks by Native Americans and a blacksmith's shop complete with period trade equipment.

ARRIVAL, GETTING AROUND AND INFORMATION   LUBBOCK

By car I-27 bisects the centre of Lubbock, while Loop 289 encircles the city and defines its outer limits.

By air Lubbock's Preston Smith Airport (☎806 775 2044, ⓦflylia.com) is a few minutes north of the city on I-27; taxis

9

BUDDY HOLLY

Lubbock's claim to world fame is as the birthplace of **Buddy Holly**. Inspired by the blues and country music of his childhood – and a seminal encounter with the young Elvis Presley, gigging in Lubbock at the *Cotton Club* – Buddy Holly was one of rock'n'roll's first singer-songwriters. The Holly sound, characterized by steady strumming guitar, rapid drumming and his trademark hiccupping vocals, was made famous by hits such as *Peggy Sue*, *Not Fade Away* and *That'll Be the Day*. Buddy was killed at 22 in the Iowa plane crash of February 3, 1959 ("The Day the Music Died"), that also claimed the Big Bopper and Ritchie Valens. Don't leave town without visiting the **Buddy Holly Center**, 1801 Crickets Ave (Tues–Sat 10am–5pm, Sun 1–5pm; $5; ⓦ buddyhollycenter.org), an impressive space that holds a collection of Holly memorabilia, including the black glasses he wore on the day he died.

Across the street from the center is the **Buddy Holly Statue**, an 8ft bronze figure that's the focal point of the Buddy and Maria Elena Holly Plaza. **Buddy's grave** is in Lubbock's cemetery at the end of 34th Street; take the right fork inside the gate, and the grave, decorated with flowers and guitar picks, is on the left.

to downtown cost around $20 (Yellow Cab; ☎ 806 765 7777). **Local buses** Citibus (☎ 806 712 2000, ⓦ citibus.com) runs commuter routes within the Loop, stopping at around

7.45pm (Mon–Sat; $1.50).
Visitor centre Sixth floor, 1500 Broadway (Mon–Fri 8am–5pm; ☎ 800 692 4035, ⓦ visitlubbock.org).

ACCOMMODATION

Baymont Inn and Suites 3901 19th St ☎ 800 337 0300, ⓦ baymontinns.com. Well-located and recently renovated chain motel (formerly the *Lubbock Inn*) with no-frills rooms, a restaurant and a pool with waterfalls. Breakfast is included. **$79**

Woodrow House B&B 2629 19th St ☎ 806 793 3330, ⓦ woodrowhouse.com. Ten rooms, each with a different theme – there's even one in a restored train carriage – in a mansion-style modern house opposite Texas Tech. There's a pool and the included breakfast is nicely prepared. **$99**

EATING AND DRINKING

Cagle Steaks 118 Inler Ave ☎ 806 795 3879. Classic Texas Plains steak restaurant where the vegetable options don't extend much beyond a baked potato or fries. A 16oz rib eye with all the trimmings costs $27. Mon–Thurs 5.30–9.30pm, Fri & Sat 5–10pm.

The Crafthouse Gastropub 3131 34th St ☎ 806 687 1466. Owned and operated by young, friendly Lubbock natives, this cute, intimate spot serves appealing soups, salads and sandwiches; its sweet onion soup ($7) and ratatouille ($9) are highlights. Tues–Thurs 11am–10pm, Fri & Sat 11am–midnight.

Gardski's 2009 Broadway ☎ 806 744 2391. Popular American restaurant for Texas Tech students and alumni, with historic photos lining the walls. The house fries ($6)

– lathered in cheese and doused with bacon bits – are filling enough, but there are plenty of other options, mostly burgers ($7–9) and sandwiches ($6.50–9). Daily 11am–10pm.

Lone Star Oyster 34th Flint Ave ☎ 806 796 0101. Beloved, well-worn dive bar that has been around for ages. As the name suggests, they serve oysters and assorted seafood dishes, but the real draws are the rock-bottom drink prices and the lively atmosphere. Mon–Fri & Sun 4pm–2am, Sat 11am–2pm.

Tom and Bingo's BBQ 3006 34th St ☎ 806 799 1514. This tiny family-run institution churns out the best chopped beef sandwich ($6) in Lubbock. When the brisket is sold out the doors close for the day. Mon–Sat 11am–3pm.

Amarillo and around

AMARILLO may seem cut off from the rest of Texas, up in the northern Panhandle, but it stands on one of the great American cross-country routes – I-40, once the legendary **Route 66**. The city's name comes from the Spanish word for "yellow", the colour of the soil characteristic to these parts. Sitting on ninety percent of the world's helium and hosting a world-class cattle market, Amarillo is a prosperous, laidback city with a nice mix of cowtown appeal, arty eccentricity and mouth-watering steaks.

Amarillo's small "**old town**" consists of a few tree-lined streets and some shabby homes. More interesting is the **Route 66 Historic District**, known locally as **Old San Jacinto**, a quirky stretch of restaurants, bars and stores that runs west along Sixth Street (the old Route 66) from Georgia for about a mile to Western Street.

Amarillo Livestock Auction

100 S Manhattan St off Third • ☎ 806 373 7464, café ☎ 806 342 9411, ⓦ amarillolivestockauction.com

Amarillo is host to the world's most stomping, snorting **livestock auction**. Held every Monday at 10am in the stockyards on the east side of town, it's a great show and a fascinating glimpse into Panhandle life. Stop in after at the on-site **café** for gut-busting plates of Texas and southern specialities; the chicken fried steak ($7.95) is legendary.

Cadillac Ranch

10 miles west of Amarillo on I-40, exit 60 (Arnot Rd)

For a classic slice of Americana, drive ten miles west of town to **Cadillac Ranch**. An extraordinary vision in the middle of nowhere, ten battered cars stand upended in the soil, their tail fins demonstrating the different Cadillac designs from 1949 to 1963. Since the cars were installed in 1974, they have been subject to countless makeovers at the hands of graffiti artists, photographers and members of the public – all encouraged by owner Stanley Marsh 3 (he eschews Roman numerals), eccentric helium millionaire and *bon vivant*, on whose land the cars are planted.

ARRIVAL AND INFORMATION

AMARILLO AND AROUND

By car I-40 cuts through Amarillo, running south of downtown; the old Route 66 (Sixth St) runs parallel, to the north.

By bus Greyhound arrives downtown at 700 S Tyler St (☎ 806 374 5371).

Destinations Albuquerque, NM (3 daily; 4hr 55min); Austin (3 daily; 12hr); Dallas (3 daily; 6hr 50min); El Paso (2 daily; 9hr 20min); Fort Worth (3 daily; 6hr); Houston (3 daily; 13hr).

By plane There's a small airport (☎ 806 335 1671) 7 miles east.

Visitor centre Civic Center, 401 S Buchanan St, Entrance No. 2 (April–Sept Mon–Fri 9am–6pm, Sat & Sun 10am–4pm; Oct–March Mon–Fri 8.30am–5.30pm, Sat noon–4pm; ☎ 806 374 8474, ⓦ visitamarillotx.com).

ACCOMMODATION, EATING AND DRINKING

Big Texan Steak Ranch and Motel 7701 E I-40, exit 75 ☎ 806 372 6000, ⓦ bigtexan.com. Rip-roaring Wild Western fun in this famed old, cavernous restaurant, which as well as serving 20oz T-bone steaks ($27) and BBQ brisket sandwiches ($10), offers the 72oz steak challenge: if you can eat it within an hour, you get it free (losers pony up around $70). For cowboy kitsch, you can't beat the attached motel, with its Texas-flag shower curtains, Texas-shaped outdoor pool, cowhide bedcovers and saloon doors. Daily 7am–10.30pm. **$79**

Golden Light Café and Cantina 2908 W 6th Ave ☎ 806 374 9237. Tasty burgers and sandwiches at good value (most around $5) at this well-located joint. The cantina side regularly draws some of the best touring musicians in Texas. Café: Mon–Wed 11am–10pm, Thurs–Sat 11am–11pm; cantina: Tues–Sat 4pm–2am.

★ **Outlaws Supper Club** 10816 SE Third Ave ☎ 806 335 1032. Practically surrounded by ranch land, this friendly, casual restaurant is a must for steak connoisseurs, with every possible cut imaginable. The 20oz-prime rib goes for $19. Mon–Fri 11am–9pm, Sat 4–9.30pm.

Palo Duro Canyon State Park

Palo Duro Canyon, twenty miles southeast of Amarillo, is one of Texas' best-kept secrets – puzzling considering it's one of the largest and most breathtaking canyons in the

---

A TEXAS-SIZED SPECTACLE

You may balk at heart-warming musical extravaganzas, but the onsite outdoor production of **TEXAS**, about the settling of the Panhandle in the 1800s, has an undeniable pull in an area not exactly throbbing with nightlife. With the dramatic prairie sky as a ceiling, a 600ft-high cliff as a backdrop and genuine thunder and lightning (June–Aug Tues–Sun 8.30pm, pre-show steak dinner 6pm; dinner $13.95, show tickets $16–30; ☎ 806 655 2181, ⓦ texas-show.com), it is a spectacle not soon forgotten.

9

country. Plunging 1000ft from rim to floor, it splits the plains wide open and offers expansive vistas and a riot of colours, especially at sunset and in spring, when the whole chasm is painted with wild flowers.

The park encompasses the most scenic part of the 120-mile canyon. You can explore the depths on **horseback** (1hr guided ride $35, 5hr ride $140; ☎806 488 2180), though backpackers and hikers may want to escape the tourist busloads by following the Prairie Dog Town fork into more remote sections of the park.

INFORMATION AND ACCOMMODATION · PALO DURO CANYON STATE PARK

Park access and fees Open daily: June–Aug 8am–10pm; Sept May 8am–8pm. Admission is $5.

Visitor centre 11450 Park Rd 5, Canyon (☎806 488 2227, ⓦ tpwd.state.tx.us/state-parks/palo-duro-canyon).

Campgrounds and cabins ☎512 389 8900. There are two full-service campsites and two primitive sites with no facilities. Camping in the backcountry is also permitted; check in at the visitor centre for directions to the designated area. There are also seven rustic cabins to choose from; the three more expensive options are worth it for their commanding rim views alone. Primitive camping $12, serviced sites $24, cabins from $60

The Davis Mountains

The temperate climate of the verdant **Davis Mountains**, south of the junction of I-10 and I-20, makes them a popular summer destination for sweltering urban Texans. The eponymous **state park**, with its pleasant hiking trails, draws the most visitors to the range, while the **McDonald Observatory** to the northwest lures with the promise of world-class celestial views. South along Hwy-17, tiny **Marfa** is a windswept art community in the middle of the West Texas desert.

Fort Davis and around

Fort Davis, at the junction of Hwy-118 and Hwy-17, is a peaceful base for exploring the Davis Mountains, and you can pick up a driving map at its visitor centre; there's precious little to do in town itself, however.

McDonald Observatory

3640 Dark Sky Drive · Daily 10am–5.30pm · Free · ☎432 426 3640, ⓦ mcdonaldobservatory.org

The glassy, starry nights facilitate the work of the **McDonald Observatory** about twenty miles northwest of Fort Davis on Hwy-118. Nocturnal "star parties" here provide a wonderful opportunity to look at the constellations for yourself and learn more about what exactly you're looking at (Tues, Fri & Sat, time depends on sunset; $14). Wear warm clothing and bring food and drink, as the café doesn't always have substantial meals available.

Davis Mountains State Park

Open year-round · $6 · ☎800 792 1112, ⓦ tpwd.state.tx.us

Davis Mountains State Park, four miles northwest of Fort Davis, offers good hiking and birdwatching opportunities, as well as being prime habitat for black bears and mountain lions. Departing just west of the campground on Park Road 3A, the **Skyline Drive** trail provides the fullest sense of the park's rugged environs as it winds through the mountains for 4.5 miles before emerging at the Fort Davis Historic Site. For a less taxing outing, take the **Indian Lodge** trail from the lodge's car park. After a somewhat steep initial stretch, the trail levels off and offers commanding views. After 1.5 miles it connects with a one-mile trail leading to a recently renovated quail-viewing platform.

ACCOMMODATION AND EATING · FORT DAVIS AND AROUND

Campgrounds Davis Mountains State Park ☎512 389 8900, ⓦ texasstateparks.org. The state park has a variety of scenic shaded campsites, both primitive and fully serviced. $8/$20

Hotel Limpia 101 Memorial Square, Fort Davis ☎432 426 3237, ⓦhotellimpia.com. Historic, characterful hotel in the heart of town with period furnishings and a small outdoor pool. Its on-site restaurant, the *Blue Mountain Bistro*, serves excellent upscale dinners (daily except Wed 7.30–10.30am, 11am–2pm & 5–9pm); choose from rich dishes such as beef bourguignon ($19). **$99**

Indian Lodge Davis Mountain State Park ☎800 792 1112. Rooms at the state park's romantic 1930s adobe-style *Indian Lodge* are clean and comfortable – and often booked up, so call in advance. There's a good-sized outdoor pool, and the breakfast buffet at the lodge's *Black Bear* restaurant (Mon 7–10am, Tues–Sun 7–10am, 11am–2pm & 5–9pm) offers a mind-boggling range of options. **$95**

Marfa

MARFA, a small, but thriving community 21 miles south of Fort Davis on Hwy-17, is the kind of place that it's at once hard to imagine existing where it is but also existing anywhere else. It is very much a desert oasis, with a respected **art scene** pulling artists and the curious from afar in increasing numbers. It's also a decidedly offbeat town, where chic designer shops and prefab galleries are offset by historic buildings that attest to its former role as a ranching centre. It all makes for a fascinating mix. Much more ethereal, the **Marfa Lights**, a few miles east of town, consistently draw crowds, even if the lights don't always cooperate.

The Chinati and Judd foundations

Just outside town is the extraordinary **Chinati Foundation** (tours Wed–Sun 10am; $25; ☎432 729 4362, ⓦchinati.org), founded by minimalist Donald Judd. The avant-garde works on display across fifteen buildings here include some of the world's largest permanent art installations, set in dramatic contexts both indoors and out. Back in town at 104 S Highland St, the **Judd Foundation** also leads tours of its modernistic art spaces (Mon–Fri 9am–5pm; ☎432 729 4406, ⓦjuddfoundation.org/marfa).

The Marfa Lights

Viewing centre at Hwy-90, 9 miles east of Marfa • Open year round

Since the 1880s, mysterious bouncing lights have been seen in the town's flat fields. Dubbed the "**Marfa Lights**", they have long attracted conspiracy theorists and alien-hunters, though their cause may be more prosaic. The town's **visitor centre** (varied opening hours), in the *Hotel Paisano*, can give advice on good vantage points to see the ghostly illuminations; if in doubt, head for the viewing centre four hours after sunset.

ACCOMMODATION   MARFA

El Cosmico 802 S Highland Ave ⓦelcosmico.com. A "magical tribe of dirt wizards" constructed this avant-garde development of painstakingly renovated Air Stream trailers and safari tents on 18 acres just outside town. Most of the trailers have outdoor showers only, but they are all pleasantly furnished. Camping **$15**, safari tent **$65**, trailer **$110**

Hotel Paisano 207 N Highland Ave ☎432 729 669, ⓦhotelpaisano.com. When James Dean's last film, the

1956 epic, *Giant*, was filmed in town, the cast stayed at this historic and swanky hotel. The public areas exude elegance, while the original rooms are cramped; the much larger suites have patios or balconies. Rooms **$99**, suites **$159**

Thunderbird Hotel 601 W San Antonio ☎877 729 1984, ⓦthunderbirdmarfa.com. A renovated motor court turned high-end hipster hotel. Clean lines define the minimalist rooms, which feature flat-screen TVs, iHomes and designer bath products. **$130**

EATING

★ **Cochineal** 107 W San Antonio St ☎432 729 3300. Understated, tucked-away spot that puts the focus squarely on a range of refined and unfussy dishes. The menu changes frequently, but can feature starters such as savoury gorgonzola soufflé ($9) and mains such as roasted barramundi ($28). There's also a cosy cocktail bar. Thurs–Tues 6pm–late.

Food Shark Shade Pavilion, Highland Ave ☎432 386 540, ⓦfoodsharkmarfa.com. Beloved far and wide, the

perennially popular *Food Shark* serves up Mediterranean-inspired dishes such as *fatoush* salad for $7.50 out of an old delivery truck. Arrive at noon on the dot or be prepared for a long wait. Thurs–Sat noon–3pm.

Future Shark 120 N Highland Ave ☎432 729 4278. Laidback offshoot of the creators of *Food Shark*, this modernistic cafeteria doles out plates with healthy ingredients such as quinoa and butternut squash and

9

home-made takes on classic TV dinners (most options $8–10). Mon–Fri 11.30am–7pm.

★ **New York Pizza Foundation** 100 E San Antonio St ☎ 432 729 3377, ⊕ pizzafoundation.com. Mercurial pizza shop that prepares its dough daily and delivers thin-crust

offerings ($15–20) to an understandably devoted following. The menu is straightforward and build-your-own pizzas are limited to four toppings, but the execution is on a par with anything you could hope to find in NYC. Cash only. Fri–Sun from 1pm until the dough runs out; usually by 8pm.

Big Bend National Park and around

The **Rio Grande**, flowing through 1500ft-high canyons, makes a ninety-degree bend south of Marathon to form the southern border of **BIG BEND NATIONAL PARK** – thanks to its isolation, one of the least visited of the US national parks.

The Apache, who forced the Chisos out 300 years ago, believed that this hauntingly beautiful wilderness was used by the Great Spirit to dump all the rocks left over from the creation of the world; the Spanish, meanwhile, called it *terra desconocida*, "strange, unknown land". A breathtaking 800,000-acre expanse of forested mountains and ocotillo-dotted desert, Big Bend has been home to ranchers, miners and smugglers, a last frontier for the true-grit pioneers of the American West.

Today, there is camping in designated areas, but much of the park remains barely charted territory. Its topography results in dramatic juxtapositions of desert and mountain, plant and **animal life**: mountain lions, black bears, roadrunners and javelinas (a bristly, grey hog-like creature with a snout and tusks) all roam free. Despite the dryness, tangles of pretty wild flowers and blossoming cacti erupt into colour each March and April. In the heightened security measures since September 11th, it has become illegal to cross the Rio Grande into **Mexico**.

HIKING, RAFTING AND HOT SPRINGS IN BIG BEND NATIONAL PARK

West of the park headquarters a spur road leads south for about six miles, up into the **Chisos Basin**, which is ringed by dramatic peaks – the one gap in the rocky wall here is called the **Window**, looking out over the Chihuahuan Desert. Several of the park's best **hikes** depart from either the road here or from the trailhead, near the store by the visitor centre.

HIKES

Lost Mine Trail An ideal morning outing in the Chisos Basin, this 4.8-mile out-and-back rises 1100ft through a series of moderate switchbacks to a ridge with breath-taking views of Juniper Canyon, the far rim and Mexico beyond.

South Rim Trail From the Chisos Basin trailhead, the 12-mile loop hike to the South Rim is one of the most popular in the park, and the views deep into the interior of Mexico are humbling. Count on a gruelling 8hr – most of which will be completely exposed – or 10hr if you elect to include the rim trails.

Marufo Vega trail For the serious (and experienced) hiker, the 13-mile loop hike to the river on the Marufo Vega trail is one of the most stunning in the entire National Park Service. It offers views of the Sierra del Carmen mountain range in Mexico and a descent into a rarely visited slick-rock canyon. Feral burros (wild donkeys) sometimes wail here at sunset, and subsistence Mexican farmers set up camps to harvest candelilla across the border. Pick up the topographical map of the

trail from one of the visitor centres and check with a park ranger about the current conditions before setting out.

Rio Grande Village Trail This gentle hour-long hike from the Rio Grande Village campsite leads past a wildlife-viewing platform before ending with expansive views of the river and nearby mountains.

RAFTING

At three separate stages within the park's boundaries the river runs through gigantic canyons. The western-most, Santa Elena, is the most common rafting trip, with mostly gentle Class II–III floats; outfitters are available at Terlingua (see opposite).

HOT SPRINGS

Driving 20 miles southeast of Panther Junction brings you to the riverside Rio Grande Village – unless you choose to detour just before, to bathe in the natural hot springs that feed into the river. The hot springs can be reached via an easy 15-mile walk along the signposted dirt Hot Springs Rd.

ARRIVAL AND INFORMATION

BIG BEND NATIONAL PARK

By car The most interesting route into Big Bend is from the west. You can't follow the river all the way from El Paso, but Hwy-170 – reached on Hwy-67 south from Marfa (see p.609) – runs through spectacular desert scenery east from Ojinaga, Mexico, which was practically wiped off the map due to floods in 2008. Before reaching the park boundary just beyond Study Butte, you pass through Big Bend Ranch State Park and the community of Terlingua (see below).

Access and entry fees Open daily 24hr. Entrance is $20/vehicle, $10/cyclists or motorcyclists.

Park headquarters In the centre of the park at Panther

Junction (daily 8am–6pm; ☎432 477 2251 ⓦnps.gov/bibe). The entrance fee is payable here (and at all of the visitor centres listed below), there are orientation exhibits and a daytime petrol station.

Visitor centres The Chisos Basin, a short drive south of Panther Junction, has a visitor centre (daily 8am–6pm; ☎432 477 2264) and a convenience store. There is also a visitor centre at the east end of Hwy-118 at Rio Grande Village (daily 8am–6pm; ☎432 477 2271), where there's also a petrol station, and at Persimmon Gap (daily 8am–6pm; ☎432 477 2666), at the park's northern boundary on Hwy-385.

ACCOMMODATION AND EATING

Most camping at the park's three **developed campgrounds** (pay at a visitor centre) is first-come, first-served, though some reservations can be made for the high season (Nov–April; ☎877 444 6777, ⓦrecreation.gov). **Primitive sites** are scattered along the many marked hiking trails. These have no facilities, and you'll need a wilderness permit ($10) from a visitor centre. The sites at Juniper Flats are only about a 3-mile hike and are located in a nice meadow. Other stunning sites in the Chisos Mountains are SE-3, SW-3 and NE-4.

Chisos Basin Campground The most popular developed campground in the park, Chisos Basin is dramatically perched at 5400ft and has the benefit of being within walking distance of numerous trails, a visitor centre and the *Chisos Mountain Lodge*'s restaurant. The sixty pitches have access to running water, though there are no hookups. Pitches $14

Chisos Mountains Lodge ☎432 477 2292, ⓦchisosmountainslodge.com. At the Chisos Basin visitor centre, the park's only roofed accommodation option offers motel-style rooms with balconies and a few stone cottages (#102 and #103 are the best). Reservations are essential. The on-site restaurant (daily 7–10am, 11am–4pm & 5–8pm) has a good all-you-can-eat salad bar for $9. Doubles **$123**, cottages **$150**

★ **Gage Hotel** 101 Hwy-90 W, Marathon ☎432 386 4205, ⓦgagehotel.com. Marathon, 40 miles north of the Persimmon Gap visitor centre, is best known for the luxurious *Gage Hotel*, which has exceedingly comfortable rooms outfitted with plush furnishings. Rooms are spread throughout the two-storey hotel and the adobe-styled *Los Portales* annexe; there are also handsome houses available for larger groups. There's a nice restaurant and a bar famed for its buffalo burger. **$130**

Terlingua

For such a small place, **TERLINGUA**, scattered across the low hills along Hwy-170, has a lot to recommend it – not least an atmospheric **ghost town**, the remnants of the Chisos Mining Company's quicksilver operation here in the early twentieth century. The whole area is free to roam around and includes shuttered mine shafts, the foundations of several buildings and a cemetery. Terlingua's proximity to Big Bend National Park and its rugged locale makes it one of the best spots in the state for **outdoor adventures**; several outfitters in town lead a variety of tours (see below).

ACTIVITIES

TERLINGUA

Tours Desert Sports (☎432 371 2727, ⓦdesertsportstx.com), on Hwy-118 at the intersection with Hwy-118, offers a variety of rafting trips (1–12 days); allow $150/person for a party of four for a full day's guided trip along Santa Elena Canyon. It also leads group hikes, rents rafts and mountain bikes, and provides shuttles into the backcountry.

Far Flung Outdoor Center (☎800 839 7238, ⓦbigbendfarflung.com), on the south side of Hwy-170 just east of the ghost town, leads a wide variety of half-day and full-day jeep tours (from $79) to otherwise inaccessible corners of the national park as well as ATV tours ($150 for drivers; $75 for riders) and rafting outings (from $72).

ACCOMMODATION

★ **Big Bend Casitas** Hwy-170, between the ghost town and the Hwy-118 intersection ☎800 839 7238, ⓦbigbendfarflung.com. Run by Far Flung (see above),

these twelve cheerful and spacious red-roofed *casitas* are each pleasantly appointed with flat-screen TVs, a/c, kitchenettes and outdoor grills. The evening starlight views

9

from the covered porches are simply stunning, and guests receive a discount on Far Flung tours. **$139**

Chisos Mining Company Motel 23280 Hwy-170 ☎ 432 371 2254, ⓦ cmcm.cc. On the east edge of town near the intersection with Hwy-118, this rustic compound holds a very basic motel with spartan double rooms, as well as colourful cabins. While it's the best budget option in town, it is decidedly bereft of creature comforts and some

rooms can get cold at night. Doubles **$59**, cabins **$101**

La Posada Milagro 100 Milagro Rd ☎ 432 371 3044, ⓦ laposadamilagro.net. At the top of a hill, three luxuriously rustic rooms in a restored dry-stack stone building, along with a four-bed bunkhouse. The views are expansive and there's on-site yoga and a coffeeshop serving comfort meals for breakfast and lunch daily. Doubles **$185**, bunkhouse **$145**

EATING AND DRINKING

Ghost Town Saloon Café 1001 Terlingua Ghost Town Rd ☎ 432 371 2512. In the ghost town, this welcoming café serves hearty home-cooked brunches like sausage biscuits and gravy ($5.25) and pork chops ($4.95). Daily 6am–2pm.

★ **La Kiva** 23222 Hwy-170 ☎ 432 371 2250, ⓦ lakiva .net. For rowdy late-night action, head to *La Kiva*, Hwy-170 at Terlingua Creek, an improbable underground bar and restaurant with cave-like rooms and an outdoor courtyard. The drinks menu is long and features several tequilas and potent house cocktails. Mon–Fri & Sun 5pm–midnight,

Sat 5pm–1am.

★ **Starlight Theatre** 631 Ivey Rd ☎ 432 371 2326, ⓦ thestarlighttheatre.com. Near Terlingua's fly-blown cemetery, this old movie house has been converted into a welcoming bar and restaurant serving crowd-pleasers including chilli ($8.95) and specials such as chicken-fried antelope ($19.95). Outside, locals linger on the porch to drink beer, gossip and marvel at the mountains. Mon–Fri 5pm–midnight, Sat 5pm–1am, Sun 11am–2pm & 5pm–midnight.

El Paso

Back when Texas was still Tejas, **EL PASO**, the second-oldest settlement in the United States, was the main crossing on the Rio Grande. It still plays that role today, its 600,000 residents joining with another 1.7 million across the river in **Ciudad Juarez**, Mexico, to form the largest binational (and bilingual) megalopolis in North America. At first sight it's not an especially pretty place – massive railyards fill up much of downtown, the belching smelters of copper mills line the riverfront and the northern reaches are taken up by the giant Fort Bliss military base. Its dramatic setting, however, where the Franklin Mountains meet the Chihuahuan Desert, gives it a certain bold pioneer edge, bearing more relation to old rather than new Mexico, with little of the pastel softness of the Southwest USA. El Paso is also the home of Tony Lama, makers of top-quality **cowboy boots**, available at substantial discounts at outlets across town.

While it's tempting to cross the border here into Mexico, remember that escalating **drug wars** have turned Juarez into one of the most dangerous cities in the world.

Ysleta del Sur and the Mission Trail

Ysleta del Sur 119 S Old Pueblo Drive • Mon–Fri 8am–5pm **Mission Trail** ☎ 915 534 0630, ⓦ visitelpasomissiontrail.com

Although El Paso is predominantly Hispanic, there is also a substantial population of **Tigua Indians**, a displaced Pueblo tribe, based in a reservation (complete with the almost statutory casino) on Socorro Road, southeast of downtown. The reservation's arts-and-crafts centre sells pottery and textiles. Adjacent to the reservation, the simple **Ysleta del Sur**, the oldest mission in the United States, marks the beginning of an eight-mile **Mission Trail**, with three missions – still active churches – set among scruffy cotton, alfalfa, chilli, onion and pecan fields.

ARRIVAL AND INFORMATION

By plane El Paso's airport is about 5 miles east of downtown; a taxi to the centre will cost about $22, although many downtown hotels offer free van rides.

By bus Greyhound buses stop at 200 W San Antonio Ave

(☎ 915 542 1355).

Destinations Albuquerque, NM (2 daily; 4hr 30min); Amarillo (2 daily; 9hr 15min); Austin (2 daily; 12hr 25min); Dallas (5 daily; 12hr 50min); Fort Worth (6 daily; 11hr 40min); Houston

THE US–MEXICO BORDER

Downtown El Paso's character is shaped by the **US–Mexico border**. In times past, outlaws and exiles from either side of the border would take refuge across the river, and today's traffic remains considerable and not entirely uncontroversial. Manual labourers come north to find undocumented jobs, and US companies secretly dump their toxic waste on the south side. Drugs are a major issue, too. The border itself, the **Rio Grande**, has caused its share of disagreements: the river changed course quite often in the 1800s, and it was not until the 1960s, when it was run through a concrete channel, that it was made permanent.

An attractive 55-acre park, the **Chamizal National Memorial**, on the east side of downtown off Paisano Drive, was built to commemorate the settling of the border dispute; it has a small museum (Tues–Sat 10am–5pm; free). Elsewhere, the small but engrossing **Border Patrol Museum**, 4315 Transmountain Drive (Tues–Sat 9am–5pm; free), explains the work of the patrollers and highlights the ingenuity of smugglers.

CROSSING INTO MEXICO

On the Rio Grande, the **Cordova Bridge** – or Bridge of the Americas – heads across **into Mexico**, where there's a larger park and a number of museums; there are no formalities, so long as you have a multiple-entry visa for the USA and don't travel more than twenty or so miles south of the border. Crossing here is free; at the three other bridges – two downtown and one near the Ysleta Mission – you have to pay a 35¢ fee.

(5 daily; 18hr 5min); San Antonio (2 daily; 10hr 20min). **By train** Amtrak (☎915 545 2247) pulls in at the Daniel Burnham-designed Union Station at 700 San Francisco St. Destinations Albuquerque, NM (2 daily; 16hr 30min); Austin (1 daily; 16hr 50min); Dallas (1 daily; 22hr 45min); Fort Worth (1 daily; 21hr 25min); Houston (1 daily; 18hr 35min); San Antonio (1 daily; 12hr 15min).

Visitor centre 1 Civic Center Plaza in the convention centre complex (Mon–Fri 8am–5pm, Sat 10am–3pm; ☎800 351 6024, ⓦ visitelpaso.com).

ACCOMMODATION

Camino Real 101 S El Paso St ☎915 534 3000, ⓦ caminoreal.com. Downtown hotel in a grand old 1912 building. The romantic lobby bar *El Domo* is topped by a colourful Tiffany glass dome and surrounded by rose and black marble, while the 357 opulent rooms and suites are all comfortably appointed. There are also two on-site restaurants, with the more informal option serving all meals daily. $115

Gardner Hotel & Hostel 311 E Franklin St ☎915 532 3661, ⓦ gardnerhotel.com. Rooms in this atmospheric hotel – where John Dillinger bedded down in the 1920s – vary from dorms, through to singles with shared bath, to simple en-suite doubles furnished with antiques. Dorms $25, doubles $60

EATING, DRINKING AND ENTERTAINMENT

Ardovino's Desert Crossing 1 Ardovino Drive, Sunland Park, NM ☎575 589 0653. Just across the state line in New Mexico and well worth the 10min drive from downtown, this enchanting restaurant serves up pasta dishes like a gnocchi with chorizo for around $15 and hosts a summer farmers' market. Tues–Fri 5–10.30pm, Sat 9am–2.30pm & 5–10.30pm, Sun 10am–2.30pm & 5–9pm.

H&H Coffee Shop & Car Wash 701 E Yandell Drive ☎833 533 1144. Quirky time-warp diner dishing up tasty Tex-Mex – reputed to be a favoured stop for George W. Bush and assorted governors. Stop by in the morning for the flavourful *huevos rancheros* ($6). Mon–Sat 9am–5pm.

The Hoppy Monk 4141 N Mesa St ☎915 307 3263. Inviting and anomalous brewpub a couple miles northwest of downtown with a stellar selection of craft ales on tap as well as better food than you might expect; try the sweet potato fries with toasted walnut aioli ($6) and the veggie monk – a black bean and pumpkin burger with provolone ($10). Mon–Thurs 3pm–2am, Fri & Sat 11am–2am.

★ **L&J Café** 3622 E Missouri Ave ☎915 566 8418. A good-value joint offering up excellent Mexican food such as chicken in a mole sauce or steak tacos (both $8.25). Mon–Wed 10am–9pm, Thurs & Fri 10am–10pm, Sat 9am–10pm, Sun 9am–9pm.

Palace Theatre 125 Pioneer Plaza ☎915 231 1100. Regal and intimate downtown venue that routinely hosts top-notch national and international rock and country acts as well as dance and orchestral performances. Hours vary.

Tap Bar and Restaurant 408 E San Antonio Ave ☎915 532 1848. A diverse local crowd hangs out at this downtown dive, which serves good, cheap Mexican-American staples, including heaped plates of nachos with shredded beef, and beers (most around $2 a bottle). Daily noon–midnight.

The Great Plains

BISON IN THEODORE ROOSEVELT NATIONAL PARK, ND

The Great Plains

The rolling hills and vast grasslands of the Great Plains have been home to adventurers, artists and outlaws for centuries, from great Sioux warriors Crazy Horse and Sitting Bull to Jesse James and Mark Twain. Stretching west through Missouri, Oklahoma, Kansas, Nebraska, Iowa, South Dakota and North Dakota, the Great Plains are often stereotyped as an expanse of unvaryingly flat corn fields, the "flyover states" of conservative "Middle American" values. On the contrary, the region is loaded with attractions, from quirky Americana on Route 66 to dynamic art and culinary scenes in Omaha, Tulsa and St Louis, and is often not flat at all – there are canyons, forests, hills and splashes of unexpected colour, as well as two of the nation's mightiest rivers: the Missouri and the Mississippi.

The Plains also share a complex, fascinating history. Once home to nomadic tribes such as the **Sioux** and a handful of hardy French traders, the region only saw US colonization really ramped up after the Civil War – by the 1880s the systematic destruction by white settlers of the awesome herds of **bison** presaged the virtual eradication of the **Plains Indians**, though their ancestors retain a significant presence in South Dakota and Oklahoma (the latter was settled primarily by tribes removed from the east). Despite harsh conditions and a series of droughts, emigrants poured into the region; after World War I **wheat** production doubled in the US, creating a boom across the Great Plains that ended with another drought in 1932 and dust storms that lasted three years; images of the devastating "Dustbowl" remain as potent as the fantasy of Dorothy and Toto being swept up from Kansas by a tornado to the land of Oz. Indeed, drama here comes in the form of such unpredictable **weather** as freak blizzards, dust devils, lightning storms and, most notoriously, "twister" **tornadoes**. Today **farming** – though still the major activity on the Plains – isn't the only game in town; the region's economy is booming thanks to **oil** and **natural gas**, especially in Oklahoma and more recently North Dakota. Though the lunar landscapes of South Dakota's **Badlands** and stately **Mount Rushmore** in the Black Hills are easily the region's most visited areas, there's plenty of entertainment elsewhere, from Kansas City **barbecue** and the birthplace of **Mark Twain**, to wicked old cowboy towns like **Deadwood** in South Dakota and **Dodge City** in Kansas.

Having a **car** is practically imperative to make the most of the Great Plains, where distances are long, roads straight and seemingly endless and the population sparse.

Missouri

Formed as a state in 1821, **MISSOURI** acted as bridge between the two halves of America for much of the nineteenth century, when cities like **St Louis** on the

NATIONAL ROUTE 66 MUSEUM, ELK CITY, OK

Highlights

❶ Gateway Arch, St Louis, MO Ride the pod-like tram (trolley) to the top of this iconic monument, or simply admire its majestic symmetry from the riverside park below. **See p.619**

❷ BBQ in Kansas City, MO Sample some of America's finest (and sauciest) brisket, hickory-smoked ribs and "burnt ends". **See p.627**

❸ Route 66, OK Oklahoma boasts 400 miles of this iconic roadway, lined with classic Americana, diners and rolling grassland scenery. **See p.630**

❹ Price Tower, Bartlesville, OK Spend the night in Frank Lloyd Wright's only skyscraper,

a stylish, copper-clad 1950s time capsule. **See p.632**

❺ Nebraska State Capitol, NE Soaring above the plains like a fantastical, Byzantine skyscraper, this has to be one of America's most enthralling capitol buildings. **See p.643**

❻ The Black Hills, SD Where the Midwest meets the West: prairie dogs, buffalo, hiking trails and caves galore, and the behemoth stone sculptures of Mount Rushmore and Crazy Horse. **See p.651**

❼ Theodore Roosevelt National Park, ND Venture further north for a look at the softly eroded, untrammelled landscape that helped inspire a rancher to the US presidency. **See p.658**

HIGHLIGHTS ARE MARKED ON THE MAP ON P.618

Mississippi and **Kansas City** and **St Joseph** astride the **Missouri** boomed as depots for cattle heading east and settlers heading west. Due to the **Missouri Compromise** of 1820, slavery was permitted in the state, though it remained within the Union during the Civil War (Confederate guerrilla forces attracted considerable support, however). Today the big cities of Missouri provide most of the allure, though the densely forested **Ozark Mountains** in the south offer a welcome contrast to the plains.

THE GREAT PLAINS

HIGHLIGHTS

1. Gateway Arch, St Louis, MO
2. BBQ in Kansas City, MO
3. Route 66, OK
4. Price Tower, Bartlesville, OK
5. Nebraska State Capitol, NE
6. The Black Hills, SD
7. Theodore Roosevelt National Park, ND

GREAT REGIONAL DRIVES

Route 66, Oklahoma Soak up the classic Americana on one of the few remaining stretches of original Rte-66, some four hundred miles from Quapaw near the Missouri border to Texola, straddling Texas.

Flint Hills National Scenic Byway, Kansas Fifty miles through rolling hills of tallgrass prairie, smothered in flowers in early summer, following Hwy-177 from Council Grove to Cassoday in east central Kansas.

Sandhills Journey Scenic Byway, Nebraska Soak up the historic towns and villages and meandering rivers of the Sandhills region on this scenic route following Hwy-2 west from I-80 at Grand Island, some 275 miles all the way to Alliance and the road to the Black Hills.

Needles Highway, Black Hills, South Dakota Short but mesmerizing section of Hwy-87 in the Black Hills, a twisting, narrow route through tunnels and pinnacles of granite.

10

St Louis and around

Perched just below the confluence of the Mississippi and Missouri river, **ST LOUIS** (pronounced, whatever Judy Garland may have suggested, "Saint Lewis") boomed in the nineteenth century as the gateway to the West, and later played a significant role in the development of jazz and the blues (Josephine Baker, Chuck Berry and Miles Davis were all born here, and Scott Joplin developed ragtime in the city's honky-tonks). As the name suggests, the roots of St Louis are **French**; originally part of Louisiana Territory, it was founded in 1764 by French fur trader Pierre Laclede and later became a major port for **steamboats**. In 1904 the **World's Fair** was held in the city at the peak of its fortunes, but beginning with an ugly race riot in 1917 the population began to fall, decreasing by two thirds in just seventy years. Once the fourth largest metropolis in the USA, today St Louis is a medium-sized suburban city, best known for the mind-bending **Gateway Arch**, one of America's most distinctive monuments, and **Forest Park**, with its bevy of free museums.

Gateway Arch

Riverside, at Market St • Daily: June–Aug 8am–10pm; Sept–May 9am–6pm • Free entry; tram rides $10; movies $7 • ☎ 877 982 1410, ⓦ gatewayarch.com

An astonishing feat of engineering, the **Gateway Arch** dominates downtown St Louis; a glittering arc of steel, its vast size is hard to appreciate until you get up close. Designed by Finnish-born architect Eero Saarinen and completed in 1965, the 630ft-high stainless-steel parabola commemorates the role of St Louis in the western expansion of the USA, especially honouring the epic **Lewis and Clark Expedition**, which set off from here in 1804, and all the pioneers that came after. It's fun to take the four-minute **tram ride** up the hollow, gently curving arch, as tiny, five-seat capsules carry you to a viewing gallery at the top, where you can linger as long as you like – the views of St Louis, the mighty Mississippi and the surrounding tree-studded plains are spectacular. To avoid lengthy waits, pick up a numbered ticket early in the day and come back at an appointed time. The rides depart from the **visitor centre**, set in a massive bunker beneath the arch. Here you can also watch an old-fashioned **film** about the construction of the monument, and another on the Lewis and Clark Expedition itself – you'll need timed tickets for both. While you wait, peruse the cavernous **Museum of Westward Expansion**, which recounts the Lewis and Clark story, drawing heavily on the pair's eminently readable journals. Down on the levee below the Arch, one-hour **cruises** (March–Nov daily noon, 2pm & 3pm; $14) aboard replica paddle-wheelers depart regularly (buy tickets at the Gateway Arch).

Old Courthouse

11 N 4th St • Daily: June–Aug 8am–4.30pm; Sept–May 9am–6pm • Free • ☎ 314 655 1700, ⓦ nps.gov/jeff

A few minutes' walk west from the Gateway Arch, the domed **Old Courthouse** was completed in 1862, a grand example of the wealth and prestige of St Louis at that time.

The Greek Revival-style interior contains museum galleries charting the development of the city from 1764 to the present day, but the most poignant section is dedicated to the watershed **Dred Scott** trial that opened here in 1846; the US Supreme Court's decision to rule against Scott eleven years later – effectively sanctioning slavery – helped move the country toward Civil War.

Cathedral Basilica of Saint Louis

4431 Lindell Blvd (Central West End) • Daily 7am–5pm; guided tours Mon–Fri 10am–4pm, Sun 1pm, after noon Mass (reservations required Mon–Fri) • Free • ☎ 314 373 8241, ⊛ cathedralstl.org

Trendy shops, wine bars and hundred-year-old mansions line the leafy thoroughfares of the **Central West End** district, three miles west of Gateway Arch, but the real treasure here is the Romanesque-Byzantine **Cathedral Basilica of Saint Louis**. Completed in 1914, the cathedral houses the world's largest collection of jaw-dropping mosaic art under one roof; the central dome, rising 143ft, is smothered with blue and gold mosaic panels dedicated to the Holy Trinity and other Biblical figures.

Forest Park

The best deal in the city (everything is free), the green expanse of **Forest Park** harbours an incredible cache of treasures, four miles directly west of downtown. In addition to its two exceptional **museums**, kids will enjoy the well-regarded **Saint Louis Zoo** and the **St Louis Science Center**, straddling I-64 along the park's southern edge.

Missouri History Museum

5700 Lindell Blvd, at DeBaliviere • Daily 10am–5pm, Tues till 8pm • Free, touring exhibits extra • ☎ 314 746 4599, ⊛ mohistory.org

The northern gateway to Forest Park is dominated by the stately Neoclassical pile of the **Missouri History Museum**, built in 1914 with proceeds from the 1904 **World's Fair**. The fair has its own gallery, and upstairs the history of the city is chronicled with an illuminating blend of artefacts, videos, photos and re-creations – don't miss Rodin's bust of local news magnate **Joseph Pulitzer** and exhibits on the landmark **Dred Scott** case. A replica of Lindbergh's *Spirit of St Louis* hangs above the main hall, but the most thought-provoking section is the dimly lit **Question Bridge**, where screens show 150 video interviews on loop of African American men mulling issues of race and gender.

Saint Louis Art Museum

1 Fine Arts Drive • Tues–Sun 10am–5pm, Fri till 9pm • Free • ☎ 314 721 0072, ⊛ slam.org

The majestic Beaux Arts-style **Saint Louis Art Museum** is the only surviving structure from the 1904 World's Fair (held in the park), offering a surprisingly comprehensive jaunt through global art history from the Bronze Age to Modernism. Highlights include the world's largest public collection of work by German Expressionist **Max Beckmann,** who taught in St Louis (1947–48), and a whole gallery dedicated to **Alexander Calder**'s seminal installation *White Lily*. One of Monet's *Water Lilies* is on show, along with *Bathers with a Turtle* by Matisse (saved from the Nazis in 1939) and Cezanne's *The Bathers*. The Asian art section (especially the early Chinese bronzes) is exceptional, and the American section includes a gallery for St Louis' very own **New Hats** movement, and an important ensemble of work from Missouri artist **George Caleb Bingham**.

Soulard Farmers Market

730 Carroll St • Wed & Thurs 8am–5pm, Fri 7am–5pm, Sat 7am–5.30pm • ☎ 314 622 4180, ⊛ soulardmarket.com

A few blocks south of downtown, the colourful **Soulard Farmers Market**, which traces its roots back to 1779, is a terrific place to pick up picnic items and fresh fruit, especially on a Saturday (the current building opened in 1929). Don't miss the Bavarian Creams and croissants at the *Soulard Bakery*.

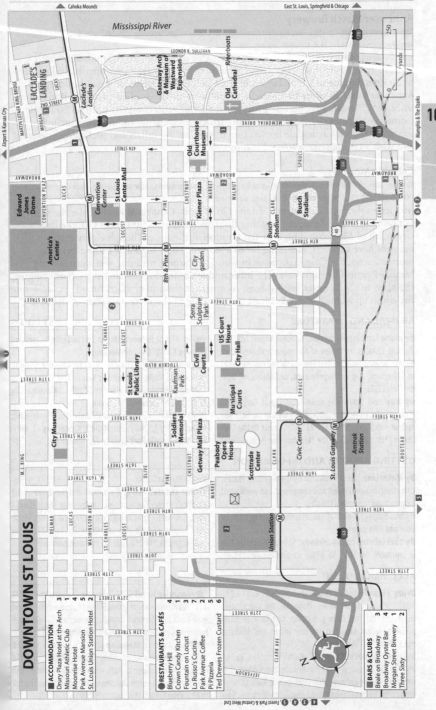

10

Anheuser-Busch Brewery

12th and Lynch sts, South City • June–Aug Mon–Sat 9am–5pm, Sun 11.30am–5pm; Sept–May Mon–Sat 10am–4pm, Sun 11.30am–4pm • Free tours • ☎ 314 577 2626, ⓦ budweisertours.com

Of the tens of thousands of Germans who came to St Louis in the mid-eighteenth century, many were skilled brewers; only one of the breweries they opened still stands, but it does happen to be the largest in the USA. The intricate red-brick buildings of the **Anheuser-Busch Brewery** have produced millions of barrels of beer (mostly Budweiser) since 1852. Locals were fiercely proud of the family-run company until its 2008 sale (some say takeover) by Belgian company InBev. Free eighty-minute **tours** include visits to see its beloved Clydesdale horses, beechwood ageing cellars and packaging lines, and end with a tasting session (over 21s only).

Cahokia Mounds

30 Ramey Drive, off Collinsville Rd (Collinsville, IL) • **Site** Daily 8am–dusk **Interpretive Center** Wed–Sun 9am–4pm • Free (donation $7) • ☎ 618 346 5160, ⓦ cahokiamounds.org • Access by car via I-70 exit 6

Just across the Mississippi from St Louis in Illinois, **Cahokia Mounds** is the site of an astonishing Native American city that flourished between 900 and 1350, the largest city north of Mexico and bigger than London at the time. Though eighty earth mounds have survived, including **Monk's Mound**, 100ft high and a mind-bending fourteen acres, the Cahokians built in wood, not stone, meaning you won't see any Mesoamerican-like ruins here. The **Interpretive Center** does an amazing job of bringing the place to life however, with videos, reconstructions and artefacts found on site, while the climb up Monk's Mound at least gives a sense of the incredible scale of the city.

ARRIVAL AND DEPARTURE   ST LOUIS

By plane Lambert-St Louis International Airport (ⓦ flystl .com) is 13 miles northwest of downtown and connected by taxi (around $40), Go Best Express shared minibus ($21 or $27 return; ⓦ gobestexpress.com) and MetroLink light rail (just $2.25).

By bus and train The main Amtrak and Greyhound terminals share the same space, a mile west of the Gateway Arch at 430 S 15th St (☎ 314 231 4485), next to the Civic Center MetroLink station. The Megabus stop is on the east side of 21st St between Market and Eugenia sts (serving Chicago, Kansas City and Memphis).

Destinations (bus) Chicago (5 daily; 6hr–6hr 55min); Hannibal (1 daily; 2hr 35min); Kansas City (3 daily; 4hr 25min); Memphis (1 daily; 5hr 55min); Oklahoma City (3 daily; 10hr 10min–11hr 25min).

Destinations (train) Chicago (5 daily; 5hr 25min–6hr); Jefferson City (2 daily; 2hr 20min); Kansas City (2 daily; 5hr 40min); Little Rock (1 daily; 7hr 10min).

GETTING AROUND AND INFORMATION

By MetroLink The St Louis area light-rail system ($2.25; ⓦ metrostlouis.org) is fast and convenient, but you'll need a car to make the best of the city.

By bus Buses ($2) go to all suburbs, though service can be slow and infrequent.

By taxi Cabs are readily available: St Louis American Cab is reputable (☎ 314 531 8766, ⓦ stlamericancab.com).

Meters start at $2.50.

Visitor centres Two at the airport and two more at the America's Center Convention Complex (Mon–Fri 8.30am–5pm, Sat 9am–3pm; ☎ 800 916 0092) and Kiener Plaza, next to the Old Courthouse (Mon–Fri 9am–5pm, Sat 9am–2pm; ☎ 314 231 1023, ⓦ explorestlouis.com).

ACCOMMODATION

Drury Plaza Hotel at the Arch 2 S 4th St ☎ 314 231 3003, ⓦ druryhotels.com. Opposite the Arch, this converted old hat factory features tastefully restored accommodation, breakfast and free snacks and drinks at the 5.30pm "kickback". $190

Missouri Athletic Club 405 Washington Ave ☎ 314 231 7220, ⓦ mac-stl.org. For historic atmosphere and bargain rates downtown, this 1903 gem is hard to beat, with comfy but worn rooms and beautiful public areas. $68

★ **Moonrise Hotel** 6177 Delmar in The Loop ☎ 314 721 1111, ⓦ moonrisehotel.com. Elegant boutique hotel a short walk from the Metrolink station; spacious rooms with sleek bathrooms, modern decor and a cool rooftop bar. $125

★ **Park Avenue Mansion** 2007 Park Ave ☎ 314 588 9004, ⓦ parkavenuemansion. Stunning B&B in an 1874 French Second Empire beauty, with a lovely private garden and five elegant suites dressed up in period style. The full champagne breakfast is superb. $139

St. Louis Union Station Hotel 1820 Market St ☎314 621 5262, ⓦstlouisunionstation.com. Rooms are fairly standard *Hilton* chain fare, but the building is anything but, a fabulous conversion of the 1894 Union Station, with a mesmerizing Grand Hall and even a small boating lake. **$98**

EATING

Downtown, your best bet for food and drink is up-and-coming **Washington Street** and **Laclede's Landing**, a section of cobbled streets and warehouses on the waterfront converted into restaurants and bars. Other targets are **Delmar Loop**, six blocks of shops, bars and restaurants along Delmar Boulevard near Washington University campus (ⓦvisittheloop.com); and **The Hill**, a small, neat Italian community of bakeries, one-room grocery stores, delis and restaurants. **Toasted ravioli** is a St Louis speciality, as is **gooey butter cake**, squares of sugary cream cheese delight.

★ **Blueberry Hill** 6504 Delmar Blvd, The Loop ☎314 727 4444, ⓦblueberryhill.com. Opening in 1972 and crammed full of blues memorabilia, this restaurant/bar boasts a justly famous burger ($6.25), all-day-breakfast ($7.50) and local Schlafly brews on tap ($4.50); there's live music every weekend downstairs, where living legend Chuck Berry drops in for monthly cameos ($35).

Crown Candy Kitchen 1401 St Louis Ave, Old North district ☎314 621 9650, ⓦcrowncandykitchen.net. A St Louis tradition since 1913, this old-fashioned soda fountain serves malts and shakes ($4.79), thick-sliced sandwiches (from $4.49), chilli ($3.99) and a vast array of sweet treats. Mon–Thurs 10.30am–8pm, Fri & Sat 10.30am–9pm, Sun 11am–5pm.

Fountain on Locust 3037 Locust St, Central West End ☎314 535 7800, ⓦfountainonlocust.com. Located inside a gorgeous Art Deco car showroom from 1916, this café is the home of the ice cream martini ($8.25) and excellent sandwiches, salads and soups (from $5.79). Tues–Thurs 11am–10pm, Fri & Sat 11am–midnight, Sun noon–9pm.

★ **Lo Russo's Cucina** 3121 Watson Rd, The Hill ☎314 647 6222, ⓦlorussos.com. The house specialities at this colourfully curtained dining room are pepper-fuelled dishes such as *ziti con vodka* and *fettucine pollo asiago*. Mains $14.95 –25.95. Tues–Thurs & Sun 5–9pm, Fri & Sat 5–10pm.

Park Avenue Coffee 417 N 10th St, downtown ☎314 231 5282, ⓦparkavenuecoffee.com. The place downtown to get decent espresso and your gooey butter cake fix, in an array of delicious flavours. Mon–Sat 7am–6pm, Sun 7.30am–6pm.

Pi Pizzeria 6144 Delmar Blvd, The Loop ☎314 727 6633, ⓦrestaurantpi.com. President Obama's favourite deep-dish pizza, with pies ranging $15.95–17.95. Mon–Sat 11am–midnight, Sun 11am–11pm.

Ted Drewes Frozen Custard 4224 S Grand Blvd (summer only), South St Louis ☎314 352 7376; also 6726 Chippewa Ave (closed Jan & Feb) ☎314 481 2652, ⓦteddrewes.com. A legendary slice of Americana since 1929, where long queues form for the "concretes" ($5) – ice cream so thick it won't budge if you turn your cup upside down. Daily 11am–midnight.

DRINKING, NIGHTLIFE AND ENTERTAINMENT

There's a concentration of tourist-oriented bars and clubs in **Laclede's Landing**, with nightly live music of all stripes, while the **Delmar Loop** attracts students and 30-somethings. Dressed-down **Soulard** hold the city's best blues and jazz pubs, while **Grand Center**, a few miles west of downtown, is its theatre district.

★ **Beale on Broadway** 701 S Broadway ☎314 621 7880, ⓦbealeonbroadway.com. Home of St Louis blues, this intimate bar drips with atmosphere, with live acts nightly including local legend Kim Massie (Thurs). Cover around $7. Daily 7pm–3am.

★ **Broadway Oyster Bar** 736 S Broadway (downtown) ☎314 261 8811, ⓦbroadwayoysterbar.com. This Cardinals fan favourite, with ramshackle beer garden and no-frills bar, serves up decent oysters, beer and a lively atmosphere on game days. Also a great live jazz and blues venue. Daily 11am–3am.

Morgan Street Brewery 721 N 2nd St ☎314 231 9970, ⓦmorganstreetbrewery.com. Laclede's Landing mainstay, a huge bar, restaurant and microbrewery offering seasonal beers, excellent burgers and pitchers for just $2 on Thursday nights. Mon 4–10pm, Tues–Sun 11am–2.30pm.

★ **Three Sixty** 1 S Broadway ☎314 641 8842, ⓦ360-stl.com. This hip rooftop bar at *Hilton St. Louis at the Ballpark* soars 400ft above downtown, offering scintillating views and a bird's-eye perch over Busch Stadium. Mon–Thurs 4pm–1am, Fri & Sat 4pm–2am, Sun 4–11pm.

Hannibal

No other place had as much influence on **Mark Twain** as his boyhood home of **HANNIBAL**, an otherwise sleepy ensemble of nineteenth-century red-brick and clapboard gently sloping towards the Mississippi. Twain, born Samuel Clemens in 1835 in Florida, Missouri, based

10

> **MARK TWAIN RIVERBOAT**
>
> Get a sense of what riverboat life used to be like in these parts aboard a one-hour sightseeing or two-hour dinner cruise on the **Mark Twain Riverboat** (100 Center St; April–Nov 1.30pm plus seasonal variations; dinner cruises late May to Oct 6.30pm; $14–37; ☎573 221 2477, ⓦmarktwainriverboat.com), a replica paddle-steamer based at the Center Street Landing, a short walk from the Twain museum.

his seminal novels *The Adventures of Tom Sawyer* and *The Adventures of Huckleberry Finn* on his early life in Hannibal, and today the short stretch of historic properties on Main Street is crammed with restaurants, gift shops and museums dedicated to his memory.

The town is 120 miles north of St Louis, squeezed between two steep bluffs; walk up to the **Mark Twain Memorial Lighthouse** to the north (accessible by 244 steps) or drive up **Lover's Leap** to the south (both sunrise–sunset; free) for killer views of the old houses and the muddy expanse of the Mississippi.

Mark Twain Boyhood Home & Museum

120 N Main St • Daily 9am–5pm • $11 • ☎573 221 9010, ⓦmarktwainmuseum.org

Hannibal was Twain's youthful stomping ground between 1839 and 1853, his time here meticulously chronicled at the illuminating **Mark Twain Boyhood Home & Museum**. Buy tickets at the **Interpretative Center**, where exhibits and videos chart Twain family history in the region, before peeking inside the humble **Huckleberry Finn House** (a reconstruction of the home of Tom Blankenship, Twain's model for Huck). The **Boyhood Home** itself on Hill Street is a simple, white clapboard house where Twain lived, its rooms restored in period style; further along Main Street is the **Mark Twain Museum**, where a hall of exhibits and videos re-create scenes from Twain's books, and original book illustrations by **Norman Rockwell** are displayed upstairs.

Mark Twain Cave

300 Cave Hollow Rd (off Hwy-79) • Daily: June–Aug 9am–8pm; April, May, Sept & Oct 9am–6pm; Nov–March 10am–4pm • $15.95 • ☎573 221 1656, ⓦmarktwaincave.com

About one mile south of town, the **Mark Twain Cave** is as much testimony to the influence of Twain's fiction as to the appeal of creepy caverns. Discovered in 1819, the cave system featured heavily in *Tom Sawyer*, and by the 1880s had already become a major attraction for fans: the smoke from their lanterns and their graffiti (as well as the signature of Jesse James) are still much in evidence. The caves themselves are an intriguing warren of narrow passages, with limestone piled up like pancakes. Note that the caves are always chilly – bring a jacket.

ACCOMMODATION AND EATING   HANNIBAL

Best Western on the River 401 N Third St ☎573 248 1150, ⓦbestwestern.com. Just a short stroll from Main St, with comfy business rooms, indoor pool in the atrium, breakfasts and wi-fi (it also has computers). **$110**

Java Jive 211 N Main St ☎573 221 1017, ⓦjavajiveonline .com. A welcoming boho space with plenty of comfy chairs, free wi-fi, tempting cakes, soups and sandwiches ($4.75–9), set in a spacious 1905 red-brick beauty. Mon–Thurs

7am–9pm, Fri & Sat 7am–10pm, Sun 8am–6pm.

Mark Twain Dinette 400 N Third St ☎573 221 5300, ⓦmarktwaindinette.com. Yes, it's touristy, but this local diner has been serving up delicious fried chicken ($7.50), "maid-rite" ground beef sandwiches ($2.95), frosty mugs of home-made root beer ($1.85), onion rings by the foot ($7.95) and Mississippi mud malts ($4.55) since 1942. Tues–Sun 6am–8pm.

Kansas City and around

Forget all those Midwest stereotypes – **KANSAS CITY** is a dynamic urban centre of more than two million people, with Art Deco skyscrapers and fountains, a fabulous art museum and a rich cultural heritage that includes jazz and an influential African

American community. Then there's **Kansas City-style barbecue**, one of America's most celebrated dishes.

Founded in 1838, the city today actually comprises two fairly distinct – and governmentally separate – cities, separated by the state border and the Missouri River. Virtually all the major points of interest sit on the Missouri side (known as "KC"), while the Kansas section ("KCK") maintains a much lower profile.

Downtown Kansas City

After a period of significant decline in the 1980s and early 1990s, **downtown** Kansas City has undergone a remarkable renaissance, with flagship projects such as the **Power & Light District** (for shopping and entertainment), the futuristic **Sprint Center** and the Moshe Safdie-designed **Kauffman Center for the Performing Arts** already completed. Just north is the **historic district** known as **River Market**, where colourful shops, cafés and a farmers' market at Fifth and Walnut streets liven up the riverside area.

Arabia Steamboat Museum

400 Grand Blvd • Mon–Sat 10am–5.30pm, Sun noon–5pm • $14.50 • ☎ 816 471 4030, ⓦ 1856.com

Discovered by archeologists in 1988, the *Arabia* was a steamboat built back in 1856 at the height of the riverboat boom, and today this remarkable find forms the core of the **Arabia Steamboat Museum**, its preserved cargo shedding light on frontier life at the time.

American Jazz Museum and Negro Leagues Baseball Museum

1616 E 18th St • Tues–Sat 9am–6pm, Sun noon–6pm • Individual museums $10; combined ticket $15 • Baseball Museum ☎ 816 221 1920, ⓦ nlbm.com; Jazz Museum ☎ 816 474 8463, ⓦ americanjazzmuseum.com

The **18th and Vine Historic Jazz District**, a couple of miles southeast of downtown, was the hub of the city's flourishing African American community during segregation, and became a hotbed for jazz from the 1930s to the 1950s. The modern complex containing the **American Jazz Museum** and the **Negro Leagues Baseball Museum** now anchors the neighbourhood.

The **jazz museum** offers an overview of the neighbourhood's role in developing America's greatest original art form, and especially local hero **Charlie Parker** (born here in 1920). Its *Blue Room* functions as a working jazz bar (Mon & Thurs–Sat 5–11pm; Fri & Sat $10 cover).

The **baseball museum** is as much an introduction to early **civil rights history** as baseball, with an enthralling collection of photographs, exhibits and game equipment that traces the turbulent progress of black baseball in America, which was segregated from the white major leagues between 1920 and 1959 – the first Negro League was founded here in Kansas City, with local team the Monarchs fielding **Jackie Robinson** in 1945 before he made his historic move to the Dodgers.

National World War I Museum

100 W 26 St • June–Aug daily 10am–5pm; Sept–May closed Mon • $14 (2-day pass) • ☎ 816 888 8100, ✇ theworldwar.org

America's only museum dedicated to the Great War, the **National World War I Museum** opened in 2006 underneath the soaring **Liberty Memorial**, completed eighty years earlier – take the elevator up the tower for the best views of the city. The museum itself charts the course of the conflict with videos, mock trenches, touch-screen displays and plenty of military equipment, and is especially good on America's road to war in 1917.

Nelson-Atkins Museum of Art

4525 Oak St • Wed 10am–4pm, Thurs & Fri 10am–9pm, Sat 10am–5pm, Sun noon–5pm • Museum and grounds free, parking $5 • ☎ 816 561 4000, ✇ nelson-atkins.org

One of the most attractive gallery spaces in the USA, the extensive **Nelson-Atkins Museum of Art** melds the original 1933 building with the stunning, contemporary Bloch Building completed in 2007. Assuming you can tear yourself away from the gorgeous **courtyard café** in the centre, the artwork more than matches the architecture: paintings from local boy **Thomas Hart Benton** vie with one of Monet's *Water Lilies* and Caravaggio's famed *John the Baptist*, his fourth in a series of eight. Don't skip the museum's remarkable **Chinese art** collection, especially its meditative Temple Room. In the grounds are 22 pieces of the giant (and iconic) *Shuttlecocks* series, created by Claes Oldenburg and Coosje van Bruggen.

Boulevard Brewing Company

2501 Southwest Blvd • Mon–Fri 8.30am–5pm; see website for tour times (tickets available only on the day of the tour) • Free • ☎ 816 474 7095, ✇ boulevard.com

Modern Kansas City icon **Boulevard Brewing Company** started making craft ales in 1989, and now knocks out more than 180,000 barrels a year. Learn all about the brewing process and taste the suds (five free drinks) on a 45-minute **tour** of the premises.

Harry S. Truman National Historic Site

219 N Delaware Ave (tickets must be obtained at the site's visitor centre, 223 N Main St), Independence • Tours daily every 15–30min (no tours on Mon Nov to late May) • $4 • ☎ 816 254 9929, ✇ nps.gov/hstr

The life of 33rd President **Harry Truman** is real American success story, celebrated at the **Harry S. Truman National Historic Site** in **Independence**, a few miles east of Kansas City. Born in rural Missouri in 1884, Truman never completed college, but rose up the political ladder to become FDR's vice-president in 1945 – when Roosevelt died soon afterwards, Truman ascended to the Oval Office just in time to drop the atomic bomb on Japan. The historic site preserves the grand nineteenth-century mansion Truman called home from 1919 until his death in 1972, though it originally belonged to the family of his wife, Bess. Tour tickets must be obtained at the **visitor centre**, where a video chronicles Truman's early life.

Harry S. Truman Library & Museum

500 W US-24, Independence • Mon–Sat 9am–5pm, Sun noon–5pm • $8 • ☎ 816 268 8200, ✇ trumanlibrary.org

A short drive north of the Truman Historic Site, the **Harry S. Truman Library & Museum** completes the autobiographical picture started at the Harry S. Truman National Historic

Site by covering Truman's time in office between 1945 and 1953. Interactive exhibits chart the many controversies of his presidency, such as entering the Korean War and the recognition of the state of Israel. Truman and his wife are buried in the courtyard outside.

ARRIVAL AND DEPARTURE
KANSAS CITY

By plane Kansas City International Airport (ⓦflykci.com) is 20 miles northwest of downtown. Metro buses ($1.50) and faster shared shuttle buses regularly head into the city; try SuperShuttle ($18; ☎800 258 3826, ⓦsupershuttle .com). The equivalent taxi ride costs around $50; call Yellow Cab (☎816 471 5000).

By bus The somewhat isolated Greyhound terminal (also used by Jefferson Lines) lies a couple of miles east of downtown at 1101 Troost Ave (☎816 221 2835). Megabus services to St Louis and Chicago arrive and depart on the east side of Grand Blvd, at 3rd St downtown.

Destinations Des Moines (4 daily; 2hr 40min–3hr 30min); Lawrence (4 daily; 55min); Omaha (2 daily; 3hr 10min–4hr); St Louis (3 daily; 4hr–4hr 30min); Topeka (4 daily; 1hr 30min); Wichita (2 daily; 4hr 10min).

By train Amtrak trains call in at Union Station, 30 W Pershing Rd.

Destinations Albuquerque (1 daily; 18hr 10min); Chicago (3 daily; 5hr 40min–7hr 30min); Dodge City (1 daily; 6hr 35min); St Louis (2 daily; 5hr 40min); Topeka (1 daily; 1hr 44min).

GETTING AROUND AND INFORMATION

By bus The Metro bus system ($1.50; ☎816 221 0660, ⓦkcata.org), offers a $3 day pass and a three-day, $10 visitor pass (buy online).

By bicycle The B-Cycle bike sharing programme (ⓦkansas city.bcycle.com) offers bikes at various city locations for $7/24hr or $15/week (rides under 30min are free; over 30min you pay $2/30min).

Visitor centre 22nd floor, City Center Square, 1100 Main St (Mon–Fri 8.30am–5pm; ☎816 221 5242, ⓦvisitkc .com).

ACCOMMODATION

Aladdin 1215 Wyandotte St, at 12th St ☎816 421 8888, ⓦhialaddin.com. This venerable hotel dating from 1926 is now run by *Holiday Inn*, with plush, contemporary designed rooms, Art Deco elements, champagne on arrival and an in-house spa. **$120**

★ **Hotel Phillips** 106 W 12th St ☎816 221 7000, ⓦhotelphillips.com. Gorgeously restored downtown 1930s luxury hotel. Rooms are spacious and relaxing, while the mezzanine above the lobby has wonderful Art Deco touches. **$120**

Hotel Savoy 219 W 9th St ☎816 842 3575, ⓦsavoy hotel.net. Opened in 1888, this Garment District landmark has been beautifully renovated into a boutique B&B offering gourmet breakfasts and spacious rooms, clawfoot tubs and original furniture. **$109**

EATING

Barbecue is an art form in Kansas City, where meats are slow-smoked with a combination of hickory and oak woods, and low-brow joints flourish on word-of-mouth popularity (85 at last count). "**Burnt ends**" is a particular Kansas speciality – tasty pieces of meat cut from the charred end of a smoked beef brisket, smothered with sauce.

Arthur Bryant's 1727 Brooklyn Ave, at 18th St ☎816 231 1123, ⓦarthurbryantsbbq.com. Kansas City's most famous barbecue joint (with roots in the 1908 business established by BBQ godfather Henry Perry), remains surprisingly low key and popular with locals, though expect long queues at peak times. Beef and ribs are smoked to perfection (from $8.95), but the secret here is the sauces: original, sweet or rich and spicy. Mon–Thurs 10am–9.30pm, Fri & Sat 10am–10pm, Sun 11am–8pm.

Gates Bar-B-Q 3205 Main St ☎816 753 0828, ⓦgatesbbq.com. A Kansas City barbecue tradition since 1946, and another place famed for lip-smacking sauces and its hickory-smoked cuts – try the burnt ends ($6.95). Mon–Thurs & Sun 10am–midnight, Fri & Sat 10am–1am.

LaMar's Donuts 3395 Main St ☎816 561 7176, ⓦlamars.com. A KC institution since 1960, now with branches in several states; this is the original, knocking out perfect, airy doughnuts from 75¢. Daily 5.30am–2pm.

★ **Oklahoma Joe's** 3002 W 47th Ave ☎913 722 3366, ⓦoklahomajoesbbq.com. Cross the state line into Kansas for this justly popular BBQ joint, where the meats are priced to please (dinners from $9.49). The perfectly smoky BBQ beans ($2.39) alone are worth a visit. Mon–Thurs 11am–8.30pm, Fri & Sat 11am–9.30pm.

DRINKING, NIGHTLIFE AND ENTERTAINMENT

Kelly's Westport Inn 500 Westport Rd ☎816 561 5800, ⓦkellyswestportinn.com. Shabby but friendly bar inside Kansas City's oldest structure, constructed around 1850. Check out the rooftop deck. Daily 11am–3am.

Manifesto 1924 Main St ☎ 816 536 1325, ⊚ theriegerkc .com/manifesto. Incredibly hip lounge bar with edgy cocktails ($12) credited for boosting the current cocktail boom in Kansas City – make a reservation. Mon–Sat 5pm–1.30am.

Midland Theatre 1228 Main St ☎ 816 283 9921, ⊚ midlandkc.com. Lovingly restored music hall that's been Kansas City's primary mid-level concert venue since 1927 (check out the gold-leaf, Czech hand-cut crystal chandeliers inside). Hours vary.

Mutual Musicians Foundation 1823 Highland Ave ☎ 816 471 5212. Landmark in the 18th and Vine district (founded in 1917 as a musician's union), and now an amazing after-hours club. Jazz jam sessions (Fri & Sat 1.30–5.30am) have been running since 1930. Hours vary.

10

St Joseph

Sixty miles north of Kansas City, overlooking the Missouri River, **ST JOSEPH** boasts an astounding collection of nineteenth-century architecture, a legacy of its boom years as supplier to Western pioneers; iconic American foodstuffs Aunt Jemima pancakes (1889) and saltine crackers (1876) also originated here. Though it's a relatively small and sleepy city these days, its sixteen museums commemorate legends of the American West such as the **Pony Express** and **Jesse James**, and it also harbours the most enticing **fine dining experience** in the state.

Pony Express Museum

914 Penn St • Mon–Sat 9am–5pm (Dec–Feb till 4pm), Sun 11am–4pm • $6 • ☎ 816 279 5059, ⊚ ponyexpress.org

St Joseph was the eastern terminus of the short-lived but fabled **Pony Express**, which delivered mail 1966 miles to Sacramento, California, in ten days via continuous horseback relay. Established in February 1860, the Pony Express was made redundant in October 1861 by the completion of the transcontinental telegraph, but riders such as Buffalo Bill Cody went on to become legends. The full story is told in dioramas and a short introductory film at the **Pony Express Museum**, set in the company's original pinewood stables.

Patee House Museum and Jesse James Home

1202 Penn St, at 12th St • April–Oct Mon–Sat 9am–4pm, Sun 1–4pm; Nov–March Sat 10am–4pm, Sun 1–4pm • $6; $4 for Jesse James Home • ☎ 816 232 8206, ⊚ ponyexpressjessejames.com

The incredibly grand Patee House Hotel, built in 1858 and the headquarters of the Pony Express, is now a vast warren of galleries forming the **Patee House Museum**, crammed with memorabilia. Highlights include a display dedicated to newscaster **Walter Conkrite** (born here in 1916), the "Western on Wood" paintings by **George Warfel** and a working **carousel** ($1.50). The museum also owns St Joseph's major claim to fame, the **Jesse James Home** (accessed from the back of the museum, though tickets are sold separately), the one-storey frame cottage in which **Jesse James** was shot in the back of the head on April 3, 1882, by Robert Ford, a 20-year-old member of his own gang who had negotiated a $10,000 reward from the governor of Missouri. James was living incognito here (he'd only moved in 100 days before). The house is decked out in period style and festooned with all sorts of information about the outlaw.

ACCOMMODATION AND EATING   ST JOSEPH

Hi Ho Bar & Grill 1817 Frederick Ave ☎ 816 233 7363, ⊚ hiho-stjoe.com. A favourite neighbourhood bar since 1910, with an Irish theme, famous pork tenderloin sandwiches (a local speciality; $7.29) and excellent live entertainment. Mon–Sat 11am–1.30am, Sun 11am–midnight.

★ **J C Wyatt House** 1309 Felix St ☎ 816 676 1004, ⊚ jcwyatt.net. This gorgeous 1891 home, festooned with period furnishings, operates as a sort of supper club, with three-course set menus (you choose the main in advance), and a reservation-only policy. Menus are seasonal (lunch is $12.95, dinner from $29.95) and American-/French-influenced, but usually include chicken salad and salmon. No alcohol, but BYOB (no corkage fee). Tues–Sat 11.30am–1.30pm & 6–11pm.

Shakespeare Chateau Inn & Gardens 809 Hall St ☎ 816 232 2667, ⊚ shakespearechateau.com. This converted B&B, in a spectacular 1885 Queen Anne mansion, features original stained-glass windows and three luxurious suites with romantic, period furnishings. $150

The Ozarks

Occupying most of southern Missouri, the **Ozark Mountains** are not particularly high (up to 2560ft), though the roads through them switch, dip, climb and swerve to provide soothing views of steep hillsides thick with oak, elm, hickory and redbud, particularly resplendent in autumn. A distinct **Ozark culture** developed here in the nineteenth century in rough, isolated backwoods communities, much like Appalachia; though it has a rich history of fiddle music, square dances and folklore, movies and literature have often explored the darker side of life here, most recently in *Winter's Bone* (2010). Along the southwest Missouri border, lakes created by damming the **White River** (Lake Taneycomo and Table Rock Lake are the most prominent), have helped fuel a tourist boom, centred on the major resort town of **Branson**.

Branson

Nestled among pristine lakes and forests, **BRANSON**, forty miles south of I-44, attracts millions of visitors each year to what's become known as the "Ozark Disneyland" for its fifty or so **live music venues** (almost all of a country or nostalgia bent), a handful of theme parks and shows exclusively geared towards families.

Branson Landing on Lake Taneycomo offers waterfront shopping, dining and entertainment. West of Hwy-65, **76 Country Boulevard** (and, increasingly, Shepherd of the Hills Expressway) is lined for miles by a wide range of neon-licked restaurants, stores and entertainment venues. The spectrum ranges from Japanese fiddler-singer **Shoji Tabuchi** and Russian comedian **Yakov Smirnoff** to **Acrobats of China** and beloved country acts like **Buck Trent** and the **Oak Ridge Boys**. Kids will enjoy the attractions (think zip-lines, IMAX and the "World's Largest Toy Museum") and variety shows, while fans of **country** will love the music – the quality is much higher than you might expect. **Tickets** for a two-hour show are fairly priced ($20–30 is typical) and there's no shortage of takers, especially in summer.

ACCOMMODATION AND EATING   BRANSON

Big Cedar Lodge 612 Devil's Pool Rd, Ridgedale ☎816 232 2667, ⓦbigcedar.com. Accommodation is easy to find in Branson itself, but to escape the mayhem drive 10 miles south to this self-contained resort, in a tranquil wooded valley on the lake. Spacious lodges or chalet-style rooms with all mod cons and plenty of activities on site. $129

Danna's BBQ & Burger Shop 963 Hwy-165 ☎417 337 5527, ⓦdannasbbq.com. Perfect place for barbecue and

burgers; try the exceptional pulled pork sandwich ($6.69). Mon–Sat 11am–8pm.

Mel's Hard Luck Diner 2800 West Hwy 76 (Grand Village Shopping Center) ☎417 332 0150, ⓦmelshardluckdiner .com. This 1950s-style diner features waiters who sing as they serve. As you might suspect, the food isn't really the main draw, so stick to the basics: burgers (from $12.99), sandwiches and Mel's root beer malts ($4.99). Mon–Thurs & Sun 11am–8pm, Fri & Sat 11am–8.30pm.

Oklahoma

Wedged between Texas to the south and Kansas to the north, **OKLAHOMA** is more West than Midwest, where ranchers sport Stetsons, Native American tribes mingle with oilmen and locals say "fixin' to" a whole lot. Created in 1907 and romanticized by Rodgers & Hammerstein in their first musical, *Oklahoma!*, the state was one of the hardest hit by Depression in the 1930s, encapsulated most famously in John Steinbeck's novel (and John Ford's film) **The Grapes of Wrath**, but also in Dorothea Lange's haunting photos of itinerant families, and in the sad yet hopeful songs of local boy **Woody Guthrie**. Today the state is a solidly Republican, conservative stronghold, the "buckle" of the Bible belt, with a booming economy largely thanks to oil and gas.

For visitors the main draws are Americana-laced **Route 66**, great **live music** and a couple of dynamic cities; artsy **Tulsa**, in the hilly and wooded northeast, and the revitalized capital, **Oklahoma City**. The state also claims a large Native American population, with 39

10

ROUTE 66: OKLAHOMA

Oklahoma contains the longest stretch of driveable Route 66 in the US (nearly 400 miles), lined with diners, quirky Americana and historic sights. Here are the highlights, driving from east to west. Tulsa (see below) and Oklahoma City (see p.632) are also en route. See ⓦ oklahomaroute66.com for more.

Waylan's Ku-Ku Burger 915 N Main St, Miami. Classic diner serving juicy burgers and fries.

The Blue Whale 2680 N Hwy-66, Catoosa (ⓦ bluewhaleroute66.com). This 80ft blue whale sculpture has been entertaining drivers since 1972.

The Golden Driller Expo Square, Yale Ave at 21st St, Tulsa. This 76ft-tall statue of an oil worker has been a symbol of Tulsa since 1953.

Rock Café 114 W Main St, Stroud (ⓦ rockcafert66.com). Home of the famed

alligator burger and German *jagerschnitzel* since 1939.

Route 66 Interpretive Center 400 E 1st St Chandler (ⓦ route66interpretivecenter.org).

Round Barn 107 E Hwy-66, Arcadia (ⓦ arcadiaroundbarn.com). Restored 1898 landmark and museum.

POPS 660 W Hwy-66, Arcadia (ⓦ pops66 .com). Modern homage to classic diners, with a giant 66ft-tall soda bottle.

Oklahoma Route 66 Museum 2229 W Gary Blvd, Clinton (ⓦ route66.org).

---

sovereign tribes (there are no "reservations" here) – "oklahoma" is the Choctaw word for "red man" – and many of its towns host museums devoted to Native American history.

Tulsa

Thanks to oil and increasingly, natural gas, **TULSA** is booming, with a robust economy and a growing regional population of around one million. The city's first oil rush funded construction of stunning **Art Deco buildings** in the late 1920s; after years of decline, downtown Tulsa is undergoing a second renaissance, with a spate of residential and commercial development including the **BOK Center** (designed like a shimmering saucer by César Pelli), numerous art galleries and independent stores and restaurants popping up on a monthly basis. It's an easy city to navigate and an essential stop for art and music lovers: the **Woody Guthrie Center**, **Philbrook Museum of Art** and **Gilcrease Museum** pack enough interest to last several days.

Woody Guthrie Center and Brady Arts District

102 E Brady St • Tues–Sun 10am–6pm • $8 • ☎ 918 574 2710, ⓦ woodyguthriecenter.org

The **Woody Guthrie Center** celebrates one of America's greatest musical legends, the folk singer who inspired Bob Dylan and countless others. Born in Okemah (65 miles south of Tulsa) in 1912, Guthrie spent much of his life on the road, and the centre commemorates his work with an introductory movie, numerous listening posts and exhibits, including Guthrie's heavily inscribed fiddle and a special section on his most famous ballad, *This Land is Your Land*.

Opposite the centre, **Guthrie Green** hosts free weekend concerts and anchors the flourishing **Brady Arts District** of bars and galleries such as **108 Contemporary** (ⓦ 108contemporary.org) and the **Philbrook Downtown**, the contemporary art wing of the Philbrook (Wed–Sat noon–7pm, Sun noon–5pm; $9, includes admission to Philbrook), converted from old warehouses.

Philbrook Museum of Art

2727 S Rockford Rd • Tues, Wed & Fri–Sun 10am–5pm, Thurs 10am–8pm • $9 • ☎ 918 749 7941, ⓦ philbrook.org

Tulsa is full of surprises, but few match the scope of the **Philbrook Museum of Art**, housed in the vast Italianate fantasy mansion built by oil tycoon **Waite Phillips** in 1927, amid an oasis of fountains and greenery. Once you've finished admiring the building (galleries in the original home blend seamlessly with the modern wing), you can focus on the permanent collection, which features everything from Native American pottery, baskets and African sculpture to American art such as *Blue Kimono* by William Merritt Chase.

Gilcrease Museum

1400 N Gilcrease Museum Rd • Tues–Sun 10am–5pm • $8 • ☎ 918 596 2700, ⊕ gilcrease.utulsa.edu

Just northwest of downtown Tulsa in the verdant, gently rolling Osage Hills, the **Gilcrease Museum** aims to tell the story of the Americas through art. Thomas Gilcrease (1890–1962), of Native American heritage, grew very rich in the 1910s once oil was discovered under his land. Though his mansion is more like a cottage compared to the Phillips' home, his private art collection is truly exceptional, best known for **art of the American West**. Inside hangs the world's largest cache of Remingtons, Russells and Morans, great Bierstadt canvases, thousands of paintings by Native American artists and a vast stash of Native American artefacts from all across the Americas, from Inuit seal-gut jackets to turtle-bone necklaces and ancient pottery of the Mississippian culture.

ARRIVAL, DEPARTURE AND GETTING AROUND   TULSA

By plane Tulsa International Airport (⊕ tulsaairports .com) lies 8 miles northeast of downtown; taxis will cost around $20 (meters start at $2). Tulsa Transit bus #203 also serves the airport (6.10am–6.35pm; $1.50).

By bus Greyhound services arrive and depart downtown at 317 S Detroit Ave (☎ 918 584 4428).

Destinations Bartlesville (1 daily; 50min); Oklahoma City (5 daily; 1hr 50min–2hr 15min); St Louis (3 daily; 7hr–8hr 25min).

Local bus Tulsa Transit (⊕ tulsatransit.org), the city's bus service, operates Mon–Sat 5am–8.30pm ($1.50; day pass $3.25).

ACCOMMODATION

Ambassador 1324 S Main St ☎ 918 587 8200, ⊕ ambassadorhotelcollection.com/tulsa. This Art Deco beauty is now a plush downtown hotel, with rooms blending original fittings with iPod docks and Italian stone baths. **$220**

★ **Campbell Hotel** 2636 E 11th St ☎ 918 744 5500, ⊕ thecampbellhotel.com. The old *Casa Loma Hotel* (1927) on Rte-66 has been reborn as this cool boutique

place, with each of the 26 rooms featuring a different design, all with Tulsa themes, from Art Deco to the lavish four-poster in the Renaissance Suite. **$139**

Cedar Rock Inn 4501 W 41st S ☎ 918 447 4493, ⊕ cedar rockinn.com. Easily Tulsa's most enticing B&B, just west of the city in a grand 1890 property; five luxurious suites with antique furnishings and huge breakfasts. **$149**

EATING, DRINKING AND NIGHTLIFE

Tulsa's **Blue Dome** district is the best place for eating and drinking downtown; you can walk from here to the equally lively **Brady Arts District**, but the free Old Urban Trolley bus (Fri & Sat 5pm–2am; 20–30min loop; ⊕ oldurbantrolley.com) is a great idea. **Live music** is a big part of the scene, with "Tulsa Sound" veterans like Leon Russell still performing.

Cain's Ballroom 423 N Main St ☎ 918 584 2306, ⊕ cainsballroom.com. Tulsa's coolest, most intimate live venue (the building dates back to 1924). Ask to see the hole in the wall punched in by Sid Vicious, on tour here with the Sex Pistols in 1978. Cover varies. Daily shows from 7pm.

Fat Guy's Burger Bar 140 N Greenwood Ave ☎ 918 794 7782, ⊕ fatguysburgers.com. The juicy, messy burgers ($5.35) here are the best in town, while the peanut butter bacon burger ($7.25) is for real troopers. Mon–Sat 11am–10pm, Sun 11am–9pm.

Spudder 6536 E 50th St ☎ 918 665 1416, ⊕ thespudder .com. Old-fashioned Tulsa steakhouse, decked out with old road signs and serving juicy slabs of meat (steaks from $29.99, ribs $24.99). Mon–Thurs 5.30–10pm, Fri & Sat 5–11pm.

The Vault 620 S Cincinnati Ave ☎ 918 948 6761, ⊕ vaulttulsa.com. Former drive-in bank from the 1960s, now a restaurant featuring quality local produce and seasonal American menus (pimento mac and cheese for $11, pork bourguignon $16). Mon–Thurs 11am–10pm, Fri 11am–11pm, Sat 4–11pm.

Bartlesville and around

The rolling green hills north of Tulsa soon give way to the flat plains around **BARTLESVILLE**, home to one of the most exceptional hotels in the US. The town was just a muddy collection of oil derricks in Indian Territory when a young, ambitious banker arrived from Iowa in 1905; in just a few years **Frank Phillips** had become a multimillionaire from drilling oil, and **Phillips Petroleum** became one of the nation's biggest companies.

Price Tower

510 Dewey Ave, at 6th St • **Art Center** Tues–Sat 10am–5pm, Sun noon–5pm • $6 **Guided tours** Tues–Thurs 11am & 2pm; Fri & Sat 11am, 1pm & 2pm; Sun 2pm • $12 • ☏ 918 336 4949, ⓦ pricetower.org

Bartlesville is dominated by the extraordinary 221ft-tall **Price Tower**, an ornate cantilevered copper-green oddity completed in 1956, the only skyscraper designed by **Frank Lloyd Wright** that the famed architect ever saw built. Today the main attraction inside is a stunningly cool **hotel** (see below). If you can't spend the night, take a look at the **Price Tower Art Center**, which shows travelling art exhibitions; **guided tours** (1hr) take in the best parts of the tower itself. You can also grab a drink at the stylish *Copper Bar* (Tues–Thurs 4–9pm, Fri & Sat 4–11pm) on its top floors. Built for the H.C. Price Company, the tower was purchased by the ubiquitous Phillips Petroleum in 1981, who donated it to the art centre in 2000.

Frank Phillips Home

1107 Cherokee Ave • Tours Wed–Fri 10am, 11am, 2pm, 3pm & 4pm; Sat also 1pm (guided tours only) • $5 • ☏ 918 336 2491, ⓦ frankphillipshome.org

The **Frank Phillips Home**, a lavish Neoclassical mansion built in 1909 by the founder of Phillips Petroleum, has been beautifully preserved to reflect the remodelling of 1930, with elegant lower rooms contrasting with the ostentation of Mrs Phillips' bedroom and bathroom upstairs, replete with gold taps, mirrored ceilings and pink marble floors.

Woolaroc Museum & Wildlife Preserve

1925 Woolaroc Ranch Rd (off Hwy-123) • June–Aug Tues–Sun 10am–5pm; Sept–May closed Tues • $10 • ☏ 918 336 0307, ⓦ woolaroc.org

Oilman Frank Phillips' beautiful former ranch, now known as the **Woolaroc Museum & Wildlife Preserve**, lies twelve miles southwest of Bartlesville in the Osage Hills, where an exceptional Western art and history collection is scattered throughout seven huge rooms. Look for the 95-million-year-old dinosaur egg, exquisite Navajo blankets, scalps taken by Native Americans and Buffalo Bill's weathered saddle.

ACCOMMODATION	BARTLESVILLE

★ **Inn at Price Tower** 510 Dewey Ave, at Sixth St ☏ 877 424 2424, ⓦ pricetower.org. Frank Lloyd Wright fantasy, all triangular shapes, copper fittings and original, tiny elevators. The rooms are gorgeous period pieces (think *Mad Men*), with comfy beds and compact 1950s showers. Take breakfast on the terrace, surrounded by copper "leaves". __$145__

Oklahoma City

The capital and the largest city in the state, **OKLAHOMA CITY** was created in a matter of hours on April 22, 1889, after a single gunshot signalled the opening of the land to white settlement; what was barren prairie at dawn had by nightfall become a city of ten thousand. Today that city is booming, its principal attractions being the cattle auctions and steakhouses of **Stockyards City**, the top-notch **Cowboy Museum** and an exceptional collection of **Dale Chihuly** glass art.

Situated right on top of the state's oil deposits, black gold has fuelled the city economy since 1928, and despite a period of decline in the 1980s, it now boasts a greater metropolitan population of 1.2 million. The horrific **bombing** of the Alfred P. Murrah Federal Building in 1995 by domestic terrorist Timothy McVeigh – which killed 168 people, nineteen of them children – tore the heart out of the city, but it has refused to be defined by it; instead the innovative, $350-million Metropolitan Area Projects (**MAPS**), funded by a one-cent sales tax, built sports, entertainment, cultural and convention facilities (the current MAPS 3 project will run till 2017 and is expected to raise $777 million).

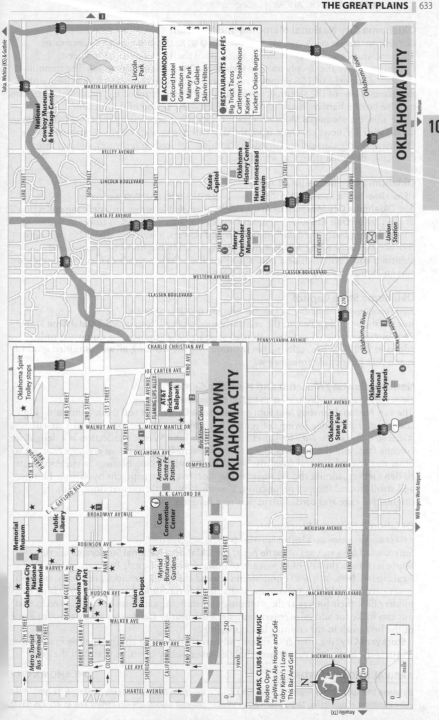

OKLAHOMA CITY

10

ACCOMMODATION
Colcord Hotel — 2
Grandison at Maney Park — 4
Rusty Gables — 3
Skirvin Hilton — 1

RESTAURANTS & CAFÉS
Big Truck Tacos — 1
Cattlemen's Steakhouse — 4
Kaiser's — 3
Tucker's Onion Burgers — 2

DOWNTOWN OKLAHOMA CITY

★ Oklahoma Spirit Trolley stops

BARS, CLUBS & LIVE-MUSIC
Rodeo Opry — 3
TapWerks Ale House and Café — 1
Toby Keith's I Love This Bar And Grill — 2

10

Oklahoma City National Memorial and Museum

620 N Harvey Ave • **Museum** Mon–Sat 9am–6pm, Sun 1–6pm • $10 • ☎ 405 235 3313, ⓦ oklahomacitynationalmemorial.org

The area where the Federal Building stood until the 1995 bombing has been transformed into the deeply moving **Oklahoma City National Memorial**. The tranquil site includes a field of 168 empty glass, bronze and stone chairs (each inscribed with the name of one of the victims), as well as a black granite reflecting pool flanked by two massive bronze barriers marking 9.01–9.03am – the period of destruction.

The adjacent **Memorial Museum** is beautifully done, recounting the tragedy in minute detail, with TV news coverage from the day, interviews with survivors, tributes to the victims and poignant debris (shredded clothing, cracked coffee mugs, twisted filing cabinets), all pulled from the wreckage.

Oklahoma City Museum of Art

415 Couch Drive • Tues–Sat 10am–5pm, Thurs till 9pm, Sun noon–5pm • $12 • ☎ 405 236 3100, ⓦ okcmoa.com

The **Oklahoma City Museum of Art** is chiefly memorable for its mesmerizing collection of glass art by **Dale Chihuly**, beginning with a 55ft-tall blown-glass tower in the lobby and including boats filled with glass balls and flowers, a walkway under his signature reef-like Persian Ceiling and stunning lilac spears. Highlights of the permanent paintings collection include a couple of Renoirs, a Peale portrait of George Washington and an iconic *Calla Lily* by Georgia O'Keeffe.

Oklahoma State Capitol

2300 N Lincoln Blvd • Mon–Fri 8am–5pm, Sat & Sun 9am–4pm • Free • ☎ 800 652 6552, ⓦ ok.gov

Just northeast of downtown, the relatively modest (by US standards) **Oklahoma State Capitol** was completed in Greco-Roman style in 1917 (though the dome was only added in 2002). What really makes it unique are the working **oil wells** studded around it and pumping crude from below.

National Cowboy Museum and Heritage Center

1700 NE 63rd St • Daily 10am–5pm • $12.50 • ☎ 405 478 2250, ⓦ nationalcowboymuseum.org

The vast **National Cowboy Museum and Heritage Center** is a real treat, combining high and popular art in one loving collection, beginning with the monumental 18ft-tall statue *The End of the Trail* by James Earle Fraser. John Wayne's collection is a delight for cowboy fans, and the memorabilia-packed Western Performers Gallery pays homage to other movie cowboys and cowgirls. Watch videos of bucking broncos in the American Rodeo Gallery, admire the *Windows to the West*, five huge triptychs by Wilson Hurley, and stroll around Prosperity Junction, a mock 1900 cattle town at dusk, with its original jail cage and cordial invitation to a hanging.

Oklahoma National Stockyards

2501 Exchange Ave • Auctions Mon & Tues from 8am • Free • ☎ 405 235 8675, ⓦ onsy.com

Surrounded by a vast sea of cattle pens, the **Oklahoma National Stockyards** auction house facilitates the sale of thousands of dollars' worth of cattle between Stetson-wearing ranchers. You won't understand a word the quick-fire auctioneer says, but you won't need to; although vegetarians and animal-lovers should steer clear, watching the bidders flick their fingers as the stomping and snorting cattle are being shunted in and out can make for addictive entertainment. Visit nearby *Cattlemen's* afterwards, for some of the best steak in the country (see opposite).

Stockyard City, the district of shops and bars that grew up around the stockyards from 1910, is the best place to buy incredibly ornate cowboy boots, hats and all the gear.

ARRIVAL AND DEPARTURE   **OKLAHOMA CITY**

By plane Will Rogers World Airport (ⓦ flyokc.com) is 10 miles southwest of downtown; Metro Transit buses serve the centre (Mon–Fri 7.47am, 11.47am & 5.02pm). A taxi will cost around $24–26 (Yellow Cab ☎ 405 236 5551).

Airport Express shuttle vans are faster and more convenient ($24; ☎405 681 3311, ⓦ airportexpressokc.com).

By bus Greyhound services call in at the Union Bus Depot at 427 W Sheridan Ave, downtown (☎405 235 6425). Destinations Albuquerque (3 daily; 10hr 20min–10hr 55min); Dallas (4 daily; 3hr 40min–5hr); Kansas City

(4 daily; 6hr 20min–7hr 30min; St Louis (3 daily; 9hr 50min–10hr 45min); Tulsa (5 daily; 1hr 50min–2hr 20min); Wichita (2 daily; 3hr).

By train The Amtrak station is at 100 South E.K. Gaylord Blvd, at the southwest corner of downtown; there's a daily service to Fort Worth (4hr 15min).

GETTING AROUND AND INFORMATION

By bus Metro Transit (☎405 235 7433, ⓦ gometro.org), operates Mon–Sat; fares are $1.50 for regular buses, while the Downtown Discovery trolley buses are free, linking downtown attractions with Bricktown (daily every 15–30min; Oct–April no service Sun).

By bike The Spokies bike-share programme (ⓦ spokiesokc

.com) charges $5/day for bikes at six kiosks across the downtown area (unlimited 30min rides; $2 each additional 30min).

Visitor centre Cox Convention Center, at the corner of Sheridan Ave and E.K. Gaylord Blvd (Mon–Fri 9am–6pm; ☎405 602 5141, ⓦ visitokc.com).

10

ACCOMMODATION

★ **Colcord Hotel** 15 N Robinson Ave ☎405 601 4300, ⓦ colcordhotel.com. Sleek boutique hotel housed in the city's first skyscraper (1910). Spacious rooms with downtown views are outfitted with modern furnishings and glass-tiled showers, while the lobby is a marbled feast for the eyes. **$175**

Grandison at Maney Park 1200 N Shartel Ave ☎405

232 8778, ⓦ grandisoninn.com. Top B&B in a romantic Victorian (1904), crammed with decorative art, maplewood floors and eight period rooms with whirlpool tubs. **$109**

Skirvin Hilton 1 Park Ave ☎405 272 3040, ⓦ skirvin hilton.com. Gorgeous 1911 hotel, completely restored in 2007 to its 1920s heyday, with exceptionally ritzy decor, comfy rooms and a superb restaurant. **$206**

EATING, DRINKING AND ENTERTAINMENT

The renovated-warehouse restaurants of **Bricktown** (ⓦ bricktownokc.com), along Sheridan and Reno avenues east of the Amtrak station, are popular with visitors and locals alike. If you're driving, be prepared to see numerous outlets of Sonic, the drive-in fast-food franchise that was founded here in 1959.

★ **Big Truck Tacos** 530 NW 23rd St ☎405 525 8226, ⓦ bigtrucktacos.com. This ex-food truck is now a must-eat experience; the "5th Amendment" taco ($3.50) contains a mystery ingredient, usually revealed at the end of the day via Twitter (anything from regular beef or duck to tongue or quail). Mon–Thurs 7.30am–10pm, Fri & Sat 7.30am–midnight.

★ **Cattlemen's Steakhouse** 1309 S Agnew Ave ☎405 236 0416, ⓦ cattlemensrestaurant.com. Evoca-tively dark restaurant founded in 1910 – expect burgundy booths, juicy steaks and specially made Double Deuce beer. Try T-bones ($27.95), rib eyes ($23) or the famed "lamb fries" (actually fried lambs' testicles from Iceland). Mon–Fri 6am–10pm, Sat & Sun 6am–midnight.

Kaiser's 1039 N Walker Ave ☎405 232 7632, ⓦ kaisers bistro.com. Old-fashioned diner and soda fountain, here

since 1918, with bar stools, malts ($4), ice cream scoops from $2 (try the salted caramel) and bison burgers ($8.95). Mon–Sat 11am–9pm, Sun 11am–5pm.

Rodeo Opry 221 Exchange Ave ☎405 297 9773, ⓦ ohfo.org. Non profit venue devoted to authentic country music shows in the style of Nashville's *Grand Ole Opry*. One show a week ($6–12). Sat 7.30pm.

TapWerks Ale House and Café 121 E Sheridan Ave ☎405 319 9599, ⓦ tapwerks.com. This popular Brick-town spot features a British-influenced menu and lays claim to the largest beer selection in the state, with hundreds available. Daily 11am–2am.

Toby Keith's I Love This Bar And Grill 310 Johnny Bench Drive ☎405 231 0254, ⓦ tobykeithsbar.com. The country crooner's joint in Bricktown is a good place for a beer and live country music (Keith was born in Clinton,

---

RED DIRT

Fans of live music should make time for the small city of **Stillwater**, seventy miles north of Oklahoma City and the home of **Red Dirt music**; a blend of folk, country, blues and rock styles, with home-grown bands Jason Boland and the Stragglers, No Justice, the Jason Savory Band and the godfather of the genre, Bob Childers (indie rockers All-American Rejects also hail from here). Check out venues such as *Eskimo Joe's* (ⓦ eskimojoes.com) and *Tumbleweed Dance Hall* (ⓦ calffry.com), or visit ⓦ stillwaterscene.com.

Oklahoma). Mon–Thurs 11am–10pm, Fri & Sat 11am–midnight, Sun 11am–9pm.
Tucker's Onion Burgers 324 NW 23rd St ☎ 405 609 2333, ⓦ tuckersonionburgers.com. Indulge in this local speciality, with shredded onions seared into the beef patty to create the main event, from $4.99 (the onion burger capital of the world is in nearby El Reno). Daily 11am–9pm.

Kansas

10

Thanks to the *Wizard of Oz*, most people have heard of **KANSAS** even if they have very little idea of what it's like beyond the movies: vast fields of corn, twisters, *Little House on the Prairie* and the boyhood home of Clark Kent (aka Superman). Indeed, Dorothy's immortal words "we're not in Kansas anymore" has made the state a sort of bellweather ever since, and what Bill Bryson called "the most quintessential of American states" has recently been the scene of much liberal hand-wringing in books like *What's the Matter with Kansas?* (the state is overwhelming conservative).

Be prepared for a few surprises; there are certainly vast, flat bits of Kansas, but the tallgrass prairies of the **Flint Hills** are beautiful, wild and rolling, and college towns such as **Lawrence** are crammed with galleries, restaurants and cool bars. Around the middle of the state you leave the Midwest behind entirely – **Dodge City** is all cowboy boots and Stetsons.

Lawrence

Confusingly, Kansas City, Missouri (see p.624) is far bigger and more interesting than Kansas City, Kansas, and your first major pit stop in the state should be **LAWRENCE** on the Kansas River (locally, the "Kaw"), forty miles further west. The town boasts enticing museums, real hills (a rare treat in these parts) and plenty of bars and restaurants, with an energy owed in part to the **University of Kansas (KU)** and the much-loved **Jayhawks** sports teams, as well as a long liberal and intellectual history. Author **William S. Burroughs** was one of the city's more colourful inhabitants – the heroin-addicted author of *Naked Lunch* lived here from 1981 till his death in 1997 (ask about the "Burroughs Trail" at the visitor centre) – while seminal African American poet **Langston Hughes** also spent his childhood here in the early 1900s.

Freedom's Frontier National Heritage Area Exhibit

200 W 9th St, Carnegie Building • Wed–Fri 10am–4.30pm • Free • ☎ 785 856 3040, ⓦ freedomsfrontier.org

Lawrence was founded by the anti-slavery New England Emigrant Aid Company in 1854. As a consequence, the town was at the centre of the "**Bleeding Kansas**" conflicts, and later in the Civil War it was the site of the 1863 massacre euphemistically known at **Quantrill's Raid**. The **Freedom's Frontier National Heritage Area Exhibit** provides an overview of this violent period, with a special room dedicated to the Kansas-Nebraska Act of 1854.

University of Kansas Natural History Museum

1345 Jayhawk Blvd • Tues–Sat 9am–5pm, Sun noon–5pm • Free, suggested donation $5 • ☎ 785 864 4450, ⓦ naturalhistory.ku.edu

Most of Lawrence's formal attractions are clustered on the KU campus, atop Mount Oread, a few blocks southwest of downtown. The **University of Kansas Natural History Museum** is a vast repository of dinosaur fossils and botanical and zoological exhibits, with the key highlights being a huge chronological tableau of North American flora and fauna (an actual installation from the Chicago World's Fair of 1893), as well as the stuffed horse **Comanche**, the lone Seventh Cavalry survivor of the Battle of Little Bighorn.

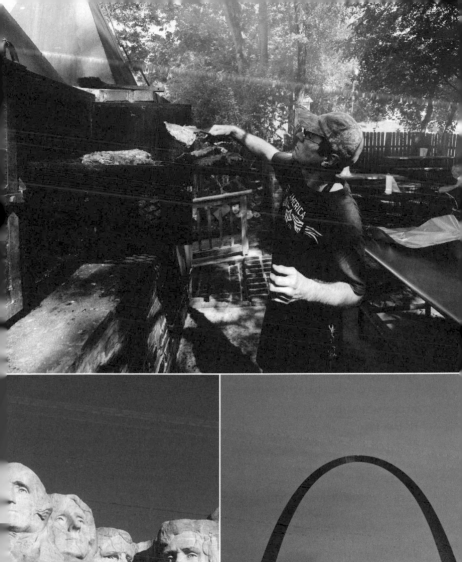

10

ROCK CHALK JAY HAWK

One of college basketball's best-known traditions, the "**Rock Chalk Chant**" has belonged to KU since 1886, though it's changed a bit since then. Hearing several thousand fans in the Allen Fieldhouse slowly intone "Rock Chalk, Jay Hawk, K-U-u-u-uuu!" before home games is spine-tingling. Check ⓦ kuathletics.com for the latest schedule. The inventor of basketball, James Naismith, came to teach at KU and died here in 1939; his **original rules of basketball** will be displayed in a specially built gallery near the stadium (probably from 2015).

Spencer Museum of Art

301 Mississippi St • Tues, Fri & Sat 10am–4pm, Wed & Thurs 10am–8pm, Sun noon–4pm • Free • ☏ 785 864 4710, ⓦ spencerart.ku.edu

With its galleries arranged thematically rather than chronologically, the **Spencer Museum of Art** offers an easily digested overview of KU's extensive art collection, which includes Dürer prints, rare photography from Diane Arbus and Aaron Siskind, the famed daguerreotype portrait of Dorothy Draper (1840), and a remarkably strong East Asian collection ranging from precious Song Dynasty scrolls to contemporary video art from Taiwan. Paintings to look out for include **Otto Dix**'s *Self-portrait*, Dante Gabriel Rossetti's *La Pia de' Tolommei* and a huge selection by **Thomas Hart Benton**.

ARRIVAL AND INFORMATION

LAWRENCE

By bus Greyhound services stop at the Pick N Pay store at 2447 W 6th St (☏ 785 843 5622).
Destinations Kansas City (1 daily; 55min); Topeka (4 daily; 35min).
By train Amtrak trains arrive at 413 E 7th St.
Destinations Dodge City (1 daily; 5hr 30min); Kansas City

(1 daily; 1hr 35min); Topeka (1 daily; 37min).
Visitor centre North of downtown in the renovated 1889 Union Pacific Depot, 402 N 2nd St (Mon–Sat 8.30am–5.30pm, Sun 1–5pm; ☏ 785 865 4499, ⓦ visitlawrence .com); a 25min film charts the city's history during the "Bleeding Kansas" years.

ACCOMMODATION

Eldridge Hotel 7th and Massachusetts sts ☏ 785 749 5011, ⓦ eldridgehotel.com. All-suite hotel with comfortable rooms. Twice burned down by pro-slavery forces (this version dates from 1925), it has been restored to its elegant heyday. **$145**

The Oread 1200 Oread Ave ☏ 785 843 1200, ⓦ theoread .com. Right next to the KU campus, with a rooftop bar, elegant, contemporary rooms and granite bathrooms. The attractive limestone building looks historic but was completed in 2010 to blend in with the campus. **$150**

EATING, DRINKING AND ENTERTAINMENT

As befits a college town, the restaurant and nightlife scene in Lawrence is especially good, with locals and students alike congregating along **Massachusetts Street**, a pleasant strip of independent stores, cafés and bars in the centre of town.

Burger Stand 803 Massachusetts St ☏ 785 856 0543, ⓦ thecasbahburgerstand.com. Best gourmet burgers in town ($7.50), served with a selection of crisp craft beers on tap. Daily 11am–2am.
Free State Brewing Co 636 Massachusetts St ☏ 785 843 4555, ⓦ freestatebrewing.com. Bar converted from an old bus station, with a huge range of microbrews and excellent food; think butternut squash ravioli or crawfish gumbo ($8–12). Mon–Sat 11am–midnight, Sun noon–11pm.
★ **Pachamama's** 800 New Hampshire St ☏ 785 841 0990, ⓦ pachamamas.com. Locally sourced farm-to-table produce and an ever-changing seasonal menu make this the top spot in town; try specialities such as

paprika-cured beef fillet and chilli-raspberry BBQ duck breast ($9–28). Tues–Thurs 11am–2pm & 5–9.30pm, Fri & Sat 11am–2pm & 5pm–midnight.
Sandbar 17 E 8th St ☏ 785 842 0111, ⓦ thesandbar .com. Fun Key West-themed bar with potent cocktails, jukebox and the campy indoor hurricane show every night 10pm (wind, rain, napkins blowing and "mermaids" on the bar). Mon–Fri 3pm–2am, Sat 1pm–2am, Sun 5pm–2am.
Teller's 746 Massachusetts St ☏ 785 843 4111, ⓦ 746mass.com. Elegant restaurant and bar converted from an 1889 bank, the first robbed by Clyde Barrow (before he hooked up with Bonnie Parker; the toilets are named after the duo). Mon–Thurs & Sun 11am–10pm, Fri & Sat 11am–11pm.

Topeka

The unassuming Kansas state capital of **TOPEKA**, 28 miles west of Lawrence, is an essential stop for students of US history; in addition to a lavish capitol building and state history museum, the **Brown v. Board of Education** site commemorates a pivotal moment in the Civil Rights movement.

Brown v. Board of Education National Historic Site

1515 SE Monroe St • Daily 9am–5pm • Free • ☎ 785 354 4273, ⓦ nps.gov/brvb

In 1951, a group of black parents in Topeka challenged segregation in local schools; in what was a crucial step for Civil Rights, the US Supreme Court eventually ruled in their favour three years later, effectively ending the practice. Named after the case, the **Brown v. Board of Education National Historic Site**, housed in the former all-black Monroe School, commemorates this event with a series of thought-provoking exhibits and an excellent video.

Kansas State Capitol

SW 10th Ave and SW Jackson St • Mon–Fri 8am–5pm • Free • ☎ 785 272 8681, ⓦ kshs.org/capitol

The incredibly opulent **Kansas State Capitol** looks like an Italian Renaissance palace. Original construction started in 1866, but wasn't complete until 1903; today the Rotunda is a mesmerizing, multistorey space, with shiny copper pillars, stained glass, murals, huge chandeliers and detailed stencilling. The House and Senate chambers (in session Jan–May) are decked out like Baroque ballrooms (with desks), while the most famous mural is the dramatic image of John Brown in *Tragic Prelude*, painted by John Steuart Curry in 1940.

Kansas State History Museum

6425 SW 6th Ave • Tues–Sat 9am–5pm, Sun 1–5pm • $8 • ☎ 785 272 8681, ⓦ kshs.org/museum

The **Kansas State History Museum** offers a comprehensive overview of the state's surprisingly rich history, from the Santa Fe Trail and the culture of the Kansa and Wichita tribes, to John Brown and the Civil War, with a full-size 1868 steam train and a 1940s diner among the attractions.

The Flint Hills

Discovery Center 315 S 3rd St, Manhattan • June–Aug Mon–Thurs 10am–8pm, Fri & Sat 10am–5pm, Sun noon–5pm; Sept–May Mon–Wed, Fri & Sat 10am–5pm, Thurs 10am–8pm, Sun noon–5pm • $9 • ☎ 785 587 2726, ⓦ flinthillsdiscovery.org

Beyond Topeka, I-70 continues west through the undulating **Flint Hills**, one of the few remaining habitats of **tallgrass prairie**, vast oceans of greens and browns that roll away to the horizon. Get oriented at the **Flint Hills Discovery Center** in the college town of **Manhattan**, a futuristic building crammed with hands-on exhibits and movies. If your curiosity is piqued, drive along Hwy-177 south of here, which cuts through pretty rural villages and the **Tallgrass Prairie National Preserve**, just north of Strong City (free; ⓦ nps.gov/tapr), where there's a small visitor centre and trails across the hills.

Abilene

The sleepy rural town of **ABILENE**, 44 miles west of Manhattan, was once a booming cattle depot, the northern terminus of the **Chisholm Trail** from Texas (Wild Bill Hickok was marshal here for a few months in 1871). The main reason for a pit stop today is the connection with **Dwight D. Eisenhower**, though Abilene still harbours an incredible cache of gorgeous nineteenth-century homes; **Old Abilene** (opposite the Eisenhower site), is an ongoing project to preserve the oldest part of town, replete with log cabins.

Eisenhower Presidential Library & Museum

200 SE Fourth St • Daily 9am–4.45pm (June & July 8am–5.45pm) • $10 • ☎ 785 263 6700, ⓦ eisenhower.archives.gov

An enlightening and moving memorial to the man who was Supreme Allied Commander in World War II and the 34th President (1953–61), the **Eisenhower Presidential Library & Museum** encompasses Ike's **boyhood home** (tour guides lead you through), with its original furnishings, an excellent introductory video in the **visitor centre** and the illuminating **museum**, which covers all the main events of his extraordinary life (and contains his famous wartime Cadillac). There are also temporary (and free) exhibits in the **library/archives building**. The former president and his wife Mamie are buried in the chapel opposite the visitor centre, dubbed **Place of Meditation**, which Ike helped design.

EATING   ABILENE

★ **Brookville Hotel Restaurant** 105 E Lafayette St (just north of I-70) ☎ 785 263 2244, ⓦ brookvillehotel .com. Family restaurant with roots in the 1870s (this is a replica built in 2000); delicious set dinners ($14.99)

comprise fried chicken, mash, gravy, creamed corn and slaw, with ice cream. Reservations recommended. Wed–Fri 5–7.30pm, Sat 11.30am–2pm & 4.30–7.30pm, Sun 11.30am–2pm & 5–7pm; Jan–March limited hours.

Wichita

The largest city in Kansas, **WICHITA** is a cowboy town with a remarkable tradition of popular culture icons, from the *Dennis the Menace* cartoon strip (set in Wichita) and **Pizza Hut** (founded here in 1958), to key members of the 1950s **Beat movement** (Allen Ginsberg wrote *Wichita Vortex Sutra* after he visited in 1966, to "see where everyone came from") and influential local billionaires the **Koch brothers**, the conservative activists Democrats love to hate. It can be hard to absorb this bewildering heritage on a short visit, but Wichita has an intriguing array of museums and galleries nonetheless.

Wichita-Sedgwick County Historical Museum

204 S Main St • Tues–Fri 11am–4pm, Sat & Sun 1–5pm • $4 • ☎ 316 265 9314, ⓦ wichitahistory.org

The three floors of **Wichita-Sedgwick County Historical Museum** provide illuminating insights into the history of the city, especially its predominant role in early aviation – Cessna was one of several companies established here, and today the city remains a global centre of **aircraft construction**. The museum is housed in **Old City Hall**, an 1892 masterpiece of Richardsonian Romanesque, a heavy stone building studded with turrets, gargoyles and arches.

Kansas African American Museum

601 N Water St • Tues–Fri 10am–5pm, Sat noon–4pm • $5.50 • ☎ 316 262 7651, ⓦ tkaamuseum.org

Many Americans (never mind foreigners) are amazed to learn that Kansas has a large and influential black population. The **Kansas African American Museum**, housed in the old 1917 Calvary Baptist Church, details the lesser-known history of Buffalo Soldiers (all-black US army regiments raised after the Civil War) and early black Wichitans.

Wichita Art Museum

1400 W Museum Blvd • Tues–Sat 10am–5pm, Sun noon–5pm • $7, Sat free • ☎ 316 268 4921, ⓦ wichitaartmuseum.org

Displays in the spacious modern galleries of the **Wichita Art Museum** often rotate, but lovers of American art will find plenty of gems in the permanent collection, from famed Western painter **Charles M. Russell** (who commands his own room here) and a good selection of American Impressionism, to the stark realism of Eakins and Hopper. Highlights include John Steuart Curry's *Kansas Cornfield* and Hopper's *Sunlight on Brownstones*; Wichita artists William Dickerson and C.A. Seward are also well represented.

Old Cowtown Museum

1865 W Museum Blvd • Tues–Sat 10am–5pm (late April to late Oct also Sun noon–5pm) • $7.75 • ☎ 316 350 3323, ⊛ oldcowtown.org

To get a feel for Wichita in its cowboy heyday, visit the fun **Old Cowtown Museum**, where a seventeen-acre riverside exhibit re-creates the buildings of the 1870s. Looking and feeling like a movie set, the area includes – along with some docile longhorns – the city's first one-room jail, a schoolroom, a store, a smithy, churches, stables and old homes.

ARRIVAL AND INFORMATION

By plane Domestic flights arrive at the Mid-Continent Airport (⊛ flywichita.org), 7 miles southwest of downtown on W Kellogg Drive; buses (#1) serve downtown (hourly Mon–Sat; $1.75; ⊛ wichitatransit.org), otherwise taxis meet most flights (Best Cabs ☎ 316 838 2233).

By bus Greyhound stops at 312 S Broadway Ave, two blocks east of Main St (☎ 316 265 7711).

Destinations Dodge City (1 daily 3hr 5min); Kansas City (2 daily; 3hr 5min–4hr 15min); Oklahoma City (2 daily; 3hr).

Visitor centre 515 S Main St, downtown (Mon–Fri 7.45am–5.30pm; ☎ 316 265 2800, ⊛ gowichita.com).

ACCOMMODATION AND EATING

Just east of downtown, the nineteenth-century brick warehouses of **Old Town** (⊛ oldtownwichita.com) were transformed in the early 1990s into an entertainment district of bars and restaurants, an area that really comes alive at weekends.

★ **Ambassador** 104 S Broadway St ☎ 316 239 7100, ⊛ ambassadorhotelcollection.com/wichita. Spacious rooms, luxurious beds and sleek bathrooms in the elegantly renovated Union National Bank Building. **$220**

Hotel at Old Town First and Mosley sts ☎ 316 267 4800, ⊛ hotelatoldtown.com. Stylish turn-of-the-twentieth-century flavour (the building dates from 1906) and excellent location combined with spacious, modern suites with full kitchens. **$160**

Old Mill Tasty Shop 604 E Douglas Ave ☎ 316 264 6500. Nostalgic soda fountain, dating back to 1933, popular for great sandwiches, desserts and blue-plate specials. Mon–Thurs 11am–3pm, Fri 11am–8pm, Sat 8am–8pm.

River City Brewing Co 150 N Mosley St ☎ 316 263 2739, ⊛ rivercitybrewingco.com. Top-notch burgers ($9–10) and own-brewed ales are available this Old Town mainstay, which hosts local bands every weekend. Mon–Tues 11am–10pm, Wed & Thurs 11am–midnight, Fri & Sat 11am–2am, Sun noon–10pm.

Dodge City

About 150 miles west of Wichita, **DODGE CITY** is perhaps the most famous of all America's frontier towns, its blend of cowboys and kitsch a must-see for any Wild West aficionado. Dodge actually had a relatively brief heyday, from 1875 until 1886. Established in 1872 along with the Santa Fe Railroad, which transported millions of buffalo hides, by 1875 the town of traders, trappers and hunters had to find a new economic base – the buffalo had been practically exterminated. The era of the great cattle drives was underway, but even then Dodge City's gambling, drinking and lawlessness – which kept busy charismatic, if morally suspect, lawmen such as Bat Masterson and Wyatt Earp – were much exaggerated, and every gunfight meticulously chronicled by the local press. In the 1980s Dodge began another boom, with TV shows like *Gunsmoke* helping to create the tourist industry that thrives today.

Boot Hill Museum

400 Front St • June–Aug daily 8am–8pm; Sept–May Mon–Sat 9am–5pm, Sun 1–5pm • $10 • ☎ 620 227 8188, ⊛ boothill.org

Dodge City's old downtown area is enveloped by a hinterland of railroad tracks and giant silos (most original buildings were destroyed by fire in 1885), and aside from the city's main annual event, July and August's **Dodge City Days and Rodeo** (⊛ www.dodgecitydays .com), the town is content to replay its movie image in the **Boot Hill Museum**. The best of several museums and attractions in the centre, it displays a mountain of artefacts from the old West, and arranges special dinners, mock gunfights and Wild West-style variety shows (see website for times). Infamous **Boot Hill Cemetery** looms above the museum, although there's just a sorry little patch of lawn on one corner of the original site, which was abandoned in 1879 after just 34 burials. The bodies were re-interred elsewhere, but wooden markers tell the stories of some of the characters once buried here.

ARRIVAL AND INFORMATION

By bus Greyhound services stop at the U-Haul dealership, 2601 Central Ave (☎620 225 0675). There's a daily service to Wichita (2hr 50min).

By train Amtrak trains come right into downtown at the 1896 Santa Fe Station, at Central Ave and E Wyatt Earp Blvd.

DODGE CITY

Destinations Albuquerque (1 daily; 11hr 30min); Kansas City (1 daily; 7hr); Lawrence (1 daily; 5hr 20min).

Visitor centre 400 W Wyatt Earp Blvd (June–Aug daily 8.30am–6.30pm; Sept–May Mon–Fri 8.30am–5pm; ☎620 225 8186, ⓦvisitdodgecity.org).

ACCOMMODATION AND EATING

Casey's Cowtown Club 503 E Trail St ☎620 227 5225, ⓦcaseyscowtown.com. Skip the chains and stuff yourself at this locally owned steakhouse, with prime aged steaks (specials from $22) and an old-time Dodge City feel. Mon–Fri 11am–10pm, Sat 4–10pm, Sun 8am–2pm.

Dodge House 2408 W Wyatt Earp Blvd ☎620 225 9900, ⓦdodgehousehotel.com. A cheaper alternative to the chains along US-50, this ageing but characterful option (with a pedigree going back to 1873) is pleasant enough and also has a decent on-site restaurant. $85

Nebraska

Anchored in the east by two of the Midwest's coolest cities, and in the west by some tantalizing monuments to the Oregon Trail, much of **NEBRASKA** is blanketed in a vast expanse of flat farmland. The two sides of the state, connected by four hundred fairly dreary miles of I-80, are well worth exploring, from hip **Omaha** and state government and university hub **Lincoln** to the rugged outcrops of **Scottsbluff**.

Nebraska Territory opened in 1854 and was settled rapidly, beginning with Omaha, a major transport crossroads. Statehood was granted in 1867, and during the 1870s and 1880s, rail companies, encouraged by grants that allowed them to accumulate one sixth of the state's land, laid down such a comprehensive network of tracks that virtually every farmer was within a day's cattle drive of the nearest halt. Thus the buffalo-hunting country of the Sioux and Pawnee was turned into high-yield farmland, which even now has few rivals in terms of beef production. Today, fiscally conservative Nebraska bans government debt by law, and is the only US state to have a unicameral legislature.

Omaha

Every year on the first weekend in May, **OMAHA**, Nebraska's largest city, becomes the unlikely centre of the financial world thanks to billionaire local boy **Warren Buffett** (aka "the Sage of Omaha"); hordes of media and Wall Street bankers fly in for the carnival-like annual shareholders' meeting of Berkshire Hathaway, Buffett's phenomenally successful investment company. Yet for the rest of the year Omaha remains one of the most fashionable cities in the Midwest, with a boho chic downtown district of shops, restaurants and bars, excellent galleries and museums and a dynamic indie music scene.

Durham Museum

801 S 10th St • Tues 10am–8pm, Wed–Sat 10am–5pm, Sun 1–5pm • $9 (free parking on site) • ☎402 444 5071, ⓦdurhammuseum.org

Omaha's most impressive sight is the **Durham Museum**, housed in the old Union Pacific Railroad station, an Art Deco gem completed in 1931. Underneath the cavernous Great Hall are galleries that explore the history of the city from its foundation in 1854, through the boom and bust years of the railroads and meatpacking stockyards to the insurance giants of the present. Fittingly enough, you can also wander through a row of vintage train cars, and there's a special exhibit on the landmark **Trans-Mississippi Exposition**, held here in 1898. The humble **Buffett Grocery Store** of 1915, owned by Warren Buffett's grandfather, is also reproduced.

ARRIVAL AND INFORMATION

OMAHA

By plane Omaha Airport (Eppley Airfield; ⓦ flyoma.com) is just 3 miles northeast of downtown. Take a taxi or shared shuttle bus (ⓦ omalink.com; $29.85).

By bus Greyhound and Burlington Trailways share the bus station at 1601 Jackson St (☎ 402 341 1906).

Destinations Chicago (3 daily; 8hr 50min–9hr 30min); Des Moines (4 daily; 2hr–2hr 15min); Kansas City (2 daily; 3hr–4hr 15min); Lincoln (1 daily; 1hr 15min).

By train The modern Amtrak station is at 1003 S Ninth St, downtown.

Destinations Chicago (1 daily; 9hr 36min); Denver (1 daily 9hr 10min); Lincoln (1 daily; 1hr).

Visitor centre 1001 Farnam St, downtown (May–Sept Mon–Fri 8am–6pm, Sat 10am–6pm, Sun 10am–4pm; Oct–April Mon–Fri 8am–4.30pm, Sat 10am–4pm; ☎ 402 444 4762, ⓦ visitomaha.com). Rent bikes here ($10/hr, $30/day).

ACCOMMODATION

Cornerstone Mansion 140 N 39th St ☎ 402 558 7600, ⓦ cornerstonemansion.com. Excellent B&B option in an 1894 home close to downtown, with period rooms, friendly, knowledgeable host (and dogs), big breakfasts and good wi-fi. $85

Hilton Garden Inn 1005 Dodge St ☎ 402 341 4400, ⓦ hiltongardeninn.hilton.com. Great location next to Old Market, but with quiet and clean rooms, super-comfy beds and free cookies and wi-fi (extra-fast internet $3.95/day). $160

EATING, DRINKING AND NIGHTLIFE

Aim to spend some time in the **Old Market** district, centred on Howard Street between 10th and 13th streets downtown, where historic warehouses now contain Omaha's most vibrant restaurants and bars. It's also worth checking out the **indie music scene**; notable local bands include Bright Eyes, Cursive, Neva Dinova and The Faint.

Bohemian Café 1406 S 13th St ☎ 402 342 9838, ⓦ bohemiancafe.net. Czech immigrants settled in "Little Bohemia" south of downtown, with this café established in 1924; employees dressed in traditional Czech outfits serve goulash ($13.45), plum dumplings ($16.45) and other favourites. Mon, Wed & Thurs 11am–8pm, Fri & Sat 11am–10pm, Sun 11am–9pm.

★ **The Slowdown** 729 N 14th St ☎ 402 345 7569, ⓦ theslowdown.com. Rock club and bar at the epicentre of Omaha's stalwart indie rock scene, serving beers from

Nebraska Brewing Co. Mon–Sat 4pm–2am.

Sokol Underground 2234 S 13th St ☎ 402 346 9802, ⓦ sokolunderground.intuitwebsites.com. Under the venerable 1926 Sokol Auditorium, this indie venue hosts many rock and hip-hop shows. See website for show times.

Upstream Brewing Company 514 S 11th St ☎ 402 344 0200, ⓦ upstreambrewing.com. Fine craft ales and lagers to pair with locally grown produce and hand-cut Omaha steaks (most mains $11–20). Mon–Thurs 11am–1am, Fri & Sat 11am–2am, Sun 10am–10pm.

Lincoln

Fifty miles southwest of Omaha, its smaller neighbour, **LINCOLN**, is another real surprise, a dynamic capital city with a thriving economy, home of University of Nebraska-Lincoln (**UNL**) and the beloved **Huskers** sports teams. The jaw-dropping **State Capitol** alone warrants a stop here, but the museums and culinary attractions are just as enticing.

Nebraska State Capitol

1445 K St • Mon–Fri 8am–5pm, Sat 10am–5pm, Sun 1–5pm • Hourly free tours • ☎ 402 471 0448, ⓦ capitol.org

Dwarfing the rest of downtown, the Art Deco tower of the 1932 **Nebraska State Capitol** protrudes 400ft into the sky like an elegant Byzantine skyscraper. The "Tower of the Plains" is topped by a golden dome and a statue of a seed sower on a pedestal of wheat and corn, but the interior is just as awe-inspiring. The soaring, mural-smothered vestibule and rotunda are as grand as a cathedral, while the unicameral chamber has a gold-stencilled ceiling. Take the elevator up to the fourteenth-floor observation deck a for a birds'-eye view of the city.

Museum of Nebraska History

131 Centennial Mall N (15th St) • Mon–Fri 9am–4.30pm, Sat & Sun 1–4.30pm • $2 suggested donation • ☎ 402 471 4754, ⓦ nebraskahistory.org

Twelve thousand years of life on the Plains are covered at the **Museum of Nebraska History**, where displays focus on Native American tribes (featuring a Pawnee earthlodge c.1865) and the political and economic struggles of the state into the early twentieth century.

University of Nebraska State Museum

14th and Vine sts • Mon–Wed, Fri & Sat 9.30am–4.30pm, Thurs 9.30am–8pm, Sun 1.30–4.30pm • $6 ($9 with planetarium) • ☏ 402 472 2642, ⓦ museum.unl.edu

In the heart of the UNL campus, the **University of Nebraska State Museum** is fun for kids and adults, with hand-on galleries of towering mammoth and mastodon skeletons (some 12.5 million years old), a video kiosk featuring Richard Dawkins, a detailed exhibit on Nebraska's Native Americans and a stuffed bison donated by Buffalo Bill in 1908. Look out for the famous **Innocent Assassins Fossil**, two sabre tooth tigers in a death struggle. Aspiring astronomers should check out the adjacent **Mueller Planetarium**.

Sheldon Museum of Art

12th and R sts • Tues 10am–8pm, Wed–Sat 10am–5pm, Sun noon–5pm • Free • ☏ 402 472 2461, ⓦ sheldonartmuseum.org

The **Sheldon Museum of Art** building, on the UNL campus, is a work of art itself, an understated masterpiece designed by Philip Johnson and completed in 1963. Half the space is devoted to travelling exhibits that change every three to four months, while the permanent collection rotates every year; the focus here is American Modern Art, with highlights including Edward Hopper's *Room in New York* and works from Georgia O'Keeffe and Mark Rothko. Nebraska artists Dale Nichols and photographer Wright Morris are also well represented.

ARRIVAL AND INFORMATION
LINCOLN

By bus Lincoln's Greyhound bus station is at 5250 Superior St (☏ 402 474 1071), 4 miles northeast of downtown.
Destinations Denver (1 daily; 8hr 45min); Omaha (1 daily; 1hr 5min).
By train Amtrak trains arrive at 277 Pinnacle Arena Drive (just west of downtown), at uncomfortably early hours;

westbound at 12.14am, and eastbound at 3.26am (☏ 402 476 1295).
Destinations Denver (1 daily; 8hr); Omaha (1 daily; 1hr 30min).
Visitor centre Lincoln Station, right next to Amtrak (Mon–Fri 9am–8pm, Sat 8am–2pm, Sun noon–4pm; ☏ 402 434 5348, ⓦ lincoln.org).

ACCOMMODATION

The Cornhusker 333 South 13th St ☏ 402 474 7474, ⓦ marriott.com. This historic *Marriott* hotel opened in 1926, with a great location downtown, spacious luxury rooms and all the extras; pool, gym and decent restaurants. **$160**

Downtown Holiday Inn 141 N St ☏ 402 475 4011, ⓦ holidayinn.com. Most budget accommodation in Lincoln lies outside the centre, but this is the best of the chains downtown, with standard, comfy rooms and a second-floor pool with skylight ceiling. **$120**

EATING, DRINKING AND NIGHTLIFE

Lincoln's compact, student-thronged downtown comes into its own after dark. Among its alphabetical array of broad boulevards, O Street (the subject of Allen Ginsberg's poem *Zero Street*) is the main drag; 13th and 14th streets are packed with bars and places to eat.

Duffy's Tavern 1412 O St ☏ 402 474 3543, ⓦ duffys lincoln.com. This popular student bar pulls in a younger crowd for its famed "fishbowl" cocktails and live rock bands (Mon is comedy night). Daily 4pm–2am.
The Green Gateau 330 S 10th St ☏ 402 477 0330, ⓦ greengateau.com. A charming restaurant that's the best weekend breakfast and brunch spot in town ($7–13), with fluffy pancakes and perfect eggs benedict.

Mon–Fri 11am–2pm & 5–9pm, Sat 8am–9pm, Sun 8am–3pm.
★ **Zoo Bar** 136 N 14th St, at P St ☏ 402 435 8754, ⓦ zoobar.com. Legendary blues bar open since 1973, attracting both local and national jazz and blues acts (Magic Slim was a regular until his death in 2013). Mon–Thurs 3pm–1am, Fri & Sat 3pm–2am, Sun 5–11pm.

> **CARHENGE**
>
> Three miles north of Alliance on Hwy-87, **Carhenge** (daily dawn–dusk; free; ⓦ carhenge.com) is classic Americana, a wacky replica of Stonehenge with 38 old cars swapped in for Salisbury Plain's famous stones. Erected in 1987 by artist Jim Reinders (who had studied the original in England), this intriguing collection of Chevys, Cadillacs and Plymouths, painted a brooding battleship grey and tilted at unusual angles, is an ingenious piece of pop art.

The Sandhills

From Lincoln, it's long, dull drive across the state on I-80 to Wyoming, but you can break the monotony by veering off the highway at Grand Island and following the **Sandhills Journey Scenic Byway** (Hwy-2) for 272 miles to **Alliance**, with its one major attraction, Carhenge (see box above). The **Sandhills** cover a quarter of the state, an otherworldly landscape carpeted with short-grass prairie and sand dunes softened by delicate wild flowers and shiny ponds. Apart from a few farmsteads, grain silos and tiny churches, all you're likely to see are lazing cattle, a few sluggish rivers and mile-long coal trains weaving their way through the hills.

The Oregon Trail landmarks

Western Nebraska is rich in **Oregon Trail** history, beginning with **Chimney Rock National Historic Site** (daily 9am–5pm; $3; ⓣ 308 586 2581) 44 miles southwest of Alliance, a spire of stone rising 480ft above the North Platte River. Chipped away by erosion and lightning since the era of westward migration, it remains one of the most recognizable and memorable landmarks in the area.

The twin towns of **GERING** and **SCOTTSBLUFF**, 23 miles further west, lie beneath the 800ft rampart of **Scotts Bluff National Monument** (daily 9am–4.30pm; $5; ⓣ 308 436 4340, ⓦ nps.gov/scbl). Trips to the top (by foot or free shuttle bus) are rewarded with a magnificent view, and the entrance fee includes the absorbing **Oregon Trail Museum**, which relates the experiences of the early emigrants.

ACCOMMODATION AND EATING THE OREGON TRAIL LANDMARKS

★ **Barn Anew** 170549 County Rd L ⓣ 308 632 8647, ⓦ barnanew.com. Follow the ruts of bygone wagon trains to this inviting B&B, 2 miles west of Scottsbluff, a converted nineteenth-century farmstead with comfy period rooms and sweeping views of the monument as it erupts from the prairie floor. **$110**

Emporium Coffeehouse & Cafe 1818 1st Ave, Scottsbluff ⓣ 308 632 6222, ⓦ emporiumdining.com. Grab a decent pasta, steak, beer or coffee at this friendly restaurant (dinner mains $12–22), with live music on the patio every Fri night. Mon 6.30am–5pm, Tues–Sat 6.30am–10pm, Sun 7am–3pm.

Iowa

Boasting undulating hills and acre upon acre of verdant pastures, **IOWA** lacks the glitz and glamour of America's more widely visited states. Indeed, Iowa represents as vivid a portrait of quintessential rural America as you're likely to find; crimson barns, big blue skies and vast fields of corn with only grain elevators breaking the horizon. Even writer Bill Bryson, who grew up in Iowa and didn't like it much in *Lost Continent* – he calls Des Moines "the most powerful hypnotic known to man" – remarks on the friendliness of the locals. There's a sense of humour too; Iowa is not only the birthplace of Hollywood cowboy king John Wayne (in 1907), but is also the "future birthplace" of one Captain James T. Kirk (expected in 2228), celebrated with a marker and annual Trekfest in the small town of Riverside.

Travellers usually experience Iowa by heading west along I-80 via **Herbert Hoover National Historic Site**, collegiate **Iowa City** and **Des Moines**, or heading north along the Mississippi to **Dubuque**.

Herbert Hoover National Historic Site

110 Parkside Drive, West Branch (I-80 exit 254) • Daily 9am–5pm • **Visitor Center** Free • ☎ 319 643 2541, ⓦ nps.gov/heho **Herbert Hoover Presidential Museum** $6 • ☎ 319 643 5301, ⓦ hoover.archives.gov

Some 46 miles west of Illinois and the Mississippi on I-80, the sleepy village of West Branch is home to the **Herbert Hoover National Historic Site**, dedicated to rehabilitating the reputation of the 31st President of the United States. History hasn't been kind to **Herbert Hoover** (1874–1964) and even today, if he's remembered at all, it's as the president who oversaw the Wall Street Crash and failed to stem the subsequent Great Depression – Franklin Roosevelt defeated him by a landslide in 1932. Yet there's more to the man than this, especially his worldwide humanitarian efforts beginning in World War I. Get oriented with the film at the **Visitor Center**, view the preserved buildings around the humble **Birthplace Cottage**, and take in the enlightening exhibits at the **Herbert Hoover Museum**. Hoover and his wife are buried on the rise nearby.

Iowa City

The collegiate heart of Iowa beats strongest in **IOWA CITY**, where residents rally around the **University of Iowa** (UI) and its student body of more than 30,000 (half the city's population). Since the state is without a major professional sports franchise, the black and gold colours of the school's fanatically supported **Hawkeyes** sports teams are a *de facto* uniform among supporters all over the state (see ⓦ hawkeyesports.com for schedules). The small, compact downtown, dominated by the university campus, makes a pleasant pit stop just off I-80, with plenty of enticing places to eat, though there's little reason to spend the night.

Old Capitol Museum

21 Old Capitol (Iowa Ave and Clinton St) • Tues, Wed & Fri 10am–3pm, Thurs & Sat 10am–5pm, Sun 1–5pm • Free • ☎ 319 335 0548, ⓦ uiowa.edu/oldcap

Now part of the UI campus, the **Old Capitol Museum** is a reminder of Iowa City's days as state capital, before government was transferred to more central Des Moines in 1857. Iowa's first capitol building was completed here in 1842, and the old Senate and House chambers upstairs have been beautifully restored, while exhibits on the first and ground floors focus on the early history of the state.

EATING AND DRINKING   IOWA CITY

⭐ **Hamburg Inn No. 2** 214 N Linn St ☎ 319 337 5512, ⓦ hamburginn.com. The essential meal stop in Iowa City since 1948, serving breakfast all day (this is a college town after all), sensational pie shakes and freshly made burgers. Daily 6.30am–11pm.

⭐ **Molly's Cupcakes** 14 S Clinton St ☎ 319 333 1297, ⓦ icmollys.com. Grab a coffee and indulge in spectacular cupcakes just across from the old Capitol; the Key Lime pie flavour is a moist, creamy sensation (cakes $2–3). Mon–Thurs 8am–10pm, Fri 8am–midnight, Sat 10am–midnight, Sun 10am–10pm.

The Amana Colonies

A short drive seventeen miles northwest of Iowa City, the **AMANA COLONIES** comprise seven rural villages along the serene Iowa River valley, communities of pretty clapboard houses, rolling meadows and woodlands. Amana was originally an experiment in communal living, founded in 1855 by the German Inspirationists (not linked to the Amish or Mennonites) – while each family lived in their own home, they all ate together and shared profits from the farms. Communal life was finally ended by mutual agreement in 1932, but members of the Colonies have retained close family ties, as well as their religious principles. Today the streets of the largest village, **Amana**, are mainly given over to tourism, and though the neat, uniform signs can make it seem a little like Toytown, many of the buildings are 1850s originals and the restaurants, craft shops, Amana Woollen Mill and several fruit wineries sell quality products – probably the most compelling reason to visit the Colonies is their undeniably excellent, old-style German food.

EATING AND DRINKING

THE AMANA COLONIES

Millstream Brewing Co 835 48th Ave, Amana ☎ 319 622 3672, ✪ millstreambrewing.com. Iowa's oldest microbrewery Is the best place for a delicious beer to drink on site (try the IPA, "Iowa Pale Ale"), or take away (six bottles $7.50). Mon–Fri 10am–4pm, Sat 10am–5pm, Sun 11am–5pm (longer hours in summer).

★ **Ox Yoke Inn** 4420 220th Trail, Amana ☎ 319 622 3441, ✪ oxyokeinn.com. Open since 1940 (in a former communal kitchen) and specializing in family-style meals of Wiener schnitzel, *spatzle* (egg noodles) and *kasseler rippchen* (smoked pork with apple sauce; mains from $9.50). Mon–Sat 8am–9pm, Sun 9am–7pm (seasonal variations).

Des Moines

The modern steel-and-glass skyline of downtown **DES MOINES** (pronounced da-MOYN) mostly shot up during the 1970s and 1980s, testimony to the city's ever-growing insurance business. Today the Iowan capital region has a population of half a million, and travelling on I-80 it makes an obvious stop, not least because it's the only major city in over a hundred miles. The central business district stands on the west bank of the Des Moines River, though there's not much to see here; downtown streets are conspicuously empty at night and at weekends, and during workdays pedestrians use the **Skywalk**, a four-mile network of temperature-controlled corridors linking twenty blocks of offices, banks, car parks, restaurants, hotels and movie theatres.

Iowa State Capitol

1007 E Grand Ave • Mon–Fri 8am–4.30pm, Sat 9am–4pm, call for tour times • Free • ☎ 515 281 5591, ✪ legis.iowa.gov

Completed in 1886, the **Iowa State Capitol** looms over downtown, its 275ft, 23-carat-gold-leafed dome shimmering in the prairie sun like a Renaissance palace. The interior is even more impressive, with a soaring rotunda adorned with murals and mosaics, and several ornate offices – you can also go to the third-floor galleries to watch sessions of the state House and Senate (usually Jan–April). Grab a map inside the entrance and walk around yourself, or join a guided tour (the only way to climb the dome).

State of Iowa Historical Museum

600 E Locust St • Mon–Sat 9am–4.30pm, Sun noon–4.30pm • Free • ☎ 515 281 5111, ✪ iowahistory.org/museum

Get to grips with Iowa's history at the impressive **State of Iowa Historical Museum**, down the slope just west of the capitol. Along with a host of temporary exhibits, a huge permanent gallery chronicles the early history of Iowa from its Native American roots through to statehood in 1846, while a second space covers the way Iowa's natural resources have been developed since then – a rare mammoth skeleton stands at the entrance.

Des Moines Art Center

4700 Grand Ave (4 miles west of downtown) • Tues, Wed & Fri 11am–4pm, Thurs 11am–9pm, Sat 10am–4pm, Sun noon–4pm • Free • ☎ 515 277 4405, ✪ desmoinesartcenter.org

One of the Midwest's under-visited gems, the **Des Moines Art Center** contains a surprising number of treasures in stylish galleries designed by lauded architects Eliel Saarinen, I.M. Pei and Richard Meier. The focus here is on modern art, from abstract Expressionism to Pop. Highlights include the stark loneliness of Hopper's *Automat*, Georgia O'Keeffe's wavy *From the Lake No. 1*, and Francis Bacon's chilling *Study after Velásquez's Portrait of Pope Innocent X*. Quality work from Picasso, Matisse, Miró, Basquiat, LeWitt, Warhol and Rothko is also on show.

10

ARRIVAL AND INFORMATION

DES MOINES

By plane Des Moines International Airport (ⓦdsmairport .com) is 7 miles southwest of downtown. Local bus #8 links with downtown three times daily Mon–Fri (ⓦridedart .com; $1.75); otherwise taxis meet all flights.

By bus Burlington Trailways (☎515 243 5283), Greyhound (☎515 243 1773) and Jefferson Lines (☎515 283 0074) buses pull in at 1107 Keosauqua Way, just north of downtown.

Destinations Chicago (4 daily; 6hr 35min–10hr 45min); Dubuque (1 daily; 6hr 20min); Iowa City (3 daily; 2hr); Kansas City (4 daily; 3hr–3hr 15min); Minneapolis (4 daily; 4hr 40min–5hr 35min); Omaha (4 daily; 2hr 10min).

Visitor centre Capitol Square (part of the Skywalk), 400 Locust St (Mon–Fri 8.30am–5pm; ☎515 256 5575, ⓦcatchdesmoines.com).

ACCOMMODATION AND EATING

Plenty of cheap **motels** surround Des Moines (especially off I-235). The **Court District** (along Court Ave) is the most enticing place to **eat** downtown, though the **East Village** just across the river and Ingersoll Avenue further to the west are also worth exploring.

Court Avenue Restaurant & Brewing Co 309 Court Ave ☎515 282 2739, ⓦcourtavebrew.com. Decent American staples (like steaks, salmon and burgers from $9.99) and local craft beers on tap. Mon–Thurs & Sun 11am–midnight, Fri 11am–2am, Sat 9am–2am.

Hessen Haus 101 4th St ☎515 288 2520, ⓦhessenhaus .com. Fun German-themed beer hall in a former railway

station, selling two-litre glass boots ("Das Boot") of beer; polka acts play live on Saturdays (6–10pm). Mon & Tues 11am–midnight, Wed–Sat 11am–2am, Sun noon–2am.

Hyatt Place Downtown 418 6th Ave ☎515 282 5555, ⓦdesmoines.place.hyatt.com. The best place to stay in the centre, with spacious, stylish rooms, excellent buffet breakfast and huge 42" flat-screens. $170

Dubuque

The small city of **DUBUQUE** ("debuke") occupies a handsome location amid rocky bluffs on the Mississippi River, 84 miles northeast of Iowa City. The city's origins lie in a small settlement established by French-Canadian pioneer **Julien Dubuque**, after the local Meskwaki people granted him rights to mine lead here in 1788 – in the nineteenth century, Dubuque became a booming river port and logging centre. Today it's developed into something of a mini-break destination, with a couple of huge casinos, resort hotels, a smattering of grand nineteenth-century buildings and plenty of attractions.

National Mississippi River Museum & Aquarium

350 E 3rd St • Daily: June–Aug 9am–6pm; Sept & Oct 9am–5pm; Nov–May 10am–5pm • $15 • ☎563 557 9545, ⓦrivermuseum.com

Dubuque's premier sight, the vast **National Mississippi River Museum & Aquarium** comprises several interlinked halls loaded with interactive exhibits, movies and tanks teeming with marine life, from beavers, otters, turtles and freshwater fish such as "Earl", a monstrously large catfish, to a less impressive saltwater exhibit. The history of Mississippi exploration is also charted, and there's an enlightening section on steamboats starting with Robert Fulton's first commercial enterprise in 1807.

St Luke's United Methodist Church

1191 Main St • Daily 7.30am–5pm • Free • ☎563 582 4543, ⓦstlukesumcdbq.org

Make time for the sensational Tiffany stained-glass windows at **St Luke's United Methodist Church** in downtown Dubuque, one of the region's lesser-known wonders.

GOING UP?

Don't miss a ride on Dubuque's **Fenelon Place Elevator**, at the end of 4th St (April–Nov daily 8am–10pm; $1.50 one-way, $3 return; ⓦdbq.com), said to be the world's shortest and steepest funicular railway; built in 1893, it trundles 296ft up a sharp bluff to a scintillating view across downtown and over the great river to Illinois and Wisconsin.

The Romanesque beauty was completed in 1897, with six major windows and more than ninety smaller pieces exhibiting Tiffany's trademark Art Nouveau brilliance.

ACCOMMODATION, EATING AND DRINKING   DUBUQUE

Candle Ready Cakes 197 Main St, at 2nd St ☎ 563 845 0794, ⓦ candlereadycakes.com. Sells excellent coffee and delicious cupcakes ($2) with a bewildering variety of toppings. Tues–Sat 10am–6pm.

Freddie's Popcorn 1086 Main St, between 10th and 11th sts ☎ 563 690 0885, ⓦ freddiespopcorn.com. Popcorn fans should make for this tiny family store, with flavours ranging from bacon cheddar cheese to cherry. Tues–Thurs 9am–5pm, Fri 9am–6pm, Sat 10am–4pm (Sat from 1pm May–Oct).

Hotel Julien 200 Main St ☎ 800 798 7098, ⓦ hoteljulien dubuque.com. Once owned by mobster Al Capone, this is the posh, historic choice downtown; mostly dating from 1915,

the renovated rooms feature plush dark-wood furnishings, iPod docks and luxury linens. $140

Pepper Sprout 378 Main St ☎ 563 556 2167, ⓦ pepper sprout.com. Specializing in "Midwest cuisine" (it isn't just a gimmick), with dishes such as venison lasagne and bison tenderloin gracing the menu (mains $18–28). Tues–Thurs 5–9pm, Fri & Sat 5–10pm.

Redstone Inn & Suites 504 Bluff St ☎ 563 582 1894, ⓦ theredstoneinn.com. This grand Victorian mansion constructed by early Dubuque benefactor A.A. Cooper in 1894 is now a charming fifteen-room B&B, decorated in period style (walnut dressers and the like). $75

10

South Dakota

The wide-open spaces of the Great Plains seemingly roll away to infinity on either side of I-90 in **SOUTH DAKOTA**. The land may be more green and fertile east of the Missouri River, but vast numbers of visitors speed straight to the spectacular "West State", home of the **Badlands** and the adjacent **Black Hills** – two of the most dramatic, mysterious and legend-impacted tracts of land in the USA. The latter is home of that most American of icons, **Mount Rushmore**, and equally monumental **Crazy Horse Mountain**, though it's the wildlife, hiking trails, mountain lakes and memorably scenic highways that often make the greatest impression.

Pierre

Straggling along the east bank of the Missouri River at the centre of South Dakota's vast, rolling grasslands, **PIERRE** (pronounced "pier") is capital of the state, despite having a population of just over thirteen thousand. Founded in 1880, the city retains a sliver of historic buildings along tiny **Pierre Street** downtown, but beyond the main strip of motels and restaurants (Sioux and Wells aves), much of Pierre feels like a small university campus. Just 35 miles north of I-90, the city is an essential stopover for anyone interested in the fascinating **history** of South Dakota before racing west to the Black Hills.

THE GREAT SIOUX NATION

Some 62,000 Native Americans call South Dakota home (10 percent of the state), almost all of them **Sioux**; no surprise that the movie *Dances With Wolves* was filmed here in the late 1980s. Known to themselves as the **Oceti Sakowin** ("seven council fires"), the **Great Sioux Nation** can be loosely divided into three dialect groups (Santee-Dakota, Yankton-Nakota and Teton-Lakota), and further divided into bands such as the Oglala and Hunkpapa (both Lakota), though there are **nine official tribes** (each with a reservation) in the state today.

For decades after **Wounded Knee** (see p.650), Sioux history and culture were outlawed; until the 1940s, it was illegal to teach or even speak their language. Today, more Sioux live on South Dakota's six reservations than dwelled in the whole state during pioneer days, but their prospects are often grim. Native American traditions are still celebrated, however, at **powwows**, held in summer on or near the reservations (especially big in Rapid City); local tourism offices offer annual dates and locations. Check also ⓦ sdtribalrelations.com.

South Dakota State Capitol Building

500 E Capitol Ave • Mon–Fri 8am–7pm, Sat & Sun 8am–5pm (open till 10pm during legislative session) • Free • ☎ 605 773 3765

American state capitols are invariably grand affairs, but the **South Dakota State Capitol Building**, completed in 1910, is especially elegant, its terrazzo-tile floors, marble staircase, murals and 161ft-tall dome reminiscent of an opulent Victorian conservatory. You'll be considering a career in local politics after viewing the gorgeous Senate and House chambers upstairs, replete with antique oak and mahogany desks and stained-glass skylights.

10

Cultural Heritage Center

900 Governors Drive • June–Aug Mon–Sat 9am–6.30pm, Sun 1–4.30pm; Sept–May Mon–Sat 9am–4.30pm, Sun 1–4.30pm • $4 • ☎ 605 773 3458, ⊛ history.sd.gov/museum

Half a mile north of the capitol, the **Cultural Heritage Center** explores the complex history of South Dakota, with videos, Native American objects, pioneer implements and prehistoric artefacts chronicling not just the European settlement of the region but also providing one of the most enlightening introductions to Sioux **culture** in the country. Highlights include a rare **Sioux horse effigy** from 1876, and the **Verendrye Plate**, an inscription on lead buried near here by French brothers in 1743.

ACCOMMODATION AND EATING   PIERRE

★ **Cattleman's Club Steakhouse** 29608 Hwy-34 (4 miles east of town) ☎ 605 224 9774, ⊛ cattlemansclub steakhouse.com. Established in 1986 by local cattleman Myril Arch, this is the place to gorge on quality steak at low prices: think $13–16 for hefty sirloin and rib eye; great steak sandwiches, too. Mon–Sat 5–10pm.

Clubhouse Hotel & Suites 808 W Sioux Ave ☎ 605 494 2582, ⊛ pierre.clubhouseinn.com. The pick of the hotels in town, with large, luxury rooms (suites come with big lounge and mini-kitchen, bedroom and bathroom), gym and pool, free wi-fi and use of computers. **$130**

★ **The Donut Shop** 1120 N Euclid Ave ☎ 605 224 7491. Local legend just north of downtown, a small shack in a residential area knocking out classic doughnuts in a variety of flavours, sliced and filled with buttercream and rolled in sugar. Tues–Sat 6am–1pm.

Badlands National Park

The spectacularly eroded layers of sand, silt, ash, mud and gravel on display in **BADLANDS NATIONAL PARK** were created more than 35 million years ago, when there was an ancient saltwater sea here. The sea subsequently dried up; over the last few million years, erosion has slowly eaten away at the terrain revealing mesmerizing gradations of earth tones and pastel colours. The crumbly earth is carved into all

---

WOUNDED KNEE

No other place represents nineteenth-century atrocities against Native Americans as potently as **Wounded Knee**, some seventy miles south of Badlands National Park. It was here, on December 29, 1890, that the US Army killed more than three hundred unarmed Sioux men, women and children. The massacre was triggered by a misunderstanding during a tribal round-up: a deaf Native American, asked to surrender his rifle along with his peers, instead held it above his head, shouting that he'd paid a lot for it; an officer grabbed at the gun, it went off and the troops started firing.

Today, the site, near the junction of highways 27 and 28 in Pine Ridge Indian Reservation, is a naked tribute to the tragedy. A simple marker details the hour of mass death, while a commemorative stone monument, surrounded by a chain-link fence on a nearby hill, marks the victims' collective gravesite.

In 1973 violence returned to Wounded Knee when members of the Oglala Sioux and the American Indian Movement (AIM) occupied the village for 71 days, a protest about a corrupt tribal official in a deeply symbolic location (after the exchange of gunfire and two deaths, the standoff with the FBI ended quietly).

manner of shapes: pinnacles, precipices, pyramids, knobs, cones, ridges, gorges – or, if you're feeling poetic, lunar sandcastles and cathedrals. The rainbow hues that colour these formations are most striking at dawn, dusk and just after rainfall (heaviest in May and June).

Among the best of the park's marked **hiking trails** is the **Door Trail**, a less than one mile excursion from the large car park about two miles north of the Ben Reifel Visitor Center, which enters the eerie wasteland through a natural "doorway" in the rock pinnacles. A longer hike along the gently undulating **Castle Trail**, which winds through buttes and grassy prairies for ten miles (return), begins from the same parking area. Remember to carry more than enough water (particularly if you venture into the backcountry), as none is available beyond developed areas.

The park is most accessible via I-90, which skirts the northern edge; a paved forty-mile road (Hwy-240, between exits 110 and 131) through the park is peppered with scenic overlooks.

10

INFORMATION   BADLANDS NATIONAL PARK

Access and entry fee Badlands National Park is open 24hr. Entry is $15/car.
Ben Reifel Visitor Center 25216 Ben Reifel Rd (daily:

mid-May to early Sept 8am–7pm; early Sept to late Oct and mid-April to mid-May 8am–5pm; late Oct to mid-April 8am–4pm; ☎ 605 433 5361, ⓦ nps.gov/badl).

ACCOMMODATION

Badlands Inn 20615 Hwy-377 ☎ 877 386 4383, ⓦ cedarpasslodge.com. This basic but clean motel (breakfast and satellite TV included) is less than 2 miles from Cedar Pass just outside the park's Interior Entrance, and managed by the same outfit. $120
Cedar Pass Campground Near Ben Reifel Visitor Center ☎ 605 433 5460, ⓦ cedarpasslodge.com. Open year-round on a first-come, first-served basis, with cold running water, flush toilets and covered picnic tables. The

primitive Sage Creek Campground (free) offers pit toilets and covered picnic tables but no water, while backcountry camping throughout the park is free (register at the visitor centre). Basic pitches $16, with hookups $28
Cedar Pass Lodge 20681 Hwy-240 ☎ 877 386 4383, ⓦ cedarpasslodge.com. The only hotel option within the park, with eco-friendly lodges freshly upgraded in 2013 and its own restaurant (free wi-fi in the lobby and restaurant). Open mid-April to mid-Oct. $137

Wall

It can be tough to understand the appeal of **WALL**, the town just north of Badlands National Park on I-90, an unashamed tourist trap but a classic, umissable slice of Americana nonetheless. You have to understand the history; **Wall Drug** (daily 7am–8pm, 7pm in winter; ☎ 605 279 2175, ⓦ walldrug.com), which opened here in 1931 as a pharmacy, was always famous because of the gimmicks, not because of the pharmacy. Right from the start, huge billboards were placed along miles of highway, and free iced water was promised to all comers – elaborate and ultimately successful ploys to attract customers. Today the tradition continues with a giant 85ft-tall dinosaur at exit 110, 5¢ coffee and cheap doughnuts, a genuinely impressive Western art gallery and a kitschy emporium that serves up to twenty thousand visitors daily.

The Black Hills

The timbered, rocky **BLACK HILLS** rise like an island from a sea of grain-growing plains, stretching for a hundred miles between the Belle Fourche River in the north and the Cheyenne to the south. For generations of Sioux, their value was and still is immeasurable, a kind of spiritual safe place where warriors went to speak with Wakan Tanka (the Great Spirit) and await visions. Even though they're mountains in the classic sense – the highest of the lot, Harney Peak, rises 7242ft – they were dubbed *Paha Sapa*, or Black Hills, as the blue spruce and Norway pine trees blanketing them seem black from a distance.

THE GEORGE S. MICKELSON TRAIL

One of the most rewarding ways to enjoy the beauty of the Black Hills is to traverse the 109-mile "rail-to-trail" **George S. Mickelson trail** on foot or by mountain bike; the crushed limestone and gravel trail follows the old Deadwood to Edgemont rail line, abandoned in 1983. Hard-core cyclists cover the trail in one day (heading south is a bit easier), but there are plenty of places to break the journey (careful planning is required if you have no car to pick you up, though). Trail passes are $15/year or $3/day; see ⓦ mickelsontrail.com.

10

Assuming the Black Hills to be worthless, the United States government drew up a treaty in the mid-nineteenth century that gave these mountains (along with most of South Dakota's land west of the Missouri River) to the Native Americans. However, once the Custer Expedition of 1874 confirmed rumours of **gold** in the hills, it wasn't long before fortune-hunters came pouring in. Today much of the region is protected within the **Black Hills National Forest**, and is easily the biggest attraction on the Great Plains (though it's really more part of the American West). South Dakota's second largest settlement, **Rapid City**, is the region's commercial centre, but apart from visiting family-oriented attractions such as nearby Reptile Gardens (ⓦ reptilegardens .com) and Bear Country USA (ⓦ bearcountryusa.com), there's little reason to base yourself here. Indeed, though there's plenty of kitsch fun in the form of theme parks, crazy golf and the like throughout the Black Hills there's also plenty of history, and no place is much farther than a ninety-minute drive from the show-stoppers of **Mount Rushmore** and its ambitious work-in-progress counterpart, the **Crazy Horse Memorial**. Yet it's the outdoor activities, rich wildlife and extraordinary scenery that make the Black Hills special, from the bison herds of **Custer State Park** to the magical caverns of **Wind Cave National Park**.

Deadwood

Few places encapsulate the mystic of the American West like **DEADWOOD**, a Gold Rush town with a spectacular setting and a pantheon of iconic former residents such as Wild Bill Hickok and Calamity Jane. Yet the truth is that Deadwood was only briefly the wild town of legend (the Gold Rush was over by 1877), and by the 1880s it was a prosperous trade and supply centre. Only in the 1920s was it consciously developed into a parody of the "Wild West", but by the 1980s Deadwood was virtually bankrupt; it was only the legalization of gaming and casinos in 1989 that saved it. Though its handsome buildings are now wonderfully preserved (most of the Wild West tack is long gone and the whole town is a **National Historic Landmark**), and elegant houses line the slopes, **casinos** now dominate business here, making it something of a year-round resort – adjust your expectations accordingly and Deadwood can still be lots of fun.

Main Street

Deadwood's **Main Street** is the best place to soak up the town's historic roots, though its otherwise stately Victorian buildings are liberally sprinkled with casinos and gift stores. Wild West ground zero is **Saloon #10** at no. 657 (see opposite), a working bar which commemorates the spot where Hickok was shot dead by Jack McCall while holding two aces, a pair of eights and the nine of diamonds – forever after christened the Dead Man's Hand. In the summer actors re-stage the shooting several times daily; the original saloon space where this actually happened is down the street at no. 624, unoccupied at the time of writing. You can also attend the re-created family-friendly **Trial of Jack McCall** at the Masonic Temple (715 Main St; late May to Aug daily 7.30pm; ⓦ deadwoodalive.com). Kids will also enjoy the staged "gunfights" on Main Street (late May to Aug daily 2pm, 4pm & 6pm; free).

Days of '76 Western Museum

18 Seventy Six Drive • Feb & March Fri & Sat 10am–4pm, April & Oct Mon–Sat 9am–5pm; May–Sept daily 9am–5pm • $5.50 • ☎ 605 578 1657, ⊛ daysof76museum.com

In 1876, a year after the discovery of **gold** in Deadwood, six thousand diggers swarmed in to stake their claims; the **Days of '76 Western Museum** commemorates this portentous event and the annual **rodeo** that began in Deadwood in 1923 (held every August), with exhibits of Western and Native American artefacts, photos and artwork.

Mount Moriah Cemetery

10 Mt Moriah Drive • Daily 8am–8pm • May–Sept $1; Oct–April free • ☎ 605 578 2600

The **Mount Moriah Cemetery** above the town is a major attraction thanks to the resting place of James Butler Hickock, aka **Wild Bill Hickok** (1837–76), spy, scout, bullwhacker, stagecoach driver, sheriff and gambler who spent just a few weeks in Deadwood prior to his murder here in 1876. Martha "**Calamity Jane**" Canary (1852–1903), an illiterate alcoholic whose chequered career included stints as scout, prostitute, nurse and even stage performer, arrived around the same time as Hickok; despite barely knowing him, she was buried 27 years later beside Hickok's bronze monument and bust.

10

GETTING AROUND AND INFORMATION   DEADWOOD

By bus The Deadwood Trolley (hourly: late May to mid-Sept Mon–Thurs & Sun 7am–1.30am, Fri & Sat 7am–3am; mid-Sept to late May Mon–Thurs & Sun 8am–midnight, Fri & Sat 7am–3am; ☎ 605 578 2622) runs to all the major

sights, hotels and casinos ($1 per ride).
History and Information Center 3 Siever St (daily 9am–5pm; ☎ 605 578 9749); offers an overview of Deadwood's past and present.

ACCOMMODATION, EATING AND DRINKING

Bullock Hotel 633 Main St ☎ 800 336 1876, ⊛ historic bullock.com. Historic hotel built around 1895, with a range of period-themed rooms from lavish suites to more affordable "full rooms", all with free wi-fi and parking included. **$155**
Deadwood Social Club 657 Main St ☎ 605 578 3346, ⊛ saloon10.com. The restaurant above the famed saloon affords an opportunity to enjoy a Kobe rib eye or filet mignon, and amazing cheesecake (mains $13–25). Daily 11am–10pm.
Lodge at Deadwood 100 Pine Crest Lane ☎ 605 584 4800, ⊛ deadwoodlodge.com. This plush hotel and casino opened in 2009 just outside town overlooking the

valley, with modern, comfy rooms and all the extras (indoor pool, fireplaces and wi-fi included). **$160**
Midnight Star 677 Main St ☎ 605 578 1555, ⊛ themidnightstar.com. Kevin Costner's three-level casino, sports bar and restaurant is festooned with memorabilia from his career in film (especially costumes), and is a great place to grab a Midnight Star Ale or "block-buster" sandwich. Daily 8am–2am.
Saloon #10 657 Main St ☎ 605 578 3346, ⊛ saloon10 .com. Grab a beer at this sawdust-floor bar that recreates the spot where Hickok died (his chair is preserved above the door). Daily 8am–2am.

Lead

In utter contrast to Deadwood just three miles north, **LEAD** (pronounced "Leed") is a quiet working town, operated and virtually controlled by Homestake Mining until 2002 and dripping with history. The Homestake gold claim was founded in 1876; **George Hearst** was the geological genius who bought it one year later. His son Randolph was the newspaper magnate and inspiration for *Citizen Kane* (see p.1048). By the time of its closure in 2002, a maze of shafts dropped 8000ft below the town,

---

STURGIS – WELCOME BIKERS

The town of **Sturgis**, about fourteen miles east of Deadwood, has come to life in a big way each August since 1938 when the **Sturgis Motorcycle Rally** (☎ 605 720 0800, ⊛ sturgis motorcyclerally.com) packs the otherwise sleepy town. An abundance of Harley-Davidson souvenirs stock the downtown stores year-round, and even if you've rolled into Sturgis on four wheels, the **Sturgis Motorcycle Museum & Hall of Fame**, 999 Main St (Mon–Fri 9am–5pm, Sat 9am–4pm, Sun 10am–4pm; $10; ☎ 605 347 2001, ⊛ sturgismuseum.com) is worth a visit.

today partly reborn as the futuristic Sanford Underground Research Facility, which operates a lab to detect dark matter.

Homestake Visitor Center

160 W Main St • **Visitor Center** Daily: Oct–April 9am–5pm, May–Sept 8am–6pm • Free • ☎ 605 584 3110, ⓦ homestaketour.com **City tours** Daily mid-May to mid Sept 10am, 11.15am, 1pm, 2.30pm, 4pm • $7.50

Start your visit to Lead at the **Homestake Visitor Center**, which offers a short video on the history of the town plus views over the mind-blowing 1250ft-deep, mile-wide **Open Cut**. **City tours** leave from here, taking in the grand 1914 **Opera House** at 309 Main St, being gradually restored after a 1984 fire, and the old hoist room for the mine (now serving the Sanford lab) – there's no actual tour of the mine itself.

Mount Rushmore National Memorial

13000 Hwy-244, Keystone • Daily: mid-May to mid-Aug 8am–10pm; mid-Aug to Sept 8am–9pm; Oct to mid-May 8am–5pm • Free; parking $11 • ☎ 605 574 2523, ⓦ nps.gov/moru

One of America's best-known monuments, the **Mount Rushmore National Memorial** is unarguably the linchpin of the Black Hills' tourist circuit. It's a beautiful fifty-mile drive south of Deadwood, though by far the most impressive approach is to follow **Iron Mountain Road** (US-16A) from Custer State Park (see opposite). This gorgeous route runs seventeen miles up via three curly twists in the road called "pigtail bridges", each an engineering and design triumph.

The memorial was created by sculptor **Gutzon Borglum**, who chose the faces and heads of four certifiably great American presidents: **George Washington**, **Thomas Jefferson**, **Abraham Lincoln** and his idol, **Theodore Roosevelt**.

Sixty years old when the project began in 1927, sculptor Borglum died shortly prior to the dedication of the last head – Roosevelt's – in 1941. An incredible engineering feat, each head is about 60ft from chin to crown – by way of comparison, the Statue of Liberty's head is just 17ft. The best times to view Rushmore are at dawn or dusk, when there are fewer people and better natural lighting.

Crazy Horse Memorial

12151 Ave of the Chiefs, Crazy Horse (Hwy-16) • Visitor centre daily: late May to mid-Oct 8am–dusk; mid-Oct to late May 8am–5pm • $10/person or $27/carload • ☎ 605 673 4681, ⓦ crazyhorsememorial.org

In 1939, prompted by the sight of the Rushmore monument, Sioux leader Henry Standing Bear wrote to **Korczak Ziolkowski**, who had just won first prize for sculpture at the New York World's Fair, telling him that Native Americans "would like the white man to know that the red man has great heroes, too". Less than a decade later, the New Englander moved permanently to the Black Hills to undertake a vastly more ambitious mission than Rushmore: the **Crazy Horse Memorial**, depicting the revered warrior Crazy Horse on horseback. The work Ziolkowski began on **Thunderhead Mountain** in 1948 didn't stop with his death in 1982; his widow, children and grandchildren continue to realize his vision. Ziolkowski refused to accept federal or state funds, instead relying entirely on admissions and contributions, a practice the memorial's foundation continues to this day: the 90ft-high face was completed in time for the fiftieth anniversary celebrations in 1998, although it will easily be another half-century before the project is completed.

The main viewing terrace at the **visitor centre** is nearly a mile from the carving itself; its 20ft scale model on display is 34 times smaller than the end result, which will be 563ft high and 641ft long.

Jewel Cave National Monument

11149 US-16 • **Visitor Centre** Daily: Sept–May 8.30am–4.30pm; June–Aug 8.30am–7pm **Cave access** By guided tour only (1hr 20min): April & Oct 3 daily; May & Sept 6 daily; June–Aug daily every 20min; Nov–March daily 10am & 2pm • Tours $8 • ☎ 605 673 8300, ⓦ nps.gov/jeca

The third longest cave in the world at 166 miles (and counting), **Jewel Cave National Monument** is a maze of passages, caverns and astounding calcite crystal formations. The tours only cover a half mile, but there are 723 steps up and down (reservations crucial in July). Discovered in 1900, this cave system contrasts radically from the Wind Cave (below), with its frostwork formations like a subterranean coral reef without water, all bubbles and a thick crust of mostly grey crystals. Look out for the famous "bacon formation", an amazing ribbon of multistriped crystal.

Custer State Park

The buffalo, pronghorn and prairie-dog rich plains of **Custer State Park** are some of the most enticing sections of the Black Hills. The **Needles Highway** (Hwy-87; closed mid-Oct to mid-April) winds for fourteen miles through pine forests and past the eponymous jagged granite spires in the park's northwestern corner, between Sylvan and Legion lakes. In the southeastern reaches of the park, the eighteen-mile **Wildlife Loop** undulates through rolling meadows rich with pronghorn antelope, deer and begging burros (tame and disarming four-legged panhandlers who'll stick their snouts through the windows of slow-moving vehicles in search of snack handouts), as well as the herd of 1300 **bison** for which the park is known (elk and bighorn sheep are harder to spot).

For a fuller appreciation of the beauty of Custer State Park, set out on one of its myriad **hiking** and **biking trails**. A good, short introductory hike is the three-mile **Lovers Leap Trail**, which begins near the park's main **visitor centre**, on Hwy-16A in the park's eastern section. One of the park's most prominent hikes is the six-mile trek from Sylvan Lake up **Harney Peak** (7242ft) where you are rewarded by expansive views from the stone lookout tower perched atop the summit.

INFORMATION   CUSTER STATE PARK

Access and entry fee The park is open daily 24hr, though scenic drives can close in winter. Entry is $15 (valid one week).

Visitor centre Late May to Aug 8am–8pm; Sept–Nov & April to late May 9am–5pm; closed Dec–March (☎605 255 4464).

ACCOMMODATION

Four hotels lie inside the park under the umbrella of Custer State Park Resorts (☎888 875 0001, ⓦ custerresorts.com); all have restaurants and are open summer only (May–Sept) There are also several campgrounds with flush toilets and showers (☎800 710 2267), four of which feature camping cabins ($47); all have standard tent sites ($24).

State Game Lodge 13389 Hwy-16A ☎605 255 4541, ⓦ custerresorts.com. Completed in 1922, this place became all the rage after President Calvin Coolidge used it as his "summer white house" in 1927. Choose from basic but comfy motel-style lodgings but also some lovely individual cabins; its restaurant offers hearty meals, including exceptional flapjacks and French toast for breakfast. $115

Wind Cave National Park

26611 US-385 • Visitor centre daily: late May to early Sept 9am–6pm; early Sept to mid-Oct & mid-April to late May 8am– 5pm; mid-Oct to mid-April 8am–4.30pm • $7–23 • ☎605 745 4600, ⓦ nps.gov/wica

Beneath wide-open rangelands, **Wind Cave National Park**, directly south of Custer State Park, comprises more than one hundred miles of mapped underground passages etched out of limestone and is one of the largest caves in the US. Rangers lead a variety of cave **tours** from the visitor centre, pointing out delicate features such as frostwork and boxwork along the way. If you come in summer, forget the standard walking tours and opt for the ones that allow you to crawl around in the smaller passages, or explore the caves by candlelight – call ahead for reservations.

If you lack the inclination to delve into the Dakotas' dank bowels, **driving** through the park is another quintessential Black Hills experience. Like Custer, its native grass prairies are home to deer, antelope, elk, coyote, prairie dogs and a sizeable herd of bison.

Hot Springs

The Black Hills' southern anchor, the pretty town of **HOT SPRINGS** became the region's first tourist destination in the 1890s thanks to its balmy, mineral-rich spring waters (a legacy maintained at **Evans Plunge** water park, ⓦevansplunge.com). Though it's surrounded by seventeen motels and counting, its downtown is (as yet) largely uncommercialized, with several dozen utilitarian yet handsome sandstone structures passed by the sprightly **Fall River** – this never freezes thanks to the spring water, with a small waterfall and trail along the river in the centre of town.

Mammoth Site

1800 Hwy-18 bypass • Mid-May to mid-Aug daily 8am–8pm; mid-Aug to mid-May check website for hours • $9 • ☎ 605 745 6017, ⓦmammothsite.com

The unique **Mammoth Site** is the only *in situ* display of mammoth fossils in the USA, with some sixty unearthed so far, from around 26,000 years ago. Inside its dome, fascinating guided **tours** explain how these ten-ton mammoths (along with camels, bears and rodents) were trapped in a steep-sided sinkhole and gradually became covered by sediment; complete skeletons are easy to pick out in the excavation site.

ACCOMMODATION AND EATING   HOT SPRINGS

Dale's 745 Battle Mountain Ave ☎605 745 3028. This classic family diner is justly popular with locals, with incredibly cheap specials (breakfast from $2.75) and a big range of comfort food. Mon–Sat 6am–7pm, Sun 6am–2pm.

Gus' Best Ice Cream 345 N River St ☎605 745 6506,

ⓦgusbesticecream.com. Shaved ice, ice cream and classic, addictive smoothies. Mon–Sat noon–8pm.

Smith Fargo Suites 321 N River St ☎605 890 0585, ⓦsmithfargosuites.com. The coolest accommodation in Hot Springs is this renovated 1910 sandstone property. Open May–Oct. $99

Black Hills Wild Horse Sanctuary

Highland Rd (3 miles off Hwy-71) • Tours daily: May & Oct–Dec 10am & 1pm; June–Sept 9am, 11am, 1pm, 3pm • $50 • ☎ 605 745 5955, ⓦwildmustangs.com

Animal lovers should visit the **Black Hills Wild Horse Sanctuary**, a fifteen square-mile preserve of more than five hundred wild mustangs (14 miles south of Hot Springs). Two-hour tours take you up close to various bands of horses, views over the Cheyenne River, the sacred Lakota Sun Dance site (the ceremony takes place in June) and ten-thousand-year-old petroglyphs.

North Dakota

Times are good in **NORTH DAKOTA**, a rural state with a booming economy thanks to the controversial but incredibly lucrative fracking oil industry (it's now the second biggest oil-producing state in the USA, after Texas). With an astounding state surplus of US$1 billion and unemployment at just three percent, ad-hoc "man-camp" settlements and sky-high property prices have become the norm, fuelling fears of a boom-bust economy. With a population of less than 700,000 and a harsh winter, for now the state's tourism industry (as in Canada, its northern neighbour) only really operates in the summer, and though drilling rigs and pumpjacks dot the landscape in the western part of the state, there's plenty here to attract visitors.

Bismarck and around

Named in honour of Germany's "Iron Chancellor", **BISMARCK** became North Dakota's capital in 1889. With its sister city of **MANDAN** it has a combined population of 100,000 but retains a mellow, small-town feel – it's not an especially attractive place, but the area is rich in Native American and US heritage, much of it related to the expedition of Lewis and Clark, who wintered along the banks of Missouri near here in 1804–05.

North Dakota State Capitol

600 E Boulevard Ave • Tours Mon–Fri 9–11am & 1–3pm (also Sat & Sun June–Aug) • Free • ☎ 701 328 2480

Though it lacks the grand domes so common in other states, locals are still proud of the nineteen-storey limestone **North Dakota State Capitol**, completed in 1934 and set at the crest of a public park studded with statues (including one of Sakakawea). The interior, a model of spatial economy and marbled Art Deco elegance, is open for guided **tours**, while the eighteenth-floor **observation deck** offers vast panoramas of the surrounding plains.

10

ND Heritage Center

612 E Boulevard Ave • Mon–Fri 8am–5pm, Sat & Sun 10am–5pm • Free • ☎ 701 328 2666, ⓦ history.nd.gov

Across the street from the capitol, the superb **ND Heritage Center** is undergoing a massive expansion that should be complete by late 2014, with four state-of-the-art galleries showcasing North Dakota history. Look out for Sitting Bull's painted robe.

Fort Abraham Lincoln State Park

4480 Fort Lincoln Rd (7 miles south of downtown Mandan via Hwy-1806) • Grounds daily 9am–5pm; visitor centre, Custer House and On-a-Slant May–Sept Mon–Fri 9am–5pm, Sat & Sun 8am–5pm • $5/vehicle, plus $6/adult (to enter buildings) • ☎ 701 667 6340, ⓦ fortlincoln.com

Just across the Missouri from Bismarck lies **Fort Abraham Lincoln State Park**, containing the reconstruction of a US army fort originally built here in 1872. Buildings include a barracks, a theatre, stables and several wooden blockhouses, but the centrepiece is the **Custer House**, an admirable reconstruction of George Custer's home (he was commander here before the Little Big Horn). The forty-minute guided tour supplies nuggets of quirky information about the brutally ambitious, indefatigable horseman (for example, he liked to eat raw onions), his wife and their household.

The park also includes six earthlodge reconstructions on the site of the once-vast **On-A-Slant Village**, occupied by the Mandan people from around 1575 to 1781, when a smallpox epidemic decimated the tribe. The park's **visitor centre** houses Mandan exhibits and artefacts as well as information on Custer and Lewis and Clark.

Lewis and Clark Interpretive Center and Fort Mandan

US-83 and Hwy-200A, Washburn • June–Aug daily 9am–5pm; Sept–May Mon–Sat 9am–5pm, Sun noon–5pm • $7.50 • ☎ 701 462 8535, ⓦ fortmandan.com

The Lewis and Clark expedition actually spent the winter of 1804–05 some 38 miles upstream of present-day Bismarck, in an improvised cottonwood stockade they grandly entitled **Fort Mandan**. The fort has been artfully reconstructed from local cottonwood (the original was already ruined by 1806), with a visitor centre and on-site guides offering context. Admission includes the **Lewis and Clark Interpretive Center**, two miles southeast, with interactive exhibits chronicling the expedition, the story of Fort Clark and the 1830s expedition of artist Karl Bodmer and German explorer Prince Maximilian.

Knife River Indian Villages National Historic Site

564 County Rd 37, Stanton • Daily: mid-May to Aug 8am–6pm; Sept to mid-May 8am–4.30pm • Free • ☎ 701 745 3300, ⓦ nps.gov/knri

After the Mandan abandoned On-A-Slant (above), they moved upstream and settled along the Knife River near three older Hidatsa villages, commemorated today at **Knife River Indian Villages National Historic Site**. It was here in 1804 that the explorers Lewis and Clark came into contact with **Sakakawea** (aka Sacajawea); the **visitor centre** explores the connection and the history of the site, while an impressively solid looking earthlodge stands outside – trails lead past the barely visible remains of the actual villages.

ARRIVAL, INFORMATION AND TOURS	BISMARCK AND AROUND

By bus The Greyhound terminal is at 3750 E Rosser Ave (☎ 701 223 6576).

Destinations Billings (2 daily; 7hr 30min–10hr); Minneapolis

(2 daily; 8hr 15min–8hr 30min).

Visitor centre 1600 Burnt Boat Drive, exit 157 I-94 (late May to Aug Mon–Fri 7.30am–7pm, Sat 8am–6pm, Sun

10am–5pm; Sept to late May Mon–Fri 8am–5pm; ☎800 767 3555, ⓦbismarckmandancvb.com).

Tours A few miles west of downtown on the Missouri River, the *Lewis & Clark Riverboat* runs hour-long historical cruises in the summer (usually Wed–Sun 3–4pm, check the website for dates; $13.75; ☎701 255 4233, ⓦlewisand clarkriverboat.com); longer cruises with meals ($23.95– 33.95) are also available.

ACCOMMODATION AND EATING

Kay's Bed & Breakfast 807 N 6th St ☎701 258 6877, ⓔkaylink@bis.midco.net. Lovely 1918 clapboard home with just two upstairs rooms that share a pink bathroom, cutesy decor and Kay Link's home-cooked breakfasts. **$125**

Laughing Sun Brewery 107 N 5th St ☎701 751 3881, ⓦlaughingsunbrewing.com. Try the "feast like a sultan" IPA or strawberry wheat beer at this local microbrewery and restaurant. Mon–Thurs 4pm–midnight, Fri–Sun 2pm–midnight.

★ **Little Cottage Café** 2513 E Main Ave ☎701 223 4949. Classic local diner, serving big breakfasts and heaps of comfort food since 1965 (mains $6–9). Daily 6am–9pm.

Peacock Alley 422 E Main St ☎701 255 7917, ⓦpeacock-alley.com. Opened in the old *Patterson Hotel* in 1933, this classic American grill and bar offers a range of local beers on tap (Mandan's Buffalo Common; $4.75), and fabulous, messy burgers such as the Dakota ($11), piled with Angus beef, bacon and mushrooms on a beer bun. Mon–Fri 11am–1am, Sat 10am–1am.

Radisson Bismarck 605 E Broadway Ave ☎701 255 6000, ⓦradisson.com. Bismarck has plenty of motels on the outskirts, but this is the only real option downtown, an ageing property but with comfortable, modern rooms, parking, airport shuttle (free) and a decent indoor pool. **$98**

Theodore Roosevelt National Park

A vast tract of multihued rock formations, rough grassland and badlands, **Theodore Roosevelt National Park** is North Dakota's premier tract of unspoiled wilderness, named after the feisty president who roamed, hunted and ranched here in the 1880s. Split into north and south units along the banks of the Little Missouri, approximately seventy miles apart, the park is at its most beautiful at sunrise or sundown – the best times to observe such fauna as mule deer, feral horses, elk, pronghorn, ever-present bison and closely knit prairie dog communities. Note that in an odd twist of raggedly drawn **time zones**, the park's north unit is on Central time, while the south unit is on Mountain time.

South Unit

Your first taste of the **south unit** is likely to be at the breathtaking **Painted Canyon**, seven miles east of Medora (just off I-94). Here and elsewhere in the park, the land is like a sedimentary layer cake that for millions of years has been beaten by hard rains, baked by the sun into a kaleidoscope of colours and cut through to its base by the river.

At the main entrance to the park, the **Medora Visitor Center** (see opposite) contains a small museum dedicated to Theodore Roosevelt; behind it sits the simple **Maltese Cross Cabin** that served as Roosevelt's first home in North Dakota in 1884. From here most visitors drive the remarkably scenic 36-mile **loop road**, which passes several sprawling prairie dog towns and overlooks. The most spectacular is the view from **Wind Canyon**, ten miles out of Medora, where a small gorge of caramel-like sandstone has been shaped smooth by the wind, and the Little Missouri makes a picturesque oxbow in the valley below. **Hiking trails** lace the park; the Petrified Forest Loop (10-mile round trip; 5–6hr) leads to a vast collection of petrified wood and tree stumps.

Medora

Tiny **MEDORA**, the southern gateway to the park, is a resort town with a split personality; between June and September it hums with activity as tourists flock in to enjoy the **Medora Musical** (opposite), while the rest of the year it reverts to sleepy mountain village, with just a handful of businesses open. Medora began life in 1883 when wealthy French nobleman **Marquis de Mores** established a cattle-processing plant here (it was named for his wife). That venture soon failed, and the town's current prosperity began when wealthy local philanthropist Harold Schafer pumped new life into it in the 1960s. Today it's the best base from which to explore the national park, whichever season you visit.

MEDORA MUSICAL AND PITCHFORK FONDUE

Medora's biggest draw by far is the long-running **Medora Musical**, a super-Americana song and dance and variety show staged beneath the stars in a marvellously sited amphitheatre, on a hillside just outside town (one segment of the show is always dedicated to Theodore Roosevelt). The extravaganza, which runs each summer (June to early Sept daily 7.30pm; $35), is preceded two hours earlier by the **Pitchfork Steak Fondue**, a fantastic feed for which hundreds of steaks are simultaneously dipped on pitchforks into giant oil vats ($28 for 12-inch rib eye and buffet). For both events call ☎ 800 633 6721 (ⓦ medora.com).

10

Chateau de Mores State Historic Site

3448 Chateau Rd • Mid-May to mid-Sept daily 8.30am–6.30pm; mid-Sept to mid-May interpretive centre only Wed–Sun 9am–5pm • Mid-May to mid-Sept $7; $3.50 mid-Sept to mid-May • ☎ 701 623 4355, ⓦ history.nd.gov

A grand summer home built by the French aristocrat Marquis de Mores in 1883, the **Chateau de Mores** was briefly a buzzing centre of Plains high society until the failure of his cattle business just three years later. The house is open summers only, but the nearby **interpretive centre** offers introductory films, an exhibition on the irascible marquis and a hall dedicated to German immigration in North Dakota.

North Unit

The park's smaller **North Unit**, just beyond the seemingly unending convoys of trucks running along Hwy-85 (it's just 15 miles south of oil-boom town **Watford City**), receives only a fraction of the south unit's visitors, though it's arguably more spectacular. Highlights include the jaw-dropping views from **River Bend Overlook**, along the park's fourteen-mile scenic drive, and similar vistas from **Oxbow Overlook**, at that same road's end, while the demanding twelve-mile **Buckhorn Trail** winds through sage-filled terrain before following steep gulches up into lofty prairies full of grazing bison.

INFORMATION

Entry fee $10/car or $5/person (on foot or bike).
North Unit Visitor Center At the North Unit entrance, Hwy-85 (mid-Nov to March Fri–Sun 9am–5.30pm; April to

THEODORE ROOSEVELT NATIONAL PARK

mid-Nov daily 9am–5.30pm; ☎ 701 842 2333).
South Unit Visitor Center Medora (daily 8am–4.30pm; ☎ 701 623 4466, ⓦ nps.gov/thro).

ACCOMMODATION AND EATING

SOUTH UNIT

Booking is essential for any stay in Medora between June and August. Note also that in Medora only *Theodore's*, *Boots Bar & Grill* and *Little Missouri Saloon* are usually open for meals between October and May.

Badlands Motel 501 Pacific Ave ☎ 800 633 6721, ⓦ medora.com. If you don't feel like camping at the national park ($10), rest your head at this utilitarian motel, with basic a/c rooms and free wi-fi. Open May to mid-Oct. <u>$135</u>

★ **Rough Riders Hotel** 301 Third Ave ☎ 800 633 6721, ⓦ medora.com. Dating back to 1884 but given a swish remodelling in 2010, this is Medora's top digs, with cosy rooms, plush bathrooms and plenty of Roosevelt memorabilia (including "Teddy" bears in each room). Open year-round. <u>$189</u>

Theodore's Rough Riders Hotel, 301 Third Ave ☎ 800 633 6721, ⓦ medora.com. Specializes in buffalo kabobs and prime rib, as well as unique appetizers such as walleye cheeks. Mains are expensive ($25–35), but there's a cheaper

pub menu of burgers and fish and chips ($13–17). Daily 7–1.30pm & 4.30–9pm.

NORTH UNIT

The closest hotels to the North Unit lie in Watford City, but are often booked full with oil workers – the roads around here are unnervingly thick with trucks and traffic, though the oil boom means the restaurants and bars in town are lively every night of the week.

Outlaws Bar & Grill 120 S Main St ☎ 701 842 6859, ⓦ outlawsbarngrill.com. The restaurant of choice in Watford City, with waits for tables even on Monday nights; worth it for great food such as beer-battered asparagus ($11), juicy steaks (from $16) and a range of burgers and salads; draught beers in the bar. Mon–Fri 11am–10pm, Sat noon–10pm.

Roosevelt Hotel 600 Second Ave SW ☎ 701 842 3686, ⓦ rooseveltinn.com. Watford City's premier hotel sports vast, comfy suites with kitchens and soft carpets, breakfast included and a strict "no muddy boots" policy. <u>$124</u>

The Rockies

SAWTOOTH NATIONAL RECREATION AREA, ID

11

The Rockies

Only when you traverse the Rocky Mountain states of Colorado, Wyoming, Montana and Idaho does the immense size of the American West really hit home. Stretching over one thousand miles from the virgin forests on the Canadian border to the deserts of New Mexico, America's rugged spine encompasses an astonishing array of landscapes – geyser basins, lava flows, arid valleys and huge sand dunes – each in its own way as dramatic as the region's magnificent snow-capped peaks. All that geological grandeur is enhanced by wildlife such as bison, bear, moose and elk, and the conspicuous legacy of the miners, cowboys, outlaws and Native Americans who struggled over the area's rich resources during the nineteenth century.

Each of the four states has its own distinct character. **Colorado**, with fifty peaks over 14,000ft, is the most mountainous and populated, as well as the economic leader of the region with a liberal, progressive reputation. Friendly, sophisticated **Denver**, the Rockies' only major metropolis, is also the most visited city, in part because it serves as gateway to some of the best ski resorts in the country. Less touched by the tourist circus is vast, brawny **Montana**, where the "Big Sky" looks down on a glorious verdant manuscript scribbled over with gushing streams, lakes and tiny communities.

Vast stretches of scrubland fill **Wyoming**, the country's least populous state, its most conservative and traditionally Western, best known for gurgling, spitting **Yellowstone**, adjacent **Grand Teton National Park** and the nearby **Bighorn Mountains**. Rugged, remote whitewater rafting hub **Idaho** holds some of the Rocky Mountains' last unexplored wildernesses, most notably the mighty **Sawtooth** range.

Attempt to rush around every national park and major town and you'll miss out on one of the Rockies' real delights – coaxing your car along the tight switchback roads that wind up and over precipitous mountain passes, especially through the majestic **Continental Divide**. At some point it's worth forsaking motorized transport, to see at least some of the area by **bike**; the Rockies contain some of the most challenging and rewarding cycling terrain on the continent. And of course, you cannot really claim to have experienced the mountains unless you embark on a hike or two.

DURANGO & SILVERTON NARROW GAUGE RAILROAD

Highlights

❶ **Durango & Silverton Narrow Gauge Railroad, CO** This steam-train ride corkscrews through spectacular mountains to the mining town of Silverton. **See p.688**

❷ **Mesa Verde National Park, CO** Explore the extraordinary cliffside dwellings, abandoned by the Ancestral Puebloans eight hundred years ago. **See p.691**

❸ **Yellowstone National Park, WY** A thermal wonderland, where wolves and bears prowl, and shaggy bison wander past towering geysers. **See p.697**

❹ **Grand Teton National Park, WY** This spectacular chain of mountains is prime

territory for hiking, biking and wildlife viewing. **See p.703**

❺ **Little Bighorn, MT** One of the most famous battlefields in America looks much as it did in 1876, when Custer faced off against Sitting Bull and Crazy Horse. **See p.709**

❻ **Going-to-the-Sun Road, Glacier National Park, MT** The hairpin turns along this fifty-mile stretch offer staggering views near the Continental Divide. **See p.720**

❼ **Sawtooth Mountains, ID** Of all Idaho's 81 mountain ranges, the Sawtooth summits make for the most awe-inspiring scenic drive. **See p.723**

HIGHLIGHTS ARE MARKED ON THE MAP ON P.664

WHEN TO VISIT THE ROCKIES

Between early June and early September you can expect **temperatures** in the high sixties all the way up to a hundred degrees Fahrenheit, depending on whether you are in the high desert of Wyoming, the plains of Idaho or the mountains of Colorado. Be prepared for wild variations in the mountains – and, of course, the higher you go the colder it gets. The altitude is high enough to warrant a period of acclimatization, while the sun at these elevations can be uncomfortably fierce. In fact, parts of Wyoming and Colorado bask in more hours of sunshine per year than San Diego or Miami Beach. Spring, when the snow melts, is the least attractive time to visit, and while the delicate golds of quaking aspen trees light up the mountainsides in early autumn, by October things are generally a bit cold for enjoyable hiking or sports. Most **ski** runs are open by late November and operate well into March – or even June, depending on snow conditions. The coldest month is January, when temperatures below 0°F are common.

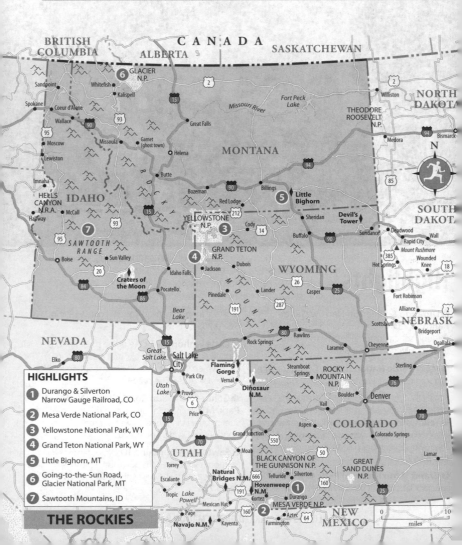

HIGHLIGHTS

1. Durango & Silverton Narrow Gauge Railroad, CO
2. Mesa Verde National Park, CO
3. Yellowstone National Park, WY
4. Grand Teton National Park, WY
5. Little Bighorn, MT
6. Going-to-the-Sun Road, Glacier National Park, MT
7. Sawtooth Mountains, ID

THE ROCKIES

Colorado

Progressive and increasingly multicultural, **COLORADO** is the snowboarding, outdoorsy mountain state that produces more beer than any other, gave us *South Park* in 1997, and in 2012, legalized marijuana – its culture is often more Californian than cowboy, albeit without the ocean. Yet Colorado remains proud of its traditional Western roots, and it's not all mountains; a third of the state is covered by plains as flat as Nebraska, and in the south the dry, desert terrain resembles New Mexico. And it's only liberal to a point; parts are still very conservative (Obama won the state in 2012, but 46 percent voted Republican), and it was here that horrific mass shootings took place in Columbine (1999) and Aurora (2012).

Beyond the trendy capital **Denver**, the obvious attraction for travellers are the Rocky Mountains, littered with ski resorts such as **Aspen** that double as hiking and biking nirvanas in the summer, and with old silver towns like **Leadville** and **Crested Butte**. The most spectacular terrain and wildlife is protected within **Rocky Mountain National Park** and around **Pikes Peak**, which towers over the state's second largest city, **Colorado Springs**. The far west of the state stretches onto the red-rock deserts of the Colorado Plateau, where the dry climate has preserved the extraordinary natural sculptures of **Colorado National Monument**, while the southwest boasts **Mesa Verde National Park**, home to remarkable cliff cities left by the ancient Ancestral Puebloans.

11

Denver

Its substantial ensemble of glittering skyscrapers marking the final transition between the Great Plains and the American West, **DENVER** stands at the threshold of the **Rocky Mountains**. Though clearly visible from downtown, the majestic peaks of the Front Range start to rise roughly fifteen miles west, and the "**Mile High City**" (at an elevation of 5280ft) is itself uniformly flat.

Denver was founded in 1858, near turgid Cherry Creek and the location of Colorado's first **gold** strike. Prospectors swiftly moved on, but Denver has remained the state's most important commercial and transport nexus and today's artsy, liberal population coexists happily with a dynamic business community.

16th Street Mall

Denver is highly unusual among the cities of the West in having a lively **downtown** core, its regeneration sparked by the opening of **Coors Field** (home of Major League baseball's Colorado Rockies) in 1995. At its heart lie the shops and restaurants of **LoDo** (Lower Downtown) and of **16th Street Mall** (ⓦ16thstreetmalldenver.com), a pedestrianized strip more than a mile in length. Sprinkled with shady trees, food carts and painted pianos (May–Sept daily 8am–10pm), free for anyone to play, the street is also served by **free MallRide buses** (Mon–Fri 5am–1.30am, Sat 5.30am–1.30am, Sun 6.30am–1.30am; every 1.5–15min) and on summer evenings in particular it's bursting with activity. It can also boast one of the best independent **bookstores** in the US:

GREAT REGIONAL DRIVES

Beartooth Hwy The most dramatic and scenic entry to Yellowstone, following US-212 from Red Lodge in Montana high across the snow-capped Beartooth Mountains.

I-70, Colorado The most spectacular interstate in the country begins to climb immediately beyond Denver, rising high into the Rockies, passing alpine ski villages and frozen lakes.

Hwy-24 to Peaks Pike, Colorado A staggeringly beautiful nineteen-mile drive up Peaks Pike, just west of Colorado Springs, with mountain views up to seventy miles distant.

Sawtooth Scenic Byway, Idaho. Drive into the heart of pristine Idaho wilderness on meandering Hwy-75, 115 miles beside the Salmon River toward jagged, snowy peaks.

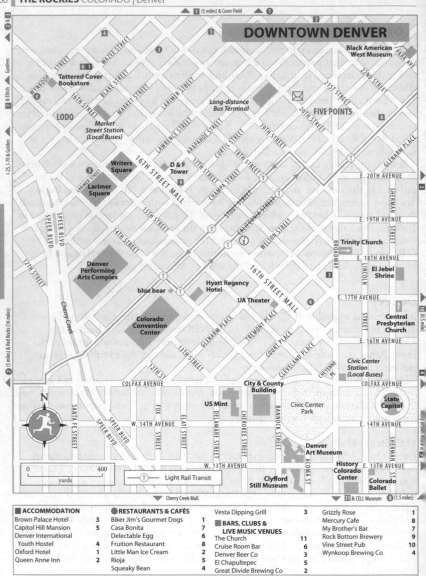

DOWNTOWN DENVER

■ ACCOMMODATION		● RESTAURANTS & CAFÉS		Vesta Dipping Grill	3	Grizzly Rose	1
Brown Palace Hotel	3	Biker Jim's Gourmet Dogs	1			Mercury Cafe	8
Capitol Hill Mansion	5	Casa Bonita	7	■ BARS, CLUBS &		My Brother's Bar	7
Denver International		Delectable Egg	6	LIVE MUSIC VENUES		Rock Bottom Brewery	9
Youth Hostel	4	Fruition Restaurant	8	The Church	11	Vine Street Pub	10
Oxford Hotel	1	Little Man Ice Cream	2	Cruise Room Bar	6	Wynkoop Brewing Co	4
Queen Anne Inn	2	Rioja	5	Denver Beer Co	3		
		Squeaky Bean	4	El Chapultepec	5		
				Great Divide Brewing Co	2		

the **Tattered Cover** (Mon–Fri 6.30am–9pm, Sat 9am–9pm, Sun 10am–9pm; ☎303 436 1070, ⓦtatteredcover.com) and café at 1628 16th St and Wynkoop, in a restored 1896 warehouse opposite the venerable Union Street train station. Further south along the mall, the 1910 **D&F Clocktower** (325ft), modelled on the Campanile in Piazza San Marco, Venice, is all that remains of a department store demolished in the 1970s. A couple of blocks west, a 40ft **blue bear** peers hopefully in through the windows of the Denver Convention Center on 14th Street; installed in 2005, and officially titled *I See What You Mean*, it has rapidly established itself as an iconic landmark.

The State Capitol

200 E Colfax Ave • Mon–Fri 7.30am–5pm; free tours every 45min; Mon–Fri 10am–3pm • ☎ 303 866 2604, ⊛ colorado.gov/capitoltour

Three blocks from the southeastern end of 16th Street, the **State Capitol** offers a commanding view of the Rockies swelling on the western horizon; the thirteenth step up to its entrance is exactly one mile above sea level. The building itself is an elegant but fairly subdued Neoclassical pile compared to other state capitols, completed in 1908 as a rather predictable copy of the Capitol in Washington DC, replete with giant murals and ornate stained glass. Climb its dome for an even better view.

Denver Art Museum

100 W 14th Ave Pkwy • Tues–Thurs, Sat & Sun 10am–5pm, Fri 10am–8pm • $13 • ☎ 720 865 5000, ⊛ denverartmuseum.org

The splendidly eclectic collections of the **Denver Art Museum** spread through two separate modern buildings, either side of 13th Avenue. The Hamilton Building holds contemporary artworks, including Sandy Skoglund's spooky installation *Fox Games*, as well as galleries of African and Oceanic works, while the North Building has a spectacular array of Native American and pre-Columbian artefacts of all kinds – its Olmec miniatures are truly extraordinary.

Clyfford Still Museum

1250 Bannock St • Tues–Thurs, Sat & Sun 10am–5pm, Fri 10am–8pm • $10 • ☎ 720 354 4880, ⊛ clyffordstillmuseum.org

When abstract painting pioneer **Clyfford Still** died in Maryland in 1980, his will stipulated that his estate be given to any American city willing to establish a museum dedicated solely to his work. It wasn't until 2004 that Denver stepped up, and in 2011 the **Clyfford Still Museum** opened next to the art museum, a wonderful space for a rotating collection of 825 paintings and 1575 works on paper. Still's abstract expressionism can be heavy going, but the giant canvases and jagged swirls of colour are incredibly absorbing.

History Colorado Museum

1200 Broadway • Mon–Sat 10am–5pm, Sun noon–5pm • $10 • ☎ 303 447 8679, ⊛ historycoloradocenter.org

The history of the state is artfully explored at the **History Colorado Museum**, not a typical museum experience: exhibits are enhanced with videos and interactive displays throughout, with permanent galleries organized by theme rather than chronology. One section recreates life in the plains town of Keota in the 1920s, while "Colorado Stories" features everything from the exploits of Kit Carson to the advent of leisure skiing.

Molly Brown House Museum

1340 Pennsylvania St • Tues–Sat 10am–4.30pm (also Mon June–Aug), Sun noon–4.30pm (tour every 30min till 3.30pm) • $8 • ☎ 303 832 4092, ⊛ mollybrown.org

The "**unsinkable Molly Brown**" has been an American icon since her survival of the *Titanic* disaster in 1912, her myth cemented by the eponymous musical and the Debbie Reynolds movie of 1964. The gorgeously preserved **Molly Brown House Museum**, purchased by Margaret Tobin Brown's rich husband in 1894, explodes many of the myths (not least the fact Margaret was never "Molly"), but tours (the only way to get inside the house) also emphasize just how remarkable and generous a life the real woman led, working tirelessly for causes such as women's suffrage and social justice. The house has been restored to its 1910 grandeur, loaded with period pieces, many of which belonged to the Browns.

Black American West Museum

3091 California St • Tues–Sat 10am–4pm • $10 • ☎ 720 242 7428, ⊛ blackamericanwestmuseum.com

Denver's black community is most prominent in the old **Five Points** district, northeast of LoDo, created to house black railroad workers in the 1870s. The **Black American West Museum** has intriguing details on black pioneers and outlaws, and debunks Western myths: one third of all nineteenth-century cowboys were black, and many were former slaves who left the South after the Civil War.

Coors Brewery Tour

1221 Ford St, at 13th St, Golden • Mon & Thurs–Sat 10am–4pm (June–Aug also Wed), Sun noon–4pm • Free • ☎ 303 277 2337, Ⓦ millercoors.com/golden-brewery-tour.aspx

Ever since 1873 the town of **Golden**, twenty miles west of downtown but essentially a Denver suburb, has been virtually synonymous with beer giant **Coors** and the world's largest single brewery facility (the company itself merged with Molson in 2005). The brewery is three blocks east of Golden's main thoroughfare, Washington Avenue, served by regular buses from Market Street Station in Denver. Self-guided tours highlight the malting, brewing and packaging processes, ending with a tasting session of such products as the much-maligned low-cal Coors Light, and the wildly successful **Blue Moon Belgian White**.

Buffalo Bill Museum

987½ Lookout Mountain Rd, Golden • May–Oct daily 9am–5pm; Nov–April Tues–Sun 9am–4pm • $5 • ☎ 303 526 0744, Ⓦ buffalobill.org

11

Among the peaks that rise sharply behind downtown Golden is Lookout Mountain, the final (and highly photogenic) resting place of **Buffalo Bill Cody**, the famed frontiersman and showman who died in Denver in 1917. Despite protests from Cody, Wyoming, the town Bill had co-founded (see p.697), Cody's wife insisted that Lookout Mountain was always his first choice (folks in Cody have argued for the body's "return" ever since). Gruesome artefacts in the comprehensive adjacent **Buffalo Bill Museum** include a pistol with a handle fashioned from human bone.

ARRIVAL AND DEPARTURE   DENVER

By plane Denver International Airport (Ⓦ flydenver.com) is 24 miles northeast of downtown; if you rent a car and are heading for Rocky Mountains National Park or Boulder, there's no need to go anywhere near the city centre. All taxi companies, including Metro (☎ 303 333 3333) charge a flat rate of $55.15 to downtown (elsewhere is on the meter). By 2016 the light rail extension should link the airport with Denver, but until then hourly RTD SkyRide buses (Ⓦ rtd -denver.com) serve downtown ($11) and Boulder ($13). Various independent shuttles, such as Big Sky (☎ 303 300 2626, Ⓦ bigskyshuttle.com), drop passengers at downtown hotels for $30–50, and also serve the ski resorts further afield.
By train Amtrak trains arrive on the northwest edge of

downtown Denver at the beautiful old Union Station on at 1701 Wynkoop St.
Destinations Chicago (1 daily; 18hr 40min); Glenwood Springs (1 daily; 5hr 48min); Grand Junction (1 daily; 7hr 52min); Omaha (1 daily; 8hr 50min); Salt Lake City (1 daily; 15hr).
By bus The Greyhound terminal (☎ 303 293 6555) is close to downtown at 1055 19th St.
Destinations Albuquerque (2 daily; 8hr 15min); Colorado Springs (5 daily; 1hr 10min–1hr 35min); Glenwood Springs (3 daily; 3hr 35min); Grand Junction (3 daily; 5hr 15min); Kansas City (2 daily; 11hr 20min); Omaha (1 daily; 9hr 40min); St Louis (2 daily; 16hr 50min); Vail (3 daily; 2hr 20min).

GETTING AROUND AND INFORMATION

By bus Free buses run up and down 16th Street Mall (see p.665), while RTD also run pay-to-ride buses throughout the city ($2.25; ☎ 303 229 6000, Ⓦ rtd-denver.com); frequent services to local sports venues and the airport leave from the Market Street Station at Market and 16th. All RTD services can carry bikes (free) and wheelchair users.
By bike The Denver Bike Sharing Program (Ⓦ denver.bcycle .com) requires access passes of $8/24hr or $20/7 days, and charges $4/30min (first 30min free, second 30min $1).

By light rail Denver's light rail system (fares $2.25–5; Ⓦ rtd -denver.com) currently links the 16th Street Mall with the Denver Broncos stadium and the Pepsi Center, but is being radically expanded by the FasTracks project, with its hub at Union Square and lines opening between 2014 and 2016.
Visitor centre Downtown at 1600 California St, entered via 16th Street Mall (May–Oct Mon–Fri 9am–6pm, Sat 9am–5pm, Sun 11am–3pm; Nov–April Mon–Fri 9am– 5pm; ☎ 303 892 1505, Ⓦ denver.org/visitdenver).

ACCOMMODATION

Brown Palace Hotel 321 17th St ☎ 303 297 3111, Ⓦ brownpalace.com. Beautiful downtown landmark dating from 1892, with elegant dining rooms and public areas, as well as impeccable rooms. The eight-storey

cast-iron atrium is stunning. $370
Capitol Hill Mansion 1207 Pennsylvania St ☎ 303 839 5221, Ⓦ capitolhillmansion.com. Luxurious, gay-friendly B&B in a turreted 1891 Richardson Romanesque sandstone

mansion on a leafy street near the State Capitol. Each of its eight antique-furnished rooms is delightful, and several include large whirlpool tubs. $134

Denver International Youth Hostel 630 E 16th Ave ☏ 303 832 9996, ⓦyouthhostels.com/Denver. Solid budget option near downtown, much improved in recent years; each dorm has a kitchen, shower, TV and three bunks, with shared computers (free internet). Dorms $19

Oxford Hotel 1600 17th St ☏ 303 628 5400,

ⓦtheoxfordhotel.com. In LoDo since 1891, this historic hotel oozes charm and offers stylish rooms featuring European antiques, Bose stereo systems and iPod docking stations. $270

★ **Queen Anne Inn** 2147 Tremont Place ☏ 303 296 6666, ⓦqueenannebnb.com. Central, eco-friendly and very hospitable 1879 B&B near a peaceful park where you can catch a carriage ride; each of the fourteen rooms and suites is tastefully and individually decorated. $135

EATING

★ **Biker Jim's Gourmet Dogs** 2148 Larimer St ☏ 720 746 9355, ⓦbikerjimsdogs.com. Originally a street vendor, Jim knocks out superb hot dogs ($6), with everything from reindeer or wild boar brats (bratwurst sausages) to spicy elk and buffalo, all perfectly charred and served with caramelized onions. Mon–Thurs & Sun 11am–10pm, Fri & Sat 11am–3am.

Casa Bonita 6715 W Colfax Ave, Lakewood ☏ 303 232 5115, ⓦcasabonitadenver.com. This Denver institution (lampooned in *South Park*), has been serving up Mexican food and kitsch family fun since 1974, aided by its 85ft tower and Tex-Mex paraphernalia. Try the "all-you-can-eat deluxe dinners" (beef or chicken $14.49). Mon–Thurs & Sun 11am–9pm, Fri & Sat 11am–10pm.

Delectable Egg 1625 Court Place ☏ 303 892 5720, ⓦdelectableegg.com. Local mini-chain knocking out the extra fluffy Denver omelette (filled with ham, green peppers and onions; $8.95), Denver sandwich (beef topped with two eggs; $8.75) and a vast range of specials, wraps and burritos. Mon–Fri 6.30am–2pm, Sat & Sun 7am–2pm.

★ **Fruition Restaurant** 1313 E 6th Ave ☏ 303 831 1962, ⓦfruitionrestaurant.com. Current gourmet trend-setter on Denver's dynamic farm-to-table scene, with seasonal menus that might include Colorado Spring lamb loin, smoked sturgeon *rillette* (pâté) and potato-wrapped

oysters. Mon–Sat 5–10pm, Sun 5–8pm.

Little Man Ice Cream 2620 16th St ☏ 303 455 3811, ⓦlittlemanicecream.com. Hugely addictive ice cream in this shop, with scoops ($2.50) of handmade flavours such as nutmeg, gingerbread and bourbon-spiked buttercream. Daily 11am–midnight.

Rioja 1431 Larimer St ☏ 303 820 2282, ⓦriojadenver .com. Creative and hugely enjoyable Mediterranean cuisine, with robust meat, fish and pasta mains ($18.50–32), and some tables outside. Mon–Thurs 5–10pm, Fri 5–11pm, Sat 10am–2.30pm & 5–11pm, Sun 10am–2.30pm & 5–10pm.

★ **Squeaky Bean** 1500 Wynkoop St ☏ 303 623 2665, ⓦthesqueakybean.net. Creative restaurant with a cult following with intriguing menus of seasonal cuisine; think barbecued celery root, venison tartare and charred onion risotto (four courses for $55). Tues–Thurs 5–10pm, Fri & Sat 5–11pm, Sun 10am–2pm.

Vesta Dipping Grill 1822 Blake St ☏ 303 296 1970, ⓦvestagrill.com. Attractive dinner-only restaurant in a renovated LoDo warehouse serving tasty food in unusual combinations; the basic concept is to dip meat or veggies in a wide spectrum of sauces (Mediterranean, Asian and Mexican). Small plates $2–12, mains $18–30. Mon–Thurs & Sun 5–10pm, Fri & Sat 5–11pm.

NIGHTLIFE AND ENTERTAINMENT

Denver's liveliest nightlife is concentrated in the LoDo district, which runs the gamut from brewpubs and sports bars to upmarket cocktail bars, while SoCo (South of Colfax) boasts eight nightclubs within four blocks (see ⓦcoclubs.com). For events listings, see the free weekly *Denver Westword* (ⓦwestword.com).

BARS AND CLUBS

The Church 1160 Lincoln St ☏ 303 832 3528. A dance club inside a gutted 1865 church that combines a downtown nightlife landmark, wine bar, sushi bar and three invariably busy dancefloors. Programming varies from hard house to garage to hip-hop, and the crowd can be equally eclectic. $5–20 cover. Thurs–Sun 9pm–2am.

Cruise Room Bar Oxford Hotel, 1600 17th St ☏ 303 628 5400. This 1933 replica of the Art Deco martini bar on the *Queen Mary* ocean liner boasts a free jukebox and excellent cocktails. Mon–Thurs & Sun 4.30–11.45pm, Fri & Sat 4.30pm–12.45am.

My Brother's Bar 2376 15th St ☏ 303 455 9991. Legendary dive bar with appropriately crabby staff, superb burgers and loyal regulars. Open since 1873, this is where Jack Kerouac hung out when visiting. Daily 11am–2am.

LIVE MUSIC AND ARTS VENUES

Denver Performing Arts Complex 1400 Curtis St ☏ 303 893 4100, ⓦartscomplex.com. Home to the Denver Center Theater Company, Colorado Symphony Orchestra, Opera Colorado and the Colorado Ballet. Facilities include eight theatres, as well as the acoustically superb, in-the-round Symphony Hall.

11

DENVER'S TOP 5 BREWPUBS

Denver Beer Co 1695 Platte St ☎303 433 2739, ⓦdenverbeerco.com. Seasonal, small-batch producer. Sample the Graham Cracker Porter, a robust stout. Mon–Thurs 3–11pm, Fri & Sat noon–midnight, Sun noon–9pm.

Great Divide Brewing Co 2201 Arapahoe St ☎303 296 9640, ⓦgreatdivide.com. Pioneer since 1994, home of Denver Pale Ale and Titan IPA. Mon, Tues & Sun noon–8pm, Wed–Sat noon–10pm.

Rock Bottom Brewery 1001 16th St ☎303 534 7616, ⓦrockbottom.com. Craft brewing chain founded in Denver. Best brew: Molly's Titanic Brown Ale. Daily 11am–2am.

Vine Street Pub 1700 Vine St ☎303 388 2337, ⓦmountainsunpub.com. Best neighbourhood pub, home of the ultra-hoppy Colorado Kind Ale. Mon 4pm–1am, Tues–Sun 11am–1am.

Wynkoop Brewing Co 1634 18th St ☎303 297 2700, ⓦwynkoop.com. The state's oldest brewpub; try the Railyard Ale, a smooth amber beer. Daily 11am–midnight.

El Chapultepec 1962 Market St ☎303 295 9126, ⓦthepeclodo.com. Tiny but popular LoDo stalwart with nightly live jazz and occasional big names. Cover $2 Fri & Sat. Daily 11am–2am.

Grizzly Rose 5450 N Valley Hwy ☎303 295 1330, ⓦgrizzlyrose.com. Huge, legendary country-music venue, 10min drive north of downtown on I-25, where nightly bands include some famous names, and there's even a mechanical bull. Cover $5–20. Tues–Fri 11am–2am, Sat & Sun 6pm–2am.

★ **Mercury Cafe** 2199 California St ☎303 294 9258, ⓦmercurycafe.com. When the *Merc*'s not hosting jazz, you'll find tango dance classes, poetry readings or some other form of entertainment. A good-value restaurant serves healthy choices (many vegetarian) as well as high tea. Tues–Thurs 5.30pm–1am, Fri 5.30pm–2am, Sat 9am–2am, Sun 9am–1am.

★ **Red Rocks Amphitheatre** 18300 W Alameda Parkway, Morrison ☎720 865 2494, ⓦredrocksonline .com. This remarkable, 9000-capacity venue, squeezed between two glowing 400ft red-sandstone rocks 15 miles west of downtown Denver, has been the setting for thousands of rock and classical concerts since 1941; U2 filmed *Under a Blood Red Sky* here in 1983. The surrounding park and visitor centre is open free of charge during the day.

Colorado Springs and around

Sprawling for ten miles alongside I-25, **COLORADO SPRINGS** was founded as a holiday spot in 1871 by railroad tycoon William Jackson Palmer. He attracted so many English gentry to the town that it earned the nickname "Little London". Today the city of more than half a million remains a tourist magnet, littered with family-friendly attractions under the shadow of **Pikes Peak**, and happily coexisting with some major defence industry contractors and a high military presence (most notably Fort Carson, Peterson Air Force Base and the US Air Force Academy).

Colorado Springs is also home to the **United States Olympic Training Center** and the **World Figure Skating Museum**. There's otherwise not much to see downtown, but **Historic Old Colorado City** is a great place to shop and eat, and the surrounding area is packed with attractions; the stretch of Hwy-24 west of downtown is especially fun for families.

Garden of the Gods

I-25 exit 146 • **Garden of the Gods** Daily: May–Oct 5am–11pm; Nov–April 5am–9pm • Free **Visitor & Nature Center** 1805 N 30th St • Daily: June–Aug 8am–8pm; Sept–May 9am–5pm • Free • ☎719 634 6666, ⓦgardenofgods.com

An attractive city park, **Garden of the Gods** is a bizarre ensemble of gnarled and warped red sandstone that looks more like arid Arizona than the Rocky Mountains that frame it. Loop roads and hiking trails lace the park (which is just over five square miles), passing finely balanced overhangs, jagged pinnacles, massive pedestals and mushroom formations; you'll find maps and exhibits on the area's geology and history at the **visitor centre** at the eastern border. Avoid summer weekends when the place is packed.

Manitou Springs

Small **Manitou Springs**, five miles west of Colorado Springs on Hwy-24, is an attractive if touristy town of stately Victorian buildings, shops, restaurants and eleven natural springs – carbonated (and cool) mineral waters that made the town famous in the 1880s. You can still safely sip the water for free; each spring has a subtly different taste, but the **Twin Spring** on Ruxton Avenue is the sweetest.

Manitou Cliff Dwellings

10 Cliff Rd (5 miles west of I 25 on Hwy-24) • Daily: May–Sept 9am–6pm; March, April, Oct & Nov 9am–5pm; Dec & Jan 10am–4pm • $9.50 • ☎ 719 685 5242, ⊛ cliffdwellingsmuseum.com

If you don't have time to visit Mesa Verde (see p.691) or any of the ancient pueblos further south, the **Manitou Cliff Dwellings** will provide a decent if slightly odd introduction to the great **Anasazi culture** of the southwest. The small on-site **museum** contains artefacts, pottery and descriptions of Anasazi life, but the centrepiece is the strip of impressive dwellings themselves, set enigmatically into the red sandstone cliffside – you can wander through them via narrow passageways. What isn't made especially clear, however, is that these dwellings are actually reconstructions, using original Anasazi bricks and stones salvaged from ruins in McElmo Canyon (close to Mesa Verde), but opened here specifically as a tourist attraction in 1907.

Pikes Peak

Toll road 5069 Pikes Peak Hwy, Cascade • Daily: Late May to early Sept 7.30am–6pm; rest of Sept 7.30am–5pm; Oct–April 9am–3pm • May–Nov $12/person up to $40/car, Dec–April $10/person up to $35/car • ☎ 719 385 7325, ⊛ pikespeak.us.com **Railway** 515 Ruxton Ave, Manitou Springs • March–Dec, see website for times • $35; reservations advised • ☎ 719 685 5401, ⊛ cograilway.com

The mind-bending, nineteen-mile drive up **PIKES PEAK**, ten miles west of Colorado Springs on Hwy-24, is one of the most spectacular roads in the country, affording (on a clear day) jaw-dropping panoramas of snow-capped Rockies to the north and west, and the immense vastness of the Great Plains to the eastern horizon; it's even possible to see Denver seventy miles north.

Though not the tallest mountain in the Rockies (or even Colorado), Pikes Peak (14,115ft) is the best known – largely because the view from its crest inspired songwriter **Katharine Lee Bates** to write the words to "*America The Beautiful*" after a visit in 1893. It's named after American army general and explorer Zebulon Pike, who mapped the summit in 1806, but failed to climb it himself.

Most visitors drive up the mountain; the **toll road** is paved all the way, with plenty of pull-outs to admire the views. An easy (if pricier) alternative is the thrilling **Pikes Peak Cog Railway**, which runs year-round and grinds its way up an average of 847ft per mile on its ninety-minute journey to the summit. Hardier souls can hike to the top via the 11.8-mile **Barr Trail**, which gains 7900ft elevation from a trailhead just beyond the cog railway depot; this is an extremely tough climb, and most hikers spend one night in Barr Camp (⊛ barrcamp.com).

However you reach it, be prepared for freezing winds and snow on the bleak and windswept peak; a gift shop and café provide welcome relief.

ARRIVAL AND DEPARTURE   COLORADO SPRINGS AND AROUND

By bus Greyhound stops at 120 S Weber St downtown (☎ 719 635 1505). Colorado Springs Shuttle runs direct to Denver Airport ($50; ☎ 719 687 3456, ⊛ coloradoshuttle .com).

Destinations Albuquerque (2 daily; 7hr); Denver (6 daily; 1hr 10min–1hr 35min).

Visitor centre 515 S Cascade Ave (Mon–Fri 8.30am–5pm; ☎ 719 635 7506, ⊛ visitcos.com).

ACCOMMODATION

★ **The Mining Exchange** 8 S Nevada Ave ☎ 719 323 2000, ⊛ wyndham.com. Well worth the splurge, with spacious, luxurious rooms, excellent staff and beautifully restored premises dating from 1901 (it was once a stock exchange for mining companies). $160

Old Town GuestHouse 115 S 26th St ☎ 719 632 9194,

11

ⓦoldtown-guesthouse.com. Rustically elegant B&B with flower-themed rooms, comfy beds, well-equipped kitchenettes and an evening wine reception. **$99**

Sunflower Lodge 3703 W Colorado Ave ☎719 520 1864, ⓦsunflowerlodge.com. Provides cosy budget accommodation in retro motel units, most with kitchenettes and all with cable TV and a/c. **$67**

EATING AND DRINKING

Airplane Restaurant 1665 N Newport Rd ☎719 570 7656, ⓦsolosrestaurant.com. Not the best food in town (burgers from $9.49), but hey, this restaurant is actually inside an old military aeroplane (a Boeing KC-97, built in 1953). The cockpit is open for kids to play in. Mon–Thurs & Sun 11am–9pm, Fri & Sat 11am–10pm.

Marigold Café 4605 Centennial Blvd ☎719 599 4776, ⓦmarigoldcoloradosprings.com. Good lunchtime sandwiches, patisserie (Mon–Sat 8am–9pm) and, in the evenings, delicious French-inspired bistro food that belies the drab exterior (mains $13–19). Mon–Sat 11am–2.30pm & 5–9pm.

Phantom Canyon Brewing Co 2 E Pikes Peak Ave ☎719 635 2800, ⓦphantomcanyon.com. Great place for craft-brewed beer and filling pub food such as artichoke dip ($8) and beer-battered fish and chips ($11). Daily 11am–2am.

Pikes Peak Chocolate and Ice Cream 125½ N Tejon St (also in Manitou Springs) ☎719 634 2626, ⓦpikes peakchocolate.com. Sweet treat central, selling chocolates, fudge and exquisite ice cream. Mon–Thurs 11am–7pm, Fri & Sat 11am–8pm, Sun noon–6pm.

Great Sand Dunes National Park

Your first sight of **GREAT SAND DUNES NATIONAL PARK** comes as a shock; far from being tucked away in crevices or sheltered in a valley, the dunes are simply a colossal pile of sand that appears to have been dumped alongside the craggy Sangre de Cristo Mountains, 170 miles southwest of Colorado Springs. Over millions of years, these fine glacial grains have eroded from the San Juan Mountains and blown east until they could drift no further; the result is an eerie and deeply incongruous fifty-square-mile area of silky, shifting trackless desert, visible from miles around.

The park's **visitor centre** is three miles beyond the park entrance. Shortly beyond that lies the goal for most visitors, the "**beach**" beside Medano Creek, which flows along the eastern and southern side of the dune mass, often mobbed by local families frolicking in the water in summer. To reach the dunes themselves, you'll have to wade across the shallow creek, but be sure to take shoes – the sand can get incredibly hot. The dunes loom very large from the moment you start walking, but depending on current drifting they may take ten minutes or so just to reach the base, which can be hugely tiring, especially when the often-high winds swirl grit into your eyes at every step. Your reward is the sheer fun of climbing up the actual dunes, and, especially, sliding back down again (bring your own dune board). The scenery is spectacular; climb the 750ft peak of **Star Dune**, the tallest in the park, for views across the whole park, but start early and take plenty of water.

ARRIVAL AND INFORMATION
GREAT SAND DUNES NATIONAL PARK

Access and entry fees The park is at 11500 Hwy-150, Mosca, and is open 24hr daily. Admission is $3 (free for kids 15 and under).

Visitor centre Three miles beyond the park entrance (daily: June–Aug 8.30am–6pm; Sept–May 9am–4.30pm; ☎719 378 6399, ⓦnps.gov/grsa).

ACCOMMODATION AND EATING

Great Sand Dunes Lodge 7900 Hwy-150, Mosca ☎719 378 2900, ⓦgsdlodge.com. The only hotel in the area is just outside the park entrance, with pleasant rooms (satellite TV included), views of the dunes, an indoor pool and outdoor gas grills. Open mid-March to late Oct. **$100**

Great Sand Dunes Oasis 5400 Hwy-150, Mosca ☎719 378 2222, ⓦgreatdunes.com. In front of the lodge, this is the only restaurant for miles around, serving burgers, frybread and Mexican specialities, and also offers showers, laundry and tent sites, as well as a small number of basic cabins (April to mid-Oct). Camping from **$25**, cabins **$55**

Pinyon Flats Campground 11500 Hwy-150 (1 mile north of the visitor centre) ☎719 378 6399, ⓦnps.gov /grsa. With a free backcountry permit, you can camp in the park's seven primitive backcountry sites; the large Pinyon

Flats Campground, with restrooms (loop 1 is first-come, first-served; loop 2 and 3 sites can be reserved), however, is accessible by car, and much more popular, usually filling with tents and RVs alike in summer. $20

Boulder

The lively college town of **BOULDER**, just 27 miles northwest of Denver on US-36, is home to a youthful population that seems to divide its time between phenomenally healthy daytime pursuits and almost equally unhealthy nocturnal activities. Sometimes referred to as "seven miles surrounded by reality", Boulder was founded in 1858 by a prospecting party who felt that the nearby Flatiron Mountains "looked right for gold"; they found little, but the community grew anyway.

Downtown centres on the leafy pedestrian mall of **Pearl Street**, lined with bustling cafés, galleries and stores – including several places where you can rent **mountain bikes**. The most obvious short excursion is to drive or hike up nearby **Flagstaff Mountain** for views over town and further into the Rockies; any road west joins up with the **Peak to Peak Highway**, which heads through spectacular scenery towards Rocky Mountain National Park (see below). For rock climbing, **Eldorado Canyon State Park** (ⓦparks.state.co.us/parks/eldoradocanyon) offers many opportunities; the excellent Neptune Mountaineering, south of town at 633 S Broadway (Mon–Fri 10am–7pm, Sat & Sun 10am–6pm; ☎303 499 8866, ⓦneptunemountaineering.com), can answer questions and provide gear.

11

ARRIVAL AND INFORMATION

BOULDER

By bus Denver's RTD (ⓦrtd-denver.com) runs regular buses from Denver ($5) and its airport ($13), to the Transit Center, 14th and Walnut sts (☎303 299 6000).

Visitor centre 2440 Pearl St (Mon–Fri 9am–5pm; ☎303 442 2911, ⓦbouldercoloradousa.com).

ACCOMMODATION, EATING AND DRINKING

Corner Bar 2115 13th St (Hotel Boulderado) ☎303 442 4560. Cool hotel bar offering reasonably priced local beers, martinis and dishes until late on the patio. Mon–Fri 11.30am–11.45pm, Sat & Sun 10am–11.45pm.

★ **Flagstaff House** 1138 Flagstaff Rd ☎303 442 4640, ⓦflagstaffhouse.com. The undisputed five-star champ of Boulder restaurants, specializing in French cuisine with Asian influences; the soft-shell crab season is justly legendary (budget for $50/head). Mon–Fri & Sun 6–10pm, Sat 5–10pm.

Foot of the Mountain Motel 200 W Arapahoe Ave ☎303 442 5688, ⓦfootofthemountainmotel.com. Friendly, log-cabin-style motel redolent of the 1950s, nine blocks west of downtown beside Boulder Creek. $90

★ **Hotel Boulderado** 2115 13th St ☎303 442 4344, ⓦboulderado.com. Gorgeous historic hotel opened in 1909, with its famous stained-glass canopy ceiling, cherrywood staircase and balcony overlooking the lobby. Rooms are decked out in Victorian grandeur, with period furniture and wallpaper. Worth a visit even if you're not staying here. $250

Laughing Goat Coffee House 1709 Pearl St ☎303 440 4628, ⓦthelaughinggoat.com. Classic Boulder boho café, with tasty coffee, wacky art, music, poetry and even local beer. Mon–Fri 6am–11pm, Sat & Sun 7am–11pm.

★ **Redstone Meadery** 4700 Pearl St ☎720 406 1215, ⓦredstonemeadery.com. Step back to the Middle Ages at this producer of genuine mead (fermented honey wine). Mon–Fri noon–6.30pm, Sat noon–5pm.

West End Tavern 926 Pearl St ☎303 444 3535, ⓦthewestendtavern.com. Nice spot for roots music, locally brewed beer and spectacular views of the Flatirons from the roof terrace. Daily 11.30am–1.30am.

Rocky Mountain National Park

To experience the full, pristine grandeur of the Rockies, and especially its wildlife, a visit to the **ROCKY MOUNTAIN NATIONAL PARK** is essential. The park straddles the Continental Divide at elevations often well in excess of 10,000ft, with large sections inhabited by elk herds, moose, black bears and bighorn sheep. A full third of the park is above the tree line, and large areas of snow never melt; the name of the **Never Summer Mountains** speaks volumes about the long, empty expanses of arctic-style tundra. The park's lower reaches, among the rich forests, hold patches of lush greenery;

you never know when you may stumble upon a sheltered mountain meadow flecked with flowers. Parallels with the European Alps spring to mind – helped, of course, by the heavy-handed Swiss and Bavarian themes of so many local motels and restaurants. Note however, that at a tenth of the size of Yellowstone, the park attracts a similar number of visitors – more than three million per year, the bulk of whom come in high summer, meaning that the one main road through the mountains can get incredibly congested.

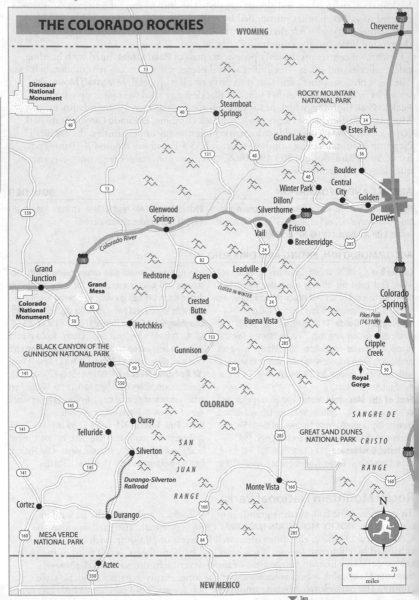

THE COLORADO ROCKIES

HIKING THE ROCKY MOUNTAIN NATIONAL PARK

As ever, the best way to appreciate the Rocky Mountain National Park is on foot. With dozens of superb **hikes** to choose from, think what kind of experience you're after – photographing a particular animal, for instance, or hiking across the Continental Divide – and enlist a ranger to help plan your excursion. Bear in mind that the delicate ecosystem makes it essential to stay on the paths, and be watchful of your own system too; plan hikes conservatively and drink plenty of water to avoid altitude sickness and dehydration.

The obvious launching point for numerous day and overnight hikes is **Bear Lake**, a pretty spot at the end of a spur road from Estes Park where the mountains are framed to perfection in its cool, still waters.

Trail Ridge Road

The showpiece of the park is **Trail Ridge Road** (open late May to mid-Oct), the 45-mile stretch of US-34 that connects the small gateway towns of Estes Park and Grand Lake. The highest-elevation paved road in any US national park (cresting at 12,183ft) it affords a succession of tremendous views, and several short trails start from car parks along the way. Majestic peaks and alpine tundra are at their most breathtaking to either side of the **Alpine Visitor Center** (see below), halfway along at Fall River Pass. If you're generally happy to admire the scenery from your car, the visitor centre is really the only requisite stop along the way, for its **exhibits** explaining the flora and fauna of the tundra and also its simple, good-value **cafeteria**. Good areas for wildlife viewing lie a little further east along Trail Ridge Road.

Old Fall River Road

An alternative scenic drive through the park follows the unpaved, summer-only **Old Fall River Road**, completed in 1920. Running east–west (one-way) along the bed of a U-shaped glacial valley, it doesn't have open mountain vistas, but it's much quieter than its paved counterpart, and there's far more chance of spotting **wildlife**: roaming the area are moose, coyote, mountain lions and black bears, which, with the park's plentiful natural food supply, tend to avoid contact with humans.

ARRIVAL AND INFORMATION   ROCKY MOUNTAIN NATIONAL PARK

Access and entry fees The park is open daily 24hr. Admission is $20/car.

By car Coming from the east on US-36 you'll arrive at the gateway town of Estes Park, 65 miles northwest of Denver. To reach the western entrance, 85 miles from Denver, turn north off I-70 onto US-40, which negotiates Berthoud Pass en route to Grand Lake. There is no public transport to the park or the gateway towns.

Visitor centres The park HQ and Beaver Meadows Visitor Center is 3 miles west of Estes Park on US-36 (daily 8am–4.30pm; ☎ 970 586 1206, ⊛ nps.gov/room). The Fall River Visitor Center is 5 miles west of Estes Park on US-34 (daily 9am–5pm). The Kawuneeche Visitor Center is a mile north of Grand Lake on US-34 (daily 8am–4.30pm). The Alpine Visitor Center (late May to early Oct daily 10.30am–4.30pm) is on Trail Ridge Rd. Note that the Moraine Park Visitor Center was closed in 2013 due to sequestration (check the website for the latest).

GETTING AROUND

By shuttle bus Free shuttle buses (late May to early Oct, daily 7am–7pm) run through the park; between Moraine Park Visitor Center (closed at the time of writing) and the Fern Lake (every 20min), and between Moraine Park Visitor Center and Bear Lake (every 15min). Free shuttles also link the Moraine Park Visitor Center with Estes Park at the entrance to the park (6.30am–8pm), every 30min–1hr.

By bike New Venture Cycling, 2050 Big Thompson Ave, Estes Park (daily 9am–4pm; ☎ 970 231 2736, ⊛ newventure cycling.com), offers rentals ($16/hr, $55/day) and tours along Trail Ridge Rd (from $75).

ACCOMMODATION AND EATING

ESTES PARK

Alpine Trail Ridge Inn 927 Moraine Ave (US-36) ☎ 970 586 4585, ⊛ alpinetrailridgeinn.com. Comfortable, standard motel accommodation, a short drive from the park entrance, with outdoor heated pool and spacious rooms. Open May to early Oct. **$112**

Baldpate Inn 4900 S Hwy-7 ☎ 970 586 5397, ⓦ baldpate inn.com. Local restaurants are generally poor, though the excellent dinner buffet at this 1917 inn includes hearty soups, freshly baked gourmet breads and a range of salads (make sure you check out the "Key Room" before you leave). Late May to mid-Oct daily 11.30am–8pm.

Stanley Hotel 333 Wonderview Ave ☎ 970 577 4000, ⓦ stanleyhotel.com. Historic inn, occupying a fantastic mountainside location since 1909. It's perhaps best known for inspiring Stephen King's *The Shining*, but don't let that put you off – the rooms and condos are ultra-luxurious and demon free. $160

GRAND LAKE

Blue Water Bakery Café 928 Grand Ave ☎ 970 627 5416. Serves fine coffee, pastries and sandwiches, as well as more exotic items like mango coconut scones. Daily 6am–5pm.

Fat Cat Café 916 Grand Ave ☎ 970 627 0900. Right on the lake, this small café knocks out a tasty breakfast buffet at weekends ($12), excellent coffee and cinnamon rolls. Mon & Wed–Fri 7am–2pm, Sat & Sun 7am–1pm.

Grand Lake Brewing Co 99921 US-34 (4 miles south of Grand Lake) ☎ 970 627 9404, ⓦ grandlakebrewing .com. This being Colorado it would be remiss to skip the

local brewpub, despite the early closing; who can resist Woolly Booger Nut Brown Ale or Stumpjumper IPA? Mon–Thurs & Sun noon–8pm, Fri & Sat noon–9pm.

★ **Shadowcliff Lodge** 100 Summerland Park Rd ☎ 970 627 9220, ⓦ shadowcliff.org. Gorgeous, log-built youth hostel, perched high in the woods, which has dorm rooms and clean, comfortable doubles, and also hosts residential workshops on environmental themes. Open June–Sept. Dorms $27, doubles $130

Western Riviera Lakeside Lodging 419 Garfield St ☎ 970 627 3580, ⓦ westernriv.com. Sixteen old-fashioned but clean rooms overlooking the lake, with microwaves and cable TV. $140

CAMPING

Campgrounds Five official campgrounds provide the only accommodation within the park ($20/night); all fill early each day in summer, when reservations are essential for Moraine Park, Glacier Basin and Aspenglen (☎ 518 885 3639, ⓦ recreation.gov), while Longs Peak and Timber Creek remain first-come, first-served.

Backcountry camping You'll need a permit (May–Oct $20; Nov–April free; ☎ 970 586 1242), valid for up to seven days and available from either park headquarters or the Kawuneeche Visitor Center (see p.675).

Winter Park

The former railroad centre of **WINTER PARK**, 67 miles northwest of Denver, may not be Colorado's trendiest resort, but it was one of the first, established by the city of Denver in 1938 and now the third largest in the state.

Its wide, ever-expanding variety of ski and bike terrain, friendly atmosphere, family attractions and good-value lodgings draw more than a million visitors a year. Its namesake **ski resort** (mid-Nov to mid-April; various passes available; ⓦ winterparkresort .com) also has exceptional facilities for kids and disabled skiers, as well as the 200-acre **Discovery Park**, an excellent, economical area for beginners. Experienced skiers, in turn, relish mogul runs on Mary Jane Mountain, the fluffy snows of the Parsenn Bowl and the backcountry idyll of Vasquez Cirque.

Summer visitors enjoy six hundred miles of excellent **mountain-biking** trails, the best of which are accessible from the chairlift, in addition to the exhilarating 1.5-mile-long **Alpine Slide** sled ride ($15), and several contemporary music festivals.

ARRIVAL AND INFORMATION   WINTER PARK

By bus Home James shuttle buses travel from Denver airport ($100 one-way; ☎ 800 359 7503, ⓦ homejames transportation.com). Once you're in town an excellent network of free shuttle buses means you don't need a car.

By train The nearest Amtrak station is at 205 Fraser Ave, 5 miles north of Winter Park in Fraser.

Chamber of Commerce 151 W Lyman Ave (Mon–Fri 8.30am–5pm, Sat 9am–3pm; ☎ 407 644 8281, ⓦ winter park.org).

Hotel reservations Hotels and condos near the ski area can be booked through Winter Park Central Reservations (☎ 970 726 1564, ⓦ winterparkresort.com).

Steamboat Springs

Surrounded by wide, snowy valleys, **STEAMBOAT SPRINGS**, 65 miles north of I-70 via Hwy-131, is where Colorado's skiing industry was born. When Norwegian ski-jump champion Karl Hovelsen moved here in 1914, it was still a ranching town, but after he designed his own ski jump locals soon caught on and today the town is home to more Winter Olympic champions than any other resort, while each February, the town's **Winter Carnival** celebrates the season with a range of fun events (details from the visitor centre).

Steamboat's top-notch **ski resort** (ⓦsteamboat.com), snuggled into Mount Werner four miles south of downtown, is boosted by dogsled expeditions, hot-air ballooning and snowmobiling. The town also benefits from its hot springs: you can soak year-round in the secluded 105°F **Strawberry Park Hot Springs** (Mon–Thurs & Sun 10am–10.30pm, Fri & Sat till midnight; $10; ⓦstrawberryhotsprings.com), seven miles north of town and only accessible by 4WD in winter; various shuttles, detailed on the website, make the trip from town. The **Old Town Hot Springs** at 136 Lincoln Ave (Mon–Fri 5.30am–9.45pm, Sat 7am–8.45pm, Sun 8am–8.45pm; pools $16, waterslides $6, fitness centre $16; ⓦsteamboathotsprings.org) has more of a water-park feel.

ARRIVAL, GETTING AROUND AND INFORMATION — STEAMBOAT SPRINGS

By plane Most winter visitors fly into Yampa Valley Regional Airport, 22 miles west of Steamboat Springs in Hayden; GO Alpine Airport Shuttle (☏970 879 2800, ⓦgoalpine.com) runs buses to the resort ($36.30 one-way; $57.20 return) and also direct from Denver Airport ($90 one-way).

By shuttle bus From town, free SST buses (daily 7am–1.45am, every 20min; ☏970 879 3717) run the 4 miles to and from the ski resort.

Visitor centre 125 Anglers Drive (June–Aug Mon–Sat 8am–6pm, Sun 10am–4pm; Sept–May Mon–Fri 8am–5pm, Sat 10am–3pm, Sun 9am–6pm; ☏970 879 0880, ⓦsteamboat-chamber.com).

ACCOMMODATION AND EATING

Café Diva 1855 Ski Time Square Drive ☏970 871 0508, ⓦcafediva.com. Fine restaurant, serving sophisticated, seasonal dishes – Boulder Valley beef tenderloin ($36) and house-cured buffalo carpaccio ($16), for example. Daily 5.30–11pm.

Hazie's 2305 Mount Werner Circle ☏970 871 5150. Expensive New American cuisine but worth it; throws in a free gondola ride up the slope with the price of a meal (three-course *prix fixe* from $36). Mid-Dec to March Mon–Wed 11.30am–2.30pm, Thurs–Sun 11.30am–2.30pm & 5–10pm; mid-June to Aug Thurs–Sat 5–10pm.

Rabbit Ears Motel 201 Lincoln Ave ☏970 879 1150, ⓦrabbitearsmotel.com. Good, friendly, family-owned motel, with spacious rooms, flat-screen TVs and microwaves. $109

★ **Strawberry Park Hot Springs** 4200 Hwy-36 ☏970 879 0342, ⓦstrawberryhotsprings.com. This hot springs resort offers quirky accommodation in bare-bones cabins and (in summer) converted wagons (must provide bedding for both) or a two-storey train carriage by the springs; camping is also available. Cabins $65, wagons $60, train carriages $115, camping $55

Summit County

The purpose-built ski resorts, old mining towns, snow-covered peaks, alpine meadows and crystal lakes that make up **Summit County** lie alongside I-70, roughly seventy miles west of Denver. This section of the interstate was one of the last in the national system to be completed, and is justly regarded as an engineering marvel: it crosses the Continental Divide via the Eisenhower Tunnel, at 11,158ft, before snaking high above Vail Pass. Beyond the simple pleasure of driving I-70, the most enticing target is the mountain town of **BRECKENRIDGE** (11 miles south of the highway at a mere 9603ft), where streets are lined with brightly painted Victorian houses, shops and cafés. This is the liveliest of Summit County's four towns; born in 1859 as a gold rush camp, it boasts a large historic district (with homes from the 1890s and early 1900s), touristy but tasteful stores, art galleries and cool restaurants.

ARRIVAL, GETTING AROUND AND INFORMATION — SUMMIT COUNTY

By bus Greyhound buses stop at the Frisco Transfer Center (☏970 668 9290), 1010 Meadow Drive, just off I-70 exit 203, from where free buses (see p.678) radiate to the surrounding ski resorts. Shuttles from Denver airport include Colorado Mountain Express, which runs to the Transfer Center for $49 and Keystone, Copper Mountain and Breckenridge for $64 (☏970 926 9800, ⓦcoloradomountainexpress.com). Summit Express serves the same destinations for slightly cheaper rates

11

SKIING AND SUMMERS IN SUMMIT COUNTY

Winter is the busiest time in Summit County. **Breckenridge Ski Resort** (☎970 453 5000, ⓦbreckenridge.com), the oldest of the area's four top-class resorts, spans four peaks and offers ideal terrain as does the plush **Keystone Ski Resort** (☎970 496 4500, ⓦkeystoneresort.com), where the biggest night-ski operation in the US permits skiing until 8.30pm. The smallest resort in the county, **Arapahoe Basin** ("A-Basin"; ☎970 468 0718, ⓦarapahoebasin.com), offers great above-tree-line bowl skiing. The slopes at **Copper Mountain** (☎970 968 2318, ⓦcoppercolorado.com) are divided into three clear ability sections.

In **summer**, mountain bikers and road-racers alike especially relish **cycling** the stretch of Hwy-9 between Frisco and Breckenridge; **Alpine Sports** at 435 N Park Ave in Breckenridge (daily 8am–5.30pm; ☎970 453 9623) is good for rental bikes (its **Vail Pass Bike Shuttle** takes you to the top of Vail Pass so you can cruise fourteen miles downhill on a paved bike path all the way back). Each resort runs a chairlift or **gondola** to the top of the mountains for access to great **hiking** and cycling trails. Keystone is particularly outstanding for its mountain-bike trails with world-class downhill and cross-country trails accessed by its lifts (mid-June to early Sept, Mon–Thurs & Sun 10am–5pm, Fri & Sat 10am–7pm; day pass $39). Breckenridge offers its Summer Fun Park (mid-June to early Sept daily 9.30am–5.30pm; all-day pass $68), featuring toboggan rides down the dry **Alpine Slide** (single ride $18), as well as trampolining ($15), mini-golf ($10) and a giant maze ($10).

($45–61; ☎970 668 6000, ⓦsummitexpress.com). Destinations (Greyhound) Denver (2 daily; 1hr 45min); Glenwood Springs (3 daily; 1hr 50min); Grand Junction (3 daily; 3hr 30min); Vail (3 daily; 35min).

By local transport Summit Stage (daily 6.30am–1.30am; ☎970 668 0999, ⓦco.summit.co.us) provides free local transport from the Frisco Transfer Center to Breckenridge, Copper Mountain and Keystone. In Breckenridge itself, the free Town Trolley (☎970 547 3140) connects downtown with the ski resort every 20min (9am–midnight) during

ski season, and every 30min in the summer. The Free Ride bus system (☎970 547 3140, ⓦbreckfreeride.com) also connects town and the Summit Stage bus station with various ski slopes (daily 6.15am–11.15pm).

Breckenbridge Welcome Center & Museum 203 S Main St (daily 10am–6pm; ☎970 453 5579, ⓦtownof breckenridge.com). Supplies all sorts of information and maps, and also contains an excellent movie and museum on the history of the town. Ask here about local hiking and biking trails.

ACCOMMODATION

Lodging rates in Summit County double in winter. Frisco, near I-70, generally has the best-priced inns and motels, while Breckenridge holds a few downtown B&Bs and a large number of expensive slopeside condos; the Breckenridge Resort Chamber (☎970 453 2918, ⓦgobreck.com) has details of package deals. Resort accommodation at both Copper Mountain and Keystone (see above) is first class, and so too are the prices. For something with a little more character, the Summit Huts Association manages four backcountry huts in the area (July–Sept & Nov–May; ⓦsummithuts.org).

Allaire Timbers Inn 9511 Hwy-9, at River Park Drive, Breckenridge ☎970 453 7530, ⓦallairetimbers.com. Cosy wooden lodge on the edge of town, with each room featuring different themes from wolves and bears to rabbits and the more whimsical "moon and stars". Choose the luxury hot tub suites for a splurge. $149

Fireside Inn 114 N French St, Breckenridge ☎970 453 6456, ⓦfiresideinn.com. Homely little B&B with floral, antique-filled bedrooms (all with private bath), plus several cramped dorm rooms that share a TV lounge, showers and kitchenette. Dorms $30, doubles winter $140, doubles summer $101

Frisco Lodge 321 Main St, Frisco ☎970 668 0195, ⓦfriscolodge.com. Creaky B&B that oozes character, built back in 1885 in a vaguely Austrian style. Units have kitchenettes and access to an outdoor hot tub, and cooked buffet breakfast and teatime snacks are served in the cluttered lounge. $104

Skiway Lodge 275 Ski Hill Rd, Breckenridge ☎970 453 7573, ⓦskiwaylodge.com. Friendly, good-value motel a short walk from Main St, with spacious rooms sporting gas fireplaces, LCD TVs and balconies. Guests have access to two outdoor hot tubs and a fire pit. $99

EATING AND DRINKING

★ **Alpenglow Stube** Keystone Resort ☎970 496 4386. The best dining experience in Summit County

– take the free gondola ride to the top of 11,444ft North Peak, don Austrian slippers and feast in beautifu surroundings on New American cuisine with a Bavarian edge. Three-course set menus run $32.95 and up. Nov to mid-April daily 5.30–10pm, mid June to Aug limited hours.

Breckenridge Brewery 600 S Main St, Breckenridge ☎ 970 453 1550, ⓦ breckbrew.com. This huge brewpub, a landmark at the southern edge of town since 1990, serves good-quality microbrews (try the Avalanche Ale) and hearty pub food (burgers $9, fish and chips $11). Daily 11am–2am.

Gold Pan Saloon 103 N Main St ☎ 970 453 5499, ⓦ thegoldpansaloon.com. The local dive bar since 1879, with real swinging doors, cheap breakfasts and decent

burgers ($8.50), live music (Thurs) and DJs (Fri & Sat). Happy hour 4–7pm. Daily 7am–1.30am.

Hearthstone 130 S Ridge St ☎ 970 453 1148, ⓦ hearthstonerestaurant.biz. Restaurant in the gorgeous 1886 Kaiser House featuring local produce and seasonal menus, with mains such as blackberry elk ($39), cedar plank organic salmon ($29) and blue-crab-stuffed rainbow trout ($29). Daily 4–11pm.

Mary's Mountain Cookies 128 S Main St ☎ 970 547 4757, ⓦ marysmountaincookies.com. Knocking out delicious, hot cookies loaded with fudge, oatmeal, M&Ms, chocolate and macadamia nuts (from $1.99). Daily 10am–9pm.

Leadville

Ringed by snow-capped mountains at an elevation of more than 10,000ft, 24 miles south of I-70 and Summit County, the atmospheric old mining town of **LEADVILLE** (officially the highest city in the US), enjoys a magnificent vista of mounts Elbert (14,440ft) and Massive (14,421ft), Colorado's two highest peaks. Leadville is rich in character and history, its old red-brick streets abounding with tales of gunfights (Doc Holliday fought his last here), miners dying of exposure and graveyards being excavated to get at the seams. Gold was discovered in 1860, but silver took over in the 1870s and later copper and zinc; by 1880 Leadville was the second largest town in Colorado. After a seventeen-year shutdown, the Climax molybdenum mine reopened in 2012, resuming Leadville's longest tradition.

National Mining Hall of Fame & Museum

120 W 9th St • Daily: Nov to late May 11am–6pm; late May to Oct 9am–5pm • $7 ($10 combined with Matchless Mine) • ☎ 719 486 1229, ⓦ mininghalloffame.org

Leadville's rich history and the story of gold mining is chronicled at the **National Mining Hall of Fame & Museum**, which also owns and operates the Matchless Mine (see below), through exhibits, nuggets of real gold and a walk-through replica of an underground mine shaft.

Matchless Mine

E 7th St (1.25 miles east of town) • Late May to late Sept daily 10am–4.30pm • $7 ($10 combined with National Mining Hall of Fame & Museum) • ☎ 719 486 1229, ⓦ matchlessmine.com

In 1878, **Horace Tabor**, a storekeeper and one-time mayor who grubstaked prospectors in exchange for potential profits, hit the jackpot when two of his clients developed a silver mine that produced $20 million within a year. Collecting his one-third share, Tabor left his wife to marry waitress "**Baby Doe**" McCourt and purchased the profitable **Matchless Mine**. However, by the time of his death in 1899, Tabor was financially ruined. Baby Doe survived him by 36 years, living a hermit-like existence in the godforsaken wooden shacks above the Matchless Mine. The buildings still stand, two miles out of town, and in the crude wooden shack in which she died, emaciated and frostbitten, guides recount Baby Doe's bizarre saga in full, fascinating detail.

Tabor Opera House

308 Harrison Ave • June–Aug Mon–Sat 10am–5pm • $5 • ☎ 719 486 8409, ⓦ taboroperahouse.net

Silver king Horace Tabor funded construction of the stately red-brick **Tabor Opera House** in 1879, its old stage, ranks of red velvet-and-gilt seats and eerie, dusty old dressing rooms mostly unchanged since then. In 1882, garbed in black velvet knee britches and diamonds, **Oscar Wilde** addressed a host of dozing miners here on the

TOP OF THE ROCKIES

By far the most spectacular way to reach Aspen from Leadville is to drive over Independence Pass via the **Top of the Rockies National Scenic Byway** (aka Hwy-82; ⓦ topoftherockiesbyway.org), a scintillating route that passes the pretty village of Twin Lakes (ⓦ visittwinlakescolorado.com) and crosses the Continental Divide at 12,095ft. On the western side the road winds along the Roaring Fork River, past Independence Ghost Town, into Aspen. The pass is generally closed between November and late May; the alternate route via I-70 and Glenwood Springs adds an extra seventy miles to the trip from Denver.

"Practical Application of the Aesthetic Theory to Exterior and Interior House Decoration with Observations on Dress and Personal Ornament".

ACCOMMODATION, EATING AND DRINKING   **LEADVILLE**

Delaware Hotel 700 Harrison Ave ☎719 486 1418, ⓦ delawarehotel.com. Gorgeous Victorian hotel opened in 1886, with comfy, antique-filled rooms and *Callaway's* restaurant offering sandwiches ($10) and platters for $14 (Thurs–Sun 11.30am–8pm). Open May–Oct. **$70**

★ **Golden Burro Café** 710 Harrison Ave ☎719 486 1239, ⓦ goldenburro.com. Classic diner since 1938, with cosy booths and friendly local ladies serving hefty breakfasts (miner's platter $7.50), fried chicken ($9.95) and a meatloaf dinner ($10.95) – it's one of those places where the menu is fun to read. Mon–Thurs 6.30am–8pm, Fri & Sat 6.30am–9pm, Sun 6.30am–2pm.

Governor's Mansion Guest Suites 129 W 8th St ☎719 486 1865, ⓦ governorsmansion.net. Built in 1881 and once the home of former governor Jesse McDonald, this wonderful property now sports two spacious and tastefully decorated guest suites, both with full kitchens. **$110**

McGinnis Cottage Inn 809 Spruce St ☎719 486 3110, ⓦ mcginniscottage.com. Friendly B&B run by the accommodating Donna McGinnis in a clapboard home dating back to 1898, with three rooms all with flat-screen TVs. **$135**

Silver Dollar Saloon 315 Harrison Ave ☎719 486 9914. Leadville's oldest bar (1879) is a wood-panelled and welcoming watering hole filled, rather incongruously given the Wild West exterior, with Irish memorabilia. Daily 11am–2am.

★ **Two Guns Distillery** 401 Harrison Ave ⓦ twoguns distillery.com. This small distillery opened with a drinking area and patio in 2013, the perfect place to sample its excellent 1880s Wild West Whiskey and Single Six Rocky Mountain Moonshine (cocktails $7 and up). Mon–Fri 5–10pm, Sat & Sun 11am–11pm.

Aspen

While there's more than a grain of truth to the image of **ASPEN**, sixty miles west of Leadville (and 160 miles west of Denver), as a celebrity hangout, it's a perfectly accessible and appealing place for ordinary folks to visit, and in summer at least the room rates are affordable for all but those on shoestring budgets. Indeed, unlike in resorts like Vail, which are often deserted out of season, affordable housing and local development have made this a real working town where ski bums really do mingle with millionaires. While spending too much time in Aspen itself is something of a waste given the virtually limitless recreation opportunities in the neighbouring mountains, hanging out around the town's leafy pedestrianized streets or browsing in the chichi stores and galleries makes a pleasant way to spend a couple of hours. Visiting in winter does require more cash, though you can save money by commuting to the slopes from Glenwood Springs (see p.684), less than fifty miles away.

Brief history

From inauspicious beginnings in 1879, this pristine, remote and mountain-locked town established itself as one of the world's top **silver** producers. By the time the silver market crashed fourteen years later, it had acquired tasteful residential palaces, grand hotels and an opera house. Ironically enough, during the 1930s, when Aspen's population had slumped below seven hundred, the anti-poverty WPA programme gave the struggling community the cash to build its first crude ski lift. Entrepreneurs seized the opportunity presented by the varied terrain and plentiful snow, and the first chairlift was dedicated on **Aspen Mountain** in 1947. In 1950, inspired by its great natural beauty, Chicago businessman Walter Paepcke created what is now the **Aspen Institute**, a respected think-tank, and also helped found the **Aspen Music Festival** (classical music concerts July & Aug; ⓦaspenmusicfestival). Skiing really drove Aspen's growth, however, and it has since spread to three more mountains – **Aspen Highlands**, **Snowmass** and **Buttermilk**, with the jet set arriving in force during the 1960s. All four mountains are now operated by **Aspen Skiing Company** (ⓣ970 925 1220, ⓦaspensnowmass.com), with Highlands and especially Snowmass (on Brush Creek Rd, off Hwy-82) featuring their own "villages" of condos, shops and restaurants.

John Denver Sanctuary
Rio Grande Park (near the visitor centre) • Daily 24hr • Free

Beloved folk singer **John Denver** moved to Aspen in 1971, and was inspired to write many of his biggest hits, such as *Rocky Mountain High*, by the surrounding countryside. Denver was killed in an air crash in 1997, and the tranquil **John Denver Sanctuary** commemorates the singer with many of his songs etched into granite rocks – fans still gather at the memorial every year, on the anniversary of Denver's death (Oct 12).

11

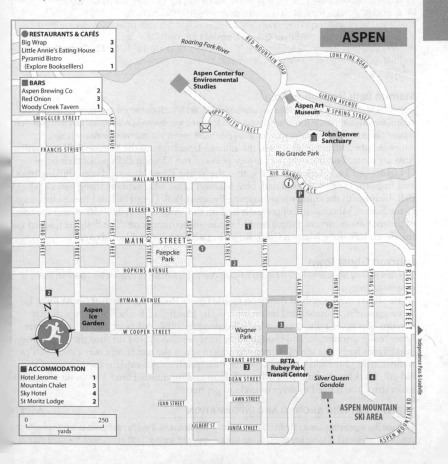

11

SKIING AND SUMMERS IN ASPEN

The mogul-packed monster of **Aspen Mountain**, looming over downtown, is for experienced skiers only. On the other hand, **Buttermilk** is great for beginners, with an excellent ski school managed by **Aspen Skiing Co** (w aspensnowmass.com; most lessons around $70) that offers a three-day guaranteed "Learn to Snowboard" programme; the wide-open runs of **Snowmass**, though mostly for intermediate skiers, feature some testing routes. **Aspen Highlands** has high-speed lifts and offers excellent extreme skiing terrain. The town's best value has to be its fifty miles of groomed **Nordic ski trails** – one of the most extensive free cross-country trail networks in the US. **Lift passes** are expensive (and feature a complicated pricing matrix); serious skiers will get better deals by buying a package with their accommodation. The "Classic Pass" generally starts at around $220 for four days, and $350 for seven days, but only for early and late season – peak-season prices will be considerably more (more than $600 for seven days). You can rent skis and snowboards at any Four-Mountain Sports stores at all four mountains for $49.95–59.95 per season.

Cycling is the main **summer** pursuit around Aspen; Timberline Bike Tours, 730 E Cooper Ave (☎ 970 274 6076, w timberlinebike.com), offers mountain bikes to rent, organized tours including multinight trips (from $85/day) and guidance on routes and difficulty levels. **Aspen Skiing Co** also rents a wide range of bikes (near the Gondola) from $63/day. The Roaring Fork River, surging out of the Sawatch Range, is excellent for **kayaking** and **rafting** during a short season that's typically over by early to mid-July. Beware, though, as sections of Class V rapids here are dangerous and every summer sees fatalities. Aspen Whitewater Rafting, 520 Durant St (☎ 970 920 3511, w aspenwhitewater.com), offers guided trips (from $80.50 for a half day).

If you fancy **walking** in the mountains, an easy way to get your bearings and enjoy great valley views is to take the **Silver Queen Gondola** from 601 Dean St to the summit of Aspen Mountain (mid-June to early Sept daily 10am–4pm; $28; ☎ 970 925 1220). **Elk Camp Gondola** (mid-June to early Sept daily 10am–4pm; $28) runs up Snowmass.

Maroon Bells Recreation Area

Maroon Creek Rd • Daily 24hr • $10/vehicle; $6 bus tour, includes admission • ☎ 970 925 3445 • From mid-June to early Sept, between 9am and 5pm, access is by bike, skates, on foot and public bus only (Castle/Maroon bus from downtown); in Sept the road opens to cars Mon–Thurs and buses only Fri–Sun; the road normally closes completely once it snows (open to cross-country skiers or snowmobile tours)

An essential excursion from Aspen, the alluring landscapes of the **Maroon Bells Recreation Area** are centred on the twin purple-grey peaks of the Maroon Bells peaks themselves (14,014ft and 14,156ft), protected within the White River National Forest. Hiking trails lead from the car park around dark blue Maroon Lake, where mesmerizing views of the Bells blend with the equally jaw-dropping Pyramid Peak (14,018ft) and the reddish crags of the Sievers Mountains. Longer trails lead up to Crater Lake (10,076ft), nearer the base of the mountains, where a small herd of moose sometimes graze. The Bells are reached via the eleven-mile-long Maroon Creek Road, but **access is limited** (see above).

Ashcroft Ghost Town

Castle Creek Rd • Daily 24hr; tours mid-June to Aug daily 9am–5pm • Mid-June to Aug tours $3, otherwise free • ☎ 970 925 3721, w aspenhistorysociety.com

Some eleven miles south of Aspen on Castle Creek Road, the **Ashcroft Ghost Town** is an enigmatic site surrounded by mountains, its handful of timber buildings all that remains of a silver mining community founded in 1880. Ashcroft and its mines were never really sustainable, and though a few hardy settlers stayed on into the 1920s, most inhabitants had gone after just five years. Even when the site is officially closed you can wander around the old buildings for free (interpretive signs explain the history of the old jail, blacksmith shop, Blue Mirror Saloon and infamous Hotel View), set along one main strip. You'll need to drive or cycle to get here.

ARRIVAL, GETTING AROUND AND INFORMATION   ASPEN

By plane Tiny Aspen-Pitkin County Airport (w aspenairport .com) lies 4 miles north of town; free buses run into Aspen

and Snowmass. If you fly into Denver, connecting flights may only cost another $100 or so, much the same price as a shuttle from Denver airport with Colorado Mountain Express ($118; ☎ 970 926 9800, ⓦ coloradomountainexpress.com).

By bus and train The nearest Amtrak and Greyhound stations are in Glenwood Springs (p.684), 40 miles from Aspen. RFTA buses (see below) run to Aspen for $7 (1hr 40min).

Local buses Free RFTA buses (☎ 970 925 8484, ⓦ rfta.com), centred on the Rubey Park transit station on Durant St in the heart of town, connect the four mountains with each other in winter, plus the airport and outlying areas (Aspen to Snowmass Village is free and runs all year). Access to Maroon Bells is limited (see opposite).

Visitor centre 425 Rio Grande Place (Mon–Fri 8.30am–5pm; ☎ 970 925 1940, ⓦ aspenchamber.org).

ACCOMMODATION

Stay Aspen Snowmass Central Reservations (☎ 970 925 9000, ⓦ stayaspensnowmass.com) runs a helpful service and doesn't balk if you ask for the cheapest available room; it also arranges package deals combining accommodation with lift tickets. Rates vary considerably even in winter, and are lowest in the "value seasons" (last week in Nov, first two weeks of Dec and first two weeks of April). Prices also reduce dramatically during the summer, when **camping** is also a good cheap option; there are nine USFS campgrounds around Aspen, of which only a handful can be reserved (☎ 518 885 3639, ⓦ recreation.gov). Several campgrounds are on Maroon Creek Road south of Aspen, while smaller options abound east of town toward Independence Pass.

Hotel Jerome 330 E Main St ☎ 970 920 1000, ⓦ hotel jerome.com. Stately downtown landmark built in 1889 at the height of the silver boom, re-fitted with the gamut of modern amenities. Luxurious rooms feature period wallpaper, antique brass and cast-iron beds. **$450**

Mountain Chalet 333 E Durant Ave ☎ 970 925 7797, ⓦ mountainchaletaspen.com. Friendly mountain lodge with large, comfortable rooms, pool, hot tub, gym and fine buffet breakfast. Some dorm-style beds are available in winter, along with more straightforward rooms. Dorms **$59**, doubles winter **$209**, doubles summer **$129**

★ **Sky Hotel** 709 E Durant Ave ☎ 970 925 6760, ⓦ theskyhotel.com. Fashionable slopeside hotel sporting chic, 1970s-style decor; playful rooms have faux-fur throws, wi-fi and game consoles. There's also a hot tub, fitness room and outdoor pool, while its *39 Degrees* bar is a choice après-ski spot. Winter **$394**, summer **$213**

St Moritz Lodge 334 W Hyman Ave ☎ 970 925 3220, ⓦ stmoritzlodge.com. A short walk from central downtown, with well-priced dorms and private rooms that tend to be booked way in advance. Facilities include a small heated pool and a comfortable common room. Continental breakfast included in winter. Dorms **$48**, doubles winter **$199**, doubles summer **$174**

EATING, DRINKING AND NIGHTLIFE

Nightlife in Aspen is at its peak in the après-ski winter season, but there's always something going on year-round. In summer, downtown hosts several top-notch festivals, including the summer-long Aspen Music Festival (☎ 970 925 9042, ⓦ aspenmusicfestival.com), when orchestras and operas feature well-known international performers, as well as promising students.

Aspen Brewing Co 304 E Hopkins Ave, ☎ 970 920 2739, ⓦ aspenbrewingcompany.com. Check out the tasting room of Aspen's very own microbrewery, serving brews such as the hoppy Independence Pass IPA, and the malty Brown Bearale (pints $4.75, pitchers $15). Daily noon–11.30pm.

Big Wrap 520 E Durant Ave ☎ 970 544 1700. Cheap eats in central Aspen? No wonder this place is so popular, with tasty, wholesome wraps at just $6.95, and nutrient-rich smoothies for $4.05. Mon–Sat 10am–6pm.

★ **Little Annie's Eating House** 517 E Hyman Ave ☎ 970 925 1098, ⓦ littleannies.com. Lively, popular and unpretentious saloon-style restaurant from 1972, serving potato pancakes ($9.95), hearty beef stews ($9.95) and salads at lunch, and huge trout, salmon, chicken, beef or rib dinner platters for $20.95–25.95. Daily 11.30am–10pm (bar open until 1.30am).

Pyramid Bistro (Explore Booksellers) 221 E Main St ☎ 970 925 5338, ⓦ pyramidbistro.com. Fantastic bookstore with a shady roof terrace and an upstairs café serving creative vegetarian dishes, organic tofu and veggie stir fries ($12), wild salmon ($18), sweet potato and parsnip gnocchi ($13) and salads ($12). Daily 11.30am–9.30pm.

Red Onion 420 E Cooper Ave ☎ 970 925 9955, ⓦ redonionaspen.com. Aspen's oldest pub, dating from 1892, delivers decent beers and burgers (from $12.50) and serves bar snacks (sliders $3) and big plates (grilled trout $18.92). Daily 11am–2am.

Woody Creek Tavern 2858 Upper River Rd, Woody Creek ☎ 970 923 4585, ⓦ woodycreektavern.com. Rustic tavern in tiny Woody Creek, 7 miles northwest along Hwy-82, where ranch hands, Aspen visitors and the occasional celebrity local (Hunter S. Thompson was a frequent patron) shoot pool, guzzle fresh lime-juice margaritas and eat good Tex-Mex. Daily 11am–10pm.

Vail

Compared to most other Colorado ski towns, **VAIL**, 97 miles west of Denver on I-70, is a new creation: just a handful of farmers lived here before the resort opened in 1962. The town sprawls eight miles or so along the narrow valley floor, with nuclei from east to west at **Vail Village** – the area's main social centre – Lionshead, Cascade Village and West Vail. Vail Resorts, which operates the ski area at Vail, owns an even more exclusive gated resort, **Beaver Creek**, eleven miles further west on I-70 (the small towns of Avon, Eagle-Vail and Edwards extend the resort area still further along the valley). Each area is pedestrianized and linked by **free shuttle buses** between them and the lifts. The villages themselves are mostly uninspiring collections of Tyrolean-style chalets and concrete-block condos, pockmarked by pricey fashion boutiques and often painfully pretentious restaurants; the real highlights are the stunning mountain scenery and activities on offer. Indeed, given the exceptional quality of the snow, and the sheer size and variety of terrain available, Vail is a formidable winter sport destination. In summer, you can use the lifts to go **mountain biking**, best at Vail, and **hiking**, best at the quieter Beaver Creek. Note, however, that unlike Aspen, Vail is essentially just a big resort, and often deserted out of season.

ARRIVAL AND INFORMATION   VAIL

By plane From Denver International Airport, several companies offer shuttles to Vail and Beaver Creek, including Colorado Mountain Express ($82; ☎970 926 9800, ⓦcoloradomountainexpress.com). More convenient (hence more expensive) flights are available to Eagle County Regional Airport (ⓦflyvail.com), just 35 miles west of Vail. Ground transport from the airport to either resort is just $4 on Eagle County Transit (ⓦeaglecounty.us/Transit/).
Visitor centre 101 Fawcett Rd, Avon (Mon–Thurs 8am–5pm, Fri 8am–4pm; ☎970 476 1000, ⓦvisitvailvalley.com).

ACCOMMODATION

Sonnenalp Hotel 20 Vail Rd Village ☎970 476 5656, ⓦsonnenalp.com. For the full Vail experience splash out on this luxury hotel bang in the centre of Vail, with an excellent spa, Alpine theme and spacious suites with Bavarian furniture, fireplaces and large bathrooms with heated floors. __$250__
Tivoli Lodge 386 Hanson Ranch Rd ☎970 476 5615, ⓦtivolilodge.com. Family-owned hotel with comfy rooms, pool, whirlpool and sauna; rates include a continental breakfast, and you can find bargains online. __$230__

EATING AND DRINKING

★ **CinéBistro (Solaris)** 141 East Meadow Drive ☎970 476 3344, ⓦcobbcinebistro.com/solaris. Cool concept: watch the latest movies while dining from a quality American bistro menu (oven-baked goat's cheese $12; buttermilk-fried chicken $16.50). Show tickets $15 (kids 3–12 $12). Doors open daily, 30min before first showtime.
★ **Little Diner** 616 W Lionshead Circle ☎970 476 4279, ⓦthelittlediner.com. Legendary 1950s style diner, best experienced over a lazy breakfast ($8–10), though you may have to wait: it only seats twenty around a U-shaped counter. There's a selection of grilled and cold sandwiches for lunch. Daily 7am–2pm.
Moe's Original BBQ 616 W Lionshead Circle ☎970 479 7888, ⓦmoesoriginalbbq.com. Genuine hot-pit Alabama barbecue; try the pulled pork sandwich, wings with special sauces and the superb mac and cheese. Daily 11am–4pm.
Terra Bistro 352 E Meadow Drive ☎970 476 6836, ⓦterrabistrovail.com. Good for a splurge, this is a little gem among many posh restaurants in Vail; organic, farm-to-table dishes include raspberry green salad ($11), and cornmeal-crusted trout fillet ($16.50). Daily 7.30–10am, 11am–2.30pm & 5–10pm.
Westside Cafe & Market 2211 N Frontage Rd W ☎970 476 7890, ⓦwestsidecafe.net. Dressed up like a Colorado mining shack with outdoor seating, this is a top breakfast spot, best known for its twists on eggs Benedict (try the crab cake version). Daily 7am–10pm.

Glenwood Springs

Bustling, touristy **GLENWOOD SPRINGS** sits at the western end of impressive Glenwood Canyon, 157 miles west of Denver on I-70 and within striking distance of both Vail and Aspen; as such, it offers those with their own vehicle a budget base for either destination. Just north of the confluence of the Roaring Fork and

Colorado rivers, the town was long used by the Ute people as a place of relaxation thanks to its **hot springs**, which became the target for unscrupulous speculators who broke treaties and established resort facilities in the 1880s. North from downtown and across the Eagle River is the town's main attraction, the huge **Glenwood Hot Springs Pool**, 410 N River St (daily: June–Aug 7.30am–10pm; Sept–May 9am–10pm; $14.25–19.25; whotspringspool.com), offering spa services in addition to two large pools, waterslides and a mini-golf course ($6.50). More intimate are the natural, subterranean steam baths of the nearby **Yampah Spa Vapor Caves**, 709 E 6th St (daily 9am–9pm; from $12; wyampahspa.com), where you can relax on cool marble benches set deep in ancient caves and enjoy a variety of classy spa treatments. Also on the north side of town is the **Glenwood Caverns Adventure Park**, 508 Pine St (summer daily 9am–9pm, hours vary at other times; day pass $48; wglenwoodcaverns.com), with thrill rides, horseback rides and caverns that extend for two miles, with chambers reaching 50ft.

ARRIVAL, GETTING AROUND AND INFORMATION — GLENWOOD SPRINGS

By bus Greyhound buses stop 2 miles west of downtown at the petrol station at 51171 US-6, just off I-70.
Destinations Denver (2 daily; 3hr 35min–3hr 45min); Grand Junction (3 daily; 1hr 35min); Vail (2 daily; 1hr 20min).
By train Amtrak services arrive at 413 7th St in the heart of downtown.

Destinations Denver (1 daily; 6hr 28min); Grand Junction (1 daily; 2hr 4min); Salt Lake City (1 daily; 9hr 12min).
Local buses RFTA buses run every 30min (daily 6.53am–7.53pm; $1; wrfta.com).
Visitor centre 802 Grand Ave (June–Aug Mon–Fri 9am–5pm, Sat & Sun 9am–1pm; Sept–May Mon–Fri 9am–5pm; t970 945 6589, wglenwoodchamber.com).

ACCOMMODATION, EATING AND DRINKING

Best Kept Secret B&B 915 Colorado Ave t970 945 8586, wbestkeptsecretbb.com. Historic B&B just off the main drag, set in a blossom-covered 1914 home with just two lovely en-suite rooms; the huge breakfasts are great but the best feature is the outdoor hot tub. **$132**
Glenwood Canyon Brewing Co Hotel Denver, 402 7th St t970 945 1276, wglenwoodcanyon.com. Cooks up reliable pub grub, great burgers and excellent handcrafted microbrews. Mon–Thurs & Sun 11am–11pm, Fri & Sat 11am–midnight.
Glenwood Motor Inn 141 W 6th St t970 945 5438, wglenwoodmotorinn.com. This good-value, family-owned

motel has clean, comfortable rooms a couple of blocks away from the hot springs. **$74**
Hotel Denver 402 7th St t970 945 6565, wthehotel denver.com. Dating back to 1914, the grandfather of Glenwood resort hotels has recently been restored with an elegant, 1920s theme, though rooms come with modern amenities. **$130**
Rosi's Little Bavarian Restaurant 141 W 6th St t970 928 9186, wrosisbavarian.com. Great breakfast joint, with Vienna crêpes, wholewheat pancakes and bratwurst plates in addition to the usual items. Don't miss the home-made Bavarian pastries. Wed–Mon 7am–1pm.

Grand Junction and around

The immediate environs of **GRAND JUNCTION**, 87 miles west of Glenwood Springs on I-70, are awash in outdoor opportunities, and within a fifty-mile stretch you can trace the transition from fertile alpine valley to full-blown desert. Although initial impressions are unfavourable – a sprawl of factory units and sales yards lines the I-70 Business Loop – the tiny **downtown** is much nicer, with leafy boulevards

---

MOUNTAIN BIKING GRAND JUNCTION

The Grand Junction area is prime mountain biking territory, with a network of local trails just outside the city; visit Ruby Canyon Cycles at 301 Main St (Mon–Fri 9am–6pm, Sat 9am–5pm; t970 241 0141, wrubycanyoncycles.com) for trail information and rentals. You can also try the smooth, rolling single-track trails in nearby Fruita; Over the Edge Sports, 202 E Aspen Ave (daily 9am–6pm; t970 858 7220, wotesports.com), in the centre of town, has trail information and rental bikes (from $49/day).

hemming in a small, tree-lined historic district dotted with sculptures and stores. Nevertheless, the main attractions lie in the surrounding rugged and spectacular high desert country.

Dinosaur Journey Museum

550 Jurassic Court, Fruita • May–Sept daily 9am–5pm; Oct–April Mon–Sat 10am–4pm, Sun noon–4pm • $8.50, kids $5.25 • ☏ 970 858 7282, ⓦ museumofwesternco.com

Although the Colorado section of Dinosaur National Monument (ⓦ nps.gov/dino) is ninety miles north of Grand Junction, the town of **Fruita**, twelve miles west of town, contains the intriguing **Dinosaur Journey Museum**. The interactive museum features robotic displays of several kinds of dinosaurs, as well as a collection of giant, locally excavated bones – all helping to create a vivid picture of these prehistoric beasts. Its Dino Digs programme (ⓦ dinodigs.org) offers half- to five-day **digs** nearby.

Colorado National Monument

1750 Rim Rock Drive, Fruita • **Monument** Daily 24hr • $10/vehicle, good for a week **Visitor centre** Daily: June–Aug 8am–6pm; Dec–Feb 9am–4pm; March–May & Sept–Nov 9am–5pm • ☏ 970 858 3617, ⓦ nps.gov/colm

Grand Junction's main attraction is the mesmerizing scenery of **Colorado National Monument**, where more than two hundred million years of wind and water erosion have gouged out rock spires, domes, arches, pedestals and balanced rocks along a line of cliffs a few miles south of the city; the colourful result makes for an enthralling painted desert of warm reds, stunning purples, burnt oranges and rich browns. The park has two entrances at either end of twisting, 23-mile **Rim Rock Drive**, which links a string of spectacular overlooks with the **visitor centre** at the north end of the park (exit 19, I-70). Short hikes along the way afford views of several monoliths, while longer treks get right down to the canyon floor.

ARRIVAL AND INFORMATION

GRAND JUNCTION

By bus Greyhound buses stop at 230 S 5th St on the edge of downtown, three blocks east of the train station.
Destinations Denver (3 daily; 4hr 20min–5hr 20min); Glenwood Springs (2 daily; 1hr 35min); Las Vegas (2 daily; 9hr 30min); Vail (2 daily; 2hr 50min).
By train The Amtrak station is at 339 South 1st St on the edge of downtown.
Destinations Denver (1 daily; 8hr 15min); Glenwood Springs (1 daily; 1hr 47min); Salt Lake City (1 daily; 6hr 55min).
Visitor centre 740 Horizon Drive (Mon–Fri 8.30am–5pm; ☏ 800 962 2547, ⓦ visitgrandjunction.com).

ACCOMMODATION AND EATING

El Palomino Motel 2400 North Ave ☏ 970 242 1826, ⓦ elpalominomotel.com. Older-style 1950s motel but great value, with clean, quiet rooms, decent continental breakfast, flat-screen TVs and pool. **$60**
Grand Junction Bed and Breakfast 3153 F Rd (I-70 exit 37) ☏ 970 261 3938, ⓦ grandjunctionbnb.com. Cosy bungalow B&B close to downtown, offering breakfast on the outdoor deck and plush, spotless rooms – owners Judy and Sam are especially friendly. **$115**
Kannah Creek Brewing Co 1960 N 12th St ☏ 970 263 0111, ⓦ kcbcgj.com. Popular brewpub with outdoor seating, which serves decent pizza (from $8.49), pastas (from $10.99), salads (from $6.49), wine and cider on tap and tasty microbrewed beers (pints $4, pitchers $14; happy hour daily 3–6pm, $3 pints, $12 pitchers). Mon–Thurs & Sun 11am–10pm, Fri & Sat 11am–11pm.
Main St Café 504 Main St ☏ 970 242 7225, ⓦ mainstreetcafegj.com. Tasty breakfasts and lunches are available at this retro 1950s diner; try the Elvis burger (green chilli burger with cheddar) for $8.50, or the veggie Reuben garden burger ($7.55). Daily 7am–4pm.

Black Canyon of the Gunnison National Park

Hwy-347 (off US-50, 15 miles east of Montrose) • Daily 24hr • **South Rim Rd** April to mid-Nov • $15/vehicle, good for a week **South Rim Visitor Center** Daily: June–Aug 8am–6pm; Sept–May 8.30am–4pm • ☏ 970 249 1914, ⓦ nps.gov/blca

Containing a narrow, precipitous gorge a mind-boggling one-mile deep, **BLACK CANYON OF THE GUNNISON NATIONAL PARK** lies seventy miles southeast of Grand

Junction. The view down into the fearsome, black rock canyon to the foaming Gunnison River below is as foreboding as mountain scenery gets. Over two million years, the river has eroded a deep, narrow gorge, leaving exposed cliffs and jagged spires of crystalline rock more than 1.7 billion years old. The one-way aspen-lined **South Rim Road** leading through the park to the top of the canyon winds uphill until the trees abruptly come to an end, the road levels out and the scenery takes a dramatic turn – stark black cliffs, with the odd pine clinging to a tiny ledge in desperation. The road is lined with **viewpoints: Gunnison Point** behind the visitor centre, the **Pulpit Rock** overlook and **Painted View Wall**, where the vast scale and height of the streaky cliffs really hits home, are the best. South Rim Road ends at **High Point** (8289ft), and the Warner Point Trail (1.5 miles return).

Crested Butte

The beautiful Victorian mining town of **CRESTED BUTTE** (pronounced like "beaut"), 153 miles east of Grand Junction and ninety miles from the Black Canyon, sits 8885ft up on a flat, alpine plain surrounded by snowy peaks. The town boomed after it was founded in the 1870s but almost died off in 1952 after its coal deposits were exhausted and the **Big Mine** closed. However, the development of 11,875ft **Mount Crested Butte**, four miles north of the town, into a world-class **ski resort** in the 1960s, and its further transformation into **mountain bikers'** paradise two decades later means that today it can claim to be the top year-round resort in Colorado (there's also fishing, hiking and kayaking in the summer). The old town is resplendent with gaily painted clapboard homes and businesses, with all the action taking place among the low-rise, historic buildings, bars and restaurants on **Elk Avenue**.

Crested Butte Mountain Resort

12 Snowmass Rd • Summer lift tickets $17 (all-day hike and bike pass $32); winter passes from $59 • ☏ 970 349 2222, ⓦ skicb.com

In skiing and snowboarding circles, **Crested Butte Mountain Resort** is best known for its extreme terrain, with lifts serving out-of-the-way bowls and faces that would only be accessible by helicopter at other resorts; unsurprisingly, the resort hosts both the US extreme skiing and snowboarding championships. That said, plenty of long beginner runs are mixed in over the mountain's one thousand skiable acres, with sixteen chairlifts linking 121 usually uncrowded runs. In summer the action switches to zip-line tours ($60), the Adventure Park ($13 per activity), mountain biking (see box below) and the trails of **Evolution Bike Park** (rental bikes $77/24hr)

ARRIVAL, INFORMATION AND GETTING AROUND   CRESTED BUTTE

By plane A 5hr drive southwest from Denver along mostly minor highways, Crested Butte is not easy to reach, though the roads are almost always open. Many skiers fly from Denver to Gunnison Airport, 28 miles south, a 40min trip to Crested Butte via the Alpine Express Shuttle ($35 one-way; ☏ 970 641 5074, ⓦ alpineexpressshuttle.com).

BIKING CRESTED BUTTE

In summer, **mountain bikes** all but outnumber cars around the town, especially during **Fat Tire Week** in late June (now officially dubbed **Crested Butte Bike Week**), one of the oldest festivals in the sport; the original evolved from a race over the rocky 21-mile Pearl Pass to Aspen in 1976, now commemorated at the **Pearl Pass Mountain Bike Tour** (Sept).

You can still ride the route to Aspen – 190 miles shorter than the road – but some of the most exciting trails are much nearer the town and include the gorgeous 401 trail with its wide-open vistas; the thickly wooded Dyke Trail; and the long, varied and occasionally challenging Deadmans. The Alpineer, 419 Sixth St (☏ 970 349 5210, ⓦ alpineer.com), rents bikes ($35/day). Aficionados can also visit the Mountain Bike Hall of Fame at 331 Elk Ave (daily: June–Sept 10am–8pm; Dec–March noon–6pm; $4; ⓦ mtnbikehalloffame.com).

By bus Dolly's Mountain Shuttle (☎970 349 2620, ⓦcrestedbutteshuttle.com) provides transport to Aspen for $60/person (6-person or $360 minimum in summer; $600 in winter); Denver is $650. Mountain Express (free; ⓦmtnexp.org) buses ply the 3 miles between the town and resort (every 15–20min, 7.10am–9.40pm).
Visitor centre 601 Elk Ave (daily 9am–5pm; ☎970 349 6438, ⓦcbchamber.com).

ACCOMMODATION

The choice of accommodation is between the ski area or downtown; in season, you're likely to flit between the two areas every day, so it's only worth staying at the generally more expensive mountainside lodgings if you're obsessed with getting first tracks. Crested Butte Mountain Resort (see p.687) can book rooms and advise on package deals – reserve well in advance during winter.

Crested Butte International Lodge & Hostel 615 Teocalli Ave ☎970 349 0588, ⓦcbhostel.com. Modern and clean, with good-value dorm beds, but poorer private rooms. Dorms $25, doubles $75

Elk Mountain Lodge 129 Gothic Ave ☎970 349 7533, ⓦelkmountainlodge.com. Compact but comfy rooms, breakfast and a shared hot tub (indoors) in this old mining boarding house built in 1919. $119

Old Town Inn 708 Sixth St ☎970 349 6184, ⓦoldtowninn.net. Standard motel rooms with great home-made breakfasts, free bikes and cookies and coffee in the afternoon. $129

★ **Purple Mountain Lodge** 714 Gothic Ave ☎970 349 5888, ⓦpurplemountainlodge.com. Extremely comfortable B&B (more blueish than purple), with bright, cheery rooms, its own day spa, a hot tub and free bikes in summer. $179

EATING AND DRINKING

Brick Oven Pizzeria & Pub 223 Elk Ave ☎970 349 5044, ⓦbrickovencb.com. Wildly popular for its outdoor patio (with bar), thirty beers on tap and decent pizza (large from $18.99) such as the "Hurricane Hanna"(sliced meatballs, bacon and mushrooms, drizzled with pesto). Daily 6.30am–10pm.

Eldo Brewery & Tap Room 215 Elk Ave ☎970 349 6125, ⓦeldobrewpub.com. The coolest place to be on a sunny afternoon, the second-floor deck of this brewpub (with five seasonal beers on tap; $4) is always packed; the Wild West timber exterior is faux but handsome, and the third-of-a-pound burgers (from $7), and veggie burgers ($8) are excellent. Mon–Sat 3–10pm, Sun 3–9pm.

Kochevars 127 Elk Ave ☎970 349 6745. Timber-frame beauty from 1891, the original saloon established by Jacob Kochevar, with cheap drinks and bar snacks. Pool tables inside. Daily 1pm–2am.

Montanya Distillers 130 Elk Ave ☎970 799 3206, ⓦmontanyarum.com. Housed in the old electric plant of 1901, this award-winning rum maker offers all sorts of cocktails, free tastings and tours along with classy shared plates of snacks and Mountain Oven breads. Daily 11am–9pm.

Wooden Nickel 222 Elk Ave ☎970 349 6350, ⓦwoodennickelcb.com. One of the oldest saloons in town (the old wooden bar dates from the 1890s); the restaurant is the focus these days, with perfect steaks and local trout ($26). Daily 4–10pm.

Durango

Thanks to a splendid setting amid the San Juan Mountains, **DURANGO**, founded in 1880 as a refining town and rail junction for Silverton, 45 miles north, has boomed to become southwest Colorado's largest town. A friendly, ebullient place, it's now home to a mixed population of teleworkers and outdoor enthusiasts, who enjoy its year-round range of activities, excellent restaurants and flourishing arts scene.

THE DURANGO & SILVERTON RAILROAD

Between May and October, the steam trains of the **Durango & Silverton Narrow Gauge Railroad** make up to three daily return trips along a spectacular route through the mountains. All trains leave the depot at 479 Main Ave, **Durango**, in the morning, with the first at 8am, and allow time for lunch in **Silverton**.

Reserve via ☎970 247 2733 or ⓦdurangotrain.com. Basic summer fares are $85, $51 for kids 5–11; for shorter winter excursions they drop to $59 and $34 respectively.

INFORMATION AND ACTIVITIES

Visitor centre 111 S Camino del Rio, near the train station on the main highway (June–Sept Mon–Fri 8am–6pm, Sat 9am–5pm, Sun 11am–4pm; Oct–May Mon–Fri 8am–5pm; ☎ 970 247 3500, ⊛ durango.org).

River-rafting Several operators run river-rafting excursions

DURANGO

on the Animas River. Full-day expeditions with Mild to Wild Rafting (☎ 970 247 4789, ⊛ mild2wildrafting.com), for example, cost from $80 upwards. If you just want a taster, brief float trips with Flexible Flyers (☎ 970 247 4628, ⊛ flexibleflyersrafting.com) start at just $18.

ACCOMMODATION

Hometown Hostel 736 Goeglein Gulch Rd ☎ 970 388 415, ⊛ durangohometownhostel.com. This appealing hillside home, 2 miles northeast of downtown, holds four bunk-bedded dorm rooms; one male, one female, and two mixed. There's also a cosy communal living room and an outdoor deck. All linens provided. Dorms $28

★ **Rochester Hotel** 721 E Second Ave ☎ 970 385 1920, ⊛ rochesterhotel.com. Charming, intimate nineteenth-century B&B, where the differing Wild West themes of

the fifteen very comfortable rooms, some of which have kitchenettes, are inspired in part by classic, locally filmed Westerns. Winter $169, summer $219

★ **Strater Hotel** 699 Main Ave ☎ 970 247 4431, ⊛ strater.com. Major downtown landmark that's bursting with frontier elegance. Mostly small, antique-furnished rooms, great buffet breakfasts and a reasonable restaurant. Winter $102, summer $177

EATING AND DRINKING

East by Southwest 160 E College Drive ☎ 970 247 5533, ⊛ eastbysouthwest.com. Ravishing pan-Asian bistro, serving a wide array of delicious Thai, Vietnamese, Indonesian and Japanese dishes. Typical mains cost around $20, sushi or sashimi platters for two more like $30. Mon–Sat 11.30am–2.30pm & 5–10pm, Sun 5–10pm.

★ **Jean-Pierre Bakery & Cafe** 601 Main Ave ☎ 970 247 7700, ⊛ jeanpierrebakery.com. Classic French bakery/restaurant offering exquisite breads and pastries, plus sandwiches, salads and quiches for $10–16, and full meals such as mussels or beef with crab for up to $30. Live music on Fri & Sat. Daily 7am–10pm.

★ **Linda's Local Food Cafe** 309 W College Drive

☎ 970 259 6729, ⊛ lindaslocalfoodcafe. Bright, exceptionally friendly little cafe, alongside Albertson's supermarket. Linda's cooking is quite phenomenal. While the menu is largely Mexican, with burritos from $9, pork or chicken tamales for $11, or a filling tortilla soup for $5, delicious daily specials draw from world cuisines. Mon–Sat 8am–9pm, Sun 8.30am–2pm.

Steamworks Brewing Co 801 E Second Ave ☎ 970 259 9200, ⊛ steamworksbrewing.com. Large brewpub, perched a block above Main Ave; enjoy wood-fired pizzas (from $10) on its sunny open-air patio, or home-brewed beer in the bustling, cavernous interior. Mon–Thurs & Sun 11am–midnight, Fri & Sat 11am–2am.

Silverton

The turnaround point for the narrow gauge railroad from Durango comes at **SILVERTON**: "silver by the ton", allegedly. Spread across a small flat valley and hemmed in entirely by the tall peaks of the San Juan Mountains, it's one of Colorado's most evocative (and secluded) mountain towns, where wide, dirt-paved streets lead off toward the surrounding heights. Silverton's zinc- and copper-mining days only came to an end in 1991, and the population has dropped since then, with those who remain generally relying on the seasonal tourist train – winters here are harsh and largely quiet. Although the false-fronted stores along "Notorious Blair Street" may remind one of the days when **Wyatt Earp** dealt cards here, the town is defined by the restaurants and gift shops that fill up around noon, when train passengers are in town.

ACCOMMODATION AND EATNG

SILVERTON

Avalanche Coffee House 1067 Blair St ☎ 970 387 5282. A welcome contrast to Silverton's run-of-the-mill steakhouses, this friendly hangout offers fresh coffee, pastries and snacks, plus more substantial pizzas. 9am–6pm; closed Wed.

Grand Imperial Hotel 1219 Greene St ☎ 970 387 5527, ⊛ grandimperialhotel.com. Very central, bright red main street hotel, with plenty of historic ambience and old-style

rooms of varying degrees of comfort. The cheapest fall well short of luxury. $79

Triangle Motel 848 Greene St ☎ 970 387 5780, ⊛ trianglemotel.com. Behind its rather ugly facade, this motel at the south end of town is very well maintained, offering good facilities for the price, with two-room suites available. $80

Ouray

The attractive mining community of **OURAY** lies 23 miles north of Silverton, on the far side of 11,018ft **Red Mountain Pass**, where the bare rock beneath the snow really is red, thanks to mineral deposits. The Million Dollar Highway twists and turns to get here, passing abandoned mine workings and rusting machinery in the most unlikely and inaccessible spots; trails and backroads into the San Juans offer rich pickings for hikers or drivers with 4WD vehicles.

Ouray itself is squeezed into a verdant sliver of a valley, with the commercially run **Ouray Hot Springs** beside the Uncompahgre River at the north end of town. A mile or so south, a one-way-loop dirt road leads to Box Canyon Falls Park (daily 8am–dusk; $4), where a straightforward 500ft trail, partly along a swaying wooden parapet, leads into narrow Box Canyon and the namesake falls that thunder through a tiny cleft in the mountain at the far end.

ACCOMMODATION AND EATING   OURAY

Bon Ton 426 Main St ☎970 325 4951, ⓦ stelmobonton .com. Snug basement restaurant that offers Ouray's most satisfying cuisine. Italian classics for around $18–20, plus signature Colorado dishes such as lamb chops with jalapeño mint sauce ($29). Mon & Thurs–Sat 5.30–9pm, Sun 9.30am–1pm & 5.30–9pm.

Box Canyon Lodge 45 Third Ave ☎970 325 4981, ⓦ boxcanyonouray.com. An old-style timber motel below the park, where guests can bathe in natural hot tubs. The guest rooms are cosy and snug, with good furnishings and fittings. **$105**

★ **Hot Springs Inn** 1400 Main St ☎970 325 7277, ⓦ hotspringsinn.com. All of the very pleasant rooms at this comfortable upscale modern inn, at the north end of town, have deck balconies facing the river, and the staff are hugely helpful with area recommendations. **$159**

Telluride

Set in a picturesque valley, at the flat base of a bowl of vast steep-sided mountains, **TELLURIDE** lies 120 miles northwest of Durango via an indirect highway route. The former mining village was briefly home to the young Butch Cassidy, who robbed his first bank here in 1889. These days, it's better known as a top-class **ski resort** that rivals Aspen for celebrity allure. Happily, it has achieved its status without losing its character, exemplified by the beautifully preserved low-slung buildings along its wide main street. Healthy young bohemians with few visible means of support but top-notch ski equipment seem to form the bulk of the twelve hundred inhabitants, while most visitors tend to stay two miles up from town in **Mountain Village**, served by a free, year-round gondola service. Summer **hiking** opportunities are excellent; one three-mile round-trip walk leads from the head of the valley, where the highway ends at Pioneer Mill, up to the 431ft **Bridal Veil Falls**, the tallest in Colorado.

ACCOMMODATION AND EATING   TELLURIDE

Baked in Telluride 127 S Fir St ☎970 728 4775. Take-out deli-bakery, just off the main drag, that's great for morning espressos and pastries, and has a nice little terrace where you can enjoy soup, sandwiches or pizza. Daily 5.30am–10pm.

Cosmopolitan Hotel Columbia, 300 W San Juan Ave ☎970 728 0660, ⓦ columbiatelluride.com. Mains at Telluride's fanciest restaurant, set in a luxury hotel near the ski lifts – mostly contemporary Southwestern, but including Thai- and Japanese-influenced options – start at well over $20. Daily 6–10.30pm.

New Sheridan Hotel 231 W Colorado Ave ☎970 728 4351, ⓦ newsheridan.com. Restored 1895 hotel in the heart of town, where the large, very luxurious rooms have stylish antique furnishings but modern bathrooms and fittings. The cheapest face inwards, but it costs little more to enjoy great mountain views. Winter **$204**, summer **$163**

Smuggler Joe's Brewpub and Grille 225 S Pine Ave ☎970 728 0919. Very lively, convivial evening hangout, with a wide-ranging menu of ordinary pub grub but some exceptional house brews, including raspberry wheat beers. Daily 11am–2am.

Victorian Inn 401 W Pacific Ave ☎970 728 6601, ⓦ victorianinntelluride.com. Despite the name, this is a smart motel rather than a historic inn, lacking a pool or a/c. The rooms are conventional and unexciting, but the location is unbeatable for the price, and it has its own sauna. Winter **$99**, summer **$124**

11

Mesa Verde National Park

The only US national park devoted exclusively to archeological remains, **MESA VERDE NATIONAL PARK** is set high on a densely wooded plateau, so remote that its extensive **Ancestral Puebloan ruins** were not fully explored until 1888, when a local rancher discovered them on his land.

During the thousand or so years up to 1300 AD, Ancestral Puebloan peoples expanded to cover much of the area now known as the "**Four Corners**". While their earliest dwellings were simple pits in the ground, they ultimately developed the architectural sophistication needed to build the spectacular multistorey apartments that characterize Mesa Verde, nestled in rocky alcoves high above the sheer canyons that bisect the southern edge of the Mesa Verde plateau. The region's inhabitants eventually migrated into what's now New Mexico to establish the pueblos where their descendants still live.

All the park's ruins are located twenty or more tortuous miles up from the roadside visitor centre. The access road forks to reach the two main constellations of remains: **Chapin Mesa** to the south, and **Wetherill Mesa** to the west.

Chapin Mesa

Ruins Road, the driving route around **Chapin Mesa** (April to late Oct, daily 8am–sunset) consists of two one-way, six-mile loops, which provide access to assorted sites including the park's two best-known attractions

Tucked 100ft below an overhanging ledge of pale rock, and the largest Ancestral Puebloan cliff dwelling to survive anywhere, **Cliff Palace** holds 217 rooms and 23 *kivas*, each thought to have belonged to a separate family or clan. Probably a ceremonial or storage centre rather than a communal habitation, it may have been home to 120 people. Guided tours (see below) offer the chance to walk through the empty plazas and peer down into the mysterious *kivas*. If you don't have a ticket you can still get a great view from the overlook where the tour groups gather.

Built around 1240, **Balcony House** was remodelled during the 1270s to make it even more impregnable; access is very difficult, and it's not visible from above. Guided tours involve scrambling up three hair-raising ladders and crawling through a narrow tunnel. It's a spectacular site, with two circular *kivas* standing side by side, but those who don't share the fearless Ancestral Puebloan attitude to heights should give it a miss.

Wetherill Mesa

The tortuous twelve-mile drive onto **Wetherill Mesa** beyond the main park road is open in summer only (daily 9am–4.15pm), and even then for ordinary sized vehicles only.

From the parking lot at the far end, a free **miniature train** loops around the tip of the mesa. Its main stop is at **Long House**, the park's second largest ruin, where hour-long tours descend sixty or so steps to reach its central plaza, then scramble around its 150 rooms and 21 *kivas*.

INFORMATION AND TOURS   MESA VERDE NATIONAL PARK

Park access and entry fees The park is 15 miles up from US-160, 10 miles east of Cortez and 35 miles west of Durango. From late May to early Sept, entry is $15/vehicle, $8 for motorcyclists, cyclists and pedestrians; early Sept to late May it's $10 and $5 respectively; valid for a week.

Visitor centre Beside US-160 at the entrance to the park, 15 miles or around 40min drive below the mesa-top sites

(daily: spring and autumn 8am–5pm; summer 7.30am–7pm; winter 8.30am–4.30pm; ☎970 529 5036, ⓦnps .gov/meve).

Ruins tours The three main ruins in the park – Balcony House and Cliff Palace on Chapin Mesa, and Long House on Wetherill Mesa – can only be visited on timed, guided tours. Buy tickets ($3/tour), at the visitor centre as soon as you arrive.

ACCOMMODATION AND EATING

Far View Motor Lodge Fifteen miles up from US-160 ☎970 564 4300, ⓦvisitmesaverde.com. Peaceful lodge offering the only rooms at Mesa Verde. Standard rooms

have private balconies, while "Kiva" rooms are more luxurious; all have wi-fi but not phones or TVs. The *Metate Room* is a pretty good restaurant that's open daily for dinner only; mains such as elk tenderloin cost up to $30. Open late April to late Oct. Standard $145, Kiva $183 **Morefield Campground** Four miles up from US-160 ☎970 564 4300, ⓦvisitmesaverde.com. The park's official campground – so large it's almost never full – is a long way down from the ruins. No reservations are necessary. Open early May to early Oct. 1 or 2 vehicles $24, hookups $34

Spruce Tree Terrace Near the Chapin Mesa museum ☎970 564 4300, ⓦvisitmesaverde.com. The one place in the park to offer food year-round, this straightforward cafeteria serves sandwiches, salads and Navajo tacos at very affordable prices, and has a pleasant shaded terrace. Daily: mid-March to May & late Aug to Oct 10am–5pm; June to late Aug 9am–6.30pm; Nov to mid-March 11am–3.30pm.

Wyoming

Pronghorn antelope all but outnumber people in wide-open **WYOMING**, the ninth largest but least populous state in the union, with just 576,000 residents. This is classic **cowboy country** – the inspiration behind *Shane*, *The Virginian* and countless other Western novels – replete with open range, rodeos and country-music dance halls. The state emblem, seen everywhere, is a hat-waving cowboy astride a bucking bronco, and the spurious "Code of the West", signed into state law in 2010 and urging residents to follow such maxims as "ride for the brand", illustrates Wyoming's ongoing attachment to the myths of the Wild West.

Unlikely as it may seem, this rowdy state was the first to grant women the right to vote in 1869 – a full half-century before the federal government, on the grounds that the enfranchisement of women would attract settlers and increase the population, thereby hastening statehood. A year later Wyoming appointed the country's first women jurors, and the "Equality State" elected the first female US governor in 1924. Today the state government is dominated by Republicans and President Obama managed just 28 percent of the vote in 2012 (only in Utah did he get less).

The mineral extraction industry and the tourism sector are the main drivers of Wyoming's modern economy. Indeed, the state is home to one of America's most famous natural attractions, the simmering geothermal landscape of **Yellowstone National Park**, along with the craggy mountain vistas of adjacent **Grand Teton National Park**. Travelling to Yellowstone from South Dakota on I-90 you will pass the helter-skelter **Bighorn Mountains**, likeable Old West towns such as **Cody** and **Buffalo**, and the otherworldly outcrop of **Devils Tower**; anyone crossing the state from Nebraska to Utah on I-80 will also pass a handful of worthy detours.

Cheyenne

The eastern approach into the capital of Wyoming, **CHEYENNE**, dropping into a wide dip in the plains, leaves enduring memories for most travellers. With the snow-crested Rockies looming in the distance and short, sun-bleached grass encircling the town, the sky appears gargantuan, dwarfing the city's outlying neighbourhoods. Even a quick exploration reveals a diverse community shaped by railroads, state politics and even nuclear arms. Union Pacific's sprawling yards and fine old terminus now mark the eastern edge of downtown, while to the west, the city's long-standing military installation was expanded in 1957 to house the first US intercontinental ballistic missile base.

Cowboy culture is big here, too, as the ranchwear stores and honky-tonks attest. In late July, the ten-day **Cheyenne Frontier Days** festival (ⓦcfdrodeo.com) attracts thousands to its huge outdoor rodeo, big-name C&W concerts, parades, chuckwagon races, air shows and cook-outs. The rest of the year, things are pretty quiet. The **Wyoming State Museum**, 2301 Central Ave, takes a sober look at Wild West history (May–Oct Mon–Sat 9am–4.30pm; Nov–April Mon–Fri 9am–4.30pm, Sat 10am–2pm; free; ☎307 777 7022, ⓦwyomuseum.state.wy.us), while the more light-hearted

Cheyenne Frontier Days Old West Museum, five minutes' drive from downtown at 4610 Carey Ave (daily 9am–5pm; $10; ⊛oldwestmuseum.org), tells the history of the Frontier Days celebrations.

ACCOMMODATION AND EATING   CHEYENNE

Freedom's Edge Brewing Co 301 W 16th St ☎307 635 9245, ⊛freedomsedgebrewing.com. Popular microbrewery in elegant premises downtown, dating from 1892; sup a pint of 1890 IPA or Wyoming Wit. No food as yet, but a tranquil patio in the summer. Tues–Thurs 3–9pm, Fri 3–11pm, Sat 11am–11pm.

Historic Plains Hotel 1600 Central Ave ☎307 638 3311, ⊛theplainshotel.com. Opened in 1911 but refurbished in 2002, this choice delivers plenty of historic ambience, though the standard ("classic") rooms remain fairly small and bare-bones (the mattresses tend to be spongy) – the "King Parlor" rooms (from $139) are much better. **$119**

Luxury Diner 1401 W Lincolnway ☎307 638 8971. Classic old diner in a converted railroad dining car serving all the home-made classics; excellent corned beef, BLTs with amazing sweet potato fries and the hefty "Luxury Burger". Daily 6am–4pm.

Nagle Warren Mansion 222 E 17th St ☎307 637 3333, ⊛naglewarrenmansion.com. This historic B&B is the pick of Cheyenne's non-motel accommodation (book ahead); built in 1888, the house contains twelve luxurious rooms decked out in elegant Victorian West style and period antiques. **$155**

Laramie

LARAMIE lies fifty miles west of Cheyenne via either I-80 or the spectacular Hwy-210 (Happy Jack Rd), the latter slicing through plains studded with bizarrely shaped boulders and outcrops. At first Laramie seems typical of rural Wyoming, but behind downtown's Victorian facades lurk vegetarian cafés, day spas and secondhand bookstores – unusual for rodeo land, and a direct by-product of the **University of Wyoming**, whose campus spreads east from the town centre. Tensions between the differing cultures were highlighted by the notorious murder of gay student Matthew Shepard in 1998, which directly led to a change in US hate crime laws to cover sexual orientation.

Wyoming Territorial Prison State Park

975 Snowy Range Rd • May–Oct daily 8am–7pm • $5 • ⊛ wyomingterritorialprison.com

The centrepiece of the ambitious **Wyoming Territorial Prison State Park**, west of town is the old **prison** itself, in business from 1872 to 1903. A touch over-restored, it nonetheless holds informative displays on the Old West and women in Wyoming, as well as huge mugshots of ex-convicts – among them Butch Cassidy, incarcerated here for eighteen months in 1896 for the common crime of cattle-rustling.

ACCOMMODATION AND EATING   LARAMIE

Gas Lite Motel 960 N 3rd St ☎307 742 6616. Rare independent motel among the chains, with a kitchsy Old West theme, ageing but adequate rooms near the centre of town and friendly owners – great value. **$55**

Lovejoy's Bar & Grill 101 E Grand Ave ☎307 745 0141, ⊛elmerlovejoys.com. Busy diner/bar in the old 1900 *Johnson Hotel* downtown, with great burgers ($8.75), buffalo meatloaf ($12.50) and tasty, locally brewed beer. Daily 11am–midnight.

Night Heron Books & Coffeehouse 107 E Ivinson St

☎307 742 9028, ⊛nightheronbooks.com. Decent coffee, cakes, quiche and sandwiches among antique books downstairs and newer books upstairs. Daily 7am–8pm.

Vee Bar Guest Ranch 2091 Hwy-130 ☎307 745 7036, ⊛veebar.com. If you're looking for a rural place to lay your head, travel about 20 miles west out of Laramie to this ranch where you can relax in a cosy creekside cabin and enjoy a hearty cooked breakfast (they offer week-long riding and ranching holidays in summer). Minimum stay three nights. **$925**

Rawlins

There would be little reason to stop at the tiny prairie town of **RAWLINS**, one hundred miles west of Laramie on I-80, but for the unmissable **Wyoming Frontier Prison**, 500 W Walnut St (hourly tours daily 8.30am–4.30pm; $8; ☎307 324 4422,

ⓦwyomingfrontierprison.org). In service from 1901 till 1981, this huge jail with dingy cells, peeling walls and echoing corridors can make for a creepy experience – not least due to the fascinating anecdotes told by the exceptional guides. The darkest moment comes as the gas chamber (in use from 1937 until 1965) is revealed.

The Wind River Range

Heading northwest to Grand Teton and Yellowstone national parks from Rawlins and I-80, roads skirt the **WIND RIVER RANGE**, the state's longest and highest mountains. No roads cross the mountains; you can either see them from the east by driving through the **Wind River Indian Reservation** on US-287, or from the less accessible west, by taking US-191 up from I-80 at Rock Springs.

Dubois

The best base to explore the Wind River Range is the former logging town of **DUBOIS** ("dew-BOYS"), squeezed into the tip of the Wind River valley north of the reservation and an oasis among the badlands. The town turned to tourism after its final sawmill closed in 1987; it doesn't hurt that it's located sixty miles southeast of Grand Teton National Park via dramatic **Togwotee Pass**. Home to the biggest herd of bighorn sheep in the lower 48 states, Dubois celebrates that fact with the impressive **National Bighorn Sheep Interpretative Center**, a half-mile northwest of town on US-26/287 (907 W Ramshorn; June–Aug Mon–Sat 9am–6pm, Sun 9am–5pm; Sept–May Mon–Sat 9am–5pm; $2.50; ☎307 455 3429, ⓦbighorn.org). Along with running five-hour 4WD sheep-spotting tours (winter only; $50, reservations required), the centre provides self-guided tours and has exhibits on the majestic mascot of the Rockies.

ACCOMMODATION, EATING AND DRINKING   DUBOIS

Cowboy Café 115 E Ramshorn St ☎307 455 2595. Masterful country breakfasts, fresh, juicy buffalo burgers and tasty home-made fries – the coconut cream pie is pretty good, too. Daily 7am–9pm.

Trail's End Motel 511 W Ramshorn St ☎307 455 2540, ⓦtrailsendmotel.com. Immaculate, peaceful log-and-pinewood motel with units on the Wind River and a riverside deck. $99

Twin Pines Lodge & Cabins 218 W Ramshorn St ☎307 455 2600, ⓦtwinpineslodge.com. Comfy rooms in the main log building or spacious rustic cabins dating from 1934 (with wi-fi and microwaves). $95

Pinedale

On the west side of the Wind River Range, a scenic 77-mile drive from Jackson on US-189/191 along the Hoback River, tiny well-to-do **PINEDALE** offers excellent access to outdoor pursuits. The **Museum of the Mountain Man**, 700 E Hennick Rd (May–Sept daily 9am–5pm; Oct Mon–Fri 9am–4pm; $5; ☎307 367 4101, ⓦmuseumofthe mountainman.com), commemorates its role as a rendezvous for fur trappers in the 1830s, as well as the legacy of the Native American trappers.

WIND RIVER RESERVATION

The **Wind River Reservation** is shared by the Eastern Shoshone and Northern Arapaho tribes; sadly, it has become known for violent crime and widespread drug usage in recent years. Poverty is endemic and the average life expectancy is 49. Other than the usual spread of casinos, the reservation is best known for the monument to **Sacagawea**, the Shoshone guide of Lewis and Clark's expedition, erected here in 1963 at **Fort Washakie**. The best and safest way to experience the local Native American culture is to attend a **powwow** – gatherings of both spiritual and social significance – held mainly in summer, and generally open to the public. Contact the **Shoshone Tribal Cultural Center** at 90 Ethete Rd in Fort Washakie (Mon–Fri 9am–4pm; ☎307 332 9106) or check ⓦwindriver.org for details.

A sixteen-mile road winds east from Pinedale past Fremont Lake to **Elkhart Park Trailhead**, from where horse-worn paths lead past beautiful **Seneca Lake** and up rugged Indian Pass to glaciers and 13,000ft peaks. More so even than in most areas of the Rockies, mosquito repellent is a necessity in the Wind River Range in summer.

ACCOMMODATION AND EATING   PINEDALE

★ **Log Cabin Motel** 49 E Magnolia St ☎370 367 4579, ⓦthelogcabinmotel.com. Rustic lodge dating from 1929 dripping in atmosphere, with old Western-style log cabins, many with kitchens and all with modern amenities (satellite TV etc). Cabins **$119**, doubles **$79**

Wind River Brewery 402 Pine St ☎307 367 2337, ⓦwindriverbrewingco.com. Serves interesting beers, cooks up good, fresh Western burgers and hosts occasional live local music. Mon–Thurs & Sun11am–11pm, Fri & Sat 11am–midnight.

To Yellowstone: the northern route

Heading west from South Dakota and the Black Hills to Yellowstone National Park, I-90 and then US-14 slices across the vast open spaces and mountain ranges of **northern Wyoming** for some 430 miles, beginning with **Devils Tower**, 25 miles northwest of I-90.

Devils Tower National Monument

Monument Daily 24hr **Visitor centre** Early April to late Nov daily 8am–7pm • $10/car (good for a week) • Camping $12/night • ☎307 467 5283, ⓦnps.gov/deto

Though Congress designated **DEVILS TOWER**, in far northeastern Wyoming, as the country's first national monument in 1906, it took Steven Spielberg's inspired use of it as the alien landing spot in *Close Encounters of the Third Kind* to make this eerie 1267ft volcanic outcrop a true national icon. Plonked on top of a thickly forested hill above the peaceful Belle Fourche River, it resembles a giant wizened tree stump; however, it can be hauntingly beautiful when painted ever-changing hues by the sun and moon. Four short **trails** loop the tower (where deer and wild turkey are often spotted), beginning from the **visitor centre** at its base, three miles from the main gate.

Buffalo

Snuggled among the southeastern foothills of the Bighorn Mountains, easy-going **BUFFALO** remains largely unaffected by the bustle of the nearby I-90/I-25 junction; winters here are mild compared to other areas of Wyoming, thus prompting locals to refer to the town as the state's "banana belt". Although Main Street, now lined with frontier-style stores, used to be an old buffalo trail, the place was actually named after Buffalo, New York. The **Jim Gatchell Memorial Museum**, 100 Fort St (Jan–May & Sept–Dec Mon–Fri 9am–4pm; June–Aug Mon–Sat 9am–6pm, Sun noon–6pm; $5; ☎307 684 9331, ⓦjimgatchell.com), houses a fine collection of Old West curiosities pertaining to soldiers, ranchers and Native Americans.

ACCOMMODATION   BUFFALO

★ **Occidental Hotel** 10 N Main St ☎370 684 0451, ⓦoccidentalwyoming.com. Wonderfully restored historic hotel dating back to 1880, where you can stay in the Owen Wister Suite, where the writer wrote a chunk of *The Virginian*.

The sumptuous lobby is a sight in itself, and many rooms feature vintage radios tuned to old-time music on the hotel's own micro-frequency. There's also bluegrass music in the bar on some nights. **$75**

The Bighorn Mountains and Bighorn Basin

Of the three scenic highways that wind through the **Bighorn Mountains**, US-14A from **Burgess Junction**, fifty miles west of **Sheridan**, is the most spectacular. The road (typically closed Nov–May due to snow), edges its way up **Medicine Mountain**, on whose windswept western peak the mysterious **Medicine Wheel** – the largest such monument still intact – stands protected behind a wire fence. Local Native American legends offer no clues as to the original purpose of these flat stones, arranged in a circular "wheel" shape with 28 spokes and a circumference of 245ft – though the pattern suggests sun worship or early astronomy.

The route down the highway's west side, with gradients of ten to twenty percent, is said to have cost more to build per mile than any other road in America. Tight hairpin bends will keep drivers' eyes off the magnificent overlooks down into the **Bighorn Basin**, a sparsely vegetated valley walled in by mighty mountains on three sides and ragged foothills to the north.

Cody

The "rodeo capital of the world", located along US-14 and the North Fork of the Shoshone River, **CODY** was the brainchild of investors who, in 1896, persuaded **"Buffalo Bill" Cody** to become involved in their development company, knowing his approval would attract homesteaders and visitors alike. Despite Bill spending much of his later life in the town, his wife had the hero buried in Golden, Colorado in 1917 (see p.668); Wyoming has argued for the body's "return" ever since. In stark contrast, the town's other famous son, painter **Jackson Pollock**, who was born here in 1912, is rarely mentioned.

In summer, tourism is huge business here, but underneath all the Buffalo Bill-connected attractions and paraphernalia, Cody manages to retain the feel of a rural Western settlement. The wide main thoroughfare, **Sheridan Avenue**, holds souvenir and ranchwear shops and hosts parades during early July's annual **Cody Stampede Rodeo** (☎307 587 5155, ⊛codystampederodeo.com). In summer the **Cody Nite Rodeo** takes place nightly at the open-air arena at 519 W Yellowstone Ave on the western edge of town (June–Aug daily 8pm; $18; same contact info).

Just east of the rodeo grounds off US-14 (at 1831 Demaris Drive), the 1890s buildings gathered at **Old Trail Town** (mid-May to Sept daily 8am–7pm; $8; ☎307 587 5302, ⊛oldtrailtown.org), include cabins and saloons frequented by Butch Cassidy and the Sundance Kid.

Buffalo Bill Historical Center

720 Sheridan Ave • May to mid-Sept daily 8am–6pm; mid-Sept to Oct daily 8am–5pm; March, April & Nov daily 10am–5pm; Dec–Feb Thurs–Sun 10am–5pm • $18 • ☎307 587 4771, ⊛bbhc.org

By far the biggest year-round attraction in Cody is the superb **Buffalo Bill Historical Center**. In addition to charting the life of William Cody and the history of Buffalo Bill's Wild West, the museum is home to the nation's most comprehensive collection of Western Americana. Never afraid to shatter prevailing myths about the West and its peoples, the huge collection interprets the history of the cowboy, the Plains Indians, Western art, firearms, dude ranching, Western conservation and frontier entrepreneurship.

ACCOMMODATION, EATING AND DRINKING   CODY

Buffalo Bill's Antlers Inn 1213 17th St ☎307 587 2084, ⊛antlersinncody.com. Clean and comfortable motel, which stands out as good value, especially in the summer; breakfast and cable TV included. **$115**
Irma Hotel 1192 Sheridan Ave ☎307 587 4221, ⊛irmahotel.com. This historic gem was built by Buffalo Bill in 1902 (named for his daughter), and retains a superb

original cherrywood bar (a gift to Bill from Queen Victoria) in its namesake downstairs restaurant. **$162**
Proud Cut Saloon 1227 Sheridan Ave ☎307 527 6905. Cowboy-style bar (with game trophies on the walls) and steakhouse serving decent bacon burgers, barbecue and steaks. Mon–Sat 11am–10pm, Sun noon–9pm.

Yellowstone National Park

America's oldest and easily its most famous national park, **YELLOWSTONE NATIONAL PARK** attracts three million visitors every year (97 percent of them in summer), for good reason; the sheer diversity of what's on offer is mind-bending. Not only does

---

PLANNING A YELLOWSTONE VISIT

The key to appreciating the park is to take your time, plan carefully and – particularly in summer – exercise patience with the inevitable crowds and traffic. While you can explore a representative proportion in a day-trip, allow for a stay of at least three days to see the park fully. The majority of Yellowstone's top sights are signposted within a few hundred yards of the 142-mile **Loop Road**, a figure-of-eight circuit fed by roads from the park's five entrances, though the traditional **North Entrance** is the one marked by the 1903 **Roosevelt Arch**. Although the speed limit is a radar-enforced 45mph, journey times are very difficult to predict. Wildlife traffic jams, usually caused by stubborn herds of bison parking themselves on the pavement, are not unusual and should be expected; also for this reason, it's advisable to avoid night driving in Yellowstone.

11

Yellowstone deliver jaw-dropping mountain scenery, from the scintillating colours of the **Grand Canyon of the Yellowstone** to the deep-azure **Yellowstone Lake** and wild-flower-filled meadows, but it's jam-packed with so much **wildlife** you might think you've arrived at a safari park. Shambling grizzly bears, vast herds of heavy-bearded bison (buffalo) and horned elk mingle with marmots, prairie dogs, eagles, coyotes and more than a dozen elusive wolf packs on the prowl. What really sets Yellowstone apart, however, is that this is one of the world's largest **volcanoes**, with thermal activity providing half the world's **geysers**, thousands of **fumaroles** jetting plumes of steam, **mud pots** gurgling with acid-dissolved muds and clays, and of course, **hot springs**. The park might not look like a volcano, but that's because the caldera is so big – 34 by 45 miles – and because, thankfully, it hasn't exploded for 640,000 years.

The following account runs clockwise around the Loop Road, beginning at Mammoth Hot Springs five miles south of the North Entrance. Of course, no trip to Yellowstone is complete without at least one **hike**, be it to a waterfall or geyser; each visitor centre has free day-hiking handouts for their areas.

Mammoth Hot Springs

The small village-like centre of **Mammoth Hot Springs**, at the northern tip of the Loop Road (with lodgings, general stores and petrol station), was once **Fort Yellowstone**, with most of the stolid buildings constructed here between 1891 and 1913 now used for park administration. Elk are often seen grazing on the grass in winter. Today, the old bachelor officers' quarters of 1909 houses the **Albright Visitor Center & Museum**, with movies and exhibits on the human history of the park and a small art gallery of Yellowstone-related paintings (some by Thomas Moran). The main attraction here, though – the **hot springs** – are clearly visible south of the centre; terraces of barnacle-like deposits cascade down a vapour-shrouded mountainside. Tinted a marvellous array of greys, greens, yellows, browns and oranges by algae, they are composed of travertine, a form of limestone which, having been dissolved and carried to the surface by boiling water, is deposited as tier upon tier of steaming stone.

Tower-Roosevelt and the Lamar Valley

The main landmark of Yellowstone's **Tower** and **Roosevelt** area, twenty miles east of Mammoth Hot Springs, is the high peak of **Mount Washburn**; its lookout tower can be reached by an enjoyable hike (5 or 6 miles return, depending on which trailhead you use) or a gruelling cycle ride. For an easier hike, take the trail that leads down to the spray-drenched base of 132ft **Tower Fall**, 2.5 miles south of Tower Junction.

From Tower Junction, the Northeast Entrance highway wanders through the meadows of serene **Lamar Valley** – often called "North America's Serengeti" for its **abundant wildlife**, where life-and-death struggles between predators (grizzlies, wolves, mountain lions) and prey (elk, pronghorn, mule deer and especially bison) play out daily. This is the most spectacular route to Montana, via the Beartooth Highway.

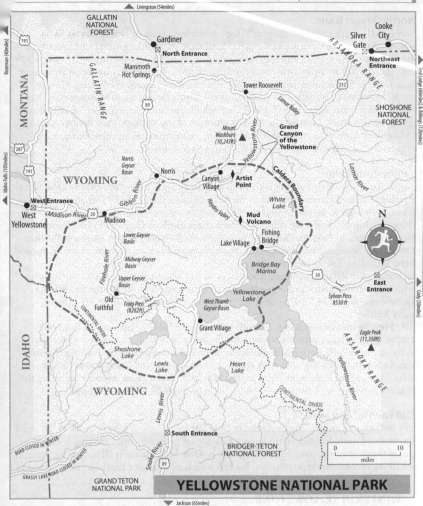

YELLOWSTONE NATIONAL PARK

The Grand Canyon of the Yellowstone

The Yellowstone River roars and tumbles for twenty miles between the sheer red, pink and golden-hued cliffs of the **Grand Canyon of the Yellowstone** (some 800–1200ft high) its course punctuated by two powerful **waterfalls**: 109ft **Upper Falls** and its downstream counterpart, thunderous 308ft **Lower Falls**. On the south rim, **Artist Point** looks down hundreds of feet to the river canyon, where frothing water swirls between mineral-stained walls. Nearby, **Uncle Tom's Trail** descends steeply to a spray-covered platform in the canyon, gently vibrating in the face of the pounding Lower Falls. A few miles south, the river widens to meander through tranquil **Hayden Valley**, one of the finest spots in Yellowstone to view wildlife from the road.

To get oriented, visit the modern **Canyon Visitor Education Center** (see p.701) in **Canyon Village**, the most visitor-friendly centre in the park; all the services, shops and restaurants are close together on a horseshoe-shaped cul-de-sac. The centre highlights the natural wonders of the park and its "supervolcano" status through multimedia exhibits and films – it's the best overall introduction to Yellowstone.

Norris Geyser Basin

Some twelve miles west of Canyon Village is the less crowded **Norris Geyser Basin**, where two separate trails explore a pallid landscape of whistling vents and fumaroles. **Steamboat** is the world's tallest geyser, capable of forcing near-boiling water over 300ft into the air; full eruptions are entirely unpredictable. The **Echinus Geyser** is the largest acid-water geyser known; every 35 to 75 minutes it spews crowd-pleasing, vinegary eruptions of 40 to 60 feet. Get oriented at the **Norris Geyser Basin Museum** (late-May to Sept daily 9am–6pm; ☎307 344 2812), which chronicles the history of Yellowstone's geothermal activity. Nearby, the modest **Museum of the National Park Ranger** (late May to late Sept daily 9am–5pm; ☎307 344 7353) charts the development of the park ranger since 1916 with exhibits and films in an old army log cabin.

Yellowstone Lake

North America's largest alpine lake, deep and deceptively calm **Yellowstone Lake** fills a sizeable chunk of the eastern half of the Yellowstone caldera. At 7733ft above sea level, it's high enough to be frozen half the year, and its waters remain perilously cold through summer. You'll see the lake sixteen miles south of Canyon Village (passing the **Mud Volcano** and **Sulphur Caldron**), where the small **Fishing Bridge Museum & Visitor Center** (see opposite) has displays on lake biology and stuffed waterbirds found around here, including Trumpeter swans.

Nearby **Lake Village** has hotels and places to eat, while rowboats ($10/hour), along with larger motorboats and powerboats, can be rented from the **Bridge Bay Marina** (May–Sept; ☎307 242 3876), also the place to catch scenic cruises (mid-June to early Sept).

At **West Thumb Geyser Basin**, 21 miles south from Lake Village, where hot pools empty into the lake's tranquil waters and fizz away into nothing, it's easy to see why early tourists would have made use of the so-called **Fishing Cone** by cooking freshly caught fish in its boiling waters. A couple of miles south, the **Grant Visitor Center** (late-May to Sept daily 8am–7pm ☎307 344 2650) has a small exhibit examining the role of forest fires in Yellowstone, using the major fires of 1988 as examples.

Old Faithful and around

For well over a century, the dependable **Old Faithful** (17 miles west from West Thumb) has erupted more frequently than any of its higher or larger rivals, making it the most popular geyser in the park – for many, this is what Yellowstone is all about. As a result, a half-moon of concentric benches, backed by a host of visitor facilities, now surround

---

WINTER IN YELLOWSTONE

Blanketed in several feet of snow between November and April, Yellowstone takes on a new appearance in **winter**: a silent and bizarre world where waterfalls freeze in mid-plunge, geysers blast towering plumes of steam and water into the crisp air and bison – beards matted with ice – stand in huddles. It's undeniably cold, and transport can require some hefty pre-planning, but crowds are nonexistent and wildlife-spotting opportunities are superb. Only the fifty-mile road from Gardiner to Cooke City via Mammoth Hot Springs is kept open (although beyond that, the Beartooth Highway is closed). The park's sole winter lodging is available at *Mammoth Hot Springs Hotel & Cabins* or *Old Faithful Snow Lodge & Cabins* (both accessible only by snowcoach and snowmobile, and closed for Nov and much of Dec).

Xanterra (see opposite) operates **snowcoach** trips and tours of the park over the closed roads from West Yellowstone, Flagg Ranch to the south, Old Faithful and Mammoth Hot Springs ($82). **Snowmobile** rental, generally cheapest in West Yellowstone, costs around $140–200 a day; only a limited number of snowmobiles are allowed in the park at any one time, so reserve ahead (see ⓦyellowstoneadventures.com). Much less expensive is **cross-country skiing** and **snowshoeing**, with groomed or blazed trails throughout the park.

t at a respectful distance on the side away from the Firehole River. On average, it "performs" for expectant crowds every 65 to 92 minutes; approximate schedules are displayed nearby. The first sign of activity is a soft hissing as water splashes repeatedly over the rim; after several minutes, a column of water shoots to a height of 100 to 180ft as the geyser spurts out a total of eleven thousand gallons. As soon as it stops, everyone leaves, and you'll suddenly have the place to yourself. The **Old Faithful Visitor Education Center** (see below) opened in 2010, with interactive exhibits explaining Yellowstone's thermal features and plenty of activities for kids. Check out also the **Old Faithful Inn** while you're here (p.702), a Yellowstone landmark built in 1904, featuring the oldest log-and-wood-frame structures in the world and a seven-storey lobby.

Two miles of boardwalks lead from Old Faithful to dozens of other geysers in the Upper Basin. If possible, try to arrive when **Grand Geyser** is due to explode. This colossus blows its top on average just twice daily, for twelve to twenty minutes, in a series of four powerful bursts that can reach 200ft. Other highlights along the banks of the Firehole River, usually lined with browsing bison, include the fluorescent intensity of the **Grand Prismatic Spring** at **Midway Geyser Basin**, particularly breathtaking in early evening when human figures and bison herds are silhouetted against plumes of mineral spray.

11

ARRIVAL, INFORMATION AND TOURS

By car Two of the five main entrances to Yellowstone are in Wyoming, via Cody to the east and Grand Teton National Park to the south. The others are in Montana: West Yellowstone (west), Gardiner (north) and Cooke City (northeast). Due to winter snow, most roads are open from early May to Oct only.

By shuttle bus Although a car is virtually essential to explore Yellowstone, Karst Stage (☎406 556 3500, ⓦ karststage.com) operates expensive shuttle buses to West Yellowstone ($51.50 one-way) and Mammoth ($157.50 one-way) from the Bozeman, Montana airport (May–Oct).

Park admission Admission ($25/car, good for a week) includes entry to adjacent Grand Teton National Park (see p.703).

Petrol You'll find petrol stations throughout the park (summer only).

Albright Visitor Center Near the north entrance at

YELLOWSTONE NATIONAL PARK

Mammoth (daily: late May to Sept 8am–7pm; Oct to late May 9am–5pm; ☎307 344 2263, ⓦ nps.gov/yell); the park's sole year-round information centre.

Summer-only visitor centres Along the main Loop Road at Canyon Village (daily: late May to Aug 8am–8pm; Sept 8am–6pm; first half of Oct 9am–5pm); Old Faithful (daily: late April to late May 9am–6pm; late May to Sept 8am–8pm; Oct 9am–5pm; ☎307 344 2751); and Fishing Bridge Visitor Center at Yellowstone Lake (late May to Sept daily 8am–7pm; ☎307 344 2450). Each hosts an exhibit on a different aspect of the park, and issues backcountry hiking permits.

Guided tours Companies that offer park tours, at more than $100 for a full day, include Xanterra (☎307 344 7901, ⓦ yellowstonenationalparklodges.com) and West Yellowstone's Buffalo Bus Tours (☎406 646 9564, ⓦ yellowstone vacations.com).

ACCOMMODATION

IN THE PARK

All indoor lodging within Yellowstone is run by Xanterra (see above). Unless otherwise indicated, all the properties listed below are open in summer only Reservations, always strongly recommended, are essential over holiday weekends. Every major "village" has a dining room (most close by 9.30pm), and sometimes a laundry, grocery store, petrol station, post office and gift shop.

Canyon Lodge & Cabins Canyon Village. Plain en-suite hotel rooms and cabins (the cheapest are simple frame types; more comfortable versions are $188), dating back to the park's first major revamp in 1957 and located half a mile from Grand Canyon of the Yellowstone. Cascade Lodge and Dunraven Lodge were added in the 1990s. Cabins (basic) $99, rooms $185

Lake Lodge Cabins Fabulous rustic log building (built 1920–26), acting as the focus for nearly 186 en-suite budget cabins close to the lake – visit the lobby even if you're not staying. The cheapest cabins have one double bed and are a very basic "pioneer" style; others have two doubles and can accommodate four people. Open Mid-June to late Sept. $75

Lake Yellowstone Hotel & Cabins Alarmingly yellow, this huge Grand Colonial-style hotel on the lake features ordinary rooms and dark, dingy en-suite cabins popular with tour groups. Its Sun Room, overlooking the lake, is a terrific spot for an evening drink. Doubles $210, cabins $141

Mammoth Hot Springs Hotel & Cabins Venerable 1937 behemoth (though the oldest wing dates from 1913), offering a range of cabins and hotel rooms. The Map Room is worth a look regardless of whether you stay, featuring a giant wall map made of more than 2500 pieces of wood. Open May to early Oct & late Dec to early March. Cabins $130, shared-bath cabins $86, doubles $123, shared-bath doubles $87

★ **Old Faithful Inn & Lodge Cabins** One of the most beautiful lodges around, this magnificent 1904 inn has a wide range of rooms, in addition to budget and en-suite cabins. You can watch Old Faithful erupt from the terrace bar. Open mid-May to mid-Oct. Cabins $115, shared-bath cabins $69, doubles $140, shared-bath doubles $103

Old Faithful Snow Lodge & Cabins This comparatively new lodge holds modern rooms, alongside attractive slightly older cabins that are well sealed against the cold. Open mid-May to mid-Oct & late Dec to early March. Cabins $99, doubles $229

Roosevelt Lodge Cabins More than eighty cabins a short drive from the Lamar Valley, from sparsely furnished to motel-like, grace this attractive, historic property, built in 1920 with log buildings designed to give a dude ranch effect – the most serene and atmospheric of all the lodges in the park. $115, shared-bath doubles $69

CAMPING

Official campgrounds Of Yellowstone's twelve camp-grounds, Xanterra operates five (rates are per night for up to six people) – Bridge Bay ($21), Canyon ($25), Grant Village ($25), Madison ($21) and Fishing Bridge (RVs only; $46), all of which can be reserved in advance (see p.701) while the park service runs the other seven on a first-come, first-served basis; arrive early in the day to get a site during summer months, as most are full by 11am. Fees for park-run tent camping range $15–20 per night. Only Mammoth campground is open year-round; the rest open any time from early May until late June and start closing in mid-Sept. All have toilet facilities, but few have showers.

Backcountry camping To camp in the backcountry, you'll need a permit – free from visitor centres, information stations and ranger stations; these can be collected no earlier than 48hr in advance of your camping trip.

EATING

IN THE PARK

Each of Yellowstone's lodges and villages boast official dining rooms, typically open May–Sept 7–10am, 11.30am–2.30pm and 5–10pm, offering similar menus of pricey but usually high-quality food: breakfast buffets ($12.75) that include fresh fruit, cereals, pastries and standard cooked items; lunches (box lunches for $10.95) such as smoked trout ($10.50); and more elaborate dinners such as bison sirloin ($27.50). Each location also usually features a workaday cafeteria open similar hours with cheaper options such as bison burgers ($14) and sandwiches ($8.25), as well as soda fountains and general stores, where burgers and fries along with ice cream and

GATEWAY TOWNS

In addition to Jackson (see p.706) and Cody (p.697) in Wyoming, the small towns just outside the park's western and two northern gates offer cheaper lodging. West Yellowstone, the largest town, is somewhat disfigured by gift stores and fast-food joints but manages to retain a certain charm. Friendly Gardiner lies just 5 miles from Mammoth Hot Springs. Less developed, the one-street town of Cooke City is 3 miles from the isolated northeast entrance on US-212, which stops just east of town in winter.

Elk Horn Lodge 103 Main St, Cooke City ☎406 838 2332, ⍟elkhornlodgemt.com. Two cabins and six motel rooms, all with full bath, TV, mini-fridges, microwaves and coffeemakers. Cabins $120, doubles $99

★ **Headwaters of the Yellowstone B&B** Hwy-89, Gardiner ☎406 848 7073, ⍟headwatersbandb.com. A fantastic B&B on the banks of the Yellowstone River, less than 4 miles north of Gardiner. All five guest rooms have their own private bathroom, while the two cabins – one sleeping up to four, the other up to six – enjoy amazing views. $125, cabins $200

Madison Hotel 139 Yellowstone Ave, West Yellowstone ☎406 646 7745, ⍟madisonhotelmotel.com. This historic 1912 hotel includes an adjacent motel (with cabin-themed rooms) and one of the few hostels in the region; the attractive, log-hewn main building includes single-sex dorm rooms that sleep up to four. Open late May to early Oct. Dorms $36, hotel doubles $75, motel doubles $89

Three Bear Lodge 217 Yellowstone Ave, West Yellowstone ☎406 646 7353, ⍟three-bear-lodge.com. Large motel housing 75 sizeable rooms and two-bedroom family units that sleep six. On-site amenities include a friendly diner, and snowmobile packages are usually available. $175

Yellowstone Village Inn 1102 Scott St, Gardiner ☎406 848 7417, ⍟yellowstonevinn.com. On the edge of town, this high-end motel has 43 tidy rooms, most themed around wildlife or Western Americana, including a John Wayne room. Substantially lower rates off-season. $139

shakes are served.

Lake House Restaurant Grant Village ☎307 344 7311. Casual dining and a decent pub-style menu (bison burgers and the like) take second place to the view: this restaurant is literally right on Lake Yellowstone. Late May to late Sept daily 6.30–10.30am & 5–10.30pm.

Roosevelt Lodge Dining Room ☎307 344 7311. The best of the resort restaurants features applewood-smoked BBQ ribs ($19.95), wild game Bolognese ($13.75) and breakfast mains for $6.75–9.25. It also does an addictive Yellowstone sundae (huckleberry ice cream with crumb-cake and berries) for $6.25. Early June to early Sept daily 7–10am & 11.30am–9.30pm.

GATEWAY TOWNS

Beartooth Café 14 Main St, Cooke City ☎406 838 2475, ⓦbeartoothcafe.com. Cooke City's best restaurant throughout the day (but no breakfast), serving buffalo burgers ($9.95), mountain trout dinners ($18.95) and sandwiches for lunch ($8.95). Late May to Sept daily 11am–9pm.

★ **Lodge Cabin Cafe** 106 Hwy-212, Silver Gate ☎406 838 2367, ⓦthelogcabincafe.com. Highly atmospheric diner and B&B since 1937, just down the road from Cooke City (near the park entrance), serving a menu rich in organic and local produce – the local trout is highly recommended, as are the pies, cakes and steaks. Mid-May to late Sept daily 6.30am–10pm.

Running Bear Pancake House 538 Madison Ave, West Yellowstone ☎406 646 7703. Serves an enjoyable breakfast and lunch, with the highlights home-made cinnamon rolls, pies, fresh soups and of course, lavish stacks of pancakes (most dishes under $10). Daily 6.30am–1.30pm.

Wild West Corral Drive-In 711 Scott St, Gardiner ☎406 848 7627. The place for burgers since 1960; the awesome "wild west burger" ($14.75) comprises two half-pound patties with bacon, onion, mushrooms and two cheeses. Daily 7am–11pm.

Grand Teton National Park

The jagged tooth-like peaks of **GRAND TETON NATIONAL PARK**, stretching for fifty miles south from Yellowstone to Jackson, are more dramatic than the mountains of its superstar neighbour park to the north. These sheer-faced cliffs make a magnificent spectacle, rising abruptly to tower 7000ft above the valley floor. A string of gem-like lakes is set tight at the foot of the mountains; the park also encompasses the broad, sagebrush-covered **Jackson Hole** river basin (a "hole" was a pioneer term for a flat, mountain-ringed valley), broken by the gently winding Snake River, rich in elk, bison and moose – it's a lot more common to see the latter here than in Yellowstone.

Colter Bay Village and around

While no road crosses the Tetons, those that run along their eastern flank were designed with an eye to the mountains, affording stunning views at every bend. Coming from Yellowstone, Hwy-89 swoops down to Jackson Lake and **Colter Bay Village** for your first taster of the jaw-dropping views to come. The "village" contains shops, a petrol station, cabins (see p.706) and a marina (summer daily 7am–7pm) where boats can be rented (see box below). The **Colter Bay Visitor Center** (see p.704) displays 35 artefacts from the David T. Vernon Indian Arts Collection, an ensemble of rare Native American artwork donated to the park by billionaire Laurance Rockefeller in 1976.

Jackson Lake Lodge and around

Five miles south of Colter Bay, **Jackson Lake Lodge** is a gorgeous park hotel, built in 1955, with fabulous views of the mountains from its bar and back terrace – stop in

---

GRAND TETON ADVENTURES

Cycling the flat roads of Jackson Hole is a joy; bikes can be rented at Adventure Sports within the Dornan's complex in Moose ($15/hr, $36/day; ☎307 733 3307, ⓦdornans.com), where an eight-mile, paved trail runs to Jenny Lake (or 12 miles south to Jackson). To admire the Tetons from **water**, rent a **canoe** or **kayak** from the same outfit ($49/day) or take a 10-mile Barker-Ewing Scenic Float Trip ($70; ☎307 7331800, ⓦbarkerewing.com) along the Snake River.

The Tetons also offer excellent **rock-climbing** opportunities; Exum Mountain Guides (☎307 733 2297, ⓦexumguides.com) runs classes and guided trips from a summer office, steps from Jenny Lake. Jackson Hole Adventure Center (ⓦdojacksonhole.com) can arrange a variety of activities, from whitewater rafting to horseback riding.

Official park activities run by Grand Teton Lodge Co (ⓦgtlc.com) include scenic Snake River float trips ($62), park bus tours ($50), horseback riding ($40/hr from Colter Bay) and 1hr 30min Jackson Lake cruises from Colter Bay ($30). Boat rentals on Jackson Lake are $17/hr for canoes and kayaks, and $40 for motorboats (also from Colter Bay). Advance reservations are highly recommended. Swimming is free and allowed in all lakes.

even if you're not staying here. Nearby **Oxbow Turnout** is a good place to spot wildlife in the early morning, while further south on Teton Park Road the narrow side road up **Signal Mountain** (7727ft) offers a breathtaking panorama of the Tetons and especially the wide valley of Jackson Hole.

Jenny Lake

From Jackson Lake Lodge, Teton Park Road continues fourteen miles south to crystal-clear **Jenny Lake**, where the timber-frame **Visitor Center** (see below), housed in a former studio built by artist Harrison Crandall in 1926, has a small exhibit on the formation of the Teton Range. Down at the boat dock, **ferries** shuttle across the lake (daily 8am–6pm, every 15min; $7 one-way, $12 return) for a face-to-face encounter with towering, partly hunchbacked 13,770ft **Grand Teton** (Wyoming's second highest mountain) and cascading **Hidden Falls** (also reachable by a two-mile hike along the south shore of the lake). You can also take one-hour scenic cruises of the lake here (mid-May to Sept 11am, 2pm & 5pm; $16; reservations recommended ☎307 734 9227).

Moose and around

Just before Teton Park Road crosses the Snake River and rejoins Hwy-89 it passes through **Moose**, eight miles south of Jenny Lake, the small park headquarters. It's also home to the beautifully designed **Craig Thomas Discovery & Visitor Center** (see below), where the park's geology, ecology and human history (including some artefacts from the Vernon Indian Art Collection) are explained through illuminating exhibits, artwork and movies (it also has free wi-fi). Nearby, **Menors Ferry Historic District** on the Snake River preserves Bill Menor's 1894 homestead cabin and store, and the 1916 **Maud Noble Cabin**, with exhibits on the portentous meeting that took place here in 1923 to discuss the formation of the park. Before exiting the park south, detour to **Mormon Row**, a short drive off Hwy-89 via Antelope Flats Road. This is where Mormon homesteaders settled in the early 1900s, and several timber barns and homes remain standing; look for the Moulton Barn, positioned photogenically with the snow-capped Tetons in the background.

ARRIVAL AND INFORMATION **GRAND TETON NATIONAL PARK**

By bus If you are prepared to hike or cycle, you don't need a car to make the most out of Grand Teton. Alltrans Park Shuttle runs from Jackson (see p.706) to all the main locations in the park six times daily for $14/day (cash only); you'll pay an additional $12/person or $25/family at the park entrance. See ⓦ alltransparkshuttle.com.

Park admission Grand Teton's entrance fee of $25/car (good for 1 week) also covers Yellowstone. The park is open 24hr daily.

Visitor centres The main visitor centre is in Moose (daily: May & Oct 8am–5pm; June–Sept 8am–7pm; Nov–April 9am–5pm; ☎307 739 3399), with smaller centres in Jenny Lake (June–Aug daily 8am–5pm; ☎307 739 3392) and Colter Bay (daily: May & Sept 8am–5pm; June–Aug 8am–7pm; ☎307 739 3594). Check the park website for the latest weather conditions (ⓦ nps.gov/grte).

GRAND TETON TOP HIKES

Hiking trails in Grand Teton National Park waste no time in getting to the highlights. To climb one of the craggy Tetons themselves you need to be an experienced mountaineer: guides can usually take fit newbies up Grand Teton in two days after two days of training – contact Exum Mountain Guides (see p.703).

Leigh Lake Easy and popular walk following the sandy beaches of Leigh Lake, where the imposing 12,605ft Mount Moran bursts out dramatically from the shore.

Bradley & Taggart Lakes Moderate hike of just over 5 miles around these lakes at the base of the Tetons; lots of wildlife and wild flowers en route.

Phelps Lake Overlook Pleasant stroll of just under 2 miles from the Death Canyon Trailhead, with views of the lake, the canyon and Jackson Hole.

Death Canyon A more adventurous, but suitably rewarding amble heads up the macabrely named Death Canyon itself, reaching a verdant plateau after 4 miles on a well-graded trail adjacent to crashing creek waters.

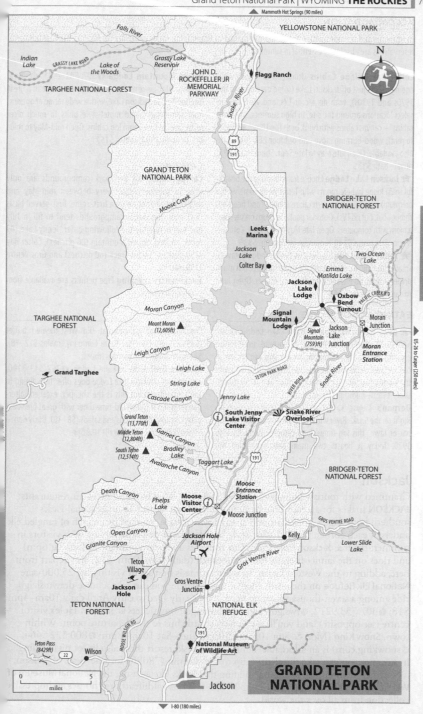

11

GRAND TETON NATIONAL PARK

ACCOMMODATION

Most rooms and activities within the park are managed by Grand Teton Lodge Company (☎ 307 543 3100, ⓦ gtlc.com); reservations are absolutely essential in summer.

Colter Bay Village Cabins Utilitarian and somewhat ageing cabins just off Jackson Lake (some date back to the 1920s and 1930s), with no a/c or TVs, and wi-fi only in select locations around the site. In high summer, $57 "tent cabins" – canvas cabins with bunk beds (bed linen available to rent), wood-burning stove and outdoor BBQ grill – are also available. Open late May to late Sept. Shared bath **$73**, private bath **$135**

★ **Jackson Lake Lodge** Choose from rooms in the beautiful main lodge (where rooms with Teton views come with a premium) or spacious, modern cabins (phones and free wi-fi throughout, but no TVs). Outdoor pool and shops on site, plus a room with computers. Open late May to early Oct. Cottages & non-view rooms **$249**, mountain-view rooms **$339**

★ **Jenny Lake Lodge** Luxurious timber lodge getaway, smaller and much quieter than the other options, but much pricier – rates do include breakfast and dinner. Open June to early Oct. Cabins **$565**

Signal Mountain Lodge ☎ 307 543 2831, ⓦ signal mountainlodge.com. Independently run lodge in a great location beside Jackson Lake, with a wide range of options, from somewhat bland motel-style units to much nicer rustic one- or two-room log cabins. Open mid-May to mid-Oct. Doubles **$194**, cabins **$157**

CAMPING

Campgrounds All five park campgrounds are only open in summer (dates vary between mid-May and mid-Oct) and operate on a first-come, first-served basis ($21/site). Individual campgrounds tend to fill in July and Aug in roughly the following order: Jenny Lake (49 tents; no RVs), Signal Mountain (86 pitches), Colter Bay (350 pitches), Lizard Creek (60 pitches) and Gros Ventre (355 pitches).

Backcountry camping Free permits are available from park visitor centres.

EATING AND DRINKING

★ **Blue Heron Lounge** Jackson Lake Lodge ☎ 307 543 3100, ⓦ gtlc.com. Be sure to earmark time for an evening drink at this hotel bar, where you can recline in comfortable chairs and ogle through huge picture windows the warm blues, greys, purples and pinks of a Teton sunset. Daily 11am–midnight (in season).

Dornan's Moose ☎ 307 733 2415, ⓦ dornans.com. Right on the Snake River with Teton views from the rooftop bar or lawn, this log-frame food complex dates back to 1920. Today it boasts two main eating options: the

Chuckwagon all-you-can eat Old West-themed buffet ($15–25) and the Pizza Pasta Company (mains $12–18). See website for the various hours.

Pioneer Grill Jackson Lake Lodge ☎ 307 543 3100, ⓦ gtlc.com. *Jackson Lake Lodge* does offer fine dining in the Mural Room but this is the cheaper, excellent alternative, laid out like an old-time diner with great breakfast plates, sandwiches, soups and salads ($8–10). Daily 6am–10pm (take-out window till 10.30pm).

Jackson

Crammed with touristy boutiques, art galleries, Old West bars and excellent restaurants, **JACKSON** makes for an enjoyable base, five miles from Grand Teton National Park's southern boundary. Centred around shady **Town Square**, marked by an arch of tangled elk antlers at each corner, the Old West-style boardwalks of **downtown** burst with visitors in summer; the free **Jackson Hole Shoot Out** recreates a Western gunfight (Mon–Sat 6pm) and rides on the family-friendly **Red Stagecoach** (daily 9am–9pm; $12) also depart from here, adding to the Western kitsch. In winter, time is best spent visiting the 25,000-acre **National Elk Refuge** on the north edge of town, where you can take a horse-drawn sleigh ride among a seven-thousand-strong herd of elk (early Dec to early April daily 10am–4pm; $18; ☎ 307 733 9212, ⓦ fws.gov/nationalelkrefuge); buy tickets at Jackson Hole's visitor centre (see opposite), and you'll be taken by shuttle bus to the departure point. Within town, **Snow King** (Mon & Sun 10am–4.30pm; Tues–Sat 10am–8pm; ☎ 800 522 5464, ⓦ snowking.com) is an affordable, family-friendly ski resort that's also lit for night skiing; in summer you can take the chairlift up to the summit (7808ft) for fine views of Jackson.

North of town on Hwy-89, in a building that looks like a castle, the **National Museum of Wildlife Art** (daily 9am–5pm; $12; ☎ 307 733 5771, ⓦ wildlifeart.org) houses an impressive collection from all over the world.

Jackson Hole Mountain Resort and Teton Village

While busiest in summer with road-tripping national park visitors, Jackson remains a year-round draw thanks to **Jackson Hole Mountain Resort** (winter season late Nov to early April; lift tickets $95; ☎307 733 2292, ⊚jacksonhole.com), where the slopes are among the finest in the US for confident intermediates and advanced skiers and boarders. Twenty minutes' drive from downtown Jackson lies **Teton Village** at the base of the resort: in the summer you can ride the **Aerial Tram** (late May to late Sept; 10min) some 4139ft straight up to Rendezvous Mountain (10,450ft) for hiking and mind-bending views, or the **Bridger Gondola** (late June to mid-Sept daily except Sat 4.30–10pm) to Gondola Summit (9095ft) for fine dining (you can also hike between the two points). There's also a popular **downhill bike park** on the slopes, while back in Teton Village kids will enjoy the pop jet fountains, climbing wall and bungee trampolines.

ARRIVAL AND GETTING AROUND JACKSON

By plane Jackson's airport, 8 miles north in Grand Teton National Park, is linked to town by AllTrans shuttle service ($16 one-way to Jackson, $29 to Teton Village; ☎307 733 3135, ⊚jacksonholealltrans.com), and $25–30 taxis. The main flights here are from Denver (United) and Salt Lake City (Delta). Rental cars are available at the airport.

By bus Salt Lake Express (⊚saltlakeexpress.com) runs the only regular public transport to Jackson, from Idaho Falls (2 daily; 1hr 55min) and Salt Lake City (1 daily; 7hr). START buses (daily 6.30am–10pm, every 30min; ⊚startbus.com), provide free transport within Jackson Hole (up to the Wildlife Art Museum), and charge $3 for trips to Teton Village.

INFORMATION AND ACTIVITIES

Visitor centre 532 N Cache St (daily: late May to late Sept 8am–7pm; late Sept to late May 9am–5pm; ☎307 733 3316, ⊚jacksonholechamber.com).

Bike tours Guided bike tours with Teton Mountain Bike Tours, 545 North Cache St (☎307 733 0712, ⊚tetonmtbike .com) start at $65/half-day.

Rafting Dozens of rafting companies, including Charlie

Sands Wild Water (☎307 733 4410, ⊚sandswhitewater .com), offer whitewater trips on the Snake River south of town; expect to pay about $67 for a half-day trip, including transport and outerwear.

Dogsled tours Dogsled tours (late Nov to early April) start at $190/half-day with Continental Divide Dogsled Adventures (☎307 455 30522, ⊚dogsledadventures.com).

ACCOMMODATION

Accommodation in Jackson is fairly expensive in summer; rates drop by around 25 percent in winter and are good value for a ski vacation. In Teton Village, on the other hand, the ski-in ski-out accommodation is at a premium come winter. Explore possibilities quickly using Jackson Hole Central Reservations (☎307 733 4005, ⊚jacksonholewy.com).

★ **The Alpine House** 285 N Glenwood St ☎307 739 1570, ⊚alpinehouse.com. You won't receive better service at five-star resorts than you'll get at this cosy, 22-room B&B on a quiet street a few blocks from the town square. Breakfasts are equally extraordinary. $145

Anvil Motel 215 N Cache St ☎307 733 3668, ⊚anvil motel.com. Situated at one of Jackson's busier inter-sections, it's not the quietest spot, but the smallish rooms are in good shape and the rates are cheap. $77

The Hostel 3315 Village Drive, Teton Village ☎307 733 3415, ⊚thehostel.us. Excellent slopeside hostel featuring a lounge with fireplace, TV and games room, laundry and ping pong and pool tables. Dorm beds and

private rooms, either with king bed or four twin beds. Dorms $34, doubles $99

The Inn at Jackson Hole 3345 W Village Drive, Teton Village ☎307 733 2311, ⊚innatjh.com. Boasts 83 mid-size rooms, along with a few lofts. Amenities include heated outdoor pool and hot tub, laundry and a popular restaurant, *Masa Sushi*. $229

The Wort Hotel 50 N Glenwood St ☎307 733 2190, ⊚worthotel.com. Built in 1941, the *Wort* is the most venerable high-end property in town, combining old-world style with modern facilities that include hot tubs. $359

EATING AND NIGHTLIFE

JACKSON

Million Dollar Cowboy Bar 25 N Cache St (Town Square) ☎307 733 2207, ⊚milliondollarcowboybar.com. Built in

the early 1930s, this watering hole is a touristy but essential pit stop, with saddles for bar stools; downstairs the *Cowboy Steakhouse* has pinewood booths and knocks out a mean buffalo rib eye, blackened steak baguette ($16) and elk burger ($15). Daily noon–1.30am (steakhouse daily 11am–2pm & 5–10pm).

Shades Café 82 S King St ☎ 307 733 2015, ⊛ shadescafejh.com. Unpretentious and affordable spot in an historic log cabin, with excellent breakfasts and light, healthy lunches (soups, sandwiches, burritos). The lovely deck is a popular hangout on mild-weather days. Daily 7.30am–3pm.

Silver Dollar Bar & Grill 50 N Glenwood St ☎ 307 733 2190, ⊛ worthotel.com. More than 300 Morgan silver dollar coins from 1921 are inlaid into the entire bar here; admire it over the potent Bartender's Margarita. The restaurant section has outdoor seating and a menu featuring Snake River Farms Kobe burger ($19), smoked pheasant soup ($8.50) and the signature bone-in rib eye ($37). Grill daily 7am–2pm & 5.30–10pm; bar daily 11.30am–2am.

Snake River Brewing Co 265 S Millward St ☎ 307 739 2337, ⊛ snakeriverbrewing.com. Great locals' brewpub a few blocks southwest of Town Square. Reasonably priced pastas and wood-fired pizzas are well worth trying (lunch deals just $7), but it's the award-winning beers that pack 'em in (order the sampler tray). Daily 11.30am–midnight.

★ **Snake River Grill** 84 E Broadway (Town Square) ☎ 307 733 0557, ⊛ snakerivergrill.com. This local favourite does Old West with elegance, offering a fresh, seasonal menu, famed beer-battered onion rings (served on a branding iron), potato pancake with smoked salmon, steak tartare pizza (most mains $21–33) and its lauded Eskimo Bars dessert (chocolate-covered bars of cake and warm caramel dipping sauce; $10). Daily 5.30–10pm.

TETON VILLAGE

★ **Couloir Restaurant & The Deck** Jackson Hole Mountain Resort ☎ 307 739 2675, ⊛ jacksonhole.com. Take the Bridger Gondola (free at night) to dine at 9095ft up the mountain; *Couloir* specializes in local farm-to-table American cooking (try the house-smoked buffalo tenderloin; four courses $95), while *The Deck* serves up drinks and bar snacks with stellar views (happy hour 5–6pm). The Deck late June to mid-Sept Sun–Fri 4.30pm–midnight; Couloir late June to mid-Sept Sun–Fri 6pm–midnight.

Mangy Moose 3285 Village Drive ☎ 307 733 4913, ⊛ mangymoose.net. Legendary ski-bum hangout, famed for its après-ski sessions that segue into evenings of live rock or reggae. The bustling upstairs dining room serves decent burgers, chicken and pasta from 5.30pm. Cover charge for live music $5–25. Daily 7am–2am.

Montana

Believe the hype: **MONTANA** really is Big Sky country, a region of snow-capped summits, turbulent rivers, spectacular glacial valleys, heavily wooded forests and sparkling blue lakes beneath a vast, deep blue sky that seems to stretch for a million miles. The Blackfeet and Shoshone once hunted bison here and today the state remains a bastion of Western culture, a land of cowboys, ranches, small cities and nineteenth-century ghost towns (when the gold ran out so did the people). In Montana, so the jokes go, locals keep snow tyres on till June, you can drive at 75mph but you'll still be passed on the highway and half the licence plates are Canadian. Cheap Charlie Russell prints line every wall, and all the railway stations are now bars, offices or restaurants. Grizzly bears, elk and bighorn sheep are found in greater numbers in Montana than just about anywhere else on the continent.

The scenery is at its most dramatic and heavily trafficked in the **western** side of the state, especially the phenomenal **Glacier National Park** and the surrounding mountain chains, landscapes that featured heavily in 1990s movies *A River Runs Through it* and *The Horse Whisperer* (both filmed in part on Dennis Quaid's Montana ranch). In contrast, the **eastern** two-thirds is dusty high prairie – sun-parched in summer and wracked by blizzards in winter – that attracts far fewer visitors.

Each of Montana's small cities has its own proud identity, and most of them are conveniently located off the east–west I-90 corridor. Enjoyable **Missoula** is a laidback college town, a glimmer of liberalism in this otherwise libertarian state; the historic copper-mining hub of **Butte** was once a union stronghold; the elegant state capital **Helena** harkens back to its prosperous gold-mining years; and **Bozeman**, just to the south, is one of the hippest mountain towns in the USA, buzzing with out-of-towners in the peak months.

Little Bighorn Battlefield National Monument

756 Battlefield Tour Rd, Crow Agency (1 mile east of I-90 exit 510, on US-212) • Daily 8am–9pm; Tour Rd daily 8am–8pm; visitor centre daily 8am–7.30pm • $10/car, $5/pedestrians and motorcycles; bus tours late May to Aug daily 10am, 11am, noon, 2pm & 3pm ($10) • ⓘ 406 638 2621, Ⓦ nps.gov/libi

With the exception of Gettysburg, no other US battle has gripped the American imagination like the **Battle of the Little Bighorn** in June 1876, the biggest defeat of US forces by Native Americans in the West and the scene of the much mythologized "Custer's Last Stand". Once seen as a tragic hero, Custer is better known today for a series of blunders leading up to the battle, and the decisive Indian victory – of combined Arapaho, Lakota Sioux and Cheyenne warriors – helped shape the legends of leaders Sitting Bull and Crazy Horse (see box below).

The monument is located on the current Crow Indian Reservation in the Little Bighorn Valley, and you can trace the course of the battle on a **self-guided driving tour** through the grasslands, between the visitor centre and Last Stand Hill itself, and the Reno-Benteen Battlefield five miles away – there are also several **hiking trails**. What makes Little Bighorn so unique is that the landscape has remained virtually unchanged since 1876; equally unusual, white headstone markers show where each cavalryman was killed (Custer himself was re-buried in 1877 at the West Point Military Academy in New York state), while red granite markers do the same for Native American warriors, making for an extremely evocative experience. The **visitor centre** only contains a small exhibit on the battle, so to get the most out of the site listen to a **ranger talk** or take a **free ranger tour**; there are also fascinating hour-long **bus tours** with Crow-operated Apsaalooke Tours, and you can also use your phone to access audio tour commentary.

11

Billings and around

With a population of around 105,000, **BILLINGS** is Montana's big city, with a booming economy and even a couple of skyscrapers (though the state's tallest building, First Interstate Tower, is a modest 272ft). Founded in 1882, Billings was originally a railroad

---

CUSTER'S LAST STAND

During an erratic career, **George Armstrong Custer** was one of the central American military icons of the mid- to late nineteenth century. Though he graduated last in his class at West Point in 1861, he became the army's youngest-ever brigadier general, seeing action at Gettysburg and national fame through his presence at the ultimate Union victory at Appomattox, with his own troops blocking the Confederate retreat. However, he was also suspended for ordering the execution of deserters from a forced march he led through Kansas, and found notoriety for allowing the murder in 1868 of almost one hundred Cheyenne women and children at the Battle of Washita River. His most (in)famous moment, though, came on June 25, 1876, at the **Battle of the Little Bighorn**, known to native tribes as the **Battle of the Greasy Grass**.

Custer's was the first unit to arrive in the **Little Bighorn Valley**. Disdaining to await reinforcements, he set out to raze a village along the Little Bighorn River – which turned out to be the largest-ever gathering of Plains Indians. As a party of his men pursued fleeing women and children, they were encircled by two thousand Lakota and Cheyenne warriors emerging from either side of a ravine. The soldiers dismounted to attempt to shoot their way out, but were soon overwhelmed; simultaneously, Custer's command post on a nearby hill was wiped out.

Although American myth up to the 1960s established Custer as an unquestioned hero, archeologists and historians have since discounted the idea of **Custer's Last Stand** as a heroic act of defiance in which Custer was the last cavalryman left standing; the battle lasted less than an hour, with the white soldiers being systematically and effortlessly picked off. This most decisive Native American victory in the West – led by Sitting Bull and warriors like Crazy Horse – was also their final great show of resistance. With a total 268 US combatants killed, an incensed President Grant piled maximum resources into a military campaign that brought about the effective defeat of all Plains Indians by the end of the decade.

town; today the nearby Bakken and Heath shale oil fields continue to fuel the city's explosive growth. **Downtown**, bounded on its north side by the 400ft crumpled sandstone cliffs of the **Rimrock** (or just "the Rims"), centres on the tent-like **Skypoint** structure covering the intersection of Second Avenue and Broadway. While there are plenty of shops and restaurants here, this isn't likely to be the version of Montana you've come to experience – make time instead for the city's cultural attractions and the intriguing historic sites nearby.

Moss Mansion

914 Division St • Tues–Sat 10am–4pm, Sun 1–4pm (1hr tours on the hour till 3pm) • $10 • ☎ 406 256 5100, ⓦ mossmansion.com

The most prominent historical property downtown is the **Moss Mansion**, a sturdy 1903 red-sandstone manse built for **P.B. Moss** (1863–1947), an entrepreneur who made a fortune running most of the businesses and utilities in Billings from the 1890s. His daughter lived in this house virtually unaltered until it became a museum in 1984, so the contents are in mint condition, lavishly furnished and decorated in various styles, from a Moorish-themed entrance hall and sombre English oak dining room to a pretty pink French parlour.

Yellowstone Art Museum

401 N 27th St • Tues, Wed & Sat 10am–5pm, Thurs & Fri 10am–8pm, Sun 11am–4pm • $6 (free parking on site) • ☎ 406 256 6804, ⓦ yellowstone.artmuseum.org

The modest **Yellowstone Art Museum**, partly housed in the town's 1910 jail, is mostly filled with travelling art exhibits, but the excellent permanent collection galleries on the ground floor specialize in Montana art from the mid-twentieth century on; work rotates here, but highlights include the Western books, paintings and posters by cowboy illustrator **Will James** (1892–1942), who lived here in later life, and contemporary works from **Theodore Waddell**, who was born in Billings in 1941 (ironically, both spent time in the jail's drunk tank). Make time also for the **Visible Vault** across the road (included), where all 7000 plus items in the permanent collection are stored and you can view resident artists at work.

Pompeys Pillar National Monument

Exit 23, I-94 • Daily: May to early Sept 8am–8pm; early Sept to early Oct 9am–4pm • $7 • ☎ 406 875 2400, ⓦ pompeyspillar.org

Just 28 miles northeast of Billings, overlooking the Yellowstone River, **Pompeys Pillar National Monument** would just be a 150ft-tall sandstone outcrop with modest appeal if not for its fascinating historical connections: the rock was named by explorer **William Clark** for Sacagawea's son when he passed here in 1806, but he also **carved his signature** into its stone flanks. It's now protected by glass (surrounded by graffiti going back to the 1880s and reached via a boardwalk), but history buffs will get chills being up close to the only physical evidence of the Corps of Discovery's 1804–06 expedition. The excellent **visitor centre** provides details of the expedition.

ARRIVAL AND INFORMATION

BILLINGS AND AROUND

By plane Billings Logan International Airport (ⓦ fly billings.com) is just 2 miles northwest of downtown. Taxis meet most flights.

By bus The Greyhound bus station is downtown at 2502 First Ave N.

Destinations Bismarck (2 daily; 7hr 15min–10hr 30min);

Bozeman (2 daily; 2hr 35min); Butte (2 daily; 4hr 10min); Missoula (2 daily; 6hr 14min–6hr 40min).

Visitor centre 815 S 27th St, downtown (late May to Aug Mon–Sat 8.30am–5pm, Sun noon–4pm; Sept to late May Mon–Fri 8.30am–5pm; ☎ 406 252 4016, ⓦ visitbillings.com).

ACCOMMODATION AND EATING

C'mon Inn 2020 Overland Ave S ☎ 406 655 1100, ⓦ cmon inn.com. Fun place to stay, with lush garden courtyard with waterfalls and spacious rooms with fireplaces, jacuzzis, flat-screen TVs and fridges, plus continental breakfast. $129

Josephine B&B 514 N 29th St ☎ 406 248 5898, ⓦ thejosephine.com. Five cosy rooms and suites in a

home dating from 1912, which has the added draw of fresh fruit and sourdough pancakes for breakfast. $95

★ **Stella's Kitchen and Bakery** 2525 1st Ave N ☎ 406 248 3060. Local favourite for its hearty breakfasts and pastries, especially the hefty pancakes, cinnamon buns and apple pie. Mon–Sat 5.30am–5pm, Sun 7am–1am.

Überbrew 2305 Montana Ave ☎ 406 534 6960. With ten breweries in the metro area, Billings has more craft beer makers than any other community in Montana. Get acquainted at this superb brewpub, with excellent *hefeweizen* (wheat beer) and bar food such as bison burgers. Daily 11am–9pm.

Red Lodge and the Beartooth Scenic Highway

The small but popular resort town of **RED LODGE** lies along Bear Creek, sixty miles south of Billings at the foot of the awe-inspiring **Beartooth Mountains** – whose jagged peaks and outcrops contain some of the oldest rocks on earth – and in winter acts as a base for skiers using the popular **Red Lodge Mountain**, six miles west on US-212 (☎ 406 446 2610, ⓦ redlodgemountain.com). Originally founded to mine coal for the transcontinental railroads, Red Lodge's future was secured by the construction of the 65-mile **Beartooth Scenic Highway** (usually open late May to early Oct) connecting to Cooke City at the northeastern entrance to Yellowstone National Park (see p.697), a jaw-dropping ride of tight switchbacks, steep grades and vertiginous overlooks (allow 2–3hr to the park entrance). Even in summer the springy tundra turf of the 10,940ft **Beartooth Pass** is covered with snow that (due to algae) turns pink when crushed. All around are gem-like corries, deeply gouged granite walls and huge blocks of roadside ice.

11

ACCOMMODATION   RED LODGE

★ **Pollard Hotel** 2 N Broadway ☎ 406 446 0001, ⓦ thepollard.com. Handsome 1893 brick hotel with some of the cheery, Victorian-themed rooms offering jacuzzis and balconies, plus pool, sauna and a comfortable old library. $95

Red Lodge Inn 817 S Broadway ☎ 406 446 2030, ⓦ theredlodgeinn.com. Budget option south of town;

it looks like an old-fashioned cabin-style motel, but the rooms are clean and modern with new bathrooms, cable TV and a/c. Basic breakfast included. $95

Yodeler Motel 601 S Broadway ☎ 406 446 1435, ⓦ yodelermotel.com. Offers a quirky Bavarian-German theme to go with its clean and basic motel rooms; most of the water is heated by solar power. $79

EATING AND DRINKING

Bridge Creek Backcountry Kitchen 116 S Broadway ☎ 406 446 9900, ⓦ eatfooddrinkwine.com. Great place to try the local "mountain cuisine", with Montana-grown and -raised ingredients: steaks, fresh seafood, wild game and creative pasta dishes (mains $19–34). Tues–Sat 11am–3pm & 5–10pm (limited winter hours).

Café Regis 501 S Word Ave, at 16th St W ☎ 406 446 194, ⓦ caferegis.com. Best place in town for breakfast, with local ingredients and home-baked goods; wholesome salads, wild salmon and tasty corn cakes feature. Wed–Sun 6am–2pm.

Más Taco 304 N Broadway ☎ 406 446 3636. Popular, family joint on the northern edge of town, serving authentic tacos; pork "al Pastor", *carne asada*, slow-roasted

chicken and shrimp (everything under $10). Tues–Sat 11am–5pm.

Red Box Car 1300 S Broadway ☎ 406 446 2152. A must-try experience on the southern edge of town, this 100-year old boxcar has been a diner since 1972, knocking out tasty, cheap burgers (from $3) and exquisite "box burgers" (all-steak patties) from $4.50 – great shakes, onion rings and Indian tacos. Sit outside overlooking the river. Daily 11am–10pm.

Red Lodge Ales (Sam's Tap Room) 1445 N Broadway ☎ 406 446 0243, ⓦ redlodgeales.com. The local micro-brewery knocks out some excellent ales, from its highly drinkable IPA to some intriguing seasonal beers, as well as deli sandwiches. Daily 11am–9pm.

Bozeman

Founded in 1864, **BOZEMAN** lies at the north end of the lush Gallatin Valley some 145 miles west of Billings, a small, affluent college town of around 40,000 with a pleasant, lively **Main Street** and a couple of worthwhile museums. The city is also a gateway to Yellowstone (just 90 miles south), and home to **Montana State University** (MSU), whose **Bobcats** sports teams enjoy enthusiastic support among locals. The biggest game of the year is the (American) football match with bitter rivals Missoula-based University of Montana, dubbed the "**Brawl of the Wild**" (usually in Nov; see ⓦ msubobcats.com).

BOZEMAN AND THE BIG OUTDOORS

Though the natural wonders of Yellowstone and Glacier national parks beckon, Bozeman offers plenty of scenic and energetic attractions of its own, particularly in rugged Hyalite Canyon just south of town, which has top-notch hiking and mountain biking in summer and excellent ice climbing December to March. In winter, try the challenging local ski area, **Bridger Bowl** (☎406 587 2111, ⓦbridgerbowl.com). An hour's drive south down the beautiful Gallatin Valley is the much pricier **Big Sky Resort** (☎406 995 5900, ⓦbigskyresort.com), popular for its top-quality powder and steep slopes on 11,166ft Lone Mountain. For details on more outdoor activities, check with the **visitor centre** in Bozeman (see below).

Museum of the Rockies

600 W Kagy Blvd (off S 7th Ave) • June–Aug daily 8am–8pm; Sept–May Mon–Sat 9am–5pm, Sun 12.30–5pm (Living History Farm: late May to Aug daily 9am–5pm) • $14 • ☎406 994 2251, ⓦmuseumoftherockies.org

South of downtown, the huge **Museum of the Rockies** is best known for its exceptional **dinosaur** collection, almost all of it obtained from digs in Montana. Among the many highlights is the world's largest-known skull of a *T.rex*, a large ensemble of giant *Triceratops* skulls and skeletons and landmark *Deinonychus* finds (the nasty little ancestor of the *Velociraptor*) that revolutionized the way scientists thought about dinosaurs (that modern-day birds are direct descendants of dinosaurs is a big theme of the museum). The section on Native American culture of the northern Rockies is comprehensive but a bit drier, and there is also a section of pioneer history, a decent planetarium showing movies throughout the day (included) and, in summer, the **Living History Farm**, an 1889 farmhouse and blossom-filled garden manned by costumed guides.

Pioneer Museum

317 W Main St • June–Aug Mon–Sat 10am–5pm; Sept–May Tues–Sat 11am–4pm • $5 • ☎406 522 8122, ⓦpioneermuseum.org

The small **Pioneer Museum** is crammed with all sorts of historical bits and pieces relating to the history of Bozeman and Gallatin County, from exhibits on MSU and Gary Cooper (who went to high school here), to city founder, gambler and womanizer John Bozeman and **Fort Ellis**, the army camp that operated near Bozeman 1867 to 1886. The museum occupies the old jail of 1911 (in operation till 1982), with several of the old cells still intact; you can also see the gallows where the jail's one execution took place in 1924.

ARRIVAL AND INFORMATION
BOZEMAN

By plane Bozeman Yellowstone International Airport (ⓦbozemanairport.com) is 7 miles northwest of downtown; in addition to taxis, Karst Stage (ⓦkarststage.com) offers shuttles to West Yellowstone ($51.50 one-way) and Mammoth Hot Springs ($157.50 one-way).

By bus The Greyhound terminal is at 1205 E Main St, about a mile from the centre.

Destinations Billings (2 daily; 2hr 35min); Bismarck (1 daily; 15hr 5min); Butte (2 daily; 1hr 30min); Missoula (2 daily; 3hr 40min–4hr).

Visitor centre 222 E Main St (Mon–Fri 9am–5pm; ☎406 586 4008, ⓦdowntownbozeman.org). See also ⓦbozeman chamber.com.

ACCOMMODATION

Howlers Inn 3185 Jackson Creek Rd ☎406 587 5229, ⓦhowlersinn.com. True to its name, this delightful hotel sits next to a small wolf sanctuary and features a jacuzzi, sauna and modern rooms with DVD-players and microwaves. **$120**

★ **Lehrkind Mansion** 719 N Wallace Ave ☎406 585 6932, ⓦbozemanbedandbreakfast.com. Occupies a gorgeous Queen Anne home built in 1897 by a German beermaker, offering nine rooms and suites richly appointed with Victorian antiques and Old West-styled furniture. **$159**

EATING AND DRINKING

Cateye Café 23 N Tracy St, off Main St ☎406 587 8844, ⓦcateyecafe.com. Cool, quirky, friendly little place, knocking out classic American comfort food such as chicken

pot pie with corn bread ($8.75) and honey-fried chicken ($9.75). Mon–Fri 7am–2.30pm, Sat & Sun 7am–2pm.

Community Food Co-op 44 E Main St, at Black Ave

☎ 406 922 2667, ⊚ bozo.coop. Spacious, clean self-serve café (buffet priced at $8.49/lb), with terrific vegetarian dishes, deli sandwiches, salads, curries and mouth-watering desserts. Mon–Sat 8.30am–9pm, Sun 8.30am–8pm.

Copper Whiskey Bar & Grill 101 E Main St, at Black Ave ☎ 406 404 1700 ⊚ coppermontana.com. Hoppin' bar and restaurant serving interesting dishes such as grouper sandwich ($17) and steak frites ($15), along with 100 types of whisky. Daily 4pm–2am.

★ **Granny's Gourmet Donuts** 3 Tai Lane, at W Lincoln St ☎ 406 922 0022. This tiny hole-in-the-wall near the MSU campus has garnered something of a cult following for its freshly made donuts, just 75¢ each, from the addictive

chocolate flavour to the zingy strawberry. Cash only. Tues–Fri 7am–2pm, Sat & Sun 8am–2pm.

★ **Montana Ale Works** 611 E Main St ☎ 406 587 7700, ⊚ montanaaleworks.com. Offers dozens of quality local microbrews along with solid steaks and bison burgers, sandwiches and dumplings. Mon–Thurs & Sun 4–10pm, Fri & Sat 4–11pm.

Ted's Montana Grill 105 W Main St ☎ 406 587 6000, ⊚ tedsmontanagrill.com. The place to go for a splurge, with high-quality steaks (from $25), bison pot roast ($19), the ubiquitous bison burgers ($13) and scrumptious salt-and-pepper onion rings ($7). Mon–Thurs 11am–10pm, Fri & Sat 11am–11pm, Sun 11am–9pm.

Butte and around

11

Eighty miles west of Bozeman, the former copper-mining colossus of **BUTTE** (rhyme with "mute") burst into life after gold was discovered here in 1862. Set on the slopes of a steep hill, today it sports massive black steel headframes – "gallus frames" (gallows frames) to miners – grand architecture, Cornish pasties and Irish and Serbian churches, all a legacy of its turbulent mining heyday. Though mining still takes place here, Butte's population has been reducing for years, with 34,500 current inhabitants and large areas of the centre boarded up or simply empty lots. The historical section is known as **Uptown**, while below Front Street lies **The Flats**, where most people live today. At dusk it's all oddly attractive, when the golden light casts a glow on the mine-pocked hillsides, and the old neon signs illuminate historic brick buildings.

Berkeley Pit Viewing Stand

300 Continental Drive · Mid-May to Sept Mon–Sat 8am–8pm, Sun 9am–6pm · $2 · ☎ 406 723 3177, ⊚ pitwatch.org

In 1954 Anaconda Mining decided to open up the **Berkeley Pit**, an incredibly productive move that led to some 320 million tons of copper being extracted before the mine closed in 1982 (thanks to the collapse in copper prices). Unfortunately, the company had to demolish half of Butte to create this giant hole, 1800ft deep, one mile wide and 1.25 miles long; and when the whole thing flooded after closing, it became some of the most toxic water in the US. At the viewing stand you can take in the vast size of it all, and learn about the long-term efforts to clean it up.

World Museum of Mining

155 Museum Way (at the end of West Park St) · April–Oct daily 9am–5pm (underground mine tours daily 10.30am, 12.30pm & 3pm) · $8.50; tours $12, combined ticket $17 · ☎ 406 723 7211, ⊚ miningmuseum.org

The excellent **World Museum of Mining**, on the far side of the Montana Tech of the University of Montana campus, is packed with fascinating memorabilia, and outside, beyond the scattered collection of rusting machinery – from jackhammers to mine carts – the museum's fifty-building **Hell Roarin' Gulch** re-creates a cobbled-street mining camp of the 1890s, complete with saloon, bordello, church, schoolhouse and Chinese laundry. Above it all looms the 100ft headframe of the 3200ft-deep **Orphan Girl** mineshaft, which closed in 1955; below it all you can take in an **underground tour** (1hr 30min) of some of the rickety old facilities, walking through tunnels 65ft below ground (the mine is completely flooded below 100ft).

Copper King Mansion

219 W Granite St · Tours (1hr) April Sat & Sun 9am–4pm; May–Sept daily 9am–4pm · $7.50 · ☎ 406 782 7580, ⊚ thecopperkingmansion.com

Few mining baron estates are grander than the 34-room **Copper King Mansion**, completed for copper magnate **William A. Clark** in 1888. Clark was already a successful businessman when he came to Butte in 1872, but his investments in copper made him a multimillionaire. Along with frescoed ceilings, handcrafted mahogany and birds-eye maple chandeliers and fireplaces, the "modern Elizabethan"-style mansion has been restocked with an incredible collection of period antiques, dolls, toys, clocks, paintings and carpets; it also has the draw of being a B&B (see below).

Charles W. Clark Chateau

321 W Broadway • June–Sept Fri–Sun 1–4pm (if staff are available) • Tours $6 • ☎ 406 491 5636, ⓦ bsbarts.org

Charles W. Clark, the eldest son of William Clark (see p.713), built the 26-room **Charles W. Clark Chateau** in 1898, a mock-French castle with a splendid spiral staircase, exotic-wood-inlaid rooms and wrought-iron decor. It now holds Victorian furniture and antiques, as well as a rotating selection of contemporary regional art. Opening is dependent on volunteers, so call ahead to check.

Mai Wah Museum

17 W Mercury St • June–Sept Tues–Sat 10am–4pm • $5 • ☎ 406 723 3231, ⓦ maiwah.org

Hard to imagine today, but Butte once had a thriving Chinese community, at its peak in the 1910s and commemorated at the **Mai Wah Museum**. The museum occupies two historic buildings; the **Wah Chong Tai**, erected in 1899 and a general store operated by the Chinn family until 1941; and the **Mai Wah Noodle Parlour**, built in 1909. In 2013 the Wah Chong Tai section reopened, crammed with all its original contents frozen in time (a collector had bought the shop's whole stock in 1941 hoping to open his own museum). There's also an excellent exhibit on the 2007 excavations across the street, and a detailed section on Butte's Chinatown, which emerged around here in the 1870s. Despite considerable anti-Chinese prejudice from the 1890s on, the community thrived until the mining declined – by the 1940s most Chinese had gone and many nearby buildings were demolished.

ARRIVAL, INFORMATION AND TOURS

By bus Greyhound buses drop off downtown at 1324 Harrison Ave.
Destinations Billings (2 daily; 4hr 10min); Bozeman (2 daily 1hr 30min); Missoula (2 daily; 1hr 50min).
Chamber of Commerce Just off I-90, exit 126, at 1000 George St (Mon–Sat 8am–8pm, Sun 9am–6pm; ☎ 406 723 3177, ⓦ buttecvb.com).

BUTTE AND AROUND

Walking tours For more on the town's colourful history, take a 90min walking tour with Old Butte Historical Adventures, 117 N Main St (April–Oct Mon–Sat 10am–4pm; $15; ☎ 406 498 3424, ⓦ buttetours.info), which covers the area's architecture, mines, railway lines, a speakeasy and even journeys to the region's ghost towns (prices vary; by appointment only).

ACCOMMODATION

★ **Copper King Mansion** 219 W Granite St ☎ 406 782 7580, ⓦ thecopperkingmansion.com. Staying at this historic B&B really is like staying in a museum (see p.713); checkout is 9am to allow tours of the rooms to begin, and much of the interior – bedrooms and bathrooms – contain exhibits. Sleeping here is a spellbinding experience; the place drips with history and the breakfasts are excellent.

No TVs or wi-fi in rooms, and one shared shower (most rooms have old-style baths). $75
Toad Hall Manor 1 Green Lane ☎ 406 494 2625, ⓦ toadhallmanor.com. Stylish B&B in a stately neo-Georgian house, whose four units variously come with jacuzzis, fridges, microwaves and courtyards. $140

EATING AND DRINKING

★ **Joe's Pasty Shop** 1641 Grand Ave ☎ 406 723 9071. This small diner has been serving up the hearty, meat-and-potato-filled Cornish dish ($5.25) since 1947 – order it with gravy ($6.50) for an extra treat. Mon–Fri 7am–7pm, Sat 7am–6pm.
★ **Matt's Place** 2339 Placer St ☎ 406 782 8049. This classic drive-in diner opened in 1930 (the counter is from 1936 and lighting fixtures are 1950s originals), with malts

and shakes with home-made ice cream, and good, old-fashioned cheeseburgers with hand-cut fries. Mid-March to Dec daily 7am–2.30pm.
Pekin Café & Lounge 117 S Main St ☎ 406 782 2217. The last of Butte's historical Chinese noodle parlours, this gem has been going strong since 1911; inside is a line of pink wooden booths, with curtains for privacy – and the food is cheap and solid American Chinese, Cantonese and

Sichuan fare (noodles $4.95–8.95; set dinners from $8.25). Mon & Sun 5–10pm, Wed & Thurs 5–11pm, Fri & Sat 5pm–midnight.

Pork Chop John's 8 W Mercury St ☎406 782 0812, ⓦporkchopjohns.com. For more rib-stuffing, lunch-bucket fare, head to another old-time favourite (since 1932) for its fried breaded pork sandwiches (served like burgers; $3.50), hamburgers and grilled-cheese sandwiches ($4.95). Mon–Sat 10.30am–10.30pm.

Sparky's Garage 222 E Park St ☎406 782 2301. Fun restaurant loaded with auto memorabilia and old cars; you can eat in a pickup truck. Great comfort food including brisket and catfish sandwiches. Mon–Thurs 11am–9.30pm, Fri & Sat 11am–10pm, Sun noon–9pm.

Uptown Café 47 E Broadway ☎406 723 4735, ⓦuptowncafe.com. The best place for a sit-down restaurant experience in Butte, serving pizza, pasta and sandwiches, but best known for its steak-and-seafood dinner mains and inexpensive, fixed ($15–20) five-course meals. Mon–Fri 11am–2pm & 5–10pm, Sat & Sun 5–10pm.

Helena

Some seventy miles north of Butte on I-15 and framed by the Rocky Mountains, **HELENA** is Montana's relaxed, tiny state capital, founded in 1864 when a party of gold prospectors hit the jackpot at Last Chance Gulch. During the boom years, more than $20 million of gold was extracted from the gulch, and fifty successful prospectors remained here as millionaires. **Last Chance Gulch** is now the town's attractive main street (the water still runs underground), whose stately Victorian buildings are home to gift shops, diners and bars. Contrast this with the far more modest digs southwest of town in **Reeder's Alley** (ⓦreeders alley.com), a collection of miners' bunkhouses, wooden storehouses and other humble stone and brick structures built between 1875 and 1884, now refurbished into smart shops and restaurants. Helena has an unexpected Hollywood connection, too: **Gary Cooper** was born here in 1901 and almost became a real cowboy before heading to Hollywood in the 1920s to play one on screen, while actress **Myrna Loy** lived here as a child.

State Capitol Building

1301 E Sixth Ave • Mon–Sat 8am–5pm, Sun 11am–5pm (tours Mon–Sat 9am–2pm, hourly) • Free • ☎406 444 4789, ⓦvisit-the-capitol.mt.gov

The Montana legislative branch has worked since 1902 out of the elegant **State Capitol Building**, covered with a copper-clad dome and featuring an ornate, French Renaissance interior adorned with stained-glass skylights and numerous murals. The most famous artwork lies in the House Chamber, where a huge mural completed by Montana artist **Charles M. Russell** in 1911 depicts a dramatic encounter between native tribes and Lewis and Clark.

Montana's Museum

225 N Roberts St • Mon–Sat 9am–5pm, Thurs closes 8pm • $5 • ☎406 444 2694, ⓦmontanahistoricalsociety.org

The illuminating **Montana's Museum**, opposite the capitol, chronicles the history of the state in great detail with clear explanations and rare artefacts from each period. It's especially good on prehistory and the region's Native American cultures, as well as having a modern, family-friendly hall depicting Montana at the time of Lewis & Clark's 1805 expedition. Don't miss the small gallery dedicated to Western artist Charles M. Russell, and upstairs "Big Medicine", the rare (and revered) white buffalo that died and was preserved here in 1959.

ARRIVAL AND INFORMATION   HELENA

By plane Helena Regional Airport (ⓦhelenaairport.com) is 2 miles northeast of downtown; you'll need to call a taxi (☎406 449 5525) or arrange a hotel shuttle.

By bus Long-distance buses stop at Helena's transit centre at 1415 N Montana Ave, northeast of downtown. There's one daily service to Butte (1hr 15min).

Visitor centre 225 Cruse Ave (☎406 447 1530, ⓦgohelena.com).

ACCOMMODATION

Barrister Bed & Breakfast 416 N Ewing St ☎406 443 7330, ⓦthebarristermt.tripod.com. Gorgeous 1874 Victorian mansion near the cathedral and originally used as priests' quarters, now offering five graceful rooms. $122

Comfort Suites 3180 N Washington St ☎406 495 0505, ⓦcomfortsuiteshelena.com. This is by far the best

11

value of the modern chain hotels on the outskirts, with spacious suites (with seating area), huge workspaces, TVs and great breakfasts. **$110.**

Sanders B&B 328 N Ewing St ☎406 442 3309,

ⓦsandersbb.com. Justly popular B&B in a home from 1875, whose seven old-fashioned rooms come with Western decor and antiques, some with clawfoot tubs and fireplaces. **$130**

EATING AND DRINKING

★ **Big Dipper Ice Cream** 58 N Last Chance Gulch ☎406 513 1051, ⓦbigdippericecream.com. Local gem – the original is in Missoula (see opposite) – with unusual and delicious concoctions such as strawberry pink peppercorn sorbet (scoops $2.50, shakes $4). Daily 11am–10pm.

Lewis and Clark Brewing Co 1517 Dodge Ave ☎406 442 5960, ⓦlewisandclarkbrewing.com. Stop at the local microbrewery beer hall for a burger and a highly rated Tumbleweed IPA. Daily 2–8pm.

★ **Old Miners Dining Club at the Caretaker's Cabin** 212 S Park Ave ☎406 449 6848, ⓦoldminersdiningclub .com. Exceptional dining experience in an 1865 cabin, with a carefully crafted menu of barbecue seafood, steaks ($25.95), home-made cheesecake and Australian lobster. Wed–Sat 5–11pm (call ahead to confirm times).

Windbag Saloon 19 S Last Chance Gulch ☎406 443 9669. Big old barn of a place – and former brothel – that serves rib-stuffing seafood, burgers and steaks. Mon–Thurs 11am–9.30pm, Fri 11am–10pm, Sat noon–9.30pm.

Gates of the Mountains

Some 25 miles north of Helena off Hwy-287 • June–Sept hours vary, generally hourly Mon–Fri 11am–2pm or 3pm, Sat & Sun 10am–4pm • $16 • ☎406 458 5241, ⓦgatesofthemountains.com

One of the region's more worthwhile excursions is the two-hour guided **boat tour** through the stunning **Gates of the Mountains**. This dramatic stretch of the Missouri River, also known as Great White Rock Canyon, is a six-mile gorge between sheer 1200ft-tall limestone cliffs named by explorer Meriwether Lewis. While not as grand as Glacier National Park, the gentle cruise does offer plenty of raw, scenic splendour not to mention an eye-opening array of wildlife, including resident pelicans and bald eagles, bighorn sheep and occasionally mountain lions and black bears (August is the best time for the latter).

Missoula and around

Framed by the striking Bitterroot and Sapphire mountains, vibrant and friendly **MISSOULA** is full of contrasts – bookstores, continental cafés and gun shops – a place where students from the local University of Montana provide much of the town's energy. Founded in 1866, it's now the second biggest city in Montana.

OUTDOOR ACTIVITIES AROUND MISSOULA

Missoula is a particularly good base for outdoor activities. Worthwhile hikes traverse the 60,000 acres of the **Rattlesnake National Recreation Area**, which, despite the name, claims to be serpent-free; find more information at the local **ranger station**, at Fort Missoula, Building 24 (Mon–Fri 7.30am–4pm; ☎406 329 3750, ⓦfs.usda.gov/lolo). Missoula is excellent for cycling, too, and another good source of information and **trail maps** is the Adventure Cycling Association, 150 E Pine St (☎406 721 1776, ⓦadventurecycling.org); the Bicycle Hangar, 1801 Brooks St (Mon–Sat 10am–6pm; March–Aug also Sun 11am–5pm; ☎406 728 9537, ⓦbicycle-hangar.com), rents out good-quality bikes.

The most developed of the city's small ski areas is **Montana Snowbowl**, twelve miles northwest, which has a range of slopes for all abilities (lift tickets $43) and boasts a summer **chairlift** (July to early Sept daily noon–5pm; $8, $2 for bikes; ☎406 549 9777, ⓦmontana snowbowl.com). For state-park **camping** you'll need to backtrack east, either 25 miles on I-90 to small **Beavertail Hill** (May–Oct; day-use fee $5, camping $28; ☎406 542 5500), which also has two replica tepees to stay in ($35), or forty miles on Hwy-200 and a brief jog on Hwy-83 north to **Salmon Lake** (same info and phone), which is great for its fishing and swimming in the Clearwater River.

Missoula Art Museum

335 N Pattee St • May–Aug Tues–Sat 10am–4pm, Sun noon–4pm; Sept–April Wed–Fri 10am–5pm, Sat & Sun10am–3pm • Free •
📞 406 728 0447, 🌐 missoulaartmuseum.org

One sign of Missoula's dynamism is its **Missoula Art Museum**, which displays challenging contemporary work in digital photography, painting and sculpture (especially work related to the American West), and a range of eye-opening pieces by contemporary Native American artists.

Montana Museum of Art & Culture

Main Hall, University of Montana • Sept–May Tues, Wed & Sat noon–3pm, Thurs & Fri noon–6pm; June–Aug Wed, Thurs & Sat
noon–3pm, Fri noon–6pm • Free • 📞 406 243 2019, 🌐 umt.edu/montanamuseum

On the university campus, the **Montana Museum of Art & Culture** boasts an incredibly rich collection of art highlighted by interesting Renaissance-era Flemish tapestries, paintings and prints by Rembrandt, Delacroix, Joan Miró, Picasso and Toulouse-Lautrec, and American art from Frederic Remington, Warhol, Rockwell and many others.

Elk Country Visitor Center

5705 Grant Creek Rd • Jan–April Mon–Fri 8am–5pm, Sat 10am–5pm; May–Dec Mon–Fri 8am–6pm, Sat & Sun 9am–6pm • Free •
📞 406 523 4545, 🌐 rmef.org

Operated by the pro-conservation/pro-hunting Rocky Mountain Elk Foundation just outside town, the **Elk Country Visitor Center** provides exhibits about the prodigious, especially horned, creatures in the region, with a short walking trail providing on-site examples of a few of the creatures you can expect to see on more rugged hikes.

Smokejumper Center

5765 W Broadway • **Visitor centre** Late May to Aug daily 8.30am–5pm • Free • 📞 406 329 4934, 🌐 smokejumpers.com

Fires are common in this part of the country during the dry season, and the associated dangers are highlighted at the Forest Service **Smokejumper Center**, ten miles out of town on US-93. A small **visitor centre** explains methods used to train smokejumpers here – highly skilled firefighters who parachute into forested areas to stop the spread of wildfires. Free guided tours (45min) are also given of the parachute loft and training facilities.

ARRIVAL AND INFORMATION   MISSOULA

By plane Missoula International Airport (🌐 flymissoula .com) is just 4 miles northwest of downtown on W Broadway; taxis and Mountain Line public buses (Mon–Fri 11 daily; $1; 🌐 mountainline.com) serve the airport.

By bus Greyhound pulls in at 1660 W Broadway, on the edge of downtown.

Destinations Billings (2 daily; 6hr 30min); Bozeman (2 daily;

3hr 45min); Butte (2 daily; 1hr 50min); Seattle (2 daily; 10hr 30min); Spokane (2 daily; 4hr 20min).

Visitor centre 101 E Main St (late May to Aug Mon–Fri 9am–7pm, Sat 9am–3pm, Sun 10am–2pm; Sept to late May Mon–Fri 9am–5pm; 📞 406 532 3250, 🌐 destination missoula.org).

ACCOMMODATION

Doubletree Missoula-Edgewater 100 Madison St 📞 406 728 3100, 🌐 doubletree.com. Best of the chain hotels, near the university right on the Clark Fork River – on which you can conveniently fly-fish – with nice rooms and suites and gym, pool and hot tub. $159

Goldsmith's Inn 809 E Front St 📞 406 728 1585, 🌐 missoulabedandbreakfast.com. Quaint 1911 Victorian

B&B with nice riverside views, whose seven rooms and suites variously offer balconies and fireplaces. $124

Ruby's Inn 4825 N Reserve St 📞 406 721 0990, 🌐 erckhotels.com/rubys. Friendly old-school motel which has simple rooms plus free high-speed internet, outdoor pool, spa and laundry. $89

EATING AND DRINKING

⭐ **Big Dipper Ice Cream** 631 S Higgins 📞 406 543 5722, 🌐 bigdippericecream.com. Local icon, serving innovative ice cream flavours such as huckleberry and El Salvador coffee

(scoops $2.50, shakes $4). Daily 10.30am–10pm.

Kettlehouse Brewing Co 602 Myrtle St 📞 406 728 1660, 🌐 kettlehouse.com. Lovingly known as the "K-hole", this tap room doesn't serve food, just quality handcrafted beers such as Cold Smoke Scotch Ale. Daily noon–8pm.

★ **Red Bird** 111 N Higgins St ☎ 406 549 2906, Ⓦ redbirdrestaurant.com. Famed for its eclectic decor, and delicious, pricey, nouveau Western eats, such as local lamb with apple couscous and chilli-rubbed bison tenderloin (mains $25–37). Tues–Sat 5–9.30pm.

The Shack 222 W Main St ☎ 406 549 9903, Ⓦ theshack cafe.com. Solid breakfast option, with tasty omelettes and

moderately priced Mexican food, pasta and sandwiches for lunch. Mon–Thurs 7am–3pm, Fri–Sun 7am–9pm.

Staggering Ox 1220 SW Higgins Ave ☎ 406 542 2206, Ⓦ staggeringox.com. Offers the most bizarre take on conventional fare – "clubfoot" sandwiches baked in a can and presented vertically – but the concept works, with tasty combos such as pepperoni and cheese and lots of veggie options ($6.50). Mon–Sat 10am–8pm, Sun 11am–7pm.

Garnet Ghost Town

Garnet Range Rd (11 miles south of Hwy-200) • Summer daily 10am–5pm; rest of year Sat & Sun 11am–3pm • $3 • Ⓦ garnetghosttown.net • Road open May–Dec only

To get an in-depth look at the rugged days of the Old West, travel east from Missoula some forty miles on I-90, then another ten bumpy miles by single-lane Bear Gulch Road, to **Garnet Ghost Town**. In the late 1890s this site was home to thousands of hard-rock gold miners doing a tough, perilous job – by 1905 many of the mines were abandoned and the town's population had shrunk to about 150. By the 1940s Garnet was a ghost town, and since the buildings have been kept in their semi-decayed state, the atmosphere is quite arresting: the quiet and lonely spectre of vacant, wood-framed saloons, cabins, stores and a jail, set amid acres of rolling hills that invite a leisurely stroll.

National Bison Range

58355 Bison Range Rd (Hwy-212), Moiese • **Visitor centre** May to mid-Oct daily 9am–5pm; mid-Oct to April Mon–Fri 8am–4pm **Red Sleep Mountain Drive** Mid-May to early Oct daily 6.30am–9.30pm • $5 • ☎ 406 644 2211, Ⓦ fws.gov/refuge/national_bison_range

Conveniently located just off the route between Missoula and Glacier National Park, the 18,500-acre **National Bison Range** lies near the town of Moiese, twenty miles west of St Ignatius on Hwy-212. Beyond the small **visitor centre** the nineteen-mile **Red Sleep Mountain Drive** loop road rises into the hills for stellar views of the surrounding mountains, before dropping down to plains that harbour small herds of 350–500 bison – you might also see black bears, and plenty of pronghorn and deer. Note that it's strictly forbidden to leave your car, except on two marked hiking trails.

Flathead Lake and around

The alpine charms of 28-mile-long **Flathead Lake** provide a welcome diversion on the long route north toward Glacier National Park, reached by following US-93 north from I-90. Between **Polson** in the south and **Somers** in the north, US-93 follows the lake's curving western shore, while the narrower Hwy-36 runs up the east below the **Mission Mountains**, and is the summer home to countless roadside cherry and berry vendors. Surrounded by low-lying mountains, both routes offer handsome views of the deep blue waters, and the lake is a great place for hiking, boating or just lazing on the shore for a few hours, though there are plenty of amusements in the nearby towns: the small resort of **Bigfork** in the northeast is the most pleasant place to stay.

Wild Horse Island State Park

US-93 is closest to **Wild Horse Island** (daily dawn–dusk; $3; ☎ 406 849 5256), the lake's largest island, which you can reach by boat. Hiking on its terrific range of moderate-to-steep trails, which lead past knolls and buttes up to fine lookouts over the lake, you're apt to see mule deer and the odd group of bighorn sheep – though the eponymous untamed equines are few and rarely visible (there are just five). To visit the island rent a boat or contact Pointer Scenic Cruises in Big Fork (Ⓦ wildhorseislandboattrips.com).

11

ACCOMMODATION AND EATING

Bridge Street Cottages 309 Bridge St, Bigfork ☎406 837 2785, ⒲ bridgestreetcottages.com. Ten cosy, luxurious self-catering one-bedroom cottages and smaller cottage suites close to town and the Swan River, with fully equipped kitchens (washer and dryer) and fireplaces. Rates halve in winter. Suites $185, cabins $250

Candlewycke Inn 311 Aero Lane, Bigfork ☎406 837 6406, ⒲ candlewyckeinn.com. An antique-laden B&B whose five pleasant units variously come with jacuzzis, skylights and fridges. $155

FLATHEAD LAKE AND AROUND

Echo Lake Cafe 1195 Hwy-83 ☎406 837 4252, ⒲ echolakecafe.com. Best place for breakfast or lunch, serving up solid omelettes and burgers, with some veggie options, too (most mains $9–12). Daily 6.30am–2.30pm.

★ **Eva Gates** 456 Electric Ave, Bigfork ☎406 837 4356, ⒲ evagates.com. For souvenirs and picnic items don't miss the fudges, jams and sweets made with huckleberries at this local institution, established in 1949. Mid-June to Aug daily 9am–7pm; Sept to mid-June Mon–Fri 9am–5pm.

Whitefish

The old logging town of **WHITEFISH**, just 25 miles west of Glacier National Park, is now one of the most popular resorts in Montana, perched on the south shore of beautiful **Whitefish Lake** in the shade of the **Whitefish Mountain Ski Resort** (☎406 862 2900, ⒲ skiwhitefish.com). As one of the area's big-name winter-sports draws, the resort is also excellent for **hiking** in summer, when you can trudge four hard miles up to a restaurant on top of the mountain and take a free chairlift ride for the descent (uphill it's $12), or **cycle** the roads around the lake and foothills – bikes can be rented from Glacier Cyclery, 326 E 2nd St ($30–55/day; ☎406 862 6446, ⒲ glaciercyclery.com).

11

ACCOMMODATION

WHITEFISH

Grouse Mountain Lodge 2 Fairway Drive ☎406 862 3000, ⒲ grousemountainlodge.com. Large, luxurious modern hotel with a lodge theme, open all year-round, with a golf course on site and useful shuttle service (free) to take you into town or up the mountain. $150

Hidden Moose Lodge 1735 E Lakeshore Drive ☎406 862 6516, ⒲ hiddenmooselodge.com. Charming

timber-chic B&B, excellent for its outdoor hot tub, hearty breakfasts and rooms with jacuzzis or private decks. $99

North Forty Resort 3765 Hwy-40 W ☎406 862 7740, ⒲ northfortyresort.com. Stay at one of these 22 homely log cabins (minimum 5 people), which come equipped with fireplaces, kitchens, DVD players, free wi-fi and outdoor BBQs. $219

EATING AND DRINKING

Great Northern Brewing Co (Black Star Draught House) 2 Central Ave ☎406 863 1000, ⒲ greatnorthern brewing.com. This being Montana it would be remiss not to sample the local microbrewery, with its own tasting room serving all the seasonal beers plus a selection of snacks and sandwiches ($9). Daily: June–Aug & Dec–March 11am–11pm; April & May 4–10.30pm; Sept–Nov 2–10pm.

Loula's 300 2nd St E ☎406 862 5614, ⒲ loulaswhitefish .com. Great local café, best known locally for its sumptuous pies, such as the freshly made coconut cream and the huckleberry peach combo. Mon & Tues 7am–3pm, Wed–Sun 7am–3pm & 5.30–9.30pm.

Montana Coffee Traders 110 Central Ave ☎406 862 7667, ⒲ coffeetraders.com. Cool boho café with the best

espresso in the state (made with Costa Rican beans). Coffee from $1.50, but also sandwiches ($5.50), and a killer savoury bacon scone ($2). Mon–Sat 8.30am–5.30pm, Sun 9am–5pm.

★ **Sweet Peaks Ice Cream** 419½ 3rd St ☎406 862 4668, ⒲ sweetpeaksicecream.com. Irresistible in summer, when you might end up visiting daily for the luscious huckle-berry, salty caramel and maple bacon flavours. Mon–Thurs & Sun 12.30–9pm, Fri & Sat 12.30–9.30pm.

★ **Tupelo Grille** 17 Central Ave ☎406 862 6136, ⒲ tupelogrille.com. The most esteemed dining experience in town, giving your stomach a (pricey) Southern treat with crawfish cakes, creole chicken and good ol' shrimp and grits (most mains $14–32). Daily 5.30–10pm.

Glacier National Park

Two thousand lakes, a thousand miles of rivers, thick forests, breezy meadows and awe-inspiring peaks make up one of America's finest attractions, **GLACIER NATIONAL PARK** – a haven for bighorn sheep, mountain goats, black and grizzly bears, wolves and mountain lions. Although the park does hold 25 small (and rapidly retreating) glaciers, it really takes its name from the huge flows of ice that carved these immense valleys 20,000 years ago. In the summer months this is prime **hiking** and **whitewater rafting** territory, while **huckleberries** litter the slopes in autumn. Outside of summer, the crisp air, icy-cold waterfalls and copious snowfall give the impression of being close to the Arctic Circle; in fact, the latitude here is lower than that of London.

Note that Glacier is one of the few national parks you can happily explore without a car; Amtrak runs up to the park entrance, where shuttle buses ply up and down the mind-bending **Going-to-the-Sun Road**.

Going-to-the-Sun Road

The fifty-mile **Going-to-the-Sun Road** across the heart of Glacier National Park is one of the most awe-inspiring scenic drives in the country, and driving it from west to east can take several hours, creating the illusion that you'll be climbing forever – with each successive hairpin bringing a new colossus into view. Beginning at **West Glacier**, the road runs east along ten-mile **Lake McDonald** before starting to climb, as snowmelt from waterfalls gushes across the road, and the winding route nudges over the **Continental Divide** at **Logan Pass** (6680ft) – a good spot to step out and enjoy the views.

The most popular **trail** in the park begins at Logan Pass, following a boardwalk for a mile and a half across wild-flower-strewn alpine meadows framed by towering craggy peaks, en route to serene **Hidden Lake**. Four miles on, there's an overlook at **Jackson Glacier**, one of the few glaciers visible from the roadside. From here the road descends to **St Mary Lake** and the east gate at St Mary, right on the edge of the Great Plains.

Many Glacier

If you have time, explore some of the more remote park sections of the park by car, bike or on foot, beginning with **Many Glacier**, twenty miles northwest of St Mary. At Swiftcurrent Lake an easy two-mile loop trail runs along the lakeshore, and an exciting five-mile, one-way trail heads to Iceberg Lake, so called for the blocks of ice that float on its surface even in midsummer. Another popular option is to take the trip to the foot of the **Grinnell Glacier** via two boat trips and two hikes ($24.95; ⓦglacierparkboats.com).

Southern loop

US-2 runs around the **southern border** of the park, for 85 miles between West Glacier and St Mary. It's not as dramatic as Going-to-the-Sun Road, but still very scenic; you'll pass **Goat Lick Overlook**, a good place to spot mountain goats, the remote village of **East Glacier Park** and the entrance to the **Two Medicine** section of the park, a less crowded centre for hiking and boating.

ARRIVAL AND INFORMATION   GLACIER NATIONAL PARK

By car The park's main, western entrance is at West Glacier, 25 miles east of Whitefish and just 35 miles south of the Canadian border. The east gate is at St Mary. Going-to-the-Sun Rd is the one through-road between the two entrances, usually passable between early June and mid-Oct, though in recent years road closures for constructions have made travel more intermittent. The southern border of Glacier is skirted by US-2, which remains open all year and is an attractive alternative drive.

By train Amtrak trains follow the route of US-2, stopping at West Glacier, a short walk from the west gate; East Glacier Park, 30 miles south of St Mary (1hr 40min by train from West Glacier); and Essex (summer only), in between (40min from West Glacier).

Park admission The park itself is open year-round. May–Oct the entrance fee is $25/vehicle (or $12/individual on foot, bike or motorcycle), and Nov–April the rate is $15/car ($10 for other visitors); both are good for 7 days.

Visitor centres There are several visitor centres (all ☎406 888 7800, ⓦnps.gov/glac). One is at the park's main, western entrance at Apgar (daily: mid-May to mid-June 9am–4.30pm; mid-June to Aug 8am–5.30pm; first 2 weeks Sept 8.30am–3pm), and another at the east gate at St Mary (daily: late May to late June & late Aug to mid-Sept 8am–5pm; late June to late Aug 8am–6pm). The Logan Pass (daily: mid-June to Aug 9am–7pm, first 2 weeks Sept 9.30am–4pm) visitor centre stands at the top of Going-to-the-Sun Rd.

WHITEWATER RAFTING IN GLACIER

Several companies now compete for the excellent **whitewater rafting** trips in and around Glacier National Park, mostly based at West Glacier. The Glacier Raft Company is a reputable operator offering half-day ($52) and full-day ($105) excursions (☎406 888 5454, ⓦglacierraftco.com).

GETTING AROUND AND TOURS

By "jammer bus" Travellers arriving by public transport can travel around the park via the bright-red 1936 "jammer" buses (so called because of the need to jam the gears into place) that provide narrated sightseeing tours from the main lodges (June–Sept; ☎406 892 2525, ⓦglacierparkinc.com; 2–8hr; $30–90).

By Glacier Shuttles Free Glacier Shuttles operate on two routes: one between Apgar Transit Center, several miles from the park gate, and Logan Pass (7.30am–7pm every 15–30min; 1hr 30min–2hr trip), and one between Logan

Pass and St Mary Visitor Center (7.30am–7pm, every 40min–1hr; 1hr); both run at least every 30min, and July to early Sept only.

Guided tours Sun Tours (June–Sept; ☎406 226 9220, ⓦglaciersuntours.com) offers daily half-day guided tours led by members of the Blackfeet tribe ($40 from St Mary).

Boat tours and rentals Tour boats explore all of the large lakes, ranging $12–24.25 for 1hr trips. Kayak rental starts at $15/hr. Contact Glacier Park Boat Co (☎406 257 2426, ⓦglacierparkboats.com).

ACCOMMODATION

WITHIN THE PARK

Accommodation within the park is run by Glacier Park Inc (all reservations at ☎406 892 2525, ⓦglacierparkinc. com), and most of the lodges are open from June into Sept. None have TVs in the rooms; wi-fi is now available in hotel lobbies (note there is limited mobile [cell] phone service in the park).

Lake McDonald Lodge Ten miles from western entrance. This grand hotel opened in 1914 with an ideal shoreline location and a picturesque Swiss chalet design, offering simple 1950s motel rooms, more spacious lodge rooms or small rustic cabins outside the complex. Motel rooms $79, lodge rooms $191, cabins $137

Many Glacier Hotel Twelve miles west of Babb and US-2. Stately, alpine-style lodge built in 1915, right on Swiftcurrent Lake, with pricey suites and value rooms for half that price. Doubles $163, suites $336

Rising Sun Motor Inn 5.5 miles west of St Mary. Near the shores of St Mary Lake, 7 miles in from the east gate at St Mary, this 1941 inn is more rustic than the big lodges, but closer to the trails and Logan Pass. $134.

Swiftcurrent Motor Inn Many Glacier, 13 miles west of Babb and US-2. The park's cheapest accommodation, featuring cabins dating from the 1930s with or without bathrooms, and good for its access to trails on the northeast side. Cabins $80, en suite $101

Village Inn at Apgar Apgar Village. Fronting Lake McDonald with overlooking the mountains and the water, a 1950s hotel with just 36 rooms; the views are the main draw. $146.

CAMPING

The park's thirteen campgrounds ($10–23) often fill up by late morning during July and Aug; ask at any visitor centre for locations and availability or call ☎406 888 7800. Most

are open from June to mid-Sept, though St Mary and the Apgar Picnic area open year-round (no charge Dec–March). All sites are first-come, first-served, with the exception of Fish Creek and St Mary, which you can reserve six months in advance ($23; ☎518 885 3639, ⓦrecreation.gov). There are showers available at the Rising Sun and Swiftcurrent campstores (St Mary and Fish Creek campgrounds have free showers for guests only).

Backcountry camping Strictly regulated by advanced reservation request lottery – visit the website on details of how to apply (the camping fee is $5/person per night).

OUTSIDE THE PARK

Backpacker's Inn 29 Dawson Ave ☎406 226 9392, ⓦserranosmexican.com. At the back of *Serrano's* Mexican restaurant, with three cosy cabins: two are private with bathrooms and a third offers shared dorm space. Open May–Sept. Dorms $15, cabins $40

Belton Chalet 12575 US-2, West Glacier (2 miles outside the western entrance) ☎406 888 5000, ⓦbeltonchalet.com. This quaint 1910 lodge offers simple yet elegant digs, though the three-bedroom cottages have fireplaces and balconies; no phone or TV. Open late June to late Sept (cottages also available Oct–May). Doubles $155, cottages $325

★ **Glacier Park Lodge** East Glacier Park (close to the Amtrak station) ☎406 892 2525, ⓦglacierparkinc.com. Wide range of cosy lodge rooms, but best known for the massive Douglas-fir and cedar columns (bark still attached) in its huge, phenomenal lobby, brought over from the Pacific Northwest in 1913 by Great Northern Railway (non-guests are welcome to look). $152

Izaak Walton Inn 290 Izaak Walton Inn Rd, Essex ☎406 888 5700, ⓦizaakwaltoninn.com. Halfway between the east and west park gates is Essex, where this atmospheric 1939 inn is the site of the Amtrak stop. As well as cosy wood-panelled rooms, it provides four fun, remodelled train cabins, and has a serviceable restaurant for fish and burgers. Doubles $99, cabins $189

North Fork Hostel 80 Beaver Drive, Poleridge ☎ 406

888 5241, @ nfhostel.com. Up in Polebridge, 28 miles north of the park's west entrance, largely via gravel road, this laidback, extremely cosy hostel offers camping pitches, dorm beds, small private chalets and log cabins. Free wi-fi. Camping $15, dorm $20, chalets $50, cabins $80

EATING AND DRINKING

Serrano's 29 Dawson Ave, East Glacier Park ☎ 406 226 9392, @ serranosmexican.com. The decent Mexican food served in this historic 1909 cabin makes a pleasant change (tacos $3.25, *chiles rellenos* $14.95), and it also serves local microbrews. May–Sept daily 5–10pm.

Two Sisters Café Hwy-89, Babb ☎ 406 732 5535, @ twosisterscateringmontana.com. This multicoloured roadhouse, famous for its outlandish decor, is great for

home-made pie, lemonade, burgers, chilli and desserts. Late May to Aug daily noon–2.30pm & 5–10pm.

Whistle Stop 1024 Hwy-49, East Glacier Park ☎ 406 226 9292. Best of a cluster of places here, worth a stop for its famous huckleberry pie (all berries, with a thin crust), with adequate meaty dinners, burgers and even better breakfasts. June to mid-Sept daily 7am–10pm.

11

Idaho

Declared a state in 1890 after much political wrangling, **IDAHO** was the last of the Western regions to be penetrated by white settlers – in 1805, **Lewis and Clark** described central Idaho's bewildering labyrinth of razor-edged peaks and wild waterways as the most difficult leg of their epic trek. Though much of its scenery deserves national park status, it has always lacked the major showstoppers (and therefore the crowds) of its neighbouring states, a situation its famously conservative citizens have long been happy to maintain.

Nevertheless, you'd be remiss to skip Idaho; the state capital, **Boise**, is surprisingly urbane and friendly, but above all, this is a destination for the outdoors enthusiast. The state is laced with incredibly **scenic highways**, especially through the jaw-dropping **Sawtooth Mountains**, with Red Fish Lake offering some of the most mesmerizing scenery in the Rockies. Other natural wonders include **Hells Canyon**, America's deepest river gorge, and the black, barren **Craters of the Moon**. Hikers and backpackers have the choice of some eighty mountain ranges, interspersed with virgin forest and lava plateaus, while the mighty **Snake** and **Salmon rivers** offer endless **fishing** and especially **whitewater rafting**. And you'll eat well here: the **fresh trout** is superb, and the state is also known for hops (and therefore microbrews), lamb and of course, fine potatoes.

Craters of the Moon National Monument

US-20, 18 miles west of Arco • Daily 24hr; visitor centre daily late May to Aug 8am–6pm; Sept to late May 8am–4.30pm • $8/car, $4/bicycle and pedestrian (good for 7 days); Lava Flow campground $10 (May–Nov) • ☎ 208 527 1300, @ nps.gov/crmo

The eerie, 83-square-mile **Craters of the Moon National Monument**, ninety miles west of Idaho Falls, comprises a surreal cornucopia of lava cones, tubes, buttes, craters, caves and splatter cones, with trees battered by the fierce winds into bonsai-like contortions. These arose from successive waves of lava pouring from wounds in the earth's crust throughout the millennium; the most recent event occurred two thousand years ago.

The park **visitor centre** is on US-20. A seven-mile **loop road**, open late April to mid-November, takes you around myriad lava fields, where trails of varying difficulty lead past assorted cones and monoliths – don't stray from the paths, as the rocks are razor-sharp and can reach oven-like temperatures. Highlights include the one-mile trail past hollow **tree moulds** where the ancient wood ignited, leaving craggy holes; the steep half-mile trek to the top of the **Inferno Cone**, with commanding views of the region; and the eight-mile **Wilderness Trail** (free wilderness permit required, from the visitor centre), which leads deep into the backcountry past cinder cones, ropy lava flows and the blown-out expanse of **Echo Crater**.

Sun Valley

Some 160 miles east of Boise, in wonderfully scenic country, **Sun Valley** is the common label for the entire Wood River Valley area – though technically it is just the name of a **ski resort** (wsunvalley.com). Here in the gentle foothills of the Sawtooths near the old sheep-ranching village of **KETCHUM**, the world's first chairlift was built in 1936, and the resort attracted the likes of Clark Gable and Gary Cooper, who came to hunt and fish. **Ernest Hemingway** completed *For Whom the Bell Tolls* as a guest of the resort in 1939, and lived in Ketchum for the last two years of his life before his shotgun suicide (his simple grave can be found in the town cemetery). The resort has information on events commemorating him in late summer.

Sun Valley is based around **Bald Mountain**, the 9100ft peak on which most of the serious skiing occurs, and **Dollar Mountain**, the 6600ft peak with easier runs for beginner skiers. The **season** runs from late November to April; as well as downhill skiing, you can also set off cross country. Ketchum itself is a lively little town with plenty of accommodation, and even a bit of nightlife. Among **summer** outdoor activities are **cycling** along thirty miles of excellent trails, as well as **mountain biking** on the superb lift-accessed trails on Bald Mountain (lift ticket $25/day) and **rafting** on the rivers to the north.

11

ARRIVAL, GETTING AROUND AND INFORMATION SUN VALLEY

By shuttle Sun Valley Express (☎ 208 342 7750, wsunvalley express.com) runs daily shuttles from Boise to Sun Valley (2hr 45min) for $65.
By bus Mountain Rides buses link Sun Valley resort with

Ketchum and other locations in the valley (rides free; ☎ 208 788 7433, wmountainrides.org).
Visitor centre 491 Sun Valley Rd E (daily 9am–5pm; ☎ 208 726 3423, wvisitsunvalley.com).

ACCOMMODATION

Inn at Ellsworth Estate 702 Third Ave S, Hailey (13 miles south of Sun Valley) ☎ 208 788 6354, wellsworthestate .com. Nine clean and tasteful B&B rooms with smart modern furnishings, some with fireplaces and DVD players. $119
Lift Tower Lodge 703 S Main St, Ketchum ☎ 208 726 5163. Simple and functional, with basic motel units that include complimentary breakfast. $85
Sun Valley Inn 1 Sun Valley Rd ☎ 208 622 4111,

wsunvalley.com. Resort lodgings opened in 1937, offering a mock-Swiss Alps design but relatively new, remodelled rooms. $204
★ **Sun Valley Lodge** 1 Sun Valley Rd ☎ 208 622 4111, wsunvalley.com. This luxurious 600-room resort, built in 1936, is as expensive as you'd expect, with flat-screen TVs, high-speed internet and DVD players, and suites with parlours and fireplaces. $234

EATING, DRINKING AND NIGHTLIFE

Cristina's 520 Second St E ☎ 208 726 4499, wcristinas ofsunvalley.com. This charming wooden shack actually turns out to be an expensive breakfast-and-lunch hangout (sandwiches $13.75), which also offers a nice Sunday brunch and good omelettes ($14.50). Mon–Sat 7am–5.30pm, Sun 9am–3pm.
Ketchum Grill 520 East Ave ☎ 208 726 4460, wketchumgrill.com. Inspired, tasty and eclectic options, from pasta and hamburgers to braised Lava Lake lamb and peppered duck breast (mains $9.25–19.95). Daily

5–9.30pm.
Roundhouse ☎ 208 622 2371, wsunvalley.com. Perched 7700ft on Bald Mountain, only accessible by gondola or chairlift, this is the ultimate place for the après-ski or a posh meal of wild salmon and the like (mains $16–18). Summer & winter seasons daily 10am–4pm.
Whiskey Jacques 251 N Main St, Ketchum ☎ 208 726 5297, wwhiskeyjacques.com. Fun local bar, with live music by mid-level national acts, and a solid range of pizzas and burgers. Daily 4pm–2am.

The Sawtooth Mountains

North of Ketchum and Sun Valley, Hwy-75 climbs through rising tracts of forests and mountains to top out after twenty miles at the spectacular panorama of **Galena Summit** (8701ft). Spreading out far below, the meadows of the Sawtooth Valley stretch northward. The winding road – dubbed the **Sawtooth Scenic Byway** – meanders beside the young **Salmon River**, whose headwaters rise in the forbidding icy peaks to the

IDAHO'S BIG RIVER ADVENTURE

Taking a five-day rafting trip down the Middle Fork of the **Salmon River** is perhaps the most exhilarating and unforgettable experience in Idaho; by the time you've finished you'll feel like one of Lewis and Clark's team. The river drops 3000ft during its 105-mile journey through the isolated and spectacular River of No Return Wilderness. Trips usually begin in Stanley and end in Salmon, Idaho and cost from $1665. See ⓦ rowadventures.com.

south, as the serrated ridge of the **Sawtooth Mountains** forms an impenetrable barrier along the western horizon. The main highlight along this stretch is **Red Fish Lake** (just off the highway, 60 miles north of Ketchum), beautifully framed by Mount Heyburn and Grand Mogul peaks, home to sockeye salmon and plenty of hiking and camping opportunities.

At tiny **STANLEY**, seven miles north of the lake, the main activity in summer is organizing **rafting trips**. Operators include the River Company (ⓣ 208 788 5775, ⓦ therivercompany.com), which charges $75–91.

Salmon River Scenic Byway

Thirteen miles west of Stanley at the town of **Sunbeam**, you begin the 45-mile section of the **Salmon River Scenic Byway** that leads into the historic settings preserved at the **Land of the Yankee Fork State Park**, whose **interpretive centre** (summer daily 9am–5pm; free; ⓣ 208 879 5244) at the park's eastern junction, near Challis at the intersection of highways 75 and 93, gives you the opportunity to try your luck panning gold. Along the way you can find opportunities for camping, rafting, fishing and cross-country skiing, or exploring the preserved ghost towns of **Custer** and **Bonanza**. Also worth a look is the **Yankee Fork Gold Dredge**, a 112ft, nearly thousand-ton barge that mined gold from stream gravel, and the **Custer Motorway** (also known as Forest Road 070), an old, rustic toll road, curving northwest away from Hwy-75, with numerous historic attractions and rugged trails leading off from it.

INFORMATION   THE SAWTOOTH MOUNTAINS

Visitor centre Pick up details of camping sites and hiking trails at the Sawtooth National Recreation Area headquarters, 8 miles north of Ketchum at 5 North Fork Canyon Rd (daily 8.30am–5pm; ⓣ 208 727 5000, ⓦ fs.fed.us/r4/sawtooth).

ACCOMMODATION AND EATING

★ **Sawtooth Hotel** 755 Ace of Diamonds St, Stanley ⓣ 208 721 2459, ⓦ sawtoothhotel.com. Iconic log cabin hotel since 1931, with nine old-country style rooms (5 with private bathrooms) and world-class dining. Shared bathrooms $70, private bathrooms $90

Stanley Baking Co & Café 250 Wall St, Stanley ⓣ 208 774 2981, ⓦ stanleybakingco.com. Simple wooden lodge serving good breakfasts and lunches, both featuring delectable home-baked goods (cinnamon rolls, sticky buns, croissants, muffins and coffee cake). Daily 7am–2pm.

Stanley High Country Inn 21 Ace of Diamonds St, Stanley ⓣ 208 774 7000, ⓦ highcountryinn.biz. Rustic lodge, with spacious rooms and suites with kitchenettes, satellite TV and a free continental breakfast (computer with internet access available). $120

Boise

The verdant, likeable capital of Idaho, **BOISE** (pronounced *BOY-see*; never *zee*) straddles I-84, just fifty miles east of the Oregon border, and was established in 1862 for the benefit of pioneers using the Oregon Trail. After adapting (or misspelling) the name originally given to the area by French trappers – *les bois* (the woods) – the earliest residents boosted the town's appearance by planting hundreds more trees.

Today Boise is a friendly, cosmopolitan and outdoorsy city of some 205,000, with great skiing, biking and floating along the Boise River (the favourite way for locals to cool off in the summer), all within paddling distance of a host of excellent independent stores, restaurants and bars. Downtown is centred on the fountains at **Grove Plaza**, where the annual "**Alive after Five**" concert series sees different food and drink vendors take over the square (June–Sept every Wed).

Boise is also unique in having the largest **Basque** population in the world outside of the Basque heartland (in Spain and France), and is the home of **Boise State University** (BSU), whose football team the **Broncos** (with its famed all-blue field, lined with blue-painted turf) receives fanatical support from locals – their rivalry with snooty University of Idaho in Moscow (who are reputed to consider the Broncos uncouth drunks) goes back a long way, though the two teams rarely meet these days. But perhaps Boise's best feature is the **Greenbelt**, a 25-mile bike path and hiking trail that crisscrosses the tranquil **Boise River**, linking various parks right in the heart of the city.

Idaho State Capitol

700 W Jefferson St • Mon–Fri 6am–6pm, Sat & Sun 9am–5pm • Free • ☎ 208 332 1012, ⍟ capitolcommission.idaho.gov

The centrepiece of downtown Boise is the **Idaho State Capitol**, with a fairly typical grand Neoclassical domed exterior completed in 1912, but an unusual, striking interior clad in white marble with green veining (the Corinthian columns are actually scagliola, fake marble, but almost everything else is the real deal). Get maps for a self-guided tour in the basement, where exhibits on the potentially dry subject of the history and structure of Idaho state government are surprisingly entertaining. Nearby, the **Old Boise Historic District** (⍟ oldboise.com) is an elegant area of stone-trimmed brick restaurants and shops (built mostly 1903–10).

Basque Museum and Cultural Center

611 Grove St • Tues–Fri 10am–4pm, Sat 11am–3pm • $5 • ☎ 208 343 2671, ⍟ basquemuseum.com

The **Basque Museum and Cultural Center**, on the "Basque Block" of Grove Street, traces the heritage of the Basque shepherds of mountainous central Idaho through illuminating antiques, relics, photographs and key manuscripts.

The site includes the charming Cyrus Jacobs-Uberuaga boarding house, built in 1864. The international Basque **Jaialdi Festival** attracts people from all over the world, and has been held here several times (the next will be in July 2015; ⍟ jaialdi.com).

Idaho Historical Museum

610 N Julia Davis Drive • May–Sept Tues–Fri 9am–5pm, Sat & Sun 10am–5pm; Oct–April Tues–Fri 9am–5pm, Sat 10am–5pm • $5 • ☎ 208 334 2120, ⍟ history.idaho.gov

The **Idaho Historical Museum** displays artefacts from Native American and Basque peoples, details the difficult experience of the Chinese miners of the 1870s and 1880s, and describes the lives of Idahoans from furriers to gold miners and ranchers. Included in the museum admission, the outdoor **Pioneer Village** preserves cabins and houses dating from as early as 1863, among them an adobe that belonged to the mayor in the 1870s.

Old Idaho Penitentiary

2445 Old Penitentiary Rd, off Warm Springs Ave • Daily: late May to Aug 10am–5pm; Sept to late May noon–5pm • $5 • ☎ 208 334 2844, ⍟ history.idaho.gov

On the edge of town, the grim **Old Idaho Penitentiary** is an imposing sandstone citadel that remained open from 1870 until a major riot in 1973 finally persuaded the

---

THE BARD IN BOISE

Just outside town in a specially built outdoor theatre, at 5657 Warm Springs Ave, the **Idaho Shakespeare Festival** (June–Sept; most tickets $29–39; ☎ 208 336 9221, ⍟ idahoshakespeare .org) offers inspired performances, and tickets are usually cheap and available. Around five plays are presented per season, with two or three of them penned by the Bard. A small restaurant provides food and booze, but you can also bring your own.

authorities to build modern facilities – some shared cells still had slop buckets instead of toilets. Exhibits include confiscated weapons and mugshots of former inmates, including one Harry Orchard, who murdered the state governor in 1905. You can also wander the prison yard and explore the old buildings, including the cramped solitary-confinement unit, and the gallows where the last hanging in Idaho was carried out in 1957. There's also the **J.C. Earl Weapons Exhibit**, with a comprehensive if equally macabre collection of knives, swords and guns from rare Iranian Bronze Age arrowheads to modern M16s.

ARRIVAL AND INFORMATION BOISE

By plane Boise Airport (ⓦ iflyboise.com) is 3 miles south of downtown, just off I-84; get into town by taxi ($12) or Valley Ride public bus (Mon–Fri every 30min, Sat every hour; $1; ⓦ valleyride.org).

By bus Greyhound buses stop at 1212 W Bannock St, just west of downtown.

Destinations Lewiston (1 daily; 5hr 46min); Moscow (1 daily; 6hr 50min); Portland, OR (2 daily; 9hr 45min); Salt Lake City (2 daily; 6hr 50min–7hr 25min); Spokane (1 daily; 8hr 35min); White Bird (1 daily; 3hr 55min).

Visitor centre Concierge Corner on Grove Plaza (Mon–Fri 10am–4pm; ☎ 208 336 8900, ⓦ boise.org).

ACCOMMODATION

Grove Hotel 245 S Capitol Blvd ☎ 208 333 8000, ⓦ grovehotelboise.com. Solid-value, elegant rooms, many offering great views of the city and mountains, with 32-inch flat-screens. Indoor pool. **$140**

Hotel 43 981 Grove St ☎ 208 342 4622, ⓦ hotel43.com. This is Boise's celebrity boutique, the kind of place that visiting superstars spend the night; rooms offer chic, contemporary style with all the extras. **$230**

★ **Idaho Heritage Inn** 109 W Idaho St ☎ 208 342 8066, ⓦ idheritageinn.com. Handsome pile built in 1904

that was the residence of Governor Chase Clark in the 1940s, with six cosy period rooms and suites. **$75**

★ **The Modern** 1314 W Grove St ☎ 208 424 8244, ⓦ themodernhotel.com. Revamped *Travelodge* turned boutique motel, which has a smart 1950s themed design and rooms with minimalist designer decor and HDTVs. **$105**

Red Lion Downdowner 1800 Fairview Ave ☎ 208 344 7691, ⓦ redlion.com. Huge hotel with pool, a handy shuttle that will take you anywhere in town and pick you up and spacious, comfy business-style rooms. **$120**

EATING AND DRINKING

Boise claims to have invented "fry sauce" (though Utah also makes a good case), a delicious combo of mayonnaise, ketchup and spices; almost every restaurant has its own version. Less prosaically, Boise is close to Idaho's southwest wine country – try some of the very decent local Pinot Gris vintages before you leave (see ⓦ wine.idaho.gov).

★ **Bar Gernika** 202 Capitol Blvd ☎ 208 344 2175, ⓦ bargernika.com. Old Basque-style pub, excellent for its authentic Basque specialties – particularly the range of stews and lamb dishes, and its famous beef tongue (most mains under $10). Mon 11am–11pm, Tues–Thurs 11am–midnight, Fri 11am–1am, Sat 11.30am–1am.

★ **Barbacoa** 276 Bobwhite Court ☎ 208 338 5000, ⓦ barbacoa-boise.com. This whimsical place boasts a mad eclectic interior with giant wire sculptures, crazy chandeliers and even a Moroccan theme, though the cuisine is mostly contemporary American; steak sandwich ($18), seafood pasta ($23) and Idaho trout ($25). Daily 4pm–late.

Bittercreek Alehouse 246 N 8th St ☎ 208 345 1813, ⓦ bcrfl.com/bittercreek. With 39 drafts from craft brewers all over the West and decent burgers ($9.50) this is a smart place to spend an evening. Mon–Thurs & Sun 11am–10pm, Fri & Sat 11am–midnight.

★ **Boise Fry Co** 111 Broadway ☎ 208 495 3858, ⓦ boisefrycompany.com. Fittingly for a state so associated with potatoes, this local mini-chain knocks out some of the best fries anywhere; you choose from six types of potatoes,

then the size (small from $2.49), and then the style (curly, home-style, shoestring and so on). Add up to nine sauces and eight types of salt. The "bourgeois" is fried in duck fat and sprinkled with truffle salt ($6). Daily 11am–9pm.

Chandlers 981 W Grove St ☎ 208 383 4300, ⓦ chandlersboise.com. Try this posh steakhouse for great, expertly grilled cuts of beef ($31–43), but also the "ten-minute martinis" ($12; it takes that long to freeze the glass with water, chip away at the ice and make the cocktail). Daily 4–11.30pm.

Fork 199 N 8th St ☎ 208 287 1700, ⓦ boisefork.com. Cool farm-to-table hotspot, with the menu listing where all the produce is sourced; highlights include the addictive rosemary-parmesan fries ($4.95), and the "grown-up grilled cheese" (with onion jam; $7.95). Daily 11.30am–10pm.

Goldy's 108 S Capitol Blvd ☎ 208 345 4100, ⓦ goldys breakfastbistro.com. Modern diner serving up a range of savoury items from salmon cakes to biscuits 'n' gravy and the celebrated sweet potato hash browns, and where you can create your own excellent breakfast combos for less than $12. Daily 6.30am–2pm.

JET-BOATING HELLS CANYON

The most exhilarating way to experience Hells Canyon is via a **jet-boat** ride – you won't easily forget the soaring cliffs, whitewater rapids, bald eagles, black bears and gorgeous scenery. On the Idaho side, Kilgore Adventures is a reputable outfit, based in the small town of White Bird, thirty miles north of Riggins (☎ 208 839 2255, ⓦ killgoreadventures.com); 5–6hr tours are $175. Stops include Kirkwood Historical Ranch Museum, Sheep Creek Cabin and the Indian Petroglyph writings, with lunch at the Dam Visitor Center.

Hells Canyon

From the busy little watersports and ski resort of **McCALL**, 110 miles north of Boise, Hwy-55 climbs steadily to merge with US-95 and follow the turbulent **Little Salmon River**. Just south of the hamlet of **Riggins**, thirty miles on, comes a good opportunity to see **Hells Canyon** from Idaho. With an average depth of 5500ft this is the deepest river gorge in the US, though you wouldn't guess so due to its broad expanse and lack of sheer walls. Nevertheless, it is impressive, with Oregon's Wallowa and Eagle Cap ranges rising behind it and the river glimmering far down below. **Heaven's Gate Overlook** is the best viewpoint into the canyon from Idaho; from the south end of Riggins, allow a half-day to reach the overlook on a very steep and winding gravel road (Forest Road 517), best tackled in a 4WD. The canyon is also accessible by road from Oregon and by jet-boat trip (see box above).

Moscow

The thirty miles of US-95 between Lewiston, at the north end of Hells Canyon, and **MOSCOW**, wind through the beautiful rolling hillsides of the fertile Palouse Valley. Moscow itself is a fun, friendly town that makes a good overnight stop, and is the site of the **University of Idaho**. Bookstores, galleries, bars and cafés line the tree-shaded **Main Street**, while theatre, music and independent cinema are on offer throughout the year, along with a sprinkling of arts festivals: the **Moscow Artwalk** (☎ 208 883 7036) brings together dozens of artists, galleries and the public for diverting summertime exhibits, and the **Lionel Hampton Jazz Festival** (☎ 208 885 6765, ⓦ uidaho.edu/jazzfest) showcases big names new and old.

Idaho Panhandle

The narrow, rugged, northern section of Idaho is known as the **Idaho Panhandle**, more easily accessed from Washington and Montana on I-90 – which follows the Coeur d'Alene River and its South Fork – than the southern part of the state. Though **Wallace** makes for an enticing historical attraction, this region really is all about the outdoors. Note that the Panhandle observes Pacific Time (1hr behind the rest of the state, on Mountain Time).

Coeur d'Alene

Now a major resort and the capital of the Panhandle, **COEUR D'ALENE** ("Core da Lane") lies fifty miles north of Moscow on the shores of lovely 25-mile-long **Lake Coeur d'Alene**, which stretches into the mountains. Poised on the lake is the expensive **Coeur d'Alene Resort**, which dominates the unremarkable downtown, where **cruises** (mid-June to Aug daily 11.30am–1pm & 2–3.30pm; $32.75; ⓦ cdaresort.com) give you a closer view.

ACCOMMODATION AND EATING   **COEUR D'ALENE**

★ **Beverly's** Coeur d'Alene Resort, 115 S 2nd St ☎ 208 765 4000, ⓦ beverlyscda.com. Chic choice with

amazing lake views, with fine seafood and beef, king crab and bison carpaccio (mains $20–40). Mon–Sat

11

11

THE NEZ PERCÉ

The first whites to encounter the **Nez Percé** people were the weak, hungry and disease-ridden Lewis and Clark expedition in 1805. The natives gave them food and shelter, and cared for their animals until the party was ready to carry on westward.

Relations between the Nez Percé (so called by French-Canadian trappers because of their shell-pierced noses) and whites remained agreeable for more than fifty years – until the discovery of gold, and white pressure for property ownership led the government to persuade some renegade Nez Percé to sign a treaty in 1863 that took away three quarters of tribal land. As settlers started to move into the hunting grounds of the Wallowa Valley in the early 1870s, the majority of the Nez Percé, under **Chief Joseph**, refused to recognize the agreement. In 1877, after much vacillation, the government decided to enact its terms and gave the tribe thirty days to leave.

Ensuing skirmishes resulted in the deaths of a handful of settlers, and a large army force began to gather to round up the tribe. Chief Joseph then embarked upon the famous **Retreat of the Nez Percé**. Around 250 warriors (protecting twice as many women, children and old people) outmanoeuvred army columns many times their size, launching frequent guerrilla attacks in a series of narrow escapes. After four months and 1700 miles, the Nez Percé were cornered just thirty miles from the safety of the Canadian border. Chief Joseph then (reportedly) made his legendary speech of surrender, "From where the sun now stands I will fight no more forever". Today some 1500 live in a reservation between Lewiston and Grangeville – a minute fraction of their original territory.

Nez Percé National Historic Park, with 38 separate sites, is spread over a huge range of north-central Idaho, eastern Oregon and western Montana. At the visitor centre in Spalding, ten miles east of Lewiston (daily 8am–4.30pm, summer closes 5pm; free; ☎ 208 843 7001, ⓦ nps.gov/nepe), the Museum of Nez Percé Culture focuses on tribal arts and crafts, while the White Bird Battlefield, seventy miles further south on US-95, was where the tribe inflicted 34 deaths on the US Army, in the first major battle of the Retreat.

11am–2.30pm & 5–10pm, Sun 5–10pm.

Bistro on Spruce 1710 N 4th St ☎ 208 664 1774, ⓦ bistroonspruce.com. Mid-priced, scrumptious items such as seared ahi tuna, duck confit and wild salmon, with huckleberry crème brûlée for dessert (mains $15–19). Mon–Fri 11am–2.30pm & 5–9pm, Sat 9am–3pm & 5–9pm, Sun 9am–3pm.

Flamingo Motel 718 E Sherman Ave ☎ 208 664 2159, ⓦ flamingomotelidaho.com. Aside from the Coeur d'Alene Resort, you can stay at this cheap and clean option, which offers kitschy theme rooms kitted out in classic cowboy, tropical cabana and ultra-patriotic stylings. **$100**

Roger's Ice Cream & Burgers 1224 E Sherman Ave ☎ 208 930 4900, ⓦ rogersicecreamburgers.com. Addictive, home-made flavours such as huckleberry heaven and moose tracks, as well as hand-cut French fries from Idaho potatoes and juicy burgers ($5.50). Mon–Thurs 10.30am–10pm, Fri–Sun 10.30am–11pm.

Silver Mountain

610 Bunker Ave, Kellogg • ☎ 208 783 1111, ⓦ silvermt.com

About forty miles east of Coeur d'Alene on I-90, you'll come to Kellogg and the surprisingly good ski resort of **SILVER MOUNTAIN**. It boasts the world's longest single-stage **gondola** (3.1 miles, rising 3400ft in 16min; rides $18), the **Silver Rapids Waterpark** (for guests at the resort), fine skiing in winter, and some good mountain biking (rental $25/day) and hiking in summer.

Wallace

Twelve miles east of Silver Mountain lies the authentic, undeveloped Western mining town of **WALLACE**, established by one Colonel Wallace in 1884 and briefly the silver mining capital of the world. Those days are long gone, and the town has struggled to survive in recent years, despite being extremely picturesque (the 1997 movie *Dante's Peak* was filmed here) – its shabby, historic streets are some of the most memorable in the Rockies. Get acquainted with the town's turbulent history on the **Sierra Silver Mine Tour**, a 75-minute trolley-car ride departing 420 N Fifth St (June–Aug daily every

> ### ROUTE OF THE HIAWATHA
>
> One of the highlights of the Idaho Panhandle is hiking or biking the **Route of the Hiawatha Bike Trail** (ⓦ ridethehiawatha.com), the former fifteen mile stretch of rail line between Roland and Pearson that runs through ten tunnels and travels over seven high trestles; the 1.7 mile-long St. Paul Pass tunnel is the highlight. Trail passes are $10; there is a shuttle between Pearson and Roland that costs $9. The equally spectacular **Trail of the Coeur d'Alenes** runs 73 miles from Mullan to Plummer (see ⓦ parksandrecreation.idaho.gov/parks /trail-coeur-d-alenes).

30min 10am–4pm, May & Sept till 2pm; $14, bus only $6; ☎208 752 5151, ⓦ silverminetour.org), which lets you descend 1000ft to appreciate the hard labour endured by miners a century ago.

To find out more, drop by the **Wallace District Mining Museum** at 590 Bank St (May, June & Sept daily 10am–5pm; July & Aug daily 9am–5pm; Oct & April Mon–Sat 10am–5pm; Nov–March Mon–Fri 1–5pm; $3; ☎208 556 1592, ⓦ wallaceminingmuseum.org), which has replicas, photos and artefacts from the gold and silver heydays from the 1880s to the 1940s. To see what miners did on their days off, visit the **Oasis Bordello Museum** at 605 Cedar St (May–Oct Mon–Sat 10am–5pm, Sun 11am–3pm; $5; ☎208 753 0801), chronicling the colourful hundred-year history of a certain local "institution".

ACCOMMODATION AND EATING   WALLACE

Red Light Garage 302 5th St ☎208 556 0575, ⓦ redlightgarage.com. This diner drips with character, smothered with old signs; it's best known for its amazing huckleberry shakes ($4.25), but also serves up a mean burger ($5.50). Mon–Thurs & Sun 7am–8pm, Fri & Sat 7am–9pm.

Smokehouse BBQ 424 6th St ☎208 659 7539, ⓦ smokehousebbqsaloon.com. This quirky local gem features a huge old bar, ramshackle interior, some outdoor tables, great barbecue plates ($12) and specials such as salmon and trout burgers. The building dates from 1890,

and once served as courthouse and jail. Mon–Thurs 11.30am–9pm, Fri & Sat 11.30am–10pm.

Wallace Brewing Co 610 Bank St ☎208 660 3430, ⓦ wallacebrewing.com. Local brewpub located in another 1890 building, purveyors of such gems as Jackleg Stout and Huckleberry Lager. Tues–Thurs 1–6pm, Fri & Sat 1–8pm.

Wallace Inn 100 Front St ☎208 752 1252, ⓦ thewallace inn.com. Best place to stay in town, with a pool, hot tub, sauna and gym, with the comfy, spacious rooms featuring a modern, neat style. $136

Sandpoint

Forty-four miles north of Coeur d'Alene, the pretty little town of **SANDPOINT** lies at the northwestern end of 43-mile long **Lake Pend Oreille** (pronounced "PON-duh-ray"), with its downtown overlooking placid Sandy Creek but its main attractions somewhat further out. At the south end of the lake, **Farragut State Park**, 13400 Ranger Rd (☎208 683 2425), has four thousand acres for boating, hiking, camping ($24–26) and the like. To the northeast, the spiky Selkirk Mountains hold the **Schweitzer Mountain Resort** (☎208 263 9555, ⓦ schweitzer.com), northern Idaho's best ski resort, with plenty of spacious, comfortable lodging. In summer you can use one of the lifts for hiking and mountain biking ($12/ride or all day for $20).

The
Southwest

JOHN FORD POINT, MONUMENT VALLEY

The Southwest

The Southwestern desert states of New Mexico, Arizona, Utah and Nevada stretch from Texas to California, across an elemental landscape ranging from towering monoliths of red sandstone to snowcapped mountains, on a high desert plateau that repeatedly splits open to reveal yawning canyons. This overwhelming scenery is complemented by the emphatic presence of Native American cultures and the palpable legacy of America's Wild West frontier.

Each of the four Southwestern states remains distinct. New Mexico bears the most obvious traces of long-term settlement, the Native American pueblos of the north coexisting alongside former Spanish colonial towns like **Santa Fe**, **Albuquerque** and **Taos**. In Arizona, the history of the Wild West is more conspicuous, in towns such as **Tombstone**, site of the OK Corral. More than a third of the state belongs to Native American tribes, including the Apache, Hopi and Navajo; most live in the red-rock lands of the northeast, notably amid the splendour typified by the **Canyon de Chelly** and **Monument Valley**.

The canyon country of northern Arizona – even the immense **Grand Canyon** – won't prepare you for the compelling desertscape of southern Utah, where **Zion** and **Bryce** canyons are the best known of a string of national parks and monuments. **Moab**, between majestic **Canyonlands** and surreal **Arches** in the east, is the top destination for outdoors enthusiasts. Nevada, on the other hand, is nothing short of desolate, though gamblers are lured by the bright lights of **Las Vegas**.

You can count on warm sunshine anywhere in the Southwest for nine months of the year, with incredible sunsets most evenings. Although "snowbirds" flock to southern Arizona in winter, elsewhere summer is the peak tourist season, despite air temperatures topping 100°F, and the awesome thunderstorms that sweep through in late summer, causing flash floods and forest fires. By October, perhaps the best time to come, the crowds are gone and in the mountains and canyons the leaves turn red and gold. Winter brings snow to higher elevations, while spring sees wild flowers bloom in the desert.

The Southwest's backcountry wildernesses are ideal for **camping** and backpacking expeditions. It's vital to be prepared for the harshness of the desert: always carry water and if you venture off the beaten track let someone know your plans.

Unless you have your own vehicle, many of the most fascinating corners of the region are utterly inaccessible. Scheduled public **transport** runs almost exclusively between the big cities – which are not at all the point of visiting the region.

Brief history

Among the earliest inhabitants of the Southwest were the **Ancestral Puebloans**. While their settlements and cliff palaces, abandoned More than seven centuries ago, are now evocative ruins, their descendants, the **Pueblo** peoples of New Mexico and the **Hopi** in Arizona, still lead similar lifestyles. From the fourteenth century onwards, the incoming **Navajo** and **Apache** appropriated vast tracts of territory, which they in turn were soon defending

12

MUSEUM HILL, SANTA FE

Highlights

❶ **Santa Fe, NM** Great museums, fascinating history, atmospheric hotels – New Mexico's capital is a must on any Southwest itinerary. **See p.737**

❷ **La Posada, AZ** Glorious old restored hotel, straight from the heyday of Route 66, that's a great reason to spend a night in Winslow. **See p.763**

❸ **The Havasupai Reservation, AZ** Glorying in its turquoise waterfalls, this little-known offshoot of the Grand Canyon remains home to its original Native American inhabitants. **See p.771**

❹ **Monument Valley, AZ/UT** Though the eerie sandstone monoliths of Monument Valley are familiar the world over, they still take every visitor's breath away. **See p.773**

❺ **Canyon de Chelly, AZ** Ancestral Puebloan "cliff dwellings" pepper every twist and turn of this stupendous sheer-walled canyon. **See p.775**

❻ **Scenic Hwy-12, UT** Crossing the heart of Utah's red-rock wilderness, Hwy-12 is perhaps the most exhilarating drive in the USA. **See p.784**

❼ **Delicate Arch, UT** This freestanding natural arch is the crowning glory of Arches National Park. **See p.790**

❽ **Cirque du Soleil, Las Vegas, NV** Currently staging eight different, dazzling shows, this postmodern Canadian troupe has redefined Las Vegas spectacle. **See p.796**

HIGHLIGHTS ARE MARKED ON THE MAP ON PP.734–735

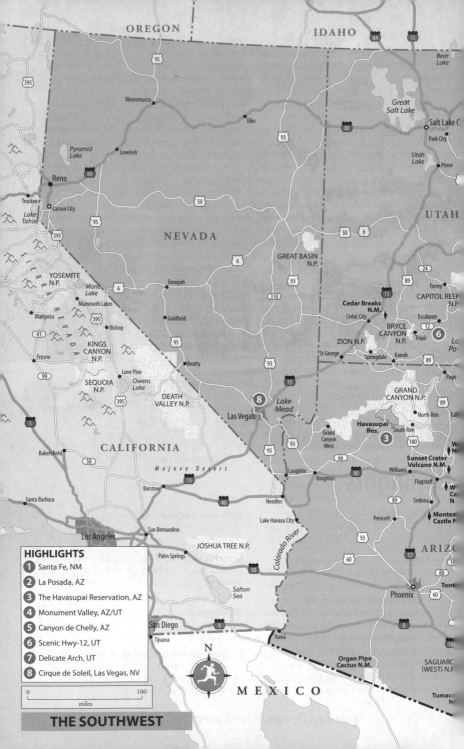

HIGHLIGHTS

1. Santa Fe, NM
2. La Posada, AZ
3. The Havasupai Reservation, AZ
4. Monument Valley, AZ/UT
5. Canyon de Chelly, AZ
6. Scenic Hwy-12, UT
7. Delicate Arch, UT
8. Cirque de Soleil, Las Vegas, NV

0 — 100
miles

THE SOUTHWEST

GREAT REGIONAL DRIVES

The High Road, northern NM Time-forgotten Hispanic villages in the rolling hills between Santa Fe and Taos.

Hwy-12, southern UT Stupendous desert wilderness, crossed by rivers and dotted with waterfalls.

Road between the Rims, northern AZ The 215-mile drive between the North and South Rims of the Grand Canyon leads past dramatic red-rock cliffs, and across the Colorado River.

Route 66, northern NM and AZ The legendary "Mother Road" to California motors through towns like Albuquerque, Winslow and Flagstaff, and is still very much the place to get your kicks.

Self-drive route, Monument Valley, UT/AZ Teasing a reluctant rental car through the red sands of Monument Valley, passing legendary movie locations, is one of the Southwest's greatest thrills.

---

against European immigrants. The first such, in 1540, were Coronado's **Spanish** explorers, fruitlessly searching for cities of gold. Sixty years later, Hispanic colonists founded **New Mexico**, an ill-defined province that extended into much of modern California and Colorado. Not until 1848 was the region taken over by the **United States**. Almost immediately, outsiders began to flock through on their way to Gold Rush California.

Thereafter, violent confrontations increased between the US government and the Native Americans. The entire **Navajo** population was rounded up and forcibly removed to barren eastern New Mexico in 1864 (though they were soon allowed to return to northeastern Arizona), while the **Apache**, under warrior chiefs Cochise and Geronimo, fought extended battles with the US cavalry. Though the nominal intention was to open up lands to newly American settlers, few ever succeeded in extracting a living from this harsh terrain.

One exception were the **Mormons**, whose flight from persecution brought them by the late 1840s to the alkaline basin of Utah's **Great Salt Lake**. Through sheer hard work, they established what amounted to an independent country, with outlying communities all over the Southwest. They still constitute more than sixty percent of Utah's population and dominate the state's government.

New Mexico

Settled in turn by Native Americans, Spaniards, Mexicans and Yankees, **NEW MEXICO** remains hugely diverse. Each successive group has built upon the legacy of its predecessors; their histories and achievements are intertwined, rather than simply dominated by the white American latecomers.

New Mexico's indigenous peoples – especially the **Pueblo Indians**, heirs to the **Ancestral Puebloans** – provide a sense of cultural continuity. After the **Pueblo Revolt** of 1680 forced a temporary Spanish withdrawal into Mexico, proselytizing padres co-opted the natives without destroying their traditional ways of life, as local deities and celebrations were incorporated into Catholic practice. Somewhat bizarrely to outsiders, grand churches still dominate many Pueblo communities, often adjacent to the underground ceremonial chambers known as *kivas*.

The Americans who arrived in 1848 saw New Mexico as a wasteland. Apart from a few mining booms and range wars – such as the Lincoln County War, which brought **Billy the Kid** to fame – New Mexico was relatively undisturbed until it became a state in 1912. Since World War II, when the secret **Manhattan Project** built the first atomic bomb here, it has been home to America's premier weapons research outposts. By and large, people work close to the land, mining, farming and ranching.

The mountainous **north** is the New Mexico of popular imagination, with its pastel colours, vivid desert landscape and adobe architecture. Even **Santa Fe**, the one real city, is hardly metropolitan in scale and the narrow streets of its small historic centre retain the feel of bygone days. The amiable frontier town of **Taos**, 75 miles northeast, is remarkable chiefly for the stacked dwellings of neighbouring **Taos Pueblo**.

While most travellers simply race through **central New Mexico**, it does hold isolated pockets of interest. Dozens of small towns hang on to remnants of the winding old "Chicago-to-LA" **Route 66**, long since superseded by I-40. **Albuquerque**, New Mexico's largest city, sits dead centre. The area to the **east**, stretching toward Texas, is largely desolate, but the mountainous region **west** offers more – above all **Ácoma Pueblo**, the mesa-top "Sky City".

In wild, wide-open **southern New Mexico**, deep **Carlsbad Caverns** and the desolate dunes of **White Sands** are the main attractions, and elsewhere you can still stumble upon mining and cattle-ranching towns barely changed since the end of the Wild West.

Santa Fe

One of America's oldest and most beautiful cities, **SANTA FE** was founded by Spanish adventurers and missionaries in 1610, a decade before the Pilgrims reached Plymouth Rock. Spread across a high plateau at the foot of the stunning **Sangre de Cristo** mountains, New Mexico's capital still glories in the adobe houses and baroque churches of its original architects, while its newer museums and galleries attract art-lovers from all over the world. The busiest season is **summer**, when temperatures usually reach into the eighties Fahrenheit; in winter, daytime highs average a mere 42°F, though with snow on the mountains the city looks more ravishing than ever.

As upward of a million and a half tourists descend yearly upon a town of just seventy thousand inhabitants, Santa Fe has inevitably grown somewhat overblown. There's still a lot to like, however. Despite the summer crowds, the downtown area still has the peaceful ambience of a small country town, while holding an extraordinary array of cultural and historic treasures. The rigorous insistence that every building should look like a seventeenth-century Spanish colonial palace takes a bit of getting used to, but above all else, it's rare indeed for it to be such fun simply to stroll around a Southwestern city.

Once you've got your bearings, the best places to get a sense of local history and culture are the **Palace of the Governors** and the **New Mexico Museum of Arts** downtown and the museums of **Indian Arts and Culture** and **Folk Art** a couple of miles southeast. Alternatively, set about exploring Santa Fe's distinct neighbourhoods, such as the old **Barrio Analco** just southeast of downtown, home to the **San Miguel Mission**; the **Canyon Road** arts district, just beyond; and funkier **Guadalupe Street** to the west, with its new **Railyard** development.

The plaza

The main focus of life in Santa Fe is still the central **plaza** – especially when filled with buyers and craftspeople during the annual **Indian Market**, on the weekend after the third Thursday in August, and during the first weekend in September for the **Fiestas de Santa Fe**. Apart from an influx of art galleries and restaurants, the surrounding web of narrow streets has changed little. When the US took over in 1848, the new settlers

12

ADOBE

The single most defining feature of New Mexico is its **adobe architecture**, as seen on homes, churches and even shopping malls and motels. A sun-baked mixture of earth, sand, charcoal and chopped grass or straw, adobe bricks are set with a similar mortar, then plastered over with mud and straw. The soil used dictates the colour of the final building, so subtle variations are apparent everywhere. These days, most of what looks like adobe is actually painted cement or concrete, but even this looks attractive enough in its own semi-kitsch way, while hunting out such superb genuine adobes as the remote **Santuario de Chimayó** on the "High Road" between Taos and Santa Fe, the formidable church of **San Francisco de Asis** in Ranchos de Taos or the multitiered dwellings of **Taos Pueblo**, can provide the focus of any enjoyable New Mexico tour.

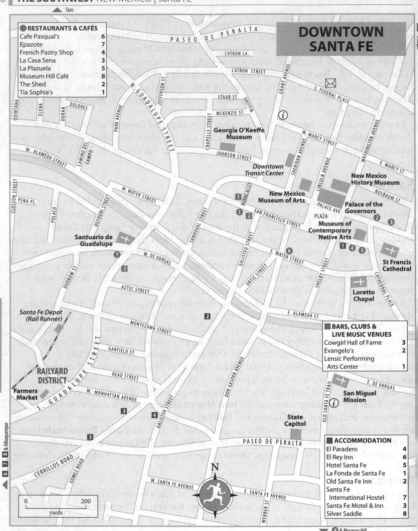

DOWNTOWN SANTA FE

12

chose to build in wood, but many of the finer adobe houses have survived. Since the 1930s, almost every non-adobe structure in sight of the plaza has been designed or redecorated to suit the Pueblo Revival mode, with rounded, mud-coloured plaster walls supporting roof beams made of thick pine logs.

Palace of the Governors

105 W Palace Ave • Mon–Thurs, Sat & Sun 10am–5pm, Fri 10am–8pm; closed Mon in winter • $9, free Fri 5–8pm; under-17s free • ① 505 476 5100, ⓦ palaceofthegovernors.org

Set behind an arcaded veranda that serves as a market for Native American crafts-sellers, the low-slung, initially unprepossessing **Palace of the Governors** fills the entire northern side of Santa Fe's plaza. Originally sod-roofed, the oldest public building in the USA was constructed in 1610 as the headquarters of Spanish colonial administration. Until 1913, it looked like a typical, formal, territorial building, with a square tower at each corner;

THE MUSEUMS OF NEW MEXICO

A combination ticket, costing $20 and valid for four days, grants admission to five leading **Santa Fe museums**: the Palace of the Governors, the Museum of Fine Arts, the Museum of Indian Arts and Culture, the Museum of International Folk Art and the Museum of Spanish Colonial Art. Alternatively, a $15 one-day ticket entitles you to visit *either* the Palace of the Governors and the Museum of Fine Arts, *or* the museums of Indian Arts and International Folk Art.

---

its subsequent adobe "reconstruction" was based on pure conjecture. The well-preserved interior, organized around an open-air courtyard, holds excellent historical displays and a well-stocked bookstore.

A sensitively integrated extension immediately behind holds the very visual exhibits of the **New Mexico History Museum** (same hours and ticket), including letters from Billy the Kid.

New Mexico Museum of Arts

107 E Palace Ave • Mon–Thurs, Sat & Sun 10am–5pm, Fri 10am–8pm, closed Mon in winter • $9, free Fri 5–8pm, under-17s free • ☎ 505 476 5072, ✆ nmartmuseum.org

Housed in an attractive adobe on the northwest corner of the plaza, Santa Fe's **Museum of Fine Arts** focuses around a beautiful garden courtyard, and concentrates on changing exhibits of painting and sculpture by local artists. Selections from the permanent collection, displayed upstairs, usually include an O'Keeffe or two, and one room is devoted to painter and printmaker Gustave Baumann.

Georgia O'Keeffe Museum

217 Johnson St • Mon–Thurs, Sat & Sun 10am–5pm, Fri 10am–7pm • $12, under-19s free • ☎ 505 946 1000, ✆ okeeffemuseum.org

The ten galleries of the showpiece **Georgia O'Keeffe Museum** house the world's largest collection of O'Keeffe's work. Highlights include many of the desert landscapes she painted near **Abiquiu**, forty miles northwest of Santa Fe, where she lived from 1946 until her death in 1986. Most of the museum is given over to touring exhibitions devoted to differing aspects of O'Keeffe's work, so there's little guarantee as to which pieces may be displayed at any one time. The first two rooms, however, feature selections from the permanent collection, which may include early New York cityscapes that make a surprising contrast among the more familiar sun-bleached skulls and iconic flowers.

Museum of Indian Arts and Culture

Museum Hill, 2 miles southeast of downtown • Daily 10am–5pm; closed Mon in winter • $9, under-17s free • ☎ 505 827 6344, ✆ miaclab.org

The excellent **Museum of Indian Arts and Culture** provides comprehensive coverage of all the major Southwest tribes, including the 'O'odham, Navajo, Apache, Pai, Ute and Pueblo peoples. Myth and history are explained in copious detail, while ancient artefacts ranging from pots and pipes to bells, whistles and spearthrowers are drawn from sites that extend as far south as the Casas Grandes ruins in Mexico. Different sections explain how native peoples have thrived in such differing terrains as canyons, river basins, mesas and deserts. There's also a comprehensive array of Native American pottery, from pristine thousand-year-old Ancestral Puebloan and Mimbres pieces up to the works of twentieth-century revivalists.

Museum of International Folk Art

Museum Hill, 2 miles southeast of downtown • Daily 10am–5pm; closed Mon in winter • $8, under-17s free • ☎ 505 827 6344, ✆ moifa.org

The delightful **Museum of International Folk Art** centres on the huge **Girard Collection** of paintings, textiles and especially, **clay figurines**, gathered from all over the world. These are arranged in colourful dioramas that include a Pueblo Feast Day, complete with dancing *kachinas* and camera-clicking tourists, and street scenes from countries such as Poland, Peru, Portugal and Ethiopia featuring fabulously ornate churches and cathedrals.

12

ARRIVAL AND DEPARTURE

By plane Santa Fe's small airport, 10 miles southwest of downtown, is only served by flights from LA, Denver and Dallas/Fort Worth.

By Rail Runner From the Santa Fe Depot, half a mile southwest of downtown, the Rail Runner train line connects Santa Fe with downtown Albuquerque (1hr 40min; $9 one-way,

$10 all-day pass; ☎ 866 795 7245, ⌨ nmrailrunner.com).

By Amtrak Daily trains between Chicago and LA stop at Lamy, 17 miles southeast, where they're met by Lamy Shuttle vans ($28 one-way; ☎ 505 982 8829).

Destinations Chicago (daily; 25hr); Flagstaff (daily; 7hr 30min); Los Angeles (daily; 19hr 30min).

INFORMATION AND TOURS

New Mexico Department of Tourism 491 Old Santa Fe Trail (daily: June–Aug 8am–7pm; Sept–May 8am–5pm; ☎ 505 827 7336, ⌨ newmexico.org). The best place to pick up maps, brochures and information on Santa Fe and the whole state.

Walking tours Historic Walks of Santa Fe run regular 1hr 45min walking tours of downtown, starting from hotels

including *La Fonda*, at 100 E San Francisco St (March–Dec; schedules vary; $14; ☎ 505 986 8388).

Bus tours The Loretto Line, based at the Loretto Chapel, 207 Old Santa Fe Trail, runs bus tours of the city, taking in Museum Hill and Canyon Rd as well as the plaza area (mid-March to Oct daily 10am, noon & 2pm; $15; ☎ 505 983 3701, ⌨ toursofsantafe.com).

ACCOMMODATION

In summer, when every bed in town is frequently taken, you're unlikely to find a room within walking distance of downtown Santa Fe for under $125. **Cerrillos Road** (US-85), the main road in from I-25, holds most of Santa Fe's **motels** and its one **hostel**.

El Paradero 220 W Manhattan Ave ☎ 505 988 1177, ⌨ elparadero.com. Converted Spanish-era farmhouse near Guadalupe St. The rooms are relatively plain and simple and furnished with folk art; thirteen are en suite, the remaining two share a bathroom. Good breakfast and helpful hosts. **$130**

★ **El Rey Inn** 1862 Cerrillos Rd, at St Michael's Drive ☎ 505 982 1931, ⌨ elreyinnsantafe.com. This white-painted adobe compound offers the most character and best value of the Cerrillos Road motels, with stylish, distinctive and large Southwestern rooms adorned with Art Deco tiles, semi-private patios, some nice suites, complimentary breakfasts, a pool and a large garden. **$105**

Hotel Santa Fe 1501 Paseo de Peralta, at Cerrillos Rd ☎ 505 982 1200, ⌨ hotelsantafe.com. Run by Picuris Pueblo, this attractive, elegant and very comfortable adobe hotel on the edge of downtown is within walking distance of the plaza, and has its own good restaurant, *Amaya*. **$199**

★ **La Fonda de Santa Fe** 100 E San Francisco St ☎ 505 982 5511, ⌨ lafondasantafe.com. Gorgeous old inn on the southeast corner of the plaza, marking the end of the Santa Fe Trail, and featuring hand-painted murals and stained glass throughout. Each lavishly furnished room is different, with some lovely suites, and there's a delightful restaurant plus rooftop bar. **$189**

Old Santa Fe Inn 320 Galisteo St ☎ 505 995 0800,

⌨ oldsantafeinn.com. Former Rte-66 motor court, now an appealing inn; many of its tasteful, Mexican-themed rooms have their own gas fireplaces. Avoid the few rooms in the inadequately soundproofed two-storey buildings. Rates include breakfast. **$224**

Santa Fe International Hostel 1412 Cerrillos Rd, at Alta Vista ☎ 505 988 1153, ⌨ hostelsantafe.com. Old-fashioned hostel, in a ramshackle former motel a couple of miles southwest of the plaza. Some travellers find the staff unfriendly, the owner a control freak and the rooms poorly furnished and dirty; others seem satisfied, and don't mind the compulsory chores. In winter the whole place can be damp and cold. Dorms **$18**, shared-bath doubles **$35**, en-suite doubles **$45**

★ **Santa Fe Motel & Inn** 510 Cerrillos Rd ☎ 505 982 1039, ⌨ santafemotel.com. To call this delightfully stylish yet inexpensive little adobe complex a "motel" barely does it justice; even its most conventional rooms are appealingly furnished, and some have their own kitchens, while there are several gorgeous *casitas*. The rates, great for such a quiet, central location, include a cooked breakfast. **$139**

Silver Saddle 2810 Cerrillos Rd, at Siler Rd ☎ 505 471 7663, ⌨ santafesilversaddlemotel.com. Busy, down-to-earth Western-themed motel, in the finest Rte-66 tradition. Each room has a little patio, some have cooking facilities, and all feature fun cowboy trappings. **$62**

EATING

Cafe Pasqual's 121 Don Gaspar Ave ☎ 505 983 9340, ⌨ pasquals.com. Lovely lively, and ever-innovative Old/New Mexican restaurant that serves top-quality organic food in an attractive tiled dining room. Dinner mains range from

vegetarian enchiladas ($24), via a Mexican mixed plate ($28), to chilli-rubbed *filet mignon* ($39). Appetizers include spicy Vietnamese scallops ($14). Mon–Thurs & Sun 8am–3pm & 5.30–9.30pm, Fri & Sat 8am–3pm & 5.30–10pm.

★ **Epazote** 416 Agua Fria ☎ 505 988 5991, ⓦ epazote santafe.com. Wonderful, very stylish Mexican restaurant. Chef Fernando Olea takes an infectious delight in good food; forget the menu, and let him cook whatever he fancies – whether it's spiced corn truffles with cheese, slow-cooked lamb in banana leaves, or even *chapulines* (grilled grasshoppers). Be sure to sample his three distinct *mole* sauces. Full dinners around $30. Mon–Wed 5.30–9pm, Thurs–Sat 5.30pm–1am.

French Pastry Shop La Fonda de Santa Fe, 100 E San Francisco St ☎ 505 983 6697. Though it looks and feels more like a diner than a coffeehouse, this hotel café serves fabulous pastries and coffees, along with breakfasts, sandwiches and crêpes sweet and savoury. Daily 6.30am–5pm.

La Casa Sena 125 E Palace Ave ☎ 505 988 9232, ⓦ lacasasena.com. Lovely courtyard restaurant, a block from the plaza; zestful Southwestern lunches, with most mains $12–16, are the best deal; the $14 seafood sampler plate is great value. Dinner mains cost $17–28. At the adjoining, cheaper *La Cantina*, staff perform Broadway show tunes during dinner (Wed–Sun only). Daily 11am–3pm & 5.30–10pm.

★ **La Plazuela** La Fonda de Santa Fe, 100 E San Francisco St ☎ 505 982 5511, ⓦ lafondasantafe.com. Delightful, beautifully furnished Mexican restaurant, which feels like an open-air courtyard even though it's covered by a glass ceiling. All the usual Mexican dishes are nicely prepared and sold for reasonable prices, with mains at $11–19 at lunchtime, and ranging, for pricier items such as lamb shank, up to $35 in the evening. Mon–Fri 7am–2pm & 5.30–10pm, Sat & Sun 7am–3pm & 5.30–10pm.

Museum Hill Café 705 Camino Lejo ☎ 505 984 8900, ⓦ museumhillcafe.net. Spacious café, enjoying fabulous mountain views from a terrace between the folk art and Indian arts museums, and offering free wi-fi. Inexpensive but good sandwiches – turkey, tuna and steak all cost around $11 – plus tacos, flautas, burgers, pasta specials and salads, and a large Sunday brunch. Tues–Sun 11am–3pm.

The Shed 113 E Palace Ave ☎ 505 982 9030, ⓦ sfshed .com. Mexican-flavoured local restaurant in a pleasant garden courtyard, serving a steady diet of chilli enchiladas, blue-corn tortillas and even low-fat specialities. There's little over $10 on the lunch menu, but dinner works out a bit more expensive. Mon–Sat 11am–2.30pm & 5.30–9pm.

Tia Sophia's 210 W San Francisco St ☎ 505 983 9880. Spicy, very inexpensive Mexican diner, a block or two west of the plaza, that's hugely popular with lunching locals. Daily breakfast and lunch specials for under $10. Mon–Sat 7am–2pm, Sun 8am–1pm.

NIGHTLIFE AND ENTERTAINMENT

Cowgirl Hall of Fame 319 S Guadalupe St ☎ 505 982 2565, ⓦ cowgirlsantafe.com. Very busy country-themed restaurant and bar, with karaoke on Mondays and live music every other night. Mon–Thurs & Sun 11am–11pm, Fri & Sat 11am–midnight.

Evangelo's 200 W San Francisco St ☎ 505 982 9014. The only good bare-bones bar in easy walking range of the plaza, with a pool table and a jukebox, plus occasional live music. Be sure to check out the *Underground* dive bar downstairs. Daily noon–midnight.

Lensic Performing Arts Center 211 W San Francisco St ☎ 505 988 1234, ⓦ lensic.org. All year round, this strikingly converted "Pueblo Deco" theatre downtown hosts musical and theatrical performances, by touring artists as well as local groups.

Santa Fe Opera Seven miles north of Santa Fe, 1.4 miles northeast of US-84 exit 168 ☎ 505 986 5900 or ☎ 800 280 4654, ⓦ santafeopera.org. In its much-anticipated summer season, from late June through August, the Santa Fe Opera stages five separate productions in a magnificent purpose-built amphitheatre. Ticket prices start at $30.

Bandelier National Monument

Ten miles south of Los Alamos, a total of 50 miles northwest of Santa Fe • Access to Frijoles Canyon by car Dec–Feb only; March–Nov free shuttle from car park at White Rock, on Hwy-4 in White Rock • $12/vehicle • ☎ 505 672 3861, ⓦ nps.gov/band

Around 1300 AD, itinerant Ancestral Puebloan groups, seeking sanctuary from drought and invasion, gathered at the edge of the forested mesas of the Pajarito Plateau to build what's now **Bandelier National Monument**, a community that amalgamated their assorted cultures.

A paved 1.5-mile trail leads through the prime site, **Frijoles Canyon**. Not far from its beginning, a side path from the circular, multistorey village of **Tyuonyi** leads up to dozens of **cave dwellings**, their rounded chambers scooped out of the soft volcanic rock; you can scramble up to and even enter, some, to peer out across the valley. The main trail continues to the **Long House**, an 800ft series of two- and three-storey houses built against the canyon wall. Rows of petroglyphs are visible, carved above the holes that held the roof beams. Half a mile beyond, protected by a rock overhang 150ft above the canyon floor and accessible only via rickety ladders and steep stairs, a reconstructed *kiva* sits in **Alcove House**.

12

THE ANCESTRAL PUEBLOANS

Few visitors to the Southwest are prepared for the awesome scale and beauty of the desert cities and cliff palaces left by the **Ancestral Puebloans**, as seen all over the high plateaus of the "**Four Corners**" region, where Colorado, New Mexico, Arizona and Utah now meet.

Although the earliest humans reached the Southwest around 10,000 BC, the Ancestral Puebloans first appeared as the **Basketmakers**, near the San Juan River, two thousand years ago. Named for their woven sandals and bowls, they lived in pits in the earth, roofed with logs and mud. Over time, the Ancestral Puebloans adopted an increasingly settled lifestyle, becoming expert farmers and potters. Their first freestanding houses on the plains were followed by multistoreyed **pueblos**, in which hundreds of families lived in complexes of contiguous "apartments". The astonishing **cliff dwellings**, perched on precarious ledges high above remote canyons, which they began to build around 1100 AD, were the first Ancestral Puebloan settlements to show signs of defensive fortifications. Competition for scarce resources became even fiercer toward the end of the thirteenth century and it's thought that warfare and even cannibalism played a role in their ultimate dispersal. Moving eastward, they joined forces with other displaced groups in a coming-together that eventually produced the modern **Pueblo Indians**. Hence the recent change of name, away from "Anasazi", a Navajo word meaning "ancient enemies", in favour of "Ancestral Puebloan".

Among the most significant **Ancestral Puebloan sites** are:

Mesa Verde Magnificent cliff palaces, high in the canyons of Colorado; see p.691.

Bandelier National Monument Large riverside pueblos and cave-like homes hollowed from volcanic rock; see p.741.

Chaco Canyon The largest and most sophisticated freestanding pueblos, far out in the desert; see p.750.

Canyon de Chelly Superbly dramatic cliff dwellings in a glowing sandstone canyon now owned and farmed by the Navajo; see p.775.

Hovenweep Enigmatic towers poised above a canyon; see p.792.

Wupatki Several small pueblo communities near the edge of the Painted Desert, built by assorted groups after an eleventh-century volcanic eruption.

Walnut Canyon Numerous homes set into the canyon walls above lush Walnut Creek, just east of Flagstaff.

Betatakin Canyon-side community set in a vast rocky alcove in Navajo National Monument; visible from afar, or close-up on guided hikes.

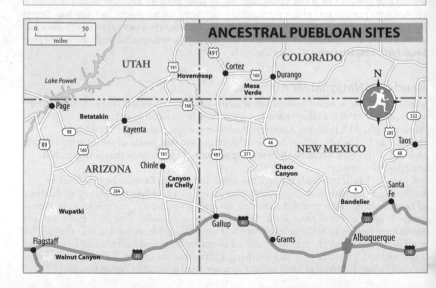

ANCESTRAL PUEBLOAN SITES

The High Road

The quickest route between Santa Fe and Taos follows US-84 as far as the Rio Grande, then follows the river northeast on Hwy-68. US-84 passes through the heartland of the **northern pueblos**, a cluster of tiny Tewa-speaking communities, but unless your visit coincides with a feast day, there's little to see.

However, a circuitous route known as the "**High Road**" leaves US-68/84 a dozen miles north of Santa Fe, near Nambe Pueblo. Leading high into the wooded **Sangre de Cristo Mountains**, it passes a number of pueblos and Hispanic villages.

Santuario de Chimayó

Daily: May–Sept 9am–6pm; Oct–April 9am–5pm; Mass Mon–Sat 11am, Sun 10.30am & noon • ☎ 505 351 9961, ⓦ elsantuariodechimayo.us

The quaint mountain village of **CHIMAYÓ**, 25 miles north of Santa Fe at the junction of Hwy-503 and Hwy-76, is the site of the 1816 **Santuario de Chimayó**. Known as the "Lourdes of America" for the devotion of its many pilgrims, this round-shouldered, twin-towered adobe beauty sits behind an enclosed courtyard; a pit in the floor of a side room holds the "holy dirt" for which the site is venerated.

ACCOMMODATION AND EATING	THE HIGH ROAD

Hacienda Rancho de Chimayó Hwy-98 ☎ 505 351 2222, ⓦ ranchodechimayo.com. Immediately across from the *Rancho* restaurant, and run by the same management, this peaceful B&B inn offers seven appealing en-suite rooms, arranged around a shared courtyard; several have their own patio space. **$79**

★ **Rancho de Chimayó** Hwy-98 ☎ 505 351 4444,

ⓦ ranchodechimayo.com. The best traditional New Mexican restaurant in the state, serving superb *flautas* and a mouthwatering *sopaipilla*, stuffed with meat and chillis and costing $8 for lunch, $12 in the evening, on a lovely sun-drenched outdoor patio. May–Oct Mon–Fri 11.30am–9pm, Sat & Sun 8.30am–10.30am & 11.30am–9pm; Nov–April Tues–Sun 11.30am–9pm.

Taos

Still home to one of the longest-established Native American populations in the USA, though transformed by becoming first a Spanish colonial outpost and more recently a hangout for bohemian artists, Hollywood exiles and New Age dropouts, **TAOS** (which rhymes with "mouse") is famous out of all proportion to its size. Not quite six thousand people live in its three component parts: **Taos** itself, around the plaza; sprawling **Ranchos de Taos**, three miles to the south; and the Native American community of **Taos Pueblo**, two miles north.

Beyond the usual unsightly highway sprawl, Taos is a delight to visit. Besides museums, galleries and stores, it still offers an unhurried pace and charm and the sense of a meeting place between Pueblo, Hispanic and American cultures. Its reputation as an **artists' colony** began at the end of the nineteenth century, and new generations of artists and writers have "discovered" Taos ever since. English novelist **D.H. Lawrence** visited in the 1920s, while **Georgia O'Keeffe** stayed for a few years soon afterwards.

Taos plaza

The old Spanish **plaza** at the heart of Taos is now ringed by jewellery stores, art galleries and restaurants; all conform to the predominant Pueblo motif of rounded brown adobe. Specific sights are few – a small **gallery** in the *Fonda de Taos* holds a collection of sexy but amateurish paintings by D.H. Lawrence, and the tree-filled square itself is often animated by guitar-toting buskers – but the surrounding streets are perfect for an aimless stroll.

Governor Bent House and Museum

117 Bent St • Daily: April–Oct 9.30am–5pm; Nov–March 10am–4pm • $2 • ☎ 505 758 2376

Bent Street, a block north of the plaza, takes its name from the first American governor of New Mexico, Charles Bent, whose former home is now the **Governor Bent House**

THE RIO GRANDE PUEBLOS

The first Spaniards to explore what's now New Mexico encountered 100,000 so-called **Pueblo Indians**, living in a hundred villages and towns (*pueblo* is Spanish for "village"). Resenting the imposition of Catholicism and their virtual enslavement, the various tribes banded together in the 1680 **Pueblo Revolt** and ousted the entire colonial regime, killing scores of priests and soldiers and sending hundreds more south to Mexico. After the Spanish returned in 1693, the Pueblos showed little further resistance and they have coexisted ever since, accepting aspects of Catholicism without giving up their traditional beliefs and practices. New Mexico is now home to around forty thousand Pueblo Indians; each of its nineteen autonomous pueblos has its own laws and system of government.

The Pueblos celebrate Saints' days, major Catholic holidays such as Easter and the Epiphany and even the Fourth of July with a combination of Native American traditions and Catholic rituals, featuring elaborately costumed dances and massive communal feasts. The spectacle of hundreds of costumed, body-painted tribal members of all ages, performing elaborate dances in such timeless surroundings, is hugely impressive.

However, few pueblos are quite the tourist attractions they're touted to be. While the best known, **Taos** and **Ácoma**, retain their ancient defensive architecture, the rest tend to be dusty adobe hamlets scattered around a windblown plaza. Unless you arrive on a feast day or are a knowledgeable shopper in search of Pueblo crafts, visits are liable to prove disappointing. In addition, you'll be made very unwelcome if you fail to behave respectfully – don't "explore" places that are off-limits to outsiders, such as shrines, *kivas* or private homes.

Fifteen of the pueblos are concentrated along the Rio Grande north of Albuquerque, with a long-standing division between the seven **southern pueblos**, south of Santa Fe, most of which speak Keresan and the group to the north, which mostly speak Tewa (pronounced *tay-wah*). Visitors to each are required to register at a visitor centre; some charge an admission fee of \$3–10 and those that permit such activities typically charge additional fees of \$5 for still photography, \$10–15 for video cameras and up to \$100 for sketching. There's no extra charge for feast days or dances, but photography is usually forbidden on special occasions.

and Museum. The imposition of American rule was resented by Taos's Hispanic and Indian population alike, and Bent was killed here by an angry mob on January 19, 1847. A ramshackle museum of frontier Taoseño life, his house holds Indian artefacts, antiquated rifles and even an eight-legged lamb.

Kit Carson Home and Museum

113 Kit Carson Rd • Daily 11am–4pm • \$5 • ⓣ 575 758 4945, ⓦ kitcarsonhomeandmuseum.com

The dusty but evocative adobe home of "mountain man," mason, and part-time US cavalry officer **Kit Carson** stand just east of the plaza. Born in Kentucky in 1809, Carson left home to join a wagon train to Missouri in 1826, and spent the ensuing winter in Taos. He was to return repeatedly throughout his life, in between escapades such as scouting for the 1840s Frémont expeditions and campaigning against the Navajo in the 1860s (see p.773).

Millicent Rogers Museum

1504 Millicent Rogers Rd, 4 miles north of the plaza • April–Oct daily 10am–5pm; Nov–March Tues–Sun 10am–5pm • \$10, under-17s \$2 • ⓣ 505 758 2462, ⓦ millicentrogers.org

Focusing on both Native American and Hispanic art, and tracing how those cultures have been perceived, the **Millicent Rogers Museum** is one of New Mexico's best galleries. Millicent Rogers herself – a former fashion model, granddaughter of a founder of Standard Oil and "close" to Cary Grant – lived here until her death in 1953. Her collection includes superb Ancestral Puebloan and Mimbres pottery; the more recent black-on-black ceramics of San Ildefonso Pueblo potter Maria Martínez; and beautiful Navajo blankets.

San Francisco de Asis

In the small unpaved plaza of Ranchos de Taos, the mission church of **San Francisco de Asis** turns its broad shoulders, or more accurately its massive adobe buttresses, to the passing traffic on Hwy-68. Built around 1776, it's one of colonial New Mexico's most splendid architectural achievements, with subtly rounded walls and corners that disguise its underlying structural strength.

Hacienda Martínez

708 Hacienda Way, off Lower Ranchitos Rd, Ranchos de Taos, 2 miles west of Hwy-68 • April–Oct Mon–Sat 10am–5pm, Sun noon–5pm; Nov–March Mon, Tues & Thurs–Sat 10am–4pm, Sun noon 4pm • $8 • ☏ 575 758 0505, ⦿ taoshistoricmuseums.org

One of the few Spanish haciendas to be preserved in something like its original state, the **Hacienda Martínez** was built in 1804 by Don Antonio Martínez, an early mayor of Taos. Within its thick, windowless, adobe walls – the place could be sealed like a fortress against then still-prevalent Indian raids – two dozen rooms are wrapped around two separate patios, holding animal pens and a well. Trade goods of the kind Don Antonio once carried south along the Rio Grande are displayed alongside tools, looms and simple furnishings of the era, plus a fine collection of Hispanic religious art.

Taos Pueblo

Just over 2 miles north of Taos plaza, along either of two separate approach roads off Hwy-68 • Mon–Sat 8am–4pm, Sun 8.30am–4pm, but closed mid-Feb to March, and also frequently closed for tribal events • $10/person, plus $6 per still or video camera, including cellphones • ☏ 505 758 1028, ⦿ taospueblo.com

Continuously inhabited for nearly one thousand years, the two multistorey adobes at **Taos Pueblo** jointly constitute the most impressive Native American dwelling place still in use. Hlauuma, the north house, and Hlaukwima, the south house, are separated by the Rio Pueblo de Taos, which flows down from the sacred Blue Lake, inaccessible to outsiders. Pueblo residents make few concessions to the modern world, living without toilets, running water or electricity. Paying the entry fee entitles you to join guided **walking tours** led by Pueblo residents.

For most of the year, Pueblo life continues with scant regard for the intrusion of tourists, but summer feast days and dances, like the **Corn Dances** in June and July and the **Feast of San Gerónimo** at the end of September, can be spectacular.

ARRIVAL AND INFORMATION   TAOS

By bus Taos Express buses connect with Rail Runner trains to and from Santa Fe, at weekends only (departs Taos Fri 4.30pm, Sat & Sun 8am & 4.30pm; journey time 2hr; return $10, reservations required; ☏ 505 751 4459, ⦿ taosexpress.com).

Visitor centre 1139 Paseo del Pueblo Sur, 2 miles south of the plaza at the intersection of hwys 68 and 585 (June–Aug daily 9am–5pm; Sept–May Mon–Sat 9am–5pm; ☏ 505 758 3873, ⦿ taos.org). Brochures, maps and free wi-fi.

TOURS AND ACTIVITIES

Cottam's Rio Grande Rafting Full-day whitewater rafting trips through the Taos Box Canyon of the Rio Grande (April–midsummer only, Mon–Fri $104, Sat & Sun $114; ☏ 505 758 2822, ⦿ cottamsoutdoor.com). They also arrange biking, kayaking and, in winter, snowmobiling expeditions.
Far Flung Adventures Half- and full-day rafting trips on the Rio Grande from Pilar, south of Taos (half-day $55;

one-day trips Mon–Fri $105, Sat & Sun $125; ☏ 505 758 2628, ⦿ farflung.com).
Taos Trolley Tours In summer, open-air tram (trolley) tours visit the main attractions (May–Oct daily 10.30am & 2pm from visitor centre, 10.45am & 2.15pm at plaza; ☏ 505 550 5612, ⦿ taostrolleytours.com; $33, including entry fees).

ACCOMMODATION

El Pueblo Lodge 412 Paseo del Pueblo Norte ☏ 505 758 8700, ⦿ elpueblolodge.com. Southwestern-themed 1940s fake-adobe motel, half a mile north of downtown near Taos Pueblo, where the nicely furnished rooms have extra-large bathrooms and there's a decent outdoor pool

and hot tub. **$110**
★ **Historic Taos Inn** 125 Paseo del Pueblo Norte ☏ 505 758 2233, ⦿ taosinn.com. Gorgeous, romantic central Taos landmark, consisting of several ancient adobes welded together to create an atmospheric and very

12

Southwestern hotel. Each room plays some variation on the Pueblo theme, with varying degrees of luxury; the cosy, convivial lobby area was once an open courtyard. $105

La Doña Luz 114 Kit Carson Rd ☎ 505 758 9000, ⊛ stayintaos.com. Hispanic-flavoured rooms of differing sizes, prices and standards – all have en-suite facilities, some have fully equipped kitchens and/or hot tubs – in a peaceful adobe B&B a very short walk east of the plaza. $84

La Fonda de Taos 108 South Plaza ☎ 505 758 2211, ⊛ lafondataos.com. Vintage 1930s hotel on the plaza that has been totally modernized to hold 24 luxurious suites, with Southwestern furnishings and tiled bathrooms. The lobby even holds a gallery of D.H. Lawrence paintings. $149

★ **Mabel Dodge Luhan House** 240 Morada Lane ☎ 505 751 9686, ⊛ mabeldodgeluhan.com. This 200-year-old adobe B&B complex, not far northeast of the plaza, isn't the most luxurious option, but its historic associations are impressive, with lovely guestrooms named in honour of guests like Willa Cather and Ansel Adams. Two rooms, including the light-filled solarium, share a bathroom painted by D.H. Lawrence; the cheaper lodge annexe has more modern fittings. $105

EATING AND DRINKING

Bent Street Deli & Cafe 120 Bent St ☎ 505 758 5787, ⊛ bentstreetdeli.com. Open in daytime only, this airy, partly outdoor place is always buzzing with locals and day-trippers. Good-value breakfasts are followed by sandwich or pasta lunches, with plenty of options for under $10. Mon–Sat 8am–4pm, Sun 10am–3pm.

Doc Martin's Historic Taos Inn, 125 Paseo del Pueblo Norte ☎ 505 758 1977, ⊛ taosinn.com. Delicious, inventive New Mexican food in romantic old adobe inn. Typical lunchtime burgers and burritos cost $10–15, while dinner mains, such as piñon-crusted salmon or roast chicken, range up to $30. Unusual options on the weekend brunch menu include the Kit Carson – poached eggs on yam biscuits. Mon–Fri 11am–10pm, Sat & Sun 7.30am–2.30pm.

Graham's Grille 106 Paseo del Pueblo Norte ☎ 505 751 1350, ⊛ grahamstaos.com. This popular central bistro stretches a long way back from the highway; a large, well-shaded patio complements its copious indoor seating. Tasty lunchtime sandwiches, or "small plates" such as tamales, or mussels with chorizo, cost $6–8, while almost all the dinner steaks, pasta or Mexican mains are under $20. Mon–Fri 7am–10.30am, 11.30am–2.30pm & 5–9pm, Sat & Sun 8am–2.30pm & 5–9pm.

Michael's Kitchen 304C Paseo del Pueblo Norte ☎ 505 758 4178, ⊛ michaelskitchen.com. Inexpensive Mexican and Southwestern dishes in an old adobe kitchen, plus fresh-baked pastries, cinnamon rolls and coffee in the morning. Mon–Thurs 7am–2.30pm, Fri–Sun 7am–8pm.

Tiwa Kitchen 328 Veterans Hwy, Taos Pueblo ☎ 505 751 1020. Indian-run, largely organic restaurant on the road into Taos Pueblo, serving strong chilli-flavoured stews, traditional *horno*-baked bread and Indian frybread, all costing under $10, plus lots of blue corn meal. June–Aug 11am–7pm; Sept–May 11am–5pm; closed Tues.

Albuquerque

Sprawling at the heart of New Mexico, where the east–west road and rail routes cross both the Rio Grande and the old road south to Mexico, **ALBUQUERQUE** is, with half a million people, the state's only major metropolis. The "**Duke City**" may have grown a bit fast for comfort, but the original Hispanic settlement is still discernible at its core

ROUTE 66 IN THE SOUTHWEST

If you do ever plan to motor west, there's still one definitive highway that's the best. Eighty-five years since it was first completed, 75 since John Steinbeck called it "the mother road, the road of flight" in *The Grapes of Wrath* and 65 since songwriter Bobby Troup set it all down in rhyme, what better reason to visit the Southwest could there be than to get hip to this timely tip and get your kicks on **Route 66**?

The heyday of Route 66 as the nation's premier cross-country route – winding from Chicago to LA – lasted barely twenty years, from its being paved in 1937 until it began to be superseded by freeways in 1957. It was officially rendered defunct in 1984, when Williams, Arizona, became the last town to be bypassed. Nonetheless, substantial stretches of the original Route 66 survive, complete with the motels and drive-ins that became icons of vernacular American architecture. Restored 1950s roadsters and the latest Harley Davidsons alike flock to cruise along the atmospheric, neon-lit frontages of towns such as Albuquerque and Flagstaff, or through such empty desertscapes as those between Grants and Gallup in New Mexico or Seligman and Kingman in Arizona.

and its diverse population gives it a rare cultural vibrancy. Even if its architecture is often uninspired, the setting is magnificent, sandwiched between the Rio Grande and the glowing **Sandia Mountains**. Specific highlights include the intact **Spanish plaza**, the neon-lit **Route 66** frontage of Central Avenue and the excellent **Indian Pueblo Cultural Centre**, while every October Albuquerque hosts the nation's largest **hot-air balloon** rally. Although the huge international popularity of TV's **Breaking Bad** has certainly boosted tourism, no specific locations from the series are worth visiting – not that that's stopped local entrepreneurs from offering tours, or indeed selling "blue meth" bath salts and candies.

Old Town

Once you've cruised up and down **Central Avenue**, looking at the flashing neon and 1940s architecture of this twenty-mile stretch of Route 66, most of what's interesting about Albuquerque is concentrated in **Old Town**, the heart of the Spanish city. As the interstate billboards rightly proclaim, "it's darned old and historic". The tree-filled **main plaza** is overlooked by the twin-towered adobe facade of **San Felipe de Neri church**; it's a pleasant place to wander or have a meal, even if there's not a whole lot to do.

Albuquerque Museum of Art and History

2000 Mountain Rd • Tues–Sun 9am–5pm • $4, free Sun 9am–1pm • ☎ 505 743 7255, ⊕ cabq.gov/museum

The **Albuquerque Museum of Art and History**, a couple of blocks northeast of the plaza, makes a great introduction to the city's story. Besides an impressive array of the armour and weaponry carried by the Spanish conquistadors, it holds delicate religious artefacts, plus paintings and photos showing Albuquerque through the centuries.

New Mexico Museum of Natural History and Science

1801 Mountain Rd NW • Daily 9am–5pm; closed Mon in Jan & Sept • $8 • ☎ 505 841 2800, ⊕ nmnaturalhistory.org

With its full-scale models of dinosaurs and a replica of a Carlsbad-like snow cave, the **New Mexico Museum of Natural History and Science** is aimed primarily at kids. Its fascinating "Start Up" exhibition uses Microsoft's origins in Albuquerque in 1977 as the springboard for a history of the computer revolution. Albuquerque was where the first Altair personal computer was developed, prompting an incredibly young-looking Bill Gates and Paul Allen to move here in 1977 and establish "Micro-Soft" to write software for the first generation of home-based programmers.

ABQ BioPark

June–Aug Mon–Fri 9am–5pm, Sat & Sun 9am–6pm; Sept–May daily 9am–5pm • $12.50 • ☎ 505 768 2000, ⊕ cabq.gov/culturalservices/biopark

In the **ABQ BioPark**, alongside but not quite within sight of the Rio Grande, the **Albuquerque Aquarium** offers such diverse experiences as eating in a restaurant beside a glass-walled tank filled with live sharks, and walking through a tunnel surrounded on all sides by fierce-eyed moray eels. The whole place has been designed with a great eye for aesthetics. Across the park's central plaza, the **Botanic Garden** consists of two large conservatories plus a series of formal walled gardens.

Indian Pueblo Cultural Centre

2401 12th St NW • **Museum** Daily 9am–5pm • $6 **Gift store** Daily 9am–5.30pm • Free • ☎ 505 843 7270, ⊕ indianpueblo.org

The **Indian Pueblo Cultural Centre** is a stunning museum and crafts market, cooperatively owned and run by Pueblo Indians. As well as explaining the shared Ancestral Puebloan heritage at the root of Pueblo culture, the museum explores the impact of the Spanish conquistadors. There's also a good explanation of a topic rarely discussed with outsiders: how indigenous religion has managed to coexist with imported Catholicism. Videos illustrate modern Pueblo life and the stores upstairs sell pottery and jewellery, while a good-quality **café** serves Pueblo specialities.

12

National Museum of Nuclear Science and History

601 Eubank Blvd SE • Daily 9am–5pm • $8 • ☎ 505 245 2137, ⓦ nuclearmuseum.org

The **National Museum of Nuclear Science and History**, immediately outside Albuquerque's huge Kirtland Air Force Base, used to stand within the base, until the threat of terrorism rendered that location inappropriate. Displays range from the early discoveries of Madame Curie to a 1953 *Life* magazine cover reading "we are in a life and death bomb race". You'll be soothed to learn how much more precise and sophisticated today's weapons are compared with the "primitive city-busting concepts" of the Cold War era, just how safe nuclear waste disposal can be and a host of other little-known facts. A gift store sells space-age novelties.

The Sandia Mountains

Sandia Peak Tramway June–Aug daily 9am–9pm; May–Sept Mon & Wed–Sun 9am–8pm, Tues 5–8pm • $20 • **Ski season** Mid-Dec to mid-March • Lift tickets $50 • ☎ 505 242 9052, ⓦ sandiapeak.com

The forested **Sandia Mountains** tower 10,500ft over Albuquerque to the east; views from the summit are especially beautiful at and after sunset, when the city lights sparkle below. In summer it's a good 25°F cooler up here than in the valley, while in winter you can go downhill or cross-country **skiing**.

The world's longest tramway, the 2.7-mile **Sandia Peak Tramway**, climbs to the top from the end of Tramway Road a dozen miles northeast of town. During the uppermost 1.5 miles of its exhilarating fifteen-minute climb, not a single support tower interrupts its progress.

12

ARRIVAL AND DEPARTURE

ALBUQUERQUE

By plane Buses connect Albuquerque's International Sunport, 4 miles southeast of downtown, with the Rail Runner network, while a taxi into town with Albuquerque Cab (☎ 505 883 4888, ⓦ albuquerquecab.com) costs $15 and up.

By bus Long-distance Greyhound buses use the Alvarado Transportation Center.

Destinations Denver (2 daily; 8hr); Flagstaff (3 daily; 6hr); Phoenix (3 daily; 9hr)

By train One daily train in each direction on Amtrak's Southwest Chief service calls at the Alvarado Transportation Center, at First and Central.

Destinations Chicago (1 daily; 26hr 30min); Flagstaff (1 daily; 6hr); Los Angeles (1 daily; 18hr).

GETTING AROUND AND INFORMATION

By bus and train Albuquerque has its own light-rail system, Rail Runner (from $2; ☎ 866 795 7245, ⓦ nmrailrunner.com). Commuter trains from its downtown Albuquerque station, in the Alvarado Transportation Center, run south to Belen and north to Santa Fe (see p.737). Connecting buses from the

airport run to the downtown station (Mon–Sat).

Visitor centres 303 Romero St NW, in the Old Town (daily: April–Oct 10am–6pm; Nov–March 9.30am–4.30pm; ☎ 505 842 9118, ⓦ itsatrip.org), and at the airport (Mon–Fri 9.30am–8pm, Sat 9.30am–4pm).

ACCOMMODATION

The 20-mile length of **Central Avenue**, the old Route 66, is lined with the flashing neon signs of $50-per-night **motels**. Try to have a good look in daylight, to spot those that may turn scary at night.

Andaluz 125 Second St NW ☎ 505 242 9090, ⓦ hotel andaluz.com. Historic, elegant hotel, built in Mexican style by Conrad Hilton in 1939 and now exquisitely re-vamped, that's downtown's most appealing upscale option. Beautiful wood-panelled lobby, top-class restaurant and cosy bar. $159

Casas de Sueños 310 Rio Grande Blvd SW ☎ 505 247 4560, ⓦ casasdesuenos.com. Beautifully furnished, exotic and friendly B&B, very close to Old Town, with themed adobe *casitas* (cottages) and smaller rooms of varying degrees of luxury – some have kitchenettes and whirlpool baths. Rooms $129, hot-tub suites $159

La Quinta Inn Albuquerque Airport 2116 Yale Blvd SE ☎ 505 243 5500, ⓦ lq.com. Large, relatively upscale motel, served by frequent shuttles from the nearby airport, and offering accommodation that's far from memorable but safe, good-value and quiet; rates include breakfast. $75

★ **Monterey Non-Smokers Motel** 2402 Central Ave SW ☎ 505 243 3554, ⓦ nonsmokersmotel.com. Clean, fifteen-room motel, two blocks west of Old Town, run by a friendly Polish couple, and offering a pool and laundry as well as of course a strict nonsmoking policy. $72

Route 66 Hostel 1012 Central Ave SW ☎ 505 247 1813, ⓦ rt66hostel.com. Albuquerque's only hostel, a friendly place between Old Town and downtown, offers dorm beds and very plain but bargain-priced private doubles, plus kitchen facilities and abundant books and board games. Office hours daily 7.30–10.30am & 4–11pm. Dorms $20, shared-bath doubles $30, en-suite doubles $35

EATING

66 Diner 1405 Central Ave NE ☎ 505 247 1421, ⓦ 66diner .com. Classic Fifties diner, with white-capped waiting staff, a soda fountain and a lively late-night clientele. Mon–Fri 11am–11pm, Sat 8am–11pm, Sun 8am–10pm.

Artichoke Café 424 Central Ave SE ☎ 505 243 0200, ⓦ artichokecafe.com. Simple but classy restaurant in the heart of downtown, serving a good, varied menu of California-influenced modern American cuisine; typical mains cost $12–15 at lunch, $20–30 for dinner. Mon–Fri 11am–2.30pm & 5.30–10pm, Sat 5.30–10pm, Sun 5–9pm.

Flying Star 3416 Central Ave SE ☎ 505 255 6633, ⓦ flyingstarcafe.com. Lively, crowded café serving eclectic international cuisine to a largely student clientele. Blue-plate specials such as Vietnamese noodles, mac cheese or pasta pomodoro for $10. Other branches throughout northern New Mexico. Mon–Thurs & Sun 6am–11pm, Fri & Sat 6am–midnight.

Frontier 2400 Central Ave SE ☎ 505 266 0550, ⓦ frontierrestaurant.com. Legendary diner across from the university – no longer (quite) open around the clock – where an unceasing parade of characters chow down on burgers, burritos and great vegetarian enchiladas. Daily 5am–8am.

The Grove Cafe & Market 600 Central Ave SE ☎ 505 248 9800, ⓦ thegrovecafemarket.com. With its emphasis on fresh organic ingredients, this lively Rte-66 cafe-deli makes a great spot for breakfast, lunch or a bit of both. Poached eggs with ham and fresh fruit costs $9, a lunch-time salad or sandwich more like $11. Tues–Sat 7am–4pm, Sun 8am–3pm.

Pueblo Harvest Cafe Indian Pueblo Cultural Center, 2401 12th St NW ☎ 505 843 7270, ⓦ indianpueblo.org. While still serving Pueblo specialities such as Indian frybread at lunchtime, this unusual Native American restaurant is also open both for breakfast (try the $10 cornmeal pancakes) and for fine dining in the evening, when braised bison ribs are among its good $20–30 mains. Mon–Thurs 8am–8.30pm, Fri & Sat 8am–9pm, Sun 8am–4pm.

DRINKING AND NIGHTLIFE

The Anodyne 409 Central Ave NW ☎ 505 244 1820, ⓦ theanodyne.com. Downtown's most popular bar, tucked away upstairs, offers pool tables, pinball, a good jukebox and an eclectic mix of customers, from beer guzzlers to martini sippers. Mon–Fri 4pm–1.30am, Sat 7pm–1.30am, Sun 7–11.30pm.

Caravan East 7605 Central Ave NE ☎ 505 265 7877, ⓦ caravaneast.com. Enormous honky-tonk, where tenderfeet can do the two-step with throngs of urban cowboys and the live music includes plenty of mariachi and conjunto as well as country. Tues, Fri & Sat 5pm–2am, Sun 6pm–midnight.

Effex 420 Central Ave SW ☎ 505 842 8870, ⓦ effexabq .com. Huge, multistorey and very central gay club, across the street from the landmark KiMo Theater, with masses of room for shirtless posing as well as dancing. Tues–Sat 7pm–7am.

KiMo Theater 423 Central Ave NW ☎ 505 768 3544, ⓦ cabq.gov/kimo. Gorgeous, city-owned "Pueblo Deco" theatre that puts on an eclectic programme of opera, dance and theatre performances, kids' movies and everything from burlesque to Beethoven, as well as live bands.

The Launchpad 618 Central Ave SW ☎ 505 764 8887, ⓦ launchpadrocks.com. Dance and live music space that showcases touring indie and world music bands; besides the fabulous space-age decor, there's also a cluster of pool tables.

12

Ácoma Pueblo

Twelve miles south of I-40, 50 miles west of Albuquerque • Cultural Center mid-Feb to mid-Nov daily 8am–7pm; mid-Nov to mid-Feb Sat & Sun 9.30am–4pm; last Sky City tour leaves 1hr before closing; Entire pueblo closed to all visitors June 24, June 29, July 9–14, July 25, first and/or second weekend in Oct, first Sat of Dec • Tours $23, plus $13 for photo permit, no camcorders or video • ☎ 505 470 0181, ⓦ sccc.acomaskycity.org

The amazing **Ácoma Pueblo** encapsulates a thousand years of Native American history. Its focus is the ancient village known as "**Sky City**", perched 367ft high atop a magnificent isolated mesa. Probably occupied by Chacoan migrants between 1100 and 1200 AD, when the great pueblos of Chaco Canyon were still in use, Ácoma has adapted to repeated waves of invaders ever since. Although visitors seldom feel the awkwardness possible at other pueblo communities, Ácoma is the real thing, and its sense of unbroken tradition can reduce even the least culturally sensitive traveller to awestruck silence.

To visit Sky City, you have to join one of the hour-long guided **tours** that leave regularly from the excellent visitor centre and museum at the base of the mesa. The main stop is at the striking **San Esteban del Rey** mission, a thick-walled adobe church completed in 1640. Rather than follow its architectural example, the Ácomans went on constructing the multistorey stone and adobe houses around which the tour then proceeds. Only thirteen families live permanently on the mesa; most Ácomans reside down below, where they can get electricity, running water and jobs. Villagers do, however, come up during the day to sell pottery and frybread.

El Morro National Monument

Hwy-53, 25 miles east of Zuni Pueblo and 42 miles west of Grants · Daily: summer 8am–7pm; spring & autumn 9am–6pm; winter 9am–5pm · $3/person · ☎ 505 783 4226, ⓦ nps.gov/elmo

Hidden away south of the Zuni Mountains, 42 miles west of Grants, **El Morro National Monument** feels far off the beaten track. Incredibly, however, this pale-pink sandstone cliff was a regular rest stop for international travellers before the Pilgrims landed at Plymouth Rock, thanks to a perennial pool of water that collects beneath a tumbling waterfall. This spot was first recorded by Spanish explorers in 1583; in 1605, Don Juan de Oñate, the founder of New Mexico, carved the first of many messages that earned it the American name of **Inscription Rock**.

Chaco Canyon

Reached by 20-mile dirt roads from either Seven Lakes, 18 miles northeast of Crownpoint, or Nageezi, on US-550 36 miles south of Bloomfield · Daily 7am–sunset · $8/vehicle or $4/individual · ☎ 505 786 7014, ⓦ nps.gov/chcu

Few visitors brave the long, bumpy ride to **Chaco Canyon**, north of I-40 between Grant and Gallup. Although **Chaco Culture NHP** holds North America's **largest pre-Columbian city**, for beauty and drama it can't match such sites as Canyon de Chelly (see p.775) and the low-walled canyon itself is a mere scratch in the scrubby high-desert plains.

However, Chaco still holds plenty to take your breath away. Thirteen separate sites are open to visitors. Six, arrayed along the canyon's north wall, are so-called **Great Houses** – self-contained pueblos, three or four storeys high, whose fortress-like walls concealed up to eight hundred rooms.

Both routes to Chaco Canyon entail driving twenty miles over rough but passable dirt roads, not to be attempted in poor weather. Whether you approach from the south or the north, you enter the park at its southeast corner, close to the **visitor centre**. The basic first-come, first-served *Gallo* campground ($10), a short way east, usually fills by 3pm.

The major stop along the canyon's eight-mile one-way **loop road** (daily dawn–dusk) is at the far end, where **Pueblo Bonito** ("beautiful town") can be explored on an easy half-mile trail. Work on this four-storey D-shaped structure started in 850 AD and continued for three hundred years; it remained the largest building in America until 1898. Entering the ruin via its lowest levels, the path reaches its central plaza, which held at least three **Great Kivas** – ceremonial chambers used by entire communities rather than individual clans or families.

Gallup

As the largest town in I-40's three-hundred-mile run between Albuquerque and Flagstaff, the famous Route 66 stop of **GALLUP**, 25 miles east of the Arizona state line, might be expected to offer a diverting break in a long day's drive. Don't get your hopes up; cheap motels make it a handy overnight pit stop, but there's nothing to hold your interest.

The Navajo and other Native Americans come together in Red Rock State Park, four miles east of Gallup, on the second weekend in August for the **Inter-Tribal Indian Ceremonial**, the largest such gathering anywhere (☎505 863 3896, ⌨theceremonial .com). Four days of dances and craft shows have as their highlight a Saturday morning parade through the town.

ACCOMMODATION AND EATING   GALLUP

Coffee House 203 W Coal Ave ☎505 726 0291. If you're passing through Gallup and simply want a snack or a cappuccino, head for this lively, arty coffee bar, a block off the main drag in the heart of town. Mon–Fri 9am–5pm, Sat 9am–3pm.

★ **El Rancho Hotel and Motel** 1000 E 66 Ave ☎505 722 2885, ⌨elranchohotel.com. Sumptuous Rte-66 roadhouse built in 1937 by the brother of movie mogul D.W. Griffith. From the murals in its opulent Spanish Revival

lobby to the gallery of signed photos of celebrity Hollywood guests, it's bursting with atmosphere, though the guest rooms are small, and the bathrooms even smaller. Some rooms are in a less characterful two-storey motel building alongside. The decorative dining room (daily 6.30am–10pm) serves burgers named after John Wayne and Humphrey Bogart, and the usual barbecue, steaks and shrimp at around $13, while the bar stays open until 1am. **$102**

Carlsbad Caverns National Park

In **CARLSBAD CAVERNS NATIONAL PARK**, the Guadalupe Mountains are so riddled with underground caves and tunnels as to be virtually hollow. Tamed in classic park service style with concrete trails and electric lighting, this subterranean wonderland is now a walk-in gallery, where tourists flock to marvel at its intricate limestone tracery. Summer crowds can get intense, but that's part of the fun – Carlsbad feels like a throwback to the great 1950s boom in mass tourism.

At three hundred miles southeast of Albuquerque, however, the park is a *long* way from anywhere else. To reach it from the unenthralling town of Carlsbad itself, which holds the nearest accommodation and dining, drive twenty miles southwest on US-62/180, then seven miles west from White's City.

Almost all visitors confine their attention to **Carlsbad Cavern** itself, the only cave covered by the entrance fee. Direct elevators drop to the Cavern's centrepiece, the **Big Room**, 750ft below the visitor centre, but you can walk down instead via the **Natural Entrance Route** (last entry summer 3.30pm; rest of year 2pm). This steep footpath switchbacks into the guano-encrusted maw of the cave, taking fifteen minutes to reach the first formation and another fifteen to reach the Big Room. All visitors must ride the elevator back out.

Measuring up to 1800ft long and 250ft high, the Big Room is festooned with stalactites, stalagmites and countless unnameable shapes of swirling liquid rock. All are a uniform stone grey; rare touches of colour are provided by slight red or brown mineral-rich tinges, improved with pastel lighting. It takes an hour to complete the level trail around the perimeter. Whatever the weather up top – summer highs exceed 100°F – the temperature down here is always a cool 56°F.

Adjoining the Big Room, the **Underground Lunchroom** is a vast formation-free side cave, paved in the 1950s to create a diner-cum-souvenir-shop that sells indigestible lunches in polystyrene containers, plus Eisenhower-era souvenirs including giant pencils and Viewmaster reels.

Guided tours explore beautiful side caves such as the **King's Palace**, filled with translucent "draperies" of limestone (2–4 tours daily; $8). Additional tours can take you along the **Left Hand Tunnel** route down from the visitor centre ($7), or on a much more demanding descent into either **Spider Cave** or the **Hall of the White Giant** (both $20).

12

Entry $6 for three days, under-16s free; national park passes cover up to four adults; optional tours extra.
Visitor centre Daily: June to late Aug 8am–7pm; late

Aug to May 8am–5pm (☏ 575 785 2232, tour reservations ☏ 877 444 6777, ⓦ nps.gov/cave, tour reservations ⓦ recreation.gov).

Best Western Stevens Inn 1829 S Canal St ☏ 575 887 2851, ⓦ bestwesternnewmexico.com. This large, old-fashioned roadside motel complex, a mile south of central Carlsbad, has recently received a thorough makeover. The rooms are generally big but otherwise unremarkable, and there's an outdoor pool. Rates include a breakfast buffet at the *Flume Room*, which is as good a place to eat as you're likely to find (Mon–Sat 6am–10pm, Sun 6am–9pm). **$132**
Blue House Bakery 609 N Canyon St ☏ 575 628 0555. Set on a broad and very sleepy residential road, this

popular cottage café/bakery serves early-morning coffee and pastries, then salads and sandwiches later on. Mon–Fri 6am–2pm, Sat 6am–noon.
★ **Trinity Hotel** 201 S Canal St ☏ 575 234 9891, ⓦ thetrinityhotel.com. An unexpected find for this part of New Mexico, this former bank in downtown Carlsbad has been beautifully converted into a boutique hotel. Most rooms have walk-in showers, and there's an excellent restaurant, open for all meals but, unlike the hotel itself, closed on Sundays. **$149**

Roswell

Seventy-five miles north of Carlsbad, an alien spaceship supposedly crash-landed outside the small ranching town of **ROSWELL** on July 4, 1947. The commander of the local air-force base announced that they had retrieved the wreckage of a flying saucer and despite a follow-up denial the story has kept running, with TV series like *X-Files*, *Roswell* and *Taken* stoking the imaginations of UFO theorists.

Despite the wishful thinking of the truly weird visitors who drift in from the plains, the **International UFO Museum**, 114 N Main St (daily 9am–5pm; $5; ☏ 575 625 9495, ⓦ roswellufomuseum.com), inadvertently exposes the whole tawdry business as transparent nonsense. By way of contrast, the **Roswell Museum**, 100 W 11th St (Mon–Sat 9am–5pm, Sun 1–5pm; free; ☏ 575 624 6744, ⓦ roswellmuseum.org), boasts an excellent, multifaceted collection, with a section celebrating pioneer rocket scientist Robert Goddard (1882–1945).

Farley's 1315 N Main St ☏ 575 627 1100, ⓦ farleys pub.com. Lively sci-fi-themed pub and diner, not far up the hill from the Roswell Museum, with lots of gleaming chrome and neon; things can get noisy, but the food and drink keeps flowing, and it's reasonably priced. Mon–Thurs noon–11pm, Fri & Sat 11am–midnight,

Sun 11am–9pm.
La Quinta Inn 200 E 19th St ☏ 575 622 8000, ⓦ lq.com. Very dependable motel, just off the main through highway north of the centre; new, clean and well managed, with an indoor pool and free breakfasts. **$109**

Lincoln

Better known as **Billy the Kid**, Brooklyn-born William Bonney first came to fame as an 18-year-old in 1878, when the **Lincoln County War** erupted between rival groups of ranchers and merchants in the frontier town of **LINCOLN**, on Hwy-380 halfway between Carlsbad and Albuquerque. Since those days, no new buildings have joined the venerable false-fronted structures that line Main Street and the entire town is now the **Lincoln State Monument**. Visitors can stroll its length at any time and visit various historical sites.

Displays in the **Historic Lincoln Visitors Centre** (daily 8.30am–5pm) cover Hispanics, cowboys and Apaches, as well as the Lincoln County War. Billy the Kid's most famous jailbreak is commemorated at the **Lincoln County Courthouse** (daily 8.30am–5pm), at the other end of the street; waiting here under sentence of death, he shot his way out and fled to Fort Sumner, where Sheriff Pat Garrett eventually caught up with him.

12

On the first weekend of August the streets echo with gunfire once again, during the three-day **Old Lincoln Days** festival.

ARRIVAL, INFORMATION AND ACCOMMODATION   LINCOLN

Entry Each site $3.50, joint admission to all sites $5; not all sites remain open throughout the winter (☎ 575 653 4372, ⓦ nmmonuments.org).

Wortley Hotel US-380 ☎ 575 653 4300, ⓦ wortley hotel.com. Once owned by Pat Garrett, this old-style roadside hotel offers seven plain but appealing rooms, furnished with functional Victorian antiques. Its dining room serves breakfast and lunch Wed–Sun only. April to mid-Oct only. **$95**

White Sands National Monument

US-70, 14 miles west of Alamogordo • **Visitor centre** Daily: June–Aug 8am–7pm; April, May, Sept & Oct 9am–6pm; Nov–March 9am–5pm • $3/person • ☎ 575 479 6124, ⓦ nps.gov/whsa

Filling a broad valley west of Ruidoso and the Sacramento Mountains, the **White Sands** are 250 square miles of glistening, three-storey-high dunes, not of sand, but of finely ground gypsum eroded from the nearby peaks. Most of the desert valley is used as a missile range and training ground; only the southern half of the dunes is protected within **White Sands National Monument** (and even that is often closed for an hour or two at a time while missile tests are under way). The **visitor centre**, just off US-70, illuminates the unique local plants and animals. An eight-mile paved road stretches into the heart of the dunes, where you can scramble and slide in the sheer white landscape.

Silver City

Almost entirely wilderness, the semi-arid, forested, volcanic **Mogollon** and **Mimbres mountains** of southwest New Mexico soar to 10,000ft above the high desert plains and remain little altered since Apache warrior **Geronimo** was born at the headwaters of the Gila River.

Halfway up the mountains, the biggest settlement, **SILVER CITY**, lies 45 miles north of I-10. The Spanish came here in 1804, sold the Mimbreño Indians into slavery and opened the **Santa Rita copper mine**, just east of town below the Kneeling Nun monolith. The town was re-established in 1870 as a rough-and-tumble silver camp – **Billy the Kid** spent most of his childhood here. Ornate old buildings stand scattered along elm-lined avenues and across the hills. The **Western New Mexico University Museum**, 12th and Alabama (Mon–Fri 9am–4.30pm, Sat & Sun 10am–4pm; free; ☎ 575 538 6386, ⓦ wnmuseum.org), holds the world's finest collection of beautiful **Mimbres pottery**, produced locally around 1100 AD.

ACCOMMODATION AND EATING   SILVER CITY

Diane's Restaurant and Bakery 510 N Bullard St ☎ 575 538 8722, ⓦ dianesrestaurant.com. Welcoming downtown restaurant where the menu ranges from steak and meatloaf via Italian seafood stews to Thai green curries, pretty much all at $14–20; there are lots of wines by the glass, and they have their own bakery across the street. Tues–Fri 11am–2pm & 5.30–9pm, Sat 5.30–9pm, Sun noon–4pm.

Javelina Coffee House 210 N Bullard St ☎ 575 388 1350. Bright, friendly community rendezvous in the heart of downtown, open daily from very early indeed, and attracting arty types to drink coffee, eat pastries and use the free wi-fi. Mon–Thurs 6am–9pm, Fri & Sat 6am–10pm, Sun 6am–7pm.

Murray Hotel 200 W Broadway ☎ 575 956 9400, ⓦ murray-hotel.com. The biggest building in downtown Silver City, this Art Deco beauty opened in 1938, but was defunct for twenty years before being reopened by sympathetic new owners in 2012. The guest rooms have been refurbished with a knowing retro touch – the en-suite bathrooms are particularly tasteful – and the public spaces remain impressive. **$149**

Palace Hotel 106 W Broadway ☎ 575 388 1811, ⓦ silvercitypalacehotel.com. Small nineteenth-century hotel downtown, nicely restored to suit budget travellers. Some rooms have showers instead of baths, and they all have historic rather than contemporary fittings. The lack of a/c can be a problem in high summer, as can weekend noise from nearby bars. Doubles **$51**, suites **$82**

12

Arizona

The tourism industry in **ARIZONA** has, literally, one colossal advantage – the **Grand Canyon** of the Colorado River, the single most awe-inspiring spectacle in a land of unforgettable geology. Several other Arizona destinations have a similarly abiding emotional impact, however, thanks to the sheer drama of human involvement in this forbidding but deeply resonant desert landscape.

Over a third of the state still belongs to **Native Americans**, who outside the cities form the majority of the population. In the so-called **Indian Country** of northeastern Arizona, the **Navajo Nation** holds the stupendous **Canyon de Chelly** and dozens of other **Ancestral Puebloan ruins**, as well as the stark rocks of **Monument Valley**. The Navajo surround the homeland of the stoutly traditional **Hopi**, who live in remote **mesa-top villages**. The third main group, the **Apache**, in the harshly beautiful southeastern mountains, were the last Native Americans to give in to the overwhelming power of the American invaders.

The **southern** half of the state holds ninety percent of its people and all its significant cities. State capital **Phoenix**, a five-hundred-square-mile morass of shopping malls and tract-house suburbs, is larger and duller than lively **Tucson**, while there's some great frontier Americana in the southeast corner, especially in **Tombstone**.

Tucson

The former Spanish and Mexican outpost of **TUCSON** (pronounced *too-sonn*), a mere sixty miles north of Mexico, has grown into a modern metropolis of 900,000-plus people without entirely sacrificing its historic quarters. Equal parts college town and retirement community, it suffers from the same Sunbelt sprawl as Albuquerque and Phoenix, but has a compact centre, some enjoyable restaurants and pretty good nightlife. Some superb landscape lies within easy reach, from the forested flanks of **Mount Lemmon** to the rolling foothills of **Saguaro National Park**.

Tucson Museum of Art

140 N Main Ave • Wed, Fri & Sat 10am–5pm, Thurs 10am–8pm, Sun noon–5pm • $10, under-19s free; free first Sun of month • ☎ 502 624 2333, ⓦ tucsonmuseumofart.org

The **Tucson Museum of Art**, the highlight of **downtown Tucson**, devotes its main building to changing exhibitions of modern painting and sculpture. An adjoining adobe, the **Palice Pavilion**, displays magnificent pre-Columbian artefacts, including Mochica ceramics from northern Peru, with extraordinarily life-like faces; textiles from the later Peruvian Chancay culture; and gold from Colombia and Costa Rica.

Arizona State Museum

1013 E University Blvd • Mon–Sat 10am–5pm • $5, under-18s free • ☎ 520 621 6302, ⓦ statemuseum.arizona.edu

In the **Arizona State Museum**, on the campus of the **University of Arizona**, a mile east of downtown, the Pottery Project traces the history of Southwestern ceramics. A stunning case is devoted to fabulous "burden carrier" pots made by the Hohokam between 850 and 1000 AD. The large **Paths of Life** exhibition illuminates the cultures of the major native peoples of the Southwest and northern Mexico.

UA Museum of Art

1031 N Olive Rd • Tues–Fri 9am–5pm, Sat & Sun noon–4pm • Free • ☎ 520 621 7567, ⓦ artmuseum.arizona.edu

Treasures at the eclectic **UA Museum of Art** include a morbid altarpiece from the cathedral of Spanish city of Ciudad Rodrigo, along with prints, drawings and canvases by Rembrandt, Picasso and Warhol; a solitary O'Keeffe; and some fine Cubist sculpture by Jacques Lipchitz.

HERE
LIES
LesterMoore
FOUR SLUGS
FROM A 44
NO LES
NO MORE

Arizona-Sonora Desert Museum

2021 N Kinney Rd, 14 miles west of downtown • March–May & Sept daily 7.30am–5pm; June–Aug Mon–Fri & Sun 7.30am–5pm, Sat 7.30am–10pm; Oct–Feb daily 8.30am–5pm • June–Aug $12, kids 4–12 $4; Sept–May $14.50, kids 6–12 $5 • ☎ 520 883 2702, ⓦ desertmuseum.org

Part zoo, part garden, the **Arizona-Sonora Desert Museum** makes a hugely satisfying adjunct to nearby Saguaro National Park. Displays in the museum proper explain regional geology and history, while dioramas are filled with tarantulas, rattlesnakes and other creepy crawlers. In enclosures along the loop path beyond – a hot walk in summer – bighorn sheep, mountain lions, jaguars and other seldom-seen desert denizens prowl in credible simulations of their natural habitats.

Saguaro National Park

In two sections: Tucson Mountain District is 15 miles west of downtown Tucson, Rincon Mountain District is 17 miles east of downtown • Visitor centres at both daily 8am–5pm • Admission to either or both section, valid for a week, costs $10/vehicle • ☎ 520 733 5158, ⓦ nps.gov/sagu

Flanking Tucson to either side, the two sections of **Saguaro National Park** offer visitors a rare opportunity to stroll through desert "forests" of monumental, multilimbed **saguaro** (*sa-wah-row*) cactuses. Each saguaro can grow 50ft tall and weigh eight tons, but takes around 150 years to do so. They're unique to the Sonora Desert and encountering them en masse is a real thrill. Both segments of the park can be seen on short forays from the city: in summer, it's far too hot to do more than pose for photographs and there is no lodging or even permanent campground.

The **Tucson Mountain District** stretches north from the Desert Museum west of downtown Tucson, on the far side of the mountains. Beyond the **visitor centre**, the nine-mile **Bajada Loop Drive** loops through a wonderland of weird saguaro, offering plentiful short hiking trails. Signal Hill is especially recommended, for its petroglyphs and superb sunset views.

In the **Rincon Mountain District**, east of town, short trails lead off the eight-mile **Cactus Forest Drive** (daily: April–Oct 7am–7pm; Nov–March 7am–5pm). The saguaro cactuses thin out almost as soon as you start climbing the Tanque Verde Ridge Trail, which leads in due course to a hundred-mile network of remote footpaths through thickly forested canyons.

San Xavier del Bac

1950 W San Xavier Rd, 9 miles south of downtown Tucson, just west of I-19 • Daily: church 7am–5pm, museum 8am–4.30pm • Donation • ⓦ sanxaviermission.org

The **Mission San Xavier del Bac** – the best-preserved mission church in the USA – stands south of downtown Tucson on the fringe of the vast arid San Xavier Indian Reservation, home to the Akimel O'odham people. It was built for the Franciscans between 1783 and 1797 and even today its white-plastered walls and towers seem like a dazzling desert mirage. No one can name the architect responsible for its Spanish Baroque, even Moorish, lines – it consists almost entirely of domes and arches, making only minimal use of timber – let alone the O'odham craftsmen who embellished its every feature. Sunday morning masses draw large congregations from the reservation.

ARRIVAL AND INFORMATION   TUCSON

By plane Tucson's airport, 10 miles south of downtown and served mainly by regional flights, is served by the $25 shuttle vans of Arizona Stagecoach (☎ 520 889 1000, ⓦ azstagecoach.com).

By train The Amtrak station is at 400 E Toole Ave; connecting Amtrak buses run north to Phoenix.

Destinations Los Angeles (3 weekly; 10hr); New Orleans (3 weekly; 37hr).

By bus Greyhound buses stop at 471 W Congress St (☎ 520 792 3475).

Destinations Las Cruces (2 daily; 5hr 30min); Los Angeles (5 daily; 10hr); Phoenix (6 daily; 2r).

Visitor centre 100 S Church Ave (Mon–Fri 9am–5pm, Sat & Sun 9am–4pm; ☎ 520 624 1817, ⓦ visittucson.org).

12

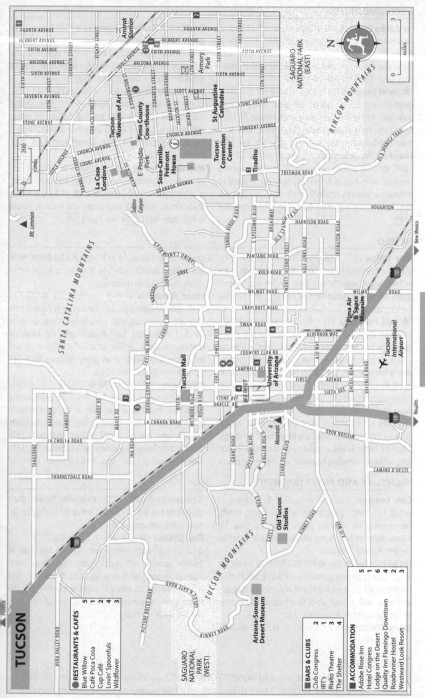

TUCSON

● RESTAURANTS & CAFÉS

Blue Willow	5
Café Poca Cosa	1
Cup Café	2
Lovin' Spoonfuls	4
Wildflower	3

■ BARS & CLUBS

Club Congress	2
IBT's	1
Rialto Theatre	3
The Shelter	4

■ ACCOMMODATION

Adobe Rose Inn	5
Hotel Congress	1
Lodge on the Desert	6
Quality Inn Flamingo Downtown	4
Roadrunner Hostel	2
Westward Look Resort	3

ACCOMMODATION

⭐ **Adobe Rose Inn** 940 N Olsen Ave ☎ 520 318 4644, ⓦ aroseinn.com. Charming, great-value B&B in a peaceful residential area near the university. Six attractive en-suite rooms plus a courtyard pool and copious communal breakfasts. June–Aug $90, Sept–May $135

⭐ **Hotel Congress** 311 E Congress St ☎ 520 622 8848, ⓦ hotelcongress.com. Central, bohemian hotel, a short walk from Amtrak and Greyhound, with vintage Art Deco furnishings. Forty plain en-suite guest rooms, with loud music and dancing at night. June–Aug $69, Sept–May $89

Lodge on the Desert 306 N Alvernon Way ☎ 520 320 2000, ⓦ lodgeonthedesert.com. 1930s adobe resort a couple of miles east of downtown, tastefully restored to resemble a Mexican hacienda, with large, comfortable rooms and a good restaurant. June–Aug $109, Sept–May $199

Quality Inn Flamingo Downtown 1300 N Stone Ave ☎ 520 770 1910, ⓦ flamingohoteltucson.com. A much-loved Tucson fixture, barely a mile north of downtown, the revamped Western-themed *Flamingo* motel looks straight out of the 1950s – Elvis slept here. $60

Roadrunner Hostel 346 E Twelfth St ☎ 520 940 7280, ⓦ roadrunnerhostelinn.com. Small and very central independent hostel in easy walking distance of eating and nightlife. Six-bed dorms or private doubles, with a communal kitchen and patio. Closed noon–3pm daily. Dorms $22, doubles $45

Westward Look Resort 245 E Ina Rd ☎ 520 297 1151, ⓦ westwardlook.com. Fancy but very affordable resort, in attractive landscaped grounds north of the city, which holds almost 250 extra-large rooms and suites in private *casitas*. June–Sept $104, Oct–May $169

EATING

Blue Willow 2616 N Campbell Ave ☎ 520 327 7577, ⓦ bluewillowtucson.com. Tasty, fruity breakfasts, with nothing priced over $9, and light lunches and dinners (mains like their signature meatloaf cost $15), on a pleasant garden patio. Mon–Fri 7am–9pm, Sat & Sun 8am–9pm.

⭐ **Café Poca Cosa** 110 E Pennington St ☎ 520 622 6400, ⓦ cafepocacosatucson.com. Popular and stylish downtown café that serves tasty but inexpensive Mexican – or to be more precise, Sonoran – cuisine with contemporary Southwestern flair. Typical highlights on the blackboard menu include shredded beef, or cod with clams. Lunch mains around $10; at dinner they're more like $20. Tues–Thurs 11am–9pm, Fri & Sat 11am–10pm.

Cup Café Hotel Congress, 311 E Congress St ☎ 520 798 1618, ⓦ hotelcongress.com. Jazzy downtown café, straight out of the 1930s. As well as making a good morning rendezvous, with eggy breakfasts for around $12, it offers lunchtime

sandwiches and salads for $11–14, and a full dinner menu that includes fish'n'chips for $16. Mon–Thurs & Sun 7am–10pm, Fri & Sat 7am–midnight.

Lovin' Spoonfuls 2690 N Campbell Ave ☎ 520 325 7766, ⓦ lovinspoonfuls.com. Far and away Tucson's best vegetarian restaurant, with a totally vegan menu – even the $11.25 "country fried chicken" and the breakfast chorizo-and-bacon "deluxe scramble" contain soya and tofu. More importantly, it all tastes delicious. Mon–Sat 9.30am–9pm, Sun 10am–3pm.

Wildflower 7037 N Oracle Rd ☎ 520 219 4230, ⓦ foxrc .com. Stylish mall restaurant, well north of the centre, serving fusion New American cuisine. Dine on the spacious patio, or nestle into the plush indoor seating, to enjoy appetizers like edamame dumplings with shiitake mushrooms ($9); mains include lemongrass scallops with forbidden rice ($23). Mon–Thurs & Sun 11am–9pm, Fri & Sat 11am–10pm.

NIGHTLIFE AND ENTERTAINMENT

Club Congress Hotel Congress, 311 E Congress St ☎ 520 622 8848, ⓦ hotelcongress.com. Hectic, trendy, late-opening bar with live music, including some big names, three or four nights weekly, and club nights on the rest. Nightly until late.

IBT's 616 N Fourth Ave ☎ 520 882 3053, ⓦ ibtstucson .com. Tucson's premier gay downtown dance club features contemporary DJs most nights and also puts on drag acts and revue, with a huge dance floor indoors and another on the patio outside. Daily noon–2am.

Rialto Theatre 318 E Congress St ☎ 520 740 1000,

ⓦ rialtotheatre.com. 1920s vaudeville theatre that's reincarnated as Tucson's hottest venue for touring bands. Hours vary, showtime usually 8pm.

The Shelter 4155 E Grant Rd ☎ 520 326 1345, ⓦ thesheltercocktaillounge.com. Take a trip back to groovier times in this round, windowless "go-go boot-wearing lounge"; all lava lamps, pinball machines and velvet paintings. It's barely changed since 1961, but still shakes up a mean martini and has occasional live music and DJs. Daily 3pm–2am.

Tombstone

The legendary Wild West town of **TOMBSTONE** lies 22 miles south of I-10 on US-80, 67 miles southeast of Tucson. More than a century has passed since its mining heyday, but "The Town Too Tough to Die" clings to an afterlife as a tourist theme park. With its dusty streets, wooden sidewalks and swinging saloon doors, it's barely changed. The moody gunslingers who stroll the streets these days are merely rounding up customers to watch them fight, but there's enough genuine rivalry between groups to give the place an oddly appealing edge. The ideal time to visit is during **Helldorado Days** in late October, a bonanza of parades and shoot-outs, when the air is cooler and the sun less harsh.

OK Corral

Allen St, between Third and Fourth sts • Daily 9am–5pm; gunfights Tues–Thurs 2pm & 4pm, Fri–Mon 2pm & 5pm • $6, or $10 with gunfight • ⓦ ok-corral.com

Tombstone began life as a silver boomtown in 1877 and by the end of the 1880s it was all but deserted again. On October 26, 1881, however, its population stood at more than ten thousand. At 2pm that day, **Doc Holliday**, along with sheriff **Wyatt Earp** and his brothers Virgil and Morgan, confronted a band of suspected cattle rustlers, the Clantons, in the **Gunfight at the OK Corral**. Within a few minutes, three of the rustlers were dead. The Earps were accused of murder, but charges were eventually dropped.

Although the real gunfight in fact took place on Fremont Street, the **OK Corral** itself remains a big attraction. The first thing you see on entering is the hearse that took the victims away. Crude dummies in the second of two baking-hot adobe-walled courtyards beyond show the supposed locations of the Earps and the Clantons.

ACCOMMODATION AND EATING   TOMBSTONE

Big Nose Kate's 417 E Allen St ☎ 520 457 3107, ⓦ bignosekates.info. Very fancy Wild-West saloon, where the waitresses wear period costume and country musicians entertain most afternoons. Prices on menu of burgers, pizzas and calzones start around $8. Daily 10am–midnight.

Landmark Lookout Lodge 781 N US-80 ☎ 520 457 2223, ⓦ lookoutlodgeaz.com. Chain motel with classy, tasteful Western-themed rooms and splendid mountain views, a mile north of downtown. **$99**

★ **Larian Motel** 410 E Fremont St ☎ 520 457 2272, ⓦ tombstonemotels.com. Much the best of the old-style motels in the middle of old Tombstone. Clean, well-maintained rooms and exceptionally friendly and helpful owners. **$79**

Phoenix

Arizona's state capital and largest city, **PHOENIX** holds relatively little appeal for tourists. It began life in the 1860s, as a sweltering little farming town in the heart of the Salt River Valley, with a ready-made irrigation system left by ancient Native Americans (the name Phoenix honours the fact that the city rose from the ashes of a long-vanished **Hohokam** community). Within a century, however, Phoenix had acquired the money and political clout to defy the self-evident absurdity of building a huge city in a waterless desert. Now the sixth largest city in the US, it has filled the entire valley; more than 1.5 million people live within its boundaries, while four million people inhabit the twenty separate incorporated cities, such as **Scottsdale**, **Tempe** and **Mesa**, which make up the metropolitan area.

Above all, Phoenix is hot; summer daytime highs average over 100°F, making it the hottest city outside the Middle East. Even in winter, temperatures rarely drop below 65°F, making the Phoenix/Scottsdale area popular with snowbirds looking to warm their bones in the luxury resorts and spas, play a round of golf, or hike through the mountain and desert preserves.

Phoenix Art Museum

1625 N Central Ave • Wed 10am–9pm, Thurs–Sat 10am–5pm, Sun noon–5pm • $15, kids 6–17 $6 • ☎ 602 257 1222, ⓦ phxart.org

The permanent collection at the vast and hugely rewarding **Phoenix Art Museum**, a mile north of dowtown, is rooted in an extensive array of Western art. Anish Kapoor's black sculpture *Upside Down Inside Out* is another highlight, and temporary exhibitions range through all eras and styles. A top-quality gift store stocks Mexican crafts and jazzy modern ceramics.

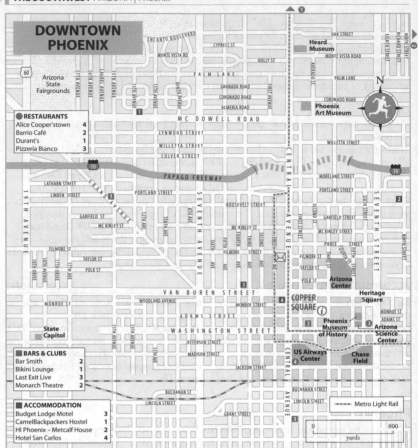

Heard Museum

2301 N Central Ave • Mon–Sat 9.30am–5pm, Sun 11am–5pm • $18, kids 6–12 $7.50 • ☎ 602 252 8848, ⓦ heard.org

Now greatly enlarged but still showcasing its lovely original buildings, the **Heard Museum** provides a wonderful introduction to the **Native Americans** of the Southwest. A sumptuous pottery collection includes stunning Mimbres bowls (see p.753), clay dolls made by the Quechan and Mohave peoples as souvenirs for nineteenth-century railroad passengers, and modern Hopi ceramics. You'll also find a complete Navajo *hogan* (see p.774), some fine old Havasupai baskets, Apache beadwork, painted buffalo-skin shields from New Mexican pueblos and a great collection of Hopi kachina dolls. The museum also holds a superb store and a good café.

Desert Botanical Garden

1201 N Galvin Pkwy • Daily: May–Sept 7am–8pm; Oct–April 8am–8pm • $18, kids 3–12 $8 • ☎ 480 941 1225, ⓦ dbg.org

In **Papago Park**, at the south end of Scottsdale, the fascinating **Desert Botanical Garden** is filled with an amazing array of cactuses and desert flora from around the world. Prime specimens include spineless "totem pole" cactuses from the Galápagos Islands and "living stone" plants from South Africa that at a glance you'd never suspect were alive. Separate enclaves are devoted to **butterflies** – seen at their best in August and September – and to **hummingbirds**, of which Arizona boasts fifteen indigenous species.

Taliesin West

114th St and Frank Lloyd Wright Blvd, 12 miles northeast of downtown Scottsdale • Oct–May daily 10am–4pm; June & Sept daily 9am–4pm; July & Aug Mon & Thurs–Sun 9am–4pm; see website for tour schedules • Panorama Tour $24, Insight Tour $32, Behind The Scenes Tour $60 • ☎ 480 860 2700, ✆ franklloydwright.org

Frank Lloyd Wright came to Phoenix to work on the *Biltmore Hotel* in 1934, and returned to spend most winters here until his death in 1959. His studio, **Taliesin West**, is now an architecture school and design studio, with multimedia exhibits of his life and death.

Taliesin West remains a splendidly isolated spot, where Wright's trademark "organic architecture" makes perfect sense. Blending seamlessly into the desert, the complex can only be seen on guided visits. The expertise and enthusiasm of the guides makes the experience well worth the relatively high prices.

ARRIVAL AND DEPARTURE
PHOENIX

By plane Sky Harbor International Airport, 3 miles east of downtown, is connected by free shuttles with the Metro Light Rail station at 44th and Washington (✆ valleymetro .org). SuperShuttle (☎ 602 244 9000, ✆ supershuttle.com) operates local shuttle services, while Arizona Shuttle Services runs to other towns in Arizona (☎ 520 795 6771, ✆ arizonashuttle.com)

By train Amtrak trains don't serve Phoenix, though buses coincide with services to Tucson (see p.754) and Flagstaff (p.763).
By bus Greyhound buses arrive at 2115 E Buckeye Rd (☎ 602 389 4200), close to the airport.
Destinations Las Vegas (2 daily; 8hr 30min); Los Angeles (8 daily; 7hr 30min); Tucson (6 daily; 2hr).

GETTING AROUND AND INFORMATION

By car Phoenix is so vast that it's much easier to drive than to use public transport – even driving, it can take hours to get across town.
By light rail The Metro Light Rail System (one-way ride $2, one-day pass $4; ☎ 602 253 5000, ✆ valleymetro .org) follows a 20-mile route, with stations in downtown Phoenix and Tempe, but it's much more useful for

commuters than visitors.
Phoenix visitor centre 125 N Second St, downtown (Mon–Fri 8am–5pm; ☎ 602 254 6500 or ☎ 877 225 5749, ✆ visitphoenix.com).
Scottsdale visitor centre 4343 N Scottsdale Rd (Mon–Fri 8am–5pm; ☎ 480 421 1004 or ☎ 800 782 1117, ✆ scottsdalecvb.com).

12

ACCOMMODATION

Metropolitan Phoenix is so huge that it's essential to stay near the places you want to visit. Downtown Phoenix is relatively inexpensive, with cheap options a few blocks north of the centre. Room rates are considerably more expensive in **winter**, when snowbirds from all over the USA fill the upscale **resorts** of Scottsdale in particular.

CENTRAL PHOENIX

Arizona Biltmore Resort & Spa 2400 E Missouri Ave ☎ 602 955 6600, ✆ arizonabiltmore.com. Extraordinarily lavish 1930s resort, retaining its Art Deco trimmings and extravagant gardens. Two golf courses, four restaurants, eight pools, plus afternoon teas, tennis and spa. Oct–April $327, May–Sept $167

Budget Lodge Motel 402 W Van Buren St ☎ 602 254 7247, ✆ blphx.com. This unexciting motel offers the best deal within walking distance of the downtown core; you won't want to walk here after dark, though. $69

CamelBackpackers Hostel 1601 N 13th Ave ☎ 602 258 4143, ✆ camelbackpackers.com. Clean, friendly hostel in a former private home on the northern fringes of downtown. Two mixed dorms (6–8-bed), plus one private room and a shared lounge and kitchen. Check in 3–8pm, free (basic) breakfasts and wi-fi. Dorms $26, double $60

HI Phoenix – Metcalf House 1026 N Ninth St above

Roosevelt St ☎ 602 254 9803, ✆ hiusa.org/phoenix. Dorm beds in a slightly run-down residential district. No phone reservations, but space is usually available in the ten-bed men's dorm and four-bed "ladies" dorm. No curfew, plus use of kitchen and laundry; rates include breakfast. Closed July. Dorms $23.50

Holiday Inn Express Phoenix Airport 3401 E University Drive ☎ 602 453 9900, ✆ hiexpress.com. Good-value motel whose large modern rooms make a handy stop before or after a flight from nearby Sky Harbor – connected by free shuttles. Pool and complimentary breakfast. Oct–April $136, May–Sept $106

Hotel San Carlos 202 N Central Ave ☎ 602 253 4121, ✆ hotelsancarlos.com. To appreciate this very central 1920s hotel, you have to prefer an old-fashioned, frazzled and often noisy hotel to a new, deathly quiet motel. That said, the rooms are tastefully furnished, if small, and there's a nice Vietnamese restaurant and rooftop swimming pool. Oct–April $189, May–Sept $119

SCOTTSDALE

Motel 6 Scottsdale 6848 E Camelback Rd ☎ 480 946 2280, ⓦ motel6.com. Cut-price lodgings are few and far between in Scottsdale, so this totally unremarkable budget motel is well worth considering. Oct–April **$86**, May–Sept **$52**

The Phoenician 6000 E Camelback Rd ☎ 480 941 8200, ⓦ thephoenician.com. Gorgeous 250-acre resort, spread out at the base of Camelback Mountain and offering every conceivable luxury, with golf course, waterfalls and lush gardens as well as lavish rooms and restaurants. Oct–April **$479**, May–Sept **$249**

EATING

CENTRAL PHOENIX

Alice Cooper'stown 101 E Jackson St ☎ 602 253 7337, ⓦ alicecooperstown.com. Barbecue restaurant-cum-sports bar, owned by the rock star and local resident. While far from fine dining, the food's better than you might expect, with barbecue sandwiches at $9 and mixed plates for $14, and the atmosphere is fun, with waiters in full Alice make-up. Mon–Thurs 11am–9.30pm, Fri & Sat 11am–11pm, Sun noon–8pm.

Barrio Café 2814 N 16th St ☎ 602 636 0240, ⓦ barrio cafe.com. Reservations are not taken at this wildly popular little local Mexican place, but it's worth the wait – you can always bide your time sampling the huge array of tequilas, and there's live music Thurs–Sun – to enjoy authentic southern Mexican food, including succulent *cochinita pibil* (pork) for $12. Tues–Thurs 11am–10pm, Fri 11am–10.30pm, Sat 5–10.30pm, Sun 11am–9pm.

Durant's 2611 N Central Ave ☎ 602 264 5967, ⓦ durantsaz.com. Old-style downtown restaurant that's a venerable institution, complete with red-leather banquettes and velvet wallpaper, and specializing in rich all-American food such as oysters Rockefeller ($17.50) and steaks at $33 and up. Locals drop in for late-night drinks at the central bar. Mon–Thurs 11am–midnight, Fri 11am–1am, Sat 5pm–1am, Sun 4.30pm–midnight.

Pizzeria Bianco Heritage Square, 623 E Adams St ☎ 602 258 8300, ⓦ pizzeriabianco.com. High-quality brick-oven pizzas at $12–16, in a very convenient downtown location, with ultra-fresh ingredients including home-made mozzarella. No reservations. Mon 11am–9pm, Tues–Sat 11am–10pm.

SCOTTSDALE

Arcadia Farms 7014 E First Ave ☎ 480 941 5665, ⓦ arcadiafarmscafe.com. The most popular lunch rendez-vous in Scottsdale's Old Town – salads, sandwiches and mains, including specials like crêpes and crab cakes, cost $13–16 – also serves healthy Southwestern breakfasts, and there's open-air courtyard seating. Daily 8am–3pm.

Bandera 3821 N Scottsdale Rd ☎ 480 994 3524, ⓦ hillstone.com. Chicken cooked in the wood-burning oven ($17) is the speciality in this busy, inexpensive rotisserie on the southeast edge of downtown, though other meats and fish are almost as good. Mon–Thurs & Sun 4.30–10pm, Fri & Sat 4.30–11pm.

Cowboy Ciao 7133 E Stetson Drive, at Sixth ☎ 480 946 3111, ⓦ cowboyciao.com. This hip downtown option serves "modern American food with global influences". At lunchtime, a burger or seared tuna sandwich costs $13–19; the $13 "Stetson" chopped salad is also available in the evening, when a "mucho mushrooms" stir-fry is $25 and the cumin-rubbed pork shank is $33. Mon–Thurs & Sun 11.30am–2.30pm & 5–10pm, Fri & Sat 11.30am–2.30pm & 5–11pm.

NIGHTLIFE AND ENTERTAINMENT

Bar Smith 130 E Washington St, Phoenix ☎ 602 229 1265, ⓦ barsmithphoenix.com. The best thing about this stylish downtown bar and lounge is its fabulous outdoor dancefloor, upstairs. Mon–Wed 11am–2pm, Thurs & Fri 11am–2pm & 9.30pm–2am, Sat 9.30pm–2am.

Bikini Lounge 1502 Grand Ave, Phoenix ☎ 602 252 0472, ⓦ thebikinilounge.com. A gem of a dive bar, this veteran tiki bar attracts a fascinating, eclectic mix of local characters. Daily 3pm until late.

Last Exit Live 717 S Central Ave, Phoenix ☎ 602 271 7000, ⓦ lastexitlive.com. This rock-oriented live music venue, downtown, programmes acts ranging from country-rock to local punks. Hours vary.

Monarch Theatre 122 E Washington St, Phoenix ☎ 602 692 9633, ⓦ facebook.com/monarchtheatre. Downtown Phoenix's hottest new club, in a former night-club space overhauled with a huge dance floor and stage, puts on the biggest names in electronica. Hours vary.

Petrified Forest National Park

Straddling I-40, 108 miles east of Flagstaff • Visitor center daily: early May to late Sept 8am–6pm; late Sept to early May 8am–5pm • $10/vehicle, or $5 for motorcyclists, cyclists and pedestrians • ☎ 928 524 6228, ⓦ nps.gov/pefo

At **Petrified Forest National Park**, erosion continues to unearth a fossilized prehistoric forest of gigantic trees. The original cells of the wood have been replaced by multicoloured crystals of quartz, cross sections of which, cut through and polished, look stunning. On the ground, however, along the trails that set off from the park's 27-mile **Scenic Drive**, the trees are not always all that exciting. Segmented, crumbling and very dark, they can seem like a bunch of logs lying in the sand; the best viewing is when the setting sun brings out rich red and orange hues.

The park's northern section – site of the main visitor centre – is renowned for its views of the **Painted Desert**, an undulating expanse of solidified sand dunes, which at different times of day take on different colours (predominantly bluish shades of grey and reddish shades of brown).

Winslow

On I-40, 56 miles east of Flagstaff, **WINSLOW** is a Route 66 town kept alive by transcontinental truckers. It's the closest the interstate comes to the Hopi mesas (see p.776), which jut from the desert across sixty miles of butte-studded wilderness to the north. If you only know of it thanks to the line about "standin' on the corner in Winslow, Arizona", in the Eagles' *Take It Easy*, you'll be glad there's an official **Standin' on the Corner Park** at Kinsley Avenue and Second.

ACCOMMODATION AND EATING

WINSLOW

★ **La Posada** 303 E Second St ☎ 928 289 4366, ⓦ laposada.org. Winslow's grandest accommodation option, the last and greatest of the Southwest's railroad hotels, is totally magnificent – a worthy candidate for the best hotel in the world. The whole enormous complex oozes earthy Southwestern style. Doors from the lobby lead straight to the old railroad platform, while the guest rooms hark back to the heyday of transcontinental travel. All have en-suite baths or even whirlpool tubs, but not phones. **$119**

★ **Turquoise Room** La Posada, 303 E Second St ☎ 928 289 2888, ⓦ theturquoiseroom.net. La Posada's showcase restaurant is irresistible in terms both of its decor and contemporary Southwestern cuisine. Dinner mains range from chilli-tinged south-of-the-border specialities such as grilled chicken breast with tomatillo sauce ($19) to Colorado elk medallions with huckleberries ($34). Daily 7am–9pm.

Flagstaff

Northern Arizona's liveliest and most attractive town, **FLAGSTAFF** occupies a dramatic location beneath the San Francisco Peaks. Poised halfway between New Mexico and California, it's much more than just a way station for tourists en route to the Grand Canyon, eighty miles northwest. Ever since it was founded, in 1876, Flagstaff has been a diverse place, with a strong black and Hispanic population and Navajo and Hopi heading in from the nearby reservations.

Downtown, where barely a building rises more than three storeys, oozes Wild West charm. Filled with cafés, bars and stores selling Route 66 souvenirs and Native American crafts, as well as outdoors outfitters, it's a fun place to stroll around, but holds no significant tourist attractions. Its main thoroughfare, Santa Fe Avenue, used to be **Route 66** and before that the pioneer trail west. The tracks of the Santa Fe Railroad still cut downtown in two, so life remains punctuated by the mournful wail of passing trains.

Museum of Northern Arizona

3101 N Fort Valley Rd, 3 miles northwest of downtown Flagstaff on US-180 • Daily 9am–5pm • $10, kids 10–17 $6 • ☎ 928 774 5213, ⓦ musnaz.org

Flagstaff's **Museum of Northern Arizona** makes an essential first stop for any visitor to the Colorado Plateau. Although it covers local geology, geography, flora and fauna, its main emphasis is on documenting **Native American** life. It starts with an excellent run-through of the Ancestral Puebloan past, then turns to contemporary Navajo, Havasupai, Zuni and Hopi cultures, with rooms devoted to pots, rugs, *kachina* dolls and silver and turquoise jewellery.

ARRIVAL AND INFORMATION

By bus Greyhound, 880 E Butler Ave (☎ 928 774 4573). Destinations Albuquerque (3 daily; 6hr); Las Vegas (2 daily; 5hr 30min); Los Angeles (6 daily; 11hr); Phoenix (5 daily; 2hr 45min).

By train Amtrak's Southwest Chief stops in the heart

FLAGSTAFF

of town. Destinations Albuquerque (1 daily; 6hr); Chicago (1 daily; 20hr); Los Angeles (1 daily; 11hr 30min).

Visitor centre 1 E Rte-66 (Mon–Sat 8am–5pm, Sun 9am–4pm; ☎ 928 774 9541, ⊕ flagstaffarizona.org).

ACCOMMODATION

DuBeau International Hostel 19 W Phoenix Ave ☎ 928 774 6731, ⊕ dubeauhostel.com. Welcoming independent hostel just south of the tracks, whose spotless en-suite motel rooms serve as four-person dorms, or private en-suite doubles, but the common areas can get noisy. Free breakfast and wi-fi, plus Grand Canyon tours ($85; March–Oct Tues, Thurs & Sat; Nov–Feb Wed & Sat). Dorms $20, doubles $56

Grand Canyon International Hostel 19 S San Francisco St ☎ 928 779 9421, ⊕ grandcanyonhostel .com. Independent hostel, under the same friendly management as the similar nearby *DuBeau* but significantly quieter. Four-bed dorms plus eight private rooms, sharing bathrooms. Rates include breakfast. Dorms $24, doubles $52

Hotel Weatherford 23 N Leroux St ☎ 928 779 1919, ⊕ weatherfordhotel.com. Restored downtown hotel

with elegant wooden fittings. The finest rooms offer tasteful accommodation, with antique furnishings and clawfoot tubs plus phones and TVs; five more en-suite rooms are smaller and cheaper; and three large but basic ones share a bathroom. Shared-bath doubles $49, en-suite doubles $89

★ **The Inn at Four Ten** 410 N Leroux St ☎ 928 774 0088, ⊕ inn410.com. Bright Craftsman-style B&B, a short walk from downtown. All nine rooms are en suite, most with fireplaces and three with whirlpool tubs; superb breakfasts. $165

Monte Vista 100 N San Francisco St ☎ 928 779 6971, ⊕ hotelmontevista.com. Attractive landmark 1920s hotel. Don't expect luxury, let alone tranquillity; the ambience is more like a hostel than a hotel. Many of the guests are young international travellers. Weekend rates typically rise by $20. $65

EATING AND NIGHTLIFE

Beaver Street Brewery 11 S Beaver St ☎ 928 779 0079, ⊕ beaverstreetbrewery.com. Popular microbrewery that also serves inventive and inexpensive food, including fondues. Mon–Wed & Sun 11am–1am, Thurs–Sat 11am–2am.

Criollo 16 N San Francisco St ☎ 928 774 0541, ⊕ criollolatinkitchen.com. Smart restaurant, serving Latin American food worth lingering over. Tapas as well as substantial dishes such as pork belly tacos ($10), *ropa vieja* (braised beef; $12) and paella with fish, shellfish and chorizo ($18). Mon–Thurs 11am–10pm, Fri 11am–midnight, Sat 9am–midnight, Sun 9am–10pm.

Diablo Burger 120 N Leroux St ☎ 928 774 3274, ⊕ diabloburger.com. Stylish central joint, with outdoor seating on Heritage Square, and $10–13 burgers using

beef from hormone-free cattle from the Diablo ranch. Cash only. Mon–Wed 11am–9pm, Thurs–Sat 11am–10pm.

Macy's European Coffee House & Bakery 14 S Beaver St ☎ 928 774 2243, ⊕ macyscoffee.net. Not merely superb coffee, but heavenly pastries to go with it, in a chaotic but friendly, student-oriented atmosphere. Substantial mains (all vegetarian) include black bean pizza ($8), and there's even couscous for breakfast ($5). Daily 6am–10pm.

The Museum Club 3404 E Rte-66 ☎ 928 526 9434, ⊕ themuseumclub.com. This log-cabin taxidermy museum, popularly known as "The Zoo", somehow transmogrified into a classic Rte-66 roadhouse, saloon and country music venue – live bands typically Thurs–Sat – that's a second home to hordes of dancing cowboys. Daily 11am–2am.

Sedona

There's no disputing that the New Age resort of **SEDONA**, 28 miles south of Flagstaff, enjoys a magnificent setting, amid definitive Southwestern canyon scenery. Sadly, however, the town adds nothing to the beauty of its surroundings, with mile upon mile of ugly red-brick sprawl interrupted only by hideous malls. While Europeans tend to be turned off by Sedona, many American travellers love its luxurious accommodation, fancy restaurants and almost limitless opportunities for active outdoor holidaying.

Since author Page Bryant "channelled" the information in 1981 that Sedona is in fact "the heart *chakra* of the planet" and pinpointed her first **vortex** – a point at which psychic and electromagnetic energies can supposedly be channelled for personal and planetary harmony – the town has achieved its own personal growth and blossomed as a focus for **New Age** practitioners of all kinds. Whether you love it or hate it may depend on whether you share their wide-eyed awe for angels, crystals and all matters mystical – and whether you're prepared to pay over-the-odds prices for the privilege of joining them.

You can see most of the sights, albeit from a distance, from US-89A; the best parts are south along Hwy-179 within Coconino National Forest. The closest **vortex** to town is on **Airport Mesa**; turn left up Airport Road from US-89A as you head south, a mile past the downtown junction known as the "**Y**" and it's at the junction of the second and third peaks. Further up, beyond the precariously sited airport, the **Shrine of the Red Rocks** looks out across the entire valley.

ACCOMMODATION AND EATING   SEDONA

⭐ **The Canyon Wren** 6425 N US-89A ☎928 282 6900, ⓦcanyonwrencabins.com. Four large and hugely comfortable, private two-person cabins, each with a kitchen and a whirlpool tub, 6 miles north of Sedona in Oak Creek Canyon; they're especially cosy in winter. No wi-fi. **$155**

Coffee Pot Restaurant 2050 W Hwy-89A ☎928 282 6626, ⓦcoffeepotsedona.com. Sedona's largest, oldest diner serves a hundred kinds of omelettes ($7–12), and all the burgers ($7–10), Mexican dishes ($8–10) and fried specials you could hope for. Daily 6am–2pm.

Heartline 1610 W Hwy-89A ☎928 282 0785, ⓦheartlinecafe.com. Tasteful white-table-linen restaurant, with an attractive garden courtyard, that serves determinedly healthy Southwestern cuisine. Dinner mains such as pecan-crusted trout cost $25–30, a "Sedona Sunrise" salmon breakfast $10.50. Daily 8am–9.30pm.

Sedona Motel 218 Hwy-179 ☎928 282 7187, ⓦthesedonamotel.com. Small, amazingly inexpensive motel, in an ideal and attractive location, with a friendly atmosphere on its shared communal deck. **$89**

12

Williams

Although Flagstaff is generally regarded as the obvious base for visitors to the Grand Canyon's South Rim, **WILLIAMS**, 32 miles west, is in fact the closest interstate town to the national park. While it can't boast half the charm or pizzazz of its neighbour, it's a nice enough little place, filled with Route 66-era motels and diners and retaining a certain individuality despite the stream of tourists.

ARRIVAL AND INFORMATION   WILLIAMS

By train Amtrak's *Southwest Chief* stops at Williams Junction, 3 miles east of town, twice daily.
Destinations Albuquerque (1 daily; 7hr); Chicago (1 daily; 21hr); Los Angeles (1 daily; 10hr 30min).
Visitor centre 200 W Railroad Ave (daily: June–Aug

8am–6.30pm; Sept–May 8am–5pm; ☎928 635 1418, ⓦexperiencewilliams.com).
Grand Canyon Railway The Grand Canyon Railway (☎303 843 8724, ⓦthetrain.com) sets off daily, usually at 9.30am, from the Williams Depot in the centre of town.

ACCOMMODATION AND EATING

Canyon Motel & RV Park 1900 E Rodeo Rd ☎928 635 9371, ⓦthecanyonmotel.com. The word "motel" hardly does this restored Rte-66 relic, east of downtown, justice. Accommodation is in individual brick cottages and converted railroad cars; two 1929 cabooses sleep five to six each, while a larger carriage holds three separate en-suite units. Don't expect luxury, but it's a memorable experience, and there are also fifty RV spaces. RV sites **$38**, motel rooms **$79**, carriage rooms **$105**, cabooses **$159**

Grand Canyon Railway Hotel 1 Fray Marcos Blvd ☎928 635 4010, ⓦthetrain.com/hotel. The Grand Canyon Railway's flagship hotel opened in 1908 as the *Fray Marcos*. Rebuilt and renamed, it lacks character, though

the large open lobby is pleasant enough, and there's also an indoor pool, spa and saloon. All rooms provide two queen beds. **$169**

The Lodge on Route 66 200 E Rte-66 ☎877 563 4366, ⓦthelodgeonroute66.com. Restored Rte-66 motor-court motel in the heart of town, with spotless and very comfortable rooms and friendly management. **$90**

⭐ **Pine Country Restaurant** 107 N Grand Canyon Blvd ☎928 635 9718, ⓦpinecountryrestaurant.com. Traditional, very central diner with friendly staff, where you can get a full dinner, such as pork chops or country fried steak, for $11. The home-made pies, including raspberry cream cheese, are irresistible. Daily 6.30am–9pm.

The Grand Canyon

Although almost five million people visit **GRAND CANYON NATIONAL PARK** every year, the canyon itself remains beyond the grasp of the human imagination. No photograph, no statistics, can prepare you for such vastness. At more than one mile deep, it's an inconceivable abyss; varying between four and eighteen miles wide, it's an endless expanse of bewildering shapes and colours, glaring desert brightness and impenetrable shadow, stark promontories and soaring sandstone pinnacles. Somehow it's so impassive, so remote – you could never call it a disappointment, but at the same time many visitors are left feeling peculiarly flat. In a sense, none of the available activities can quite live up to that first stunning sight of the chasm. The **overlooks** along the rim all offer views that shift unceasingly from dawn to sunset; you can **hike** down into the depths on foot or by mule, hover above in a **helicopter** or raft through the **whitewater rapids** of the river itself; you can spend a night at **Phantom Ranch** on the canyon floor or swim in the waterfalls of the idyllic **Havasupai Reservation**. And yet that distance always remains – the Grand Canyon stands apart.

The vast majority of visitors come to the **South Rim** – it's much easier to get to, it holds far more facilities (mainly at **Grand Canyon Village**) and it's open year round. There is another lodge and campground at the **North Rim**, which by virtue of its isolation can be a lot more evocative, but at 1000ft higher it is usually closed by snow from mid-October until May. Few people visit both rims; to get from one to the other demands either a tough two-day hike down one side of the canyon and up the other or a 215-mile drive by road.

The South Rim

When someone casually mentions visiting the "Grand Canyon", they're almost certainly referring to the **South Rim**. To be more precise, it's the thirty-mile stretch of the South Rim that's served by a paved road; and most specifically of all, it's **Grand Canyon Village**, the small canyon-edge community, sandwiched between the pine forest and the rim, that holds the park's **lodges**, **restaurants** and **visitor centre**. Nine out of every ten visitors come here, however, not because it's a uniquely wonderful spot from which to see the canyon, but simply because tourist facilities just happen to have been concentrated here ever since the railroad arrived a century ago.

Exploring the South Rim

Most South Rim visits start at **Mather Point** near the Canyon View Information Plaza, where the canyon panorama is more comprehensive than any obtainable from Grand Canyon Village. The views to the east in particular are consistently stupendous; it's hard to imagine a more perfect position from which to watch the **sunrise** over the canyon.

Various vantage points along the rim-edge footpath nearby offer glimpses of the Colorado River. Walk west for around ten minutes – turn left along the rim from the information plaza – and you'll come to **Yavapai Point**. From here, you can see two tiny segments of the river, one of which happens to include both the suspension footbridge across the Colorado and *Phantom Ranch* (see p.770). Nearby, the **Yavapai Geology Museum** (daily: summer 8am–8pm; winter 8am–5pm; free) has illuminating displays on how the canyon may have formed.

Two separate roads extend along the South Rim for several miles in either direction from the information plaza and Grand Canyon Village, paralleled to the west in

---

GRAND CANYON ADMISSION PRICES

Admission to Grand Canyon National Park, valid for seven days on either rim, costs $25 for one private, noncommercial vehicle and all its passengers, or $12 per pedestrian or cyclist. All the park-service **passes** (see p.41) are sold and valid.

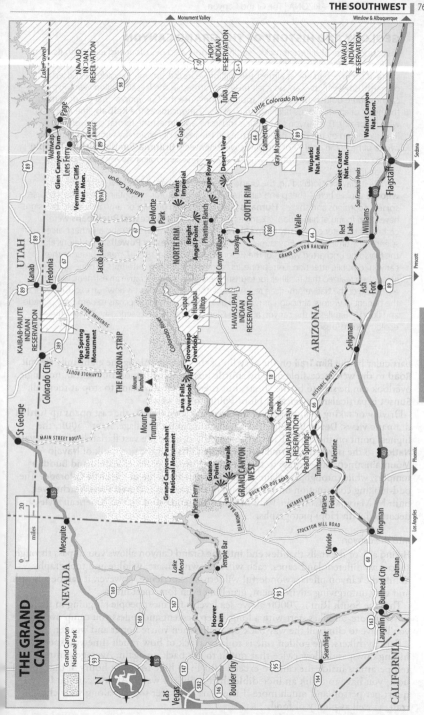

THE GRAND CANYON

Grand Canyon National Park

12

GEOLOGY AND HISTORY OF THE GRAND CANYON

Layer upon layer of different rocks, readily distinguished by colour and each with its own fossil record, recede down into the Grand Canyon and back through time. Although the strata at the riverbed are, at almost two billion years old, among the oldest exposed rocks on earth, however, the canyon itself has only formed in the last six million years, Experts cannot agree quite how that has happened, because the Colorado actually cuts through the heart of an enormous hill (known to Native Americans as the **Kaibab**, "the mountain with no peak"). The canyon's fantastic sandstone and limestone formations were not literally carved by the river, however; they're the result of erosion by wind and extreme cycles of heat and cold. These features were named – **Brahma Temple**, **Vishnu Temple** and so on – by Clarence Dutton, who wrote the first Geological Survey report on the canyon in 1881.

While it may look forbidding, the Grand Canyon is not a dead place. All sorts of desert **wildlife** survive here – sheep and rabbits, eagles and vultures, mountain lions and, of course, spiders, scorpions and snakes. **Humans** have never been present on any great scale, but signs have been found of habitation as early as 2000 BC and the **Ancestral Puebloans** were certainly here later on. A party of **Spaniards** passed through in 1540 and a Father Garcés spent some time with the Havasupai in 1776, but **John Wesley Powell**'s expeditions along the fearsome uncharted waters of the Colorado in 1869 and 1871–72 really brought the canyon to public attention. Entrepreneurs made a few abortive attempts to mine different areas, then realized that facilities for tourism were a far more lucrative investment. With the exception of the Native American reservations, the Grand Canyon is now run exclusively for the benefit of visitors, although as recently as 1963 there were proposals to dam the Colorado and flood 150 miles of the canyon and the Glen Canyon dam has seriously affected the ecology downstream.

12

particular by the **Rim Trail** on the very lip of the canyon. Along the eight-mile **Hermit Road** to the west, accessible only by shuttle bus or bike for most of the year, no single overlook can be said to be the "best", but there are far too many to stop at them all. **Sunset** is particularly magical at Hopi Point, to the west.

Driving or taking a shuttle bus along Desert View Drive to the east opens up further dramatic views. **Desert View** itself, 23 miles out from the village, is, at 7500ft, the highest point on the South Rim. Visible to the east are the vast flatlands of the **Navajo Nation**; to the northeast, **Vermillion** and **Echo Cliffs** and the grey bulk of **Navajo Mountain** ninety miles away; to the west, the gigantic peaks of **Vishnu** and **Buddha temples**, while through the plains comes the narrow gorge of the **Little Colorado**. The odd-looking construction on the very lip of the canyon is **Desert View Watchtower**, built by Mary Jane Colter in 1932 in a conglomeration of Native American styles and decorated with Hopi pictographs.

Into the canyon

Hiking any of the trails that descend **into the Grand Canyon** allows you to pass through successive different landscapes, each with its own climate, wildlife and topography. While the canyon offers a wonderful wilderness experience, however, it can be a hostile and very unforgiving environment, gruelling even for expert hikers.

That the South Rim is 7000ft above sea level is for most people fatiguing in itself. Furthermore, all hikes start with a long, steep descent and unless you camp overnight you'll have to climb all the way back up again when you're hotter and wearier.

For day-hikers, the golden rule is to keep track of how much time you spend hiking down and allow twice that much to get back up again. Average summer temperatures inside the canyon exceed 100°F; to hike for eight hours in that sort of heat, you have to drink an incredible thirty pints of water. Always carry at least a quart per person and much more if there are no water sources along your chosen trail, as well as plenty of food.

Bright Angel Trail

The **Bright Angel Trail**, which starts from the village, switchbacks for 9.6 miles down to **Phantom Ranch**. Under no circumstances should you try to hike down and back in a single day; the longest feasible day hike is to go as far as **Plateau Point** on the edge of the arid Tonto Plateau, an overlook above the Inner Gorge from which it is not possible to descend any further. That twelve-mile round trip usually takes at least eight hours. In summer, water can be obtained along the way.

Miners laid out the first section of the trail a century ago, along an old Havasupai route. It has two short tunnels in its first mile. After another mile, the **wildlife** starts to increase (deer, rodents and ravens) and there are a few **pictographs**, all but obscured by graffiti.

At the lush **Indian Gardens** almost five miles down, site of a ranger station and campground with water, the trails split to Plateau Point or down to the river via the **Devil's Corkscrew**. The latter route leads through sand dunes scattered with cactuses and down beside **Garden Creek** to the Colorado, which you then follow for more than a mile to *Phantom Ranch* (see p.770).

ARRIVAL AND INFORMATION

THE SOUTH RIM

By car Most visitors reach the park entrance at Tusayan by driving north from I-40, either for 52 miles from Williams or 75 miles from Flagstaff.

Amtrak Amtrak trains come no closer to the South Rim than the stations at Flagstaff and Williams. Arizona Shuttle buses (☎928 226 8060, ⓦarizonashuttle.com; one-way $29) connect Flagstaff's Amtrak station, via Williams, with *Maswik Lodge* in Grand Canyon Village.

Grand Canyon Railway Restored railroad, operated by steam engines in summer, connect a station in the heart of Williams with Grand Canyon Village (☎928 773 1976, ⓦthetrain.com). While you don't see the canyon from the train, it's a fun way to make a short visit to the park. Services operate daily all year, typically leaving Williams at 9.30am and reaching the canyon at 11.45am, and then leaving the canyon at 3.30pm to arrive back in Williams at 5.45pm. Return fares range from $75 in Coach Class (under-13s $45) up to $199 (under-13s not permitted) in the Luxury Parlor Car.

Grand Canyon Visitor Center Canyon View Information Plaza, immediately north of the spur road that heads west into the village from Hwy-64 (daily: May to mid-Oct 8am–6pm; mid-Oct to April 9am–5pm; ☎928 638 7888, ⓦnps.gov/grca).

12

SHUTTLE ROUTES

Grand Canyon Village is always accessible to private vehicles and so is the road **east** from the village to Desert View. Both the road **west** from the village to Hermit's Rest, however, and the short access road to **Yaki Point**, east of Mather Point, are only open Dec–Feb. At other times, you have to use the park's free **shuttle buses**.

SOUTH RIM TOURS

Xanterra (contact the transportation desk in any lodge or call ☎888 297 2757) runs at least two short daily **coach tours** along the rim to the west ($28) and east ($47) of the village, **sunrise** and **sunset** trips ($21.50) and **mule** rides to Abyss Overlook, at rim level ($123), and *Phantom Ranch*, down by the river (from $507).

Multiday **whitewater rafting trips** in the canyon proper – such as those run by Western River Expeditions (ⓦwesternriver.com) or Canyoneers (ⓦcanyoneers.com) – are often booked up years in advance, while no **one-day** raft trips are available within Grand Canyon National Park. For a trip along the river at short notice, there are, however, two alternatives, at either end of the canyon. Colorado River Discovery, based in Page, Arizona, offers one-day trips that start below **Glen Canyon Dam** and take out at **Lees Ferry** ($89; ☎928 645 9175 or ☎888 522 6644; ⓦraftthecanyon.com), while further west, the tribal-run Hualapai River Runners arrange pricey one-day trips on the Hualapai Reservation, starting at Diamond Creek (March–Oct, $381; ☎928 769 2636, ⓦgrandcanyonwest.com).

Aeroplane tours cost from around $100 for 30min up to as long as you like for as much as you've got. Operators include Grand Canyon Airlines (☎928 638 2359 or ☎866 235 9422, ⓦgrandcanyonairlines.com). **Helicopter tours**, from more like $150 for 30min, are offered by Maverick (☎928 638 2622, ⓦmaverickhelicopter.com) and Papillon (☎928 638 2359, ⓦpapillon.com). All the companies are in **Tusayan**.

Village Route Loops between Grand Canyon Village and Canyon View Information Plaza, stopping at *Bright Angel*, *Maswik* and *Yavapai* lodges and *Mather Campground*, as well as Yavapai Point.

Kaibab Trail Route Connects Canyon View Information Plaza with Yaki Point, off Desert View Drive a couple of miles east of the village.

Hikers' Express Early-morning service to Yaki Point from *Bright Angel Lodge*, via the information plaza, for hikers using the South Kaibab Trail.

Hermits Rest Route Between March and Nov, this route follows Hermit Road 7 miles west of the village.

Tusayan Route Regular 20min runs between Tusayan and Canyon View Information Plaza.

ACCOMMODATION

Roughly two thousand **guest rooms** are available close to the South Rim: half of them in and around **Grand Canyon Village** – where the very few rooms that enjoy canyon views tend to be booked up to two years in advance – and a further thousand in **Tusayan**, an unattractive strip-mall 7 miles south.

LODGES AND HOTELS

Best Western Grand Canyon Squire Inn 100 Hwy-64, Tusayan ☎ 928 638 2681, ⓦ grandcanyonsquire.com. Tusayan's most lavish option bills itself as the canyon's "only resort hotel", with an outdoor pool, indoor spa and bowling alley. Most rooms are spacious and very comfortable, if unremarkable; paying extra gets you an enormous deluxe room with oval bath. $230

★ **Bright Angel Lodge** Grand Canyon Village same-day ☎ 928 638 2631, advance ☎ 303 297 2757 or ☎ 888 297 2757, ⓦ grandcanyonlodges.com. An imposing central lodge and a westward sprawl of rustic but delightful detached log cabins. Though reasonably sized and appealingly furnished, many lodge rooms share bathrooms and/or toilets; a few offer private showers. Lodge rooms $72, cabins $120

★ **El Tovar** Grand Canyon Village same-day ☎ 928 638 2631, advance ☎ 303 297 2757 or ☎ 888 297 2757, ⓦ grandcanyonlodges.com. Log-construction rim-side hotel that combines rough-hewn charm with elegant sophistication. Only three suites offer canyon views; the rest of the 78 tastefully furnished rooms come in two different sizes, but are otherwise very similar. Almost all provide just one bed. Rooms $183, suites $348

Kachina and Thunderbird Lodges Grand Canyon Village same-day ☎ 928 638 2631, advance ☎ 303 297 2757 or ☎ 888 297 2757, ⓦ grandcanyonlodges.com. Anonymous but perfectly adequate motel-style rooms, each with two queen-size beds and full bath, set in a low and utterly undistinguished two-storey block just yards from the rim. $180

Maswik Lodge Grand Canyon Village same-day ☎ 928 638 2631, advance ☎ 303 297 2757 or ☎ 888 297 2757, ⓦ grandcanyonlodges.com. Large complex, a few hundred yards back from the rim, with two distinct blocks of motel-style rooms plus a cluster of basic summer-only cabins, each holding two double beds. Cabins $94, Maswik South $92, Maswik North $176

★ **Phantom Ranch** Colorado River ☎ 303 297 2757 or ☎ 888 297 2757, ⓦ grandcanyonlodges.com. Located at river level, *Phantom Ranch* can only be reached on foot or mule. First call on its individual cabins goes to mule riders (see p.769), but hikers can sleep in four ten-bunk, single-sex dormitories. Reservations are essential, but cancellations are handed out first-come, first-served at *Bright Angel Lodge* early each morning. Family-style meals in its restaurant cost $21 for breakfast, $28–44 for dinner. Dorms $46, cabins $149

Seven Mile Lodge AZ-64, Tusayan ☎ 928 638 2291. The last remaining little roadside motel in Tusayan. Reservations are not accepted; rooms are simply doled out from 9am daily. Despite the slight premium charged for housing three or four guests in the same room, it's still great value for groups of (close) friends. $99

Yavapai Lodge Grand Canyon Village same-day ☎ 928 638 2631, advance ☎ 303 297 2757 or ☎ 888 297 2757, ⓦ grandcanyonlodges.com. The largest in-park lodge, set back in the woods half a mile from the rim. The rooms themselves offer perfectly decent motel-style accommodation, most with twin beds. $125

CAMPING

★ **Bright Angel Campground** Phantom Ranch area, Colorado River; details on ⓦ nps.gov/grca reserve via Backcountry office PO Box 129, Grand Canyon, AZ 86023. Accessible only on overnight backpacking trips, this campground, amid the cottonwoods, holds 32 sites, each with its own picnic table. Camping by backcountry permit only. $5

Desert View Campground Desert View ⓦ nps.gov /grca. Simple campground, set back from the rim 25 miles east of Grand Canyon Village, open May to mid-Oct only, on a first-come, first-served basis, with no RV hookups. $12

Mather Campground Grand Canyon Village, south of the main road not far from Market Plaza ☎ 928 638 7851, advance reservations ☎ 877 444 6777, ⓦ recreation.gov. Year-round tent and RV camping (without hookups). Sites holding up to two vehicles and six people should be reserved well in advance in summer; in winter, they're first-come, first-served. Walk-in sites for hikers and bikers year round. Walk-in sites $6, vehicle sites March to mid-Nov $18, mid-Nov to Feb $15

EATING AND DRINKING

Arizona Room Bright Angel Lodge ⓦgrandcanyon lodges.com. Informal, plain but good-quality restaurant, a few yards from the rim. The open kitchen serves conventional meat and seafood meals, with sandwiches, salads and simple main dishes costing $8–12 at lunchtime, and typical dinner prices including a slab of baby back ribs for $26. Daily 11.30am–3pm (March to mid-Sept only) & 4.30–10pm; closed early Jan to mid-Feb.

Bright Angel Dining Room Bright Angel Lodge ⓦgrandcanyonlodges.com. Straightforward, windowless diner that serves pretty much anything you might want, from snacks and salads for around $10 to steaks at up to $26. No reservations. Daily 6am–10pm.

Canyon Cafe Yavapai Lodge ⓦgrandcanyonlodges .com. Locals prefer the *Yavapai's* large cafeteria to the

Maswik's for its salad bar and fried chicken, and slightly lower prices. All main dishes cost under $10, with daily specials at $9 and a two-piece chicken dinner for $6.50. Summer daily 6am–10pm; spring & autumn daily 6am–9pm; shorter hours and closures in low season.

★ **El Tovar** El Tovar Hotel ☎ 928 638 2631 ext 6432, ⓦgrandcanyonlodges.com. Very grand, very classy dark-wood dining room, with great big windows – though only the front tier of tables have actual canyon views. The food itself is rich and expensive, especially at dinner, when main dishes such as roast duck or salmon tostada cost around $26, and steaks more like $35. Lunchtime sandwiches, tacos and so on $10–15. Daily 6.30am–11am, 11.30am–2pm & 5–10pm.

The Havasupai Reservation

92 miles north of I-40 exit 123, via AZ-66 and Arrowhead Hwy-18, then 8 miles on foot, horseback or helicopter • No entry to reservation without advance lodging reservation; entrance fee $35 • ☎ 928 448 2121, ⓦ havasupaifalls.net

The **Havasupai Reservation** really is another world. Things have changed a little since a 1930s anthropologist called it "the only spot in the United States where native culture has remained in anything like its pristine condition", but the sheer magic of its turquoise waterfalls and canyon scenery makes this a very special place.

Havasu Canyon is a side canyon of the Grand Canyon, 35 miles as the raven flies from Grand Canyon Village, but almost two hundred miles by road. Turn off the interstate at Seligman or Kingman, onto AZ-66, then follow Arrowhead Hwy-18 to **Hualapai Hilltop**. An eight-mile trail zigzags down a bluff from there, leading through the stunning waterless Hualapai Canyon to the village of **SUPAI**. Riding down on horseback with a Havasupai guide costs $70 one way, $120 return and there's often a helicopter service as well ($85 one-way; ☎623 516 2790). Hiking is free, but all visitors pay a $35 entry fee on arrival at Supai.

Beyond Supai the trail leads to a succession of spectacular **waterfalls**, starting with two dramatic cascades, New Navajo Falls and Rock Falls, created by a flash flood in 2008. Beyond those lie Havasu Falls, great for swimming, and Mooney Falls, where a precarious chain-ladder descent leads to another glorious pool.

ACCOMMODATION AND EATING   THE HAVASUPAI RESERVATION

Havasu Campground Havasu Canyon ☎ 928 448 2121, ⓦ havasupaifalls.net. Facilities in this creekside campground are primitive in the extreme. Tents can be pitched to either side of the creek, which is crossed by makeshift footbridges, and reservations are compulsory. **$23.70**

Havasupai Lodge Supai Village ☎ 928 448 2111, ⓦ havasupaifalls.net. Set slightly apart from things on the edge of the village, this simple two-storey motel

holds plain but comfortable a/c rooms, without phones or TVs. All sleep four people. Advance bookings compulsory. **$159.50**

Tribal Café Main Plaza, Supai Village ☎ 928 448 2981. The only place to get a meal in Supai. Fried breakfasts, and a lunch or dinner of beef stew, Indian frybread or burritos, cost around $9, or more with grated cheese. Daily: May–Sept 6am–7pm; Oct–April 8am–5pm.

The Hualapai Reservation: Grand Canyon West

Inhabited like the Havasupai reservation immediately east by descendants of the Pai people, the **Hualapai Reservation** spreads across almost a million acres, bounded to the north by a 108-mile stretch of the Colorado River.

Fifty miles northwest of the reservation's only town, **PEACH SPRINGS**, itself 35 miles northwest of **Seligman** on Route 66, a cluster of overlooks above the Colorado river is cannily promoted as **Grand Canyon West** of the Grand Canyon. This is the closest spot

12

to Las Vegas where it's possible to see the canyon and most of its visitors are day-trippers who fly here unaware that they're not seeing the canyon at its best. The massive Hualapai programme to attract tourists culminated in 2007 in the unveiling of the **Skywalk** (ⓦgrandcanyonwest.com) a horseshoe-shaped glass walkway which despite the hype does not extend out over the canyon itself, but above a side arm, with a vertical drop of just 1200ft immediately below. It's so extraordinarily expensive, limited in scope and time-consuming to visit – unless you pay for an air tour from Las Vegas (from $170; Scenic Airlines, ☎702 638 3300, ⓦscenic.com), you have to drive a minimum of forty miles on rough remote roads from the nearest highway and pay at least $88 per person to reach and walk on the Skywalk – that it can't be recommended over a trip to the national park.

The road between the rims

The 215-mile route by road from Grand Canyon Village to the **North Rim** follows AZ-64 along the East Rim Drive to Desert View, then passes an overlook into the gorge of the Little Colorado, before joining US-89 fifty miles later at **CAMERON**.

Seventy barren miles north of Cameron, the direct route to the North Rim, now US-89A, crosses **Navajo Bridge** 500ft above the Colorado River. Until the bridge was built, a ferry service operated six miles north at **LEES FERRY**. Established in 1872 by Mormon pioneer John D. Lee, it was the only spot within hundreds of miles to offer easy access to the banks of the river on both sides. Now the sole launching point for **whitewater rafting** trips into the Grand Canyon, the ferry site stands close to the atmospheric remains of Lee's Lonely Dell ranch.

Back on US-89A, beneath the red of the **Vermilion Cliffs**, a succession of **motels** all have their own restaurants. The turning south to get to the North Rim, off US-89A onto AZ-67, comes at **JACOB LAKE**, from where it's 41 miles to the canyon itself, along a road that's closed in winter.

ACCOMMODATION AND EATING	THE ROAD BETWEEN THE RIMS

Cameron Trading Post 466 US-89, Cameron ☎928 679 2231, ⓦcamerontradingpost.com. Large, smart motel complex, where rooms on the upper floors have large balconies that look out across the Little Colorado. A pleasant dining room with tin ceiling and large fireplace serves all meals (daily: May–Sept 6am–10pm; Oct–April 7am–9.30pm). RVs **$25**, rooms **$109**

Jacob Lake Campground US-89A, just west of intersection ☎928 643 7395, ⓦfs.usda.gov/kaibab. Lovely wooded ForestService campground that caters to tent campers only. Closed mid-Oct to mid-May. **$17**

Jacob Lake Inn Intersection of US-89A and AZ-67, Jacob Lake ☎928 643 7232, ⓦjacoblake.com. Sprawling

complex of simple motel rooms and log cabins plus a petrol station, a general store, an old-fashioned diner counter and a restaurant where chicken, trout or steak mains cost well under $20. Cabins **$107**, rooms **$139**

Marble Canyon Lodge US-89A, not far west of Navajo Bridge, just past the turnoff for Lees Ferry ☎928 355 2225, ⓦmarblecanyoncompany.com. More than fifty conventional motel-style rooms, with TVs but no phones, in low-slung buildings in a romantic desert-outpost setting at the foot of the cliffs. In the adequate but unexciting restaurant, open for all meals daily, main dishes cost $8–14, and a Navajo taco salad is $9. **$80**

The North Rim

Higher, more exposed and far less accessible than the South Rim, the **NORTH RIM** of the Grand Canyon receives less than a tenth as many visitors. A cluster of venerable Park Service buildings stand where the main highway reaches the canyon and a handful of rim-edge roads allow drivers to take their pick from additional lookouts. Only one hiking trail sees much use, the **North Kaibab Trail**, which follows Bright Angel Creek down to *Phantom Ranch*.

The park itself remains open for day-use only after mid-October, but no food, lodging or gas is available and visitors must be prepared to leave at a moment's notice. It's shut down altogether by the first major snowfall of winter.

ARRIVAL AND INFORMATION

THE NORTH RIM

Transcanyon Shuttle The only public transport to serve the North Rim is a daily shuttle that leaves *Grand Canyon Lodge* at 7am daily, and the South Rim at 1.30pm (4hr; $85 one-way; ☎ 602 638 2820, ⓦ trans-canyonshuttle.com).

Visitor centre At the entrance to *Grand Canyon Lodge* (mid-May to mid-Oct daily 8am–6pm; ☎ 928 638 7864, ⓦ nps.gov/grca).

ACCOMMODATION AND EATING

★ **Grand Canyon Lodge** ☎ 480 337 1320, ⓦ grand canyonlodgenorth.com. Cabins and larger motel-style blocks, mostly ranged over the quiet, well-wooded hillside beside the approach road. Western Cabins have full-size bathrooms and porches and sleep up to four people; just four stand close enough to the rim to offer canyon views. Frontier Cabins accommodate three guests and have smaller bathrooms, while Pioneer Cabins have two separate bedrooms. Reservations for all are available up to thirteen months in advance, and are absolutely essential. Motel rooms $\overline{\$124}$, Pioneer & Frontier Cabins $\overline{\$129}$, Western Cabins $\overline{\$195}$
Lodge Dining Room Grand Canyon Lodge ☎ 928 638 2611 or ☎ 928 645 6865 out of season,

ⓦ grandcanyonlodgenorth.com. The room itself, with its soaring timber ceiling, is elegant and impressive, and window tables enjoy awesome canyon views. Dinner mains such as blackened salmon cost around $20, lunch options more like $10. Dinner reservations essential. Daily 6.30–10am, 11.30am–2.30pm & 4.15–9.45pm.
★ **North Rim Campground** One mile north of Grand Canyon Lodge ☎ 877 444 6777 or ☎ 515 885 3639, ⓦ recreation.gov. Very pleasant forest campground with 87 car-camping sites, but no RV hookups. Although all vehicle sites are often reserved in advance, additional room is always available for backpackers. Closed mid-Oct to mid-May. Tents $\overline{\$5}$, vehicle sites $\overline{\$16}$

Monument Valley

Straddling the Arizona–Utah state line, 24 miles north of Kayenta and 25 miles southwest of Mexican Hat • Car park daily 24hr; visitor centre daily: May–Sept 6am–8pm; Oct–April 8am–5pm • $5 • ☎ 435 727 5870, ⓦ navajonationparks.org

The classic southwestern landscape of stark sandstone buttes and forbidding pinnacles of rock, poking from an endless expanse of drifting red sands, is an archetypal Wild West image. Only when you arrive at **MONUMENT VALLEY** – which straddles the Arizona–Utah state line, 24 miles north of Kayenta – do you realize how much your perception of the West has been shaped by this one spot. Such scenery does exist elsewhere, of course, but nowhere is it so perfectly distilled. While moviemakers have flocked here since the early days of Hollywood, the sheer majesty of the place still takes

12

THE NAVAJO NATION

The largest Native American reservation in the US, popularly known as the **NAVAJO NATION**, covers much of northeastern Arizona and extends into both western New Mexico and Monument Valley in southernmost Utah. Everyone can speak English, but Navajo, a language so complex that it served as a secret code during World War II, is still the lingua franca. The reservation follows its own rules over Daylight Savings; in frontier-style towns like Tuba City, the time varies according to whether you're in an American or a Navajo district.

When the Americans took over this region from the Mexicans in the mid-nineteenth century, the Navajo – who call themselves *Dineh*, "The People" – almost lost everything. In 1864, Kit Carson rounded up every Navajo he could find and packed them off to Fort Sumner in desolate eastern New Mexico. A few years later, however, the Navajo were allowed to return. Most of the 300,000-plus Navajo today work as shepherds and farmers on widely scattered smallholdings, though craftspeople also sell their wares from roadside stands and tourist stops.

As you travel in this region, respect its people and places. Though the Ancestral Puebloans are no longer present, many of the relics they left behind are on land that holds spiritual significance to their modern counterparts. Similarly, it is offensive to photograph or intrude upon people's lives without permission.

On a practical note, don't expect extensive **tourist facilities**. Most towns are bureaucratic outposts that only come alive for tribal fairs and rodeos and hold few places to eat and even fewer hotels and motels. For information online, visit ⓦ discovernavajo.com and ⓦ explorenavajo.com.

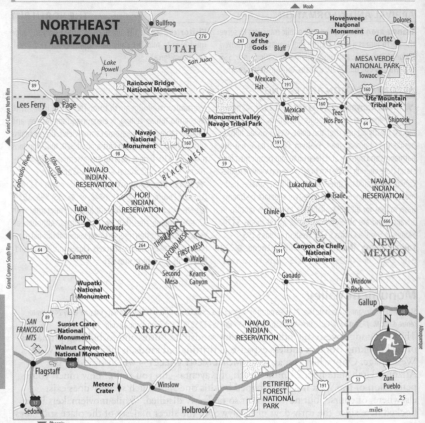

your breath away. Add the fact that it remains a stronghold of **Navajo** culture and Monument Valley can be the absolute highlight of a trip to the Southwest.

The biggest and most impressive pair of monoliths are **The Mittens**; one East and one West, each has a distinct thumb splintering off from its central bulk. More than a dozen other spires spread nearby, along with **rock art panels** and assorted minor **Ancestral Puebloan ruins**.

You can see the buttes for free, towering alongside US-163, but the four-mile detour to enter **Monument Valley Tribal Park** is rewarded with much closer views. A rough, unpaved road drops from behind the visitor centre and *View* hotel to run through Monument Valley itself. The seventeen-mile **self-drive route** makes a bumpy but bearable ride in an ordinary vehicle and takes something over an hour (daily: May–Sept 6am–8.30pm; Oct–April 8am–4.30pm). However, the Navajo-led **jeep** or **horseback tours** into the backcountry are very much recommended; a ninety-minute jeep trip costs from around $50 per person if arranged on the spot, with plenty of longer and potentially much more expensive alternatives. As well as stopping at such movie locations as the **Totem Pole**, most tours call in at a Navajo *hogan* (eight-sided dwelling) to watch weavers at work.

ACCOMMODATION AND EATING   MONUMENT VALLEY

Goulding's Lodge Two miles west of US-163, across from the park approach road ☎ 435 727 3231, ⓦ gouldings.com. A former trading post that now incorporates an upscale motel with dramatic, long-range valley views, an indoor pool, a general store, a petrol station, a museum of movie memorabilia and a campground. Tents $26, RV spaces $45, rooms $209

Mitten View Campground Monument Valley Tribal Park ☎ 435 727 5870, ⓦ navajonationparks.org. The park's exposed campground, half a mile down the unpaved road in to the valley itself, is first-come, first-served. Water is available in summer only, and rates are charged per person, for anyone aged over 6. $5

★ **The View Hotel** Monument Valley Tribal Park ☎ 928 727 3470, ⓦ monumentvalleyview.com. All of the luxurious rooms in this stunning Navajo-owned hotel, alongside the tribal park visitor centre, have private balconies that command a magnificent panorama. $209

The View Restaurant Monument Valley Tribal Park ☎ 928 727 3470, ⓦ monumentvalleyview.com. The only eating option in the tribal park enjoys a prime position overlooking the valley, with some irresistible outdoor tables. The food is good but not exceptional, with authentic Navajo dishes such as mutton stew ($14) and blue-corn frybread ($5) alongside more conventional burgers and salads. Daily 7am–2pm & 5pm until late.

Canyon de Chelly National Monument

A short distance east of **Chinle**, 87 miles southeast of Monument Valley and seventy miles north of I-40, twin sandstone walls emerge abruptly from the desert floor, climbing at a phenomenal rate to become the awesome 1000ft cliffs of **CANYON DE CHELLY NATIONAL MONUMENT**. Between these sheer sides, the meandering cottonwood-fringed Chinle Wash winds through grasslands and planted fields. Here and there a Navajo *hogan* stands in a grove of fruit trees, a straggle of sheep is penned in by a crude wooden fence or ponies drink at the water's edge. And everywhere, perched on ledges in the canyon walls and dwarfed by the towering cliffs, are the long-abandoned adobe dwellings of the **Ancestral Puebloans**.

Two main canyons branch apart a few miles upstream: **Canyon de Chelly** (pronounced *de shay*) to the south and **Canyon del Muerto** to the north. Each twists and turns in all directions, scattered with vast rock monoliths, while several smaller canyons break away. The whole labyrinth threads its way northward for thirty miles into the Chuska Mountains.

Canyon de Chelly is a magnificent place, on a par with the best of the Southwest's national parks. Its relative lack of fame owes much to the continuing presence of the **Navajo**, for whom the canyon retains enormous symbolic significance (although they did not build its cliff dwellings). Visitors are largely restricted to peering into the canyon from above, from overlooks along the two rim drives. There's no road in and apart from one short trail you can only enter the canyons with a Navajo guide.

The view from above: the rim drives

Each of the two rim drives is a forty-mile round-trip, with a succession of spectacular overlooks that takes two to three hours to complete.

Junction Overlook, four miles along the **South Rim Drive**, stands far above the point where the two main canyons branch apart; as you scramble across the bare rocks you

12

CANYON DE CHELLY JEEP TOURS

With the exception of the White House Trail (see p.776), the only way to get a close-up view of Canyon de Chelly's amazing Ancestral Puebloan remains is to take a **guided tour** with a Navajo guide. A typical half-day tour will get you to and from White House Ruin; continuing beyond to see Spider Rock takes a full day.

Canyon de Chelly Tours ☎ 928 674 5433, ⓦ canyon dechellytours.com. Jeep tours with Navajo guides. Scheduled 3hr tours to White House Ruin, starting from *Chinle Holiday Inn*, March–Oct daily 9am, 1pm & 4pm; $75, under-13s $50.

Thunderbird Lodge ☎ 928 674 5841, ⓦ tbirdlodge .com. For most of the year, these popular "shake'n'bake" tours zigzag into either or both canyons in open-top flatbed trucks; in winter they carry on in glass-roofed army vehicles. Half-day trips daily: summer 9am & 2pm; winter 9am & 1pm; adults $51.50, under-13s $40. Full-day tours late spring to late autumn only: daily 9am; $83, no reductions.

can see Canyon de Chelly narrowing away, with a *hogan* immediately below. Two miles further on, by which time the canyon is 550ft deep, **White House Overlook** looks down on the highly photogenic **White House Ruins**. This is the only point from which unguided hikers can descend to the canyon floor, taking perhaps thirty to 45 minutes to get down and a good hour to get back up. The beautiful if precarious trail, at times running along ledges chiselled into the slick rock, culminates with a close-up view of the ruins; the most dramatic dwellings, squeezed into a tiny alcove 60ft up a majestic cliff, were once reached via the rooftops of now-vanished structures. Visitors can only walk a hundred yards or so in either direction beyond the site. Back up on the South Rim Drive, twelve miles along, the view from **Sliding House Overlook** reveals more Ancestral Puebloan ruins seemingly slipping down the canyon walls toward the ploughed Navajo fields below, while eight miles further on the road ends above the astonishing **Spider Rock**, where twin 800ft pinnacles of rock come to within 200ft of the canyon rim.

The **North Rim Drive** runs twenty miles up Canyon del Muerto to **Massacre Cave** – really just a pitifully exposed ledge – where a Spanish expedition of 1805 killed a hundred Navajo women, children and old men. Visible from the nearby **Mummy Cave Overlook** is the striking **House Under The Rock**, with its central tower in the Mesa Verde style. Of the two viewpoints at **Antelope House Overlook**, one is opposite Navajo Fortress, an isolated eminence atop which the Navajo were besieged by US troops for three months in 1863, while the other looks down on the twin ruined square towers of Antelope House. In the **Tomb of the Weaver** across the wash, the embalmed body of an old man was found wrapped in golden eagle feathers.

12

INFORMATION	CANYON DE CHELLY NATIONAL MONUMENT

Entry Free 24hr access, but to rim drives only, not valley floor; ☎ 928 674 5500, ⓦ nps.gov/cach.

ACCOMMODATION AND EATING

Chinle Holiday Inn Rte-7, Chinle ☎ 928 674 5000, ⓦ holiday-inn.com/chinle-garcia. Smart, adobe-fied motel, with a hundred comfortable, well-equipped rooms. The cosy, colourful on-site dining room is nothing exceptional, but it's the best you'll find in Chinle, with $14 specials such as glazed pork chops. $154

Cottonwood Campground At the start of South Rim Drive ☎ 928 674 2106, ⓦ navajonationparks.org. First-come, first-served tent-only campground among the

trees beside *Thunderbird Lodge*; each of the ninety sites accommodates up to four for no additional fee. No showers. Cash only. $10

Thunderbird Lodge At the start of South Rim Drive ☎ 928 674 5841, ⓦ tbirdlodge.com. Conventional, clean if somewhat faded motel rooms surrounding a century-old trading post, which houses a large and reasonably priced self-service cafeteria (daily 6.30am–9pm). $122

The Hopi Mesas

Almost uniquely in the United States, the **Hopi** people have lived continuously in the same place for more than eight hundred years. Some invaders have come and gone in that time, others have stayed; but the villages on **First**, **Second** and **Third mesas** have endured, if not exactly undisturbed then at least unmoved.

To outsiders, it's not immediately obvious why the Hopi chose to live on three barren and unprepossessing fingers of rock poking from the southern flanks of **Black Mesa** in the depths of northeast Arizona. There are two simple answers. The first lies within the mesa itself: its rocks are tilted to deliver a tiny but dependable trickle of water and also hold vast reserves of coal. The second is that the Hopi used to farm and hunt across a much wider area and were only restricted to their mesa-top villages when their Navajo neighbours encroached. While the Hopi are celebrated for their skill at "**dry farming**", preserving enough precious liquid to grow corn, beans and squash on hand-tilled terraces, this precarious and difficult way of life has nonetheless been forced upon them.

By their very survival and the persistence of their ancient beliefs and ceremonies, the Hopi have long fascinated outsiders. While visitors are welcome, the Hopi have no desire to turn themselves into a tourist attraction. Although stores and galleries make it easy to buy crafts such as pottery, basketwork, silver overlay jewellery and hand-carved *kachina* dolls, tourists who hope for extensive sightseeing – let alone spiritual revelations – are likely to leave disappointed and quite possibly dismayed by what they perceive as conspicuous poverty.

The modern, mock-Pueblo **Hopi Cultural Centre** below Second Mesa holds a **museum** (July & Aug Mon–Fri 8am–5pm, Sat & Sun 9am–3pm; Sept–June Mon–Fri 8am–5pm; $3; ☎928 734 6650, ⍉hopiculturalcenter.com). Unless your visit coincides with one of the very few social events that's open to tourists, the only way to see the mesa-top villages is on a **guided tour**. These are currently available at **WALPI** on First Mesa, where visitors assemble at the road's-end community centre in nearby **SICHOMOVI** (daily 9am–3pm; $13; ☎928 737 2670) and at **SIPAULOVI** on Second Mesa, which has its own small visitor centre (Mon–Fri 9am–4pm; $15; ☎928 737 5426, ⍉sipaulovihopiinformationcenter.org). All tours offer plenty of opportunity to ask questions and to buy pottery, *kachina* dolls and fresh-baked *piiki*, a flatbread made with blue cornflour.

ACCOMMODATION AND EATING   THE HOPI MESAS

Hopi Cultural Center Motel Second Mesa ☎928 734 2401, ⍉hopiculturalcenter.com. Built in a faux-Pueblo architectural style, this motel offers 34 plain but acceptable rooms that are usually booked solid in summer. The cafeteria serves good, substantial meals, including local delicacy *noqkwivi*, lamb stewed with hominy ($9.25). **$105**

12

Utah

With the biggest and most beautiful landscapes in North America, **UTAH** has something for everyone: from brilliantly coloured canyons, across desert plains, to thickly wooded and snow-covered mountains. Almost all of this unmatched range of terrain is public land, making Utah *the* place to come for **outdoor pursuits**, whether your tastes run to hiking, mountain biking, whitewater rafting or skiing.

In **southern Utah**, especially, the **scenery** is stupendous, a stunning geological freak show where the earth is ripped bare to expose cliffs and canyons of every imaginable hue. The region holds so many **national parks**, it has often been suggested that the entire area should become one vast park. The most accessible parks – such as **Zion** and **Bryce Canyon** – are by far the most visited, but lesser-known parks like **Arches** and **Canyonlands** are every bit as dramatic. Huge tracts of this empty desert, in which fascinating pre-Columbian pictographs and Ancestral Puebloan ruins lie hidden, are all but unexplored; seeing them requires self-sufficiency and considerable planning.

Although **northern Utah** holds less appeal for tourists, **Salt Lake City**, the capital, is by far the state's largest and most cosmopolitan urban centre, and makes an attractive and enjoyable stopover.

TOP DAY-HIKES IN UTAH

Calf Creek Falls, Grand Staircase-Escalante (p.784)		4hr
Delicate Arch Trail, Arches (p.790)		2hr
Hickman Bridge Trail, Capitol Reef (p.786)		2hr
Horseshoe Canyon, Canyonlands (p.788)		5hr
Mesa Arch Trail, Canyonlands (p.787)		1hr
Navajo Loop Trail, Bryce Canyon (p.783)		2hr
West Rim Trail, Zion (p.780)		1 day
White House Trail, Canyon de Chelly (p.775)		2hr 30min

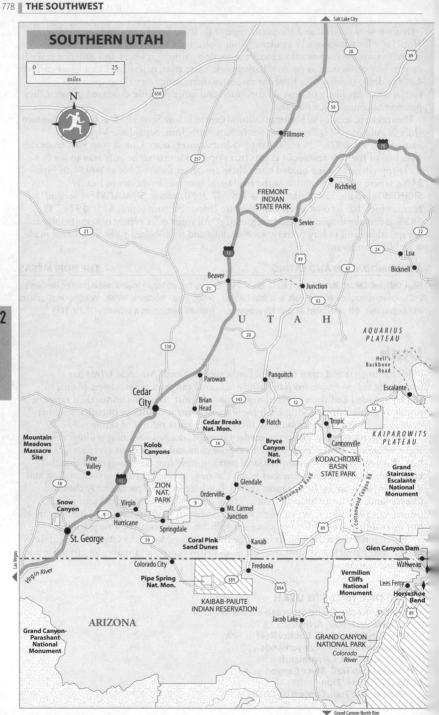

SOUTHERN UTAH

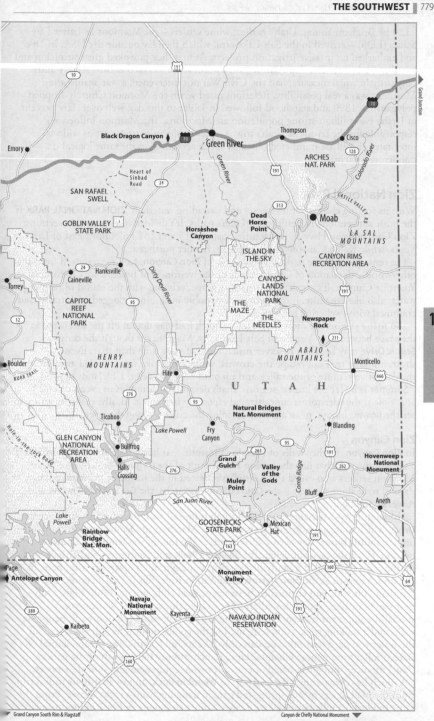

Led by Brigham Young, Utah's earliest white settlers – the **Mormons** or Latter Day Saints (LDS) – arrived in the Salt Lake area, which then lay outside the USA, in 1847 and embarked on massive irrigation projects. At first they provoked great suspicion and hostility back East. The Republican Convention of 1856 railed against slavery and polygamy in equal measure; had the Civil War not intervened, a war against the Mormons was a real possibility. Relations eased when the Mormon Church dropped polygamy in 1890 and statehood followed in 1896; to this day, well over sixty percent of Utah's two-million-strong population are Mormons. The Mormon influence is responsible for the layout of Utah's towns, where residential streets are as wide as interstates and all are numbered block by block according to the same logical if ponderous system.

Zion National Park

With its soaring cliffs, riverine forests and cascading waterfalls, **ZION NATIONAL PARK** is the most conventionally beautiful of Utah's parks. It's divided into two main sections: Zion Canyon is on Hwy-9, thirty miles east of I-15 and 158 miles northeast of Las Vegas, while Kolob Canyons is just off I-15, further northeast.

The centrepiece of the park, the lush oasis of **Zion Canyon**, feels far removed from the otherworldly desolation of Canyonlands or the weirdness of Bryce. Like California's Yosemite Canyon, it's a spectacular narrow gorge, echoing with the sound of running water; also like Yosemite, it can get claustrophobic in summer, clogged with traffic and crammed with sweltering tourists.

Too many visitors see Zion Canyon as a quick half-day detour off the interstate as they race between Las Vegas and Salt Lake City. Magnificent though the canyon's **Scenic Drive** may be, Zion deserves much more of your time than that. Even the shortest hiking trail can escape the crowds, while a day-hike will take you away from the deceptive verdure of the valley and up onto the high-desert tablelands beyond.

Summer is by far the busiest season. That's despite temperatures in excess of 100°F and violent thunderstorms concentrated especially in August. Ideally, come in spring to see the flowers bloom, or in autumn to enjoy the colours along the river.

Zion Canyon

In **Zion Canyon**, mighty walls of Navajo sandstone soar half a mile above the box elders and cottonwoods that line the loping North Fork of the **Virgin River**. The awe of the Mormon settlers who called this "Zion" is reflected in the names of the stupendous slabs of rock along the way – the **Court of the Patriarchs**, the **Great White Throne** and Angel's Landing.

Although Hwy-9 remains open to through traffic all year, the paved six-mile **Scenic Drive**, which branches north off it, is from late March until October only accessible on free **shuttle buses**. The Scenic Drive ends at the foot of the **Temple of Sinawava**, beyond which the easy but delightful **Riverside Walk** trail continues another half-mile up the canyon, to end at a sandy little beach. For eight miles upstream from here, in the stretch known as the **Zion Narrows**, the Virgin River fills the entire gorge, often less than 20ft wide and channelled between vertical cliffs almost 1000ft high. Only devotees of extreme sports should attempt to hike this ravishing "slot canyon"; specialist equipment is essential, including waterproof, super-grip footwear, neoprene socks and a walking stick, complemented in the cooler months by a drysuit, plus all the water you need to drink. You can only hike its full length downstream, a total of sixteen miles from remote Chamberlain's Ranch, twenty miles north of the park's East Entrance; Springdale-based operators provide equipment and shuittle services.

A much less demanding hike leads up to **Weeping Rock**, an easy half-hour round trip from the road to a gorgeous spring-fed garden dangling from a rocky alcove. From the same trailhead, a mile beyond *Zion Lodge*, a more strenuous and exciting route cuts

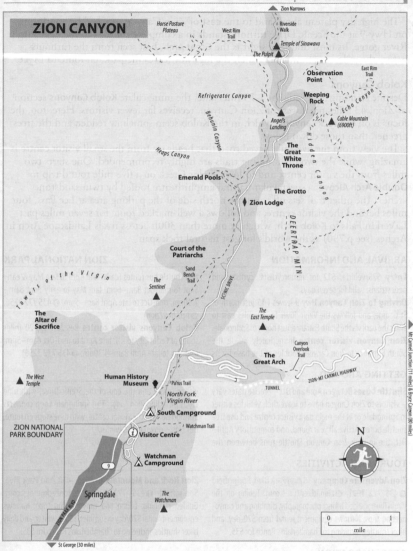

ZION CANYON

Zion Narrows
Horse Pasture Plateau
West Rim Trail
Riverside Walk
Temple of Sinawava
The Pulpit
Observation Point
East Rim Trail
Refrigerator Canyon
Weeping Rock
Echo Canyon
Cable Mountain (6900ft)
Angel's Landing
Behunin Canyon
Heaps Canyon
The Great White Throne
Hidden Canyon
Emerald Pools
The Grotto
Zion Lodge
DEERTRAP MTN.
Court of the Patriarchs
Sand Bench Trail
Towers of the Virgin
The Sentinel
The East Temple
12
The Altar of Sacrifice
Canyon Overlook Trail
The Great Arch
The Great Arch
ZION-MT CARMEL HIGHWAY
Mt Carmel Junction (11 miles) & Bryce Canyon (80 miles)
The West Temple
Human History Museum
Pa'rus Trail
TUNNEL
North Fork Virgin River
South Campground
Watchman Trail
ZION NATIONAL PARK BOUNDARY
Visitor Centre
9
Watchman Campground
Springdale
The Watchman
0   1
mile
N
St George (30 miles)

through narrow **Hidden Canyon**, whose mouth turns into a waterfall after a good rain. Directly across from the lodge a short and fairly flat trail (2-mile return) winds up at the **Emerald Pools**, a series of three clearwater pools, the best (and furthest) of which has a small sandy beach at the foot of a gigantic cliff.

The single best half-day **hike** climbs up to **Angel's Landing**, a narrow ledge of whitish sandstone protruding 1750ft above the canyon floor. Starting on the Emerald Pools route, the trail switchbacks sharply up through cool **Refrigerator Canyon** before emerging on the canyon's west rim; near the end you have to cross a heart-stopping 5ft neck of rock with only a steel cable to protect you from the sheer drops to either side. That round trip takes a good four hours, but backpackers can continue another twenty miles to the gorgeous Kolob Canyons district (see p.782).

The high dry plateau above and to the **east** of Zion Canyon, reached by continuing on Hwy-9 at the Scenic Drive turnoff, stands in a complete contrast to the lush Virgin River gorge. Its most dramatic sight is the **Great Arch**, best seen from the turnouts before the mile-long **tunnel** via which the highway leaves the park, en route to Bryce.

Kolob Canyons

Despite standing alongside the I-15 interstate, the immaculate **Kolob Canyons** section of Zion, 43 miles northwest of Zion Canyon, receives far fewer visitors. Here, too, the focus is on **red-rock canyons**, which in the Kolob seem somehow redder, and the trees greener, than those down below.

The view from the five-mile paved road that heads up from the small **visitor centre** is amazing, while the two main hiking trails are highly recommended. One starts two miles from the visitor centre and follows Taylor Creek on a five-mile round trip to **Double Arch Alcove**, a spectacular natural amphitheatre roofed by twin sandstone arches. The other trail sets off from the north side of the parking area at Lee Pass, four miles beyond the visitor centre, and follows a well-marked route for seven miles past LaVerkin Falls to **Kolob Arch**, which at more than 300ft across rivals Landscape Arch in Arches (see p.790) as the world's longest natural rock span.

ARRIVAL AND INFORMATION   ZION NATIONAL PARK

Entry $25/vehicle, $12 for motorcyclists, cyclists and pedestrians; valid for seven days.

Driving to Zion Canyon Hwy-9 leaves I-15 just north of St George, and follows the Virgin River for 30 miles east to enter the park via the South Entrance, just north of Springdale.

Zion Canyon visitor centre Immediately inside the South Entrance to Zion Canyon; doubles as the base for its

two shuttle bus routes (daily: late April to late May & early Sept to mid-Oct 8am–6pm; late May to early Sept 8am–7.30pm; mid-Oct to late April 8am–5pm; ☎ 435 772 3256, ⓦ nps.gov/zion).

Kolob Canyons visitor centre Beside I-15, 20 miles south of Cedar City (daily: late April to mid-Oct 8am–5pm; mid-Oct to late April 8am–4.30pm; ☎ 435 772 3256).

GETTING AROUND

Shuttle buses Between April and Oct – precise dates vary – visitors to Zion Canyon have to leave their vehicles either in Springdale or at the main park visitor centre and use free shuttle buses. Active all year round, and compulsory April–Oct, the in-park Zion Canyon Shuttle runs between the

visitor centre and the end of the Scenic Drive, with nine stops including *Zion Lodge*. The Springdale Loop connects Springdale with the visitor centre, with nine stops en route, but closes down in the winter.

TOURS AND ACTIVITIES

Zion Adventure Company 36 Zion Park Blvd, Springfield ☎ 435 772 1001, ⓦ zionadventures.com. Tubing on the Virgin River; guided biking, photography, climbing and canyoneering trips; Narrows equipment rental from $20/day; and hiker shuttles, including to Chamberlain's Ranch for $35.

Zion Rock and Mountain Guides 1458 Zion Park Blvd, Springfield ☎ 435 772 3303, ⓦ zionrockguides.com. Guided climbing, biking and canyoneering trips; Narrows equipment rental $20/day in summer, $35 in winter; and daily hiker shuttles, including to Chamberlain's Ranch for $35.

ACCOMMODATION

Apart from *Zion Lodge* in Zion Canyon itself, accommodation and eating facilities are concentrated in the pleasant community of Springdale, just outside the park's South Entrance.

HOTELS

Best Western Zion Park Inn 1215 Zion Park Blvd ☎ 435 772 3200, ⓦ zionparkinn.com. Modern, refurbished hotel at Springdale's southern end, offering spacious rooms with panoramic windows, plus a heated swimming pool. **$149**

★ **Desert Pearl Inn** 707 Zion Park Blvd ☎ 435 772 8888, ⓦ desertpearl.com. Gorgeous hotel, ranged alongside the Virgin River just outside the park, with superb

views. Stylish rooms with high ceilings, wooden floors, huge windows and balconies, facing either riverside lawns or a lovely turquoise pool with hot tubs. **$168**

Terrace Brook Lodge 990 Zion Park Blvd ☎ 435 772 3932. Springdale's one remaining budget motel offers run-down but acceptable motel rooms with no redeeming features other than price and a convenient central location. **$120**

12

Zion Lodge Scenic Drive, Zion Canyon Advance ☎303 297 2757, same-day ☎435 772 7700, ⓦzionlodge .com. Appealing if often overcrowded complex of low-slung wooden buildings, a couple of miles up the Scenic Drive, which offers the only food and lodging within the canyon. En-suite cabins have gas fireplaces and private porches; the motel rooms are plainer, but still have porches or balconies. Rooms $186, cabins $193

CAMPING

South Campground Zion Canyon ☎435 772 3256, ⓦnps.gov/zion. Arrive early for this first-come,

first-served riverside campground, just north of the visitor centre; it tends to fill by noon. Flushing toilets and cold running water, but no showers. Open early March to early Nov $16

Watchman Campground Reservations ☎877 444 6777 or ⓦrecreation.gov. Large campground, amid the cottonwoods south of the visitor centre, with flushing toilets and cold running water, but no showers. Eighteen walk-in, tent-only sites; the rest can hold one RV or two ordinary cars. Reservations March to early Nov only. Basic sites $16, with hookup $18, riverside sites $20

EATING

Bit & Spur 1212 Zion Park Blvd, Springdale ☎435 772 3498, ⓦbitandspur.com. Hectic dinner-only Mexican restaurant and bar, facing the red-rock cliffs, where the food has a creative edge, and the margaritas are top-notch. Chilli-rubbed steak costs $26, the Zuni lamb-and-corn stew $18, and a *chile relleno* (stuffed chilli) just $14. Daily 5–10pm.

Red Rock Grill Zion Lodge, Scenic Drive, Zion Canyon ☎435 772 7760, ⓦzionlodge.com. The river views from the lodge's bright, cool, upstairs dining room will probably linger longer in your mind than its standard breakfasts and lunches, both $8–12. Dinners are slightly

more sophisticated, with mains such as steak or trout at $16–24. Daily: May–Sept 6.30–10.30am, 11.30am–3pm & 5–10pm; Oct–April 7–10am, 11am–2pm & 5.30–8pm.

Spotted Dog Cafe Flanigan's Inn, 428 Zion Park Blvd, Springdale ☎435 772 3244, ⓦflanigans.com. Reasonably priced restaurant, attached to a motel at the park end of town, that's larger than it looks – the open-air patio is just the tip of the iceberg. Dinner mains such as braised lamb shank ($22) or trout ($18) have a zesty, continental feel; they also offer a substantial breakfast buffet. Daily 7–11am & 5–10pm.

12

Bryce Canyon National Park

The surface of the earth can hold few weirder-looking spots than **BRYCE CANYON**, just south of US-89 86 miles northeast of Zion Canyon. Named for Mormon settler Ebenezer Bryce, who declared that it was "a helluva place to lose a cow", it is not in fact a canyon at all. Along a twenty-mile shelf on the eastern edge of the thickly forested **Paunsaugunt Plateau**, 8000ft above sea level, successive strata of dazzlingly coloured rock have slipped and slid and washed away to leave a menagerie of multihued and contorted **stone pinnacles**.

In hues of yellow, red and flaming orange, the formations here have been eroded out of the muddy sandstone by a combination of icy winters and summer rains. The top-heavy pinnacles known as **"hoodoos"** form when the harder upper layers of rock stay firm as the lower levels wear away beneath them. **Thor's Hammer**, visible from Sunset Point, is the most alarmingly precarious. These hoodoos look down into technicolour ravines, all far more vivid than the Grand Canyon and much more human in scale. The whole place is at its most inspiring in winter, when the figures stand out from a blanket of snow.

The two most popular viewpoints into **Bryce Amphitheatre**, at the heart of the park, are on either side of *Bryce Canyon Lodge*: the more northerly, **Sunrise Point**, is slightly less crowded than **Sunset Point**, where most of the bus tours stop. **Hiking trails** drop abruptly from the rim down into the amphitheatre. One good three-mile trek, a great extension of the shorter **Navajo Loop Trail**, starts by switchbacking steeply from Sunset Point through the cool 200ft canyons of **Wall Street**, where a pair of 800-year-old fir trees stretch to reach daylight. It then cuts across the surreal landscape into the **Queen's Garden** basin, where the stout likeness of Queen Victoria sits in majestic condescension, before climbing back up to Sunrise Point. A dozen trails crisscross the amphitheatre, but it's surprisingly easy to get lost, so don't stray from the marked routes.

Sunrise and Sunset points notwithstanding, the best view at both sunset and dawn (the best time for taking pictures) is from **Bryce Point**, at the southern end of the amphitheatre. From here, you can look down not only at the Bryce Canyon formations but also take in the grand sweep of the whole region, east to the **Henry Mountains** and north to the Escalante range. The park road then climbs another twenty miles south, by way of the intensely coloured **Natural Bridge**, an 85ft rock arch spanning a steep gully, en route to its dead end at **Rainbow Point**.

GETTING AROUND AND INFORMATION

Entry $25/vehicle, $12 for motorcyclists, cyclists and pedestrians; valid for seven days.

Visitor centre Hwy-63, 1.5 miles beyond park entrance station (daily: May–Sept 8am–8pm; April & Oct 8am–6pm; Nov–March 8am–4.30pm; ☎ 435 834 5322, ⓦ nps .gov/brca).

BRYCE CANYON NATIONAL PARK

Shuttle buses Although visitors can drive to all the scenic overlooks year round, the park runs free shuttle buses to reduce traffic congestion. These shuttles don't go as far south as Rainbow Point, which is normally served by two daily bus tours from the visitor centre (☎ 435 834 5322).

ACCOMMODATION AND EATING

INSIDE THE PARK

Lodge at Bryce Canyon 100 yards from the rim ☎ 435 834 8700, ⓦ brycecanyonforever.com. The only accommodation option within the park itself, this 1920s stone-and-timber lodge consists of a handful of luxurious suites, a row or two of rough-hewn but comfortable cabins and seventy ordinary motel rooms. All are en suite. Lunchtime salads and sandwiches in its high-ceilinged and reasonably high-quality dining room, open for all meals, cost around $12; dinner mains like slow-cooked short ribs up to $30. Open mid-Nov to March. Rooms $175, cabins $203, suites $244

North Campground Near visitor centre, Bryce Canyon ☎ 877 444 6777, ⓦ recreation.gov (reservations) & ⓦ nps.gov/brca (information). Year-round campground that accepts reservations for thirteen of its 99 sites only, between early May and Sept only. It's usually fully occupied by early afternoon. RVs can stay, but there are no hookups or showers; sites hold up to ten people, in two vehicles. $15

Sunset Campground Across from Lodge, Bryce Canyon ☎ 877 444 6777, ⓦ recreation.gov (reservations) & ⓦ nps.gov/brca (information). Seasonal campground near Sunset Point. Only twenty of its 100 sites can be reserved in advance; all hold up to ten people, in two vehicles, and are first-come, first-served, so all tend to be

taken by early afternoon. RVs can stay, but there are no hookups. Open April to mid-Oct. $15

NEAR THE PARK

Half a dozen accommodation options loiter just outside the park along highways 12 and 63, in what's known as Bryce Canyon City, while there is a further cluster in the small town of Tropic, 8 miles east along Hwy-12.

Best Western Plus Bryce Canyon Grand Hotel 30 N 100 East, Bryce Canyon City ☎ 435 834 5700, ⓦ best westernutah.com. Large new chain motel, just off Hwy-63 a mile short of the park, with good comfortable rooms and an outdoor pool and hot tub. $160

Bryce Canyon Inn 21 N Main St, Tropic ☎ 435 679 8502, ⓦ brycecanyoninn.com. Standard motel rooms, plus eighteen large, newer log cabins, available in summer only. Rates include continental breakfast. Rooms $70, cabins $99

Ruby's Inn 26 S Main St, Bryce Canyon City ☎ 435 834 5341, ⓦ rubysinn.com. Large, unattractive motel complex on Hwy-63, a mile or so outside the park. Fifty of the 368 rooms feature whirlpool baths, and there's a heated indoor swimming pool. The food in the dining room, open for all meals, is consistently atrocious. $117

Grand Staircase-Escalante National Monument

East of Bryce Canyon, Hwy-12 curves along the edge of the Table Cliff Plateau before dropping into the remote canyons of the **Escalante River**, the last river system discovered within the continental US and site of some wonderful **backpacking** routes. The Escalante region is the focus of the vast **Grand Staircase-Escalante National Monument**, the main visitor centre for which is at the west end of **ESCALANTE**, 38 miles east of Tropic.

The most accessible highlight is **Calf Creek**, sixteen miles east of Escalante, where a trail leads just under three miles upstream from a nice undeveloped **campground** ($7) to a gorgeous shaded dell replete with a 125ft waterfall. More ambitious trips start from trailheads along the dusty but usually passable **Hole-in-the-Rock Road**, which

turns south from Hwy-12 five miles east of Escalante. A trio of slender, storm-gouged **slot canyons**, including the delicate, graceful Peek-a-Boo Canyon and the downright intimidating Spooky Canyon, can be reached by a mile-long hike from the end of Dry Fork Road, 26 miles along. From **Hurricane Wash**, 34 miles along, you can hike five miles to reach Coyote Gulch and then a further five miles, passing sandstone bridges and arches, to the Escalante River. Under normal conditions, two-wheel-drive vehicles should go no further than **Dance Hall Rock**, 36 miles down the road, a superb natural amphitheatre sculpted out of the slickrock hills.

Thirty miles beyond Escalante, at **BOULDER**, the Burr Trail, almost all of which is paved, heads east through the southern reaches of **Capitol Reef National Park** and down to **Lake Powell**.

INFORMATION   GRAND STAIRCASE-ESCALANTE NATIONAL MONUMENT

Entry No admission fee or opening hours.
Escalante information centre 755 W Main St, Escalante (mid-March to mid-Nov daily 7.30am–5.30pm; mid-Nov to mid-March Mon–Fri 8am–4.30pm; ☎ 435 826

5499, ⓦ ut.blm.gov/monument).
Kanab information centre 745 E US-89, Kanab (mid-March to mid-Nov daily 8am–4.30pm; mid-Nov to mid-March Mon–Fri 8am–4.30pm; ☎ 435 644 4680).

ACCOMMODATION AND EATING

Circle D Motel 475 W Main St, Escalante ☎ 435 826 4297, ⓦ escalantecircledmotel.com. Basic old-style motel, perched at the west end of town, with assorted rooms arrayed a long wooden veranda; ask for one of the newer ones. $74
Escalante Outfitters 310 W Main St, Escalante ☎ 435 826 4266, ⓦ escalanteoutfitters.com. Hikers' and campers' supply store where seven attractive little log cabins have heating but no phone or TV, and share use of

a bathhouse. There's also an espresso and snack bar. Open mid-March to Nov. Tents $16, cabins $45
★ **Kiva Koffeehouse** Mile 73.86, Hwy-12 ☎ 435 826 4550, ⓦ kivakoffeehouse.com. Solitary little cafe, perched on a rocky eminence. Fabulous views along the Escalante River plus simple snacks such as granola, sandwiches or enchiladas (served daily except Tues 8.30am–4.30pm) and two very comfortable guest rooms. Open April–Oct. $170

Capitol Reef National Park

CAPITOL REEF might sound like something you'd find off the coast of Australia, but its towering ochre-, white- and **red-rock walls** and deep **river canyons** are of a piece with the rest of the Utah desert. The outstanding feature, a multilayered, 1000ft-high reef-like wall of uplifted sedimentary rock, looms above Hwy-24, eleven miles east of Torrey, and 120 miles northeast of Bryce Canyon. Stretching over a hundred miles north to south, but only a few miles across, the seemingly impenetrable barrier of the **Waterpocket Fold** was warped upward by the same process that lifted the Colorado Plateau and its sharply defined sedimentary layers display two hundred million years of geological activity. The Fold is repeatedly sliced through by deeply incised river canyons – some just 20ft wide, but hundreds of feet deep – often accessible only on foot.

Motorists who stick to the park's paved through road, Hwy-24, which follows the canyon of the **Fremont River** across the northern half of the Fold, do not incur an entrance fee. Beneath the **Castle**, an enormous rock outcrop, you'll find the park's visitor centre and campground. To the west, the **Goosenecks Overlook** gazes down 500ft into the entrenched canyons cut by Sulphur Creek. Further east, beyond Fruita's former schoolhouse, some extraordinary **Fremont petroglyphs** of bighorn sheep and stylized space-people were chipped into the varnished red rock a thousand years ago. Another four and a half miles along, a beautiful **day-hike** heads up along the gravelly riverbed through **Grand Wash** – a cool canyon where Butch Cassidy and his gang used to hide out.

If you prefer a more energetic hike, try the supremely rewarding two-mile, two-hour **Hickman Bridge Trail** that climbs out up from the main road to reach a towering, 100ft natural bridge. Alternatively, you can reach several more superb trailheads by following the paved **Scenic Drive**, which heads eight miles south from the visitor centre, passing the top of Grand Wash, to reach **Capitol Gorge**.

The nearest food and lodging to Capitol Reef is around **Torrey**.

INFORMATION CAPITOL REEF NATIONAL PARK

Entry $5/vehicle, for Scenic Drive only.
Visitor centre 52 Scenic Drive (daily: summer 8am–6pm; spring & autumn 8am–5pm; winter 8am–4.30pm; ☎ 435 425 3791, ⓦ nps.gov/care).

ACCOMMODATION AND EATING

★ **Café Diablo** 599 W Main St, Torrey ☎ 435 425 3070, ⓦ cafediablo.net. Inventive modern restaurant, offering a slight Southwestern twist to meats and fish, with marinated lamb loin at $29 and rattlesnake patties for $9. Reserve ahead. Mid-April to Oct daily 11.30am–10pm.

Capitol Reef Inn & Cafe 360 W Main St, Torrey ☎ 435 425 3271, ⓦ capitolreefinn.com. Long-established but crisply maintained little motel, facing south to Boulder Mountain and holding a good, well-priced diner (April–Oct daily 7am–9pm). $65

★ **Rim Rock Inn** 2523 E Hwy-24 ☎ 435 425 3398, ⓦ therimrock.net. Modern, wood-built hotel, 3 miles east of Torrey, and offering good-value rooms plus the recommended *Rim Rock* restaurant (daily noon–10pm). $64

Canyonlands National Park

$10/vehicle, $5 for motorcyclists, cyclists, and pedestrians; valid for seven days • ☎ 435 719 2100, ⓦ nps.gov/cany

Utah's largest and most magnificent national park, **CANYONLANDS NATIONAL PARK** is as hard to define as it is to map. Its closest equivalent, the Grand Canyon, is by comparison simply an almighty crack in a relatively flat plain; Canyonlands is a bewildering tangle of canyons, plateaus, fissures and faults, scattered with buttes and monoliths, pierced by arches and caverns and penetrated only by a paltry handful of dead-end roads.

Canyonlands focuses on the Y-shaped confluence of the **Green** and **Colorado rivers**, buried deep in the desert forty miles southwest of Moab. The only spot from which you can see the rivers meet, however, is a five-mile hike from the nearest road. With no road down to the rivers, let alone across them, the park therefore splits into three major sections. The **Needles**, east of the Colorado, is a red-rock wonderland of sandstone pinnacles and hidden meadows that's a favourite with hardy hikers and 4WD enthusiasts, while the **Maze**, west of both the Colorado and the Green, is a virtually inaccessible labyrinth of tortuous, waterless canyons. In the wedge of the "Y" between the two, the high, dry mesa of the **Island In The Sky** commands astonishing views, with several overlooks that can easily be toured by car. Getting from any one of these sections to the others involves driving at least a hundred miles.

Canyonlands does not lend itself to a short visit. With no lodging and little camping inside the park, it takes a full day to have even a cursory look at a single segment. Considering that summer temperatures regularly exceed 100°F and most trails have no water and little shade, the Island In The Sky is the most immediately rewarding option. On the other hand, for a long day-hike you'd do better to set off into the Needles.

Island In The Sky

Visitor centre Hwy-313, 22 miles southwest of US-191 • Daily: March–Oct 8am–6pm; Nov–Feb 9am–4pm • ☎ 435 259 4712, ⓦ nps.gov/cany

Reached by a good road that climbs steadily from US-191, 21 miles south of I-70, the **Island In The Sky** district looks out over hundreds of miles of flat-topped mesas that drop in 2000ft steps to the river. Four miles along from its **visitor centre**, the enjoyable **Mesa Arch Trail** loops for a mile around the mesa-top hillocks to the edge of the abyss, where long, shallow Mesa Arch frames an extraordinary view of the **La Sal Mountains**, 35 miles northeast. The definitive vantage point, however, is **Grand View Point Overlook**, another five miles on at the southern end of the road. An agoraphobic's nightmare, it commands an endless prospect of layer upon layer of bare sandstone, here stacked thousands of feet high, there fractured into bottomless canyons.

12

The Island In The Sky's only developed **campground**, the first-come, first-served and waterless *Willow Flat* ($10), is just back from the **Green River Overlook**, along the right fork shortly after the Mesa Arch trailhead.

Dead Horse Point State Park

Drive 20 miles southwest of US-191 on Hwy-313, then 7 miles southeast • Daily: May–Sept 8am–6pm; Oct–April 8am–5pm • $10/vehicle, National Parks passes not valid • ☎ 435 259 2614, ⊚ stateparks.utah.gov/parks/dead-horse

A turnoff on the road towards the Island In The Sky cuts south to the smaller but equally breathtaking **Dead Horse Point**, located at the tip of a narrow mesa, which looks straight down 2000ft to the twisting Colorado River. Cowboys used the mesa as a natural corral, herding up wild horses then blocking them in behind a piñon pine fence that still marks its 90ft neck. One band of horses was left here too long and died – hence the name.

The Needles

Drive 40 miles south from Moab on US-191, then 35 miles west on Hwy-211 • **Visitor centre** March–Oct daily 8am–5pm; Nov & second half of Feb daily 9am–4pm; closed Dec to mid-Feb • ☎ 435 259 4711, ⊚ nps.gov/cany

Taking its name from the colourful sandstone pillars, knobs and hoodoos that punctuate its many lush canyons and basins, the **Needles** district allows an intimate look at the Canyonlands environment, where you're not always gazing thousands of feet downward or scanning the distant horizon. The pretty 35-mile drive into the region from US-191 winds along Indian Creek through deep red-rock canyons lined by pines and cottonwoods.

A demanding eleven-mile round-trip hike from mushroom-shaped hoodoos at the road's-end **Big Spring Canyon Overlook** offers the only access to the **Confluence Overlook**, 1000ft above the point where the Green River joins the muddy waters of the Colorado, to flow together toward fearsome **Cataract Canyon**. Among the best of the shorter walks that head away from the road is **Pothole Point**, a mile earlier. A longer day-trip or a good overnight hike leaves from near the *Squaw Flat* **campground** ($15) to the green meadow of **Chesler Park**, cutting through the narrow cleft of the Joint Trail.

The Maze and Horseshoe Canyon

Some 46 miles east of Hwy-24, 66 miles south of Green River • **Hans Flat Ranger Station** Daily 8am–4.30pm • ☎ 435 259 2652, ⊚ nps.gov/cany

Filling the western third of Canyonlands, on the far side of the Colorado and Green rivers, the harsh and remote **Maze** district is noted for its many-fingered box canyons, accessible only by jeep or by long, dry hiking trails.

Tree-lined **Horseshoe Canyon**, reached halfway down a long, long dirt road that loops south from Green River itself to join Hwy-24 just south of Goblin Valley, contains some fabulous **ancient rock art**. Allowing at least an hour's driving from the highway both before and after, plus five hours for the six-mile round-trip hike into the canyon itself, you'll need to set aside a full day, but it's well worth the effort, both for the joy of the walk and for the "**Great Gallery**" at the far end. Hundreds of mysterious, haunting pictographs – mostly life-sized human figures, albeit weirdly elongated or draped in robes and adorned with strange, staring eyes – were painted onto these red-sandstone walls, probably between 500 BC and 500 AD.

It was from the Horseshoe Canyon trailhead, incidentally, that **Aron Ralston** set off on the 2003 hike to Blue John Canyon, beyond Horseshoe Canyon, which culminated in his having to cut off his right arm, as immortalized in **127 Hours**.

Arches National Park

US-191, 5 miles northwest of central Moab • $10/vehicle, $5 for motorcyclists, cyclists, and pedestrians; valid for seven days • **Visitor centre** Daily: early March to Oct 7.30am–6.30pm; mid-Nov to early March 8am–4.30pm • ☎ 435 719 2299, ⊚ nps.gov/arch

The writer Edward Abbey, who spent a year as a ranger at **ARCHES NATIONAL PARK** in the 1950s, wrote that its arid landscape was as "naked, monolithic, austere and unadorned as the sculpture of the moon". Apart from the single ribbon of black asphalt that snakes through the park, there's nothing even vaguely human about it. Massive fins of red and golden sandstone stand to attention out of the bare desert plain and more than eighteen hundred natural arches of various shapes and sizes have been cut into the rock by eons of erosion. The narrow, hunching ridges are more like dinosaurs' backbones than solid rock, and under a full moon you can't help but imagine that the landscape has a life of its own.

While you could race through in a couple of hours, it takes at least a day to do Arches justice. A twenty-mile road cuts uphill sharply from US-191 and the **visitor centre**. The first possible stop is the south trailhead for **Park Avenue**, an easy trail leading one mile

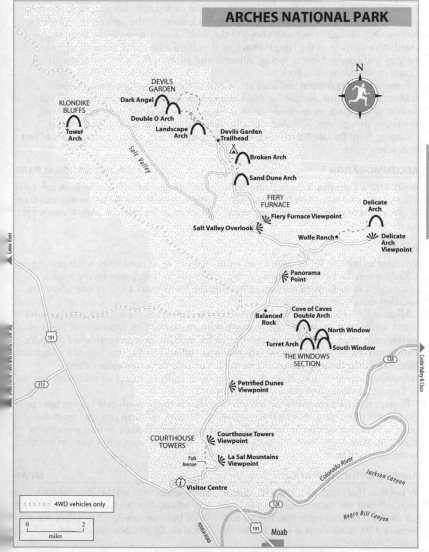

ARCHES NATIONAL PARK

12

down a scoured, rock-bottomed wash. If you stay on the road, the **La Sal Mountains Viewpoint** provides a grandstand look at the distant 12,000ft peaks, as well as the huge red chunk of **Courthouse Towers** closer at hand.

From **Balanced Rock** beyond – a 50ft boulder atop a slender 75ft pedestal – a right turn winds two miles through the **Windows** section, where a half-mile trail loops through a dense concentration of massive arches, some more than 100ft high and 150ft across. A second trail, fifty yards beyond, leads to **Double Arch**, a staunch pair of arches that together support another.

Further on, the main road drops downhill for two miles past Panorama Point and the turnoff to **Wolfe Ranch**, where a century-old log cabin serves as the trailhead for the wonderful three-mile round-trip hike up to **Delicate Arch**. Crowds congregate each evening beside the arch, a freestanding crescent of rock perched at the brink of a deep canyon, for the superb sunset views; coming back down in the dark can be a little hair-raising, though. Three miles beyond the Wolfe Ranch turnoff, the deep, sharp-sided mini-canyons of the **Fiery Furnace** section form a labyrinth through which rangers lead regular hikes in spring, summer and autumn ($10; reserve at the visitor centre or via ⓦrecreation.gov).

From the **Devil's Garden** trailhead at the end of the road, an easy one-mile walk leads to a view of the astonishing 306ft span of **Landscape Arch**, now too perilously slender to approach more closely. Several other arches lie along short spur trails off the route, though one, Wall Arch, finally collapsed in 2008. Seeing them all and returning from **Double O Arch** via the longer primitive trail requires a total hike of just over seven miles.

ACCOMMODATION   ARCHES NATIONAL PARK

Devil's Garden Campground Devil's Garden ☎518 885 3639, ⓦrecreation.gov. Arches' only campground, 18 miles north of the visitor centre, remains open all year; all its fifty sites, which hold up to ten people each, can be reserved between March and Oct; between Nov and Feb, 24 of them are first-come, first-served. No showers. $20

Moab

Founded in the late 1800s, **MOAB** was hardly a speck until the 1950s, when prospector Charlie Steen discovered uranium nearby. When the mining boom finally waned, the town threw in its lot with tourism to become the Southwest's number one adventure-vacation destination.

Moab still isn't a large town, though – the population has yet to reach ten thousand – and neither is it attractive. The setting is what matters. With two national parks on its doorstep, plus millions more acres of public land, Moab is an ideal base for outdoors enthusiasts. At first, it was a haven for **mountain bikers** lured by the legendary **Slickrock Bike Trail**. Then the **jeep** drivers began to turn up and the **whitewater-rafting** companies moved in, too. These days it's almost literally bursting, all year, with legions of Lycra-clad vacationers from all over the world.

Perhaps the main reason Moab has grown so fast is that out-of-state visitors tend to find Utah's other rural communities so boring. As soon as Moab emerged from the pack, it became a beacon in the desert, attracting tourists ecstatic to find a town that stayed up after dark – even if it does amount to little more than a few miles of motels, restaurants and bars.

ARRIVAL AND INFORMATION   MOAB

By bus Moab Luxury Coach (☎435 940 4212, ⓦmoab luxurycoach.com) runs shuttle services to Moab from Salt Lake City (1 daily, continues to Bluff; $159 one-way/person) and the Amtrak station at Grand Junction, CO (2 daily; $180/vehicle).

Visitor centre Center and Main (daily: mid-March to Oct Mon–Sat 8am–7pm, Sun 9am–6pm; Nov to mid-March Mon & Thurs–Sun 9am–5pm, Tues 1–5pm, Wed 9am–2pm; ☎435 259 8825, ⓦdiscovermoab.com).

ACCOMMODATION

Adobe Abode 778 W Kane Creek Blvd ☏ 435 259 7716, ⓦ adobeabodemoab.com. Attractive, low-slung, Pueblo-style home, which despite being a few hundred yards from downtown Moab feels like it's way out in the desert. All its six B&B rooms are comfortable and tastefully furnished, and the breakfasts are superb. **£139**

Best Western Greenwell Inn 105 S Main St ☏ 435 259 6151, ⓦ bestwesternmoab.com. Central, modern hotel that offers spacious good-value rooms with tasteful furnishings and fittings. **$140**

Lazy Lizard International Hostel 1213 S Hwy-191 ☏ 435 259 6057, ⓦ lazylizardhostel.com. This laidback independent hostel, a mile south of the centre, is nothing special, but backpackers appreciate its six-person dorms, private rooms and cabins, and it also has a hot tub, kitchen and wi-fi. Dorms **$10**, rooms **$30**, cabins **$34**

★ **Red Rock Lodge** 51 N 100 West ☏ 435 259 5431, ⓦ red-rocklodge.com. Though lacking the flair of Moab's fancier inns, this simple traditional motel offers clean rooms in a quiet central location. **$70**

Red Stone Inn 535 S Main St ☏ 435 259 3500, ⓦ moabredstone.com. Modern motel, a few blocks south of the centre, where the plain good-value rooms have kitchenettes, and guests can use a nearby pool. **$105**

Slickrock Campground 1301 N Hwy-191 ☏ 435 259 7660, ⓦ slickrockcampground.com. Moab's largest site, a mile north of town, is a pleasant spot, with plenty of trees and grass. Its fourteen cabins sleep three to four people each, and it offers a pool and hot tub. Tents **$26**, RVs **$33**, cabins **$53**

EATING

★ **Buck's Grill House** 1394 N Hwy-191 ☏ 435 259 5201, ⓦ bucksgrillhouse.com. Belying its stockade-like exterior, this is actually a sophisticated affair, serving rich, classy Southwestern food at reasonable prices. Most mains cost $16–19, though steaks and chops range up to $30. Mon–Sat 11.30am–9.30pm, Sun 10am–9.30pm.

Desert Bistro 36 S 100 West ☏ 435 259 0756, ⓦ desertbistro.com. Dinner-only restaurant, with outdoor seating. On the Mediterranean-influenced menu, mains such as smoked rabbit *agnolotti* or buffalo mignon cost up to $44. Tues–Sun 5.30–10pm.

Red Rock Bakery & Net Cafe 74 S Main St ☏ 435 259 5941. Small café-bakery opposite the visitor centre, with good coffee, breads and pastries, plus free wi-fi. Mon–Thurs 7am–4pm, Fri & Sat 7am–9pm, Sun 7am–3pm.

12

The San Juan River

From Natural Bridges, Hwy-261 runs south for 25 miles to the edge of Cedar Mesa, high above the eerie sandstone towers of the **Valley of the Gods**. It then turns to gravel and drops more than 1000ft in little over two twisting, hairpin-turning miles down the "**Moki Dugway**". Six miles from the foot of the switchbacks, the barely marked Hwy-316 branches off to the aptly named **Goosenecks State Reserve** (open 24hr; free), high above the **San Juan River**. A thousand feet below, the river snakes in such convoluted twists and turns that it flows six miles in total for every one mile west.

Back on Hwy-261, sleepy **MEXICAN HAT**, just twenty miles north of Monument Valley, takes its name from a riverside **sandstone hoodoo** that looks like a south-of-the-border sombrero.

The rafts you may see emerging from the water at Mexican Hat went in at **BLUFF**, twenty miles upstream. US-163 connects the two towns, well away from the river but still an enthralling drive, while the backstreets of Bluff hold **Mormon pioneer houses**.

ACTIVITIES   THE SAN JUAN RIVER

★ **Wild Rivers Expeditions** ☏ 435 672 2365, ⓦ rivers andruins.com. Fabulous one-day float trips from Bluff to Mexican Hat, with visits to ancient ruins and plentiful wildlife spotting, including eagles (adults $175, under-13s $133).

ACCOMMODATION AND EATING

★ **Cottonwood Steakhouse** 409 W Main St, Bluff ☏ 435 672 2282, ⓦ cottonwoodsteakhouse.com. Open-air barbecue, with wooden tables arranged around a giant cottonwood. A great place to enjoy beer and steaks (priced at up to $25) beneath the stars – though the menu's a bit short if you're not a beef-eater. Daily: April, May & Oct

5–9pm; June–Sept 6–10pm.

Desert Rose Inn 701 W Main St, Bluff ☏ 435 672 2303, ⓦ desertroseinn.com. Modern timber-built motel, holding thirty attractively designed and well-furnished rooms, plus individual cabins of similar standard. **$119**

Kokopelli Inn 161 E Main St, Bluff ☏ 435 672 2322,

ⓦkokoinn.com. Friendly, quiet roadside motel, adjoining a gas station and grocery with a deli counter. $82

★ **Mexican Hat Lodge** US-163, Mexican Hat ☎ 435 683 2222, ⓦwww.mexicanhat.net. Mexican Hat's northernmost motel – a former dance hall – with thirteen rooms of differing sizes. Its open-air *Swingin Steak* restaurant (daily 6–9pm) is everything you could wish for from a cowboy steakhouse, grilling huge perfect steaks over a fire of sweet-smelling wood, at $21 for an 8oz steak, $36 for an 18oz. Open Feb–Oct. $84

Hovenweep National Monument

Hidden in the no-man's-land that straddles the Utah–Colorado border, the remote **Ancestral Puebloan ruins** at **Hovenweep National Monument** offer a haunting sense of timeless isolation. While it preserves six distinct conglomerations of ruins, all sprouting from the rims of shallow desert canyons, easy access is restricted to **Little Ruin Canyon**, behind the **visitor centre**. A mile-long loop trail offers good views of the largest ruins, including the grandly named **Hovenweep Castle**, constructed around 1200 AD. No accommodation, petrol or food is available.

ARRIVAL AND INFORMATION   HOVENWEEP NATIONAL MONUMENT

By car Drive 25 miles east on Hwy-262, which branches off US-191 halfway between Bluff and Blanding in Utah, or 35 miles west from Cortez, Colorado, along County Road G.

Visitor centre Little Ruin Canyon (daily: April & Oct 8am–5pm; May–Sept 8am–6pm; Nov–March 9am–5pm; ☎ 970 562 4282, ⓦnps.gov/hove).

ACCOMMODATION

Hovenweep Campground Little Ruin Canyon ☎ 970 562 4282, ⓦnps.gov/hove. First-come, first-served 31-site campground, close to the visitor centre. It has a few

RV spaces, but no hookups. Running water in summer only. No reservations. $10

Lake Powell and Glen Canyon Dam

The mighty rivers and canyons of southern Utah come to an abrupt and ignoble end at the Arizona border, where the **Glen Canyon Dam** stops them dead in the stagnant waters of **Lake Powell**. Ironically, the lake is named for John Wesley Powell, the first person to run the Colorado River through the Grand Canyon. The roaring torrents that he battled, along with magnificent Glen Canyon itself, are now lost beneath these placid blue waters and the blocked-up Colorado, Green, Dirty Devil, San Juan and Escalante rivers have become a playground for houseboaters and waterskiers. The construction of the dam in the early 1960s outraged environmentalists and archeologists and created a peculiar and utterly unnatural landscape, the deep and tranquil lake a surreal contrast with the surrounding dry slickrock and sandstone buttes.

Lake Powell has 1960 miles of shoreline – more than the entire US Pacific coast – and 96 water-filled side canyons. The water level fluctuates considerably, so for much of the time the rocks to all sides are bleached for many feet above the waterline, with a dirty-bath tidemark sullying the golden sandstone. Many summer visitors bring their own boats or rent a vessel from one of the marinas that fringe the lake.

GLEN CANYON DAM itself, on US-89, two miles northwest of Page, Arizona, can be seen from the **Carl Hayden Visitor Centre** (daily: March–April & Oct 8am–5pm; May–Sept 8am–6pm; Nov–Feb 8.30am–4.30pm; ☎ 928 608 6404, ⓦnps.gov/glca) on the west bank, which also arranges $5, 45-minute dam tours.

Salt Lake City

Disarmingly pleasant and easy-going, **SALT LAKE CITY** is well worth a stopover of a couple of days. Its setting is superb, towered over by the **Wasatch Front**, which marks the dividing line between the comparatively lush eastern and the bone-dry western halves of northern Utah. The area offers great hiking and cycling in summer and autumn and, in

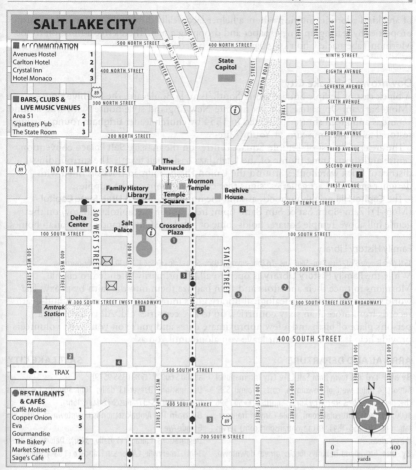

SALT LAKE CITY

ACCOMMODATION
Avenues Hostel	1
Carlton Hotel	2
Crystal Inn	4
Hotel Monaco	3

BARS, CLUBS &
LIVE MUSIC VENUES
Area 51	2
Squatters Pub	1
The State Room	3

RESTAURANTS
& CAFÉS
Caffè Molise	1
Copper Onion	3
Eva	5
Gourmandise
The Bakery	2
Market Street Grill	6
Sage's Café	4

TRAX

12

winter, superb **skiing**. Outsiders still tend to imagine Salt Lake City as decidedly short on fun, but so long as you're willing to switch gears and slow down, its unhurried pace and the positive energy of its people can make for an enjoyable experience.

Temple Square

50 E North Temple St • Daily 9am–9pm • ☎ 801 240 1706, ⓦ visittemplesquare.com

The geographical – and spiritual – heart of Salt Lake City is **Temple Square**, the world headquarters of the **Mormon Church** (or the Church of Jesus Christ of Latter-Day Saints – LDS). Its focus, the very plain granite **Temple** itself, was completed in 1893 after forty years of intensive labour. Only confirmed Mormons may enter the Temple and then only for the most sacred LDS rituals – marriage, baptisms and "sealing", the joining of a family unit for eternity.

The northern of the two **visitor centres** that lie within the gates of Temple Square holds a model of Jerusalem in 33 AD and dioramas of Jesus preaching in North America. Its southern counterpart concentrates on the story of Salt Lake City's first Mormon settlers. As soon as you show the slightest interest, you'll be shepherded to join a free 45-minute **tour** or at least ushered into the odd oblong shell of the **Mormon Tabernacle**. No images of any kind adorn its interior, where a helper laconically displays its remarkable acoustic properties by tearing up a newspaper and dropping a nail. There's free admission to the Mormon Tabernacle Choir's 9.30am Sunday broadcast and its rehearsals on Thursday evenings at 8pm.

Downtown Salt Lake City

A block east of Temple Square along South Temple Boulevard, the **Beehive House** (Mon–Sat 9am–9pm; free) is a plain white New England-style house, with wraparound verandas and green shutters. Erected in 1854 by church leader **Brigham Young**, it's now restored as a small museum of Young's life.

The area southwest of Temple Square centres on the massive **Salt Palace** convention centre and sports arena (home of the Utah Jazz basketball team). The surrounding district of brick warehouses around the Union Pacific railroad tracks is filled with designer shops and art galleries, signs that even Mormons can be yuppies.

The **Capitol Hill** neighbourhood, around the imposing, domed **Utah State Capitol** (Mon–Fri 7am–8pm, Sat & Sun 8am–6pm; free; ⍟ utahstatecapitol.utah.gov) on the gentle hill above Temple Square, holds some of Salt Lake City's grandest Victorian homes.

Family History Library

35 N West Temple Blvd • Mon 8am–5pm, Tues–Fri 8am–9pm, Sat 9am–5pm • Free • ☏ 866 406 1830, ⍟ familysearch.org

While the **Family History Library** is open to all, it's primarily intended to enable Mormons to trace their ancestors and then baptize them into the faith by proxy. The world's most exhaustive genealogical library gives immediate access to birth and death records from more than sixty countries, up to five centuries old. All you need is a person's place of birth and a few approximate dates and you're on your way; volunteers provide help if you need it, but leave you alone until you ask.

ARRIVAL AND DEPARTURE	SALT LAKE CITY

By air A taxi into town from Salt Lake City International Airport, 4 miles west of downtown, costs around $25; cheaper shuttle vans are run by Xpress Shuttles (☏ 801 596 1600, ⍟ xpressshuttleutah.com), while Canyon Transportation (☏ 801 255 1841, ⍟ canyontransport.com) serves the ski areas.

By bus Greyhound-Trailways buses arrive downtown, at 300 S 600 W (☏ 801 355 9579).
Destinations Denver (3 daily; 10hr 30min); Las Vegas (2 daily; 8hr); San Francisco (2 daily; 15hr).

By train The Amtrak station is downtown at 320 S Rio Grande Ave.
Destinations Chicago (1 daily; 34hr); Denver (1 daily; 14hr); Emeryville, CA, for San Francisco (1 daily; 16hr).

GETTING AROUND AND INFORMATION

By bus and tram Local buses and TRAX trams (trolleys) are operated by the Utah Transit Authority (☏ 801 743 3882, ⍟ rideuta.com); journeys within the downtown area are free.

Visitor centre Downtown at 90 S West Temple Blvd (daily 9am–5pm; ☏ 801 534 4490, ⍟ visitsaltlake.com).

ACCOMMODATION

Avenues Hostel 107 F St ☏ 801 539 8888, ⍟ saltlakehostel.com. Simple hostel a short way east of downtown, with communal kitchen and living room, where not all guests are necessarily travellers. Dorm $18, doubles $45

Carlton Hotel 140 E South Temple Blvd ☏ 801 355 3418, ⍟ carltonhotel-slc.com. Friendly, old-fashioned hotel, at the budget end of the spectrum, offering good-value rooms with kitchen facilities very close to downtown.

Rates include breakfast. $89

Crystal Inn 230 W 500 South ☏ 801 328 4466, ⍟ crystalinnsaltlake.com. Spacious, well-equipped and very reasonably priced hotel close to downtown, with large buffet breakfasts included and free airport shuttle. $97

Hotel Monaco 15 W 200 South ☏ 801 595 0000, ⍟ monaco-saltlakecity.com. Stylish, very upscale downtown hotel, housed in a former bank. $229

EATING

Caffè Molise 55 W 100 South ☏ 801 364 8833, ⍟ caffemolise.com. Authentic, high-quality, great-value

Italian food downtown, with tables in a nice little courtyard in summer and jazz on Fridays. Mon–Thurs

11.30am–9pm, Fri & Sat 11.30am–10pm, Sun 10am–9pm.

Copper Onion 111 E Broadway ☎801 355 3282, ⓦ thecopperonion.com. Hip downtown bistro, a couple of blocks south of Temple Square, with lunchtime burgers and salads for $13–15, and meatloaf or skillet chicken at dinner for around $20. Mon–Thurs 11.30am–3pm & 5–10pm, Fri 11.30am–3pm & 5–11pm, Sat 10.30am–11pm, Sun 10.30am–10pm.

Eva 317 S Main St ☎801 359 8447, ⓦ evaslc.com. Hip downtown restaurant-cum-wine bar; while it's not exactly a tapas bar, the menu consist of small plates, typically priced at $6–12, drawn from assorted Mediterranean cuisines and extending from risotto and pasta to Greek-style *spanakopita* or pork chops. Mon–Fri 4pm–midnight, Sat 5pm–midnight, Sun 5–10pm.

Gourmandise The Bakery 250 S 300 East ☎801 328 3330. It's the pastries that draw downtown devotees in droves, but this hugely popular café also does great, cheap, lunchtime salads, sandwiches and specials. Mon–Thurs 7am–1pm, Fri & Sat 7am–11pm.

Market Street Grill 48 W Market St ☎801 322 4668, ⓦ marketstreetgrill.com. As close as Salt Lake City comes to a New York City bar and grill, with fresh seafood, especially oysters, plus steaks in all shapes and sizes. $11 lunch specials, full dinners $22–30. Mon–Thurs 6.30am–2pm & 5–9pm, Fri 6.30am–2pm & 5–9.30pm, Sat 8am–noon & 4–9.30pm, Sun 9am–3pm & 4–9pm.

Sage's Café 473 E 300 South ☎801 322 3790, ⓦ sages cafe.com. Salt Lake's finest vegetarian restaurant, with an all-organic menu that ranges from pizza to raw salads. Mon–Fri 11.30am–10pm, Sat & Sun 10am–10pm.

DRINKING AND NIGHTLIFE

Salt Lake City doesn't roll up the sidewalks when the sun goes down. To find out about the broad range of **fringe** art, music and clubland happenings, pick up the free *City Weekly* (ⓦ slweekly.com).

Area 51 400 W 451 South ☎801 534 0891, ⓦ area51slc .com. Named for Nevada's notorious alien zone, Salt Lake's largest club caters to young and old alike, with contemporary dance music as well as 80s goth and indie in post-industrial surroundings. Tues–Sat 9pm–2am.

Squatters Pub 147 W 300 South ☎801 363 2739, ⓦ squatters.com. This casual, friendly place is the pick of Salt Lake's brewpubs, with a dozen good beers of its

own and a decent menu of burgers, salads, steaks and curries. Mon–Thurs 11am–midnight, Fri 11am–1am, Sat 10am–1am, Sun 10am–midnight.

The State Room 638 S State St ☎800 501 2885, ⓦ thestateroomslc.com. The top local live music venue, attracting big-name touring acts, and offering a dancefloor as well as auditorium seating. Hours vary.

12

Nevada

Desolate **NEVADA** consists largely of endless tracts of bleak, empty desert, its flat sagebrush plains cut intermittently by angular mountain ranges. Apart from the huge acreages given over to mining and grazing, much of Nevada is used by the **military** to test aircraft and weapons systems.

By far the most compelling reason to visit Nevada is to see the surreal oasis of **Las Vegas**. While its eye-popping architecture, lavish restaurants, decadent nightclubs and amazing shows offer an unforgettable sensory overload, the experience remains rooted in **gambling**. Even the smaller and more down-to-earth settlements of **Reno** and state capital **Carson City** revolve around the casino trade.

In the **Great Basin**, where the rivers and streams have no outlet to the ocean, Nevada has an eerie beauty. The main cross-state route, **I-80**, shoots from Salt Lake City to Reno, skirting bizarrely named little towns scattered with casinos, bars, brothels and motels. The other significant road, **US-50**, has a reputation as the loneliest highway in America. Older and slower, it follows much the same route as the Pony Express of the 1860s, but many towns have faded away altogether.

Las Vegas

A dazzling desert oasis, entirely devoted to thrilling its visitors, **LAS VEGAS** is not like other destinations. Without its tourists, Las Vegas wouldn't even exist; everything, from its spectacular architecture to its world-class restaurants and showrooms, is designed to sate their every appetite. Not only does Las Vegas hold almost all the world's largest hotels, but that's pretty much all it holds; it's the hotels themselves that forty million people a year come to see. Each is a neighbourhood in its own right, crammed full of places to eat, drink, dance and play, and centring on an enormous casino, crammed with slot machines and table games.

Most visitors see no more of Las Vegas than two short, and very different, linear stretches. **Downtown**, the original centre, now amounts to four brief blocks of Fremont Street, while **the Strip** starts a couple of miles south, and runs for four miles. The Strip is the real centre of the action, with each colossal mega-casino vying to out-do the next with some outlandish theme, be it an Egyptian pyramid, a Roman extravaganza, a fairytale castle or a European city.

In 1940, Las Vegas was home to just eight thousand people. It owes its extraordinary growth to its constant willingness to adapt. Far from remaining kitsch and old-fashioned, as you might expect, it's forever re-inventing itself. Entrepreneurs race to spot the latest shift in who has the money, and what they want to spend it on. A few years back, the casinos realized that modern gamblers were happy to pay premium prices to eat good food; top chefs now run gourmet restaurants in places like *Bellagio* and the *Cosmopolitan*. More recently, demand from younger visitors has prompted casinos like *Wynn Las Vegas* to open high-tech nightclubs to match those in Miami and LA.

The reputation Las Vegas still enjoys, of being a quasi-legal adult playground where (almost) anything goes, dates back to its early years. Most of its first generation of luxury resorts, like the *Flamingo*, the *Sands* and the *Desert Inn*, were controlled by the Mob, in an era when illegal profits could be easily "skimmed" off, and respectable investors steered clear of casinos. Then as now, visitors loved to imagine that they were rubbing shoulders with gangsters. Mob rule has however long since come to an end, with the city now under the sway of massive corporations.

The Strip

In the old days, the casinos along Las Vegas's legendary **Strip** were cut-throat rivals. Each stood a long way back from the road, and was a dark, low-ceilinged labyrinth, in which it was all but impossible to find an exit. During the 1980s, however, visitors started to explore the Strip on foot. Mogul Steve Wynn cashed in by placing a flame-spouting volcano outside his new *Mirage*. As the casinos competed to lure in pedestrians, they filled in those daunting distances from the sidewalk and between each casino and the next.

With Las Vegas booming in the 1990s, gaming corporations bought up first individual casinos, and then each other. The Strip today is dominated by just two colossal conglomerates, MGM Resorts and Caesars Entertainment, each of which owns a string of neighbouring casinos. Once you own the casino next door, there's no reason to make each a virtual prison. The Strip has therefore opened out, so that much of its central portion now consists of pedestrian-friendly open-air terraces and pavilions housing bars and restaurants.

Mandalay Bay

3950 Las Vegas Blvd S • ☎ 702 632 7777, ⓦ mandalaybay.com • **Shark Reef** Daily 10am–10pm • $18 • ☎ 702 632 4555, ⓦ sharkreef.com

The southernmost mega-casino, **Mandalay Bay**, consists of two golden skyscrapers towering over a huge, vaguely tropical-themed complex. Its high-end array of dining and entertainment options include the first-ever Cirque du Soleil nightclub, and a Cirque show celebrating Michael Jackson. At the back of the property, the **Shark Reef** aquarium focuses on dangerous marine predators, prowling through tanks designed to resemble an ancient temple that's sinking into the sea.

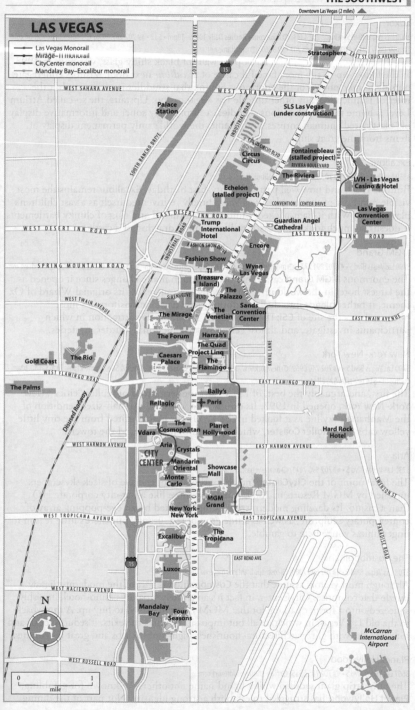

Downtown Las Vegas (2 miles)

LAS VEGAS

- ●—● Las Vegas Monorail
- ●—● Mirage–TI monorail
- ●—● CityCenter monorail
- ●—● Mandalay Bay–Excalibur monorail

The Stratosphere

SLS Las Vegas
(under construction)

Palace Station

Circus Circus

Fontainebleau
(stalled project)

The Riviera

LVH - Las Vegas
Casino & Hotel

Echelon
(stalled project)

Las Vegas
Convention
Center

Trump
International
Hotel

Guardian Angel
Cathedral

Fashion Show

Encore

TI
(Treasure
Island)

Wynn
Las Vegas

The Palazzo

The Mirage

The Venetian

Sands
Convention
Center

The Forum

Harrah's

The Quad

Project Linq

The Flamingo

Caesars
Palace

Gold Coast

The Rio

The Palms

Bellagio

Bally's

Paris

The
Cosmopolitan

Planet
Hollywood

Vdara

Aria

Crystals

CITY
CENTER

Mandarin
Oriental

Monte
Carlo

Showcase
Mall

Hard Rock
Hotel

New York-
New York

MGM
Grand

Excalibur

The
Tropicana

Luxor

Mandalay
Bay

Four
Seasons

McCarran
International
Airport

WEST SAHARA AVENUE — EAST SAHARA AVENUE

EAST ST LOUIS AVENUE

WEST DESERT INN ROAD — EAST DESERT INN ROAD

SPRING MOUNTAIN ROAD

WEST TWAIN AVENUE — EAST TWAIN AVENUE

WEST FLAMINGO ROAD — EAST FLAMINGO ROAD

WEST HARMON AVENUE — EAST HARMON AVENUE

WEST TROPICANA AVENUE — EAST TROPICANA AVENUE

EAST RENO AVE

WEST HACIENDA AVENUE

WEST RUSSELL ROAD

SOUTH RANCHO DRIVE

INDUSTRIAL ROAD

CIRCUS CIRCUS BLVD

THE STRIP

LAS VEGAS BOULEVARD SOUTH

CONVENTION CENTER DRIVE

RIVIERA BOULEVARD

PARADISE ROAD

SANDS AVENUE

KOVAL LANE

SWENSON ST

Disused Roadway

N

0   1
      mile

12

Luxor

3900 Las Vegas Blvd S • ☎ 702 262 4444, ⓦ luxor.com • **Bodies** Daily 10am–10pm • $32 • ☎ 702 262 4400, ⓦ bodiestheexhibition.com
Titanic Daily 10am–10pm • $32 • ☎ 702 492 3960, ⓦ rmstitanic.net

The huge **Luxor** pyramid, with its sloping walls of black shiny glass, was built in 1993 as the follow-up to the more fanciful castle of *Excalibur* next door. Visitors congregate outside to take photos of the enormous Sphinx that straddles its driveway, but the interior is much like any other upscale Las Vegas casino. Upstairs, the so-called Atrium Level is home to two exhibitions – **Bodies**, a surprisingly sober and informative display of "plastinated" human corpses, and **Titanic**, the world's only permanent display of items from the great ship.

Excalibur

3850 Las Vegas Blvd S • ☎ 702 597 7777, ⓦ excalibur.com

Built in 1990, and now well past its twenty-first birthday, **Excalibur** remains the most visible reminder of the era when Las Vegas briefly re-invented itself as a vast children's playground. With its jam-packed, multicoloured turrets and ring of clunky battlements it doesn't so much look like a castle as like a child's drawing of a castle.

MGM Grand

3799 Las Vegas Blvd S • ☎ 702 891 7777, ⓦ mgmgrand.com • **CSI: The Experience** Daily 9am–9pm • $28 • ☎ 702 891 7006, ⓦ csiexhibit.com

The enormous **MGM Grand** casino has been through many changes since it opened as the largest hotel in the world in 1993. Having long since lost its original Wizard of Oz theme, it rather blends into the background these days. For visitors, it's most noteworthy as the site of **CSI: The Experience**, an interactive attraction in which participants investigate, and almost certainly solve, fictional murder mysteries.

New York–New York

3790 Las Vegas Blvd S • ☎ 702 740 6969, ⓦ newyorknewyork.com • **Roller Coaster** Mon–Thurs & Sun 11am–11pm, Fri & Sat 10.30am–midnight • $14 one ride, $25 all-day pass

The first, and arguably the best, of Las Vegas's modern breed of replica "cities", **New York–New York**, opened in 1997. Its exterior – a squeezed-up, half-sized rendition of the Manhattan skyline as it looked in the 1950s – is best admired from the tiny little yellow cabs of its **Roller Coaster**, which speed at 67mph around the towers.

Aria

3730 Las Vegas Blvd S • ☎ 702 590 7111, ⓦ arialasvegas.com

The focal point of the **CityCenter** "neighbourhood", an enclave of sleek skyscrapers unveiled by MGM Resorts in 2009, **Aria** looks more like a big-city corporate HQ than a casino. Its dazzling modernism is complemented by an eye-popping array of contemporary sculpture, as well as a fine crop of restaurants, but there's little reason to linger unless you're here to gamble.

The Cosmopolitan

3708 Las Vegas Blvd S • ☎ 702 698 7000, ⓦ cosmopolitanlasvegas.com

Although most visitors assume that the **Cosmopolitan** is part of the modernist jigsaw puzzle that comprises CityCenter, in fact it's an entirely separate casino-hotel, impishly squeezed onto a former parking lot that MGM never managed to buy up. A throwback to the old Las Vegas, in which it's all but impossible to find the exits, it seduces locals and tourists alike with glitzy architectural flourishes, high-profile clubs and great restaurants.

Planet Hollywood

3667 Las Vegas Blvd S • ☎ 702 785 5555, ⓦ planethollywoodresort.com

The only Strip giant saddled with a brand name not otherwise known for gambling, **Planet Hollywood** has struggled to establish a strong identity. Not part of the dining chain, it opened in 2000 as a new version of the long-established *Aladdin*. The main attraction within is the large **Miracle Mile** shopping mall; the actual casino is relatively small, and largely targeted at "hip" young visitors.

Paris

3655 Las Vegas Blvd S • ☎ 877 603 4386, ⓦ parislasvegas.com **Eiffel Tower** Daily 9.30am–12.30am • $10.50 daytime, $15.50 evening • ☎ 888 727 4758

Designed by the architects responsible for *New York–New York*, and opened just before the millennium, **Paris** represented the final flourish of the Las Vegas craze for building miniature cities. Its exterior remains one of the Strip's most enjoyable spectacles, and pleasing Parisian touches continue inside. Half the height of the Seine-side original, the **Eiffel Tower** that surmounts it towers 540ft tall. Its summit offers great views, with the prime time to come being the evening, when it makes the perfect vantage point to watch the *Bellagio* fountains.

Bellagio

3600 Las Vegas Blvd S • ☎ 702 693 7111, ⓦ bellagio.com

Ranking high among Las Vegas's absolute must-see casinos, **Bellagio** surveys the Strip across the graceful dancing fountains of a broad, semicircular lake. Unveiled in 1998, this cream-coloured vision of Italian elegance was the handiwork of entrepreneur Steve Wynn, who aimed to build the greatest hotel the world had ever seen. While Wynn himself is no longer at the helm, *Bellagio* is still going strong, now an integral component of CityCenter and racking up the highest turnover and biggest profits in the city.

The two main attractions are the **fountains**, which erupt in regular balletic extravaganzas between early afternoon and midnight daily, and the magnificent **Conservatory**, where gardeners arrange themed displays that include bizarre whimsical props amid an extraordinary array of living plants.

Caesars Palace

3570 Las Vegas Blvd S • ☎ 702 227 5938, ⓦ caesarspalace.com

Still a Las Vegas headliner in its own right, **Caesars Palace** remains arguably the biggest name on the Strip. Cobbled together for just $24 million, it opened in 1966, complete with clerks dressed as Roman centurions and cocktail waitresses kitted out like Cleopatra. White marble Classical statues are still everywhere you look, from Julius Caesar forever hailing a cab on the main driveway to the Winged Victory of Samothrace guarding a row of gently cascading pools. While the central bulk of *Caesars Palace* is set back around 150 yards from the Strip, all the intervening space has been built over, most notably by the vast **Forum** mall, in which a domed false-sky ceiling cycles between "day" and "night" at hourly intervals.

The Mirage

3400 Las Vegas Blvd S • ☎ 702 791 7111, ⓦ mirage.com **Secret Garden** Daily 10am–7pm • $20 • ☎ 702 791 7188, ⓦ miragehabitat.com

Built as entrepreneur Steve Wynn's first Strip venture, in 1989, the **Mirage** can justly claim to have changed the city overnight. Proving that by investing in luxury, glamour and spectacle – and adding an artificial volcano – casinos could bring back the crowds, it spawned such a host of imitators that now, ironically, it no longer stands out from the pack. There's still plenty to like about the *Mirage*, from its glassed-in atrium, complete with towering tropical trees, via its well-judged array of restaurants and bars, to its huge complex of pools and gardens. Amid the foliage, the **Secret Garden and Dolphin Habitat** holds cages containing everything from black leopards to white tigers, and two pools of bottlenose dolphins.

12

The Venetian and the Palazzo

Venetian 3355 Las Vegas Blvd S • ☎ 702 414 1000, ⓦ venetian.com **Palazzo** 3325 Las Vegas Blvd S • ☎ 702 607 7777, ⓦ palazzo.com
Madame Tussauds Mon–Thurs & Sun 10am–9.30pm, Fri & Sat 10am–10.30pm • $26 • ☎ 866 841 3739, ⓦ mtvegas.com

The hugely successful **Venetian** opened in 1999 as a re-creation of owner Sheldon Adelson's honeymoon trip to Venice. Around a dozen of the city's landmarks squeeze side-by-side into the casino's Strip facade, while the principal echo of Venice in the opulent interior is the **Grand Canal** upstairs, where singing gondoliers take paying customers on short gondola rides ($16). There's also an outlet of **Madame Tussauds** waxwork museum, where you're free to take unlimited photos of, and with, your new-found waxy friends.

Although Adelson insists that the adjoining **Palazzo** is a distinct entity, it's effectively the same building as the *Venetian*, reached by broad internal walkways. Counted as a single unit, with more than seven thousand rooms, this would be the largest hotel in the world. Considered on its own, on the other hand, the *Palazzo* is among the least interesting casinos in town.

Wynn and Encore

Wynn 3131 Las Vegas Blvd S • ☎ 702 770 7000, ⓦ wynnlasvegas.com **Encore** 3121 Las Vegas Blvd S • ☎ 702 770 8000, ⓦ encorelasvegas.com

Steve Wynn, the man credited with inventing the new Las Vegas by opening first the *Mirage* and then *Bellagio*, built his own self-named resort, **Wynn Las Vegas**, in 2005. Having swiftly complemented it with **Encore** next door, he now runs two nominally distinct resorts on the same site.

Matching bronze crescents, soaring skywards, the two buildings are breathtaking. Wynn loves to fill his casinos with dazzling swathes of colour, so plush red carpets sweep through their interiors, meeting in a flower-packed central garden where trees are bedecked with fairy lights and lanterns. *Wynn's* most unusual feature is the **Lake of Dreams**, an expanse of water illuminated at night with changing projections, and peopled by mysterious mannequins. *Encore* is best known for its indoor-outdoor, day-night **Encore Beach Club**.

Circus Circus

2880 Las Vegas Blvd S • ☎ 702 734 0410, ⓦ circuscircus.com **Adventuredome** Daily 10am–midnight during school hols, otherwise Mon–Thurs 11am–6pm, Fri & Sat 10am–midnight, Sun 10am–9pm • Rides $5–8, all-day $28

The candy-striped big top of **Circus Circus** has loomed beside the Strip for half a century, but with its neighbours closing down and pedestrian traffic having dwindled to nothing, the casino these days feels all but forgotten. It does however hold Las Vegas's largest theme park, the **Adventuredome**, housed in a giant pink enclosure at the back and aimed very much at children.

The Stratosphere

2000 Las Vegas Blvd S • ☎ 702 380 7777, ⓦ stratospherehotel.com **Tower** Mon–Thurs & Sun 10am–1am, Fri & Sat 10am–2am • $18
Thrill Rides Mon–Thurs & Sun 11am–1am, Fri & Sat 11am–2am • X-Scream, Big Shot & Insanity $15 each; combination tickets including tower admission up to $34; SkyJump $110, minimum age 14 • ☎ 702 380 7711

A colossal landmark at the Strip's northern limit, the 1149ft **Stratosphere** is the tallest structure west of the Mississippi. Two observation decks offer fabulous views, while the top also serves as the launching point for several terrifying **Thrill Rides**. X-Scream is a giant boat that tips its passengers upside down; Insanity, a crane that spins riders out over the abyss; and Big Shot a glorified sofa that free falls hundreds of feet. Worst of all is the **SkyJump**, in which harnessed jumpers step off a platform to fall 855ft.

Downtown

Amounting as far as visitors are concerned to little more than three or four blocks, **downtown** is where Las Vegas started out when the railroad arrived in 1905, and also held its first casinos back in the 1930s. Although more recently the area has been overshadowed by the Strip, many visitors nonetheless prefer downtown, feeling that by

12

offering serious gambling, plus cheap bars, restaurants and buffets, its no-nonsense casinos represent the "real" Las Vegas. With its old-style neon signs and garish arrays of multicoloured lightbulbs, **downtown** also looks much more like the Las Vegas of popular imagination than does the high-tech Strip. In the artificial sky of the **Fremont Street Experience**, a canopy that covers four city blocks and lights up after dark in a dazzling light show of monsters and mayhem, it boasts a genuine must-see attraction.

The Mob Museum

300 Stewart Ave • Mon–Thurs & Sun 10am–7pm, Fri & Sat 10am–8pm • $18 • ☎ 702 229 2734, ⊛ themobmuseum.org

Opened in 2012, Las Vegas's **Mob Museum** is the latest bid by former mayor Oscar Goodman – who as a lawyer defended many underworld figures – to revitalize downtown as a tourist destination. It offers a fascinating chronicle of both the mobsters who once controlled the city and the lawmen who eventually brought them down.

Hoover Dam

Thirty miles southeast of the Strip • **Parking** Daily 8am–6.15pm; $7 **Visitor Center** Daily: April–Sept 9am–6pm; Oct–March 9am–5pm • $8 **Powerplant Tour** April–Sept 9.25am–4.55pm; Oct–March 9.25am–3.55pm • $11 including visitor centre **Dam Tour** April–Sept Mon–Thurs 9.30am–4pm, Fri & Sat 9.30am–4.30pm; Oct–March daily 9.30am–3.45pm • All-inclusive fee $30, no reductions, minimum age 8 • ☎ 702 494 2517, ⊛ usbr.gov/lc/hooverdam

Just under an hour's drive southeast of Las Vegas, the mighty **Hoover Dam** straddles the Colorado River. While this graceful 726ft-tall concrete marvel does not, as many visitors imagine, supply a significant proportion of the electricity that keeps Las Vegas running, its construction during the 1930s triggered the growth spurt, and the gambling boom, that created the modern city.

The main highway to Arizona, US-83, crosses the Colorado on a new bridge, slightly downstream from the dam. To see the dam itself, leave the highway via the spur roads at either end, park in the multistorey garage on the Nevada side, and walk down to the Visitor Center. Displays there explain the story and inner workings of the dam, but paying just a little extra entitles you to join a **Powerplant Tour**, and ride an elevator down to its base. The hour-long **Dam Tour** takes you right into its bowels, exploring its dank and mysterious tunnels.

ARRIVAL AND DEPARTURE   LAS VEGAS

By plane McCarran International Airport is a mile east of the southern end of the Strip, and 4 miles from downtown. Bell Trans (☎ 702 739 7990, ⊛ bell-trans.com) runs minibuses to the Strip ($7.50) and downtown ($10). Taxis typically charge around $20 to reach casinos at the southern end of the Strip, $30 or more for casinos further north or downtown.

By bus Long-distance Greyhound buses arrive at 200 S Main St downtown.

Destinations Albuquerque (2 daily; 13hr); Flagstaff (2 daily; 5hr 45min); Los Angeles (8 daily; 5hr 15min); Phoenix (2 daily; 9hr); Salt Lake City (2 daily; 8hr).

GETTING AROUND AND INFORMATION

On foot Traffic is so bad in Las Vegas that it's not worth renting a car just to explore the Strip. Be warned, though, that on summer days it's too hot to walk more than a couple of blocks.

By bus Both the most useful routes on the RTC network (⊛ catride.com) – the Deuce on the Strip (daily 24hr) and the faster Strip & Downtown Express or SDX (daily 9am–12.30am) – run the full length of the Strip and connect with downtown. Buy tickets before you board;

2hr pass $5, 24hr pass $7, three-day pass $20.

By monorail The overpriced and less-than-convenient Las Vegas Monorail runs along the eastern side of the Strip from the *MGM Grand* to the defunct *Sahara* (Mon–Thurs 7am–2am, Fri–Sun 7am–3am; single trip $5, one-day pass $12; ⊛ lvmonorail.com), but doesn't go to the airport or downtown.

Visitor centre 3150 Paradise Rd, east of the Strip, but not worth visiting (Mon–Fri 8am–5pm; ☎ 877 847 4858).

ACCOMMODATION

The fundamental choice for Las Vegas visitors is whether to stay one of the colossal mega-casinos on the Strip, which is home to twenty of the world's 27 largest hotels. Between them, these hold over 75,000 high-quality, and often very luxurious, rooms, but stays inevitably entail long queues to check in, a lack of personal service and endless walking to and fro. Downtown is smaller and on a more manageable scale, while finding a room elsewhere in the city is not recommended for anyone hoping to experience all that makes Las Vegas unique. Note that every room changes in **price** every night. A room that costs $49 on Wednesday may well be $199 on Friday and Saturday, so it's best to visit during the week rather than the weekend. Most hotels also charge so-called "resort fees", which cover internet access, phone calls and the like, and all hotel bills are also subject to an additional room tax of twelve percent on the Strip, and thirteen percent downtown.

THE STRIP

Aria 3730 Las Vegas Blvd S ☎ 866 359 7757 or ☎ 702 590 7111, ⓦ arialasvegas.com. If you're a modernist rather than a traditionalist, CityCenter's focal resort is the place for you. The rooms are classy rather than opulent, with great big beds and walk-in showers as well as tubs, but check-in tends to be slow. Resort fee $25. Mon–Thurs & Sun $169, Fri & Sat $259

Bellagio 3600 Las Vegas Blvd S ☎ 888 987 6667 or ☎ 702 693 7111, ⓦ bellagio.com. *Bellagio's* opulent rooms epitomize luxury, while its location and amenities can't be beaten. The premium rooms overlook the lake and its fountains, but the views from the back, over the pool are great too. Resort fee $25. Mon–Thurs & Sun $199, Fri & Sat $269

Caesars Palace 3570 Las Vegas Blvd S ☎ 866 227 5938, ⓦ caesarspalace.com. Contemporary comfort wins out over kitsch at *Caesars Palace* these days. The sheer scale can be overwhelming, but with its top-class dining and shopping, plus a fabulous pool and spa, it still has a real cachet. For serious luxury, pay extra to stay in the newer Augustus and Octavius towers. Resort fee $25. Mon–Thurs & Sun $209, Fri & Sat $299

Circus Circus 2880 Las Vegas Blvd S ☎ 800 634 3450 or ☎ 702 734 0410, ⓦ circuscircus.com. While *Circus Circus* is showing its age, if you don't plan to linger in your room, and have a car, its rock-bottom rates may prove irresistible. Pay a few dollars extra to stay in its two renovated towers, as opposed to the dingy Manor section. Resort fee $9. Mon–Thurs & Sun $29, Fri & Sat $94

★ **The Cosmopolitan** 3708 Las Vegas Blvd S ☎ 702 698 7000, ⓦ cosmopolitanlasvegas.com. Stylish contemporary casino where the guest rooms are classy and comfortable, with colossal beds, and all except the cheapest have Strip-view outdoor balconies. Resort fee $25. Mon–Thurs & Sun $180, Fri & Sat $270

Excalibur 3850 Las Vegas Blvd S ☎ 877 750 5464 or ☎ 702 597 7777, ⓦ excalibur.com. Cross the drawbridge to enter the Disney-esque castle, wheel your bag through the casino full of kids, and, so long as you pay a little extra for a renovated "wide-screen" room, you've found yourself a nice place to stay. Resort fee $15. Mon–Thurs & Sun $36, Fri & Sat $120

Luxor Las Vegas 3900 Las Vegas Blvd S ☎ 877 386 4658 or ☎ 702 262 4444, ⓦ luxor.com. It can still be a thrill to stay in one of the sizeable original rooms of this futuristic black-glass pyramid, but there's a reason rooms in the newer tower next door cost a little more – they're in much better condition, and have baths and/or jacuzzis

rather than showers. Resort fee $18. Mon–Thurs & Sun $65, Fri & Sat $125

Mandalay Bay 3950 Las Vegas Blvd S ☎ 877 632 7800 or ☎ 702 632 7777, ⓦ mandalaybay.com. Effectively a self-contained resort, well south of the central Strip. If you're happy to spend long days by its extravagant pool, and while away your evenings in its fine restaurants, bars, clubs and theatres, then it's well worth considering. Certainly the rooms are exceptionally comfortable, with both baths and walk-in showers. Resort fee $25. Mon–Thurs & Sun $90, Fri & Sat $160

MGM Grand 3799 Las Vegas Blvd S ☎ 877 880 0880 or ☎ 891 7777, ⓦ mgmgrand.com. The *MGM Grand* feels a bit too big for its own good; once you've queued to check in, and walked half a mile to your room, you may not feel up to venturing out to explore. Accommodation has been largely upgraded at the expense of its former character. Resort fee $25. Mon–Thurs & Sun $89, Fri & Sat $179

The Mirage 3400 Las Vegas Blvd S ☎ 800 374 9000 or ☎ 702 791 7111, ⓦ mirage.com. The casino that re-defined Las Vegas luxury now seems like a relatively modest choice, in that its rooms are smaller than the current norm, and the bathrooms even smaller. They're still more than comfortable, though, and enjoy excellent on-site amenities. Resort fee $25. Mon–Thurs & Sun $125, Fri & Sat $240

★ **New York–New York** 3790 Las Vegas Blvd S ☎ 866 815 4365 or ☎ 702 740 6969, ⓦ newyorknewyork.com. Las Vegas's own Big Apple makes a more appealing prospect than most of its larger, less compact neighbours. The guest rooms are attractive and readily accessible, with some nice Art Deco touches, and the casino holds some excellent bars and restaurants. Resort fee $18. Mon–Thurs & Sun $85, Fri & Sat $170

★ **Paris–Las Vegas** 3655 Las Vegas Blvd S ☎ 877 796 2096 or ☎ 702 946 7000, ⓦ parislasvegas.com. An ideal compromise – stay in a big-name property, with excellent amenities plus "only in Vegas" features like the Eiffel Tower outside your window – without paying premium prices for opulent fittings you don't really need. Resort fee $20. Mon–Thurs & Sun $93, Fri & Sat $201

Planet Hollywood 3667 Las Vegas Blvd S ☎ 866 919 7472 or ☎ 702 785 5555, ⓦ planethollywoodresort .com. Rooms in a style they call "Hollywood Hip" – which means black and gold carpets and wallpaper; movie stills on the wall; and walk-in showers as well as baths – in a great-value central location. Resort fee $20. Mon–Thurs & Sun $79, Fri & Sat $159

The Stratosphere 2000 Las Vegas Blvd S ☎ 800 998 6937 or ☎ 702 380 7777, ⓦ stratospherehotel.com. Too far to walk to from either the Strip or downtown, but at least something of a destination in its own right, even if its simple but sizeable rooms aren't in the 1000ft tower. Resort fee $7.50. Mon–Thurs & Sun $39, Fri & Sat $99

The Venetian 3355 Las Vegas Blvd S ☎ 866 659 9643 or ☎ 702 414 1000, ⓦ venetian.com. In the very top tier of Strip hotels, in terms of amenities in the property as a whole, as well as the sheer comfort in the guest rooms. All are suites; step down from the sleeping area, with its huge bed, to reach a sunken living space closer to the panoramic windows. Resort fee $20. Daily $209

Wynn Las Vegas 3131 Las Vegas Blvd S ☎ 877 321 9966 or ☎ 702 770 7000, ⓦ wynnlasvegas.com. The super-large rooms in Las Vegas's most definitively opulent property are tastefully decorated and equipped with ultra-luxurious linens, while the bathrooms feature marble tubs, walk-in showers and even TVs. Resort fee $25. Mon–Thurs & Sun $259, Fri & Sat $399

DOWNTOWN AND ELSEWHERE

The D 301 E Fremont St ☎ 702 388 2400, ⓦ thed.com. This central downtown hotel is a real bargain. All its rooms have had a top-to-bottom makeover and the amenities downstairs are much improved. No resort fee. Mon–Thurs & Sun $39, Fri & Sat $99

El Cortez 600 E Fremont St ☎ 800 634 6703 or ☎ 702 385 5200, ⓦ ecvegas.com. Long renowned as Las Vegas's cheapest casino, a short but potentially intimidating walk from the heart of Fremont Street. The "Vintage" rooms are no better than faded motel rooms, but the "Cabana" suites, across the street, are much more appealing. No resort fee. Mon–Thurs & Sun $28, Fri & Sat $68

The Golden Nugget 129 E Fremont St ☎ 800 846 5336 or ☎ 702 385 7111, ⓦ goldennugget.com. Downtown's classiest option is the only hotel hereabouts with amenities – like its amazing pool – to match the Strip giants. The actual rooms, at their freshest but loudest in the Rush Tower, are smart and comfortable, if not all that exciting. No resort fee. Mon–Thurs & Sun $69, Fri & Sat $129

Hard Rock Hotel 4455 Paradise Rd ☎ 800 473 7625, ⓦ hardrockhotel.com. If you're coming to mix with partying see-and-be-seen twenty-somethings, around the pool, bars and nightlife venues, then the *Hard Rock* will suit you perfectly. The rooms are cool and comfortable, and you can even open the floor-to-ceiling windows. It's too far from the Strip, though, to make a good base for the city as a whole. Resort fee $22. Mon–Thurs & Sun $62, Fri & Sat $249

Las Vegas Hostel 1322 E Fremont St ☎ 800 550 8958 or ☎ 702 385 1150, ⓦ lasvegashostel.net. Popular with young travellers, this converted motel is a mile east of downtown in an area where walking is unadvisable. Adequate bare-bones accommodation includes four-, six- and eight-bed single-sex and mixed dorms, and en-suite private rooms. There's a pool and hot tub, and the management organize tours. Dorms $13, doubles $36

EATING

Las Vegas used to be a byword for bad food, with just the occasional mobster-dominated steakhouse to relieve the monotony of pile'em-high buffets. Those days have gone. Every major Strip casino now holds half a dozen or more high-quality restaurants, run by top chefs from all over the world. Prices have soared, to a typical minimum spend of $50 per head at big-name places, but so too have standards, and you could eat a great meal in a different restaurant every night in casinos such as *Aria*, *Bellagio*, the *Cosmopolitan* and the *Venetian*.

BUFFETS

Bacchanal Buffet Caesars Palace, 3570 Las Vegas Blvd S ☎ 702 731 7778, ⓦ caesarspalace.com. The Strip's latest gourmet buffet, much the best at any Caesars-owned property, opened in 2012. It features 500 freshly-made items daily, from sushi, dim sum and phô soup to fresh oysters and wood-fired pizzas, prepared by chefs at nine "show kitchens". Dinner queues tend to be long, so it's best to come for lunch. Breakfast $20; lunch $25; champagne brunch $32; dinner $35, or $40 at weekends. Breakfast Mon–Fri 7–11am; lunch Mon–Fri 11am–3pm; champagne brunch Sat & Sun 7am–3pm; dinner daily 3–10pm.

Buffet Bellagio Bellagio, 3600 Las Vegas Blvd S ☎ 702 791 7111, ⓦ bellagio.com. The first "gourmet buffet" in town sparked standards and, less happily, prices to rise all over Las Vegas, and still features high-quality food for all meals. Even for breakfast ($17), besides the expected bagels, pastries and eggs, you can have salmon smoked or baked, fruit fresh or in salads, and omelettes cooked to order, with fillings such as crabmeat; lunch costs $20, and dinner $30, or $37 at weekends. Breakfast Mon–Fri 7–11am; lunch Mon–Fri 11am–4pm; brunch Sat & Sun 7am–4pm; dinner daily 4–10pm.

★ **The Buffet at Wynn** Wynn Las Vegas, 3131 Las Vegas Blvd S ☎ 702 770 7000, ⓦ wynnlasvegas.com. Buffets are always a high priority for Steve Wynn, and this is among the best in the city. In a plush room that oozes Belle Epoque excess, it's buffet food at its finest, with dishes from lamb osso buco and smoked duck salad, to cucumber and scallop ceviche and sushi rolls. On weekdays, breakfast costs $20 and lunch $23; weekend brunch is $32; and dinner is $37, rising to $40 on Fri & Sat. Breakfast Mon–Fri 8am–11am; lunch Mon–Fri 11am–3.30pm; brunch Sat

12

12

& Sun 8am–3.30pm; dinner Mon–Thurs & Sun 3.30–10pm, Fri & Sat 3.30–10.30pm.

★ **Le Village Buffet** Paris, 3655 Las Vegas Blvd S ☎702 946 7000, ⓦparislasvegas.com. Unique in focusing on a single cuisine – or rather, on French cuisine from Brittany to Provence – *Le Village* offers the most satisfying meal of any casino buffet. If you're partial to French meat or fish, or simply fancy a fresh baguette and all the cheese you can eat in a playful themed setting, don't miss it. Breakfast costs $19 on weekdays, $22 at weekends; weekday lunch is also $22; and both the weekend champagne, and dinner daily, cost $31. Breakfast Mon–Fri 7–11am, Sat & Sun 7–10am; lunch Mon–Fri 11am–3.30pm; brunch Sat & Sun 10am–3.30pm; dinner daily 3.30–10pm.

RESTAURANTS

Beijing Noodle No. 9 Caesars Palace, 3570 Las Vegas Blvd S ☎877 346 4642, ⓦcaesarspalace.com. Approached via aquariums that hold a thousand goldfish, and resembling a mysterious underwater cavern, this Chinese noodle shop is one of Las Vegas's most enjoyable places to eat. Fortunately, the food matches the setting, though with dim sum buns and dumplings at around $12, and the (large) noodle dishes more like $20, so too do the prices. Daily 11am–10.30pm.

★ **Bouchon** Level 10, Venezia Tower, The Venetian, 3355 Las Vegas Blvd S ☎702 414 6200, ⓦbouchon bistro.com. Thomas Keller's scrupulous evocation of a French bistro may not have the novelty value of the city's showier restaurants, but it's a lovely, relaxed spot, with plentiful outdoor seating and food that's nothing short of *magnifique*. Brunch is the best value, with sandwiches or quiche for under $20; dinner mains like steak frites or sole marinière cost $37. Mon–Fri 7am–1pm & 5–10pm, Sat & Sun 8am–2pm & 5–10pm.

Gordon Ramsay Steak Paris, 3655 Las Vegas Blvd S ☎702 946 7000, ⓦparislasvegas.com. For his first Las Vegas venture, perfectionist pottymouth Gordon Ramsay played it safe, opening a high-class steakhouse near *Paris's* main entrance. Diners select from a trolley laden

with marbled, aged slabs of prime meat; a superbly cooked veal chop costs $50, a strip steak $63, and the $125 tasting menu includes Beef Wellington. Daily 5–10.30pm.

Jean Phillippe Patisserie Bellagio, 3600 Las Vegas Blvd S ⓦjpchocolates.com. It takes rare self-discipline to walk past this extraordinary bakery without swooning at its central feature. The world's largest chocolate fountain swirls around the entire room, cascading through endless funnels and pipettes. The urge to stop for a $5 mug of hot chocolate, if not a coffee, crêpe, smoothie or pastry, is all but overwhelming. Mon–Thurs 7am–11pm, Fri–Sun 7am–midnight.

★ **Mon Ami Gabi** Paris, 3655 Las Vegas Blvd S ☎702 944 4224, ⓦmonamigabi.com. Among the first Las Vegas restaurants to offer alfresco dining, right on the Strip, this exuberant evocation of a Paris pavement brasserie remains the city's premier lunchtime pick. For a real taste of France, you can't beat a $13 croque madame (ham, cheese and egg sandwich) for breakfast; moules frites (mussels and chips) for lunch ($22); or steak frites for dinner ($25). Mon–Thurs & Sun 7am–11pm, Fri & Sat 7am–midnight.

★ **Oscar's Beef * Booze * Broads** The Plaza, 1 Main St ☎702 386 7227, ⓦplazahotelcasino.com. Perched in a glass bubble, staring down Fremont Street, this shameless cash-in by former mayor Oscar Goodman is a huge favourite with all who remember the old Las Vegas with affection. Primarily a New York-style steakhouse, serving top-quality filet mignon or bone-in steaks ($40-plus), it also has a full Italian-heavy menu of pasta, chicken and fish. Mon–Thurs & Sun 5–10pm, Fri & Sat 4.30pm–midnight.

★ **Scarpetta** Level 3, Cosmopolitan, 3708 Las Vegas Blvd S ☎877 893 2003, ⓦcosmopolitanlasvegas.com. It comes as a pleasant shock to pass through *Scarpetta's* unassuming entrance and find yourself confronted with panoramic windows overlooking the *Bellagio* fountains. Thanks to "new Italian" chef Scott Conant, the food is even better than the view. *Le tout* Las Vegas has flocked to enjoy appetizers like his $18 tuna "susci", and mains including short rib and marrow agnolotti ($25) or black cod ($32). For the full works, go for the $110 set menu. Daily 6–11pm.

DRINKING AND NIGHTLIFE

Every Las Vegas casino offers free drinks to gamblers. Sit at a slot machine or gaming table, and a cocktail waitress will find you and take your order; tips are expected. In addition, the casinos hold bars and lounges of all kinds; very few tourists venture further afield to drink. Strip bars tend to be themed, as with the Irish pubs of New York–New York; downtown they're a bit more rough-and-ready. A new generation of visitors is responsible for the spectacular growth in the city's **clubbing** scene. Casinos like the *Cosmopolitan* and *Wynn Las Vegas* now boast some of the world's most spectacular – and expensive – clubs and ultra-lounges.

Chandelier Cosmopolitan, 3708 Las Vegas Blvd S ☎702 698 7000, ⓦcosmopolitanlasvegas.com. Beneath the dazzling, dangling canopy of the eponymous two-million-crystal chandelier, the *Cosmopolitan's* centrepiece bar soars through three separate levels. On the enclosed middle floor,

reached via a glass elevator, where the action is, DJs entertain an excited, buzzy and generally young crowd. Casino level open 24hr, other levels hours vary.

Encore Beach Club Encore, 3121 Las Vegas Blvd S ☎702 521 4005, ⓦencorebeachclub.com. This luxurious multilevel complex of pools, patios, bars and private bungalows is the definitive expression of Las Vegas's craze for DJ-fuelled daytime poolside parties. Escape the crowds – bigger than ever thanks to Prince Harry's 2012 antics – either on pristine white "lily pads" out in the water, or in your own cabana, but the pounding music will follow you everywhere. Expect ultra-high prices for drinks, let alone table service. Cover $20–60. Late April to Oct Fri noon–7pm, Sat & Sun 11am–7pm.

Krave Massive Neonopolis, 450 Fremont St ☎702 836 0830, ⓦkravelasvegas.com. As *Krave*, the world's largest gay nightclub was until 2012 based on the Strip. It added *Massive* when it became downtown's first major club, taking over this colossal space in the Neonopolis mall. Its sheer scale is unbelievable; a former 14-screen movie theatre has been re-divided to feature four dance floors, including one devoted to hip-hop and one to Latin music, as well as three bars. Cover varies. Wed–Sat 10pm–4am.

★ **Marquee** Cosmopolitan, 3708 Las Vegas Blvd S ☎702 333 9000, ⓦmarqueelasvegas.com. Cutting-edge indoor-outdoor combination of a nightclub with a pool-centred "dayclub", created by the TAO group, with a 50ft-high main floor, home to regular gigs by the world's hottest DJs. Add in drinks, let alone table service, and you can expect to spend hundreds of dollars. The dayclub is smaller and more squashed-up than at *Encore*, but attracts bigger-name DJs and celebs. Cover varies $20–80. Nightclub Mon & Thurs–Sat 10pm–4am; dayclub daily 10am–7pm.

Minus5 Ice Lounge Mandalay Bay, 3930 Las Vegas Blvd S ☎702 740 5800, ⓦminus5experience.com. Funny, gimmicky bar that's exactly what it says it is – a bar in which every single thing is made of ice, from the walls to the glasses. Customers are loaned jackets, gloves and boots to tolerate the sub-zero temperature – yes, it's minus 5. Cover varies, typically $25 including one drink. Mon–Thurs & Sun 11am–2am, Fri & Sat 11am–3am.

Parasol Up, Parasol Down Wynn Las Vegas, 3131 Las Vegas Blvd S ☎702 770 7000. A quintessential example of the Wynn way with design, these twin upstairs-downstairs bars are festooned with richly coloured umbrellas. A cocktail or two, and you'll feel you're right at Las Vegas's absurd and exhilarating heart. Mon–Thurs & Sun 11am–4am, Fri & Sat 11am–5am.

ENTERTAINMENT

12

The Strip is once more riding high as the entertainment epicentre of the world. While Elvis may have left the building, headliners such as Celine Dion and Elton John attract thousands of big-spending fans night after night, and all the major touring acts pass through. Meanwhile the old-style feathers-and-sequins revues have been supplanted by a never-ending stream of jaw-droppingly lavish shows by the Cirque du Soleil, plus the postmodern likes of the Blue Men.

Big Elvis Harrah's, 3475 Las Vegas Blvd S ☎702 369 5000, ⓦharrahslasvegas.com. Las Vegas's biggest and best-loved Elvis impersonator, Pete Vallee, has a mastery of Elvis' repertoire and easy audience rapport that makes this the best free show in town. Free. Mon, Tues & Thurs–Sun 2–6pm.

Human Nature The Venetian, 3355 Las Vegas Blvd S ☎702 414 1000, ⓦhumannaturelive.com. The unlikely mission of this wholesome Australian vocal quartet, to add a down-under twist to the Motown sound, enjoys the personal blessing of Smokey Robinson himself. And no wonder – with their fabulous voices and very likeable energy, they really are superb. A smokin' live band plays the music, and the boys simply soar. $73–117. Mon & Thurs–Sun 7pm.

★ **Jubilee** Bally's, 3645 Las Vegas Blvd S ☎800 237 7469, ⓦballyslasvegas.com. Don't come to *Jubilee* expecting cutting-edge class. Come to enjoy the illusion that the last forty or so years never happened, and that high-kicking showgirls in ostrich feathers – and, for the late shows, no bras – still represent the pinnacle of world entertainment. There's nothing quite like it left, anywhere else in the city. $58–118. Mon–Thurs, Sat & Sun 7.30pm & 10.30pm (topless).

★ **Love** The Mirage, 3400 Las Vegas Blvd S ☎702 792 7777, ⓦcirquedusoleil.com. A genuinely triumphant collaboration in which Cirque perform superbly choreographed dancing and acrobatics to a crystal-sharp Beatles soundtrack, *Love* is much more than just another "jukebox musical". There's no story, and no attempt to depict the Beatles as actual people – though eerily we hear their voices in retrieved studio chatter – just a dazzling celebration of their music. $79–180. Mon & Thurs–Sun 7pm & 9.30pm

★ **Mystère** TI, 3300 Las Vegas Blvd S ☎702 894 7722, ⓦcirquedusoleil.com. Twenty years since it opened, Las Vegas's original Cirque du Soleil show is still arguably the best – you can see why it changed the Strip's entertainment scene forever, overnight. Pure spectacle, from the gorgeous costumes and billows of cascading silk to the jaw-dropping circus skills and phenomenal feats of strength. $69–119. Sat–Wed 7pm & 9.30pm.

★ **O** Bellagio, 3600 Las Vegas Blvd S ☎702 693 8866, ⓦcirquedusoleil.com. With no disrespect to the astonishing skills of Cirque du Soleil's divers and acrobats, the real star of this phenomenal long-running show is the theatre itself, which centres on a metal-mesh stage, all or any part of which can suddenly disappear underwater, making possible a dazzling array of death-defying leaps and heart-stopping plunges. $98.50–155. Wed–Sun 7.30pm & 10pm.

Terry Fator Mirage, 3400 Las Vegas Blvd S ☎ 702 792 7777, ⓦ mirage.com. Even if you dread seeing a ventriloquist, make an exception for Terry Fator. Yes, this ordinary middle-American guy swaps corny jokes with soft toys, but he also has an extraordinary talent – an astonishing

five-octave singing voice that delivers perfect impressions of artists from Aaron Neville to Garth Brooks, and Ozzy Osbourne to Etta James, all without moving his lips. $66–143. Tues–Sat 7.30pm.

Great Basin National Park

Lehman Caves visitor centre Daily: summer 8.30am–4pm; winter 9.30am–3pm • 1hr tours $8, 1hr 30min tours $10 • ☎ 775 234 7331, ⓦ nps.gov/grba

Just across the border from Utah, **Great Basin National Park** encapsulates the scenery of the Nevada desert, from angular peaks to high mountain meadows cut by fast-flowing streams. Guided tours from the visitor centre at **Lehman Caves**, five miles west of tiny **Baker**, explore limestone caves that are densely packed with intriguing formations. Beyond the caves, a twelve-mile road climbs the east flank of the bald, usually snowcapped **Wheeler Peak**, where trails lead past alpine lakes and through a grove of gnarled, ancient bristlecone pines to the 13,063ft summit. Off-track cross-country skiing is excellent in winter.

Elko

ELKO, the self-proclaimed last real cowtown in the West, straggles alongside I-80 a hundred miles west of Utah. Amid huge open cattle ranges, it's a fitting home for January's annual **Cowboy Poetry Gathering** (ⓦ westernfolklife.org), a get-together that celebrates folk culture and aims to keep alive the traditions and tales of the Wild West.

This area having been extensively settled by Basque shepherds in the nineteenth century, each Fourth of July weekend sees the 72-hour **National Basque Festival** (ⓦ elkobasque.com), in which hulking men throw huge logs at each other amid a whole lot of carousing and downing of platefuls of Basque food.

ACCOMMODATION AND EATING   **ELKO**

Star Hotel 246 Silver St ☎ 775 753 8696, ⓦ elkostarhotel.com. Two blocks south of the main drag, this simple family restaurant, steeped in local history, serves Basque cuisine such as cod for $18 as well as American staples including grilled steaks from $23. Mon–Fri 11am–2pm & 5–9.30pm, Sat 4.30–9.30pm.

Thunderbird Motel 345 Idaho St ☎ 775 738 7115, ⓦ thunderbirdmotelelko.com. Traditional, old-fashioned Western motel in the heart of downtown Elko, offering conventional but comfortable rooms plus a pool, at very reasonable rates. $59

> ### BURNING MAN
>
> Nevada's legendary **Burning Man Festival** is celebrated in a temporary, vehicle-free community known as **Black Rock City**, way out in the Black Rock Desert, twelve miles north of tiny Gerlach, which is itself a hundred miles north of Reno. It takes place at the end of August each year, in the week leading up to Labor Day. That's a very, very hot time to be out in the Nevada desert, particularly if, like perhaps half of the fifty thousand revellers, you're completely naked.
>
> The festival takes a different theme each year, always with a strong emphasis on spontaneity and mass participation. An exhilarating range of performances, happenings and art installations culminates in the burning of a giant human effigy on the final Saturday. After that, in theory at least, Black Rock City simply disappears without trace.
>
> For full information and the latest ticket prices, for which the standard rate is around $380 for the week, access ⓦ burningman.com. All visitors must buy tickets in advance; you can't pay at the gate. Only those who can prove total self-sufficiency are admitted; that means you have to bring all your water, food and shelter. The site holds no public showers or pools and its economy is almost entirely based on barter. No money can change hands, other than for coffee and ice.

12

Reno

The "biggest little city in the world", **RENO**, on I-80 near the California border, is a somewhat downmarket version of Las Vegas, with miles of gleaming slot machines and poker tables, along with tacky wedding chapels and quickie divorce courts. While the town itself may not be much to look at, its setting – at the foot of the snowcapped **Sierra Nevada**, with the Truckee River winding through the centre – is superb. The **casinos** are concentrated downtown, along Virginia Street on either side of the railroad tracks.

ARRIVAL AND DEPARTURE   RENO

By plane Reno-Tahoe International Airport is a couple of miles southeast of downtown. North Lake Tahoe Express (📞 866 216 5222, 🌐 northlaketahoeexpress.com) is among several local shuttle operators.

By bus Greyhound buses arrive at 155 Stevenson St.

Destinations Salt Lake City (2 daily; 10hr); San Francisco (5 daily; 5hr).

By train Amtrak trains call at 280 N Centre St downtown. Destinations Salt Lake City (1 daily; 10hr); San Francisco (1 daily; 9hr).

ACCOMMODATION AND EATING

Atlantis 3800 S Virginia St 📞 775 825 4700, 🌐 atlantis casino.com. Tower-block casino near the Convention Center, with rooms of all degrees of luxury and a dozen restaurants including *Toucan Charlie's* buffet, where lunch costs $13–15 and dinner $19–30. Mon–Thurs & Sun **$80**, Fri & Sat **$130**

Silver Legacy 407 N Virginia St 📞 775 325 7401, 🌐 silverlegacyreno.com. Among the older casino/hotels in downtown Reno, offering good-value rooms and dining and a flavour of old-style Nevada. Mon–Thurs & Sun **$70**, Fri & Sat **$100**

Carson City

Nevada state capital **CARSON CITY** stands thirty miles south of Reno, as you follow US-395 along the jagged spires of the **High Sierra** towards **Death Valley**. Named after frontier explorer Kit Carson in 1858, it holds a number of elegant buildings and a handful of world-weary casinos. The excellent **Nevada State Museum**, 600 N Carson St (Tues–Sun 8.30am–4.30pm; $8; 📞 775 883 6129), covers the geology and natural history of the Great Basin.

ACCOMMODATION AND EATING   CARSON CITY

Bliss Bungalow 408 W Robinson St 📞 775 230 0641, 🌐 blissbungalow.com. Comfortable, antiques-filled B&B in a restored Arts and Crafts house downtown, with five very pleasant en-suite rooms; the owners don't live on site, so you put together your own breakfast. **$75**

Hardman House 917 N Carson St 📞 775 882 7744, 🌐 hardmanhousehotel.com. A very decent budget option, with 62 bright, colourful motel rooms and friendly, helpful staff. **$55**

12

California

VIEW FROM BERNAL HEIGHTS PARK, SAN FRANCISCO

13

California

Publicized and idealized all over the world, California has a formidable reputation as a terrestrial paradise of sun, sand and surf, also boasting fast-paced, glitzy cities, primeval old-growth forests and vast stretches of deserts. While it's been the source of some of the country's most progressive movements, from the protests of the Sixties to modern environmentalist, civil rights and various reform activities, its economy has only just started to recover from the 2008–12 state budget crisis, bankruptcy narrowly avoided. Nonetheless, California's GDP remains bigger than that of most European countries, and regardless of its economic ups and downs, the "Golden State" retains an unbreakable grip on the world's imagination, thanks in large part to Hollywood.

California is far too large to be fully explored in a single trip – much will depend on what you're looking for. **Los Angeles** is easily the biggest and most stimulating city: a maddening collection of diverse neighbourhoods, from the Mexican and Japanese enclaves downtown and family fun of Disneyland to the glitz of Beverly Hills and craziness of Venice Beach, knitted together by miles of traffic-clogged freeways. To the south, the more conservative metropolis of **San Diego** has broad, welcoming beaches, great food and a renowned zoo, while further inland, the **deserts**, most notably **Death Valley**, make up a barren and inhospitable landscape of volcanic craters and saltpans that in summer becomes the hottest place on earth. Heading north, the **central coast** is a gorgeous run that takes in lively small towns such as **Santa Barbara** and **Santa Cruz**.

California's second city, **San Francisco**, is a European-styled jewel whose wooden Victorian houses and steep hills make it one of the world's most distinctive and appealing cities. To the east, mesmerizing national parks include **Yosemite**, where waterfalls cascade into a sheer glacial valley, and **Sequoia/Kings Canyon** with its gigantic trees, as well as the ghost towns of the **Gold Country**. North of San Francisco the countryside becomes wilder, wetter and greener, peppered with volcanic tablelands and verdant mountains.

As you might expect, a **car** is necessary for exploring much of California. A city such as Los Angeles couldn't exist without the automobile, and in any case driving down the coastal freeways in a sleek convertible is too much fun to resist. And if you plan to do any long-distance **cycling**, travelling from north to south can make all the difference – the wind blows this way in the summer, and the ocean side of the road offers the best views.

HWY-1

Highlights

❶ **San Diego food trucks** The city's lauded food truck scene offers everything from gourmet lobster and salmon tacos to hickory-smoked barbecue and Korean street food. **See p.821**

❷ **Venice Beach** LA's wacky seaside town is a real slice of California. **See p.836**

❸ **Joshua Tree National Park** The eerily twisted "arms" of Joshua trees beckon visitors to explore this long-abandoned desert mining country. **See p.850**

❹ **Mono Lake** A strange and remote sight that's well worth the trip – prime birdwatching

territory amid blue waters and gnarled tufa columns. **See p.855**

❺ **Yosemite National Park** Giant sequoias, towering waterfalls, the sheer face of Half Dome – your eyes will hardly get a rest. **See p.860**

❻ **Hwy-1** A thrilling, circuitous drive along the West Coast, with pounding Pacific surf and dramatic cliffside vistas. **See p.868**

❼ **Alcatraz** Eerie, legendary one-time maximum-security prison stuck out on "the Rock" in San Francisco Bay. **See p.882**

HIGHLIGHTS ARE MARKED ON THE MAP ON P.812

13 | ## Brief history

Spaniard **Juan Cabrillo** first sighted San Diego harbour in 1542, naming it **California** after an imaginary island from a Spanish novel, but in 1602 **Sebastián Vizcáino** bestowed most of the place names that still survive; his exaggerated description of **Monterey** as a perfect harbour led later Spanish colonizers to make it the region's military and administrative centre. Father **Junípero Serra** first established a small Catholic mission and *presidio* (fort) at San Diego, and by 1804 a chain of 21 missions, each a long day's walk from the next along the dirt path of *El Camino Real* (The Royal Road), ran from San Diego to San Francisco. Native Americans were either forcibly converted to Catholicism or executed, with disease killing off those who managed to survive the Spanish onslaught.

HIGHLIGHTS

1. San Diego food trucks
2. Venice Beach
3. Joshua Tree National Park
4. Mono Lake
5. Yosemite National Park
6. Hwy-1
7. Alcatraz

0 — 100 miles

CALIFORNIA

CALIFORNIA CLIMATES

The **climate** in **southern California** features seemingly endless days of sunshine and warm, dry nights, with occasional bouts of winter flooding. **Coastal** mornings can be hazy or overcast, especially in May and June. In **San Francisco** it can be chilly all year, and fog rolls in to spoil many a sunny day, though you can expect extreme variations in the **Bay Area** as a whole (you'll soon see why the locals talk about "microclimates" around here). Much more so than in the south, winter in **northern California** can bring rain for weeks on end. Most hiking trails in the **mountains** are blocked between October and June by the snow that keeps California's ski slopes among the busiest in the nation.

California becomes American

Mexico gained its independence in 1821, taking control of California, but **Americans** were already starting to arrive, despite the immense difficulty of getting to the Mexican state – three months by sea or four months by covered wagon. The growing belief that it was the **Manifest Destiny** of the United States to cover the continent from coast to coast, evident in the imperialist policies of President James K. Polk, soon led to the brief **Mexican-American War**. By January 1847 the Americans controlled the entire West Coast, and Spanish-speaking *Californios* were gradually marginalized. In 1850 California became the **31st state**.

The Gold Rush and the boom years

The **Gold Rush** of 1849 made not just California, but insured that the American West would be colonized in a matter of decades. A mere nine days before the signing of the treaty that ended the Mexican-American war, flakes of **gold** were discovered in the Sierra Nevada, leading to a rush of prospectors from all parts of the world. It took just fifteen years to pick the land clean of visible gold, and the **transcontinental railroad** was completed in 1869, linking the gold fields to the rest of the USA. Due to cut-rate rail prices and the lure of a dry, toasty climate and bountiful citrus groves, hordes of newcomers came from the Great Plains to Southern California and helped make Los Angeles the state's biggest city. Thanks to this migration, along with periodic real-estate booms and the rise of the **film industry**, California became the nation's fastest-growing state. Heavy industry followed during **World War II**, in the form of shipyards and aeroplane factories.

California in the modern world

As home to the **Beats** in the 1950s and the **hippies** in the 1960s, California was at the leading edge of global cultural change. The economic counterpart of this shift also developed when **Proposition 13**, in 1978, augured a national trend to dramatically cut taxes at the cost of government solvency (not resolved until the passage of **Proposition 30** in 2012 signalled a dramatic reversal). The 1980s saw further right-wing gains, with a string of laissez-faire Republican governors, and the 1990s crash-landed in economic scandal, a depressed housing market, rising unemployment, gang violence and race riots in LA – compounded by **earthquakes**, **drought** and **flooding**.

Some of the glow has further come off the golden state in the twenty-first century, but countless new **migrants** – many from Latin America – continue to arrive. One of these immigrants, Austrian **Arnold Schwarzenegger**, had the good fortune to become a well-paid action movie hero before taking his place as 38th California governor, and the misfortune to rule during the recent, severe economic recession, which helped weaken the state's economy and pop the unemployment rate above twelve percent. By 2013 the Democrats had a majority in both houses of the state legislature, and **Jerry Brown**, the Democratic governor who replaced Schwarzenegger in 2011, signed a balanced budget for the state, its first in years, ushering in what Californians hope will be the beginning of a sustained recovery.

13 # San Diego

Relatively free from smog and overbuilt freeways, **SAN DIEGO** is the second most populous city in California – affluent and libertarian, but also easy-going and friendly. In 1769 it was the site of the first Spanish mission in California, but the city only really took off with the arrival of the Santa Fe Railroad in the 1880s. During World War II the US Navy made San Diego its Pacific Command Center, but since the end of the Cold War the military sector had reduced dramatically; San Diego has since become a biotech industry hub and is home to telecommunications giant Qualcomm, founded here in 1985. However, it is San Diego's reputation as an ocean-oriented "resort city" that provides much of its current appeal, its long white beaches, sunny weather and bronzed bodies giving rise to the city's well-deserved nickname, "Sandy Ego".

Downtown San Diego

Loosely bordered by the curve of San Diego Bay and the I-5 freeway, **downtown** is, for those not headed straight to the beach, the inevitable nexus of San Diego and the best place to start a tour of the city. Various preservation and restoration projects have improved many of the older buildings, resulting in several pockets of stylish turn-of-the-century architecture. The tall Moorish archways of the **Santa Fe Railroad Depot**, at the western end of Broadway, are contiguous with the downtown branch of the **Museum of Contemporary Art**, or MCA San Diego, 1001 Kettner Blvd (daily except Wed 11am–5pm; $10; ☎858 454 3541, ⓦmcasd.org), a fine first stop for anyone interested in contemporary art with a California twist. Further east, **Broadway** slices through the middle of downtown, at its

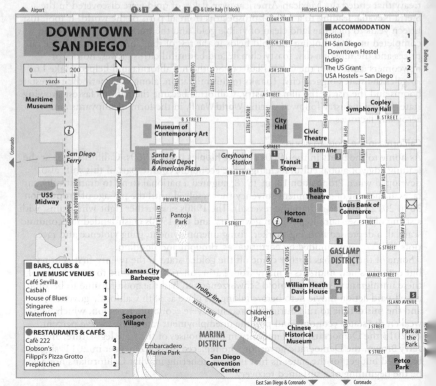

most lively between Fourth and Fifth avenues. Many visitors linger around the fountains on the square outside **Horton Plaza**, between First and Fourth avenues, south of Broadway (Mon–Fri 10am–9pm, Sat 10am–8pm, Sun 11am–6pm; ⓦwestfield.com/hortonplaza), a giant roofless mall of some 140 stores and, for better or worse, San Diego's de facto city centre. The complex's whimsical, postmodern style, loaded with quasi-Art Deco and Southwestern motifs, is inevitably a colossal tourist draw. A half-mile north of Broadway along India Street is the **Little Italy** district (ⓦlittleitalysd.com), mostly worth visiting for its restaurants and occasional festivals such as the late-May Sicilian Festival (ⓦsicilianfesta ,com) and mid-October Festa.

Gaslamp District

South of Broadway, a few blocks from Horton Plaza, lies the sixteen-block **Gaslamp District**, San Diego's original city centre, which later became a notorious red-light district, but is now filled with charming cafés, antique stores, art galleries and, of course, "gas lamps" – powered by electricity. A tad touristy it may be, but its late nineteenth-century buildings are dazzling and grandiose, best appreciated – and the area's general history gleaned – during the ninety-minute **walking tour** (Sat 11am; $15; ☎619 233 4692, ⓦgaslampquarter.org/saturday-walking-tours) that begins from the small cobbled square at Fourth and Island avenues. The square is within the grounds of the **William Heath Davis House**, 410 Island Ave (Tues–Sat 10am–5pm, Sun noon–4pm; $5; ☎619 233 4692, ⓦgaslampquarter.org), whose owner founded modern San Diego and had his New England saltbox-style home designed in modules in 1850 and shipped here via Cape Horn. Filled with photographs, each room commemorates a different historical period.

The bayfront

Along San Diego's curving, enjoyable **bayfront**, the pathway of the **Embarcadero** runs a mile or so along the bay, curling around to the western end of downtown; along this stretch, **Kansas City Barbecue** at 600 W Harbor Drive (daily 11am–2am; ☎619 231 9680, ⓦkcbbq.net) shamelessly milks the fact that the bar scenes from the popular 1986 movie *Top Gun* were filmed here. Beyond this lies the grey bulk of giant aircraft carrier **USS Midway**, 910 N Harbor Drive (daily 10am–5pm, last admission 4pm; $19; ☎619 544 9600, ⓦmidway.org), which shows off its formidable collection of naval hardware and weapons to the public, along with flight simulators and 29 restored planes, from Dauntless dive bombers to F-4 Phantoms.

Maritime Museum

1492 N Harbor Drive • Daily: June–Aug 9am–9pm; Sept–May 9am–8pm • $16 • ☎619 234 9153, ⓦsdmaritime.org

San Diego's **Maritime Museum** offers an enlightening look at shipping of past eras, with a collection of nine boats including the 1863 *Star of India*, the world's oldest active iron sailing ship, which began its career on the Isle of Man and then hauled working-class immigrants to New Zealand; the **Californian**, a modern replica of an 1847 US Revenue cutter; the **HMS Surprise**, a replica of an eighteenth-century, 24-gun frigate that served in the film *Master and Commander*; and an actual Soviet diesel submarine, the creaky old **B-39**.

Balboa Park

Buses #3, #7 and #120 from downtown; Balboa Park tram trolley (July–Oct Mon 8.15am–6.30pm, Tues–Sun 8.15am–8pm; Nov–June daily 8.15am–5.15pm; 8–40min; free) runs frequently between the main museums and the Inspiration Point car park on Park Blvd (also free)

Less than two miles northeast of downtown, sumptuous **Balboa Park** is one of the largest **museum enclaves** in the USA, as well as a delight for its landscaping, traffic-free promenades, and stately Spanish Colonial-style buildings. Near the centre, the **Spreckels Organ Pavilion** (concerts Sun 2–3pm; free; ⓦsosorgan.com) is worth a look as the home

13

BALBOA PARK MUSEUMS – SIX OF THE BEST

The **Balboa Park Passport**, a week-long pass that allows one-time admission to all fourteen of the park's museums and its Japanese garden (plus the San Diego Zoo, for an extra $35), is available for $53 from the visitor information centre (daily 9.30am–4.30pm; ☎619 239 0512, ⓦbalboapark.org), located in the House of Hospitality at 1549 El Prado.

Automotive Museum 2080 Pan American Plaza (daily 10am–5pm; $8.50; ☎619 231 2886, ⓦsdautomuseum.org). Classic motorcycles and cars, among them a 1948 Tucker Torpedo – one of only fifty left.

Museum of Man 1350 El Prado (daily 10am–4.30pm; open Sat–Sun till 5.30pm late-May to Aug; $12.50; ☎619 239 2001, ⓦmuseumofman.org). Huge anthropological museum containing Maya and Native American artefacts and Egyptian relics.

Natural History Museum 1788 El Prado (daily 10am–5pm; $17; ☎619 232 3821, ⓦsdnhm .org). Fabulous collection of fossils, hands-on displays of minerals and exhibits on dinosaurs and crocodiles.

Reuben H. Fleet Science Center 1875 El Prado (daily 10am–6pm; $13, kids 3–12 $11; including IMAX film $17/$14; ☎619 238 1233, ⓦrhfleet.org). Vast child-oriented museum of science-lite amusements with an IMAX theatre.

San Diego Museum of Art 1450 El Prado (Mon, Tues, Fri & Sat 10am–5pm, Thurs 10am–9pm, Sun noon–5pm; $12, Sculpture Court and Garden free; ☎619 232 7931, ⓦsdmart.org). Containing a solid stock of European paintings, from the Renaissance to the nineteenth century; highlights includeHals and Rembrandt.

Timken Museum of Art 1500 El Prado (Tues–Sat 10am–4.30pm; Sun noon–4.30pm; free; ☎619 239 5548, ⓦtimkenmuseum.org). Gallery containing a stirring collection of Russian icons and paintings including Rembrandt's *Saint Bartholomew*, Jacques-Louis David's portrait of Cooper Penrose and *Cranberry Harvest*, a masterpiece by Eastman Johnson.

---

of one of the world's largest organs, with some 4500 pipes. Most of the major museums (see box above) flank El Prado, the pedestrian-oriented road that bisects the park.

San Diego Zoo

2920 Zoo Drive • Daily: mid-June to early Sept 9am–9pm; early Sept to mid-June 9am–5pm • Day ticket including bus tours and Skyfari $44, kids (3–11) $34; combined ticket including Safari Park $79, kids $61; including SeaWorld $143, kids $113 • ☎619 231 1515, ⓦsandiegozoo.org

Easily one of the city's biggest and best-known attractions, **San Diego Zoo** lies immediately north of the main museums in Balboa Park and is generally regarded as the country's premier zoo. It's an enormous place, and you can easily spend a full day or more here, checking out major sections devoted to the likes of chimps and gorillas, sun and polar bears, lizards and lions, and flamingos and pelicans. There's also a **children's zoo**, with walk-through birdcages and an animal nursery, and the **Koalafornia Adventure**, highlighting Australian animals, added in 2013. Take a **guided bus tour** early on to get an idea of the layout, or survey the scene on the vertiginous **Skyfari**, an overhead tramway. Bear in mind that the zoo's beloved giant **pandas** Bai Yun, Gao Gao and their offspring spend a lot of time sleeping or being prodded by biologists in the park's Giant Panda Research Station. If you have access to a car you might want to consider visiting the associated **San Diego Safari Park** at Escondido (35 miles north; ⓦsdzsafaripark.org) – combo tickets are available.

Old Town

Old Town State Historic Park: 4002 Wallace St • Daily: May–Sept 10am–5pm; Oct–April 10am–4pm (tours daily 11am & 2pm) • Free • ☎619 220 5422, ⓦparks.ca.gov • Site is opposite the Old Town Transit Center, with Coaster, Trolley and MTS Bus service to downtown; by car, take I-5 and exit on Old Town Ave (exit 19), following the signs or from I-8 turn off onto Taylor St and left onto Juan St

Some four miles north of downtown, **OLD TOWN** is where the city of San Diego began. The area was preserved beginning in 1968, much of it within the **Old Town State Historic Park**, an illuminating (and free) living museum that commemorates San Diego in the Mexican and early American periods of 1821 to 1872. Featuring 25 structures, some of them original **adobes** displaying many of their original furnishings, the park has a working blacksmith shop, friendly burros and several small museums including the **Casa de Estudillo**, completed by the Mexican commander of the town, José Maria de Estudillo, in 1829.

Presidio Hill and around

In 1769, Spanish Franciscan friar Junípero Serra chose what's now **Presidio Hill** as the site of the first California mission, the **Mission San Diego de Alcalá**. The Spanish-style building now atop the Presidio Hill on the edge of Old Town is only a rough approximation of the original mission, but its **Junípero Serra Museum**, 2727 Presidio Drive (June to early Sept Fri–Sun 10am–5pm; early Sept to May Sat & Sun 10am–4pm; $6; ☎619 232 6203, ⊛sandiegohistory.org), offers an intriguing examination of the Franciscan padre who led the Spanish Catholic conversion of California. The **Mission Basilica San Diego de Alcalá** itself was relocated in 1774 six miles north to 10818 San Diego Mission Rd (daily 7am–7pm; free; ☎619 283 7319, ⊛missionsandiego.com), to be near a water source and fertile soils – and to be safer from attack. The present building is still a working parish church, while a small **museum** (daily 9am–4.45pm; free) holds a collection of Native American crafts and artefacts from the mission.

Ocean Beach and Point Loma

OCEAN BEACH, six miles northwest of downtown, is a fun and relaxed seaside suburb whose quaint, old-time streets and shops have preserved some of their funky 1960s character, though ongoing development has worn away some of their ramshackle appeal. The two big hangouts include **Newport Street**, where backpackers slack around at snack bars and surf and skate rental shops, and **Voltaire Street**, which true to its name has a good range of independent-minded local businesses. There is often good surf, and the beach itself can be quite happening – especially on weekends, when the local party scene gets cranking. South from the pier rise the dramatic **Sunset Cliffs**, a prime spot for twilight vistas.

Cabrillo National Monument

1800 Cabrillo Memorial Drive • Daily 9am–5pm, last entry 4.30pm • Seven-day pass $5/vehicle, $3/pedestrian or cyclist • ☎619 557 5450, ⊛nps.gov/cabr • From downtown, take bus #923 and switch to #28 in Ocean Beach

South of Ocean Beach, at the southern end of the hilly green peninsula of **Point Loma**, the **Cabrillo National Monument** marks the spot where Juan Cabrillo and crew became the first Europeans to land in California, albeit briefly, in 1542. The startling views from this high spot, across San Diego Bay to downtown and down the coast to Mexico, easily repay a trip here. A platform atop the western cliffs of the park makes it easy to view the November to March **whale migration**, when scores of grey whales pass by en route to their breeding grounds off Baja California. The nearby visitor centre (same as park hours) contains more information, and lies near the 1855 **Old Point Loma Lighthouse** (same hours), whose interior contains replica equipment from the 1880s.

SeaWorld San Diego

500 Sea World Drive • Daily: hours vary seasonally (at least 11am–5pm); mid-June to Aug 9am–11pm • $79, children (3–9) $71, parking $15; with San Diego Zoo & Safari Park $143 (kids $113) • ☎800 257 4268, ⊛seaworldparks.com

The giant amusement park of **Seaworld**, the San Diego branch of an entertainment colossus that stretches from California to Texas to Florida, is the city's most popular attraction for its undeniable kid-friendly appeal and especially its ensemble of ten **killer whales**. Along with various thrill rides, some of its spectacles include "Shamu Rocks", an unfortunate pairing of whales with flashing lights and rock music; Forbidden Reef,

13

stocked with moray eels and stingrays; the Wild Arctic, populated by walruses, beluga whales and polar bears; and the Shark Encounter, where sharks circle menacingly around visitors walking through a viewing tunnel.

Mission Beach and Pacific Beach

The biggest-name public beaches in San Diego are **Mission Beach**, the peninsula that separates Mission Bay from the ocean, and its northern extension, **Pacific Beach** – nightlife central for coastal San Diego. Enjoy nursing a beer at one of the many beachfront bars, or rollerblade or bike down **Ocean Front Walk**, the concrete boardwalk running the length of both beaches. A mile north of Pacific Beach's Crystal Pier, **Tourmaline Surfing Park**, La Jolla Boulevard at Tourmaline Street, is reserved exclusively for the sport, as well as windsurfing – but no swimmers are allowed. If you don't have a board, a good alternative is a few miles north at **Windansea Beach**, a favourite surfing hot spot that's also fine for swimming and hiking alongside the oceanside rocks and reefs.

Belmont Park

3146 Mission Blvd • June–Aug Mon–Thurs & Sun 11am–11pm, Fri & Sat 11am–midnight; March–May, Sept & Oct Mon–Thurs & Sun 11am–8pm, Fri & Sat 11am–10pm; Nov & Dec Mon, Thurs & Sun 11am–6pm, Fri & Sat 11am–10pm; Jan & Feb Fri & Sat 11am–10pm, Sun 11am–8pm • Most rides $2–6; unlimited park pass $26.95/day • ☎ 858 228 9283, ⓦ belmontpark.com

Near the southern end of Ocean Front Walk in Mission Beach, once-derelict **Belmont Park** has been renovated with modern rides, though the two main attractions are both from 1925: the **Giant Dipper** roller coaster (with a 73ft drop; $6), one of the few of its era still around, and the heated **Plunge Pool** ($7/day), once the setting for famous celluloid swimmers Johnny Weissmuller and Esther Williams.

La Jolla and farther north

Attracting the rich and famous since the 1950s, **La Jolla** (pronounced "La Hoya") remains an elegant beach community, thirteen miles northwest of downtown San Diego, though it's far less stuffy and more welcoming these days. Stroll its immaculate, gallery-filled streets, fuel up on California cuisine at one of the many street cafés, or visit the local branch of San Diego's **Museum of Contemporary Art**, 700 Prospect St (daily except Wed 11am–5pm; $10; ☎858 454 3541, ⓦmcasd.org), which has a huge, regularly changing stock of paintings and sculptures from 1955 onwards, and is especially good on California pop and minimalism. Nearby is the popular **La Jolla Cove** on Coast Boulevard (daily 9am–dusk; free), much of it an ecological reserve whose clear waters make it perfect for snorkelling (if you can find a parking space; aim for the $4/hr Coast Walk public parking on Coast Blvd, just off Prospect St).

Further north, the **Birch Aquarium at Scripps**, 2300 Expedition Way, off N Torrey Pines Rd (daily 9am–5pm; $17, teens [13–17] $14, kids [3–12] $12.50; parking free for 3hr; ☎858 534 3474, ⓦaquarium.ucsd.edu), has a wide range of highlights including the Hall of Fishes, a huge tank with a thick kelp forest home to countless sea creatures, and the smaller but revamped "ElasmoBeach" tank, displaying a range of fearsome leopard sharks and rays.

Torrey Pines State Natural Preserve

12600 N Torrey Pines Rd • Preserve Daily 7.15am–sunset (5–8pm) • Free (parking $12–15) **Visitor centre** Daily: May–Sept 10am–6pm; Oct–April 10am–4pm; guided nature walk Sat & Sun 10am & 2pm • ☎ 858 755 2063, ⓦ torreypine.org

Some eight miles north of La Jolla, Torrey Pines Road provides the only access (via a steep path) to **Torrey Pines City Beach Park** (aka **Black's Beach**), part of the **Torrey Pines State Natural Reserve**. It's the region's premier clothing-optional beach and one of the best and most daunting surfing beaches in Southern California, known for its huge barrelling waves during big swells. The state preserve protects the country's rarest species of pine, the Torrey Pine – one of two surviving strands. Thanks to salty conditions and stiff ocean breezes, the pines contort their 10ft frames into a variety of tortured, twisted shapes.

ARRIVAL AND DEPARTURE

SAN DIEGO

By plane San Diego International Airport (ⓦsan.org) is just 3 miles northwest of downtown. Metropolitan Transit System's Bus #992 (daily 5am–11.30pm; every 15min Mon–Fri, every 30min Sat & Sun; $2.25) connects with downtown and the Trolley, Coaster and Amtrak stations. Taxis are always available ($10–12 to downtown), and all major car rental desks are represented at the terminals.

By bus The Greyhound bus terminal is at 1313 National Ave (ⓣ619 515 1100), just east of Petco Park and conveniently located next to the 12th & Imperial Transit Center (for tram trolley and bus connections). Note that all

journeys to San Francisco (12–14hr) and Santa Barbara (6–7hr) require a change in Los Angeles.

Destinations Las Vegas, NV (1 daily; 8hr 40min); Los Angeles (17 daily; 2hr 10min–2hr 55min); Phoenix, AZ (2 daily; 8hr 20min–8hr 30min); Tijuana, Mexico (18 daily; 1hr 10min); Tucson, AZ (1 daily, 7hr 45min).

By train Amtrak trains use the Santa Fe Railroad Depot, close to the western end of Broadway at 1050 Kettner Blvd. Destinations Los Angeles (11 daily; 2hr 45min–3hr); San Juan Capistrano (11 daily; 1hr 24min–1hr 39min); Santa Barbara (4 daily; 5hr 35min–5hr 45min).

GETTING AROUND

Despite its size, **getting around** San Diego without a car is slow but not too difficult. Travelling can be harder at night, with most public transport routes closing down around 11pm or midnight. **Taxis** are also an affordable option: meters start at $2.80 and the average fare is anywhere from $6 for a jaunt around Downtown to $20–25 to get up to the more northerly beaches (Ocean, Mission or Pacific).

BUSES

The Metropolitan Transit System (MTS; ⓣ619 595 4555, ⓦsdmts.com) runs San Diego's bus system. One-way fares are $2.25–2.50; the exact fare is required when boarding (dollar bills are accepted).

Day Tripper Transit Pass These provided unlimited rides on most bus and trolley (see below) routes for one- to four-day visits ($5, $9, $12 and $15 respectively), available from the Transit Store (see below).

Transit Store 102 Broadway, at First Ave (Mon–Fri 9am–5pm; ⓣ619 234 1060); local bus timetables, free regional transport guides and travel passes. If you know your point of departure and destination, you can get automated bus information on ⓣ619 685 4900.

THE TRAM (TROLLEY)

Complementing county bus lines is the San Diego Trolley, often called the "Tijuana Trolley" because it travels to the US–Mexico border in San Ysidro. One-way tickets are $2.50. Of the three routes, the Blue Line is the more visitor-oriented, starting at Old Town and heading south to Little Italy and downtown San Diego, then on to the Mexican border. From the transfer station at Imperial and 12th, the trolley's Orange Line usefully loops around downtown, but offers little else of interest to visitors, darting out toward the eastern suburbs. The newer Green Line also reaches these suburbs, starting at Old Town, but is really only useful for visitors headed to Mission San Diego or Qualcomm Stadium.

Trams leave every 15min during the day (starting around 5am); the last service back from San Ysidro leaves at 1am, so an evening of south-of-the-border revelry and a return to San Diego the same night is quite possible.

THE COASTER

The North San Diego County coast is linked to downtown via a commuter light-rail system called The Coaster (ⓣ800 262 7837, ⓦgonctd.com/coaster). On weekdays, eleven trains run southbound from Oceanside to downtown (Santa Fe Depot), with the same number returning northbound (and an extra two trains on Friday night), while six trains make the trip on Saturday and just four on Sundays and holidays. Fares (from downtown) are $4 to Old Town, $5 to Sorrento Valley and $5.50 to all other stations ($12 for a day pass).

CYCLING

San Diego is a fine city for cycling, with many miles of bike paths. You can carry bikes on the San Diego Bay ferry and certain city bus routes for no charge. Board at any bus stop displaying a bike sign and fasten your bike securely to the back of the bus. See the ⓦthemappything.com, ⓦsdmba.com and ⓦsdcbc.org for an introduction to the scene.

Rental shops Bicycle Discovery, 742 Felspar St, Pacific Beach (Mon–Sat 10am–7.30pm, Sun 10am–5.30pm; $7/hr, $25/day; ⓣ858 272 1274, ⓦbicycle-discovery.com); Cheap Rentals, 3689 Mission Blvd, Mission Beach (daily 9am–7pm; $5/hr, $12/day; ⓣ858 488 9070, ⓦcheap-rentals.com).

INFORMATION

Visitor centre 1140 N Harbor Drive, in front of the B Street Cruise Ship Terminal (daily: June–Sept 9am–5pm;

Oct–May 9am–4pm; ⓣ619 236 1212, ⓦsandiego.org).

13

ACCOMMODATION

HOTELS, MOTELS AND B&BS

Beach Cottages 4255 Ocean Blvd, Mission Beach ☎ 858 483 7440, ⓦ beachcottages.com. Right on the beach, three blocks south of the pier, this relaxing spot offers a wide range of accommodation, from simple and rather frayed motel units to more elaborate cottages. Most have kitchenettes; all have fridges. Motel rooms $150, studios $240, cottages and apartments $295

Bed & Breakfast Inn at La Jolla 7753 Draper Ave ☎ 800 582 2466, ⓦ innlajolla.com. Designed in 1913 by early modernist Irving Gill, this is a collection of fifteen themed rooms – topped by the $425-a-night Irving Gill Penthouse, inexplicably decorated in Victoriana – with tranquil gardens and great service. It's close to the beach and art museum, too. $199

★ **Bristol** 1055 First Ave, downtown ☎ 619 232 6141, ⓦ thebristolsandiego.com. Excellent value at this friendly, central boutique hotel with stylish modern decor and tasteful amenities, plus iPod docks and flat-screen TVs. $135

Britt Scripps Inn 406 Maple St ☎ 888 881 1991, ⓦ brittscripps.com. Fetching Victorian inn located in a marvellously restored 1887 Queen Anne mansion near Balboa Park, with nine plush rooms offering antiques, flat-screen TV and some modern boutique touches, too. $205

Dolphin Motel 2912 Garrison St ☎ 866 353 7897, ⓦ dolphin-motel.com. The epitome of the roadside motel, in this case offering small, clean rooms with queen beds, and a good location roughly between Ocean Beach and Point Loma, within easy reach of the airport. Off-season rates can drop as low as $50. $80

Indigo 509 Ninth Ave, downtown ☎ 619 727 4000, ⓦ hotelinsd.com. Smart boutique digs in the Gaslamp District at a newish property that offers the usual business-class amenities plus special touches such as local art on the walls and rooftop terrace bar with a fire pit. $190

La Pensione 606 W Date St at India St, Little Italy ☎ 619 236 8000, ⓦ lapensionehotel.com. Good-value hotel within walking distance of the city centre. Minimalist-modernist rooms are small but equipped with microwaves, fridges and cable TV, and there's an on-site laundry. $120

The US Grant 326 Broadway, downtown ☎ 800 237 5029, ⓦ usgrant.net. Across from Horton Plaza, this has been downtown's poshest address since 1910, with grand Neoclassical design, chandeliers, marble floors and cosy but comfortable rooms and more capacious suites. The elegant ballrooms and swanky conference rooms are also worth a peek. $250

HOSTELS

HI-San Diego Downtown Hostel 521 Market St, at Fifth Ave, downtown ☎ 619 525 1531, ⓦ sandiego hostels.org. Centrally located, especially good for the Gaslamp District and Horton Plaza. Free breakfast and wi-fi, plus a library, kitchen and various organized trips to Tijuana and other places. Dorms $25, doubles $80

Ocean Beach International Hostel 4961 Newport Ave, Ocean Beach ☎ 619 223 7873, ⓦ californiahostel.com. Lively spot a block from the beach, offering barbecues, bike and surfboard rentals, airport transport and nightly movies. Free wi-fi, sheets, showers and continental breakfast. Dorms $20, doubles $105

★ **USA Hostels – San Diego** 726 Fifth Ave, between F and G sts, downtown ☎ 619 232 3100, ⓦ usahostels .com/sandiego. This well-placed hostel on the edge of the Gaslamp District is a converted 1890s building, with six to eight beds per room. Sheets, breakfast and wi-fi included, plus organized tours to Tijuana; this is one of the city's best hostels. Dorms $25, doubles $85

CAMPING

Campland on the Bay 2211 Pacific Beach Drive ☎ 800 422 9386, ⓦ campland.com. Of the city's half-dozen RV-oriented campgrounds, very few accept tents. This is the best option; basic pitches are available, starting at $45; pitches at larger, more elaborate sites with more amenities can run to $450. Pools and hot tubs, as well as a marina, activity rentals and a general store on site. $45

EATING

★ **Cafè 222** 222 Island Ave at Second Ave, downtown ☎ 619 236 9902, ⓦ cafe222.com. Hip café serving some of the city's best breakfasts and lunches, with excellent pancakes, French toast and pumpkin-and-peanut-butter waffles, and inventive twists on traditional sandwiches and burgers (including vegetarian), at reasonable prices (most mains $7–10). Daily 7am–1.45pm.

Dobson's 956 Broadway Circle, downtown ☎ 619 231 6771, ⓦ dobsonsrestaurant.com. This elegant restaurant in an old two-tier building is a San Diego institution, loaded with business types in power ties. The cuisine leans toward continental, from crab hash and oyster salad to flatiron steak and rack of lamb (mains $16–39). Owner Paul Dobson is actually a professional bullfighter (fights are still held in Tijuana). Mon–Fri 11.30am–10pm, Sat 5–10pm.

Filippi's Pizza Grotto 1747 India St, Little Italy ☎ 619 232 5094. A good spot for affordable favourites like thick, chewy pizzas and pasta dishes, including a fine lasagne ($8–10). Meals are served in a small room at the back of an Italian deli. Daily 11am–10pm.

★ **Hodad's** 5010 Newport Ave, Ocean Beach ☎ 619 224 4623, ⓦ hodadies.com. In business in one spot or another since 1969, this is one place in town you can get

SAN DIEGO'S GOURMET FOOD TRUCKS

Don't leave San Diego without sampling the city's dynamic **food truck** scene; these ain't your average kebab vans. Always check Twitter feeds (listed on the websites) for the latest locations, times and menus (see also Ⓦ sdfoodtrucks.com).

Devilicious Ⓦ deviliciousfoodtruck.com. Already a San Diego institution, with its signature butter-poached lobster grilled cheese sandwich a real treat.
Miho Gastrotruck Ⓦ mihogastrotruck.com. Top-quality farm-to-table truck, with an ever-changing menu that might feature Californian salmon tacos and fried chicken with biscuits.

Super Q Food Truck Ⓦ superqfoodtruck.com. Hickory-smoked BBQ comes to San Diego; magnificent brisket, pulled pork and crispy sweet potato fries.
Tabe BBQ Ⓦ tabebbq.com. Some of the best Asian-fusion street food in the whole country: think char-grilled pork or beef marinated in a traditional, spicy Korean sauce.

a damn fine burger, whether it comes straight up (from $5.25) or includes cheese ($6.75), tuna or veggies (both $6.25). Fries and rings complete a meal at this cheap, justly popular spot. Mon–Thurs & Sun 11am–9pm, Fri & Sat 11am–10pm.

★ **Karl Strauss Brewery & Restaurant** 1044 Wall St, La Jolla ☎ 858 551 2739, Ⓦ karlstrauss.com. La Jolla's neighbourhood brewpub knocks out excellent craft beers to wash down perfectly grilled burgers ($12.50) and beer-brined chops ($19.95). Daily 11am–10pm.

Marketplace Deli 2601 Fifth Ave ☎ 619 239 8361. Just south of Hillcrest near the entrance to Balboa Park, this is a winner for its prime pizzas and sandwiches ($5–7), and especially the Reuben, with pastrami, sauerkraut and cheese on rye bread. Also offers good tuna melts and pasta salads, at easy-to-swallow prices. Daily 11am–3pm.

Old Town Mexican Café 2489 San Diego Ave, Old Town ☎ 619 297 4330, Ⓦ oldtownmexcafe.com. Among the better Mexican diners in Old Town, where the crowds queue up for the likes of pozole soup and *carne asada*

tacos; apart from at breakfast, you'll probably have to wait for a table. Tacos are just $2 on "Taco Tuesdays" (margaritas $2.50). Mon–Thurs & Sun 7am–11pm, Fri & Sat 7am–2am.

Point Loma Seafoods 2805 Emerson St, Point Loma ☎ 619 223 1109, Ⓦ pointlomaseafoods.com. Mid-priced counter serving up San Diego's freshest fish in a basket, with good platters and seafood cocktails, along with mean crab cake and scallop sandwiches (from $8.80). With views across the bay to Downtown, this popular joint is packed at weekends; don't even try to find an adjacent parking spot. Mon–Thurs 9am–7pm, Fri & Sat 9am–8pm, Sun 10am–8pm.

★ **Prepkitchen** 1660 India St, Little Italy ☎ 619 398 8383, Ⓦ prepkitchen.com. Part of another local mini-chain specializing in creative small plates, from bacon-wrapped dates ($9.75) to local fish tacos ($12.25). Mon–Thurs 11.30am–3pm & 5–10pm, Fri 11.30am–3pm & 5–10.30pm, Sat 10am–3pm & 5–10.30pm, Sun 10am–3pm & 5–10pm.

NIGHTLIFE AND ENTERTAINMENT

San Diego has a respectable range of **bars**, with the Gaslamp District being a good place to get dressed up for cocktails or for pure sports-bar swilling. The beach communities offer a more rowdy atmosphere, abetted by plenty of beer and loud music. Since the 1990s the city and surrounding area has also developed a reputation for **microbreweries** (or "craft beer") – if you like beer make sure you check out the local brews.

BARS AND CLUBS

★ **AleSmith Brewing Co** 9368 Cabot Drive (I-15 exit 14) ☎ 858 549 9888, Ⓦ alesmith.com. A bit of a hike (it's 9 miles inland from La Jolla), but this is a top-notch microbrewery with a huge selection of Belgian-style ales on tap; organize transport in advance (free tours of the brewery every Sat at 2pm). Tues–Thurs 2–8pm, Fri noon–9pm, Sat 11am–8pm, Sun 11am–6pm.

The Alibi 1403 University Ave, Hillcrest ☎ 619 295 0881. The place to hit when you just want to get drunk – a classic dive bar with potent drinks, pool tables, occasional live acts and grungy but cosy decor. Daily 8am–2am.

Café Sevilla 353 Fifth Ave, downtown (Gaslamp District)

☎ 619 233 5979, Ⓦ cafesevilla.com. Traditional Spanish cuisine and tapas upstairs, hip Latin American-style club downstairs, with salsa and Spanish grooves to dance to, and flamenco performances to keep you entertained. Mon 5pm–midnight, Tues–Fri 5pm–1.30am, Sat 11.30am–1.30pm & 5pm–1.30am, Sun 11am–11pm.

Stingaree 454 Sixth Ave, downtown (Gaslamp District) ☎ 619 544 9500, Ⓦ stingsandiego.com. Three-storey luxury club in a historic warehouse, with restaurant, floor-to-ceiling waterfalls and cool, jungly rooftop bar. To party with the likes of the Kardashians you'll need to glam up and pay up ($12 for drinks). Fri & Sat cover $20–30. Mon & Wed–Sat 5pm–2am.

13

Waterfront 2044 Kettner Blvd, Little Italy ☎619 232 9656, ⊕waterfrontbarandgrill.com. A mixed bag of working-class boozers and slumming hipsters are drawn to this old-time Little Italy joint for burgers, fish'n'chips and bar food, and a festive atmosphere. An essential stop to see the real drinker's San Diego. Daily 6am–2am.

LIVE MUSIC VENUES

Brick by Brick 1130 Buenos Ave, Mission Bay (6 miles north of downtown) ☎619 675 5483, ⊕brickbybrick .com. Cool lounge that's one of the better-known indie spots around town, attracting a broad mix of local indie rock, metal, hip-hop and burlesque acts. Most shows $5–10. Wed–Sun 2pm–2am.

★ **Casbah** 2501 Kettner Blvd, Little Italy ☎619 232 4355, ⊕casbahmusic.com. If you're up for a night of hipstering, this is a good spot to begin – a grungy joint that nevertheless hosts a solid, varying roster of blues, funk, reggae, rock and indie bands. Despite the cramped interior, it's popular with locals. Daily 8pm–midnight.

Dizzy's 4275 Mission Bay Drive, Pacific Beach ☎858 270 7467, ⊕dizzysjazz.com. As the name suggests, this joint is devoted to straight-up jazz and little else – literally, because gigs are held in the San Diego Jet Ski Rentals showroom, forcing you to focus on the music instead of chatting over dinner and cocktails. Cover $15–20 (cash only). See website for show times.

House of Blues 1055 Fifth Ave, downtown ☎619 299 2583, ⊕houseofblues.com. The heavyweight on the local concert scene, drawing big-name rock and pop acts. The environment's a little too well scrubbed – as are the bands – but you can sometimes see a good show here. Don't miss the Bead Wall, an entire wall covered in Mardi Gras beads from New Orleans. Daily 4–11pm.

Humphrey's by the Bay 2421 Shelter Island Drive, Point Loma ☎619 220 8497, ⊕humphreysconcerts .com. Also including a restaurant, this mainstream concert venue draws a range of mellow, agreeable pop, blues, jazz, country, folk and lite-rock acts, often of national calibre. Times vary according to show.

Los Angeles

Thanks to Hollywood, most people on the planet have at least heard of **LOS ANGELES**. The City of Angels, Tinseltown or just "La-La Land" is the home of the world's movie and entertainment industry, the palaces of Beverly Hills, Sunset Strip, the original Disneyland, the Dodgers and the Lakers and a beach culture that inspired California's modern surfing boom in the 1950s. Yet first-time visitors should expect some surprises, beginning with the vast size of the place, hard to absorb until you actually get here. LA is only America's second biggest city in terms of population, but stitched together by an intricate network of freeways crossing a thousand square miles of widely varying architecture, social strata and cultures. Beyond the skyscrapers, **downtown LA** actually has an historic Mexican heart and is a traffic-clogged sixteen miles from the hip ocean enclaves of **Santa Monica** and **Venice Beach** – and thanks to high crime and gangster rap, South Central LA and Compton have become bywords for violence and gangs such as the Crips and the Bloods. West from downtown, **Hollywood** has streets imbued with movie myths and legends – and adjoining **West LA** is home to the city's newest money, shown off in Beverly Hills and along the Sunset Strip.

Suburban **Orange County**, to the southeast, holds little of interest apart from **Disneyland**, a few museums and a handful of libertine beach towns. On the far side of the northern hills lie the **San Gabriel and San Fernando valleys**, or simply "the Valley", where tract homes and strip malls are enlivened by occasional sights of interest, many of them in genteel **Pasadena**.

Downtown LA

Since the opening of the **Staples Center** in 1999, **Downtown LA** has been experiencing something of a renaissance, with many of its graceful old banks and hotels turned into apartments and the enormous **LA Live** complex opening in 2008. It remains a diverse neighbourhood however, with, in the space of a few blocks, adobe buildings and Mexican market stalls, **skid row** (one of the highest concentrations of homeless people in the USA), Japanese shopping plazas and avant-garde art galleries.

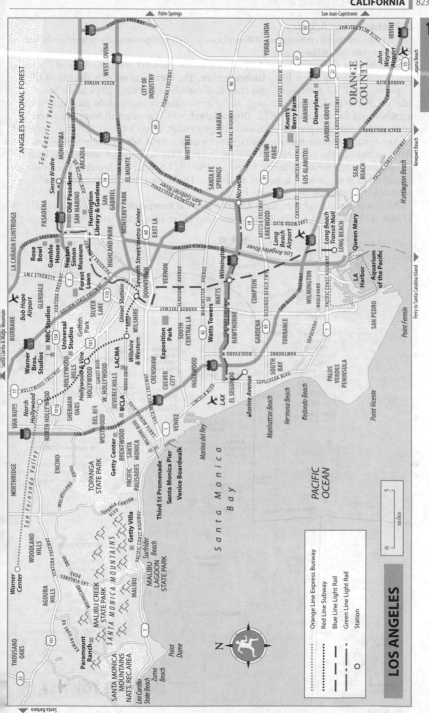

LOS ANGELES

Palm Springs ▲

San Juan Capistrano ▲

Santa Barbara ▲

Santa Clarita & Magic Mountain ▲

Ferry to Santa Catalina Island ▲

Laguna Beach ▶
Newport Beach ▶
Huntington Beach ▶

ANGELES NATIONAL FOREST

ORANGE COUNTY

Legend:
· · · · · · Orange Line Express Busway
· · · · · · Red Line Subway
— — — Blue Line Light Rail
- ○ - Green Line Light Rail
○ Station

0 miles 5

N

13 El Pueblo de Los Angeles

Paseo de la Plaza, and N Main St · **Visitor centre** E 10 Olvera St · Free · ☎ 213 628 1274, ⓦ elpueblo.lacity.org **Tours** Tues–Sat 10am, 11am & noon; 50min · Free · ⓦ lasangelitas.org

LA was born at **El Pueblo de Los Angeles**, an historic district centred on the old plaza just across Alameda Street from **Union Station**. The **Plaza** was roughly the site of the city's original 1781 settlement, and the plaza church **La Placita**, 535 N Main St (daily 6.30am–8pm; ⓦ laplacita.org), is the city's oldest, a small adobe structure with a gabled roof dating back to 1822. **Olvera Street**, which runs north from the plaza, contrived in part as a pseudo-Mexican village market, offers a cheery collection of food and craft stalls. Among the historic structures here is **Avila Adobe** (daily 9am–4pm; free), technically the city's oldest building (from 1818), although it was almost entirely rebuilt out of reinforced concrete following the 1971 Sylmar earthquake. The house is furnished as it might have appeared in the late 1840s, and the courtyard outside contains the **visitor centre** (see p.841).

Other worthwhile sights include **América Tropical Interpretive Center** in Sepulveda House, 125 Paseo de La Plaza (enter from Olvera St; Tues–Sun 10am–3pm; free;

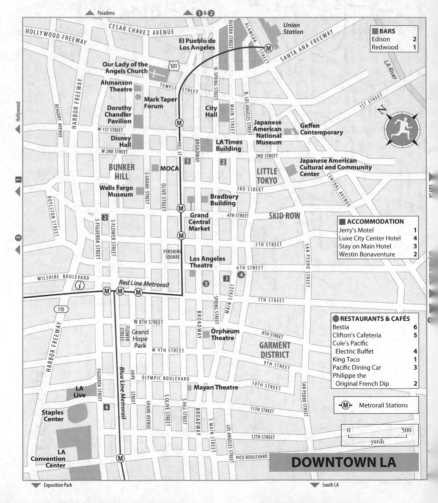

213 485 6855, ⓦamericatropical.org), which preserves and interprets the epic 80ft-by-18ft *América Tropical* mural by David Siqueiros, one of the greatest Mexican artists of the twentieth century, and the **Garnier Building**, now the **Chinese American Museum**, 425 N Los Angeles St (Tues-Sun 10am-3pm; suggested admission $3; ☎213 485 8567, ⓦcamla.org). Inside, local Chinese history, society and culture is detailed, including revealing letters, photos and documents, as well as a smattering of contemporary art and the re-creation of a Chinese herb shop from c.1900.

Civic Center

South from the Plaza, across the Santa Ana Freeway, the municipal-government core of the **Civic Center** offers three of the city's most notable buildings. **City Hall**, 200 N Spring St (public entrance at 201 Main St; observation deck Mon–Fri 9am–5pm; free; ☎213 978 1059, ⓦlacity.org) is an iconic, classically styled tower that's been visible in films from *Dragnet* to *Superman*. You can get a good look at the inside of the building for free, including its 28th-storey 360-degree observation deck. To the west, **Walt Disney Concert Hall**, First Street at Grand Avenue, is Frank Gehry's grand spectacle of modern architecture, a 2300-seat acoustic showpiece with a curvaceous, stainless-steel exterior and an interior with rich, warm acoustics and a mammoth, intricate pipe organ. Self-guided **audio tours** (1hr; narrated by actor John Lithgow) are the easiest way to explore the hall and are offered most days from 10am to 2pm for free; days vary for the free one-hour **guided tours**, which run at noon and 1pm. Visit ⓦmusiccenter.org for the latest schedule. Note that no tours include the actual auditorium – for that you'll have to see a show.

Bunker Hill

Until a century ago the area south of the Civic Center, **Bunker Hill**, was LA's most elegant neighbourhood, but after a half-century of decay, 1960s urban renewal transformed it into the imperious **Financial District**, with colossal new towers. At the base of the towering Wells Fargo Center at 333 S Grand Ave sits the **Wells Fargo History Museum** (Mon–Fri 9am–5pm; free; ☎213 253 7166, ⓦwellsfargohistory.com) charting the history of Wells Fargo & Co, the banking colossus that was founded in Gold Rush California, with old mining equipment, antiques, photographs, a two-pound chunk of gold, a re-created assay office from the nineteenth century and a simulated stagecoach journey from St Louis to San Francisco. Two blocks south at 633 W 5th St, the **US Bank Tower** (1018ft), completed in 1989, is still the tallest building on the West Coast.

Museum of Contemporary Art

250 S Grand Ave • Mon & Fri 11am–5pm, Thurs 11am–8pm, Sat & Sun 11am–6pm • $12; free Thurs 5–8pm; includes admission to the Geffen Contemporary at MOCA • ☎213 626 6222, ⓦmoca.org

The main highlight in the Financial District today is the **Museum of Contemporary Art** (MOCA), which was designed by showman architect Arata Isozaki as a vivid array of reddish geometric blocks. In addition to work by Mark Rothko, Robert Rauschenberg and Claes Oldenburg, and some eye-opening temporary exhibits, it features an impressive selection of **Southern California artists**, ranging from Lari Pittman's spooky, sexualized silhouettes to Robert Williams' feverishly violent and satiric comic-book-styled paintings.

Little Tokyo and around

East of Bunker Hill, **Little Tokyo** is an appealing collection of historic sites, restaurants and galleries, centred around the **Japanese Village Plaza** (most stores daily 9am–6pm; ⓦjapanesevillageplaza.net), a touristy outdoor mall at 335 E 2nd St and Central Avenue. Nearby, the comprehensive **Japanese American National Museum**, 100 N Central Ave (Tues, Wed & Fri–Sun 11am–5pm, Thurs noon–8pm; $9; ☎213 625 0414, ⓦjanm.org), houses exhibits on everything from origami to traditional furniture

13

and folk craftwork to the story of the internment of Japanese Americans during World War II. Just north and set in a former police garage renovated by Frank Gehry, the **Geffen Contemporary at MOCA**, 152 N Central Ave (Mon & Fri 11am–5pm, Thurs 11am–8pm, Sat & Sun 11am–6pm; $12; free Thurs 5–8pm; includes admission to MOCA; ☎213 626 6222, ⓦmoca.org), is used for the edgier temporary shows of the Museum of Contemporary Art.

Broadway

Broadway was once LA's most fashionable shopping and entertainment district, but today it's largely taken over by the hustle and bustle of Hispanic clothing and trinket stores, all to a soundtrack of blaring salsa music. You can sample a vivid taste of the area at the **Grand Central Market**, between Third and Fourth streets (daily 9am–6pm; ⓦgrandcentralsquare.com), where you'll find everything from apples and oranges to pickled pig's feet and ice cream. Right alongside, the whimsical terracotta facade of the 1918 **Million Dollar Theater** mixes buffalo heads with bald eagles. It was seen in the film *Blade Runner*, as was the neighbouring 1893 **Bradbury Building**, no. 304 (lobby open Mon–Sat 9am–5pm; free), featuring a magnificent sunlit atrium surrounded by stylish wrought-iron balconies and open-cage elevators.

LA Live and the Grammy Museum

800 W Olympic Blvd • ☎213 763 6030, ⓦlalive.com

The southwest corner of downtown LA is dominated by the Staples Center arena and retail behemoth **LA Live**, a $2.5-billion shopping and entertainment complex that features cinemas, sports facilities and broadcast studios, upper-end hotels, a central plaza, a bowling alley and numerous arcades, restaurants and clubs. It also contains the absorbing **Grammy Museum** (Mon–Fri 11.30am–7.30pm, Sat & Sun 10am–7.30pm; $12.95, $8 after 6pm; ☎213 765 6800, ⓦgrammymuseum.org), not just devoted to the Grammy Awards (America's most prestigious music awards), but recorded music in general, with interactive displays over four floors including the Songwriters Hall of Fame, stage outfits and exhibits on Ray Charles and Sam Cooke, personal artefacts from Elvis Presley, Miles Davis and Neil Diamond, and a real recording studio.

South LA

South LA comprises such notable neighbourhoods as **Watts**, **Compton** and **Inglewood**, but beyond the **USC campus** and **Exposition Park** hardly ranks on the tourist circuit – especially since it burst onto the world's TV screens as the focal point of the April 1992 **riots**. It's better known as **South Central**, but LA City Council voted to change the name in 2003 in the hopes of disassociating the area with connotations of gang violence and economic depression. It's generally a place to visit with caution or with someone who knows the area, though it's safe enough in daytime around the main drags.

Exposition Park

700 Exposition Park Drive • Free (parking $10/day) • ☎213 744 7458, ⓦexpositionpark.org

Across Exposition Boulevard from the fortress-like USC campus, **Exposition Park** incorporates lush landscaped gardens and a number of enticing museums. The family-oriented **California Science Center**, off Figueroa Street at 700 State Drive (daily 10am–5pm; free; ☎323 724 3623, ⓦcaliforniasciencecenter.org), contains enjoyable working models and thousands of gadgets to keep the children distracted, with an **IMAX Theatre** ($8.25, kids $5) and since 2012 the retired **Space Shuttle Endeavour**, with an excellent accompanying exhibition (timed tickets required; free). On the east side of the park, the **California African American Museum**, 600 State Drive (Tues–Sat 10am–5pm, Sun 11am–5pm; free; parking $10; ☎213 744 7432, ⓦcaamuseum.org), has stimulating exhibits on the history and culture of America's black communities.

13

Natural History Museum of Los Angeles County

900 Exposition Blvd • Daily 9.30am–5pm • $12, kids (3–12) $5; parking $8 • ☎ 213 763 3466, Ⓦ nhm.org

The **Natural History Museum of Los Angeles County**, with its echoey domes and travertine columns, has a tremendous stock of dinosaur skeletons, which include the skull of a Tyrannosaurus rex and the frame of a huge flightless bird. In the fascinating **California History Hall** the creation and development of LA is charted with a series of dioramas from the 1930s and Walt Disney's animation stand from 1923. The seasonal **Butterfly Pavilion** (mid-April to early Sept) and **Spider Pavilion** (mid-Sept to early Nov) require timed tickets (both an extra $15).

The Watts Towers

1765 E 107th St • Tours (30min) every 30min Thurs–Sat 10.30am–3pm, Sun 12.30–3pm • $7 • ☎ 213 847 4646, Ⓦ wattstowers.org • Metro Blue Line to 103rd St/Watts Towers

The neighbourhood of **Watts** provides a compelling reason to delve deeper into South LA (but only during the day): the fabulous, Gaudí-esque **Watts Towers**. Constructed from iron, stainless steel, old bedsteads and cement, and decorated with fragments of bottles and around seventy thousand crushed seashells, these seventeen striking pieces of street art were built by Italian immigrant Simon Rodia, who had no artistic training but laboured over the towers' construction from 1921 to 1954. Once finished, he left the area, refused to talk about the towers and faded into obscurity, dying in 1965. Entry is by **guided tour** only, but you can still see the towers through the fence if you visit when it's closed.

Hollywood

Hollywood encapsulates the LA dream of glamour, money and overnight success, with millions of tourists arriving on pilgrimages every year. Although many of the big film companies long ago relocated to blander digs in Burbank, and you're still more likely to see a homeless person than a movie star, recent attempts at renovation have added a bit of the old glitz to the previously shabby streets.

Hollywood & Highland Center and Dolby Theatre

6801 Hollywood Blvd • **Hollywood & Highland Center** Mon–Sat 10am–10pm, Sun 10am–7pm • Free (parking $2/2hr) • Ⓦ hollywoodandhighland.com **Dolby Theatre** Tours (30min) every 30min daily 10.30am–4pm • $17 (March–May $15) • ☎ 323 308 6300, Ⓦ dolbytheatre.com

The hub of **Central Hollywood** is the corner of Hollywood Boulevard and Highland Avenue, where, amid the flashy neon tourist traps, the modern **Hollywood & Highland Center** hosts a major hotel and chic restaurants, plus colossal pseudo-film-set architecture and the **Dolby Theatre**, where the Oscars are held annually (the fun **guided theatre tours** take in the posh Dolby Lounge and the chance to see a real statuette). Tucked into the western side of the centre, **Madame Tussauds Hollywood** (daily 10–7pm; extended hours seasonally, see website; $27.95, discounts online); ☎ 323 798 1670, Ⓦ madametussauds.com/hollywood) provides the usual (but pricey) scarily life-like wax models representing the gamut of Hollywood movies.

TCL Chinese Theatre

6925 Hollywood Blvd • Tours (20min) every 15–30min daily 10am–9.30pm • Tours $13.50 • ☎ 323 464 8111, Ⓦ tclchinesetheatres.com

Also incorporated in the Hollywood & Highland Center is the historic **TCL Chinese Theatre**, which opened in 1927 and has since been expanded into a multiplex, its main auditorium restored to its gloriously kitschy origins. It's an odd version of a classical Asian temple, replete with dubious Chinese motifs and upturned dragon-tail flanks; the lobby's Art Deco splendour and the grand chinoiserie of the auditorium certainly make for fascinating viewing. After a **guided tour** linger in the theatre's forecourt to see the **handprints** and **footprints** left in cement by Hollywood's big names. You'll probably

13

encounter plenty of celebrity impersonators in the forecourt – Elvis, Marilyn and *Star Wars* characters among them – along with low-rent magicians, smiling hawkers and assorted oddballs vying for your amusement and money.

Hollywood and Vine

The most legendary intersection on Hollywood Boulevard is **Hollywood and Vine** – the mythical place for budding stars to be "spotted" by big-shot directors and whisked off to fame and fortune – in the shadow of the iconic "record stack" of the **Capitol Records Building**. Few aspiring stars actually loiter in this gritty environment, but many visitors do come to trace the **Walk of Fame** (1.3 miles from N Gower St to N La Brea Ave; and Vine St from Yucca St to Sunset Blvd), a series of gold-inset stars honouring famous and forgotten names of radio, TV and movies.

Egyptian Theatre

6712 Hollywood Blvd • Tours 1 monthly, Sat 10.30am; documentary Sat 11.40am • Tours $9; documentary $9; combo tickets $15; films $11 • ☎ 323 466 3456, ⊚ americancinemathequecalendar.com

The venerable **Egyptian Theatre** was the site of the very first Hollywood premiere (*Robin Hood*, an epic swashbuckler starring Douglas Fairbanks Sr) in 1922. Financed by impresario **Sid Grauman**, the Egyptian was a glorious fantasy in its heyday, modestly seeking to re-create the Temple of Thebes, with usherettes dressed as Cleopatra. Movie-lovers should make a special trip here to view an art-house, foreign or indie film, or to take one of the excellent monthly one-hour **guided tours** (see the website for dates); afterwards you can opt to see **Forever Hollywood**, an absorbing documentary celebrating the history of movie-making.

El Capitan Theatre

6838 Hollywood Blvd • ☎ 866 546 6984, ⊚ elcapitan.go.com

A few blocks west of the Egyptian Theatre, across from the Hollywood and Highland Center, the similarly impressive **El Capitan Theatre** is a colourful 1926 movie palace, with Baroque and Moorish details and a wild South Seas-themed interior of sculpted angels and garlands. Today it hosts Disney premieres (Disney owns it), while the old Masonic Temple next door hosts the TV talk show of comedian **Jimmy Kimmel** (which tapes at 4.30pm Mon–Thurs; for free tickets visit ⊚ 1iota.com or call ☎ 866 546 69849).

Hollywood Museum

1660 N Highland Blvd, at Hollywood Blvd • Wed–Sun 10am–5pm • $15 • ☎ 323 464 7776, ⊚ thehollywoodmuseum.com

Just south of Hollywood Boulevard, the **Hollywood Museum** exhibits the fashion, art design, props and special effects taken from a broad swathe of movie history, including spectaculars such as the *Harry Potter* series. However, the museum is mostly filled with a hotchpotch of memorabilia, from Elvis' bathrobe to Rocky's boxing gloves; hopes are high that the **Academy Museum** (⊚ oscars.org/academymuseum) will be the definitive Hollywood showcase when it opens in 2017 (see p.832).

Hollywood Forever Cemetery

6000 Santa Monica Blvd • **Grounds** Daily 8am–9pm (Cathedral Mausoleum daily 10am–2pm) • Free • ☎ 323 469 1181, ⊚ hollywood forever.com **Tours** Sat 10am, noon or 2pm (2hr) • $15 • ☎ 818 517 5988, ⊚ cemeterytour.com

Given its location a few blocks south of Sunset Boulevard, it's fitting that the **Hollywood Forever Cemetery** is the final resting place of more of Hollywood's stars than anywhere else, including Rudolph Valentino, Cecil B. DeMille, George Harrison (of the Beatles), director John Huston, Terry the dog (Toto in *The Wizard of Oz*) and Douglas Fairbanks Sr, as well as more unexpected grave markers, such as Dee Dee Ramone and Johnny Ramone playing one last guitar riff.

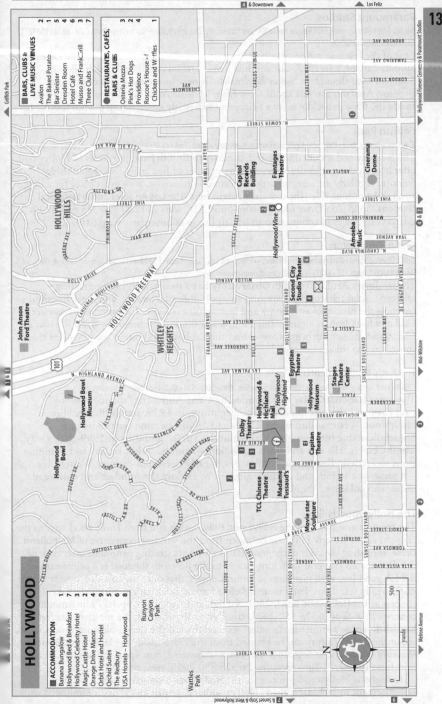

HOLLYWOOD

ACCOMMODATION
Banana Bungalow 1
Hollywood Bed & Breakfast 7
Hollywood Celebrity Hotel 3
Magic Castle Hotel 2
Orange Drive Manor 4
Orbit Hotel and Hostel 9
Orchid Suites 5
The Redbury 6
USA Hostels - Hollywood 8

**BARS, CLUBS &
LIVE MUSIC VENUES**
Avalon 2
The Baked Potato 1
Bar Sinister 5
Dresden Room 6
Hotel Café 3
Musso and Frank Grill 7

**RESTAURANTS, CAFÉS,
BARS & CLUBS**
Osteria Mozza 3
Pink's Hot Dogs 2
Providence 4
Roscoe's House of Waffles
Chicken and Waffles 1

13

Paramount Studios

Melrose Gate Visitor Entrance, 5555 Melrose Ave, at Windsor Blvd • Tours (2hr) daily 9.30am–2pm, every 30min • $48 • ☎ 323 956 1777, Ⓦ paramountstudiotour.com

One of the few true movie-making attractions remaining in Hollywood, the **Paramount Studios** date back to 1917. The original iconic arched entrance – which Gloria Swanson rode through in *Sunset Boulevard* – is now inside the complex opposite Bronson Ave (you can just about see it from Melrose Ave), but the only way to get inside the 65-acre backlot is on a pricey but extremely entertaining **guided tour**.

Griffith Park

4730 Crystal Springs Drive • Daily 5am–10.30pm, mountain roads close at dusk • Free • ☎ 323 913 4688, Ⓦ laparks.org/dos/parks/griffithpk

The greenery and mountain slopes that make up **Griffith Park**, northeast of Hollywood, offer lush gardens, splendid views and many miles of fine trails – though hillside wildfires regularly menace the park in summer. Otherwise, it's a great place for a long stroll, hike or bike ride. The one major sight here, the **Los Angeles Zoo & Botanical Gardens**, 5333 Zoo Drive (daily 10am–5pm; $18, kids 2–12 $13; ☎ 323 644 4200, Ⓦ lazoo.org), pales in comparison to its San Diego counterpart (see p.816).

Griffith Observatory

2800 E Observatory Rd • **Observatory** Tues–Fri noon–10pm, Sat & Sun 10am–10pm • Free **Planetarium** Tues–Fri 12.45–8.45pm, Sat & Sun 10.45am–8.45pm • $7 • ☎ 213 473 0800, Ⓦ griffithobservatory.org

The landmark Art Deco **Griffith Observatory** has a twelve-inch Zeiss refracting telescope, solar telescopes for viewing sunspots and solar storms, and modern exhibits covering the history of astronomy and human observation. The observatory has been used as a backdrop in innumerable Hollywood films, most famously *Rebel Without a Cause*, and the site offers great views over the LA basin and out to sea (provided the smog isn't too thick).

The Autry National Center

4700 Western Heritage Way • Tues–Fri 10am–4pm, Sat & Sun 10am–5pm • $10 • ☎ 323 667 2000, Ⓦ theautry.org

The **Autry National Center** was founded by Gene Autry, the "singing cowboy" who cut more than six hundred discs beginning in 1929, starred in blockbuster Hollywood Westerns during the 1930s and 1940s, became even more of a household name through his TV show in the 1950s, and died in 1999 after a very lengthy career. His **arts and crafts collection** – from buckskin jackets and branding irons to Frederic Remington's sculptures of early twentieth-century Western life – represents a serious and credible attempt to explore the mindset and culture of those who colonized the West.

The Hollywood Hills

The canyons and slopes of the **Hollywood Hills**, which run from Hollywood west to the canyons above Beverly Hills, are best seen from the winding concourse of **Mulholland Drive**, threading the crest of the mountains. With its striking panorama after dark of the illuminated city-grid stretching nearly to the horizon, the road is a prime axis for the LA good life, with mansions so commonplace that only the half-dozen fully blown castles really stand out. For a more up-close look at landmark architecture, take in a concert at the **Hollywood Bowl**, 2301 N Highland Ave (Los Angeles Philharmonic concerts July–Sept; ☎ 323 850 2000, Ⓦ hollywoodbowl.com), the massive concrete bandshell whose summer music offerings tend toward the crowd-pleasing variety. More about the Bowl's history can be gleaned from the video inside the **Hollywood Bowl Museum** (mid-June to Sept Tues–Sat 10am–showtime, Sun 4pm–showtime; Oct to mid-June Tues–Fri 10am–5pm; free; ☎ 323 850 2058) near the entrance.

Throughout Hollywood you can see the **Hollywood Sign**, erected as a property advertisement in 1923 (it spelled "Hollywoodland", until 1949) and illuminated with four thousand light bulbs. Nowadays, infrared cameras and radar-activated zoom lenses have been installed to catch graffiti writers. Curious tourists who can't resist a close look are liable for a steep fine. The **best views** can be had from the Griffith Observatory (opposite). For a much simpler look, see ⓦ hollywoodsign.org.

West LA

West LA begins immediately beyond Hollywood, roughly bordered by the foothills of the Hollywood Hills to the north and the Santa Monica Freeway (I-10) to the south. West LA is the place where the city's nouveau riche flaunt their fortunes most conspicuously, from the trendy confines of West Hollywood and shadowy wealth of Bel Air to the high-priced shopping strips of Beverly Hills.

Museum Row

The **Miracle Mile**, the 1.5-mile section of Wilshire Boulevard between Fairfax and Highland avenues, was the premier property development of the 1930s, although recent public investment has created a "**Museum Mile**" in its place, also known as **Museum Row**. The first is sited at the **La Brea Tar Pits** at 5801 Wilshire Blvd (park daily sunrise–sunset; free), where for thousands of years, animals who tried to drink from the thin layer of water covering this rank pool of tar became stuck fast and preserved for posterity. It's now surrounded by life-sized replicas of such victims as mastodons and sabre-toothed tigers, some of them reconstructed at the park's impressive **Page Museum** (daily 9.30am–5pm; $12, parking $7–9; ☎ 323 934 7243, ⓦ tarpits.org). Across the street, the **Craft and Folk Art Museum**, 5814 Wilshire Blvd (Tues–Fri 11am–5pm, Sat & Sun noon–6pm; $7; ☎ 323 937 4230, ⓦ cafam.org) has a small selection of handmade objects – rugs, pottery, clothing and so on – with rotating exhibitions featuring the likes of handmade tarot cards, ceramic folk art and highly detailed Asian textiles. At the intersection with Fairfax Avenue, the **Petersen Automotive Museum**, 6060 Wilshire Blvd (Tues–Sun 10am–6pm; $15, parking $2/30min; ☎ 323 930 2277, ⓦ petersen .org), pays homage to motorized vehicles of all kinds on three floors, with rotating exhibits such as the Golden Age of customizing, Hollywood prop cars and "million-dollar" vehicles.

LA County Museum of Art

5905 Wilshire Blvd • Mon, Tues & Thurs 11am–5pm, Fri 11am–8pm, Sat & Sun 10am–7pm • $15 • ☎ 323 857 6000, ⓦ lacma.org

The enormous **LA County Museum of Art (LACMA)** is not the best art collection in the city, but it is the biggest and most diverse. The **Ahmanson Building** opens with some rare Polynesian artefacts, but also contains a compelling collection of vivid **German Expressionism** and **Abstract** art from the likes of Kandinsky, Picasso (look out for the startling *Women of Algiers, after Delacroix*) and Warhol. Floor 3 provides an overview of **European art** from Greek and Roman sculpture and medieval religious imagery to a rather unfashionable collection of Renaissance and Mannerist works, though you should seek out El Greco's *The Apostle Saint Andrew*, an uncommonly reserved portrait, and Rembrandt's probing *Portrait of Marten Looten*. Floor 4 contains a moderately interesting sample of **Islamic Art** and sculptures and artefacts from **South and Southeast Asia**.

Most big-budget temporary exhibitions take place in the **Hammer Building**, on the northeast side of the site, though the second and third floors are crammed with **Chinese and Korean artworks**. Level 3 also houses the new **African Art** gallery, opened in 2013. The exceptional **Pavilion for Japanese Art** was created by iconoclastic architect Bruce Goff to re-create the effects of traditional shoji screens, filtering varying levels and qualities of light through to the interior. Displays include painted scrolls, ceramics and lacquerware, viewable on a ramp spiralling down to a small, ground-floor waterfall that trickles pleasantly amid the near-silence of the gallery.

13

The **Art of the Americas Building** is home to the museum's small collection of American art, while **modern art** is showcased in the **Broad Contemporary Art Museum**, which houses some of the West Coast's largest paintings. Among the more prominent are works by Abstract Expressionists such as Mark Rothko and Franz Kline, as well as the splashy, colourful paintings of Sam Francis. Finally, the **Resnick Pavilion**, a huge, glass-and-marble showpiece designed by Renzo Piano, houses flexible open galleries to accommodate works of any size. Note that the new **Academy Museum** (ⓦoscars.org /academymuseum) should be opening next door in 2017.

West Hollywood

The **West Hollywood** neighbourhood is synonymous with social tolerance and upmarket trendiness, with a sizeable gay contingent, seen most prominently along the chic blocks of **Santa Monica Boulevard**, from Doheny Drive to La Cienega Boulevard. Just south, **Melrose Avenue** is LA's most fashionable shopping street and one of the unmistakeable symbols of southern California, where neon and flashy signs abound among a fluorescent rash of designer and secondhand boutiques, antique shops and high-end diners. **La Brea Avenue** runs perpendicular to the east side of the Melrose district, offering more space, fewer tourists, chic clothiers, upscale restaurants and even trendier galleries.

On the north edge of West Hollywood, on either side of La Cienega Boulevard, is the two-mile-odd amalgam of restaurants, hotels, billboards and nightclubs on Sunset Boulevard known as the **Sunset Strip**, one of LA's best areas for nightlife. The scene hit its stride in the 1960s around the landmark **Whisky-a-Go-Go** club, no. 8901, which featured seminal psychedelic rock bands such as The Doors, Love and Buffalo Springfield. The music venues (see p.845) are still worth a visit, whether you want to rock, headbang or just dance, and, like the streets noted above, Sunset Boulevard makes for a lively night-time walk.

Beverly Hills and around

Beverly Hills is one of the world's wealthiest residential areas, patrolled by more cops per capita than anywhere else in the USA. Glorified by the elite shops of **Rodeo Drive**, squeaky-clean streets and ostentatious displays of wealth, the city is undoubtedly the height of LA pretension. Luckily, there are a number of decent and unassuming spots for visitors interested in things other than commodities. The **Paley Center for Media**, 465 N Beverly Drive (Wed–Sun noon–5pm; free, suggested donation $10, parking free; ☎310 786 1000, ⓦpaleycenter.org), is one such place, vividly chronicling eighty years of our media-saturated age, and best for its voluminous library of shows, where you can take in everything from *I Love Lucy* to *The Simpsons*. For an overview of Beverly Hills' shopping and the area's art and architecture, take a trip on the **Beverly Hills Trolley** (40min ride; hourly Sat & Sun 11am–4pm; also July, Aug & Dec Tues–Sun same hours; $5; ☎310 285 2442), departing hourly from the corner of Rodeo and Dayton Way.

Greystone Mansion

905 Loma Vista Drive • Park daily 10am–5pm • Free • ☎ 310 285 6830, ⓦ greystonemansion.org

The grounds of the biggest house in Beverly Hills, **Greystone Mansion**, are now maintained as a public **park** by the city. The 50,000-square-foot manor was built in 1928 by oil titan Edward Doheny. Normally you can't go inside, but you can admire the mansion's limestone facade and intricate chimneys, then stroll through the sixteen-acre park, with its koi-filled ponds and expansive views of the LA sprawl.

Westwood and UCLA

West of Beverly Hills and north of Wilshire Boulevard, **Westwood** is the home of the **University of California at Los Angeles (UCLA)**, and is known to many as "Westwood

Village". Though it's lost some of its eminence, Westwood remains the most densely packed movie-theatre district in town and its 1931 **Westwood Village Theater**, crowned with a grand neon spire at 961 Broxton Ave, is still used for Hollywood premieres and "sneak previews" to gauge audience reactions. Art lovers shouldn't miss a trip to the **UCLA Hammer Museum**, 10899 Wilshire Blvd (Tues–Fri 11am–8pm, Sat & Sun 11am–5pm; $10, free Thurs; ☎ 310 443 7000, ⓦ hammer.ucla.edu), where there are some impressive early American works from Gilbert Stuart, Thomas Eakins and John Singer Sargent, and insightful, sometimes risk-taking contemporary and avant-garde exhibits.

The UCLA campus

The highlights of the **UCLA campus** include the central **quadrangle**, a green space bordered by UCLA's most graceful buildings, including **Royce Hall**, modelled on Milan's Church of St Ambrosio, with high bell towers, rib vaulting and grand archways; and the **Powell Library** (hours vary; during term time Mon–Thurs 9am–11pm, Fri 7.30am–6pm, Sat 9am–5pm, Sun 1–10pm; free; ☎ 310 825 1938, ⓦ library.ucla.edu), featuring a spellbinding interior with lovely Romanesque arches, columns and stairwell. The **Fowler Museum**, 308 Circle Drive N (Wed–Sun noon–5pm, Thurs closes 8pm; free; ☎ 310 825 4361, ⓦ fowler.ucla.edu), offers an immense range of multicultural art – including ceramics, religious icons, paintings and musical instruments. The **Murphy Sculpture Garden**, in the northeast corner of campus at Charles E Young Drive (daily 24hr; free), is LA's best outdoor display of modern sculpture, featuring pieces by Henry Moore, Barbara Hepworth, Henri Matisse, Jacques Lipchitz and Isamu Noguchi.

The Getty Center

1200 Getty Center Drive (main entrance on N Sepulveda Blvd) • Mon–Fri & Sun 10am–5.30pm (June–Aug Fri 10am–9pm), Sat 10am–9pm • Free; parking $15 • ☎ 310 440 7300, ⓦ getty.edu • MTA line #761 from UCLA after taking line #2 or #302 from downtown, or line #720 from Santa Monica

Towering over the surrounding area, the **Getty Center** is Richard Meier's Modernist temple to high art, clad in acres of travertine, its various buildings devoted to conservation, acquisition and other philanthropic tasks, and its surrounding gardens arranged with geometric precision.

The quality of the **exhibits** is extraordinary. In the rooms devoted to decorative arts, you can see a formidable array of ornate French furniture from the reign of Louis XIV, with clocks, chandeliers, tapestries and gilt-edged commodes filling several overwhelmingly opulent chambers. The painting collection features all the major names from the thirteenth century on, including Van Gogh's **Irises** and a trio of evocative Rembrandts: *Daniel and Cyrus before the Idol Bel*, in which the Persian king tries foolishly to feed the bronze statue he worships; *An Old Man in Military Costume*, the exhausted, uncertain face of an old soldier; and *Saint Bartholomew*, showing the martyred saint as a quiet, thoughtful Dutchman – the knife that will soon kill him visible in the corner of the frame. Elsewhere in the museum, photography is well represented by Man Ray, Moholy-Nagy and other notables, and there's also a rich assortment of classical, Renaissance and Baroque sculpture – highlighted by Bernini's **Boy with a Dragon**, depicting a plump, possibly angelic toddler bending back the jaw of a dragon with surprising ease.

13

Santa Monica and around

Friendly and liberal, **Santa Monica** is a great spot to visit, a compact, accessible bastion of oceanside charm that, incidentally, has traditionally attracted a large contingent of British expats (though many have recently left "Little Britain", as it's called, in search of cheaper rents).

Santa Monica reaches nearly three miles inland, but most spots of interest are within a few blocks of the Pacific Ocean, notably **Palisades Park**, the pleasant, cypress-tree-lined strip along the top of the bluffs that makes for striking views of the surf below. Two blocks east of Ocean Avenue, the **Third Street Promenade**, a pedestrianized stretch between Wilshire Boulevard and Broadway with street vendors, buskers and itinerant evangelists, is the closest LA comes to having a dynamic urban energy, and by far the best place to come for alfresco dining, beer-drinking and people-watching, especially after dark. Further south, another good stretch is **Main Street**, where the visitor centre is located (see p.841), and which boasts a serviceable array of fine restaurants, bars, shops and a few galleries.

Down below Palisades Park, the crowded **beach** is better for sunbathing than swimming, and the refurbished **Santa Monica Pier** (daily 24hr; free; ☎310 458 8901, ⓦsantamonicapier.org) boasts a well-restored 1922 wooden **carousel** (Mon & Thurs 11am–5pm, Fri–Sun 11am–7pm; July & Aug also Tues 3–7pm; $2 a ride, kids $1; ☎310 394 8042). Although the tired rides of **Pacific Park** (hours vary, usually summer daily 11am–11pm, Sat & Sun closes 12.30am; unlimited rides $22.95; ⓦpacpark.com) may catch your eye, save your money for the **Santa Monica Pier Aquarium** (Tues–Fri 2–6pm, Sat & Sun 12.30–5pm; suggested $3–5, kids under 12 free; ⓦhealthebay.org/smpa), below the pier at 1600 Ocean Front Walk, where you can get your fingers wet touching sea anemones and starfish.

Getty Villa

17985 PCH • Wed–Mon 10am–5pm, by reservation only • Free; parking $15 • ☎ 310 440 7300, ⓦ getty.edu

If you really want to indulge in some serious (ancient) art, head five miles north of Santa Monica along the beautiful, curving **Pacific Coast Highway (PCH)** to the opulent **Getty Villa**. Built by oil tycoon J. Paul Getty in 1974 adjacent to his home, in the style of a Roman country house, it now serves as the Getty Foundation's spectacular showcase for its wide array of Greek, Etruscan and Roman antiquities. Athenian vases are well represented, many of them the red-ground variety, as are ancient *kylikes*, or drinking vessels, and ceremonial amphorae, or vases, given as prizes in athletic contests. Not to be missed is a wondrous Roman *skyphos*, a fragile-looking blue vase decorated with white cameos of Bacchus and his friends, properly preparing for a bacchanalia.

Malibu

Twenty miles north of Santa Monica, **Malibu** is synonymous with luxurious celebrity isolation, along with hillside wildfires, which routinely smoke those same celebrities out of their gilded confines. Malibu's **Surfrider Beach** was the surfing capital of the world in the 1950s and early 1960s, and is still a big attraction (the surf is best in late summer; check the surfing report at ⓦsurfrider.org). The beach is part of **Malibu Lagoon State Park** (daily 8am–dusk), a nature reserve and bird refuge, and nearby is the **Adamson House**, 23200 PCH (tours Wed–Sat 11am–3pm; last tour at 2pm; 1hr; $7; ☎310 456 8432, ⓦadamsonhouse.org), a stunning, historic Spanish Colonial-style home built in 1929, featuring opulent decor and colourful tilework. The adjoining **Malibu Lagoon Museum** (Wed–Sat 11am–3pm; $7, includes Adamson House tour), formerly the Adamsons' five-car garage, chronicles the history of the area from the days of Chumash people to the "gentlemen" ranchers and the birth of modern surfing.

CLOCKWISE FROM TOP SEAWORLD, SAN DIEGO (P.817); JOSHUA TREE NATIONAL PARK (P.850); WALT DISNEY CONCERT HALL, DOWNTOWN LA (P.825) >

13

Venice

Immediately south of Santa Monica via Main Street or the boardwalk, **Venice** is the eccentric, loopy version of Los Angeles, home to outlandish skaters, brazen bodybuilders, panhandlers, streetballers, buskers and street-side comedians. It's been this way since the 1950s and 1960s, when the Beats and then bands like the Doors bummed around the beach, and though gentrification has definitely had an impact in recent years, Venice retains an edgy feel in parts, with a gang culture that has never really been eradicated.

It wasn't always like this. Venice was laid out in the marshlands of Ballona Creek in 1905 by developer **Abbot Kinney** as a romantic replica of the northern Italian city. His twenty-mile network of canals and waterfront homes never really caught on, although a later remodelling into a low-grade version of Coney Island postponed its demise for a few decades. **Windward Avenue** is Venice's main artery, running from the beach into what was the Grand Circle of the canal system – now paved over – and the original Romanesque arcade, around the intersection with Pacific Avenue, is alive with health-food shops, trinket stores and rollerblade rental stands.

Nowhere else does LA parade itself quite so openly as along the wide pathway of **Venice Boardwalk**, packed year-round at weekends and every day in summer with musicians, street performers, trinket vendors and many others; it's lively and fun during the day, but strictly to be avoided after dark, when shades of the creepy old Venice appear. South of Windward is **Muscle Beach**, a legendary outdoor weightlifting centre where serious-looking dudes (and a few muscular women) pump serious iron and budding basketballers hold court on the concrete.

The South Bay and Long Beach

South from LA along PCH is an eight-mile coastal strip of quiet **South Bay** beach towns: **Manhattan Beach**, **Hermosa Beach** and **Redondo Beach**. Each has a beckoning strip of white sand, and Manhattan and Hermosa are especially well equipped for surfing and beach sports; a good time to come is during the **Fiesta Hermosa** (w fiestahermosa.com), a three-day event held on Memorial Day and Labor Day. They're also well connected by the regular bus lines to downtown LA. To the south are **Long Beach** and the natural gem of **Santa Catalina Island**, 22 miles long and twenty miles offshore. Trips run several times daily from Long Beach Downtown Landing to **Avalon** (July & Aug 7–8 daily; $72.50 return; 1hr) with Catalina Express (t 800 481 3470, w catalinaexpress.com).

Long Beach

One of the largest ports in the world, **Long Beach** is well off the tourist trail, though its downtown section does offer an enjoyable stretch of restored architecture and antique stores around **Pine Avenue**, linked by the Blue Line light rail to downtown LA (see p.840). Running from Ocean Boulevard to 3rd Street, the three-block strip known as the **Promenade** is lined with touristy restaurants and stores that can get busy on weekend nights.

Queen Mary

1126 Queens Hwy • Mon–Thurs 10am–6pm, Fri–Sun 10am–7pm • $24.95 self-guided tours (includes Ghosts & Legends Show), kids $13.95 • t 562 499 1050, w queenmary.com

Long Beach's most famous attraction is, of course, the mighty **Queen Mary**, the 1936 Art Deco ocean-liner purchased by the city of Long Beach in 1967. Now a luxury hotel, the ship is also open for exhibits that include extravagantly furnished lounges and luxurious first-class cabins, and a wealth of gorgeous Art Deco details in its glasswork, geometric decor and chic streamlining. Various add-ons can increase the price of admission: **Diana: Legacy of a Princess A Royal Exhibition** ($27.95) and the themed **Haunted Encounters** tour ($27.95).

13

Aquarium of the Pacific

100 Aquarium Way • Daily 9am–6pm • $25.95, kids (3–11) $14.95 • ☎ 562 590 3100, ⓦ aquariumofpacific.org

The most popular family attraction in Long Beach is the entertaining **Aquarium of the Pacific**, which exhibits more than eleven thousand marine species. The aquarium's interactive **Shark Lagoon** is especially fun (kids can touch the gentle bamboo and epaulette sharks), while visitors can also feed the tropical Australian parrots in **Lorikeet Forest**. The equally popular **Behind the Scenes Tour** (extra $19) takes you into the "wet side" of the aquarium, and includes feeding some of the fish.

Orange County

Throughout the USA, **Orange County** is synonymous with anodyne, white suburbia – most famously as the site of **Disneyland** – but in recent years it's begun to change, with many new Hispanic arrivals and more cultural (and culinary) diversity. Still, most tourists come just for the theme parks and for the easy-going, upscale beach towns of the **Orange County coast**.

Disneyland

1313 Harbor Blvd, Anaheim • Hours vary, usually June–Aug daily 8am–midnight; Sept–May Mon–Fri 10am–6pm, Sat 9am–midnight, Sun 9am–10pm • $92, kids (3–9) $86, parking $16 • ☎ 714 781 4565, ⓦ disneyland.com

The pop-culture colossus of **Disneyland** is one of America's most iconic sights, as well as one of its most expensive – most of the park's hotels are ridiculously overpriced and there's little quality cuisine in the area. The park is 45 minutes by **car** from downtown LA on the Santa Ana Freeway. Arrive early, as traffic and rides quickly become nightmarishly busy, especially in summer.

Disneyland's best **rides** are in **New Orleans Square** and adjacent **Adventureland**: the Indiana Jones Adventure, an interactive archeological dig and 1930s-style newsreel show leading up to a giddy journey along 2500ft of skull-encrusted corridors; the Pirates of the Caribbean, a boat trip through underground caverns full of singing rogues; and the Haunted Mansion, a riotous "doom buggy" tour in the company of the house spooks. Other themed areas include **Frontierland**, with mainly lower-end Wild West attractions; **Fantasyland**, with low-tech fairy-tale rides, notably the treacly It's a Small World; and **Toontown**, a cartoonish zone aimed at the kindergarten set.

It's more worthwhile to zip right through to **Tomorrowland**, Disney's vision of the future, where the Space Mountain roller coaster plunges through the darkness of outer space and the late Michael Jackson is celebrated in the *Captain EO Tribute*, a seventeen-minute 3-D film juiced up with special effects.

Disney California Adventure Park

The **Disney California Adventure Park** is technically a separate park but is connected to the main one in architecture and style – although it's much less popular. Aside from its slightly more exciting roller coasters and better food, the California Adventure is really just another "land" to visit, albeit a much more expensive one – you'll have to shell out $92, or $137 for a one-day pass that covers both (same hours).

Knott's Berry Farm

8039 Beach Blvd (off the Santa Ana Freeway), Buena Park • Hours vary, usually June–Aug Mon–Thurs & Sun 10am–11pm, Fri & Sat 10am–midnight; Sept–May Mon–Fri 10am–6pm, Sat 10am–10pm, Sun 10am–7pm • $62, kids (3–11) $33; parking $15 • ☎ 714 220 5200, ⓦ knotts.com

If you're a bit fazed by the excesses of Disneyland, you might prefer **Knott's Berry Farm**, four miles northwest, whose roller coasters are far more exciting than anything at its rival. Knott's also has its own adjacent water park, **Soak City USA** (June–Sept only, hours vary but generally daily 10am–5pm or 7pm; $34.99, kids $24.99; ⓦ soakcityoc .com), offering dozens of drenching rides of various heights and speeds.

13

Orange County coast

Stretching from the edge of Long Beach to the border of San Diego County 35 miles south, the **Orange County coast** is chic suburbia with a shoreline, the ambience easy-going, libertarian and affluent. As the names of the main towns suggest – **Huntington Beach, Newport Beach** and **Laguna Beach** – most of the good reasons to come here involve sea and sand, though a handful of other sights can also make for an interesting trip. Check out the **International Surfing Museum**, 411 Olive Ave, Huntington Beach (Mon & Sun noon–5pm, Tues noon–9pm, Wed–Fri noon–7pm, Sat 11am–7pm; free; ☎714 960 3483, ⓦsurfingmuseum.org), loaded with famous legends of the waves; Newport Beach's excellent **Orange County Museum of Art**, 850 San Clemente Drive (Wed–Sun 11am–5pm, Thurs until 8pm; $12; ☎949 759 1122, ⓦocma.net), focusing on modern California art and presenting regular lectures, events and art and architecture tours; and Laguna Beach's incredibly popular **Pageant of the Masters** at 650 Laguna Canyon Rd, Hwy-133 (July daily shows begin at 8.30pm; tickets $15–150; ☎949 497 6582, ⓦfoapom.com), a strangely compelling spectacle in which participants dress up as characters from famous paintings. To the far south, **San Juan Capistrano** merits a stop as the site of the best kept of all the Californian **missions**, 26801 Ortega Hwy at Camino Capistrano in the centre of town (daily 9am–5pm; $9; ☎949 234 1300, ⓦmissionsjc.com).

The San Gabriel and San Fernando valleys

The northern limit of LA is defined by two long valleys, the **San Gabriel** and **San Fernando**, lying over the hills from the central basin. Starting close to one another a few miles north of downtown, spanning outwardly in opposite directions – east to the deserts, west to the Central Coast – they feature a few worthwhile points of interest, the highlight of which is undoubtedly the old-money hamlet of **Pasadena**.

The San Gabriel Valley

Ten miles northeast of downtown LA, the **San Gabriel Valley**'s main appeal is **Pasadena**, best known for its annual **Rose Parade** and **Rose Bowl Game** at the stadium west of town, both held on January 1. Particularly distinctive is the historic shopping precinct of **Old Pasadena** along Colorado Boulevard, now fashionable for its restaurants and boutiques (and accessible on the Gold Line light rail), but also worthy for its century-old architecture in various historic revival styles.

Pasadena's other best offerings are the splendid collection of the **Norton Simon Museum**, 411 W Colorado Blvd (Wed, Thurs & Sat–Mon noon–6pm, Fri noon–9pm; $10; ☎626 449 6840, ⓦnortonsimon.org), one of LA's best but least-known art institutions, with a prime selection of Old Masters including Rubens and Rembrandt and modern works by Klee and Picasso – works that match up to anything at the Getty Center, though the crowds here are much more manageable; and the **Gamble House**, 4 Westmoreland Place (1hr tours every 20–30min Thurs–Sun noon–3pm; $13.75; 20min tours Tues 12.15pm & 12.45pm; $8; ☎626 793 3334, ⓦgamblehouse.org), a 1908 Arts and Crafts style mansion with striking Japanese-inspired design elements – one of many works in the vicinity built by Craftsman masters Charles and Henry Greene. The engaging **Pacific Asia Museum**, a mile east at 46 N Los Robles Ave (Wed–Sun 10am–6pm; $10; ☎626 449 2742, ⓦpacificasiamuseum.org), is modelled after a Chinese imperial palace, showcasing historical treasures from Korea, China and Japan, including decorative jade and porcelain, swords and spears, and a large amount of paintings and drawings.

Huntington Library

1151 Oxford Rd, off Huntington Drive, San Marino • Daily except Tues 10.30am–4.30pm • Mon & Wed–Fri $20, Sat & Sun $23 • ☎626 405 2100, ⓦhuntington.org

Three miles southeast of Pasadena, in dull, upper-crust **San Marino**, the **Huntington Library** is a combined library and **art gallery** complex set off by many acres of themed

botanical gardens and handsome buildings. It definitely rates a visit, as it contains some key historic documents and rare books, such as a Gutenberg Bible and the *Ellesmere Chaucer* – the latter an illuminated manuscript of **The Canterbury Tales** dating from around 1410. Notable paintings include the finest collection of British portraits outside of the UK, including Gainsborough's **Blue Boy**, **Pinkie** by Thomas Lawrence and Reynolds' **Mrs Siddons as the Tragic Muse**, and a few signature works from Constable, Turner, Blake and van Dyck.

Forest Lawn Cemetery

1712 S Glendale Ave, Glendale • Daily 8am–5pm • Free • ☎ 323 254 3131, ⓦ forestlawn.com

The **San Fernando Valley**, spreading west of the San Gabriel Valley, is a vast, uninspiring sprawl of tract homes, mini-malls and fast-food diners, but merits a trip to see **Forest Lawn Cemetery** in Glendale, a fascinating, often kitschy, display of death Hollywood-style. Those buried here include Errol Flynn, Walt Disney, Nat King Cole, Clark Gable and Jean Harlow, among other notables, many under grave markers so garish and tacky they must be seen to be believed.

Burbank and the studios

In the heart of the "Valley", the otherwise dull city of **Burbank** is the place where many movie and TV studios relocated from Hollywood in the 1950s through to the 1970s; today it's still home to media giants such as the Walt Disney Company, Warner Bros Entertainment, Warner Music Group and Nickelodeon. Although you can't get into Disney, **Warner Bros**, 3400 W Riverside Drive (tours 2hr 15min; Mon–Sat 8.15am–4pm; $52, parking $7; ☎877 492 8687, ⓦvipstudiotour.warnerbros.com) does offer worthwhile "VIP" insider **tours** of its sizeable facilities and active backlot, where *Friends* was filmed in the 1990s.

Universal Studios Hollywood

100 Universal City Plaza, Universal City • Hours vary, usually June–Aug daily 8am–10pm; Sept–May daily 10am–6pm • 1 day pass $84.99 (2 days for $93), kids $76.99; parking $10–15 • ☎ 818 508 9600, ⓦ universalstudioshollywood.com • Metro Red Line to Universal City

The largest of the Burbank backlots belongs to **Universal Studios**, though the section you get to visit is essentially a theme park. Admission includes the **studio tour** (every 5–10min; 45min) with the first half featuring a tram ride through a make-believe set where you can see the house from *Psycho* and the shark from *Jaws*, have a close encounter with King Kong (a 3-D experience created by Peter Jackson) and encounter the plane crash from *War of the Worlds*. You'll also see the Wisteria Lane set from hit series *Desperate Housewives*.

Six Flags Magic Mountain

26101 Magic Mountain Pkwy, Valencia • Hours vary, usually June–Aug daily 10am–10pm; Sept–May Sat & Sun 10am–8pm • $66.99, kids $41.99 (discounts on website); parking $18 • ☎ 661 255 4100, ⓦ sixflags.com/magicmountain

Some 25 miles north of Burbank, **Six Flags Magic Mountain** boasts some of the wildest roller coasters and rides in the world – highlights include the Viper, a huge orange monster with seven loops; Full Throttle, which speeds through a record-breaking 160ft loop – it's the tallest and fastest looping roller coaster in the world – and Green Lantern: First Flight, one of the newest "fifth dimension coasters", where your seat pivots and pitches independently of the direction of the track, and is utterly terrifying. Of the other rides, Lex Luthor: Drop of Doom stands out for its 400ft freefall, the tallest drop tower ride in the world.

ARRIVAL AND DEPARTURE   **LOS ANGELES**

BY PLANE
Los Angeles International Airport (LAX) Sixteen miles southwest of downtown LA (☎ 310 646 5252, ⓦ lawa.org).

To travel between LAX and downtown's Union Station ($7 one-way), the UCLA campus in Westwood (at parking structure 32 on Kinross Ave), or the La Brea Avenue station ($7

13

one-way) of the Metro Expo Light Rail Line, the LAX Flyaway service (☎ 866 435 9529) uses buses in freeway carpool lanes to provide the most direct airport access on public transport. Buses run every 30min, 24hr, except at Westwood, which runs 6am–11pm ($8 weekends, $11 weekdays one way). Super-Shuttle (☎ 800 258 3826, ⍟ supershuttle.com) and Prime Time Shuttle (☎ 800 733 8267, ⍟ primetimeshuttle.com) run all over town around the clock and take 30–60min depending on your destination; fares are around $16 to downtown and the Westside, up to $40 for more outlying areas.

Taxis Metered taxis will cost around $50 from LAX to West LA, $55 to Hollywood, $40 to Santa Monica, around $100 to Disneyland, and a flat $46.50 to downtown; a $4 surcharge applies for all trips starting from LAX. All trips from the airport cost a minimum of $19 (⍟ taxicabsla.org for more information).

BY BUS

The main Greyhound bus terminal, at 1716 E 7th St (☎ 213 629 8401), is in a seedy section of downtown, though access is restricted to ticket holders and it's safe enough inside.

Destinations Bakersfield (12 daily; 2hr 10min–2hr 35min); Las Vegas (10 daily; 5hr–7hr 55min); Palm Springs (3 daily; 2hr 30min–3hr 30min); Phoenix (8 daily; 6hr 50min–8hr 35min); Sacramento (8 daily; 7hr 15min–9hr 45min); San Diego (19 daily; 2hr 10min– 2hr 55min); San Francisco (10 daily; 7hr 25min–12hr 5min); Santa Barbara (4 daily; 2hr 10min–2hr 40min); Tucson (5 daily; 10–11hr 40min).

BY TRAIN

Amtrak's Union Station lies on the north side of downtown at 800 N Alameda St (☎ 213 624 0171); from here you can reach Metrorail and Metrolink lines and also access the nearby Gateway Transit Centre, which offers connections to bus lines. To get to San Francisco (10hr 30min) you'll need to change trains in San Luis Obispo or switch to a bus in Santa Barbara.

Destinations Fullerton (for Disneyland; 11 daily; 29min); Portland, OR (1 daily; 29hr 22min); Sacramento (1 daily; 13hr 49min); San Diego (11 daily; 2hr 45min–2hr 55min); Santa Barbara (6 daily; 2hr 35min–2hr 44min); Tucson (2 daily; 9hr 30min).

GETTING AROUND

The bulk of LA's public transport is operated by the LA County Metropolitan Transit Authority (MTA or "Metro"). Its massive Union Station/Gateway Transit Center, on Chavez Avenue at Vignes Street, serves many thousands of daily commuters travelling by Metrorail, Metrolink, Amtrak and the regional bus systems. On the east side of the station is the Patsaouras Transit Plaza, where you can hop on a bus.

BY METRORAIL

LA's Metrorail (⍟ metro.net) subway and light-rail system encompasses six major lines, though extensions are planned in coming years. Trains run daily from 5am to 12.30am, about every 5min during peak hours and every 10–15min at other times. No smoking, eating or drinking is allowed on board. The system connects with the Metro Liner bus rapid transit system (the Orange Line for the San Fernando Valley and Silver Line for San Gabriel Valley):

• **Expo Line** Light rail connecting Culver City with downtown LA (7th Street/Metro Center). Santa Monica extension slated for 2015.

• **Red Line** Subway connecting Union Station in downtown LA with North Hollywood, via 7th Street/Metro Center, Hollywood/Vine and Universal City.

• **Purple Line** Subway connecting Union Station in downtown LA with Wilshire/Western (following the same route as the Red Line to Wilshire/Vermont). An extension is planned to Westwood, but this won't be open till at least 2023.

• **Green Line** Light-rail line between Redondo Beach and Norwalk, via Long Beach and LAX.

• **Blue Line** Light-rail line running north–south route between Long Beach and downtown LA (7th Street/Metro Center) via South LA, Watts and Compton.

• **Gold Line** Light rail from Pasadena (Sierra Madre Villa) to East LA (Atlantic) via downtown LA (Union Station),

Little Tokyo, Chinatown, Heritage Square, Southwest Museum and Mission.

• **Silver Line (Metro Liner bus)** Runs west from the El Monte Station in the San Gabriel Valley to downtown LA (Union Station), then south to the Harbor Gateway Transit Center in South LA.

• **Orange Line (Metro Liner bus)** Runs from Chatsworth in the San Fernando Valley and the Warner Center in the Woodland Hills to the North Hollywood Red Line Metro Station.

Fares On Metro Rail and the Metro Orange Line (Silver Line single fares are $2.45), single fares must be loaded on a TAP stored-value card ($1); purchase your fare before you board at self-service TAP vending machines. Rates are $1.50 one way, with day passes available for $5, and seven-day passes $20 (all on TAP cards).

BY METROLINK

Metrolink commuter trains (☎ 800 371 5465; ⍟ metrolink trains.com) ply primarily suburban-to-downtown routes on weekdays, which can be useful if you find yourself in far-flung districts, among them places in Orange, Ventura, Riverside and San Bernardino counties. The system reaches as far as Oceanside in San Diego County, where you can connect to that region's Coaster (see p.819) and Sprinter commuter rail. Metrolink one-way fares cost $5.50–15.

BY BUS

Buses on the major arteries between downtown and the coast run roughly every 15–25min, 5am–2am; other routes, and the all-night services along the major thoroughfares, are less frequent, sometimes only hourly. At night, be careful not to get stranded downtown waiting for connecting buses.

Fares On buses, you can pay for a single ride with cash using exact change or a TAP stored-value card (see opposite). Standard one-way fare is $1.50, but express buses (a limited commuter service) and any others using a freeway are usually $2.20–2.90. A seven-day pass is $20, also accepted on the Metro.

DASH DASH buses operate through the LA Department of Transportation, or LADOT (☎ 213 808 2273, ⍟ ladottransit .com), with a flat fare of 50¢ for broad coverage throughout downtown and very limited routes elsewhere in the city. The LADOT also operates quick, limited-stop routes called commuter express, though these cost a bit more ($1.50–4.25 depending on distance).

BY TAXI

You can find taxis at most terminals and major hotels. Among the more reliable companies are Independent Cab (☎ 323 666 0050, ⍟ taxi4u.com), Checker Cab (☎ 818 488 5088, ⍟ ineedtaxi.com), Yellow Cab (☎ 877 890 4562, ⍟ layellowcab.com) and United Independent Taxi (☎ 323 653 5050, ⍟ unitedtaxi.com). Fares start at $2.85, plus $2.70 for each mile (or 30¢ per 37 seconds of waiting time), with a $4 surcharge if you're picked up at LAX. If you encounter problems visit ⍟ taxicabsla.org.

BY BIKE

Cycling in LA may sound perverse, but in some areas it can be one of the better ways of getting around. There is an excellent beach bike path between Santa Monica and Redondo Beach, and another from Long Beach to Newport Beach, as well as many equally enjoyable inland routes, notably around Griffith Park and the grand mansions of Pasadena. For maps and information, contact the LA Department of Transportation, 100 S Main St, 9th Floor (☎ 213 972 4962, ⍟ bicyclela.org).

Rentals Santa Monica Bike Rentals (☎ 310 980 2873, ⍟ santamonicabikerental.com), on the Santa Monica Bike Path between Bicknell Ave and Bay St rents bikes for $10/hr, $25/5hr and $40/day (10hr).

INFORMATION

VISITOR CENTRES

Downtown The LA Tourism & Convention Board, at the North Entrance ticket booth of the Natural History Museum, 900 Exposition Blvd (daily 9.30am–5pm; ☎ 213 763 3466, ⍟ discoverlosangeles.com).

Hollywood Hollywood & Highland Center, 6801 Hollywood Blvd (Mon–Sat 10am–10pm, Sun 10am–7pm; ☎ 323 467 6412, ⍟ discoverlosangeles.com).

Beverly Hills 9400 S Santa Monica Blvd (Mon–Fri 9am–5pm, Sat & Sun 10am–5pm; ☎ 310 248 1015, ⍟ lovebeverlyhills.com).

Santa Monica 1920 Main St, Suite B, between Pico Blvd and Bay St (Mon–Fri 9am–5.30pm, Sat & Sun 9am–5pm; ☎ 310 393 7593). There's an information kiosk at 1400 Ocean Ave, in Palisades Park (daily: late May–Aug 9.30am–5.30pm; Sept to late May 9.45am–4.30pm; ☎ 310 393 0410, ⍟ santamonica.com).

ACCOMMODATION

HOTELS, MOTELS AND B&BS

DOWNTOWN AND AROUND

★ **Jerry's Motel** 285 Lucas Ave ☎ 213 481 8181, ⍟ jerrysmotel.com; map p.824. Hip, remodelled motel with neat, stylish rooms, free parking, large flat-screen TVs and loads of satellite channels; just outside downtown, this is a bargain. **$79**

Luxe City Center Hotel 1020 S Figueroa St ☎ 213 748 1291, ⍟ luxecitycenter.com; map p.824. Chic, downtown chain that offers sleek, contemporary decor, soothing tones and a host of amenities, use of local Gold's gym and in-room Nintendo games for the truly bored. **$150**

Westin Bonaventure 404 S Figueroa St ☎ 213 624 1000, ⍟ westin.com; map p.824. Modernist luxury hotel with five glass towers that resemble cocktail shakers, a six-storey atrium with a "lake", and elegant cone-shaped rooms. A breathtaking exterior elevator ride ascends to a rotating cocktail lounge. **$209**

HOLLYWOOD AND WEST HOLLYWOOD

★ **Hollywood Bed & Breakfast** 1701 N Orange Grove Ave ☎ 323 874 8017, ⍟ hollywoodbandb.com; map p.829. Fun, convenient place to stay: a quirky B&B in a 1912 home that looks a little like something out of Dr Seuss, close to all the action, with four cosy rooms and a small pool. **$140**

Hollywood Celebrity Hotel 1775 Orchid Ave ☎ 323 850 6464, ⍟ hotelcelebrity.com; map p.829. Good choice on the affordable boutique scene, with a great location in central Hollywood and rooms with charming furnishings and free breakfast. **$159**

★ **Magic Castle Hotel** 7025 Franklin Ave ☎ 323 851 0800, ⍟ magiccastlehotel.com; map p.829. Justly popular hotel boasting single rooms (with queen beds) and spacious one- and two-bedroom suites in a neat, modern style – with heated pool, breakfast and free soda, candy, chocolate, crackers, nuts, granola bars and cookies 24 hours a day. **$189**

13

Orchid Suites 1753 Orchid Ave ☎800 537 3052, ⓦorchidsuites.com; map p.829. Roomy, if spartan, suites with cable TV, kitchenette, laundry room and heated pool. Very close to the most popular parts of Hollywood and adjacent to the massive Hollywood & Highland mall. **$159**
The Redbury 1717 Vine St ☎323 962 1717, ⓦtheredbury.com; map p.829. Hollywood's most stylish boutique hotel; the theme is "bohemian counterculture" but with a sort nineteenth-century, European elegance (more Byron than Beats) – they even call their luxurious suites "flats", with full kitchens and washer-dryers. **$329**

WEST LA AND BEVERLY HILLS

Beverly Hills Hotel 9641 Sunset Blvd ☎310 276 2251, ⓦbeverlyhillshotel.com. The classic Hollywood resort, with a bold colour scheme and Mission-style design, and surrounded by its own exotic gardens. Features marbled bathrooms, VCRs, jacuzzis and other such luxuries, as well as the famed *Polo Lounge* restaurant. **$610**
Beverly Hilton 9876 Wilshire Blvd ☎310 274 7777, ⓦhilton.com. This prominent, geometric white hotel at the corner of Wilshire and Santa Monica boulevards has a pool and gym, plus in-room plasma TVs, boutique decor and balconies. Also has one of the few remaining *Trader Vic's* bars. **$295**
Beverly Laurel 8018 Beverly Blvd ☎323 651 2441. The coffee shop, *Swingers*, attracts the most attention here; the motel has nice retro 1960s touches, though the rooms are plain. Good location, not far from the Fairfax District and Beverly Hills. **$158**
★ **Farmer's Daughter** 115 S Fairfax Ave ☎323 937 3930, ⓦfarmersdaughterhotel.com. Conveniently located across from (naturally) the Farmers' Market, this is a handsome boutique property with internet access, DVD players, flat-screen TVs and elements of "country styled" Midwestern kitsch. **$199**

SANTA MONICA AND MALIBU

★ **Ambrose** 1255 20th St, Santa Monica ☎310 315 1555, ⓦambrosehotel.com. Best choice for inland Santa Monica, with Arts-and-Crafts-styled decor and boutique rooms that include continental breakfast. **$289**
Cal Mar 220 California St, Santa Monica ☎310 395 5555, ⓦcalmarhotel.com. Good for its central location, and the garden suites have CD/DVD players and dining rooms, kitchens and balconies. There's a heated pool,

fitness room and airport shuttle, too. **$230**
Casa Malibu Inn 22752 Pacific Coast Hwy, near Malibu ☎310 456 2219. Located right on Carbon Beach and featuring worn, but comfy 1950s-esque rooms – facing a courtyard garden or right on the beach with the sound of pounding waves. Some rooms with fireplace, jacuzzi and balcony. **$220**

HOSTELS

Banana Bungalow 5920 Hollywood Blvd, Hollywood ☎877 977 5077, ⓦbananabungalow.com; map p.829. Large, popular hostel, just east of the heart of Hollywood, with airport shuttles, tours to Venice Beach and theme parks, and in-room kitchens and many other amenities. There's a similarly priced branch in West Hollywood at 603 N Fairfax Ave (☎323 655 2002). Dorms **$32**, doubles **$89**
HI-Santa Monica 1436 2nd St at Broadway, Santa Monica ☎310 393 9913, ⓦhilosangeles.org. A few blocks from the beach and pier, the building was LA's Town Hall from 1887–89, and retains its historic charm, with a pleasant inner courtyard, internet café, movie room – and 260 beds. Reservations essential in summer. Dorms **$46**
Orange Drive Manor 1764 N Orange Drive, Hollywood ☎323 850 0350, ⓦorangedrivehostel.com; map p.829. Centrally located hostel (right behind the Chinese Theatre), offering tours to film studios, theme parks and homes of the stars. Dorms **$36**, doubles **$80**
Orbit Hotel and Hostel 603 N Fairfax Ave, West Hollywood ☎323 655 1510, ⓦorbithotel.com; map p.829. Retro 1960s hotel and hostel with sleek Day-Glo furnishings and modern decor, offering complimentary breakfast, movie-screening room, patio, café, private baths in all rooms, and shuttle tours. Dorms **$35**, doubles **$95**
Stay on Main Hotel 636 S Main St, downtown LA ☎213 213 7829, ⓦstayonmain.com; map p.824. Lodging near a dicey section of the Old Bank District, offering wi-fi access and clean, simple but stylish accommodation, with shared bunk rooms and private rooms with and without private bath. Dorms **$32**, doubles **$55**
USA Hostels – Hollywood 1624 Schrader Ave, Hollywood ☎323 462 3777, ⓦusahostels.com; map p.829. A block south of the centre of Hollywood Blvd, near major attractions, and with a games room, private baths, bar, wi-fi access and garden patio, as well as airport and train shuttles. Dorms **$48**, doubles **$120**

EATING

DOWNTOWN AND AROUND

★ **Bestia** 2121 7th Place ☎213 514 5724, ⓦbestia.com; map p.824. Incredibly creative multiregional Italian restaurant. Menus based on more than sixty different house-cured meats and charcuterie, and Neapolitan pizzas baked in wood-fired ovens. Mon–Thurs & Sun 6–11pm, Fri & Sat 6pm–midnight.

Clifton's Cafeteria 648 S Broadway ☎213 627 1673, ⓦcliftonscafeteria.com; map p.824. Classic 1935 cafeteria with bizarre decor: redwood trees, waterfall and mini-chapel. The food is traditional meat-and-potatoes American, and cheap, too. Daily 6.30am–7.30pm.
Cole's Pacific Electric Buffet 118 E 6th St ☎213 622 4090; map p.824. In the same seedy spot since 1908, this

is LA's oldest restaurant – and restored in 2008. The decor and food haven't changed much, and the rich, hearty French-dip sandwiches are still loaded with steak, pastrami or brisket – a dish supposedly invented at this very spot, a claim challenged by *Philippe*'s (see below). Mon–Wed & Sun 11am–10pm, Thurs 11am–11pm, Fri & Sat 11am–1am.

★ **King Taco** 2904 N Broadway ☎323 222 8500, ⓦkingtaco.com; map p.824. The most centrally located diner in a chain of ultra-cheap shops around downtown (this one north of Chinatown), with many varieties of savoury tacos, tamales, quesadillas and burritos. Mon–Thurs & Sun 8.30am–11pm, Fri & Sat 8.30am–2am.

Pacific Dining Car 1310 W 6th St ☎213 483 6000, ⓦpacificdiningcar.com; map p.824. Would-be English supper club, here since 1921, located inside an old railroad carriage where the downtown elite used to cut secret deals. Very expensive and delicious steaks. Breakfast is the best value. Daily 24hr.

★ **Philippe the Original French Dip** 1001 N Alameda St ☎213 628 3781, ⓦphilippes.com; map p.824. This 1908 sawdust-floored café serves up the eponymous sandwich with turkey, ham, lamb, pork or beef dipped in roasting pan juices – an amazingly good and filling treat for $6.75. Cash only. Daily 6am–10pm.

HOLLYWOOD AND WEST HOLLYWOOD

Barney's Beanery 8447 Santa Monica Blvd ☎323 654 2287, ⓦbarneysbeanery.com; map p.829. Hundreds of bottled beers and hot dogs, hamburgers and bowls of chilli served in a hip, grungy environment since 1927 Angelenos can be divided up by those who love or hate the place – everyone knows it. Mon–Fri 10am–2pm, Sat & Sun 9am–2am.

Osteria Mozza 6602 Melrose Ave ☎323 297 0100, ⓦosteriamozza.com; map p.829. Italian fine dining culinary star (from the Mario Batali stable) with an amazing mozzarella bar showcasing handcrafted varieties from cream-filled burrata to spongy bufala. Mon–Fri 5.30–11pm, Sat 5–11pm, Sun 5–10pm.

★ **Pink's Hot Dogs** 709 N La Brea Ave ☎323 931 7594, ⓦpinkshollywood.com; map p.829. Depending on your taste, these monster hot dogs – topped with anything from bacon and chilli cheese to pastrami and Swiss cheese – are lifesavers or gut bombs, served here since 1939. Mon–Thurs & Sun 9.30am–2am, Fri & Sat 9.30am–3am.

★ **Providence** 5955 Melrose Ave ☎323 460 4170, ⓦprovidencela.com; map p.829. Near the top of the LA pricey-restaurant scale, and for good reason: the place is swarming with foodies, who come for the black sea bass, foie gras ravioli, lump blue crab and plenty of other tremendous choices. Mon–Thurs 6–10pm, Fri noon–2pm & 6–10pm, Sat 5.30–10pm, Sun 5.30–9pm.

Roscoe's House of Chicken and Waffles 1514 N Gower

St ☎323 466 7453, ⓦroscoeschickenandwaffles.com; map p.829. This diner – a soul food restaurant chain founded in 1975 by Herb Hudson, a Harlem native – attracts all sorts for its fried chicken, greens and thick waffles. Mon–Thurs & Sun 8.30am–midnight, Fri & Sat 8am–4am.

WEST LA

★ **The Apple Pan** 10801 W Pico Blvd ☎310 475 3585. Grab a spot at the U-shaped counter and enjoy freshly baked apple pie with vanilla ice cream and nicely greasy hamburgers (from $8). An old-time joint that opened in 1947, and was supposedly the inspiration for the *Johnny Rockets* chain. Daily 11am–midnight.

Nate 'n' Al's 414 N Beverly Drive ☎310 274 0101, ⓦnatenal.com. The best-known deli in Beverly Hills since 1945, popular with movie people and one of the few reasonably priced places in the vicinity. Get there early to grab a booth. Daily 7am–9pm.

★ **Nobu Matsuhisa** 129 N La Cienega Blvd ☎310 659 9639, ⓦnobumatsuhisa.com. The biggest name in town for sushi, charging the highest prices. Essential if you're a raw-fish aficionado with a wad of cash; combo lunches $21–26, or fixed-price meals $75–110. Mon–Fri 11.45am–2.15pm & 5.45–10.15pm, Sat & Sun 5.45–10.15pm.

★ **Nyala** 1076 S Fairfax Ave ☎323 936 5918, ⓦnyala-la.com. One of several favourites in Little Ethiopia, serving staples such as *doro wat* (marinated chicken) and *kitfo* (chopped beef with butter and cheese) with the delightfully spongy *injera* bread. Mon–Sat 11.30am–10.30pm, Sun 12.30–9.30pm.

Tsujita 2057 Sawtelle Blvd ☎310 231 7373, ⓦtsujita-la.com. One of the hottest ramen noodle shops in the city, with mouth-watering *tsukemen*, dipping noodles with an incredible pork broth ($9.95), served at lunch only. Daily 11am–midnight.

SANTA MONICA AND VENICE

Chaya Venice 110 Navy St ☎310 396 1179, ⓦthechaya.com/venice. Elegant mix of Japanese and Mediterranean foods in an arty sushi bar, with plenty of Cal-cuisine elements, excellent service and a suitably snazzy clientele. Mon–Thurs 11.30am–2.30pm & 6–10.30pm, Fri 11.30am–2.30pm & 6–11pm, Sat 6–11pm, Sun 6–10pm.

Espresso Cielo 3101 Main St ☎310 314 9999, ⓦsm.espressocielo.com. Beautifully crafted coffees from Vancouver's lauded 49th Parallel roasters, in a sunny setting near the beach. Also serves a good range of teas and excellent locally made pastries. Daily 7am–7pm.

★ **Father's Office** 1018 Montana Ave ☎310 736 2224, ⓦfathersoffice.com. If you're as interested in celebrity-spotting as in chowing down, check out this chic gastropub opened back in 1953, where the craft beers and the "Office Burger" ($12.50) have garnered a loyal

13

following. Mon–Thurs 5pm–1am, Fri 4pm–2am, Sat noon–2am, Sun noon–midnight.

⭐ **Rae's Diner** 2901 Pico Blvd. Classic diner since 1958, with heavy, tasty comfort food. Its turquoise-blue facade and interior have been seen in many films, notably *True Romance*, Steve Martin's *Bowfinger* and the remake of *Starsky and Hutch*. Eat for under $6, cash only. Daily 6.30am–4pm.

⭐ **Umami Burger** 500 Broadway ☎310 451 1300, ⓦumami.com. Home of the truffle burger ($12), spicy bird burger ($12), truffle fries ($5.50) and several other artful creations, this mini-chain has become a major coast-to-coast fad. Mon–Wed 11am–10pm, Thurs–Sat 11am–11pm, Sun noon–10pm.

SOUTH BAY AND LONG BEACH

Johnny Reb's 4663 N Long Beach Blvd ☎562 423 7327, ⓦjohnnyrebs.com. The waft of BBQ ribs, catfish and hush puppies alone may draw you to this prime Southern spot, where the portions are large and the prices low. Daily 7am–8.30pm.

⭐ **Pann's** 6710 La Tijera Blvd, Inglewood ☎323 776 3770, ⓦpanns.com. One of the all-time great Googie diners since 1958, where you can't go wrong with the classic burgers or biscuits and gravy (mains $10–12). Daily 7am–9pm.

⭐ **Randy's Donuts** 805 W Manchester Ave, Inglewood ☎310 645 4707, ⓦrandys-donuts.com. This Pop Art fixture is hard to miss, thanks to the colossal doughnut sitting on the roof built in 1953. Excellent for its piping-hot treats ($0.75–1.10), which you can pick up at the drive-through on your way to or from LAX. Daily 24hr.

ORANGE COUNTY

Angelo's Hamburgers 511 S State College Blvd, Anaheim ☎714 533 1401. Straight out of *Happy Days*,

a drive-in complete with roller-skating car-hops, neon signs, vintage cars and, incidentally, good cheeseburgers for just $1.75. Mon–Wed & Sun 8am–11pm, Thurs–Sat 8am–1am.

Heroes Bar & Grill 125 W Santa Fe Ave, Fullerton ☎714 738 4356, ⓦheroesbarandgrill.net. The place to come if you're starving after hitting the theme parks. Knock back one of the hundred beers available or chow down on hamburgers, chilli, ribs or meatloaf. Daily 11am–midnight.

Ruby's 1 Balboa Pier, Newport Beach ☎949 675 7829, ⓦrubys.com. The first and finest of the retro-streamline 1940s diners in this chain – in a great location at the end of Newport's popular pier. Mostly offers the standard fare of burgers, fries and soda. Daily 8am–8pm.

THE SAN GABRIEL AND SAN FERNANDO VALLEYS

⭐ **Dr Hogly Wogly's Tyler Texas BBQ** 8136 Sepulveda Blvd, Van Nuys ☎818 780 6701, ⓦhogly wogly.com. You could be in for a long wait for some of the best chicken, sausages, ribs and beans in LA since 1969, despite the long drive to the middle of nowhere. Daily 11am–10pm.

Fair Oaks Pharmacy & Soda Fountain 1526 Mission St, South Pasadena ☎626 799 1414, ⓦfairoaks pharmacy.net. Restored soda fountain with many old-time drinks like lime rickeys, root beer floats, milkshakes and egg creams – a historic 1915 highlight along the former Route 66. Mon–Sat 9am–9pm, Sun 10am–7pm.

⭐ **Porto's Bakery** 315 N Brand Blvd, Glendale ☎818 956 5996, ⓦportosbakery.com. Top-notch café serving Cuban flaky pastries (90¢) and sandwiches, rum-soaked cheesecakes, muffins, Danishes, croissants, tarts and cappuccino. Mon–Sat 6.30am–8pm, Sun 7am–6pm.

NIGHTLIFE

BARS

⭐ **Dresden Room** 1760 N Vermont Ave, Hollywood ☎323 665 4294, ⓦthedresden.com; map p.829. One of the neighbourhood's classic bars and restaurants, perhaps best known for its evening show (Tues–Sat 9pm–1.15am), in which the husband-and-wife lounge act of Marty and Elayne take requests from the crowd of old-timers and hipsters. Mon–Sat 4.30pm–2am, Sun 4.30pm–midnight.

⭐ **Edison** 108 W 2nd St, downtown LA ☎213 613 0000, ⓦedisondowntown.com; map p.824. One of LA's best über-chic bars, with stunning antique industrial decor (it's located in downtown's first power plant, dating from 1910), retro lounge music, upmarket food, a nice (though pricey) range of cocktails and a smart dress code. Wed–Fri 5pm–2am, Sat 7pm–2am.

El Carmen 8138 W 3rd St, West LA ☎323 852 1552, ⓦelcarmenrestaurant.com. Faux dive bar with a

south-of-the-border theme pushed to the extreme, with black-velvet pictures of Mexican wrestlers, steer horns, stuffed snakes and much tongue-in-cheek grunge, as well as signature margaritas and a good range of tequilas. Daily 5pm–2am.

Hinano Café 15 W Washington Blvd, Venice ☎310 822 3902. Low-attitude chill bar by the beach – an untouristy place for a drink, with pool tables, good and cheap burgers, shambling decor and a mostly local crowd. Daily 10am–2am.

HMS Bounty 3357 Wilshire Blvd, Koreatown ☎213 385 7275, ⓦthehmsbounty.com. An authentic dive experience, this grungy bar, advertising "Food and Grog", is a hot spot for hipsters and grizzled old-timers – they come for the dark ambience, cheap and potent drinks and kitschy nautical motifs. Mon–Thurs & Sun 11am–1am, Fri & Sat 11am–2am.

Library Alehouse 2911 Main St, Santa Monica ☎310 314 4855, ⊛libraryalehouse.com. Presenting the choicest brews from West Coast microbreweries and beyond, this is a good spot to select from a range of well known and obscure labels while munching on a decent selection of food. Daily 11.30am–midnight.

★ **Musso and Frank Grill** 6667 Hollywood Blvd, Hollywood ☎323 467 7788, ⊛mussoandfrank.com; map p.829. If you haven't had a drink in this landmark bar, open since 1919 (located in the centre of the district), you haven't been to Hollywood. It also serves pricey diner food. Tues–Sat 11am–11pm.

Redwood 316 W 2nd St, downtown LA ☎213 680 2600, ⊛theredwoodbar.com; map p.824. Solid choice for serious drinking and cheap all-American grub since 1943, now remade into a "pirate bar" featuring skull-and-crossbones decor and live rock and rockabilly music most nights (sometimes $10 cover). Daily 11am–2am.

CLUBS

The Abbey 692 N Robertson Blvd, West Hollywood ☎310 289 8410, ⊛abbeyfoodandbar.com; map p.829. West Hollywood party central: a crazy, busy club scene in the heart of gay WeHo that nonetheless caters to a mixed crowd for its great people-watching, go-go dancers and buzzing atmosphere. Daily 9am–2am.

★ **Avalon** 1735 N Vine St, Hollywood ☎323 462 8900, ⊛avalonhollywood.com; map p.829. Major dance club spinning old-school faves, along with the usual techno and house, with the occasional big-name DJ dropping in. Prices are among the most expensive in town. Cover $10–20. Fri 9.30pm–5am, Sat 9.30pm–7am.

Bar Sinister 1652 N Cherokee, Hollywood ☎323 462 1934, ⊛barsinister.net; map p.829. Sprightly dance beats most nights of the week, then memorably spooky Goth music and anaemic-looking vampire types on Sat. Connected to *Boardner's* bar. Cover $10–15. Sat 10pm–3am.

Circle Bar 2926 Main St, Santa Monica ☎310 450 0508, ⊛circle-bar.com. Old-fashioned dive (based on the original 1949 oval-shaped bar) that mainly draws a crowd of high-fiving party dudes who get plastered on the pricey but potent drinks and struggle to keep the beat on the dance floor. No cover. Daily 9pm–2am.

Three Clubs 1123 N Vine St, Hollywood ☎323 462 6441, ⊛threeclubs.com; map p.829. Dark, perennially trendy bar and club where the usual crowd of hipsters drops in for retro, rock and funk music, and gets pleasingly plastered. Colourless exterior and lack of good signage makes the joint even hipper. Mon & Fri 6pm–3am, Tues, Wed & Sat 6pm–2am, Thurs 6pm–1.30am, Sun 5pm–2am.

LIVE MUSIC

The Baked Potato 3787 Cahuenga Blvd W, Studio City ☎818 980 1615, ⊛thebakedpotato.com; map p.829.

A small but near-legendary contemporary jazz spot since 1970, where many reputations have been forged. Daily 7pm–2am.

The Echo 1822 Sunset Blvd, Echo Park ☎213 413 8200, ⊛theecho.com. An Echo Park club with scrappy indie-rock bands playing in a dark, intense little hole for a crowd of serious hipsters. A good place to catch what's bubbling up on the underground music scene. Open daily, see website for times and cover.

Harvelle's 1432 4th St, Santa Monica ☎310 395 1676, ⊛harvelles.com. A stellar blues joint near the Third Street Promenade, open since 1931. It offers different performers nightly and a little funk, R&B and burlesque thrown in too. Daily 8pm–2am.

★ **Hotel Café** 1623 N Cahuenga Blvd, Hollywood ☎323 461 2040, ⊛hotelcafe.com; map p.829. Comfortable spot for acoustic acts and singer-songsmiths, as well as indie bands. Usually has the best line-up in town for this sort of thing. Daily, shows usually from 7pm.

Key Club 9039 Sunset Blvd, West Hollywood ☎310 274 5800. A hot spot in the liveliest section of the strip, attracting a young, hip group for its regular concerts in the rock, punk and metal vein, with occasional lighter fare as well. Also has DJ and club nights. Wed–Sun 6pm–1am.

The Roxy 9009 W Sunset Blvd, West Hollywood ☎310 276 2222, ⊛theroxyonsunset.com. Among the top showcases for the music industry's new signings, intimate and with a great sound system, on the western – but still frenetic – end of the strip. Punk and hip-hop dominate. Hours vary, see website for upcoming shows.

Rusty's Surf Ranch 256 Santa Monica Pier ☎310 393 7437, ⊛rustyssurfranch.com. Offers not only surf music – and displays of old-time long boards – but also rock, pop, folk and even karaoke. Always a popular spot for tourists, near the end of the pier. Mon–Fri noon–2am, Sat & Sun 11am–2am.

The Troubadour 9081 Santa Monica Blvd, West Hollywood ☎310 276 6168, ⊛troubadour.com. An old 1957 mainstay that's been through a lot of incarnations in its fifty years. It used to be known for folk and country rock, then metal, and now for various flavours of indie rock. Hours vary, see website for upcoming shows.

The Viper Room 8852 Sunset Blvd, West Hollywood ☎310 358 1881, ⊛viperroom.com. Great live acts – expect almost any musician to show up on stage. Partly owned by Johnny Depp until 2004, and the place where River Phoenix died of a drug overdose in 1993. Hours vary, shows usually daily from 8pm.

★ **Whisky-a-Go-Go** 8901 Sunset Blvd, West Hollywood ☎310 652 4202, ⊛whiskyagogo.com. Legendary spot since 1964, and still important for LA's rising music stars. Mainly hard rock and metal, though you might catch an alternative act now and then. Daily 10am–2am.

13

ENTERTAINMENT

CLASSICAL MUSIC, OPERA AND DANCE

Disney Hall 1st St at Grand Ave, downtown LA ☎323 850 2000, ⓦlaphil.com. LA's most renowned cultural attraction, which hosts the LA Philharmonic in a striking Frank Gehry building.

Greek Theatre 2700 N Vermont Ave, Griffith Park ☎323 665 1927, ⓦgreektheatrela.com. Outdoor, summer-only venue (May–Oct) hosting mainstream rock and pop acts and seating for five thousand. Parking can be a mess, so come early.

The Hollywood Bowl 2301 N Highland Ave, Hollywood ☎323 850 2000, ⓦhollywoodbowl.org. A famed band-shell (see p.830) that hosts the LA Philharmonic and summer open-air concerts, usually of the pops variety.

Los Angeles Ballet 11755 Exposition Blvd, West LA (venues rotate) ☎310 998 7782, ⓦlosangelesballet.org. Features a Nov–May programme with standards like the *Nutcracker* and a good number of new and modern works.

Los Angeles Chamber Orchestra 350 S Figueroa St, downtown LA (venues rotate) ☎213 622 7001, ⓦlaco .org. Presents a range of chamber works, not all canonical, from different eras. Prices vary widely.

COMEDY

Comedy & Magic Club 1018 Hermosa Ave, Hermosa Beach ☎310 372 1193, ⓦcomedyandmagicclub.info. Notable South Bay comedy space where Jay Leno some-times tests material. Tickets can run up to $30, depending on the performer. Tues–Sun 8pm–midnight.

The Comedy Store 8433 W Sunset Blvd, West LA ☎323 656 6228, ⓦthecomedystore.com. LA's premier comedy showcase and popular enough to be spread over three rooms – which means there's usually space, even at week-ends. Daily 7pm–2.30am.

★ **Groundlings Theatre** 7307 Melrose Ave, West LA ☎323 934 4747, ⓦgroundlings.com. Pioneering venue where only the gifted survive (Lisa Kudrow and Kristen Wiig among them), with furious improv events and high-wire comedy acts that can inspire greatness or groans. No alcohol. Shows usually start Mon–Sat 8pm, Sun 7.30pm.

The Improv 8162 Melrose Ave, West LA ☎323 651 2583, ⓦimprov.com. Long-standing brick-walled joint that spawned a national chain. Still known for hosting some of the best acts working in both stand-up and improv. One of LA's top comedy spots – so book ahead. Daily 6pm–2am.

The Laugh Factory 8001 Sunset Blvd, West Hollywood ☎323 656 1336, ⓦlaughfactory.com. Stand-ups of varying reputations, with the odd big name and regular ensemble shows. Daily 7pm–2am.

Second City Studio Theater 6560 Hollywood Blvd, Hollywood ☎323 464 8542, ⓦsecondcity.com. Ground-breaking comedy troupe with numerous branches in LA, hosting nightly improv and sketch comedy sometimes built around lengthy routines and theme performances. Shows usually Mon–Fri 8pm, Sat 3.30pm, Sun 1.30pm.

THEATRE

★ **The Actors' Gang** 9070 Venice Blvd, Culver City ☎310 838 4264, ⓦtheactorsgang.com. A cross between a major and an alternative theatre; having fewer than a hundred seats keeps it cosy, though it does host the odd spectacular production that features semi-famous names from film or TV.

Ahmanson Theatre Music Center, 135 N Grand Ave, downtown LA ☎213 628 2772, ⓦcentertheatregroup .org. A 2000-seat theatre hosting colossal travelling

---

PRO SPORTS IN LA

Baseball The LA Dodgers (☎323 224 1500, ⓦlosangeles.dodgers.mlb.com) play at Dodger Stadium, 1000 Elysian Park Ave, near downtown; the LA Angels of Anaheim (☎714 940 2000, ⓦlosangeles.angels.mlb.com) at Angel Stadium of Anaheim at 2000 Gene Autry Way, Anaheim in Orange County; seats for both $15–150.

Basketball The Lakers (tickets $25–260; ☎213 480 3232, ⓦnba.com/lakers), Clippers ($20–250; ☎213 742 7430, ⓦnba.com/clippers), and women's Sparks ($10–55; ☎213 742 7340, ⓦwnba. com/sparks) all play at the Staples Center, 1111 S Figueroa St in downtown LA.

Football The 102,000-seat Rose Bowl (☎626 577 3100, ⓦrosebowlstadium.com) is the site of Pasadena's New Year's Day college football game, but LA hasn't had a pro franchise since the Raiders moved back to Oakland in 1994.

Hockey The Kings are based at Staples Center ($25–135; ☎213 742 7100, ⓦkings.nhl.com), and Orange County's Anaheim Ducks play at Honda Center, 2695 East Katella Ave, Anaheim ($20–175; ☎714 704 2500, ⓦducks.nhl.com).

Soccer The Galaxy ($20–125; ☎310 630 2200, ⓦlagalaxy.com) and CD Chivas USA ($15–100; ☎310 630 2000, ⓦcdchivasusa.com) both play at the StubHub Center, 18400 Avalon Blvd, in the South Bay city of Carson.

shows from Broadway. If you've seen a major production advertised on TV and on the sides of buses, it's probably playing here.

★ **The Complex** 6476 Santa Monica Blvd, Hollywood ☎ 323 465 0383, ✆ complexhollywood.com. A group of alternative companies revolving around five small theatres, where you're likely to see any number of dynamic productions.

Geffen Playhouse 10886 Le Conte Ave, Westwood ☎ 310 208 5454, ✆ geffenplayhouse.com A 500-seat, quaint Spanish Revival building that often hosts one-person shows. There's a decidedly Hollywood connection, evident in the crowd-pleasing nature of many of the productions.

Hudson Theatres 6539 Santa Monica Blvd, Hollywood ☎ 323 856 4252, ✆ hudsontheatre.com. Socially conscious "message" plays alternate with more satirical, comedic works at this venue for upcoming actors. Complex consists of three stages, plus a café and art gallery.

Open Fist Theatre 6209 Santa Monica Blvd, Hollywood ☎ 323 882 6912, ✆ openfist.org. As you might expect from the name, biting and edgy works are often the focus at this small theatre company, employing a limited cast of spirited unknowns.

Pantages Theatre 6233 Hollywood Blvd, Hollywood ☎ 323 468 1770, ✆ hollywoodpantages.com. Quite the stunner: an exquisite, atmospheric Art Deco theatre in the heart of historic Hollywood, hosting major touring Broadway productions.

Theatre West 3333 Cahuenga Blvd West, Hollywood ☎ 323 851 7977, ✆ theatrewest.org A classic venue that's always a good spot to see inventive, sometimes odd, productions with a troupe of excellent young up-and-comers.

FILM

Arclight 6360 Sunset Blvd, Hollywood ☎ 323 464 1478, ✆ arclightcinemas.com. All-reserved seats in fourteen theatres, top-of-the-line projection, good sightlines, wide seats and – best of all – the iconic Cinerama Dome, a white hemisphere that has the biggest screen in California.

Egyptian 6712 Hollywood Blvd, Hollywood ☎ 323 466 3456, ✆ egyptiantheatre.com. Has showings of revival, experimental and art films, and has been lovingly restored as a kitschy masterpiece of the Egyptian Revival – all grand columns, winged scarabs and mythological gods (see p.828).

TCL Chinese Theatre 6925 Hollywood Blvd, Hollywood ☎ 323 464 8111, ✆ tclchinesetheatres.com. With its forecourt thick with tourists and wild chinoiserie design, this Hollywood icon shows relentlessly mainstream films, but is still worthy of all the postcard images (see p.827).

Nuart 11272 Santa Monica Blvd, West LA ☎ 310 281 8223, ✆ landmarktheatres.com. Shows rarely seen classics, documentaries and edgy foreign-language films, and is the main option for independent filmmakers testing their work. Sometimes offers brief December previews of Oscar contenders.

Village 961 Broxton Ave, Westwood ☎ 310 248 6266, ✆ regencymovies.com. One of the best places to watch a movie in LA, with a giant screen, fine seats and good balcony views, and a frequent spot for Hollywood premieres. The marvellous 1931 exterior features a white spire.

★ **Warner Grand** 478 W 6th St, San Pedro ☎ 310 548 7672, ✆ grandvision.org/warner-grand.asp. Restored 1931 Zigzag Moderne masterpiece with dark geometric details, great columns and sunburst motifs – a style that almost looks pre-Columbian. Now a repertory cinema and performance hall.

The deserts

The hot and forbidding landscape of California's **deserts** exerts a powerful fascination for adventurous travellers. The two distinct regions are the **Low Desert** in the south, the most easily reached from LA, containing the opulent oasis of **Palm Springs** and the primeval expanse of **Joshua Tree National Park**; and the **Mojave** or **High Desert**, dominated by **Death Valley** and stretching along Hwy-395 to the sparsely populated **Owens Valley**, infamous as the place from which LA stole its water a hundred years ago.

It is impossible to do justice to this area without a car. Palm Springs can be reached on public transport from LA, but only the periphery of Joshua Tree is accessible and it's a long hot walk to anywhere worth seeing. You can get as far as dreary Barstow on Greyhound and Amtrak, but no transport traverses Death Valley, understandably so in the summer.

Palm Springs and around

Amid farmland replete with golf courses, condos and millionaires, **PALM SPRINGS** embodies a strange mix of Spanish Colonial and the "**Desert Modern**" architecture of

13

the 1950s. Massive Mount San Jacinto looms over its low-slung buildings, casting a welcome shadow over the town in the late-afternoon heat. Most Angelenos come for **"the Season"**, the delightfully balmy months from January to May when all the golf and tennis tournaments are held. In recent years, the city has also become a major **gay and lesbian** resort (Ⓦvisitgaypalmsprings.com has a list of options).

Downtown Palm Springs stretches for half a mile along **Palm Canyon Drive** from Tamarisk to Ramon roads, much of it a wide, bright and modern strip of chain stores that has engulfed the town's quaint Spanish Colonial-style buildings.

Village Green Heritage Center

219 S Palm Canyon Drive • **Heritage Center** Mid-Oct to May Wed & Sun noon–3pm, Thurs–Sat 10am–4pm • $2 • Ⓣ 760 323 8297; Ⓦ palmsprings.com/history **Agua Caliente Cultural Museum** June–Aug Fri–Sun 10am–5pm; Sept–May Wed–Sun 10am–5pm • Free • Ⓣ 760 778 1079, Ⓦ accmuseum.org

The early history of Palm Springs is preserved at the **Village Green Heritage Center**, comprising two historic properties: the **McCallum Adobe**, the oldest building in Palm Springs, was built in 1884, while **Miss Cornelia's Little House** was built in 1893 from railroad ties and is now furnished with antiques from the pioneer era. Also on the plaza, the **Agua Caliente Cultural Museum** charts the history and culture of the local Agua Caliente Band of Cahuilla Indians, with a small but absorbing collection of basketry and pottery.

Palm Springs Art Museum

101 Museum Drive • Tues, Wed & Fri–Sun 10am–5pm, Thurs noon–8pm; June–Sept closed Tues • $12.50; free Thurs 4–8pm • Ⓣ 760 322 4800, Ⓦ psmuseum.org

Don't skip the **Palm Springs Art Museum**, where the obvious wealth of its benefactors has been put to superb use. The focus is on both older and contemporary art, principally from California, though with wider-ranging Native American and Southwestern art too. Galleries with diverting exhibits surround a large central space, dotted with works by major sculptors such as Henry Moore, Barbara Hepworth and Alexander Calder.

Indian Canyons

38500 S Palm Canyon Drive • Oct–June daily 8am–5pm; July–Sept Fri–Sun 8am–5pm • $9 • Ⓣ 760 323 6018, Ⓦ indian-canyons.com

The best-known and most accessible of the Palm Springs canyons are Palm Canyon, Andreas Canyon and Murray Canyon, known collectively as **Indian Canyons**, on part of the Agua Caliente Indian Reservation that lies to the south of downtown. The most popular target is fifteen-mile long **Palm Canyon**, which comes choked with palms beside a seasonal stream along which runs the easy 1.5-mile Palm Canyon Trail. A one-mile loop visits the best of **Andreas Canyon**, noted for its rock formations and more popular than **Murray Canyon**, which is difficult to reach but offers a 12ft waterfall as a reward for those prepared to hike two miles. The **Palm Canyon Trading Post**, 380 N Palm Canyon Drive (same hours as canyons; Ⓣ760 323 6018), is a gift shop that serves as the visitor centre.

Palm Springs Aerial Tramway

1 Tram Way, at N Palm Canyon Drive • Mon–Fri 10am–9.45pm, Sat & Sun 8am–9.45pm • $23.95; $36 with dinner at Pines Café • Ⓣ 888 515 8726, Ⓦ pstramway.com

When the desert heat becomes too much to bear, you can travel up from the arid desert floor to (sometimes) snow-covered alpine hiking trails atop Mount San Jacinto by riding the **Palm Springs Aerial Tramway** on the northern edge of Palm Springs. Every thirty minutes large cable cars glide up to the Mountain Station at 8516ft – a rise of almost 6000ft. From here you can summit the nearby peak of 10,834ft **Mount San Jacinto** itself (5.5 miles one way), or explore a number of other shorter forest trails.

13

Palm Desert

Some fourteen miles southeast of downtown Palm Springs, **PALM DESERT** is, like rest of the **Coachella Valley**, littered with golf courses and elite resorts, with the added treat of the mile-long **El Paseo**, a boutique-rich strip known for its kitschy Halloween golf-cart parade (ⓦgolfcartparade.com). For more cultured pursuits, you'll find the **Palm Springs Art Museum in Palm Desert** (Tues, Wed & Fri–Sun 10am–5pm; Thurs noon–8pm; $5; ☏760 322 4800, ⓦpsmuseum.org) where El Paseo meets Hwy-111 (western end), this outpost of the original (see opposite) opened in 2012 to showcase rotating exhibitions of contemporary sculpture, painting, photography and new media.

Palm Desert is also home to the **Living Desert**, a combination garden and zoo at 47900 Portola Ave (daily: June–Sept 8am–1.30pm; Oct–May 9am–5pm; $17.75; ☏760 346 5694, ⓦlivingdesert.org), rich with cactus and palm gardens, but throwing in incongruous African desert animals such as giraffes, zebras, cheetahs and warthogs.

ARRIVAL AND DEPARTURE   PALM SPRINGS

By plane Several airlines serve Palm Springs International Airport, 3400 E Tahquitz Canyon Way (☏760 318 3800), where you can take a taxi, or catch bus #24 then transfer to the #111 into town. Tickets are often expensive, and if you're flying to California it is usually cheaper to fly into Los Angeles and rent a car from there.

By train Amtrak trains arrive at a desolate platform 3 miles north of Palm Springs at North Indian Drive, half a mile south of I-10. A taxi to downtown will cost around $20.

Destinations Houston (3 weekly; 32hr 34min); Los Angeles (3 weekly; 3hr 33min); New Orleans (3 weekly; 43hr 4min); San Antonio (3 weekly; 26hr 14min); Tucson (3 weekly; 6hr 52min).

By bus Greyhound buses stop at the Amtrak station north of town (see above).

Destinations Calexico (Mexican border; 3 daily; 3hr 5min); Los Angeles (3 daily; 2hr 30min–3hr 25min).

GETTING AROUND AND INFORMATION

By bus For all major destinations in the Coachella Valley, SunLine Transit (☏800 347 8628, ⓦsunline.org) operates daily 6am–8pm (until 11pm on some routes) and charges $1/ride, plus an extra 25¢ for transfers (unlimited within

2hr of purchase); a day pass costs $3.

Visitor centre 2901 N Palm Canyon Drive (daily 9am–5pm; ☏800 347 7746, ⓦvisitpalmsprings.com).

ACCOMMODATION

A Place in the Sun Hotel 754 San Lorenzo Rd ☏760 325 0254, ⓦaplaceinthesunhotel.com. Built in the early 1950s as a retreat for the production crew of

the film *A Place in the Sun*, starring Elizabeth Taylor, this is a popular (pet-friendly) option set around a palm-fringed saltwater pool, with comfy studios and

---

COACHELLA

Since 1999 the **Coachella Valley Music and Arts Festival** (commonly known simply as "Coachella"), has been held across several stages at the Empire Polo Club south of downtown Indio at 81-800 Ave 51 (25 miles southeast of Palm Springs). The massive three-day rock and alternative music festival is packed with big-name artists and is wildly popular, despite the high cost of attending. The **Stagecoach Festival** (ⓦstagecoachfestival.com) is the outdoor country music festival "cousin" of Coachella, typically taking place one week later at the same venue,

PRACTICALITIES

First you need to purchase a **festival pass** (from $349/person online); passes are only good for the dates of the weekend you choose (you must buy two passes to attend both weekends), and there are no one-day passes. **Advance sales** typically take place a year before the festival, so make sure you check the website (ⓦcoachella.com) for updates.

Thousands of festival-goers **camp** on the polo field adjacent to the venue grounds ($85/car or pitch, in addition to the festival pass). Plenty of nearby **resorts** offer packages, which include festival shuttle buses, but these can start at over $2500 (see ⓦvalleymusictravel.com). If you want to stay somewhere cheaper but don't want the hassle of driving every day, you can still take one of the festival shuttle buses for $60 (for three days).

13

bungalows featuring rattan furniture and bright, snappy colours. **$129**

Casa Cody Inn 175 S Cahuilla Rd ☎760 320 9346, ⓦcasacody.com. Built in the 1920s by glamorous Hollywood pioneer Harriet Cody, this historic B&B offers tastefully furnished Southwestern-style rooms, a shady garden, great pool and tasty buffet breakfasts in a good location two blocks from downtown. All options but the "rooms" have a kitchen. Families and small groups should go for the gorgeous two-bedroom adobe cottage ($429). **$99**

★ **Desert Riviera Hotel** 610 E Palm Canyon Drive ☎760 327 5314, ⓦdesertrivierahotel.com. Palm Springs' most popular hotel for good reason, a 1951 gem with lush gardens, mountain views, heated pool, jacuzzi and simple but cosy rooms with a host of nice little extras (like a welcome basket of tasty treats). **$149**

★ **Orbit In** 562 W Arenas Rd ☎877 996 7248, ⓦorbitin.com. Modernist nirvana with two nearly adjacent locations: the super-stylish nine-room *Orbit In* itself, built in 1957 with its boomerang bar beside a chilled pool (where complimentary Orbitinis are served); and the more secluded 1940s *Hideaway* with lawns, a fire pit and guest kitchen/lounge. Cruise town on the free bikes, relax in rooms equipped with DVD and CD player and relax over a continental breakfast. It's adults-only and a two-night stay is required. *Orbit In* **$149**, *Hideaway* **$169**

EATING AND DRINKING

Cheeky's 622 N Palm Canyon Drive ☎760 327 7595, ⓦcheekysps.com. *The* place for breakfast, using seasonal, local and organic ingredients for the likes of a veggie-rich green frittata ($10), or one of their half-dozen types of bacon – or even a bacon flight ($4). Also inventive lunches. Wed–Mon 8am–2pm; closed Wed June–Sept.

★ **Johannes** 196 S Indian Canyon Drive ☎760 778 0017, ⓦjohannesrestaurants.com. The best of the modern, downtown restaurants, this unpretentious place offers superb-quality food ranging across international styles but with the occasional Austrian dish – schnitzel is a speciality ($13 at the bar). Mains might include crispy roasted half duck ($29) or even Thai curry ($21). Daily 5–10pm.

Las Casuelas Terraza 222 S Palm Canyon Drive ☎760 325 2794, ⓦlascasuelas.com. *Las Casuelas* opened its original establishment in 1958, but you can't beat this Spanish Colonial-style sister restaurant for its bustling atmosphere, stacks of mist-cooled outdoor seating centred on a palm-roofed bar, and usually some live entertainment. The food suffers from north-of-the-border blanding but is still tasty, and with combination plates for $12–16 and $5.50 margaritas it's not too expensive. Daily 11am–10pm.

★ **Tyler's Burgers** 149 S Indian Canyon Drive ☎760 325 2990, ⓦtylersburgers.com. Awesome old-fashioned burgers, fries and classic coleslaw at modest prices (from $6.75), either inside or on the patio. Cash only. Mon–Sat 11am–4pm.

Joshua Tree National Park

Covering a vast area where the high Mojave meets the lower Colorado Desert, **JOSHUA TREE NATIONAL PARK** is one of the most magical and intriguing of California's national parks. Almost 1250 square miles have been set aside for the park's ragged and gnarled namesakes, which aren't trees at all, but a type of **yucca**, similar to an agave. Named by Mormons in the 1850s, who saw in their craggy branches the arms of Joshua pointing to the promised land, Joshua trees can rise up to 40ft tall, and somehow manage to flourish despite the extreme aridity and rocky soil.

This unearthly landscape is ethereal at sunrise or sunset, when the desert floor is bathed in red light; at noon it can be a furnace, with temperatures topping 125°F in summer. Still, the park attracts campers, day-trippers and rock-climbers for its unspoiled beauty, gold-mine ruins, ancient petroglyphs and striking rock formations.

Visiting the park

A visit to **Keys Ranch** (by guided tour only; Oct–May daily 10am & 1pm; $5; reservations recommended on ☎760 367 5555) provides a testament to the difficulty of making a life in such a difficult environment, but if you'd rather wander around the national park by yourself, there are many options: one of the easiest hikes (3 miles, foot-travel only) starts one and a half miles from Canyon Road, six miles from the Twentynine Palms visitor centre, at **49 Palms Oasis**. West of the oasis, quartz boulders tower around the **Indian Cove** campground; a trail from the eastern branch of the campground road heads to **Rattlesnake Canyon**, where, after rainfall, the streams and waterfalls break an otherwise eerie silence among the monoliths.

13

Moving south into the main body of the park brings you to the **Wonderland of Rocks**, which features rounded granite boulders that draw rock-climbers from around the world. One fascinating trail climbs four miles past abandoned mines to the antiquated foundations and equipment of **Lost Horse Mine**, which produced around five million dollar's worth of gold and silver between 1894 and 1931 (in today's money). You can find a brilliant desert panorama of badlands and mountains at the 5185ft **Keys View** nearby, from where Geology Tour Road leads down to the east through the best of Joshua Tree's **rock formations** and, further on, to the **Cholla Cactus Garden**, a quarter-mile loop through an astonishing concentration of the "jumping" **cholla** cactus.

ARRIVAL AND INFORMATION   JOSHUA TREE NATIONAL PARK

Access and entry fees The park is open daily 24hr; admission is $15/vehicle for seven days, $5/cyclist or hiker (☎ 760 367 5500, ⓦ nps.gov/jotr).

By car Visiting the park without your own transport is not really an option. The park is less than an hour's drive north-east from Palm Springs, and best approached along Hwy-62, which branches off I-10; you can enter the park via the West Entrance at the town of Joshua Tree, or the North Entrance at Twentynine Palms (both with visitor centres).

Cottonwood Visitor Center Eight miles north of I-10 and the South Entrance at Cottonwood Spring (Mon–Fri 9am–4pm, Sat & Sun 8am–4pm). Exhibits here cover the park's natural history and desert ecology. Rangers can provide advice and maps, there's a bookstore and videos

are shown on demand.

Joshua Tree Visitor Center (West Entrance) 6554 Park Blvd, Joshua Tree, a block south of Hwy-62 (daily 8am–5pm). This is the busiest visitor centre, but the rangers do their best to field questions. Exhibits cover park geology, but also the human history of the region, plus sections on rock-climbing and hiking. Café and bookstore on site, videos shown on demand.

Oasis Visitor Center (North Entrance) 74485 National Park Drive, Twentynine Palms, at the junction of Utah Trail (daily 8am–5pm). The main visitor centre has displays on the natural formation of the park, and especially its two types of desert environment. Park videos shown on request 11am–3pm.

ACCOMMODATION AND EATING

Joshua Tree National Park has nine **campgrounds**, all concentrated in the northwest except for one at Cottonwood by the southern entrance. All have tables, fire rings (bring your own wood) and vault toilets, but only two (*Black Rock* and *Cottonwood*) have water supplies and flush toilets. All pitches are first-come, first-served, though *Black Rock* and *Indian Cove* can be reserved from Oct–May. More than eighty percent of the park is designated wilderness where **backcountry camping** is permitted, provided you register before you head out.

★ **29 Palms Inn** 73950 Inn Ave (off National Park Drive), Twentynine Palms ☎ 760 367 3505, ⓦ 29palmsinn.com. Built in 1928 and the best place in town, where an array of cosy adobe bungalows and wood-framed cabins are set around attractively arid grounds and gardens, and a central pool area contains a restaurant and bar. It's worth upgrading to a bungalow or even the lovely 1930s *Irene's Historic Adobe*, which sleeps four. Cabins $70, bungalows $85, *Irene's* $220

Black Rock Reservations on ☎ 877 444 6777. A large

campground (100 sites; 4000ft) only accessible from outside the park. Water available. $15

Indian Cove Reservations on ☎ 877 444 6777. Another large campground (101 sites; 3200ft) only accessible from outside the park. It's set among granite boulders and a trail from the eastern section of the campground road leads to Rattlesnake Canyon – its streams and waterfalls (depending on rainfall) breaking an otherwise eerie silence among the monoliths. No water. $15

Death Valley National Park

DEATH VALLEY – famously known as the hottest place on earth – is a place where sculpted rock layers form deeply shadowed, eroded crevices at the foot of silhouetted hills, their exotic minerals turning ancient mud flats into rainbows of sunlit iridescence. Throughout the summer, the **temperature** averages 112°F and the hot ground can reach near boiling. Better to come in spring, when wild flowers are in bloom and it's generally mild and dry. The central north–south valley contains two main outposts, **Stovepipe Wells** and **Furnace Creek**, site of the **visitor centre** (see p.852).

Dante's View, 21 miles south on CA-190 and ten miles along a very steep access road, offers a fine morning vista in which the pink-and-gold Panamint Mountains are

13

highlighted by the rising sun. Near Stovepipe Wells, some thirty miles northwest of Furnace Creek, spread fifteen rippled and contoured square miles of ever-changing **sand dunes**. The most popular sight, though, is the surreal **Scotty's Castle** (50min tours: early Nov to mid-April hourly 9am–4pm; late April to late May hourly 10am–4pm; late May to early Nov 10am, noon, 2pm & 4pm; $15; reservations ☎877 444 6777), forty miles north of Stovepipe Wells, built in the 1920s as a luxury desert retreat; tours take in the decorative wooden ceilings, indoor waterfalls and a remote-controlled player piano.

When travelling through this shadeless, desiccated area, be careful about heading out in the middle of the day (when the danger of heatstroke is at its worst), and always carry plenty of water for both car and body.

ARRIVAL AND INFORMATION

DEATH VALLEY NATIONAL PARK

By car Be sure to top up your tank before you head in, as petrol is notoriously expensive in the park. There's no scheduled public transport into the park.

Entrance Entrance to the park (good for seven days) is $20/vehicle, or $10/person if you're mad enough to walk or cycle. There are no staffed entrance stations, so pay at one of the self-serve machines near park entrances or at the visitor centre.

Visitor centre Furnace Creek is right in the heart of the valley and has an excellent visitor centre (daily: early Oct to mid-June 8am–5pm: mid-June to early Oct 9am–6pm; ☎760 786 3200, ⓦnps.gov/deva).

ACCOMMODATION AND EATING

Campgrounds in the park cost anywhere from nothing to $18 a night; most sites can't be reserved, and very few have shade. Free **backcountry camping** is allowed in most areas of the park, provided you keep 2 miles away from any roads (paved or otherwise) and 200 yards from water sources. No permits are required, but voluntary backcountry **registration** is strongly recommended and you'll probably need to carry in your own water. **RV drivers** will only find hookups inside the park at Stovepipe Wells and Panamint Springs, though most surrounding towns have facilities for RVs.

The Inn at Furnace Creek ☎7760 786 2345, ⓦfurnacecreekresort.com. Though only open in the more fashionable cooler months, this beautiful Mission-style adobe hotel, built amid date palms and tended lawns, is *the* place to stay in the park. Rooms are modern but tastefully done, many with great views. The gourmet dining room is set in a beautiful room that's hardly changed since the 1920s; just be prepared to dress up a bit, as shorts and T-shirts aren't allowed. It's also a great spot for afternoon tea or an evening cocktail; breakfast is also available. **$365**

The Ranch at Furnace Creek ☎760 786 2345, ⓦfurnacecreekresort.com. Functional, family-oriented and cheaper than the *Inn at Furnace Creek*, the *Ranch* lacks much of its atmosphere. The comfortable motel rooms are rather overpriced, but at least you get free access to the chlorine-free mineral swimming pool. Cabins **$142**, motel **$17**

The High Sierra and Owens Valley

The towering **eastern** peaks of the **HIGH SIERRA** drop abruptly to the barren landscape of **OWENS VALLEY**, sixty miles west of Death Valley. Almost this entire section of the Sierra Nevada is wilderness: well-maintained roads lead to trailheads at above 8000ft, providing access to the stark terrain of spires, glaciers and clear mountain lakes.

US-395 is the lifeline of the area and connects its several small towns, all with plenty of budget motels. As there is virtually no public transport in this area, except for CREST and YARTS (see p.854), you'll really need a car to get around.

Mount Whitney and Lone Pine

Rising out of the northern Mojave Desert, the mountainous backbone of the Sierra Nevada announces itself with a bang two hundred miles north of Los Angeles at 14,497ft **Whitney**, the highest point in the contiguous 48 US states. A silver-grey ridge of pinnacles forms a nearly sheer wall of granite, dominating the small roadside town of **LONE PINE** well over 10,000ft below.

13

Many early Westerns were filmed in the **Alabama Hills** to the west, named after Confederate sympathizers during the Civil War, a rugged expanse of bizarrely eroded sedimentary rock. Some of the oddest formations are linked by the **Picture Rocks Circle**, a paved road that loops around from Whitney Portal Road, passing rocks shaped like bullfrogs, walruses and baboons.

Two thousand eager souls make the strenuous 22-mile round-trip **hike** (12–16hr; 6100ft ascent) to the summit of Mount Whitney each summer and autumn (generally snow-free June–Oct), some doing it in one very long day, others sleeping along the way at one of two trail camps. The excellent **Mount Whitney Trail** passes a few lakes before following roughly one hundred switchbacks up to 13,600ft Trail Crest Pass; it then weaves through an often-windy landscape of jagged boulders to the epic summit.

INFORMATION

MOUNT WHITNEY AND LONE PINE

Visitor Center Two miles south of town on US-395 at the junction of CA-136 (daily 8am–5pm; ☎760 876 6222).

Permits Mount Whitney trail permits ($15) are awarded by lottery, and you're required to carry all food (and anything else with a scent) in a bear-proof food canister:

applications are available at ⓦr5.fs.fed.us/info and are only accepted in Feb. Free last-minute permits can be obtained from the visitor centre (see above) a day in advance of your planned ascent after 11am; try to avoid weekends, when demand is highest.

ACCOMMODATION AND EATING

Alabama Hills Cafe & Bakery 111 W Post St ☎760 876 4675. Stop in for some of the finest pancakes around (from $5.50), then take away some own-baked goods for later. Mon–Thurs 5.30am–2pm, Fri–Sun 7am–2pm.

Dow Villa Motel 310 S Main St (US-395) ☎760 876 5521, ⓦdowvillamotel.com. Sizeable complex featuring an older section built in 1923 to house movie-industry visitors, although John Wayne always requested Room 20

in the newer motel section. There's an impressive range of accommodation here, from basic bathless rooms to plush motel units. __$82__

Whitney Portal Family Campground ☎877 444 6777, ⓦrecreation.gov. Lovely 43-site campground at the base of the Mount Whitney Trail (8100ft). Open late May to late Oct. __$19__

Big Pine and the White Mountains

About fifty miles from Lone Pine, hikes lead from the end of Glacier Lodge Road, ten miles west of nondescript **BIG PINE**, up to **Palisades Glacier**, the southernmost glacier in the Northern Hemisphere. Along the opposite wall of five-mile-wide Owens Valley, the ancient, bald and dry **White Mountains** are home to gnarled **bristlecone pines**, the oldest living things on earth, some first sprouting over four thousand years ago.

The most accessible trees are in 10,000ft **Schulman Grove**, 24 miles east of Big Pine in **Ancient Bristlecone Pine Forest** ($3/person or $6/car; ☎760 873 2500, ⓦr5.fs.fed .us/inyo). The mile-long **Discovery Trail** passes some photogenic examples, while the four-mile **Methuselah Trail** loops by but (intentionally) fails to identify the oldest tree, the 4750-year-old Methuselah; both radiate out from the stylish, eco-friendly visitor centre (June–Sept daily 10am–5pm; Oct call for hours).

ACCOMMODATION

BIG PINE AND THE WHITE MOUNTAINS

Keough's Hot Springs Keough's Hot Springs Rd ☎760 872 4670, ⓦkeoughshotsprings.com. The area's prime hot springs resort has a variety of accommodation options, from bathless tent cabins and a so-called modular retreat

(a two-bedroom mobile home) to RV and tent sites. Pool fees are included in all roofed-accommodation rates. Tent cabins __$75__, modular retreat __$115__, RVs __$28__, tents __$23__

Bishop

The largest town (population 3500) in Owens Valley, **BISHOP** is an excellent base for cross-country skiing, fly-fishing and especially rock climbing. There are many **adventure travel specialists** based in town, including Sierra Mountain Center at 174 W Line St (☎760 873 8526, ⓦsierramountaincenter.com).

13

INFORMATION BISHOP

Visitor centre 690 N Main St (Mon–Fri 10am–5pm, Sat & Sun 10am–4pm; ☏ 888 395 3952, ⊛ bishopvisitor.com).
Ranger station 798 N Main St (June–Sept daily 8am–5pm; Oct–May Mon–Fri 8.30am–4.30pm; ☏ 760 873 2500); for specific questions on hiking and camping in the area.

ACCOMMODATION AND EATING

Creekside Inn 725 N Main St ☏ 760 872 3044, ⊛ bishopcreeksideinn.com. A modern, upscale hotel in the centre of town offering large rooms (some with kitchenette for $10–20 extra), complimentary breakfast and an outdoor pool. $140

Erick Schat's Bakkerÿ 736 N Main St (US-395) ☏ 760 873 7156. This bustling, pseudo-Dutch bakery has dozens of own-made breads on offer, as well as outdoor tables for tucking into good sandwiches (about $8). Don't leave without a loaf of round pecan pullaway bread ($7.50) – essentially an enormous cinnamon roll. Mon–Thurs 6am–6pm, Fri 6am–8pm, Sat & Sun 6am–6.30pm.

Mammoth Lakes

Forty miles north along US-395 from Bishop, then three miles west on CA-203, the resort town of **MAMMOTH LAKES** is home to the state's premier ski slopes outside of the Lake Tahoe Basin; in summer, it hosts on- and off-road bike races. To ski **Mammoth Mountain** (☏ 800 626 6684, ⊛ mammothmountain.com), which looms up behind the resort, pick up **lift tickets** ($99 a day) from the Main Lodge on Minaret Road, where you can also rent **equipment** and book **lessons**. In summer, fifty miles of snow-free slopes transform into the 3500-acre **Mammoth Mountain Bike Park**; a basic "pedal-only" fee ($15) gives you access to the trails; in addition, bike rentals are available for two hours ($30), four hours ($39) and full days ($50).

Devil's Postpile National Monument

Shuttle bus: late June to early Sept daily 7.30am–7pm (last bus leaves Devils Postpile 7.45pm), every 20–40min from Mammoth Mountain Main Lodge Adventure Center • Entrance free; shuttle bus day pass $7/person • ☏ 760 934 2289, ⊛ nps.gov/depo

One appealing summer-only destination is **Devil's Postpile National Monument**, seven miles southwest of Mammoth Mountain. This collection of slender, blue-grey basaltic columns, some as tall as 60ft, was formed as lava from a volcanic eruption cooled and fractured into columnar forms. From here, a two-mile hike along the San Joaquin River leads to 101ft **Rainbow Falls**, which refract the midday sun perfectly.

ARRIVAL AND INFORMATION MAMMOTH LAKES

By bus Year-round ESTA buses stop four times a week in the *McDonald's* parking lot on CA-203. There's also a seasonal YARTS service to Tuolumne Meadows and Yosemite Valley (July & Aug once daily; June & Sept Sat & Sun only; ⊛ yarts.com), which departs from *Mammoth Mountain Inn*, opposite the Main Lodge, at 7am and returns that evening around 9pm.

Visitor centre 2510 Main St (CA-203; daily 8am–5pm; ☏ 760 924 5500, ⊛ visitmammoth.com). The best source of practical information for the area, 0.5 mile east of the centre.

ACCOMMODATION

Cinnamon Bear Inn 113 Center St ☏ 800 845 2873, ⊛ cinnamonbearinn.com. A reasonably priced, 22-room B&B inn done in New England colonial style, with comfortable rooms; also on offer is a hot tub, wine-and-nibbles happy hour on arrival and a full breakfast. $119

Convict Lake Campground Just west of US-395, about 4 miles south of the Mammoth turnoff. This wooded, lakeside national forest campground boasts the longest open season in the area. Open late April to Oct. $20

Sierra Nevada Resort 164 Old Mammoth Rd ☏ 760 934 2515, ⊛ sierranevadalodge.com. With a terrific lobby that recalls a Southwestern hunting lodge, this renovated hotel has great-value rooms, some with fireplace ($80 extra). Rates include continental breakfast, access to a pool and hot tub and even a mini-golf course. $119

EATING AND DRINKING

Lakefront Restaurant Tamarack Lodge ☏ 760 934 2442. Superb lake views accompany equally outstanding dishes from a menu with French-Californian leanings that might include wild mushroom strudel ($12), walnut-crusted

chicken breast ($23) and a sumptuous selection of desserts and ports. Daily 11am–2pm (summer only) & 5.30–9.30pm.
The Stove 644 Old Mammoth Rd ☎760 934 2021.

A longstanding Mammoth favourite for its traditional country cooking, *The Stove* serves egg, waffle and pancake breakfasts (around $9), sandwiches, and full dinners – all in large portions. Daily 6.30am–2pm & 5–9pm.

Mono Lake

The vitreous blue expanse of **Mono Lake** sits in the midst of a volcanic desert tableland in the eastern shadow of Yosemite National Park. This science-fiction landscape holds two large islands – one light-coloured (Paoha), the other black (Negit) – surrounded by salty, alkaline water. Strange sandcastle-like formations of **tufa** – calcium deposited from springs – were exposed after Los Angeles extended an aqueduct carrying water diverted from the lake's feeder streams into the Mono Basin through an eleven-mile tunnel. Mono Lake is the primary nesting ground for the state's **California gull** population – twenty percent of the world's total – and a prime stopover for hundreds of thousands of grebes and phalaropes.

INFORMATION   MONO LAKE

Mono Lake Committee Information Center US-395 at Third St, in the adjacent town of Lee Vining (daily 9am–5pm; ☎760 647 6595, ⓦmonolake.org).

Mono Basin Scenic Area Visitor Center (June–Aug daily 8am–5pm; Sept–May call for hours; ☎760 647 6323, ⓦr5.fs.fed.us/info).

ACCOMMODATION AND EATING

El Mono Motel US-395, at Third St ☎760 647 6310, ⓦelmonomotel.com. This seasonal motel (it generally opens and closes with Tioga Pass) is the cheapest in town and has rooms that are small (and lack TVs and phones), but well kept and cheerfully decorated. **$69**
Whoa Nellie Deli CA-120, at US-395 ☎760 647 1088.

Inside the unlikely setting of *Tioga Gas Mart*, you'll find a lively atmosphere as this deli's kitchen dishes out great tortilla soup, jambalaya ($13), fish tacos ($12), pizza slices, burgers and steaks, along with espresso, microbrews and margaritas. May–Oct daily 6.30am–9pm.

Bodie State Historic Park

Daily: mid-May to late Oct 9am–6pm; late Oct to mid-May 10am–3pm • $7 • ☎760 647 6445, ⓦparks.ca.gov

North of Mono Lake, in a remote, high desert valley accessed by three miles of hardscrabble road, stands a well-preserved relic of the gold-mining glory days of the late nineteenth century. **Bodie State Historic Park** is perhaps the most evocative **ghost town** in the USA, with most of its structures preserved in their decay, but not renovated. Boasting sixty saloons and dance halls and a population of nearly ten thousand at its peak, it was among the wildest of Western mining camps; more than 150 wooden buildings survive around the town centre, littered with old bottles, bits of machinery and stagecoaches. Note that this is one of the coldest places in California, with snow often preventing vehicular access between December and April; call ahead for road conditions.

Bakersfield and the San Joaquin Valley

The vast **interior** of California is split down the middle by the **Sierra Nevada** (Spanish for "snowy range"), or High Sierra, a sawtooth range of snow-capped peaks that stands high above the semi-desert of the Owens Valley. The wide **San Joaquin Valley** in the west was made fertile by irrigation projects during the 1940s, and is now almost totally agricultural.

The flat, colourless oil town of **BAKERSFIELD** is the unlikely home of the country's largest community of **Basque** descent, and one of the liveliest **country music** scenes in the nation. During the late 1950s and 1960s it become known for its distinctive "**Bakersfield Sound**", a far less slick and commercial affair than its Nashville, Tennessee

13

counterpart, epitomized by the gutsy honky-tonk of local artists such as Merle Haggard and Buck Owens. Even today the city serves as something of an alternative to the glossy country pop coming from Tennessee, and Bakersfield's honky-tonks are jumping every weekend night, when Stetson hats and fringy shirts are the required apparel and audiences span generations.

ARRIVAL AND INFORMATION   BAKERSFIELD AND THE SAN JOAQUIN VALLEY

By train The Amtrak station is downtown at 601 Truxtun Ave, the southern terminus of Amtrak's San Joaquin route from Sacramento and Oakland (onward connections to LA via Thruway bus).
Destinations Fresno (6 daily; 2hr); Oakland (4 daily; 6hr 10min); Sacramento (2 daily; 5hr 15min).
By bus The Greyhound bus station is downtown at 1820

18th St (☎ 661 327 5617).
Destinations Los Angeles (13 daily; 2hr 10min–2hr 30min); San Francisco (3 daily; 6hr 15min–7hr).
Visitor centre 515 Truxtun Ave, right by the Amtrak station (Mon–Fri 8am–5pm; ☎ 661 852 7282, ⊚ bakers fieldcvb.org).

ACCOMMODATION, EATING AND NIGHTLIFE

★ **Buck Owens' Crystal Palace** 2800 Buck Owens Blvd ☎ 661 328 7560, ⊚ buckowens.com. Very much a showpiece for Buck Owens' music and memorabilia, though the master himself died in 2006. It's a cabaret-style setup (Tues–Thurs free, Fri & Sat $5) with burgers and grills available while local and touring bands perform on Wednesday and Thursday; Tuesday is karaoke night. Buck's old band, The Buckeroos (sometimes fronted by his son Buddy), perform on Friday and Saturday nights at 7.30pm. Tues–Thurs 11am–10pm, Fri & Sat 11am–midnight, Sun 10am–2am.

★ **Noriega Hotel** 525 Sumner St ☎ 661 322 8419, ⊚ noriegahotel.com. The most authentic Basque restaurant in town is this 1893 place where louvered shutters and ceiling fans cool diners at long, communal tables. They serve an all-you-can-eat set menu of soup, salad, beans, pasta, a meat dish and cheese to finish, along with a jug of wine to keep you going. There are three sittings ($10 breakfast; $15 lunch; $20 dinner), and reservations are recommended for dinner, which

will include meaty stews and the Basque speciality of pickled tongue. Tues–Sun 7–9am, noon–2.30pm & 7–9.30pm.

★ **Padre Hotel** 1702 18th St ☎ 888 443 3387, ⊚ thepadrehotel.com. Wonderful conversion of a classic hotel from 1928, now given the boutique treatment with large flat-screen TVs, teak furnishings and super-stylish bathrooms. Icons of Bakersfield life are referenced in bespoke wallpaper featuring oil derricks and steer skulls – all very *There Will Be Blood*. There are also iPod docking stations. Doubles $120, suites $180

★ **Trout's** 805 N Chester Ave ☎ 661 399 6700, ⊚ therockwellopry.webs.com. One country venue not to be missed – and the last of the genuine old honky-tonks – is a slightly seedy country-music bar a couple of miles north of downtown that's been in business since 1931. There's live music nightly on a couple of dancefloors and you can get up to speed with evening line-dance lessons (Tues–Fri). There's a small cover charge for live sets (around $5). Daily 11am–2am.

Sequoia and Kings Canyon national parks

The southernmost of the Sierra Nevada national parks are Sequoia and Kings Canyon. As you might expect, **Sequoia National Park** contains the thickest concentration – and the biggest specimens – of giant sequoia trees found anywhere, something that tends to overshadow its assortment of meadows, peaks, canyons and caves. **Kings Canyon National Park** has comparatively few big trees, but compensates with a gaping canyon gored out of the rock by the Kings River as it cascades down from the High Sierra.

Sequoia National Park

The scenery is quite varied in **SEQUOIA NATIONAL PARK** – paths lead through copious forests and meadows, while longer treks rise above the tree line to the barren peaks of the High Sierra. Soon after entering the park from the south, CA-198 becomes the **Generals Highway** and climbs swiftly into the dense woods of the aptly labelled

Giant Forest, where displays in the modern **Giant Forest Museum** (daily: mid to late May 9am–5pm; late May to mid-Oct 9am–6pm; free) explain the life cycle and ecosystem of the sequoias and the means of protecting the remaining groves. From here you can explore along Crescent Meadow Road, where a loop road leads to the formidable granite monolith of **Moro Rock** (a 3-mile marked trail leads from Giant Forest), which streaks upward from the green hillside. A short, but steep hike to the flat summit can reveal 150-mile views on a rare clear day.

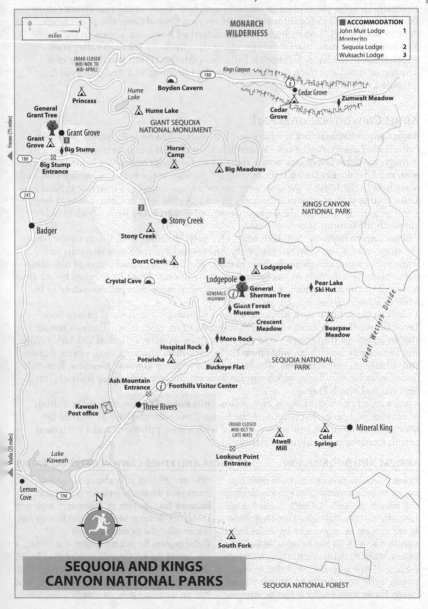

ACCOMMODATION	
John Muir Lodge	1
Montecito	
Sequoia Lodge	2
Wuksachi Lodge	3

SEQUOIA AND KINGS CANYON NATIONAL PARKS

13

As you continue east, a perimeter trail around sequoia-rimmed **Crescent Meadow** leads to **Tharp's Log**, a cabin hollowed out of a fallen sequoia by Hale Tharp, who was led here by Native Americans in 1856. Just north of Giant Forest, and accessible via the Generals Highway, is the biggest sequoia of them all, the 275ft-tall **General Sherman Tree**, estimated to be between 2300 and 2700 years old and with a base diameter of 36.5ft.

Whatever your plans, stop at **Lodgepole Village**, three miles north of the General Sherman Tree, for the geological displays and film shows at the fine **visitor centre** (see below), as well as for information on touring **Crystal Cave**, the park's single cave (3 miles long), among hundreds of unmarked ones, that's open to the public. You can also explore a glacial canyon along the two-hour **Tokopah Valley Trail**, which leads to the base of Tokopah Falls, beneath the 1600ft **Watchtower** cliff. The top of the Watchtower is accessible by the fatiguing, but straightforward, six-mile **Lakes Trail**.

Kings Canyon National Park

Kings Canyon National Park is wilder and less visited than Sequoia, with a maze-like collection of canyons and a few isolated lakes. To reach the canyon proper, pass through the **Grant Grove** area, where there's a useful **visitor centre** (see below), along with the 2.5-mile **Big Stump Trail** showing off remains at the hands of logging that took place here in the 1880s – the trees were shipped cross-country to convince cynical East Coasters that such enormous trees really existed. A mile west of Grant Grove, a large stand of sequoias contains the **General Grant** and **Robert E. Lee** trees, which closely approach the General Sherman in size.

Kings Canyon Highway (CA-180; May–Oct only) descends from Grant Grove into the steep-sided Kings Canyon, cut by the furious forks of the Kings River. Its wall sections of granite and gleaming blue marble, and the yellow pockmarks of blooming yucca plants (particularly in late spring), are magnificent. Don't be tempted by the clear waters of the river, for people have been swept away even when paddling close to the bank in a seemingly placid section.

Once in the national park proper, the canyon sheds its V-shape and gains a floor. **Cedar Grove Village** is named for its proliferation of incense cedars. There's a **ranger station** across the river (late May to early Sept Tues–Sun 9am–5pm; ☎559 565 3793), and the scenery is rich with **wild flowers** – leopard lilies, shooting stars, violets, lupine and others – as well as **birdlife**. Wander around evergreen **Zumwalt Meadow**, four miles from Cedar Grove Village, which spreads beneath the forbidding grey walls of Grand Sentinel and North Dome.

Just a mile further on, Kings Canyon Road hits **Roads End**; beyond, the multitude of canyons and peaks that constitute the Kings River watershed are networked by **hiking paths**, almost all best enjoyed armed with a tent, provisions and a wilderness permit from the trailhead ranger station.

ARRIVAL AND INFORMATION   SEQUOIA AND KINGS CANYON NATIONAL PARKS

By bus The national parks are accessible by public transport via the Sequoia Shuttle ($7.50 each way, including park entrance fee; ☎877 404 6473, ⌨sequoiashuttle.com), which runs from Visalia to Giant Forest in 2hr 30min.

By car The parks are easy to reach by car. The fastest approach is along CA-180 from Fresno via the Big Stump Entrance, though it's slightly shorter to take CA-198 from Visalia, a 55-mile drive that nonetheless includes a tortuous 15-mile ascent after the Ash Mountain Entrance. Consider looping in one entrance and out the other, and

make sure you stock up in advance on cash and petrol, though some of both is available in or near the parks.

Entrance fees The parks are always open: entry costs $20/car or $10/hiker or biker, and is valid for seven days. Fees are collected at the entrance stations.

Visitor centres The park headquarters is at Foothills, a mile beyond the Ash Mountain Entrance along CA-198 (daily 8am–4.30pm; ☎559 565 3341, ⌨nps.gov/seki), with other centres located at Lodgepole, Giant Forest Museum, Grant Grove and Cedar Grove.

ACCOMMODATION

Inside and between the parks, much of the **accommodation** is managed by Delaware North Companies (☎877 436 9615, ⓦvisitsequoia.com). Space is at a premium in summer, when booking a couple of months in advance is advisable. Price and availability force many to stay just **outside the parks**: there's limited choice along CA-180, but Three Rivers, on CA-198, has a good selection. Except during public holidays, there's always plenty of **camping** space in the parks and adjacent national forests.

Big Meadows Three miles east of Generals Hwy, midway between Lodgepole and Grant Grove Village. Free, sprawling, under utilized National Forest Service campground. Open snowmelt to first snowfall. No water.

Grant Grove Cabins and John Muir Lodge The parks' widest selection of ways to sleep under a roof: canvas roofed tent cabins (late May to early Sept); ageing, rustic cabins (May–Oct); modernized bath cabins (late April to late Oct); or the swanky, modern and year-round *John Muir Lodge*, with very comfortable hotel rooms and wi-fi. Tent cabins $62, rustic cabins $87, bath cabins $129, *John Muir Lodge* $191

Lodgepole Four miles north of Giant Forest ☎800 444 6777, ⓦrecreation.gov. The largest and busiest of all the national park campgrounds, 4 miles north of Giant Forest

and close to all Lodgepole facilities (market, snack stand, laundry, showers). Open early May to early Dec; reservations essential late May to late Sept. $20

Sheep Creek, Sentinel and **Moraine** ☎800 444 6777, ⓦrecreation.gov. National Park Service-operated campgrounds set very near one another and the Cedar Grove visitor centre; all have flush toilets. *Sheep Creek* is open late May to mid-Oct, *Sentinel* early July to early Sept and *Moraine* late May to early Sept. $18

Wuksachi Lodge Directly competing with the *John Muir Lodge* for the best rooms in the parks, the *Wuksachi* is the newest lodging option around (it opened in 1999) and consists of several blocks of rooms scattered in the woods around an elegant central lounge and restaurant. Open year-round. $224

EATING

There are **food** markets and fairly basic summer-only cafeterias at Lodgepole (the most extensive), Stony Creek and Cedar Grove, while nearby Three Rivers offers the best selection outside the parks. The restaurants inside the parks offer mostly diner-style fare, with the exception of the classy restaurant at *Wuksachi Lodge*.

Montecito Sequoia Lodge ☎800 227 9900. This family-style restaurant serves hearty buffet breakfasts ($9), lunches ($10) and dinners ($20) at long tables in an enormous room. Daily 8–9am, noon–1pm & 6–7pm.

Wuksachi Lodge Dining Room ☎559 565 4070. The finest restaurant in the parks, with Reuben sandwiches

and the like ($10) at lunch and more formal dinners such as seared trout ($20) and steaks ($25) served in a modern, baronial-style room. There's also a full buffet breakfast (continental $8; full $13). Daily 7–10am, 11.30am–2.30pm & 5–10pm (bar open until 11pm).

Sierra National Forest

Sierra National Forest, sited between Kings Canyon and Yosemite national parks, offers a chance to hike and camp in near-complete solitude. Planning is essential, though – public transport is nonexistent, and roads and trails can often close due to bad weather.

The popular Shaver Lake and Huntington Lake area, rich in campgrounds, soon give way to the isolated alpine landscapes beyond 9200ft Kaiser Pass. The sheer challenge posed by the rugged, unspoiled terrain of adjoining **John Muir Wilderness** can make the national parks look like holiday camps, though the area can get surprisingly busy (for a wilderness) in the summer. You can bathe outdoors at nearby **Mono Hot Springs**, or head for *Mono Hot Springs Resort*, near Edison Lake, which has indoor mineral baths along with primitive cabins.

INFORMATION SIERRA NATIONAL FOREST

Ranger stations High Sierra office, along CA-168 in Prather, en route to Shaver Lake (daily 8am–4.30pm; ☎559 855 5355); Bass Lake office, in the hamlet of North

Fork at the southern end of Bass Lake (Mon–Fri 8am–4.30pm; ☎559 877 2218). Each location can issue overnight permits for wilderness camping.

13

ACCOMMODATION

Mono Hot Springs Campground Reserve on ☎877 444 6777, ⓦ recreation.gov. Fairly well-used campground flanking *Mono Hot Springs Resort* with some shaded sites. No water; pit toilets. Open June–Oct. **$19**

Mono Hot Springs Resort ☎559 325 1710, ⓦ mono hotsprings.com. Right on the banks of the San Joaquin River, this resort offers accommodation ranging from simple cabins to more commodious en-suite options with kitchen; there's also a small lunch-and-dinner restaurant, a limited general store and a post office. All cabin prices include complimentary use of the therapeutic mineral pools and on-site spa. Open May–Oct. **$109**, with kitchen **$125**

Yosemite National Park

Put simply, **Yosemite Valley**, nestled in **YOSEMITE NATIONAL PARK**, and created by glaciers gouging through the canyon of the Merced River, is one of the world's most dramatic geological spectacles. Just seven miles long and less than one mile across, it's walled by 3000ft near-vertical cliffs, streaked by tumbling waterfalls and topped by domes and pinnacles that form a jagged silhouette against the sky. At ground level, grassy meadows are framed by oak, cedar and fir trees; deer, coyotes and black bears abound. You can visit any time of year – even in winter when the waterfalls ice over and most trails are blocked by snow.

In 1864, President Abraham Lincoln signed into law the landmark Yosemite Grant, which set aside Yosemite Valley and the Mariposa Grove for public use and preservation. In 1890, Yosemite became the third national park in the USA, thanks in great part to the campaigning work of naturalist **John Muir**, a Scottish immigrant who spearheaded the conservation movement that led to the founding of the Sierra Club.

Yosemite Valley

Three roads from San Joaquin Valley converge on **Yosemite Valley**, roughly in the centre of the park's 1200 square miles and home to its most dramatic scenery. Unsurprisingly, this is also the busiest part of Yosemite, with **Yosemite Village** holding the fine **visitor centre** (see p.862) and many services.

El Capitan, Half Dome and the Mist Trail to Vernal Fall

Yosemite Valley's cliffs are like few you'll see anywhere else. At 3600ft, **El Capitan** is one of the world's biggest slabs of exposed granite, so large that rock-climbers on its face are virtually invisible to the naked eye. The truncated face of **Half Dome** is the sheerest cliff in North America, just seven degrees off the vertical. The sixteen-mile round-trip journey understandably attracts a great deal of interest, so you'll need to reserve a permit ($8) if you want to day-hike to the rounded summit during the high season (May–Oct); plan to start at the crack of dawn, if not before.

The popular **Mist Trail to Vernal Fall** (3 miles round trip; 2–3hr; 1100ft ascent) winds up so close to the sensual waterfall that during the annual snowmelt period hikers are drenched by the spray but rewarded by vivid rainbows.

Upper Yosemite Fall

An early start is recommended for the trail to **Upper Yosemite Fall** (7 miles round trip; 4–7hr; 2700ft ascent), which leads up along a steep switchback path from behind the *Camp 4* campground, near *Yosemite Lodge*. This almost continuous ascent provides fine views over the valley on the way up and, after about two miles, a chance to appreciate the power of the water as it crashes almost 1500ft in a single cascade.

Glacier Point and the Four-Mile Trail

The most spectacular views of Yosemite Valley are from **Glacier Point**, the top of a 3200ft near-sheer cliff, 32 miles by road from the valley. It's possible to get there on foot via the vertiginous **Four Mile Trail** (4.8 miles one way; 3–4hr; 3200ft ascent), though many prefer to take the bus up (see p.862) and the trail down. The valley floor lies directly beneath the viewing point, which affords tremendous views across to Half Dome and the snow-capped summits of the High Sierra in the distance.

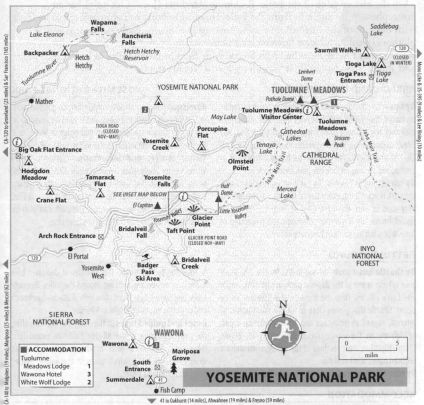

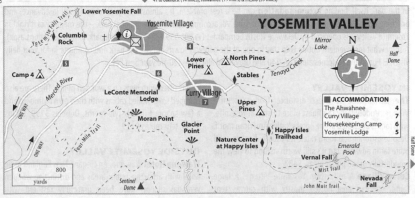

13

Outside Yosemite Valley

Mariposa Grove, close to the park's South Entrance, is the biggest and best of Yosemite's groves of **giant sequoia** trees, accessed by a 2.5-mile loop trail. The most renowned of the grouping is the **Grizzly Giant**, thought to be more than 2700 years old. Though the access road is closed from November to April, you can hike here at any time of the year; in fact, that's the only way to get into the other sequoia stands, at Tuolumne and Merced groves, near Crane Flat (2–3 miles on foot).

On the eastern edge of the park, **Tuolumne Meadows** (June–Oct only) has an atmosphere quite different from the valley; here, at 8600ft, you almost seem to be level with the tops of the surrounding snow-covered mountains. Early summer reveals a plethora of colourful wild flowers. It's a better starting point than the valley for backcountry hiking into the High Sierra, with eight hundred miles of trails, both long and short, crisscrossing their way along Sierra Nevada ridges.

ARRIVAL AND INFORMATION   YOSEMITE NATIONAL PARK

By bus In an effort to encourage visitors to arrive by public transport, the National Park Service and local authorities maintain the efficient YARTS bus system (☎1 877 989 2787, ⍟yarts.com), which operates routes along CA-140, CA-120 and US-395. Tickets can be bought on board or online, and all fares include the park entrance fee.

By car Getting to Yosemite by car is straightforward, and the park is open 24hr, every day of the year – though the only road in from the east, CA-120 from Lee Vining, is closed from early November to around the beginning of June. Gas is not available in Yosemite Valley.

Admission Park entry is $20/vehicle including passengers, or $10 for each cyclist and hiker, and is valid for seven days. Pay at the ranger stations when you enter or leave, or if they're closed, at the visitor centre in Yosemite Valley.

Visitor centres and information Yosemite Valley Visitor Center (daily 10am–6pm; ☎209 372 0299) is the park's main recorded information outpost; other visitor centres and information stations are found at Big Oak Flat, Tuolumne Meadows and Wawona. The park can also be contacted on ☎209 372 0200, ⍟nps.gov/yose.

GETTING AROUND

By shuttle bus If you're driving in just for the day, leave your vehicle in one of the day-use parking lots at Yosemite and Curry villages, then use the free and frequent Valley Visitor Shuttle that passes close to all the main points of interest, as well as trailheads and accommodation areas. In high season, the service runs roughly every 10–20min (7am–10pm) to most sections of the valley, with slightly reduced hours at other times.

By bike Although bicycles are not allowed off paved surfaces

in Yosemite, cycling around the 12 miles of dedicated bike paths is an excellent way to get around the valley. *Yosemite Lodge* and *Curry Village* (April–Nov only, 8.30am–8pm) both rent city bikes for about $10/hr or $26/day.

Buses and guided tours Of the many bus tours on offer, the most engaging is the all-day Yosemite Grand Tour (May–Nov; $82, $95 with lunch; ☎209 372 4386, ⍟yosemitepark.com), which takes in the valley, Glacier Point and Mariposa Grove.

ACCOMMODATION

In the park itself, finding **accommodation** can be a real problem. It's almost essential to book well in advance, and anything other than camping can be quite expensive. All accommodation in the national park – the majority of it right in Yosemite Valley – is operated by Delaware North Companies (☎801 559 4884, ⍟yosemitepark.com/Reservations.aspx). A somewhat inconvenient option is to stay in one of the gateway towns outside the park and commute in for your daily visits; El Portal and Midpines along CA-140 and Groveland along CA-120 are your best bets.

IN YOSEMITE VALLEY

The Ahwahnee A short distance from Yosemite Village. Undoubtedly the finest place to stay in Yosemite, with rooms decorated in the hotel's Native American motif. Despite astronomical room rates, it's usually booked solid quite far in advance, but it's still worth visiting to view the wonderfully grand public areas. **$487**

Curry Village A mile from Yosemite Village. A large family-oriented area dotted mostly with canvas tent

cabins fitted with beds on a wooden plinth. There are also cramped solid-walled cabins with their own bathroom and a few spacious motel-style rooms. Doubles **$199**, cabins **$150**, tent cabins **$129**

OUTSIDE YOSEMITE VALLEY

Wawona Hotel Wawona. An elegant, New England-style hotel with attractive public areas and distinctive wooden verandas. Rooms have been gracefully restored with old-style furniture, Victorian patterned wallpaper and ceiling fans – though those in the main lodge are fairly small and lack bathrooms. **$159**, en-suite **$235**

White Wolf Lodge About halfway between Yosemite Valley and Tuolumne Meadows. Spacious four-berth tent cabins each fitted with wood-burning stove and candles. Four motel-style cabins are also available. Open July–Sept. Motel-style cabins **$156**, tent cabins **$124**

CAMPING

To camp anywhere in the backcountry, you must obtain a wilderness permit ($5/person; details at ⓦ nps.gov /yose/planyourvisit/wildpermits.htm). If you hope to stay in one of Yosemite Valley's crowded campgrounds, it's almost essential to book beforehand (☎ 877 444 6777, ⓦ recreation.gov).

EATING

Ahwahnee Dining Room The Ahwahnee ☎ 209 372 1489. A baronial restaurant that's one of the most beautiful in the USA, and where the food is the best (and priciest) in Yosemite: eggs benedict ($19), spinach salad with pork belly ($12) and grilled steelhead ($33); the Sunday brunch ($43) is equally marvellous. Casual dress is permitted during the day, but in the evening men need long trousers, collared shirt and closed shoes; women should be similarly smartly attired. Daily 7am–2pm & 5.30–9pm.

Degnan's Deli Yosemite Village. Some of the best takeaway food in the valley: bowls of soup and chilli ($4–5), as well as massive, freshly made sandwiches and salads for around $8. Daily 7am–6pm.

Pizza Deck and Curry Bar Curry Village. Very much the place to repair to on a balmy evening after a day on the trail. Jostle for an outdoor table while you wait for a decent, build-your-own pizza (from $23 for 12 slices) and enjoy an elegant 23oz schooner of draft beer ($8), or even a daiquiri or margarita ($9). June–Sept daily noon–10pm.

The Central Coast

Between Los Angeles and San Francisco, the four hundred or so miles of the **Central Coast** are home to a few modestly sized cities and lined by clean, sandy beaches and dramatic stretches of cliffs and capes. Of the various highlights, **Big Sur** is one of the most rugged and beautiful stretches of coastline in the world, **Santa Barbara** is a wealthy resort full of old and new money, and **Santa Cruz** is a coastal town with multiple identities. In between, languorous **San Luis Obispo** makes a good base for visiting **Hearst Castle**, the hilltop palace of publishing magnate William Randolph Hearst. Almost all of the towns grew up around the original Spanish Catholic **missions**, many of which feature their original architecture – **Monterey**, 120 miles south of San Francisco, was California's capital under Spain and Mexico, and briefly the state capital in 1850.

Santa Barbara

Beautifully sited on gently sloping hills above the Pacific Ocean, **SANTA BARBARA**'s low-slung Spanish Revival buildings feature red-tiled roofs and white stucco walls, while its wide, golden beaches are lined by palm trees along a curving bay. **State Street**, the main drag, is home to an appealing assortment of diners, bookshops, coffeehouses and nightclubs.

El Presidio de Santa Barbara

123 E Canon Perdido St • Daily 10.30am–4.30pm • $5 • ☎ 805 965 0093, ⓦ sbthp.org/presidio.htm

Santa Barbara's few remaining genuine mission structures are preserved as **El Presidio de Santa Barbara**. The centre of the complex is the barracks of the old fortress El Cuartel, the second oldest building in California, now housing historical exhibits and a scale model of the small Spanish colony.

Santa Barbara Historical Museum

136 E De la Guerra St • Tues–Sat 10am–5pm, Sun noon–5pm • Donation • ☎ 805 966 1601, ⓦ santabarbaramuseum.com

Built around an 1817 adobe, the **Santa Barbara Historical Museum** presents an array of middling local artworks and rotating exhibits on Spanish- and Mexican-era life, as well

13

as other aspects of the city's past – from Ice Age geology to artefacts from native settlements on through modern photographs.

Santa Barbara County Courthouse

1100 Anacapa St • Grounds Mon–Fri 8am–5pm, Sat & Sun 10am–4.30pm; tours Mon, Tues & Fri 10.30am & 2pm, Wed, Thurs & Sat 2pm • Free • ☎ 805 962 6464, ⓦ santabarbaracourthouse.org

Three blocks north of El Presidio, the still-functional **County Courthouse** is a Spanish Revival gem, an idiosyncratic 1929 variation on the Mission theme with striking murals, tilework and fountain. Enjoy a free tour or take a break in the sunken gardens, explore the quirky staircases or climb the 70ft-high "El Mirador" clock tower for a nice view out over the town.

Karpeles Manuscript Library

21 W Anapamu St • Wed–Sun noon–4pm • Free • ☎ 805 962 5322, ⓦ rain.org/~karpeles/sbafrm.html

The beautifully decorated **Karpeles Manuscript Library** is home to a diverse array of original documents on display in temporary exhibitions. At any given time, the collection may include such notable items as the Constitution of the Confederate States of America, Napoleon's battle plans for his Russian invasion, or the manuscripts of famous figures such as Mark Twain and Thomas Edison.

Stearns Wharf and Ty Warner Sea Center

Ty Warner Sea Center: daily 10am–5pm • $8, teens (13–17) $7, kids (2–12) $5 • ☎ 805 962 2526, ⓦ sbnature.org/twsc/2.html

At the foot of State Street, take a stroll among the pelicans along **Stearns Wharf**, built in 1872 and the oldest wooden pier in California. The wharf is lined with knick-knack shops, seafood restaurants, ice cream stands and the **Ty Warner Sea Center**, offering a tot-friendly selection of touch tanks, interactive exhibits, whale bones and tide pools.

Mission Santa Barbara

2201 Laguna St • Daily 9am–4.30pm • $5 • ☎ 805 682 4713, ⓦ sbmission.org

The city takes its name from the "Queen of the Missions", **Mission Santa Barbara**, whose imposing twin-towered facade combines Romanesque and Mission styles to give it a formidable character. The present structure, built to replace a series of three adobe churches that had been destroyed by earthquakes, was finished and dedicated in 1820 by Franciscan friars. A small **museum** displays artefacts from the mission's archives, while the adjacent cemetery contains the remains of some four thousand Native Americans, many of whom helped build the original complex. The mission's first incarnation included aqueducts, waterworks, a grist mill and two reservoirs; today, you can view the old pottery kiln and tanning vats in ruin.

ARRIVAL, GETTING AROUND AND INFORMATION	SANTA BARBARA

By bus Greyhound buses arrive from Los Angeles and San Francisco every few hours, stopping near the Amtrak station at 224 Chapala St.
Destinations Los Angeles (7 daily; 3hr); San Francisco (4 daily; 10hr).
By train Amtrak trains stop at 209 State St, one block south of US-101.
Destinations Los Angeles (1 daily; 2hr 30min); San Luis

Obispo (1 daily; 2hr 50min); Salinas (1 daily; 5hr 45min); San Jose (1 daily; 7hr 45min); Oakland (1 daily; 8hr 30min).
Local shuttle bus Exploring Santa Barbara mainly involves walking and short drives, though there's a 50¢ shuttle that loops between downtown and the beach, and from the harbour to the zoo.
Visitor centre 1 Garden St (Mon–Sat 9am–5pm, Sun 10am–5pm; ☎ 805 965 3021, ⓦ santabarbara.com).

ACCOMMODATION

Blue Sands Motel 421 S Milpas St ☎ 805 965 1624, ⓦ bluesandsmotel.com. It may look like your average roadside motel at first, but the *Blue Sands* is actually the

city's best deal for accommodation: clean rooms with gas fireplaces, kitchenettes and flat-screen TVs – along with a heated pool. **$167**

YOSEMITE NATIONAL PARK (P.860) >

13

Carpinteria State Beach Campground Twelve miles east of Santa Barbara ☎800 444 7275, ⓦreserve america.com. A campground on one of the better stretches of sand in these parts, with tidepools and regular winter sightings of whales and sea lions. $45

Cheshire Cat 36 W Valerio St ☎805 569 1610, ⓦcheshirecat.com. Loaded with twee Victorian decor, this B&B has twelve rooms, two cottages and a coach house, and features a hot tub, bikes for guests' use and an *Alice in Wonderland* theme – certain rooms have names such as Tweedle Dee and Mad Hatter. $219

Santa Barbara Tourist Hostel 134 Chapala St ☎805 963 0154, ⓦsbhostel.com. Santa Barbara's top hostel is pricey, but centrally located near the beach, train and bus stations and State St. Bicycle rentals are available, as well as internet access and complimentary breakfast. Dorms $44, doubles $135, en-suite $145

Spanish Garden Inn 915 Garden St ☎805 564 4700, ⓦspanishgardeninn.com. Probably the finest boutique lodging you'll find in Santa Barbara, the *Spanish Garden Inn* offers elegant rooms with designer furnishings and fireplaces, with access to an on-site fitness centre. $309

EATING, DRINKING AND NIGHTLIFE

Arigato Sushi 1225 State St ☎805 965 6074. The main draw for sushi in town is this boutique Japanese spot that's a bit on the pricey side, with the requisite modernist chic and hipster diners. Daily 5.30–9.30pm.

Bouchon 9 W Victoria St ☎805 730 1160. Among the town's top choices for elite dining, this California cuisine favourite presents such rotating items as rack of lamb, venison, maple-glazed duck breast and a full selection of fresh seafood ($20–32), all served amid bright and cheery environs. Mon–Thurs & Sun 5–9pm, Fri & Sat 5–10pm.

Ca' Dario 37 E Victoria St ☎805 884 9419. Expect a fine set of cheeses and excellent pastas, plus mains that may span roasted quail, veal chops, crêpes and fresh fish. Mains $15–32. Mon–Thurs 11.30am–10pm, Fri & Sat 11.30am–10.30pm, Sun 5–10pm.

Restaurant Roy 7 W Carrillo St ☎805 966 5636. A stylish little restaurant where the likes of bacon-wrapped filet mignon ($30), rack of lamb ($30) and handmade pastas ($20–25) dominate the menu. There's also original art on display, and backgammon contests from time to time. Daily 6pm–midnight.

SOhO 1221 State St ☎805 962 7776, ⓦsohosb.com. Santa Barbara's best place for eclectic bookings, with blues, funk, rock or reggae bands performing on any given night; the occasional big jazz name even comes through from time to time. Daily 6pm–midnight.

Tupelo Junction Cafe 1218 State St ☎805 899 3100. A top place for breakfast. *Tupelo Junction's* morning menu features mushroom-and-truffle scrambles ($14), crab cake and potato hash ($16) and vanilla French toast ($13). Equally fine lunches and dinners are also on offer. Mon 8am–2pm, Tues–Sun 8am–2pm & 5–9pm.

Wildcat Lounge 15 W Ortega St ☎805 962 7970, ⓦwildcatlounge.com. Santa Barbara's main hot spot for dancing, as well as catching electronica DJs and various bands. The chic atmosphere brings in a mix of locals, students and out-of-towners. Cover $5–10. Check website for hours.

San Luis Obispo

SAN LUIS OBISPO, 95 miles north of Santa Barbara along US-101 and roughly halfway between Los Angeles and San Francisco, is a few miles inland, but makes a good base for exploring the coast. The vibrant university town holds a smattering of nineteenth-century architecture, especially around **Buchon Street**, as well as good restaurants, pubs and accommodation.

The compact core of San Luis Obispo is eminently walkable, centred on the late eighteenth-century **Mission San Luis Obispo de Tolosa**, 751 Palm St (daily: early March to early Nov 9am–5pm; early Nov to early March 9am–4pm; free; ☎805 543 6850, ⓦmissionsanluisobispo.org), which was the prototype for the now-ubiquitous red-tile-roof church. Between the mission and the visitor centre, **Mission Plaza**'s terraces step down along San Luis Creek, along which footpaths meander, crisscrossed by periodic bridges and overlooked by shops and outdoor restaurants. **Higuera Street**, one block south of Mission Plaza, is the town's main drag and springs to life every Thursday night for a **Farmers' Market** (6–9pm; free), when the street is closed to cars and filled with vegetable stalls, barbecues and street musicians. Another highlight, the **Dallidet Adobe & Gardens**, 1185 Pacific St (Fri 10am–1pm, Sun 1–4pm; donation; ☎805 543 0638), is a handsome 1860s residence and one of the area's oldest buildings, with a pleasant garden sitting in the shadow of a pair of 125ft-tall redwoods.

ARRIVAL AND INFORMATION

By bus At the time of writing, San Luis Obispo's Greyhound stops were at 1460 Calle Joaquin St and 202 Tank Farm Rd; check ⓦ greyhound.com for updates.
Destinations Los Angeles (6 daily; 4–5hr); San Francisco (4 daily; 7hr).

By train Amtrak trains stop several times each day at the end of Santa Rosa St, one-half mile south of the town centre. This is the northern terminus of the *Pacific Surfliner* route, from which you can transfer to *Coast Starlight* trains

covering the entire coast.
Destinations Los Angeles (1 daily; 5hr 20min); Oakland (1 daily; 5hr 40min) and connecting to San Francisco via shuttle bus; Salinas (1 daily; 2hr 55min); San Jose (1 daily; 4hr 55min); Santa Barbara (1 daily; 2hr 50min).

Visitor centre 1039 Chorro St (Mon–Wed & Sun 10am–5pm, Thurs–Sat 10am–7pm; ☎805 781 2670, ⓦ visitslo.com).

ACCOMMODATION

Rates for accommodation here are generally low, though if you want a nice view of the ocean, you're better off taking a short drive south to Pismo Beach, a beach town that makes a pleasant stopover.

Garden Street Inn 1212 Garden St ☎805 545 9802, ⓦ gardenstreetinn.com. This very central B&B is in a restored 1887 home and features comfortable, mildly themed rooms and suites (Emerald Isle, Walden, etc). **$169**

Hostel Obispo-HI 1617 Santa Rosa St ☎805 544 4678, ⓦ hostelobispo.com. A tidy, comfortable hostel set about one block from the train station. There's a lounge and patio, as well as bike rentals and pancake breakfasts. Dorms **$27**, doubles **$60**

Madonna Inn 100 Madonna Rd ☎805 543 3000, ⓦ madonnainn.com. The raft of standard "theme" rooms, cottages and suites – from fairy-tale cutesy to Stone Age caveman – at this kitsch monstrosity can

come as a disappointment to some, and its imposingly shocking-pink, chalet-style lobby may be enough to satiate your curiosity. Still, it's an essential landmark for many visitors. **$189**

Petit Soleil 1473 Monterey St ☎805 549 0321, ⓦ petitsoleilslo.com. This very stylish French-themed B&B offers modern decor in each uniquely designed room; there's also an even more elegant "Joie de Vivre" suite, and exceptionally tasty continental breakfasts. **$169**

San Luis Creek Lodge 1941 Monterey St ☎800 593 0333, ⓦ sanluiscreeklodge.com. With 25 pleasant rooms spread across three buildings – each in a vaguely Greek Revival, Tudor or Craftsman style – this centrally located inn is a smart option. **$139**

EATING, DRINKING AND NIGHTLIFE

★ **Big Sky Cafe** 1121 Broad St ☎805 545 5401. This airy, modern spot cooks with an emphasis on both vegetarian fare and seafood. It's popular for items such as *pozole* stew, paella ($18.50) and ginger noodles, as well as carnivore-friendly choices such as braised lamb shank ($17.50) and sirloin sandwiches. Mon–Thurs 7am–9pm, Fri 7am–10pm, Sat 8am–10pm, Sun 8am–9pm.

Linnaea's 1110 Garden St ☎805 541 5888, ⓦ linnaeas .com. San Luis Obispo's original coffee bar serves good espresso and regularly offers live music – from indie rock to folk to piano blues – on its small stage. Free, but donations to performers appreciated. Mon–Wed

6.30am–10pm, Thurs & Fri 6.30am–11pm, Sat 7am–11pm, Sun 7am–10pm.

Mo's Smokehouse BBQ 1005 Monterey St ☎805 544 6193. Go for the tender pulled pork or ribs at this moderately priced joint, and pair your wonderfully greasy meat with a side of beans, slaw or fried green tomatoes. Mon–Wed 11am–9pm, Thurs–Sat 11am–10pm.

SLO Brew 1119 Garden St ☎805 543 1843, ⓦ slobrewingco.com. The major music venue on the local scene includes a pair of bars spread over two floors; shows featuring local and touring bands are booked several times weekly. Tickets $8–17. Mon 4pm–2am, Tues–Sun 11.30am–2am.

Hearst Castle

The visitor centre is well signed off CA-1, 8 miles north of Cambria • ☎805 927 2020, ⓦ hearstcastle.com

Forty-plus miles northwest of San Luis Obispo along coastal Hwy-1, hilltop **HEARST CASTLE** is one of the most extravagant estates in the world. The former holiday home of publisher **William Randolph Hearst** brings in more than one million visitors a year. Its interior combines walls, floors and ceilings torn from European churches and castles with Gothic fireplaces and Moorish tiles – Hearst's buying

13

sprees were legendary for their cost and breadth, and nearly every room is bursting with Greek vases and medieval tapestries. Even the extravagant pools are lined with works of art.

Work on Hearst's nearly four-hundred-square-mile ranch began in 1919, but the castle was never truly completed: rooms were gutted as soon as they were finished to accommodate more booty. The main facade, a twin-towered copy of a Mudejar cathedral, stands atop steps curving up from the world's most photographed swimming pool, the **Neptune Pool**, lined by a Greek colonnade and marble statues – the height of aesthetic glory or irredeemably vulgar, depending on your taste.

The most dramatic time to visit is morning, when coastal fog often enshrouds the slopes below the castle, making it resemble **Citizen Kane**'s eerily evocative Xanadu, which was modelled on the estate. Four different 45-minute guided **tours** – which are essential, as are reservations – leave from the visitor centre just off Hwy-1 and showcase different aspects of the estate, from the Grand Rooms Tour ($25) to the Upstairs Suites Tour ($25). The Evening Tour (1hr 40min; $36), offered only in spring and autumn, features docents in period dress eerily speaking of Hearst in the present tense. If you arrive early for your scheduled tour, you can pass time in the visitor centre's mildly diverting **museum** (daily 9am–5pm; free).

Big Sur

While not an official geographical designation, wild and craggy **BIG SUR** is the de facto regional name for the ninety miles of rocky cliffs and crashing seas along the California coast between Hearst Castle and the Monterey Peninsula; the breathtakingly unspoilt area extends inland for about twenty miles, well into the Santa Lucia Mountains. Running through this striking terrain is exhilarating **Hwy-1**, carved out of bedrock cliffs hundreds of feet above the frothing ocean and opened in 1937. Resist the temptation to bust through Big Sur in a single day, though; the best way to enjoy its perfect isolation and beauty is slowly. Leave the car behind as often as you can and wander through its numerous parks, where a mere ten-minute walk can completely remove you from any hint of the built environment.

Julia Pfeiffer Burns State Park

Day use $10 • ☎ 831 667 2315, ⓦ parks.ca.gov

Julia Pfeiffer Burns State Park has some of the best day-hikes in Big Sur. The most popular walk here is an easy, ten-minute jaunt that begins at the parking area, then heads through a tunnel under the highway, along the edge of a cliff and, finally, to an overlook of spectacular **McWay Falls**, which crashes colourfully onto a beach below Saddle Rock. A less-travelled path leads down from Hwy-1 two miles north of the waterfall (at milepost 37.85) through a 200ft-long tunnel to the wave-washed remains of a small wharf at **Partington Cove**, one of the few places in southern Big Sur where you can actually reach the seashore itself.

Nepenthe and Pfeiffer Beach

Dawn–dusk • $5/car • ☎ 831 667 2315

The dramatically sited complex of **Nepenthe**, which consists of a gallery, café and restaurant – as well as a bookstore full of Henry Miller's works – is named for the mythical drug that induces forgetfulness. Just over a mile north, you'll find the region's post office, as well as a **petrol station** selling absurdly expensive fuel. Nearby, unmarked Sycamore Canyon Road leads a mile west to Big Sur's finest strand, **Pfeiffer Beach**, a white-sand, sometimes windy stretch that's part of Pfeiffer Big Sur State Park (see opposite) and is dominated by a charismatic hump of rock whose colour varies from brown to red to orange in the changing light.

Pfeiffer Big Sur State Park

Day use $10 • ☎ 831 667 2315, ⓦ parks.ca.gov

13

Plumb in the middle of the Big Sur River's valley, **Pfeiffer Big Sur State Park** is one of the most beautiful and enjoyable parks in all of California, with miles of hiking trails and excellent river swimming. In late spring and summer, the river's crystal-clear waters run highest, creating deep swimming holes among the large boulders plunked along the bottom of its narrow, steep-walled gorge. Since the park is sheltered a few miles inland, its weather is warmer and sunnier than elsewhere in Big Sur. The park's most popular hiking trail leads to 60ft **Pfeiffer Falls**, one-half mile up a narrow canyon shaded by redwood trees.

ARRIVAL, GETTING AROUND AND INFORMATION

BIG SUR

By car Most visitors will need a car to follow CA-1's dramatic path through Big Sur between San Luis Obispo and the Monterey Peninsula.

By bus The only public transport through Big Sur is Monterey-Salinas Transit (MST) bus #22 ($3.50), which departs from Monterey Transit Plaza and runs as far south as *Nepenthe*. Its schedule varies throughout the year – call ☎ 888 678 2871 or check ⓦ mst.org.

Visitor centres Be sure to stop at Big Sur Station (☎ 831 667 2315; hours vary seasonally), the region's finest repository of park information. The Chamber of Commerce (Mon, Wed & Fri 9am–1pm; ☎ 831 667 2100, ⓦ bigsur california.org) has information on area accommodation and restaurants.

ACCOMMODATION

In keeping with Big Sur's backwoods qualities, most **accommodation** is in rustic lodges, with scattered affordability. Note that the relatively few places on offer are full most nights in summer (especially weekends), so book well in advance. The following listings are ordered from south to north.

Deetjen's Big Sur Inn Hwy-1, 7 miles north of Julia Pfeiffer Burns State Park ☎ 831 667 2377, ⓦ deetjens .com. Built by a Norwegian immigrant, this laidback compound (with great restaurant and bar), spread across several buildings, offers comfortably rustic lodging. Ski lodge-style log cabins feature fireplaces, rocking chairs, old-fashioned leaded windows and lots of wood panelling. $\overline{\underline{\$105}}$

Pfeiffer Big Sur State Park Campground ☎ 800 444 7275, ⓦ reserveamerica.com. Big Sur's biggest and most popular campground has spacious and well-shaded sites, many situated among the redwoods. Showers, a well-stocked store and even a laundry are all available. Drive-in $\overline{\underline{\$35}}$, walk-in $\overline{\underline{\$5}}$

Riverside Campground & Cabins Hwy-1, just over half a mile north of Pfeiffer Big Sur State Park ☎ 831 667 2414, ⓦ riversidecampground.com. True to its name, this friendly, privately operated campground boasts a number of sites right next to the Big Sur River; a dozen cabins of varying sizes are also available, as well as showers and an on-site store. Tents $\overline{\underline{\$45}}$, cabins with shared bath $\overline{\underline{\$95}}$, cabins with private bath $\overline{\underline{\$140}}$

EATING

Nepenthe Hwy-1, 3 miles south of Pfeiffer Big Sur State Park ☎ 831 667 2345. Definitely not for the thrifty, this high-profile steak-and-seafood restaurant boasts a warm amber mood, unforgettable views (sunset whale-watching is possible in season) and an après-ski-like atmosphere. Mains $27–42. Daily 11.30am–4.30pm & 5–10pm (10.30pm in July & Aug).

Redwood Grill Hwy-1, just over half a mile north of Pfeiffer Big Sur State Park ☎ 831 667 2129. This budget diner (all things relative in Big Sur) at *Fernwood Resort* serves good salads and sandwiches for around $15, while pork ribs ($17–26) and pizzas ($19–24) are available at dinner. Daily 11.30am–9pm.

Monterey Peninsula

Immediately north of Big Sur are the rocky headlands of the **Monterey Peninsula**, where gnarled cypress trees mark the collision between cliffs and sea. The provincial harbour town of **Monterey** was the capital of California under the Spanish, and briefly under the Mexicans and Americans, and retains many old adobes and historic structures (alongside scores of tourist traps). **Carmel**, on the other hand, three miles to the south, is a self-consciously quaint village of million-dollar holiday homes and art galleries, while pleasant **Pacific Grove** is known mainly for its lighthouse and resident butterflies.

13

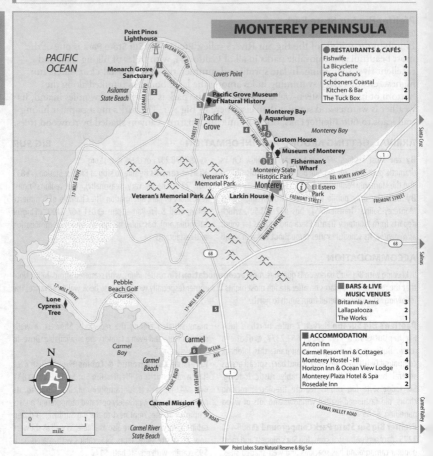

MONTEREY PENINSULA

Point Pinos Lighthouse
PACIFIC OCEAN
Monarch Grove Sanctuary
Asilomar State Beach
Lovers Point
Pacific Grove Museum of Natural History
Pacific Grove
Monterey Bay Aquarium
Monterey Bay
Custom House
Museum of Monterey
Fisherman's Wharf
Monterey State Historic Park
Monterey
Veteran's Memorial Park
Veteran's Memorial Park
Larkin House
El Estero Park
DEL MONTE AVENUE
FREMONT STREET
17-MILE DRIVE
68
Pebble Beach Golf Course
Lone Cypress Tree
Carmel Bay
Carmel Beach
Carmel
OCEAN AVE
JUNIPERO AVE
SCENIC ROAD
Carmel Mission
RIO ROAD
CARMEL VALLEY ROAD
Carmel River State Beach
N
0   mile   1
Point Lobos State Natural Reserve & Big Sur

● **RESTAURANTS & CAFÉS**
Fishwife 1
La Bicyclette 4
Papa Chano's 3
Schooners Coastal
  Kitchen & Bar 2
The Tuck Box 4

■ **BARS & LIVE
MUSIC VENUES**
Britannia Arms 3
Lallapalooza 2
The Works 1

■ **ACCOMMODATION**
Anton Inn 1
Carmel Resort Inn & Cottages ... 5
Monterey Hostel - HI 4
Horizon Inn & Ocean View Lodge ... 6
Monterey Plaza Hotel & Spa ... 3
Rosedale Inn 2

Santa Cruz
Salinas
Carmel Valley

Monterey

Named by Spanish merchant and explorer Sebastian Vizcaíno in 1602, **MONTEREY** went from a Spanish and Mexican military and administrative centre to, after the USA took over in 1846, the site of the negotiating and writing of the state constitution. It then became the first capital of California before ultimately being superseded by Sacramento. The compact centre still features some of the best vernacular **buildings** of California's Hispanic past, most sitting within a few blocks of the waterfront and part of sprawling **Monterey State Historic Park**.

Mid-September's **Monterey Jazz Festival** (ⓦmontereyjazzfestival.org), the oldest continuous festival in the world, draws crowds from afar to annually shake the Monterey Peninsula out of its otherwise tranquil mood.

Museum of Monterey

5 Custom House Plaza • June–Aug Tues–Sat 10am–7pm, Sun noon–5pm; Sept–May Wed–Sat 10am–5pm, Sun noon–5pm • $5 • ⓣ 831 372 2608, ⓦ montereyhistory.org

Though not part of Monterey State Historic Park, the most prominent building near the wharf is the **Museum of Monterey**, which reopened in 2011 after an extensive renovation. The museum hosts a rotation of temporary exhibitions that focus on historical art and artefacts of the region, as well as striking multimedia exhibits on whales.

Custom House

Custom House Plaza • Mon, Sat & Sun 10am–4pm • $3

Custom House, the oldest government building on the West Coast, once acted as California's main port of entry; portions of it were built by Spain in 1814, Mexico in 1827 and the USA in 1846. The balconied building has been restored and now displays 150-year-old crates of coffee and liquor in a small museum inside.

Larkin House

464 Calle Principal • Mon, Sat & Sun 10am–4pm • Free

The best place to get a feel for life in Old Monterey is **Larkin House**, half a mile south of Custom House Plaza, where the first two-storey adobe in California is filled with many millions of dollars' worth of antiques and is surrounded by lush gardens. Thomas Larkin – the first and only American Consul to California – is credited with developing the now-familiar Monterey style of architecture, which combines local adobe walls and the balconies of Southern plantation homes with a puritan Yankee's taste.

Cannery Row

One-time Ocean View Avenue was renamed **Cannery Row** after John Steinbeck's evocative 1945 portrait of the rough-and-ready men and women who worked in and around the thirty-odd fish canneries here. During World War II, Monterey was the sardine capital of the western world, catching and canning some 200,000 tonnes each year. However, overfishing ensured that by the time Steinbeck's celebrated novel was published, the sardines were more or less all gone; today, the canneries are shopping centres and flashy restaurants, many with names adopted from Steinbeck's stories.

Monterey Bay Aquarium

886 Cannery Row • Generally daily 10am–6pm, but check website for seasonally varying hours • $35 • ☎ 831 648 4800, ⊛ montereybay aquarium.org

At the western end of Cannery Row sits the magnificent **Monterey Bay Aquarium** – one of the largest, most stunning displays of underwater life in the world. The aquarium's eastern end is largely devoted to the **Outer Bay** section, an enormous tank with vast windows providing matchless views of the species that populate the deep waters just beyond the bay. Lazy hammerhead sharks glide among foul-tempered tuna, while hungry barracuda dart about and massive sunfish make their stately circuit of the tank's perimeter.

Towards the middle of the building, the **sea otters** always draw a crowd, particularly at feeding time (10.30am, 1.30pm & 3.30pm). These playful critters are now relatively common out in the bay, but were once hunted nearly to extinction for their uncommonly soft fur.

At the western end of the aquarium, habitats close to shore are presented in the **kelp forest**, where mesmerizing, ever-circling schools of silver anchovies avoid the sharks. The complex also opens directly onto the bay, allowing you to step out and peer into **wild tide pools** after observing the bevy of captive tanks.

Pacific Grove

Hugging the tip of the Monterey Peninsula, **PACIFIC GROVE** – or "Butterfly Town USA", as it likes to call itself – began as a nineteenth-century campground and Methodist retreat, and still holds ornate wooden **cottages** from those long-forgotten days, along 16th and 17th streets, and a good number of preserved Victorian homes throughout town.

Pacific Grove Museum of Natural History

165 Forest Ave • Tues–Sun 10am–5pm • $3 donation • ☎ 831 648 5716, ⊛ pgmuseum.org

The engaging **Pacific Grove Museum of Natural History** is home to an informative collection of local wildlife, including lots of butterflies, more than four hundred stuffed

13

birds, a relief model of the Monterey Peninsula and Big Sur, and exhibits on the ways of life of the native Costanoan and Salinan peoples.

Lovers Point and Point Pinos Lighthouse

Ocean View Boulevard circles the town along the coast, passing the headland of **Lovers Point** – originally called Lovers of Jesus Point – where preachers used to hold sunrise services. Surrounded in early summer by colourful red-and-purple blankets of blooming ice plants, it's one of the peninsula's finest beaches, where you can lounge and swim along the intimate, protected strand. Ocean View Boulevard runs another mile along the coast out to the tip of the peninsula, where the c.1855 **Point Pinos Lighthouse** (90 Asilomar Blvd; Mon & Thurs–Sun 1–4pm; $2 donation; ⓦpointpinos .org) is the oldest continuously operating lighthouse on the California coast.

Monarch Grove Sanctuary

250 Ridge Rd • Dawn–dusk • Free

A couple of blocks southeast from Point Pinos Lighthouse, you'll want to visit Pacific Grove's **Monarch Grove Sanctuary**, especially between early November and late February when you can easily spot giant brown clumps of monarchs congregating high in the eucalyptus treetops.

17-Mile Drive

Daily dawn–dusk • $9.75/car; motorcycles prohibited

If you have time, take **17-Mile Drive**, a privately owned, scenic toll road that loops along the coast south to Carmel and provides beautiful vistas of rugged headlands and the glistening shore. One other highlight along the way is the **Lone Cypress Tree**, whose solitary silhouette has been the subject of many a postcard image in these parts for decades.

Carmel

Set on gently rising bluffs above a rocky shore, the precious town of **CARMEL** is well known for its genteel air, inflated real-estate prices, neat rows of boutiques and miniature homes, and a largely untouched coastline. **Carmel Beach** (dawn–dusk; free), at the foot of Ocean Avenue, is a tranquil cove of emerald-blue water bordered by soft, blindingly white sand and cypress-covered cliffs, while around the tip of Carmel Point, idyllic, mile-long **Carmel River State Beach** (dawn–dusk; free) includes a bird sanctuary on a freshwater lagoon, as well as the mouth of the Carmel River.

About one mile from Carmel River State Beach at 3080 Rio Road, sandstone **Carmel Mission** (Mon–Sat 9.30am–5pm, Sun 10.30am–5pm; $6.50; ☎831 624 1271, ⓦcarmelmission.org) has undergone a painstakingly authentic restoration, making the whimsically ornate structure the most romantic mission in the entire chain.

Point Lobos State Natural Reserve

Daily 8am–dusk • $10 • ☎ 831 624 4909, ⓦ parks.ca.gov

Spread over two square miles just south of Carmel on Hwy-1, **Point Lobos State Natural Reserve** has more than 250 bird and animal species along its hiking trails, and the sea here is one of the richest underwater habitats in California. Grey whales are often seen offshore, migrating south in January and returning with young calves in April and early May. Because Point Lobos itself juts so far out into the ocean it contains some of the earth's most **undisturbed views** of the sea, as craggy granite pinnacles reach out to jagged blue coves.

ARRIVAL AND INFORMATION   MONTEREY PENINSULA

By bus Amtrak and Greyhound avoid the Monterey Peninsula entirely, so you'll have to arrive by bus or train at the inland agricultural city of Salinas. From there, Monterey-Salinas Transit bus #20 ($3.50) makes the 55min trip to Monterey several times daily from the Transit Center at 110 Salinas St.

Visitor centres Lake el Estero visitor centre, 401 Camino el Estero, Monterey (Mon–Sat 9am–6pm, Sun 9am–5pm; ☎ 888 221 1010, ⓦ seemonterey.com); Chamber of Commerce, 584 Central Ave, Pacific Grove (Mon–Fri 9.30am–5pm, Sat 10am–3pm; ☎ 831 373 3304, ⓦ pacificgrove.org).

ACCOMMODATION

MONTEREY

HI-Monterey Hostel 778 Hawthorne St ☎ 831 649 0375, ⓦ montereyhostel.org. Right near Cannery Row, this well-managed hostel has a spacious common room and pleasant dorms. Call for private room rates. Dorms **$30**

Monterey Plaza Hotel & Spa 400 Cannery Row ☎ 831 646 1700, ⓦ montereyplazahotel.com. Sited amid Cannery Row's tourist-geared action – it's just three blocks from the Monterey Bay Aquarium – this four-star waterfront hotel boasts plush rooms, outstanding views and *Schooners Coastal Kitchen & Bar* (see below). **$299**

Veteran's Memorial Park Campground Jefferson St, 1 mile west of downtown ☎ 831 646 3865, ⓦ monterey.org/rec. The Monterey Peninsula's only campground, in the hills above town, is the picturesque site of John Steinbeck's fictional *Tortilla Flat*. It's set among trees with picnic tables and fire rings at all forty sites, which are available on a first-come, first-served basis. **$27**

PACIFIC GROVE

Anton Inn 1095 Lighthouse Ave ☎ 888 242 6866, ⓦ antoninn.com. The clean lines and understated modern decor at this classy inn mark a refreshing change from the overabundance of Victoriana in Pacific Grove. All rooms have electric fireplaces, while some boast hot tubs. **$219**

Rosedale Inn 775 Asilomar Blvd ☎ 831 655 1000, ⓦ rosedaleinn.com. The cabin-like exteriors of the rooms at this delightful inn hide refreshingly modern interiors, featuring ceiling fans, pine furniture, fireplaces and jacuzzi baths. The real standout, though, is the affable service. **$150**

CARMEL

Horizon Inn & Ocean View Lodge Junipero St and Third Ave ☎ 800 350 7723, ⓦ horizoninncarmel.com. A relatively affordable choice in Carmel, this inn is set a few blocks north of the town centre and features cosy rooms, a continental breakfast basket delivered to your door and access to an outdoor hot tub. **$199**

EATING, DRINKING AND NIGHTLIFE

MONTEREY

Lallapalooza 474 Alvarado St ☎ 831 645 9036. A smooth martini bar (with reasonable American-cuisine restaurant attached) featuring olive-themed art on the walls, a small sidewalk terrace and a stylish oval bar – the dressiest place in town to imbibe. Daily 4pm–midnight.

Papa Chano's 462 Alvarado St ☎ 831 646 9587. One of Monterey's great bargains, *Papa Chano's* is the place to go for authentic Mexican specialities. In true California taqueria style, everything's under $10. Daily 10am–10pm.

Schooners Coastal Kitchen & Bar Monterey Plaza Hotel & Spa, 400 Cannery Row ☎ 831 646 1706. This dignified restaurant, set in one of Monterey's finest hotels, claims stunning views over the bay and an adventurous seafood menu ($15–28) at dinner; breakfast and lunch are also available. Daily 6.30am–9.30pm.

PACIFIC GROVE

Fishwife 1996 Sunset Drive ☎ 831 375 7107. Peerless, Caribbean-tinged California cuisine in a friendly, down-to-earth setting. Try the delicious "Prawns Belize" ($18.50)

– large prawns sautéed with red onions, chillies, lime juice and cashews. Mon–Thurs & Sun 11am–9pm, Fri & Sat 11am–10pm.

The Works 667 Lighthouse Ave ☎ 831 372 2242, ⓦ theworkspg.com. The best hangout in otherwise somnolent Pacific Grove, this relaxed bookshop and café also hosts live music and comedy most Saturday evenings (tickets $12–15). Café Mon–Sat 7am–6pm, Sun 8am–5pm; bookshop Mon & Wed–Sat 10am–6pm, Sun noon–5pm.

CARMEL

La Bicyclette Dolores St and Seventh Ave ☎ 831 622 9899. Wooden tables and ceiling-hung copper pots help set a suitably rustic tone for this delightful, country-style French/Italian restaurant. Mains are $14–28; the menu changes daily. Daily 8–11am & 11.30am–10pm.

The Tuck Box Dolores St and Seventh Ave ☎ 831 624 6365. Breakfast, lunch and afternoon tea are served at this half-timbered, mock-Tudor Olde England cottage. It's costly and kitsch (and cash-only), but fun. Daily 7.30am–2.30pm.

Santa Cruz

The quintessential California beach town, **SANTA CRUZ**, 75 miles south of San Francisco, is sited at the foot of thickly wooded mountains beside clean, sandy beaches. Its strong hippie vibe and university-town status provides a sharp contrast to the upscale resort sophistication of Monterey Peninsula across the bay.

13

Santa Cruz Beach Boardwalk

Hours vary seasonally • All-day unlimited rides $32, individual rides $3–6 • ☎ 831 423 5590, ⓦ beachboardwalk.com

Dominating the main beach area is the **Santa Cruz Beach Boardwalk**, which stretches for half a mile along the edge of the sand and is the best surviving beachfront amusement park on the West Coast, packed solid on summer days with day-tripping families and teenagers on the prowl. While the latest thrill is the Undertow – a 50ft-tall spinning-car roller coaster unveiled in 2013 – the star attraction will always be the **Giant Dipper**, a wild wooden roller coaster (c.1924) that's jolted the bones of more than sixty million people and is the fifth oldest such thrill ride in the USA; you may recognize it from films such as *Sudden Impact* or *The Lost Boys*.

Steamer Lane

West of the Beach Boardwalk, along West Cliff Drive, the shore is pounded by some of the state's biggest waves, not least at Cowell Beach's **Steamer Lane**. If you want to get in the water and give it a shot, try Club Ed (☎ 831 464 0177, ⓦ club-ed.com). In the beach car park, they offer rentals (surfboard and wetsuit $18/hr, $35/day) and lessons ($85/2hr).

Santa Cruz Surfing Museum

701 W Cliff Drive • June–Aug daily except Tues 10am–5pm; Sept–May Mon & Thurs–Sun noon–4pm • Donation requested • ☎ 831 420 6289, ⓦ santacruzsurfingmuseum.org

Ghosts of surfers past are animated at the evocative **Santa Cruz Surfing Museum**, housed in the old red-brick lighthouse building at Lighthouse Point near Cowell Beach. The tiny museum holds surfboards ranging from 12ft redwood planks used by the sport's local pioneers to modern, multifinned cutters.

Natural Bridges State Beach

Daily 8am–sunset • $10 • ☎ 831 423 4609, ⓦ santacruzstateparks.org

Both a cliffside bicycle path and West Cliff Drive run two miles west from Lighthouse Point to **Natural Bridges State Beach**. Near the sands, waves have cut holes through coastal cliffs to form delicate arches in the remaining stone; three of the four bridges after which the park was named have since collapsed, however, leaving large stacks of stone protruding from the surf.

ARRIVAL, GETTING AROUND AND INFORMATION   SANTA CRUZ

By bus Greyhound buses stop several times daily at the Metro Center, 920 Pacific Ave.
Destinations Los Angeles (5 daily; 9–10hr); Oakland (3 daily; 2hr); San Francisco (4 daily; 2hr 45min); San Jose (4 daily; 1hr).
Local buses Santa Cruz has an excellent bus system, based around the Metro Center and operated by the

Santa Cruz Metropolitan Transit District (☎ 831 425 8600, ⓦ scmtd.com). Basic fares are $2; an all-day pass costs $6.
Bike rental Santa Cruz Family Cycling Center, 914 41st Ave (☎ 831 475 3883, ⓦ familycycling.com), rents hybrids and cruisers for $30/day and mountain bikes for $50–75.
Visitor centre 303 Water St (Mon–Sat 9am–5pm, Sun 10am–4pm; ☎ 831 425 1234, ⓦ santacruz.org).

ACCOMMODATION

Big Basin Redwoods State Park Campground ☎ 831 338 8860, ⓦ santacruzstateparks.org. This enormous, marvellously lush park in the nearby Santa Cruz Mountains has a large campground adjacent to its visitor centre and several trailheads, as well as a couple of free walk-in campgrounds in the backcountry. **$35**
Capitola Venetian Hotel 1500 Wharf Rd, Capitola ☎ 831 476 6471, ⓦ capitolavenetian.com. A 6-mile drive east of downtown Santa Cruz, this quirky, ageing beachfront hotel is just across the bridge from Capitola's

lively esplanade. All rooms have kitchens with gas stoves; some are two-bedroom suites. **$229**
Cliff Crest Bed & Breakfast Inn 407 Cliff St ☎ 831 427 2609, ⓦ cliffcrestinn.com. An eclectically furnished Queen Anne-style Victorian home with five guestrooms and a self-contained carriage house, all set among lovely gardens. It's within walking distance of downtown and the Beach Boardwalk. Rates include a full breakfast served in the solarium. Doubles **$195**, carriage house **$265**

HI-Santa Cruz Hostel 321 Main St ☎831 423 8304, ⓦhi-santacruz.org. As informal as Santa Cruz itself, this hostel is set in a series of 1870s cottages just a couple of blocks from the beach and includes dorms and private rooms. Dorms $28, doubles $65

EATING, DRINKING AND NIGHTLIFE

The Catalyst 1011 Pacific Ave ☎831 423 1338, ⓦcatalystclub.com. The main venue in town for big-name touring artists, this medium-sized club has something happening almost nightly. Beware of brusque staff from time to time. Tickets $12–30. Hours vary.

The Crêpe Place 1134 Soquel Ave ☎831 429 6994. This longtime local favourite cooks up its namesake item with savoury and sweet fillings, all for about $12. The flower-filled back garden is a delightful spot to eat on a warm summer's evening, and there's regular live entertainment. Mon–Thurs 11am–midnight, Fri 11am–1am, Sat & Sun 9am–midnight.

★ **Davenport Roadhouse** 1 Davenport Ave, Davenport ☎831 426 8801. A 15min drive up CA-1 from Santa Cruz brings you to this village gem and its unique dishes, many of them organic: artichoke leek lasagne ($14), pan-seared king salmon ($28) and wood-fired pizzas ($9–13), plus more conventional pasta, burger and chowder options. Mon 8.30am–3pm, Tues–Fri 8.30am–9pm, Sat 8am–9pm, Sun 8am–8.30pm.

Kuumbwa Jazz 320 Cedar St ☎831 427 2227, ⓦkuumbwajazz.org. The city's showcase for traditional and modern jazz, this club boasts a friendly and intimate garden setting tucked down a small alley. Don't be surprised to see a big name or two (Bobby Hutcherson, Larry Carlton) come through each month. Tickets $12–28. Hours vary.

Saturn Cafe 145 Laurel St ☎831 429 8505. Santa Cruz's wackiest diner is set in a round building and decked out with red vinyl banquettes, Formica tables and a space-age theme. The vegetarian menu ranges from burgers and sandwiches to vegan breakfasts, and just about everything's under $11. It's also one of the few late-night dining options in town. Mon–Wed 11am–1am, Thurs & Fri 11am–3am, Sat 10am–3am, Sun 10am–1am.

San Francisco

SAN FRANCISCO proper occupies just 47 hilly square miles at the tip of a slender peninsula along the Northern California coast. Arguably the most beautiful, and probably the most progressive major city in the USA, it remains true to itself: an individualistic place whose residents pride themselves on living in a city like few – if any – others in the world. It's a surprisingly compact and approachable place, where downtown streets rise on impossible gradients to reveal stunning views, and where **fog** rolls in on a moment's notice to envelop everything in mist. This is not the California of monotonous blue skies and slothful warmth – the temperature rarely exceeds 80°F and usually hovers in the 60s between May and August, until summer weather finally arrives in autumn's early weeks.

San Francisco is a city of distinct neighbourhoods. It's second in the USA to only New York in terms of population density – commercial square-footage is surprisingly small and mostly confined to the downtown area, so the rest of the city is primarily residential with street-level shopping districts easily explored on foot. You could try to plough through much of it in a day or two, but the best way to get to know San Francisco is to dawdle.

Brief history

The original inhabitants of this area, the **Ohlone Indians**, were all but wiped out within a few years of the establishment in 1776 of the **Mission Dolores**, the sixth in the chain of Spanish Catholic missions that ran the length of California. Two years after the Americans replaced the Mexicans in 1846, the discovery of gold in the Sierra foothills precipitated the rip-roaring **Gold Rush**. Within a year, fifty thousand pioneers had come from the Midwest and East Coast (or from China), turning San Francisco from a muddy village and wasteland of sand dunes into a thriving supply centre and transit town. By the time the **transcontinental railroad** was completed in 1869, San Francisco was a lawless, rowdy boomtown of bordellos and drinking dens, something the moneyed elite – who hit it big on the much more dependable silver Comstock Lode in

DOWNTOWN SAN FRANCISCO
Alcatraz (1½ miles)
0 500 yards
BARS, CLUBS & LIVE MUSIC VENUES
22111 Minna 8
Amsterdam Café 10
Bottom of the Hill 22
Café du Nord 21
Cat Club 16
Edinburgh Castle 9
Great American Music Hall 11
Hemlock Tavern 7
Latin American Club 25
Lexington Club 24
Li Po Cocktail Lounge 4
Lucky 13 19
Martuni's 17
Mighty 20
Royal Cuckoo 26
SFJazz Center 14
Specs Twelve Adler Museum Café 3
The Café 23
The End Up 13
The Fillmore 12
The Independent 15
The Saloon 2
The Wild Side West 27
Tonga Room & Hurricane Bar 5
Tony Nik's 1
Tunnel Top 6
Zeitgeist 18
ACCOMMODATION
Good Hotel 7
HI-Fisherman's Wharf 1
Hotel Diva 4
The Inn San Francisco 9
Parker Guest House 8
Phoenix Hotel 6
Queen Anne Hotel 3
USA Hostel 5
Washington Square Inn 2
RESTAURANTS & CAFÉS
Arizmendi 20
Bi-Rite Creamery 21
Borobudur 10
Brothers Korean BBQ 12
Burgermeister 17
Dosa 23
Frascati 4
Gary Danko 2
Goood Frikin Chicken 25
Gordo Taqueria 19
Great Eastern 7
Greens 1
Grubstake 9
Hog Island Oyster Co. 6
Just for You 27
Kokkari 5
La Espiga de Oro 26
Le P'tit Laurent 22
Little Star Pizza 14
Nopa 15
Papalote 24
Pluto's 18
Rosamunde Sausage Grill 16
Saigon Sandwich 13
Shalimar 11
Sociale 8
Trattoria Contadina 3
San Francisco Bay
FISHERMAN'S WHARF
Sea Lion Platforms
Aquarium of the Bay
Musée Méchanique
Boudin Museum & Bakery
Fish Alley
San Francisco Maritime National Historic Park
Ghirardelli Square
Fort Mason Center
Magic Theatre
FORT MASON
San Francisco Art Institute
Lombard Street
Coit Tower
TELEGRAPH HILL
RUSSIAN HILL
NORTH BEACH
CHINATOWN
NOB HILL
FINANCIAL DISTRICT
THEATER DISTRICT
PACIFIC HEIGHTS
Exploratorium
Ferry Building
Embarcadero Center
Transamerica Pyramid
Bank of America Center
Chinatown Gate
Cable Car Museum and Powerhouse
Grace Cathedral
Fairmont Hotel
National Shrine of St. Francis of Assisi
Saints Peter & Paul Church
Condor Club
Haas-Lilienthal House
Lafayette Park
Rincon Center
Transbay Terminal
Cupid's Span
Powell-Hyde Line
Powell-Mason Line
California Line
F-MARKET Historic Streetcar
THE EMBARCADERO
VAN NESS AVENUE
MARKET ST

13

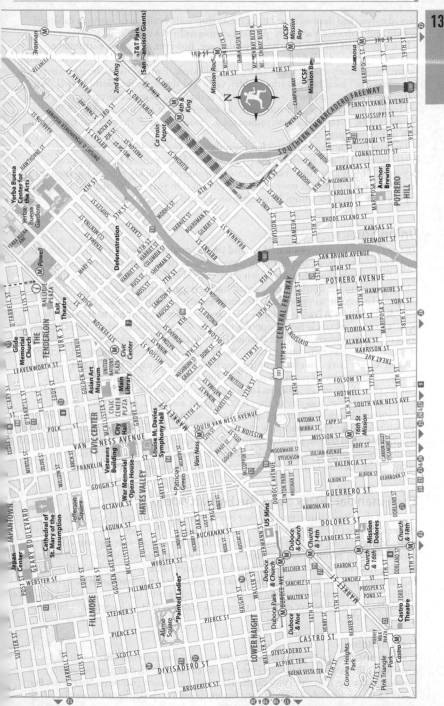

13

Nevada – worked hard to mend by constructing wide boulevards, parks, a cable-car system and elaborate Victorian redwood mansions by century's end.

In the midst of the San Francisco's golden age, however, a massive **earthquake**, followed by three days of fire, wiped out three-quarters of the city in 1906. Rebuilding began immediately and in the decades that followed, many of its landmarks were built, including both local **bridges** (the Golden Gate and the Bay). By World War II, San Francisco had been eclipsed by Los Angeles as the West Coast's most populous, but it achieved a new cultural eminence with the emergence of the Beats in the 1950s, hippies in the 1960s and a newly liberated gay population all throughout the second half of the twentieth century.

Since the 1990s, San Francisco has been the scene of the dot-com revolution's meteoric rise, fall and recovery; the resultant wealth has pushed housing prices sky-high. This is a city in a constant state of evolution, quickly gentrifying itself into one of the most high-end towns on earth – thanks, in part, to the disposable incomes pumped into its coffers from its sizeable singles and gay contingents.

Union Square

The city's retail heart can be found around **Union Square**, located north of Market Street and bordered by Powell and Stockton streets; it takes its name from its role as gathering place for stumping speechmakers during the Civil War. Cable cars clank past throngs who gravitate to the district's many smart hotels, department stores, boutiques and theatres. The square witnessed the attempted assassination of President Gerald Ford outside the **Westin St Francis Hotel** in 1975 and was also the location of the legendary opening scene of Francis Ford Coppola's film *The Conversation*, in which Gene Hackman spies on strolling lovers. Many of **Dashiell Hammett**'s detective stories are set partly in the *Westin St Francis*; in fact, during the 1920s, he worked there as a Pinkerton detective.

Along Geary Street, not far from the south side of the square, the **Theater District** is a pint-sized Broadway of restaurants, tourist hotels and, naturally, theatres. On the eastern side of the square, **Maiden Lane** is a chic urban walkway that, before the 1906 earthquake and fire, was one of the city's roughest areas, where prostitution ran rampant and homicides averaged around ten a month. Nowadays, aside from some prohibitively expensive boutiques, the main feature is San Francisco's only **Frank Lloyd Wright-designed building**, an intriguing circular space at no. 140 that, when it opened in 1948, was a prototype for the Guggenheim Museum in New York. Today it's occupied by Xanadu Gallery, which specializes in premium Asian art pieces.

The Financial District and the Embarcadero

North of the city's main artery, Market Street, the glass-and-steel skyscrapers of the **Financial District** form the city's only real high-rise area. Workers clog the streets and coffee kiosks during business hours, but the canyons of skyscrapers quieten down considerably by evening. Along Montgomery Street, the grand pillared entrances and banking halls of the post-1906 earthquake buildings jostle for attention with a mixed bag of modern towers, of which the most recognizable is the **Transamerica Pyramid**, still one of the tallest buildings in the world. The off-white, once-controversial structure resembles a squared-off rocket more than an actual pyramid and opened to business tenants in 1972.

Ferry Building

Farmers' Market Sat 8am–2pm, Tues & Thurs 10am–2pm • ☎ 415 291 3276, ⓦ ferryplazafarmersmarket.com

Once cut off from the rest of San Francisco by the double-decker Embarcadero Freeway – damaged in the 1989 earthquake and torn down two years later – the **Ferry Building**, at the foot of Market Street, was modelled on the cathedral tower in Seville,

CABLE CARS

It was the invention of the **cable car** that put the high in San Francisco's high society, as it made life on the hills both possible and practical. Since 1873, these trams (trolleys) have been an integral part of life in the city, supposedly thanks to Scotland-born Andrew Hallidie's concern for horses. Having watched a team struggle and fall, breaking their legs on a steep San Franciscan street, Hallidie designed a **pulley system** around the thick wire rope his father had patented for use in the California mines (the Gold Rush was slowing, so the Hallidies needed a new market for their product). Despite locals' initial doubts, a transport revolution followed. At their peak, just before the 1906 earthquake, hundreds of cable cars travelled 110 miles of track throughout the city; over the years, usage dwindled and, in 1964, nostalgic citizens voted to preserve the last seventeen miles (now just 10) as a National Historic Landmark.

The cars fasten onto a moving two-inch cable that runs beneath the streets, gripping on the ascent, then releasing at the top and gliding down the other side. You can see the huge motors that still power these cables at the excellent **Cable Car Museum and Powerhouse**, 1201 Mason St, at Washington (daily: April–Sept 10am–6pm; Oct–March 10am–5pm; free; ☎ 415 474 1887, ⓦ cablecarmuseum.org).

Spain. Before the bridges were built in the 1930s, it was the arrival point for fifty thousand cross-bay commuters daily. After decades of misguided modifications that resulted in colourless workspaces and a dwindling emphasis on ferry service, it has emerged immaculately restored, now boasting deluxe offices, an airy gourmet marketplace in its grand nave and a revitalized commuter service. The best time to stop by is during the **Ferry Plaza Farmers' Market**, with local produce sold from numerous stalls around the building.

The Embarcadero

Since its namesake freeway was pulled down, the **Embarcadero**, which whizzes by the Ferry Building, has experienced a dramatic renaissance from an area of charmless office blocks into a swanky waterfront district with fine restaurants and hotels making the most of the bay views. Its wide bayside promenade is one of the city's most popular paths for walking, running and skating.

Exploratorium

Pier 15 • Tues–Sun 10am–5pm, plus Thurs 6–10pm for ages 18-plus • $25, kids $19, free first Wed of month • ☎ 415 528 4360, ⓦ exploratorium.edu

Settled into its sparklingly new bayside home as of 2013, the hugely popular **Exploratorium** is the best participatory science museum in the Bay Area – and one of the best in the USA – with hundreds of hands-on exhibits that engagingly explain scientific principles such as electricity and sound waves. A major draw is the Tactile Dome (reservations essential), a complete sensory-deprivation space explored on hands and knees that's huge fun for anyone who is not claustrophobic.

Jackson Square and around

At the turn of the twentieth century, the eastern flank of the Financial District formed part of the **Barbary Coast**. This area of landfill appeared thanks to the hundreds of ships that lay abandoned by sailors heading for the Gold Rush; enterprising San Franciscans repurposed the dry ships as hotels, bars and stores. At the time, the district was a rough-and-tumble place known as "Baghdad by the Bay", packed with saloons and brothels, where hapless young males were forcibly taken aboard merchant ships and pressed into involuntary servitude. William Randolph Hearst's *Examiner* newspaper lobbied frantically to shut down the quarter, resulting in a 1917 California law prohibiting prostitution.

13

Remains of this tumultuous era can be seen in **Jackson Square Historic District**, not an actual square but an area bordered by Washington, Columbus, Sansome and Pacific streets. These were the only buildings downtown to escape the catastrophic 1906 fire unharmed, and today Jackson Street and Pacific Avenue in particular provide glimpses of what early San Francisco looked like.

Chinatown

The oldest such enclave in the USA, bustling and noisy **Chinatown** is shoehorned into several densely populated blocks and is home to one of the largest Chinese communities outside Asia. It has its roots in the arrival of Chinese sailors keen to benefit from the Gold Rush of 1849, and the migration of Chinese labourers to the city after the completion of the transcontinental railroad twenty years later. The city didn't extend much of a welcome: Chinese immigrants were met by a tide of vicious racial attacks and the 1882 Chinese Exclusion Act (the only law in American history aimed at a single racial group), which prevented Chinese immigration and naturalization. Nowadays, Chinatown bristles with activity despite its increasingly elderly population base and, in sharp contrast to the districts that surround it, a clear lack of wealth.

Enter through **Chinatown Gate** at the intersection of **Grant Avenue** (the district's tourist thoroughfare) and Bush Street. Gold-ornamented portals and brightly painted balconies sit above Grant's crass souvenir stores – some of the tackiest emporia in the city. A few blocks up, **Old St Mary's Cathedral**, 660 California St at Grant Ave, was one of the few San Francisco buildings to survive the 1906 earthquake and fire, and there's a good photo display of the damage to the city in its entranceway.

Portsmouth Square

One half-block east of Grant between Washington, Clay and Kearny streets stands **Portsmouth Square**, San Francisco's first real city centre in the mid 1800s and now, for all intents and purposes, Chinatown's living room. When John Montgomery came ashore in 1846 to claim the land for the United States, he raised his flag here and named the square after his ship; the spot where he first planted the US flag is marked today by the one often flying in the square. The plaza is primarily worth visiting to simply absorb everyday Chinatown life, with spirited card games played atop makeshift tables and neighbourhood children enjoying the playground.

Stockton Street

Parallel to Grant Avenue, **Stockton Street** is the commercial artery for Chinatown locals, its public housing tenements looming overhead and streets full to bursting with locals on the hunt for that day's meat, fish and produce. **Ellison Enterprises**, 805 Stockton St at Sacramento St, is known as Chinatown's best-stocked herbal pharmacy, where you'll find clerks filling orders the ancient Chinese way – with hand-held scales and abaci – from drug cases filled with dried bark, roots, cicadas, ginseng and other restorative staples.

Golden Gate Fortune Cookie Factory

56 Ross Alley • Daily 9am–7pm • Free • ☎ 415 781 3956

Anyone with even a moderately sweet tooth will want to duck into fragrant **Golden Gate Fortune Cookie Factory**, where, true to its name, the cramped plant has been churning out 20,000 fresh fortune cookies a day since 1962 – all by hand. A bag of forty cookies is no more than a few dollars, but it costs 50¢ to snap a photo.

North Beach and Telegraph Hill

Resting in the hollow between Russian and Telegraph hills, and bisected by busy Columbus Avenue, **North Beach** has always been a gateway for immigrants. Italian immigration to the neighbourhood was ignited, unsurprisingly, by the Gold Rush, although it gained momentum at the end of the nineteenth century, when this area began to develop the characteristics – focaccia bakeries, delis – of a true *Piccola Italia*.

City Lights

261 Columbus Ave, at Broadway • Daily 10am–midnight • ☎ 415 362 8193, ⓦ citylights.com

North Beach became a centre of alternative culture after the 1953 opening of **City Lights**, the first paperback bookstore in the USA and still owned by poet and novelist Lawrence Ferlinghetti. The **Beat Generation** briefly made the store (and the city) the literary capital of America, achieving overnight notoriety when charges of obscenity were levelled at Allen Ginsberg's epic poem *Howl* in 1957.

Condor Club

560 Broadway, at Columbus Ave • Daily noon–2am • ☎ 415 781 8222, ⓦ condorsf.com

At the crossroads of Columbus and Broadway, poetry meets porn in a neon-lit assembly of strip joints, the most famous of these being the **Condor Club**. It was here that a well-endowed waitress named Carol Doda slipped out of her top one night and kickstarted the concept of topless waitressing in 1964.

Washington Square Park and around

The soul of North Beach is **Washington Square Park**, a grassy gathering spot and public backyard that plays host to dozens of older, local Chinese each morning practising tai chi. On the north side of the park, the white lacy spires of **Saints Peter and Paul Church**, 666 Filbert St at Powell St, look like a pair of fairytale castles rising from the North Beach flats.

Coit Tower

Daily 10am–6.30pm, mural tours Wed & Sat 11am • Lobby free, elevator to top $5 • ☎ 415 362 0808

Immediately east of North Beach looms Telegraph Hill, atop which sits the prominent lookout of **Coit Tower**, a 210ft-tall concrete pillar built in 1933. Provided there isn't too long a line for the cramped elevator, the trip to the open-air viewing platform is well worth it – a stunning panorama with unimpeded vistas in every direction. Also take time to admire the **frescoes** draped around the interior's base, painted by students of **Diego Rivera** during the Depression.

Filbert and Greenwich steps

A pair of beautifully lush pedestrian paths that cling to Telegraph Hill's steep eastern flank, the **Filbert and Greenwich steps** pass between oversized bungalows and gardens both wild and manicured. As you stroll, look and listen for the famed flock of parrots – two hundred strong, and counting – that now calls this side of the great hill home.

Russian Hill

Rising a few blocks west of Columbus, **Russian Hill** was named for six unknown Russian sailors who died here on an expedition in the early 1800s. In the summer, there's always a long queue of cars waiting to drive down the tight curves of **Lombard Street** from the precipitous perch on Hyde Street. Surrounded by palatial dwellings and herbaceous borders, Lombard is an especially thrilling drive at night, when most visitors are gone and the city lights twinkle below.

Fisherman's Wharf

If the districts of San Francisco are a family, then **Fisherman's Wharf** is the boisterous uncle who showed up at the reunion in a ghastly shirt, put a lampshade on his head and

13

ALCATRAZ

Before the rocky islet of **Alcatraz** became America's most dreaded **high-security prison** in 1934, it had already served as a fortress and military jail. Surrounded by the bone-chilling water of San Francisco Bay, it made an ideal place to hold the nation's most wanted criminals – men such as Al Capone and Machine Gun Kelly. The conditions were inhumane: inmates were kept in solitary confinement, in cells no larger than 9ft by 5ft, most without light. They were not allowed to eat together, read newspapers, play cards or even talk; relatives could visit for just two hours each month. Escape really was impossible: nine men managed to get off "the Rock", but none gained his freedom, and the only two to reach the mainland (using a jacket stuffed with inflated surgical rings as a raft) were soon apprehended.

Due to its massive running costs, the prison finally closed in 1963. The island remained abandoned until 1969, when a group of Native Americans staged an occupation as part of a peaceful attempt to claim the island for their people, citing treaties that designated all federal land not in use as automatically reverting to their ownership. Using all the bureaucratic trickery it could muster, the US government finally ousted them two years later, claiming the operative lighthouse qualified it as active.

At least 750,000 tourists each year take the excellent hour-long, self-guided audio **tour** of the abandoned prison, which includes sharp anecdotal commentary as well as re-enactments of prison life featuring improvised voices of the likes of Capone and Kelly. **Ferries** to Alcatraz leave from Pier 33 (frequent departures 9am–3.55pm; night tour departs at 6.10pm and 6.50pm mid-May to late Oct, 4.20pm late Oct to mid-May; day tour $28, night tour $35; ☎415 981 7625, ⓦalcatrazcruises.com); allow at least three hours for a visit, including cruise time. Advance **reservations** are essential – in peak season, it's nearly impossible to snag a ticket for a same-day visit.

---

never left. The city doesn't go dramatically out of its way to court and fleece tourists, but the scores of tacky souvenir shops and overpriced restaurants that crowd Fisherman's Wharf expose this area's mission of raking in disposable tourist dollars. The district flourished as a serious fishing port well into the twentieth century, although these days the few fishermen that can afford the exorbitant mooring charges have usually finished their trawling by early morning and are gone by the time most visitors arrive.

The most endearing attraction here is the large colony of barking **sea lions** that often take over a number of floating platforms between piers 39 and 41. Another entertaining pick is the **Musée Mécanique** on Pier 45 (Mon–Fri 10am–7pm, Sat & Sun 10am–8pm; free; ☎415 346 2000, ⓦmuseemechanique.org), which houses an extensive collection of vintage arcade machines and 1980s video games.

San Francisco Maritime National Historic Park

Visitor centre 499 Jefferson St, at Hyde St • Daily: June–Aug 9.30am–5.30pm; Sept–May 9.30am–5pm • ☎415 447 5000, ⓦnps.gov/safr

Immediately west of Fisherman's Wharf is **San Francisco Maritime National Historic Park**, a low-key complex that includes restored sailing vessels, curving jetties, impressive nautical architecture and a sandy spit. Drop into the fine **visitor centre**, which sells tickets for touring the park's docked ships along the adjacent Hyde Street Pier.

Civic Center and the Tenderloin

While certain areas of San Francisco can almost seem like an urban utopia, the adjoining districts of **Civic Center** and the **Tenderloin** are reminders that not everybody has it so easy. Civic Center's Beaux Arts-style federal and municipal buildings can't help but look at loggerheads with San Francisco's quirky wooden architecture – little wonder, as they're the sole remnant of a grand architectural plan to transform downtown into a boulevard-dotted, Paris-inspired place after the original buildings were levelled by the 1906 earthquake.

City Hall

Mon–Fri 8am–8pm; tours (free) Mon–Fri 10am, noon & 2pm • ☎ 415 554 6139, ⓦ sfartscommission.org/tours

It was at the huge, golden-domed **City Hall**, across from grassy Civic Center Plaza, that Mayor George Moscone and Supervisor Harvey Milk were assassinated in 1978. The best way to see its grand interior is on one of the regularly offered **tours** – simply show up at the Docent Tour kiosk on the rear side of the main building facing Van Ness Avenue.

13

Asian Art Museum

200 Larkin St, at McAllister St • Tues, Wed & Fri–Sun 10am–5pm, plus Feb–Sept Thurs 10am–9pm, Oct–Jan Thurs 10am–5pm • $12, $5 after 5pm Thurs, free first Tues of month • ☎ 415 581 3500, ⓦ asianart.org

The **Asian Art Museum** is home to more than ten thousand paintings, sculptures, ceramics and textiles from all over Asia; since it's so overwhelming in size and scope, it's worth picking up an audio guide to navigate its numerous highlights. The sizeable museum's most precious holding is undoubtedly the oldest-known Chinese Buddha image, dating back to 338 AD.

South of Market

Formerly one of San Francisco's least desirable neighbourhoods, **South of Market** has taken a surprising upswing in the last few decades, thanks in part to internet start-up companies attracted to the district. The centrepiece is lovely **Yerba Buena Gardens** (daily dawn–10pm; free; ⓦ yerbabuenagardens.com).

AT&T Park

Tours 10.30am & 12.30pm (non-game days only) • $17.50 • ☎ 415 972 2400, ⓦ sfgiants.com

Its name may not be pretty, but **AT&T Park**, the San Francisco Giants' baseball park, is one of the finest venues of its kind. Brilliantly sited along the water in one of the sunniest parts of town, its outfield opens onto the bay, with concession stands featuring the ballpark's signature garlic fries.

The Mission

Vibrant, hip and ethnically mixed, the **Mission** is San Francisco's most exciting district. It's also home to generally pleasant weather, for when much of the rest of the city is shrouded in spring and summer fog, the remarkably flat Mission can be bright and (relatively) warm. After California's annexation, the area became home to succeeding waves of immigrants: first Scandinavians, followed by a significant Irish influx, then a sizeable Latin American population, who remain its dominant group today. The neighbourhood is rich in trendy bars and restaurants – notably along Valencia Street – that jostle for space with old taquerias.

MISSION DISTRICT MURALS

The hundreds of **murals** around the Mission underscore a strong sense of community pride and Hispanic heritage. The greatest concentration of work can be found on Balmy Alley, an unassuming back way between 24th, Harrison, 25th and Treat streets in the neighbourhood's southern section, where's there barely an inch of wall unadorned. While some of the murals are more heartfelt than either skilled or beautiful, it's still worth stopping by for a peek, although the heavy-handed political imagery can be wearying.

For an informed tour of the artwork, contact Precita Eyes Mural Arts and Visitors Center, 2981 24th St at Harrison St (tours Sat & Sun 1.30pm; 2hr 15min; $20; ☎ 415 285 2287, ⓦ precitaeyes .org), which has sponsored most of the paintings since its founding in 1971; the organization also sells maps of the neighbourhood's murals.

13

Mission Dolores

3321 16th St, at Dolores St • Daily: May–Oct 9am–4.30pm; Nov–April 9am–4pm • $5 donation • ☎ 415 621 8203, ⓦ missiondolores.org

The Mission neighbourhood takes its name from **Mission Dolores**, the oldest building to survive the 1906 earthquake and fire. It was founded in 1776 as Spain staked its claim to California; the graves of the Native Americans it tried to "civilize" can be seen in the atmospheric cemetery next door (made famous in Hitchcock's *Vertigo*), along with those of white pioneers.

The Castro

Progressive and celebratory, but also increasingly comfortable and wealthy, the **Castro** is the city's centre of gay culture. Some people maintain it's still the wildest place in town, others insist it's a shadow of its former self. Many of the same hangouts remain from its 1970s heyday as portrayed in the 2009 film *Milk*, but these days they're host to a slightly more conservative breed as cute shops and restaurants lend a boutique-like feel to the place. A visit to the district and its adjacent steep, manicured residential streets is a must if you're to get any idea of just what San Francisco is all about – the liveliest time to stroll around is on Sunday afternoons, when the streetside cafés are packed.

Castro Theatre

429 Castro St, at 17th St • ☎ 415 621 6120, ⓦ castrotheatre.com

The neighbourhood's major sight is the **Castro Theatre**, a stunning example of the Mediterranean Revival style, and flagged by the neon sign that towers above surrounding buildings. Inside, its wall-mounted busts of heroic figures and massive ceiling ornamentation lend an air of affirmed glamour, though you'll have to come for a movie showing to get in.

Haight-Ashbury (Upper Haight)

Two miles west of the city's downtown core, **Haight-Ashbury** – invariably known among locals these days as the **Upper Haight**, or simply "the Haight" – lent its name to an entire era, receiving in return a fame on which it has traded mercilessly ever since. Centred on the junction of Haight and Ashbury streets, the neighbourhood was a run-down Victorian neighbourhood until being transformed into the hub of counterculture cool in the mid-1960s. These days, it's as overtly capitalistic as anywhere else in the city, a tie-dyed theme park of sorts where shops sell hippie-themed souvenirs, secondhand vintage clothes and Grateful Dead Beanie Babies, with a number of brightly coloured, youthful clothing boutiques interspersed. It also remains a hot spot for runaway youths, so expect to be repeatedly hit up for spare change as you roam Haight Street's increasingly menacing streets.

Lower Haight

Toward the eastern end of Haight Street, around Fillmore Street, is the **Lower Haight**, a far more authentic area than the neighbouring Upper Haight. Primarily an African American neighbourhood since World War II, it seems perfectly happy to lurk in the shadow of the higher-profile Mission as San Francisco's second hippest neighbourhood.

Golden Gate Park

The largest and most diverse green space in a city rich in parklands, **Golden Gate Park** is the one above all that's not to be missed. Stretching three miles west from the Haight all the way to the Pacific Ocean, it was constructed in the late 1800s on what was then an area of wild sand dunes buffeted by sea spray. Today, despite throngs of daily visitors (particularly in its museum-rich eastern reaches), you can always find some solitude among its hidden meadows and quiet paths.

Don't miss the **Japanese Tea Garden** (daily: March–Oct 9am–6pm; Nov–Feb 9am–4.45pm; $7, free Mon, Wed & Fri before 10am, ☎ 415 752 1171, ☀ japanese teagardensf.com), which features carp-filled ponds, bonsai and cherry trees and sloping bridges that all lend a tranquil feel. Nearby, the immaculate **Conservatory of Flowers** (Tues–Sun 10am–4.30pm; $7; ☎ 415 831 2090, ☀ conservatoryofflowers.org) and 75-acre **San Francisco Botanical Garden** (daily: March–Sept 9am–6pm; Oct & Feb 9am–5pm; Nov–Jan 10am–4pm; $7; ☎ 415 661 1316, ☀ sfbotanicalgarden.org) are both worthwhile destinations for exotic foliage and quiet reflection.

de Young Museum

Tues–Thurs, Sat & Sun 9.30am–5.15pm, Fri 9.30am–8.45pm • $10, free first Tues of month • ☎ 415 750 3600, ☀ deyoung.famsf.org

The **de Young Museum** lends almost as much space to major touring shows as to its own varied holdings, which include an impressive collection of American art from colonial times up to the present day. Its striking structure vies for equal attention – be sure to visit the ninth-floor observation tower for sweeping views across the park and city.

California Academy of Sciences

Mon–Sat 9.30am–5pm, Sun 11am–5pm • $30, check website for free days • ☎ 415 379 8000, ☀ calacademy.org

Across the Music Concourse from the de Young, the **California Academy of Sciences** is the park's most popular destination. Inside the grand, glass-walled entrance, exhibits from the planetarium, natural history museum and aquarium are smartly intertwined and make for an entertainingly educational day's visit; its so-called Living Roof, meanwhile, includes a variety of native wild flowers and seven grassy hillocks that pay homage to San Francisco's seven major hills.

Golden Gate Bridge

The orange towers of the **Golden Gate Bridge**, San Francisco's signature architectural symbol, are visible from almost every high point in the city. Its colour was originally intended as a temporary undercoat before a grey topcoat was to be applied, but locals liked the primer so much upon the bridge's 1937 opening that it's remained ever since. Driving or bicycling across it is a genuine thrill, while the walk across its 1.7-mile span allows you to take in its enormous size and absorb the views of the Marin headlands, as well as those of the city itself. The view is especially beautiful at sunset, when the waning glow paints the city a delicate pink – unless of course everything's shrouded in fog, when the bridge takes on a patently eerie quality.

ARRIVAL AND DEPARTURE	SAN FRANCISCO

BY PLANE

SAN FRANCISCO INTERNATIONAL AIRPORT
Most international and domestic flights arrive at San Francisco International Airport (SFO; ☎ 650 821 8211, ☀ flysfo.com), about 15 miles south of the city. There are several ways of getting into the centre from here, each of which is clearly signed at baggage-reclaim areas.
BART The most popular option is BART (☀ bart.gov), whose electric trains whisk you from the airport to the heart of downtown for $8.25 in under 40min, with regular departures.
Minibus shuttles The top option among these is SuperShuttle (☎ 800 258 3826, ☀ supershuttle.com), which departs every 5–10min and charges $17/person (but only $10 for each additional person in your party).

Taxi and rental car You can expect a taxi from SFO to any downtown location to cost $45–55 (plus customary 15 percent tip). The usual car-rental agencies operate free shuttle buses from the upper level to their car lots.

OAKLAND INTERNATIONAL AIRPORT
Several domestic airlines fly into compact Oakland International Airport (OAK; ☎ 510 563 3300, ☀ oakland airport.com) across the bay. It's efficiently connected with San Francisco via BART's new airport connector tram (scheduled to open in autumn 2014), which drops you at the Coliseum/Oakland Airport BART station; once there, board BART for San Francisco to complete your 35min journey (about $9).

13

BY BUS

All of San Francisco's Greyhound services use the temporary Transbay Terminal, bound by Main, Folsom, Beale and Howard sts, two blocks south of Market St; the new terminal is scheduled to open a few blocks away by 2017.

Destinations Eureka (daily; 6hr 45min); Los Angeles (12 daily; 7hr 25min–11hr 50min); Redding (4 daily; 5hr 45min–9hr 50min); Reno (6 daily; 5hr 10min–6hr 35min); Sacramento (9 daily; 2hr–2hr 40min); Salinas (6 daily; 2–4hr); San Diego (6 daily; 10hr 30min–12hr 45min); San Jose (9 daily; 1hr–1hr 45min); San Luis Obispo (4 daily;

7hr); Santa Barbara (3 daily; 8hr 40min–9hr 20min); Santa Cruz (3 daily; 2hr 50min); Santa Rosa (daily; 1hr 45min).

BY TRAIN

Amtrak Trains stop across the bay in Richmond (the most efficient BART transfer point) and continue to Emeryville, from where free shuttle buses run across the Bay Bridge to downtown San Francisco.

Destinations Fresno (daily; 4hr 20min); Los Angeles (daily; 8hr 50min); Reno (daily; 7hr 20min); Sacramento (daily; 2hr 20min); Salinas (daily; 4hr 20min); San Diego (daily; 11hr 40min).

GETTING AROUND

San Francisco's **public transport** system, **Muni** (☎ 511, ⓦ sfmta.com), may often be maligned by locals for its unpredictable schedule, but it covers every neighbourhood relatively inexpensively. If you can budget the time, **walking** is often your best bet, with each turn revealing surprises. For a wealth of information on all forms of Bay Area transport, including real-time traffic maps, visit ⓦ 511.org.

By bus, streetcar or cable car Muni operates a comprehensive network of buses, streetcars and cable cars that trundle up and around (and tunnel through) the city's hills. The flat fare is $2 on buses and trains (exact change only); with each ticket you buy, make sure you get a free transfer – good on all lines (except cable cars) for at least 90min from the time you receive it. Muni streetcars run until about 1am nightly; after that, owl buses run sporadically between 1–5am. A single cable car fare is as steep as the hills the vessels climb: $6, with no free transfers.

By electric rail BART – short for Bay Area Rapid Transit (☎ 415 989 2278, ⓦ bart.gov) – is the region's electric rail transport system. Tickets aren't cheap ($1.75–10.90 one way, depending how far you ride), but the system boasts clean and comfortable trains that follow a fixed schedule. Tickets can be bought on the station concourse, or you can use Clipper (see box below); save your ticket after entering the station, as you'll also need it when exiting your destination station. Note that the system shuts down for

maintenance each night between about 1–5am.

By taxi Taxis ply San Francisco's streets, although they can be quite expensive and difficult to find outside of downtown, especially at weekends. If you're phoning ahead, try Veteran's Cab (☎ 415 648 1313) or Yellow Cab (☎ 415 333 3333). Fares are roughly $5 for the first mile, plus a customary 15 percent tip.

By bike Cycling is an option for exploring the city, though you'll need to be continually alert for wayward drivers and have strong legs to tackle the city's punishing hills. The handiest option for rentals is Blazing Saddles (☎ 415 202 8888, ⓦ blazingsaddles.com), with more than half a dozen locations around the central area of the city – two of the most convenient are at 1095 Columbus Ave at Francisco St in North Beach, and Pier 41 at Fisherman's Wharf. Rates for a standard bike are $32/day, but check the company's website for coupons. Bikes are allowed on Muni buses equipped with bicycle racks (on the front of the bus) and on BART (except during peak hours).

INFORMATION AND TOURS

San Francisco Visitor Information Center 900 Market St, at Powell St (Mon–Fri 9am–5pm, Sat & Sun 9am–3pm; Nov–April closed Sun; ☎ 415 391 2000, ⓦ sanfrancisco.travel). Set on the lower level of Hallidie

Plaza and well-served by BART and Muni buses, trains and cable cars, the sizeable information centre has free maps of the city and the Bay Area, and can help with lodging and travel plans. Its free *San Francisco Book* provides detailed, if

---

SAN FRANCISCO TRANSPORT PASSES

The **Muni Passport** is well suited for city visitors staying a few days, allowing unlimited rides on Muni buses, trains and cable cars; it's available in one- ($14), three- ($22) or seven-day ($28) denominations. If you'll be using multiple transport services during a shorter visit, you may want to consider purchasing an electronic **Clipper** card (☎ 877 878 8883, ⓦ clippercard.com), available for $3 via vending machines on the concourse of Market Street Subway stations. It's accepted by all major Bay Area transport agencies (excluding Blue & Gold Fleet ferries), making for hassle-free transfers.

selective, information about accommodation, entertainment, exhibitions and shopping. You can also buy all transport passes and a handy Muni map ($3) here.

City Pass The good value City Pass ($94) m citypass.com /san-francisco) pays for entry into several top local museums – California Academy of Sciences and the Exploratorium, among others – and also acts as a seven-day Muni pass, including cable car fares. It's available at the San Francisco Visitor Information Center.

Bus tours City Sightseeing San Francisco (☎415 440 8687, ⓦcity-sightseeing.us; from $28) and its red open-top double-decker buses trundle along several routes around the city.

Bay cruises Blue & Gold Fleet (☎415 705 8200, ⓦblue andgoldfleet.com) operates bay cruises from Pier 39,

though be warned that everything may be shrouded in fog, making the price ($26) less than worth it.

Walking tours The best among San Francisco's considerable choice of walking tours include City Guides (free, but small donation requested; ☎415 557 4266, ⓦsfcityguides.org), which features a sprawling roster of fun ambles; Cruisin' the Castro ($30; ☎415 255 1821, ⓦcruisinthecastro.com), offering absorbing and witty tours of the gay community; and the free, self-guided Barbary Coast Trail (☎415 454 2355, ⓦsfhistory.org), highlighting the oldest parts of the city and marked by bronze medallions set in the street. There are also tours of Mission murals (see p.883) that take in the district's distinctive street art.

ACCOMMODATION

San Francisco residents complain frequently about skyrocketing rents, and it's no different for visitors. Expect **accommodation** to cost upwards of $200 per night in a reasonable hotel or motel, less out of high season, and keep in mind that rates can fluctuate wildly at any time based on demand. To get the best deal, be sure to reserve well in advance, especially for summer and early autumn visits. The **San Francisco Visitor Information Center** (see opposite) can help with finding accommodation, while **San Francisco Reservations** (☎800 677 1500, ⓦhotelres.com) regularly offers cut-price rates on lodging. For B&Bs, contact **Bed and Breakfast San Francisco** (☎415 899 0060, ⓦbbsf.com). If funds are particularly tight, look into one of the many excellent **hostels** (see p.888), where lodging rates start around $29. Bear in mind that all quoted room rates are subject to a 14 percent local occupancy tax. Finally, other than one group-only site, there's nowhere legal to **camp** in San Francisco itself, so if you're determined to sleep underneath the stars, head to any number of parks in the East Bay, down the Peninsula or in Marin County.

HOTELS, MOTELS AND B&BS
DOWNTOWN AND AROUND
Hotel Diva 440 Geary St, at Mason St, Union Square ☎415 885 0200, ⓦhoteldiva.com. Trendy, modern art hotel with spacious rooms, as well as sleek metal and leather furniture. Particularly well positioned if you're planning to see theatre, with A.C.T. and the Curran directly across the street. $239

Phoenix Hotel 601 Eddy St, at Larkin St, Tenderloin ☎415 776 1380, ⓦjdvhotels.com/phoenix. A favourite with touring bands, this raucous retro motel conversion feels more Los Angeles than San Francisco and features a small pool. Its 44 rooms are eclectically decorated in tropical colours with a rotation of local artwork on the walls. $199

Washington Square Inn 1660 Stockton St, at Union St, North Beach ☎415 981 4220, ⓦwsisf.com. This B&B-style hotel overlooking Washington Square has large, airy rooms decorated in modern shades of taupe and cream; staff are friendly and amenable. $249

PACIFIC HEIGHTS
Queen Anne Hotel 1590 Sutter St, at Octavia St ☎415 441 2828, ⓦqueenanne.com. Gloriously restored Victorian building enjoying its second life as a boutique B&B. Each room is stuffed with gold-accented Rococo

furniture and bunches of silk flowers, while some have fireplaces; the parlour (where afternoon tea and sherry is served) is packed with museum-quality period furniture. $195

SOUTH OF MARKET, THE MISSION AND THE CASTRO
Good Hotel 112 Seventh St, at Mission St, South of Market ☎415 621 7001, ⓦthegoodhotel.com. Fun, eco-aware hotel within walking distance of several museums, featuring pet-friendly accommodation and free bicycle rental. $179

The Inn San Francisco 943 S Van Ness Ave, at 20th St, Mission ☎415 641 0188, ⓦinnsf.com. Superb, sprawling B&B spread across two adjoining Victorians. The 1872 mansion has fifteen dark and stylish rooms; the 1904 extension next door holds six more. The breakfast buffet, redwood hot tub, on-site parking and rooftop sun deck with stunning views all help make for a delightful stay. $195

★ **Parker Guest House** 520 Church St, at 17th St, Castro ☎888 520 7275, ⓦparkerguesthouse.com. Popular with gay visitors, this 21-room converted mansion is set amid beautiful gardens and features ample common areas (including a living room with fireplace), a sunny breakfast room and a sauna. $159

13

HOSTELS

★ **HI-Fisherman's Wharf Hostel** Building 240, Fort Mason ☎ 415 771 7277, ⓦ sfhostels.com/fishermans -wharf. High above the waterfront between the Golden Gate Bridge and Fisherman's Wharf, this is a choice option for the outdoorsy traveller, mostly thanks to its location on the edge of Fort Mason's rolling meadow. Be aware that although public transport connects the hostel with the city's main sights, it's nonetheless a little out of the way. Dorms $42, doubles $90

USA Hostel 711 Post St, at Jones St, Union Square ☎ 415 440 5600, ⓦ usahostels.com. A friendly and fun place with a 45-seat cinema (with complimentary popcorn) on site, along with free all-you-can-make pancakes and oatmeal in the morning. Large lockers and wi-fi are available. Dorms $47, doubles with shared bath $113, en-suite $122

EATING

San Francisco has long been known for its fine dining restaurants, and more recently for its wealth of low-end marvels including taquerias, dim sum joints and street food carts. Indeed, the greatest asset of the city's food scene is its staggering variety – not only in types of cuisine, but in price ranges and overall experiences.

DOWNTOWN AND AROUND

★ **Borobudur** 700 Post St, at Jones St, Union Square ☎ 415 775 1512. Indonesian powerhouse that fuses Indian and Thai influences with often extraordinary results. Don't pass up the *roti prata* (grilled, flaky bread) and curry dipping sauce appetizer. Mains about $10. Mon–Thurs 11.30am– 10pm, Fri & Sat 11.30am–11pm, Sun 1–10pm.

★ **Frascati** 1901 Hyde St, at Green St, Russian Hill ☎ 415 928 1406. Vividly romantic, two-level bistro on a prime Russian Hill corner. Uniquely paired California dishes such as maple-leaf duck breast with herb and huckleberry sauce retain a level of comfort, and the wine list is extensive. Mains $20–30. Mon–Sat 5.30–9.45pm, Sun 5.30–9pm.

Gary Danko 800 North Point St, at Hyde St, Fisherman's Wharf ☎ 415 749 2060. Don't let the location put you off – this understated oasis regularly vies for the title of best restaurant in food-obsessed San Francisco. Granted, the performance food served with a flourish, but its five-course *prix fixe* menus ($73–107) are utterly splurge-worthy. Reserve well ahead. Daily 5.30–10pm.

Great Eastern 649 Jackson St, at Kearny St, Chinatown ☎ 415 986 2500. Elegant and traditional restaurant serving favourites such as sautéed squab with Chinese broccoli. Most mains about $20. Daily 10am–1am.

Greens Building A, Fort Mason Center ☎ 415 771 6222. San Francisco's original vegetarian restaurant remains popular thanks to its continually inventive menu, picturesque pier setting and airy interior. It's surprisingly casual, given the quality and price of the food. Mains $18–23. Tues–Fri 11.45am–2.30pm & 5.30–9pm, Sat 11am–2.30pm & 5.30–9pm, Sun 10.30am–2pm & 5.30–9pm.

Grubstake 1525 Pine St, at Polk St, Polk Gulch ☎ 415 673 8268. Its dining counter set in an old railcar, this classic diner dishes out all the American basics (and breakfast all night); what really sets it apart, however, are all the Portuguese specialities on the menu, including *caldo verde* soup. Mains $8–15. Daily 5pm–4am.

Hog Island Oyster Co. Ferry Building Marketplace, The Embarcadero ☎ 415 391 7117. This outpost of the Tomales Bay (Marin County) farm hosts mollusc devotees who sit elbow to elbow at the wrap around granite bar. The lists of available oysters (about $18 for six, $30 for a dozen), wines and beers are equally impressive, while the creamy oyster stew is a perennial hit. Mon–Fri 11.30am–8pm, Sat & Sun 11am–6pm.

★ **Kokkari** 200 Jackson St, at Front St, Jackson Square ☎ 415 981 0983. This bustling restaurant's Greek influence runs deep, relying as it does on Hellenic staples such

---

SAN FRANCISCO'S SUPER BURRITO

Philadelphia has its cheesesteaks, New York its pastrami sandwiches and Texas its barbecue. In San Francisco, the **super burrito** is not only the premier bargain food, but truly a local phenomenon. The city is home to well over 150 **taquerias** – informal Mexican restaurants specializing in tacos, quesadillas, tortas and, of course, burritos – and locals are often heard debating their favourites effusively. A San Francisco super burrito stuffs a jumbo tortilla with any number of grilled or barbecued meats, Spanish rice, beans (choices include whole pinto, black or refried), melted cheese, *pico de gallo* (a splashy mix of diced tomato, onion, jalapeño and coriander), guacamole or slices of avocado, a splatter of salsa and even sour cream. And with its emphasis on vegetables, grains and legumes, the burrito also easily lends itself to vegetarian and vegan variants. Most San Francisco taquerias wrap their goods in aluminum foil for easy handling, as most locals eat burritos by hand. Expect to pay $6–10 for a super burrito and to not have much of an appetite for hours afterward. Forego the utensils, order a Mexican beer or non-alcoholic *agua fresca* (fruit drink) with your foiled meal, and you'll fit right in.

as lamb and aubergine. Its huge open fireplace heats two dazzling dining rooms decorated with oriental rugs and goatskin lampshades. Mains $20–30. Mon–Thurs 11.30am–2.30pm & 7.30–10pm, Fri 11.30am–2.30pm & 5.30–11pm, Sat 5–11pm, Sun 5–10pm.

Saigon Sandwich 560 Larkin St, at Eddy St, Tenderloin ☏ 415 474 5698. Cupboard-sized, lunch-only shop selling sizeable, made-to-order *banh mi* (Vietnamese sandwiches) for no more than $3.50; ask the hardworking ladies behind the counter to add lashings of fresh carrot and bundles of coriander (cilantro). Expect a queue out the door every afternoon. Daily 7am–5pm.

★ **Shalimar** 532 Jones St, at O'Farrell St, Tenderloin ☏ 415 928 0333. The chicken tikka masala is the main attraction at this austere South Asian joint, although the lamb saag is just as exceptional (and generous in its portion). Afterwards, expect to smell as if you yourself have been doused in spices and baked in the tandoor oven. Mains under $10. Daily noon–midnight.

Trattoria Contadina 1800 Mason St, at Union St, North Beach ☏ 415 982 5728. Family-owned, warm and charming, with white cloth-swathed tables and photograph-covered walls. The rigatoni with aubergine and smoked mozzarella is a top option, and the Powell-Mason cable car will drop you off steps from the front door. Mains under $20. Mon–Thurs 5–9pm, Fri 5–9.30pm, Sat 10am–2pm & 5–9.30pm, Sun 10am–2pm & 5–9pm.

SOUTH OF MARKET, THE MISSION AND AROUND

Bi-Rite Creamery 3692 18th St, at Dolores St, Mission ☏ 415 626 5600. Tiny, inexpensive ice cream shop that hits all the right notes with its artisanal flavours. Usual suspects like mint choc-chip share freezer space with unique concoctions such as toasted coconut and honey lavender. Mon–Thurs & Sun 11am–10pm, Fri & Sat 11am–11pm.

Dosa 995 Valencia St, at 21st St, Mission ☏ 415 642 3672. *Dosa's* crêpe-like namesake item – and its close cousin, the thicker *uttapam* – dominate its South Indian menu, while the terracotta dining room is welcoming and not too noisy. Mains $12–22. Mon–Wed 5.30–10pm, Thurs 5.30–11pm, Fri 5.30pm–midnight, Sat 11.30am–3.45pm & 5.30pm–midnight, Sun 11.30am–3.45pm & 5.30–10pm.

Goood Frikin Chicken 10 29th St, at Mission St, Mission ☏ 415 970 2428. Superbly seasoned poultry that warrants the extra "o" in this airy restaurant's goofy name. The dining room is cast in various earth tones, with the ceiling and walls covered in soothing landscape murals. The best bet is the rotisserie half-chicken, served with tasty sides for less than $10. Daily 11am–10pm.

★ **Just for You** 732 22nd St, at Third St, Potrero Hill ☏ 415 647 3033. This out-of-the-way gem produces some of the fluffiest (and largest) beignets outside New Orleans.

All breads are house-made (try the raisin cinnamon toast), while the enormous pancakes are the stuff of legend; lunches are equally burly and delicious. Mains about $10. Mon–Fri 7.30am–2pm, Sat & Sun 8am–3pm.

La Espiga de Oro 2916 24th St, at Florida St, Mission ☏ 415 826 1363. As authentic a place as you'll find in San Francisco's Latino stronghold, this informal, open-air spot makes its own delectable tortillas; when grilled, they're often the best part of any meal here. Daily 5am–7pm.

★ **Le P'tit Laurent** 699 Chenery St, at Diamond St, Glen Park ☏ 415 334 3235. Carnivores won't want to miss *Laurent's* meaty cassoulet (complete with full leg of duck) and memorable desserts; the service and overall vibe are equally warm. Conveniently, it's steps from the Glen Park BART station. Mains from $20. Mon–Thurs & Sun 5.30–9.30pm, Fri & Sat 5.30–10.30pm.

★ **Papalote** 3409 24th St, at Valencia St, Mission ☏ 415 970 8815. Peerless Cal-Mex cuisine – there's nary a poor menu choice to be made, from the top-grade nachos to anything that includes the perfectly grilled *carne asada*. The warm chips and otherworldly salsa make for an ideal pairing. Most things $10 or less. Mon–Sat 11am–10pm, Sun 11am–9pm.

WESTERN ADDITION AND AROUND

Burgermeister 86 Carl St, at Cole St, Cole Valley ☏ 415 566 1274. Popular spot bang on the N-Judah streetcar line that broils excellent gourmet half-pound burgers. All the mainstream choices are available, as well as a handful of unusual options (such as the mango burger) for the adventurous. Most hover around $10 or so. Daily 11am–10pm.

★ **Little Star Pizza** 846 Divisadero St, at McAllister St, Western Addition ☏ 415 441 1118. One of San Francisco's top pizzerias, dimly lit and packed nightly with hipsters enjoying its lively bar and jukebox blasting American and British indie rock. The kitchen bakes deep-dish and thin-crust pizzas ($19–25) with equal aplomb. Mon–Thurs 5–10pm, Fri & Sat noon–11pm, Sun noon–10pm.

Nopa 560 Divisadero St, at Hayes St, Western Addition ☏ 415 864 8643. Buzzing, impossibly popular hot spot that leans on a number of cuisine styles, from New American (country pork chop, rotisserie herbed chicken) to further afield (Moroccan vegetable *tagine*, baked pastas). Mains under or about $20. Mon–Fri 5pm–1am, Sat & Sun 11am–1am.

Rosamunde Sausage Grill 545 Haight St, at Fillmore St, Lower Haight ☏ 415 437 6851. Tiny storefront serving terrific, inexpensive grilled sausages on sesame rolls (under $7). Options range from Hungarian pork to tequila-smoked chicken *habanero*. Mon–Wed & Sun 11.30am–10pm, Thurs–Sat 11.30am–11pm.

★ **Sociale** 3665 Sacramento St, at Spruce St, Presidio Heights ☏ 415 921 3200. Intimate, pricey Italian bistro worth seeking out at the end of its verdant pedestrian lane.

13

Go for the heated dining courtyard, cosy atmosphere and fontina cheese-crammed fried olives appetizer ($9). Mon 5.30–10pm, Tues–Sat 11.30am–2.30pm & 5.30–10pm.

THE SUNSET AND THE RICHMOND

★ **Arizmendi** 1331 Ninth Ave, at Irving St, Inner Sunset ☎ 415 566 3117. The daily rotation of artisanal breads and pastries are reason enough to head to this small, earthy and inexpensive bakery, but its gourmet pizza slices ($2.50) are the true surprise treat. Tues–Fri 7am–7pm, Sat & Sun 7.30am–6pm.

Brothers Korean BBQ 4128 Geary Blvd, at Sixth Ave, Inner Richmond ☎ 415 387 7991. The decor here isn't anything to get excited about, but the moderately priced feasts of marinated meats and myriad, pungent side dishes are worth the visit. Certain tables have sunken *hibachis* on which you can cook your own meats. Mains $13–25. Daily 11am–midnight.

Gordo Taqueria 1233 Ninth Ave, at Lincoln Way, Inner Sunset ☎ 415 566 6011. Efficient burrito shop that lives up to its name (which translates as "fat" in English) by specializing in hefty, stumpy slabs on a par with any in town. The menu's as simple as can be, including only tacos, burritos and quesadillas, and everything's around $6. Daily 10am–10pm.

Pluto's 627 Irving St, at Seventh Ave, Inner Sunset ☎ 415 753 8867. Custom salads are the big draw here, as they're among the biggest, best and cheapest anywhere (about $7.50); elsewhere on the menu, the turkey and stuffing is a soul-warming option any day of the year. Daily 11am–10pm.

NIGHTLIFE AND ENTERTAINMENT

San Francisco offers visitors no shortage of things to do come nightfall. While justly famous for its restaurants, it also boasts a huge number of **bars**, ranging from comfortably scruffy jukebox joints to chic watering holes and everything in between. Its **gay bars** are many and varied, ranging from cosy cocktail lounges to no-holds-barred leather-and-chain hangouts. The city doesn't have nearly the number of lesbian bars it once did, but a small handful of good ones still exist around town, particularly in Bernal Heights. San Francisco's **live music** scene reflects the character of the city: laidback, eclectic and not a little nostalgic. Options for shows are wide and the scene is strong, with the city regularly spawning good young bands. San Francisco's **nightclub** scene may not exactly be globally recognized, but the upside is that you won't have to endure high cover charges, ridiculously priced drinks, feverish posing or long lines. Also, most clubs here close at 2am, so you can usually be sure of finding things well under way by 10pm. The Sunday edition of the *San Francisco Chronicle* (🖰 sfgate .com), along with the free weeklies *San Francisco Bay Guardian* (🖰 sfbg.com) and *SF Weekly* (🖰 sfweekly.com), are the best sources for **listings**.

BARS

Amsterdam Café 937 Geary St, at Larkin St, Tenderloin ☎ 415 409 1111. San Francisco's smartest destination for craft beer aficionados has innumerable brews available in bottles and on draught. Try to snag one of the covered outdoor tables flanking the entrance. Mon noon–midnight, Tues, Wed & Sun noon–1am, Thurs–Sat noon–2am.

Edinburgh Castle 950 Geary St, at Polk St, Tenderloin ☎ 415 885 4074. Evocative Scottish pub filled with Highland memorabilia and plenty of beer and whiskey behind the lengthy bar. Arrive early on Tuesday for trivia night. Daily 5pm–2am.

★ **Latin American Club** 3286 22nd St, at Valencia St, Mission ☎ 415 647 2732. Cosy place with a warm vibe great for an early chat over drinks before the crowds arrive later in the evening. The loft space above the entrance is full of piñatas, Mexican streamers and assorted trinkets. Mon–Thurs 6pm–2am, Fri 5pm–2am, Sat 3pm–2am, Sun 2pm–2am.

Li Po Cocktail Lounge 916 Grant Ave, at Jackson St, Chinatown ☎ 415 982 0072. Named after the Chinese poet, charmingly grotty *Li Po* is one of the few places to drink in Chinatown. Enter through the false cavern front and grab a drink among the many regulars. Daily 2pm–2am.

Lucky 13 2140 Market St, at Church St, Castro ☎ 415 487 1313. Straight bar on the outskirts of the Castro with an extensive selection of international beers. It's filled with pool-players chomping on free popcorn; there's a loud jukebox inside and a humble patio out back. Daily 11am–2am.

★ **Royal Cuckoo** 3202 Mission St, at Valencia St ☎ 415 550 8667. Dimly lit nightspot where a live organ player sits in five nights a week (Wed–Sun), sometimes with an accompanying vocalist; other nights see all-vinyl DJs manning the lo-fi house stereo. The drink menu is suitably sophisticated: lots and lots of craft cocktails ($6–12), plus the requisite wine and beer. Mon–Thurs 4pm–2am, Fri–Sun 3pm–2am.

Specs Twelve Adler Museum Café 12 Saroyan Place, at Columbus Ave, North Beach ☎ 415 421 4112. Known locally as simply "Specs", this friendly dive set just off North Beach's main drag is known for its chatty bar staff and is decked out with loads of oddities from the high seas. Its regulars may be older eccentrics, but it's popular with just about everybody. Mon–Fri 4.30pm–2am, Sat & Sun 5pm–2am.

Tonga Room & Hurricane Bar The Fairmont, 950 Mason St, at California St, Nob Hill ☎ 415 772 5278. Ultra-campy bar styled like a Polynesian village, complete with pond, simulated rainstorms and grass-skirted band murdering jazz and pop covers upon a floating raft. Cocktails are predictably overpriced, but the happy hour buffet (about $10) helps make up for it. Wed, Thurs & Sun 5–11.30pm, Fri & Sat 5pm–12.30am.

★ **Tony Nik's** 1534 Stockton St, at Union St, North Beach ☎ 415 693 0990. A legendary watering hole in a neighbourhood full of them, *Tony Nik's* dim, sulky interior and stiff drinks have been summoning North Beach denizens for ages. The bar area is the liveliest spot, while the even darker back area is great for intimate chats. Daily 4pm–2am.

Tunnel Top 601 Bush St, at Stockton St, Union Square ☎ 415 722 6620. Fun spot atop the Stockton Tunnel where you can expect stiff drinks, a terrific balcony and nightly entertainment (usually DJs). Daily 5pm–2am.

Zeitgeist 199 Valencia St, at Duboce St ☎ 415 255 5505. This cyclist bar is a Mission institution, with an enormous outdoor beer garden that's wildly popular on sunny afternoons. Come for punk tunes, tattooed bartenders, afternoon cook-outs at weekends, famously powerful Bloody Marys and lots of beer on tap. Daily 9am–2am.

GAY AND LESBIAN BARS

The Café 2369 Market St, at 17th St, Castro ☎ 415 861 3846, ⓦ cafesf.com. With its mainstream house DJs, cheap cover and nightly happy hour until 9pm, this longtime staple of the Castro club scene remains a crowd-pleaser. It's classic out-and-proud Castro, from the thumping beats to the rainbow-coloured socks strategically placed on male dancers. Mon–Fri 5pm–2am, Sat & Sun 3pm–2am.

Lexington Club 3464 19th St, at Lexington St, Mission ☎ 415 863 2052. One of the few places in the city where the girls outnumber the boys – men must be accompanied by a woman to enter – this bustling lesbian bar attracts all sorts with its no-nonsense decor, friendly atmosphere and excellent jukebox. Mon–Thurs 5pm–2am, Fri–Sun 3pm–2am.

Martuni's 4 Valencia St, at Market St, Mission ☎ 415 241 0205. Serving kitschy drinks on the edge of the Mission, Castro and Hayes Valley, this two-room piano bar attracts a fun and diverse crowd, with many keen to sing along to classics by Judy, Liza and Edith. Daily 2pm–2am.

★ **The Wild Side West** 424 Cortland Ave, at Andover St, Bernal Heights ☎ 415 647 3099. Unpretentious and friendly tavern at the centre of the Bernal Heights lesbian scene, with plenty of kitsch Americana to gaze at. There's a lovely, quirky art-filled garden out back, but without heat lamps, you'd be well advised to stay inside on a cold evening. Daily 2pm–2am.

LIVE MUSIC: ROCK, BLUES AND JAZZ

Bottom of the Hill 1233 17th St, at Missouri St, Potrero Hill ☎ 415 621 4455, ⓦ bottomofthehill.com.

Well off the beaten path, San Francisco's celebrated indie-rock stronghold draws crowds nightly for local and nationally touring acts. $8–15. Hours vary.

Café du Nord 2170 Market St, at Sanchez St, Castro ☎ 415 861 5016, ⓦ cafedunord.com. This old subterranean speakeasy is a terrific place to enjoy touring or local rock bands, with the occasional swing and folk act booked for good measure. The amber-walled Swedish American Hall upstairs also regularly features shows. $10–20. Hours vary.

The Fillmore 1805 Geary Blvd, at Fillmore St, Western Addition ☎ 415 346 6000, ⓦ thefillmore.com. This ballroom auditorium was at the heart of 1960s counter-culture, masterminded by legendary local promoter Bill Graham. It's still a terrific spot for catching up-and-comers and longtime favourites alike – the sort of place bands love to perform. $20 and up. Hours vary.

★ **Great American Music Hall** 859 O'Farrell St, at Polk St, Tenderloin ☎ 415 885 0750, ⓦ gamh.com. A former bordello converted long ago into a beloved venue for rock, blues and international acts. The ornately moulded balcony offers seats with terrific views for those who arrive early. $15 and up. Hours vary.

Hemlock Tavern 1131 Polk St, at Post St, Polk Gulch ☎ 415 923 0923, ⓦ hemlocktavern.com. A variety of hipster-approved music is performed in the shoebox-sized room inside this popular bar, from underground pop to arty noise to electro-punk-disco to ukulele country. Free–$8. Hours vary.

The Independent 628 Divisadero St, at Hayes St, Western Addition ☎ 415 771 1421, ⓦ theindependentsf .com. This mid-sized club with friendly staff and exceptional sound books top acts from near (Rogue Wave) and far (Vieux Farka Toure). $10–20. Hours vary.

The Saloon 1232 Grant Ave, at Vallejo St, North Beach ☎ 415 989 7666, ⓦ sfblues.net/Saloon.html. Lively, lowbrow hardcore blues venue that's wonderfully anachronistic among the encroaching boutiques along upper Grant's shopping and dining strip. $3 and up. Hours vary.

SFJazz Center 201 Franklin St, at Fell St, Hayes Valley ☎ 866 920 5299, ⓦ sfjazz.org. With incomparable acoustics and a central location adjacent to the Civic Center, this newly opened venue has instantly drawn major figures in jazz (Bill Frisell and Brad Mehldau, among many others) to its stage for multinight residencies. $20 and up. Hours vary.

CLUBS

★ **111 Minna Gallery** 111 Minna St, at Second St, South of Market ☎ 415 974 1719, ⓦ 111minnagallery .com. Combination bar, art gallery and DJ venue set a short way down an alley. It gets busier, noisier and more raucous as the evening wears on. Free–$8. Hours vary.

13

Cat Club 1190 Folsom St, at Eighth St, South of Market ☎415 703 8965, ⓦsfcatclub.com. With free karaoke every Tuesday and dancing every other night of the week in a pair of separate rooms, there's something for practically every clubgoer here: electro, darkwave, goth, Britpop. Free–$10. Hours vary.

The End Up 401 Sixth St, at Harrison St, South of Market ☎415 646 0999, ⓦtheendup.com. Best known as the home of Sunday's all-day T-Dance party (6am–8pm), this stalwart club attracts a mixed bag of hardcore clubbers for after-hours dancing on the cramped dancefloor; if you need a break from the beat assault, head for outdoor patio with plenty of seating. $5 and up. Hours vary.

Mighty 119 Utah St, at 15th St, Potrero Hill ☎415 762 0151, ⓦmighty119.com. Huddled close to the freeway, this converted warehouse space is a combination art gallery, performance venue, club and lounge. As for the music, it's mostly live funk or DJs spinning old-school classic house. $5 and up. Hours vary.

ENTERTAINMENT

San Francisco has a top reputation for embracing the highbrow arts: patrons flock to **opera** and **classical music** performances, while the city's symphony orchestra is considered among the best in the USA. **Theatre** in San Francisco is accessible and much less costly than elsewhere, but most of the major venues – barring a couple of exceptions – are mediocre, forever staging Broadway reruns; you'd do better to explore the more interesting fringe circuit. **Tickets** can be purchased either through the individual theatre's box offices or often through Ticketmaster (☎415 421 8497, ⓦticketmaster.com); for last-minute bargains, try the Tix booth (daily 10am–6pm; ☎415 430 1140, ⓦtixbayarea.org) located on the west side of Union Square plaza.

BALLET, OPERA AND CLASSICAL MUSIC

San Francisco Ballet War Memorial Opera House, 301 Van Ness Ave, at Grove St, Civic Center ☎415 865 2000, ⓦsfballet.org. The city's ballet company, the oldest and one of the largest in the USA, puts on an ambitious annual programme (Jan–May) of both classical and contemporary dance. Tickets begin at around $40, while standing-room tickets are sometimes sold 2hr before performances at a deep discount.

San Francisco Opera War Memorial Opera House, 301 Van Ness Ave, at Grove St, Civic Center ☎415 864 3330, ⓦsfopera.org. A typical season (Sept–Dec, with a short run June & July) for this internationally regarded company offers a mixture of avant-garde stagings by composers such as John Adams or André Previn, along with acclaimed productions of perennial favourites by Wagner or Puccini. Tickets start at around $40, with prices rising dramatically from there.

★ **San Francisco Symphony** Louise M. Davies Symphony Hall, 201 Van Ness Ave, at Grove St, Civic Center ☎415 864 6000, ⓦsfsymphony.org. Since the 1995 arrival of conductor Michael Tilson Thomas, this once-musty institution has catapulted to the first rank of American symphony orchestras. Though Thomas' relentless self-promotion can be off-putting, his emphasis on the works of twentieth-century composers has added considerable vibrancy to the company's programming. The season runs Sept–May and tickets range from $40 far upwards, with day-of-performance rush tickets sometimes available for $20.

THEATRE

American Conservatory Theater (ACT) 415 Geary St, at Taylor St, Theater District ☎415 749 2228, ⓦact-sf.org. Leading resident group that mixes newly commissioned works and innovative renditions of the classics, with inventive set design and staging. Tickets $30–70, although preview shows can cost as little as $10.

★ **BATS Improv** Bayfront Theater, Fort Mason Center ☎415 474 6776, ⓦimprov.org. Celebrated long-form improv company (its titular acronym stands for Bay Area Theatresports) that stages shows such as *Improvised Elvis: The Musical* year-round. Tickets $17–20.

★ **Beach Blanket Babylon** Club Fugazi, 678 Green St, at Powell St, North Beach ☎415 421 4222, ⓦbeach blanketbabylon.com. This locally legendary musical revue has been running continuously since 1974, though it regularly incorporates new spoofs of current events. Expect celebrity impersonations and towering hats, and be sure to reserve in advance. Tickets $25–130.

Exit Theatre 156 Eddy St, at Taylor St, Tenderloin ☎415 673 3847, ⓦtheexit.org. One of the best spots in town for cutting-edge theatre, the Exit is best known

---

STERN GROVE FESTIVAL

The **Stern Grove Festival** (☎415 252 6252, ⓦsterngrove.org) presents free, open-air performances by San Francisco's symphony orchestra, opera and ballet companies (with jazz, blues, hip-hop and rock acts also booked) on summer Sundays at 2pm at its namesake park at 19th Ave and Sloat Blvd. Arrive early to secure a spot on the lawn; public transport (Muni lines #K, #L, #M, #23 and #28) is recommended.

for its women-centric plays and spring DivaFest season; it's also a central location for the annual San Francisco Fringe Festival. Tickets $10–20.

The Marsh 1062 Valencia St, at 22nd St, Mission ☎800 838 3006, ⓦthemarsh.org. This long-standing alternative space hosts fine solo shows, many with an offbeat bent. Monday nights are test nights ($7) for works in progress; other nights typically run $15–30.

Theatre Rhinoceros Eureka Theatre, 215 Jackson, at Battery St, Jackson Square ☎800 838 3006, ⓦtherhino.org. The city's prime LGBT company presents productions that range from heartfelt political drama to raunchy cabaret acts. Formerly based in the Mission, it's currently in search of a new permanent home. Tickets $15–25.

The Bay Area

Of the nearly seven million people who live in the vicinity of San Francisco, only one in eight lives in the city itself. Everyone else is spread around the **Bay Area**, a sharply contrasting patchwork of mostly rich and some poor towns dotted down the peninsula or across one of the three impressive bridges that span the chilly waters of the exquisite natural harbour. In the **East Bay** are hard-working Oakland and intellectual Berkeley, while south of the city, the **Peninsula** holds the gloating wealth of Silicon Valley. To the north across the Golden Gate Bridge is the woody, leafy landscape and rugged coastline of **Marin County**, a combination of ostentatious luxury and copious natural beauty.

The East Bay

The largest and the second-most-travelled bridge in the USA, the **Bay Bridge** connects downtown San Francisco to the East Bay. Currently being replaced along half its span in an over-budget and delayed project, it is crossed by a hundred million vehicles each year. The heart of the East Bay is **Oakland**, a resolutely blue-collar city that spreads north to the progressive university town of **Berkeley**; the two communities merge into one conurbation, and the hills above them are topped by a twenty-mile string of forested **regional parks**.

Oakland

OAKLAND, the workhorse of the Bay Area, is one of the largest ports on the West Coast. It has also been the breeding ground of revolutionary **political movements**. In the Sixties, the city's fifty-percent black population found a voice through the militant Black

---

SPORTS IN THE SAN FRANCISCO BAY AREA

Advance tickets for all major Bay Area sports events are available through Ticketmaster (☎415 421 8497, ⓦticketmaster.com) or direct from the teams – although you can get often snare day-of tickets, at least for baseball.

Baseball The Oakland Athletics play at the usually sunny Oakland Coliseum (☎510 638 4900, ⓦoaklandathletics.com), which has its own BART station. The San Francisco Giants play at gleaming AT&T Park, where home runs sometimes land in the bay (☎415 972 2000, ⓦsfgiants.com).

Football By the time you read this, the resurgent San Francisco 49ers (☎415 656 4900, ⓦsf49ers.com) will have relocated to Santa Clara in the South Bay, where you may have to pay around $100 per seat. The struggling Oakland Raiders share the Oakland Coliseum (☎510 864 5000, ⓦraiders.com) with the Athletics.

Basketball The Golden State Warriors play at Oracle Arena (☎510 986 2200, ⓦnba.com/warriors) in Oakland, next door to the Oakland Coliseum.

Ice hockey The formidable San Jose Sharks (☎408 287 7070, ⓦsharks.nhl.com) play at the SAP Center in San Jose.

Soccer The San Jose Earthquakes (☎408 985 4625, ⓦsjearthquakes.com), draw respectable crowds at collegiate Buck Shaw Stadium in Santa Clara.

13

Panthers and in the Seventies the Symbionese Liberation Army, kidnappers of heiress Patty Hearst, obtained a ransom of free food for the city's poor. It's not all hard graft, though: the climate is often sunny and mild when San Francisco is cold and dreary, and there's great hiking in the redwood- and eucalyptus-covered hills above the city.

There's not much to see within Oakland itself. The major concession to the tourist trade is the waterfront Jack London Square, an aseptic cluster of chains that have nothing to do with the writer. At the far eastern end of the promenade, however, is **Heinhold's First and Last Chance Saloon**, a tiny slanting bar built in 1883 from the hull of a whaling ship (see p.897). Jack London really did drink here and the collection of yellowed portraits of him on the wall are the only genuine thing about the writer you'll find on the square. A half-mile north up Broadway from the waterfront, Oakland's restored downtown is anchored by chain stores and the gargantuan open-air **City Center** complex of offices and fast-food outlets. Beside it, at Broadway and 14th Street, **Frank Ogawa Plaza** is a pleasant place to eat lunch outdoors, while further east on 10th and Oak streets, the **Oakland Museum of California** (Wed–Sun 11am–5pm, Fri till 9pm; $12, free first Sun of month; ☎510 238 2200, ⓦmuseumca.org) has good exhibits of California's ecology and history, including the Beat Generation.

Writer **Gertrude Stein** was born in Oakland at around the same time as the macho and adventurous London, but she's barely commemorated anywhere because she harshly criticized her home town. Oakland residents cite in its defence the small, trendy community of **Rockridge** and the lively neighbourhoods around Piedmont and Grand avenues, the latter near pleasant **Lake Merrit**.

Joaquin Miller Park, the most easily accessible of Oakland's hilltop parks, stands above East Oakland (take AC Transit bus #64 from downtown) and includes a small white cabin called The Abbey, former abode of the "Poet of the Sierras", Joaquin Miller. Also in the nearby hills but reached by AC Transit bus #53, the **Chabot Space & Science Center**, 10000 Skyline Blvd (Tues–Sun 10am–5pm, Fri & Sat till 10pm; $15.95; ☎510 336 7300, ⓦchabotspace.org) features excellent interactive displays and a fine planetarium.

Berkeley

BERKELEY (named after the English philosopher-theologian George Berkeley) is dominated by the **University of California**, one of America's most famous places of learning, especially known for progressive politics. The very name of Berkeley conjures up images of dissent and it remains a solidly left-wing oasis, although today the campus prides itself on its high academic rankings and Nobel-laureate-laden faculty. **Sproul Plaza**, in front of the school's entranceway, Sather Gate, is where the Free Speech Movement began. Stroll the campus's tree-shaded pathways or join the free student-led **tours** that leave from the elegant **Campanile** (Mon–Sat 10am, Sun 1pm).

The campus's grand buildings and thirty thousand students give off an energy that spills south down raucous **Telegraph Avenue**, where dishevelled vendors peddle rainbow bracelets in front of vegetarian restaurants, pizza joints and book- and music stores. Just off it is the now-quiet **People's Park**, a site of almost-daily pitched battles between protestors and police in the Sixties and early Seventies, part of the revolt against the Vietnam War.

Older academics congregate in **Northside**, popping down from their woodsy hillside homes to partake of goodies from Gourmet Ghetto – the restaurants, delis and bakeries on Shattuck Avenue, including the renowned *Chez Panisse* (see p.897). North of here, on the hills, **Tilden Regional Park** has good trails and a fine rose garden. Along the bay itself, at the **Berkeley Marina**, you can rent windsurfing boards and sailboats, or just watch the sun set behind the Golden Gate.

ARRIVAL AND DEPARTURE   THE EAST BAY

By plane Flights direct to the East Bay touch down at Oakland Airport, just outside town (☎510 563 3300 or ☎800 992 7433 for automated flight info, ⓦoakland airport.com). The AirBART shuttle van (every 15min; $3;

13

☎ 510 569 8300) runs to the Coliseum BART (see below) station. There are numerous door-to-door shuttle buses from the airport, such as A1 American (☎ 877 378 3596, ⓦ a1americanshuttle.com) – expect to pay around $20 to downtown Oakland, $30–40 to San Francisco.

By bus The Greyhound bus station is in a slightly dodgy part of northern Oakland on San Pablo Ave at 21st St. Destinations Oakland to: Eureka (1 daily; 6hr 15min); Los Angeles (12 daily; 6hr 55min–11hr 45min); Reno (5 daily; 4hr 40min–6hr 5min); Sacramento (8 daily; 1hr

30min–2hr); San Jose (8 daily; 1hr–1hr 35min); Santa Barbara (3 daily; 8hr 10min–8hr 50min); Santa Cruz (3 daily; 2hr 20min).

By train Amtrak trains terminate at 2nd Street near Jack London Square, after stopping in Richmond and Emeryville. Destinations Oakland to: Los Angeles (10 daily; 8hr 30min–12hr 40min); Reno (5 daily; 5hr 15min–7hr); Sacramento (10 daily; 2–3hr); San Jose (8 daily; 1hr–1hr 55min); Santa Barbara (10 daily; 7hr 50min–9hr 20min); Truckee (5 daily; 5hr 15min–5hr 50min).

GETTING AROUND AND INFORMATION

By underground train The underground BART system links the East Bay with San Francisco (see p.886).

By bus AC Transit ($2.10 one-way; ☎ 510 891 4777, ⓦ actransit.org) buses cover the entire East Bay area, with a more limited service running to Oakland and Berkeley from the Transbay Terminal in San Francisco; the only option for crossing the Bay when BART shuts down for the night.

Oakland CVB 463 11th St (Mon–Fri 8.30am–5pm; ☎ 510 839 9000, ⓦ oaklandcvb.com).

Visit Berkeley 2030 Addison St (Mon–Fri 9am–1pm & 2–5pm; ☎ 510 549 7040, ⓦ visitberkeley.com).

UC Berkeley visitor centre 101 Sproul Hall (☎ 510 642 5215, ⓦ berkeley.edu).

ACCOMMODATION

The East Bay's motels and hotels are generally better value for money than their San Francisco counterparts, especially in Oakland, making it worth considering as a base for visiting the city.

OAKLAND

Jack London Inn 444 Embarcadero West ☎ 510 444 2032, ⓦ jacklondoninnoakland.com. Kitschy but great-value 1950s-style motor lodge next to Jack London Square. The rooms are fully modernized, plus there's a decent restaurant and seasonal outdoor pool. $65

Waterfront Hotel 10 Washington St ☎ 510 836 3800, ⓦ jdvhotels.com. Plush, modern hotel with brightly decorated rooms, moored on the best stretch of the Oakland waterfront. Outdoor pool, plus complimentary wine and cheese hour. $259

BERKELEY

★ **Bancroft Hotel** 2680 Bancroft Way ☎ 510 549 1000, ⓦ bancrofthotel.com. Small, welcoming boutique hotel – just 22 well-appointed rooms – in a classy building with a great location and service. Views of campus and the Bay from upper rooms. Breakfast included. $119

★ **The Claremont Resort & Spa** 41 Tunnel Rd ☎ 510

843 3000, ⓦ claremontresort.com. The lap of luxury among Berkeley hotels in a 1915 building. Even the basic rooms are a treat, but you'll pay for the privilege. Spa sessions start around $100/hr for facials or massages. $254

Downtown Berkeley YMCA 2001 Allston Way, at Milvia St ☎ 510 848 9622, ⓦ baymca.org. Berkeley's best bargain accommodation, especially for singles, just one block from the BART stop. Rates include use of gym and pool. $85

The French Hotel 1538 Shattuck Ave ☎ 510 548 9930, ⓦ french-hotel-berkeley.com. There's a touch of European class about this small and comfortable hotel with eighteen simple but pleasant rooms in the heart of Berkeley's Gourmet Ghetto. $105

Rose Garden Inn 2740 Telegraph Ave ☎ 800 992 9005, ⓦ rosegardeninn.com. Forty stylishly decorated rooms of varying sizes but all with fireplaces, in a mock-Tudor mansion near the university. Hot buffet breakfast included. $158

EATING

As befits the birthplace of California cuisine, the East Bay offers a choice of good restaurants. Berkeley is both an upmarket diners' paradise and a student town where you can eat cheaply and well, especially on and around Telegraph Avenue. Oakland is much more a heartland of classic American cuisine, with a good spread of ethnic restaurants too.

OAKLAND

★ **Bay Wolf** 3853 Piedmont Ave ☎ 510 655 6004, ⓦ baywolf.com. Chic restaurant whose menu is influenced by the cuisine of Tuscany, Provence and the Basque country. Specialities such as Liberty Ranch Duck with smoked

chorizo cost $20–25. Cheaper menu on Monday. Mon–Thurs & Sun 5.30–9pm, Fri & Sat 5.30–10pm.

La Furia Chalaca 310 Broadway ☎ 510 451 4206, ⓦ lafuriachalaca.com. Great range of seafood pasta in various Peruvian sauces for around $15, plus meat dishes such as pork stew. Mon–Thurs 11.30am–3pm & 5–10pm, Fri & Sat 11.30am–10pm, Sun 11.30am–9pm.

★ **Le Cheval** 1007 Clay St ☎ 510 763 8595, ⊛ lecheval .com. Huge downtown Vietnamese place serving exquisitely spiced food for $10–15 in comfortable, stylishly decorated surroundings. Mon–Thurs 11am–9pm, Fri & Sat 11am–9.30pm, Sun 4–9pm.

BERKELEY

Brennan's 700 University Ave ☎ 510 841 0960, ⊛ brennansberkeley.com. Great simple self-service meals such as roast beef and mash for $7–12. It's also a solidly blue-collar hangout, great for drinking inexpensive beers and watching sports on TV, including European football (soccer). Mon–Wed & Sun 11am–9.30pm, Thurs–Sat 11am–10.30pm; bar till 2am.

Cha-Am 1543 Shattuck Ave ☎ 510 848 9664, ⊛ chaamberkeley.com. Climb the stairs to this unlikely, always crowded small restaurant for deliciously spicy Thai food such as *gaeng massaman* curry for $9.50. Mon–Thurs 11.30am–9.30pm, Fri & Sat 11.30am–10pm, Sun noon–9.30pm.

The Cheeseboard Collective 1512 Shattuck Ave ☎ 510 549 3055, ⊛ cheeseboardcollective.coop. Incredibly good gourmet pizza at $2.50 a slice. Often has live music in the afternoon. Great cheese and baked goods at the attached shop. Tues–Sat 11.30am–3pm & 4.30–8pm.

★ **Chez Panisse** 1517 Shattuck Ave ☎ 510 548 5525, ⊛ chezpanisse.com. The first and still the best of the California cuisine restaurants, overseen by legendary chef

Alice Waters. The main restaurant's *prix fixe* menu costs $65–100 depending on the day of the week. The café upstairs is comparatively inexpensive. Reservations recommended for the café, essential for the main restaurant. Restaurant sittings Mon–Sat 6pm & 8.30pm; café Mon–Thurs 11.30am–2.45pm & 5–10pm, Fri & Sat 11.30am–3pm & 5–11.30pm.

Gather 2200 Oxford St ☎ 510 809 0400, ⊛ gather restaurant.com. Trendy restaurant with menus based on local produce and sustainability, half vegetarian, half top-quality meat and fish. Great lunch deals for $12. Mon– Fri 11.30am–2pm & 5–10pm, Sat & Sun 10am–2.30pm & 5 10pm.

Kirala 2100 Ward St ☎ 510 549 3486, ⊛ kiralaberkeley .com. Many argue that *Kirala* serves the best sushi in the Bay Area, if not the whole USA. Moderate pricing, too – expect to pay around $20 to get your fill. Mon–Fri 11.30am–2pm & 5.30–9.30pm, Sat 5.30–9.30pm, Sun 5–9pm.

Tikka Korner 2101 University Ave ☎ 510 981 1734, ⊛ tikkakorner.com. Surprisingly good-quality Pakistani buffet, costing only $7.95 and featuring a range of nicely spiced veg and non-veg curries, plus plenty of naan. Mon–Wed & Sun 11am–11pm, Thurs 11am–1am, Fri & Sat 11am–2am.

★ **Vik's Chaat Corner** 2390 4th St ☎ 510 644 4432, ⊛ vikschaatcorner.com. Fantastic daytime spot, where you can feast on authentic South Indian dishes such as masala dosa for well under $10 in a huge, saffron-coloured self-service canteen. Mon–Thurs 11am–6pm, Fri–Sun 11am–8pm.

DRINKING, NIGHTLIFE AND ENTERTAINMENT

The many bohemian cafés in Berkeley are full from dawn to near midnight; for serious drinking you're better off in one of the many **bars**, particularly in rough-hewn Oakland. Nightlife is where the East Bay really comes into its own. Though traditional **clubs** are virtually nonexistent, there are plenty of **live music venues**. The range of **films** screened here is also top-notch. Berkeley's Pacific Film Archives at 2575 Bancroft Ave ($9.50; ☎ 510 642 5249, ⊛ bampfa.berkeley.edu for tickets) is one of the finest film libraries in California. The free *East Bay Express* has the most comprehensive **listings** of what's on.

OAKLAND

The Alley 3325 Grand Ave ☎ 510 444 8505. Ramshackle black-timber piano bar, decorated with business cards, where local old-timers come specifically to sing the blues from 9pm. Tues–Sat 4pm–2am, Sun 6pm–midnight.

Coffee Mill 3363 Grand Ave ☎ 510 465 4224. Delicious coffee and pastries are available at this café near Lake Merritt, which doubles as an art gallery and often hosts poetry readings, too. Daily 7am–6pm.

Eli's Mile High Club 3629 Martin Luther King Jr Way ☎ 510 594 0666, ⊛ elismilehigh.com. Hidden under raised freeways, this gem of a venue has been revamped in minimalist style and hosts obscure, punk, hardcore and psychobilly acts. Cover $8–20. Daily, hours vary.

Heinhold's First and Last Chance Saloon 56 Jack London Square ☎ 510 839 6761, ⊛ heinolds.com. Tiny and authentic waterfront bar whose interior has hardly changed since around 1900, when Jack London drank here. Small outdoor patio too. Mon 3–11pm, Tues–Thurs & Sun noon–11pm, Fri & Sat noon–1am.

Pacific Coast Brewing Co 906 Washington St ☎ 510 836 2739, ⊛ pacificcoastbrewing.com. The only real microbrewery downtown, featuring a good selection of ales, which you can wash down with ample portions of pub grub. Mon–Thurs 11.30am–midnight, Fri & Sat 11.30am–1am, Sun 11.30am–11pm.

The White Horse Inn 6551 Telegraph Ave, at 66th St ☎ 510 652 3820, ⊛ whitehorsebar.com. Oakland's oldest gay bar – a small, friendly place with mixed dancing

13

for men and women, plus comedy nights. Wed–Sun 1pm–2am.

Yoshi's World Class Jazz House 510 Embarcadero W ☎510 238 9200, ⊚yoshis.com. The centrepiece of Oakland's revived Jack London Square, this combination jazz club and sushi bar routinely attracts the biggest names in jazz. Cover $10–50. Restaurant Mon–Wed 5.30–9pm, Thurs–Sat 5.30–10pm, Sun 4–9pm; bar & shows till late.

BERKELEY

924 Gilman 924 Gilman St ☎510 525 9926, ⊚924 gilman.org. On the outer edge of the hardcore punk, indie and experimental scene, this institution helped launch Green Day and Sleater-Kinney. No alcohol, all ages. Cover $5–10. Fri–Sun, hours vary.

Ashkenaz 1317 San Pablo Ave ☎510 525 5054, ⊚ashkenaz.com. World music and dance café hosting acts from modern Afro-beat to the best of the Balkans. Kids and under-21s welcome. Cover $10–20. Tues–Sun, hours vary.

Caffè Mediterraneum 2475 Telegraph Ave ☎510 841 5634, ⊚caffemed.com. Berkeley's oldest café, straight out of the Beat Generation archives: beards and berets optional, battered books de rigueur. Pavement seating. Daily 7am–midnight.

Freight and Salvage 2020 Addison St ☎510 644 2020, ⊚freightandsalvage.org. Singer-songwriters perform in a smooth coffeehouse setting. Tickets mostly under $20, open-mic nights $5. Daily, hours vary.

★ **Pub (Schmidt's Tobacco & Trading Co)** 1492 Solano Ave ☎510 525 1900. This small, relaxed bar lures a mixture of bookworms and game players with a good selection of beers. Its other speciality is tobacco, so it even gets away with a semi-open smoking area out back. Mon–Wed & Sun noon–midnight, Thurs–Sat noon–1am.

Triple Rock Brewery 1920 Shattuck Ave, Berkeley ☎510 843 2739, ⊚triplerock.com. Lively student bar with fine burgers and beers, including cask-conditioned ales at weekends. Mon–Wed 11.30am–1am, Thurs–Sat 11.30am–2am, Sun 11.30am–midnight.

The Peninsula

The city of San Francisco sits at the tip of a neck of land commonly referred to as the **Peninsula**. Home of old money and new technology, the Peninsula stretches south from San Francisco through fifty miles of relentless suburbia along the Bay side, winding up in the futuristic roadside landscape of Silicon Valley near **San Jose**. There was a time when the region was largely agricultural, but the computer boom – spurred by Stanford University in **Palo Alto** – has replaced the orange groves and fig trees with office complexes and car parks. Most of the land along the **coast** – separated from the bayfront sprawl by a ridge of redwood-covered peaks – remains rural; it also contains some of the best **beaches** in the Bay Area.

Palo Alto

Palo Alto, home of preppy, conservative **Stanford University**, has become something of a social centre for Silicon Valley's nouveau riche and wealthy students, as evidenced by the trendy cafés and chic restaurants along its main drag, **University Avenue**. The town itself doesn't offer much to see other than Spanish Colonial homes, but the plush campus is a pleasant place to take a stroll or free student-led tour (daily 11am & 3.15pm; ☎650 723 2560, ⊚stanford.edu).

ACCOMMODATION AND EATING   PALO ALTO

Bistro Elan 2363A Birch St ☎650 327 0284, ⊚bistro elan.com. Elegant California cuisine such as duck confit and pan-seared scallops goes for well over $20 at this swanky place. Tues–Fri 11.30am–2pm & 5.30–11pm, Sat 5.30–11pm.

Cardinal Hotel 235 Hamilton Ave ☎650 323 5101, ⊚cardinalhotel.com. Reasonably affordable and comfortable rooms, the cheaper ones with shared bathrooms, are available at this downtown institution with a posh lobby. $95

Cowper Inn 705 Cowper St ☎650 327 4475, ⊚cowper inn.com. Restored Victorian house with attractive and cosy

rooms, some with shared bathrooms, close to University Ave. Excellent hot buffet breakfast included. $135

Evvia 420 Emerson St ☎650 326 0983, ⊚evvia.net. California-style Greek dishes such as braised lamb shank with *myzithra* cheese cost around $30. Mon–Fri 11.30am–2pm & 5.30–10pm, Sat 5–11pm, Sun 5–9pm.

Oren's Hummus 261 University Ave ☎650 752 6492, ⊚orenshummus.com. Excellent new Middle Eastern restaurant, serving filling wraps and huge wads of fluffy pitta bread with which to mop up a plethora of dips, mostly under $10. Mon–Thurs & Sun 11am–11pm, Fri & Sat 11am–midnight.

San Jose

Burt Bacharach could easily find **SAN JOSE** today by heading south from San Francisco and following the heat and smog that collects below the Bay. Although one of the fastest-growing cities in California, it is not strong on identity – though in area and population it's close to twice the size of San Francisco. Sitting at the southern end of the peninsula, San Jose has over the last three decades emerged as the civic heart of Silicon Valley. Ironically, it's also acknowledged as the first city in California, though the only sign of this is the unremarkable eighteenth-century **Mission Santa Clara de Asis**, on the pleasant campus of the Jesuit-run Santa Clara University.

The area's most famous landmark is the relentlessly hyped **Winchester Mystery House**, 525 S Winchester Blvd, just off I-280 near Hwy-17 (daily 9am–5pm, till 7pm in summer; various tours $27–40; ☎408 247 1313, ⊛winchestermysteryhouse.com), a folly of a mansion built by Sarah Winchester, heiress to the Winchester rifle fortune following her husband's death in 1884, to appease the spirits of those killed with the weapons. The **Rosicrucian Egyptian Museum**, 1660 Park Ave (Wed–Fri 9am–5pm, Sat & Sun 10am–6pm; $9; ☎408 947 3636, ⊛rosicrucian.org), houses a brilliant collection of Assyrian and Babylonian artefacts, while the revamped **Tech Museum of Innovation** (daily 10am–5pm; $15; ☎408 294 8224, ⊛thetech.org), downtown at 201 S Market St, contains hands-on displays of high-tech engineering as well as an IMAX theatre ($10, $5 with museum entry).

INFORMATION   SAN JOSE

Visitor centre Inside the huge Convention Center complex at 408 S Almaden Blvd (Mon–Fri 8am–5pm, Sat & Sun 11am–5pm; ☎408 295 9600, ⊛sanjose.org). Geared more to business people than travellers.

ACCOMMODATION, EATING AND DRINKING

71 Saint Peter 71 N San Pedro St ☎408 971 8523, ⊛71saintpeter.com. Patio dining and oyster bar centred on a menu of filet mignon, pork loin, chicken and salads. A hot spot with the in-crowd. Mon–Thurs 11.30am–2pm & 5–9pm, Fri 11.30am–2pm & 5–10pm, Sat 5–10pm.

Cafe Stritch 3/4 S First St ☎480 280 6161, ⊛cafestritch .com. This up-and-coming place does a decent line in beers, cocktails and bar snacks. Also features live pop and rock shows some nights. Mon & Tues 4–10pm, Wed–Fri 4pm–1am, Sat 10am–1am, Sun 10am–10pm.

Hotel De Anza 233 W Santa Clara St ☎408 286 1000, ⊛hoteldeanza.com. Smart business hotel in one of the livelier parts of town, which offers good online deals, especially at weekends. $99

Original Joe's 301 S First St ☎408 292 7030, ⊛originaljoes.com. San Jose institution, serving quality Italian specialities such as sauteed calf's liver in the $15–30 range, plus cheaper snacks. Daily 11am–1am.

Valley Inn 2155 The Alameda ☎408 241 8500, ⊛valley innsanjose.com. An above-average motel with compact, well-kept and brightly decorated rooms. Conveniently located for the Rosicrucian Museum and the western suburbs. $89

The Peninsula coast

The **coastline** of the Peninsula south from San Francisco is a world away from the bayside: mostly undeveloped, with a few small towns, and countless beaches that run 75 miles down to the mellow cities of Santa Cruz and Capitola. Just south of San Francisco, Hwy-1 hugs the precipitous cliffs of Devil's Slide, passing the decent mini-resort of **Pacifica** en route to the clothing-optional sands of **Gray Whale Cove State Beach** (daily 8am–sunset; ☎650 728 5336, ⊛parks.ca.gov). Two miles further on Hwy-1, the red-roofed buildings of the 1875 **Point Montara Lighthouse**, set among the windswept Monterey pine trees at the top of a steep cliff, have been converted into a youth hostel (see p.900). Just beyond the hostel, down California Street, the **Fitzgerald Marine Reserve** (free; ☎650 728 3584) has three miles of diverse oceanic habitat, peaceful trails and, at low tide, the best tidal pools.

A few miles further south on Hwy-1 is **Princeton-by-the-Sea**, whose busy harbour nestles below the protruding headland of **Pillar Point**. On either side of the headland lie the wonderful strands of **Mavericks** and **Miramar**, both renowned for superb surfing conditions. The next town is constantly expanding **Half Moon Bay**, which is highly appealing and boasts the best facilities on the coast. Further south lie a succession of wild

13

coves, the tiny hamlet of **Pescadero** and **Año Nuevo State Reserve** (tours Dec–March hourly 8am–4pm; $7/person, $10 parking; ☎800 444 4445, ⊛parks.ca.gov), renowned for the mating rituals of its northern elephant seals.

ACCOMMODATION	THE PENINSULA COAST

Costanoa Coastal Lodge & Camp 2001 Rossi Rd, just south of Pescadero ☎650 879 1100, ⊛costanoa.com. Offers a pampered night under the stars with accommodation ranging from modest cabins to luxury suites. Cabins $95, suites $350

Goose & Turrets 835 George St, Montara ☎650 728 5451, ⊛gooseandturretsbandb.com. Quirky and cosy Victorian house run by an engaging older couple. Great gourmet breakfasts and afternoon tea included. $175

★ **HI-Point Montara Lighthouse** Off Hwy-1, Montara ☎650 728 7177, ⊛norcalhostels.org. Dorms and rooms are in the converted outhouses of an 1875 lighthouse; SamTrans bus #294 from Pacifica. Office hours 7.30am–10pm. Dorms $30, doubles $74

Old Thyme Inn 779 Main St, Half Moon Bay ☎650 726 1616, ⊛oldthymeinn.com. A Victorian house with cosy and beautifully furnished rooms, the pricier ones with hot tubs. It's an easy walk to the town's restaurants and facilities. $159

EATING AND DRINKING

★ **Cetrella** 845 Main St, Half Moon Bay ☎650 726 4090, ⊛cetrella.com. The classiest option in town is this award-winning Mediterranean restaurant, with delights such as braised Australian lamb shank for around $25; live jazz Sat & Sun eves. Tues–Thurs & Sun 5.30–9.30pm, Fri & Sat 5.30–10pm; bar opens later; Sun brunch 10.30am–2.30pm.

Duarte's Tavern 202 Stage Rd, Pescadero ☎650 879 0464, ⊛duartestavern.com. Open since 1894 and still one of the best places to eat on the Peninsula, where you can feast on artichoke soup and huge portions of fish ($20–25) in a down-home atmosphere. Great breakfasts too. Daily 7am–9pm.

★ **La Costanera** 8150 **Cabrillo Hwy** (Hwy-1), Montara ☎650 728 1600, ⊛lacostanerarestaurant .com. One of the most highly rated venues on the coast,

serving traditional Peruvian cuisine and lovely pisco sours in the smart interior or on the breezy deck. Tues–Thurs & Sun 5–9pm, Fri & Sat 5–9.30pm.

Nick's Seashore Restaurant 101 Rockaway Beach Ave, Pacifica ☎650 359 3903, ⊛nicksrestaurant.net. An all-purpose joint providing cheap breakfasts, moderate pasta options, and pricier steak/seafood dishes for $22–32. Mon–Thurs 11am–10pm, Fri 9am–10pm, Sat & Sun 8am–10pm, bar till 1am.

Sam's Chowder House 4210 Cabrillo Hwy (Hwy-1), Princeton-by-the-Sea ☎650 712 0245, ⊛samschowder house.com. *Sam's* has established itself as one of the Peninsula's prime restaurants, serving New England-style seafood, as well as meat dishes, for $20–30. Mon–Thurs 11.30am–9pm, Fri 11.30am–9.30pm, Sat 11am–9.30pm, Sun 11am–9pm.

Marin County

Across the Golden Gate from San Francisco, **Marin County** is an unabashed introduction to Californian self-indulgence in wonderful natural surroundings: a pleasure zone of conspicuous luxury and abundant natural beauty, with sunshine or fog, sandy beaches, high mountains and thick redwood forests. Though in the past the region served as logging headquarters, the county is now one of the wealthiest in the USA, attracting young professionals to its swanky waterside towns.

The Marin Headlands

The largely undeveloped **Marin Headlands**, across the Golden Gate Bridge from San Francisco and far more rugged, afford some of the most impressive views of the bridge and the city behind. Heading west on Bunker Hill Road takes you up to the brink of the headlands before the road snakes down to Fort Barry and wide, sandy **Rodeo Beach**, from which numerous hiking trails branch out.

Sausalito

Attractive, smug little **SAUSALITO**, along the Bay below US-101, was once a gritty community of fishermen and sea traders, full of bars and bordellos. Now exclusive restaurants and pricey boutiques line its picturesque waterfront promenade and expensive, quirky houses climb the ridges above central Bridgeway Avenue.

The town has a one-of-a-kind exhibit in the **Bay Model Visitor Center**, 2100 Bridgeway (Sept–May Tues–Sat 9am–4pm; June–Aug Tues–Fri 9am–4pm, Sat & Sun 10am–5pm; donation; ☎415 332 3870, ⊛spn.usace.army.mil/bmvc), where elevated walkways in a huge building lead you around a scale model of the entire bay, surrounding deltas and its aquatic inhabitants, offering insight on the diversity of this area.

Mount Tamalpais and Muir Woods

Mount Tamalpais dominates the skyline of the Marin peninsula, looming over the cool canyons of the rest of the county and dividing it into two distinct parts: the wild western slopes above the Pacific Coast and the suburban communities along the calmer bay frontage. The Panoramic Highway branches off from Hwy-1 along the crest above Mill Valley, taking ten miles to reach the centre of **Mount Tamalpais State Park** (daily 8am–sunset; parking $8; ☎415 388 2070, ⊛mttam.net), which has some thirty miles of hiking trails and many campgrounds.

Muir Woods National Monument

Daily 8am–sunset • $5 • ☎415 388 2595, ⊛nps.gov/muwo

While most of the redwood trees that once covered its slopes have long since been chopped down, one towering grove remains, protected as the **Muir Woods National Monument**. It's a tranquil and majestic spot, with sunlight filtering 300ft down from the treetops to the laurel- and fern-covered canyon below. Being so close to San Francisco, Muir Woods is often packed with coach-tour hordes; more secluded hiking paths include the Matt Davis Trail, leading south to Stinson Beach and north to Mount Tamalpais.

Mill Valley

From the east peak of Mount Tamalpais, a quick two-mile downhill hike follows the Temelpa Trail through velvety shrubs of chaparral to the town of **MILL VALLEY**, the oldest and most enticing of the inland towns of Marin County. For many years the playground and often residence of high-profile hippies like Grace Slick and Phil Lesh, Mill Valley hosts October's annual **Mill Valley Film Festival**, a world-class event that draws Bay Area stars and up-and-coming directors alike.

Point Reyes National Seashore

The westernmost tip of Marin County comes at the end of the **Point Reyes National Seashore**, a near-island of wilderness bordered on three sides by more than fifty miles of isolated coastline – pine forests and sunny meadows hemmed in by rocky cliffs and sandy, windswept beaches. This wing-shaped landmass is a rogue piece of the earth's crust that has been drifting steadily northward along the San Andreas Fault, having started out some six million years ago as a suburb of Los Angeles. This was the epicentre of the great earthquake of 1906, when the land here shifted more than 16ft in an instant.

Eight miles west of **Inverness**, a small road leads down to **Drake's Beach**, the presumed landing spot of Sir Francis Drake in 1579. Appropriately, the coastline resembles the southern coast of England – cold, wet and windy, with chalk-white cliffs rising above the wide sandy beach. The road continues southwest another four miles to the very tip of Point Reyes, where a precarious-looking **lighthouse** (Thurs–Sun 10am–4.30pm; tours first and third Sat of each month; free; ☎415 669 1534) is an excellent spot for watching sea lions and, from mid-March to April and late December to early February, migrating grey whales.

ARRIVAL AND DEPARTURE   **MARIN COUNTY**

By bus Golden Gate Transit (☎415 923 2000 in San Francisco, ☎415 455 2000 in Marin, ⊛goldengate.org) offers a comprehensive bus service around Marin County

and across the Golden Gate Bridge from the Transbay Terminal in San Francisco.

By ferry There are frequent connections by smart modern

13

ferries to Sausalito, Larkspur and Tiburon from San Francisco. These are run by Golden Gate Ferry from $9.50 each way (see p.901) from the Ferry Building and by Blue & Gold Fleet ferries $11 each way (see p.887) from Pier 39 at Fisherman's Wharf.

INFORMATION

Marin County Visitors Bureau Signposted off US-101 at 1 Mitchell Blvd (Mon–Fri 9am–5pm; ☎415 925 2060, ⊛visitmarin.org).
Sausalito Chamber of Commerce 780 Bridgeway Ave (Tues–Sun 11.30am–4pm; ☎415 332 0505, ⊛sausalito.org).
Mill Valley Chamber of Commerce & Visitor Center 85 Throckmorton Ave (Tues–Fri 10am–4pm; ☎415 388 9700, ⊛millvalley.org).

ACCOMMODATION, EATING AND NIGHTLIFE

Marin has relatively few **hotels** and most charge well in excess of $100 a night; **motels** are also scarce in the best parts of the county, though there are a couple of attractively faded ones along the coast. If you want to stay in a B&B, contact the **Marin Bed and Breakfast** service (☎415 485 1971, ⊛marinbedandbreakfast.com). Marin has a wide variety of restaurants encompassing most cuisines and all budgets. Nightlife is mostly low key but there are a few lively bars and a handful of splendid music venues.

SAUSALITO

Casa Madrona 801 Bridgeway Ave ☎415 332 0502, ⊛casamadrona.com. Deluxe, all mod cons hotel with an extension spreading up the hill above the Bay. All rooms are tastefully decorated. Spa facilities available. **$279**

★ **Fish** 350 Harbor Drive ☎415 331 3474, ⊛331fish .com. This place makes a point of serving sustainable fish and seafood in undoubted style. Follow the Portuguese red chowder with a tuna melt for just $14. Daily 11.30am–4.30pm & 5.30–8.30pm.

No Name Bar 757 Bridgeway Ave ☎415 332 1392. An ex-haunt of the Beats, which hosts live music, mostly jazz, nightly from 8pm and on Sundays 3–7pm. Mon–Fri 11am–midnight, Sat & Sun 10am–1am.

Tommy's Wok 3001 Bridgeway ☎415 332 5818, ⊛tommyswok.com. This Chinese spot specializes in organic vegetables, free-range meats and fresh seafood, cooked in Mandarin, Hunan and Szechuan recipes. Most items under $10. Mon–Thurs 11.30am–3pm & 4–9pm, Fri & Sat 11.30am–3pm & 4–9.30pm, Sun 4–9pm.

MARIN HEADLANDS

HI-Marin Headlands Building 941, Fort Barry ☎415 331 2777, ⊛norcalhostels.org. Worth the effort for its setting, in cosy old army barracks near the ocean. On Sundays and holidays only, MUNI bus #76 from San Francisco stops right outside. Closed 10am–3.30pm, except for check-in. Dorms **$26**, doubles **$72**

MILL VALLEY

★ **Avatar's Punjabi Burritos** 15 Madrona St ☎415 381 8293, ⊛enjoyavatars.com. A dastardly simple cross-cultural innovation: burritos stuffed with delicious spicy curries for around $8. Does a brisk takeaway trade, as there are just two tables inside. Daily 11am–8pm.

Mill Valley Inn 165 Throckmorton Ave ☎415 389 6608, ⊛millvalleyinn.com. One of the county's top establishments, this gorgeous European-style inn offers elegant rooms, lavishly furnished in period style, as well as two private cottages. **$249**

Small Shed Flatbreads 17 Madrona St ☎415 383 4200, ⊛smallshed.com. Unusual place that serves a tasty range of cheesy toppings on organic stoneground flatbreads, as well as burgers and quiches, all around $14. Mon–Wed & Sun 11am–9pm, Thurs 11am–9.30pm, Fri & Sat 11am–10pm.

Sweetwater Music Hall 19 Corte Madera Ave, Mill Valley ☎415 388 3850, ⊛sweetwatermusichall.com. Finally relocated back to Mill Valley in an old theatre, this legendary Marin venue has live rock, folk and blues most nights. Hours vary.

POINT REYES NATIONAL SEASHORE

★ **HI-Point Reyes Point Reyes National Seashore** 1390 Limantour Spit Rd, 6 miles west of the visitor centre ☎415 663 8811, ⊛norcalhostels.org. Located in an old ranch house and surrounded by meadows and forests. Office hours 7.30–10am & 4.30–9pm; no check-in after 9.30pm. Dorms **$25**, doubles **$82**

Point Reyes Seashore Lodge 10021 Hwy-1, Olema ☎415 663 9000, ⊛pointreyesseashore.com. Attractive, largely wooden lodge that's the size of a hotel but with the personal touch of a B&B. All rooms overlook the garden and brook. **$145**

Vladimir's Czech Restaurant 12785 Sir Francis Drake Blvd, Inverness ☎415 669 1021. This relic of rural Bohemia in the far West has been serving up tasty items such as Moravian cabbage roll, roast duckling and apple strudel since 1960. Main courses $20–30. Tues–Sun 11am–9pm.

MOUNT TAMALPAIS

Mountain Home Inn 810 Panoramic Hwy ☎415 381 9000, ⊛mtnhomeinn.com. Romantically located on the crest of Mount Tamalpais, this B&B offers great views and endless hiking. Some rooms with hot tubs. Ample cooked breakfasts included and a great restaurant. **$195**

The Gold Country

Around 150 years before techies from all over the world rushed to California in search of Silicon gold, rough-and-ready "forty-niners" invaded the **GOLD COUNTRY** of the Sierra Nevada, about 150 miles east of San Francisco, in search of the real thing. The area ranges from the foothills near Yosemite to the deep gorge of the Yuba River two hundred miles north, with **Sacramento** as its largest city. Many of the mining camps that sprang up around the Gold Country vanished as quickly as they appeared, but about half still survive. Some are bustling resorts, standing on the banks of whitewater rivers in the midst of thick pine forests; others are just eerie ghost towns, all but abandoned on the grassy rolling hills. Most of the mountainous forests along the Sierra crest are preserved as near-pristine wilderness, with excellent hiking and camping. There's also great skiing in winter, around the mountainous rim of **Lake Tahoe** on the border between California and Nevada.

Sacramento

California's state capital, **SACRAMENTO**, in the flatlands of the Central Valley, was founded in 1839 by the Swiss John Sutter. He worked hard for ten years to build a busy trading centre and cattle ranch, only to be thwarted by the discovery of gold at a nearby sawmill in 1848. His workers quit their jobs to go prospecting and thousands more flocked to the goldfields of the Central Mother Lode, without any respect for Sutter's claims to the land. Sacramento became the main supply point for the miners and remained important as the western headquarters of the transcontinental railroad. Flashy office towers and hotel complexes have now sprung from its rather suburban streetscape, enlivening the flat grid of leafy, tree-lined blocks.

There's not a great deal to see, though the wharves, warehouses, saloons and stores of the historic core along the **riverfront** have been restored and converted into the touristy shops and restaurants of **Old Sacramento**. On the northern edge of the old town, the **California State Railroad Museum** (daily 10am–5pm; $10; ☎916 445 6645, ⓦcsrmf.org) brings together a range of lavishly restored 1860s locomotives, with "cow-catcher" front grilles and bulbous smokestacks.

A mile or so east of downtown, the dome of the **State Capitol** (☎916 324 0333, ⓦcapitolmuseum.ca.gov) stands proudly in a spacious green park. Restored to its original elegance, the luxurious building brims over with finely crafted details. There are free hourly **tours** (daily 10am–4pm); ID is required to enter the building. Further east at 27th and L streets, **Sutter's Fort State Historic Park** (daily 10am–5pm; $5; ☎916 445 4422, ⓦsuttersfort.org) is a re-creation of Sacramento's original settlement. An adobe house displays relics from the Gold Rush, and on summer weekends costumed volunteers act out scenes from the 1850s.

ARRIVAL AND DEPARTURE

SACRAMENTO

By plane Sacramento International airport (☎916 874 0700, ⓦsacairports.org), 12 miles northwest of downtown, is served by most major domestic airlines. SuperShuttle Sacramento vans (☎800 258 3826, ⓦsupershuttle.com) can take you directly to any downtown destination for $15.

By bus Frequent Greyhound buses pull into the bus depot at 715 L St, a block from the K Street Mall.

Destinations Los Angeles (7 daily; 7hr 20min–9hr 45min); Reno (5 daily; 2hr 45min–3hr 30min); San Francisco (8 daily; 2hr–2hr 45min); Truckee (2 daily; 2hr–2hr 40min).

By train Trains pull in at the Amtrak station at 4th and I sts, near Old Sacramento.

Destinations Oakland/Emeryville (12–16 daily; 1hr 55min–3hr); Reno (1 daily; 4hr 45min); Truckee (1 daily; 3hr 30min).

INFORMATION

Visitor centres 1002 2nd St in Old Sacramento (daily 10am–5pm; ☎916 442 7644, ⓦdiscovergold.org) and 1608 I St, near the State Capitol (Mon–Fri 8am–5pm;

☎916 808 7777). Both offices hand out plenty of brochures and an informative self-guided walking tour guide.

13

Listings A useful website is ⓦsacramento365.com. For events and entertainment, check out the free *Sacramento News & Review* (ⓦnewsreview.com) or *Ticket*, the Friday supplement to the *Sacramento Bee* newspaper (ⓦsacbee.com). The city's gay and lesbian scene is covered by *Outword* (ⓦoutwordmagazine.com).

ACCOMMODATION

HI-Sacramento 925 H St, downtown ☏916 443 1691, ⓦnorcalhostels.org. This hostel is housed in a rambling 1885 mansion with all the usual facilities, plus free bike rental, but there's a daytime lockout and 11pm curfew. Dorms $30, doubles $79

Vagabond Inn 909 3rd St, Old Town ☏800 522 1555, ⓦvagabondinn.com. Motor lodge-style accommodation near the river and Old Sacramento: there's a pool and free shuttle to public transport hubs. $89

Vizcaya Mansion 2019 21st St, Midtown ☏916 594 9285, ⓦvizcayasacramento.com. A lavish, historic property with elegantly furnished rooms and marble-tiled bathrooms. Decent breakfast included. Very good value. $106

EATING, DRINKING AND NIGHTLIFE

★ **Ma Jong's** 1116 15th St, downtown ☏916 442 7555, ⓦmajongs.com. Great value pan-Asian diner set in the modern Park Downtown complex. You can get a choice of meat, prawns or veg in different styles such as Thai basil special or Mongolian, all $10 or less. Mon–Thurs & Sun 11am–9pm, Fri & Sat 11am–2.30am.

Old Ironsides 1901 10th St, downtown ☏916 443 9751, ⓦtheoldironsides.com. A good spot for offbeat live music, mostly indie rock. Also has open-mic and dance-club nights, plus there's decent food. Most nights entry is free, though a few events cost $5–7. Mon–Fri 8pm–2am, Sat 6pm–2am.

Paesano's 1806 Capitol Ave, midtown ☏916 447 8646, ⓦpaesanos.biz. Brick-walled pizzeria also serving hearty portions of pasta and oven-baked sandwiches. Items $8–21. Mon–Wed 11.30am–9.30pm, Thurs 11.30am–10pm, Fri 11.30am–10.30pm, Sat noon–10.30pm, Sun noon–9.30pm.

River City Brewing Company 545 Downtown Plaza, downtown ☏916 447 2739, ⓦrivercitybrewing.net. This slick, modern brewpub at the west end of the K Street Mall serves standard American food for $10–15, enhanced by tasty beers (some brewed on site). Daily noon–2am.

★ **Tapa the World** 2115 J St, Midtown ☏916 442 4353, ⓦtapatheworld.com. Choose from twenty different tapas such as *chorizo con papas*, all $4–8, or enjoy a full meal of paella, lamb or fresh fish, while being serenaded by flamenco guitar. Daily 11.30am–midnight.

The Mines

In the romantically rugged landscape of the Gold Country, overshadowed by the 10,000ft granite peaks of the Sierra Nevada, fast-flowing rivers cascade through steeply walled canyons. During the autumn, the flaming reds and golds of poplars and sugar maples stand out against an evergreen background of pine and fir. The camps of the **southern mines** were the liveliest and most uproarious of all the Gold Rush settlements: Wild West towns full of gambling halls, saloons and gunfights in the streets. Freebooting prospectors in these "placer" mines sometimes panned for nuggets of gold in the streams and rivers; further **north**, the diggings were far richer and more successful, but the gold was (and still is) buried deep underground, so had to be pounded out of hardrock ore.

The southern mines

The hub of the southern mining district is **SONORA**, set on steep ravines roughly a hundred miles east of San Francisco. This friendly and animated logging town boasts Victorian houses and false-fronted buildings on its main Washington Street.

Sonora's one-time arch-rival, **COLUMBIA**, three miles north on Parrots Ferry Road, is now a ghost town designated as a state historic park, with a carefully restored Main Street that gives an excellent idea of what Gold Rush life might have been like. In 1854 it was California's second largest city and missed becoming the state capital by two votes, but by 1870 the gold had run out and it was abandoned.

In **JAMESTOWN**, three miles south of Sonora, the **Railtown 1897 State Historic Park** (daily: April–Oct 9.30am–4.30pm; Nov–March 10am–3pm; $5; ☏209 984 3953, ⓦrailtown1897.org), on the corner of 5th and Reservoir streets, holds an impressive collection of old steam trains, including the one used in *High Noon*, and offers rides at weekends in season (April–Oct; $15).

INFORMATION

Visitor centre 385 S Washington St, Sonora (April–Sept Mon–Fri 9am–7pm, Sat 10am–6pm, Sun 10am–5pm; Oct–March Mon–Fri 9am–6pm, Sat 10am–6pm; ☎ 800 446 1333, ⓦ tcvb.com).

ACCOMMODATION

Columbia City Hotel 22768 Main St, Columbia ☎ 209 532 1479, ⓦ briggshospitalityllc.com. Subtly refurbished to maintain its nineteenth-century character while providing luxurious and well-appointed rooms. Continental buffet breakfast included. $137

Columbia Inn Motel 22646 Broadway, Columbia ☎ 209 533 0446, ⓦ columbiainnmotel.net. Basic but spotless motel with reasonable-sized rooms, a small pool and cheery staff. Set in the leafy suburbs but an easy stroll to the state park. $65

Gunn House 286 S Washington St, Sonora ☎ 209 532 3421, ⓦ gunnhousehotel.com. The expanded old adobe house of the Mother Lode's first newspaper proprietor, Dr Gunn, has large, slightly dark rooms. Full breakfast included. $79

★ **National Hotel** 18183 Main St, Jamestown ☎ 800 894 3446, ⓦ national-hotel.com. All nine rooms are furnished with antiques and decorated with period flock wallpaper. There is also a casually elegant restaurant and an atmospheric saloon bar. $140

EATING AND DRINKING

Smoke Café 18191 Main St, Jamestown ☎ 209 984 3733. Unpretentious place that serves tasty Southwestern-style Mexican food and huge margaritas in a touristy atmosphere; lunch specials hover around $8 and there's live music most nights. Mon–Thurs & Sun 11am–midnight, Fri & Sat 11am–2am.

Sonora Thai 51 S Washington St, Sonora ☎ 209 532 2355. All the Siamese favourites from stir fries to spicy red and green curries can be enjoyed at this simple place for $10–15. Mon–Thurs 11am–9pm, Fri & Sat 11am–9.30pm.

Zane Iron Horse Lounge 97 S Washington St, Sonora ☎ 209 532 4482. This is the best place to find a hint of the Wild West and drink with the locals. The beers are unremarkable but the spirits are cheap and strong. Daily noon–late.

Grass Valley and Nevada City

The compact communities of **GRASS VALLEY** and **NEVADA CITY**, four miles apart in the Sierra Nevada Mountains, were the most prosperous and substantial of the gold-mining towns. Since the 1960s, artists and craftspeople have settled in the elaborate Victorian homes of the surrounding hills. In Grass Valley, the **North Star Mining Museum** (May–Oct daily 10am–5pm; donation; ☎ 530 273 4255) at the south end of Mill Street is housed in what used to be the power station for the North Star Mine. Its giant water-driven **Pelton wheel**, fitted with a hundred or so iron buckets, once powered the drills and hoists of the mine. Grass Valley's most colourful gold-era resident was **Lola Montez**, an Irish entertainer and former mistress of Ludwig of Bavaria, who retired here after touring America with her provocative "Spider Dance" and kept a grizzly bear in her front yard.

Towns don't get much quainter than Nevada City. Amid all its shops and restaurants, the lacy-balconied and bell-towered **Firehouse Museum #1**, 214 Main St (May–Oct Tues–Sun 1–4pm; Nov–April by appointment; donation; ☎ 530 265 5468, ⓦ nevadacountyhistory.org) describes the social history of the region.

Empire Mine State Park

10791 E Empire St • Daily 10am–5pm; cottage tour times vary • $7 • ☎ 530 273 8522, ⓦ empiremine.org

The last mine in California to shut down was its richest, the **Empire Mine**, now preserved as a pine-forested state park a mile southeast of Grass Valley off Rte-49. It closed in 1956, after more than six million ounces of gold had been recovered, when the cost of getting the gold out of the ground exceeded $35 an ounce, the government-controlled price at the time. Machinery sold off when the mine closed has been replaced from other disused workings and now augments the excellent **museum** at the entrance.

By bus Grass Valley is connected to Nevada City every 30min by the Gold Country Stage minibus (Mon–Fri 8am–7pm, Sat 10am–5pm; $1.50, $4.50 for a day pass; ☎888 660 7433, ⓦgoldcountrystage.com).

Grass Valley Chamber of Commerce 128 E Main St

(Mon–Fri 10am–5pm, Sat & Sun 10am–3pm; ☎530 273 4667, ⓦgrassvalleychamber.com).

Nevada City tourist office 132 Main St, a block north of Hwy-49 (Mon–Fri 9am–5pm, Sat 11am–4pm; ☎800 655 6569, ⓦnevadacitychamber.com).

ACCOMMODATION

Coach N Four Motel 628 S Auburn St, Grass Valley ☎530 273 8009, ⓦcoachn4.webs.com. Handy for Empire State Park, this clean and comfortable motel with neatly furnished rooms offers the best rates around. **$60**

Holbrooke Hotel 212 W Main St, Grass Valley ☎530 273 1353, ⓦholbrooke.com. Right in the centre of town, this historic hotel, where Mark Twain once stayed, has stylish rooms, an opulent lobby and highly rated bar-cum-restaurant. **$75**

★ **National Hotel** 211 Broad St, Nevada City ☎530 265 4551, ⓦthenationalhotel.com. The oldest continuously operated hotel in the West and a state historic

landmark, with plenty of Gold Rush charm in the rooms and lobby, which boasts original photographs, musty wallpaper and a grand staircase. **$81**

Outside Inn 575 E Broad St, Nevada City ☎530 265 2233, ⓦoutsideinn.com. Quiet 1940s motel with a wide range of simple but comfortable rooms and a swimming pool, just a 10min walk from the centre of town. **$79**

Swan-Levine House 328 S Church St, Grass Valley ☎530 272 1873, ⓦswanlevinehouse.com. Attractively decorated, sunny en-suite rooms in an old Victorian hospital. There's original artwork on display and the friendly owners give printmaking lessons. **$100**

EATING AND DRINKING

Café Mekka 237 Commercial St, Nevada City ☎530 478 1517. Relaxed, fabulously decorated coffee shop – from exposed piping to trompe l'oeil wallpaper – popular with teenagers, trendies and ex-hippies. Mon–Thurs 7am–11pm, Fri 7am–midnight, Sat 8am–midnight, Sun 8am–10pm.

Diegos 217 Colfax Ave, Grass Valley ☎530 477 1460, ⓦdiegosrestaurant.com. Stunningly decorated with colourful wall mosaics, this Central and South American restaurant serves tasty delights such as *achiote de pollo* for $14.95. You can wash your meal down with Latin beers or sangria. Daily 11am–9pm.

★ **Friar Tuck's** 111 N Pine St, Nevada City ☎530 265 9093, ⓦfriartucks.com. Quality American, European and Pacific Rim cuisine, including fondue dinners for $25–30, is served at this classy establishment. Live, mostly acoustic

music every night. Daily 4–10pm.

★ **Marshall's Pasties** 203 Mill St, Grass Valley ☎530 272 2844. Mind-boggling array of fresh filled Cornish pasties for around $5, a legacy of the immigrant Cornish miners. Only several cramped tables inside so best for takeaway. Mon–Fri 9.30am–6pm, Sat 10am–6pm.

Sopa Thai 312 Commercial St, Nevada City ☎530 470 0101, ⓦsopathai.net. Wonderful, tasty and moderately priced Thai food, served with a smile in a pleasantly decorated dining room. The green curry is superb for $13.95. Daily 11am–3pm & 5–9.30pm.

South Pine Café 102 Richardson St, Grass Valley ☎530 274 0261, ⓦsouthpinecafe.com. Relaxing, bright place that specializes in fine eggy breakfasts, including a Mexican one with meat and vegetarian options such as the Thai scramble for $8.95. Daily 8am–3pm.

Lake Tahoe

One of the highest, deepest, cleanest and coldest lakes in the world, **Lake Tahoe** is perched high above the Gold Country in an alpine bowl of forested granite peaks. Longer than the English Channel is wide, and more than 1000ft deep, it's so cold that perfectly preserved cowboys who drowned more than a century ago have been recovered from its depths. The lake straddles the Nevada state line as well and lures weekenders with sunny beaches in the summer, snow-covered slopes in the winter and bustling casinos year-round.

South Lake Tahoe and around

In **SOUTH LAKE TAHOE**, the lakeside's largest community, ranks of restaurants, modest motels and pine-bound cottages stand cheek by jowl with the high-rise gambling dens of **Stateline**, just across the border in Nevada. If you happen to lose your money at the tables and slot machines, you can always explore the beautiful hiking trails, parks and beaches in the surrounding area.

The **Heavenly Gondola**, in the heart of town, rises to an elevation of 9136ft (summer daily 10am–5pm; $32). From there, enjoy breathtaking views from East Peak Lake, East Peak Lookout or Sky Meadows. Hikes are graded from easy to strenuous. Closer to the water, the prettiest part of the lake is along the southwest shore, at **Emerald Bay State Park**, ten miles from South Lake Tahoe, which has a number of good shoreline **campgrounds**. A mile from the car park, **Vikingsholm** is a reproduction of a Viking castle, built as a summer home in 1929 and open for hourly tours (summer daily 10am–4pm; $8). In **Sugar Pine Point State Park**, two miles north, the huge **Ehrman Mansion** (daily 11am–4pm; $8) is decorated in Thirties-era furnishings; the extensive lakefront grounds were used as a location in *The Godfather II*.

The rest of the 75-mile **drive** is lovely enough, though certainly not the "most beautiful drive in America", as locally produced brochures claim. Another way to see the lake is to take a paddlewheel **boat cruise** on the MS *Dixie II* from Zephyr Cove in Nevada, reached on a free shuttle from South Lake Tahoe, or *Tahoe Queen* from Ski Run Marina in South Lake Tahoe itself (timetable varies; $39–75; ☎775 589 4906, ⓦzephyrcove.com). The more expensive cruises include dinner.

Tahoe City

TAHOE CITY, the hub on the lake's northwestern shore, manages to retain a more relaxed small-town attitude than South Lake Tahoe. Hwy-89 meets Hwy-28 at Lake Tahoe's only outlet, the **Truckee River**. At the mouth of the river, the **Gatekeeper's Museum** (May–Sept daily except Tues 10am–5pm; Oct–April Sat & Sun 11am–3pm; $5; ☎530 583 1762, ⓦnorthtahoemuseums.org), contains a well-presented hodgepodge of artefacts from the nineteenth century, and a good collection of native basketware. **Rafting** down the Truckee is a common activity in summer, with raft rental companies (prices start around $35/person) clustered at the junction of highways 28 and 89.

Squaw Valley, the site of the 1960 Winter Olympics, is situated five miles west of Tahoe City off Hwy-89, although the original facilities (except the flame and the Olympic rings) are now swamped by the rampant development that has made this California's largest ski resort (see box below).

LAKE TAHOE SKIING

Lake Tahoe rivals the Rocky Mountains in offering some of the best **downhill skiing** and **snowboarding** in North America. Although skiing is not cheap – lift passes can cost well over $60/day and ski/snowboard rental $30–35 – most resorts offer decent-value pass/rental/lesson packages or multiday discounts, especially if booked in advance online. **Cross-country skiing** is also popular, with rentals around $20 and trail passes in the region of $15–30.

DOWNHILL SKIING

Heavenly Reachable by shuttle from Southshore, 2 miles from the casinos, or via the gondola on Hwy-50, next to the state line ☎775 586 7000, ⓦskiheavenly.com. Prime location and sheer scale (85 runs and 29 lifts) make this one of the lake's most frequented resorts, and it also offers the highest vertical skiing served by a lift in the area.

Squaw Valley USA Squaw Valley Rd, halfway between Truckee and Tahoe City ☎530 583 6955, ⓦsquaw.com. Thirty-three lifts service more than 4000 acres of unbeatable terrain at the site of the 1960 Winter

Olympics. Non-skiers can take the cable lift and use the ice-skating/swimming pool complex for the day.

CROSS-COUNTRY SKIING

Royal Gorge Soda Springs, 10 miles west of Truckee ☎530 426 3871, ⓦroyalgorge.com. The largest and best of Tahoe's cross-country resorts has 204 miles of groomed trails.

Spooner Lake Nevada, at the intersection of Hwy-50 and Hwy-28 ☎775 749 5349, ⓦspoonerlake.com. The closest cross-country resort to South Lake Tahoe has lake views and 63 miles of groomed trails.

13

ARRIVAL AND DEPARTURE

LAKE TAHOE

By train or bus The nearest you can get to Lake Tahoe on Greyhound or Amtrak from San Francisco and Sacramento is Truckee, 15 miles north (see opposite). From there, local TART buses (☎ 800 736 6365, ⓦ laketahoetransit.com) run to Tahoe City and around but, frustratingly, not onwards to South Lake Tahoe.

By plane There are shuttles from both ends of the lake to the nearest airport at Reno: North Lake Tahoe Express (☎ 866 216 5222, ⓦ northlaketahoeexpress.com) and South Tahoe Express (☎ 166 898 2463, ⓦ southtahoe express.com); prices vary according to the number of passengers.

GETTING AROUND AND INFORMATION

By bus or tram (trolley) Transport around the south shore is provided by BlueGo buses and trams (☎ 530 541 7149, ⓦ bluego.org), while the north shore is covered by TART (see above).

Visitor centres There are four official visitor centres

around the lake: the two in California are at 3066 US-50, South Lake Tahoe (daily 9am–5pm; ☎ 800 288 2463, ⓦ tahoesouth.com) and 100 N Lake Blvd, Tahoe City (daily 9am–5pm; ☎ 888 824 6348, ⓦ gotahoenorth.com).

ACCOMMODATION

There are dozens of bargain motels along the Southshore, though weekday rates from $50 can easily more than double on weekends and in summer. In Tahoe City, there are fewer budget choices. If you're stuck, any of the visitor centres will try to help.

★ **Basecamp Hotel** 4143 Cedar Ave, South Lake Tahoe ☎ 530 208 0180, ⓦ basecamphotels.com. Slick sports hotel created out of an old motel, with smart, imaginatively designed rooms and a convivial bar where guests are encouraged to mingle. Quality continental breakfast and advice on outdoor activities are complimentary. **$95**

Camp Richardson Resort Hwy-89 between Emerald Bay and South Lake Tahoe ☎ 800 544 1801, ⓦ camp richardson.com. Hotel-style rooms and comfortable cabins with full kitchens on a 150-acre resort that also has campsites from $35. In summer, cabins are available by the week only. **$95**

River Ranch Lodge Hwy-89 and Alpine Meadows Rd, Tahoe City ☎ 530 583 4264, ⓦ riverranchlodge.com.

Historic lodge on the Truckee River with a casual atmosphere and one of the lake's best restaurants. Great value for the north lake. **$110**

★ **Sunnyside** 1850 W Lake Blvd, 1 mile south of Tahoe City ☎ 530 583 7200, ⓦ sunnysideresort.com. Large, comfortable mountain lodge right on the lakeshore. Unbeatable views from many rooms and a popular restaurant and cocktail deck on the ground floor. **$140**

Tamarack Lodge 2311 N Lake Blvd, 1 mile northeast of Tahoe City ☎ 530 583 3350, ⓦ tamarackattahoe .com. You'll get more for your money at this comfortable and clean lodging, nestled on a pleasant wooded knoll, than almost anywhere else on the lake. Some larger cabins, too. **$70**

EATING AND DRINKING

★ **The Brewery at Lake Tahoe** 3542 Lake Tahoe Blvd, South Lake Tahoe ☎ 530 544 2739, ⓦ brewery laketahoe.com. Microbrewery with decent ales ranging from pale to porter, including its signature Bad Ass, plus food specials such as beer-steamed shrimp and quality New York steaks for $35. Daily 8am–late.

Bridgetender Bar & Grill 65 W Lake Blvd, Tahoe City ☎ 530 583 3342, ⓦ tahoebridgetender.com. Friendly, rustic bar with good music, a fine range of beers and huge portions of ribs, burgers and more for $9–15. Mon–Thurs & Sun 11am–11pm, Fri & Sat 11am–midnight.

Nephele's 1169 Ski Run Blvd, South Lake Tahoe ☎ 530 544 8130, ⓦ nepheles.com. Long-standing restaurant at the foot of the Heavenly ski resort, with a great selection of California cuisine: grilled meat, fish and pasta dishes cost $22–37. Daily 2pm–2am.

River Ranch 2285 River Rd, Tahoe City ☎ 530 583 4264, ⓦ riverranchlodge.com. Great curved dining room to maximize the Truckee River views and an outdoor patio in summer. A delicious pepper steak will set you back $33 but the quality of the cuisine is a cut above the Tahoe average. Daily noon–10pm.

★ **Soule Domain** 9983 Cove Ave, King's Beach ☎ 530 546 7529, ⓦ souledomain.com. Typical Tahoe rustic elegance in unexpected surroundings. Lots of seafood and ethnic dishes, such as curried cashew chicken, plus other seafood and meaty delights for $20–30. Daily 6–11pm.

Tep's Villa Roma 3450 Lake Tahoe Blvd, South Lake Tahoe ☎ 530 541 8227, ⓦ tepsvillaroma.com. South Shore institution serving up generous portions of hearty Italian food, including several simple yet superb vegetarian pasta dishes for about $10–20. Daily 5–10pm.

Truckee

13

Fifteen miles north of Tahoe City, the pleasant town of **TRUCKEE** is not only a jumping-off point for Lake Tahoe, but a developing tourist destination in its own right. It is well placed for outdoor excursions and it retains a fair amount of nineteenth-century wooden architecture along its main drag, Donner Pass Road, still referred to as Commercial Row by locals.

★ **Cedar House Sport Hotel** 10918 Brockway Rd ☎530 582 5655, ⊛cedarhousesporthotel.com. The rustic Alpine style of the building gives way to San Francisco chic in the snazzy designed rooms of this trendy sport hotel. A lavish buffet breakfast is included and there's a fine restaurant too. **$180**

Dragonfly 10118 Donner Pass Rd ☎530 587 0557, ⊛dragonflycuisine.com. A refreshingly modern place providing a mixture of Pacific Rim, Southeast Asian and American dinners for $23–34 on its rooftop terrace. Full sushi bar too. Daily 11.30am–2.30pm & 5.30pm–midnight.

★ **Mellow Fellow Pub** 10192 Donner Pass Rd ☎530 214 8927, ⊛mellowfellowpub.com. Truckee's newest watering hole has a huge range of fine draught ales, bottled beers and tasty snacks such as sausages. There's a dartboard, too. Mon–Thurs 3–10pm, Fri & Sat noon–midnight, Sun noon–10pm.

Truckee Hotel 10007 Bridge St ☎800 659 6921, ⊛truckeehotel.com. Decked out in Victorian B&B style, this venerable hotel near the train station offers bargain rooms and live music several times a week in the popular bistro. **$79**

Donner Lake

Several miles west of Truckee, **Donner Lake**, surrounded by alpine cliffs of silver-grey granite, was the site of a gruesome tragedy in 1846, when the **Donner Party**, heading for the Gold Rush, found their route blocked by early snowfall. They stopped and built crude shelters, hoping that the snow would melt; it didn't. Fifteen of their number braved the mountains in search of help from Sutter's Fort in Sacramento; only two men and five women made it, surviving by eating the bodies of the men who died. The horrific tale is recounted in the small **Emigrant Trail Museum** (daily: June–Aug 9am–5pm, Sept–May 9am–4pm; donation; ☎530 582 7892), just off Donner Pass Road in Donner State Park (parking $8 and camping May–Sept; camping $35, hike/bike in $7; ☎800 444 7275, ⊛parks.ca.gov).

The Wine Country

The warm and sunny hills of **Napa** and **Sonoma valleys**, which run almost parallel to each other an hour north of San Francisco, are by reputation at the centre of the American wine industry. In truth, less than five percent of California's wine comes from the region, but what it does produce is America's best. In summer, cars jam the main arteries as visitors embark on a day's hectic tasting.

The Napa Valley

Thirty miles of gently landscaped hillsides, the **Napa Valley** looks more like southern France than a near-neighbour of the Pacific Ocean. The one anomaly is the town of **Napa** itself, a sprawling, ungainly city of 60,000, best avoided in favour of the wineries and small towns north on Hwy-29. The first of these, nine miles north, is **YOUNTVILLE**, anchored by **V Marketplace 1870**, 6525 Washington St (daily 10.30am–5.30pm; ☎707 944 2451, ⊛vmarketplace.com), a shopping complex in a converted winery that contains a range of touristic emporia.

At the northern end of the valley, beyond the pretty village of **St Helena**, lies homey **CALISTOGA**, which is as well known for its mud baths, whirlpools and mineral water as its wineries. A mile further up the road, the **Old Faithful Geyser** (daily: June–Aug

13

NAPA VALLEY WINERIES

Almost all of Napa Valley's **wineries** offer tastings, though not all have tours. There are more than three hundred wineries in all, producing wines of a very high standard, so your taste should ultimately determine the ones you visit.

Beringer Vineyards 2000 Main St, St Helena ☎707 963 7115, ⓦberinger.com. Napa Valley's most famous piece of architecture, the gothic "Rhine House", modelled on the ancestral Rhine Valley home of Jacob Beringer, graces the cover of many a wine magazine. Expansive lawns and a grand tasting room, heavy on dark wood, make for a regal experience. Tasting $20, tours $25–40. Daily: June–Aug 10am–6pm; Sept–May 10am–5pm.

Chateau Montelena 1429 Tubbs Lane, 2 miles north of Calistoga ☎707 942 9105, ⓦmontelena .com. Smaller but highly rated winery, nestled below Mount St Helena. The Cabernet Sauvignon in particular is acquiring a fine reputation. Tasting $20, tour $30. Daily 9.30am–4pm.

Clos Pégase 1060 Dunaweal Lane, Calistoga ☎707 942 4981, ⓦclospegase.com. A flamboyant upstart at the north end of the valley, this high-profile winery amalgamates fine wine and fine art, with a sculpture garden around buildings designed by postmodern architect Michael Graves. Tasting $15. Daily 10.30am–5pm; free tours at 11.30am and 2pm.

★ **Goosecross Cellars** 1119 State Lane, east of Yountville ☎800 276 9210, ⓦgoosecross.com. It's well worth taking time to locate this friendly family-run winery, tucked away off Yountville Cross Rd. Crush-time is fun and its Chardonnay especially good. Tasting $20, tours by appointment ($30). Daily 10am–4.30pm.

Robert Mondavi 7801 St Helena Hwy, Oakville ☎888 766 6328, ⓦrobertmondavi.com. Long the standard-bearer for Napa Valley wines ("Bob Red" and "Bob White" are house wines at many California restaurants), they have one of the most informative and least hard-sell tours. Tasting from $30, tours from $15. Tours and tasting daily 10am–5pm, reservations recommended.

9am–6pm; Sept–May 5pm; $10; ☎707 942 6463, ⓦoldfaithfulgeyser.com), discovered during oil drilling here in the 1920s, spurts boiling water 60ft into the air at forty-minute intervals.

ARRIVAL, GETTING AROUND AND INFORMATION THE NAPA VALLEY

Bus tours From San Francisco there are daily Gray Line bus tours ($80; ☎800 472 9546, ⓦgrayline.com) to the Wine Country; otherwise you will need a car.

Visitor centres 1310 Napa Town Center, off First St, in Napa (daily 9am–5pm; ☎707 226 7459, ⓦnapavalley .com). This is the main office, but most towns have their own information outlet.

ACCOMMODATION AND EATING

ST HELENA

Ambrose Bierce Inn 1515 Main St ☎707 963 3003, ⓦambrosebiercehouse.com. Luxury accommodation in the 1872 house once inhabited by Bierce, a nineteenth-century author, himself. Breakfast is washed down with complimentary champagne. $239

El Bonita Motel 195 Main St ☎707 963 3216, ⓦelbonita.com. Old roadside motel done up to hotel standard in Art Deco style, with a pool and hot tub. Surrounded by a 2.5-acre garden, the rooms here contain microwaves and refrigerators. $120

CALISTOGA

★ **Calistoga Inn** 1250 Lincoln Ave ☎707 942 4101, ⓦcalistogainn.com. Relaxing, excellent-value rooms with one bed, most with private bath, in a landmark building with its own restaurant and microbrewery right on the main street, creating a lively atmosphere. $119

Dr Wilkinson's Hot Springs 1507 Lincoln Ave ☎707 942 4102, ⓦdrwilkinson.com. Legendary health spa and hotel downtown. Choose from a variety of spacious, well-lit rooms with sparse furnishings, facing the courtyard or pool patio. A/c and TV standard. $149

The Sonoma Valley

On looks alone, the crescent-shaped **Sonoma Valley** beats Napa hands down. This altogether more rustic valley curves between oak-covered mountain ranges from the Spanish Colonial town of **SONOMA** to **Glen Ellen**, a few miles north along Hwy-12. It's far smaller than Napa, and many of its wineries are less formal, family-run businesses.

Mission San Francisco Solano de Sonoma

Daily 10am–5pm • $3 • ☎ 707 935 6832, ⓦ sonomaparks.org

The restored **Mission San Francisco Solano de Sonoma** in Sonoma State Historic Park, just east of the spacious plaza in Sonoma, was the last and northernmost of the California missions. The plaza was also the site of the Bear Flag Revolt, the 1846 action that propelled California into independence from Mexico and then statehood.

Jack London State Historic Park

Daily 9.30am–5pm; June–Aug till 7pm • $8/car • ☎ 707 938 5216, ⓦ jacklondonpark.com

A half-mile up London Ranch Road from Sonoma State Historic Park, **Jack London State Historic Park** sits on the 140 acres of ranchland owned by the famed author of *The Call of the Wild*. Here you'll find the author's final resting place, along with a decent museum that houses a collection of souvenirs.

ARRIVAL AND INFORMATION   THE SONOMA VALLEY

By bus Public transport to the valley is available on Golden Gate Transit (see p.901) buses from San Francisco to Petaluma and Santa Rosa.

Visitor centre 453 1st St E on Sonoma Plaza (Mon–Sat 9am–5pm, Sun 10am–5pm; ☎ 707 996 1090, ⓦ sonomavalley.com).

ACCOMMODATION AND EATING

★ **The Girl & The Fig** 110 W Spain St, Sonoma ☎ 707 938 3634, ⓦ thegirlandthefig.com. This renowned restaurant offers French dinners with delights such as duck confit for $15 or wild flounder moulière for $25. Mon–Sat 11.30am–10pm, Sun 10am–10pm.

Glen Ellen Inn 13670 Arnold Drive, Glen Ellen ☎ 707 996 6409, ⓦ glenelleninn.com. Husband-and-wife team (not called Glen and Ellen) cook and serve Califonia-style gourmet dishes such as Wine Country Cioppino for $18.95 in a small, romantic dining room. Mon, Tues & Thurs–Sun 11.30am–9pm, Wed 5.30–9pm.

Jack London Lodge 13740 Arnold Drive, Glen Ellen ☎ 707 938 8510, ⓦ jacklondonlodge.com. Modern motel near Jack London State Park, with comfy rooms and a pool. The friendly saloon is a popular local hangout. **$124**

Swiss Hotel 18 W Spain St, Sonoma ☎ 707 938 2884, ⓦ swisshotelsonoma.com. A 70-year-old landmark building situated right on the plaza, with a fine restaurant. The five cramped rooms have four-poster queen-size beds and views of either the garden patio or the plaza. **$150**

SONOMA VALLEY WINERIES

Nearly fifty **wineries** are scattered across the Sonoma Valley but there's a good concentration in a well-signposted group a mile east of Sonoma Plaza, down East Napa Street. Some are within walking distance but often along quirky back roads, so take a winery map from the tourist office and follow the signs closely.

Bartholomew Park Winery 1000 Vineyard Lane ☎ 707 935 9511, ⓦ bartpark.com. This lavish Spanish Colonial building is surrounded by some great topiary in the gardens and extensive vineyards. The wines are relatively inexpensive vintages that appeal to the pocket and palate alike. There's a good little regional history museum, too, that also provides an introduction to local viticulture. Tasting $10. Self-guided tours and tasting daily 11am–4.30pm.

Benziger Family Winery 1883 London Ranch Rd, Glen Ellen ☎ 888 490 2739, ⓦ benziger.com. Beautiful vineyard perched on the side of an extinct volcano next to Jack London State Park. There are five or six daily tram tours through the fields ($15) with an emphasis on viticulture, or a self-guided tour introducing trellis techniques. Tasting $10–20; tour

$40. Daily 10am–5pm. Tours 11.15am, 12.45pm & 2.15pm.

Buena Vista Carneros 18000 Old Winery Rd ☎ 800 926 1266, ⓦ buenavistacarneros.com. Oldest and grandest of the wineries, founded in 1857, whose wine has re-established a good reputation after some slim years. The tasting room, a restored state historical landmark, features a small art gallery. Tasting $10 including glass, tours from $30. Daily 10am–5pm.

Ravenswood 18701 Gehricke Rd, Sonoma ☎ 707 933 2332, ⓦ ravenswood-wine.com. Noted for its "gutsy, unapologetic" Zinfandel and advertising a "no wimpy" approach to the wine business, this unpretentious winery is particularly friendly and easy-going. Well-known to locals for its summer BBQs. Tasting $15, tour $15. Daily 10.30am–4.30pm, tours at 10.30am.

13

The northern coast

The fog-bound towns and windswept, craggy beaches of the **northern coast** that stretches all the way to the Oregon border is better suited for hiking and camping than sunbathing, with cool temperatures year-round and a huge network of national, state and regional parks preserving magnificent **redwoods**, the tallest and among the oldest trees on earth.

The Sonoma Coast and Russian River Valley

Despite the weekend influx from San Francisco, the villages of the **Sonoma Coast** and **Russian River Valley** seem all but asleep for most of the year. Tucked along the slow, snaking Hwy-1, coastal towns include **BODEGA BAY**, where Hitchcock filmed *The Birds*. From here, a great thirteen-mile hike leads along the rugged cliffs to a prime seal- and whale-watching spot, **Goat Rock Beach**, where the Russian River joins the ocean. The inland valley, centred on the town of **Guerneville**, has a constantly growing reputation for fine wineries.

Guerneville

About ten miles inland on Hwy-116, along the warm and pastoral Russian River Valley, **GUERNEVILLE** is a well-established and primarily gay resort, though welcoming to all comers. **Johnson's Beach** (mid-May to early Oct daily 10am–6pm; free) on a placid reach of the river in the centre of town, is the prime spot, with canoes, pedal boats and tubes for rent at reasonable rates.

The **Armstrong Redwoods State Reserve** ($8/car), two miles north, contains 750 very dense acres of enormous redwoods interspersed by trails. Guided expeditions run by Horseback Adventures (☎707 887 2939, ⊛redwoodhorses.com) vary in length from several hours ($100) to expensive three-day pack trips ($1500) with tented accommodation.

ACCOMMODATION AND EATING   **GUERNEVILLE**

Creekside Inn and Resort 16180 Neely Rd ☎707 869 3623, ⊛creeksideinn.com. Extremely comfortable self-catering units in a rambling set of two-storey buildings amid the redwoods on the opposite side of the river. Swimming pool and upstairs hot tub. $98

Johnson's Beach and Resort 16241 1st St ☎707 869 2022, ⊛johnsonsbeach.com The resort that runs the beach (see above) has simple rustic cabins and modest-sized tent pitches. Tents $25, cabins $60

Taqueria la Tapatia 16632 Hwy-116. This is an excellent, authentic and cheap Mexican joint, with the usual brightly painted interior and a great range of filling tacos, tamales and burritos, most for well under $10. Daily 11am–10pm.

Trio 16225 Main St ☎707 604 7461, ⊛triorussianriver.com. Garishly painted grill serving sandwiches, some Mexican food and delicious baby back ribs for $19. Has live music every night. Tues & Wed 5–10pm, Thurs–Sun noon–10pm; bar till 1.30am.

The Mendocino coast

The coast of **Mendocino County**, starting 150 miles north of San Francisco, is an even more dramatic extension of the Sonoma coastline. **MENDOCINO** itself looks like a transplanted New England fishing village, just without the fishing boats: weathered and charming, it offers plenty of art galleries and boutiques instead. Less than ten miles north, its sister town of **Fort Bragg** is far more down to earth and consequently less expensive.

Van Damme State Park

1.5 miles south of Mendocino on Hwy-1 · $8/car · ☎707 937 5804 · ⊛parks.ca.gov

Just south of town, hiking and cycling trails weave through the unusual **Van Damme State Park**, on Hwy-1, where the ancient trees of the Pygmy Forest are stunted to waist height because of poor drainage and soil chemicals. Two-hour sea cave tours through the park are available through Kayak Mendocino (3 daily; $60; ☎707 964 7480, ⊛kayakmendocino.com).

Beachcomber Motel 1111 N Main St, Fort Bragg ☎707 964 2402, ⓦbeachcombermotel.com. Set just as the coast starts getting wilder again north of town, the smart and spacious rooms here enjoy splendid ocean views. Simple breakfast included. **$109**

★ **Little River Inn** Two miles south of Mendocino on Hwy-1 at Little River ☎888 466 5683, ⓦlittleriver inn.com. Wonderful spot with views over a bay full of

sea stacks. Accommodation ranges from cosy rooms to spacious seafront cottages. The restaurant/bar is excellent, too. **$130**

Mendocino Hotel 45080 Main St ☎800 548 0513, ⓦmendocinohotel.com. Luxurious, antique-filled rooms, the cheaper ones with shared bath, and some truly outstanding garden suites, lend an air of class to this popular hotel. **$186**

EATING AND DRINKING

955 Ukiah St 955 Ukiah St, Mendocino ☎707 937 1955, ⓦ955restaurant.com. High quality main courses such as rosemary-scented lamb stew ($25) follow equally delicious starters like duck and chickpea wontons in the elegant dining room. Thurs–Sun 6–10pm.

Café Beaujolais 961 Ukiah St, Mendocino ☎707 937 5614, ⓦcafebeaujolais.com. The town's premier restaurant, whose founder wrote a book on organic California cuisine and which serves up a frequently changing menu of innovative main courses such as pan-roasted sturgeon fillet for around $20–35. Mon & Tues 5.30–10pm, Wed–Sun 11.30am–2.30pm & 5.30–10pm.

★ **Mendo Bistro** 301 N Main St, Fort Bragg ☎707 964 4974, ⓦmendobistro.com. This genteel option, upstairs in the converted old Union Lumber Store complex, serves excellent, imaginative international cuisine, including gourmet pasta dishes, for $15–25. It also has a sleek downstairs bar called *Barbelow*. Daily 5–9pm.

Patterson's Pub 10485 Lansing St, Mendocino ☎707 937 4782, ⓦpattersonspub.com. Extremely friendly local joint with a range of fine ales, cocktails and a fairly buzzing atmosphere. Chunky sandwiches and filling pasta dishes go for $13–15. Daily noon–2am.

The Humboldt coast

Humboldt is by far the most beautiful of the coastal counties: almost entirely forest, overwhelmingly peaceful in places, in others plain eerie. The impassable cliffs of **King Range** prevent even the sinuous Hwy-1 from reaching the "Lost Coast" of its southern reaches. To get there you have to detour inland via US-101 through the deepest redwood territory as far as **Garberville**, a one-street town with a few good bars that is the centre of the "Emerald Triangle", which produces the majority of California's largest cash crop, marijuana.

Humboldt Redwoods State Park

Open 24hr • Free • ☎707 946 2409, ⓦhumboldtredwoods.org

Redwood country begins in earnest a few miles north of Garberville, at the **Humboldt Redwoods State Park**, California's largest redwood park. The serpentine **Avenue of the Giants** weaves for 33 miles through trees that block all but a few strands of sunlight, with numerous access points to US-101. This is the habitat of *Sequoia sempervirens*, the coastal redwood, with ancestors dating back to the days of the dinosaurs; some are over 360ft tall.

Eureka and around

Many people bypass **EUREKA**, the largest town on the north coast, but the Old Town is worth a wander, especially during the Arts Alive! nights on the first Saturday of each month, when almost a hundred businesses open their doors for arts – much of it performing – along with plenty of drinking and frivolity. Tiny **Samoa**, a few minutes by car over the bay from sprawling Eureka, holds the last remaining cookhouse in the West. Lumbermen used to flock to the still functioning *Samoa Cookhouse* (see p.914) to eat gargantuan portions of red meat on long trestle tables after a day of felling redwoods.

Arcata, seven miles north of Eureka, a small college town with an alternative vibe and mellow pace, has a grassy central plaza surrounded by good restaurants, and some excellent windswept white sand beaches to the north.

13

BIGFOOT COUNTRY

Willow Creek, forty miles east of Arcata, is the self-proclaimed gateway to "**Bigfoot Country**". Reports of giant 350- to 800-pound humanoids wandering the forests of northwestern California have circulated since the late nineteenth century, fuelled by long-established Native American legends, but weren't taken seriously until 1958, when a road maintenance crew found giant footprints. Thanks to their photos, the Bigfoot story went worldwide. However, in 2002, the bereaved family of Ray L. Wallace claimed he made the 1958 footprints, a hoax they had promised to keep secret until after his death. But the number and variety of prints (more than forty, since 1958) still points to a Bigfoot mystery, and the small **Willow Creek-China Flat Museum** (mid-April to Oct Wed–Sun 10am–4pm; Oct to mid-April by appointment; free; ☎ 530 629 2653, ⓦ bigfootcountry.net) in Willow Creek has details of Bigfoot's alleged activities, as well as local Native American artefacts.

ACCOMMODATION AND EATING

EUREKA AND AROUND

★ **Carter House Inns** 301 L St, Eureka ☎ 800 404 1390, ⓦ carterhouse.com. All rooms are top quality within this enclave of four Victorian buildings arranged around a quiet junction. There's also the private $625-a-night Carter Cottage and the superb *Restaurant 301*. Gourmet breakfast included. **$389**

Hotel Arcata 708 9th St, Arcata ☎ 707 826 0217, ⓦ hotelarcata.com. Right on the town's main square, this hotel exudes a quaint old-fashioned charm with flock wallpaper and patterned carpets in its cosy rooms. **$89**

Jambalaya 915 H St, Eureka ☎ 707 822 4766, ⓦ jambalayaarcata.com. The town's best-value bar/restaurant with a saucy Cajun touch – the jambalaya itself is only $8

– and an additional nightly diet of R&B, jazz and rock bands. Mon–Fri 5pm–2am, Sat noon–2am, Sun 9pm–2am.

★ **Lost Coast Brewery and Café** 617 4th St, Eureka ☎ 707 445 4480, ⓦ lostcoast.com. Serves a superb range of beers and large, hearty meat and fish dishes for $10–15 to a rambunctious crowd of discerning microbrew drinkers and sports fans. Mon–Thurs & Sun 11am–10pm, Fri & Sat 11am–11pm.

Samoa Cookhouse Off Cookhouse Rd, Samoa ☎ 707 442 1659, ⓦ samoacookhouse.net. Eating massive portions of red meat at the long tables here is pure entertainment; you're served as much as you can eat of the three daily fixed menus ($10–15) with a smile and a bit of history. Daily 7am–9pm.

Redwood National Park

Nearly forty miles north of Arcata, the small town of **ORICK** marks the southern limit and busiest section of the **Redwood National Park**. **Tall Trees Grove** here is home to one of the world's tallest trees – a mighty 367-footer. Many visitors hike to it on the 8.5-mile trail from Bald Hill Road near Orick, but check with the **Kuchel information centre** (see below) if the access road to the closest trailhead has reopened.

Of the three state parks within the Redwood National Park area, **Prairie Creek** is the most varied and popular. Highlights include the meadows of **Elk Prairie**, where herds of Roosevelt Elk – massive beasts weighing up to twelve hundred pounds – wander freely.

Spectacular coastal views can be had from trails in the Klamath area, especially the **Klamath Overlook**, two miles up Requa Road and about three quarters of a mile above the sea. You can jump over, lumber under or glide through all the naturally contorted and sculpted **Trees of Mystery** (daily: summer 8am–7pm; winter 9am–5pm; $15; ☎ 800 638 3389, ⓦ treesofmystery.net), except the impressive **Cathedral Tree**, where nine trees have grown from one root structure to form a spooky circle.

INFORMATION AND ACCOMMODATION

REDWOOD NATIONAL PARK

Park headquarters 1111 Second St, Crescent City (June–Aug daily 9am–5pm; Sept–May Mon–Sat 9am–5pm; ☎ 707 464 6101, ⓦ nps.gov/redw). There are a number of other visitor centres all over the park.

Kuchel information centre Two miles north of Orick, at the southern entrance to the park (June–Aug 9am–6pm; Sept–May 9am–4pm; ☎ 707 464 6101).

Campgrounds ☎ 800 444 7275, ⓦ reserveamerica .com. There are developed campgrounds at Jedediah Smith, Mill Creek Gold Bluffs Beach and Elk Prairie, which should be booked in advance during summer. Free permits for backcountry camping are available at the visitor centres (see above). Hiker/biker **$5**, vehicle **$35**

The northern interior

13

The remote **northern interior** of California, cut off from the coast by the **Shasta Cascade** range and dominated by forests, lakes and mountains, is largely uninhabited. I-5 leads through the heart of this near-wilderness, forging straight through the unspectacular farmland of **Sacramento Valley** to **Redding** – the region's only buses follow this route. Redding makes a good base for the **Whiskeytown-Shasta-Trinity area** and the more demanding **Lassen Volcanic National Park**. Mountaineers and the spiritually minded flock to **Mount Shasta**, which is close enough to the volcanic **Lava Beds** at the very northeastern tip of the state for them to be a long but feasible day's car trip.

Redding and around

With strip malls lining the I-5 that bisects it, **REDDING** appears to be an anomaly amid the natural splendour of the northern interior. The region's largest city, with more than 70,000 people, it has acted as a northern nexus since the late nineteenth century. Today it remains a crossroads but the superb **Turtle Bay Exploration Park**, 800 Auditorium Drive (mid-March to mid-Sept daily 9am–5pm; mid-Sept to mid-March Wed–Sat 9am–4pm, Sun 10am–4pm; $14; ☎530 243 8850, ⊕turtlebay.org), full of fascinating interactive exhibits, and stunning Sundial Bridge, designed by Spanish architect Santiago Calatreva, have greatly enhanced the town's image.

Shasta

SHASTA, just four miles west of Redding and not to be confused with Mount Shasta, is something of a ghost town. The row of half-ruined brick buildings here represent a once booming gold-mining town. The **Courthouse** has been turned into a museum (Thurs–Sun 10am–5pm; $3), full of historical California artwork and mining paraphernalia, while the gallows and prison cells are a grim reminder of the daily executions that went on here.

ACCOMMODATION AND EATING　　　　　　　　　　　**REDDING AND AROUND**

Best Western Hilltop Inn 2300 Hilltop Drive ☎800 336 4880, ⊕bestwestern.com. This comfortable franchise – with its pool, sauna, buffet breakfasts and convivial grill – makes you feel you're staying somewhere more personal than your average chain. Specials available most of the year. **$125**

★ **Janya's Thai Cuisine** 630 N Market St ☎530 243 7682, ⊕janyasthaicuisine.com. This gem, hidden behind its rather uninspiring strip mall frontage, offers a huge menu from spicy papaya salad to excellent stir-fries and curries, mostly $10–15. Mon–Fri 11am–3pm & 4–9pm, Sat & Sun 11.30am–9pm.

Market Street Steakhouse 1777 Market St ☎530 241 1777, ⊕marketstreetsteakhouse.com. As the name suggests, succulent steaks costing $20–35 are the speciality here, and the bar is a buzzing meeting place in its own right. Mon–Wed 11am–9pm, Thurs 11am–10pm, Fri 11am–11pm, Sat 4–11pm.

Tiffany House 1510 Barbara Rd ☎530 244 3225, ⊕tiffanyhousebb.com. Run by a genteel and welcoming couple, the *Tiffany* is a plush yet good-value B&B in a converted Victorian house, with a pricier detached cottage behind. **$125**

Lassen Volcanic National Park

About fifty miles over gently sloping plains east from Red Bluff on Hwy-36, or forty miles east from Redding on Hwy-44, the 106,000 acres that make up the pine forests, crystal-green lakes and boiling thermal pools of the **LASSEN VOLCANIC NATIONAL PARK** are among the most unearthly parts of northern California's forbidding landscape, which receives up to 50ft of snowfall each year, keeping the area pretty much uninhabited outside the brief summer season. **Mount Lassen** itself last erupted in 1915, when the peak blew an enormous mushroom cloud some seven miles skyward, tearing

13

the summit into chunks that landed as far away as Reno; scientists predict that it is the likeliest of all the West Coast volcanoes to blow again.

The thirty-mile tour of the park along Hwy-89 from **Manzanita Lake** in the north should take no more than a few hours but is often not fully open until the snows have melted in June. The Mount Lassen explosion denuded the devastated area, ripping out every tree and patch of grass, and a large area of desolation remains amid the reforestation. Marking the halfway point, **Summit Lake** is a busy camping area set around a beautiful icy lake, close to the most manageable hiking trails. From a parking area to the south (8000ft up), the steep, five-mile ascent to Lassen Peak begins. Experienced hikers can do it in four hours, but wilderness seekers will have a better time pushing east to the steep trails of the **Juniper Lake** area.

Continuing south along Hwy-89, Lassen's indisputable show-stealers are **Bumpass Hell** and **Emerald Lake**, the former (named after a man who lost a leg trying to cross it) a steaming valley of active pools and vents that bubble away at a low rumble. The trails are sturdy and easy to manage, but you should never venture off them; the crusts over the thermal features are often brittle, and breaking through could plunge you into very hot water. From **Sulphur Works**, an acrid cauldron of steam vents near the south entrance, a magnificent but gruelling trail leads for a mile around the site to the avalanche-prone summit at **Diamond Peak**, which affords great views over the entire park and forest beyond.

INFORMATION AND ACCOMMODATION

LASSEN VOLCANIC NATIONAL PARK

Access and entry fees The park is open 24hr. Access is $10/vehicle, valid for seven days.

Lassen visitor centre At the southern entrance on Hwy-89 (daily: June–Aug 9am–6pm; Sept–May 9am–5pm; ☏ 530 595 4480, ⦿ nps.gov/lavo), where you can get free maps and information, including the *Lassen Park Guide*; there's also a smart café.

Manzanita Lake visitor centre Just inside the northern entrance (June–Aug daily 9am–5pm; ☏ 530 595 4444 ext 5180). Includes the Loomis Museum, which documents the park's eruption cycle.

Lassen campgrounds ☏ 877 444 6777, ⦿ recreation

.gov. All of the park's developed campgrounds should be booked well in advance during summer, even though night temperatures can drop to freezing. Primitive camping requires a free wilderness permit obtainable in advance from the park visitor centres and entrance stations. Developed sites from $12

Manzanita Lake Camping Cabins Manzanita Lake ☏ 530 840 6140, ⦿ lassenrecreation.com. Newly constructed pine cabins, simply furnished and some with bunk beds. All have picnic tables outside, ideal for enjoying the views. There's a nearby store for provisions. $59

Mount Shasta and around

Roughly sixty miles north of Redding, the almost conical bulk of 14,162ft **MOUNT SHASTA** rises imperiously towards the clouds. Still considered active despite not having erupted for two hundred years, this lone peak dominates the landscape for a hundred miles around. Its alleged mystical "energies" attract New Agers by the score, especially to **Mount Shasta City**, right below the mountain's western flank. If you want to climb to the summit (10hr; crampons and ice axe needed most of the year), or simply to explore the lower reaches of the mountain along the many trails, you must obtain a free permit from the **ranger district office**, 204 W Alma St (April–Oct Mon–Sat 8am–4.30pm; Nov–March Mon–Fri same hours; ☏ 530 926 4511), or you can self-issue one at the main trailheads. The small nearby towns of **Dunsmuir** and **McLoud** make equally good bases for the Mount Shasta region.

ARRIVAL AND INFORMATION

MOUNT SHASTA AND AROUND

By bus The nearest Greyhound stop is at Weed, 7 miles north of Mount Shasta City, connected by local STAGE buses (☏ 530 842 8295).

By train The nearest Amtrak station is at Dunsmuir, 6 miles south of Mount Shasta City and also connected

by STAGE buses.

Chamber of Commerce 300 Pine St, Mount Shasta City (daily: June–Aug 9am–5.30pm; Sept–May 10am–4pm; ☏ 530 926 3696, ⦿ mtshastachamber.com).

ACCOMMODATION

Cold Creek Inn 724 N Mount Shasta Blvd, Mount Shasta City ☎800 292 9421, ⓦcoldcreekinn.com. Nicely refurbished motel, an easily walkable few blocks from downtown. Some of the simple but spacious rooms have mountain views. $88

Lake Siskiyou Resort & Camp 4239 W. A. Barr Rd, 4 miles southwest of Mount Shasta City ☎530 926 2618, ⓦreynoldsresorts.com. The most picturesque campground in the area is this woodland option, where you can

picnic, bathe and go boating. Open April–Oct. Tent sites $20, cabins $65

★ **Railroad Park Resort** 100 Railroad Park Rd, Dunsmuir ☎530 235 0420, ⓦrrpark.com. The most unique lodging in the area, most of the accommodation options are fashioned out of old railway cabooses, though there are also some cabins and RV hookups. Popular dining car restaurant, too. $125, RVs $37

EATING

Black Bear Diner 401 W Lake St, Mount Shasta City ☎530 926 4669, ⓦblackbeardiner.com. The original location of this ever-growing family diner chain, a great place for heaped breakfasts or classic American dinners for around $10. Daily 6am–10pm.

Dogwood Diner 5841 Sacramento Ave, Dunsmuir ☎530 678 3502, ⓦthedogwooddiner.com. Extremely busy most of the time for good reason, this trendy spot serves up fine

breakfasts and gourmet burgers ($11). Mon–Thurs & Sun 7.30am–9pm, Fri & Sat 7.30am–10pm.

★ **Trinity Café** 622 N Mt Shasta Blvd, Mount Shasta City ☎530 926 6200. The best place for quality international cuisine made from local produce. The menu changes weekly and fine microbrewed ales are available on tap. Most main courses are over $20. Tues–Sat 5–9pm, Sun 9am–2pm.

Lava Beds National Monument

Lava Beds National Monument, in the far north of the state, is one of the most remote and alluring of California's parks. The human history of these volcanic caves and huge black lava flows is as violent as the natural forces that created them. Before the Gold Rush the area was home to the **Modoc** Indians, but repeated bloody confrontations with miners led to them being forced into a reservation with the Klamath, their traditional enemy. When the Modocs drifted back to the area in 1872, the army was sent in. Fifty-five Modoc warriors, under the leadership of "Captain Jack", held back an army ten times the size for five months from a natural fortress of passageways now known as **Captain Jack's Stronghold**, at the park's northern tip.

The bulk of the lava tube caves are close to the **visitor centre** (see below), where you can take the free ranger tours (times vary) or borrow a torch and helmet for free to explore the caves alone. Immediately north and west of Lava Beds, the **Klamath Basin National Wildlife Refuge** hosts millions of birds migrating along the Pacific Flyway. Surprisingly, the best way of spotting the wildlife is by driving along designated routes. The nearest town to both sights is sleepy **Tulelake** to the northeast.

INFORMATION   LAVA BEDS NATIONAL MONUMENT

Access and entry fees The park is open 24hr. Access is $10/vehicle, valid for seven days.

Lava Beds visitor centre Just inside the southwestern entrance (daily: June–Aug 8am–6pm; Sept–May 8am–5pm;

☎530 667 8113, ⓦnps.gov/labe

Klamath Basin visitor centre Off Hill Rd, near the northwest entrance for the Lava Beds (Mon–Fri 8am–4.30pm, Sat & Sun 10am–4pm; ☎530 667 2231).

ACCOMMODATION AND EATING

Captain Jack's Stronghold Five miles south of Tulelake on Hwy-139 ☎530 664 5566. The area's best restaurant does excellent soups, salads, sandwiches, pasta and some international dishes, such as chicken teriyaki, all in the $12–20 range. Tues–Sun 9am–8pm.

Fe's B&B 660 Main St, Tulelake ☎877 478 0184, ⓦfesbandb.com. Very welcoming place with cosy rooms and a good breakfast to get you started. The knowledgeable owner also runs tours of the area. $80

The Pacific Northwest

CRATER LAKE NATIONAL PARK, OR

The Pacific Northwest

The eco-friendly, liberal and ruggedly independent Pacific Northwest states of Washington and Oregon are well known as the wet green pocket in America's upper-left corner, similar in climate, topography and environmental politics, and with a passion for farm-to-table produce, organic wineries and local microbreweries. Oregon is especially progressive, with no sales tax, an easy-going lifestyle, and "urban-growth boundaries" around its larger cities. Yet that's not that whole story. Both states are split by the great north–south spine of the Cascade Mountains; on the west side lies the Pacific Northwest of popular imagination, forming a cultural block with hippie northern California to the south, but to the east, the conservative farmers of the arid, ranching badlands of both states have more in common with Idaho and Montana than their liberal cousins on the coast.

The region only contains two big cities, **Seattle** and **Portland**, but visiting the Pacific Northwest is really about the great outdoors; you can hike, bike, kayak and climb in some of the nation's most mesmerizing national parks. From the isolated rainforests and hot springs of **Olympic** and the stately peaks of **North Cascades** to the vast massif of **Mount Rainier** and the still lava-scraped landscapes of **Mount St Helens**, Washington seems especially blessed with jaw-dropping vistas, at least when it's not raining. And while few states are so set up for mountain biking as Oregon, just rounding the rim of **Crater Lake** and peering down on that perfectly blue cone is a truly magical experience.

While the Vancouver, Seattle and Portland corridor is well covered by public transport, you'll need a **car** to explore the parks, mountains and more isolated eastern parts of the region.

Washington

Smothered with dense forests of fir, cedar and cypress, WASHINGTON really is the "**Evergreen State**", rich in natural beauty, national parks and – inconveniently – heavy rain that sweeps in from the Pacific, at least west of the Cascades. Likeable

PIKE PLACE MARKET, SEATTLE

Highlights

❶ Pike Place Market, Seattle, WA Venerable seafood diners, flying salmon, fresh fish and produce vendors, street entertainers, gum alley and Rachel, the brass pig. **See p.923**

❷ San Juan Islands, WA These bucolic islands make for a great summertime trip by ferry, with charming towns, culinary treats and the chance to see killer whales. **See p.934**

❸ Cascade Loop, WA Series of highways that snake back and forth across the mighty Cascade Mountains, passing pristine alpine lakes and snow-capped peaks. **See p.944**

❹ Mount St Helens, WA The most infamous volcano in North America remains a haunting sight more than three decades after it blew its top. **See p.946**

❺ Portland, OR Sample the food carts, coffeeshops, microbreweries and eclectic culture of one of America's most bike-friendly and plain kookiest cities. **See p.949**

❻ Columbia River Gorge, OR U-shaped valley carved from colossal Ice Age floods, home to precipitous waterfalls and historic highways. **See p.956**

❼ Crater Lake, OR Cradled in what's left of a hollowed-out volcano, this sheer-blue lake is a staggeringly beautiful sight. **See p.964**

HIGHLIGHTS ARE MARKED ON THE MAP ON P.922

and vibrant, Seattle contains some of the state's most popular attractions, though its greatest asset may be its proximity to glorious **Puget Sound**, the deep-water inlet around which much of the population of Washington lives. To the west is the **Olympic Peninsula**, whose mountains are home to elk and lush vegetation that merges into rainforest, and whose rustic beaches have remained pristine and protected. A few hours south lies the awe-inspiring peak of **Mount Rainier** and the eye-opening volcanic scenery of **Mount St Helens**.

Dry and desolate, the sprawling prairie-plateau that makes up most of **eastern Washington** is a great, bleak expanse enlivened by the pleasant city of **Spokane** and the colossal **Grand Coulee Dam**. Otherwise you're only likely to come out here if you're

HIGHLIGHTS

1. Pike Place Market, Seattle, WA
2. San Juan Islands, WA
3. Cascade Loop, WA
4. Mount St Helens, WA
5. Portland, OR
6. Columbia River Gorge, OR
7. Crater Lake, OR

PACIFIC NORTHWEST

> ### GREAT REGIONAL DRIVES
>
> **Hwy-101** This great coastal route follows the Pacific Ocean from the Californian border, skirting the best Oregon beaches and dunes to Astoria and on into Washington, where it cuts into the rainforests of Olympic National Park.
>
> **Hurricane Ridge Rd, WA** Spectacular, seventeen-mile climb to the top of the Olympic Mountain Range, where deer graze, flowers bloom and incredible vistas of snowy peaks roll away in all directions.
>
> **Cascade Loop** Take a leisurely ride through the mighty Cascades, from alpine meadows to the semi-arid grasslands and lakes of eastern Washington.
>
> **Journey Through Time Scenic Byway, OR** This combination of highways 26 and 7 in Oregon connects the richly coloured landscapes of the John Day Fossil Beds with the remote, snow-capped Blue Mountains.

travelling the Cascade loop, a spectacular four-hundred-mile round-trip drive through the snow-capped **Cascade Mountains**.

Seattle

Few people outside the Pacific Northwest knew much about **SEATTLE** before 1991, and it was considered a distant, rainy backwater even by most Americans. Since **Nirvana** and **grunge rock** exploded that year, things have never been the same: Hollywood quickly jumped on the bandwagon with *Sleepless in Seattle*, *Frasier* and *Grey's Anatomy*, and today the tourists and Alaska cruise ships flock in to soak up the city's famously picturesque setting, lively **Pike Place Market**, stunning **Chihuly Garden and Glass**, fun coffeehouses and slew of excellent museums, framed by a modern skyline of shiny skyscrapers and the snowy peak of Mount Rainier in the distance.

Yet the 1990s wasn't the first time Seattle made a global impact. Founded in 1851, the city was really put the map after the **Klondike Gold Rush** in the late 1890s, Seattle's population doubling and economy booming as it served as the main port of embarkation for hopeful miners; in 1962 the **World's Fair** saw the construction of the iconic **Space Needle** and brief attention again thanks to Elvis in *It Happened at the World's Fair*. From the beginning of the twentieth century, **Boeing** was crucial to the city's economic strength, and more recent success stories have included global corporate icons **Microsoft**, **Starbucks** and **Amazon.com**, all based here. One Seattle stereotype that remains true: it still **rains** a lot here, especially from October to May.

Pike Place Market

Pike St and First Ave • Mon–Sat 10am–6pm, Sun 11am–5pm • Free • ☎ 206 682 7453, ⓦ pikeplacemarket.org

Few cities in America have anything like **Pike Place Market**, founded in 1907 overlooking the waterfront and the oldest continuously working public market in the USA; countless stalls offer piles of lobsters, crabs, salmon, vegetables, fruit and flowers. Though it's often mobbed by tourists in the summer, locals still shop here and having saved it from demolition in the 1970s remains a source of pride. The covered complex is a labyrinth of thirteen buildings on a triangular lot covering nine acres, holding three hundred produce and fish vendors, bakeries, craft stalls, touristy shops and small retailers.

At the main entrance on Pike Street the fishmongers of **Pike Place Fish Co** hurl the catch of the day back and forth to the amusement of tour groups while street entertainers play to rapt crowds. Here also is the brass statue of "**Rachel the pig**", a large, actual piggy bank, with receipts going to charity. Even if you have no interest in buying salmon or fresh fruit, there are some classic **places to eat** here, as well as the original **Starbucks** (see box, p.924). Don't leave without taking a peek at the slightly gross **Gum Wall**, an alley along the side of the market plastered with used chewing gum, some if it strung out like stalactites (seriously).

14

THE ORIGINAL STARBUCKS?

Love it or loathe it, **Starbucks** has become a truly global coffee chain, as familiar to Asians and Europeans as Americans. Pike Place is where it all began; the original store opened near here in 1971, and the original logo (now way too racy for the brand) is maintained at the often-packed 1912 Pike St branch (Mon–Fri 6am–9pm, Sat & Sun 6.30am–9pm; ☎206 448 8762, ⓦstarbucks .com) across the street from the market entrance (don't confuse this with the much newer branch at Pike and First). Inside you'll find a variety of special drinks and merchandise only available at this store, though the coffee is standard Starbucks stuff. Note however that Starbucks moved to this location in 1977; the first branch was actually not far away at 2000 Western Ave (now torn down).

Seattle Aquarium and the Waterfront

1483 Alaskan Way (Pier 59) • Daily 9.30am–5pm • $21.95, kids (4–12) $14.95 • ☎206 386 4300, ⓦseattleaquarium.org

A steep walk down to the waterfront from Pike Place Market lies **Seattle Aquarium**, with its hundreds of species of fish, birds, plants and mammals and a special focus on marine life of the Puget Sound. Highlights include a functional salmon hatchery and fish ladder, the ever-popular **otters** (sea and river) and the **fur seals**. From the aquarium it's possible to stroll along the **Waterfront** north or south: just to the south lies more family fun at **Miner's Landing** (Pier 57) and the **Seattle Great Wheel** (a 175ft-high Ferris wheel; Mon–Thurs & Sun 10am–11pm, Fri & Sat 10am–midnight; $13, kids 4–11 $8.50; ⓦseattlegreatwheel.com).

The Seattle Art Museum

1300 First Ave • Wed & Fri–Sun 10am–5pm, Thurs 10am–9pm • Suggested donation $17, free first Thurs of month • ☎206 654 3100, ⓦseattleartmuseum.org

Art aficionados will enjoy a rainy afternoon in the **Seattle Art Museum**, though it lacks real show-stoppers – check the current line-up of temporary exhibitions before you go. The permanent collection serves up a little of everything, from ancient Greek vases and Maya statues to American paintings and a collection of contemporary **Australian Aboriginal** art. **The Porcelain Room** is definitely worth checking out, an installation of more than one thousand pieces arranged in a stunning, thematic display, and the American galleries contain works by Bierstadt, Hassam, Copley and Singer Sargent, as well as key Seattle artists of the 1930s and 1940s.

However, the museum is best known for its ethnic art, such as **Native American** totem poles, rattles and canoes, along with colourful headdresses, masks, baskets and woven fabrics; and contemporary and traditional **African art**, with surprising pieces like *Mercedes-Benz Shaped Coffin* by Ghana's Kane Kwei, a mix of tradition and postmodernism.

Columbia Center

701 Fifth Ave • Observation deck open daily 10am–8pm • $9 • ☎206 386 5564

Looming high above downtown, **Columbia Center** is a shiny glass skyscraper of offices completed in 1985 – at 1049ft high, it's the second tallest building on the West Coast. Head to the 73rd-floor **Sky View Observatory** (via the 4/F lobby) for a predictably jaw-dropping panorama of the city and surrounding mountains, or grab a coffee at the fortieth-floor Starbucks (p.930).

Frye Art Museum

704 Terry Ave • Tues, Wed & Fri–Sun 11am–5pm, Thurs 11am–7pm • Free • ☎206 622 9250, ⓦfryemuseum.org

Five blocks east of Columbia Center in the First Hill neighbourhood, the **Frye Art Museum** holds works by Winslow Homer, John Singer Sargent and Thomas Eakins, as well as a fine selection of the **Munich school**, focusing on the Belle Epoque between 1870 and 1900. Recent exhibits have broadened the museum's focus to include more contemporary work, including multimedia, performance and installation art.

Pioneer Square

A few blocks south of modern downtown, **Pioneer Square** is Seattle's oldest district, where the original settlement began in the 1850s and still rich with appealing bookshops and galleries amid the old red-brick and wrought-iron buildings. The name refers to an area; there are parks and squares here (Occidental Park and Pioneer Place), but no plaza itself called Pioneer Square. There are also a number of rough-around-the-edges clubs and bars, and more than a few homeless people adding to the diverse

14

DOWNTOWN SEATTLE

ACCOMMODATION

Ace Hotel	4
Alexis	11
Green Tortoise	8
HI-Seattle at the American Hotel	12
Hotel Andra	5
Hotel Five	3
Hotel Vintage Park	9
Inn at the Market	7
Monaco	10
Pensione Nichols	6
Shafer Baillie Mansion	2
University Inn	1

RESTAURANTS & CAFÉS

The 5 Spot	2
Bauhaus Books & Coffee	7
Café Flora	11
Caffè Ladro	1
Canlis	4
Dahlia Lounge	9
Dick's Drive-In	6
Espresso Vivace	5
Ivar's Acres of Clams	12
Paseo Caribbean	3
Phnom Penh Noodle House	15
Pike Place Chowder	10
Pike Street Fish Fry	8
Salumi	13
Zeitgeist Coffee	14

BARS, CLUBS & LIVE MUSIC VENUES

5 Point Café	1
Alibi Room	10
Central Saloon	14
Comet Tavern	5
Dimitriou's Jazz Alley	2
Elysian Brewing	4
Highway 99 Blues Club	12
Il Terrazzo Carmine	7
Kells Irish Pub	6
Lava Lounge	4
Neumo's	3
Pike Pub & Brewery	11
Showbox at the Market	9
Trinity Nightclub	13
Triple Door	8

N

0   200
yards

environs. Kids will love the **Waterfall Garden** (daily 8am–3.45pm; free) at 219 Second Ave South.

Smith Tower

506 Second Ave • April–Oct daily 10am–dusk; Nov–March Sat & Sun 10am–4pm • $7.50 • ☎ 206 622 4004, ⓦ smithtower.com

The elegant white-terracotta **Smith Tower** was the city's first skyscraper in 1914, as well as its long-time visual icon well before the arrival of the Space Needle. These days, it's best for the prime views from its 35th-floor **observation deck** and the adjacent **Chinese Room**, with carved teak ceiling and blackwood furniture.

Underground Tour

Entrance at 608 First Ave • Hours vary, often daily on the hour 11am–5pm • $17, kids (7–12) $9 • ☎ 206 682 4646, ⓦ undergroundtour.com

The city's seamy past is on display in the ninety-minute **Underground Tour**, which details how, after a disastrous 1889 fire, this area was rebuilt with the street level raised by one storey, so what used to be storefronts are now underground, linked by subterranean passageways. The tours start at the entrance to the passages on First Avenue, but the tour takes place entirely under the streets of Pioneer Square.

Klondike Gold Rush National Historical Park

319 Second Ave S • Daily 9am–5pm • Free • ☎ 206 220 4240, ⓦ nps.gov/klse

Seattle's 1890s boom is chronicled at **Klondike Gold Rush National Historical Park**, a visitor centre recalling the days when Seattle was the gateway to Yukon gold, prospectors streamed in and traders – and con artists – made their fortunes. The centre occupies the old *Cadillac Hotel* building, dating from 1889 – most of the actual park is in Alaska.

Seattle Center

305 Harrison St • Free • ☎ 206 684 7200, ⓦ seattlecenter.com

North of downtown, the **Seattle Center** was built for the 1962 Seattle World's Fair and since then the 74-acre complex has become the city's cultural hub, the site of museums, sporting events, concerts and festivals (see p.931).

Families with bored kids might consider the **Pacific Science Center** (ⓦ pacsci.org), full of science-related exhibits for children, and the **Children's Museum** (ⓦ thechildrensmuseum .org), offering attractions like an artificial mountain forest, where kids crawl through logs or simulate a rock climb.

Space Needle

400 Broad St • Daily 8am–midnight • $21, two trips in 24hr $29 • ☎ 206 905 2100, ⓦ spaceneedle.com

The **monorail** from Westlake Center to Seattle Center (see above) drops you next to the **Space Needle**, Seattle's 605ft-high Space Age icon completed in 1962, which is most appealing at night when it's lit up. The panoramic view from the 520ft observation deck is always a major draw.

Chihuly Garden and Glass

305 Harrison St • Mon–Thurs 10am–10pm, Fri–Sun 10am–11pm • $19 • ☎ 206 753 4940, ⓦ chihulygardenandglass.com

Next door to the Space Needle, the astounding **Chihuly Garden and Glass** opened in 2012 to showcase Dale Chihuly's extravagant creations, from the Persian Ceiling to towering forests of blue glass: though you can spy some of the Tacoma-boy turned art celebrity's biggest installations from over the hedge, you'll only really appreciate the spectacle from the inside.

EMP Museum

325 Fifth Ave N • Daily 10am–7pm, winter closes 5pm • $20, kids (5–17) $14 • ☎ 206 770 2700, ⓦ empmuseum.org

To get to grips with Seattle's musical legacy, visit the Frank Gehry-designed **EMP Museum,** a crazy, giant burst of coloured aluminium that houses special exhibits dedicated to rock legend **Jimi Hendrix**, who was born here in 1942, and an especially moving section on seminal Seattle band **Nirvana** and lead singer **Kurt Cobain** (who committed suicide in Seattle in 1994). Elsewhere there's the *If Vi was IX* installation by artist Trimpin, a tower of more than 700 guitars and instruments, a psychedelic "Sky Church" auditorium and even a science fiction hall of fame, with associated horror movie memorabilia.

Capitol Hill

A fifteen-minute bus ride east of downtown takes you to the mildly counterculture-flavoured **Capitol Hill**, an electric neighbourhood of historic mansions and a thriving LGBT community. The main drag is **Broadway**, which offers a solid choice for dining, buying music, clubbing and drinking coffee, while the section between E Roy Street and E Highland Drive contains **Harvard-Belmont Historic District**, sprinkled with huge Neoclassical piles and sprawling period-revival homes; for a tour, contact the Seattle Architectural Foundation (April–Dec Thurs–Sat, times vary; $25; ☎ 206 667 9184, ⓦ seattlearchitecture.org).

Seattle Asian Art Museum

1400 E Prospect St (Volunteer Park) • Wed & Fri–Sun 10am–5pm, Thurs 10am–9pm • Suggested donation $7 • ☎ 206 654 3100, ⓦ seattleartmusem.org

Located within the green expanse of Volunteer Park at the northern end of Capitol Hill, the **Seattle Asian Art Museum** is home to one of the most extensive collections of East Asian art in the USA, spread across many centuries and dynasties, and highlighted by meticulously crafted Japanese landscape scrolls and the grim, early Chinese statues of tomb guardians, court attendants and warriors.

The University District

Some five miles from downtown, north of Lake Union, the **University District**, or the "U" District, is a busy hodgepodge of coffeehouses, cinemas and boutiques catering to the University of Washington's 40,000 students. The area centres on University Way, known as "**The Ave**", and is lined with inexpensive ethnic restaurants and a handful of decent book- and record stores.

On campus, the **Henry Art Gallery**, 15th Ave NE and NE 41st St (Wed, Sat & Sun 11am–4pm, Thurs & Fri 11am–9pm; $10; ☎ 206 543 2280, ⓦ henryart.org), houses American and European paintings and photography from the last two centuries, and imaginative contemporary exhibits, while the **Burke Museum**, 17th Ave NE and NE 45th St (daily 10am–5pm; $10; ☎ 206 543 5590, ⓦ burkemuseum.org), holds the USA's largest collection of Native American art and artefacts west of the Mississippi – and presents selections from its huge collection of 2.75 million fossils and Ice Age skeletons, including the remains of a 12,000-year-old sloth.

Fremont

The "independent Republic" of **Fremont** is a self-consciously hip area five miles north of downtown, with a spate of boutiques, bookshops and cafés around Fremont Avenue N from N 34th to N 37th streets. Just off N 34th Street, the **Fremont Sunday Market**

GOODBYE TO THE DRAGON

A steady stream of martial arts fans make their way to historic Lakeview Cemetery, just northeast of Capitol Hill at 1554 15th Ave E, to pay their respects to movie star **Bruce Lee** (1940–73), buried here with his son **Brandon Lee** (1965–93). Bruce was born in San Francisco but raised in Hong Kong, later becoming an iconic kung-fu movie star (his wife Linda was from Seattle, and chose to bury him here). The two relatively modest marble tombstones are often littered with flowers. The cemetery is open daily 9am– sunset.

(Sun 10am–5pm; free; ☎206 781 6776, ⓦfremontmarket.com) hosts 150 vendors of street food, secondhand jewellery, furniture, clothing, trinkets and music. Fremont's other main draws are its quirky **public artworks**, most notably the **Fremont Troll**, lurking under the Aurora Bridge, 36th St and Aurora Ave (this section was renamed Troll Ave in its honour), and emerging from the gloom with an actual VW Bug in its clutches. At the triangular corner of N 36th Street and Fremont Place, a Slovakia-built statue of **Lenin** thrusts forth toward passing motorists, surrounded by blocky flames.

14

Future of Flight Aviation Center & Boeing Tour

Entrance is on Hwy 526, a few miles west of exit 189 off I-5 • Daily 8.30am–5.30pm (tours 9am–3pm) • April–Sept $20; Oct–March $18 • ☎425 438 8100, ⓦfutureofflight.org

Some 25 miles north of Seattle, the last major suburb along I-5, **Everett**, is home to the 747 manufacturing plant for **Boeing**, site of the popular **Future of Flight Aviation Center & Boeing Tour**. Visit the interactive exhibits and displays in the Aviation Center Gallery before taking a ninety-minute tour of the Boeing plant itself, where 747s, 777s and 787s are in various phases of gestation. The 98-acre factory is listed in the *Guinness Book of World Records* as the largest building in the world by volume (472 million cubic feet).

The Museum of Flight

9404 E Marginal Way (I-5 exit 158) • Daily 10am–5pm; Airpark daily 10am–5pm (select planes open June–Aug Fri–Sun 11am–3pm) • $18, kids (5–17) $10 • ☎206 764 5720, ⓦmuseumofflight.org • Take #124 bus (20min)

Boasting one of the biggest and best ensembles of historic aircraft in the USA, the **Museum of Flight** encompasses two giant galleries filled with planes – from John Glenn's 1962 Mercury space capsule and an SR-71 Blackbird spy plane to Spitfires and Messerschmitts. The galleries surround the restored 1909 "**Red Barn**" that was the original **Boeing** manufacturing plant, now displaying relics from the early days of flight. You can also have a go on several flight simulators ($6), while more icons are on display outside in the museum's expansive **Airpark**, which has a walk-in collection of planes that include the 737 and 747, as well as a Concorde and the first jet Air Force One.

ARRIVAL AND DEPARTURE   SEATTLE

By plane Sea-Tac Airport (☎206 787 5388, ⓦportseattle .org/sea-tac), is 14 miles south of downtown Seattle. Shuttle Express has a shared door-to-door service (daily 24hr; ☎425 981 7000, ⓦshuttleexpress.com) for $18 to downtown. Taxis charge by the meter; expect to pay around $40 for downtown (taxis charge a flat rate of $40 to go back to the airport from downtown). Much cheaper, and the best option overall, the Link Light Rail takes you to the central Westlake station downtown (Mon–Sat 5am–1am, Sun 6am–midnight, every 7–15min; $2.75; ☎206 398 5000, ⓦsoundtransit.org) in under 40min. Metro bus #124 also travels to downtown Seattle ($2.25–3) every 30min.

By bus Greyhound buses arrive at 811 Stewart St at Eighth Ave, on the northeastern edge of downtown. Bolt Bus (ⓦboltbus.com) stops at Fifth Ave S and S King St, with departures to Portland (5 daily) and Vancouver, Canada (4 daily) for as low as $14.

Destinations Olympia (4 daily; 1hr 35min); Port Angeles (2 daily; 2hr 40min–3hr); Portland (4 daily; 3hr 45min–4hr 25min); Port Townsend (2 daily; 2hr 10min–2hr 25min); Spokane (4 daily; 5hr 30min–7hr 35min); Tacoma (6 daily; 45min–1hr); Vancouver, Canada (4 daily; 4hr 10min).

By train Trains arrive at the Amtrak terminal in King Street Station at 303 S Jackson St; just to the east along Jackson St, the International District Station is a hub for frequent Metro buses going downtown (see above).

Destinations Portland (5 daily; 3hr 40min–4hr 15min); Spokane (1 daily; 8hr 5min); Tacoma (5 daily; 43–46min); Vancouver, Canada (2 daily; 4hr); West Glacier (1 daily; 14hr 36min).

THE FREMONT FAIR

The **Fremont Fair & Solstice Parade** (☎206 297 6801, ⓦfremontfair.org), in mid-June, is Seattle's jolliest celebration, with hundreds of food stalls and arts vendors, plus a parade of naked bicyclists and human-powered floats, followed by a pageant at the end of the route in Gas Works Park.

GETTING AROUND

By bus Seattle's mass transit system, known as the Metro (☎ 206 553 3000, ⊛ metro.kingcounty.gov), runs bus routes throughout the city. Customer service stations are available at King Street Center, 201 S Jackson St (Mon–Fri 8am–5pm), and at Westlake Station, near Fourth Ave and Pike St (Mon–Fri 9am–5.30pm); both offer maps and schedules and sell ORCA cards, stored-value cards valid on buses, trains and ferries (you can also purchase them at ⊛ orcacard.com). Buses run weekdays from 5am or 5.30am to midnight or 1am, though some routes may end service as early as 7pm; typically, weekend hours start an hour or two later and end an hour earlier; fares are $2.25, or up to $3 during rush hour (Mon–Fri 6–9am & 3–6pm). ORCA cards cost $5; you can then add $5–300 in stored value.

By monorail Westlake Center mall, 400 Pine St, is the southern terminus of the 1.3-mile monorail (Mon–Fri 7.30am–11pm, Sat & Sun 8.30am–11pm, every 10min; one-way fare $2.25, kids (5–12) $1; ⊛ seattlemonorail .com) to Seattle Center. Cash only (no ORCA cards).

By light rail Central Link runs 15.6 miles between downtown Seattle's Westlake Station and Sea-Tac Airport, making eleven stops along the way (Mon–Sat 5am–1am, Sun 6am–midnight, every 7.5–15min; ⊛ soundtransit .org). Fares range $2–2.75 depending on how far you travel (ORCA cards are accepted). The link north to the University of Washington and Capitol Hill is expected to open in 2016.

By ferry Washington State Ferries (☎ 206 464 6400, ⊛ wsdot.wa.gov/ferries) services from Bainbridge Island and Bremerton dock at Pier 52 on downtown's waterfront. Ferry routes from Vashon Island and Southworth connect at Fauntleroy in West Seattle, at 4829 SW Barton.

14

INFORMATION AND TOURS

Visitor centre Inside the Washington State Convention and Trade Center, Seventh Ave at Pike St (Mon–Fri 9am–5pm; also Sat & Sun 9am–5pm June–Aug; ☎ 206 461 5840, ⊛ visitseattle.org); also in Pike Place Market (daily 10am–6pm; same number).

Tours Let's Tour Seattle (☎ 206 632 1447, ⊛ letstourseattle .com) organizes 4hr bus tours (from $49) of the city, while Argosy Cruises runs year-round sightseeing trips around the harbour ($23.50; ☎ 206 623 1445, ⊛ argosycruises.com).

ACCOMMODATION

★ **Ace Hotel** 2423 First Ave ☎ 206 448 4721, ⊛ theace hotel.com. Modern white minimalist rooms in the heart of Belltown (just north of downtown), with hardwood floors, lofty ceilings and shared bathrooms, plus some more comfortable and well-appointed suites with private bathrooms. Doubles __$109__, suites __$199__

Alexis 1007 1st Ave, downtown ☎ 206 624 4844, ⊛ alexishotel.com. Hotel featuring plush decor, spa and steam room, just south of Pike Place Market. Nearly half the rooms are suites, the largest with luxurious touches including fireplaces and dining rooms. __$310__

Green Tortoise Hostel 105 Pike St, Downtown ☎ 206 340 1222, ⊛ greentortoise.net. Conveniently located hostel right across from Pike Place Market, with dorms sleeping from four to eight and some private doubles. Free breakfast, internet terminals and pickups at Amtrak, Greyhound or ferries; also summer walking tours of the city. Dorms __$32__, doubles __$58__

HI-Seattle at the American Hotel 520 S King St ☎ 206 622 5443, ⊛ hiusa.org/seattle. Conveniently located hostel in a 1926 building, close to Amtrak, with comfy dorms and private rooms, with all the usual shared amenities: wi-fi, laundry, TV room and kitchen. Non HI members pay $3/night extra. Dorms __$35__, doubles __$86__

Hotel Andra 2000 Fourth Ave ☎ 206 448 8600, ⊛ hotel andra.com. An intimate boutique hotel in the Belltown neighbourhood, with chic, modern units featuring designer furnishings – more than half of them suites. __$310__

★ **Hotel Five** 2200 Fifth Ave ☎ 206 441 9785, ⊛ hotel fiveseattle.com. Hip boutique hotel with a bright, Pop Art theme, free daily coconut-and-pineapple cupcakes and coffee (3–7pm) and free bicycles. Parking on-site is $15/day. __$185__

Hotel Vintage Park 1100 Fifth Ave ☎ 206 624 8000, ⊛ hotelvintagepark.com. Stylish boutique hotel with rooms themed around wine-drinking and vineyards; amenities may include fireplaces, jacuzzis, flat-screen TVs, stereos and, of course, nightly tastings of vino. __$255__

Inn at the Market 86 Pine St ☎ 206 443 3600, ⊛ innat themarket.com. If you want close proximity to Pike Place Market, this luxury boutique hotel is a top choice for its floor-to-ceiling views of the market, city or bay, and its tasteful decor and rooftop deck. __$269__

Monaco 1101 4th Ave, downtown ☎ 206 621 1770, ⊛ monaco-seattle.com. Luxurious hotel with designer furnishings, plus a striking lobby, gym and elegant suites with CD players and flat-screen TVs – some with jacuzzis, too. __$288__

Pensione Nichols 1923 1st Ave, Belltown ☎ 206 441 7125, ⊛ pensionenichols.com. Classy little B&B with small but clean rooms, shared bathrooms and simple, tasteful decor in a 1908 office building (though lacking an elevator, TVs and a/c). Two-night minimum during summer. __$160__

Shafer Baillie Mansion 907 14th Ave E, Capitol Hill ☎ 206 322 4654, ⊛ sbmansion.com. Oak-panelled 1914 Tudor Revival mansion-turned-B&B that offers three rooms

and two suites (plus three units in a subdivided ballroom) with antique tubs and refrigerators, plus DVD players and flat-screen TVs. **$189**
University Inn 4140 Roosevelt Way NE, University District ☎ 206 632 5055, ⓦ universityinnseattle.com.
Trendy hotel close to the University of Washington with free coffee and cupcakes every afternoon and a bright, contemporary design. All rooms have microwaves and come with complimentary breakfast; there's also a pool and spa. **$169**

EATING

Seattle has many fine **restaurants**, from the funky diners of Capitol Hill and ethnic restaurants of the University District to the delicious fish of Pike Place Market. Moreover, local **coffeehouses** host an engaging cultural scene, and are inexpensive choices for whiling away the time or surfing the internet. **Seafood** dominates menus: try the salmon (a lot of it comes from Alaska these days), Dungeness crabs (named after Dungeness in Washington, not the one in Kent, England) and oysters from the Puget Sound.

BELLTOWN

★ **Dahlia Lounge** 2001 4th Ave ☎ 206 682 4142, ⓦ tomdouglas.com. Gourmet restaurant best known for its seafood, featuring delicious main courses such as Yukutat salmon with cherries and Dungeness crab cakes. If you can't afford to drop a wad on dinner (mains $22–37), try the adjoining, excellent *Dahlia Bakery* for a freshly made doughnut. Mon–Thurs 11.30am–2.30pm & 5–10pm, Fri 11.30am–2.30pm & 5–11pm, Sat 9am–2pm & 5–11pm, Sun 9am–2pm & 5–9pm.

CAPITOL HILL

Bauhaus Books & Coffee 301 E Pine St ☎ 206 625 1600, ⓦ bauhauscoffee.net. A stylish hangout for the hipster set, with large tables, a used-book section – focusing on art and architecture volumes – and good coffee and tea. Mon–Fri 6am–1pm, Sat 7am–1am, Sun 8am–1am.
Café Flora 2901 E Madison St ☎ 206 325 9100, ⓦ cafeflora.com. The city's best vegan and vegetarian restaurant, attracting even devout carnivores for its creative soups, salads and mains, such as yam fries and white-bean pizza (dinner mains $15–19). Mon–Fri 9am–10pm, Sat 9am–2pm & 5–10pm, Sun 9am–2pm & 5–9pm.
Dick's Drive-In 115 Broadway Ave E ☎ 206 323 1300, ⓦ ddir.com. Long-standing fast-food institution founded in 1954 and serving up sloppy but serviceable burgers ($2.70), rich shakes ($2.15) and fries with just the right crunch. One of six citywide locations. Daily 10.30am–2am.
★ **Espresso Vivace** 532 Broadway E ☎ 206 860 2722, ⓦ espressovivace.com. A fine haunt for serious java-drinkers and truly run by "espresso roasting and preparation specialists"; their sidewalk coffee bar at 321 Broadway

E is the prime people-watching perch in the area. Daily 6am–11pm.
Pike Street Fish Fry 925 E Pike St ☎ 206 329 7453, ⓦ pikestreetfishfry.net. Hole-in-the-wall for excellent fish and chips with fresh catfish, cod, halibut and home-made tartare sauces. Mon–Wed & Sun 11.30am–midnight, Thurs–Sat 11.30am–2.30am.

DOWNTOWN & PIONEER SQUARE

Ivar's Acres of Clams 1001 Alaskan Way (Pier 54) ☎ 206 624 6852, ⓦ ivars.com. Posh restaurant right on the waterfront since 1938 ($32 for salmon, $15 for cod and chips), but also the no-frills *Fish Bar* takeaway counter where cod and chips is $8.29, and salmon and chips $8.99. Mon–Thurs & Sun 11am–10pm, Fri & Sat 11am–11pm.
Phnom Penh Noodle House 660 S King St (south of Pioneer Square) ☎ 206 748 9825, ⓦ phnompenhnoodles.com. Like the name says, an authentic Cambodian noodle joint that doles out rich helpings of noodles in various sauces, as well as traditional favourites such as spicy soups and fish cakes. Mon, Tues & Thurs 9am–8pm, Fri 9am–8.30pm, Sat 8.30am–8.30pm, Sun 8.30am–8pm.
Pike Place Chowder 1530 Post Alley (near Pike Place Market) ☎ 206 267 2537, ⓦ pikeplacechowder.com. Humble cafeteria that cooks up award-winning clam chowder (from $4.95), heavy on the clams, as well as seared scallops and fish and chips; expect a short wait in line. Daily 11am–5pm.
★ **Salumi** 309 Third Ave S, Pioneer Square ☎ 206 621 8772, ⓦ salumicuredmeats.com. Old-fashioned sausages served on delicious home-made bread, featuring oxtail, prosciutto, lamb and assorted hog parts. Expect long waits during peak hours. Tues–Fri 11am–4pm.

COFFEE WITH A VIEW

Unbeknown to most visitors, the **best café views** in Seattle can be had from a humble Starbucks (Mon–Fri 4.30am–6.30pm; ☎ 206 447 9934) on the 40th floor of the soaring Columbia Center (see p.924). You don't pay a cent to ride the elevator, and for the price of a cup of coffee you can enjoy stunning views of downtown Seattle for as long as you like.

PIKE PLACE MARKET: FIVE TO TRY

Athenian 1517 Pike Place ☎206 624 7166, ⓦathenianinn.com. Open since 1909, this venerable seafood restaurant featured in *Sleepless in Seattle*. Mon–Sat 6.30am–9pm, Sun 9am–4pm.

Beecher's Handmade Cheese 1600 Pike Place ☎206 956 1964, ⓦbeechershandmadecheese.com. Quality cheeses, sandwiches and exceptional mac & cheese ($5). Daily 9am–7pm.

Lowell's 1519 Pike Place ☎206 622 2036, ⓦeatat lowells.com. Legendary breakfast spot since 1957, with spectacular views of the harbour from three floors.

Daily 7am–7pm.

Piroshky Piroshky 1908 Pike Place ☎206 441 6068, ⓦpiroshkybakery.com. Russian bakery knocking out "piroshkies", pies with fillings such as smoked salmon or rhubarb. Mon–Fri 7.30am–6.30pm, Sat & Sun 7.30am–7pm.

Three Girls Bakery 1514 Pike Place ☎206 622 1045. Market institution since 1912, serving huge sandwiches and freshly baked shortbreads, hazelnut-chocolate cookies and *rugelach*. Daily 6am–6pm.

14

Zeitgeist Coffee 171 S Jackson St ☎206 583 0497, ⓦzeitgeistcoffee.com. Excellent espresso coffee ($1.90), cappuccino ($2.50), some sandwiches, the occasional, mind-blowing strawberry rhubarb pie ($5), and copious modern artworks are found at this pleasant haunt in the heart of Pioneer Square's gallery scene. Mon–Fri 6am–7pm, Sat 7am–7pm, Sun 8am–6pm.

FREMONT AND AROUND

Canlis 2576 Aurora Ave N (south of Fremont) ☎206 283 3313, ⓦcanlis.com. Designed with local stone and cedar in 1950 (with a nod to Lloyd Wright) and featuring creative nouveau Northwest cuisine, highlighted by wild-nettle pasta, Kobe tenderloin and Maine lobster (set three courses from $85). Dress up and book ahead. Mon–Fri 5.30–10pm, Sat 5–10pm.

Paseo Caribbean 4225 Fremont Ave N ☎206 545 7440, ⓦpaseoseattle.com. Extremely hip Fremont sandwich joint, which despite the hype, really does deliver on

fabulous, juicy, messy baguette sandwiches with slow-roasted pork ($8.50) and marinated chicken thighs ($8.50). Tues–Fri 11am–9pm, Sat 11am–8pm.

QUEEN ANNE (SEATTLE CENTER)

The 5 Spot 1502 Queen Anne Ave N ☎206 285 7768, ⓦchowfoods.com. Quirky Southern-style diner whose affordable meals may include red beans and rice, fried chicken dipped in buttermilk and honey, and brisket with Coca-Cola marinade (mains $10–11). The decor changes regularly to highlight different US cities. Mon–Fri 8.30am–midnight, Sat & Sun 8.30am–3pm & 5pm–midnight.

Caffè Ladro 600 Queen Anne Ave N ☎206 282 1549, ⓦcaffeladro.com. Near the Seattle Center, this coffeeshop has an arty flair, with a range of light meals (and some veggie options) in addition to hearty coffees that many swear by. Seven other citywide branches. Mon–Thurs & Sun 5.30am–9pm, Fri & Sat 5.30am–10pm.

DRINKING AND NIGHTLIFE

Though the buzz has cooled somewhat since the 1990s, Seattle still boasts a vibrant nightlife and live music scene, at its most frenetic in Pioneer Square, but other prime turf for hearing music can be found in Capitol Hill, downtown and Belltown.

BARS AND CLUBS

★**5 Point Café** 415 Cedar St ☎206 448 9991, ⓦthe5pointcafe.com. Classic 24hr dive bar and diner with the memorable motto "alcoholics serving alcoholics since 1929"; they also serve great burgers and breakfast at all hours. Daily 24hr (bar 6am–2am).

Alibi Room 85 Pike St (Post Alley) ☎206 623 3180, ⓦseattlealibi.com. Swanky bar tucked in an alley behind the Pike Place Market. Excellent food in café-type rooms upstairs, DJs spinning tunes on the dancefloor downstairs and a happy hour that starts in the middle of the afternoon. Daily noon–2am.

Central Saloon 207 First Ave S, Pioneer Square ☎206 622 0209, ⓦcentralsaloon.com. Seattle's oldest bar was established in 1892, and is consistently crowded, filled

with a mix of slumming tourists and slumming scenesters. Live music ranges from alt-rock to blues and metal. Daily 11.30am–2am.

Comet Tavern 922 E Pike St, Capitol Hill ☎206 323 9853, ⓦcomettavern.com. The oldest bar on Capitol Hill and a grunge institution – not surprisingly a scruffy dive and a rocker's hangout, too, with regular shows by hard-rockers and head-bangers. Try to avoid the toilets. Mon–Fri 3pm–2am, Sat & Sun 1pm–2am.

★**Elysian Brewing** 1221 E Pike St, Capitol Hill ☎206 860 1920, ⓦelysianbrewing.com. Brewpub of one of the best local microbreweries, based within a 1919 warehouse with flavourful oddities such as the Immortal IPA, Dragonstooth Stout and Avatar Jasmine IPA, a fragrant brew dry-hopped with jasmine. The menu is pretty good,

14

too, including sandwiches and tacos. Mon–Fri 11.30am–2am, Sat & Sun noon–2am.

Kells Irish Pub 1916 Post Alley, Pike Place Market ☎ 206 728 1916, ⓦ kellsirish.com/seattle. Spirited Irish bar and restaurant in a central location, with patio seating and performances by Irish-oriented folk and rock groups. Crowd is mostly tourists and business-district types. Daily 11.30am–2am.

Lava Lounge 2226 2nd Ave, Belltown ☎ 206 441 5660. All 1950s lounge-revival kitsch, with tiki-inspired decor and eclectic live music and DJs at night, happy hour from 3 to 7pm and shuffleboard to pass the time. Daily 3pm–2am.

Pike Pub & Brewery 1415 1st Ave, downtown ☎ 206 622 6044, ⓦ pikebrewing.com. Small craft brewery serving its own beers, as well as numerous bottled brands; however, only adequate food and a touristy atmosphere (it is near Pike Place Market, after all). Daily 11am–midnight.

Trinity Nightclub 111 Yesler Way, Pioneer Square ☎ 206 697 7702, ⓦ trinitynightclub.com. Giant, two-level dance club with the Chinese-themed Card Room lounge, state-of-the-art sound, acclaimed DJs and two spacious dancefloors. Wednesday sees one of the biggest Bollywood and bhangra nights in the USA. Wed–Sat 8pm–2am.

MUSIC VENUES

★ **Dimitriou's Jazz Alley** 2033 6th Ave, Belltown ☎ 206 441 9729, ⓦ jazzalley.com. Best big-name jazz spot in town, showcasing international acts across a range of styles, as well as up-and-coming talent. Tickets start around $20. Tues–Sun 5.30–11pm.

Highway 99 Blues Club 1414 Alaskan Way, downtown ☎ 206 382 171, ⓦ highwayninetynine.com. Rootsy joint showcasing regional and national performers in blues, rockabilly and R&B, in a fun, convivial atmosphere with a dancefloor and Louisiana-style food. Cover $10–20 Fri & Sat. Wed & Thurs 6pm–1am, Fri 4pm–2am, Sat 6pm–2am.

Moore Theater 1932 2nd Ave, Belltown ☎ 206 467 5510, ⓦ stgpresents.org. This 1907 former vaudeville auditorium sometimes hosts exciting up-and-coming bands, but more often you'll find established names in pop and rock, along with comedians, dancers, kids' shows and so on. Box office opens 90min prior to the performance (or get tickets at the Paramount Theatre Box Office at 9th Ave and Pine St, Mon–Fri 10am–6pm).

Neumo's 925 E Pike St, Capitol Hill ☎ 206 709 9442, ⓦ neumos.com. A hard-thrashing venue that has clawed its way up (almost) to the top of the "rawk" heap. The bands are of the punk, goth, rock and alt-anything variety, and the crowd will mosh you into oblivion if you let them. Shows typically start at 8pm daily, but check website.

Showbox at the Market 1426 1st Ave, downtown ☎ 206 628 3151, ⓦ showboxpresents.com. This thousand-person hall across from Pike Place Market is the best place to catch touring acts that have yet to make the bigger arenas, along with well-regarded regional bands, usually with an indie slant. Hours vary.

Sunset Tavern 5433 Ballard Ave NW, Ballard ☎ 206 784 4880, ⓦ sunsettavern.com. Along with being a colourful bar and karaoke spot, the *Sunset's* also a good venue for catching aggressive young rockers and various eclectic acts in cheap nightly performances. Daily 5pm–2am.

Tractor Tavern 5213 Ballard Ave NW, Ballard ☎ 206 789 3599, ⓦ tractortavern.com. Solid joint in Ballard with great character, stuffed with a mix of hipsters and burnouts, good microbrewed beers and roots music of all kinds – zydeco, Irish, blues, bluegrass, alt-country. Box office Mon–Fri noon–4pm, see website for current showtimes.

Triple Door 216 Union St, downtown ☎ 206 838 4333, ⓦ thetripledoor.net. Attractive venue that's good for folk, roots, alt-country and blues; the Mainstage has major players and up-and-comers, while the Musicquarium mixes things up with DJs and more experimental fare – it's also free. Mon–Wed & Sun 4pm–midnight, Thurs–Sat 4pm–2am.

ENTERTAINMENT

Benaroya Hall 200 University St ☎ 206 215 4747, ⓦ seattlesymphony.org. This glass-walled venue downtown is the home of the Seattle Symphony Orchestra (entrance at the corner of Second Ave and Union St). The

season runs Sept–July.

Fifth Avenue Theatre 1308 5th Ave ☎ 206 625 1900, ⓦ 5thavenue.org. Seattle's tradition of hosting big-name musicals is maintained at this 1926 downtown venue; hit

---

SEATTLE FESTIVALS

Seattle's biggest events are **Bumbershoot**, hosting hundreds of artists on dozens of stages around town on Labor Day weekend in early September (☎ 206 281 7788, ⓦ bumbershoot.org), and the **Northwest Folklife Festival** (☎ 206 684 7300, ⓦ nwfolklife.org), a Memorial Day (late May) event at the Seattle Center drawing folk musicians from around the world. In late May and early June, the Seattle **International Film Festival** (☎ 206 464 5830, ⓦ siff.net) centres on classic moviehouses in Capitol Hill, and in July and early August, **Seafair** (☎ 206 728 0123, ⓦ seafair.com) is a colourful celebration held all over town with aeroplane spectacles, hydroplane events and milk-carton boat races.

production Hairspray actually opened here before Broadway.
Intiman Theatre 201 Mercer St ☎206 441 7178, ⓦintiman.org. Place to catch high-quality classics and premieres of innovative works, especially during the Intiman Theatre Festival (June–Sept).

Marion Oliver McCaw Hall 321 Mercer St ☎206 733 9725, ⓦmccawhall.com. Sleek modern facility in the Seattle Center that hosts the Seattle Opera (☎206 389

7676, ⓦseattleopera.org) and the Pacific Northwest Ballet (☎206 441 2424, ⓦpnb.org) – the latter puts on around ten programmes from Sept–June.

Seattle Repertory Theatre 155 Mercer St (Seattle Center) ☎206 443 2222, ⓦseattlerep.org. Home to Seattle's longest-established small troupe and two stages: the Bagley Wright Theatre and the more intimate Leo Kreielsheimer Theatre.

Whidbey Island

With its sheer cliffs and craggy outcrops, rocky beaches and rambling countryside, **WHIDBEY ISLAND** is the second largest island in the continental USA – nearly fifty miles in length from north to south, it forms the northern boundary of **Puget Sound**, some thirty miles north of Seattle.

Just a few miles away from where the ferry docks in Clinton, the town of **Langley**, established by German immigrants in 1890, is a well-heeled seaside village with a stretch of wooden storefronts, antique stores and galleries set on a picturesque bluff overlooking the water.

The middle part of the island contains **Ebey's Landing National Historic Reserve** (daily 8am–dusk; free; ⓦnps.gov/ebla), whose late nineteenth-century military garrisons Fort Casey and Fort Ebey have been converted into evocative state parks, peppered with haunting gun batteries and eerie, bomb-shelter-like bunkers.

Nearby, charming little **Coupeville** features several preserved Victorian mansions, and its Front Street is where you'll find most of the shops and restaurants. Scenes from the movie *Practical Magic* (1998) were shot here, though it was supposed to be set in New England.

On the northern edge of the island, **Deception Pass State Park**, 5175 N Hwy-20 (daily 8am–dusk; $10/day per vehicle; ☎360 675 2417) sprawls over four thousand acres of rugged land and sea that's great for hiking, fishing, birdwatching and scuba diving.

ARRIVAL, INFORMATION AND GETTING AROUND   WHIDBEY ISLAND

By ferry The quickest route from Seattle is to drive 30 miles north to Mukilteo and catch the ferry to Clinton on Whidbey's southern tip (daily 5am–12.30am; 20min trip; foot passengers $4.65, vehicle and driver $6.35–7.75). From Port Townsend on the Olympic Peninsula (see p.940) another ferry goes to Coupeville (6.30am–8.30pm; 30min; foot passengers $3.10, vehicle and driver $10.20–12.70; ⓦwsdot.wa.gov/ferries).

By bus Sea Tac Shuttle (ⓦseatacshuttle.com) buses connect Sea-Tac Airport with all the major towns on Whidbey (9 daily;

$36–37 one-way).

Chambers of Commerce 905 Northwest Alexander St, Coupeville (Mon–Fri 9am–5pm; ☎360 678 5434, ⓦcoupevillechamber.com); 208 Anthes Ave, Langley (daily 11am–4pm; ☎360 221 6765, ⓦvisitlangley.com).

Local buses Whidbey's bus system, Island Transit (Mon–Fri 3.45am–7.45pm, Sat 7.15am–7pm; ☎360 678 7771, ⓦislandtransit.org), offers ten free routes that collectively run along the length of the island.

ACCOMMODATION AND EATING

Anchorage Inn 807 N Main St, Coupeville ☎877 230 1313, ⓦanchorage-inn.com. Justly popular Victorian B&B, with seven period-style rooms, tranquil wraparound deck, tasty breakfasts and friendly owners. $99

Braeburn 197 2nd St, Langley ☎360 221 3211, ⓦbraeburnlangley.com. Laidback island diner with outdoor patio, serving old-fashioned meatloaf and coleslaw, pot roast, pancakes and omelettes. Mon–Fri 8am–4pm, Sat & Sun 7am–4pm.

Christopher's 103 NW Coveland St, Coupeville ☎360

678 5480, ⓦchristophersonwhidbey.com. Enticing seafood restaurant, with fresh salmon and local clams on the menu, as well as pasta, pork tenderloin and hearty stews. Mon–Fri 11.30am–2pm & 5–9pm, Sat & Sun noon–2.30pm & 5–10pm.

Country Cottage of Langley 215 6th St, Langley ☎360 221 8709, ⓦacountrycottage.com. Six rustic but cosy cottages set around a restored 1920s farmhouse, all units with CD players and fridges, some with jacuzzis and fireplaces. $139

14

Kapaws Iskreme 21 NW Front St, Coupeville ☏ 360 929 2122. Luscious bowls of ice cream (3 scoops for $3; add $1 for waffle cone), with long, though fast-moving, queues in summer; try the fresh huckleberry flavour. Daily 11.30am–5pm.

Useless Bay Coffee Co 121 2nd St, Langley ☏ 360 221 4515, ⊚ shop.uselessbaycoffee.com. Best coffee on the island, and a good place for a quick, tasty breakfast – locals go here, while tourists tend to frequent the *Braeburn*. Daily 7.30am–4.30pm.

The San Juan Islands

North and west of Whidbey Island, midway between Seattle and Vancouver, Canada, the unspoiled **SAN JUAN ISLANDS** are scattered across the northern reaches of Puget Sound, with plenty of small-town charm, culinary treats and killer whales offshore. Every summer brings lots of visitors, especially on the largest islands, San Juan and Orcas, so you're well advised to book your stay and transport in advance. Ferries depart Anacortes on the mainland, eighty miles north of Seattle, where you can also catch services to Sidney in Canada.

Orcas Island

Horseshoe-shaped **ORCAS ISLAND** offers a bucolic getaway with rugged hills that tower over its fetching farm country, craggy beaches and abundant wildlife. The island's highlight is **Moran State Park** (daily 8am–sunset; $10/per vehicle) off Horseshoe Highway southeast of Eastsound (the main island settlement), where more than thirty miles of hiking trails wind through dense forest and open fields to freshwater lakes and to the summit of **Mount Constitution** – the San Juans' highest point at 2409ft – crowned with a medieval-style stone observation tower.

San Juan Island

SAN JUAN ISLAND is best known as the site of, at the southern tip, **San Juan Island National Historical Park**, where the **American Camp** (visitor centre June–Aug daily 8.30am–5pm; Sept to mid-Oct daily 8.30am–4.30pm; mid-Oct to May Wed–Sun 8.30am–4.30pm; free; ☏ 360 378 2902, ⊚ nps.gov/sajh), once played a role in the so-called "Pig War", a rather absurd 1859 border confrontation between the USA and Britain (no shots were fired, and the island was officially ceded to the USA in 1872). More appealing is **English Camp**, to the west (same entry as American Camp), where forests overlook rolling fields and maple trees near the shore, and four buildings from the 1860s and a small formal garden have been restored.

Friday Harbor is a small and attractive resort village with cafés, shops and a waterfront that make for pleasant wandering. Its small **Whale Museum**, 62 First St N (daily: June–Aug 9am–6pm; rest of year 10am–5pm; $6; ⊚ whalemuseum.org), has a set of whale skeletons and displays explaining their migration and growth cycles, as well as a listening booth for whale and other cetacean songs. To see the real thing, head past the coves and bays on the island's west side to **Lime Kiln Point State Park**, 6158 Lighthouse Rd (daily 8am–sunset; $10/vehicle), named after the site's former lime quarry. Orca ("killer") whales come here in summer to feed on migrating salmon, and there's usually at least one close sighting a day.

ARRIVAL AND DEPARTURE   THE SAN JUAN ISLANDS

By ferry Washington State Ferries sails to the islands from the harbour a few miles west of Anacortes. The town is reachable via Airporter Shuttle (6am–11.30pm; 3hr trip; $33 one-way, $61 return; ☏ 866 235 5247, ⊚ airporter.com), which runs from Sea-Tac Airport (11 daily) and downtown Seattle (3 daily). The ferry runs 12–18 times daily; and stops at Lopez, Shaw and Orcas islands before ending at Friday Harbor on San Juan Island (5.30am–10.45pm; ☏ 888 808 7977, ⊚ wsdot.wa.gov/ferries). Motorists should get to the port early, as there's often an hour's wait or more to get vehicles onto a summer crossing. Return fares to any of the islands – $12.45 for foot passengers and $23.95–45.75 for a car and driver, depending on the destination and season – are collected only on the westbound journey, and there is no charge for foot passengers on inter-island trips (bringing a bike costs an extra $2).

By catamaran The Victoria Clipper (☎ 206 448 5000, ⓦ clippervacations.com), a high-speed passenger-only catamaran, runs once daily from Seattle's Pier 69 to San Juan's Friday Harbor ($42.50 one-way, $85 return; 3hr 30min), with a 5hr layover.

By plane Kenmore Air (☎ 866 435 9524, ⓦ kenmoreair .com) has several seaplane flights daily from Seattle's Lake Union and Boeing Field airports to Friday Harbor and Orcas Island (both $142.50 one-way).

GETTING AROUND, TOURS AND INFORMATION

ORCAS ISLAND
By shuttle bus San Juan Transit (☎ 360 378 8887, ⓦ sanjuantransit.com) offers summertime transportation (5–6 daily, Fri–Mon only; late June to early Sept) around Orcas Island, serving Eastsound, Moran State Park and the Ferry Landing. Tickets are $5 per trip (exact change only).
By bike Rent bicycles from Wildlife Cycles, 350 N Beach Rd in Eastsound (May–Sept daily 10am–6pm; Oct–Dec & Feb–April Tues–Sat 10am–5pm; $35/day; ☎ 360 376 4708, ⓦ wildlifecycles.com).
Kayaking tours Orcas is a renowned kayaking centre. Guided tours are provided by Shearwater Kayak Tours at 138 N Beach Rd in Eastsound (3hr; $75; ☎ 360 376 4699, ⓦ shearwaterkayaks.com) and Spring Bay Kayak Tours (2hr tour by naturalists; $40/person) at 464 Spring Bay Trail, 20 miles from the Ferry Landing (☎ 360 376 5531, ⓦ springbayonorcas.com).
Chamber of Commerce 65 N Beach Rd, Eastsound

(Mon–Sat 10am–3pm; ☎ 360 376 2273, ⓦ orcasisland chamber.com).

SAN JUAN ISLAND
By shuttle bus From mid-May to mid-Sept, San Juan Transit stops at most of the island's principal attractions ($5 one-way, $15 for a day pass; ☎ 360 378 8887, ⓦ sanjuan transit.com).
By bike Rent bikes at Island Bicycles, 380 Argyle St, Friday Harbor ($10–13/hr, $40–52/day; mid-June to early Sept daily 10am–5.30pm; early Sept to mid-June Wed–Sat; ☎ 360 378 4941, ⓦ islandbicycles.com).
Chamber of Commerce 135 Spring St (daily 10am–4pm; ☎ 360 378 5240, ⓦ sanjuanisland.org).
Tours San Juan Safaris (☎ 360 378 1323, ⓦ sanjuansafaris .com) is one of several companies offering 3hr whale-watching cruises (April–Oct only; $85), plus sea-kayaking trips (June–Sept) for the same price.

ACCOMMODATION

ORCAS ISLAND
Beach Haven Resort 684 Beach Haven Rd, Eastsound ☎ 360 376 2288, ⓦ beach-haven.com. Beachfront apartments and very rustic log cabins lining a gorgeous, densely wooded, sunset-facing cove; in summer they're only available by the week. Kitchens but no TV or wi-fi and very patchy mobile phone reception. $125
Orcas Hotel 18 Orcas Hill Rd, Orcas Village ☎ 360 376 4300, ⓦ orcashotel.com. The best spot to stay near the ferry landing is this restored Victorian inn from 1904, whose plushest rooms have jacuzzis, balconies and harbour views, though not the cheaper ones. $89
★ **Outlook Inn on Orcas Island** 171 Main St, Eastsound ☎ 360 376 2200, ⓦ outlookinn.com. One of the best places to stay on the island, with a range of cosy rooms from luxurious suites to standard rooms with shared bathrooms and no TV. Reservations crucial. $79

SAN JUAN ISLAND
★ **Bird Rock Hotel** 35 First St, Friday Harbor ☎ 360 378 5848, ⓦ birdrockhotel.com. Boutique-like hotel with designer furnishings, flat-screen HDTVs, iPod docks and some units with jacuzzis (the cheapest rooms have shared bath). $127
Lakedale Resort 4313 Roche Harbor Rd, Friday Harbor ☎ 360 378 2350, ⓦ lakedale.com. Large resort which has everything from elegant lodge rooms to canvas-walled cabins and log-framed cabins that sleep up to six. Cabins May–Sept only. Rooms $269, canvas-walled cabins $179, log-framed cabins $399
★ **Trumpeter Inn** 318 Trumpeter Way, Friday Harbor ☎ 360 378 3884, ⓦ trumpeterinn.com. Gorgeous modern B&B, with six comfy rooms, a concierge service, full gourmet breakfast and freshly baked afternoon treats. $179

EATING

ORCAS ISLAND
New Leaf Café 171 Main St (Outlook Inn), Eastsound ☎ 360 376 2200, ⓦ newleafcafeorcas.com. Fresh, seasonal and French-inspired Northwest food, ocean views and exquisite dishes such as smoked salmon pasta ($22) make this one of the more popular restaurants on the island. Mon, Tues & Thurs 8–11am & 5.30–9.30pm, Fri 8–11am & 5.30–10pm, Sat 8am–1pm & 5.30–10pm,

Sun 8am–1pm & 5.30–9.30pm.
Tee-Jay's 112 Haven Rd (Odd Fellows Hall basement), Eastsound (Madrona Point) ☎ 360 376 6337. Locals love this Mexican hole-in-the-wall for its sensational fish tacos (salmon and cod), as well as bacon-wrapped jalapeno poppers (stuffed and deep-fried peppers) and home-made salsas; eat on the patio outside. Thurs–Sun 11am–8pm.

14

14

SAN JUAN ISLAND

Bakery San Juan 775 Mullis St, Friday Harbor ☎ 360 378 5810, ⓦ bakerysanjuan.com. Superb place to stock up on freshly baked sourdough bread, but also knocks out excellent pizza slices ($5), key lime pies that often sell out early and some of the tastiest cinnamon rolls anywhere. Mon–Fri 8am–5pm.

★ **Duck Soup Inn** 50 Duck Soup Lane (near Lakedale Resort), Friday Harbor ☎ 360 378 4878, ⓦ ducksoupinn

.com. The best gourmet restaurant on the island, specializing in quality fresh fish, stews, rack of lamb and other prime Northwest cuisine (mains $29–35). July & Aug Tues–Sun 5–10pm; April to mid-May & Oct Fri–Sun 5–10pm; mid-May to June & Sept Thurs–Sun 5–10pm.

Rocky Bay Café 225 Spring St, Friday Harbor ☎ 360 378 5051. Beloved local favourite for its all-American breakfasts of omelettes, eggs Benedict and biscuits and gravy. Daily 6.30am–2.30pm.

Tacoma

Thirty miles south of Seattle via I-5 but increasingly part of the greater metro sprawl, **TACOMA** is an old industrial city that has transformed itself since the 1990s with new museums, theatres and restaurants. Flagship projects include the massive blue-and-white **Tacoma Dome**, a major concert venue just off the freeway (☎ 253 272 3663, ⓦ tacoma dome.org) and the **Broadway Center for the Performing Arts**, 901 Broadway (☎ 253 591 5890, ⓦ broadwaycenter.org), whose two stunning former moviehouses are landmarks with terracotta facades and much historic-revival decor. Most of Tacoma's attractions lie on nearby **Pacific Avenue**, though much of the allure comes from the connection with glass-art celebrity **Dale Chihuly**, born here in 1941.

Museum of Glass

1801 E Dock St • June–Aug Mon–Sat 10am–5pm, Sun noon–5pm; Aug–May Wed–Sat 10am–5pm, Sun noon–5pm • $12 (parking $2/hr) • ☎ 253 284 4750, ⓦ museumofglass.org

High-quality rotating exhibits of glass art grace the **Museum of Glass**, which sticks out like a shiny Space Age kiln above the Dock Street Marina. The kiln section actually contains the **Hot Shop**, an open workshop surrounded by seating where you can observe resident glass-blowers in action (with commentary). The galleries in the main building usually feature three or four temporary exhibits that change every six months. Dale Chihuly's glittering work often features and permanently adorns the plaza outside, as well as the adjacent pedestrian overpass, the **Bridge of Glass** (daily dawn–dusk; free; ⓦ chihuly.com/bridgeofglass), framed by two crystalline blue spires and lined with the Venetian Wall, choc-a-block with glass vases and other vitreous curiosities.

Union Station and the Tacoma Art Museum

Union Station 1717 Pacific Ave • Mon–Fri 8am–5pm • Free • ☎ 253 863 5173 • **Tacoma Art Museum** 1701 Pacific Ave • Wed–Sun 10am–5pm • $10 • ☎ 253 272 4258, ⓦ tacomaartmuseum.org

On the west side of the Bridge of Glass is the copper-domed 1911 **Union Station**, redesigned as a courthouse in 1992 with the main hall now a display space for some of Dale Chihuly's more flamboyant works – especially the orange-hued glass butterflies of the **Monarch Window**. You'll need photo ID to get in. One block north, the **Tacoma Art Museum** shows changing exhibits of predominantly Northwestern, contemporary art, as well as some permanent Chihuly glass installations.

Washington State History Museum

1911 Pacific Ave • Tues–Sun 10am–5pm • $9.50 (parking $4/2hr) • ☎ 253 272 9747 ⓦ washingtonhistory.org

On the south side of Union Station, the absorbing **Washington State History Museum** charts the history of the state thematically, with especially illuminating exhibits on the Native American population, the milieu of frontier towns and the early logging industry. The transformation of the Columbia River into a giant hydropower asset is covered in detail, as is the Great Depression of the 1930s, which was especially rough up here.

CLOCKWISE FROM TOP FRIDAY HARBOR ON SAN JUAN ISLAND, WA (P.934); MULTNOMAH FALLS, OR (P.956); TOUTLE RIVER VALLEY, MOUNT ST HELENS, WA (P.946) >

14

Karpeles Manuscript Library Museum and around

407 S G St • Tues–Fri 10am–4pm • Free • ☎ 253 383 2575, ⓦ karpeles.com

One of the region's little-visited gems, the astounding **Karpeles Manuscript Library Museum** occupies a small Neoclassical American Legion hall completed in 1931. Thanks to the Karpeles Library (based in Santa Barbara), the space shows a mind-blowing array of original documents, letters and manuscripts, from the concluding page of Darwin's *Origin of Species* and a page of Karl Marx's *Das Kapital* to the Japanese surrender document from 1945 and the *Enola Gay* logbook. Exhibits are usually thematic and change every four months.

Point Defiance Park

5400 N Pearl St, off Ruston Way • Daily sunrise–sunset • Free • **Fort Nisqually** June–Aug daily 11am–5pm; Sept & May Wed–Sun 11am–5pm; Oct–April Wed–Sun 11am–4pm • $6.50 • ☎ 253 591 5339, ⓦ fortnisqually.org

Four miles north of downtown Tacoma lies picturesque **Point Defiance Park**, its **Five-Mile-Drive** loop offering fine vistas of Puget Sound and many appealing hiking trails. Family-friendly park highlights include an on-site zoo and aquarium, but especially **Fort Nisqually**, a reconstruction of the fur-trading post Hudson's Bay Company set up in 1833, seventeen miles south of here, with homes and storehouses manned by costumed volunteers illustrating the stark lifestyles of denizens of the original fort, circa 1850s.

ARRIVAL, INFORMATION AND GETTING AROUND — TACOMA

By bus The Greyhound bus station is at 510 Puyallup Ave (☎ 253 383 4621), 1 mile south of downtown. Destinations Olympia (4 daily; 40min); Portland (4 daily; 2hr 50min–3hr 30min); Seattle (6 daily; 45min–1hr 15min).

By train The Amtrak station is at 1001 Puyallup Ave, 1.5 miles southeast of downtown. Destinations Portland (5 daily; 3hr); Seattle (5 daily; 1hr 6min).

By light rail You can easily get around the downtown core on the free Tacoma Link Light Rail system (Mon–Fri 5am–10pm, Sat 8am–10pm, Sun 10am–6pm; ☎ 206 398 5000, ⓦ soundtransit.org), which links Tacoma Dome with Union Station and the Broadway Center.

Visitor centre Inside the *Courtyard by Marriott*, 1516 Pacific Ave (April–Oct Mon–Sat 9am–5pm, Sun noon–5pm; Nov–March Tues–Sat 9am–5pm; ☎ 253 284 3254, ⓦ traveltacoma).

ACCOMMODATION

Geiger Victorian Bed & Breakfast 912 North I St ☎ 253 383 3504, ⓦ geigervictorian.com. Beautifully restored 1889 home loaded with all the chintz and antiques you'd expect, plus a fireplace and clawfoot tubs in the three rooms. **$129**

★ **Hotel Murano** 1320 Broadway Plaza ☎ 253 986

8083, ⓦ hotelmuranotacoma.com. If you're sufficiently fired up by all the glass art in town, make a night of it with a stay at this hip boutique hotel, which apart from its designer digs, flat-screen TVs and the like, has corridors and public spaces loaded with shimmery artworks. **$189**

EATING AND DRINKING

Engine House No 9 611 N Pine St ☎ 253 272 3435, ⓦ ehouse9.com. The "E-9" occupies an old 1907 firehouse that drips with historic character (check out the old horse stalls) and offers loads of local microbrews, decent pizza and fish tacos – the rest of the food menu is just so-so. Mon–Wed 11am–1am, Thurs & Fri 11am–2am, Sat 10am–2am, Sun 10am–1am.

Frisko Freeze 1201 Division Ave ☎ 253 272 6843. Old burger dive and drive-in knocking out old-fashioned burgers, triple cheeseburgers, super-thick shakes and fat onion rings since 1956. Mon–Thurs & Sun 10am–11pm, Fri & Sat 10am–1am.

★ **Southern Kitchen** 1716 6th Ave ☎ 253 627 4282, ⓦ southernkitchen-tacoma.com. Delicious gumbo, cat-fish, hush puppies, candied yams and fried okra (mains from $9.95) are about as close to Dixie as you're going to get in the Pacific Northwest. Mon–Thurs 8am–8pm, Fri & Sat 8am–9pm, Sun 8am–7pm.

Swiss Restaurant & Pub 1904 S Jefferson Ave ☎ 253 572 2821, ⓦ theswisspub.com. This place has nothing to do with Switzerland, the food is OK and the beers are better, but it's the wacky decor that rewards a visit; the 1913 building boasts Chihuly's glass "Eight Venetians" above the bar, along with stuffed animals and accordions. Daily 11am–2pm.

Olympia and around

Chosen as Washington's territorial capital in 1853 and state capital in 1889, liberal and laidback **OLYMPIA** has a neat, compact downtown area, though the most attractive part of the city lies just to the south in the Washington State Capitol Campus, littered with grand Neoclassical piles.

Legislative Building

416 Sid Snyder Ave SW • Mon–Fri 7.30am–5pm, Sat & Sun 11am–4pm; tours Mon–Fri on the hour 10am–3pm (Sat & Sun 11am–3pm) • Free • ☎ 360 902 8880, ⓦ leg.wa.gov

Though it doesn't sport the lavish artwork of other US capitols, the grand Neoclassical **Legislative Building** merits a look for its vast central rotunda space alone, the interior lavishly finished in white Alaskan marble throughout. The sandstone edifice was completed in 1928, its dome soaring 287ft and six gargantuan bronze entry-doors decorated with scenes from state history; check out also the large circular walnut table in the State Reception Room, whose base was carved from a single walnut tree trunk in the shape of eagles' legs.

Wolf Haven International

3111 Offut Lake Rd SE, Tenino • April–Sept Mon & Wed–Sat 10am–4pm, Sun noon–4pm; Oct–Jan & March Sat 10am–4pm, Sun noon–4pm (last tours always at 3pm) • $12 • ☎ 360 264 4695, ⓦ wolfhaven.org

Ten miles south of Olympia along Old Hwy-99, **Wolf Haven International** is a nonprofit organization offering sanctuary to wolves unable to survive in the wild. Not to be missed is "**A Midsummer's Night**" event, which offers just 25 visitors the chance to interact much more closely with the wolves during an overnight camp-out (Aug Sat & Sun; $75).

ARRIVAL, GETTING AROUND AND INFORMATION   OLYMPIA AND AROUND

By bus The Greyhound station is at 107 Seventh Ave SE at Capitol Way (☎ 360 357 5541), just north of the Capitol Campus.
Destinations Portland (4 daily; 2hr 2hr 40min); Seattle (4 daily; 1hr 35min); Tacoma (4 daily; 40min).
Local buses Intercity Transit ($1.25 ticket, one-day pass $2.50; ☎ 360 786 1881, ⓦ intercitytransit.com); also provides a free DASH shuttle service between downtown, the Farmers' Market and the Capitol Campus (Mon–Fri 7am–6pm; also Sat April–Aug; every 10–15min).
Visitor centre 103 Sid Snyder Ave SW, on the Capitol Campus (Mon–Fri 9am–5pm, Sat 10am–3pm; ☎ 360 704 7544, ⓦ visitolympia.com)

ACCOMMODATION

Inn at Mallard Cove 5025 Meridian Rd NE ☎ 360 491 9795, ⓦ theinnatmallardcove.com. Half-timbered Tudor Revival estate whose three lovely rooms variously come with fireplaces, private decks and jacuzzis. **$179**
Phoenix Inn Suites 415 Capitol Way N ☎ 360 570 0555, ⓦ phoenixinnsuites.com. Plush business hotel with big flat-screens, fridges and microwaves in each room, plus an on-site pool, jacuzzi and gym. **$159**
Swantown Inn 1431 Eleventh Ave SE ☎ 360 753 9123, ⓦ swantowninn.com. Four luxurious rooms in a striking 1887 Queen Anne-style mansion, with CD players, delicious gourmet breakfast and views of the Capitol. **$129**

EATING, DRINKING AND NIGHTLIFE

5th Avenue Sandwich Shop 117 Fifth Ave SE ☎ 360 705 3393, ⓦ 5thavesandwich.com. Convenient, quick and expertly crafted sandwiches, with the classic Reuben ($8.95) an especially memorable creation, stuffed with corned beef and sauerkraut. Mon–Fri 10am–4pm, Sat 11am–4pm.

OLYMPIA FARMERS' MARKET

The covered **Olympia Farmers' Market**, 700 N Capitol Way (April–Oct Thurs–Sun 10am–3pm; Nov–Dec Sat & Sun only; ⓦ olympiafarmersmarket.com), is a great place to stock up on fresh fruits, vegetables, herbs and handicrafts. Cheap food stalls include Curry in a Hurry and Dingey's (crab cakes and fish and chips from $8.99).

14

14

OLYMPIA ROCKS

Though it's a small city and firmly in Seattle's shadow, Olympia is regarded as one of the founding fathers of the US **indie rock** scene, starting with the creation of K Records in 1982 and blossoming in the 1990s. Local bands with a modicum of fame have included Dub Narcotic Sound System, Beat Happening, Bikini Kill and Some Velvet Sidewalk. Current trendsetters include the acoustic punk band Hail Seizures, country "outlaws" Rodeo Kill and low-fi Mount Eerie/Microphones, with the area around East Fourth Avenue prime territory for live music; always a good bet is the **Brotherhood Lounge**, 119 Capitol Way N (daily 4pm–2am; ☎ 360 352 4153, ⓦ thebrotherhoodlounge.com).

Batdorf & Bronson 516 S Capitol Way ☎ 360 786 6717, ⓦ batdorfcoffee.com. Superb coffee – espresso and cappuccino ($2.95) – breakfasts, pastries and quiches. Free wi-fi, too. Mon–Fri 6.30am–6pm, Sat & Sun 7am–6pm.

Eastside Club Tavern 410 Fourth Ave E ☎ 360 357 9985, ⓦ theeastsideclub.com. Divey pub since 1942, justly popular for its range of quality beers on tap. Food is

supplied by *Al Forno Olympia Pizza* via a pass-through window. Mon–Fri noon–2am, Sat & Sun 1pm–2am.

Iron Rabbit Restaurant & Bar 2103 Harrison Ave NW ☎ 360 956 3661, ⓦ ironrabbit.net. Menus of fresh, local produce, great burgers and Northwest beef, as well as root beer made on the premises and decent craft beers on tap. Mon–Thurs 11am–10pm, Fri 11am–11pm, Sat 9am–11pm, Sun 9am–9pm.

The Olympic Peninsula

Some thirty miles from Seattle, the far northwest corner of Washington State ends at the **Olympic Peninsula**, a largely untouched wilderness of great snow-capped peaks, tangled rainforests and the pristine beaches of the Pacific edge, as well as being home to **eight Native American tribes**. As every tween will inform you, this is also the moody, vampire-laced landscape of Stephenie Meyer's **Twilight** series – though the films were mostly shot in Oregon, the books are set in **Forks**, just outside **Olympic National Park**. Fringed with logging communities such as this, it's the magnificent national park where you should spend most of your time, with its superb hiking trails, campgrounds and lodges.

Port Townsend and around

With its multicoloured mansions overlooking the water, convivial cafés and compact scale, **PORT TOWNSEND** is a handsome relic from the 1890s. Perched on the peninsula's northeastern tip across from Whidbey Island, Port Townsend's physical split – half on a bluff, half at sea level – reflects nineteenth-century social divisions, when wealthy merchants built their houses **Uptown**, far above the clamour of the working-class port below. The **Downtown** area lies at the base of the hill on **Water Street**, which sports an attractive medley of Victorian brick-and-stone commercial buildings, now home to restaurants, boutiques and especially art galleries.

Jefferson Museum of Art & History

540 Water St • Daily 11am–4pm • $4 • ☎ 360 385 1003, ⓦ jchsmuseum.org

Port Townsend's rich history is detailed in the **Jefferson Museum of Art & History**, based in the old City Hall of 1892, which has an eclectic assortment of items, from a photographer's chair draped with bear and buffalo skins to antique farm and nautical implements, and unusual late nineteenth- and early twentieth-century two-necked harp guitars.

Fort Worden State Park

200 Battery Way • **Park** Daily sunrise–sunset • $10/vehicle (Discovery Pass) **Guardhouse Visitor Center** April–Oct daily 10am–4pm; March Mon–Thurs 10am–3.30pm; Nov & Dec Thurs–Mon 10am–4pm • ☎ 360 344 4400, ⓦ fortworden.org

In the late 1890s the area north of Port Townsend was designated a military base, the remains of which today form bucolic **Fort Worden State Park**, home to several museums, Point Wilson Lighthouse and a small beach (seals sometimes lounge here) – not to mention dozens of good hiking trails that lead to the massive concrete gun emplacements of Artillery Hill. Get oriented at the 1904 **Guardhouse Visitor Center**, where you'll also learn about the much-loved 1982 romantic drama *Officer and a Gentleman*, filmed in Port Townsend and the by then decommissioned Fort Worden. The 1908 **Coast Artillery Museum** (daily 11am–4pm; $4; ☎360 385 0373) chronicles the history of the site, while the 1904 **Commanding Officer's Quarters Museum** (March & April, Oct & Nov Sat & Sun noon–4pm; May–Sept daily noon–5pm; $4) is an old base house furnished to reflect officer life in 1910. Down by the beach the **Marine Science Center** (Sept to mid-June Fri–Sun noon–4pm; mid-June to Aug Wed–Mon 11am–5pm; Sept–March Fri–Sun noon–4pm; $5; ☎360 385 5582) has exhibits on local seals and killer whales.

14

ARRIVAL AND INFORMATION

By ferry Although Port Townsend, 125 miles from Seattle, is easily accessed by road, you can also get there by Washington State Ferries from Coupeville (see p.933). The ferry terminal is just south of downtown, off Water St.

Visitor centre 440 12th St (Mon–Fri 9am–5pm, Sat 10am–4pm, Sun 11am–4pm; ☎360 385 2722, ⌂enjoypt.com).

ACCOMMODATION

Bishop Victorian 714 Washington St ☎360 385 6122, ⌂bishopvictorian.com. Built in 1890 by British sailor and builder William Bishop, this creaky old hotel with period rooms just off the main drag features breakfasts brought to rooms each morning and cable TV. **$140**

Manresa Castle Seventh and Sheridan sts ☎360 385 5750, ⌂manresacastle.com. Quasi-Prussian castle from 1892 (built by the town's first mayor, Charles Eisenbeis), with thirty rooms ranging from affordable cosy single units to swanky suites in the tower. **$109**

Old Consulate Inn 313 Walker St ☎360 385 6753, ⌂oldconsulate.com. Romantic B&B in the 1889 Hastings House, with spiky tower, wraparound veranda and seven plush suites (plus one rather tiny room). **$110**

Palace Hotel 1004 Water St ☎360 385 0773, ⌂palace hotelpt.com. This Richardson Romanesque charmer has seen better days (the 1889 property was an old rooming house), but still has antique decor, clawfoot tubs and excellent views of the Sound (the cheapest rooms have shared bathrooms). **$99**

EATING AND DRINKING

★ **Fountain Café** 920 Washington St ☎360 385 1364. Housed in a pretty clapboard building a short walk from the waterfront, this restaurant crafts high-quality seafood and pasta ($16–18), with specialities such as local pan-fried oysters ($14) and paella ($27). Mon–Thurs & Sun 11am–3pm & 5–9pm, Fri & Sat 11am–3pm & 5–9.30pm.

Port Townsend Brewing Co 330 10th St ☎360 385 9967, ⌂porttownsendbrewing.com. Local brewery with no-frills taproom and quirky little beer garden for live music and lounging – on the edge of the marina a mile or so south of downtown, this is where the locals hang out. Mon–Tues, Thurs, Sat & Sun noon–7pm, Wed noon–8pm, Fri noon–9pm.

Silverwater Café 237 Taylor St ☎360 385 6448, ⌂silverwatercafe.com. Gourmet restaurant serving fresh seafood such as salmon fillets ($24), hazelnut halibut ($28) and coriander (cilantro)-ginger-lime prawns ($22.50); also does the best local fish and chips ($13). Mon–Thurs 11.30am–2.30pm & 5–10pm, Fri & Sat 11.30am–11pm, Sun 10am–10pm.

Sirens 823 Water St (2/F) ☎360 385 1100, ⌂sirenspub .com. This gastropub is the most inviting place in town, with an outdoor terrace on the second floor, overlooking the water; local microbrews on tap ($4.50) and decent burgers ($12.50). Come for happy hour (daily 4–6pm; $1 off drinks). Daily noon–2am.

Port Angeles

Fifty miles west of Port Townsend, **PORT ANGELES** is the most popular point of entry into Olympic National Park, a few miles to the south. Its harbour is backed by soaring mountains, but there are few reasons to linger at this workaday stopover – other than

---

FESTIVE PORT TOWNSEND

Though bustling year-round, Port Townsend is busiest during its **summer festivals** – principally the **Festival of American Fiddle Tunes** held at Fort Worden State Park in early July, **Jazz Port Townsend** in late July (see ⌂centrum.org for information on both), and the **Wooden Boat Festival** in early September (☎360 385 4742, ⌂woodenboat.org).

14

BOATS TO CANADA

Black Ball Ferry Line (☎ 360 457 4491, ⓦ cohoferry.com) car ferries link Port Angeles with historic Victoria, Canada, 23 nautical miles across the Strait of Juan de Fuca (March–Dec 2–4 ferries daily; 90min trip; one-way fares $17 walk-on, $60.50/car and driver).

---

the town's having the peninsula's best transport links and the biggest choice of motels, supermarkets and cheap places to eat.

ARRIVAL AND INFORMATION   PORT ANGELES

By bus The Greyhound/Olympic Bus Lines depot (☎ 360 565 8015) is beside the waterfront at 111 E Front St. Destinations Port Townsend (2 daily; 25min); Seattle (2 daily; 2hr 50min–3hr 20min); Sea-Tac Airport (2 daily; 3hr 50min–4hr 15min).

Visitor centre 121 E Railroad St, beside the ferry terminal (Mon–Fri 9am–5pm; ☎ 360 452 2363, ⓦ portangeles .org).

ACCOMMODATION AND EATING

Domaine Madeleine 146 Wildflower Lane ☎ 360 457 4174, ⓦ domainemadeleine.com. B&B with a lovely five-acre garden and five art-themed rooms, which variously come with jetted tubs, fireplaces and balconies. **$195**

Michael's Seafood & Steakhouse 117 E 1st St ☎ 360 417 6929, ⓦ michaelsdining.com. The tasty, well-presented food at this moderate to expensive spot

features paella, oysters, pizza, pasta and especially steak (mains $18–30). Mon–Thurs & Sun 4–10pm, Fri & Sat 4–11pm.

Olympic Bagel Co 802 E 1st St ☎ 360 452 9100. Serves the town's best bagels (with ten flavours of cream cheese), coffee, home-made soups, omelettes and panini. Free wi-fi. Mon–Fri 6am–3pm, Sat & Sun 7am–3pm.

Olympic National Park

Magnificent **OLYMPIC NATIONAL PARK**, comprising the colossal Olympic Mountains in the heart of the peninsula plus a separate, isolated sixty-mile strip of Pacific coastline farther west, is one of Washington's prime wilderness destinations, with raging rivers, alpine meadows, sizeable tracts of moss-draped rainforest and boundless opportunities for spectacular hiking and wildlife watching. **Black-tailed deer** are fairly common and quite relaxed around people wielding cameras; black bears, Roosevelt elk and cougars are rarer to spot.

Around 95 percent of the park is designated wilderness and inaccessible by car; no roads go through the middle but instead enter the interior from its edge like spokes on a wheel. Get oriented and check latest conditions at the main visitor centre in Port Angeles (see p.941) before driving seventeen miles (one way) up to **Hurricane Ridge**, which at 5242ft affords mesmerizing views of the jagged peaks and sparkling mountain glaciers around **Mount Olympus** (7980ft), the park's highest point (its peak is only accessible to professional mountaineers).

Sol Duc Hot Springs and Lake Crescent

An essential park highlight is **Sol Duc Hot Springs**, some 36 miles (1hr drive) west of Port Angeles, where there is a tranquil resort (opposite), hiking trails up to the moss-covered rocks and gentle cascades of **Sol Duc Falls** and the **hot springs** themselves – three outdoor pools (and one unheated swimming pool) with mineral-rich waters bubbling up at 99 to 104°F (May–Oct daily 9am–9pm; $12 extra for day-visitors, free for resort guests). On the way to Sol Duc (20 miles from Port Angeles), US-101 skirts picturesque twelve-mile-long **Lake Crescent**, hemmed in by densely wooded mountains and another popular place to stay (see opposite). The lakeside and trails here, including the easy 1.8-mile round-trip hike to **Marymere Falls**, is the only section of the park accessible for free.

Coastal and Quinault sections

With more time you can explore the wild **beaches** of the Pacific coast section of the park, where black rocks jut out of the sea at **Rialto Beach** and appealing **Ruby Beach** is named for its red-and-black-pebbled sand. The far western portion of the park contains the **Hoh Rain Forest** (88 miles and a 2hr drive from Port Angeles), and **Quinault Rainforest**, the most beautiful of all the peninsula's rainforests, set around the shores of glacier-carved **Lake Quinault**, some 128 miles and more than three hours' drive from Port Angeles.

INFORMATION

OLYMPIC NATIONAL PARK

Entry Olympic National Park is open 24hr, although some roads, campgrounds and other visitor facilities close in winter. Seven-day park passes are $5 for individuals, or $15/car, payable at entry booths at the park boundaries.
Visitor centres The main centre, just outside Port Angeles at 3002 Mount Angeles Rd (hours vary, often daily

9am–4pm, summer till 6pm; ☎ 360 565 3100, ⊕ nps.gov /olym), has exhibits, useful trail maps and information on trail conditions. There are smaller visitor centres on Hurricane Ridge and at the Hoh Rain Forest. Note that it often rains in the park – there's even a fair amount of snow as late as June.

ACCOMMODATION AND EATING

Campgrounds The park has sixteen excellent NPS-operated campgrounds ($10–18; ☎ 360 565 3130, ⊕ recreation.gov); try Heart o' the Hills, 6 miles south of Port Angeles, along Hurricane Ridge Rd, or further west, Altair – though this is closed from mid-Sept to mid-May along with several others. From $10
Lake Crescent Lodge 416 Lake Crescent Rd ☎ 360 928 3211, ⊕ olympicnationalparks.com. Historic inn built in 1916, beautifully positioned amid dense forest on the lake's south shore, offering simple rooms (no TVs, phones or wi-fi) and elegant cottages in the surrounding woods. Excellent on-site restaurant. Open May–Dec. $160
★ **Lake Quinault Lodge** 345 South Shore Rd ☎ 360

288 2900, ⊕ olympicnationalparks.com. Charming 1926 lodge perched on the shores of Lake Quinault, offering rooms with fireplaces or lakeside views (no phones, but TVs and free wi-fi), and an on-site pool and sauna. $125
Sol Duc Hot Springs Resort 12076 Sol Duc Hot Springs Rd ☎ 866 476 5382, ⊕ olympicnationalparks.com. Set deep in the park 12 miles off US-101, this resort sports 26 comfy wooden cabins with bathrooms (no TV, phone signal or wi-fi), and pricier three-bedroom suites with kitchens. The resort provides free guest access to the hot springs (opposite) and there's the high-quality *Spring Restaurant* on site (daily in season 7.30–10pm & 5.30–10pm; dinner mains $16–32). Open March–Oct. $140

The southwest coast

Heading south on US 101 from Lake Quinault, leaving the national park and Olympic Peninsula, it's about forty hilly miles to industrial **Aberdeen** (where Kurt Cobain and other Nirvana band members grew up), from where there's a choice of routes: US-12/Hwy-8 lead east towards Olympia (see p.939), while US-101 pushes south over the hills, threading along the shore of muddy Willapa Bay and the **southwest coast** of Washington. The bay is home to the 15,000-acre **Willapa National Wildlife Refuge** (daily sunset–sunrise; free; ☎ 360 484 3482, ⊕ fws.gov/willapa), whose various dunes, forests, marshes and mudflats shelter some two hundred species of migrating shorebirds.

Long Beach Peninsula

Seven miles southwest of Willapa National Wildlife Refuge, the **Long Beach Peninsula** is something of a low-rent resort area, but merits a trip to the northern tip, where the ghost town of **OYSTERVILLE** is a forested collection of rusting old buildings. This is the home of **Oysterville Sea Farms** (Mon–Tues & Fri–Sun 9.30am–5pm; ☎ 360 665 6585, ⊕ willabay.com), recognizable by its piles of discarded shells and renowned for its fresh clams and smoked oysters. Also tasty is the **Pacific Coast Cranberry Museum**, 2907 Pioneer Rd in the town of Long Beach (April to mid-Dec 10am–5pm; free; ☎ 360 642 5553, ⊕ cranberrymuseum.com), where you can wander through a cranberry bog and purchase berry-flavoured treats.

Cape Disappointment State Park

Hwy-100, Ilwaco · Daily 6.30am–sunset · $10/vehicle · ☎ 360 642 3078, ⊕ parks.wa.gov

Down at the far southwestern tip of Washington, near the mouth of the Columbia River on a craggy headland, lies scenic **Cape Disappointment State Park**. Take in the weathered (but still functional) 1898 **North Head Lighthouse** (May–Sept daily noon–4pm; tours $2.50) or visit the **Lewis and Clark Interpretive Center** (March–Nov daily 10am–5pm; Dec–Feb closed Mon & Tues; $5), which recounts the whole history of the celebrated 1804–06 expedition but especially the hazards of navigating the Columbia River and the bleak winter the party spent near here in 1805. Fortunately, you'll be spared such difficulties as you travel south on US-101 over the sweeping 1966 span of the **Astoria–Megler Bridge**, crossing the state boundary into Oregon (see p.960).

14

ACCOMMODATION	THE SOUTHWEST COAST

Cape Disappointment State Park Hwy-100, Ilwaco ☎ 888 226 7688. Accommodation in the park ranges from a variety of campgrounds, some with electricity and water, to fourteen yurts within walking distance of the beach, each furnished with bunk beds that sleep three, and a heater. There are also three rustic cabins on the shore of Lake O'Neil. Camping from $12, cabins $74

The North Cascades and the Cascade Loop

The central part of Washington State is dominated by the mighty Cascade ranges, best experienced from the **Cascade Loop Scenic Highway** (☎ 509 662 3888, ⓦ cascadeloop.com), an entrancing four-hundred-mile route through the mountains – though the full trip is only feasible during the summer, since at other times snow closes the mountain passes.

The loop begins on Hwy-20 (aka the North Cascades Highway), which runs east from I-5 at Burlington for sixty miles up the Skagit River Valley into the majestic peaks of **North Cascades National Park** (☎ 360 854 7200, ⓦ nps.gov/noca). Ask about current road and **hiking trail** conditions at the visitor centre in tiny **Newhalem**, Hwy-20, milepost 120 (daily: July–Aug 9am–6pm; May, June, Sept & Oct 9am–5pm ☎ 206 386 4495). Beyond the high passes of the national park, Hwy-20 runs thirty miles down the Methow Valley into the dry, rolling hills of central Washington and one-street **WINTHROP**, an old mining town officially founded in 1891 and now forever decked out solely in Wild West buildings thanks to a local ordinance.

The fetching resort of **CHELAN**, sixty miles south of Winthrop, nestles at the foot of **Lake Chelan**, whose glacially deep waters fill a glacially carved trough nestled in the mountains. At the Chelan end the vegetation and low-lying hills are arid and

---

LAKE CHELAN AND STEHEKIN

To appreciate the size and beauty of **Lake Chelan** you'll need to take the **ferry service** that shoots fifty miles all the way to the head of the lake at **STEHEKIN**, a tiny, former mining port and isolated village otherwise accessible only by seaplane. As you cruise north the mountains get bigger and the vegetation changes back from desert to alpine. Most visitors, just come for the day, with a couple of hours to look around before the ferry heads back; you can visit **Rainbow Falls**, a spectacular 312ft plume of water three miles from the dock (45min bus tours meet the ferries and charge $8), though it's only at full force in the spring. There's also the **House That Jack Built** craft shop, a fixture near the dock since 1977 (daily 10.30am–2.30pm), and the visitor centre (hours vary, summer daily 8.30am–5pm; ☎ 360 854 7365, ⓦ stehekin.com).

ARRIVAL AND DEPARTURE

By ferry The Lake Chelan Boat Company, 1418 W Woodin Ave in Chelan (☎ 509 682 4584, ⓦ ladyofthe lake.com), runs the passenger-ferry service to Stehekin from the jetty a mile west of town (May to mid-Oct daily 8.30am; 90min in Stehekin; departs 2pm to arrive in Chelan 6pm; $24 one-way, $40.50 return). A faster boat (mid-June to mid-Sept daily 8.30am; arrives 11am, 1hr layover; departs noon; $3 one-way, $61 return) reaches Stehekin in half the time. Combo day trips mean departing on the express and leaving on the slower boat, giving you 3hr in Stehekin.

By seaplane Chelan Seaplanes ($89 one-way, $178 return; ☎ 509 682 5555, ⓦ chelanseaplanes.com) flies between Lake Chelan and Stehekin daily (30min).

desert-like, and the hotels and small beaches along the lake are hot in summer, making this prime holiday territory.

ACCOMMODATION AND EATING   THE NORTH CASCADES AND THE CASCADE LOOP

★ **Campbell's Resort** 104 W Woodin Ave, Chelan 509 682 2561, campbellsresort.com. The grande dame of Lake Chelan resorts since 1901 dominates the lakefront in the heart of town, with spacious suites and rooms facing the water, hot tubs, pools, beach access and all modern amenities. The *Pub & Veranda* (daily 7am–11pm) serves excellent seafood from Seattle and local beers and produce (lamb burger $14, prawn buckets $21. **$257**

North Cascades Mountain Hostel 209 Castle Ave,

Winthrop 509 699 0568, northcascadesmountain hostel.com. Clean, modern hostel offering dorms, communal kitchen and bathrooms, laundry, free wi-fi and use of hostel bikes. **$25**

Old Schoolhouse Brewery 155 Riverside Ave, Winthrop 509 996 3183, oldschoolhousebrewery.com. Grab a local microbrew and take in the scene from the deck of this excellent pub; tasty snacks include the trout spinach dip. Mon–Thurs & Sun noon–9pm, Fri & Sat noon–10pm.

Leavenworth

Forty miles south of Chelan, the Cascade Loop turns west along US-2 just north of the apple-producing town of Wenatchee and winds its way 22 miles to pocket-sized **LEAVENWORTH**. Founded in the 1860s as a mining supply town, in 1965, after thirty years of depression, Leavenworth voted to "go alpine" to boost tourism. Today it sports a cutesy **Bavarian** theme that just about works, buildings decked out in high gables and half-timbered woodwork. The town is a fun place to eat, and is also a good base for taking in the outdoor activities in the spectacular mountain surroundings.

INFORMATION AND TOURS   LEAVENWORTH

Visitor centre 940 US-2 (Mon–Fri 9am–5pm; 509 548 5807, leavenworth.org).

Tours and activities River Rider, 10860 US-2, at milepost 102 (206 448 7238, riverrider.com) is a dependable

outfit offering tubing on the Wenatchee River ($20/person) and kayaking and rafting excursions ($55–75) on a range of Cascade rivers.

ACCOMMODATION AND EATING

★ **Andreas Keller** 829 Front St 509 548 6000, andreaskellerrestaurant.com. Top-notch restaurant doling out hefty helpings of hearty German cuisine such as pickled herring, schnitzel and spaetzle. Mon–Thurs & Sun 11.30am–9pm, Fri & Sat 11.30am–10pm.

Enzian Inn 590 US-2 509 548 5269, enzianinn .com. The rooms at this stylish hotel feature hand-carved Austrian furnishings and come with the dubious pleasure of being serenaded by an actual alphorn at the free breakfast buffets. **$120**

Hotel Pension Anna 926 Commercial St 509 548 6273, pensionanna.com. Another Austrian-style B&B, rooms decked out in cheerful Teutonic kitsch, with suites containing fireplaces and jacuzzis. **$160**

Icicle Brewing Co 935 Front St 509 548 2739, iciclebrewing.com. The local microbrewery offers fine German-style ales and Hefeweizen (wheat beer) and bar food such as ploughman's platter and turkey sandwiches. Mon–Fri noon–11pm, Sat & Sun 11am–11pm.

Snoqualmie Falls

6501 Railroad Ave SE (Hwy-202) • Daily sunrise–sunset • Free • snoqualmiefalls.com

West of Leavenworth, US-2 crosses the mountains over Stevens Pass, but the principal east–west highway, I-90, lies further south, connecting Seattle with the Yakima Valley. Just three miles north of I-90 exit 25 is the strikingly beautiful, 270ft-tall torrent of **Snoqualmie Falls**, and behind it the luxurious *Salish Lodge* (salishlodge.com), built in 1919 but best known as posing as the *Great Northern Hotel* in the David Lynch cult TV series *Twin Peaks* in the early 1990s.

Mount Rainier National Park

Set in its own national park, glacier-clad **MOUNT RAINIER** (14,410ft) is the highest peak in the Cascades (the seventh highest in the USA), and a major Washington landmark.

Not until June does the snow melt enough for roads to open, and then the deer and mountain goats appear, dazzling wild flowers illuminate the alpine meadows and the mountain makes for some perfect hiking.

If you only have a day to explore, visit the south and east sides, entering on Hwy-706 at the Nisqually entrance and stopping at **Longmire** eight miles further on, site of the area's first resort in the 1880s and a small **museum** (daily: May & June 9am–4.30pm; July & Aug 9am–5pm; free; ☎360 569 6571). Nine miles from here is stunning **Narada Falls**, a 168ft plunge of water right next to the road, before the last two miles of highway rises to the main visitor centre at **Paradise** (see below). Note that **climbing** Mount Rainier peak itself is extremely hazardous and should only be undertaken by experienced climbers (permits $44).

ARRIVAL AND INFORMATION | MOUNT RAINIER NATIONAL PARK

By car The park is some 60 miles southeast of Tacoma by way of Hwy-7 and a transfer onto minor Hwy-706.

Entrances The park has four entrances: Nisqually in the southwest corner, Stephen's Canyon in the southeast, White River in the northeast and Carbon River in the northwest. Only the Nisqually entrance is open year-round (for cross-country skiing); the others open June–Sept.

Admission $15/vehicle or $5/pedestrian, for a one-week pass.

Visitor centres For map and trail conditions, stop by the visitor centres at Longmire (see above), Sunrise (July & Aug daily 10am–6pm) and, the most useful, Paradise (daily: early May to mid-June 10am–5pm; mid-June to Aug 10am–7pm; ☎360 569 6571, ⊚nps.gov/mora). The smaller Wilderness & Climbing Information Centers are usually open longer hours: Paradise (Mid-May to Sept Mon–Thurs & Sun 6am–3pm, Fri & Sat 6am–5pm; ☎360 569 6641) and White River (late May to Aug Mon–Thurs & Sun 7.30am–5pm, Fri 7am–7pm, Sat 7am–5pm; ☎360 569 6670).

ACCOMMODATION AND EATING

★ **Mounthaven** 38210 Hwy-706, Ashford ☎360 569 2594, ⊚mounthaven.com. Just 5 miles outside the park, this rustic resort has nine cabins, most with fireplaces, kitchenettes, fridges, wood stoves and porches. No TVs or mobile phone coverage, but free wi-fi available. **$120**

National Park Inn Longmire ☎360 569 2275, ⊚mtrainierguestservices.com. This classic timber lodge inside the park is open year-round with 25 cosy rooms, a restaurant and plenty of chairs on the veranda to lounge on. No TVs, wi-fi or mobile phone reception. **$116**

Paradise Inn Paradise Valley Rd S ☎360 569 2275, ⊚mtrainierguestservices.com. Staying in this gorgeous 1916 rustic lodge near the peak (at 5420ft) is an experience in itself, especially when snow still blankets the surrounding forests and wood fires glow in the magnificent cedar lobby. Rooms are old and small and there are no TVs, phones or wi-fi, but the food in the restaurant is excellent (there's also a small café). Make reservations well in advance. Open late May to early Oct. **$115**

Mount St Helens

The looming volcanic mound of **MOUNT ST HELENS** erupted on May 18, 1980, its blast wave flattening 230 square miles of surrounding forests, creating a massive mudflow that sent an avalanche of debris down the river valleys and killed 57 people. Since then, the forests and animals have re-emerged through the scarred landscape (despite minor eruptions in 2004 and 2005), with the surrounding privately managed forests especially well recovered. The mountain itself is protected within **Mount St Helens National Volcanic Monument**, managed by the Forestry Service, and accessed via three entry routes (though the peak itself is not accessible by car).

Spirit Lake Memorial Highway (Hwy-504)

First-time visitors should approach Mount St Helens along **Spirit Lake Memorial Highway** (Hwy-504), off I-5 roughly halfway between Olympia and Portland. The road snakes through dark green forests for 52 miles from Castle Rock to Johnson Ridge (4200ft), though the 1980 post-blast moonscape is largely gone; only the barren Toutle River valley and tree stumps overgrown by grass speak to its violent

> ## CLIMBING MOUNT ST HELENS
> Mountain **permits** are required for those interested in **climbing** above 4800ft anywhere in Mount St Helens National Volcanic Monument. From April to October, the time you'll most likely want to make the effort, only one hundred permits per day are given out, a fee is charged ($22), and you must reserve your permit ahead of time online at ⓦ mshinstitute.org, which also arranges guided climbs ($175). Most reasonably fit people can make the ascent (the height gain is 4500ft in 5 miles), with round-trips completed within 7–12 hours.

14

past. Start at the **Mount St Helens Visitor Center** (below), five miles from the interstate in Silver Lake, which has a big exhibit on the history of the explosion and the region. From here it's 22 miles to the smaller **Hoffstadt Bluffs Visitor Center** (daily 10am–4pm; free; ⓦhoffstadtbluffs.com) at 1400ft, which contains a restaurant, gift shop and an exhibit on the old Spirit Lake resort, destroyed by the 1980 eruption. The devastation of local forests and their subsequent recovery is the focus at the **Forest Learning Center** (mid-May to Sept daily 10am–4pm; free; ☎360 274 7750), six miles further up (at 2650ft) with enlightening exhibits on the replanting work conducted by Weyerhaeuser in the 1980s – some trees will be ready to harvest in the 2020s. Outside you can sometimes see elk herds down on the river plain. From here it's another ten miles to beautiful Clearwater Lake and a final nine-mile climb to the **Johnson Ridge Observatory** (mid-May to Oct daily 10am–6pm; $8; ☎360 274 2140), which focuses on the eruption itself via an excellent film and exhibits, backed by jaw-dropping views of the still-steaming lava dome (presuming the weather cooperates; prepare for disappointment).

Mount St Helens: southside and eastside
You can also visit the south and east sides of the mountain via forest roads 83 and 99 (open late June to Oct) respectively, featuring Lava Canyon and the nearby Ape Cave lava tubes, views of Spirit Lake as well as ashen lahars and **Windy Ridge** (4170ft) on the northeast side (2hr from Lava Canyon), where entire slopes are still denuded of foliage, and colossal tree husks lie scattered like twigs. Note that driving from Johnston Ridge to Lava Canyon takes around three hours (4hr to Windy Ridge).

ARRIVAL AND INFORMATION   MOUNT ST HELENS

Entry passes Driving the Spirit Lake Hwy is free, though some of the visitor centres require admission (see above) and you'll need to buy a one-day Monument Pass ($8) to hike the trails around Coldwater Lake and the Johnston Ridge Observatory; for the south and east side of the mountain you'll need a National Forest Recreation Pass ($5/day), available by putting money in drop boxes at site car parks.

Visitor centre Hwy-504, 5-mile marker (mid-May to mid-Sept daily 9am–5pm; call ahead for winter hours; exhibits $5; ☎360 274 0962, ⓦmountsthelens.com). See also ⓦfs.usda.gov/mountsthelens.

ACCOMMODATION

Eco Park Resort 14000 Spirit Lake Hwy ☎360 274 7007, ⓦecoparkresort.com. Rustic resort on the western side of Mount St Helens, with cosy two- and four-person timber cabins (shared bathrooms), as well as cheaper yurts and tent sites. Limited mobile phone coverage, no TVs or wi-fi. Tents **$20**, yurts **$75**, cabins **$100**

Lone Fir Resort 16806 Lewis River Rd, Cougar ☎360 238 5210, ⓦlonefirresort.com. Very convenient to the south side of Mount St Helens, with spacious but ageing rooms with microwaves and fridges. No phones or mobile phone service, but they do have free wi-fi. **$75**

Spokane
Arid eastern Washington offers little in the way of major attractions, though you might want to break the long, dreary journey on I-90 at **SPOKANE** ("spo-CAN"), the region's only real city of any size, just a few miles from the Idaho border. The city's

14

GRAND COULEE DAM

Eighty miles west of Spokane, the immense **Grand Coulee Dam** is the country's largest concrete structure. Constructed between 1933 and 1942 on the Columbia River, the dam was one of the cornerstones of FDR's New Deal, and remains one of the world's top generators of hydroelectricity. Heroic tales of power production are detailed in the **visitor centre**, on Hwy-155 on the west side of the dam (daily: June & July 8.30am–11pm; Aug 8.30am–10.30pm; Sept 8.30am–9.30pm; Oct–May 9am–5pm; free; ☎ 509 633 9265, ⓦ usbr.gov/pn/grandcoulee), which also runs free 50min tours (April–Oct daily) of the dam and one of its massive generating plants.

---

family-friendly hub, hundred-acre **Riverfront Park**, was the site of the 1974 World's Fair and sprawls over two islands in the middle of the Spokane River, which tumbles down the rocky shelves of **Spokane Falls**. The park attractions (hours vary, often Mon–Fri 11am–6pm, Sat & Sun until 8pm; day passes $20; ⓦspokaneriverfrontpark.com) include an IMAX Theatre ($8.50), ice-skating rink (Oct–March; $4.50), carousel ($2) and the **Spokane Falls SkyRide** ($7.75), a cable car that rises above the falls to take in a commanding view of the area.

The city was established in the 1870s, and most of the relics of Spokane's early grandeur can be found several blocks southwest of Riverfront Park on West Riverside Avenue, where Neoclassical facades cluster around Jefferson Street. The **Northwest Museum of Art and Culture**, 2316 W 1st Ave (Wed–Sun 10am–6pm; $7; ☎ 509 456 3931, ⓦnorthwestmuseum.org), focuses on regional history and artwork, Native American culture and fine arts from WPA-era paintings to items from nineteenth-century Japan and seventeenth-century Holland. Make sure to drop by the adjacent **Campbell House** (tours on the hour Wed–Sun noon–3pm; free with museum admission), a Tudor Revival confection dreamed up for a silver baron in 1898.

ARRIVAL AND INFORMATION   SPOKANE

By bus and train Greyhound and Amtrak share the transit centre at 221 W First St.
Destinations (bus) Boise (1 daily; 10hr 15min); Coeur d'Alene (3 daily; 40–45min); Portland (1 daily; 6hr 35min); Seattle (4 daily; 5hr 30min–7hr 45min).

Destinations (train) Portland (1 daily; 7hr 25min); Sandpoint (2 daily; 1hr 5min); Seattle (1 daily; 8hr 10min); West Glacier (2 daily; 5hr 46min).
Visitor centre 201 W Main Ave (Mon–Fri 9am–5pm, also summer Sat & Sun; ☎ 509 747 3230, ⓦ visitspokane.com).

ACCOMMODATION AND EATING

★ **Davenport Hotel** 10 S Post St ☎ 509 455 8888, ⓦ davenporthotelcollection.com. A stately 1914 treasure with a wildly ornate lobby and spacious, well-designed suites. **$120**

★ **Frank's Diner** 1516 West 2nd Ave ☎ 509 747 8798, ⓦ franksdiners.com. Classic diner in an old train carriage dating back to 1906 (it was turned into a diner in 1931); superb, filling breakfasts ($5–12), cramped booths and no-nonsense waitresses. Daily 6am–9pm.

Hotel Lusso N One Post St ☎ 509 747 9750, ⓦ davenport hotelcollection.com. Stylish hotel whose spacious, well-appointed rooms have HDTVs, just two blocks from Riverfront Park. No breakfast. **$120**

Milford's Fish House 719 N Monroe St ☎ 509 326 7251, ⓦ milfordsfishhouse.com. Serves chic seafood such as pan-fried oysters, lobster tail, Thai catfish and Manila clams (most dishes $25–29). Mon & Sun 4–9pm, Tues–Sat 5–10pm.

Oregon

For nineteenth-century pioneers on the arduous Oregon Trail, the rich and fertile **Willamette Valley** was the promised land of OREGON, and it's still the heart of the state's social, political and cultural life. **Portland**, the biggest city, is alternative, creative and one of the coolest cities in the USA right now; **Salem**, the state capital, maintains a small-town air; and **Eugene** is a lively, outdoorsy college community.

East of Portland, waterfalls cascade down mossy cliffs along the **beautiful Columbia River Gorge**, south of which looms the imposing silhouette of **Mount Hood**. Central Oregon is based around the popular recreation hub of **Bend**, while further south the liberal hamlet of **Ashland** offers a splash of culture with its annual Shakespeare Festival. The **Oregon coast**'s most northerly town, **Astoria**, enjoys a magnificent setting strewn with imposing Victorian homes, while farther south, wide expanses of pristine sand are broken by jagged black monoliths and pale lighthouses look out from stark headlands over sheltered coves. Finally, the rugged deserts and lava fields of **Eastern Oregon** are much more remote, and some small towns still celebrate their cowboy roots with annual rodeos.

14

Portland

Long overshadowed by West Coast hot spots San Francisco and Seattle, eco-friendly, organic **PORTLAND** is increasingly matching its rivals in the hipster cool stakes, with booming arts, culinary, coffee and microbrew scenes, an inexplicably large number of indie cinemas serving beer and an alternative, outdoorsy culture lampooned in cult US TV show *Portlandia*. Celebrated local writer **Chuck Palahniuk**, who started his career here, describes the city in his travelog *Fugitives and Refugees*; while there are no major show-stoppers, its eccentric characters, cafés and markets, leafy parks and eclectic neighbourhoods make it the most enticing destination in the state. The city is famous for its **bicycling** culture, and visit in June and you'll see why it's also known as the "**City of Roses**", with public gardens overflowing with blooms. The **Willamette** (pronounced "wuh-LAM-it") **River** bisects Portland into its east and west sides, with the **downtown core** between the river's west bank and the I-405 freeway, but to really get to grips with the city you'll need to sample the **neighbourhoods**.

The city was actually named after Portland, Maine, following a coin toss between its two East Coast founders in 1845 ("Boston" was the other option). Today Portland is booming, with the likes of Nike and Columbia Sportswear based here, Intel a major employer and Adidas making the city its North American headquarters. That's not to say things are perfect; as you'll soon realize, Portland has a major homeless problem, with some estimates claiming up to two thousand minors on the streets at any one time.

Pioneer Courthouse Square

Named after the adjacent **Pioneer Courthouse**, a Neoclassical 1868 structure that still maintains its judicial function, **Pioneer Courthouse Square** is the indisputable centre of Portland. Surrounded by **downtown**'s historic white terracotta buildings, the square's curving brick terraces are regularly filled with music and people – the information centre is also here (see p.953).

KOOKY CITY – PORTLAND'S HIDDEN GEMS

Darcelle XV Showplace 208 NW Third Ave (⊛darcellexv.com). Portland's last true classic burlesque/drag show, established 1967.

Hippo Hardware 1040 E Burnside (⊛hippohardware.com). An institution since 1976, a fancy junk store with a focus on salvaged architecture from the 1850s to 1960s.

Kidd's Toy Museum 1300 SE Grand Ave (⊛kiddstoymuseum.com). Antique toys from 1869 to 1939, the eccentric collection of one Frank Kidd.

Mill Ends Park Middle strip of SW Naito Pkwy, at Taylor St. Officially the smallest park in the world, the size of a large dinner plate.

Rocky Horror Picture Show Clinton Street Theater, 2522 SE Clinton St. This movie has been showing every Saturday night here, at midnight, since 1978; it's an "interactive" presentation, so be warned. Entry $6.

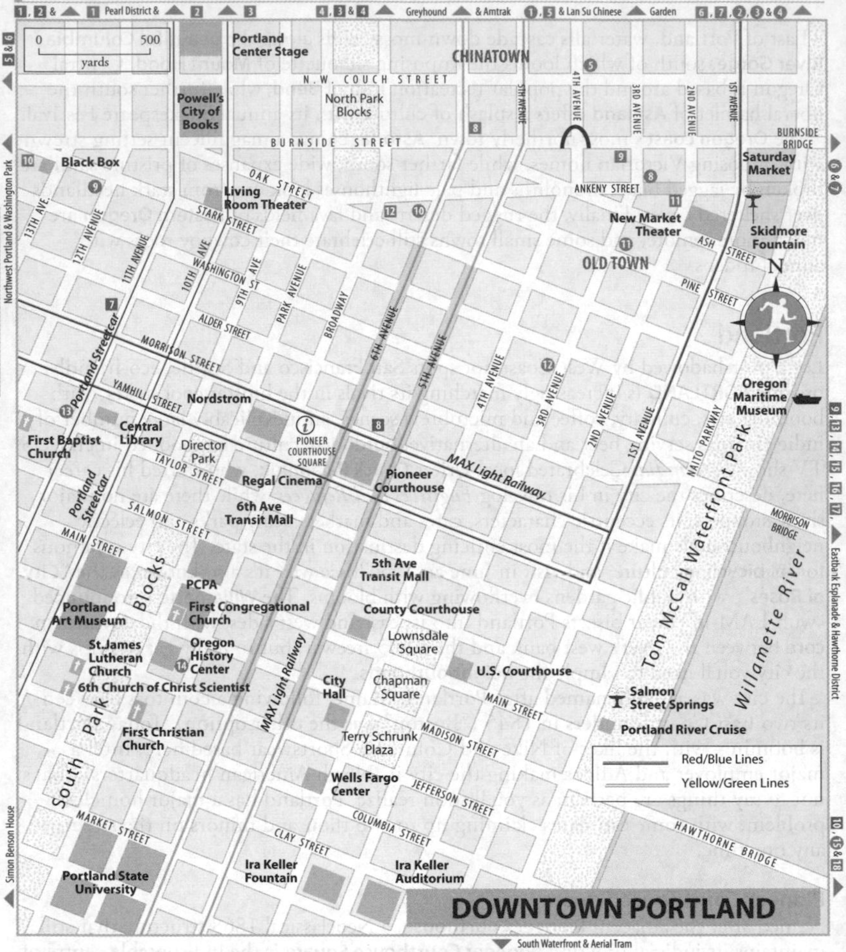

Pearl District &
Greyhound
& Amtrak
& Lan Su Chinese
Garden
0
500
yards
Portland Center Stage
CHINATOWN
N.W. COUCH STREET
Powell's City of Books
North Park Blocks
5TH AVENUE
4TH AVENUE
3RD AVENUE
2ND AVENUE
1ST AVENUE
BURNSIDE STREET
BURNSIDE BRIDGE
Black Box
Saturday Market
OAK STREET
ANKENY STREET
Living Room Theater
STARK STREET
New Market Theater
Skidmore Fountain
13TH AVE.
12TH AVENUE
11TH AVENUE
10TH AVE
WASHINGTON ST
9TH AVE
PARK AVENUE
BROADWAY
6TH AVENUE
5TH AVENUE
ASH STREET
OLD TOWN
PINE STREET
N
ALDER STREET
MORRISON STREET
Portland Streetcar
YAMHILL STREET
Nordstrom
Oregon Maritime Museum
Central Library
First Baptist Church
Director Park
PIONEER COURTHOUSE SQUARE
TAYLOR STREET
Regal Cinema
Pioneer Courthouse
MAX Light Railway
NAITO PARKWAY
Tom McCall Waterfront Park
Portland Streetcar
6th Ave Transit Mall
SALMON STREET
MORRISON BRIDGE
MAIN STREET
5th Ave Transit Mall
PCPA
Park Blocks
Portland Art Museum
First Congregational Church
County Courthouse
St.James Lutheran Church
Oregon History Center
Lownsdale Square
U.S. Courthouse
6th Church of Christ Scientist
City Hall
Chapman Square
MAIN STREET
Willamette River
Salmon Street Springs
MAX Light Railway
First Christian Church
South Park
MADISON STREET
Terry Schrunk Plaza
Portland River Cruise
Red/Blue Lines
Yellow/Green Lines
Wells Fargo Center
JEFFERSON STREET
MARKET STREET
COLUMBIA STREET
HAWTHORNE BRIDGE
CLAY STREET
Ira Keller Fountain
Ira Keller Auditorium
Portland State University
DOWNTOWN PORTLAND
Northwest Portland & Washington Park
Simon Benson House
Eastbank Esplanade & Hawthorne District
South Waterfront & Aerial Tram

ACCOMMODATION
- Edgefield 9
- Governor 7
- Heron Haus 6
- HI-Portland Hawthorne 10
- HI-Portland Northwest 1
- Hotel deLuxe 5
- Inn at Northrup Station 2
- Kennedy School 3
- The Nines 8
- White Eagle 4

RESTAURANTS & CAFÉS
- Beast 2
- Bunk Sandwiches 10
- Higgins 14
- Huber's Café 12
- Jake's Famous Crawfish 9
- Leo's Coffee Shop 13
- Le Pigeon 6
- Noble Rot 7
- Old Town Pizza 1
- Pine State Biscuits 3
- Ping 5
- Podnah's Pit 4
- Pok Pok 15
- Stumptown Roasters 11
- Voodoo Doughnut 8

BARS, CLUBS & LIVE MUSIC VENUES
- Bridgeport Brewing 1
- Cascade Brewing Barrel House 16
- Crystal Ballroom 10
- Dan & Louis Oyster Bar 11
- Dante's 9
- Deschutes Brewery 2
- Dot's Café 18
- Gasthaus Pub 5
- Gilt Club 4
- Goodfoot 15
- Hair of the Dog Brewing Co 17
- Holocene 13
- Jimmy Mak's 3
- Pied Cow 14
- Roseland Theater 8
- Saucebox 12
- Upright Brewery 6
- Wonder Ballroom 7

Portland Art Museum

1219 SW Park Ave • Tues, Wed & Sat 10am–5pm, Thurs & Fri 10am–8pm, Sun noon–5pm • $15 • ⓣ 503 226 2811, ⓦ portlandartmuseum.org

With a huge collection spanning two buildings, the **Portland Art Museum** is a vast trove of international artwork, with the main building displaying a wide-ranging selection of Northwest Native American artefacts, Japanese silk screens and ancient Chinese earthenware. On the second floor, the **American Art** collection includes a room dedicated to the early Modernism of **C.S. Price**, who moved to Portland in 1929, a gallery of Mount Hood landscapes and work from American Impressionists Childe Hassam and J. Alden Weir. There's also one of Rembrandt Peale's "porthole portraits" of George Washington. The **European Art** collection is dominated by a rather unfashionable ensemble of Baroque pieces, Italian Mannerism and French Rococo work from the likes of Boucher and Fragonard, but there is a small *Joan of Arc* by Millais and a Van Dyck portrait of *Cardinal Rivarola*.

In the adjacent **Mark Building**, reached via an underground passage, the focus is mostly on Modernist and contemporary art. There's a provocative gallery of work by Dutch artist **Folkert de Jong** (including the gruesome *Operation Harmony*), pieces by Rothko and Pollock and couple of iconic Jean-Michel Basquiat scribbles, while the usual crowd-pleasers can be found in the **Impressionist** section; Degas, Monet (with one of his ubiquitous *Water Lilies*), Renoir and Cezanne are all well represented, and there's an intriguing Van Gogh, *Charette de Boeuf*.

14

Oregon History Museum

1200 SW Park Ave • Mon–Sat 10am–5pm, Sun noon–5pm • $11 • ☎ 503 222 1741, ⓦ ohs.org

Facing the art museum on the other side of the South Park Blocks and decorated with huge trompe l'oeil pioneer murals, the **Oregon History Museum** presents imaginative exhibits exploring different facets of the state's history. The "Oregon My Oregon" galleries upstairs takes a chronological approach, beginning with the region's Native American peoples, while "Oregon Voices" is more thematic, tackling issues such as homelessness in Portland and the Green movement from 1950 to the present.

Old Town

Old Town, the area around and just south of the **Burnside Bridge**, is where Portland was founded in 1843, and where legend has it hapless drunks were once regularly kidnapped, or "shanghaiied", to be indentured servants on Asia-bound ships via underground tunnels. These days, missions for the homeless coexist with galleries, brewpubs, boutiques and, especially, clubs. The **Weekend Market** (March–Dec Sat 10am–5pm, Sun 11am–4.30pm; ⓦ portlandsaturdaymarket.com) packs the area with arts and crafts stalls, eclectic street musicians, spicy foods and lively crowds.

Chinatown

North of Burnside, the ornamental gate at Fourth Avenue marks **Chinatown**, the second largest Chinese community in the USA until the 1880s, when racist attacks forced most to leave. There's still enough of a community here to support a range of cheap ethnic restaurants and the enticing **Lan Su Chinese Garden**, 239 NW Everett St at NW 3rd (daily: April–Oct 10am–6pm; Nov–March 10am–5pm; $9.50; ⓦ lansugarden .org), a large Suzhou-style garden completed by Chinese craftsmen in 2000, with traditional vegetation, ponds and walkways (Suzhou is one of Portland's sister cities).

Washington Park

SW Park Place • Daily 5am–10pm • Free • ☎ 503 823 252, ⓦ washingtonparkpdx.org

Three miles southwest of downtown, the 160-acre **Washington Park** is home to a number of family-friendly attractions. These include the lovely **International Rose Test Garden** (daily 7.30am–9pm; free), featuring a huge array of bright

---

CITY OF BOOKS

On the northern edge of downtown is one of Portland's biggest draws, the famed **Powell's City of Books**, 1005 W Burnside St (daily 9am–11pm; ⓦ powells.com). With more than a million new, used and rare books on four floors, Powell's occupies an entire block, as well as separate branches around town, and provides free colour-coded maps so customers don't get lost.

14

PORTLAND BY CABLE CAR

The sleek **Portland Aerial Tram** (mid-May to mid-Sept Mon–Fri 5.30am–9.30pm, Sat 9am–5pm; Sun 1–5pm, every 6min; $4 return; ⓦgobytram.com) connects the South Waterfront terminal at 3303 SW Bond Ave (downtown) with the upper terminal at Kohler Pavilion on Oregon Health & Science University's main campus, 500ft up the hillside – it's a three-minute ride that's perfect for viewing Portland, and on a clear day, Mount Hood.

early-summer blooms; the tranquil **Japanese Garden** (Mon noon–7pm, Sun & Tues–Fri 9am–7pm, Sat 9am–9pm; $9.50; ☎503 223 1321, ⓦjapanesegarden.com), actually a collection of five traditional gardens with ponds, bridges, foliage and sand designs; and the **Oregon Zoo** (daily: May–Sept 9am–6pm; Oct–April 9am–4pm; $11.50; ⓦoregonzoo.org), with the requisite primates, penguins and, especially, elephants ever since "Packy" was born here in 1962 (he's currently the oldest male Asian elephant in North America).

The Eastside

Since the end of the nineteenth century, most of Portland's population has lived on the **Eastside**. Perhaps the best reason to venture across the river is to walk or bike the three-mile loop of the **Eastbank Esplanade**, which connects from the Hawthorne to the Steel bridges on floating walkways and cantilevered footpaths, offering striking views of downtown. Near the loop's south end in what's known as **Central Eastside**, the interactive exhibits, planetarium, IMAX and high-tech toys of the **Oregon Museum of Science and Industry (OMSI)**, 1945 SE Water Ave (Mon–Thurs & Sun 9.30am–7pm, Fri & Sat 9.30am–9pm; reduced hours in winter; $13, kids 3–13 $9.50; ⓦomsi.edu), are bright and kinetic, though primarily geared toward children and adults with only a sketchy knowledge of science. Otherwise the coolest thing on display here is the **USS Blueback**, the US Navy's last non-nuclear submarine, used in the movie *Hunt for Red October* (1990). Tech geeks will love the special two-hour guided tours by actual submarine veterans (extra $15). Two miles east from the river, the **Hawthorne District** is Portland's free-spirited hub of counterculture, sprinkled with Victorian and Arts and Crafts bungalows and quirky places to eat and drink.

ARRIVAL AND DEPARTURE   PORTLAND

By plane Portland International Airport (PDX; ⓦpdx .com) is 13 miles northeast of downtown, accessed at Terminal C by the MAX Red Line light rail (every 5–20min, 5am–midnight; $2.50), which shuttles passengers on a 40min trip downtown. A cab from the airport to downtown will cost around $40–45 (trips go by the meter).

By bus Greyhound buses stop at 550 NW 6th Ave (☎503 243 2361), near the train station.

Destinations Astoria (2 daily; 2hr 40min); Eugene (4 daily; 2hr 25min–3hr 15min); Sacramento (4 daily; 12hr 25min–15hr); Salem (4 daily; 1hr–1hr 15min); Seattle (4 daily; 4hr 5min).

By train Union Station is at 800 NW 6th Ave, within walking distance of the centre; if you arrive at night, take a cab – this part of town can be dicey after dark.

Destinations Eugene (3 daily; 2hr 35min); Salem (3 daily; 1hr 7min); Seattle (5 daily; 3hr 40min–4hr 25min); Spokane (1 daily; 7hr 30min); Vancouver, Canada (1 daily; 8hr 5min).

GETTING AROUND AND INFORMATION

By light rail MAX (short for Metropolitan Area Express) light rail system (standard fare $2.50) channels riders around central downtown and Old Town, connecting to the western and eastern suburbs on the Red and Blue lines; north Portland on the Yellow Line; and the far eastern and southern suburbs on the Green Line.

By bus Tri-Met buses are based at the downtown transit mall along Fifth and Sixth avenues. The Tri-Met Ticket Office in Pioneer Square (Mon–Fri 8.30am–5.30pm; ☎503 238 7433, ⓦtrimet.org) offers free transport maps and sells all-zone day tickets ($5), regular fares ($2.50) and other passes.

By streetcar Portland Streetcar line runs between the south waterfront, Pearl District and Northwest Portland, covering many downtown sights on NW and SW 10th and 11th streets – and will connect to the Eastside in coming years. Fares are $1 (see ⓦ portlandstreetcar.org).

By taxi Taxis don't stop in the street; pick up one at a hotel or call Broadway Cab (☎ 503 333 3333) or Portland Taxi (☎ 503 256 5400).

By bike The city boasts an impressive, extensive network of cycling paths and trails; the most central place to rent a bike is Waterfront Bicycles, 10 SW Ash St (Mon–Fri 10am–6pm, Sat & Sun 9am–6pm; $9/hr or $28/half-day; ☎ 503 227 1719, ⓦ waterfrontbikes.com).

Visitor centre In Pioneer Square at 701 SW 6th Ave (Mon–Fri 8.30am–5.30pm, Sat 10am–4pm, Sun 10am–2pm; ☎ 503 275 8355, ⓦ travelportland.com).

14

ACCOMMODATION

★ **Edgefield** 2126 SW Halsey St ☎ 503 669 8610, ⓦ mcmenamins.com/edgefield. East of town in the suburb of Troutdale, this unique brewery-resort built in 1911 has restaurants, bars, winery and tasting room, distillery, cinema and golf course (no TVs or phones and limited free wi-fi, though). In the same building, there's also a comfy hostel section. The cheapest doubles have shared baths. Dorms $30, doubles $70

Governor 611 SW 10th Ave ☎ 503 224 3400, ⓦ governorhotel.com. Stylish 1909 pile rich with elegant rooms and suites with fireplaces, spas, sofas and period decor, plus an on-site pool and fitness centre. A block from MAX and streetcar lines. $113

Heron Haus 2545 NW Westover Rd ☎ 503 274 1846, ⓦ heronhaus.com. Charming 1904 Tudor B&B, with some large suites featuring fireplaces, spas and cosy sitting areas. Excellent continental breakfast and close hiking access to Portland's expansive Forest Park. $170

HI-Portland Hawthorne 3031 SE Hawthorne Blvd ☎ 503 236 3380, ⓦ portlandhostel.org. Classy Victorian house in the Hawthorne District, offering free wi-fi, tours of local sights, cheap bike rental and occasional live music. Dorms $28 (non HI members $31), private rooms $60

HI-Portland Northwest 425 NW 18th Ave ☎ 503 241 2783, ⓦ nwportlandhostel.com. Located in a gorgeous 1889 mansion in Northwest Portland. Contains espresso bar, free wi-fi, kitchen and fireplace. Dorms $20, private rooms $65

★ **Hotel deLuxe** 729 SW 15th Ave ☎ 503 219 2094, ⓦ hoteldeluxeportland.com. Boutique treasure with a theme based on Hollywood's golden, glamorous era, offering smart decor and on-site gym, plus iPod stations and HDTVs. Outdoor movies on the roof every Thursday night in summer. Well placed along the MAX tracks, just west of downtown. $179

★ **Inn at Northrup Station** 2025 NW Northrup St ☎ 503 224 0543, ⓦ northrupstation.com. Cute boutique hotel on the trolley line in Northwest Portland, offering colourful suites with splashy designs, some with kitchens, patios and in-room bars. $169

Kennedy School 5736 NE 33rd Ave ☎ 503 249 3983, ⓦ mcmenamins.com/kennedyschool. Artsy rooms in a refurbished 1915 schoolhouse with chalkboards and cloakrooms, plus modern amenities. There's an on-site brewpub, cinema, outdoor bathing pool and "detention bar". $115

The Nines 525 SW Morrison ☎ 877 229 9995, ⓦ thenines .com. The most central hotel in Portland, hovering above Pioneer Courthouse Square and offering visitors posh designer furnishings, DVD players, iPod docks and an on-site ballroom and gym. $299

White Eagle 836 N Russell St ☎ 503 335 8900, ⓦ mcmenamins.com/452-white-eagle-home. Ultra-cheap 1905 hotel and hip brewpub north of downtown, famed for its nightly live rock shows – so early sleepers beware. Rooms are clean and simple, with shared baths; there are "bunk rooms" (dorms) too. Dorms $45, doubles $65

EATING

Portland's Northwest cuisine provides a mix of international cooking and fresh regional produce, and the city is becoming nationally famous for its many excellent dining options – after all, this was the birthplace of influential food critic James Beard (1903–85). Downtown, the **Pearl District** (northwest of downtown, a gentrified zone thick with lofts, galleries and boutiques) and **Northwest Portland** (aka Nob Hill, stretching between Burnside and Pettygrove streets along NW 23rd and 21st avenues), all have swanky cocktail bars, upscale bistros and fun brewpubs, while the **Eastside** harbours many of the city's best new restaurants.

PORTLAND FARMERS' MARKET

The southern end of South Park Blocks (within the Portland State University campus) hosts the popular **Portland Farmers' Market** (mid-March to mid-Dec Sat 8.30am–2pm; also Wed at Salmon St; ⓦ portlandfarmersmarket.org) that draws local fruit and vegetable growers, and other vendors of artisanal bread, pastries, candles and handicrafts.

14

PORTLAND'S FOOD TRUCK SCENE

The humble food truck (or food cart as they are known here) has been elevated to an art form in Portland (there are more than 700 licensed carts in the city), with gourmet meals offered for under $10. Most are organized into groups dubbed "pods", notably at SW 3rd and Washington (featuring some of the best Mexican carts), SW 5th at Stark and SW 9th at Alder, the largest lot in the city. See ⓦfoodcartsportland.com for the latest maps.

FIVE TO TRY

Burgatroyd SE 2nd Ave and SE Oak St ⓦburgatroyd .com. Sumptuous burgers for $6. Mon–Sat 11am–7pm.

Honkin' Huge Burritos Pioneer Courthouse Square. Portland's oldest cart and still some of the best burritos. Mon–Fri 11.30am–2.30am.

Nong's Khao Man Gai SW 10th Ave and Alder St ⓦkhaomangai.com. Thai chicken and rice perfection ($7). Mon–Fri 10am–4pm.

Portland Soup Co SW 4th Ave and Hall St ⓦportlandsoupco.com. Seasonal soups ($6) from one of the most beautiful carts in town. Mon–Fri 11am–3pm.

Tábor SW 5th Ave and Stark St ⓦschnitzelwich .com. Authentic Czech cuisine famed for the "schnitzelwich" ($8), a breaded and pan-fried pork loin served in a ciabatta roll. Mon–Fri 10am–3pm.

DOWNTOWN

Bunk Sandwiches 211 SW 6th Ave ☎503 972 8100, ⓦbunksandwiches.com. The pork belly Cubano sandwich ($9) here is one of the culinary highlights of the city. Be prepared for long queues at lunchtime. Daily 8am–3pm.

Higgins 1239 SW Broadway ☎503 222 9070, ⓦhigginsportland.com. Fine, expensive, farm-to-table pioneer of Northwest cuisine. The menu rotates, but watch for the Alaskan halibut, salmon risotto and "whole pig" plate that features a festival of pork. Mon–Fri 11.30am–midnight, Sat & Sun 4pm–midnight.

Huber's Café 411 SW 3rd Ave ☎503 228 5686, ⓦhubers.com. Established in 1879, this is Portland's oldest restaurant; in addition to historic charm it specializes in roast turkey ($16.95) and "Spanish coffee" (rum, Bols, Kahlua, coffee and fresh whipped cream). Mon–Thurs 11.30am–10pm, Fri & Sat 11.30am–11pm, Sun 4–10pm.

Jake's Famous Crawfish 401 SW 12th Ave ☎503 226 1419. A landmark since 1892, with a staggering, expensive choice of fresh local seafood such as sturgeon and Dungeness crab, and spicy crawfish cakes. Terrific desserts, too. Mon–Thurs 11.30am–10pm, Fri & Sat 11.30am–midnight, Sun 3–10pm.

★ **Leo's Coffee Shop** 837 SW 11th Ave, at Taylor St ☎503 228 1866. Bargain breakfasts and lunches served in an old-fashioned mom-and-pop diner, with booths and bar stools; hefty breakfast plates from $4.75, with burgers $4.20 and grilled cheese sandwiches just $2.95. Cash only. Daily 6.30am–3pm.

★ **Voodoo Doughnut** 22 SW 3rd Ave ☎503 241 4704, ⓦvoodoodoughnut.com. Cult doughnut shop where there's usually a queue for the addictive, gut-busting creations (from $0.95). Daily 24hr.

CHINATOWN

Old Town Pizza 226 NW Davis St ☎503 222 9999, ⓦoldtownpizza.com. Touristy but fun place to eat pizza ($15), though the food takes second place to the resident ghost, Nina, supposedly a nineteenth-century prostitute that died here. Also serves its own microbrews at the bar. Mon–Thurs & Sun 11.30am–11pm, Fri & Sat 11.30am–midnight.

Ping 102 NW 4th Ave ☎503 229 7464, ⓦpingpdx.com. Looks like nouveau Chinese fare, but is actually based on Asian street-vendor cooking – including fried pork knuckles, stewed duck leg and many different, very tasty skewers – though for higher-end prices. Tues–Fri 11am–10pm, Sat 2–10pm.

EASTSIDE

Beast 5425 NE 30th Ave ☎503 841 6968, ⓦbeastpdx .com. Top showcase for all things beef, and anything from pork-trotters osso buco to chicken-liver mousse and quail-egg toast. There are only two seatings per night, so reserve ahead. Wed–Sat 6pm & 8.45pm, Sun 10am & noon.

★ **Le Pigeon** 738 E Burnside St ☎503 546 8796, ⓦlepigeon.com. Locals argue constantly about whether this is Portland's – or the Northwest's – best restaurant, for its pricey but outstanding French-influenced beef-cheek bourguignon, duck crêpes and sweetbreads. Daily 5–10pm.

Noble Rot 1111 E Burnside St ☎503 233 1999, ⓦnoble rotpdx.com. The real highlight here is the gorgeous view of the city, though the wine flights, onion tarts and justly celebrated macaroni and cheese add to the appeal. Mon–Thurs 5–10pm, Fri & Sat 5–11pm, Sun 5–9pm.

Pine State Biscuits 2204 NE Alberta St ☎503 477 6605, ⓦpinestatebiscuits.com. Amazing breakfast experience mainly thanks to its decadent Southern-style biscuit sandwiches (try the Reggie, $8). Mon–Wed 7am–3pm, Thurs & Sun 7am–11pm, Fri & Sat 7am–1am.

Podnah's Pit 1625 NE Killingsworth St ☏ 503 281 3700, ☏ podnahspit.com. Classic barbecue comes to Portland; try the mouth-watering smoked trout, BBQ brisket, pulled pork and ribs. Mon–Fri 11am–10pm, Sat & Sun 9am–10pm.

★ **Pok Pok** 3226 SE Division St ☏ 503 232 1387, ☏ pokpokdiv.com. One of the nation's best spots for Thai food – scrumptious curry noodles, green papaya salad and pad thai. The Vietnamese fish-sauce wings are legendary. Daily 11.30am–10pm.

NIGHTLIFE

Portland is a beer-drinker's paradise, boasting 51 microbreweries at last count – the Oregon Brewers Festival is held annually here at the end of July (☏ oregonbrewfest.com). The city also has a dynamic **indie music** scene, with the late Elliott Smith one of its biggest successes (bands such as Blind Pilot, The Shins, Helio Sequence and Menomena lead the scene today).

BARS AND COFFEEHOUSES

Dot's Café 2521 SE Clinton St, Eastside ☏ 503 235 0203. Hip late-night spot decked out in garage-sale decor, offering good brews, classic burgers, cheese-and-jalapeno fries, and, unexpectedly, fabulous martini cocktails. Daily 2pm–2.30am.

Gilt Club 306 NW Broadway, Pearl District ☏ 503 222 4458, ☏ giltclub.com. Sexy cocktail lounge and late-night restaurant with expertly crafted cocktails, cool booths and romantic drapes. Tues–Thurs 5pm–1am, Fri & Sat 5pm–2am.

Pied Cow 3244 SE Belmont Ave ☏ 503 230 4866. An Eastside favourite for its coffee, tea and desserts. Set in a gorgeous Victorian house, it offers late-night hours, garden seating and the chance to puff fruit-flavoured tobacco from a hookah pipe. Mon–Thurs 4pm–midnight, Fri 4pm–1am, Sat noon–1am, Sun noon–midnight.

Saucebox 214 SW Broadway, downtown ☏ 503 241 3393, ☏ saucebox.com. Great pan-Asian cuisine, colourful cocktails and nightly music that attracts black-clad poseurs and serious hipsters in the loft, and more serious diners in the front room. Tues–Fri 4.30pm–2am, Sat 5pm–2am.

★ **Stumptown Roasters** 128 SW 3rd Ave, downtown ☏ 503 295 6144, ☏ stumptowncoffee.com. Widely acknowledged as the city's best coffee, made from a blend of seven different types and organically certified (espresso $2.50). The most convivial and central branch of a local chain. Mon–Fri 6am–7pm, Sat & Sun 7am–7pm.

LIVE MUSIC AND CLUBS

Crystal Ballroom 1332 W Burnside St, downtown ☏ 503 225 0047, ☏ mcmenamins.com. Two levels above the *Ringlers* bar, a nineteenth-century dance hall with a "floating" floor on springs. Bands tend toward great national indie rockers; also retro-DJs in "Lola's Room" on the floor in between. Hours vary.

Dante's 350 W Burnside St ☏ 503 226 6630, ☏ dantes live.com. Cabaret acts and live music mix with the club's signature "Sinferno" Sunday strip shows ($8) and "Karaoke from Hell" Mondays (plus cool pizza window). Daily 11am–2.30am.

BEST OF THE BREWERS

★ **Bridgeport Brewing** 1313 NW Marshall St ☏ 503 241 3612, ☏ bridgeportbrew.com. Purveyors of an excellent IPA best drunk fresh from its bustling brewpub in the city's Pearl district. Oldest craft brewer in the state. Tues–Thurs 11.30am–11pm, Fri & Sat 11.30am–midnight, Sun & Mon 11.30am–10pm.

Cascade Brewing Barrel House 939 SE Belmont St ☏ 503 265 8603, ☏ cascadebrewingbarrelhouse.com. Award-winning, barrel-aged and sour beers. Mon & Sun noon–10pm, Tues–Thurs noon–11pm, Fri & Sat noon–midnight.

Deschutes Brewery 210 NW 11th Ave ☏ 503 296 4906, ☏ deschutesbrewery.com. Outpost of the lauded Bend microbrewery, with a vaguely Scottish theme and eighteen taps. Mon–Thurs & Sun 11am–11pm, Fri & Sat 11am–midnight.

★ **Gasthaus Pub (Widmer Brothers)** 955 N Russell St ☏ 503 281 3333, ☏ widmerbrothers.com. Sample Widmer Brothers' Alchemy Ale or their Pitch Black IPA. Mon–Thurs & Sun 11am–10.30pm, Fri & Sat 11am–11pm.

Hair of the Dog Brewing Co 61 SE Yamhill St ☏ 503 232 6585, ☏ hairofthedog.com. Specializes in high-alcohol, bottle-conditioned beers. Tues–Thurs & Sun 11.30am–8pm, Fri & Sat 11.30am–10pm.

★ **Upright Brewery** 240 N Broadway ☏ 503 735 5337, ☏ uprightbrewing.com. Specializes in French and Belgian farmhouse-inspired beers but made with local ingredients and added Pacific Northwest flavours. Fri 4.30–9pm, Sat & Sun 1–6pm.

14

Goodfoot 2845 SE Stark St, Eastside ☎ 503 239 9292, ⓦ thegoodfoot.com. Frenetic live music joint and dance club, always sweaty, noisy and packed on weekends – but worth it to hear top-notch DJs spinning funk and retro-soul. Daily 5pm–2am.

Holocene 1001 SE Morrison St, Eastside ☎ 503 239 7639, ⓦ holocene.org. Packed with hipsters posing at point-blank range and an essential stop for local DJs and bands, *Holocene* mixes a range of cocktails and even broader spectrum of musical styles. Cover usually $5–10. Wed, Thurs & Sat 8.30pm–2am, Fri 5pm–2am.

Jimmy Mak's 221 NW 10th Ave, downtown ☎ 503 295 6542, ⓦ jimmymaks.com. One of the few choices for nightly jazz in a town not known to swing. Come by to hear

local Mel Brown or visiting name acts. Mon–Thurs 5pm–midnight, Fri & Sat 5pm–1am.

Roseland Theater 8 NW 6th Ave, downtown ☎ 503 224 2038, ⓦ roselandpdx.com. Located in one of the city's dicier corners, but a top spot for rock and alternative acts – often the last affordable venue for fans before the groups start touring stadiums. Hours vary.

Wonder Ballroom 128 NE Russell St, Eastside ☎ 503 284 8686, ⓦ wonderballroom.com. A specially renovated old ballroom from 1914 that plays host to some of the more intriguing national and international acts in indie rock and other alternative styles. Just off a gritty stretch of MLK Blvd, so drive or take a cab. Hours vary.

ENTERTAINMENT

Portland Center for the Performing Arts 1111 SW Broadway ☎ 503 248 4335, ⓦ pcpa.com. Multivenue complex which includes the Arlene Schnitzer Concert Hall, a sumptuously restored 1928 vaudeville and movie house that presents musical extravaganzas, dance and theatre, hosting performances by the Oregon Symphony (☎ 503 228 1353, ⓦ orsymphony.org). The centre also includes the

1917 Keller Auditorium, 222 SW Clay, home to the Portland Opera (☎ 503 241 1407, ⓦ portlandopera.org) and Oregon Ballet Theater (☎ 503 222 5538, ⓦ obt.org).

Portland Center Stage 128 NW 11th Ave ☎ 503 445 3700, ⓦ pcs.org. Premier theatre company that offers new and classic works in the stylishly renovated Gerding Theater at the Armory, built in 1891.

The Columbia River Gorge and Mount Hood

East of Portland the **Columbia River Gorge** cuts through the snowy peaks of the Cascades for 75 miles, an important corridor between east and west for thousands of years. Scoured into a wide U-shape by huge Ice Age-era floods, the gorge is a nationally protected scenic area (ⓦ fs.usda.gov/crgnsa), where waterfalls tumble down sheer cliffs, and fir and maple trees turn fabulous shades of gold and red in the autumn.

Historic Columbia River Highway

Although the gorge looks enchanting from both sides of the river (Washington state lies on the northern bank), the Oregon side offers the most interest. Heading east from Portland, leave I-84 at junction 17 for the **Historic Columbia River Highway** (US-30), a narrow, winding two-lane road that boasts several excellent vantage points, particularly at **Crown Point**, where the 1918 **Vista House** (daily: mid-March to April, Sept & Oct 10am–4pm; May–Aug 9am–6pm; free; ☎ 503 695 2230, ⓦ vistahouse.com) – perched 733ft above the gorge about 25 miles east of downtown Portland – has been restored to its original German Art Nouveau glory. Inside you'll find exhibits on the history of the highway, built between 1913 and 1922.

Further east, the highway passes some of the most jaw-dropping **waterfalls** in the region, beginning with the two-tier torrent of **Bride's Veil**, 4.5 miles from Vista House. Another four miles on is the spectacular, and hugely popular, **Multnomah Falls** (daily dawn–dusk; free; ☎ 503 695 2372), the second tallest year-round waterfall in the USA, whose waters plunge 542ft down a rock face, collect in a pool, and then drop another 70ft. This is an extremely busy bottleneck in the summer, so be prepared for crowds and a carnival-like atmosphere.

A few miles east the highway rejoins I-84; drive nine miles and cross the river on the 1926 **Bridge of the Gods** ($1) and head towards **Stevenson** (WA), where the **Columbia Gorge Interpretive Center Museum** (daily 10am–5pm; $10; ☎ 509 427 8211, ⓦ columbiagorge.org) chronicles the history of the gorge through videos and illuminating exhibits – there's a special focus on the **Cascades Portage**, which once bypassed seven

---

SKIING MOUNT HOOD

Mount Hood boasts six **ski areas**: Timberline Lodge, Mount Hood Meadows, Ski Bowl, Cooper Spur, Snow Bunny and Summit. Timberline offers the only year-round lift-served skiing in North America (lift tickets $60/day; ☎ 503 272 3158; ⓦ timberlinelodge.com). Mount Hood Meadows ($59; ⓦ skihood.com) and Ski Bowl ($49; ⓦ skibowl.com) are the best alternatives, though without the handsome lodge (see below).

---

miles of rapids near here (the rapids were submerged in 1940 after the Bonneville Dam was completed). Some 23 miles east of Stevenson, back on the Oregon side of the river via the rickety 1924 Hood River Bridge ($1), lies the attractive town of **Hood River**. Hordes of **kitesurfers** and **windsurfers** bound over its choppy river in the summer, while the snowy peak of Mount Hood provides a romantic, mist-shrouded backdrop, best observed from **Panorama Point** off Hwy-35, just south of the town.

ACCOMMODATION AND EATING

Bridal Veil Lodge 46650 E Historic Columbia River Hwy, Corbett ☎ 503 695 2333, ⓦ bridalveillodge.com. Cute B&B right next to the Bridal Veil Falls, dating back to 1926 and offering four clean, cosy rooms with bathrooms (some with TVs). $129

★ **Full Sail Brewing Co** 506 Columbia St, Hood River ☎ 541 386 2247, ⓦ fullsailbrewing.com. Fine local microbrewery; enjoy a cask-conditioned Imperial Stout ($4.25) while looking out over Hood River and the Columbia Valley,

HISTORIC COLUMBIA RIVER HIGHWAY

and munch on superb half-pound burgers ($12) or beer cheese soup ($6). Free brewery tours daily (1pm, 2pm, 3pm & 4pm). Daily 11am–9pm.

Tad's Chicken 'n Dumplings 1325 E Historic Columbia River Hwy, Troutdale ☎ 503 666 5337, ⓦ tadschicdump .com. Old-fashioned roadhouse with its delicious "original chicken 'n dumplins" ($15), and plenty of local seafood. Mon–Fri 5–10pm, Sat & Sun 4–10pm.

Mount Hood

Dominating the horizon south of the Columbia River and the town of Hood River, **Mount Hood** (11,240ft) is a mesmerizing dormant volcano and the tallest peak in Oregon, sprinkled with eleven active glaciers. The **Mount Hood Scenic Loop** – a combination of highways 35 and 26 – links the mountain and the Columbia Gorge while passing numerous orchards along the way, which in the spring and summer offer great opportunities to sample fresh fruit, juice and desserts (see ⓦ hoodriverfruitloop .com). One of the other joys of the area is to explore the mountain via trails radiating out from its slopes, most of them protected within the **Mount Hood National Forest**; ranger centres (see below) can supply more information. Note that there are no trails to the summit of Mount Hood; only experienced mountaineers should tackle the technical climb to the top (free permits required).

Near the intersection of highways 35 and 26, a turnoff leads to the grand, New Deal-era **Timberline Lodge** (see below), which Stephen King fans might recognize as the exterior set for the hotel in Stanley Kubrick's **The Shining**.

INFORMATION AND ACCOMMODATION

Hood River Ranger Station 6780 Hwy-35, Parkdale (Mon–Fri 8am–4.30pm; ☎ 541 352 6002).

★ **Timberline Lodge** 27500 W Leg Rd, Government Camp ☎ 503 272 3311, ⓦ timberlinelodge.com. Solidly built in rough-hewn stone and timber, and featuring an interior loaded with Arts and Crafts-style wooden furniture

MOUNT HOOD

and antique fittings. The rooms at this 1937 gem are really cosy, with a heated outdoor swimming pool open year round. $130

Zigzag Ranger Station 70220 E Hwy-26, Zigzag, 45 miles southeast of Portland (daily 7.45am–noon & 1–4.30pm; ☎ 503 622 3191).

The Willamette Valley

South of Portland, the **Willamette Valley** (pronounced Will-A-Mette) has been the heart of Oregon since settlers poured in along the Oregon Trail in the 1840s, a fertile paradise compared to what they'd seen en route. It still boasts a diverse agricultural economy, but is best known today for its New England-style **covered bridges** and especially its grapes. The scenic route through wine country, Hwy-99 W, accesses dozens of acclaimed **wineries**, most of which pour superb Cabernets, Rieslings and Pinot Noirs. Pick up a wine-country tour map from any local visitor centre (or visit Ⓦoregonwine.org).

14

Salem

Most visitors assume that Portland is the capital of Oregon, but that honour belongs to **SALEM**, a leafy city of 155,000 some 45 miles south on the banks of the Willamette River. The main reason to stop is to view the unusual, Art Deco **Oregon State Capitol**, 900 Court St NE (Mon–Fri 7.30am–5pm; free; ☏503 986 1388, Ⓦleg.state.or.us), completed in 1938 from Vermont marble, its 166ft cupola topped by a large gold-leaf pioneer, axe in hand. Also worth a look is the **Willamette Heritage Center**, 1313 Mill St SE (Mon–Sat 10am–5pm; $6; ☏503 585 7012, Ⓦwillametteheritage.org), a collection of nine well-preserved pioneer buildings, including those associated with the Methodist Mission to Oregon in the 1840s and 1850s, and the gloomy Thomas Kay Woollen Mill, built in the 1890s.

ACCOMMODATION AND EATING   SALEM

Betty's Bed & Breakfast 965 D St NE ☏503 399 7848, Ⓦsalemoregonbedandbreakfast.com. This charming 1922 Arts and Crafts-style home lies within walking distance of downtown with two simple, cosy rooms; Betty's breakfasts are a real treat. **$110**

Grand Hotel in Salem 201 Liberty St SE ☏503 540 7800, Ⓦgrandhotelsalem.com. Classy hotel in the heart of downtown with a huge range of comfy, spacious rooms, free parking, small gym and pool. **$129**

Sassy Onion 1244 State St ☏503 378 9180 Ⓦsassyonion.com. Local mini-chain, with this branch close to the Capitol, perfect for a breakfast of "world famous French toast" ($6.49) or quarter-pound burgers ($8.99) for lunch. Mon–Fri 6am–3pm, Sat & Sun 7am–3pm.

Eugene

Oregon's second largest city, 110 miles south of Portland, **EUGENE** is a liberal enclave and energetic cultural centre, to which the **University of Oregon** (UO) lends a youthful bohemian feel, especially along 13th Avenue just west of campus (cult 1970s movie *Animal House* was filmed here). The college football team, the **Ducks**, has a loyal following in the city (Ⓦgoducks.com), and their rivalry with Oregon State University's Beavers, aka the "Civil War", is especially fierce. Indeed, Eugene has a strong sporting heritage: **Nike** was established at the university in 1964, and in the 1970s local runner (and athletics hero) **Steve Prefontaine** set US records in every race from the 2000m to the 10,000m. Prefontaine's tragic death in a car crash in 1975 is commemorated at legendary **Hayward Stadium**, where the US Olympic trials took place in 2012 (and will again in 2016).

Jordan Schnitzer Museum of Art

1430 Johnson Lane (UO campus) • Tues–Sun 11am–5pm, Wed closes 8pm • $5 • ☏541 346 3027, Ⓦjsma.uoregon.edu

The UO ("you-vo") campus is worth visiting for its **Jordan Schnitzer Museum of Art**, which only displays five percent of its 13,000 artworks at any one time. Much of the gallery space is taken up by high-quality travelling exhibits, and even the permanent

THE OREGON COUNTRY FAIR

Ten miles west of Eugene on US-126, little **Veneta** hosts the **Oregon Country Fair** (tickets $24–28; ☏541 343 4298, Ⓦoregoncountryfair.org) in July, a long-standing hippie festival of music, art, food and dancing. Traffic can be heavy, and even if you have a car it's easier to go by bus – the LTD (see opposite) has special services.

ASHLAND AND THE SHAKESPEARE FESTIVAL

The progressive hamlet of **ASHLAND**, 180 miles south of Eugene, is the unlikely home of one of the world's best tributes to Shakespeare, the **Oregon Shakespeare Festival**, actually a repertory theatre company, founded in 1935. Its season runs from February to early November, offering eleven different plays; four by Shakespeare and seven by other classic, modern and contemporary writers. Performances take place in the half-timbered **Elizabethan Theatre** (early June to mid-Oct) and adjacent to it, the **Angus Bowmer Theatre**, which stages both classical and more recent works, and the austere **Thomas Theatre**, which has a mostly modern repertoire. The three theatres share the same box office, 15 S Pioneer St (tickets $25–115; ☎541 482 4331, ⓦosfashland.org).

If you come in the summer, head twenty miles northwest to the preserved Old West hamlet of **Jacksonville** for the annual **Britt Festival** (June–Aug; most tickets $28–44; ☎541 773 6077, ⓦbrittfest.org), to hear the top names in Jazz, pop, rock and country music.

Ashland has more than sixty B&Bs, many of which are in charming Victorian homes; see Ashland B&B Network (☎800 944 0329, ⓦabbnet.com).

galleries rotate, but the **Asian collections** are especially good: Japanese, Chinese and Korean contemporary art, as well as traditional scrolls, textiles and ceramics. There's also an intriguing collection of Russian Orthodox icons and always a strong showing of Pacific Northwest art and photography. Don't miss the tranquil **garden courtyard**.

Museum of Natural & Cultural History

1680 E 15th Ave • Wed–Sun 11am–4pm • Free • ☎541 346 3024, ⓦnatural-history.uoregon.edu

The handsome cedar-frame **Museum of Natural & Cultural History**, on the UO campus, is a real gem, with displays and artefacts shedding light on Oregon's archeological and indigenous history; check out the 10,000-year old sandal, and the even rarer 15,000-year old specimen of desiccated human faeces.

ARRIVAL, GETTING AROUND AND INFORMATION   EUGENE

By bus Greyhound buses stop at 987 Pearl St, downtown. Destinations Portland (4 daily; 2hr 25min–3hr 10min); Sacramento (4 daily; 9hr 45min–11hr 35min); Salem (4 daily; 1hr 20min–1hr 45min).

By train The Amtrak station is at 433 Willamette St. Destinations Portland (3 daily; 2hr 35min); Salem (3 daily; 1hr 12min).

Local buses Eugene has a terrific bus system, the LTD

($1.75; ☎541 687 5555, ⓦltd.org), offering day passes for $3.50.

Visitor centres Downtown at 754 Olive St (Mon–Fri 8am–5pm; ☎541 484 5307, ⓦeugenecascadescoast.org). The branch across in Springfield (3312 Gateway St, I-5 exit 195A; daily 9am–6pm; ☎541 484 5307) has slightly more information.

ACCOMMODATION

Campbell House 252 Pearl St ☎541 343 1119, ⓦcampbellhouse.com. An elegant 1892 Victorian home turned luxurious B&B with thirteen handsome rooms in the main house and six suites in the Carriage House. **$129**

Eugene Whiteaker International Hostels 970 W 3rd Ave ☎541 343 3335, ⓦeugenehostels.com. Built in 1930 and located in the hip Whiteaker area with male and

female dorms, single rooms and one family suite. Shared kitchen, laundry, free local calls, free wi-fi and daily continental breakfast. Dorms **$23**, rooms **$46**, family suite **$36**

Excelsior Inn 754 E 13th Ave ☎541 342 6963, ⓦexcelsior inn.com. Small hotel near the University of Oregon with fourteen rooms and suites themed around classical music. **$135**

EATING AND NIGHTLIFE

Newman's Fish Co 1545 Willamette St ☎541 344 2371, ⓦnewmansfish.com. Fine seafood house where you can fill up on fish 'n' chips, clam chowder and shrimp skewers for less than $10. Mon–Fri 9am–7pm, Sat 9am–6.30pm.

★ **Ninkasi Brewing Co** 272 Van Buren St ☎541 344 2739, ⓦninkasibrewing.com. The first and still the best of the local microbreweries, producing quality, hoppy beers in the artsy Whiteaker neighbourhood. Mon–Wed & Sun noon–9pm, Thurs–Sat noon–10pm.

Prince Pückler's 1605 E 19th Ave ☎ 541 344 4418, ⓦ princepucklers.com. Rich, creamy gourmet ice cream near the UO campus, with fresh fruit flavours in the summer and always tempting fudge sundaes. Daily noon–11pm.

WOW Hall 291 W 8th Ave ☎ 541 687 2746, ⓦ wowhall.org. Old venue dating from 1932 that showcases up-and-coming rockers, indie rock and punk; most shows start at 9pm and cover is $15–20. Hours vary.

The Oregon coast

The **Oregon coast** offers four hundred beautiful, moody and often secluded miles of stunning terrain, almost all of it public land, where parks and campgrounds abound, and the extensive beaches are open for hiking, beachcombing, shell fishing and whale-watching.

Astoria and around

Set dramatically on a hilly peninsula at the mouth of the Columbia River, the port of **ASTORIA** has recently been transformed into a shabby-chic town of boutiques, brewpubs, restaurants and antique stores, despite remaining a little rough around the edges. Downtown lies close to the water, overlooking the spectacular four-mile cantilever bridge across to Washington State (see p.944). The town is named for tycoon John Jacob Astor, who founded a fur trading post here in 1811 (he never visited personally); a small memorial to his **Fort Astoria**, complete with blockhouse, lies on Exchange Street behind the Fort George Brewery (the fort was handed over to the Brits in 1813 and renamed Fort George).

Flavel House and Oregon Film Museum

Easily the most striking edifice in town, **Flavel House**, 441 8th St (daily May–Sept 10am–5pm; Oct–April 11am–4pm; $5; ☎ 503 325 2203, ⓦ cumtux.org)was the grand Queen Anne-style home of influential sea captain George Flavel, completed in 1886 and today featuring main rooms set up as dioramas with period furniture and elaborate decor. The **Oregon Film Museum** around the corner at 732 Duane St (daily: May–Sept 10am–5pm; Oct–April 11am–4pm; $4; ⓦ oregonfilmmuseum.com), in the historic jail featured in *The Goonies* (1985), is dedicated to movies shot in the state.

Columbia River Maritime Museum

1792 Marine Drive • Daily 9.30am–5pm • $12 • ☎ 503 325 2323, ⓦ crmm.org

Exhibits from Astoria's seafaring past are on display at the **Columbia River Maritime Museum**, which also has impressive displays of native artefacts and ships such as the *Lightship Columbia*, as well as walrus-tusk Inuit sculptures once sold to sailors as scrimshaw. Look out for the oldest items in the museum, a rare wooden block and chunk of beeswax from a seventeenth-century Spanish galleon wrecked on Nehalem Spit.

Astoria Column

Astor Park • Daily 5am–10pm (column closes at 9pm) • Free, parking $1 • ⓦ astoriacolumn.org

From Marine Drive, numbered streets climb up towards fancy Victorian mansions and eventually the top of Coxcomb Hill, where the handsome 125ft-tall **Astoria Column**, completed in 1926 and decorated with a winding mural depicting pioneer history, offers stunning views for anyone willing to climb its 164 cramped spiral stairs (the views are almost as good from the car park below).

Fort Clatsop

92343 Fort Clatsop Rd • Daily: mid-June to early Sept 9am–6pm; early Sept to mid-June 9am–5pm • $3 • ☎ 503 861 2471, ⓦ nps.gov/lewi

Less than ten miles south of Astoria, **Fort Clatsop** is a replica of Lewis and Clark's winter camp, built somewhere near here in 1805; no remains have ever been found, but written descriptions make this site seem most likely. The exhibits in the visitor centre and fort, reconstructed in aromatic cedar and surrounded by huge Sitka spruce, make it well worth seeking out. The fort forms part of the **Lewis & Clark National Historical Park**, with several other sites in Washington state.

Fort Stevens State Park

100 Peter Iredale Rd, Hammond • Daily sunrise–sunset • $5 for 7 days • ☎ 503 861 1671, ⓦ oregonstateparks.org

Nine miles west of Astoria, off US-101, **Fort Stevens State Park** offers many good hiking trails and miles of beaches. Along with remnants of the 1865 earthen fort itself, you can also see the iron carcass of the **Peter Iredale**, run aground in 1906 and slowly sinking into the sand, one of the few shipwrecks you can actually clamber about on.

14

ARRIVAL AND INFORMATION

ASTORIA AND AROUND

By bus The Astoria Transit Center is at 900 Marine Drive, downtown.
Destinations Cannon Beach (2 daily; 45min); Portland (2 daily; 2hr 10min–2hr 20min); Seaside (2 daily; 25min).

Visitor centre 111 W Marine Drive (May–Aug daily 8am–6pm; Sept–April Mon–Fri 9am–5pm; ☎ 503 325 6311, ⓦ oldoregon.com)

ACCOMMODATION

★ **Cannery Pier Hotel** 10 Basin St ☎ 503 325 4996, ⓦ cannerypierhotel.com. Enticing boutique property housed on a waterfront pier right over the water, whose sleek modern rooms have fireplaces and balconies. **$269**

Hotel Elliott 357 12th St ☎ 503 325 2222, ⓦ hotel elliott.com. Wonderfully historic 1924 structure with luxury amenities in its rooms and suites, some with fireplaces and jacuzzis, all right in the centre of the action. **$149**

EATING

Bowpicker Fish & Chips 1634 Duane St ☎ 503 791 2942, ⓦ bowpicker.com. Simple takeaway with two tables and some of the tastiest fish and chips anywhere (beer-battered fresh albacore tuna, uniquely; $8–10). April–Oct Wed–Sun 11am–4pm; Nov–March Thurs–Sun 11am–dusk.
Columbia River Coffee Roaster (Three Cups Coffee House) 279 W Marine Drive ☎ 503 325 7487, ⓦ thundermuck.com. Best coffee in town, roasted in small batches in a historic structure with views of the river. Mon–Sat 7am–5pm, Sun 8am–4pm.
Drina Daisy Bosnian Restaurant 915 Commercial St

☎ 503 338 2912, ⓦ drinadaisy.com. Worth a visit just for the experience of trying home-cooked Bosnian food in Oregon; think whole-roasted lamb, pickled vegetables and rich, tasty stews. Wed–Sun 11am–10pm.
★ **Fort George Brewery** 1483 Duane St ☎ 503 325 7468, ⓦ fortgeorgebrewery.com. Local microbrewer in a 1924 warehouse (pints $4.25, pitchers $15) also serving decent burgers ($8.95), house-made sausages ($8.50), rock fish tacos ($10.95) and pan-seared oysters ($12.50). Mon–Thurs 11am–11pm, Fri & Sat 11am–midnight, Sun noon–11pm.

Cannon Beach

Seventeen miles south of Astoria, **Seaside** is a drab resort of carnival rides and chain motels, but another nine miles on, more attractive **CANNON BEACH** is best known for its enticing four-mile strip of sand and 235ft-tall **Haystack Rock**, a massive black monolith rising out of the beach and crowned with nesting seagulls and tufted puffins. Its tide pools are accessible at low tide, though the rock itself is definitely not climbable. There's no parking or beach access at the rock itself; you'll have to park at Hemlock and Gower Street in Midtown (signposted "Haystack Parking") and walk, or take the bus from Cannon Beach's pretty "**downtown**" (actually just a single stretch of Hemlock Street lined with shops and restaurants), several miles north.

To escape the tourists, head four miles north to **Ecola State Park** (dawn–dusk; $5/vehicle) where dense conifer forests decorate the basaltic cliffs of Tillamook Head (you might see elk here), or south to **Oswald West State Park** (dawn–dusk; free), named after the pioneering governor who helped preserve most of the state's coastline, where there's a beautiful beach, rocky headland and rainforest.

Tillamook and the Three Capes Scenic Loop

Forty miles south of Cannon Beach, **TILLAMOOK** is famous mainly for the **Tillamook Cheese Factory**, just north of town on US-101 (daily 8am–6pm, mid-June to early Sept till 8pm; free; ⓦtillamookcheese.com), where on a self-guided tour you can watch cheese evolve from milky liquid in huge vats to yellow bricks on conveyor belts, and sample quality ice cream in the process. South of Tillamook, US-101 curves around bucolic inland valleys, but better is the lengthier alternative of the **Three Capes Scenic Loop**, which leads you on a circuitous trip lurching around picturesque bays and jagged promontories, across lowlands and around hillsides, until the road merges with US-101 west of the coastal **Siuslaw National Forest**.

Newport

Some 44 miles south of Tillamook, there's no avoiding **Lincoln City**, the ugliest town on the Oregon coast, sprawling along the highway for seven congested, dreadful miles, but hold out for another thirty miles and you'll reach **NEWPORT**, which makes a fine base for visiting the central coast. The **Historic Bayfront** along Bay Boulevard is the obvious first stop – with its souvenir shops, seafood diners and sea lions wallowing on the wharves – along with pleasant **Nye Beach**, a quiet oceanside gem further west. To the south, across the bridge at 2820 SE Ferry Slip Rd, the impressive **Oregon Coast Aquarium** (daily: June–Aug 9am–6pm; Sept–May 10am–5pm; $18.95; ☏541 867 3474, ⓦaquarium.org) is home to marine mammals such as sea otters and seals, seabirds such as tufted puffins, and a whopping octopus in a glass-framed sea grotto, but its highlight is Passages of the Deep, a shark-surrounded underwater tunnel. Just north of town at 750 NW Lighthouse Drive, Newport's other top attraction is scenic **Yaquina Head** (daily 7am–9pm; three-day pass $7/vehicle; ☏541 574 3100), with an informative Interpretive Center (daily 9.30am–5pm), striking 93ft-tall cape lighthouse (free tours daily except Wed 10am–4pm), man-made tidepools and frisky seals and sea lions playing on the shoreline rocks.

ARRIVAL AND INFORMATION   NEWPORT

By bus Newport's bus station is at 956 SW 10th St (☏541 265 2253). To get to Portland (1 daily; 5hr) or other destinations you must change in Corvallis or Salem.

Chamber of Commerce 555 SW Coast Hwy (☏541 265 8801, ⓦnewportchamber.org).

ACCOMMODATION, EATING AND DRINKING

Café Stephanie 411 NW Coast St ☏541 265 8082. Great place to go for sandwiches, fish tacos and salmon chowder, with filling breakfasts, too. Daily 7.30am–3pm.

★ **Chowder Bowl** 728 NW Beach Drive (on Nye Beach) ☏541 265 7477, ⓦnewportchowderbowl .com. Despite its unexceptional look, this small canteen really does serve the best bowl of chowder ($6.25) in town. Mon–Thurs & Sun 11am–8pm, Fri & Sat 11am–9pm.

Rogue Ales Public House 748 SW Bay Blvd ☏541 265 3188, ⓦrogue.com. Liveliest spot for food and beer, and also offers one- and two-bedroom "Bed and Beer" hotel

units ($105, plus two complimentary bottles; ☏541 961 0142) so you don't have to risk driving away drunk. Mon–Thurs & Sun 11am–midnight, Fri & Sat 11am–1am.

Sylvia Beach Hotel 267 NW Cliff St (Nye Beach) ☏541 265 5428, ⓦsylviabeachhotel.com. This well-worn favourite features twenty rooms each bearing the name of a famous writer, from Melville to Amy Tan. No TVs, radios, phones or wi-fi. **$115**

★ **Tyee Lodge** 4925 NW Woody Way ☏541 265 8953, ⓦtyeelodge.com. This 1940s tree-framed beach home offers six luxurious and modern B&B units with expansive oceanfront views. **$195**

SEA LION CAVES

Some 38 miles south of Newport, US-101 passes the extraordinary **Sea Lion Caves** (daily 9am–7pm; $14; ☏541 547 3111, ⓦsealioncaves.com), America's largest sea cave system and often crammed with hundreds of lounging, barking sea lions – you'll smell them before you see them. The caves are accessed via a 225ft elevator; you're most likely to see sea lions in autumn and winter (they are often perched on the rocks outside in summer).

RIDING AND SURFING THE DUNES

The **Oregon dunes** are famous for their OHV (off-highway vehicle) opportunities, with special areas set aside for all manner of thrills and spills (get maps from the visitor centre). Various sand buggies, ATVs and dirt bikes can be rented at Sun Dunes Frontier, four miles south of Florence on US-101 (March–Sept; ☎541 997 3544, ⊛sanddunesfrontier.com), while the art of sandboarding (surfing on the dunes) can be mastered at Sand Master Park, 5351 US-101 in Florence (☎541 997 6006, ⊛sandmasterpark.com), with board rentals from $10/24hr.

14

Oregon Dunes National Recreation Area

Daily 24hr • $5/vehicle • **Visitor centre** 855 Highway Ave, Reedsport, US-101 (20 miles south of Florence) • Mid-July to early Sept Mon–Sat 8am–4.30pm; early Sept to mid-July Mon–Fri 8am–4.30pm • ☎541 271 6000

Beginning at the town of Florence, fifty miles south of Newport, colossal sand dunes dominate the coast for another 42 miles, punctuated with dramatic pockets of forest and lake, and rising up to an incredible 500ft high. Though frequently invisible from US-101, about half of the dunes are accessible to the public in the **Oregon Dunes National Recreation Area**. The US Forest Service, which manages the dunes, maintains evocative **hiking trails** that are, for the most part, free of ATVs and proceed through a variety of terrains.

Port Orford to the California border

Towns are fewer and farther apart going south on US-101, with the coastline at its prettiest beyond **Port Orford**, 100 miles south of Florence, where forested mountains sweep smoothly down to the sea. These mountains mark the western limit of the **Siskiyou National Forest**, a vast slab of remote wilderness best explored by boat along the turbulent Rogue River from workaday **GOLD BEACH**. Here, the visitor centre has details of rafting and powerboat excursions. Starting seven miles south of Gold Beach are a trio of very appealing state parks (all open daily sunrise–sunset and free): **Cape Sebastian**, which has a fine viewpoint perched 200ft above the surging waves, as well as trails through flowery meadows and ocean bluffs; **Pistol River**, best known for its fabulous collection of sea stacks – monstrous, gnarled behemoths scattered amid the waters – and regular **windsurfing** competitions; and **Samuel H. Boardman**, a twelve-mile coastal strip rich with viewpoints, picnic areas and scenic paths. Finally, at the state's far southwestern corner, **Brookings** is a retirement-oriented town with a warm climate, and is best used as a base for exploring northern California's **Redwood National Park**, with the park's headquarters just 25 miles south in Crescent City (see p.914).

Bend and around

A booming city of 80,000, **BEND** makes a fun base for exploring the arid hills of central Oregon, giving access to prime outdoor activities and packed with good restaurants, sports shops and a mind-boggling array of **microbreweries**. Though the outskirts are a sprawl of strip malls and highways, downtown is a compact, pleasant district, separated from the Deschutes River by **Drake Park**, a popular half-mile stretch of greenery with shady paths, Deschutes River Trail and an outdoor stage overlooking a fetching stretch of the river known as **Mirror Pond**. Beyond recreation, Bend's main attraction is the **High Desert Museum**, five miles south of downtown on US-97 (daily: May–Oct 9am–5pm; Nov–March 10am–4pm; May–Oct $15, Nov–March $12; ☎541 382 4754, ⊛highdesertmuseum.org), a fascinating collection of artefacts from Native American and pioneer history, along with displays of regional flora and fauna – river otters, porcupines and so forth – and a reconstructed pioneer homestead and sawmill.

14

INFORMATION

BEND AND AROUND

Visitor centre 750 NW Lava Rd, Suite 160, at Oregon Ave (June–Aug Mon–Fri 9am–5pm, Sat & Sun 10am–4pm; Sept–May closed Sun; ☎ 541 382 8048, ⓦ visitbend.com).

ACCOMMODATION, EATING AND DRINKING

★ **The Blacksmith** 211 NW Greenwood Ave ☎ 541 318 0588, ⓦ bendblacksmith.com. Pricey but delicious Northwest cuisine such as perfectly charred BBQ rib eye steak, Idaho trout and king salmon fillets (mains $14–36). Mon–Thurs 4–10pm, Fri & Sat 4pm–midnight, Sun 4–9pm.

★ **Deschutes Brewery** 1044 NW Bond St ☎ 541 382 9242, ⓦ deschutesbrewery.com. Serves some of the Northwest's best beers; try the beautifully balanced Black Butte porter, or the Mirror Pond pale ale, along with locally sourced sausages, burgers, breads and mustard. Mon–Thurs 11am–11pm, Fri & Sat 11am–midnight, Sun 11am–10pm.

Goody's 957 NW Wall St ☎ 541 389 5185, ⓦ goodys chocolates.com. A sweet treat institution in Bend, selling hand-crafted chocolates, popcorn and incredible ice cream. Mon–Thurs & Sun 10am–10pm, Fri & Sat 10am–10.30pm.

Lara House 640 NW Congress St ☎ 541 388 4064, ⓦ larahouse.com. Romantic B&B featuring six beautiful rooms in a 1910 Arts and Crafts estate, with flat-screen TVs, shared sunroom and candlelit front porch. $194

★ **Old St Francis School** 700 NW Bond St ☎ 541 382 5174, ⓦ mcmenamins.com. Charming former 1936 Catholic school that offers plush hotel rooms and free on-site cinema admission, an on-site pub and the chance to stay in a nunnery, friary or parish house. $135

Pine Tavern 967 NW Brooks St ☎ 541 382 5581, ⓦ pine tavern.com. Established in 1936, this restaurant and bar serves a huge selection of regional microbrewed ales, plus moderately priced seafood, steak and sandwiches, overlooking the river. Daily 11.30am–11pm.

Newberry National Volcanic Monument

The so-called **Lava Lands** cover a huge area of central Oregon, but especially in the Bend area at **Newberry National Volcanic Monument**. Dating back seven thousand years to the eruption of Mount Newberry, the monument is actually a caldera – a huge, gently sloping crater laced with hiking paths, nature trails, campgrounds and prime fishing spots. Some of the highlights (most of them free with monument admission) include the chilly, mile-long **Lava River Cave** (lantern rentals $5), an eerie subterranean passage made from a hollow lava tube that remains a steady 42°F; the **Lava Cast Forest** – circular, basalt holes of tree trunks burnt by lava before they could fall; and the surreal landscape of the **Big Obsidian Flow**, huge hills of volcanic black glass that native tribes throughout the area once used to make arrowheads. The **Lava Lands visitor centre** (see below) is an excellent source of maps and information on hiking trails, and provides access to the monument's other major sight, **Lava Butte**, a massive 500ft-tall cinder cone, whose narrow rim you can reach by car and traverse in a short walk.

INFORMATION

NEWBERRY NATIONAL VOLCANIC MONUMENT

Admission The monument is open May–Sept dawn–dusk, and a day pass is $5/vehicle.

Visitor centre 58201 S Hwy-97 (11 miles south of Bend; June–Aug daily 9am–5pm; May & Sept closed Tues & Wed; ☎ 541 593 2421).

Crater Lake National Park

Just over a hundred miles south of Bend, the blown-out shell of Mount Mazama holds the hypnotically beautiful **CRATER LAKE**, formed after an explosion 42 times greater than that of Mount St Helens. You won't forget the first time you peer over the volcano rim: the biggest island on the lake, **Wizard Island**, is actually the tip of a still-rising cinder cone, and the so-called **Phantom Ship** is a jagged volcanic dyke that, in dim light or fog, resembles a mysterious clipper on the water. In its snowy isolation, the lake, at a depth of nearly 2000ft, is awe-inspiring; in summer, wild flowers bloom along its high rim.

Regular **boats** cruise the lake (see opposite), reached via the sheer, mile-long **Cleetwood Cove trail** (June–Oct) which provides the only access to the lake surface

(700ft down). The trail is on the north edge, but visitor facilities are clustered on the south edge at tiny **Rim Village**. Other activities include **scuba diving** (June–Sept; free permits) into the depths of the deep, blue lake.

ARRIVAL, INFORMATION AND TOURS

By car You'll need a car to get to the park, though only the southern route (US-62 from Medford) is open year-round. The northern access road (via Hwy-138) is more exciting, emerging from the forests to cut across a bleak pumice desert, though it's closed from mid-Oct to June, as is the spectacular "Rim Drive" around the crater's edge.

Admission A seven-day pass costs $10/car ($5/motorcycles, bicycles and pedestrians).

Visitor centres The park headquarters is at the Steel

CRATER LAKE NATIONAL PARK

Visitors Center, 3 miles south of Crater Lake off Hwy-62 (daily: late April to early Nov 9am–5pm; early Nov to late April 10am–4pm; ☎541 594 3100, ⓦnps.gov/crla). The Rim Visitor Center, 3 miles further along West Rim Drive and overlooking the lake, is open late May to late Sept daily 9.30am–5pm.

Boat tours Regular boats cruise the lake from Cleetwood Cove (mid-July to mid-Sept daily 9.35am–3.30pm; 2hr; $35; ☎888 774 2728, ⓦcraterlakelodges.com).

ACCOMMODATION

Cabins at Mazama Village Off Hwy-62 (7 miles from the crater) ☎303 297 2757, ⓦcraterlakelodges.com. Clean but simple rooms with one or two queen beds and private bathrooms, but no TVs, telephones, wi-fi or a/c. Open late May to mid-Sept. **$140**

★ **Crater Lake Lodge** ☎303 297 2757, ⓦcraterlake

lodges.com. Grand 1915 hotel on the lake's south side, with a magnificent Great Hall, complete with Art Deco flourishes and simple but pleasant rooms – get either a corner room or one overlooking the lake. Free wi-fi is available here. Open mid-May to mid-Oct. **$165**

Journey Through Time Scenic Byway

The sagebush steppe, spartan hills and stark rock formations of eastern Oregon have an austere beauty that's more like Arizona than the cooler coastal areas, and culturally, this region is more Wild West than west coast, characterized by ranches and small towns. Driving the eastern section of the **Journey Through Time Scenic Byway** (a combination of highways 26 and 7), from the unexpected colours of the John Day Fossil Beds to the remote, snow-capped Blue Mountains ranges provides a decent taster, best broken up into two or three days.

John Day Fossil Beds National Monument

East of Bend and the Ochoco Mountains on US-26, the first major highlight is the **John Day Fossil Beds National Monument**, a dry-sounding prospect that is quite the opposite, with stunning mountain landscapes preserving a mind-boggling array of plant and mammal fossils from between 45 million and five million years old. There are three fossil sites, the first of which is the **Painted Hills Unit**, ten miles northwest of **Mitchell**, just off US-26. Striped in shades of beige, rust and brown, the surfaces of these evocative, sandcastle-like hills are quilted with rivulets worn by draining water. Mitchell itself is worth a look, a virtually abandoned, genuine Old West town with the atmospheric *Little Pine Café*.

Sheep Rock and Clarno units

Thirty miles east of Mitchell is the **Sheep Rock Unit**, on Hwy-19, two miles from its junction with US-26 and at the end of spectacular **Painted Gorge**, lined by basalt columns thrusting out of the earth like ancient ruined castles. Here, the **Condon Paleontology Center** (daily 10am–5pm, closed some Mondays; Free; ☎541 987 2333, ⓦnps.gov/joda) provides a superb introduction to the fossil beds region. Short trails loop out from the centre, while nearby the **Cant Ranch Historic Home** (Mon–Thurs 9am–4pm; Free) was built in 1917 by the Cant family, now housing exhibits on the region's human history. A mile north is the **Blue Basin Area**, a natural, blueish-tinted amphitheatre where the mile-long **Island in Time Trail** loops past various fossil replicas, including that of a sabre-toothed cat and a tortoise that hurtled to its death millions of years ago.

The last national monument site, the **Clarno Unit**, is eighteen miles west of the town of Fossil, which is sixty miles northwest of Mitchell and US-26. It doesn't have a visitor centre, but does offer the quarter-mile **Trail of the Fossils**, the only place where you can see up-close fossils in situ (mostly plants), along with huge **palisades** that loom over the setting – massive pillars of rock created by volcanic mudflows some 44 million years ago.

14

John Day and Prairie City

Some forty miles east of the fossil beds along US-26, the small workaday town of **JOHN DAY** acts as the commercial centre for the John Day River valley, though it was once far more important. In its nineteenth-century gold-boom years this was a major city, with the third largest Chinatown in America. Learn about this bizarre heritage at the **Kam Wah Chung State Heritage Site** (signposted at the west end of town at 125 Canton Rd), which preserves the old store and home of a Chinese merchant and his business partner, a traditional Chinese medicinal healer. The two arrived in the 1880s and stayed the rest of their lives; the **Interpretation Center** (May–Oct daily 9am–5pm; free; ☎ 541 575 2800) tells their fascinating story and that of other Chinese immigrants to Oregon. The only way to visit the house itself, its exotic interior preserved like a 1940s time capsule, is to take a guided tour (30–45min; free, on the hour till 4pm).

Continue thirteen miles east along US-26 and the John Day River to tiny but attractive **PRAIRIE CITY**, with its Old West style buildings and several good places to eat and drink. From here the scenic byway winds its way through the southern reaches of the **Wallowa-Whitman National Forest**, and over a couple of moderate mountain passes – though the views are mostly obscured by dense ponderosa pines.

Baker City

Gold was discovered on the Powder River in 1861, giving rise three years later to the boomtown of **BAKER CITY**, whose **Main Street** features stylish old piles mostly built of local stone in a potpourri of European styles – from gothic through to Renaissance Revivals – little changed since those heady days. It's a quiet, old-fashioned place, despite the plethora of motels on the outskirts, with downtown home to small independent stores and cafés.

Oregon Trail Interpretative Center

22267 Hwy-86 (I-84 exit 302) • Daily: April–Oct 9am–6pm; Nov–March 9am–4pm • April–Oct $8, Nov–March $5 • ☎ 541 523 1843, ⓦ blm.gov/or/oregontrail

Set dramatically on top of an arid, wind-blown hill (the old Flagstaff gold mine), five miles east of downtown, the **Oregon Trail Interpretative Center** chronicles pioneer life on the Oregon Trail from the 1840s with dioramas, replicas, relics and audiovisual displays, and a preserved thirteen-mile section of the trail itself, revealing actual wagon ruts and other points of interest.

PENDLETON'S ROUND-UP RODEO

North of Baker City, 95 miles away on I-84, the city of Pendleton is best known as the home of the popular, week-long **Pendleton Round-Up** in September ($15–25/event; ☎ 541 276 2553, ⓦ pendletonroundup.com), combining traditional rodeo with extravagant pageantry since 1910; the **Round-Up Hall of Fame**, 1114 SW Court Ave (June–Sept Mon–Sat 10am–4pm; $5; ☎ 541 276 0815, ⓦ pendletonhalloffame.com), is stuffed with memorabilia, and around town you can pick up a cowboy hat or fringy shirt at one of the many Western boutiques.

ACCOMMODATION AND EATING

Barley Brown's Brewpub 2190 Main St ☎541 523 4266, ⓦ barleybrowns.com. Dependable pub fare and good handcrafted microbrews; try the shredder's wheat, a dark, sweet beer. Mon–Sat 4–10pm.

Bridge Street Inn 134 Bridge St ☎541 523 6571, ⓦ bridgestreetinn.net. Independently owned motel, with clean and simple rooms with cable TV, kitchenettes and microwaves. Great deal. $55

★ **Geiser Grand** 1996 Main St ☎541 523 1889, ⓦ geisergrand.com. Dating back to 1889 but thoroughly restored in the 1990s, this historic "Italianate Renaissance Revival" gem drips with character, its spacious rooms finished in period style and modern amenities. The café and bar is a decent choice for breakfast or dinner. $109

Oregon Trail Motel Restaurant 211 Bridge St ☎541 523 5044, ⓦ oregontrailmotelandrest.com. Dependable diner, just off Main St, full of locals enjoying the cheap breakfast plates and gut-busting strawberry waffles – don't expect Portland-standard coffee, however. Daily 6am–8pm.

York's Covered Wagon 1549 Campbell St ☎541 523 2577, ⓦ yorkscoveredwagon.com. Soak up the Americana kitsch at this 1925 landmark, part souvenir and supplies store (check out the huge mural of the Oregon Trail), part deli, with big burgers ($4.99), hot turkey ($5.99) and all-you-can-eat chilli (4–7pm) for $5.99. Daily 6am–8pm.

14

Alaska

MOOSE IN DENALI NATIONAL PARK

Alaska

The sheer size of Alaska is hard to grasp. Superimposed onto the Lower 48 states, it would stretch from the Atlantic to the Pacific, while its coastline is longer than that of the rest of the mainland US combined. All but three of the nation's twenty highest peaks are found here and one glacier alone is twice the size of Wales. In addition, not only does it contain America's northernmost and westernmost points, but because the Aleutian Islands stretch across the 180th meridian, it contains the easternmost point as well. Wildlife may be under threat elsewhere, but here it is abundant, with bears standing 12ft tall, moose stopping traffic in downtown Anchorage, wolves prowling national parks, bald eagles circling over the trees and rivers solid with fifty-pound-plus salmon.

Travelling here demands a spirit of adventure and to make the most of the state you need to enjoy striking out on your own and roughing it a bit. Binoculars are an absolute must, as is bug spray; the **mosquito** is referred to as "Alaska's state bird" and only industrial-strength repellent keeps it away. On top of that, there's the **climate** – though Alaska is far from the giant icebox people imagine (see box, p.973).

The state's southernmost town, **Ketchikan**, rich in Native heritage, makes a pretty introduction, while **Sitka** retains a Russian influence. Further north are swanky **Juneau**, the capital; **Haines**, with its mix of old-timers and arty newcomers; **Skagway**, redolent of gold-rush days; and **Glacier Bay National Park**, an expensive side-trip from Juneau that penetrates one of Alaska's most stunning regions.

To the west, **Anchorage** is the state's main population centre and transport hub, while south of here are the stunning **Kenai Peninsula** and **Prince William Sound**. Interior and northern Alaska is the quintessential "great land" – a rolling plateau divided by the glacier-studded Alaska and Brooks ranges, crisscrossed by rivers and with views of imposing peaks, above all **Mount McKinley**, the nation's highest – tiny **Talkeetna** offers great views. The mountain is at the heart of **Denali National Park**, while to the east is the untrammelled vastness of **Wrangell-St Elias National Park**. **Fairbanks**, Alaska's diverting second city, serves as the hub of the North, with roads fanning out to **hot springs** and five hundred miles north to the Arctic Ocean at **Prudhoe Bay**.

GETTING TO ALASKA

Alaska is a long way from the rest of the United States, and however you get there it's going to be expensive. Having accepted that, however, there is no question as to the most enjoyable method – the memorable ferry trip on the Alaska Marine Highway, which runs 3500 miles from Alaska to Washington almost entirely in sheltered waters. You'll see plenty of marine wildlife and spend at least two nights on board bonding with fellow passengers.

BY PLANE

Most flights from the Lower 48 are routed via Seattle. The most frequent service is operated by Alaska Airlines (☎ 800 252 7522, ⊛ alaskaair.com); you'll pay $500–800 return to Anchorage with optional stopoffs at Ketchikan, Juneau, Sitka and Cordova at little extra cost.

ST MICHAEL'S ORTHODOX CATHEDRAL, SITKA

Highlights

❶ Sitka Russian influence, blended with Native heritage and fabulous coastal scenery, make this one of Alaska's most diverting towns. **See p.976**

❷ The Chilkoot Trail Follow in the (frozen) footsteps of the Klondike prospectors on this demanding 33-mile trail near Skagway. **See p.980**

❸ Talkeetna Every Alaska visitor's favourite small town is the base for superb flightseeing trips around Mount McKinley. **See p.991**

❹ Denali National Park Alaska's finest park offers superb mountain scenery and incomparable wildlife-spotting around the highest peak in North America. **See p.992**

❺ Aurora borealis The spectacular after-dark displays of the Northern Lights are at their best around Fairbanks from mid-September to mid-March. **See p.997**

❻ Dalton Highway This lonely 500-mile road leads north from Fairbanks, climbing through the Brooks Range to the Arctic Ocean. **See p.997**

HIGHLIGHTS ARE MARKED ON THE MAP ON P.972

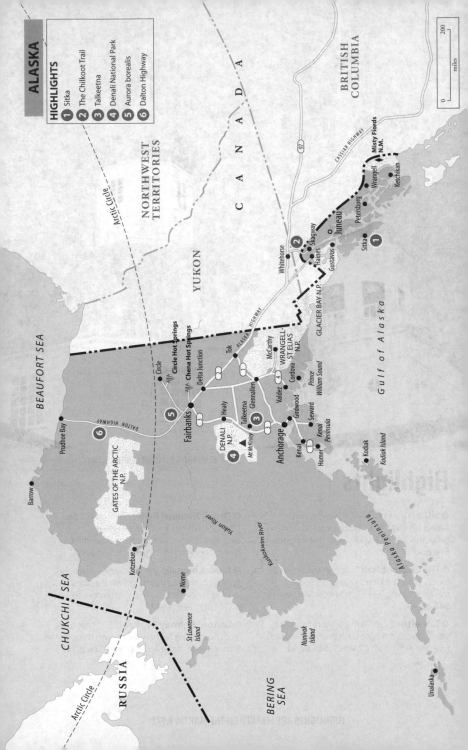

PLANNING A VISIT: COST AND CLIMATE

Alaska is more expensive than most other states and major cities. There's little budget accommodation and **eating** and **drinking** will set you back at least twenty percent more than in the Lower 48 (perhaps fifty percent in more remote regions). Still, experiencing Alaska on a **low budget** is possible, though it requires planning and off-peak travel. From June to August room prices are crazy; May and September, when tariffs are relaxed and the weather only slightly chillier, are equally good times to go, and in April or October you'll have the place to yourself, albeit with a smaller range of places to stay and eat. Ground **transport**, despite the long distances, is reasonable, with backpacker shuttles between major centres, although it is often easier to combine a car rental with flights. **Winter**, when hotels drop their prices by as much as half, is becoming an increasingly popular time to visit, particularly for the dazzling **aurora borealis** (see box, p.997).

While winter **temperatures** of -40°F are commonplace in Fairbanks, the most touristed areas – the southeast and the Kenai Peninsula – enjoy a maritime climate (45–65°F in summer) similar to that of the Pacific Northwest, meaning much more rain (in some towns 180-plus inches per year) than snow. Remarkably, the summer temperature in the Interior often reaches 80°F.

15

BY FERRY

The ferries of the state-run Alaska Marine Highway System (☎800 642 0066, ⍟ferryalaska.com), reaching many places that cars can't, operate in two separate regions with only an occasional link.

Southeast route via Inside Passage The popular southeast route runs 1000 miles from Bellingham, north of Seattle, through a wonderland of pristine waters, narrow fjords and untouched forests to Skagway, at the northern end of the Inside Passage, stopping at Ketchikan, Wrangell, Sitka, Juneau and Haines. The whole trip takes three days and costs $363 for walk-on passengers, $478 for a small car, $58 for a bicycle and $89 for kayaks. It is possible to sleep – and even to pitch a tent – on the "solarium", a covered, heated upper deck, while a two-berth cabin costs from $337.

Southwest route The southwest ferry system connects the Kenai Peninsula and Prince William Sound to Kodiak and the Aleutians, and the two systems are linked by "Cross-Gulf" ferries from Juneau to Whittier and Kodiak twice a month in summer. Intermediate fares vary with distance: $45 from Sitka to Juneau; $83 from Sitka to Ketchikan; or $221 from Juneau to Whittier. While it's a bargain for foot passengers prepared to rough it, an extended voyage with vehicle and a cabin (both of which should be reserved in advance) becomes expensive. If you're driving up from the Lower 48, consider boarding a ferry at Prince Rupert in British Columbia, two days' drive north of Seattle. This saves one day at sea without missing much of the natural spectacle.

BY CAR

For many people the drive up through Canada is one of the major highlights of a visit to Alaska. The only road is the 1500-mile Alaska Highway from Dawson Creek in British Columbia to Fairbanks, which was built by the military in just eight months. It has a fearsome reputation but is now fully paved with petrol stations, campgrounds and hotels along the way.

BY BUS

No direct buses run to Alaska, though for around $150 (booking 21 days ahead) you can hop on a Greyhound in Seattle and, after a few transfers over two gruelling days, reach Whitehorse in the Yukon. From there Alaska Direct (☎800 770 6652, ⍟alaskadirectbusline.com) make the run to Anchorage ($220) or Fairbanks ($200).

GETTING AROUND

Getting around Alaska on the cheap can be tough; public transport is limited and many areas are only accessible by boat (see above) or plane, which is invariably pricey.

By bus Anchorage is the hub of Alaska's bus network, with several bus companies running to major destinations: Seward with The Park Connection ($65; ☎800 266 8625, ⍟alaska coach.com); Homer with Stage Line ($90; ☎907 868 3914, ⍟stagelineinhomer.com); Talkeetna with Denali Overland ($95/person, min 4 passengers; ☎907 733 2384, ⍟denali overland.com) and Denali ($75) and Fairbanks ($99) with

Alaska/Yukon Trails (☎907 888 5659, ⍟alaskashuttle.com).
By train The Alaska Railroad (☎800 321 6518, ⍟akrr .com) runs nearly 500 miles from Seward north through Anchorage to Fairbanks, with a spur to Whittier for cruise liners and ferries to Valdez and Juneau. One-way summer fares from Anchorage are: Denali $150, Fairbanks $216, Whittier $74 and Seward $79.

By car Driving around Alaska in summer requires no special skills, though minor routes are often gravel, requiring caution. Wildlife, especially moose, can be a danger any time, even on city streets. In spring and autumn you should be prepared for snow, and it is wise to carry a survival kit, particularly in winter, as traffic can be sparse even on major routes. Road conditions can change rapidly – call ☎ 511 or ☎ 866 282 7577 or see ⓦ 511.alaska.gov.

By plane Travel by plane is not always more expensive than other methods. Alaska Airlines (see p.970) flies to most major communities and uses partners such as ERA Aviation (☎ 800 866 8394, ⓦ flyera.com) and PenAir (☎ 800 448 4226, ⓦ penair.com) to get to smaller towns. Chartering a plane might sound extravagant but can be inexpensive for groups of four or more and may be the crowning glory of an Alaska vacation. To arrange this contact any "bush plane" operator (every town has at least one). Rusts Flying Services in Anchorage (☎ 800 544 2299, ⓦ flyrusts.com) and K2 Aviation in Talkeetna (☎ 800 764 291, ⓦ flyk2.com) are excellent and very reliable starting points.

The Alaskapass Foot passengers planning to travel up the Inside Passage to Anchorage, Denali and Fairbanks may make considerable savings by purchasing the AlaskaPass (ⓦ alaskapass.com), covering the Alaska Marine Highway ferries, the Alaska Railroad, and the White Pass & Yukon Railroad. There are three passes: fifteen consecutive days of travel ($879); eight travel days out of twelve ($749); and twelve days out of 21 ($899). Kids (2–11) travel half-price. Add on an extra $85 booking fee, which is charged per itinerary (not/person).

Ketchikan

KETCHIKAN, almost seven hundred miles north of Seattle, is the first port of call for cruise ships and ferries and its historic downtown, wedged between water and forested mountains, becomes saturated in summer. Beyond the souvenir shops it's delightful, built into steep hills and partly propped on wooden pilings, dotted with boardwalks, wooden staircases and totem poles.

By 1886, the town's numerous canneries made it the "salmon capital of the world", while forests of cedar, hemlock and spruce fed its sawmills. Ketchikan now looks to tourism as its saviour, with the nearby **Misty Fiords National Monument** as the prime draw. The state's fourth largest city is a strong contender for the nation's wettest; annual precipitation averages 165 inches, but the perennial drizzle and sporadic showers won't spoil your visit.

The bulk of Ketchikan's historic buildings lie on **Creek Street**, a picturesque boardwalk along Ketchikan Creek. This was a red-light district until 1954; the bordellos now house gift shops and galleries. **Dolly's House**, 24 Creek St, once the home and workplace of Dolly Arthur, the town's most famous madam, is now a preserved brothel stuffed with saucy memorabilia (generally daily 8am–4pm; $5).

Most of the totem poles around town are authentic replicas, but the **Totem Heritage Center**, 601 Deermount St (daily 8am–5pm; $5), exhibits the USA's largest collection of original totem poles: 33 mostly nineteenth-century examples recovered from abandoned Native villages. The Tlingit-run **Saxman Totem Park**, two miles south of town (hourly bus), displays the world's largest standing collection of poles and an authentic tribal house. For $3 you can see the poles and exterior of the buildings, but you'll need to join the **Saxman Native Village Tour** (May–Sept daily; 1hr; $35; ☎ info@capefoxtours.com; no phone) to see sculptors at work and a dance performance in the clan house.

TONGASS NATIONAL FOREST

For a true outdoor adventure, you can rent a **cabin** in the huge Tongass National Forest – which encompasses most of southeast Alaska – for around $35/night. Get details from the visitor centres in Juneau and Ketchikan, or at the **Southeast Alaska Discovery Center**, 50 Main St (May to mid-Sept daily 8am–3pm; ☎ 907 228 6220, ⓦ fs.fed.us/r10/tongass), a striking cedar-framed building which houses absorbing displays ($5) of the region's natural habitats and native culture, or through ⓦ recreation.gov.

Fourteen of the best replica totem poles and a rebuilt tribal house stand in **Totem Bight State Park**, breathtakingly set between the forest and the Tongass Narrows, an arm of the sea/channel, ten miles north of town on the Tongass Highway. On the way back take some time out to walk the easy but enjoyable boardwalk up to **Perseverance Lake**, starting on Ward Lake Road, four miles north of town.

ARRIVAL AND INFORMATION KETCHIKAN

By plane The airport is on an island reached by ferries (every 30min; $5 return).

By ferry Ferries dock 2 miles north of downtown on Tongass Hwy.

By bus City buses run through town twice an hour during summer peak months; ⓦborough.ketchikan.ak.us/bus/info.htm has current schedules.

Visitor centre 131 Front St (daily 8am–5pm; ☎907 225 6166, ⓦvisit-ketchikan.com).

ACCOMMODATION

Alderhouse 420 Alder St ☎907 247 2537, ⓦalderhousebnb.com. Very welcoming B&B close to the AMHS ferry dock and to buses running between downtown and Totem Bight. Attention to detail makes everything, especially the breakfast, a treat. The lovely outdoor patio enjoys views of Tongass Narrows. Open June–Sept; two-night minimum. **$137**

Eagle View Hostel 2303 5th Ave ☎907 225 5461, ⓦeagleviewhostel.com. Suburban house with great views of the Narrows. Single-sex dorms (and one double room) including bed linen, towel and use of kitchen and barbecue. No lockout or curfew. Take Jefferson off Tongass Hwy then right onto 5th. Open April–Oct. Dorms **$25**, double **$50**

Ketchikan Youth Hostel United Methodist Church, 400 Main St ☎907 225 3319, ⓔketchikanhostel @gmail.com. Very basic hostel with nineteen beds in male and female dorms; bring your own sleeping bag or rent bedding. Guests have access to the church kitchen. Open June–Aug. **$20**

The New York Hotel 207 Stedman St ☎866 225 0246, ⓦthenewyorkhotel.com. Tastefully refurbished hotel in the heart of Ketchikan, with cosy rooms, a good café and gorgeous views of the harbour. **$149**

Ward Lake Recreation Area Eight miles north on Ward Lake Rd ☎800 280 2267. The closest campground to town, with picnic tables, trails and a lake. **$10**

EATING AND DRINKING

Chico's 435 Dock St ☎907 225 2833. Bargain authentic Mexican food and pizza. Dinners start at $10, or you can just grab a $7 burrito to eat in or take away. Daily lunch specials for $10. Daily 11am–9pm.

Diaz Café 335 Stedman St ☎907 225 2257. Great inexpensive diner food with some tasty Filipino dishes. Tues–Sat 11.30am–2pm & 4–8pm, Sun noon–730pm.

First City Saloon 830 Water St ☎907 225 1494. Straightforward boozing bar (though with free wi-fi),

occasionally featuring bands and shows. The likeliest place for a little dancing. Daily 11am–2am.

★ **Ketchikan Coffee Company** 211 Stedman St ☎907 247 2326, ⓦketchikancoffee.com. Attractive coffeeshop with a daytime menu of tasty bagels, excellent soups, delicious sandwiches and salads (mostly $9–13), plus desserts and microbrews. Daily 7am–4pm; lunch served 10.30am–3pm.

Misty Fjords National Monument

Twenty-two miles east of Ketchikan on the mainland, the awe-inspiring **MISTY FJORDS NATIONAL MONUMENT** consists of 2.3 million acres of deep fjords flanked by sheer 3000ft glacially scoured walls topped by dense rainforest. As befits its name, the monument is at its most atmospheric when swathed in low-lying mists.

ARRIVAL AND ACCOMMODATION MISTY FJORDS NATIONAL MONUMENT

Access Charter a floatplane with Taquan Air (☎800 770 8800, ⓦtaquanair.com) or kayak with Southeast Sea Kayaks (☎907 225 1258, ⓦkayakketchikan.com) – both operate out of Ketchikan.

Tours The best way to experience this area is on a tour by Misty Fiords Cruise and Fly (☎907 225 3845,

ⓦmistyfjordscruisefly.com); its 5hr cruise ($179) and excellent 75min flightseeing tour ($229) depart from the waterfront.

Cabins Thirteen rustic cabins are scattered through the park, managed by the Forestry Service (☎877 444 6777, ⓦreserveusa.com). From **$25**

15

Sitka

Shielded by islands from the Pacific Ocean, **SITKA** is one of Alaska's prettiest and most historic towns. The Russians established a fort here in 1799 and Sitka subsequently became the capital of Russian America, witnessing transfer of ownership to the USA in 1867. Sitka today earns its keep mostly from fishing and tourism and offers a wealth of great outdoor activities.

The best place to get a grasp of Sitka's Russian past is diminutive **Castle Hill**. It's a two-minute stroll to **St Michael's Orthodox Cathedral** (Mon–Fri 9am–4pm; $2), a typically Russian church completed in 1848 and rebuilt after a disastrous fire in 1966. Nearby is the large, mustard-coloured 1842 **Russian Bishop's House** (daily 9am–5pm; $4). Guided tours take in the restored chapel, schoolroom and living quarters. Four blocks east at 104 College Drive, the **Sheldon Jackson Museum** (daily 9am–5pm; $4) houses a compact but extensive display of Native artefacts accumulated by missionary and educationalist Sheldon Jackson.

Nearby, the site of a decisive battle between the Tlingit and the Russians is now the **Sitka National Historic Park** with its evocative collection of vividly painted **totem poles**, copies of nineteenth-century originals. A **visitor centre** (May–Sept daily 8am–5pm; $4) features good displays plus working craftspeople.

Sitka's **trail system** ranges from coastal strolls to harder climbs up Gavan Hill and steep Mount Verstovia: for more information visit the **Forest Service office**, 204 Siganaka Way (☎907 747 6671).

ARRIVAL, INFORMATION AND TOURS

By ferry Traditional and fast ferries (around 5 weekly) dock 7 miles northwest of town; Sitka Tours shuttles ($8 each way; ☎907 747 8443) run in.

By plane Sitka's airport is a 30min walk from downtown, again served by Sitka Tours shuttles.

Visitor centre 303 Lincoln St (daily 9am–5pm; ☎907 747 5940, ⓦsitka.org).

SITKA

Town tours Sitka Tours offers informative 2hr town tours ($12) covering most of the historical buildings.

Kayak rental and tours Sitka Sound Ocean Adventures rents out kayaks ($50/half-day, double $65; ☎907 752 0660, ⓦssoceanadventures.com) and organizes the full-day guided Wild Coast Paddling Tour ($209).

ACCOMMODATION, EATING AND DRINKING

★ **Backdoor** 104 Barracks St ☎907 747 8856. Very popular spot at the back door of Old Harbour's Bookstore, serving up excellent coffee and tasty home-made lunches, including a good chicken pot pie. Cash only. Mon–Sat 6.30am–5pm, Sun 9am–2pm.

★ **Ludvig's Bistro** 256 Katlian St ☎907 966 3663, ⓦludvigsbistro.com. Not to be missed – expensive but excellent Spanish and Moroccan-influenced dishes using local and organic ingredients. Mon–Sat 5–9pm.

Pioneer Bar 212 Katlian St ☎907 747 3456. Down-to-earth boozing spot lined with hundreds of black-and-white photographs of fishing boats. Daily 11am–2am.

Sitka Hotel 118 Lincoln St ☎907 747 3288,

ⓦsitkahotel.net. This historic hotel offers a touch of old-fashioned style, though some rooms come without bathrooms. **$124**

Sitka International Hostel 109 Jeff Davis St ☎907 747 8661, ⓦsitkahostel.org. Comfortable, clean and basic accommodation in a building that is nearly a century old, with 23 beds and a communal kitchen. Dorms **$24**

Starrigavan Less than a mile north of the ferry dock on Halibut Point Rd ☎877 444 6777. There are 34 primitive pitches, and some rustic cabins, set among old growth hemlock-spruce forest, with access to some nearby hiking trails. Camping **$12**, cabins **$50**

Juneau and around

The sophisticated and vibrant city of **JUNEAU** is the only state capital in the nation not accessible by road. It is exceptionally picturesque, wedged between the **Gastineau Channel** and the rainforested hills behind. In 1880, Joe Juneau made **Alaska's first gold strike** here, and until the last mine closed in 1944 this was the world's largest producer of low-grade ore – all the flat land in Juneau, stretching from downtown to the airport, is waste rock from the mines. Today, state government provides much of the employment, and tourism plays its part with the drive-to **Mendenhall Glacier** and the watery charms of **Tracy Arm fjord** as temptation.

Many original buildings stand in the **South Franklin Street Historic District** – Juneau managed to avoid the fires that destroyed many other gold towns in Alaska. The onion-domed **St Nicholas Russian Orthodox Church**, 326 Fifth St (Mon 9am–6pm, Tues & Thurs 9am–5pm, Fri 10am–noon & 3–5pm, Sat 11am–3pm, Sun 1–5pm; $2 suggested donation), contains icons and religious treasures, while the well-presented **Alaska State Museum**, 395 Whittier St (daily 8.30am–5.30pm; $7), covers Native culture, Russian heritage and the first gold strikes. Its pride and joy is the logbook in which Bering reported his first sighting of Alaska. The smaller **Juneau-Douglas City Museum**, at Main and Fourth streets (Mon–Fri 9am–6pm, Sat & Sun 10am–5pm; $6), displays relics from the mining era. The best views of town are from the top of the **Mount Roberts Tramway** (May–Sept Mon 11am–9pm, Tues–Sun 8am–9pm; $31), which rises 1800ft from the cruise-ship dock to a nature centre and some easy trails.

15

ARRIVAL, INFORMATION AND ACTIVITIES   JUNEAU

By boat Ferries dock 14 miles northwest of downtown at Auke Bay; they often arrive at unearthly hours, so getting into town can be a problem. The only alternative to a $35 taxi ride (sharing encouraged) is walking 1.5 mile south to DeHarts grocery, served by Capital Transit buses (Mon–Sat hourly 8am–10.30pm, Sun 9am–5pm; $2; ☎ 907 789 6901).

By plane Buses pick up near the busy airport, 9 miles north of downtown.

Visitor centre 800 Glacier Ave, Suite 201 (Mon–Fri 8.30am–5pm, Sat & Sun 9am–5pm; ☎ 888 581 2201, ⓦ traveljuneau.com) has stacks of brochures about the Tongass National Forest, Glacier Bay and around.

Mountain biking Driftwood Lodge (☎ 907 586 2280) rents out mountain bikes for $20/day.

ACCOMMODATION

Alaskan Hotel and Bar 167 S Franklin St ☎ 800 327 9374, ⓦ thealaskanhotel.com. The oldest operating hotel in southeastern Alaska is pleasant place with a salacious past, and the least expensive choice in town. Shared bath $60, en suite $90

Juneau Hostel 614 Harris St ☎ 907 586 9559, ⓦ juneauhostel.net. Clean, comfortable and relaxed hostel, in an old home near downtown, with dorm beds and a family room, but an inconvenient daytime lockout (9am–5pm) and an 11pm curfew. Dorms $12, family room per person $12

Mendenhall Lake Campground Montana Creek Rd, 13 miles from downtown. A gorgeous Forest Service campground within sight of the Mendenhall Glacier and with space for RVs ($26) and some lovely lakeside walk-in tent sites. Open mid-May to Sept. Tent sites $10, RV sites $26

★ **Silverbow Inn** 120 2nd St, downtown ☎ 800 586 4146, ⓦ silverbowinn.com. Attractive little hotel with smallish but nicely furnished rooms, each with TV and phone, and with a good continental breakfast included. The owners also run a bakery next door. $89

GLACIER BAY NATIONAL PARK

Sixteen glaciers spill into the 65-mile-long **Glacier Bay**, northwest of Juneau. Brown and black bears, moose, mountain goats, sea otters, humpback whales, porpoise, seals and a colourful array of birds call the area home.

ARRIVAL AND ACCOMMODATION

By plane or boat It's going to cost you to get here. Either fly with Alaska Airlines from Juneau (about $100 one way) or join a day-cruise (8hr; $200) from Bartlett Cove, 9 miles north.

Accommodation You'll also need a bed for at least one night. At Bartlett Cove you can camp for free or stay at Glacier Bay Lodge, with tasteful rooms and a good restaurant (☎ 888 229 8687, ⓦ visitglacierbay.com; $219). In central Gustavus there's accommodation at Homestead B&B (☎ 907 697 2777, ⓦ homestead bedbreakfast.com; $145).

EATING AND DRINKING

Alaskan Hotel Bar 167 S Franklin St. Great old bar with live music most nights, especially toward the weekend. Daily 11am–2am.

The Hanger on the Wharf Merchants Wharf ☎907 586 5018. Former floatplane hangar with great waterfront views and more than twenty beers on tap, plus pool tables and live music at weekends. Wraps and burgers at lunch and the likes of jambalaya and halibut tacos ($13–14) at dinner. Mon–Fri & Sun 11am–1am, Sat 11am–3am.

★ **Paradise Café and Bakery** 245 Marine Way ☎907 586 2253. Stylish little café and bakery with excellent soups, salads and wraps. A little pricey but worth it.

Gluten-free options available. Tues–Fri 7am–4pm, Sat & Sun 8am–3pm.

Rainbow Foods 224 4th St ☎907 586 6476, ⓦrainbow-foods.org. Wholefood and organic grocery serving a limited selection of light lunches (Mon–Fri), plus a deli and salad bar. Try the home-made cookies and espresso. Mon–Fri 9am–7pm, Sat & Sun 10am–6pm.

Silverbow Bakery 120 2nd St ☎907 586 4146. Relaxed eat-in bakery and coffee bar with bagels, freshly baked bread, challahs, hot and cold deli sandwiches ($7–11), soups and superb pastries. Mon–Fri 6.30am–6pm, Sat 7.30am–4pm, Sun 8am–4pm.

15 Haines

Tiny **HAINES** sits on a peninsula at the northern end of the longest and deepest fjord in the US, Lynn Canal. Somewhat overshadowed by its brasher neighbour, Skagway, it remains a slice of real Alaska with an interesting mix of locals and urban escapees. The Tlingit fished and traded here for years before 1881, when the first missionaries arrived. Today, the town survives on fishing and tourism, hosting in mid-August the cook-outs, crafts and log-rolling of the **Southeast Alaska Fair**.

The **Sheldon Museum & Cultural Center**, 11 Main St (Mon–Fri 10am–5pm, Sat & Sun 1–4pm; $5; ⓦsheldonmuseum.org), shows how Haines fits into its Chilkat environment and the wider Tlingit world, exhibiting fine examples of woodwork, clothing and the distinctive yellow and black Chilkat blanket in wolf, raven and killer whale designs.

Half a mile away, grassy **Fort William H. Seward** was established in 1903 to contain Gold Rush lawlessness and territorial disputes with Canada. It is now home to **Alaska Indian Arts** (Mon–Fri 9am–5pm; free), where you can meet carvers working on huge totem poles.

Nearby, the natural history museum of the **American Bald Eagle Foundation**, 113 Haines Hwy at Second Ave (daily 10am–6pm; $3), has a fine exhibit of dioramas and museum specimens that depict the rich biodiversity of this region. The centre also features live eagle feedings (10.30am & 2.30pm) as well as hosting numerous presentations throughout the year.

In mid-November, this area is home to the world's largest gathering of **bald eagles**. More than three thousand birds – as many as two dozen to a tree – gather along a five-mile stretch of the Chilkat River that runs parallel to the Haines Highway; the **Chilkat Bald Eagle Preserve** between miles 18 and 24 is the best place from which to observe them feasting on a late salmon run.

ARRIVAL, INFORMATION AND TOURS

By ferry Haines' AMHS ferry terminal is 5 miles north of town, with daily services to and from Juneau and Skagway. A convenient passenger-only fast ferry ($35 one-way; ☎888 766 2103, ⓦhainesskagwayfastferry .com) runs between Haines and Skagway from a dock near Fort Seward.

Visitor centre 122 Second St (Mon–Fri 8am–6pm, Sat & Sun 9am–5pm; ☎800 458 3579, ⓦhalnes.ak.us).

Tours Haines is a popular starting point for rafting trips: Chilkat Guides on Beach Rd (☎907 766 2491, ⓦraftalaska .com) runs 4hr float trips ($94) down the Chilkat River, ideal for viewing eagles and other wildlife.

ACCOMMODATION

Bear Creek Cabins and Hostel Small Tracts Rd ☎907 766 2259, ⓦbearcreekcabinsalaska.com. A good hostel over a mile south of Fort Seward with coin-op laundry and no lockout nor curfew. Campers can use hostel facilities.

Camping $14, dorms $20, cabins $68

Hotel Halsingland Fort Seward ☎907 766 2000, ⓦhotelhalsingland.com. Located across the grassy parading grounds in Fort Seward, this large Victorian building was once home to Fort Seward's commanding officers. Today, it offers quiet rooms, private baths and an on-site restaurant and lounge. **$119**

Port Chilkoot Campground Mud Bay Rd ☎ 800 542 6363, ⓦ hotelhalsingland.com. Central campground with a handful of flat-ground sites, pay-showers and a laundry. Basic RVs & tents with vehicle **$16**, hookups **$25**

Portage Cove State Recreation Site Beach Rd, half a mile southeast of Fort Seward. A small site for backpackers and cyclists only, by the beach with great views, fire sites and potable water. No overnight parking. **$5**

★ **Summer Inn B&B** 117 2nd Ave ☎ 907 766 2970, ⓦ summerinnbnb.com. Immaculate downtown B&B with shared bathrooms and a good cooked breakfast. It has a very homely feel with clawfoot baths, quilts and fresh flowers. **$110**

EATING AND DRINKING

Bamboo Room 11 2nd St near Main ☎ 907 766 2800. Standard diner popular for its well-prepared meals (especially the local halibut and chips, $25), and freshly baked pies. Breakfast served until 3pm. Tues–Thurs & Sun 7am–9pm, Fri & Sat 7am–10pm.

Chilkat Restaurant and Bakery 5th Ave at Dalton St ☎ 907 766 3653. A great spot for baked goods with an espresso coffee, or more substantial fare – everything from tasty breakfasts, salads and halibut sandwiches to Thai lunches for $11, all beautifully cooked. Mon, Tues, Fri & Sat 7am–3pm & 5–8pm, Wed, Thurs & Sun 7am–3pm.

★ **Mosey's Cantina** 31 Tower Rd, Fort Seward ☎ 907 766 2320. Serving up authentic Mexican home-made cuisine (dinner mains from $16) in a cosy setting, up the road from the cruise ship terminal. All seafood is locally caught and the restaurant closes in October so staff can pick, peel and roast their own chilli peppers in New Mexico. Mon & Wed–Fri 11.30am–2.30pm & 5–8.30pm, Sat & Sun 5–8.30pm.

★ **Mountain Market** 151 3rd Ave, at Haines Hwy ☎ 907 766 3340. Combined natural-food grocery, deli and espresso bar that's one of the best places in town for a $6 bagel breakfast, a $7 tortilla wrap, or just a freshly baked treat with your mocha. A fun place to meet fellow travellers and colourful locals. May–Oct daily 7am–7pm; Nov–April Mon–Fri 7am–7pm, Sat 8am–7pm, Sun 9am–5pm.

15

Skagway

SKAGWAY, the northern terminal of the southeast ferry route, sprang up overnight in 1897 as a trading post serving **Klondike Gold Rush** pioneers setting off on the five-hundred-mile ordeal. Having grown from one cabin to a town of twenty thousand in three months, Skagway, rife with disease and desperado violence was reported to be "hell on earth". It boasted more than seventy bars and hundreds of prostitutes and was controlled by criminals, including **Jefferson "Soapy" Smith**, notorious for cheating hapless prospectors out of their gold.

By 1899, the Gold Rush was over but the completion in 1900 of the White Pass and Yukon Route railway from Skagway to Whitehorse, the Yukon capital, ensured Skagway's survival. Today the town's eight hundred residents have gone to great lengths to maintain (or re-create) the original appearance of their home, much of which lies in the **Klondike Gold Rush National Historic Park**, and in summer as many as five cruise ships a day call in to appreciate the effort.

Skagway is very compact, and most of the sights can easily be seen on foot. Strolling up Broadway you can't miss the eye-catching facade of the 1899 **Arctic Brotherhood Hall**, decorated with almost nine thousand pieces of driftwood and housing the visitor centre (see p.980).

The *Skagway Trail Map*, available from the visitor centre and at ⓦ skagway.com/skagway trailmap.pdf, details local **hikes**, including the **Dewey Lakes trails**, which pass pretty subalpine lakes and tumbling waterfalls, and the tougher scramble up AB Mountain.

Klondike Gold Rush National Historic Park

Visitor centre: Broadway, at Second Ave • Daily 8am–6pm • Free • ☎ 907 983 2921, ⓦ nps.gov/klgo

Many of the buildings hereabouts form part of the **Klondike Gold Rush National Historic Park**, notably the **Mascot Saloon** on Broadway (daily 8am–6pm; free), and **Moore Homestead**, Fifth Ave at Spring St (daily 10am–5pm; free), a museum **devoted** to

Skagway's founder, with photos of the Gold Rush. There's further detail in the **City of Skagway Museum** (Mon–Fri 9am–5pm, Sat & Sun 1–5pm; $2), which contains Soapy's Derringer pistol and good Tlingit artefacts.

The park's visitor centre has historical displays, talks, walking tours and an impressive movie about the Gold Rush, as well as maps and information on the Chilkoot Trail.

White Pass and Yukon Route railway

Early May to late Sept 2–3 departures daily • $115 return to White Pass summit • ☎ 800 343 7373, ⓦ wpyr.com

A lazy way to take in the scenery is on the **White Pass and Yukon Route** railway, which follows the gushing Skagway River past waterfalls and ice-packed gorges and over a 1000ft-high bridge, stopping at the White Pass summit. There's no shortage of riders, so get there early and grab a seat on the left-hand side going up. The company also offers a bus connection to Whitehorse.

15

ARRIVAL, INFORMATION AND ACTIVITIES   SKAGWAY

By ferry AMHS ferries and an independent operator arrive daily from Haines and Juneau on the edge of downtown just a block from the WP & YR train station (see below).
By bus or train Yukon Alaska Tourist Tours (reservations essential on ☎ 866 626 7383, ⓦ yatt.ca), run a bus from Skagway to Whitehorse ($65) and a train–bus combo ($135 return).
Visitor centre Arctic Brotherhood Hall, Broadway between Second and Third aves (daily 8am–6pm; ☎ 888

762 1898, ⓦ skagway.com).
Mountain biking Sockeye Cycles, Fifth Ave and Broadway (☎ 907 983 2851, ⓦ cyclealaska.com), rents out well-maintained mountain bikes for $25/4hr and also offers a variety of cycling tours.
Backpacking supplies The Mountain Shop, 4th Ave and State (☎ 907 983 2544, ⓦ packerexpeditions.com), rents and sells everything you'll need.

ACCOMMODATION

★ **At the White House** 475 8th Ave, at Main St ☎ 907 983 9000, ⓦ atthewhitehouse.com. High-standard B&B in a restored historic home with modernized rooms, private baths and substantial breakfasts. $135
★ **Cindy's Place** Mile 0.2 Dyea Rd ☎ 800 831 8095, ⓦ alaska.net/~croland. Three log cabins in the woods 2 miles from downtown, one budget, two more luxurious with food provided and private bathrooms (one with a wood-burning stove), phone and cooking equipment. There's free use of the hot tub plus thoughtful touches such as a dozen varieties of tea and coffee in the cabins, fresh baking and

home-made jams. Cabins: budget $65, luxury $135
Skagway Home Hostel 3rd Ave and Main St ☎ 907 983 2131, ⓦ skagwayhostel.com. In-with-the-family hostel in a century-old building with single-sex and mixed dorms. There's a communal feel, ample supplies for cooking (honesty box) and an 11pm curfew. Mixed dorms $15, single-sex $20
Skagway Mountain View RV Park Broadway, at 12th Ave ☎ 888 323 5757, ⓦ bestofalaskatravel.com. Large RV-dominated spot with all the expected facilities, water and electricity hookup and a few wooded tent sites) that are in high demand. Tent sites $29, RV sites $49

EATING AND DRINKING

Corner Café State St, at 4th Ave ☎ 907 983 2155. A basic daytime diner popular with locals for its salads, soups, sandwiches and pizza. Mon–Sat 9am–6pm.
Red Onion Saloon Broadway, at 2nd Ave ☎ 907 983 2222. An 1898 bar and former bordello with heaps of character, draft beers and excellent soups, hot sandwiches and pizzas. Daily 10am–2am.
Skagway Brewing Company Broadway, at 7th Ave

☎ 907 983 2739. Good brews and a varied menu of sandwiches, "Alaskan tapas" and (after 5pm) more substantial dinner/pub food. Daily 11am–10pm.
★ **Starfire** 4th Ave, at Spring St ☎ 907 983 3663. Authentic, delicious Thai food, with mains averaging $15 and patio dining in summer. It's very popular with locals and cruise-ship passengers, so call ahead for reservations in the peak summer season. Daily 5–9 pm.

The Chilkoot Trail

Alaska's most famous hike, the 33-mile **CHILKOOT TRAIL**, is one huge wilderness museum following in the footsteps of the original Klondike prospectors. Starting in

Dyea, nine miles from Skagway and ending in **Bennett** in Canada, the trail climbs through rainforest to tundra strewn with haunting reminders of the past, including ancient boilers that once drove aerial tramways and several collapsed huts. The three- to five-day hike is strenuous, especially the ascent from Sheep Camp (1000ft) to Chilkoot Pass (3550ft). You must carry food, fuel and a tent and be prepared for foul weather.

ARRIVAL, INFORMATION AND ACCOMMODATION THE CHILKOOT TRAIL

By bus or train Shuttles run to Dyea, and the White Pass and Yukon Railway runs a service for hikers returning to Skagway (Mon, Tues & Fri; $95).
Hiking info and permits The hiking season runs from July to early Sept, with a quota system administered by Parks Canada (W wpc.gc.ca/eng/lhn-nhs/yt/chilkoot/index .aspx). First visit the Skagway Trail Center, Broadway at 1st

Ave (early June to early Sept daily 8.30am–4.30pm), where rangers brief you on the challenges and dangers, and can advise on weather conditions and bus and train schedules for the trip back to Skagway. While here, you must also pay Can $50 for a permit.
Camping Campgrounds along the trail have shelters with stoves and firewood; not all have bear-proof lockers for food.

15

Anchorage

Wedged between Cook Inlet and the imposing Chugach Mountains, **ANCHORAGE** is home to more than forty percent of Alaska's population and is the state's transport hub. A sprawling city on the edge of one of the world's great wildernesses, it is often derided as "just half an hour from Alaska". However, it has its attractions and, with its beautiful setting, can make a pleasant one- or two-day stopover.

Downtown Anchorage

Apart from the **Anchorage Museum**, downtown sights are fairly modest: the 1915 **Oscar Anderson House Museum**, 420 M St (June–Sept Tues–Sun noon–4pm; $10; ☎907 274 2336), illustrates early Anchorage life, and the **Alaska Experience Theatre**, 333 West 4th Ave (daily 10am–6pm; ☎907 272 9076, W alaskaexperiencetheatre.com), presents films of the Northern Lights and of Alaska's best scenery (every 30min; $10), and of the devastating 1964 Good Friday **earthquake** that levelled much of downtown – North America's strongest-ever quake at magnitude 9.2 (every 15min, $6); a combined ticket for both films is $13.

The Anchorage Museum
6th Ave, at C St • May–Sept daily 9am–6pm; Oct–April Tues–Sat 10am–6pm, Sun noon–6pm • $15 • W anchoragemuseum.org
Your first stop in town should be the **Anchorage Museum**, which provides a fascinating overview of the state and its history alongside beautiful examples of carved ivory and basketware. There's a fine collection of art, including the iconic painting of Mount McKinley by Alaska's best-known painter, Sydney Laurence, and contemporary works, as well as numerous self-discovery science displays, a planetarium and a touch tank containing some of the marine invertebrates that inhabit the nearby tidal flats. A relatively new extension houses the Smithsonian's **Arctic Studies Center**, a superb collection of First Nation artefacts and ceremonial dress.

Alaska Native Heritage Center
Off the Glenn Hwy, at Muldoon Rd • May–Sept daily 9am–5pm • $25 • W alaskanative.net • A free shuttle runs four times a day from the Anchorage Museum and the visitor centre
Seven miles east of the town centre lies the **Alaska Native Heritage Center**. Although pricey, it gives an excellent introduction to the state's five main ethnic groups, each represented by a typical house where native guides interpret their culture. There are also performances and films in the auditorium.

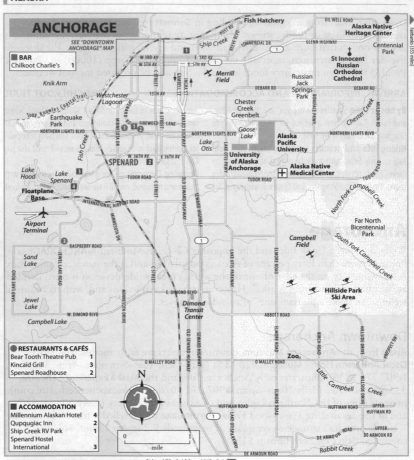

ANCHORAGE

SEE "DOWNTOWN
ANCHORAGE" MAP

■ **BAR**
Chilkoot Charlie's **1**

Knik Arm

Tony Knowles Coastal Trail

Earthquake
Park

Lake
Hood

Lake
Spenard

Floatplane
Base

Airport
Terminal

Sand
Lake

Jewel
Lake

Campbell Lake

● **RESTAURANTS & CAFÉS**
Bear Tooth Theatre Pub **1**
Kincaid Grill **3**
Spenard Roadhouse **2**

■ **ACCOMMODATION**
Millennium Alaskan Hotel **4**
Qupqugiac Inn **2**
Ship Creek RV Park **1**
Spenard Hostel
International **3**

Fish Hatchery

Ship Creek

Merrill
Field

Westchester
Lagoon

SPENARD

Lake
Otis

Goose
Lake

University
of Alaska
Anchorage

Chester
Creek
Greenbelt

Alaska
Pacific
University

Alaska Native
Medical Center

Campbell
Field

Hillside Park
Ski Area

Dimond
Transit
Center

Zoo

Little Campbell Creek

OIL WELL ROAD

Alaska Native
Heritage Center

Centennial
Park

St Innocent
Russian
Orthodox
Cathedral

Russian
Jack
Springs
Park

Chester Creek

Far North
Bicentennial
Park

South Fork Campbell Creek

North Fork Campbell Creek

Rabbit Creek

N

0 _____ 1
mile

Girdwood (25 miles) & Seward (115 miles) ▼

Fairbanks (355 miles) ►

**DOWNTOWN
ANCHORAGE**

Tony Knowles
Coastal Trail

Cycle
Route

Oscar Anderson
House Museum **6**

Elderberry
Park

■ **ACCOMMODATION**
Bent Prop Inn **8**
Copper Whale Inn **6**
Historic Anchorage Hotel **5**
Oscar Gill House **9**
Voyager Hotel **7**

Captain Cook Monument

Public Lands
Information
Center
(APLIC) **5**

Oomingmak
Musk Ox
Producers' Co-op

★
Transit
Center

Train
Station

Hilton
Hotel

Egan
Center

Performing
Arts Center

Town
Square
Park

Weekend Market

Bronze
Dog Sled
Statue

Alaska
Experience
Theater

Cyrano's
Off-Center
Playhouse

Anchorage
Museum

Federal
Building

● **RESTAURANTS & CAFÉS**
Ginger **8**
Glacier Brewhouse **7**
The Marx Bros. Café **4**
New Sagaya's City Market **9**
Sack's Café and Restaurant **5**
Snow City Café **6**

■ **BARS**
Darwin's Theory **2**
Humpy's **3**

N

0 _____ 200
yards

Delaney Park (aka The Park Strip)

▼ **9** (50 yards)   ▼ **9** (200 yards)

15

Tony Knowles Coastal Trail and Chugach State Park

On long summer days it is good to stay outside, perhaps strolling (or biking) along the **Tony Knowles Coastal Trail**, which offers restorative views of Turnagain Arm, or exploring the mountains and lakes of the 495,000 acre **Chugach State Park**, just fifteen minutes' drive east from Anchorage. Challenging trails include the scramble up 4500ft Flattop Mountain, giving spectacular views of the city and Cook Inlet.

ARRIVAL AND INFORMATION   ANCHORAGE

By plane Anchorage International Airport (☎ 907 266 2526), 5 miles southwest of town, is served by the city's People Mover bus #7A ($1.75 flat fare or $5 day pass from the driver). Alaska Shuttle (☎ 907 338 8888) charges $50 (1–5 passengers) to take you downtown and taxis cost around $30. An Alaska Rail Station terminal in the airport has a direct service to the downtown core. Many hotels offer free airport shuttles.
By train The station is downtown at 411 W 1st Ave (☎ 800 544 0552, ⊕ akrr.com).
Visitor centres The Log Cabin Visitor Center, downtown at 4th and F (daily 8am–7pm; ☎ 907 274 3531, ⊕ anchorage .net), is across the street from the Alaska Public Lands Information Center (daily 9am–5pm; ☎ 907 644 3661, ⊕ alaska centers.gov), which has excellent natural history displays plus maps and brochures. Staff will help plan back-country trips, and make reservations both for accommodation and shuttle buses in Denali National Park – vital in summer. It's also the only place in town with public washrooms.
Shopping There are no sales taxes in Anchorage, so visitors can enjoy a tax-free retail experience.

ACCOMMODATION

There are plenty of accommodation choices in Anchorage, though inexpensive places can be hard to find, especially in summer. All hotels in Anchorage charge a twelve-percent hotel tax.

Bent Prop Inn 700 H St ☎ 907 276 3635, ⊕ bentprop inn.com. Functional and very central hostel with daytime lockout and evening curfew; reserve well ahead in summer. Facilities include a communal kitchen and dining area, free wi-fi and coin-operated washing machines. Dorms **$30**, doubles **$65**

★ **Copper Whale Inn B&B** 440 L St ☎ 907 258 7999, ⊕ copperwhale.com. A charming inn conveniently located on the edge of the downtown core. Rooms offer private or shared baths and all guests are treated to an excellent breakfast in the main lobby with views across the Cook Inlet and onto the Alaska Range Mountains. One of the few historic buildings to survive the 1964 earthquake. Shared bath **$189**, en suite **$229**

★ **Historic Anchorage Hotel** 330 E St ☎ 907 272 4553, ⊕ historicanchoragehotel.com. Located in the downtown core, built in 1916 and restored to its original grandeur in 1989. The comfortable rooms all come complete with restored original sinks and bathtubs, and the hallways are decorated with black-and-white photos of Alaska in the early 1900s. Free continental breakfast. **$219**

★ **Millennium Alaskan Hotel** 4800 Spenard Rd ☎ 907 243 2300, ⊕ millenniumhotels.com/usa/millennium anchorage. A 5min drive from the airport, this contemporary hotel, on the shores of scenic Lake Spenard, offers cosy yet spacious rooms with private bathrooms, two on-site restaurants and seasonal watering hole *The Deck at Lake Hood*, where you can sit outside and enjoy the midnight sun or simply watch the seaplanes come and go from Lake Hood, the world's largest and busiest seaplane base. Free airport shuttle and shuttle to the downtown core. **$197**
Oscar Gill House 1344 W 10th Ave ☎ 907 279 1344, ⊕ oscargill.com. Lovely B&B in a 1913 house, restored with understated elegance. Two rooms share a bath while one has its own jacuzzi, all tastefully done and managed by very welcoming hosts. Shared bath **$115**, en suite **$135**
Qupqugiac Inn 640 W 36th Ave, midtown ☎ 907 563 5633, ⊕ qupq.com; bus #9 from downtown passes a block away on Arctic Blvd. Great budget hotel with clean, simple rooms with phone and satellite TV, and a communal lounge with kitchen. Shared bath **$85**, en suite **$100**
Spenard Hostel International 2845 W 42nd Ave ☎ 907 248 5036, ⊕ alaskahostel.org. Friendly suburban independent hostel with a nearby mall just 1.5 miles from the airport (bus #7A), and less than a block from Anchorage's famous bike trail system. Cheap bike rental, no curfew or lockout. Dorms **$25** cash, **$27** if using credit card
Voyager Hotel 501 K St, at 5th Ave ☎ 907 277 9501, ⊕ thevoyagerhotel.com. The best of the mid-to upper-range hotels, featuring spacious rooms (with kitchenette) and most of the facilities of a business hotel at much lower cost. Reserve well ahead in summer. **$190**

15

EATING, DRINKING AND NIGHTLIFE

Nowhere in Alaska will you find a more diverse range of places to eat than in Anchorage. You wouldn't make a special journey for its culinary wonders, but after weeks in the wilds the city can seem like heaven. Carr's supermarket at the junction of Northern Lights Boulevard and Minnesota Drive (bus #3 or #36) has groceries and a strong deli section.

Good **bars** abound, both downtown and in the lively (and somewhat edgy) strip of Spenard Road between Northern Lights Boulevard and International Airport Road.

RESTAURANTS AND CAFÉS

Bear Tooth Theatre Pub 1230 W 27th Ave ☎ 907 276 4200, ⓦ beartooththeatre.net. Splendid cinema with attached restaurant, where you can enjoy pizzas ($14–22), Caesar salads ($7), burritos and tacos ($11–14) while watching art-house movies ($3). There's takeaway too, and excellent microbrews. Grill Mon–Fri 11am–11.30pm, Sat & Sun 10am–11.30pm.

Ginger 425 W, at 5th Ave ☎ 907 929 3680, ⓦ ginger alaska.com. Great food, excellent service and a warm ambience in a place specializing in Pacific Rim cuisine – curries, seafood, poultry and beef (mains $25). Mon–Fri 11.30am–2pm & 5–10pm, Sat & Sun 11am–2.30pm & 5–10pm.

Glacier Brewhouse 737 W 5th St ☎ 907 274 2739, ⓦ glacierbrewhouse.com. Hugely popular restaurant, bar and microbrewery serving wonderful food and drink. Half a dozen tasty house-brewed beers accompany alderwood-baked pizza ($11), wood-grilled New York steak ($30) or steamed king crab legs ($37). Mon 11am–4pm, Tues–Thurs 11am–10pm, Fri & Sat 11am–11pm, Sun 10am–9.30pm. Bar closes 1hr after restaurant.

Kincaid Grill 6700 Jewel Lake Rd ☎ 907 243 0507, ⓦ kincaidgrill.com. Small and intimate restaurant, strong on Alaskan regional cuisine, local hospitality and outstanding service. The salmon prepared with truffle hollandaise, mushroom-leek ragout and scallion potatoes is unmissable. Tues–Sat 5–10pm.

The Marx Bros. Café 627 W 3rd Ave ☎ 907 278 2133, ⓦ marxcafe.com. The best all-round fine dining downtown served up in a historic house with views of the water. Start with Alaskan oysters with pepper vodka and ginger sorbet ($14.50) or Neapolitan seafood mousse ($15), followed by baked halibut in macadamia-nut crust ($38). Tues–Sat 5.30–10pm.

New Sagaya's City Market 900 W 13th Ave, at I St ☎ 907 274 6173. Trendy and expensive grocery, deli and café with a great selection ranging from organic vegetables and great cheeses to pizza, wraps, Thai dishes and good coffee. Mon–Sat 6am–10pm, Sun 8am–9pm.

Sacks Café and Restaurant 328 G St, between 3rd and 4th aves ☎ 907 274 4022, ⓦ sackscafe.com. Innovative cuisine in a casual, yet sophisticated atmosphere featuring fresh Alaskan seafood, knockout appetizers, innovative mains and unique sandwiches, salads and desserts. There's a small outdoor patio. Mon–Thurs 11am–9.30pm, Fri 11am–10pm, Sat 10am–10pm, Sun 10am–9.30pm.

Snow City Café 1034 W 4th Ave ☎ 907 272 2489, ⓦ snowcitycafe.com. The best place for breakfast – eggs Benedict or Florentine for $12, yogurt, fruit and granola for $6 – or relaxing over a pot of Earl Grey and a slice of cake. Lunch options include soups, salads, pesto chicken pasta ($13), and meatloaf with mac and cheese ($13). Mon–Fri 7am–3pm, Sat & Sun 7am–4pm.

★ **Spenard Roadhouse** 1049 West Northern Lights Blvd ☎ 907 770 7623. A popular place among locals and visitors alike serving a variety of delicious contemporary comfort food (mains $15), with plenty of gluten-free options. Ask about the monthly bacon special. Mon–Fri 11am–11pm, Sat & Sun 9am–11pm.

BARS AND LIVE MUSIC VENUES

Alaska Center for the Performing Arts 621 W 6th Ave ☎ 907 263 2787. Three-theatre downtown complex that hosts shows, plays, opera and concerts of all stripes.

Chilkoot Charlie's 2435 Spenard Rd ☎ 907 272 1010, ⓦ koots.com. Sawdust-strewn barn that packs them in nightly for pricey drinks, pool, foosball, two floors of DJ-led dance, and live music from 9.30pm. Mon–Fri 10.30am–2.30am, Sat & Sun 10.30am–3am.

Darwin's Theory 426 G St, at 4th Ave ☎ 907 277 5322. A straightforward bar good for inexpensive boozing and encounters with colourful local characters. Mon–Fri 10.30am–2.30am, Sat & Sun 10.30am–3am.

Humpy's 610 W 6th Ave ☎ 907 276 2337, ⓦ humpys.com. Popular watering hole with live music and a strong college-bar feel. The likes of charbroiled salmon ($19), burgers ($10–15), soups, and salads ($5–15) slip down with local microbrews plus English and Belgian bottled beers, and over thirty single malts. Restaurant Mon–Fri 10.30am–1am, Sat & Sun 10am–1am; bar closes 1hr after restaurant.

Kenai Peninsula

South of Anchorage, the Seward Highway hugs the shore of **Turnagain Arm** past **Girdwood** and the **Alyeska ski resort**. Just beyond, a side road heads past the ever-popular **Portage Glacier** and through a tunnel to **Whittier**, little more than a ferry dock giving access to Prince William Sound (see p.988). Beyond Portage, the Seward Highway enters the **Kenai Peninsula**, "Anchorage's playground", which at more than nine thousand square miles is larger than some states. It offers an endless diversity of activities and scenery, based around communities such as **Seward**, the base for cruises into the inspirational **Kenai Fjords National Park** and artsy **Homer**, where the waters and shorelines of the glorious **Kachemak Bay State Park** are the main destination. Most Alaskans come to the peninsula to fish: the Kenai, Russian and Kasilof rivers host "combat fishing", thousands of anglers standing elbow to elbow using strength and know-how to pull in thirty-pound-plus king salmon. **Campgrounds** along the rivers fill up fast, especially in July and August.

Girdwood and Portage Glacier

GIRDWOOD, 37 miles south of Anchorage, lies two miles inland in the shade of the **Alyeska Resort**, Alaska's largest winter sports complex and the world's lowest-elevation ski resort, starting just 270ft above sea level. Downhill runs (some lit at night) are open from November to mid-April (lifts $65/day), and in summer you can ride the Alyeska Tramway ($20) up to stunning views and good hiking territory.

Eleven miles south of Girdwood, a road leads to Whittier, past the active, frequently calving **Portage Glacier**, a popular day-tour from Anchorage aboard the *Ptarmigan* (☎800 544 2206, ☻portageglaciercruises.com). The ninety-minute cruise departs from Portage Glacier Day Lodge on Portage Lake ($34), or there's a combo bus/boat tour (5hr 30min; $74) from Whitehorse.

15

GETTING AROUND AND INFORMATION

By bike You can explore the town and coastal cycle path on bikes from Girdwood Ski and Cyclery, Mile 1.5 Alyeska Hwy (Wed–Sun 10am–7pm; $30/day; ☎907 783 2453, ☻girdwoodskicyclery.com).

GIRDWOOD AND PORTAGE GLACIER

Begich-Boggs Visitor Center Mile 5.5 Portage Glacier Rd (May–Sept daily 9am–6pm; ☎907 277 5581). A great place to stop, surrounded by breathtaking scenery and with up-to-date info, exhibits and films.

ACCOMMODATION AND EATING

Alyeska Hostel 227 Alta Drive ☎907 783 2222, ☻alyeskahostel.com. A basic hostel with a selection of accommodation options, and linen available for a fee. Dorms $25, rooms $67, private cabin $85

Alyeska Resort 1000 Arlberg Rd ☎907 754 1111, ☻alyeskaresort.com. This luxurious hotel, at the base of Alyeska Ski Resort, is *the* place to fully experience the outdoor activities year round. Some rooms have stunning views of the Chugach Mountains. $260

★ **The Bake Shop** Olympic Circle Drive at the base of the ski lifts ☎907 783 2831, ☻thebakeshop.com. Tasty, inexpensive eats: delicious and hearty breakfasts, a variety of home-made soups and sandwiches on

sourdough. You can eat on the patio in summer. Mon–Fri & Sun 7am–7pm, Sat 7am–8pm.

Carriage House B&B Mile 0.2 Crow Creek Rd ☎888 961 9464, ☻thecarriagehousebandb.com. Close to the ski resort, this gorgeous timber-framed B&B is quietly set among hemlocks and spruce trees, and boasts elegant furnishings, tasty breakfasts and welcoming staff. $100

★ **Double Musky Inn** Crow Creek Rd ☎907 783 2822, ☻doublemuskyinn.com. A favourite with Anchorage folk, this busy place has a diverse menu of Cajun-influenced meals and is well worth the wait. Plan on $50 a head and a meal to remember. Tues–Thurs 5–10pm, Fri–Sun 4.30–10pm.

Seward

SEWARD, 127 miles south of Anchorage, sprang to life in 1903 after this ice-free port was declared the ideal starting point for a railroad to the Interior. It's still a key freight terminal, but tourism – particularly cruises into Kenai Fjords National Park – is now its most conspicuous business.

Seward's main activities are enjoying the scenery and visiting the waterfront **SeaLife Center** (May–Sept daily 9am–7pm; $20; ☻alaskasealife.org), a successful marriage of research, education and tourism partly funded by the *Exxon Valdez* oil spill settlement. It offers the chance to watch ongoing research and marvel at the underwater antics of Steller sea lions, harbour seals and puffins. You can also tackle the trail to Race Point on **Mount Marathon** (4hr return), scene of an annual Fourth of July race, thanks to two pioneers who, in 1909, bet each other to run up and down the 3022ft climb – the current record is 43 minutes 23 seconds.

Seward's two hubs of activity, the small boat harbour and downtown, are joined by the mile-long Fourth Avenue.

ARRIVAL AND INFORMATION   SEWARD

By boat Alaska Marine Hwy ferries (see p.973) run to Seward from several locations throughout the state.
By train or bus Get here from Anchorage by train on the Coastal Classic (a lovely journey; $79 one-way, $125 return; ☎ 800 544 0552) or Seward Bus Lines (☎ 907 224 3608;

$40 one-way).
Visitor centre Mile 2 Seward Hwy, just as you enter the city (May–Sept daily 9am–6pm; ☎ 907 224 8051, ⓦ seward.com).

ACCOMMODATION

★ **Alaska's Treehouse** 7 miles north on the Seward Hwy (take Timber Lane Drive then Forest Rd) ☎ 907 224 3867, ⓦ virtualcities.com/ak/treehouse.htm. A lovely timber-frame house hidden among 2 acres of spruce and hemlock bush, with cosy beds, forest trails, delicious home-cooked breakfasts and a hot tub on the deck. A great place to spend a few days amid breathtaking scenery. $120
Moby Dick Hostel 432 3rd ☎ 907 224 7072, ⓦ mobydick hostel.com. In the heart of downtown, a choice of comfortable options ranging from dorm-style bunks (with discounts for paying cash) to private cabins with kitchens and baths – all at budget rates. Bunks $25, cabins from $70
Murphy's Motel 911 Fourth Ave ☎ 800 686 8191, ⓦ murphysmotel.com. Conveniently located near the

small-boat harbour and within walking distance of several restaurants. Cosy rooms with views of harbour and mountains, a gas BBQ and a freezer to store your catch of the day. $109
Waterfront Park Off Ballaine Blvd, downtown ☎ 907 224 4055. An excellent site with quiet spots – you can almost fish from your tent. Open mid-April to Sept. Tents $10, basic RV sites $15, hookups $30
Windsong Lodge Mile 0.5 Exit Glacier Rd ☎ 907 265 4501, ⓦ sewardwindsong.com. Set in a small forest lot, the *Windsong Lodge* offers a tranquil setting in which to begin or end an adventure in Seward. The rooms are fitted with pine furnishings and Alaskan art, and there are stunning views of the river valley from the balcony. Open May–Sept. $255

EATING, DRINKING AND NIGHTLIFE

Food in Seward is fairly expensive given that all produce must be delivered from the south. There are, however, several excellent options in town well worth the extra dollars.

★ **Chinooks Waterfront Restaurant** On the waterfront at the small boat harbour ☎ 907 224 2207. This charming place, popular with locals and visitors alike, serves up a scrumptious menu of fresh, locally caught seafood including Alaskan King Crab, razor clams, grilled salmon and halibut, with non-seafood dishes also available. Upstairs dining affords stunning views while the downstairs bar/bistro hosts live musicians on occasion. Daily 11am–10pm.
Resurrect Art Coffee House 320 3rd Ave ☎ 907 224 7161, ⓦ resurrectart.com. This converted church is *the* place in town to enjoy an espresso or latte with board games, wi-fi, art and events. Daily 7am–10pm.

Resurrection Roadhouse Mile 0.5 Exit Glacier Rd ☎ 907 224 716, ⓦ sewardwindsong.com. One of the better places to eat in Seward, nestled in a forest and overlooking the river and mountains – a perfect setting to enjoy breakfast or speciality pizzas or simply to quench your thirst with a selection of great brews. May–Sept daily 6am–2pm & 5–10pm.
Yukon Bar 201 4th Ave, at Washington St ☎ 907 224 3063. This boisterous pub is well worth a visit. A great selection of beers, and live music in summer (usually with a set or two from Kenai legend Hobo Jim on Sun) mean it's a great way to end the day. Daily 11am–2am.

Kenai Fjords National Park

Most visitors to Seward also drive thirteen miles out to **Exit Glacier** (24hr; free), one of the few in the state you can approach on land. From the **nature centre** at the end of the road (summer daily 9am–8pm; free), it's under a mile to the still-active glacier, though signs warn you back from the ice wall and its inviting blue clefts. Exit Glacier is part of **KENAI FJORDS NATIONAL PARK**, a magnificent 669,983-acre region of peaks, glaciers and craggy coastline. The prodigious three-hundred-square-mile Harding Icefield feeds three dozen glaciers, now retreating and exposing more of the dramatic fjords after which the park is named. Eight "tidewater" glaciers "calve" icebergs into the sea with thunderous booms and the fjords also hold a wealth of **marine wildlife** – sea otters, porpoises, orcas, seals, Steller sea lions, plus grey, humpback and minke whales – as well as the sea-bird rookeries of the Chiswell Islands.

ARRIVAL, INFORMATION AND TOURS	KENAI FJORDS NATIONAL PARK

By bus A shuttle bus (☎ 907 224 5569; $15 return) runs hourly from the small boat harbour to Exit Glacier.

Visitor centre 1212 Fourth Ave by Seward's small boat harbour (mid-May to early Sept daily 8.30am–7pm; ☎ 907 224 2125); provides maps, film shows and details on regional hikes.

Catamaran cruises Fast catamaran cruises ($59–189) are operated by Major Marine Tours (☎ 800 764 7300, ⓦ majormarine.com) and Kenai Fjords Tours (☎ 888 478

3346, ⓦ kenaifjords.com); pay out for the longer day-tours that go right up to the calving glaciers. For a once-in-a-lifetime opportunity to kayak or SUP (stand-up paddle) amid ancient glaciers and icebergs, spend a day or two with the excellent Liquid Adventures (☎ 907 224 9225, ⓦ liquid -adventures.com). All tours include hearty lunches, snacks, use of kayaks or paddle boards; tents and sleeping bags are included for longer tours.

Homer and around

HOMER is the end of the road, 226 miles south of Anchorage. The town sits beneath low bluffs with a four-mile finger of land – **The Spit** – slinking out into Kachemak Bay, framed by dense black forest and crystalline glaciers. As there are plenty of outdoor activities, spirited nightlife and a busy arts community, you'll probably want to linger a few days.

Russians, in pursuit of sea otters, were the first whites to reach the area; at the end of the 1800s coal mining and fish-salting brought American settlers. In 1896, **Homer Pennock**, a gold-seeker from Michigan, set up the community that still bears his name. In summer hordes of young people arrive from the Lower 48 to work on the halibut boats, many living in an impromptu tent city on the Spit.

Most hotels, restaurants and shops are in town, while fishing charter and tour operators can be found along the twee boardwalks of the Spit. There is no public transport between the town and the Spit.

Alaska Islands & Ocean Visitor Center and Pratt Museum

Your first stop should be the new **Alaska Islands & Ocean Visitor Center**, 95 Sterling Hwy (May–Sept daily 9am–5pm; free; ☎ 907 235 6961, ⓦ islandsandocean.org), showcasing the Alaska Maritime National Wildlife Refuge through dioramas and interactive exhibits. Also worth a visit is the excellent **Pratt Museum**, 3779 Bartlett St (daily 10am–6pm; $8; ☎ 907 235 8635, ⓦ prattmuseum.org), which brilliantly covers the cultural and natural history of Kachemak Bay and also operates a couple of cameras trained on nesting sea birds and the salmon-feeding bears.

The Spit

Many of Homer's most popular activities revolve around the **Spit**. To Alaska anglers, Homer is "**Halibut Central**": a day's fishing excursion with any of the charter companies begins at around $225. If you don't mind the crowds, it's cheaper and simpler to visit the **Fishing Hole**, on the Spit, which is stocked with salmon and offers good fishing from mid-May to mid-September.

Kachemak Bay State Park

The *Danny J* ferry (☎ 907 226 2424, ⓦ halibut-cove-alaska.com) makes two daily trips to Halibut Cove via Gull Island rookery, for $57.50 return, $34.50 if you book in for an evening meal

The prime tourist attraction in the Homer area is **Kachemak Bay State Park**, directly across the bay, with nearly 400,000 acres of forested mountains, glaciers and fjords. Birds here include puffin, auklets, kittiwakes and storm petrels, and marine mammals

15

such as seals, sea otters and whales are also plentiful. The most popular destination is the gorgeous hamlet of **Halibut Cove**, where boardwalks link art galleries and *The Saltry* restaurant (see below).

Pick up the park's **hiking trails** leaflet ($2) and other information from the visitor centre in Homer. The most-travelled route, up to **Grewingk Glacier**, is an easy three-and-a-half-mile trek above the forest to the foot of the glacier, from where you get splendid views of the bay.

ARRIVAL, GETTING AROUND AND INFORMATION   HOMER AND AROUND

By bus The Stage Line (☎907 868 3914, ⓦstagelinein homer.com) runs between Anchorage and Homer for $90 each way.
By bike Rental from Cycle Logical, 3585 East End Rd #8

($25/day; ☎907 226 2925).
Visitor centre 201 Sterling Hwy (May–Sept Mon–Sat 9am–6pm, Sun 10am–6pm; ☎907 235 7740, ⓦhomer alaska.org).

ACCOMMODATION

★ **Driftwood Inn** 135 W Bunnell Ave ☎907 235 8019, ⓦthedriftwoodinn.com. A rambling older hotel with an extensive and varied range of rooms, RV parking and a communal TV lounge with video library. There's free tea and coffee and breakfast is available for a fee. Shared bath $99, en suite $109
★ **Homer Hostel** 304 W Pioneer Ave ☎907 235 1463, ⓦhomerhostel.com. Central hostel with mixed and single-sex dorms (5- to 6-beds), two private rooms, and a big lounge with a great view. There's no curfew or lockout and they have cheap bike and rod rental. Dorms $27, rooms $68
Homer Spit Campground ☎907 235 8206. The classic

Homer experience, in various sites with wash blocks and fish-cleaning tables nearby. Tents $8, basic RV sites $20, hook-ups $50
Old Town B&B 106 W Bunnell Ave ☎907 235 7558, ⓦoldtownbedandbreakfast.com. Three-room B&B in a 1936 building with wooden floors, antiques, quilted bed covers and old-fashioned bathroom fittings; two have tremendous sea views. Shared bath $110, en suite $130
Seaside Farm Hostel Mile 5 East End Rd ☎907 235 7850, ⓦxyz.net/~seaside. Small farm hostel with slightly cramped bunks and a lovely range of rooms, plus small cabins dotted around the property. Open May–Sept. Camping $10, dorms $20, rooms & cabins $75

EATING AND DRINKING

Café Cups 162 W Pioneer Ave ☎907 235 8330, ⓦcafe cupsofhomer.com. Relaxing yet vibrant place serving up fabulous local seafood, steak and pasta dinners (mains $28), with an extensive wine list. Tues–Sat 4.30–9pm.
Fresh Sourdough Express 1316 Ocean Drive ☎907 235 7571, ⓦfreshsourdoughexpress.com. Fine local and organic produce at this friendly bakery-restaurant, noted for its breakfasts ($9), burgers and seafood dinners. Daily 6am–4pm.
★ **La Balenine Café** The Spit Rd ☎907 299 6672. Superb little café where an executive pastry chef prepares delicious dishes using local ingredients; there's a hearty box lunch ($15) for those heading out to sea for the day, while the Salmon Bowl ($10) is highly recommended for lunch. Tues–Sun 5am–4pm.
The Saltry 9 W Ismilof Rd, Halibut Cove ☎907 226

2424, ⓦhalibut-cove-alaska.com/saltry.htm. A great, intimate place serving local seafood dishes (mains $30) prepared in a variety of ways. There's an outdoor patio for when the weather behaves. Reservations are essential as the only way to reach this restaurant is by boat ($30 return). Daily 11am–9pm.
Salty Dawg The Spit ☎907 235 6718. No self-respecting drinker should pass up a few jars in the *Dawg* with its dark interior, life preservers and thousands of signed dollar bills pinned to the wall, and what seems to be the only surveyor's benchmark located in a US bar. Daily 11am–5am.
Two Sisters Bakery 233 E Bunnell Ave ☎907 235 2280. Great little spot for that morning coffee, either inside or at tables out on the deck. Also pizza, soups and quiches at moderate prices. Mon–Fri 7am–6pm, Sat 7am–4pm, Sun 9am–2pm.

Prince William Sound

Prince William Sound, a largely unspoiled wilderness of steep fjords and mountains, glaciers and rainforest, sits between the Kenai Peninsula to the west and the Chugach Mountains to the north and east. Teeming with marine mammals, the Sound has a relatively low-key tourist industry. The only significant settlements, spectacular **Valdez**, at the end of the trans-Alaska pipeline, and **Cordova**, a fishing community only accessible by sea or air, are the respective bases for visiting the **Columbia** and **Childs glaciers**.

The Chugach and Eyak people were displaced by Russian trappers in search of sea otter pelts, and then by American miners and fishers. The whole glorious show was very nearly spoiled forever on Good Friday 1989, when the **Exxon Valdez** spilled eleven million gallons of crude oil. Although 1400 miles of coast were befouled and some 250,000 birds died, and the long-term effects are still unclear, today no surface pollution is visible.

Valdez

VALDEZ (pronounced *val-Deez*), 300 miles from Anchorage and the Western Hemisphere's northernmost ice-free port, has a stunning backdrop of mountains, glaciers and waterfalls and a record annual snowfall of more than 40ft. It offers great hiking, rafting, sea kayaking, wildlife-viewing and, of course, fishing.

Brief history

In the 1890s **Gold Rush** Valdez became a base for prospectors crossing the deadly Valdez and Klutina glaciers to the Yukon. Only three hundred of the 3500 miners who set out on the Valdez Trail made it to the goldmines – those that did not perish from frostbite and starvation gave up. Valdez came to depend on fish canneries, logging and the military for its survival, but nature conspired to finish it off on Good Friday 1964: the epicentre of North America's largest **earthquake** was just 45 miles away. The ground turned to quivering jelly, shattering roads and buildings and killing 33 residents. Refusing to be intimidated, the survivors moved sixty-odd buildings four miles to the more stable present site.

The town's fortunes rose again during the 1970s, when oil was found beneath Prudhoe Bay, and Valdez became the southern terminus of the eight-hundred-mile **trans-Alaska pipeline**, carrying close to a million barrels of oil per day. Winds and tides kept the *Exxon Valdez*'s oil away from Valdez in 1989, and in fact the city profited as base for the massive **clean-up**. The operation cost Exxon three billion dollars, with eleven thousand workers in more than one thousand boats and three hundred planes scouring the beaches. All seems pristine now, though many species have still not fully recovered their former numbers.

The town museums

The **Valdez Museum**, 217 Egan Drive (May–Sept daily 9am–5pm; $7), carries just enough detail on the Gold Rush, oil terminal, glaciation and the *Exxon Valdez* oil spill. The entry price covers you for its **annexe**, at 436 S Hazelet Ave (same hours), which covers the 1964 earthquake at length.

The **Maxine & Jesse Whitney Museum** at the Community College, 303 Lowe St (May–Sept daily 9am–7pm; free), has an astounding collection of carved ivory and an assortment of dead beasts, including a couple of moose hides with Alaskan scenes burned into them by an early pioneer. There's also an instructive documentary on the Alaska Pipeline.

Columbia Glacier

You should take a cruise out into Prince William Sound, principally to see the spectacular **Columbia Glacier**, three miles wide at its face and towering 300ft above the sea. Unfortunately it is receding rapidly and the fjord is now so choked with ice that you can't get close to the face. Weather permitting, you can see it at long range from the AMHS ferries between Valdez and Whittier, but for a closer look go with Stan Stephens Glacier & Wildlife Cruises (see p.990), who pick their way through a floating ice field and point out such sights as Bligh Reef, where the *Exxon Valdez* grounded.

15

ARRIVAL AND DEPARTURE

By car One of the most exciting things about Valdez is getting here. The Richardson Hwy holds epic scenery: alpine meadows, mountain glaciers, icy Thompson Pass and waterfall-fringed Keystone Canyon.

By ferry Ferries from Cordova or Whittier dock at the

VALDEZ

end of Hazelet Ave (☎ 907 835 4436); it's a gorgeous journey.

By plane ERA Aviation (see p.995) flies twice daily from Anchorage (from $308 return) to the airport 4 miles east, from where taxis (☎ 907 835 2500) downtown cost around $10.

INFORMATION, TOURS AND ACTIVITIES

Visitor centre On Fairbanks Drive at Chenega St (May–Sept Mon–Fri 8am–7pm, Sat 9am–6pm, Sun 10am–5pm; ☎ 907 835 4636, ⊚ valdezalaska.org).

Kayak tours and rentals Pangaea Adventures, 107 N Harbor Drive (☎ 907 835 8442, ⊚ alaskasummer.com), offer sea-kayaking trips to Duck Flats; $69 (3hr), or a more ambitious coastal paddle to Gold Creek; $99 (6hr). It is worth making the effort to reach distant paddling destinations (accessed by water taxi), principally Shoup

Glacier (8hr; $199) and Columbia Glacier (10hr; $249). They also offer kayak rentals (single $55/day, double $75, $5/day less after the first day), and glacier hikes (half-day $99).

Cruises Stan Stephens Glacier & Wildlife Cruises (☎ 866 867 1297, ⊚ stanstephenscruises.com) to Columbia Glacier: choose between the 6hr cruise ($120) and the 9hr cruise that also visits the Meares Glacier ($155). Light lunches are served on both sailings.

ACCOMMODATION AND EATING

Valdez's accommodation gets snapped up pretty quickly and there's no hostel, but a free phone outside the visitor centre connects with some of the fifty-plus B&Bs, or see ⊚ valdezbnbnetwork.com.

Alaska Halibut House 208 Meals Ave ☎ 907 835 2788. Family-run establishment serving up various seafood dishes; the battered halibut and home-made clam chowder are tasty. Mon–Sat 11am–8pm.

Bear Paw RV Park 101 N Harbour Drive ☎ 907 835 2530, ⊚ bearpawrvpark.com. Centrally located in town and very busy, this campground offers both tent and RV sites, along with a laundry, hot showers and cable TV. Tents $12, RVs $30

L&L's B&B 533 W Hanagita St ☎ 907 835 4447, ⊚ lnlalaska.com. Cosy B&B with five comfortable shared

bathrooms a 10min walk from the centre, with free bikes and good breakfasts. $75

Valdez Glacier Campground Five miles out of town at 1200 Airport Rd ☎ 907 873 4058. Despite its inconvenient location, this campground offers good fishing and great views of the surrounding mountains. Tents $10, basic RV sites $25, hookups $30

Valdez Harbor Inn 100 N Harbor Drive ☎ 907 835 3434, ⊚ valdezharborinn.com. A renovated *Best Western*, with a great waterside location, where rooms have cable TV, DVD player, microwave and fridge. $180

Cordova

Far quieter than Valdez, and only accessible by sea or air, **CORDOVA** is an unpretentious fishing community on the southeastern edge of the Sound. In 1906 Cordova was chosen as the port for the copper mined in Kennicott, a hundred miles northeast, gambling on cutting a path between two active glaciers for the proposed Copper River and Northwestern Railroad – the CR&NW – ridiculed at the time as the "Can't Run & Never Will". Nonetheless, in 1911 it was completed when the "**Million Dollar Bridge**" spanned the Copper River. However the mines lasted just 27 years and Cordova shifted its dependency to fishing, in turn dealt a potentially fatal blow by the *Exxon Valdez* in 1989. For the next two seasons, the community reeled from the effects of the **oil spill**; since then fortunes have slowly improved.

Cordova itself has few sights; the **small-boat harbour** is the core of the town's activity, particularly in summer. The **Cordova Museum**, 622 First St (May–Sept Mon–Sat 10am–6pm, Sun 2–4pm; $1 suggested donation), has quirky exhibits on local history, including the tiny **ice worm** that lives in the glaciers and the funky festival that celebrates its existence each February. The **Ilanka Cultural Center**, by the harbour at 110 Nicholoff Way (May–Sept Mon–Fri 10am–5pm; donation; ☎ 907 424 7903, ⊚ ilankacenter.org), has a complete orca skeleton hanging over the entrance, plus local native arts and crafts and a fine bookshop.

The Copper River Delta

Today the "Million Dollar Bridge", battered by the 1964 earthquake, cuts a lonely figure at the end of the Copper River Highway, a 48-mile gravel road across the wetlands of the Copper River Delta, a major stopover for migratory birds backed by the Chugach Mountains. It is a tranquil spot for fishing, birdwatching or **hiking** along excellent trails, such as the one to Saddlebag Glacier. The road ends just over the bridge beside the incredibly active **Childs Glacier**.

ARRIVAL, GETTING AROUND, INFORMATION AND TOURS   CORDOVA

By plane There is no road access to Cordova; daily flights from Anchorage and Juneau land at the airport 12 miles down the Copper River Hwy, to be met by a shuttle ($12).

By ferry Near daily ferries from Valdez and Whittier dock a mile north of town.

By car By far the best way to make the journey to the Million Dollar Bridge is in a rental car (from around $80/day, unlimited mileage) from Chinook Auto Rentals, in the

Airport Depot Diner or at the *Northern Nights Inn* (☎ 877 424 5279, ⓦ chinookautorentals.com).

Chamber of Commerce 404 First St (Mon–Fri 9am–5pm; ☎ 907 424 7260, ⓦ cordovachamber.com).

Tours Copper River and Northwest Tours (☎ 907 424 5356) run occasional day-trips to the Million Dollar Bridge ($85 including lunch).

15

ACCOMMODATION

Cordova Lighthouse Inn 112 Nicholoff Way ☎ 907 424 7080, ⓦ cordovalighthouseinn.com. This cosy, recently renovated inn offers a choice of rooms with shared kitchen and private bath, and suites with kitchen; some have stunning views of the small-boat harbour. Rooms **$155**, suites **$349**

Reluctant Fisherman Inn 407 Railroad Ave ☎ 907 424 3272, ⓦ reluctantfisherman.com. Lovely, recently spruced-up waterfront inn and restaurant; rooms have either a mountain or harbour view. You could easily while away the afternoon on the balcony watching the fishing boats sail by. **$130**

Talkeetna

A hundred miles from Anchorage, the eclectic hamlet of **TALKEETNA** has a palpable small-town Alaska feel, but is lent an international flavour by the world's mountaineers, who come here to scale the 20,320ft **Mount McKinley**, usually referred to in Alaska by its Athabascan name **Denali**, "the Great One". Whatever you choose to call it, North America's highest peak rises from 2000ft lowlands, making it the world's tallest from base to peak (other major peaks such as Everest rise from high terrain). The mountain is best seen from the **overlook** just south of Talkeetna, which reveals the peak's transcendent white glow, in sharp contrast to the warm colours all around.

From mid-April to mid-July, climbers mass in Talkeetna to be flown to the mountain: only half of the 1200 attempting the climb each year succeed, usually due to extreme weather.

ARRIVAL, INFORMATION AND TOURS   TALKEETNA

By bus Bus services avoid Talkeetna except for Alaska Park Connection (daily from Anchorage; $65; ☎ 800 266 8625, ⓦ alaskacoach.com).

By train Daily trains from Anchorage to Denali and Fairbanks stop half a mile south of town.

Talkeetna Ranger Station B St (May–Sept daily

8am–5.30pm; ☎ 907 733 2231).

Flight tours Air-taxi companies such as K2 Aviation (☎ 800 764 2291, ⓦ flyk2.com) run flightseeing trips to Mount McKinley, ranging from a spectacular 1hr ($205) flight to the full 90min grand tour ($290) all around the mountain, which includes a glacier landing in a plane fitted with skis.

MOOSE DROPPING FESTIVAL

Talkeetna's famed **Moose Dropping Festival** falls on the second weekend of July; little brown balls sell fast (with a sanitary coat of varnish) for use in earrings or necklaces. In addition to these highly desirable lumps of Alaskana, the festival features dancing, drinking, a moose-dropping throwing competition and some more drinking.

ACCOMMODATION

For a town of just three hundred, Talkeetna teems with excellent accommodation, much of it on Main Street. Reservations are advised between May and September when it teems with climbers from around the world.

Talkeetna Alaskan 12.5 miles along Talkeetna Spur Rd just south of town ☎ 907 733 9500, ⓦ talkeetna lodge.com. Easily the fanciest hotel in the area, with a variety of rooms, a few private suites and an on-site restaurant and bistro. This is the place to sit back and enjoy the sunset over Mount McKinley. Doubles $285, suites $479

★ **Talkeetna House of Seven Trees Hostel** Main St ☎ 907 733 7733, ⓔ house7trees@gmail.com. Travellers the world over return each year to this charming and welcoming hostel in the heart of this tiny town. It offers a variety of private and family rooms, as well as dorm beds.

Dorms $25, private rooms $75

Talkeetna River Park Western end of Main St ☎ 907 733 2231. This place offers a good selection of camping sites, though many people stroll another hundred yards west and (unofficially) pitch by the river. $10

Talkeetna Roadhouse ☎ 907 733 1351, ⓦ talkeetna roadhouse.com. Dating from 1917, the central *Talkeetna Roadhouse* bolsters its old-style Alaskan atmosphere with great home cooking and offers bunks, doubles with shared bathrooms and rustic cabins. Dorms $21, doubles $68, cabins $110

15

Denali National Park

The six-million-acre **DENALI NATIONAL PARK**, 240 miles north of Anchorage, is home to **Mount McKinley**, which is often shrouded in cloud. The mountain is far from the park's only attraction, however. Shuttle buses offer a glimpse of a vast world of tundra and taiga, glaciers, huge mountains and abundant wildlife – the Park Service reports that 95 percent of visitors see **bears**, **caribou** and **Dall sheep**, 82 percent moose, and more than one-fifth **wolves**, along with porcupine, snowshoe hare, red foxes and more than 160 bird species. Visiting Alaska without trying to see Denali is unthinkable for most travellers, and therein lies a problem. In high summer, the visitor centre and service areas out on the Parks Highway are a stream of RVs, tour buses and the like. Things pick up in the park itself, and backcountry hiking, undertaken by only a tiny fraction of visitors, remains a wonderfully solitary experience.

In **winter**, Denali is transformed into a ghostly, snow-covered world. Motorized vehicles are banned and travel, even for park personnel, is by snowshoe, skis or dogsled as temperatures dive and northern lights glitter over the snows.

Toklat River and Wonder Lake

Shuttle buses run to the Savage River at Mile 15 (free); **Toklat River** at Mile 53 ($24), where rangers lead one-hour tundra tours each day at 1.30pm; the Eielson Visitor Center at Mile 67 ($31); and the aptly named **Wonder Lake** at Mile 84 ($42). Return take two, six, eight and eleven hours, respectively. The shuttle drivers don't give guided tours, but with forty pairs of watchful eyes on board, you're almost guaranteed to see

---

BACKCOUNTRY HIKING AND CAMPING

Backcountry camping is the best way to appreciate Denali's scenery and its inhabitants. Don't expect it to be easy though, as there are no formal trails and with thick spongy tundra and frequent river crossings even hardy hikers find themselves limited to five miles a day. The park is divided into 87 units with only a limited number of campers allowed in 41 of them. Free permits are available one day in advance from the **Backcountry Information Center** (daily 9am–6pm), facing the Wilderness Access Center, though high demand means you should be prepared to hike in the less popular areas. The BIC will also teach you about avoiding run-ins with bears and issue you with bear-resistant food containers. Camper buses reserved for those with campground or backcountry permits cost $31. These also carry bikes; cyclists can be dropped anywhere, but are obliged to keep to the road.

the big mammals. You can also hop off at any point for a day-hike (no permits required), returning to the road to flag down the next bus back, if it has room.

ARRIVAL

By car Denali Park is about 5hr from Anchorage or 3hr from Fairbanks.

By bus Buses from Anchorage are run by The Park Connection (☏ 800 266 8625, ⱳ alaskacoach.com) and Alaska/Yukon Trails (☏ 800 770 2267, ⱳ alaskashuttle .com), charging $75–90, with the latter continuing to Fairbanks ($60).

By train Trains (daily in summer) leave at 8.15am from

DENALI NATIONAL PARK

both Anchorage ($121) and Fairbanks ($53), dropping you at 4pm and 12.30pm respectively at the train station 1.5 mile inside the park entrance.

By shuttle bus Free shuttles run from the hotels outside the park gate to the Denali Visitor Center (8am–6pm daily) opposite the train station.

Admission Park entry costs $10/person and is valid for a week.

GETTING AROUND

By shuttle bus The only vehicles allowed on Denali's narrow, unpaved 90-mile road are a few tour buses and green shuttle buses, which you should book well in advance (☏ 800 622 7275, ⱳ nps.gov/dena) or up to two days ahead at the Wilderness Access Center (see below). Buses run at least

hourly in season, with more to pick up stragglers at day's end.

By camper bus Camper buses, reserved for those with campground or backcountry permits, cost $31. These also carry bikes; cyclists can be dropped anywhere, but are obliged to keep to the road.

INFORMATION, ACTIVITIES AND TOURS

Wilderness Access Center Just inside the park entrance (May–Sept daily 5am–8pm; ☏ 907 683 9274, ⱳ nps.gov /dena/index.htm); you can pick up a free copy of the *Alpenglow* paper and a wide range of literature here or at the visitor centre (daily 8am–6pm), near the train station

Ranger-led activities Short hikes and the popular, and free, dogsled demonstrations are held daily at various times and locations.

Narrated bus tours Another option is to join a narrated tour (☏ 800 208 0200) along the park road: either the

5hr Natural History Tour ($77.50) or the full-day Tundra Wilderness Tour ($154.50), which reaches at least Mile 53, stopping frequently to observe wildlife.

Rafting Just outside the park entrance, several rafting companies offer 2hr trips down the Nenana River: all offer a gentle "scenic float" and an 11-mile "Canyon Run" through Class III and IV rapids – they cost around $87 individually and $173 for a full-day trip. Denali Outdoor Center (☏ 888 303 1925, ⱳ denalioutdoorcenter.com) charges a few dollars more than some others, but offers a quality experience.

ACCOMMODATION

The best way to experience Denali up close is to camp, with most of the park's six campgrounds open from mid-May to mid-September; all sites are bookable at the main visitor centre, by phone or online (☏ 800 622 7275, ⱳ reservedenali.com) and all require a one-time $5 reservation fee (without which you may have to wait a day or two to get a spot). With the exception of several exclusive lodges deep in the heart of the park, there are no **hotels** in Denali, so your choice is between $160-a-night gaggle of summer-only hotels a mile north of the park entrance or the cheaper offerings either 10 miles further north in the little coal-mining town of **Healy**, or spots a few miles south along the highway.

Denali Rainbow Village RV Park Mile 238.6 ☏ 907 683 7777, ⱳ denalirv.com. The only cheap option by the park entrance, with tents and RV sites. Tents or basic RV sites $25, hookups $42

Denali Mountain Morning Hostel Mile 224.5 ☏ 907 683 7503, ⱳ hostelalaska.com. The only real hostel hereabouts is this excellent spot in the woods 13 miles

south, with a free shuttle to the park. There are spacious dorms and fixed tents (both $32/person), one double room and cabins, an efficient kitchen, all manner of games and friendly hosts. Dorms & tents $32, double $80, cabins $80

Earth Song Lodge Mile 4, Stampede Rd ☏ 907 683 2863, ⱳ earthsonglodge.com. Lovely place with a cluster of cabins with great views and a café on site. $165

EATING

Black Bear Coffee House Mile 238.5, Parks Hwy ☏ 907 683 1656, ⱳ blackbeardenali.com. Home-cooked breakfasts, lunches and dinners in a cosy setting. Mid-May to mid-Sept daily 6.30am–10pm.

Lynx Creek Pizza and Pub Mile 238.6 Parks Hwy ☏ 907 683 2547. Salads, sandwiches, pizza and draft microbrews. Mid-May to mid-Sept daily 11am– midnight.

15

Wrangell-St Elias National Park

As Denali becomes more crowded, people are increasingly making the trip to the more remote **WRANGELL-ST ELIAS NATIONAL PARK** in the extreme southeast corner of the Interior, where four of the continent's great mountain ranges – the Wrangell, St Elias, Chugach and Alaska – cramp up against each other. Everything is writ large: glacier after enormous glacier, canyon after dizzying canyon, and nine of the sixteen highest peaks in the US, all laced together by braided rivers and idyllic lakes where mountain goats, Dall sheep, bears, moose and caribou roam.

The first whites in the area came in search of gold but instead hit upon one of the continent's richest copper deposits. The mines closed in 1938, after 27 frantic years of production, and today **McCarthy** and **Kennicott**, with more than thirty creaking, disused buildings, are ghost towns. You can visit the mill complex in Kennicott on fascinating two-hour **walking tours** run by St Elias Alpine Guides ($25; ☎888 933 5427, ⓦsteliasguides.com), who also run a number of hikes, ice-climbing trips, mountain-bike rides, raft trips and even glacier skiing adventures out into the virtually trailless park.

15

ARRIVAL AND INFORMATION — WRANGELL-ST ELIAS NATIONAL PARK

Getting to McCarthy Half the fun is getting to McCarthy along 58 rugged miles of the McCarthy Road, following the abandoned railroad that once linked the Kennicott mill to the port at Cordova. Take it slow and stop often to admire the scenery and abandoned trestle bridges. At the end of the road you cross the Kennicott River on a footbridge and continue half a mile to the village of McCarthy on foot. If you haven't got a vehicle you can go with Backcountry

Connection (☎800 770 6652, ⓦkennicottshuttle.com), which charges $109 for same-day return and $149 for next-day return from Glennallen. From McCarthy, a shuttle bus runs along 4 miles of dirt road to Kennicott.

Visitor centre Just south of Glennallen at Mile 107 on the Richardson Hwy (May–Sept daily 9am–7pm; ☎907 822 5234, ⓦnps.gov/wrst).

ACCOMMODATION AND EATING

Kennicott Glacier Lodge Kennicott ☎800 582 5128, ⓦkennicottlodge.com. Upmarket place with comfortable rooms, warm hosts and delicious meals at the restaurant which opens for breakfast, lunch and dinner (dinner reservations essential). $185

Kennicott River Lodge and Hostel Near the road end

☎907 554 4441, ⓦkennicottriverlodge.com. This place has four-bunk cabins and nice common areas along with several private cabins. Bunks $35, cabins $115

Lancaster's Backpacker's Hotel McCarthy ☎907 554 4402, ⓦmccarthylodge.com. Simple rooms with shared bathrooms, with some singles at $30 less. $98

Fairbanks

FAIRBANKS, 360 miles north of Anchorage and at the end of the Alaska Highway from Canada, is somewhat bland but makes a great base for exploring a hinterland of gold mines, hot springs and limitless wilderness, and for journeys along the **Dalton Highway** to the Arctic Ocean oilfield of **Prudhoe Bay**.

Fairbanks suffers remarkable extremes of climate, with winter temperatures dropping to -70ºF and summer highs topping 90ºF. Proximity to the Arctic Circle means more

FESTIVALS AND EVENTS IN FAIRBANKS

The spectacular **aurora borealis** (see p.997) is a major winter attraction, as is the **Ice Alaska Festival** in mid-March, with its ice-sculpting competition and dogsled racing on frozen downtown streets. Summer visitors should try to catch the three-day **World Eskimo-Indian Olympics** (ⓦweio.org) in mid-July when contestants from around the state compete in dance, art and sports competitions, as well as some unusual ones like ear-pulling, knuckle hop, high kick and the blanket toss.

than 21 hours of sunlight in midsummer, when midnight baseball games take place under natural light, and 2am bar evacuees are confronted by bright sunshine.

Brief history

Alaska's second largest town was founded accidentally, in 1901, when a steamship carrying trader E.T. Barnette ran aground in the shallows of the Chena River, a tributary of the Yukon. Unable to move his supplies any further, he set up shop in the wilderness, catering to the few trappers and prospectors in the area. The following year **gold** was found, a tent city sprang up and Barnette made a mint. In 1908, at the height of the rush, Fairbanks had a population of 18,500, but by 1920 it had dwindled to just 1100. During World War II several huge **military bases** were built and the population rebounded, getting a further boost in the mid-1970s when it became the construction centre for the **trans-Alaska pipeline**.

Downtown

The main point of interest **downtown** is the small **Fairbanks Community Museum**, 410 Cushman St at 5th Ave (Mon–Fri 10am–4pm; free), displaying trapping, mining and dogsled racing equipment. A similarly wintry theme is pursued at the **Ice Museum**, 500 2nd Ave at Lacey St (summer daily 10am–9pm; $12), a year-round taster of the Ice Sculpting competition by way of a slide show and walk-in refrigerators housing some small carvings.

Pioneer Park

A couple of miles west of downtown on the banks of the Chena River, the touristy **Pioneer Park** (mostly free) celebrates Alaskan history though various pioneer museums, the only large wooden sternwheeler left in the USA, and a miniature railway encircling the entire park; there's plenty to amuse the kids.

Creamer's Field and Museum of the North

College Road heads west past **Creamer's Field**, thick with sandhill cranes and Canada geese, especially in spring and autumn, to the University of Alaska Fairbanks' attractive campus. Here UAF's superb modern **Museum of the North** (May–Sept daily 9am–7pm; $12; ⓦuaf.edu/museum) displays eclectic collections of Native and contemporary art, as well as natural and human history displays.

ARRIVAL AND DEPARTURE   FAIRBANKS

By plane Alaska Airlines flies frequently from Anchorage to Fairbanks Airport, 4 miles southwest; the MACS Yellow Line bus (Mon–Sat; $1.50) runs downtown, but the long wait between services means you'll probably want to grab a taxi (around $15). Most hotels offer shuttles to the airport or rail depot. The airport is also a gateway for flights into the bush; Era Aviation (see p.990) operates a reliable service.

By bus Alaska/Yukon Trails buses from Anchorage (daily May–Sept; $99; ☏800 770 7275, ⓦalaskashuttle.com) drop off at the airport and major hostels and hotels.
By train Trains from Anchorage (May–Sept daily; Oct–April weekly) stop beside the Johansen Expressway, inconveniently far from downtown.

GETTING AROUND, INFORMATION AND TOURS

By bike and bus The best way to get around town is by car, but there's a good riverside cycle trail and the six Fairbanks MACS City bus lines (☏907 459 1011; $1.50/ride or $3/day pass) provide a reasonable service.
Visitor centre 101 Dunkel St (May–Sept daily 8am–9pm; ☏800 459 3701, ⓦexplorefairbanks.com); dispenses

information on lodging and activities, with free films, cultural events, internet access and an excellent historical display. Also houses the Alaska Public Land Information Center (APLIC; daily 8am–6pm; ☏907 459 3730, ⓦalaska centers.gov/fairbanks.cfm) for information on backcountry activities and the area's parks, including Denali.

15

15

River cruises Unashamedly touristy but fun and very popular is a 4hr cruise down the Chena River on the "Riverboat Discovery" ($60; ☎ 866 479 6673, ⓦ riverboatdiscovery.com), which includes a visit to a mock Native village.

Wilderness tours Several companies can whisk you off into the surrounding bush and fly you to the Arctic Circle; the widest choice is with the Northern Alaska Tour Company (☎ 907 474 8600, ⓦ northernalaska.com).

ACCOMMODATION

Downtown motels and hotels tend to be either quite pricey or pretty dodgy. B&Bs are plentiful, with rooms from $80 a night; the visitor centre offers free phone calls and all the brochures. Thankfully, there are several good hostels and a couple of decent campgrounds.

Ah, Rose Marie 302 Cowles St ☎ 907 456 2040, ⓦ akpub.com/akbbrv/ahrose.html. Small but justly popular B&B where a hearty breakfast is served on the glassed-in porch. **$90**

Billie's Backpackers Hostel 2895 Mack Blvd ☎ 907 479 2034, ⓦ alaskahostel.com. Welcoming though somewhat cramped hostel, in a nice area and handily placed on the bus routes between downtown and the university. There's a kitchen and bikes for guest use. No curfew. Dorms **$30**, camping **$20**

Golden North Motel 4888 Old Airport Way ☎ 907 479 6201, ⓦ goldennorthmotel.com. Friendly and spotlessly clean motel near the airport with cable TV. Free pickups are available and the Yellow and Blue buses pass nearby. **$97**

GoNorth Base Camp Hostel and Campground 3500 Davis Rd ☎ 907 479 7272, ⓦ gonorth-alaska.com.

A kind of outdoors hostel in a forested area, with large fixed tents with five beds. There's also camping, space in a tipi and reasonably priced bike and canoe rental. Dorms **$28** (**$25** with own sleeping bag), tents **$12**, tipis **$20**

Minnie Street B&B Inn 345 Minnie St ☎ 907 456 1802, ⓦ minniestreetbandb.com. Top-line B&B with every luxury, and a spacious deck with a hot tub. Some rooms have a jacuzzi and there's a full breakfast. Shared bath **$139**, private bath **$179**, premium suite with jacuzzi **$239**

Tanana Valley Campground 1800 College Rd, at Aurora Drive ☎ 907 456 7956. Conveniently located next to the fairgrounds and right on the MACS red bus route. Each site has a picnic table, fire pit and free wi-fi, and there are showers and a coin-operated laundry. Tents **$16**, basic RV sites **$20**, hookup **$26**

EATING AND NIGHTLIFE

Fairbanks' **eating** options are varied, with good Thai particularly prevalent. They're also well scattered, with downtown and College Road, toward the university, having the greatest concentrations. Nowhere downtown sells groceries: the closest places are Safeway and Fred Meyer at the eastern end of College Road. Fairbanks has its decent **nightspots**, though none in hard-drinking downtown.

Alaska Coffee Roasting Co. West Valley Plaza, 4001 Geist Rd ☎ 907 457 5282, ⓦ alaskacoffeeroasting.com. Fairbanks' best coffee, roasted daily on the premises, served in a cosy café hung with local art. There's a good selection of wraps, cakes and muffins, too. Mon–Fri 7am–10pm, Sat & Sun 8am–10pm.

Blue Loon Mile 353.5, Parks Hwy ☎ 907 457 5666, ⓦ theblueloon.com. Late-closing hot spot 5 miles west of Fairbanks that's always good for a convivial drink. Hosts local and touring bands (sometimes a DJ) several nights a week, summer outdoor concerts and movies most nights (5.30pm & 8pm). Tues–Sat 5pm–2am, Sun 4pm–2am.

The Diner 244 Illinois St ☎ 907 451 0613. A local favourite for breakfast and brunch, offering reliable diner food at good prices (from $16). Mon–Fri 6am–7pm, Sat & Sun 6am–6pm.

Gambardella's Pasta Bella 706 2nd Ave, downtown ☎ 907 457 4992, ⓦ gambardellas.com. Fairbanks' best Italian, and not wildly expensive, with a pleasant outdoor area for those endless summer evenings. Tasty salads, the

best pizza in town and most scrumptious lasagne anywhere in Alaska. Mains average $25. Mon–Fri 11am–10.30pm, Sat & Sun noon–10.30pm.

Howling Dog Saloon Mile 11, Old Steese Hwy, Fox ☎ 907 456 4695, ⓦ howlingdogsaloon.alaskansavvy.com. It's 11 miles north of town, but this is perhaps the north's best bar – unassuming, unpretentious and fun. Live rock and R&B bands perform. Daily 5pm–3am.

The Marlin 3412 College Rd ☎ 907 479 4646. Poky wood-panelled cellar bar with cutting-edge bands – blues, jazz and rock – most evenings from around 9pm and only a small cover charge, if any. Mon–Thurs 4pm–2am, Fri & Sat 4pm–3.30am.

Pump House 796 Chena Pump Rd ☎ 907 479 8452, ⓦ pumphouse.com. A local favourite in a historic pumphouse, stuffed with gold-mining paraphernalia and with a deck by the Chena River. Great for steak, seafood and burgers, and also pulls in a substantial drinking crowd. Mains $30. Tues–Sat 4pm–midnight, Sun 10am–2pm & 4pm–midnight.

THE NORTHERN LIGHTS

The **aurora borealis**, or "Northern Lights", an ethereal display of light in the uppermost atmosphere, give their brightest and most colourful displays in the sky above Fairbanks. For up to one hundred winter nights, the sky appears to shimmer with dancing curtains of colour ranging from luminescent greens to fantastic veils that run the full spectrum. Named after the Roman goddess of dawn, the aurora is caused by an interaction between the earth's magnetic field and the **solar wind**, an invisible stream of charged electrons and protons continually blown out into space from the sun. The earth deflects the solar wind like a rock in a stream, with the energy released at the magnetic poles – much like a neon sign.

The Northern Lights are at their most dazzling from December to March, when nights are longest and the sky darkest, but late September can be good for summer visitors. They are visible pretty much everywhere, but the further north the better, especially around Fairbanks.

Second Story Café 3525 College Rd ☏907 474 9574. Pleasant spot above Gulliver's Bookstore, serving wraps, sandwiches, bagels, biscotti and coffee, all at reasonable prices. Free wi-fi as well. Mon–Sat 9am–7pm, Sun 11am–5pm.

Thai House 412 5th Ave, downtown ☏907 452 6123. A small but ever-popular restaurant serving the usual range of Thai dishes, but all done to perfection and modestly priced at around $15. Mon–Sat 9am–9pm.

Around Fairbanks: Chena Hot Springs

Chena Hot Springs, the most accessible and developed resort in the area, stands sixty miles east of Fairbanks amid a bucolic swath of **muskeg** (grassy swampland) and forest traversed by good hiking trails and teeming with moose. For $10 a day non-guests can use the hot pools and large outdoor "rock pool" (free for guests); the resort also rents out canoes and mountain bikes, as well as offering rafting float trips.

The Dalton Highway

Built in the 1970s to service the **trans-Alaska pipeline**, the mostly gravel Dalton Highway, or Haul Road, runs from Fairbanks five hundred miles to the oil facility of Prudhoe Bay on Alaska's north coast, some three hundred miles beyond the Arctic Circle. It is a long, bumpy and demanding drive, so take spare tyres, petrol, provisions and, ideally, a sturdy 4WD: most regular rentals aren't permitted up here. Not far from Fairbanks you start to parallel the pipeline, snaking up hills and in and out of the ground. At 188 miles, a sign announces that you've just crossed the **Arctic Circle**.

The highway plugs on north through increasingly barren territory, finally dispensing with trees as you climb through the wilderness of the **Brooks Range**, a 9000ft chain mostly held within the **Gates of the Arctic National Park**. From Atigun Pass you descend through two hundred miles of grand glaciated valleys and blasted Arctic plains to the end of the road at dead-boring **Deadhorse**. You can't stroll by the ocean or camp here, so your choices are confined to staying in one of the $190-per-night hotels and taking a $39 tour past the adjacent – and off-limits – **Prudhoe Bay** oil facility to dip a toe (or your full body) into the Arctic Ocean.

ARRIVAL AND GETTING AROUND   **THE DALTON HIGHWAY**

The **Northern Alaska Tour Company** (☏800 474 1986, ⊛northernalaska.com) will drive you up in a minibus and either drive you back to Fairbanks ($189; a long arduous day) or fly you back ($359). It also runs a three-day fly/drive tour to Prudhoe Bay for $989.

Hawaii

HANAUMA BAY, OAHU

Hawaii

With their fiery volcanoes, palm-fringed beaches, verdant valleys, glorious rainbows and awesome cliffs, the islands of Hawaii boast some of the most spectacularly beautiful scenery on earth. Despite their isolation, two thousand miles out in the Pacific, they belong very definitely to the United States. Pulling in more than seven million tourists per year, the fiftieth state can seem at times like a gigantic theme park.

Honolulu, on **Oahu**, is by far the largest city in Hawaii, while Waikiki, its resort annexe, is the main tourist centre. Three other islands attract sizeable numbers of visitors: **Hawaii** itself, also known as the **Big Island** in a vain attempt to avoid confusion, **Maui** and **Kauai**. All the islands share a similar topography and **climate**. Ocean winds shed their rain on their northeast, **windward** coasts, keeping them wet and green; the southwest, **leeward** (or "Kona") coasts can be almost barren, and so make ideal locations for big resorts. While temperatures remain consistent all year at between 70°F and 85°F, rainfall is heaviest from December to March, which nonetheless remains the most popular time to visit. Although a visit to Hawaii doesn't have to cost a fortune, the one major expense you can't avoid, except possibly on Oahu, is car rental.

Brief history

Each of the Hawaiian islands was forced up like a vast mass of candle drippings by submarine volcanic action. The "hot spot" that fuelled them all has remained stationary as the Pacific plate drifts above. That process continues at Kilauea on the Big Island, where lava explodes into the sea to add new land day by day, while the oldest islands are now mere atolls way to the northwest. Until two thousand years ago, these unknown specks were populated only by the few plants, birds and animals carried here by wind or wave. The first known human inhabitants were the **Polynesians**, who arrived in two principal migrations: from the Marquesas from around 200 AD, and another from Tahiti several centuries later.

No western ship chanced upon Hawaii until **Captain Cook** reached Kauai in 1778. He was amazed to find a civilization sharing a culture – and language – with the peoples of the South Pacific. Although Cook himself was killed on the Big Island in 1779, his visit started an irreversible process of change. In reshaping the islands to suit their needs, Westerners decimated the indigenous flora and fauna – as well as the Hawaiians themselves. Cook's men estimated that there were a million islanders; the population today is roughly the same, but barely eight thousand **pure-blood Hawaiians** are left.

Within a few years of Cook's arrival, **Kamehameha** became the first king to unite all the islands. However, exposure to the world economy swiftly devastated Hawaii's traditional way of life. White advisers and ministers soon dominated the government, and the descendants of the first missionaries from New England became Hawaii's most powerful class. As the US grew increasingly reliant on Hawaiian-grown **sugar**, Hawaii moved inexorably towards annexation. In 1887 an all-white group of "concerned businessmen" forced King David Kalakaua to surrender power, and subsequently called in a US warship and declared a provisional republican government. US President Cleveland (a Democrat) responded that "Hawaii was taken possession of by the United

---

Getting to and around Hawaii p.1002	Whale-hunting and whale-watching
Sea sports and safety p.1007	p.1013
Molokini snorkel cruises p.1012	

NAPILI BAY, MAUI

Highlights

❶ Waikiki Beach, Oahu Learn to surf, or just sip a cocktail, on the world's most famous beach. **See p.1004**

❷ Pearl Harbor, Oahu View a reminder of December 7, 1941 – the "date that will live in infamy" – by visiting the sunken *USS Arizona*. **See p.1005**

❸ Kilauea eruption, Big Island The Big Island gets bigger day by day, thanks to the spectacular eruption of its youngest volcano, Kilauea. **See p.1010**

❹ Lahaina, Maui This early nineteenth-century whaling port ranks among the most historic towns in Hawaii. **See p.1012**

❺ Lumahai Beach, Kauai This superb beach has been featured in countless movies, but beware the treacherous waters. **See p.1015**

❻ Kalalau Trail, Kauai Admire the magnificent Na Pali coastline of Kauai from one of the world's greatest hiking trails. **See p.1015**

HIGHLIGHTS ARE MARKED ON THE MAP ON P.1002

GETTING TO AND AROUND HAWAII

Honolulu, just under six hours by plane from the West Coast, is one of the world's busiest centres for air traffic; return fares from **LA**, **San Francisco** and **Seattle** start at around $350. Direct flights from the mainland also serve Maui, the Big Island and Kauai.

Hawaiian Airlines (Ⓦ hawaiianair.com) connects all the major islands several times per day, with standard one-way fares of around $120. A budget competitor, Go! (Ⓦ iflygo.com), offers less frequent services at lower rates. There are **no ferry services** between the major islands.

States forces without the consent or wish of the government of the islands…(It) was wholly without justification…not merely a wrong but a disgrace".

On August 12, 1898, Hawaii was formally **annexed** as a territory of the United States. Its ultimate integration into the American mainstream was hastened by its crucial role in the war against Japan, and the expansion of tourism thereafter. The islands finally became the fiftieth of the United States in 1959, after a plebiscite showed a seventeen-to-one majority in favour. The only group to oppose statehood were the few remaining native Hawaiians.

Modern Hawaii

Roughly sixty percent of the 1.4-million modern Hawaiians were born here. Around 38 percent are of Asian descent and 26 percent Caucasian, with 150,000 claiming at least some Hawaiian ancestry. With agriculture in decline, the need to import virtually all the basics of life results in a high **cost of living**.

Few vestiges of **ancient Hawaii** remain. What is presented as "historic" usually postdates the missionary impact. Ruined temples (*heiaus*) to the old gods still stand in some places, but Hawaii's "old towns" are pure nineteenth-century Americana, with false-front stores and raised wooden boardwalks. While authentic **hula** is a powerful art form, you're most likely to encounter it bastardized in a *luau*. Primarily tourist money-spinners, these "traditional feasts" provide an opportunity to sample Hawaiian **foods** such as *kalua* pig, baked underground, and local fish such as *ono*, *ahi*, *mahi-mahi* and *lomi-lomi* (raw salmon).

The Hawaiian **language** endures primarily in place names and music. At first glance it looks unpronounceable – especially as its written form uses just twelve letters (the five

HAWAII

0 ——— 50
miles

N

HIGHLIGHTS

1. Waikiki Beach, Oahu
2. Pearl Harbor, Oahu
3. Kilauea eruption, Big Island
4. Lahaina, Maui
5. Lumahai Beach, Kauai
6. Kalalau Trail, Kauai

vowels, plus *h, k, l, m, n, p,* and *w*) – but each letter is enunciated individually, and long words break down into repeated sounds, such as "*meha-meha*" in "Kamehameha".

Oahu

Almost three quarters of Hawaii's population live on **OAHU**, which has monopolized the islands' trade and tourism since European sailors realized that **Honolulu** offered the safest in-shore anchorage for thousands of miles. Well over half of all visitors to Hawaii arrive in Honolulu, and many remain for their entire vacation. Oahu effectively confines tourists to the tower-block enclave of **Waikiki**, just east of downtown Honolulu; there are few rooms anywhere else.

While over-development makes it hard to recommend Oahu over its neighbours, it can still give a real flavour of Hawaii. Oahu has some excellent **beaches**, with those on the North Shore a haven for **surfers** and campers, and the **cliffs** of the windward side are awesome.

Honolulu

Until the Europeans came, there was no significant settlement on the site of modern **HONOLULU**; soon so many foreign ships were frequenting its waters that it had become Kamehameha's capital, and it remains the economic centre of the archipelago. While the city covers a long (if narrow) strip of southern Oahu, **downtown** is a manageable size, and a lot quieter than its glamorous image might suggest. The tourist hotels are concentrated in the skyscrapers of the distinct suburb of **Waikiki**, a couple of miles east.

While its setting is beautiful, right on the Pacific and backed by dramatic cliffs and extinct volcanoes, most visitors are here simply to enjoy the sheer **hedonism** of shopping, eating and generally hanging out in the sun.

16

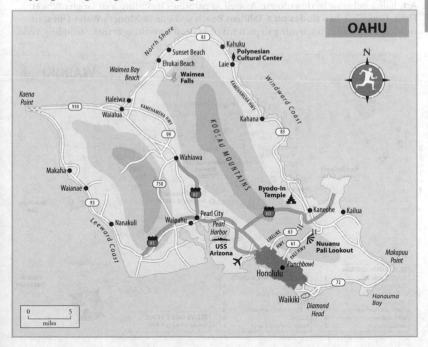

Waikiki

Built on a reclaimed swamp, two miles east of downtown Honolulu, **Waikiki** is very nearly an island, all but separated from the city between the sea and the Ala Wai canal. The site may be venerable, but these days its *raison d'être* is rampant commercialism. You could, just about, survive here with very little money, but there would be no point – there's nothing to see, and the only thing to do apart from surf and sunbathe is to stroll, and shop, along the seafront **Kalakaua Avenue**.

In places, the parallel **Waikiki Beach** narrows to just a thin strip of sand, but it's still a wonderful place to spend a lazy day, and there's always something going on, from surf lessons to outrigger canoe rides. The pedestrian walkway along its edge, lined with pleasant gardens, makes it a refuge from the frenzy nearby, and usually you only have to walk a little west of the centre to find a more secluded spot.

Iolani Palace

364 S King St • Guided tours Tues–Thurs 9–10am, Fri & Sat 9–11.15am, self-guided tours Mon 9am–4pm, Tues–Thurs 10.30am–4pm, Fri & Sat noon–4pm • Guided tours $22, self-guided tours $15 • ☎ 808 522 0832, ⓦ iolanipalace.org

The imposing **Iolani Palace**, still the focal point of downtown Honolulu, was built for King David Kalakaua in 1882. It later became a prison for his sister and deposed successor Queen Liliuokalani, who was tried for treason here for allegedly supporting her own restoration, and sentenced to house arrest. It now serves as a memorial to and museum of the Hawaiian monarchy; there's an impressive collection of ancient artefacts in the basement, including feathered royal cloaks. Across the road stands a flower-bedecked, gilt statue of Kamehameha the Great.

Honolulu Museum of Art

900 S Beretania St • Tues–Sat 10am–4.30pm, Sun 1–5pm • $10, under-18s free • ☎ 808 532 8700, ⓦ honolulumuseum.org

Oahu residents take great pride in the stunning fine art at the Honolulu **Museum of Art**, half a mile east of downtown. As well as paintings including Van Gogh's **Wheat Field**, Gauguin's **Two Nudes on a Tahitian Beach** and one of Monet's **Water Lilies**, the Academy also holds fascinating depictions of Hawaii by visiting artists, including vivid,

16

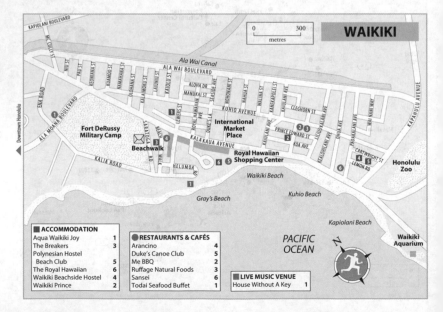

WAIKIKI

Ala Wai Canal

Fort DeRussy Military Camp

International Market Place

Royal Hawaiian Shopping Center

Beachwalk

Waikiki Beach

Gray's Beach

Kuhio Beach

Kapiolani Beach

Honolulu Zoo

Waikiki Aquarium

PACIFIC OCEAN

■ ACCOMMODATION

Aqua Waikiki Joy	1
The Breakers	3
Polynesian Hostel Beach Club	5
The Royal Hawaiian	6
Waikiki Beachside Hostel	4
Waikiki Prince	2

● RESTAURANTS & CAFÉS

Arancino	4
Duke's Canoe Club	5
Me BBQ	2
Ruffage Natural Foods	3
Sansei	6
Todai Seafood Buffet	1

■ LIVE MUSIC VENUE
House Without A Key | 1

stylized studies of Maui's Iao Valley and Hana coast by Georgia O'Keeffe, plus magnificent ancient **Chinese** ceramics and bronzes.

Chinatown

Just five minutes' walk west of downtown Honolulu, the faded green-clapboard storefronts of **Chinatown**, lining the narrow streets that lead down to Nuuanu Stream, seem like another world. Some of Chinatown's old walled courtyards are now malls, but the businesses remain much the same as ever, and you can still find herbalists weighing out dried leaves in front of vast arrays of bottles. Pig snouts and salmon heads are among the food specialities at **Oahu Market**, on N King and Kekaulike streets.

Bishop Museum

1525 Bernice St • Daily except Tues 9am–5pm • $20 • ☎ 808 847 3511, ⓦ bishopmuseum.org • TheBus #2 from Waikiki

The anthropological collection at the **Bishop Museum** – well away from the ocean and downtown, near the foot of the Likelike Highway – showcases real Polynesian culture. Three floors of its beautifully restored Hawaiian Hall display ancient carved stone and wooden images of gods, magnificent feather **leis** and cloaks, and a full-sized **hale** (traditional hut) from Kauai, in addition to a full-sized sperm whale. The Pacific Hall alongside considers the peoples of the rest of Polynesia, with a superb exhibit on traditional navigation.

National Memorial Cemetery of the Pacific

2177 Puowaina Drive • Daily: March–Sept 8am–6.30pm; Oct–Feb 8am–5.30pm • Free • ☎ 808 532 3720, ⓦ cem.va.gov/cems/nchp/nmcp.asp •
TheBus #15

High above Honolulu, lush lawns in the caldera of the extinct Punchbowl volcano – once home to an ancient sacrificial temple – are the setting for the **National Memorial Cemetery of the Pacific**. More than 25,000 casualties from all US Pacific wars, including Vietnam, lie buried here, while a central memorial commemorates almost 29,000 further service personnel still considered missing in action.

Pearl Harbor

Nine miles west of downtown Honolulu • **Visitor centre** Daily 7am–4.30pm, tours 8am–3pm • Free • ☎ 808 422 0561, ⓦ nps.gov/usar **USS Missouri** Daily: June–Aug 8am–5pm; Sept–May 8am–4pm • Tours $22–47 • ☎ 808 455 1600, ⓦ ussmissouri.com • TheBus #20 from Waikiki

Almost the whole of **Pearl Harbor**, the principal base for the US Pacific fleet, is off-limits to visitors. However, the surprise Japanese attack of December 7, 1941, which an official US inquiry called "the greatest military and naval disaster in our nation's history", is commemorated by a simple white memorial set above the wreck of the battleship **USS Arizona**, still discernible in the clear blue waters. More than 1100 of its crew lie entombed there.

Free tours of the memorial operate between 8am and 3pm each day, but it can be two or three hours after you pick up your numbered ticket before you're called to board the ferry that takes you there. The visitor centre does at least offer long-range views of the memorial, which was partly financed by Elvis Presley's 1961 Honolulu concert, his first show after leaving the army.

The huge **USS Missouri**, which survived the attack and was the scene four years later of the ceremony in Tokyo Harbor that ended World War II, is moored alongside the *Arizona*. Guided visits, by bus from alongside the Pearl Harbor visitor centre, include the actual surrender site as well as sweeping views of the harbour from the *Missouri*'s bridge.

Diamond Head

Trail daily 6am–6pm • $5/vehicle or $1/hiker • ⓦ hawaiistateparks.org • TheBus #22 or #58 from Waikiki

Waikiki's most famous landmark is the craggy 762ft pinnacle of **Diamond Head**, an extinct volcano that looms immediately east. The lawns of the crater interior are oddly bland, but a straightforward hiking trail, passing through a network of tunnels built during World War II, leads up a mile or so to the summit, and a panorama of the whole coast.

16

Hanauma Bay Nature Preserve

Ten miles east of Waikiki • June–Aug daily except Tues 6am–7pm, 2nd and 4th Sat of month 6am–10pm; Sept–May daily except Tues 6am–6pm, 2nd Sat of month 6am–10pm • $7.50, under-13s free • ☎ 808 396 4229, ⓦ www1.honolulu.gov/parks/facility/index.htm • TheBus #20 from Waikiki

The magnificent crescent-shaped **Hanauma Bay**, formed when the wall of a crater collapsed and let in the sea, is Oahu's best place to **snorkel**. Thanks to strict conservation measures, which include closing the entire bay to visitors every Tuesday, the sea abounds in brightly coloured fish.

ARRIVAL AND INFORMATION

By plane Honolulu's International Airport (ⓦ hawaii.gov /hnl) is west of downtown, a total of 10 miles west of Waikiki. Driving to Waikiki takes anything from 25min–1hr 15min, with typical taxi fares at $35–40. Speedishuttle offers a shuttle service to any Waikiki hotel (from $13; ☎ 877 242 5777, ⓦ speedishuttle.com). Regular buses #19 and #20 also head to Waikiki, but don't allow large bags, cases or backpacks.

Information There is no useful visitor centre in Honolulu or Waikiki, but the Hawaii Visitors Bureau maintains a strong online presence at ⓦ gohawaii.com.

GETTING AROUND

TheBus Honolulu is the centre of an exemplary bus network that covers the entire island (☎ 808 848 5555, ⓦ thebus.org). All journeys cost $2.50, with free transfers onto any connecting route; a four-day pass is $25. The most popular routes with Waikiki-based tourists are #2 to downtown, #8 to Ala Moana, #20 to Pearl Harbor, #22 to Hanauma Bay, and the bargain "Circle Island" buses (#52 clockwise and #55 counterclockwise), which take 4hr to loop around the central valley and the east coast, passing the legendary North Shore surf spots.

By car Although car rental outlets abound, at the airport and in Waikiki, driving is not a convenient option for Waikiki-based visitors, who are liable to pay very hefty parking fees.

Tours Polynesian Adventure Tours run city and island bus tours, costing anything from $25 up to $120 for a full day, as well as off-island packages (☎ 888 206 4531, ⓦ polyad.com).

ACCOMMODATION

All the accommodation listed below is in or near **Waikiki**; very little is available in central Honolulu. Waikiki accommodation covers a wide range and the highest rates will bring absolute luxury, but it's possible to find comfortable lodging for much less. Though an ocean view costs at least $50 extra, nothing is far from the Pacific.

Aqua Waikiki Joy 320 Lewers St ☎ 808 923 2300, ⓦ aquawaikikijoy.com. Good-value little hotel, with quirky pastel decor, from the airy garden lobby through to the spacious upgraded rooms, all of which have balconies and whirlpool baths. $\underline{176}$

The Breakers 250 Beach Walk ☎ 808 923 3181, ⓦ breakers-hawaii.com. Small, old-fashioned Polynesian hotel on the western edge of central Waikiki; all rooms have kitchenettes and TV, and there's a bar and grill beside the pool. $\underline{140}$

Polynesian Beach Club Hostel 2584 Lemon Rd ☎ 808 922 1340, ⓦ polynesianhostel.com. This safe, reasonably clean hostel is really nothing fancy, but it's a great price for staying a block from the sea. A/c dorms of assorted sizes; those with four beds also have en-suite bathrooms. "Semi-private" rooms share bathrooms, while studios are en suite. Van tours offered. Dorms from $\underline{20}$, semi-private doubles $\underline{65}$, studios $\underline{95}$

★ **The Royal Hawaiian** 2259 Kalakaua Ave ☎ 808 923 7311, ⓦ royal-hawaiian.com. The 1920s "Pink Palace", commanding the beach, is one of Waikiki's best-loved landmarks. Its original building, looking out across terrace gardens to the sea, remains irresistible. $\underline{375}$

Waikiki Beachside Hostel 2556 Lemon Rd ☎ 808 923 9566, ⓦ waikikibeachsidehostel.com. Small hotel block near the park in eastern Waikiki – not literally "beachside" – that has been converted into a popular, lively private hostel, with dorms that can also be booked in their entirety to create private rooms. Dorms from $\underline{18}$, semi-private twins $\underline{70}$

Waikiki Prince 2431 Prince Edward St ☎ 808 922 1544, ⓦ waikikiprince.com. Very central budget hotel, offering bright if unremarkable en-suite a/c rooms with balconies but lacking phones or daily maid service. The "standard" and "economy" units have basic cooking facilities. Seventh night free March–Dec. $\underline{70}$

EATING

Both Honolulu and Waikiki offer an enormous range of **dining** options. Excellent and well-priced stalls in the **Maunakea Marketplace** on Maunakea Street in Chinatown sell all sorts of international cuisines; there's a large fast-food mall in the **Ala Moana Center**; and Waikiki's Kuhio Avenue is lined with snack outlets and noodle bars.

Arancino 255 Beach Walk, Waikiki ☎ 808 923 5557, ⓦ arancino.com. Italian trattoria in the heart of Waikiki. Appetizers to share cost $12–20, while pasta and pizza mains range from $11 up to the tasty *spaghetti alla pescatore* ($29), with all kinds of fish swimming in olive oil and garlic. Daily 11.30am–2.30pm & 5–10pm.

Chef Mavro 1969 S King St, Honolulu ☎ 808 944 4714, ⓦ chefmavro.com. Standout gourmet restaurant, where the Greek-born chef offers delicate and delightful contemporary Hawaiian on *prix-fixe* menus costing from $85 for four courses up to $175 for eleven. Tues–Sun 6–9pm.

Duke's Canoe Club Outrigger Waikiki, 2335 Kalakaua Ave, Waikiki ☎ 808 922 2268, ⓦ dukeswaikiki.com. Crowded chain restaurant, right on the beach, with a feast of retro tiki and surf styling, and good-value buffets for breakfast ($17) and lunch ($16), plus pricier dinners and Hawaiian music on weekends. Daily 6.30am–midnight.

★ **Indigo** 1121 Nuuanu Ave, Honolulu ☎ 808 521 2900, ⓦ indigo-hawaii.com. Chinatown's classiest option, a lovely space with indoor and outdoor seating, serves delicious "Eurasian" crossover food. In addition to the good-value $16 lunch buffet, you can select from a broad range of dim sum ($7–12), while dinner mains include a whole steamed fish for $27. Tues–Fri 11.30am–9pm, Sat 4–9pm.

Me BBQ 151 Uluniu Ave, Waikiki ☎ 808 926 9717. Tiny diner serving tasty Korean barbecue; tangy beef ribs cost less than $10, but you can also get eggs and Portuguese sausages. Mon–Sat 7am–9pm.

Ruffage Natural Foods 2443 Kuhio Ave, Waikiki ☎ 808 922 2042. Tiny, inexpensive wholefood grocery with take-away counter and limited seating; healthy vegetarian food in the day for less than $10, including great smoothies, and sushi in the evening. Daily 9am–10.30pm.

★ **Sansei** Waikiki Beach Marriott, 2552 Kalakaua Ave, Waikiki ☎ 808 931 6286, ⓦ sanseihawaii.com. Wonderful, dinner-only Japanese-inspired restaurant, serving superb sushi at around $10 for a speciality roll, and a full Pacific Rim menu with mains at $16–40. Mon–Thurs & Sun 5.30–10pm, Fri & Sat 5.30pm–1am.

Todai Seafood Buffet 1910 Ala Moana Blvd, Waikiki ☎ 808 947 1000, ⓦ todai.com. Stylish all-you-can-eat Japanese buffet in western Waikiki. Lunch costs $16 and dinner $32, but the range and quality of the food, including sushi, shrimp, crab and lobster, makes it a real bargain. Mon–Thurs 11.30am–2pm & 5.30–9pm, Fri 11.30am–2pm & 5.30–9.30pm, Sat 11.30am–2.30pm & 5–9.30pm, Sun 11am–2.30pm & 5.30–9.30pm.

16

NIGHTLIFE AND ENTERTAINMENT

Honolulu's **nightlife** is concentrated in Waikiki, where fun-seeking tourists set the tone. On the whole, the available entertainment is on the bland side. Hawaii tends to be off the circuit for touring musicians, so if you enjoy live music you'll probably have to settle for lesser-known local performers.

Hawaii Theatre 1130 Bethel St, Honolulu ☎ 808 528 0506, ⓦ hawaiitheatre.com. Check the programme at this beautifully restored Chinatown landmark as soon as you know your dates; performances of hula or Hawaiian music here, especially, are truly memorable.

★ **House Without A Key** Halekulani, 2199 Kalia Rd, Waikiki ☎ 808 923 2311, ⓦ halekulani.com. Romantic open-air beach bar, blessed with spectacular ocean sunsets, where the no-cover evening cocktail hour features gentle,

old-time Hawaiian classics performed by top-notch musicians and hula dancers. Daily 7am–9pm.

★ **La Mariana Sailing Club** 50 Sand Island Access Rd ☎ 808 848 2800, ⓦ lamarianasailingclub.com. This quirky waterfront restaurant, hidden away amid Honolulu's docks, has a strong claim to be Hawaii's last genuine tiki bar; the food may be a little overpriced, but the ambience, with classic Hawaiian music on Friday evenings and live piano (nightly except Mon), is priceless. Daily 11am–9pm.

SEA SPORTS AND SAFETY

The nation that invented **surfing** remains its greatest arena. The sport was popularized early in the twentieth century by Olympic swimmer Duke Kahanamoku, using a 20ft board; these days most are around 6ft. As a rule, the best surfing beaches are on the north shore of each island. **Windsurfing** and **kitesurfing**, too, are hugely popular, in similar locations, while smaller **boogie boards** make an exhilarating initiation. **Snorkelling** and **diving** are top-quality, although Hawaii's **coral** has fewer brilliant hues than those seen in warmer equatorial waters.

Bear in mind, however, that **drownings** in Hawaii are all too common. Waves can sweep in from two thousand miles of open ocean onto beaches that are unprotected by any reef. Not all beaches have lifeguards and warning flags, and unattended beaches are not necessarily safe. Watch the sea carefully before going in, and never take your eyes off it thereafter. If you get swept out, don't fight the big waves; allow yourself to be carried out of the danger zone, then when the current dies down swim back to shore.

Windward Oahu

The most spectacular moment on a tour of Oahu comes as you leave Honolulu on the **Pali Highway** (Hwy-61), and cross the Koolau Mountains to see the sheer green cliffs of the windward side, veiled by swirling mists. The highest spot, four miles northeast of Honolulu, is the **Nuuanu Pali Lookout**. Kamehameha the Great finalized his conquest of Oahu here in 1795, forcing hundreds of enemy warriors over the edge of the cliffs. Down on the coast beyond, **Kailua**, the main windward town, has a beautiful beach; President Obama holidays here each winter.

Polynesian Cultural Center

Laie, 35 miles north of Waikiki • Mon–Sat noon–9pm • Basic admission $50, children 3–11 $36; dinner packages start at $70/$55 • ☎ 808 293 3333, ⊗ polynesia.com • TheBus #52 from Waikiki

The **Polynesian Cultural Center** – Oahu's leading paying attraction, with one million annual visitors – stands ten miles short of the island's northernmost tip. A haphazard mixture of real and bogus Polynesia, in which the history veers firmly towards the latter, it's owned and run by the Mormon Church. After touring "villages" modelled on assorted Polynesian islands, you can stay into the evening for a *luau* and/or dance performances, plus dinner.

North Shore Oahu

Although the **surfing beaches** of northern Oahu are famous the world over, they're minimally equipped for tourists. **Waimea**, **Sunset** and **Ehukai** beach parks are all laidback roadside stretches of sand, where you can usually find a quiet spot to yourself. In summer, the tame waves may leave you wondering what all the fuss is about; see them at full tilt in the winter and you'll have no doubts. **HALEIWA**, the main surfers' hangout, combines alternative shops and cafés with upfront tourist traps.

The Big Island

Although the **Big Island of Hawaii** could hold all the other islands with room to spare, it has the population of a medium-sized town, with just 185,000 people (perhaps half what it held in Captain Cook's day). Visitation remains lower than at Oahu and Maui; despite its fair share of restaurants, bars and facilities, this is basically a rural community, where sleepy old towns have remained unchanged for a century. The few resorts are built on the barren lava flows of the Kona coast to catch maximum sunshine.

Thanks to the **Kilauea** volcano, which has destroyed roads and even towns, and spews out pristine beaches of jet-black sand, the Big Island is still growing, its southern shore inching ever further out to sea. **Hawaii Volcanoes National Park**, which includes **Mauna Loa** as well as Kilauea (though not **Mauna Kea**, further to the north and higher than either), is absolutely compelling; you can explore steaming craters and cinder cones, venture into the rainforest, and at times approach within feet of the eruption itself.

As befits the birthplace of King Kamehameha, more of the ancient Hawaii survives on the Big Island than anywhere else, with temples and historic sites including the **Puuhonua O Honaunau** in the southwest, and lush **Waipio Valley** in the northeast.

The Kona and Kohala coasts

Hawaii's leeward, western shoreline divides into two distinct areas: the verdant, fertile **Kona coast**, to either side of its only sizeable community, **Kailua**, and the **Kohala coast** further north, where barren lava trails down to the sea, and the luxury resorts stand out as incongruous green patches alongside its superb beaches.

16

Kailua

The little town of **KAILUA**, sometimes also referred to as **Kona**, has played a major part in Hawaiian history. It has therefore been more impacted by tourism than any other Big Island community, and its constant row of fast food restaurants and souvenir shops could be almost anywhere.

King Kamehameha's funeral rites were performed in the ancient temple of **Ahuena Heiau**, poised beside a little beach at the northern end of the bay. A short way south, **Hulihee Palace** (Tues–Sat 10am–3pm; $6) faces out to sea from the centre of Kailua. Built as the governor's residence in 1838, it was damaged in an earthquake in 2006, but you can still inspect the massive *koa*-wood furnishings inside, made to fit the considerable girth of its royal Hawaiian residents.

Kealakekua Bay

Kealakekua Bay, a dozen miles south of Kailua in the prime coffee-growing district of South Kona, is where Captain Cook was killed on February 14, 1779, during his second visit to Hawaii. Once a major population centre, it's now barely inhabited, and the white **obelisk** on the death site – legally a small piece of England – is all but inaccessible. You can only get to within a mile of the obelisk by car, at **Napoopoo Beach**. The bay itself is the best place on the Big Island for **snorkelling**.

Puuhonua O Honaunau

Four miles south of Kealakekua Bay • Daily 7am–sunset • $5/vehicle • ☎ 808 328 2326, ⓦ nps.gov/puho

Puuhonua O Honaunau National Historical Park, the single most evocative historical site in all the Hawaiian islands, juts into the Pacific on a small peninsula of jagged black lava. The grounds include a lovely little beach, backed by a fishpond and three *heiaus* (temples), guarded by carved effigies. An ancient "place of refuge" lies protected behind the mortarless masonry of the sixteenth-century Great Wall. Anyone who broke the intricate system of *kapu* (taboo) – perhaps by treading on the shadow of a chief, or fishing in the wrong season – could expect summary execution unless they fled to such a sanctuary. As chiefs lived on the surrounding land, transgressors had to swim through shark-infested seas. If successful, they would be absolved and released overnight.

The Kohala coast

The best of the Big Island's spectacular sandy **beaches** – safe for summer swimming, though with tempestuous winter surf – lie north of Kailua along the **Kohala coast**.

For idyllic seclusion, head for the turquoise lagoons of **Kiholo Bay**, reached via an unmarked and very bumpy dirt road halfway between mile-posts 82 and 83 on Kamehemeha Highway, just under thirty miles from Kailua. Immediately north of there, three separate self-contained oases – Waikoloa, Mauna Kea and Mauna Lani – have been carved from the inhospitable lava desert, each holding two or three hotels, a beach or two, and nothing else. Just beyond, you reach the most famous strand of all, ravishing **Hapuna Beach**.

Windward Hawaii

Almost all the rain that falls on Mauna Kea flows down the eastern side of the Big Island. As a result, myriad streams and waterfalls nourish dense jungle-like vegetation, so the main road north along the coast from Hilo is alive with flowering trees and orchids.

Hilo

Although it's the Big Island's capital and largest town, just 45,000 people live in **HILO**, which remains endearing and unpressured. Mass tourism has never taken off here, mainly because it rains too much. However, America's wettest city blazes with tropical blooms against a backdrop of rainbows.

With its modest streets and wooden stores, Hilo's **downtown** looks appealingly low-key. Sadly, that's largely because all the buildings that stood on the seaward side of Kamehameha Avenue were destroyed by two tsunami, in 1946 and 1960. The story is told in the **Pacific Tsunami Museum**, 130 Kamehameha Ave (Mon–Sat 9am–4pm; $8; ⓦtsunami.org). A scale model shows how the city looked before 1946; contemporary footage and letters bring home the impact of the tragedy.

The **Lyman Museum**, based in the 1830s home of early missionaries at 276 Haili St (Mon–Sat 10am–4.30pm; $10; ⓦlymanmuseum.org), holds a fascinating display of ancient weapons and documents Hawaii's various ethnic groups, including the Portuguese who arrived in 1878 from the volcanic Azores, bringing with them what became the ukulele.

North from Hilo

The **Belt Road** (Hwy-19) follows the **Hamakua coast** north of Hilo, clinging to the hillsides and crossing ravines on slender bridges. For a glimpse into the interior, head into the mountains after fifteen miles to the 450ft **Akaka Falls**. A short loop trail through the forest, festooned with wild orchids, offers views of Akaka and other waterfalls.

Highway-240, which turns north off the Belt Road at **HONOKAA**, comes to an abrupt end after nine miles at the edge of **Waipio Valley**. As the southernmost of six successive sheer-walled valleys, this is the only one accessible by land, though the one road in is too steep for cars, and makes a gruelling half-hour hike. Waipio is as close as Hawaii comes to the classic South Seas image of an isolated and self-sufficient valley, dense with fruit trees and laced by footpaths leading down to the sea.

Hawaii Volcanoes National Park

Visitor centre Daily 7.45am–5pm **Jaggar Museum** Daily 8.30am–5pm • $10/vehicle • ☎ 808 967 7311, ⓦnps.gov/havo

The Big Island's southernmost volcanoes, **Mauna Loa** and **Kilauea**, jointly constitute **HAWAII VOLCANOES NATIONAL PARK**, thirty miles from Hilo and eighty from Kailua. The park's dramatic landscapes include desert, arctic tundra and rainforest, besides two active volcanoes.

Evidence is everywhere of the awesome power of the volcanoes to create and destroy; no map can keep up with the latest whims of the lava flow. Whole towns have been engulfed, and once-prized beachfront properties lie buried hundreds of yards back from the sea.

Kilauea Caldera

The main focus of the park is **Kilauea Caldera**, the summit crater of Kilauea, twenty miles up from the ocean. Close to the rim, both the **visitor centre** and the fascinating **Jaggar Museum** of geology offer basic orientation. Kilauea is said to be the home of the volcano goddess **Pele**, who has followed the "hot spot" from island to island. When Mark Twain came here in 1866, he observed a dazzling lake of liquid fire; after a huge explosion in 1924 it became shallower and quieter, a black dusty expanse dotted with hissing steam vents. Volcanic activity in the caldera resumed in 2008, however, so visitors currently can only admire the merging plumes of smoke from a distance.

It's still possible to **hike** nearby. The five-mile **Kilauea Iki Trail** explores an adjoining crater, where you pick your way from cairn to cairn across an eerie landscape of cracked and jagged lava, while the mile-long **Devastation Trail** is a boardwalk laid across the scene of a 1959 eruption.

Chain of Craters Road

Chain of Craters Road winds down to the sea from Crater Rim Drive, sweeping around cones and vents in an empty landscape where the occasional dead white tree trunk or flowering shrub pokes up. Fresh sheets of lava constantly ooze down the slopes to cover the road, so it now comes to a dead end a short way along the coast, a fifty-mile round-trip from the park entrance (with no facilities along the way). Depending on where current volcanic activity is concentrated, it is possible at times to walk across the congealed lava from the end of the road to see molten rock gush from the earth – sometimes directly into the sea.

ARRIVAL AND GETTING AROUND   THE BIG ISLAND

Kona International Airport Largely open-air, and offering all the usual car-rental places. Speedi Shuttle shared vans (☏ 877 242 5777, ☏ speedishuttle.com) cost around $25/person to Kailua, 9 miles south, or $52 to the Waikoloa resorts, 20 miles north.

Hilo International Airport On the eastern outskirts of Hilo; a taxi into downtown costs around $15.
Hele-On Bus Circle-island bus network, connecting Hilo and Kailua with all the main towns and resorts (flat fare $2; ☏ 808 961 8744, ☏ heleonbus.org).

ACCOMMODATION

KAILUA

★ **King Kamehameha's Kona Beach Hotel** 75-5660 Palani Rd ☏ 808 329 2911, ☏ konabeachhotel.com. Rooms at this veteran resort hotel have been beautifully renovated, making it great value for such a superb location, facing a picturesque beach in the heart of Kailua. **$144**

Kona Tiki Hotel 75-5968 Ali'i Drive ☏ 808 329 1425, ☏ konatikihotel.com. Simple, fifteen-room motel, inches from the ocean, that's a gem for budget travellers. All the clean, comfortable rooms have balconies; some have kitchenettes; and rates include breakfast beside the small pool. No TVs or phones. **$94**

KOHALA COAST

★ **Hapuna Beach Prince Hotel** 62-100 Kauna'oa Drive, Kohala Coast ☏ 808 880 1111, ☏ hapunabeach princehotel.com. Low-slung luxury hotel, at the north end of Hapuna Beach, offering opulent accommodation in an idyllic situation. **$199**

Waikoloa Beach Marriott 69-275 Waikoloa Beach Drive, Waikoloa ☏ 808 886 6789, ☏ marriotthawaii.com. Classy and very elegant hotel, facing lovely Anaehoomalu

Beach, with its own lagoon and pool complex. All 500-plus rooms have private balconies. **$179**

HILO

★ **Dolphin Bay Hotel** 333 Iliahi St ☏ 808 935 1466, ☏ dolphinbayhilo.com. Very friendly little hotel, just across the river from downtown. All the spotlessly clean studios and suites have TV, bathroom, and kitchen, but no phones. Reduced rates for more than one night. **$139**

Hilo Bay Hostel 101 Waianuenue Ave ☏ 808 933 2771, ☏ hawaiihostel.net. Smart, clean, safe and very welcoming hostel, in an attractive and central historic building. Dorms **$27**, doubles **$67**, en-suite doubles **$77**

HAWAII VOLCANOES NATIONAL PARK

★ **Hale Ohia** Volcano ☏ 808 967 7986, ☏ haleohia .com. Delightful B&B, just outside the park, consisting of several cabins and cottages in gorgeous rainforest gardens south of the highway across from Volcano village. **$195**

Volcano House 1 Crater Rim Drive ☏ 808 756 9625, ☏ hawaiivolcanohouse.com. Historic, newly restored lodge, alongside the edge of Kilauea crater inside the national park, with spectacular views, and good food in the evening. **$285**

EATING

KAILUA

Island Lava Java 75-5799 Ali'i Drive ☏ 808 327 2161, ☏ islandlavajava.com. Seafront mall café that's perfect for a light ocean-view breakfast or inexpensive lunch or dinner; burgers and sandwiches $13, pizzas $17–23, steak or lamb up to $28. Daily 6.30am–9.30pm.

SOUTH KONA

★ **The Coffee Shack** 83-5799 Mamalahoa Hwy, Captain Cook ☏ 808 328 9555, ☏ coffeeshack.com. The quintessential South Kona café, perched above gorgeous gardens just north of mile marker 108, and enjoying staggering views. Wonderfully fresh coffee, sensational smoothies, plus cooked breakfasts, pizzas, salads and colossal sandwiches. Daily 7.30am–3pm.

KOHALA COAST

★ **Roy's Waikoloa Bar & Grill** Kings' Shops, Waikoloa ☏ 808 886 4321, ☏ roysrestaurant.com. Flamboyant Pacific Rim dinners, best enjoyed on the lakeside terrace. Dim-sum-style appetizers, designed to share, at $10–15, and mains such as *shutome* (swordfish) with lemongrass and Thai curry and Waikoloa roast duck at $30–40. Daily 5–9.30pm.

HILO

★ **Hilo Bay Café** 315 Makaala St ☏ 808 935 4939, ☏ hilobaycafe.com. Smart, good-value mall café, well south of the ocean. Most dishes are pretty rich, from the French onion soup ($7) and the "Blue Bay Burger" ($12) to mains like sautéed shrimp ($25). Mon–Thurs 11am–9pm, Fri & Sat 11am–9.30pm, Sun 5–9pm.

16

The Seaside Restaurant 1790 Kalanianaole Ave ☎808 935 8825, ⓦseasiderestaurant.com. Two miles south of downtown, this plain but lively restaurant boasts thirty-acre fishponds full of trout, mullet and catfish. The fish is great, whether steamed or fried as a main course, or sushi-style as an appetizer, and you'd be hard pressed to spend more than $25 on a full fish supper. Tues–Thurs 4.30–8.30pm, Fri & Sat 4.30–9pm.

Maui

The island of **MAUI**, the second largest in the Hawaiian chain, is Oahu's principal rival, attracting roughly a third of all visitors to the state. Some say that things have gone too far, with formerly remote, unspoiled beaches, around **Kaanapali** (north of Lahaina) and **Kihei** for example, now swamped by sprawling resorts. On the other hand, the crowds come to Maui for the good reason that it's still beautiful. This is the best equipped of all the islands for **activity** holidays – whale-watching, windsurfing, diving, sailing, snorkelling and cycling. Temperatures along the coast can be searing, but it's always possible to escape to somewhere cooler. **Upcountry Maui**, on the slopes of the mighty **Haleakala** volcano, is a delight, while the waterfalls and ravines along the tortuous road out east to **Hana** outclass anything on Oahu.

Kahului and Wailuku

The twin towns of **KAHULUI** and **WAILUKU** occupy the northern side of the low-lying "neck" that connects its two mountainous sections. Kahului is the main commercial centre; Wailuku is one of the few towns on Maui that feels like a genuine community, with budget accommodation and restaurants to make it a good central base.

Although there's no sightseeing to speak of in either Kahului or Wailuku, Wailuku's Main Street heads straight into the **West Maui Mountains**, stopping three miles in at **Iao Needle**, a stunning 1200ft pinnacle of green-clad lava that stands, head usually in the clouds, at the intersection of two lush valleys. Kamehameha won control of Maui here in 1790, in a battle determined by a cannonade directed by two European gunners.

Lahaina

The only real town along the green but sunny shoreline of West Maui, **LAHAINA** is one of Hawaii's prettiest communities. Back in the nineteenth century it was capital of the entire Kingdom of Hawaii, but it has barely grown since then, and still resembles a peaceful tropical village. Its main oceanfront street is lined with timber-frame buildings; coconut palms sway to either side of the mighty central banyan tree; surfers swirl into the thin fringe of beach to the south; and the mountains of West Maui dominate the skyline.

South Maui

South of Kahului, across the isthmus, the resort area known as South Maui starts at **KIHEI**. The road is heavily built-up on both sides, but the hotels, malls and condos thin

---

MOLOKINI SNORKEL CRUISES

Maui's best-known **snorkelling** and **diving** spot is the tiny crescent of **Molokini**, poking above the sea – all that's left of a once-great volcano. There's no beach or landfall, but you do see a lot of fish, including deep-water species. Countless cruises leave early each morning (to avoid the heat) from Maalea Harbor on the south shore of the central isthmus; snorkellers can pay anything from $60 to $120 for a morning trip, and from $40 for a shorter afternoon jaunt. Recommended boats include *Four Winds II* (☎800 736 5740, ⓦfourwindsmaui.com) and the smaller *Paragon II* (☎808 244 2087, ⓦsailmaui.com).

WHALE-HUNTING AND WHALE-WATCHING

Whaling ships first arrived in Hawaii in 1820, the same year as the missionaries – and had an equally dramatic impact. Whales were never actually hunted here, but Hawaii swiftly became the centre of the industry and was such a paradise that up to fifty percent of each crew deserted here, to be replaced by native Hawaiians. Decline came with the Civil War – when many ships were deliberately sunk to blockade Confederate ports – and an 1871 disaster, when 31 vessels lingered in the Arctic too long, became frozen in, and had to be abandoned. Ironically, the waters off western Maui now rate among the world's best areas for whale-watching and between roughly December and April, **humpback whales** are often visible from the shore, although whale-watching trips can take you much closer. Operators include the nonprofit Pacific Whale Foundation (from $25; ☎ 800 942 5311, ⊛ pacificwhale.org).

---

out beyond the manicured lawns of **WAILEA**, near some superb beaches. **Paluea Beach** is ideal for families, while **Little Beach**, reached by a trail from the gorgeous, enormous **Makena (Big) Beach**, is famous for (illegal) nudism.

Upcountry Maui

Hawaii is not always a land tarnished by civilization. **Central Maui** has been turned into a pastoral idyll, thanks to an ingenious system of irrigation channels. The highway to the top of **Haleakala** climbs higher, at a faster rate, than any road on earth. Starting in rich meadows, it climbs past purple-blossoming jacaranda, firs and eucalyptus to reach open ranching land, and then ascends in huge curves to the volcanic desert and the crater itself.

Haleakala

Visitor centre Daily dawn–3pm • $10/vehicle • ☎ 808 572 4400, ⊛ nps.gov/hale

Though **HALEAKALA** – "the House of the Sun" – is the world's largest dormant volcano, you may not appreciate its full 10,000ft majesty until you're at the top. Shield volcanoes are not as dramatic as the classic cones, as lava oozes from fissures along broad flanks to create a long, low profile and the summit is often obscured by clouds. That it hasn't erupted for two hundred years doesn't necessarily mean it won't ever again.

The higher reaches of the mountain are a **national park**; the road up remains open around the clock. Manhattan would fit comfortably into the awe-inspiring **crater**, almost eight miles across, which was for the ancient Hawaiians a site of deep spiritual power. The most popular time to come is for the **sunrise**; with a full day, you can enjoy some tremendous hiking trails across the crater floor.

The road to Hana

The rains that fall on Haleakala cascade down Maui's long windward flank, covering it in thick, jungle-like vegetation. Convicts in the 1920s hacked out a **road** along the coast that has become a major tourist attraction, twisting in and out of gorges, past innumerable waterfalls and across more than fifty tiny one-lane bridges. All year round, and especially in June, the route is ablaze with colour from orchids, rainbow eucalyptus and orange-blossomed African tulip trees.

The former sugar town of **Hana** at the far end of the road is a pleasant enough little community that isn't especially interested in attracting tourists. The usual day's excursion continues ten miles further to gorgeous **Oheo Gulch**, where waterfalls tumble down the hillside to oceanfront meadows. That makes a total of just over fifty miles (3hr) each way from Kahului.

ARRIVAL

Kahului Airport Two miles east of central Kahului. Speedi Shuttle (☎ 877 242 5777, ⊕ speedishuttle.com) charges $30/

MAUI

person to Kihei, $50 to Lahaina.

ACCOMMODATION

★ **Banana Bungalow** 310 N Market St, Wailuku ☎ 808 244 5090, ⊕ mauihostel.com. Friendly independent hostel, open to non-Maui residents only, not far from central Wailuku. Beds in four- and six-bed dorms, and basic private rooms, without en-suite facilities. Free island excursions. Dorms $33, doubles $84

Best Western Pioneer Inn 658 Wharf St, Lahaina ☎ 800 457 5457, ⊕ pioneerinnmaui.com. Maui's oldest hotel, splendidly positioned on the seafront in the centre of Lahaina. All the tastefully furnished rooms have private baths and a/c, and open onto lovely balconies. No on-site parking. $154

Maui Sunseeker 551 S Kihei Rd, Kihei ☎ 808 879 1261, ⊕ mauisunseeker.com. Small hotel-cum-condo, catering to a predominantly gay clientele. Great-value rooms and suites, all with kitchen facilities and ocean views. $155

★ **The Mauian** 5441 Lower Honoapiilani Rd, Napili ☎ 808 669 6205, ⊕ mauian.com. Very friendly, laidback little resort, in vintage architectural style, on ravishing Napili Beach a few miles north of Lahaina. $186

Old Wailuku Inn 2199 Kahookele St, Wailuku ☎ 808 244 5897, ⊕ mauiinn.com. Luxurious plantation-style B&B, in landscaped gardens. Tasteful 1930s-era furnishings, private patios and baths; guests share a living room and veranda. $165

EATING

★ **Cilantro Fresh Mexican Grill** 170 Papalaua Ave, Lahaina ☎ 808 667 5444, ⊕ cilantrogrill.com. Simple but very appetizing Mexican diner. The food is uniformly tasty and fresh, with enchiladas, burritos and so on for $7–15, and whole rotisserie chickens for $15. Mon–Sat 11am–9pm, Sun 11am–8pm.

★ **The Feast at Lele** 505 Front St, Lahaina ☎ 866 244 5353, ⊕ feastatlele.com. An inspired cross between a *luau* and a gourmet restaurant, in a romantic beachfront setting. Five excellent and unusual courses of Polynesian food, plus sunset music and hula performances. The $115 adult charge includes unlimited cocktails; for children, it's $85. Reservations essential. April–Sept daily 6pm; Oct–March daily 5.30pm; schedules may vary.

Soup Nutz and Java Jazz 3350 Lower Honoapiilani Rd, Honokowai ☎ 808 667 0787, ⊕ javajazz.net. This funky mall hangout, north of Lahaina, is more than a juice and espresso bar, serving good food all day, with lots of comfy seating and a steady jazz soundtrack. Daily 6am–9pm.

Kauai

Although no point on the tiny island of **KAUAI** is as much as a dozen miles from the sea, the variety of its landscapes is quite incredible. This is the oldest of the major islands, and erosion has had more than six million years to sculpt it into fantastic shapes. The mist-shrouded extinct volcano **Mount Waialeale** at its heart is the world's wettest spot, draining into a high landlocked swamp. Nearby is the chasm of **Waimea Canyon**, while the north shore holds the vertiginous green cliffs of the awe-inspiring **Na Pali** coast, familiar from films such as *Jurassic Park* and *South Pacific*, but the sole preserve of adventurous **hikers**. Kauai is a place to be active, on sea and land; if you take only one **helicopter** flight in your life, this is the place to do it.

East Kauai

Kauai's principal town, **LIHUE**, stands slightly inland of little Nawiliwili Harbor at Kauai's southeast corner. Roughly at the midpoint of the one main road that encircles the island (prevented from completing a loop by the Na Pali cliffs), as a base it's undistinguished. The population is just five thousand, and downtown consists of a few tired plantation-town streets set well back from the sea.

Most Kauaians live between Lihue and the overlapping communities of **WAILUA**, **WAIPOULI** and **KAPAA**, whose malls, condos and hotels blend into each other a few miles north of the capital. All the way along there's an exposed thin strip of beach; only Wailua is especially scenic, and you have to head further north for good swimming or snorkelling.

The North Shore

The most beautiful region in the entire Hawaiian archipelago, Kauai's stupendous **North Shore** is lined with superb beaches, most of which are lashed by heavy waves ideal for surfers – for much of the year, and only safe for swimming in summer.

To reach the easternmost of these, long, golden **Secret Beach**, drive up Hwy-56 from the south, pass **Kilauea**, and then turn right at Kalihiwai. Take the second right onto a dirt track and the beach is a ten-minute walk down through the woods. At the far end, a waterfall of beautiful fresh mountain water cascades down the cliffs, and there are often spinner dolphins just offshore, especially around the picturesque 1913 Kilauea **lighthouse**. The cliffs above are a bird sanctuary.

Major development stops beyond the resort of **Princeville**, mainly because the road then crosses seven successive one-lane bridges. The first is over the Hanalei River, where endangered Hawaiian ducks, coots and stilts are protected by the preservation of their major habitats – natural wetlands and taro ponds.

The small town of **HANALEI** itself, set around a magnificent bay, has some low-key apartments for rent, but otherwise little formal accommodation. Gorgeous **Lumahai Beach**, just beyond the western edge of the bay, has starred in countless movies, among them *South Pacific*, but is far too treacherous for swimming in winter. All the roadside beaches from here on, however, are good for snorkelling. The road finally comes to an end at **Kee Beach**, perhaps the most delightful spot of all, with safe inshore swimming.

The Na Pali coast

Despite the rampant resort-building elsewhere on the island, the lush valleys of Kauai's **Na Pali coast** remain inviolate – though accessible enough by canoe to sustain large Hawaiian populations, their awesome walls shield them from any attempt to build roads. Separated each from the next by knife-edge ridges of rock thousands of feet high but just a few feet thick, they make Kauai one of the world's great hiking destinations.

The **Kalalau Trail** along the shore, which starts alongside Kee Beach, is unforgettable. The full eleven-mile trek to Kalalau Valley is arduous and gets progressively more dangerous; in places you have to scramble along a precipitous (and shadeless) wall of crumbly red rock.

However, the first two miles of the trail, to **Hanakapiai Beach**, are the most beautiful. They're steep but straightforward, passing through patches of dense vegetation where you clamber over the gnarled root systems of the splay-footed **hala** (pandanus) tree. From the beach, a further hour's arduous hike (off the main trail) leads inland to the natural amphitheatre of the towering **Hanakapiai Falls**. It takes at least four and a half hours to get to the falls and back from the trailhead.

South and West Kauai

POIPU, Kauai's largest beach resort, lies on the south coast roughly ten miles west of Lihue, where sunshine is more consistent and there's great surfing and snorkelling.

Two of Hawaii's major scenic attractions – the gorge of **Waimea Canyon**, and **Kokee State Park** at its far end – can only be reached from the **west coast** of Kauai. The coast itself, however, is nondescript. **WAIMEA**, the largest town, is just one short street at the foot of the poorly marked road up to the canyon. The statue of **Captain Cook**, which commemorates his "discovery" of Hawaii here on January 20, 1778, is an exact replica of one in Cook's home town of Whitby, England.

Waimea Canyon

It's not unreasonable to call **Waimea Canyon** the "Grand Canyon of the Pacific". At 3000ft, it may not be quite as deep as its Arizona rival, but the colours – all shades of green against the bare red earth – are absolutely breathtaking. The road from Waimea climbs beside the widening gorge, until after eight miles the mile-wide canyon can be seen in all its splendour.

16

Kokee State Park

Explore **Kokee State Park**, atop Kauai beyond Waimea Canyon, as early in the day as possible; by late morning the valleys may be filled with mist and clouds. At the end of the road, eighteen miles up from the town of Waimea, **Kalalau Lookout** stands over the valley where the Kalalau Trail ends.

The **Pihea Trail** follows the course of a lunatic attempt to extend the road along the ridge beyond. At times it narrows to a few feet, with precipitous drops to either side, and visibility can drop to nothing as the clouds siphon across the ridges. Inland lies the **Alakai Swamp**, where the heaviest rainfall on earth collects in the rock; the few humans who manage to penetrate the mists are assailed on all sides by the shrills, whistles and buzzes of a jungle without mammals or snakes. Kauai is the only island where mongooses have not killed off most native **birds**, and at this height mosquitoes are no threat either, so some of the world's rarest species survive here and nowhere else.

The trail through the swamp consists of a boardwalk for almost its entire six-mile length, though in places the planks just rest on cloying black mud. Giant ferns dangle above the trail and orchids gleam from the undergrowth. If you make it all the way to the end, you're rewarded with a stupendous panorama of Hanalei Bay.

ARRIVAL AND DEPARTURE   KAUAI

Lihue Airport All flights to Kauai land at Lihue's airport, 2 miles east of downtown. Speedi Shuttle (☎ 877 242 5777, ⓦ speedishuttle.com) charges $17/person to Kapaa, $39 to Poipu.

ACCOMMODATION

EAST KAUAI

Garden Island Inn 3445 Wilcox Rd, Lihue ☎ 808 245 7227, ⓦ gardenislandinn.com. Good-value motel, dripping with purple bougainvillea, near the beach. All the simple but appealing rooms have fridges and microwaves. **$119**

Plantation Hale Suites 484 Kuhio Hwy, Wailua ☎ 808 822 4941, ⓦ plantation-hale.com. Comfortable, inexpensive suites, each with kitchen and living room, facing across lawns to the sea. **$95**

THE NORTH SHORE

The Cliffs at Princeville 3811 Edward Rd, Princeville ☎ 808 826 6219, ⓦ cliffsatprinceville.com. Large, newly upgraded and nicely furnished suites in Princeville's biggest condo complex, with a clifftop setting next to the golf course. **$269**

★ **Hanalei Colony Resort** 5–7130 Kuhio Hwy, Haena ☎ 808 826 6235, ⓦ hcr.com. Oceanfront resort in a fabulous location 6 miles west of Hanalei. Each unit has two bedrooms, plus a kitchen, living room, bathroom and lanai, though no phones or TVs. **$249**

Hanalei Inn 5–5468 Kuhio Hwy, Hanalei ☎ 808 826 9333, ⓦ hanaleiinn.com. Small-scale inn a block from the bayfront, offering four very simple studio apartments, each with a kitchen and private bathroom. **$169**

SOUTH AND WEST KAUAI

★ **Grand Hyatt Kauai Resort** 1571 Poipu Rd, Poipu ☎ 808 742 1234, ⓦ kauai-hyatt.com. Arguably the nicest tropical resort in Hawaii, sprawling along the seafront at the east end of Poipu. Top-of-the-range bedrooms and great sea views, plus amazing pools and landscaping. **$289**

Waimea Plantation Cottages 9400 Kaumualii Hwy, Waimea ☎ 808 338 1625, ⓦ waimea-plantation.com. Former sugar-plantation homes, gathered in a coconut grove and fully renovated with luxurious bathrooms and linen draperies – an absolute delight, even if the sea here isn't safe for swimming. **$168**

EATING

EAST KAUAI

Caffé Coco 4-369 Kuhio Hwy, Wailua ☎ 808 822 7990, ⓦ caffecocokauai.com. Attractively ramshackle dinner-only bistro, with a laidback feel, where almost all the tables are outdoors. The menu is largely vegetarian, with lots of spicy, wholesome tofu dishes, plus chicken and fish specials, with most mains $20–28. Daily 5–9pm.

Hamura Saimin 2956 Kress St, Lihue ☎ 808 245 3271. Family-run diner, serving good-value Japanese-style fast food at communal U-shaped counters. Just grab a seat if you spot one free. The speciality is heaped bowls of *saimin* (noodle soup), costing $5–6, or $7 with shrimp tempura. Mon–Thurs 10am–10pm, Fri & Sat 10am–midnight, Sun 10am–9pm.

★ **Hanamaulu Restaurant** 3-4253 Kuhio Hwy, Hanamaulu ☎ 808 245 2511. Far Eastern-style teahouse, complete with fishponds, a mile from central Lihue, and serving both Chinese and Japanese cuisine; three set dinner menus for under $25, plus sushi in the evening only. Tues–Fri 10am–1pm & 4.30–8.30pm, Sat & Sun 4.30–8.30pm.

16

THE NORTH SHORE

Hanalei Gourmet Hanalei Center, Hanalei ☎ 808 826 2524, ⓦ hanaleigourmet.com. Breezy former schoolhouse offering tasty deli sandwiches ($10–14), salads, fish dips, or boiled shrimp, as well as dinner specials like panfried crab cakes for up to $30. Daily 8am–10.30pm.

SOUTH AND WEST KAUAI

★ **The Beach House** 5022 Lawai Rd, Poipu ☎ 808 742 1424, ⓦ the-beach-house.com. Fashionable Pacific Rim restaurant in an irresistible oceanfront setting, with good-value lunches for around $15 and fine dinners to match its spectacular sunsets. Appetizers such as *ahi* bruschetta cost $12–18; mains like the mint coriander rack of lamb up to $40. Daily 11am–10pm.

Kalaheo Café & Coffee Co 2 2300 Kaumualii Hwy, Kalaheo ☎ 808 332 5858, ⓦ kalaheo.com. On the main circle-island highway just west of Poipu, this handy café serves local coffee from Kauai and beyond, plus cooked breakfasts, burgers and salads later on, and $20 dinner mains like crispy aubergine (eggplant) parmesan or fresh catch. Mon 6.30am–2.30pm, Tues–Thurs 6.30am–2.30pm & 5–8.30pm, Fri & Sat 6.30am–2.30pm & 5–9pm, Sun 6.30am–2pm.

16

Contexts

History

There is much more to the history of North America than the history of the
United States alone. In these few pages, however, there's little room to do
more than survey the peopling and political development of the disparate
regions that now form the USA.

First peoples

The true pioneers of North America, nomadic hunter-gatherers from Siberia, are
thought to have reached what's now **Alaska** around 14,000 years ago. Thanks to the
last ice age, when sea levels were 300ft lower, a "**land-bridge**" – actually a vast plain,
measuring six hundred miles north to south – connected Eurasia to America.

Alaska was at that time separated by glacier fields from what is now Canada, and thus
effectively part of Asia rather than North America. Like an air lock, the region has
"opened" in different directions at different times; migrants reaching it from the west,
unaware that they were leaving Asia, would at first have found their way blocked to
the east. Several generations might pass, and the connection back towards Asia be
severed, before an eastward passage appeared. When thawing ice did clear a route into
North America, it was not along the Pacific coast but via a corridor that led east of the
Rockies and out onto the Great Plains.

This migration may well have been spurred by the pursuit of large mammal species,
and especially **mammoth**, which had already been harried to extinction throughout
almost all of Eurasia. A huge bonanza awaited the hunters when they finally
encountered America's own indigenous "**megafauna**", such as mammoths, mastodons,
giant ground sloths and enormous long-horned bison, all of which had evolved with no
protection against human predation.

Filling the New World

Within a thousand years, ten million people were living throughout both North and
South America. Although that sounds like a phenomenally rapid spread, it would
only have required a band of just one hundred individuals to enter the continent,
and advance a mere eight miles per year, with an annual population growth of
1.1 percent, to achieve that impact. The mass **extinction** of the American megafauna
was so precisely simultaneous that humans must surely have been responsible,
eliminating the giant beasts in each locality in one fell swoop, before pressing on in
search of the next kill.

The elimination of large land mammals precluded future American civilizations from
domesticating any of the animal species that were crucial to Old World economies.
Without cattle, horses, sheep or goats, or significant equivalents, they lacked the
resources to supply food and clothing to large settlements, provide draft power to
haul ploughs or wheeled vehicles, or increase mobility and the potential for conquest.
What's more, most of the human diseases that were later introduced from the rest of

c.60 million BC	15,000 BC	11,000 BC
Two mighty islands collide, creating North America as a single landmass, and throwing up the Rocky Mountains	First nomadic peoples from Asia reach Alaska	Almost all North America's large mammals become extinct, possibly due to over-hunting

the world originally evolved in association with domesticated animals; the first Americans developed neither immunity to such diseases, nor any indigenous diseases of their own that might have attacked the invaders.

At least three distinct waves of **migrants** arrived via Alaska, each of whom settled in, and adapted to, a more marginal environment than its predecessors. The second, five thousand years on, were the "**Nadene**" or Athapascans – the ancestors of the Haida of the Northwest, and the Navajo and Apache of the Southwest – while the third, another two thousand years later, found their niche in the frozen Arctic and became the **Aleuts** and the **Inuits**.

Early settlements

The earliest known settlement site in the modern United States, dating back 12,000 years, has been uncovered at Meadowcroft in southwest Pennsylvania. Five centuries later, the Southwest was dominated by the so-called **Clovis** culture, while subsequent subgroups ranged from the Algonquin farmers of what's now New England to peoples such as the Chumash and Macah, who lived by catching fish, otters and even whales along the coasts of the Pacific Northwest.

Nowhere did a civilization emerge to rival the wealth and sophistication of the great cities of ancient Mexico. However, the influence of those far-off cultures did filter north; the cultivation of crops such as beans, squash and maize facilitated the development of large communities, while northern religious cults, some of which performed human sacrifice, owed much to Central American beliefs. The **Moundbuilders** of the **Ohio** and **Mississippi** valleys developed sites such as the Great Serpent Mound in modern Ohio and Poverty Point in Louisiana. The most prominent of these early societies, now known as the **Hopewell** culture, flourished in the first four centuries AD. Later on, **Cahokia**, just outside present-day St Louis, became the largest pre-Columbian city in North America, centred on a huge temple-topped mound, and peaking between 1050 and 1250 AD.

In the deserts of the **Southwest**, the **Hohokam** settlement of Snaketown, near what's now Phoenix, grappled with the same problems of water management that plague the region today. Nearby, the **Ancestral Puebloan** "Basketmakers" developed pottery around 200 AD, and began to gather into the walled villages later known as pueblos, possibly for protection against Athapascan invaders, such as the Apache, who were arriving from the north. Ancestral Puebloan "cities", such as Pueblo Bonito in New Mexico's Chaco Canyon – a centre for the turquoise trade with the mighty Aztec – and the "Cliff Palace" at Mesa Verde in Colorado, are the most impressive monuments to survive from ancient North America. Although the Ancestral Puebloans dispersed after a devastating drought in the twelfth century, many of the settlements created by their immediate descendants have remained in use ever since. Despite centuries of migration and war, the desert farmers of the **Hopi Mesas** in Arizona (see p.776), and the pueblos of **Taos** and **Ácoma** in New Mexico, have never been dispossessed of their homes.

Estimates of the total indigenous population before the arrival of the Europeans vary widely, but an acceptable median figure suggests around fifty million people in the Americas as a whole; perhaps five million of those were in North America, speaking around four hundred different languages.

c.2500 BC	900 AD	1001–02	1050
Agriculture reaches North America from Mexico	Mississippian settlements – city-like conglomerations of earthen mounds – appear throughout the Southeast	Leif Eiriksson sails from Greenland to establish Vinland, in northern Newfoundland	Ancestral Puebloan culture reaches its peak at Chaco Canyon in the Southwest

European contacts

The greatest seafarers of early medieval Europe, the **Vikings**, established a colony in Greenland around 982 AD. Under the energetic leadership of Eirik the Red, this became a base for voyages along the mysterious coastline to the west. **Leif Eiriksson** – also known as Leif the Lucky – spent the winter of 1001–02 at a site that has been identified with L'Anse aux Meadows in northern Newfoundland. Climatic conditions may well have been much better than today, though it remains unclear what "grapes" led him to call it **Vinland**. Expeditions returned over the next dozen years, and may have ventured as far south as Maine. However, repeated clashes with the people the Vikings knew as **Skraelings** or "wretches" – probably Inuit, also recent newcomers – led them to abandon plans for permanent settlement.

Christopher Columbus

Five more centuries passed before the crucial moment of contact with the rest of the world came on October 12, 1492, when **Christopher Columbus**, sailing on behalf of the Spanish, reached the Bahamas. A mere four years later the English navigator John Cabot officially "discovered" Newfoundland, and soon British fishermen were setting up makeshift encampments in what became **New England**, to spend the winter curing their catch.

Over the next few years various expeditions mapped the eastern seaboard. In 1524, the Italian **Giovanni Verrazano** sailed past Maine, which he characterized as the "Land of Bad People" thanks to the inhospitable and contemptuous behaviour of its natives, and reached the mouth of the Hudson River. The great hope was to find a sea route in the Northeast that would lead to China – the fabled **Northwest Passage**. To the French **Jacques Cartier**, the St Lawrence Seaway seemed a promising avenue, and unsuccessful attempts were made to settle the northern areas of the Great Lakes from the 1530s onwards. Intrepid trappers and traders ventured ever further west.

Spanish explorations

To the south, the Spaniards started to nose their way up from the Caribbean in 1513, when **Ponce de Leon**'s expedition in search of the Fountain of Youth landed at what's now Palm Beach, and named **Florida**. Following the lucrative conquest of Mexico, the Spanish returned in 1528 under Panfilo de Narvaez, who was shipwrecked somewhere in the Gulf. A junior officer, **Cabeza de Vaca**, survived, and with three shipmates spent the next six years on an extraordinary odyssey across Texas into the Southwest. At times held as slaves, at times revered as seers, they finally got back to Mexico in 1534, bringing tales of golden cities deep in the desert, known as the **Seven Cities of Cibola**.

One of Cabeza de Vaca's companions was a black African slave called **Estevanico the Moor**. Rather than re-submit to slavery, he volunteered to map the route for a new venture; racing alone into the interior, with two colossal greyhounds at his side, he was killed in Zuni Pueblo in 1539. The following year, **Francisco Vázquez de Coronado**'s larger expedition proved to everyone's intense dissatisfaction that the Seven Cities of Cibola did not exist. They reached as far as the Grand Canyon, encountering the Hopi along the way. Hernán Cortés, the conqueror of the Aztec, had meanwhile traced the outline of Baja California, and in 1542 Juan Cabrillo sailed up the coast of California, failing to spot San Francisco Bay in the usual mists.

1492	1528	1565
Christopher Columbus makes landfall in the Bahamas	A Spanish expedition is shipwrecked in Florida; Cabeza de Vaca and three survivors, including Esteban, a black African, take eight years to walk to Mexico City	Pedro Menéndez de Avilés founds St Augustine in Florida

Although no treasures were found to match the vast riches plundered from the Aztec and Inca empires, a steady stream of less spectacular discoveries – whether new foodstuffs such as potatoes, or access to the cod fisheries of the northern Atlantic – boosted economies throughout Europe. The Spanish established the first permanent settlement in the present United States when they founded **St Augustine** on the coast of Florida in 1565, only for Sir Francis Drake to burn it to the ground in 1586. In 1598 the Spanish also succeeded in subjugating the Pueblo peoples, and founded **New Mexico** along the Rio Grande. More of a missionary than a military enterprise, the colony's survival was always precarious due to the vast tracts of empty desert that separated it from the rest of Mexico. Nonetheless, the construction of a new capital, **Santa Fe**, began in 1609 (see p.737).

The growth of the colonies

The sixteenth-century rivalry between the English and the Spanish extended right around the world. Freebooting English adventurers-cum-pirates contested Spanish hegemony along both coasts of North America. Sir Francis Drake staked a claim to California in 1579, five years before **Sir Walter Raleigh** claimed **Virginia** in the east, in the name of his Virgin Queen, Elizabeth I. The party of colonists he sent out in 1585 established the short-lived settlement of **Roanoke**, now remembered as the mysterious "Lost Colony" (see p.357).

The Native Americans were seldom hostile at first encounter. To some extent the European newcomers were obliged to make friends with the locals; most had crossed the Atlantic to find religious freedom or to make their fortunes, and lacked the skills to make a success of subsistence farming. Virginia's first enduring colony, **Jamestown**, was founded by Captain John Smith on May 24, 1607. He bemoaned "though there be Fish in the Sea, and Foules in the ayre, and Beasts in the woods, their bounds are so large, they are so wilde, and we so weake and ignorant, we cannot much trouble them"; six in every seven colonists died within a year of reaching the New World.

Gradually, however, the settlers learned to cultivate the strange crops of this unfamiliar terrain. As far as the English government was concerned, the colonies were commercial ventures, to produce crops that could not be grown at home, and the colonists were not supposed to have goals of their own. Following failures with sugar and rice, Virginia finally found its feet with its first **tobacco** harvest in 1615 (the man responsible, John Rolfe, is better known as the husband of Pocahontas). A successful tobacco plantation requires two things in abundance: land and labour. No self-respecting Englishman came to America to work for others; when the first **slave** ship called at Jamestown in 1619, the captain found an eager market for his cargo of twenty African slaves. By that time there were already a million slaves in South America.

New England

The 102 **Puritans** remembered as the "**Pilgrim Fathers**" were deposited on Cape Cod by the *Mayflower* in late 1620, and soon moved on to set up their own colony at Plymouth (see p.182). Fifty died that winter, and the whole party might have perished but for their fortuitous encounter with the extraordinary **Squanto**. This Native American had twice been kidnapped and taken to Europe, only to make his way home;

1579	1607	1610	1619
Francis Drake claims California, generally believed to be an island, for England	English colonists establish Jamestown in Virginia	Santa Fe is founded as capital of New Mexico; horses begin to spread across the Southwest	Twenty African slaves arrive in Virginia on a Dutch ship

he had spent four years working as a merchant in the City of London, and had also lived in Spain. Having recently come home to find his entire tribe exterminated by smallpox, he threw in his lot with the English. With his guidance, they finally managed to reap their first harvest, celebrated with a mighty feast of Thanksgiving.

Of greater significance to New England was the founding in 1630 of a new colony, further up the coast at Naumkeag (later Salem), by the Massachusetts Bay Company. Its governor, **John Winthrop**, soon moved to establish a new capital on the Shawmut peninsula – the city of **Boston**, complete with its own university of Harvard. His vision of a Utopian "City on a Hill" did not extend to sharing Paradise with the Native Americans; he argued that they had not "subdued" the land, which was therefore a "vacuum" for the Puritans to use as they saw fit. While their faith helped individual colonists to endure the early hardships, the colony as a whole failed to maintain a strong religious identity (the Salem witch trials of 1692 did much to discredit the notion that the New World had any moral superiority to the Old), and breakaway groups left to create the rival settlements of Providence and Connecticut.

Between 1620 and 1642, sixty thousand migrants – 1.5 percent of the population – left England for America. Those in pursuit of economic opportunities often joined the longer-established colonies, thereby serving to dilute the religious zeal of the Puritans. Groups hoping to find spiritual freedom were more inclined to start afresh; thus **Maryland** was created as a haven for Catholics in 1632, and fifty years later **Pennsylvania** was founded by the Quakers.

The English were not alone, however. After Sir Henry Hudson rediscovered Manhattan in 1609, it was "bought" by the **Dutch** in 1624 – though the Native Americans who took their money were passing nomads with no claim to it either. The Dutch colony of New Amsterdam, founded in 1625, lasted less than forty years before being captured by the English and renamed **New York**; by that time, a strong Dutch presence dominated the lower reaches of the Hudson River.

Venturing west

From their foothold in the Great Lakes region, meanwhile, the **French** sent the explorers Joliet and Marquette to map the Mississippi in 1673. Upon establishing that the river did indeed flow into the Gulf of Mexico, they turned back, but they'd cleared the way for the foundation of the huge and ill-defined colony of **Louisiana** in 1699. The city of **New Orleans**, at the mouth of the Mississippi, was created in 1718.

While the Spanish remained ensconced in Florida, things went less smoothly in the Southwest. The **Pueblo Revolt** of 1680 drove the Spanish out of New Mexico altogether, though they returned in force a dozen years later. Thereafter, a curious synthesis of traditional and Hispanic religion and culture evolved, and the Spanish presence was not seriously challenged.

Things were also changing in the unknown hinterland. The frontier was pushing steadily westwards, as colonists seized Indian land, with or without the excuse of an "uprising" or "rebellion" to provoke them into bloodshed. The major killer of indigenous peoples, however, was **smallpox**, which worked its way deep into the interior of the continent long before the Europeans. As populations were decimated, great migrations took place. The original inhabitants of the region had been sedentary farmers, who also hunted buffalo by driving them over rocky bluffs. With

1620	1664	1682
A hundred Puritan colonists reach New England aboard the *Mayflower*, and settle at Plymouth	The Dutch settlement of New Amsterdam, captured by the English, becomes New York City	Quaker settlers found Philadelphia. The Sieur de la Salle claims the Mississippi valley for France as Louisiana

the arrival of **horses** on the Great Plains (probably captured from the Spanish, and known at first as "mystery dogs"), an entirely new, nomadic lifestyle emerged. Groups such as the Cheyenne and the Apache swept their rivals aside to dominate vast territories, and eagerly seized the potential offered by the later introduction of firearms. Increasing dependence on trade with Europeans created a dynamic but fundamentally unstable culture.

The American Revolution

The American colonies prospered during the **eighteenth century**. Boston, New York and Philadelphia in particular became home to a wealthy, well-educated and highly articulate middle class. Frustration mounted at the inequities of the colonies' relationship with Britain, however. The Americans could only sell their produce to the British, and all transatlantic commerce had to be undertaken in British ships.

Full-scale independence was not an explicit goal until late in the century, but the main factor that made it possible was the economic impact of the pan-European **Seven Years' War**. Officially, war in Europe lasted from 1756 to 1763, but fighting in North America broke out a little earlier. Beginning in 1755 with the mass expulsion of French settlers from Acadia in Nova Scotia (triggering their epic migration to Louisiana, where the **Cajuns** remain to this day), the British went on to conquer all of Canada. In forcing the **surrender of Québec** in 1759, General Wolfe brought the war to a close; the French ceded Louisiana to the Spanish rather than let it fall to the British, while Florida passed briefly into British control before reverting to the Spanish. All the European monarchs were left hamstrung by debts, and the British realized that colonialism in America was not as profitable as in those parts of the world where the native populations could be coerced into working for their overseas masters.

There was also another major player – the **Iroquois Confederacy**. Iroquois culture in the Great Lakes region, characterized by military expansionism and even human sacrifice, dates back around a thousand years. Forever in competition with the Algonquin and the Huron, the southern Iroquois had by the eighteenth century formed a League of Five Nations – the Seneca, Cayuga, Onondaga, Oneida and Mohawk, all in what's now upstate New York. Wooed by both the French and British, the Iroquois charted an independent course. Impressed by witnessing negotiations between the Iroquois and the squabbling representatives of Pennsylvania, Virginia and Maryland, Benjamin Franklin wrote in 1751 that "It would be a very strange thing if …ignorant savages should be capable of forming a scheme for such a union…that has subsisted ages and appears indissoluble; and yet that a like union should be impracticable for ten or a dozen English colonies".

An unsuccessful insurrection by the Ottawa in 1763, led by their chief **Pontiac**, led the cash-strapped British to conclude that, while America needed its own standing army, it was reasonable to expect the colonists to pay for it. In 1765, they introduced the **Stamp Act**, requiring duty on all legal transactions and printed matter in the colonies to be paid to the British Crown. Arguing for "no taxation without representation", delegates from nine colonies met in the Stamp Act Congress that October. By then, however, the British prime minister responsible had already been dismissed by King George III, and the Act was repealed in 1766.

1692	1718	1759	1764
Eighteen supposed witches are executed in Salem, Massachusetts	The Sieur de Bienville founds New Orleans	British General James Wolfe forces the surrender of Quebec, ending the French and Indian War	New England responds to British legislation with the cry "no taxation without representation"

However, in 1767, Chancellor Townshend made political capital at home by proclaiming "I dare tax America", as he introduced legislation including the broadly similar Revenue Act. That led Massachusetts merchants, inspired by **Samuel Adams**, to vote to boycott English goods; they were joined by all the other colonies except New Hampshire. Townshend's Acts were repealed in turn by a new prime minister, Lord North, on March 5, 1770. By chance, on that same day a stone-throwing mob surrounded the Customs House in Boston; five people were shot in what became known as the **Boston Massacre**. Even so, most of the colonies resumed trading with Britain, and the crisis was postponed for a few more years.

In May 1773, Lord North's **Tea Act** relieved the debt-ridden East India Company of the need to pay duties on exports to America, while still requiring the Americans to pay duty on tea. Massachusetts called the colonies to action, and its citizens took the lead on December 16 in the **Boston Tea Party**, when three tea ships were boarded and 342 chests thrown into the sea.

The infuriated British Parliament thereupon began to pass legislation collectively known as both the "Coercive" and the "Intolerable" Acts, which included closing the port of Boston and disbanding the government of Massachusetts. Thomas Jefferson argued that the acts amounted to "a deliberate and systematical plan of reducing us to slavery". To discuss a response, the first **Continental Congress** was held in Philadelphia on May 5, 1774, and attended by representatives of all the colonies except Georgia.

The Revolutionary War

War finally broke out on April 18, 1775, when General Gage, the governor of Massachusetts, dispatched four hundred British soldiers to destroy the arms depot at **Concord**, and prevent weapons from falling into rebel hands. Silversmith **Paul Revere** was dispatched on his legendary ride to warn the rebels, and the British were confronted en route at Lexington by 77 American "Minutemen". The resulting skirmish led to the "shot heard 'round the world".

Congress set about forming an army at Boston, and decided for the sake of unity to appoint a Southern commander, **George Washington**. One by one, as the war raged, the colonies set up their own governments and declared themselves to be states, and the politicians set about defining the society they wished to create. The writings of pamphleteer Thomas Paine – especially *Common Sense* – were, together with the Confederacy of the Iroquois, a great influence on the **Declaration of Independence**. Drafted by Thomas Jefferson, this was adopted by the Continental Congress in Philadelphia on July 4, 1776. Anti-slavery clauses originally included by Jefferson – himself a slave-owner – were omitted to spare the feelings of the Southern states, though the section that denounced the King's dealings with "merciless Indian Savages" was left in.

At first, the Revolutionary War went well for the British. General Howe crossed the Atlantic with twenty thousand men, took New York and New Jersey, and ensconced himself in Philadelphia for the winter of 1777–78. Washington's army was encamped not far away at Valley Forge, freezing cold and all but starving to death. It soon became clear, however, that the longer the Americans could avoid losing an all-out battle, the more likely the British were to over-extend their lines as they advanced through the vast and unfamiliar continent. Thus, General Burgoyne's expedition, which set out from Canada to march on New England, was so harried by rebel guerrillas that he had

1770	1773	1775
In the Boston Massacre, British sentries fire on a mob and kill five colonists	In the Boston Tea Party, two hundred colonists respond to British duties by tipping tea into the sea	The Revolutionary War begins with the "shot heard 'round the world"; George Washington assumes command of the Continental Army

to surrender at Saratoga in October 1777. Other European powers took delight in coming to the aid of the Americans. Benjamin Franklin led a wildly successful delegation to France to request support, and soon the nascent American fleet was being assisted in its bid to cut British naval communications by both the French and the Spanish. The end came when Cornwallis, who had replaced Howe, was instructed to dig in at Yorktown and wait for the Royal Navy to come to his aid, only for the French to seal off Chesapeake Bay and prevent reinforcement. Cornwallis surrendered to Washington on October 17, 1781.

The ensuing **Treaty of Paris** granted the Americans their independence on generous terms – the British abandoned their Native American allies, including the Iroquois, to the vengeance of the victors – and Washington entered New York as the British left in November 1783. The Spanish were confirmed in possession of Florida.

The victorious US Congress met for the first time in 1789, and the tradition of awarding political power to the nation's most successful generals was instigated by the election of George Washington as the first **president**. He was further honoured when his name was given to the new capital city of **Washington DC**, deliberately sited between the North and the South.

THE CONSTITUTION

As signed in 1787 and ratified in 1788, the **Constitution** stipulated the following form of government:

All **legislative** powers were granted to the **Congress of the United States**. The lower of its two distinct houses, the **House of Representatives**, was to be elected every two years, with its members in proportion to the number of each state's "free Persons" plus "three fifths of all other persons" (meaning slaves). The upper house, the **Senate**, would hold two Senators from each state, chosen by state legislatures rather than by direct elections. Each Senator was to serve for six years, with a third of them to be elected every two years.

Executive power was vested in the **President**, who was also Commander in Chief of the Army and Navy. He would be chosen every four years, by as many **"Electors"** from each individual state as it had Senators and Representatives. Each state could decide how to appoint those Electors; almost all chose to have direct popular elections. Nonetheless, the distinction has remained ever since between the number of "popular votes", across the whole country, received by a presidential candidate, and the number of state-by-state "electoral votes", which determines the actual result. Originally, whoever came second in the voting automatically became **Vice President**.

The President could **veto** acts of Congress, but that veto could be overruled by a two-thirds vote in both houses. The House of Representatives could **impeach** the President for treason, bribery or "other high crimes and misdemeanors", in which instance the Senate could remove him from office with a two-thirds majority.

Judicial power was invested in a **Supreme Court**, and as many "inferior Courts" as Congress should decide.

The Constitution has so far been altered by 27 **Amendments**. Numbers **14** and **15** extended the vote to black males in 1868 and 1870; **17** made Senators subject to election by direct popular vote in 1913; **19** introduced women's suffrage in 1920; **22** restricted the President to two terms in 1951; **24** stopped states using poll taxes to disenfranchise black voters in 1964; and **26** reduced the minimum voting age to 18 in 1971.

1776	**1777**	**1781**	**1787**
The Declaration of Independence is signed on July 4	General Washington takes up winter quarters at Valley Forge	Surrounded by land and sea, British commander Lord Cornwallis surrenders at Yorktown	The Constitution is signed in Philadelphia

The nineteenth century

During its first century, the territories and population of the new **United States of America** expanded at a phenomenal rate. The white population of North America in 1800 stood at around five million, and there were another one million African slaves (of whom thirty thousand were in the North). Of that total, 86 percent lived within fifty miles of the Atlantic, but no US city could rival Mexico City, whose population approached 100,000 inhabitants (both New York and Philadelphia reached that figure within twenty years, however, and New York had passed a million fifty years later).

It had suited the British to discourage settlers from venturing west of the Appalachians, where they would be far beyond the reach of British power. However, adventurers such as **Daniel Boone** started to cross the mountains into Tennessee and Kentucky during the 1770s. Soon makeshift rafts, made from the planks that were later assembled to make log cabins, were careering west along the Ohio River (the only westward-flowing river on the continent).

The Lousiana Purchase

In 1801, the Spanish handed Louisiana back to the French, on condition that the French would keep it forever. However, Napoleon swiftly realized that attempting to hang on to his American possessions would spread his armies too thinly, and chose instead to sell them to the United States for $15 million, in the **Louisiana Purchase** of 1803. President Thomas Jefferson swiftly sent the explorers **Lewis and Clark** to map out the new territories, which extended far beyond the boundaries of present-day Louisiana. With the help of Sacagawea, their female Shoshone guide, they followed the Missouri and Columbia rivers all the way to the Pacific; in their wake, trappers and "mountain men" came to hunt in the wilderness of the Rockies. The **Russians** had already reached the Pacific Northwest, and established fortified outposts to trade in beaver and otter pelts.

British attempts to blockade the Atlantic, primarily targeted against Napoleon, gave the new nation a chance to flex its military muscles. British raiders succeeded in capturing Washington DC, and burned the White House, but the **War of 1812** provided the USA with a cover for aggression against the Native American allies of the British. Thus **Tecumseh** of the Shawnee was defeated near Detroit, and **Andrew Jackson** moved against the Creek of the southern Mississippi. Jackson's campaign against the Seminole won the USA possession of Florida from the Spanish; he was rewarded first with the governorship of the new state, and later by his election to the presidency. While in office, in the 1830s, Jackson went even further, and set about clearing all states east of the Mississippi of their native populations. The barren region that later became Oklahoma was designated as "Indian Territory", home to the "Five Civilized Tribes". The Creek and the Seminole, and the Choctaw and Chickasaw of Mississippi were eventually joined by the Cherokee of the lower Appalachians there, after four appalling months on the forced march known as the "**Trail of Tears**".

Manifest Destiny and the Mexican War

It took only a small step for the citizens of the young republic to move from realizing that their country might spread across the whole continent to supposing that it had a quasi-religious duty – a "**Manifest Destiny**" – to do so. At its most basic, that doctrine

1789	1803	1814
George Washington is inaugurated as the first President of the United States	President Thomas Jefferson buys Louisiana west of the Mississippi for $15 million	British soldiers advance on Baltimore after burning the White House, but are repelled

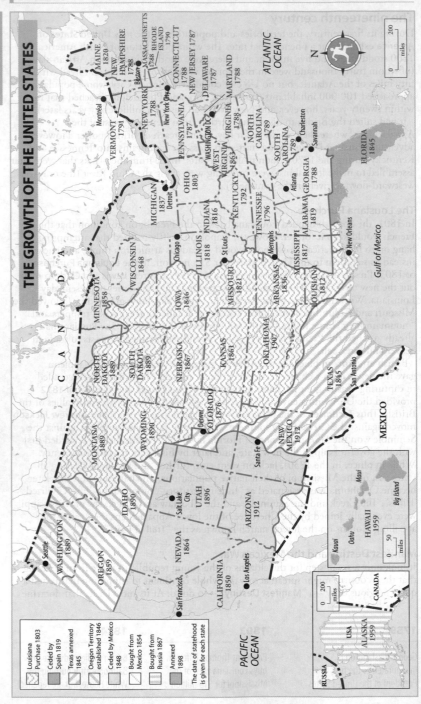

THE GROWTH OF THE UNITED STATES

N

0 — 200 miles

ATLANTIC OCEAN

MAINE 1820

NEW HAMPSHIRE 1788

VERMONT 1791

MASSACHUSETTS 1788

RHODE ISLAND 1790

CONNECTICUT 1788

NEW YORK 1788

NEW JERSEY 1787

PENNSYLVANIA 1787

DELAWARE 1787

MARYLAND 1788

WASHINGTON DC

VIRGINIA 1788

WEST VIRGINIA 1863

NORTH CAROLINA 1789

SOUTH CAROLINA 1788

GEORGIA 1788

FLORIDA 1845

OHIO 1803

KENTUCKY 1792

TENNESSEE 1796

ALABAMA 1819

MICHIGAN 1837

INDIANA 1816

ILLINOIS 1818

WISCONSIN 1848

MINNESOTA 1858

IOWA 1846

MISSOURI 1821

ARKANSAS 1836

MISSISSIPPI 1817

LOUISIANA 1812

NORTH DAKOTA 1889

SOUTH DAKOTA 1889

NEBRASKA 1867

KANSAS 1861

OKLAHOMA 1907

TEXAS 1845

MONTANA 1889

WYOMING 1890

COLORADO 1876

NEW MEXICO 1912

IDAHO 1890

UTAH 1896

ARIZONA 1912

NEVADA 1864

CALIFORNIA 1850

OREGON 1859

WASHINGTON 1889

CANADA

MEXICO

PACIFIC OCEAN

Gulf of Mexico

Montréal

Detroit

Chicago

St Louis

Memphis

New Orleans

San Antonio

Santa Fe

Denver

Salt Lake City

Los Angeles

San Francisco

Seattle

New York City

Boston

Charleston

Savannah

Atlanta

Louisiana Purchase 1803

Ceded by Spain 1819

Texas annexed 1845

Oregon Territory established 1846

Ceded by Mexico 1848

Bought from Mexico 1854

Bought from Russia 1867

Annexed 1898

The date of statehood is given for each state

Kauai

Oahu

Maui

Big Island

HAWAII 1959

0 — 50 miles

0 — 200 miles

RUSSIA

USA

ALASKA 1959

CANADA

amounted to little more than a belief that might must be right, but the idea that they were fulfilling the will of God inspired countless pioneers to set off across the plains in search of a new life.

Mexico was by now independent of Spain. The Spanish territories of the Southwest had never quite become full-fledged colonies, and as American settlers arrived in ever-increasing numbers they began to dominate their Hispanic counterparts. The Anglos of **Texas** rebelled in 1833, under General Sam Houston. Shortly after the legendary setback at the **Alamo** (see p.593) in 1836, they defeated the Mexican army of Santa Anna and Texas became an independent republic in its own right.

The ensuing **Mexican War** was a bare-faced exercise in American aggression, in which most of the future Civil War generals received their first experience fighting, on the same side. The conflict resulted in the acquisition not only of Texas, but also of Arizona, Utah, Colorado, Nevada, New Mexico and finally California, in 1848. A token US payment of $15 million to Mexico was designed to match the Louisiana Purchase. Controversy over whether slavery would be legal in the new states was rendered academic by the simultaneous discovery of gold in the Sierra Nevada of California. The resultant **Gold Rush** created California's first significant city, **San Francisco**, and brought a massive influx of free white settlers to a land that was in any case unsuitable for a plantation-based economy.

Proponents of Manifest Destiny seldom gave much thought to the **Pacific Northwest**, which remained nominally part of British Canada. However, once the Oregon Trail started to operate in 1841 (see p.948), American settlers there swiftly outnumbered the British. In 1846, a surprisingly amicable treaty fixed the border along the 49th parallel – the line it already followed across eastern Canada – and left the whole of Vancouver Island to the British.

The Civil War

From its inception, the unity of the United States had been based on shaky foundations. Great care had gone into devising a **Constitution** that balanced the need for a strong federal government with the aspirations for autonomy of its component states. That was achieved by giving Congress two separate chambers – the **House of Representatives**, in which each state was represented in proportion to its population, and the **Senate**, in which each state, regardless of size, had two members. Thus, although in theory the Constitution remained silent on the issue of **slavery**, it allayed the fears of the less populated Southern states that Northern voters might destroy their economy by forcing them to abandon their "peculiar institution".

However, the system only worked so long as there were equal numbers of "Free" and slave-owning states. The only practicable way to keep the balance was to ensure that each time a new state was admitted to the Union, a matching state taking the opposite stance on slavery was also admitted. Thus the admission of every new state became subject to endless intrigue. The 1820 **Missouri Compromise**, under which Missouri joined as a slave-owning state and Maine as a Free one, was straightforward in comparison to the prevarication and chest-beating that surrounded the admission of Texas, while the Mexican War was widely seen in the North as a naked land grab for new slave states.

1831	1836	1847	1848
Nat Turner leads a slave revolt in Virginia	Texas declares itself independent; Mexican general Santa Anna massacres the defenders at the Alamo four days later	Mormon settlers found Salt Lake City	Mexico cedes California and New Mexico to the USA for $18.25 million

Abolitionist sentiment in the North was not all that great before the middle of the nineteenth century. At best, after the importation of slaves from Africa ended in 1808, Northerners vaguely hoped slavery was an anachronism that might simply wither away. As it turned out, Southern plantations were rendered much more profitable by the development of the cotton gin, and the increased demand for manufactured cotton goods triggered by the **Industrial Revolution**. However, the rapid growth of the nation as a whole made it ever more difficult to maintain a political balance between North and South.

Matters came to a head in 1854, when the **Kansas-Nebraska Act** sparked guerrilla raids and mini-wars between rival settlers by allowing both prospective states self-determination on the issue. That same year, the **Republican Party** was founded to resist the further expansion of slavery. Escaped former slaves such as Frederick Douglass were by now spurring Northern audiences to moral outrage, and Harriet Beecher Stowe's *Uncle Tom's Cabin* found unprecedented readership.

In October 1859, **John Brown** – a white-bearded, wild-eyed veteran of Kansas's bloodiest infighting – led a dramatic raid on the US Armory at Harpers Ferry, West Virginia, intending to secure arms for a slave insurrection (see p.359). Swiftly captured by forces under Robert E. Lee, he was hanged within a few weeks, proclaiming that "I am now quite certain that the crimes of this guilty land will never be purged away but with blood".

The Republican presidential candidate in 1860, the little-known **Abraham Lincoln** from Kentucky, won no Southern states, but with the Democrats split into Northern and Southern factions he was elected with 39 percent of the popular vote. Within weeks, on December 20, South Carolina became the first state to secede from the Union; the **Confederacy** was declared on February 4, 1861, when it was joined by Mississippi, Florida, Alabama, Georgia, Louisiana and Texas. Its first (and only) president was **Jefferson Davis**, also from Kentucky; his new vice president remarked at their joint inauguration that their government was "the first in the history of the world based upon the great physical and moral truth that the negro is not equal to the white man". Lincoln was inaugurated in turn in March 1861, proclaiming that "I have no purpose, directly or indirectly, to interfere with the institution of slavery in the States where it exists. I believe I have no lawful right to do so, and I have no inclination to do so". He was completely inflexible, however, on one paramount issue: the survival of the Union.

The coming of war

The **Civil War** began just a few weeks later. The first shots were fired on April 12, when a federal attempt to resupply Fort Sumter, off Charleston, South Carolina, was greeted by a Confederate bombardment that forced its surrender. Lincoln's immediate call to raise an army against the South was greeted by the further secession of Virginia, Arkansas, Tennessee and North Carolina. Within a year, both armies had amassed 600,000 men; Robert E. Lee had been offered command of both and opted for the Confederacy, while George McLellan became the first leader of the Union forces. Although the rival capitals of Washington DC, and Richmond, Virginia, were a mere one hundred miles apart, over the next four years operations reached almost everywhere south of Washington and east of the Mississippi.

1858	1859	1860
Abraham Lincoln declares "A house divided against itself cannot stand"	Anti-slavery activist John Brown seizes the federal arsenal and armory at Harpers Ferry, Virginia, and is later executed	Lincoln's election as president prompts South Carolina and other Southern states to secede and form the Confederacy

Tracing the ebb and flow of the military campaigns – from the early Confederate victories, via Grant's successful siege of Vicksburg in 1863 and Sherman's devastating March to the Sea in 1864, to Lee's eventual surrender at Appomattox in April 1865 – it's easy to forget that it was not so much generalship as sheer economic (and man-) power that won the war. The **Union** of 23 Northern states, holding more than 22 million people, wore down the **Confederacy** of eleven Southern states, with nine million. As for potential combatants, the North initially drew upon 3.5 million white males aged between 18 and 45 – and later recruited blacks as well – whereas the South had more like one million. In the end, around 2.1 million men fought for the Union, and 900,000 for the Confederacy. Of the 620,000 soldiers who died, a disproportionate 258,000 came from the South – one quarter of its white men of military age. Meanwhile, not only did the North continue trading with the rest of the world while maintaining its industrial and agricultural output, it also stifled the Confederacy with a devastating **naval blockade**. The Southern war effort was primarily financed by printing $1.5 billion of paper currency, which was so eroded by inflation that it became worthless.

Even so, the Confederacy came much closer to victory than is usually appreciated. The repeated out-manoeuvring of federal forces by General **Robert E. Lee**, and his incursions into Union territory, meant that in each of three successive years, from 1862 to 1864, there was a genuine possibility that Northern morale would collapse, allowing opponents of the war to be elected to power and agree to peace. After all, the Revolutionary War had shown how such a war could be won: for the Union to triumph, it had to invade and occupy the South, and destroy its armies, but for the South to win it had only to survive until the North wearied of the struggle.

The dashing tactics of Confederate generals Lee and Jackson, forever counter-attacking and carrying the fight to the enemy, arguably contributed to the Southern defeat. The grim, relentless total-war campaigning of Grant and Sherman eventually ground the South down. Ironically, had the Confederacy sued for peace before Lee gave it fresh hope, a negotiated settlement might not have included the abolition of slavery. In the event, as the war went on, with Southern slaves flocking to the Union flag and black soldiers fighting on the front line, emancipation did indeed become inevitable. Lincoln took the political decision to match his moral conviction by issuing his **Emancipation Proclamation** in 1862, though the **Thirteenth Amendment** outlawing slavery only took effect in 1865.

Reconstruction

Lincoln himself was assassinated within a few days of the end of the war, a mark of the deep bitterness that would almost certainly have precluded successful **Reconstruction** even if he had lived. For a brief period, after black men were granted the vote in 1870, Southern states elected black political representatives, but without a sustained effort to enable former slaves to acquire land, racial relations in the South swiftly deteriorated. Thanks to white supremacist organizations such as the Ku Klux Klan, nominally clandestine but brazenly public, Southern blacks were soon effectively disenfranchised once more. Anyone working to transform the South came under attack either as a "carpetbagger" (a Northern opportunist heading South for personal profit) or a treacherous "scalawag" (a Southern collaborator).

1861	1862	1865
The artillery bombardment of Fort Sumter in South Carolina marks the start of the Civil War	President Lincoln's Emancipation Proclamation declares that all slaves in states or areas of states still in rebellion to be free	General Robert E. Lee of the Confederacy surrenders to Union General Ulysses Grant on April 9; five days later, Lincoln is assassinated

The aftermath of the Civil War can almost be said to have lasted for a hundred years. While the South condemned itself to a century as a backwater, the rest of the re-United States embarked on a period of expansionism and prosperity.

The Indian Wars

With the completion of the transcontinental railroad in 1867, Manifest Destiny became an undeniable reality. Among the first to head west were the troops of the federal army, with Union and Confederate veterans marching under the same flag to battle the remaining Native Americans. Treaty after treaty was signed, only to be broken as soon as expedient (usually upon the discovery of gold or precious metals). When the whites overreached themselves, or were driven to desperation, the Native Americans fought back. The defeat of **General George Custer** at Little Bighorn in 1876, by **Sitting Bull** and his Sioux and Cheyenne warriors (see p.709), provoked the full wrath of the government. Within a few years, leaders such as **Crazy Horse** of the Oglala Sioux and **Geronimo** of the Apache had been forced to surrender, and their people confined to reservations. One final act of resistance was the visionary, messianic cult of the **Ghost Dance**, whose practitioners hoped that by ritual observance they could win back their lost way of life, in a land miraculously free of white intruders. Such aspirations were regarded as hostile, and military harassment of the movement culminated in the massacre at **Wounded Knee** in South Dakota in 1890.

A major tactic in the campaign against the Plains Indians was to starve them into submission, by eliminating the vast herds of bison that were their primary source of food. As General Philip Sheridan put it, "For the sake of a lasting peace…kill, skin and sell until the buffalo are exterminated. Then your prairies can be covered by the speckled cow and the festive cowboy". More significant than the activities of the much-mythologized cowboys, however, was the back-breaking toil of the miners up in the mountains, and the homesteading families out on the plains.

Industry and immigration

The late nineteenth century saw massive **immigration** to North America, with influxes from Europe to the East Coast paralleled by those from Asia to the West. As in colonial times, national groups tended to form enclaves in specific areas – from the Scandinavian farmers of Minnesota and the northern Plains to the Basque shepherds of Idaho and the Cornish miners of Colorado. In the Southwest, where individual hard work counted for less than shared communal effort, the **Mormons** of Utah had fled persecution to become the first white settlers to eke a living from the unforgiving desert.

The fastest growth of all was in the nation's greatest **cities**, especially New York, Chicago and Boston. Their industrial and commercial strength enabled them to attract and absorb migrants not only from throughout Europe but also from the Old South – particularly ex-slaves, who could now at least vote with their feet.

Stretching "from sea to shining sea", the territorial boundaries of the USA had almost reached their current limits. In 1867, however, Secretary of State William Seward agreed to buy **Alaska** from the crisis-torn Russian government for $7.2 million. The purchase was at first derided as "Seward's Folly", but soon gold was discovered there as well.

1870	1876	1876	1881
Senator Hiram P. Revels of Mississippi becomes the first black man to sit in Congress	Sioux warriors defeat the Seventh Cavalry, and kill General George Custer, at Little Bighorn	Mark Twain's *The Adventures of Tom Sawyer* is the first book to be written on a typewriter	Pat Garrett kills Billy the Kid in Fort Sumner, New Mexico; shoot-out at OK Corral, in Tombstone, Arizona

The various presidents of the day, from the victorious General Grant onwards, now seem anonymous figures compared to the industrialists and financiers who manipulated the national economy. These **"robber barons"** included such men as John D. Rockefeller, who controlled seventy percent of the world's oil almost before anyone else had realized it was worth controlling; Andrew Carnegie, who made his fortune introducing the Bessemer process of steel manufacture; and J.P. Morgan, who went for the most basic commodity of all – money. Their success was predicated on the willingness of the government to cooperate in resisting the development of a strong labour movement. Strikes on the railroads in 1877, in the mines of Tennessee in 1891 and in the steel mills of Pittsburgh in 1892 were forcibly crushed.

The nineteenth century had also seen the development of a distinctive American voice in **literature**, which rendered increasingly superfluous the efforts of passing English visitors to "explain" the United States. From the 1830s onwards, writers explored new ways to describe their new world, with results as varied as the introspective essays of Henry Thoreau, the morbid visions of Edgar Allan Poe, the all-embracing novels of Herman Melville and the irrepressible poetry of Walt Whitman, whose endlessly revised *Leaves of Grass* was an exultant hymn to the young republic. Virtually every leading participant in the Civil War wrote at least one highly readable volume of memoirs, while public figures as disparate as Buffalo Bill Cody and the showman P. T. Barnum produced lively autobiographies. The boundless national self-confidence found its greatest expression in the vigorous vernacular style of **Mark Twain**, whose depictions of frontier life, fictionalized for example in *Huckleberry Finn*, gave the rest of the world an abiding impression of the American character.

Many Americans saw the official "closure" of the Western frontier, announced by the Census Bureau in 1890, as tantamount to depriving the country of the Manifest Destiny that was its *raison d'être*, and sought new frontiers further afield. Such **imperialist ventures** reached a crescendo in 1898, with the annexation of the Kingdom of **Hawaii** – which even then-President Cleveland condemned as "wholly without justification…not merely wrong but a disgrace" – and the double seizure of Cuba and the Philippines in the **Spanish-American War**, which catapulted **Theodore Roosevelt** to the presidency. Though he took the African proverb "speak softly and carry a big stick" as his motto – and was hardly, if truth be told, noted for being soft-spoken – Roosevelt in office did much to heal the divisions within the nation. While new legislation reined in the worst excesses of the robber barons, and of rampant capitalism in general, it alleviated popular discontent without substantially threatening the business community or empowering the labour movement. A decade into the twentieth century, the United States had advanced to the point that it knew, even if the rest of the world wasn't yet altogether sure, that it was the strongest, wealthiest country on earth.

The twentieth century

The first years of the twentieth century witnessed the emergence of many features that came to characterize modern America. In 1903 alone, Wilbur and Orville Wright achieved the first successful powered **flight** and Henry Ford established his Ford Motor Company. Ford's enthusiastic adoption of the latest technology in mass production

1892	1896	1901	1906
New York's Ellis Island opens; twelve million immigrants pass through before it closes in 1954	Ruling in *Plessy v Ferguson*, the Supreme Court creates the doctrine of "separate but equal" provision for whites and blacks	Following the assassination of President McKinley, the 42-year-old Theodore Roosevelt becomes the youngest-ever president	A massive earthquake devastates San Francisco

– the assembly line – gave Detroit a head start in the new **automobile** industry, which swiftly became the most important business in America. Both **jazz** and **blues** music first reached a national audience during that same period, while Hollywood acquired its first **movie** studio in 1911, and its first major hit in 1915 with D.W. Griffith's unabashed glorification of the Ku Klux Klan in *Birth of a Nation*.

This was also a time of growing **radicalism**. Both the NAACP (National Association for the Advancement of Colored People) and the socialist International Workers of the World ("the Wobblies") were founded in the early 1900s, while the campaign for women's suffrage also came to the forefront. Writers such as Jack London and Upton Sinclair, who exposed conditions in Chicago's stockyards in *The Jungle*, proselytized to the masses.

Though President Wilson kept the USA out of the **Great War** for several years, American intervention was, when it came, decisive. With the Russian Revolution illustrating the dangers of anarchy, the USA also took charge of supervising the peace. However, even as Wilson presided over the negotiations that produced the Treaty of Versailles in 1919, isolationist sentiment at home prevented the USA from joining his pet scheme to preserve future world peace, the League of Nations.

Back home, the 18th Amendment forbade the sale and distribution of alcohol, while the 19th finally gave all American women the vote. Quite how **Prohibition** ever became the law of the land remains a mystery; certainly, in the buzzing metropolises of the Roaring Twenties, it enjoyed little conspicuous support. There was no noticeable elevation in the moral tone of the country, and Chicago in particular became renowned for the street wars between bootlegging gangsters such as Al Capone and his rivals.

The two Republican presidents who followed Wilson did little more than sit back and watch the Roaring Twenties unfold. Until his premature death, **Warren Harding** enjoyed considerable public affection, but he's now remembered as probably the worst US president of all, thanks to the cronyism and corruption of his associates. It's hard to say quite whether **Calvin Coolidge** did anything at all; his laissez-faire attitude extended to working a typical four-hour day, and announcing shortly after his inauguration that "four fifths of our troubles would disappear if we would sit down and keep still".

The Depression and the New Deal

By the middle of the 1920s, the USA was an industrial powerhouse, responsible for more than half the world's output of manufactured goods. Having led the way into a new era of prosperity, however, it suddenly dragged the rest of the world down into economic collapse. The consequences of the **Great Depression** were out of all proportion to any one specific cause. Possible factors include American over-investment in the floundering economy of postwar Europe, combined with high tariffs on imports that effectively precluded European recovery. Conservative commentators at the time chose to interpret the calamitous **Wall Street Crash** of October 1929 as a symptom of impending depression rather than a contributory cause, but the quasi-superstitious faith in the stock market that preceded it showed all the characteristics of classic speculative booms. On "Black Tuesday" alone, enough stocks were sold to produce a total loss of ten thousand million dollars – more than twice the total amount of money in circulation in the USA. Within the next three years, industrial production was cut by half, the national income dropped by 38 percent, and, above all, unemployment rose from 1.5 million to 13 million.

1919	1925	1927	1929
The 18th Amendment heralds the introduction of Prohibition; the 19th Amendment gives women the vote	F. Scott Fitzgerald, who dubs this era the Jazz Age, publishes *The Great Gatsby*	*The Jazz Singer*, starring Al Jolson, becomes the first commercially successful "talkie"	The Wall Street Crash plunges the USA into economic turmoil

National self-confidence, however shaky its foundations, has always played a crucial role in US history, and President Hoover was not the man to restore it. Matters only began to improve in 1932, when the patrician **Franklin Delano Roosevelt** accepted the Democratic nomination for president with the words "I pledge myself to a new deal for America", and went on to win a landslide victory. At the time of his inauguration, early in 1933, the banking system had all but closed down; it took Roosevelt the now-proverbial "Hundred Days" of vigorous legislation to turn around the mood of the country.

Taking advantage of the new medium of radio, Roosevelt used "Fireside Chats" to cajole America out of crisis; among his earliest observations was that it was a good time for a beer, and that the experiment of Prohibition was therefore over. The **New Deal** took many forms, but was marked throughout by a massive growth in the power of the federal government. Among its accomplishments were the National Recovery Administration, which created two million jobs; the Social Security Act, of which Roosevelt declared "no damn politician can ever scrap my social security program"; the Public Works Administration, which built dams and highways the length and breadth of the country; the Tennessee Valley Authority, which by generating electricity under public ownership for the common good was probably the closest the USA has ever come to institutionalized socialism; and measures to legitimize the role of the unions and revitalize the "Dust Bowl" farmers out on the plains.

Roosevelt originally saw himself as a populist who could draw support from every sector of society. By 1936, however, business leaders – and the Supreme Court – were making their opinion clear that he had done more than enough already to kick-start the economy. From then on, as he secured an unprecedented four consecutive terms as president, he was firmly cast as the champion of the little man.

After the work-creation programmes of the New Deal had put America back on its feet, the deadly pressure to achieve victory in **World War II** spurred industrial production and know-how to new heights. Once again the USA stayed out of the war at first, until it was finally forced in when the Japanese launched a pre-emptive strike on Hawaii's Pearl Harbor in 1941. In both the Pacific and in Europe, American manpower and economic muscle eventually carried all before it. By dying early in 1945, having laid the foundations for the postwar carve-up with Stalin and Churchill at Yalta, Roosevelt was spared the fateful decision, made by his successor Harry Truman, to use the newly developed atomic bomb on Hiroshima and Nagasaki.

The coming of the Cold War

With the war won, Americans were in no mood to revert back to the isolationism of the 1930s. Amid much hopeful rhetoric, Truman enthusiastically participated in the creation of the **United Nations**, and set up the **Marshall Plan** to speed the recovery of Europe. However, as Winston Churchill announced in Missouri in 1946, an "**Iron Curtain**" had descended upon Europe, and Joseph Stalin was transformed from ally to enemy almost overnight.

The ensuing **Cold War** lasted for more than four decades, at times fought in ferocious combat (albeit often by proxy) in scattered corners of the globe, and during the intervals diverting colossal resources towards the stockpiling of ever more destructive arsenals. Some of its ugliest moments came in its earliest years; Truman was still in

1932	1941	1945	1954
Franklin D. Roosevelt pledges "a new deal for the American people"	A surprise Japanese attack on Pearl Harbor precipitates US entry into World War II	President Truman's decision to drop atomic bombs on Hiroshima and Nagasaki marks the end of World War II	The Supreme Court declares racial segregation in schools to be unconstitutional

office in 1950 when war broke out in **Korea**. A dispute over the arbitrary division of the Korean peninsula into two separate nations, North and South, soon turned into a standoff between the USA and China (with Russia lurking in the shadows). Two years of bloody stalemate ended with little to show for it, except that Truman had by now been replaced by the genial **Dwight D. Eisenhower**, the latest war hero to turn president.

The Eisenhower years are often seen as characterized by bland complacency. Once Senator **Joseph McCarthy**, the "witch-hunting" anti-Communist scourge of the State Department and Hollywood, had finally discredited himself by attacking the army as well, middle-class America seemed to lapse into a wilful suburban stupor. Great social changes were taking shape, however. World War II had introduced vast numbers of women and members of ethnic minorities to the rewards of factory work, and shown many Americans from less prosperous regions the lifestyle attainable elsewhere in their own country. The development of a **national highway system**, and a huge increase in automobile ownership, encouraged people to pursue the American Dream wherever they chose. Combined with increasing mechanization on the cotton plantations of the South, this led to another **mass exodus** of blacks from the rural South to the cities of the North, and to a lesser extent the West. **California** entered a period of rapid growth, with the aeronautical industries of Los Angeles in particular attracting thousands of prospective workers.

Also during the 1950s, **television** reached every home in the country. Together with the LP record, it created an entertainment industry that addressed the needs of consumers who had previously been barely identified. **Youth culture** burst into prominence from 1954 onwards, with Elvis Presley's recording of *That's All Right Mama* appearing within a few months of Marlon Brando's moody starring role in *On the Waterfront* and James Dean's in *Rebel Without a Cause*.

The civil rights years

Racial segregation of public facilities, which had remained the norm in the South ever since Reconstruction, was finally declared illegal in 1954 by the Supreme Court ruling on *Brown v. Topeka Board of Education*. Just as a century before, however, the Southern states saw the issue more in terms of states' rights than of human rights, and attempting to implement the law, or even to challenge the failure to implement it, required immense courage. The action of Rosa Parks in refusing to give up her seat on a bus in Montgomery, Alabama, in 1955, triggered a successful mass boycott (see p.459), and pushed the 27-year-old **Rev Dr Martin Luther King, Jr** to the forefront of the civil rights campaign. Further confrontation took place at the Central High School in Little Rock, Arkansas, in 1957 (see p.471), when the reluctant Eisenhower had to call in federal troops to counter the state's unwillingness to integrate its education system.

The election of **John F. Kennedy** to the presidency in 1960, by the narrowest of margins, marked a sea-change in American politics, even if in retrospect his policies do not seem exactly radical. At 43 the youngest man ever to be elected president, and the first Catholic, he was prepared literally to reach for the moon, urging the USA to victory in the Space Race in which it had thus far lagged humiliatingly behind the Soviet Union. The two decades that lay ahead, however, were to be characterized by disillusion, defeat and despair. If the Eisenhower years had been dull, the 1960s in particular were far too interesting for almost everybody's liking.

1955	**1962**	**1963**
Black seamstress Rosa Parks refuses to change her seat on a bus in Montgomery, Alabama	John Glenn becomes the first US astronaut to go into orbit; President Kennedy faces down the Russians in the Cuban Missile Crisis	Rev. Martin Luther King, Jr delivers "I Have a Dream" speech; President Kennedy is assassinated

Kennedy's sheer glamour made him a popular president during his lifetime, while his assassination suffused his administration with the romantic glow of "Camelot". His one undisputed triumph, however, came with the **Cuban missile crisis** of 1962, when the US military fortunately spotted Russian bases in Cuba before any actual missiles were ready for use, and Kennedy faced down premier Khrushchev to insist they be withdrawn. On the other hand, he'd had rather less success the previous year in launching the abortive **Bay of Pigs** invasion of Cuba, and he also managed to embroil America deeper in the ongoing war against Communism in Vietnam by sending more "advisers" to Saigon.

Although a much publicized call to the wife of Rev Martin Luther King, Jr during one of King's many sojourns in Southern jails was a factor in Kennedy's election success, he was rarely identified himself with the **civil rights** movement. The campaign nonetheless made headway, lent momentum by television coverage of such horrific confrontations as the onslaught by Birmingham police on peaceful demonstrators in 1963. The movement's defining moment came when Rev King delivered his electrifying "I Have a Dream" speech later that summer. King was subsequently awarded the Nobel Peace Prize for his unwavering espousal of Gandhian principles of nonviolence. Perhaps an equally powerful factor in middle America's recognition that the time had come to address racial inequalities, however, was the not-so-implicit threat in the rhetoric of **Malcolm X**, who argued that black people had the right to defend themselves against aggression.

After Kennedy's assassination in November 1963, his successor, **Lyndon B. Johnson**, pushed through legislation that enacted most of the civil rights campaigners' key demands. Even then, violent white resistance in the South continued, and only the long, painstaking and dangerous work of registering Southern black voters en masse eventually forced Southern politicians to mend their ways.

Johnson won election by a landslide in 1964, but his vision of a "**Great Society**" soon foundered. He was brought low by the war in **Vietnam**, where US involvement escalated beyond all reason or apparent control. Broad-based popular opposition to the conflict grew in proportion to the American death toll, and the threat of the draft heightened youthful rebellion. San Francisco in particular responded to psychedelic prophet Timothy Leary's call to "turn on, tune in, drop out"; 1967's "Summer of Love" saw the lone beatniks of the 1950s transmogrify into an entire generation of hippies.

Dr King's long-standing message that social justice could only be achieved through economic equality was given a new urgency by riots in the ghettoes of Los Angeles in 1965 and Detroit in 1967, and the emergence of the Black Panthers, an armed defence force in the tradition of the now-dead Malcolm X. King also began to denounce the Vietnam War; meanwhile, after refusing the draft with the words "No Vietcong ever called me nigger", **Muhammad Ali** was stripped of his title as world heavyweight boxing champion.

In 1968, the social fabric of the USA reached the brink of collapse. Shortly after Johnson was forced by his plummeting popularity to withdraw from the year-end elections, Martin Luther King was gunned down in a Memphis motel. Next, JFK's brother **Robert Kennedy**, now redefined as spokesman for the dispossessed, was fatally shot just as he emerged as Democratic front-runner. It didn't take a conspiracy theorist to see that the spate of deaths reflected a malaise in the soul of America.

1968	1969	1974	1980
With the nation polarized by war in Vietnam, Rev. Martin Luther King, Jr, and Robert Kennedy are assassinated	Neil Armstrong becomes the first man to walk on the moon	Embroiled in the Watergate scandal, Richard Nixon resigns	With Iranian students holding the US embassy in Tehran, Ronald Reagan defeats President Jimmy Carter

Richard Nixon to Jimmy Carter

Somehow – perhaps because the brutally suppressed riots at the Chicago Democratic Convention raised the spectre of anarchy – the misery of 1968 resulted in the election of Republican **Richard Nixon** as president. Nixon's conservative credentials enabled him to bring the USA to a rapport with China, but the war in Vietnam dragged on to claim a total of 57,000 American lives. Attempts to win it included the secret and illegal bombing of Cambodia, which raised opposition at home to a new peak, but ultimately it was simpler to abandon the original goals in the name of "peace with honor". Perceptions differ as to whether the end came in 1972 – when Henry Kissinger and Le Duc Tho were awarded the Nobel Peace Prize for negotiating a treaty, and Tho at least had the grace to decline – or in 1975, when the Americans finally withdrew from Saigon.

During Nixon's first term, many of the disparate individuals politicized during the 1960s coalesced into **activist groupings**. Feminists united to campaign for abortion rights and an Equal Rights Amendment; gay men in New York's *Stonewall* bar fought back after one police raid too many; Native Americans formed the American Indian Movement; and even prisoners attempted to organize themselves, resulting in such bloody debacles as the storming of Attica prison in 1971. Nixon directed various federal agencies to monitor the new radicalism, but his real bugbear was the antiwar protesters. Increasingly ludicrous covert operations against real and potential opponents culminated in a botched attempt to burgle Democratic National Headquarters in the **Watergate** complex in 1972. It took two years of investigation for Nixon's role in the subsequent cover-up to be proved, but in 1974 he **resigned**, one step ahead of impeachment by the Senate, to be succeeded by **Gerald Ford**, his own appointee as vice president.

With the Republicans momentarily discredited, former Georgia governor **Jimmy Carter** was elected president as a clean-handed outsider in the bicentennial year of 1976. However, Carter's enthusiastic attempts to put his Baptist principles into practice on such issues as global human rights were soon perceived as naive, if not un-American. Misfortune followed misfortune. He had to break the news that the nation was facing an **energy crisis**, while after the Shah of Iran was overthrown, staff at the US embassy in Tehran were taken hostage by Islamic revolutionaries. Carter's failed attempts to arrange their release all but destroyed his hopes of winning re-election in 1980. Instead he was replaced by a very different figure, the former movie actor **Ronald Reagan**.

From Reagan to Clinton

Reagan was a new kind of president. Unlike his workaholic predecessor, he made a virtue of his hands-off approach to the job, joking that "they say hard work never killed anybody, but I figured why take the risk?" That laissez-faire attitude was especially apparent in his domestic economic policies, under which the rich were left to get as rich as they could. The common perception that Reagan was barely aware of what went on around him allowed his popularity to remain undented by scandals that included the labyrinthine **Iran-Contra** affair.

Reagan's most enduring achievement came during his second term, when his impeccable credentials as a Cold Warrior enabled him to negotiate **arms-control** agreements with **Mikhail Gorbachev**, the new leader of what he had previously called the "Evil Empire".

1987	1991	1993	1995
Speaking in front of the Berlin Wall, Reagan challenges: "Mr Gorbachev, tear down this wall!"	Following the Iraqi invasion of Kuwait, the Gulf War begins	Seven people are killed, and a thousand injured, in a bombing of the World Trade Center	A truck bomb in Oklahoma City kills 168

In 1988, **George H.W. Bush** became the first vice president in 150 years to be immediately elected to the presidency. Despite his unusually broad experience in foreign policy, Bush did little more than sit back and watch in amazement as the domino theory suddenly went into reverse. One by one, the Communist regimes of eastern Europe collapsed, until finally even the Soviet Union crumbled away. Bush was also president when **Operation Desert Storm** drove the Iraqis out of Kuwait in 1991, an undertaking that lasted one hundred hours and in which virtually no American lives were lost.

However, the much-anticipated "**peace dividend**" – the dramatic injection of cash into the economy that voters expected to follow the end of the arms race – never materialized. With the 1992 campaign focusing on domestic affairs rather than what was happening overseas, twelve years of Republican government were ended by the election of Arkansas Governor **Bill Clinton**.

Although Clinton's initial failure to deliver on specific promises – most obviously, to reform the healthcare system – enabled the Republicans to capture control of Congress in 1994, the "Comeback Kid" was nonetheless elected to a second term. Holding on to office proved more of a challenge in the face of humiliating sexual indiscretions, but the Senate ultimately failed to convict him in **impeachment** proceedings.

The twenty-first century

When Clinton left the presidency, the economy was **booming**. His former vice president, however, **Al Gore**, contrived to throw away the 2000 presidential election, a closely fought tussle for the centre ground that ended in a **tie** with his Republican opponent, **George W. Bush**. With the final conclusion depending on a mandatory re-counting of votes in Florida, where various irregularities and mistakes complicated the issue, the impasse was ultimately decided in Bush's favour by the conservative **Supreme Court**. At the time, the charge that he had "stolen" the election was expected to seriously overshadow his presidency, while the authority of the Supreme Court was also threatened by the perception of its ruling as partisan.

Within a year, however, the atrocity of **September 11, 2001** drove such concerns into the background, inflicting a devastating blow to both the nation's economy and its pride. More than three thousand people were killed in the worst terrorist attack in US history, when two hijacked planes were flown into the World Trade Center in New York City and one into the Pentagon. The attacks were quickly linked to the al-Qaeda network of Saudi Arabian terrorist Osama bin Laden, and within weeks President Bush declared an open-ended "War on Terror".

Confronting a changed world, Bush set about rewriting the traditional rule-book of diplomacy and international law. In 2002, he declared that the USA had a right to launch pre-emptive attacks: "If we wait for threats to fully materialize, we will have waited too long…We must take the battle to the enemy, disrupt his plans, and confront the worst threats before they emerge."

A US-led invasion of **Afghanistan** in 2001 was followed by a similar incursion into **Iraq** in 2003, ostensibly on the grounds that Iraqi dictator Saddam Hussein was developing "weapons of mass destruction". Although Saddam was deposed, apprehended, and in due course executed, it became universally acknowledged that no such weapons existed, and Iraq degenerated into civil war.

1998	2000	2001	2005
President Clinton proclaims "I did not have sex with that woman"	The Supreme Court rules George W. Bush to have been elected President	On September 11, more than three thousand people die in the worst terrorist attack in US history	Hurricane Katrina slams into the Gulf Coast, devastating New Orleans

Despite a wave of financial scandals, spearheaded by the collapse of the mighty energy firm Enron, Bush was elected to a second term in 2004. The country remained polarized, however, and the Bush administration was lambasted for the appalling inadequacy of its response when **Hurricane Katrina** and consequent floods devastated New Orleans and the Gulf Coast in 2005.

That the Democrats regained control of both Senate and House in 2006 was due largely to the deteriorating situation in Iraq. Similarly, the meteoric rise of Illinois Senator **Barack Obama** – and his hard-fought victory over Hillary Clinton in the 2008 Democratic primaries – owed much to his being almost unique among national politicians in his consistent opposition to the Iraq war. However, while Obama's message of change and optimism, coupled with his oratorical gifts and embrace of new technologies, especially resonated with young and minority voters, his ultimate triumph over John McCain in the presidential election later that year was triggered by the abrupt impact of a new **recession**. After bankers Lehman Brothers filed for bankruptcy in September 2008 – the largest bankruptcy in US history – it was clear that no element of the economy was safe from the consequences of reckless "subprime" mortgage lending.

The national exhilaration over Obama's achievement in becoming the first black US president did not take long to fade. Despite managing to achieve at least some measure of reform of the **healthcare** system, Obama was seen as failing to deliver on many of his original campaign pledges. In particular, his initiatives in the Middle East had little impact, and he seemed to be wrong-footed when the so-called "Arab Spring" toppled governments in Tunisia, Egypt and Libya in 2011. Direct involvement in the war in Afghanistan – the longest conflict in US history – was due to end when this book went to press, but no great credit seems likely to accrue to Obama, whose one moment of genuine national acclaim came when US forces finally found, and killed, Osama bin Laden in 2011. His comfortable re-election in 2012 owed much to the role of the Tea Party in drawing the Republican party ever further to the right. The Republican majority in the House of Representatives, however, remained sufficiently determined to impede President Obama's agenda that it was prepared to precipitate the **US government shutdown** of late 2013.

2008	2010	2013
Barack Obama wins election as the first black President	An explosion causes a massive oil spill in the Gulf of Mexico	The National Security Agency is revealed to be working with technology companies to monitor all electronic communications in the USA

Books

Space not permitting a comprehensive overview of American literature, the following list is simply an idiosyncratic selection of books that may appeal to interested readers. Books tagged with the ★ symbol are particularly recommended.

HISTORY AND SOCIETY

Dee Brown *Bury My Heart at Wounded Knee*. Still the best narrative of the impact of white settlement and expansion on Native Americans across the continent.

Bill Bryson *Made in America*. A compulsively readable history of the American language, packed with bizarre snippets.

★ **Mike Davis** *City of Quartz*. City politics, neighbourhood gangs, unions, film noir and religion are drawn together in this award-winning, leftist, hyperbolic history of Los Angeles.

John Demos *The Unredeemed Captive*. This story of the aftermath of a combined French and Native American attack on Deerfield, Massachusetts, in 1704 illuminates frontier life in the eighteenth century.

★ **W.E.B. DuBois** *The Souls of Black Folk*. Seminal collection of largely autobiographical essays examining racial separation at the start of the twentieth century.

Brian Fagan *Ancient North America*. Archeological history of America's native peoples, from the first hunters to cross the Bering Strait up to initial contact with Europeans.

Tim Flannery *The Eternal Frontier*. "Ecological" history of North America that reveals how the continent's physical environment has shaped the destinies of all its inhabitants, from horses to humans.

Shelby Foote *The Civil War: a Narrative*. Epic, three-volume account containing anything you could possibly want to know about the "War Between the States".

John Kenneth Galbraith *The Great Crash 1929*. An elegant and authoritative interpretation of the Wall Street Crash and its implications.

David Halberstam *The Best and the Brightest*. Still-relevant, gut-wrenching examination of how America's finest, most brilliant Ivy Leaguers plunged the nation into the first war it ever lost, disastrously.

Aldo Leopold *Sand County Almanac*. A meditation on natural history and landscape by the father of conservation ecology.

Meriwether Lewis and William Clark *The Original Journals of the Lewis and Clark Expedition, 1804–1806*. Eight volumes of meticulous jottings by the Northwest's first inland explorers, scrupulously following President Jefferson's orders to record every detail of flora, fauna and native inhabitant.

Magnus Magnusson and Herman Pálsson (trans) *The Vinland Sagas*. If you imagine stories that the Vikings reached America to be no more than myths, here's the day-to-day minutiae to convince you otherwise.

James M. McPherson *Battle Cry of Freedom*. Extremely readable history of the Civil War, which integrates and explains the complex social, economic, political and military factors in one concise volume.

Clyde A. Milner II, Carol A. O'Connor and Martha A. Sandweiss *The Oxford History of the American West*. Fascinating collection of essays on Western history, covering topics ranging from myths and movies to art and religion.

James Mooney *The Ghost Dance Religion and The Sioux Outbreak of 1890*. An extraordinary Bureau of Ethnology report, first published in 1890 but still available in paperback. Mooney persuaded his Washington superiors to allow him to roam the West in search of first-hand evidence and even interviewed Wovoka, the Ghost Dance prophet, in person.

Edmund Morgan *American Slavery, American Freedom*. Complex and far-reaching historical account of the cunning means by which white working-class conflict was averted by rich Virginia planters through the spread of black slavery.

Roderick Frazier Nash *Wilderness and the American Mind*. Classic study of the American take on environmental and conservation issues over the past couple of hundred years. Especially good sections on John Muir and his battles to preserve Yosemite.

Stephen Plog *Ancient Peoples of the Southwest*. Much the best single-volume history of the pre-Hispanic Southwest, packed with diagrams and colour photographs.

Marc Reisner *Cadillac Desert*. Concise, engaging account of the environmental and political impact on the West of the twentieth-century mania for dam-building and huge irrigation projects.

David Reynolds *Waking Giant: America in the Age of Jackson*. Rousing new portrait of America in the first half of the nineteenth century, from its clumsy attempt to take Canada in the War of 1812 to its successful Mexican land grab three decades later, with the figure of Andrew Jackson providing the touchstone throughout.

Hampton Sides *Blood And Thunder*. Hugely readable re-telling of the exploits of Kit Carson and his role in the campaigns against the Navajo.

★ **Billy Sothern** *Down in New Orleans: Reflections from a Drowned City*. Death penalty lawyer/activist Sothern's personal account of Katrina is moving, but it is his uncompromising report of the dirty secrets the floods revealed that truly shock. Yet he miraculously manages to imbue the horror with humanism and hope.

★ **Alan Taylor** *American Colonies*. Perhaps the best book on any single era of American history – a superb account of every aspect of the peopling of the continent, from remote antiquity until the Declaration of Independence.

Henry David Thoreau *Walden*. Few modern writers are more relevant than this nineteenth-century stalwart, whose Walden imagined environmentalism one hundred years early, and whose *Civil Disobedience* provided the template for modern activism.

★ **Mark Twain** *Roughing It, Life on the Mississippi* and many others. Mark Twain was by far the funniest and most vivid chronicler of nineteenth-century America. *Roughing It*, which covers his early wanderings across the continent, all the way to Hawaii, is absolutely compelling.

Geoffrey C. Ward, with Ric and Ken Burns *The Civil War*. Illustrated history of the Civil War, designed to accompany the TV series and using hundreds of the same photographs.

Richard White *It's Your Misfortune And None of My Own*. Dense, authoritative and all-embracing history of the American West, which debunks the notion of the rugged pioneer by stressing the role of the federal government.

Juan Williams *Eyes on the Prize*. Informative and detailed account of the civil rights years from the early 1950s up to 1966, with lots of rare, and some very familiar, photos.

Edmund Wilson *Patriotic Gore*. Fascinating eight-hundred-page survey of the literature of the Civil War, which serves in its own right as an immensely readable narrative of the conflict.

Bob Woodward and Carl Bernstein *All the President's Men* and *The Final Days*. Although Woodward continues to crank out Washington exposés, his Nixon-era books still can't be beaten for their portrait of diligent young journalists bringing down a corrupt president, and that president's own unique mania.

BIOGRAPHY AND ORAL HISTORY

Muhammad Ali, with Hana Yasmeen Ali *The Soul of a Butterfly: Reflections on Life's Journey*. Thought-provoking and moving autobiography, in the course of which the iconic boxer's third daughter helps him describe his career and embrace of Sufi Islam.

Maya Angelou *I Know Why the Caged Bird Sings*. First of a five-volume autobiography that provides an ultimately uplifting account of how a black girl transcended her traumatic childhood in 1930s Arkansas.

Donald A. Barclay, James H. Maguire and Peter Wild (eds) *Into the Wilderness Dream*. Gripping collection of Western exploration narratives written between 1500 and 1800; thanks to any number of little-known gems, the best of many such anthologies.

Taylor Branch *America in the King Years*. Brilliant three-volume series showing the immense and long-overdue changes that enveloped America in the civil rights struggle of the 1950s and 60s through the lens of Martin Luther King, Jr.

William F. Cody *The Life of Hon. William F. Cody, Known as Buffalo Bill*. Larger-than-life autobiography of one of the Wild West's greatest characters, treasurable for the moment when he refers to himself more formally as "Bison William".

Jill Ker Conway (ed) *Written by Herself*. Splendid anthology of women's autobiographies from the mid-1800s to the present, including sections on African Americans, scientists, artists and pioneers.

Frederick Douglass, et al *The Classic Slave Narratives*. Compilation of ex-slaves' autobiographies, ranging from Olaudah Equíano's kidnapping in Africa and global wanderings to Frederick Douglass's eloquent denunciation of slavery. Includes Harriet Jacobs' story of her escape from Edenton, North Carolina.

★ **U.S. Grant** *Personal Memoirs*. Encouraged by Mark Twain, the Union general and subsequent president wrote his autobiography just before his death, in a (successful) bid to recoup his horrendous debts. At first the book feels oddly downbeat, but the man's down-to-earth modesty grows on you.

Edmund Morris *The Rise of Theodore Roosevelt, Theodore Rex* and *Colonel Roosevelt*. Thoroughly engaging and superbly researched three-volume biography of Theodore Roosevelt, tracing the energetic and controversial president's astonishing trajectory to the White House and his far-reaching achievements.

Luc Sante *Low Life*. Rip-roaring look at New York vice in the nineteenth century, and how gangsters, prostitutes, machine politicians and saloon thugs all contributed to the colour and character of the city.

Joanna L. Stratton *Pioneer Women*. Original memoirs of women – mothers, teachers, homesteaders and circuit riders – who ventured across the plains from 1854 to 1890. Lively, superbly detailed accounts, with chapters on journeys, homebuilding, daily domestic life, the church, the cowtown, temperance and suffrage.

★ **Frank Waters** *Book of the Hopi*. Extraordinary insight into the traditions and beliefs of the Hopi, prepared through years of interviews and approved by tribal elders.

★ **Malcolm X, with Alex Haley** *The Autobiography of Malcolm X*. Searingly honest and moving account of Malcolm's progress from street hoodlum to political leader, which traces the development of his thinking before and after his split from the Nation of Islam. The conclusion, when he talks about his impending assassination, is extremely painful.

Gary Younge *Stranger In A Strange Land* and *No Place Like Home*. Black British journalist Gary Younge is an acute observer of contemporary America; his experiences in the self-proclaimed New South make fascinating reading.

ENTERTAINMENT AND CULTURE

Kenneth Anger *Hollywood Babylon*. A vicious yet high-spirited romp through Tinseltown's greatest scandals, amply illustrated with gory and repulsive photographs, and always inclined to bend the facts for the sake of a good story. A shoddily researched second volume covers more recent times.

★ **Thomas Brothers** *Louis Armstrong's New Orleans*. A vivid account not only of the wildly talented trumpeter but also of his contemporaries and their cultural context. A brilliant evocation of the exciting hotbed of creativity that fired early-twentieth-century New Orleans.

Bob Dylan *Chronicles: Volume One*. Far from the kind of stream-of-consciousness he wrote in his younger days, Dylan focuses in almost microscopic detail on three distinct moments in his life, including Greenwich Village in the early 1960s and New Orleans in the 1980s. The result is a compelling testament to his place at the epicentre of America's cultural life.

Robert Evans *The Kid Stays in the Picture*. Spellbinding insider's view of the machinations of Hollywood after the demise of the studio system, written with verve by one of LA's biggest egos, the head of Paramount at its peak.

★ **Peter Guralnick** *Lost Highways*, *Feel Like Going Home* and *Sweet Soul Music*. Thoroughly researched personal histories of black popular music, packed with obsessive detail on all the great names. His twin Elvis biographies, *Last Train to Memphis* and *Careless Love*, trace the rise and fall of the iconic star, while also managing to evaluate him seriously as a musician.

Gerri Hershey *Nowhere to Run: the History of Soul Music*. Definitive rundown of the evolution of soul music from the gospel heyday of the 1940s through the Memphis, Motown and Philly scenes to the sounds of the early 1980s. Strong on social commentary and political background and studded with anecdotes and interviews.

Michael Ondaatje *Coming through Slaughter*. Extraordinary, dream-like fictionalization of the life of doomed New Orleans cornet player Buddy Bolden, written in a lyrical style that evokes the rhythms and pace of jazz improvisation.

Robert Palmer *Deep Blues*. Readable history of the development and personalities of the Delta Blues.

★ **Geoffrey C. Ward, Ken Burns, et al** *Jazz: a History of America's Music*. While the story peters out somewhat after bebop, this highly readable volume boasts hundreds of rare photographs, first-hand accounts and lively essays to provide a beautifully drawn picture of America's home-grown music and its icons.

TRAVEL WRITING

Edward Abbey *The Journey Home*. Hilarious accounts of whitewater rafting and desert hiking trips alternate with essays by the man who inspired the radical environmentalist movement Earth First! All of Abbey's books, especially *Desert Solitaire*, a journal of time spent as a ranger in Arches National Park, make great travelling companions.

James Agee and Walker Evans *Let Us Now Praise Famous Men*. A deeply personal but also richly evocative journal of travels through the rural lands of the Depression-era Deep South, complemented by Evans' powerful photographs.

Bill Bryson *The Lost Continent*. Using his boyhood home of Des Moines in Iowa as a benchmark, the author travels the length and breadth of America to find the perfect small town. Hilarious, if at times a bit smug.

Alistair Cooke *Alistair Cooke's America*. The author's thorough, eloquent overview of American life and customs touches on the complexity of its culture and politics.

J. Hector St-John de Crèvecoeur *Letters from an American Farmer and Sketches of Eighteenth-Century America*. A remarkable account of the complexities of Revolutionary America, first published in 1782.

Charles Dickens *American Notes*. Amusing satirical commentary about the USA from a jaded British perspective that's still lighter in tone than the author's later, more scabrous *Martin Chuzzlewit*.

Robert Frank *The Americans*. The Swiss photographer's brilliantly evocative portrait of mid-century American life from coast to coast, with striking images contextualized by an introductory essay from Jack Kerouac.

★ **Ian Frazier** *Great Plains*. An immaculately researched and well-written travelogue containing a wealth of information on the people of the American prairielands from Native Americans to the soldiers who staff the region's nuclear installations.

William Least Heat-Moon *Blue Highways*. Account of a mammoth loop tour of the USA by backroads, in which the author interviews ordinary people in ordinary places. A good overview of rural America, with lots of interesting details on Native Americans.

Jack Kerouac *On the Road*. This definitive account of transcontinental beatnik wanderings now reads as a curiously dated period piece.

James A. MacMahon (ed) *Audubon Society Nature Guides*. Attractively produced, fully illustrated and easy-to-use guides to the flora and fauna of seven different US regional ecosystems, covering the entire country from coast to coast and from grasslands to glaciers.

Virginia and Lee McAlester *A Field Guide to American Houses*. Well-illustrated and engaging guide to America's rich variety of domestic architecture, from pre-colonial to postmodern.

John McPhee *Encounters with the Arch Druid*. In three interlinked narratives, the late environmental activist and Friends of the Earth founder David Brower confronts developers, miners and dam-builders, while trying to protect three different American wilderness areas – the Atlantic shoreline, the Grand Canyon and the Cascades of the Pacific Northwest.

Bernard A. Weisberger (ed) *The WPA Guide to America*. Prepared during the New Deal as part of a make-work programme for writers, these guides paint a fairly comprehensive portrait of 1930s and earlier America.

Edmund White *States of Desire: Travels in Gay America*. A revealing account of life in gay communities across the country, focusing heavily on San Francisco and New York.

FICTION

GENERAL AMERICANA

★ **Raymond Carver** *Will You Please Be Quiet Please?* Stories of the American working class, written in a distinctive, sparse style that perhaps owes something to Hemingway and certainly influenced untold numbers of contemporary American writers. The stories served as the basis for Robert Altman's film *Short Cuts*.

Don DeLillo *White Noise* and *Underworld*. The former is his best, a funny and penetrating pop culture exploration, while the latter is one of those typically flawed attempts to pack the twentieth-century American experience into a great big novel. Worthwhile, though.

William Kennedy *Ironweed*. Terse, affecting tale of a couple of down-on-their-luck drunks haunted by ghosts from a chequered past; excellent evocation of 1930s America, specifically working-class Albany, New York.

★ **Herman Melville** *Moby-Dick*. Compendious and compelling account of nineteenth-century whaling, packed with details on American life from New England to the Pacific.

★ **John Dos Passos** *USA*. Hugely ambitious trilogy that grapples with the USA in the early decades of the twentieth century from every possible angle. Gripping human stories with a strong political and historical point of view.

E. Annie Proulx *Accordion Crimes*. Proulx's masterly book comes as close to being the fabled "Great American Novel" as anyone could reasonably ask, tracing a fascinating history of immigrants in all parts of North America through the fortunes of a battered old Sicilian accordion. The Wyoming-set short stories collected in *Close Range* – which include *Brokeback Mountain* – are also recommended.

NEW YORK CITY

Paul Auster *New York Trilogy*. Three Borgesian investigations into the mystery and madness of contemporary New York. Using the conventions of the detective novel, Auster unfolds a disturbed and disturbing picture of the city.

Truman Capote *Breakfast at Tiffany's* and *In Cold Blood*. The first of these two uniquely American and very different stories is about a fictional social climber in New York called Holly Golightly; the second concerns the true-life stories of two serial killers in the heartland.

Michael Chabon *The Amazing Adventures of Kavalier & Clay*. Pulitzer Prize-winning novel charting the rise and fall of comic-book-writing cousins in New York City – one a refugee from World War II Prague, the other a closeted Brooklynite.

F. Scott Fitzgerald *The Great Gatsby*. Perhaps the most American of American novels, from the definitive author of the Jazz Age.

★ **Chester Himes** *Cotton Comes to Harlem, Blind Man with a Pistol* and many others. Action-packed and uproariously violent novels set in New York's Harlem, starring the much-feared detectives Coffin Ed Johnson and Grave Digger Jones.

Grace Paley *Collected Stories*. Shrewd love-hate stories written over a lifetime by the daughter of Russian-Jewish immigrants, who published dead-on accounts of New York life in three instalments, which came out in the 1950s, the early 1970s and the late 1980s respectively.

★ **J.D. Salinger** *The Catcher in the Rye*. Classic novel of adolescence, tracing Holden Caulfield's sardonic journey through the streets of New York.

NEW ENGLAND

Emily Dickinson *The Cambridge Companion*. It took many decades for the innovative work of this pre-eminent poet, which touches on dark emotional themes, to be recognized. This anthology is a good place to start.

Nathaniel Hawthorne *The House of the Seven Gables*. A gloomy gothic tale of Puritan misdeeds coming back to haunt the denizens of a cursed mansion.

John Irving *The Cider House Rules*. One of Irving's more successful sprawling novels, weaving themes of love, suffering and the many facets of the abortion debate against a Maine backdrop.

H.P. Lovecraft *The Best of H.P. Lovecraft: Bloodcurdling Tales of Horror and the Macabre*. Creepy New England stories from the author Stephen King called "the twentieth century's greatest practitioner of the classic horror tale".

THE SOUTH

William Faulkner *The Reivers*. The last and most humourous work of this celebrated Southern author. *The Sound and the Fury*, a fascinating study of prejudice, set like most of his books in the fictional Yoknatapawpha County in Mississippi, is a much more difficult read.

Zora Neale Hurston *Spunk*. Short stories celebrating black culture and experience from around the country, by a writer from Florida who became one of the bright stars of the Harlem cultural renaissance in the 1920s.

Harper Lee To Kill a Mockingbird. Classic tale of racial conflict and society's view of an outsider, Boo Radley, as seen through the eyes of children.

Cormac McCarthy Suttree. McCarthy is better known for "modern Western" works like Blood Meridian and All the Pretty Horses, but this beautifully written tale, of a Knoxville, Tennessee, scion opting for a hard-scrabble life among a band of vagrants on the Tennessee River, is his best.

Carson McCullers The Heart is a Lonely Hunter. McCullers is unrivalled in her sensitive treatment of misfits, in this case the attitude of a small Southern community to a deaf-mute.

Margaret Mitchell Gone With the Wind. Worth a read even if you know the lines of Scarlett and Rhett by heart.

★ **Toni Morrison** Beloved. Exquisitely written ghost story by the Nobel Prize-winning novelist, which recounts the painful lives of a group of freed slaves after Reconstruction, and the obsession a mother develops after murdering her baby daughter to spare her a life of slavery.

Flannery O'Connor A Good Man is Hard to Find. Short stories, featuring strong, obsessed characters, that explore religious tensions and racial conflicts in the Deep South.

Alice Walker In Love and Trouble. Moving and powerful stories of black women in the South, from the author of The Color Purple.

Eudora Welty The Ponder Heart. Quirky, humorous evocation of life in a backwater Mississippi town. Her most acclaimed work, The Optimist's Daughter, explores the tensions between a judge's daughter and her stepmother.

LOUISIANA

James Lee Burke The Tin Roof Blowdown. Louisiana resident Burke's 27th crime novel, written in the immediate aftermath of Katrina, is a bleak, angry and miserable vision of the flood-ravaged and lawless city of New Orleans.

George Washington Cable The Grandissimes. Romantic saga of Creole family feuds, written c.1900 but set during the Louisiana Purchase. Superb evocation of steamy Louisiana, the Creole lifestyle and the resistance of New Orleans to its Americanization. Apparently shocking at the time for its sympathetic portrayal of blacks.

★ **Kate Chopin** The Awakening. Subversive story of a bourgeois married woman whose fight for independence ends in tragedy. The swampy Louisiana of a century ago is portrayed as both a sensual hotbed for her sexual awakening and as her eventual nemesis.

Valerie Martin Property. A bleak but wonderfully written tale of the brutalizing effects, on both mistress and slave, of slavery on a Louisiana sugar plantation.

Anne Rice Feast Of All Saints. Rice's vampire novels are great fun, but her finest portrait of nineteenth-century New Orleans comes in this sensitive examination of race, sexuality and gender issues in the antebellum period.

★ **John Kennedy Toole** A Confederacy of Dunces. Anarchic black tragicomedy in which the pompous and repulsive anti-hero Ignatius J. Reilly wreaks havoc through an insalubrious and surreal New Orleans.

★ **Robert Penn Warren** All The King's Men. This fascinating fictionalized saga of Louisiana's legendary "King-fish", Huey Long, is a truly great American novel.

THE GREAT LAKES AND THE GREAT PLAINS

★ **Willa Cather** My Ántonia. Stunning book set in Nebraska that provides a great sense of the pioneer hardships on the Great Plains.

Louise Erdrich The Beet Queen. Offbeat tale of passion and obsession among poor white North Dakota folk – particularly women – against the 1940s backdrop of a changing culture.

Garrison Keillor Lake Wobegon Days. Wry, witty tales about a mythical Minnesota small town, poking gentle fun at the rural Midwest.

Mari Sandoz Old Jules. Written in 1935, this fictionalized biography gives a wonderful insight into the life of the author's pioneer Swiss father on the Nebraskan plains.

Upton Sinclair The Jungle. Documenting the horrific unsanitary conditions in Chicago's meat-packing industry, Sinclair's compelling Socialist-tract-cum-novel, first serialized in 1905, ranks among the most influential books in US history.

Laura Ingalls Wilder Little House in the Big Woods. A fascinating and delightful insight into pioneer life in the wilderness of nineteenth-century Wisconsin, the first of a series.

Daniel Woodrell The Outlaw Album. These dozen compelling short stories, by a contemporary Missouri author, evoke the dark undercurrents at work in the rural hinterland of the Ozarks.

Richard Wright Native Son. The harrowing story of Bigger Thomas, a black chauffeur who accidentally kills his employer's daughter. The story develops his relationship with his lawyer, the closest he has ever come to being on an equal footing with a white.

THE ROCKIES AND THE SOUTHWEST

Willa Cather Death Comes for the Archbishop. A magnificent evocation of the landscapes and cultures of nineteenth-century New Mexico.

A.B. Guthrie Jr Big Sky. When published in the Thirties it shattered the image of the mythical West. Realistic historical fiction at its very best, following desperate mountain man and fugitive Boone Caudill, whose idyllic life in Montana was ended by the arrival of white settlers.

Tony Hillerman The Dark Wind, and many others. The adventures of Jim Chee of the Navajo Tribal Police on the reservations of northern Arizona, forever dabbling in dark and mysterious forces churned up from the Ancestral Puebloan past.

Barbara Kingsolver *Pigs in Heaven*. A magnificent evocation of tensions and realities in the contemporary Southwest, by a writer who ranks among America's finest stylists.

Norman MacLean *A River Runs Through It*. Unputdownable – the best ever novel about fly-fishing, set in beautiful Montana lake country.

CALIFORNIA AND THE WEST

★ **Raymond Chandler** *The Big Sleep* and *Farewell My Lovely*. The original incarnations of archetypal tough guy and iconic private eye Philip Marlowe are far more complex and beautifully written than the related movies lead you to expect. Pulp fiction at its finest – written by an American raised in London.

David Guterson *Snow Falling on Cedars* and *East Of the Mountains*. Two gripping novels that capture the flavour of the Pacific Northwest; the first is an atmospheric mystery centring on postwar interracial tensions, the second features a dying man looking back on his life.

Jack London *The Call of the Wild*. London's classic tale, of a family pet discovering the ways of the wilderness while forced to pull sleds across Alaska's Gold Rush trails, still makes essential reading before a trip to the far north.

Armistead Maupin *Tales of the City*. Long-running saga comprising sympathetic and entertaining tales of life in San Francisco, which also work surprisingly well as suspenseful standalone novels. That many of its key characters are gay meant that over the years the series became a chronicle of the impact of AIDS on the city.

Thomas Pynchon *The Crying of Lot 49*. Short, funny and accessible, this novel of techno-freaks and potheads in Sixties California reveals, among other things, the sexy side of stamp collecting.

John Steinbeck *The Grapes of Wrath*. The classic account of a migrant family forsaking the Midwest for the Promised Land. Steinbeck's lighthearted but crisply observed novella *Cannery Row* captures daily life on the prewar Monterey waterfront. The epic *East of Eden* updates and resets the Bible in the Salinas Valley and details three generations of familial feuding.

Nathanael West *The Day of the Locust*. West wrote dark novels wholly vested in the American experience; this one, set in LA, is an apocalyptic story of fringe characters at the edge of the film industry.

Film

The list below focuses on key films in certain genres that have helped define the American experience – both the light and the dark. Those tagged with the ★ symbol are particularly recommended.

MUSIC/MUSICALS

Calamity Jane (David Butler, 1953). The Western gets a rumbustious musical twist with tomboy Doris Day bringing thigh-slapping gusto to the title role and Howard Keel as the rugged hero who (almost) tames her.

Gimme Shelter (Albert and David Maysles, 1969). Excellent documentary about the ill-fated Rolling Stones concert at Altamont; a searing look at homegrown American violence and Vietnam-era chaos at the end of the 1960s.

The Girl Can't Help It (Frank Tashlin, 1956). Pneumatic, pouting Jayne Mansfield defined the blonde bombshell for the Atomic generation. And Tashlin, who spent years as a madcap Looney Tunes animator, knew just how best to display her cartoonish, candy-sweet charms. The rock'n'roll plot delivers some fab musical moments, too, with numbers from Eddie Cochran, Little Richard and the wonderful Julie London.

Gold Diggers of 1933 (Mervyn LeRoy/Busby Berkeley, 1933). In which genius choreographer Berkeley pioneered his trademark overhead-crane shots of flamboyantly trompe l'oeil dance numbers featuring lines of glamorous chorines. See also *42nd Street* and *Footlight Parade*.

Meet Me in St Louis (Vincente Minnelli, 1944). Most famous for its Judy Garland number *The Trolley Song*, this charming piece of nostalgia celebrates turn-of-the-century America through the ups and downs of a St Louis family during the 1903 World's Fair.

★ **Singin' in the Rain** (Stanley Donen/Gene Kelly, 1952). Beloved musical comedy about Hollywood at the dawn of the sound era, featuring memorable tunes like *Make 'Em Laugh* and the title song, along with energetic performances by star Kelly, sidekick Donald O'Connor and a pixieish Debbie Reynolds.

Viva Las Vegas (George Sidney, 1964). One of Elvis's finer musicals, partly due to the effervescent presence of Ann-Margret – of all the King's co-stars only she could match him for sheer animal sexuality. The two were having an affair during the shoot, and the chemistry drips from the screen.

Woodstock (Michael Wadleigh, 1969). *Gimme Shelter's* upbeat counterpart, documenting the musical pinnacle of the hippie era, showing half a million flower children peacefully grooving to Jimi Hendrix, The Who and Sly and the Family Stone while getting stoned, muddy and wild on an upstate New York farm.

SILENT ERA

Birth of a Nation (D.W. Griffith, 1915). Possibly the most influential film in American history, both for its pioneering film technique (close-ups, cross-cutting and so on) and appalling racist propaganda, which led to a revival of the KKK.

★ **The General** (Buster Keaton, 1926). A fine introduction to Keaton's acrobatic brand of slapstick and inventive cinematic approach; the Great Stone Face chases down a stolen locomotive during the Civil War.

The Gold Rush (Charlie Chaplin, 1925). Chaplin's finest film: the Little Tramp gets trapped in a cabin during an Alaska blizzard in an affecting story that mixes sentiment

and high comedy in near-perfect balance.

Greed (Erich von Stroheim, 1923). An audacious scene-by-scene adaptation of Frank Norris's novel *McTeague*, a tragic tale of love and revenge in San Francisco. Slashed from ten to two and a half hours by MGM, the film remains a cinematic triumph for its striking compositions, epic drama and truly bleak ending.

Sunrise (F.W. Murnau, 1927). Among the most beautiful Hollywood productions of any era. *Sunrise's* German émigré director employed striking lighting effects, complex travelling shots and emotionally compelling performances in a tale of a country boy led astray by a big-city vamp.

WESTERNS

McCabe and Mrs Miller (Robert Altman, 1971). Entrepreneur Warren Beatty brings prostitution to a Washington town and tries to reinvent himself as a gunslinger in this now-classic anti-Western.

Once Upon a Time in the West (Sergio Leone, 1968). The quintessential spaghetti Western, filmed in Spain by an Italian director, but steeped in mythic American themes.

Red River (Howard Hawks, 1948). Upstart Montgomery Clift battles beef-baron John Wayne on a momentous cattle drive through the Midwest. Prototypical Hawks tale of clashing tough-guy egos and no-nonsense professionals on the range.

★ **The Searchers** (John Ford, 1956). Perhaps Ford's most iconic Western, with vivid cinematography and epic scale; John Wayne relentlessly hunts down the Native American chief who massacred his friends and family.

The Wild Bunch (Sam Peckinpah, 1969). A movie that says as much about the chaotic end of the 1960s as it does about the West, featuring a band of killers who hunt for women and treasure and wind up in a bloodbath unprecedented in film history.

AMERICANA

Breakfast at Tiffany's (Blake Edwards, 1961). Manhattan never looked more chic, and Audrey Hepburn, dressed in Givenchy, gives a quintessentially stylish performance as vulnerable kept woman Holly Golightly. The theme tune, too, *Moon River*, penned by Henry Mancini, shines. Author Truman Capote originally wanted Marilyn Monroe to play Golightly.

★ **Citizen Kane** (Orson Welles, 1941). Often called the greatest American movie, and one that subverts the rags-to-riches American Dream: a poor country boy finds nothing but misery when he inherits a fortune.

E.T. The Extra-Terrestrial (Steven Spielberg, 1982). Reagan-era blockbuster and sentimental variation on 1950s monster flicks, imbued with the director's ongoing interest in absentee fathers, suburban fantasies and otherworldly saviours. A fine example of American cinema's never-ending quest for lost innocence.

★ **Gone with the Wind** (Victor Fleming, 1939). Possibly the most popular movie of all time, this lush, affecting and elegiac look at the Old South provides three hours of expertly wrought historical melodrama. Vivien Leigh dazzles as rebellious Southern belle Scarlett O'Hara, while Hattie McDaniel, as her mammy, was the first African American ever to be awarded an Oscar.

Mr. Smith Goes to Washington (Frank Capra, 1939). Tub-thumping populist film that still resonates for its rosy belief in the goodness of the common man, dark view of political elites and earnest hope for America's future. Capra's *Meet John Doe* offers a grimmer variation on the tale, while *It's a Wonderful Life* provides a Christmas take on the same themes.

North by Northwest (Alfred Hitchcock, 1959). Not only an exciting chase film, in which international criminal James Mason hunts down ad-man Cary Grant, but also a

---

ON LOCATION

Although many memorable sights are off-limits to the public or exist only on the backlot tours of movie-studio theme parks, countless filmmaking locations are at least prepared to accommodate visitors. This list provides an overview of notable films.

2001: A Space Odyssey (Stanley Kubrick, 1968). Monument Valley, Arizona. See p.773.

Back to the Future (Robert Zemeckis, 1985). Gamble House, Pasadena. See p.838.

Badlands (Terrence Malick, 1973). Badlands National Park, South Dakota. See p.650.

Being There (Hal Ashby, 1979). Biltmore Estate, Asheville, North Carolina. See p.402.

The Birds (Alfred Hitchcock, 1963). Bodega Bay, California. See p.912.

Blade Runner (Ridley Scott, 1982). LA: Union Station, Bradbury Building. See p.840.

The Bridges of Madison County (Clint Eastwood, 1995). Winterset, Iowa.

Chinatown (Roman Polanski, 1974). LA: Santa Catalina Island (see p.836).

Citizen Kane (Orson Welles, 1941). The inspiration for "Xanadu" was Hearst Castle, California. See p.867.

Close Encounters of the Third Kind (Steven Spielberg, 1978). Devils Tower, Wyoming. See p.696.

Easy Rider (Dennis Hopper, 1969). New Orleans (see p.536); Sunset Crater, Arizona.

Five Easy Pieces (Bob Rafelson, 1970). San Juan Islands, Washington (see p.934).

Galaxy Quest (Dean Parisot, 1999). Goblin Valley, Utah. See p.788.

Grapes of Wrath (John Ford, 1940). Petrified Forest, Arizona. See p.762.

Greed (Erich von Stroheim, 1923). Death Valley, California. See p.851.

High Plains Drifter (Clint Eastwood, 1972). Mono Lake, California. See p.855.

Intolerance (D.W. Griffith, 1916). "Babylon" set, Hollywood, California. See p.827.

Jaws (Steven Spielberg, 1975). Martha's Vineyard, Massachusetts. See p.191.

Little Big Man (Arthur Penn, 1970). Custer State Park, South Dakota. See p.655.

Manhattan (Woody Allen, 1978). Central Park (see p.77); Brooklyn Bridge. See p.67.

Midnight in the Garden of Good and Evil (Clint Eastwood, 1998). Savannah, Georgia. See p.424.

Mr. Smith Goes to Washington (Frank Capra, 1939). Lincoln Memorial. See p.324.

Mystery Train (Jim Jarmusch, 1989). *Arcade*, Memphis, Tennessee. See p.444.

Nashville (Robert Altman, 1975). Parthenon (see p.449); Grand Ole Opry. See p.448.

fun travelogue that starts on New York's Madison Avenue and ends on the cliff-face of Mount Rushmore.

Prairie Home Companion (Robert Altman, 2006). It's fitting that Altman, no stranger to nostalgia, came up with this impeccable movie as his swansong: a musical about the (fictional) final broadcast of the (real-life) down-home radio show from author Garrison Keillor. Altman's typically star-studded ensemble cast, and a smart screenplay from Keillor – who plays himself – create a wry, melancholy and beautiful tribute to lost dreams.

Rebel Without a Cause (Nicholas Ray, 1955). The apotheosis of adolescent angst, with James Dean lamenting the hypocrisies of family life and engaging in all manner of fisticuffs, deadly drag races and night-time battles with the cops.

There Will Be Blood (Paul Thomas Anderson, 2007). This unsettling epic saga of America's turn-of-the-century oil boom differs from Upton Sinclair's novel, *Oil!* in unexpected ways to become dominated by Daniel Day-Lewis, whose magisterial performance as monstrous prospector Daniel Plainview raises disturbing questions about the American Dream.

★ **The Way We Were** (Sidney Pollack, 1973). The kind of Hollywood movie they don't make any more – a political film made by political people about a political time. Barbra Streisand is superb as the fiery left-wing intellectual who falls hard for Robert Redford's blonde WASP in the 1930s; the desperately romantic film then follows their relationship against decades of huge social and cultural change.

★ **The Wizard of Oz** (Victor Fleming, 1939). A cinematic institution and Technicolor extravaganza that shows Hollywood at its zenith, romanticizing small-town life in the Midwest and offering eye-popping fantasies of good and evil witches, scary flying monkeys and a wide-eyed Judy Garland sporting ruby slippers on a yellow-brick road.

ROAD MOVIES

Badlands (Terrence Malick, 1973). Midwest loner-loser Martin Sheen and girlfriend Sissy Spacek tour the heartland while on a random murder spree. Life on the road as a metaphor for existential futility.

Easy Rider (Dennis Hopper, 1969). Hippies Peter Fonda and director Hopper take to the road while riding a groovy set of wheels, pick up nerdy Jack Nicholson on the way, have a bad trip in a New Orleans cemetery and meet

North by Northwest (Alfred Hitchcock, 1959). United Nations, NYC (see p.76); Mount Rushmore, South Dakota. See p.654.

On the Town (Stanley Donen/Gene Kelly, 1949). American Museum of Natural History, NYC. See p.80.

Paper Moon (Peter Bogdanovich, 1973). St Joseph, Missouri. See p.266.

The Parallax View (Alan J. Pakula, 1974). Space Needle, Seattle. See p.926.

Planet of the Apes (Franklin J. Schaffner, 1968). Lake Powell, Utah. See p.792.

Poseidon Adventure (Ronald Neame, 1972). *Queen Mary*, Long Beach, California. See p.836.

Rebel Without a Cause (Nicholas Ray, 1955). Griffith Observatory, LA. See p.830.

Return of the Jedi (Richard Marquand, 1983). Redwood National Park, California. See p.914.

Rocky (John G. Avildsen, 1976). Philadelphia Museum of Art, Pennsylvania (see p.131).

The Searchers (John Ford, 1956). Monument Valley, Arizona. See p.773.

Shane (George Stevens, 1953). Wyoming: Grand Teton National Park (see p.703); Jackson Hole. See p.707.

The Shining (Stanley Kubrick, 1980). *Timberline Lodge*, Oregon. See p.957.

Singin' in the Rain (Stanley Donen/Gene Kelly, 1952). *Chinese Theatre*, Hollywood. See p.847.

Some Like It Hot (Billy Wilder, 1959). *Coronado Hotel*, San Diego.

The Sting (George Roy Hill, 1973). Santa Monica Pier, California. See p.834.

A Streetcar Named Desire (Elia Kazan, 1951). New Orleans, Louisiana. See p.536.

Sunset Boulevard (Billy Wilder, 1950). Hollywood: Paramount Studios (see p.830); Sunset Boulevard. See p.832.

Thelma and Louise (Ridley Scott, 1991). Arches National Park, Utah. See p.788.

The Thing (Christian Nyby/Howard Hawks, 1951). Glacier National Park, Montana. See p.719.

Touch of Evil (Orson Welles, 1958). Venice, California. See p.836.

Twin Peaks (David Lynch/ABC-TV, 1990–91). Snoqualmie Falls/*Salish Lodge*, Washington. See p.945.

Vertigo (Alfred Hitchcock, 1958). San Francisco: Golden Gate Bridge (see p.885); *Fairmont Hotel*, Nob Hill.

Witness (Peter Weir, 1985). Lancaster County, Pennsylvania. See p.135.

Zabriskie Point (Michelangelo Antonioni, 1969). Death Valley, California. See p.851.

a futile fate. Melancholy and yearning, it's a haunting piece of cinema.

★ **Thelma and Louise** (Ridley Scott, 1991). The road movie as feminist manifesto, in which two friends (Susan Sarandon and Geena Davis) wind up on the run after one kills a would-be rapist. At last it's the girls who get to tote the guns and swig the whiskey – and Scott provides stunning images of the American Southwest.

FILM NOIR AND GANGSTER FILMS

Bonnie and Clyde (Arthur Penn, 1967). Warren Beatty and Faye Dunaway play Depression-era gangsters in a film that did much to destroy Hollywood's censorship code by ushering in an era of open sexuality and unmitigated blood and violence.

Chinatown (Roman Polanski, 1974). Film noir Seventies-style, with Jack Nicholson as Jake Gittes, a morally aloof private eye whose dogged investigations reveal municipal corruption, racism and incest in LA.

Double Indemnity (Billy Wilder, 1944). The quintessential film noir: insurance salesman Fred MacMurray is corrupted by femme fatale Barbara Stanwyck, with stylishly dark photography and a memorably fatalistic ending.

★ **The Godfather** (Francis Ford Coppola, 1972). The film that revived the gangster genre for modern times, avoiding the cartoonish mobsters and G-men of its predecessors and focusing instead on the family hierarchy of organized crime and its deep connections to all levels of American society. *The Godfather II* is if anything, even better, tracing both the genesis of the Corleone family and its inevitable decline.

Klute (Alan J. Pakula, 1971). This feminist film noir marked the transformation of Jane Fonda from sex kitten into radical firebrand. She offers a nuanced portrayal of a fiercely independent New York hooker who refuses to be rescued by Donald Sutherland's PI.

Mildred Pierce (Michael Curtiz, 1945). Half film noir, half mother-daughter melodrama, with a barnstorming performance from arch diva Joan Crawford in the title role. Both femme fatale and long-suffering heroine, she's as ambiguous as any character you'll find in the noir canon.

INDEPENDENT AND CULT MOVIES

Be Kind Rewind (Michel Gondry, 2008). With his back catalogue of pop music, MTV videos and Levis commercials, Gondry is sometimes accused of pretension, but despite its quirks this hilarious film, about a group of misfits who accidentally wipe all the videos in their store and have to remake them – is a yearning hymn to cinephilia, community and popular memory.

Blue Velvet (David Lynch, 1986). A young man (Kyle MacLachlan) peeps beneath the cheery facade of apple-pie America and finds a sinister netherworld of tortured lounge singers, vicious sex games and gas-inhaling perverts.

Bowling for Columbine (Michael Moore, 2002). Maverick director Moore bagged an Oscar for this eye-opening documentary into US gun culture.

Fargo (Joel Coen, 1996). Set amid the snowy landscapes of northern Minnesota and North Dakota, a quirky tale of a scheming car salesman whose plan to kidnap his own wife and keep the ransom money goes terribly wrong.

★ **Mystery Train** (Jim Jarmusch, 1989). Shock-haired indie darling Jarmusch offers a deeply atmospheric and typically skewed portrayal of the crumbling, melancholic music city of Memphis, with four stories revolving around different guests in a gothic motel. Includes cameos from musical icons Rufus Thomas, Screamin Jay Hawkins and Tom Waits.

Pulp Fiction (Quentin Tarantino, 1994). A touchstone for American independent cinema, composed of three interlocking vignettes and directed with stylish verve and audacity.

Slacker (Richard Linklater, 1990). Emblematic of Generation X ennui in the 1990s, this indie great also manages to highlight 96 characters with episodic monologues over the course of 24 hours in Austin, Texas.

★ **Taxi Driver** (Martin Scorsese, 1976). Robert De Niro does a memorable turn as Travis Bickle, a psychotic loner and would-be assassin whose infatuation with a teen prostitute (Jodie Foster) inspired a real-life assassination attempt on Ronald Reagan five years later.

★ **When the Levees Broke** (Spike Lee, 2006). No one does righteous anger like Spike Lee, and this powerful documentary – the full four hours of it – was the first to ram the point home that the catastrophe that hit New Orleans in 2005 was not a natural disaster, but a man-made, entirely preventable event. Telling the story via news footage, interviews, home movies and punditry, and with a haunting jazz soundtrack, this is an intense and brave work of art.

Small print and index

A ROUGH GUIDE TO ROUGH GUIDES

Published in 1982, the first Rough Guide – to Greece – was a student scheme that became a publishing phenomenon. Mark Ellingham, a recent graduate in English from Bristol University, had been travelling in Greece the previous summer and couldn't find the right guidebook. With a small group of friends he wrote his own guide, combining a highly contemporary, journalistic style with a thoroughly practical approach to travellers' needs.

The immediate success of the book spawned a series that rapidly covered dozens of destinations. And, in addition to impecunious backpackers, Rough Guides soon acquired a much broader readership that relished the guides' wit and inquisitiveness as much as their enthusiastic, critical approach and value-for-money ethos.

These days, Rough Guides include recommendations from budget to luxury and cover more than 120 destinations around the globe, as well as producing an ever-growing range of eBooks.

Visit **roughguides.com** to find all our latest books, read articles, get inspired and share travel tips with the Rough Guides community.

Rough Guide credits

Editor: Ann-Marie Shaw
Layout: Nikhil Agarwal
Cartography: Lokamata Sahu, Ed Wright
Picture editor: Natascha Sturny
Proofreader: Samantha Cook
Managing editor: Mani Ramaswamy
Senior editor: Alice Park
Assistant editor: Dipika Dasgupta
Production: Charlotte Cade

Cover design: Wif Matos, Nikhil Agarwal
Photographers: Dan Bannister, Tim Draper, Curtis Hamilton, Angus Oborn, Anthony Pidgeon, Martin Richardson, Greg Roden, Susannah Sayler, Greg Ward, Paul Whitfield
Editorial assistant: Olivia Rawes
Senior pre-press designer: Dan May
Operations coordinator: Helen Blount
Publisher: Joanna Kirby
Publishing director (Travel): Clare Currie

Publishing information

This eleventh edition published April 2014 by
Rough Guides Ltd,
80 Strand, London WC2R 0RL
11, Community Centre, Panchsheel Park,
New Delhi 110017, India
Distributed by Penguin Random House
Penguin Books Ltd,
80 Strand, London WC2R 0RL
Penguin Group (USA)
345 Hudson Street, NY 10014, USA
Penguin Group (Australia)
250 Camberwell Road, Camberwell,
Victoria 3124, Australia
Penguin Group (NZ)
67 Apollo Drive, Mairangi Bay, Auckland 1310,
New Zealand
Penguin Group (South Africa)
Block D, Rosebank Office Park, 181 Jan Smuts Avenue,
Parktown North, Gauteng, South Africa 2193
Rough Guides is represented in Canada by Tourmaline
Editions Inc. 662 King Street West, Suite 304, Toronto,
Ontario M5V 1M7
Printed in Singapore by Toppan Security Printing Pte. Ltd.

1072pp includes index
A catalogue record for this book is available from the
British Library
ISBN: 978-1-40933-893-2
The publishers and authors have done their best to
ensure the accuracy and currency of all the information in
The Rough Guide to the USA, however, they can accept
no responsibility for any loss, injury, or inconvenience
sustained by any traveller as a result of information or
advice contained in the guide.
1 3 5 7 9 8 6 4 2

MIX
Paper from
responsible sources
FSC™ C018179

Help us update

We've gone to a lot of effort to ensure that the eleventh
edition of **The Rough Guide to the USA** is accurate
and up-to-date. However, things change – places get
"discovered", opening hours are notoriously fickle,
restaurants and rooms raise prices or lower standards. If
you feel we've got it wrong or left something out, we'd like
to know, and if you can remember the address, the price,
the hours, the phone number, so much the better.

Please send your comments with the subject line
"**Rough Guide the USA Update**" to ✉ mail@uk
.roughguides.com. We'll credit all contributions and send a
copy of the next edition (or any other Rough Guide if you
prefer) for the very best emails.

Find more travel information, connect with fellow
travellers and plan your trip on ⊕ roughguides.com

Acknowledgements

Nick Edwards would like to thank the following people at the various tourist authorities, as well as the accommodations they helped organise: Sheree Allqood & Amber Potter (Cincinnati), Scott Peacock (Columbus), Lexi Hotchkiss & April Ingle (Cleveland), Susan Dallas (Louisville), Pete Burakowski (Buffalo), Michelle Blackley (Niagara), Patti Donoghue (Rochester), Lisa Burns (Livingston Co), Meg Vanek (Auburn), Lisa Berg (Ulster Co), Rick Dunlap (Harrisburg), Kelly Chamberlin (Half Moon Bay), Nina Laramore (Wine Country), Heather Noll (Mendocino), Richard Stenger (Eureka/Humboldt), Jeff Parmer (Crescent City), Laurie Baker & Chris Han (Redding/Shasta Cascade), Wrenn Johns & Tom Lawrenson (Truckee) and Barbara Hillman & Dam Marengo (Berkeley). Special thanks to Meg Columbo (MAG, Rochester), Christine & Todd (Doubleday Inn, Gettysburg), Mark Carter (Carter House Inns, Eureka), Christian Strobel (Basecamp Hotel, South LakeTahoe) and Brenna Meastas (Bancroft Hotel, Berkeley). Well done to Ann-Marie Shaw for the mammoth edit and Alice Park at RG for overseeing. Cheers to the following friends for hospitality and/or great company: Minette & Ken, Janine, Pam, Brendan, Nick P, Bob, Blake, Dean & Ashley, Clint (on both sides of the country!), Steve W, Zora, Charles D, Charles H, Laramie & Wendi, Annie & Drew and Nicki & Eric. To Maria, lovely to be in the 'Burgh again together.

Max Grinnell thanks Ann-Marie Shaw and Mani Ramaswamy of Rough Guides for their support during this project. I'd also like to thank the people of Illinois, Wisconsin, Minnesota, Indiana, Michigan, Delaware, Virginia, the District of Columbia, Maryland and West Virginia for their hospitality and kindness.

Charles Hodgkins thanks Annie Shaw for yet another successful run as my editor; Nick Edwards and Stephen Keeling for their collaborative spirit; RG's cartographers, picture editors, and typesetters for their crucial contributions; Alice Park and Mani Ramaswamy for keeping the work coming; Andrew, Gregory and Jeff for getting me into this mess in the first place; and Chenery Street for being a real nice place to work on a book.

Steven Horak thanks Charles, Sam, and Far Flung Outdoor Center for their helpful suggestions. Many thanks as well to Annie Shaw for her excellent editing and enthusiasm, Alice Park for her support, and the entire Rough Guides crew in Delhi and London who made this edition possible.

Sarah Hull would like to thank Stephen Keeling for the mental health meet-ups, Annie Shaw for her patience, kindness and editing dexterity and Alice Park for steering the ship. I couldn't have done it without Jeff Richard at the Louisiana Office of Tourism, Christine Decuir at the New Orleans CVB, Elizabeth Barrow at the Crystal Coast Tourism Authority, Sundae Horn at the Ocracoke Civic and Business Association, Connie Nelson at the Wilmington CVB, Fiona Clarke at Hills Balfour, the wonderful Carey Ferarra at Georgia Department of Economic Development, Hannah Smith at the Athens CVB, Vickie Ashford at the Greater Birmingham CVB, the unbeatable Meg Lewis at the Montgomery Chamber of Commerce, lovely Mary Allyn Hedges at Oxford CVB, Sandy Bynum at Mississippi Development Authority, Jonathan Lyons (a lifesaver) at the Memphis CVB, Katherine Roberts (a champ!) at the Nashville Convention and Visitor's Corp., Shelda Rees at the Chattanooga CVB, divine Amanda Marr at the Sevierville (TN) Chamber of Commerce, Cat Kessler at the Asheville CVB and Wright Tilley at Boone (NC) Tourism. Laura Prensner is a dear old friend and was a huge help in Atlanta. The hilarious Michael Wommack saved me in the Golden Isles. As ever, a shout out goes to Molly Hamill, for the New England love and her general amazingness. During the writing stage, Julia McBee was ally extraordinaire, keeping me in pudding, cigarettes and turkey sandwiches and standing by me through numerous personal fires. Amanda Huhn lent me her wheels and gave me Bob Wills; she also stayed on the phone with me during the terrible two hours – thanks beyond words. This time, though, my most fervent gratitude goes to saint Sabrina Canfield, who harboured me in New Orleans when my heart was broken in the Delta, making jokes, procuring fried shrimp and being a wise and unceasing wonder.

Stephen Keeling would like to thank Glenda Purkis in Abilene, KS; John Cohen and Nancy Richardson in Boise (especially for the camera!); Lori Hogan in Cheyenne; Becca Krapfl in Dubuque; Meg Trendler and Debbie Williamson in Eugene; Sandy Dobmeier in Grand Forks, ND; Donnie Sexton in Helena; Lisa Weigt at Kansas/Oklahoma Travel & Tourism; Toni Alexander in Kansas City; Lisa Cooper and David Ezra at KBC PR & Marketing; Christine Metz Howard and Christina Phelps in Lawrence, KS; Phyllis Fleming in Lead, SD; Shannon Peterson, Ellie Connot and Priscilla Grew in Lincoln, NB; Karen Hibbard in Manhattan, KS; Sara Stewart and Stacey Malstrom at Maxwell PR; Jenna Herzig in Medora, ND; Stephanie Lynch at the Missouri Division of Tourism; Fred Walker at North Dakota Tourism; Elisa Milbourn and Brittany White in Oklahoma City; Judiaann Woo in Portland, Oregon; Ali Cotterill for the Portland tips; Kim Birrell at Rocky Mountain International; Brad Jones in Seattle; Maureen Droz and Vicky Engelhaupt at the South Dakota Department of Tourism; Beth Carmichael in St. Joseph, MO; Melissa Kershner in Topeka; Vanesa Masucci and Zach Fort in Tulsa; Doug Bolken in Watford City, ND; fellow trooper Sarah Hull; Alice Park and Annie Shaw for all their hard work and editing back in the UK; and lastly to Tiffany Wu, whose love and support made this possible.

Todd Obolsky would like to thank Tracy Belcher at PAMM and Suzie Sponder at the GMCVB. And I have to acknowledge my top-notch editors at Rough Guides, Alice Park and Annie Shaw – it was a pleasure working with both of you.

Andrew Rosenberg would like to thank Annie Shaw – great to work with an old friend and colleague again – and Alice Park.

Claus Vogel would like to send a heartfelt thank you to Brittany Harding, Jack Bonney, Terri Hendricks, Cindy Clock, Dee Buchanon and Deborah Hansen for their fabulous assistance and generosity throughout this journey. Special thanks also to Carole Tallman, Chris Mautino, Pamela Sousa, Sarah Stokey, Linda Hall, Nicholas Hammond, Barbara Gayer, Jennifer Pastrick and Tim Sullivan for their wonderful support and northern hospitality. You all were so kind in introducing me to your beautiful state of Alaska. Finally, I would also like to thank my editors Alice Park and Ann-Marie Shaw for their continued support, patience, encouragement, and for entrusting me to introduce our readers to this beautiful corner of our planet. What a thrill the last few months have been!

Greg Ward would like to thank Sam Cook for twenty years of adventures writing this book together; Alice, Jake and the girls for a great weekend in San Francisco; Annie for making the editing process a joy; and Allan Affeldt, John Anderson, Marcus Buck, Kerstin Busse, Bernie Caalim, Marian DeLay, John Douponce, Robin Palmer, Callie Tranter, Alana Yamamoto, and John Young for much-appreciated help on the road.

Readers' updates

Thanks to all the readers who have taken the time to write in with comments and suggestions (and apologies if we've inadvertently omitted or misspelt anyone's name):

Alessandro Arcangeli; Revis Bell; Claire Bowden-Dan; Marko Bucik; Jonathan Callaway; Paul Cavanagh; Barbara Cummins; Carol Dane; Mike David; Randall Dinwiddie; Ben Evans; Najma Flückiger; Matthew Fransioli; Shelley

Gillespie; Nel and Peter de Haan; Russell Harland; Doug Hooper; Alfred Jacobsen; Eric Lacy; Peter Laverick; Katja Lehmann; Paul Phillips; Alison Rowlings; Katy Sage; Esther Schouten; Tom Shortland; Martin Westlake; Carol Wilson.

Photo credits

All photos © Rough Guides except the following:
(key: t-top; c-centre; b-bottom; l-left; r-right)

p.1 Corbis: Owaki-Kulla (t)
p.4 Robert Harding Picture Library: Neale Clark (t)
p.5 Alamy: age fotostock (b)
p.9 Alamy: dbimages (b)
p.11 Corbis: Karl Weatherly (t); Robert Harding Picture Library: Andy Selinger (b)
p.13 Robert Harding Picture Library: Eurasia (t); Michael Nolan (c); Alamy: Prisma Bildagentur AG (b)
p.14 Alamy: Prisma Bildagentur AG (b)
p.15 Alamy: All Canada Photos (t); Nikreates (c); Wolfram's DC Stock Images (b)
p.16 Alamy: Peter Phipp/Travelshots.com (tl); Robert Harding Picture Library: Ellen Rooney (tr); Doug Berry (c); Corbis: Chicago Sports Review-Wimmer (b)
p.17 Robert Harding Picture Library: Neale Clarke (t)
p.18 Alamy: Jon Arnold Images Ltd (t); Corbis: Jen Maler/Retna Ltd (b)
p.19 Alamy: Danita Delimont (tl); Robert Harding Picture Library: Douglas Peebles (tr); Latitude: Bill Bachmann (br)
p.20 Alamy: Jim Zuckerman (cr); Corbis: Danny Lehman (b)
p.21 Robert Harding Picture Library: Raga Jose Fuste (t); Alamy: Peter Tsai Photography (c); Corbis: Lance Murphey/epa (b)
p.22 Alamy: Jeff Greenberg (t); Robert Harding Picture Library: Alvaro Leiva (c)
p.23 Nigel Francis (tl); Robert Harding Picture Library: Alvaro Leiva (tr); Michele Falzone (b)
p.24 Alamy: Phil Gould (tl); Robert Harding Picture Library: Ruth Tomlinson (tr)
pp.56–57 Corbis: Radius Images
p.97 Richard Levine (t); Alamy: Alberto Paredes (br)
pp.102–103 Getty Images: AFP
p.105 Corbis: Kent Kobersteen/National Geographic Society (t)
p.125 Richard Cummins (t); Corbis: Bob Krist (bl)
pp.156–157 Corbis: Amanda Hall/Robert Harding World Imagery
p.219 Alamy: Daniel Dempster Photography (bl)
pp.238–239 Corbis: Russel KORD/Photononstop
p.241 Alamy: Dennis MacDonald (t)
p.271 Alamy: Ian Dagnall (t); Corbis: Walter Bibikow (br)

p.297 Alamy: aaronpeterson.net (t)
pp.314–315 Corbis: Grant Smith/VIEW
p.316 Corbis: G. Jackson/Arcaid
p.365 Alamy: John Norman (bl); Pat & Chuck Blackley (br)
pp.382–383 Corbis: Russel KORD/Photononstop
p.386 Alamy: Pat & Chuck Blackley
p.411 Getty Images: Scott Olson (t); Alamy: ZUMA Press, Inc. (b)
p.457 Corbis: Gavin Hellier
p.479 Corbis: Marco Simoni/Robert Harding World Imagery
p.503 Corbis: Russel KORD/Photononstop (bl)
pp.534–535 Corbis: Paul Souders
p.537 Corbis: Julie Dermansky
p.549 Irene Abdou (t); Alamy: Cindy Hopkins (c); Cosmo Condina North America (b)
pp.568–569 Corbis: Will van Overbeek/National Geographic Society
p.571 Corbis: J. Dennis Thomas
p.591 Corbis: Ian Shive
pp.614–615 Getty Images: Gallo Images
p.617 Getty Images: age fotostock RM
p.637 Corbis: Larry W. Smith (t); Getty Images: Gallo Images (br)
pp.660–661 Corbis: Tim Fitzharris/MINDEN PICTURES
p.663 Alamy: Inge Johnsson
p.733 Robert Harding Picture Library: Riccardo Lombardo/Cubo Images
p.811 Corbis: Jon Hicks
p.835 Alamy: Reinhard Dirscherl (t); Robert Landau (bl)
pp.918–919 SuperStock: CCOphotostock-KMN
p.921 Alamy: D. Hurst
p.937 Nik Wheeler (t); Alamy: Luc Novovitch (bl); Corbis: Kevin Schafer (br)
pp.968–969 SuperStock: Alaska Stock

Front cover Bald eagle © Getty Images/Michael Melford
Back cover Zabriskie Point, Death Valley National Park, CA © Alamy/Ian Dagnall (t); Detail of Chrysler Building, NYC © Corbis/George Hammerstein (bl); French Quarter building, New Orleans, LA © Inge Johnsson (br)

Index

Maps are marked in grey

O

Map symbols

The symbols below are used on maps throughout the book

✈	International airport	⬧	Point of interest	⚔	Battle site
✕	Domestic airport/airfield	⚲	Viewpoint/lookout	⚑	Hindu/Jain temple
★	Transport stop	⌂	Campsite	⛷	Ski
Ⓜ	Metro/subway	♁	Museum	⌒	Mountain range
Ⓣ	Tram stop	🏛	Monument/memorial	▲	Mountain peak
P	Parking	⚘	Waterfall	⚶	Swamp/marshland
✉	Post office	⊤	Fountain/garden	♣	Tree
@	Internet access	⋔	Spring	⋈	Gorge
ⓘ	Information center	⊠	Gate/park entrance	⌣	Bridge
✚	Hospital/medical center	✪	State capital	⌒	Arch
⌓	Cave	⚲	Lighthouse	⛴	Boat

⊙	Statue
♀	Church (regional maps)
▪	Building
⊡	Church (town maps)
⬯	Stadium
⊞	Cemetery
▢	Park/forest
□	Beach
⬒	Indian reservation
═	National Parkway

Listings key

- ▪ Accommodation
- ● Restaurants & cafés
- ▪ Bars & live music venues
- ● Shops